A
GAZETTEER
OF THE
TERRITORIES UNDER THE GOVERNMENT
OF THE
EAST-INDIA COMPANY,
AND OF THE
NATIVE STATES ON THE CONTINENT OF INDIA

A GAZETTEER OF THE TERRITORIES UNDER THE GOVERNMENT OF THE EAST-INDIA COMPANY, AND OF THE NATIVE STATES ON THE CONTINENT OF INDIA

COMPILED BY THE AUTHORITY OF THE HON COURT OF DIRECTORS AND CHIEFLY FROM DOCUMENTS IN THEIR POSSESSION

BY

EDWARD THORNTON, ESQ.

AUTHOR OF THE "HISTORY OF THE BRITISH EMPIRE IN INDIA

GYAN

Published by

GYAN

Gyan Publishing House
5, Ansari Road
Daryaganj, New Delhi-110002
Phone: 011-47034999, 9811692060
E-mail: books@gyanbooks.com

Distribution Network
gyanbooks.com
India, USA, Canada, UK, Australia, France

ISBN : 978-81-212-2166-5 (HB)
First Published, 1858

2nd Impression 2021

Printed at: Gyan Press, Delhi.

A
Gazetteer of the Territories Under The Government
of the
East-India Company, and of the
Native States on The Continent of India
Author: Edward Thornton

A
GAZETTEER
OF THE
TERRITORIES UNDER THE GOVERNMENT
OF THE
EAST-INDIA COMPANY,
AND OF THE
NATIVE STATES ON THE CONTINENT OF INDIA.

COMPILED BY THE AUTHORITY OF THE HON. COURT OF DIRECTORS, AND CHIEFLY FROM DOCUMENTS IN THEIR POSSESSION,

BY

EDWARD THORNTON, ESQ.
AUTHOR OF THE "HISTORY OF THE BRITISH EMPIRE IN INDIA."

Corrected to the Latest Period by the Author.

LONDON:
Wm. H. ALLEN & CO. 7, LEADENHALL STREET.
1858.

PREFACE.

THE desire repeatedly expressed in the GENERAL COURTS of the EAST-INDIA COMPANY that an authentic *Gazetteer of India* should be offered to the British public in a cheap and convenient form, has led to the publication of the present edition. The work has been compiled by the authority of the Court of Directors, and though comprised within a single volume, it will be found to contain the great mass of information comprehended in the four volumes of the "Gazetteer of India," published by the same author in 1854.

This result has been obtained by retrenching some few redundancies, and by adopting an enlarged page and distributing the matter into two separate columns. By these means space has been also acquired for the insertion of much new matter, rendered necessary by the political and territorial changes which have more recently taken place within our Eastern possessions. On the character of the work a few remarks will be sufficient. Its chief objects are,—1st, To fix the relative position of the various cities, towns, and villages, with as much precision as possible, and to exhibit with the greatest practicable brevity all that is known respecting them; and, 2ndly, To note the various countries, provinces, or territorial divisions, and to describe the physical characteristics of each, together with their statistical, social, and political circumstances. To these have been added minute descriptions of the principal rivers and chains of mountains; thus presenting to the reader, within a brief compass, a mass of information which could not otherwise be obtained, except from a multiplicity of volumes and manuscript records.

The volume, in short, may be regarded as an epitome of all that has yet been written and published respecting the territories under the government, or political superintendence, of the British power in India. Its merits have been frequently discussed in the General Courts of the East-India Company, where successive Chairmen have borne ample testimony to the utility of the publication, and where it has been characterized by the best-informed among the Proprietors as "*a complete history of India, untainted in any degree by political bias.*"

A GAZETTEER,

&c.

ABOO.—A mountain in the territory of Serohee, in Rajpootana, connected with the Aravulli range, but rising far above any other summit. The top of the mountain is extremely irregular, terminating in numerous peaks. The circuit of the base is estimated at from forty to fifty miles. The highest summit, called Guru Sikra, is terminated by a small platform inclosed by a low rampart. The elevation above the sea assigned to it is 5,000 feet. It is a celebrated place of pilgrimage, especially for the Jains, who have a very magnificent place of worship at Dilwara, situate about the middle of the mountain, and five miles south-west of Guru Sikra, the highest summit. The group consists of four temples, arranged in the form of a cross, the principal being that most westerly, dedicated to Richabdeo. Colonel Tod says, "Beyond controversy, this is the most superb of all the temples in India, and there is not an edifice besides the Taj Mahal that can approach it." It has been erected on the site of temples dedicated to Siva and Vishnu, and, according to tradition, the founder purchased the site from the ruler of Serohee, by covering as much ground as was requisite with silver coin, and paying it as the price. In the centre of the court forming the outer part of the building is the pagoda containing a colossal statue of the deified coryphæus of the Jains, composed of an alloy of several metals. Before the temple is an equestrian statue of the founder, Bimul Sah, a Jain merchant of Anhulwara. "The whole of this temple is said to have occupied a period of fourteen years in building, and to have cost eighteen crores of rupees (18,000,000*l.*) besides fifty-six lacs (560,000*l.*) spent in levelling the side of the hill on which it is built." The second temple, dedicated to Nemninath, appears, from an inscription on it, to have been founded in 1236; the two other temples are of later date, being not quite 400 years old, and are much inferior to the former two. All have symptoms of decay. One of the most singular circumstances concerning these extraordinary buildings is, that the vast quantities of marble of which they are constructed must have been brought from a distance, there being none on the mountain. Near the group is a small but beautiful lake, called the Nuki Talao. The summit of the mountain is situate forty miles north-east of the British cantonment of Deesa, to which it was thought it might afford the site for a useful and excellent sanatarium. The suggestion was favourably entertained. In 1847, about sixty ladies and gentlemen, with a number of children, were assembled here, and a hundred European invalids were also sent to partake of the presumed restorative powers of the climate. Its value in this respect must be tested by further experience. Lat. 24° 45′, long. 72° 49′.

ABOUNUGUR, in the British district of Futtehpore, Lieut.-Gov. N. W. Provinces, a small town on the route from Calpee to the town of Futtehpore, and one mile north-west of the latter. Lat. 52° 56′, long. 80° 52′.

ABOOPOOR, in the British district of Meerut, Lieut.-Gov. N. W. Provinces, a village on the route from Delhi to the town of Meerut, and twenty-three miles north-east of the former. Lat. 28° 48′, long. 77° 35′.

ABOR.—A mountain tribe, occupying a tract of country bordering the district of Upper Assam, and intersected by the river Sanpoo or Dihong, the remotest feeder of the Brahmapootra. The centre of the tract is in lat. 28° 10′, long. 95° 20′.

ABRAKONUNE.—A town in the native state of Nepal, distant north-west from Khatmandoo 178 miles. Lat. 28° 46′, long. 82° 41′.

ABRANG.—A town in the native state of Kashmere, or the dominions of Gholab Singh, distant north from Simla 180 miles. Lat. 33° 40′, long. 76° 42′.

ACESINES RIVER.—See CHENAUB.

ACHALGANJ, in the district of Bainswarra, territory of Oude, a town four miles north-east of the left bank of the Ganges. Population 5,000, of whom 500 are Mussulmans, the rest Hindoos. Lat. 26° 25′, long. 80° 35′.

ACHEEN.—A native state in the north-western part of the island of Sumatra. In 1819, a treaty was concluded between the E. I. Company and the sovereign of Acheen, on the occasion of the recovery by the latter of his throne after a temporary expulsion from it; but in 1824, all the British possessions on the island of Sumatra were surrendered to the king of the Netherlands, in consideration of certain cessions made on the part of that sovereign to the British. In the course of the negotiations preliminary to the withdrawal of the latter from Sumatra, a confident expectation was expressed that no hostile measures would be adopted by their successors towards the king of Acheen; and this was met by the plenipotentiaries of the king of the Netherlands in a spirit of cordiality and tolerance. The chief town, Acheen, is situate on a river about a league from the sea. The port is but indifferent. The number of houses, which are of rude construction, is estimated at 8,000. Lat. 5° 35′, long. 95° 45′.

ACHERA, or UCHRA, in the British district of Furruckabad, Lieut.-Gov. N. W. Provinces, a village on the route from the cantonment of Alligurh to that of Futtehgurh, and twenty-two miles west of the latter. Lat. 27° 26′, long. 79° 22′.

ACHORA.—A town in the native state of Kashmere, or dominions of Gholab Singh, distant north from Sirinagur thirty-eight miles. Lat. 34° 36′, long. 74° 56′.

ADAM'S BRIDGE.—A narrow ridge of sand, nearly closing the Gulf of Manaar on the north and north-east. Its western extremity joins the eastern point of the island of Rameswaram, near the continent of India; its eastern extremity joins the eastern point of the island of Manaar, lying near the coast of Ceylon; and its length is about thirty miles, the direction being from south-east to north-west. It is partly above and partly below water; but when covered, has nowhere, it is said, above three or four feet of water, even at high tides. It is by the Brahmins called the Bridge of Rama, as along it, according to their mythology, Rama, the renowned deity and king of Oude, aided by Hanuman with his host of monkeys, marched, when invading Ceylon, to take vengeance on Ravana, the demon giant, who had carried off his wife Sita. Lat. 9° 5′, long. 79° 30′.

ADAM'S ISLAND, off the coast of Arracan, situate between the islands of Amherst and Paget, and ten miles from the mainland. Lat. 18° 45′, long. 94° 4′.

ADANADA, in the British district of Malabar, presidency of Madras, the residence of the Alvangheri Tamburacul, or chief of the Namburis,—a Brahminical class of which some account will be found under the article MALABAR. Distance from Calicut, S.E., thirty-five miles. Lat. 10° 54′, long. 76° 5′.

ADDALUR, in the British district of Coimbatoor, presidency of Madras, a town on the route from Trichinopoly to Seringapatam, ninety-two miles north-west of the former. Lat. 11° 25′, long. 77° 34′.

ADDANKI, in the British district of Nellore, presidency of Madras, a town on the route from Ongole to Hyderabad, twenty-six miles north of the former. Lat. 15° 52′, long. 80°.

ADDAR, in the British district of Chota Nagpoor, Lieut.-Gov. of Bengal, a town on the route from Chaibassa to Palamow, forty-seven miles south-east of the latter. Lat. 23° 20′, long. 84° 30′.

ADDOOE.—A town in the native state of Cutch, under the political superintendence of the presidency of Bombay, distant east from Bhooj fifty miles. Lat. 23° 23′, long. 70° 29′.

ADDUMDIDGEE, in the British district of Bograh, Lieut.-Gov. of Bengal, a town on the route from Pubna to Dinajepoor, fifty-nine miles north of the former. Lat. 24° 49′, long. 89° 2′.

ADEN.—A town and seaport of Arabia Felix, in the province of Yemen, and included among the possessions governed by the East-India Company. The territory of Aden consists of a mountainous peninsula, connected with the mainland by a narrow isthmus of sand, which is nearly covered at high water, spring tides. The town is situate on the eastern shore, and surrounded by an amphitheatre of lofty mountains. Opposite to, and commanding the town, is the island of Seerah, 1,200 yards in length by 700 in breadth. The geological formation of Aden is of igneous origin, the whole peninsula being little more than a huge mass of volcanic rocks. Aden has been not inappropriately styled the "Eye of Yemen," and, from its position, it may be justly regarded as the key to the Red Sea. Its harbour is represented as the finest in Arabia. Since its possession by the British, the port has been declared free, and no customs-duties are now levied there. Its trade is steadily increasing, and under British management the settlement bids fair to regain its former prosperity, and to surpass in the extent of its commerce any of the ports of the Red Sea. As a military post of great strength, an admirable harbour for steamers, a depôt for coals, or as the entrepôt for an extensive commerce, it has no rival. A brief sketch of the incidents which led to its occupation by the British may not prove uninteresting. In January, 1837, a Madras ship, sailing under British colours, was wrecked on the coast of Aden. The inhabitants of the town plundered the vessel, and refused to land the crew, or to supply them with provisions; in consequence of which several perished. Such as succeeded in reaching the shore were robbed, and some Mahomedan ladies, bound on a pilgrimage to Mecca, suffered brutal indignities. The government of Bombay felt bound not merely to demand redress for the outrage, but to take such further precautions as should preclude the recurrence of similar enormities. Captain Haines, of the Indian navy, was accordingly deputed to Aden, and obtained from the sultan an assurance of reparation for the plunder of the vessel, and, moreover, a formal consent to the transfer of the peninsula to the British, in consideration of an annual stipend. But before the treaty could be signed, or the promise of compensation confirmed, a plot had been formed by the sultan's son for the seizure, at the parting interview, of the person and papers of the British agent. Intelligence of the meditated treachery being conveyed to the British, the interview was evaded. After the lapse of a few months, Captain Haines reappeared before Aden, authorized by his government to enforce the completion of the stipulated arrangement. He forthwith addressed the sultan, demanding the fulfilment of the contract; but his requisition was met on the part of the sultan's son by language and conduct the most violent and insulting. "I am," so writes the young sultan, "above you and above my father. If you come to the gate, I will permit you to enter, and then be upon your head: this is the law of the Bedouins." It was obvious that further negotiation must prove futile. The place was attacked by a combined naval and military force, commanded by Captain Smith, R.N., and Major Bailie, of the Bombay army, and captured on the 17th January, 1849, with trifling loss on the part of the victors. A line of works has been thrown across the isthmus, for defence against any attack from the Arabs. The ramparts are about thirty feet high, with ample flanking defences, connecting together the spurs of the heights of Aden, which project forward on the isthmus, and are scarped to an equal height with the ramparts. These defences form a position which is considered to be unassailable by a native force. Lat. 12° 45′, long. 45° 3′.

ADJUMPOOR.—A town in the territory of Mysore, under the administration and control of the government of India, distant northwest from Seringapatam 103 miles. Lat. 13°46′, long. 76° 2′.

ADJUNTA, in Hyderabad, or the territory of the Nizam, a decayed town on the southern declivity of a pass over the mountains forming the southern boundary of the valley of the Taptee, or province of Candeish. On the northern slope of the pass towards Candeish, in a deep glen penetrating the inmost recesses of the mountain, is an extensive group of cavern-temples, the most elaborately and skilfully executed of any yet explored in India. Twenty-seven of them have been surveyed, and ascertained to have been intended for Buddhist purposes, either of worship or asceticism. They are generally spacious, hewn with indefatigable toil in the solid rock of amygdaloid, and decorated on the inside with a vast profusion of Buddhistic sculptures or paintings. These generally represent, in brilliant colours in fresco, gay and festive scenes and subjects, apparently marriage processions, or joyous domestic incidents, in which beautiful female figures are depicted, with complexions as fair as those of Europeans. These specimens of art exhibit perfect decorum, and are unpolluted by the revolting grossness and obscenity so prominently obtruded in Brahminical works of similar description. Captain Gill, an officer of the Madras establishment, has been for some time employed by the government in taking copies of the paintings, several of which have been transmitted to the Museum of the East-India Company in London. These cave-temples are excavated in the face of a cliff about 300 feet high, and the series of openings extends along the front of the precipice for the length of about 500 yards. Adjunta is distant from Aurungabad, N.E., 55 miles; Ahmednuggur, N.E., 122; Poona, N.E., 190; Bombay, N.E., 222. Lat. 20° 32′, long. 75° 49′.

ADJYGURH, in Bundlecund, a hill fort on an isolated summit at the north-western edge of the Bindachal plateau, and separated from its brow by a narrow but very deep and impassable ravine. Granite forms the great body of Adjygurh, presenting all round a perpendicular face of rock to the height of between thirty and fifty feet, and constituting a natural barrier of defence. North-east of this, and separated from it by a deep ravine, is the hill of Bihonta, of nearly equal elevation, having on its summit a plateau, which, though of a smaller area, affords space for the formation of batteries in position to act effectually against the fortress on the principal hill, the whole summit of which, about a mile in circuit, is inclosed by a rampart running round the bold brow of the rock. Within the inclosure are two great masses of ruins of temples, resembling in architectural character those of Southern India, and covered with most intricate and elaborate sculptures. The whole surface of the plateau is overspread with shattered images and fragments of fine carvings in stone, the sound and durable character of which material defies the prolonged action of the mountain air; and the carving, though overspread by a minute black lichen, being as sharp as when first chiselled. The temples are built of the same materials, viz. greywacke, and of similar proportions. On the northern declivity of the hill, and within the defences of the gate of the fort, is a natural well, or chasm, in the rock, filled with water; the depth is unascertained, but it is said to be several hundred feet. There are two ways from the plain to the summit. One is a footpath ascending obliquely up the eastern declivity; the other, a difficult road up the northern side. From the spot where the extreme steepness bars farther progress without artificial assistance, the ascent is continued by vast flights of stairs formed in the rock. The way on the north side is flanked by five gateways, situate in succession one above the other; that on the east side by four. Adjygurh seems to find no place in the history of India till towards the close of the eighteenth century, when it was wrested from a Bundela chief, named Bukht Singh, by Ali Bahadur, a descendant from an illegitimate branch of the house of the Peishwa. Shumsheer Bahadur, his son and successor, appears to have acceded in 1803 to the cession made by the Peishwa, of parts of Bundelcund to the East-India Company, and to have sent an order to the Mahratta commandant of Adjyghur for the evacuation of that place; a British force being at the same time despatched to take possession. This force, after repelling a fierce attack from the troops of Luchmun Singh Dowa, a neighbouring zemindar, arrived before Adjyghur; but the killadar refused to relinquish possession except on the receipt of 13,000 rupees, to discharge arrears of pay. It was agreed to advance this sum, but Luchmun Singh Dowa privately making an offer of 18,000 rupees, the killadar permitted him to enter, and the British detachment was obliged to retire from the place. Luchmun Singh Dowa retained possession of his purchase till the beginning of 1809, when Adjyghur was invested by a strong British force under Lieutenant-Colonel Martindell. Previously, on the 22nd of January, the steep and high hill of Regowli, situate eight miles north-west of Adjygurh, strongly fortified and garrisoned by 500 chosen men, was stormed by the British, who, however, met with an obstinate resistance, having twenty-eight of their number killed, and 115 wounded. Of the defenders about sixty were killed, many wounded, and the remainder fled. On the 7th of February, the hill of Bihontah, situate immediately north of Adjyghur, was stormed by the British; and strong batteries being formed on commanding points, such impression was made on the defences of the fort, that Luchmun Singh Dowa surrendered the place on condition of receiving an equivalent in lands in the plain. In the following June, Luchmun Singh Dowa secretly, and without notice, repaired to Calcutta; and the authorities at Adjygurh, alarmed at the measure, determined to remove into the fort his family, whom he had left residing at Tirowni, in the immediate vicinity of Adjygurh. An old man, the father-in-law of the fugitive chief, being directed to make arrangements for removing the females of the family, entered their residence, fastening the door after him. After a considerable time, no sound of life being heard, an entrance was effected by the roof, when all the inmates, women, children, and the old man himself, were found with their throats cut. As those who watched without had not heard any noise, it is plain that the sufferers had made no resistance. On the subjection of this territory by the arms of the British, the legitimate rajah, Bukht Singh, attached himself to the victors, and received, in the first instance, a money allowance for his support, which was subsequently superseded by a grant of Adjygurh. On the recovery of the portion of country possessed by Luchmun Singh Dowa, that also was granted to Bukht Singh, subject to the payment (for the whole) of an annual tribute of 7,750 rupees. Bukht Singh was succeeded, in 1837, by his son Madho Singh, on the occurrence of whose death without issue, some years afterwards, an attempt was made by the widow of the deceased prince to resist the succession of his brother, but without effect. Towards the close of the year 1853, a youth of thirteen years of age succeeded to the throne. Two years afterwards the minor rajah died without a lineal heir by birth or adoption, and the question as to the disposal of the territory is under consideration. The family are Hindoo (Bondela Rajpoots). The territory, which is estimated to have an area of 340 square miles, is bounded on the north by the native state of Churkaree and the British district of Banda; south and east by the native state of Punnah, and west by Chutterpore. It extends from lat. 24° 47′ to 25° 5′, and from long. 80° 8′ to 80° 31′. In 1832 it was stated to contain 608 villages, and a population of 45,000. The latest accounts give the revenue at 325,000 rupees, or 32,500*l*. The military force in 1847 consisted of 200 cavalry, 1,200 infantry, and eighteen artillerymen. Politically, Adjygurh is one of the states connected with the administration of the agent of the lieutenant-governor of the North-West Provinces. The residence of the rajah is at Naushah, a town at the northern base of the hill of Adjygurh. The population of this town is estimated at 5,000, and it is a neat, regularly-built place, but subject to virulent malaria. This great evil is not, however, found on the plateau on the summit, which has been proved to be a remarkably healthy station. According to barometrical observations, the mean elevation of the plateau on the summit is 1,340 feet above the sea, 860 above the town at its base, or the general level of the surrounding country. Distance of the town of Adjyghur S. from Banda, forty-seven miles; S.W. from Allahabad, 130; N.W. from Calcutta, by Allahabad, 625. Lat. 24° 52′, long. 80° 20′.

ADONI, or ADWANNY, in the British district of Bellary, under the presidency of Madras, a town near the north-western frontier, towards the territory of the Nizam. It is described by the Mahomedan historian as "situated on the summit of a high hill, and containing many ponds and fountains of clear and sweet water, with numerous princely structures." It was considered impregnable, being fortified with eleven ramparts, one within another, and continued to be of great importance until 1786, when it was surrendered, either through treachery or cowardice, to Tippoo Sultan, of Mysore, who lost no time in completely dismantling it. Distance from Bellary, N.E., forty-one miles; Madras, N.W., 270. Lat. 15° 38′, long. 77° 20′.

ADRAMPATAM, in the British district of Tanjore, presidency of Madras, a town on the coast of Palk Straits, thirty-four miles west of Point Calimere. Lat. 10° 22′, long. 79° 27′.

ADUMPOOR, in the British district of Azimgurh, Lieut.-Gov. N.W. Provinces, a town on the route from Ghazeepoor to Goruckpoor, forty-three miles north of the former. Lat. 26° 10′, long. 83° 41′.

ADUSUMALLI, in the British district of Guntoor, presidency of Madras, a town on the route from Ongole to Guntoor, twenty-three miles south-west of the latter. Lat. 16° 2′, long. 80° 21′.

ADWANNY.—See ADONI.

AENG.—A village of Arracan, situate on the left bank of the river bearing the same name, and forty-five miles from its mouth. It was formerly a place of some importance on account of the trade between Ava and Arracan, and is represented to have been of considerable size; at the period of Pemberton's visit, however, it contained only 150 houses, built of bamboo, and constructed in the manner usually adopted by the Mughs,—that of raising them on piles two or three feet from the ground. The population, taking on an average five persons to each house, would amount only to 750 souls. The inhabitants consist of Mughs and Burmese. The neighbouring country is fertile, and the plains in its vicinity afford good crops of grain. During the spring tides the river is navigable as far as the village, and at other tides within a few miles of it, and then the cargoes are transferred from the larger boats to the smaller craft, which convey the goods to the town. This place is celebrated as being the commencement of the great route over the Yoomadoung mountains to Ava, and which derives its appellation from this circumstance. At first the route lies through a very level and fertile country, but the scenery is soon changed, and it proceeds over a succession of low hills till it reaches the village of Sarowah, situate fifteen miles from Aeng. During this part of the route it crosses the Aeng river several times: when not fordable, the river is passed by wooden bridges. From Sarowah, which place is 147 feet above the sea, commences the ascent of the pass. For the first few miles it is gradual, but the last mile or two is excessively steep, and the path is conducted in a zigzag manner to the summit. This part of the road passes through much forest and thick jungle; about half-way there is a stream very conveniently situated, but the deficiency of water in most places is very great. The stockade of Nariengain is situate on the summit of the pass. It had been strengthened by the Burmese during the war of 1852, and was deemed impregnable. The removal of the British battalion from the vicinity had, however, induced its occupants to relax from their accustomed vigilance, and on the 7th of January, 1853, a small force, under the command of Captains Nuttall and Sunderland, succeeded in capturing the fortification by surprise. The distance of the summit from Sarowah is eighteen miles, and the ascent being 4,517 feet, the average rise is 250 feet in the mile. The altitude of Nariengain is 4,664 feet above the sea, and is stated by all travellers of this route to command a most beautiful and extraordinary view. It is thus described by one:—"Here a most splendid panorama presented itself; for on one side, at a distance perhaps of sixty miles, like a reflector, interspersed by numerous blemishes, lay the bay of Combermere, with all its connected estuaries, resembling streaks of silver on an emerald ground; above and about us rolled vast volumes of murky clouds, obedient to the sightless couriers of the air, ever and anon unveiling the mountainous region below to our wondering gaze." The most difficult portion of the pass is the descent on the eastern side of the mountain, which is much steeper than the other. The distance to Kheng Khyong, the next halting-place, is eight miles, and the descent being 3,777 feet, the average declination is 472 feet in the mile. The second division of the route extends to Maphe Myoo, following generally the course of the Man river, which it crosses many times. This stream, even in the season of inundation, is generally fordable at the place where crossed. Obstacles in the shape of boulders of rock at times present themselves, but do not create much difficulty. After passing the village of Dho, which is situate at the foot of the pass, the remainder of the road to Maphe Myoo runs through an open and well-cultivated country. This village has been justly designated as the "key to the whole position." From Maphe Myoo the route proceeds over a thickly-wooded country, and passes through several small villages to Tsedo, a distance of sixteen miles, where it separates, one branch running in a south-easterly direction to the village of Memboo, on the Irawaddy river, a distance of twenty-two miles; and the other forty-six miles, over a fertile and highly-cultivated country, to Shembegwen Ghaut. This route is by far the best of those between Ava and Arracan, and a considerable trade was carried on by means of it. It was not traversed by foreigners, at least till the end of the first Burmese war; and the first persons who crossed it were the officers and men from a detachment of Sir Archibald Campbell's army, under Captain Ross, in March, 1826, who effected the journey from Shembegwen Ghaut to Aeng, a distance of 125 miles, in eleven days. Since that, several others have accomplished it; among whom was Mr. Pemberton, whose account of it has generally been followed in the above narration. The village of Aeng is situate in lat. 19° 49′, long. 94° 9′.

AENG RIVER.—A river of Arracan, which rises in the central ridge of the Yoomadoung mountains, in about lat. 20° 2′, long. 94° 15′, and after flowing, principally in a southerly direction, a distance of about sixty miles, discharges itself into Combermere Bay, fifteen miles east of Khyouk Phyoo.

AFGHANISTAN, the name given to the northern portion of the region lying between India and Persia. This country being situate beyond the continent of India, no notice of it in this work can be properly required, although political relations subsist between its ruler and those of the British empire in the East. It may, however, be desirable to give a brief sketch of its history, brought down to the period of its invasion and subsequent abandonment by the British. The dominant power in Afghanistan in later times has been exercised by the tribe of Dooranees. Ahmed Shah, the founder of their government, after experiencing many vicissitudes in contests with the Persians and his own countrymen, procured himself to be crowned at Kandahar in the year 1747: at his death, the dominions which acknowledged his sovereignty extended from the west of Khorassan to Sirhind, and from the Oxus to the sea. His son and successor, Timur Shah, seems to have had no desire as to empire beyond that of preserving the dominions which he inherited. He did not succeed even in this limited object of ambition, having suffered from the encroachments of the king of Bokhara, against whom he was ultimately induced to march with an immense army. This movement, however, produced only a peace, by which that prince was allowed to retain all the fruits of his aggressions. By Timur the chief seat of government was removed to Kabool. He was succeeded by Zemaun Shah, a younger son, who repeatedly threatened India with invasion, the last time in the year 1800, when his design was arrested by apprehensions for the safety of his own dominions on the west. He was finally compelled to yield to his elder brother, Mahmood, by whom, in accordance with Asiatic precedent, he was imprisoned and deprived of sight. Zemaun Shah had inflicted the like penalties on his elder brother, Hoomayon. Mahmood did not enjoy his success undisturbed. His possession of the throne was contested by another brother, named Shoojah-ool-Moolk, and after a severe struggle the latter became master of the prize in dispute, and of the person of his rival. On this occasion Shoojah-ool-Moolk exercised unusual clemency. He imprisoned his brother, but he spared his sight. This humanity was but ill rewarded. In the course of the intrigues and convulsions which marked the reign of Shoojah, in common with all eastern princes, Mahmood obtained his freedom, and reappeared in arms against his competitor. The result was disastrous to Shoojah, who fled to Lahore, where he was confined and plundered by Runjeet Singh. He ultimately escaped, and found a retreat in the British territory. Mahmood owed his success to the talents of his vizier, Futteh Khan; but Kamram, the son of Mahmood, having taken an aversion to the minister, prevailed on his father to imprison him and put out his eyes. Eventually Futteh Khan was murdered with great cruelty. This treatment of the vizier laid the foundation of another revolution, in which the brothers of that personage were the chief actors. Mahmood fled to Herat, where he died, and was succeeded in the portion of authority which he had been able to retain by his son Kamram. The rest of the country passed into the hands of the brothers of Futteh Singh, the most able and active of them being Dost Mahomed Khan. Shoojah made two attempts to recover his lost throne, but failed, and was compelled again to seek refuge beyond the limits of the dominions which he claimed. About the year 1837, the conduct of certain agents of Russia in the countries lying to the westward of India, excited the apprehensions of the British government. It was consequently desired to establish an alliance with the ruling powers of Afghanistan, and overtures were made to Dost Mahomed Khan. They failed: the attention of the British authorities was then turned to the exiled prince Shah Shoojah, and an expedition from British India on a large scale was prepared for the purpose of restoring him to the throne from which he had been expelled. At this time Dost Mahomed held Kabool and a considerable portion of the Huzareh country. The three brothers of Dost Mahomed, Kohen Dil Khan, Rehem Dil Khan, and Meher Dil Khan, held Kandahar with the surrounding country. Herat, the fourth subdivision of Afghanistan, continued to be held by Kamram. The British force destined to act in Scinde and Afghanistan was furnished partly from Bengal, partly from Bombay, and consisted of 28,350 men. These were to be aided by a Sikh force amounting to 6,000, and by a force nominally assigned to the Shazadah (Shoojah's eldest son), of 4,000; while a Sikh army of observation, amounting to 15,000, was to assemble in Peshawur. The chief command was held by Sir John Keane, commander-in-chief of the army under the presidency of Bombay. The march of the invading force was attended by many difficulties and privations, but it was successfully pursued to Kandahar, where, on the 8th of May, 1839, Shah Shoojah was solemnly enthroned. On the 21st of the same month, the British army was before Ghuznee; on the 23rd the gates of that place were blown in, and the fortress successfully stormed. On the 7th of August the victors entered the city of Kabool (Dost Mahomed having previously quitted it), and the war was regarded as at an end. A few months dispelled this illusion. The British troops, though engaged in maintaining the throne of the prince, who from the chief city of eastern Afghanistan claimed to exercise the power of a sovereign, found that they were virtually in an enemy's country. The wild tribes manifested the most inveterate hostility; and the 2nd of November, 1841, was signalized by a fearful outbreak at Kabool, in which several distinguished British officers were massacred. Among them was Colonel Sir Alexander Burnes. From that time the situation of the British force at Kabool was one of continued danger and suffering. Akbar Khan, son of Dost Mahomed Khan, arrived to co-operate with the desperate bands previously engaged against them; and late in the month of December, Sir William Macnaghten, envoy in Afghanistan, unfortunately agreed to hold a conference with him. At this meeting the British representative and several officers were treacherously murdered. A convention, under which the British were to evacuate Afghanistan, was subsequently concluded: in the belief that its terms would be observed, the remnant of the army began to move. They were attacked on the road, exposed to miserable hardships from cold, hunger, and fatigue, as well as from the annoyances of the enemy, into whose hands many fell, some as ordinary prisoners, others (including the high-minded Lady Sale and several of her countrywomen) by arrangement with Akbar Khan. The remainder pushed on for Jelalabad, which was held by Sir Robert Sale; but only one European (Dr. Bryden, of the Bengal army), and four or five natives succeeded in reaching it. Such was the fate of a force which, about two months before, numbered 5,000 fighting men, with an array of camp-followers more than three times as many. Other disasters followed, and Ghuznee, so recently and so brilliantly won, returned by surrender into the hands of the enemy. The course of events thus direful to the British army was not less so to the prince in whose behalf it was engaged. Shah Shoojah met the fate which had overtaken so many of his English supporters, and died by the hands of assassins. Gloomy as were now the fortune and prospects of the British in Afghanistan, the darkness was relieved by many displays of brilliant and successful valour. General Nott at Kandahar, and Sir Robert Sale at Jelalabad, must be especially named as having nobly maintained the honour and interests of their country. Preparations were also in progress for vindicating them on a larger scale, before finally abandoning a spot where so much of treachery had been encountered, and so much of disaster incurred. A force of 12,000 men was assembled under General Pollock, and this army, having successfully advanced through the Khyber Pass, joined the force under Sir Robert Sale at Jelalabad. General Pollock subsequently advanced towards Kabool; he was joined by the army under General Nott from Kandahar, and on the 15th of September, 1842, the British national anthem, pealed forth by the band of her Majesty's 9th foot, with three vociferous cheers from the soldiery, marked the elevation of the British colours upon the spot from which they had not long before been driven under circumstances of treachery and murderous cruelty. One of the most gratifying results of this success was the rescue of the European prisoners from the hands of Akbar Khan. It was not intended to retain possession of Kabool, and after destroying the fort, the magnificent bazaar, the principal mosque, and some other buildings, the British army withdrew, leaving Afghanistan to the anarchy which it seemed destined long to endure. Dost Mahomed Khan had surrendered in the course of the war, and it was apparently intended to keep him permanently under *surveillance* within the British dominions; but on the abandonment of Afghanistan he was set at liberty. Overtures, at a subsequent period, were made by the Dost, soliciting the establishment of amicable relations with the British, which were met in a friendly spirit by the Indian Government, and resulted in the conclusion of a treaty of alliance with the ruler of Kabool. The treaty bears date the 30th March, 1855.

AFZULPOOR.—A town in one of the sequestrated districts of the native state of Hyderabad, or dominions of the Nizam, distant west from Hyderabad 141 miles. Lat. 17° 11′, long. 76° 26′.

AGAI, in the district of Sultanpoor, territory of Oude, a village eleven miles north-west of Sultanpoor cantonment, and eighty south-east of Lucknow. Population 400, all Hindoos. Lat. 26° 20′, long. 81° 57′.

AGAPOOR, in the jaghire of Rampoor, in Rohilcund, a village on the route from Bareilly to Moradabad, and sixteen miles south-east of the latter. Lat. 28° 47′, long. 79° 3′.

AGAWALLEE.—A town in the native state of Dewas, in Malwa, distant north from Oogein thirty-one miles. Lat. 23° 35′, long. 75° 36′.

AGHAGANJ, in the district of Aldemau, territory of Oude, a village close to the eastern frontier, towards the British district of Goruckpoor. Population 200. Lat. 26° 24′, long. 82° 50′.

AGLAR, a small river of Gurwhal, rises on the northern declivity of the Surkanda Peak, and about lat. 30° 32′, long. 78° 23′, at an elevation of 7,130 feet above the sea. It flows rapidly to the westward through a deep and narrow valley, and after a course of about twenty-three miles, falls into the Jumna on the left side, in lat. 30° 35′, long. 78° 3′.

AGNEAPULLEE.—A town in Hyderabad, or dominions of the Nizam, distant north-east from Hyderabad 155 miles. Lat. 18° 5′, long. 80° 46′.

AGOADA.—A town in the Portuguese territory of Goa. It is situated on the sea-coast, at the entrance of the river leading to the town of Goa, in lat. 15° 30′, long. 73° 50′.

AGOREE, in the British district of Mirzapore, a town on the right or south bank of the river Sone. The town contains some remarkable Hindu temples, fine views of which are given in Daniell's "Oriental Scenery." Distance forty-eight miles south-east of Mirzapore. Lat. 24° 32′, long. 83° 1′.

AGOUTUH, in the British district of Boolundshuhur, Lieut.-Gov. N.W. Provinces, a town on the route from Boolundshuhur to Muzufurnugur, situate nine miles north of the former. Lat. 28° 31′, long. 77° 57′.

AGRA.—A British district within the limits of the Lieut.-Gov. N.W. Provinces, and denominated from the city of the same name. It is bounded on the north by the British district of Muttra; on the east, by the British districts of Mynpooree and Etawa; on the south, by the territories of Dholpore and Gwalior; and on the west, by the territory of Bhurtpore. It lies between lat. 26° 46′—27° 24′, long. 77° 29′—78° 55′; is eighty-five miles in length from east to west, and thirty-eight in breadth. Its area comprises 1,864 square miles. The elevation above the sea of the average water-line of the Jumna at Agra might be estimated at about 650 feet, and it is probable that, with the exception of the summits of the sandstone hills at Futtehpore Sikri, no spot in the district has an elevation much exceeding 700 feet. The district, though bounded and intersected by several noble rivers, suffers on the whole from the want of water. Neither the Chumbul, flowing along the frontier in a depressed channel, beset with deep and difficult ravines, nor the scanty and uncertain torrents of Rajpootana, are much available for irrigation, while the channel of the Jumna is much too deep to allow water to be profitably raised and distributed over the surface of the adjacent country. The elevated banks of the Jumna are generally thinly peopled, and barren, or scantily cultivated. The soil is sandy, and its arid character, as well as that of the climate, indicated by the natural produce, consisting of a species of tamarisk, mimosa, capparis, and tamarind. The water of the wells is frequently brackish; in some the contamination is but slight, in others so considerable as to render the water deleterious. In some seasons the rains have nearly failed, and in 1837-38 so completely as to produce famine to an appalling extent. Much of the aridity no doubt results from the neglect or wilful destruction of those noble works constructed by the early princes of the Timurian dynasty, for the purposes of irrigation. The existence of the vast tank, above twenty miles in circumference, which Akbar constructed at Futtehpore Sikri, can now be traced only in the scattered ruins of the embankment. The most important object presented to the geologist in this district is the well-marked early sandstone of the hills of Futtehpore Sikri, on the western frontier. They are thus described by Voysey, in the fifteenth volume of the As. Res.—"On the Building Stones and Mosaic of Agra:"—"This low range runs in a nearly north-east and south-west direction, and the dip of the strata, which are very distinct, varies from an angle of 25° to 50°, nearly at right angles to the direction of the hill, in a south-south-westerly direction. It is remarkable that a range of hills, south of Futtehpoor, of the same rock, dips in a contrary direction, the precipitous face being to the southward, and the dip to the northward." The fort of Agra, the mausoleum of Akbar, the great mosque, and a considerable proportion of the Taj Mahal, are built of this stone, though it is of a disagreeable brick-colour, and but of indifferent quality for the purposes of masonry, decomposing very readily, especially some slaty varieties which contain much mica and iron. The red colour frequently passes into a variety of a grey hue, sometimes abruptly, sometimes gradually; and a considerable quantity of the latter variety has been used in erecting the edifices of Agra. The climate has a wide range of temperature. In mid-winter the night frosts and hailstorms sometimes cut off or check the cotton crop, which is the only commercial crop of importance, occupying, on an average, a tenth of the cultivable area. The population, according to census 1852, consisted of 572,226 Hindoos agricultural; 323,812 Hindoos not agricultural; 25,072 Mahomedans and others not Hindoo, belonging to the agricultural class; and 80,851 non-agricultural; making a total of 1,001,961, and giving an average of 537 persons to each square mile. The chief routes through the district are:—1. That from south-east to north-west, from Cawnpore through Etawa, running in some measure parallel to the left bank of the Jumna, which it crosses at Agra by ferry during the rains, and for the rest of the year by a bridge of boats; and then proceeds in nearly the same direction to Muttra, and subsequently to Delhi. 2. From east to west, from Futtehgurh, by Mynpooree, crossing the Jumna at Agra, and thence by Bhurtpore and Jeypoor to Ajmere. 3. From north-east to south-west, from Bareilly, by Khasganj, to Agra, crossing the Jumna there, and thence carried on to Kotah and Neemuch. 4. From south to north, from Mhow (the Bombay and Agra road) to Agra, and thence continued across the Jumna to the grand trunk-road from Calcutta at Allyghur. Several lines proceed from Agra to various places west and south-west of the Jumna. The Jumna is also used as a channel of transport, communication, and travelling, but is ill suited for the purpose. In addition to these routes, the district is intersected by the East-Indian Railway. It is intimated by Ferishta that the arms of Persia had been felt in this part of India previously to the time of Alexander, and that subsequently no foreign power penetrated so far until Mahmood of Ghuznee, in 1017, marched against Kunnoj, and sacked Muhabun, within a few miles of the place where Agra now stands. In 1193, Shahabaddin Mohammad Ghori defeated the army of Jaya Chandra, the rajah of Kunnoj and Benares, the action taking place near Agra, and close to Chandwar, now called Ferozabad. Sikandar Lodi, Afghan sovereign of Delhi, who reigned from

1488 to 1517, regarding this part of his dominions as of great importance, took measures for strengthening his power in it, and making Agra his residence. This prince ended his days there. In 1526 the city fell into the hands of Baber, but his bravery, military talents, and resources were put to the test in overpowering the obstinate resistance of the Afghan population of the country, who subsequently, under Shere Shah, succeeded in dethroning his son and successor Humayon. After the restoration of Humayon, his son Akbar recovered the country about Agra in 1559, fortified the city, and in a great measure made it the seat of government, until that distinction was transferred to Delhi by Aurungzebe, in 1658. On the dismemberment of the empire, consequent on the battle of Paniput, in 1761, Agra, with its territory, fell under the dominion of the Jat chief of Bhurtpore, from which power it passed, in 1774, to Nujeef Khan, the powerful minister of Shah Allum. Subsequently to the death of Nujeef Khan, Madajee Scindia, the Mahratta chief, seized the territory under colour of a grant from Shah Allum. Dowlut Rao Scindia, the nephew and successor of Madhajee, assigned this tract to the French adventurer Perron, for the purpose of supplying resources to maintain the large force under his command. In 1803, during the war between the East-India Company and Scindia, Agra was held for Perron by Hessing, an adventurer of Dutch descent, who, after a brief show of resistance, surrendered it to General Lake, in October of that year, and it was formally ceded to the British by the second article of the treaty of Serjee Anjenjaum.

AGRA, a celebrated city, the principal place of the British district of the same name, is situate on the right bank of the Jumna, here to be crossed by the East-Indian Railway. That river, during the season of low water, is dry in the channel next the town; the deeper channel, through which the entire stream then passes, stretching under the opposite bank, distant nearly half a mile. The river spreads most widely opposite the fort, and in that part its extreme breadth during the rains is about half a mile. A fine strand-road, eighty feet wide, was constructed by the labour of the destitute poor during the dreadful famine of 1838, and extends about two miles from the custom-house nearly to the Taj Mahal. Public-spirited natives have adorned it with ghauts, or passages of stone giving access to the river, which is much frequented for the purposes of bathing and ritual ablution. The material for the roads is kunkur, or calcareous conglomerate, which readily settles into a hard and durable surface. The old walls of the city remain, and mark out a space extending along the river about four miles in length, with a breadth of three; and as the outline does not much deviate from the rectangular, the area is about eleven square miles: but of this not one-half is at present occupied. There is one fine wide street, running from the fort in a north-westerly direction, and nearly bisecting the city. The houses are built chiefly of red sandstone from the hills of Futtehpore Sickree, and many are three or four stories high. Most of the other streets are narrow and irregular, but kept clean. "The shops contain very few articles; many of them are small cabins of about eight feet square, and contain goods in proportion" with their insignificant dimensions. The city boasts of numerous large structures, memorials of the resources and magnificence of the sovereigns of the Timurian dynasty of Hindostan. The fort, built by Akbar in the latter part of the sixteenth century, is of an irregular form, but having for its general outline the sides of a scalene triangle, the base of which, about five furlongs in length, extends along the river. The south-western side is slightly concave towards the interior, and is about three furlongs in length: the north-western side is in like manner concave towards the interior, and is about two furlongs in length. The total circuit exceeds a mile. In 1803 this place was invested by the army of Lord Lake, and after some abortive attempts to negotiate, a battery of eight eighteen-pounders being completed, and together with two enfilading batteries, one of four twelve-pounders, the other of two and four howitzers, brought to bear on the south-east bastion, produced such terrible effects, that in the course of a day the Mahratta force, amounting to between five and six thousand men, were compelled to capitulate. On that occasion 164 pieces of ordnance were taken, and treasure to the amount of 264,000*l*. The buildings most worthy of note within the fortress are the palace of Shahjehan, his hall of audience, and the Motee Masjid, or Pearl Mosque. The palace is small, and contains only two chambers of tolerable size. Their interior surface is entirely overlaid with white marble, ornamented with arabesques and carvings of flowers. The even surfaces are decorated with mosaics, and the columns with fillets of yellow or black marble. The parts more in relief were enriched with gilding, of which some vestiges remain. Adjoining is the harem, a suite of small chambers, directly accessible only through the imperial apartments. One more highly ornamented than the rest is said to have lodged the favourite consort of the sovereign. It commands a view of the river, through a screen-work of marble, pierced in one place by a cannon-ball, discharged during the siege by the British army. Many of the chambers were refreshed by fountains which played through orifices in the mosaic pavements. Every practicable contrivance was requisite for mitigating the heat, which during the sultry months is so great that the palace is then uninhabitable for Europeans. Here Shahjehan ended his days in a splendid but vigilantly-guarded captivity, to which he was consigned by his son Aurungzebe. In the court before this building Tavernier saw a bath forty feet in diameter, hollowed out of one mass of grey stone. Contiguous is Shahjehan's audience-chamber, equal in size to his whole palace. Originally it was inclosed merely by arcades, occasionlly hung with tapestry. The British authorities have walled up the arches, leaving a few openings to serve as windows, and thus formed a large room, used as an arsenal. Although the excessive heat during the sultry season prevents Europeans from permanently inhabiting it, an officer with a company of sepoys is daily on duty in the fort, for the protection of the armory, the medical depôt, and the treasure belonging to the collectorate of the district. Adjacent is the Motee Masjid, or Pearl Mosque, styled so on account of its architectural beauty. The exterior is of the red sandstone of which the buildings of the fort are generally constructed, but within nothing is seen but white marble. A quadrangular court, having in the midst a large basin for ritual ablution, is inclosed on three sides by arcades. On the fourth, facing the entrance, and raised some steps above the level of the court, is a large vestibule, the roof of which is supported by a great number of pillars. Above is a terrace, surmounted by a noble dome, and on each side of this is one similar in shape, but of less size. A large and elegant kiosk rises at each extremity of this front, and in the interval between these are seven others, equidistant. The view of the spectator, completely secluded within the precincts of this building, rests undisturbed on a scene of tranquil solemnity. The interior of the mosque is of an oblong shape, well proportioned and highly embellished. The celebrated Taj Mahal, or mausoleum of Shahjehan and his consort Arjimand Banoo, surnamed Mumtazi Mahal, is situate on the right bank of the Jumna, outside the city, and about a mile east of the fort, with which it communicates by a recently-constructed road. As the intervening ground was covered with ruins of great size and excellent workmanship, much labour and cost were required to level the way, it being frequently necessary to cut it through walls of solid masonry eight or ten feet thick, and so well cemented that it was found requisite to blast them with gunpowder. The extreme outline of the Taj Mahal is a vast rectangle formed by a great wall of red sandstone. The quadrangle is from east to west 964 feet, and from north to south 329. One of the longer faces has a northern aspect, and rises directly from the river; its red hue forms a disagreeable contrast to the dazzling whiteness of the rest of the building. At each extremity of this face, but within the quadrangle, and filling up its north-eastern and north-western angles respectively, is a mosque, or at least a building in the usual style of such edifices. They are constructed principally of red sandstone, but have interspersed embellishments of white marble, and are each surmounted by three domes of the same material. Only that on the western side, however, is used as a mosque, the other having been built entirely for the sake of uniformity. The Taj Mahal, or actual mausoleum of the imperial couple, is situate on the north side of the quadrangle, looking down upon the river. The whole area before it "is laid out in square parterres, planted with flowers and shrubs in the centre, and with fine trees, chiefly the cypress, all round the borders, forming an avenue to every road." Above the level of this extensive inclosure, and ascended by a noble flight of marble steps, rises the terrace of white marble, on which is situate the sepulchral edifice. This terrace, about 400 feet square, and 60 high, has for its upper surface a platform paved with large slabs of the same material with the steps by which it is reached, highly polished, and formed into regular squares, having the seams marked by narrow streaks of black marble neatly inlaid. At each angle of the terraced platform is a minaret about 100 feet high, surmounted by a light kiosk or cupola, supported on eight pillars, and commanding a grand view of the Jumna, the surrounding country, the fort, the city, and a striking expanse of ruins. The great dome is represented to be 70 feet in diameter, and 260 in height, from the foundation of the lower terrace. It is crowned by two gilt globes, one above the other, a gilt crescent surmounting the whole. The sepulchral apartment in the interior is a regular octagon, each side of which is twenty-four feet in length. Here repose the remains of the Padshah Shahjehan, and by their side those of his consort Arjimand Banoo, surnamed Mumtazi Mahal and Mumtazi Zemani. The actual tomb or sarcophagus of the empress is covered with arabesques, fanciful mouldings, flowers, and other decorations, displaying the exercise of an invention fertile but capricious. Interlaced with the flowers and arabesques are numerous inscriptions taken from the Koran. The tomb of Shahjehan is a little higher than that of his consort, and less profusely decorated. These tombs are within a common inclosure of marble railing, or lattice-work, of extraordinary lightness. The ceiling is dome-shaped; over it is the spacious apartment under the principal dome, and around are several corridors and smaller apartments. On the floor of the upper one are two cenotaphs, corresponding to those below, and surrounded by a screen-work of marble six feet high, loaded with elaborate wrought mosaics. Above rises the great dome, which "is so profusely clustered with fruits, flowers, and foliage of the same splendid description, as to have the appearance of a blooming bower; and there can be little doubt that it was intended to convey an idea of the blissful seats of Paradise." So curious is the workmanship of the mosaics said to be, that "a single flower in the screen around the tombs or sarcophagi contains a hundred stones, each cut to the exact shape necessary, and highly polished; and in the interior of the building there are several hundred flowers, each containing a like number of stones," of twelve different kinds. Exclusively of the materials of the mosaics, the terrace, the minarets, and the principal buildings, are altogether externally and internally constructed of white marble, or at least overlaid with it, so that no other is seen. It is represented to have been brought from Jeypoor, 130 miles to the west, and, as well as the other materials, except the sandstone, to have been presented as tribute. According to Tavernier, who had an opportunity of observing the progress of the work, 20,000 men were incessantly employed on it for twenty-two years.—(See Voyages, vol. iii. p. 94.) To the northeast of the city, higher up the river, and on the left or opposite side of it, is the Rambagh, a sort of pleasure-ground, laid out in a style similar to that in front of the Taj Mahal. It is chiefly remarkable for an antique mausoleum of great dimensions and elaborate workmanship, known by the name of the tomb of Itimad-ud-daulat. It is, however, now much decayed; and its coating of stone having in many places fallen off, the internal structure of crude brick and mud appears. Adjoining the fort on the north-west, is the Jama Masjid, or Great Mosque, an immense pile of building, in general in the same style as that of the interior of the fort. Of modern buildings the most worthy of note is a college, situate on the west of the city, and consisting of a fine quadrangle, having a turret at each corner, and two principal entrances. The Metcalfe Testimonial is considered to possess some architectural beauty. The character of the "testimonial," however, seems remarkable; the building consisting of a dancing-room and refectory, with some subordinate offices. Adjacent to the city, on the west, is the Government-house, the official residence of the Lieutenant-Governor of the North-West Provinces. The civil lines are on the north-west of the city, and inclose various offices of government. The magistrate's cutchery is to the south of the town, between the civil lines and the cantonments; and opposite to it is a printing-office, called the Agra Press. There is also a banking establishment, carrying on business under the name of the Agra Bank. The church is a handsome building, but not capable of containing above a thousand persons; and a new one is about to be erected in the civil station. There are two places of worship for Romanists, and one for Baptists. Among the benevolent establishments of the place may be noticed the Orphan Institution, which originally supported 2,000 children, but now not above a tenth of that number. The Church Missionary Society has a branch here, but on a small scale. Agra, being the seat of the subordinate government of the Upper or North-West Provinces, has revenue and judicial establishments, corresponding with those at Calcutta, which control those branches of administration throughout the Lower Provinces. The military lines are outside the city wall, and a mile and a half south of the fort, and about the same distance from the right bank of the Jumna. This station is within the Meerut military division, and is usually occupied by a considerable body of European and native infantry and artillery. The climate of Agra is considered healthy from November till the end of March. During the hot winds which prevail in April, May, and the early part of June, the climate is distressing and prejudicial to the European constitution; producing apoplexy, dysentery, dyspepsia, fevers, acute and intermittent, and severe ophthalmia. The rainy season, from the latter part of June to the middle of September, is still more unhealthy; yet even then the average amount of disease is rather below than in excess of that of the generality of stations in the North-West Provinces. The only decidedly unhealthy locality in Agra or its neighbourhood is the fort; and this, in consequence of its position on the bank of the Jumna, where a slimy deposit takes place at the end of the rains, which, aided by the high walls, dense mass of buildings, and deep stagnant ditch, becomes a fertile source of disease during the hot and rainy months. The markets are supplied with poultry, butchers' meat, and such vegetables as are in request by Europeans. Peas, greens, asparagus, cauliflower, French-beans, and artichoke, succeed well in the cold season. Much cotton is sent in boats down the Jumna to the lower provinces from Agra, the produce either of the district, or of the neighbouring one of Muttra, or of the adjacent territories of Bhurtpore or Dholpore, and Gwalior. Salt is a still more important article of commerce, as none is prepared in the Doab; and being principally brought from Rajpootana, it passes in large quantities through Agra. The population of the city of Agra, including the suburbs and cantonment, has been returned, according to the census of 1852, at 125,262. Agra is N.W. from Calcutta 783 miles, N.W. from Allahabad 288, N.W. from Cawnpore 179, S.E. from Delhi, by Allyghur, 139. Elevation above the sea probably about 650 feet. Lat. 27° 10′, long. 78° 5′.

AGRAHAUT, in the British district of Cuttack, lieut.-gov. of Bengal, a town on the route from Cuttack to Ballasore, nine miles north of the former. Lat. 20° 34′, long. 85° 59′.

AGROHA, in the British district of Hurriana, lieut.-gov. N.W. Provinces, a town on the route from Hissar to Sirsuh, twelve miles north of the former. Lat. 20° 18′, long. 75° 44′.

AGUR, in the territory of Gwalior, or possessions of Scindiah's family, a large town on the route from Oojein to Kota, forty-one miles north-east of former, 101 south of latter. It is situate in an open plain on the north-east of an extensive and fine tank. It has a rampart of stone, and within it a well-built fort. In 1820 it had a population of about 30,000, and an armed force consisting of 1,200 swordsmen and spearsmen, 250 matchlockmen, and 200 cavalry. Elevation above the sea 1,598 feet. Lat. 23° 41′, long. 76° 2′.

AGUSTMOONDI, in the British district of Kumaon, lieut.-gov. N.W. Provinces, a village with Hindoo temple, on the route from Sireenuggur to the temple of Kedarnath, and twenty-five miles south of the latter. It is situate on the left bank of the Mundagnee, at an elevation of 2,561 feet above the sea. Lat. 30° 23′, long. 79° 5′.

AHAR, in the British district of Boolundshuhur, lieut.-gov. N.W. Provinces, a town on the route from Boolundshuhur to Moradabad, twenty-two miles east of the former. Lat. 28° 27′, long. 78° 18′.

AHEERWARREE, in the British district of Sholapoor, presidency of Bombay, a town on the route from Sholapoor to Beejapoor, eleven miles south of the former. Lat. 17° 30′, long. 76° 1′.

AHEERWAS.—See AIRWAS.

AHEREE.—A town in the territory of Nagpore, distant south-east from Nagpore 130 miles. Lat. 19° 27′, long. 80° 3′.

AHERWA, in the British district of Cawnpore, lieut.-gov. N.W. Provinces, a village on the route from the cantonment of Cawnpore to Futtehpoor, and seven miles south-east of the former. Lat. 26° 23′, long. 80° 28′.

AHIRO.—See UHROW.

AHLADGANJ, in the territory of Oude, a province named from one of its towns. It lies between lat. 25° 36′—25° 58′, long. 81° 8′—81° 47′; is about twenty-five miles in length from south-east to north-west, and eighteen in breadth. It contains the following subdivisions:—1. Ahladganj; 2. Bihar; 3. Manikpur; 4. Rampur. Ahladganj, the town from which it is named, is situate two miles south-west of the route from Banda to Partabgarh, twenty-two miles south-west of the latter, 114 east of the former. Lat. 25° 56′, long. 81° 38′.

AHMADGANJ, in the British district of Futtehpoor, lieut.-gov. N.W. Provinces, a village on the route from Allahabad to the town of Futtehpoor, and thirty-six miles south-east of the latter. Lat. 25° 47′, long. 81° 12′.

AHMEDABAD.—A British collectorate within the jurisdiction of the presidency of Bombay: it is bounded on the north by the Guicowar's dominions; on the east by the British district of Kaira, and the territory and gulf of Cambay; and on the south and west by Kattywar. It extends from lat. 21° 22′ to lat. 23° 30′, and from long. 71° 26′ to long. 72° 50′; and is 148 miles in length from north to south, and sixty-two miles in breadth. It contains seven talooks or subdivisions, with an area of 4,356 square miles, and a population of 650,223. The district is traversed from north to south by the river Sabur Muttee. The general appearance of the country is almost that of a perfect level, the land appearing as if it had been abandoned by the sea at no very remote period, according to the reckoning of geologists. A tract running from the head of the Gulf of Cambay to the Runn of Cutch is still subject to be covered with water. In the Gogo pergunnah, lat. 21° 40′, there are some rocky hills; but from these, as far north as the town of Ahmednuggur, in Guzerat, lat. 23° 31′, there is no hill larger than a sandhill, and no rock or stone to be met with, except on the verge of the two points taken. Beyond Ahmednuggur commences the hill country, whence was brought most of the stone employed in Mahomedan architecture, the fine remains of which still adorn the city and neighbourhood of Ahmedabad. The surface of the country being thus level, there are no ghauts or passes. The roads even in the fine weather are heavy, as the soil is such as to fall into deep sand when much trodden over. The want of material is the great drawback to the construction of roads in this collectorate. In the rains they are impassable for wheeled carriages; in many places they form the drains of the country, and in wet weather, should an inquiry be made as to the locality of the cart-road, a small river or lake would probably be pointed out. An improvement in this respect may, however, be shortly looked for, as the district is about to be traversed by the Bombay and Baroda Railway. The climate during the hot season is dreadfully sultry. The state of the collectorate, as regards the circumstances of the people, is represented to be very superior to the general condition of the inhabitants of the Deccan. The villages for the most part consist of substantial houses of brick and tiles, with only a small proportion of huts. In some of the larger villages there are houses with upper stories, and the appearance of the inhabitants indicates them to be in possession of every ordinary comfort. They are generally well clothed, not excepting even the lower classes. Their food is grain of various qualities, from rice to bajree, according to their means. A disposition to apply native energy and capital to the development of the resources of this district has recently manifested itself among the population of one of its towns. It being suggested that greater facility of communication between the town of Dhollera and the port of the same name would conduce to the prosperity of those places, a company of native speculators undertook to effect the object by means of a tramway. The distance to be traversed is four miles. Sanguine expectations are entertained that the scheme will prove highly profitable to its projectors; and if this be the result, the investment of native capital in works of public utility may be looked for in other quarters of the presidency. The revision of the government land assessment is in progress, but this collectorate is not yet in a condition for the strict enforcement of a revenue system adapted to more settled districts. The country is inhabited by a race only recently reclaimed from lawless habit, who are yet to be confirmed in a course of peaceful industry, to which, however, it is stated, they are gradually becoming more devoted. At present the chief object sought is to induce permanency and regularity of cultivation by light rates of assessment, the utmost simplicity of system, and a total abstinence from all vexatious interference with existing immunities.

AHMEDABAD, in the presidency of Bombay, the principal place in the British collectorate of the same name, is situate on the east or left bank of the river Saburmuttee. An English observer says: "From being formerly one of the largest capitals in the East, it is now only five miles and three-quarters in circumference, surrounded by a high wall, with irregular towers every fifty yards, in the usual style of Indian fortifications: there are twelve principal gates, and several smaller sallyports." At the commencement of the seventeenth century, a very florid description of its glories was given by a native writer: "The houses of Ahmedabad are in general built of brick and mortar, and the roofs tiled. There are 300 different mohullas (wards), each mohulla having a wall surrounding it. The principal streets are sufficiently wide to admit of ten carriages abreast. It is hardly necessary to add that this is, on the whole, the handsomest city in Hindoostan, and perhaps in the world." Its condition in 1780 is thus described by a judicious military historian of our own country: "The walls of Ahmedabad are of immense extent, and, for so vast a city, were remarkably strong. Though this ancient capital was considered in a comparatively deserted condition, even at this period it was supposed to contain upwards of 100,000 inhabitants." Its present decayed state, however, affords indications of its former grandeur, when the mosques and palaces were numerous and magnificent, the streets regular and spacious, and many aqueducts, fountains, and seraes, or public lodging-houses, conduced to the convenience and comfort of the inhabitants and visitors. The noblest architectural relic is the Jumma Musjed, or great mosque, built by Ahmed Shah, of Guzerat, the founder of the city. Near this superb structure is the mausoleum of the founder and his sons, and adjoining is the cemetery of the less eminent members of his family. Another noble structure is the mosque of Sujaat Khaun, which, though less magnificent, is more elegant than Sultan Ahmed's. Next worth notice is the ivory mosque, which, though built of white marble, has obtained that distinction from being curiously lined with ivory, and inlaid with a profusion of gems, to imitate natural flowers, bordered by a silver foliage on mother-of-pearl. Near the city wall is a beautiful tank, or small lake, called Kokarea, a mile in circumference, lined with hewn stone, and a flight of steps all round. There are four entrances, through gateways, adorned with cupolas supported on pillars. In the middle of the lake is an island, in which are a summer palace and small pleasure-ground. Access to this retreat was gained by a bridge of forty-eight arches, now dilapidated. Two miles from the city, on the banks of the Saburmuttee, is the Shahbagh, or royal garden, a summer palace, built by Shahjehan, when he governed Guzerat as viceroy of his father Jehangir. It is an extensive structure, of complicated plan; and though now little more than a collection of ruins, plainly appears to have been constructed with great cost, and in an elegant taste. The gardens everywhere had abundance of the finest water, from fountains and aqueducts supplied by the Saburmuttee; and though they are much defaced, they still contain a great number of fine shrubs, and trees of great age and size. Ahmedabad was formerly celebrated for its commerce and manufactures in cloths of gold and silver, fine silk and cotton fabrics, articles of gold, silver, steel, enamel, mother-of-pearl, lacquered ware, and fine wood-work. Excellent paper was also made here; and there were many artists in portrait-painting and miniatures. The trade in indigo, cotton, and opium was very great. But all this prosperity was swept away by the rapacity of the Mahrattas; and the competition of British goods, so much lower in price than those of India, must effectually prevent the revival of the manufacturing industry of this place. In other respects, this city may yet attain its former flourishing condition, as the Bombay and Baroda Railway is destined to pass close to its walls.

The city was founded in the year 1412, by Ahmed Shah, of Guzerat, on the site of the more ancient city of Yessavul. In 1572 it was, with the rest of Guzerat, subjugated by Akbar. The decay of the realm of Delhi, and the rise of the Mahrattas, led to further changes. As early as 1737 the authority of the court of Delhi in Guzerat was no more than nominal, and various leaders, Mussulman and Mahrattas, contended for the possession of Ahmedabad. In the year last named, it fell into the hands of two of these combatants, who, though of different creeds, had united their army for the promotion of their personal interests, and now exercised an equal share of authority, and divided the revenues between them. The Mahratta chief (Dammajee Guicowar) having subsequently been imprisoned by the Peishwa, the agent of his Mogul partner took advantage of his absence, to usurp the whole power of the city, permitting Dammajee's collector to realize his master's pecuniary claims. Dammajee, on obtaining his liberty, united his forces with those of Ragonath Rao (a name well known in the history of that period), who was engaged in an expedition for establishing the Peishwa's claims in Guzerat; and the combined armies gained possession of Ahmedabad in 1755. In 1780 it was stormed and captured by a British force under General Goddard. The British, however, did not then retain it. The place returned to the Mahrattas, with whom it remained until 1818, when, on the overthrow of the Peishwa, it reverted to the British government. On its present condition there is little more to remark. The city walls, which have been already noticed, were thoroughly repaired in 1834, at a cost of 250,000 rupees. An ample supply of water is raised from the river, and distributed throughout the city by means of pipes. The population is said to amount to 130,000 inhabitants. One of the government English schools has been established in this town, which was opened on the 1st January, 1846, under a native instructor, who obtained high distinction at the examination of the Elphinstone Institution in 1845. The inhabitants of Ahmedabad had particularly distinguished themselves by their exertions to erect a schoolhouse; and having raised a sum of 4,397 rupees, which, with the addition of a small grant from the Board of Education, was sufficient for the purpose, the building was completed, under the superintendence of the government engineer. Government vernacular schools have also been established in this town. In 1848 a new church was constructed, at an expense of about 12,000 rupees. Ahmedabad is distant from Bombay, N., 290 miles; from Poona, N.W., 320; from Delhi, S.W., 490; from Calcutta, W., 1,020. Lat. 23°, long. 72° 36′.

AHMED KHAN, in the British district of Kurrachee, in the province of Scinde, presidency of Bombay, a town on the route from Kurrachee to Sehwan, seventy miles northeast of the former. Lat. 25° 26′, long. 67° 54′.

AHMEDNUGGUR. — A British collectorate within the jurisdiction of the presidency of Bombay. Including the sub-collectorate of Nassick, it is bounded on the north by Candeish, on the east by the Nizam's dominions, on the south-east by Sholapoor, on the south and south-west by Poona, and on the west by Tannah and by some of the petty states tributary to the Guicowar. It extends from lat. 18° 16′ to 20° 30′, and from long. 73° 29′ to 75° 37′, and is 179 miles in length from northwest to south-east, and 100 miles in breadth; it contains an area of 9,931 square miles, and has a population of 995,585. The principal geographical feature of this tract is the chain of ghauts which runs along a considerable portion of its western boundary, throwing out numerous spurs or ridges from its eastern side. Between the ridges are table-lands of greater or less extent, descending in vast terraces of various degrees of elevation above the sea. Those terraces have a general and gradual inclination towards the south-east, indicated by the courses of the rivers, which take that direction. The Great Indian Peninsula Railway traverses the north-eastern section of the collectorate. It is also intersected by the Bombay and Agra road, which enters the Ahmednuggur district at the Tull Ghaut, and quits it at the Chandore Ghaut. There is also a road connecting Poona, *viâ* Seroor, with the town of Ahmednuggur, and continued thence for some distance towards Malligaum; another between Poona and Narrayengaum, which is to be carried on to Nassick. There are besides various cross-roads, connecting different towns throughout the collectorate. With a view to the production of wool of superior character, sheep-farms were established by the government in 1835, in the neighbourhood of Ahmednuggur; but after the lapse of eleven years, during which period the experiment had been in progress, it became obvious that it was attended with little advantage, and the farms were ordered to be abolished. Except in the town of Yeola, celebrated for its silk fabrics, of which it exports annually to the value of about 50,000 rupees, the only manufacture consists of the coarse cloths of the country.

AHMEDNUGGUR.—The principal town of the British collectorate of the same name, presidency of Bombay. The town, or petta, is surrounded by a wall of no great height, and within it by an immense prickly-pear hedge, about twenty feet high. "No human being can pass it without cutting it down, and this is a matter of the utmost difficulty, as it presents on every side the strongest and most pointed thorns imaginable. Being full of sap, fire will not act upon it, and the assailants, while employed in clearing it, would be exposed to the enemy's matchlocks from behind, so that it is stronger than any abbatis or other barrier that can be conceived." The fort is about 1,000 yards from the town, and is built entirely of stone. It is of an oval ground-plan, about a mile in circumference, with a vast number of large round towers. The town contains an English church. In 1849 a commodious dhurmsalah, or place for the accommodation of travellers of all persuasions, capable of containing 250 persons, was erected by funds raised from the subscriptions of the native and European inhabitants. A good supply of water is obtained by means of aqueducts. An English school and several vernacular seminaries have been established in the town by the government.

Ahmednuggur was founded in 1494 by Ahmud Nizam Shah, originally an officer of the Bahmani state, who, on the breaking up of that government, assumed the title and authority of a sovereign, and fixed his capital at this place, named after its founder. It was built on the site of a more ancient town, called Bingar. Ahmud Nizam Shah died in 1508, and was succeeded by his son Boorhan Nizam Shah. In his reign the state attained high prosperity, until he met with a great defeat in 1546, from Ibrahim Adil Shah, king of Beejapoor. Boorhan Nizam Shah died in 1553, and was succeeded by his son Husain Nizam Shah. This prince, in 1562, also suffered a very severe defeat from the king of Beejapoor, and lost several hundred elephants and 660 pieces of cannon; amongst them was the great gun now at Beejapoor, and considered to be one of the largest pieces of brass ordnance in the world. This king of Ahmednuggur was subsequently confederated with the kings of Beejapoor, Golkonda, and Beedur, against Rajah Ram of Bijayanagar, who, in 1564, was defeated, made prisoner, and put to death in cold blood at Talikot, in the present British district of Belgaum. Husain Nizam Shah died in 1565, and was succeeded by his son Murtaza Nizam Shah, nicknamed Divana, or the Insane, from the extravagance of his conduct. He was in 1588 cruelly murdered by his son Miran Husain Nizam Shah, who, having reigned ten months, was deposed and put to death. He was succeeded by his nephew Ismail Nizam Shah, who, after a reign of two years, was deposed by his own father, who succeeded by the title of Burhan Nizam Shah II. To this prince, who died in 1594, succeeded his son Ibrahim Nizam Shah, who, after a reign of four months, was killed in battle against the king of Beejapoor, and Ahmud, a reputed relative, was raised to the throne; but as it was soon after ascertained that he was not a lineal descendant, he was expelled the city, and Bahadur Shah, the infant son of Ibrahim Nizam Shah, was placed on the throne under the influence of his great-aunt Chand Bibi (widow of Ally Adil Shah, king of Beejapoor, and sister of Murtaza Nizam Shah, of Ahmednuggur), a woman of heroic spirit, who, when the city was besieged by Murad, the son of Akbar, in person defended the breach which had been made in the rampart, and giving the assailants a sanguinary repulse, compelled them to raise the siege. These events took place in 1595. In 1599, Prince Daniel Mirza, son of Akbar, at the head of that monarch's forces, besieged the city of Ahmednuggur, and after Chand Bibi had been murdered in a sedition, stormed the place, massacred most within it, and made prisoner the infant king, who was confined in the fort of Gwalior. Though the capital was thus taken, nominal kings of Ahmednuggur continued to hold feeble and precarious sway until 1636, when Shahjehan totally and finally uprooted the monarchy. In 1759 the city was, for a sum of money, betrayed to the Peishwa by the commandant holding it for the government of Delhi. In 1797 it was ceded by the Peishwa to the Mahratta chief Dowlut Row Scindia. In 1803 it was invested by a British force under General Wellesley, and surrendered after a feeble resistance of two days. It was, however, shortly after given up to the Peishwa, but the fort was again occupied by the British in 1817, by virtue of the treaty of Poona. On the fall of the Peishwa, Ahmednuggur became the seat of the local government of the collectorate of the same name. The city of Ahmednuggur in 1819 was reputed to have a population of above 20,000 persons, and its prosperity has been rapidly progressive since it has been under British rule. Distant from Bombay, E., 122 miles; from Poona, N.E., 71; Mhow, S.W., 250; Hyderabad, N.W., 280; Nagpore, S.W., 325; Calcutta, by Nagpore, S.W., 930; Delhi, by Mhow, 680. Lat. 19° 6′, long. 74° 46′.

AHMEDNUGGUR, in the British district of Allyghur, lieut.-gov. of the N.W. Provinces, a town on the route from Coel to Furruckabad, thirty-three miles south-east of the former; it has a population amounting to 6,740. Lat. 27° 44′, long. 78° 38′.

AHMEDNUGGUR.—A Rajpoot district of the Myhee Caunta, in the province of Guzerat, politically connected with the presidency of Bombay. In the year 1790, the then ruler of Edur severed this tract of territory from the remainder of his dominions, and bestowed it as a separate principality upon his second son Sugram Sing. The revenue of the petty state, including that of the feudal chieftains, was estimated in 1847 at 7,000*l*. per annum, of which the rajah's share amounted to 5,000*l*. The British connection with this state commenced in the arrangement made with the Baroda government in 1820, under which the Guicowar stipulated to withdraw his troops from the Myhee Caunta, and the British government engaged to collect the Guicowar's dues free of expense to that prince. The amount of tribute from Ahmednuggur is 895*l*. per annum. In 1835, the death of the rajah gave rise to a case of suttee, performed at midnight, in defiance of the representations of the political commission; the British troops were fired upon, and their European officer, Lieutenant Lewis, wounded. The rite of suttee has been since formally abolished in the Myhee Caunta. The rajah of Joudpore dying in the year 1841 without male issue, led to numerous intrigues in regard to the succession, which finally terminated in the election of Tukht Sing, the rajah of Ahmednuggur, to the throne of Marwar or Joudpore. His possessions in the Myhee Caunta were thereupon claimed by the ruler of Edur, the representative of the senior branch of the family, both as the feudal superior, and as the nearest collateral heir. The validity of the claim was recognised by the British government, and the possessions of Ahmednuggur are now merged in the state of Edur.

AHMEDNUGGUR.—The principal town of the district of the same name, in the Myhee Caunta division of Guzerat, presidency of Bombay. It is situated on the banks of the stream named the Haut Muttee, in an extensive plain, and surrounded by the remains of a fine old stone wall. There is a fort within the area, but it has been allowed to fall to ruin. *Population 9,000. Distant north from* Baroda ninety-one miles. Lat. 23° 34′, long. 73° 1′.

AHMEDPOOR.—A town in the Sinde Sagur Doosb division of the Punjab, situated on the right bank of the Chenaub, thirty-seven miles north-east of Mooltan. Lat. 30° 34', long. 71° 48'.

AHMEDPOOR.—A town in the native state of Bhawulpoor. It is sometimes called Barra, or "the great," to distinguish it from Ahmedpoor Chuta, or "the little," in the same country. There is a large and lofty mosque, with four tall minarets; but the private houses are in general meanly built of mud. Ahmedpoor has manufactures of matchlocks, gunpowder, cotton, and silk. The population is estimated by Hough at 30,000. Lat. 29° 10', long. 71° 21'.

AHMEDPOOR CHUTA, or "THE LITTLE."—A town in the native state of Bhawulpoor. Before the annexation of Subzulcote to the Bhawulpoor territory in 1843, Ahmedpoor was the frontier town towards Sinde. Distant south-west from Bhawulpoor 129 miles. Lat. 28° 16', long. 70° 13'.

AHMOOD, in the British district of Broach, presidency of Bombay, a town twenty-one miles north of Broach, and thirty miles south-west of Baroda. Lat. 21° 59', long. 72° 53'.

AHMUDGURH.—A town with a fort in the British district of Boolundshuhur, lieut.-gov. of the N.W. Provinces, sixty miles south-east of Delhi. Lat. 28° 14', long. 78° 11'.

AHOO, or AHU.—A small river of Malwa, rising about lat. 24° 5', long. 76° 1'. It holds a sinuous course, but generally in a northerly direction; and forming a junction with the small river Amjar, at a short distance below the confluence, falls into the Kali Sindh, on the left side, at Gagroun, in lat. 24° 36', long. 76° 19'. The Ahoo is crossed by means of a ford, on the route from Neemuch to Saugor, at Bulwara.

AHRORAH.—The principal place of the pergunnah of the same name, in the British district of Mirzapore, a town twelve miles south-east of Chunar, twenty south of Benares. Lat. 25° 2', long. 83°.

AHTOOR, in the British district of Salem, presidency of Madras, a town on the route from Salem to Cuddalore, thirty miles east of the former. Lat. 11° 36', long. 78° 39'.

AIKOTA, in the territory of the native state of Cochin, a town at the northern extremity of the island of Vaipu, or Vipeen, bounded for the most part by the Backwater, as the British denominate the extensive shallow lake or estuary formed by numerous streams flowing from the Western Ghauts. It is described by Bartolomeo as "a fortified town, with a very ancient harbour, where, according to tradition, St. Thomas once landed." In the latter part of the eighteenth century it was held by the Dutch. On occasion of the war in 1790, between Tippoo Sultan and the British, this place was garrisoned by the forces of the East-India Company. Distance from Cochin, north, fifteen miles; from Bangalore, south-west, 220. Lat. 10° 10', long. 76° 15'.

AIRWAS, or AHEERWAS, in the territory of Indore, or possessions of Holkar's family, a decayed town with ruinous fort, in Malwa, on the southern frontier, towards the Dhar territory, held by a petty Goond rajah. It is situate in a rugged tract, amidst deep and scarcely penetrable jungle and forest; and from this circumstance, as well as from the expectation of succour from the fellow-feeling of the rajah, it was sought as the last lurking-place of Cheetoo, the notorious Pindaree chief, after he had been hunted from his other places of concealment by the indefatigable pursuit of the British in 1816; and here "he met a most appropriate end, being slain in the jungles by a tiger." Airwas is distant north of Bombay 350 miles. Lat. 22° 31', long. 76° 31'.

AJEE, a river in Kattywar, rising in lat. 22° 10', long. 70° 52', and flowing in a north-westerly direction, falls into the Gulf of Cutch: the total length of its course is about sixty miles.

AJEETMALL, in the British district of Etawa, lieut.-gov. of the N.W. Provinces, a town twenty-five miles south-east of Etawa. Supplies and water are abundant. Lat. 26° 33', long. 79° 23'.

AJI, or HADJEE.—A river rising in the British district Ramgurh, about lat. 24° 32', long. 86° 10'. It takes a course south-east for twenty-five miles through that district, and for six miles through Mongheer, and subsequently passes into the British district Beerbhoom, through which it continues in a southerly direction for sixty miles, when it takes a course east, which it continues to hold along the southern boundary for ninety miles, until it falls into the Bhagruttee, on the right side, at Cutwa, in lat. 23° 39', long. 88° 9'. The upper part of its course lies through a tract rich in coal and iron. It is navigable for about ten weeks during the periodical rains of autumn; and advantage is taken of that favourable time to send down coal and iron to Calcutta. According to popular notion, "whatever man bathes in its waters thereby becomes unconquerable."

AJMERE.—The principal place of the British district of the same name, a city of great antiquity and celebrity. It is situate in a valley, or rather basin, which, though rocky, is very picturesque and beautiful, and surrounded by hills. On the base and lower slope of one of the hills the town is built. It is surrounded by a wall of stone. There are five lofty and strong gateways in a beautiful style of architecture, all on the north and west sides. The town contains several mosques and temples, built in a massive style of architecture. The houses of the wealthy are very spacious and well built, and some of the streets are wide and handsome; but the generality are narrow and greatly deficient in cleanliness, though in this respect the place has the advantage over the towns of native states; and on the whole the habitations of the poorer classes are more commodious than ordinary. Beyond the city walls are the remains of an antique Jain temple, on the lower part of Taragurh, a mountain rising over the town on the north-east. South of the town is an extensive piece of artificial water, called the Ana-Sagar, formed by damming up some torrents by means of a bund 600 yards long by 100 yards broad. In the rainy season the circumference of the Ana-Sagar is upwards of six miles. Until within the last few years, unless the periodical rains were heavy, the lake was not invariably filled. In 1846, measures for increasing the supply were completed, by turning into the lake the stream from the Ajeipall hills; and no inconvenience has been subsequently experienced from the scarcity of water. The river Looni, the name implying "salt," has its origin in this lake; its stream is not, however, salt at its egress. The bund, or dyke, was constructed by Ana Deva, sovereign of Ajmere, probably about the close of the eleventh century. Visola Deva, who reigned about a century earlier, excavated the Beesila Talao, another artificial lake, situate a mile north-east of the former, and half a mile east of the city of Ajmere. The form is a regular oval, the bank of which, originally faced all round with stone, is two miles and a half in circumference. Beyond the city wall is the ruinous palace of Shah Jehan. Another, of Akbar, has been converted into an arsenal, the powder-magazine of which, amply stored, must, in the event of explosion, produce the most awful consequences to the town. Ajmere is the seat of a British political agency. The city, on account of the inclination of its site, has peculiar facilities for drainage, but the habits of the population defy the efforts for enforcing cleanliness made by the police, though active and vigilant. The jail, an old Mahomedan building, some hundred yards outside the town-wall, but in an airy and healthy situation, contains, it is said, on an average, 150 prisoners, generally of the predatory tribes: they are employed on the public works, but the result of their labour is trifling. The climate of the town and its environs, though in the end of spring and the beginning of summer very hot, is in general healthy. Small-pox sometimes prevails to a wide and fatal extent, its desolating effects being increased by the inattention of the people to cleanliness, and their neglect of vaccination. The hospital is a small building near the magazine, and has a central ward thirty feet by twenty. There is no recent return of the population of this town: in 1837 it was stated to be upwards of 23,000, and it is believed that the place has been progressively improving since it came under British rule, a course still in operation. Passing from legend to history, we find it recorded that the rajah of Ajmere confederated, in the year 1008, with those of Lahore, Oojein, Gwalior, Kalinjer, Kanowj, and Delhi, to repel the invasion of Mahmood of Ghuzni, by whom the allied army was utterly routed. At the time of the Mussulman invasion in 1191, under Muhammed Shahabuddin, monarch of Ghoor, Prithwi Rao, who held the combined rule of Ajmere and of Delhi, was the most powerful sovereign of India. He, at the head of a vast army, met the invader near Thanesur, and overthrew him with great slaughter, Muhammed himself escaping from the field with much difficulty, and severely wounded. The Mussulman, however, subsequently renewing the invasion, with the advantages of greater experience, and an army better disciplined, was met by Prithwi Rao at Tirouri, near Thanesur, where a desperate battle took place, in which the Hindoos were routed with great loss, and their rajah, being made prisoner, was, it is said, put to death. The conqueror, following up his success, took the city of Ajmere, put numbers of the inhabitants to the sword, and enslaved the rest, assigning the devastated country to a relative of the overthrown rajah, under stipulation of a heavy tribute. Akbar acquired Ajmere, in 1559, without a battle, or any resistance, and under his territorial, fiscal, and military arrangements, the city became the principal place of a very extensive province of the same name, which, according to the Ayeen Akbery, included Mewar, or the present state of Oodeypore; Marwar, or the present state of Joudpore; and Haraoti, including the present states of Boondee and Kota. On the dismemberment of the empire of Delhi, subsequent to the invasion of Ahmed Shah Durani, Ajmere shared in the confusion of the general struggle, and ultimately fell into the hands of the Mahrattas. In 1809, Doulut Rao Sindia conferred its government on the brother of Bappoo Sindia, and it became the head-quarters of plundering operations in Jeypore and Joudpore. In 1817, at the commencement of the war, a British force was ordered to Ajmere, and the town and territory were afterwards formally ceded to the East-India Company. Ajmere is distant from Bombay, N., by Mhow and Neemuch, 677 miles; from Delhi, S.W., by Nusserabad, 258; from Calcutta, N.W., by Allahabad, 1,039. Lat. 26° 29′, long. 74° 43′.

AJMERE.—A British district under the lieut.-gov. of the N.W. Provinces. It is bounded on the east by the Rajpoot states of Kishengurh and Jeypore; on the south by the territory of Mewar; on the west and north-west by British Mairwara and Joudpore. It lies between lat. 25° 43′—26° 42′, long. 74° 22′—75° 33′; is 80 miles in length from south-east to north-west, and 50 in breadth. The area is 2,029 square miles. The south-east part is in general sandy and rather level, yet not without inequalities in some places, forming irregular ranges of no great height or length. In the north, the north-west, and the west, are many hills and mountains, either connected with the great Aravulli range, or forming part of it. They are considered of primitive formation, and are schistose in the greatest proportion, the strata lying obliquely, dipping from east to west. The summit, rising above the city of Ajmere, and having an estimated elevation of more than 1,000 feet above the valley at its base, or upwards of 3,000 feet above the sea, is probably the loftiest in that part of the range. The mountain of Taragurh contains lodes of carbonate of lead, worked from time immemorial by the natives. The demand for the article is, however, so small, that little if any profit is derived from the working. There are also ores of manganese in the same mountain, and indications of copper, besides some lodes of ore of that metal *in situ*. Iron ore is abundant, and yields a metal of good quality. The soil in many places is much impregnated with mineral salts, especially carbonate of soda. From this cause, the water of the Koree, the only river, cannot be used for drinking, or any alimentary purposes, except during the periodical rains, at which time only it becomes a wide stream. Rising in the territory of Mewar or Oodeypore, about lat. 25° 32′, long. 73° 58′, it takes a course generally east, flows along the southern boundary of the district for about thirty miles, and subsequently through it for the same distance, and joins the Banas on the eastern frontier. The other streams are mere rain-torrents, very full and impetuous in wet weather, but soon subsiding. The Looni, which falls into the Gulf of Cutch, may be said to have its origin in an artificial lake or tank called the Ana-Sagar. The stream, under the name of the Sagar-Mutti, flows first to the Besila Talao, another artificial piece of water. Thence it flows on, till at Govindghur it is joined by the Sarasvati from Poshkur, a third artificial lake, and at this confluence takes the name of Looni. There are no natural lakes in Ajmere, but tanks or artificial bodies of water abound. The principal are those just named; the Ana-Sagar and the Besila Talao, at the city of Ajmere, and the lake of Poshkur, three or four miles to the north-west of it. The general elevation of the plain of Ajmere has been estimated at 2,000 feet above the sea. The entire population, as returned by a recent census (1848), amounts to 224,891; something more than 110 to the square mile. Of the above number, 118,533 are returned as Hindoo agricultural; 79,070 as Hindoo non-agricultural; 7,172 Mahomedans and others not being Hindoos, agricultural; and 20,116 non-agricultural. The superintendent reports that the population was taken by native officers, and that it "may be considered as an approximation to the truth."

AJRA.—A town in the native state of Kolapore, under the administration and control of the presidency of Bombay; distant south from Kolapore forty miles. Lat. 16° 8′, long. 74° 17′.

AKAR.—A town in the territory of Nagpore, distant north from Konkeir forty miles. Lat. 20° 50′, long. 81° 32′.

AKAYA.—A village situate on the left bank of the Kuladyne river, twenty miles west of the town of Arracan. Lat. 20° 49′, long. 93° 7′.

AKBARPOOR, in the British district of Mundlaisir, within the territory of Indore, a town on the route from Bombay to Indore, forty-three miles south-west of the latter. Lat. 22° 8′, long. 75° 33′.

AKBARPOOR, in the British district of Cawnpore, the principal place of the pergunnah of the same name, a town on the route from Cawnpore to Etawa, and twenty-eight miles west of the former; population 6,330. The road in this part of the route is rather good. Lat. 26° 22′, long. 80°.

AKBARPOOR, in the British district of Shahjahanpoor, lieut.-gov. of the N.W. Provinces, a village on the route from Bareilly to the cantonment of Futtehgurh, and forty-two miles south-east of the former. The road in this part of the route is rather good, the country open, level, and cultivated. Lat. 27° 48′, long. 79° 43′.

AKBERPOOR, in the district of Aldemau, territory of Oude, a village situate on the river Tons (eastern), thirty-five miles south-east of Faizabad, 105 south-east of Lucknow. Butter estimates the population at 1,000, of whom two-thirds are Mussulmans, most of them weavers. Lat. 26° 28′, long. 82° 35′.

AKBURABAD, in the native state of Rampoor, lieut.-gov. of the N.W. Provinces, a town on the north-eastern route from the town of Rampoor to Nugina, and twenty miles north of the former. Lat. 29° 5′, long. 79° 4′.

AKBURABAD, in the British district of Allygurh, lieut.-gov. of the N.W. Provinces, a town on the route from Allahabad to Coel, twelve miles south-east of the latter. Lat. 27° 48′, long. 78° 21′.

AKBURPOOR, in the British district of Goorgaon, lieut.-gov. of the N.W. Provinces, a village at the eastern base of a rocky range of hills of sandstone formation, largely intermixed with quartz. Distance south from Delhi 56 miles. Lat. 27° 52′, long. 77° 10′.

AKBURPOOR, in the British district of Muttra, lieut.-gov. of the N.W. Provinces, a village on the route from Muttra cantonment to Delhi, and sixteen miles north-west of the former. The road in this part of the route is rather heavy. Lat. 27° 39′, long. 77° 37′.

AKDIRAH, in the Rajpoot state of Joudpore, on the route from Nusseerabad to Deesa, and 141 miles south-west of the former. The surrounding country is gravelly, and though occasionally diversified with a few small hills, is in general level. The road in this part of the route is firm and good. Lat. 25° 23′, long. 73° 17′.

AKHA.—A tribe inhabiting the mountainous country situated on the northern boundary of Assam, and the eastern boundary of Bhotan. The centre of the tract is about lat. 27° 10′, long. 92° 40′.

AKHUNDI, in the Rajpoot state of Joudpore, a village on the route from Balmer to the city of Joudpore, and fifty-two miles east of the former. It is situate six miles north of the right bank of the river Loni, in a low swampy country, liable to be laid under water by the inundation of that river during the rainy season, when the road becomes deep and difficult. Lat. 25° 59′, long. 72° 14′.

AKKAWARRUM.—A town in Hyderabad, or dominions of the Nizam. Distant east from Hyderabad 59 miles. Lat. 17° 15′, long. 79° 26′.

AKKERI.—See EEKAIREE.

AKLI, in the Rajpoot state of Joudpore, a village on the route from Pokhurn to Balmer, and twenty-six miles north of the latter place. The road in this part of the route is good, being over a plain, though barren, country. Lat. 26° 4′, long. 71° 24′.

AKLONEE.—A town in the native state of Gwalior, or possessions of Scindia, distant south-east from Agra fifty miles. Lat. 26° 35′, long. 78° 37′.

AKLOOJ, in the British territory of Sattara, presidency of Bombay, a town on the right bank of the Neera river, seventy miles east of Sattara. Lat. 17° 52′, long. 75° 5′.

AKNUR, in the Northern Punjab (territory of Gholab Singh), is situate on the banks of the Chenaub, here a very large river. At the beginning of August, when largest, it was found by Broome and Cunningham to have seven channels, the broadest 920 yards wide, some of the others breast-deep, and all having very rapid streams. The Chenaub is navigable downwards from a point a short distance above Aknur to the sea. The town, though mostly in ruins, has a very fine and picturesque appearance when viewed from without, the remains of the old palace being strikingly contrasted with the buildings of the new fort. Here is a ferry over the river. Aknur is situated at the base of the lowest or most southern range of the Himalaya, where it first rises above the plain of the Punjaub. Lat. 32° 50′, long. 74° 50′.

AKOAT.—A town in Hyderabad, or dominions of the Nizam, situate in one of the recently-sequestrated provinces of the kingdom. Distant west from Ellichpoor thirty-two miles. Lat. 21° 3′, long. 77° 9′.

AKOLAH.—A town in Hyderabad, or dominions of the Nizam, distant north from Jaulnah twenty miles. Lat. 20° 6′, long. 76° 2′.

AKORAH, in the British district of Peshawur, one of the divisions of the Punjab, a town situated on the right bank of the Kabool river, a tributary to the Indus, and on the route from Attock to Peshawur, twelve miles north-west of the former. Lat. 34°, long. 72° 10′.

AKOREE, in Bundelcund, in the British territory of Jaloun, a small town on the route from Calpee to Jhansi, thirty-five miles south-west of the former. It has water and supplies in abundance. Lat. 25° 57′, long. 79° 20′.

AKOUNAH.—A town in the territory of Oude, distant north from Oude fifty miles. Lat. 27° 29′, long. 82°.

AKOWLAH, in Hyderabad, or the territory of the Nizam, a town in one of the recently ceded districts, on the route from Nagpore to Aurungabad, 142 miles south-west of former, 122 north-east of latter. It is a considerable place, with high and handsome walls, and the numerous ruins contiguous to it indicate that it must have formerly been much more considerable. Distance from Hyderabad, north-west, 250 miles; from Bombay, north-east, 300. Lat. 20° 40′, long. 77° 2′.

AKRA.—A town in the Daman division of the Punjab: it is situated on the left bank of the small river Gombela, a tributary of the Indus, fifty-seven miles north from Dera Ismael Khan. Lat. 32° 36′, long. 70° 33′.

AKRAUNEE PERGUNNAH.—A tract of British territory under the presidency of Bombay, situate between the two branches of the Satpoora mountains, bounded on the north by the Nerbudda; on the east by the Burwani state and Torun Mal; on the south by the Soottampore and Kookurmoonda pergunnahs; and on the west by the state of Raj Peepla. It extends from lat. 21° 39′ to lat. 22° 4′, and from long. 73° 48′ to long. 74° 30′. It is about fifty miles in length from east to west, and about twenty at its greatest breadth.

AKULKOTE, within the political jurisdiction of the government of Bombay, a town, with annexed territory, in the southern Mahratta country, held in jaghire from the East-India Company by a petty chief styled rajah, who was formerly tributary to the rajah of Sattara. This prince is bound to furnish a contingent of cavalry to the British government. A proposal made by the latter to commute the obligation for a pecuniary payment has been met by a refusal on the part of the rajah. Distant from Bombay, S.E., 250 miles. Lat. 17° 30′, long. 76° 16′.

AKYAB, or ARRACAN PROPER.—A district of Arracan, bounded on the north by Chittagong, on the west by the Bay of Bengal, on the east by the Yoomadoung mountains, and on the south by the island of Ramree and numerous creeks and estuaries. It lies between lat. 20°—21° 33′, long. 92° 12′—94°. Its area is about 6,000 miles, and it is the largest of the three provinces of Arracan. It is in general flat, but along the sea-shore some low ridges of hills run parallel with the sea, and to the north and east its boundary is formed by high ranges, over which are several passes to Chittagong and Ava. The valley, which constitutes the principal part of the province, is intersected by numerous streams and tide nullahs, besides the larger rivers Myoo, Coladyne, and Lemyoo, which run through it, and in the rainy season completely inundate the neighbouring country, and insulate the villages in their vicinity. The soil is peculiarly adapted for the cultivation of rice, which is carried to a greater extent here than in any other district in Arracan. The numerous streams and nullahs which intersect the valley are by artificial means turned to the purposes of irrigation. The population of the district amounts, it is stated, to about 177,585.

AKYAB.—The chief town of the district of the same name, as well as the whole province of Arracan. It was formerly called Tset-twe, and is still known by that name among the Mugh inhabitants. The designation of Akyab was derived, Lieutenant Phayre supposes, from a pagoda situate near this spot, which was called Akhyab-dau-kun (royal jawbone hillock), from a jawbone of Gautama's being buried there. It is situate on the eastern side of the island of Akyab, which is at the south-western extremity of the district, and at the mouth of the Coladyne or Kuladyne river. The island is separated from the mainland by the Roozeekeea creek, which connects the river Kuladyne with Tekmyoo. It is of late years only that this town has been at all flourishing, for previously to the Burmese war it was a paltry village, consisting only of a few ill-constructed bamboo huts. It is now the most important town in the province, certainly in a commercial point of view, though, as a military station, it is superseded by Khyouk Phyoo. The houses are well built and more substantial than the generality of Mugh residences, and the streets, which are broad and regular, are built at right angles to one another. Further improvements are in progress. There is a plentiful supply of all kinds of grain in the shops; and articles for clothing, cutlery, glass, are imported from Bengal, and exposed for sale. Its situation is extremely well suited for a commercial town, and it is to this circumstance, probably, that its present prosperity is owing. Being placed at the entrance of the chief river of the province, which has an uninterrupted inland navigation, and near a fertile country, where much grain is produced, and having a good harbour, it possesses every facility for carrying on an export and import trade, which it in consequence possesses to a considerable extent. Lighthouses and other works, projected for the benefit of navigation and commerce, have been erected in the vicinity of the town. The climate of this town is considered as healthy as Khyouk Phyoo or Sandoway. The population amounts to about 5,000 souls. Lat. 20° 10′, long. 92° 54′.

ALADIN ISLANDS.—A cluster of islands to the south-west of the Tenasserim provinces, about thirty-four miles distant from the mainland of Siam. Lat. 9° 40′, long. 98° 8′.

ALAKANANDA.—See ALUKNUNDA.

ALAMBARAI, ALLEMBADDY, or ALLUMKADDY, in the British district Coimbatore, presidency of Madras, a town on the right bank of the river Cauvery. In the history of Mysore it is mentioned as a place of importance in 1624; and in the ill-planned British campaign of 1768 it was occupied by a small British garrison, which was dispossessed by the troops of Hyder Ali. Distance from Seringapatam, east, sixty-five miles; from Madras, south-west, 185. Lat. 12° 9′, long. 77° 49′.

ALAMPOOR, in the Rajpoot state of Jeypore, a decayed town on the old route from Agra to Mow, 141 miles south-west of former, 274 north-east of latter. In consequence of the distractions and devastations in this part of India during the latter part of the last and the early part of the present century, most of the inhabitants deserted this town, and took refuge in the neighbouring stronghold of Naushahur or Madhupur. Water is obtainable here from numerous wells; but supplies must be collected from the neighbourhood. Lat. 25° 57′, long. 76° 25′.

ALAPOOR, in the British district of Goorgaon, lieut.-gov. of the N.W. Provinces, a village on the route from Delhi to Muttra, and thirty-eight miles south of the former. The road in this part of the route is good. Lat. 28° 16′, long. 77° 7′.

ALATPOOR, in the British district of Mynpooree, lieut.-gov. of the N.W. Provinces, a village on the route from the city of Agra to the cantonment of Mynpooree, and eighteen miles west of the latter. The road in this part of the route is laid under water to the depth of from one to three feet during the periodical rains in the latter part of summer; at other times it is tolerably good: the country is level, and partially cultivated. Lat. 27° 10′, long. 78° 50′.

ALAYGYAN PASS.—A pass over the Youmadoung mountains, leading from Sandoway, in the British district of Arracan, to the town of Prome, in the British territory of Pegu. The crown of the pass is about eleven miles north-east from Sandoway. Lat. 18° 31′, long. 94° 39′.

ALBAK.—A town in Hyderabad, or dominions of the Nizam, distant north-west from Rajahmundry 110 miles. Lat. 18° 10′, long. 80° 47′.

ALDEMAU, in the territory of Oude, a district denominated from the village of that name. It is bounded on the north-west by the district Pachamrat; on the north-east by the river Ghogra, separating it from the British district Goruckpoor; on the south-east by the British district Azimgurh; and on the west by Sultanpoor. It lies between lat. 26°—26° 40′, long. 82° 15′—83° 6′.

ALDEMAU, in the territory of Oude, an ancient village whence is denominated the district of the same name. It is situate four miles from the right bank of the river Ghogra. Close to it is a small mud fort, mounted with two cannon, the station of the local officer of police. There are many shops for cloth and other merchandise kept by Hindoo traders. Butter estimates the population at 400, of whom 300 are Mussulmans. Distant fifty miles S.E. from Faizabad; 120 E. from Lucknow; thirty-five N.W. from Azimgurh. Lat. 26° 27′, long. 82° 55′.

ALEEPOOR, in the British district of Delhi, lieut.-gov. of the N.W. Provinces, a village on the route from the city of Delhi to Kurnal. It is situate on the Delhi Canal, from which it is supplied with water. There is a police-station here. The road in this part of the route is good in dry weather, and supplies for troops may be obtained in abundance on due notice. Lat. 28° 48′, long. 77° 12′.

ALEPPI.—See AULAPOLAY.

ALI BAUG, in the British district of Tannah, presidency of Bombay, a town on the sea-coast, nineteen miles south of Bombay. Lat. 18° 40′, long. 72° 58′.

ALI BUNDER, in Sinde, a small town on the Gonnee, one of the offsets of the Indus to the east. Here is a dam made in 1799 by Futteh Ali, one of the ameers of Sinde. This, according to Pottinger, was "the only work of public utility ever made by one of the reigning family," being intended to retain the water of the river for the purposes of irrigation, and to exclude the salt-water, which, sent upwards by the tide, rendered sterile the surrounding country. This barrier had the natural consequence of causing in the channel of the Gonnee a deposit of alluvial matter, which is gradually filling it; so that, though formerly navigable throughout the year, this branch of the Indus had in 1809 become so shallow, that boats could ply only during four months of the inundation between Ali Bunder and Hyderabad. The channel below Ali Bunder has also become nearly obliterated, though formerly by far the greatest estuary of the Indus. The contiguous part of Cutch also suffered the most disastrous consequences from the water being cut off; the district of Sayra, formerly remarkable for fertility, ceasing to yield a blade of vegetation, and becoming part of the Runn, or Great Salt Desert, on which it bordered. Ali Bunder is in lat. 24° 22′, long. 69° 11′.

ALIGANJ, or SEWAN ALIGANJ, in the British district of Sarun, lieut.-gov. of Bengal, a town on the route from Dinapore to Goruckpore, fifty-four miles N.W. of former, seventy-four S.E. of latter. It has a good bazaar, and water and supplies are abundant. It is stated that the population are principally Mussulmans. Lat. 26° 8′, long. 84° 24′.

ALIGANJ, in the district of Sultanpore, territory of Oude, a village twelve miles north-west of the cantonment of Sultanpore, seventy south-east of Lucknow. Butter estimates its population at only 100, all Hindoos; yet adds, "there is a bazaar of sixty shops, and a market, attended by between 300 and 400 shopkeepers." Lat. 26° 24′, long. 82°.

ALIGUNJ.—A town in the territory of Oude, distant north from Lucknow ninety-one miles. Lat. 28° 9′, long. 80° 40′.

ALIPOORA, in the British district of Allahabad, lieut.-gov. of the N.W. Provinces, a village on the right bank of the Ganges, 766 miles north-west of Calcutta by the river route, forty-two miles south-east of Allahabad by the same. Lat. 25° 12′, long. 82° 14′.

ALIPORA.—See ALLYPOORA.

ALIPORE.—A town in British district of the Twenty-four Pergunnahs, lieut.-gov. of Bengal, on the route from Fort William to Fulta, by Tolly's Nullah, four miles south-east of Fort William, twenty-one north-west of Fulta. The official residence of the lieut.-governor of Bengal has been fixed in this town. Heber describes it as a large village, in the vicinity of which are several houses belonging to Europeans, and considered remarkably healthy and dry. In this town is situate the great jail of Alipore, built in 1810, at a cost of 10,000*l.*, exclusive of the labour of the prisoners employed upon the work. Convicts sentenced to long periods of imprisonment in Bengal are usually confined in this jail. The number of prisoners in 1848 amounted to 991. Lat. 22° 30′, long. 88° 27′.

ALIWAL.—A village near the left bank of the Sutlej, and within a short distance of the town of Loodianah. It is within the tract of country subject to the commissioner and superintendent of the Cis-Sutlej territories. Here, on the 28th January, 1846, Sir Harry Smith attacked, defeated, and drove back a large body of Sikhs, which had crossed the Sutlej from Philour, on its right bank, and threatened Loodianah. The movements of the officer commanding in this action were marked by the most consummate tact and judgment, and the object of them was completely accomplished. Lat. 30° 57′, long. 75° 36′.

ALLAHABAD.—A British district under the lieut.-gov. of the N.W. Provinces, named from its principal place. It is bounded on the north by the territory of Oude; on the east by the British districts Jounpore and Mirzapore; on the south-west by the territory of Rewah and the British district of Banda; and on the west by the British district of Futtehpore. It lies between lat. 24° 49′—25° 44′, long. 81° 14′—82° 26′; is eighty-five miles in length from south-east to north-west, and fifty in breadth. The area is 2,788 square miles. Four of the subdivisions called pergunnahs, amounting to about a third of the district, are comprised within the Doab, extending upwards from its south-eastern angle, marked by the confluence of the Jumna and Ganges. The general slope of the surface is to the south-east, as evidenced by the descent of the Ganges and of the smaller streams in the same direction. There is, besides, a declivity from the south-west to the north-east, indicated by the descent in that direction of the Jumna and Tons, discharging themselves into the Ganges, the bed of which is the channel of drainage for the whole district. The elevation above the sea of the average water-mark at the confluence of the Jumna and Ganges, is about 340 feet. The plain of the Doab is estimated to be in this part about sixty feet higher, or 400 feet above the sea; and probably no part of the district within the rivers has an elevation of 500 feet. The part stretching along the left bank of the Ganges has doubtless a less elevation, in consequence of the general slope of the surface to the south-east. The country to the right of the same river, and extending towards the rugged region of Rewah, must have some more elevated spots. The district is well furnished with the means of irrigation, as, in addition to those offered by watercourses and tanks, there are 60,000 wells, of which 9,000 are pukka, or lined with brick. The climate of this district is considered more moist than that of the adjacent tracts; rains are more frequent, and the hot winds thereby mitigated. The vegetation likewise is more luxuriant. The country is overspread with a vigorous growth of timber, and yields an abundant return to the cultivator of even the choicest products of the European garden. The British residents in the district are now making zealous and successful efforts for the improvement of agriculture. The best kinds of maize, cotton, and flax, have been introduced. Some dye-stuffs, besides indigo, are cultivated to considerable extent, especially kussum, or kusumtha (Carthamus tinctorius), or safflower, for yielding a bright orange or deep red colour. The most important articles of traffic are salt, cotton, indigo, and sugar. The population, according to the census of 1853, amounts to 1,379,788. A comparison with the area shows that the average number of persons to each square mile rather exceeds 490. The towns and villages, classified according to population, are as follow:—Number containing less than 1,000 inhabitants, 3,319; ditto more than 1,000, and less than 5,000, 233; ditto more than 5,000, 3. The East-Indian Railway traverses the district, which is also intersected by the great trunk road from Calcutta to the North-Western Provinces, proceeding through Benares, and thence north-westerly along the left bank of the Ganges to Allahabad, having previously crossed the river close to it. From Allahabad it proceeds still in a north-westerly direction nearly parallel to the Ganges, and at a short distance from its right bank crosses the north-western frontier of the district of Allahabad to Futtehpore. The earlier history of this province is involved in the obscurity which hangs over the history of India generally until a comparatively recent period. In 1194 it was subjugated by the Patans under Mohamed Shahab-ud-deen, of Ghor, and wrested from that race by Baber about 1529. On the dismemberment of the empire of Delhi it became a field of contention, on which the emperor, the vizier of Oude, the English, and the Mahrattas acted conspicuous parts. In the arrangements of the English with the emperor, a portion of this province was assigned for the support of the latter; but on that prince throwing himself into the hands of the Mahrattas, the territory was regarded as having escheated, and was thereupon transferred to the vizier, from whom, under the treaty of 1801, it passed with other districts to the East-India Company.

ALLAHABAD, the principal place of the district of the same name, is situate at the south-eastern extremity of the Doab, on the tongue of land formed by the confluence of the Ganges and Jumna rivers, the latter of which is here crossed by the East-Indian Railway. The fort on the east and south rises directly from the banks of the confluent rivers, which render it nearly impregnable in that direction. It is about 2,500 yards in circuit, is built of red stone, and, according to Von Orlich, is now "a bastioned quinquangle; the ancient walls with semicircular bastions face the two streams; the land side is quite regular, and consists of two bastions, and a half-bastion with three ravelins," and stands higher than any ground in face of it. Heber observes, "It has been a very noble castle, but has suffered in its external appearance as much as it has probably gained in strength by the modernization which it has undergone from its present masters, its lofty towers being pruned down into bastions and cavaliers, and its high stone ramparts topped with turf parapets, and obscured by a green sloping glacis. It is still, however, a striking place; and its principal gate, surmounted by a dome with a wide hall beneath, surrounded by arcades and galleries, and ornamented with rude but glowing paintings, is the noblest entrance I ever saw to a place of arms." The exterior has been modernized in the Italian style, but the interior retains its antique and striking character. An ancient and spacious palace, overlooking the Jumna, has been fitted up for the residence of the superior officers; and the rest of the Europeans of the garrison are lodged in well-constructed barracks. The arsenal, situate in the fort, is one of the largest in India; it contains arms for 30,000 men, and thirty pieces of cannon. Altogether it is a place of great strength, probably impregnable to native powers, and requiring for its reduction a regular siege according to European tactics. It is said to have cost 1,750,000*l*. Among the finest structures of Allahabad, is that called the Serai of Khusru, the ill-fated son of Jehangir. It is a fine quadrangle surrounded by an embattled wall, along the inside of which are a series of lodges for the gratuitous reception of travellers. Adjoining is a garden or pleasure-ground, containing some fine old mango-trees, and three mausoleums, in a rich, magnificent, yet solemn style of architecture. Heber states that they were raised over two princes and a princess of the imperial family, but does not specify their names. In the middle of the fort stands an antique stone column, popularly styled *Gada*, or Club of Bhim Sen, a hero who figures in the romantic legends of Hindostan. It is mentioned by Tieffenthaler as standing in his time; was pulled down during some alterations made in the fort in 1798, and has lately been replaced. The length is forty-two feet seven inches; the shape nearly cylindrical, yet slightly tapering, the lower diameter being three feet two and a quarter inches; the upper, two feet two inches. It bears two Sanskrit inscriptions of considerable length, and obviously of remote antiquity; but notwithstanding the endeavours of Prinsep, Troyer, and Mill, no certain conclusion can be drawn as to their date. The present town of Allahabad is situate principally west of the fort, and extending along the Jumna. Its position is advantageous, but it is, nevertheless, an ill-built, poverty-stricken place. Heber observes, "The city of Allahabad is small, with very poor houses and narrow irregular streets, and confined to the banks of the Jumna." The Jumma Masjit, or great mosque, is a solid, stately building, but without much ornament. It is advantageously situate on the banks of the Jumna, and on one side adjoins the city, on the other an esplanade before the glacis of the fort. After the conquest of the province by the East-India Company, it was fitted up as a residence of the general of the station; subsequently, to the purposes of an assembly-room; and ultimately restored to its former destination. The Mussulmans, however, regarding it as polluted, displayed a contemptuous indifference on the subject. Below the fort is a subterraneous temple, entered by a long passage sloping downwards. Its shape is square, and the roof supported by pillars; in the middle is a linga or phallic emblem, and at one end a dead forked tree, continually watered with great care by the attendant priests, who maintain that it still retains its sap and vitality; but Tieffenthaler describes it as leafless in his time, a century ago. The place is a close, loathsome den, rendered more hideous by obscene and monstrous figures of Mahadeva, Ganesh, and other objects of worship; and is damp from water trickling from its rocky walls. This insignificant moisture is alleged by the superstitious to be the outlet of the river Sarasvati, which is lost in the sands near Thannesur, in Sirhind, upwards of 400 miles to the north-west. Wilford observes: "The confluence of the Ganga and Yamuna [Ganges and Jumna] at Prayaga is called Triveni by the Pauranics, because three rivers are supposed to meet there; but the third is by no means obvious to the sight. It is the famous Sarasvati, which comes out of the hills to the west of the Yamuna, passes close to Thaneser, loses itself in the great sandy desert, and reappears at Prayag, humbly oozing from one of the towers of the fort, as if ashamed of herself. Indeed she may blush at her own imprudence, for she is the goddess of learning and knowledge, and was then coming down the country with a book in her hand, when she entered the sandy desert, and was unexpectedly assailed by numerous demons with frightful countenances, making a dreadful noise. Ashamed of her own want of forethought, she sank into the ground, and reappeared at Prayaga or Allahabad." Close to the wall of the fort, outside this revered cavern, is the actual confluence of the Jumna and Ganges, visited by great numbers of pilgrims of both sexes, anxious to bathe in the purifying waters. Formerly it was not uncommon for devotees of either sex to cause earthen vessels to be fastened round their waists or to their feet, and having proceeded in a boat to the middle of the stream, then precipitate themselves, to rise no more, supposing that by this self-immolation they secured eternal bliss. At present the meetings here appear to have abated somewhat of their more gloomy and murderous character. According to the description of Skinner, who visited the place on the 14th of December, 1826, "it was a religious fair, and took place on the very spot of the confluence of the two streams. There did not seem to me to be anything sold; bathing and praying were the great occupations. A great number of platforms, about eight or ten feet square, with long legs to them, stood in the water; they had canopies above them, and were as booths in English fairs, for in them people frequently sat as if to rest themselves after having waded through the river to reach them. The Brahmins, however, seemed to be the peculiar masters of each, for they never moved from their seats; but occupying the centre, with their rosaries in their hands, remained at their posts to administer to the spiritual wants of those who visited them. It was a very pretty scene; the women had their holiday clothes on, and shone in rosy scarfs among the crowd." The military cantonment is on the north-west side of the fort, in a delightful situation, having some picturesque variety of surface, and being finely wooded. This town is the seat of the civil establishment for the district of Allahabad, which consists of the usual functionaries, European and native. The population of the city and suburbs, according to the census of 1853, amounts to 72,093. There is reason to conclude that the prosperity of the place is on the advance, in part, probably, from the growing importance of the North-West Provinces, and partly from the introduction of steam-navigation on the Upper Ganges. In 1839 a grant from government of 5,000 rupees was sanctioned to aid in the erection of a church, the remaining funds to be supplied by private subscription.

Some have on very slender grounds maintained this place to be the Palibothra of Greek and Roman geographers, but the best authorities consider that city identical with Patna. Probably the first authentic mention of it is by Baber, who styles it Piag. The fort was built by Akber, who changed the name of the city to Allahabad. On the dismemberment of the empire of Delhi, it was seized in 1753 by Safder Jang, the vizier of Oude. It had three years previously (1750) been sacked by the Patans of Furruckabad. In 1765 it was taken by the British, and assigned as the residence of Shah Alum, the titular emperor of Delhi, who was, however, so infatuated as to leave this place of refuge in 1771. In consequence it was resumed by the donors, and transferred to the nawaub of Oude by the treaty of 1773. In 1801 it was ceded by the nawaub to the East-India Company. So completely was it ruined, either by violence or gradual decay, that Hodges, who visited it in 1782, describes it as consisting merely of thatched huts, with scarcely a vestige of any considerable house remaining. Its desolation, as well as the great number of fakirs, or mendicants under religious garb, who resort to it, caused it to be called Fakirabad. Elevation above the sea about 340 feet. Distance N.W. from Calcutta by land 496 miles; in the same direction from Benares, 75; S.E. from Lucknow, 128; in similar direction from Cawnpore, 124; from Calpee, 153; from Agra *viâ* Etawa, 288, or by grand trunk road, 302; from Delhi, 391. Lat. 25° 26′, long. 81° 55′.

ALLAPOOR, in the British district of Budaon, lieut.-gov. of the N.W. Provinces, a town on the route from Shahabad to Budaon, ten miles south-east of the latter. Lat. 27° 55′, long. 79° 20′.

ALLATORI, in the British district of Trichinopoly, presidency of Madras, a town on the route from Trichinopoly to Seringapatam, eight miles west of the former. Lat. 10° 49′, long. 78° 39′.

ALLEEGUNJE, in the British district of Purneah, lieut.-gov. of Bengal, a town on the right bank of the river Ronkee, forty miles north of Purneah. Lat. 26° 19′, long. 87° 48′.

ALLEE MOHUN, ALLEERAJPOOR, or RAJPOOR ALI.—A small district in Malwa, under the political superintendence of the Governor-General's resident at Indore. It lies between lat. 22° 2′ and 22° 30′, long. 74° 16′ and 74° 44′, and extends from north to south about thirty-four miles; its extreme breadth from east to west being about thirty-two. Its area is 708 square miles. The political connection between the British government and Allee Mohun commenced by the interposition of the former, for the purpose of rendering less humiliating the nature of the rajah's dependence on the neighbouring state of Dhar. Allee Mohun was an ancient tributary of the rulers of Dhar, and the tribute had been commuted by a cession of certain customs-duties which were collected by the officers of the Dhar state. The authority thus exercised in Allee Mohun by the servants of a foreign government was not only attended with considerable inconvenience, but was calculated to lessen the dignity of the rajah in the estimation of his own subjects; and, at his request, an arrangement was made in 1821, under which the Dhar state transferred to the British government its right to the Allee Mohun tribute, in consideration of an equivalent, and the rajah of Allee Mohun agreed to collect the duties, and to pay to the British government an annual sum, which amounts to 12,000 rupees. The rajah is a Hindoo. The population was estimated by Malcolm at 69,384. The revenue appears to have fluctuated within thirty years, according to the management. The latest account gives it at 35,000 rupees, or 3,500*l*. The military establishment consists but of thirty horsemen and 100 sebundies.

ALLEE MOHUN.—A town in Malwa, the chief place of the petty district of the same name, but not the place of residence of the present rajah, who has fixed his abode at Rajpoor. Lat. 22° 12′, long. 74° 24′.

ALLEH, in the British district of Poonah, presidency of Bombay, a town on the left bank of the Kokree river, fifty miles north of Poonah. Lat. 19° 11′, long. 74° 5′.

ALLEHGUNJ, in the British district of Furruckabad, lieut.-gov. of the N.W. Provinces, a town on the left bank of the Ramgunga river, eleven miles N.E. of Furruckabad. Allehgunj contains 5,383 inhabitants. Lat. 27° 33′, long. 79° 45′.

ALLEMBADY.—See ALAMBARAI.

ALLIGAUM.—A town situate on the left bank of the river Bheema, in the British district of Ahmednuggur, presidency of Bombay. Soon after the acquisition of the Deccan by the British, it was observed that the horses of the south of India were rapidly declining in respect to the qualities constituting the perfection of the animal. In the hope of restoring the former character of the Deccan breed, a government stud was established in this place in 1827; but though some good specimens were occasionally turned out, the majority proved greatly inferior to the horses imported from the Persian Gulf and the Cape. The establishment was nevertheless maintained for a series of years. Additional experience, however, resulted only in continued disappointment, and at length, in 1842, all hope of ultimate success being then abandoned, the stud was ordered to be abolished. Distant east from Poonah thirty-two miles. Lat. 18° 35′, long. 74° 23′.

ALLIGAUM, in Hyderabad, or territory of the Nizam, a town near the northern frontier, towards the British district Saugor and Nerbudda, on the northern declivity of the range of mountains bounding the valley of the Taptee on the south. Distance from Ellichpoor, south-west, 71 miles; Aurungabad, north-east, 100. Lat. 20° 24′, long. 76° 53′.

ALLIPOOR.—A town in the territory of Nagpore, distant south-west from Nagpore 50 miles. Lat. 20° 33′, long. 78° 44′.

ALLIYARKA TANDA, in the British district of Hyderabad, province of Scinde, a town on the route from Hyderabad to Oomerkote. It is situate at the intersection of the two great routes from Hyderabad eastward, and from Cutch to Upper Scinde and the Punjaub. It has some manufactures, principally in cotton and dyeing. Population 5,000. Lat. 25° 27′, long. 68° 48′.

ALLOOR.—A town in the territory of Nagpore, distant south-east fram Nagpore 170 miles. Lat. 19° 49′, long. 81° 20′.

ALLOOR.—A town in Hyderabad, or dominions of the Nizam, distant west from Hyderabad 29 miles. Lat. 17° 20′, long. 78° 8′.

ALLOWALLEEA.—A title belonging to certain Seik chiefs, whose possessions on the left bank of the Sutlej were confiscated by the British government in 1848, in consequence of the non-performance of their feudatory obligations during the Lahore war.

ALLUMPOOR, in the British district of Midnapoor, lieut.-gov. of Bengal, a town 30 miles north-west of Midnapoor. Lat. 22° 30′, long. 86° 57′.

ALLYGUNJ.—See ULLEEGUNJE.

ALLYGURH.—A British district under the lieut.-gov. of the N.W. Provinces. It is bounded on the north by the British district Bolundshuhur; on the east by the British districts of Budaon and Mynpooree; on the south by the British districts of Mynpooree and Muttra; and on the west by the British districts Muttra and Goorgaon. It lies between lat. 27° 27′—28° 11′, long. 77° 32′—78° 47′, and embraces an area of 2,149 square miles. Like the rest of the Doab between the Jumna and the Ganges, this district is generally level; but there is a prolonged elevation of surface in the centre, between the two great rivers. The crest of this elevation slopes to the south-east, as indicated by the respective amounts of altitude on the course of the Ganges Canal, which is laid down along the ridge with a view to diffusing more effectually the benefits of irrigation on each side of it. The staple alimentary crops are wheat, barley, millet, and pulse: rice is little cultivated. The chief commercial crops are indigo, cotton, tobacco, and sugar. The population, according to the census of 1853, amounts to 1,134,565. The following classification of the towns and villages of the district is obtained from the official statement prepared in 1853.—Number containing less than 1,000 inhabitants, 1,747; ditto more than 1,000 and less than 5,000, 214; ditto more than 5,000 and less than 10,000, 8; ditto more than 10,000 and less than 50,000, 3; ditto more than 50,000, 1.

At the commencement of the present century this territory was the principal seat of the short-lived power of the French adventurer Perron. Perron's force being either dispersed or destroyed in the campaign of 1803 (principally by the events of the siege of Allyghur and the battle of Delhi), its leader surrendered to the British. In 1804 the district suffered from the devastating incursion of Holkar, the Mahratta chief, who was, however, severely chastised, suffering the loss of his host of cavalry, which was surprised and cut to pieces by the British, under General Lake, at Furruckabad. An incursion, made in the next year by Ameer Khan the Patan, had nearly a similar result; that freebooter losing nearly all his followers, and himself escaping with difficulty across the Jumna. The widely-spread dangers which threatened the British power in India at the commencement of the Pindarree and Mahratta war, in 1817, encouraged, among others, the chief of Hatrass, in this district, to revolt; but a vigorous bombardment of a few hours so shattered the place, that after a great number of its defenders were destroyed, a part of the survivors took to flight, and the rest surrendered the fortress, which was immediately dismantled. A complete pacification of the district speedily ensued.

ALLYGURH.—A fort in the British district of the same name, situate near the route from Agra to Delhi, and fifty-five miles north of the former place. The vicinity is interspersed with marshes and shallow pieces of water, which become so much swollen during the rains as to have rendered the place inaccessible, and consequently secure from attack, at that season. The outline of the works at the time of the capture by the British was a polygon, of probably ten sides, having at each angle a bastion, with a renny or fausse-braie, well provided with cannon. Outside this line of defence was a ditch, above 100 feet wide, thirty feet deep from the top of the excavation, and having ten feet of water. Across this ditch was no passage but by a narrow causeway, defended by a traverse, mounted with three six-pounders. Perron, the French adventurer, who held the fort with a Mahratta force, made demonstrations, at the head of about 20,000 men, of an intention to give battle under its walls; but after a brief and weak resistance, fled to Agra. At daylight on the 4th September, 1803, the British storming party took the traverse before its guns could be discharged, and hurrying forward a twelve-pounder, blew in the first gate, being exposed during this operation to a destructive fire; and here the assailants suffered their chief loss. The inner gates were subsequently blown in; and entrance having been finally made by forcing the wicket of another, the ramparts were mounted, and the place taken possession of after a vigorous defence of an hour, during which fifty-nine of the assailants were killed (including six officers), and 206 wounded. Above 2,000 of the garrison fell, and many more, who had swum the ditch, were destroyed by the British cavalry, in attempting to fly across the country. A medal, commemorative of the storming of the fort, was struck in London in the year 1851, and presented, under the sanction of the Queen, to the surviving officers and soldiers who took part in its capture. The civil and fiscal establishments, as well as the military cantonment and bazaar, are located towards Coel, a short distance south of the fort. In 1844 a proposal for converting the fort of Allyghur into a jail for 1,400 prisoners was sanctioned; but in 1847, in consequence of the alleged unhealthiness of the fort, arising as well from its construction as its position, it was determined to abandon the undertaking. Elevation above the sea 740 feet. Distance S.E. from Delhi 84 miles; N.W. from Calcutta 803. Lat. 27° 56′, long. 78° 8′.

ALLYPOOR, in the British district of Futtehpoor, lieut.-gov. of the N.W. Provinces, a village on the route from Cawnpore to the town of Futtehpoor, and six miles north-west of the latter. The road in this part of the route is good; the country level, and partially cultivated. Lat. 25° 57′, long. 80° 50′.

ALLYPOORA, or ALIPORA, in Bundelcund, a jaghire or feudal possession, named after its principal place. It lies between lat. 25° 8′—25° 21′, long. 79° 14′—79° 24′. It is bounded on the north by the British district Humerpoor; on the east and south by the lapsed state of Jeitpore; and on the west by the native state of Jhansee; and is estimated "to comprise an area of eighty-five square miles, and to contain twenty-eight villages, with a population of 9,000 souls." The revenue of the jaghire is estimated at 45,000 rupees (4,500*l.*), and the jaghiredar, or dewan as he is called, is stated to maintain a small force of seventy-five infantry. The grant was made in 1808 to the chief found by the British authorities in possession, and whose descendant now holds the jaghire.

ALLYPOORA, or ALIPORA, in Bundelcund, the principal place of the jaghire or feudal possession of that name, situate on the route from Gwalior to Chutterpore, 100 miles S.E. of the former, 24 N.W. of the latter. Lat. 25° 10′, long. 79° 24′.

ALLYPOOR PUTTEE, in the British district of Mynpooree, lieut.-gov. of the N.W. Provinces, a town on the route from Cawnpoor to Coel, 76 miles south-east of the latter. Lat. 27° 20′, long. 79° 13′.

ALMACOOR, in the British district of Kurnool, presidency of Madras, a town on the route from Kurnool to Guntoor, 38 miles east of the former. Lat. 15° 52′, long. 78° 40′.

ALMELEH, in the British district of Sholapoor, presidency of Bombay, a town situate five miles from the right bank of the river Beemah, forty-four miles south-east of Sholapoor. Lat. 17° 5′, long. 76° 16′.

ALMORA, the principal place of the British district of Kumaon, within the territories subject to the lieut.-gov. of the N.W. Provinces, is situate on the crest of a ridge which runs from east to west, and consists principally of one street, three-quarters of a mile long, forming two bazaars, divided from each other by Fort Almora, and by the site of the ancient palace of the rajahs of Kumaon, now occupied by a jail. Detached houses, chiefly inhabited by Europeans and Brahmins, are scattered along each face of the mountain below the town. The houses have each a ground story of stone, and that part in the trading quarter of the town is occupied by a shop. The upper stories, of which there are sometimes two, are constructed of timber, and are covered with a sloping roof of heavy grey slate, on which small stacks of hay are sometimes piled for winter consumption. The stone-built story is generally whitewashed, and tricked out with grotesque paintings. The main street, secured by a gate at each end, has a natural pavement of slate-rock, and is kept in very neat order. At the western extremity, and immediately adjoining the town, are the lines of the regular troops, and in the rear of them the fortification called Fort Moira. The defence on the north-eastern side is a small martello tower called St. Mark's. There are several Hindoo temples, but none meriting particular notice. The Cutcherry, or public office of the district, is at Almora, but the houses of the civil officers are at Hawelbagh, five miles north of it, and there the provincial battalion is stationed. This town, which had been fast decaying under the Goorkha sway, has much improved since it has become a British station. At Sittolee, close to Almora, was fought the battle which decided the fate of the war between the British and the Goorkhas. In advancing to the attack, the British had to cross by ford the river Kosila, flowing at the bottom of a deep ravine. Having accomplished the passage, the heights and town of Almora were successively carried in the most rapid and brilliant manner, and the result was the conclusion of a convention, by which the whole of the district of Kumaon was ceded to the British. Elevation above the sea, of Fort Moira, 5,520 feet; of the town, 5,337. Distance N.W. from Calcutta, by Lucknow and Bareilly, 910 miles. Lat. 29° 35′, long. 79° 42′.

ALOT.—A town of Malwa, in the native state of Dewas, distant north from Oojein thirty-two miles. Lat. 23° 44′, long. 75° 34′.

ALSIR, in the Rajpoot state of Bikaneer, a small town situate about two miles north of the route from Ruttungurh to the town of Bikaneer, and sixty-five miles east of the latter. Lat. 27° 56′, long. 74° 24′.

ALUKNUNDA.—A river in the territory of British Gurhwal, formed by the junction of two considerable streams; the Doulee, flowing from the north-east; the Vishnoo or Bishenganga, from the north-west. The confluence of those rivers is at Vishnooprag, in lat. 30° 33′, long. 79° 38′, where, at the end of May, when the mountain-streams are fullest, Raper found the Doulee to have a breadth of about thirty-five or forty yards, with a rapid current, and the Vishnoo a breadth of twenty-five or thirty yards, also with a rapid current. The elevation of the confluence above the sea is 4,743 feet. The Aluknunda, or united stream, flows south-westward for thirty-four miles to Kurnprag, where it on the left side receives the Pindur, a considerable river flowing from the east. From that confluence it flows westward sixteen miles to Roodurprag, where on the right side it receives the Mundagnee, another considerable river, having a direction from north to south, and coming from the celebrated fane of Kedarnath. It thence takes a direction south-westward for thirty miles, passing by Sireenuggur, the capital of Gurhwal, to Deoprag, where on the right side it is joined by the Bhageerettee; the stream from this confluence downwards being called the Ganges. The Bhageerettee rushes with great force and rapidity down a steep declivity, roaring and foaming over large rocks scattered over its bed. Its breadth is 112 feet, and it rises forty feet during the melting of the snow. The Aluknunda, flowing with a smooth unruffled surface, gently winds round the point of confluence. It is 142 feet in breadth, and rises forty-six feet at the same period. The breadth of the united stream is 240 feet. The Aluknunda abounds with fine fish, some of which, of the rohu (Cyprinus denticulatus) species, are four or five feet in length; another kind, called soher, a beautiful and finely-flavoured fish, attains the length of six or seven feet. Gold in small quantities has been obtained by searching the sands of this river; but the remuneration resulting has been so scanty that the search is nearly discontinued.

ALUMKHAN, in the Daman division of the Punjab, a town situated on the right bank of the Indus, distant north-west from Mooltan forty-eight miles. Lat. 30° 25′, long. 70° 49′.

ALUMPARVA, in the British district of Chingleput, presidency of Madras, a town on the coast of Coromandel, thirty miles south of the town of Chingleput. Lat. 12° 17′, long. 80° 6′.

ALUMPOOR.—A town in Hyderabad, or dominions of the Nizam, situated on the left bank of the Toongabudra, distant east from Kurnool seven miles. Lat. 15° 52′, long. 78° 11′.

ALUNG.—A town in the Guicowar's possessions, in the peninsula of Kattywar, under the political management of the presidency of Bombay, distant south from Gogo twenty miles. Lat. 21° 23′, long. 72° 9′.

ALUNIAWAS, in the Rajpoot state of Joudpore, a village on the route from the town of Joudpore to that of Ajmeer, and twenty-two miles west of the latter. It has 600 houses, the inhabitants of which are of notoriously bad character. Lat. 26° 32′, long. 74° 24′.

ALVAR TINNEVELLY, in the British district of Tinnevelly, presidency of Madras, a town on the right bank of the river Chindinthoora, nineteen miles south east of Tinnevelly. Lat. 8° 36′, long. 78°.

ALWUR, or MACHERY.—A Rajpoot state under the control of the Governor-General's agent for the states of Rajpootana. Tijarra included, it may be described as bounded on the north by the British district of Goorgaon and the native district of Kot Quasin; on the east by Goorgaon and the territory of Bhurtpore; on the south by the territory of Jeypore; on the west by the same territory and that of Jhujhur; and lies between lat. 27° 4′—28° 13′, long. 76° 7′—77° 14′. It is about eighty miles in length from north to south, and sixty-five in breadth. Its area is stated to be 3,573 square miles. The valley into which falls the principal drainage of this tract may, on satisfactory grounds, be taken to have an elevation of at least 900 feet above the sea. Alwur fort is 1,200 feet above the more depressed tracts, or more than 2,000 above the level of the sea. The hills for the most part form continuous ranges, inclosing valleys, or rather plains, of small extent, from which in many places insulated peaks and clusters of peaks rise abruptly, each suggesting by its sharp outline the notion of a tooth. Each of these eminences is usually surmounted by a small fort. The inhabitants, under the name of Mewatti, are described by Rennell as "most savage and brutal." Fraser, who about the year 1820 traversed the country through almost its whole length, and Jacquemont, who took nearly the same route in 1832, received no molestation, though the latter appears to have been rather discountenanced by the rajah, in accordance with his then usual conduct towards Europeans. The marked displeasure which the Governor-General and other British authorities have shown to the Rao Raja, in consequence of this ostentatiously-displayed aversion to the natives of Europe, appears to have produced an amendment in his conduct, as, in 1843, he acted with great politeness to Von Orlich, and cordially invited him to visit Alwur. The population of the Alwur state is computed at 280,000. The annual revenue of the Rao Raja is estimated by Colonel Sutherland at 180,000*l.*; but he has been constrained by the British government, with reference to an engagement concluded in 1826, to grant an annual allowance, and certain districts in Tijarra, to an illegitimate son of his uncle and predecessor. The grant, however, is understood to have lapsed, on the failure of direct heirs on the part of the chief of Tijarra. Jacquemont, who saw a muster of the troops or followers of the Rao Raja, computed their number at 30,000: of these not more than a fourth had arms, such as they were, the best of them being muskets rejected from the British service as damaged. The men, generally natives of Oude, were ill paid, and in all respects badly treated. Never had he seen more wretched troops; and he adds, that a few hundred horsemen of Runjeet Singh would find no difficulty in putting them all to the sword. It is ascertained, however, from official documents, that the entire force of the rajah amounts to about 4,000 cavalry and 3,000 infantry, irrespective of sebundies employed for the purposes of police and the collection of the revenue. Of these there are about 8,000. The rajah is also stated to possess about 360 cannon (50 of them, however, unserviceable), and 500 camel-swivels. He is bound to assist the East-India Company with his entire force in the event of war.

The Mewattis played a prominent and important part in the time of the early Mahomedan kings of Delhi, making predatory inroads even to the gates of their capital, until the fearful chastisement inflicted, as already mentioned, by Gheias-ood-deen Bulbun, in 1265. Early in the fifteenth century they ventured again to brave the power of the sovereigns of Delhi, but, in 1429, they were subdued by Mobarik Shah. About 1720, the rajah of Amber, or Jeypore, taking advantage of the distracted state of the empire of Delhi, wrested from it several possessions, including Mewat, or the country of the Mewattis, of which the present state of Alwur, or Macherry, is part. Pertaub Singh, who held Macherry as a jaghire from the ruler of Jeypore, assisted Nujuf Khan, the ostensible commander-in-chief of the emperor of Delhi, to expel the Jauts from Agra in 1774, and on that event received an imperial sunnud, or grant, constituting him Rao Raja of Macherry, to be held directly from the crown, and independently of Jeypore. The Rao Raja soon after wrested the fort of Alwur, and some other places, from the rajah of Bhurtpore. Towards the close of the last century, nearly the whole territory was overrun by the Mahrattas, who conferred some parts of it on the well-known adventurer George Thomas, and employed him in enforcing their power over the rest. On the 1st November, 1803, this territory was the scene of a signal triumph of the British arms, the particulars of which will be found under the article Laswaree. On the conclusion of peace in 1803, Tijarra and some other districts were made over by the British government to the Rao Raja of Macherry, in consideration of services performed during the war, and a treaty concluded between him and the East-India Company. In the war with the Mahratta leader Holkar, the predatory attacks of the Mewattis caused some inconvenience and loss to the army of Lord Lake. In spite of every precaution, they constantly succeeded in making booty of numbers of camels and horses, and murdering such men as ventured from the camps singly or in small parties. Still, notwithstanding the lawlessness of these people, the conduct of their rajah was considered so satisfactory to the British government, that, in 1805, it granted to him an additional territory out of that resumed from the rajah of Bhurtpore, in consequence of his treachery during the war with Holkar. In many instances, however, the Rao Rajas, though deeply indebted to the generosity of the British authorities, have shown little cordiality towards their benefactors, and occasionally energetic measures have been necessary to coerce or chastise them. The Rao Raja having, in 1808, made an embankment across the Mahnas Ny, or stream running by Laswaree, and thus prevented the water from flowing into the Bhurtpoor territory, where it served extensive purposes of irrigation, the British government interfered, but the dispute, as already mentioned, was not finally settled till after the lapse of many years. In 1812, the Rao Raja commenced hostilities against the state of Jeypore, and seized two forts, with the territory belonging to them, though such aggression was in direct contravention of his treaty with the East-India Company; nor did he, when required, make restitution, until a British force advanced within a day's march of the capital, when he reluctantly yielded. In 1826, Lord Combermere marched against Alwur, in consequence of the refusal of that state to give up certain persons charged with an attempt to assassinate Ahmed Buksh Khan, the nawaub of Ferozpore; but the Rao Raja, by ultimate though somewhat tardy compliance, averted the danger with which he was threatened. In 1831, discovery was made of a negotiation by which the Rao Raja preposterously sought to become anew the vassal of the weak state of Jeypore, and soon after his refusal to redress some wrongs done to the nawaub of Ferozpore, was punished by the infliction of a fine by the British government.

ALWUR.—The capital of the Rajpoot state of that name, situate at the base of a rocky range of quartz and slate, and estimated by Fraser to rise 1,200 feet above the adjacent country. It is an ill-built town, of no great size, and is surrounded by a wretched mud wall, with gates defended by bastions. Within the inclosure are temples, erected by the Hindoo inhabitants, but in a style imitated from Mahomedan structures. The palace of Rao Raja, which is surrounded by a small garden, is of cubical shape, having its wall pierced with a great number of small windows, and covered with rude and glaring paintings, representing the fights of elephants, processions of the chief and his court, and scenes drawn from Hindoo mythology. On the summit of the mountain is a fort, built in a very ornamental style, and serving as a retreat for the Rao Raja in the sultry season, and as a place of refuge in time of danger. The wall of the town, extending up the steep side of the mountain, incloses also the fort. At the foot of the mountain a very deep tank was excavated by the late Rao Raja, and near it he built a pavilion of white marble, of great size, and in a very elegant and highly finished style. Troops may obtain supplies and water in abundance here. Distance S.W. from Delhi, by Ferozpore 110 miles, by Rewari 108; N.W. from Calcutta, *viâ* Muttra, Agra, Etawah, and Allahabad, 900 miles. Lat. 27° 34′, long. 76° 40′.

ALYUNNOOR, in the British district of Madura, presidency of Madras, a town on the left bank of the river Goondar, twenty-two miles west of Ramnad. Lat. 9° 17′, long. 78° 32′.

AMAIN, or AMYNE, in the territory of Gwalior, or possessions of Scindia's family, a town near the left bank of the river Sindh, forty miles E. of Gwalior fort, sixty-five W. of Calpee. Lat. 26° 20′, long. 78° 52′.

AMAIT, in the Rajpoot state of Oodeypore or Mewar, a town on the route from Neemuch to Joudpore, ninety miles N.W. of former, 102 S.E. of latter. It is situate in a fine valley, nearly surrounded by hills; is walled, and has a good bazaar. Lat. 25° 15′, long. 73° 58′.

AMALLAPOORUM, in the British district of Rajahmundry, presidency of Madras, a town in the delta of the Godavery river, twenty-four miles S.W. of Coringa. Lat. 16° 34′, long. 82° 4′.

AMANIGANJ, in the district of Sultanpoor, territory of Oude, a village on the route from Lucknow cantonment to Partabgarh, seventy miles south-east of the former, forty north-west of the latter. About 500 people frequent the market held here, and much cotton is purchased from traders, who bring it on bullocks or carts. Water is abundant, and supplies may be had. The road in this part of the route is good. Butter states the population at 300, all Hindoos. Lat. 26° 24′, long. 81° 36′.

AMARAH, in the territory of Oude, district of Bainswarra, a village near the left bank of the Ganges, on the route from Cawnpore to Pertabgurh, thirty-nine miles south-east of the former. Lat. 26° 4′, long. 80° 56′.

AMARAKANTAK, in the British district of Ramgurh, territory of Saugor and Nerbudda, under the lieut.-gov. of the N.W. Provinces, a famous Hindoo shrine on a jungly table-land, crowning a mountain of considerable elevation. According to the account received by Blunt from some intelligent Brahmins who had visited the temple, it is situate in the midst of the table-land, and is a building about forty feet high, containing a great number of images, mostly representing Bhavani or Parbati, considered by the Brahmins as the consort of Siva, and worshipped here with unusual fervour. Close to the temple is a basin, inclosed with masonry, and about eight yards long and six wide, whence flows water, considered by the natives the head of the Nerbudda; and according to an improbable statement, the head-water of the Son issues from the same basin, in an opposite direction. According to the more probable account of Tieffenthaler, the Son rises half a mile from the basin. This place is one of considerable resort for Hindoo pilgrims, though the surrounding country is in general a wild and nearly pathless jungle, regarded by the natives as the "abode only of wild beasts, demons, and savage Goonds." The spot, formerly the subject of conflicting claims, was adjudged within the British territory, in 1826, by the treaty of Nagpore. Though only 120 miles south-east of the British station of Jubbulpore, it has been so imperfectly explored, that no tolerable approximation has been made to ascertain its elevation above the sea. According to one estimate, it is 5,000; according to another, more probable, 3,500 feet. The height, however, is sufficient to render the climate much cooler than in the country about Jubbulpore, which has an average elevation of 1,500 feet above the sea. At Amarakantak the temperature seldom exceeds 95° at the hottest time of the year. Lat. 22° 40′, long. 81° 50′.

AMARAPOORA.—See UMMERAPOORA.

AMARPATAN.—A town in the native state of Rewah or Baghelcund, distant south-west from Rewah twenty-four miles. Lat. 24° 18′, long. 81° 3′.

AMARPOOR.—A town in the native state of Nepal, distant south-east from Khatmandoo 113 miles. Lat. 26° 47′, long. 86° 47′.

AMBA.—A town in the native state of Indore, or possessions of Holkar, distant S.W. from Indore ninety-six miles. Lat. 21° 25′, long. 75° 16′.

AMBA.—A river rising on the western declivity of the Western Ghauts, about lat. 18° 40′, long. 73° 23′, and flowing first south-westerly for twenty miles, and then north-westerly thirty, falls into the Indian Ocean about lat. 18° 50′, long. 73°.

AMBA BHOWANNEE.—A town in the Rajpoot state of Oodeypoor or Mewar, distant south-west from Oodeypoor sixty-one miles. Lat. 24° 22′, long. 72° 51′.

AMBAGUR.—A town in the territory of Nagpore, distant north-east from Nagpore thirty-nine miles. Lat. 21° 29′, long. 79° 40′.

AMBAH.—A town in Hyderabad, or dominions of the Nizam, distant N.W. from Hyderabad 167 miles. Lat. 18° 44′, long. 76° 30′.

AMBAITA, or UMBUHTUH, in the British district of Suharunpoor, lieut.-gov. of the N.W. Provinces, a village on the route from Kurnal to Suharunpoor, and fifteen miles south-west of the last-mentioned place. It is situate in a level and cultivated country, well supplied with water. The road in this part of the route is in general very good, but much under water during the rainy season. Distance N. from Calcutta 995 miles. Lat. 29° 51′, long. 77° 24′.

AMBALA.—See UMBALLA.

AMBEANHULLY, in the district of North Canara, presidency of Madras, a village near the Darmany Ghaut, on the road from Dharwar to the port of Coompta, where a toll has been established for the purpose of keeping the road over the ghaut in good repair. Lat. 14° 31′, long. 74° 37′.

AMBER, in the Rajpoot state of Jeypoor, a decayed city four miles north-east of the city of Jeypoor. It is situate on the margin of a small lake, in a valley or rather basin, on all sides surrounded by hills; and its temples, houses, and streets are scattered among numerous ravines, furrowing the slopes of the surrounding hills and opening on the lake. Those streets, intricate and gloomy by site and the shade of numerous trees, are now nearly uninhabited, except by ghastly Hindoo ascetics, with their hair in elf-knots, and their faces covered with chalk, sitting, naked and hideous, amidst tombs and ruined houses. On the slope of the hill, rising west from the margin of the lake, is situate the vast and gorgeous palace of Amber. Its style is massive and solid, resembling those primeval ruins to be seen in Kashmir. Both Jacquemont and Heber observe that they had never viewed a scene so striking, picturesque, and beautiful. Higher up on the slope of the hill, and in general gloomy in the exterior, but crowned with four elegant kiosks, is the zenana; and higher up still, and communicating with the palace by a succession of towers and gateways, is a huge, gloomy castle, with high towers, machicollated battlements, and many loopholes, and rendered more striking by one tall minaret rising above the whole cluster. Besides the purposes of defence, it serves as a treasury and a state prison. Here is a small temple where a goat is daily offered up to Kali, being substituted for the human being sacrificed here every morning (according to local tradition) during the darker and more unmitigated sway of paganism. Amber was the capital of the state of Amber previously to the foundation of the city of Jeypoor by Jai Singh. Lat. 26° 59′, long. 75° 58′.

AMBERWARRA.—A town in the territory of Nagpore, distant north from Nagpore eighty miles. Lat. 22° 20′, long. 79° 10′.

AMBGAON.—A town in the territory of Nagpore, distant S.E. from Nagpore 100 miles. Lat. 19° 56′, long. 80°.

AMBGAON.—A town in the territory of Nagpore, distant E. from Nagpore eighty-five miles. Lat. 21° 24′, long. 80° 28′.

AMBOH.—A town in Keunjur, a native state on the south-west frontier of Bengal, distant S.W. from Balasore fifty-six miles. Lat. 21° 7′, long. 86° 14′.

AMBOOR, in the British district of North Arcot, presidency of Madras, a town on the route from Bangalore to Madras, seventy-nine miles E. of the former. Lat. 12° 47′, long. 78° 47′.

AMBOOR DROOG, in the British district of North Arcot, presidency of Madras, a town on the route from Bangalore to Madras, seventy-five miles E. of the former. Lat. 12° 50′, long. 78° 44′.

AMBORA.—A town in the territory of Nagpore, distant E. from Nagpore thirty-one miles. Lat. 21° 3′, long. 79° 39′.

AMBOYNA.—An island in the Eastern Archipelago, lying to the south-west of the large island of Ceram. It was captured by the British in 1796, and again in 1810, under the vigorous administration of Lord Minto, but finally restored to the Dutch after the peace of Paris, in 1814. The town is in south lat. 3° 35′, long. 128°.

AMEE.—A river rising in the British district of Goruckpore, lieut.-gov. of the N.W. Provinces, in lat. 27° 8′, long. 82° 38′, and taking a south-easterly course, for the first thirty-six miles of which it is "a small marshy channel, which in the rainy season overflows its banks to a considerable extent." At that point, and about lat. 26° 55′, long. 83°, on the right side, it is joined by the Burar or Budh, of nearly equal size; and Buchanan states, "Below the junction the channel is about sixty yards wide, while in the beginning of January the water extended from side to side, and was so deep as to require my elephant to swim. The water was, however, nearly stagnant." Above the junction he describes it as a small river, fed entirely from springs in the plains of this district, but containing a copious supply of water for agricultural purposes. Continuing a south-easterly course, it expands, about seventy miles from its source, into a small lake, and sends off a lateral stream, which, rejoining the lake, forms a triangular island, containing the town of Maguhar, in lat. 26° 41′, long. 83° 10′. Close to this it is crossed by the route from the cantonment of Goruckpoor to Lucknow, and is there so considerable, that the passage must be made by ferry or by temporary bridge. It continues its south-easterly course; and at Onaula, twenty-five miles below this place, "the channel of the Ami may be thirty or forty yards wide, and in March is filled with water from side to side. It is deep, but nearly stagnant." At that place it is crossed by the route from Azimgurh to the cantonment of Goruckpoor, the passage being made by bridge. A few miles below this place, it falls into the Rapti, on the right side, in lat. 26° 30′, long. 83° 29′. Throughout its course it receives numerous small streams, right and left, and by lateral channels communicates with several of the watercourses and small lakes which abound in this level alluvial tract.

AMEENGURH, in the British district of Belgaum, presidency of Bombay, a town on the route from Kuladgee to Moodgul, thirty-two miles south-east of the former. Lat. 16° 2′, long. 76° 1′.

AMEERGONG, in the British district of Bulloah, lieut.-gov. of Bengal, a town twenty-eight miles east from Bulloah. Lat. 22° 55′, long. 91° 21′.

AMEER KHAN'S POSSESSIONS.—See TONK.

AMERCOTE.—See OOMERKOTE.

AMETHI, in the district of Partabgarh, territory of Oude, a town with a small fort. Butter estimates the population at 10,000, all cultivators, and one-fourth Mussulmans. Lat. 26° 8′, long. 82° 2′.

AMHERST, or JUGGOO ISLAND, situate off the southern extremity of the island of Ramree. Its greatest length is about six miles; its width about half as much. At the eastern part of the island there is a harbour, and to the north-west cantonments bearing the name of Haye's Cantonments.

AMHERST.—A town situate at the entrance of the Saluen or Martaban river, in a district of the same name, within the province of Tenasserim, and so called in honour to the governor-general during whose administration it was founded. The site was fixed upon by commissioners employed to choose the most eligible spot in the province for a commercial town. The ceremony of hoisting the British flag and naming the future town took place on the 6th April, 1826. On the following day the ground was measured, plans drawn out, and operations commenced; these movements being accompanied by a proclamation to the native inhabitants, which, after declaring that those who chose to take up their abode in the new town should receive the protection and support of the British government, concluded in these terms: "Whoever desires to come to the new town, or the villages beyond the Saluen river, under the English government, may come from all parts and live happy, and those who do not wish to remain may go where they please without hindrance." The town is protected by a battery built on a promontory commanding the entrance of the harbour. Its situation for a commercial town is eligible, being accessible by ships of any burden, and means of inland communication being afforded by rivers in its vicinity. The harbour, however, though large, is somewhat difficult of access, and during the south-west monsoon dangerous. The surrounding country is dry and elevated, and exposed to the influence of the north-west and south-west monsoons, which renders it remarkably healthy, and suited to European constitutions. There are large forests of good teak in the upper course of the rivers, and this place is the emporium of the trade for timber from these parts. Shortly after its settlement the number of houses amounted to 230, and the population 1,200 souls. It is about 100 miles S.E. of Rangoon, and 30 south of Moulmein. Lat. 16° 4′, long. 97° 40′.

AMILEA, in the British district of Shahjehanpur, lieut.-gov. of the N.W. Provinces, a village on the route from Bareilly to Seetapore, fifty-two miles south-east of the former. Lat. 28° 3′, long. 80° 10′.

AMILEA, in the British district of Etawa, lieut.-gov. of the N.W. Provinces, a village on the route from the cantonment of Etawa to Calpee, and twenty-eight miles south-east of the former. The road in this part of the route is heavy and bad, the country level and cultivated. Lat. 26° 33′, long. 79° 24′.

AMIL GOT.—A village in Sinde, near a ferry over the Indus, on the route from Subzulcote to Shikarpoor, and about twenty miles east of the latter place. It is situate about a mile from the right bank of the Indus, in a fine plain. At this ferry the army of Shah Shoojah, amounting to 6,000 men, passed in January, 1839. The passage occupied seven days. Lat. 27° 53′, long. 68° 56′.

AMINAGUR, in the British district of Pooralia, lieut.-gov. of Bengal, a town on the right bank of the river Coosy, fifty miles north-west of Midnapoor. Lat. 22° 54′, long. 86° 51′.

AMJAR, a small river of Malwa, rises in the Mokundara range, about twelve miles west of the Mokundara pass, and in lat. 24° 37′, long. 75° 44′. It holds a course first north-east for twenty-five miles, and then south-easterly for about fifteen miles, and flowing by the south-western entrance of the Mokundara pass, falls into the Aou about ten miles above its confluence with the Kali Sindh, at Gagroun.

AMJHERRA.—A petty Rajpoot state in Malwa, under the superintendence of the political resident at Indore. It is bounded on the north-east, the east, and south-east, by Dhar; on the south by Dhar and the district of Baug; on the south-west by Allee Rajpoor; and on the north-west by Jabooah. It lies between lat. 22° 16′—22° 47′, long. 74° 40′—75° 15′, and extends from north-east to south-west about forty-two miles, and from south-east to north-west about thirty-three. The area is 584 square miles. In addition to opium, which is extensively cultivated, the staple crops are Indian corn, cotton, gram, sugar-cane, jowar, and bajra. When British supremacy was first established in Malwa, this petty state was labouring beneath a twofold oppression. The pay of the Arab soldiers and other foreign mercenaries had been suffered to fall in arrear, and the rajah consequently found it impossible either to control or to discharge them; while Scindia, under pretence of satisfying his demand for tribute, held military occupation of the country, and inflicted severe exactions upon the inhabitants. From this state of thraldom the state was rescued through the intervention of the British government. By its aid the bands of mercenaries were paid off and dismissed, and the guarantee of the paramount power for the punctual payment of Scindia's tribute (35,000 rupees per annum) was made conditional on the removal of the troops of that chief. Under these auspices the revenues of the state increased from 40,000 rupees in 1819, to 100,000 rupees in 1829, and have subsequently continued at that amount. The military force maintained by the rajah consists of 1,000 infantry; and the fund for the maintenance of the Malwa Bheel corps is aided by a contribution from this state to the extent of 4,000 rupees per annum. The population was estimated many years since at 57,232, and is perhaps now larger; but the administration of the country is not reported in favourable terms.

AMJHERRA, in Malwa, the principal place of the native state of the same name, is situate in an extensive valley inclosed by low hills on all sides except the north, towards which the valley stretches out in open expanse. The small river which runs by the town becomes dry in the hot season, but a fine tank lies to the eastward, where also there is an encamping-ground. According to Malcolm, the town contained in 1820, 500 houses, with good bazaars well supplied. Elevation above the sea 1,890 feet. Distant S.W. from Oojein sixty miles, W. from Dhar twelve miles. Lat. 22° 32′, long. 75° 10′.

AMLA.—A town of Malwa, in the native state of Dhar, distant north from Dhar thirty miles. Lat. 23°, long. 75° 20′.

AMLEE.—A town in the Rajpoot state of Oodeypoor or Mewar, distant N.E. from Oodeypoor sixty miles. Lat. 25° 20′, long. 74° 20′.

AMMANAIKOOR, in the British district of Madura, presidency of Madras, a town on the route from Dindigul to Madura, fifteen miles south of the former. Lat. 10° 22′, long. 77° 59′.

AMMANIMA CHUT, in the British district of Coimbatore, presidency of Madras, a town on the route from Seringapatam to Dindigul, fifty-one miles south of the former. Lat. 11° 44′, long. 77° 3′.

AMNEIR.—A town in the territory of Nagpore, distant N.W. from Nagpore forty-seventy miles. Lat. 21° 23′, long. 78° 29′.

AMOOD, in the British district of Humerpore, lieut.-gov. of the N.W. Provinces, a village on the route by Keitah from Jubbulpore to Calpee, thirty-five miles south-east of the latter. Water is abundant; but supplies must be collected from the surrounding country. Lat. 25° 43′, long. 79° 45′.

AMORHA, in the British district of Goruckpore, lieut.-gov. of the N.W. Provinces, a town, the principal place of the pergunnah of the same name. It is situate on the route from Goruckpore cantonment to the city of Lucknow, sixty-eight miles west of the former, ninety-eight miles east of the latter. The Ramrekha, a small feeder of the Koyane, flows close to the town, and though of small width, has depth and volume of water, requiring to be crossed by ferry. Buchanan states the number of dwellings at 100; and consequently, six persons being allowed to each, the population may be estimated at 600. Provisions and wood are plentiful. The road in this part of the route is sandy, heavy, and bad. Distant N.W. from Benares 108 miles; N.E. from Allahabad ninety-five miles. Lat. 26° 43′, long. 82° 27′.

AMPATA, or OMPTA, in the British district Hooghly, under the lieut.-gov. of Bengal, a town on the river Damooda. As the river is navigable at all times for considerable craft, from the great channel of the Hooghly, as far up as this place, it is a town of some importance, being the great depôt for the coal brought down by boats in the rainy season from the fields of Burdwan and Bancoora. Distance from Calcutta, W., twenty-two miles; from Burdwan, S., forty-five. Lat. 22° 35′, long. 88° 4′.

AMRABAD.—A town in Hyderabad, or dominions of the Nizam, distant S. from Hyderabad eighty-one miles. Lat. 16° 23′, long. 78° 55′.

AMRAPOOR, in the British district of Bellary, presidency of Madras, a town on the route from Chittel Droog to Chittoor, forty miles east of the former. Lat. 14° 8′, long. 77° 2′.

AMREE.—A village in Sinde, on the route from Kotree, near Hyderabad, to Sehwan, and twenty-four miles south-east of this latter place. Amree is situate on the right bank of the Indus; it is a small and apparently a poor village, but there is much cultivation near it. Lat. 26° 7′, long. 68° 2′.

AMREELI, or UMREYLEE.—A town within the peninsula of Kattywar, situate on the river Thobee, a tributary of the Setroonjee, which, seventy miles lower down, falls into the Gulf of Cambay. "The town of Umreylee has rather a striking appearance on approaching it, presenting a solid circumvallation, with round towers of good dimensions, inclosing about 2,000 houses, with a small stream (the Thobee) winding round the northern face." The town, with the tallook or subdivision annexed to it, contains a population of 32,000, residing in ninety-nine villages and towns; and pays an annual tribute of 1,760 rupees to the Guicowar, and a zortulubee of 4,966 rupees to the nawaub of Joonagurh. Distance from Ahmedabad, S.W., 132 miles; Baroda, S.W., 139 miles. Lat. 21° 36′, long. 71° 15′.

AMRITSIR, a walled city of the Punjab, is situate nearly half-way between the rivers Beas and Ravee. It owes its importance to a *Tulao* or reservoir, which Ram Das, the fourth *Guru*, or spiritual guide of the Sikhs, caused to be made here in 1581, and named Amrita Saras, or "fount of immortality." It thenceforward became a place of pilgrimage, and bore the names Amritsir and Ramdaspoor. Nearly two centuries after, Ahmed Shah, the founder of the Durani empire, alarmed and enraged at the progress of the Sikhs, blew up the shrine with gunpowder, filled up the holy *Tulao*, and causing kine to be slaughtered upon the site, thus desecrated the spot, which was drenched with their gore. On his return to Kabool, the Sikhs repaired the shrine and reservoir, and commenced the struggle which terminated in the overthrow of Mahomedan sway in Hindostan. The *Tulao* is a square of 150 paces, containing a great body of water, pure as crystal, notwithstanding the multitudes that bathe in it, and supplied apparently by natural springs. In the middle, on a small island, is a temple of Hari or Vishnu; and on the bank a diminutive structure, where the founder, Ram Das, is said to have spent his life in a sitting posture. The temple on the island is richly adorned with gold and other costly embellishments, and in it sits the sovereign *Guru* of the Sikhs, to receive the presents and homage of his followers. There are five or six hundred Akalees or priests attached to the temple, who have erected for themselves good houses from the contributions of the visitors. Amritsir is a very populous and extensive place. The streets are narrow, but the houses in general are tolerably lofty and built of burnt brick. The apartments, however, are small; but on the whole Amritsir may claim some little architectural superiority over the towns of Hindostan. It has considerable manufactures of coarse cloths, inferior silks, and shawls, made in imitation of the Kashmir fabric, in which great quantities of goats' wool from Bokhara are consumed. There is besides a very extensive transit-trade, as well as considerable monetary transactions with Hindostan and Central Asia, the prosperity of the place having, in these respects, resulted from the decay of Shikarpoor and Mooltan. Rock salt is brought on the backs of camels from a mine near Mundi, about 120 miles to the eastward of Lahore, a large and solid lump, resembling a block of unwrought marble, being slung on each side of the animal. Runjeet Singh constructed a canal from the Ravee, a distance of thirty-four miles; but it is a mean and inexpensive work. Provision is made for an ample supply of water to the town from the Baree Doab Canal, now in course of construction. The most striking object at Amritsir is the huge fortress Govindghur, built by Runjeet Singh in 1809, ostensibly to protect the pilgrims, but in reality to overawe their vast and dangerous assemblage. Its great height and heavy batteries, rising one above the other, give it a very imposing appearance. It contained, at the time of Hügel's visit, the treasure of Runjeet Singh. Measures have been taken by the British for adding to its security. This city was selected for the establishment of the first mission of the Church of England to the Punjab; and in 1854 subscriptions for a new church had been collected to the amount of 8,000 rupees. Population 80,000 or 90,000. Lat. 31° 40′, long. 74° 45′.

AMROWLI, or UMROWLEE, in the British district of Furruckabad, lieut.-gov. of the N.W. Provinces, a village on the route from the cantonment of Allyghur to that of Futtehghur, and twenty-six miles north-west of the latter. The road in this part of the route is bad for wheeled carriages; the country is level, and cultivated in some parts, in others overrun with bush-jungle. Lat. 27° 28′, long. 79° 18′.

AMULNAIR, in the British district of Ahmednuggur, presidency of Bombay, a town on the route from Ahmednuggur to Darroor, forty-one miles south-east of the former. Lat. 18° 56′, long. 75° 21′.

AMULNEIR, in the British district of Khandeish, presidency of Bombay, a town on the left bank of the river Borai, twenty-one miles north-east of Dhoolia. Lat. 21° 3′, long. 75° 1′.

AMURGURH.—A fortress in the north of the Punjab, situate in the dominions of Gholab Singh, two or three miles to the right of the route from Lahore to Kashmir. It formerly belonged to Dyhan Singh, a powerful vassal of the maharaja of the Sikhs. The jealous aversion of its proprietor prevented any European from closely surveying it, but Vigne, who at a distance examined it by means of a telescope, states it to be built on the precipitous bank of a ravine to the westward of it. The outline is rectangular, and though built of stone and of very solid masonry, it must fall before a regular attack, being commanded from other eminences at no great distance. Lat. 32° 57′, long. 74° 18′.

AMURNATH.—A cave amidst the mountains bounding Kashmir on the north-east. It is a natural opening in a rock of gypsum, and is, according to Vigne, about thirty yards high and twenty deep; but Moorcroft states it to be 100 yards wide, thirty high, and 500 deep. It is believed by the Hindoos to be the residence of the deity Siva, and is hence visited by great crowds of both sexes and all ages. A great number of doves inhabit the cave, and these, being frightened by the shouts and tumultuous supplications of the pilgrims, fly out, and are considered thus to be evidence of a favourable answer to the prayers offered; the deity being supposed to come forth in the shape of one of these birds. Amongst other fables, it is asserted that those who enter the cave can hear the barking of the dogs in Thibet. It is mentioned by Hügel under the name of Oumrath. Lat. 34° 15′, long. 75° 49′.

AMWA.—A town of Bundelcund, in the native state of Punnah, distant N.W. from Rewah thirty-one miles. Lat. 24° 53′, long. 81° 6′.

ANAGAON.—A town in Hyderabad, or dominions of the Nizam, distant N.W. from Hyderabad ninety-eight miles. Lat. 18° 21′, long. 77° 30′.

ANAJEE, in the territory of Mysore, a town, the principal place of a pergunnah or subdivision of the same name, situate on the north bank of a large artificial lake on the route from Chittel Droog to Savanoor, twenty-eight miles N.W. of the former, sixty-three S.E. of the latter. Lat. 14° 28′, long. 76° 7′.

ANAKAPILLI, in the British district of Vizagapatam, presidency of Madras, a town on the route from Rajahmundry to Vizianagrum, forty miles south-west of the latter. Lat. 17° 40′, long. 83° 5′.

ANANDPOOR, in the hill state of Kuhloor, a small town situate in the narrow peninsula or tongue of land formed by a remarkable flexure of the Sutlej, and about five miles from either side. It is built at the base of the peak of Nina Devi, stated by Vigne to attain an elevation of about 3,000 feet above the town, or more than 4,000 feet above the sea. That traveller describes it as containing "several large brick buildings with flat roofs and windowless walls, that gave it a sombre but rather imposing aspect." Distant N.W. from Calcutta 1,107 miles. Lat. 31° 17′, long. 76° 36′.

ANANTAWARAM.—A town in Hyderabad, or dominions of the Nizam, distant N.W. from Rajahmundry forty-seven miles. Lat. 17° 21′, long. 81° 16′.

ANCHITTY, in the British district of Salem, presidency of Madras, a town seven miles E. from Seringapatam, and fifty-nine miles N.W. of Salem. Lat. 12° 22′, long. 77° 47′.

ANDAMANS.—See NICOBARS.

ANDARY, in the British territory of Saugor and Nerbudda, a town thirty-nine miles S.W. from Jubbulpoor, 116 miles N. of Nagpoor. Lat. 22° 49′, long. 79° 34′.

ANDOOREE.—A town in the territory of Nagpore, distant S.W. from Nagpore fifty-nine miles. Lat. 20° 33′, long. 78° 32′.

ANDREW BAY, on the coast of Arracan, fourteen miles south of the entrance of the Sandoway river. The centre of the bay is about lat. 18° 16′, long. 94° 16′.

ANDRYTEE, in Bussahir, a feeder of the river Pabur, has its rise on the southern declivity of the Shatul pass, in lat. 31° 24′, long. 78° 1′. It is a powerful and rapid mountain torrent, which holds a southerly course for about fifteen miles to its junction with the Pabur at Chergaon, in lat. 31° 13′, long. 77° 56′. It appears to be mentioned by Hodgson under the name of Indravati.

ANDUR, in the British district of Sarun, lieut.-gov. of Bengal, a town on the route from Dinapoor to Goruckpoor, fifty-eight miles N.W. of the former. Lat. 26° 4′, long. 84° 22′.

ANEAMSAGUR.—A town in Hyderabad, or dominions of the Nizam, distant N.E. from Hyderabad sixty-five miles. Lat. 18° 9′, long. 79° 4′.

ANEE, or URNEE, in the British district of Allygurh, lieut.-gov. of the N.W. Provinces, a village on the route from Meerut to Muttra, and thirty miles north-east of the latter. The road in this part of the route is good, the country open and well cultivated. Lat. 27° 52′, long. 77° 54′.

ANGADDYPOORAM, in the British district of Malabar, presidency of Madras, a town fifty miles W. from Coimbatoor, and thirty-eight miles S.E. of Calicut. Lat. 10° 58′, long. 76° 17′.

ANGEY KYOUNG, off the coast of Arracan, a long and narrow island running parallel with Penekeong island, in Hunter's Bay. It is about twenty miles in length, and three in breadth, and is described as "mountainous, woody, rugged, without any appearance of inhabitants or cultivation." Lat. 19° 47′—20° 4′, long. 93° 10′.

ANGHARAH.—A town in the native state of Nepal, distant N.E. from Almora 121 miles. Lat. 29° 58′, long. 81° 40′.

ANGOOL.—One of the petty native states on the south-west frontier of Bengal, known as the Cuttack Mehals, which became tributary to the British government upon the conquest of the province of Cuttack in 1804. Angool, the principal place, is situate in lat. 20° 48′, long. 84° 53′.

ANG-TONG, in the territory of Siam, a town situated on the left bank of the river Me-nam, fifty-three miles N. of the town of Siam, 248 miles S.E. from Amherst. Lat. 15° 35′, long. 101° 20′.

ANGTSOO.—A town in the native state of Nepal, distant N.E. from Almora 129 miles. Lat. 29° 52′, long. 81° 50′.

ANHUT.—See AMHERST ISLAND.

ANIAH, in the British district of Bolundshuhur, lieut.-gov. of the N.W. Provinces, a village on the route from Allygurh cantonment to that of Delhi, and twenty-one miles north-east of the former. The road in this part of the route is good; the country open, with a sandy soil, scantily cultivated. Lat. 28° 6′, long. 77° 58′.

ANIGEEREE, in the British district of Dharwar, presidency of Bombay, a town on the route from Dharwar to Bellary, twenty-nine miles east of the former. Lat. 15° 25′, long. 75° 30′.

ANIKUL, in territory of Mysore, a town on the S.E. frontier, "situate on the eastern verge of the tract of woody hills extending from Savendy Droog to the Cavery." It was formerly a place of strength and importance, where Hyder Ali found refuge when driven from Seringapatam by insurrection. Distance from Seringapatam, N.E., 75 miles; Bangalore, S.E., 20; Madras, W., 178. Lat. 12° 44′, long. 77° 44′.

ANJAR, in the native state of Cutch, under the political superintendence of the Bombay government, a town, the chief place of a district of the same name. As a friendly return for the assistance rendered to the rajah of Cutch in recovering certain alienated possessions, the town and district of Anjar were ceded by him, in 1816, to the East-India Company. In 1822 the arrangement was modified by a new treaty, under which the cession was restored, on condition of an annual money payment. The condition, however, not being satisfactorily fulfilled, the subject was reconsidered, and in 1832 the claim both as to arrears and prospective payments was relinquished. Lat. 23° 6′, long. 70° 3′.

ANJE-DIVA, or ANJADEEPA.—An island distant about two miles from the coast of North Canara. "It is about a mile in length, and possessed by the Portuguese. It appears on the outside barren and rocky, but of a pleasant aspect on the opposite side, next the main, where it is fortified by a wall and some towers. In case of necessity, a ship may find shelter under this island from the S.W. monsoon." Distant S.E. from Goa fifty-one miles. Lat. 14° 45′, long. 74° 10′.

ANJENGAUM, or UNJENGAUM, in Hyderabad, or the territory of the Nizam, a town near the north-western frontier, towards the British districts of Saugor and Nerbudda. It is situate at the southern base of the range of mountains bounding the valley of the Taptee on the south. Distance from Nagpore, S.W., 90 miles; Ellichpore, S.E., 42; Hyderabad, N., 231; Bombay, N.E., 350. Lat. 21° 40′, long. 77° 51′.

ANJENGO, in the territory of Travancore, a town on the seacoast, situate on a narrow strip of land running from north-west to south-east, having on the south-west the Indian Ocean, and on the north-east an extensive shallow estuary or back-water. It consists of two rows of houses, arranged parallel to each other; the Portuguese church and English burying-ground being at the north-western extremity, the fort at the south-eastern. There is no shelter for shipping, which must anchor at sea, "in eleven or twelve fathoms mud, off shore a mile and a half or two miles;" and the intercourse with the shore is, in consequence of the extreme violence of the surf, very difficult and dangerous, even in the fine season, when it is practicable only in country boats, and is totally impracticable during the monsoon, which is here excessively boisterous, and dangerous to shipping; so that the coast is not frequented during the south-west monsoon. Most of the inhabitants of Anjengo profess to be Christians: they are of the Romish Church, either descended from the Portuguese, or converted natives of Malabar. With few exceptions, they are poor, subsisting by fishing or manufacturing cordage from coir or cocoa-nut fibre. The East-India Company had here formerly a factory of some importance, but latterly discontinued. The district of Anjengo, in which the town is situate, is now, however, under the British government. Distance from Cannanore, S.E., 240 miles; from Madras, S.W., 390. Lat. 8° 40′, long. 76° 49′.

ANKOLA.—See UNKOLA.

ANKREE.—A town in Hyderabad, or dominions of the Nizam, distant N. from Hyderabad 129 miles. Lat. 19° 14′, long. 78° 27′.

ANNADARAROOPAD, in the British district of Rajahmundry, presidency of Madras, a town thirteen miles N.W. from Rajahmundry, forty-five miles N.E. of Ellore. Lat. 17° 7′, long. 81° 40′.

ANNANTAGHERRY.—A town in Hyderabad, or dominions of the Nizam, distant N.W. from Guntoor sixty miles. Lat. 17° 3′, long. 80° 3′.

ANNANTAPOOR.—A town in the native state of Mysore, under the administration and control of the government of India, distant N.W. from Seringapatam 150 miles. Lat. 14° 3′, long. 75° 15′.

ANNAVARAM, in the British district of Vizagapatam, presidency of Madras, a town twenty-five miles N.W. from Vizagapatam, and thirty-nine miles S.W. of Vizianagrum. Lat. 17° 50′, long. 83°.

ANNAWUTTY.—A town in Mysore, under the administration and control of the government of India, distant N.W. from Seringapatam 180 miles. Lat. 14° 33′, long. 75° 12′.

ANNUTRAM, in the British district of Etawa, lieut.-gov. of the N.W. Provinces, a village on the route from the cantonment of Etawa to Calpee, and 20 miles south-east of the former. Lat. 26° 36′, long. 79° 18′.

ANOOPSHUHUR, in the British district of Bolundshuhur, lieut.-gov. of the N.W.

Provinces, a town on the route from Bareilly to Delhi, and 73 miles south-east of the latter. It is situate on the right bank of the Ganges, the channel of which is here about a mile wide, only one-fifth of that space being occupied by the stream in the dry season, when it is limpid, and still so deep as to be unfordable, and crossed either by ferry or bridge of boats. The right bank, on which the town is situate, is about thirty feet above the channel, the left bank low, and, in consequence, the country on that side is extensively flooded in high inundations. At the time of Tennant's visit, in 1798, it was surrounded by a mud wall between twenty and thirty feet thick, and at the northern extremity was a large antique residence of the zemindar or proprietor of that part of the country; on the south a large fort built of brick, and so strong as to be impregnable to a native force. The town has a bazaar, and though of no great extent, is populous, but ill-built, the houses being either of mud or ill-cemented brick. Population 8,947. Lat. 28° 20′, long. 78° 21′.

ANOPGURH, in the Rajpoot state of Bikaner, a town near the north-west frontier, towards Bahawulpoor. It is situate in a country of great sterility, in lat. 29° 14′, long. 73° 26′.

ANTOWRAH, in the territory of Oude, a town on the route from the cantonment of Futtehgurh to that of Seetapoor, 38 miles north-east of the former, 44 west of the latter. It has a bazaar; water is plentiful, and supplies may be collected from the surrounding country, which is level, and partially cultivated, though in many places overrun with jungle. The road in this part of the route is bad. Lat. 27° 40′, long. 80° 6′.

ANTREE, in the territory of Gwalior, a small town on the route from the fort of Gwalior to Saugor, 18 miles S.E. of former, 184 N.W. of latter. It is situate at the southern entrance of a rocky ravine, so narrow that only one wheeled carriage can pass at once along the road, which is very narrow, rocky, and bad. Salt is manufactured here by washing the saline earth in the vicinity, and by the heat of the sun evaporating the brine thus obtained. Tieffenthaler describes it, about eighty years ago, as a town once tolerably handsome, but much decayed, and having at its west side a fort with four very strong towers. Here, at the close of December, 1843, the Mahratta force was posted to oppose the British advancing from Bundelcund under the command of General Grey. The British commander marched westward to turn their position, and the Mahrattas, marching by a parallel route, gave battle at Punniar, and were totally defeated. Lat. 26° 3′, long. 78° 16′.

ANUNDPOOR.—A town in the native state of Jutt, one of the Sattara jaghires, distant S.E. from Sattara 89 miles. Lat. 16° 54′, long. 75° 9′.

ANUNDPORE, in the British district of Midnapoor, lieut.-gov. of Bengal, a town 15 miles N.E. from Midnapoor. Lat. 22° 35′, long. 87° 30′.

ANWULKHERA, or UMURKHERA, in the British district of Agra, lieut.-gov. of the N.W. Provinces, a town on the route from the city of Agra to Bareilly by Khasgunge, and 15 miles north-east of the former. It has a small bazaar; indifferent water may be had from wells, and supplies may be obtained from the neighbourhood. The road in this part of the route is bad, the country cut up with ravines, and very partially cultivated. Lat. 27° 19′, long. 78° 12′.

AONGTHA, in the Burman empire, a town situate on the left bank of the river Khyendwen, and 90 miles N.W. of Ava. Lat. 22° 39′, long. 94° 58′.

AONLAGANJ, or AOUNLAH, in the British district of Bareilly, a town on the route from Allygurh to Bareilly, 80 miles N.E. of former, 21 S.W. of latter. It has a large bazaar, and water is abundant. Population 7,649. Lat. 28° 16′, long. 79° 13′.

AOUGASEE.—The principal place of the pergunnah of the same name, in the British district of Banda, lieut.-gov. of the N.W. Provinces, a town on the right bank of the Jumna, 30 miles north-east of the town of Banda. Lat. 25° 40′, long. 80° 50′.

AOUNG, or AOON, in the British district of Futtehpore, lieut.-gov. of Agra, a village on the route from Cawnpore to the town of Futtehpore, and 22 miles north-west of the latter. Water is obtained from wells, but supplies are scarce. The road in this part of the route is bad. Lat. 26° 9′, long. 80° 38′.

AOUNLAH.—See AONLAGANJ.

API.—A town in the native state of Nepal, distant N.E. from Almora eighty-two miles. Lat. 30°, long. 81°.

APPAROWPETT.—A town in Hyderabad, or dominions of the Nizam, distant N. from Hyderabad 132 miles. Lat. 19° 16′, long. 78° 14′.

APPOOWA.—A village in Arracan, situate on the right bank of the Coladyne river. Lat. 20° 50′, long. 93° 1′.

APTA, in the British district of Tannah, presidency of Bombay, a town on the route from Callianee to Nagotna, twenty-two miles north of the latter. Lat. 18° 51′, long. 73° 12′.

ARABUL, in Kashmir, a beautiful cataract on the Veshau, one of the principal tributaries of the Behut or Jhelum. Lat. 33° 37′, long. 74° 52′.

ARACHI, in the British district of Salem, presidency of Madras, a town twenty-eight miles N.W. from Trichinopoly, and forty-one miles S.E. of Salem. Lat. 11° 7′, long. 78° 30′.

ARAIL, in the British district of Allahabad, lieut.-gov. of the N.W. Provinces, the principal place of the pergunnah of the same name, a small town on the right bank of the Ganges, at the confluence of the Jumna, and opposite the city of Allahabad, from which it is distant about a mile. Lat. 25° 25′, long. 81° 56′.

ARAUN.—A river of Hyderabad, rising in lat. 20° 10′, long. 77° 12′, near the town of Bassim, and flowing easterly for fifty miles, and south-east for sixty miles, falls into the Payne Gunga river on the left or north side, in lat. 19° 54′, long. 78° 20′.

ARAVACOORCHY, in the British district of Coimbatore, presidency of Madras, a town on the route from Dindigul to Salem, thirty miles N. of the former. Lat. 10° 47′, long. 77° 58′.

ARAVULLI, in Western India, a range of mountains extending in a direction N.E. from the vicinity of Champanere, about lat. 22° 40′, long. 74°, where, though low and not strongly marked, it joins the W. extremity of the Vindhya. It extends along the S.W. frontier of the territory of Banswarra, Dongurpoor, and the S.W. and N.W. of Mewar or Odeypore, dividing it from the lower region of Marwar or Joudpoor; and, proceeding into the districts of Mairwarra and Ajmere, becomes confounded with the low rocky ranges of Shekhawati and Delhi. Its N.E. extremity may, perhaps, be assumed in lat. 26° 50′, long. 75°. On the N.W. side, or towards Marwar, it is very bold and precipitous, less so on the S.E.; but according to Tod, there is no pass over it practicable for wheeled carriages from Edur, near its S.E. extremity, to Ajmere, a distance of 220 miles. The most elevated summit is Mount Aboo, 5,000 feet above the sea.

ARAWUD, in the British district of Khandeish, presidency of Bombay, a town forty-eight miles S.W. from Boorhaunpoor, sixty-one miles N.E. of Dhoolia. Lat. 21° 10′, long. 75° 39′.

ARCOT (Southern Division).—A British district under the presidency of Madras. It is bounded on the north by the British districts northern division of Arcot and Chingleput; on the east by Pondicherry and the Bay of Bengal; on the south by the British districts of Tanjore and Trichinopoly, and on the west by the British district of Salem. It lies between lat. 11° 11′—12° 39′, long. 78° 42′—80° 4′. The area, according to official authority, is 7,600 square miles. The general surface of the country forms part of the great slope from the Eastern Ghauts to the coast of the Bay of Bengal. In its eastern part, or towards the sea, it is low and level, but in the interior, towards the ghauts, rises into hills, not forming continuous ranges, but in general isolated. The principal rivers intersecting or bounding the district are the Southern Penna or Panar, and the Coleroon. The former falls into the Bay of Bengal a little north of Cuddalore. It is devoid of water during the dry season, and such also is the condition of most of the other streams of this district, which fall either into the Penna or into the Bay of Bengal. The Coleroon, however, which forms the southern boundary towards Tanjore, is abundantly supplied with water during the greater part of the year. Pursuing its course in a north-eastern direction, the Coleroon falls into the Bay of Bengal, near Devicottah. From Devicottah, at the mouth of the Coleroon, the seacoast extends in a northern direction for forty-five miles to lat. 12°, long. 79° 55′; thence, in a north-easterly direction twenty-two miles, to lat. 12° 15′, long. 80° 4′; the total length of the seacoast of this district being sixty-seven miles. Porto Novo, nine miles north of Devicottah, is at the mouth of the Vellaur, a river rising towards the base of the Eastern Ghauts, and having a considerable length of course, with an annicut or dam thrown across it in this district, by means of which its waters are rendered available for the purposes of irrigation. It is at all times too small at its mouth to admit of any but coasting craft; but ships may anchor two miles off shore in six fathoms, with good holding-ground of mud, and protected from southerly winds by the Coleroon shoal lying in that direction. The seacoast is sandy, with small hills, which, viewed from a distance, appear to be islets. About fifteen miles beyond Porto Novo, in the same direction, is Cuddalore, at the mouth of the Southern Penna. The climate is exempt from sudden vicissitudes of temperature, and storms are less frequent here than in most other places on the Coromandel coast. In the vicinity of the shore the temperature is comparatively moderate during the prevalence of the sea-breezes; but when they give place to the land-winds during spring, the heat becomes very distressing, and is accompanied by great aridity, against which neither glass nor wood is proof, the former breaking suddenly from the expansive power of the heat, and the latter from the same cause warping, cracking, and splitting. The thermometer sometimes reaches 115° in the shade, and according to some reports it occasionally rises as high as 130°. The mineral wealth of this district is small, with the exception of a rich mine of iron-ore in the south-eastern part, furnishing metal of excellent quality, which is reduced at Porto Novo by a company of European capitalists. No satisfactory information is accessible as to either the botany or zoology of the district, nor indeed as to any branch of natural history. According to the census taken in 1851, the population amounted to 1,006,005. Assuming the area at 7,600 square miles, and the population as above stated, the result will show a relative density of 132 to the square mile. The proportion of Mussulmans and others is stated to be about one twenty-fifth part of the whole; the remainder of the population being Hindoos. Cuddalore is the seat of the civil establishment of the district; Trinomalee, and the French settlement of Pondicherry, also locally within the limits of this district, are described under their respective names in the alphabetical arrangement.

ARCOT (Northern Division). — A British district under the presidency of Madras. It is bounded on the north by the British district of Nellore, on the east and south-east by the British district Chingleput, on the south by the British district of Arcot (southern division) and Salem, and on the north-west by Mysore and the British district of Cuddapah; and lies between lat. 12° 22′—14° 11′, long. 78° 17′—80° 12′. The area is estimated by one authority at 5,571 square miles; according to another, at 5,790. The principal river is the Palar, which, rising in the territory of Mysore, pursues a direction generally easterly, and entering this district about lat. 12° 58′, long. 78° 30′, flows through it, continuing its easterly course for about 102 miles, passing close to the towns of Vellore and Arcot, and subsequently crossing into the British district of Chingleput. Though a considerable torrent during the rainy season, it is at other times dry on the surface of its channel, though water may at all times be obtained by digging therein. There are several smaller streams, such as the Poiney, the Soonarmukai, and some others, all devoid of water in the dry season, but during the periodical rains flowing freely, and replenishing the tanks and channels for irrigation. Tanks, or artificial pieces of water, are very numerous, and the dimensions of some are surprisingly great. That of Cauverypak is eight miles long and three broad. Besides many channels for irrigation, a canal has been made from the southern extremity of Pulikat lake to Madras, distant twenty miles; and by this communication that city receives abundant supplies of charcoal, firewood, vegetables, grain, fish, and other articles of consumption. The soil on the plains is for the most part sandy, mixed with loam and gravel: it is extensively cultivated, principally with rice and other grains; and even in the mountainous tracts there is a considerable portion of fertile ground. Cotton is the principal commercial crop. The population according to the latest official return is 1,485,873, an amount which, compared with the area furnished by the same authority (5,790 square miles), indicates a relative density of about 257 to the square mile. The language spoken in this collectorate is the Tamul. The lines of the Madras Railway Company traverse this district. The other routes are—1. From east to west, from Madras through Arcot to Bangalore. 2. From north-east to south-west, from Madras through Arcot to Coimbatore. 3. From north to south, from Chittoor to Arcot. Arcot, the principal place, Vellore, Chittoor, are described under their respective names in the alphabetical arrangement.

ARCOT, the principal place of the northern division of the British territory bearing the same name, is situate on the right side of the river Palar, and on the line of railway from Madras to Beypoor. The site is advantageous and salubrious, being on a gentle eminence, sloping down to the bank. The bed of the river is about half a mile wide; but in the dry season the stream is not sufficient to turn a mill, and the channel is sometimes even totally dry. Water of good quality can, however, always be obtained by sinking pits into the sands which form the bed. The military cantonment can accommodate three regiments; one of European, and two of native cavalry. There is an extensive barrack for Europeans, built of brick and lime mortar; and contiguous are three hospitals, well constructed, well ventilated, and in all respects commodious; besides other buildings requisite for such an establishment. There is a neat Protestant Episcopal church adjoining. The old fort has been nearly demolished; but its outline can still be traced almost throughout its entire extent, which was once very considerable. In the town are the ruins of the palace of the nawaub of Arcot, besides the remains of various buildings erected by Mussulmans, and some mosques, still in a state of repair. The town, with the talook or subdivision annexed, is stated officially to have a population of 53,474, inhabiting 10,042 houses.

Arcot occupies a prominent place in the history of the contests waged in this part of India during the earlier part of the eighteenth century. Here Clive confirmed the military reputation which he had previously acquired by some adventurous exploits in other quarters. The English having previously taken but feeble measures to support their ally, the well-known Mahomet Ali, Clive suggested an attack upon Arcot, then held by a rival power, and offered himself as the commander of the expedition. His suggestion and offer were accepted; but the force placed at his disposal was altogether disproportioned to the service for which it was destined. It consisted but of 300 sepoys and 200 Europeans, with three field-pieces; and with this small force an attack was to be made upon a fortress garrisoned by 1,100 men. On approaching the place, a violent storm of thunder and rain fell; an event which might certainly be regarded as a misfortune rather than an advantage. It proved, however, the latter; for Clive, marching his small force through this war of the elements, a thing regarded as unparalleled in India, was looked upon as an assailant whom it would be vain to resist; the garrison accordingly abandoned the fort, and Clive took possession of it. The enemy, however, having received large reinforcements, under Rajah Sahib, son of the celebrated Chunda Sahib, became in turn the assailants, and Clive was called upon to defend the place which had so remarkably passed into his hands. This task he performed with consummate skill, though his force was so small that he was obliged to husband his resources with the greatest care. Being summoned to surrender, he replied in terms of haughty defiance. At length, on the 14th November, 1751, the enemy commenced the attack long threatened, and from which nothing short of complete success was anticipated. This attempt, and its results, are thus recorded in a modern historical work :—"The day of attack was one among the most distinguished in the Mahometan calendar. Happy was the Mussulman to whom it brought death from the sword of the unbeliever, for his fall was regarded as but a sudden introduction to the highest paradise. By this belief the enthusiasm of the enemy's troops was wrought up almost to madness, and it was further increased by the free use of an intoxicating substance called bang. The morning came, and with it the expected movement. Clive was awakened, and found his garrison at their posts, according to the disposition which he had previously made. On the enemy's side a vast multitude were in motion, bringing ladders to every part of the wall that was accessible. Besides these desultory operations there were others in progress, all directed to the same end. Four principal divisions of the enemy's troops marched upon the four points where an entrance to the fort seemed the more likely to be effected—the two gates and the two breaches which had been made in the wall. The parties who attacked the gates drove before them several elephants, armed with plates of iron on their foreheads, with which it was expected they would beat down the obstacles which stopped the course of the assailants; but the device was more disastrous to those who employed it than to those against whom it was directed. The elephants, wounded by the musketry of the British force, turned and trampled upon those who were urging them forward. At the north-west breach, as many as it was capable of admitting rushed wildly in, and passed the first trench before their opponents gave fire. When given, it was with terrible effect. A number of muskets were loaded in readiness, which those behind delivered to the first rank as fast as they could discharge them. Every shot did execution, while three field-pieces contributed effectually to thin the number of the assailants. In a few minutes they fell back: but the attempt was only suspended, not abandoned. Another and another party followed, and were driven off as had been those who preceded them. To approach the south-west breach, the enemy embarked seventy men on a raft, who thus attempted to cross a ditch, and had almost gained their object, when Clive, observing that his gunners fired with bad aim, took the management of one of the field-pieces himself. This he worked with such precision and effect that a few discharges threw the advancing party into confusion. The raft was overset, and those on board thrown into the water, where some were drowned. The remainder saved themselves by swimming back, abandoning the unfortunate raft which was to have borne them to the breach. These various attacks occupied about an hour, and cost the enemy in killed and wounded about 400 men. After an interval employed by the assailants in endeavouring, under much annoyance, to carry off their dead, the firing upon the fort was renewed, both with cannon and musketry. This was again discontinued. A formal demand of leave to bury the dead was complied with, and a truce of two hours agreed upon. At the expiration of the prescribed time the firing once more recommenced, and lasted until two o'clock on the following morning, when it ceased, never to be renewed. At daybreak the gallant defenders of the fort learned that their besiegers had precipitately abandoned the town. The garrison immediately marched into the enemy's quarters, where they found several pieces of artillery and a large quantity of ammunition. These spoils were forthwith transferred to the fort, and thus ended a siege of fifty days. Military history records few events more remarkable than this memorable siege. Its conduct at once placed Clive in the foremost rank of distinguished commanders. Justly has it been said that he was 'born a soldier.' At the time when with a handful of men, most of them unpractised in the operations of war, he defended the fort of Arcot against a force several thousand strong, his military experience was small, while of military education he was entirely destitute. His boyhood had passed in idleness, or in the reckless perpetration of mischief, while the few years which he had numbered of manly life had, for the most part, been occupied with the details of trade. Deprived of all the means by which, in ordinary cases, men are gradually prepared for the duties of military service or command, he showed himself a perfect master of the arts of war. Like all other eminent commanders, he communicated to those under him a spirit of devotedness and self-abandonment, which is among the most graceful as well as the most valuable qualities of a soldier. An instance of this occurred among the native troops employed in the defence of Arcot, which is alike honourable to them and to their commander. When provisions became scarce, and there was ground for apprehending that famine would compel a surrender, the sepoys proposed that their diet should be restricted to the thin gruel in which the rice was boiled, and that the whole of the grain should be given to the Europeans, as they required more nourishment. With such a spirit pervading his little garrison, Clive might well look forward to a successful termination of his brave defence of Arcot; but that spirit his own military virtues had fostered and called forth." On the evening of the memorable day, reinforcements, dispatched from Madras for the support of Clive, entered the town, and a few days afterwards Clive left the place, for a field where his services were more pressingly required. Arcot was taken by Hyder Ali when that invader ravaged the Carnatic; and beyond these facts there is little in its history of interest or importance. Distance from Madura, N.E., 220 miles; Tanjore, N., 145; Cuddalore, N., 88; Bangalore, E., 118; Vellore, E., 14; Madras, W., 65. Lat. 12° 54′, long. 79° 24′.

ARCULGODE.—A town in Mysore, under the administration and control of the government of India, distant N.W. from Seringapatam 49 miles. Lat. 12° 46′, long. 76° 7′.

ARDANJI, in the British district of Tanjore, presidency of Madras, a town on the route from Tripatoor to Negapatam, twenty-eight miles east of the former. Lat. 10° 11′, long. 79° 3′.

ARDYSIR.—A town in the native state of Cutch, under the political superintendence of the presidency of Bombay, distant N.E. from Bhooj seventy-five miles. Lat. 23° 38′, long. 70° 50′.

AREEJAW, in Sinde, a large village on the route from Schwan to Larkhana, in the fertile island inclosed between the Indus and its offset the Narra. It is situate eight miles south from Larkhana, the same distance west of the Indus, and one mile east of the Narra. Lat. 27° 24′, long. 68° 9′.

AREENG, or AURUNG.—The principal place of the pergunnah of the same name, in the British district of Muttra, lieut.-gov. of the N.W. Provinces, a small town on the route from Muttra to Deeg, and nine miles west of the former. Here the army of Holkar, the Mahratta chief, was encamped Oct. 7, 1804, and being attacked by the British under General Lake, sought safety in a precipitate flight, in which their chief led the way. About thirty of their number were killed, and several made prisoners. Lat. 27° 29′, long. 77° 36′.

AREEPADGAH, in the British province of Arracan, lieut.-gov. of Bengal, a town 63 miles N.W. of Arracan. Lat. 21° 6′, long. 92° 33′.

AREEPORE, or HAREEPOOR, in the British district of Ghazeepoor, lieut.-gov. of the N.W. Provinces, a town 32 miles N.E. of Ghazeepoor, 40 miles W. of Chupra. Areepore has a population of 6,382. Lat. 25° 49′, long. 84° 2′.

ARGAUM, in Hyderabad, or territory of the Nizam, a village near the northern frontier, towards the British territory of Saugor and Nerbudda, some distance southward of the range of mountains bounding the valley of the Taptee on the south. This place is rendered memorable by having been the site of an action which took place on the 28th November, 1803, between the British army commanded by Major-General Wellesley (afterwards duke of Wellington), and that of the Mahrattas commanded by Scindia and Munny Bappoo, brother of the rajah of Berar, in which the latter was defeated with great loss. A medal in commemoration of the victory was struck in London, in 1851, and presented, under the sanction of the Queen, to the surviving officers and soldiers who were engaged in the action. It is situated in a plain much cut up by water-courses, and on the route from Ellichpoor to Aurungabad. Distance 40 miles S.W. of the former, 135 N.E. of the latter. Lat. 21° 2′, long. 77° 2′.

ARIANCOOPAN.—See PONDICHERRY.

ARKAIRY.—A town in Hyderabad, or dominions of the Nizam, distant S.W. from Hyderabad 104 miles. Lat. 16° 50′, long. 77° 6′.

ARMEGON, in the British district of Nellore, presidency of Madras, a village situate on the coast opposite to a shoal of the same name, between "the inner edge of which and the coast there is a space from three to four miles wide, now called Blackwood Harbour." One of the earliest settlements of the East-India Company in the Carnatic was founded at this place, where a factory was erected in 1628, defended by twelve pieces of cannon. Distance N. of Madras 66 miles. Lat. 14° 2′, long. 80° 12′.

ARMOREE.—A town in the territory of Nagpore, distant S.E. from Nagpore 74 miles. Lat. 20° 28′, long. 80° 2′.

ARMOYAMCOTTA, in the British district of Madura, presidency of Madras, a town situate twenty miles N. from Ramnad, and fifty-three miles S.E. of Madura. Lat. 9° 40′, long. 78° 56′.

ARNALLA.—An island off the coast of the Northern Concan, presidency of Bombay, situate one mile from the mainland, the intervening channel being navigable for vessels of considerable burthen. On the island is a fort, which, in 1781, was taken by the British army under General Goddard. Distant N. from the city of Bombay thirty-five miles. Lat. 19° 28′, long. 72° 47′.

ARNEE.—A town in Hyderabad, or dominions of the Nizam, distant S. from Omrawuttee fifty-five miles. Lat. 20° 4′, long. 78° 4′.

ARNEE, in the British district of Arcot, northern division, a town with British cantonment. Its site is rather low and flat, yet with a sufficient declivity towards a small river about a quarter of a mile distant, to carry off the rain thither even during the monsoon. The river being fed by springs, affords an unremitting supply of excellent water. The country round is open, the nearest hills, which consist of granite and syenite, being six miles distant; and there is scarcely any vegetation, except a few straggling palms and some patches of stunted jungle. The soil of the plain consists of disintegrated granite, mixed with sand or clay, and in many places is impregnated with impure saline matter, chiefly salts of soda, which during the dry season cause a white efflorescence on the surface. This place, formerly a strong fortress, is now much decayed. It is a station for European troops, the cantonment of which is within the now dilapidated rampart, but for some years past has only been occasionally occupied as a temporary depôt. Immediately opposite to it are two bomb-proof ranges of buildings, forming the officers' quarters; behind these, and about three hundred yards distant, are the barracks, calculated to accommodate one European regiment. These are also bomb-proof, and are spacious and strongly built, forming three sides of a square; the fourth side being occupied by a wall with a gateway. Contiguous is a commodious hospital. Elevation above the sea 400 feet. Distance from Madura, N.E., 207 miles; Tanjore, N., 131; Bangalore, E., 119; Vellore, S.E., 20; Arcot, S., 17: Madras, S.W., 74. Lat. 12° 40′, long. 79° 21′.

AROOA.—See OOMRAWUH.

AROUL, in the British district of Mynpooree, lieut.-gov. of the N.W. Provinces, a small town or village on the route from Muttra cantonment to that of Mynpooree, and twenty-three miles west of the latter. Water is plentiful, and supplies may be collected from the surrounding country. The road in this part of the route is tolerably good in dry weather, but during the rains in the latter part of summer, is in many places under water to the depth of from one to three feet: the country is level and partially cultivated. Lat. 27° 8′, long. 78° 45′.

ARPEILLEE.—A town in the territory of Nagpore, distant S. from Nagpore 110 miles. Lat. 19° 44′, long. 79° 58′.

ARRACAN PROPER.—See AKYAB.

ARRACAN, a province of India, situate to the east of the Bay of Bengal, is bounded on the north by Chittagong, from which it is divided by the Naaf river and the Waili hills; on the east by the Yoomadoung range of mountains, which separates it from Ava; on the south by a portion of the British province of Pegu; and on the west by the Bay of Bengal. It lies between lat. 18° and 21° 33′, long. 92° 10′—94° 50′. Its extreme length from the Kintalee pass to its northern extremity is about 290 miles. Its greatest breadth is at the north, where it measures ninety miles from Ramoo to the central ridge of the Yoomadoung mountains; eighty miles further south it is seventy miles broad, measuring from the mouth of the Kuladyne river to the summit of the mountains. For some leagues south of this, the coast is very much interrupted by bays and creeks; and thence onward to its most extreme point at Cape Negrais (beyond the recently-defined boundaries of Arracan), the mainland is a very narrow strip, measuring rarely more than twenty miles, and on an average not more than fifteen miles across. The area of the province is 13,484 square miles. The coast is skirted by many islands, the more important of which are Ramree, Cheduba, and Shapuree. That part of the coast lying between the Naaf and Arracan rivers is lined by shoal banks, stretching in some parts two or three miles from the shore. Further south the coast is lined by a number of rocky islands, of which those called the Broken Islands and the Terribles are the larger; but neither of these groups has the slightest appearance of cultivation. The remainder of the coast from Ramree to Kintalee is excessively rugged and rocky, indented by bays which afford no shelter for ships, studded by islands, and beset by various sources of peril. "Between the Kuladyne and Sandoway rivers," says Pemberton, "the whole coast consists of a labyrinth of creeks and tide-nullahs, all of which terminate at the foot of the lower ranges, and receive the contributions of numerous small streams." The physical aspect of this country is very diversified; hilly, but having extensive flats and valleys, the latter of which are generally fertile and highly cultivated, being intersected by numerous small rivers. There is, however, abundance of low marshy land, overrun with thick jungle, and so much cut up by rivers and tide-nullahs, as to render communication by land very difficult, in some instances almost impracticable; the principal intercourse between the stations and villages being carried on by water. Along the whole line of the eastern frontier, the boundary between Arracan on the one side, and Ava and the newly-acquired British province of Pegu on the other, is formed by the Yoomadoung mountains. This range is a portion of the great chain which, running from the south of Assam, in lat. 26° 30′, extends to Cape Negrais. The height of the mountains varies, averaging at this part from three to four thousand feet. The Blue Mountain, in lat. 22° 37′, long. 93° 11′, is said to be upwards of 8,000 feet above the level of the sea. The inhabitants of these mountainous tracts consist of several independent tribes, who have never submitted to any government. They lead a life of hardship and danger, especially the women, who are stoutly made, though diminutive in size. The cultivation consists in clearing away the thick forests and shrubs which clothe the mountain-sides, and preparing the ground for the seed. Rice and cotton are the principal productions; but tobacco and some esculent vegetables are planted by the sides of streams. Over this range there are several passes; but that called the Aeng route is superior to all others, and is an excellent road, by means of which, before the Burmese war of 1825, a great trade was carried on between Arracan and Ava, in which it is said 40,000 men were annually employed. Subsequently, however, this commerce declined, on account of the want of confidence in the Burmese government and people. There are several low ranges of hills stretching along the coast, but all are considered ramifications of the great chain. They abound in forests. The principal rivers of Arracan are the Myoo, Kuladyne or Arracan river, Lemyo, Talak, and Aeng. The sources of the three former are among the mountains to the north of Arracan, about lat. 22° 30′. They flow in a southerly direction, and are on an average not more than twenty miles distant from each other; after a course of about 150 miles they disembogue into Hunter's Bay, where they are connected by numerous creeks, and by which the communication in this part is carried on. The Talak river is for many miles nothing more than a mountain torrent, and is only navigable for the last twenty-five miles of its course. The Aeng river during the spring tides is navigable up to the town of that name, which is forty-five miles from its mouth. Both this river and the Talak take their rise in the Yoomadoung mountains, and empty themselves into Combermere Bay, twenty-five miles east of the town of Khyouk Phyoo. There are no lakes in the province. The climate of Arracan has generally been considered very injurious to Europeans, as well as to the natives of other parts of India; and the great mortality of the troops engaged in the first Burmese war afforded melancholy illustration of the truth of this belief. It is only the interior, however, which is characterized by the great degree of unhealthiness; Akyab, Sandoway, and Khyouk Phyoo, situate on the seashore, have long been known to be far more favourable to the retention of health than most parts of the province, while the town of Arracan and the village of Talak, situate inland, are peculiarly injurious. There are various indications of a volcanic nature in Arracan. Along the coast, and in the islands of Ramree and Cheduba, are situated "earthy cones covered with a green sward," from which issue springs of muddy water, emitting bubbles of gas. Two severe earthquakes have taken place in the province; one in 1763, the other in 1833. By the latter four hills were rent asunder to the width of from thirty to sixty feet; and in the plains its effects were shown by "the earth opening in several places and throwing up water and mud of a sulphurous smell." From Nayadong mountain, near Khyouk Phyoo, in the island of Ramree, vapour and flame were seen to issue to the height of several hundred feet. Of the mineral resources of this country very little is known. In some parts, however, iron-ore is found, and in Ramree some iron-mines were once worked; but the working has long been discontinued, the quality and price of the product rendering competition with that imported from Great Britain hopeless. In the island of Cheduba iron is found, but in such small quantities as to be of no value. Coal has been found in the Sandoway district, and in the island of Ramree, near Khyouk Phyoo. Favourable reports have been made of its quality, but it has not been extensively worked. There are several petroleum-wells in the islands of Ramree and Cheduba, and the oil found is of excellent quality, though not produced in great quantities. A profusion of fine forests deck the summits and sides of the mountains: the principal trees are the oak and teak, masses of which clothe those forming the northern and eastern frontier. The creeks and nullahs which intersect the numerous valleys and alluvial plains, being dammed up, and turned to the purposes of irrigation, render the country peculiarly suited for the cultivation of rice, its staple produce, and of which it yields the richest crops in India, and affords a large surplus for exportation. No manure enriches the ground, the irrigation it receives rendering its application unnecessary. There are various other products in Arracan. The chief of these are tobacco, sugar, cotton, indigo, and black and red pepper. Arracan possesses no manufacture of any importance; but salt is produced to some extent in parts of the province near the coast, and in the island of Ramree, especially at the harbour of Khyouk Phyoo. It is obtained entirely by solar evaporation, is of excellent quality, and forms an article of exportation. A kind of coarse cloth is woven by the women, but it is worn only by the people of the province. One of the many advantages accruing to this province from British administration is the steady increase of commerce since it has come into the possession of that government. Rice and salt constitute the chief articles of exportation; the others are tobacco, sugar, wood-oil, betel-nut, buffalo-hides and horns, elephants' teeth, dried fish, and edible birdnests. Akyab is the principal port of the province, and the trade is there considerable. The province is divided into three districts. The first and largest is Akyab, or Arracan proper. It consists of a valley running parallel to the seashore, and is very low and flat. The second, Sandoway, comprehending the mainland between the eighteenth and nineteenth degrees of latitude, is mountainous, and intersected by rivers running across from west to east. The capital town is Sandoway, and is considered the most healthy station of the province. The third, Ramree, which includes Aeng and the islands of Ramree and Cheduba. The first of these is considerable, and is separated from the mainland by a narrow and navigable channel. Cheduba is separated from Ramree by a channel some miles broad, and its capital, Khyouk Phyoo, is situate on the northern extremity of the island. It is considered healthy. The aboriginal inhabitants of Arracan are termed Mughs. When the province came into the possession of the British, the population was only about 100,000. In 1831 it had increased to 173,000, and in 1839 to 248,000. It is now upwards of 321,000. In 1839 the Mughs amounted to more than half the population. This is probably the case still, though the comparative numbers must have been in some measure affected by the immigration consequent on the increase of commercial prosperity. Education to a certain extent is very general throughout the province; and there are few persons to be found who cannot read. The instruction of the children is part of the duty of the priest, who is employed in this description of labour a great part of the day. The boys assemble in the monasteries, and go generally at the age of ten years. They are taught reading, writing, and arithmetic. There is no difference between the education of the rich and the poor. The alphabet contains thirty-six letters, which are written from left to right; they use either the palm-leaf or a kind of paper manufactured from the bark of a tree. The vernacular language of the Mugh is similar to the Burmese. The character is just the same. Seven government English schools have been established in the province; three in the town of Akyab, and four in that of Ramree. Several youths have recently been placed in the Medical College at Calcutta. Previous to admission into this institution, they undergo a course of instruction in the English language, and are then drafted into the college, where they receive the necessary training, with a view to future employment in the medical service in their native country.

The history of Arracan, till the year 1184, comprises an account of the reigns of 120 princes. We are informed by the only document possessed by the Mughs which pretends to be an historical record (called by them *Radzawang*,—History of Kings), that the first of these rulers died after a long and happy reign, in the Mugh era 63, corresponding with A.D. 701. The period of which this history treats does not fail to exhibit those scenes of treachery, usurpation, dethronement, and assassination so characteristic of the history of an Indian native state, and there can be no reason for doubting that in this respect at least the picture bears some resemblance to the truth, whatever degree of authenticity it may display in general. In 1783 Arracan was invaded and conquered by the Burmese. Thenceforward the history of the country becomes part of that of Ava, under which head its continuation will be found. The first war between that state and the British government ended in the transfer to the latter of certain portions of the Burmese territory, of which Arracan was one. The annexation of this province was considered necessary, not so much from its resources or the fertility of its soil (for a large part was swamp and jungle), as from the barrier afforded by the Yoomadoung mountains against any aggression upon the British territory in that quarter. Since, however, this province has been included in the catalogue of British possessions, a sterile and unprofitable tract has been transformed into a highly-cultivated country, trade has increased to an extent that could not be contemplated, and the variety and quality of the productions of Arracan have been found to equal those of almost any other part of India. The benefits accruing to the inhabitants from these changes may be truly estimated by considering that, instead of being engaged in incessant feuds and quarrels, they are now a peaceable, contented, and happy people, engaged in the ordinary operations of life.

ARRACAN.—Formerly the capital town of the province of the same name, but which, long decreasing in importance, is now comparatively of little consequence, and only interesting on account of its old associations. It is situate in a valley on the banks of a small branch of the Arracan or Kuladyne river, and is about fifty miles from the sea. This valley is intersected by numerous streams and nullahs, all of which overflow, and "convert it into a noisome swamp." It is surrounded on all sides by hills varying in height from 200 to 500 feet: the hollows between them consist of swamps and jungles. On the summits of these hills many temples and pagodas have been erected, which at a distance give a lively and picturesque appearance to the scene. None are of any importance, except to the worshippers of Gautma, of which deity each contains an image. The town is straggling, and the houses are poor and small, constructed of bamboo, and raised several feet from the ground, to protect them from the water, which in the time of inundation flows under them. The principal street lies along the bank of the stream which divides the town, and over which several ill-constructed wooden bridges are thrown. Before the war the place was much larger, and contained at one time, it is said, 18,000 houses; but the number of those inhabited must be fearfully decreased, for, according to Pemberton, the population in 1835 amounted only to 8,000 or 10,000. The town contains but one place of any particular interest, and that is the ancient fort of Arracan, which is now in a state of ruinous decay. The British succeeded in taking this fort by assault, on the 1st April, 1825. There is one bazaar in the town, where provisions of all kinds are procurable, and the shops are well supplied with muslins, cloths, and other articles of British manufacture, including glass, crockery, and cutlery; which articles are generally imported from Calcutta. The position of Arracan, in a swampy valley, and surrounded with hills, is "particularly calculated to engender that condition of the surrounding atmosphere which long experience has shown to be productive of febrile disease." Arracan has been the grave of many of the British troops, who fell victims to the insalubrity of the climate. From this cause, and from its inconvenient situation in a commercial point of view, it is matter neither of surprise nor regret that it should have been superseded by the towns of Akyab and Khyouk Phyoo. This place was taken by the Burmese in 1783; and its capture, in 1825, by the British under General Morrison, was followed by the subjugation of the whole province. Lat. 20° 42′, long. 93° 24′.

ARRACAN RIVER. — A large stream discharging the waters of the Coladyne, and other rivers of Arracan, into the Bay of Bengal. "The entrance of this river is low, and has some rocks near it called the 'Fakiers,' covered at high water." Lat. 20° 5′, long. 92° 57′.

ARRAH, in the British district of Shahabad, lieut.-gov. of Bengal, a town on the route from Dinapore to Ghazeepore, 25 miles W. of former, 75 E. of latter. Supplies and water are abundant, the surrounding country being fertile and well cultivated, and a large and beautiful lake being close to the town. There is a government school here. According to Buchanan, the town contains 2,775 houses. Lat. 25° 31′, long. 84° 43′.

ARRIATOOR, in the British district of Trichinopoly, presidency of Madras, a town on the route from Tanjore to Cuddalore, 24 miles N. of the former. Lat. 11° 8′, long. 79° 8′.

ARRULL.—A town in the native state of Cutch, under the political superintendence of the presidency of Bombay, distant N.W. from Bhooj 39 miles. Lat. 23° 26′, long. 69° 11′.

ARUL, in Sinde, is a watercourse, or channel, proceeding from the south-eastern part of Lake Manchur (an expansion of the Narra), and discharging its water into the Indus, on the western side, about four miles below Sehwan, after a course of about twelve miles. At Sehwan it is a deep, sluggish stream 200 feet wide. The Narra, the lake, and the Arul form a continuous channel communicating at both extremities with the Indus, and running for above 100 miles nearly parallel to it on the western side. As the current is very moderate in this channel during the inundation, it is then more frequented than the main stream. It falls into the Indus in lat. 26° 24′, long. 67° 55′.

ARUN, the principal tributary to the Coosy river, rises in Thibet, in several streams, situate between lat. 87° and lat. 88°, and about long. 28° 45′, and flows upwards of 200 miles through Thibet, first in a south-easterly, and then in a westerly direction, to the great snowy range of the Himalayas, where, in lat. 28° 12′, long. 86° 53′, "it passes between their mighty peaks, and receives the torrents which rush from their northern face." The Arun then flows in a southerly direction for 110 miles through Nepal, to its junction with the Coosy, in lat. 26° 58′, long. 86° 57′.

ARUNDAWULL.—A town in the native state of Jeypoor, one of the hill zemindarries, under the political superintendence of the government of Madras, distant W. from Vizianagrum 85 miles. Lat. 18° 24′, long. 82° 12′.

ARUNG. — A town in the territory of Nagpoor, distant E. from Nagpoor 184 miles. Lat. 21° 11′, long. 82°.

ARWAL.—See Urwul.

ARWAPULLY.—A town in Hyderabad, or dominions of the Nizam, distant E. from Hyderabad 70 miles. Lat. 17° 20′, long. 79° 34′.

ARWEE.—A town in the territory of the rajah of Nagpore, distant W. from Nagpore 48 miles. Lat. 20° 57′, long. 78° 27′.

ASAMOW, or HUSESMOW, in the British district of Cawnpore, lieut.-gov. of the N.W. Provinces, a village on the route from the cantonment of Cawnpore to that of Calpee, and thirteen miles north-east of the latter. The road in this part of the route is excellent; the country well cultivated, and studded with small villages. Lat. 26° 15′, long. 79° 55′.

ASHTA, in the British territory of Sattara, presidency of Bombay, a town on the route from Meeruj to Sattara, 20 miles N.W. of former. Lat. 16° 57′, long. 74° 28′.

ASHTA.—A town in Hyderabad, or dominions of the Nizam, distant N.W. from Hyderabad 203 miles. Lat. 19° 22′, long. 76° 19′.

ASHTA, in Malwa, in the territory of Bhopal, a town on the route from Saugor to Mhow, 158 miles S.W. of former, 79 N.E. of latter. It is situate on the right or east bank of the river Parbutty, crossed near the town by ford. Here is a fort with a large tank, and supplies are abundant. Malcolm states the number of houses at 500, an amount which assigns a population of about 2,500 persons. It is the chief place of a pergunnah, stated to contain 244 khalsa villages, or such as belong to the government, and seventy-three allotted as jagirs or fiefs. When Hunter passed in 1792, it was held by a Mahratta chief; but having been subjugated by the British government, was by treaty, in 1818, granted, with four other pergunnahs, to the nawaub of Bhopal, to mark the approbation of his zeal and fidelity, and to enable him to maintain the contingent force, as he had stipulated. Distant S.E. from Oojein 59 miles, S.W. from Allahabad 373, S. from Agra 310. Lat. 23°, long. 76° 41′.

ASHTEE, or ASHTA, in the British collectorate of Sholapore, presidency of Bombay, a small town or village near the eastern frontier, towards the territory of the Nizam. Here, in February 1818, the Peishwa, in his hopeless flight after the battle of Poona, was surprised by a British force commanded by General Smith; and though Gokla, the Mahratta commander, made a gallant and skilful attempt to secure the fortune of the day by turning the right flank of the British, and charging their rear, he was overthrown and slain, and the Peishwa compelled to hasten his flight. The titular rajah of Sattara and some of his family were thereupon rescued from the thrall of the Peishwa, and subsequently invested with a limited dominion. Ashtee is distant S.E. from Poona 112 miles. Lat. 17° 50′, long. 75° 29′.

ASHTEH. — A town in Hyderabad, or dominions of the Nizam, distant S.E. from Ahmednuggur 39 miles. Lat. 18° 49′, long. 75° 15′.

ASHWAPOOR.—A town in Hyderabad, or dominions of the Nizam, distant E. from Hyderabad 160 miles. Lat. 17° 50′, long. 80° 54′.

ASHWAROWPETTA.—A town in Hyderabad, or dominions of the Nizam, distant E. from Hyderabad 175 miles. Lat. 17° 15′, long. 81° 11′.

ASKOT, in the British district of Kumaon, lieut.-gov. of the N.W. Provinces, a town 42 miles E. of Almora. Lat. 29° 46′, long. 80° 22′.

ASMAH, in the British district of Mymunsing, lieut.-gov. of Bengal, a town 52 miles E. from Jumalpoor, 61 miles W. of Silhet. Lat. 24° 53′, long. 90° 53′.

ASOPHGURH, in the British district Bijnour, lieut.-gov. of the N.W. Provinces, a village and fort on the route from Moradabad to Hurdwar, and fifteen miles south of the latter. It is situate on the left bank of the Ganges, in a site which is described by Mundy as very unfavourable. "Asofghur, which must be the depôt of malaria and jungle-fever, is hemmed in on all sides by forests, intersected by spacious swampy plains, covered with the rankest and most luxuriant grass and rushes. The appearance of the country, and the very smell of the air, were enough to give a fit of the ague." Nearly opposite the village is a ferry over the Ganges, there 300 yards wide, rapid, and with a stony bottom. Lat. 29° 45′, long. 78° 15′.

ASPOOR, *in the British district of* Bareilly, lieut.-gov. of the N.W. Provinces, a village on the route from the town of Bareilly to Pilleebheet, and seven miles N.E. of the former. Lat. 28° 26′, long. 79° 33′.

ASSAM.—An extensive province at the north-eastern extremity of British India. It is bounded on the north-west and north by Bhotan; on the north-east by Thibet; on the south-east by Burmah and the Naga tribes; on the south by Cachar, Tuleram Senaputtee's country, Jynteah, and the country inhabited by the Cossyah tribes; and on the west by the British zillah Goalpara. It may be stated to extend from lat. 25° 49′ to 28° 17′, and from long. 90° 40′ to 97° 1′. The area is returned as 21,805 square miles. On the north, south, and east, Assam is bordered by mountains of great elevation. The face of the country within presents to the eye an immense plain, studded with numerous clumps of hills rising abruptly from the general level. In the number of its rivers Assam is said to exceed every country in the world of similar extent. The existence of sixty-one has been ascertained, and there are many others of less importance. The chief among them is the Brahmapootra, which traverses the entire length of the valley, and divides it into two parts, the northern and the southern. The climate is said to bear some resemblance to that of Bengal, but its local position, and other modifying circumstances, render it far more temperate and equal. The degree of heat, even at the warmest season, is but moderate, and the nights are cool and refreshing throughout the year. The mean annual temperature is about 67°; the mean temperature of the four months when the heat is greatest, about 80°; that of the winter about 57°. The rains are of long continuance, commencing in March, and lasting until the middle of October. Earthquakes are frequent in Assam: few months pass without one or two shocks being experienced; but as in most countries where such occurrences are common, they are little regarded, and soon forgotten. The remembrance of one, apparently of extraordinary severity, in 1607, is preserved. By this convulsion a number of hills are stated to have been rent asunder, leaving wide and open chasms, and a few entirely disappeared; the earth opened in various places, throwing up water and mud; in other parts tracts of ground suddenly sunk, and a number of lives were lost. One of much less violence was officially reported to have taken place in 1847 at Nowgong, when several government buildings sustained considerable injury. Of the geology of Assam, it is said little is known in detail. Among the most useful of the mineral productions of the country, coal must be noticed. It has been discovered in a great variety of places on the north side of the Brahmapootra, and is believed to exist to a very great extent all along the southern side of the valley. The quality has not been sufficiently tested; but much of a tolerably fair character has been found, and it is believed that some much superior may be expected to reward the labour of further search. Iron-ore is met with in various places. In certain parts of Assam are brine-springs, from which salt is manufactured. The produce is said to be superior to that imported from Bengal; but, from various causes, it is fully as expensive. Gold-dust is washed down the rivers from the neighbouring hills; the deposits are richer in the upper parts of their respective courses, and fresh supplies are found at every monsoon. Most of the streams yield this much-valued produce in greater or less degree. Upon the zoology of Assam, it may be observed that the forests and mountains abound with wild animals. Elephants wander in large herds, and are very destructive. Many are killed in the forests, for the sake of the ivory which they furnish; and it is calculated that not less than 500 are annually caught in the province, and transported to different parts of India. Still their numbers are stated not to be perceptibly diminished. The mode of catching the wild elephant differs from that pursued in Chittagong. There large herds are surrounded by a mass of hunters, and a barricade of trees being formed, with the addition of a trench, a number of tame elephants are sent into the inclosure, which is called a keddah, and the wild elephants are secured with ropes. In Assam a single elephant is selected from the herd, and fairly run down, when the animal is entangled by ropes attached to tame elephants, and thus rendered helpless. The rhinoceros inhabits the denser parts of the forest; it is also found in high grass-jungle, near miry swamps, where it is sought by the huntsman for the sake of its skin and horn. These animals are easily tamed, and may be seen at Gowhatty, harmless as cows, attended by a single man. Tigers abound, notwithstanding the large sums paid by government in the form of rewards for their destruction. Bears are numerous, as are also leopards, wild buffaloes, and wild hogs. The fox and the jackal are met with. Wild game is abundant, and the rivers teem with fish. The tea-plant was known to be indigenous in Upper Assam before that country was in our possession. It subsequently became an article of culture and preparation, under the management of natives of China skilled in those arts, and brought from that country at the instance of government. The subject naturally attracted notice in England, the great centre of commercial enterprise; and the formation of the Assam Tea Company, now some years in operation, was the result. The intercourse between Assam and Bengal proper is almost entirely maintained by water, the facilities afforded by the Brahmapootra and Ganges, with their connecting branches, being available throughout the year. The voyage upward, hitherto tedious, is about to be rendered prompt and facile by the establishment of river-steamers on the Brahmapootra. The population of Assam is returned at 710,000. They are chiefly Hindoos; but there is a proportion of Mussulmans, which has been estimated at a sixth of the whole. A commixture of various tribes and races seems to have composed the aggregate; irruptions of the hill people, and stragglers from other districts, aiding to form the mass. Education was little known previously to the efforts of the British government to extend it. There are now government schools, where English is taught as well as the vernacular. The schools devoted solely to the latter are rather numerous. There are considerable differences in the state of the different schools; but on the whole they appear tolerably efficient. The cost for each pupil is far less than in Bengal; but this is certainly a minor consideration in comparison with the successful results of expenditure. In addition to what is done by government, the American Baptist missionaries appear to have taken up the business of education with energy and success.

That the Assamese were a warlike people may be inferred, not only from their conquest of the country, but from their successful resistance of various attempts made on their independence by the rulers of the Mogul empire while in the height of its vigour and military renown. The decline of the country dates from the latter part of the last century. In 1770 a rebellion broke out, which terminated in the expulsion of the rajah. Through the intervention of the British government, the rajah recovered his territories, and a British detachment was located in Assam, with the view of preserving the peace of the country. But the endeavour to effect a reconciliation between the prince and his disaffected chiefs proving fruitless, the force was withdrawn after the expiration of a few months. The government was then seized by the minister, who for a time permitted the nominal sovereignty to remain with the royal family. From this period Assam seems to have been abandoned to anarchy. In 1815 the minister expelled the rajah and usurped his dominions. In this emergency the ex-rajah sought the aid of the Burmese, who replaced him upon the throne, but after a brief reign again deposed him, and made Assam a dependency of Ava. On the breaking out of the first Burmese war, Assam was conquered by the British, and under the treaty with Ava, dated in February, 1826, the possession of the province was confirmed to them. A portion of Upper Assam was then constituted into a separate principality, and conferred upon Poorunder Singh, the rajah who had been expelled by the Burmese, and the remainder of the country became incorporated with the British dominions. The misgovernment, however, of Poorunder Singh, and his utter incapacity for the duties of his position, shortly led to the resumption of his territory, and in 1838 the whole province was placed under British administration. Under British rule the country has decidedly improved, and there can be no doubt that the arts of civilization will gradually extend. The cultivation of the tea-plant will give occupation to the industry of the people, and conduce to their increased prosperity. The government, however, have been constantly annoyed by the hill tribes, whose apparently irreclaimable habits of marauding have furnished occasion for very serious discussions on the means of restraining them. In dealing with such persons, severe measures would obviously be the first to present themselves to the mind; but the home authorities, always reluctant to resort to such measures, have recommended the exercise of that personal influence which has been so successful in similar cases occurring in other parts of India, and the adoption of a course of conciliation, tempered, however, by a judicious firmness, that will not suffer crime to be perpetrated with impunity.

ASSAPOOR.—A town in the native state of Indoor, or possessions of Holkar, distant S.W. from Indoor 30 miles. Lat. 22° 18′, long. 75° 39′.

ASSAYE, in Hyderabad, or territory of the Nizam, a village on the south or right bank of the Juah, in the doab or tongue of land inclosed between that river and the Kaitna, flowing more to the south. Both rivers are fordable, except in the height of the rainy season. Here on the 23rd September, 1803, Major-General Wellesley, subsequently duke of Wellington, gained a brilliant victory over a combined Mahratta force of immense superiority in point of numbers. The British troops engaged amounted only to about 4,500 men, while the Mahratta force, in addition to 10,500 men disciplined and commanded by European officers, consisted of irregular infantry of about the same amount, and a body of cavalry estimated at not less than 30,000; the whole constituting an army of upwards of 50,000 men. A medal, struck in commemoration of the victory, was presented in 1851, with the sanction of the Queen, to the surviving officers and soldiers who took part in the action. Distance from the city of Hyderabad N.W. 261 miles, from Aurungabad N.E. 43. Lat. 20° 18′, long. 75° 55′.

ASSEAGAUM.—A town in Hyderabad, or dominions of the Nizam, distant S. from Ellichpoor 75 miles. Lat. 20° 9′, long. 77° 22′.

ASSEERGURH.—A hill-fort at the north-eastern angle of the presidency of Bombay. It is situate on an isolated mountain, detached from the Satpoora range, dividing the valley of the Taptee from that of the Nerbudda, and its site is estimated to be 750 feet above the base of the mountain. The extreme length of the fortified summit from east to west is about 1,100 yards, the breadth from north to south about 600. In consequence of the great irregularity of the outline, the area is small in proportion to those dimensions, being not more than 300,000 square yards. According to Ferishta, Asseergurh was first made a place of strength in the fourteenth century, by Asa, a zemindar, surnamed Ahir, or "cow-herd," from his great wealth in cattle; and that author adds, that the family had previously possessed the mountain for nearly seven centuries. The troops of Nasir Khan, sovereign of Candeish, having by a base stratagem obtained entrance to the fort, murdered Asa and all his family; and the rulers of Candeish retained possession until 1599, when it was blockaded by Akbar, to whom it was surrendered. Subsequently to the dismemberment of the empire of Delhi, it fell into the power of Madhajee Scindia, from whom it was taken by the British, under Colonel Stevenson, in 1803; but in the same year was restored by the treaty of Serji Anjengaum. In 1819 it was besieged by a British force under Brigadier-General Doveton, to whom it surrendered on the 9th April, after a vigorous resistance; and has ever since remained in the occupation of a British garrison. A medal, struck in commemoration of its capture in 1803, was in 1851 presented, under the sanction of the Queen, to the surviving officers and soldiers who took part in the siege. Distant S.E. from Mow 99 miles, N.E. from Bombay 290. Lat. 21° 26′, long. 76° 26′.

ASSOORILLEE.—A town in Hyderabad, or dominions of the Nizam, distant N.E. from Hyderabad 142 miles. Lat. 18° 40′, long. 80° 13′.

ASSYE.—See ASSAYE.

ASUN, a small river of the British district of Dehra Doon, has its source from a spring rising close under a temple a short distance north-west of the town of Dehra. This source is in lat. 30° 20′, long. 78° 4′, and at the elevation of 2,148 feet above the sea. The Asun, collecting several rivulets, the greater part from the south-western declivity of the mountains of Gurwhal, holds a north-westerly course of about twenty-six miles, and falls into the Jumna on the left side, a short distance below Rajghat, and at the elevation of 1,469 feet above the sea; thus falling a little more than twenty-six feet a mile. The confluence is in lat. 30° 26′, long. 77° 43′.

ASUN, or AHSIN, in the territory of Gwalior, a small river rising about lat. 25° 59′, long. 77° 38′. It takes a direction generally north-east, and in lat. 26° 36′, long. 78° 28′, joins the Kooaree, a small river, which, sixty-five miles lower down, or farther to the S.E., falls into the river Sindh. The total length of course of the Asun is about eighty miles. At thirty miles from its source, and in lat. 26° 28′, long. 78° 6′, it is crossed by means of an easy ford on the route from Agra to Gwalior.

ATALMALICA.—A town in the native state of Keunjur, one of the Cuttack mehals, under the political superintendence of the government of India, distant E. from Sumbulpoor 80 miles. Lat. 21° 14′, long. 85° 12′.

ATER, in the territory of Gwalior, a town on the right bank of the Chumbul, 46 miles N.E. of the fort of Gwalior. It is situate among quicksands and jungly ravines, and is consequently difficult of access. Before its subjugation by the Mahrattas, it was the residence of a petty rajah, whose dwelling was a castle on the west of the town, inclosed with a rampart having towers. Lat. 26° 44′, long. 78° 43′.

ATHGATH, in the British district of Agra, lieut.-gov. of the N.W. Provinces, a town on the route from Etawah to Agra, 20 miles W. of the former. Lat. 26° 47′, long. 78° 47′.

ATKA, in the British district of Ramgurh, lieut.-gov. of Bengal, a town on the route from Calcutta to Sherghotty, 70 miles S.E. of the latter. Lat. 24° 6′, long. 85° 49′.

ATORNI, in the British district of Agra, lieut.-gov. of the N.W. Provinces, a village on the route from the city of Agra to that of Muttra, and ten miles north-east of the former. The road in this part of the route is wide and in general good; the country level, and well cultivated. Lat. 27° 13′, long. 77° 58′.

ATPAREE, in the British district of Sattara, presidency of Bombay, a town 65 miles S.E. from Sattara, and 65 miles S.W. of Sholapoor. Lat. 17° 26′, long. 75°.

ATROWBA TELHENEE, in the British district of Azimgurh, lieut.-gov. of the N.W. Provinces, a town the principal place of the pergunnah of the same name, is situate on the route from the town of Azimgurh to Faizabad, in Oude, and 24 miles N.W. of the former, in lat. 26° 20′, long. 82° 56′.

ATROWLEE, the principal place of the pergunnah of the same name, in the British district of Allygurh, lieut.-gov. of the N.W. Provinces, on the route from Futtehghur to Meerut, by Bolundshuhur, and 101 miles N.W. of the former. It is a large open town, with a bazaar; and water and supplies may be had in abundance. Population 12,722. Lat. 28° 2′, long. 78° 20′.

ATROWLEEA, in the British district of Azimgurh, lieut.-gov. of the N.W. Provinces, a town on the route from Azimgurh to Sultanpoor, 25 miles N.W. of the former. Lat. 26° 17′, long. 83° 1′.

ATTA, in Bundelcund, in the British territory of Jaloun, a town on the route from Calpee to Jhansi, 11 miles S.W. of the former. It has a bazaar, and supplies and water are abundant. Lat. 26° 3′, long. 79° 40′.

ATTAIA, in the British district of Mymunsing, lieut.-gov. of Bengal, a town on the route from Dacca to Bograh, 49 miles N.W. of the former. Lat. 24° 11′, long. 89° 53′.

ATTANAGAR, in the district of Salon, territory of Oude, a town situate on the river Sai, 65 miles S.E. of Lucknow, 55 N.W. of Allahabad. Butter estimates the population at 6,000, all cultivators, of whom two-thirds are Mussulmans. Lat. 26° 6′, long. 81° 20′.

ATTARAN, a river in the Amherst district of the Tenasserim provinces, formed by the junction of two streams, the Zimme and the Weingo, in lat. 16° 8′, long. 98° 9′. The united current flows for forty-five miles in a north-westerly direction, and falls into the Moulmein river about three miles above the town of Moulmein, and in lat. 16° 31′, long. 97° 44′.

ATTARAN, in the British district of Amherst, Tenasserim provinces, a town 39 miles S.E. from Moulmein, and 30 miles N.E. of Amherst. Lat. 16° 9′, long. 98° 10′.

ATTAUREE.—A village in the Punjab, five miles from the right bank of the Sutlej. Lat. 30° 34′, long. 73° 56′.

ATTOCK.—A fort and small town in the Punjab, on the left or east bank of the Indus, 912 miles from the sea, and close below the place where it receives the water of the Kabool river, and first becomes navigable. The name, signifying *obstacle*, is supposed to ave been given to it under the presumption that no scrupulous Hindoo would proceed westward of it; but this strict principle, like many others of similar nature, is little acted on. Some state that the name was given by the emperor Akbar, because he here found much difficulty in crossing the river. The river itself is at this place frequently by the natives called Attock. Here is a bridge, formed usually of from twenty to thirty boats across the stream, at a spot where it is 537 feet wide. In summer, when the melting of the snows in the lofty mountains to the north raises the stream so that the bridge becomes endangered, it is withdrawn, and the communication is then effected by means of a ferry. The banks of the river are very high, so that the enormous accession which the volume of water receives during inundation scarcely affects the breadth, but merely increases the depth. The rock forming the banks is of dark-coloured slate, polished by the force of the stream, so as to shine like black marble. Between these "one clear blue stream shot past." The depth of the Indus here is thirty feet in the lowest state, and between sixty and seventy in the highest, and runs at the rate of six miles an hour. There is a ford at some distance above the confluence of the river of Kabool; but the extreme coldness and rapidity of the water render it at all times very dangerous, and, on the slightest inundation, quite impracticable. On the right bank, opposite Attock, is Khyrabad, a fort, built according to some by the emperor Akbar, according to others by Nadir Shah. The fortress of Attock was erected by the emperor Akbar in 1581, to command the passage; but though strongly built of stone on the high and steep bank of the river, it could offer no effectual resistance to a regular attack, being commanded by the neighbouring heights. Its form is that of a parallelogram; it is 800 yards long and 400 wide. The town, which is inclosed within the walls of the fort, was formerly considerable, but has now gone greatly to decay. The population is estimated by Burnes at 2,000. Runjeet Singh obtained possession of Attock with his characteristic trickery, having by a bribe induced the Afghan commander to surrender it to him. Lat. 33° 54′, long. 72° 20′.

ATTREE.—A large watercourse sent off by the Teesta, in the British district of Dinajepore, presidency of Bengal, in lat. 26° 22′, long. 88° 48′. The great stream of the Teesta, deriving its origin from the mountains of Nepal, separates in two branches, the Attree proceeding south; the other, continuing to bear the name of Teesta, flows south-east. The Attree, proceeding from the point of divergence for forty-seven miles, through the districts of Dinajepore and Rungpoor, throws off at that distance a branch termed the Purnababa. Thence it continues its course in a southerly direction through Dinajepore for sixty miles, when it forms the boundary between this district and Bograh for twenty miles. It then passes into the British district Rajshahye, through which it flows south and south-east for seventy-five miles, before passing into the British district Pubna, through which it continues to flow S.E. for fifty miles, expanding into numerous marshes and jhils, or small lakes, and ultimately falling into the Konaie (an offset of the Brahmapootra), in lat. 23° 59′, long. 89° 45′, having had a total length of course of about 252 miles. Like other Indian rivers, it is differently denominated in different parts of its course, and towards its mouth is known by the name of Balasar. It communicates right and left with many other rivers; and so gentle is the slope of its waterway, from the alluvial level character of the tract which it traverses, that it may justly be compared to a channel through the Soonderbunds. It is navigable throughout during the rainy season for boats between thirty and forty tons burthen, but in the dry season the navigation is much impaired.

ATUK.—A town in the native state of Bhawulpoor, distant W. from Bhawulpoor 28 miles. Lat. 29° 25′, long. 71° 20′.

ATUVA, in the British district of Vizagapatam, presidency of Madras, a town 23 miles S.W. from Vizianagrum, and 23 miles N.W. from Vizagapatam. Lat. 17° 59′, long. 83° 10′.

AUCKLAND BAY.—A bay on the coast of the district of Mergui, in the Tenasserim provinces. The entrance is surrounded by islands and rocks, forming the Mergui Archipelago. The centre of the bay is in lat. 12° 5′, long. 98° 40′.

AUKLAH.—A town in Hyderabad, or dominions of the Nizam, distant S.W. from Nagpoor 90 miles. Lat. 20° 8′, long. 78° 19′.

AULAPOLAY, or ALEPPI, in the native state of Travancore, a town on the seacoast, having a considerable trade in timber, betel-nut, coir or cocoanut-fibre, pepper, cardamoms. There is no shelter for shipping, but large ships may anchor in five or five and a half fathoms, and smaller in four fathoms, about four miles from the shore. The land has here encroached on the sea, and having in front a soft mud-bank, a ship may ride in this locality with less risk than on any other part of the coast. Bartolomeo describes this place, about 1788, as "of considerable size, inhabited by a large number of Pagans, Mahometans, and Christians of St. Thomas." It communicates southward with Quilon and Trivandrum, the capital of Travancore; northwards with the town of Cochin, by means of canals dug parallel to the sandy seacoast, and connecting the series of lakes or backwaters. Between these and the sea is a communication by a wide creek or inlet, through which is floated the timber for exportation, as hither is conveyed for disposal the produce of the rajah's forests, extending over the valleys and declivities of the Western Ghauts. The rajah has also here an establishment for building small craft. Distance from Cochin city, S., 33 miles; Cannanore, S.E., 178; Mangalore, S.E., 255; Bangalore, S.W., 255; Madras, S.W., 366. Lat. 9° 30′, long. 76° 24′.

AULATODDY, in the British district of South Canara, presidency of Madras, a town 46 miles S.E. from Mangalore, and 36 miles N. of Cannanore. Lat. 12° 20′, long. 75° 16′.

AURAG RIVER.—A feeder of the Mahanuddy, rising in lat. 21° 20′, long. 82° 43′, in the native state of Phooljer, on the south-west frontier of Bengal, and flowing in an easterly direction for 100 miles through the native states of Bora Samba, Patna, and Sonepoor, falls into the Tell Nuddee on the left side, in lat. 20° 51′, long. 83° 54′, seventeen miles before its junction with the Mahanuddy.

AURUNG.—See Areeng.

AURUNGABAD, in the British district of Muttra, lieut.-gov. of the N.W. Provinces, a town on the route from the city of Agra to the cantonment of Muttra, and four miles south-west of the latter. Here, October 4th, 1804, a British convoy, consisting of a party of sepoys in charge of a hundred camels loaded with grain, were surrounded by a large detachment of Mahratta horse, who made booty of the cattle and grain, and made prisoners of the troops and camp-followers. The road in this part of the route is heavy and sandy in parts; the country is cut up by ravines, and partially cultivated. Lat. 27° 26′, long. 77° 47′.

AURUNGABAD, in the British district of Moorshedabad, lieut.-gov. of Bengal, a town on the route from Burhampore to Rajmahal, 31 miles S.E. of the latter. Lat. 24° 37′, long. 88° 2′.

AURUNGABAD, in the territory of Oude, a town on the route from Seetapoor cantonment to that of Shahjehanpoor, 28 miles N.W. of the former, 34 E. of the latter. Tieffenthaler describes it as having a brick-built palace, inclosed with a wall, and adjoining a fort of quadrangular ground-plan, and having low hexagonal towers. At present it has a bazaar, and is supplied with water from wells. The road in this part of the route is bad, the country open and waste. Lat. 27° 47′, long. 80° 27′.

AURUNGABAD, in Hyderabad, or the territory of the Nizam, a city near the north-western frontier, towards the British district Ahmednuggur. It is situate on the river Doodna, a tributary of the Godavery. Approached from the east, the view is pleasing, trees being interspersed among the houses, and a tall mausoleum rearing its dome and minarets above the other buildings. There is a wall of the kind common in India, low, but strengthened with round towers. The palace, built by Aurungzebe, originally a structure of no great dimensions or architectural beauty, is now in so decayed a state that it is unsafe to pass through the ruins. The chief ornament of the city is the mausoleum, also built by Aurungzebe, to receive, it is said, the remains of a favourite daughter. It bears some resemblance to the famous Taj Mahal of Agra, but is in every respect greatly inferior. Aurungabad was formerly the capital of the extensive soobah or province of the same name, comprehending a considerable proportion of the ancient Deccan kingdom of Ahmednuggur. It is now described as an expanse of ruined buildings. The town is amply supplied with water, and has been selected for one of the stations of the army of the Nizam. Of the present amount of population there is no correct account; but in 1825 it was estimated at 60,000; at the present time it most probably falls far short of that number. Distance from Ahmednuggur, N.E., 68 miles; Poona, N.E., 138; Bombay, N.E., 175; Hyderabad, N.W., 270; Nagpoor, S.W., 263. Lat. 19° 51′, long. 75° 21′.

AUTANCURRAY, in the British district of Madura, presidency of Madras, a town on the seacoast of Palk Strait, 11 miles S.E. of Ramnad. Lat. 9° 20′, long. 79° 4′.

AUTERIAH.—A town in the territory of Nagpore, distant S.E. from Ramgurh 40 miles. Lat. 22° 23′, long. 81° 26′.

AUTGAWN.—A town in the native state of Patna, one of the petty states on the south-west frontier of Bengal, distant S. from Sumbulpoor 60 miles. Lat. 20° 40′, long. 83° 39′.

AUTGURH.—One of the petty native states on the south-west frontier of Bengal, known as the Cuttack Mehals, which became tributary to the British government upon the conquest of the province of Cuttack in 1804. Autgurh, the principal town, is situate 20 miles W. of Cuttack. Lat. 20° 31′, long. 85° 40′.

AUTMALLIK.—A petty native territory on the south-west frontier of Bengal, forming one of the group of districts known as the Cuttack Mehals. It extends from lat. 20° 34′ to lat. 21° 4′, and from long. 84° 16′ to long. 84° 50′. It contains an area of 648 miles, with a population amounting to 29,160.

AUTOOR, in the British district of Madura, presidency of Madras, a town 31 miles N.W. from Madura, and 10 miles S.E. of Dindigul. Lat. 10° 18′, long. 77° 55′.

AUTUNKULL.—A town in the native state of Travancore, distant S.E. from Quilon 20 miles. Lat. 8° 41′, long. 76° 52′.

AVA, the capital of the Burmese empire, is situate on the left bank of the Irawaddy, and on an island formed by that river, which flows along the northern face of the city, and two of its confluents, the Myit-nge and the Myit-tha; the former joining it above the town, at the north-eastern angle, and the latter below it, at the western extremity. In addition to the natural defences presented by these broad and rapid streams, the city is surrounded by a brick wall, fifteen feet in height and ten in thickness, strengthened by an interior bank of earth, on the top of which is a terre-plein. The wall, however, except at certain points, is stated to be ill constructed and out of repair. Between the wall and the river is a ditch, which, though broad and deep in some places, is fordable in the dry season. Within the walls, which measure five and a half miles in circumference, are comprised the larger and the lesser town. The latter occupies the north-eastern quarter, and contains the royal palace, the hall of justice, the council-chamber, the arsenal, and the houses of several officers of distinction; the whole being inclosed by a strong, well-constructed wall, twenty feet in height, and defended on the exterior by a teak-wood stockade, of equal elevation. The palace is of modern date, and, as might be expected, is less remarkable in its architecture for harmony of proportion, or grandeur of design, than for richness and beauty in details. In the larger town the houses of the better class are, for the most part, constructed of planks, and tiled, few being built of brick; while those of the lower orders are mere huts: but even these, in point of airiness, elevation, and mode of construction, are represented as constituting better habitations for the poor than are to be met with in other Asiatic countries. In Bengal the sleeping-apartments of the larger portion of the population are level with the ground, while throughout the Ava territories the dwelling of every man is elevated in proportion to his means; and even those of the poorer classes are raised three feet above the ground. Though the country round Ava is well cultivated, there is little of bustle or activity within the town; and its stillness and tranquillity indicate no great extent of industry or amount of population. The latter has been estimated at from 25,000 to 30,000. Distant from Prome, N.E., 221 miles. Lat. 21° 52′, long. 96° 1′. For an account of the territory of which this place is the capital, see BURMAH.

AVANJAH.—A town in Hyderabad, or dominions of the Nizam, distant S.W. from Hyderabad 48 miles. Lat. 16° 42′, long. 78° 19′.

AVINASI, in the British district of Coimbatore, presidency of Madras, a town on the route from Coimbatore to Salem, 24 miles N.E. of the former. Lat. 11° 11′, long. 77° 19′.

AVUDERCOVIL, in the British district of Tanjore, presidency of Madras, a town 50 miles S. of Tanjore, and 50 miles N. of Ramnad. Lat. 10° 5′, long. 79° 5′.

AWEIN, in the British district of Amherst, one of the Tenasserim provinces, a town nine miles N.W. of the town of Ye, and 63 miles S.E. of Amherst. Lat. 15° 20′, long. 98°.

AWUN.—A town in the Rajpoot state of Jeypoor, distant S. from Jeypoor 80 miles. Lat. 25° 48′, long. 75° 47′.

AYAGUDY, in the British district of Coimbatore, presidency of Madras, a town 29 miles N.W. from Dindigul, and 20 miles S. of Darapooram. Lat. 10° 28′, long. 77° 38′.

AYAH, in the British district of Futtehpore, lieut.-gov. of the N.W. Provinces, a town which with that of Sah gives name to the pergunnah of Ayah Sah. It is miscalled Teah by Rennell, and is situate nine miles S.W. of the town of Futtehpore. Lat. 25° 51′, long. 80° 42′.

AYEWARRA.—A town in the territory of Nagpore, distant N. from Nagpore 96 miles. Lat. 22° 33′, long. 79° 20′.

AYNOOR.—A town in Mysore, distant N.W. from Seringapatam 139 miles. Lat. 14°, long. 75° 31′.

AYRWA, in the British district of Furruckabad, lieut.-gov. of the N.W. Provinces, a town 33 miles S.W. from Futtygurh, 28 miles N.E. of Etawah. Lat. 26° 54′, long. 79° 30′.

AZEEMABAD, in Sirhind, a town on the route from Kurnal to Lodiana, and nine miles N.W. of the former place. Its site is slightly elevated above the neighbouring plain, which is under water in the rainy season. The town is surrounded by a high brick wall, pierced with loopholes for musketry, and having bastions surmounted with towers. Water is at all times obtainable from a large tank, rendered accessible by a flight of brick-built stairs. At the north of the town is a large caravansera, inclosed with a lofty embattled wall, having a handsome tower at each corner, and surrounded by a deep ditch capable of being filled with water. Azeemabad is often in the maps mentioned with the alias of Tirowlee. Distant N.W. from Calcutta 1,098 miles. Lat. 29° 48′, long. 77°.

AZEEZPOOR, a village in Sinde, lies on the route from Subzulcote to Shikarpoor, and 18 miles a little south of west of the latter place. It is situate on the east bank of the Indus, over which is a ferry called Azeezpoor Patan. By treaty of November, 1842, it was ceded, together with Subzulcote and several other towns, to Mahomed Bhawlkhan, and in the following February it was transferred accordingly. Lat. 27° 52′, long. 69° 2′.

AZGURPOOR, in the British district of Bolundshuhur, lieut.-gov. of the N.W. Provinces, a village on the route from Meerut to Muttra, and 54 miles N.E. of the latter. The road in this part of the route is good, the country open and partially cultivated. Lat. 28° 12′, long. 77° 55′.

AZIMGHUR.—A British district subject to the lieut.-gov. of the N.W. Provinces, and named from its principal place. It is bounded on the north-west by the territory of Oude; on the north by the British district of Goruckpore; on the north-east by Sarun; on the south-east by the British district of Ghazeepore, and on the south-west by the British district of Jounpore. It lies between lat. 25° 36′—26° 24′, long. 82° 45′—84° 12′, and has an area of 2,520 square miles. The principal rivers are the Gogra, the Tons (north-eastern), and the Chota or Lesser Surjoo. The population is returned at 1,653,251. Populous towns are unknown. There are only three within the district containing more than 10,000 inhabitants. The principal routes through the district are—1. From north to south, from Goruckpore to Ghazeepore. 2. From north-east to south-west, from Goruckpore to Azimghur, and continued thence to Jounpore cantonment. 3. From south-east to north-west, from Ghazeepore to Azimghur, thence, in the same direction, to Faizabad, and from that place to Secrora. 4. From south-east to north-west, from Ghazeepore to Lucknow. The country was early subdued by the Rajpoots: an inscription at Deogano proves that in the middle of the twelfth century it was subject to the sovereign of Canouj, and on the subversion of that kingdom by the defeat and slaughter, in 1194, of Jaya Chandra, by Mohammed of Ghor, became part of the Patan kingdom of Delhi, with which, in 1528, it was by the conqueror Baber transferred to the Timurian or Mogul dynasty founded by him in Hindostan. On the dismemberment of the empire consequent on the invasion of Hindostan, in 1760, by Ahmed Shah Dooranee, the tract comprised within the present district of Azimghur was, with Oude and some other possessions, appropriated by Shooja-ud-dowlah, the nawaub vizier of Oude. By the treaty of the 10th November, 1801, it, with other districts, was ceded in commutation of subsidy, by the nawaub vizier Saadut Ali, to the East-India Company.

AZIMGHUR.—The principal place of the district of the same name, a town situate on the river Tons (north-eastern), here traversed by a bridge of boats, and navigable downwards to its confluence with the Surjoo. Azimghur was founded about 1620, by Azim Khan, a powerful zemindar, inheriting an extensive tract of country conferred on one of his ancestors by the imperial court of Delhi. Little respecting the town is stated by any European except Hamilton, who mentions that "a considerable quantity of cotton goods are manufactured and exported from this place and its vicinity." Population, including the cantonment, 13,322. Distant from Calcutta, N.W., *viâ* Ghazeepore, 448 miles; from Benares, N., by Jounpore, 81; from Allahabad, N.E., 109; from Lucknow, S.E., 171. Lat. 26°, long. 83° 14′.

AZOEZPOOR, in the British district of Muttra, lieut.-gov. of the N.W. Provinces, a village on the route from the cantonment of Muttra to Delhi, and 27 miles N.W. of the former. The road in this part of the route is good. Lat. 27° 46′, long. 77° 31′.

AZUMPOOR.—A town in the British district of Bijnour, lieut.-gov. of the N.W. Provinces, distant N.W. from Calcutta 890 miles; E. from Meerut 28 miles. Lat. 29°, long. 78° 14′.

B.

BABOOBUND, in the British district of Sumbulpoor, on the south-west frontier of Bengal, a town on the route from Sumbulpoor to Nagpoor, 11 miles W. of the former. Lat. 21° 22′, long. 83° 52′.

BABRA.—A town in the province of Guzerat, or territory of the Guicowar, distant S.W. from Deesa 70 miles. Lat. 23° 50′, long. 71° 6′.

BABRIAWAR, in the peninsula of Kattywar, province of Guzerat, a district named from the Babria tribe of Coolies, who formerly possessed the adjacent districts of Kattywar and Gohilwar, but have latterly been driven by the invading Kattis into this comparatively small tract. It is bounded on the north-west and north by the district of Kattywar; on the east by that of Gohilwar; on the south-east and south by the Arabian Sea; and on the south-west and west by the district of Sorath. It lies between lat. 20° 47′—21° 10′, long. 71° 3′—71° 33′. The district contains thirty-three tallooks or subdivisions, seventy-one towns and villages, and a population estimated at 18,468, paying annually to the Guicowar a tribute of 10,677 rupees; besides which sum, the nawaub of Joonaguih, in consequence of a claim made by him over the district, extorts considerable sums as a sort of black-mail. Jaafarabad, the only collection of dwellings which can with propriety be denominated a town, is described in its place in the alphabetical arrangement.

BABRIGOTE, in the British district of Hyderabad, province of Sinde, a town on the left bank of the main branch of the river Indus, 30 miles S. of Tatta. Lat. 24° 20′, long. 67° 55′.

BACHMEYEE, in the British district of Mynpooree, lieut.-gov. of the N.W. Provinces, a village on the route from the cantonment of Allygurh to that of Mynpooree, and forty-nine miles south-east of the former. The road in this part of the route is bad, the country level, and partly covered with jungle, partly cultivated. Lat. 27° 42′, long. 78° 50′.

BACHOONDA.—A town in the Rajpoot state of Joudpore, distant S. from Joudpore 55 miles. Lat. 25° 31′, long. 73° 10′.

BACKERGUNGE (including Deccan Shabazpore).—A British district named from the town formerly the locality of its civil establishment, and within the limits of the lieut.-gov. of Bengal. It is bounded on the north by the British districts Deccan, Jelalpoor, and Dacca; on the north-east and east by the British district of Bulloa, from which it is separated by the Meghna; on the south by the Bay of Bengal; on the south-west by the Sunderbunds; and on the west by the British district of Jessore. It lies between lat. 22° 2′—23° 13′, long. 89° 49′—91°, and has an area, according to official return, of 3,794 square miles. It is throughout a level alluvial country, watered by the two great rivers the Ganges and the Meghna, or Lower Brahmapootra, and by many streams or watercourses, offsets from those main rivers. The climate is regarded as generally healthy, being cooled by the numerous streams, so that the thermometer has not been known to rise above 88° in the shade. To guard against the widely-extending inundations, the houses of the natives are built on mounds, raised by excavating the ground for materials; and the depressions thus made serve as tanks, which in some parts of the district are very numerous and useful, as the water of the rivers is brackish. The soil is in general a rich alluvial mud, deposited by the streams, which often produce very violent effects, sweeping away land in some places and depositing it in others, where it is soon cultivated, and yields rich and abundant crops of rice. The jungles abound in wild beasts, including the rhinoceros, wild buffalo, tiger, leopard, wild swine, deer of various kinds, monkeys, and birds in vast variety and numbers. Besides rice, the principal crops are sugar-cane, cotton, wheat, pulse, mustard-seed, other oil-seeds, pease, and other pulse. The population, according to official statement, is 733,800, an amount which, compared with the area, shows a relative density of 193 to the square mile. It embraces a small number of native Christians, descendants from persons of half-blood between Portuguese and Hindoos. These Christians are of the Romish persuasion, and have a church at Seebpore. There are also some converts recently made by Baptist missionaries.

BACKERGUNGE, a town in the British district of the same name, lieut.-gov. of Bengal, is situate on the offset from the Ganges called Backergunge Creek. It was the seat of the civil establishment of the district previously to its removal to Burrisol, the present locality. Distance from Burrisol, S., 12 miles; Calcutta, E., 125. Lat. 22° 33′, long. 90° 22′.

BACOTEE, or BUKOTHE, in the British district of Cawnpore, lieut.-gov. of the N.W. Provinces, a village on the route from the cantonment of Futtehghur to that of Cawnpore, and 36 miles N.W. of the latter. Lat. 26° 53′, long. 80° 6′.

BADAMEE, in the British district of Belgaum, presidency of Bombay, a town and hill fort on the route from Kuladgee to Bellary. The fort was taken by storm in 1818, by a detachment under Sir Thomas Munro. Distant 22 miles S.E. of Kuladgee. Lat. 15° 55′, long. 75° 45′.

BADANPOOR.—A town of Central India, in the native state of Meyhar, distant S.W. from Rewah 40 miles. Lat. 24° 9′, long. 80° 54′.

BADAPULLY.—A town in Hyderabad, or the dominions of the Nizam, distant S.W. from Hyderabad 49 miles. Lat. 16° 45′, long. 78° 11′.

BADARKA, in the district of Bainswara, territory of Oude, a town situate four miles east of the left bank of the Ganges, distant five miles E. of Cawnpore, 42 S.W. of Lucknow. Butter estimates the population at 8,000, of whom only fifty are Mussulmans. Lat. 26° 28′, long. 80° 30′.

BADERHAT, in the British district of Moorshedabad, lieut.-gov. of Bengal, a town 11 miles W. from Moorshedabad, 52 miles S. of Rajmahal. Lat. 24° 16′, long. 87° 59′.

BADHEE, or **BUDDEEA**, in the Pinjor Dhoon, a village on the Baladh, a small stream tributary to the Sursa. It is situate on an excellent military road leading from Pinjor to Malown and Belaspoor. Lat. 30° 55′, long. 76° 53′.

BADINOO, in the Rajpoot state of Bikaneer, a village on the route from Rutungurh to the town of Bikaneer, and 30 miles E. of the latter. It contains 200 houses, supplied with tolerably good water from a well 271 feet deep. Lat. 27° 54′, long. 73° 51′.

BADLEE, in the jaghire of Jujhur, lieut.-gov. of the N.W. Provinces, a village on the north-eastern frontier, towards the British district of Delhi. Lat. 28° 33′, long. 76° 51′.

BADOWAS.—See BHARAWAS.

BADRAJ, a summit of the mountain bounding the Dehra Dun on the north, rises over the left bank of the Jumna, a short distance above its confluence with the Tons. It was a station in the trigonometrical survey of the Himalaya. Elevation above the sea 7,510 feet. Lat. 30° 29′, long. 78° 1′.

BADRAJ DEVI, in the British district of Jaunsar, a halting-place on the ascent to the fort of Bairat, in the mountains between the rivers Jumna and Tons. It was a station in the trigonometrical survey of the Himalaya. Elevation above the sea 6,043 feet. Lat. 30° 33′, long. 77° 56′.

BADRAJ MASRAS, in Gurwhal, a summit on a ramification from the great Manin Peak between the Jumna and Bhageerettee. It was a station in the trigonometrical survey of the Himalaya. Elevation above the sea 7,344 feet. Lat. 30° 32′, long. 78° 7′.

BADRINATH, in the British district of Gurwhal, lieut.-gov. of the N.W. Provinces, a town on the route from Serinagar to the Mana Pass, 25 miles south of the latter, and 55 north-east of the former. It is situate on the right bank of the Bishengunga, or Vishnugunga, a feeder of the Aluknunda, in the middle of a valley about four miles long and one broad; and is equidistant from two lofty mountains, one rising to the east, the other to the west. The bank on which it stands is sloping; that opposite is bolder, its brow being on a level with the top of the temple of Badrinath, situate in the highest part of the town, and rising between forty and fifty feet from the ground. The building is of conical form, with a small cupola, covered with plates of copper, and surmounted by a golden ball and spire. The original establishment is reported to be of very great antiquity; the present temple has, however, a modern appearance, several former ones having been overwhelmed by avalanches, and an earthquake having shaken the present erection so seriously as to render necessary an almost entire restoration. A short distance below the temple is the Tapta Kund, a tank about thirty feet square, covered with a roof of planks, supported on wooden posts. It is supplied from a thermal spring, by means of a subterraneous communication, terminated by a spout in the form of a dragon's head. A thick smoke or steam, of a strong sulphureous smell, is sent forth by the water, which is so hot as to be scarcely endurable to the feel until the temperature is reduced by the admixture of cold water from another spring. In this manner a bath is formed, in which the sexes bathe indiscriminately. The ablution, accompanied by due adoration of the idol, and liberal fees to the attendant Brahmins, is considered so efficacious in cleansing from past offences, that from forty-five to fifty thousand pilgrims visit the shrine every twelfth year, when the Kumbh Mela is celebrated. They assemble at Hurdwar, and as soon as the fair there is closed, towards the middle of April, proceed on their round of pilgrimage in the mountains, by Devaprayag, Rudraprayag, Kedarnath, Badrinath, and home by Nanaprayag and Karnprayag. In ordinary years the number of pilgrims is considerably less. Much attention is ostensibly paid to the comforts and enjoyments of the deity, who is daily provided with a dinner, which is placed before the idol, and the doors of the sanctuary then closed, to leave him uninterrupted during his meal and subsequent repose. The doors are opened after sunset; and at a late hour, his bed being prepared, he is again inclosed, and left in solitude. The vessels in which he is served are of gold and silver, and a large establishment of servants is kept up. The temple is closed in November, and the treasure and valuable utensils buried in a vault beneath; and every human being connected with the establishment then proceeds to Josimath, or some other more genial wintering-place, Badrinath and its vicinity being at that season covered with deep snow. Some mountaineers once took advantage of a sudden thaw, and making their way to the treasury, plundered it of 900 pounds weight of gold and silver. They were, however, discovered and put to death. In former times the rajahs of Gurwhal frequently made free with the treasure, borrowing sums, and making over villages as security, which were never subsequently redeemed. From this and other sources, the institution obtained possession of 226 villages in Gurwhal and Kumaon, which, however, according to Traill, yield collectively an annual income of only 200*l.*; and as the annual expenditure sometimes exceeds the income derived from the offerings of votaries and the rents of the assigned lands, the deficiency is supplied by loan, to be repaid in years when the offerings of the pilgrims prove unusually large. The priests (Brahmins from the Deccan) are under the control of one of their own caste, called Rawul. As there are no women of their caste here, they live in a state of perfect celibacy, but are in truth a very profligate set; notwithstanding which, it is believed that through their mediation the deity holds forth an unqualified remission from transmigration. West of the temple about twelve miles is a group of six summits, called the Badrinath Peaks, having the elevations respectively of 23,441, 23,236, 22,934, 22,754, 22,556, and 21,895; and six miles to the south-west is a summit having an elevation of 21,385 feet above the sea. Elevation of the temple above the sea 10,294 feet. Lat. 30° 44′, long. 79° 32′.

BADROOAH.—A town in the province of Guzerat, or dominions of the Guicowar, distant N. from Baroda 19 miles. Lat. 22° 30′, long. 73° 10′.

BADSHAHNAGUR, in the British district of Shahjehanpoor, lieut.-gov. of the N.W. Provinces, a town on the route from Futtygurh to Shahjehanpoor, seven miles S. of the latter. Lat. 27° 48′, long. 80°.

BADSHAPOOR, in the British district of Jounpoor, the principal place of the pergunnah of the same name, a town on the route from Allahabad to Jounpoor, 30 miles N.E. of the former, 36 S.W. of the latter. It has a large bazaar and water, and supplies are abundant and good. Lat. 25° 40′, long. 82° 10′.

BADULWALA, in the British district of Hurriana, lieut.-gov. of the N.W. Provinces, a village near the southern frontier, towards Shekhawati. Lat. 28° 49′, long. 75° 54′.

BAGAPAR, in the British district of Goruckpoor, lieut.-gov. of the N.W. Provinces, a town 32 miles N. of Goruckpoor. Lat. 27° 9′, long. 83° 35′.

BAGEHWAREE, in the British district of Sholapoor, presidency of Bombay, a town on the route from Beejapoor to Moodgul, 26 miles S.E. of the former. Lat. 16° 33′, long. 76° 3′.

BAGESUR, in the British district of Kumaon, lieut.-gov. of the N.W. Provinces, a small town at the confluence of the rivers Surjoo and Gaomati. It has a bazaar containing forty-two shops, all belonging to merchants permanently residing in the town of Almora, and frequenting this place for two months only in the year during the briskness of the trade with Tartary. There are two considerable fairs in the year for the purposes of that trade, which has latterly been greatly on the increase. According to native tradition, the inhabitants of this place and its vicinity are the descendants of Moguls, left in Kumaon by Tamerlane's orders; and numerous tombs, substantially formed of large flat tiles, are, according to Traill, the memorials of that race. The elevation is something more than 3,000 feet above the sea. Distance N.E. of Almora 17 miles; N.W. from Calcutta, by Almora, 911 miles. Lat. 29° 50′, long. 79° 49′.

BAGHAT, or BUGHAT, a district among the Cis-Sutlej hill states, is bounded on the north by a detached portion of Pateeala and by Burrowlee; on the east by Keyonthul; on the south-east and south by outlying possessions of Pateeala; and on the west by Beja, Kothar, and Subatoo. It is about nine miles long in a direction from south-east to north-west, and six in breadth; its area being about thirty square miles. Its centre is in lat. 30° 55′, long. 77° 7′. On the expulsion of the Goorkhas, in 1815, the British government sold six pergunnahs of the ten which it comprised, to the rajah of Pateeala, for 13,000*l.*, and conferred the remaining four on the rana, or chief, although from his unfriendly conduct he had little claim to consideration. The population, assuming the average of the neighbouring country (114 to the square mile), would be about 3,420. On the death of the rana without heirs, in 1839, his territory was regarded as having escheated to the East-India Company, and the rajah of Pateeala offered to purchase it for 15,000*l.* Between 1839 and 1842, allotments of land were granted to individuals for locations, and a cantonment for an European regiment built on the hills. The annual land revenue was estimated at 285*l.*, out of which 128*l.* was paid to the relatives of the late rana. Doubts, however, were expressed at home as to the propriety of the resumption; and the question was referred by the then governor-general, Lord Ellenborough, to Sir George Clerk, at that time envoy at the court at Lahore, on whose report the escheat was set aside, and a younger brother of the deceased formally recognised as successor. This prince died in the beginning of the year 1849, and a claim to the succession was then preferred by a first cousin of the last two chiefs. The claim was not allowed; but a discretional authority was given to the local government, either to resume the estate, or if more expedient, to bestow it on the claimant by a new sunnud, under proper conditions. The former alternative was adopted, and Baghat is now a British possession.

BAGHEL, in the British district of Goruckpore, lieut.-gov. of the N.W. Provinces, a small town near the south-eastern frontier, towards British district Sarun. According to Buchanan, it contains 100 houses, an amount which would assign it a population of about 600 persons. Distant S.E. from Goruckpore cantonment 45 miles. Lat. 26° 22′, long. 83° 57′.

BAGHIN.—A small river rising in Bundelcund, in the table-land surmounting the range of Panna, and in lat. 24° 45′, long. 80° 23′. It takes a course north-east for about twenty miles, and falls over the brow of the ridge in a cascade, the elevation of which is estimated by Jacquemont at 100 yards. Running north it enters the British district of Banda, and flows along the western base of Kalleenjur; a few miles beyond which it turns N.E., in which direction it continues until its fall into the Jumna on the right side, in lat. 25° 33′, long. 81° 5′. Its total length of course is about ninety miles. It is called Bagun by Garden, who mentions that it is crossed forty miles from its source by the route from Banda to Kalleenjur.

BAGHONDEE, in the Rajpoot state of Joudpore, a village on the route from Balmer to the town of Joudpore, and forty-nine miles east of the former. It is situate in the fertile low country on the north or right bank of the Loni, and near the confluence of the Leek, a torrent flowing from the north. Lat. 25° 56′, long. 72° 12′.

BAGHPUT, in the British district of Meerut, lieut.-gov. of Agra, a town the principal place of the pergunnah of the same name, with a population of 6,494 persons. Lat. 28° 56′, long. 77° 17′.

BAGLUNG CHAUR.—A town in the native state of Nepal, distant N.W. from Katmandoo 137 miles. Lat. 28° 23′, long. 83° 15′.

BAGMUTTEE.—A river rising in Nepal, and, according to Kirkpatrick, on the northern declivity of the mountain Shipuri, in lat. 27° 53′, long. 85° 29′, about eighteen miles direct N.E. from the city of Katmandoo. Taking a winding course, but generally southwest, it passes along the east side of Katmandoo, separating it from the contiguous town of Patn, situate on the left or east bank; and in this part of its course it assumes the appearance of a "respectable stream." Its meandering course in the mountain-gorges between the source and those towns is probably double the direct distance. Continuing its course generally southerly, it passes from the valley of Nepal into the Terrai, or jungly plain, at the foot of the mountains, and thence becomes navigable. Continuing its course in the same direction, it traverses or bounds in its course the British districts of Sarun, Mongheer, and Tirhoot; when, passing from the latter, it proceeds to its confluence with the Ganges, in lat. 25° 23′, long. 86° 34′, and about eight miles below Mongheer, but on the opposite side of the river. Its total length of course is about 285 miles. In its course through the plain it receives numerous streams right and left, and among them the lesser Gunduck; whence the united stream is frequently denominated the Gunduck.

BAGNAN, in the British district of Hooghly, lieut.-gov. of Bengal, a town on the route from Calcutta to Midnapoor, 25 miles W. of the former. Lat. 22° 28′, long. 88° 1′.

BAGNEE.—A river of Bhotan, rising to the north of the main range of the Himalayas, about lat. 28° 5′, long. 89° 31′, and flowing in a southerly direction through Bhotan for 150 miles, joins the Guddada in lat. 26° 18′, long. 89° 50′; the joint streams finally falling into the Brahmapootra.

BAGNUGGUR.—See Bakhira.

BAGNUGOUR, in the British district of Goruckpore, lieut.-gov. of the N.W. Provinces, a town on the route from Goruckpore to Bansee, 21 miles N.W. of the former. Lat. 26° 54′, long. 83° 8′.

BAGORE.—A town in the Rajpoot state of Oodeypoor, distant N.E. from Oodeypoor 67 miles. Lat. 25° 20′, long. 74° 30′.

BAGROD, in territory of Gwalior, or possessions of Scindia's family, a town on the route from Saugor to Asseergurh, 39 miles S.W. of former, 245 N.E. of latter. It has a bazaar, and is provided with water from wells. Lat. 23° 44′, long. 78° 13′.

BAGUL, or BHAGUL.—A small hill state, bounded on the north by Sooket, from which it is separated by the Sutlej; on the east by Bhugee and Dhamee, and an outlying portion of Pateeala; on the south-east by Koonear, and on the west by Hindoor, Kuhloor, and Mangul. It is about eighteen miles long from north to south, and ten in breadth from east to west; containing probably a hundred square miles. The central part is situate about lat. 31° 13′, long. 77° 1′. Its surface has in general considerable elevation, especially in the west, which consists of a mountainous tract, containing the summit of Bahadurgarh, 6,233, and Bara Devi, 7,003 feet above the sea. The drainage of Bhagul is principally to the southward, in which direction several small streams and torrents flow and discharge themselves into the river Gunbur. A stream, called in the trigonometrical survey the Seer, flows in a north-westerly direction, and discharges itself into the Sutlej. Bhagul comprises twelve pergunnahs or districts, and has a population estimated at 40,000, and an annual revenue computed at 5,000*l.* sterling; out of which a tribute of 360*l.* is paid to the British government. This state was, on the expulsion of the Ghoorkas in 1815, restored by the British to the hereditary rajah, subject to the condition of maintaining 100 beegarrees, of making roads through the district, and in case of war, of joining the British troops with his forces. His armed retainers are about 3,000.

BAGULKOTA, in the British district of Belgaum, presidency of Bombay, a town on the route from Belgaum to Moodgul, 50 miles W. of the latter. Lat. 16° 10′, long. 75° 46′.

BAGUR.—A hilly tract comprising the eastern part of Guzerat and the western of Malwa, and containing the small states of

Banswara and Doongurpoor, and their numerous petty tributaries. It is a very rough country, consisting of numerous ranges running N. and S., and covered with thick jungle; yet its general elevation is inferior to that of Malwa, though greater than that of Guzerat. The boundaries are probably not very accurately defined; but this tract is laid down in Walker's Map of Western India as lying between lat. 23° 10′—24° 10′, long. 73° 45′—74° 58′.

BAGURPOOR, in the British district of Moradabad, lieut.-gov. of the N.W. Provinces, a village on the route from the town of Moradabad to Meerut, and 23 miles W. of the former. Lat. 28° 54′, long. 78° 29′.

BAH, in the British district of Agra, lieut.-gov. of the N.W. Provinces, giving with Pinnahut name to the pergunnah of Bah Pinnahut. It is situate three or four miles from the right bank of the Jumna, 40 miles S.E. of Agra. Lat. 26° 52′, long. 78° 40′.

BAHA, in the British district of Agra, lieut.-gov. of the N.W. Provinces, a town 16 miles S.W. of the city of Agra. Lat. 27° 2′, long. 77° 53′.

BAHADERPOOR, in Guzerat, or territory of the Guicowar, a town on the route from Dhuboi to Mow, six miles N.E. of former, 150 W. of latter. Lat. 22° 9′, long. 73° 34′.

BAHADERPOOR, in the British district of Mirzapoor, lieut.-gov. of the N.W. Provinces, a village on the right bank of the Ganges, 14 miles N.W. of Mirzapoor, or, higher up the stream, 735 N.W. of Calcutta by water, or 912 if the Sunderbund passage be taken. Lat. 25° 16′, long. 82° 22′.

BAHADERPOOR, in the Rajpoot territory of Alwur, a village on the route from Delhi to the town of Alwur, and 11 miles N.E. of the latter. The road to the north, or towards Delhi, lies through the Kishengurh Pass, and is bad; to the south-west it is good. Lat. 27° 40′, long. 76° 48′.

BAHADERPOOR.—A town in the province of Guzerat, or territory of the Guicowar, distant S.E. from Baroda 20 miles. Lat. 22° 10′, long. 73° 30′.

BAHADOORGANJ, or BAHADOORPOOR, in the British district of Ghazeepoor, lieut.-gov. of Agra, a town on the route from Ghazeepoor cantonment to that of Goruckpoor, 26 miles N. of the former, 75 S. of the latter. It is situate on the right bank of the Tons (north-eastern), called in this part of its course the Surjoo. Lat. 25° 48′, long. 83° 21′.

BAHADOORGANJ, in the British district of Bareilly, lieut.-gov. of the N.W. Provinces, a village on the route from Bareilly to Petoragarh, and 42 miles N.E. of the former. Lat. 28° 44′, long. 79° 53′.

BAHADOORGUNJE, in the British district of Purneah, lieut.-gov. of Bengal, a town 36 miles N.E. from Purneah, 69 miles N.W. of Dinajepore. Lat. 26° 12′, long. 87° 51′.

BAHADOORGURH.—A jaghire, or feudal possession under the political superintendence of the lieut.-gov. of the N.W. Provinces. It is bounded on the east and south by the British district of Delhi, and on the north and west by that of Rohtuk, and extends from lat. 28° 37′ to 28° 49′, and from long. 76° 54′ to 77° 1′. The length of the estate from north to south is fourteen miles, and its breadth from east to west six miles, containing an area of forty-eight square miles. The population, if assumed at the average of the adjacent state of Rohtuk (300 to the square mile), would amount to 14,400. This jaghire, though comprehended in the grant made by the British government to the nawaub of Jhujur in 1806, was specified in the schedule thereto annexed as the portion conferred upon Mohummud Ismael Khan, the brother of the nawaub. For a time it constituted the sole possession of Bahadoor Jung Khan, the present nawaub of Bahadoorgurh; the separate pergunnah of Dadur, which was held by his father on the condition of military service, having been retained by the nawaub of Jhujur, who agreed to furnish the quota of horse for whose maintenance the fief had been bestowed. By recent accounts it appears, however, that Dadur has again reverted to Bahadoor Jung Khan. The nawaub of Bahadoorgurh is a Mahometan. His revenue amounts to 13,000*l.* per annum, and the military force maintained by him consists of 150 horse and foot.

BAHADOORGURH, on the route from Delhi to Hansi, and 18 miles W. of the former, is a considerable walled town, the capital of the jaghire or feudal territory of the same name. Lat. 28° 40′, long. 76° 58′.

BAHADOORGURH, in the Cis-Sutlej hill state of Hindoor, a fort on a ridge forming the boundary between that state and Bagul. Elevation above the sea 6,233 feet. Lat. 31° 13′, long. 76° 56′.

BAHADOORPOOR, in the territory of Gwalior, or possessions of Scindia's family, a fortified village on the route from Etawah to Gwalior fort, 67 miles S.W. of former, 17 N.E. of latter. Lat. 26° 16′, long. 78° 23′.

BAHADOORPOOR, in the British district of Budayon, lieut.-gov. of the N.W. Provinces, a village on the route from Allyghur to Moradabad, and 33 miles S.W. of the latter. Lat. 28° 29′, long. 78° 28′.

BAHAR.—See Behar.

BAHAR.—A town in the territory of Oude, distant S. from Lucknow 41 miles. Lat. 26° 17′, long. 80° 52′.

BAHAWULPORE, a state of Western India, is bounded on the north-west for a short distance by Sinde, and for the rest of the long frontier in that direction by the Punjaub; on the east, south-east, and part of the south, by the British district of Bhutteeana and the Rajpoot states of Bickaneer and Jessulmere; and on the south-west angle by Sinde. It is a long narrow tract, of shape approaching to that of an elongated oval, lying between lat. 27° 41′—30° 25′, long. 69° 30′—73° 58′. It is 310 miles in length from north-east to south-west; 110 in breadth at the widest part, measured at right angles to the line of its length; and 22,000 square miles in superficial extent; of which, however, only about a sixth part is capable of cultivation. The north-western frontier is formed by a river-line, consisting in its successive parts of the Ghara, the Punjnud, and the Indus. Bahawulpore is a remarkably level country, there being no considerable eminence within its limits, as the occasional sand-hills, seldom exceeding fifty or sixty feet in height, cannot be considered exceptions. The cultivable part extends along the river-line for a distance of about ten miles in breadth, from the left or eastern bank. In the sandy parts of the desert beyond this strip of fertility, both men and beasts, leaving the beaten path, sink as if in loose snow. The transition from the desert to the cultivated tract is very abrupt and striking. In the course of half a mile, or less, the country changes from a howling wilderness to a scene where thick and verdant groves, green fields, and luxuriant crops delight the eye, and offer supplies for all the wants of man. The population of Bahawulpore consists chiefly of Jets of Hindoo descent; of Hindoos of more recent settlement in the country; of Beloochees, and Afghans. The large admixture of the blood of the hardy mountaineers of the west causes the people to differ widely in appearance and constitution from the more eastern Hindoos. They are bulky, strong, dark-complexioned, and harsh-featured, with long hair and beards. The upper classes use the dress and language of Persia. The language of the bulk of the people is a *patois* of Hindostani, mixed with Pushtoo and Belooche, and is rendered disagreeable to strangers by the nasal drawling tone in which it is uttered. The khan and a great majority of the inhabitants are Mahomedans, but Hindoos are treated with much toleration. The dominant race is that generally known in the country by the name of Daudputrees, or sons of David; having been first collected, as is supposed, by David, a man of note, though of the weaver caste, at Shikarpoor, in Sinde, who, being driven thence, found refuge in the present location of those who bear his name. Bhawl Khan, one of his descendants, founded the capital, and called it after himself, Bahawulpore. The present khan is the lineal descendant of the founder of the race. The annual revenue is about a million and a half of rupees.

The rulers of Bahawulpore were, during the flourishing state of the Durani monarchy, nawaubs, or deputy-governors, for that power. On its dismemberment, consequent on the expulsion of Shah Shoojah, the nawaub of that time, without a struggle, became independent, and assumed the title of khan. On the rise of Runjeet Singh, the late ruler, Mahomed Bhawl Khan, in alarm for his own safety, tendered his allegiance to the British, and solicited their protection. It being the policy of the British government to make the Sutlej the boundary of Runjeet Singh's dominions, the khan's request was complied with as regarded his Cis-Sutlej territories. In 1838, upon the proposed restoration of Shah Shoojah to the throne of Cabool, it became expedient to fix the future relations of the nawaub, both with respect to the British and the restored king; and a treaty was accordingly concluded, by the terms of which Bahawulpore was released from allegiance to Cabool, and placed under the protection of the British government. The khan invariably acted as the steady friend of the British, and the support given by him to their troops in the wars in Sinde and Afghanistan was rewarded in February, 1843, by the annexation to his territories of a portion of the northern part of Sinde, including Subzulcote and the fertile district of Bhoong Bara. At the commencement of the Mooltan rebellion in 1848, the khan volunteered to the British government the services of the whole of his military force. At the latter end of May, his troops, amounting to about 9,000 horse and foot, crossed the Sutlej, and effecting a junction with Capt. Edwardes and General Courtlandt, sustained an attack at the village of Kineyree from the army of Moolraj, amounting to 8,000 men with ten guns, which resulted in the complete discomfiture of the latter. For this service the khan, in addition to the reimbursement of his military expenditure, received a pension for life of 10,000*l.* per annum. In 1844 the nawaub readily ceded a strip of land on the Sutlej which was essential to the British for the continuance of a frontier customs-line to that river. Bhawl Khan died in 1852, and his eldest son Hajee Khan having been disinherited and imprisoned, the vacant throne fell to a younger son, Sadik Khan. Hajee subsequently escaped from prison, and being joined by many of the chiefs and people, and ultimately by the troops, succeeded in possessing himself of the country, and of the person of his brother. No part was taken in the contest by the British government. Upon its termination in favour of Hajee, they recognised the title of the candidate who, it appeared, was most acceptable to the population, and interfered no further than to obtain for the deposed nawaub a fitting stipend, with permission to reside within the British dominions. The total population of Bahawulpore has been rated at 600,000, but this estimate probably errs in excess. The principal towns are Bahawulpore the capital, Ahmedpoor, Ooch, and Khanpoor.

BAHAWULPORE, the capital of the state of the same name, is situate on a branch of the Ghara, about two miles from the main stream, and fifty miles above its confluence with the Chenaub. It is surrounded by a ruinous wall of mud, which is about four miles in circuit; but part of the inclosed space is occupied by groves of trees. The houses are built, some of burnt, some of sun-dried bricks, but they are in general mean. The residence of the khan, like the rest, is in a very plain style of architecture. Population about 20,000. A good road has been recently constructed from this town through the territory of Bikaneer to Sirsu, in Bhutteana. Lat. 29° 24′, long. 71° 47′.

BAHILI, in the native state of Bussahir, a mountain-ridge proceeding in a north-westerly direction to the left bank of the Sutlej from Moral-ke-kanda, a lofty range stretching south-westward from the Himalaya. On the summit is situate a fort, which, at the time of Fraser's visit, was a square redoubt, surrounded by an excellent stockade. Below it, but at a great depth, runs the Nowgurreekhola, a considerable stream, flowing from the east, and falling into the Sutlej on the left side. Lat. 31° 22′, long. 77° 42′.

BAHMEIR, in the British district of Candeish, presidency of Bombay, a town 92 miles E. from Surat, 40 miles N.W. of Malligaum. Lat. 21° 4′, long. 74° 17′.

BAHMINGAWN.—A town in the native state of Nepal, distant N.W. from Khatmandoo 240 miles. Lat. 29° 7′, long. 81° 40′.

BAHNSDI, in the British district of Ghazeepoor, lieut.-gov. of the N.W. Provinces, a town six miles S.W. of the right bank of the river Ghogra, 47 N.E. of Ghazeepoor cantonment. Lat. 25° 53′, long. 84° 12′.

BAHR.—A village in the petty hill state of Beja, at the base of the range of hills bounding the Pinjor Dun on the north-east, and consisting in this part of slate, clay, sandstone, and trap. It is situate on the route from Pinjor to Subathu, and six or eight miles north of the former place. When visited by Lloyd, in 1822, it was a small hamlet, with one shop and a storehouse. It is now, however, more considerable, being the station where, in the road from the plains to Subathu, Simla, and Kotgurh, wheeled carriages, tents, and similar bulky articles are deposited, previously to resuming the journey with the aid of jampans, or mountain-sedans. The ascent to Bahr from Pinjor commences about three miles from the former place, and is very gradual and by a good road. From Bahr, in the direction of Subathu, there is an excellent road, originally made for military purposes. It is impracticable, however, for beasts of burthen loaded as in the plains; yet even camels, which are those least suited for hill-service, can proceed as far as Subathu with half-loads. Bahr is supplied with water by means of a small artificial channel cut from a mountain-stream. Elevation above the sea 2,500 feet. Distance N.W. from Calcutta 1,060 miles. Lat. 30° 53′, long. 77°.

BAHREH.—See Bara River.

BAHUL, in the British district of Hurriana, lieut.-gov. of the N.W. Provinces, a town on the route from Beekaneer to Hansee, 40 miles S.W. of the latter. Lat. 28° 38′, long. 75° 40′.

BAICULL, in South Canara, within the territories subject to the presidency of Madras, a town and fort, the latter situate on a high point projecting southwards into the sea. The town, which stands to the northward of the fort, is very small and irregularly built. The tract within which this place is situate, is supposed at the remotest period of its history to have formed part of the realm ruled by the Cadumba dynasty, which was overthrown, it has been conjectured, in the second century of the Christian era. It subsequently became part of the great realm of Vijayanagar, on the destruction of which by the Mussulman confederacy at the battle of Telikot, in 1565, it was seized by the rajah of Bednor. On the conquest of that state by Hyder Ali, in 1763, it fell to that adventurer, and on the overthrow of his son Tippoo, in 1799, was incorporated with the dominions of the East-India Company. The town of Baicull is distant S.E. from Mangalore 37 miles; S.E. from Bombay 480; W. from Bangalore 177; W. from Madras 358. Lat. 12° 24′, long. 75° 6′.

BAIJNATH.—A town of the Punjaub, in the native state of Mundi, one of the hill states north of the Sutlej, distant N.W. from Mundi 29 miles. Lat. 32°, long. 76° 43′.

BAILA.—A town in the territory of Nagpore, distant S. from Berar 25 miles. Lat. 20° 48′, long. 79° 5′.

BAILA, or BYLA, in the British district of Jaunsar, a village on a high mountain close to the left bank of the Tons. Here was a secondary station during the great trigonometrical survey of the Himalayas. Elevation above the sea 6,318 feet. Lat. 30° 45′, long. 77° 47′.

BAILAMAN.—A town in the native state of Mohurbunge, situate on the south-west frontier of Bengal, distant W. from Midnapoor 85 miles. Lat. 22° 29′, long. 86° 4′.

BAILEY ISLAND.—One of the group of islands forming the Mergui archipelago, off the Tenasserim coast. Lat. 12° 9′, long. 97° 50′.

BAILGAON.—A town in the territory of Nagpore, distant N.E. from Nagpore 91 miles. Lat. 21° 58′, long. 80° 16′.

BAIMLEY.—A town in Hyderabad, or the dominions of the Nizam, distant N.E. from Sholapoor 40 miles. Lat. 18° 9′, long. 76° 16′.

BAING, a river of the Tavoy district of the Tenasserim provinces, rises in lat. 13° 27′, long. 98° 51′, and flowing in a northerly direction for sixty-five miles, falls into the river Tenasserim in lat. 14° 14′, long. 98° 35′.

BAINPORE, in the British district of Midnapore, lieut.-gov. of Bengal, a town 29 miles N.W. from Midnapore, 46 miles S. of Bancoora. Lat. 22° 35′, long. 87°.

BAINROH, in Sirhind, a village on the route from Hansi to Loodiana, and 45 miles S. of the latter town. Distant N.W. from Calcutta 1,067 miles. Lat. 30° 20′, long. 75° 57′.

BAINSWARA, an extensive district of Oude, is bounded on the north-west and north-east by the district of Lucknow; on the south-east by the districts of Sultanpoor, Salon, and Ahladganj; on the south-west by the Ganges, dividing it from the British districts Allahabad, Futtehpore, Cawnpore, and Furrukhabad—lies between lat. 25° 55′—26° 48′, long. 80° 20′—81° 35′, and is about seventy-five miles in length from east to west, and fifty-eight in breadth. It contains the following pergunnahs or subdivisions:—1. Ranjit Purua; 2. Harha; 3. Ateha; 4. Mauhranwa; 5. Kumranwa; 6. Daundia-khera; 7. Hasnganj; 8. Majranow; 9. Haidargarh; 10. Rae Bareli; 11. Dalamau; 12. Sarendi; 13. Bardar.

BAINTGHUR, in the British district of Hijellee, lieut.-gov. of Bengal, a town on the river Russoolpoor, 43 miles S.E. of Midnapoor. Lat. 21° 55′, long. 87° 47′.

BAIRAT, in the British district of Jaunsar, N.W. Provinces, a fort on a summit of the range between the Tons and Jumna, and near the right bank of the latter river. It was a station of the large series of triangles in the great trigonometrical survey of the Himalayas. Elevation above the sea 7,599 feet. Lat. 30° 35′, long. 78°.

BAIRCHUE.—A town in the native state of Gwalior, or possessions of the Scindia family, distant E. from Oojein 34 miles. Lat. 23° 14′, long. 76° 20′.

BAIREA, or BYRIAH, in the British district of Ghazeepoor, lieut.-gov. of the N.W. Provinces, a town on the left bank of the Ganges, six miles by water S. of Ghazeepoor cantonment, N.W. of Calcutta 607 by water, or 784 taking the Soonderbund channel. Lat. 25° 29′, long. 83° 32′.

BAIRKAIRA, in the British territory of Saugor and Nerbudda, under the lieut.-gov. of the N.W. Provinces, a town on the river Nerbudda, 39 miles W. of Jubbulpoor. Lat. 23° 6′, long. 79° 26′.

BAIROOR.—A town in Hyderabad, or dominions of the Nizam, distant S.E. from Hyderabad 71 miles. Lat. 16° 46′, long. 79° 26′.

BAIRSEAH.—A district in Central India, bounded on the north, north-east, and east by Scindia's territory; on the south by Bhopal, and on the west by Omutwarra. It extends from lat. 23° 26′ to 23° 52′, and from long. 77° 10′ to 77° 40′, and has an area of 456 square miles. It was formerly a dependency of Dhar, but overrun by the Pindarries previously to the dispersion of those plunderers by the British government under the administration of the marquis of Hastings. At the termination of the war it was ostensibly restored to Dhar by the treaty of 1819, but was to remain in the possession of the British for a term of five years, for the purpose of liquidating a loan; after which period it was still to continue under the management of the British government, which was thenceforward to account to the Dhar state for the revenue and produce of the district. This arrangement was probably suggested by the remoteness of Bairseah from the territory of Dhar and the seat of its government. In 1821 the district was ceded to the British government on condition of the annual payment of a lac of rupees; but the bargain being found a losing one, the state of Dhar was prevailed upon to take it back. This step was not approved by the home authorities, who expressed an opinion that Dhar had not been liberally dealt with. In consequence, the former relations were reverted to, and Bairseah is now a British possession, subject to the payment above mentioned.

BAIRSEAH.—A town in Malwa, the chief place of the British district of the same name. Lat. 23° 37′, long. 77° 27′.

BAITMUNGALUM. — A town in the native state of Mysore, under the administration and control of the government of India, distant N.E. from Seringapatam 110 miles. Lat. 13°, long. 78° 16′.

BAITOOL, or BEITOOL, in the British territory of Saugor and Nerbudda, lieut.-gov. of the N.W. Provinces, a town the principal place of the pergunnah of the same name, on the route from Nagpore to Mhow, 112 miles N.W. of former, 185 S.E. of latter. It is situate on the small river Machna, a tributary of the Towa, and in a pleasant valley at the south base of the Satpoora range. There is a fort here. The pergunnah of Baitool contains seams of coal, but of no very good quality. The population of the pergunnah, by the last returns, was 93,441. The town of Baitool, originally under the dominion of the Goond rajah of Kerla, appears to have been subjugated about a century ago by the Bhonsla rajah of Nagpore or Berar; and in 1818 was, with the rest of Saugor and Nerbudda territory, ceded to the British government. Distant S.E. from Saugor 150 miles; S. from Agra 370; S.W. from Allahabad 356; W. from Calcutta 677; N.E. from Bombay 390. Lat. 21° 50′, long. 77° 58′.

BAJAROW, or BUGREE, in the Rajpoot state of Jeypoor, a large village with a fort built on a rock, 50 miles S.E. of the city of Jeypoor. Lat. 26° 25′, long. 76° 27′.

BAJEE, in Bussahir, a ruined fort on a summit of a ridge stretching north-eastward from the peak of Whartoo to the outer Himalaya. Elevation above the sea 9,105 feet. Lat. 31° 15′, long. 77° 37′.

BAJETPORE, in the British district of Mymunsing, lieut.-gov. of Bengal, a town 46 miles N.E. of Dacca, and 75 miles S.W. of Silhet. Lat. 24° 12′, long. 90° 56′.

BAJPOOR, in Guzerat, or the territory of the Guicowar, a town on the right bank of the river Taptee, distance from the city of Surat, N.E., 60 miles. Lat. 21° 22′, long. 73° 48′.

BAJUNI, in the hill state of Hindoor, a village on the route from Subathu to Bilaspoor, and 22 miles N.W. of the former town. It is situate near the Gamrara river, at the eastern base of the ridge of Malown; the fortress of which is built on the summit, 2,000 feet above it. Lat. 31° 12′, long. 76° 52′.

BAKAH.—A town in the territory of Nagpore, distant E. from Nagpore 104 miles. Lat. 21° 2′, long. 80° 47′.

BAKHIRA, or BAGNUGGUR, in the British district of Goruckpoor, lieut.-gov. of the N.W. Provinces, a small town on the western bank of the Bukra lake. Buchanan, describing its condition nearly fifty years ago, states, "Bakhira contains 250 houses, surrounded by a ditch, rampart, and bamboo hedge, still very inaccessible, although not in repair." Allowing six persons to each house, the population may be estimated at 1,500 persons. It has a market. Distance N.W. from Goruckpoor cantonment 19 miles. Lat. 26° 55′, long. 83° 4′.

BAKHIRA JHIL, or BUDANCH TAL, in the British district of Goruckpoor, lieut.-gov. of the N.W. Provinces, so called from the small town of Bakhira, situate on its western bank, is thus described by Buchanan. "It is certainly the finest piece of fresh water that I have seen in India, but it will not bear a comparison in beauty with European lakes." He adds, that though generally known to Europeans by the name of Bakhira Jhil, the natives generally call it Barachi; and a nawaub of Oude, accustomed to hunt on its bank, called it Moti Jhil, or "Pearl of Lakes." Distant 13 miles N.W. of the cantonment of Goruckpore. Lat. 26° 53′, long. 83° 5′.

BAKRA.—A town in the Rajpoot state of Joudpore, distant N.W. from Joudpore 73 miles. Lat. 26° 44′, long. 72° 3′.

BAKROO.—A town in the Rajpoot state of Joudpore, distant S.W. from Joudpore 83 miles. Lat. 25° 18′, long. 72° 30′.

BAKUH.—A town in the territory of Nagpore, distant N. from Nagpore 74 miles. Lat. 22° 12′, long. 79° 2′.

BAKUL, or PAKUL, in the British district of Goorgaon, lieut.-gov. of the N.W. Provinces, a village situate at the eastern base of a low rocky range of hills, partly of sandstone, partly of quartzose formation. Distance S. from Delhi 20 miles. Lat. 28° 21′, long. 77° 17′.

BALA.—A town in the Rajpoot state of Joudpore, distant E. from Joudpore 35 miles. Lat. 26° 10′, long. 73° 41′.

BALABET.—A town in the native state of Gwalior, or possessions of Scindia's family, distant N.W. from Saugor 40 miles. Lat. 24° 20′, long. 78° 30′.

BALAGHAT DISTRICTS.—This name designates a large tract of elevated country in the south of India, extending from the rivers Toombuddra and Krishna in the north, to the extremity of Mysore in the opposite direction. The area, excluding that part which forms the state of Mysore, is 28,669 square miles. The name Balaghat implies "above the ghauts," as Payenghat indicates "below the ghauts." The district formed part of the ancient Hindoo kingdom of Bijyanagar, or Carnata. It was conquered by the Mahomedans, and upon the fall of the Mogul empire was split into various states, more or less powerful and independent; some of them originating in the claims of official rank, some in local possession, and others in undisguised usurpation. The notorious Hyder Ali conquered, but did not tranquillize the country; the petty chiefs, called poligars, continuing to disturb it; these men, while exacting from the cultivators all that they could, being engaged in constant struggles with the government, to evade or withhold any payment on their own part. Hyder was succeeded by his son Tippoo Sultan, whose headstrong perverseness led him into hostilities with the British, which subjected him in the first instance to the deprivation of half his dominions, and ultimately to the loss of the whole. On his defeat and death, the country was partitioned. The chief of Kurnool was permitted to retain his patrimony, which was of ancient tenure. The remainder was shared among the rajah of Mysore (restored by the conquerors), the British, and the Nizam; but the whole is now either nominally or actually British. In 1800 the Nizam ceded his portion in commutation of subsidy. In 1841, the nawaub of Kurnool, by misconduct, incurred the penalty of forfeiture; and Mysore, though not formally British territory, has long been under British management. Excluding Mysore, the country is divided into three districts, Bellary, Cuddapah, and Kurnool. Under the above heads more detailed information will be found.

BALAGUTCH, in the British district of Tirhoot, lieut.-gov. of Bengal, a town on the route from Mongheer to Hajepoor, 50 miles W. of the former. Lat. 25° 29′, long. 85° 43′.

BALAHARA, in the Rajpoot state of Jeypore, a village with a fort, on the route from Agra to Ajmere, 78 miles W. of former, 150 E. of latter. It is situate close to a pass through a chain of rocky hills running north and south. At the close of the last century the fort was bombarded, and partially demolished by Duboigne, the general of Scindia. Lat. 26° 57′, long. 76° 47′.

BALAN.—A town in the Rajpoot state of Joudpore, distant S.E. from Beekaneer 51 miles. Lat. 27° 19′, long. 73° 44′.

BALANA, in the Rajpoot state of Jessulmer, a town in the desert, 35 miles N.E. of the city of Jessulmer. Lat. 27° 13′, long. 71° 29′.

BALAONEE, in the British district of Sattara, presidency of Bombay, a town 45 miles S.E. from Sattara, 29 miles N.W. of Meeruj. Lat. 17° 11′, long. 74° 32′.

BALAPOOR.—A town in Hyderabad, or dominions of the Nizam, distant S. from Hyderabad four miles. Lat. 17° 18′, long. 78° 33′.

BALARAMPOOR.—See BULRAMPOOR.

BALASINORE.—A petty native state or jaghire in the province of Guzerat, politically connected with the government of Bombay. It is bounded on the north by the Myhee Caunta; on the south-east by the Rewa Caunta; on the south-west and west by the British district of Kaira. It extends from lat. 22° 53′ to 23° 17′, and from long. 73° 17′ to 73° 40′, and contains an area of about 258 square miles. The jaghire is held by a Mussulman nawaub, a scion of the powerful family of Babi. Joonaghur, in the peninsula of Kattywar, and Theraud, in Guzerat, are in the possession of other branches of the same family. The nawaub of Balasinore has an income of 4,154*l.*, out of which he pays annually a tribute of 1,000*l.* to the British government. The population is about 19,000. The jaghire was originally a grant from the government of Delhi, but in 1768 it became tributary to the Peishwa, by whose fall, in 1818, the claim passed to the British government. The estate was some years ago placed under attachment, in consequence of the murder of a state creditor, whose debt had been guaranteed by the British government, and was retained under British management pending the minority of the rajah, but restored to him in a flourishing condition in the year 1846, upon his attaining the age of nineteen. The nawaub maintains a small military force, consisting of fifty peons and eight horsemen, who are employed indiscriminately in revenue, police, and miscellaneous duties.

BALASINORE.—A town the chief place of the petty state bearing the same name. It lies on the route from Neemuch to Baroda, and supplies and water are abundant. It is surrounded by a wall, and is rather a thriving place. Distant from Neemuch, S.W., 147 miles; from Baroda, N., 49; from Ahmedabad, E., 49; from Mhow, W., 160; from Bombay, N., 280. Lat. 22° 58′, long. 73° 20′.

BALASORE, in the British district of Cuttack, within the lieut.-gov. of Bengal, a town situate near the Boorahbullung, a small river falling into the Bay of Bengal a short distance to the eastward. The sea rises on the bar from twelve to fifteen feet in common spring tides, but there is not more than a depth of two or three feet on the bar at low water in the dry season. Balasore is provided with dry docks, to which vessels can be floated during the spring tides. It is frequented chiefly by vessels from the Maldives, and by craft engaged in taking rice and salt to Calcutta. The situation of the town is unfavourable, being on a low dreary plain, deformed by numerous unsightly ridges and sandhills. The trade of the place was formerly extensive and important, but is now much decayed. The Portuguese and Dutch, in the early period of European intercourse, held possessions here, and a factory belonging to the Danes, with adjoining lands, was ceded to the British government in 1846 for a pecuniary consideration. As large ships cannot enter the river, they must be anchored in Balasore Roads, where they are in some degree sheltered, and may lie over good holding-ground five or six miles off shore. Balasore Roads form an extensive bay, which stretches from Point Palmyras to the south-westernmost banks at the mouths of the Hooghly. This town is the locality of the civil establishment of the northern division of Cuttack. Distance from Madras, N.E., 730 miles; Cuttack, N.E., 100; Nagpore, E., 507; Calcutta, S.W., 116. Lat. 21° 30′, long. 87°.

BALBEEGA, in the British district of Behar, lieut.-gov. of Bengal, a town on the route from Calcutta to Shergotty, 15 miles E. of the latter. Lat. 24° 30′, long. 85° 6′.

BALCHA, a pass on the frontier separating Gurwhal from Bussahir, lies over a crest of the ridge dividing the valleys of the rivers Tons and Pabur. This ridge is covered with lofty and dense forests, abounding in the celebrated deodar, considered identical with the cedar of Lebanon. Elevation of the pass above the sea 8,898 feet. Lat. 31° 4′, long. 78°.

BALCHORAH.—See BALZORA.

BALCONDAH.—A town in the native state of Hyderabad, or dominions of the Nizam, distant N. from Hyderabad 100 miles. Lat. 18° 51′, long. 78° 20′.

BALDHI, in Thibet, a town on the northern shore of the great lake of Yarbrough Youmtso, distant N. from Durrung 191 miles. Lat. 29° 3′, long. 91° 14′.

BALDOOM CHITTY, in the British district of Chota Nagpoor, lieut.-gov. of Bengal, a town 95 miles E. from Sirgoojah, and 63 miles S.E. of Palamow. Lat. 23° 4′, long. 84° 37′.

BALEHBA.—A town in the Rajpoot state of Joudpore, distant W. from Joudpore 139 miles. Lat. 25° 56′, long. 71°.

BALIBANG.—A town in the native state of Nepal, distant W. from Khatmandoo 120 miles. Lat. 27° 49′, long. 83° 21′.

BALING, in the British district of Kumaon, lieut.-gov. of the N.W. Provinces, a village on the right bank of the river Dhouli. Elevation above the sea 11,000 feet. Lat. 30° 12′, long. 80° 35′.

BALIYA, in the district of Sultanpoor, territory of Oude, a town 87 miles S.E. of Lucknow. It is situate in an extensive jungle, seven miles north of the left bank of the river Sai. Butter estimates the population at 6,000, all Hindoos and cultivators. Lat. 25° 55′, long. 82° 5′.

BALKISSEN, in the British district of Burdwan, lieut.-gov. of Bengal, a town 11 miles N. from Burdwan, and 27 miles W. of Nuddya. Lat. 23° 22′, long. 87° 56′.

BALLAIRAI DROOG.—A town in Mysore, distant N.E. from Seringapatam 100 miles. Lat. 13° 9′, long. 75° 29′.

BALLAMGARH.—See BULUBGURH.

BALLAPOOR.—A town in Mysore, distant N. from Bangalore 23 miles. Lat. 13° 17′, long. 77° 36′.

BALLAPOOR.—A town in Mysore, distant N.E. from Seringapatam 99 miles. Lat. 13° 26′, long. 77° 47′.

BALLAPOOR, in the territory of Oude, a town on the route from Cheetapoor to Sekrora, 30 miles S.E. of the former, 50 N.W. of the latter, 35 N. of Lucknow. Lat. 27° 22′, long. 81° 6′.

BALLARY.—See BELLARY.

BALLASAR.—See ATTREE.

BALLAVEDDER.—A town in Mysore, distant N.W. from Seringapatam 152 miles. Lat. 14° 27′, long. 75° 52′.

BALLEABERA, in the British district of Midnapoor, lieut.-gov. of Bengal, a town situate to the south of the route from Midnapore to Sumbulpore, 27 miles S.W. of the former. Lat. 22° 16′, long. 87°.

BALLIAPUDDA, in the British district of Cuttack, lieut.-gov. of Bengal, a town on the river Mahanuddy, 24 miles E. of Cuttack. Lat. 20° 27′, long. 86° 19′.

BALLIAREE, in the British district of Hyderabad, province of Sinde, a town on the northern boundary of the great western Runn of Cutch, 108 miles S.E. of Hyderabad. Lat. 24° 21′, long. 69° 46′.

BALLPOOR, in the territory of Oude, a town on the route from the cantonment of Sekrora to that of Sultanpore, seven miles S.E. of the former, 76 N.W. of the latter, 50 N.E. of Lucknow. Lat. 27° 3′, long. 81° 45′.

BALMER, in the Rajpoot state of Joudpore, a town of about six hundred houses, built principally of stone, with a small fort occupying the summit of a conical hill three hundred feet high, at the foot of which is the town. Distant S.W. from Joudpore 119 miles. Lat. 25° 47′, long. 71° 22′.

BALOAMOODRUM, in the British district of Madura, presidency of Madras, a town 31 miles W. from Dindigul, 54 miles N.W. of Madura. Lat. 10° 25′, long. 77° 34′.

BALOTRA, in the Rajpoot state of Joudpore, a town on the route from Balmer to the city of Joudpore, and 62 miles S.W. of the latter. It is situate on the right bank of the Loonee, and on the high road from Joudpore to Dwarka, a celebrated place of pilgrimage at the western extremity of Guzerat. There is, consequently, a great thoroughfare of pilgrims and other devotees, and of those requisite to minister to their wants; so that the bazaar is crowded with passengers, and filled with goods of various kinds. The town is supplied with good water from 125 wells, lined with masonry. The population consists of 6,750 Hindoos and 525 Mussulmans. Lat. 25° 52′, long. 72° 21′.

BALOUN.—A river rising in lat. 26° 41′, long. 86° 22′, in the Terai or marshy lands at the base of the Sub-Himalaya range. At the distance of eight miles from its source, it flows over the northern boundary of the British district of Tirhoot, and holding a course southerly for sixty miles, falls into the Gogaree in lat. 25° 50′, long. 86° 16′.

BALOWAL, in the Sungurh district of the Damaun division of the Punjab, a town 60 miles N. of Dera Ghazee Khan, 70 miles S.W. of the town of Dera Ismael Khan. Lat. 30° 53′, long. 70° 31′.

BALUMBA, in the peninsula of Kattywar, province of Guzerat, a town in the north-eastern quarter of the district of Hallar, and eight miles from the coast of the Gulf of Cutch. Distance from Ahmedabad, W., 139 miles; Baroda, W., 180. Lat. 22° 42′, long. 70° 30′.

BALUNG.—A town of Bonei, one of the petty native states on the south-west frontier of Bengal, under the political superintendence of the government of India, distant N.E. from Sambulpoor 50 miles. Lat. 21° 42′, long. 84° 46′.

BALWA.—See BAUTWA.

BALZORA, or BALCHORAH, in the territory of Oude, a fort and trading station near the northern frontier, towards Nepal. For two months every summer a mart is held at Balzora, the mountaineers bringing their native products to exchange for the wares of the plains. Distant N. from Lucknow 120 miles. Lat. 28° 34′, long. 81° 12′.

BAMANWALA, or BUNYAWALA.—A village, with a Hindoo temple, in the British district of Dehra Doon. Here was one of the stations for the series of small triangles in the great trigonometrical survey of the Himalaya. Elevation above the sea 2,220 feet. Lat. 30° 19′, long. 78° 1′.

BAMBHOLA, or BOMBOLA, in the native state of Kishengurh, in Rajpootana, a town on the route from Agra to Nusseerabad, 195 miles S.W. of former, 28 N.E. of latter. It has a bazaar, and water is abundant. Lat. 26° 27′, long. 75° 12′.

BAMBHORA, or **BHANIBORA**, in Bussahir, a fort in the district of Chooara, on a lofty summit rising about two miles north of the right bank of the Pabur. Elevation above the sea 9,844 feet. Lat. 31° 14′, long. 77° 50′.

BAMINGOLAH, in the British district of Dinajepore, lieut.-gov. of Bengal, a town 36 miles S.W. from Dinajepore, 15 miles N.E. of Maldah. Lat. 25° 7′, long. 88° 21′.

BAMNEE.—A town in Hyderabad, or dominions of the Nizam, distant E. from Jaulnah 49 miles. Lat. 19° 47′, long. 76° 41′.

BAMO MYO, in Burmah, a town situated on the left or eastern bank of the Irawaddy river, 174 miles N.E. of Ava. Lat. 24° 14′, long. 97°.

BAMOULLI, or **BAMBOLEE**, in the Rajpoot state of Alwur, a village on the route from Muttra to the town of Alwur, and 12 miles S.E. of the latter. Lat. 27° 29′, long. 76° 48′.

BAMOURI, or **BUMBOUREE**, in the British district of Pillibheet, lieut.-gov. of the N.W. Provinces, a police and trading station on the route from Bareilly to Almora, and 42 miles south of the latter. It is situate near the right bank of the Goula, or Bullea, which here passes from the mountains to the plain by an extensive ravine. The road, though a much-frequented channel of communication between the district of Kumaon and the plains, is, according to Heber, so difficult as not to be passable for horses accustomed only to the plain. Bamouri has an elevation above the sea of upwards of 1,700 feet. Lat. 29° 13′, long. 79° 35′.

BAMRA.—See Bombra.

BAMSARU, in Gurwhal, a pass over a mountain proceeding from the cluster of the Jumnotri peaks, separating the Ganges from the Jumna. Its summit enters within the limit of perpetual congelation, as a British party, which crossed it at the end of August, found it then covered with deep snow. Elevation above the sea 15,447 feet. Lat. 30° 56′, long. 78° 36′.

BAMUNGAON.—A town in the native state of Indore, or the possessions of the family of Holkar, distant S.W. from Mhow 41 miles. Lat. 22° 6′, long. 75° 20′.

BAMUNGAON.—A town in the Rajpoot state of Boondee, distant N.E. from Boondee 33 miles. Lat. 25° 46′, long. 76° 5′.

BAMUNHATEE.—A town of Mohurbunge, one of the petty native states on the south-west frontier of Bengal, under the political superintendence of the government of India. Distant W. from Midnapore 80 miles. Lat. 22° 16′, long. 86° 10′.

BAMUNWAS, in the Rajpoot state of Jeypore, a town on the route from Agra to Nusserabad, 102 miles S.W. of former, 118 N.E. of latter. It is of considerable size, has a bazaar, and water and supplies, except firewood, are abundant. Lat. 26° 34′, long. 76° 37′.

BANAAR, an offset of the Brahmapootra river, leaving the parent stream opposite the town of Jumalpoor, in lat. 24° 51′, long. 90° 4′, and flowing in a southerly direction for 120 miles, to lat. 23° 37′, long. 90° 31′, where it falls into the Dulasseree river, about seven miles above its junction with the Megna.

BANAGANPILLY, in the British district of Cuddapah, presidency of Madras, a town on the route from Bellary to Guntoor, 90 miles E. of the former. Lat. 15° 19′, long. 78° 17′.

BANAIRA.—A town of Rajpootana, in the native state of Oodeypoor, distant N.E. from Oodeypoor 88 miles. Lat. 25° 30′, long. 74° 45′.

BANAPOOR.—A town in the territory of Nagpore, distant N.E. from Nagpore 92 miles. Lat. 22° 10′, long. 78° 14′.

BANAS (Eastern).—A river of Rajpootana, rising on the western frontier of Mewar, amidst a cluster of summits of the Aravulli range, five miles S.W. of the station or encamping-ground of Saimur, and in lat. 24° 47′, long. 73° 28′. The word is significant in Sanscrit, and means "Hope of the forest;" having been, according to the local legend, originally the name of a "chaste shepherdess, who, while disporting in the waters of this natural fountain, espied to her horror an intruder gazing on her charms," and praying for aid to the guardian divinity of the place, was metamorphosed into the stream. Holding its course through Mewar for 120 miles, it is joined by the river Beris, or Beruch. Having received the Beris on the right, and a few miles beyond that confluence the Botaseri on the left, it continues its north-easterly course, receiving on the left the river of Ajmer, and subsequently several torrents flowing from the territory of Jeypore in the rainy season. At the town of Tonk, and about 235 miles from its source, its direction changes, first to south-east, and sweeping round the hills in which are situate the stronghold of Rintambor, it falls into the Chumbul, in lat. 25° 54′, long. 76° 50′, after a total course of about 320 miles. The route of the British army under Monson, flying before Holkar, in 1804, lay across the river in this part of its course; and on the 22nd of August the stream was so swollen from flood as to be for two days impassable for the army.

BANASA, in Gurwhal, a village in the valley of the Jumna, and seven miles below the source of that river. It is situate on the left bank of the Jumna, at the confluence of the Banasa torrent, and on a natural ledge of rock, a series of which, in that part of the valley, rise over each other on the side of the mountain. The site is picturesque and sublime in the highest degree. The Banasa is at the confluence about two-thirds the size of the Jumna. In 1816, half the village of Banasa was overwhelmed and destroyed by the fall of a precipice. In the vicinity are numerous thermal springs, the waters of which are too hot to be borne by the touch. Lat. 30° 56′, long. 78° 27′.

BANAWARAM, in the territory of Mysore, a town situate in a fine open country on the side of a large tank, which, when visited by Buchanan, was dry. After various vicissitudes, it was, in 1694, taken in a night assault by Chika Deo, rajah of Mysore. Hyder Ali, in establishing his ascendancy over the posterity of that prince, made himself master of Banawaram in the latter part of the eighteenth century. At the time of his making this acquisition, it is said there were about two thousand houses in the place, but most of the inhabitants were removed, with those of five other towns, to Nagapuri, which Hyder had recently founded in the vicinity. The new town, however, being found extremely unhealthy, the surviving inhabitants, who had been drawn from Banawaram, were allowed to return home. Distance from Seringapatam, N.W., 76 miles; Bangalore, N.W., 100; Madras, W., 280. Lat. 13° 24′, long. 76° 13′.

BANCANEER. — A town in the native state of Gwalior, or territory of the Scindia family, distant S.W. from Mhow 40 miles. Lat. 22° 13′, long. 75° 14′.

BANCOORAH, a British district within the territories subject to the lieut.-gov. of Bengal, and having its name in common with its principal place. It is also called West Burdwan. It is bounded on the north by the British district Beerbhoom, on the east by the British district Burdwan, on the south by the British district Midnapore, and on the west by the British districts Pooralia and Pachete. It lies between lat. 22° 53′—23° 46′, long. 87°—87° 39′; is 60 miles in length from N. to S., and 42 in breadth. The area is 1,476 square miles. It is generally a level tract, yet with gentle undulations, and inclining gradually towards the south-east, the streams all flowing in that direction. Among these may be mentioned the Hadjee and the Damoodah. Both streams are navigable for about ten weeks during the periodical rains of autumn, and are then the channels for the conveyance of iron and coal to Calcutta and its vicinity. The communication, however, though quick, is precarious and difficult, and will shortly be superseded by a branch from the Calcutta railway, diverging from the main line in the vicinity of Burdwan, and proceeding to Raneegunje. The Dalkisore, flowing from the British district Pachete, crosses the western boundary of Bancoorah, and flowing by the town of that name, holds through the district a course in a direction easterly, or south-easterly, for forty-five miles, to a point where it passes the eastern frontier into the British district Burdwan. The population is stated at 480,000. Bancoorah contains some Mussulmans, but the great majority are Brahminists, divided into numerous castes and classes. This district was formerly part of Burdwan. The northern part was obtained by the British from Meer Cossim, in 1760, the cession being confirmed by Shah Alum in 1765, at which time the southern part was also acquired from the last-named authority.

BANCOORAH. — A town, the principal place of the district of the same name, on the route from Calcutta to Benares, 101 miles N.W. of the former, and 327 S.E. of the latter. It is situate on the left bank of the river Dalkisore, has a bazaar and a spacious public building for the accommodation of travellers. Distant S.W. from Berhampore 115 miles. Lat. 23° 14′, long. 87° 6′.

BAND. — A town of Bundlecund, in the native state of Tehree, distant E. from Tehree 15 miles. Lat. 24° 44′, long. 79° 8′.

BANDA. — A British district in Bundlecund, under the lieut.-gov. of the N.W. Provinces, named from its principal place. It is bounded on the north by the British district Futtehpoor; on the north-east by the British districts Futtehpoor and Allahabad; on the south-east by the territory of Rewah; on the south and south-west by some of the petty native states of Bundlecund; and on the west and north-west by the British district of Humeerpoor. It lies between lat. 24° 53′—25° 54′, long. 80° 3′—81° 35′, and has an area of 2,878 square miles. The rivers which bound or intersect the district are the Jumna, the Cane or Keyn, the Runj or Baghin, and the Pysunnee. The climate is productive of ague to Europeans, who sometimes can be freed from its attacks only by removal to purer air; but the natives enjoy at least the usual average of health. The black soil of the plains is noted for fertility, producing in great abundance and perfection wheat, barley, maize, millet of various sorts, and pulse. Sugar also, and indigo, are successfully cultivated; but of commercial crops by far the most important is cotton, for which the district is so celebrated that the produce is distinguished in commerce by the prefix of its name. It is mostly exported in its raw state by way of Calpee and Chilatara, on the Jumna, there being scarcely any manufacture, except of coarse cloth, dyed red with a colour obtained from the root of a plant called al (Morinda multiflora). The population is officially stated to be 743,872. The towns and villages are classed as follows: Number containing less than 1,000 inhabitants, 948; more than 1,000 and less than 5,000, 192; more than 10,000 and less than 50,000, one; making a total of 1,143. Under the recent revenue-settlement of the North-West Provinces, the government demand on the lands of this district has been fixed for a term of years, and is not liable to be increased until the year 1874.

Possession of the tract comprised within this district appears to have been much contested in the struggles for dominion in Hindostan. In 1023 Kalleenjur was in vain besieged by Mahmood of Ghizni; but in 1196 it was taken by Kotb-ood-deen, an officer of Mohammed Sultan of Ghor. It seems to have been partially retained by the Patans, when most other parts of the possessions of Delhi had submitted to Baber, or his son Humaion; as the latter besieged Kalleenjur in 1532 without success. Its rajah probably aimed at independence; as in 1545 he defended Kalleenjur against Humaion's Patan rival, the renowned Shir Shah, who succeeded in taking it, though mortally wounded in the attack; breathing his last at the moment of its capture. About 1735 the rajah of this part of Bundlecund transferred it by will to Bajee Rao, the Peishwa; and by the treaty of Bassein in 1802, and the supplementary treaty of 1803, it was ceded to the East-India Company.

BANDA, the principal town of the district of the same name, is situate on the right side of the river Cane, or Keyn, which here is described as having steep banks, sandy bottom, and usual depth of water from November to June from one and a half to two feet. The town is of considerable size, but straggling and ill built; the houses being of mud, though there is abundance of excellent building-stone procurable. The habitation of the nawaub, or titular prince of the place, is an exception; being at the time of Jacquemont's visit, in 1830, new, spacious, and built with solidity; but in vile taste, partly Indian, partly European; wretchedly furnished, and having a profusion of gross sculptures. This nominal prince has, however, an annual income equal to 40,000*l.*, which his father, the late nawaub, is said to have expended in conviviality and genial enjoyment. This provision is secured to the family by an engagement with the East-India Company, concluded in 1812. In lieu of the military force maintained by his father, the present rajah has been allowed to retain only a suitable retinue. In a commercial point of view, Banda is considered a thriving place, being a great mart for cotton. The population amounted in 1847 to 33,464. Distant S.W. from Allahabad 95 miles; N.W. from Calcutta 560; S.E. from Agra 190. Lat. 25° 28′, long. 80° 23′.

BANDA CHHOTA, or BANDA THE LESS, in the British district of Banda, lieut.-gov. of the N.W. Provinces, a village on the route from the town of Banda to Rewa, six miles S. of the former. Lat. 25° 24′, long. 80° 25′.

BANDAIR.—A range of hills to the northward of the valley of the Nerbudda, commencing about lat. 24° 30′, long. 80° 48′, in a south-westerly direction. Its termination does not appear to be very precisely ascertained. The formation of the range is, according to Franklin, altogether of sandstone, horizontally stratified.

BANDAJAN.—A pass over the range of the Himalaya, forming the southern boundary of Koonawar. It consists of gneiss, and is covered with perennial snow, which extends in an unbroken sheet to the river Sipun, a depth of 1,200 feet. The summit of the pass is 14,854 feet above the sea. Lat. 31° 22′, long. 78° 4′.

BANDE.—A town in the native state of Sawunt Warree, under the administration and control of the government of Bombay, distant E. from Vingorla 15 miles. Lat. 15° 49′, long. 73° 56′.

BANDERPOOR, in the British district of Futtehpoor, lieut.-gov. of the N.W. Provinces, a town on the right bank of the Ganges, 869 miles from Calcutta by the river; 61 miles above Allahabad; 32 miles S.E. of the town of Futtehpoor. Lat. 25° 48′, long. 81° 18′.

BANDHUA HASNPOOR, in the district of Sultanpoor, territory of Oude, a village with a fort 78 miles S.E. of Lucknow. Lat. 26° 16′, long. 82° 4′.

BANDOOGURH, in the territory of Rewa, in Baghelcund, a fortified post near the south-west frontier, and 60 miles S. of the town of Rewah. Lat. 23° 41′, long. 81° 6′.

BANDORA.—A town of the island of Salsette, situate at the southern point, where the island is connected with that of Bombay by the causeway and arched stone bridge constructed by the local government from funds principally contributed by the Parsee merchant Sir Jamsetjee Jejeebhoy. Distant N. of Bombay fort nine miles. Lat. 19° 1′, long. 72° 55′.

BANDRA, in the Rajpoot state of Joudpore, a village two miles N. of the route from Balmer to the town of Joudpore, and 10 miles N.E. of the former place. It contains 150 houses. Lat. 25° 52′, long. 71° 28′.

BANGA BAZAR, in the British district of Silhet, lieut.-gov. of Bengal, a town 22 miles W. of Silchar, and 41 miles E. of Silhet. Lat. 24° 50′, long. 92° 30′.

BANGALORE, in the territory of Mysore, a town, the principal place of the district of the same name, and the chief station of the British military force in the territory, is situate on a high ridge of primary formation, the rock being generally granite or gneiss. The fort, of an oval ground-plan, constructed of strong masonry, with round towers and powerful cavaliers, was nearly dismantled by Tippoo Sultan, on his finding it incapable of resisting the assault of a British army; but in 1802 it was put in thorough repair by Purneah, the minister of the rajah of Mysore. The town is tolerably well built, has a good bazaar, and is inclosed by a wall, a ditch, and a broad fence of thorns and bamboos. The present importance of the place results from its being the locality of the great British military establishment for the territory of Mysore. The cantonment, on an elevated ridge of ground, running longitudinally east and west, and sloping north and south, is nearly two miles and a half in length, and one mile in breadth. It is two miles east of the fort. The dragoon barracks consist of eight ranges of buildings, parallel to each other, and one hundred and twenty-six feet apart, each extending two hundred and twenty-four feet in length, forty-three in breadth, and being twelve in height, all tiled, and built of brick, and the whole inclosed by a wall of the same material, nine feet high. The European infantry barracks are sufficient for eight hundred men. The native troops live in huts; the officers in detached bungalows or lodges, the compounds or inclosures of which are separated from each other by hedges of aloes or euphorbia; and the profusion of planting, though perhaps carried to an insalubrious excess, gives a delightful appearance to the cantonment, strikingly contrasted with the bare aspect of the surrounding country. The gardens produce the usual vegetables of Europe in great abundance, and the products of the flower-garden are remarkably varied, vivid, and luxuriant. Water is good and abundant, there being eight large tanks in and about the place, besides several of smaller dimensions. Bangalore may be considered one of the finest climates in India, being cool and pleasant throughout the greater part of the year. The sun is generally powerful; but in the shade and in the house it is always cool.

Bangalore, from time immemorial, was a place of importance; but the foundation of the present fort was laid by a descendant of Kempe-Goud, a husbandman of the neighbouring country, who, probably in the sixteenth century, had left his native village to avoid the tyranny of the wadeyar of that place, and settled on a spot a few miles to the north of Bangalore. To the peaceful occupation of a farmer he added that of a warrior, and his first exploit was the conquest of this place, where, and at Savendroog, his family subsequently erected fortresses. Bangalore, with other possessions, was, however, wrested from them by Beejapore. Somewhat later we find it enumerated among the jaghires of Shahjee, father of Sevajee, the founder of the Mahratta sway; and at an early period of his career in the service of the Beejapore state, that adventurer seems to have fixed his residence there. It appears to have passed into the possession of Vencojee, one of the sons of Shahjee; but he having occupied Tanjore, deemed Bangalore too distant, especially under the circumstances of the times, to be safe. He accordingly, in 1687, entered into a bargain for its sale to Chick Deo, rajah of Mysore, for three lacs of rupees; but before it could be completed, Kasim Khan, commander of the forces of Aurungzebe, marched upon the place, and entered it almost without resistance. This event, however, had no other result than to transfer the stipulated price from one vender to another; for that general, not coveting the possession, immediately delivered it over to Chick Deo, on payment of the three lacs. In 1758, Nunjeraj, the powerful minister of the rajah, caused Bangalore to be granted, as a jaghire or fief, to Hyder Ali, afterwards usurper of Mysore, who greatly enlarged and strengthened the fort, which, in 1760, on his expulsion from Seringapatam, served as his refuge from destruction. In 1791 it was stormed by a British army commanded by Lord Cornwallis. Distance direct from Seringapatam, N.E., 71 miles; Mangalore, E., 185; Bellary, S., 155; Madras, W., 185. Lat. 12° 58′, long. 77° 38′.

BANGAON, in the British district of Shahjehanpoor, lieut.-gov. of the N.W. Provinces, a town 29 miles S.W. from Shahjehanpoor, 18 miles N. of Furruckabad. Lat. 27° 39′, long. 79° 38′.

BANGAON, in the British district of Nuddea, lieut.-gov. of Bengal, a town on the route from Calcutta to Jessore, 39 miles N.E. of the former. Lat. 23°, long. 88° 50′.

BANGARAH, one of the numerous outlets by which the Ganges discharges its waters into the Bay of Bengal. Lat. 21° 50′, long. 89° 42′.

BANGERMOW, in the territory of Oude, a town on the route from Lucknow to Nanamow Ghat, 43 miles W. of the former, four E. of the left bank of the Ganges. Distant N. from Cawnpore, by Nanamow Ghat, 47 miles. Lat. 26° 53′, long. 80° 16′.

BANGHEYA.—A town in the native state of Nepal, distant N.W. from Khatmandoo 230 miles. Lat. 28° 55′, long. 81° 46′.

BANGSEE.—See Bansee.

BANGUNGA, a river rising in the territory of Nepal, from a source which, though as yet unexplored, is probably in about lat. 27° 43′, long. 82° 55′. It takes a southerly course, crosses the northern frontier of the British district of Goruckpore, through which it continues for twenty-three miles, and joins the Booree Rapti on the left side of the latter. It is probably the greater of the two; and hence the united stream often bears the name of Bangunga. Below the confluence the united stream has a channel a hundred yards wide, with a considerable volume of water, scarcely fordable even in the dry season. Above the confluence the Bangunga is navigable, and a considerable quantity of timber is floated down by it.

BANGUNGA, a river rising near the north-western frontier of the Rajpoot state of Jeypoor. For a considerable distance it is merely a channel for water in the rainy season, and quite dry at other times. At Maunpoor, eighty miles from its source, it is described by Boileau, after the commencement of the rainy season in August, with a channel 600 yards wide, and nearly dry. Forty miles lower down, the same traveller, a few days later, found it, after heavy rains, fordable for camels. Twenty miles beyond this point it is joined by the torrent Gumbeer, and thence is called generally by the latter name. Thirty-three miles to the east of the junction, and 173 from its source, it is crossed on the route from Agra to Gwalior, and even at that point has only a small rill of clear water in the dry season; but its sandy bed, 130 yards wide, indicates that the body of water may be considerable during the rains. Its final discharge is into the Jumna, on the right side, in lat. 27°, long.

78° 32′; the total length of channel being about 220 miles. It is sometimes called the Ootungun.

BANGURSIR, in the Rajpoot state of Jessulmer, a village on the route from Bahawulpoor to Bap, and 120 miles S.E. of the former. Bangursir is in lat. 27° 59′, long. 72° 34′.

BANIA CHUNG, in the British district of Silhet, lieut.-gov. of Bengal, a town 83 miles N.E. from Dacca, and 40 miles S.W. of Silhet. Lat. 24° 32′, long. 91° 22′.

BANIHAL, in the Northern Punjab, is a pass over the mountains of the same name, bounding Kashmir on the south. The ascent is much more considerable on the southern than on the northern side, where it descends into Kashmir, which country has a greater elevation than that part of the Punjab lying to the south. Though by no means the highest, being but 8,500 feet above the sea, it is one of the most difficult passes into Kashmir, and is seldom attempted with horses, though Vigne passed it in that way. Forster entered Kashmir on foot through this pass. The pergunnah, or district, also bears the name of Banihal. Lat. 33° 21′, long. 75° 20′.

BANKEE.—A town in the territory of Oude, distant N.E. from Lucknow 93 miles. Lat. 28° 4′, long. 81° 43′.

BANKOTE, in the British district of Rutnagherry, presidency of Bombay, a town with a small haven at the mouth of the river Savitree. Fort Victoria, situate on a high barren hill of red colour, is on the south side of the entrance. On the north side is Harissa Hill. The anchorage is in five fathoms low water, abreast of the fort. Bankote is 68 miles S. of Bombay. Lat. 17° 58′, long. 73° 8′.

BANKY, one of the native mehals in the district of Cuttack, lieut.-gov. of Bengal, paying an annual tribute of 4,162 rupees to the British government. Its centre is in lat. 20° 18′, long. 85° 35′.

BANMOWTEE, or BUROTI, in the British district of Allyghur, lieut.-gov. of the N.W. Provinces, a village on the route from Meerut to Muttra, and 39 miles N.E. of the latter. Lat. 27° 59′, long. 77° 55′.

BANNAWASSI, in North Canara, within the territory subject to the presidency of Madras, a town once of much celebrity, but subsequently greatly decayed. Here is a temple of Siva or Mahadeva, which had formerly very large endowments, and although a very mean building, was kept in good repair and very much frequented. Distance (direct) from Soonda, S.E., 20 miles; from Bombay, S.E., 340; Madras, N.W., 370. Lat. 14° 33′, long. 75° 5′.

BANOULI.—A town in Hyderabad, or dominions of the Nizam, distant N. from Hyderabad 109 miles. Lat. 18° 50′, long. 78° 5′.

BANS, in the British district of Kumaon, lieut.-gov. of the N.W. Provinces, a village on the route from Almora to Petoragarh, and 43 miles N.E. of the former. Lat. 29° 40′, long. 80° 13′.

BANSDA, or BAUNSDA. — A petty native state, under the political superintendence of the government of Bombay. It is bounded on the west and north by the British collectorate of Surat; on the east by the Daung; and on the south by the native state of Dhurrumpore. It extends from lat. 20° 35′ to 21°, long. 73° 8′ to 73° 28′, and contains an area of 325 square miles, and a population of 24,050. During the minority of the young chief, the management of the district was assumed by the British government, and under its auspices considerable improvement has taken place, both in regard to the increase of revenue and the diminution of crime. The British officer in charge was also assiduous in training the young rajah to such habits of business as might fit him for the administration of his affairs, when it should become expedient to intrust it to him. The present amount of revenue is 47,000 rupees, or 4,700*l.* per annum, subject to the deduction of 780*l.* per annum for chouth, or tribute, to the British government, which was transferred to it by the Peishwa in 1802, under the treaty of Bassein. A small military force is kept at the cost of the chief, but it is not superintended or controlled as to discipline by the British government. The town of Bansda, distant from Surat, S.E., 45 miles, is in lat. 22° 44′, long. 73° 25′.

BANSEE, or BANGSI, in the British district of Goruckpore, lieut.-gov. of the N.W. Provinces, a town the principal place of the pergunnah of the same name, is situate on the river Raptee, having there a channel 200 yards wide, with low banks, inundated to great extent during the rainy season. It has a market, and 600 houses, and allowing six persons to each, the population may consequently be estimated at 3,600. Distant N. from Benares 130 miles, N.E. from Allahabad 136. Lat. 27° 7′, long. 82° 58′.

BANSEE, in the British district of Allahabad, lieut.-gov. of the N.W. Provinces, a town 23 miles S. of Allahabad, 51 miles E. of Mirzapoor. Lat. 25° 4′, long. 81° 50′.

BANSKERA.—See BAUSHKERA.

BANSRORE, or BYNSRORE, in the territory of Kota, in Rajpootana, a fort situate in the angle of confluence where the river Bhamuni falls into the Chumbul. Its site is the summit of a great rock, from 300 to 700 feet above the average height of the surface of the water in the river, which is here 500 yards wide, and even in the dry season forty feet deep. The stream is very rapid and violent, there being a fall of between thirty and forty feet above the fort, and another of equal depth below. The base of the rock is washed on all sides except the north, and is there only accessible; but the rock has been artificially scarped. The fort, however, could without much difficulty be reduced by shells; and even before the introduction of artillery, was taken by Alauddin, the Patan sovereign of Delhi, who reigned from 1295 to 1316. Distant direct from Kota, S.W., 22 miles; from Oojein, N., 127. Lat. 24° 58′, long. 75° 36′.

BANSWADDY.—A town in Hyderabad, or dominions of the Nizam, distant N.W. from Hyderabad 81 miles. Lat. 18° 23′, long. 77° 57′.

BANSWARRA.—A petty Rajpoot state in the western quarter of Malwa, bordering on the province of Guzerat, and politically under the Governor-General. It is bounded on the north by Dongurpoor and Oodeypoor, or Mewar; on the north-east and east by Pertaubgurh; on the south by the dominions of Holkar and Jaboos; and on the west by the Rewa Caunta. It extends from lat. 23° 10′ to 23° 48′, and from long. 74° 2′ to 74° 41′; it is about forty-five miles in length from north to south, and thirty-three in breadth from east to west, and has an area of 1,440 square miles. The population may be assumed at 144,000. The ruling family of this petty state is a branch of that of Oodeypore. It was dependent on the empire of Delhi until the ascendancy of the Mahrattas, by whom it was fearfully oppressed. In 1812 the ruler of this principality made overtures to the British government, and sent an agent to Baroda with the draft of a treaty, offering to become tributary, on condition of the expulsion of the Mahrattas; but it was not till 1818 that a treaty was concluded. With the treaty thus negotiated the chief was dissatisfied, and about two months afterwards it was replaced by another. Most of the articles in this, the existing treaty, are of the usual character; but the advice of the British government was to be followed in settling the affairs of the principality: the British government was not only to defend the country from external attacks, but also, if necessary, to afford to the chief aid in reducing his refractory connections and relations to obedience. The chief stipulated to pay tribute to the British government. In 1829 Captain Spears proceeded to Banswarra to effect certain necessary reforms, in the course of which a certain officer of police was dismissed. After repeatedly importuning the good offices of the British agent, which that functionary deemed it proper to withhold, the wretch formed the design of destroying the man who stood, as he believed, between him and profitable employment; and the crime was effected through the instrumentality of a Mahomedan servant. No doubt, it is said, existed as to the guilt of the accused parties, yet they were sentenced only to transportation; probably because the evidence against them was altogether circumstantial. Even this lenient punishment the principal criminal found means to elude, having succeeded in making his escape on the way to Bombay. In 1835, a large balance was due to the British government for tribute, nearly the whole of the revenues of the country having been expended by the chief and his minister in wasteful extravagance and shameless debauchery. The reiterated exhortations of the British agent for a reform of the administration had been wholly disregarded. Strong remonstrances on the part of the British government were made, and the consequences which must follow perseverance in the reckless course pursued by the rawul and his minister, distinctly pointed out. Some effect was thereby produced; part of the arrears of tribute were paid; the minister was dismissed, and an arrangement was made with the rajah of Pertaubghur for co-operation in the suppression of plunderers. The career of the prince whose misconduct had given rise to the evils thus sought to be abated, was not long protracted; and his death raised the question, often productive of confusion in Oriental states, of the right to the succession. He left no direct male heirs; and females in Rajpoot states have no claim to succeed. The difficulty, however, was happily got over without disturbance. The chiefs were called together, with the sanction of the political agent, and proceeded in conformity with usage, as was understood, to an election. The result was the installation of Bahadoor Singh, a member of the family, who it appeared had in all respects the best claim. The tributary thakoors of this state are thirty-three in number, and their forces, with those of the state, amount to about 525, inclusive of the military police establishment. The practice of suttee has been recently abolished in Banswarra.

BANSWARRA, on the route from Mhow to Deesa, 123 miles N.W. of the former, 178 S.E. of the latter, a town the principal place of the small Rajpoot state of the same name. It is situate eight miles west of the left bank of the river Mahye, and has a rampart inclosing a considerable area; much, however, of the inclosed space being occupied by gardens. The palace, or residence of the rawul or chief, is a large, turreted, battlemented building, on a rising ground overlooking the town, and near a beautiful tank overhung with trees, access to the water being gained by a fine ghaut, or flight of steps. Within the town are some handsome Hindoo temples and an extensive bazaar. The majority of the inhabitants are Brahminists, but there is a considerable number of Mussulmans. Distance direct from Neemuch, S.W., 76 miles; from Nusserabad, S., 200; from Oojien, N.W., 91; from Bombay, N.E., 330; from Agra, S.W., 350. Lat. 23° 30′, long. 74° 24′.

BANTER, in the district of Bainswara, territory of Oude, a town five miles N.E. of the left bank of the Ganges, eight miles E. of

Cawnpore, 30 S.W. of Lucknow. Butter estimates the population at 5,000, of whom 150 are Mussulmans. Lat. 26° 29′, long. 80° 32′.

BAONEE, or BOWNEE, in Bundelcund, a jaghire or feudal possession held under the East-India Company. It is inclosed on all sides by the British territories, except on the south-eastern corner, where it adjoins the small state of Behree, and lies between lat. 25° 54′—26° 7′, long. 79° 44′—80° 1′. Its length from north to south is about fifteen miles, and its breadth is of similar extent. Its area is stated to be 127 miles, and it "is estimated to contain fifty-two villages, with a population of 18,800 souls, and to yield a revenue of one lac of rupees (10,000*l.*) per annum." It was originally granted about the middle of the last century to Ghaziud din Khan, at one time the vizier of Alumgir II., emperor of Delhi, by the Peishwa. The grant was confirmed by the British government on obtaining possession in 1802, and the Mahomedan descendant of the original grantee still holds the jaghire. He resides at Calpee, and maintains fifty horse and 300 foot. In the large map of India published by Horsburgh, 1827, it is denominated "Bownie of Calpie."

BAP, in the Rajpoot state of Jessulmere, a small town close to the eastern frontier towards Joudpore, on the route from the town of Beekaneer to that of Jessulmere, and 100 miles N.E. of the latter. Bap is in lat. 27° 22′, long. 71° 26′.

BAPIOO.—A town in the Rajpoot state of Beekaneer, distant S.E. from Beekaneer 48 miles. Lat. 27° 50′, long. 74° 8′.

BARA.—A small but important river of Afghanistan, in the province of Peshawur. It rises in Tirah, or the hilly tract lying between Sufeid Koh and the Salt Range. From the benefits which it confers on the country through which it flows, it has, in conformity with oriental feelings, become an object of veneration. The length of the river is about sixty miles. It enters the plain of Peshawur in lat. 33° 53′, long. 71° 30′. The rice grown in this plain is considered superior to any other, and so highly esteemed, that in the tripartite treaty of 1838, Runjeet Singh stipulated to supply a certain quantity of it yearly to Shah Shoojah.

BARA, or BAREH, in the British district of Ghazeepore, lieut.-gov. of the N.W. Provinces, a town on the route from Chupra to Ghazeepore, 17 miles E. of the latter. It contains a population of 7,042. Lat. 25° 30′, long. 83° 51′.

BARABUTTEE.—A fort in the province of Cuttack, lieut.-gov. of Bengal, situate about a mile from the town of Cuttack. It was stormed in October, 1803, by a British force under Colonel Harcourt, and its capture was followed by the submission of the province. Lat. 20° 29′, long. 85° 56′.

BARA DEVI, in the hill state of Hindoor, a peak, ten miles south of the left bank of the Sutlej, of the lofty range of mountains extending from north-west to south-east through the western part of that state. On the summit is a small temple. Elevation above the sea 7,003 feet. Lat. 31° 11′, long. 76° 57′.

BARAGHEE.—A town in the raj of Odeipoor, one of the petty states on the south-west frontier of Bengal, distant N. from Odeipoor seven miles. Lat. 22° 44′, long. 83° 22′.

BARAGU POINT.—The southernmost point of land on the coast of Pegu. Lat. 15° 44′, long. 95° 30′.

BARAH, in the British district of Cawnpore, lieut.-gov. of the N.W. Provinces, a town on the route from the cantonment of Cawnpore to that of Calpee, and 26 miles N.E. of the latter. It has a bazaar, and is well supplied with water. The road in this part of the route is excellent; the country partially cultivated. Lat. 26° 23′, long. 80° 5′.

BARAH, in the British district of Allahabad, lieut.-gov. of the N.W. Provinces, a town on the route from Bandah to Mirzapoor, 90 miles E. of the former. Lat. 25° 14′, long. 81° 49′.

BARAHAUT, in the native state of Gurwhal, a town on the right bank of the Bhagerettee, as the Ganges is called in the upper part of its course. Barahaut is in lat. 30° 43′, long. 78° 29′.

BARAHULLY.—A town in Hyderabad, or dominions of the Nizam, distant N.W. from Hyderabad 111 miles. Lat. 18° 34′, long. 77° 23′.

BARAI, in the Punjab, a town situate in the Jetch Dooab, 106 miles N.W. of the town of Lahore. Lat. 32° 30′, long. 72° 40′.

BARAK.—A considerable feeder of the Megna river, and an offset from the Jeeree, which it leaves in lat. 24° 43′, long. 93° 13′, and flowing first westerly through Cachar and Silhet for ninety miles, and then south-westerly for 110 miles, falls into the Megna in lat. 24°, long. 90° 59′.

BARA LACHA PASS, in the Punjab, a pass leading over the Himalaya mountains from the British district of Lahul, into the dominions of Gholab Singh. The crown of the pass is about lat. 32° 44′, long. 77° 31′.

BARA LOHAKUR, in the British district of Bolundshuhur, lieut.-gov. of the N.W. Provinces, a village on the route from Allyghur cantonment to that of Delhi, and 40 miles N.W. of the former. Lat. 28° 22′, long. 77° 49′.

BARAMAHAL.—A subdivision of southern India, situate within the presidency of Madras. The tract was annexed to the dominions of Mysore by Hyder Ali. It was ceded to the British in 1792 by Tippoo Sultan, under the treaty of Seringapatam, and now constitutes the northern portion of the British district of

Salem. Its centre is in lat. 12° 30′, long. 78° 20′.

BARAMULA, in Kashmir, is a gorge in the mountains forming the south-western boundary of the valley. Through this aperture the Jhelum flows, draining the whole of this extensive basin. The town is situate on the west or right bank of the river, here crossed by a bridge of eight piers. Baramula is in lat. 34° 10′, long. 74° 30′.

BARAMUTTEE, in the British district of Poonah, presidency of Bombay, a town 55 miles S.E. from Poonah, and 50 miles N.E. of Sattara. Lat. 18° 10′, long. 74° 39′.

BARANDA.—See BURENDA PASS.

BARASET.—A British district under the lieut.-gov. of Bengal. It is named from its principal place. On the north it is bounded by the British district of Nuddea; on the east by the British district of Jessore; on the south by the Sunderbunds; on the south-west by the Twenty-four Pergunnahs; and on the west by the river Hooghly, separating it from the British district Hooghly. It lies between lat. 22° 16′—22° 59′, long. 88° 25′—89° 22′; is about sixty-three miles in length from south-east to north-west, and in breadth about thirty-one. The area is about 1,424 square miles. The population has been returned at 522,000. The rivers intersecting or bounding the district are the Hooghly, the Isamuttee or Jaboona, and the Kubbuduk. A great number of other streams and watercourses, offsets of the Ganges, traverse the country in various directions, especially during the periodical rains, and in many places lay the surface extensively under water, particularly in the south-eastern part, where the Baira jhil or lake extends over about a fifth of the district during the rains, and is at other times a mere swamp. This redundant moisture, and the pestilential atmosphere resulting from its action on the alluvial soil and decayed vegetation, appear to have prevented the full development of the natural resources of the district, which, under adequate culture, might be expected to yield more abundantly sugar, cotton, indigo, and rice. The district is traversed by the road from Calcutta to Dacca.

BARASET.—A town the principal place of a district of the same name, under the lieut.-gov. of Bengal, is situate three miles north-east of an offset from the Hooghly to the Sunderbunds, and eight miles east of the main stream. It is an insignificant place, little deserving notice. Lat. 22° 43′, long. 88° 33′.

BARASHEE.—The name given to one of the numerous streams intersecting the delta of the Ganges. In the upper part of its course it bears the name of Koomar, and in lat. 23° 28′, long. 89° 38′, separates into two channels, the eastern branch receiving the name of Barashee, which it retains until it divaricates into the Attara Banka and the Balissore.

BARATHOR.—A town in the native state of Nepal, distant N.W. from Khatmandoo 94 miles. Lat. 28° 30′, long. 84° 4′.

BARAUNSA, in the district of Sultanpoor, territory of Oude, a village 80 miles S.E. of Lucknow. Butter estimates the population at 300, including 100 Mussulmans. Lat. 26° 21′, long. 82° 12′.

BARCOOR, or BARKURU.—A town, the principal place of a subdivision of the same name, in the British district of South Canara, presidency of Madras. It is situate in a fertile well-watered country. The town is now much ruined, as is the fortress, which, according to Buchanan, was founded by Hari Hara, rajah of Vijayanagar, who reigned from 1367 to 1391. Lat. 13° 28′, long. 74° 49′.

BARDOLEE.—A town of Wusravee, one of the petty native states of the Rewa Caunta, under the political superintendence of the presidency of Bombay, distant E. from Surat 20 miles. Lat. 21° 4′, long. 73° 10′.

BAREE, in the native state of Gurwhal, a village on the left bank of the Jumna, has belonging to it a few fertile patches of soil, yielding good crops of grain and of potatoes, the cultivation of which has recently been introduced here from the British settlements. There is here a petty manufacture of woollen cloth, the material being supplied by the native flocks and worked up by the men, the women being otherwise employed. "It is strange," as Skinner observes, "to meet in these wild passes with men, each sturdy enough to make a Hercules, armed with a distaff and a work-basket." Baree is in lat. 30° 55′, long. 78° 26′.

BAREE, in the native state of Dholpoor, a town, the principal place of a small district of the same name, situate among hills in the south-west part of the territory. The rana of Gohud, having by treaty, in 1805, relinquished Gohud and some other districts to the East-India Company, was granted the districts of Dholpoor, of Baree, and of Rajakhera, which he now holds with the title of rana of Dholpoor. It appears to have been little visited by Europeans. Distant W. of Dholpoor 18 miles, S.W. of Agra 44. Lat. 26° 38′, long. 77° 42′.

BAREE, in the territory of Bhopal, a large town, the principal place of a pergunnah of the same name. It is situate in a mountainous country on the north or left bank of the river Jamneer. Distant S.E. of the town of Bhopal 46 miles. Lat. 23° 3′, long. 78° 4′.

BAREE, in the British district of Ghazeepoor, lieut.-gov. of the N.W. Provinces, a town on the right bank of the Ganges, at the confluence of the Karamnasa. Distant N.W. from Calcutta 400 miles. Lat. 25° 32′, long. 83° 52′.

BAREE.—A town in the territory of Oude, distant N. from Lucknow 29 miles. Lat. 27° 15′, long. 80° 53′.

BAREE DOOAB.—One of the natural sections into which the Punjab is divided. It lies between the river Ravee on the north-west, and the Ghara or Sutlej, and the Beas rivers, on the south-east. Its length is 370 miles, and its average breadth about forty-five. Though not the most extensive, this dooab is one of the most important of those of the Punjab, both in a commercial and agricultural point of view. It contains the towns of Lahore, Mooltan, and Amritsir, and is traversed from north-east to south-west by the great canal (now under construction), which, diverging from the Ravee at Mahadeopoor, proceeds to Tibri, a distance of twenty seven miles, whence, throwing out branches at various intervals for the supply of the adjacent districts, it pursues its course to the vicinity of Chichawutni, where it rejoins the parent stream. Its total length, inclusive of its branches, will be about 480 miles. The cost is estimated at 527,697*l*.

BAREILLY.—A British district within the jurisdiction of the lieut.-gov. of the N.W. Provinces. The portion of country now included within it was formerly divided into two districts; one bearing the name of Bareilly, the other called Pillibeet. The district, as at present constituted, is bounded on the north by Kumaon; on the east by Oude and the British district of Shahjehanpore; on the south by Shahjehanpore and Budaon; and on the west by Budaon, the Rampoor territory, and the British district of Moradabad. It lies between lat. 28° 2′ and 29° 19′, long. 79° 4′ and 80° 12′; contains twenty-three pergunnahs, and has an area of 2,937 square miles. It is a level country, watered by the Western Ramgunga, the Goulah, the Gurrah or Deoha, and the Gogra or Surju, which latter for a short distance forms the north-eastern boundary towards Oude. The climate is fine, suffering little from the hot winds, though colder in winter than might be expected from the latitude and elevation. The soil is fertile, and, except in a part of the northern division, highly cultivated, producing excellent wheat, the original seed of which was brought from England, very fine rice, cotton, sugar, tobacco, barley, maize, millet, pulse, plantains, dates, walnuts, grapes, strawberries, apples, and pears. The population, according to official return, is 1,378,268. The number of towns containing less than 1,000 inhabitants is 3,152; more than 1,000 and less than 5,000, 165; more than 5,000 and less than 10,000, 3; more than 10,000 and less than 50,000, 1; more than 50,000, 1: making a total of 3,322. The union of the district of Pillibeet with Bareilly was arranged in 1842. In 1846 the incorporation of the two was complete, and under the existing settlement of the North-West Provinces, the government demand on account of the land revenue has been fixed, and is not liable to increase until the year 1867.

The Rohilla Patans, formerly the ruling race, are numerous, and are easily distinguished by their superior stature and fairer complexions, as well as by their arrogant air. In 1815 a serious riot, fomented, if not originally excited, by the more fanatical Mahometans, endangered the safety of the city of Bareilly, and was suppressed only by resorting to strong military measures. In this disturbance the Patan portion of the population were the chief actors. The principal routes are that proceeding northwards from Bareilly, by Bamouri, to Almora, in Kumaon; another, also from south to north, but east of the former, proceeding from Bareilly, by the town of Pillibeet and the Birindeo Pass, to Petoragarh, in Kumaon; another, in a direction from south-east to north-west, from the town of Pillibeet to Nugina; another, in a direction from west to east, and leading from Roodurpore to Birindeo. The Bereilly district forms part of the country called Rohilcund, deriving its name from the Rohilla Patans, sprung from the Yusufzai Afghans, who settled in the tract about 1720, and the character of whose descendants has been adverted to in the course of this article. Though often obliged to struggle against the supremacy of the sovereigns of Delhi, they maintained a precarious and ill-defined independence until 1774, when a body of British troops, under the command of Colonel Champion, acting in co-operation with Shujah ud Dowlah, the nawaub vizier of Oude, totally defeated the confederated Rohillas at Tessunah, a short distance from the town of Bareilly, and hence named Futtygunge, or "Place of Victory." In 1796, a disputed succession to a Rohilla jaghire again called for the interference of the British, whose army, under the command of Sir Robert Abercrombie, defeated the Rohillas close to the village of Betoura, a few miles from Bareilly. A village, now situate on the field of battle, also bears the name of Futtygunge, from the result. By these events a large tract of territory, of which Bareilly formed part, passed into the hands of the nawaub vizier. In 1801, both Bareilly and Pillibeet were included in the cessions made by that prince, in commutation of subsidy, to the East-India Company.

BAREILLY, the principal place of the British district of the same name, is situate in a pleasant and well-wooded country on the left bank of the Jooa, a tributary of the Western Ramgunga. It is a considerable town, and though somewhat ruinous, has a brisk and lucrative commerce, and some manufactures. The total population in 1853 was stated to be 111,332. Elevation above the sea 470 feet. Distance N.W. from Calcutta 788 miles, E. from Delhi 152. Lat. 28° 23′, long. 79° 28′.

BARENGEE, in the British district of Cuttack, lieut.-gov. of Bengal, a town 40 miles W. of Point Palmyras, and 40 miles N.E. of Cuttack. Lat. 20° 40′, long. 86° 30′.

BAREWELLEE.—A town in Hyderabad, or dominions of the Nizam, distant S.W. from Hyderabad 95 miles. Lat. 16° 4′, long. 78°.

BARGA, in Koonawur, a pass leading across the range of the Himalaya bounding that district on the south. This, with three other passes, occurs in a space of little more than a mile. Of these Barga is the lowest, and probably has not an elevation of more than 15,000 feet above the sea. Lat. 31° 16′, long. 78° 19′.

BARGAUT, in the British district of Saugor and Nerbudda, under the lieut.-gov. of the N.W. Provinces, a town on the route from Ruttunpoor to Jubbulpoor, 60 miles W. of the former. Lat. 22° 29′, long. 81° 11′.

BARIPOOR, in the British district of Mirzapoor, lieut.-gov. of the N.W. Provinces, a village on the left bank of the Ganges, close to the frontier towards the British district of Benares, distant N.W. from Calcutta, by the river, 749 miles; S.E. from the city of Allahabad, by the same course, 77. Lat. 25° 16′, long. 82° 15′.

BARKALOOR, in the British district of North Canara, presidency of Madras, a town once of great celebrity, but now so ruined that its name has disappeared from the maps of India. Faria y Sousa, in his Annals for A.D. 1581—1584, observes:—"Bracalor, a city seated on the coast of Canara, in almost 14 degrees of latitude, was once one of the most noted places of trade in India, in the form of a commonwealth, but much decayed since the Portuguese built a fort there." It is not given in the accurate and comprehensive Trigonometrical Survey Map of India; but in that work, the name of "Colloor" is set down in a site corresponding to that of the ancient town. Horsburgh mentions, "Barsalor Peak, in lat. 13° 50′, long. 74° 54′, is a round mountain, about three and a quarter leagues inland, having the high chain of Bednore mountains for its base." This site corresponds almost exactly with that of Colloor in the trigonometrical survey; so that it may be concluded that Colloor of the present maps is identical with Barkalur or Barcelor of the earlier. Colloor is distant (direct) from Mangalore, N., 68 miles; Bombay, S.E., 380; Bangalore, N.W., 195; Madras, W., 370.

BARKAROONDEE.—A town in the territory of Nagpore, distant S.E. from Nagpore 90 miles. Lat. 20° 27′, long. 80° 20′.

BARODA, a city of Guzerat, and the capital of the territory of the prince called the Guicowar, is situate near the river Biswamintri, which is there crossed by a stone bridge, consisting of two ranges of arches, one over the other. The fortifications of the town are of no great strength, consisting of slight walls, with towers at irregular intervals, and several double gateways. The town is intersected and divided into four equal quarters, by two spacious streets, meeting in the centre, at a market-place, containing a square pavilion, with three bold arches on each side, and a flat roof, adorned with seats and fountains. The houses are in general very high, and built of wood, with sloping tiled roofs. The palace, or residence of the Guicowar, is a building of the same sort, having wooden galleries projecting one over another; and though the edifice is large, it is but of mean appearance. The house of the British resident may be characterized in like terms. The British cantonment is outside the town, and consists of "a number of small brick houses, with trellis, wooden verandahs, sloping tiled roofs, and upper stories, each surrounded by a garden with a high green hedge of the milk-bush. The church is a small, but convenient and elegant Gothic building, accommodating about 400 persons. The population some years since was reported at 140,000. The dominions of the Guicowar, over which the government of India exercise political superintendence, are described in the article on Guzerat. His annual revenue is estimated at 668,744*l*. The military establishment of this prince, in addition to his regular troops, amounting to 6,059 cavalry and infantry, comprises also the subsidiary force at the disposal of the British government, which consists of five regiments of infantry, completed to 800 men each, two regiments of cavalry, and a company of artillery. He also maintains a contingent force of 3,000 cavalry, paid and equipped agreeably to the suggestions of the British government, and a corps of irregulars, known as the Guzerat Irregular Horse, commanded by British officers. The state of Baroda was a branch of the great Mahratta confederacy, and its ruler, the Guicowar, one of the princes who acknowledged the puppet rajah of Sattara, the descendant of Sevajee, as their chief. Pelajee Guicowar succeeded his uncle Dunnajee Guicowar as second in command of the Mahratta armies in 1721, and by predatory excursions gradually extended his authority over Guzerat. Bajee Rao, the first Peishwa, conferred upon him the title of "Leader of the Royal Troops." Pelajee was murdered in 1732 by the rajah of Joudpore, and succeeded by his son Damajee, who still further extended the authority of his family. Damajee then threw off allegiance to the Peishwa, and joined a conspiracy in favour of his rival; but being treacherously made prisoner, he was not allowed to obtain his liberty but at the sacrifice of half his possessions, and under acknowledgment that he held the other half in fief to the Peishwa. Damajee dying in 1768, the succession was disputed by two of his sons, and finally decided in favour of Syajee, a prince of weak intellect, to the exclusion of Govind Rao, his elder brother. Syajee died without issue in 1792, and was succeeded by his elder brother, Govind Rao, whom he had supplanted in 1768. In 1800 the government devolved upon Annund Rao, a prince of weak intellect. His illegitimate brother Canojee usurped the administration, but was speedily ejected by Rawajee, the minister of the late Govind Rao. Shortly afterwards Rawajee solicited the assistance of the British government, for the purpose of reducing Mulhar Row, a relative of the late prince, who, advancing with a force in support of Canojee, had commenced hostilities against the Guicowar. A body of troops was detached by the government of Bombay, to prevent the subversion of Annund Rao's authority, and Mulhar Rao professed submission; but while negotiation was in progress, he availed himself of an opportunity to make a treacherous attack upon the British detachment, which was, however, successfully repelled, and on the arrival of reinforcements under Sir William Clark, Mulhar Rao was entirely defeated, and compelled to surrender at discretion. During these proceedings, a convention was concluded between the government of Bombay and Rawajee, on behalf of Annund Rao. This was signed on the 15th March, 1802. Thus, the British government, by treating with the Guicowar as a substantive state, secured his independence of the Peishwa. Under the treaty, the Guicowar had agreed to receive a British subsidiary force; and the Arab soldiers in his service being no longer required, it was resolved to disband them. These foreign mercenaries had for some time ruled at Baroda; and, alarmed at the prospect of reduction, they placed the Guicowar in confinement, and refused to release him till their claims were satisfied. They permitted Canojee to escape from Baroda, and serious disorders were apprehended. Major Walker called in the aid of an European regiment from Bombay, which, with the subsidiary force under Colonel Woodington, invested the town of Baroda, and after a siege of ten days, a practicable breach having been made, the garrison surrendered. Other engagements between the Guicowar and the British government followed, and on the 21st April, 1805, the stipulations of the existing agreements were consolidated in a definitive treaty of general defensive alliance. The Guicowar thereby agreed to receive a permanent subsidiary force, and to provide funds for their payment, as well as the liquidation of certain advances of money made for the benefit of the Guicowar state, and the interest thereon. Henceforward there is little to notice in the history of the Guicowar state till disputes between the Guicowar and the Peishwa, in regard to certain territorial claims, gave rise to a series of events which dissolved the great Mahratta confederacy, and hurled its leader from sovereignty to captivity. To enter minutely into these disputes is here neither necessary nor practicable. It may suffice to state, that with a view to their termination, Gungadhur Shastry, an able and upright servant of the Guicowar, proceeded to Poona, whence he was seduced to Punderpore, under pretence of devotion, and there treacherously murdered by the contrivance of a wretch named Trimbuckjee Dainglia, a prime favourite of the Peishwa. This led to a succession of hostile operations between the British government and the Peishwa, terminating first in the humiliation of the latter, and ultimately in the destruction of his state and power. When, as a result of his first discomfiture, the Peishwa yielded to the British government his rights in Guzerat, the Guicowar received an accession of territory; and a new treaty, supplemental to the former, was concluded by the resident, Captain Carnac. Annund Rao died in 1819, and was succeeded by Syajee Rao. The rite of suttee was abolished throughout the Guicowar's dominions, by proclamation dated the 12th February in the year 1840. The reigning prince has it in contemplation to connect his capital by railway with Tunkaria, on the coast of the Gulf of Cambay, a distance of about forty miles. The city of Baroda is distant from Ahmedabad, S.E., 68 miles; from Surat, N., 81; from Bombay, N., 231; from Poona, N., 263; from Mhow, W., 166; from Calcutta, W., 980. Lat. 22° 16′, long. 73° 14′.

BARODA.—A town in the native state of Gwalior, or possessions of Scindia, distant S.W. from Gwalior 103 miles. Lat. 25° 30′, long. 76° 49′.

BARONDA.—A town in the native state of Rewah, in the province of Bundlecund, under the political superintendence of the government of India, distant S. from Rewah 30 miles. Lat. 24° 6′, long. 81° 18′.

BAROO, in the Rajpoot state of Jessulmeer, a village 71 miles N.E. of the town of Jessulmeer. Lat. 27° 20′, long. 71° 59′.

BAROO BARYE, in the British territory of Saugor and Nerbudda, lieut.-gov. of the N.W. Provinces, a town 75 miles S. from Saugor, 70 miles E. of Hoshungabad. Lat. 22° 46′, long. 78° 49′.

BAROWNDA, in the British district of Mirzapoor, lieut.-gov. of the N.W. Provinces, a village on the route from the city of Mirzapoor to Rewa, and 25 miles S.W. of the former. The road in this part of the route is excellent, having been laid down under the superintendence of the East-India Company's engineers. Elevation above the sea 500 feet. Lat. 24° 57′, long. 82° 12′.

BARR, in the British district of Patna, lieut.-gov. of Bengal, a town on the right bank of the Ganges, on the route from Berhampore to Dinapore, 246 miles N.W. of former, 44 E. of latter. The houses are scattered over a considerable extent. Lat. 25° 27′, long. 85° 47′.

BARRA, in the British district of Tannah, presidency of Bombay, a town on the river Vyturna, 30 miles N. of Callianee. Lat. 19° 40′, long. 73° 11′.

BARRABHOOM, a British district within that part of the presidency of Bengal which is under the political agent for the south-west frontier, and named from its principal place. It is bounded on the north by the British district of Pachete; on the east and south by that of Pooralia; and on the west by Singboom and the British district of Pachete: it lies between lat. 22° 48′—23° 10′, long. 86° 9′—86° 52′; is forty-six miles in length from east to west, and thirty-five in breadth. The area is 860 square miles.

BARRACKPOOR.—A town with military cantonment, in the British district of the Twenty-four Pergunnahs, lieut.-gov. of Bengal, on the left bank of the river Hooghly, here about three-quarters of a mile in width. Several regiments of native infantry are usually stationed at this place, hutted in commodious lines, and adjoining are the bungalows or lodges of their European officers. There are also other lodges, the residences of European families, "attracted hither by the salubrity of the air, the vicinity of the Governor-General's residence, or the beauty and convenience of the river." The house of the Governor-General is handsome and commodious, but not very spacious. It is situate in a park of about 250 acres, laid out with great taste and picturesque effect, the surface being artificially varied in elevation with much judgment, and offering as beautiful a display of turf, tree, and flowering shrub, as any scene in the world can produce. Distance N. from Calcutta 16 miles. Lat. 22° 46′, long. 88° 26′.

BARRACKUR.—A river of Bengal, rising in lat. 24° 4′, long. 85° 27′, in the British district of Ramgurh, through which it flows in a circuitous course for 120 miles, and, passing into the district of Beerbhoom, which it traverses for thirty-five miles, falls into the Dammoodah in lat. 23° 40′, long. 86° 51′.

BARRAH, in the Rajpoot state of Kotah, a town on the route from Calpee to the city of Kotah, 275 miles S.W. of former, 46 E. of latter. It has a bazaar, and supplies and water are abundant. Lat. 25° 7′, long. 76° 33′.

BARREEAH, or DEOGHUR BARREEAH.—A petty Rajpoot state of the Rewa Caunta, in the province of Guzerat, under the political superintendence of the government of Bombay. The tract of country composing it stretches from lat. 22° 21′ to lat. 22° 58′, and from long. 73° 41′ to long. 74° 18′. It is bounded on the north by the districts of Loonawarra and Soauth; on the south by Oodepoor; on the east by Dohud and Jabboah; and on the west by Godra and Champaneer. The area is 870 square miles. The connection existing between the British government and the Barreeah state commenced in 1803, when Scindia's districts in Guzerat were taken possession of by a British force under Colonel Murray. The success of that campaign appears to have been materially facilitated by the good-will displayed towards the British by the rajah of Barreeah, whose conduct throughout called forth the warmest praises of the commanding officer; and a treaty was entered into by the British, subsidizing a detachment of the Barreeah Bheels at a monthly expense of eighteen hundred rupees. This secured the friendship and co-operation of this tribe, and enabled our troops to pass through the country without molestation. In the year 1824, the sovereign of Barreeah consented to make payment of 12,000 rupees to the British government in consideration of its protection, liable to a future increase in proportion to any subsequent improvement in the amount of the revenue of the state. The arrangement was ratified by the Governor-General, under date 20th April, 1824. The amount is partly appropriated to defray the expense of maintaining a chain of police thanahs from Baroda to Neemuch; and with reference to this tribute, the expense of a military force sent a few years ago to suppress the Naikra disturbances, was borne by the British government. The revenue of the state is estimated at 57,651 rupees, or about 5,765*l.* The population, estimated at seventy-four to the square mile, would amount to 64,380. The military force at the disposal of the rajah, including the feudatory troops, amounts to 416 men, a small portion only being cavalry. Three field-guns constitute his artillery.

BARREEAH, in Guzerat, a town giving name to the small territory so called. Distance from Baroda, N.E., 50 miles; Ahmedabad, S.E., 81. Lat. 22° 42′, long. 73° 51′.

BARSEE.—A town in an outlying section of the British district of Sholapoor, presidency of Bombay, entirely surrounded by the Nizam's territories. Inconvenience having been experienced from the levy of duties by the native government on goods in transit between Barsee and the British frontier, it was proposed to the Nizam to abandon his right, in consideration of a pecuniary compensation, or to cede for an equivalent a portion of territory sufficient to unite Barsee with the remainder of the collectorate. The question has been settled by the recent cessions of territory for the maintenance of the Nizam's military contingent. Distant 43 miles N. from Sholapoor, 128 miles E. of Poonah. Lat. 18° 16′, long. 75° 46′.

BARUMGULA, a town in the north of the Punjab, and on the southern slope of the Pir Panjal, which bounds Kashmir on the south, is situate in the Pir Panjal, or Nandan Sar Pass from the Punjab into Kashmir. The situation is beautiful and picturesque, at the extremity of a dark and deep defile, through which the Punch river flows. The height above the sea is 6,800 feet. Lat. 33° 36′, long. 74° 40′.

BARUT.—A town in Hyderabad, or dominions of the Nizam, distant N.E. from Nandair 10 miles. Lat. 19° 14′, long. 77° 31′.

BARWAH, in the British district of Ganjam, presidency of Madras, a town on the seacoast, 48 miles S.W. of Ganjam, 94 miles

N.E. of Vizianagrum. Lat. 18° 53′, long. 84° 40′.

BASANTGANJ, in the district of Salon, territory of Oude, a walled town on the western boundary, towards the district of Bainswara, 65 miles S.E. of Lucknow, 70 S.E. of Cawnpore, 55 N.W. of Allahabad. Butter estimates its population at 6,000, of whom half are Mussulmans. Lat. 26°, long. 81° 20′.

BASANTPOOR.—A town in the territory of Oude, distant S.E. from Lucknow 29 miles. Lat. 26° 42′, long. 81° 28′.

BASHTA, in the British district of Bijnour, lieut.-gov. of the N.W. Provinces, a town on the route from Meerut to Chilkea, 31 miles E. of the former. Lat. 29° 3′, long. 78° 18′.

BASNEE, in the Rajpoot state of Joudpore, a village on the route from Pokhurn to the town of Joudpore, and 12 miles N. of the latter. It is situate on the banks of a torrent, which in the rainy season discharges itself into the river Loni. Wells are numerous; but the water which they yield is brackish. Lat. 26° 27′, long. 73° 12′.

BASODA, or BASONDA, in territory of Gwalior, or possessions of Scindia's family, a town on the route from Tehree to Ougein, 78 miles S.W. of former, 188 N.E. of latter. It is situate on a stream tributary to the Betwa, and is the principal place of a pergunnah of the same name. Population about 10,000. Lat. 23° 51′, long. 77° 58′.

BASOUDEMTSO.—A large lake in Thibet, sixty miles in circumference. The centre of the lake is about lat. 29° 40′, long. 94° 35′.

BASSEIN, in the British province of Pegu, a town the principal place of the district of the same name, is situate on the left or eastern bank of one of the main arteries by which the waters of the Irrawaddy discharge themselves into the sea. The offset, which in this part of its course is called the Bassein River, leaves the parent stream in lat. 17° 45′, long. 95° 14′, and flowing in a southerly direction for eighty-five miles, reaches the town of Bassein, where its deep channel affords a safe passage for ships of the largest burthen. Below the town the river takes the name of Negrais, and flows in the same direction for seventy-five miles, to lat. 15° 55′, long. 94° 25′, where it falls into the Bay of Bengal a few miles south of Cape Negrais. Bassein occupies an important position in the military occupation of the country, from its complete command of the navigation of the river on which it is situate. It was captured by the British with trifling loss, on the 19th May, 1852, in the first campaign of the second Burmese war. Lat. 16° 45′, long. 94° 50′.

BASSEIN, in presidency of Bombay, a decayed town on an island separated by a narrow channel from the mainland of the Northern Concan. The island lies between lat. 19° 20′ and 19° 28′, long. 72° 48′ and 72° 54′; is about eleven miles in length from south-east to north-west, and three in breadth, and has an area probably of about thirty-five square miles. It appears to be of very irregular surface, and has some rugged eminences of considerable elevation; amongst others, "one very high hill of table form, and another, not quite so elevated, rising in a conical peak." Bassein early attracted the notice of the Portuguese, as the river or strait separating the island from the mainland was a convenient rendezvous for shipping engaged in hostile operations in the neighbouring quarters. In 1534 it was ceded to the Portuguese by Bahadur Shah of Guzerat. The Portuguese, who were bound to have ceded it to the English authorities, as part of the dowry of the Infanta on her marriage with Charles II., retained it until 1765, when it was invested by the forces of the Peishwa; and, though well maintained, the defences having been rendered untenable, it was surrendered on good conditions. It was in 1780 invested by a British force commanded by General Goddard, who, "owing to the great strength of the place," made regular approaches with "a very powerful artillery, principally twenty-four pounders, and one battery of twenty mortars, at the distance of 500 yards, which did great execution;" and after a siege of twelve days the place surrendered. It was restored to the Mahrattas by the humiliating treaty of Salbye. Here, in 1802, was concluded the important treaty by which the Peishwa agreed to maintain a British subsidiary force, thus virtually and formally dissolving the Mahratta confederacy. On the final overthrow of the Peishwa in 1818, Bassein was incorporated with the presidency of Bombay. The town of Bassein is distant N. from Bombay 28 miles. Lat. 19° 20′, long. 72° 52′.

BASSIM.—A town in Hyderabad, or dominions of the Nizam, distant S. from Ellichpoor 80 miles. Lat. 20° 8′, long. 77° 11′.

BASSWARAJE DROOG, in the British district of North Canara, presidency of Madras, called by the British navigators Fortified Island, from the defences erected on it by an ancient Mysorean rajah. Distant direct from Mangaloor, N., 105 miles; from Bombay, S., 340. Lat. 14° 18′, long. 74° 29′.

BASTENDA, in the British district of Goalpara, in the north-east quarter of the lieut.-gov. of Bengal, a town on the route from Rungpore to Goalpara, 38 miles W. of the latter. Lat. 26°, long. 90° 5′.

BASTI.—See Bustee.

BASUNEE.—A town in the Rajpoot state of Joudpore, distant N.E. from Joudpore 98 miles. Lat. 27° 16′, long. 74° 15′.

BASUNEE, in the Rajpoot state of Joudpore, a village on the route from Balotra to the town of Joudpore, and eight miles S. of the latter. Lat. 26° 13′, long. 73° 7′.

BASUNGPEER, in the Rajpoot state of Jessulmere, a village on the route from the town of Bikaneer to that of Jessulmere, and 11 miles E. of the latter. It is situate at the base of rocky hills rising above it on the north and west, and contains thirty houses, supplied with water from a tank. Lat. 26° 55′, long. 71° 7′.

BASUTEA, in the British district of Hijellee, lieut.-gov. of Bengal, a town on the route from Calcutta to Kedjeree, nine miles N. of the latter. Lat. 22°, long. 88° 2′.

BASWAPATAM.—A town in the territory of Mysore, distant W. from Chittel Droog 40 miles. Lat. 14° 11′, long. 75° 52′.

BATALA.—A town of the Punjaub, in the Baree Doab division, situate on the left bank of the Kussoor Nullah, distance N.E. from Amritsur 24 miles. Lat. 31° 49′, long. 75° 14′.

BATCULL, in the British district of Canara, presidency of Madras, a town situate on a small stream which a mile and a half lower down falls into the Arabian Sea, or North Indian Ocean. The town has two mosques, though the majority of the inhabitants are Brahminists. The total population is estimated at 3,000. Distance direct from Mangaloor, N., 80 miles; Madras, N.W., 390. Lat. 13° 59′, long. 74° 36′.

BATE ISLAND.—See Beyt Island.

BATEL, in the Punjaub, a town in the Daman, situate 31 miles N.W. of the town of Dera Ghazee Khan. Lat. 30° 20′, long. 70° 25′.

BATESAR, in the British district of Agra, lieut.-gov. of the N.W. Provinces, a town on the right bank of the Jumna, 35 miles S.E. of the city of Agra. It is described by Bacon as "chiefly remarkable for the exceeding beauty of the scenery around it, and the broad lake-like appearance of the river as it meanders quietly through its precipitous banks." Lat. 26° 56′, long. 78° 36′.

BATHERI, in the native state of Gurwhal, a village on the right bank of the Bhagirathi, as the Ganges is called in the upper part of its course. It is situate 300 feet above the stream, and close to the confluence of the Retal Nadi, a torrent falling into the Bhagirathi on the right side. Lat. 30° 59′, long. 78° 36′.

BATINDA.—A town in the native state of Patialah, one of the protected Sikh states, distant W. from Patialah 90 miles. Lat. 30° 10′, long. 75°.

BAT KOOCHEE, in the British district of Durrung, in Lower Assam, lieut.-gov. of Bengal, a town on the northern boundary of the district, 20 miles N. of Durrung. Lat. 26° 40′, long. 91° 59′.

BATTA, or BHUTAH, in Sirmor, a stream draining the Kyarda Doon, the waters of which it discharges into the Jumna. It rises seven miles S.E. of Nahun, and collecting the various torrents of the Doon, holds first an easterly and then a southerly course of about eighteen miles to its fall into the Jumna, close to the spot where that river commences its passage through the Sewalik range. The Bhutah for part of its course is dry in the hot season, and then forms part of the route from Hurdwar to Nahun.

BATTANA, in the British district of Tannah, presidency of Bombay, a town on the route from Bhewndy to Damaun, 18 miles N.W. of the former. Lat. 19° 30′, long. 73°.

BAUG, in the raj or small state of Amjherra, a town with a fort, situate on a sandstone hill, in a wild, rugged, jungly tract, and at the confluence of the small rivers Wagrey and Girna. Here are furnaces for smelting the iron-ore raised in the neighbouring hills. It is surrounded by a low mud wall, and is stated to contain 400 houses; from which amount, according to the usual average, the population appears to be about 2,000 persons. In a range of hills extending N.E. and S.W., and in a spot about three and a quarter miles S.E. of the town, are four remarkable caves excavated in the N.W. face of the rock. According to the fabulous tradition of the Hindoos, they were excavated by the Panch Pandoos, those celebrated heroes of Hindoo mythology to whom all wonders are referred. The learned Erskine, however, has determined that the temples are Buddhist. Baug is the principal place of a pergunnah of the same name, containing seventy-six villages, twenty-seven of which are deserted. Though included within the limits of Amjherra, it appears to have fallen to the share of Scindia, who granted it, with its estimated annual revenue of 9,000 rupees, to one of his relatives. Baug is situate on the road from Guzerat to Malwa by what is termed the pass of Oodeypore. Two roads diverge from Baug; one the Tanda ghat, having a N.E. direction; the other the Tirrella ghat, leading to Indore and Oojein: this last is by far the best carriage-road. Distance S.W. from Mow 61 miles. Lat. 22° 23′, long. 74° 51′.

BAUG-CHEENEE.—A town in the native state of Gwalior, or possessions of Scindia, distant N.W. from Gwalior 27 miles. Lat. 26° 28′, long. 77° 56′.

BAUGDA, in the British district of Nuddea, lieut.-gov. of Bengal, a town 26 miles S.E. of Kishungur, and 23 miles W. of Jessore. Lat. 23° 12′, long. 88° 50′.

BAUGLEE, in the territory of Gwalior, a town in Malwa, belonging to a petty rajah tributary to the Scindia family, situate on the Kalee Sind river. It has a small well-built fort, and about 500 houses, with a population of about 3,000. Distant 54 miles S.E. from Oojein. Lat. 22° 38′, long. 76° 24′.

BAUG NUDDEE.—A small river rising in the Cuttack Mehals, in lat. 20° 16′, long. 84° 14′, and flowing north for about sixty miles, principally through the petty state of Boad, falls into the Mahanuddy river near the town of Sonepoor, in lat. 20° 55′, long. 84° 9′.

BAUJPOOR.—A town in the native state of Wusravee, presidency of Bombay, 58 miles N.E. from Surat, and 34 miles E. from Wusravee. Lat. 21° 22′, long. 73° 48′.

BAULAPOOR, in Hyderabad, or territory of the Nizam, a town on the route from Ellichpoor to Aurungabad, 65 miles S.W. of former, 102 N.E. of latter, on the river Mun, a tributary of the Taptee. Lat. 20° 43′, long. 76° 50′.

BAULEA, a town in the British district Rajeshahye, and the seat of the civil establishment of the district, is situate near the left bank of the Podda, or great eastern branch of the Ganges, on the route from Berhampore to Jumalpore. It has a bazaar and considerable traffic. One of the government English schools was opened here in 1837. The civil station of the district was formerly at Nator, but as the spot was low, and very unhealthy, the establishment was, in 1822, removed to Baulea, which is built on a ridge of clay and kunkur. Distance from Calcutta, N., 122 miles; from Berhampore, N.E., 47; from Jumalpoor, S.W., 136. Lat. 24° 22′, long. 88° 36′.

BAUMEE. — A pass leading from the southern portion of Arracan into Pegu. The crown of the pass is about lat. 17° 25′, long. 94° 50′.

BAUN, or OOTUNGHUN. — A river rising in the Rajpoot state of Jeypoor, in lat. 27° 20′, long. 76° 3′, near the town of Munohurpoor; and flowing 215 miles, first south and afterwards west, passing in its course through the states of Bhurtpore, Dholpoor, and the British district of Agra, it falls into the Jumna on its right side, in lat. 26° 58′, long. 78° 31′.

BAUNDA, in the Reechna Dooab division of the Punjab, a town 58 miles N.E. of the town of Mooltan. Lat. 30° 46′, long. 72° 3′.

BAUNK, in the native state of Korea, on the S.W. frontier of the presidency of Bengal, a small town or village among the mountains of Gondwana, 44 miles N.W. of the town of Sirgooja, 108 S. of Mirzapoor, 360 W. of Calcutta. Lat. 23° 34′, long. 82° 42′.

BAUNSDA.—See BANSDA.

BAUNTWA, in Guzerat, a town of Kattywar, in the district of Soruth. It is the principal place of a tallook or subdivision containing fifty-four villages and a population estimated at 20,000. A tribute of 1,200*l.* annually is paid to the British government. The chiefs of Bauntwa, younger branches of the family of the second nawaub of Joonagurh, by whom it was alienated in 1740, have an aggregate income which has been estimated at about 100,000 rupees. Distance from Ahmedabad, S.W., 190 miles. Lat. 21° 30′, long. 70° 10′.

BAUSHKERA, in the British district of Moradabad, lieut.-gov. of the N.W. Provinces, a village on the route from the town of Moradabad to Almora, and 27 miles N. of the former. Lat. 29° 10′, long. 79°.

BAUSUR.—A town in the territory of Hyderabad, or dominions of the Nizam, distant N. from Hyderabad 110 miles. Lat. 18° 53′, long. 78°.

BAYPOOR.—See BEYPOOR.

BAYTEE, in the British district of Allahabad, lieut.-gov. of the N.W. Provinces, a village on the route by the left bank of the Ganges from Allahabad cantonment to that of Benares, 30 miles S.E. of the former, 44 W. of the latter. Lat. 25° 18′, long. 82° 22′.

BAZAAR, in the Punjaub, a town of the district of Bunnoo, situate on the right bank of the Khoorum river, 60 miles N. of Dera Ismail Khan. Lat. 32° 39′, long. 70° 42′.

BAZAR, in the district of Peshawur, a division of the Punjab, a town situate 50 miles N.E. of the town of Peshawur. Lat. 34° 33′, long. 72° 10′.

BAZPOOR.—A town in the British district of Moradabad, lieut.-gov. of the N.W. Provinces. Lat. 29° 9′, long. 79° 10′.

BEARA, in the native state of Wusravee, under the political superintendence of the government of Bombay, a town on the route from Boorhanpoor to the city of Surat, 190 miles W. of former, 39 E. of latter. Population about 4,000. Lat. 21° 4′, long. 73° 26′.

BEAS, one of the great rivers of the Punjab, rises on the southern verge of the Rotang pass, in Lahoul, a Himalayan region north-east of the Punjab, and at a point 13,200 feet above the sea, in lat. 32° 24′, long. 77° 11′. The river takes a southerly course of about eighty miles to Mundi, and has there a considerable body of water, and a width of from 150 to 200 yards, with a depth of twelve feet. The depth, however, in the warm season constantly varies, beginning to swell in the evening, attaining its maximum by morning, and declining through the day, losing about one-third of its water. This periodical change results from the melting of the snow diurnally by the heat of the sun. From Mundi the Beas takes a course of fifty miles, chiefly westerly, to Nadaun, where Vigne found it in the low season 150 yards wide, twelve feet deep, and running at the rate of three miles and a half an hour. Forster, who crossed the Beas a short distance below Nadaun, states that he found it to have a rapid stream about 100 yards wide; but the breadth frequently varies, and Moorcroft, about a quarter of a mile above the town, found it only 100 feet wide, and running at the rate of five miles an hour. B. Von Hügel describes it here as an unfordable clear rapid stream, running between steep and lofty banks, access being obtained to the water by large and well-constructed stairs. From Nadaun it takes a wide sweep of about eighty miles to the north-west, and having entered the plain of the Punjab, it turns southward, a course which it holds for about eighty miles further, to its confluence with the Sutluj. A short distance below Nadaun it receives the river of Kunyar, flowing from the south. Macartney measured it at the ferry of Bhyrawul, about twenty miles above the confluence, and there found it 740 yards wide, and so rapid that, in crossing, the boats were driven ten or twelve miles down the stream. This was in August, at a season when the river is at its greatest height. In the low or cold season it is fordable in most places. By the competent observer last quoted, the Beas is regarded as larger than the Sutluj, though in length of course it is greatly inferior to that river. But Burnes states, that though they have the same breadth each, about 200 yards, the Sutluj has the greater volume of water. The confluence of the Beas with the Sutluj takes place at Endreesa, near the village Hurekee, and in lat. 31° 10′, long. 75° 4′, after a course by the former river of 290 miles. The Beas is considered to be identical with the Hyphasis of Arrian, the Greek name being a corruption of *Beypasha*, given it by the natives. The united stream below the confluence bears the name of the Ghara until the confluence with the Chenaub.

BEAWR, or BEOUR, in the British district of Ajmere, a town of Mairwara, 30 miles S.W. of Nusseerabad cantonment. It is situate in an extensive valley, which is likewise the site of the cantonment of the Mhair corps, a force of 1,000 men raised from the Mhairs, a tribe inhabiting that part of the Aravulli range. The only public building at this place is the prison, a well-regulated establishment, the expenses of which are defrayed by the labour of the prisoners. Lat. 26° 10′, long. 74° 26′.

BECHORE.—See Pichore.

BECTALUNG, in the British district of Sylhet, lieut.-gov. of Bengal, a town on the left bank of a small rivulet running into the river Barak, 52 miles S.W. of Sylhet. Lat. 24° 25′, long. 91° 12′.

BEDER, in Hyderabad, or the territory of the Nizam, a large town near the right bank of the Manjera, a considerable tributary of the river Godavery. Its site is on a table-land 2,359 feet above the sea, and about 100 feet above the level of the adjacent country. It is surrounded by lofty walls, and is still a large city, though greatly declined from its former state, when it was the capital of a principality and the residence of kings. It is at present chiefly noted for the manufacture called Bidari ware, used particularly for the bottoms or bowls of *hookas* or tobacco-pipes, and for vessels to hand round betel to guests. The material is an alloy, consisting of twenty-four parts of tin and one of copper. The ware is coloured black with a preparation for which this place is celebrated, and which is made by mixing equal parts of muriate of ammonia and saltpetre-earth with water, compounding them into a paste. The colour is said to be very durable; and if it become impaired, it is restored by the application of oil or butter. The sable hue of the articles thus fabricated is relieved by silver ornaments. Beder is 75 miles N.W. of the city of Hyderabad. Lat. 17° 53′, long. 77° 36′.

BEDNOR.—A town in the Rajpoot state of Oodeypoor, distant N.W. from Oodeypoor 93 miles. Lat. 25° 51′, long. 74° 20′.

BEDNORE, or NUGGUR, in the native state of Mysore, under the administration of the government of India, a city, the principal place of a district of the same name, situate in the midst of a basin or depression in a rugged table-land on the Western Ghats, and at an elevation estimated at more than 4,000 feet above the sea. The town does not appear to have been at any time fortified, its defence having been injudiciously intrusted to the line of posts erected on the summits of the surrounding hills. On a bold eminence within the lines of defence are the citadel and the ruined palace of the rajah. The town is favourably situate for commerce, on the road leading from Mangalore, through Hosso Angadi, one of the best passes through the Western Ghats. Originally a village, this place in 1645 became the seat of government of the rajah of Ikeri, who thenceforward was denominated rajah of Bednore, and its prosperity rapidly advanced, so that the population soon exceeded 100,000 persons. In 1763 it was taken by Hyder Ali, the usurper of Mysore, who pillaged it of property of the estimated value of 12,000,000*l.*, and subsequently made it the seat of his government, and, in honour of himself, called it Hyder-nuggur, or Hyder's Town, subsequently abbreviated popularly into Nuggur, by which name it is at present generally known. Early in 1783 General Matthews occupied this town, at the head of a considerable British force; but being soon after attacked by Tippoo with a vastly superior force, all attempts at resistance were quickly overpowered; and the British force having surrendered, General Matthews and the other principal officers were put to death, and the rest of the force imprisoned and very cruelly treated. Bednore is distant from Seringapatam, N.W., 150 miles; Bangaloor, N.W., 183; Mangaloor, N., 70; Madras, W., 360. Lat. 13° 50′, long. 75° 6′.

BEEANS, in the British district of Kumaon, lieut.-gov. of the N.W. Provinces, a Bhoti subdivision or collection of hamlets on the upper part of the course of the river Kalee, bounded on the north and north-east by South-western Thibet; on the south-east by the territory of Nepal; on the south by the mehal of Choudans; and on the west and north-west by the mehal of Dharma; and situate between lat. 30° 8′—30° 28′, long. 80° 42′—80° 57′; and having an area of about 200 square miles. The pass on the northern frontier of this subdivision, forming a communication with South-western Thibet, has an elevation of about

15,000 feet. The peak of Beeans Rikhi, a summit of the Himalayas on the same frontier, rises to the height of 20,000 feet.

BEEAS, in the British district of Rajeshaye, lieut.-gov. of Bengal, a town on the route from Dacca to Bograh, 26 miles S. of the latter. Lat. 24° 29', long. 89° 18'.

BEEBAMEYOO, in the British district of Etawah, lieut.-gov. of the N.W. Provinces, a town on the route from Etawah to Agra, 16 miles N.W. of the former. Lat. 26° 56', long. 78° 53'.

BEEBEEPOOR, in the British district of Cawnpore, lieut.-gov. of the N.W. Provinces, a village on the route from the cantonment of Futtehgurh to that of Cawnpore, and 32 miles N.W. of the latter. Lat. 26° 49', long. 80° —.

BEEBREE, in the British district of Mynpooree, lieut.-gov. of the N.W. Provinces, a village on the route from the cantonment of Allygurh to that of Mynpooree, and 30 miles N.W. of the latter. Lat. 27° 30', long. 78° 46'.

BEECHA KOH.—A town in the native state of Nepal, distant S.W. from Khatmandoo 32 miles. Lat. 27° 17', long. 85° 1'.

BEEDASIR, or BIDASIR, in the Rajpoot state of Bikaner, a town near the south-eastern frontier, towards Joudpore. About five miles south-east of the town, during the rainy season, is a piece of water about four miles long and half that breadth, with a depth of four or five feet. It dries up in the hot season, leaving a thick crust of salt, which is taken off both for home use and exportation. The number of houses, according to Tod, is 500. The adjacent country is the least sterile part of the territory of Bikaner, in consequence of the nearness of water to the surface. Lat. 27° 48', long. 74° 26'.

BEEGOH.—A town in the native state of Beekaneer, distant E. from Beekaneer 52 miles. Lat. 28° 4', long. 74° 13'.

BEEGHUR, in the British district of Hurriana, lieut.-gov. of the N.W. Provinces, a village on the route from Hansi to Bhutneer, and 42 miles N.W. of the former. It is a poor place, being scantily supplied even with water. Lat. 29° 22', long. 75° 34'.

BEEHEE, in the British district of Shahabad, lieut.-gov. of Bengal, a town on the route from Dinapoor to Benares, 39 miles W. of the former. Lat. 25° 30', long. 84° 31'.

BEEHUR, a river of the district of Boghelkhund, or territory of Rewah, rises in lat. 24° 15', long. 81° 5', about 25 miles S.W. of the town of Rewah. The elevation above the sea, of its source, must considerably exceed 1,000 feet, as at the Chachye Fall, fifty miles farther north, or down the stream, the bed has an elevation of 990 feet. At the Chachye Fall, the stream, passing from the plateau of Rewah to the more depressed country farther to the north-east, is precipitated down the face of the bounding ledge a depth of 200 feet. Two miles below this it falls into the Tons, on the right side, in lat. 24° 48', long. 81° 22'. At Rewah, thirty miles from its source, it is crossed by the route from Allahabad to Saugor, and at that point is fordable in the dry season, the stream being then fifteen yards wide, and knee-deep: the bed is eighty yards wide. Jacquemont describes it in the same place as a torrent flowing down a wide and deep channel over irregular calcareous masses.

BEEHUT, in territory of Gwalior, a town on the route from Kalpee to the fort of Gwalior, 94 miles W. of former, 30 E. of latter. There is here a fort of masonry on an eminence. A small business is driven in smelting and selling the iron raised from the sandstone hills a short distance to the south. Lat. 26° 13', long. 78° 37'.

BEEJAPOOR.—A ruined town in Sattara, near the eastern frontier, towards Hydrabad, or the territory of the Nizam. Duff gives the following account of its condition: "The walls, which are of hewn stone and very lofty, are to this day entire, and being surmounted by the cupolas and minarets of the public buildings, still present to a spectator from without the appearance of a flourishing city; but within all is solitude, silence, and desolation. The deep moat, the double rampart, and the ruins of the splendid palaces in the citadel, attest the former magnificence of the court. The great mosque is a grand edifice, and the tomb of Ibrahim Adil Shah is remarkable for its elegant and graceful architecture. But the chief feature in the scene is the mausoleum of Muhummud Adil Shah, the dome of which fills the eye from every point of view; and though in itself entirely devoid of ornament, its enormous dimensions and austere simplicity invest it with an air of melancholy grandeur, which harmonizes with the wreck and desolation that surround it. When viewed as mere ruins, the remains of that city as they at present exist are exceedingly grand, and as a vast whole, far exceed anything of the kind in Europe." Among the various wonders of this ruined capital of the extinct kingdom of Beejapoor, not the least remarkable is the vast gun called Malik i Maidan, or "the King of the Plain," one of the largest pieces of brass ordnance in the world. The muzzle is four feet eight inches in diameter, the calibre two feet four inches, the length nearly fifteen feet, the weight forty tons. Its removal to England has been suggested by the Bombay government; but as the expense of its conveyance to the coast was estimated at 30,000 rupees, the home authorities expressed an opinion, that the object proposed was not of sufficient importance to justify the expense.

The founder of the Mussulman state of Beejapoor was, according to Ferishta, a son of Murad II., the Osmanli sultan; on whose death, his successor, Muhammad II., gave orders that all his brothers should be strangled. From this fate one only, named Yusuf, escaped, by a stratagem of his mother. After many adventures, Yusuf is stated to have entered into the service of the king of Ahmedabad Bieder, in which he raised himself to the highest offices of the state. On the king's death, he withdrew from Ahmedabad to Beejapoor, and declared himself its king; the people at the same time acknowledging his claim. Yusuf reigned with great prosperity, and extending his dominions westward to the seacoast, took Goa from the Portuguese. His resources must have been great, as he built the vast citadel of Beejapoor. He died in 1510, and was succeeded by his son Ismael, who died in 1534, after a brilliant and prosperous reign. The fate of his son and successor Mulu Adil Shah was widely different, he having been deposed and blinded, after a disastrous and inglorious reign of only six months; thus making way for his younger brother Ibrahim, a profligate man, who died 1557, and was succeeded by his son Ali Adil Shah. This king confederated with the kings of Ahmednuggur and of Golconda, against Raja Ram, the rao or sovereign of Bijyanagar, and, with the exception of the padshah of Delhi, by far the greatest potentate of India. Raja Ram was, in 1564, defeated in a great battle, at Talikot, on the river Krishna, and being made prisoner, was put to death in cold blood, and his capital taken and sacked. The wall of Beejapoor, the Jama Masjit or great mosque, the aqueducts, and some other great works of the city, were constructed by Ali Adil Shah, whose death occurred in 1579. The throne, on this event, passed to his nephew Ibrahim Adil II., an infant, whose interests were managed by Chaund Bibi, widow of the late king, a woman celebrated for her determination, talents, and energy. On Ibrahim arriving at years of discretion, and assuming the government, he ruled with ability; and dying in 1626, after a reign of forty-seven years, was succeeded by Muhammad Adil Shaw, under whose reign Sevajee, the notorious founder of the Mahratta sway, rose into notice. Shahjee, the father of Sevajee, had been an officer in the service of the king of Beejapoor; and the first aggressions of Sevajee were made at the expense of that state, from which, in the interval between 1646 and 1648, he wrested several forts: soon afterwards he took possession of the greater part of the Concan. Muhammad, however, had a more formidable enemy in Shah Jehan, whose son Aurungzebe, in obedience to the imperial mandate, besieged the city of Beejapoor, and was on the eve of taking it, when he precipitately marched away to Agra, whither he was drawn by intelligence of some court intrigues, which he feared might end in his destruction. After his departure, the power of Sevajee rapidly increased, and that of the king of Beejapoor proportionally declined. Muhammad died in 1660, and was succeeded by Ali Adil II., who, on his decease in 1672, left the kingdom, then fast descending to ruin, to his infant son Secunder Adil Shah, the last of the race who occupied the throne, as, in 1686, Aurungzebe took Beejapoor, and put an end to its existence as an independent state. Those vast and wonderful ruins passed, with the adjoining territory, to the Mahrattas during the decline of the realm of Delhi, in the early part of the eighteenth century. On the overthrow of the Peishwa, in 1818, they passed into the hands of the British government, and were included within the territory assigned by that government to the rajah of Sattara. The late ruler of that state manifested much anxiety for the preservation of the splendid remains of Mahomedan grandeur in Beejapoor, and adopted measures for repairing and upholding them; and since its escheat, the Bombay government has acted in the same laudable spirit, having taken measures, with the approbation of the home authorities, for arresting the further progress of dilapidation in the buildings, as well as for collecting and preserving the relics of manuscripts, coins, copper-plate inscriptions, and other curious and interesting relics of the past. Distance from Sattara, S.E., 130 miles; from Poona, S.E., 170; from Bombay, 245. Lat. 16° 50′, long. 75° 48′.

BEEJAPORE, in Guzerat, or territory of the Guicowar, a town on the route from Mow to Deesa, 200 miles N.W. of former, 60 S.E. of latter. Population 12,000. Lat. 23° 32′, long. 72° 45′.

BEEJEE.—See Bhujee.

BEEJEEPOOR. — A town of Purlakemedy, one of the Koond states, on the north-east frontier of the Madras presidency, distant S.W. from Goomsoor 50 miles. Lat. 19° 33′, long. 84°.

BEEJUL.—A river of Baghelcund, rising in Rewah, about lat. 24° 10′, long. 82° 30′, and flowing in a north-easterly direction for thirty miles through Rewah, and twenty-five miles through Mirzapore, falls into the river Sone on the right bank, in lat. 24° 32′, long. 83° 2′.

BEEJWAR, in the Rajpoot state of Alwur, a town near the left bank of the Saubie Nulla, a torrent dry from November to July, but widely spreading during the rains. Distance S.W. from Delhi 65 miles. Lat. 27° 58′, long. 76° 35′.

BEEJWAR, in Central India, a town in the native state of Tonk, or possessions of Ameer Khan, distant N.E. from Tonk 18 miles. Lat. 26° 20′, long. 75° 44′.

BEEKANEER, or **BIKANEER**, a state of Rajpootana, is bounded on the north by the British district of Butteeanah; on the east by that of Hurriana and by Shekawuttee; on the south-east by Shekawuttee; on the south by Joudpore; and on the west by Jessulmere and Bahawulpore. It lies between lat. 27° 30′ – 29° 55′, long. 72° 30′—75° 40′. It is 160 miles across, in a direction from north to south, and 200 in a direction at right angles with the former. The area is 17,676 square miles. The climate is characterized by extraordinary extremes of temperature, according as the sun may be above or below the horizon. There is the unexceptionable evidence of Elphinstone respecting this point, at least as regards the closing part of the year. Proceeding to the capital at the beginning of November, the members of his mission suffered great mortality. "Thirty sepoys," he states, "without reckoning followers, were taken ill in the course of one day at Nuttoosir, and forty persons of all descriptions expired during the first week of our halt at Bikaneer. The great difference between the temperature of the days and nights no doubt contributed to this mortality. Even the English gentlemen used to suffer from cold during the night-marches, and were happy to kindle a large fire as soon as we reached our ground; yet the sun became powerful so early in the morning, that we always woke with a feverish heat, which lasted till sunset." Boileau found the weather piercingly cold in winter, and even in the beginning of February ice was formed in considerable quantities on the ponds, and the different vessels of water in his camp were completely frozen. But on the 9th May the temperature was 120° at noon; 123° at 1 P.M.; 119° at 2 P.M.; 116° at 3 P.M., in the same tent. Yet under this great heat the air was not found unhealthy, and there was not a sick man in camp; so that a comparison with the effects of the season encountered by Elphinstone, would seem to show that the more sultry is the more healthy part of the year. Under the wretched agriculture of this country, the crops are a sort of millet, bajra (Holcus spicatus), moth (Phaseolus aconitifolius); and in some situations, where the rains fall abundantly and seasonably, the produce is considerable. Wheat, barley, and the better kinds of pulse, are of necessity imported. Some of the cucurbitaceous tribe succeed well, especially the water-melon. Elphinstone observes: "In the midst of so arid a country, the water-melon, the most juicy of fruits, is found in profusion. It is really a subject of wonder to see melons three or four feet in circumference growing from a stalk as slender as that of a common melon, in the dry sand of the desert. They are sown, and perhaps require some cultivation, but they are scattered about, to all appearance, as if they grew wild." The natives assert that a large melon suffices to allay the thirst of a horse and his rider.

The majority of the population are by descent Jauts, a people inhabiting from a very remote period a widely-extended country on the east of the Indus from the Himalaya to the Indian Ocean. To that ancient stock it is believed about three-fourths of the people of Beekaneer belong. The predominant race are Rajpoots of the Rahtore tribe, of which class is the rajah, a descendant from Bika, the founder of the state and capital. Brahmins of the Sarsote (Sarasvati) tribe are numerous, and are said to be peaceable and industrious; lax in practising the tenets of their religion, as they eat flesh of various kinds, smoke tobacco, and trade in kine. There is also a considerable number of Jains. The Charuns, of Rajpoot origin, are an influential class, who, by the assertion of the loftiest pretensions and the exercise of the most wily arts of priestcraft, contrive to hold the minds and properties of the community at their mercy. But slight regard is paid to the prejudices of caste by the Rajpoots of the desert, eating and drinking with little either of scruple or discrimination. Tod, whose admiration of them appears to be far more ardent than judicious, says, "They would make the best soldiers in the world if they would submit to discipline, as they are brave, hardy, easily satisfied, and very patient." Formerly great numbers of wretched women were burned alive with the corses of their deceased husbands. It is related that one corse "was accompanied to the pyre by eighty-four victims, another had eighteen, others less and less, until at last the late Maharajah Soorut Singh was gathered to his fathers without a single suttee sharing the funeral pile." At the last sacrifice of this kind that occurred in the Bika family, the departed rajah's second son, an exceedingly fine young man, was burned "with the widow Deep-jee, a princess of the house of Oodepoor, who was in the prime of eastern widowhood, being reported about sixteen or seventeen years of age at the time of this cruel sacrifice." This was in the Hindoo year 1882, corresponding with A.D. 1825. The language of the country is a dialect of Hindee. The annual revenue of the rajah is stated at 65,000*l.*, the half of which is derived from the land. With such moderate resources, the rajah is reported by Elphinstone to have contrived to maintain some degree of decent state. The military force, maintained partly by feudal arrangements, amounted in the year 1848 to upwards of 5,000 regulars, horse and foot. The population is stated to amount to 539,250. In 1799 Beekaneer was invaded by the adventurer George Thomas, who forced the rajah to pay 20,000*l.* as compensation for alleged wrongs. Subsequently, with the view of securing himself against the neighbouring state of Bahawulpoor, as well as of coercing his own feudatories, the rajah sought English protection, and in 1818 entered into a treaty with the East-India Company.

BEEKANEER, or BIKANEER, the capital of the Rajpoot state of the same name, is situate in a singularly desolate tract, the soil being hard, stony, and totally unfit for cultivation. Viewed from without, it presents the appearance of a great and magnificent city, having a fine wall surmounted by many round towers, and crowned with the usual Indian battlements. So imposing is its appearance, that when approached by Elphinstone's mission, there were disputes among his followers whether it or Delhi were the more extensive. Boileau states the population at nearly 60,000, which coincides with the estimate of Tod, who states the number of houses at 12,000, and assigns five persons to each house; but it seems scarcely credible that a country so sterile should be able to furnish the necessaries of life to a town having a population of 60,000 persons. Distance of Beekaneer N.W. from Calcutta 1,175 miles, from Ajmere 130 miles. Lat. 28°, long. 73° 22′.

BEEKASUR, in the Rajpoot state of Bickaneer, a village on the route from Nagor to the city of Bickaneer, and 25 miles S.E. of the latter. It contains sixty houses, supplied with water from a well. Lat. 27° 40′, long. 73° 30′.

BEELARA.—A town in the native state of Marwar, or Joudpore, distant E. from Joudpore 42 miles. Lat. 26° 11′, long. 73° 49′.

BEELKAW.—A town in the peninsula of Kattywar, forming part of the possessions of the Guicowar, but placed under the political management of the presidency of Bombay, distant S. from Rajkote 61 miles. Lat. 21° 27′, long. 70° 40′.

BEELUN, in the Baree Doonb division of the Punjab, a town situated on the left bank of the Chenaub, five miles N. of the town of Mooltan. Lat. 30° 11′, long. 71° 31′.

BEEMA.—A river rising about lat. 19° 5′, long. 73° 33′, in the table-land of the district of Poona, presidency of Bombay, at an elevation of 3,090 feet above the level of the sea. It takes a south-easterly direction, and traversing, during a course of 380 miles, the districts of Poona, Ahmednuggur, Sholapore, and the territory of Sattara, enters the dominions of the Nizam, and after a further course of 130 miles, falls into the Kistnah river in lat. 16° 24′, long. 77° 20′.

BEEOR.—A village in the jaghire of Jhughur, lieut.-gov. of the N.W. Provinces. Lat. 28° 11′, long. 76° 19′.

BEERBHANWALLA, in the British district of Bijnour, lieut.-gov. of the N.W. Provinces, a village three miles from the right bank of the Ramgunga (western). Lat. 29° 32′, long. 78° 42′.

BEERBHOOM, a British district in the lieut.-gov. of Bengal, is bounded on the north by the British district of Bhaugulpore; on the east by the British districts Moorshedabad and Nuddea; on the south by the British districts Burdwan, Bancoora, and Pachete; and on the west by the British districts Ramgurh, Pachete, and Monghyr. It lies between lat. 23° 32′—24° 40′, long. 86° 25′—88° 30′. The area is 4,730 square miles. The district is traversed by numerous torrents descending from the highlands, which take a direction east or south-east until, discharging themselves into the channels either of the Bhagruttee or Damooda, their contents find their way to the estuary of the Ganges. Of these torrents the chief are the Hadjee and the Barakar. Coal and iron-ore in vast quantities and excellent quality exist along the courses of the Damooda and Hadjee, in the southern and western parts of the district. The population is stated to be 1,040,876. Beerbhoom was acquired by the East-India Company in 1765, by virtue of the firman of Shah Allum, padshah of Delhi, granting the dewanny of Bengal, Behar, and Orissa.

BEERCOOL, in the British district Midnapore, lieut.-gov. of Bengal, a town two miles N. of the shore of the Bay of Bengal, distant from the town of Midnapore, S., 54 miles; from Calcutta, S.W., 85. Lat. 21° 38′, long. 87° 32′.

BEERGUNJE, in the British district of Dinajepore, lieut.-gov. of Bengal, a town on the route from Dinajepore to Darjeeling, 17 miles N. of the former. Lat. 25° 48′, long. 88° 36′.

BEERKOOR.—A town in Hyderabad, or dominions of the Nizam, distant N.W. from Hyderabad 89 miles. Lat. 18° 28′, long. 77° 52′.

BEEROOL, in the British district of Nuddea, lieut.-gov. of Bengal, a town on the route from Hooghly to Jessore, 40 miles S.W. of the latter. Lat. 23°, long. 88° 35′.

BEERPOOR, in the presidency of Bombay, a town of Guzerat, on the route from Mow to Deesa, 180 miles N.W. of former, 146 S.E. of latter. It has a bazaar, and is well supplied with water, and belongs to the nawaub of Balasinore, a descendant of Osman Khan, who received it from Shahjehan, padshah of Delhi. Lat. 23° 10′, long. 73° 29′.

BEERPOOR, in the British district of Bareilly, lieut.-gov. of the N.W. Provinces, a village on the route from the city of Agra to Bareilly, and 24 miles S.W. of the latter. Lat. 28° 15′, long. 79° 13′.

BEERPOOR, in the British district of Tirhoot, lieut.-gov. of Bengal, a town on the route, along the left bank of the Ganges, from Mongheer to Patna, 19 miles E. of the latter. Lat. 25° 32′, long. 85° 33′.

BEERPORE, in the British district of Furruckabad, lieut.-gov. of the N.W. Provinces, a village on the route from the cantonment of Allygurh to that of Futtehgurh, and 17 miles N.W. of the latter. Lat. 27° 26′, long. 79° 26′.

BEERUMSIR, a village of the Rajpoot state of Bickanere, on the eastern frontier, towards Shekhawati, is situate on the route from Patun to the town of Bickanere, and 97 miles E. of the latter. Lat. 28° 2′, long. 74° 53′.

BEESOO, in the Rajpoot state of Joudpore, a village on the route from Pokhurn to Balmer, and 43 miles N. of the latter. Lat. 26° 16′, long. 71° 24′.

BEESULNUGGUR, or BISANAGAR, in Guzerat, or territory of the Guicowar, a town on the route from Mow to Deesa, 220 miles N.W. of former, 50 S.W. of latter. It has considerable transit-trade, in sending iron and some other heavy goods to Marwar; and the manufacture of cotton cloths is carried on to a considerable extent. Population 18,000. Distance from Ahmedabad, N., 45 miles. Lat. 28° 40′, long. 72° 33′.

BEESULPOOR, in the Rajpoot state of Joudpore, a town on the route from the city of Joudpore to that of Ajmeer, and 18 miles E. of the former. It contains 800 houses, and a bazaar of 100 shops, and is supplied with good water from seventy wells lined with brick, and from fifteen to twenty feet deep. Population 4,050. Lat. 26° 16′, long. 73° 26′.

BEESULPOOR.—A town in the British district Bareilly, lieut.-gov. of the N.W. Provinces, and on the route from the town of Bareilly to Seetapoor, being 25 miles S.W. of the former place. It has a good bazaar, and is abundantly supplied with water. Population 7,245. Lat. 28° 18′, long. 79° 52′.

BEETHNOK.—A town in the Rajpoot state of Beekaneer, distant S.W. from Beekaneer 40 miles. Lat. 27° 50′, long. 72° 46′.

BEETUREE, in the Rajpoot state of Joudpore, a village on the route from Jessulmere *viâ* Nagor to Nusseerabad, and 202 miles N.W. of the latter. It is supplied with good water from two wells 200 feet deep. Lat. 27° 5′, long. 72° 25′.

BEGERWAL, in Sirhind, a village on the route from Hansee to Lodiana, and 75 miles N. of the former town. It is situate in a level, fertile, well-cultivated country. Distant N.W. from Calcutta 1,051 miles. Lat. 30° 6′, long. 75° 53′.

BEGH, in the British district of Furruckabad, lieut.-gov. of the N. W. Provinces, a village on the route from the cantonment of Allyghur to that of Futtehgurh, and 13 miles N.W. of the latter. Lat. 27° 26′, long. 79° 30′.

BEGIEGHAT, in the British district of Suharunpoor, lieut.-gov. of the N.W. Provinces, a village on the route from Kurnal to Suharunpoor. It is situate on the left bank of the Jumna, crossed here by ferry. Distant N.W. from Calcutta 976 miles. Lat. 29° 45′, long. 77° 13′.

BEGOKE, in the British district of Bhuttiana, lieut.-gov. of the N.W. Provinces, a village on the route from Hansee to Bhutnair, and 80 miles N.W. of the former. Lat. 29° 31′, long. 75° 3′.

BEGUMABAD, in the British district of Meerut, lieut.-gov. of the N. W. Provinces, a town on the route from Delhi to the town of Meerut, and 28 miles N.E. of the former. It has a serai, or lodge for travellers, and a bazaar. Lat. 28° 51′, long. 77° 38′.

BEGUMGUNJ, in the territory of Oude, a village on the route from Azimgurh to Fyzabad, 66 miles N.W. of the former, 20 S.E. of the latter. Lat. 26° 39′, long. 82° 22′.

BEGUMGUNJE, in the British district of Bulloah, lieut.-gov. of Bengal, a town on the route from Bulloah to Tipperah, 15 miles N.E. of the former. Lat. 22° 56′, long. 91° 9′.

BEGUMPOOR, in the British district of Allahabad, lieut.-gov. of the N.W. Provinces, a village on the route by Rajapoor ferry from the cantonment of Allahabad to Banda, and 13 miles W. of the former. Lat. 25° 24′, long. 81° 46′.

BEHADARPOOR, in the British district of Mozuffurnuggur, a village on the route from Meerut to Saharunpoor, and six miles S.E. of the town of Mozuffurnuggur. Lat. 29° 24′, long. 77° 50′.

BEHAR.—A British district under the lieut.-gov. of Bengal, so called from a town of the same name. It lies between lat. 24° 12′—25° 22′, long. 83° 25′—86° 6′; is 165 miles in length from north-east to south-west, and sixty-eight in breadth. The area is 5,694 square miles. It is bounded on the north by the British district of Patna; on the east and north-east by that of Mongheer; on the south by Ramghur and Palamow; on the west by Mirzapore; and on the north-west by Shahabad. It is a well-watered tract, being traversed or bounded by numerous rivers; among which may be enumerated the Son, the Phalgu, and the two Punpuns. With respect to the climate of Behar, it may be observed, that autumn is marked by the periodical rains usual in this part of India. The nights in winter are cool, and frosts sometimes injure the crops. The heat is excessive in the latter part of spring and early part of summer, and the annoyance resulting is increased by dust, there being then no vestige of verdure. Gaya, about the middle of the district, is considered the most sultry place within it; partly in consequence of the radiation from the extensive sands of the rivers; partly from the same effects caused by the bare rocks around the town. Rice, throughout the district, is generally the most important crop; the grain, which is very fine, is largely exported, being much in demand in the Calcutta market. Wheat is next in importance; then barley; then maruya, maize, jowar, and various kinds of millet, melons, cucumbers, and other cucurbitaceous growths of various sorts. The potato, introduced by Europeans, is now cultivated to great extent. The cabbage, cauliflower, lettuce, turnip, and most other European garden vegetables succeed well in the cold season. Of the commercial crops the most important is opium; and this article forms a productive source of revenue to government. Sugar and cotton are also extensively produced. Tobacco, indigo, and kusum or safflower, are raised, but in no great quantity; and the betel-leaf, though considered the finest in India, is not cultivated to any great extent. The manufacturing industry is rather important, being employed in producing fabrics of cotton, blankets, silk fabrics, carpets, tents, tape, thread, ropes, paper, torches, glass, coarse jewellery, coarse cutlery and hardware, turnery, leather, saddlery, shields and other fabrics in leather; fabrics of horn; ornaments in lac and glass, and in gold, silver, and other metals; ink, soap, sugar, nitre, pottery, tiles, and bricks. Ardent spirits are distilled in large quantities, especially from the mahua flowers. Perfumes from sandalwood, roses, and jasmine, are also made to a considerable extent. Dyeing is largely practised, but with no great skill. The population is estimated at 2,500,000. Of routes, first, the great trunk-road from Calcutta to the North-West Provinces traverses the south-west of the district, in a direction from south-east to north-west. Second, a route proceeds from north to south, from Patna to Gaya, where it takes a south-western direction to Shergotty, whence it is continued in the same direction to Palamow. With respect to the roads in general, Buchanan observes that he has seen no country, at all civilized, so ill provided with them. It must be observed, however, that the innumerable torrents traversing and inundating the country during the rainy season, render it very difficult either to make good roads or to keep them in repair.

The present British district of Behar comprises a portion only of the south-west half of the great soobah or province which bore the same name among the chief divisions of the empire of Delhi. Previously to the comparatively clear accounts derivable from the Moslem annals, this soobah appears in the legendary lore of the Hindoos to have been comprised within the realm of Magadha. Wilford observes, "It is universally acknowledged that the court of the kings of Magadha, now the province of Bahar, was one of the most brilliant that ever existed." Its meridian greatness has been conjectured to have continued for above two thousand years, during which "the kings of Magadha were lords paramount and emperors of India." In the time of Kutbuddin, viceroy of Mohammed, the Mussulman sultan of Ghor, it formed part of the dominions of Jaichand, king of Kannouj. Jaichand was in 1194 defeated and slain by the Mussulman general, and Behar and Bengal added to the dominion of Delhi, from which capital governors were thenceforward appointed. One of these governors was in 1340 slain by Malek Fakhr-uddin, who assumed the title of king of Bengal and Behar. The power of the dynasty which he founded was weakened by Baber, who wrested from it Behar, and was finally overthrown by Shir Shah, the Patan, who dethroned Humayon, the son of Baber, and expelled him from India. Bengal subsequently revolted, but was again united by Akbar to the empire of Delhi, of which it thenceforward remained a part until 1765, when, being virtually in the possession of the East-India Company, it was formally granted to that body by the firman of Shah Alum, the padshah of Delhi. The tract thus conferred comprised not only the present British districts of Behar, Patna, and Shahabad, on the right bank of the Ganges, but an extent nearly equal on the left bank of that river, and at present coextensive with the British district of Tirhoot and Sarun.

BEHAR, in the British district of the same name, lieut.-gov. of Bengal, a place now much decayed, the original city being nearly deserted, and the present town consisting of a collection of dwellings dispersed around its remains. The whole is divided into twenty-four mahalls or wards, containing houses interspersed with fields, gardens, and groves. From the old city a bazaar extends southward. It is roughly paved, and altogether a wretched street, though there are a few good houses in the rear, right and left of it. There are some ruins of mosques originally well-built structures. During the Mahomedan sway in this part of India, the town is stated to have surrounded the old ditch on every side for at least a mile. Its ruin dated from its sack by the Mahrattas, when they invaded Bengal and Behar, about 1742, Ali Verdi Khan being nawaub of the province; and all relics of prosperity were swept away by a dreadful famine which occurred some years subsequently. The number of inhabited houses, however, was estimated by Buchanan, fifty years ago, at 5,000; which, according to the usually admitted ratio of persons to dwellings, would denote a population of 30,000 persons. Distant S.E. from Patna 37 miles, N.W. from Calcutta 255. Lat. 25° 10′, long. 85° 35′.

BEHAR.—A town in the native state of Coosh Behar, in North-Eastern India, distant N.E. from Rungpore 41 miles. Lat. 26° 16′, long. 89° 29′.

BEHAREE, in the British district of Cawnpore, lieut.-gov. of the N.W. Provinces, a village on the route from the cantonment of Etawah to that of Cawnpore, and 36 miles W. of the latter. Water is obtained from wells. Lat. 26° 21′, long. 79° 55′.

BEHAREE, in the British district of Ghazeepoor, lieut.-gov. of the N.W. Provinces, a town on the route from Ghazeepoor cantonment to Jounpoor, 30 miles W. of the former, and 30 S.E. of the latter. Lat. 25° 35′, long. 83° 5′.

BEHLA, in the British district of Poona, presidency of Bombay, a town on the left bank of the Kokree river, 39 miles W. of Ahmednuggur. Lat. 19° 8′, long. 74° 11′.

BEHLAPOOR, in the British district of Ahmednuggur, presidency of Bombay, a town on the left bank of the river Paira, 35 miles N. of Ahmednuggur. Lat. 19° 36′, long. 74° 39′.

BEHRAH.—A town of Rajpootana, in the district of Godwar, distant S.W. from Ajmeer 136 miles. Lat. 25° 4′, long. 73° 15′.

BEHREE, in Bundelcund, a jaghire or feudal possession, named from its principal place. It is bounded by the British district of Hummerpore on every side, except for two or three miles on the west, where it adjoins the petty chieftainship of Bownee: its centre is in lat. 25° 55′, long. 79° 59′; and it comprises thirty square miles, five villages, with a population of 2,500 souls, and yields a revenue of 2,300*l*. The jaghiredar or feudatory, a Bhoondela Rajpoot, maintains twenty-five horse and 100 foot. In 1811, this jaghire was granted to be held in perpetuity of the East-India Company, as a reward to the jaghiredar for services rendered to the British government.

BEHREE, in Bundelcund, the principal place of the feudal possession of the same name, is situate on the left bank of the Betwa, 20 miles S.E. of Calpee. Lat. 25° 54′, long. 79° 58′.

BEHUR, in the British district of Bijnour, lieut.-gov. of the N.W. Provinces, a town 39 miles E. from Bijnour, and the same distance N. of Moradabad. Lat. 29° 21′, long. 78° 50′.

BEHUT.—A town in the territory of Gwalior, or possessions of Scindia, distant S. from Gwalior 82 miles. Lat. 25° 1′, long. 78° 30′.

BEHUT, in Bundelcund, a small town on the right bank of the river Deesaun, 54 miles S.W. of Calpee. It is the principal place of a jaghire or feudal grant, made in 1817, by the East-India Company to a descendant of one of the Kalleenjur Cowbeys, or Brahminical possessors of that fortress, who, in 1812, surrendered it on conditions to the British arms. It is stated to comprise fifteen square miles, to contain seven villages, with a population of 2,500 souls, and to yield a revenue of 1,550*l*. per annum. The military strength of this small domain corresponds with its limited extent; amounting to only sixty-one men, ten of whom are cavalry. The jaghiredar of Behut holds the mouzah of Lohargaon under the British government, subject to the payment of a revenue of 1,400 rupees per annum. Behut is in lat. 25° 25′, long. 79° 25′.

BEIRWAL, or BHAIRIWALA, in Sirhind, a village on the route from Hansi to Lodiana, and 39 miles S. of the latter town. Distant N.W. from Calcutta 1,071 miles. Lat. 30° 24′, long. 75° 58′.

BEJA.—An insignificant hill state in the Cis-Sutlej territory, bounded on the north by Kothar, on the east by the lapsed territory of Bughat, on the south by Pateeala, and on the west by Mhilog. It is barely five miles long from north-east to south-west, and not more than two at its greatest breadth. Its centre is in lat. 30° 56′, long. 77° 2′. It comprises only three pergunnahs, supposed to contain a population of 3,000, and yields a revenue of 400*l*., out of which a tribute of 18*l*. is paid to the British government. This state was, on the expulsion of the Goorkas in 1815, conferred on the rajah, on condition of subordinate military co-operation. He employs about 200 armed retainers.

BEJAGURH.—A town in the native state of Indoor, or possessions of the Holkar family, distant S.W. from Indoor 75 miles. Lat. 21° 40′, long. 75° 32′.

BEJAURA.—A town in the native state of Sirgoojah, on the south-west frontier of Bengal, distant N.E. from Sirgoojah 36 miles. Lat. 23° 16′, long. 83° 40′.

BEJEYGERH.—See BIDJEYGURH.

BEJIGURH, in the British district of Aligurh, lieut.-gov. of the N.W. Provinces, a town with a fort on a route from the cantonment of Aligurh to that of Futtehgurh, and 18 miles S.E. of the former. Elevation above the sea 713 feet. Lat. 27° 43′, long. 78° 17′.

BEJOURA, in the British district of Allahabad, lieut.-gov. of the N.W. Provinces, a village on the right bank of the Ganges, 783 miles N.E. of Calcutta by the river route, and 25 miles S.E. of the city of Allahabad by the same. Lat. 25° 16′, long. 82° 5′.

BELA, in the British district of Behar, lieut.-gov. of Bengal, a town on the route from Gayah to Patna, 45 miles S. of the latter. Lat. 24° 58′, long. 85° 3′.

BELAH, or BEYLUH, in the British district of Etawa, lieut.-gov. of the N.W. Provinces, is a small town on the route from the cantonment of Etawa to Lucknow by Nanamowghat, and 40 miles E. of the former. It has a bazaar, and supplies and water are abundant. Lat. 26° 49′, long. 79° 44′.

BELANOO, in the jaghire or feudal possession of Jujhur, lieut.-gov. of the N.W. Provinces, a village on the route from Chooroo, in Bikanere, to Kanond, and five miles W. of the latter place. Lat. 28° 15′, long. 76° 8′.

BELASPOOR, in the jaghire of Rampoor, lieut.-gov. of the N.W. Provinces, a town on the route from Almorah to Moradabad, by Bamouree and Rampoor, 72 miles S.W. of Almorah fort, 18 miles N.E. of Rampoor town, 35 miles E. of Moradabad cantonment. It is a place of considerable size, and has a good supply of water and provisions. Elevation above the sea 560 feet. Lat. 28° 53′, long. 79° 20′.

BELASPOOR.—The principal place of the small mountain state of Kuhloor, and the residence of the rajah. It has a picturesque site on the left or eastern bank of the Sutluj. At the time of Forster's visit in 1783 it was a flourishing town, well built, with a degree of regularity unusual in that country. The houses were constructed of stone and lime mortar, and the streets paved strongly, though roughly; but at the time of Moorcroft's visit in 1820 it was in a ruinous condition, in consequence of having been twice sacked by the Gorkhas. The bazaar is now much dilapidated, and slenderly stocked; the inhabited houses are reduced to a few hundred, and the only ornament of the town is the residence of the rajah, a building of moderate size, but neat, and decorated with flowers in fresco. The Sutluj, a deep and rapid river, and running at the rate of five miles an hour, is crossed about two miles above the town by a much-frequented ferry, forming a communication with the Punjab. Elevation above the sea 1,465 feet. Lat. 31° 19′, long. 76° 50′.

BELASPOOR.—See BILLASPOOR.

BELEEGAON.—A town in the native state of Bhotan, distant N.E. from Behar, the capital town of Cooch Behar, 69 miles. Lat. 27° 10′, long. 89° 53′.

BELEEN, in the British district of Pegu, presidency of Bengal, a town 20 miles from the left bank of the river Sittang, 62 miles S.E. of Pegu. Lat. 17° 22′, long. 97° 10′.

BELERIAGANJ, in the British district of Azimgurh, lieut.-gov. of the N.W. Provinces, a small town on the route from the town of Azimgurh to that of Goruckpore, and 10 miles N. of the former. Distant N. from Benares 63 miles. Lat. 26° 11′, long. 83° 12′.

BELGAUM, a British collectorate in the presidency of Bombay, is bounded on the north by the territory of Sattara, the Southern Mahratta jaghires, and the British collectorate of Sholapore; on the east by the dominions of the Nizam; on the south by the British collectorates of Dharwar and North Canara; and on the west by the Portuguese territory of Goa and the native states of Sawunt Warree and Colapore. It extends from lat. 15° 23′ to 16° 39′, and from long. 74° 2′ to 76° 23′; it is 160 miles in length from east to west, and 89 in breadth, and contains an area of 5,405 square miles, with a population of 1,025,882. Formerly the district of Belgaum constituted a portion of the collectorate of Dharwar; but in 1836, owing to the great extent of the latter, it was distributed into two divisions, the northern receiving the appellation of Belgaum, and the southern retaining its former name. The principal routes are from west to east, from the port of Vingorla, through the towns of Belgaum and Kuladgee, to Moodgul, in the Nizam's territory; and from north-west to south-east, from Colapore, through the towns of Nepanee and Belgaum, to Dharwar. Canarese is the language of the people. The district of Belgaum formed part of the territorial cession made by the Peishwa, under the treaty of June, 1817, for the maintenance of a subsidiary force to be provided by the British government.

BELGAUM.—A town, the principal place of the British collectorate of the same name, situate on the route from Dharwar to Colapore. In 1818, after the overthrow of the Peishwa, the place was invested by a British force. The fort is of an oval ground-plan, about 1,000 yards in length, 700 in breadth, and surrounded by a broad and deep wet ditch, cut in very hard ground. After a feeble resistance for twenty-one days, the garrison, consisting of 1,600 men, capitulated, having lost twenty killed and fifty wounded; while the loss of the British amounted only to eleven killed and twelve wounded. Within the last few years considerable improvements have been made in the town. In 1848 the principal inhabitants formed themselves into a committee, and in the course of four months, aided solely by the voluntary subscriptions of the townsmen, effected a complete reconstruction of the roads and lanes of the town, extending in the aggregate to a length of between nine and ten miles. The example thus set was followed in several towns and villages of the district; and the sense entertained by the government of the public spirit of the inhabitants of Belgaum was testified by the grant of 600*l.* to be expended in the further improvement of the town. Additional importance has been conferred upon this place, from its selection as the site of the educational institution for the instruction of the sons of natives of rank. This institution is supported by subscriptions from the chiefs and native gentry of the Southern Mahratta country, amounting annually to about 600*l.* A separate grant was made by the British government for the erection of the building; and the funds required for supplying the school with furniture, books, &c., were raised by private subscription. At a more recent period it was deemed desirable to throw open the institution to the sons of the middle classes of the country; and the number of pupils rapidly increased; in February, 1853, it exceeded fifty. Great apathy was at first evinced by the higher class sirdars, none of whom availed themselves of the proffered means of instruction; this, however, has been succeeded by a better spirit, and the list of pupils now contains the names of two of the descendants of the late chief of Sanglee, while the young chief of that state has himself condescended to receive instruction from the head master. Belgaum, which is situate on the plain east of the Ghauts, is 2,500 feet above the level of the sea. It is distant N.W. from Dharwar 42 miles. Lat. 15° 50′, long. 74° 36′.

BELGRAM, in the territory of Oude, a town on the route by Shahabad from Shahjehanpore to Lucknow, 75 miles N.W. of the latter. Heber, who passed through it in 1824, describes it as a small town with "marks of having been much more considerable, but still containing some large and good, though old, Mussulman houses." At present it has a bazaar, and is well supplied with water. The road in this part of the route is very sandy and bad. Lat. 27° 10′, long. 80° 5′.

BELHA, in the district of Pertabgurh, territory of Oude, a town on the left bank of the Sai, five miles east of the town of Pertabgurh. Butter states its population to be 3,000, all Hindoos. Distant E. of Lucknow 115 miles, N. of Allahabad 33. Lat. 25° 50′, long. 82°.

BELHA, in the British district of Tirhoot, lieut.-gov. of Bengal, a town 36 miles N.E. from Durbunga, 69 miles N. of Mongheer. Lat. 26° 18′, long. 86° 30′.

BELHA, in the British district of Azimghur, lieut.-gov. of the N.W. Provinces, a town the principal place of the pergunnah called Belhabans, is situate close to the southern frontier, in a swampy tract, much cut up by watercourses, some discharging themselves into the Ganges, others into the north-eastern Tons. It is 20 miles S. of Azimghur, 26 N.W. of Ghazeepoor, 34 N.E. of Benares, and in lat. 25° 48′, long. 83° 13′.

BELHARI, in the British district of Saugor and Nerbudda, a town on the north-east frontier towards Bundelcund, on the route from Allahabad to Jubbulpoor, 220 miles S.W. of former, 52 N.E. of latter. It is situate in a plain, amidst extensive ruins, proofs of its former prosperity, from which it has miserably declined, having been almost totally ruined by the predatory attacks of the Pindarees and other freebooters. There are, however, still some fine Hindoo temples in the town and its environs. Lat. 23° 44′, long. 80° 22′.

BELHIR.—A town in the territory of Oude, distant N.W. from Lucknow 32 miles. Lat. 27° 14′, long. 81° 20′.

BELHUTTEE.—A town in the native state of Sanglee, one of the Southern Mahratta jaghires, under the political superintendence of the presidency of Bombay, distant S.E. from Dharwar 53 miles. Lat. 15° 4′, long. 75° 47′.

BELJOOREE, or BAILJOOREE, in the British district of Moradabad, lieut.-gov. of the N.W. Provinces, a town on the route from Kasheepoor to Dehra, two miles N.W. of the former. Beljooree has a population of 7,354. Lat. 29° 14′, long. 79°.

BELLAMKONTA, in the British district of Guntoor, presidency of Madras, a town on the route from Guntoor to Nelgoondah, 32 miles N.W. of the former. Lat. 16° 30′, long. 80° 4′.

BELLARY.—A British district of the presidency of Madras, named from its principal place. It is bounded on the north by the territory of the Nizam, from which it is separated by the river Toongabudra or Tumbudda; on the east by the forfeited jaghire of Kurnool and the British district Cuddapah; on the south-west and south by the territory of Mysore; and on the west by the British district Dharwar. It lies between lat. 13° 40′—15° 58′, long. 75° 44′—78° 19′. Its area, according to official return, is 13,056 square miles. The country is altogether a highland, the most elevated part of which is to the west, where the surface rises towards the culminating range of the Western Ghauts, and to the south, where it rises to the elevated table-land of Mysore. The principal rivers are the Tumbudda or Toongabudra, the Vedavutty or Hugry, and the Northern Penna or Pennair. The climate is characterized by great aridity, the vapours of the ocean driven by the south-west monsoon being arrested, condensed, and precipitated in enormous quantities on the seaward or western sides, and on the summits of the Western Ghauts, so that but a small quantity reaches the central or eastern parts of the district, which, being also remote from the Bay of Bengal on the east, is beyond the influence of the north-east monsoon; so that less rain, on an average, falls in Bellary than in any place in Southern India. The population, according to a recent official statement, amounted to 1,229,599; indicating a relative density of ninety-four to the square mile. It is composed of a great variety of castes. People of two different tongues, the Teloogoos and Canarese, meet as it were in the centre of the district. The Teloogoo language is spoken in the eastern part of the district, and the Canarese in the western; the line of separation lying half-way between Bellary and Ghooty. In addition to the lines of railway which will intersect the district, the principal routes are, first, from south-east to north-west, from Madras, through Cuddapah, to the cantonment of Bellary, and thence, through the villages of Hospett and Humpsagur, to Dharwar and Belgaum; second, from south to north, from the military cantonment of Bangalore to that of Bellary; third, from south-west to north-east, from the military station of Hurryhur to Bellary, and thence to Hyderabad; fourth, a new trunk-road from Madras, through Chittoor and Palmanair, to Bellary. The Ceded Districts came into the possession of the East-India Company in the year 1800, by a treaty entered into with the Nizam, subsequent to the fall of Tippoo Sultan and the partition of his dominions. The collectorate of Bellary forms the western division of the districts so called.

BELLARY.—The principal place of the British district of the same name, under the presidency of Madras. It is the chief seat of the judicial and revenue establishments for the district, and the head-quarters of the military force of the Ceded Districts, consisting of Bellary and Cuddapah. The fort or fortified rock, round which the cantonment is situate, is a hill of bare granite of semi-elliptical form, the length of which, in a direction from north-east to south-west, is about 1,150 feet. "It rises abruptly from the plain to the height of 450 feet, and is about two miles in circumference." At the distance of a few hundred yards to the northward, is a long ridge of bare rugged rocks of similar formation, and at a short distance to the eastward are several lesser elevations of the same character. The summit of this hill being flat, and surrounded by a rampart of granite, constitutes what is styled the Upper Fort, which might be rendered impregnable; but having no accommodations for a garrison, is unoccupied by troops, except a small guard having custody of prisoners detained there. It contains several tanks or cisterns, excavated in the rock, from its south-western to its north-eastern corner; and outside this turreted rampart are a ditch and covered way. The lower fort is half a mile in diameter, and contains barracks for a regiment of the Crown and for the East-India Company's European artillery, the arsenal and commissariat stores, a Protestant church, and several bungalows, or lodges for officers. On the south-east of the lower fort is the pettah or native town, to which, at considerable expense to government, the inhabitants were removed in 1816, having previously inhabited the forts. About half a mile south-west of the base of the rock on which the fort is situate, is the cantonment, with its bazaar, native barracks, and officers' houses. The total native population, exclusive of military, is stated to have been, in 1836, 30,426. Elevation above the sea 1,600 feet. Distance from Bombay, S.E., 380 miles; Mangalore, N.E., 210; Calicut, N.E., 280; Bangalore, N., 160; Madras, N.W., 270. Lat. 15° 8′, long. 76° 59′.

BELLAT UNGADY, in the British district of South Canara, presidency of Madras, a town on the route from Mangalore to Chittel Droog, 30 miles N.E. of the former. Lat. 12° 59′, long. 75° 20′.

BELLOOD.—A town in the territory of Nagpoor, distant E. from Nagpoor 124 miles. Lat. 20° 45′, long. 81° 1′.

BELLOOR, in the territory of Mysore, a large town, with a fort strongly fortified with a mud rampart and ditch. There was formerly a similar defence round the town, but it is at present ruinous. Distant from Seringapatam, N., 38 miles; from Bangalore, W., 58. Lat. 12° 58′, long. 76° 48′.

BELLOOR, in the territory of Mysore, a town the principal place of a subdivision of the same name. It is situate a mile from the right or west bank of the river Yagachi or Bhadri, and on the north margin of a large tank. It has a good fort built of stone, and a large temple in repair. Distant from Seringapatam, N.W., 76 miles; Bangalore, W., 118. Lat. 13° 9′, long. 75° 55′.

BELLUBUTTI.—A town in Hyderabad, or possessions of the Nizam, distant E. from Beejapoor 60 miles. Lat. 16° 46′, long. 76° 42′.

BELLUNDA, in the British district of Futtehpoor, lieut.-gov. of the N.W. Provinces, a small town with bazaar, on the route from Allahabad to Cawnpore, and 75 miles N.W. of the former. Lat. 25° 54′, long. 80° 59′.

BELMAREA, in the British district of Rajeshaye, lieut.-gov. of Bengal, a town on the route from Pubna to Rampore, 20 miles N.W. of the former. Lat. 24° 11′, long. 89°.

BELOUT, in the British district of Alligurh, lieut.-gov. of the N.W. Provinces, a village on the route from the cantonment of Alligurh to that of Muttra, and 17 miles S.W. of the former. Lat. 27° 40′, long. 78° 2′.

BELOWREE, in the British territory of Sattara, presidency of Bombay, a town on the left bank of the Kistnah river, 58 miles S.E. of Sattara. Lat. 16° 59′, long. 74° 33′.

BELOWTEE, in the British district Shahabad, lieut.-gov. of Bengal, a small town on the route from Dinapoor to Ghazeepore, 40 miles W. of former, 52 E. of latter. The town is in lat. 25° 33′, long. 84° 28′.

BELPUR VILLAPOORAM, in the British district of South Arcot, presidency of Madras, a town on the route from Trichinopoly to Madras, 98 miles N.E. of the former. Lat. 11° 57′, long. 79° 33′.

BELUN, or BELUND.—A small river rising in the south-western part of Boghelkhand, about lat. 24° 35′, long. 81° 55′. It first runs about twenty-five miles eastward, then about an equal length northwards, and then turning westward falls into the Tons on the right side, in lat. 25° 5′, long. 81° 50′, after a total course of about ninety miles. It traverses the plateau lying between the Tara range and the Kutra, at an elevation of between 500 and 600 feet above the sea, and is probably in the dry season a very insignificant stream, as Jacquemont, who then crossed it, classes it among the petty brooks which flow through the country.

BELWIN, in the British district of Mirzapoor, lieut.-gov. of the N.W. Provinces, a village on the route from Chunar to the city of Mirzapoor, 10 miles W. of the former, 11 E. of the latter. It is situate on the Belwin, a small river with a bed forty yards wide, and a stream in the dry season ten yards wide and knee-deep. Lat. 25° 7′, long. 82° 50′.

BENARES, under the lieut.-gov. of the N.W. Provinces, a British district, named from its principal place. It is bounded on the north by the British district Jounpore; on the north-east by Ghazeepoor; on the south-east by Shahabad; on the sout hand south-west by Mirzapoor; and on the west by Mirzapoor and Jounpore. It lies between lat. 25° 7′—25° 32′, long. 82° 45′—83° 38′; is fifty-five miles in length from east to west, and thirty in breadth, and embraces an area of 994 square miles. The principal rivers which touch upon or traverse the district are the Ganges, the Karamnassa, and the Goomtee. There are several smaller streams, of which the Gurohee and the Nand are the principal. Lakes and tanks are numerous, but of small size; the principal one, which is twenty miles east of the city of Benares, not exceeding a mile in circuit. The elevation of the city of Benares above the sea is estimated by James Prinsep at 270 feet; and as the surface of the district is remarkably level, probably no part of it has a greater elevation than 300 feet. The climate, though this tract is scarcely beyond the tropics and little elevated above the sea, is in winter cool and rather arid; frosts sometimes at that season occurring in such severity as materially to injure the rubbee or early crop. On the whole, however, the mean temperature is greater than might be supposed. According to James Prinsep, the mean temperature is 77°. The staple products are wheat, barley, pulse of various kinds, millet, maize, oil-seeds, tobacco, safflower, opium, and most of the esculent vegetables of Europe. The crops, sown late in the spring, and reaped in autumn, consist of rice, various descriptions of pulse, hemp, cultivated for its intoxicating products, indigo, ginger, turmeric, and maize. One of the most important exchangeable products is furnished by the sugar-cane; this district, in the article of sugar, whether regard be had to abundance of produce or excellence of quality, surpassing nearly every other part of British India. Opium and indigo are likewise cultivated with success, and the produce in these two commodities has been considered to be of equal value with that of sugar. According to the census of 1853, the population of the district, excluding the city of Benares, cantonments, and civil station, amounts to 656,111; and if that of the city, &c., be added, the number would be increased to 851,757. The population of the different places in the district is thus represented:—Number of towns containing less than 1,000 inhabitants, 1,840; ditto more than 1,000 and less than 5,000, 104; ditto more than 5,000 and less than 10,000, one; ditto more than 10,000 and less than 50,000, one; ditto more than 50,000, one. The principal routes are: 1. From south-east to north-west, from Calcutta to the city of Benares, and thence in a westerly direction to Allahabad. 2. A continuation of the Calcutta route through the city of Benares and the Sekrol cantonment, in a north-westerly direction, to Jounpore. 3. From north-east to south-west, from the cantonment of Ghazeepore, by that of Sekrol, to that of Mirzapore. 4. From north east to south-west, from the city of Benares and the Sekrol cantonment to Chunar. The district is also traversed by the East-Indian Railway. The tract comprised within the present district of Benares was at a very remote period the seat of an independent Hindoo state, founded, it is said, by a Kasi rajah, represented as the sixth in descent from Buddha, about 1,200 years before the Christian era. It subsequently formed part of the dominions of the Rajpoot sovereigns of Canouj, and early fell under the Mussulman yoke, having in 1193 been taken by Mahomed, the Afghan king of Ghor. About 1529 it was wrested from the Patan sovereign of Delhi by the victorious Baber. On the dismemberment of the empire, consequent upon the repeated invasions of Ahmed Shah Durani, it formed part of the prey seized by Sufdar Jung, the nawaub vizier of Oude, by whose grandson, Asof-ul-Dowlah, it was ceded to the East-India Company, under Article V. of the treaty of 1775, and has since remained an integral part of the British dominions in India. At the time of the cession, the city of Benares, with a rich and extensive tract annexed to it, was held by Cheyt Singh, the grandson and successor of Munsaram, who early in the same century had by a deep-laid course of intrigue succeeded in becoming zemindar, or feudatory holder of extensive possessions, which were greatly increased by his son Bulwunt Singh. Cheyt Singh engaged to pay to the British government the same rent for his zemindary that he had previously paid to the Nabob vizier. When the Governor-General, Warren Hastings, became pressed for pecuniary resources to carry on the extensive warlike operations in which he was engaged, he made demands on the rajah of Benares, as Cheyt Singh was styled, for contributions exceeding the stipulated payments. After repeated attempts at evasion, the demands were met by determined resistance, and Cheyt Singh, resorting to arms, cut off two companies of sepoys in Benares, and inflicted other losses and disgrace on the British. His career of success was, however, cut short by the arrival of reinforcements, the ultimate results being his overthrow, deprivation, and flight to Gwalior, where he died in 1810.

BENARES, the principal place of the British district of the same name, is situate on the left bank of the Ganges. "The depth of water in front of the town in the dry season is more than fifty feet, and the freshes of September add forty-two to this level. The breadth of the Ganges is 600 yards at low water, and a little more than half a mile in the rains. This splendid stream forms a bay indenting the front of the town, so as to display its picturesque beauties to great advantage." The measured length of the city "along the banks of the river by survey, is barely three miles, and the average depth does not exceed one mile." Access is obtained to the water by ghats or flights of broad steps, elaborately and solidly constructed of the fine freestone of Chunar and its vicinity, often in a highly ornamented style. "Upon the ghats are passed the busiest and happiest hours of every Hindoo's day; bathing, dressing, praying, preaching, lounging, gossiping, or sleeping, there will be found. Escaping from the dirty, unwholesome, and confined streets, it is a luxury for him to sit upon the open steps and taste the fresh air of the river; so that on the ghats are concentrated the pastimes of the idler, the duties of the devout, and much of the necessary intercourse of business." They extend nearly along the whole length of the river's bank in the city, though in some places interrupted by temples reaching down to the water's edge. Around these are posted hideous fakirs, and other ascetics of revolting appearance, "offering every conceivable deformity which chalk, cow-dung, disease, matted locks, distorted limbs, and disgusting and hideous attitudes of penance can show." Of these ghats the Ugneswur, Ghoosla, Madhoray, Punchgunga, Munikurnika, Brukma, Rajrajeswuri, Shridur, Munshi, Dusaswumedh, and the Rajghat, are selected by Prinsep as peculiarly worthy of delineation by his pencil. A fine view of the Dusaswumedh ghat is also given by Daniell. Some narrow ghats are appropriated to the burning of dead bodies, the ashes and unconsumed bones of which are thrown into the river; and here suttee was performed until the practice was forbidden by the British government. At the time of Heber's visit, about thirty years ago, self-immolation by drowning in the Ganges was frequent. The city rises from the line of ghats so as to form a vast amphitheatre, presenting a picturesque and noble view to spectators on the opposite side of the river. Above the numerous and crowded houses, in varied and striking styles of architecture, are seen the pinnacles of Hindoo pagodas, and above all the minarets and domes of the great mosque of Aurungzebe, the most remarkable structure in Benares, though neither of imposing dimensions or striking architectural beauty. The mosque rises from the platform over the Madhoray ghat, and was erected on the site of the temple of Bindh Madhu, or Vishnu, described by Tavernier as in his time covering a great extent of ground. This Aurungzebe demolished, and to signalize the triumph of Islam over Brahminism, employed the materials in the building of the mosque. "The minars have been deservedly admired for their simplicity and boldness of execution. They are only eight and a quarter feet in diameter at the base, and the breadth decreases to seven and a half feet, while they have an altitude of 147 feet two inches from the suhun or terraced floor of the Musjid, to the kulsa or pinnacle. The terrace is elevated about eighty feet above the river at low-water level." Though so slender, they have staircases inside; but the ascent is not devoid of hazard, as they each lean fifteen inches from the perpendicular, and one of them was in a state of very hazardous decay, until repaired some years ago under the direction of James Prinsep. There are few mosques in the centre of the city, or along the river's bank; but they are numerous in the north-eastern quarter. They are generally elegant little edifices marked by small slender minarets, and usually stand in gardens planted with tamarinds; but they seem little frequented. Most of them were, like the great mosque, constructed on the sites of demolished Hindoo fanes, and with the materials of those structures. The total number of mosques was ascertained in 1829 to be 333. The number of Sivalas, or Hindoo temples, was 1,000; which can scarcely be regarded as large, since religion "is the staple article of commerce, through which the holy city flourishes and is enriched." Benares, long regarded as the centre of Hindoo religion and science, has of late considerably declined in this respect. Prinsep says, "The schools and hallowed retirements of the Benares pundits are sought after as the fountain-heads of Brahminical learning, and are consequently filled with pupils; but from a prevailing idea that the receiving of remuneration would destroy the merit of teaching the Vedas, the pundits in most cases accept of nothing from their scholars, trusting to donations and stipends from rajahs and men of rank. In the present day encouragement from such quarters is becoming more and more precarious, and Sanscrit learning is consequently on the decline; while the great success of the new colleges in Calcutta, in which the study of European literature is united with that of India, will tend further to eclipse the *alma mater* of rigid Hindooism." A Sanscrit college was instituted by the British government at Benares in 1792, in which an English department was at a later period established. The subjects in which competitors for scholarships in the English department were required to qualify themselves in 1854, comprised English poetry and history, political economy, and mathematics. The languages taught are Persian, Hindee, Sanscrit, and English. A new government college has just been completed in this city, at a cost of 13,200*l*. The streets of Benares, as Prinsep observes, "are confined, crooked, and so narrow that even narrow seems a term too wide." They might more properly be styled alleys: so confined are they as not to admit a wheeled carriage of any description; and they indeed scarcely afford room for the passage of any sort of beasts, whether under the saddle or bearing a burthen. The thoroughfare is sunk considerably below the basement story of the houses, which have generally an arched passage in front, behind which is a shop and a store-room. The houses are, with little exception, built of stone, and they are generally lofty; some are two stories high only, but most of them are of three, and not a few have four, five, and even six; the upper in many instances projecting beyond the lower. It is not uncommon for a house on one side of the street to be in its upper part connected with another at the opposite side. The windows are small, to exclude strong light, heat, and the inquisitive glances of strangers, of which the inmates are very impatient. Most of the fronts are stained deep red, or else are fantastically painted in gaudy colours, to represent "flowerpots, men, women, bulls, elephants, gods and goddesses, in all their many-headed, many-handed, and many-weaponed varieties." During the fine season the hours of sleep among the higher classes are passed "in light screened inclosures of carved stone, elevated on the most prominent points of the roof, open to the sky above, and to the gentle night-breeze on the four sides." The same writer adds, "The universal practice of sleeping on the roofs of houses in the hot season gives the town somewhat of a *diable boiteux* appearance, when viewed from the summit of the minarets at daybreak." The gaudy festivals here celebrated give incredible delight to this childish people. Of these the principal is the Ram Lila, representing the triumph of the incarnate deity Ram over the gigantic demon Ravan, who is personated by a huge ogre-like figure, filled with explosive combustibles, and blown up at the conclusion of the performance. The concluding ceremony, styled the Bhurut Melao, is still more splendid, forming a picture to which it has been said no description can do justice. Wonderfully splendid also is the Duwallee, celebrated with a universal illumination. "The city appears like the creation of the fire-king; the view from the water affording the most superb and romantic spectacle imaginable. The outlines of a whole city are marked in streams of fire, and the coruscations of light shoot up into the dark blue sky above, and tremble in long undulations on the rippling waves below." The mercantile year finishes on this festival with much propriety, if it be devoted to the goddess of wealth; those engaged in commerce then carefully cleanse and decorate the exteriors of their houses; and the credit of a merchant who should neglect to do so would be seriously shaken. The population of the city and suburbs of Benares, but exclusive of the cantonment, amounted in 1853 to 185,984. The number of houses in Benares proper was 30,205; of which 12,000 were brick or stone: the number in Secrole was 3,000. In 1850 the city was visited by an awful calamity, attended with great destruction of life and property. A fleet of boats, laden with 3,000 barrels of gunpowder, and manned by 500 sailors, in proceeding from Calcutta to Allahabad, had been detained at Benares, and on the 1st May were lying off the Raj ghat, within a few yards of the river-bank, when an explosion took place, causing death or injury to 348 individuals, and the damage of property to the extent of 17,000*l.* Immediately preceding the accident, the powder-boats had been approached by a pinnace, a spark from which, it was conjectured, had caused the explosion. In the suburbs of this city a tragical occurrence took place in 1799, when the British agent Mr. Cherry, and other Englishmen, were murdered by Vizier Ali, the deposed ruler of Oude, who had been permitted to reside at Benares. Benares, though its pretensions to architectural distinction are recent, is probably a town of great antiquity. It was *originally known by the name of Kasi and* Kasika, and, according to Hamilton, by that of Ksethra, said to be derived from Kshetra Briddha, the first rajah of Kasi of whom there is any certain notice, and who is conjectured to have reigned about sixteen centuries before the Christian era. The learned writer says, "Kasi continued to have kings of its own until the Mohammedan invasion; and considerable ruins of these princes' palaces still remain." It was first subjected to the Mohammedan sway, probably about 1198, by Mohammad Sultan of Ghor, in Afghanistan. It was subjected by Baber, taken from him by his Patan opponents in 1529, and immediately regained. Falling a prey to the Nawaub vizier of Oude on the dissolution of the empire of Delhi, about 1760, it was by treaty of 1775 ceded by him to the East-India Company. The Calcutta Railway passes close to the city. Elevation above the sea 270 feet. Distant N.W. from Calcutta 421 miles, by the Ganges 669, or 846 if the Soonderbund passage be taken; E. of Allahabad by land 74; S.E. from Delhi 466. Lat. 25° 17′, long. 83° 4′.

BENCOOLEN, formerly the chief establishment possessed by the East-India Company in the island of Sumatra, on the south-western coast, but ceded to the king of the Netherlands in 1825, with all the other British possessions on the island, in exchange for the Dutch settlements on the continent of India. S. lat. 3° 47′, long. 102° 19′.

BENDA, in the British district of Cawnpore, lieut.-gov. of the N.W. Provinces, a village on the route from Allahabad to Calpee, and 24 miles E. of the latter. Lat. 26° 9′, long. 80° 10′.

BENEER.—See Booneere.

BENEEGUNJ.—A town in the territory of Oude, distant N.E. from Lucknow 41 miles. Lat. 27° 18′, long. 80° 31′.

BENGAL.—The chief presidency of British India, containing Calcutta, the seat of the supreme government, and surpassing each of the other two presidencies in area, population, and resources. Exclusive of the native states which are retained under the control and political supremacy of the government of India, the territories embraced within the limits of this presidency have been distributed into several subdivisions, subject to the authority of separate functionaries. Among these may be mentioned the two lieutenant-governors, one of the North-West and the other of the Lower Provinces of Bengal; the commissioners of Pegu, Nagpore, the Punjab, the Tenasserim provinces, &c. In the present article it is proposed to treat only of the Lower Provinces, or that portion which has been committed to the charge of the lieutenant-governor of Bengal. The remaining subdivisions will be found noticed in their proper places in the alphabetical arrangement. The tract included within the lieutenant-governor*ship of Bengal extends from the northern frontier of the province of Pegu, in lat. 19° 15′,* to the northern frontier of Assam, in lat. 28° 16′; and west to east, from the south-eastern boundary of the district of Mirzapoor, to the western frontier of Burmah. It is bounded on the north by Nepaul, Sikkim, and Bhotan; on the north-east by Thibet; on the east by Burmah; on the south by the Bay of Bengal and Pegu; on the south-west by the petty independent states on that frontier; and on the west by the territory under the lieutenant-governorship of the North-West Provinces. The area is 195,985 square miles. The seacoast of the presidency comprises a considerable portion of the north-western shore of the Bay of Bengal, its innermost or northern recess, and a great extent of its eastern coast. Commencing at Prighi, on the coast of Orissa, in lat. 19° 27′, long. 85° 15′, it proceeds thence in a direction north-east, across the openings of the river Mahanuddy, for 130 miles, to False Point, where it is indented westward, forming a bay, terminated to the north, at a distance of thirty-five miles, at Point Palmyras. No ships of burthen can enter any of the mouths of that great river, though coasting and river craft of considerable tonnage may navigate it. From Point Palmyras the coast makes a more considerable indentation to the westward, forming the bay called Balasore Roads, the shore of which extends north-east to the mouth of the Hoogly, a distance of 130 miles. This bay, or great roadstead, is of high importance, as having excellent anchorage for shipping frequenting the Hoogly; but the coast is low, and large shipping can seldom approach it nearer than three or four miles. From the mouth of the Hoogly the coast turns nearly eastward for 180 miles along the shore of the Soonderbunds, being indented with numerous inlets, the estuaries of various offsets from the Ganges insulating many low tracts of land. Few of those inlets are frequented by shipping, though the Hooringotta estuary is large enough to admit vessels of four or five hundred tons. Off the mouth of the Hoogly, and about twenty-five miles from land, is a depression in the bottom of the sea, where are no soundings. This remarkable depression is about fifteen miles across, and is known by the name of the "Swatch of no Ground." From Rabnabad island the coast has a direction north 50 miles, and subsequently east for 65, to Chittagong, where it takes a direction south. This conformation of the coast makes a bay, which on its northern side receives the great estuaries of the main streams of the Ganges and Brahmapootra, which appear, however, to have been little explored. In its northern part this gulf is "interspersed with islands, some of which rival in size and fertility our Isle of Wight. The water at ordinary times is hardly brackish at the extremities of these islands, and in the rainy season the sea, or at least the surface of it, is perfectly fresh to the distance of many leagues out." From Chittagong the coast takes a south-east direction for 300 miles to lat. 19° 15′, where the coast of the recently constituted British province of Pegu commences.

With the exception of a part of Orissa and Chittagong, and other districts extending along the north-eastern and eastern coasts of the Bay of Bengal, the territories of this lieutenant-governorship are situate in the basins of the rivers Ganges and Brahmapootra, and comprise the entire of the great delta formed by the joint waters of those two rivers. From the Himalayas, stretching along its northern frontier, the general slope of the surface is southward; from the mountains of Assam, Sylhet, and Tipperah it is westward and south-westward; and from the highlands connecting the Vindhya range with the Western Ghauts, the slope is eastward and south-eastward. No tract of the same extent in the world is traversed by so great a number of rivers and watercourses. The Ganges, flowing from the British district of Ghazeepoor, in the lieutenant-governorship of the North-West Provinces, touches on the western boundary of the Lower Provinces of Bengal at Chowsa, in lat. 25° 27′, long. 83° 58′, and for seventy miles holds a circuitous course, but generally in a direction north-east, to the confluence of the Gogra, flowing from the north-west, and joining it on the left side, with a volume of water not inferior to that of the Ganges itself. At that confluence the Ganges passes into the Bengal territory, and turning to the south-east, receives, twenty miles lower down, on the right side, the Sone, another very large river flowing from the south-west. From this confluence it assumes a direction nearly east, and at a distance of twenty miles, it on the left side, at Hajeepoor, receives the Gunduck, flowing from the north. From that confluence its course is sinuous, but generally easterly, for 160 miles, to the confluence of the Coosy, flowing from the north, which it receives on the left side, at Kuttree. This accession gives the Ganges its greatest volume of water, as at a short distance lower down it begins to send off numerous branches to the left, which by meandering courses traverse the country in various directions, and ultimately rejoin the main stream, or are lost by evaporation, or absorbed in the purposes of irrigation. Below the last-named confluence, and in lat. 24° 44′, long. 87° 59′, it throws off on the right side the Bhagruttee, and at this point commences the great delta of the joint streams of the Ganges and Brahmapootra, the whole country towards the sea being an extraordinary reticulation of watercourses. Below the divergence of the Bhagruttee, the main stream of the Ganges, called in this part of its course the Podda or Pudda, continues its course south-easterly, and seventy miles lower down throws off on the same side the Jellinghee, which subsequently uniting with the Bhagruttee, forms the river Hoogly, which flowing southward by Calcutta, falls into the sea at Saugor Island, and is almost the only estuary, with the exception of that of the Hooringottah, frequented by large ships. The Podda continuing its course in a direction south-east for 100 miles to Juffergunje, there unites with the Konaie, a great branch of the Brahmapootra; and the combined stream flowing in a southerly direction for 150 miles, falls into the Bay of Bengal in lat. 22° 15′, long. 90° 43′. The Brahmapootra touches the Bengal territories near Soom, at the north-east extremity of the valley of Assam, about lat. 27° 51′, long. 96° 48′. In lat. 27° 48′, long. 95° 27′, it is joined by the Dihong, the name given at this part of its course to the Sanpoo, a river having its source north of the Himalayas. From this confluence the course of the river is very sinuous as far as Mehindergunje, where it divaricates into two great branches, that to the right, or south, and of the greater size, being called the Konaie, and that to the left, or east, retaining the name Brahmapootra.

The Konaie holds a course nearly due south, to its communication, by means of an offset, with the Ganges at Juffergunje, and subsequently south-east, under the name of the Dulasseree, to its reunion with the parent stream. The Brahmapootra takes a wide circuit to the south-east, as far as Bairubbazar, in lat. 24°, long. 90° 59′, where it turns to the south-west, being in this part of its course denominated the Megna, and thus flows to its junction, as above stated, with the Dulasseree, and thence onward to its confluence with the Kirtynassa, a considerable offset of the Ganges. At this point it again turns south-east, and divides into three branches; the first, called the Hattia, falls into the Bay of Bengal in lat. 22° 25′, long. 91° 22′; the second, known as the Shabazpore, enters the bay in lat. 22° 20′, long. 91° 8′; and the third forms a junction with the Ganges. Of the other rivers which drain the waters of the southern face of the Himalaya, and of northern Bengal, into the Ganges and Brahmapootra, the principal are, the Teesta, falling into the Brahmapootra near Mehindergunje; the Ataree, falling into the Konaie four or five miles above Juffergunje. Those of less dimensions are very numerous. The hill country to the right, or south-west side of the Ganges, supplies it with few perennial tributaries; that of most considerable magnitude, besides the Sone, being the Dammoodah, which, rising in the highlands of Ramgurh, takes a course south-eastward, and falls into the Hoogly a few miles above Fort Mornington, in lat. 22° 13′, long. 88° 7′. The Coossy, rising in Ramgurh, takes a south-easterly course, in some measure parallel to that of the Dammoodah, and falls into the Hoogly near Basutea, in lat. 22°, long. 88° 4′. The Soobunreeka rises in Chota Nagpoor, and taking a course south-east, falls into the Bay of Bengal a few miles below the town of Peeply, and in lat. 21° 35′, long. 87° 23′. The Byeturnee, under the names of the Sunk and Coel rivers, rises in the same district, and passing through the native states on the south-west frontier, enters the district of Cuttack, and flows south-east to Point Palmyras, where, under the name of the Dumrah, it falls into the Bay of Bengal, in lat. 20° 50′, long. 87° 3′. The Braminy rises in the district of Palamow, and taking a direction south-east, and, like the Byeturnee, flowing for the greater part of its course through the native states on the south-west frontier, it subsequently enters the district of Cuttack, and falls into the Bay of Bengal at Point Palmyras. The Mahanuddy enters the same district from the Cuttack Mehal states, in lat. 20° 24′, long. 85° 38′, and holds an easterly course to the town of Cuttack, where it parts into several branches, the principal of which falls into the Bay of Bengal near False Point, in lat. 20° 20′, long. 86° 50′. The inland navigation, at all times considerable, is vastly increased during the periodical rains, when "all the lower parts of Bengal contiguous to the Ganges and Brahmapootra are overflowed, and form an inundation of more than a hundred miles in width, nothing appearing but villages and trees, except very rarely the top of an elevated spot, the artificial mound of some deserted village, appearing like an island." A vast increase of the facilities for navigation at the same season takes place throughout the streams traversing any parts of the level alluvial tracts of the presidency. Rennell computed the number of persons employed in this inland navigation, when he wrote, about seventy years ago, at 30,000; and it is no improbable conjecture that, in consequence of the increase of traffic resulting from the greater security of property conveyed by water, and the more extensive use of that mode of conveyance for military and other purposes, the number is now quadrupled. Jhils, or extensive shallow lakes, are very numerous, but their limits are generally ill-defined; in the dry season their extent is greatly diminished, and several are totally dried up. The most extensive and remarkable are the Monda jhil, the Dulabari jhil, and the Chullum jhil, in the British district of Rajeshahi; the Aka jhil, in the district Jessore; and the Great jhil, in the district Backergunge. "The boats used in this extensive commerce are of various forms and construction, influenced by local circumstances. The patella, or baggage-boat of Hindoostan, is of saul-wood, clinker-built, and flat-bottomed, with rather slanting outsides, and not so manageable as a punt or London barge. Its great breadth gives it a very light draught of water, and renders it fittest for the cotton and other up-country products, which require little better than a dry and secure raft to float them down the stream. The oolak, or common baggage-boat of the Hoogly and central Bengal, has a sharp bow and smooth rounded side: this boat is the best for tracking and sailing before the wind, and is tolerably manageable with the oar in smooth water. The Dacca pulwar is more weatherly, although, like the rest, without keel, and the fastest and most handy boat in use for general traffic. The salt-boats of Tumlook are another distinct class. The light boats which carry betel-leaf, the wood-boats of the Sunderbuns, of various forms and dimensions, from the burthen of one hundred to that of six thousand maunds; the Calcutta bhur, or cargo-boat of the port; the Chittagong boats; the light Mug boats, with floors of a single hollowed piece of timber, and raised sides, neatly attached by sewing, with strips of bamboo over the seams; and an almost endless variety of others might be enumerated, besides the small dinghee and the panswee, the common canoe, and the ketch-rigged pinnace, the budgerow, and the bauleah; the three last employed by Europeans for their personal conveyance. A native traveller, according to his degree and substance, engages a dinghee or a panswee, a pulwar or an oolak; the man of wealth puts his baggage and attendants in these, and provides a budgerow or a pinnace for his personal accommodation. Officers of high standing in the civil or military service, travelling with a large retinue of servants and a quantity of baggage, seldom have less than five or six boats (one of them a cooking-boat, another fitted with an oven for baking bread), and sometimes as many as fifteen when they carry their horses and equipages, and the materials of housekeeping for their comfortable establishment on arrival."

No part of the great culminating ridge of the Himalaya is situate within the limits of the territory subject to the lieut.gov. of Bengal, though in the extreme north-eastern corner of Assam, a spur from it, closing in the northern branch of the Brahmapootra for a short distance, forms the northern boundary of the British territory. The greatest elevation probably within the presidency is Dupha Boom, separated from the spur just mentioned by the valley of the Brahmapootra, to the south of which it rises. Its summit is 14,540 feet above the level of the sea. Some of the summits of the mountainous tract on the east of Bengal are stated to have an elevation of 5,000 feet. The geological formation there appears to be granite overlaid with carboniferous sandstone, abounding with coal and iron-ore, intermixed with limestone of excellent quality. In the great mountain-tract in the west (where in some localities it attains an elevation of about 3,000 feet above the sea), granite is found to be overlaid with carboniferous sandstone, containing iron and coal in great abundance, the localities of this last mineral being found at wide intervals through a tract probably of no less extent than the whole of England, extending from the vicinity of Rajmahal on the north-east, about lat. 25° 5′, long. 87° 45′, to the banks of the river Son on the north-west, about lat. 24° 30′, long. 83° 20′, and southward as far as Talcher, in Orissa, lat. 21°, long. 85° 10′; and throughout the tract the distribution of iron appears to be equally extensive. Gold is obtained in the form of dust at Sumbulpore, in Orissa, which locality moreover contains diamonds. Gold is also met with in considerable quantity in the sand of streams in Assam; but altogether lower Bengal does not appear to be very rich in the precious metals. Rennell, describing the alluvial nature of the soil of the delta, observes, "There is no appearance of virgin earth between the Tiperah hills on the east and the province of Burdwan on the west, nor on the north till we arrive at Dacca and Bauleah. In all the sections of the numerous creeks and rivers in the delta nothing appears but sand and black mould, in regular strata, till we arrive at the clay that forms the lower part of their beds. There is not any substance so coarse as gravel, either in the delta, or nearer the sea than 400 miles, where a rocky point, a part of the base of the neighbouring hills, projects into the river." The enormous depth of alluvial deposit at Calcutta was ascertained in the unsuccessful attempt to form, by boring, an Artesian well, between the years 1835 and 1840, when the borer, after penetrating through alternating strata of peat, sand, and clay, reached a depth of from 400 to 481 feet, when "fine sand, like that of the seashore, intermixed largely with shingle, composed of fragments of primary rocks, quartz, felspar, mica, slate, limestone, prevailed; and in this stratum the bore has been terminated."

The climate is characterized by great humidity, in consequence of the moisture swept over it from the ocean and the Bay of Bengal, and precipitated in the form of the periodical rains. These prevail in summer and autumn, and in some seasons are very heavy, the annual rain-fall at Calcutta ranging from fifty to eighty-five inches. In the office of the surveyor-general at Calcutta, a register of meteorological facts is carefully kept, and the following is an abstract of the mean annual summaries for the ten years commencing 1841 and ending 1850:—

Annual Mean Temperature—Fahrenheit.

Years.	At Sunrise.	At 2 40 P.M.	At Sunset.
	Degrees.	Degrees.	Degrees.
1841	72.7	89.0	82.4
1842	73.3	88.0	82.1
1843	73.3	87.6	82.5
1844	72.7	87.6	82.3
1845	73.7	86.9	82.3
1846	74.3	86.3	81.9
1847	73.2	86.1	81.1
1848	74.1	87.4	82.5
1849	73.6	86.7	81.8
1850	73.1	86.1	81.4
Mean....	73.4	87.2	82.0

The stormy weather of the south-west monsoon, a strong aerial current, sets in early in June, and continues with little intermission until the middle of September, bringing with it the periodical rains of that time of the year. The north-east monsoon follows, setting in either in October or early in November; and in the course of December is followed by more settled weather, which continues through January, and brings the cold marking that season. During February, March, and April, the prevailing wind is from the south. In May the air is for the most part still, there being little steady wind, though at the commencement there are occasionally violent unsteady gusts.

The zoology of Bengal is extensive, varied, and interesting: wild elephants are numerous in the forest zone along the southern base of the Sub-Himalaya, and in the extensive uncultivated wilds of Assam and Chittagong. The rhinoceros frequents the same locality, and both are found in small numbers in the British district of Bhaugulpore, on the right or south-west side of the Ganges. The rhinoceros is also found in the southern part of Bengal, toward the Sunderbunds. Bears are numerous and very dangerous; both the black bear (*Ursus indicus*) and the species analogous to the ursine sloth of tropical America. The tiger infests the dense jungle, and checks the increase of herbivorous quadrupeds, as those mark by their surprising abundance the extraordinary luxuriance of the vegetation. The leopard and lynx are also of common occurrence; as is the wild buffalo in close marshy coverts. The gayal, a huge bovine quadruped, is met with in the range of mountains that form the eastern boundary of the provinces of Arracan, Chittagong, Tipperah, and Sylhet. The stag, elk, antelope, and deer of various kinds, are abundant; as are also wild swine. Monkeys and lemurs, and some other quadrumanous creatures, harbour in most of the woods; and the former, favoured by popular superstition, infest many of the habitations and some of the towns. The canine genera are numerous, and comprise the hyena, wolf, jackal, fox, and wild dog of two varieties.

The Sunderbunds produce great quantities of wood, but seldom of very large growth or first-rate quality; but the sal (Shorea robusta) and some other trees attain great size, and afford excellent timber in the belt of the forest which extends along the base of the Sub-Himalaya. An abundance of fine timber is produced in the western highlands and in Orissa; but in most places the distance from navigable streams diminishes its value.

The principal alimentary crop is rice, though wheat and other cerealia are grown largely in the more elevated and northern parts. In the fertile and irrigated tracts, two crops of rice are usually produced from the same ground in one year. The other grains most commonly cultivated are bajra (Holcus spicatus) and jowar (Holcus Sorghum). Oil-seeds are largely cultivated; the consumption of oil among the natives being very great. The principal crops of this kind are mustard, til or sesame, and ricinus or castor-oil plant. Ginger, turmeric, capsicum, and chillies, are largely grown for condiments. The esculent vegetables comprise most of those usual in Europe. Of fruits the principal are the mango, jak (Artocarpus integrifolia), orange, lime, shaddock, citron, cocoanut, tamarind, plantain, betelnut, guava, and mulberry, which is cultivated more for the sake of its leaves, used in feeding silkworms, than on account of its fruit.

The principal commercial crops are cotton, indigo, coffee, safflower, hemp, flax, tobacco, sugar, rice, and the opium-poppy. In Assam the genuine tea-plant abounds, and some of its produce of fine quality has found a ready market in London; but the dense population, indefatigable industry, and long experience which the Chinese tea-districts possess, must for a long time insure them a superiority in supplying this important article, unless political events should arrest their prosperity. The manufacturing industry of the country has everywhere waned before the influence of British competition. The extensive manufactures of muslins of Dacca, formerly so much prized, have nearly ceased, and that of the cotton goods of Balasore has had a similar fate. The principal manufactures are now conducted in Calcutta and its vicinity, and consist of coarse cottons, sailcloth, rope-making, iron-work, sugar-refining, tanning, and distillation of rum. The Cossipore iron-foundry, on the left bank of the river Hoogly, three miles north of Calcutta, when in full work, annually turns out 200 pieces of ordnance. Nearly all the export and import trade of the presidency is conducted through the port of Calcutta. The principal articles of export are cotton, indigo, sugar, rum, rice, saltpetre, lac, silk, opium, and limited quantities of coffee and tobacco; those of import are British cotton goods, salt, iron, copper, and hardware. The value of the foreign export trade in 1834-35 amounted to 4,158,598*l.*, and in 1853-54 to 10,571,216*l.* The value of the foreign import trade at the same periods was 2,645,355*l.* and 7,759,352*l.* Six principal sources supply the government revenue, amounting to ten millions sterling per annum. These are the land, opium, salt, stamps, excise, and customs. A list of the government colleges and schools, and an account of the number and religion of the pupils receiving instruction therein at the date of the latest returns, are contained in the following statement:—

Institutions.	Christians.	Mahomedans.	Hindoos.	Other Persuasions.	Total.
Hindu College	..	..	488	..	488
————, Pautshala	..	..	215	..	215
————, B. School	..	..	453	..	453
Sanscrit College	..	..	299	..	299
Calcutta Mudrissa	..	280	..	..	280
Hoogly College	7	5	395	..	407
————, B. School	..	1	165	..	166
————, Mudrissa	1	151	30	..	182
————, Mukhtub	..	22	11	..	33
Seetapore Mudrissa	..	40	..	..	40
Dacca College	32	26	328	..	386
Kishnagur College	1	4	195	..	200
Chittagong School	18	9	98	..	125
Commillah ,, ...	4	10	69	..	83
Sylhet ,, ...	3	19	110	..	132
Bauleah ,, ...	2	..	80	..	82
Midnapore ,, ...	..	4	113	..	117
Cuttack ,, ...	19	13	89	1	122
Patna ,, ...	..	..	..	..	61
Bhaugulpore ,, ...	..	15	70	30	115
Moozufferpore ,, ...	1	22	34	..	57
Gyah ,, ...	1	19	83	..	103
Jessore ,, ...	1	5	80	..	86
Burdwan ,, ...	..	2	64	..	66
Bancoorah ,, ...	..	..	70	..	70
Baraset ,, ...	..	1	146	..	147
Howrah ,, ...	2	3	139	..	144
Ooterparah ,, ...	..	..	208	..	208
Beerbhoom ,, ...	..	..	..	..	87
Barrackpore ,, ...	..	1	88	..	89
Russapugiah ,, ...	..	37	14	..	51
Assam (72 schools)	..	..	..	..	4,025
Arracan (2 schools)......	3	75	..	72	150
Tenasserim (2 schools) ..	9	23	1	74	107
S.W. Frontier (3 schools)	..	9	18	12	39
Vernacular Schools......	..	..	..	..	1,904
Grand total	104	796	4,153	189	11,319

The presidency contains the undermentioned British districts, having the areas and population stated below :—

Districts.	Area. Square Miles.	Population.
Jessore	3,512	381,744
Twenty-four Pergunnahs	2,277	701,182
Burdwan	2,224	1,854,152
Hoogly	2,007	1,520,840
Nuddea	2,942	298,736
Bancoorah	1,476	480,000
Baraset	1,424	522,000
Bhaugulpore	7,803	2,000,000
Dinajpore	3,820	1,200,000
Monghyr	3,592	800,000
Poorneah	5,712	1,600,000
Tirhoot	6,114	2,400,000
Maldah	1,288	431,000
Cuttack	3,061	1,000,000 (Cuttack and Pooree)
Pooree	1,768	
Balasore	1,876	556,395
Midnapore and Hidgellce	5,029	666,328
Koordah	930	571,160
Moorshedabad	1,856	1,045,000
Bagoorah	2,160	900,000
Rungpore	4,130	2,559,000
Rajshaye	2,084	671,000
Pubna	2,606	600.000
Beerbhoom	3,114	1,010,876
Dacca	1,960	600,000
Furreedpore and Deccan Jelalpore	2,052	855,000
Mymensing	4,712	1,487,000
Sylhet, including Jyntea	8,424	380,000
Bakergunge, including Deccan Shabazpore	3,794	733,800
Shahabad	4,403	1,600,000
Patna	1,828	1,200,000
Behar	5,694	2,500,000
Sarun, with Chumparan	6,394	1,700,000
Chittagong	2,717	1,000,000
Tipperah and Bulloah	4,850	806,950 600,000
The Sunderbunds, from Saugor Island on the west to the Ramnabad Channel on the east	6,500	Unknown.
Cossya Hills	729	10,935
Cachar	4,000	60,000
Taleram (Senaputty Territory)	2,160	5,015
Lower Assam — Camroop	2,788	300,000
Lower Assam — Nowgong	4,160	70,000
Lower Assam — Durrung	2,000	80,000
Upper Assam — Joorhat (Seebpoor)	2,825	200,000
Upper Assam — Luckimpoor	2,950	30,000
Upper Assam — Sudya, including Mutruck	6,942	30,000
Goalpara	3,506	400,000
Arracan	15,164	321,522
Sumbulpore	4,693	274,000
Ramgurh or Hazareebah	8,524	372,216
Lohurdugga — Chota Nagpore	5,308	482,900 (Chota Nagpore and Palamow)
Lohurdugga — Palamow	3,468	
Singhboom	2,944	200,000
Maunbhoom — Pachete	4,792	772,340 (Pachete and Barabhoom)
Maunbhoom — Barabhoom	860	
Total	203,946	40,871,091

Bengali, Hindostanee or Oordoo, Ooriya, Assamese, and the Burmese, are the languages spoken.

Of the early history of Bengal little is known, and not only is fact mixed with fable, but, as is the case with the early history of every part of India, the fabulous portion is by far the larger. In passing to the period when India began to attract the attention of Mahomedan invaders, we come to firmer ground. At the death of Shahab-oo-Deen, which took place in 1206, Bengal, if not entirely subdued, was in the process of absorption into the dominions of that conqueror. The commander, however, by whom it was reduced, took the not unusual course of disclaiming the authority under which he had served. He was, however, compelled to succumb, and deprived of the province of Behar, but was allowed to retain that of Bengal in feudal subordination Making, however, an attempt to recover what he had lost, he perished in battle in 1225. A subsequent governor, named Togral, commenced resistance by refusing to share with the throne of Delhi booty which he had acquired in a successful expedition, and pursued his contumacious course by assuming in 1279 the title of king. Having defeated two armies sent against him in succession, he was compelled to fly before a third, led by the emperor in person, and being overtaken, paid the price of his ambitious daring with his life. A son of the emperor appears to have succeeded to the government, and to have held it for a very long series of years. In 1340, during the reign of Mohammed Toghluk, the province again revolted from the empire, and thenceforward almost every ruler claimed independence, but rarely enjoyed it for any lengthened period, the kings of Delhi from time to time asserting their supremacy by the despatch of an army to overrun the country; the only measure by which they could enforce recognition of their superiority. In 1356, Ferose the Third of Delhi received an embassy from Bengal, an act which would seem an acknowledgment of the independence of its monarch. War was renewed, however, with his successor, and the Delhi sovereign marched an army to the extreme south-eastern point of Bengal. Amicable relations, or at least relations apparently amicable, after a time were again established, by the revival of the treaty concluded with the predecessor of the then reigning monarch of Bengal. In 1528 we find the king of Bengal engaged in hostilities with Baber. Shortly after Bengal was conquered, and its king expelled by the bold and adventurous Shir Khan, who assumed the title of king, and being opposed by Humayon, son of Baber, compelled that sovereign to retire; a movement which was attended by the loss of the greater part of that prince's army. The subsequent fortune of Shir Khan, or Shir Shah, brought Bengal again under the rule of the throne of Delhi. Under the emperor Mohammed Shah Sur Adili, who usurped the throne in 1553, the governor of Bengal, Mohammed Sur, like former governors, revolted. He was successfully opposed by Hemu, the able minister to whom Adili had intrusted his affairs, and perished in the conflict which terminated his rule. Another pretender, however, appeared, and in contest with him the emperor Adili lost his life. A few years later the good fortune of Akbar reunited the province to the empire. A mutiny, caused by the introduction of financial reforms, followed, and was not suppressed without difficulty. An insurrection of the Affghan settlers, who were very numerous, and were naturally attached to the Affghan chiefs who had in succession held sway in Bengal, succeeded the mutiny; and it was not till after fifteen years of disturbances that the royal authority was finally established. In 1624, Shah Jehan, flying from his father Jehangir, against whom he had rebelled, possessed himself temporarily of Bengal, but was speedily driven out. The eighteenth century was marked in India by the breaking up of the empire of Delhi; the progress of the Mahrattas, who had risen into notice in the preceding century; the wars between the French and English, and the final triumph of the latter. Among the factories established by the English East-India Company for carrying on their trade, was one at Hooghly, and another at Cossimbazar. That of Hooghly in the year 1700 was transferred to Calcutta, then a new British settlement, and destined shortly to become the capital of British India. In 1756, the nabob of Bengal having taken possession of the factory at Cossimbazar, proceeded to attack Calcutta, which surrendered after a brief siege. The Company's servants became prisoners, and were treated with barbarous cruelty. The details are too well known to require notice. Calcutta was retaken by Clive, and peace restored; but subsequent disputes led to a renewal of hostilities, which terminated in the battle of Plassy. From this time the fortunes of the British rose in the ascendant, and in the year 1765 the emperor of Delhi conferred upon the East-India Company the provinces of Bengal, Behar, and Orissa. Thus did this part of India become British, and in this manner originated that mighty dominion which in less than ninety years has been matured into the British empire in the East.

BENGSOLLEE.—A town in the native state of Bhotan, distant N.W. from Goalpara 36 miles. Lat. 26° 36′, long. 90° 23′.

BENKAR, or TASS-GONG.—A town in the native state of Bhotan, distant N.E. from Goalpara 95 miles. Lat. 27° 19′, long. 91° 29′.

BENKYPOOR.—A town in the territory of Mysore, distant N.W. from Seringapatam 120 miles. Lat. 13° 50′, long. 75° 46′.

BENNOOR.—A town in Hyderabad, or possessions of the Nizam, distant E. from Bejapoor 60 miles. Lat. 16° 56′, long. 76° 41′.

BENTINCK ISLAND.—One of the group forming the Mergui archipelago. It is about twenty miles in length from north to south, and six in breadth: its centre is in lat. 11° 45′, long. 98° 9′.

BEOUR.—See BEAUR.

BERAH, or BURAH, in the British district Budaon, lieut.-gov. of the N.W. Provinces, a village on the route from the city of Agra to Bareilly, and 39 miles S.W. of the latter. Lat. 28° 5′, long. 79° 6′.

BERAHERAPOOR, in the British district of Mynpoorie, lieut.-gov. of the N.W. Provinces, a village on the route from the cantonment of Allygurh to that of Mynpoorie, and 33 miles N.W. of the latter. Lat. 27° 35′, long. 78° 42′.

BERAI GUNGA, in the native state of Gurwhal, a feeder of the Jumna, rises on the south-western foot of the great snowy peak of Banderpuch, in lat. 30° 59′, long. 78° 35′, and at the elevation of 12,489 feet above the sea. It holds a circuitous course first in a southerly direction, for about four miles, and then westerly for nine more, and unites with the Jumna on its left side, in lat. 30° 55′, long. 78° 27′.

BERANAH, in the Baree Dooab division of the Punjab, a town situated on the route from Lahore to Loodhianah, 22 miles S.E. of the town of Lahore. Lat. 31° 29′, long. 74° 30′.

BERAR.—See NAGPORE.

BERAR.—A valley of Hyderabad, or the dominions of the Nizam, bounded on the north by the Sautpoora range of mountains, dividing it from a detached portion of Scindia's territory and the Nerbudda provinces; on the south by the Maiker Bassim and Mahur districts of the Nizam's country; on the east by the territory of the rajah of Nagpore; and on the west by Candeish. It lies between lat. 20° 15′ and 21° 40′, long. 76° and 78° 2′, with an area estimated at from 8,500 to 9,000 square miles. The Poornah river, a branch of the Taptee, running from east to west, affords with its numerous tributary streamlets an ample supply of water to the valley, the soil of which is peculiarly suitable to the cultivation of cotton. Ellichpore is the chief town, but as a place of trade, Oomrawuttee, the depôt for the raw cotton of the district, is the most flourishing town in this part of India. The valley of Berar is included in the territory recently assigned by the Nizam to the British for the maintenance of the military force termed the "Nizam's Contingent." Under the new administration, the district lands will be subjected to a moderate assessment, and the trade at once relieved from the oppressive system of transit-duties in force throughout the remainder of Hyderabad. If to these encouragements be added facility of transport to the western coast, —and this boon also is about to be conceded by the construction of a railway from the cotton districts to the port of Bombay,—no further interference by the government in the agriculture or trade of the country can be needed, and sanguine expectations may be entertained that the produce of the great cotton-field of India will at length be enabled to compete with America for the supply of cotton to the British market.

BERARU, in the British district of Bareilly, lieut.-gov. of the N.W. Provinces, a village on the route from Bareilly to Petoragurh, and 49 miles N.E. of the former. Supplies may be had from the neighbouring country, and water is abundant, though unwholesome in the hot season. Lat. 28° 50′, long. 79° 57′.

BEREE, in the British district of Rohtuk, lieut.-gov. of the N.W. Provinces, a town having a population of 9,397, on the route from Hansi to Goorgaon, and 50 miles S.E. of the former. It was comprehended in the grant made by the Mahrattas to the adventurer George Thomas, whose occupation of it was resisted by a strong garrison, principally of Rajpoots and Jats. It was, however, after an obstinate resistance, stormed, and the defenders put to the sword, except a few who escaped into the neighbouring jungles. Thomas states that the petty district of Beree, before it was desolated by the Mahrattas, had twenty-four villages and a revenue of 3,000*l.*; at the time of its acquisition by him, sixteen villages, and a revenue of 1,000*l.* Water and supplies may be obtained, and there is good encamping-ground. The road in this part of the route is good. Lat. 28° 40′, long. 76° 40′.

BERGANWAN, in the British district of Hummerpore, lieut.-gov. of the N.W. Provinces, a small town on the route from Calpee to Jhansee, 46 miles S.W. of the former. Lat. 25° 53′, long. 79° 13′.

BERGAWAH, in the territory of Gwalior, a village on the route from Etawa to the fort of Gwalior, 23 miles S.W. of former, 60 N.E. of the latter. It is situate on the small river Coharry, on the right bank of which is room for encampment, though rather rough. Lat. 26° 39′, long. 78° 44′.

BERHAMPOOR.—A town in the native state of Nepal, distant S.E. from Khatmandoo 60 miles. Lat. 26° 54′, long. 85° 40′.

BERHAMPORE.—See BURHAMPORE.

BERHAMPORE, in the British district of Ganjam, presidency of Madras, a town with military cantonment; the latter situate on a rocky ledge of ground, in the midst of a cultivated plain of considerable extent to the south and east, but on the west and north bounded by hills at the distance of from five to ten miles. The western hills, which are of considerable height, are covered with jungle of bamboos and brushwood, and have a bold continuous outline. Those to the north are less elevated, and have an undulating outline. The plain is studded with numerous tanks; but there are no perennial streams, though several nullahs, usually dry, become torrents during the rainy season, when they convey the water from the Western Hills to the Ganjam river. Water, however, is abundant throughout the year, being readily obtainable from wells of the depth of ten or twelve feet. The soil of the cantonment is dry and gravelly, and in many places granite rocks protrude from the surface. The native town is adjacent to the sepoys' lines, but lies somewhat lower. It is reputed to have a population of 20,000. The streets are narrow, and, like those of the majority of Indian towns, dirty. The houses are mean, a few constructed with bricks, but mostly of mud only. There are, however, well-supplied bazaars, in which the necessaries of life and some of its luxuries are met with in abundance. Silk and cotton cloths are manufactured here to some extent, and sugar and sugar-candy in large quantities. The south-western monsoon sets in at the beginning of June, and continues until September, when it is succeeded by the north-east, which usually terminates its visitation by the close of October. The weather from that time until the end of February is both pleasant and healthy, the sky being clear and the air cool and bracing: the dews at night are heavy. The thermometer at this season ranges from 50° to 75°. April and May are hot and unhealthy: the thermometer then ranges from 75° to 90°, and fevers and rheumatism prevail. Distance from Chicakol, N.E., 90 miles; Vizagapatam, N.E., 150; Masulipatam, N.E., 325; Madras, N.E., 525; Ganjam, S.E., 20; Cuttack, S.E., 108; Calcutta, S.E., 325. Lat. 19° 20′, long. 84° 50′.

BERIS, BERUCH, or **BAIRAS**, a river tributary to the Banas, rises in Mewar, in the Aravulli range, a few miles west of the town of Gogonda, in lat. 24° 34′, long. 73° 42′, and flowing first north-east and subsequently in a south-easterly direction, during which it receives the waters of two small streams issuing from the tank at the city of Oodeypoor, it passes that city, and enters the artificial lake of Udaia on the west, and emerging from the south-east angle of its embankment, pursues a very sinuous course, but principally north-easterly, to the town of Chittorgurh, receiving in this interval several small streams, the chief of which is the Western Gumbhir, falling into it on the right side. From Chittorgurh it takes a course rather more northerly, and finally falls into the Banas on the right side, in lat. 25° 18′, long. 75° 6′, having flowed 120 miles. Jacquemont, who crossed it near the confluence of the Gumbhir, mistakes it for the Banas, and Blumenthal's map to the work is still more incorrect. Heber, who also crossed it at the same place, erroneously designates it the Bunass. He states that in this place it "runs with a considerable stream of very bright and beautiful water. On our left hand were the ruins of a long, lofty, and handsome bridge, of eight Gothic arches, and one semi-circular one in the centre, with a ruined tower and gateway at each end. The ford was deep, with a sharp gravelly bottom." He does not mention what we learn from Garden, that the ruined bridge which he describes was not over the stream which he crossed, but over the Gumbhir, the confluence of which is close to the ford.

BERLO.—A village in the jaghire or feudal possession of Jujhur, lieut.-gov. of the N.W. Provinces. Lat. 28° 32′, long. 76° 5′.

BERMA.—A river rising in the states of Bundelcund, in lat. 25°, long. 79° 36′, near the town of Logassi, and flowing in a north-easterly direction for about eighty miles, principally through the British district of Humeerpore, falls into the Betwa on the right side, in lat. 25° 53′, long. 79° 59′.

BERMYA, in the British district of Dacca, lieut.-gov. of Bengal, a town 35 miles N. of the city of Dacca. Lat. 24° 13′, long. 90° 30′.

BEROUNDA, or BURROUNDA, in Bundelcund, a town or stronghold at a difficult ghat or pass, by which lies a route from Banda to Rewa, 35 miles S.E. of the former, 77 N.W. of the latter. It is the principal place of a chieftainship, "possessed by a family of the Rajbunsee caste, and totally unconnected with the chieftains of the province. How the family obtained the raj is not ascertainable, and the succession does not seem to have descended in a direct line." On obtaining supremacy in Bundelcund, in 1802, by the treaty of Bassein, the British government found the present family in possession; and in 1807 confirmed its claims by a sunnud, or written grant. "The raj is estimated to yield 45,000 rupees per annum. It comprises 275 square miles, and contains seventy-five villages, with a population of 24,000 souls," and maintains a force of forty horse and 200 foot, with one gun. Berounda is in lat. 25° 4′, long. 80° 43′.

BERUMBAH.—One of the petty native mehals of Cuttack which became tributary to the British upon the conquest of that district in 1803. Berumbah Gurh, the principal place, is distant W. from Cuttack 38 miles. Lat. 20° 23′, long. 85° 22′.

BESSERAH, or BISEORA, in the British district of Mirzapoor, lieut.-gov. of the N.W. Provinces, a small town on the route, by the right bank of the Ganges, from Allahabad cantonment to that of Mirzapoor, 45 miles S.E. of the former, 16 W. of the latter. It has a bazaar, and is well supplied with water. Lat. 25° 15′, long. 82° 20′.

BESSONA, or BUSSOAH, in the native state of Macherry, a small town on the route from Delhi to the Rajpoot town of Jeypore, 50 miles N.E. of latter. It is situate amongst some isolated rocky hills rising from a sandy plain, and is surrounded by a strong mud rampart. Lat. 27° 9′, long. 76° 40′.

BESTHAR, in the district of Bainswara, territory of Oude, two miles N.E. of the left bank of the Ganges, 12 S.E. of Cawnpore, 40 S.W. of Lucknow. Butter estimates its population at 4,000, of whom 600 are Mussulmans. Lat. 26° 25′, long. 80° 30′.

BESULEE.—A river of Gwalior, rising in lat. 26° 9′, long. 78° 21′. It flows in a circuitous but generally north-easterly direction for 63 miles, to lat. 26° 24′, long. 79° 1′, when it falls into the Sinde river.

BETAUL.—A town in the native state of Nepal, distant W. from Khatmandoo 107 miles. Lat. 27° 37′, long. 83° 34′.

BETAWUD, in the British district of Khandeish, presidency of Bombay, a town on the left bank of the river Panjur, 20 miles N.E. of Dhoolia. Lat. 21° 8′, long. 74° 52′.

BETHYAN.—A town in the native state of Kashmir, or dominions of Gholab Singh, distant N.W. from Jamoo 33 miles. Lat. 33° 4′, long. 74° 43′.

BETIGANOW, in the district of Ahladganj, in the territory of Oude, a village on the left bank of the Ganges, 88 miles S.E. of Cawnpore, 90 S. of Lucknow. Butter states it to be the unhealthiest spot in Southern Oude. Lat. 25° 42′, long. 81° 24′.

BETOURA, in the British district of Bareilly, lieut.-gov. of the N.W. Provinces, a village on the route from the town of Bareilly to Moradabad, and 13 miles N.W. of the former. The road in this part of the route is good; the country open, flat, and cultivated. Lat. 28° 28′, long. 79° 22′.

BETTADAPOOR.—A town in the territory of Mysore, distant W. of Seringapatam 41 miles. Lat. 12° 29′, long. 76° 9′.

BETTIAH, or BETIYA, in the British district of Sarun, lieut.-gov. of Bengal, a town on the route from Goruckpoor to Mullye cantonment, 82 miles E. of former, 67 W. of latter. It is the principal place of Champaran, or the north-east division of the district, and that portion is thence frequently denominated Bettiah. Supplies are abundant here; and a mile and a half E. of the town is an encamping-ground, on a grassy plain. Tieffenthaler, mentioning its state about eighty years ago, describes it as a populous town, having a large fort of masonry, with a ditch and towers, and containing several tanks within its circuit. Distant N.W. from Patna 95 miles. Lat. 26° 46′, long. 84° 34′.

BETWA, or BETWANTI.—A river rising in Malwa, in the raj or principality of Bhopal, one mile and a half S. of the large tank at the town of Bhopal, and in lat. 23° 14′, long. 77° 22′. From its source it flows in a south-easterly direction, parallel to the road leading from Bhopal to Hosingabad, for twenty miles, to Suttapoor, whence it takes a north-easterly course through the raj for about thirty-five miles, and in lat. 23° 28′, long. 77° 48′, near Bhilsa, crosses the northern frontier into the territory of Gwalior, through which it continues to flow nearly in the same direction for about 115 miles, to lat. 24° 58′, long. 78° 17′, where it arrives in the province of Bundelcund, which it does not leave for the rest of its circuitous course of 190 miles to its junction with the Jumna at Humeerpoor, in lat. 25° 57′, long. 80° 17′; its total length of course being about 360 miles, generally in a north-easterly direction. It receives many small streams right and left. Of these, the Dhasan, the principal, falls into it on the right side, in lat. 25° 48′, long. 79° 28′; the Jamni eighty miles higher up, on the same side; and still higher up, the Beena. The route from Neemuch to Saugor crosses it near Bhilsa by a good ford; fifty miles lower down, or more north-east, it is also crossed by the route from Goonah to Saugor, and it has there a "bed 220 yards wide; bottom rock and stone; banks sloping at the ghat (ford); stream thirty yards wide, and two deep;" again, ninety miles further down, and in lat. 25° 23′, long. 78° 46′, by the route from Agra to Saugor, where it has a bed 600 yards wide, full of rocks and loose stones; and 110 miles farther down, by the circuitous course of the river, and in lat. 25° 52′, long. 79° 52′, by the route from Banda to Calpee, where it has a "bed 550 yards, and stream in the dry season 180 yards wide; bottom sand and gravel." Jacquemont, who saw it in the beginning of spring, or dry season, states it to be then, at its junction with the Jumna, half a mile wide, and in some parts not fordable. He styles it an enormous river, being during the periodical rains from one to two miles wide, with a current of six, seven, or nine miles an hour. It is, however, not navigable in any part of its course. Baber erroneously states that it falls into the Ganges.

BEWAR, in the British district of Hummerpore, lieut.-gov. of the N.W. Provinces, a town on the route from Banda to Calpee, 35 miles N.W. of former. It has a bazaar, and is well supplied with water. Lat. 25° 46′, long. 80°.

BEWUR, in the British district Mynpooree, the principal place of the pergunnah of the same name, is a small town half a mile from the right bank of the Kali Nadi (east), on the route from the cantonment of Futtehgurh to that of Mynpooree, and 15 miles E. of the latter. It has a bazaar, and water is plentiful. The country is low, level, and cultivated. Lat. 27° 13′, long. 79° 21′.

BEYLA.—A town in the native state of Cutch, under the political superintendence of the presidency of Bombay, distant N.E. from Bhooj 75 miles. Lat. 23° 50′, long. 70° 40′.

BEYLA, in British district Sarun, lieut.-gov. of Bengal, a town on the route from Dinapoor to Khatmandoo, 106 miles N. of former, 91 S. of latter. Lat. 26° 52′, long. 84° 52′.

BEYLUH.—See Belah.

BEYPOOR, or BAIPOOR, in the British district of Malabar, presidency of Madras, a seaport, situate at the north side of the estuary of the Sharapoya, or river of Beypoor, which rises in the Western Ghats. Vessels drawing fourteen feet water may, when the tide is in, be floated over the bar by means of casks; and within there is good depth of water. The situation of the town is very beautiful, but it has little trade, except in timber, the greater part of the teak, the growth of the forests on the ghats to the eastward, being floated down the river for exportation at this place. This circumstance induced some projectors to prepare accommodations for building ships of war here; but the small depth of water on the bar rendered the selection absurd for such a purpose. With similar views saw-mills were constructed here, but wind, which was employed as the motive power, was found too precarious and feeble for the purpose. From the great abundance of wood for fuel, steam might obviously be advantageously employed for this purpose; and competent judges are of opinion that there are encouraging indications of coal on the banks of the river below high-water mark. Iron-ore is found in the neighbourhood, and smelted at the iron-works established here. Purchases of the article have recently been made by the government for the service of the gun-carriage department, and favourable reports of its quality transmitted to the home authorities. When connected with the city of Madras by the railway now under construction, Beypoor will doubtless become a thriving port. Distance S.E. from Cannanore 56 miles, from Bombay 570, from Calicut six. Lat. 11° 10′, long. 75° 51′.

BEYPOOR.—A river deriving its origin from the Neilgherry Mountains. The head of this stream is formed by the drainage of the elevated tabular mass of hills which occur to the north-west of the group at Neddiwuttum; and though it descends the face of the hills at no great distance from the fall of the Moyaar, the intervention of a sharp spur diverts its course into an exactly opposite direction, forcing it over the ridge called the Carcoor or Yellamullay Hills, to find its way to its embouchure on the western coast at Beypoor, near Calicut.

BEYREAH, in the British district of Ghazeepoor, lieut.-gov. of the N.W. Provinces, a town on the left bank of the Ganges, 58 miles N.E. of Ghazeepoor. Lat. 25° 44′, long. 84° 32′.

BEYRUDONI.—A town in Hyderabad, or territory of the Nizam, distant S.W. from Hyderabad 120 miles. Lat. 16° 16′, long. 77° 10′.

BEYT, or BET, in Guzerat, or territory of the Guicowar, an island at the entrance of a bay, an inlet of the Gulf of Cutch, and indenting the north-east coast of the district of Okamundul, in the peninsula of Kattywar. The castle or fort, formerly called Kullorkot, is on the west side of the island, and is compact and imposing, having lofty massive towers mounted with iron ordnance, and with its narrowest and most efficient face towards the water. It formerly belonged to a Rajpoot pirate, but now belongs to the Guicowar. The whole island singularly abounds with temples and shrines in honour of Crishna; and the population, principally consisting of Brahmins, is mainly supported by the resort of pilgrims. The place is also called Sankhodwara, or "the Door of the Shell;" a great number of fine conch shells being obtained from the various banks off the shore, and exported to all parts of the world, principally for the purpose of being carved into ornaments. The fort is distant from Ahmedabad, W., 225 miles; Baroda, 265. Lat. 22° 28', long. 69° 10'.

BEZWARRA, in the British district of Masulipatam, presidency of Madras, a town on the route from Guntoor to Ellore, 20 miles N.E. of the former. The trunk-road from Madras to Calcutta is by the ferry of Bezwarra, which is well provided with the means of transit. Lat. 16° 31', long. 80° 41'.

BHADARSA, in the district of Pachhamrat, territory of Oude, a town nine miles S. of Faizabad, 75 E. of Lucknow, situate on the river Tons (eastern). Here is an eleemosynary establishment with an annual income of 15,000 rupees, the endowment of the nawaub vizier Asaf ud Daulah. The establishment is under the care of a Seiad, or descendant of Fatima, and the proceeds of the endowment are distributed indiscriminately among Mussulman and Hindoo religious mendicants. According to Butter, the population of the place is 5,000, of whom 2,000 are Mussulmans. Lat. 26° 38', long. 82° 8'.

BHADER.—A river rising in the peninsula of Kattywar, province of Guzerat, about lat. 22° 10', long. 71° 18', and flowing in a south-westerly direction for 135 miles, falls into the Indian Ocean near the town of Poorbunder, in lat. 21° 38', long. 69° 46'.

BHADINYA, in the district of Sultanpoor, territory of Oude, a town on the right bank of the river Goomtee, 15 miles S.E. of Sultanpoor cantonment, 98 S.E. of Lucknow. Here is a ruined fort, formerly held out, by a refractory zemindar or landholder, against the officers of the Oude government, two of whom were killed in the attempt to take it. The British troops under Colonel Faithfull subsequently captured it, and gave it up to the government of Oude, through the supineness of which the zemindar was allowed to reoccupy and repair it. An officer of the Oude government succeeded in taking it in 1836, when it was dismantled; and since that time it has remained in ruins. After the destruction of the fort, the cultivators of the surrounding country emigrated in great numbers. Butter estimates the population at 2,000, including 100 Mussulmans. Lat. 26° 10', long. 82° 18'.

BHADOWRA.—A town in the native state of Gwalior, or possessions of Scindia, distant S.W. from Gwalior 110 miles. Lat. 24° 47', long. 77° 28'.

BHADREZ, in the Rajpoot state of Joudpore, a village on the route from Pokhurn to Balmeer, and 12 miles N.W. of the latter. It is situate at the eastern base of a range of rocky hills, stretching about twenty miles in a direction from north-west to south-east. The road in this part of the route is sandy and uneven. Lat. 25° 52', long. 71° 16'.

BHADRI, in the district Ahladganj, territory of Oude, a town close to the south-east frontier, towards the British district of Allahabad. Jag Mohun Singh, the zemindar or landholder of this place and of the surrounding country, held out against the Oude government, until in 1834 all the disposable forces of the kingdom, with 100 pieces of artillery, were brought against him. Attempting to escape with ten cannon across the Ganges, he was overtaken, killed, and his head carried off in triumph: the estate, however, was given to his son. Distant N. of Allahabad 22 miles, S.E. of Lucknow 90. Lat. 25° 47', long. 81° 45'.

BHADRINATH.—See BADRINATH.

BHADU.—A town in the native state of Kashmeer, or possessions of Gholab Singh, distant E. from Jamoo 36 miles. Lat. 32° 30', long. 75° 36'.

BHAGA PURANA, in Sirhind, a village on the route from Ferozpoor to Simla, and 43 miles S.E. of the former town. It is supplied with water from three wells, each 150 feet deep. The surrounding country is wild, and overrun with jungle. The road is in general good, but in a few places sandy and heavy. Distant N.W. from Calcutta 1,081 miles. Lat. 30° 40', long. 75° 5'.

BHAGEERETTEE.—The name by which the Ganges is designated in the upper part of its course. The stream first issues from the mountains of Gurwhal, in lat. 30° 54', long. 79° 7', and holds a direction north-west to Gangotri, and thence to Bhairogati, where it receives the Jahnuvi. The course of the united stream is then south-westerly to Sookhee, where it breaks through the "Himalaya Proper." After a further course of ninety miles, during which it is joined by the Julkar and the Bhillung, it unites at Deoprag, in lat. 30° 8', long. 78° 39', with the Aluknunda, and from this confluence the stream is called the Ganges. Upwards of 1,000 miles below Hurdwar, where the Ganges first enters the plains, it throws off an extensive branch, which is regarded by Hindoos as the genuine stream of the sacred river; for the particulars of which see BHAGRUTTEE.

BHAGELKHUND.—See REWA.

BHAGMARA, in the British district of Durrung, province of Assam, lieut.-gov. of Bengal, a town on the route from Bisnath to Luckimpoor, 10 miles N. of the former. Lat. 26° 49', long. 93° 12'.

BHAGRUTTEE.—A large branch of the Ganges, and regarded by the natives as the genuine stream of the sacred river, which at Jagotnathpur, in lat. 24° 40', long. 88° 7', separates into two branches, the right, or western, being denominated the Bhagruttee, the eastern bearing the name of Podda, and conveying the greatest volume of the water to form a junction by various channels with the Brahmapootra. Taking a course very sinuous, but generally south, for 135 miles, it at Naddya, in lat. 23° 25′, long. 88° 22′, unites with the river of Jellinghee, an offset of the Ganges, sent off from the main stream more to the east. The united stream flowing by Calcutta to the sea is called the Hoogly. Through this channel the passage made to Rajmahal and the North-West Provinces is 177 miles less than that by the Soonderbunds passage, more to the east; and hence is followed for the greater part of the year; but in spring, the depth of water being reduced to one foot, navigation of large craft through this channel is at that season precluded. It is by Rennell denominated the Cossimbazar river, from the circumstance of its flowing by that place.

BHAGUL.—See BAGUL.

BHAGULPORE.—A British district under the lieut.-gov. of Bengal, and named from its principal place. It is bounded on the north by the kingdom of Nepaul and the British district of Purnea; on the east by the districts of Purnea and Maldah; on the south by the British district of Beerbhoom; and on the west by the British districts of Monghyr and Tirhoot. It lies between lat. 24° 17′—26° 20′, long. 86° 15′—88° 3′; is 150 miles in length from north to south, and 108 in breadth, and has an area of 5,806 square miles. The district is intersected by the Ganges, which, running west and east, divides it into two parts, the northern division being in extent about a fourth of the whole. The other rivers which intersect or skirt the district are the Gogaree, and the Douse or Ejara. On the south side of the Ganges, numerous torrents of great size rush down from the hills during the rains, and discharge themselves into that river; but though their channels are in general of great width, they become devoid of water during the dry season. Bhagulpore being nearly intertropical, and the elevation above the sea inconsiderable, the heat in the dry season, comprising spring and the early part of summer, is great, and more so in the hills than in the plains, the reflection of the sun's rays, and radiation of heat from the rocks of the highlands, greatly increasing the temperature. The winters are mild, though slight frosts sometimes occur, and ice is occasionally obtained by exposing boiled water to the night air. The winds prevailing from February to June bring aridity; those which prevail during the remainder of the year are moister; but, altogether, the climate is drier here than in the tracts more to the north and east. The periodical rains of the close of the summer and early part of autumn are heavy. Wild elephants infest the woods and jungly valleys of the hills in the eastern and south-eastern parts of the district, and issuing thence, commit great ravages among the crops. The rhinoceros is sometimes met with. Wild hogs are most numerous and troublesome on the northern side of the Ganges. The gaur, or gayal, a great bovine quadruped, is sometimes met with. There are besides, the wild buffalo, the nylgau (Antilope picta), various other species of antelopes, deer, porcupines, monkeys in great numbers, and hares. The beasts of prey are tigers, leopards, bears, hyænas, wolves, jackals, foxes. Of birds there are cranes, peafowl, parrots, paroquets, partridges, quails, ortolans, ducks, teal, and snipes. The boa constrictor, or some other huge snake, lurks in the rocky recesses of the jungles, but it is not dreaded by the natives, who state that it preys on deer and wild swine. Venomous serpents are, however, very numerous, and, if native report may be trusted, destroy annually a very considerable number of individuals. In the Ganges, and other large streams, both the blunt-snouted crocodile and the long-snouted are numerous. Large tortoises abound, some being five or six feet in length. Fish are abundant, and many are of fine quality. The trade of the fisherman is pursued by numbers, according to Buchanan amounting to many thousands. Honey-bees abound in the woods, and their produce is largely gathered, but consumed by the people on the spot, and not made an article of commerce. Rice is the staple crop; next in importance is wheat; then barley, maize, maruya (Eleusine corocana), various kinds of millet, jowar (Holcus Sorghum), bajra (Holcus spicatus), oil-seeds and pulse in great abundance and variety, and cucurbitaceous plants. The potato is cultivated to a considerable extent, as also are carrots, onions, asparagus, and some other European esculent vegetables during the cool season. The sugar-cane is widely cultivated, and thrives remarkably well; cotton and indigo are grown largely, and are of good quality; the opium-poppy and tobacco receive little attention; kusum or safflower, for dyeing, is an important object of culture, as is the jujube, being used as food for the lac-producing insect. Iron-mining and smelting are carried on. The principal manufactures are glass, pottery, works in gold, silver, copper, and iron, tanning and shoemaking, cotton-spinning and weaving, dyeing to considerable extent, silk-winding and weaving; but much of the manufacturing industry of the district has decayed before the competition of British manufactures. A few years since, search was made for coal, and though some was found, it was of such inferior quality as to discourage the pursuit. The population is stated at 2,000,000, of whom the Mussulmans are reputed to be about twenty-three in the hundred, the remainder being Brahminists. The civil establishment is located at the town of Bhagulpore, and comprises about eleven Europeans, with a considerable staff of native functionaries. The eastern portion of the district is traversed by the East-Indian Railway.

The territory of Bhagulpore, considered to have been originally part of the great realm of Magadha, became part of the Mahomedan kingdom of Gour, and, subsequently subjugated nominally by Akber, was by him declared part of the dominions of the monarch of Delhi. In 1763, Cossim Ali attempted to make a stand against the British forces at Udanala, in the south-eastern part of this province; but his intrenchments were forced with great slaughter, and all within them fell into the hands of the victors. It passed to the East-India Company by the grant of Shah Alum, emperor of Delhi, in 1765.

BHAGULPORE.—The principal place of the British district of the same name, a town on the right bank of the Ganges, here seven miles in width during the rains. It lies on the route from Berhampore to Dinapore, 150 miles north-west of the former, 143 east of the latter. Though represented to be two miles in length, and a mile in width, it is a poor place, consisting of scattered market-places, meanly built, and, owing to the declivities of the ground, very inconveniently situated. It is, however, ornamented by many handsome houses of European residents, and also by mosques. There is also a Romish chapel. The cavalry barracks are now only occasionally occupied; but four miles from them are the barracks of a native corps formed of the highlanders of the Rajmahal wilds. There are also a court of justice and a jail, "a very neat and creditable building," and which has lately been well ventilated and otherwise improved. An educational institution, in which English instruction is afforded, has been established in the town by the British government. The number of pupils in 1852 amounted to 115. Adjacent to the town are the Cleveland monuments, erected to the memory of a meritorious civil functionary of that name, who filled the office of judge and magistrate about the year 1780; one in the Hindoo style, raised by native subscription; the other erected at the cost of the East-India Company. In the vicinity are two round towers, each about seventy feet high. The names of their founders are unknown, as are also the era and object of their erection; but they closely resemble the *pyrethra*, so numerous in Affghanistan, Persia, and Syria, as well as the round towers of Ireland. The site of the ancient Palibothra has been conjectured to be contiguous to this town. Bhagulpore is distant N.W. from Calcutta, by Berhampoor and Moorshedabad, 268 miles; by the course of the Ganges, 326. Lat. 25° 11′, long. 87°.

BHAGULPORE, in the British district of Goruckpore (N.W. Provinces), a small town which formerly gave name to a pergunnah or subdivision. It is situate on the left bank of the river Ghoghra, and was reported by Buchanan to contain a hundred and twenty-five huts, but to be neater, cleaner, and more thriving than most native towns of its size. One of the streets is wide, and has a row of sheds for the hucksters on the market-days. Many of the huts are very neatly roofed with tiles. It is said to have been the birth-place and residence of Parasu Rama, an incarnation of Vishnu, and highly famed in Hindoo legendary lore. In the neighbourhood are several ruins, but none that would seem worthy of so extraordinary a personage. A stone pillar, attributed by some to Parasu Rama, by others to Bhim, the son of Pandu, is generally popularly known by the name of the Staff (lath). Bhagulpore is 50 miles S.E. of the cantonment of Goruckpore. Lat. 26° 10′, long. 83° 52′.

BHAGWANGOLA.—See BOGWANGOLA.

BHAGWEE, in Central India, in the jaghire of Jujhur, lieut.-gov. of the N.W. Provinces, a town on the route from Rohtuk to Narnol, and 25 miles S. of the former. Lat. 28° 35′, long. 76° 27′.

BHAINEE, in Sirhind, a village on the route from Ferozpoor to Simla, and 72 miles S.E. of the former place. Distant N.W. from Calcutta 1,098 miles. Lat. 30° 35′, long. 76° 36′.

BHAIROGATI, in Gurwhal, the confluence of the river Jahnevi with the Bhageerettee, as the Ganges is called in the upper part of its course. Hodgson describes it as "a most terrific and really awful-looking place," and adds, that he had seen nothing to be compared with it in horror and extravagance. Both rivers are confined within high perpendicular walls of solid granite, and in the acute angle formed by the confluence a lofty massive rock projects downwards between the streams like an enormous wedge. The Jahnevi, the larger stream, is beautifully clear, with a bluish tinge; the Bhageerettee of a dingy hue. Hodgson compares this scene of terrific sublimity to "the appearance that the ruins of a Gothic cathedral might have to a spectator within them, supposing that thunderbolts or earthquakes had rifted its lofty and massy towers, spires, and buttresses; the parts left standing might then, in miniature, give an idea of the rocks of Bhairoghati." The Bhageerettee, where forty-five feet wide and rather deep, is traversed by a sanga or wooden bridge, sixty feet above the stream. Hence is the name of the place, signifying the ghat or pass of Bhairo, some mythological personage, worshipped in a small temple near the spot. Elevation above the sea 8,511 feet. Lat. 31° 2′, long. 78° 54′.

BHAIROWAL, in the Baree Doab division of the Punjab, a town situated on the right bank of the Beas river, 31 miles S.E. of the town of Amritsir. Lat. 31° 26′, long. 75° 14′.

BHAKURI, in the British district of Allygurh, lieut.-gov. of the N.W. Provinces, a village on the route from the cantonment of Allygurh to that of Delhi, seven miles N.W. of the former. The road in this part of the route is in many places heavy, and confined between sand-drifts; the country is open, sandy, and partially cultivated. Lat. 27° 59′, long. 78° 3′.

BHALKEE, in Hyderabad, or territory of the Nizam, a town on a stream a feeder of the river Manjera, distant from the city of Hyderabad, N.W., 98 miles. Lat. 18° 3′, long. 77° 17′.

BHALOD, in Guzerat, or territory of the Guicowar, a town on the left or south bank of the river Nerbudda, 35 miles S. of Baroda, 55 N. of Surat. Lat. 21° 48′, long. 73° 15′.

BHALOT.—A town in the Rajpoot territory of Shekawutee, distant S.W. from Delhi 82 miles. Lat. 28° 10′, long. 76° 6′.

BHALTHA.—A town in the Rajpoot state of Jhalawar, distant E. from Neemuch 100 miles. Lat. 24° 17′, long. 76° 30′.

BHAMANIKHERA, in the British district of Goorgaon, lieut.-gov. of the N.W. Provinces, a village on the route from Delhi to Muttra, and 47 miles S. of the former city. The vicinity, now ill cultivated, appears to have been once populous and prosperous, as it abounds in the remains of small mosques and ornamented tombs. Water is supplied from tanks and wells, and supplies are procurable from the surrounding country. The road in this part of the route is good. Lat. 28° 4′, long. 77° 24′.

BHAMGURH.—A town in the native state of Gwalior, or Scindia's possessions, distant S.E. from Mhow 72 miles. Lat. 21° 48′, long. 76° 35′.

BHAMONCALLEE, in the British district of Jessore, lieut.-gov. of Bengal, a town on the route from Jessore to Fureedpore, 12 miles N.E. of the former. Lat. 23° 15′, long. 89° 21′.

BHAMON, or **BHAMUNNAGRA**, in the British district of Budaon, lieut.-gov. of the N.W. Provinces, a village on the route, by Khasgunj, from Bareilly to Allyghur cantonment, and 30 miles S.E. of the latter, 56 N.E. of Delhi. The road in this part of the route is generally good, but in some places heavy; the country open and partially cultivated. Lat. 27° 51′, long. 78° 34′.

BHANDUK.—A town in the territory of Nagpoor, distant S. from Nagpoor 70 miles. Lat. 20° 8′, long. 79° 12′.

BHANEYRUH, in the British district of Allyghur, lieut.-gov. of the N.W. Provinces, a village on the route from Meerut to Muttra, and 33 miles N.E. of the latter. The road in this part of the route is tolerably good, the country open and well cultivated. Lat. 27° 54′, long. 77° 54′.

BHANGURH.—A town in the Rajpoot state of Alwur, distant S.W. from Alwur 38 miles. Lat. 27° 7′, long. 76° 22′.

BHANPOOR, in the British district of Goruckpoor, lieut.-gov. of the N.W. Provinces, a small town 58 miles N.W. of the cantonment of Goruckpoor. Buchanan states the number of its houses at 100; and consequently, allowing five persons to each, the population may be estimated at 500. Lat. 27° 6′, long. 82° 37′.

BHANPOORA, in territory of Indore, or possessions of Holkar's family, a town on the route from Neemuch to Kota, 60 miles E. of former, 60 S. of latter. It is situate on the river Rewa, at the base of a ridge of hills, and has a fort built of stone, but not finished. "There is a fine palace in the inside, which is also unfinished. Both of these were commenced by Jeswunt Row Holkar, of whom there is a beautiful cut-marble statue in the palace; and on the walls and gateway are several figures of animals of various descriptions. The city is surrounded by a wall." It is the principal place of a pergunnah containing seventy villages. Population 20,000. Elevation above the sea 1,344 feet. Lat. 24° 30′, long. 75° 45′.

BHANPOOR THANA, in the British district of Goruckpoor, lieut.-gov. of the N.W. Provinces, a town on the left bank of the Koana river, 49 miles N.W. of Goruckpoor. Lat. 26° 59′, long. 82° 43′.

BHANRA, in the district of Sooltanpoor, territory of Oude, a village a mile from the right bank of the river Goomtee, five miles N.W. of Sooltanpoor cantonment, 77 S.E. of Lucknow. Butter estimates its population at 400, all Hindoos. Lat. 26° 20′, long. 82° 4′.

BHANSTON.—A town in the Rajpoot state of Kotah, distant E. from Kotah 60 miles. Lat. 25° 7′, long. 76° 49′.

BHAOON, in the British district of Boolundshuhur, lieut.-gov. of the N.W. Provinces, a town on the route from Anoopshuhur to Meerut, and 26 miles S.E. of the latter. Lat. 28° 38′, long. 78° 1′.

BHAPOORUH, or **BOPRU**, in the British district of Paneeput, lieut.-gov. of the N.W. Provinces, a village on the route from the city of Delhi to Kurnool, and 46 miles N.W. of the former. The road in this part of the route is good. Lat. 29° 14′, long. 77° 4′.

BHARATGANJ, in the British district of Allahabad, lieut.-gov. of the N.W. Provinces, a small town on the route by the Kuttra Pass, from the cantonment of Allahabad to Rewa, and 40 miles S.E. of the former city. It has a bazaar, and supplies and water are abundant. The road in this part of the route is rather good, the country level, well cultivated, and studded with small villages. Lat. 25° 4′, long. 82° 15′.

BHARAWAS, in the British district of Goorgaon, lieut.-gov. of the N.W. Provinces, a town on the route from Delhi to Rewari, and 50 miles S.W. of the former. It has a small bazaar; there is water from wells, and supplies are procurable from the vicinity of Rewari, five miles distant. The old cantonment of Rewari is a mile N.W. of Bharawas. The road in this part of the route is good, the adjacent country open. Lat. 28° 8′, long. 76° 39′.

BHARERA, in the British district of Shahjehanpoor, lieut-gov. of the N.W. Provinces, a village on the route from Futtehgurh to the cantonment of Shajehanpoor, and 15 miles S.W. of the latter. The road in this part of the route is indifferent, the country open, level, and partially cultivated. Lat. 27° 46′, long. 79° 50′.

BHAROLE, in the British district of Mynpooree, lieut.-gov. of the N.W. Provinces, a small town or village on the route from the city of Agra to the cantonment of Mynpooree, and 23 miles W. of the latter. The road in this part of the route is laid under water to the depth of from one to three feet during the periodical rains in the latter part of summer, at other times it is tolerably good. The country is flat and partially cultivated. Lat. 27° 8′, long. 78° 46′.

BHASEYPOOR, in the British district of Tirhoot, lieut.-gov. of Bengal, a town 28 miles N.E. from Mozufferpoor, 32 miles N.W. of Durbunga. Lat. 26° 30′, long. 85° 39′.

BHASOUR, in Sirhind, a village on the route from Hansee to Lodiana, and 36 miles S. of the latter town. It is situate in a country with a slightly undulating surface, moderately fertile and partially cultivated. The road in this part of the route is generally good, but liable to become miry in heavy rains. Distant N.W. from Calcutta 1,074 miles. Lat. 30° 25′, long. 76°.

BHATGONG, in the native state of Nepaul, one of the chief towns of the kingdom, and the favourite residence of the Brahmins of the country. "Its palace and buildings in general are of more striking appearance; and its streets, if not much wider, are at all events much cleaner than those of Khatmandoo." Lat. 27° 37′, long. 85° 22′.

BHATNEER.—See BHUTNEER.

BHATTIES.—See BHUTTEEANA.

BHAUBEIR.—A small district in the north-west of Guzerat, having a population composed entirely of coolies. It is bounded on the north by Deodur; on the south by Radhunpore; on the east by Therwarra; and on the west by Soorgaum. It is about fourteen miles long and twelve broad, and consists of a flat jungle-country; the soil being principally sandy, and producing only one crop of the commoner grains yearly. The population does not exceed 500; and the revenue is little more than 1,200 rupees. Four-fifths of the population are described as armed men. The district pays no tribute to any government. It became connected with the British government in 1819, upon the expulsion of the Kosas from Guzerat; and a further agreement was entered into in 1826. The policy observed towards it is that of non-interference with its internal affairs, but control in its external relations, which are superintended by the government of Bombay. The town of Bhaubeir is distant W. from Deesa 39 miles. Lat. 24° 7′, long. 71° 30′.

BHAUBRA.—A town of Malwa, in the native state of Jabboah, distant S.W. from Jabboah 18 miles. Lat. 22° 33′, long. 74° 25′.

BHAUGULPORE.—See BHAGULPORE.

BHAUL, in the British district of Khandeish, presidency of Bombay, a town on the left bank of the Girna, 31 miles E. of Malligaum. Lat. 20° 35′, long. 75°.

BHAWALPOOR, in the British district of Etawa, lieut.-gov. of the N.W. Provinces, a village on the route from the cantonment of Etawa to Allahabad, and 24 miles S.E. of the former. Lat. 26° 34′, long. 79° 22′.

BHAWULPOOR.—See BAHAWULPOOR.

BHAWUR.—See JAUNSAR.

BHAYNSEEA, in the British district of Bareilly, lieut.-gov. of the N.W. Provinces, a village on the route by Nanakmath and Ruderpoor, from the town of Pillibheet to that of Kasheepoor, 23 miles S.E. of the latter. Lat. 29° 2′, long. 79° 19′.

BHEEAMOW, or BETIMOW, in the British district of Futtehpoor, lieut.-gov. of the N.W. Provinces, a town on the right bank of the Ganges, 10 miles N. of the town of Futtehpoor. Lat. 26° 3′, long. 80° 51′.

BHEEGA, in the British district of Ramgur, lieut.-gov. of Bengal, a town on the main trunk-road from Calcutta to Benares, 30 miles N. of Hazareebagh. Lat. 24° 24′, long. 85° 20′.

BHEEKUNGHAM.—A town in the native state of Indoor, or territory of Holkar's family, distant S. from Indoor 60 miles. Lat. 21° 51′, long. 76° 8′.

BHEELS.—See CANDEISH.

BHEELWARA.—A town in the Rajpoot state of Oodeepoor, distant S. from Ajmeer 80 miles. Lat. 25° 20′, long. 74° 44′.

BHEEMAR, in the Rajpoot state of Joudpore, a village on the route from Pokhurn to Balmer, and 56 miles N. of the latter. It is a prosperous little place, inhabited by Charuns, a singular Rajpoot tribe, combining the avocations of priestcraft and trade, and retaining by their artifices a wonderful influence over their superstitious countrymen. Water is obtained from two wells about 180 feet deep. The road eastward, or towards Pokhurn, is good, but in the other direction indifferent. Lat. 26° 19′, long. 71° 33′.

BHEEM GHORA, in the British district of Saharunpoor, a place of Hindoo pilgrimage, about a mile north-east of Hurdwar. It is in a small recess of the mountain bounding the Dehra Doon on the south, and in a perpendicular rock about 350 feet high. Here is a kunda or pool supplied with water from a small branch of the Ganges, and frequented by pilgrims to practise the ablution which they consider efficacious to wash away their sins. According to the legend, Bheema was posted here to prevent the Ganges foom taking another course. Immediately above the bath is a small cave or artificial excavation in the rock. It is pointed out as a miraculous indenture made by the kick of the horse on which Bheema was mounted, and though only five feet square, affords shelter to a fakir. Raper states that his associate, Webb, took the height of Bheema Ghora, and found it to be 407 feet; but as the Kunda is supplied with water from one of "the small channels of the river," it must be almost exactly on the same level as the Ganges, if by the expression of "the river" that great stream be meant. Perhaps the elevation ascertained by Webb is that of the summit of Bheema Ghora above the river. Hurdwar is 1,024 feet above the sea. Lat. 29° 58′, long. 78° 14′.

BHEENDAH.—A town in the Rajpoot state of Oodeypoor, distant S.E. from Oodeypoor 30 miles. Lat. 24° 29′, long. 74° 16′.

BHEENMAL.—A town in the Rajpoot state of Joudpore, distant S.W. from Joudpore 100 miles. Lat. 25° 5′, long. 72° 20′.

BHEENPOOR.—A town in Hyderabad, or dominions of the Nizam, distant N. from Hyderabad 167 miles. Lat. 19° 46′, long. 78° 35′.

BHEER.—A town in Hyderabad, or dominions of the Nizam, distant N.W. from Hyderabad 206 miles. Lat. 19°, long. 75° 55′.

BHEERJORA, in the British district of Goalpara, lieut.-gov. of Bengal, a town 21 miles N.W. from Goalpara, 95 miles N.E. of Rungpore. Lat. 26° 27′, long. 90° 32′.

BHEERNAGUR, in the British district of Purneah, lieut.-gov. of Bengal, a town on the right bank of the river Coosy, 29 miles N.W. of Purneah. Lat. 25° 59′, long. 87° 10′.

BHEETAH, in the British district of Allahabad, lieut.-gov. of the N.W. Provinces, a town on the route from Mirzapore to Banda, 11 miles S. of Allahabad. Lat. 25° 17′, long. 81° 52′.

BHEKORAEE, in the Rajpoot state of Joudpore, a village on the route from Pokhurn to Balmer, and 32 miles S. of the former. It is inhabited by Charuns, a tribe of Rajpoots, who by priestcraft have acquired an extraordinary influence over their countrymen. There are about a hundred houses, generally supplied with water from a large tank, which fails in the dry season, and then recourse is had to two wells, one of fresh, the other of brackish water. There is a small fort or tower for the defence of the village. The road is tolerable on the north, or towards Pokhurn, but in the other direction sandy and bad. Lat. 26° 30′, long. 71° 50′.

BHENTPOOR, in the British district of Pooree, lieut.-gov. of Bengal, a town nine miles W. of Juggurnaut, 47 miles S. of Cuttack. Lat. 19° 50′, long. 85° 47′.

BHERACOLE.—One of the petty native states on the south-west frontier of Bengal. It contains an area of about 200 square miles, and its centre is in lat. 21° 5′, long. 84° 20′.

BHEREE.—A village in the British district of Hurriana, lieut.-gov. of the N.W. Provinces. Lat. 29° 29′, long. 75° 56′.

BHETAEE.—A town in the native state of Nepal, distant W. from Khatmandoo 132 miles. Lat. 27° 46′, long. 83° 10′.

BHEWANNEE, or BOWANI, in the British district of Rohtuck, lieut.-gov. of the N.W. Provinces, a town with a fort, which was taken by the British in 1809, in consequence of hostile acts committed by the chief who possessed it. The population is returned at 29,442. Lat. 28° 45′, long. 76° 14′.

BHEWNDY, in the British district of Tannah, presidency of Bombay, a town on the route from Bombay to Nassick, 29 miles N.E. of the former. The town is supplied with water by means of an aqueduct constructed by the inhabitants, the government having contributed 500*l.* in aid of its cost. The population and mercantile importance of this place are officially stated to be on the increase. Lat. 19° 19′, long. 73° 9′.

BHIDANWALA, in Sirhind, a village situate on a high bank, beneath which flows a large offset of the Sutlej, issuing from that river on the left, a short distance below its junction with the Beas. About three miles below the junction is a ghat, communicating with Harikepatan, in the Punjaub, and distinguished as being an important channel of traffic. Lieutenant Mackeson thus describes the scene :—"Thirty-two boats, with three men to each, were unceasingly employed from morn to night in transporting loaded hackeries and beasts of burthen of every description across the river. I observed little difference one day from another; it was a scene of constant activity and bustle." Bhidanwala is within the territory formerly belonging to the Alawala Sikh chief, one of those under the control and protection of the British, but who, failing in his allegiance, incurred the penalty of forfeiture of his dominions. Distant N.W. from Calcutta 1,167 miles. Lat. 31° 10′, long. 75°.

BHIKAREEPOOR, in the British district of Bareilly, lieut.-gov. of the N.W. Provinces, a village on the route from Bareilly to Petoragurh, and 40 miles N.E. of the former. Water and supplies for troops are here abundant. The road in this part of the route is bad; the country level, open, and cultivated. Lat. 28° 42′, long. 79° 52′.

BHILKHET, in the British district of Kumaon, lieut.-gov. of the N.W. Provinces, a halting-place on the route from Pillibheet to Petoragurh cantonment, 62 miles N.E. of the former. It is situate on the river Ludhia, here fordable, and on the bank of which is encamping-ground for a regiment. Supplies must be collected from the adjacent country, as there is no village. The road to the south-west, or towards Pillibheet, is bad, stony, and has a steep declivity; in the other direction, or towards the north-east, it is better, but with steep ascent. Lat. 29° 11′, long. 80° 6′.

BHILLUNG, in the native state of Gurwhal, a considerable feeder of the Bhageerettee, as the Ganges is called in the upper part of its course. It rises in lat. 30° 46′, long. 78° 55′, and taking a south-westerly course of about fifty miles, falls into the Bhageerettee on the left side, in lat. 30° 23′, long. 78° 31′. The elevation of the confluence is 2,278 feet above the sea. Raper, who crossed it by means of a jhula or rope-bridge, about five miles above the mouth, found the stream there, in the beginning of May, between sixty and seventy feet wide. It abounds with fish, called by Moorcroft trout, which are taken by snaring. Herbert estimates the length of course of the continuous stream of the Bhillung and the part of the Bhageerettee below the confluence, measured from the source of the former to the point at which the latter passes into the plains near Hurdwar, at a hundred and fifty miles. More recent information leads to the conclusion that this estimate is in excess of the true distance, which may be computed at one hundred and twenty miles. The Bhillung is considered a sacred stream by the Hindoos.

BHILSA, in the territory of Gwalior, or the possessions of Scindia's family, a town the principal place of a pergunnah of the same name. It is situate on a trap rock on the right or eastern bank of the river Betwa, and has a fort, inclosed by a wall of stone, furnished with square towers and a ditch. The suburb outside has some spacious streets, containing good houses. Here is a gun, "measuring nineteen feet and a half in length, with a bore of ten inches, in elegant proportions, and highly ornamented. It is of the finest brass, and cast with the appearance of a network over it, and has on it large rings held by dolphins." It is alleged to have been made by order of Jehangir. At Sanchi Kanckhera, four miles and a half south-west of Bhilsa, on a detached hill on the left bank of the river Betwa, are some vast monuments of antiquity. The principal is a hemisphere, constructed of thin layers of freestone, arranged in steps, without any cement, and overlaid with a coat of mortar four inches thick. It has on the summit a level horizontal area, thirty-five feet in diameter, and was formerly surmounted by a cupola, the fragments of which remain. The hemisphere stands on a base twelve feet high, and extending all round seven feet from the termination of the hemisphere to the outside. The circumference of the building, measured round the base, is 554 feet. A line drawn from the base to the centre of the crown measures 112 feet; the height from the ground to the summit is between seventy and eighty feet. Facing each of the cardinal points is a vast gateway. The north, east, and west gateways are forty feet high; their sides and upper parts being masses of stonework, carved in the most elaborate manner into the forms of elephants, human beings, and other shapes. Opposite each of these gateways, and resting against the face of the circular basement, is a figure of Buddha. The southern gateway is plain. Around are scattered numerous ruins and shattered sculptures; and at a short distance is a hemisphere similar to that already described, but unornamented, and of less dimensions, being only 246 feet in circumference. These buildings have been conjectured to be monuments raised to enshrine some relic consecrated by Buddhist superstition. From a shaft sunk lately from the summit, thirty feet below the foundation, it has been ascertained that the inner part of the building is solid brickwork, without any chamber. On many parts of these buildings are numerous inscriptions in the Pali character, commemorating gifts made by various parties, for the raising, decoration, or maintenance of the work. Bhilsa was taken in 1230 from the Hindoos by Samsuddin Altamsh, sovereign of Delhi. It appears, however, to have soon again fallen into the power of the Hindoos, as in 1293 it was wrested from them by an officer of Jelaluddin Ferose, sovereign of Delhi; and it must have again passed to the Hindoos, as in 1528 Baber states that it belonged to Pagans. It was a few years after taken by his son Humayoon, and subsequently seized by his successful Affghan rival Shir Shah. It was finally (A.D. 1570) incorporated with the empire of Delhi by Akbar. Bhilsa and its annexed pergunnah are stated to yield at present an annual revenue of 325,000 rupees. The tobacco produced in the vicinity of the town is considered the finest in India. The space, however, producing the very fine sort is very circumscribed, not exceeding three acres. "The chief, if not the only cause of the goodness of the tobacco of this single spot, is the very careful and high cultivation applied." The sorts produced in the neighbouring fields are of ordinary quality. Population about 30,000. Distant E. from Oojein 134 miles, S. from Gwalior 190. Lat. 23° 30′, long. 77° 50′.

BHIMBUR, in the Punjab, a town on the route from Lahore to Kashmir, through the Baramula Pass. It is situate on a small stream, which falls into the Chenaub, from which river the town is distant about forty miles. The houses are low and flat-roofed. Their number is estimated at 1,000, and that of shops at 150. Lat. 32° 59′, long. 74° 6′.

BHIM TAL, in the British district of Kumaon, lieut.-gov. of the N.W. Provinces, a small lake near the southern frontier, about ten miles above Bhumowree, on the Almorah road. It is situate in the bottom of a valley about three miles long, and is itself 3,000 feet in length and 2,400 in breadth, and the depth in the middle has been ascertained by sounding to be sixty-four feet. It is described by Heber as "a very beautiful place. It is a little mountain valley, surrounded on three sides by woody hills, and on the fourth by a tract of green meadow, with a fine lake of clear water. A small and very rude pagoda, of grey stone, with a coarse slate roof, under some fine peepul-trees, looked like a little church; and the whole scene, except that the hills were higher, so strongly reminded me of Wales, that I felt my heart beat as I entered it." Near, and connected with it by a stream, is a piece of water of considerable extent, but shallow and overgrown with aquatic vegetation. Both appear to be in course of being filled up by detritus brought down by streams from the higher grounds. Their waters are emptied by a torrent falling into the Goula, a feeder of the Ramgunga. Elevation above the sea 4,271 feet. Lat. 29° 19′, long. 79° 41′.

BHINAY.—See BUNAEE.

BHIND, in the territory of Gwalior, a town on the route from Etawa to Gwalior fort, 29 miles S.W. of former, 54 N.E. of latter. Though now much decayed, it was once important and populous, with a fort surrounded by a double rampart, the inner of masonry, the outer of mud, and strengthened by towers. In an inclosed pleasure-ground, near the town, are three fine buildings, supported on columns and arches of stone. Lat. 26° 33′, long. 78° 52′.

BHINDUS, in the jaghire of Jujhur, lieut.-gov. of the N.W. Provinces, a village situate on the left bank of the Hansoutee Nullah, a torrent dry for a great part of the year, but spreading widely during the rains. Lat. 28° 32′, long. 76° 37′.

BHINGA.—A town in the territory of Oude, distant N. from Oude 61 miles. Lat. 27° 40′, long. 82° 1′.

BHINGREE, in the British district of Goruckpore, lieut.-gov. of the N.W. Provinces, a small town on the south-eastern frontier, towards the British district of Sarun, situate equidistant between the rivers Chhota Gunduk and Jhuraie, and about six miles from each. According to Buchanan, it contains 100 houses, an amount which would assign it a population of 600. Distant S.E. from Goruckpore cantonment 50 miles. Lat. 26° 22′, long. 84° 4′.

BHIRANUH.—A village of the British district Hurriana, lieut.-gov. of the N.W. Provinces. Lat. 29° 33′, long. 75° 33′.

BHITARGANAW, in the district of Bainswara, territory of Oude, a town 25 miles S. of Lucknow, 34 E. of Cawnpore. Butter estimates the population at 4,000, of whom fifty are Mussulmans. Lat. 26° 29′, long. 80° 54′.

BHITREE, in the British district of Ghazeepore, lieut.-gov. of the N.W. Provinces, the principal place of the pergunnah of the same name, a small town or village on the route from Benares to Ghazeepoor, 28 miles N.E. of the former, 17 W. of the latter, and four N. of the left bank of the Ganges. Lat. 25° 35′, long. 83° 17′.

BHOELEE, in the British district of Mirzapore, lieut.-gov. of the N.W. Provinces, a town the principal place of the pergunnah of the same name, on the river Karamnasa, 10 miles E. of Chunar, 15 S. of Benares. Lat. 25° 6′, long. 83° 3′.

BHOGNEEPOOR, in the British district of Cawnpore, the principal place of the pergunnah of the same name, a small town with a bazaar, on the route from Calpee to Cawnpore, and eight miles N.E. of the former. The road in this part of the route is good, the country well cultivated and studded with villages. Lat. 26° 12′, long. 79° 51′.

BHOGPOOR, or BAUGPOOR, in the British district of Saharunpoor, lieut.-gov. of the N.W. Provinces, a village on the route from Moradabad to Hurdwar, and 13 miles S. of the latter. It is situate on the right bank of the Ganges, which here, according to Davidson, "is split up into innumerable small and rapid streams, each perhaps eighty yards wide." About three miles below the village is a ferry over the river, there 300 yards wide, rapid, and with a stony bottom. Nearly opposite the village, the Ganges becomes in February fordable for elephants and camels; and in 1828, the laden cattle of Lord Combermere's army forded it there. Bhogpoor was formerly fortified, and three ruinous bastions are yet remaining. Lat. 29° 48′, long. 78° 13′.

BHOJPOOR, in the district of Bainswara, territory of Oude, a town five miles from the left bank of the Ganges, 50 S. of Lucknow. Butter estimates its population at 9,000, of whom 150 are Mussulmans. Lat. 26° 8′, long. 81° 6′.

BHOJPOOR, in the British district of Moradabad, lieut.-gov. of the N.W. Provinces, a town on the route from the town of Moradabad to Almora, and nine miles N. of the former. It has a bazaar and a mosque; a proportion of the inhabitants being Mahometans. It was once a flourishing place, but was ruined in the Rohilla war, though still cottons are manufactured and dyed here to a considerable extent. The surrounding country is open, level, and fertile, producing the sugar-cane in perfection. Lat. 28° 57′, long. 78° 53′.

BHOJPOOR, in the British district of Shahabad, lieut.-gov. of Bengal, a town a mile to the right of the route from Dinapoor to Ghazeepoor, 59 miles W. of former, 40 E. of latter. It has 200 houses; and assuming the usually received average of five inmates to each, the population appears to be about 1,000. It is the principal place of a pergunnah of the same name. Lat. 25° 32′, long. 84° 11′.

BHOKAREREE, in the British district of Muzuffurnugur, lieut.-gov. of the N.W. Provinces, a village on the route from Moradabad to the town of Muzuffurnugur, and 14 miles E. of the latter. It is situate near the right bank of the Ganges, in a country partially cultivated. The road in this part of the route is bad. Distant N.W. from Calcutta 942 miles. Lat. 29° 30′, long. 78°.

BHOKUR.—See KERIALL.

BHONGAON, the principal place of the pergunnah of the same name, in the British district of Mynpooree, lieut.-gov. of the N.W. Provinces, is on the route from Futtehgurh cantonment to that of Mynpooree, and seven miles E. of the latter. It has a bazaar, and "the remains of a mosque, bespeaking the once respectability of the place," and is well supplied with water. The road in this part of the route is good; the country level, open, and but partially cultivated. Lat. 27° 15′, long. 79° 14′.

BHONTA, in Rajpootana, a town in the native territory of Godwar, distant S.W. from Ajmeer 91 miles. Lat. 25° 36′, long. 73° 39′.

BHONTEE.—A town of Central India, in the native state of Jhansee, distant W. from Jhansee 31 miles. Lat. 25° 20′, long. 78° 11′.

BHOOJ.—The capital of the native state of Cutch, a town situate at the base of a fortified hill, and containing about 20,000 inhabitants. Macmurdo observes, that "the town, when viewed from the north, has an imposing appearance; and the number of white buildings, mosques, and pagodas, interspersed with plantations of date-trees, give a stranger an idea of the respectability of the town, which is removed on entering the gates." A Chinese appearance is communicated to the rajah's palace, which is a castle of good masonry, by a coat of enamel which is spread over the cupolas and roofs. A large tank has been excavated to the west of the city. In 1819 a dreadful earthquake took place, which destroyed the fort and principal buildings, and occasioned great loss of life. Lat. 23° 13′, long. 69° 44′.

BHOOM.—A town in Hyderabad, or dominions of the Nizam, distant N.W. from Hyderabad 200 miles. Lat. 18° 29′, long. 75° 42′.

BHOOMPOORA.—A town in the native state of Gwalior, or possessions of Scindia, distant W. from Gwalior 49 miles. Lat. 26° 23′, long. 77° 30′.

BHOOMUH, in the British district of Mozuffurnuggur, lieut.-gov. of the N.W. Provinces, a town, the principal place of the pergunnah of the same name, situate in lat. 29° 16′, long. 78°.

BHOON, in the British district of Ghurwhal, lieut.-gov. of the N.W. Provinces, a town 38 miles S. of Sireenugur, and 41 miles W. of Almora. Lat. 29° 44′, long. 79° 1′.

BHOONAGEER, or BHONGIR, in the territory of Hyderabad, a town at the southwest base of a mountain, distant N.E. from the city of Hyderabad 32 miles. Close to the westward of it is a tank of considerable size, and in the same direction beyond the tank extends a well-cultivated, populous country. Lat. 17° 30′, long. 78° 58′.

BHOONG BARA.—A pergunnah or district of Sinde, in the vicinity of Subzulcote. It contains fifteen villages, and when subject to the Talpoor ameers of Khyerpoor, yielded an annual revenue of 60,000 rupees. This territory had been wrested by the ameers from the khan of Bhawlpoor, but in the beginning of 1843 the British authorities in Sinde transferred it to Mahomed Bhawl Khan, the ruler of Bhawlpoor, as a reward for his zealous and long-tried friendship. The principal place, Bhoong, is situate on the left bank of the Indus, in lat. 28° 24′, long. 69° 50′.

BHOORA.—A town in the British territory of Nagpoor, distant N.E. from Nagpoor 85 miles. Lat. 21° 50′, long. 80° 17′.

BHOORPAH, in the British district of Kumaon, lieut.-gov. of the N.W. Provinces, a village in the Bhotia subdivision of Juwahir, on the route to Hiundes, and 17 miles S. of the Juwahir Pass. It is situate on the left bank of the river Goree, which runs 140 feet below, and is crossed by a bridge close to the village. Elevation of the village above the sea 10,836 feet. Lat. 30° 22′, long. 80° 13′.

BHOORS PEAK, in Sirmoor, a summit of the lower Himalayas, commanding an extensive prospect. On the top is a small Hindoo temple. Elevation above the sea 6,439 feet. Lat. 30° 46′, long. 77° 12′.

BHOOSKEE, in the British district of Patna, lieut.-gov. of Bengal, a town on the route from Bhagulpore to Patna, 15 miles S.E. of the latter. Lat. 25° 27′, long. 85° 27′.

BHOOSNUGRA, in the British district of Allyghur, lieut.-gov. of the N.W. Provinces, a village on the route from the city of Agra to Allyghur cantonment, 28 miles N. of the former. The road in this part of the route is excellent, the country highly cultivated. Lat. 27° 34′, long. 78° 6′.

BHOPAL.—A native state in Malwa, presidency of Bengal, under the political superintendence of the Governor-General. It is bounded on the north by Gwalior, or the possessions of Scindia, and the British district of Bairseah; on the north-east and south-east by the Saugor and Nerbudda territory; on the south-west by the possessions of Holkar and of Scindia; and on the north-west by Scindia's districts and Omutwarra. It lies between lat. 22° 32′ and 23° 46′, and long. 76° 25′ and 78° 50′; is 157 miles in length from east to west, and 76 in breadth from north to south. The area is estimated at 6,764 square miles. The extreme southern part of the territory is a portion of the valley of the Nerbudda, from which river the ground rises northward to the Vindhya range. The greater part of Bhopal lies on the other side of the range, and is a table-land sloping northward from it. The principal rivers which intersect or skirt this territory are the Nerbudda, the Dhasan, the Betwa, the Parbutti, and the Newuj. A considerable portion of the population, as well as the nawaub or sovereign, are of Patan lineage, descended from a colony settled in the territory in the time of Aurungzebe. With these are intermixed Patans, but the great mass of the population is Hindoo. If the relative density of the population be taken at the rate assumed by Malcolm for Central India generally—ninety-eight to the square mile,—the aggregate will amount to 662,872. Bhopal is ruled by a sovereign having the title of nawaub; his revenues in 1848 amounted to 220,000*l*. A school has been established at Sehore, a town distant 20 miles from Bhopal, in which a number of youths now in public employ have been educated. It is proposed to introduce into it the study of English literature.

The state of Bhopal was founded by Dost Mahommad Khan, an Affghan adventurer, who, having obtained the government of a district in Malwa by the favour of Aurungzebe, succeeded, in 1723, in expelling several Hindoo proprietors. Thereupon he fortified the town of Bhopal, built for his residence the fort of Futtyghur adjoining it, and on the death of Aurungzebe he assumed the title of Nawaub. In 1778, when the British army commanded by General Goddard marched across the greater part of Hindostan, the state of Bhopal was the only Indian power which manifested a friendly spirit; and in 1809, when another British expedition, commanded by General Close, appeared in that part of India, the nawaub of Bhopal earnestly, but in vain, petitioned to be received under British protection. The siege of Bhopal, which followed in 1813, by divisions of Scindia's and the Nagpore army, amounting to fifty or sixty thousand men, is one of the most remarkable in later days; and the conduct of the chief, whose garrison at the commencement of the siege did not exceed eight or ten thousand men, is the theme of praise and the admiration of the Mahomedans of India. The siege lasted nine months, and after it was raised the state appeared destined to enjoy but little repose. In the same year a movement by the disciplined Mahratta battalions of General Baptiste was directed against Bhopal; but the meditated attack was abandoned, and it is believed through the intervention of the British government. These friendly offices led the way to the treaty of 1818. Most of the articles of this treaty are of the usual character,—protection by the British government, and acknowledgment of its supremacy by that of Bhopal, with an understanding for subordinate co-operation. By the last article, excepting that formally announcing its conclusion, and containing the engagement for the ratification, the British government, on account of the zeal and fidelity of the nawaub, gratuitously bestowed on him in perpetuity the district of Ashta and four others. These districts, which had been taken from the Peishwa, were of considerable value. The prince with whom this treaty was negotiated lived but a short time after its conclusion, having met his death from a pistol accidentally discharged by a child. His nephew, an infant, was thereupon declared his successor, and betrothed to the infant daughter of the deceased prince. An attempt subsequently made to disturb the succession was put down by an intimation that the British government was prepared to maintain his claim, if necessary, by force. "During the minority of the prince," says Sutherland, "the form of administration was somewhat remarkable. The widow of the late nawaub was considered the head of the administration; the other influential persons being a Mahomedan, a Hindoo, and a Christian." Of the last Sir John Malcolm thus speaks:—"Shahzed Musseah, or Belthazzar Bourbona, with whom I am well acquainted. This person, who is an able man and a brave soldier, is the descendant of a Frenchman called Bourboun, who had come to India in the time of the emperor Akber." By the treaty of 1818, article six, it was stipulated that the state of Bhopal should furnish a contingent of 600 horse and 400 infantry, for the service of the British government. In 1824, an arrangement was effected, by which the proportions of the contingent were altered to 300 cavalry and 673 infantry, with two six-pounders manned by twenty gunners. This change was made with the view of operating as an inducement for allowing the force to be placed under European command. According to the latest returns, the contingent at present consists of three troops of cavalry, numbering 259 men; six companies of infantry, 522 men; forty-eight artillerymen, and four European officers. In addition to the contingent, the military force at the disposal of the state, inclusive of the quotas of the jaghiredars, or feudal chieftains, consists of 4,246 men of all arms of the service. In 1827 a new dispute arose. The nawaub had attained an age when he might expect to be admitted to the unrestricted exercise of his authority, but the begum (widow of the late nawaub) refused to surrender it, on the ground, that as the right of the claimant resulted from her adoption of him, it remained in abeyance during her life. She also refused to sanction his marriage with her daughter, and declared the betrothal void, assigning a reason not necessary to be here discussed. The British government expressed an opinion in favour of the claim of the young nawaub, and in opposition to that of the begum, but did not attempt to enforce its views by the only arguments which seemed likely to be effective. The results were, that the begum triumphed, and the once adopted, but now rejected heir, was compelled to forego his pretensions both to the government and to the begum's daughter, resigning them in favour of a younger brother. When this new candidate attained an age to assert his claims, the begum appeared as unwilling to yield to them as to those of the unfortunate aspirant who had preceded him. On various pleas she postponed the intended marriage of the prince with her daughter, and was evidently determined to retain him as long as possible in a state of pupilage. The marriage, however, at length took place; but this event wrought no change in the feelings of the begum, or, if any, it was that of inflaming her animosity towards the young nawaub. The contest for power continued until the ultimate mode of arbitration was resorted to, and the collision ended in favour of the nawaub. Under this prince an additional sum was set apart for the support of the contingent. But his reign was brief, and on his death the succession passed to his daughter, a child then only six years of age, but who has recently been recognised as the eventual ruler of Bhopal. A regency was of course appointed, and was subsequently replaced by another, including the begum, under which various useful reforms have been effected.

BHOPAL.—The principal place of the territory of the same name. The town is surrounded by a wall of masonry about two miles in circuit, within which is a fort also of masonry, but all much dilapidated. Outside the town is a large gunge or commercial quarter, with wide straight streets, but manifesting like appearances of decay. On the south-west of the town, and on a huge solid rock, is a fort called Futtygurh, having a rampart of masonry with square towers, all much dilapidated, though the residence of the nawaub, the sovereign of the state. On the south-west of the fort is a lake about four miles and a half in length, and a mile and a half in breadth; and on the east of the town another, two miles in length. Both appear to be artificial, yet have considerable depth, and abound in fish and alligators. From the former issues the Bess river; from the latter the Patra. Bhopal is the seat of the British political residency. The place is said to have derived its name from its Rajpoot founder, the minister to the celebrated Hindoo rajah Bhoj. Being noted for its fine tank, it is often denominated Bhopal Tal, or Bhopal's Lake. Distant S.W. from Allahabad 325 miles; S. from Agra, by Saugor, 335; N.W. from Calcutta, by Sumbulpore and Nagpore, 790. Lat. 23° 14′, long. 77° 33′.

BHOPALPOOR.—A town of Omutwarra, in Malwa, tributary to Scindia, situate on the route from Neemuch to Saugor, 157 miles E. of former, 149 W. of latter. It is situate on the right or east bank of the river Newuj, and appears to have been a British cantonment, subsequently done away with, as Garden styles it "old cantonment." Lat. 23° 48′, long. 76° 56′.

BHOPAWAR, in the territory of Gwalior, or possessions of Scindia, a ruinous town containing about 130 houses. It is held by the petty rajah of Amjerrah, who pays an annual tribute of 2,000 rupees. Distant S.W. of Oojein 64 miles, S.W. of Gwalior 330. Elevation above the sea 1,836 feet. Lat. 22° 35′, long. 75° 1′.

BHOPRA, in the British district of Hydrabad, province of Scinde, a town on the left bank of the river Seer, 42 miles S.E. of Tatta. Lat. 24° 12′, long. 68° 19′.

BHOPRA.—See Bapooruh.

BHORANEE.—A town in the Rajpoot state of Joudpore, distant S.W. from Joudpore 56 miles. Lat. 25° 37′, long. 72° 43′.

BHORASO, in the native territory of Gwalior, a considerable town on the left or west bank of the river Betwa, facing the town of Koorwaee, on the opposite bank. Lat. 24° 8′, long. 78° 1′.

BHOREE.—A town in the British province of Nagpoor, distant S. from Nagpoor 15 miles. Lat. 20° 56′, long. 79° 3′.

BHORE GHAUT, in the North Concan, or collectorate of Tannah, presidency of Bombay, a pass through the ghauts on the route from Bombay to Poona, 40 miles S.E. of the town of Bombay, and about the same distance N.W. of the town of Poona. It was considered the key of the Deccan in the early wars of the East-India Company with the Mahrattas of Poona; and in 1781, General Goddard, under such an impression, proposed to fortify it; but the proposal fell to the ground, being disapproved by the governor and council of Bombay. The pass is now traversed by an excellent road connecting the cities of Bombay and Poona. Sir John Malcolm, to whom the merit of this work is due, observes, "It is impossible for me to give a correct idea of this splendid work, which may be said to break down the wall between the Concan and the Deccan. It will give facility to commerce, be the greatest convenience to troops and travellers, and lessen the expense of European and other articles to all who reside in the Deccan." Tolls are levied at this pass according to rates prescribed by law, and which are to be limited to the amount necessary for keeping the road over the ghaut in good repair. Lat. 18° 48′, long. 73° 24′.

BHOREKPOOR, in the British district of Furruckabad, lieut.-gov. of the N.W. Provinces, a town on the route from Etawa to Futtehgurh, and 14 miles S.W. of the latter. The road in this part of the route is very bad; the country fertile and highly cultivated. Lat. 27° 12′, long. 79° 34′.

BHORUH, in the British district of Goorgaon, lieut.-gov. of the N.W. Provinces, a town on the route from Delhi to Rewaree, 35 miles S.W. of the former. Lat. 28° 17′, long. 76° 54′.

BHORUNPOOR, in the British district of Ghazeepoor, lieut.-gov. of the N.W. Provinces, a town on the left bank of the Ganges, 522 miles N.W. of Calcutta by water, or by land 425; E. of Ghazeepoor cantonment 50. Lat. 25° 45′, long. 84° 33′.

BHOTAN.—A native territory on the north-eastern frontier of Bengal, situate among the mountains forming the southern slope of the Himalayas. It is bounded on the north by Thibet; on the east by tracts inhabited by uncivilized mountain tribes; on the south by the British districts of Assam and Goalpara, and by the native state of Cooch Behar; and on the west by the native state of Sikkim. It extends from lat. 26° 18′ to lat. 28° 2′, and from long. 88° 32′ to long. 92° 30′. Its greatest length from east to west is 230 miles, its breadth 120, and it contains an area of 19,000 square miles. Little appears to be known regarding the political existence of this native state until late in the last century. In 1772, the territory of Cooch Behar being invaded and ravaged by the Booteahs, its ruler had recourse to the British government for military aid, which being granted, the Booteahs were expelled, pursued, and attacked within their own dominions. The Booteahs in their turn solicited the mediation of the authorities of Thibet, who, proposing a cessation of hostilities, a treaty of peace was in 1774 concluded between the British and the rajah of Bhotan. From this period little intercourse appears to have taken place with Bhotan, until the occupation by the British of Assam. In the interim, the Booteahs, taking advantage of the weakness of the native government of Assam, had seized upon several tracts of low lands lying at the foot of the mountains, called Dooars or Passes; and these were used as the means of committing depredations within the British territories. The mission of Captain Pemberton, for the purpose of putting an end to these grievances, having failed in its object, and all other means of obtaining redress and security proving alike unsuccessful, it became necessary to attack the Dooars, and measures were accordingly taken, by which they were brought under British management.

BHOTIYA COOSY.—One of the principal tributaries of the river Coosy. It rises on the southern face of the main Himalaya range, about lat. 28° 28′, long. 86° 15′, and flowing through Nepal in a southerly direction for 100 miles, falls into the San Coosy about lat. 27° 28′, long. 85° 41′.

BHOUNRAHA, in the British district of Bareilly, lieut.-gov. of the N.W. Provinces, a village on the route from the town of Bareilly to Seetapoor, and 17 miles S.W. of the former. It is situate on the right bank of the river Gurra, the bed of which is 250 yards wide, and fordable from November to June; the depth of water in that interval being usually about two feet. After the rains have set in, the passage must be made by ferry. The road in this part of the route is good; the country open, fertile, and cultivated. Lat. 28° 18′, long. 79° 49′.

BHOUPURUH, or BHOPERA, in the British district of Meerut, lieut.-gov. of the N.W. Provinces, a village on the route from Delhi to the town of Meerut, and nine miles N.E. of the former. Lat. 28° 42′, long. 77° 24′.

BHOUROOPOOR, in the British district of Mirzapoor, lieut.-gov. of the N.W. Provinces, a village on the right bank of the Ganges, 38 miles N.W. of the city of Mirzapoor. Lat. 25° 12′, long. 82° 15′.

BHOVANI.—A river taking its rise amongst the southern spurs of the Koondah group of the Neilgherries, about lat. 11° 15′, long. 76° 4′. At the Madoor, or Shoondaputty Ghaut, it receives a considerable tributary, and swelling into a large stream, continues an easterly course, and forming a junction with the Moyaar near Danaikencotta, it flows into the Cauvery near the town of Bovanikudal, after a course of about 120 miles.

BHOWANEEPORE, in the British district of Purneah, lieut.-gov. of Bengal, a town five miles from the right bank of the Coosy river, 30 miles S.W. of Purneah. Lat. 25° 34′, long. 87° 9′.

BHOWANEEPORE.—One of the southern suburbs of Calcutta, and the locality of the asylum in which destitute European and country-born lunatics are maintained at the expense of government. In sanctioning the establishment of a new public asylum of this character, the home authorities have suggested the selection of a more convenient and salubrious site for the building. Lat. 22° 31′, long. 88° 25′.

BHOWANNY.—See BHEWANNEE.

BHOWAPAR, in the British district of Goruckpore, lieut.-gov. of the N.W. Provinces, a town, the principal place of a pergunnah, on the eastern route from Azimgurh to Goruckpore cantonment, 53 miles N. of the former, 12 S. of the latter. It is situate on the river Raptee, here crossed by ferry. Buchanan, in his report, made forty years ago, states, "Bhowapar, where the office of police stands, contains 125 houses, huddled together, and buried in a thicket, the remains of a hedge by which the town was defended." It has a market; and, allowing six persons to each house, the population appears to be 750. Lat. 26° 40′, long. 83° 20′.

BHOWDA, or BHOURA. — A jaghire or feudal dependency of Colapore, within the presidency of Bombay. Its centre is in lat. 26° 33′, long. 73° 53′. The climate is unhealthy, and the country wild and rugged, a great part being overrun with thick jungle. The people are hardy, and of a warlike temperament; and until lately, travelling through the tract was attended with danger. A line of road intended to traverse it will materially conduce to its improvement.

Where cultivated, the products are rice and the inferior grains. The forests supply the adjacent parts with wood, which is floated down the streams after the monsoon. The revenue is something more than 50,000 rupees, and the military force of the chief amounts to about 500 men.

BHOWGAON, in the British district of Mirzapoor, lieut.-gov. of the N.W. Provinces, a village on the left bank of the Ganges, six miles N. of Mirzapoor, or lower down the stream; 714 N.W. of Calcutta by water, or 891 if the Sunderbund passage be taken. Lat. 25° 14′, long. 82° 32′.

BHOWNUGGUR, in the British district of Ahmedabad, in the peninsula of Kattywar, a town near the west coast of the Gulf of Cambay. It is situate on a small stream which falls into the gulf at a few miles' distance, and is converted by the tide into a good and safe harbour for shipping; and in consequence is a place of extensive trade. Though under the jurisdiction of the British district of Ahmedabad, it is the residence of the rana or chief of Gohilwar, hence called thakoor of Bhownuggur. Distance from Ahmedabad, S.W., 90 miles; Bombay, N., 200. Lat. 21° 45′, long. 72° 10′.

BHOWPOOR, in the British district of Agra, a village on the route from the town of Agra to Jeypore, and 27 miles W. of the former. The road in this part of the route is generally good, though in a few places heavy; the country rather fertile, and highly cultivated. Lat. 27° 3′, long. 77° 40′.

BHOWRA.—A town in the native state of Bhopal, distant S.W. from Bhopal 44 miles. Lat. 22° 55′, long. 76° 50′.

BHOWREH, in the British district of Poonah, presidency of Bombay, a town on the right bank of the river Beema, 85 miles S.E. of Poonah. Lat. 17° 58′, long. 75° 1′.

BHOWURGURREE.—A town in Nagpoor, distant S.E. from Nagpoor 170 miles. Lat. 19° 11′, long. 80° 43′.

BHUBEEGHUR, in the British district of Allyghur, lieut.-gov. of the N.W. Provinces, a town with a fort close to the left bank of the Kalee Nuddee (east), 10 miles E. of Allyghur cantonment, 52 miles N.E. of Agra. Lat. 27° 57′, long. 78° 18′.

BHUDDAWUR.—Formerly the designation of a jaghire on the banks of the Chumbul, from which the rajahs of that name derive their title. During the disastrous retreat of Colonel Monson before Holkar, in 1804, the chief of Bhuddawur afforded valuable assistance to Lord Lake's division; and in acknowledgment of past services, the family hold several grants of rent-free land in the district of Agra. The present chief, being a minor, is a ward of the British government, under whose arrangements a suitable education is being bestowed upon the young prince.

BHUDDUR, or PUDHOR, in Sirhind, a town thirty-six miles from the left bank of the Sutlej. It belongs to a Sikh chief, who has been deprived of independent authority in consequence of non-performance of feudatory obligations; and with the annexed territory, yields him an annual revenue estimated at 5,000*l.* Distant N.W. of Calcutta, by way of Delhi, 1,060 miles. Lat. 30° 27′, long. 75° 19′.

BHUDLEE.—A town in the peninsula of Kattywar, or territory of the Guicowar, under the political management of the presidency of Bombay, distant S.E. from Rajkote 46 miles. Lat. 22°, long. 71° 30′.

BHUDOEE, in the British district of Mirzapoor, lieut.-gov. of the N.W. Provinces, a town 20 miles N. from Mirzapoor, 29 miles W. of Benares. Lat. 25° 23′, long. 82° 38′.

BHUDOUSA, in the British district of Banda, lieut.-gov. of the N.W. Provinces, a small town situate on the Bhagee, a tributary of the Jumna, 32 miles S.W. of the right bank of the latter river, 25 miles S.E. of the town of Banda, 80 miles W. of Allahabad. Lat. 25° 15′, long. 80° 42′.

BHUDOWLEE, in the British district of Mirzapoor, lieut.-gov. of the N.W. Provinces, a town on the right bank of the Ganges, on the route from the cantonment of Mirzapoor to that of Benares, six miles N.E. of the former, 21 S.W. of the latter. The route here crosses the river by ferry. Distant N.W. from Calcutta by water 705 miles. Lat. 25° 13′, long. 82° 40′.

BHUDRUCK, in the British district of Balasore, lieut.-gov. of Bengal, a town on the route from Balasore to Cuttack, 41 miles S.W. of the former. Lat. 21°, long. 86° 39′.

BHUDWAS, in the British district of Allygurh, lieut.-gov. of the N.W. Provinces, a village on the route from the cantonment of Mynpooree to that of Allygurh, and 34 miles S.E. of the latter. It has water from wells. Lat. 27° 38′, long. 78° 35′.

BHUJEE, or BEEJEE, a small hill state, is bounded on the north by Sooket, in the Punjab, from which it is separated by the Sutlej; on the east by the petty chieftainship of Goond, tributary to the state of Keonthal; on the south by Kothee Dhami and a detached district of Pateeala; and on the west by Bhagul. It is about twenty miles in length from east to west, and seven in its greatest breadth from north to south. Its area is about seventy miles, its centre lying in about lat. 31° 13′, long. 77° 16′. It is a long narrow strip of land, extending along the left bank of the Sutlej, and up the declivity of the mountains which rise south of that river. Previously to the invasion of the Goorkhas, it was one of the twelve lordships occupying the country between the rivers Tonse and Sutlej; and on the expulsion of those aggressors, was by the British government conferred on the present family. It comprises ten pergunnahs, having a population, estimated, perhaps too highly, at 25,000, and a revenue of 3,000*l.*; out of which a tribute of 144*l.* is paid to the East-India Company. The rana has about 1,000 armed retainers.

BHUGOO, or BHUGGU, in the Rajpoot state of Joudpore, a village on the route from Nagor to Bickaneer, and 22 miles N.W. of the former. Lat. 27° 27′, long. 73° 37′.

BHUGWANPOOR, in the British district of Bareilly, lieut.-gov. of the N.W. Provinces, a village on the route from the town of Bareilly to Shahjehanpoor, and 15 miles S.E. of the former place. Lat. 28° 10′, long. 79° 38′.

BHUGWAN TALAO, in the British district of Mirzapoor, lieut.-gov. of the N.W. Provinces, a village on the route from Mirzapoor cantonment to Saugor, 13 miles S.W. of the former, 74 N.E. of the latter. The route in this part is an excellent made road. Lat. 25° 4′, long. 82° 27′.

BHUGWUNPOOR, in the British district of Suharunpoor, lieut.-gov. of the N.W. Provinces, a town on the route from Suharunpoor to Hurdwar, and 18 miles E. of the former town. Distant N.W. from Calcutta 963 miles. Lat. 29° 56′, long. 77° 53′.

BHUGWUNTGURH, in the Rajpoot state of Jeypore, a village on the route from Agra to Boondee, 130 miles S.W. of former, 67 N.E. of latter. It is situate at the base of a hill, on the top of which is a fort. Lat. 26° 9′, long. 76° 24′.

BHUKRA, in the British district of Allygurh, lieut.-gov. of the N.W. Provinces, a village on the route from the cantonment of Allygurh to that of Muttra, and five miles S.W. of the former. Lat. 27° 49′, long. 78° 7′.

BHUMAL, in Sirhind, a village on the route from Loodiana to Ferozpoor, and 23 miles W. of the former town. It is situate a mile and a half from the left bank of the Sutlej, in an open country, partially cultivated, and having in general a sandy soil. Distant N.W. from Calcutta 1,125 miles. Lat. 30° 56′, long. 75° 32′.

BHUMREE.—A town in the territory of Oude, distant N. from Oude 53 miles. Lat. 27° 34′, long. 82° 22′.

BHUNDRI, in Sirhind, a village on the route from Loodiana to Ferozpoor, and 20 miles W. of the former town. It is situate on the left bank of the Sutlej, and seems likely soon to be swept away by the violence of the current. It is meanly built of mud, the roofs of the houses being either of the same material or of thatch. There are a few shops and a mosque; most of the population consisting of Mussulmans, of Rajpoot descent. The population is about 600. Distant N.W. from Calcutta 1,122 miles. Lat. 30° 58′, long. 75° 38′.

BHUNEEANA, in the Rajpoot state of Joudpoor, a small town on the route from Pokhurn to Balmeer, and 22 miles S. of the former. It is situate in a depressed tract, traversed by a torrent, the bed of which is devoid of water in the dry season; but in the rainy season there is a considerable current, which was formerly collected by an embankment, so as to form a very large tank. In 1822 the violence of the stream made a breach in the embankment, so that the tank was emptied, and though repaired in the following year at an expense of 400*l.*, it was again, in 1824, rendered useless by a fresh flood, which, making its way through all obstacles, swept over the country and destroyed a village several miles lower down. The tank has not since been repaired; but an abundant supply of good water is obtained from twenty-four wells, most of which are twenty feet deep, and some not more than ten. There is a fort thirty yards long and twenty yards broad, with four bastions, the whole being built of sun-dried brick. The population is about 2,000. Lat. 26° 39′, long. 71° 53′.

BHUNGAR, or MINUS, in Sirmoor, a stream rising on the eastern declivity of the Chur Peak, in lat. 30° 44′, long. 77° 38′. After a course of about fifteen miles in a north-easterly direction, it falls into the Tons, in lat. 30° 46′, long. 77° 46′.

BHUNOOR.—A town in the territory of Hyderabad, or dominions of the Nizam, distant S.W. from Hyderabad 138 miles. Lat. 15° 59′, long. 77° 6′.

BHURHILA, in the British district of Bareilly, lieut.-gov. of the N.W. Provinces, a village on the route from the town of Bareilly to Shahjehanpoor, and four miles S.E. of the former. Lat. 28° 17′, long. 79° 33′.

BHURKHORA, in the British district of Sarun, lieut.-gov. of Bengal, a town six miles W. of the route from Chupra to Bettiah, 22 miles N. of the former. Lat. 26° 5′, long. 84° 46′.

BHURMSIR, in the Rajpoot state of Jessulmeer, a considerable village in the great desert, 100 miles N.E. of Jessulmeer. Lat. 27° 42′, long. 72° 10′.

BHUROKHAREE, in the British district Kumaon, lieut.-gov. of the N.W. Provinces, a fort on the route from Almora to Bareilly, and 30 miles S. of the former. It is situate on the right bank of the river Bullea or Goula, which here flows to the plain down a beautiful and well-wooded valley. Elevation above the sea 1,709 feet. Lat. 29° 15′, long. 79° 36′.

BHUROLE.—A town in Guzerat, or dominions of the Guicowar, distant N.W. from Deesa 40 miles. Lat. 24° 31′, long. 71° 30′.

BHURTAPOOR, in the territory of Oude, a town near the northern frontier towards Nepaul. It is situate in a low swampy expanse or island, at the confluence of some large streams, which, flowing from Nepaul, fall into the Gogra at this place. Tieffenthaler mentions, that in his time (eighty years ago) it was surrounded by a wall. Distant 100 miles N. of Lucknow. Lat. 28° 20′, long. 81° 3′.

BHURTPOOR, in the British district of Tirhoot, lieut.-gov. of Bengal, a town on the left bank of the river Byar, 24 miles S. of Mozufferpoor. Lat. 25° 44′, long. 85° 32′.

BHURTPORE.—A native state, named from its principal place, and politically connected with the government of India. It is bounded on the north by the British district Goorgaon; on the north-east by Muttra, and on the east by Agra; on the south and south-west by the Rajpoot states of Kerowlee and Jeypore; on the west by that of Macherry or Alwur; and lies between lat. 26° 43′—27° 50′, long. 76° 54′—77° 49′. It is about seventy-seven miles in length from north to south, and fifty in breadth. The area is stated to be 1,978 square miles. The northern part of the territory appears to be for the most part depressed, so as to form an extensive irregular and shallow basin, bounded by low hills, and receiving torrents from Alwur, terminating in the jhils or small lakes of Deeg and its vicinity. The only perennial streams appear to be the Manisni in the north, and the Baun river, with its tributary the Gumir, in the south; but the two latter are mere rills during the dry season. The country suffers from want of water; yet the soil, though in many places sandy, is rendered highly productive by the indefatigable industry of the inhabitants in promoting its irrigation from numerous wells, some of them very deep. Heber says, "The crops of corn now on the ground were really beautiful; that of cotton, though gone by, showed marks of having been a very good one; what is a sure proof of wealth, I saw several sugar-mills and large pieces of ground whence the cane had just been cleared." He adds, that the whole presented a picture of prosperous industry superior to anything which he had been led to expect, or which he had seen in the British territories since leaving the southern parts of Rohilcund. A far less favourable account is, however, given by Sleeman of the aspect and productiveness of the territory; but he appears to have believed that the immediate vicinity of the town of Bhurtpore was improving. The population may be estimated at 600,000 souls. The rajah and most of his people are Jauts, professing Brahminism, with considerable latitude. The revenue of the rajah is stated at about 170,000*l.* per annum. The military force maintained by the rajah consists of 1,500 cavalry, armed with matchlock and sword, 200 artillery, and 1,500 infantry, with a sebundy corps of about 2,200, maintained for purposes of police and revenue. A few field-pieces in addition complete the military strength of the state.

Probably the first authentic information respecting the remote ancestors of the present possessor of Bhurtpore is to be found in Ferishta, who states, that in 1026 a horde of Jauts or Juts molested Mahmood of Ghuznee on his return from Guzerat, and was nearly exterminated by him. In 1397, Tamerlane, marching towards Delhi, fell in with and massacred a horde of the same race, then, as well as others of their lineage long after, noted freebooters. In 1525, the army of Baber was harassed by them in his march through the Punjab. Perhaps no race more distinctly exhibits the physical traits of Hindoo lineage, and they may with probability be regarded as the aboriginal population of the plains lying along the Indus and its tributaries. Tod, in *Journal Asiatique*, May, 1827, maintains that the Jauts are of the same stock as the Getæ and Massagetæ of the classical writers, the Jutes of Jutland in Denmark, and, consequently, as the Anglo-Saxon conquerors of England. He does not, however, adduce any even slightly plausible grounds for so improbable a notion. In the reign of Muhammad Shah, of Delhi, and in the year 1720, Chooraman, the elected leader of the Jauts, supported the cause of the Seiads Husan Ali Khan and Abdullah, who had revolted. He was rewarded for his aid with 200,000 mohurs; but the Seiads being overcome, Chooraman incurred the enmity of the padshah. After the death of Chooraman, his son, growing in audacity, disdained to preserve any semblance of subordination towards the court of Delhi. A considerable army was despatched against him, but it was utterly defeated, and a rich booty gained by the Jaut victor. Sooraj Mal, grandson of Chooraman, was favoured by the rajahs of Jeypore, by whose aid the forts of Deeg and Koombher were built, probably about the year 1730. Bhurtpore is noticed as a place of strength about the same time, or perhaps a few years later. Sooraj Mal bore an important part in the distraction which marked the fall of the empire of Delhi. In 1754 he was enabled, by the strength of his forts, to baffle the confederated forces of the Vizier Ghazi-uddin, the Mahrattas, and the Rajpoots of Jeypore, but thought it expedient to soothe his enemies by a payment equal to 70,000*l.* In 1756 he received the title of rajah. Subsequently the power and resources of the Jauts became so considerable, that in 1760, their ruler, Sooraj Mal, rajah of Bhurtpore, as he was now called, joined with 30,000 men the great army of Hindoos, confederated under Sedasheo Bhao, to oppose Ahmed Shah Dooranee in his invasion of Hindostan. Alarmed at the misconduct, and irritated at the insolence of Sedasheo Bhao, Sooraj Mal seceded from the confederacy, and thus escaped the carnage of the ensuing defeat at Paniput. It was during the confusion resulting from this battle, and probably in 1761, that Sooraj Mal obtained possession of Agra, by bribing the commander of the garrison; and having thus brought the power of the Jauts to the greatest height which it ever attained, he was soon after killed in action against Nujeeb ad Dawlah, commander of the forces of Delhi. Agra was in 1774 wrested from Nawal Singh, the son of Sooraj Mal, by

Nujeef Khan, nominally the commander-in-chief of the army of Delhi, but in reality an independent potentate. Rennell observes, that previously to this reverse, the Jauts of Bhurtpore "appear to have possessed a tract of country along both sides of the Jumna river, from the neighbourhood of Gwalior to that of Delhi, in length about 160 miles, and fifty broad." After a period of great distraction, in which several rulers rose and passed away by assassination or casualty, Runjeet Singh, one of the offspring of Sooraj Mal, became rajah of Bhurtpore about the close of the eighteenth century. The first political relations between the British government and Bhurtpore appear to have commenced under the rule of this rajah, with whom, in September, 1803, a treaty offensive and defensive was concluded, with proviso, that no tribute should be demanded from him, neither should there be any interference with the internal affairs of his raj; and in the same year the favourable feeling of the British government towards the ruler of Bhurtpore was shown by a gratuitous grant of twenty pergunnahs in the district of Agra. They were ill bestowed; for in 1804, after some less overt acts of hostility, the artillery of the rajah mounted on the fortifications of Deeg opened on the British troops engaged beneath its walls against the Mahratta army of Holkar. The cavalry of the rajah had also joined that of the Mahratta chief. In consequence of this hostile demonstration, the fortress of Deeg was, towards the close of the year, besieged by the British army under General, afterwards Lord Lake, and carried by storm. In January, 1805, Lake invested the fort of Bhurtpore, in which, according to native report, were 8,000 men. A breaching-battery of six eighteen-pounders, and one of four eight-inch and four five-and-half-inch mortars, were the means of offence with which operations were commenced against defences of vast size, massive proportions, and singular tenacity. Four successive attempts at storming were with little difficulty repelled by the well-prepared Jauts; and the British army, after a loss of 388 killed, 1,894 wounded, and fifty-two missing,—a total of 2,334, was compelled to retire. Though victorious, the rajah was obviously alarmed by the pertinacity of the besiegers, and his success was followed by overtures for peace. A treaty was accordingly concluded on the 17th April, 1805. The rajah's territory was guaranteed to him; mutual aid was stipulated for, when required by either government; the rajah was bound to pay to the East-India Company twenty lacs of rupees (200,000*l.*), of which three lacs were to be paid immediately, two more in two months, three more in April, 1806, the same amount in the succeeding year, four in 1808, and the remaining five in 1809. As a bonus on good behaviour, the payment of the last instalment was to be remitted in case the rajah's conduct should prove satisfactory; but the territory granted in 1803 to the rajah was resumed by the British government. In 1825, the death of Rajah Buldeo Singh gave occasion to a dispute respecting the succession. The more powerful party maintained the claim of Doorjun Sal, the deceased rajah's brother. Sir David Ochterlony, the British political agent for Rajpootana, favoured the supporters of Buldeo Singh, the infant son of the late rajah, and to carry his views into effect assembled a well-appointed army of 15,000 men, with a train of 100 pieces of artillery, and marched towards Bhurtpore; but his operations were peremptorily countermanded by the chief government, though subsequently, towards the close of the same year, indications of hostile feelings in Doorjun Sal appeared to point out the expediency of his deposal and the establishment of the infant Buldeo Singh in his place. To effect this purpose, Lord Combermere, commander-in-chief, invested the town with an army computed to exceed 20,000 men, with 112 pieces of ordnance, besides fifty belonging to the horse-artillery. The fire of the besieging batteries, though maintained with great vigour, being found not to make a satisfactory impression on the defences, which were constructed of mud, supported and bound by beams and logs, recourse was had to mining; and on the 18th January, 1826, a mine of great dimensions having been sprung with good effect, the place was stormed and taken, after a desperate resistance made for an hour by the garrison, of whom 6,000 are reported to have been killed. The garrison was computed at the commencement of the siege to amount to 20,000 men; and all who escaped the carnage were made prisoners. The total loss on the part of the British was 103 killed, 466 wounded, and nine missing. Doorjun Sal, attempting to escape, was taken prisoner, with his wife and two sons. The ordnance captured amounted to 133 serviceable pieces, and two broken and dismounted. The amount of prize-money distributed was 481,100*l.* The other Jaut forts, Biana, Waer, Koombher, Deeg, and Kama, were forthwith surrendered. The fortifications of the city of Bhurtpore were completely dismantled, the infant Bulwunt Singh was established as rajah, and a treaty concluded, by which the indemnification of the British government for the expenses of the war was stipulated for, and the admission of a resident political agent agreed to. Doorjun Sal was deported to Benares, where, until his death, which occurred in 1851, he received from the British government an allowance of 50*l.* per month, his mother and son having an allowance of the same amount for their support. Some years after these transactions, the rajah, Buldeo Singh, on attaining competent age, was admitted to the exercise of the sovereign authority. The British troops were withdrawn; but the reconstruction of the fortifications of Bhurtpore was interdicted. Buldeo Singh, who was conspicuous for the efficiency of his administration, and for the personal kindness which he manifested in his intercourse with his subjects, died in 1854, when arrangements were made by the British government for carrying on the administration during the minority of his infant son.

BHURTPORE, the principal place of the territory of the same name, is a rather large town, being three miles in length, one and a quarter in breadth, and about eight in circumference. Its site is somewhat depressed; and this circumstance, in a military point of view, contributes to its strength, as the water of a neighbouring jhil, or small lake, being higher than the ditch of the town, can be discharged into it in such a volume as to render it unfordable. This precaution having been taken on the occasion of Lord Lake's attack in 1805, the difficulty of gaining the breaches was one of the main causes of the ill success of that attempt. A movement to flood the ditch at the commencement of the siege by Lord Combermere in 1825, was rendered abortive by the promptness of a British detachment, which took post so as effectually to prevent the opening of a passage for the flow of water from the jhil. The defences of the town and of the fort within it having been dismantled, those celebrated works are now shapeless piles of mud, and the town itself is merely a great collection of hovels, presenting nothing interesting to the traveller. The dismantled fort, or citadel, contains the palace of the rajah, consisting of "three detached buildings; one for the chief, another for the females of his family, and the third for his court of justice." Tieffenthaler, writing of its state about seventy years ago, describes it as a town recently built by the Jat ruler, who in a short time converted it from an insignificant place into a populous city, inclosed with a wall and ditch. Notwithstanding the prejudicial effects produced by its capture in 1826, and the meanness of its buildings, Bhurtpore is considered to be still a thriving place, owing probably to its having considerable transit-trade, especially in the salt of the Sambur Lake, in Rajpootana. The population has been estimated at 100,000, which seems a large number for the capital of so small a state, yet may appear the less improbable when the great extent of the town itself is taken into consideration. The place was, after Lord Lake's attack, much enlarged, so that the fort, of which one side then overlooked the country, was subsequently quite inclosed within the city walls. Bhurtpore was probably founded in the early part of the eighteenth century, when the Jats of this part of India were becoming powerful, and was perhaps named after Bharat, a legendary character of great note in Hindoo lore. It is considered to be under the tutelary influence of Krishna, and during the first siege, in 1805, some of the native soldiers in the British service declared that they distinctly saw the town defended by that divinity, "dressed in yellow garments, and armed with his peculiar weapons, the bow, mace, conch, and pipe." Distant W. from Agra 34 miles, S.W. from Muttra 22, S. from Delhi 119, N.W. from Calcutta by Agra 817. Lat. 27° 12′, long. 77° 33′.

BHURWAREH, in the British district of Tirhoot, lieut.-gov. of Bengal, a town six miles N. of the route from Mozufferpoor to Purneah, 23 miles N.E. of the former. Lat. 26° 12′, long. 85° 49′.

BHURWAROO, in the British district of Humerpore, lieut.-gov. of the N.W. Provinces, a town on the route by Keitha from Jubbulpore to Calpee, 65 miles S. of the latter. Lat. 25° 23′, long. 79° 37′.

BHUTEURA, a village in the hill state of Joobul, Cis-Sutlej territory, is situate on the route from Chepal to Deohra, and four miles N. of the former place. It is laid down in the trigonometrical survey under the name of Briteowry. Lat. 30° 58′, long. 77° 40′.

BHUTNEER, or BHUTNAIR.—A town at present belonging to the rajah of Bikaneer, but formerly the principal place of Bhuttiana, or the country of the Bhattis or Bhuttis. Tod gives it as his opinion, that "to a colony of this race Bhutnair owes its name, though not its existence." This emigration of the Bhatti Rajputs is stated by Thomas to have taken place about six centuries ago. They permanently established themselves as the predominant class, though the majority are Jats, supposed to be the aboriginal population of the country. Though the surrounding country is now a desert, and water can seldom be met with outside the town at a less distance than twelve miles, it was formerly well watered, cultivated, and populous, as appears from the numerous sites of towns and villages built of excellent brick. The universal desolation and depopulation is attributed by Colvin to the want of water, caused by the inhabitants of the protected Sikh states further north, who, for the purposes of irrigation, dam up the Gagur and other rivers, and cause them to spread over the country, where they are lost by absorption and evaporation. Sharifuddin, however, describing its attack by Tamerlane in 1397, mentions that the surrounding country was then a desert, and that the town was supplied with water from a great lake filled by inundations. He adds, that the transit-trade had rendered it very wealthy. It surrendered to the invaders, who, however, finding occasion for quarrel, began to plunder and massacre the inhabitants; and they in despair having slaughtered their women and children, rushed on the Moguls, great numbers of whom fell, until the Bhattis were slain to a man, and the place so utterly demolished, that no trace remained of human habitation. It was subsequently rebuilt and fortified, and belonged to the maharajah of Bickaner in 1800, when it was attacked by the bold adventurer George Thomas, to whom it capitulated after the rampart had been breached. The Bhattis at that time formed a collection of hordes of freebooters, who held the tract now forming the northern part of Bahawulpoor and of Bickaner, the southern of Sirhind, and that part of the British district of Hurriana west of Hansee. Thomas reported them as "cruel in their nature, savage and ferocious in the highest degree; that they have an utter abhorrence of all the usages of civilized life, are thieves from their birth, and scruple not, in their predatory incursions into the neighbouring districts, though unresisted, to add murder to robbery." The greater part of Bhuttiana is now comprised in the British district of that name. Bhutneer is distant N.W. from Calcutta 1,094 miles, N.W. from Delhi 207. Lat. 29° 34′, long. 74° 26′.

BHUTORA, or BETOURA, in the British district of Futtehpoor, lieut.-gov. of the N.W. Provinces, a town on the right bank of the Ganges, eight miles N. of the town of Futtehpoor. It is a place of some note, and is mentioned by Heber as the station of the civil magistrate of the district at the time when he wrote, about thirty years ago. Distant N.W. from Calcutta, by land 592 miles, by the course of the Ganges 906. Lat. 26° 2′, long. 80° 56′.

BHUTOWLAH, in the British district of Moradabad, lieut.-gov. of the N.W. Provinces, a village on the route from Allygurh to the town of Moradabad, and 29 miles S.W. of the latter. Lat. 28° 33′, long. 78° 32′.

BHUTTEEAREE, in the British district of Chittagong, lieut.-gov. of Bengal, a town on the route from Chittagong to Tipperah, 12 miles N.W. of the former. Lat. 22° 30′, long. 91° 49′.

BHUTTIANA.—A British district in Northern India, subject to the jurisdiction of the lieut.-gov. of the N.W. Provinces, and so called from having been the possession of the Bhuttis or Bhattis, of Rajpoot descent. It is bounded on the north by the territories of Bahawulpore and the protected Sikh states; on the east by the British district of Hurriana; on the south by the state of Bickaner; and on the west by that of Bahawulpoor. It lies between lat. 29° 12′—30° 29′, long. 73° 1′—75° 22′, and extends from the borders of Hurriana to the river Sutlej. Its outline, which is very irregular, incloses an area of 3,017 square miles. The western part, being the northern skirt of the great sandy desert, is nearly waste and uninhabited. In the middle and eastern parts, the soil, when properly watered, is very productive. The numerous ruins of towns and villages throughout Bhuttiana prove it to have been once prosperous and populous, probably when the river Guggur, flowing by the town of Bhutneer, made its way to the Sutlej above Bahawulpoor. That this tract was formerly less arid, is proved by the fact stated by Sharifuddin, that at the time of Tamerlane's invasion, at the close of the fourteenth century, Bhutneer was supplied with water from an extensive lake. George Thomas, when at Bhutneer, was informed that the Guggur formerly ran along the north side of that place, but that "its channel had been choked up by vast quantities of earth forced down from the mountains; and, according to the prevailing opinion of the natives, though now lost in the sands west of the city, it formerly extended as far as the Sutluj, which it joined in the vicinity of Ferozepore." Measures are in progress for the improvement of the irrigation of the district, by means of channels connected with this river. The Chitang, a river running in some measure parallel to the Guggur, but a little farther east, formerly united with it near Raneah; and a few years ago a canal was made by British engineers, to draw from the canal of Feroz Shah a supply of water to replenish the Chitang, which in this part of its course had been nearly obliterated. The population of this thinly-peopled tract is reckoned at 112,974, of whom 65,363 are Hindoos, and 47,611 Mahometans and others.

The cessions made by Scindia in 1803, under the treaty of Serjee Anjengaum, brought the British into immediate and intimate connection with this country, which they made great efforts to improve; but the lawless and predatory habits of the people long resisted all their attempts. In 1810 it became necessary to march into the country a military force, under Colonel Adams, when the chief, Bahadur Khan, was expelled; but his son, Zabeta Khan, having submitted unconditionally, the greater part of the country was placed under him. It however remained in an unquiet and unsettled state, and within a very few years it became necessary formally to undertake the task of defining its boundaries and those of the neighbouring states; disturbance and confusion having produced their usual effects in obliterating them. A strip of land on the Sutlej, required for the continuation of the British customs line to that river, was readily ceded by the rajah of Bahawulpore in 1844, and constitutes the north-western angle of Bhuttiana.

BHYNS, in the British district of Muttra, lieut.-gov. of the N.W. Provinces, a village on the route from the city of Agra to Bareilly, and 19 miles N.E. of the former. Lat. 27° 22′, long. 78° 15′.

BHYNTHUREE, in the native state of Nepal, a fort on the summit of a mountain two miles E. of the left bank of the Kalee (eastern), 14 miles. E. of Petorabgurh cantonment. Elevation above the sea 5,615 feet. Lat. 29° 34′, long. 80° 30′.

BHYRAH, in the British district of Tirhoot, lieut.-gov. of Bengal, a town on the route from Patna to Carraree, 64 miles N.E. of the former. Lat. 25° 51′, long. 86° 16′.

BHYROWALAH.—A village in the Punjab, at a ferry over the Beas river, here found to be 740 yards wide when crossed by the British mission under Elphinstone, in the end of July, at which season the water is highest. The current was so rapid on that occasion, that several of the boats employed were swept ten miles down the stream. Though the river is so formidable, the boats are wretched craft, no better than small rafts, with a plank one foot high all round, and draw only six inches water. Lat. 31° 25′, long. 75° 13′.

BHYRVEE.—A river of Nepal, rising in lat. 29° 16′, long. 81° 58′, and, flowing in a south-westerly direction for about seventy miles, falls into the Kurnalli in lat. 28° 38′, long. 81° 17′, on the borders of Oude.

BHYS, or BHAIS.—A small river, the head-water of which is supplied from the tank of Bhopal, in lat. 23° 14′, long. 77° 22′. Flowing north-east for forty-five miles, it falls into the Betwa, on the left side, near the town of Bhilsa, and in lat. 23° 32′, long. 77° 50′.

BHYSONDAH.—See BYNSONT.

BIANA, in the territory of Bhurtpore, a town on the route from Agra to Mhow, 50 miles S.W. of the former. It is situate on an eminence in a small plain, between two ranges of hills, running in some measure parallel to each other, and in a direction from north-east to south-west. The town contains many temples, and the whole ridge of the hill is covered with the remains of large buildings; among which, the most remarkable is a fort containing a high pillar of stone, called Bhim Lat, or the Staff of Bhim, conspicuous for a great distance through the country. This place was formerly of much greater importance; its downfall was hastened by the rajah of Bhurtpoor, who, in the middle of the last century, expelled from it a considerable number of its Mussulman inhabitants of Afghan descent. Latterly, however, it appears to have revived; it is now of considerable size, and possesses some large well-built houses of stone. It is mentioned by Ferishta as a place of importance in 1491, when it stood a siege against Sikandar Lodi, the Patan monarch of Delhi. Baber describes it in 1526 as one of the most famous forts in India. It was at that time held by an Afghan chief, who surrendered it to Baber. In the following year a very sanguinary and obstinately-contested battle was fought near this town, between Baber and Rana Sanka, the Rajpoot prince of Oodeypoor, who was ultimately defeated with great slaughter. Biana is distant N.W. from Calcutta 851 miles. Lat. 26° 57′, long. 77° 20′.

BIANS.—See BEEANS.

BIARMI, or BEARMA.—A river rising amidst the Vindhya range, in the Saugor and Nerbudda territory, at an elevation of 1,700 feet above the sea, and in lat. 23° 20′, long. 79° 3′, and taking a north-east course of about 110 miles, falls into the Sonar, on the right side, in lat. 24° 20′, long. 79° 55′. About ten miles lower down, or farther north-east, the united stream falls into the Cane. The slope of its channel is 700 feet.

BICCAVOLE, in the British district of Rajahmundry, presidency of Madras, a town 18 miles E. from Rajahmundry, 16 miles N.W. of Coringa. Lat. 16° 57′, long. 82° 6′.

BICHNEE.—See BIKAIRI.

BICHOLIM, in the Portuguese territory of Goa, a town on the route from the seaport of Agoada to Belgaum, distant N.E. from the former 14 miles, N. from Goa 8 miles. Lat. 15° 36′, long. 74° 1′.

BICKANEER.—See BEEKANEER.

BICKRAMPOOR, in the British district of Southern Cachar, lieut.-gov. of Bengal, a town 52 miles E. from Sylhet, 13 miles N.W. of Silchar. Lat. 24° 55′, long. 92° 42′.

BIDDREE.—A town in the Southern Mahratta jaghire of Jamkundee, presidency of Bombay. It is situated on the north or left bank of the river Kistnah, 14 miles E. from the town of Jamkundee. Lat. 16° 32′, long. 75° 31′.

BIDHNOO, in the British district of Cawnpore, lieut.-gov. of the N.W. Provinces, a town on the route from the cantonment of Banda to that of Cawnpore, and 11 miles S. of the latter. Lat. 26° 20′, long. 80° 19′.

BIDJEY GURH, or BIJIGARH, in the British district of Mirzapore, lieut.-gov. of the N.W. Provinces, a ruinous fortress "on the top of a high mountain, covered from its base to its summit with wood," and most difficult of access. In the autumn of 1781, Cheyt Singh, the refractory zemindar of Benares, took refuge in this fort, where he had previously placed his family and the greater part of his treasure; but Major Popham having advanced to invest it, the zemindar took to flight, with everything valuable which he could remove. The place was, however, defended for a time in the names of the wife and mother of the fugitive, who remained, but finally surrendered. The fort is situate nine miles N. of the left bank of the river Son, and 50 S. of Benares. Lat. 24° 34′, long. 83° 9′.

BIDJWASIN, in the British district of Delhi, lieut.-gov. of the N.W. Provinces, a village on the route from Delhi to Rewari, and 15 miles S.W. of the former. Lat. 28° 30′, long. 77° 7′.

BIDOULEE, a small town in the British district of Muzuffernuggur, lieut.-gov. of the N.W. Provinces, is situate on the route from Kurnal to Meerut, and 13 miles S.E. of the former. It has a bazaar, and is abundantly supplied with water. Lat. 29° 34′, long. 77° 10′.

BIGAHPOOR, in the district of Bainswara, territory of Oude, a town four miles N.E. of the left bank of the Ganges, 40 S.W. of Lucknow. Butter estimates the population at 6,000, including 100 Mussulmans. Lat. 26° 24′, long. 80° 33′.

BIGANBAREE, in the British district of Mymunsing, lieut.-gov. of Bengal, a town on the left bank of the Kunkas river, 19 miles N. of Jumalpoor. Lat. 25° 10′, long. 90°.

BIGGAREE.—A canal of irrigation, in the Shikarpoor district of the province of Sinde, issuing from the Indus in lat. 28° 3′, long. 69° 6′, and having a course of about thirty miles.

BIGHEURA, in the British district of Purneah, lieut.-gov. of Bengal, a town on the right bank of the river Nagore, 32 miles S.E. of Purneah. Lat. 25° 32′, long. 88°.

BIGROULI, in the hill state of Joobul, Cis-Sutlej territory, under British protection, a considerable village on the route from Chepal to Deohra, and five miles N. of the former. It has a romantic site on the right bank of a stream called the Nar, and is inhabited by Brahmins. Lat. 31° 1′, long. 77° 38′.

BIHAR, or BAHADURGANJ.—A town and fort in the territory of Oude, 75 miles S. from Lucknow, and 44 miles N.W. from Allahabad. Population 10,000. Lat. 25° 50′, long. 81° 24′.

BIHTA, in the district of Bainswara, territory of Oude, a village on the left bank of the river Sai, 55 miles S.E. of Lucknow, 60 N.W. of Allahabad. It is noted for its manufacture of salt. Lat. 26° 10′, long. 81° 20′.

BIJAHUREE, in the British district of Allygurh, lieut.-gov. of the N.W. Provinces, a village on the route from the city of Agra to Allygurh cantonment, and 15 miles S. of the latter. Lat. 27° 42′, long. 78° 9′.

BIJAWUR, in Bundelcund, the principal place of the small territory of the same name, is situate in a mountainons tract 23 miles S. of Chutterpore, 70 N.E. of Saugor, and in lat. 24° 37′, long. 79° 31′. The small raj or state of which it is the capital lies between lat. 24° 22′ and 25°, long. 78° 58′ and 79° 50′, and was supposed, in 1832, to contain 920 square miles and 344 villages, with a population of 90,000 souls. In 1849 it was reported to yield a revenue of 22,500*l*. This state pays no tribute, but maintains a force of 100 horse and 1,300 foot. The right of the rajah, a Boondela Rajpoot, results from his descent from Dewan Beer Singhe Deo, natural son of Juggut Raj, son of Chuttur Sal, the founder of the short-lived independence of Bundelcund. After the acquisition of Bundelcund by the East-India Company, a grant was made in 1811, confirming the right of Rutten Singh, then rajah; on whose death without issue, in 1833, his nephew succeeded.

BIJAYANAGAR.—A ruined city, formerly the metropolis of the Brahminical realm of Bijayanagar, or Carnata, the power of which was destroyed in 1565, at the battle of Talicot, by a confederacy of the Mussulman kings of the Deccan. Lat. 15° 19′, long. 76° 32′.

BIJBAHAR, or VIGIPARA, in Kashmir, the largest town in the valley, after the capital, is situate on the banks of the Jailum, about 25 miles S.E. of the city of Kashmir. Over the river here is one of those singular and simply-constructed timber bridges, which, notwithstanding the apparently frail nature of their fabric, have endured for centuries, in consequence of the exemption of the country from storms or inclement weather. There is nothing else worthy of notice except a considerable bazaar. Lat. 33° 47′, long. 75° 13′.

BIJEYPOOR, in the British district of Mirzapoor, lieut.-gov. of the N.W. Provinces, a town three miles S. of the route from Mirzapoor to Allahabad, 15 miles W. of the former. Lat. 25° 8′, long. 82° 24′.

BIJIPOOR.—A town in the native state of Gwalior, or possessions of Scindia, distant S.W. from Gwalior 52 miles. Lat. 26° 2′, long. 77° 28′.

BIJNA, in Bundelcund, a town on the route from Banda to Jhansi, 95 miles W. of the former, 40 E. of the latter. It is the principal place of a jaghire or feudal possession, which, despoiled of several villages by the state of Jhansi, is now comprised within an area of twenty-seven miles, containing six villages, with a population of 2,800 souls, and yields a revenue of 8,000 rupees (800*l*.). This jaghire was formerly tributary to Jhansi, but in 1821 the obligation for the annual payment of 2,500 rupees was cancelled in consideration of the value of the resumed villages. The military force maintained consists of 125 foot and fifteen horse, with two guns. The grant was made by the East-India Company in April, 1823, in favour of the Dewan Soorjun Singh and Dewan Beejye Bahadoor. Bijna is in lat. 25° 27′, long. 79° 5′.

BIJNEE.—A town in the native state of Bhotan, the principal place of a subdivision of territory of the same name, distant N.E. from Goalpara 20 miles. Lat. 26° 23′, long. 90° 50′.

BIJNOUR, in the territory of Oude, a town on the route from Allahabad to Lucknow, 114 miles N.W. of the former, 14 S. of the latter. Lat. 26° 44′, long. 80° 59′.

BIJNOUR, a British district, lieut.-gov. of the N.W. Provinces, is bounded on the north-east by the British district of Gurhwal; on the east and south-east by the British district of Moradabad; on the west by the British districts Meerut, Mozuffurnugur, and Saharunpore; and lies between lat. 28° 54′—29° 58′, long. 78° 1′—78° 53′. The area is stated to be 1,904 square miles. The soil and climate are well suited to the growth of the sugar-cane, the produce of which is in much demand, and is considered little inferior to that of the West Indies. Cotton is cultivated to considerable extent, as is also wheat for exportation, especially to the west. Under the existing revenue settlement of the North-West Provinces, no increase of the land assessment in this district can take place until the year 1866. The rivers are the Koh and the Ramgunga. The amount of population, according to the returns of 1853, is 695,521.

Bijnour is part of the territory bearing the name of Rohilcund, from the Rohilla Patans, who in the last century held sway there. In 1774 their power was broken by the defeat which they received from the British, and the country became subordinate to the nawaub of Oude. Finally, in 1802, it was ceded to the East-India Company by the ruler of Oude, and embodied with the British territories.

BIJNOUR, the station of the civil authorities in the British district of Bijnour, lieut.-gov. of the N.W. Provinces, is situate on the route from Moradabad to Mozuffurnugur, and 31 miles S.E. of the latter town. Distant N.W. from Calcutta 800 miles. The population is returned at 11,745 inhabitants. Lat. 29° 22′, long. 78° 11′.

BIJOLEE, in the territory of Gwalior, a village on the route from Calpee to the fort of Gwalior, 16 miles E. of latter, 112 W. of former. Lat. 26° 13′, long. 78° 24′.

BIJOLLEE.—A town in the Rajpoot state of Oodeypore, distant N.E. from Oodeypore 101 miles. Lat. 25° 7′, long. 75° 20′.

BIJOWLEE, in the British district of Allahabad, lieut.-gov. of the N.W. Provinces, a village on the left bank of the Ganges, 774 miles N.W. of Calcutta by the river route, 34 S.E. of the city of Allahabad by the same. Lat. 25° 18′, long. 82° 11′.

BIJOWLEE, in the British district of Etawa, lieut.-gov. of the N.W. Provinces, a village on the route from the cantonment of Etawa to Calpee, and 12 miles S.E. of the former. Lat. 26° 41′, long. 79° 13′.

BIKAIRI, in the British territory of Saugor and Nerbudda, lieut.-gov. of the N.W. Provinces, a village on the route from Mirzapoor to Saugor, 235 miles S.W. of former, 27 E. of latter. Elevation above the sea 1,263 feet. Lat. 23° 53′, long. 79° 13′.

BIKANPOOR, in the British district of Meerut, lieut.-gov. of the N.W. Provinces, a village on the route from Delhi to the town of Meerut, and 18 miles N.E. of the former. Lat. 28° 45′, long. 77° 31′.

BIKARAH, in the British district of Etawa, lieut.-gov. of the N.W. Provinces, a town on the route from Lucknow, in Oude, by Nanamow Ghat, to Etawa, and 30 miles E. of the latter. Lat. 26° 45′, long. 79° 39′.

BIKEEAKEE SYN, in the British district of Kumaon, lieut.-gov. of the N.W. Provinces, a town on the left bank of the *Ramgunga* river, 22 miles N.W. of Almora. Lat. 29° 42′, long. 79° 20′.

BIKONTPORE, in the British district of Dinajepore, lieut.-gov. of Bengal, a town on the right bank of the Teesta river, 78 miles N. of Dinajepore. Lat. 26° 43′, long. 88° 36′.

BIKRAMPOOR, in the British district of Beerbhoom, lieut.-gov. of Bengal, a town on the route from Burhampoor to Kishnugur, 32 miles S. of the former. Lat. 23° 37′, long. 88° 23′.

BIKUMPOOR, in the Rajpoot state of Jessulmere, a fort in the sandy desert, 95 miles N.E. of the town of Jessulmere. It has a wall of rubble-stone twenty-five feet high and a hundred yards square, with very small bastions, and occupies the whole of an eminence in such a manner that the flat summit is level with the terre-plein of the rampart, and the exterior acclivity of the eminence gives the defence a rather stiff section. On the north-east angle is a round tower of considerable height, extensively overlooking the surrounding country. There are four guns mounted in various parts of the fort, which is garrisoned by a force not exceeding 100 men, in the service of the rawul of Jessulmere. The place, though having a rather imposing appearance, has little real strength, being completely commanded by sandhills at a short distance. At the south-east of the fort is a small town, containing about 220 houses. Population 965. Lat. 27° 43′, long. 72° 16′.

BILAREE, in the British district of Moradabad, lieut.-gov. of the N.W. Provinces, a town on the route from Coel to Moradabad, 14 miles S. of the former. Lat. 28° 36′, long. 78° 53′.

BILARIMOW, in the British district of Cawnpore, lieut.-gov. of the N.W. Provinces, a village on the route from the cantonment of Etawa to that of Cawnpore, and 39 miles W. of the latter. Lat. 26° 21′, long. 79° 51′.

BILGY, in the British district of North Canara, presidency of Madras, is situate on a stream a tributary of the river Tudri. The surrounding country is mountainous, being a rugged plateau formed by an expansion of the ghats, here of less elevation than in most other parts. Contiguous to the town is a difficult part of the route from Canara to Mysore, and hence denominated the Passes of Bilgy. The area of the tallook of Bilgy is 256 square miles, and the population, according to official return, 17,345, indicating a relative density of 67 to the square mile. The town of Bilgy is distant from Bombay, S.E., 340 miles; from Madras, W., 380. Lat. 14° 23′, long. 74° 52′.

BILHAWALLA, or BILLABAREE, in the British district of Moradabad, lieut.-gov. of the N.W. Provinces, a village on the route from the town of Moradabad to Almora, and 20 miles N. of the former. Heber, who mentions it under the name of Belagary, observes, "I was pleased with the appearance of the houses, which, though very humble, were all in good repair, showed abundance of buffaloes in their little courtyards, and were kept with a degree of cleanliness and smartness." Lat. 29° 5′, long. 78° 58′.

BILHEKI, in the British district of Bareilly, lieut.-gov. of the N.W. Provinces, a town on the route by the Bhurindeo Pass from Bareilly to Petoragurh, and 43 miles S. of the latter. Its elevation above the sea is 740 feet. Lat. 28° 59′, long. 80° 5′.

BILHOUR, or BILOUR.—A considerable town in the British district of Cawnpore, lieut.-gov. of the N.W. Provinces, on the route from Cawnpore to Futtehgurh, and 34 miles N.W. of the former. The town contains a population of 5,045. Lat. 26° 50′, long. 80° 9′.

BILLASPOOR, in Sirhind, a village on the route from Suharunpoor to Subathoo, and 33 miles N.W. of the former place. It is a poor collection of mud-built houses, though the principal place of a small district yielding an annual revenue of 1,300*l.*, which has lately escheated to the East-India Company, in consequence of the failure of heirs to the late Sikh proprietor. Distant N.W. from Calcutta 991 miles. Lat. 30° 20′, long. 77° 22′.

BILLOWNAN, in the British district of Aligurh, lieut.-gov. of the N.W. Provinces, a village on the route from Futtehgurh to Meerut, and 83 miles N.W. of the former. Lat. 27° 52′, long. 78° 32′.

BILLOWTEE, or BILOTHE, in the British district of Muttra, lieut.-gov. of the N.W. Provinces, a village on the route from Muttra cantonment to Delhi, and 17 miles N.W. of the former. Lat. 27° 40′, long. 77° 36′.

BILOHI, or BOWLEE, in the British district of Mirzapore, lieut.-gov. of the N.W. Provinces, a village on the route from Mirzapore to the town of Rewa, and 48 miles S.W. of the former. It is remarkable for a cascade of the Sunpaira, a small river, which, tumbling over the brow of the Kutra range, falls nearly perpendicularly from a height of 398 feet in its course, to discharge itself into the Adh, a tributary of the Bilund. Elevation above the sea 1,128 feet. Lat. 24° 41′, long. 82° 19′.

BILRAM, or BILGRAM, in the British district of Budaon, lieut.-gov. of the N.W. Provinces, a town on the route from Futtehgurh to Meerut, and 70 miles N.W. of the former. Lat. 27° 49′, long. 78° 39′.

BILSEE, in the British district of Budaon, lieut.-gov. of the N.W. Provinces, a town on the route from Futtygurh to Moradabad, containing a population of 5,206. Distant 13 miles N.W. of Budaon. Lat. 20° 9′, long. 79°.

BILWA, or BELAWA, in the British district of Goruckpore, lieut.-gov. of the N.W. Provinces. Buchanan describes it as a small, poor place, with a petty fort, consisting of a ditch and an earthen rampart, with a strong hedge of thorny bamboos on the counterscarp. Distant S.E. of Goruckpore cantonment 20 miles. Lat. 26° 36′, long. 83° 43′.

BIMCHUTUR, in Bussahir, a halting-place on the southern declivity of the Yoosoo Pass. It is situate amidst groves of pine, oak, and birch trees, in a beautiful sequestered glen, sheltered from the chilling winds, and ending on the north-east in a bare, rocky, and steep mountain. Elevation above the sea 11,950 feet. Lat. 31° 20′, long. 78° 6′.

BIMLIPATAM, in the British district of Vizagapatam, presidency of Madras, a town on the coast of the Bay of Bengal, 16 miles N.E. of Vizagapatam. Lat. 17° 52′, long. 83° 30′.

BINDACHAL, in the British district of Mirzapore, lieut.-gov. of the N.W. Provinces, a town on the route from Allahabad cantonment to that of Mirzapore, 53 miles S.E. of the former, and eight W. of the latter. The town is situate on the right bank of the Ganges, 456 miles N.W. of Calcutta. Lat. 25° 10′, long. 82° 30′.

BINDACHAL.—A range of mountains in and adjacent to Bundelcund, of the locality of which Franklin gives the following description:—"They commence at Kesogar, five miles north of Seunda, on the Sindh river, and making a circuitous sweep by Narawar, Chandri, Hirapur, Rajghar, Ajeyghar, and Calanjara, they cease near Barghar to belong to Bundelcund, and continue their course by Bindhyavasini and Tara, until they approach the Ganges at Surajghara, and again at Rajmahal." The appearance of the plain of Bundelcund, partially inclosed by these barriers, is said to be highly picturesque, resembling a vast bay of the sea indenting the land, but bounded and restrained by the heights by which it is skirted. Towards the south-east, the south, and south-west, the table-land is bounded by mountains rising above it to a moderate height, and denominated the Panna range.

BINDIA NOWAGURH. — See NOWAGURH.

BINDKEE KHAS, in the British district of Futtehpoor, lieut.-gov. of the N.W. Provinces, a small town on the route from Futtehpoor to Calpee, and 17 miles N.W. of the former. The surrounding country is level and cultivated. Lat. 26° 3′, long. 80° 40′.

BINDORE, in the British district of Dinajepore, lieut.-gov. of Bengal, a town on the route from Dinajepore to Purneah, 30 miles N.W. of the former. Lat. 25° 43′, long. 88° 10′.

BINDOUR, in the British district of Futtehpoor, lieut.-gov. of the N.W. Provinces, a town on the left bank of the Jumna, at the confluence of the small river Rind, 17 miles W. of the town of Futtehpoor. Lat. 25° 54′, long. 80° 34′.

BINDRABAN, in the British district of Muttra, lieut.-gov. of the N.W. Provinces, a town beautifully situate on the right bank of the Jumna, and four miles E. of the route from Muttra to Delhi. The water of the river being held sacred by the Hindoos, numerous devotees visit it for the purpose of ritual ablution, access being afforded to the stream by numerous fine ghats or flights of steps, constructed of red stone, brought from Jeypore, nearly 150 miles distant. These ghats extend for nearly a mile along the river, and are provided with numerous dewasthans, or fanes, for the more convenient performance of rites by the devotees. The ground-plan of the principal temple is cruciform, resembling that of a Gothic church, but of no great dimensions. From its vaulted roof depend numerous idols, rudely carved in wood, and the supporting pillars and walls are covered with coarse sculptures. Two other buildings, being cylindrical towers rounded off at the top, resemble in shape the celebrated black pagoda of Juggernath and the temples of Bhobaneser, but are inferior in dimensions to those extraordinary structures. There are a great number of other edifices connected with Hindoo mythology; and these become continually more numerous, as various rajahs, or other wealthy persons, from time to time build and dedicate fanes of costly and elaborate workmanship to the varied objects of their superstitious reverence. Crowds of pilgrims from all parts of India frequent this town to offer their devotions, especially to Krishna, who, according to the legend, here slew the great serpent Kaliya Naga, which, lying across the Jumna, stopped its course and poisoned the water. Here also he spent his youthful years, sporting with the Gopis or milkmaids, and playing on musical instruments. A tree is still pointed out, at the foot of which he sat, and among the branches of which the marks of his flute are said to be seen. In honour of the divinity, a festival is held from the tenth day of the light half of Kuar (September and October) to the day of the full moon, at Bindabran, where a stone platform or stage has been built for the exhibition of the mimic dance, in a square near the river-side. Here also was a favourite resort of Rama, who conquered Ravana, the giant tyrant of Lanka or Ceylon, with the aid of Hanuman, the monkey-shaped divinity, and his grotesque followers; and in recognition of those auxiliary services, the monkeys which crowd the luxuriant groves around the town are regularly fed and protected by the Brahmins, principally from a fund provided from an endowment made by the celebrated Mahratta chieftain Madhajee Scindia. One of those creatures was treated with peculiar attention, as its lameness, caused by an accidental hurt, was considered a point of resemblance to their benefactor Madhajee, who, in his flight from the battle of Paniput, was overtaken by an Afghan, who with a battle-axe gave him so severe a cut on the right knee, that he was for life deprived of the use of the leg of that side. The population of the town has been returned at 19,776 inhabitants. It was sacked in 1757 by a detachment of 25,000 Affghan cavalry, sent by Ahmed Shah Dooranee, under the command of Jahan Khan, who put many of the inhabitants to the sword, burned many in their houses, drove off others into slavery, and slaughtering kine, defiled the temples of the Hindoos with the blood of those animals, regarded sacred by them. Distant N.W. from Calcutta 823 miles, S. from Delhi 92. Lat. 27° 34′, long. 77° 45′.

BINEKA, in the British territory of Saugor and Nerbudda, lieut.-gov. of the N.W. Provinces, a town on the route from Saugor to Shahgurh, 20 miles N.E. of the former. Lat. 24° 4′, long. 78° 55′.

BINJOLEE.—A town in the British territory of Nagpore, distant N.E. from Bustar 15 miles. Lat. 19° 18′, long. 82° 10′.

BINOA, a river in the Northern Punjab, rises near the southern bank of the Ravee, and, flowing south-east for about fifty miles, falls into the Beas, east of Tira, and opposite Kumla Gurh, in lat. 31° 48′, long. 76° 33′. Like all the streams of the Himalaya, it varies greatly in volume, according to the season, being fordable in cold weather, but in the hot season, in consequence of the melting of the snow, becoming a deep and rapid stream.

BINSUR PEAK, in the British district of Kumaon, lieut.-gov. of the N.W. Provinces, a summit of the Sub-Himalaya, or range south of the main chain. Distant N.E. of Almorah nine miles. Elevation above the sea 7,969 feet. Lat. 29° 42′, long. 79° 48′.

BIRAHNA, in the British district of Aligurh, lieut.-gov. of the N.W. Provinces, a village on the route from the cantonment of Aligurh to that of Muttra, and 12 miles N.E. of the latter. Lat. 27° 34′, long. 77° 54′.

BIRCHIGUNG, in the British district of Kumaon, lieut.-gov. of the N.W. Provinces, an elevated pass on the route from Almorah fort, by the course of the river Goree and Unta Dhura Pass, to South-western Tibet, 114 miles N.E. of Almorah. It lies over the skirts of two great summits of the main range of the Himalaya, designated in Webb's survey peaks Nos. 16 and 17, and having respectively the heights above the sea of 18,166 and of 19,225 feet. The elevation of the crest itself of the pass is estimated by Manson at 15,000 feet. He describes the conformation of the rock as clayslate, talc, slate, and greywacke, and near the top of the pass a few blocks of quartz, all totally bare of vegetation. Lat. 30° 12′, long. 80° 17′.

BIRIMDEO, in the British district of Kumaon, lieut.-gov. of the N.W. Provinces, a town on the right bank of the river Kalee, 47 miles S.E. of Almora. Elevation above the sea 798 feet. Distant N.W. from Calcutta, by Bareilly, 842 miles. Lat. 29° 7′, long. 80° 13′.

BIRJOO, in the British district of Kumaon, lieut.-gov. of the N.W. Provinces, a village in the Bhotia subdivision of Juwahir, on the route to Hiundes, and 14 miles S. of the Juwahir Pass. It is situate on the left bank of the Goree, about a mile below its confluence with the Gunkha. Elevation above the sea 11,314 feet. Lat. 30° 23′, long. 80° 12′.

BIRKOOTE, in the British district of Beerbhoom, lieut.-gov. of Bengal, a town on the line of railway now under construction from Burdwan to Rajmahal, 83 miles N. of the former. Lat. 24° 24′, long. 87° 48′.

BIRMEE, in the British district of Ramgur, lieut.-gov. of Bengal, a town on the left bank of the Barrachur river, 42 miles N.E. of Hazareebagh. Lat. 24° 17′, long. 86°.

BIRMSIR.—A town in the Rajpoot state of Jessulmeer, distant N.W. from Jessulmeer 11 miles. Lat. 27° 3′, long. 70° 53′.

BIRSILPOOR, in the Rajpoot state of Jessulmere, a small town on the route from Bahawulpoor to Bap, and distant 90 miles S.E. of the former. It has a fort situate on a small eminence, rising to the height of about twenty feet. The town, situate at the south and east faces of the fort, contains 400 houses, many shops, and eleven wells sixty feet deep, but with water so salt as to be scarcely usable; so that the inhabitants are generally supplied from reservoirs of fresh water on the north-west side of the town. A high sandhill, a mile south-west, completely commands the whole place. On the top of it the emperor Humayun is said to have encamped nearly 400 years ago, but was refused admission into the fort. The place is of great antiquity, having been built, according to native report, in the second century of the Christian era. The chief, professing a nominal subjection to the rawul of Jessulmere, in 1835 civilly received Boileau, a British officer of engineers engaged on a mission in those regions. Birsilpoor has a population of 2,005 persons. Lat. 28° 11′, long. 72° 20′.

BIRSINGPOOR, in Bundelcund, a town on the route by the Kuttra Pass and Rewa, from Mirzapoor to Loharganow, 100 miles S.W. of Mirzapoor. It belongs to the rajah of Punnah. Elevation above the sea 1,064 feet. Lat. 24° 48′, long. 81° 1′.

BIRSINGPOOR, in the British district of Cawnpore, lieut.-gov. of the N.W. Provinces, a town on the right bank of the river Rind, 17 miles S. of the cantonment of Cawnpore. Lat. 26° 13′, long. 80° 21′.

BISALA, in the Rajpoot state of Joudpore, a small town on the route from Pokhurn to Balmer, and 16 miles N. of the latter. It is situate at the base of a rocky ridge of considerable height, stretching southward for about twenty miles. It has a small hill-fort, and contains above two hundred houses, supplied with water from wells. Lat. 25° 55′, long. 71° 23′.

BISANUH, in the British district of Allyghur, lieut.-gov. of the N.W. Provinces, a village on the route from the city of Agra to Allyghur cantonment, and 25 miles N. of the former. Lat. 27° 29′, long. 78° 7′.

BISARO, in the British district of Allyghur, lieut.-gov. of the N.W. Provinces, a village on the route from Meerut to Muttra, and 42 miles N.E. of the latter. Lat. 28° 1′, long. 77° 57′.

BISAUT, in the native state of Gurwhal, a village on the western declivity of the mountain bounding the fertile valley of Banal on the eastern side. Lat. 30° 50′, long. 78° 16′.

BISENTAUR, in the Peshawur division of the Punjab, a town situated on the route from Jhelum to Rawul Pindee, 30 miles N.W. of the town of Jhelum. Lat. 33° 24′, long. 73° 20′.

BISEORA.—See BESSERAH.

BISHENPORE, in the British district Bancoora, lieut.-gov. of Bengal, a town on the route from Berhampore to Midnapore, 95 miles S.W. of former, 48 N. of latter. It is a large town, and has a bazaar, and is situate on the right bank of the river Dalkisore, 20 miles S.E. of the town of Bancoora. Lat. 23° 4′, long. 87° 21′.

BISHWUR.—A town in Hyderabad, or dominions of the Nizam, distant N.W. from Hyderabad 212 miles. Lat. 19° 59′, long. 76° 51′.

BISKOHUR, in the British district of Goruckpoor, lieut.-gov. of the N.W. Provinces, a town on the route from Goruckpoor to Buraech, 66 miles N.W. of the former. Lat. 27° 19′, long. 82° 38′.

BISNATH, in the British district of Durrung, lieut.-gov. of Bengal, a town on the right bank of the Brahmapootra, on the route from Durrung to Luckimpoor, 70 miles N.E. of the former. Lat. 26° 40′, long. 93° 10′.

BISOWLEE.—A town in the British district of Budaon, lieut.-gov. of the N.W. Provinces, 22 miles N.W. of Budaon. Lat. 28° 18′, long. 79°.

BISRAMGUNGE, in Bundelcund, a village in the native state of Punna, on the route from Banda to Jubbulpoor, 50 miles S. of the former, 181 N. of the latter. It is beautifully situate in a wooded gorge, through which the ascent commences from the plains of Bundelcund to the plateau on the summit of the range styled by Franklin the Pannah Hills. Lat. 24° 50′, long. 80° 19′.

BISSEE.—A town in the British territory of Nagpore, distant S.E. from Nagpore 42 miles. Lat. 20° 38′, long. 79° 29′.

BISSEMCUTTACK.—A town in the hill zemindarry of Jeypoor, on the north-east frontier of the presidency of Madras, distant N. from Ryaguddah 23 miles. Lat. 19° 30′, long. 83° 35′.

BISSLY, in the territory of Mysore, a small town on the south-west frontier, towards Coorg, situate in a pass through the Western Ghats, on the route from Bangaloor to Mangaloor, 136 miles W. of former, 60 E. of latter. Lat. 12° 45′, long. 75° 45′.

BISSOWER, or **BUSAWUR**, in the territory of Bhurtpore, a town on the route from

Agra to Ajmer, 63 miles W. of former, 165 E. of latter. Heber, who calls it Peshawer, describes it as very prettily situated on the side of a little rocky eminence, with a ruinous palace on its summit. There is a bazaar. The transit-trade is considerable, especially in cottons sent from Malwa and Rajpootana eastward, towards the Jumna. Lat. 27° 2′, long. 77° 7′.

BISSOWLEE.—See BISULI.

BISTH JULINDER. — See JULINDER DOAB.

BISULI, or BISSOWLEE.—A town in the north-east of the Punjab, and on one of the southern ranges of the Himalaya, situate on the river Ravee, which is here about eighty yards wide. There is a large irregularly-built bazaar, but the place is chiefly remarkable for the huge palace of the rajah, regarded by Vigne as the finest building of the kind in the East; "exhibiting in its square turrets, open and embattled parapets, projecting windows, Chinese-roofed balconies, and most-like tank in front," a striking likeness to the great baronial mansions which in some parts of Europe remain as memorials of the feudal ages. Lat. 32° 33′, long. 75° 28′.

BISWAH, in the territory of Oude, a town on the route from Seetapoor to Sekrora, 20 miles S.E. of the former, 60 N.W. of the latter, 45 N. of Lucknow. Lat. 27° 29′, long. 81° 5′.

BISWUK, in the British district of Patna, lieut.-gov. of Bengal, a town on the route from Behar to Gayah, 20 miles W. of the former. Lat. 25° 8′, long. 85° 18′.

BITHOOR, in the British district of Cawnpore, lieut.-gov. of the N.W. Provinces, is situate on the right bank of the Ganges, 12 miles N.W. of Cawnpore cantonment. It has numerous Hindoo temples, and several ghats or flights of steps, giving access to the sacred stream, to which the Brahmins and their followers frequently resort for the purpose of ritual ablution. Brahma is particularly reverenced here. At the principal ghat, denominated Brahmavertta Ghat, he is said to have offered an aswamedha on completing the act of creation. The pin of his slipper, left behind him on the occasion, and now fixed in one of the steps of the ghat, is still worshipped there; and on the full moon of Agrahayana (November-December), a very numerously-attended mela or meeting, that mixes piety with profit, is annually held at that place. Upon the death of Maharajah Bajee Row, in 1851, the jaghire, situate close to the town, which had been bestowed upon him during pleasure, lapsed to the government, and was subjected to the general regulations in force in Cawnpore. The population of Bithoor is returned at 13,580. Lat. 26° 37′, long. 80° 20′.

BITTER STREAM.—A torrent rising in the Sulieman range, lat. 31° 30′, long. 69° 58′, and flowing through Daman about forty miles, loses itself in the sands before reaching the Indus.

BLACK ROCK.—Situate a few miles off the shore of Arracan, and to the north of Cape Negrais. Lat. 16° 11′, long. 94° 16′.

BLACKWOOD'S HARBOUR, on the coast of Coromandel, situate to the north of Point Pondy, and sheltered by the Armegon Shoal. According to Horsburgh "between the inner edge of the shoal and the coast is a space from three to four miles wide, called Blackwood Harbour, with soundings from four and a half fathoms near the shore, to six or seven fathoms contiguous to the edge of the shoal." Lat. 14° 1′, long. 80° 14′.

BLIUVANUGIRI, in the British district of South Arcot, presidency of Madras, a town on the route from Tranquebar to Vicravandy, 32 miles N.W. of the former. Lat. 11° 28′, long. 79° 43′.

BLUE MOUNTAIN.—A lofty peak rising to the height of 8,000 feet above the level of the sea, and forming part of the range of the Youmadoung Mountains. Lat. 22° 37′, long. 93° 10′.

BLUFF POINT.—A bold headland on the coast of Amherst, one of the districts of the Tenasserim provinces. Lat. 15° 47′, long. 97° 45′.

BOAD.—One of the Cuttack mehals, in the district of Cuttack, under the political control of the government of India. It became subject to British supremacy upon the conquest of the province in 1804. Its area is 1,377 square miles, and its population has been estimated at 61,965 persons. The town is situate on the river Mahanuddy, navigable for river craft of considerable burthen from the sea to this place, a distance of 190 miles. It was formerly a more important place than at present; as there are numerous ruined temples; but it is still the residence of a petty rajah tributary to the British government, and is described as a large fenced village. Distant from Cuttack, W., 100 miles; Nagpore, E., 330; Calcutta, S.W., 285. Lat. 20° 53′, long. 84° 20′.

BOANUH, in the British district of Delhi, lieut.-gov. of the N.W. Provinces, a town on the Western Jumna Canal, 17 miles N.W. of Delhi. Lat. 28° 48′, long. 77° 5′.

BOBEENA.—A town of Bundlecund, in the native state of Jhansi, distant S.W. from Jhansi 18 miles. Lat. 25° 15′, long. 78° 33′.

BOBILEE.—See DOBBILI.

BODEGAUM.—A town in Hyderabad, or dominions of the Nizam, distant N.E. from Ahmednuggur 50 miles. Lat. 19° 20′, long. 75° 30′.

BODEN.—A town in Hyderabad, or dominions of the Nizam, distant N.W. from Hyderabad 100 miles. Lat. 18° 40′, long. 77° 57′.

BODWUR, in the British district of Khandeish, presidency of Bombay, a town on the route from Aurungabad to Boorhanpoor, 80 miles N.E. of the former. Lat. 20° 51′, long. 75° 59′.

BODYNAIKENOOR, in the British district of Madura, presidency of Madras, a town 52 miles W. of Madura, 49 miles S.W. of Dindigul. Lat. 10° 1′, long. 77° 24′.

BOENCHIE, in the British district Hooghly, under the lieut.-gov. of Bengal, a town on the route from Calcutta to Burdwan. It has a bazaar, and water may be obtained in abundance from a large tank. Distant from Calcutta, N.W., 46 miles; from Burdwan, S.E., 35. Lat. 23° 6′, long. 88° 15′.

BOGAREA, in the British district of Bhagulpore, lieut.-gov. of Bengal, a town on the route from Burhampoor to Bhagulpore, 22 miles S. of the latter. Lat. 24° 54′, long. 86° 55′.

BOGOORAH, or **BOGRAH**, within the territory subject to the lieut.-gov. of Bengal, a district named from its principal place. It is bounded on the north by the British districts Dinajpore and Rungpore; on the east by the river Konai, a branch of the Brahmapootra, separating it from the British district Mymensing; on the south by the British districts Mymensing and Pubna; on the south-west by the British district Rajeshaye; and on the west by the British district Dinajpore. It lies between lat. 24° 36′—25° 19′, long. 88° 45′—89° 48′, and has an area of 2,160 square miles. It is traversed or skirted by numerous rivers, among which may be mentioned the Konaie, the Goggot, the Kurateea, the Jamuna, and the Attree. The climate is extremely hot before the rains set in, about the middle of June. They continue until October, when the cool season commences, during which warm clothing and fires at morning and evening are indispensable to comfort. Bogoorah is, throughout, a level alluvial tract. Rice is the principal crop; the sugar-cane is also grown to considerable extent in the north-western quarter of the district. Mulberry plantations are extensive, and the trees constitute a great ornament of the country, besides yielding the food of the silkworm, the produce of which, though coarse, is strong and durable, and finds a ready market, at remunerating prices. Hemp is cultivated on account of the narcotic and intoxicating qualities of its resinous sap. Cotton is grown to some extent; indigo to a still greater. The amount of the population will be found under the article BENGAL. The district was acquired in 1765 by the East-India Company, by virtue of the firman or grant from Shah Allum, of the dewanny of Bengal, Behar, and Orissa.

BOGOORAH, or **BOGRAH**, in the British district of the same name, a town on the route from Berhampoor to Jumalpoor, 129 miles N.E. of the former, and 54 S.W. of the latter. It is situate on the Kurattea, a large river, navigable for craft, during the rainy season, of the largest size employed in inland navigation. It has a bazaar, and supplies are abundant; but it is a place of no importance otherwise than as the seat of the civil establishment. Distant N.E. from Calcutta 247 miles. Lat. 24° 50′, long. 89° 22′.

BOGSADALLEE.—A town in the native state of Bhotan, distant N.W. from Behar 41 miles. Lat. 26° 32′, long. 88° 53′.

BOGWANGOLA, in the British district Moorshedabad, lieut.-gov. of Bengal, a town on the right bank of the Ganges, the channel of which is here subject to such great and sudden changes as sometimes to sweep away the towns situate on its banks. From this circumstance, Bogwangola, though a thriving place, and a great mart for grain, with which it supplies the neighbouring town of Moorshedabad, has "more the appearance of an encampment than a town." It has, however, a pleasing aspect, consisting of neat though humble cottages, with sides of matting, and "scattered very prettily over a large green common, fenced off from the river by a high grassy mound." Distance N. from Calcutta 120 miles. Lat. 24° 20′, long. 88° 20′.

BOHAN DEVI, in the native state of Gurwhal, a village amidst the mountains near the south-western frontier, and between the Jumna and Bhagirathi, as the Ganges is called in the upper part of its course. The village is so called from a temple dedicated to a deity named Bohan. Lat. 30° 30′, long. 78° 18′.

BOHANEEGUNJ, in the district of Abladganj, territory of Oude, a town 32 miles N.W. of Allahabad, 77 S.W. of Oude. Butter estimates the population at 6,000, of whom a third are Mussulmans. Lat. 25° 48′, long. 81° 34′.

BOHAURY, in the British district of Broach, presidency of Bombay, a town on the route from Surat to Baunsda, 36 miles S.E. of the former. Lat. 20° 56′, long. 73° 22′.

BOHELLAH.—A town in Nagpore, distant W. from Konkeir 40 miles. Lat. 20° 18′, long. 81° 9′.

BOHROOPAH, in the British district of Cuttack, lieut.-gov. of Bengal, a town on the route from Ganjam to Cuttack, five miles S. of the latter. Lat. 20° 24′, long. 85° 53′.

BOILCOONTLA, in the British district of Kurnool, presidency of Madras, a town on the route from Kurnool to Ongole, 48 miles S.E. of the former. Lat. 15° 24′, long. 78° 40′.

BOIRONEE, in the British district of Ganjam, presidency of Madras, a town situate 25 miles N.W. of Ganjam. Lat. 19° 35′, long. 84° 50′.

BOJAPOMAH.—A town of Eastern India, situated in the territory inhabited by the Naga tribes, 60 miles N. from Muneepoor, 81 miles

S.E. from Nowgong. Lat. 25° 40′, long. 93° 50′.

BOKER, BILUND, or BEYLUN.—A river rising in the British district of Mirzapore, lieut.-gov. of the N.W. Provinces, among the mountains of Gondwana, and about lat. 24° 40′, long. 83° 20′. It takes a westerly course, and, passing from the frontier of the district of Mirzapore into that of Allahabad, falls into the river Tons (south-western), in lat. 25° 2′, long. 81° 53′, after a total length of course of about 138 miles. It is the Belund of the surveyor-general's map; Bailan of Franklin; Belun of Garden, who mentions it as crossed in lat. 24° 57′, long. 82° 18′, by the route from Allahabad to Jubbulpoor, by the Kutra Pass.

BOKERDHUN.—A town in Hyderabad, or dominions of the Nizam, distant N.E. from Aurungabad 42 miles. Lat. 20° 18′, long. 75° 50′.

BOKOWLI, in territory of Bhurtpore, a village on the route from Agra to Mow, 32 miles S.W. of former. Indifferent water may be had from wells, and supplies may be collected from the surrounding country. Lat. 27° 1′, long. 77° 36′.

BOKPYN CREEK.—An inlet of the sea on the coast of Mergui, one of the Tenasserim provinces. Its mouth is in lat. 11° 17′, long. 98° 50′.

BOKRAWALI, in the British district of Allygurh, lieut.-gov. of the N.W. Provinces, a village on the route from the cantonment of Allygurh to that of Delhi, and five miles N.W. of the former. Lat. 27° 56′, long. 78° 5′.

BOKUR.—A town in Hyderabad, or dominions of the Nizam, distant E. from Nandair 23 miles. Lat. 19° 12′, long. 77° 43′.

BOLACOLE, in the British district of Pubna, lieut.-gov. of Bengal, a town on the right bank of the river Konaie, 36 miles E. of Pubna. Lat. 24° 6′, long. 89° 45′.

BOLAN PASS, in Beloochistan, on the great route from Northern Sinde, by Shikarpoor and Dadur, to Kandahar and Ghuznee. It is not so much a pass over a lofty range, as a continuous succession of ravines and gorges, commencing near Dadur, and first winding among the subordinate ridges stretching eastward from the Hala chain of mountains, the brow of which it finally cross-cuts, and thus gives access from the vast plain of Hindostan to the elevated and uneven tract extending from the Hindoo Koosh to the vicinity of the Indian Ocean. Its commencement on the eastern side, from the plain of Cutch Gundava, is about five miles west of Dadur, and in lat. 29° 30′, long. 67° 35′; the elevation of the entrance being about 800 feet above the level of the sea, and that of its outlet at the western extremity, 5,793 feet. There is no descent on the western side, as the route opens on the Dasht-i-Bedowlut, a plain as high as the top of the pass. The total length is between fifty-four and fifty-five miles; the average ascent ninety feet in the mile. The Bengal column of the Army of the Indus in 1839 spent six days in marching through the pass, entering it on the 16th, and leaving it on the 21st of March. Its artillery, including eight-inch mortars, twenty-four-pounder howitzers, and eighteen-pounder guns, was conveyed without any serious difficulty. The eminences bounding the pass have in general no great height above it, in most places not exceeding 500 feet; but at Beebee Nanee, twenty-six miles from the entrance, they are very lofty. The Bolan Pass, though very important in a military point of view, as forming the great communication between Sinde and Khorasan, is inferior in a commercial interest to the Gomul, farther north, through which the Lohani Afghans, in their annual migrations, conduct the main portion of the traffic between Hindostan on the one point, and Afghanistan and Central Asia on the other. The western extremity and highest point of the Bolan Pass is in lat. 29° 56′, long. 67° 6′.

BOLAPILLY, in the British district of Cuddapah, presidency of Madras, a town 80 miles N. of Cuddapah, 61 E. of Kurnool. Lat. 15° 40′, long. 79°.

BOLARUM, in the territory of the Nizam, a military cantonment for the troops in the service of that prince, a short distance from the city of Hyderabad. It is situate on an elevated ground of granitic formation, six or eight miles in circumference, and having on its summit an open plain extending to the east of the cantonment. The lines can accommodate two battalions of infantry, a risalah or troop of irregular horse, and 250 artillery. There is a well-constructed hospital in an airy situation, having accommodation for 150 patients. The gardens produce in abundance and excellence the usual kinds of European vegetables, besides the common Indian fruits. Mangoes attain great perfection. Grapes, pine-apples, and strawberries, also thrive well; and a few peaches have been grown, but not of good quality. No rank vegetation is permitted to spring up in the cantonment; the hedgerows are annually cut down to a certain height: the place is consequently open, and thus rendered in a great measure free from the sources of noxious exhalations. It is one of the healthiest stations in the Deccan, and invalids resort to it from various places. The medical school formerly existing in this place was abolished in 1847, and a new school of medicine substituted at Hyderabad, in which are taught anatomy, chemistry, pharmacy, the practice of medicine and surgery. On the 21st September, 1855, a mutiny broke out in one of the cavalry regiments of the Hyderabad force, when Brigadier Colin Mackenzie, commanding the southern division of the contingent, was desperately wounded, and narrowly escaped with his life. Elevation above the sea 1,890 feet. Distance from Hyderabad, N., 11 miles; Secunderabad, N., six. Lat. 17° 30′, long. 78° 34′.

BOLAVY, in the British district of North Canara, presidency of Madras, a town on the left bank of the Cauly Nuddy, 41 miles N. of Honahwar. Lat. 14° 53′, long. 74° 22′.

BOLEPORRA, in the British district of Cuttack, lieut.-gov. of Bengal, a town on the left bank of the Mahanuddy river, 50 miles E. of Cuttack. Lat. 20° 24′, long. 86° 40′.

BOLIMA, a town in the native state of Kashmere, or dominions of Gholab Singh, distant N. from Jhelum 41 miles. Lat. 33° 37′, long. 73° 38′.

BOLL GHUR, in the British district of Pooree, lieut.-gov. of Bengal, a town 44 miles S.W. from Cuttack, 45 miles N.W. of Juggernaut. Lat. 20° 10′, long. 85° 20′.

BOLONGO, or BORONGO ISLAND.—The most westerly of a group known by the name of the Broken Islands, lying at the entrance of the Arracan river. Between this island and Middle Bolongo there is good anchorage, sheltered from all winds but the south. The island is mountainous, woody, rugged, and without any appearance of inhabitants or cultivation : its centre is about lat. 20°, long. 93°.

BOMBAY.—One of the three British presidencies of India, and so denominated from its principal place, the city of that name. Exclusive of the subordinate territories of native princes, over which the East-India Company exercises paramount political sway, and of Sinde, which, though recently placed under the government of Bombay, may properly be regarded as a distinct territory, the tracts subject to the Bombay presidency form a narrow strip, of irregular outline, stretching for a considerable distance from north to south. This territory is bounded on the north by the possessions of the Guicowar and by Indore, belonging to the family of Holkar ; on the east by part of the possessions of the Scindia family, by Indore, by the dominions of the Nizam, and by the territories subject to the presidency of Madras ; on the south by the Madras territories, by the Portuguese possessions attached to Goa, and by Mysore ; and on the west by the Arabian Sea, the Gulf of Cambay, and Guzerat. Its greatest length, in a direction nearly from south-east to north-west, is about 660 miles ; its greatest breadth, from Oolpar, in the district of Surat, to a point near Boorhanpoor, on the Taptee, 240. The area of the country within the above limits which is directly subject to the British government, is 67,945 square miles : if the territories administered by or on behalf of native princes, including those of the Guicowar, be included, the area will be 124,265 square miles : if Scinde be added, the entire area will be 176,385. In proportion to its area, the Bombay territory has the advantage of an extensive seacoast, reaching from south to north, from near Vingorla, adjoining the Goa frontier, in lat. 15° 44′, to Cambay, at the head of the gulf of the same name, in lat. 22° 16′, a distance of 480 miles ; in addition to which, along the western side of the Gulf of Cambay, is a seacoast of eighty miles. This large extent of coast is well supplied with havens, including Dewghur, Geriah, Jygurh, Rajapur, Choul, Bombay, Bassein, Damaun, Surat, Broach, and several others of less importance. None of these, however, with the exception of that of Bombay, can be approached or quitted with safety during the prevalence of the south-west monsoon. A continuation of that bold lofty range of mountains known by the name of the Western Ghauts, though that name is appropriated more peculiarly to the southern part of the range, the more northern being called by the natives the Siadri Mountains, runs in some measure parallel to the coast, and, on an average, about forty-five miles from it.

The climate at Bombay Island, and generally along the coast, is sultry, the average temperature of the whole year being about 80°, and the lowest not under 70°. The greatest heat, however, falls considerably below that of many other parts of India, and seldom exceeds 100°. The quantity of rain is for the most part very great ; in one year (1831) it amounted at Bombay to 99.64 inches. This, however, is considerably in excess of the usual amount. In 1838 the fall was only 50.78 inches ; and the result of a series of observations, commencing with the former year and terminating with the latter, was to exhibit various fluctuations between the two extremes which have been quoted. In some later years, however, the fall seems to have been much greater than an average framed upon such data, and even considerably beyond the highest amount in the above series. A statement more recently published gives the fall in one year at Mahabuleshwar at 248 inches ; at Rutnagherry, 130 ; and at Tanna, 106 inches. A statistical memoir, published some years ago, gives the average fall of rain at Bombay at 80 inches. The zoology of this part of India appears to have received but little attention. A curious species of maneless lions is found in Guzerat, along the banks of the Saburmuttee, near Ahmedabad : tigers and leopards are numerous in various parts, and very destructive. There are also wolves, hyænas, jackals, wild swine, wild buffaloes, porcupines, the nylgau, monkeys, and other quadrumanous animals. Among domestic animals the horse formerly held a high place. The horses of Kattywar shared the celebrity of those of the Deccan, whence the supplies for mounting the vast cavalry establishments of the native princes were obtained. The extinction of the authority of some of those princes, together with the decline of others, and the establishment of general peace under the paramount influence of the British government, have probably been the cause of the declension which has taken place in the quality of the native horses, which are now of an inferior description. The East-India Company have made various efforts to restore their character, especially by the establishment, in the year 1827, of a stud at Alligaum; but the experiment having been carried on for some years, at great expense, and without any advantage, it was ultimately abandoned, and the stud establishment abolished. The other domestic animals to be enumerated are buffaloes, camels, kine, swine, and sheep. A series of experiments, extending over several years, were carried on by government for the improvement of this last description of animal, by the introduction of the superior breeds of Europe and the Cape; but with little effect. Wool, however, is one of the exports of Bombay. The staple crops are rice, bajra, jowar, barley, gram, kodroo, and some inferior grains. Cotton of the indigenous species is extensively grown in various parts of the presidency. The American varieties have been introduced with much advantage, especially in the collectorate of Dharwar and other parts of the Southern Mahratta country. The native sugar-cane flourishes in some of the collectorates. In the zillah of Poonah the cultivation of the Mauritius cane has greatly diminished, the cause being attributed to the poverty of the Deccan soil north of the Krishna. Wheat is produced generally in the northern parts of the presidency, and is extensively cultivated in the provinces of Guzerat, where it may be seen even to the border of the sea. It is stated, however, to deteriorate during a sea-voyage, and to be unsuitable to the English market. Coffee flourishes in Belgaum; but for its successful culture neither the soil nor climate of the Deccan north of that collectorate is well fitted. The other products are chiefly tobacco, oil-plants, and indigo. Complete success has attended the introduction of the potato in the collectorates of Poona and Kaira. The chief markets for the root are Bombay, Poona, Dhoolia, Aurungabad, Jaulna, and Hingolee. Experiments for the cultivation and preparation for the English market, of flax and the Syrian tobacco, have proved unsuccessful. The mulberry was some time since introduced in the elevated tract about Poona, with a view to the production of silk, but the experiment has altogether failed.

Among the trees found in the Bombay territories are the teak, bombax, Adansonea Dalbergia, Suritenia febrifuga, acacias of various kinds, especially the catechu, the Bassia latifolia or mhowa, bearing a vast profusion of flowers, the petals of which, when dried, resemble raisins in appearance and taste, and are largely consumed as food as well as for distillation, by which process a spirit is obtained which furnishes the most usual intoxicating beverage of the natives. The importance of trees, in so far as they furnish articles of food, or timber for the various purposes to which that article is applied, are too obvious to have been overlooked in any age, however low its rank in point of information. The indirect advantages of those beautiful productions of nature have been ascertained and admitted only at a period comparatively modern. Humboldt, and subsequently other writers, have shown that trees perform important functions in regard to the productive powers of the soil and the character of the climate, as well in influencing the supply of one of the first and most indispensable necessaries of animal existence,—water. In every place where trees have heedlessly been extirpated, the supply of water has been reduced, the fertility of the soil has been diminished, and the character of the climate has deteriorated. Their preservation is consequently an object deserving attention, not only on the ground of their direct utility, but as possessing perhaps even a stronger claim on account of the indirect blessings of which they are the instruments. The authorities of India have not been insensible to these claims upon their notice. In March, 1844, the Court of Directors authorized the unappropriated surplus of the annual grant of 5,000 rupees to the Agri-horticultural Society of Western India to be devoted to the plantation of useful trees in different parts of the presidency. In June, 1845, a scheme was drawn up for carrying out the measure under the above sanction, and operations were commenced in April, 1846. A public notice was also issued, in which, after assuring the people of the interest taken by the government in the promotion of measures tending to their amelioration and comfort, rules were promulgated pointing out the evils arising from the scarcity of trees, and encouraging individuals, by the offer of rewards and other marks of public approbation, to plant trees on their own lands. Besides roadside trees and scattered plantations, the Bombay territory possesses many wooded tracts of sufficient magnitude to be termed forests. The position of the port of Bombay as a great naval depôt would naturally direct attention to such descriptions of timber as might be beneficially employed in shipbuilding; and the conservation of the forests within the presidency was formerly deemed an object of importance, and officers were appointed for this duty by the local government. About the year 1824 the conservator's establishment was broken up, probably in consequence of the discontinuance at Bombay of building line-of-battle ships for the Crown. After the lapse of twenty years, however, the want of such an institution became apparent; an establishment for the conservation and management of the forests of the Bombay presidency was then organized, and Dr. Gibson, superintendent of the Botanical Gardens, was in 1847 appointed conservator of forests.

Manufactures, of which there were formerly some of importance, have generally yielded to the competition of the cheaper fabrics of Britain. Surat, long celebrated for its cotton goods, now produces scarcely any. Boorhanpoor has from the same cause lost the silk manufacture, which it formerly carried on to a considerable extent. Paper is made at Poona. The manufactures of the presidency may, however, be regarded as of slight importance in a commercial point of view, being restricted to such branches as are indispensable in each locality; and cotton and other raw materials being shipped for Britain to be manufactured, and sent back for the use of those inhabiting the place where the article was raised.

The trade with other parts of India, as well as with Great Britain and foreign countries, is considerable. The principal articles of export are cotton, wool, Cashmere shawls, opium from Malwa, coffee, pepper, ivory, and gums. The chief imports are piece-goods, thread, twist, and yarn (of all which the quantities imported from Great Britain are very large), metals, raw silk from China and the eastward, tea, wine, and beer. The value of the foreign export trade of Bombay has more than doubled in the last twenty years, and now amounts to about 7,000,000*l.* sterling. Several sources contribute to the supply of the government revenue: among these the principal are the land assessment, customs duties, salt-excise, and opium passes or permits for the transit of the drug from Malwa to Bombay. The government revenue from all sources is returned at about four millions and a half sterling.

Considerable efforts have been made of late years by the government to improve the means of communication. The principal roads are—1. From Bombay over the Bhore Ghaut to Poona, and thence diverging in various directions, to Sattara, Sholapore, Ahmednuggur, and Narrayengaum. 2. The Bombay and Agra road, traversing the presidency in a north-easterly direction, and affording facilities for the exchange of the produce of Berar and the northern parts of the Deccan for that of the more western districts. 3. The route northward from Bombay to Surat, Broach, and Baroda. 4. From the port of Vingorla, *viâ* Belgaum, to Dharwar, and continued thence to Hooblee, one of the great cotton marts of the Southern Mahratta country; beyond which it joins the road leading to the port of Coomta, in North Canara. In furtherance of the comprehensive system of railways which has been projected for India, a line was some time since commenced from Bombay in a north-easterly direction, under the auspices of the Great Indian Peninsula Company. A portion of the line has been opened. It proceeds towards the Ghauts, where it crosses the mountains by two separate branches, one of which is destined to join the line from Calcutta, and the other that from Madras. The former will communicate by a branch line with the cotton district of Berar. A second line is also under construction, under the superintendence of the Bombay, Baroda, and Central India Railway Company. The works are at present confined to the section between Surat, Baroda, and Ahmedabad, but it is contemplated to extend this line southerly to Bombay, and northerly to Delhi. Mordee Bay, now inundated by the sea, has been pointed out as the most eligible site for the terminus of the railway at Bombay. A project has been accordingly sanctioned for recovering this locality from the sea; and a portion of the space reclaimed is to be appropriated for the purposes of the railway.

The population of the southern part of the presidency of Bombay is principally Mahratta, and consists generally of cultivators of the soil. The branches of the Ghauts, stretching out to the eastward from the main range south of the town of Sattara, are held by Ramosees, a hill-tribe more civilized and subdued than the Bheels. They do not extend further south than Colapore, or further east than Beejapoor, and have no language but that of the Mahrattas, whom they resemble in dress and manners. In the Southern Concan the majority of the population is Mahratta; that tract, and a portion of the Ghauts and Deccan to the east of it, being the original and peculiar seat of the race. The north-eastern portion of the Bombay dominions, comprising the greater part of the valley of the river Taptee, including the extensive basin or valley of Candeish, is partly inhabited by the Bheels, who are considered to be an eighth of the whole population of that district. Farther west and north-west, in the collectorates of Broach, Ahmedabad, Surat, and Kaira, this aboriginal population is found intermingled with some other rude tribes, denominated Coolies, Doonjas, Chowdrias, Dooblas, and Koonbies, besides Grasias, sunk still lower in barbarism than the original race, and Brahminists, Jains, Bhoras, a peculiar class of Mussulmans; Mussulmans of other descriptions, generally descended from Arabians; Sindhians, Beloches, or Mekranis. In the city of Bombay and its vicinity, besides the Brahminists and Mussulmans constituting the bulk of the population, there are Christians of the Romanist, Protestant, and Armenian persuasions; a considerable number of Parsees, and some Jews.

For the superintendence and good government of the ministers of the United Church of England and Ireland, in the presidency of Bombay, the Crown was empowered, under the act of 3 & 4 Wm. 4, c. 85, to constitute the bishopric of Bombay, subject to the ecclesiastical jurisdiction of the bishop of Calcutta as metropolitan of India. The ecclesiastical establishment of this presidency consists of a bishop, an archdeacon, who is also a chaplain, seven chaplains, inclusive of the archdeacon, and sixteen assistant-chaplains, stationed in various parts of the presidency. The ecclesiastical jurisdiction of the bishop of Bombay extends over all places under the control of the governor of Bombay and his political agents, including Cutch, Sinde, and Aden. There are two ministers of the Church of Scotland at the presidency, appointed and paid by the East-India Company under the provisions of the act of Parliament above noticed. Mahratta and Canarese are the two languages prevailing in the south and south-eastern parts of the presidency; Guzeratti in the northern. Persian and Oordoo are employed to some extent as the languages of business and of etiquette. Marwari, Portuguese, and Arabic, are also in use. The government is vested in the governor and three councillors, styled "the Governor in Council of Bombay," subject, however, to the "superintendence, direction, and control" of the Governor-General of India in Council. Civil and criminal justice are both administered in the territories subject to the government of Bombay by the courts of the East-India Company, in addition to the Supreme Court, in which the judges are appointed by the Crown. In the former class the functionaries are appointed by the local government, and the law administered is embodied in the regulations of that government, and the legislative acts of the government of India; in the latter, the modes of procedure are assimilated to those of the courts at Westminster. The jurisdiction of this court is, however, limited to the presidency town, except in regard to British subjects. The most convenient mode of considering the details of area and population will be to follow the revenue division into collectorates, which are as follows :—

	Area in Square Miles.		Population.	
Surat	1,629		492,684	
Broach	1,319		290,984	
Admedabad	4,356		650,223	
Kaira	1,869		580,631	
Khandeish.........	9,311		778,112	
Tannah or Northern Concan	5,477		815,849	
Poonah	5,298		666,006	
Ahmednuggur, including the sub-collectorate of Nassick	9,931		995,585	
Sholapore	4,991		675,115	
Belgaum	5,405		1,025,882	
Dharwar..........	3,837		754,385	
Rutnagherry, or South Concan ..	3,964		665,238	
Bombay Island, including Colaba..	18		566,119	
Kolaba Territory..	318		58,721	
Sattara	10,222		1,005,771	
		67,945		10,021,305
Sinde :—				
Shikarpore........	6,120		350,401	
Hyderabad	30,000		551,811	
Kurrachee........	16,000		185,550	
		52,120		1,087,762
Native States within the Bombay Territories :—				
Baroda (Guicowar)	4,399		325,526	
Khyrpore (Sinde)..	5,000		105,000	
Kattywar	19,850		1,468,900	
Kolapore	3,445		500,000	
Sawunt Warree ..	800		120,000	
Cutch	6,764		500,536	
Mahratta jaghiredars............	3,775		419,025	
Petty States in Guzerat	16,617		1,030,938	
		60,650		4,469,925
		180,715		15,578,992

An armed maritime force has long been maintained at this presidency, such a provision being peculiarly called for by the necessity of being prepared to quell and overawe the native pirates, as well as those of Arabia. This force is maintained at an annual cost of about a quarter of a million sterling. Several steam-vessels are employed in maintaining the semi-monthly communication between Bombay and Suez. It may be here stated, however, that the East-India Company are about to relinquish the duty of conveying the mails between Suez and India so soon as arrangements can be made for its transfer to other hands.

The military force of the presidency consists of a regiment of artillery, comprising one brigade of horse and four battalions of foot, a corps of engineers, three regiments of native light cavalry, three regiments of European infantry, twenty-nine regiments of native infantry, and a marine battalion, affording an aggregate, according to a recent parliamentary return, of something more than 34,000 regular troops. There are, besides, a regiment of Poona irregular horse, a Guzerat provincial battalion, the Guzerat irregular horse, Candeish Bheel corps, Kolapore local corps, Rajpootan field force, Sawuntwaree local corps, the Belooch battalions (two), the Scinde irregular horse (two regiments), Cutch irregular horse, Southern Mahratta irregular horse, Rutnagherry Rangers, the native veteran battalion, and two police corps, furnishing an aggregate of nearly 18,000 men, the whole constituting a standing force of nearly 52,000. The forces of the Crown at the same period, placed under the control of the military authorities in the presidency, were something above 6,000, making a grand total of military force in the East-India Company's service in this presidency, exclusive of 3,711 Madras troops then serving within it, of more than 59,000 men. The educational institutions are divided into two principal classes: the first comprises all the vernacular schools, in which elementary instruction is conveyed through the medium of the native languages; the second class embraces the Elphinstone Institution and the various schools in which the English tongue and the literature and sciences of Europe are imparted.

The wonderful cave-temples, excavated in the rocks at Karli, Elephanta, Bag, Ellora, and some other places, indicate, from their characteristics, that formerly the population and rulers of this part of India were of the Buddhist persuasion. At the commencement, however, of the Mussulman invasion, Brahminism appears to have been universally prevalent; and the wealth and flagrant idolatry of the Sivaists of Somnath Patan drew down upon them, in the year 1024, the exterminating attack of Mahmood of Ghuzni. The Concan appears to have first been conquered by the Mussulmans, under Mahomed Shah, the Bahmany king of the Deccan, in the year 1470; forty years having been spent in the obstinately-resisted conquest of that rugged tract, which, after all, remained but imperfectly subjugated. The tract more to the east and south-east, comprising the present collectorates of Dharwar and Belgaum, and the province of Sattara, was part of the Brahminical realm of Bijayanagar, whose resources in an expedition against the king of Beejapoor, in the early part of the sixteenth century, are described with more than oriental exaggeration by the annalist of the Portuguese. This power was in 1565 destroyed by a confederacy of Mussulman kings of the Deccan; and the districts of Belgaum, Dharwar, Colapore, and Sattara, incorporated with the dominions of Beejapoor, the ruler of which was one of the confederated princes. The more central part of the presidency, comprising the present collectorates of Ahmednuggur and Poona, was first invaded by the Mussulman armies, by the command of Alla-ood-Deen Khiljy, the Patan monarch of Delhi, about the year 1308; and its conquest appears to have been completed in 1318, by his immediate successor Mobarik Khiljy. The general revolt of the Deccan against Mahomed Toghluk occurred in 1350, and towards the close of the following century (1490), upon the extinction of the Bahmany dynasty, this tract was formed into a Mussulman state, under the denomination of Ahmednuggur, by Ahmed, the founder of the Nizam Shahi dynasty. Candeish, in the valley of the Taptee, appears to have been first reduced under the sway of the Mussulmans by Alla-ood-Deen, about the commencement of the fourteenth century, and, after various vicissitudes and struggles, formed into an independent state by Malik Raja. The remainder of the territory of the East-India Company under this presidency, or that portion lying about the Gulf of Cambay, formed part of the ancient kingdom of Guzerat, which, invaded, overrun, and immediately relinquished by Mahmood of Ghuzni in the early part of the eleventh century, was conquered, in 1297, by the troops of Alla-ood-Deen, of Delhi. Subsequently to the general revolt of the Deccan, it became the scene of anarchy and bloodshed, until 1391, when it was formed into an independent Mussulman state by Muzuffur Khan, a Rajpoot converted to Islam. The islands of Bombay and Salsette formed part of the dominions of Guzerat in 1429, and though temporarily lost, were recovered and retained to the time of the arrival of the Portuguese in India at the close of the fifteenth century. The Portuguese appear to have commenced their commercial and warlike operations on the coast of this presidency about 1508. Diu seems to have been their earliest permanent settlement, and there, by leave of the native sovereign, they built a factory, which was fortified in 1534. Bombay was first visited by the Portuguese in 1509, when they took a Mussulman ship; and it appears to have soon become one of their permanent possessions, as in 1531 the Portuguese expedition destined against Goa rendezvoused thereat. In 1534, Bahadur Shah, king of Guzerat, ceded the island of Bassein to the Portuguese in perpetuity. The first British establishment within the limits of this presidency was made at Surat in 1601. In the latter part of the sixteenth century, the territories now subject to the presidency of Bombay were, in a great measure, reunited to the realm of Delhi, by the power of Akbar; but the resumption was not completed until 1637, under the reign of Shah Jehan. The East-India Company in the mean time pushed its commercial concerns in western India; its affairs being under the management of a governor and council residing at Surat, and whose jurisdiction was styled "the Presidency of Surat." In 1661, the island of Bombay was by the crown of Portugal ceded to the crown of England, as part of the portion of the infanta Catherine of Portugal on her marriage with Charles II. The Portuguese local authorities, however, for some time evaded the transfer, and at length but partially complied; and Charles, either from vexation or some worthier motive, in 1669 granted the island to the East-India Company; but the Portuguese, who continued to retain the islands of Salsette and Karanja, long pursued a course of annoyance and hostility highly prejudicial to the British settlement. In 1676, the English crown granted to the East-India Company authority to establish a mint at Bombay, and, notwithstanding many adverse circumstances, the prosperity of this settlement was rapidly on the increase. In 1683, Bombay was declared by the Court of Directors the seat of the presidency, and also their principal station in the East Indies. In the same year Captain Keigwin, the commander of the East-India Company's military forces in the island, revolted, and repudiating the local authority of the East-India Company, proclaimed that of the Crown. The state of the settlement at this time bore testimony to the great efforts made for its improvement by the East-India Company, during the short time which had elapsed since its acquisition. They "had expended the large sum of 300,000*l.* on fortifications and improvements; had constructed an excellent harbour, to become the resort of English trade. The garrison of Bombay consisted of 505 men, and the island was supported by its own revenue." Next year arrived the mandate of the Crown, that the island should be forthwith restored to the Company, who accordingly resumed possession; but the precarious state of their affairs and the strength of the mutineers caused an unconditional pardon to be granted. The intended change was now, in 1685, carried into effect, and the seat of the presidential government transferred from Surat to Bombay. In the succeeding year, the president was declared Governor-General of India, and the establishment at Surat reduced to an agency. The ambition of the sovereigns of Delhi had overthrown the Mussulman kingdoms of the Deccan, which had been the bulwarks of their faith against the Brahminists in that part of India; and the tyranny and intolerance of Aurungzebe excited a spirit of resistance and retaliation among the Mahratta Brahminists, which, fomented and directed by their notorious leader Sevajee, ultimately overthrew the Mussulman sway, and in its place established the various Mahratta powers that have in turn succumbed beneath British supremacy. During this struggle, from the middle to the close of the seventeenth century, the Mahrattas extended their dominion over nearly the whole of the tract governed by the presidency of Bombay; and the managers on behalf of the East-India Company having the sagacity to foresee the probability of the ultimate success of the Mahrattas, on being more immediately exposed to their hostility, adopted the perilous policy of forming treaties with Sevajee and his successor; thus incurring the enmity of Aurungzebe, whose forces in 1688 invaded the island of Bombay, and besieged the town, but soon after withdrew, on the payment of a sum of money. The East-India Company became, likewise, frequently embroiled with that monarch, in consequence of the outrages of English pirates, who took several ships belonging to his subjects. The extension of the dominions of the East-India Company on this side of India was long very slow, being almost confined to Bancoote and Fort Victoria, acquired in 1756 from the Mahrattas in exchange for Gheriah, to the island of Bombay and the factories of Surat, Broach, and Ahmedabad, until 1774, when the British authorities, taking advantage of disputes among the Mahrattas, captured the islands of Salsette and Karanja, having stormed the fort of Tanna, the main defence of the former island. Both were formally ceded to the British by the treaty concluded on the 6th March, 1775, with Ragoba, who was recognised by the Bombay government as Peishwa. In virtue of this treaty, Ragoba had been supported with a force of 1,500 men of all arms, including 450 Europeans, and at Arass a battle was fought, the result of which, though little decisive, inclined to the British. The supreme government disapproved of the treaty and connection with Ragoba, and deputed their agent to Poona to treat with the ministerial party without the intervention of the Bombay government. The treaty of Poorunder, concluded on the 1st March, 1776, was the result. Ragoba was now left to his fate. Peace was concluded with his enemies, the ministers at Poona conducting the regency during the minority of Maderow Narrain, the infant Peishwa, who was a posthumous son of Narrain Rao, one of the nephews of Ragoba. By this treaty the British obtained possession of the pergunnah and city of Broach. In 1777, war with France impending, a ship belonging to that nation put into Choul, a port of the Concan, about thirty miles south of Bombay, and in the territory of the Mahrattas, whose views appeared so unequivocally hostile to the British, that the supreme government determined on reinstating Ragoba in power, and vigorously prosecuting the war against his rivals, the party at Poona opposed to the British interests. In 1779, a force consisting of 3,900 men, destined to act against Poona, was despatched from Bombay. It entered the Deccan through the Bhore Ghat, and advanced to Tullygaon, within eighteen miles of Poona. There being encountered, harassed, and nearly surrounded by a Mahratta force reputed to consist of 50,000 men, the British army became panic-struck, destroyed the greater part of their stores, threw the heavy guns into a tank, and took to flight, closely urged by their active enemies. The managers of this wretched expedition concluded at Wargaum, about ten miles above the Bhore Ghat, a convention, by which, as the price of the release of the forces from their hopeless position, Salsette, the adjacent islands, and some other places, were to be ceded to the Mahrattas. These concessions were disavowed by the governor of Bombay, and a force, consisting of six battalions of infantry, a proportionate detail of artillery, and some cavalry, which had been despatched by the Bengal government, and placed under the command of Colonel Goddard, continued its course from the vicinity of the Jumna across Northern Hindostan to Surat. In the commencement of the year 1780, Colonel Goddard took Dubhoy and Ahmedabad, while other portions of the British force made acquisitions in the Concan. In the close of the same year, Bassein was taken by Goddard in person. That officer, in 1781, advanced on the road to Poona to the foot of the Bhore Ghat; but the movement appears to have been merely with a view to intimidation, and, being vigorously attacked by the Mahrattas, he made a disastrous retreat to Panwell, the port at which troops were generally embarked for Bombay. Both parties being tired of those harassing and indecisive operations, a treaty was, in 1782, concluded at Salby, on terms somewhat humiliating to the British government, which engaged to abandon the interests of Ragoba, and surrendered Bassein and the acquisitions in Guzerat, with the exception of Broach, which was subsequently made over to the Mahratta chief Scindia. On the death of the nawaub of Surat, in 1799, the British authorities at Bombay obtained from Govind Rao Guicowar a grant of the town of Surat and the adjacent territory belonging to it, guaranteeing to the family a competent pension for the relinquishment of their claim. At the same time a British subsidiary force was formed for the support of the Guicowar, whose authority was established against his opponents, after a few smart actions. In 1790, a treaty of offensive and defensive alliance against Tippoo Sultan had been concluded between the English government, the Peishwa, and the Nizam; and the Peishwa was also a party to the treaty of peace concluded with Tippoo in 1792. In 1795, the young Peishwa, Maderow Narrain, died. To secure a continuance of his own power, Nana Furnavese (one of the Mahratta ministers) endeavoured to exclude the legitimate heir, Bajee Rao, the son of Ragoba. But Nana's views were frustrated by Scindia, who arrived at Poona with a large force, and placed Bajee Rao upon the vacant throne. Scindia's influence became paramount at Poona, and he soon annihilated the independence of the Peishwa's government. In 1802, a contest took place between Scindia and Holkar. The Peishwa joined the former, whose army sustained a signal defeat near Poona, on the 25th October. The Peishwa fled to Bassein, having previously intimated to the British resident at his court his desire to enter into a defensive alliance with the Company on the basis of that of Hyderabad, and his readiness to cede territory for the maintenance of a subsidiary force. These overtures were favourably received by Lord Wellesley, and after a short negotiation a treaty was concluded at Bassein, by which the Peishwa engaged to receive, and the East-India Company to furnish, "a permanent subsidiary force of not less then six thousand regular native infantry, with the usual proportion of field-pieces and European artillerymen attached, and with the proper equipment of warlike stores and ammunition," to be stationed in perpetuity in his highness's dominions. The charge for maintaining this force was estimated at 25,00,000 rupees, or 250,000*l.* annually. To meet possible deficiencies, an additional annual sum of 100,000 rupees was allowed, the whole charge being defrayed by ceding to the British lands estimated to yield a revenue to that amount. "The conclusion of this treaty is to be regarded as an important step in the extension of the salutary influence of the British government in India." By a supplemental article, it was agreed that a native cavalry regiment should be added to the subsidiary force, and that the province of Bundelcund, belonging to the Peishwa, should be made over to the British, in lieu of the southern districts of his dominions which had been ceded by the treaty of Bassein. In 1803, certain districts were ceded by Scindia, under the treaty of Serji Anjengaum, to the allies engaged in the war against him; and by the partition treaty of Poona, a portion of the cession, comprehending the fort and territory of Broach, was assigned to the British. By the treaty of Baroda, in 1805, explaining, confirming, and consolidating former treaties, the Guicowar ceded to the British various districts now forming constituent parts of the collectorates of Ahmedabad and Kaira. In 1812, the island and harbour of Malwan, or Sindidroog, were obtained by treaty from the rajah of Kolapore, and in the same year the fort of Vingorla, and that of Gunaramo Tembe, with their respective ports, were similarly obtained from the rajah of Sawuntwarree. In 1815, the murder at Punderpoor of Gungadhur Shastree, the Guicowar's minister and envoy, who had repaired thither under the sanction and protection of the British government, and with the view of forwarding some political objects entertained by it, was a prominent indication of the hostile intentions of Bajee Rao, the Peishwa, by whose minister, Trimbukjee, the atrocity was perpetrated. On this supervened, in 1817, the general confederacy of the Mahratta states against British supremacy, and the Peishwa entering into it, was in the same year defeated in the engagement at Kirkee, and in 1818 at Ashti. He was subsequently deposed and pensioned by the East-India Company, and the greater part of his dominions incorporated with the presidency of Bombay. The territory acquired on that event comprises the present collectorates of Tannah and Rutnagherry, Poona, Candeish, Dharwar, Belgaum, Sattara, and the southern jagheers, containing collectively an area of 47,214 square miles. A portion of this territory, lying within the general line of the territory of the Nizam, was conveyed to that prince in exchange for his acquisitions under the treaty of Serji Anjengaum and the partition treaty of Poona. These were situated on the right bank of the river Seena, and in the district of Ahmednuggur, and being transferred to the Company, formed another addition to the Bombay presidency.

BOMBAY.—The principal place of the presidency of the same name. The island on which the city is situate, extends from north-east to south-west eight miles, with an average breadth of three, and landlocks the harbour lying between it and the mainland, protecting it from the violence of the Arabian Sea. To the south, this natural seaward bulwark is continued and strengthened by a couple of rocky islets. The more northern, which is joined to the island of Bombay by a causeway overflowed at high water, is called Old Woman's Island; the other, or more southern, is called Colaba, or Lighthouse Island; and this is united to Old Woman's Island by a causeway overflowed at high water spring tides, as the latter island is connected with Bombay. Thus the three islands, linked by causeways, form a continuous breakwater, extending from north-east to south-west a distance of nearly ten miles. Bombay is likewise connected with the large island to the northward, called Salsette, by a causeway and arched stone bridge from Mahim to Bandora, more recently constructed by government, aided by a munificent contribution from Sir Jamsetjee Jejeebhoy, a Parsee merchant of immense wealth, but of far greater liberality; the latter of which, indeed, appears almost boundless. Bombay owes him so much, that it would be almost criminal to pass over his name in any account of that settlement. His case affords an illustration of the value and utility of honorary distinctions. Wealth he needed not; but the honour of knighthood, conferred on him by the British sovereign, was an evidence to himself and to all his fellow-citizens, that his public spirit was neither overlooked nor disregarded. The honour could not fail to be the more gratifying, from the fact that he was the first native of India who ever received it. On approaching Bombay from the seaward, the view is very beautiful; the background in the distance beyond the harbour being formed by the range of Western Ghauts, and exhibiting the boldest, most picturesque, and varying outlines imaginable. Bombay "is formed by two ranges of rock of unequal lengths, running parallel to each other on opposite sides of the island; and these ranges are united at their extremities by hills of sandstone, which are only a few feet above the level of the sea. The interior of the island was formerly liable to be overflowed by the sea, which is now prevented by substantial works and embankments. The lower parts of the island are, however, still subject to the influence of the heavy rains, which in their season reduce them to a swamp; so that, during the continuance of the rainy monsoon, the houses are separated from each other by water, sometimes for several months. Bombay Island in coming from seaward appears very low, excepting Malabar Hill, which is of middling height, having a regular oblong appearance sloping a little towards the sea, and is covered with trees. Among these some white buildings are interspersed, with a signal-post and flagstaff at the point near Mazagon Hill, which is situated to the northward of Bombay town, and is of middling height, not easily known until well up the harbour. Parell Hill, farther northward, is a round mount, having on it a flagstaff; but this and an oblong hill near it, covered with trees, are not perceived until far up the harbour. Suree Fort is on a point of land near these hills." The area of the island is estimated at eighteen and a quarter square miles. The harbour is probably as large an expanse of water as is found anywhere landlocked; and its area may be estimated with tolerable safety at about fifty square miles, or if the shallow bight running towards the north of Salsette be included, at about eighty. On its east side this noble sheet of water is rendered picturesque by the islands Karanga, Elephanta, and Derwedi, called by British sailors Butcher Island. The lighthouse is situate at the southern extremity of Colaba island: its lantern is 150 feet above the level of the sea. There are six or seven fathoms water at the entrance of the harbour, and the tide rises sufficiently for the supply of wet docks which have been constructed at the pier or causeway connecting Colaba with Old Woman's Island. The greatest height which the tide rose in 1832 was seventeen feet eleven inches. Several excellent line-of-battle ships have been built here. Independently of its advantageous position with respect to the rest of India, as well as to Persia, Arabia, Africa, and more remotely Europe, the great excellence of the harbour of Bombay and its facilities for ship-building, as well as for commerce, give it a superiority over any other in India. An authority intimately acquainted with the subject thus testifies:—"In Bombay alone two ships of the line, or one ship and two frigates, can be produced to the British navy every eighteen months. The docks of Bombay are capable of containing ships of any force. Situated as Bombay is, between the forests of Malabar and Guzerat, she receives supplies of timber with every wind that blows. Flax of good quality is also the produce of our territories in India. It is calculated that every ship in the navy of Great Britain is renewed every twelve years. It is well known that teakwood-built ships last fifty years and upwards. Many ships Bombay-built, after running fourteen or fifteen years, have been bought into the navy, and were considered as strong as ever. The *Sir Edward Hughes* performed eight voyages as an Indiaman before she was purchased for the navy." The *Wellesley*, a seventy-four gun ship, the fire of which in 1839 destroyed the defences of Kurrachee, and which was in other instances instrumental in gaining important successes in India, was built at Bombay. More recently the *Meeanee*, of eighty guns, and the brigs *Jumna* and *Nerbudda*, have been built at this port for her majesty's government.

It has been remarked, that "the advantages of Bombay consist in its commercial site, importance, and resources, its unequalled harbour and means of naval accommodation, and its situation on the western coast, considered relatively to Europe and to the Poona Mahrattas." The old town or fort is situate on the southern extremity of the island, towards Old Woman's Island, and is about two miles in circuit, strongly fortified, "battery above battery completely commanding the harbour." On the land side it was formerly incapable of being defended against an attack made by regular approaches, as a bombardment of a few hours must have fired the whole town; the houses being arranged closely together, generally built of wood, and lofty; and in such a conflagration the magazines must have inevitably exploded. The formation of an extensive esplanade, and some other precautionary measures, have, however, of late years greatly added to the security of the place. Still more recently, the increase of the calibre of the guns employed has completed the means of defence, rendering them adequate to an effectual resistance of an attack likely to be made from any quarter. In the old town or fort the streets are very narrow; but great improvements have been lately made, and more are contemplated. New streets are projected; a better system of drainage has been introduced, and a plan devised for securing to the town an ample supply of wholesome water. Among the remarkable buildings is the Government House, extending along one side of a square planted with trees: it has a fine colonnade, and contains the government offices, a saloon, and library. There is a large and handsome church within the fort, and a Presbyterian place of worship; and a church has been recently built on the island of Colaba, where there are considerable cantonments. About a mile north-west of the fort is the

Black Town, the situation of which is so low that during the monsoon rains it is in many places flooded, and the communication between the houses cut off. Few Europeans inhabit either of those towns, their residences being for the most part dispersed over the island. Besides the Government House within the fort, there are two other government residences in the island; one at Parell, six miles north of the fort, and another at Malabar Point.

Like most Eastern towns, Bombay has suffered severely from the casualty of fire. A very destructive conflagration took place in October, 1845, commencing in the shop of a manufacturer of fireworks. Upwards of 190 houses were destroyed, and the loss of property was estimated at seven lacs of rupees (about 70,000*l.*). The extent of the conflagration and loss would doubtless have been much greater, but for the exertions of one of the magistrates, Mr. Edward Danvers, in superintending and directing, amidst much personal danger, the force at his disposal while engaged in attempts to stop the progress of the flames. The men employed in this duty were obtained by draughts from one of her majesty's regiments, from the marine battalion, and from various ships lying in the harbour. Some of the seamen distinguished themselves by one of those acts of cool and deliberate daring, in utter disregard of apparently impending death, which seem almost ordinary events to the hardy sons of the ocean. During the conflagration information was given to the police, that on the lower floor of a house, the upper part of which was on fire, there were deposited a number of barrels of gunpowder. A party of sailors immediately volunteered to remove them, and actually brought out the entire quantity, amounting to several thousand pounds weight, while fragments of burning materials were falling around them.

Bombay is the seat of a Supreme Court of justice, constituted under letters patent from the Crown, under powers granted by act of Parliament, and consisting of a chief justice and one puisne judge; from whose decision an appeal, subject to certain limitations and conditions, lies to the Queen in Council. The powers of this court are very extensive, embracing not only the civil and criminal jurisdiction exercised by the judges at home, whether in their courts at Westminster or on circuit, but also the functions of the courts of equity, the ecclesiastical and admiralty courts, and the adjudication of cases of insolvency. Such is the present constitution, and such the powers of the Supreme Court; but the act 16 & 17 Vict. c. 95, recently passed, appears to contemplate some changes in the judicial institutions of India, the nature of which cannot of course be anticipated. The chief court of the Company is termed the Sudder Adawlut: its functions are to hear appeals from the district courts throughout the presidency, and to exercise a general supervision over those courts. Among the public establishments at Bombay may be enumerated the Chamber of Commerce; the Bank of Bombay; the Oriental Bank, of which the chief Indian branch is here situate, the head office being in London; a branch of the Agra and United Service Bank; the government Savings Bank; several insurance companies; the Bombay Steam Navigation Company; the Bombay branch of the Royal Asiatic Society; the native general library; the Bombay Geographical Society; the Medical and Physical Society of Bombay; the Agri-horticultural Society of Western India, and the Bombay Diocesan Library. There are also various associations for the promotion of benevolent and religious objects. Amusements, especially those of a national character, are much encouraged by Europeans; and the climate has not prevented the formation of clubs for the practice of the Scottish game of golf and the English one of cricket. A Yacht Club also furnishes opportunity for the indulgence of the nautical taste so prevalent at home. The Elphinstone Institution has already been referred to in the notice of the educational establishments given under the article "Bombay presidency."

The population is composed of various elements. According to a census of the islands of Bombay and Colaba, taken on the 1st May, 1849, the numbers of the various castes, including the military and the floating population of the harbour, were as under:—

Jains, Lingaehs, or Boodhists ...	1,902
Brahmins	6,936
Hindoos of other castes	289,995
Mussulmans	124,155
Parsees	114,698
Jews	1,132
Native Christians	7,456
Indo-Britons	1,333
Indo-Portuguese	5,417
Pure European	5,088
Seedee, Negro, African	889
Other castes	7,118
Total	566,119

The pursuits and occupations of the people are of course various, and, as in all other great cities, there is a proportion whose avocations will not sustain minute inquiry without damage to their reputation. In 1843 an extensive and most extraordinary system of plunder was discovered, and some of those concerned in it brought to justice. This scheme was organized with all the precision that might be looked for in a plan for prosecuting any lawful object devised and conducted by men habituated to business and well acquainted with its details. The number of persons engaged in it amounted to two or three hundred, and its operations had been carried on without interruption, and down to a very late period before the discovery, without suspicion on the part of the superior officers of government, for upwards of thirty years. The chief scene of plunder was the harbour, where the goods were unlawfully but quietly transferred from one boat to another, then landed in the ordinary way, with as much coolness as though they had been legally acquired, conveyed in open day from the shore to the godowns or warehouses of persons of apparent substance and credit, and there brought to sale without any attempt at concealment. This traffic constituted the principal business of the gang, who, however, it was believed, occasionally varied it by suggesting and encouraging piracies, though they did not actively engage in them, and by participating in the profits of robberies and burglaries committed in the town. It was feared, indeed, that crimes of deeper tinge than those against property might be charged upon the gang. Though this herd of plunderers continued to exercise their craft for nearly a third of a century without drawing upon themselves the notice of the government, their existence and occupations were known to many not associated with them, but whose silence was secured by that powerful spring of conduct in India, respect for caste, or by a resort to intimidation. These men were indeed said to be more dreaded by those who knew them and their pursuits than was the power of the government. The staff of the association was perfect and well organized. It had a chief director, superintendents under him, a cashier and a numerous body of inferior officers afloat and ashore. A regular set of books were kept with the most scrupulous accuracy, and the division of profits was made with the strictest nicety. Such a body, united for such purposes, could scarcely in these days exist in any part of Europe for any long period; and it may be regarded as pretty certain, that those who exercise the profession of plunder in that quarter of the globe do not conduct their business or apportion their unlawful gains with the precision which marked the proceedings of this body of marauders. Its existence affords a curious illustration of the peculiar nature of Indian society as compared with that found at home. The temperature is moderate in proportion to the latitude, being diminished by the sea-breezes. The climate was formerly considered very unhealthy; but it has of late years greatly improved, the proportion of deaths to the population in ordinary seasons now closely approximating to that of London. Bombay is distant from Calcutta, W., 1,040 miles; from Madras, N.W., 645; from Delhi, S.W., 730; from Hyderabad, N.W., 390; from Ahmedabad, S., 285; from Poona, N.W., 75. Lat. 18° 57′, long. 72° 52′.

BOMBRA.—A raj in the country superintended by the political agent for the south-west frontier of Bengal. It is bounded on the north by Bonie, on the south by Bheracole and Pallera, on the east by Keunjur, and on the west by Sumbhulpore. It extends from lat. 21° 11′ to 21° 38′, and from long. 84° 11′ to 85° 11′; is sixty-four miles in length from east to west, and thirty in breadth. The area is 1,244 square miles. The value of the raj has been estimated at 10,000 rupees per annum. The tribute is nominally 340 rupees; but it is diminished by 300 rupees allowed in consequence of the Raepore road passing through the estate. The people, estimated at about 56,000, are said to be savages, and their ruler to be no better.

BOMEEGUTEH, in the British district of Dharwar, presidency of Bombay, a town five miles W. of the route from Coomta to Dharwar, 24 miles S. of the latter. Lat. 15° 6′, long. 75° 3′.

BOMINI, in the British district of Allahabad, lieut.-gov. of the N.W. Provinces, a village on the route by the Kutra Pass, from Allahabad to Rewa, and 34 miles S.E. of the former city. Lat. 25° 9′, long. 82° 15′.

BOMOREE, in Bundlecund, in the raj or principality of Oorcha or Tehree, a town on the route from Agra to Saugor, 180 miles S.E. of former, 93 N.W. of latter. It is situate on a rising ground, and is a rather pleasant place, the streets being wide and clean. Here is an extensive jhil or mere, formed by a vast artificial mound, constructed across the extremity of a valley, receiving the water of a stream. It is a noble sheet of water, about four miles long and two wide, deep and clear, abounding with fish, and very extensively available for the purposes of irrigation. On a rocky ridge overlooking the lake is the ruined palace of the rajah who made it. Lat. 25° 8′, long. 79° 10′.

BOMUNPILLEE.—A town in Hyderabad, or dominions of the Nizam, distant N.E. from Hyderabad 150 miles. Lat. 18° 20′, long. 80° 34′.

BONDSDORA. — A river rising in lat. 19° 39′, long. 83° 27′, in the native state of Calahandy, on the south-west frontier of Bengal, and discharging itself into the Bay of Bengal in lat. 18° 21′, long. 84° 12′.

BONHAT, in the British district of Beerbhoom, lieut.-gov. of Bengal, a town on the route of the railroad from Burdwan to Rajmahal, 60 miles S. of the latter. Lat. 24° 10′, long. 87° 47′.

BONICUT.—A town in the native state of Cashmere, or dominions of Gholab Singh, distant N. from Sirinagur 29 miles. Lat. 34° 28′, long. 74° 51′.

BONIE.—A raj under the political agent for the south-west frontier. It is bounded on the north by Chota Nagpore, on the east by Keunjur and Singbhoom, on the west by Sumbhulpoor and Gangpore, and on the south by Bombra. Its area is 1,057 square miles. The centre is in lat. 22°, long. 85° 8′. The people are represented to be savages, and the native government bad. The revenue of the country, as computed by the British agent, is 6,000 rupees. The annual tribute is 200 rupees. The population is estimated at upwards of 47,000.

BONYTEE DEBEE, in Sirmour, a summit of the ridge extending from Bus Peak to Nahun. It is surmounted by a small Hindoo temple and the remains of a stone fort held by the Goorkhas during their occupation of the country, and was a station of the small series of triangles during the trigonometrical survey of the Himalayas. Elevation above the sea 5,120 feet. Lat. 30° 38′, long. 77° 19′.

BOOCHEYKEE, in the Reechna Dooab division of the Punjab, a town situated on a feeder of the Ravee river, 45 miles S.W. of the town of Lahore. Lat. 31° 18′, long. 73° 30′.

BOOCHKAL, in Bussahir, a pass on the route from Rampoor to the Shatool Pass. It is the highest and most northern limit of the forest on this declivity of the Himalaya. Elevation above the sea 11,800 feet. Lat. 31° 21′, long. 77° 59′.

BOODAGAON.—A town in the territory of Nagpore, distant N.E. from Nagpore 90 miles. Lat. 21° 52′, long. 80° 20′.

BOODAWUL, or BOORAWUL. — The name of a district in Candeish, presidency of Bombay, formerly belonging to a native chief. In 1855 the territory escheated to the British government, from failure of heirs on the part of the late chief. Distant E. from Dhoolia 65 miles. Lat. 21° 3′, long. 75° 43′.

BOODGOWARRA, in the British territory of Saugor and Nerbudda, lieut.-gov. of the N.W. Provinces, a town on the left bank of the Weingunga river, 31 miles N.E. of Seuni. Lat. 22° 9′, long. 80° 9′.

BOODHANUH, in the British district of Muzuffurnugar, lieut.-gov. of the N.W. Provinces, a town on the route from Kurnoul to Meerut, and 43 miles S.E. of the former. It is of considerable size, has a bazaar, and supplies are abundant. The road in this part of the route is good; the country wooded and well cultivated. Population 6,750. Lat. 29° 16′, long. 77° 32′.

BOODUHREYEE, or BURURAEE, in the British district of Mynpooree, lieut.-gov. of the N.W. Provinces, a village on the route from the city of Agra to the cantonment of Mynpooree, and 30 miles W. of the latter. Lat. 27° 7′, long. 78° 40′.

BOODYGERRY.—A town in the territory of Mysore, distant N.E. from Seringapatam 86 miles. Lat. 13° 9′, long. 77° 49′.

BOODYHAUL.—A town in the territory of Mysore, distant N. from Seringapatam 82 miles. Lat. 13° 36′, long. 76° 29′.

BOOGODAH, in the British district of Ganjam, presidency of Madras, a town 10 miles S.E. of Goomsoor. Lat. 19° 50′, long. 84° 51′.

BOOJAN, in the British district of Kumaon, lieut.-gov. of the N.W. Provinces, a village on the route from Almora to Kasheepoor, 12 miles S.W. of the former. Lat. 29° 30′, long. 79° 31′.

BOOKAPATAM, in the British district of Bellary, presidency of Madras, a town on the right bank of the Chittrawutty river, 90 miles S.E. of Bellary. Lat. 14° 12′, long. 77° 53′.

BOOLEE, or BUDI, in the British district of Kumaon, lieut.-gov. of the N.W. Provinces, a village on the route from Ascot, up the valley of the river Kalee, to the Beans Pass, into Hiundes or South-western Tibet. Boolee is in lat. 30° 6′, long. 80° 52′.

BOOLUNDSHUHUR.—A British district under the lieut.-gov. of the N.W. Provinces, bounded on the north by the British district Meerut, on the east by the British districts Moradabad and Budaon, on the south by the British district Allygurh, and on the southwest and west by the British districts Goorgaon and Delhi and the jaghire of Bulubgurh. It lies between lat. 28° 3′—28° 43′, long. 77° 28′—78° 32′; is eighty miles in length from south-east to north-west, and fifty-seven in breadth from north-east to south-west. The climate is liable to considerable extremes, as rather sharp frosts are not unknown in winter, the thermometer falling a few degrees below the freezing-point, and water becoming congealed under shelter of a tent; yet in the latter part of spring and the beginning of summer, when the hot winds set in from Rajpootana and Southern Sirhind, the temperature becomes very high. The surface of the country has a general slope from north-west to southeast, as indicated by the descent of the slopes of the Jumna and Ganges in that direction, and also of those of the Hindun and East Kali Nuddee, the courses of which lie between those two great rivers, and in some measure parallel to them. The country, though remarkably level, has a gradual and very gentle elevation about midway between the Ganges and Jumna, rising in that part into a slight ridge, along which the channel of the Ganges Canal holds its course. Cotton appears to be the staple production of the soil, for commercial purposes, and might, it is believed, become a rich source of profit to the cultivator, merchant, and manufacturer. As in other parts of the Doab, the soil here produces indigo, sugar, tobacco, wheat, barley, millet, and various kinds of pulse. Domestic quadrupeds are scarcely one half the size of those in Bengal and Behar. Under the existing revenue settlement of the North-West Provinces, the demand of the government on the lands of this district has been fixed for a term of years, and is not liable to be increased until 1859. The population of the district is returned at 778,342. It appears, moreover, that by far the largest portion of the people are Hindoo; the respective numbers being Hindoos, 633,696; Mussulmans and others, 144,646. The following is a classification of the towns and villages in the district:—

Number containing less than 1,000 inhabitants..	1,346
Ditto more than 1,000 and less than 5,000......	121
Ditto more than 5,000 and less than 10,000	6
Ditto more than 10,000 and less than 50,000....	5
Total..........................	1,478

This district formed part of the territory acquired by Perron, a French adventurer in the service of Scindia, who, arriving in India in no higher capacity than that of a common sailor, succeeded, by a series of fortunate intrigues, in obtaining the chief command under the Mahratta chief above named, and ultimately in elevating himself to the rank of a petty sovereign. The Franco-Mahratta state thus formed was marked by the sagacious policy of the Marquis Wellesley as an excrescence on the face of India, to be extirpated with the least possible delay, and Lord Lake was ordered to regard its annihilation as a primary object. Perron, who seems to have been more anxious for the preservation of his moveable property than of his dignity or power, after a feeble attempt at resistance, abandoned both his territory and his troops, and made his peace with the British government. The victory gained by Lord Lake in the vicinity of Delhi over the fragmentary remains of the French force, gave the final blow to the short-lived state which had sprung up and been cut down with almost unparalleled rapidity. The territory was included in the cessions made by Scindia to the East-India Company, under the second article of the treaty of Serjee Angengaum, concluded 30th December, 1803.

BOOLUNDSHUHUR, or BURRUN, the principal town of a pergunnah in the British district of the same name, is situate on the right bank of the Kali Nuddi, there passed in the dry season by a good ford, and during the rains by ferry. It lies on the route from Bareilly to Delhi, and 40 miles S.E. of the latter. There is a bazaar here, and supplies are abundant. The town contains a population of 15,005 inhabitants. Elevation above the sea 784 feet. Distance N.W. from Calcutta 780 miles. Lat. 28° 24′, long. 77° 56′.

BOOMIDAIRAH.—A town in the territory of Nagpore, distant N.W. from Bustur 46 miles. Lat. 19° 33′, long. 81° 23′.

BOONDEE, in Rajpootana, a small territory named from its principal place, and under the political superintendence of the Governor-General. It is bounded on the north by the state of Jeypore; on the east by the state of Kotah; on the south by Scindia's dominions; and on the west by the state of Oodeypoor. It is eighty-five miles in length, and fifty in breadth, and lies between lat. 24° 58′ and 25° 55′, long. 75° 23′ and 76° 30′. The area is 2,291 square miles. A range of mountains, running from north-east to south-west, divides it into two nearly equal portions of level expanse; that on the south-east extending to the river Chumbul, and that on the north-west reaching to the base of the mountains towards Ajmere. The only river of importance is the Chumbul, which first touches on the territory in lat. 25° 17′, long. 75° 58′, holds a course north-east for sixty miles, forming for that distance the boundary between this state and that of Kotah, and is navigable during the rains for craft of considerable burthen. The Mej or Nej, a small river flowing from the Oodeypore territory or Mewar, takes a course in a direction north-east, through Boondee, for about eighty miles, and falls into the Chumbul. The other streams are unimportant. Iron abounds in the neighbourhood of the town of Boondee, which is celebrated for its manufactures in this metal. The climate is deemed unhealthy; fevers and rheumatism, ophthalmic and bronchial affections, are said to prevail in most parts. The sovereign, his feudatories, and the dominant portion of the people, are Rajpoots of the Hara tribe; but the greater part of the population, especially in the mountains, are Meenas, considered to be the indigenous inhabitants. These are indefatigable freebooters, and when Scindia overran this part of India in 1809, so incessantly harassed his army, that he found it necessary to march away, though no regular resistance was offered in the field. The military force at the disposal of the state, including the troops of the feudal chiefs and the police force, amounts to 6,170 men. The only fort of importance in Boondee is Nynwah. Bulwunt Sing obtained possession of it in 1806 by bribery, and retained it for several months, though many fruitless attempts were made for its reduction. The amount of the revenue of Boondee from land-assessment, transit-duties, and a few minor sources, has been computed to be five lacs of rupees, or 50,000*l*. The population may probably be assumed, at the average of British Rajpootana, 100 to the square mile; at which rate it would be 229,100. The rajah of Boondee, by lineage of the Hara subdivision of the Chauhan tribe of Rajpoots, originally ruled over the whole of Haraoti, so named from its population. According to Tod, the city and state of Boondee were founded in the year 1342, by Rao Dewa, in a site which he wrested from the indigenous Meenas, a great number of whom he ruthlessly put to the sword. In 1569, Rao Soorjun, the sovereign of Boondee, held the celebrated fortress of Rintimpoor for the rajah of Mewar, and surrendered it to Akbar on condition of receiving an extensive government, and a high command in the army of the Padshah. The territory of Boondee was dismembered by Jehangir, the son and successor of Akbar, who granted the portion south-east of the Chumbul to Madhu Singh, the great-grandson of Rao Soorjun, and declared him Rao of Kota, the capital of that tract. Chutter Sal, the ruler of Boondee at the time of the contest between Dara and Aurungzebe, espoused the cause of the former, and was slain in the battle of Samaghar. At the battle of Jajau, in 1707, where Azim and Moazzim, the sons of Aurungzebe, contended for the succession, the Haras of Boondee supported the cause of the latter, and succeeded in placing him on the throne. In 1804, during the disastrous retreat of the British force under Colonel Monson before Holkar, the rajah of Boondee showed himself a firm supporter of the British cause; not only giving the retiring force unmolested passage through his territory, but aiding them to the extent of his ability, and thus drawing on himself the determined enmity of Holkar, to which he was given up by the pusillanimous policy of that period, the Mahrattas taking military occupation of his capital. On the commencement, in 1817, of the Mahratta and Pindarree wars, the ruler of Boondee came forward with alacrity to further the British views, and at the conclusion of peace was rewarded by a remission of the tribute previously paid to Holkar, and which by the result of the war had fallen to the disposal of the British government. At the same time the lands held by Holkar within the state of Boondee were restored; the fidelity of the rajah being thus tardily acknowledged. The tribute paid to Scindia was continued, but transferred to the British government. This tribute amounted to 80,000 rupees; but 40,000 of the sum were on account of two-thirds of the pergunnah of Patun, which was to have been recovered from Scindia. The recovery was not, however, effected, and the claim of the British government to tribute was on this account reduced to one-half the contemplated amount. By the treaty of Gwalior, in January, 1844, the management of Scindia's share of Patun was made over to the British government. The treaty between Boondee and the East-India Company was made in 1818. The rajah, who had so strongly and repeatedly manifested his regard for British alliance, died in 1821, about three years after the conclusion of the treaty, and was succeeded by his son, then about eleven years of age. A council of regency, consisting of four persons of station and influence, was named, but did not long maintain its authority. The mother of the infant rajah intimated her opinion, that "the system would not work; that four English gentlemen might conduct state affairs in concert, but that four natives never could." Upon this lady the exercise of the powers of the regency was thereupon conferred; but it soon became evident that the choice was an unfortunate one. The interests of the country were neglected; the training of the young prince for the duties of his position was unattended to, and the queen-mother was even suspected of ministering to his vices, with the view of prolonging the period of her own power. The evil influences of this woman were to some extent counteracted by an able and sincere minister, who extricated the state from a mass of financial difficulties, and by regularity of payment rendered the military force efficient and contented. The useful life of this valuable state-servant was, however, cut short by assassination. The young rajah had married a sister of the rajah of Joudpore, who was about twice his own age. Some points in the treatment of this lady gave offence to her family, and a band of conspirators from Joudpore perpetrated the dark deed above related. Having accomplished their object, they fortified themselves in their house, and prepared for defence. There they were cannonaded from the hill-fort. A party of their friends outside the walls made demonstrations of an intention to relieve them, but took no effectual steps for the purpose. Other parties from Joudpore were approaching; but two leaders of the conspiracy were captured in an attempt to make their escape, and publicly executed. A third met death in a less formal mode; and these disheartening circumstances, combined with the firmness and energy displayed by the British representative, who had proceeded to the spot, probably averted a war between Boondee and Joudpore, which might readily have become general among the Rajpoot states.

BOONDEE.—The capital of the Rajpoot state of the same name, a town situate in a valley, or rather basin, nearly surrounded on all sides by rocky hills. The palace is situate on the slope of the hill above the town, with which it communicates by a road running in a zigzag direction on the face of the steep acclivity. According to Tod, this splendid residence "is an aggregate of palaces, each having the name of its founder; and yet the whole so well harmonizes, and the character of the architecture is so uniform, that its breaks or fantasies appear only to arise from the peculiarity of the position, and serve to diversify its beauties. The Chuttermahl, or that built by Rajah Chuttersall, is the most extensive and most modern addition. It has two noble halls, supported by double ranges of columns of serpentine." Indeed it seems generally admitted, that the palace is well entitled to the distinction which it has acquired in Rajpootana of unsurpassed beauty; and though some structures have been erected in imitation of it, such as the Castle of Indarghur, none, it is said, can compete with the original. The town contains few edifices of any size or beauty; but the two principal bazaars are of good width, clean, and occupied by many traders. As Boondee, however, has no pretensions to commerce, it offers no inducement to merchants on a large scale. A wall environs the town, the entrances to which are by three several massive gates, which continue closed from sunset to sunrise. The population consists principally of native Haras, a few leading Hindoo foreigners, and a small proportion of Mahomedans. Distant direct from Kotah, N.W., 22 miles; Bombay, N.E., 490; Agra, S.W., 195; Delhi, S.W., 245. Lat. 25° 26′, long. 75° 43′.

BOONDEE KA GOTRA.—A town in the Rajpoot state of Boondee, distant N. from Boondee 15 miles. Lat. 25° 40′, long. 75° 46′.

BOONEERE, in Northern Afghanistan, is the tract lying north-west of the Indus, and north of the Kabool river, and bearing the general name of the Eusufzai country. It is inclosed by the Indus on the south-east, the Hindoo Koosh on the north; on other sides by mountains separating it from Suwat on the west, and on the south from the country held by the Khuttuk and Eusufzai tribes, on the lower course of the Kabool river. In its general character it is rugged, being composed of a number of small valleys, opening into one larger, through which flows the Burrindoo, a stream falling into the Indus on the west side, a little below Torbela. Booneere lies between lat. 34°—34° 40′, long. 72°—73°.

BOONGUL.—A town in Hyderabad, or dominions of the Nizam, distant S.W. from Hyderabad 31 miles. Lat. 16° 59′, long. 78° 17′.

BOORAH, in the British district of Mynpooree, lieut.-gov. of the N.W. Provinces, a village on the route from the city of Agra to the cantonment of Mynpooree, and 34 miles W. of the latter. Lat. 27° 7′, long. 78° 36′.

BOORAHBULLUNG.—A river rising in Mohurbunge, one of the Cuttack mehals, in lat. 22° 7′, long. 86° 30′, and, flowing in a south-easterly direction, falls into the Bay of Bengal in lat. 21° 28′, long. 87° 7′, eight miles S.E. of the town of Balasore.

BOORAI, in the British district of Midnapoor, lieut.-gov. of Bengal, a town five miles E. of the trunk road from Midnapoor to Cuttack, 40 miles S. of the former. Lat. 21° 50′, long. 87° 24′.

BOORAINEE, in the British district of Ghazeepoor, lieut.-gov. of the N.W. Provinces, a town on the right bank of the Ganges, 620 miles N.W. of Calcutta by water. Lat. 25° 25′, long. 83° 30′.

BOORBARORE, in the British district of Meerut, lieut.-gov. of the N.W. Provinces, a village on the route from Delhi to the town of Meerut, and nine miles S.W. of the latter. Lat. 28° 54′, long. 77° 42′.

BOOREAH, in Sirhind, a town on the right bank of the canal or watercourse of Firoz Shah. The population consists principally of Sikhs. It has a bazaar, and is of some importance on account of the ferry in the vicinity over the Jumna, by which the route proceeds from Ambala to Saharunpoor. The canal of Firoz, two and a half or three feet deep, is crossed by a ford. The territory of which this is the principal place, constitutes one of the protected Sikh states. It contains an area of 80 square miles, and a population of 11,920 persons. The town is distant N.W. from Calcutta 1,005 miles. Lat. 30° 9′, long. 77° 25′.

BOOREE DEHING.—A river of Assam, and a considerable feeder of the Brahmapootra; it is an offset of the Noh Dihing, from which it diverges in lat. 27° 29′, long. 96° 11′, and flowing in a westerly direction through Assam for 121 miles, during which course it receives several smaller rivers, falls into the Brahmapootra in lat. 27° 15′, long. 94° 41′.

BOOREE LOHIT.—The name of one of the two streams into which the Brahmapootra divides in its passage through the valley of Assam. It diverges from the main stream about lat. 21° 7′, long. 94° 30′, and flowing south-west for fifty-nine miles, rejoins it about lat. 26° 45′, long. 93° 42′.

BOORHATH, in the British district of Seebpoor, in Upper Assam, a town on the left bank of the Disang river, 43 miles N.E. of Seebpoor. Lat. 27° 9′, long. 95° 20′.

BOORHAUNPOOR, in the territory of Gwalior, or possessions of Scindia's family, a town situate on the north or right side of the river Taptee, the banks of which are here bold, and rise sixty or seventy feet above the average height of the stream. It is surrounded by a weak rampart of brickwork, which is highest along the lofty bank of the river; and, seen from the south bank, the place has a striking appearance. The ground-plan of the rampart is a semicircle, the diameter extending along the Taptee, and half-way between the extremities is a palace built by Akbar. This edifice is styled the Lal Kilah, or Red Fort, from the colour of its bricks. Though much dilapidated, it still contains a ruinous mosque, halls embellished with white marble, gardens or pleasure-grounds, and other relics of imperial magnificence. A rampart, separating it from the town, gave it the character of a fortress. The only other building worth notice is the Jamamasjit, or great mosque, built by Aurungzebe. Notwithstanding that the Brahminical population is numerous, they have no temples, their rudely-sculptured idols being placed under trees, or in ill-built niches. A few of the wealthier merchants have good and commodious houses, built of teak, profusely decorated with carvings. The most wealthy and influential of the trading community are the Borahs, a Mahomedan tribe, descended from the Hassannee, so dreaded in the time of the crusades. The Borahs, with their families, inhabit a distinct ward, which they shut up at night, excluding all other persons; and they have a peculiar mosque. There are still here, principally in the hands of Borahs, considerable manufactures of muslins, flowered silks, and brocades, for which the place was formerly so famous, that in the time of Tavernier, about the year 1665, they were exported in great quantities to Persia, Egypt, Turkey, Russia, and Poland; but even at that time the place was much decayed. In 1849 this town was the scene of a desperate and sanguinary affray, which took place between the Mahomedans and the Hindoos, upon the occasion of one of the religious festivals of the latter.

Boorhaunpoor is mentioned in the Ayeen Akbery as a large city. Its governor was one of the greatest officers of the court of Delhi, and usually an uncle, a brother, or a son of the Padshah. Previously to its subjugation by Akbar, in 1599, it was a place of much importance, being the capital of the sovereigns of Candeish, one of whom, Malik Nasir, founded it about A.D. 1414. Hence the sovereigns of Candeish are often denominated sultans of Boorhaunpoor. It was visited in 1611 by Sir Thomas Roe, on his embassy to the Great Mogul; in 1685, under the reign of Aurungzebe, it was plundered by the troops of Sumbhajee, the Mahratta leader under the command of Humbeer Rao; and in 1720 was wrested from the government of Delhi by Asaf Jah, or Nizam-ul-mulk, who there defeated the army brought against him by the Padshah's officer. It appears to have been subjugated by Madhajee Scindia in his rapid course of aggrandizement in the latter part of the eighteenth century, and was occupied in 1803 by the British under Colonel Stevenson, but was restored in the same year by the sixth article of the treaty of Serji Anjengaum. Its present assessment to the exchequer of Scindia is 45,000 rupees annually. Distant N.E. from Bombay 280 miles, S.E. from Oojein 132, N.E. from Poona 250. Lat. 21° 18′, long. 76° 20′.

BOOROO, in the British district of Ahmedabad, presidency of Bombay, a town on the route from Cambay to Rajkote, 22 miles N.W. of the former. Lat. 22° 24′, long. 72° 19′.

BOOSUN, in the jaghire of Jujhur, lieut.-gov. of the N.W. Provinces, a village on the route from Delhi to Narnol, and five miles E. of the latter. Lat. 28° 2′, long. 76° 16′.

BOOTEA.—A petty native state on the south-west frontier of the presidency of Bengal. Its centre is in lat. 21° 55′, long. 82° 45′.

BOOZROOK.—A town in Hyderabad, or dominions of the Nizam, distant W. from Hyderabad 122 miles. Lat. 17° 13′, long. 76° 42′.

BOPALPUTNAM.—A town in Nagpoor, distant S.E. from Nagpoor 180 miles. Lat. 18° 51′, long. 80° 30′.

BOPLEE, in the British territory of Saugor and Nerbudda, lieut.-gov. of the N.W. Provinces, a town 18 miles S.E. from Seuni, 63 miles N.E. of Nagpoor. Lat. 21° 50′, long. 79° 51′.

BORAI.—See Boree.

BORAI.—A river rising in lat. 21° 8′, long. 74° 3′, at the northern extremity of the Syadree range of mountains, and, flowing through Khandeish for 64 miles, falls into the Taptee river on its southern or left bank, in lat. 21° 20′, long. 74° 51′.

BORARA.—A town in the Rajpoot state of Kishengurh, distant S.E. from Ajmeer 30 miles. Lat. 26° 16′, long. 75° 10′.

BORA SAMBA.—A small raj within the jurisdiction of the political agent for the south-west frontier of Bengal. It is bounded on the north by Phooljee, on the east and south by the petty state of Patna, and on the west by that of Kerrial. Its central point is in lat. 20° 55′, long. 83° 10′. Its form is angular and very regular, being nearly oblong. Its area is 622 square miles. The country is wild, and the people savage, even beyond their neighbours. When visited by the British agent, the rajah and his relations lived in an almost inaccessible valley, where they afforded refuge to many lawless plunderers. The agent compelled the surrender of some rebel subjects of the rajah of Nagpore, and the restoration of a number of cattle stolen by them. On an elevated table-land in this country the temperature is said to be so moderate that the orange-tree grows well. The annual revenue of the country was estimated at about 4,000 rupees. The tribute, which is only 160 rupees, was regularly paid. The population is estimated at about 28,000.

BORE, or BHORE.—A town in one of the Southern Mahratta jaghires of the same name, in political connection with the presidency of Bombay, distant S. from Poona 25 miles. Lat. 18° 9′, long. 73° 53′.

BOREE.—A river of Khandeish, rising in lat. 20° 47′, long. 74° 18′, and flowing first east for fifty miles, and then north for forty more, falls into the Taptee opposite the town of Thalnair, in lat. 21° 14′, long. 75° 4′.

BOREE, or BORAI.—A petty district, the patrimony of a Bheel chief, in the territory of Malwa, under the political superintendence of the Governor-General's agent at Indore. The revenue of the rajah amounts to 14,000 rupees, or 1,400*l.* per annum, and a small body of infantry and cavalry, consisting of about forty-five men in the whole, is maintained in his service. The town of Borai is in lat. 22° 30′, long. 74° 44′.

BOREE.—A town in Nagpoor, distant N.W. from Nagpoor 96 miles. Lat. 22° 21′, long. 78° 23′.

BOREE, in the British district of Tannah, presidency of Bombay, a town on the route from Bombay to Damaun, 79 miles N. of the former. Lat. 20° 6′, long. 72° 46′.

BOREGAUM.—A town in Nagpoor, distant S.W. from Nagpoor 60 miles. Lat. 20° 40′, long. 78° 24′.

BOREGAUM.—A town in the native state of Gwalior, or Scindia's possessions, distant N.E. from Boorhanpoor 21 miles. Lat. 21° 35′, long. 76° 30′.

BORENAR, in the British district of Khandeish, presidency of Bombay, a town on the right bank of the Girna river, 42 miles E. of Dhoolia. Lat. 20° 50′, long. 75° 25′.

BORI GUNDUK.—The most considerable feeder of the Gunduck river. Rising on the northern face of the great snowy range of the Himalayas, about lat. 28° 58′, long. 85° 50′, it flows in a south-westerly direction for fifty miles, during the latter part of which it passes through a gorge in the Himalayas, and enters the territory of Nepal, which it traverses for sixty miles, and then takes the name of Trisul Gunga. From this point, turning south-west, it holds a course of seventy miles, and joins the Gunduck near the town of Nayacot, in lat. 27° 30′, long. 84° 5′.

BORKHEREE.—A town in the native state of Joura, in Central India, distant N.E. from Joura 30 miles. Lat. 23° 50′, long. 75° 29′.

BOSOMPOEE-MAH.—A town on the south-eastern borders of Assam, inhabited by the Naga tribes, situated 54 miles N.W. of Muneepoor, and 79 miles S.E. of Nowgong. Lat. 25° 29′, long. 93° 32′.

BOTEH, in the British district of Poonah, presidency of Bombay, a town on the right bank of the Moola river, 18 miles E. of Jooneer. Lat. 19° 16′, long. 74° 10′.

BOUME KEUNE.—A town of Pegu, in the British district of Bassein, on the route from Cape Negrais to Sandoway, 60 miles N.E. of the former. Lat. 16° 52′, long. 94° 30′.

BOUNLEE.—A town in the Rajpoot state of Jeypoor, distant S.E. from Jeypoor 50 miles. Lat. 26° 20′, long. 76° 21′.

BOUTI, or BOULEE, in Bundelcund, in the territory of Rewa, a village near the route from Mirzapoor to the town of Rewa, and 58 miles S.W. of the former. It is remarkable for a very picturesque cascade, formed by a small river flowing some miles farther north into the Chutenea, a tributary of the Bilund. The fall is 400 feet down a rock, the base of which is of sandstone of a green colour, having above it a variegated or mottled stratum, overlaid by a purple stratum, which becomes more and more light-coloured, so as to approach salmon-colour before reaching the surface. Elevation above the sea 1,000 feet. Lat. 24° 41′, long. 81° 59′.

BOVANIKUDAL, or BHAWANI, in the British district of Coimbatore, presidency of Madras, a town situate at the confluence of the rivers Bhawani and Cauvery. It has a ruinous fort and two very celebrated temples, one sacred to Siva, the other to Vishnu, built by the poligar of the place, who held it as a feudatory to the rajahs of Madura. Distance from the town of Coimbatore, N.E., 58 miles; Madras, S.W., 213. Lat. 11° 26′, long. 77° 44′.

BOWAH, or BAOOHA, in the British district of Futtehpore, lieut.-gov. of the N.W. Provinces, a town on the route from Banda to the town of Futtehpore, and 15 miles S.W. of the latter. It has a bazaar, and is supplied with water from wells and a tank. Lat. 25° 52′, long. 80° 40′.

BOWAL, in the British district of Dacca, lieut.-gov. of Bengal, a town on the route from Dacca to Jumalpoor, 18 miles N. of the former. Lat. 23° 57′, long. 90° 30′.

BOWANA.—See BURANA.

BOWANEEGUNJE, in the British district of Rajeshaye, lieut.-gov. of Bengal, a town on the route from Rampore to Dinajepore, 20 miles N.E. of the former. Lat. 24° 35′, long. 88° 50′.

BOWANNEE, in the Reechna Dooab division of the Punjab, a town situated on the left bank of the Cheenaub river, 80 miles W. of the town of Lahore. Lat. 31° 37′, long. 72° 50′.

BOWARA, in the British district of Tirhoot, lieut.-gov. of Bengal, a town on the left bank of the river Baloun, 18 miles N.E. of Durbunga. Lat. 26° 17′, long. 86° 10′.

BOWERGURH, in the British territory of Saugor and Nerbudda, lieut.-gov. of the N.W. Provinces, a town 33 miles S. of Hoshungabad, 30 miles N. of Baitool. Lat. 22° 16′, long. 77° 51′.

BOWLEE.—See BILOHI.

BOWNEE.—See BAONEE.

BOWPHUT, in the British district of Backergunje, lieut.-gov. of Bengal, a town on the right bank of the Ganges, 20 miles S.E. of Backergunje. Lat. 22° 23′, long. 90° 38′.

BOWRA.—See BHOWDA.

BOWRI, or BHUOREE, in the British district of Mozuffurnugur, lieut.-gov. of the N.W. Provinces, a village on the route from Kurnoul to Meerut, and 30 miles S.W. of the former. Lat. 29° 24′, long. 77° 26′.

BOWUR.—A division of the native state of Gurwhal, situated in the north-west corner of that district: its centre is about lat. 30° 55′, long. 78° 10′.

BRAHMAPOOTRA.—One of the principal rivers of Hindostan, rising in Thibet, at the eastern extremity of the snowy range of the Himalayas, about lat. 28° 30′, long. 97° 20′. Taking a south-westerly direction for about sixty-three miles to the village of Soom, it touches upon the British province of Assam, whence flowing in a direction generally west for forty-three miles, it for that distance forms the boundary between the British territory and Thibet. It then enters Assam, and continuing a westerly course, divides the province into two nearly equal portions, the districts of Luckimpoor, Durrung, and the greater portion of Camroop lying to the north, and those of Seebpoor and Nowgong to the south. In this part of its course it is joined by many tributary streams. Among these may be noticed the Digaroo, a small river flowing from the north-east, and somewhat lower down two others,—the Dibong and the Dihong. The last-mentioned river, which is known through the greater part of its course as the Sanpoo, and which is the remotest feeder of the Brahmapootra, rises on the northern face of the Himalayas, in lat. 30° 25′, long. 82° 5′, a few miles to the eastward of the sources of the Sutlej and Indus, and pursuing a course in a reverse direction, winds its way through Thibet, and washes the borders of the territory of Lassa. After a total course of about 1,000 miles, it turns suddenly to the south, and enters Assam at the north-eastern angle, where, under the name of the Dihong, it falls into the Brahmapootra, as above mentioned. From the point of junction, the river flows for seventy-five miles to lat. 27° 10′, long. 94° 30′, where it diverges into two streams, the northern denominated the Booree Lohit, the southern bearing the name of the Dihing. These again unite, after a separate course of about sixty-five miles. The Brahmapootra thence flowing for the distance of 220 miles, during which it passes the towns of Durrung and Gowhatty, finally leaves the province of Assam near the town of Goalpara. From Goalpara, the river, keeping a south-westerly direction, traverses the district of the same name for about sixty miles, when making a circuit round the western point of the Garrow Mountains, it forms for fifty miles the boundary between the British district of Rungpore on the west, and the districts of Goalpara and Mymensing on the east. In lat. 25° 10′, long. 89° 43′, it throws off the Konaie, and after a further course in a south-easterly direction of 130 miles, changes its name of Brahmapootra to that of Meghna. Proceeding thence south-west for fifty miles, it recovers a portion of the waters of its offset the Konaie, through the channel of the Dulasseree, and twenty-five miles lower down it receives a considerable portion of the waters of the Ganges through the channel of Kirtynassa. Then flowing east for ninety miles, it falls into the Bay of Bengal through three mouths; the Hattia river to the east, the Shabazpore in the centre, and the Ganges to the west. The total length of this river, from its source in the north-eastern range of the Himalayas to its discharge into the Bay of Bengal, measures 933 miles. Its branches, together with those of the Ganges, intersect the territory of Bengal in such variety of direction as to form a complete system of inland navigation.

BRAHMINY.—A river rising in the district of Palamow, about lat. 23° 25′, long. 84° 13′. Taking a south direction for 240 miles, and easterly for sixty more, during which it flows through the petty native states in Orissa to the western boundary of the British district of Cuttack, which it touches in about lat. 20° 50′, long. 86°, and continuing its direction south-east for about 110 miles, falls into the Bay of Bengal near Point Palmyras, and in lat. 20° 43′, long. 87° 6′.

BREMAHDASUM, in the British district of Tinnevelly, presidency of Madras, a town 17 miles W. from Tinnevelly, 49 miles E. of Anjengo. Lat. 8° 45′, long. 77° 30′.

BRITEOWRY.—See Bhuteura.

BROACH, a British collectorate subject to the presidency of Bombay, is bounded on the north by the Myhee river and the Guicowar's territories; on the east by the Guicowar's and the Rajpeepla rajah's territories, and by Wusravee; on the south by the Keem river, which separates it from the Surat collectorate; and on the west by the Gulf of Cambay. Its length from north to south is about fifty-seven miles, and its breadth from east to west forty-one miles. It lies between lat. 21° 22′—22° 11′, and long. 72° 30′—73° 10′, and contains an area which is calculated at 1,319 square miles. Two rivers intersect this collectorate; viz., the Nerbudda, running from east to west from the Rajpeepla territory, along the walls of the town of Broach, to the sea, and which is always navigable for boats of fifty tons burthen; and the Dhadur, which runs in a similar direction, and empties itself in the sea at Tunkaria Bunder. The chief products are jowaree (Holcus Sorghum) and cotton, the former being the principal food of the cultivators, and is only sold when their cotton crop is inadequate to meet their expenses. The principal crop of jowaree is sown in August and reaped in February. Cotton is sown in June, and the first picking takes place in March; the second picking succeeds in about fifteen days, and the whole crop is not cleared off till the end of April. From its value in the market, it has become a primary object of cultivation in this collectorate, and the prices would, it is said, be much increased if the cultivators could be persuaded to devote more attention to the picking, and to divest themselves of some prejudices in regard to the storing of it. The government experiments for improving the cultivation of cotton in Broach are stated to have been unsuccessful; the American species (New Orleans and Georgian) having been found to degenerate in the course of a few seasons. Wheat is grown to some extent. In some parts of the district rice is cultivated; but its quality is coarse, except in the Hansote pergunnah, where, by the aid of irrigation, in a few villages a very superior grain is produced: in other parts of the district the produce is dependent entirely on the rains to bring it to maturity. Tobacco thrives upon the alluvial grounds.

The climate of Broach is considered as healthy as any part of Guzerat. The rains are moderate; the average fall being thirty-three inches, while the quantity at Bombay is computed at eighty. According to Colonel Williams, it is so cold in the months of December, January, and February, that Fahrenheit's thermometer sometimes falls to 40° in the open air at daybreak. From the beginning of March until the rains commence, there are hot winds from the north-east and east, but only occasionally; perhaps once a fortnight: during their prevalence the barometer will rise to 108° in the house. From the middle of April the prevailing wind is from the westward or southward. The population is given under the article BOMBAY.

In regard to the means of communication, it may be observed that there are no macadamized roads in the district, nor any material wherewith to construct them; yet so little is the want of these felt, that nowhere throughout the presidency is communication so well kept up. The level of the district, observes the collector, favours a partiality for wheeled vehicles; and during nine months of the year the whole zillah is intersected with rough but practicable lines of communication, so perfect that it would be difficult to devise a mode of improvement in so far as the requirements of commerce are concerned. There is a small manufacture of leather in Broach, which is considered superior to that of the adjoining districts. Coarse native paper is made in the town of Unklesur; and these articles, with the fabrication of cotton cloths, so far as it has not been superseded by that of Britain, seem to form the whole of the manufactures of the zillah.

BROACH, in the British collectorate of the same name, presidency of Bombay, is a large and ancient town, the principal place in the collectorate, and the seat of the civil establishment. It is situate on the north or right side of the river Nerbudda, about thirty miles from its mouth. The river is here a noble sheet of water, two miles wide at ebb-tide, but shallow for the most part even at flood-tide, when, however, there is a deep but intricate channel, admitting vessels of considerable burthen. The state of the river is such, however, as to prevent the town from becoming an extensive port for large vessels, it appearing that it is at all times navigable only for boats of fifty tons burthen. Broach was formerly a flourishing town, with a large population. Subsequently its commerce and manufactures fell away, and it became a poor and dilapidated place. More recent returns, however, show a considerable increase in its exports and imports, and indicate a revival of its former prosperity. Broach is situate on an elevated mound, supposed to be artificial, raised about eighty feet above the level of the sea, on the banks of the river. The town itself is surrounded by a wall, which on the river-face has been placed in repair, but on every other side is very much dilapidated. It contains about 3,341 houses, inhabited by 12,971 souls of different castes. The most substantial and spacious of the houses are occupied by the Muzmoodars of the Broach district, Hindoo bankers and merchants, a few Parsees and Mahomedans. The suburbs are extensive, and the number of the inhabitants is calculated to be about 18,361. They chiefly consist of shopkeepers, artisans of every kind, Dhobees, and fishermen; and the houses are generally of an inferior order to those in the town. The suburbs have a bazaar, and on the outskirts are the cotton-warehouses. The town of Broach was long famous for its manufacture of cloth, consisting of fine dotees and doreeas, chequered cloths, table-cloths, &c. The weavers were capable of imitating almost any pattern of Scotch plaid. Coarse piece-goods were also made up in considerable quantities, and still continue to be produced; but the manufacture of the finer description of cloths has fallen off largely, in consequence of the importation of English goods. Many of the weavers were Parsees, which class are known to have been located in Broach for six centuries. The destruction of that branch of manufacture has greatly affected their numbers and prosperity; but those who remain, though most of them poor, retain their character for industry. A few of the more opulent are ship-owners and brokers. One remarkable vestige of the former commercial importance of Broach is a Dutch burying-ground, in which the members of the factory belonging to that nation were interred. The tombs are yet in good preservation, and the inscriptions on them legible. They date back as far as 1646, and come down to 1770. Here is an hospital for animals, containing horses, dogs, cats, monkeys, peacocks, as well as a variety of insects. It is ostensibly attended by certain religionists, who derive a good income from lands devoted to the purpose. Few places are better supplied with provisions than Broach. Meat of all kinds is excellent and cheap; there is no want of poultry; the bazaars are well supplied with fruits and vegetables from the neighbouring villages; and the Nerbudda affords a variety of fish, exclusive of that brought in by the fishing-boats from the sea. The carp in the river are uncommonly large, sometimes weighing fifty pounds. One of the government English schools has been established in this place. This town is thought, with some appearance of probability, to have been the Barygaza of Ptolemy and Arrian. After the subjugation of Guzerat by the Musulmans, and the subsequent formation of the state of that name, Broach formed part of the new kingdom. On its overthrow by Akbar, in 1583, this place became included within the kingdom of Delhi, and was governed by a petty nawaub. It was taken in 1685 by the Mahrattas. The nawaub held it subordinate to the Peishwa until 1772, when it was captured by a British force under General Wedderburn, who was killed in the assault. In 1783, it was by the treaty of Poona ceded to Scindiah, in acknowledgment of certain services. It was stormed in 1803 by a British force commanded by Colonel Woodington, and finally ceded to the East-India Company by Scindiah, under the treaty of Serji Anjengaum. Distance of the town N. from Bombay 190 miles, S. from Ahmedabad 95, S.W. from Mhow 188, S.W. from Delhi, by Mhow, 624. Lat. 21° 42′, long. 73° 2′.

BROANG, in Bussahir, a village in the district of Koonawur, is situate on the left bank of the Buspa, two miles from its confluence with the Sutluj. It gives name to the Broang, or Burenda Pass, distant about eight miles south; the intervening tract being a wood principally of luxuriant plane-trees, horse-chestnuts, birches, and rhododendrons. Broang is 7,411 feet above the sea. Lat. 31° 28′, long. 78° 14′.

BROKEN POINT.—A prominent headland on the coast of Arracan, 90 miles N.E. of Cape Negrais. Lat. 17° 19′, long. 94° 35′.

BRUMMAWARA, in the British district of South Canara, presidency of Madras, a town on the route from Mangalore to Bednore, 40 miles N. of the former. Lat. 13° 26′, long. 74° 49′.

BUBEROO, in the British district of Banda, lieut.-gov. of the N.W. Provinces, a town 24 miles E. of Banda, 72 miles W. of Allahabad. Lat. 25° 33′, long. 80° 47′.

BUBOORA, in the British district of Mirzapoor, lieut.-gov. of the N.W. Provinces, a village on the right bank of the Ganges, nine miles N.W. of the city of Mirzapoor, or higher up the stream. Lat. 25° 12′, long. 82° 26′.

BUBREE.—A town in the territory of Oude, distant N.E. from Lucknow 11 miles. Lat. 27°, long. 81° 8′.

BUCHOWRA, in the British district of Furrukhabad, lieut.-gov. of the N.W. Provinces, a village on the route from the cantonment of Allygurh to that of Futtehgurh, and 35 miles N.W. of the latter. Lat. 27° 30′, long. 79° 11′.

BUCHRAON, in the district of Bainswara, territory of Oude, a town 28 miles S.E. of Lucknow, 85 N.W. of Allahabad. Butter estimates the population at 5,000; of whom only 100 are Mussulmans. Lat. 26° 28′, long. 81° 7′.

BUCKEA.—A river rising in lat. 27° 6′, long. 85° 40′, on the northern face of the Sub-Himalayas: it flows in a southerly direction for thirty-five miles through Muckwanee, a district of Nepal, and for twenty miles forms the boundary between Nepal and the British district of Tirhoot, which latter district it traverses for fifty miles previous to its fall into the Bagmuttee river, in lat. 26°, long. 85° 56′.

BUCKRANEE.—A village in Sinde, on the route from Sehwan to Larkhana, and seven miles south of the latter place. It is situate in the extensive island contained between the Indus and its offset the Narra, being distant four miles from the left bank of the former, and about half a mile from a ferry over the latter, known as the ferry of Buckranee. From this ferry to the ford opposite Tonia Hassem, the distance is about a mile and a half. The neighbourhood is fertile and well cultivated. Lat. 27° 25′, long. 68° 12′.

BUDAON.—A British district in the Rohilcund division of the lieut.-gov. of the N.W. Provinces. It is bounded on the north by the British district of Moradabad; on the north-east by the British district of Bareilly; on the south-east by that of Shahjehanpore; on the south by Furruckabad and Mynporee; and on the west by Allyghur and Bolundshuhur. It lies between lat. 27° 38′—28° 29′, long. 78° 21′—79° 35′, and contains an area of 2,368 square miles. It is a low, level, and in general fertile tract, watered in its south-western part throughout its whole length by the Ganges, in its eastern for some distance by the Ramgunga, and in the intermediate space by the Yarwuffadar, or Sote, and the Muhawa. That portion of the district situate south-west of the Ganges will participate in the benefits of navigation and irrigation to be derived from the branch canal proposed to be made from the Ganges Canal to the river Ganges above Furruckhabad. The official returns show the population to amount to 1,019,161, of which number 877,509 are Hindoos, and 141,652 Mahometans and others. Hence it appears that nearly six-sevenths of the whole are Hindoo. The following classification of the towns and villages in the district is also furnished by the official returns:—Number containing less than 1,000 inhabitants, 2,050; ditto more than 1,000 and less than 5,000, 173; ditto more than 5,000 and less than 10,000, 5; ditto more than 10,000 and less than 50,000, 3; total, 2,231. The principal routes are—1. From Furruckhabad, in a north-westerly direction, to Suhuswan, whence a route proceeds northerly to Moradabad, and another north-westerly to Hurdwar. 2. From Agra to Bareilly, in a direction from south-west to north-east. 3. From Allyghurh cantonment to Moradabad, and in a direction nearly parallel to the last. 4. Nearly from east to west, from Delhi to Bareilly. Under the revenue settlement of the North-Western Provinces, the government demand on the lands of this district has been fixed for a term of years, and is not liable to be increased until the year 1866.

BUDAON.—A town giving name to a British district under the lieut.-gov. of the N.W. Provinces. The population is not inconsiderable, having, in 1848, been officially ascertained to amount to 21,369. Lat. 28° 2′, long. 79° 11′.

BUDDAPOODY, in the British district of Nellore, presidency of Madras, a town five miles E. of the route from Nellore to Guntoor, 48 miles N. of the former. Lat. 15° 9′, long. 80°.

BUDDAUM PUHAR.—A town in Mohurbunge, one of the native states on the south-west frontier of Bengal, distant S.W. from Midnapoor 76 miles. Lat. 22° 5′, long. 86° 14′.

BUDDOOR.—A town in Hyderabad, or dominions of the Nizam, distant N.E. from

Ellichpoor 53 miles. Lat. 21° 30′, long. 78° 19′.

BUDDUNPOOR, in the British district of Muttra, lieut.-gov. of the N.W. Provinces, a village on the route from the cantonment of Meerut to that of Muttra, and 25 miles N. of the latter. Lat. 27° 47′, long. 77° 51′.

BUDEEAR, in the native state of Gurwhal, a considerable feeder of the Jumna, rises on the south-eastern declivity of Kedar Kanta, in lat. 31°, long. 78° 17′, and, after a course of about eighteen miles, falls into the Jumna on the right side, in lat. 30° 49′, long. 78° 19′, at an elevation of 4,000 feet above the sea. The Budeear, at the confluence, is as wide as the Jumna, but not so deep.

BUDEENA, in the British district of Hyderabad, province of Scinde, a town 56 miles S.E. from Hyderabad, 57 N. of Luckput, in Scinde. Lat. 24° 39′, long. 68° 52′.

BUDGE BUDGE, in the British district known as the Twenty-four Pergunnahs, lying within the jurisdiction of the lieut.-gov. of Bengal, a town on the left bank of the Hooghly, and on the route from Calcutta to Midnapore, 12 miles S.W. of the former, 56 E. of the latter. The fort, formerly occupying an important site here, as commanding the river, is now completely in ruins. Lat. 22° 28′, long. 88° 15′.

BUDHAN DHOORA, in the British district of Kumaon, lieut.-gov. of the N.W. Provinces, a mountain of the Sub-Himalaya, and forming part of the Ghagar range. Elevation above the sea 8,502 feet. Lat. 29° 28′, long. 79° 24′.

BUDHAORA, in the Rajpoot state of Jessulmeer, a village on the route from the town of Bikaneer to that of Jessulmeer, and 100 miles N.E. of the latter. Lat. 27° 20′, long. 72° 22′.

BUDI.—See Boolee.

BUDLAPOOR, in the British district of Tannah, presidency of Bombay, a town on the route from Tannah to Poonah, 20 miles E. of the former. Lat. 19° 10′, long. 73° 21′.

BUDLAPOOR, in the British district of Jounpore, lieut.-gov. of the N.W. Provinces, a town on the route from Jaunpore cantonment to that of Sultanpoor, in Oude, 17 miles N.W. of the former, 37 S.E. of the latter. Lat. 25° 52′, long. 82° 32′.

BUDLEGOOSSEE, in the British district of Bograh, lieut.-gov. of Bengal, a town on the route from Dinagepoor to Pubna, 30 miles N.W. of Bograh. Lat. 24° 59′, long. 88° 55′.

BUDNAWUR, in Malwa, in the raj or territory of Dhar, a town the principal place of a pergunnah of the same name. It is surrounded by a mud wall in bad repair, and has a fort. In 1820 it contained 734 houses and 2,654 inhabitants, and the pergunnah contained 7,735 houses and 31,119 inhabitants. It had been usurped by Daulat Rao Scindia; but on occasion of the pacification with him in 1817, the British government insisted on its restoration to the rajah of Dhar. Distance N.W. from Mow 46 miles, S.W. from Oojein 36. Lat. 23° 3′, long. 75° 18′.

BUDOERCOOT, in the British district of Ganjam, presidency of Madras, a town on the southern shore of the Chilka Lake, 14 miles N.E. of Ganjam. Lat. 19° 31′, long. 85° 18′.

BUDOKHUR, or BEROKHERA, in the British district of Banda, lieut.-gov. of the N.W. Provinces, a village on the route from the town of Banda to Rewa, seven miles S. of the former. Lat. 25° 21′, long. 80° 26′.

BUDRA.—A river rising in Mysore, about lat. 13° 15′, long. 75° 14′. Its course is at first easterly, in which direction it flows for about thirty miles, thence northerly for forty-three more, and subsequently north-easterly for thirty-eight miles, when it unites with the Tum, or Tunga, in lat. 14°, long. 75° 43′; the total length of course being 111 miles. From the confluence the united stream bears the name of Tunga Budra, or Tumbudra.

BUDRAWAR.—A town in the Northern Punjab, on the southern slope of the Himalaya, near the left bank of the river Chenaub, and on one of its feeders. The neighbouring country is beautiful, picturesque, fertile, and well cultivated. There is a large and well-supplied bazaar. The population is probably about 2,000, of whom a considerable portion are Kashmirian weavers of shawls, employing about 250 looms. There is a large square fort, built of stone. It is about 5,000 feet above the sea. Lat. 33° 3′, long. 75° 45′.

BUDROL, or BOODRA, in Bussahir, a peaked summit of a mountain proceeding in an easterly direction from the great range connecting Wartoo and the Chur. There is a ruined fort on its declivity. This peak was one of the stations for the series of small triangles in the trigonometrical survey of the Himalaya. Elevation above the sea 8,762 feet. Lat. 31° 8′, long. 77° 45′.

BUDUREA, in the British district of Budaon, lieut.-gov. of the N.W. Provinces, a town on the route from Budaon to Allygurh, 26 miles S.W. of the former. Lat. 27° 54′, long. 78° 50′.

BUDVAIL, in the British district of Cuddapah, presidency of Madras, a town on the route from Cuddapah to Ongole, 24 miles N.E. of the former. Lat. 14° 44′, long. 79° 8′.

BUFFALO MOUNTAINS.—In the Amherst province of Tenasserim, the highest ridge of the sandstone range of hills running through the plain in a direction N.N.W. to S.S.E., and attaining a height of 1,543 feet. They are about seventy miles from Moulmein.

BUGCHOOR.—See Bugudyar.

BUGDOWDEE, in the British district of Cawnpore, lieut.-gov. of the N.W. Provinces, a village on the route from the cantonment of

Cawnpore to that of Futtehgurh, and 11 miles N.W. of the former. Lat. 26° 34′, long. 80° 16′.

BUGGAUR, in Sinde, is one of the two western branches of the Indus, diverging a little below Tatta, at the head of the delta, the Sata being the eastern branch. In 1699, when visited by Hamilton, it was a very great stream, navigable as high as Lahoreebunder, twenty miles from the mouth, for vessels of 200 tons; but now, except during the inundation, it has scarcely any stream, in consequence of a sand-bank five or six feet above the level of the water stretching across the channel at the place of divarication. Where forded by the British army during the season of low water, in 1839, it was two feet and a half deep, and fifty yards wide; lower down, the channel was completely dry. When the stream was greater, it parted into four branches, entering the sea by the Pittee, the Pintianee, the Joah, and the Richel mouths. These have all become merely inlets of the sea, containing salt-water, excepting during the inundation. The word Buggaur signifies *destroyer*, a name given in consequence of the effect of the river on the lands through which it flowed. Its main course is generally westerly, extending about eighty miles from the place of divergence, in lat. 24° 40′, long. 68° 1′, to the Pittee mouth, in lat. 24° 42′, long. 67° 12′.

BUGGELWARA.—A town in the native state of Bhopal, distant S.E. from Bhopal 60 miles. Lat. 22° 53′, long. 78° 15′.

BUGGHOO CHEK, in the Reechna Dooab division of the Punjab, a town situated on the route from Amritsir to Wazeerabad, eight miles S.E. of the latter. Lat. 32° 23′, long. 74° 2′.

BUGGREEA.—A town in the native state of Talcheer, one of the Cuttack mehals, distant N.W. from Cuttack 90 miles. Lat. 21° 3′, long. 84° 41′.

BUGGUSRA, in the peninsula of Kattywar, province of Guzerat, a town in the vicinity of the Gir or wild highlands in the middle of the district of Kattywar. It is the principal place of a subdivision containing sixteen villages and a population estimated at 7,452, and paying the Guicowar an annual tribute of 3,114 rupees. Distance from Ahmedabad, S.W., 152 miles; Baroda, S.W., 160; Surat, W., 127; Bombay, N.W., 212. Lat. 21° 30′, long. 70° 59′.

BUGHA.—A town in the territory of Oude, distant N. from Lucknow 18 miles. Lat. 27° 5′, long. 80° 56′.

BUGHAT.—See BAGHAT.

BUGHRUH, in the British district of Muzufurnugur, lieut.-gov. of the N.W. Provinces, a town on the route from Meerut to Roorkee, 32 miles N. of the former. Lat. 29° 28′, long. 77° 40′.

BUGOLOH, in the British district of Goorgaon, lieut.-gov. of the N.W. Provinces, a village on the route from Delhi to Muttra, and 36 miles S. of the former. Lat. 28° 12′, long. 77° 22′.

BUGRA.—A town in the native state of Sirgoojah, on the south-east frontier of Bengal, distant N. from Sirgoojah 51 miles. Lat. 23° 50′, long. 83° 20′.

BUGRAEE.—See BIGROULI.

BUGRAYUH, or BUGGIHAR, in the British district of Allyghur, lieut.-gov. of the N.W. Provinces, a village on the route from the cantonment of Allygurh to that of Etawa, and 24 miles S. of the former. Lat. 27° 35′, long. 78° 15′.

BUGREE.—See BAJAROW.

BUGROH, or BUGROO, in the Rajpoot state of Jeypoor, a town with bazaar, on the route from Agra to Ajmere, 174 miles S.W. of former, 65 N.E. of latter. Lat. 26° 49′, long. 75° 38′.

BUGUDYAR, or BUGDWAR, in the British district of Kumaon, lieut.-gov. of the N.W. Provinces, an encamping-station at a sangha or spar-bridge over the Bugdwar torrent, on the route up the course of the Goree, by the Oonta Dhoora pass, from Almorah fort to Hiundes, or South-eastern Tibet, 114 miles S.E. of Almorah. Elevation above the sea 8,028 feet. Lat. 30° 13′, long. 80° 15′.

BUGUR.—A town in the Rajpoot state of Shekawutee, distant N.E. from Jhoonjhnoo 10 miles. Lat. 28° 13′, long. 75° 38′.

BUGWA, in Bundlecund, a town in the native state of Bijawur, distant S.W. from Bijawur 21 miles. Lat. 24° 32′, long. 79° 12′.

BUGWAH, in the British district of Rungpore, lieut.-gov. of Bengal, a town on the right bank of the Brahmapootra, on the route from Rungpore to Goalpara, 30 miles E. of the former. Lat. 25° 40′, long. 89° 44′.

BUGWARA, in the British district of Surat, presidency of Bombay, a town on the route from Bombay to Surat, 50 miles S. of the latter. Lat. 20° 25′, long. 72° 59′.

BUGWATPOOR, in the British district of Allahabad, lieut.-gov. of the N.W. Provinces, a village on the route by Rajapoor ferry from the city of Allahabad to that of Banda, and 11 miles W. of the former. Lat. 25° 24′, long. 81° 44′.

BUHADOORGURH, in the British district of Meerut, lieut.-gov. of the N.W. Provinces, a small fortified town on the route from Gurmuktesar to Anopshuhur, and 10 miles S. of the former. Lat. 28° 41′, long. 78° 13′.

BUHADOORGURH, in the hill state of Hindoor, a fort on a lofty summit of the range stretching in the Cis-Sutlej territory from north-west to south-east, in the eastern part of that state. Elevation above the sea 6,233 feet. Lat. 31° 13′, long. 76° 56′.

BUHADOORGURH.—See BAHADOORGURH.

BUHADRA, in the Rajpoot state of Jessulmeer, a village on the route from the town of Bickaneer to that of Jessulmeer, and 45 miles N.E. of the latter. A mile south-west of it, the British mission deputed to the western states of Rajpootana crossed in the middle of March the dry bed of a river 100 yards broad. Buhadra is in lat. 27° 6′, long. 71° 38′.

BUHADURPOOR.—A town in the native state of Gwalior, or possessions of Scindia's family, distant S. from Gwalior 130 miles. Lat. 24° 19′, long. 78°.

BUHAOWPOOR, or **BHOWPOOR**, in the British district of Cawnpore, lieut.-gov. of the N.W. Provinces, a village on the route from Allahabad to Etawa, and 51 miles S.E. of the latter. Lat. 26° 25′, long. 79° 36′.

BUHEREE, in the British district of Moradabad, lieut.-gov. of the N.W. Provinces, a village on the route from Moradabad to Almora, and 17 miles N. of the former. Lat. 29° 2′, long. 78° 56′.

BUHEREE, or **BUHOREE**, in the British district of Moradabad, lieut.-gov. of the N.W. Provinces, a small town, with fort, on the route from Moradabad cantonment to Kasheepoor 10 miles. N. of the former. It is situate two miles east of the left bank of the small river Dhundi, and a mile west of the right bank of the Dhela, both feeders of the Ramgunga. Lat. 28° 59′, long. 78° 51′.

BUHIRWA, in the British district of Benares, lieut.-gov. of the N.W. Provinces, a town on the route from Allahabad to the city of Benares, 59 miles E. of the former, 15 W. of the latter. Lat. 25° 16′, long. 82° 42′.

BUHLAPOOR, in the British district of Boolundshuhur, lieut.-gov. of the N.W. Provinces, a village on the route from the cantonment of Aligurh to that of Moradabad, and 12 miles N.E. of the former. Lat. 28° 4′, long. 78° 11′.

BUHNDERA, in the territory of Bhurtpoor, a village on the route from Agra to the city of Bhurtpoor, 30 miles W. of the former, 9 S.E. of the latter. It has a few shops, and water may be obtained from wells. Lat. 27° 9′, long. 77° 37′.

BUHOONAH.—A village in the British district of Hurriana, lieut.-gov. of the N.W. Provinces. Lat. 29° 33′, long. 75° 42′.

BUHORUNPOOR, in the British district of Moradabad, lieut.-gov. of the N.W. Provinces, a village on the route from the town of Moradabad to Almora, and 22 miles N. of the former. Lat. 29° 6′, long. 78° 58′.

BUHRAECH.—The principal place of the district of that name, in the territory of Oude. Tieffenthaler, describing it about the year 1770, states it to be "an ancient town of considerable extent, of greater length than breadth, the houses being built of mud and covered with thatch, except the mausoleums, mosques, and residences of the merchants, which are of brick and lime-mortar." It is situate in a pleasant wooded plain, on the left bank of the Sarju (eastern). North-east of the town is the tomb of Selar, a reputed Mussulman saint. In May there is a great concourse of pilgrims to his tomb, the small town close to which is, in honour of the deceased, called Great Buhraech, while the principal town is called Little Buhraech. Buhraech is 65 miles N.W. of Faizabad, 65 N.E. of Lucknow. Lat. 27° 34′, long. 81° 33′.

BUHREABAD, in the British district of Ghazeepore, lieut.-gov. of the N.W. Provinces, a town on the north-west frontier towards Azimgarh, 20 miles N.W. of Ghazeepore cantonment. Lat. 25° 43′, long. 83° 15′.

BUHUL, in the British district of Hurriana, lieut.-gov. of the N.W. Provinces, a town in lat. 28° 38′, long. 75° 35′.

BUHURIABAD, in the British district of Ghazeepoor, lieut.-gov. of the N.W. Provinces, a town 20 miles N.W. of Ghazeepoor, 38 miles E. of Jounpoor. Lat. 25° 40′, long. 82° 20′.

BUJANA.—See BIANA.

BUJEE.—See BHUJEE.

BUJHERA, in the British district of Shahjehanpoor, lieut.-gov. of the N.W. Provinces, a town six miles W. of the route from Shahjehanpoor to Bareilly, 24 miles N.W. of the former. Lat. 28° 3′, long. 79° 37′.

BUJJAUNA, in the peninsula of Kattywar, province of Guzerat, a town in the subdivision of Jhalawur or Rajcote. It is situate on the southern border of the Runn, or great Salt-marsh, and is the principal place of a subdivision containing twenty-six villages and a population estimated at 9,320. The chief of Bujjauna is by descent of the Jat tribe, but the family has for some generations conformed to Islam. He pays an annual tribute of 8,615 rupees to the British government. Distance from Ahmedabad, W., 55 miles. Lat. 23° 3′, long. 71° 43′.

BUJRUNGURH, in the territory of Gwalior, or possessions of Scindia's family, a town on the route from Goonah to Mow, 11 miles S. of the former. It was formerly a place of greater importance than at present, having been the stronghold of Jai Singh, rajah of Raghwagarh, the redoubted enemy of Doulut Rao Scindia. In A.D. 1816 Bujrungurh was taken by Baptiste, an officer of Doulut Rao Scindia. It is by some denominated Jainaagar Bujrungurh. Lat. 24° 34′, long. 77° 18′.

BUKERAH, in the territory of Oude, a village on the route from Lucknow to Shahjehanpoor, 30 miles S. of the latter. Lat. 27° 27′, long. 80° 3′.

BUKEYWAR, in the British district of Etawa, lieut.-gov. of the N.W. Provinces, a town on the route from Calpee to the cantonment of Etawa, and 14 miles S.E. of the latter. Lat. 26° 40′, long. 79° 15′.

BUKHOREE, in the British district of Tirhoot, lieut.-gov. of Bengal, a town 30 miles N.W. of Durbunga, 22 miles N.E. of Mozufferpoor. Lat. 26° 25′, long. 85° 37′.

BUKKUR.—A town of the Punjaub, in the Sinde Sagur Dooab, situated on a watercourse running parallel with the Indus, 19 miles S.E. of the town of Dera Ismael Khan. Population 5,000. Lat. 31° 35′, long. 71° 1′.

BUKKUR, in Sinde, a celebrated fortress on an island in the Indus, between the towns of Roree on the eastern, and Sukkur on the western bank. The eastern channel, dividing it from Roree, on the left bank, is 400 yards wide and thirty feet deep in the middle, with a current of four miles an hour; the western, dividing it from Sukkur, on the right bank, is ninety-eight yards wide, and fifteen feet deep in the middle, with a current of three miles an hour. Such is the measurement when the river is lowest, and made in a right line across the island from the eastern to the western shore of the Indus; but at some distance to the north of this right line, a spit of land from the island of Bukkur projects westward into the river, leaving between its extremity and the western shore a channel only fifty yards wide, seven feet deep in the middle, and with a current of four miles an hour. In the beginning of 1839, the engineers of the Bengal army, marching to Afghanistan, threw here a bridge of boats over the Indus. The number of boats employed for this purpose was nineteen for the western or narrower channel, and fifty-five for the eastern; and on this the army, with its baggage and battering-train, passed over. Soon afterwards the bridge was swept away. Macmurdo states that the water in the western channel disappears in the season when the river is lowest; and Burnes, that the eastern is said to have been once forded in the same season. Wood, however, found the former seven feet deep, and the latter thirty, in the dry season. The isla d of Bukkur is a rock of limestone interspersed with flint, of an oval shape, 800 yards long, 300 wide, 1,875 in circuit, and about thirty feet high. Almost the whole of it is covered by the fortress, which, in 1839, was ceded by the ameers of Khyerpoor to the British, to remain occupied by their garrison during the then existing war. Its ultimate destination was determined by the battle of Meeanee, and the consequent annexation of Sinde to the British dominions. Lat. 27° 39′, long. 68° 56′.

BUKLAHUR.—A town in the native state of Nepaul, distant W. from Khatmandoo 47 miles. Lat. 27° 38′, long. 84° 31′.

BUKLANA.—A village in the British district Hurriana, lieut.-gov. of the N.W. Provinces. Lat. 29° 8′, long. 76° 18′.

BUKOLEE, or **BUTULI**, in the hill state of Bussahir, a fort on the right bank of the Pabur, situate on a lofty rock prominently standing out from a mountain rising behind it. Elevation above the sea 5,607 feet. Lat. 31° 13′, long. 77° 54′.

BUKRA, in the British district of Goruckpoor, lieut.-gov. of the N.W. Provinces, a town four miles N. of the route from Patna to Goruckpore, 20 miles E. of the latter. Lat. 26° 37′, long. 83° 43′.

BULAHRA, in the Rajpoot territory of Shekhawutee, a town with a fort, and a place of some importance before the establishment of British supremacy. The fort is of masonry, sixty yards long and thirty broad, with very high bastions, and a fausse-braie of masonry, with a narrow but deep ditch. Being a stronghold of freebooters, it was dismantled by the British in 1835. Distance S.W. from Delhi 140 miles. Lat. 27° 53′, long. 75° 15′.

BULAMEEN, in the Bunnoo division of the Punjab, a town situated on the route from Peshawur to Ghuznee, 103 miles S.W. of the former. Lat. 33° 14′, long. 70° 11′.

BULBUDDURPOOR, in the British district of Pooree, lieut.-gov. of Bengal, a town on the south-eastern shore of the Chilka lake, 25 miles S.W. of Juggurnaut. Lat. 19° 40′, long. 85° 32′.

BULBUDDURPOOR, in the British district of Pooree, lieut.-gov. of Bengal, a town 19 miles N.W. from Juggurnaut, 39 miles S.W. of Cuttack. Lat. 19° 59′, long. 85° 40′.

BULCHA.—A pass over a high ridge, extending nearly east and west, and appearing to be the last or most northern of the ridges forming the mountainous tract which extends northwards or north-eastwards from the main range of the Himalaya, and beyond which the plains of Tibet stretch in the direction of Central Asia. Bulcha is situate within the Chinese frontier, and about eight miles north of the parallel range of Oonta Dhura, within the British frontier. The road from Almorah fort, in Kumaon, by the Juwahir valley to Tibet, lies over the Oonta Dhura and Bulcha passes. Bulcha is distant 164 miles N. of Almorah. Lat. 30° 38′, long. 80° 14′.

BULCHEEA GHAT, in the British district of Kumaon, lieut.-gov. of the N.W. Provinces, a ferry over the river Kalee (eastern), forming a communication between the territory of the East-India Company and that of Nepal. Lat. 29° 21′, long. 80° 20′.

BULDEO MUNDIT, in the British district of Muttra, lieut.-gov. of the N.W. Provinces, a town on the route from the cantonment of Muttra to Mynpooree, and 12 miles S.E. of the former. It has a bazaar, and supplies are abundant. Lat. 27° 25′, long. 77° 54′.

BULKOONREA, in the British district of Goruckpoor, lieut.-gov. of the N.W. Provinces, a town 43 miles N.E. of Goruckpoor, 39 miles S.W. of Bettiah. Lat. 26° 57′, long. 84° 1′.

BULLARY, in the British district of South Canara, presidency of Madras, a town on the route from Mangalore to Mercara, 40 miles S.E. of the former. Lat. 12° 40′, long. 75° 27′.

BULLEA, in the British district of Purneah, lieut.-gov. of Bengal, a town a mile from the left bank of the Gonkor river, 23 miles S.E. of Purneah. Lat. 25° 34′, long. 87° 52′.

BULLEEA, in the British district of Bareilly, lieut.-gov. of the N.W. Provinces, a town on the route from Budaon to Bareilly, 12 miles S. of the latter. Lat. 28° 13′, long. 79° 26′.

BULLIAH, in the British district of Ghazeepore, lieut.-gov. of the N.W. Provinces, a town situate on the left bank of the Ganges, on the route from Ghazeepore cantonment to Chuprah, 42 miles E. of the former, 40 W. of the latter. It is situate on the river Kutehur, a branch of the Tons, traversed by ferry during the rains, and at other seasons by a bridge of boats. Supplies and water are abundant here, and the road in this part of the route is good. Distant N.W. of Calcutta by water 552 miles. Lat. 25° 41′, long. 84° 12′.

BULLIAH, in the British district of Ramgurh, lieut.-gov. of Bengal, a town four miles E. of the route from Hazareebagh to Midnapoor, 15 miles S. of the former. Lat. 23° 49′, long. 85° 20′.

BULLINGEE, in the British district of Sirgooja, lieut.-gov. of Bengal, a village situate among the mountains of Gondwana, close to the northern frontier, towards the British district of Mirzapoor. Distant S. of the city of Mirzapore 90 miles, N.W. of Calcutta by Hazareebagh 355. Lat. 23° 53′, long. 82° 52′.

BULLOAH.—A British district in the lieut.-gov. of Bengal, comprising, in addition to its area on the mainland, several very considerable islands, lying at the mouth of the Megna river. It is situate between lat. 22° 21′—23° 23′, long. 90° 35′—91° 41′; is eighty miles in length from north-west to south-east, and sixty in breadth. The area of the district is included in that of Tipperah. For the amount of population see the article BENGAL.

BULLOAH, in the British district of the same name, lieut.-gov. of Bengal, a town on the left bank of the Hattia river, 160 miles E. of Calcutta. Lat. 22° 53′, long. 90° 56′.

BULLOOA, in the British district of Benares, lieut.-gov. of the N.W. Provinces, a village on the left bank of the Ganges, 653 miles N.W. of Calcutta by water. Lat. 25° 26′, long. 83° 10′.

BULLOORGEE.—A town in the territory of Hyderabad, or dominions of the Nizam, distant W. from Hyderabad 143 miles. Lat. 17° 19′, long. 76° 22′.

BULODA.—A town of Phooljer, one of the native states on the south-west frontier of Bengal, distant W. from Sumbulpoor 71 miles. Lat. 21° 11′, long. 82° 56′.

BULOGEREE, in the British district of Goalpara, lieut.-gov. of Bengal, a town 26 miles S.W. of Goalpara, 77 miles E. of Rungpore. Lat. 25° 47′, long. 90° 29′.

BULPHAEE.—A town of north-eastern India, in the native state of Bhotan, distant N. from Gowhatty 75 miles. Lat. 27° 10′, long. 91° 26′.

BULRAMPOOR.—A town in the native state of Nepal, distant W. from Khatmandoo 200 miles. Lat. 28° 10′, long. 82° 9′.

BULRAMPOOR, in the territory of Oude, near the northern frontier towards Nepal. It is situate on the river Raptee, in a pleasant plain, and is of considerable size, with mud-built houses covered with thatch. There is a noble view of Dhawalagiri, or the White Mountain of the Himalayas, probably the most elevated summit of the surface of the globe. It is distant about 120 miles N.E. of Bulrampoor. The town is situate on one of the most frequented routes from Lucknow to Nepal, and in spring and summer great numbers of traders descend from the mountains, bringing the products of Tibet to exchange for the wares of Hindustan. Distant 89 miles N.E. from Lucknow. Lat. 27° 24′, long. 82° 15′.

BULRAMPORE, in the British district of Midnapore, lieut.-gov. of Bengal, a town on the right bank of the Coosy river, 30 miles N.W. of Midnapoor. Lat. 22° 40′, long. 87° 2′.

BULRUMMER.—A town in the native state of Bombra, on the south-west frontier of Bengal, distant E. from Sumbulpoor 19 miles. Lat. 21° 30′, long. 84° 19′.

BULSAR, in the British district of Surat, presidency of Bombay, a town on the estuary of the small river of the same name. The estuary is obstructed by a bar covered by a depth of two or three feet at low water. It is a thriving place, having manufactures of cloths and considerable commerce in salt, grain, and sugar. The population is 7,000, many of whom are weavers and sailors, some cultivators. Distance from Bombay, N., 115 miles; Surat, S., 40. Lat. 20° 36′, long. 72° 58′.

BULSUN.—A small hill state between the Sutlej and the Tonse, under the superintendence of the political agent for the Cis-Sutlej states. It is bounded on the north by Komharsin, Kothkaee, and the petty lordship of Goond; on the east by Poondur; on the south and south-west by Sirmour; and on the west by Keonthul. It extends from lat. 30° 57′ to 31° 7′, long. 77° 26′ to 77° 39′; is about twelve miles in length from south-east to north-west, and eight in breadth at the opposite angles. The area is sixty-four square miles. The population is estimated at about 5,000, and the annual revenue at about 600*l.*; out of which a tribute of 108*l.* is paid to the British government. The rana has about 500 armed retainers. Part of Burrowlee, originally a portion of this small state, was retained by the East-India Company after its conquest from the Goorkhas, for the use of the military cantonment at Subathoo; but the greater portion of Burrowlee was conferred on the rajah of Hindoor and his heirs, in perpetuity, under a sunnud dated 20th November, 1815, in lieu of the fort of Malown, retained as a post for British troops.

BULTHAR, in the British district of Sarun, lieut.-gov. of Bengal, a town 19 miles N. of Bettiah, 81 miles N.E. of Goruckpoor. Lat. 27°, long. 84° 41′.

BULTI, or BULTISTAN.—A small state, north of the valley of Cashmere, forming part of the dominions of Gholab Singh, and bearing also the name of Little Tibet, by which prefix it is distinguished from Middle Tibet or Ladakh, and Great Tibet or Southern Tartary. Bulti is also sometimes called Iskardoh, from the name of its capital. It is bounded on the north by Chinese Tartary, from which it is separated by the Mustag or Mooz-Taugh (icy mountains) and the Karakorum Mountains, prolongations of the Hindoo Koosh to the eastward. On the east it has Ladakh or Middle Tibet; on the south Deotsuh and other elevated and desert tracts, which separate it from Cashmere; on the west, Ghilgit, Yessen, and Astor, small independent states. Its limits have varied with circumstances, and at no time have they been well defined; but as the result of the safest estimate of them, Bulti may be stated to lie between lat. 34° 30′—36°, long. 75°—77°. The ancestors of Ahmed Shah, the late rajah, are said to have ruled here uninterruptedly for fourteen generations; but, ten or twelve years ago, Iskardoh and the other strongholds of Bulti were seized by the present ruler of Cashmere.

BUL-TUL, or KANTAL, in Kashmir, a pass over the range of mountains inclosing that valley on the north-east. It forms the water-summit between Kashmir and Little Thibet, as from its northern declivity the Duras river flows northward to the Indus, and from its southern flows southward a feeder of the small river Sinde, a tributary of the Jailum. Its elevation above the level of the sea is 10,500 feet. It is also called the Shur-ji-La, generally pronounced Zoj-i-La; and in old maps this summit bears the name Kantal, signifying "lofty hill." Lat. 34° 14′, long. 75° 33′.

BULUBGURH, or BALLAMGARH, is the principal place of a jaghire of the same name, called also Furreedabad, which is politically under the lieut.-gov. of the N.W. Provinces. This town is situate on the route from Delhi to Muttra, and 29 miles S. of the former city. The surrounding country is well cultivated, and has a pleasing appearance; the road-sides being planted with trees. The town, though not ill built, is small and crowded; "with narrow streets, tall houses, many temples, and a sufficient number of Brahminy bulls to show the pure Hindoo descent of the ruler." The palace of the rajah is small, but very neat, and is arranged around a small court, with a marble fountain in the middle, and an open arched hall. The whole place is surrounded by a high brick wall, with mud bastions and a deep ditch. The rajah is of the Jaut tribe. His jaghire extends twenty-six miles along the right bank of the Jumna, between lat. 28° 13′—28° 33′, long. 77° 17′—77° 36′. It is bounded on the north-west by Delhi; on the north-east and east by Boolundshuhur; on the south and south-west by Goorgaon. The area is 190 square miles. Estimating the population at the average of the adjacent district Goorgaon (300 to the square mile), its amount will be 57,000. At the period of the British entrance into Delhi, this jaghire appears to have been held by two persons, in virtue of the offices of foujdar of the environs of the imperial city, and killadar of the fort of Bulubgurh. One of them was expelled in 1804, by Sir David Ochterlony; the other, named Bahadour Singh, was established in possession of the jaghire and fort, as well as the office of foujdar of the environs of Delhi. Some obscurity seems to attach to another grant, subsequently made to the same party, to cover the expense of a police establishment on the road between Delhi and Pulwul; but in 1827 this grant was resumed, the magistrate of Delhi undertaking the duties for the discharge of which it was bestowed; and the rajah of Bulubgurh now holds his jaghire on the sole condition of maintaining the road-police within the limits of his jurisdiction, namely, from Boorea-ka-pool to Mooza Phuthalla, between Sikree and Pulwul, on the high Muttra road. It appears to have been intended to assign this district to the chief in perpetuity; but no sunnud was ever prepared. Notwithstanding this omission, the jaghire has been allowed to descend on the usual principles of inheritance, the son succeeding the father, except in one instance, where, the chief dying in infancy, the possession passed to his uncle. On the death of this chief, in 1829, his infant son succeeded, and during his long minority the district, through contention and mismanagement, fell into confusion. Ultimately the interference of the British government was sought, and after a modified system had been tried and had failed, the jaghire was taken under British management. The young chieftain, however, having attained majority, remonstrated against this arrangement, and the territory was given up to him. The measure of independence rightfully belonging to the chief is not by any means clearly defined; but the British government has never interfered in civil or criminal affairs, except in the instance above mentioned. The revenue of the state is estimated at 1,60,000 rupees, and the annual disbursement at 1,80,000 rupees. The chief maintains a small force, consisting of 100 cavalry and 350 infantry. The town of Bulubgurh is in lat. 28° 20′, long. 77° 23′.

BUMROWLEE, in the British district of Bareilly, a town on the route from Bareilly to

Seetapore, and 36 miles S.E. of the former. It has a bazaar and market. Lat. 28° 12′, long. 80°.

BUMTA, a village in the Cis-Sutlej state of Poondur, a tributary of Keonthul, under British protection, is situate on the route from Chepal to Deohra, and about six miles N. of the former. Here was formerly a fort, with a strong rampart and towers, on a situation commanding the vale below, but itself commanded by a hill above it. At the time of Fraser's visit it was in ruins, having been burned some time before ; but the rajah was busy in building a residence for himself, and a Hindoo temple embellished with sculptures. Lat. 31° 1′, long. 77° 40′.

BUMUNGA, in the British district of Kumaon, lieut.-gov. of the N.W. Provinces, a village two miles W. of the right bank of the Kalee (eastern), 13 S.E. of Champawut cantonment. Lat. 29° 14′, long. 80° 18′.

BUNAEE, or BHINAY, in the British district of Ajmere, lieut.-gov. of the N.W. Provinces, a fortress, with a village at its base, on the route from Nusseerabad to Boondee, 20 miles S. of former, 70 N.W. of latter. Its site is picturesque on the summit of an isolated steep craggy hill, covered with cactus. Here resides a chief or petty rajah of the Rahtore tribe of Rajpoots, who, according to a high authority, owes allegiance to the rajah of Joudpore, as well as to the British. The place is styled by Heber a good-sized town, containing two very elegant little temples. The pergunnah of which it is the principal place contains ninety-three villages and a population of 27,340 persons. Lat. 26° 3′, long. 74° 50′.

BUNAL, in the native state of Gurwhal, a valley extending between seven and eight miles, in a direction nearly from N.W. to S.E., between lat. 30° 49′—31°, and long. 78° 9′—78° 14′. The north-western end is closed by a rocky mountain, on the declivity of which rises the Bunal stream, that waters the valley and falls into the Jumna.

BUNASS (Eastern).—A river of Rewah, in Bundlecund, rising on the south-eastern boundary, in lat. 23° 31′, long. 82° 2′, and, flowing in a north-westerly direction through Rewah for seventy miles, falls into the Sone, in lat. 24° 14′, long. 81° 33′, near the town of Rampoor.

BUNASS (Western), a river of Western India, rises in the Aravulli Mountains, on the common confines of the territories of Oodeypoor and Godwar, in Joudpore, about forty miles north-west of the city of Oodeypoor, and in lat. 24° 58′, long. 73° 20′. It takes a south-west direction, and after a course of about 180 miles, is lost in the Runn of Cutch, in lat. 23° 40′, long. 71° 15′, terminating in several intricate and small channels. The British cantonment of Deesa is situate on its left bank.

BUNBASSA.—A town in the territory of Oude, distant S. from Lucknow 115 miles. Lat. 28° 30′, long. 81° 7′.

BUNCHANEGAON, in the native state of Gurwhal, a village on the left bank of the Budeear, a feeder of the Jumna. It is situate in a fertile expanse, rising with gentle acclivity up the side of a mountain. Elevation above the sea 6,034 feet. Lat. 30° 52′, long. 78° 19′.

BUNCHAREE, in the British district of Goorgaon, lieut.-gov. of the N.W. Provinces, a village on the route from Hansee to Muttra, and 34 miles N.W. of the latter. Lat. 27° 56′, long. 77° 25′.

BUNCHOOLA FORT, in the British district of Kumaon, lieut.-gov. of the N.W. Provinces, a town on the left bank of the Gaomutee river, 17 miles N. of Almora. Lat. 29° 50′, long. 79° 50′.

BUNDA.—A town in Hyderabad, or dominions of the Nizam, distant S.E. from Kuladgee 75 miles. Lat. 15° 20′, long. 76° 12′.

BUNDARA, in the British province of Nagpore, a town on the route from Midnapore to the city of Nagpore, 612 miles W. of former, 34 E. of latter. It has a bazaar ; and being situate on the right bank of the river Waingunga, water is abundant. Elevation above the sea 892 feet. Lat. 21° 11′, long. 79° 41′.

BUNDARREE.—A town in the native state of Purlahkemedy, one of the Cuttack mehals, distant N.W. from Berhampoor, in Ganjam, 61 miles. Lat. 19° 39′, long. 83° 59′.

BUNDELCUND, or the Bundela country, is an extensive tract, bounded on the west and north-west by Gwalior ; on the north-east by the Jumna, dividing it from the British districts Etawah, Cawnpore, Futtehpoor, and Allahabad, in the Doab ; on the east by Bhagelkhand, or territory of Rewa ; and on the south by the British territory of Saugor and Nerbudda. It lies between lat. 23° 52′—26° 26′, long. 77° 53′—81° 39′ ; is 200 miles in length from south-east to north-west, 155 in breadth in the direction of the opposite angles ; and has an area of 18,099 square miles. The plains of Bundelcund are diversified by mountains, which have been classed into three ranges, —the Bindyachal, the Punna, and the Bandair. From these numerous streams flow towards the Jumna, among which may be enumerated the Sindh and its tributary the Pohooj, the Betwa, the Dhasan, the Berma, the Cane, the Baghin, the Paisuni, and the Tons. The mineral resources of this tract appear to be considerable, though very imperfectly developed. Punna contains diamonds, and contiguous are inexhaustible deposits of iron-ore ; while farther to the north-east, towards Kalleenjer, Franklin considered that he had found indications of coal. The climate is sultry in the plains. Calpee, notwithstanding its extra-tropical latitude, has been represented as one of the hottest places in India ; and the heat at Banda is also stated to be very great. That by the natives the climate is not found insalubrious, is indicated by their healthy appearance; but Europeans are frequently affected severely, and even fatally, by ague and other complaints resulting from malaria. Portions of the western part, between the Betwa and Sindh, are represented to be "notoriously unhealthy;" and there, in 1817, the British army under the marquis of Hastings experienced the ravages of cholera to a most frightful extent. There seems, however, great diversity in regard to the salubrity of particular spots, not explainable by any known laws. The British cantonments of Keita have been abandoned on account of their fatal air; but the elevated fortresses of Ajegurh and Callinger have been found uncommonly healthy, though such situations are usually throughout India the seats of deadly malaria. The principal towns of Bundelcund—Calpee, Banda, Jhansi, Duttea, Oorcha, Jaloon, Chatarpoor, Mahoba, Tehari—are noticed under their respective names in the alphabetical arrangement. Besides the British districts of Banda and Hummerpoor, the lapsed territory of Jeitpore and Jaloun, the pergunnahs of Duboi and Gurota, ceded by Jhansi to the British government, and the confiscated jaghire of Chirgaon, the province of Bundelcund contains several native states, and a variety of petty jaghires. Those belonging to the former class are, Adjyghur, Bijawur, Churkaree, Chutterpoor, Dutteeah, Jhansi, Oorcha or Terree, Punnah, Sumpthur. The British districts in Bundelcund are—Banda, Hummerpoor and Calpee, Jaloun, Jeitpore, Churgaon, ceded pergunnahs of Duboi and Gurota.

The several districts, British and foreign, contain in the aggregate, as already noticed, a total area of 18,099 square miles. Franklin estimated the population at 2,400,000. More recent inquiries afford a result of 2,260,714. In the British district of Banda the population was officially reported in 1847 as 552,526; in Humeerpore and Calpee the total was 452,091; in Jaloun the number was roughly returned at 176,297; in the Jhansi ceded pergunnahs and Churgaon, the numbers were stated to be 70,000. Jeitpore is stated to have 16,000 inhabitants, and the lapsed jaghire of Khuddee 2,800. The judicial and fiscal management of the British districts appertains to the lieut.-gov. of the N.W. Provinces. The political superintendence of the remainder forms part of the charge of the Governor-General's agent for Scindia's dominions and Bundelcund. With the principal native states of Bundelcund the British government have engagements, varying on minor points according to circumstances, but all recognising its supremacy, and binding the dependent state to the relinquishment of all political relations except with the superior. Some are tributary, some exempt from that incident. In aid of the services of the regular troops stationed in this tract, a force styled the Bundelcund Legion was formerly supported by contributions from the states of Jhansi and Jaloun. Subsequently Jaloun became a British possession, and Jhansi ceded territory in lieu of its contribution to the support of the legion. The legion itself has now ceased to exist, the British government having resolved to restore to the army-list the number of the 34th regiment Bengal Native Infantry, which had been struck out, and to form the new regiment of the volunteers from the infantry of the Bundelcund Legion.

The earliest paramount power in Bundelcund of which there is any certain record, were the Chundel Rajpoots, deriving their origin from Muhoba and its vicinity, where their rule was established by Chandra Varma. As Parmal Deo, the twentieth ruler in succession from Chandra Varma, was, in the year 1183, overthrown by Pirthi Rajah, ruler of Ajmeer and Delhi, if fifteen years be allowed on an average to each ruler, the time of Chandra Varma will be placed in the latter part of the ninth century of our era. During the age of the supremacy of the Chundel Rajpoots was the period of the greatest splendour of this country, the dominion of those princes extending from the Jumna to the Nerbudda; and Ferishta relates, that in the year 1021 their rajah marched at the head of 36,000 horse, 45,000 foot, and 640 elephants, to oppose Mahmud of Ghuzni, whom, however, he was obliged to conciliate by rich presents. After the overthrow of Parmal Deo, the country remained in ruinous anarchy until the close of the fourteenth century, when the Bundelas, a spurious subdivision of the Garhwa tribe of Rajpoots, established themselves on the right bank of the Jumna, under the conduct of Hurdeo. Pretap Hrad, tenth in descent from that chief, greatly extended and consolidated the Bundela sway, and in 1531 founded the town of Oorcha. His great-grandson Birsing Deo succeeded in still farther aggrandizing the Bundela state, chiefly through the favour of Jehangir, the padshah of Delhi, whom he had conciliated by the murder of the celebrated Abulfazl, the minister of Akbar, father of Jehangir; the latter prince hating and dreading that minister as inimical to his interests. The predatory character of the Bundela chief earned for him the name of Dangi, or robber, which has attached to all his countrymen, and to their native soil, not uncommonly known by the name of Dangaya or Thieves-land. His eldest son and successor, Jajhar Singh, revolting against the court of Delhi, was driven into exile, and disappeared finally among the wilds of Gondwana, when the country was incorporated with the empire. This arrangement, however, lasted but six years, as the violent struggles of the Bundelas for independence compelled the emperor to withdraw his forces and admit the insurgents in the western part to the relation of feudatories, on condition of military service. The eastern Bundelas, under the conduct of the rajah Chatrasal, supported by the Mahrattas, successfully made head against the forces of Delhi; but being hard pressed by Ahmed Khan Bangush, the Patan chief of Furruckabad, in 1734, solicited the aid of the Peishwa, who, succeeding in rescuing the Bundela rajah from his perilous position, was rewarded by a fort and district in the neighbourhood of Jhansi, and by a devise of the third part of Eastern Bundelcund. The Peishwa made over his portion, subject to a moderate tribute, to a Brahmin called Kasi Pandit, whose descendants held it until it recently lapsed to the East-India Company. About the same time Jhansi was wrested by the Peishwa from the rajah of Oorcha, and intrusted to a soubahdar, whose descendant retains it. The remainder of the country, from various causes, gradually became parcelled out into numerous small chieftainships. The anarchy and incessant petty wars resulting from this circumstance, encouraged the Mahrattas, under Ali Behaudar, to attempt, in 1792, the subjugation of the province. Their purpose, however, was but partially effected. Ali Behaudar spent three years in a series of desultory and harassing exertions, and ten years more in endeavours to reduce the stronghold of Callinger. He died without attaining his object, and almost immediately afterwards the state of affairs became altogether changed by the flight of the Peishwa from his capital to Bassein, and the treaty there concluded with him on the part of the East-India Company, under which and the subsequent arrangements the latter acquired the present British districts of Hummerpore and Banda. Of the two principal chiefs, who, ostensibly yielding obedience to the Peishwa, substantially held the ceded tract, Himmat Bahadur supported the views of the British authorities. His services were acknowledged by his being permitted to retain possession of his lands during his life, and by the grant of pensions to his relatives on his death, which took place in 1804. The other chief, Shamshir Bahadur, made common cause with Scindia and his Mahratta confederates against the British; but after a brief and ill-sustained attempt at resistance, was defeated by a detachment under Colonel Pouell, at Capsah, near the left bank of the river Cane, where the Mahrattas had drawn together about 12,000 men. Shamshir Bahadur ultimately submitted, on condition of receiving an annual pension of 400,000 rupees for himself and family. Further military operations have, however, from time to time been found necessary to establish firmly the British power in Bundelcund. In 1809, in consequence of the refractory conduct of the rajah of Ajegarh, that fortress was besieged by a British force, and evacuated by the enemy after having been battered for a few hours. In 1812, the possessor of the celebrated hill-fort of Callinger having set the British authorities at defiance, his stronghold was invested by a British force, which suffered a severe repulse in an attempt to storm; but the place was surrendered a few days afterwards. In 1817 the Peishwa, by the treaty of Poona, ceded to the East-India Company all his rights, interests, and pretensions, feudal, territorial, or pecuniary, in the province of Bundelcund. The power thus transferred has been exercised with strict regard to the just claims of those interested in the transfer, and the British possessions remain studded with a variety of petty dependencies, whose rights are rigidly respected. To this is probably to be attributed the peaceful state of the country under the present settlement. With the exception of the brief and unsuccessful revolt of the jaghiredar of Chirgaon, in 1841, Bundelcund has of late years been as tranquil as any part of British India. A valuable series of drawings of the cave-temples of Callinger, together with a memoir illustrative of the antiquities of Sanchi, near Bhilsa, have been recently prepared by Lieut. Maisey, portions of which have been published by the Asiatic Society of Bengal.

BUNDIPUR, or BUNDURPUR, in Cashmere, a village at the commencement of the route to Iskardoh, over the range bounding the valley of Cashmere on the north. Close to it two considerable streams flow into the Wulur Lake from the north. The water of the lake formerly reached to the village, but at present is a mile distant, in consequence of its outlet, the river Jhelum, continually deepening its bed. Bundurpur is in lat. 34° 25′, long. 74° 49′.

BUNDOEE, or BUNDOOREE, in the British district of Allahabad, lieut.-gov. of the N.W. Provinces, a village on the route, by Rajapoor ferry, from the cantonment of Allahabad to Banda, and 27 miles W. of the former. Lat. 25° 26′, long. 81° 28′.

BUNDWA, in the British district of Futtehpoor, lieut.-gov. of the N.W. Provinces, a village near the left bank of the Jumna, on the route from Banda to the town of Futtehpore, and 20 miles S.W. of the latter. Lat. 25° 50′, long. 80° 38′.

BUNDY ATMACOOR, in the British district of Kurnool, presidency of Madras, a town three miles E. of the route from Cuddapah to Kurnool, 35 miles S.E. of the latter. Lat. 15° 35′, long. 78° 34′.

BUNEHUR.—A town in the native state of Bhopal, distant E. from Bhopal 28 miles. Lat. 23° 10′, long. 77° 50′.

BUNEEPARA, in the British district of Cawnpore, lieut.-gov. of the N.W. Provinces, a town on the route from Hummerpore to Mynpooree, and 70 miles S.E. of the latter. Lat. 26° 32′, long. 80° 57′.

BUNGALA BUL.—A town in the native state of Cashmere, or dominions of Gholab Singh, distant N. from Sirinagur 42 miles. Lat. 34° 41′, long. 74° 59′.

BUNGANAPILLY.—A jaghire or feudal possession in the British district of Cuddapah, presidency of Madras, extending from lat. 15° 2′ to 15° 29′, and from long. 78° 8′ to 78° 27′, and containing an area of about 100 square miles. When visited by Dr. Heyne in 1808, it belonged to a feudal chief of the Nizam. In 1843 it was deemed necessary to invest a British agent with the administration of civil and criminal justice and police, and the superintendence of revenue matters in this jaghire; but in 1848 the authority of the British agent was withdrawn, and the possession restored to the jaghiredar.

BUNGBO.—A short tributary of the Teesta, rising about lat. 27° 21′, long. 88° 51′, and flowing south-west for twenty-one miles, separating the territory of Bhotan from that of Sikkim, falls into the Teesta near the town of Burmiok, in lat. 27° 10′, long. 88° 36′.

BUNGEET.—A small river rising in lat. 27° 11′, long. 88° 3′, on the eastern face of a spur of the Himalayas, uniting the Sub-Himalaya with the great snowy range. It flows in an easterly direction for about forty miles, separating the native state of Sikhim from the British territory of Darjeeling, and falls into the Teesta river in lat. 27° 4′, long. 88° 35′.

BUNGONG, in the British district of Chota Nagpoor, lieut.-gov. of Bengal, a town on the route from Lohadugga to Odeipoor, 51 miles S.W. of the former. Lat. 23° 3′, long. 84° 3′.

BUNIHAR.—A town in the native state of Cashmere, or dominions of Gholab Singh, distant W. from Sirinagur 39 miles. Lat. 34° 7′, long. 74° 22′.

BUNKOULEE, in Gurwhal, is situate on the declivity of a mountain near the right bank of the Jumna, and 3,000 feet above the bed of the river. It contains about a score of houses and 150 inhabitants. Lat. 30° 45′, long. 78° 8′.

BUNNEE.—See CUTCH.

BUNNEE, in the British district of Bhuttiana, lieut.-gov. of the N.W. Provinces, a village on the route from Hansi to Bhutneer, and 23 miles E. of the latter. Lat. 29° 31′, long. 74° 38′.

BUNNEE CHOWKEE, on the eastern boundary of Keonthul, a halting-place with a wooden house for the accommodation of travellers, on the route from Simla to Kotgurh, and 11 miles E. of the former post. Elevation above the sea 8,107 feet. Lat. 31° 5′, long. 77° 22′.

BUNNOO.—A fertile plain, south-west of the Kala or Salt Range, in the Punjaub. It is well watered by the river Kurum, and produces abundant crops of wheat, rice, barley, maize, and other grain, sugar-cane, tobacco, and ginger. Its centre is in lat. 32° 40′, long. 70° 30′.

BUNOWL, in the British district of Tirhoot, lieut.-gov. of Bengal, a town 22 miles N.W. of Durbunga, 20 miles N.E. of Mozufferpoor. Lat. 26° 21′, long. 85° 41′.

BUNSHEEAREE, in the British district of Dinajepore, lieut.-gov. of Bengal, a town two miles from the west bank of the river Tangon, 22 miles S.W. of Dinajepore. Lat. 25° 21′, long. 88° 21′.

BUNSI RIVER.—An offset of the Brahmapootra, diverging from that river about lat. 24° 52′, long. 89° 53′. It flows in a south-easterly direction through the British district of Mymunsing for sixty miles: subsequently dividing the district of Dacca from that of Deccan Jelalpore for eighteen miles, it falls into the Dulaseree in lat. 23° 52′, long. 90° 11′.

BUNTWALLA, in the British district of South Canara, presidency of Madras, a town the principal place of the subdivision of the same name. It is situate on the north or right bank of the river Naitravutty, a considerable stream, descending from the Western Ghats, and falling into the Arabian Sea, or North Indian Ocean, eighteen miles below the town of Mangalore. Though small, Buntwalla appears to be a place of considerable trade. During the war with Tippoo Sultan, it suffered much from the rajah of Coorg, who destroyed about two hundred houses, and led one-half of the population into captivity. Distance from Mangalore, E., 14 miles; Bombay, S.E., 445; Bangalore, W., 172; Madras, W., 355. Lat. 12° 53′, long. 75° 6′.

BUNUT, in the British district of Muzufurnugur, lieut.-gov. of the N.W. Provinces, a town on the route from Paneeput to Suharunpoor, 25 miles E. of the former. Lat. 29° 28′, long. 77° 27′.

BUNYAWALA.—See BAMANWALA.

BUO, in the British district of Behar, lieut.-gov. of Bengal, a town 19 miles S. of Behar, 38 miles N.E. of Gayah. Lat. 24° 56′, long. 85° 36′.

BURADEEL, or BURADIL.—A station on the route from Chittagong to Akyab. It is situate near the shore, and about 20 miles N. of Tek Naaf. Lat. 21° 2′, long. 92° 15′.

BURAECH.—A town in the territory of Oude, distant N.E. from Lucknow 63 miles. Lat. 27° 34′, long. 81° 40′.

BURAEE.—A town in the Rajpoot state of Shekawuttee, distant S.E. from Jhoonjhnoo 25 miles. Lat. 27° 51′, long. 75° 51′.

BURAGAON, in the British district of Jounpore, lieut.-gov. of the N.W. Provinces, a village on the route from Azimgurh to Sultanpoor, in Oude, 36 miles W. of the former, 42 S.E. of the latter. Lat. 26° 1′, long. 82° 42′.

BURAGAON, in the British district Shahjahanpoor, lieut.-gov. of the N.W. Provinces, a town, the principal place of the pergunnah of the same name, in lat. 28° 3′, long. 80° 8′.

BURAGAON, in the British district of Allygurh, lieut.-gov. of the N.W. Provinces, a village on the route, by Khasgunj, from Futtehgurh to Meerut, and 86 miles N.W. of the former. It has a few shops. Water is obtained from wells, and from the Nim Nuddi, a small river flowing about half a mile to the west. Lat. 27° 53′, long. 78° 30′.

BURAGAUM.—A town in the native state of Gwalior, or possessions of Scindia, distant N.E. from Oojein 52 miles. Lat. 23° 45′, long. 76° 20′.

BURAGONG, in the British district of Ghazeepoor, lieut.-gov. of the N.W. Provinces, a town on the right of the route from Ghazeepoor cantonment to Chupra, 34 miles E. of the former, 48 W. of the latter. It is situate on the right bank of the Tons (north-eastern), here called the Surjoo, and traversed by means of ferry during the rains, and ford at other seasons. Lat. 25° 46′, long. 84° 3′.

BURAGONG, in Bundlecund, a town in the native state of Tehree, distant S.E. from Tehree 16 miles. Lat. 24° 35′, long. 79° 6′.

BURAHA.—A town in the territory of Oude, distant S. from Lucknow 56 miles. Lat. 26° 3′, long. 81° 10′.

BURAL, in the British district of Mozuffurnugur, lieut.-gov. of the N.W. Provinces, a village near the southern boundary towards Meerut. Lat. 29° 15′, long. 77° 25′.

BURAMEE, or BRAMEE, in the Rajpoot state of Joudpore, a village on the route from Nusseerabad to Deesa, and 139 miles S.W. of the former. Lat. 25° 22′, long. 73° 23′.

BURANA, in the jaghire of Jujhur, lieut.-gov. of the N.W. Provinces, a small town on the route from Hansi to Neemuch, and 61 miles S. of the former. The water, which is brackish, is obtained from wells. Lat. 28° 21′, long. 76° 17′.

BURAPOORA, in the British district of Bijnour, lieut.-gov. of the N.W. Provinces, a town on the route from Bijnour to Sireenagur, 26 miles N.E. of the former. Lat. 29° 31′, long. 78° 38′.

BURA PUHARA, in the territory of Gwalior, a town on the route by Jhansi, from Calpee to Goona cantonment, 158 miles S.W. of former, 35 N.E. of latter. Water is abundant from a small stream, and supplies may be had. Lat. 25° 4′, long. 77° 54′.

BURAR, in the British district of Cawnpore, lieut.-gov. of the N.W. Provinces, a town 12 miles W. of the right bank of the Ganges. Lat. 26° 33′, long. 80° 10′.

BURAREE, in the British district of Etawah, lieut.-gov. of the N.W. Provinces, a village on the route from the cantonment of Etawah to Calpee, and eight miles S.E. of the former. Lat. 26° 44′, long. 79° 11′.

BURARYA, in the British district of Tirhoot, lieut.-gov. of Bengal, a town on the right bank of the Coosy river, 56 miles N.W. of Purneah. Lat. 26° 31′, long. 87° 11′.

BURASOO, in the British district of Boolundshuhur, lieut.-gov. of the N.W. Provinces, a town on the route from Khasganj to Meerut, and 58 miles S. of the latter. Lat. 28° 15′, long. 78° 6′.

BURASS, in the British district of Paneput, lieut.-gov. of the N.W. Provinces, a town on the route from Kurnal to Kythul, 111 miles W. of the former. It has a population of 30,056. Lat. 29° 45′, long. 76° 49′.

BURDA, or JAITWAR, in the peninsula of Kattywar, province of Guzerat, a division bounded on the north and north-east by the district of Hallar; on the east by that of Soruth; on the south-west by the Arabian Sea. It lies between lat. 21° 11′—21° 57′, long. 69° 30′—70° 7′. There is no official return of the area, but 570 square miles may be regarded as a probable approximation to the fact. The seacoast extends in a direction from north-west to south-east for sixty-three miles, and in that distance comprehends the ports Meednee, at the north-western extremity, on the estuary of the Boortoo; Poorbunder, twenty miles south-east of it; and Nurvee Bunder, still further south-east, and sixteen miles from the last-mentioned port. The river Boorto flows for some miles along its northern frontier; and the Bhader, the largest in the peninsula of Kattywar, having for some distance formed its south-western boundary, subsequently enters the district, and falls into the sea at Nurvee Bunder. The district belongs to the chief denominated the Rana of Poorbunder, from his residing at that town: he is of the Jaitwa tribe of Rajpoots. Besides the three seaports mentioned above, the district contains 103 villages; and the population is estimated at 46,980. The rana is subordinate to the Guicowar, to whom, according to a recent statement, he pays an annual tribute of 8,775 rupees. To the British government he pays a tribute of 22,890 rupees; and that government receives in addition a share of the custom duties of Poorbunder, amounting to 26,001 rupees, ceded to the East-India Company in 1809, for the maintenance of a small military force at that place.

BURDAPOOR.—A town in Hyderabad, or dominions of the Nizam, distant N.W. from Hyderabad 160 miles. Lat. 18° 39′, long. 76° 33′.

BURDHEE.—A town in the native state of Rewah, situate on an abrupt eminence on the right or south bank of the river Sone, at the confluence of the Goput. The district of which this town is the principal place formerly constituted a portion of the territory of the rajah of Singrowly, a tributary of the rajah of Rewah, by whom he was dispossessed of the north-western portion of his dominions. Distant E. from Rewah 68 miles. Lat. 24° 32′, long. 82° 29′.

BURDWAN.—A district under the presidency of Bengal, named from its principal place. It is bounded on the north by the British district of Beerbhoom; on the north-east and east by the British district Nuddea; on the south by the British districts of Hoogly and Midnapore; on the west by the British district Bancoorah. It lies between lat. 22° 52′—23° 40′, long.

87° 21′—88° 23′; is about seventy miles in length from north-east to south-west, and sixty in breadth. The area is 2,224 square miles. The district abounds in rivers, the most important of which are the Hadjee, Bhaggruttee, Jellinghee, Damooda, and Dalkissore. The Hadjee and Damooda are navigable during the periodical rains of autumn, and serve as channels for the conveyance of coal, iron, and other bulky or heavy goods, to Calcutta. The Bhaggruttee and Hooghly are navigable at all times. The smaller watercourses and torrents are numerous; and as most of the streams of this district are subject to be greatly swollen in the periodical rains, the country suffers sometimes from dreadful inundations, "the water rushing down as from a sluice, in a body from one to three or four feet in perpendicular height." In 1823 a dreadful and general inundation took place, and in many places quite changed the aspect of the country, obliterating fine villages, tanks, and other useful monuments of industry, and converting a scene of rich cultivation into a sandy waste. Such frightful calamities are not of uncommon recurrence, notwithstanding that bunds or embankments are maintained in various places, to the total extent of 308 miles. The climate, though very sultry during the hot season, is considered not insalubrious, and the town of Burdwan enjoys a peculiarly high reputation in this respect. This is one of the most productive parts of India, yielding fine and plentiful crops of rice, sugar, potatoes, indigo, oil-seeds, tobacco, cotton, and some others of less importance. The refining of sugar is one of the most important objects of manufacture, being conducted extensively, and with considerable skill. A large proportion of the iron and coal sent down to Calcutta under the name of Burdwan is not raised here, but in the adjoining district of West Burdwan or Bancoorah, and principally at Raneegunje, in the north-west of the last-mentioned district. This coal, though incomparably cheaper, is stated to be less suitable to steam purposes than English coal. The other wares exported are coarse silks, hides, horns, lac, and timber. The population is given under the article BENGAL.

Many of the natives of Burdwan possess large estates. The principal among them is the titular rajah of Burdwan. The present rajah is the adopted son of his predecessor, who died a few years ago; a morose miser and very rich, having an annual income of 130,000*l.*, and a vast sum accumulated by himself and his ancestors; of which hoarded wealth he took the most extraordinary care. Soon after his decease, a pretender to the raj of Burdwan presented himself, in the person of Aluk Shah, professing to be Pertaub Chund, the rightful rajah, who died fourteen years before. Aluk Shah applied for assistance to some of the neighbouring native chiefs, and, refusing to disband his followers, was arrested as a disturber of the peace, and sentenced to imprisonment. The present rajah, who succeeded to the title upon attaining his majority in 1840, in several instances has manifested a better spirit than his predecessor, by bestowing liberal donations for useful public objects. A gift of 25,000 rupees, made about the year 1843, was applied, under the sanction of the government, partly to the extension of a branch of the Medical College, and the remainder to the foundation of scholarships in the Hindoo College, called the Rajah of Burdwan's Scholarships. A previous sum of 12,600 rupees, contributed partly by the rajah and partly by other persons, was devoted to the establishment of a school at Burdwan.

The great military route, denominated the Great Trunk Road from Calcutta to Benares and the North-Western Provinces, proceeds through this district, passing through the town of Burdwan: the old line through Bancoora traverses the south-western corner of the district. There is also a route from north to south, from Cutwa to Hooghly, along the right bank of the Bhaggruttee; and another from north-east to south-west, from Berhampore, in Moorshedabad, to Midnapur, through the town of Burdwan; and another from north-west to south-east, from Sooree, in the British district Beerbhoom, to the town of Burdwan. The district is bisected by the railway now under construction from Calcutta to Rajmahal, and intersected also by the branch line proceeding from the vicinity of Burdwan to the collieries at Raneegunje. The tract comprised within this district was acquired by the East-India Company, under treaty with Meer Cossim, in 1760, and confirmed by the emperor Shah Alum in 1765.

BURDWAN, the principal place of the British district of the same name, under the presidency of Bengal, is situate on the left bank of the river Damooda, and on the route from Calcutta to Benares, nearly 74 miles N.W. of the former, about 346 S.E. of the latter. Jacquemont describes it as consisting of an assemblage of crowded suburbs, of wretched huts, with walls of mud, and covered with thatch, having no temples of striking aspect, and few handsome houses. The residence of the titular rajah is a great collection of buildings of various sizes and colours, without symmetry or regularity, and surrounded by extensive gardens in equally bad taste. Contiguous to the town is an artificial piece of water of great extent, its area being estimated at thirty acres. The earth excavated from it has been formed into a causeway surrounding it, and an ornamented porch gives access to the water, which is much frequented by the natives for the purpose of bathing. The population of the town and suburbs was found in 1814 to occupy 9,805 houses. Of this number, 7,651 were then inhabited by Hindoos, and 2,154 by Mussulmans; and the average ratio of inmates to dwellings being stated at eleven to two, the number of inhabitants appears to have then been 53,927. Here is located the civil *establishment of the district, consisting of the* ordinary European functionaries and native assistants. One of the government English schools has been established in the town: there is also here an English school under the direction of the Church Missionary Society. Lat. 23° 12′, long. 87° 56′.

BURENDA, or BROANG PASS, in Bussahir, across the most southern range of the Himalaya, which has a direction from east-south-east to west-north-west. It is reached from the south by travelling up the course of the Pabur river nearly to its source. Elevation above the sea 15,095 feet. Lat. 31° 23′, long. 78° 12′.

BURENG.—A valley of Cashmere, extending in a direction from south-east to north-west, between lat. 33° 20′—33° 30′, long. 75° 10′—75° 26′. Its upper extremity reaches nearly to the summit of the Snowy Panjal mountain, bounding Cashmere on the east; and the route by the Mirbul Pass, over that ridge, proceeds up the valley, which is drained by the river Bureng. The whole of the valley appears (as Vigne expresses it) honeycombed by caves and subterraneous water-channels, and in consequence abounds in springs of great volume and force. Of these the principal are the intermitting fountain of Sondibreri, and the vast spring of Echibul, which last is supposed to be the efflux of the engulfed water of the Bureng river.

BURENG RIVER, in Cashmere, flowing through a valley of the same name, is formed by the junction of two streams, one having its source in a large spring near the summit of the Wurdwun Pass, and flowing southwards; the other rising on the western declivity of the Snowy Panjal, and flowing north-west. After their junction, a great part of the water sinks suddenly by an opening in the rocky bed of the stream; the rest is saved by means of a canal, and conveyed north-westward toward Islamabad, beyond which, in lat. 33° 42′, long. 75° 14′, it joins the Lidur river, forming one of the principal feeders of the Jhelum. The length of the course of the Bureng is about forty miles.

BURGATCHEE, in the British district of Rajeshaye, lieut.-gov. of Bengal, a town on the route from Rampore to Dinajepore, 16 miles N.W. of the former. Lat. 24° 27′, long. 88° 22′.

BURGAUM, in the British district of Candeish, presidency of Bombay, a town on the left bank of the Girna river, 48 miles E. of Malligaum. Lat. 20° 40′, long. 75° 12′.

BURGHAUT.—A town of Bombra, one of the native states on the south-west frontier of Bengal, under the political superintendence of the government of India, distant E. from Sumbulpoor 38 miles. Lat. 21° 30′, long. 84° 36′.

BURGOONDA.—A town in the native state of Indore, or territory of Holkar, distant S. from Indore 19 miles. Lat. 22° 26′, long. 75° 49′.

BURGOW.—A town in the native state of Sirgoojah, on the south-west frontier of Bengal, distant S. from Sirgoojah 16 miles. Lat. 22° 54′, long. 83° 12′.

BURGOWA, in the district of Burdhee, in the native state of Rewa, a town among the northern mountains of Gondwana, 30 miles S. of the town of Burdhee, 68 S. of Mirzapoor, 400 W. of Calcutta by Hazareebagh. Lat. 24° 10′, long. 82° 30′.

BURGUDDA, in the British district of Mirzapore, lieut.-gov. of the N.W. Provinces, a village on the left bank of the Ganges, 771 miles N.W. of Calcutta by the river route, 37 miles S.E. of the city of Allahabad by the same. Lat. 25° 16′, long. 82° 12′.

BURGUDOOA.—A town in the territory of Oude, distant N.E. from Oude 55 miles. Lat. 27° 27′, long. 82° 42′.

BURGUR, in the British district of Palamow, lieut.-gov. of Bengal, a town on the right bank of the river Kunher, 30 miles S.W. of Palamow. Lat. 23° 38′, long. 83° 35′.

BURGUR, in the British district of Sumbulpoor, on the south-west frontier of Bengal, a town on the route from Sumbulpore to Nagpore, 22 miles S.W. of the former. Lat. 21° 20′, long. 83° 40′.

BURGURH.—A small raj within the country superintended by the political agent for the south-west frontier of Bengal. Its centre is in lat. 21° 53′, long. 83° 5′: its area is 399 square miles. The effect of a rebellion some years ago was to render the country a desert; but it was expected to improve under the rajah of Ryegurh, the south-western part of whose raj it adjoins, and by whom it is now held. Its annual value has been estimated at about 10,000 rupees. The tribute is 320 rupees. The population is estimated at about 18,000. Burgurh, the principal place, is in lat. 22° 1′, long. 83° 9′.

BURHAMPORE, in the British district of Moorshedabad, lieut.-gov. of Bengal, a town situate on the left bank of the river Bhagruttee, a great offset of the Ganges, and on the route from Calcutta to Moorshedabad. The depressed and moist site rendered it extremely unhealthy, and the prevalence of dreadful mortality was painfully brought to view by the extent and crowded state of the European burial-ground. Among the endemic diseases, cholera especially prevailed. Hence the station was regarded with great apprehension and dislike by those consigned to it by the exigencies of the civil or military service. Latterly, however, sanitary measures have been introduced with so high a degree of success, that the climate of the station, so far from proving baneful to the troops now located there, is reported to be second to none in Bengal for salubrity. Nature and art have combined to give this place an exterior in many respects attractive. Stately houses arise in convenient spots in the neighbourhood, for the accommodation of those whose residence partakes of the character of permanence, and give the station an air of grandeur and importance. This place is the seat of the civil establishment, consisting of the usual European and native functionaries. The want of a well-conducted public seminary in this town has long been felt; and a project is on foot to establish a college of the same character as those of Kishnaghur and Hooghly. The military cantonments command the notice of the traveller. The grand square, a spacious quadrangle, inclosing an excellent parade-ground, is particularly striking; and the quarters of the European officers are handsome edifices, built of brick, and stuccoed, and forming ranges of considerable extent. In the arrangements of the Bengal army, this place is included within the presidency division, and usually is occupied by a body of infantry and a detail of artillery. Distance N. from Calcutta by land 118 miles, by water 161; from Moorshedabad, S., five miles. Lat. 24° 5′, long. 88° 17′.

BURHAMPOREE.—A town in Nagpore, distant S.E. from Nagpore 60 miles. Lat. 20° 39′, long. 79° 55′.

BURHIAH, in the territory of Oude, a village on the route from Seetapoor cantonment to that of Shahjehanpoor, 45 miles N.W. of the former, 17 miles E. of the latter. Lat. 27° 50′, long. 80° 14′.

BURHIN, or BURHUL, in the British district of Goruckpore, lieut.-gov. of the N.W. Provinces, a town on the route from Azimgurh to Goruckpore cantonment, 32 miles N.E. of the former, 33 S.E. of the latter. It has a bazaar, and is situate on the left bank of the Gogra, here a great river running in one channel, and crossed by ferry. Lat. 26° 15′, long. 83° 34′.

BURHUD.—A town in the native state of Gwalior, or possessions of Scindia, distant N.E. from Gwalior 31 miles. Lat. 26° 28′, long. 78° 40′.

BURKAGURH, in the British district of Chota Nagpoor, lieut.-gov. of Bengal, a town on the route from Hazareebagh to Midnapoor, 46 miles S. of the former. Lat. 23° 20′, long. 85° 19′.

BURKAIRA, in the territory of Gwalior, or possessions of Scindia, a village on the route from Goona to Mow, 28 miles S.W. of former, 157 N.E. of latter. Water is abundant here, and supplies may be obtained. Lat. 24° 17′, long. 77° 9′.

BURKELE.—A town in the native state of Bora Samba, on the south-west frontier of Bengal, distant S.W. from Sumbulpoor 75 miles. Lat. 21°, long. 82° 59′.

BURKOT, in Gurhwal, a village on a ridge overhanging a torrent, which about two miles to the north-west falls into the Jumna on the left side. The scenery is of very great beauty. Skinner, who states that he visited nearly all the celebrated prospects of Europe, considers them surpassed by those of this sequestered tract. The rajah of Tirhee has a palace here, but in a style much at variance with the noble character of the scenery. Lat. 30° 47′, long. 78° 17′.

BURKUTUH, in the British district of Muzuffurnugar, lieut.-gov. of the N.W. Provinces, a village on the route from Kurnoul to Meerut, and 47 miles S.E. of the former. Lat. 29° 15′, long. 77° 32′.

BURLUHJUT, or BURLAH, in the British district of Muzuffurnugar, lieut.-gov. of the N.W. Provinces, a village on the route from Kurnoul to Meerut, and 32 miles S.E. of the former. Lat. 29° 25′, long. 77° 25′.

BURMAH.—An independent kingdom, situate between Eastern India and China. Previous to the year 1825 the Burmese empire was one of considerable extent and importance; but, stripped since that period of some of its richest provinces by the results of war, its territory now falls within very moderate limits, and its power has become proportionately circumscribed. It is bounded on the north by Assam and Thibet, from which it is separated by the Himalayas; on the east by China; on the south by the recently-acquired British province of Pegu; and on the west by mountain-ranges dividing it from Arracan, Tipperah, and Munneepore. It extends from lat. 19° 25′ to 28° 15′, and from long. 93° 2′ to 100° 40′, measuring 540 miles in length from north to south, and 420 in its greatest breadth; and contains an area of 96,000 square miles. Little more than a vague guess can be made of the number of the inhabitants. According to Mr. Crawfurd's estimate of twenty-two to the square mile, the population would scarcely exceed 2,000,000, and appears to be chiefly concentrated on the banks of the Irawaddy, where the principal towns are built. The general slope of the surface of the country is to the south, as indicated by the descent of its rivers. The Irawaddy, deriving its source from the snowy range of the Himalayas, in lat. 28° 5′, long. 97° 58′, and flowing in a direction for the most part due south, nearly bisects the Burmese territory, and crosses into the British district of Pegu at some distance above the town of Prome. In its course it flows by the town of Ummerapoora, and a few miles below passes the city of Ava. From this point it bends to the westward, and upon resuming its original direction, it receives on the right side its great confluent the Khyendwen, flowing also from the north. The only remaining river of any magnitude is the Salwein, which has its origin in the same range of mountains as the Irawaddy, and flowing in a direction parallel to that river, but more to the eastward, enters the British territory in nearly the same latitude, after a course of equal length.

The physical aspect of the territory from its southern frontier to the latitude of the capital is characterized by unevenness and general elevation; and beyond this, to its northern limit, it is decidedly mountainous. The plains, however, and more especially the valleys near the rivers, are remarkably fruitful. The principal products are wheat, rice, sugar-cane, tobacco, indigo, and cotton. Tea is cultivated on the hills by the mountain tribes. Horticulture is almost wholly neglected among the Burmese. Green vegetables form a considerable portion of their diet; but these for the most part are collected from the forests and marshes, and are not the result of cultivation. The seasons are regular; and although the heat which immediately precedes the rains be intense, it is of brief duration. Of the general salubrity of the climate, the best evidence perhaps is afforded in the vigour and activity of the natives. Our acquaintance with the forest productions of Burmah is not proportioned to the importance of the subject. Among them teak holds a distinguished place; and the tracts covered by this timber are unquestionably the most extensive of those in India. The Mimosa catechu, a tree rising to the height of thirty or forty feet, is widely disseminated, and yields the drug known as the catechu, or terra Japonica. Burmah, as might be expected from its mountainous character, abounds in mineral wealth. Gold is discovered in the beds of streams descending from the Himalayas. Silver-mines are wrought in one place in the eastern territory of Lao, and the inferior minerals,—iron, tin, lead, antimony, and others,—are met with in abundance, more particulary on the eastern frontier towards China. Quarries of statuary marble are worked in the neighbourhood of Ummerapoora. Traces of coal have been discovered on the banks of the Irawaddy, in the vicinity of the petroleum-wells of Renangyaong. Precious stones, consisting of the sapphire and ruby species, abound; and so highly are they esteemed, that the ownership of the mines appears to constitute the chief glory of the sovereign. When Colonel Burney was the resident in Ava, official communications were addressed to him under the authority of the "Founder of the great golden city of precious stones; the possessor of mines of gold, silver, rubies, amber, and noble serpentine."

In a country much of which still remains to be brought under the dominion of man, wild animals may be expected to be numerous. The most remarkable are the elephant, rhinoceros, tiger, spotted leopard, and several species of wild cat. It is worthy of notice, that while the feline species abounds, none of the canine family, so frequent in the neighbouring country of Hindostan, are, so far as we are acquainted, to be met with in Burmah. According to Crawfurd, "there are neither wolves, jackals, foxes, nor hyænas; and this zoological feature is said to extend to all the countries of tropical Asia lying east of Bengal." Of domestic quadrupeds, the chief are the ox, buffalo, and horse. The latter rarely exceeds thirteen hands in height: his chief use is for the saddle, being rarely employed for draught or as a beast of burthen. The camel is unknown. That so rude a people should have made little progress in the useful arts, can excite no surprise. The manufactures of the country are restricted to articles required for home-consumption, and few find their way to foreign markets. Cotton and silk goods are worked at Ummerapoora and Ava, as are also coarse species of pottery and cutlery; and if to these be added gold and silver ornaments of rude fabrication, the list of Burmese manufactures may be considered as nearly complete. Passing to the religion of the country, it may be noticed that the Burmese, though Hindoos, are not Brahmins, but Bhuddists. Their government is despotic, and their laws, like their religion, are Hindoo.

A degree of uncertainty hangs over the precise period of the arrival of the British in Burmah. It seems, however, to have been of early date, as at the commencement of the seventeenth century certain agents of the East-India Company were included in the general expulsion of Europeans from Ava. The edict of banishment did not, however, extend to the prohibition of commercial relations, its object being simply the deportation from the country of foreign residents; and trade continued to be carried on as usual by British ships with the principal ports of Burmah. In 1687 the British took possession of the island of Negrais, situate at the mouth of the western branch of the Irawaddy. Hitherto British intercourse with Burmah was purely of a commercial character; and such continued to be the case for seventy years later. Towards the close of this interval, a civil war had broken out between the Burmese and the Peguers, which in 1752 terminated in favour of the latter; but their yoke was of brief duration, and the Burmese, under their chief Alompra, succeeded in recovering their political independence. Alompra's success, according to cotemporary authority, was promoted through the covert assistance of the British factory at the entrance of the Irawaddy; and the subsequent cession of Negrais to the British, together with the grant of a piece of land at Bassein for the purposes of a factory, afford plausible grounds for accrediting the rumour. From the date of Alompra's triumph over the Peguers, every enterprise of the Burmese, for the space of more than half a century, appears to have been crowned with success. Siam felt the force of their arms in 1766. Formidable invasions of their territory by the Chinese in the three following years were triumphantly repulsed. Arracan merged into the empire in 1783. Ten years later they extorted from the Siamese the cession of the whole coast of Tenasserim; and the limits of the empire were subsequently extended by the annexation of Munneepore and Assam. About the year 1794, a party of Mugh robbers from Arracan taking refuge in the adjoining British province of Chittagong, a military force was sent by the Burmese across the frontier, in pursuit of the fugitives, without any reference to the British government. A detachment under General Erskine forthwith proceeded to Chittagong, to repel the irruption into the British territories; and upon an amicable arrangement between the general and the Burmese commander, the troops of the latter were withdrawn. On the retirement of the aggressors, the fugitive robbers were secured by the British authorities, tried, found guilty, and delivered over to the Burmese. The act was attributed by the latter to timidity. It was followed up, on the part of the British, by successive missions, in the hope of obtaining political and commercial advantages; but in each instance the British representative experienced humiliating neglect or studied insult, and no beneficial results ensued. In 1811 a Mugh chief, named Khynberring, who, it appears, had fled into Chittagong upon the subjugation of his country by the Burmese, collected a number of followers, and invaded Arracan, with the intention of expelling the Burmese from that province. He was joined on his arrival by several of his countrymen, who readily seized an opportunity to avenge themselves upon their conquerors for the tyranny and oppression which they had experienced from them. Success for a short time attended their efforts. They were, however, in the end completely defeated, and compelled again to seek refuge in Chittagong. This irruption the Burmese believed to have been instigated and supported by the British. In order to remove the suspicion, another mission was determined on, and Captain Canning was deputed to Ava to afford explanation. The embassy, like those which had preceded it, was exposed to insult and danger; and having experienced much contumelious treatment from the authorities at Rangoon, was compelled to return without reaching its destination. Khynberring still continued at large; and the refusal to deliver up the chief and his associates to the Burmese, incensed the latter, and was the means of aggravating the unfriendly relations between the people and the British. At length a formal demand was preferred by the Burmese rajah of Ramree for the surrender of the Mugh fugitives. A reply was addressed to the Burmese sovereign, based upon the principle maintained by the British government, of refusing to deliver up those who had sought its protection. In a few months a second letter was received, demanding the cession of the elephant-grounds of Ramoo, together with Chittagong, Moorshedabad, and Dacca, stated to be Burmese dependencies; and the demand was accompanied by a threat to commence hostilities, if the claim were not complied with. An answer was returned to the Burmese sovereign, to the effect that the Governor-General regarded the letter as an unauthorized act on the part of the rajah of Ramree, and trusted that such an unwarranted proceeding would receive the punishment it merited. This communication remained unnoticed, and thus matters rested. At this period Assam became the scene of civil dissension; and the Burmese, interfering on behalf of one of the candidates for power, succeeded in placing him on the throne. It was not intended, however, that he should permanently occupy this position, and he was shortly after deposed by his former supporters, who set up one of their own chiefs in his place. The Burmese thus became neighbours to the British on the northern as well as on the southern frontier; and availing themselves of their favourable position, committed several acts of aggression on villages within the British territory. Upon explanation and satisfaction for these outrages being demanded, the Burmese government affirmed that the villages had been attacked by mistake. But aggression was not restricted to the territories bordering on the newly-acquired possessions. For some time the Burmese had been gradually encroaching on the frontier of Chittagong, and had claimed jungles which were frequented by British elephant-hunters, many of whom had been detained on the pretence that they were trespassing on Burmese territory. Among other instances of outrage and treachery practised by this nation, was an assault upon a Mugh boat proceeding to the island of Shahpooree, laden with rice; the crew of which were killed. It was considered necessary, in consequence, slightly to increase the guard on the island. Its withdrawal, and the surrender of the island, were forthwith demanded by the governor of Arracan; and the requisition being followed up by the despatch of 1,000 troops under the rajah of Ramree, the place was attacked and captured on the 24th September, 1823, three of the thirteen men who composed the guard stationed on the island being killed. It was at the same time intimated, that any attempt on the part of the British to retake the island would be resented by attacking the cities of Moorshedabad and Dacca. The island was, notwithstanding, shortly again occupied by the British; and upon the occurrence of further acts of encroachments and outrage by the Burmese, the British government, in February, 1824, declared war. In March a large force, which had been despatched from the presidencies of Bengal and Madras, reached the Burmese dominions, under the command of Sir Archibald Campbell. This officer commenced operations on the Rangoon river, and took possession of the town of that name on the 12th May. He afterwards attacked and reduced the principal forts at the mouth of the Irawaddy. In January of the following year a force of 11,000 men was assembled in Chittagong, under the command of General Morrison. Its first object was to be the reduction of the province of Arracan; after which it was intended to form a junction with the army of Sir Archibald Campbell on the Irawaddy. One of these objects was accomplished by the capture of the capital, and the occupation of the entire province of Arracan; but the junction with the main army was frustrated by the impracticability of crossing the Yoomadoung Mountains, the Aeng route being then unknown to the British. In the early part of May the rains set in, and with them commenced a season of sickness, privation, and distress. Fever and dysentery broke out to an alarming extent, and many, both officers and men, who had escaped the sword of the enemy, were struck down by disease. At length the maladies which had afflicted the troops became universal, and it was evident that the only chance of preventing the whole force from falling a sacrifice to the climate was to withdraw it from the pestiferous influence to which it was subjected. A few divisions were readily transferred to more salubrious situations on the islands of Cheduba, Ramree, and Sandoway, and the remainder of the troops were recalled to Calcutta. In the mean time Sir Archibald Campbell, who had been twice disappointed in the hope of bringing affairs to an amicable and satisfactory termination, was prosecuting the war with vigour. He had taken possession of Prome; Mellore had been carried by force; and several brilliant and successful exploits were achieved under circumstances of great difficulty and discouragement. The Burmese proved by no means contemptible enemies; it was only when beaten at every point that they became alarmed for the safety of their capital, which the British army was rapidly approaching; and under the influence of this feeling they at length consented to terms of peace. A treaty was concluded at Yandaboo on the 26th of February, 1826, in which, among other stipulations, it was provided that the coast of Tenasserim, together with the province of Arracan, and its dependencies the islands of Ramree, Cheduba, and Sandoway, which had been conquered by the British, should be retained by them; that the king of Ava should renounce all claims upon the principality of Assam and the adjoining states of Cachar, Jyntea, and Munneepore, and that an accredited minister from each nation should reside at the court of the other.

Amicable relations being thus restored between the two countries, a British resident was deputed to the court of Ava. No indisposition appears to have been manifested on the part of the Burmese to the maintenance of these friendly arrangements during the reign of the king by whom the treaty had been ratified; but in 1837 this potentate was deposed, and his brother, Prince Therawaddi, usurped the throne. The new monarch evinced great repugnance to the residence of a British officer at his court; and in deference to the royal prejudice, the British minister obtained the permission of his government to remove to Rangoon. But the change of locality effected no alteration in the unfriendly conduct of the king, and it was ultimately determined altogether to withdraw the British residency from Burmah. This took place in 1840. Twelve years later, intelligence reached Calcutta that the commanders of two British vessels had been exposed to certain unwarrantable and oppressive acts by order of the governor of Rangoon; and Commodore Lambert was deputed to the place to demand reparation for the injuries which had been sustained. The Burmese authorities met the requisition by a refusal of compensation, accompanied by marked indignities towards the British officers; whereupon Commodore Lambert placed the principal ports in a state of blockade, and returned to Calcutta. There was now little room for hesitation in choosing the course which the British government ought to pursue. The question was, whether it should abandon its subjects and acknowledge its inability to protect them, or seek redress by force of arms; and there can be no doubt that it decided rightly in preferring the latter branch of the alternative. It was determined, however, not to have recourse to war except in the last resort, and only when all other means for the peaceable arrangement of existing differences had been tried and failed. Accordingly, the ultimatum of the British government was formally laid before the governor of Rangoon, in which compliance with three conditions was declared indispensable to the preservation of peace: the transmission of an apology for the insult offered to the British officers acting under Commodore Lambert; prompt payment of the sum of 990*l.* as compensation to the commanders of the two British vessels whose rights had been outraged; and the reception of a British agent under the provisions of the existing treaty. These terms being rejected, war was declared. This took place in 1852, and no want of energy was evinced in its effective prosecution. Early in April Martaban fell an easy conquest. The storming of Rangoon, which occurred a few days later, afforded a better opportunity for the display of British valour; but its capture was not effected without considerable loss both of officers and men. Bassein was the next in succession of the Burmese towns which fell to the arms of the British, and with Rangoon and Martaban constituted an excellent base for future operations. Prome followed, falling into the hands of the British almost without subjecting them to the necessity of an effort. The city of Pegu, previously taken and abandoned, was a second time occupied, and with more permanent success. A determined attempt on the part of the Burmese was made to recover it once more; but it was met by the officer in command (Major Hill, of the Madras fusiliers) with a union of decision and skill which enabled him to maintain it, though under great difficulties, until relief arrived. The lower portion of the Burmese territories was now actually in the hands of the British, and the formal annexation of the conquest was announced in the following proclamation:—"The court of Ava having refused to make amends for the injuries and insults which British subjects had suffered at the hands of its servants, the Governor-General of India in Council resolved to exact reparation by force of arms. The forts and cities upon the coast were forthwith attacked and captured; the Burman forces have been dispersed wherever they have been met; and the province of Pegu is now in the occupation of British troops. The just and moderate demands of the government of India have been rejected by the king; the ample opportunity that has been afforded him for repairing the injury that was done, has been disregarded; and the timely submission, which alone could have been effectual to prevent the dismemberment of his kingdom, is still withheld. Wherefore, in compensation for the past, and for better security in the future, the Governor-General in Council has resolved, and hereby proclaims, that the province of Pegu is now, and shall be henceforth, a portion of the British territories in the East. Such Burman troops as may still remain within the province shall be driven out; civil government shall immediately be established; and officers shall be appointed to administer the affairs of the several districts. The Governor-General in Council hereby calls on the inhabitants of Pegu to submit themselves to the authority, and to confide securely in the protection of the British government, whose power they have seen to be irresistible, and whose rule is marked by justice and beneficence. The Governor-General in Council, having exacted the reparation he deems sufficient, desires no further conquest in Burmah, and is willing to consent that hostilities should cease. But if the king of Ava shall fail to renew his former relations of friendship with the British government, and if he shall recklessly seek to dispute its quiet possession of the province it has now declared to be its own, the Governor-General in Council will again put forth the power he holds, and will visit with full retribution aggressions which, if they be persisted in, must of necessity lead to the total subversion of the Burman state, and to the ruin and exile of the king and his race." The ruler of Ava declined acceding to any formal treaty, but it was understood that he professed to abstain from active hostilities.

BURMIOK.—A town in the native state of Sikhim, distant N.E. from Darjeeling 19 miles. Lat. 27° 10′, long. 88° 34′.

BURNAH.—A small river rising in the British district of Allahabad, about 13 miles E. of the city of that name, and in lat. 25° 23′, long. 82° 8′. It takes a north-easterly course through the district for about twenty-five miles, when, turning south-east, it for fifty miles forms the boundary between the districts of Mirzapore and Jounpore; continuing its course in the same direction, it enters the district of Benares, through which it flows for thirty miles, passing the cantonment of Sikroul, and along the north side of the city of Benares, and falls into the Ganges on the left side, in lat. 25° 18′, long. 83° 7′; its total length of course being about 105 miles. During the periodical rains it is navigable for boats of considerable tonnage.

BURNAH, in the British district of Furruckabad, lieut.-gov. of the N.W. Provinces, a town on the left bank of the Kalee Nuddee, 38 miles W. of Furruckabad. Lat. 27° 26′, long. 79° 2′.

BURNAWA, in the British district of Meerut, lieut.-gov. of the N.W. Provinces, a town, the principal place of the pergunnah of the same name, on the right bank of the Hindun. Lat. 29° 7′, long. 77° 29′.

BURNUGGUR, in Guzerat, or territory of the Guicowar, a town 52 miles N. of the city of Ahmedabad. It has considerable trade, conducted principally by wealthy Brahmins, of whom many reside here. Population 12,000. Lat. 23° 48′, long. 72° 38′.

BUROD.—A town in the native state of Gwalior, or possessions of Scindia's family, distant N. from Oojein 40 miles. Lat. 23° 44′, long. 75° 49′.

BURODA, in the British district of Agra, lieut.-gov. of the N.W. Provinces, a village on the route from the city of Agra to Jeypore, and 11 miles W. of the former. The road in this part of the route is good, the country highly cultivated. Lat. 27° 8′, long. 77° 55′.

BUROOA, in the British district of Moradabad, lieut.-gov. of the N.W. Provinces, a village on the route from Almora to the town of Moradabad, and 58 miles N. of the latter. It is situate on the Dubha river, at the northern frontier of the district, towards Kumaon. Lat. 29° 21′, long. 79° 12′.

BUROONDA, in the Rajpoot state of Joudpore, a village on the route from the town of Joudpore to that of Ajmere, and 59 miles N.E. of the former. It contains 350 houses, supplied with good water from a tank and four wells, and is situate in an open grassy country; population 1,645. Lat. 26° 20′, long. 74° 4′.

BUROREE, or BUROWA, in the territory of Gwalior, or possessions of Scindia's family, a town one mile to the W. or right of the route from the fort of Gwalior to Saugor; nine miles S. of former, 178 N.W. of latter. Lat. 26° 8′, long. 78° 10′.

BUROS, in the British district of Muttra, lieut.-gov. of the N.W. Provinces, a village on the route from the city of Agra to Allygurh, and 15 miles N. of the former. Lat. 27° 20′, long. 78° 6′.

BUROTA, in Gurhwal, a village on the right bank of the Bhagirathi, as the Ganges is called in the upper part of its course. It is situate eighty feet above the stream, in a country cultivated to a considerable extent, especially for opium. Lat. 30° 36′, long. 78° 23′.

BUROTI.—See Banmowtee.

BUROULUH, in the British district of

Goorgaon, lieut.-gov. of the N.W. Provinces, a village on the route from Delhi to Muttra, and 45 miles S. of the former. Lat. 28° 5′, long. 77° 25′.

BUROUN, in the British district of Furruckabad, lieut.-gov. of the N.W. Provinces, a village on the route from the cantonment of Aligurh to that of Futtehgurh, and eight miles N.W. of the latter. It has water from wells. Lat. 27° 25′, long. 79° 30′.

BUROUR, or BURHOUL, in the territory of Oude, a village on the route from Bareilly to Seetapoor, 71 miles S.E. of the former, 34 N.W. of the latter. Water is plentiful there, and supplies are procurable. The road in this part of the route is rather good, the country open and cultivated. Lat. 27° 50′, long. 80° 24′.

BUROUR, or BUROURAH, in the British district of Bareilly, lieut.-gov. of the N.W. Provinces, a village on the route from the city of Agra to Bareilly, and 27 miles S.W. of the latter. It is situate in a level, fertile, well-watered, and well-cultivated country. Lat. 28° 12′, long. 79° 10′.

BUROUT, in the British district of Allahabad, lieut.-gov. of the N.W. Provinces, a village on the route from the city of Allahabad to Benares, and 28 miles E. of the former. Lat. 25° 21′, long. 82° 15′.

BUROUTH, in the British district of Meerut, lieut.-gov. of the N.W. Provinces, a town the principal place of the pergunnah of the same name. It contains a population of 12,350. Lat. 29° 6′, long. 77° 20′.

BUROUTUH, in the British district of Paneeput, lieut.-gov. of the N.W. Provinces, a village on the route from the city of Delhi to Kurnoul, and 20 miles N.W. of the former. Lat. 28° 54′, long. 77° 8′.

BUROWLA, in the British district of Boolundshuhur, lieut.-gov. of the N.W. Provinces, a town on the route from Khasganj to Meerut, and 64 miles S.E. of the latter. Lat. 28° 11′, long. 78° 10′.

BUR PANEE.—A river rising in lat. 25° 46′, long. 92°, in Kyrim, one of the Cossya states. It flows in a north-easterly direction for sixty miles, principally through the British territory of Jynteah, shortly after leaving which, it turns north-west, and flows for twenty miles to its junction, near Raha, with the Kullung river, a considerable offset of the Brahmapootra.

BURPETA, in the British district of Camroop, Lower Assam, a town 12 miles S.E. of Bijnee, in Bhotan, 48 miles W. of Gowhatty. Lat. 26° 18′, long. 91°.

BURPOORA, or BURREYPOORA, in the British district of Etawa, lieut.-gov. of Agra, a town, the principal place of the pergunnah of the same name, in lat. 26° 44′, long. 78° 58′.

BURPOORA, in the jaghire of Rampoor, lieut.-gov. of the N.W. Provinces, a town on the north-eastern route from the city of Rampoor to Nugina, and nine miles N. of the former. Lat 28° 55′, long. 79° 5′.

BURRABOOM, in the British district of the same name, lieut.-gov. of Bengal, a town 48 miles W. of Bancoora, 80 miles N.W. of Midnapoor. Lat. 23° 4′, long. 86° 24′.

BURRABOOM.—See BARRABHOOM.

BURRA CHACHUR, in Sinde, a thriving village on the route from Hyderabad to Sehwan, and 62 miles N.W. of the former place. It has a large mosque, in front of which are numerous tombs. The village is situate in a well-cultivated country, on a small watercourse discharging itself into the Indus a mile to the east. Lat. 26° 10′, long. 68° 6′.

BURRAGAON, in the British district of Agra, lieut.-gov. of the N.W. Provinces, a town on the right bank of the Jumna, 42 miles S.E. of the city of Agra. Lat. 26° 52′, long. 78° 42′.

BURRA GURRAWARRA, in the British territory of Saugor and Nerbudda, lieut.-gov. of the N.W. Provinces, a town 76 miles W. of Jubbulpoor, 71 miles E. of Hoosungabad. Lat. 22° 55′, long. 78° 50′.

BURRA LAMBA, in the Rajpoot state of Jeypoor, a town on the route from Nusserabad to Gwalior, 29 miles E. of former, 212 W. of latter. It is of considerable size, and is surrounded by a mud wall and ditch. Lat. 26° 20′, long. 75° 14′.

BURRAN.—A river in Sinde, which takes its rise in the Keertar Mountains, in lat. 25° 56′, long. 67° 45′, and, after a south-easterly course of sixty-five miles, falls into the Indus, in lat. 25° 14′, long. 68° 21′. In the uppper part of its course it is called the Dhurwal. For a mile before its confluence with the Indus it has a large body of water.

BURRAPUDDA.—A town in the native state of Mohurbunge, one of the Cuttack mehals, under the political superintendence of the government of India, distant N.W. from Balasore 35 miles. Lat. 21° 59′, long. 86° 48′.

BURREE MUTTANA, in the British district of Shahjehanpoor, lieut.-gov. of the N.W. Provinces, a small town on the route from Bareilly to the cantonment of Futtehgurh, and 38 miles S.E. of the former. It has a bazaar, and water and supplies for forces may be obtained in abundance. Lat. 27° 53′, long. 79° 45′.

BURREYPOORUH.—See BURPOORA.

BURRISOL, in the British district of Backergunje, lieut.-gov. of Bengal, a town situate on the right bank of a large offset of the Ganges, with which it also communicates by means of a channel called the Chittagong Passage, distant 11 miles N. of Backergunje, 82 miles S.E. of Jessore. It is the seat of the civil establishment of the district, which, in

1801, was removed to this place from the town of Backergunje. Lat. 22° 44′, long. 90° 23′.

BURROD.—A town in the Rajpoot state of Kotah, distant N.E. from Kotah 40 miles. Lat. 25° 21′, long. 76° 28′.

BURROUNDA.—See BEROUNDA.

BURSANA, in the British district of Muttra, lieut.-gov. of the N.W. Provinces, a town on the route by way of Kosy from Delhi to Deeg, and 14 miles N. of the latter. Lat. 27° 39′, long. 77° 26′.

BURSANKER, in the raj of Burrounda, in Bundelcund, a ghat or pass on the route from Banda to Rewa, 43 miles S.E. of the former, 69 N.W. of the latter. The route here passes from the plains of Bundelcund to the plateau on the summit of the hills styled by Franklin the Bindachal Range. Lat. 24° 56′, long. 80° 36′.

BURSEE, or BURSAK, in the British district of Allygurh, lieut.-gov. of the N.W. Provinces, a village on the route from the city of Agra to Allygurh cantonment, and 20 miles S. of the latter. Lat. 27° 40′, long. 78° 8′.

BURSOOAH, in the British district of Budaon, lieut.-gov. of the N.W. Provinces, a village on the route from the city of Agra to Bareilly, and 41 miles S.W. of the latter. Lat. 28° 4′, long. 79° 5′.

BURUJ, in the British district of Goruckpore, lieut.-gov. of the N.W. Provinces, a small town near the south-eastern frontier, towards the British district of Sarun. According to Buchanan, it contains 200 houses, an amount which would assign it a population of 1,200 persons. Distant S.E. from Goruckpore cantonment 40 miles. Lat. 26° 16′, long. 83° 43′.

BURWALLA, in the British district of Ahmedabad, presidency of Bombay, a town on the left bank of the Oolowtee river, 79 miles S.W. of Ahmedabad. Lat. 22° 10′, long. 71° 50′.

BURWALLA, in the British district of Hurreeana, lieut.-gov. of the N.W. Provinces, a town, the principal place of the pergunnah of the same name, distant N. from Hansee 20 miles. Lat. 29° 22′, long. 75° 59′.

BURWANEE, in the province of Nimar, territory of Malwa, a hilly district, the patrimony of a Bheel chief. Politically, it is under the superintendence of the Governor-General's agent at Indore. This tract extends along the left or south bank of the river Nerbudda, and is situate within the Sautpoora range of mountains. It lies between lat. 21° 41′ and 22° 9′, long. 74° 29′ and 75° 22′. Its length from east to west may be computed at sixty miles, and its breadth from north to south at thirty. Its area is about 1,380 square miles. The country abounds in fine timber; it is well watered by mountain-streams; but, notwithstanding this advantage, is only partially cultivated. The principality pays no tribute, and there are but few dependent thakoors or feudatories within its limits. The population is scanty. A small force (not exceeding seventy-five men, infantry and cavalry) is kept up by the rajah, and the revenues of the country are estimated at 30,000 rupees, or 3,000*l*. per annum. The chief town, which bears the same name with the district, is situate two miles from the south or left bank of the Nerbudda. It is surrounded by a double wall, with a ditch to the outer one. Lat. 22° 5′, long. 75°.

BURWANNUGUR, in the British district of Chota Nagpoor, lieut.-gov. of Bengal, a town on the route from Oodeipoor to Lohadugga, 36 miles S.W. of the latter. Lat. 23° 9′, long. 84° 19′.

BURWAY.—A town in the native state of Gwalior, or possessions of Scindia's family, distant S.E. from Mhow 39 miles. Lat. 22° 13′, long. 76° 7′.

BURWUR SAGAR, in Bundelcund, a town with bazaar on the route from Banda to Gwalior, 121 miles W. of former, 83 S.E. of latter. It is situate at the base of a long and high ridge of rocks, on the extremity of which is a picturesque old fort overlooking the town. East of this is a fine jhil or small lake, about two miles long and one and a half wide. In the middle are two rocky wooded islets of strikingly picturesque appearance. This piece of water is formed by closing up the lower gorge of an extensive valley by a mound of masonry sixty feet broad and a mile in length, having several ghats or flights of steps to the water's edge. It abounds with fine fish, and a stream which flows from it extensively diffuses the benefits of irrigation. Lat. 25° 23′, long. 78° 48′.

BUSAI, or BUSSYE, in the British district of Agra, lieut.-gov. of the N.W. Provinces, a town on the route from Agra to Etawah, 40 miles E. of the former. Bussai has a population of 12,754. Lat. 27° 8′, long. 78° 9′.

BUSALEE, in the Peshawur division of the Punjab, a town situated on the route from Wazeerabad to Rawul Pind, 16 miles S. of the latter. Lat. 33° 27′, long. 73° 6′.

BUSAOO.—A town in the Rajpoot state of Shekawutee, distant N.W. from Jhoonjhnoo 22 miles. Lat. 28° 14′, long. 75° 11′.

BUSEE, in the British district of Boolundshuhur, lieut.-gov. of the N.W. Provinces, a town on the right bank of the Ganges, E. of Delhi 60 miles. Lat. 28° 36′, long. 78° 15′.

BUSEENAGUR.—A town in the district of Singboom, on the south-west frontier of Bengal, distant N.W. from Chaibassa 40 miles. Lat. 22° 49′, long. 85° 11′.

BUSHEY, in the British territory of Saugor and Nerbudda, lieut.-gov. of the N.W. Provinces, a town on the right bank of the Johila river, 37 miles S.E. of Sohagpoor. Lat. 22° 55′, long. 81° 47′.

BUSKARIE, in the territory of Oude, a town on the route from Azimgurh to Faizabad,

34 miles N.W. of the former, 52 S.E. of the latter. Lat. 26° 25′, long. 82° 45′.

BUSPA, a river in Koonawur, and a feeder of the Sutlej, rises in Tartary, on the north-east declivity of the outer range of the Himalaya, in about lat. 31° 13′, long. 78° 11′. It is a fine stream, running smoothly down a romantic valley, bounded on the south-west by the outer range of the Himalaya, and on the north-east by the huge Ruldung range. According to native tradition, this valley was formerly a lake; and present appearances render the statement probable. The channel of the river is wide, and the stream forms many islands of sand and pebbles, overgrown with barberries and willows. The level space of the valley is frequently almost a mile wide, and is beautifully laid out in fields, and diversified with groves of apricot, peach, and walnut trees. The mountains inclosing it on the north-east and south-west are very abrupt, and for the most part formed of a bare rock. At Chetkool bridge, about eighteen miles from the source, and where the elevation of the bed of the river is 11,275 feet above the sea, its width is sixty-six feet; at some bridges lower down, the width is from seventy-seven to eighty-three feet. It receives numerous feeders on both the right and left side, and after a course of about forty-five miles in a north-westerly direction, falls into the Sutlej in lat. 31° 29′, long. 78° 15′, at an elevation of 5,945 feet above the level of the sea. The valley of the Buspa is productive in grain and pulse. The vine, though successfully cultivated in parts farther north, does not bring its fruit to maturity in this valley, in consequence of its position within the limits of the periodical rains.

BUSSAHIR, in Northern India, a considerable hill state, bounded on the north by the British district of Spiti; on the east by Chinese Tartary; on the south by Gurwhal; and on the west and south-west by various districts of the adjacent hill states. It is about ninety-five miles in length from north-east to south-west, and fifty-five miles in breadth from south-east to north-west; has an area of about 3,000 square miles, and is situate between lat. 30° 56′—32° 8′, and long. 77° 34′—78° 52′. It is one of the most mountainous and elevated countries in the world. Nirt, on the left bank of the Sutlej, is 3,087 feet; Raien, on the left bank of the Pabur, 4,932 feet above the sea: and these two places, being respectively situate at the points where the rivers cross the frontier, are the lowest positions in the territory, most parts being from 7,000 to 12,000 feet above the sea. The Sutlej intersects the country from east to west, and divides the territory into two parts, that on the north being called Koonawur, and that on the south Bussahir.

Very extensive and rich deposits of copper-ore have been discovered in Koonawur. Iron is very abundant, both in the form of ironstone and in numerous and extensive beds of the better-defined ores. These ores are extensively extracted and reduced in the pergunnah to Nawa, and at the village of Sheel, both near the south-west frontier. The ore appears to be of the sort called in England "specular iron," and has the appearance of shining metallic particles, like mica, interspersed through sandstone. The mines are in the form of adits and galleries, some of which extend half a mile into the mountain, but have no perpendicular shafts. The ore is at once reduced to the state of wrought iron without previous casting, by means of charcoal of oak or pine. That of Sheel is considered the finest, being much valued for making sabres, knives, and hatchets. The ore, as extracted from the mine, yields from thirty to fifty per cent. of the particles of specular iron, and about two-thirds of the weight of these are found to be waste in the process of reduction.

The climate varies from the nearly intertropical character of that of the banks of the Sutlej at Rampoor, 3,260 feet above the sea, and near the southern frontier, to that of regions untrodden by human foot, and rising above the limit of perpetual congelation. The most genial climate is that of the Chooara district, or the valley of the Pabur, having an elevation varying upwards from about 4,800 feet, and which is described as a beautiful and fertile tract. The productions of the earth vary from the intertropical character of those on the banks of the Sutlej at Rampoor, where bamboos and some of the tropical fruits thrive, to that of the expiring vegetation on the borders of perpetual snow. The very rapid elevation of the surface of the Sub-Himalaya and Himalaya greatly circumscribes this portion of the territory, which is stated by Dr. Royle to terminate at the height of between four thousand and five thousand feet above the sea. That scientific botanist observes: "In proportion as we ascend these mountains, the plants of India disappear, and we are delighted at finding the increase in number and variety of those belonging to European genera. At first we see only a few straggling, towards the plains, which in a more temperate climate would be their favourite resort; and it is not until we have attained a considerable elevation, that, having apparently lost all traces of tropical vegetation, we enter a forest of pines or oaks, and lofty rhododendrons, where none but European forms are recognisable." Dr. Royle, writing before Moorcroft's Travels had appeared, hoped to see the slopes of the Himalaya covered, and the edges of the terraced flats surrounded with plantations of the tea-plant. Moorcroft, however, in the course of his inquiries respecting the tea-trade of Ladakh, ascertained that a vegetable product used as tea is imported largely into that district from Bussahir, where it grows most abundantly on the banks of the Sutlej, and near Lipi, in the valley of the Pejur. Both the black and green sorts are gathered, dried, and rolled, in imitation of the Chinese teas. About eight thousand pounds weight are annually brought to Le, the capital of Ladakh, where, however, it is not so much esteemed as the Chinese tea, with which it is mixed by the poorer people. Moorcroft adds, "It was the opinion of Mohsin Ali, a wholesale dealer in tea to a large extent, that the teas of Bussahir differed from the coarser teas of China only in the mode of preparing them for the market." In Koonawur, beyond the limit of the periodical rains, the vine is an important object of rural economy, the grapes being sometimes consumed when fresh, sometimes dried in the sun for future use, and sometimes converted into wine or spirits. The great productiveness of the vine in these parts is proved by the extraordinary cheapness of both raisins and fresh grapes; the former being sold at the rate of from thirty to forty pounds for a rupee (about two shillings), the latter at from sixty to seventy pounds for the same sum. There are eighteen different kinds: some are rich and luscious; some, when neglected and ill supplied with water, produce small berries without stones, somewhat resembling the currants of Europe. Fraser draws a very gloomy picture of the character of the population of the lower or southern part of Bussahir at the time of its liberation from the Goorkha yoke. "They are revengeful and treacherous, deficient in all good qualities, abandoned in morals, and vicious in their habits. As a proof of the savage indifference with which they look on the life of another, and on the act of shedding human blood, it is said that mere wantonness or a joke will induce the crime of putting a fellow-creature to death, merely for the satisfaction of seeing the blood flow, and of marking the last struggles of their victim; and some facts, which came under our observation, of a tantamount nature, give too much reason for believing the assertion to be founded in truth. Female chastity is here quite unknown; and murder, robbery, and outrage of every kind are here regarded with indifference." The more frightful of these traits of character are said to be no longer observable; and there can be no doubt that some amelioration has resulted from British influence. European travellers have repeatedly, either singly or in small and defenceless parties, traversed the wildest parts of the country without molestation. Something, indeed, is to be attributed to the *prestige* of the European name; but Gerard, a veteran in adventurous travels, says of those persons whom he employed, "they looked not unlike banditti, which, indeed, they formerly were; but we knew well that they could be trusted;" and they were found invariably trustworthy. The people had the good sense to appreciate the advantages of their liberation from Goorkha tyranny; and such is the testimony of Fraser, who passed the severe judgment on their character just quoted. "They hail the success and coming of the British as a revolution in the world, as the dawn of their civil happiness. The people think that they will become good, free, and happy, as by inspiration; that it is the necessary result of the British power and government." "From the rajah to the peasant, there was not one who did not talk thus with confidence and enthusiasm, and uniformly concluded with saying, 'Now we shall live and improve, and be raised from beasts to men.'" In physical character they form a transition-step from the Hindoo of the plains southwards, to the vast Mongolian family farther north. "All the inhabitants of this region," observes Fraser, "as well as those near the plains, are Hindoos; their features for the most part, although gradually altered by the climate as we leave the low country, and also perhaps by country customs, and possibly by the remaining mixture of an ancient indigenous race, still retain traces that point to the chief original stock in the plains." The inhabitants of Koonawur, north of the Indo-Gangetic range, are sometimes of strongly-marked Mongolian features; and travellers agree in representing them as hardy, brave, persevering, honest, frank, and hospitable. "Thieves and robbers are unknown, and a person's word may be implicitly relied upon in anything regarding money matters. They have not the least distrust or suspicion." The inhabitants of that district, of all the highlanders, offered the only serious resistance to the warlike Goorkhas, whom they defeated in battle, and baffled by destroying the bridges and manning the fastnesses, so that the invading general was glad to make a convention, and consent to receive an annual tribute of about 750*l.*, on condition of abstaining from entering the district. They thus secured the safety of the ruling family, who had taken refuge with them. Gerard, speaking of the Tartar or Mongolian population on the northern frontier, says, "They are muscular, well made, and tall. I saw few under five feet ten, and many were six feet or more. Their strong, athletic forms were remarkably contrasted with the puny, diminutive figures of my attendants, several of whom were inhabitants of the plains; their countenance is ruddy, and they have small oblong eyes, high cheek-bones, thin eyebrows, and very few have either moustaches or beards, which they admire much." Of their moral character his report is highly favourable. "Cheating, lying, and thieving are unknown, and they may be trusted with anything. They have the nicest notions of honesty of any people on the face of the earth." He elsewhere states, that "the Tartars of Spiti were the finest fellows he ever met with."

The Bussahir females are fond of loading themselves with trinkets; wearing the nath depending from the cartilage of the nose, ear-rings, heavy circlets of brass, pewter, or more precious metals round the ancles; bangles or bracelets of similar materials; numerous rings on the toes and fingers, and round the neck; and on the breast a profusion of glass beads and trinkets, of every description of metal within their means. The bridegroom purchases the bride from her father, the price varying according to the station and means of the parties; the customary charge to a peasant or small landholder being from one to two pounds. Fraser gives the poverty of the population as the cause of polyandry, so universal in this country. "The difficulty of raising this sum, and the alleged expense of maintaining women, may in part account for, if it cannot excuse, a most disgusting usage which is universal over the country. Three or four or more brothers marry and cohabit with one woman, who is the wife of all. They are unable to raise the requisite sum individually, and thus club their store and buy this one common spouse." The surplus female population left unmarried from this abominable system, in the northern part of the country, take refuge in the Lamaic convents, becoming anis or nuns; in the southern part they are frequently without ceremony sold to the best bidders, who convey them to the plains and there dispose of them as slaves. According to Jacquemont, polyandry is so prevalent in Koonawur, that no man, except among the most wealthy, has a wife exclusively to himself. He inquired frequently how the offspring of the woman living in polyandry was affiliated, and was invariably answered that she never made a mistake in that respect. Jealousy, he was assured, was unknown. Indeed, a feeling necessarily implying some degree of attachment, could scarcely find place under circumstances which must annihilate every feeling which in the intercourse of the sexes raises man above the level of the brute creation. This accursed spot on the character of the people must tend greatly to lower the effect of the panegyrical estimates of their morals which have been quoted.

The rajah and upper classes in the southern part are Rajpoots; the other principal classes are Brahmins, Kunnoits, and Coolies, or Chumars; but notwithstanding their Hindoo origin and partial observances of Brahminism, the diet of all is very indiscriminate, consisting of wild hogs and other game, sheep, goats, and every sort of fish or flesh, except that of the cow, which is strictly prohibited in all parts of the territory of Bussahir. The people indulge in spirituous liquors, and in smoking tobacco; and the northern mountaineers are remarkably fond of tea, which they drink flavoured with salt and butter. They burn their dead on the summits of hills, commemorating the rite by raising a pile of stone on the spot. Before the British conquests in the hills, human sacrifices to the goddess Kalee, and the practice of burning the living with the corpses of the dead, were not uncommon; but (at least in the instance related by Fraser) that horrible cruelty was not perpetrated exclusively on the gentler and more helpless sex. He says, "At the death of the late rajah of Bussahir, twenty-two persons of both sexes burnt themselves along with his body: of these twelve were females, including three ranees (lawful consorts of the rajah); one or two of his wuzzeers and his first chobedar (mace-bearer) were also among the number." The religion of the more southern mountaineers is a corrupt Brahminism. They worship, under innumerable names, the chief Hindoo deities, as Siva, Ganesa, and Kalee; but have an infinite variety of deities of their own, to whom they erect shrines and altars on the hill-tops. In proceeding northwards, Brahminism is found to give way to Lamaic Buddhism, which is the exclusive faith in the northern part. According to Gerard, "there are no fewer than five distinct tongues spoken in Koonawur." In Hungrung, the most northern district, the language is Tibetan. Bussahir is governed by a rajah of Rajpoot extraction, which origin is also claimed by all the men of rank. He holds the dignity by virtue of a grant from the East-India Company, made on the expulsion of the Goorkhas in 1815, and dated the 6th of November in that year. The late rajah died in 1850. An arrangement was then made by the British government for the administration of the country during the young rajah's minority, differing in some degree from the ordinary form of government, which consisted of three hereditary ministers of equal rank, having subordinate to them a number of local magistrates. Hutton states that "there is no standing army, or any regular soldiery, since the British government extended its protection to Bussahir; and even before that time it resembled a half-armed mob, rather than a military force, having no uniform, and each man being armed according to circumstances; some with matchlocks, some with swords, and others, who possessed neither, arming themselves with sticks and branches of trees." A considerable proportion bear bows and arrows. The force which Bussahir brought forward in 1815, to aid in the expulsion of the Goorkhas, amounted to about 3,000 men; of whom probably 1,000 had matchlocks. The tribute from Bussahir to the Goorkha government was equal to 8,000*l.*; that at present paid to the East-India Company is 1,500*l.* The revenue enjoyed by the rajah, paid principally in kind, and consisting of agricultural produce, metals, blankets, and other coarse manufactures, is estimated at 150,000*l.* a year. The population is computed at *150,000*; an amount probably rather above than below the reality. On the expulsion of the Goorkhas in 1815, the East-India Company conferred the territory, as at present constituted, on Mohender Singh, the reigning chief, though his legitimacy was questioned. On the occasion of the grant, the thakoors of Koteghur and Koombarsain were dismembered from the state, and declared dependent on the East-India Company, who, moreover, reserved the forts of Ramghur, Suludan, Wartoo, Bagee, and Kurangool, as convenient military posts, together with the pergunnahs of Raden and Sundoch, on the left bank of the Pabur river. By existing arrangements, the rajah is bound to co-operate in military affairs, and to supply labourers for making roads.

BUSSANA.—A village in the British district Rohtuk, lieut.-gov. of the N.W. Provinces. Lat. 28° 53′, long. 76° 26′.

BUSSEAH, in the British district of Chota Nagpoor, lieut.-gov. of Bengal, a town on the left bank of the river Coel, 40 miles S. of Lohadugga. Lat. 22° 51′, long. 84° 54′.

BUSSEAN, in Sirhind, a small town on the route from Ferozpoor to Simla, and 70 miles S.E. of the former place. This place belongs to the British. Lat. 30° 38′, long. 75° 33′.

BUSSEE.—A town in the Rajpoot state of Shekawuttee, distant S.E. from Jhoonjhnoo 31 miles. Lat. 27° 58′, long. 76° 1′.

BUSSEE, in Sirhind, a small town near the base of the Sub-Himalaya. It has a fort, which "consists of a large square, with lofty towers at the angles; the whole beautifully built of a very small hard brick." It belongs to a Sikh sirdar, and is usually garrisoned by twenty or thirty men. Distance N.W. from Calcutta, by way of Meerut and Saharunpoor, 1,075 miles. Lat. 30° 35′, long. 76° 55′.

BUSSERHAT, in the British district of Baraset, lieut.-gov. of Bengal, a village, with police-station, near the southern frontier, towards the Sunderbunds. Distance from Calcutta, by Baraset, 40 miles. Lat. 22° 40′, long. 88° 54′.

BUSSEYE, in the British district of Muttra, lieut.-gov. of the N.W. Provinces, a village on the route from the cantonment of Allygurh to that of Etawah, and 40 miles S.E. of the former. Lat. 27° 20′, long. 78° 26′.

BUSSOMBA, or BYSOOMUH, in the British district Mozuffurnuggur, lieut.-gov. of the N.W. Provinces, a village on the route from the town of Meerut to that of Bijnour, and 22 miles N.E. of the former. Lat. 29° 12′, long. 78° 2′.

BUSSUNDAR, or DOOLOO.—A town in the native state of Nepal, distant S.W. from Jemlah 36 miles. Lat. 28° 59′, long. 81° 13′.

BUSSUNTPOOR, in the British district denominated the Twenty-four Pergunnahs, lieut.-gov. of Bengal, a town, with a police-station. Distance from Calcutta, S., 30 miles. Lat. 22° 10′, long. 88° 27′.

BUSTAR, or JUGDULPOOR, in the British territory of Nagpoor, a town near the eastern frontier, towards Orissa, on the river Inderowty, the bed of which at that place is very rocky, and the stream at no time fordable. The fort is situated in a peninsula, formed by the winding of the river; and a deep ditch having been dug across the narrow neck of land, it is considered a strong situation; but in the rainy season the river overflows its banks, and forms a very extensive lake on all sides. The zemindar or landholder of Bustar, who is improperly called rajah, has an extensive territory, containing forty-eight pergunnahs or subdivisions. The rajah, though often refractory, had been ostensibly tributary to the ruling power, and assessed nominally at 10,000 rupees annually; but as this sum could never be actually realized, the British authorities, after they had undertaken the temporary management of the revenues of Nagpore, in 1818, reduced the amount to 5,000 rupees annually. Bustar is also called Jugdulpoor. Distance from Nagpoor city, S.E., 225 miles; Masulipatam, N., 220; Madras, N., 440. Lat. 19° 13′, long. 81° 58′.

BUSTEE, in the British district of Goruckpore, lieut.-gov. of the N.W. Provinces, the principal place of the pergunnah of the same name, on the route from Goruckpoor cantonment to Lucknow, 43 miles W. of the former, 123 E. of the latter. It has a bazaar, and is well supplied with good water. Distant N.E. from Allahabad 110 miles, N. from Benares 105. Lat. 26° 49′, long. 82° 44′.

BUSWA.—A town in the Rajpoot state of Jeypoor, distant N.E. from Jeypoor 50 miles. Lat. 27° 7′, long. 76° 40′.

BUSWAR, or BUSSOHUR, in the British district of Allahabad, lieut.-gov. of the N.W. Provinces, a village on the route by Rajapoor ferry from the cantonment of Allahabad to Banda, 23 miles W. of the former. Lat. 25° 23′, long. 81° 32′.

BUSWUNTHUGGUR.—A town in Hyderabad, or dominions of the Nizam, distant S.E. from Jaulnah 91 miles. Lat. 19° 20′, long. 77° 14′.

BUTCHER ISLAND.—A low island in the harbour of Bombay, situate between the town of Bombay and the island of Elephanta. It has recently been selected as the site of a school for teaching gunnery to the men and officers of the Indian navy. Lat. 18° 56′, long. 72° 58′.

BUTCHITHULLY.—A town in the territory of Mysore, under the control and management of the government of India, distant N.E. from Seringapatam 110 miles. Lat. 13° 31′, long. 77° 56′.

BUTCHOW.—A town in the native state of Cutch, territory of Bombay, distant E. from Bhooj 44 miles. Lat. 23° 20′, long. 70° 23′.

BUTHULPOOR FORT, in the British district of Gurhwal, lieut.-gov. of the N.W. Provinces, a town on the route from Bijnour to Sireenuggur, 50 miles N.E. of the former. Lat. 29° 49′, long. 78° 49′.

BUTORA, in Bhugee, a village on the left bank of the Sutlej, at the confluence of a small feeder of that river. Elevation above the sea 2,281 feet. Lat. 31° 15′, long. 77° 21′.

BUTROWLEE, in the British district of Mynpoorie, lieut.-gov. of the N.W. Provinces, a village on the route from the city of Agra to the cantonment of Mynpoorie, and 10 miles W. of the latter. Lat. 27° 13′, long. 78° 57′.

BUTSURA, in the British district of Sarun, *lieut.-gov. of Bengal, a town on the left bank* of the river Gunduk, 36 miles N.W. of Bettiah. Lat. 27° 7′, long. 84° 9′.

BUTTATOA, or **BHUTTA THOWA**, in Sirhind, a village on the route from Loodiana to Ferozpore, and 14 miles W. of the former town. It is situate two miles from the left bank of the Sutlej, in an open country, well supplied with water, but scantily cultivated. Distant N.W. from Calcutta 1,116 miles. Lat. 30° 56′, long. 75° 41′.

BUTTEEGUAM.—A town in Nagpore, distant N. from Jeypoor, in Orissa, 20 miles. Lat. 19° 20′, long. 82° 20′.

BUTTELLY.—A town in the native state of Jeypoor, on the south-west frontier of Bengal, distant S.E. from Ryaguddah 29 miles. Lat. 19°, long. 83° 52′.

BUTWA.—A river rising in Nepal, in lat. 26° 42′, long. 87° 45′, on the southern slope of the Sub-Himalaya, and, flowing in a southerly direction through Nepal for twenty miles, and the British district of Purneah for fifty-four miles, it falls into the Mahananda river, a tributary of the Ganges, in lat. 25° 45′, long. 87° 50′.

BUXAR.—A town in the British district of Shahabad, lieut.-gov. of Bengal, situate on the right bank of the Ganges. It is a large town, and has several handsome mosques, a large and neat bazaar, and some respectable European bungalows. The fort is still in good order, and strong enough to resist any native force. The view from the summit is very fine. Buxar is remarkable in Indian history for having been the scene of the victory gained here by Sir Hector Munro over the allied forces of Meer Cossim and the vizier of Oude. Munro arrived at Buxar from Patna on the 22nd October, 1764, and found the enemy intrenched before the village, with the Ganges on their left. He immediately encamped for the night beyond range of the enemy's guns. The next morning, about eight o'clock, the enemy were found advancing; preparations were then made to receive them, and a general action ensued, which lasted about three hours, and ended in the defeat of the enemy, who retreated leisurely, blowing up several tumbrils and magazines of powder as they proceeded. Upon an attempt being made by the British to pursue them, the vizier ordered a bridge of boats which had been constructed over a stream two miles from the field of battle to be destroyed before his rear had passed over, so that 2,000 were drowned or lost. By this sacrifice, however, the remainder of his army was preserved, as the English could continue the pursuit no farther. The British force amounted to 7,072 men; consisting of 857 Europeans, 5,297 sepoys, and 918 native cavalry; also a train of artillery and twenty field-pieces. The enemy's force was estimated by some at 60,000, by others at only 40,000. Of these 2,000 were left dead on the field, and as many more perished in the nullah: they also lost 133 pieces of cannon. The British loss was not inconsiderable, amounting to 847. The population, some years since, was estimated at 3,000. Distance from Dinapore, W., 70 miles; Benares, N.E., 62; Calcutta, N.W., by Hazareebagh and Sasseram, 398; by the river, 566. Lat. 25° 32′, long. 84° 3′.

BUXA DWAR.—A town in the native state of Bhotan, distant N. from Coosh Behar 36 miles. Lat. 26° 48′, long. 89° 34′.

BUXEE, in the British district of Silhet, lieut.-gov. of Bengal, a town on the left bank of the Barak river, 22 miles S.W. of Silhet. Lat. 24° 37′, long. 91° 41′.

BUXEEPOOR, in the British district of Nuddea, lieut.-gov. of Bengal, a town on the left bank of the Jellinghee, 30 miles N. of Kishnugur. Lat. 23° 50′, long. 88° 30′.

BUXEEPORE, in the British district of Jessore, lieut.-gov. of Bengal, a town on the right bank of the Koomar river, 46 miles N.W. of Jessore. Lat. 23° 47′, long. 88° 58′.

BUXWAHO, in Bundelcund, in the territory of Punnah, a town on the route from Calpee to Jubbulpore, 159 miles S. of the former. It has a bazaar, and supplies and water are abundant. Lat. 24° 15′, long. 79° 20′.

BYANG, in the British district of Balasore, lieut.-gov. of Bengal, a town five miles S.E. of the route from Balasore to Cuttack, 46 miles S.W. of the former. Lat. 20° 55′, long. 86° 39′.

BYANGKHOLA.—A town in the native state of Nepal, distant N.W. from Khatmandoo 150 miles. Lat. 28° 39′, long. 83° 9′.

BYAR RIVER rises in the British district of Tirhoot, in lat. 26° 8′, long. 85° 1′, through which it flows in a south-easterly direction for eighty miles. Crossing from that district into that of Mongheer, which it traverses for the distance of twenty-five miles, it falls into the Ganges in lat. 25° 20′, long. 86° 6′.

BYDESSUR, or **BIDISSUR**.—A town in the British district of Pooree, or southern division of Cuttack, lieut.-gov. of Bengal. It is situate at the foot of a steep mountain, at the top of which is a plain, to which, before the occupation of the district by the British, the inhabitants were wont to retire with their effects upon any alarm. Distant 32 miles W. of Cuttack. Lat. 20° 22′, long. 85° 36′.

BYDOOR, in the British district of North Canara, presidency of Madras, a town on the route from Mangalore to the port of Coompta, 70 miles N. of the former. Lat. 13° 52′, long. 74° 41′.

BYE DERU, in the Baree Doab division of the Punjab, a town situated on the left bank of the river Ravee, 39 miles S.W. of the town of Lahore. Lat. 31° 10′, long. 73° 45′.

BYETURNEE.—A river of Orissa, inconsiderable in size, but sacred in the Hindoo mythology, more especially at its source, near Lohadugga, in lat. 23° 29′, long. 84° 55′. After a course of about two hundred and seventy-five miles, it crosses the western boundary of the British district of Cuttack, in lat. 21° 3′, long. 86° 13′, and communicating with the Mahanuddee and Brahmunee, flows through that district for seventy miles, for the last ten of which it assumes the name of the Dhumrah river, when it falls into the Bay of Bengal, in lat. 20° 49′, long. 87° 2′.

BYETURNEE.—A town in Keunjur, one of the petty states on the south-west frontier of Bengal, distant W. from Balasore 90 miles. Lat. 21° 35′, long. 85° 39′.

BYGHOOL, or BHAGUL.—A river rising at the southern base of the Sub-Himalaya, in lat. 29° 5′, long. 79° 45′, in the British district of Pilleebheet, lieut.-gov. of the N.W. Provinces. It holds a southerly course of 130 miles, and falls into the Western Ramgunga, on the left side, in lat. 27° 43′, long. 79° 40′. The route from Bareilly to Pilleebheet crosses it by ford eighteen miles north-east of the former. At certain periods of the year the stream is dammed up, to throw the water over the adjacent cultivated grounds, and must then be crossed by ferry.

BYGONBAREE, in the British district of Mymunsing, lieut.-gov. of Bengal, a town on the right bank of the river Brahmapootra, 19 miles S.E. of Jumalpore. Lat. 24° 47′, long. 90° 18′.

BYJOOA, in the British district of Sarun, lieut.-gov. of Bengal, a town on the left bank of the Gunduck, 11 miles S.W. of Bettiah. Lat. 26° 40′, long. 84° 26′.

BYLA.—See BAILA.

BYNSONT, or BHYSONDAH, in Bundelcund, a petty jaghire, containing an area of eight square miles, the patrimony of a Boondela Rajpoot chief. The population is about 2,000. This jagheer, comprising twelve villages, was divided in 1817 between the original jaghiredar and the widow of Bherit Jeo Chobey. The first grant from the East-India Company took place in 1812, and the deed of partition is dated in 1817. The estate is now held by the son of Chowbey Nowul Kishore, and is estimated to yield 9,000 rupees, or 900*l.* per annum. A force of about 136 men is maintained by the jaghiredar. Bynsont, the chief town, is in lat. 25° 17′, long. 80° 53′.

BYNSROLE.—A town in the Rajpoot state of Kotah, distant S.W. from Kotah 22 miles. Lat. 24° 49′, long. 75° 37′.

BYNSRORE.—See BANSRORE.

BYRAGPOOR, in the British district of Allahabad, lieut.-gov. of the N.W. Provinces, a village on the route, by the Rajpoor ferry, from the cantonment of Allahabad to Banda, and 24 miles W. of the former. Lat. 25° 25′, long. 81° 22′.

BYRAM GHAT, in the territory of Oude, a ferry-station on the right bank of the river Ghogra, and abreast of the town of Nawaub-Gunj, situate on the left bank, on the route from Lucknow to Sekrora, 19 miles N.E. of the former, 37 S.W. of the latter. Lat. 27° 8′, long. 81° 28′.

BYRAMNUGUR, in the British district of Boolundshuhur, lieut.-gov. of the N.W. Provinces, a village on the route from Allygurh cantonment to Moradabad, and 16 miles N. of the former. Lat. 28° 7′, long. 78° 13′.

BYRAMPORE, in the British district of Jessore, lieut.-gov. of Bengal, a town on the southern boundary of the district, 40 miles S. of Jessore. Lat. 22° 37′, long. 89° 20′.

BYRAN DROOG.—A town in the territory of Mysore, distant N.E. from Seringapatam 56 miles. Lat. 13° 6′, long. 77° 13′.

BYRAT.—A town in the Rajpoot state of Jeypoor, distant N.E. from Jeypoor 41 miles. Lat. 27° 27′, long. 76° 14′.

BYREE.—A town in the Rajpoot state of Jeypoor, distant S.E. from Jeypoor 50 miles. Lat. 26° 17′, long. 76° 14′.

BYRIAH.—See BAIREA.

BYROD, in the Rajpoot territory of Alwur, a small town on the route from Delhi to Mhow, and 32 miles S.W. of the former. It is situate at the southern extremity of a ridge of hills, among which the road winds to the N.E., and is in consequence rough and much cut up with ravines. There is a bazaar in the town, and water is obtainable from wells. Lat. 27° 55′, long. 76° 27′.

BYRONDA, in Malwa, a town in the native state of Bhopal, distant S. from Bhopal 40 miles. Lat. 22° 40′, long. 77° 15′.

BYRUMPOOR, in the British district of Allahabad, lieut.-gov. of the N.W. Provinces, a village on the route by the Rajapoor ferry from Allahabad to Banda, and 43 miles W. of the former city. Lat. 25° 24′, long. 81° 12′.

BYSAH.—A town in Hyderabad, or dominions of the Nizam, distant N. from Hyderabad 128 miles. Lat. 19° 7′, long. 78° 1′.

BYZAPOOR.—A town in Hyderabad, or dominions of the Nizam, distant W. from Aurungabad 40 miles. Lat. 19° 56′, long. 74° 47′.

BYZNATH, in Kumaon, a village with a Hindoo temple of considerable celebrity, in a valley about twenty-two miles north of Almora. Byznath is situate on the left bank of the Gaomuttee, which lower down joins the Surjoo, a principal feeder of the Kalee. Elevation above the sea 3,800 feet. Lat. 29° 54′, long. 79° 39′.

C.

CABEGHERRY, in the British district of Nellore, presidency of Madras, a town 50 miles S.W. from Ongole, 35 miles N.W. of Nellore. Lat. 14° 53′, long. 79° 46′.

CABOSSA, in the Mergui Archipelago, "a moderately high island, having a small islet or rock near it on the north side." It is one of the first of the cluster met with on approaching Mergui from the north-west. Lat. 12° 48′, long. 97° 58′.

CACHAR.—A British district of Eastern India, presidency of Bengal, bounded on the north by the Nowgong division of Assam; on the east by Munneepoor; on the south by independent Tipperah; and on the west by Jyntea and Silhet. It extends from lat. 24° 13′ to 25° 50′, and from long. 92° 24′ to 93° 28′, and is 110 miles in length from north to south, and sixty-five in breadth. The district is traversed by a navigable river, the Barak, flowing in a westerly direction, and receiving in its course the Juru and other tributaries. Tigers infest the plains to a serious extent, and large rewards are offered by government for their destruction. The principal crops are coffee and sugar. Large tracts are covered by the mulberry. Upon the death of Kishen Chunder, in 1813, his brother, Rajah Govind Chunder, succeeded to the chief power in Cachar. Subsequently the province became the arena of contention between the princes of the neighbouring principality of Munneepoor, one of whom, Gumbeer Singh, obtaining the ascendancy, expelled the reigning prince. Cachar was afterwards invaded by the Burmese, who in their turn were expelled by the British, when the legitimate rajah, Govind Chunder, was restored, and his country placed under British protection. This took place in 1824. Govind Chunder's authority was, however, resisted in the northern part of the province by Toola Ram Seenaputtee; and with a view to the speedy pacification of his dominions, the rajah was induced to assign to that individual the hilly tracts of which he was already in possession. In 1830 Govind Chunder was assassinated; and there being no descendants, either lineal or adopted, Cachar lapsed to the British, who conferred a portion upon the rajah of Munneepore, and annexed the remainder to their own dominions. Toola Ram Senaputtee's territory has subsequently lapsed to the British.

CADAVAUD, or CARWAR, in the British district of North Canara, presidency of Madras, a ruined city on the south side of the estuary of the Cauly Naddy, "a very wide and deep inlet of the sea. The passage into it is intricate, but at the height of the tide contains twenty-five feet water." Outside the river's mouth is Carwar Bay, a roadstead sheltered by islets, called by our sailors Oyster Rocks, but by the natives Coormagur, and having depths from four to seven fathoms. At the south side of the bay the shelter is best, and the bottom is of soft mud; and running from that part is a small but safe cove, with a bottom of soft mud, where Indiamen used formerly to careen. This town was once an important place of commerce, where the East-India Company had a factory in the year 1663, from which a contribution was levied in the year 1665 by Sevajee, the renowned founder of the Mahratta sway. During the time that it was subject to Hyder Ali and his son Tippoo, it progressively fell into its present ruinous state. Distance direct from Goa, S.E., 50 miles; from Bombay, S.E., 295; from Bangalore, N.W., 260. Lat. 14° 50′, long. 74° 15′.

CAKAJA.—A town in the native state of Odeipoor, on the south-west frontier of Bengal, distant N.E. from Odeipoor 35 miles. Lat. 22° 58′, long. 83° 49′.

CAKSA, in the British district of Bancoorah, lieut.-gov. of Bengal, a town situate on the line of railway from Calcutta to Raneegunje, 26 miles S.E. of the latter. Lat. 23° 26′, long. 87° 30′.

CALAHANDY.—One of the hill zemindaries belonging to a Khoond rajah, bounded on the north-west by the petty state of Patna, on the south-west frontier of Bengal; on the east by that of Boad, the independent hill tribes of Cuttack, and by the petty hill state of Jeypoor, which also bounds it on the south-west; and on the west by Berar and Keriall. It lies between lat. 19° 3′—20° 30′, and long. 82° 49′—83° 50′; is 105 miles in length from north to south, and forty-six in breadth.

CALASTRY, in the British district of North Arcot, presidency of Madras, a town on the right bank of the river Sornamooky, 60 miles N.W. of Madras. Lat. 13° 45′, long. 79° 47′.

CALCAUD, in the British district of Tinnevelly, presidency of Madras, a town 16 miles S.W. from Tinnevelly, 40 miles E. of Trivandrum. Lat. 8° 32′, long. 77° 36′.

CALCUTTA.—The principal place of the presidency of Bengal, and the metropolis of British India. It is situate on the left bank of the river Hoogly, a branch of the Ganges, regarded by Hindoos as the continuation of the sacred stream, and is distant by the river's course about a hundred miles from the sea. Its extent along the river-bank from north to south is about four miles and a half, and its breadth from thence to the Circular Road measures about a mile and a half; the entire site, which comprises an area of nearly eight square miles, being inclosed between the river and the line of the old intrenchment known as the Mahratta Ditch. This circumvallation, now almost obliterated, was intended as a defence against the incursions of the Mahrattas, and was commenced in 1742. It issued from the river on the north, and proceeding in an easterly course for the distance of half a mile, curved to the south-east, in which direction it was carried for about three miles and a half, when, taking a south-westerly direction, it was designed again to communicate with the river, and thus entirely to invest the city on the land side. The section of the ditch at the south-western angle was, however, never completed. Beyond the Mahratta Ditch, running parallel with the present Circular Road, the environs of Calcutta are studded with numerous suburbs, the principal of which are Chitpore, on the north; Nundenbagh, Bahar-Simlah, Sealdah, Entally, and Ballygunge, on the east and south-east; and Bhowaneepore, Allipore, and Kidderpore, on the south. On the opposite side of the river lie the villages of Seebpore, Howrah, and Sulkea, containing the salt-golahs or warehouses of the government, and several extensive manufactories, but depending for their prosperity chiefly upon their dockyards and ship-building establishments.

The approach to Calcutta by the river from the sea is marked by a series of elegant mansions at Garden Reach, surrounded by lawns which descend to the water's edge. Off this point anchorage is afforded to the magnificent steamers plying between Suez and Calcutta, by means of which the semi-monthly communication with Europe is carried on. A little to the north of Garden Reach are situate the government dockyards; above these, the canal designated Tolly's Nullah forms a junction with the river. To this succeeds the arsenal, and still higher up is Fort William. From this point the appearance of Calcutta becomes grand and imposing. Heber, writing thirty years ago, describes the scene from the fort as striking, "having on the left the Hoogly, with its forest of masts and sails seen through the stems of a double row of trees. On the right is the district called Chowringhee, lately a mere scattered suburb, but now almost as closely built as, and very little less extensive than Calcutta. In front is the Esplanade, containing the Town Hall, the Government House, and many handsome private dwellings, the whole so like some parts of Petersburg that it was hardly possible to fancy myself anywhere else." Above the Esplanade, on the river-bank, is Chandpaul Ghaut, the principal landing-place of the city; and from this point a noble strand extends northwards, along which are many fine buildings, including the Custom-house, the New Mint, and other government offices. Many ghauts, or landing-places, communicate with various parts of the town, and finally the Circular Canal bounds the metropolis at its northern extremity, and separates it from the suburb of Chitpore. A line intersecting the city eastward from Bebee Ross Ghaut, on the river-bank, to the Upper Circular Road, may be regarded as the boundary between the native and the European divisions; the northern portion including the area appropriated to the native population, and the southern comprehending the space occupied by the European community. One point of difference, however, observable in the two localities is, that a considerable part of the European division is inhabited by "natives, chiefly Mussulmans and the lower castes of Hindoos, while very few Christians have their abode in the native quarter." In this last-mentioned division the streets, as in most oriental towns, are narrow, though the houses of the wealthier classes are lofty. Some few are built in the form of a hollow square, with an area of from fifty to a hundred feet each way, which, when lighted up on the occasion of festivals, has a handsome appearance. The other division is European in character and appearance, as well as in population. It has its city and its court end, the one intersected by several noble streets, and the other adorned with the residences of government functionaries and opulent merchants. In this latter quarter, which is called Chowringhee, the houses are constructed in the Grecian style of building, ornamented with spacious verandahs; and from their imposing exterior Calcutta has not unusually been dignified by the appellation of "The City of Palaces." Between Chowringhee and the river an extensive space intervenes, designated the Esplanade, on which is situate Fort William. This fort is stated to surpass every other in India in strength and regularity. Its form is octagonal, five of its sides being landward, and three facing the river. Its foundations were laid by Clive, who commenced the works soon after the battle of Plassey; and its completion dates from the year 1773. The fort mounts 619 guns. Owing to its brackish character, the water of the river is generally unfit for general use, and the chief dependence for a wholesome supply of this necessary of life rests upon artificial tanks, which obtain their stores from the periodical rains. The number of these reservoirs, public and private, which have been constructed in various parts of the city, amounts to 1,043. Fifteen of them are public tanks. The largest and best of this class is situate in Tank Square, and is replenished from the river during the freshes, in the month of September, when the water is sweet to the sea: the majority of the remainder are filled during the rains. The supply required for watering the streets, and other purposes, is raised from the river by means of a steam-engine. Attempts have been made, from time to time, to obtain water by boring through the strata in search of subterranean springs, but none were reached at a depth of 481 feet; and at this point the boring operations terminated.

No accurate census of the population appears to have been taken until the year 1850. Various estimates were made from time to time, differing widely from each other, and bearing in no instance even a tolerable approximation to the truth. According to the census of May, 1850, taken by order of the chief magistrate, the population is as follows:—

Europeans	6,233
Eurasians (progeny of white fathers and native mothers)	4,615
Americans	892
Chinese	847
Asiatics	15,342
Hindoos	274,335
Mahomedans	110,918
	413,182

The number of residences amounts to 62,565; consisting of 5,950 one-storied houses, 6,438 of two stories, 721 of three, ten of four, and one of five stories; and 49,445 huts. Among the public buildings are the Government House, erected by the Marquis Wellesley in 1804, at a cost of 130,000*l.*; the Town Hall on the Esplanade, built in the Doric style of architecture; the Supreme Court of Judicature; the Madrissa and Hindoo colleges; La Martinière, an institution in which twenty boys and thirty girls are educated from funds bequeathed by General Claude Martin, originally a common soldier in the French army, but subsequently a major-general in the East-India Company's service; Metcalfe Hall, erected by subscription, as a public testimonial of the estimation in which the character of the late Lord Metcalfe was held by the population of Calcutta; the Ochterlony Monument, raised in honour of Sir David Ochterlony, and designed in the Saracenic style, to mark the friendly feeling which the general always showed towards the followers of the Prophet. At the south-west angle of the fort is a ghat, erected to perpetuate the memory of James Prinsep, one of the most eminent men of his age; and at a short distance from it is the monument commemorative of the victories of Maharajpore and Punniar, constructed from the cannon captured on those fields. There are also the rooms of the Asiatic Society, an institution founded in 1784 by Sir William Jones; St. Paul's Cathedral, recently erected, through the exertions and munificence of Bishop Wilson, aided by the grant of 15,000*l.* from the East-India Company; the Scotch church in Tank Square; Writers' Buildings in the same locality; and the theatre in Park Street, Chowringhee. In Calcutta are also located the Bank of Bengal, the Union Bank, and the Bengal Chamber of Commerce. On the opposite side of the river, and facing Garden Reach, is Bishop's College, situate to the north of the Botanical Gardens. This institution was founded for the purpose of instructing native youths and others in the doctrine and discipline of Christianity, in order to their becoming preachers, catechists, and schoolmasters, under the Society for the Propagation of the Gospel in Foreign Parts. The Hindoos have 167 buildings devoted to their religion; the Mahomedans 74. There is also a Chinese temple. Other religious denominations, holding a faith and practising worship more or less pure, have also places of assemblage. The Jews have a synagogue; there is one Greek and one Armenian church, three Baptist chapels, and two belonging to Independents not Baptists; while the adherents to the Church of Rome have five. Of the places of worship connected with the national churches, the Church of England has eight, the Established Church of Scotland one, and the Free Church of the latter country one. Among the charitable institutions are St. James' Schools, instituted by Bishop Middleton; the European Female Orphan Asylum, established for the education of female European orphans; the Benevolent Institution, designed for the instruction of indigent Christian children; the Free School and Church; the Church Missionary Almshouses; the Leper Asylum; and the General Assembly's Institution. About three miles below Calcutta are situate the Botanical Gardens, occupying the north-west bank of the Hoogly at Garden Reach. These gardens were established in the latter part of the last century, for the purpose of improving the botanical productions of India and promoting the interchange of plants with other countries.

The highest spring tide in the Hoogly at Calcutta, between the 1st November, 1844, and the 30th November, 1847, appears to have occurred on the 28th August, 1847, when it rose twenty-three feet and a quarter above the silt of the entrance-dock at Kidderpore. Under the influence of storms and hurricanes, the tide in the Hoogly has occasionally greatly exceeded its ordinary level. An instance occurred on the 20th and 21st May, 1833, when the embankments of the river were destroyed, and great devastation ensued. In the beginning of March the river is at its lowest; and the freshes are at their height in September, when the tides are scarcely visible, and the river-water is sweet to the sea. Should there be any foundation for the suspicion that the channel of the Hoogly is gradually silting up, and will ultimately cease to be navigable, it has been suggested that the river Mutwal, flowing about twenty-five miles more to the eastward, is well calculated to supply its place, and might be connected with Calcutta by a ship-canal or railway. The most elevated part of Calcutta is in Clive Street, where it is thirty feet above the sea-level at low water. Immediately opposite Clive Street and the Custom-house, but on the opposite bank of the river, and in the suburb of Howrah, is the terminus of the East-India Railway. At this point the width of the river barely exceeds that of the Thames at Waterloo Bridge, and a ferry has been found to suffice for the maintenance of the more limited communication which has hitherto subsisted between the city and its western suburbs. But a different state of things is about to spring up. A section of the railway has been opened, and a stream of population daily pours into Calcutta, while another seeks egress from the city; and a less tedious mode of crossing the river has been found indispensable. Railways and a ferry are not links of the same chain. The latter is to give way, and its place is to be shortly occupied by a substantial bridge thrown over the river Hoogly in the immediate vicinity of the terminus. A company has been formed for the purpose of providing the chief cities of India with gas. Calcutta is to be the starting-point for its operations; and it may be confidently expected that a very brief period will be permitted to elapse before the present defective system of lighting the city with oil-lamps is entirely superseded. The mean temperature at Calcutta is about 66° in January, 69° in February, 80° in March, 85° in April and May, 83° in June, 81° in July, 82° in August and September, 79° in October, 74° in November, and 66° in December. The annual fall of rain during six years, commencing with 1830, averaged sixty-four inches. In 1852 an act was passed, authorizing an assessment on the owners of houses and landed proprietors, and directing the appointment of commissioners, to be elected by the rate-payers, to apply the proceeds in cleansing, improving, and embellishing the town.

Calcutta owes its origin to Governor Charnock, who transferred the Company's factory from the town of Hoogly to the opposite side of the river. In 1700, certain villages, occupying the site whereon Calcutta now stands, were assigned to the Company, in recognition of a present made by them to Azim, a son of Aurungzebe. They were forthwith fortified, and the new British settlement, in compliment to the then reigning king of England, received the name of Fort William. Calcutta was the name of one of the villages transferred; and hence the appellation by which the capital of British India has since been known: thus humble was its origin in the last year of the seventeenth century. At the commencement of the succeeding century, it was the place whence strangers from a far-distant country gave law to a large part of India, and half a century more brought the entire country under their control. For a long period no one expected such a result, and circumstances gave little promise of it. In 1756, Sooraj-oo-Dowlah, the then soubahdar or nawaub of Bengal, whose hatred of the English was extreme, having captured the English factory at Cossimbazar, proceeded to attack Calcutta, which, little prepared for such an assault, and abandoned by some who ought to have been foremost in its defence, yielded after two days' siege. The Company's servants of course became prisoners of war, and were treated with a degree of barbarity hardly to be expected from such a ruler as was the soubahdar of Bengal. It will be unnecessary to give details; the horrors of the Black-hole have obtained a place in Indian history, which will not allow of their being forgotten. Vengeance, however, followed from Madras, though somewhat tardily. Clive had just arrived there from England, and on him happily devolved the duty of commanding the force despatched for the recovery of Calcutta, it being no less happily aided by a squadron under the command of Admiral Watson. Calcutta was retaken, and peace with the soubahdar restored. The disputes between the English and French, however, caused the renewal of war not long after, and the well-known battle of Plassey terminated in a manner fatal to the hopes of the soubahdar. From this time the English continued to increase in power and influence. In 1765 the emperor of Delhi conferred upon the East-India Company the dewanny of the three provinces of Bengal, Behar, and Orissa. The duties of dewanny consisting in the collection and management of the revenues, the gift of the dewanny was substantially the gift of the provinces. Thus did this part of India become absolutely British, and in this manner originated that mighty empire which in less than ninety years has been matured into that which it is now seen to be. Calcutta is in lat. 22° 34′, long. 88° 25′.

CALICUT, in the British district of Malabar, a seaport town. It is situate on the open beach, there being neither river nor haven, and ships must anchor in the open sea; large ones two or three miles from land, in five or six fathoms water; smaller ones within a rocky bank abreast of the town, having on it three fathoms water. Formerly a place of great importance, few vestiges of its grandeur remain. The successors of the Tamuri rajah or zamorin, who once lived here in great splendour, are no longer independent princes, but stipendiaries of the East-India Company. The haven, said to have been once capacious, has been filled up by drifted sand. It was visited by Vazco de Gama in 1498, being the first place in India touched at, either by him or any other European navigator. It then contained many stately buildings, especially a Brahminical temple, not inferior to the greatest monastery in Portugal. In 1510, the Portuguese, commanded by Albuquerque, landed, burned the town, and plundered the palace of the zamorin, who, however, rallying his followers, put them to flight, and made them sail away, having suffered heavy loss. In 1513 the zamorin concluded a peace with the Portuguese, and permitted them to build a fort, or rather a fortified factory here. In 1616 the English East-India Company established a factory at Calicut.

According to native tradition and accounts, a prince called Cheruman, having divided Malabar among the ancestors of the present chieftains, had nothing remaining to bestow on Tamuri, from whom descended the chief whom the Portuguese found in possession. Thereupon he gave that personage his sword, "with all the territory in which a cock crowing at a small temple here could be heard. This formed the original dominions of the Tamuri, and was called Colicodu, or the Cock-

crowing." Notwithstanding this scanty domain, the *Tamuri rajah* or *zamorin* became by far the most powerful chieftain of Malabar; and the family enjoyed great prosperity until the Mysorean invasion of the country, in 1766, when the individual who was zamorin at that juncture, having endeavoured to propitiate Hyder Ali by submission, but finding, subsequently, that no reliance could be placed on that unprincipled adventurer, barricaded his house, fired it, and perished in the flames. Calicut, having with other parts of Malabar cast off the yoke of Hyder, was, in 1773, reconquered by the Mysorean ruler, whose forces were, however, in 1782, driven out by the British. Tippoo Sultan retook the place in 1789, and treated the inhabitants with a studied and detestable cruelty, thus described by Bartolomeo, who was then in the vicinity:—"He was preceded by 30,000 barbarians, who butchered every person who came in their way, and by his heavy cannon, under the command of General Lally, at the head of a regiment of artillery. Then followed Tippoo Sultan himself, riding on an elephant, and behind marched another corps, consisting of 30,000 men also. The manner in which he behaved to the inhabitants of Calicut was horrid. A great part of them, both male and female, were hung. He first tied up the mothers, and then suspended the children from their necks. The cruel tyrant caused several Christians and heathens to be brought out naked, and made fast to the feet of his elephants, which were then obliged to drag them about till their limbs fell in pieces from their bodies." Such of the men as were not immediately massacred, whether Brahminists or Christians, were forcibly subjected to the initiatory rite of Mahomedanism, or at best had the option of submitting thereto or being hanged. The foreign merchants and factors were expelled; and with the view of utterly ruining it, the cocoanut-trees and sandal-trees in the adjoining country were cut down, and the pepper-vines torn up by the roots. The city was almost completely demolished, and most of the materials taken to Nellura, six miles to the south-eastward, where they were used to build a fort and town called by Tippoo Sultan, Furruckabad, or Fortunate Town, "a fancy," says Colonel Wilks, "which afterwards nearly proved fatal to his troops, by leaving them the choice of a ruin or an unfinished work as points of retreat and rendezvous." In the latter part of 1790, the Mysorean force, having been concentrated in the neighbourhood of Calicut, was attacked by a British detachment commanded by Colonel Hartley, and totally defeated; Tippoo's general was made prisoner with 900 of his men, and 1,500 more laid down their arms at the "fortunate town," whither they had been pursued by the conquerors. Under the treaty concluded in 1792, which deprived Tippoo of half his dominions, Calicut fell to the share of the East-India Company, and was formally incorporated with the British dominions. After this event the scattered survivors of the population returned and rebuilt their dwellings; and Buchanan, at the time of his visit in 1800, found the number of houses considerable, and the prosperity and population rapidly on the increase. Distance from Bombay, S.E., 566 miles; Mangalore, S.E., 130; Cannanore, S.E., 50; Cochin, N.W., 96; Bangalore, S.W., 170; Madras, S.W., 335. Lat. 11° 15′, long. 75° 50′.

CALIMERE POINT.—A headland, forming the south-eastern extremity of the British district of Tanjore. "It is low, and covered with cocoanut-trees." Distant 50 miles S. of Tranquebar. Lat. 10° 17′, long. 79° 56′.

CALLIAN DROOG, in the British district of Bellary, presidency of Madras, a town six miles W. of the route from Madras to Bellary, 41 miles S. of the latter. Lat. 14° 34′, long. 77° 9′.

CALLIANEE, in the British district of Tannah, presidency of Bombay, a town situate on the line of the Great Indian Peninsula Railway, distant 28 miles N.E. of Bombay. Lat. 19° 14′, long. 73° 12′.

CALLIAUD, in the British district of Malabar, presidency of Madras, a town on the route from Cannanore to Seringapatam, 20 miles N.E. of the former. Lat. 12° 1′, long. 75° 40′.

CALLINGER.—See KALLEENJUR.

CALLWA, in the British district of Kurnool, presidency of Madras, a town 19 miles S.E. of Kurnool, 90 miles N.W. of Cuddapah. Lat. 15° 38′, long. 78° 16′.

CALPANNEE, in the British district of Rungpore, lieut.-gov. of Bengal, a town on the left bank of the Goggot river, 30 miles N.W. of Rungpore. Lat. 26° 1′, long. 89°.

CALPEE, the principal place of the pergunnah of the same name, a town on the right bank of the Jumna. The channel of the river is here a mile and a half wide; but during the dry season the width of the stream, which then flows under the right bank, is only half a mile, the remainder of the bed being a heavy sand. The town, situate among rugged ravines, is in general meanly built, the houses being chiefly of mud, though some of a better kind are of kunkur or calcareous conglomerate. A small fort is situate between the river and town, above which its elevation is about fifty feet. The site of the fort is naturally strong, having on all sides precipitous ravines, but the works are weak and ill-contrived, and could not resist a serious attack. So slight is the opinion entertained by the natives of the strength of the place, that in 1825, a zemindar in the vicinity, arming his tenants and labourers to the number of about 500 men, attempted to take it, in the hope of carrying off a considerable treasure there, belonging to the British authorities. The attempt was, however, defeated, with the loss of a few lives on the side of the assailants, and the zemindar taken prisoner. Calpee was formerly a more considerable place than at present, and had a mint; now its principal business is the receipt of the cotton of Bundlecund, to be transmitted by the Jumna to the lower provinces. Efforts have not been wanting on the part of the government to extend the cultivation of the American species of cotton to this part of India, but the experiments were unsuccessful. Paper is manufactured here, and the refining of sugar carried on to such perfection, that the natives boast, with some reason, that it is the finest in the world, and so pure, as to resemble the diamond in appearance. It is, however, too high-priced to be in general demand. The temperature of the atmosphere during the hot winds in the early part of summer is very great, probably in consequence of the stagnation of air in the deep, narrow ravines, and the powerful radiation from the calcareous rocks inclosing them. The population in 1853, as ascertained by actual enumeration, amounted to 21,812. Calpee is recorded to have been founded by Basdeo or Vasudeva, who reigned at Cambay from the year 330 to 400. The Mussulmans took it in 1196, under the conduct of Kutbuddin Aibuk, the viceroy of Muhammud, the sovereign of Ghor; and in 1527 it passed, by surrender, from the Patan dynasty of Delhi to Baber. On the dissolution of the empire of Delhi, consequent on the invasion of Ahmed Shah Dooranee in 1761, it appears to have been in the hands of the Mahrattas, from whom, in 1778, it was taken by the British, but subsequently relinquished by them. It was transferred to the East-India Company in 1802 by the Peishwa, under the treaty of Bassein; but Nana Govind Rao, the jaghiredar of Jaloun, who possessed the place, assuming an attitude hostile to the British government, Calpee was besieged on the 4th December, 1803, and, after a few hours' resistance, yielded. By subsequent engagement in 1806, Nana Govind Rao surrendered all claim on Calpee to the East-India Company. Distance S.E. from Agra 130 miles, S.W. from Cawnpore 46, N.W. from Allahabad 153, N.W. from Calcutta 648. Lat. 26° 7′, long. 79° 48′.

CALPEE.—See KULPEE.

CALVENTURA ISLANDS, off the coast of Arracan, consist of two divisions. The centre of these groups is about lat. 16° 53′, long. 94° 20′.

CAMAPURAM.—A town in the native state of Travancore, in political connection with the presidency of Madras, distant N. from Quilon 30 miles. Lat. 9° 18′, long. 76° 30′.

CAMBAY.—An ancient city, the capital of a small compact territory in the province of Guzerat, comprehended between the rivers Myhee and Saburmutty on the east and west, and bounded by the British collectorate of Kaira on the north, and the Gulf of Cambay on the south. The district extends from lat. 22° 9′ to 22° 41′, and from long. 72° 20′ to 73° 5′, and contains an area of about 500 square miles. The population is 37,000. It is under the political superintendence of the government of Bombay. The city is situate at the head of the gulf of the same name, on the north or right side of the estuary of the river Myhee, here having from two to four fathoms water, and a tide so rapid, that if a vessel take the ground, it must inevitably overset. This decayed city is now only three miles in circumference, surrounded by a brick wall perforated for musketry, flanked with fifty-two irregular towers, without fosse or esplanade; the works are out of repair, and the cannon of the towers of little consequence. The palace of the nawaub is in good repair, but built in a style of architecture little attractive to the eye of taste. The Jumna Mosseid, or principal mosque, a handsome building, was formerly a Brahminical temple, and was converted to its present purpose when the Mussulmans subjugated Guzerat.

Cambay was formerly a place of great trade, and Tieffenthaler in 1751 reckoned seventy vessels at anchor here. It was long celebrated for its manufactures of chintz, silk, and gold stuffs; but when the place was visited by Forbes, the weavers were few and poor, and no merchants or traders of consequence, except the English brokers, were to be found there. Its decline is attributed partly to the oppression of the nawaub, and partly to the fact of access to it by water having become more difficult. It, however, still has some celebrity for agates, cornelians, and onyxes, which are wrought into a great variety of ornaments. The best agates and cornelians are found in peculiar strata, about thirty feet below the surface, in a small tract among the Rajpeepla hills, on the banks of the Nerbudda. They are not met with in any other part of Guzerat, and are generally cut and polished in Cambay. The following account of the processes to which they are subjected is given by a writer of the latter part of the last century:—"On being taken from their native bed, they are exposed to the heat of the sun for two years (the longer they remain in that situation, the brighter and deeper will be the colour of the stone); fire is sometimes substituted for the solar ray, but with less effect, as the stones frequently crack, and seldom acquire a brilliant lustre. After having undergone this process, they are boiled for two days, and sent to the manufacturers at Cambay. The agates are of different hues: those generally called cornelians are black, white, and red, in shades from the palest yellow to the deepest scarlet." Cambay is a very ancient place, and has had a variety of names at different periods. "Its last transition was to Cambayet or Khumbavati," the origin of which name is ascribed to a tradition too trivial to be mentioned. After the erection of the Mussulman kingdom of Guzerat, at the close of the fourteenth century, it became the principal place of the surrounding district. Early in the sixteenth century it appears to have been a remarkably well-built city, in a fertile country, filled with merchants of all nations, and with artisans and manufacturers like those of Flanders. The present nawaub of Cambay is a descendant of Momin Khan, the second of that name, who was chief of Cambay in 1746, and who, about ten years afterwards, seized upon Ahmedabad, from which, however, after sustaining a long siege, he was expelled by the Mahrattas. That marauding nation established in Cambay, as in various other places, their claim to chouth. This tribute seems to have been a subject of dispute between the Guicowar and the Peishwa, the latter of whom, however, succeeded in appropriating it; but by the treaty of Bassein it was ceded to the East-India Company. The Company are also entitled to half the customs-duties of the port. The revenue of the nawaub is estimated at 3,00,000 Company's rupees, or 30,000*l.* The Company's tribute was rated in the schedule annexed to the treaty at 60,000 rupees, or 6,000*l.*, and their share of the customs realized in 1825 34,096 rupees, or 3,409*l.* The military establishment of the nawaub consists of 1,700 peons and horsemen, who are employed indiscriminately in revenue, police, and miscellaneous duties: a few pieces of ordnance complete the return of military strength. The city of Cambay is distant from Bombay, N., 230 miles; from Ahmedabad, S., 52; from Mhow, W., 202. Lat. 22° 18′, long. 72° 39′.

CAMBAY, GULF OF, extends between lat. 21°—22° 10′, long. 71° 50′—72° 40′, having a length from north to south of about eighty miles, and a breadth, on an average, of twenty-five. It is shallow, and abounds in shoals and sand-banks. Numerous and considerable rivers flow into it. Of those, the Saburmuttee, running in a south-westerly direction from the Aravulli Mountains, enters the gulf at its head, in lat. 22° 10′, long. 72° 23′; the Myhee, flowing from the same range, and having a direction south-westerly, enters the gulf in nearly the same latitude as the former river, but more to the east. Lower down, and also on the east side, in lat. 21° 33′, the gulf receives the great river Nerbudda; still lower down, on the same side, in lat. 21° 3′, the Taptee; and on the west side the less considerable streams of the Gooma, Oolowtee, Gelya, and Setroonjee, flowing from Kattywar. The tides, which are very high, rising upwards of thirty feet, rush in with great rapidity, causing much danger to shipping; and this hazard is greatly increased by the continually shifting shoals, caused by the frequent inundations of the rivers. It is, however, an important inlet, being the channel by which the abundant and valuable produce of central Guzerat, and the districts of Ahmedabad and Broach, is exported.

CAMROOP.—A British district, one of the divisions of Lower Assam. It lies between lat. 25° 47′—26° 39′, long. 90° 40′—92° 10′; is ninety-two miles in length from east to west, and fifty-two in breadth; and contains an area of 2,788 square miles, with a population of 300,000. Limestone has been recently found in the Ranska Dooar, within this district. The discovery is regarded as important, and experimental measures for testing its quality are in progress, under the authority of the government.

CAMULAPOOR, in the British district of Cuddapah, presidency of Madras, a town on the right bank of the river Pennar, 13 miles N.W. of Cuddapah. Lat. 14° 36′, long. 78° 43′.

CANACON.—A town in the Portuguese territory of Goa, on the route from Goa to Honahwar, 32 miles S.E. of the former. Lat. 15° 2′, long. 74° 8′.

CANARA, a British district under the presidency of Madras, is a tract of territory of some length, but of inconsiderable breadth. The name applied to this country is unknown to the natives, and is considered to be a European corruption of Carnata, the name of one of the ancient Hindoo kingdoms of the Deccan. The district now denominated Canara is bounded on the north by the Portuguese territory of Goa and the Bombay presidency; on the east by the Bombay presidency, the territory of the rajah of Mysore, and the British district of Coorg; on the south by Coorg and the British district of Malabar; and on the west by the Indian Ocean and the territory of Goa. It lies between lat. 12° 11′—15° 30′, long. 74° 9′—75° 44′, and has an area of 7,720 square miles. It is popularly divided into North and South Canara.

NORTH CANARA may be regarded as that part of the district lying between lat. 13° 35′—15° 30′, long. 74° 9′—75° 10′. The seacoast of North Canara has scarcely any sinuosities, and is a hundred miles in length, but within its whole extent there is hardly a landlocked or tolerably safe station for square-rigged vessels. There are, however, numerous creeks and inlets. The sheet of water forming the estuary or backwater of Mirji or Mirjan, by which the Toodry passes to the sea, is represented as capable of being formed into a useful harbour. The advantages of the place are thus enumerated by the collector of the district and Captain F. Cotton, of the engineers:—"It presents a large natural harbour, forming the mouth of a considerable river, which runs down from the Western Ghats, and is navigable for about fifteen or twenty miles, as far as a place named Oopenputten. Its entrance, which is protected by high hills on each side, has a depth of water over the bar, which, as far as could be judged by two measurements, is about sixteen or seventeen feet at high tide, and may be increased during the spring tides to about nineteen or twenty feet. The depth inside the harbour is much greater, being about twenty-five feet, and in some places more; and this so close to the shore, that vessels of a large size might lie so near as to be laden from the bank without the use of boats at all; and there is ample room for almost any number of vessels to ride in deep water." Captain Cotton seems to consider that it presents greater natural advantages as a port than any one on this coast, between Bombay and Cochin.

SOUTH CANARA is the portion lying between lat. 12° 11′—13° 39′, long. 74° 45′—75° 42′. It has the advantage of a seacoast of upwards of a hundred miles in length, with numerous inlets available for fishing-boats, and one seaport, Mangalore, now accessible only to vessels of small burthen, but capable of being improved so as to admit ships of large draught. There is great diversity in the classes of the population of this district, of which the Brahminists are supposed to be the most numerous. The Jains, who have nearly vanished from many other parts of India, are here still numerous. The residue is composed of natives professing Christianity, descendants of those converted by the Portuguese, and of course of the Romish church, and Mussulmans and a few Jews. There were formerly many slaves by birth, adscripti glebæ, and considered as a sort of live-stock inseparable from the soil. Of those oppressed beings the principal were the Corars, who, like the Helots of Laconia, were the descendants of those who once possessed and ruled the country. British India, however, by a recent act of its government, has abrogated slavery throughout every part of its widely-spread dominions. The population of the two tracts constituting the district will be found under the article MADRAS.

The early history of the country known as Canara is obscure. Soon after the middle of the last century, it fell into the hands of the adventurer Hyder Ali; and on the fall of his son Tippoo, in 1799, it passed to the East-India Company. The principal towns, viz., in North Canara, Condapoor, Batcull, Honahwar, Coomta, Mirjan, Unkola, Sedashevagurh; in South Canara, Mangalore, Buntwalla, Oodapee, Barkoor, Karkull, and Jamalabad, are noticed under their names in the alphabetical arrangement.

CANARAC, in the British district of Pooree, or southern division of Cuttack, presidency of Bengal, a town on the north-western coast of the Bay of Bengal, in this part called the Orissa coast. The land here is rather low, having a level and barren aspect, with a steep sandy beach, which may be approached to within one and a half mile by large ships. Five or six miles south from Canarac are the remains of the celebrated temple of the sun, popularly denominated by the British the Black Pagoda. This extraordinary structure will, however, probably soon be quite demolished, as the rajah of Koorda has lately been employing workmen to pull down the finest sculptures, and remove them to embellish the temple of Juggernauth at Pooree. Distance from Pooree, N.W., 19 miles; Cuttack, S., 43; Calcutta, S.W., 235. Lat. 19° 54′, long. 86° 10′

CANCANHULLY.—A town in Mysore, distant E. from Seringapatam 48 miles. Lat. 12° 33′, long. 77° 28′.

CANCOOPA.—A town in Mysore, distant N. from Seringapatam 150 miles. Lat. 14° 33′, long. 76° 22′.

CANDEISH.—A British collectorate of the presidency of Bombay. It is bounded on the north by the Akraunee pergunnah, the native state of Burwanee, and by Holkar's territory; on the east by a detached portion of Scindia's dominions, and one of the recently sequestrated districts of the Nizam; on the south by the Nizam's dominions and the Ahmednuggur collectorate; and on the west by various petty states, forming the southern portion of Guzerat. It extends from lat. 20° 10′ to 21° 58′, and from long. 73° 37′ to 76° 20′; its greatest length from east to west is 175 miles, its extreme breadth from north to south 128. The area is estimated at 9,311 square miles. This district was combined with that of Ahmednuggur until 1849, when it was detached and formed into a separate zillah. It is a great valley, or rather basin, traversed by the Taptee, flowing from east to west, and flanked on the north side throughout its whole extent by the Sautpoora range; on the south by the range on which are the fort of Chandore and the ghaut of Adjunta; and on the south-west by the expansion of the Syadree range, or Western Ghauts. On the south-east the bounding surface is but slightly elevated, sinking gradually to the more depressed territory of the valley of Berar, in the dominions of the Nizam. The lower part of Candeish is in general fertile, the soil consisting principally of a rich mould of a dark reddish-brown colour, formed, apparently, for the most part, of the disintegration of the trappean rock. There is, indeed, a considerable portion of sand, as well as hard unkindly soil mixed with gravel; yet the better descriptions predominate. Much of the cultivable tract is now covered by jungle; but the former prosperity of the province is attested by numerous remains of tanks and buildings. In its existing condition, the collectorate presents the features of a province partially recovered from a state of depopulation; the villages being scattered and small, and the cultivated lands bearing but a very small proportion to the entire area. The scantiness of the population, and the remains of former magnificence and grandeur in decayed and ruined mansions, dismantled towns, and dilapidated walls, spread an indescribable air of desolation over the face of the country. The district, moreover, is infested by beasts of prey. Among them tigers abound in an extraordinary degree. Amidst the hills and coverts where these animals find shelter, they can rarely be attacked with success, except with the aid of elephants. An establishment is accordingly maintained by government for their extirpation, and private efforts for their destruction are stimulated by the offer of rewards. By means of these two systems no less than seventy-three tigers were destroyed in Candeish in one year. The inhabitants are principally Mahrattas, described about thirty years ago "as peaceable and inoffensive, but timid, helpless, unenterprising, and sunk under the oppression and the multiplied calamities to which they were so long exposed." A portion of the population was at the same time represented as bold and restless, from which the predatory forces of Jeswunt Rao Holkar were formerly recruited. Still more restless and less removed from barbarism were the Bheels, a tribe of plunderers supposed to have been the aborigines of Guzerat and the adjacent quarters of Hindostan, and who have been recognised from remote ages as a distinct people. The earliest notice of the race occurs in the celebrated Hindoo poem of the Mahabhurat. In the Mahomedan history of Malwa and Guzerat, they are described as a nation inhabiting the jungles and hilly districts of Meywar and Oodipoor; and the ancient records of Candeish advert to the residence of the tribe in that portion of the province which lies north of the Taptee. Their settlements are still in the same localities; and in Candeish the Bheels are estimated to form one-eighth of the entire population of the province.

During the struggle between the Mahomedans and the Mahrattas, the excesses of the Bheels rose to a great height; yet it would appear that Candeish was in a flourishing condition up to the year 1798, when Bajee Rao succeeded, on the death of Nana Furnavese, to the free exercise of authority as Peishwa. The decline of this rich province is to be dated from the year 1802, when it was ravaged by Holkar's army. This blow was followed by the famine of 1803, and its ruin was subsequently consummated by the rapacity and misgovernment of the Peishwa's officers. A portion of the population abandoned the plains; organized bands of robbers started up in every direction; the surrounding country was laid waste; and on the occupation of the province by the British government, in 1818, anarchy and oppression had reached a fearful height. Successive measures were resorted to for the pacification of the province, some conceived in a mild, others in a harsher spirit; but all proved alike unsuccessful. At length, in 1825, it was determined to adopt a conciliatory line of policy, and to make a more systematic effort for the restoration of tranquillity. A military corps was raised, into which were draughted the more unruly spirits, who disdained any occupation but that of arms. The men received five rupees per mensem, with an additional rupee as batta when on outpost duty. Clothing was furnished by government, and, armed with fusils, the levy was drilled as light infantry. At the commencement of the second season of its service, the first opportunity was afforded for testing the discipline and courage of the Bheel corps. The village of Boorwarree had been attacked and plundered; and emissaries from the gang engaged in the work were going about among the hills to collect the disaffected, when a small detachment of the Bheel corps arrived at sunset near the scene of their operations. Captain, now Colonel Outram, who commanded this small force, arrived, after a tedious night's march, on the eminence to which the gang had retired, when he was immediately assailed by showers of arrows and stones. A jemadar and many of the recruits were wounded; but the men fought on steadily, and the enemy was eventually driven from the commanding position. Fatigued, however, with the night-march, and indisposed to subject his followers to the severe exertion of following the gang from hill to hill, a retreat was feigned by Captain Outram, and the enemy by this ruse drawn down into the open plain. Here they were charged and dispersed at the point of the bayonet; the plunder of the village was recovered; arms and other property were captured; the marauding chief, with many of his followers, killed; and the gang entirely dispersed. The subsequent reception of the corps in the camp of Malligaum, by the 23rd regiment Bombay Native Infantry, was eminently calculated to conciliate their feelings and secure their attachment. Men of high caste visited, and presented them with betelnut, to the no small amazement of the guests. The regiment was complimented by the government on this manifestation of good feeling. At the close of the monsoon of 1827, the corps was reviewed by the brigadier of the district, whose high commendation of their skill and steady performance of intricate manœuvres was announced in general orders. The results of the conciliatory and enlightened system pursued by the government have been summed up as follows:—"Roads," says Captain Graham, "formerly hazardous for armed parties, are traversed in safety at all hours by single unarmed passengers; the formidable list of crimes has dwindled down to the report of a few petty thefts; and the Bheels, from outcasts, have become members of civil society, daily rising in respectability, and becoming useful and obedient subjects of the state." As an illustration of the degree to which confidence and the sense of security prevailed, it is related by the same authority, that in a village near the Sautpoora range a petty theft had been committed by a few boys, who carried off the cooking-utensils from two houses. The patell and the inhabitants who suffered were asked how it happened that the articles had been taken without awakening them, and the answer was, "That since the government settlement had been made, none in the village ever thought of fastening up their houses at night, considering themselves in perfect security." The population of Candeish is given under the article BOMBAY.

A circumstance which can scarcely fail to attract the attention of the traveller in this district, is the frequent intersection of his route by excellent cart-roads. Candeish in a remarkable degree enjoys the advantage of cart-traffic. Independently of the great arteries which traverse the province from the Chandore to the Sautpoora range, from Malligaum to the confines of the Daung, on the line to Surat, and from Malligaum and Dhoolia to Sowda and Asseerghur, many districts enjoy the advantage of a passable and often an excellent cart-road from village to village, throughout their entire extent. That portion of the main Bombay and Agra road which traverses this collectorate is in excellent order; that from Malligaum to Surat is in tolerable condition, though the extent of traffic on it has not been considered sufficient to warrant any great outlay in its constant repair. The road from Malligaum and Dhoolia to Sowdah, leading to Asseerghur and the Berar provinces, which has been marked out and cleared, is a good fair-weather road, though heavy after much rain. The province will also be traversed by one of the lines of the Great Indian Peninsula Railway Company. The collectorate abounds with fine cattle; and carts of an improved construction, for the transit both of goods and travellers, are in general use. The introduction of these, like the improvement of the roads, has been the work of government. Horses and camels are rare. Among the experimental sheep-farms established by government in different parts of the territory subject to the presidency of Bombay, with a view to the improvement of the native breeds, and the production of wool of superior character, was one in this province; but it shared the fate of the rest, on the results appearing unsatisfactory, and in 1847 was abolished.

The earliest mention of Candeish in authentic history is probably that by Ferishta, who states that in the year 1370 a great part of it was granted in jaghire by Feroze Toghluk, padshah of Delhi, to Mullik Raja, an adventurer, whose power so rapidly grew, that in a few years he had an army of 12,000 horse, and levied contributions extensively in Malwa and Rajpootana. Mullik, dying in 1399, was succeeded by his son Mullik Nusseer Khan, who by a vile and sanguinary stratagem acquired the strong hill-fort Asseerghur; but his ambition inducing him to enter on undertakings above his strength, his affairs were brought to utter ruin, and in 1437 he died broken-hearted. He was succeeded by his son Meeran Adil Khan, who sat on the throne till 1441, when he was assassinated by his son. Meeran Moobarik Khan then succeeded; and he dying in 1457, the throne passed to his son Adil Khan, under whose rule Candeish is said to have attained its greatest prosperity. Of this there are many monuments, and among them the remains of the citadel and of several magnificent palaces in Borehaunpoor survive. Candeish was, however, obliged to yield tribute to Mahmund Shah, of Guzerat. Adil Khan died in 1503, and was succeeded by his younger brother, Daud Khan; who dying in 1510, his son Ghizing Khan was placed upon the throne, but fell by poison after a reign of only two days. The direct line of the family failing, a relative, named Alam Khan, was raised to the throne, but displaced by a rival, Adil Khan, the grandson of Nusseer Khan, who was supported by his maternal grandfather, the king of Guzerat. Adil Khan died in 1520. To him succeeded his son Meeran Mahomed, who, on the throne of Guzerat becoming vacant, was raised to it by the chief people of that state, but died in 1535, not long after his elevation, and was followed on the throne of Candeish by his brother Meeran Moobarik, who was, however, excluded from the throne of Guzerat. In his reign, the forces of Akbar, emperor of Delhi, expelled Baz Bahadur, king of Malwa, from that country, and pursuing the fugitive into Candeish, sacked the great and wealthy town of Borehaunpoor, but were soon after attacked and routed with great slaughter by Moobarik, who died in 1566, after a prosperous reign of thirty-two years. He was succeeded by his son Meeran Mahomed Khan, who died in 1576, after a perilous and troubled reign. His death made way for his brother Raja Ali: this prince, joining his forces with those of Murad Marza, son of Akbar, was in 1596 killed in battle waged against the king of Ahmednuggur. His son Bahadar Khan filled his place until, defying the power of Akbar, he was besieged by the forces of the emperor in Asseerghur, and after a long blockade, being obliged to surrender, was in 1599 sent prisoner to the fortress of Gwalior, and his kingdom, under the denomination of Dandis, reduced into the form of a province of the realm of Delhi. Shah Jehan in 1634 made a new arrangement, adding some districts to Candeish, and constituting the whole a soobah or province of his empire. During the fierce contests for power and dominion between the families of Holkar and Scindia, at the close of the eighteenth and the commencement of the present century, Candeish was reduced nearly to the state of a desert by the predatory troops of Jeswant Rao Holkar; and on the final overthrow of the Peishwa in 1818, it was annexed to the British dominions.

CANDEYAN.—A town in the territory of Mysore, under the administration and control of the government of India, distant N.W. from Seringapatam 101 miles. Lat. 13° 23′, long. 75° 36′.

CANE, a river of Bundelcund, rises among the hills on the southern frontier, towards the Saugor and Nerbudda territory, at an elevation of 1,700 feet above the sea, and in lat. 23° 54′, long. 80° 13′. It first takes a north-easterly course, and at Pipereah Ghaut, in lat. 24° 15′, long. 80° 23′, about thirty-five miles from its source, it forms a cataract falling over the northern brow of the Bandair range. It then takes a westerly direction, and, flowing parallel to the base of the range, receives in succession the Putna and the Sonar, joining it on the left side; the Meerhausser, on the right side; and still lower down the Oormel and the Chundrawul, on the left side. The course is generally northerly, inclining to the east; and after running 230 miles, it falls into the Jumna on the right side, at Chilatara, in lat. 25° 47′, long. 80° 35′. It has numerous rapids, and in some places cataracts; according to Jacquemont, some not less than 300 feet high; and altogether, "the bed of the river is too rocky for all the efforts of art or labour ever to render it navigable. It is well stocked with a great variety of fish, and the pebbles which are found in its bed are so exquisitely beautiful as to be in great request for ornaments." They are, however, merely water-rolled fragments of basalt. Though the river cannot be rendered navigable at all seasons, small craft of little draught proceed in the rainy season from the Jumna as far up as the town of Banda, a distance of thirty-five miles. The water of this river is by the natives considered unwholesome.

CANISTERS, the name given to three islands of the Mergui Archipelago, lying in the course of vessels approaching the harbour of Mergui from Calcutta. The Great Canister, the largest of the three, is in lat. 12° 56′, long. 98° 19′.

CANKJARA, in the British district of Goalpara, lieut.-gov. of Bengal, a town 15 miles from the right or northern bank of the river Brahmapootra, 29 miles N. W. of Goalpara. Lat. 26° 23′, long. 90° 17′.

CANNANORE, in the British district of Malabar, presidency of Madras, a seaport town and British military cantonment, situate on the north shore of a small bay, open to the south, but sheltered on the west, or towards the Arabian Sea, by a bluff headland running north and south, and surmounted by a fort and some other buildings, which render it easily distinguishable at sea. Ships may anchor abreast of the fort in five or five and a half fathoms water; but a close approach is dangerous, as the water shoals, with rocky bottom, on which some fine ships have been wrecked. It is a populous place, but very irregularly built; yet has many good houses, especially that of the Moplai or Mussulman family, proprietors of the town. This residence is described by Buchanan as large, and one of the best native houses which he had seen. The possessions of the Moplai proprietor of Cannanore are confined to the town and a small tract about two miles round it on every side. For these possessions an annual rent of 14,000 rupees is paid to the East-India Company. Some of the Laccadive islands are also subject to this family; yet so scanty withal is their revenue, that they are compelled to resort to commerce, and carry on trade with Arabia, Bengal, Sumatra, and some other places; the customs of Cannanore are, however, all received by the East-India Company. A proposal has been recently made to the Beebee for the transfer to the British government of the Laccadive islands, in consideration of a pecuniary equivalent. It is a port of considerable trade, principally in pepper, grain, timber, and cocoanuts; vast quantities of the last of which are exported to the countries northwards, where none are produced. The soil and climate in the vicinity are peculiarly favourable to the growth of this species of palm, which is so abundant that the whole country in every direction appears covered with forests of it. The British cantonment is situate close to the seashore, and to the north-west face of the fort, which, since its acquisition by the East-India Company, has been improved and strengthened according to regular rules of fortification. The cantonment has barracks for a European regiment and two native regiments, and a regiment of native foot artillery, with an extensive and well-arranged hospital. There is a jail here. Cannanore is a place of great antiquity; but the present Moplai family acquired it at a comparatively late period, by purchase from the Dutch, who had wrested it from the Portuguese. On the invasion of Malabar by Hyder Ali, in the year 1768, he found ready submission and aid from Ali Raja, the Moplai chief of Cannanore. In the year 1784, in the war with Tippoo Sultan, it was garrisoned by the British; but on the conclusion of the treaty of Mangalore, was given up to the Moplai family. It soon fell into the hands of Tippoo Sultan; and in the year 1791, having been besieged by a British force under General Abercromby, it was, after a brief resistance, unconditionally surrendered; since which time it has been the principal British station in Malabar. Distance from Mangalore, S.E., 79 miles; Bombay, S.E., 615; Cochin, N.W., 148; Bangalore, S.W., 168; Madras, S.W., 345. Lat. 11° 52′, long. 75° 26′.

CANOUJ.—See KUNNOUJ.

CANTALBAREE.—A town in the native state of Bhotan, distant N. from Rungpore 63 miles. Lat. 26° 36′, long. 89° 9′.

CAP.—An island "forming the west side of the Tavoy river's entrance. It is moderately high, bluff, covered with trees, and may be easily known by the cap, a small round bushy islet, bearing from it W. by S. about 1⅔ miles." Lat. 13° 32′, long. 98° 13′.

CAP ISLAND.—A small island, or rather rock, situate about a mile from the island of Ramree (coast of Arracan), on which coal has been discovered. The rock is constituted chiefly of sandstone, and runs up to a peak. The coal is found to the seaward point of the rock, and barely above high-water mark. It has never been worked. Lat. 19° 23′, long. 93° 32′.

CAPTAINGUNJ, or KAPTANGUNJ, in the British district of Goruckpore, lieut.-gov. of the N.W. Provinces, a town on the route from the cantonment of Goruckpore to Bettiah, 22 miles N.E. of the former, 60 W. of the latter. According to Buchanan's description of it at the time of his survey, forty years ago, it "contains about 250 houses, or rather huts; but some of them are tiled; and for its size it carries on a good deal of trade." Distant N.W. from Dinapore 115 miles. Lat. 26° 56', long. 83° 42'.

CAPTAINGUNJ, or KUPTAIN GUNJ, in the British district of Goruckpore, lieut.-gov. of the N.W. Provinces, a small town on the route from the cantonment of Goruckpore to Lucknow, 55 miles W. of the former. Buchanan describes it as having "only twenty-five shops." Lat. 26° 46', long. 82° 34'.

CAPTAINGUNJ, or KUPTAINGUNJ, in the British district of Azimgurh, lieut.-gov. of the N.W. Provinces, a town on the route from the town of Azimgurh to that of Secrora, in Oude, and 12 miles N.W. of the former. Lat. 26° 12', long. 83° 4'.

CARAGOLA, in the British district of Purneah, lieut.-gov. of Bengal, a town on the left bank of the river Ganges, 30 miles S. of Purneah. Lat. 25° 20', long. 87° 25'.

CARAMNASSA.—See KURUMNASSA.

CARANGOOLY, in the British district of Chingleput, presidency of Madras, a town on the route from Madras to Trichinopoly, 49 miles S.W. of the former. It was taken by surprise by a British force under Captain Davis, in 1780. Lat. 12° 32', long. 79° 57'.

CARANJA ISLE.—See KARANGA.

CARIHULLY.—A town in the territory of Mysore, under the administration and control of the government of India, distant E. from Seringapatam 56 miles. Lat. 12° 26', long. 77° 33'.

CARLEE.—See KARLEE.

CARNATIC.—A division of Southern India. Its limits were probably at no time very accurately defined. According to Rennell, it anciently comprised all that part of the peninsula which lies south of the Gundlacama river, and of the river Tumbudra, from the coast of Coromandel eastward, to the Western Ghauts on the opposite coast. These limits would comprise the present territory of Mysore, Poodoocottah, and the British districts of Bellary, Cuddapah, Nellore, Chingleput, North and South Arcot, Salem, Coimbatoor, Trichinopoly, Madura, Tanjore, and Tinnivelly. According to Wilks, the ancient name of the Carnatic was Canara; and the "Canara language is only found within a district bounded by a line beginning near the town of Beder, about sixty miles north-west of Hyderabad, waving south-east by the town of Adoni; thence by Anantpore and Nundidroog, along the Eastern Ghauts, to the pass of Gujjelhutty; thence by the chasm of the Western Hills between the towns of Coimbatoor, Palatchi, and Palgaut, northwards, along the skirts of the Western Ghauts, to the source of the Kistna; and thence eastward to Beder." The tract thus defined appears in the first instance to have been comprised within the boundaries of the Hindoo kingdom of Carnata or Bijganagar. Upon the subversion of this monarchy, its territory was partitioned between the Mahomedan kingdoms of Beejapore and Golconda; and upon the annexation of these realms to the empire of Delhi, in the reign of Aurungzebe, the whole of the Carnatic merged into the soubah of the Deccan. By Hamilton, the Carnatic is said to commence at the south frontier of Guntoor, and to extend to Cape Comorin; and this writer ascribes to it an average breadth of only seventy-five miles. By Hamilton also it is divided into the Southern, the Central, and the Northern Carnatic. The first name is by him assigned to the country south of the river Coleroon, which comprises the native state of Poodoocottah and the British districts of Tinnevelly, Madura, part of Trichinopoly, and Tanjore. To the Central Carnatic he assigns the country between the Coleroon and the Pennar rivers, comprising the larger portion of the district of Trichinopoly, and the districts of North and South Arcot, Chingleput, and a section of Nellore. The Northern Carnatic he limits by the river Pennar on one extremity, and Guntoor on the other; including within it the remainder of Nellore. Modern custom seems to incline rather to Hamilton's view of the limits of the Carnatic, which may be understood to extend from lat. 8° 10' to lat. 16°, and from the sea on the east to long. 77° 20' on the west. This country was the theatre in which, during the last century, the French and English governments contended for mastery in India. The notorious Mahomed Ali bore the title of Nabob of the Carnatic; but in 1801 that title became merely nominal in his successors, the British government obtaining all actual power, of which indeed it had long exercised the chief portion. The last nabob dying in 1855 without heirs, the titular dignity of his house expired, and thus perished one more of the Mahometan dynasties of India.

CAROOR, in the British district of Coimbatoor, presidency of Madras, a town situate on the left or north bank of the river Ambrawutty, and on a gentle rising ground, near which are the ruins of a considerable fort, containing a large temple. Distance from Calicut, E., 160 miles; Mangalore, S.E., 256. Lat. 10° 58', long. 78° 9'.

CARRAREE, in the British district of Tirhoot, lieut. gov. of Bengal, a town on the route from Durbunga to Purneah, 32 miles E. of the former. Lat. 26° 7', long. 86° 29'.

CARRICAL.—See KARICAL.

CARUNAPALE, on the seacoast of the territory of Travancore, a small town at the northern extremity of an extensive inlet communicating with the Indian Ocean. Distance from Cochin city, S.E., 60 miles. Lat. 9° 16', long. 75° 28'.

CARWAR.—See CADAVAUD.

CASHMERE.—The name now given to the extensive tract of country in Northern India, constituting the dominions of Gholab Singh. It is bounded on the north by the Karakorum Mountains, separating it from Thibet, which also forms its eastern frontier; on the south by the British districts of Spiti and Lahoul, and by the Punjaub; and on the west by the Punjaub and the Huzareh country. It extends from lat. 32° 17′ to lat. 36°, and from long. 73° 20′ to 79° 40′; its extreme length from east to west being 350 miles, and its breadth about 270. The area is about 25,000 square miles, and the population has been estimated at 750,000. Within its limits are included the valley of Cashmere, the provinces of Jamu, Bulti or Iskardoh, Ladakh, Chamba, and others of less consequence. The more important among them form the subject of separate articles, which will be found under their respective names. The remainder of this notice will be restricted to a description of Cashmere proper. The valley of Cashmere is a tract inclosed by lofty mountains, having in the centre a level expanse, and in all other parts a very uneven surface, formed by numerous ridges and gorges, extending from the plain to the surrounding highlands. If its limits be considered as determined by the culminating ridge of the tortuous range of mountains which on every side inclose it, Cashmere will be found to be 120 miles long, from the Snowy Panjal on the south-east, to the Durawur ridge in the north; and sixty-five miles broad, from the Futi Panjal on the south, to Shesha Nag at the north-east. The superficial extent is about 4,500 square miles, or a little less than four-fifths of the size of Yorkshire. The shape of the outline is irregular, but has a remote resemblance to an oval. The tract thus defined lies between lat. 33° 15′—34° 35′, long. 74° 10′—75° 40′. Hügel estimates the plain forming the bottom of the valley to be seventy-five miles long and forty miles broad, having a superficial extent of about 2,000 square miles. The general aspect of Cashmere is simple and easily comprehended, it being a basin bounded on every side by lofty mountains, in the inclosing range of which are several depressions, called popularly passes, as they afford means of communication between the valley and the adjacent countries. In the middle is the extensive alluvial tract intersected by the Jhelum and its numerous tributaries, which flow down from the mountains, and are fed by the abundant snow and rains falling in those elevated regions. All these streams find their way by the sole channel of the Jhelum through the Baramula Pass, to the plain of the Punjab, in their course to the ocean. With the exception of one summit south of Bultul Pass, the elevation of the inclosing range falls far short of that attained by the summits of the Himalaya or of the Hindoo Koosh. The number of the passes into Cashmere over the mountains is very variously stated; by Abul Fazel at twenty-six, Ferishta at three, Elphinstone at seven. Hügel mentions twelve, and adds that the four following of these are practicable at all times of the year: 1. The Nabog, on the eastern frontier; 2. the Banihal, on the southern frontier; 3. the Baramula Pass, southwards, or Punch Pass, on the western frontier; 4. Baramula Pass, westward, or Dubb Pass, on the same frontier. Vigne enumerates twenty, and adds, that "an active mountaineer could enter the valley in many places besides the regular passes." Eleven of these passes are said to be practicable for horses. There is no carriage-way into the valley, but the Mogul emperors frequently brought elephants by the Pir Panjal Pass, or that through which the Bimber road lies. These huge animals, being wonderfully sure-footed and capable of making their way in difficult places, were used to convey the females of the household. The Sikhs invaded the valley through the Baramula Pass, and took with them a six-pounder, slung on poles and borne by thirty-two men at a time. That European skill and perseverance could make these passes practicable for artillery, cannot be doubted. When the Mogul emperor Akbar visited Cashmere in 1587, he appointed seven maleks, or chieftains, as hereditary wardens, one for each of the passes considered to be the most important, and allotted to each a revenue, from lands and villages, proportioned to the support of an armed force deemed requisite to defend the post committed to his care. The descendants of these maleks retain the titles, but their revenues and powers are now little more than nominal. The grandeur and splendour of Cashmirian scenery results from the sublimity of the huge inclosing mountains, the picturesque beauty of the various gorges, extending from the level alluvial plain to the passes over the crest of the inclosing range; the numerous lakes and fine streams, rendered often more striking by cataracts; the luxuriance and variety of the forest-trees, and the rich and multiform vegetation of the lower grounds. The attractiveness of the scenery, the mildness of the climate, and the fertility of the soil, make Bernier conclude that it was actually the site of the garden of Eden; and Abul Fazel describes it "as a garden in perpetual spring."

The zoology of Cashmere does not appear to be rich. Bears, both brown and black, are very numerous. They are said at particular seasons to descend from the mountains and rob the fruit-trees. The wolf is rare. Vigne mentions the hyæna, but doubts its existence. A panther, or sort of leopard, of a white colour with small black spots, is common in the mountains. The other beasts of prey are the jackal, fox, otter, mongoose or ichneumon, and stoat. A large and fine variety of stag occurs wild in the more retired valleys, and sometimes in severe weather great herds enter from the neighbouring wilds, and commit great havoc in the cultivated grounds. The gazelle, ibex, wild goat, musk-deer, and some other species of deer frequent the wilder parts. Though of inferior size, Hügel represents the horse as strong, lively, of great bottom, and very tractable. It is represented as amusing to see one of them mounted by a native, dash at a gallop across a shallow river, over the bed of which, covered with loose stones, no other horse could venture but with the greatest caution. Hügel has known these hardy creatures carry each a weight of 300 pounds during the course of a day nearly forty miles across the elevated pass of Pir Pinjal. The climate, in its effect on vegetation, is described by Jacquemont as wonderfully resembling that of Lombardy, and we consequently are not surprised at finding its flora bearing a strong affinity to that of Europe. Of the character of the vegetation, an accomplished naturalist, Dr. Royle, remarks, that there is "so great an extension of the herbaceous parts as well as of the flowers of plants, that many of them rival in luxuriance those of tropical climates." Of trees, the *deodar*, or Himalayan cedar, merits notice. Its botanical range extends from 7,000 to 12,000 feet above the level of the sea, and in its most congenial locality attains a great height and a circumference of above thirty feet. So durable is its timber, that some used in the building of one of the wooden bridges over the Jhelum was found little decayed, after exposure to the weather for above 400 years. The forests of Cashmere also contain the Pinus longifolia, and two other species of pine, a species of fir, one of yew, and one of juniper. The chunar (Platanus orientalis) is also considered an exotic, but is probably nowhere found more abundant or luxuriant than in Cashmere. By order of the Mogul emperors, a grove, composed of chunars and poplars, was planted in every Cashmirian village; and these, now arrived at their full growth, are among the greatest ornaments of the valley. Most of these are ascribed to the philanthropic governor of Cashmere, Ali Mirdhan Khan, who exercised his office under Shah Jehan from 1642 to 1657. So tastefully have they been disposed, that, according to Hügel, a judicious landscape-gardener could scarcely wish one to be added or removed throughout the whole valley. Hügel does not mention the oak. Dr. Royle states, on the authority of Falconer, "that few, if any, oaks descend on the northern side of the Pir Panjal into the valley." The maple, willow, and white thorn are common. Birch and alder trees approach the limit of perpetual congelation.

The most celebrated manufacture of Cashmere is that of shawls. The wool used for this purpose is of two kinds: one called pashm shal (or shawl-wool), and obtained from the tame goat; the other, the fleece of the wild goat, wild sheep, and other animals, named asali tus. In all instances it is a fine down, growing close to the skin under the common coat, and is found not only on the animals just mentioned, but also on the yak or grunting ox, and on the dog of the intensely cold and arid tracts of Tibet. The greater part is supposed to be produced in Chan Than, a tract in the west of Tibet, and is in the first instance sold at Rodokh, a fort near the frontier towards Ladakh, to which it is conveyed on the backs of sheep, there usually employed as beasts of burden. It is purchased by the Cashmirians at Le, the chief place of Ladakh, and carried thence to Cashmere, either on men's shoulders or on the backs of horses. There is also some brought by Moguls from Pamir, or from the vicinity of Yarkund. There is much division of labour in this manufacture: one artisan designs the patterns; another determines the quality and quantity of the thread required for executing them; a third apportions and arranges the warp and woof (the former of which is generally of silk) for the border. Three weavers are employed on an embroidered shawl, of an ordinary pattern, for three months; but a very rich pair will occupy a shop for eighteen months. Of late years the annual value of the shawl-manufacture of Cashmere has been declining, the decay of this branch of trade being attributable to several causes. In Hindostan, British officers have to a great extent superseded the class of natives with whom this sort of manufacture was in chief demand. The reduced prosperity of the Ottoman and Persian nations has also greatly contracted the supply to those quarters. In Europe the taste for these costly articles is on the wane, and generally throughout the world shawls of British manufacture are displacing those of Cashmere. The essential oil, or celebrated attar of roses, made in Cashmere, is considered superior to any other; a circumstance not surprising, as, according to Hügel, the flower is here produced of surpassing fragrance as well as beauty. A large quantity of rose-water twice distilled is allowed to run off into an open vessel, placed over-night in a cool running stream, and in the morning the oil is found floating on the surface in minute specks, which are taken off very carefully by means of a blade of the sword-lily. When cool it is of a dark-green colour, and as hard as resin, not becoming liquid at a temperature below that of boiling water. Between 500 and 600 pounds weight of leaves are required to produce one ounce of the attar.

The greater part of the population are Mahometans, of whom the Sunis, or those considered the orthodox class, are much more numerous than the Shias, or votaries of Ali. The population of the valley is calculated at present not to exceed 200,000 persons, to which number it has been in thirty years reduced from 800,000 by the awful dispensations of earthquake, pestilence, and famine. In 1828 a dreadful earthquake destroyed 1,200 persons, and was in two months followed by the cholera, by which 100,000 perished in the course of forty days. In 1833 an unseasonable fall of snow caused the failure of four-fifths of the rice-crop. The roads were covered with the corpses of those who perished of want in attempting to emigrate. Parents frequently sold a child for a rupee, to prolong existence for two or three days; mothers killed and devoured their own offspring. Pestilence followed; and from these successive calamities resulted the almost unexampled depopulation stated above. The population of the capital, Serinagur, which was estimated by Elphinstone at from 150,000 to 200,000, is now not more than 40,000. The other towns, besides the capital, are Islamabad, Shupeyon, Pampur, Sopur, Bijbahar, Baramula, Shahbad.

The early history of Cashmere, which lies rather within the province of the oriental antiquarian than the limits of the present work, has been drawn from darkness, and methodized by the varied learning and cultivated judgment of Professor Wilson. Still there is much uncertainty regarding it until the reign of Shumsud-Din, who ascended the throne in 1315, and introduced Mahometanism. In 1586 the country was conquered by the Mogul emperor Akbar, and became an integral part of his vast empire. In 1752 it was subjugated by the Afghan Ahmed Shah, the founder of the Durani empire, and remained under Afghan sway until 1819, when it was conquered by the Sikhs. From that time it was ruled by a governor appointed by the maharajah of the Punjaub until the year 1845. An unprovoked aggression on the British territory by the Sikh army, in the month of December of that year, led to hostile operations, which resulted in the occupation by the British of Lahore, where a treaty was concluded, under which the hill-country between the Beas and the Indus, including the province of Cashmere, was ceded to them as indemnification for the expenses of the war. The larger portion of this territorial cession was at once transferred, in independent possession, to its present ruler, Gholab Singh, in consideration of a pecuniary equivalent. By the terms of the treaty, Gholab Singh acknowledges the supremacy of the British government, and binds himself to assist them with troops, under certain contingencies; in return, he is to be aided in defending himself from his enemies. According to the returns of 1848, the military force maintained by the ruler of Cashmere consisted of 1,200 artillery, 1,972 cavalry, and 20,418 infantry, exclusive of an irregular force furnished by his feudal chiefs; but an intimation had been received by the British government of his intention, at a fitting opportunity, to effect a reduction in the strength of his army.

CASIMABAD, in the British district of Ghazeepoor, lieut.-gov. of the N.W. Provinces, a town on the route from Ghazeepoor to Goruckpoor, 15 miles N. of the former. Lat. 25° 45′, long. 83° 43′.

CASSAWARUM PETTA, in the British district of North Arcot, presidency of Madras, a town five miles N. of the projected line of railroad from Madras to Menil, 10 miles N.E. of the latter. Lat. 13° 10′, long. 79° 41′.

CASSEAHGOW.—A town in the native state of Nepal, distant N. from Jemlah 25 miles. Lat. 29° 40′, long. 81° 49′.

CASSERGURJE, in the British district of Mymunsing, lieut.-gov. of Bengal, a town on the left bank of the Brahmapootra, 25 miles S.E. of Jumalpore. Lat. 24° 47′, long. 90° 26′.

CATCHOOA, in the British district known as the Soonderbunds, lieut.-gov. of Bengal, a town on the route from Backergunje to Jessore, 32 miles W. of the former. Lat. 22° 37′, long. 89° 52′.

CATMANDHOO.—See KHATMANDOO.

CATTYWAR.—See KATTYWAR.

CAUDWIN.—A town in Nagpore, distant N.W. from Bustur 28 miles. Lat. 19° 24′, long. 81° 36′.

CAULY NUDDY.—A river of Western India, rising in lat. 15° 33′, long. 74° 47′, in Belgaum, twenty miles north-west from the town of Dharwar, and flowing southerly for eleven miles, through the collectorate of Belgaum, and fifty miles through that of North Canara, it turns west, in which direction it flows for thirty miles, and falls into the Indian Ocean near the town of Sedashevaghur, in lat. 14° 51′, long. 74° 11′.

CAUSERGODE, in the British district of South Canara, presidency of Madras, a town on the route from Mangalore to Cannanore, 26 miles S.E. of the former. Lat. 12° 30′, long. 75° 3′.

CAUVERIPURAM, in the British district of Coimbatoor, presidency of Madras, a town on the right bank of the Cauvery, 80 miles N.E. of Coimbatoor. Lat. 11° 54′, long. 77° 48′. The pass of Cauveripuram, which is thirty miles in length, winding through two lofty ranges of mountains, was traversed in 1799 by the detachment under Colonel Read on the march to Seringapatam.

CAUVERY, a river of Southern India, rises in the British district of Coorg, in lat. 12° 25′, long. 75° 34′, and taking an easterly direction for thirty-three miles, turns north-east for eight miles, at which point it touches on the territory of Mysore, and for twenty miles forms its boundary towards Coorg, still flowing north-easterly. It then enters Mysore, through which it flows in a direction generally south-easterly for ninety-five miles, to Tullacaud, from whence, its course being first north-easterly, and subsequently easterly, it becomes the bounding line between the Mysore territory and that of the British district Coimbatore for forty miles, when it finally leaves Mysore. Taking a direction south-east for forty-seven miles, it then makes its way, at the pass of Caveripuram, through the range of the Eastern Ghats, and continues to hold a course generally southerly for forty-seven miles, to Yirodu, where it turns south-east. It subsequently turns east, and after a further course of ninety miles to the vicinity of Trichinopoly, divides into several streams, embracing a delta seventy miles in length from the apex to the sea, and having a base of eighty miles. The most considerable branch is the Coleroon, the course of which is the furthest to the north. The length of the Coleroon is ninety-two miles, and the length of course from the source of the parent river, in Coorg, to the mouth by which the Coleroon enters the sea, is 472 miles. The branch which continues to bear the name of the Cauvery is of inferior magnitude, much of its volume of water being drawn off to irrigate the neighbouring lands. The principal tributaries of the Cauvery are the Hennavutty, flowing from the north-west, and joining it on the left side close to Kistnarajpoor; the Lechman-Teert, which, flowing from the south-west, joins it about eight miles lower down, but on the opposite or right side; the Cubbany, a considerable stream, also flowing from the south-west, and joining it on the right side; the Shimska, flowing from the north, and joining it on the left side; the Arkavati, flowing also from the north, and joining it on the left side; the Bhowani, descending from the Neilgherry group, flowing east, and falling into it on the right side; the Noyel river, running a course nearly parallel to that last mentioned, and joining the Cauvery on the right side; the Ambrawutty, which, flowing north-east, falls into the Cauvery on the right side. There are many others of less importance, and which, though large and rapid during the monsoon rains, are at other times totally or nearly devoid of water. Such is the case with the Cauvery itself in the low country during March, April, and part of May; but, replenished by the south-west monsoon, the volume of water early in July becomes considerable, and in August the inundation is great. The course of the Cauvery is over an extensive and generally barren surface of granitic rocks, with scarcely any woods or jungle on its banks. It consequently brings down no vegetable alluvium, but a rich clay, rendering the plains of Tanjore the most fertile portion of the south of India. During the inundation, the river is navigable through the low country for craft. Those in use are represented to be "circular baskets, from nine to fourteen feet in diameter, covered with buffalo leather." In these cotton, sandal-wood, saltpetre, and other wares, are brought down the river; and as the violence of the current precludes their upward navigation, they are taken to pieces, the basket-work abandoned, and the leather taken back on men's heads. The Cauvery passes from the tableland of Mysore to the low country by two falls; the upper, or that of Gungan Zooka, being 370 feet; the lower, or that of Burr Zooka, 460. During the periodical inundations, the vast body of water and enormous falls, combined with the sublime scenery adjacent, render these cataracts inferior to none in grandeur. Various public works connected with the Cauvery have of late years been undertaken by the government. An expenditure estimated at 50,000*l.* was sanctioned in 1841, for completing certain annicuts or dams thrown across the river, to collect the waters for purposes of irrigation; and a sum of between 2,000*l.* and 3,000*l.* at a later period was assigned to the construction of a bridge over the river at Frazerpet, being on the main line of communication between Bangalore and the western coast.

CAUVERYPAUK, in the British district of North Arcot, presidency of Madras, a town situate on the route from Madras to Arcot, and in the midst of a fertile district, artificially irrigated by means of one of the most magnificent tanks in the south of India, 11 miles E. of the latter. Lat. 12° 54′, long. 79° 33′.

CAUZEE, in the British district of Silhet, lieut.-gov. of Bengal, a town on the south or left bank of the Soormah river, 10 miles W. of Silhet. Lat. 24° 54′, long. 91° 42′.

CAWNPORE, under the lieut.-gov. of the N.W. Provinces, a British district named from its principal town. It is entirely within the limits of the Doab, extending from the Jumna to the Ganges, the latter river forming its north-eastern boundary, and dividing it from the territory of Oude; the former, the south-western boundary, separating it from the British districts of Humeerpoor and Calpee, and from the Bundela state of Bownee. On the north-west it is bounded by the British districts Etawah and Furruckhabad, on the south-east by the British district Futtehpore. Cawnpore lies between lat. 25° 55′ and 27°, long. 79° 34′—80° 37′; is seventy-five miles in length from north to south, and sixty-five in breadth; and has an area of 2,337 square miles. The population in 1853, as ascertained by actual enumeration, was 1,174,556; of whom 1,085,132 were Hindoos, and 89,424 Mahometans. The following classification of towns and villages is furnished by official returns:—Number containing less than 1,000 inhabitants, 3,314; ditto more than 1,000 and less than 5,000, 214; ditto more than 5,000 and less than 10,000, 6; ditto more than 10,000 and less than 50,000, 1; ditto more than 50,000, 1; total, 3,536. The greater part of this district lies on the scarcely perceptible slope, extending westward or south-westward, from the slightly elevated crest of the Doab; and consequently the Urrund or Rhind, and the Kurun or Singur, the only streams of much importance, flow towards the Jumna, and ultimately discharge themselves into it. The Esun flows in a direction from north-west to south-east twenty miles, through the north-eastern angle of the district. The Pandoo traverses the whole district in the same direction, and falls into the Ganges at the south-eastern corner. In addition to the means afforded by the Esun, the Jumna, and the Ganges (all of which are navigable in their course through this district), a farther channel of water-carriage will soon be opened in the prolongation of the Ganges Canal, which leaves that river on the right side, at Kan Khal, about two miles below Hurdwar, and, proceeding down the Doab, is intended to rejoin the main stream at Cawnpore. Besides the inclination of the surface of the country towards the Jumna, a general slope from north-west to south-east is indicated by the direction of the courses of the two great rivers in that direction.

Rice is scarcely cultivated, though some may be observed about the cantonment of Cawnpore, in the valley of the Esan, and a few other places; the alimentary crops being chiefly wheat, barley, maize, pulse, oil-seeds, sugar, and potatoes. Millet is cultivated, not so much for its grain, which is small and meagre, as on account of its straw, which is ten feet long, and an inch in circumference. Sugar-cane and maize thrive luxuriantly, growing to the height of eight or ten feet, and grow so closely as to exclude the light of the sun. Indigo, considered indigenous in this tract, and found wild in great luxuriance and of fine quality, is cultivated, but to no great extent; more land being now cropped for seed, which is exported, than for preparing the dye. The poppy, which has been but recently introduced, thrives well, and its culture is likely to contribute to the prosperity of the district. Safflower (Carthamus tinctorius) is also extensively cultivated for dyeing cottons a rose-colour. The cotton-plant thrives well, and is an important crop. An excellent judge on this subject says, "The cotton-plants which I saw in many places from Agra to Allahabad seemed more prolific than any which I have seen elsewhere." The soil and climate are well suited for producing fine tobacco, which is especially cultivated in the vicinity of Kanauj. Under the existing revenue settlement of the North-West Provinces, the lands of this district are not liable to any increased assessment on the part of government until the year 1870.

Schools in this district are numerous. The scholars are exclusively males, except in one of the missionary schools, called the Native Female Orphan Asylum, which contains fifty girls, who are maintained as well as educated. The schools are classed as Persian, Arabic, Hindee, Sanscrit, and English. It is stated that the desire for instruction has increased. This is attributed to the general encouragement afforded to education by government, as well as to a supply of useful vernacular books from the same quarter. In facilities of communication this district has many advantages. Besides those afforded by the great rivers, and the East-Indian line of railway, it possesses others in a number of excellent roads. The great trunk road connecting the north of India with the capital passes completely across the district: it is metalled and kept in admirable repair. From the city of Cawnpore to Calpee, there is another metalled road, completed about five years since. Besides these, the district is intersected in every direction by convenient roads, annually repaired at the close of the rains. While these prevail, the roads are in some places flooded, and consequently for a time impassable. To remedy this, bridges are gradually constructed as funds are available; the whole management of the roads (with the exception of the great trunk road) being vested in a committee composed of Europeans and natives. The great trunk road is under the charge of an officer of engineers.

The tract comprised within this district was, in 1195, subdued by the Mahomedans, under Shahabuddin Ghori. In 1529, Baber subdued and added it to his dominions; and in 1540 it was the scene of the arduous struggles of his son Humayon with the Patan chief Sher Khan, by the event of which the former was expelled from the sovereignty of Delhi, which passed over to his rival. In the dismemberment of the empire, in the eighteenth century, it came into the hands of Sufder Jung, nawaub of Oude. By the treaty of Fyzabad, concluded 1775, between the East-India Company and Asuf-ud-dowlah, the then nawaub of Oude, the former stipulated to supply a regular brigade for the defence of the latter, and Cawnpore was selected as the station of this force. Subsequently, in 1801, the subsidy stipulated by the nawaub for the maintenance of the auxiliary British force was commuted by the cession of the provinces of the Southern Doab and some others; and in virtue of this treaty, the tract comprised in the present district of Cawnpore was embodied with the territory of the East-India Company.

CAWNPORE, the principal place of the district of the same name, is situate in the pergunnah or subdivision of Jaujmau. The site is on the right bank of the Ganges, stated by Von Orlich to be here 500 yards wide in the season when the stream is lowest; when swollen by the periodical rains, in the latter part of summer, it was found to be about a mile wide, and very rapid; but on that occasion the river was unusually low, in consequence of the small quantity of rain which had fallen that season. The city covers an area of 690 acres, contains about 11,000 houses of all descriptions, and nearly 59,000 inhabitants. The population of the cantonments amounts to 49,975; making a total of 108,796, exclusive of the military. The commerce at the ghat or landing-place is busy and important, the Ganges being navigable downwards to the sea, a distance of above 1,000 miles, and upwards to Sukertal, a distance of 300. The scene is vividly described by Skinner:—"Every description of vessel that can be imagined was collected along the bank: the pinnace, which, with its three masts and neat rigging, might have passed for a ship; budgerows—the clumsiest of all clumsy things—with their sterns several times higher than their bows; and bauleahs, ugly enough, but lightly skimming along like gondolas, compared with the heavy craft about them; the drifting haystacks, which the country boats appear to be when at a distance, with their native crews straining every nerve upon their summits, and cheering themselves with a wild and not unfrequently a sweet song; panchways shooting swiftly down the stream, with one person only on board, who sits at the head steering with his right hand, rowing with his foot, and in the left hand holding his pipe. A ferry-boat constantly plying across the stream adds to the variety of the scene, by its motley collection of passengers — travellers, merchants, and faquirs, camels, bullocks, and horses, all crowded together. The vessels fastened to the shore are so closely packed, that they appeared to be one mass, and, from their thatched roofs and low entrances, might easily pass for a floating village." The commerce of Cawnpore must gain a great increase, on the completion of the navigable canal projected to proceed from it up the middle of the Doab, and rejoin the river on the right side, two miles below Hurdwar. The immediate environs of the place, though on a sandy plain, broken occasionally into ravines, are so much embellished by art as to have considerable picturesque beauty. "On the right bank of the Ganges, many hundred bungalows, the barracks of the troops, and the bazaars, extend in a semicircle for nearly five miles, which imparts to the whole a striking and splendid appearance." The bungalows or lodges of the officers and residents are large and commodious, and though either tiled or thatched, and individually, perhaps, unsightly, have, upon the whole, a striking and pleasing appearance amidst their *compounds,* or inclosures, which are usually handsomely planted. These *compounds* or gardens, intermixed with forest-trees, give the place a very luxuriant appearance during the season favourable to verdure. The gardens are considered some of the finest in India, and produce in abundance, and of excellent quality, most European vegetables, grapes, peaches, mangoes, shaddocks, plantains, melons, oranges, limes, guavas, custard-apples. In the centre of the cantonments, and on the highest ground, are two stone buildings, of very imposing exterior—the Assembly-rooms and the theatre. A church also was built some years since, when the government granted a sum of 5,000 rupees in aid of a private subscription, and allotted a piece of ground for its erection. In the cold season horse-races are held in an extensive piece of open ground to the north-west of the cantonments. The native town is ill built and dirty, yet has a pleasing appearance as seen from without. The bazaars are well supplied with the wares of Europe, China, and India; the jewellers are considered excellent workmen, and the place is celebrated for the manufacture of leather, and of the articles fabricated from that material. Butcher's meat, poultry, fish, and vegetables, are abundant and excellent, and game abounds; the feathered kinds consisting chiefly of quails, snipes, and wild ducks. During the hot winds ortolans come in such great flights, that fifty or sixty will drop at a single shot. In midwinter the cold at night is sufficient to freeze water exposed to the atmosphere in shallow earthen pans. The ice thus formed is carefully collected and stored in an ice-house, and the quantity obtained suffices throughout the year for the supply of the European families. In the dry season the friable nature of the soil causes the dust to be a very serious annoyance, especially during the exercising of troops. Bacon, describing a military review, observes, "Arriving upon the ground just after the evolutions had commenced, the only evidence I had of the military operations going forward was in the trampling of horses, the rattling of accoutrements, and the discharges of artillery; not one single man or horse of the whole martial array did I behold until after the display, and then a light breeze springing up, by great good-fortune, carried off the huge white curtain of dust which had hitherto hung over the scene." These exercises take place on an extensive piece of open ground adjoining the town, and on which, in the cool part of the year, corresponding to the midwinter of more northern climes, the infantry of the cantonment encamp. "Regular streets and squares of canvas stretch over an immense tract: each regiment is provided with its bazaar; in the rear and far beyond the lines, the almost innumerable camp-followers, of every description, form their bivouacs." The artillery encamp on another piece of ground, beyond some ravines. The cantonments are six miles long by about half a mile broad, and contain an area of upwards of ten square miles. These in themselves form a town, having a population of about 50,000, exclusive of the military and European gentry. There is accommodation for 7,000 troops. The climate does not appear to be complained of by the residents, as they assured Heber, "that, during the rains, it was a very desirable situation; that the cold months were remarkably dry and bracing; and that the hot winds were not worse than in most other parts of the Doab." It is said to be inferior in salubrity to Meerut, to which place it has been determined to remove the head-quarters of the artillery. Heber remarks, that "there are many handsome mosques, and the view of the town from the course gives quite the idea of a city;" and adds, "On the whole, it is in many respects one of the most considerable towns which I have seen in Northern India; but being of merely modern origin, it has no fine ancient buildings to show. The European architecture is confined to works of absolute necessity only, and marked by the greatest simplicity; and few places of its size can be named where there is so absolutely nothing to see." The importance of this place is, indeed, altogether of recent date, and resulting from its selection, in A.D. 1777, as a military cantonment by the British authorities. It does not appear to be mentioned by Baber in his narrative of military operations in the Doab, and it is passed over in the Ayeen Akbery. The first notice of it is perhaps that by

Rennell. The elevation above the sea is probably about 580 feet. The distance N.W. from Calcutta is 628 miles by land, 954 by water. From Delhi it is distant, S.E., 266 miles. Lat. 26° 29′, long. 80° 25′.

CEYLON.—A large and fertile island lying at the entrance of the Bay of Bengal, and separated from the continent of India by the Gulf of Manaar and Palk Strait. In strictness it does not fall within the compass of this work, which is intended to embrace only continental India, with such oceanic appendages as are under the government of the East-India Company. Ceylon is not under that government, but is subject to the colonial department of the British administration; an arrangement strongly opposed by that great Indian statesman the Marquis Wellesley, when it was first made. The extreme length of the island is about 270 miles; its breadth varies greatly, but the average is 100 miles. It lies between lat. 5° 56′ and 9° 46′, long. 79° 36′—81° 58′. The early history of Ceylon is mixed up with the mythological absurdity which distinguishes that of other eastern nations, and which, destitute of the beauty which pervades that of Greece and Rome, is not less repulsive than despicable. The Portuguese arrived here early in the sixteenth century. In the following they were succeeded by the Dutch, who contrived to expel their predecessors; but the permanent acquisitions of those nations were restricted to the maritime parts of Ceylon. During the war originating in the French revolution, the Dutch settlements fell to the British, in whose possession they have ever since remained. The centre of the island was occupied by the native kingdom of Candy. With that kingdom the British, in 1803, became embroiled; but the war was productive of neither honour nor advantage to either party engaged in it. It was most unsatisfactorily terminated by what has been termed "a tacit suspension of hostilities." A number of British prisoners had been massacred in cold blood; but all effort to obtain either redress or vengeance was discontinued. In 1815, however, the British government suddenly saw reason to change its course. A force despatched against the Candian dominions took possession of them almost without resistance, the movement being aided by the unpopularity of the ruling monarch with his subjects. Some disturbances a few years afterwards were very readily suppressed, as were others still more recent, occurring during the government of Viscount Torrington.

CHACHLA.—A town in the native state of Cutch, in political connection with the presidency of Bombay, distant N.W. from Bhooj 31 miles. Lat. 23° 36′, long. 69° 26′.

CHACHOWRA, in Gwalior, or the possessions of Scindia, a town on the route from Goonah to Mhow, 40 miles S.W. of former, 145 N.E. of latter. It has a good bazaar, and water is abundant from wells. In the early part of the present century it was taken by Baptiste, one of Doulut Rao Scindia's generals, and since that time has fallen into great decay. Lat. 24° 10′, long. 77°.

CHACHUR.—A town in the native state of Bahawulpoor, in political connection with the government of India, distant S.W. from Bahawulpoor 81 miles. Lat. 28° 53′, long. 70° 34′.

CHACHYE, in the territory of Rewa, or Baghelcund, a village on the direct route from Mirzapore to the diamond-mines of Panna, and 71 miles W. of the former. It is remarkable for a cascade of 362 feet, formed by the Beher, a stream which, three or four miles farther down, falls into the Tons. Elevation above the sea 990 feet. Lat. 24° 47′, long. 81° 21′.

CHACKI, in the British district of Mongheer, lieut.-gov. of Bengal, a town on the route from Mongheer to Raneegunge, 52 miles S. of the former. Lat. 24° 35′, long. 86° 26′.

CHAHIN, in the Rajpoot state of Jessulmere, a village on the route from the town of Bikaneer to that of Jessulmeer, and 62 miles N.E. of the latter. The inhabitants are notorious marauders, making frequent forays to carry off cattle and other plunder. It contains 100 houses, supplied with water from five wells 180 feet deep. Lat. 27° 13′, long. 71° 53′.

CHAHIR, in Sirhind, a village on the route from Hansi to Loodiana, and 68 miles N. of the former town. It is situate in a country slightly undulated in low sandy swells, and in some places overspread with jungle, but in general cultivated. Distance N.W. from Calcutta 1,044 miles. Lat. 30° 2′, long. 75° 59′.

CHAH-MAH.—A town in the British territory of Assam, inhabited by the Naga tribes, distant 90 miles S.E. from Nowgong. Lat. 25° 34′, long. 93° 52′.

CHAIBASSA, in the British district Singhbhoom, lieut.-gov. of Bengal, a town the seat of the civil establishment, and probably the only place in the district to which the name of town can with propriety be applied. There is a jail; and here also is stationed a detachment of the Ramgurh light infantry and some local horse. Distant S. from Hazaribagh 100 miles. Lat. 22° 36′, long. 85° 45′.

CHAIL, in the British district of Allahabad, lieut.-gov. of the N.W. Provinces, a town 13 miles W. of the city of Allahabad. It is situate in the pergunnah or subdivision of Allahabad, which from it is sometimes called that of Chail. Lat. 25° 25′, long. 81° 43′.

CHAKKI.—A river of the Punjaub, rising in lat. 32° 15′, long. 76° 5′, and falling into the Beas in lat. 31° 43′, long. 75° 33′.

CHAKSOO, in the Rajpoot state of Jeypore, a town on the route from Agra to Nusseerabad, 142 miles S.W. of former, 80 E. of latter. It is of considerable size, and has a bazaar. Lat. 26° 36′, long. 76°.

CHALA, in the British district of Sudiya, in Assam, lieut.-gov. of Bengal, a town four miles from the left bank of the river Brahmapootra, 40 miles E. of Sudiya. Lat. 27° 48′, long. 96° 22′.

CHALADOKPO, in Bussahir, a torrent of the district of Koonawur. It rises in Chinese Tartary, about lat. 32°, and after a north-west course of between twenty and thirty miles, falls into the Li, or river of Spiti, on the left side, in lat. 32° 2′, long. 78° 39′, at an elevation of about 10,600 feet above the sea. About three miles above its mouth Gerard crossed it on a sango or wooden bridge, sixty-one feet above the stream, which is there a rapid, violent mountain-torrent.

CHALAIN MEW, in Burmah, an old town on the route from Sembew Ghewn, in Burmah, to Aeng, in Arracan. Around it are the remains of a lofty brick wall, at some places fifty feet high. This town is said to have been built above 1,500 years ago. It was almost destroyed by fire during the first war with the Burmese. It contained 10,000 inhabitants, and is the capital of the district of Chalain. The country around is fertile, and highly cultivated, chiefly with rice. Lat. 20° 34′, long. 94° 32′.

CHAMBA.—A town in the southern division of the kingdom of Cashmere, or dominions of Gholab Singh, situate among the southern mountains of the Himalaya, on the river Ravee, at the foot of a lofty peak covered with snow. Its situation is very picturesque and beautiful. The number of houses is estimated at 1,000. They are built of wood, and ranged about a rectangular open space, 500 yards long and eighty broad. Chumba is the residence of the rajah of the neighbouring country. The population is probably about 5,000. It appears to have decayed since the time of Forster, who calls it Jumbo, and describes it as "a mart of the first note in this part of the country." The division of which this is the principal place is one of the provinces transferred by the British to Gholab Singh in 1846. Its area is 4,500 square miles. Lat. of the town 32° 29′, long. 76° 10′.

CHAMBURGOONDY, in the British district of Nassick, presidency of Bombay, a town on the route from Sholapoor to Seroor, 28 miles S.E. of the latter. Lat. 18° 38′, long. 74° 44′.

CHAMORERIL.—A lake in Ladakh, in the elevated table-land of Rupshu, situate between the valley of the Sutluj and that of the Indus, called by Trebeck, Tsummureri. It is 15,000 feet above the level of the sea, and is surrounded by mountains, which rise in some places 5,000 feet above the surface of the water. The general breadth is about two miles and a half; the length, which is in a direction from north to south, is about fifteen miles; the circumference about forty. The water is brackish, of a blue colour, and Trebeck conjectures it deep. Lat. 32° 55′, long. 78° 15′.

CHAMPAMUTTEE.—A river rising on the southern slope of the great snowy range of the Himalayas, in lat. 27° 58′, long. 90° 5′: it flows in a southerly direction for 120 miles through the native state of Bhotan, and twenty-five miles through the British district of Goalpara, and falls into the Brahmapootra on its north or right bank, in lat. 26° 11′, long. 90° 22′.

CHAMPANEER, in the British district of Ajmere, lieut.-gov. of the N.W. Provinces, a town on the route from Oodeypoor to Kishengurh, 40 miles S. of the latter. Lat. 26°, long. 74° 58′.

CHAMPANEER.—A hill fort of Guzerat, situate on an isolated rock of great height. The fortifications inclose a space about three-quarters of a mile in length and three furlongs in breadth; and within the inclosure are two forts, an upper and a lower. The upper is the smaller but stronger, being, according to the notions of the natives, impregnable. It contains a famous Hindoo temple, dedicated to the female divinity Kali. The lower fort is also very difficult of access, and in all respects of great natural strength, and contains some curious Hindoo monuments of remote antiquity. There are no other buildings within the fort but a small gateway, with apartments for a commanding officer; so that there appears to be no accommodation for a strong garrison; and when Captain Miles visited the place in 1812, the force holding it did not exceed 300 men. At the base of the mountain is a poor straggling town, containing about 2,000 inhabitants; but everywhere around, amidst the dense jungle, now infested with tigers and other wild animals, are the remains of temples, fine houses, good tanks, and mosques. Previously to the invasion of this part of India by the Mussulmans, Champaneer was held by a Chouhan succession of Rajpoot rajahs, the last of whom, stated to have 60,000 followers, was, after a blockade of twelve years, obliged to surrender to Mahmood, king of Guzerat, who reigned from 1459 to 1511. This event took place in 1484; and from the capture of this fort and that of Joonagarh, according to popular tradition, Mahmood received the surname of Bigarrah; "the number two in the Guzerat language being called *bi*, and the name of a fort *garrah*." The kings of Guzerat retained Champaneer until 1534, when Humayon, emperor of Delhi, in person surprised the fort, ascending the precipitous rock by means of great iron spikes driven into its face, and opening the gate, admitted the main body of his troops advancing to storm. On the dismemberment of the empire of Delhi, in the latter part of the eighteenth century, it was seized by the Mahrattas, and ultimately fell into the hands of Madhajee Scindia; but was so neglected by his successor, Dowlut Rao Scindia, that on the 17th of September, 1802, it surrendered to a small British detachment under the command of Colonel Woodington.

It was subsequently, with unaccountable facility, restored in 1803 to Dowlut Rao Scindia, by the treaty of Serjee Anjengaum. It is also called Pawangarh, from its exposure to the winds, in consequence of its elevation. Distant N. from Bombay 250 miles; E. of Mhow, *vid* Dhar, Bhopawar, and Baroda, 240. Lat. 22° 30′, long. 73° 30′.

CHAMPAPORE.—A town in the British district of Bograh, lieut.-gov. of Bengal, 16 miles S.W. of Bograh. Lat. 24° 43′, long. 89° 9′.

CHAMPAWUT, or KALEE KEMAON, in the British district of Kumaon, lieut.-gov. of the N.W. Provinces, a town near the south-eastern extremity of the district, containing about sixty houses. Though its elevation above the sea is considerable, it is surrounded by much higher grounds; so that it lies in a valley, which, during the rainy season, is under water for a considerable time; and hence the locality is very unhealthy at that season. On that account, the cantonment which was formerly at this place has been abolished, and the troops removed to Lohughat, six miles farther north. Elevation above the sea 5,467 feet. Distance N.W. from Calcutta, by Lucknow and Pillibit, 858 miles. Lat. 29° 20′, long. 80° 8′.

CHAMTANG.—A town in the native state of Nepal, distant E. from Khatmandoo 100 miles. Lat. 27° 50′, long. 86° 53′.

CHANAYAPALEM, in the British district of Nellore, presidency of Madras, a town on the route from Nellore to Ongole, 36 miles N. of the former. Lat. 14° 59′, long. 80° 6′.

CHANCE ISLAND.—One of the most southern islands of the Mergui Archipelago. "It has a high peak, that may be seen ten or twelve leagues off," and may be considered as one of the Aladin group. Lat. 9° 24′, long. 98° 1′.

CHANDA, in the British district of Bareilly, lieut.-gov. of the N.W. Provinces, a village on the route from Bareilly to Petoragarh, and 70 miles N.E. of the former. It is well supplied with water. Lat. 29°, long. 80° 5′.

CHANDAH, in the territory of Nagpore, a town on the south-western frontier, towards the territory of the Nizam, and situated on the left bank of the river Eraee, near its junction with the Wurda. It is of considerable extent, the walls being six miles round. Their direction is frequently broken, and they are surmounted by a high parapet. They are built of cut stone, are from fifteen to twenty feet high, and flanked with round towers, large enough for the heaviest guns. Within the place, and equidistant from the north and south faces, but nearer the eastern than the western wall, is a citadel; and the rest of the interior consists of straggling streets, detached houses, and plantations. Chanda is distant from the city of Nagpore, S., 85 miles; Hyderabad, N., 187; Madras, N., 480; Bombay, E., 430. Lat. 19° 57′, long. 79° 23′.

CHANDAN, in the British district of Bhaugulpore, lieut.-gov. of Bengal, a town 43 miles S.W. of Bhaugulpore, 95 miles N.E. of Hazareebagh. Lat. 24° 39′, long. 86° 41′.

CHANDAOS, in the British district of Allygurh, lieut.-gov. of the N.W. Provinces, a town the principal place of the pergunnah of the same name. It is on the route from Muttra to Meerut, and 46 miles N. of the former. It has a bazaar and a market, and is abundantly supplied with water. Lat. 28° 5′, long. 77° 55′.

CHANDEORA.—See CHANDSIRA.

CHANDERI.—See CHANDHAIREE.

CHANDERNAGORE.—A French settlement, with a small adjoining territory, on the right bank of the river Hoogly, and surrounded by the territory of the British district of Hoogly, presidency of Bengal. It is delightfully situate in the extremity of a recess of a beautiful reach of the river, the bank of which on this side is considerably more elevated than on that opposite. It has an air of ruined greatness, its fine quay, and well-built streets opening on it, being now overgrown with grass, and nearly devoid of life; while the ancient residence of the governor is in ruins, the present chief officer occupying a less-assuming residence. Adjoining the French town is the native one; a collection of huts and humble dwellings huddled together; among which are many Brahminical temples, having in front ghats, or flights of stairs, giving access, for the purposes of ritual ablution, to the waters of this most revered branch of the Ganges. The Hoogly here had formerly sufficient depth of water to allow the navigation of ships of the line. The French establishment here consisted in 1840 of four juridical or police officers, a medical officer, a chaplain, two military officers, and a sort of council of management. This petty territory consists of 2,330 acres, and contains some villages, as well as the town. The authorities at Chandernagore are subject to the jurisdiction of the governor, who resides at Pondicherry, and to whom is confided the general government of the French possessions in India. The total population is estimated at 32,670; of whom 218 are Europeans, and 435 of mixed descent; the rest of unmixed native lineage. In consideration of the revenue derived by the British government from the consumption of salt in Chandernagore, an annual payment is made to the local French authorities; and under an agreement executed in Paris by the British and French authorities, the limits of this settlement have been defined, whereby sundry obstacles which retarded the construction of a portion of the Calcutta Railway have been removed.

Chandernagore appears to have been in the occupation of the French as early as 1700, the year in which Calcutta first became a British settlement. Forty years later, while the metropolis of British India continued in a state of comparative insignificance, the French settlement, under the influence of Dupleix, had attained a high degree of opulence and splendour, and which it retained until its capture by Clive in 1757. France recovered Chandernagore, with the rest of her factories in India, under the treaty with England of 1763. It was again taken by the British in 1793, upon the breaking out of the republican war, and finally restored to its present possessors at the general peace of 1816. Distance from Calcutta, N., 17 miles. Lat. 22° 50′, long. 88° 23′.

CHANDERPOOR.—One of the districts in the British territory of Nagpore. Its centre is about lat. 20° 10′, long. 79° 40′.

CHANDGURH. — A town in the native state of Gwalior, or possessions of Scindia's family, distant S.E. from Indore 60 miles. Lat. 22° 16′, long. 76° 40′.

CHANDHAIREE, in the territory of Gwalior, or possessions of Scindia's family, a town in Malwa, in a hilly and jungly tract, yet with a considerable quantity of fertile ground. It is at present much decayed, in consequence of Mahratta oppression, the desolations of war, and the diminution of its manufactures, undersold by the cheaper fabrics of Britain; but the extent and number of its ruins, and architectural excellence displayed in them, indicate its splendour and importance in former ages, when, according to the Ayeen Akbery, it contained "fourteen thousand stone houses, three hundred and eighty-four markets, three hundred and sixty caravanseras, and twelve thousand mosques." The fort of Chandhairee consists of a strong rampart of sandstone, flanked by circular towers, and situate on a high hill, and was formerly considered impregnable. Nearly forty years ago it was taken by blockade, by Baptiste, one of Scindia's generals. Among many remains of former greatness is a pass, cut through a solid rock 100 feet high: it bears an inscription, stating that the lofty gate of Goomtee and Keroli, near the tank, was made in 1301, by order of Ghiyasuddin, sovereign of Delhi. During the period of the independence of Malwa, it was a place of great importance; and its chief, a feudatory of Mahmood Khilji, the king, having revolted, was besieged by that prince in Chandhairee, which surrendered after a siege of eight months. Rana Sanka, the formidable Rajpoot adversary of Baber, had wrested Chandhairee from Ibrahim, the Patan sovereign of Delhi, about the year 1526, and gave it in feudal grant to one of his followers. Baber, in 1528, coveting the place, vowed to wage a holy war against it; and entering it by escalade, the Rajpoots, after performing their fearful rite of juhar, by the massacre of all their women and children, rushed naked and desperately on the Mussulmans, until they were slain to a man. As already mentioned, Baptiste, Scindia's general, about the year 1816, took Chandhairee from the Boondela chief who at that time held it. With the surrounding territory, it, under Mahratta sway, became a haunt of freebooters, very troublesome to the neighbouring tracts under British rule or protection; and on the conclusion of the treaty of 1844, it was, among other lands, assigned for the maintenance of the increased Gwalior contingent, commanded by British officers. Distant S. of Gwalior fort 105 miles, S. of Agra 170, S. of Delhi 280, S.W. of Calpee 140. Lat. 24° 41′, long. 78° 12′.

CHANDIAH.—A town in the native state of Rewah, or province of Baghelcund, distant S.W. from Rewah 72 miles. Lat. 23° 39′, long. 80° 47′.

CHANDINA KOLLI, in the Damaun division of the Punjab, a town situated on the right bank of the river Indus, 32 miles S. of the town of Dera Ismael Khan. Lat. 31° 20′, long. 70° 49′.

CHANDIPOOR, in the district of Aldemau, territory of Oude, a fort situate on the right bank of the river Ghoghra, 40 miles S.E. of Faizabad, 115 E. of Lucknow. Lat. 26° 33′, long. 82° 45′.

CHANDKOH, in Sinde, a district stretching along the right bank of the Indus, between lat. 26° 40′—27° 20′, and long. 67° 25′—68°. It is intersected by the Narra, the great western offset of the Indus, and several other watercourses; it is level, and extensively flooded during the season of inundation. From the latter circumstance and the nature of the soil (a rich mud deposited by the river), it has a fertility scarcely anywhere exceeded. Under the Talpoor dynasty, it belonged to the Hyderabad ameers, and yielded a considerable proportion of their revenue. It is called Chandkoh from being principally held by the Belooche tribe of that name. Pottinger, who mentions it under the name of Chandookee, estimates the revenue derived from it by the ameers at 100,000*l.* per annum; but there can be little doubt that this is an exaggeration.

CHANDKOWTA, in the British district of Sholapoor, presidency of Bombay, a town 52 miles S. of Sholapoor, 29 miles E. of Beejapoor. Lat. 16° 56′, long. 76° 11′.

CHANDNA.—A town in the Rajpoot state of Joudpore, 82 miles S.W. from Joudpore, and 80 miles N.E. from Deesa. Lat. 25° 11′, long. 72° 47′.

CHANDNUGAR, in the British district of Moradabad, lieut.-gov. of the N.W. Provinces, a village on the route from the town of Moradabad to Meerut, and 27 miles W. of the former. Lat. 28° 52′, long. 78° 27′.

CHANDODE, in Guzerat, a town situate on the right bank of the river Nerbudda. Distance from Baroda, S.E., 30 miles. Lat. 21° 58′, long. 73° 30′.

CHANDORE, in the British district of Ahmednuggur, presidency of Bombay, a town on the route from Mhow to the local capital, 215 miles S.W. of the former, 148 N.E. of the latter. It is a flourishing place, and contains a population of about 7,000. Holkar holds the patelship of the town, and some of the family appear to have formerly resided here, in a magnificent building called the Rung Muhall, erected by them in the centre of the town. The fort is situate on a nearly inaccessible summit of one of the hills of the Chandore range, and commanding an important ghat or passage on the route from Candeisb to Bombay. Its natural strength is thus described by the British commander Wallace, to whom it surrendered in 1804 :—"The hill on which it stands, or rather which forms the fort, is naturally the strongest I ever saw, being quite inaccessible everywhere but at the gateway, where alone it is fortified by art, and where it is by no means weak. There is but one entrance of any kind." Restored by the subsequent capitulation with Holkar, it was, in 1818, surrendered to a detachment sent against it by Sir Thomas Hislop, in pursuance of its cession by Holkar, under the sixth article of the treaty of Mundisore. Distance from Hyderabad, N.W., 350 miles; from Nagpore, W., 330. Lat. 20° 20′, long. 74° 14′.

CHANDPOOR, in the British district of Bijnour, lieut.-gov. of the N.W. Provinces, a town on the route from Moradabad to Mosuffernuggur, and 42 miles N.W. of the former place. It is of considerable size, having a population of 11,491 persons. Distant N.W. from Calcutta 930 miles. Lat. 29° 8, long. 78° 20′.

CHANDPOOR, in Malwa, a town in the native state of Bhopal, distant E. from Bhopal 43 miles. Lat. 23° 24′, long. 78° 4′.

CHANDPOOR.—A town in the territory of Nagpore, distant N.E. from Nagpore 51 miles. Lat. 21° 31′, long. 79° 50′.

CHANDPOOR, in the British territory of Saugor and Nerbudda, lieut.-gov. of the N.W. Provinces, a town on the route from Saugor to Jubulpoor, 20 miles S.E. of former, 65 N.W. of latter. Elevation above the sea 1,575 feet. Lat. 23° 36′, long. 79° 3′.

CHANDPOOR, in Sirmoor, a peak in the mountains between the Giree and Tons rivers, and about four miles from the right bank of the latter. It it surmounted by a small Hindoo temple, which was a station of the large series of triangles in the trigonometrical survey of the Himalayas. Elevation above the sea 8,561 feet. Lat. 30° 43′, long. 77° 43′.

CHANDPOOR, in the territory of Gwalior, or dominions of Scindia, a small town or village on the route from Gwalior fort to Saugor, 38 miles S.E. of former, 162 N.W. of latter. It is situate on the left bank of the river Sindh, which has here a channel "about 200 yards wide, and sandy; breadth of stream in dry season forty yards, and from one and a half to two feet deep; banks steep and cut into deep ravines." Lat. 25° 51′, long. 78° 27′.

CHANDPOOR, or CHUNDUNPOOR, in the British district of Furruckabad, lieut.-gov. of the N.W. Provinces, a village on the route from Bareilly cantonment to that of Futtehgurh, and six miles N.E. of the latter. Lat. 27° 27′, long. 79° 42′.

CHANDPORE.—A town in the British district of Bulloah, lieut.-gov. of Bengal, 32 miles N.W. of Bulloah. Lat. 23° 16′, long. 90° 39′.

CHANDRA RIVER.—See CHENAUB.

CHANDRAGIRI.—See CHUNDERGERRY.

CHANDSIRA, or CHANDEORA, in the Rajpoot state of Joudpore, a village on the route from Balmeer to the city of Joudpore, and 39 miles E. of the former. It is situate on the southern boundary of the Little Desert, where it is terminated by the well-watered and fertile tract along the course of the river Loonee. It contains 100 houses, supplied with water from some shallow wells rudely excavated, and unprovided with brick lining. Lat. 25° 52′, long. 72° 2′.

CHANDSUMA.—A town in the province of Guzerat, or territories of the Guicowar, distant S. from Deesa 45 miles. Lat. 23° 37′, long. 72° 4′.

CHANDUN, in the Rajpoot state of Jessulmere, a village on the route from the town of Bikaneer to that of Jussulmere, and 24 miles N.E. of the latter. Lat. 26° 59′, long. 71° 20′.

CHANDWAR, in Malwa, a town in the native state of Bhopal, distant N.W. from Bhopal 26 miles. Lat. 23° 32′, long. 77° 9′.

CHANEE SOOPE, in the British district of Kumaon, lieut.-gov. of the N.W. Provinces, a village with a temple, on the route from Almora to Petoragarh, eight miles N.E. of the former. Lat. 29° 39′, long. 79° 48′.

CHANENI.—A town in the native state of Cashmere, or Gholab Singh's dominions, 75 miles S. from Sireenagur, and 30 miles N.E. from Jamoo. Lat. 33° 1′, long. 75° 18′.

CHANGAMAH, in the British district of South Arcot, presidency of Madras, a town 53 miles S.W. of Arcot, 61 miles N.E. of Salem. Lat. 12° 19′, long. 78° 51′.

CHANGO, in Bussahir, a collection of four hamlets in Koonawur, on the left bank of the Lee, or river of Spiti. It is situate in an alluvial plain, or rather on the level bottom of a valley, down which a stream holds its course and falls into the Lee. Lat. 31° 58′, long. 78° 38′.

CHANGREZHING, in Bussahir, a hamlet of Koonawur, near the north-eastern frontier, dividing that district from Chinese Tartary, is situate three miles east of the left bank of the Lee, or river of Spiti. It forms the remotest limit to the attempts of Europeans to penetrate into Chinese Tartary in this direction, as the Chinese population of the adjacent country to the eastward vigilantly and effectually interfere to prevent their progress. Close to this place Gerard was stopped by these people, who, however, showed a mild and hospitable disposition, insisting on his receiving some grain and a fat sheep, as marks of their good-will, and would receive no money in return. Elevation above the sea 12,500 feet. Lat. 32° 8′, long. 78° 40′.

CHANGSHEEL, or CHASHIL, in Bussahir, a lofty ridge of mountains, proceeding in a south-westerly direction from the Himalayan range, forming the southern boundary of Koonawur. Its crest forms the dividing limit between the waters of the Pabur to the west and those of the Rupin to the east. It stretches about twenty miles, between lat. 30° 56′—31° 20′, long. 77° 55′—78° 12′, and is traversed by numerous passes, having elevations of between 13,000 and 14,000 feet above the sea.

CHANIRGHUR, in the territory of Oude, a small town on the route from Allahabad to Lucknow, 24 miles N.W. of the former, 104 S.E. of the latter. Lat. 25° 40′, long. 81° 35′.

CHANMUHUN.—See CHOMOOA.

CHANPOOR.—A town in the native state of Nepal, distant S. from Khatmandoo 109 miles. Lat. 26° 52′, long. 85° 14′.

CHAOOPOOR, in the British district of Budaon, lieut.-gov. of the N.W. Provinces, a village on the route from Allygurh to Moradabad, and 37 miles N. of the former. It is situate near the left bank of the Ganges. Lat. 28° 20′, long. 78° 23′.

CHAORAS, in British Gurhwal, a village on a feeder of the Tons, and distant about six miles from the right bank of that river. It was a secondary station in the great trigonometrical survey of the Himalaya. Elevation above the sea 6,568 feet. Lat. 31° 2′, long. 78° 1′.

CHAPADONE.—A river of Tenasserim, rising in lat. 15° 45′, long. 98° 10′, and, flowing generally in a south-westerly direction for forty miles, falls into the Bay of Bengal in lat. 15° 33′, long. 79° 49′.

CHAPANER, in the British territory of Saugor and Nerbudda, a town on the right bank of the river Nerbudda, 30 miles S.W. of Hoshungabad. Lat. 22° 33′, long. 77° 20′.

CHAPEIRA.—A town in the native state of Rajgurh, distant N.W. from Nursingurh 44 miles. Lat. 23° 58′, long. 76° 28′.

CHAPORA, in the Portuguese territory of Goa, a town on the seacoast, 12 miles N.W. of Goa. Lat. 15° 36′, long. 73° 49′.

CHAPRA.—See CHRYAKOT.

CHARAMAEE, in Bussahir, a lake near the summit of the Burenda Pass, in lat. 31° 23′, long. 78° 11′, and at an elevation of 13,839 feet. It gives rise to the river Pabur, whose stream immediately precipitates itself over a ledge of rock in a curve of a hundred feet, and is instantly buried in the snows piled along its rugged course for a mile, when it reappears, gliding in crystalline brightness under arching vaults of snow. Above the lake, upon a ridge, is a massive bed of snow, at least eighty feet in thickness, which topples over, and will eventually fall into it.

CHARCHUT.—See CHARSHUT.

CHARCOLLEE.—A town in the British district of Backergunje, lieut.-gov. of Bengal, 23 miles S.W. of Backergunje. Lat. 22° 28′, long. 90°.

CHAREE.—A town in the native state of Bhotan, distant N.E. from Darjeeling 78 miles. Lat. 27° 39′, long. 89° 23′.

CHARGAON, in the British territory of Saugor and Nerbudda, lieut.-gov. of the N.W. Provinces, a town 80 miles S.W. of Jubbulpore, 76 miles E. of Hoshungabad. Lat. 22° 40′, long. 78° 56′.

CHARRATTA, in the Punjab, a small town in the Derajat, about 12 miles W. of the Indus, and nine miles W. of Dera Ghazee Khan. It lies in a low country intersected by canals from the Indus. Population about 1,000. Lat. 30° 3′, long. 70° 42′.

CHARSHUT.—A small district of Jareegah Rajpoots, in the north-western part of the province of Guzerat, situate between lat. 23° 45′ and 24°, and long. 71° 20′ and 71° 25′. Charshut pays a species of black mail to Radhunpore. The population amounts to about 2,500. It depends for protection on the British government. Its connection with that government commenced on the expulsion of the numerous hordes of plunderers from Guzerat in 1819; and subsequently, in 1826, an agreement was signed between the parties. The policy observed towards Charshut is that of non-interference with its internal affairs, the protecting government exercising control over the external relations only of the protected territory. The district is divided among four chiefs.

CHARUNG PASS, in Bussahir, traverses a mountain in the district of Koonawur. The ridge is a prolongation of the huge summit of Ruldung, and rises between the valley of the Buspa river and that of the Tidung. Its passage by Gerard, in the beginning of July, appears to have been one of the most adventurous, perilous, and arduous exploits anywhere recorded. Having departed from Shulpeea, in the valley of the Buspa, and at the highest limit of vegetation, and the elevation of 14,300 feet, he held his way sometimes amidst fragments, chasms, and precipices of gneiss, sometimes through loose or half-melted snow, in which the lower limbs sank to the thighs. He reached to where, "about the height of 16,300 feet, there commenced the perpetual snow in continuous beds; the next half-mile was also on a gentle acclivity over the snow, which gave way to the depth of two feet; and lastly we ascended the steep slope to the pass. It was scarcely half a mile, but it surpassed in terror and difficulty of access anything I have yet encountered. The angle was 37½°, of loose stones, gravel, and snow, which the rain had soaked and mixed together, so as to make moving laborious and miserable; and it was so nearly impracticable, that although I spread myself on all fours, thrusting my hands into the snow to hold by it, I only reached the crest by noon, and then under great exhaustion." The danger and horror of the scene were heightened by the incessant fall of great masses of rock, one of which, of immense size, bounded down the steep within a few feet of the traveller. At the crest of the pass the mercury of the barometer gave symptoms of congelation, losing its lustre and adhering to the cup and fingers, as if amalgamated. It snowed heavily all the way, and the traveller describes his sufferings as dreadful. "I actually thought at every step I should leave a foot in the snow; my hands had passed through the stages of torpor and freezing several times, and that reaction of returning warmth which you know is worse than the contact of solid ice." The crest of the pass has an elevation of 17,348 feet above the sea. Lat. 31° 24′, long. 78° 35′.

CHARUNG LAMA, in Bussahir, a pass on the north-eastern boundary of Koonawur, and on the route from Chang to Changrezhing, being about six miles from each. The rock formations in the vicinity are limestone and clay-slate, but the crest of the pass itself consists of pebbles, imbedded in clay, and bearing marks of the action of water, though the bed of the Spiti or Lee, the nearest river, is 3,000 feet below it. The pass is at the elevation of 12,600 feet above the sea. Lat. 32° 1′, long. 78° 38′.

CHARWAH.—A town in the native state of Gwalior, or possessions of Scindia, distant S.E. from Indore 80 miles. Lat. 22° 2′, long. 76° 56′.

CHASHIL PASS, in Bussahir, over the Changshil Chashil range, has an elevation of 12,870 feet. Lat. 31° 13′, long. 78° 3′.

CHASS, in the British district of Pachete, lieut.-gov. of Bengal, a small town or village on the route from Bankoora to Hazareebagh, 71 miles N.W. of former, 67 S.E. of latter. It has a bazaar. Lat. 23° 34′, long. 86° 12′.

CHATARI, in the British district of Allygurh, lieut.-gov. of the N.W. Provinces, a small town on the route from the cantonment of Allygurh to that of Moradabad, and 14 miles N.E. of the former. It is supplied with water from wells; has a bazaar, and is surrounded by a mud wall and ditch. Lat. 28° 6′, long. 78° 13′.

CHATELI.—A town in the native state of Sukhet (Trans-Sutlej territory), 10 miles S.W. from Sukhet, and 36 miles N.W. from Simla. Lat. 31° 28′, long. 76° 49′.

CHATMAY.—A village situate on the sea-coast of Arracan. About two miles from the shore are the small islands called North Round Island and Rocky Island, three miles distant from each other. Lat. 18° 50′, long. 94° 10′.

CHATNA.—A town in the native state of Nepal, distant N.E. from Khatmandoo 30 miles. Lat. 27° 58′, long. 85° 39′.

CHATNA.—A town in the British district of Pachete, lieut.-gov. of Bengal, eight miles N.W. of Bancoora. Lat. 23° 20′, long. 87°.

CHATOOR, in the British district of Tinnevelly, presidency of Madras, a town on the route from Tinnevelly to Madura, 47 miles N. of the former. Lat. 9° 21′, long. 77° 59′.

CHATRO.—A town in the native state of Cashmere, or dominions of Gholab Singh, 89 miles W. from Sirinagur, and 34 miles N.E. from Rawul Pind. Lat. 34°, long. 73° 30′.

CHATTUR, in the British district of Ramgurh, lieut.-gov. of Bengal, a town on the right bank of the Dammoodah river, five miles S.E. of Ramgurh. Lat. 23° 39′, long. 85° 36′.

CHATTWYE, or CHETWA, in the British district of Malabar, presidency of Madras, a town on an island or strip of land extending for twenty-seven miles, nearly from south-east to north-west, between lat. 10° 9′—10° 32′, long. 76° 6′—76° 17′, with a breadth varying from two to four miles. Wrested from the Portuguese by the Dutch, it was in 1776 taken from the latter by Hyder Ali, and ceded to the British, under the pacification of 1792, by his son Tippoo Sultan. Distance from Cochin, N.W., 41 miles; Calicut, S.E., 54; Madras, S.W., 340. Lat. 10° 32′, long. 76° 6′.

CHATUH, in the British district of Muttra, lieut.-gov. of the N.W. Provinces, a small town on the route from the cantonment of Muttra to Delhi, and 22 miles N.W. of the former. Here is a large fortress, of fine exterior appearance, but in the interior exhibiting nothing but decay. There is a bazaar in the town. Lat. 27° 43′, long. 77° 34′.

CHAUNDOO, in the Reechna Doaab division of the Punjab, a town situated on the left bank of the river Chenaub, 50 miles S.W. of the town of Ramnegurh. Lat. 31° 55′, long. 72° 59′.

CHAUNG LAMA.—See CHOUGBA PASS.

CHAWPARRAH, in the British district of Saugor and Nerbudda, a town on the route from Jubulpoor to Nagpoor, 67 miles S. of former, 89 N. of latter. It is situate on the north or left bank of the Wyne-Ganga, here passed by ford. Lat. 22° 24′, long. 79° 40′.

CHAWULPATA, in the British territory of Saugor and Nerbudda, lieut.-gov. of the N.W. Provinces, a town on the right bank of the Nerbudda river, 60 miles S.W. of Dumoh. Lat. 23° 3′, long. 79° 4′.

CHAYANAPOOR.—A town in the native state of Nepal, distant S.E. from Khatmandoo 50 miles. Lat. 27° 21′, long. 85° 59′.

CHAYANPOOR.—A town the chief place of a district of the same name, in the native state of Nepaul, distant E. from Khatmandoo 115 miles. Lat. 27° 20′, long. 87° 3′.

CHEBOO, in the British district of Bandah,

a town 56 miles E. of the town of Bandah, 43 W. of Allahabad. Lat. 25° 18′, long. 81° 11′.

CHEDING, CHADON, or SADING.—A village standing on a headland on the seacoast of Mergui, in lat. 11° 23′, long. 98° 45′. It has only been established of late years, and owes its origin to Commissioner Maingy, who induced a Malay chief with his followers to settle here, for the purpose of populating and cultivating the country.

CHEDOO.—A station on the top of the Youmadoung Mountains, on the road from Ramree to Burmah by the Talak Pass, distant N.E. from Aeng 50 miles. Lat. 20° 30′, long. 94° 24′.

CHEDUBA.—An island situate to the west of the coast of Arracan, and south-west of the island of Ramree. It was anciently called Inaon. When the Burmese took the province of Arracan, its name, from what reason does not appear, was changed to Mekawuddee, and it is now known by that at the head of this article. Cheduba constitutes part of the district of Ramree, and is subordinate to the jurisdiction of its functionaries. It lies between lat. 18° 40′—18° 56′, long. 93° 31′—93° 50′. It is about twenty miles from north to south, and seventeen from east to west, and contains an area of about 250 square miles. The climate of Cheduba is considered more favourable than that of Arracan; being an island, it has the advantage of the cool sea-breezes, and it is, moreover, generally free from the mists which prevail on the continent. The eastern quarter of the island is the least healthy, being less exposed to the sea, and the air being in some measure contaminated by that from the mainland. The general character of its soil is rich and productive. Rice, tobacco, cotton, sugar-cane, pepper, hemp, and indigo, are among the productions of the island; but the first-mentioned is the staple produce, being of excellent quality, and grown as well in the valleys as in the fertile plains, which extend round the hills to within a short distance of the beach. It is trodden out by buffaloes, and the husking is performed by a wooden mill, put in motion by two men, which it is said will clean about thirty maunds in a day. Hemp and indigo are cultivated to a more limited extent, as is also tobacco, which, however, is of excellent quality. The geology is said to afford some curious instances for study. Along the coast are situate numerous earthy cones, from whose summits are emitted mud and gas. The mineral productions of the island are various, but exist in small quantities. Specimens of copper, iron, and silver ore have been found; but the principal mineral production is petroleum. The mode of collecting it is remarkable. The spot where it is known to exist being fixed upon, a space of about twenty yards square is dug to a depth of two feet, which becomes filled with water. In a short time the surface of the pool is covered with oil of a greenish colour, which is skimmed off with bamboos, and put into pots. In the dry season the water disappears, and the opportunity is then taken of turning up the soil, which by this means yields an increased quantity of the article. The oil possesses a strong, pungent smell, and is a useful ingredient in the composition of paint, as it possesses the property of preserving timber from insects, especially the white ant. Trees do not abound: those which exist are limited for the most part to the hill tracts, where they attain considerable size. The trade, as may be imagined, is not extensive, the only articles exported being oil and rice. The amount of the latter is pretty considerable, and many vessels from the western shores of Bengal, from Sandoway, Ramree, and even Bassein, return laden with this article of merchandise. The extent of the population of the island has not been ascertained, but it probably amounts to above 9,000. The inhabitants are of the Mugh persuasion. They are quiet and peaceably inclined, simple, cheerful, contented, and possess many good traits of character. Their customs and habits so closely resemble their continental neighbours, that it will be needless again to notice them. An account will be found under the article "Arracan." Its history is also comprised under that of Arracan: with that province it fell into the possession of the Burmese in the latter part of the last century, and with it, in 1824, was relieved from Burmese oppressors, by its occupation by the English.

CHEEAPUT, in Sinde, a small town between Hyderabad and Khyerpoor, and 50 miles S. of the latter place. It is important as forming, with the contiguous town of Dingee, a commanding post in the communication of Khyerpoor and Emaum-Ghur with the part of the desert adjoining this last fort. Cheeaput is in lat. 26° 55′, long. 68° 20′.

CHEEARAH.—A town in the British district of Midnapore, lieut.-gov. of Bengal, 21 miles S.W. of Midnapore. Lat. 22° 15′, long. 87° 6′.

CHEECHAWUTNEE, in the Baree Dooab division of the Punjab, a town situated on the left bank of the Ravee river, 72 miles N.E. of the town of Mooltan. Lat. 30° 30′, long. 72° 39′.

CHEEHUN, in the British district of Tannah, presidency of Bombay, a town on the seacoast, 63 miles N. of Bombay. Lat. 19° 53′, long. 72° 43′.

CHEEKLEE, in the British district of Surat, presidency of Bombay, a town 34 miles S.E. from Surat, 120 miles N. of Bombay. Lat. 20° 42′, long. 73° 6′.

CHEELA, in the Rajpoot state of Joudpore, a village on the route from Jessulmere, *viâ* Nagor, to Nusseerabad, and 184 miles N.W. of the latter. It is supplied with good water from three wells 300 feet deep. The surrounding country is open and barren. Lat. 27° 2′, long. 72° 35′.

CHEEMPA.—A town in the native state of Bhotan, distant N.E. from Darjeeling 80 miles. Lat. 27° 36′, long. 89° 26′.

CHEEMULGA, in the British district of Sholapoor, presidency of Bombay, a town on the left bank of the Kistnah river, 30 miles S. of Beejapoor. Lat. 16° 22′, long. 75° 54′.

CHEERAEEDOONGORREE, in the British territory of Saugor and Nerbudda, lieut.-gov. of the N.W. Provinces, a town 58 miles S.E. of Jubbulpore, 58 miles N.E. of Seuni. Lat. 22° 25′, long. 80° 28′.

CHEERAKA.—A town in the native state of Cutch, presidency of Bombay, distant N.W. from Bhooj 27 miles. Lat. 23° 30′, long. 69° 25′.

CHEERTROREE.—A town in the native state of Cutch, presidency of Bombay, distant E. from Bhooj 58 miles. Lat. 23° 25′, long. 70° 36′.

CHEERUNG.—A town in the native state of Bhotan, distant E. from Darjeeling 100 miles. Lat. 26° 57′, long. 89° 56′.

CHEETAPOOR.—A town in the territory of Oude, 52 miles N. from Lucknow, and 69 miles E. from Futtygurh. Lat. 27° 35′, long. 80° 45′.

CHEETUL, in the peninsula of Kattywar, province of Guzerat, a town situate on the Tobi, a stream tributary to the river Sitronjee. Distance from Ahmedabad, S.W., 130 miles; Bombay, N.W., 220. Lat. 21° 44′, long. 71° 14′.

CHEHERUT, in the British district of Allygurh, lieut.-gov. of the N.W. Provinces, a village on the route from Allyghur cantonment to Moradabad, and four miles N.E. of the former. Lat. 27° 58′, long. 78° 9′.

CHELLOOR, in the British district of Rajahmundry, presidency of Madras, a town on the route from Rajahmundry to Coringa, 19 miles E. of the former. Lat. 16° 50′, long. 82° 3′.

CHELLUMBRUM, in the British district of South Arcot, presidency of Madras, a considerable town on the seacoast, on the route from Tranquebar to Arcot, 29 miles N. of the former. It was captured by the British in 1760, during the war in the Carnatic; and in 1781, during the war with Hyder Ali, it was unsuccessfully attacked by Sir Eyre Coote. Lat. 11° 25′, long. 79° 45′.

CHEMRA.—A town in the native state of Bombra, on the south-west frontier of Bengal, 25 miles E. from Sumbulpore, and 35 miles N.W. from Bombra. Lat. 21° 30′, long. 84° 25′.

CHENAUB.—A river in the Punjab, and generally considered the largest of the five by which that country is traversed. Moorcroft, who ascended, as he conjectured, to within thirty miles of its source, supposes it to rise about lat. 32° 48′, long. 77° 27′, in Lahoul, south of Ladakh, or Middle Tibet. The source must be very elevated, as the river holds its course through the Ritanka Pass, which is 13,000 feet high. The spot from which it proceeds is, according to Vigne, a small lake, called Chandra-Bhaga, or the Garden of the Moon, and in the upper part of its course the river is called the Chandra. At Tandi it is joined by the Surajbhagha, a stream of less magnitude, running from the north; and thenceforward the river is known by the name of the Chenaub or Chinab, and sometimes of Chandra-Bhaga. The length of the streams contributing to its formation varies from forty miles in the case of the Surajbhagha, to eighty-five in that of the Chandra-Bhaga. After their confluence, Moorcroft found the stream about 200 feet broad, with a full, steady current. It takes a north-west course of about 130 miles to Kishtawar, and there receives the Muruwurdwun, or Sinund, a considerable tributary from the north. Vigne calculates the height of Kishtawar at 5,000 feet; and consequently, the Chenaub must have descended 8,000 feet in less than 200 miles, or at the rate of above forty feet in the mile. At Kishtawar, Vigne found the Chenaub flowing in a deep rocky channel twenty-five yards wide. The river thence proceeds south-west, by a very tortuous course, through a rugged country, to Riasi, a distance of about ninety miles, where it leaves the mountains, and flows into the lower ground of the Punjab. It is here about 200 yards wide, deep and tranquil, yet rapid. At Aknur, about fifty miles lower down, it becomes navigable, at least for timber-rafts, which are despatched from it down the Punjab. It continues a south-westerly course to Vazeerabad, about seventy miles lower down, where Von Hügel found the stream unfordable, and half a mile wide. Macartney measured it there in the month of July, when nearly at the fullest, and found it one mile three furlongs and twenty perches wide, with a depth of fourteen feet, and a current running five miles an hour. From this point it holds a south-west course for about thirty miles, to Ramnuggur, where, in the middle of February, and consequently the low season, it was found 300 yards wide, and with a depth of nine feet where greatest; the current running a mile and a half an hour. Hough states that it is fordable near this place in the season; but there is much reason to question this statement. It thence pursues a south-west course for about 150 miles, to its confluence with the Jhelum, a little above the ferry of Trimo. Arrian describes the turbulence of the confluence as terrific; but Burnes, who visited it at midsummer, when the streams are usually highest, found it free from violence or danger. The total length of the course of the river to this point is about 605 miles. Below the confluence with the Jhelum, the Chenaub flows south-west for about fifty miles, to its confluence with the Ravee, a much smaller river, which joins it through three mouths, close to each other.

The Chenaub was here, at the end of June, the season of the greatest height of water, three-quarters of a mile wide, and above twelve feet deep. From this place it continues its course south-west for 110 miles, to the confluence of the Ghara. At the intervening ferry opposite Mooltan, Burnes found it 1,000 yards wide at midsummer, the season of greatest inundation. The meeting of the Chenaub and Ghara is very tranquil: the water of the former is red, that of the latter pale; and these respective colours may be distinguished for some miles downwards in the united stream, the red on the right or western, the pale on the left or eastern side. The total length of course from the source to this confluence is about 765 miles. There the united stream is called Punjnud (five rivers), a name which it bears to its fall into the Indus. The ancient name of Chenaub is admitted unquestionably to have been Acesines.

CHENDRAVADAH.—A town in Hyderabad, or dominions of the Nizam, distant S.W. from Aurungabad 14 miles. Lat. 19° 40′, long. 75° 17′.

CHENGBANG.—A town of Eastern India, in the native state of Muneepoor, distant N.W. from Muneepoor 26 miles. Lat. 25° 5′, long. 93° 42′.

CHENGOOR.—A town in the native state of Bhotan, distant N. from Goalpara 80 miles. Lat. 27° 18′, long. 90° 31′.

CHENNAPUTTEN, or CHINAPATAM, in the territory of Mysore, an open town, having adjacent a handsome stone fort. The town has some manufactures, especially of glass, and of steel wire for the strings of musical instruments. This ware is much esteemed, and is sent to all parts of India. Chennaputten is distant N.E. from Seringapatam 38 miles. Lat. 12° 40′, long. 77° 16′.

CHENNOOR, in the British district of Cuddapah, presidency of Madras, a town on the route from Cuddapah to Hyderabad, five miles N. of the former. Lat. 14° 33′, long. 78° 52′.

CHENNUMPULLY, in the British district of Bellary, presidency of Madras, a town 48 miles E. of Bellary, 48 miles S.W. of Kurnool. Lat. 15° 19′, long. 77° 40′.

CHEPAL, in the Cis-Sutlej hill state of Joobul, a fort on a ledge of land projecting from the south-eastern declivity of a mountain extending from the Chour to the Wartoo peak. It was surrendered to the British by the Ghoorka garrison almost immediately after being invested by the irregular troops in the service of the East-India Company, aided by the mountaineers of Joobul. Lat. 30° 57′, long. 77° 39′.

CHERACUL, a town in the British district of Malabar, presidency of Madras. The rajah of this district, formerly a powerful chief, was a scion of the Kolastri family, one of those among whom Cheruman Permal, the achiever of the independence of Malabar, divided the country. The country was in 1789 dreadfully devastated by Tippoo Sultan, and the rajah, dreading to be forcibly circumcised by the order of that bigoted tyrant, met death by inducing one of his followers to shoot him through the head. The town is two miles from the seacoast, and three miles N. of Cannanore. Lat. 11° 55′, long. 75° 25′.

CHERAJOLEE, in the British district of Durrung, in Assam, a town on the route from Durrung to Bishnath, 29 miles N.E. of Durrung. Lat. 26° 40′, long. 92° 27′.

CHERAND, in the British district of Sarun, a town on the left bank of the river Ganges, 16 miles N.W. of Dinapoor. Lat. 25° 42′, long. 84° 53′.

CHERCHANPOOR.—A town in the territory of Nagpore, distant S.E. from Nagpore 100 miles. Lat. 20° 40′, long. 80° 39′.

CHERGAON, in Bussahir, a village on the right bank of the Pabur, immediately below the confluence of the Andrytee. Elevation above the sea 5,985 feet. Lat. 31° 13′, long. 77° 56′.

CHERGAON, called also THOLANG, in Koonawur, a district of Bussahir, is a small town near the right bank of the Sutluj, and on a small stream flowing into it. There are between fifty and sixty families, living in substantial houses, covered with roofs of tempered clay overlying layers of birch bark, supported on horizontal beams. Here are several temples, dedicated to various divinities. The rajah of Bussahir resided here when the Goorkhas had possession of the rest of his territory. Opposite to this place, and on the right side of the Sutluj, was fought an action between the Koonawaris and Goorkhas, in which the latter were defeated, and subsequently stipulated not to enter Koonawur as long as an annual tribute of 700*l.* was paid. Elevation above the sea 7,300 feet. Lat. 31° 31′, long. 78° 7′.

CHERPELCHERRY, in the British district of Malabar, presidency of Madras, a town 28 miles E. of Ponany, 43 miles W. of Coimbatore. Lat. 10° 53′, long. 76° 23′.

CHETEROWN, in Sirmoor, a summit of the mountains between the Tons and Giree, and about two miles from the left bank of the latter. It is surmounted by a Hindoo temple, which was a station of the series of small triangles during the trigonometrical survey of the Himalaya. Elevation above the sea 7,048 feet. Lat. 30° 50′, long. 77° 24′.

CHETKOOL, in Bussahir, a village situate in the upper extremity of the valley of the Buspa, and on the right bank of the river of that name. Chetkool is the residence of a lama or Tibetan priest, who subsists by writing and printing sacred texts and ejaculations for the praying-mills of the villagers. Those singular instruments of superstition consist of drums or hollow cylinders, each set up horizontally on an iron axle. Inside the wheel are deposited the scrolls inscribed with prayers or pious exclamations, and the act of devotion consists in making the machine revolve, and its contents whirl about, either by the hand, by wind, or by water. Chetkool is at the elevation of 11,480 feet above the sea. Lat. 31° 20′, long. 78° 31′.

CHETPOLL, in the British district of Coimbatoor, presidency of Madras, a town on the route from Darapooram to Polachy, 11 miles W. of the former. Lat. 10° 43′, long. 77° 26′.

CHETTAPORE, in the British district of Ganjam, presidency of Madras, a town on the route from Berhampoor to Ganjam, four miles S.W. of the latter. Lat. 19° 22′, long. 85° 3′.

CHETTULWANO.—A town in the Rajpoot state of Joudpore, distant S.W. from Joudpore 140 miles. Lat. 24° 53′, long. 71° 37′.

CHETTYPOLLIAM, in the British district of Coimbatoor, presidency of Madras, a town on the route from Coimbatoor to Dindigul, nine miles S.E. of the former. Lat. 10° 55′, long. 77° 7′.

CHEWLEEA, in the British territory of Saugor and Nerbudda, lieut.-gov. of the N.W. Provinces, a town on the route from Jubbulpore to Sumbulpoor, 22 miles S. of the former. Lat. 22° 50′, long. 80° 10′.

CHEYLAR, in the British province of Scinde, presidency of Bombay, a town on the route from Oomerkote to Deesa, 29 miles S.E. of the former. Lat. 25°, long. 70°.

CHICACOLE, in the British district of Ganjam, presidency of Madras, a town with a military cantonment on the left or north bank of the river Naglaudee. The town is built in an irregular straggling manner, with narrow crooked streets, which in rainy weather are overflowed to a considerable depth. Population about 50,000. Distance from Vizagapatam, N.E., 58 miles; Madras, N.E., 435; Calcutta, S.W., 415. Lat. 18° 18′, long. 83° 58′.

CHICHACOTTA.—A town in the native state of Bhotan, distant S.E. from Darjeeling 81 miles. Lat. 26° 32′, long. 89° 30′.

CHICHEROULY, in Sirhind, a town, the principal place of a protected Seik state of the same name, on the route from Suharunpore to Subathoo, and 27 miles N.W. of the former place. It is situate in an open, level, well-cultivated country, and is surrounded by a mud wall. There is a bazaar. Distant N.W. from Calcutta 981 miles. The petty state of Chicherouly contains an area of sixty-three square miles, with a population of 9,387. Lat. 30° 15′, long. 77° 25′.

CHICHERRY, in the British district of Palamow, lieut.-gov. of Bengal, a town on the route from Palamow to Chaibassa, 30 miles S. of the former. Lat. 23° 24′, long. 84° 12′.

CHICHOLEE, in the British territory of Saugor and Nerbudda, lieut.-gov. of the N.W. Provinces, a town 22 miles N.W. of Baitool, 50 miles S. of Hoshungabad. Lat. 22° 1′, long. 77° 40′.

CHICKA MALLINHULLY.—A town in Mysore, distant N. from Chittel Droog 21 miles. Lat. 14° 32′, long. 76° 34′.

CHICKLEE.—A petty native state in Western India, under the superintendence of the agent for the Bheel chiefs in Candeish, presidency of Bombay. The young chief was sent for education to the government college at Poona. His conduct and attention to study were at first commendable, but he subsequently became refractory and inattentive, and finally absconded. Chicklee, the principal place, is in lat. 22° 19′, long. 74° 41′.

CHICKLEE.—A town in Hyderabad, or dominions of the Nizam, distant N.E. from Jaulnah 42 miles. Lat. 20° 19′, long. 76° 20′.

CHICKMOOGLOOR.—A town in Mysore, distant N.W. from Seringapatam 88 miles. Lat. 13° 19′, long. 75° 51′.

CHICKNAIGHULLY, or CHICA NAYAKANA HULLI, in the territory of Mysore, a town of considerable size, distant from Bangalore, N.W., 73 miles; from Seringapatam, N., 69. Lat. 13° 25′, long. 76° 41′.

CHICKROWLEE.—See CHICHEROULY.

CHIKIGURH.—A town of Malwa, in the native state of Bhopal, distant E. from Bhopal 48 miles. Lat. 23° 5′, long. 78° 8′.

CHIKULDIE.—A town of Malwa, in the native state of Bhopal, distant S. from Bhopal 33 miles. Lat. 22° 47′, long. 77° 20′.

CHIKULWAHUL, in the British district of Candeish, presidency of Bombay, a town on the route from Nassick to Dhoolia, 22 miles S.W. of the latter. Lat. 20° 35′, long. 74° 36′.

CHILACULLNERP.—A town in Mysore, distant N.E. from Bangalore 58 miles. Lat. 13° 38′, long. 78° 8′.

CHILBULA, in the British district of Allahabad, lieut.-gov. of the N.W. Provinces, a village on the route by the Kutra Pass, from Allahabad to Rewa, and 36 miles S.E. of the former city. Lat. 25° 10′, long. 82° 11′.

CHILKA.—An extensive lake dividing the British district of Ganjam, in the Madras presidency, from that of Pooree, in the presidency of Bengal. It is forty-two miles in length from north-east to south-west, and fifteen in breadth, and bounded towards the east and south by a narrow strip of sand, and on the north-west by the mountains which extend from the Mahanuddy to the Godavery: it receives the waters of one branch of the Mahanuddy, and communicates with the sea by a very narrow and deep outlet, in lat. 19° 42′, long. 85° 40′. The lake is studded with several islands, and its waters are salt and shallow.

CHILKALURPADU, in the British district of Guntoor, presidency of Madras, a town 23 miles S.W. of Guntoor, 41 miles N. of Ongole. Lat. 16° 6′, long. 80° 13′.

CHILKANA, in the British district of Suharunpoor, lieut.-gov. of the N.W. Provinces, a small ruinous town on the route from Suharunpoor to Sidowra, and 10 miles N.W. of the former town. The surrounding country is level, open, and slightly cultivated; and the road in this part of the route is good. Distant N.W. from Calcutta 1,000 miles. Lat. 30° 5′, long. 77° 32′.

CHILKAUREE, in Guzerat, a town in the petty native state of Saunte, in the division of Rewa Caunta, presidency of Bombay. Distance from Ahmedabad, N.E., 97 miles. Lat. 23° 20′, long. 74° 2′.

CHILKEEA, in the British district of Moradabad, lieut.-gov. of the N.W. Provinces, a place of considerable trade on the northern frontier, towards Kumaon, situate in the Dikkalee Pass, or gorge by which the river Kosila flows to the plain. Heber describes it, at the time of his visit, in the beginning of December, as a wretched assemblage of cottages, half-buried in high grass; and adds, "The first appearance of the inhabitants of Chilkea was not prepossessing. They had the same yellow skins; the same dull, yet fierce look; the same ragged and scanty clothing; the same swords and shields, as those in the other parts of these inhospitable plains." In summer the air is so pestilential that it is then entirely abandoned. Elevation above the sea 1,076 feet. Lat. 29° 21′, long. 79° 10′.

CHILKORE, in the British district of Bhagulpore, lieut.-gov. of Bengal, a town on the route from Bhagulpore to Calcutta, 14 miles S. of the former. Lat. 25°, long. 86° 57′.

CHILLAHTARA, in the British district of Banda, lieut.-gov. of the N.W. Provinces, a small town on the route from the town of Futtehpore to that of Banda, and 22 miles N.W. of the latter. It is situate on the right bank of the Jumna, here crossed by ferry. Though a small place, much business is done here in shipping cotton, which is largely grown in the neighbouring districts, and conveyed down the river to the lower provinces. The river Cane empties itself into the Jumna on the right side, immediately above the town. Its water is considered unwholesome by the natives, who take much trouble to obtain their supply from the Jumna above the confluence. Distant N.W. from Allahabad 105 miles, from Calcutta 600. Lat. 25° 47′, long. 80° 36′.

CHILLAKAR, in the British district of Nellore, presidency of Madras, a town on the route from Madras to Nellore, 21 miles S.W. of the latter. Lat. 14° 8′, long. 79° 55′.

CHILLERA, or CHULERA, in the British district of Boolundshuhur, lieut.-gov. of the N.W. Provinces, a village on the route from the cantonment of Allyghur to that of Delhi, and 12 miles S.E. of the latter. Lat. 28° 34′, long. 77° 24′.

CHILLIANWALLA, in the Jetch Doab division of the Punjaub, a village situate five miles from the left bank of the river Jhelum. The place has acquired celebrity from a sanguinary battle which took place there on the 13th January, 1849, between a British force under Lord Gough and the army of the Sikhs. On both sides the greatest determination and most heroic bravery were displayed; on both sides the loss was frightfully severe; and though the British remained in possession of the field, the victory was dearly purchased. The annals of Indian warfare do not record a fiercer or more arduous conflict. An obelisk erected here, by order of government, preserves the memory of those who fell in the Sutlej and Punjaub campaigns. Chillianwalla is 85 miles N.W. of Lahore. Lat. 32° 40′, long. 73° 39′.

CHILLOO CHUNGEE, in the Peshawar division of the Punjab, a town situated on the route from Jhelum to Attock, eight miles W. of the town of Rawul Pind. Lat. 23° 40′, long. 72° 54′.

CHILMAREE, in the British district of Rungpoor, lieut.-gov. of Bengal, a town 36 miles S.E. of the town of Rungpoor. It is situate on the right or west bank of the Brahmapootra, amidst luxuriant groves and fine gardens; but it is an ill-built place, containing no building of any importance. Lat. 25° 25′, long. 89° 46′.

CHIMALI, in Gurwhal, a village on the right bank of the Bhageerettee, as the Ganges is called in the upper part of its course. It is situated in a fertile tract, cultivated principally for the growth of the opium-poppy. Elevation above the sea 2,942 feet. Lat. 30° 34′, long. 78° 23′.

CHIMARY, in the British district of Ahmedabad, presidency of Bombay, a town on the route from Deesa to Rajkote, 40 miles N.W. of Ahmedabad. Lat. 23° 19′, long. 72° 4′.

CHIMMAPOODY.—A town in Hyderabad, or dominions of the Nizam, distant E. from Hyderabad 116 miles. Lat. 17° 22′, long. 80° 18′.

CHIMOOR.—A town in the territory of Nagpore, distant S. from Nagpore 49 miles. Lat. 20° 30′, long. 79° 29′.

CHINA BUKEER.—The name given to one of the rivers forming the delta of the Irawady: it falls into the Bay of Bengal in lat. 16° 19′, long. 96° 10′.

CHINALGARH, in Sirmoor, a village on a picturesque site, on the summit of a rock overhanging a feeder of the river Julal. Here, in 1814, an irregular force in the service of the East-India Company was defeated by the Goorkhas in the war with that power. Lat. 30° 42′, long. 77° 16′.

CHIN AMMAPETTA, in the British district of Masulipatam, presidency of Madras, a town 29 miles N. of Ellore, 60 miles W. of Rajahmundry. Lat. 17° 3′, long. 80° 57′.

CHINAT CHOKEE, in the territory of Oude, a village on the route from Goruckpoor cantonment to Lucknow, seven miles E. of the latter. The road in this part of the route is heavy, sandy, and bad. Lat. 26° 53′, long. 81° 2′.

CHINCHLEE, in the British district of Belgaum, presidency of Bombay, a town on the right bank of the river Kistnah, 52 miles N.E. of Belgaum. Lat. 16° 34′, long. 74° 53′.

CHINDGOOR.—A town in Hyderabad, or dominions of the Nizam, distant N.E. from Hyderabad 150 miles. Lat. 18° 33′, long. 80° 26′.

CHINDWARA, in the territory of Nagpore, a town on the route from Saugor to the city of Nagpore, 82 miles S. of the former, 167 N. of the latter. It is situate in the mountainous tract called Deogur, above the Ghats, on an elevated table-land, having an open space of ground free from jungle on the summit, of about four and a half miles in circumference. In consequence of its considerable elevation, its climate is one of the most agreeable and salubrious in India; and from this advantage it has many visitors in search of health or recreation. Elevation above the sea 2,100 feet. Lat. 22° 3′, long. 78° 58′.

CHINEANE, in the Northern Punjab, on the southern slope of the Himalaya. It is situate on the Taui river, which, about fifty miles lower down, falls into the Chenaub. Chineane is a place of considerable size, is neatly built, and has a palace still belonging to the deposed rajah of the town and district, though his possessions have been seized by Gholab Singh, the present ruler of Cashmere. Chineane is in lat. 33° 5′, long. 75° 22′.

CHINEEALEE.—See CHIMALI.

CHINEPOOR.—A town in the native state of Bhopal, distant S.E. from Bhopal 52 miles. Lat. 23° 3′, long. 78° 12′.

CHINGLEPUT.—A British district within the limits of the presidency of Madras, named from its principal place. It is bounded on the north by the British district of Nellore; on the east by the Bay of Bengal; on the south by the British district of South Arcot; and on the north-west and west by the British district of North Arcot. It lies between lat. 12° 14′ and 14°, long. 79° 35′—80° 25′. Locally situate within its limits, is a small tract containing the city of Madras and the portion of territory within its municipal jurisdiction, extending about eight miles from north to south along the seashore, with an average breadth of four, and having an area of thirty square miles. Exclusive of this area, the district of Chingleput contains, according to official return, 2,993 square miles. In proportion to its area, the extent of seacoast is considerable, being about 120 miles. The only considerable river is the Palar, which, rising near Jungumcotta, in Mysore, holds its course first south-eastward, subsequently eastward, through the British districts of Salem and North Arcot, and entering this district on its western frontier, continues its easterly course through it for about sixty-three miles, to its fall into the Bay of Bengal, about four miles south of Sadras. The climate during the dry season is characterized by great heat, the thermometer having been known to reach 115° in the shade. In the vicinity of the sea it is, however, considerably mitigated by the refreshing sea-breeze. The population of the district is given under the article MADRAS. Madras, Chingleput, Conjeveram, Sadras, Walajahabad, Pallavaram, and other of the principal towns, are described under their respective names in the alphabetical arrangement. The chief routes are—1. From east to west, from Madras, through Arcot, to Bangalore. 2. From north-east to south-west, from Madras to the town of Chingleput. 3. From north to south, from Madras to Cuddalore. 4. From south to north, from Madras to Nellore. The district is also traversed by one of the lines of the Madras Railway Company.

CHINGLEPUT.—A large town in the British district of the same name, within the presidency of Madras. The fort of Chingleput is situate at the northern extremity of a valley upwards of a mile broad, and is bounded on the eastern and greater part of the northern faces by a tank or artificial lake, two miles long and one broad, from which the ditch is supplied with water. The fort is 400 yards in length from north to south, and 280 in breadth from east to west, and is divided into two parts by a rampart and ditch. The eastern part is considerably elevated, and forms what is called the inner fort. The entire western face, and part of the northern, are bounded by rice-fields, irrigated from the lake, the water of which is retained by an embankment 1,000 yards in length. On the top of this bank runs the high road leading from Madras southward. The town of Chingleput consists of one long street, and is half a mile to the south-east of the fort, equidistant from which, in a different direction, is another town, or collection of dwellings, called Nullam. The river Palar, flowing to the south-west, affords the means of drainage, and during the greater part of the year an abundant supply of water, but during the dry season the latter totally ceases; even the tank is nearly exhausted, and the decayed weeds and slime in its bed taint the air with offensive and pestiferous exhalations. The public buildings of the district are within the rampart of the fort, and consist of the court of justice, the jail, place of arms, and hospital. The civil establishment comprises a judge, a collector, and magistrate, and an adequate number of officials, European and native. A detachment, consisting generally of two companies of native infantry, stationed here, live in huts on high grounds about a quarter of a mile to the south. Notwithstanding the malaria caused by the tank, it is in general considered a remarkably healthy place. There is a manufacture of pottery here, which in 1848 attracted the attention of government, with a view to its improvement: for the purpose of prosecuting experiments with this object, a grant of 2,000 rupees per annum for two years was made. Distance from Tanjore, N., 145 miles; Cuddalore, N., 65; Bangalore, E., 162; Arcot, E., 45; Madras, S.W., 36. Lat. 12° 41′, long. 80° 2′.

CHINGONG, in Bundelcund, a town in the native state of Jhansee, 19 miles N.E. from Jhansee, and 60 miles S.E. from Gwalior. Lat. 25° 34′, long. 78° 54′.

CHINI, in Bussahir, a village of the district of Koonawur, about a mile from the right bank of the Sutluj. It is situate in a slight depression on the southern slope of a lofty mountain, down which numerous rills flow, and, watering the soil, discharge themselves into the Sutluj, which runs about 1,500 feet below the village. The intervening space is covered in the season with thriving crops and vineyards, loaded with a profusion of large and finely-flavoured grapes. The cattle are generally a hybrid breed, between the yak and common kine, than which they are stronger and hardier, with longer and thicker hair, great horns, and large bushy tails. They are invariably black, and less wild than the yak. Chini is a considerable village, connected with seven or eight others of less extent, and was the favourite residence of Lord Dalhousie, the Governor-General of India, during his sojourn in the hills. Elevation above the sea 8,770 feet. Lat. 31° 31′, long. 78° 19′.

CHINNA HURRY.—A river rising in the Mysore territory, in lat. 14° 10′, long. 76° 25′, about four miles S.W. of the town of Chittel Droog. It flows in a north-easterly direction through Mysore and the British district of Bellary, and falls into the Hugry, a feeder of the Toongabudra, in lat. 14° 56′, long. 77° 7′.

CHINNA SALEM, in the British district of South Arcot, presidency of Madras, a town on the route from Salem to Cuddalore, 50 miles E. of the former. Lat. 11° 39′, long. 78° 56′.

CHINNOOR, in Hydrabad, or territory of the Nizam, a town belonging to the rajah of Palensha, a feudal holder of an extensive tract on both banks of the river Godavery, in the vicinity of the confluence of the Pranheeta. Distance from Hydrabad, N.E., 136 miles; Madras, N., 410. Lat. 18° 55′, long. 79° 47′.

CHINRAIAN DROOG.—A town in Mysore, distant N. from Bangalore 50 miles. Lat. 13° 36′, long. 77° 16′.

CHINRAIPATAM, in the territory of Mysore, a town situate on the side of an extensive tank. It has a fort, well built of stone and lime, and a temple dedicated to Vishnu. There is here a weekly fair, but no trade of moment. Distance from Seringapatam, N.W., 38 miles. Lat. 12° 54′, long. 76° 27′.

CHINSURA.—A town with a small annexed territory, on the right bank of the river Hooghly, formerly belonging to the Dutch, and a place of considerable trade. It was among the cessions on the continent of India made by the king of the Netherlands in 1824, in exchange for the British possessions on the island of Sumatra, and is now included within the British district of Hooghly, presidency of Bengal. It is described by Rennell, about seventy years ago, as a very neat and pretty large town; and by another authority, as requiring at the period in question three-quarters of an hour to walk round it. Its site is said to be better than that of Calcutta, and it is considered one of the healthiest places in the lower provinces of Bengal. The government has established here an extensive military depôt for Europeans, with magnificent barracks and an immense hospital. Within the town is the government educational establishment denominated the Hooghly College; and in the vicinity is the field where Colonel Forde, under the order of Clive, defeated the Dutch troops in 1759. Forde had applied to Clive for written authority to commence the attack. Clive was playing at cards when he received the note, and without quitting his seat, wrote in pencil,—"Dear Forde, fight them immediately, and I will send you the order of council to-morrow." Distance from Calcutta, N., 20 miles. Lat. 22° 53′, long. 88° 23′.

CHINTACOONTA, in the British district of Cuddapah, presidency of Madras, a town on the route from Cuddapah to Bellary, 36 miles N.W. of the former. Lat. 14° 42′, long. 78° 24′.

CHINTALAPOODY, in the British district of Masulipatam, presidency of Madras, a town on the route from Ellore to Kummummett, 23 miles N. of the former. Lat. 17° 4′, long. 81° 5′.

CHINTAMUN, in the British district of Dinajepoor, lieut.-gov. of Bengal, a town on the route from Dinajepoor to Bograh, 21 miles S.E. of the former. Lat. 25° 22′, long. 88° 56′.

CHINTAPILLY, in the British district of Guntoor, presidency of Madras, a town on the right bank of the Kistnah, 35 miles N.W. of Guntoor. Lat. 16° 43′, long. 80° 11′.

CHINTOLI.—A town in Hyderabad, or dominions of the Nizam, distant N. from Moodgul 49 miles. Lat. 16° 42′, long. 76° 32′.

CHINTOMNIPETT.—A town in Mysore, distant N.E. from Bangalore 43 miles. Lat. 13° 23′, long. 78° 6′.

CHIOMOK.—A town in the native state of Cashmere, or dominions of Gholab Singh, 88 miles S.W. from Sirinagur, and 28 miles N.E. from Jhelum. Lat. 33° 20′, long. 73° 50′.

CHIPLOON, in the British district of Rutnagherry, presidency of Bombay, a town on the route from Kolapoor to Bombay, 108 miles S.E. of the latter. Lat. 17° 30′, long. 73° 36′.

CHIPURAPILLE, in the British district of Vizagapatam, presidency of Madras, a town on the north-west coast of the Bay of Bengal, 16 miles S.W. of Vizagapatam. Lat. 17° 34′, long. 83° 10′.

CHIRGONG, or CHURGAON, in Bundelcund, a small town on the route from Calpee to Goonah, 81 miles S.W. of the former, and 124 N.E. of the latter. It was formerly the principal place of a jaghire, "stated, in 1832, to comprise twenty-five square miles, and to contain ten villages, with a population of 3,800 souls, and to yield a revenue of 25,000 rupees." It was subject to a money payment of 7,500 rupees to the state of Jhansi. In 1841, the jaghiredar became contumacious; his followers committed depredations; and on remonstrance, he assumed such an attitude of defiance, that military operations were commenced against his fort of Churgaon, which he had the temerity to defend. In April in that year, the place was invested by a force amounting to about 2,000 men. The garrison assembled by the jaghiredar was conjectured by the British commander to have amounted to 4,000: native report made their numbers much greater. After cannonading the fort for two days, it was determined to attack a position without the wall, where the enemy had thrown up a stockade for the protection, as it subsequently appeared, of some wells. On the approach of the British detachment, they were received by a vigorous discharge of matchlocks, seconded by rockets and firepots. Ultimately a hand-to-hand contest decided the fate of the stockade, which was carried, though not without considerable loss. Preparations were made for establishing a breaching-battery on the captured position. These were nearly completed, when it was ascertained that the enemy had evacuated the fort, of which the British forthwith took possession. The fugitive jaghiredar lost his life in the following year, having, whilst marauding, fallen in with some British troops. His jaghire was confiscated, and transferred to the British district of Jaloun. The revenue is now estimated at from 40,000 rupees to 50,000 rupees, subject to the annual payment to Jhansi of 7,500 rupees. Lat. 25° 34′, long. 78° 53′.

CHIRING, in the British district of Gurwhal, lieut.-gov. of the N.W. Provinces, a village with small fort, formerly held by the Goorkas, at the southern base of a ridge of the Himalaya. It is situate on the right bank of the Pindur, a considerable feeder of the Aluknunda, 40 miles N.W. of Almorah fort, 39 E. of Sireenuggur. Lat. 30° 7′, long. 79° 28′.

CHIRKANWAN, in the British district of Behar, lieut.-gov. of Bengal, a town 23 miles W. of Gayah, 19 miles N.W. of Sherghotty. Lat. 24° 49′, long. 84° 41′.

CHIRKAREE, in Bundelcund, a town the principal place of a small native state of the same name, on the route from Gwalior to Banda, 41 miles S.W. of the latter. It is rather large, and occupies a picturesque site at the base of a lofty rocky hill, surmounted by a fort accessible only by a flight of steps cut in the rock, but of such size, and of so gentle an acclivity, that they are practicable for elephants. The fort is, however, commanded by two elevations at no great distance. Below the town is a fine lake swarming with fish. The raj or territory of Chirkaree is estimated to "comprise 880 square miles, and to contain 259 villages, with a population of 81,000 souls." The estimated annual revenue is 460,830 rupees. The rajah pays to the East-India Company an annual tribute of 9,484 rupees, and maintains a force of 300 cavalry, thirty artillery, and 1,000 infantry. The Peishwa having by the treaty of Bassein, in 1803, ceded to the East-India Company his sovereign claims over a portion of Bundelcund, within which Chirkaree was comprised, the British government confirmed in the raj Bikramajit, who then occupied it in right of his descent from Chuttursal, the founder of Boondela independence. Bikramajit died in 1834, and was succeeded by his illegitimate grandson Ruttun Singh, whose claim was recognised by the British authorities. The succession was disputed by Dewan Khait Singh, the representative of a junior branch of the reigning family; and his claim appears to have been well founded. His pretensions were, however, satisfied by a grant in the first instance of 1,000 rupees per mensem, and subsequently, in 1842, by the raj of Jeitpore, which was then bestowed on him. The family is Hindoo, and claims Rajpoot descent. The practice of suttee has been abolished in Chirkaree. The town of Chirkaree is in lat. 25° 24′, long. 79°·49′.

CHIRRA POONJEE, in Eastern India, a town situate on the Cossya Hills, in lat. 25° 14′, long. 91° 45′. It was formerly the site of a British sanatarium, which, after due experiments, proving unsuccessful, was abolished in 1834. The station has an elevation of 4,200 feet above the level of the sea. Its average temperature throughout the year is stated to be twelve degrees of Fahrenheit below that of the plains of Bengal, while during the hot months the difference increases to twenty degrees. Coal exists in all parts of the hills, of superior quality and in profuse abundance. The mines have been transferred by the government to lessees, who, however, would appear to have exhibited no great amount of enterprise in the speculation. Iron-ore is equally abundant, and it is believed that works might be established in those hills for the manufacture of iron and steel on a very extensive scale, and under a favourable combination of circumstances.

CHIRTAOL, in the British district of Muzuffurnugur, lieut.-gov. of the N.W. Provinces, a town the chief place of the pergunnah of the same name, with a population of 5,111. Lat. 29° 33′, long. 77° 39′.

CHIRWAKKUM, in the British district of South Arcot, presidency of Madras, a town on the route from Trichinopoly to Arcot, 52 miles N. of the former. Lat. 11° 32′, long. 79° 3′.

CHIT, in the British district of Agra, lieut.-gov. of the N.W. Provinces, a town 17 miles S.W. of the city of Agra. Lat. 26° 59′, long. 77° 54′.

CHITEA, in the British district of Bareilly, lieut.-gov. of the N.W. Provinces, a village on the route from Bareilly to Seetapore, and 37 miles S.E. of the former. Lat. 28° 11′, long. 80° 1′.

CHITIALLA.—A town in Hyderabad, or dominions of the Nizam, distant S.E. from Hyderabad 80 miles. Lat. 16° 38′, long. 79° 30′.

CHITMAPOOR, in the British district of Mynpooree, lieut.-gov. of the N.W. Provinces, a village on the route from the cantonment of Allygurh to that of Mynpooree, and 20 miles N.W. of the latter. Lat. 27° 24′, long. 78° 52′.

CHITOR, in the territory of Cochin, a town the principal place of a subdivision of the country of the same name, distant from the city of Cochin, N.E., 62 miles. Lat. 10° 43′, long. 76° 48′.

CHITRACOOTAM.—A town in the hill zemindarry of Jeypoor, in Orissa, under the political superintendence of the government of Madras, distant 25 miles S. from Jeypoor, and 80 miles N.W. from Vizianagrum. Lat. 18° 40′, long. 82° 24′.

CHITRAKOTE, or CHATARKOT, in the British district of Banda, lieut.-gov. of the N.W. Provinces, a town on the river Paisuni, 50 miles S.E. of the town of Banda. Though latterly scarcely noticed by any writer, it is described by Tieffenthaler, between seventy and eighty years ago, as the resort of all India, being the residence of Rama and his wife Sita, after they had left Ayodha. It is crowded with temples and shrines of Rama and his brother Lakshmana. The clear river Paisuni here expands into a small shallow lake, inclosed by a border of masonry, having numerous ghats or flights of stairs, to give votaries access to the water, ablution in which is deemed to absolve from offences. Lat. 25° 12′, long. 80° 47′.

CHITRIYA.—A town in the native state of Nepal, distant E. from Khatmandoo 101 miles. Lat. 27° 32′, long. 86° 56′.

CHITTA, in the British district of Jaunsar, lieut.-gov. of the N.W. Provinces, a village in the hilly tract on the right of the Jumna, and four miles west of that river. Skinner describes it as situate in a most delightful country, and having to the north a sublime view of the Himalaya. Chitta is in lat. 30° 37′, long. 78° 2′.

CHITTAGONG. — One of the districts within the presidency of Bengal, bounded on the north by independent Tipperah; on the east by the Youmadoung range of mountains, separating it from Burmah; on the south by Arracan; and on the west by the Bay of Bengal. It extends from lat. 20° 45′ to 23° 25′, and from long. 91° 32′ to 93°; its length from north to south is 185 miles, and its extreme breadth 100; containing an area (irrespective of the elevated and woody tract on the eastern frontier, inhabited only by hill tribes) of 2,717 square miles. The mountainous tract is a portion of the great chain which, running from Assam southwards, extends to Cape Negrais, and attains in the Blue Mountain, on the frontier of Chittagong, an elevation of upwards of 8,000 feet above the level of the sea. Its inhabitants are wild tribes, who have never submitted to any government. It sends forth several rivers, the most important of which is the Kurrumfoolee, which, taking a westerly direction, passes the town of Chittagong, or Islamabad, and discharges itself into the Bay of Bengal. Elephants abound in the forests of Chittagong, and large numbers are annually caught for the use of government. The mode of catching them consists in surrounding a herd of these animals by a numerous body of hunters, and a barricade of trees being formed, with the addition of a trench, a number of tame elephants are sent into the inclosure, which is called a keddah, and the wild elephants are secured by ropes attached to the tame ones. Of agricultural products rice is the staple article; the other crops are sugar-cane, hemp, oats, tobacco, mustard, and betel-nut. The population of the district is given under the article BENGAL.

Towards the close of the seventeenth century, this district was wrested from the rajah of Arracan by Aurungzebe and added to the imperial dominions. It was ceded to the East-India Company by the nabob of Bengal in 1760, and confirmed to them by the grant of Shah Alum, emperor of Delhi, in 1765. Previous to the Burmese war of 1824, its cession was demanded by the king of Ava, on the ground of its being an ancient dependency of Arracan, then a portion of the Burmese dominions.

CHITTAGONG, or ISLAMABAD.—The principal place of the British district of the same name, situate on the river of the same name, about seven miles from its mouth. It was formerly a place of considerable trade, and noted for its shipbuilding establishments. This, however, is no longer the case. Rice, the great article of export, is now sought in the ports of Arracan, where it is obtained at a cheaper rate; and large vessels have ceased to be built in its marine-yard, Moulmein having supplanted it in that respect. A succession of small round hills, planted with coffee, pepper-vines, and bamboos, and surmounted by the villas of the English residents, give to the surrounding country an interesting and romantic appearance. The climate is not considered healthy. Owing to the great extent of uncleared land, and the influence of the neighbouring mountains, continual fogs prevail during the rainy and the winter season, engendering ague and asthma; but during the hot months the air is cooler than that of Calcutta. Lat. 22° 20′, long. 91° 54′.

CHITTAIR.—A river rising within the presidency of Madras, in lat. 14°, long. 78° 45′, and flowing in a north-easterly direction for seventy-five miles, through the British district of Cuddapah, falls into the Pennar in lat. 14° 26′, long. 79° 13′.

CHITTAPET, in the British district of South Arcot, presidency of Madras, a town on the route from Arcot to Cuddalore, 30 miles S. of the former. Lat. 12° 30′, long. 79° 25′.

CHITTAVAIL, in the British district of Cuddapah, presidency of Madras, a town situate 40 miles S.E. from Cuddapah, 46 miles S.W. of Nellore. Lat. 14° 10′, long. 79° 24′.

CHITTLEDROOG.—A town with a fort, on the summit of one of a circular range of hills inclosing a basin or plain ten miles in length and four in breadth. The range is covered with small stunted trees and jungle. Chittledroog was formerly a place of some strength, having made an obstinate, though ineffectual resistance, to the power of Hyder Ali, by whom it was taken in 1779. The town, which is situate in the plain, at the foot of the rock on which the fort is built, is of considerable size, and so strongly fortified by Hyder Ali as to be impregnable to native attack. The fort was used by Tippoo as a state prison, in which, among many other captives, native and British, General Matthews was incarcerated. A mutiny took place in 1809 among the British troops stationed in this place. Seizing the public treasure, they deserted the post intrusted to their care, and marched in the direction of Seringapatam, to join the disaffected garrison of that place, but were intercepted and completely routed by a detachment under Colonel Gibbs. Chittledroog is the principal place of a division of the same name. Distant from Seringapatam, N., 128 miles; Bangalore, N.W., 120; Bellary, S., 70; Mangalore, N.E., 141; Madras, N.W., 275. Lat. 14° 14′, long. 76° 27′.

CHITTOOR, in the British district of Arcot (northern division), presidency of Madras, a town with a fort, situate on the south side of the river Puni, a feeder of the Palar. The river during the monsoon rains is four hundred yards in width, and then several tanks are replenished from it; but in the dry season the stream shrinks to a small rivulet. Elevation above the sea 1,100 feet. Distance from Bangalore, E., 104 miles; Vellore, N., 20; Arcot, N.W., 28; Cuddalore, N.W., 112; Madras, W., 80. Lat. 13° 12′, long. 79° 9′.

CHITTOR, or CHITTORGURH, in Rajpootana, in territory of Oodeypoor or Mewar, an ancient town with fortress, formerly of great importance, but now much decayed. The site is conspicuous from a considerable distance, by the high rock on which the fortress stands, and which, from its scarped sides and the buildings scattered along its crest, sufficiently denotes its nature. The town is situate on the river Biruch, or Beris, here traversed by a fine bridge of nine arches, that in the middle being semicircular, having four Gothic arches at each side. Within the inclosure of the fortress are several antique buildings; one of which, called Nolakha Bindar, is a small inner citadel, with massy and lofty walls and towers; another, a palace of the rana, is a plain building, but spacious, and in good taste, its crenated battlements having a fine effect. There are also two vast temples, dedicated to Krishna. Near those temples are two tanks or reservoirs, each one hundred and twenty-five feet long, fifty wide, and fifty deep, constructed of large blocks of stone. On the crest of the hill is a large temple, dedicated to the destroying powers, having the trident of Siva erected before the entrance. The style of architecture is good and the masonry excellent. The most remarkable building is the Kheerut Khumb, or Pillar of Victory, erected in 1439, to commemorate a victory gained over the combined armies of Malwa and Guzerat by Rana Khumbo, who reigned in Mewar from 1418 to 1468. It stands on a terrace forty-two feet square; is one hundred and twenty-two feet in height, and each of the four faces is, at the base, thirty-five feet in length. There are nine stories, and on the summit a cupola. The whole is one mass of the most elaborate sculpture, executed in white marble, and representing various subjects of Hindoo mythology. About the centre of the hill-top is a curious Jain pillar, built in 896. According to native report, there are eighty-four cisterns within the fortress; but when Heber visited the place, in an unusually dry season, but twelve retained water. One of those is fed by a perennial spring. At the south-western extremity of the hill on which the fort is built, but quite detached from it, is a small hill which would completely cover an attacking force on that side from the fire of the garrison; and in this part the hill is easiest of access. Chittoor was taken in 1303, by Alauddin, the Patan monarch of Delhi, who, however, subsequently granted it to the nephew of the former ruler, on condition of his payment of tribute, and furnishing an armed contingent of 5,000 horse and 10,000 foot. Bahadur Shah, king of Guzerat, took it in 1533, but was soon after expelled by Humaon, padshah of Delhi, who reinstated the Rajpoot prince. It was taken by storm by Akbar in 1567; the Rajpoots, when they considered their circumstances desperate, slaughtering their wives and children, and rushing on the enemy, were almost to a man cut off. It appears to have been subsequently recovered by the chief of Mewar; but about 1676 surrendered to the forces of Aurungzebe. It reverted to the Rajpoots on the dismemberment of the empire of Delhi, in the latter part of the eighteenth century. Distance direct from Neemuch, N.W., 30 miles; Nusseerabad, S., 100; Agra, S.W., 270; Mhow, N.W., 175. Lat. 24° 52′, long. 74° 41′.

CHITTRA, in the British district of Ramgurh, lieut.-gov. of Bengal, a town in a wild and hilly tract, overrun with forest and jungle. Chittra is distant from Hazareebagh, N.W., 32 miles; from Calcutta, N.W., by Hazareebagh, 250. Lat. 24° 13′, long. 84° 57′.

CHITTRAVUTTY.—A river rising in the eastern division of Mysore, in lat. 13° 35′, long. 77° 54′. It flows first in a southerly direction for twenty-two miles through Mysore, and fifty through the British district of Bellary; then turning north-east, it continues its course for fifty miles through the districts of Bellary and Cuddapah, and falls into the Pennar in lat. 14° 47′, long. 78° 45′.

CHITTUNG, in Sirhind, a small river or torrent, which passes off from the Sursooty about lat. 30° 15′, long. 77° 15′, and takes a south-west direction. It is important in an agricultural point of view, as a few miles west of Suffedun, and in lat. 29° 23′, long. 76° 32′, it is joined by the celebrated canal of Ferozshah, the water of which it conveys westward to Hissar, and thence proceeds in the same direction, "winding among the sandhills of Bhikanir, or, more properly speaking, along the northern boundary of the sandy desert," until it is lost in the plains of Bhuttiana, about thirty-seven miles west of Hissar; its total length of course being about 150 miles.

CHITTUR.—See CHITOR.

CHOBALINGAPOORAM, in the British district of Madura, presidency of Madras, a town situate 29 miles S. of Madura, 51 miles W. of Ramnad. Lat. 9° 30′, long. 78° 9′.

CHOBANA, in the Sinde Sagur Dooab division of the Punjab, a town situated 30 miles S.E. of Leia, 43 miles N. of the town of Mooltan. Lat. 30° 45′, long. 71° 30′.

CHOBEE-KE-SERAI, in the British district of Futtehpoor, lieut.-gov. of the N.W. Provinces, a small town on the route from Allahabad to the town of Futtehpoor, and 26 miles S.E. of the latter. It has a bazaar, and water from wells. The country is level and cultivated. Lat. 25° 50′, long. 81° 10′.

CHOBIPOOR, in the British district of Cawnpore, lieut.-gov. of the N.W. Provinces, a town on the route from the cantonment of Cawnpore to that of Futtehgurh, and 16 miles N.W. of the former. There is a bazaar. Lat. 26° 37′, long. 80° 15′.

CHOCHUKPOOR, in the British district of Ghazeepoor, lieut.-gov. of the N.W. Provinces, a village on the left bank of the Ganges, 26 miles S.W. of Ghazeepoor cantonment by water, 10 by land; 625 N.W. of Calcutta by water. Lat. 25° 30′, long. 83° 23′.

CHODHON, in the Rajpoot state of Joudpore, a village on the route from the town of Joudpore to that of Ajmeer, and 27 miles E. of the former. It contains 150 houses. Lat. 26° 19′, long. 73° 33′.

CHOGDA.—A town in the British district of Nuddea, lieut.-gov. of Bengal: it is situate on the left bank of the Hoogly river, 37 miles N. from Calcutta. This place was formerly celebrated for human sacrifices by drowning; it is still a famous place for burning the dead, and corpses are conveyed to it for that purpose from great distances. Lat. 23° 5′, long. 88° 30′.

CHOHAGAON.—A town in the native state of Nepal, distant S.W. from Khatmandoo 20 miles. Lat. 27° 34′, long. 85° 1′.

CHOILNA.—A town in the peninsula of Kattywar, province of Guzerat, distant S. from Rajkote 90 miles. Lat. 21° 2′, long. 70° 40′.

CHOKA, in the British territory of Saugor and Nerbudda, lieut.-gov. of the N.W. Provinces, a town 20 miles S.W. from Saugor, 45 miles N.E. of Bhilsa. Lat. 23° 40′, long. 78° 31′.

CHOKHUN, in the British district of Kumaon, lieut.-gov. of the N.W. Provinces, a town eight miles S.E. of Almora, 62 miles N. of Pilleebheet. Lat. 29° 30′, long. 79° 49′.

CHOLAWARUM, in the British district of Masulipatam, presidency of Madras, a town on the left bank of the river Kistnah, 20 miles S.W. of Masulipatam. Lat. 15° 59′, long. 81°.

CHOLUH, in the British district of Boolundshuhur, lieut.-gov. of the N.W. Provinces, a village on the route from Allyghur cantonment to that of Delhi, and 37 miles N.W. of the former. Lat. 28° 20′, long. 77° 50′.

CHOMOOA, in the British district of Agra, lieut.-gov. of the N.W. Provinces, a village on the route from the city of Agra to that of Muttra, and 15 miles N.W. of the former. Lat. 27° 15′, long. 77° 54′.

CHONDA, in the territory of Gwalior, a small town or village 18 miles N.W. of the fort of Gwalior. This place and Maharajpoor were the two keys of the position of the Mahratta army in its engagement with the British under Sir Hugh Gough, on 29th of December, 1843. The Mahrattas, who probably mustered about 15,000 men, with a numerous and well-appointed artillery, were attacked by the British, little inferior in number, and being driven from all points of their position, fled to the fort of Gwalior, having lost fifty-six guns and all their ammunition-waggons. The British loss was 106 killed, 684 wounded, and seven missing. Lat. 26° 27′, long. 78°.

CHONGBA PASS, in Bussahir, near the north-eastern boundary of the district of Koonawur, is over a ridge rising on its eastern side with a gentle acclivity; and on its western, sloping down to the left bank of the Lee, or river of Spiti. The river there is from 120 to 130 feet broad, but in one place narrows to ninety-two feet, and is at that point crossed by a sango or rude wooden bridge. Elevation above the sea 11,900 feet. Lat. 32°, long. 78° 37′.

CHOOHURPOOR, in the British district of Allyghur, lieut.-gov. of the N.W. Provinces, a village on the route from the cantonment of Allyghur to that of Delhi, and 11 miles N.W. of the former. Lat. 28°, long. 78° 3′.

CHOOKANEEPARA, in the British district of Camroop, in Assam, a town 34 miles S.E. of Goalpara, 45 miles S.W. of Gowhatty. Lat. 25° 52′, long. 91° 5′.

CHOOLERA, in the British district of Bareilly, lieut.-gov. of the N.W. Provinces, a village on the route from the city of Agra to Bareilly, and 28 miles S.W. of the latter. It is situate in a well-watered, fertile, level, and well-cultivated country. Lat. 28° 13′, long. 79° 10′.

CHOOMBI.—A town in a slip of territory belonging to Thibet, lying between the north-western boundary of Bhotan and the eastern boundary of Sikhim, distant N.E. from Darjeeling 53 miles. Lat. 27° 30′, long. 89°.

CHOONAPANEE, in the British district of Kumaon, lieut.-gov. of the N.W. Provinces, a village and small military station on the route from Birm Deo guard-house to Chumpawut, and four miles N.W. of the former. Elevation above the sea 1,500 feet. Lat. 29° 8′, long. 80° 9′.

CHOONGA.—A village in Bahawulpore, on the route from Subzulcote to Shikarpoor, and 60 miles S.W. of the former place. It is situate on the east bank of a deep and extensive *dund*, or pool of water, replenished by the inundations of the Indus. Choonga, by the draft treaty of November, 1842, was to have been transferred to Bahawulpore. Subsequently, the limits of the cession were altered, and the village was not included within them. Lat. 27° 48′, long. 69° 4′.

CHOONHURUH.—See CHOOLERA.

CHOORCHIN, in the British district of Kumaon, lieut.-gov. of the N.W. Provinces, a halting-place on the route, by the Unta Dhura Pass, from Almorah fort to Hiundes, or South-western Tibet, 156 miles N.E. of Almorah. The Chinese frontier is marked by a low wall, about a mile north of this place. Elevation of encampment about 15,000 feet. Lat. 30° 35′, long. 80° 17′.

CHOOREEA, in the British district of Chota Nagpoor, lieut.-gov. of Bengal, a town three miles from the right bank of the river Dammoodah, 23 miles N.E. of Lohadugga. Lat. 23° 31′, long. 85° 7′.

CHOORHA, in the British district of Bareilly, lieut.-gov. of the N.W. Provinces, a village on the route from the town of Bareilly to Seetapoor, and 18 miles E. of the former. Lat. 28° 18′, long. 79° 45′.

CHOORHUT.—A town in the native state of Rewah or Baghelcund, distant E. from Rewah 23 miles. Lat. 24° 24′, long. 81° 45′.

CHOOROO, a town in the Rajpoot state of Beekaneer, on the eastern frontier towards Shekhawuttee, lies on the route from Kanound to the town of Beekaneer, and 105 miles E. of the latter. It is situate on the eastern border of the desert, in a tract of extreme desolation. Elphinstone, who visited it in 1808, thus describes its state at that time:—"It is near a mile and a half round, without counting its large but mean suburbs; and though situate among naked sandhills, it has a very handsome appearance. The houses are all terraced, and both they and the walls of the town are built of a kind of limestone of so pure a white that it gives an air of great neatness to everything composed of it. It is, however, soft, and crumbles into a white powder, mixed here and there with shells. It is found in large beds in many parts of the desert. The chief of Chooroo is a dependant, rather than a subject, of the rajah of Beekaneer." Chooroo was formerly a flourishing place, but at the time of the British mission to Beekaneer in 1835, Boileau found that its commerce had been lost, from causes which he does not distinctly specify. Its merchants had removed, its bazaars had become desolate, and its fortifications had fallen to ruin. Lat. 28° 14′, long. 75° 1′.

CHOPALLA, in the Peshawur division of the Punjab, a town situated on the route from Jhelum to Pind Dadun Khan, eight miles S.W. of the town of Jhelum. Lat. 32° 57′, long. 73° 30′.

CHOPRA, in the British district of Candeish, presidency of Bombay, a town about eight miles from the right bank of the river Taptee, 51 miles N.E. of Dhoolia. Lat. 21° 14′, long. 75° 27′.

CHOPRAKOT, in the British district of Gurwhal, lieut.-gov. of the N.W. Provinces, a town 30 miles S.E. from Sireenuggur, 39 miles N.W. of Almora. Lat. 29° 59′, long. 79° 14′.

CHOPRA TUCKEA, in the British district of Paneeput, lieut.-gov. of the N.W. Provinces, a village on the route from the city of Delhi to Kurnoul, and 27 miles S.E. of the latter. Lat. 29° 19′, long. 77° 3′.

CHORE, in the British province of Scinde, presidency of Bombay, a town on the route from Hyderabad to Jessulmeer, 90 miles E. of the former. Lat. 25° 30′, long. 69° 55′.

CHORLA, a small river of Scinde, rises in the Keertar range of mountains, about lat. 25° 55′, long. 67° 50′. It has a course generally northerly of about thirty-five miles, and is lost in the arid tract west of Sehwan, in lat. 26° 20′, long. 67° 45′. In the upper part of its course it is called the Mulleeree, lower down, the Joorunb, and finally, the Chorla. It is dry for the greater part of the year, but water may be always obtained by digging in the bed.

CHORWAUR, in the peninsula of Kattywar, province of Guzerat, a town lying on the south-west coast, where the small river Vriddi falls into the Arabian Sea. It is stated to contain 1,500 houses, but far from being fully inhabited. Distance from Ahmedabad, S.W., 210 miles; Baroda, S.W., 215. Lat. 21° 2′, long. 70° 16′.

CHOTA BHOWANEE, in the British district of Hurriana, lieut.-gov. of the N.W. Provinces, a village on the route from Hansee to Neemuch, and 11 miles S. of the former. Lat. 28° 56′, long. 76° 7′.

CHOTA BULLEAH, in the British district of Mongheer, lieut.-gov. of Bengal, a town on the route from Mongheer to Chupra, 10 miles N.W. of the former. Lat. 25° 24′, long. 86° 22′.

CHOTADEKOTE, in the Mooltan division of the Punjab, a town situated 10 miles from the west or right bank of the river Indus, 13 miles S. of the town of Dera Ghazee Khan. Lat. 29° 52′, long. 70° 49′.

CHOTA KALLEE SIND.—The name of one of the principal feeders of the Chumbul. It rises in lat. 22° 50′, long. 76° 15′, in the territory of Dewas, and, flowing in a south-westerly direction for 104 miles through the territories of Dewas, Gwalior, Holkar's territory, and Jhalawur, falls into the Chumbul on the right side, in lat. 23° 59′, long. 75° 33′.

CHOTA NAGPORE, or NAGPORE THE LESS.—A British district of Bengal, under the control and management of an officer designated the Political Agent for the South-west Frontier and Commissioner of Chota Nagpore, to whose jurisdiction it was transferred in 1833, having previously been part of the zillah of Ramgurh. It is bounded on the north by the British districts Palamow and Ramgurh; on the east by the British districts Pachete and Singhboom; on the south by the British district of Singhboom and the native states of Bonei, Gangpoor, and Jushpoor; on the west by the native states of Odeipore and Sirgooja; and lies between lat. 22° 28′—23° 40′, long. 83° 54′—85° 56′. The area is 5,308 square miles. The country is but very imperfectly known, and trustworthy notices respecting it are scanty. It is represented as for the most part being a table-land, with an elevation of about 3,000 feet above the sea; but the surface undulates. The north-eastern part of the district is drained by numerous tributaries of the Soobun Reeka, flowing to the south-east, and falling into the Bay of Bengal: the south and west parts are drained by the Coel and other tributaries of the Byturnee, holding a course nearly south. Much of this district, especially the hilly part, is overrun by jungle and forests, abounding in fine timber, among which the sal (Shorea robusta) and teak are the best. There are, besides, the sissoo, various descriptions of palm, ebony, and many others. An experimental coffee-plantation was formed in this district by the British government in 1844, but was subsequently disposed of to a native planter.

The climate is little modified by the great general elevation of the surface. The range of the thermometer in the plains "may be said to be from 72° to 88° in the twenty-four hours during the rainy season; from 78° to 98° in the hot season; and from 66° to 32° in the cold season;" at which last time, in January, the thermometer has been known to fall to 28°. Coal is found in many situations in Chota Nagpore, but the veins are said to be deficient in thickness. It is conjectured that some better worth the cost of working might be discovered; but the remoteness of good markets and the want of good roads would for some time preclude any extensive or certain demand for the commodity. Iron probably exists, but the district does not appear to be rich in mineral productions. The population is given under the article BENGAL. The military head-quarters are at Dorunda, where is stationed the principal force of the Ramgurh light infantry and four guns, together with two companies of local horse. The principal routes are—1. From north to south, from Hazareebagh, through Kishenpore and Dorunda, to Sumbulpore. 2. From north-east to south-west, from Hazareebagh, through Lohardugga, to the city of Nagpore.

In 1832 serious disturbances broke out in this district, and rapidly extended to the adjacent district of Palamow. A state of complete disorganization ensued; and it was only by the employment of a strong military force, and after considerable resistance, that order was at length restored. The disturbed districts, previously parts of a collectorate under the ordinary regulations, were thereupon placed under a system of administration, which, judging from the results, is better suited to their condition; and thenceforward were tranquil.

CHOTA OODEPOOR.—See OODEPOOR.

CHOTA ORAMPAD, in the British district of Cuddapah, presidency of Madras, a town on the route from Cuddapah to Madras, 41 miles S.E. of the former. Lat. 14° 3′, long. 79° 20′.

CHOTA SERYE, in the territory of Gwalior, a village on the route from Agra to Gwalior fort, 40 miles S. of former, 31 N.W. of latter. It is a small place, ill supplied with water from one well, and has a mud fort at the head of deep ravines, extending north to the channel of the Chumbul. Lat. 26° 37′, long. 77° 57′.

CHOTEE, in the Mooltan division of the Punjab, a town situated 38 miles S.W. of Dera Ghazee Khan, 65 miles N. of the town of Mithun Kote. Lat. 29° 52′, long. 70° 19′.

CHOTEYLA, in the peninsula of Kattywar, province of Guzerat, a town near the northern frontier. It is situate close to a mountain of considerable elevation, denominated from the town, and is the principal place of a subdivision having a population of 1,840 persons, and paying a tribute of 252 rupees to the British government. Distant from Ahmedabad, S.W., 100 miles. Lat. 22° 24′, long. 71° 11′.

CHOTUN.—A town in the Rajpoot state of Joudpore, distant S.W. from Joudpore 141 miles. Lat. 25° 31′, long. 71° 3′.

CHOUBEPOOR, in the British district of Benares, lieut.-gov. of the N.W. Provinces, a village on the route from the city of Benares to Ghazeepoor, 12 miles N. of the former, 34 S.W. of the latter. Lat. 25° 28′, long. 83° 5′.

CHOUCHUCK, in the Baree Dooab division of the Punjab, a town situated on the left bank of the river Ravee, 60 miles S.W. of the town of Lahore. Lat. 31°, long. 73° 28′.

CHOUDANS, in the British district of Kumaon, lieut.-gov. of the N.W. Provinces, a small Bhoti mahall or subdivision lying between the rivers Kalee (Eastern) and Dhoulee, and extending upwards from the bifurcation at their confluence. It is about twelve miles in length from north to south, and eight in breadth, and lies between lat. 29° 57′—30° 8′, long. 80° 37′—80° 47′; containing probably between eighty and ninety square miles of area, all consisting of lofty and steep mountains or rugged ravines, as it is situate among the summits of the main chain of the Himalaya.

CHOUDHA.—See Chodhon.

CHOUDWAN, in the Damaun division of the Punjab, a town situated 49 miles S.W. of Dera Ismael Khan, 56 miles N.W. of the town of Leia. Lat. 31° 26′, long. 70° 14′.

CHOUGUL.—A town in the native state of Cashmere, or dominions of Gholab Singh, 34 miles N.W. from Sirinagur, and 111 miles N.E. from Jhelum. Lat. 34° 23′, long. 74° 31′.

CHOUL.—See Chowul.

CHOUMOOH, in the Rajpoot state of Jeypoor, a town 18 miles N. of the city of Jeypore, the principal place of a zemindarry or fief estimated to yield an annual revenue of 115,000 rupees. Lat. 27° 12′, long. 75° 50′.

CHOUNTERA, in the Peshawr division of the Punjab, a town situated 26 miles N.W. of Kala Bagh, 70 miles S.W. of the town of Peshawur. Lat. 33° 4′, long. 71° 10′.

CHOUPUKHEEA, in the British district Kumaon, lieut.-gov. of the N.W. Provinces, a village with a temple and a small military station, five miles E. of Petoragurh cantonment. Lat. 29° 35′, long. 80° 20′.

CHOUR, a remarkable peak on the northern boundary of Sirmoor, is the most elevated summit among the mountains rising over Hindostan to the south of the Himalayas, with which range it is connected by a transverse ridge running nearly north and south a distance of above fifty miles. The Chour forms a striking object as seen from the plains of Sirhind, and affords a noble prospect from its summit. "Nothing," observes Royle, "could be more magnificent than the view from this culminating point, having the plains of India indefinitely extended to the southward, and on the north the snowy peaks of the Himalaya towering even above this great height." Elevation above the sea 12,149 feet. Lat. 30° 52′, long. 77° 32′.

CHOURAR.—A petty district of Jareegah Rajpoots, in the north-western part of the province of Guzerat. During the rains, when the Runn fills, Chourar is almost an island. It lies between lat. 23° 35′ and 23° 56′, and long. 70° 53′ and 71° 11′; and is bounded on the north and south by the Runn; on the east by Warye; and on the west by Cutch. It is about twenty-five miles long and seventeen broad. The country is flat and open. Salt is found in large quantities. The great road from Pallee and Hindostan, which is also the line of transit from all parts of Northern Guzerat to the Mandavie Bunder and the whole of Cutch, passes through this district. The population amounts to about 2,500. The chiefs entertain twenty-five soldiers for their own protection, but, like the neighbouring districts, look for support from foreign invasion to the British government. The revenues average about 9,000 rupees per annum. Chourar pays no tribute to any government. The connection of Chourar with the British government first took place in 1819, upon the expulsion by the latter of the marauders from Guzerat. Further engagements were entered into in 1826. In its internal affairs no interference is exercised by the protecting power.

CHOURASS, in the district of Pertabgurh, territory of Oude, a town 13 miles W. of the town of Pertabgurh, 85 S.E. of Lucknow. Butter estimates the population at 4,000, all Hindoos and cultivators. Lat. 25° 56′, long. 81° 47′.

CHOUSALLA.—A town in Hyderabad, or dominions of the Nizam, distant S. from Jaulnah 80 miles. Lat. 18° 42′, long. 75° 46′.

CHOUTHKA BURWARA.—A town in the Rajpoot state of Jeypoor, 65 miles S.E. from Jeypoor, and 22 miles S.E. from Tonk. Lat. 26° 3′, long. 76° 19′.

CHOWBEESA, in the British territory of Saugor and Nerbudda, lieut.-gov. of the N.W. Provinces, a town on the left bank of the Nerbudda river, 58 miles E. of Jubbulpore. Lat. 23°, long. 80° 55′.

CHOWDHERA, in the British district of Boolundshuhur, lieut.-gov. of the N.W. Provinces, a village on the route from Allygurh cantonment to that of Moradabad, and 18 miles N. of the former. Lat. 28° 9′, long. 78° 14′.

CHOWGONG.—A town in the British district of Rajeshaye, lieut.-gov. of Bengal, 16 miles N.E. of Natore. Lat. 24° 33′, long. 89° 12′.

CHOWHAREE, in the British district of Allahabad, lieut.-gov. of the N.W. Provinces, a village on the route by the Kutra Pass from Allahabad to Rewa, and 37 miles S.E. of the former city. Lat. 25° 9′, long. 82° 14′.

CHOWKA, a tributary of the great river Ghoghra, rises in the British district of Bareilly, about lat. 28° 59′, long. 80° 4′. It takes a south-easterly direction through the districts of Bareilly and Shahjehanpore, and at the distance of forty miles from the source, and in lat. 28° 43′, long. 80° 15′, it on the left side is joined by an offset from the river Ghoghra. At the distance of 100 miles lower down, it, in lat. 27° 41′, long. 81° 7′, receives on the right side the Woel or Ool, a river of smaller size. Continuing a south-easterly course for about forty miles farther, it falls into the Ghoghra on the right side, in lat. 27° 9′, long. 81° 30′. It is navigable throughout the year. Buchanan signifies this river by the Bhakosa, which he mentions falls into the Ghoghra about forty miles below the confluence of the Setiganga.

CHOWKAAD, or **CHAUGAT**, in the British district of Malabar, presidency of Madras, a town on an inlet of the Arabian Sea, communicating with the estuary of a considerable stream descending from the Western Ghats. Distance from Chattwye or Chitwa, N., three miles; Calicut, S.E., 51. Lat. 10° 35′, long. 76° 6′.

CHOWKY.—A town in the territory of Nagpore, distant N. from Nagpore 82 miles. Lat. 22° 12′, long. 78° 31′.

CHOWMHAN, in the British district of Muttra, lieut.-gov. of the N.W. Provinces, a village on the route from Muttra cantonment to Delhi, and 13 miles N.W. of the former. Lat. 27° 37′, long. 77° 39′.

CHOWNDIA, in the Rajpoot state of Joudpore, a village containing thirty houses, on the route from the town of Joudpore to that of Ajmere, and 36 miles N.W. of the latter. Lat. 26° 34′, long. 74° 15′.

CHOWREGURH, in the British territory of Saugor and Nerbudda, lieut.-gov. of the N.W. Provinces, a fort among the Mahadeo Mountains. During the great Mahratta war in 1818, it was held by a garrison for the rajah of Berar or Nagpore, and evacuated on the approach of a British detachment, which took possession of it. In the same year it was ceded, with the rest of the Saugor and Nerbudda territory, to the British government by the treaty of Nagpore. In the close of the same year, a party of 2,000 Gonds attempted to retake it. The garrison consisted of only thirty men, commanded by a native officer. But these, maintaining a good countenance, deterred the besiegers from an assault by the constant fire of their guns, until a relief appeared, when the enemy were repulsed with great slaughter. Distant S.W. from Jubbulpore 70 miles. Lat. 22° 45′, long. 79°.

CHOWRYE.—A town in the territory of Nagpore, distant N. from Nagpore 60 miles. Lat. 22° 3′, long. 79° 16′.

CHOWSA, or **CHOUNSA**, in the British district of Shahabad, lieut.-gov. of Bengal, a town on the right bank of the Ganges, at the confluence of the Kurumnassa. Heber describes it as "a large town, with some neat mosques and the remains of a fort." It, however, appears to be at present in a ruinous state. Here, in 1539, the fate of the empire was decided in a battle between Humaion, the padshah of Delhi, and his Afghan rival Sheer Shah. Nearly the whole of the army of Humaion was driven into the river and drowned; and Humaion himself was saved from the same fate by floating upon a water-bag, which had been inflated for the purpose by one of the fugitives. Baber mentions that he visited Chowsa. Distant N.W. from Calcutta 574 miles by the river's course; 399 by land, *viá* Sasseram and Buxar. Lat. 25° 27′, long. 83° 58′.

CHOWUL, or **CHOUL**, in the British district of Tannah, presidency of Bombay, a town and seaport of the Northern Concan, 23 miles S. of Bombay. Lat. 18° 34′, long. 72° 59′.

CHOYAH NUDDEE.—A river of Sirhind, rising in lat. 30° 48′, long. 76° 50′, and, flowing in a south-westerly direction for twenty miles through the British district of Umballa, and seventy miles through the native territories of Patialah and Nabha, becomes absorbed in Patialah, about lat. 30° 4′, long. 75° 50′.

CHRYAKOT, or **CHERIAKOT**, in the British district of Azimgurh, lieut.-gov. of the N.W. Provinces, the principal place of the pergunnah of the same name, is on the route from the town of Azimgurh to that of Ghazeepoor, 20 miles S.E. of the former, 24 N.W. of the latter, 45 N.E. of Benares, and in lat. 25° 53′, long. 83° 24′.

CHUASI.—A town in the Trans-Sutlej hill state of Sukhet, 28 miles S.E. from Sukhet, and 20 miles N.E. from Simla. Lat. 31° 23′, long. 77° 20′.

CHUBRAMOW, in the British district of Furruckabad, a large straggling town on the trunk road from Calcutta to Delhi, and 18 miles S.W. of Futtehghur. It is mentioned by Tieffenthaler under the name of Zebramao, and probably in the Ayeen Akbery under the name of Clupramow. Lat. 27° 9′, long. 79° 32′.

CHUCH, an extensive plain to the east of Attock, and, from its proximity to that place, sometimes called the Plain of Attock. Its extent from east to west is, according to Vigne, twenty miles, and from north to south about fifteen miles. Its centre is in lat. 33° 50′, long. 72° 25′.

CHUCK, in the British province of Scinde, presidency of Bombay, a town on the left bank of the Indus, 29 miles W. of Subzulcote. Lat. 28° 15′, long. 69° 30′.

CHUCKEREEA.—A town in the British district of Chittagong, lieut.-gov. of Bengal, 49 miles S. of Chittagong. Lat. 21° 42′, long. 92° 10′.

CHUCKURDUPOOR. — A town in the British district of Singboom, on the south-west frontier of Bengal, 20 miles N.W. from Chaibassa, and 69 miles S.E. from Lohadugga. Lat. 22° 41′, long. 85° 28′.

CHUCKWADEE.—A town in the British district of Ramgurh, lieut.-gov. of Bengal, 70 miles N.E. of Hazareebagh. Lat. 24° 20′, long. 86° 25′.

CHUHKOWAL, in the Peshawar division of the Punjab, a town situated on the route from Attock to Pind Dadun Khan, 60 miles S. of the town of Attock. Lat. 33° 3′, long. 72° 37′.

CHUKA.—A town in the native state of Bhotan, distant E. from Darjeeling 68 miles. Lat. 27° 3′, long. 89° 23′.

CHUKDEHA, in the British district of Allahabad, lieut.-gov. of the N.W. Provinces, a village on the route by the Kutra Pass from Allahabad to Rewa, and 37 miles S.E. of the former city. Lat. 25° 14′, long. 82° 11′.

CHUKHERA, in the British district of Futtehpoor, lieut.-gov. of the N.W. Provinces, a village on the route from Calpee to the town of Futtehpoor, and seven miles N.W. of the latter. Lat. 25° 59′, long. 80° 43′.

CHUKSANA, in the native state of Bhurtpore, a village on the route from Agra to the city of Bhurtpore, 23 miles W. of the former, 11 E. of the latter. Lat. 27° 11′, long. 77° 43′.

CHUKUN, in the British district of Poonah, presidency of Bombay, a town on the route from Poonah to Narrayungaum, 20 miles N. of the former. Lat. 18° 48′, long. 73° 51′.

CHUKURPOOR, in the British district of Cawnpore, lieut.-gov. of the N.W. Provinces, a village on the route from Calpee to the cantonment of Cawnpore, and 12 miles W. of the latter. Lat. 26° 26′, long. 80° 15′.

CHULERA.—See CHILLERA.

CHULEYSUR, in the British district of Agra, a village on the route from the city of Agra to Mynpooree, and seven miles N.E. of the former. Lat. 27° 13′, long. 78° 10′.

CHULGULLY. — A town in the native state of Sirgoojah, 23 miles N.E. from Sirgoojah, and 51 miles S.W. from Palamow. Lat. 23° 20′, long. 83° 28′.

CHUMALARI.—A lofty peak in the snowy range of the Himalayas, having an elevation of 23,929 feet. Distant N.E. from Darjeeling 80 miles. Lat. 27° 49′, long. 89° 19′.

CHUMARPOORA, in the British district of Moradabad, lieut.-gov. of the N.W. Provinces, a village on the route from Bareilly to Delhi, and 42 miles W. of the former. Lat. 28° 27′, long. 78° 52′.

CHUMATANG. — A town in the native state of Cashmere, or dominions of Gholab Singh, 205 miles S.E. from Sirinagur, and 173 N.E. from Simla. Lat. 33° 20′, long. 78° 27′.

CHUMBA, in Gurwhal, a summit in the ridge stretching from Surkanda to the right bank of the Bhagerettee, as the Ganges is called in the upper part of its course. During the time the Goorkahs occupied the country, 1,000 of their troops held the stockade constructed here. It was a secondary station in the trigonometrical survey of the Himalaya. Elevation above the sea 5,567 feet. Lat. 30° 20′, long. 78° 28′.

CHUMBAGURH, in the Cis-Sutlej hill state of Hindoor, a fort on the steep ridge which, rising over the left bank of the Sutlej, is continued in a south-east direction to Ramgurh, and joins the Sub-Himalaya. Elevation above the sea 4,400 feet. Lat. 31° 13′, long. 76° 48′.

CHUMBALLA.—A strong stockade situate on the Arracan river, about 16 miles S. of the town of Arracan. The fortification formed an object of contest during the Burmese war in 1825. Lat. 20° 28′, long. 93° 20′.

CHUMBELA, or CHUMBLA.—A river rising in the Vindhya Mountains, near the town of Dhar, and in lat. 22° 40′, long. 75° 14′. It holds a northerly course of about seventy miles, in some degree parallel with the Chumbul, into which it falls on the left side, in lat. 23° 24′, long. 75° 28′. It is confounded by Ritter with the Chumbul.

CHUMBUL RIVER, a considerable tributary of the Jumna, rises in Malwa, in lat. 22° 26′, long. 75° 45′, about eight or nine miles south-west of the British station of Mhow, the elevation of which above the sea is 2,019 feet. The source is four miles south-east of the town of Hasulpoor, and two miles west of Burgoonda, and on the north side of the line of waterheads which determines the flow of the streams rising on that side towards the Jumna; those rising on the south side taking their courses to the river Nerbudda. The cluster of summits of the Vindhya range, amidst which the Chumbul rises, has the local appellation of Janapava. Malcolm considers this merely the nominal source, observing, "This part of the river is dry in the hot season, during which it owes its waters to other tributary streams." Such is probably the case but for a very short distance, as the Chumbul, where crossed by the route from Mhow to Dhar, at Achana Munana Ghat, about fifteen miles from its source, is sixty yards wide, with steep banks, small stream throughout the year, and sandy bottom, according to Garden, who is likely to be correctly informed. Flowing northerly, it, after a course of about eighty miles, receives on the left side the Chambela, or Chumbla, a river of nearly equal length and size with itself, and which holds like it a northerly course. About ten miles below it, on the same side, the Chumbul receives the river Waugeri, flowing from the south-west. At the town of Tal, fifteen miles lower down, the river turns to the north-west, and five or six miles farther, receives on the left side the Molanee, a tributary of greater extent of course than that of the Wageri. Thence winding with a strongly-marked detour round the fortress of Nagutwara, it flows to the south-east for ten miles, at which distance it turns to the north-east, and on the right side, fifteen miles lower down, receives the Seepra, a stream like itself flowing from the Vindhya range, and little inferior in length of course or volume of water. The Chumbul, eight miles below the confluence of the Seepra, receives, also on the right side, the Chota Kallee Sind, so called in contradistinction to a more considerable river, the Kali Sind, holding its course farther east. From the confluence of the Chota Sind, the Chumbul takes a north-westerly course, and, twenty miles farther, it receives on the left side the Sow, and on the same side, five miles farther down, the Sarde, both inconsiderable streams. Thence turning to the north-east, it finds its way through the gorges of the Mokundara range to the more depressed tract of Harouti. Previously to entering this rugged tract, it is crossed at the Gujrut Ghat, on the route from Neemuch to the Mokundara Pass. It is there "fordable after the first of November, and during the rains there is a ferry-boat in attendance. The banks of the river are steep, and its bed of rock and loose stones." At the entrance into the elevated tract or irregular plateau of Mokundara, it is stated by Tod, on hearsay report, to be seventy yards wide, and confined between cliffs perfectly perpendicular. About forty miles farther down, and two hundred and nine from the source of the river, which still holds a course either northerly or north-easterly, the stream expands into a lake, from the other extremity of which it flows through a deep and narrow channel in the rock. The scene is thus described by Tod:—"Nothing seemed to disturb the unruffled surface of the lake until we approached the point of outlet, and beheld the deep bed which the river has excavated in the rock. This is the commencement of the falls. Proceeding along the margin, one rapid succeeds another, the gulf increasing in width, and the noise becoming more terrific, until you arrive at a spot where the stream is split into four distinct channels; and a little farther an isolated rock appears, high over which the whitened spray ascends, the sunbeams playing on it. Here the separated channels, each terminated in a cascade, fall into an ample basin, and again unite their waters, boiling around the masses of black rock, which ever and anon peeps out and contrasts with the foaming surge rising from the whirlpools (choolis) beneath." The width of the stream is in one place only three yards; and consequently its depth and velocity must be very great, as a few hundred yards lower down the width is five hundred yards, and when visited by Tod in the middle of February, during the dry season, the depth in the same part was forty feet. The fall is estimated by Tod to be "under two hundred feet" in the mile intervening between the lake and the isolated rock, the descent of the principal cascade being about sixty feet. At the city of Kotah, about fifty miles farther down than this remarkable scene, and two hundred and fifty-nine from the source, the Chumbul is at all seasons a large deep stream, which must be crossed by ferry, even elephants making the passage by swimming; but six miles lower down the stream, Hunter crossed it in the end of March by a ford, which is described as "stony, uneven, and slippery." Twenty-five miles lower down the stream, it is crossed, at the ford of Paranor, by the route from Agra to Mhow, at a point where, during part of the year, the "river is about three hundred yards wide, the bed of heavy sand, banks steep and cut into deep ravines. During the dry season, the stream is usually about thirty yards wide, and from two to two and a half feet deep." "The bed of the Chumbul, for some distance above and below the Paranor ford, is sandy, and is known to the natives by the name of Koosuk." Ten miles farther down, it receives on the right side the Kali Sind (the larger river of that name), a considerable stream, flowing from the Vindhya range; and about thirty-five miles farther down, on the same side, the Parbati, rising also in the Vindhya, a few miles to the east of the source of the Kali Sind, and flowing nearly parallel to it. From this confluence, the course of the Chumbul, hitherto northerly, turns north-east, and twelve miles farther down receives on the left side its greatest tributary, the Banas, which, rising in the Aravulli range, drains or fertilizes a large portion of Rajpootana. The Chumbul, after this junction, is a great river, probably in few places fordable; and continuing a north-easterly course forty-five miles farther down, it is crossed by a ferry on the route from Nusserabad to Gwalior. Continuing to flow in the same direction about fifty-five miles further, it passes by the city of Dholpore, situate on its north-western or left bank, where it is so deep as to be passable by ferry only, yet fordable at Khitora, nearly four miles higher up, though there three-quarters of a mile broad in the dry season. "In the rainy season, when the channel is full, the prospect of such a body of running water, bounded by hills, which rise in a variety of fantastic shapes, forms a landscape peculiarly interesting."

At Dholpore the Chumbul is a beautiful clear stream, flowing gently over a bed of fine sand. In the close of April, 1805, it was forded in this vicinity, probably at Khetri, by the British army under General Lake, marching from Bhurtpore to Gwalior; and on that occasion the approaches to the stream were found so difficult, that it was necessary to make a road for the passage of the troops, who amounted to 30,000 fighting men. About forty-five miles below this city it takes a south-easterly direction, and forty-three miles lower down, in the vicinity of Birgowah, on the route from Etawah to Gwalior, is crossed by ferry; but is fordable for elephants and camels in December. Continuing in a south-easterly course for thirty-five miles, it falls into the Jumna on the right side, in lat. 26° 30′, long. 79° 19′. Its total length of course by the windings of the stream is 570 miles, described in a form nearly semicircular; the diameter being about 330 miles, from the source near Mhow to the mouth, forty miles below Etawah. Its average volume of water is said to be so considerable, that on its junction with the Jumna the Chumbul has been known, when flooded, to raise the united stream seven or eight feet in twelve hours. Bacon, however, who saw the Chumbul in the end of December, and during the dry season, states it then to have but a small volume of water. It does not appear to be used for navigation, which is probably incompatible with the average declivity of its bed, amounting to nearly two feet and a half per mile, and still more so with the general rugged and rocky character of its channel. In the early wars waged by the Mogul dynasty of Delhi for the establishment or extension of their power, it seems to have been an important military frontier, and is repeatedly mentioned by Baber.

CHUMKOOR, in Sirhind, a village on the route from Ropur to Lodiana, and seven miles S.W. of the former place. It is situate on the western brow of a high bank, formerly apparently the left bank of the Sutlej, which now flows four miles farther north. The tract intervening between the village and the river is level, low, much intersected by watercourses, and in consequence always moist, and covered with luxuriant grass and jungle. Lat. 30° 54′, long. 76° 30′.

CHUMMOO, in the Rajpoot state of Joudpore, a village on the route from Pokhurn to the town of Joudpore, and 46 miles N.W. of the latter. It is supplied with water from a well 150 feet deep. Lat. 26° 40′, long. 72° 42′.

CHUMMOOREA, in the British district of Camroop, in Assam, a town 39 miles E. of Goalpara, 34 miles S.W. of Gowhatty. Lat. 26°, long. 91° 11′.

CHUMORA, in the British district of Kumaon, lieut.-gov. of the N.W. Provinces, a village near the right bank of the Ramgunga (Eastern), and on the route from Almorah cantonment to Serakot, 30 miles N.E. of the former. Lat. 29° 47′, long. 80° 10′.

CHUMPAPOOR, in the British district of Sarun, lieut.-gov. of Bengal, a town 21 miles N.E. of Bettiah. Lat. 26° 53′, long. 84° 54′.

CHUMPAWUT.—See CHAMPAWUT.

CHUMUR.—A town in the native state of Cashmeer, or territory of Gholab Singh, 136 miles N.E. from Simla. Lat. 32° 40′, long. 78° 35′.

CHUNAHULLY.—A town in Mysore, under the administration and control of the government of India, distant N. from Seringapatam 50 miles. Lat. 13° 9′, long. 76° 56′.

CHUNAR, or CHUNARGURH, in the British district of Mirzapoor, lieut.-gov. of the N.W. Provinces, a town with fort, on a sandstone rock, close to the right or south-eastern bank of the Ganges, here at all times navigable for craft of fifty or sixty tons, completely commanded by the batteries. The rocky eminence rises abruptly from the edge of the stream to the height of 104 feet, but attains its greatest elevation about 200 yards farther south-east, where it is 146 feet high. The space inclosed by the rampart is 750 yards in length from north to south, its greatest breadth (about 300 yards) being at its northern face, fronting the Ganges: the circuit measured round the rampart is 1,850 yards. At short intervals there are many towers along the rampart, which is from ten to twenty feet high. A great part of this inclosure is generally merely an open space under grass, and a few fine trees, amongst which are the bungalows or lodges of the officers; and in some interior inclosures are the governor's house, the hospital, and the state prison, in which was confined Trimbukji Dainglia, an active instigator and promoter of the Mahratta confederacy, in 1817-18, against the British power. In the midst of this inclosure, and on the highest point of the rocky eminence, is the antique Hindoo palace, a massy vaulted edifice, containing a well fifteen feet in diameter, sunk to a very great depth in the solid rock, and always containing water, but of so indifferent quality that is not to be used except in case of emergency. Here is also a subterranean dungeon now used only as a cellar. In a small square court overshadowed by a pipal-tree, is a large slab of black marble, on which, according to Hindoo belief, "the Almighty is seated personally, though invisibly, for nine hours every day, removing during the other three hours to Benares;" and hence the sepoys conclude, that the fort cannot be taken except between the hours of six and nine in the morning. The exterior rampart is of no strength, as was proved in the course of its siege by the British in 1764, when it was in a few hours breached by a slender battering-train. The steepness of the face of the rock would, however, make storming very hazardous; and a number of large rudely-made stone cylinders are stored in all parts of the fortress, for the garrison to roll down on storming parties. The citadel, or principal stronghold, is in the north-eastern part of the greater inclosure. It mounts many cannon, and has a fine bomb-proof powder-magazine. Outside the fortifications, and on a slope to the east of them, is the native town, with houses all of stone, generally two stories high, with verandas in front, let out into shops. The population is returned at 11,058. Behind, and lower down the slope, are the European dwellings and gardens. The English church, which belongs to the Church Missionary Society, is built in a good and solid style, and embellished with a Gothic steeple. There is also here a chapel erected at the cost of the government, aided by private subscriptions, for the use of soldiers of the Roman Catholic persuasion. Chunar is a principal invalid station for European troops, though the intense heat felt here during the sultry season seems ill calculated to qualify it for such a purpose. The number of troops located here amounted in 1849 to 280, exclusive of British officers. Outside the town is the tomb of a certain Kaseem Soliman, and of his son, reputed as saints by the Mussulmans, and whose memory has been honoured by one of the sovereigns of Delhi with a splendid mausoleum and mosque. "The buildings, and the grove in which they stand, are very solemn and striking; and the carving of the principal gateway, and of the stone lattice with which the garden is inclosed, is more like embroidery than the work of the chisel."

Chunar was a place of importance as early as 1529, when it was held by a garrison of Baber, who then visited the place, and mentions that its vicinity was infested by the elephant, tiger, and rhinoceros. It soon after fell into the hands of Shir Khan, the Patan aspirant to the sovereignty of Delhi; as Ferishta mentions, that in 1532 he refused to deliver it to Humaion, the son and successor of Baber. It was taken by Humaion in 1539, but almost immediately retaken by Shir Khan; after whose death, Chunar, with the rest of the empire of Delhi, returned under the power of his rival. On the dissolution of the empire of Delhi, subsequently to the invasion of Ahmed Shah Durani, in 1760, it was seized by the nawaub of Oude. In the course of the war between the nawaub and the East-India Company, it was besieged by the troops of the latter, under General Carnac, who was repulsed in a night attack; but the rampart being breached in the south-western quarter, the garrison surrendered. In 1768, the fort, with its territory, was formally ceded by treaty to the East-India Company, and was for some time the principal depôt for artillery and ammunition for the North-Western Provinces. Elevation above the sea 280 feet. Distant E. from Mirzapoor, by land, 21 miles; by water, along the course of the Ganges, 30; S.W. from Benares 16; N.W. from Calcutta 437. Lat. 25° 5′, long. 83°.

CHUNDA.—A town in the native state of Korea, on the south-west frontier of Bengal, 21 miles N. from Korea, and 53 miles N.W. from Sirgoojah. Lat. 23° 24′, long. 82° 20′.

CHUNDALLEA, in the Rajpoot state of Joudpore, a village on the route from Pokhurn to the town of Joudpore, and 34 miles N.W. of the latter. Lat. 26° 35′, long. 72° 53′.

CHUNDA PERTABPOOR, in the territory of Oude, a town on the route from the cantonment of Jounpore to that of Sultanpoor, 36 miles N.W. of the former, 20 S.E. of the latter. Lat. 26° 5′, long. 82° 18′.

CHUNDA TAL, in the British district of Goruckpore, lieut.-gov. of the N.W. Provinces, a small lake which in the rainy season attains a length of about three miles, with a breadth of two; but its dimensions somewhat contract in the dry season. Distant from the town of Goruckpore, W., 43 miles. Lat. 26° 45′, long. 82° 38′.

CHUNDAWUL, in the Rajpoot state of Joudpore, a village on the route from Nusseerabad to Deesa, and 61 miles S.W. of the former. It is of considerable size, and contains twenty shops. Lat. 26°, long. 73° 55′.

CHUNDEEPOOR, in the British district of Futtehpoor, lieut.-gov. of the N.W. Provinces, a village on the route from Cawnpore to the town of Futtehpoor, and five miles N.W. of the latter. Lat. 25° 58′, long. 80° 46′.

CHUNDEPOOR.—A town in the territory of Nagpore, distant N.E. from Nagpore 171 miles. Lat. 22°, long. 81° 40′.

CHUNDERGERRY, or CHANDRAGIRI, in the British district of Malabar, presidency of Madras, a large square fort on an elevated site on the south side of the Chandragiri river, the northern boundary of Malabar. It was built by Sivuppa Nayaka, who reigned in Ikeri from the year 1648 to 1670, and was the first rajah of that state who made conquests in Malabar. The Chandragiri river descends from the Western Ghauts, and during the monsoon is a great torrent, but in the dry season is shallow, but very wide, and expands into an extensive estuary communicating with a salt-water lake. Distance from Cannanore, N.W., 50 miles; Mangalore, S.E., 30. Lat. 12° 27′, long. 75° 4′.

CHUNDERGHERRY, in the British district of North Arcot, presidency of Madras, a town on the route from Chittoor to Nellore, 30 miles N.E. of the former. Lat. 13° 36′, long. 79° 21′.

CHUNDERGOOTYPUTNUM.—A town in Hyderabad, or dominions of the Nizam, distant S. from Hyderabad 86 miles. Lat. 16° 10′, long. 78° 58′.

CHUNDERPOOR.—A desolated town of Burgun, one of the petty states on the south-west frontier of Bengal, situate on the left bank of the Mahanuddee. The place is memorable only as having been, sixty or seventy years since, the scene of one of those extraordinary tragedies which are not altogether unusual in India, when the females of the establishment of the rajah of Sumbhulpore, to avoid the Mahrattas, who took and sacked the town, deliberately threw themselves from the battlements of the fort (now in ruins) into the river below, having previously decked themselves with their choicest jewels and ornaments. Since that period the town has remained deserted, and the surrounding country, which is represented as extremely beautiful, and is be-

lieved to have formerly been in a high state of cultivation, has been greatly neglected. Lat. 21° 38′, long. 83° 5′.

CHUNDITULLA.—A town in the British district of Hoogly, lieut.-gov. of Bengal, 10 miles N.W. of Calcutta. Lat. 22° 40′, long. 88° 19′.

CHUNDKA, in the British district of Mirzapoor, lieut.-gov. of the N.W. Provinces, a town on the right bank of the Ganges, seven miles higher up the stream than Chunar; 699 N.W. of Calcutta by the river. Lat. 25° 7′, long. 82° 48′.

CHUNDLAH, in Bundelcund, a town on the route from Calpee to Adjygurh, 77 miles S. of the former. Davidson describes it as a "thriving place, with a population of 3,000 souls, and situated exactly at the base of a jet-black granitic rock, covered with enormous masses of granite blocks and a few stunted trees." Radiation from the rocks causes the heat to be almost intolerable, even in the night-time. Lat. 25° 4′, long. 80° 15′.

CHUNDOUR, in the British district of Goruckpoor, lieut.-gov. of the N.W. Provinces, a town 14 miles N. of Goruckpoor. Lat. 26° 54′, long. 83° 25′.

CHUNDOWSEE, in the British district of Moradabad, lieut.-gov. of the N.W. Provinces, a town on the route from Bareilly to Delhi, and 45 miles W. of the former. It is of considerable size, has a bazaar, and is surrounded by a low mud wall. Population 20,921. Lat. 28° 27′, long. 78° 50′.

CHUNDRAGHAT BERIKOT.—A town in the native state of Nepal, 242 miles N.W. from Khatmandoo, and 136 miles N. from Lucknow. Lat. 28° 45′, long. 81° 31′.

CHUNDRAGOONDA.—A town in Hyderabad, or dominions of the Nizam, distant E. from Hyderabad 144 miles. Lat. 17° 24′, long. 80° 40′.

CHUNDRAWUL.—A river rising in Bundelcund, in lat. 25° 18′, long. 79° 53′. It holds a course generally north-easterly for about sixty miles, and falls into the river Cane on the left side, in lat. 25° 46′, long. 80° 29′.

CHUNDROWTEE, in the British district of Benares, lieut.-gov. of the N.W. Provinces, a town on the left bank of the Ganges, five miles S. of the confluence of the Goomtee, 648 miles N.W. of Calcutta by water; 16 N.E., or lower down the stream, than the city of Benares. Lat. 25° 29′, long. 83° 6′.

CHUNDUNNUGGUR.—A town in the British district of Cuttack, lieut.-gov. of Bengal, 53 miles E. of Cuttack. Lat. 20° 34′, long. 86° 44′.

CHUNDUNPOOR.—A town in the territory of Oude, distant N. from Oude 70 miles. Lat. 27° 48′, long. 82° 3′.

CHUNDUNPOOR.—See CHANDPOOR.

CHUNDURGOOTY DROOG.—A town in Mysore, distant N. from Bedenore 44 miles. Lat. 14° 27′, long. 75° 1′.

CHUNDWUK, in the British district of Jounpoor, lieut.-gov. of the N.W. Provinces, a village on the route from the cantonment of Jounpoor to that of Ghazeepoor, 23 miles S.E. of the former, 37 W. of the latter. Lat. 25° 36′, long. 82° 59′.

CHUNGRUNG, in Bussahir, a pass in the district of Koonawur, over a ridge dividing the valley of the Pejur from that of the Mulgun. Elevation above the sea 9,527 feet. Lat. 31° 38′, long. 78° 25′.

CHUNGSA KHAGO, a pass over a lofty ridge between Bussahir and Gurwhal, leads up the stream forming the most remote feeder of the river Buspa. The journey is one of great danger and difficulty, as it lies over the snow, and rain setting in during the attempt would probably cause the destruction of the travellers. Some time before the visit of Gerard to this vicinity, in 1821, eighteen people perished at once in this pass; and since that calamity few travellers venture it. Gerard tried in vain, by extravagant offers, to induce a guide to conduct him by this route, which, however, seems occasionally to be pursued by Koonawari freebooters, in their forays into Gurwhal. As that intrepid traveller, a few days after, crossed the Charung Pass, having an elevation of 17,348 feet, some notion may be formed of the great elevation of Chungsa Khago, which was at the same time deemed impracticable. In the great trigonometrical survey of the Himalaya, a cone, having an elevation of 21,178 feet, is laid down in lat. 31° 13′, long. 78° 35′; and a comparison of this position with that assigned to the pass by approximation in the Map of Koonawur by Gerard, will indicate that the cone is about two miles south-west of the pass, and, consequently, forms a strong evidence of the vast elevaton of the ridge in that part. The position is laid in Gerard in lat. 31° 14′, long. 78° 33′.

CHUNNEE.—A town in the native state of Cashmere, or dominions of Gholab Singh, 11 miles S.W. from Jamoo, and 19 miles N.E. from Sealkote. Lat. 32° 37′, long. 74° 50′.

CHUNSHULAPET.—A town in Hyderabad, or dominions of the Nizam, distant N.E. from Hyderabad 145 miles. Lat. 19° 5′, long. 79° 49′.

CHUPPRA, in Malwa, a town with bazaar, on the route from Nusseerabad to Saugor, 197 miles S.E. of former, 153 N.W. of latter. It, with the surrounding territory, was granted to Ameer Khan by Holkar, and guaranteed to him by the East-India Company by treaty in 1818. (See TONK.) It is considered to yield an annual revenue of 100,000 rupees. Lat. 24° 37′, long. 76° 51′.

CHUPPUGHATEE, in the British district of Cawnpore, lieut.-gov. of the N.W. Provinces, a village on the route from Allahabad to Etawa, and 74 miles S.E. of the latter. It is situate on the Seengoor, or Kurun, here crossed by ford. Lat. 26° 10′, long. 79° 59′.

CHUPRA.—The principal place of the British district of Sarun, lieut.-gov. of Bengal, a town on the left bank of a channel of the Ganges, and on the route from Dinapore to Goruckpore, 24 miles N.W. of the former, and 124 S.E. of the latter. It contains a good many large handsome native houses. There is only one street, however, passable for wheeled vehicles; and even that is so narrow that it is difficult for small conveyances, while the other thoroughfares are scarcely practicable for palkies or litters. With the exception of the spacious dwellings of the Mahajans, or wealthy tradesmen, the houses are built of mud, with tiled roofs. The town has little breadth, but extends a mile along the river, "uniting with Sahibgunge on the east, which again joins Govingunge: this unites with Cheraied and Doonegunge, from which place to Revelgunge, a distance of fourteen miles, the appearance from the river resembles that of a long straggling town." It lies low, being but a very few feet above the level of the river, which is separated from the main channel by an extensive swampy island, and is navigable during the rains; but from October to July is impracticable for craft of any kind. The civil station is outside the town, and north of it. Chupra appears, from recent accounts, to be a populous place, well adapted for the comfortable residence of Europeans, in consequence of the salubrity of the air, the intercourse by means of the river with Dinapore, Patna, Benares, and more remotely with Calcutta and many other great towns. The population, variously reported, is, without doubt, considerable. Tieffenthaler, about eighty years ago, describes Chupra as extending half a mile along the Ganges; consisting of straw-roofed buildings, and containing French, English, and Dutch factories. Distant N.E. from Benares 118 miles; from Allahabad, E., 180. Lat. 25° 45′, long. 84° 48′.

CHUPROULEE, in the British district of Meerut, lieut.-gov. of the N.W. Provinces, a town the principal place of the pergunnah of the same name. The town, containing a population of 13,878, is situate on the left bank of the Jumna, in lat. 29° 12′, long. 77° 15′.

CHUPROWA, in the British district of Bareilly, lieut.-gov. of the N.W. Provinces, a village on the route from Bareilly to Seetapore, and 40 miles S.E. of the former. It is situate on the Kunhout, a stream here forty yards wide and four feet deep, with muddy banks and sandy bottom. The ford, which is the only mode of crossing it, is in consequence very difficult. Lat. 28° 10′, long. 80° 2′.

CHURCH ROCKS, or ST. JOHN'S ROCKS.—Four rocks distant about four leagues from the coast of Arracan, the largest being about sixteen feet high. They receive their name from the circumstance of the largest of the four, when viewed from a particular direction, very much resembling a country church. Lat. 17° 28′, long. 94° 23′.

CHURDA.—A town in the territory of Oude, 75 miles N.E. from Lucknow, and 26 miles N. from Buraech. Lat. 27° 58′, long. 81° 41′.

CHUREEDAHA, in the British district of Sarun, lieut.-gov. of Bengal, a town 16 miles N. of Chupra, 44 miles W. of Mozufferpoor. Lat. 25° 58′, long. 84° 46′.

CHURGAON.—See CHIRGONG.

CHURKHAREE.—See CHIRKAREE.

CHUROWLEE, in the British district of Etawa, lieut.-gov. of the N.W. Provinces, a village on the route from Calpee to the cantonment of Etawa, and 36 miles S.E. of the latter. Lat. 26° 29′, long. 79° 32′.

CHUSHUT.—A town in the native state of Cashmere, or dominions of Gholab Singh, 220 miles E. from Sirinagur, and 196 miles N.E. from Simla. Lat. 33° 35′, long. 78° 43′.

CHUSMA, in the Peshawar division of the Punjab, a town situated four miles from the right bank of the Indus, 11 miles N.E. of the town of Kala Bagh. Lat. 33° 7′, long. 71° 41′.

CHUTNAHULLI.—A town in Mysore, distant S.W. from Seringapatam 20 miles. Lat. 12° 12′, long. 76° 36′.

CHUTRAIL, in the Rajpoot state of Jessulmere, a halting-place on the route from Roree, in Sinde, to the town of Jessulmere, from which it is distant 15 miles N.W. Water is obtainable. The road towards Sinde is good, but stony towards the town of Jessulmere. Lat. 26° 58′, long. 70° 45′.

CHUTTERPORE, in Bundelcund, and the principal place of the territory of the same name, lies on the route from Banda to Saugor, 70 miles S.W. of the former, and 10 N.E. of the latter. It is situate to the west of a deep jhil or mere, of about two miles in breadth, and amidst high hills, forming romantic and picturesque groups. It is on the whole a thriving place, having manufactures of paper, and of coarse cutlery, made from iron mined from the adjacent hills. The rajah has lately built a handsome and extensive serae, or lodging-house for travellers, containing numerous chambers arranged along the sides of a court, into which each opens. The most striking architectural objects here, however, are the ruins of the extensive palace of Chutter Saul, the founder of the short-lived independence of Bundelcund, and in whose honour the town received its name. Adjacent is his mausoleum, a large structure, of massive proportions and elaborate workmanship, surmounted by five domes. Most of the houses in Chutterpore are low, and the streets narrow; but a few of the residences of the more wealthy inhabitants are spacious and well built, in a costly and elaborate style of architecture.

The town had formerly considerable transit-trade, but this has much decayed. It is still a good halting-place for troops, having a bazaar, and being well supplied with water. According to De Cruz, the territory of which this is the chief place contains 1,240 square miles and 354 villages, with a population of 120,000 souls. The annual revenue was stated in 1848 to be 300,000 rupees (30,000*l*.). This state maintains a military force, consisting of 100 cavalry, 1,000 infantry, and ten artillery. It pays no tribute. At the close of the last century, this raj was claimed, rather than possessed, by Sernaid Singh, in right of his descent from Chutter Sal, who had wrested it, with the remainder of Bundelcund, from the empire of Delhi. Sernaid Singh, at his death, left an infant son to the guardianship of Seoni, one of his officers, a man of low origin, who succeeded in usurping the raj, in which he was confirmed by the British, who found him in possession on the cession of Bundelcund by the Peishwa, under the treaty of Bassein, in 1802. The family are Hindoo, and consequently recognise the rite of suttee. Spry gives an affecting account of an instance of this occurring a few years since, in which the daughter-in-law of the rajah was the victim. The murderous rite has now, however, been suppressed in all the native states of Bundelcund. The town of Chutterpore is in lat. 24° 55′, long. 79° 39′.

CHUTTRUM, in the British district of Malabar, presidency of Madras, a town on the route from Ponany to Coimbatoor, 20 miles S.W. of the latter. Lat. 10° 39′, long. 76° 48′.

CHYKOA, in the British district of Sudiya, in Assam, a town on the left bank of the river Brahmapootra, eight miles S.W. of Sudiya. Lat. 27° 46′, long. 95° 36′.

CHYLARA.—A town in the territory of Oude, 64 miles S.E. from Lucknow, and 52 miles N. from Allahabad. Lat. 26° 8′, long. 81° 38′.

CHYLUH, in the British district of Boolundshuhur, lieut.-gov. of the N.W. Provinces, a village on the route from the cantonment of Allyghur to that of Delhi, and nine miles S.E. of the latter, is situate close to the left bank of the Jumna. Lat. 28° 36′, long. 77° 21′.

CHYNEPORE, or CHAYANPOOR, in the British district of Shahabad, lieut.-gov. of Bengal, a town at the northern base of the hill-tract in the south of the district. Here is a quadrangular fort, 390 feet in length from north to south, 369 from east to west. The place belongs to a family now Mussulman, but formerly professing Brahminism, having changed its profession of faith to prevent confiscation of its possessions. Distant S.E. from Benares 39 miles, N.W. from Calcutta 350. Lat. 25°, long. 83° 34′.

CHYNPORE BAREE.—See Baree.

CICILLY.—A town in the British district of South Canara, presidency of Madras, 45 miles E. of Mangalore. Lat. 12° 54′, long. 75° 34′.

CIRCARS, (THE FIVE NORTHERN).—An antiquated division of the presidency of Madras. The tract formerly comprised within the Circars lies between lat. 15° 40′—20° 17′, long. 79° 12′—85° 20′. Its seacoast commences at Motapilly, in lat. 15° 40′, long. 80° 17′, and holds a direction north-east for 450 miles, to the vicinity of Ganjam, and lat. 19° 35′, long. 85° 20′. Its greatest width is towards the south-west, where it extends about 100 miles in breadth inland, but in one part, towards the north-eastern extremity, the breadth is not more than eighteen miles. The Five Northern Circars were formerly Chicacole, Rajahmundry, Ellore, Condapilly, and Guntoor; but the tract comprised within them is at present divided into the British districts lying along the coast, and occurring in proceeding from south-west to north-east in the following order:—1. Guntoor; 2. Masulipatam; 3. Rajahmundry; 4. Vizagapatam; 5. Ganjam: detailed accounts of which are given under their respective names in the alphabetical arrangement. The Circars were obtained by the French in 1753, and continued in their possession till 1759, when they were seized by Clive, who thus deprived his adversaries of the means of carrying on the war in the Carnatic.

CIS-SUTLEJ TERRITORY.—See Sirhind, and Hill States.

CIVITAL.—A town in one of the recently sequestrated districts of Hyderabad, or dominions of the Nizam, 22 miles N.E. from Moodgul, and 69 miles N. from Ballary. Lat. 16° 6′, long. 76° 50′.

CLAIRALEA.—A town in the British district of Pachete, lieut.-gov. of Bengal, 36 miles N. of Bancoora. Lat. 23° 46′, long. 87° 9′.

CLARA.—One of the islands of the Mergui Archipelago, situate about 36 miles west of the mainland. It is high, "having small peaks, the southern one very sharp, like a sugar-loaf." Its centre is in lat. 10° 54′, long. 98° 4′.

CLOSEPETT.—A town in Mysore, 45 miles N.E. from Seringapatam, and 23 miles S.W. from Bangalore. Lat. 12° 44′, long. 77° 21′.

COADLYPETTA.—A town in Mysore, 60 miles N.W. from Seringapatam, and 70 miles E. from Mangalore. Lat. 12° 48′, long. 75° 56′.

COCHIN.—A raj, or native state, politically connected with the presidency of Madras, and so denominated from the town of the same name, formerly its capital, but now a British possession, and considered within the limits of the district of Malabar. That district bounds the Cochin raj on the west, north, and north-east sides; a small portion at the south-west angle is bounded by the Arabian Sea, and farther south is an isolated strip of territory of about thirty miles in length, bounded on the south-west by the same sea. On the south and part of the east, Cochin is bounded by the territory of Travancore: it lies between lat. 9° 48′—10° 50′, long. 76° 5′—76° 58′. The area is estimated at 1,988 square miles. A considerable portion of this raj is mountainous, extending over the Western Ghauts. The most striking physical feature of the country is furnished by the series of shallow lakes called by the British backwaters, receiving the drainage of the numerous streams descending from the Western Ghauts, and from this circumstance liable to rise enormously as these feeders swell, and to fall as they shrink or dry up. One of these feeders, the Alwye, has been known to rise nearly sixteen feet in twenty-four hours. This affects the backwater in the like degree, which sometimes continues swollen for months, but in the dry season shoals in many places to two feet, and even to six inches at the northern and southern extremities. The limits of the Cochin backwaters, distant north and south about 120 miles, pass considerably beyond the boundary of the state: the greatest breadth is about ten miles, but in some places the breadth is not more than a few hundred yards. The form is exceedingly irregular, branching into a great number of intricate and shallow channels, inclosing various low alluvial islands. The communication with the sea is at three points: one at the city of Cochin, another at Kodungaloor or Cranganore, and a third at Chetuwaya or Chatwye. Though in most places rather shallow, the backwater is navigable at all times from Cochin to Cranganore, and from Cochin to Aleppi or Aulapolay, both for passage and cargo-boats. During the rains it is everywhere navigable for flat-bottomed boats; but for the coneyance of small merchandise, canoes drawing little water are preferred. All the lands washed by this great estuary, whether islands or inclosing banks, are low and swampy, and liable to be flooded during the monsoon inundations. They are in general densely covered with luxuriant and productive cocoanut-palms, and in such places as are embanked great quantities of rice are grown; but this state of the land, and the sluggishness of the water, which has scarcely any current, render the atmosphere very damp, and sometimes very offensive to the smell, though it is not found particularly unhealthy. The average annual fall of rain during the prevalence of the monsoon is as much as seventy-two inches. This season is very long, beginning about the end of May, and lasting to the end of September. During its continuance, the average temperature is 78°; in the dry season it is about 85°. Even during the latter, though called dry, the air is moist, and frequent showers of rain reduce the temperature, so that a continued drought is almost unknown. In a commercial point of view, the timber of this state is amongst the most valuable of its productions. It grows principally in Iruari, a considerable tract in the north-east, covered with dense forests of teak of enormous size, but less durable and elastic than timber of the same kind produced in Travancore and Malabar. It is consequently more in demand for building houses than for ships, for which latter purpose it is also rendered less suitable by being cut into short junks, in order that it may the more easily be dragged to the torrents which sweep it down to the backwater, whither it is carried with such extreme violence that it is often shaken to such an extent as to be unfit for purposes requiring timber of large dimensions. Another valuable description of timber is the peon, probably a sort of pine, which furnishes excellent masts. Besides the above, there are black-wood, angely, jack, ben-teak, and bastard-cedar. The vegetable productions are rice, pepper, cardamoms, betelnut, ginger, yams, sweet potatoes, and arrowroot. Coffee of excellent quality is produced to a small extent; and it is believed that the culture might with great success be considerably increased, the chief obstacle being the apathy of the natives. Cotton is grown, but in small quantities, and is considered of inferior quality. The sugar-cane is also cultivated, but only to a trifling extent: the natives, not having the skill to make sugar, convert it into jaggery or molasses.

The zoology of the country is rich, but has not been adequately investigated. The list of wild animals comprises elephants and tigers of enormous size, buffaloes, swine, deer of various kinds, monkeys and apes in great number and variety, parrots of many kinds, and other birds of several descriptions. Snakes are very numerous and deadly, and the rivers swarm with alligators. The principal exports are rice, pepper, cardamoms, and timber. The rajah has the monopoly of pepper and cardamoms, which he buys at the lowest price at which they can be brought to market, and sells at a great advance. The forests belong to him, and the timber sold from them brings him an average income of 80,000 rupees annually. In consequence of the great extent and facility of water-carriage, and also, in the low country, from the impediments presented by torrents, lakes, inlets of the sea, or backwater, the construction of roads until of late has been little regarded. The longest and most important road is nearly parallel to the seashore, and on an average about a mile from it. This forms the principal military and official route between Travancore and Malabar. Its continuity, however, must be greatly broken by the numerous pieces of water which intersect its course. In the less swampy parts, about Trichoor, there are some excellent portions of road, for making which, laterite, there the prevailing formation, is well suited. The principal towns in the native territory—Trichoor, Cranganore, Chittoor, Vullarapullai, Verapoli, Vaipu, Aikota, Edapali, Tiripunaitorai — are noticed under their respective names in the alphabetical arrangement.

Cochin contains eight talooks or subdivisions, called respectively, Cochin, Cannanore, Moogoondaparum, Trichoor, Tallapilly, Chittoor, and Cranganore. The number of houses in 1836 was stated to be 53,720, and that of the population 288,176. The number of people, compared with the area, shows a relative density of 145 to the square mile. The population is much divided and subdivided into castes and classes, the principal of whom are, first, Namboories or Brahmins, composing the priesthood, and having wonderful influence over the Brahminical population in general. Contrary to the usual Brahminical practice, they discourage marriage in their families, only the eldest male in each being allowed the privilege of marrying. Second, Nairs, being of the Sudra or servile class, yet exclusively holding power and military station in the country, and treating all other classes except the Namboori Brahmins with great disdain. The marriage ceremony amongst this caste is very simple, and consists merely of the bridegroom, in the presence of his friends and relatives, purposely assembled, presenting a cloth to the bride, and tying a string round her neck. The engagement is as easily dissolved as formed; for on either party becoming dissatisfied with the other, they separate, and the relationship of husband and wife ceases from that moment, each being then at liberty to enter into a new engagement. The military avocations of this class having been terminated by the establishment of British supremacy, the Nairs are now maintained either by employment in the few public offices of government, or by agriculture. Third, there are several other denominations of the population, mostly outcasts of Brahminism; such as Chagowias and Kanakas, gatherers of fruit and drawers of toddy or fermented sap from the palm; Mooguas, or fishermen. This race is rather numerous, as fish abound in the backwater and the rivers, and are much in request for diet among the majority of the population. Pellers, or slaves, are either attached to the soil, and salable with it, or else unconnected with the soil, and salable at the will of those who are regarded as their owners. Fourth, Christians; of whom there are two denominations, viz., the Syrian or Jacobite Christians, who acknowledge as their spiritual head the patriarch of Antioch, and who generally adhere to a tradition that their church was founded by St. Thomas the Apostle, who landed at Cranganore, or Kotunglur, for the purpose of disseminating the gospel; and Romanist descendants of Portuguese, or of natives converted by them. Fifth, Jews; comprising Black Jews, settled in the country from time immemorial, and White Jews, descended from a colony much more recently planted here. Sixth, Mussulmans, whose number is not great. Besides those above enumerated, "there is a race of people inhabiting the mountains and jungles, called hill-people. They are regarded with abhorrence and contempt, even by the Pellers (polers or slaves), who consider themselves defiled by coming in contact with them. These wretched outcasts from society reside altogether in jungles, and rarely visit the villages; but are often seen by travellers on the roadside. Their appearance and gestures are scarcely human, and they subsist chiefly on fruits, roots, and such animals as they succeed in entrapping." There does not appear to be any official return of the relative proportion of the respective classes of the population; but some estimate may be formed from the return of the places of worship for each class; being, Brahminical, 2,734; Mussulman, 31; Jewish, 8; Christian, 108. The number of places of education respectively are, English, 5; Malayalam, 69; Tamil, 9; Maharatta, 1; Sanscrit, 7; Hebrew, 4: total, 95.

The rajah of Cochin claims to hold the territory in right of descent from Cheruman Permal, who governed this country as viceroy about the beginning of the ninth century, and who became its independent ruler by successful revolt. Whether or not the line of succession has been interrupted, is a question neither easy of solution nor necessary to be discussed; but it is certain that neither the state nor its rulers have escaped reverses. Cochin early succumbed to the Portuguese, who built a fort there. In 1599 their archbishop of Goa convened a synod at Udiampoor, in which assembly he caused the tenets of the Syrian Christians to be declared heretical, and their condemned books to be publicly and judicially burned. In 1662 the town of Cochin was taken from the Portuguese by the Dutch, under whose management it attained a high prosperity. The rajah, who retained the rest of the country, was in 1759 attacked by the rajah of Calicut, called by Europeans the Zamorin, who was expelled by the rajah of Travancore; and as a reward for the service performed on that occasion, certain portions of territory were transferred from Cochin to Travancore. In 1776, the state of Cochin was conquered by Hyder Ali, the celebrated adventurer, who had raised himself to the sovereignty of Mysore. It remained tributary and subordinate to Hyder, and subsequently to his son Tippoo Sultan, until the peace concluded by the latter with the British in 1792, when the claims of Mysore were transferred to the East-India Company. A treaty had previously been concluded (1791) between the rajah and the East-India Company; by which he had agreed to become tributary to that body, and pay a subsidy of 100,000 rupees annually. This treaty was followed by another in 1809; by which the rajah agreed to pay annually to the East-India Company, in addition to the usual subsidy of one lac of rupees, an annual sum equal to the expense of one battalion of native infantry, or 176,037 Arcot rupees; making an aggregate payment annually, in six equal instalments, of 276,037 rupees; the disposal of the amount of subsidy, as well as the distribution of the force maintained by it, whether stationed within or without the territories of the rajah of Cochin, being left unreservedly to the Company. The rajah engaged to hold no correspondence with any foreign state, without the knowledge and sanction of the Company; to admit no Europeans to his service, nor allow any to remain within his territory, without the consent and concurrence of the Company, which power might dismantle or garrison any fortresses or strong places in his dominions. On the other hand, the Company undertook to defend the territories of the rajah against all enemies whatever. Subsequently, the annual payment to the British government was reduced to 2,40,000 rupees, being one-half of the estimated amount of the revenue. Under the influence of the protecting power, many changes have been effected, calculated to advance the wealth and promote the happiness of the people. The inconvenient and vexatious imposts known as transit-duties were abolished in 1836; and in 1848, by the mutual consent of the British and Cochin authorities, the custom-house stations of both parties on the frontier were removed, thus, among other advantages, facilitating the passage of merchandise from Malabar and Coimbatore to the port of Cochin. The enlightened policy pursued by her majesty's government at home will doubtless afford additional stimulus to the productive powers of the country, as by a late order the trade of Cochin has been placed, as regards the United Kingdom, on the same footing, with certain specified exceptions, as that of the British possessions in India. In 1839 the misconduct of the reigning prince rendered it necessary to limit his personal expenditure, and intrust the administration of the government to a minister in communication with the British resident. The result has been highly successful. The existing difficulties were in a very short time surmounted, and the flourishing state of the revenue permitted an addition to be made to the personal income of the rajah. Improvement continues. In all the elements of prosperity Cochin is rapidly advancing; an outlay not inconsiderable has been incurred in the construction of roads, bridges, canals, and other works of public utility; yet, at the date of the latest information, the revenue had been found sufficient not only to meet all the demands upon it, but to afford an ample and increasing surplus. The abolition of predial slavery has recently been recommended by the British government, and will in all probability be effected at no very distant period. The present rajah of Cochin, who succeeded to the throne upon the death of his brother, is in the twenty-fourth year of his age: his installation took place in 1853.

COCHIN.—A town which, though giving name to a small raj or native state, belongs to the East-India Company, and is included within the district of Malabar, under the presidency of Madras. It is situate at the northern extremity of a piece of land about twelve miles in length from north to south, but in few places more than a mile, and in many not more than a quarter of a mile, in breadth, and which is nearly insulated by inlets of the sea and estuaries of streams flowing from the Western Ghauts. These salt-water inlets, and the estuaries communicating with them, form what is technically called by seamen frequenting the coast the Backwater of Cochin. The river or estuary, on the southern side of which the town is situate, is the principal channel of communication between this extensive inland navigation and the sea. Outside the mouth of the river is a bar, practicable for ships drawing fourteen or fifteen feet water. Notwithstanding this depth, there is a surf on the bar in particular states of the weather. After passing the bar and entering the river under the old walls of the fort, the depth of water is about twenty-five or thirty feet. In addition to the impediment of the bar, the port of Cochin is injuriously affected by the south-west monsoon, during the prevalence of which (several months) vessels can neither enter it nor depart from it in safety. Cochin is the only port south of Bombay where large ships can be built; and here, in 1820 and 1821, were built three frigates for the royal navy. Smaller vessels for the Indian navy have also been built here; and many ships, from 500 to 1,000 tons burthen, for the merchant service. The principal material is teak, produced of excellent quality in the forests of the Western Ghauts, but frequently so much injured in the passage down the torrents, rushing in numerous rapids and cataracts, as to be unfit for the construction of any but small craft of from fifty to 250 tons burthen, and called patemas, dows, or botillas.

The town of Cochin is a mile in length, and half a mile in width. It was a prosperous and fine town when in possession of the Dutch, and probably also previously, when held by the Portuguese, who, with their usual religious zeal, embellished it, among other buildings, with a fine cathedral. This, on the capture of the place by the Dutch, in 1663, was converted into a warehouse for the Dutch East-India Company. Bartolomeo, describing it about 1788, says, "This edifice is now employed for preserving the sugar which the Company obtains from Batavia, and the cinnamon they receive from Ceylon, together with nutmegs, cloves, iron, copper, cordage, rice, pepper, and various other articles of merchandise, which they bring hither from foreign countries, and sell, partly to the Indian princes, and partly to the Arabian as well as other native and foreign merchants. Cochin is intersected by beautiful streets; the arsenal is well provided with all kinds of military stores, and the citadel is strongly fortified. The latter, in the year 1778, was supplied with new ditches, bridges, batteries, and bastions." About the same time Forbes describes it as a place of great trade, "a harbour filled with ships, streets crowded with merchants, and warehouses stored with goods from every part of Asia and Europe, marked the industry, the commerce, and the wealth of the inhabitants." This prosperity was, temporarily at least, impaired by the fall of the dominion of the Dutch. In 1796 Cochin was taken by the British, and in 1806 the fortifications and public buildings, under orders from the British authorities, were destroyed by blowing them up with gunpowder. The effects of the explosions so shattered the private houses that scarcely one of any size or value remained standing. On this severe visitation, such Dutch families as had adequate means left the place, and those who were unable to remove sunk into abject beggary, though some formerly possessed titles, and held high rank and station. Under Dutch sway, Cochin was very populous, containing, besides some Europeans, Moplas or native Mussulmans, Hindoos, Arabians, Persians, Christians, comprising Armenians, Romanists, and those denominated Syrian Christians. The Portuguese Christians are described as singularly depraved, grossly and abominably superstitious; and their clergy as corrupt, licentious, and ignorant. There was formerly a Dutch church, which, after the place, passed into the hands of the English. The Jews are of two kinds: the fair Jews, of more recent arrival and settlement in the country; and the black Jews, who reside apart in a village outside the town. The latter have a synagogue here. Distance from Calicut, S.E., 95 miles; from Cannanore, S.E., 155 miles; from Mangalore, S.E., 225 miles; from Bombay, S.E., 665 miles; from Bangalore, S.W., 230 miles; from Madras, S.W., 350 miles. Lat. 9° 58′, long. 76° 18′.

CODYCONDA.—A town in the British district of Bellary, presidency of Madras, 109 miles S.E. of Bellary. Lat. 13° 50′, long. 77° 50′.

COEL, in the British district of Allygurh, lieut.-gov. of the N.W. Provinces, a town on the route from Cawnpore to Delhi, four miles S. of Allygurh. It appears to have been a place of some importance so early as the year 1193, when it was captured by the Mussulmans, under Kutb-u-din. It is the seat of the civil establishment of the district, and has in its immediate vicinity the military cantonment and bazaar. Elevation above the sea 734 feet. Population of the town 36,181. Lat. 27° 52′, long. 78° 9′.

COEL RIVER.—See BYETURNEE RIVER.

COGLASS, in the British district of Seuni, Saugor and Nerbudda territory, lieut.-gov. of the N.W. Provinces, a town on the route from Nagpore to Jubbulpoor, 68 miles S. of the latter. Lat. 22° 15′, long. 79° 40′.

COHUR.—A town in the native state of Sirgoojah, on the south-west frontier of Bengal, 49 miles N. from the town of Sirgoojah, and 72 miles W. from Palamow. Lat. 23° 48′, long. 82° 52′.

COILLE.—A town in the British district of Tirhoot, lieut.-gov. of Bengal, 23 miles N.W. of Durbunga. Lat. 26° 24′, long. 85° 43′.

COIMBATORE, within the territories subject to the presidency of Madras, a British district, named from its principal place. It is bounded on the north and north-west by the territory of Mysore; on the north-east by the British district of Salem; on the east by the British districts of Salem and Trichinopoly; on the south-east by the British district of Madura; on the south by Madura and the territory of Travancore; and on the west by the British district of Malabar and the native territory of Cochin. It lies between lat. 10° 14′—12° 19′, long. 76° 36′—78° 16′; and according to official return, has an area of 8,280 square miles. The general physical aspect of the district is that of a great recess opening to the east, in which direction it communicates with the vast plain of the Carnatic. The general surface is level, having at its western extremity, or towards the base of the Ghats, an average elevation of 800 or 900 feet above the sea. This district is inclosed on the north by the mazy group of mountains bordering the table-land of Mysore; on the south by the Pulnai or Vurragiri Mountains, and by the Animali range. Beyond the deep gap of Palghatcheri, it has on its north-western side the Kundah and Neilgherry groups. The gap of Palghatcheri, which divides the Animali group from that of the Kundahs, and which completely intersects the great range of the Ghats from east to west, is about twenty miles wide, having near the centre an elevation, stated, as a rough approximation, to be 970 feet above the sea. The principal rivers of the district are the Cauvery, Bhovani, Noyel, and Ambrawutty. Those principal streams receive right and left a great number of torrents, flowing briskly during the periodical rains, but at other times they are almost devoid of water. Much of the irrigation requisite for the production of crops is effected by means of wells. Near the mountains in the southern and western parts of this district are several extensive morasses, and the villages in the vicinity of such places are noted for insalubrity. The climate, in general, however, may be concluded, on scientific principles, to have greatly the advantage over the maritime parts of the Carnatic, partly in consequence of greater elevation, and partly from the volume of cool and fresh air introduced from the Indian Ocean through the great Palghat gap. The rains are principally brought by the north-east monsoon, which prevails from the beginning of November to the end of December; and then the Cauvery, Noyel, Bhovani, Ambrawutty, and their numerous feeders, as well as the tanks, are replenished, and the low grounds become deluged with water. For a month or six weeks after the end of the monsoon, the season is comparatively cool, delightful, and healthful, the north-east wind proving cheering and bracing to weakly constitutions. The midday temperature, however, is high; the range of the thermometer in the shade being from 62° to 80° or 82°.

Towards the end of January and throughout February, dews fall heavily, and fogs occasion intermittent fevers and catarrhs. After the end of March the north-east winds cease, and are succeeded by occasional calms and variable breezes; southerly and south-east winds succeed, and continue to about the middle of May. During April the weather gradually becomes hotter, and the average range of the thermometer for the month is from 76° to 93°. In May it rises as high as 96° or 98° in the shade, and seldom falls below 79°. From the interposition of the Ghats, the south-west monsoon is but little felt, except in the rise of the Cauvery, replenished on the table-lands of Coorg and Mysore.

The only mineral of importance is iron-ore, either a brown hæmatite or a black oxide, found in the form of sand. Beryl is found in considerable abundance, and some specimens are of very fine quality. Saltpetre abounds, but is considered to be of inferior quality. It is procured by washing the earth; and a coarse culinary salt for domestic purposes is obtained by the same process.

The zoology of this district has not been described, though, from the physical circumstances of the tract, it may be inferred to be rich. Elephants are very numerous about the bottom, and in the secluded valleys of the Ghauts, as well as in the Animali or Animalaya group, which has received its name, meaning Elephant Hill, from the great number of those animals which harbour in it. In the course of four years immediately preceding 1843, between 700 and 800 elephants were destroyed by the public establishment maintained for this purpose. The price of the largest and finest pair of tusks is from 8*l.* to 9*l.*, and of those of smaller size from 4*l.* to 6*l.* The vegetable productions consist chiefly of dry grains. The principal alimentary crops are gram (Cicer arietinum), various sorts of panic, as Panicum miliaceum, Panicum italicum, Panicum spicatum; various kinds of millet, Holcus spicatus, Holcus saccharatus, Curcuma longa or turmeric. Of commercial crops, the castor-oil plant (Ricinus communis) is much cultivated, and its produce consumed at home, and exported largely. Experiments have been conducted by the government for the introduction and cultivation of the Mauritius sugar-cane, and favourable reports have been received of their progress. Cotton is produced, and manufactured into coarse fabrics for home wear, and for exportation to Trinchinopoly, Salem, Mysore, and Malabar. One of the experimental farms established by the government, with the view of introducing the American species of cotton, was located in this district. In 1849 it was discontinued; the object for which it was formed having, it is said, been fully attained by "demonstrating that the soil and climate are capable of producing cotton suitable to the British market." The district is noted for the abundance and excellence of the tobacco which it produces. Its superiority is "attributable to the richness and suitableness of the soil for its culture, to its being irrigated from wells containing much saltpetre, and to the attention paid to its cultivation." The sandal-tree grows freely in the jungly forests round the base of the hills, and the wood is exported in considerable quantities. The extensive forests in the neighbourhood of the Animali Hills contain abundance of teak and other valuable timber. The population is given under the article MADRAS. The language spoken is the Tamil. The routes, generally speaking, between Coimbatore and the adjoining districts are good, having lately been much improved. The trunk road is from north-east to south-west, from Salem, through the towns of Coimbatore and Palghat, to the western coast at Ponany. One of the lines of the Madras Railway Company will also traverse the district. The principal places are Coimbatore, Palaghat, and Darampoor.

COIMBATOOR, the principal place of the British district of the same name, is situate near the left bank of the river Noyel, a tributary of the Cauvery, in a dry and well-cultivated country, on the declivity, and near the base of the great mountain-group of Neilgherry, and on the north side of the remarkable depression which traverses the Ghauts from east to west. From this latter circumstance it is admirably ventilated by the currents of air incessantly sweeping that great gorge. The streets are wide, airy, and neatly built; but the salubrity of the place is impaired by the bad quality of the water, which is obtained from wells, and is for the most part brackish. The European quarter is eastward of the town, and detached from it. The advantages of education have been secured to this town through the meritorious efforts of the local community, whereby an English and vernacular school has been established. The jail for the district is situate in the south-eastern part of the town, and is a large square building, capable of containing 275 prisoners. A detachment of native infantry is stationed here. The huts of the sepoys are near the town. On its south side is a tank, never less than three miles in length, and during the rains increasing to a lake of considerable extent. In the time of Hyder Ali the town is said to have contained 4,000 houses; but it suffered much in the wars between the British government and Mysore. The railway from Madras to Beypoor passes by the town. Elevation above the sea 1,483 feet. Distance from Calicut, E., 80 miles; Mangalore, S.E., 196; Bombay, S.E., 600; Seringapatam, S., 100; Bangalore, S., 140; Madras, S.W., 268. Lat. 11°, long. 77° 1′.

COLABA.—This name is given to the southern part of Lighthouse Island, the northern being called by the British Old-woman's Island. These two parts are connected by a causeway, overflowed at spring tides. Lighthouse Island is likewise connected with Bombay Island by a causeway. In 1838, a spot of ground at the northern extremity of the island, which was usually covered by the sea at high water, was granted to a company of European and native merchants, for the purpose of constructing a wharf and line of warehouses for the deposit of merchandise, and of excavating a canal, to insure constant smooth water for boats lying alongside the wharf. Colaba is the seat of an observatory, one of sixty now in operation in various parts of the world, for the purpose of magnetic and meteorological observation, whereat the instruments are read hourly, day and night, without interruption. The erection of a church at Colaba was commenced in 1848. The construction of this edifice was the result of a desire to establish some permanent memorial of the gallantry and endurance of those who fell in Scinde and Affghanistan; and the mode chosen, was selected on the ground of combining a record of the departed brave, with a purpose of the highest spiritual utility. The cost of the building was estimated at 70,000 rupees, or about 7,000*l*. Towards this sum the government contributed 30,000 rupees, the remainder to be supplied by private subscription. But the estimate having been considerably exceeded, the government has been authorized to contribute a further sum, equal to a moiety of the balance required. Colaba is the seat of barracks, which formerly were subject to the inconveniences arising from an unsatisfactory supply of water. To provide a remedy for this evil, was an object combined with the construction of the causeway connecting Colaba with Bombay Island; and a sufficient extent of iron pipes were forwarded from England to enable the project to be completed. The centre of the island is about lat. 18° 53′, long. 72° 52′.

COLABA (Angria's lapsed territory).—See KOLABA.

COLA BERA.—A town in the British district of Sumbulpoor, on the south-west frontier of Bengal, 35 miles N.E. of Sumbulpoor. Lat. 21° 54′, long. 84° 18′.

COLADYNE RIVER.—See KOLADYNE.

COLAHNELLY.—A town in the British district of Coimbatoor, presidency of Madras, 61 miles E. of Coimbatoor. Lat. 11° 10′, long. 77° 53′.

COLAIR, in the district of Masulipatam, presidency of Madras, a large lake, formed by the drainage of the three rivers Weyairoo, Tumulairoo, and Boodamair. It contains an area of about 160 square miles. A considerable outlay has been recently sanctioned for its drainage, by which the bed would be made available as arable land, capable of supporting a population of 7,000. Its centre is about lat. 16° 40′, long. 81° 20′.

COLAPORE.—See KOLAPORE.

COLAR.—A town in the native state of Mysore, 40 miles E. from Bangalore, and 66 miles W. from Chittoor. Lat. 13° 8′, long. 78° 10′.

COLEAPOLL.—A town in the British district of Pooralia, lieut.-gov. of Bengal, 56 miles N.W. of Midnapoor. Lat. 22° 51′, long. 86° 40′.

COLEHAN.—A native jaghire within the British district of Singbhoom, under the jurisdiction of the political agent for the south-west frontier of Bengal. Its revenue is returned at 10,000 rupees, a portion of which is paid to the British government as tribute. Its centre is about lat. 22° 5′, long. 85° 55′.

COLEROON RIVER.—See CAUVERY.

COLES.—See ORISSA.

COLGONG, in the British district of Bhagulpore, lieut.-gov. of Bengal, a town on the right bank of the Ganges, on the route from Berhampore to Dinapore, 130 miles N.W. of the former, 163 E. of the latter. It has a small bazaar, and a fort, now in a ruinous state. Abreast of it, in the river, are three insulated masses, consisting of huge blocks of rocks, having their crevices and rifts filled with stunted trees, and fifty or sixty feet above the water. Distant N.W. from Calcutta by Berhampore, 245 miles; by the course of the river, 309. Lat. 25° 13′, long. 87° 17′.

COLLACHULL, in the territory of Travancore, a small town on the seacoast, in a diminutive bay. The land here is rather high and bold, differing from the generality of the coast, which is low, and in most places sandy. Distance from Trivandrum, S.E., 30 miles; Cananore, S.E., 287. Lat. 8° 10′, long. 77° 18′.

COLLOOR.—See BARKALOOR.

COMALDA, in Gurwhal, a river rising in the mountains inclosing the Rama Serai valley on the north, and in lat. 30° 57′, long. 78° 7′. It has a course of about seventeen miles, generally in a south-easterly direction, to its confluence with the Jumna, on the right side, in lat. 30° 47′, long. 78° 10′. It is one of the largest streams which the Jumna receives above the confluence of the Tons. Hodgson crossed it in the beginning of April, a little above its mouth, when it was seventy feet wide, two and a half deep, and very rapid.

COMAREALLWA.—A town in the British district of Cuddapah, presidency of Madras, 29 miles S.W. of Cuddapah. Lat. 14° 16′, long. 78° 30′.

COMBAKONUM, in the British district of Tanjore, a town the principal place of a large and valuable tallook or subdivision which bears the same name. It is situate in a low level tract between two considerable branches or outlets of the river Cauvery, and extends about two miles in length from north to south, and one mile in breadth from east to west. The houses are built in the usual native style, and some in the chief streets have two stories. The bazaar forms a long and tolerably wide street, and is well supplied with provisions.

There are several celebrated pagodas here, and consequently a considerable number of Brahmins, who live on the revenues of those establishments. Many devotees resort hither to visit the pagodas. There is also considerable traffic; but the exercise of manufacturing art is chiefly confined to weaving. The weavers are said to be very industrious, but, like those engaged in the same employment in most other places, very poor. Notwithstanding its slight elevation above the sea, this place is remarkably healthy both for Europeans and natives. The lines for the small detachment of native infantry stationed here, are situate on a sandy piece of ground near the river, where are also the court-house, the jail, and the hospital. The jail is constructed to contain three hundred prisoners. Distance from Tanjore, N.E., 20 miles; Madura, N.E., 112; Bangalore, S.E., 186; Madras, S.W., 160. Lat. 10° 58′, long. 79° 26′.

COMBERMERE BAY, situate between the mouths of the Talak and Aeng rivers, on the coast of Arracan, and abounding with shoals, rocks, and sandbanks. Its centre is about lat. 19° 35′, long. 93° 35′.

COMERCOLLY, in the British district of Pubna, lieut.-gov. of Bengal, a town situate on the route from Berhampore to Dacca, 77 miles S.E. of former, 95 W. of latter. It is situate on the Goraee, a large offset flowing south-eastward from the Ganges, and often denominated by the British the river of Comercolly. The river is described by Heber as having the width of the Thames at Vauxhall. Distance from Calcutta, N.E., 104 miles. Lat. 23° 52′, long. 89° 14′.

COMORIN (CAPE), in the native state of Travancore, the most southern point of what is called the Peninsula of India. "It is formed of a circular low sandy point, not discernible above the distance of three and a half or four leagues from the deck of a large ship. Within two or three cables' length of the south-east part of the point lies a sloping rocky islet, high above water, with other rocks about it, on which the sea breaks. To the westward of this islet, the shore of the cape is sandy and barren, but to the eastward it abounds with trees, having a fort and village among them close to the sea." The land is bold and safe to approach within about a mile and a half or two miles, the depth of water in some places increasing towards the shore. "A great way out from the cape there is a bank abounding in cod, where some ships have caught considerable numbers of those fish; but it appears to be of small extent and little known." The base of the southern extremity of the Western Ghauts is about a mile or a mile and a half from the sea. "These mountains rise in majestic sharp peaks, chained together, and forming a ridge;" and "a little detached from the end of the chain over the cape, on the east side, there is a sharp conical mountain by itself, like a sugarloaf." A bold summit, some distance north of the cape, when viewed from afar, appears isolated, and has by navigators sailing at a distance been often mistaken for the cape itself. To the eastward of the rocky islet previously mentioned, and about three miles from it, is a fort. Colonel Welsh, describing the place in 1824, says, "A few fishermen's houses, some venerated temples, and a Dutch church, now form the celebrated town of Cape Comorin." Lat. 8° 5′, long. 77° 37′.

CONCAN, in the presidency of Bombay, a narrow tract stretching from the south of Sawuntwarree, on the frontier of Goa, in lat. 15° 44′, long. 73° 45′, to the Damaun river, in lat. 20° 22′, long. 72° 52′, a length of about three hundred and thirty miles, with a breadth varying from twenty-five to fifty miles. It is bounded on the west by the Arabian Sea, and on the east by the culminating ridge of the Ghats. The eastern part, stretching up the face of the Ghats, and along their summits, is extremely rugged. The mean elevation of the western, or more depressed part, is about 100 feet; but it has many isolated hills, or short ranges, some of which have a considerable elevation. Though rugged, this tract has many fertile valleys, each of which, for the most part, affords a passage to a small river or torrent holding a westerly course from the Ghats to the Arabian Sea. The geological surface-formation is volcanic, generally trap, rising in terraces from the low country to the summit of the Ghats, and in some places overlaid by ferrugineous sandstone, which, when decomposed, forms a laterite, easily mouldering into a reddish fertile earth. But a country so rugged cannot but contain much land that is totally irreclaimable, though producing in its gorges and ravines dense jungle, infested by beasts of prey, especially tigers, here remarkably fierce and destructive. In some places, however, the rock is so hard and close as totally to preclude vegetation of any kind, and presents the appearance of a huge black mass overtopping the general outline of the mountain. This is in many instances surmounted by a formidable hill-fort. The rivers, in the upper or steeper part of their course, near the mountains, are clear and rapid; but after entering the level country, where they are affected by the tide, they are very deep and muddy, their estuaries forming small havens, which, before the establishment of British supremacy, afforded lurking-places for pirates. The most fertile spots are on the banks of streams. The rivers abound with fish, but they are also frequented by alligators. Venomous serpents are unfortunately very numerous. The climate is characterized by the great heaviness of the monsoon rains, the amount of which in one year has been known to be nearly 300 inches. The Concan abounds in thermal springs, the water of which has a temperature in no instance exceeding 110°, and is found very serviceable in cases of rheumatism. When cooled, it is pleasant and salubrious to drink. The Concan comprehends two collectorates,—Tannah and Rutnaghery, which will be found more particularly described in their proper places in the alphabetical arrangement. Of the tract south of Bombay, Mhar is the principal town. There are numerous small towns or forts along the coast, at the estuaries of the small rivers, or on the creeks or small bays, which abound. Of those places the most worthy of notice are Junjera, Rutnagheriah, Viziadroog, and Vingorla, notices of which are given under their respective names.

The Concan appears to have been little noticed in Indian history until the beginning of the sixteenth century, when its seacoasts became the scene of the daring and active operations of the Portuguese. In the middle of the seventeenth century it was conquered from the king of Beejapore by the Mahratta leader Sevajee. Aurungzebe was less successful in his attempts upon it: his son Moazzim, whom he despatched against it, lost, in 1684, nearly the whole of his horses and cattle, either from want of provisions, or from the deadly effect of the climate. It thenceforward remained under the rule of the chief of Sattara, and subsequently under that of the Peishwa, until, on the overthrow of the latter in 1818, it was incorporated with the dominions of the East-India Company.

CONDAPILLY, in the British district of Masulipatam, presidency of Madras, a hill-fort, having an elevation of about 1,700 feet above the level of the sea. It was formerly noted for its strength; but of late years, according to Hamilton, "has been suffered to crumble into ruin." Distance from Madras, N., 245 miles; Masulipatam, N.W., 52; Calcutta, S.W., 658. Lat. 16° 38′, long. 80° 37′.

CONDERPEE DROOG.—A fort in the British district of Bellary, presidency of Madras, 52 miles S. of Bellary. Lat. 14° 22′, long. 77° 6′.

CONDRAPILLY.—A town in the British territory of Nagpoor, 67 miles S.W. from Bustur, and 91 miles N. from Rajahmundry. Lat. 18° 19′, long. 81° 39′.

CONJEVERAM, in the British district Chingleput, presidency of Madras, a town on the route from Madras to Arcot. It is situate on the Wegawati, a torrent devoid of water during the dry season. The streets are wide, cross each other at right angles, and have a row of cocoanut-trees on each side. The houses are of mud; they are roofed with tiles, and are built in the form of a square, with an inclosed court in the middle: altogether they appear superior to the houses in the country towns of Bengal. The principal inhabitants are Brahmins, of whom there are about a hundred families, and a large number of dancing-girls, kept in honour of Iswara or Siva. The pagodas dedicated to that deity and his consort Kamachuma are represented as "great stone buildings, very clumsily executed both in their joinings and carvings, and totally devoid of elegance or grandeur, although they are wonderfully crowded with what are meant as ornaments." These pagodas are highly famed in the mythological lore of the Brahmins, and are amongst the most revered and frequented in Southern India. The great gateway of the pagoda, as is usually the case with such structures, is huge and lofty, and from the top, which is reached by seven flights of stairs, there is a view "extremely fine; consisting of extensive woods intersected by a large sheet of water, with numerous pagodas rising among the trees, and a magnificent range of retiring mountains in the distance." Distance from Cuddalore, N., 81 miles; Arcot, E., 27; Bangalore, E., 145; Madras, S.W., 42. Lat. 12° 50′, long. 79° 46′.

CONTAI.—A town in the British district of Hijellee, lieut.-gov. of Bengal, 65 miles S.W. of Calcutta. Lat. 21° 47′, long. 87° 47′.

COOCH BEHAR.—See Koosh Behar.

COODAM.—A town in the native state of Jeypoor, one of the hill zemindarries of Madras, 73 miles S. from Jeypoor, and 83 miles W. from Vizianagrum. Lat. 18°, long. 82° 14′.

COOGDARRA.—A town in the British district of Mymunsing, lieut.-gov. of Bengal, 52 miles N.E. of Pubna. Lat. 24° 20′, long. 90°.

COOMANDA.—A town in the native state of Kareal, on the south-west frontier of Bengal, 12 miles N. from Kareal, and 108 miles S.W. from Sumbulpoor. Lat. 20° 30′, long. 82° 44′.

COOMBACOTTA.—A town in the native state of Jeypoor, one of the hill zemindarries of Madras, 10 miles S.W. from Ryaguddah, and 69 miles N. from Vizianagrum. Lat. 19° 6′, long. 83° 20′.

COOMBARREE.—A town in Hyderabad, or dominions of the Nizam, 93 miles S.E. from Ellichpoor, and 93 miles N.E. from Nandair. Lat. 20° 4′, long. 78° 23′.

COOMBLA, in the British district of South Canara, presidency of Madras, a town situate on a high peninsula, projecting into a salt-water lake, separated from the sea by a spit of sand, and receiving the water of two rivers, one flowing from the Ghauts, the other, of less size, flowing from some hills a few miles east of the town. In the rainy season, those rivers bring down a body of water, which makes the lake or inlet quite fresh; but during the rest of the year it is as salt as the external sea. The situation of the fort is very fine. The town, once considerable, but now rather decayed, was formerly joined by a bridge to the town of Kanyapoora, situate on the south or opposite side of the narrow inlet by which the lake communicates with the sea. Coombla is distant from Mangaloor, S., 19 miles; Madras, W., 360. Lat. 12° 36′, long. 75°.

COOMBTA.—See Coombla.

COOMSEE.—A town in Mysore, 29 miles N.E. from Bednore, and 141 miles N.W. from Seringapatam. Lat. 14° 3′, long. 75° 28′.

COOMTA, in the British district of North Canara, presidency of Madras, a town on a creek on the east coast of the Indian Ocean. "It seems to have been formerly a place of some note. Its lanes are straight, and fenced with stone walls, and it has many cocoanut-gardens. Twice it had the misfortune of having Tippoo's army encamped in its vicinity, and on both occasions it was burned down by some of the irregulars." Salt is made on the banks of the cove, by evaporating the sea-water. Of late years, this place appears to have recovered its former prosperity, from being selected as the port of shipment for the raw cotton produced in the district of Bellary and in the Southern Mahratta country. A road from Dharwar, by Sircy, was opened some time since; but this affording but imperfect accommodation, another was subsequently constructed, opening a communication for wheeled carriages for the entire distance between Dharwar and Coomta. The town is situate about a mile from the port, which, however, is little more than an open roadstead, having a headland running out at its northern termination, which protects the anchorage from the north-west wind, being that which prevails nearly the whole of the trading season, and renders the bay comparatively calm during this part of the year; but it is entirely exposed to the south-west monsoon, and after this commences, it is unsafe for any country vessel to remain there. It is in contemplation to erect a lighthouse at this place, and to take measures for the improvement of the harbour. Distant N.W. from Mangalore 113 miles, S.E. from Bombay 328, N.W. from Madras 410. Lat. 14° 26′, long. 74° 29′.

COOMTY.—A town in the British territory of Nagpoor, 145 miles E. from Nagpoor, and 22 miles S.W. from Ryepoor. Lat. 21°, long. 81° 22′.

COONDADUM.—A town in the British district of Coimbatoor, presidency of Madras, 33 miles S.E. of Coimbatoor. Lat. 10° 50′, long. 77° 30′.

COONDAPOOR.—The principal place of a subdivision of the same name, in the British district of North Canara, presidency of Madras. It is situate on the south or left side of an estuary receiving five fresh-water rivers, flowing down from the Ghauts. Though this estuary is extensive, it is shallow, and navigable solely for boats and small vessels; and those which ply on it are only canoes. The surrounding country is remarkably beautiful; and an old fort, erected by the Portuguese a short distance inland of the town, commands a noble prospect. General Matthews, preparing for the disastrous expedition in which he perished, made lines around this fort. The town contains about 250 houses, and has long been stationary with respect to increase of size and prosperity. Coondapoor, and some other posts on the seashore, were in the early part of the sixteenth century seized by the Portuguese, and the more inland tract was included within the great realm of Vijayanagar until its overthrow, in 1565, by a Mussulman confederacy at Telikota; subsequently to which this territory appears to have become part of the state of Bednore; on the overthrow of which by Hyder Ali, in 1763, it became incorporated with his dominions; and when his son, in 1799, fell beneath the attack of the British, it became part of the British district of North Canara. Distance from Mangalore, N., 53 miles; Bombay, S., 390; Bangalore, N.W., 205; Madras, W., 380. Lat. 13° 38′, long. 74° 45′.

COONNAGOODY.—A town in the British district of Madura, presidency of Madras, 42 miles E. of Madura. Lat. 10° 7′, long. 78° 47′.

COONOOR, one of the minor sanitary stations on the Neilgherry Hills, in the district of Malabar, presidency of Madras, 6,000 feet above the level of the sea. It is situate on the crest of the hills, in the south-east angle of their summit; the residences of the Europeans, including an hotel, being placed on the rounded tops of a range of hills, which runs from a high mountain called "Coonoor Betta," towards the top of the pass; while the bazaar and native residences are in the hollow below, and adjacent to a masonry bridge, which spans a wide stream flowing from the Jakatalla valley, and descending the hills at this point in a large volume of water. A church has been recently erected at this place. The south-west monsoon sets in at this station in the month of June, but with less rigour than at Ootacamund, owing to the clouds, which come charged with rain from the westward, meeting with opposition from the high spurs of the Dodabetta range which intervene. The annual fall of rain here averages fifty-five inches; that at Ootacamund sixty inches. Distant N. from Coimbatoor 26 miles. Lat. 11° 21′, long. 76° 56′.

COONYGUL. — A town in Mysore, 47 miles N.E. from Seringapatam, and 36 miles W. from Bangalore. Lat. 13° 1′, long. 77° 5′.

COORG, a district of Southern India, and recently an independent raj, is bounded on the north by Mysore and the collectorate of Canara; on the east by Mysore; on the south by the collectorate of Malabar; and on the west by Malabar and Canara. While a separate raj, its limits were more extensive; but upon the subjugation of the province by the British, in 1834, the talooks of Pootoor and Umr Sooleay were annexed to the collectorate of Canara. The present district of Coorg lies between lat. 11° 56′ and 12° 45′, long. 75° 25′ and 76° 13′, and extends about sixty miles from north to south, and thirty-five from east to west. The area is estimated at about 1,420 square miles. Coorg is a very rugged, and altogether mountainous region, the lowest part being fully 3,000 feet above the sea. The tract which most nearly resembles a plain, is the valley, about eighteen miles long and thirteen broad, lying between Merkara and Naknaad, which, viewed from above, has a level appearance, but when examined more closely, is found to consist of a succession of low ridges, with small narrow valleys, or perhaps rather ravines, between them; the lowest being the bed of the great river Cauvery. The ridges are parallel to each other, and commence in a steep abutment, whence they proceed in a direction south-east, until they terminate in the plains of Mysore or Wynaad. Some of those ranges have on their summits very small table-lands, but in general their tops are sharp ridges. The whole country, with few exceptions, is covered with forests more or less dense, but seldom so overgrown by underwood as to qualify them to be called jungle. To the eastward, however, towards Mysore, in which direction the elevation of the surface diminishes, bamboos make their appearance, and the forest becomes thick jungle, filled with every variety of wild animals. The general declivity of the country is to the north-east and east, as indicated by the course of the Cauvery and its feeders, which flow in that direction, and receive the drainage of nearly four-fifths of the country.

The temperature of the atmosphere in Coorg is low, owing to the elevation of the country, the proximity of the ocean to the south-west and west, and the prevalence of winds from those points. The greatest ranges of temperature are in January and February, amounting to from 53° to 72°; and the weather then is not only cold, but excessively dry. In April and May the heat becomes oppressive during the day, but the nights are almost always cool. The monsoon commences in June, and towards the close of that month the rain falls very heavily, insomuch that from the 22nd to the 27th of that month, in the year 1835, there fell twenty-seven inches. This weather continues during July, August, and September, the air being loaded with moisture, and the sun seldom seen; at the same time the temperature is wonderfully equable, the extremes in the open air being 56° and 65°. The total fall of rain in one year (1835–1836) was 119 inches, of which 44 were in June. The climate is in general healthful for Europeans, but has an unfavourable influence on those inclined to visceral congestion, asthma, or dysentery. Notwithstanding the excessive moisture, the equability of temperature causes rheumatism, catarrh, or pneumonic affections to be little known. It is a remarkable fact, however, that the "climate appears decidedly inimical to the cure of cuts, wounds, and sores, which are often totally unmanageable without change of air." For so circumscribed a tract the zoology is varied and important. Elephants are numerous, and were more so until rewards were given for their destruction; since which, numbers have been shot or taken in pitfalls. Tigers are numerous, but are not so ferocious as in less-elevated and more sultry regions. Here also are found the leopard, the chita or hunting-leopard, and the tiger-cat. Bears are rare, but exceedingly fierce and dangerous. The wild dog, as large as a greyhound, but much more strongly built, hunts in packs of a dozen or more, is very fierce, and attacks and destroys even kine. The bison attains the enormous height of seventeen hands, and the elk harbours in the secluded wilds.

Previously to the occupation of the country by the British, in 1834, the roads, or rather paths, were very rude, the rajahs discouraging any improvement, as tending to facilitate invasion. The only route which could be considered as a road, was that commencing at Periapatam, in Mysore, proceeding through a thick jungle to Verajenderpetta, and thence by the Huggala or Hingin Ghaut, a very steep descending pass, to Cannanore, in Malabar. This is the worst ghaut in the South of India, being so steep as to be nearly impracticable for laden cattle, and totally so for wheeled carriages; neither is it capable of much improvement, the declivity being in many places one in three feet. A road, commencing also at Periapatam, proceeds westward, but to the north of that just described, through Nunjerajpet to Merkara; but this is a very bad route, and is now nearly disused. At the present time the principal road is that leading from Mysore into Coorg, and thence into Canara. It proceeds from Periapatam north-westward, through Frazerpet to Merkara, and thence by the Sulia or Sumpaji Ghaut, having an easy slope down to Canara, and terminating at Mangalore, being practicable for guns and all sorts of carriages. Another road has been more recently constructed between Canara and Mysore, which passes by the Munjeerabad Ghaut, somewhat to the north of the road by the Sumpaji Ghaut. The authorities were induced to sanction the construction of this road by regard to its advantages, as connecting Canara and the important seaport of Mangalore with the towns and districts in the west of Mysore. There are several cross-routes, but these are merely very rude paths, full of large stones, intersected with deep ruts, and passing over steep acclivities, which might, by the exercise of an ordinary portion of skill and care, be either avoided or reduced.

The men of Coorg are a handsome athletic race, usually above the middle size, and, with scarcely any exception, well-limbed. The women are not so tall in proportion, but are well made and well-looking, though rather coarse, but fair in comparison to the men. Both sexes are laborious and industrious in the practice of agriculture, their main and almost exclusive employment; except that the men shoot and hunt, partly to destroy animals injurious to their crops, and partly for the produce of the sport. They are well clad, the men wearing a turban, and a gown reaching to the feet, and being girt round the waist with a shawl or handkerchief, to which they attach the formidable Nair knife. The women wear a loose cotton wrapper, reaching from the shoulders to the knees, and a small white cloth tied round the head. Both sexes daily, after their labour, wash the whole body in warm water. A very singular and revolting custom prevails here, different from polyandry, in which each woman has exclusively a plurality of husbands. In Coorg the wives of several brothers are the wives of all. "On the marriage of an elder brother, his wife is considered the property of all the brothers jointly; and as the juniors successively marry, their wives in turn are common to all the brothers." This abominable custom, however, is falling somewhat into disrepute, and its practice becoming more circumscribed. The amount of the population in 1836 was officially returned at 65,437 persons; and the increase in that year was nearly ten per cent. on the total. Since the annexation of Coorg to the British dominions, the revenue has improved, cultivation has been extended, and the general prosperity of the country steadily increased. The only assemblages of dwellings which can with any propriety be denominated towns, are Merkara, Somwarpet, and Verajenderpett. The inhabitants of Coorg are Nairs, and consequently Brahminists of the Sudra caste; yet, in some respects, they manifest little reverence for the Brahminical code. Though a barbarous, they are an energetic and brave race, and with unflinching spirit and desperate valour they maintained their independence against the vastly superior power of Hyder Ali and his son Tippoo Sultan, severely retaliating on their oppressors in the campaign of 1791, and materially aiding in their humiliation. By the treaty of that year they were received under the protection of the British government.

In 1832, the sister of the reigning rajah, with her husband, fled from Coorg into Mysore, and claimed the protection of the British resident from the violence of their relative. Under these circumstances, it became the duty of the British authorities to afford the protection implored, without regarding the complaints of the rajah, or the military preparations which he proceeded to make. Various communications passed between those authorities and the prince, whose country, it may moreover be observed, was a prey to the most oppressive tyranny and misgovernment. At length the rajah seized and detained an emissary of the British government, who, with another native, had been despatched to Coorg, under an impression that native negotiation might be more effective than European. This act of violence the rajah defended, on the ground of reprisal for the withholding from his vengeance the fugitive victim of his tyranny. Negotiation was now relinquished; a force of 6,000 men was despatched to punish the outrage, and the government of Madras issued a proclamation to the effect, that the rajah, in consequence of oppression and cruelty to his subjects, the assumption of an attitude of hostility and menace towards the British government, the encouragement and aid afforded to its enemies, and the imprisonment of the British emissary sent to open a friendly negotiation with him, was no longer to occupy the royal seat. In the beginning of April, the British force, commanded by Colonel Lindesay, entered Coorg from Mysore, and having found the stockades made by order of the rajah deserted, advanced to Merkara, the capital, which, having been evacuated, was occupied without opposition, and the British flag hoisted. Simultaneously with the movement under Colonel Lindesay, a column under the command of Colonel Foulis marched from Cannanore, in Malabar, and ascending the course of the Burrepollai, or Stony River, penetrated into the heart of the country by the Horgullum Pass, and took the town of Verajunderpet, sixteen miles south of that of Merkara. The enemy made an abortive attempt at resistance, in which they lost about 250 men and four chiefs, the loss on the British side being comparatively insignificant. On the 13th, the wretched rajah surrendered unconditionally. During those operations, a weak column, under Colonel Jackson, marched from Mangaloor, and attempted to penetrate the country by a route to the north of that of Colonel Foulis; but, entering a deep rocky ravine, suffered from a fire so deadly and well sustained, that it was obliged to retire, after severe loss, leaving behind the wounded and the whole of its baggage. Another column, under Colonel Waugh, entered the country by a route nearly parallel to that of Colonel Lindesay, but to the north of his line of march, and penetrated to Merkara, though not without suffering very severely in forcing the passage. The country thus subdued was incorporated with the territory of the East-India Company. The annexation of his dominions to those of the British was almost unavoidable, no male branch of the royal house remaining alive to become a claimant of sovereignty. The ex-rajah is now (1856) in England, and receives an annual stipend of 60,000 rupees, subject to the deduction of 40*l.* per mensem, which he has engaged to set apart for the education of his daughter, who has become a convert to Christianity.

COORLA.—A town in the British district of Ganjam, presidency of Madras, 26 miles W. of Ganjam. Lat. 19° 29′, long. 84° 45′.

COOSSY.—A river rising in the British district of Ramghur, presidency of Bengal, about lat. 23° 35′, long. 85° 58′. It has a circuitous course, but generally S.E., of 240 miles, and discharges itself into the Hoogly on the right side, in lat. 22°, long. 88° 4′. At Ameenugur, eighty miles from its source, and in lat. 22° 56′, long. 86° 45′, it receives the Comaree, a considerable torrent. Close to the town of Midnapore, and in lat. 22° 24′, long. 87° 23′, it is crossed by the route from Cuttack to Midnapore, the passage being made by ford during the dry season, and by ferry during the rains;

and at Koilaghat, yet lower down, and only forty miles from its mouth, it is crossed by the route from Calcutta to Midnapore, the passage being effected by ford in the dry season, and ferry during the rains.

COOSY.—A large river tributary to the Ganges. Its remotest source, the Bhotiya Coosy, is, according to Buchanan, in Nepal, amidst the snowy peaks of the Himalaya, and in about lat. 28° 25′, long. 86° 11′. It takes a course first south-west for about sixty miles, then winds south and south-east for 160 more, to lat. 26° 45′, long. 87° 13′, its place of exit from the mountains, from which it descends "by three cataracts, or rather violent rapids." About thirty miles above that place, it on the left side receives the Arun, a great torrent, which, rising in Thibet, flows through a valley dividing the main range of the Himalayas, thus receiving the drainage of both faces of the Snowy Mountains. About ten miles from its junction with the Arun it also receives, on the left side, the Tambur, which rises on the southern face of the Himalaya, and flows through Nepal for about 100 miles, to its confluence. At the place of its exit from the mountains, the Coosy appears to be a greater stream than the Ganges at Hurdwar, and is nowhere fordable, in ordinary years, in its course through the plains. In the upper part of its course, near the mountains, the water, even in summer, retains considerable coolness, and the stream is subject to sudden rise and fall; but it is navigable for small boats downwards from the last cataract. It there takes a southern course, and in lat. 26° 37′, long. 87° 12′, fifteen miles lower down, it touches on the British territory, and forms the boundary between it and Nepal for ten miles, when it enters the British district of Purnea, through which it holds a course due south for eighty miles, to its confluence with the Ganges, in lat. 25° 19′, long. 87° 19′; its total length of course being about 325 miles. During its course through the level alluvial tract of Purnea, it sends off numerous branches, and receives but one considerable stream—the Gogaree, which, flowing from the N.W., joins it on the right side, ten miles above its confluence with the Ganges. Notwithstanding this great loss of volume, it is everywhere a very large stream, having a channel one and a half to two and a half miles wide, with many shoals and islands, through which the river forces its way, forming many alterations among them during its inundations. Even where narrowest, Buchanan found it, when lowest, to have a stream 1,200 feet wide and fifteen deep. From those particulars it may be concluded to be larger than the Jumna, and even the Ghogra.

COOTCOTTAH.—A town in Hyderabad, or dominions of the Nizam, 82 miles S.W. from Hyderabad, and 35 miles N. from Kurnool. Lat. 16° 20′, long. 77° 55′.

COOTUL.—A town in Hyderabad, or dominions of the Nizam, 60 miles S. from Ellichpoor, and 148 miles E. from Aurungabad. Lat. 20° 19′, long. 77° 34′.

COOTULPORE.—A town in the British district of Burdwan, lieut.-gov. of Bengal, 22 miles S.W. of Burdwan. Lat. 23°, long. 87° 40′.

COPPACHOOR.—The name of a tribe inhabiting a valley between the snowy range of the Himalaya and that known as the Sub-Himalayas. The centre of the territory inhabited by this tribe is about lat. 27° 20′, long. 93° 20′.

COPPA DROOG.—A town in Mysore, distant 120 miles N.W. from Seringapatam, and 29 miles S.E. from Bedenore. Lat. 13° 31′, long. 75° 23′.

COPUL.—A town in one of the recently ceded districts of Hyderabad, or dominions of the Nizam, 51 miles W. from Bellary, and 78 miles E. from Dharwar. Lat. 15° 21′, long. 76° 13′.

CORADA.—A town in the British district of Ganjam, presidency of Madras, 65 miles N.W. of Ganjam. Lat. 19° 56′, long. 84° 20′.

CORALLEA.—A town in the British district of Tipperah, lieut.-gov. of Bengal, 31 miles N.E. of Dacca. Lat. 23° 52′, long. 90° 53′.

CORINGA, in the British district of Rajahmundry, presidency of Madras, a town on the estuary of that branch of the Godavery which opens into Coringa Bay, and which is generally called the Coringa River, its mouth forming the harbour of Coringa. At the entrance is a bar, having twelve or fourteen feet of water at spring tides. Within the bar the depth of water is from two and a half to four fathoms; but measures are in progress for obtaining a greater depth by cutting through the bar. The town, which is a place of considerable trade, is situate on the south side of the estuary. It is the best place on this coast for building or repairing small vessels, there being a considerable number of shipwrights and calkers, who here find constant employment. The place, however, from its low situation, is subject to be overflowed by extraordinary rises of the sea, and in May, 1787, in consequence of a prolonged and very violent gale from the north-east, the sea rushed over the site of the town, swept away all the houses, and in a moment destroyed nearly the whole population, estimated at about four thousand. The deluge overspread the adjacent country for several miles inland, destroying, as is estimated, fifteen thousand people, and upwards of a hundred thousand head of cattle. A similar disaster occurred in 1832, when several vessels were carried into the fields and left aground in elevated situations; one new ship, on the stocks, was swept into the river and lost. Distance from Rajahmundry, S.E., 32 miles; Madras, N.E., 290; Calcutta, S.W., 562. Lat. 16° 49′, long. 82° 19′.

CORLAM.—A town in the British district

of Ganjam, presidency of Madras, 11 miles N.E. of Chicacole. Lat. 18° 24′, long. 84° 3′.

COROMANDEL (COAST OF).—Part of the eastern coast of Southern India, forming the shore of the Bay of Bengal. It is considered to commence at Point Calimere, in lat. 10° 17′, long. 79° 56′, and to hold a direction nearly due north as far as Gondegam, in lat. 15° 20′, long. 80° 10′. It extends across the estuaries of many rivers, and the entrance to the extensive Pulicat lake or inlet; but there is no place within its whole extent where large ships can be sheltered in all weather. Blackwood Harbour, the least objectionable, is open to the north, on which point it might be sheltered by a breakwater; the construction of such a work, however, though practicable, would be enormously expensive. Of the several other places frequented by shipping, none have havens, and ships must be anchored in the open sea, where, during the closing months of the year, they are exposed to the violence of the north-east monsoon. Consequently, the coast is then nearly deserted; and the few navigators who venture to anchor, must be prepared to weigh, cut or slip anchor, and work out to sea on the first setting in of a gale. At all times a heavy sea rolls on shore from the vast expanse of the Bay of Bengal, and causes a tremendous surf, which totally precludes communication from the ships lying at anchor with the land by means of boats constructed on the European plan. These would inevitably be dashed to pieces; and resort is therefore had to the Masula boats, which are flat-bottomed, of the same shape at stem and stern, from thirty to thirty-five feet in length, ten or eleven in breadth, and seven or eight in depth. The planks which form those boats are sewed together with coir yarns, or twine spun from the cocoanut-fibre, crossing the seams over a wadding of the same fibre, which presses on the joints and prevents leakage. The places principally frequented by shipping on the Coromandel Coast are Negapatam, Nagore, Tranquebar, Cuddalore, Pondicherry, Sadras, Madras, and Pulicat. The coast throughout is, with little exception, low and sandy, and the sea shallow near the shore, with sounding gradually increasing with the distance from land. The etymology of the name Coromandel has been variously explained; but it appears that it was originally denominated Choramandal or Cholamandal, which is considered to mean the mandal or region of the Chola, an ancient dynasty of this part of India. The Coromandel Coast comprises the sea-coasts of the British districts Tanjore, Arcot, Chingleput, and Nellore.

CORONGE.—An island about two miles in length from north to south, situate close to a rocky point off the coast of Arracan, which forms a bay, having several rocks and islets. Distant from Cape Negrais, N., 38 miles. Lat. 16° 32′, long. 94° 20′.

CORYGAUM.—A village in the British district of Poona, presidency of Bombay, on the route from Poona to Ahmednuggur, 16 miles N.E. from the former. The place is unimportant, but is associated with interesting historical recollections. On the 1st January, 1818, a British force, under the command of Captain Staunton, comprising a detail of artillery, a battalion of infantry, and a small number of auxiliary horse, occupied the village, in which they were attacked by three divisions of the Peishwa's infantry, consisting of about 1,000 men each, supported by immense bodies of horse. The action lasted from noon till nine in the evening, during which period several buildings were repeatedly taken and retaken. On both sides the loss was terrific; but the result was most honourable to the British, who remained masters of the place. In recognition of the gallantry displayed on the occasion by Captain Staunton, a grant of 500*l.* per annum was conferred upon him by the East-India Company. Lat. 18° 39′, long. 74° 8′.

CORTAGERRY.—A town in Mysore, 47 miles N.W. from Bangalore, and 84 miles N.E. from Seringapatam. Lat. 13° 31′, long. 77° 17′.

CORTAPALEYAN.—A town in the British district of Coimbatoor, presidency of Madras, 55 miles N.E. of Coimbatoor. Lat. 11° 33′, long. 77° 35′.

COSSIMBAZAR, in the British district of Moorshedabad, lieut.-gov. of Bengal, a town adjoining the city of Moorshedabad on the south, and in fact a suburb of it. The Bhagirathi, a great offset of the Ganges, here forms, by its winding, a peninsula, at one time insulated, and thence denominated the Island of Cossimbazar. The manufactures of this town were formerly of importance, especially of silk fabrics; but they have much decayed before the irresistible competition of the cheaper wares of Britain. A considerable quantity of silk being produced in the surrounding country, it is generally here prepared for market. Here was formerly a considerable factory belonging to the East-India Company. In 1756 it was taken, without resistance, by Sooraj-oo-dowla, nawaub of Bengal. By a careful census in 1829, the number of houses was stated at 1,300; of inhabitants, at 3,538; of which 1,325 Mussulman, 2,213 Brahminical. Distance N.E. from Calcutta, by land, through Berhampore, 120 miles; by water, 163. Lat. 24° 8′, long. 88° 18′.

COSSIPORE.—A manufacturing suburb of Calcutta, situate on the left bank of the river Hooghly, six miles north of Fort William. Here is located the government foundry, represented as one of the most complete and perfect to be seen in any country. During the administration of Lord Hastings, several pieces of brass ordnance cast at this place were sent to England, and submitted to the examination of a committee of artillery officers at Woolwich, who pronounced the workmanship and finish superior to those of the royal arsenal.

Young artillery officers are now required to attend at this establishment for instruction in the casting of guns. The foundry, when in full work, is capable of turning out more than 200 pieces in the year. Lat. 22° 38′, long. 88° 26′.

COSSYAH HILLS embrace the tract of country lying between Assam and Sylhet on the north and south, and Jynteah and the Garrow country on the east and west, and extend from lat. 25° to 26° 7′, and from long. 90° 52′ to 92° 11′. This mountainous region is considered to be advantageously situate as an almost impregnable military post for the north-eastern frontier, arising from its occupying the centre in a line of operations which might be directed against an eastern enemy, and from its possessing natural bulwarks, requiring little aid to render them impenetrable. The Cossyah Hills have been usually regarded as containing much mineral wealth; but the result of their recent geological survey by Professor Oldham does not favour this presumption; neither iron, stone, nor coal, appearing to be abundant. The great body of Cossyahs have not adopted the customs of the Hindoos; they eat beef, and have, apparently, few religious notions. They have neither idols nor temples; but many peculiarly-shaped stones and rocks, as well as streams and groves, are accounted holy; and sacrifices are made to them. Near the villages, on the hills, are likewise to be seen gigantic stone monuments, with doorways, that remind the English visitor of Stonehenge, and are conjectured to have been erected to the memory of departed chiefs and rajahs. In 1826, a direct communication between Assam and Sylhet being considered desirable, an agreement, concurred in by the Cossyah chiefs, was concluded with the chief of Nungklow, under which, in return for British protection against external enemies, and support in the event of internal insurrection, the rajah stipulated to afford a free passage to British troops passing between Assam and Sylhet; to furnish materials for the construction of a road, and to govern his subjects according to established laws. Teerut Singh, with whom this engagement was made, having caused Lieutenants Bedingfield and Burlton to be treacherously massacred, was deposed in 1829, when the district of Nungklow was conferred upon his nephew; and engagements were at the same time entered into with the rajah of Chirra Poonjee, and the other principal chiefs of the country. A few years later the complete establishment of tranquillity was effected in the Cossyah highlands; and the salutary change was ascribed to the substitution of mild for coercive measures, and especially to the restoration of the son of Teerut Singh to the principality forfeited by his father. See also JYNTEEA.

COTA POLOOR.—A town in the British district of North Arcot, presidency of Madras, 49 miles N.W. of Madras. Lat. 13° 45′, long. 80° 4′.

COTHA, or KOTA, in the British district of Jaunsar, a village near the right bank of the Jumna, and about 3,000 feet above its bed. At the time of Hodgson's visit in 1817, it was a poor place, containing about a dozen houses and 100 inhabitants; but it is now much improved, being a neat village, and uncommonly clean, surrounded with thriving cultivation, and possessed of much cattle. It is also a place of great thoroughfare, being on the direct route from the plains to Jumnotri, and also to Theog and Kotgurh. Lat. 30° 40′, long. 78° 6′.

COTIOTE.—See MALABAR.

COTOOR.—A town in the British district of Cuddapah, presidency of Madras, 31 miles E. of Cuddapah. Lat. 14° 26′, long. 79° 20′.

COULY DROOG.—A town in Mysore, 10 miles S.E. from Bednore, and 140 miles N.W. from Seringapatam. Lat. 13° 43′, long. 75° 10′.

COURTALLUM, in the British district of Tinnevelly, a small town at the western boundary, towards the territory of Travancore. It is situate in a small recess, in the east side of that great group of mountains in which the southern extremities of the Western and Eastern Ghauts unite; and the site of the town is surrounded on three sides by hills. At this place the group is traversed by a deep narrow valley, allowing an easy communication between the Carnatic and Malabar. The dryness of the air and its low temperature, arising from local peculiarities, have deservedly acquired for this spot a character for salubrity; and it is, consequently, much frequented by invalids during the hot weather. In addition to more substantial advantages, it may be mentioned that the scenery is described as being rich and varied, and the whole enlivened with a series of beautiful waterfalls, forming a *tout ensemble*, the contemplation of which is highly grateful to the eye and soothing to the feelings. The lowest and most conspicuous of the series of waterfalls is nearly 200 feet in height, the water of which being much broken in its descent, forms a favourite bathing-place, where the bathers enjoy the benefit of a shower-bath on the grandest scale. Elevation above the sea 700 feet. Distance from Tinnevelly town, N.W., 32 miles; Madras, S.W., 350. Lat. 8° 56′, long. 77° 20′.

COVELONG, in the British district of Chingleput, presidency of Madras, a town on the Coromandel Coast. It is of dangerous approach from the south and south-east, in consequence of a rocky shoal projecting upwards of a mile into the sea in that direction. Here are the ruins of a fort, formerly belonging to the Imperial East-India Company of Ostend, but subsequently acquired by the English, who dismantled it. The locality of Covelong appears to be peculiarly favourable for the production of salt, and it is stated that a pure white description of this article may be manufactured here at the low rate of four shillings and sixpence per ton. Distance from Cuddalore, N.E., 80 miles; Arcot, E., 62; Madras, S., 21. Lat. 12° 47′, long. 80° 18′.

COVILPUTTY.—A town in the British district of Tinnevelly, presidency of Madras, 36 miles N.E. of Tinnevelly. Lat. 9° 12′, long. 77° 56′.

COWLAPOOR.—A town in the British territory of Nagpoor, 152 miles S. from Nagpoor, and 115 miles W. from Bustur. Lat. 19° 10′, long. 80° 13′.

COWREAL, in the British district of Jubbulpore, Saugor and Nerbudda territory, lieut.-gov. of the N.W. Provinces, a town on the route from Jubbulpore to Punnah, 29 miles N.E. of the former. Lat. 23° 32′, long. 80° 10′.

COXE BAZAR.—A town in the British district of Chittagong, lieut.-gov. of Bengal, situate on the eastern side of the entrance to Mascal Channel, a considerable arm of the sea, flowing between the island of Mascal and the mainland. Lat. 21° 31′, long. 92° 6′.

COYELBOODAH.—A town in the British territory of Nagpoor, 151 miles S.E. from Nagpoor, and 73 miles N.W. from Bustur. Lat. 19° 50′, long. 81° 5′.

CRANGANORE.—A town of Malabar, with a fort. It is situate on the Cranganore River, called also the Aycotta River. The river has a bar at the entrance, with five or six feet water on it: inside, there are fourteen or sixteen. The place was taken, in 1662 or 1663, from the Portuguese, by the Dutch, who appear to have constructed the fort. In 1789, it was purchased from the Dutch by the rajah of Travancore; in the following year, possession of it was taken by Tippoo Sultan; and at the general pacification which closed the war provoked by the sultan's attack upon Travancore, it was ceded to the British. In this part of India are many Jews; and one section of that extraordinary people, termed White Jews, claim a peculiar connection with Cranganore. According to their account, their ancestors escaped from Jerusalem at the time of its final destruction, and after various migrations, the descendants of the fugitives made their way to the western coast of India, where, in the year of the world 4250, or 490 of the Christian era, the local sovereign granted them a settlement at Cranganore, where they were joined by others of their nation, and in which place they remained about a thousand years; but, as one of their number stated, "discord arising among ourselves, one of our chiefs called to his assistance an Indian king, who came upon us with a great army, destroyed our houses, palaces, and strongholds, dispossessed us of Cranganore, killed part of us, and carried part into captivity." According to tradition, a colony of Syrian Christians settled here in the year 345, and their establishment continued to prosper until the arrival of the Portuguese at the close of the fifteenth century. By a course of cruel persecution, the greater part of the Syrian believers were constrained to acknowledge the authority of the papal see, which is exercised by the bishop of Cranganore and vicar-general of Malabar. Distance from Cochin, N., 19 miles; Calicut, S., 75; Cananore, S.E., 126; Mangalore, S.E., 207; Bombay, S.E., 648; Bangalore, S.W., 211; Madras, S.W., 341. Lat. 10° 14′, long. 76° 16′.

CUCHEE.—A doab or narrow peninsula east of the Indus, and between it and the Punjnud. It is embodied with Dera Ghazee Khan, and with it formed one of the districts of the late Sikh government, yielding it nine lacs of rupees annually. It is everywhere permeated by watercourses from the Indus, and is remarkably well cultivated and productive. Lat. 29° 20′—30°, long. 70° 40′—71° 10′.

CUDAMPILLY.—A town in Hyderabad, or dominions of the Nizam, 59 miles S.W. from Hyderabad, and 80 miles N. from Kurnool. Lat. 16° 56′, long. 77° 47′.

CUDDABA.—A town in Mysore, 60 miles N. from Seringapatam, and 52 miles N.W. from Bangalore. Lat. 13° 14′, long. 76° 55′.

CUDDABAL.—A town in the British district of Bellary, presidency of Madras, 46 miles W. of Bellary. Lat. 15° 5′, long. 76° 17′.

CUDDALORE, the principal place of the southern division of Arcot, presidency of Madras, a town on the Coromandel Coast, situate at the estuary of the river Panar. The river, though having a considerable length of course, is small at its mouth, and closed up by a bar, so as only to admit coasting-craft of moderate size; but measures have been sanctioned for the improvement of the harbour and the erection of a pier. The site of the town is low, being not more than five feet above the sea; and, from this circumstance, the place might be supposed to be insalubrious; but such is not the case, and the new town especially is regarded as peculiarly healthy. The population are in general well lodged, and there are many good houses, arranged in broad regular streets. The old fort, now nearly demolished, is thus described:—"A quadrangle of unequal sides, with an indifferent rampart and ditch, and no outworks, excepting one advanced from its north-eastern angle: a bastion covers each of the other angles, and the curtains are furnished with the imperfect kind of flanking defence obtainable by means of a succession of bastions placed in a prolongation of one and the same straight line." The town is the principal civil station of the zillah or district. Distant from Madura, N.E., 170 miles; Tanjore, N.E., 77; Arcot, S.E., 84; Madras, S., 100. Lat. 11° 43′, long. 79° 50′.

CUDDAPAH.—A British district under the presidency of Madras, named from the principal place within it. It is bounded on the north by Kurnool and the British district of Guntoor; on the east by the British districts Guntoor and Nellore; on the south-east by the British district of Arcot (the northern division); on the south-west by the territory of Mysore; and on the west by the British district of Bellary. It lies between lat. 13° 12′—16° 19′, long. 77° 52′—79° 48′, and comprehends an area officially returned at 12,970 square miles. The mountains of this district form an uninterrupted chain of great extent, consisting of numerous parallel and continuous ridges, which rise abruptly from the plains, and traverse the whole length of the district, constituting part of the Eastern Ghauts. The general slope of the country is to the east; the plains eastward of Bellary and Gooty having an elevation of 1,182 feet, while the depression in which the town of Cuddapah is situate, is only 507 feet above the level of the sea; and the more eastern limit of the district has an average height of 450 feet. The numerous streams which intersect the district consequently flow in that direction, discharging themselves into the Bay of Bengal. The principal river is the Northern Pennar. The most prominent characteristics of the climate are great heat during the day, and oppressive closeness and stagnation of air during the night; and from these conditions of the atmosphere results its enervating influence on the European constitution.

Of trees the most remarkable and valuable are the teak, blackwood, cocoanut-palm, date-palm, palmyra, babul or Acacia arabica, nim or margosa, and bamboo. The best soil is the regur, or black cotton-ground, in some places mingled more or less with calcareous matter, imparting to it a higher colour, and more open and friable texture. The principal alimentary crops are rice, ragi (Eleusine coracana), bajra (Holcus spicatus), jowar (Holcus Sorghum), chenna (Cicer arietinum), dhal (Citysus cajan), wheat, oil-seeds, and sugar-cane. Amongst the principal commercial crops may be mentioned tobacco, indigo, and kusum (Carthamus tinctorius). "Cotton is cultivated to considerable extent in this district." The most common fruits are the mango, tamarind, plantain, and water-melon. Less abundant are the guava, peach, lime, citron, jack, pomegranate, and grape. Such manufacturing industry as is found, is employed on cotton piece-goods, muslins, blankets, and other coarse woollens; in the preparation and use of indigo and other dyes; in the working of gold, silver, and other metals; and in pottery. The exports consist of cotton piece-goods, coarse woollens, a small quantity of silken fabrics, sugar, grain, and tobacco: the imports are betel, iron, steel, copper, and some other articles of less importance. The language spoken is the Canarese. The population is given under the article MADRAS. The district is traversed by one of the lines of the Madras Railway Company. There is also a good ordinary road in a direction from south-east to north-west, and leading from Madras to Cuddapah, and thence to Bellary. There are, besides, routes of inferior description. 1. From south to north, from the cantonment of Cuddapah to Hyderabad, through the Murkondah Pass. 2. From east to west, from Nellore to the cantonment of Cuddapah. 3. From north-east to south-west, from the cantonment of Cuddapah to Bangalore. The principal places—Cuddapah, the locality of the military and civil establishments of the district, Sidhout or Siddawattan, and Rachuti or Roychoty — are described under their respective names in the alphabetical arrangement.

In 1846 this collectorate was the scene of serious disturbances, originating, it is believed, in a feeling of distrust towards the government, occasioned by the adoption of measures affecting the prescriptive rights of landed property. These, however, were speedily suppressed; and the home authorities, upon the subject being brought before them, having directed that long undisturbed possession should be regarded as sufficient evidence of the existence of such rights, the district shortly after resumed its wonted tranquillity. The Ceded Districts, of which Cuddapah forms the eastern division, came into the possession of the East-India Company in the year 1800, by a treaty concluded with the Nizam, subsequently to the partition of the dominions of Tippoo Sultan.

CUDDAPAH, situate in the British district of the same name, under the presidency of Madras, a military cantonment five miles south-west of the right bank of the Northern Pennar or Pennaur, and immediately on the banks of the river Bogawunka. The cantonment is on a declivity, rising gently from the latter river, and contains two barracks for the accommodation of Europeans, substantially built of brick and lime-mortar, lying parallel to each other, each extending about sixty feet in length by sixteen in breadth; and spacious lines for native infantry, besides an hospital, and other requisite buildings. The military force stationed here amounts to about 1,000 men. Here are also the civil establishment for the district, and the jail, which is situate nearly in the centre of an old fort, and has a slightly elevated site, considered to be salubrious. It was erected in 1813, and consists of several buildings in separate and spacious inclosures, suited for the classification of the inmates. One of the lines of the Madras Railway Company passes close to the town. Elevation above the sea 507 feet. Distance from Bellary, S.E., 138 miles; Bangalore, N.E., 134; Vellore, N., 110; Nellore, W., 78; Guntoor, S.W., 169; Madras, N.W., 139. Lat. 14° 28′, long. 78° 52′.

CUDDAPURRUM.—A town in the native state of Travancore, 31 miles N. from Quilon, and 49 miles S.E. from Cochin. Lat. 9° 20′, long. 76° 39′.

CUDDEAPUTNUM. — A town in the native state of Travancore, 31 miles S.E. from

Trivandrum, and 19 miles N.W. from Cape Comorin. Lat. 8° 9′, long. 77° 20′.

CUDDOOR.—A town in Mysore, 90 miles N.W. from Seringapatam, and 91 miles N.E. from Mangalore. Lat. 13° 33′, long. 76° 4′.

CUDDUTURITTEE.—A town in the native state of Travancore, 21 miles S.E. from Cochin, and 61 miles N. from Quilon. Lat. 9° 45′, long. 76° 33′.

CUHMUR, in the British district of Ghazeepoor, lieut.-gov. of the N.W. Provinces, a town on the route from Benares to Dinapoor, 50 miles E. of the former. Lat. 25° 26′, long. 83° 50′.

CUKKOLUM.—A town in the native state of Travancore, 30 miles S.E. from Trivandrum, and 20 miles N.W. from Cape Comorin. Lat. 8° 15′, long. 77° 22′.

CULDINDY.—A town in the British district of Masulipatam, presidency of Madras, 28 miles N.E. of Masulipatam. Lat. 16° 30′, long. 81° 21′.

CULLOOR.—A town in the British province of Nagpoor, or lapsed estate of the rajah of Berar, 89 miles N. from Rajahmundry, and 81 miles S.W. from Bustar. Lat. 18° 10′, long. 81° 22′.

CULLYCOTA.—A town in the British district of Ganjam, presidency of Madras, 20 miles N. of Ganjam. Lat. 19° 38′, long. 85° 9′.

CULNA, in the British district of Burdwan, lieut.-gov. of Bengal, a town on the right bank of the river Hooghly, on the route from Cutwa to the town of Hooghly, 26 miles E. of Burdwan. It is a place of considerable trade, its business having greatly increased in consequence of its being found a convenient station for steamers plying between Calcutta and the North-West Provinces. Culna is said to have 60,000 inhabitants, the chief part of whom are from different parts of the country carrying on trade there. Lat. 23° 14′, long. 88° 20′.

CULNA.—A town in the British district of Jessore, lieut.-gov. of Bengal, 32 miles E. of Jessore. Lat. 23° 13′, long. 89° 42′.

CULPETTA.—A town in the British district of Malabar, presidency of Madras, 34 miles N.E. of Calicut. Lat. 11° 39′, long. 76° 10′.

CUMBAKONAM.—See COMBACONUM.

CUMBUM.—A town in the British district of Madura, presidency of Madras, 59 miles W. of Madura. Lat. 9° 44′, long. 77° 20′.

CUMMADA.—A town in Nagpoor, 80 miles N.W. from Rajahmundry, and 95 miles S.W. from Bustar. Lat. 18° 1′, long. 81° 14′.

CUMMUM.—A town in the British district of Cuddapah, presidency of Madras, 79 miles N. of Cuddapah. Lat. 15° 34′, long. 79° 10′.

CUNCHAKACHERLA.—A town in the British district of Masulipatam, presidency of Madras, 49 miles W. of Ellore. Lat. 16° 41′, long. 80° 27′.

CUNCHINCULL DROOG.—A town in Mysore, 83 miles N.W. from Seringapatam, and 59 miles N.E. from Mangalore. Lat. 13° 17′, long. 75° 39′.

CUNDOOR.—A town in the British district of Cuddapah, presidency of Madras, 59 miles S. of Cuddapah. Lat. 13° 39′, long. 78° 54′.

CUNDYKAIRA.—A town in Mysore, 76 miles N. from Seringapatam, and 128 miles N.E. from Mangalore. Lat. 13° 30′, long. 76° 39′.

CURRABAGUDDY.—A town in the British district of Bellary, presidency of Madras, 81 miles S.W. of Bellary. Lat. 14° 43′, long. 75° 50′.

CURRAH.—See KURRAH.

CURREEGONG.—A town in the British district of Rungpore, lieut.-gov. of Bengal, 23 miles N.E. of Rungpore. Lat. 25° 46′, long. 89° 38′.

CURRUCKPORE.—A town in the British district of Bhagulpore, lieut.-gov. of Bengal, 30 miles W. of Bhagulpore. Lat. 25° 5′, long. 86° 32′.

CURSALEE, in the native state of Gurwhal, a village, the last and highest to be met with in ascending the valley of the Jumna towards Jumnotri, from which it is distant three miles south-west. It consists of forty or fifty houses solidly built of stone, bonded with squared beams of timber, the exterior of which is grotesquely carved with images of Hindoo deities. There are a few small patches of tolerably level and fertile ground about the village, and on those is cultivated grain sufficient for the population. Lat. 30° 57′, long. 78° 29′.

CUTCH.—A native state under the political superintendence of the government of Bombay. It is bounded on the north-west and north by the province of Sinde; on the east by the dominions of the Guicowar; on the south by the peninsula of Kattywar and the Gulf of Cutch, and on the south-west by the Indian Ocean. Its limits, inclusive of the great salt marsh termed the Runn, extend from lat. 22° 47′ to 24° 40′, and from long. 68° 26′ to 71° 45′. Its greatest length from east to west is 205 miles, and its breadth from north to south (which is nearly equal throughout its whole extent) 110 miles. The area, exclusive of the Runn, is 6,764 square miles, and its population is returned at 500,536. This long narrow tract, interposed between the desert and the sea, forms a connecting link between Guzerat and Sinde. Two mountain-ranges intersect the country. The principal, termed the Lunkhi, nearly bisects the province from east to west; the other runs in a parallel direction, but more to the northward. Both are of moderate height. The most remarkable hill of the range first mentioned is the Nunow, rising from the centre of the province, and well known to navigators from its height and sugar-loaf form. The northern chain is in like manner distinguished by the Judria, a hill of similar form, from the materials of which are fabricated the millstones of Cutch. Indications of volcanic action are observable along the bases of the hills, where an extensive surface is overlaid with basaltic eruptions, and the rocks bear evidence of having been rent asunder by the effects of fire. Earthquakes have, indeed, been experienced to a very recent period, showing that these operations have not yet ceased. In July, 1819, a severe shock was felt throughout Cutch, the effects of which were so violent that every fortification in the country was shaken to its foundations, and several hundreds of the inhabitants perished. Among the remarkable phenomena of this convulsion of nature, were the upheaving of an enormous mound of earth and sand many miles in extent, and the simultaneous submersion of an adjacent tract of country. Allah Band, or the Band of God, is the name which has been given by the natives to the mound, in allusion to its not being the work of man.

Though the province is of small dimensions, and sterile in its character, owing to the sandy nature of the soil, there are, notwithstanding, several fertile tracts. These are chiefly comprised in the valley between the two mountain-ranges already noticed, and in the extensive plain stretching south of the Lunkhi hills, nearly to the coast, where it is skirted by a border of sand extending from the Indus on the west, to the head of the Gulf of Cutch on the east. On the opposite, or northern side of the province, beyond the second range of mountains, the entire frontier is fringed by a broad belt of luxuriant pasturage, called the Bhunni. Like Sinde, of which Cutch probably once formed part, the country is characterized by a deficiency of water. During the prevalence of the south-west monsoon, numerous torrents descend from the mountains, both in a northerly and southerly direction; but there are no permanent rivers in the province, the beds of the streams becoming dry with the cessation of the rains. No reliance, moreover, can be placed upon any considerable supply from tanks or artificial lakes, inasmuch as, owing to the porous character of the subsoil, such reservoirs are quickly exhausted by filtration. Wells, however, are abundant, and excellent water is obtained by penetrating the rock underlying the more recent formations.

Some mineral productions are obtainable in Cutch. Coal and iron have both been found, the former at Jamutra and the latter in the vicinity of Bhooj. Alum is obtained in considerable quantities by boiling the waters of the mountain springs in the neighbourhood of Lukput, whence it is exported, chiefly to Bombay, for the purposes of dyeing. There is a scarcity of timber both on the mountains and in the plains: the former are covered with low brushwood; but the trunks of decayed trees, constantly met with in the Lunkhi range, induce the belief that its sides were formerly clothed with forests. Plantations of peepul and babool occasionally surround the villages; the date-tree is more common, but the mango, banyan, and tamarind are rare. Of commercial crops, cotton is the principal; the soil of the most productive tracts being peculiarly favourable to the growth of this staple article. Sugar-cane is cultivated, but its quality is represented as inferior. Jowar, bajree, and the common grains of India, are the chief alimentary products. Though the country boasts of no great variety of fruits, none surpass it in the excellence of its grapes and musk-melons. Among the domestic animals, the horse is held in high estimation: it is remarkable for a bony head and cheeks, a thin and long neck, and large sparkling eye, with small soft ears. Kine, though of inferior breed, are abundant, as are also buffaloes and camels. The wild animals are, the tiger, leopard, wolf, hyæna, jackal, and fox. The wild ass roams in the Runn. This salt marsh consists of two principal portions, the larger bounding Scinde on the south-east, and the smaller being connected at its western extremity with the Gulf of Cutch. The Great Runn extends between lat. 23° 22′—24° 42′, long. 69° 50′—71° 20′; is about 160 miles in length from east to west, and 80 in breadth from north to south. Its area is estimated by Burnes "at the enormous space of 7,000 square miles." Throughout this wide expanse there are, however, several islands, or more elevated tracts, and some of considerable extent. Burnes does not consider the term marsh a correct appellation for this singular tract. He points out that "it has none of the characteristics of one; it is not covered or saturated with water but at certain periods; it has neither weeds nor grass in its bed, which, instead of being slimy, is hard, dry, and sandy, of such a consistency as never gives way, unless a long continuance of water on any individual spot have converted it into clay, which is rare; nor is it otherwise fenny or swampy. It is in reality but the dried-up bottom of an extensive inland sea, which, from having once been overwhelmed with water, more readily receives what flows into it, from being lower than other parts of the country." Burnes conjectures that the desiccation of the bed of this conjectural sea has resulted from its elevation by the upheaving of the earth, caused by one of those earthquakes so common in this part of India. To such an origin he attributes the saltness of the Runn, as well as to numerous saline streams flowing into it from the north and north-east. "So salt is the Runn, that it is often encrusted with it an inch deep, the water having been evaporated by the sun; and even lumps of salt may be picked up as large as a man's fist, and beautifully crystallized." During the monsoon, the Runn is flooded by sea-water blown into it, as well as by fresh water derived from the rains, or discharged into it by the various swollen rivers. In the dry season, fresh water is never to be had anywhere, except on the islands or rocky elevated spots; and there it is scarce. The Runn is throughout devoid of herbage, and vegetable life is discernible only occasionally in a tamarisk-bush, growing by means of the rain-water falling near it. The sirab, or mirage, prevails here very vividly, and highly magnifies objects, so that patches of shrubs sometimes resemble forests, and wild asses, the only quadrupeds to be seen in this desolate tract, appear as large as elephants. During the dry season, when the sun shines, the Runn may be mistaken for a great expanse of water, in consequence of the reflection of light from the glazed saline surface. Flies are so numerous on the Runn, that it is almost impossible to breathe without swallowing some; and though they do not bite, it is very difficult to force a horse through their swarms. The smaller Runn is situate between the territory of Cutch and that of Guzerat, and communicates with the Great Runn, at the south-east of which it lies, by a narrow strip of similar formation. It extends between lat. 23° 5′—23° 45′, long. 70° 45′—71° 50′, and in outline approaches an isosceles triangle, the base of which extends from east to west about 70 miles, the area being about 1,600 square miles. The western extremity of the base adjoins the eastern extremity of the Gulf of Cutch. These two saline wastes differ little from each other in their physical qualities, and few tracts of similar magnitude are so totally unproductive, salt being the only valuable commodity obtainable from them.

The political relations of the East-India Company and the government of Cutch first assumed a formal character in 1809. The articles of agreement then entered into were four, relating respectively to the protection of Guzerat from aggression on the part of Cutch; the settlement of certain claims of the Rao of Cutch on territory lying on the Guzerat side of the gulf; the suppression of piracy, and the exclusion from Cutch of Europeans and Americans. Some of these articles appear to have been but inadequately observed on the part of the rulers and people of Cutch, and in 1815 it became necessary for the British government to take hostile proceedings. The result was, the conclusion, in January, 1816, of a treaty, embodying and rendering more stringent the provisions of the former articles, and containing arrangements for the limitation of the employment of Arab mercenaries in Cutch, for the receipt of military aid from the British government, and for other purposes. By one article of this treaty, the fort of Anjar, with certain villages, were conveyed to the British government; besides which, the Rao bound himself to an annual payment of a stipulated sum. By another, he engaged to make good the losses sustained from the depredations of the people of Cutch in Kattywar, and also to defray the military expenses rendered necessary by these outrages. But by a supplemental treaty, dated the 18th June, 1816, the British government released the Rao from the payment of the military charges—upwards of 80,000*l.*, and also from the annual tribute. Thus matters stood till 1819, when, in consequence of his misgovernment, the Rao was deposed, and his infant son raised to the throne. By treaty, dated the 13th October, in the last-mentioned year, the previous treaty was confirmed, so far as it was unaltered by the new one, a council of regency was appointed to act during the minority of the Rao, and, among other points, stipulations were made for the maintenance of a British force for the defence of Cutch, at the discretion of the British government; for prohibiting negotiation with any chief or state, except by permission; for the adjustment of disputes by the arbitration of the British, and for mutual freedom of trade between British ports and those of Cutch. In May, 1822, the arrangements of the treaty of 1816 were modified by a new treaty, under which the territorial cessions made by the Rao in 1816 were restored, in consideration of a pecuniary equivalent. The sum fixed, 88,000 rupees per annum, was subsequently thought too large, and in 1832 the arrears, amounting to a considerable sum, were remitted, and all future payments on this account relinquished. The subsidy thenceforward payable for the military force stationed in Cutch was fixed at 2,00,000 rupees per annum, subject to reduction in the event of a diminution of the force; and in case the latter should be altogether withdrawn, or so reduced that the charge should not exceed the amount of the Anjar compensation, viz. 88,000 rupees, then that amount only to be demandable. In December, 1835, it was discovered that a considerable traffic in slave children was carried on between Arabia and the ports of Cutch. The British government resolved to take measures for its suppression, whereupon the Rao issued a proclamation prohibiting the inhuman practice. Under the influence of British counsel, various other measures of a salutary and beneficent character have been adopted; suttee has been abolished, and the complete suppression of infanticide is anticipated. The revenue of the Rao amounts to 7,38,423 rupees, or 73,842*l.*, and the military force maintained by him consists of a body of irregular horse, in no way subject to the control of the British government. A number of feudatory chiefs, boasting descent with the Rao from a common ancestor, enjoy an amount of revenue, and exercise unlimited authority within their respective domains. Of these chiefs, the following account is given by a former governor of Bombay:—"The family of these chiefs is derived at a recent period from Tatta in Sind, and they all sprung from a common ancestor, Humeerjee, whose son, Rao Khengar, acquired the sovereignty of Cutch before the middle of the sixteenth century of our era. The number of these chiefs is at present about 200, and the whole number of their tribe in Cutch is guessed at 10,000 or 12,000 persons. This tribe is called Jhareja. It is a branch of the Rajputs. The Rao's ordinary jurisdiction is confined to his own demesne, each Jhareja chief exercising unlimited authority within his lands. The Rao can call on the Jharejas to serve him in war; but must furnish them with pay at a fixed rate while they are with his army. He is the guardian of the public peace, and as such chastises all robbers and other general enemies. It would seem that he ought likewise to repress private war, and to decide all disputes between chiefs; but this prerogative, though constantly exerted, is not admitted without dispute. Each chief has a similar body of kinsmen, who possess shares of the original appanage of the family, and stand in the same relation of nominal dependence to him that he bears to the Rao. These kinsmen form what is called the bhyaud or brotherhood of the chiefs, and the chiefs themselves compose the bhyaud of the Rao."

CUTTACK, a British province, named from its principal place, lies within the presidency of Bengal, and is divided into three districts: the northern, or Balasore; the central, or Cuttack proper; and the southern, or Pooree. It is bounded on the north by the British districts of Midnapore and Hijellee; on the north-west by the petty native states known as the Cuttack Mehals; on the west by the Mehals and the British district of Ganjam; and on the east and south-east by the Bay of Bengal. It lies between lat. 19° 40′—21° 45′, long. 85° 8′—87° 31′, and has an area of 7,635 square miles. The seacoast, forming part of the north-western boundary of the Bay of Bengal, extends in a direction generally from south-west to north-east, from Priaghy, near the southern extremity of Chilka Lake or inlet, in lat. 19° 42′, long. 85° 40′, to a point seven miles east of the mouth of the river Soobunreeka, in lat. 21° 37′, long. 87° 30′. It is by seamen called the Orissa coast. In the southern part along the shore is a low level expanse, beyond which inland appear several "saddle-hills," terminating a chain of mountains extending along the coast to the southward. Between those hills and the low sandy shore, is the extensive Chilka Lake or inlet, communicating with the sea by means of a narrow strait, in lat. 19° 42′, long. 85° 40′; at a short distance from which a sand-bank is said to project two miles into the sea, rendering dangerous the close approach of shipping to the coast. The navigator, continuing his course to the north-east, is struck by the appearance of Pooree, with its three pagodas of Juggernauth, at the mouth of the most southerly estuary of the Mahanuddee, and in lat. 19° 49′, long. 85° 54′. At this point commences the delta of the Mahanuddee, the shore of it extending north-east for eighty miles, to lat. 20° 35′, long. 86° 40′. It is low and swampy, resembling the Sunderbunds at the estuaries of the Ganges, being intersected by numerous sluggish winding streams, influenced by the tide, and infested by innumerable alligators of great size and voracity. The soil is in general a deep mud, overgrown with coarse grass and brushwood, and containing many morasses, quagmires, and quicksands, perplexing and dangerous to travellers. The Black Pagoda, another vast monument of Brahminical superstition, is seen on the coast nineteen miles north-east of the temples of Juggernauth. Further onwards is False Bay, having at its extremity two points, the southernmost known as False Point, the other as Point Palmyras, and also called True Point. Point Palmyras is a low sandy tongue of land, covered with Palmyra palms, and having on each side a channel, each the mouth of the river Brahmunnee, that to the south being navigable for small coasting craft. It does not appear that any of the numerous estuaries of the Mahanuddee are navigable for vessels of any considerable size. Above Point Palmyras, the coast takes a direction which forms the extensive bay, terminated by the south-westernmost banks at the mouth of the Hooghly, and called by European seamen Balasore Roads. This bay "affords good anchorage, the bottom being mostly stiff blue clay, intermixed with sand at times, or small stones." Inland, or westward of the low swampy maritime tract, extends the Moghalbandi, a dry tract, with a sandy soil, in general much mixed with gravel and calcareous conglomerate. It is for the most part hungry and unproductive, and large plains occur totally unfit for cultivation, where low stunted brushwood is the only specimen of vegetation. In the more favoured parts, however, there are fine groves of mango-trees, dense thickets of luxuriant bamboos, noble specimens of the banian (Ficus indica), and various wild flowering shrubs. Inland, and westward of this tract, and in some measure parallel to it, is the hill country, closing down towards the seacoast, in the vicinity of Chilka Lake, in the southern part of the district, and also at its northern extremity, where, near Balasore, a group of rocky picturesque hills project boldly to within sixteen or eighteen miles of the shore. These mountains, denominated Nilgiri or Blue Hills, were, through a whimsical corruption of sounds, called by the earlier English navigators the Nelly Green Hills. In intermediate parts between those extremes, the distance of the high land from the coast increases in some places to sixty or seventy miles. The hills visible from the low country, between Point Palmyras and the Chilka Lake, occur generally in irregular, scattered groups, having peaked and waving summits, which seem to cross each other at all angles, or are isolated, conical, and wedge-shaped hills, wholly disconnected at their bases. Iron is abundantly diffused throughout the whole of the Cuttack hills, in the state of pisiform iron-ore, earthy-red iron-ore, and ochrey-red iron-stone.

The principal rivers are the Mahanuddee, the Brahmunnee, and the Byturnee. There are many other streams and torrents flowing from the mountains, all holding a course generally south-eastward, and falling into the Bay of Bengal, into the greater streams already described, or into the Chilka Jhil or lake. This shallow but extensive piece of water stretches, in the southern part of the district, for about forty-two miles in length, from north-east to south-west, and sixteen in breadth, being for many miles divided from the sea merely by a strip of sand not more than 300 yards in width. It communicates with the sea by a narrow channel, and its water is saline, yielding, by means of solar evaporation, large quantities of culinary salt. It abounds with excellent fish. Numerous islands abridge the extent of water-surface; and where these do not intervene, the water is shallow. The general depth is only four or five feet, the greatest does not exceed six, and the lake is considered to be in the course of being rapidly filled up by the silt swept into it by the numerous torrents of which it is the reservoir.

The climate, in general, in the low alluvial tract along the seashore, is characterized by great insalubrity, resulting from the malaria of the swamps, which produces fevers and agues. The southern parts of the seacoast, however, in the vicinity of Pooree or Juggernath, and Kanarak or the Black Pagoda, having dry sandy soil, and during the greater part of the year being favoured with a brisk refreshing sea-breeze, enjoy a healthful climate, both in the hot and cold months, with a very bracing atmosphere during the latter; but in the rainy season the wind sets from the land, and renders the climate both unpleasant and unhealthy, as in most parts of India. The coast has sometimes been extensively inundated, in consequence of the level of the sea having been raised by violent hurricanes, of which one occurred in 1831, and another in the following year, when upwards of 20,000 human beings perished, and more than 50,000 head of cattle. Though the low tract along the coast is nearly devoid of timber-trees, they are numerous in the interior. The most important are the sal (Shorea robusta), which appears to be obtainable of useful size in any required quantity; the pryasal (Buchanania latifolia), the gambar (Gmelina arborea), sisu (Dalbergia Sisu), the mango, the bur (Ficus indica), the pipal (Ficus religiosa), together with a vast variety of trees and shrubs, yielding drugs, dyes, and wild fruits relished by the natives. The woodlands also produce lac, wax, honey, and various kinds of resins. In some parts of Cuttack there are wild elephants, supposed not to be indigenous, but to have sprung from domesticated individuals, which have escaped and relapsed into the wild state. Of other wild animals, there are the tiger, panther, leopard, hyæna, bear, jackal, otter, wild dog, wild swine, wild buffalo, deer, and antelope. There is also a gigantic bovine quadruped,—the gayal, larger than the bull, having huge horns; and a large kind of antelope, called by the natives the gloranga, and resembling the nylgau (Antilope picta). There are also monkeys, the porcupine, and the ichneumon. Buffaloes are the most valuable domestic animals; the others, which are kine, sheep, swine, and goats, being of diminutive breeds. The principal crops are rice, jowar (Holcus Sorghum), bajra (Holcus spicatus), raji (Eleusine coracana), oil-seeds, opium-poppy, tobacco, indigo, and cotton in small quantities. Some experimental attempts made to introduce improvement in the production of the last-named article failed, and were consequently abandoned. The manufactures are few and insignificant, being principally coarse cotton cloths, for the wear of the poor natives, a small quantity of fine muslins, and thick cotton quilts. The population is given under the article BENGAL. The majority consists of Brahminists, not more than a tenth of the whole being Mussulmans. From Balasore rice is said to be exported in favourable seasons. Some other exports take place, but their value is very small; and it appears that, during a period of five years, the imports greatly exceeded them. Cuttack is not one of the permanently settled districts, but a settlement has recently been effected for a term of years. Cuttack and Balasore, as well as Koordah, Pooree, and Kanarak, the principal towns, are described under their respective names in the alphabetical arrangement. The routes are—1. From north-east to south-west, from Calcutta, through the town of Cuttack to the Circars; 2. from the town of Cuttack to Kamptee and Nagpore; 3. from north to south, from the town of Cuttack to Pooree.

Cuttack was among the latest of the Mahomedan acquisitions in India. The decline of the ancient royal house of Orissa dates from the death, in 1524, of Rajah Pertab Rudra Deo, an event which the monarchy was not destined long to survive. Its downfall may be regarded as completed in 1592, when a lieutenant-governor arrived from the Mahomedan kingdom of Bengal to assume charge of the administration. From this time the province appears to have formed part of the possessions of the ruler of Bengal till 1750, when it was invaded by the Mahrattas, and became tributary to the rajah of Nagpore. The chout, or tribute, amounted to 40,000*l.* per annum. After the lapse of a few years, during which the resources of the country seem gradually to have decayed, difficulty was experienced in discharging the obligation; whereupon the Bengal chief proposed that he should be absolved from the stipulated payment, and that the rajah of Nagpore should take possession of the territory, and undertake its management through his own officers. The proposal being acceded to, the province of Cuttack, in 1756, passed to the Mahrattas. Under their administration it appears to have experienced the anarchy, and to have been subjected to the rapacity, which were the unfailing characteristics of their rule. During the Mahratta war of 1803, the occupation of Cuttack formed part of the Bristish plan of military operations. This service was performed by Colonel Harcourt, who, having taken possession of Juggernaut, proceeded to reduce the fort of Barabuttee, situate about a mile from the town of Cuttack. Its capture took place on the 14th October, 1803, and the victory was followed by the entire submission of the province. Among the results of the conquest was the subjection to British supremacy of the group of native states known as the Cuttack Mehals. These are eighteen in number; viz. Angool, Autgur, Banky, Berumbah, Dhenkanaul, Hindole, Kundiapurra, Neelgur, Nursingpoor, Nyagur, Runpoor, Talchur, Tiggreah, Autmallik, Boad, Duspulla, Koonjerry, and Mohurbunge. In the aggregate they contain an area of 16,929 square miles, and a population of 761,805. Within this extensive tract the land fit for tillage bears a trifling proportion to the space occupied by rock and jungle, or covered by forests producing the finest timber. The sal-tree is particularly sought after, from the size it attains, especially in the hill state of Duspulla, whence is procured the timber annually required for the car of Juggernaut. Many years since a British superintendent was appointed, with a view to establish such a control over the conduct of the rajahs as might prevent the commission of crimes and outrages. The abolition of suttee is one of the beneficial measures arising from this appointment.

CUTTACK. — The principal place of a British district of the same name under the presidency of Bengal. "The extent, appearance, and population of the town," says an observer, "are not unsuitable to its rank as the capital of a large province. Its situation on a tongue of land or peninsula near the bifurcation of the Mahanuddee is commanding in a political and commercial point of view, though these advantages have been in some degree counterbalanced by the outlay incurred in defending it by stone revetments from the encroachments of the rivers which wash two of its sides." The fortifications are in a ruinous state, and their materials are fast disappearing, the stones being carried away and used in various public works, among others in the lighthouse at False Point, and in the macadamization of the cantonment roads. This old fort, says a recent observer, "deviates little from a regular parallelogram, having its longest faces to the north and south, the river running parallel with the former, at a short distance from it. The walls were originally defended by high square bastion towers projecting at different distances: the place could never at any time have offered much resistance, as the walls were barely five feet thick on the three land faces, which a six-pound shot could have perforated." On the river face, however, they were not only of great height but of proportional thickness. "There is only one gateway, and that in the centre of the eastern face. It is narrow, and between two square towers, like the others wide at the base, and decreasing towards their summit. The archway is of comparatively modern date, and is the work of the Mogul government of the province. There was an inner gateway, which was taken down to build the lighthouse with." A broad deep moat faced with stone seems to have been greatly relied on by the natives for the defence of the place from hostile attack. On the British taking possession of the fort in 1803, this was drained, and numerous alligators which infested it, either destroyed or allowed to escape into the river. Within the fort is an old mosque, built by the former Mogul occupants. It has no architectural pretensions whatever. The town is straggling, and exhibits evident signs of decay. There are some very good houses of hewn stone and brick, but for the most part in very indifferent repair, the poverty of the inhabitants preventing them from maintaining their habitations in decent condition. In the suburbs is the "Kuddum Russool," a Mussulman building displaying neither grandeur nor elegance, but venerated from its containing some alleged sacred relics. The inclosure and the ground surrounding it are used as the common burial-place for the Moslem inhabitants; and the guardian priests make a good harvest in unhealthy seasons, by the mortuary-fees exacted for each grave. The Jama Masjit, or great mosque, in the main street, is a very clumsy, inelegant building: it is used both as a school and a place of devotion. The Brahminical temples are rude, ungraceful erections, and generally small. The only one of large dimensions, and which was commenced by a Mahratta governor, is unfinished. Very little trade now exists in Cuttack. It has manufactures of brass cooking-vessels, and shoes, which constitute the staple commodities of the place. The soil of the vicinity is poor and sandy: rice of indifferent quality is the principal crop. The population is estimated at 40,000. Distance from Madras, N.E., 635 miles; Nagpore, E., 440; Berhampore, in Ganjam, N.E., 108; Calcutta, S.W., 220. Lat. 20° 28′, long. 85° 55′.

CUTTEREAH.—A town in the British district of Bhaugulpore, lieut.-gov. of Bengal, 38 miles S.W. of Bhaugulpore. Lat. 24° 46′, long. 86° 39′.

CUTTUB MINAR.—See Delhi.

CUTWA, in the British district of Burdwan, lieut.-gov. of Bengal, a town on the route from Berhampore to Burdwan. It is situate at the confluence of the river Hadjee with the Bhagruttee, the great western branch of the Ganges, and is on the right side of both the confluent streams. In a commercial point of view, its situation is advantageous, commanding an easy communication by the course of the Bhagruttee and Ganges with the North-West Provinces, and also with Calcutta by the course of the

Bhagruttee and Hoogly. Distance N. from Calcutta, by land 80 miles, by water 120. Lat. 23° 38′, long. 88° 10′.

D.

DABLA.—A town in the Rajpoot state of Oodeypoor or Meywar, 98 miles N.E. from the town of Oodeypoor, and 55 miles S. from Ajmeer. Lat. 25° 41′, long. 74° 49′.

DABLING.—A village of Koonawar, in Northern India, situate in a belt of arable land near the left bank of the Sutlej, and four miles from the confluence of its feeder the Hopchoo, and amidst groves of poplars and orchards of apricots. The opposite bank of the Sutlej presents a perpendicular section of 6,000 or 7,000 feet of pure rock. The scanty population is, according to the description of Herbert, altogether of the Chinese Tartar type. "The head man, a Lama, came to pay his respects to us in a dress exactly similar to what is represented as the Chinese costume. His stockings were of woollen stuff sewed, and ought rather from their shape, or want of shape, to have been called bags. His shoes were exactly Chinese, the soles having a spherical shape. He wore also a Chinese skull-cap, but the other people in the village went bareheaded, and wore long tails plaited. They were all rather fair, particularly the women, who had a fine rosy colour. We were very much pleased with the appearance of the assembled village, and could hardly help thinking we had got on the high road to Pekin." Notwithstanding that the elevation of Dabling is 9,400 feet above the sea, the reverberation of the sun's rays from the rocks rising about it, caused, during the visit of Gerard, the heat to be so great, that the thermometer reached 109° in a tent. A mile to the east of Dabling, is another less village, called Doobling, the path between them being very rough, and rendered practicable by means of scaffolds or balconies fastened in some places against perpendicular faces of precipices. The vicinity is fertile, in comparison with the sterility of the mountains rising on every side, and produces walnuts, apricots (which, when dried, resemble prunes, and form an important article in the diet of the inhabitants), cherries of small size but fine flavour, deodars, and birches. Those villages are considered so connected, that they are always named together, under the appellation of Dabling-Doobling. Lat. 31° 45′, long. 78° 39′.

DABUNPOOR, in the jaghire of Jujhur, lieut.-gov. of the N.W. Provinces, a village near the eastern frontier, towards the British district of Delhi. Lat. 28° 28′, long. 76° 43′.

DABUR, in the British district of Agra, a village on the route from the city of Agra to the Rajpoot town of Jeypore, and 28 miles W. of the former. Lat. 27° 3′, long. 77° 39′.

DABUTA, in the British district of Budaon, lieut.-gov. of the N.W. Provinces, a village on the route from Allygurh to Moradabad, 45 miles S.W. of the latter place. Lat. 28° 21′, long. 78° 23′.

DACCA.—A British district, named from its principal place, and situate within the limits of the presidency of Bengal. It is bounded on the north by the British district Mymunsing; on the east by the British districts Tipperah and Bulloah; on the south by the British district Backergunge; and on the west by the British district Deccan Jelalpore, or Furreedpore. It lies betweet lat. 23° 12′—24° 17′, long. 90° 11′—90° 58′, and has an area of 1,960 square miles. It is a level depressed tract, drained by numerous rivers, and by streams of inferior dimensions. In the north-western part of the district, however, and also in its eastern angle towards the Megna, are some small ridges, generally running from north to south, and having an elevation from twenty to fifty feet above the adjacent country. The southern division of the district is the most depressed, and being, in consequence, widely inundated during the periodical rains of closing summer and commencing autumn, is generally under rice-cultivation. Of the rivers, the Megna, or lower Brahmapootra, flowing from north-west to south-east, first touches on the district at its northern boundary at Agarasonda, and continuing to hold a direction south-east for thirty miles, forms the eastern boundary as far as Byrub Bazar, where it turns to the south, and flowing in that direction forty-five miles, forms the boundary on the east side of Dacca, towards Tipperah and Bulloah, as far as Moiskondi, where it leaves the district. At the point where it turns south, it receives on the left the Gora Outra, a considerable stream, and is thence termed the Megna; fifty miles lower down, it, on the right side, receives the Dulasseree, a large offset of the Koonaie or Jabuna, and twenty-five miles lower down, on the same side, the Kirty-Nassa, a large offset from the Ganges. It also sends off and receives, right and left, many other watercourses of less importance, and several small tributaries from the Tipperah hills.

The year may be considered to be divided into three seasons—the hot, the rainy, and the cool. The first lasts from the beginning of March to the end of June, and is succeeded by the periodical rains, continuing until the early part of October, at the close of which the cool season commences, and lasts till the middle of February, when the weather gradually becomes warmer. During the cool season, ice may be obtained by exposing water to the night air in shallow, wide earthen vessels. Generally the climate is characterized by moisture, resulting as well from the great amount of rain, as from evaporation from the several great rivers. During the hot season, sickness is prevalent, and increases with the temperature. During the cool season, there are, with little intermission, either fogs or heavy dews. The mean annual temperature at noon is 79°; the greatest annual fall of rain has been found to be ninety-three inches, the least forty-six, the mean seventy. Of wild animals, Dacca possesses the elephant, buffalo, tiger, bear, and leopard. Of wild birds, there are the fishing-eagle, vulture, kite, argila or adjutant-bird, and cranes of various kinds. The porpoise is common in the large rivers, which also harbour in great numbers the ghariyal, or sharp-beaked crocodile, and the magar, or blunt-beaked crocodile (alligator). Snakes exist in great number and variety. Fish are abundant and excellent. The domestic animals are principally kine and buffaloes. Cultivation is partial and unskilful, so that the district does not supply its own consumption of grain, and that article is imported in large quantities from the neighbouring districts. Esculent vegetables are abundant, but usually not of kinds known in Europe. Sugar, betel-nut, hemp, indigo, and other plants yielding dye-stuffs, are produced in moderate quantities. Cotton was formerly produced in considerable quantities, but its culture has been much limited since the manufacture of fine muslins in the city of Dacca has ceased, the staple being too short for the manufacture of coarse strong fabrics, which alone are now made in the district. In the attempts recently made by the East-India Company to introduce the American cotton, Dacca participated; but the result was complete and total failure. The climate appears to be unsuitable for the purpose, and myriads of insects preying on the plants, destroyed the bolls and frustrated the hopes of the cultivators.

The amount of population is given under the article BENGAL. In the northern part of the district, are two tribes, denominated, the one Kunch, the other Rajbansi, apparently of different origin from the rest of the population; more robust in physical type, and more daring and resolute in character. Excluding these, the Mussulmans are considered to be more numerous than the Brahminists, but not in a great degree. Education does not appear to be greatly encouraged in Dacca, but the town has a government college in a prosperous state, of which some account will be found in the proper place. Dacca, the locality of the civil establishment and a military cantonment, Narainganj, and Islampoor, are described under their respective names in the alphabetical arrangement. There are scarcely any roads in this district, in consequence of the facility afforded by the several large rivers for communication by water, and the extreme difficulty of conducting roads across the numerous streams. There is a very indifferent route from south-west to north-east through Dacca, from Calcutta to Sylhet; another from south to north, from Dacca to Nusseerabad, in the adjoining district of Mymensing. A superior road, projected some years since, from the capital, was abandoned in consequence of the great difficulty in the way of its execution. At a recent period, a line of steam communication was established experimentally, between Calcutta and Dacca, but the result was unfavourable, the expense having greatly exceeded the receipts. The failure being attributed in some degree to the slowness with which the natives of Bengal adopt new customs, it was resolved to continue the experiment, and to extend the line to Assam. It may be noticed that the projected line of the Eastern Bengal Railway Company will intersect this district.

Under the Mahomedan rule, the affairs of Dacca were administered by an officer appointed by the nawaub of Bengal, and accountable to him for the revenues of the province. The establishment of the British authority, on the grant of the Dewanny in 1765, of course put an end to the actual power of the subordinate governor, as well as to that of the chief; but an adequate provision was made for the Dacca nawaub, and his successors continued stipendiaries of the British government until the year 1845, when the title and dignity became extinct by the death of the last possessor without heirs. The pecuniary allowances thereupon lapsed, but a small sum was allotted for the maintenance of the female connections and servants of the deceased nawaub.

DACCA, a town, the principal place of the British district of the same name, presidency of Bengal, is situate on the Burha Gunga, a considerable stream, communicating with the Dulasseree, a large offset of the Koonaie or Jabuna. The Burha Gunga is, however, here about half a mile wide in the dry season, and still wider during the rainy season. The climate is considered good, the heat being tempered by the cooling effect of the numerous rivers; and as their currents are rather rapid, they produce none of the deleterious results of stagnant water, or of water approaching to stagnancy. The city is four miles in length, and one and a quarter in breadth. It is at present a wide expanse of ruins, in many places overgrown with jungle, which, as well as the dilapidated buildings, is infested with numerous tigers, snakes, and other noxious creatures. "All its splendid buildings, the castle of its founder, Shah Jehangir, the noble mosque he built, the palaces of the ancient newaubs, the factories and churches of the Dutch, French, and Portuguese nations, are all sunk into ruin, and overgrown with jungle." Though thus comparatively desolate, its minarets, huge ruined palaces, and other monuments of departed grandeur, give it an impressive and not unpleasing aspect, during the periodical rains of closing summer and autumn, when it stands alone above a wide, watery waste. At present, the works and places of public character are fitting only to be enumerated, not described. The city and suburbs are in a recent publication stated to possess ten bridges, thirteen ghats or landing-places, seven ferry-stations, twelve bazars, three public wells, a variety of buildings for fiscal and judicial purposes, a jail and jail-hospital, a lunatic asylum, and a native hospital. Among the noticeable establishments is the elephant depôt, containing generally from two to three hundred of these animals. The religious edifices devoted to Christianity are St. Thomas's Church, the Baptist Mission meeting-house, the Romish, Armenian, and Greek churches. There are said to be a hundred and eighty Mussulman mosques, and a hundred and nineteen Brahminical temples. The English, Armenians, and Greeks, have cemeteries at this place. Here is a college subject to the control of the government, but under the management of a local committee. The committee have a secretary, and for conducting the educational duties, there are, besides a head master, superintending the whole establishment, three masters in the senior, and nine in the junior school department, of which latter six are natives. There is also a vernacular department, directed by two pundits; and attached are a librarian and a writer. The Baptist Mission maintain a number of schools here.

In 1850, the Court of Chancery pronounced its judgment in favour of the validity of the bequest contained in the will of the late Mr. Robert Mitford, for the benefit of the native inhabitants of Dacca, and the residue of the testator's estate, amounting to between eleven and twelve thousand pounds, has been accordingly paid over to the government of Bengal, to be applied to charitable purposes within the city.

The manufactures of Dacca are at this time scarcely deserving of notice. A small quantity of coarse cotton, silk, and embroidered goods, constitutes the sum of them; and even this scanty remnant of skilled industry is constantly and rapidly giving way before the competition of British fabrics. The muslins of Dacca were formerly unrivalled for fineness and every desirable quality. The spinning of the very fine thread was carried on with wonderful nicety. The operation was performed with a fine steel spindle by young women, who could only work during the early part of the morning, while the dew was on the ground; for such was the extreme tenuity of the fibre, that it would not bear manipulation after the sun had risen. The darners were so skilful, that they could remove an entire thread from a piece of muslin, and replace it by one of finer texture. The demand for those extremely beautiful fabrics was principally for the supply of the royal wardrobe at Delhi, and has declined with the decay of that court. Such muslin, from its wonderful fineness, was called abrawan, or "flowing water," and shabnam, "evening dew." The manufacture is now totally lost; and though some time ago an order was sent from China for a small quantity of such muslin, at the rate of ten rupees, or 1*l.* per square yard, no artisan could be found competent to execute it. The falling off of the general Dacca trade took place as far back as 1801, previously to which the yearly advances made by the East-India Company and private traders for Dacca muslins, were estimated at upwards of twenty-five lacs of rupees (250,000*l.*). In 1807, the Company's investments had fallen to 59,590*l.*, and the private trade to about 56,020*l.* In 1813, the private trade did not exceed 20,595*l.*, and that of the Company was scarcely more considerable. In 1817, the English commercial residency was altogether discontinued. The French and Dutch factories had been abandoned many years before. The extent of misery caused by the annihilation of the manufacture and trade of this once flourishing mart, is not readily to be conceived. The population is given under the article BENGAL. The civil establishment of the district of which this is the chief location, consists of a judge, a collector, and other European officers, with a due proportion of subordinates. For military purposes, Dacca is within the Presidency division, and the immediate vicinity of the town was usually the station of a regiment of infantry and a detail of artillery. It had, however, been alleged, that the site of the cantonment was unhealthy, and in consequence remedial measures were from time to time adopted. These, however, failed in producing the desired result, and at the latter end of 1852, it was finally determined to abandon the cantonment. Distance of the town from Furreedpore, E., 39 miles; Berhampore, E., 138; Calcutta, N.E., 150. Lat. 23° 43′, long. 90° 25′.

DACCA JELALPORE.—See FUREEDPORE.

DACHEN.—A town in the native state of Sikhim, 51 miles N. from Darjeeling, and 150 miles N. from Dinajepore. Lat. 27° 44′, long. 88° 36′.

DADANAIGPOLLIAM.—A town in Mysore, 48 miles N. from Bangalore, and 102 miles N.E. from Seringapatam. Lat. 13° 38′, long. 77° 40′.

DADECALLEE.—A town in the British district of Barasut, lieut.-gov. of Bengal, 35 miles N.E. of Calcutta. Lat. 22° 53′, long. 88° 55′.

DADNUH, in the district of Dadree, subject to the native state of Jujhur, lieut.-gov. of the N.W. Provinces, a town situate on the north-west frontier, towards Loharu. Lat. 28° 34′, long. 75° 57′.

DADOOLA.—A village in Sinde, on the route from Shikarpoor to Subzulcote, and 40 miles S.W. from the latter town. It is situate four miles from the left bank of the Indus, in a populous and well-cultivated country, and is supplied with water from three wells. Lat. 28° 2′, long. 69° 14′.

DADREE, in the British district of Boolundshuhur, lieut.-gov. of the N.W. Provinces, a town on the route from Delhi to Allygurh, 20 miles S.E. of the former. Lat. 28° 33′, long. 77° 38′.

DADREE.—A town, the principal place of

a division of the same name, in the native state of Jujhur, within the territories subject to the lieut.-gov. of the N.W. Provinces, and situate on the route from Hansee to Neemuch. Here is a large bazar, and supplies and water are plentiful. The road to the north, or towards Hansee, is sandy and heavy, but good southwards. According to De Cruz, the district of Dadree, which was originally conferred upon the nawaub of Bahadoorgurh for the support of troops, was retained by the Jujhur nawaub, who furnished the quota for whose maintenance the district had been granted; but it appears from more recent information, that the chief of Jujhur has restored the estate to the former grantee. Distance of the town from Hansee, S., 44 miles. Lat. 28° 32′, long. 76° 20′.

DADUPOOR, in the Cis-Sutlej territory of Sirhind, a small town or village five miles from the right bank of the Jumna, and close to the Delhi Canal. Elevation above the sea between 900 and 1,000 feet. Distance N. of Delhi 88 miles. Lat. 30° 12′, long. 77° 27′.

DAICHOO, in the Rajpoot state of Joudpore, a village on the route from Pokhurn to Joudpore, 28 miles S.E. of the former place. It is supplied with good water from four wells, 150 feet deep. Lat. 26° 47′, long. 72° 27′.

DAIGLOOR.—A town in Hyderabad, or dominions of the Nizam, 100 miles N.W. from Hyderabad, and 46 miles S. from Nandair. Lat. 18° 32′, long. 77° 39′.

DAILWOURA.—A town in the peninsula of Kattywar, province of Guzerat, four miles N.E. from Diu, and 106 miles S. from Rajkote. Lat. 20° 46′, long. 71° 2′.

DAJEEPOOR.—A town in the native territory of Kolapoor, presidency of Bombay, 30 miles S.W. from Kolapoor, and 53 miles N.W. from Belgaum. Lat. 16° 22′, long. 74°.

DAJEL.—A fort, town, and district of the Punjaub, on the route from Dera Ghazee Khan to Bhag, situate among the mountains of Dajel and Hurroond. The town is a small but rather flourishing place, and important as commanding the communication through the Derajat to Cutch Gundava and Beloochistan, by the Bolan Pass. Lat. 29° 37′, long. 70° 19′.

DAKHILO, in the jaghire of Jujhur, lieut.-gov. of the N.W. Provinces, a village on the left bank of the Hansoutee nullah, a torrent dry for a great part of the year, but overflowing considerably during the rains. Lat. 28° 27′, long. 76° 37′.

DAKIAT, in the native state of Gurhwal, a village at the southern extremity of the mountain bounding the fertile valley of Banal on the eastern side: it is close to the right bank of the Jumna. Lat. 30° 49′, long. 78° 18′.

DALAMOW, in the district of Banswara, in the territory of Oude, a city on the left bank of the Ganges, and presenting a striking appearance to those who navigate it. There are two large antique shiwalas, or Hindoo temples, on the bank of the Ganges, and an ancient flight of brick-built steps gives access to the river, for the purpose of the ritual ablutions of pilgrims, it being recognised as a holy place. There is besides a brick-built fort, with walls. Butter states its "population to be 10,000, of whom 250 are Mussulmans." It is mentioned in the Ayeen Akbery. Distant S. from Lucknow 56 miles, N.W. from Allahabad 68 miles, N.W. from Calcutta 563 miles. Lat. 26° 4′, long. 81° 7′.

DALKISSORE.—A river rising in the British district of Pachete, lieut.-gov. of Bengal, about lat. 23° 30′, long. 86° 34′, and, taking a south-easterly course, passes through the districts Bancoora, Burdwan, and Hoogly, when, under the name of the Roopnerain, it forms the boundary of the districts Hidjellee and Hoogly, and falls into the river Hoogly at Diamond Harbour, in lat. 22° 12′, long. 88° 7′. Its total length of course is 170 miles. At Bancoora, fifty miles from its source, it is crossed by ford, on the route from Calcutta to Hazareebagh, and at Jahanabad, sixty-five miles lower down, it is crossed by the same route by means of ford.

DALLAH.—A town in the recently acquired British district of Pegu, 42 miles S.W. of Rangoon. Lat. 16° 21′, long. 95° 47′.

DALLAH.—The name of one of the rivers forming the delta of the Irawady. It flows past the town of Dallah, and falls into the Bay of Bengal about lat. 16° 8′, long. 75° 49′.

DALPATPOOR, in the district of Pachamrat, territory of Oude, a town on the right bank of the Ghaghra, seven miles S.E. of Faizabad, 82 E. of Lucknow. In 1837, Harpal Singh, the zemindar or proprietor of the adjacent country, employed 500 men in building a mud fort of considerable extent. Lat. 26° 44′, long. 82° 14′.

DAMAKA.—A town in the British district of Camroop, in Lower Assam, 28 miles N.E. of Goalpara. Lat. 26° 27′, long. 90° 56′.

DAMAN.—A town on the coast of the Northern Concan, and belonging to the Portuguese, though included within the limits of the presidency of Bombay. It is situate on the Damunganga, or river of Daman, which rises in the Ghauts, about forty miles further east. The river has a bar at its mouth, having two feet water at low water spring tides, and eighteen or twenty feet inside. There is never less in common springs than three fathoms at high water on the bar, the rise of the tide being seventeen or eighteen feet. Outside the bar is a road, in which vessels may anchor in eight fathoms of water. The town is fortified, and has a rampart with ten bastions and two gateways. There are nine Christian churches, and a fort called the Castle of St. Hieronymus. The surrounding country is fruitful and pleasant, except in the rainy season, when it is extensively overflowed.

During the dry season, there remain some shallow jhils or ponds, abounding in fish and reptiles. The river, admitting the tide, is brackish, and when the water left by the rain is evaporated, recourse is had to wells, the water of which, however, is also in some degree brackish, and moreover, very unwholesome, causing fevers and other formidable ailments. "Provisions and vegetables are cheap and plentiful." Daman is an excellent place for small vessels to remain at during the S.W. monsoon, and for the purpose of repair, the country being well stocked with ship-timber. Many ships of from 500 to 600 tons burthen have been built in this river. Daman, described as "a town great and strong," was sacked and burned by the Portuguese in 1531. It was subsequently rebuilt, and in 1558 was taken by the Portuguese, who converted the mosque into a Christian church. The place appears from that time to have remained one of their possessions. The district of which the town is the principal place is about ten miles in length from north to south, and five in breadth. Distance of the town of Daman from Bombay, N., 101 miles. Lat. 20° 24′, long. 72° 53′.

DAMAN, or THE BORDER, so called because it stretches between the Suliman Mountains and the Indus. The tract formerly constituted a portion of Runjeet Singh's kingdom of Lahore, and is now annexed to the British province of the Punjaub. Where not under the influence of irrigation, it in general presents the appearance of a plain of smooth hard clay, bare of grass, but sprinkled with dwarfish bushes, tamarisks, and occasionally trees of larger size, but seldom exceeding the height of twenty feet, the soil or climate being unfavourable to their further growth. In place of the clay, the surface in some places consists of a loose and irreclaimable sand. The clay appears to be deposited by the waters either of the Indus or of the numerous small rivers which, during the season of the melting of the snow, stream down from the mountains, and add to the inundation. Where duly irrigated, the clay is very productive, and few countries are more fertile than the Derajat, or that part of the plain which extends along the western bank of the Indus. The Derajat, so called from the three towns, Dera Ismael Khan, Dera Fati Khan, and Dera Ghazee Khan, abounds in towns and good villages. In summer, the heat in the Daman is intense, and the productions in a great measure resemble those of India. The Daman is 300 miles long, from the Kala or Salt Range on the north, to the confines of Sinde on the south, and has an average breadth of about sixty miles. Lat. 28° 40′ to 33° 20′, long. 69° 30′ to 71° 20′.

DAMDAMA.—A town in the Rajpoot state of Kotah, 73 miles N.E. from Neemuch, and 11 miles S. from Kotah. Lat. 25°, long. 75° 56′.

DAMMOODAH.—A river rising in the British district of Ramgurh, lieut.-gov. of Bengal, about lat. 23° 55′, long. 84° 53′. It takes a south-easterly direction through the British districts Ramgurh and Pacheet, into those of Bancoora and Burdwan, and twelve miles below the principal town of the last-named district, and in lat. 23° 5′, long. 88° 1′, it turns nearly due south, a direction which it holds for the remainder of its course through the British districts Burdwan and Hoogly, until its fall into the river Hoogly on the right side, in lat. 22° 13′, long. 88° 7′; its total length of course being 350 miles. Its feeders are numerous, the most important being the Barrachur, a considerable torrent, falling into it on the left side, in lat. 23° 40′, long. 86° 51′. On the route from Calcutta to Hazareebagh, it is crossed by means of a ferry, fifty miles above its mouth. At Raneegunj, eighty-five miles higher up, and in lat. 23° 35′, long. 87° 8′, the bed of the stream is described by Jacquemont as 500 yards wide, fordable, with a rapid current, and limpid water, about one foot deep in the middle of December, or during the dry season. At Gomeah, ninety miles higher up the stream, the same traveller states the bed to be 250 yards wide, and free from obstructions, with a slender stream of very fine water. The valley of the Dammoodah, which is about to be traversed by the railway from Calcutta, is known to abound in coal and iron; and, indeed, the only doubt as to the practicability of manufacturing malleable iron in the district, arises from the absence of limestone for the reduction of the ore into metal. Limestone, however, may be imported from Sylhet and other places; and it has been estimated by competent authority, that, assuming the cost of railway bars at 10*l.* per ton, bar-iron may be manufactured in the Dammoodah valley at least twenty per cent. lower than it could be imported from England.

DAMUK.—A town in one of the recently sequestrated districts of Hyderabad, or dominions of the Nizam, 25 miles S.E. from Omraouttee, and 85 miles S.W. from Nagpoor. Lat. 20° 30′, long. 78° 1′.

DAMUNGAUM.—A town in one of the recently sequestrated districts of Hyderabad, or dominions of the Nizam, 29 miles S.E. from Omraouttee, and 66 miles S.W. from Nagpoor. Lat. 20° 45′, long. 78° 14′.

DAMUNGUNGA.—A river rising on the western slope of the Syadree range of mountains, in lat. 20° 11′, long. 73° 42′, and, flowing in a westerly direction through the native state of Peint, and dividing the British collectorates of Surat and Tannah, intersects the Portuguese territory of Damaun, and falls into the Arabian Sea in lat. 20° 23′, long. 72° 52′.

DANA.—A town in the native state of Nepal, 158 miles N.W. from Khatmandoo, and 148 miles N.E. from Oude. Lat. 28° 47′, long. 83° 3′.

DANAYAKKAN KOTTEI.—A town in the British district of Coimbatore, presidency of Madras, 30 miles N. of Coimbatore. Lat. 11° 26′, long. 77° 7′.

DANDEEAS.—See DANTIWARA.

DANDERPHUL.—A town in the British sub-collectorate of Nassick, presidency of Bombay, 39 miles S.E. of Nassick. Lat. 19° 33′, long. 74° 7′.

DANDYAUW.—A town in the native state of Nepal, 94 miles S.E. from Almora, and 36 miles S.W. from Jemlah. Lat. 29° 8′, long. 81° 10′.

DANGAUR.—A town in the native state of Sirgoojah, 27 miles S.W. from Sirgoojah, and 33 miles N.W. from Odeipoor. Lat. 22° 50′, long. 82° 53′.

DANGKHAR.—A town in the British district of Spiti, in the district of the Julinder Dooab, one of the divisions of the Punjab, 92 miles N.E. of Simla. Lat. 32° 5′, long. 78° 15′.

DANGURTHUL.—A town in the Rajpoot state of Jeypoor, 36 miles S. from Jeypoor, and 15 miles N. from Tonk. Lat. 26° 23′, long. 75° 56′.

DANOO.—A town in the British district of Tannah, presidency of Bombay, 69 miles N. of Bombay. Lat. 19° 57′, long. 72° 43′.

DANPOOR, in the British district of Aligurh, lieut.-gov. of the N.W. Provinces, a village near the northern boundary of the district. It is 65 miles S.E. of Delhi. Lat. 28° 7′, long. 78° 6′.

DANPOOR, in the British district of Boolundshuhr, lieut.-gov. of the N.W. Provinces, a small town on the route from the cantonment of Aligurh to that of Moradabad, and 22 miles N. of the former. It has a bazar, and is well supplied with water. Lat. 28° 11′, long. 78° 16′.

DANTIWARA, in the Rajpoot state of Joudpore, a village on the route from the town of Joudpore to that of Ajmeer, and 21 miles E. of the former. It contains 100 houses and five shops. Lat. 26° 16′, long. 73° 30′.

DANTOON.—A town in the British district of Midnapoor, lieut.-gov. of Bengal, 32 miles S. of Midnapoor. Lat. 21° 57′, long. 87° 20′.

DANTROEE.—A town in the Rajpoot state of Serohee, 22 miles S.W. from Serohee, and 78 miles W. from Oodeypoor. Lat. 24° 49′, long. 72° 35′.

DAODPOOR, in the territory of Oude, a village on the route from Lucknow to Sultanpoor cantonment, 12 miles W. of the latter. It has a small bazar, and is well supplied with water. Lat. 26° 18′, long. 81° 57′.

DAOOD KAYLE, in the Sind Sagur Dooab division of the Punjab, a town situated on an offset of the river Indus, six miles S. of the town of Kala Bagh. Lat. 32° 51′, long. 71° 35′.

DAOODNUGUR, in the British district Behar, lieut.-gov. of Bengal, a town on the right bank of the river Son, navigable up to this place from its confluence with the Ganges, a distance of forty-five miles. Some of the streets are straight and wide, but the greater number mere wretched lanes. Here is a spacious well-built serae, or public lodging-house, surrounded by a rampart of brick, with battlements and loopholes, and probably intended for a stronghold of the former government. There is another extensive serae, inclosed and secured by gates. The number of houses, including Ahmudgunj, has been computed at about 2,000; and, admitting the usual ratio of inmates to houses, the population appears to be about 10,000. It is a place of considerable trade, and has manufactures of setringis, or coarse cotton carpets, blankets, and cotton fabrics of various sorts. The town is 42 miles N.W. of Gya, 60 S.W. of Patna, 89 E. of Benares. Lat. 25° 3′, long. 84° 27′.

DAORALAH.—See DOURALA.

DAPOOLEE.—A town in the British district of Rutnagherry, presidency of Bombay, 55 miles N. of Rutnagherry. Lat. 17° 48′, long. 73° 16′.

DAPOOREE.—A town situate on the left bank of the Moota river, a feeder of the Bema, in the British district of Poonah, presidency of Bombay, four miles N. of Poonah. The town contains a residence for the use of the governor of Bombay, and in its vicinity are the Botanical Gardens, maintained by the government. Lat. 18° 32′, long. 73° 51′.

DARAGUNJ, in the British district of Allahabad, lieut.-gov. of the N.W. Provinces, a town on the route from the cantonment of Allahabad to Jaunpore, and communicating by ferry with the former, of which it may be considered in some measure a suburb. The Ganges, on the left bank of which it is situate, has here a bed a mile wide, the stream in the dry season occupying only a third of that space, the remainder being moist sand and mud, over which the road is difficult. It is a place of some importance. Lat. 25° 27′, long. 81° 57′.

DARAMANY GHAT.—See AMBEANHULLY.

DARANAGUR, in the British district of Allahabad, lieut.-gov. of the N.W. Provinces, a town on the route from Allahabad to the town of Futtehpoor, 40 miles S.E. of the latter place. Supplies and water are abundant. The road to the south-east, towards Allahabad, is heavy, but that to the north-west, or towards Futtehpoor, is good. The surrounding country is level and well cultivated. Lat. 25° 41′, long. 81° 25′.

DARANUGUR, in the British district of Bijnour, lieut.-gov. of the N.W. Provinces, a town on the route from Moradabad to Muzufernugur, and 40 miles S.E. of the latter place. It is situate on the left bank of the Ganges, in a level, well-cultivated country, and has a bazar. The road in this part of the route is sandy, and bad for wheeled carriages. Distant

N.W. from Calcutta 944 miles. Lat. 29° 17', long. 78° 11'.

DARAPOOR, in the Punjab, a small village about a mile from the right or west bank of the Jhelum. Close to it are extensive ruins, called Oodenuggur, which Burnes supposes to be those of Nicæa, built by Alexander to commemorate his victory on this spot over Porus. Lat. 32° 46', long. 73° 36'.

DARAPOORAM, in the British district of Coimbatore, presidency of Madras, a town situate about half a mile from the left bank of the river Amrawati, in an elevated open country. The streets are wide, and the houses in general well built. Here is a large mud fort, formerly of considerable importance during the wars between the British and the rulers of Mysore, but now in ruins. Buchanan, after mentioning the fort, gives the following curious statement:—"The commandant, according to the report of the natives, agreed to surrender the place to Col. Fullarton. As, however, he wished to make an appearance of resistance, some pioneers were sent into the ditch to undermine the wall, which they did very coolly, while over their heads the garrison kept up a tremendous fire. When the passage was open, the firing ceased, and our troops walked in quietly, without any injury being done on either side." Distance from the town of Coimbatore, S.E., 42 miles; Madras, S.W., 250. Lat. 10° 45', long. 77° 36'.

DARBARRA, in the Punjaub, a large fortress of the Daman. It is situate 12 miles N.W. of Tak, and at the mouth of a pass into the Suliman Mountains. Its walls are very lofty, but it does not appear to be otherwise of importance, and it is situate in a very barren and secluded country. Lat. 32° 15', long. 70° 20'.

DARBEE.—A town of North-Eastern India, in the native state of Bhotan, 60 miles E. from Darjeeling, and 105 miles N. from Rungpore. Lat. 27° 12', long. 89° 18'.

DARBUNG, or **ROOSHKATONG**, in Bussahir, a river of Koonawur. It rises in about lat. 31° 57', long. 78° 25', on the south-western declivity of the stupendous range of Damuk Shu, bounding that territory on the side of Ladakh. Gerard estimates the elevation of its source at about 15,000 feet above the sea. The scene, as described by him, is one of terrific desolation. After a total course of about twenty-seven miles, it falls into the Sutlej, in lat. 31° 43', long. 78° 35'.

DARICKEE.—A town in the British district of Cuttack, lieut.-gov. of Bengal, 36 miles S.E. of Cuttack. Lat. 20° 4', long. 86° 18'.

DARISHE.—A town in the British district of Nellore, presidency of Madras, 30 miles N.W. of Ongole. Lat. 15° 48', long. 79° 44'.

DARJEELING, in the British district of the same name, lieut.-gov. of Bengal, a sanatarium for troops located within the military division of Cawnpore, Allahabad, Dinapore, and Benares. It is situate "on the southern side of a great hollow or basin, being that of the Runjeet River, which falls into the Teesta a few miles east of the place. To the north, the view is open, and exhibits the usual succession of range beyond range, all irregularly ramifying in every direction, and in apparently inextricable confusion: it terminates in the Snowy Range. To the westward, the view is confined by a lofty range at the distance of about ten miles; to the eastward, appears the valley of the Teesta; and on each side of it is the confused assemblage of mountain-ridges, as to the north; to the south, Darjeeling has the Sinchul Peak, elevated about 9,000 feet, and the Gurdun-Kuttur range, which is a ramification of it. These mountains are completely clothed with forest from the top to the very bottom." In regard to natural scenery, the country round Darjeeling is described as inferior to that of Landour and Mussooree, but as contrasting favourably with that of Almora. In one respect, however, it has an advantage even over the former places, commanding as it does the most magnificent view which can probably be obtained of the Snowy Range, distant about sixty miles, in which, eminently conspicuous, appears the Kunching Jinga, rising 27,000 feet above the sea. Dr. Hooker, when on a botanical mission to this region, thus describes his first impression of the scene:—"Early next morning I caught my first view, and I literally held my breath in awe and admiration. Six or seven successive ranges of forest-clad mountains as high as that whereon I stood (8,000 feet), intervened between me and the dazzling-white pile of snow-clad mountains, among which the giant peak of Kinchin-junga rose 20,000 feet above the lofty point from which I gazed. Owing to the clearness of the atmosphere, the snow appeared to my fancy but a few miles off, and the loftiest mountain at only a day's journey. The heavenward outline was projected against a pale-blue sky, while little detached patches of mist clung here and there to the highest peaks, and were tinged golden-yellow or rosy-red by the rising sun." Gneiss is the principal formation of the rock at Darjeeling; slate occurs on the banks of the Runjeet River; at the foot of the hills, iron-ore abounds; and traces of copper are said to have been discovered.

The advantages possessed by Darjeeling, as the site for a sanatarium, in the salubrity of its climate and facility of access from the plains of Bengal, induced the British government, in 1835, to open a negotiation with the rajah of Sikkim, for its cession, in return for an equivalent in land or money. The rajah consented to an unconditional and gratuitous transfer. Several years afterwards, however, a grant of 3,000 rupees per annum was made to the rajah, as compensation for the cession, which sum at a later period was doubled. A sanatarium for Europeans has been established, and its results, as exhibited in official medical reports, are considered satisfactory. The district of which Darjeeling is the principal place, was enlarged in 1850, by the annexation of a further portion of the territory of Sikkim. The sequestration of this tract, yielding a revenue of 26,037 rupees, took place in consequence of outrages committed by the rajah against British subjects, a course of conduct which at the same time exposed him to the forfeiture of the annual payment which had been granted as compensation for Darjeeling. Lat. 27° 2′, long. 88° 19′.

DARMAPUR.—A town in the British district of Salem, presidency of Madras, 33 miles N. of Salem. Lat. 12° 9′, long. 78° 14′.

DARMOODAR.—A town in the native state of Nepal, 190 miles W. from Khatmandoo, and 103 miles N. from Oude. Lat. 28° 17′, long. 82° 19′.

DARRAH.—A town in the British district of Bhaugulpore, lieut.-gov. of Bengal, 50 miles S.W. of Rajmahal. Lat. 24° 45′, long. 87° 5′.

DARROOR.—A town in Hyderabad, or dominions of the Nizam, 185 miles N.W. from Hyderabad, and 72 miles S. from Jaulnah. Lat. 18° 50′, long. 76° 11′.

DARSHANGANJ, in the district of Pachamrat, territory of Oude, a town near the right bank of the river Ghaghra, five miles S.E. of Faizabad. It was built by Darshan Singh, a freebooter, the brother of an adventurer originally a trooper in the Company's service, but raised to the station of zemindar, or feoffee, by the favour of Saadat Ali Khan, formerly nawaub vizier. It is rather a thriving place, several merchants of considerable property residing there. Distant E. from Lucknow 80 miles. Lat. 26° 44′, long. 82° 12′.

DASNUH, in the British district of Meerut, lieut.-gov. of the N.W. Provinces, a town, the principal place of the pergunnah of the same name, situate on the route from Delhi to Ghurmukteesur, and 18 miles E. of the former. Elevation above the sea 821 feet. Lat. 28° 41′, long. 77° 36′.

DASOREE.—A town in the Rajpoot state of Joudpore or Marwar, 79 miles N. from Joudpore, and 50 miles S.W. from Beekaneer. Lat. 27° 25′, long. 72° 56′.

DASPORE.—A town in the British district of Midnapore, lieut.-gov. of Bengal, 31 miles N.E. of Midnapore. Lat. 22° 37′, long. 87° 50′.

DATCHAPULLY.—A town in the British district of Guntoor, presidency of Madras, 52 miles N.W. of Guntoor. Lat. 16° 37′, long. 79° 48′.

DATMER, in native Gurwhal, a village on the left bank of the Supin or Tonse. The village is inhabited by savage and lawless banditti, who practise their misdeeds with much impunity, in consequence of the extreme difficulty of access to their fastness. It was a secondary station in the great trigonometrical survey of the Himalaya. Elevation above the sea 8,354 feet. Lat. 31° 5′, long. 78° 20′.

DATREE, in the British district of Mynpooree, lieut.-gov. of the N.W. Provinces, a village on the route from the city of Agra to Etawah, and 29 miles N.W. of the latter. Lat. 27° 5′, long. 78° 42′.

DAUDPOOR.—A town in the native state of Calahandy, one of the hill zemindarries of Orissa, 90 miles W. from Goomsoor, and 20 miles N.E. from Joonnagudda. Lat. 19° 59′, long. 83° 19′.

DAUKORE.—A town in the British district of Kaira, presidency of Bombay, 31 miles E. of Kaira. Lat. 22° 42′, long. 73° 10′.

DAUMNUGGUR, in the peninsula of Kattywar, province of Guzerat, or territory of the Guicowar, a town on a river which, fifty miles to the eastward, falls into the Gulf of Cambay. The surrounding country is well watered and fertile, producing abundant crops of fine grain, sugar-cane, and cotton. It is fortified, and belongs to the Guicowar, and received its name from Damoji, one of the family. Distance from Ahmedabad, S.W., 120 miles; Baroda, S.W., 120; Surat, N.W., 98; Bombay, N.W., 208. Lat. 21° 40′, long. 71° 30′.

DAUNABAD, in the Reechna Doab division of the Punjab, a town situated on a feeder of the river Ravee, 60 miles S.W. of the town of Lahore. Lat. 31° 7′, long. 73° 21′.

DAUNDIAKHERA, in the district of Bainswara, territory of Oude, a town on the left bank of the Ganges, 50 miles S. of Lucknow, 30 S.E. of Cawnpore. Butter estimates the population at between 8,000 and 9,000, of whom 250 are Mussulmans. Lat. 26° 10′, long. 80° 42′.

DAUNG, THE.—A tract of country so called, situate within the limits of the presidency of Bombay, and comprising several petty native states, tributary to a chief styled the rajah of Daung. It is bounded on the north-west by the petty state of Wursavee; on the north-east and east by Candeish and the sub-collectorate of Nassick; on the south by the native state of Peint; and on the west by that of Baunsda. It extends from lat. 20° 22′ to 21° 5′, and from long. 73° 28′ to 73° 52′. Its length from north to south is fifty-two miles, and its breadth twenty-eight, comprehending an area of 950 square miles, with a population of 70,300. The country abounds in teak forests, which are rented by the British government of the Daung chiefs, who usually refer to the British representative any points of dispute among themselves.

DAUNTA, in the Myhee Caunta division of Guzerat, or the dominions of the Guicowar, a town, the chief place of the petty native territory of the same name, situate 48 miles E. of Deesa, and 139 miles N. of Baroda. The territory of Daunta is subject to the supre-

macy of the Rajpoot state of Edur, and, moreover, pays tribute to the Guicowar. In 1820, the Rana agreed to cede a fixed proportion of his revenues to the state of Pahlunpore, but the obligation was subsequently commuted for an annual payment of 500 rupees, and the district is now released from sequestration. The town of Daunta is in lat. 24° 12', long. 72° 50'.

DAUSAN.—See DEESAUN.

DAVADANAPUTTY.—A town in the British district of Madura, presidency of Madras, 33 miles N.W. of Madura. Lat. 10° 8', ong. 77° 43'.

DAVAGOODOO.—A town in the British district of Nellore, presidency of Madras, 12 miles S.W. of Ongole. Lat. 15° 20', long. 80°.

DAVANKONDA.—A town in the British district of Bellary, presidency of Madras, 52 miles N.E. of Bellary. Lat. 15° 33', long. 77° 37'.

DAVAROY DROOG.—A town in Mysore, 76 miles N.E. from Seringapatam, and 39 miles N.W. from Bangalore. Lat. 13° 22', long. 77° 16'.

DAVERCONDA, in Hyderabad, or territory of the Nizam, a town on a hill, near the left or northern side of a feeder of the river Pedawag, one of the tributaries of the Godavery. It is supplied with water from a tank of considerable size, situate on its west side. The extensive district of Daverconda, on the south side of the town, is named from it. Distant from the city of Hyderabad, S., 52 miles. Lat. 16° 42', long. 78° 59'.

DAVERHULLY.—A town in Mysore, 68 miles N.E. from Bedenore, and 126 miles N. from Seringapatam. Lat. 14° 6', long. 76° 2'.

DAVIPOOR, in the British district of Moradabad, lieut.-gov. of the N.W. Provinces, a village on the route from the town of Moradabad to Almora, and 12 miles N. of the former. Lat. 28° 59', long. 78° 54'.

DAVULGHAUT.—A town in Hyderabad, or dominions of the Nizam, 70 miles N.E. from Aurungabad, and 100 miles S.W. from Ellichpoor. Lat. 20° 30', long. 76° 11'.

DAWLUTWALLUH, in the Damaun division of the Punjab, a town situated 80 miles N.W. of Dera Ghazee Khan, 60 miles S.W. of the town of Dera Ismael Khan. Lat. 31° 10', long. 70° 20'.

DEAGANJ, in the British district of Mynpooree, lieut.-gov. of the N.W. Provinces, a village on the route from the city of Agra to Etawah, and 46 miles S.E. of the former. Lat. 27° 3', long. 78° 46'.

DEAMAH, in the district of Sultanpoor, territory of Oude, a town on the route from Pertabgurh to Sultanpoor cantonment, 13 miles S.W. of the latter. It has a bazar, and is *abundantly supplied with water from wells.* Lat. 26° 10', long. 82° 3'.

DEARY.—A town in one of the recently sequestrated districts of Hyderabad, or dominions of the Nizam, 17 miles S.E. from Ellichpoor, and 13 miles N. from Omraouttee. Lat. 21°, long. 77° 44'.

DEATPORE.—A town in the British district of Malda, lieut.-gov. of Bengal, 25 miles N.W. of Malda. Lat. 25° 12', long. 87° 52'.

DEBEEPOORA.—See DAVIPOOR.

DEBRA.—A town in the British district of Midnapoor, lieut.-gov. of Bengal, 16 miles E. of Midnapoor. Lat. 22° 23', long. 87° 39'.

DEBUR.—A considerable lake in the Rajpoot territory of Oodeypoor or Meywar: it is about nine miles in length by five in breadth, and is fed by several streams flowing from the northward. On its southern side it has an outlet by a stream flowing into the Mhye river. Distant S.E. from Oodeypoor 30 miles. Lat. 24° 12', long. 74° 4'.

DEBURA, in the British district of Goruckpoor, lieut.-gov. of the N.W. Provinces, a town on the left bank of the river Raptee, 51 miles N.W. of Goruckpoor. Lat. 27° 17', long. 82° 58'.

DECCAN, in its usual acceptation, implies the tract of country in Southern India, situate between the Nerbudda and the Kistna rivers. Properly speaking, however, it includes the whole of the territory lying south of the Vindhya Mountains, which separate it from Hindostan on the north. Taken in its latter extent, it comprehends the valley of the Nerbudda, and the narrow tract of lowland forming a belt round the coast of the Peninsula; and it occupies, in addition thereto, the vast expanse of triangular table-land, which, resting on each side upon the Eastern and Western Ghauts, is supported at its base by the sub-Vindhyan range, termed the Sautpoora Mountains. The seaward face of the table-land on the west, towards the Concans, though abrupt, is not precipitous, but consists of a succession of terraces or steps. In their northern section, the Ghauts, on this side of the Peninsula, attain an elevation seldom exceeding 3,000 feet; advancing southward, the range increases in height, Bonasson Hill being 7,000 feet above the level of the sea, and the peak of Dodapet, in the Neilgherries, having an elevation of 8,700. Near Cape Comorin, in the extreme south, and at the point of convergence with the range from the opposite coast, the Western Ghauts terminate abruptly in a peak about 2,000 feet above the sea. Their average elevation may be stated at about 4,000 feet. From the point of convergence, the Eastern Ghauts take a northerly direction. These last-mentioned mountains, at their southern extremity, may be characterized rather as detached groups and clusters of hills appearing at intervals, than as a regular range. About lat. 11° 40', they assume the character of a continuous chain.

and, running along the coast of Coromandel in a direction a little north-west of the city of Madras, form a junction at Naggery, in lat. 13° 20′, with the main ridge, which crosses the Peninsula in a south-west direction, to the Neilgherries. Thence the Eastern Ghauts continue a northerly course, and terminate in about the same latitude as their counterpart of the opposite coast. Here uniting with the Vindhya zone, which crosses the continent from east to west, they constitute one side of the triangle upon which rests the table-land of the Deccan. In regularity and grandeur, the Eastern Ghauts bear no comparison with those of Western India; their average elevation does not exceed 1,500 feet. The intermediate table-land has consequently a gradual slope to the eastward, as indicated by the drainage of the country in that direction. All the principal rivers,—the Godavery, Cauvery, Kistna, and Pennaur, though deriving their sources from the base of the Western Ghauts, find their way into the Bay of Bengal through fissures in the Eastern Ghauts. According to Captain Newbold, "the mean elevation of the table-land around Bangalore and Nundidroog above the sea is 3,000 feet; northerly, towards Hyderabad, it sinks to 1,800 feet; and a little south of Bangalore, it falls, by rather abrupt steps, to the level of the plains of Salem, viz. 1,400 feet; whence to Cape Comorin the mean height of the country is about 400 feet. The average height of the low country between the Ghauts and the sea, on both the coasts of Coromandel and Malabar, may be roughly estimated at 200 feet, rising at the base of the mountains to 800 feet." On the Coromandel side, the slope to the sea is gentle, exhibiting the alluvial deposits borne down from the higher portions of the table-land; while that of Malabar is marked by a succession of irregular hilly spurs from the Ghauts, descending to the sea in abrupt cliffs. The central part of the Deccan is composed of waving downs, which, at one time, present for hundreds of miles one unbroken sheet of green harvests; but, in the hot season, bear the appearance of a desert, naked and brown, without a tree or shrub to relieve its gloomy sameness.

A general outline of the geology of the Deccan is all that the limits of this article will permit to be sketched. A writer, already quoted, observes, "Hypogene schists, penetrated and broken up by prodigious outbursts of plutonic and trappean rocks, occupy by far the greater portion of the superficies of Southern India. They constitute the great bulk of the Western Ghauts, from between the latitudes of 16° and 17° to Cape Comorin, and from the base of the Eastern Ghauts, from beyond the north limit of the Peninsula, to their deflection at Naggery, in lat. 13° 20′. They are partially capped and fringed in the Western Ghauts by laterite, and in the Eastern Ghauts by sandstone, limestone, and laterite. From Naggery to Cape Comorin, they form, with few exceptions, the basis of the plains of the Carnatic, Arcot, the valley of Seringapatam, Salem, Trichinopoly, Coimbatore, Tanjore, Madras, Tinnevelly, and Travancore; and, intimately associated with granite, the principal hills and ranges on the low lands south of the Salem Break and valley of the Cauvery. North of this valley, and above the break, they form the basis of the table-lands of Mysore, the Baramahal, Bellary district, part of Hyderabad, and the Southern Mahratta country; and present a ground-work on which will be sketched out, as accurately as the present imperfect state of information will permit, the circumscribed areas occupied by more recent aqueous strata. Towards the north-west flank of our area, almost in a line drawn diagonally across the Peninsula from Nagpore, by Beejapore, to the western coast, the hypogene and plutonic rocks disappear, emerging only occasionally under one of the largest continuous sheets of trap in the world." Compared, then, with some other countries, the geology of Southern India is clear and distinct in its principal features. It has been ascertained, partly from observation, and partly by means of specimens obtained from various sections of the country, that the entire basis of the Peninsula, and its principal elevations, are composed wholly of granite. Overlying the granitic floor, are the stratified hypogene rocks, the usual order of superposition being gneiss resting immediately on the granite, followed by mica and hornblende schists, the two latter supporting clay-slate, statuary marble, &c. These rocks are wholly destitute of organic remains; for, although of aqueous origin, as attested by their stratified character, the sedimentary deposit has subsequently become crystallized by the effect of subterranean heat, and hence they are grouped by geologists in the metamorphic class. Ascending in the series, we next arrive at the fossiliferous strata. Here, in the order of superposition, limestone is the lowest, followed by varieties of clay and sand rocks. From various circumstances, arising chiefly from the paucity of the imbedded fossils, and from the failure of discovering among them the distinguishing genera, these varieties have not hitherto admitted of a detailed classification. These sedimentary rocks are overlaid by the trap formation, a volcanic product, fused by subterranean heat, and projected to the earth's surface, where it occasionally assumes a columnar form, but more usually may be traced in extensive sheets, covering a vast tract of country. Two rocks, of aqueous origin, peculiar to Southern India, are met with, capping trap and all other rocks, without reference to age or composition. These are laterite and regur. The former consists of an iron-clay. In its texture, it is full of cavities and pores, and contains a large quantity of iron. While in the mass, and excluded from the air, it is soft and readily cut; but upon being broken up and exposed, it soon becomes hard, and resists the effects of air and water better than brick. It is consequently one of the most valuable materials for building.

The maximum thickness of its beds does not exceed 200 feet, and these are not altogether destitute of organic remains. Regur is the black cotton clay, formerly supposed to be produced by the decomposition of trap rocks, but now regarded, and apparently more justly, as a marine deposit. One other overlying formation requires notice,—the calcareous substance termed kunkur, found on analysis to contain the elements of oolite and chalk. Its origin is referred to the action of thermal springs, charged with carbonic acid, bringing up lime in solution, and depositing it on the earth's surface. It is used as a rough building-stone, and universally employed to burn into lime.

The universal prevalence of granite and the hypogene rocks has been mentioned. It remains to describe the geographical position of the more recent and the overlying strata. Partial deposits of sand-rock, of a recent period, containing pelagic shells, are found scattered over the south-eastern extremity of the Peninsula; but the older sandstone and limestone beds are not met with south of Salem. The chief development of these older rocks lies in the district of Cuddapah, and again in Hyderabad, also in the Southern Mahratta country, and in the tract between the Godavery and the Kistna. A bed of shelly limestone occurs in the vicinity of Pondicherry, to which, from an examination of its fossils, geologists concur in assigning a more elevated position than to the limestone strata before described. The outpouring of the trap rock is distributed over a considerable portion of the Peninsula. It extends from the seashore, at the northern extremity of the Western Ghauts, to its eastern limit at Nagpore and the banks of the river Toombuddra, and terminates southward on the seacoast, in the latitude of Fort Victoria or Bancot. Within these boundaries the landscape is marked by the usual distinctive features of basaltic rock; hills of tabular form rising from the general level, sometimes abruptly, in perpendicular masses; sometimes in steps, or terraces, piled one upon another, decked with magnificent forests, and producing beautiful and romantic scenery. From the southern termination of the trap, the laterite or iron-clay succeeds as the overlying rock, to Cape Comorin, covering the base of the mountains and the narrow tract that separates them from the sea, and occasionally exhibiting a succession of low rounded hills and undulations. It exists also in detached beds on the opposite coast of the Peninsula, expanding over a large surface near the south banks of the Pennar, crowning the loftiest summits of the Ghauts, and of the table-lands in the interior. Regur, like laterite, overtops all other rocks, with the single exception of the most recent deposits. This soil is chiefly indebted for its fertility to its retentive power in regard to moisture. When its surface is dried to an impalpable powder, the substratum retains its character of a hard black clay approaching to rock, usually moist and cold. "It occupies principally the elevated table-lands of the Ceded Districts, the Hyderabad, Nagpore, and Southern Mahratta countries. It is less common in Mysore, but is again seen in continuous sheets, from six to twenty feet thick, below the Salem Break, covering the lower plain of Coimbatore, Madura, Salem, Trichinopoly, Tanjore, Ramnad, and Tinnevelly, to the vicinity of Cape Comorin."

Of the remote history of the Deccan little is known. Hindoo legend relates that it was invaded by Rama, king of Oude, when in pursuit of Ravan, the ruler of Ceylon, who had carried off his consort Siva; but the date of Rama's existence is involved in obscurity. An ancient distribution of the country into the national divisions of Dravira or the Tamul Country, Carnata, Telingana, Maharashta, and Orissa, is, however, indicated by the five corresponding languages of the Deccan, all of which are derived from an origin totally distinct from the Sanscrit. In the fifth century before Christ, the Peninsula is stated to have been partitioned between the four kingdoms of Pandya, Kerala, Cola, and Chola. Passing, however, to authentic history, we learn that the first Mahometan invasion of the Deccan was attempted in the year 1294, by Aladin, afterwards emperor of Delhi. Its object was restricted to the assault of Deogiri, the capital of Maharashta; and this was successful, the city being captured and given up to pillage. A few years later, Aladin extended his conquests over the whole of Maharashta, Telingana, and Carnata; and in 1325 the reduction of the Deccan was completed by Mohammed Togluk. But the supremacy of the emperor was not of long duration: the Hindoo rajahs of Telingana and Carnata were the first to recover their possessions. Their success was followed by the general revolt of the Deccan, in 1347, when Hasan Ganga founded the Mahomedan dynasty of Bahmani. His independence was recognised at Delhi, and the power of the empire was thus driven across the Nerbudda. In the struggles which ensued, the house of Bahmani succeeded in subverting the kingdom of Telingana, and, at a later period (1565), the fall of the monarchy of Bijayanagar or Carnata was effected, by the league of the Mussulman princes against Rajah Ram, at the battle of Talicote. Subsequent events tended to the dismemberment of the Bahmani empire; and its final dissolution gave rise to the independent Mahometan states of Beejapore, Ahmednuggur, Golconda, Bedur, and Berar. Of these the two latter, merging into one or other of the remainder, became extinct; and in the time of Shah Jehan, in 1630, the Deccan was divided into the three kingdoms of Ahmednuggur, Golconda, and Beejapore. The first of these became tributary to Shah Jehan in 1636; and in 1686, his son and successor Aurungzebe, subverting the monarchies of Golconda and Beejapore, the whole of the territory previously severed from the empire was recovered, and the Deccan once more passed under the rule of Delhi. But though Aurungzebe now grasped the universal sovereignty of India, he was not destined long to retain it. The Mahrattas, who had previously attracted little notice, had emerged from obscurity during he reign of his father, and were now about to act a conspicuous part in the history of the Deccan. In the late imperial contest with Golconda and Beejapore, they had shared the fate of the conquered; but their power and resources, though crippled, were not destroyed. The fortresses and districts of which they had been dispossessed were again fast falling into their hands; and upon Aurungzebe's retreat to Ahmednuggur, in 1706, they attacked the imperial army, and plundered its baggage. Ten years after the death of Aurungzebe, his successor concluded a peace with Saho, the Mahratta chief, and admitted his claim to levy tribute over the whole of the Deccan. The Mogul empire was now tending to its close. Asof Jah, whose descendants are known as the nizams of Hyderabad, had succeeded to the viceroyalty of the Deccan. He was subsequently promoted to the office of vizier at Delhi; but being disgusted with the court, and sensible that his power rested upon a solid foundation, he resigned his appointment, and returned to his government at Hyderabad. The Mahrattas, in the interim, had obtained a large accession of territory, and at the time of Asof's return, the chief authority of the nation was wielded by Balaji, one of Saho's principal officers, and subsequently the founder of the dynasty of the Peishwas. This able minister had laboured unremittingly to concentrate the power of the Mahrattas; and having succeeded, he usurped the authority of his master, and offered himself as a competitor for the sovereignty of the Deccan. But Asof deemed the power of his rival too formidable for resistance: he therefore applied himself to accomplish its reduction by means of dissensions among the principal chiefs; but, failing in his attempt, he finally effected a compromise with the Peishwa, and entered the lists himself as an usurper. The result was the foundation, on the part of Asof, of the Mahometan kingdom of Hyderabad, which still continues to be ruled by his descendants; and the formation, under the Peishwa, of a powerful monarchy, comprising the larger portion of the territories now included within the limits of the presidency of Bombay. The remainder of the imperial possessions in the Peninsula, with few exceptions, were held by chieftains subject to the supremacy of one or the other of these two potentates. Those north of the Toombuddra were distributed principally between the rajahs of Colapore and Berar, and Angria of Colaba, all of whom acknowledged some degree of dependence upon the Peishwa. Of the provinces south of the Toombuddra, the Carnatic and Tanjore were held under the feudal sovereignty of the Nizam. The Mysore, though previously tributary to both Moguls and Mahrattas, assumed independence during the commotions of the times, and in the sequel became the prize of the Mahometan usurper Hyder Ali. In the extreme south, the petty state of Travancore, secured from invasion by its remote position, and by the sea and mountains which surround it, appears to have long enjoyed an uninterrupted freedom from foreign sway. The nabob of Kurnoul, Rajah Tondiman, the rajah of Coorg, and other inferior rulers, seized each on his own district, and rose to the rank of petty princes, acknowledging a feudal superiority, but maintaining their own exclusive right to internal independence.

Such were the changes introduced into the native governments of the Deccan in the earlier part of the eighteenth century. The possessions of European nations within the Peninsula afforded at that time no indication of future grandeur. A few petty settlements acknowledged the dominion of France and Portugal. The English occupied a station at Surat, and another at Madras; and these, with the island of Bombay, constituted nearly the sum of British territory in Southern India. In the subsequent contests for power which ensued between the native chiefs, the English and French took opposite sides. The results of these struggles proved unfavourable to the powers whose cause had been espoused by the French. Among the men of that nation most distinguished in India, both in war and negotiation, was M. Bussy, who established the French power and influence over the Northern Circars, so often referred to in the Indian history of the middle of the eighteenth century. These possessions, however, like most of the French acquisitions, remained to them only a very short time. Clive attacked them with a force from Bengal, and though opposed by a larger force, the skill, energy, and happy fortune which marked all Clive's enterprises, triumphed, and the Circars were transferred from the French to their great rival in India. Thenceforward the interests of France rapidly declined, the influence of the British rose in the ascendant, and a new empire was established in India. Within the limits of the Deccan the French still retain Pondicherry, with other minor settlements, and the Portuguese continue undisturbed within the slender territory of Goa and Daman; but important revolutions have occurred in the native governments within the Peninsula, from which the British alone, of all the European settlers in India, reaped any advantage. The dismembered provinces of Mysore, at the close of the first war with Tippoo, formed the earliest addition to their original acquisitions. A further annexation accrued upon the death of Tippoo, and the final partition of his dominions. This was followed by the incorporation with the British empire, of the Carnatic and Tanjore. Some years later, the forfeited possessions of the Peishwa tended to swell the extent of the empire. These acquisitions, with certain cessions from the Nizam, the subsequent conquests of Kurnool and Coorg, and the lapse, from failure of heirs, of Angria's territory of Colaba, and the raj of Sattara, constitute in the aggregate a continuous territory, stretching from the banks of the Nerbudda to Cape Comorin. Its greatest length from north to south measures 1,000 miles, and its extreme breadth exceeds 800; and if Sinde and a portion of British Guzerat be excluded, the Deccan, as defined in this article, will be found to comprehend the provinces now distributed between the two presidencies of Madras and Bombay, with the several native states already enumerated.

It will be obvious that in so large a tract of country there must be a great diversity of people and great variations as to manners and character. In the countries connected with the British government of Bombay, the higher classes, everywhere in the East the most unmanageable, were in 1822 admitted by Mr. Elphinstone to certain privileges. A great dislike existed towards the courts of law, and the privileged classes, of which there were three constituted, were exempted, the first totally, the second partially, from the strict process of the Adawlut; while a third class, composed of meritorious native military officers of the rank of soubahdar, were exempted from personal arrest. A commission was appointed, which took cognizance of cases involving claims upon the first two classes, and proceeded to dispose of them in a mode which, while securing justice, should be free from offence. The commission was subsequently abolished, and its duties transferred to an officer called "agent for sirdars."

DECCAN SHABAZPORE.—See BACKERGUNJE.

DECKNALL.—A town in one of the native states known as the Cuttack Mehals, 39 miles N. from Cuttack, and 77 miles S.W. from Balasore. Lat. 21° 1′, long. 85° 55′.

DECTAUN, in a detached portion of the native state of Gwalior, a town belonging to Scindia, on the route from Mow to Baroda, 20 miles W. of former, 196 E. of latter. It is estimated to contain 1,000 houses, and about 5,000 inhabitants, and is the principal place of a pergunnah of the same name. Elevation above the sea 1,881 feet. Lat. 22° 34′, long. 75° 31′.

DEEANUTPOOR, in the British district of Allygurh, lieut.-gov. of the N.W. Provinces, a village on the route from the cantonment of Allygurh to Agra, and 21 miles S. of the former. Lat. 27° 38′, long. 78° 7′.

DEEDWANA.—A village in the Rajpoot state of Joudpore or Marwar, 112 miles N.E. from Joudpore. Lat. 27° 19′, long. 74° 30′.

DEEG, in the territory of Bhurtpore, a town situate in a lone tract, amidst numerous marshes and jhils, or small lakes, fed by the stream Manus Nye, conveying the drainage of a considerable country lying to the west. As it is nearly surrounded by water during a great part of the year, it is then almost inaccessible to an enemy. Before dismantled by the British, its outline, the outer wall, was an irregular pentagon, the southern and longest side of which towards the middle curves inwards, or towards the north. At the south-west angle is the Shah Bourj, a high rocky mount, having on its summit an area of fifty yards square, and inclosed by a rampart, having four commanding bastions facing the four cardinal points. Within the walls, the fort, an extensive building with high rampart twenty feet thick, furnished with bastions, commands the whole town. Close to the west of the fort is the palace of the rajah, with a fine garden, inclosed by a high wall. The ground-plan of the garden is rectangular, 475 feet long and 350 wide; and on each side is a remarkably beautiful building. In the middle "is an octagonal pond, with openings on four sides, leading up to the four buildings, each opening having, from the centre of the pond to the foot of the flight of steps leading into them, an avenue of jets d'eau." These beautiful buildings, which are surpassed in India for elegance of design and perfection of workmanship only by the Taj Mahal of Agra, are constructed of a fine-grained sandstone, quarried of great dimensions at Roopbas, in the south-eastern part of the Bhurtpore territory. Deeg is a place of great antiquity. "The ancient name was Diragh, or Dirghpura, and will be found mentioned in the Skand Puran, and 4th chapter of the Bhagavat Mahatama." It became early one of the chief strongholds of the Jats, from whom, in 1776, it was wrested by Nujuff Khan, the powerful minister of Shah Alum. After the death of Nujuff Khan, however, it reverted to the rajah of Bhurtpore. Here, on the 13th of November, 1804, the army of Holkar was defeated by a British force, under the command of General Fraser; and the Jats, having taken a hostile part by firing on the victors, siege was laid to the place on the 16th of December following, and on the 23rd of the same month it was carried by storm. Subsequently restored to the Jat rajah, it, after the capture of Bhurtpore by the British, commanded by Lord Combermere, was surrendered without resistance, and dismantled. Distant W. from Muttra 24 miles. Lat. 27° 29′, long. 77° 23′.

DEEGAREE, in the Rajpoot state of Joudpore, a village on the route from the town of Joudpore to that of Ajmeer, and three miles east of the former. The road in this part of the route, though sandy, is probably good, as Boileau travelled it on horseback, by moonlight, at the rapid rate of ten miles an hour. Lat. 26° 17′, long. 73° 15′.

DEEGH.—See DIG.

DEEGHYL, in the British district of Rohtuk, lieut.-gov. of the N.W. Provinces, a considerable village on the route from Kurnool to Rewaree, and 76 miles S.W. of the former.

Water is abundant, though indifferent, and supplies are plentiful. Lat. 28° 46′, long. 76° 41′.

DEEGUCHEE.—A town in the British district of Sattara, presidency of Bombay, 61 miles E. of Sattara. Lat. 17° 30′, long. 74° 59′.

DEEHA, in the British district of Allahabad, lieut.-gov. of the N.W. Provinces, a village on the right bank of the Ganges, 795 miles N.E. of Calcutta by the river route, 13 S.E. of the city of Allahabad by the same. Lat. 25° 19′, long. 82° 3′.

DEEMLA.—A town in the British district of Rungpore, lieut.-gov. of Bengal, 39 miles N.W. of Rungpore. Lat. 26° 6′, long. 88° 55′.

DEENANUGUR, in the Lahore division of the Punjab, a town situated on the right bank of the Baree Dooab Canal, 89 miles N.E. of the town of Lahore. Lat. 32° 10′, long. 75° 29′.

DEENGROO.—A halting-place on a rivulet of the same name, on the southern declivity of the Shatul Pass. It is situate just above the limit of forest, in a tract having a rich soil covered with a close sward. Elevation above the sea 12,300 feet. Lat. 31° 21′, long. 78° 1′.

DEENGURH.—A town in the native state of Bhawulpoor, 32 miles S. from Bhawulpoor, and 116 miles N.W. from Beekaneer. Lat. 28° 56′, long. 71° 49′.

DEENHUTLA.—A town in the native state of Coosh Behar, 61 miles N.E. from Dinajepore, and 10 miles S. from Behar. Lat. 26° 7′, long. 89° 26′.

DEEPLA.—A town in the British province of Scinde, presidency of Bombay, 162 miles E. of Kurrachee. Lat. 24° 30′, long. 69° 40′.

DEEROEE, a river of Assam, rises on the south-eastern boundary, in lat. 27° 10′, long. 95° 21′, and flows for about forty-five miles through the district of Seebpoor, to its junction with the Disang, a tributary of the Brahmapootra, in lat. 27° 4′, long. 94° 41′.

DEESA, in Guzerat, or dominions of the Guicowar, a town on the river Bunnass (western), the residence and possession of a petty Mussulman chief, styled the nawaub of Deesa, who is also nawaub of Pahlunpoor. There is here a British cantonment, which is situate on the left bank of the Bunnass, three miles N.E. of the town. Distance from Mhow, N.W., 301 miles; from Neemuch, W., 251; from Bombay, N., 370. Lat. 24° 14′, long. 72° 5′.

DEESAUN.—A river rising in the native state of Bhopal, a few miles north of the town of Seermow, in about lat. 23° 28′, long. 78° 30′, and at an elevation of about 2,000 feet above the sea. After a course of ten or twelve miles north, it passes into the British territory of Saugor and Nerbudda, through which it flows north-east sixty miles, to the south boundary of Bundelcund, which it enters in lat. 24° 12′, long. 78° 53′, and flows through in a sinuous direction, but generally north, for 150 miles, falling into the Betwa on the right side, in lat. 25° 48′, long. 79° 29′; its total length of course being about 220 miles. Several torrents and small rivers fall into it, right and left, but none of any importance. It is crossed by a ford on the route from Banda to Gwalior, twenty miles above its mouth, and in lat. 25° 34′, long. 79° 28′, and has there "a sandy bottom, and water about knee-deep from November to June." Franklin regards it as the boundary between his rather arbitrary divisions of eastern and western Bundlecund. It abounds in fish, and is styled by Malcolm a fine stream; but it is not navigable.

DEESOORE.—A town in the Rajpoot district of Godwar, 75 miles S.E. from Joudpore, and 110 miles S.W. from Ajmere. Lat. 25° 19′, long. 73° 39′.

DEETAUN.—See DEOTAUN.

DEGAON.—A town of Malwa, in the native state of Bhopal, 50 miles E. from Bhopal, and 56 miles S.W. from Saugor. Lat. 23° 17′, long. 78° 10′.

DEHGONG, in Guzerat, or territory of the Guicowar, a town on the route from Ahmedabad to Neemuch, 17 miles N.E. of the former, 165 S.W. of the latter. Population 8,000. Lat. 23° 8′, long. 72° 50′.

DEHPOOR.—A town in the subdivision of Nassick, British district of Ahmednuggur, presidency of Bombay, 25 miles S.E. of Nassick. Lat. 19° 53′, long. 74° 10′.

DEHRA DOON.—A fertile valley at the south-western base of the lowest and outermost ridge of the mountains of the Himalaya, and forming with the pergunnah of Jounsar Bawur, a British district under the lieutenant-governorship of the North-West Provinces. The valley is inclosed on the north by the Jumna river, separating it from Sirmour and Jounsar; on the north-east by the mountains of native Gurhwal; on the south-east by the Ganges, dividing it from British Gurhwal; and on the south-west by the Sewalik range, separating this district from that of Saharunpoor. The length of the valley in a direction nearly from south-east to north-west, or from Rikkee Kasee on the Ganges, to Rajghat on the Jumna, is forty-five miles. Its breadth varies from fifteen to twenty miles. It lies between lat. 30°—30° 32′, long. 77° 43′—78° 24′.

The mountains on the north-eastern frontier of the valley, towards Gurwhal, have an elevation of 7,000 or 8,000 feet above the sea; those of the Sewalik range from 3,000 to 3,500. The elevation of the bed of the Ganges at the confluence of the river Sooswa, at the south-eastern extremity, is 1,200 feet; that of the Jumna, at the confluence of the Asun, at the north-western extremity, is 1,469. Midway between those depressed extremities of the valley, a gently increasing elevation runs transversely from the Sewalik Mountains to those on the north-eastern boundary, and divides the valley into two basins, that on the north-west drained by the Asun, and that on the south-east by the Sooswa, discharging themselves, as already mentioned, the former into the Jumna, the latter into the Ganges. The town of Dehra, situate on this ridge, has an elevation of 2,369 feet; the source of the Asun, an elevation of 2,148; that of the Sooswa, which river takes its rise a few hundred yards from the former, has the like elevation. These rivers flow along the north-eastern base of the Sewalik range, the surface of the valley in general having a considerable slope to that part, and in consequence, nearly all the supplies to those rivers proceed from the north-eastern side of the valley. The formations of the Sewalik are recent, or tertiary in the conventional language of geologists, and for the most part are composed of calcareous sandstone, clay conglomerate, or marl, containing a vast profusion of fossil remains of mammalia, fishes, reptiles, and testacea. The more elevated range on the north and north-east frontier consists generally of what in the same language are styled transition formations, compact limestone devoid of organic remains, clay-slate, greywacke, with occasionally dykes of trap and other stone, of supposed igneous origin, with extensive overlying beds of quartzy sandstone, and in many places large beds of quartz. The transverse elevation connecting the Sewalik and north-eastern ranges, appears to be of loosely-aggregated diluvial formation, from the fact stated by Jacquemont, that the wells at the town of Dehra, situate on the crest, are nearly 200 feet deep.

The climate is marked by a range of temperature not inconsiderable. Dr. Royle states it to vary from 37° to 101°; and he adds, that snow occasionally falls in winter. In 1841 the mean heat of June, the hottest month, was 88°; of December, the coldest, 60°; and of the whole year, 74°. Other observations, made some years earlier, give results not greatly differing from these; the mean temperature of January, which in this instance was the coldest month, being 52°; that of June, the hottest, 86°; and that of the whole year, 70°. The most unhealthy months are July, August, and September, during which the periodical rains fall; and it is stated, that of the large number of individuals engaged in the extensive grants of land made by the government in 1837, not one person, European or native, escaped fever during the unhealthy period. Hopes, however, are entertained, that by clearance of the jungle and drainage of the swamps, the deadly malaria may be removed, or its effects materially mitigated. Arborescent vegetation is greatly developed, and covers the uncultivated parts with dense and almost impenetrable forests, consisting of trees, many of which are common in more southern parts of India, and arborescent species of genera of which the herbaceous ones are found in the colder parts of the world. Here also occur plants found not only in Southern India, but even under the equator. The zoology is important, comprising the elephant, wild buffalo, tiger, leopard, hyæna, lynx, jackal, wild hog, bear, deer, and the four-horned antelope. Of quadrumanous animals, there are the langur (Simia entallus) and bandur (Simia rhesus). A species of python is met with, as might be expected in a tract so congenial to the nature of those reptiles. The soil is in general a deep rich mould, though in some places composed of shingle or gravel swept down by the torrents from the mountains. For the most part, the soil and climate are adapted to the successful growth of rice, maize, gram (Cicer arietinum), cotton, sugar, opium, hemp, indigo, plantain; and, according to a statement in a late work of good authority, "every English plant thrives luxuriantly in the Dhoon, where in March, April, and May, a splendid show of English flowers is to be seen in all the gardens." The eminent botanists, Dr. Royle and Dr. Falconer, who had ample means of local information, considered the south-western declivity of the range rising north of the Dehra Doon as well suited for the successful growth of tea. The result of the experiments made in consequence has amply justified the sagacity of their conjectures. Tea has been produced of a quality which has commanded the approval of the best professional judges. According to the latest reports, the plant was thriving in different localities, extending over four degrees of latitude and three of longitude, and it was believed that in Dehra Doon alone there were 100,000 acres suitable for its growth.

In 1837 extensive grants were made by government in the Dehra Doon. The terms were a forty years' lease, under which one-fourth was to be rent-free for the whole term, and the remainder for three years; after the expiration of which the twentieth part of the rent assigned was to be paid, rising annually in twentieths, until, at the end of the twenty-third year, the maximum rent of four annas per beegah, or twelve annas per acre, should become payable. The grants in the first instance amounted to something less than 30,000 acres, and the grantees having expended large sums in conveying emigrants and cleaning and cultivating the lands, saw reason, as the year advanced, to anticipate their reward in crops of the finest quality; but on the setting in of the rains, the jungle-fever became so general, that from death, the prostration of disease disabling many who survived, and the departure of others in terrified flight, scarcely any hands remained to gather the harvest, which consequently rotted where it grew. The circumstances of the country, however, in regard to health, appear, as already intimated, to be improvable, and better results are looked for. It does not appear that the expectations of the grantees have been generally realized, as, in some instances at least, they have withdrawn from the speculation.

At the time the valley was wrested from the rajah of Gurwhal by the Goorkhas, it is said to have yielded an annual revenue of 10,000*l.*, though those invaders could never realize more than 2,000*l.* from it. Under British rule its prosperity has evidently advanced. The number of mouzahs or townships in Dehra Doon proper is 214. The area is 673 square miles, or 431,240 British statute acres.

Previously to the Goorkha invasion of the Dehra Doon, in 1803, it was regarded as the most valuable part of the dominions of the rajah of Gurwhal, who frequently resided at Dehra, and made his final stand at the village of Gurudwara, in its vicinity, where he was defeated and slain. The invasion of the valley by the British, in 1815, during the Nepaul war, was marked by the obstinate though ineffectual defence which the Goorkhas made at Kalunga or Nalapani, and the fall of General Gillespie and a considerable number of men under its walls. On the final expulsion of the Goorkhas, it became a British district.

DEHRAH, the principal place of the Dehrah Doon, is situate on the crest of a ridge of moderate height, extending from the Sewalik range to that bounding the valley on the north-east. It is situate amidst an extensive and dense grove of very luxuriant mango-trees, and surrounded by verdure, the vicinity being watered by a torrent descending from the mountains. As the intermitting nature of the stream renders the supply of water from it precarious, the town is in dry weather supplied from several wells, nearly 200 feet deep. Jacquemont describes the place as a very large village, consisting of several cottages; and in a letter bearing date May, 1842, it is mentioned as "a large town, in the neighbourhood of which are many houses, the property of Europeans." Its situation is favourable for traffic, being at the intersection of the route from Hurdwar to Sirmoor with that from Saharunpore and the plains to the British sanitary stations of Mussouree and Landour, and to Western Gurwhal. Whatever may be the present prosperity of Dehrah, it must have resulted from British rule; for in the account of the trigonometrical survey of the Himalaya, drawn up about 1820, where it is noticed as one of the stations of small triangles, the town is said to be "small and poor." Mundy, writing eight years later, describes it as inconsiderable, but with good cantonments, and a handsome temple, built of stone, and embellished externally with designs in stucco. The elevation of this place above the sea is 2,369 feet. Distance N.W. from Calcutta 974 miles. Lat. 30° 19′, long. 78° 5′.

DEHWAREE.—A town in the British district of Sattara, presidency of Bombay, 39 miles E. of Sattara. Lat. 17° 42′, long. 70° 40′.

DEIJBARA, in the British district of Broach, presidency of Bombay, a town on the headland bounding on the north the entrance of the estuary of the river Nerbudda. Distance from Surat, N., 42 miles. Lat. 21° 41′, long. 72° 34′.

DEINWAH.—A river rising in the district of Deogurh, territory of Nagpore, in lat. 22° 20′, long. 78° 35′. After a northerly course of seventeen miles, it turns westward, and falls into the Samarsee river, in lat. 22° 33′, long. 78° 6′.

DEJEEKOTE.—A fort in Sinde, belonging to Ali Moorad, ameer of Khyerpoor, from which town it is distant eleven miles south. It is built on a range of low limestone hills, proceeding in a direction from south-east to north-west, and reaching the Indus at Roree. It consists of a number of fortifications crowning several eminences, and connected by a single mud wall pierced with loopholes. Here, in January, 1843, the British army was encamped during the advance of Sir Charles Napier to destroy Emaum Ghur. Though stronger than most of the fortresses of Sinde, Dejeekote is open to capture by escalade. There is a large tower, which was intended to contain the treasure of the Ameer, and which is covered by an irregular outwork in a singular style. On the south side of the fort is a magazine and manufactory of powder. This fort is called also Ahmedabad. Lat. 27° 22′, long. 68° 48′.

DEKAR.—A town in the British territory of Nagpoor, 140 miles E. from Nagpoor, and 172 miles W. from Sumbulpoor. Lat. 21° 30′, long. 81° 20′.

DEKOOLEE.—See DEOKULLEE.

DEKTOWLI, in the British district of Mynpooree, lieut.-gov. of the N.W. Provinces, a village on the route from the cantonment of Aligurh to that of Etawah, and 34 miles N.W. of the latter. Lat. 27° 8′, long. 78° 38′.

DELHI.—A British district within the limits of the lieutenant-governorship of the North-Western Provinces, so called from the celebrated city its principal place. It is bounded on the north by the British district of Paneeput; on the east by the Jumna, separating it from the British districts of Meerut and Boolundshuhur; on the south by Bullubgurh and the British district of Goorgaon; and on the west by the district of Rhotuck, and by Buhardoorgurh and Jhujur. It lies between lat. 28° 24′—28° 54′, long. 76° 49′—77° 29′, and has an area of 789 square miles. The population in 1853 amounted to 435,744. Of this number, 171,694 are returned as Hindoo and agricultural; 144,371 as Hindoo non-agricultural; 18,917 as Mahometans, and others not Hindoo, agricultural; and 100,762 of those classes non-agricultural. Nearly one-third of the entire population of the district is concentrated in the city of Delhi; and if the suburbs be included, the proportion will be found to exceed one-third. Exclusive of the city and its suburbs, the district is divided into two pergunnahs,—northern and southern. In both pergunnahs, the Hindoo population greatly preponderates; but in the city and suburbs of Delhi, long the seat of a powerful Mahomedan monarchy, the two races exist in almost equal proportions. The eastern, northern, and north-western parts of this district are watered by the Jumna and its branches, by the Delhi Canal, or that of Ali Mardan Khan, and by the Hansouti Nullah, a torrent which, in the rainy season, expands into the Farrukhnagar Jhil, an extensive plash or shallow lake, discharging itself into the Jumna about two miles north of the city. The southern part is barren, with an uneven surface of rocky ridges. The aspect of the country is thus described by Dr. Royle:—"Delhi, the capital of Northern India, situate on the western bank of the Jumna, nearly at the upper part of the inclined slope which forms the plains of India, is elevated about 800 feet above the level of the sea. The soil is barren, and remarkable for its saline efflorescence; and the wells, for the brackishness of their water. The rocky soil, always exposed to the solar rays, absorbs much heat, and a high temperature, with considerable dryness, is produced in the hot weather; but from the openness of the country, and exposure to the winds which pass over extensive lakes in the vicinity, a greater degree of cold is produced in winter than we should otherwise expect. We do not, therefore, find in Flora round Delhi, such plants as Guttiferæ, Anonaceæ, and Strychneæ, which, requiring moisture with heat, flourish in the southern provinces of India. But the climate in general being favourable, and the minimum of cold not long-continued, we find many of the plants which are common in warmer parts of India, but which are not found at Saharunpore." The climate being in general dry, and the soil for the most part either sandy or rocky, requires consequently to be fertilized by frequent applications of moisture. The principal alimentary crops are barley, wheat, and pulse. The demand of government in this district, on account of the land revenue, amounted, in 1846-47, to 34,967*l*. The assessment has been fixed for a series of years, and is not liable to increase until the year 1870. The district is intersected by the grand trunk road from Calcutta, and is also connected with Meerut by means of an excellent road, completed some years ago. That a tract having inconsiderable natural resources, should for so long a period have contained the capital of a vast empire, seems extraordinary. It probably resulted from the progress of the conquest of Hindostan, previously to the British sway, having always been from the west to the east. Delhi, consequently, was found the best station for maintaining political and military communication between the Deccan and the great valley of the Ganges on the one side, and on the other the Punjab and Affghanistan, usually the base of operations to invaders.

DELHI.—A celebrated city, the principal place of the British district of the same name, under the lieutenant-governorship of the North-Western Provinces. The site of the present city is a low rocky range, about a mile from the right bank of the Jumna, and on an offset of that river, which leaves the main stream five miles above the town, and rejoins it two miles below. The approach from the south-east, or the direction of Agra, is very striking, from the innumerable ruinous monuments of former prosperity and grandeur. "Everywhere throughout the plain, rise shapeless half-ruined obelisks, the relics of massive Patan architecture, their bases being buried under heaps of ruins bearing a dismal growth of thorny shrubs. Everywhere one treads on overthrown walls. Brick mosaics mark the ground-plan of the humbler dwellings of the poorer classes. Among the relics of a remote age, are occasionally to be seen monuments of light and elegant style of architecture, embellished with brilliant colours, gilt domes, and minarets encased in enamelled tiles." These surprising collections of ruins are the remains of the ancient city of Delhi, which, according to Wilford, extended above thirty miles along the banks of the Jumna. The present city, founded by Shahjehan in 1631, is about seven miles in circumference, and inclosed on three sides by a fine wall, which is interrupted towards the river. Shahjehan disposed along this defence a few weak towers scarcely projecting from it; but since the acquisition of the city by the British, it has been strengthened by large bastions, each mounting nine cannon. A ditch has also been excavated and the glacis raised. As the curtains are extensive, small external martello towers have been constructed, to bring the foot of the walls under the fire of musketry. The tops of but few houses appear above the ramparts, over which rise graceful acacias, and still overtopping these, lofty detached date-trees; while the minarets of mosques, and tombs shaded with the gloomy foliage of the salvadora, are scattered over the glacis. The Jumma Musjeed, or principal mosque, and the palace, displaying a very high and extensive cluster of towers and battlements, rise above all, and render the external aspect of the place very imposing. Franklin enumerates seven gates,—the Lahore, Ajmere, Turkoman, Delhi, Moor or Mohur, Caubul, and Cashmere. Bacon, who visited the place ten or twelve years ago, gives the same number, but styles the Caubul the Agra gate. The actual number, however, appears to be eleven,—the Cashmere, Lahore, Caubul, Buddurnao, Ajmere, Turkoman, Delhi, Rajghat, Negumbod, Lall, and Kaila gates. The last four are on the river face. The Cashmere gate has casemated apartments for the accommodation of the city-guard, which is stationed there. The streets are for the most part narrow, but the Chandni Chauk, or principal street, which runs north and south from the gate of the palace to the Delhi gate of the city, a length of about three-quarters of a mile, is fifty yards wide, having good shops on both sides. It is also remarkably clean, a small raised watercourse flowing down the middle of the street in a channel of red stone. There is another large street running east and west, from the gate of the palace to the Lahore gate of the city, but it is inferior to the Chandni Chauk, though like it provided with a watercourse. The inhabitants have, however, spoiled the appearance of both by erecting houses in the centre and across the streets in some places, so that it is not without difficulty that their original course can now be traced. In the Chandni Chauk is situate the imperial palace, described by Heber as one of the noblest kingly residences he had ever seen; far surpassing the Kremlin, though not equal to Windsor. It is inclosed on three sides by a wall of red granite, a mile in circumference, and about forty feet high, flanked with turrets and cupolas. It is very beautifully built, and has two noble gateways, each defended by a barbican. On the remaining side it is defended by the river (the branch of the Jumna), over which is a narrow bridge, forming a communication with the old fort of Selimghur, on the eastern bank. That antique fort is supposed to have been raised by some early Patan sovereign, and is in a very heavy, massive style of architecture, devoid of ornaments, except a few rude carvings on the mouldings and cornices. The entrance to the palace is through a succession of noble and very lofty gateways, built of red granite highly sculptured; the principal one is described by Heber in the same terms which he applies to the palace generally. A splendid Gothic arch in the centre of the great tower is succeeded by a long vaulted aisle, like that of a Gothic cathedral, with a small open octagonal court in its centre, all of granite, and all ornamented with inscriptions from the Koran, and finely-carved flowers. The Dewani Khas, or "private council-chamber," is a pavilion of white marble, surmounted by four cupolas of the same material, and open on one side to the court of the palace, on the other to its garden. Its pillars and arches are exquisitely carved and ornamented with arabesques gilt and inlaid, flowers, and inscriptions, in the most elaborate Persian character. A rich foliage of silver, which formerly graced the ceiling, has been long since carried off. At present this splendid and tasteful hall is seldom entered by the emperor, and is in a very filthy state, being the retreat of crows, kites, and other unclean birds. The garden, though now quite neglected and desolate, was formerly extremely beautiful, and refreshed by numerous elegant fountains of white marble, supplied from an aqueduct of the same material. Within its inclosure is an octagonal pavilion of white marble, containing a fountain and an elegantly-ornamented bath, and consisting of three very large apartments surmounted by white marble domes; but all is now mutilated and defaced with dirt. The Moti-masjid, or private mosque for the court, is an elegant little building of white marble, exquisitely carved, but, like the rest, neglected and dilapidated. The Dewanee-aûm, or public hall of audience, is a large and splendid pavilion of marble, but now fallen into ruin and neglect, the throne, when seen by Heber, being nearly covered with pigeon's dung. Near the palace, and in the Chandni Chauk, is the small mosque of Roshun-a-Dowlah, from which Nadir Shah witnessed the massacre of the inhabitants of Delhi by his troops. The Jumma Musjid, or principal mosque, is situate on a small rocky eminence, of such height that the platform from which the structure rises, overtops the adjacent houses, and is thirty feet above the general level of the city. This platform or court, a square of 450 feet, is paved with red stone, and on each of three sides is entered through a large gateway, approached from below by flights of stone steps. In the middle is a marble reservoir for water, filled by several fountains supplied from a canal by means of machinery, and intended for the ablutions required in the Mahomedan ceremonial. On three sides the court is skirted by open arcades, with octagonal pavilions at convenient intervals; the west is occupied by the mosque, a splendid structure of an oblong form, 261 feet in length, and approached by another magnificent flight of stone steps. The whole front is faced with large slabs of fine white marble, and along the cornice are ten compartments, four feet long and two and a half broad, inlaid with numerous inscriptions from the Koran, in the Nuskhi character, executed in black marble. The interior is paved with flags of white marble, three feet long and a foot and a half broad; and the walls and roof are lined with the same material. The structure is surmounted by three domes of white marble intersected with black stripes, and at each extremity of the front is a minaret of considerable height, and having a winding staircase of 130 steps of red stone, by which access is obtained to the summit, whence is a fine and extensive view of the city, with its palaces, mosques, and battlemented walls, as well as of the surrounding country, widely overspread with monuments and other buildings in every stage of decay. Attached to the mosque is a large and deep well, said to be excavated in solid rock, and from which the water is raised by means of complicated machinery and a succession of reservoirs. In 1809, the machinery became so much decayed as to be unserviceable, until repaired by the British authorities. Hamilton seems to intimate that the fountains in the court of the mosque are supplied from this source, and not from a canal, as stated by Heber. The Jumma mosque was commenced by Shahjehan in the fourth year of his reign, and completed in the tenth, at an expense of about 100,000*l.* English money. Authority was given in 1851 for the repair of the building. Of the other religious buildings, the only one worthy of much notice is the Kala Masjad, or Black Mosque, so called from the dark hue given it by time. It is a structure of no great size, in a plain massive style of architecture, according to the plan of the primitive Arabian mosques, and consists of a square court, surrounded by an arcade, and surmounted by numerous small ill-shaped domes. It is generally supposed to have been built by some of the early Affghan sovereigns. Near the Cashmere gate is an English church, erected at the cost of 10,000*l.*, by the munificence of Colonel Skinner, a highly distinguished commander of irregular troops in the East-India Company's service. Though above one-half of the population of the city consists of Hindoos, their temples are mean, in consequence perhaps of the general poverty of the votaries of the Hindoo creed. The many gorgeous palaces of the nobles of Delhi, which once gave so splendid an aspect to the city, have been in a great measure demolished, the beams and other wood-work having been torn away for fuel by the Mahrattas and Rohillas. Considerable improvements have, however, taken place since the acquisition of the city by the British, who have made it more cleanly, built a court of justice, and, for the resident, a palace, which is surrounded by several fine houses in the Italian style of architecture. A great number of houses have also been built by the native inhabitants, the number of whom is considerably on the increase.

During the prosperity of the city, all parts were copiously supplied with water by means of a canal, made, at vast expense and with much skill, by Ali Murdan Khan, a munificent Persian, of great ability, and high in command under Shahjehan. Drawing its supply from the canal of Feroz Shah, near Rair, a distance of seventy miles, this great watercourse, as it approaches the city, is conducted along the summit of a prolonged artificial mound, of such an elevation that the bottom of the channel is much higher than the surrounding country; holding its course, by means of an aqueduct of masonry, over a considerable depression, and skirting the north-eastern base of the range of rocky hills stretching westward from Delhi, the stream is finally led across it, in a channel cut through the solid rock for nearly three miles, being twenty-five feet in breadth, twenty-five in depth, generally, but in one place sixty feet. It then enters the city, and, passing through it by an open channel, trăverses another long extensive aqueduct, by which it reaches the palace, throughout the whole of which it ramifies, in open or covered courses, having outlets to the Jumna; thus diffusing constant streams of fresh water. In like manner, in the space between the range of hills and the palace, numerous under-ground channels were cut, leading to the various residences of the nobles, and the different divisions of the city; yielding to the whole city and its suburbs a supply of good water, from open well-shafts connected with these subterraneous water-courses. On a review of the ancient works in Delhi connected with the canal, it is obvious that money must have been expended with a most lavish hand, to effect even that of which the existence is known; and much is yet hidden in the ruins of the neighbourhood. According to Polier, a watercourse ran through every principal street; and such a copious and pure supply was inestimable to Delhi, as the water of the Jumna in the neighbourhood of the city, impregnated with natron, is disagreeable and unwholesome. If, as stated, Ali Murdan Khan served Shahjehan from 1638 to 1656, the canal must have been made in that interval. The resulting revenue appears to have been assigned as a remuneration to the officer who provided for the requisite repairs; as Safdar Jang, the father of Shoojah-oo-dowlah, the nawaub of Oude, is alleged to have derived an annual revenue of 250,000*l.* from it. In the course of the revolt of Safdar Jang, in 1752, and the subsequent disorders and disasters of Delhi, the canal went to ruin, and the supply of water was cut off; and though subsequently restored, at a cost of 10,000*l.*, by Ahmed Shah Dooranee, in one of his temporary occupations of the city, it again became unserviceable through neglect, and the supply was interrupted, until, in 1820, the requisite repairs having been effected by the British authorities, the watercourses and conduits of the city were again set flowing, to the unspeakable joy of the inhabitants, who went out in jubilee to meet the stream, throwing flowers and other offerings into the water, and imploring blessings on the government. When the prosperity of Delhi was at its meridian, there was, near the left bank of the Jumna, opposite the palace, an imperial preserve and pleasure-ground, surrounded by numerous palaces of the nobles; and to supply these, as well as to irrigate the Doab, Ali Murdan made another canal, which, drawing its supply from the Jumna on its left side, nearly opposite the commencement of Feroz Shah's work, proceeded in a direction in some measure parallel with the parent stream, for a distance of 135 miles, and rejoined it abreast of the city. This work, known by the name of the Doab Canal, having also gone to ruin through neglect, was repaired by the British authorities, and the flow of water restored, in January, 1830.

According to a recent census, the city of Delhi contains 152,406 inhabitants; of which number 76,372 are stated to be Hindoos, and 76,034 Mahomedans. According to a table, published in the local Gazette, of the amount of traffic crossing the bridge of boats at Delhi, in 1852, the number of buffaloes is returned at at upwards of 100,000, of mules and ponies 84,000, and of hackeries 65,000. The Delhi College is under the management of a loca. committee or council, composed partly o. European and partly of native members. The college was founded in 1792. In 1829, Nawwab Itmad-ood-Dowlah, formerly minister of the king of Oude, endowed the college with the sum of 170,000 rupees, the interest of which produces 7,253 rupees per annum; and this sum, added to the government grants and assignments, raises its gross receipts to the sum of 40,580 rupees per annum. The institution is divided into four departments,—English, Arabic, Persian, and Sanscrit. At the time of Heber's visit, in 1824, the exterior of the palace of the emperor was guarded by the troops of the East-India Company, but the internal duties were performed by a provisional corps, raised in the name of the local sovereign, and nominally under his orders. During Bacon's visit, several years afterwards, one corps in the East-India Company's service was stationed within the city, the remainder of the garrison being cantoned outside the walls. The arsenal is situate on the bank of the Jumna, and at the time of the visit of Von Orlich, in February, 1843, contained 110 guns of different calibre, and other arms of various kinds, arranged with great care and taste. The powder-magazine, until a very recent period, was situate within the walls of the city. Its dangerous position was brought to notice in the year 1850, and orders were given for its removal. The surrounding country is widely overspread with vast ruins, principally of Indreput or Delhi, the seat of empire previously to the foundation of the present walled town of Shahjehanabad. This scene of desolation extends from the garden of Shahlimar, north-west of the present town, to some distance beyond the Kutb Minar, nine miles south of it. Even on the north-west, where the extent of dilapidated remains is smaller, the road is a "continued avenue of ruined tombs, gardens, serais, and palaces," up to the walls of Delhi. A few hundred paces to the south of the present city, is the Kotela, or citadel of Feroz Shah, formerly the fortress of the old city, within the north-western angle of which it is situate. The works of this citadel were very extensive; but the architecture is clumsy in style and rough in execution, and has no pretence to aught but strength. Rising from the terraced roof of a building at the bottom of the courtyard, is a pillar, popularly called the Lath or Staff of Feroz Shah, the visible part measuring thirty-seven feet in length, and ten feet four inches in girth at the base. It is a single shaft of red sandstone, without any joint, and is thought by Prinsep to have been quarried in the Sewalik Mountains at Rajpur, on the bank of the Jumna. About a mile and a half south of this is the tomb of Humayon, the emperor, who, after being driven from his kingdom, succeeded in re-establishing the Mogul dynasty on the throne of Delhi. It stands in the middle of a platform 200 feet square, supported on every side by arcades, and ascended by four great flights of stone steps. Each arch of the arcades serves as a receptacle of one or more tombs. The mausoleum of the sovereign, rising on the platform, is a noble building, of a square form, constructed of red stone, inlaid with marble, and surmounted by a large dome of the latter material, the style of architecture approaching to that usually termed Saracenic. In the interior is a large circular apartment, in the middle of which is a small white marble sarcophagus, containing the remains of Humayon; and around are smaller apartments, in which are entombed his relatives and more favoured retainers. From the top of the building, the view is striking, being on every side over a wide expanse of ruins, which to the westward extends to a range of hills seven or eight miles distant. Some hundred yards west of this mausoleum is a collection of burial-places and small mosques, the most remarkable structure being the tomb of Nizam-ood-deen, a reputed Mussulman saint, which building is ornamented with elaborate and elegant carvings in white marble. Around, most of the deceased members of the present imperial family lie buried, each within a small inclosure of elegant lattice-work, executed in white marble. Among these monuments is that of the Princess Jahanara, a daughter of Shahjehan. About two miles west of the tomb of Humayon, and four miles south of the city, is the mausoleum of Safdar Jang, vizier of the empire in the middle of the last century, and ancestor of the present king of Oude. It is composed of arcades, surrounding a large octagonal dome, built of white marble and red sandstone, arranged in alternate parallel perpendicular sections, and contains in its interior the body, deposited in a white marble sarcophagus, beautifully carved.

A few hundred paces west of the city is an observatory of enormous size, which (as well as similar structures at Jeypoor, Muttra, Benares, and Oujein, respectively) was made by Jeysingh, rajah of Amber, who was employed by the emperor Mohammed Shah to reform the calendar. Nine miles south of the city is the celebrated Kutb Minar, probably the highest column in the world. It tapers regularly from the base to the cupola, which, according to Franklin, is capable of containing a dozen persons. The exterior is for a great part of the height adorned by fluting, there being twenty-seven projections, alternately round and angular. The column is surrounded by four balconies or galleries, supported by large stone brackets, and having small battlements, which, while they have an ornamental effect, afford some slight security to those who venture on such a giddy footing. In 1803, the column was injured by lightning and earthquake; and either from those causes, or from the more gradual influence of time, many stones on the west side have been displaced, so as to cause a vertical crack in the staircase and central pillar. A British officer of engineers has repaired the damage to a considerable extent, and has performed the task with great architectural skill. According to Bacon, the undertaking was a very bold one, as a very large portion of the masonry at the base of the pillar must have been removed before the new could be substituted. "The native masons," he observes, "generally a most hardy and adventurous set, were with the greatest possible difficulty brought to put their hands to the labour." At no great distance from this column, is the burial-place of the unfortunate emperor Shah Alum, and close to it the country residence of his successors, "a large but paltry building, in a bad style of Italian architecture, and with a public road actually leading through its courtyard."

In the absence of direct observations respecting the elevation of Delhi above the sea, an approximate estimate may be safely made from careful observations at no great distance. The height of Dasna, sixteen miles due east of the channel of the Jumna, abreast of Delhi, is 821 feet. The slope of the surface from that part of the doab to the river is very gentle, and if assumed at two feet per mile, it will give the elevation of that part of the channel at about 790 feet. Farther, the elevation of Gurgaon, seventeen miles south-west of Delhi, is 817 feet, and as, during the rainy season, an extensive and nearly stagnant piece of water extends between the two places, the inclination of the surface from the former to the latter cannot be great; though undoubtedly there is some declension, as the drainage of the jhil or swamp is into the Jumna, at Delhi. The elevation of Delhi, therefore, does not probably vary much from 800 feet. A series of observations, extending over a period of three years, gives the following as the mean temperature in the daytime, of the respective months :—January, 56°; February, 61°; March, 72°; April, 83°; May, 91°; June, 92°; July, 86°; August, 83°; September, 83°; October, 77°; November, 65°; December, 58°. Delhi may be regarded as a rather arid district; the fall of rain in 1842 is reported to have been only ten inches. That year, however, was considered a very dry one, even more so than 1837, in which the deficiency of rain was productive of dreadful famine. Smart frosts during the nights of mid-winter afford the means of producing ice, to be stored for a relief during the heats of summer. The earth, which is generally impregnated with mineral salts, especially saltpetre, is moulded into round shallow pans, into which water is poured to the depth of about an inch, and they are set out in rows on layers of split bamboos or hurdles, covered with straw. The frost of the night is sufficient, under such management, to produce ice, which is carefully removed in the morning, and deposited for preservation in deep pits.

Indraprestha or Inderput, the city which formerly occupied the site of the modern city of Delhi, is alleged to have been founded by Yudisthira, whose demise, according to the extravagant chronology of the Hindoos, occurred in the year 3101 before the Christian era. It ceased for several centuries to be the seat of regal government, until re-established by the adventurer Anungpal. About the year 980, the rajah of Delhi is mentioned as a member of a Hindoo confederacy defeated by Sebektegin, the Ghaznevide, in the Punjaub; and again as a member of a similar confederacy, experiencing a like fate from Mahmood of Ghuznee, in 1008. Ferishta, however, in recounting the expedition of that ruler to Kaunouj, which was undertaken in 1017, and the subsequent expeditions by which, in 1021 and 1023, he penetrated to Kalleenjur, makes no mention of Delhi; though in all three enterprises the routes of the invader must have lain at no great distance from it. But on the invasion of India, in 1191, by Mohammed Shahab-u-din of Ghor, Delhi appears as one of the four great Hindoo powers. It was then held in union with Ajmeer, by Pirthi or Pritwi Raj, a Rajpoot prince, who having, on the plains of Sirhind, given battle at the head of a force, according to native estimate comprising 300,000 horse and 3,000 elephants, besides infantry, was defeated, made prisoner, and put to death by the invader. Kutb-oo-deen, a lieutenant of the victor, took Delhi in 1193, and established there an independent Mahomedan dynasty, known among the Oriental historians as that of "the slaves of the sultans of Ghor." In 1288, the Khiljis or Giljis, adventurers from Afghanistan, having murdered the reigning prince, Keikobad, succeeded in transferring the sovereignty to Jelal-ood-deen, one of their number, and established the Khilji dynasty, which lasted till 1321, when it was terminated by the assassination of Sultan Mobarik, and the supreme power was transferred to Gheias-ood-deen Toghluk, the founder of the Toghluk dynasty. In the reign of Mahmud, of this dynasty, the Tartar conqueror Tamerlane invaded India; and, in 1398, marched to Delhi, the operations against which he prefaced by massacring in cold blood his Hindoo prisoners, reported by native authorities to have been 100,000 in number. After a brief resistance, Mahmud, the sovereign of Delhi, took to flight, the town was plundered and burned, and the inhabitants butchered. According to the account of a panegyrist of the invader, "high towers were erected of their heads, and their carcases were left a prey to birds and beasts: never were such carnage and desolation known." The stay of Tamerlane in Delhi was only of sufficient length to enable him to complete the series of barbarities by which his visit is rendered infamously memorable; and after his departure the city and the adjoining territory remained for nearly half a century in an unsettled state, until the sovereignty was acquired, in 1450, by Behlol, of the Patan or Afghan tribe of Lodi. His grandson, Ibrahim, was, in 1526, defeated and slain, at the battle of Paniput, by the renowned Baber, whose lineal descendant, popularly called down to a late period the Great Mogul, is at present the titular sovereign. Baber's son and successor, Humaion, was, in 1540, defeated and expelled from India by Shir Khan, an adventurer of Patan descent; but receiving assistance from the king of Persia, Humaion recovered his sovereignty in 1554, by a decisive victory which he gained at Sirhind. The progress of the power of the Moguls in India was more rapid even than that of the British in the same country; as in the reign of Akbar, the son and successor of Humaion, the empire extended from Chittagong in the east, to Candahar in the west, and from Bultistan or Little Thibet in the north, to the southern boundary of Berar at the opposite point. Subsequently, the southern frontier was for a short period extended by the conquests of Aurungzebe to Tanjore. The empire was originally distributed into twelve soubahs or vice-royalties, but the number was ultimately increased to fifteen, for the purpose of comprehending the additions which were the fruits of Akbar's later conquests. The assessed revenue of Akbar, settled by him in the fortieth year of his reign for a term of ten years, amounted to 9,07,43,881 sicca rupees, or about eleven millions sterling. Elphinstone, from Abulfazl, estimates the number of persons bound to render military service at 4,400,000, but the whole number at one time actually drawn out, did not probably much exceed 200,000 cavalry, and about 20,000 infantry and artillerymen. Bernier, who considered the army which Prince Dara, the son of Shahjehan, led against his brother Aurungzebe, as inferior to none ever mustered in India, estimates it at 100,000 cavalry, 20,000 infantry, and eighty pieces of artillery. The treasure accumulated by Shahjehan amounted, according to report, to six millions sterling, exclusive of jewels and gorgeous furniture of much greater value. The harem of Akbar was maintained on a scale of great magnificence. In the Ayeen Akbery it is described as "an inclosure of such immense extent as to contain a separate room for every one of the women, whose number exceeds 5,000." By the conquests of the successors of Akbar, especially Aurungzebe, the extent and revenues of the empire were vastly increased, though perhaps with little, if any, advance of its actual power. The empire of Aurungzebe is stated to have been divided into twenty-one soubahs, assessed in the aggregate at 37,724,615*l*.

But this prosperity was only the prelude to rapid and total decay. The chiefs of Rajpootana became alienated from the throne of Delhi; a spirit of insurrection and fierce hostility pervaded the Sikhs, Mahrattas, and others; and, after the death of Aurungzebe, in 1707, his feeble successors became the helpless instruments of conflicting chiefs and parties. His grandson, Jehandar Shah, was, in 1713, deposed and strangled, after a reign of one year. Farokshir, the next in succession, met the same fate in 1719; in the course of which year two other occupants of the musnud passed thence to the grave. Rennell observes, that, "in eleven years from the death of Aurungzebe, five princes of his line who had mounted the throne, and six others who had been competitors for it, had been disposed of; and the degraded state of the regal authority during this period had introduced an incurable anarchy, and a disposition in all the governors of provinces to shake off their dependency on the head of the empire. From this time," he continues, "affairs declined very rapidly." During the reign of Mohammed Shah, who ascended the throne in 1719, the dismemberment of the empire to a vast extent took place, through the encroachments of the Mahrattas, who, in 1737, under their leader Bajee Rao, pushed their attacks to the gates of Delhi; and the usurpation of Asof Jah, the Nizam-ool-mulk, and viceroy of the Deccan, who made himself the virtually independent ruler of the spacious realm now known as the territory of the Nizam. These disruptions, and the consequent weakening of the empire, tempted the invasion of Nadir Shah, the barbarous usurper of the sovereignty of Persia, who, having overrun the greater part of Affghanistan, crossed the Indus at Attok, and marched upon Delhi. He was met, on the 13th February, 1739, at Kernaul, by the Mogul army, which there experienced so decisive a defeat, that the invader occupied Delhi without farther resistance. Whilst engaged there in levying a heavy contribution, the Persian troops were rashly attacked by the populace, who destroyed several hundreds of them. Nadir attempted to restore order, but in vain; and being placed personally in some danger, he gave orders for a general military execution, which were acted upon with terrible fidelity. The massacre of the inhabitants continued from the dawn of light till the day was far advanced. Fifty-eight days after his arrival, Nadir marched from Delhi homewards, bearing with him plunder, the amount of which could not be much less than twenty millions sterling. At the same time Mohammed Shah ceded to Persia the greater part of the province of Tatta, commensurate with the tract now called Sinde, and all the possessions of the Mogul empire west of the Indus. In other quarters, the empire was shorn of extensive provinces. Bengal disclaimed the sovereignty of the Mogul, and the Rohilla Patans, taking advantage of the disasters inflicted by Nadir, and the confusion subsequently caused by the invasions of the Dooranees, assumed independence in 1749, in the tract extending from Oude to the Jumna. Safdar Jang, the nawaub of Oude, made himself independent in that province. The Mahrattas, in addition to the encroachments in the Deccan, which have been already noticed, made themselves masters of Guzerat, Berar, and Orissa, and Malwa was divided between them and several native princes and zemindars; Ajmeer reverted to the Rajpoots, and the Punjab was, in 1752, ceded to Ahmed Shah Dooranee, of Cabul. Ahmed Shah, the Great Mogul, who had succeeded to the shattered sovereignty of Delhi on the death of his father, in 1748, was, in 1754, deposed and blinded. In his reign, the dismemberment of the empire may be regarded as completed, and on the accession of his successor, Alumghir II., nothing remained to the house of Tamerlane but the spoiled and decayed metropolis, which itself, in 1756, was taken by Ahmed Shah Dooranee, and, in 1758, by the Mahrattas. The last-named people, now aiming at the entire empire of Hindostan, collected, under the command of Sedashio Bhao, their forces, estimated at about 70,000 cavalry and 30,000 infantry, and were, in January, 1761, encountered at Paniput by Ahmed Shah Dooranee, at the head of a confederate Mahomedan army of nearly equal number, when the Mahrattas were totally routed, their commander and the greater part of their army being cut to pieces. Shah Alum, whose right to the titular sovereignty accrued on the assassination of Alumgir, in 1759, was at that time a fugitive in Bengal, and his son Jewan Bukht, a youth of thirteen years of age, was, under the name of Shahjehan, recognised shah of Delhi, by Ahmed Shah Dooranee. Shah Alum, however, assumed the title of Padshah, and coming into collision with the forces of the English East-India Company, was defeated by them at Patna, in February, 1760. Subsequently he threw himself on the clemency of the British, and in 1765, obtaining from the East-India Company an assignment of territory yielding a revenue of 260,000*l*., he made over to them the Dewanny of the provinces of Bengal, Bahar, and Orissa, which was virtually a grant of the provinces themselves. In 1771, Shah Alum, determined at all hazards to try his fate at Delhi, left Allahabad, the residence assigned him by the British authorities, and made over to the Mahrattas the territory and revenue allotted to him by the arrangement of 1765. But the proposed transfer was of no avail to the Mahrattas, as the British authorities, regarding the alienation of the districts as an abandonment, did not hesitate to resume the grants; and the short-sighted emperor, having entered Delhi on the 25th December, 1771, found himself there the destitute and helpless captive of the Mahratta chief Madhaji Scindia, who became the real sovereign of the capital and the adjoining territory. The power of Scindia being weakened by various causes, Ghulam Kadir, a Rohilla chief, son of Zabitah Khan, and grandson of Najib-ood-dowla, who had made a great figure in the affairs of Delhi during the time of Ahmed Shah Dooranee and Alumgir, gained a footing there; but his conduct to Shah Alum was more intolerable than even that of the Mahrattas, and the Shah wrote to Scindia, urging him to march to his deliverance. The correspondence having been treacherously disclosed to Ghulam Kadir, he forcibly entered the palace of the captive emperor, struck out his eyes with a dagger, seized his scanty treasures, and subjected the females of his family to plunder and outrage. This dreadful consummation of the emperor's adversity took place in 1788, when he was about sixty-five years of age, and had nominally reigned about twenty-nine years. Ghulam Kadir shortly after fell into the hands of Scindia, who put him to death with ostentatious cruelty. Under the Mahrattas, Shah Alum long suffered neglect and abject poverty; nor was his condition improved when the command of Delhi was intrusted by that power to Perron, the French adventurer; for though a sum of about a hundred thousand pounds sterling was nominally allotted for the annual expenditure of the royal household, not much more than a fifth of that sum was ever actually disbursed. On the 8th September, 1803, the British army, under General Lake, marching from Allygurh on Delhi, came in front of a superior Mahratta force, under command of Louis Bourquien, a French adventurer, and advantageously posted on the left bank of the Jumna to defend the approaches to the city. There the army of the Mahrattas was utterly routed with great slaughter, a vast number of their men being driven into the Jumna and drowned, and all their artillery and stores falling into the hands of the British. Delhi thereupon, without farther resistance, admitted the conquering army, and the Mogul emperor was taken under the protection of the East-India Company, an allowance being assigned for his support. By the twelfth article of the treaty of Serjee Anjenjaum, signed 30th December, 1803, between the East-India Company and the Mahratta leader Dowlut Rao Scindia, the latter "renounces all claims upon his majesty Shah Alum, and engages, on his part, to interfere no further in the affairs of his majesty." In October, 1804, the Mahratta chief Jeswunt Rao Holkar, having under his command about 70,000 men, with 130 pieces of cannon, laid siege to Delhi; the British force in which consisted of but two battalions and four companies of native infantry, two corps of irregular horse, two corps of irregular infantry, and a corps of matchlock-men. Most of the irregular troops deserted, yet Lieut.-Colonel Burn, in command of the garrison, took measures for maintaining, with his very inadequate force, the whole line of defences, though nine miles in circuit, and in a very ruinous state. The operations of Holkar were materially crippled by a sortie, in which the guns of his breaching-battery were rendered unserviceable, and after an ineffectual attempt at escalade, he drew off his army with such haste, that three mines, laid for the destruction of some bastions, were left unexploded. General Lake, whose approach caused the siege to be so precipitately raised, reached the city three days afterwards. The unfortunate Shah Alum died in 1806, at the age of eighty-six, and was succeeded by his son Akbar, who, dying in 1837, at the age of eighty, was succeeded by the present Padshah, Mohammed Bahadur.

The prestige of the name of the Mogul throughout India, long after the nominal ruler of Delhi had ceased to possess any real power, was remarkable, and rendered expedient a jealousy on the subject which the real condition of the latter state would not otherwise have warranted. The feelings of deference for the throne of Delhi extended to provinces very remote from the seat of its former grandeur, and to Hindoos not less than to Mahomedans. It was in fact universal. In 1813, the Tamburetty, or princess of Travancore, a Hindoo state situate near Cape Comorin, and never subject to Delhi, applied for a dress of investiture from the Padshah, for her infant son, though he was under the guardianship of the British government. It was with some difficulty that her desire was overcome; and though compelled to acquiesce in the decision of the British authorities, the applicant was by no means satisfied that the coveted investiture was unnecessary or improper. The universal respect entertained for the Mogul authority, and even for its semblance (of which the above is an instance), has rendered it necessary that the British government should discountenance as far as possible any assumption of regal or imperial dignity on the part of the representative of the great Mahomedan power which once was paramount in India, and the head of the house of Baber is fast subsiding into the station of a subject. The British government long since disallowed his pretensions to coin money, to establish weights and measures, to confer title or command, except within the limit of his own household. The pride of the Mogul is said to have been wounded by Lord Hastings, when governor-general, having remained seated during an interview. So early, however, as 1805, the presentation of nuzzur or offerings by British functionaries was subjected to check; the Marquis of Hastings and Lord Amherst restrained it still further, and a later governor-general, Lord Ellenborough, forbade it altogether, and substituted a pecuniary equivalent, which, after some hesitation, was accepted by the king. More recently an arrangement was made with the heir-apparent, by which the palace of Delhi was to be given up to the British government, the members of the royal family over whom he should continue to exercise jurisdiction (the number of such persons being considerably abridged) removing to another residence; but the heir-apparent having recently died, further arrangements with regard to the future privileges of the family will be rendered necessary. The formal title of the Delhi sovereign is Padshah or Badshah; and so late as 1806 he has been styled by Hindoos raja of Indraprestha. The official name of the city, in the documents of the Padshah, is Shahjehanabad. The number of persons connected with the Padshah, by consanguinity more or less remote, is considerable; and from the extension of their families and the withholding by the king of their due share of the allowances granted by the British government, they are said to have been sometimes subject to great distress. The king received compensation for the discontinuance of emoluments derived from nuzzur, or offerings made in recognition of his superiority, but still did not escape the pressure of debt. It was proposed a few years since, to increase the royal allowances (previously about twelve lacs per annum), by the addition of three lacs, on condition of due provision being made for claims of dependants. His majesty did not at first think fit to accept the boon on the condition annexed to it, but subsequently altered his determination. Lat. 28° 39′, long. 77° 18′.

DELLAMCOTTAH.—A town in the native state of Bhotan, 27 miles E. from Darjeeling, and 99 miles N. from Dinajepore. Lat. 26° 59′, long. 88° 44′.

DELLY MOUNT.—See Dilly.

DEMAUN.—See Daman.

DEMREE.—A river rising in Thibet, north of the great Snowy range of the Himalayas, and in lat. 28° 45′, long. 92° 11′. It flows first southerly for sixty-five miles, when, passing through a gorge of the Himalayas, it turns south-west, and flows for 115 miles through the native state of Bhotan, to its junction with the Monas, a considerable feeder of the Brahmapootra, in lat. 27° 2′, long. 91° 10′.

DENDOWRA, in the British district of Furuckabad, lieut.-gov. of the N.W. Provinces, a village on the route from Cawnpore to Futehgurh, and 36 miles S.E. of the latter. Lat. 26° 59′, long. 80° 2′.

DENDRAH.—A town in the native state of Cashmere, or territory of Gholab Singh, 21 miles N. from Jamoo. Lat. 32° 55′, long. 74° 50′.

DENKANICOTTA.—A town in the British district of Salem, presidency of Madras, 68 miles N. of Salem. Lat. 12° 32′, long. 77° 50′.

DEOBUND, in the British district of Suharunpoor, lieut.-gov. of the N.W. Provinces, a town on the route from Mozuffurnuggur to Suharunpoor, and 20 miles S.E. of the latter town. It is situate between the rivers Hindun and Kali Nuddee, in an open and cultivated country, abounding in water and supplies for troops. The population is returned at 18,638. Distant N.W. from Calcutta 987 miles. Lat. 29° 41′, long. 77° 44′.

DEOCHUNPOOR, in the British district of Ghazeepore, lieut.-gov. of the N.W. Provinces, a town on the route from Benares to Ghazeepore cantonment, 24 miles N.E. of the former. It is situate on the left bank of the Ganges, 20 miles W. of Ghazeepore. Lat. 25° 31′, long. 83° 16′.

DEO DHOORA, in the British district of Kumaon, lieut.-gov. of the N.W. Provinces, a temple on a lofty summit in the Sub-Himalaya, or mountain system south of the principal range, on the route from Chumpawut to Almora, S.E. of Fort Almora 19 miles. Elevation of summit above the sea 6,780 feet. Lat. 29° 25′, long. 79° 56′.

DEODUR.—A small independent district in the north-west quarter of the province of Guzerat, presidency of Bombay, containing an area of about eighty square miles, with a population of 2,000, consisting principally of Rajpoots and Coolies. This petty state pays no tribute to any government. Each village protects itself, depending on the British government for external defence. The first relations between Deodur and the British date from 1819, after the expulsion of the marauders who had infested the country. The protecting government exercises no interference in regard to the internal affairs of the district, but merely controls its external relations. The town of Deodur is in lat. 24° 9′, long. 71° 49′.

DEOGAON, in the British district of Azimgurh, lieut.-gov. of the N.W. Provinces, a town, the principal place of the pergunnah of the same name, nine miles from the left bank of the Goomtee, 29 miles N. of Benares, 21 S.W. of Azimgurh. Lat. 25° 44′, long. 83° 3′.

DEOGARH.—See DEWGURH.

DEOGHUR BARREEA.—See BARREEA.

DEOGONG, in the British district of Ajmeer, lieut.-gov. of the N.W. Provinces, a town 50 miles S.E. from Ajmeer, 31 miles W. of Tonk. Lat. 26° 10′, long. 75° 26′.

DEOGUR.—A town in the British district of Bhaugulpore, lieut.-gov. of Bengal, 77 miles S.W. of Rajmahal. Lat. 24° 31′, long. 86° 42′.

DEOGUR.—A town, the principal place of a district of the same name, in the British province of Nagpoor, 55 miles N.W. from Nagpoor, and 52 miles E. from Baitool. Lat. 21° 53′, long. 78° 46′.

DEOGURH.—A town in the native state of Gwalior, or possessions of Scindia, 26 miles S.E. from Gwalior, and 56 miles S.W. from Etawah. Lat. 26° 5′, long. 78° 39′.

DEOGURH.—A town in the Rajpoot state of Oodeypoor or Meywar, 62 miles N. of the town of Oodeypoor. Lat. 25° 31′, long. 73° 58′.

DEOGURH, or OOTGIR.—A village in the Rajpoot state of Kerowly, 29 miles S.W. of Kerowly. Lat. 26° 5′, long. 77°.

DEOGURH, in the Rajpoot state of Joudpore, a village on the route from Pokhurn to the town of Joudpore, and seven miles N. of the latter. Lat. 26° 25′, long. 73° 8′.

DEO GURH.—A town of Bombra, one of the native states on the S.W. frontier of Bengal, 50 miles E. from Sumbulpore. Lat. 21° 32′, long. 84° 47′.

DEOHRA.—A village in the hill state of Bussahir. It is situate in a fertile valley inclosed by mountains, rising with a gentle declivity, formed into numerous terraces, covered with soil, and carefully cultivated under rice and other grains. The houses are dispersed in a straggling manner, amidst cultivated spots along the high banks of a feeder of the river Pabur. The residence of the Rana, situate on the summit of an isolated eminence, is a collection of buildings five or six stories high, communicating in the upper part by galleries and balconies of wood. The lower part of each building is constructed of large blocks of stone, bonded with great beams, of which the surrounding forests yield abundant supplies. The eaves of the roofs project greatly, and the outer surfaces are concave, in the Chinese style. It is totally without defence against assault. Elevation above the sea 6,550 feet. Lat. 31° 6′, long. 77° 44′.

DEOHURI, in the British district of Bareilly, lieut.-gov. of the N.W. Provinces, a village close to the route from Bareilly to Almora, and 34 miles N. of the former. Lat. 28° 53′, long. 79° 31′.

DEOJANA.—See DOOJANUH.

DEO KHAS.—A town in the British district of Behar, lieut.-gov. of Bengal, 39 miles S.W. of Gayah. Lat. 24° 40′, long. 84° 29′.

DEOKULTEE, in the British district of Ghazeepore, lieut.-gov. of the N.W. Provinces, a village on the route from Benares cantonment to that of Ghazeepore, 29 miles N.E. of the former, 17 W. of the latter. It is situate three miles north of the left bank of the Ganges, and on the river Gungee, traversed here by a bridge of masonry. Lat. 25° 33′, long. 83° 18′.

DEOLEE.—A town in the British province of Nagpoor, 52 miles S.W. from Nagpoor, and 50 miles S.E. from Omraouttee. Lat. 20° 40′, long. 78° 32′.

DEOLEEA, in the British district of Ajmeer, lieut.-gov. of the N.W. Provinces, a town on the route from Oodeypoor to Kishengurh, 46 miles S. of the latter. Lat. 25° 54′, long. 74° 53′.

DEONELLY, in Mysore, a town with an important fort, near the eastern frontier, towards the British district of North Arcot. It was here, in 1749, when the place was besieged by Nundiraj, a man notorious in the history of those times, that Hyder Ali, subsequently tyrant of Mysore, and a formidable enemy to the British and other powers of that part of India, first distinguished himself. Here, also, in 1753, was born his son Tippoo Sultan. Deonelly is 22 miles N.E. of Bangalore, 90 N.E. of Seringapatam. Lat. 13° 15′, long. 77° 46′.

DEONTHUL.—A village on the route from Subhatoo to Simla, and 3½ miles N. of the former station. It is pleasantly situate in a narrow and romantic glen on the banks of the river Gumbur, and amidst cultivated terraces, laboriously formed and overspread with soil, on the steep sides of the mountains. It should not be confounded with another place distant fifteen miles to the north-west, where a decisive action took place during the Goorkha war. The village of Deonthul is situate 2,200 feet above the sea, in lat. 31° 1′, long. 77° 2′.

DEONTUL, in the hill state of Hindoor, a summit of the Malown ridge, celebrated as the spot where the obstinately-contested Goorkha war was virtually decided. It is about a mile and a quarter S. of Malown, and is situate between that fortress and Surujgarh, both held by the Goorkhas at the beginning of April, 1815, when General Ochterlony advanced to attempt their reduction. With a view to cut off the communication between those forts, and to facilitate the formation of a breaching-battery, a British detachment, under Colonel Thompson, took possession of Deontul, where it was furiously attacked by about 2,000 Goorkhas, who, however, were utterly defeated, with the loss of 700 men, including their commander. After this defeat the Goorkhas offered no further serious opposition, and soon after concluded the convention for ceding the hill states to the East-India Company. Lat. 31° 11′, long. 76° 53′.

DEOOR.—A town in the British district of Sattara, presidency of Bombay, 16 miles N.E. of Sattara. Lat. 17° 51′, long. 74° 12′.

DEOPRAG.—See DEVAPRAYAGA.

DEORALIO.—A town in the native state of Nepal, 56 miles N. from Khatmandoo, and 140 miles E. from Malebum. Lat. 28° 29′, long. 85° 31′.

DEORALLEE, or DEVALI, in Gurhwal, a village on the western declivity of the mountain inclosing the fertile valley of Bunal on the east. Lat. 30° 50′, long. 78° 17′.

DEOREE.—A town in the British district of Behar, lieut.-gov. of Bengal, 100 miles W. of Gayah. Lat. 24° 30′, long. 83° 32′.

DEORI, or BURADEORI, in the British territory of Saugor and Nerbudda, lieut.-gov. of the N.W. Provinces, a town with bazaar on the route from Saugor to Gurrah, 44 miles S.E. of former, 41 N.W. of latter. It appears to have been scarcely noticed by travellers, though once a considerable place, as it is stated, that when burned down by a freebooter some years ago, nearly 30,000 persons perished in the conflagration. Elevation above the sea 1,705 feet. Lat. 23° 22′, long. 79° 4′.

DEOSA.—See DOWSAH.

DEOSIH.—A village in the dominions of Gholab Singh, 56 miles N. from Sirinagur. Lat. 34° 53′, long. 75° 2′.

DEOTAN, in the British district of Baitool, Saugor and Nerbudda territory, lieut.-gov. of the N.W. Provinces, a town on the route from Baitool to Mhow, 16 miles N.W. of the former. Lat. 21° 59′, long. 77° 46′.

DEOTHAN, in the British district of Muttra, lieut.-gov. of the N.W. Provinces, a village on the route from the cantonment of Muttra to Delhi, and 25 miles N.W. of the former. Lat. 27° 45′, long. 77° 32′.

DEPALPOOR, in the territory of Indore, or possessions of the Holkar family, a town on the route from Mow to Neemuch, 27 miles N.W. of former, 128 S.E. of latter. It is situate on the west side of a large tank or small lake, and in 1820 contained 1,035 houses, and about 4,000 persons. The pergunnah, of which it is the principal place, contained at the time just mentioned 7,489 houses, and a population of 30,466. Distance S.W. from Oojein 27 miles. Lat. 22° 50′, long. 75° 34′.

DERA, in the district of Ahladganj, territory of Oude, a town 30 miles N. of Allahabad, 80 S.E. of Lucknow. Butter estimates the population at 8,000, all Hindoos. Lat. 25° 49′, long. 81° 37′.

DERA, in the Peshawur division of the Punjab, a town situated on the left bank of the river Indus, 83 miles N.E. of the town of Peshawur. Lat. 34° 24′, long. 72° 59′.

DERA DEEN PUNAH.—A town in the Punjab, situate near the left bank of the Indus, on the route from Mooltan to Leia, and 40 miles N.W. of the former place. Attached to it is a small but fertile district, which, at the time of Elphinstone's visit, yielded 150,000 rupees to the Afghan chief, who held it in jaghire. Lat. 30° 25′, long. 71° 3′.

DERA DEEN PUNAH.—A town of the Derajat, on the right or west bank of the Indus. It was nearly destroyed by the great earthquake of 1819 and the overwhelming floods which at the same time descended from the Suliman Mountains. Lat. 30° 40′, long. 70° 52′.

DERA FUTTI KHAN, a town of the Derajat, is situate in a very fertile country, on a small western branch of the Indus, and at no great distance from the main stream. The crops in the vicinity are principally cotton, grain of various kinds, indigo, and some sugar and opium. Lat. 31° 9′, long. 70° 50′.

DERA GHAZEE KHAN.—The most southern and also the most important of the three towns which contribute to give to the Derajat its name. It is a large, populous, and commercial place, situate in a low alluvial tract, four miles from the right or west bank of the Indus, and contains numerous ruins of mosques, and of the extensive and well-constructed residences of the former Durani governors and officers. It carries on considerable transit-trade; an advantage attributable to its being situate at the point where one of the great routes from Eastern India and the Punjab into Beloochistan and Khorasan intersects the great route from north to south into Sinde. The bazaar contains 1,600 shops, the inmates of 530 of which are engaged in weaving and selling cloth. It is in other respects well supplied with goods, but ill-built and dirty. Some manufactures are carried on here in silk, cotton, and mixed fabrics of silk and cotton, called loongees, intended for scarfs and waistbands. Coarse cutlery is also manufactured to a considerable extent. The surrounding country is very unhealthy during the hot season, but remarkably fertile, being well irrigated, and producing grain, fruits in abundance and of fine quality, sugar, cotton, and much indigo, in which a considerable traffic is driven. Both the transit and the direct carrying trade are conducted almost exclusively by the Lohani Afghans, who are at once a pastoral and a mercantile tribe. Dera Ghazee Khan, in consequence of its advantageous position, has been recommended by Burnes and others as the best site for a great annual fair, to be held under the protection of the British government, commanding, as it does, such important routes and the navigation of the Indus north and south. It was a dera, post, or camp of Ghazee Khan, who, about three centuries ago, figured as an adventurer here, and being wrested from the Durani empire by the Sikhs, fell to the British upon the conquest of the Punjaub in 1849. Lat. 30° 4′, long. 70° 54′.

DERA ISMAEL KHAN.—A considerable town of the Derajat, built a short distance from the right or west bank of the Indus, to replace the former town, which, having been situate only a hundred yards from the river, was, a few years ago, swept away by it so completely that not a vestige was left. The town is well laid out, but is ill built of unburnt brick, and in general has an air of desolation, though in spring there is much business, it being then crowded by the Afghans of the Lohani tribe, who purchase great quantities of goods to transport by their caravans for the supply of Afghanistan and Central Asia. The most important article of commerce is white cotton cloth, of which two millions of yards are yearly sold here, and eighteen millions of yards taken through, in transit from Hindostan to the north and west of this place. There is also a considerable trade, by way of the Indus, southward, in grain and salt, from Kala Bagh. The position of Dera Ismael Khan is important, being situate on one of the great routes from the north to Sinde and the Southern Punjab, and also in the vicinity of the ferry at Kaharee, one of the most frequented over the Indus. There is another ferry over that river three miles to the eastward of the town. About three centuries ago, there was here a dera, post, or encampment of Ismael Khan, an adventurer in this country; and hence the name which the town bears. It was wrested from the Durani empire by the Sikhs, and became incorporated with the British dominions upon the conquest of the Punjaub in 1849. Its population is stated to be 8,000. Lat. 31° 50′, long. 70° 58′.

DERAJAT.—See DAMAN.

DERAPOOR, in the British district of Cawnpore, lieut.-gov. of the N.W. Provinces, a town on the right bank of the Seyngur Nuddee, 35 miles W. of Cawnpore. Lat. 26° 26′, long. 79° 51′.

DERBEND.—A British military post, on the north-west frontier of the Punjab. It is situate on the left bank of the Indus, where the stream, previously straitened in its passage through the mountains, expands on entering into the plain; and hence probably the name of Derbend, which signifies the place of a dam or strait. In its neighbourhood, in 1827, Sheer Singh, the Sikh commander, defeated Saiyid Ahmed, the fanatic Afghan, who had excited a religious war against the Sikhs. Lat. 34° 18′, long. 72° 55′.

DERESURA, in the British district of Muttra, lieut.-gov. of the N.W. Provinces, a village on the route from the cantonment of Meerut to that of Muttra, and 21 miles N. of the latter. Lat. 27° 45′, long. 77° 51′.

DERIABAD, in the territory of Oude, a town on the route from Goruckpore to Lucknow, 123 miles W. of the former, 43 E. of the latter. Provisions and water are good and abundant, but firewood very scarce. Lat. 26° 54′, long. 81° 34′.

DERIAPOOR, in the British district of Moradabad, lieut.-gov. of the N.W. Provinces, a village on the route from the town of Meerut to that of Moradabad, and 44 miles S.E. of the former place. It is situate in an open and partially cultivated country. Distant N.W. from Calcutta 888 miles. Lat. 28° 51′, long. 78° 21′.

DERRIAPOOR.—A town in one of the recently sequestrated districts of Hyderabad, or the dominions of the Nizam, 28 miles W. from Omraouttee, and 29 miles S.W. from Ellichpoor. Lat. 20° 50′, long. 77° 23′.

DERRO.—A town in the British district of Shahabad, lieut.-gov. of Bengal, 23 miles S.W. of Arrah. Lat. 25° 17′, long. 84° 27′.

DERWANEE, or DURWANEE, in the British district of Rungpoor, lieut.-gov. of Bengal, a town, the principal place of an extensive pergunnah of the same name. Distant N.W. from the town of Rungpoor 30 miles, N. from Berhampoor, by Dinajpur, 125. Lat. 25° 50′, long. 88° 50′.

DESNOK.—A town in the Rajpoot state of Beekaneer, 15 miles S. of the town of Beekaneer. Lat. 27° 48′, long. 73° 23′.

DESSOOR.—A town in the British district of North Arcot, presidency of Madras, 33 miles S. of Arcot. Lat. 12° 28′, long. 79° 32′.

DEVAPRAYAGA, in Gurwhal, a town at the confluence of the Aluknunda and Bhageerettee. The former flows from the east, the latter from the north, and at the vertex of the right angle formed by their junction the town is situate. According to the graphic description of Raper, "The contrast of the two streams is very remarkable; the former (Bhageerettee) runs down a steep declivity with a rapid force, roaring and foaming over large stones and fragments placed in its bed, while the placid Aluknunda, flowing with a smooth unruffled surface, gently winds round the point." The banks of both rivers are composed of hard black rock; but while those of the Aluknunda are almost perpendicular, to the height of eighty or a hundred feet, those of the Bhageerettee are shelving and expanded. The Aluknunda, the deeper and more considerable river, is, at the season of low water, 142 feet in breadth, and in the rainy season rises forty-six or forty-seven feet. It abounds with fish of the rohu species, four or five feet in length, regarded sacred, and so tame as to take food from the hand. The Bhageerettee is, at the season of low water, 112 feet in breadth, and rises forty feet in the rainy season. Each river is crossed by a jhula or rope bridge. The united stream having a breadth of eighty yards, receives below the confluence the name of the Ganges. The town is built 100 feet above the water, on the scarp of a mountain rising behind it about 800 feet. A flight of steps cut in the rock gives access to the town from the water's edge. The houses are arranged so as to form two rows of unequal length, joined at a right angle, the longer row facing the Bhageerettee, the other the Aluknunda. They are generally two stories high, built of large stones, cemented with lime mortar, and having sloping roofs, covered with shingles. In the upper part of the town stands a temple, sacred to Ramachandra. It is situate on a terrace from twenty to thirty yards square, and six feet high, and is built of large blocks of cut stone piled on each other, without cement, so as to form a pyramid, bulging in the middle, and decreasing rapidly towards the summit, which is surmounted by a white cupola; and over all is a square sloping roof, composed of plates of copper, crowned above with a golden ball and spire. The entrance is on the western side, in a portico, from the roof of which are hung bells of various sizes. Under the shelter thus provided, the worshippers perform their devotions. The image of Ramachandra, about six feet high, carved in black stone, but painted red, except the face, is seated opposite the door, and under the eastern part of the cupola. Before the idol, and opposite the portico, is the brazen image of a Garuda. One knee is bent on the ground, and his hands are joined in the attitude of prayer. The whole height of the building is between seventy and eighty feet. Under the terrace is a temple, sacred to Mahadeva. The only information which the Brahmins professed to be able to vouch for, when questioned respecting the age or founders of the building, was, that it had stood for 10,000 years, which is certainly a very respectable degree of antiquity. It is a peculiarly sacred place of pilgrimage for the superstitious Hindoos, being one of the five principal Prayags or confluences mentioned in the Shastras. The grand rite is ablution, which takes place at the confluence, in three kundas or basins, excavated in the rock, at a level a little lower than the surface of the current, which here is so rapid and violent as to sweep away any attempting to bathe in it. The names of the pilgrims are registered on their making sufficient disbursements to the officiating Brahmins, on account of dues and oblations. The annual revenue of these functionaries, exclusive of such contributions, does not exceed 120*l.*, derived from twenty-five villages, granted for the purpose by the rajah of Gurwhal; and notwithstanding the holy celebrity of the place, the Brahmins are compelled to eke out a subsistence by the practice of trade. The temple, as well as the rest of the town, was much shattered by an earthquake in 1803, but subsequently repaired by Brahmins sent thither for the purpose by Daulat Rao Sindia. The town contains between 200 and 250 houses, inhabited principally by Brahmins from the Deccan. The heat is sometimes very great, exceeding 100° at noon in the shade. Elevation above the sea, of the town, 2,266 feet; of the stream, 1,953. Lat. 30° 8′, long. 78° 39′.

DEVEEKOTE, in the Rajpoot state of Jesulmeer, a small town on the route from the city of Jesulmeer to Balmeer, and 22 miles S.E. of the former. Lat. 26° 44′, long. 71° 17′.

DEVIAPATAM.—A town in the British district of Madura, presidency of Madras, nine miles N.E. of Ramnad. Lat. 9° 28′, long. 78° 58′.

DEVIKOTTA, within the British district of Tanjore, presidency of Madras, a town on the Coromandel Coast, at the mouth of the Coleroon, or great northern branch of the Cauvery. The entrance of the river is difficult, and dangerous of access, from a bank called Coleroon Shoal, which stretches four or five miles to the south-east. Devikotta was taken by the British about the middle of the last century, and their possession was confirmed to them by the rajah of Tanjore. Devikotta is distant from Tranquebar N. 24 miles, Madras S. 122. Lat. 11° 22′, long. 79° 52′.

DEVUPALLI.—A town in the British district of Vizigapatam, presidency of Madras, 13 miles N.W. of Vizianagrum. Lat. 18° 16′, long. 83° 21′.

DEWAH RIVER.—See GOGRA.

DEWAN.—A town in the British district of Moorshedabad, lieut.-gov. of Bengal, 15 miles N. of Moorshedabad. Lat. 24° 24′, long. 88° 16′.

DEWANGARI.—A town in the native state of Bhotan, 53 miles N. from Gowhatty, and 50 miles N.W. from Durrung. Lat. 26° 51′, long. 91° 27′.

DEWANGUNJE.—A town in the British district of Hoogly, lieut.-gov. of Bengal, 40 miles N.W. of Calcutta. Lat. 22° 49′, long. 87° 50′.

DEWANGUNJE.—A town on the left bank of the river Coosy, in the British district of Purneah, lieut.-gov. of Bengal, 49 miles N.W. of Purneah. Lat. 26° 24′, long. 87° 14′.

DEWAS.—A town of Baghelcund, in the native state of Rewah, 21 miles N.E. from Rewah, and 50 miles S.W. from Allahabad. Lat. 24° 46′, long. 81° 35′.

DEWAS, in Malwa, a town, the principal place of a small territory of the same name, situate between lat. 22° 30′ and 23° 2′, long. 75° 53′ and 76° 27′, and embracing an area of 256 square miles. This petty raj or state is held conjointly by two chiefs of the lineage of the Puar or Pramara Rajpoots, now greatly humiliated, but at a remote period so powerful that "the world is the Pramar's," was an ancient saying, denoting their extensive sway.

Their dynasty is recorded to have ruled over Malwa for 1,058 years. In more recent times, we find one of the ancestors of the present rajahs, a military commander in the service of Sevajee, the founder of the Mahratta power, and his two sons, Tukajee and Jewajee, accompanying Bajee Rao, subsequently Peishwa, when appointed soubahdar of Malwa in 1735, and receiving from him Dewas and some other possessions. During the distracted state of Central India which followed, the dominions of the rajahs of Dewas were incessantly overrun by Mahrattas, Pindarries, and other freebooters, their towns and villages sacked, and themselves and families reduced to misery; but since the British protection has been extended to them, their dominions have been restored to order and prosperity. The treaty under which this was granted, is dated in 1818. By its engagements, the rajahs are bound to maintain a contingent force, to be at the disposal of the British government. This force, since the date of the treaty, has been considerably increased, and now consists of 400 infantry, forming part of the Malwa united contingent. The military force of the state consists of 175 horse and 500 foot. The rajahs have agreed to act by a union of authority, and to administer their affairs through one public minister. The revenue amounts to 400,000 rupees, or about 40,000*l.* The population is estimated at about 25,000. The town of Dewas is distant S.E. from Oojein 21 miles. Lat. 22° 58′, long. 76° 4′.

DEWGURH, or DEOGARH, on the coast of the collectorate of Rutnagherry, Southern Concan, presidency of Bombay, a town with a harbour having three or four fathoms of water, and sheltered towards the sea by an island, on which is a fort. In this harbour disembogues the river Seo, flowing W. from the Ghats. Distant S. from Bombay 180 miles. Lat. 16° 22′, long. 73° 25′.

DEWLE.—A town in the British district of Rutnagherry, presidency of Bombay, 25 miles E. of Rutnagherry. Lat. 17°, long. 73° 40′.

DEWRA.—A town of Bundelcund, in the native state of Chutterpore, 10 miles S.E. from Bijawur, and 23 miles S. from Chutterpore. Lat. 24° 34′, long. 79° 40′.

DEWUD.—See DOHUD.

DEWULLEE.—A town on the south-west frontier of Bengal, in the native state of Mohurbunge, 37 miles S.W. from Midnapoor, and 37 miles N. from Balasore. Lat. 22° 3′, long. 86° 58′.

DEWULMURREE.—A town in the British province of Nagpoor, on the left bank of the Prenheta or Weingunga river, and 140 miles S. from Nagpoor. Lat. 19° 20′, long. 80° 1′.

DEYVULPULLY.—A town in Hyderabad, or dominions of the Nizam, 79 miles S.E. from Hyderabad, and 73 miles N.W. from Guntoor. Lat. 16° 50′, long. 79° 35′.

DHABA.—A town in Nagpoor, 30 miles S.E. from Chanda, and 111 miles S. from Nagpoor. Lat 19° 39′, long. 79° 41′.

DHABADDY.—A town in Hyderabad, or dominions of the Nizam, 30 miles N.E. from Aurungabad, and 18 miles N.W. from Jaulnah. Lat. 20° 2′, long. 75° 46′.

DHABREE.—See DATREE.

DHADREE.—A town in a detached portion of the native state of Dhar, on the right bank of the river Nerbudda, and 49 miles S.E. from Mhow. Lat. 22° 17′, long. 76° 28′.

DHALGAON.—A town in the native state of Meeruj, one of the Southern Mahratta jaghires, 75 miles S.E. from Sattara, and 53 miles N.W. from Beejapoor. Lat. 17° 9′, long. 75° 1′.

DHAMA.—A town in the British district of Sumbulpoor, on the south-west frontier of the presidency of Bengal, 16 miles S. of Sumbulpoor. Lat. 21° 15′, long. 84° 5′.

DHAMEE, a small hill state, is bounded on the north by Bhugee; on the east and south by the territories belonging to the rajah of Pateeala; and on the west by Bhagul. Its length probably does not exceed five or six miles, its breadth may be taken to be nearly equal, and its area about twenty-five square miles. Its centre is in lat. 31° 12′, long. 77° 8′. It is throughout a collection of summits of considerable height, with intervening valleys, and is drained northward by a stream which discharges itself into the Sutlej, and southward and westward by a few insignificant streams, feeders of the small river Gumbur. The general elevation of this small territory probably exceeds 4,000 feet. The left bank of the Sutlej at Soomee, to the north, and much lower than the greater part of the country, is 2,283 feet above the sea. It is one of the Barah Thakoorai, or "twelve lordships," which were in the tract between the Sutlej and the Tonse, until the divisions were obliterated by the Gorkha invasion. Dhamee belongs to a petty Hindoo rana or prince, who received it from the British government on the expulsion of the Gorkhas in 1815. It contains seven pergunnahs or subdivisions, estimated to have a population of 3,000, and to yield an annual revenue of 350*l.*, out of which a sum of 72*l.* is paid as tribute to the East-India Company.

DHAMORA.—A river rising in lat. 26° 51′, long. 86° 28′, in the range of the Sub-Himalayas: it flows in a south-easterly direction for fifty miles, through the Terai of Nepal to the boundary of the British district of Tirhoot, from whence it maintains a southerly course for seventy miles, for the greater part of which it either intersects or bounds the district of Bhagulpore, and falls into the Gogaree in lat. 25° 31′, long. 86° 48′.

DHAMONI, or DHAMOUNI, in the British territory of Saugor and Nerbudda, lieut.-gov. of the N.W. Provinces, a town on the frontier towards Bundelcund. The fort of Dhamouni is of triangular ground-plan, and is situate on an eminence, to the eastern brow of which the rampart on that side conforms. The rampart is in general fifty feet high, and in most parts fifteen feet thick, with large round towers. There are besides interior works, strengthening the defences of the eastern quarter, where are the magazines and the residence of the commandant. Westward of the fort is the town, surrounded by a weak wall of loose stones, and to the south-west of the town is a large tank. In 1818, after the defeat and flight of Apa Sahib, rajah of Nagpore, or of Berar, it was invested by a British force under General Marshall, who, having to no purpose offered the garrison 10,000 rupees in payment of arrears, on condition of immediate evacuation, opened batteries against the place with such effect, that in six hours it was yielded unconditionally. Lat. 24° 10′, long. 78° 49′.

DHAMPOOR, in the British district Bijnour, lieut.-gov. of the N.W. Provinces, a town on the route from Moradabad to Hurdwar, and 37 miles N.E. of the former. It contains a good number of old substantial houses, and has a bazar. Elevation above the sea 754 feet. Lat. 29° 19′, long. 78° 34′.

DHAMSALA, or DHURRUMSALA.—A sanatarium for troops in the Jullundur Doab, 92 miles N.W. from Simla, 126 miles N.E. from Lahore. Lat. 32° 13′, long. 76° 22′.

DHANA, in the British territory of Saugor and Nerbudda, lieut.-gov. of the N.W. Provinces, a town 11 miles S.E. from Saugor, 39 miles W. of Dumoh. Lat. 23° 43′, long. 78° 55′.

DHANAPOOR, in the British district of Ghazeepoor, lieut.-gov. of the N.W. Provinces, a town on the right bank of the river Ganges, 19 miles S.W. of Ghazeepoor. Lat. 25° 24′, long. 83° 24′.

DHANNI, in the jaghire of Rampoor, lieut.-gov. of the N.W. Provinces, a village on the route from the town of Bareilly to Almora, and 41 miles N. of the former. Lat. 28° 49′, long. 79° 26′.

DHANRA, in the British district of Gurhwal, lieut.-gov. of the N.W. Provinces, a town on the left bank of the Vishnoo river, 64 miles N.E. of Sireenugur. Lat. 30° 56′, long. 79° 30′.

DHANROWAL.—See BHYROWALAH.

DHAONEE.—See DHANNI.

DHAP, in the British district of Rungpoor, lieut.-gov. of Bengal, a town the principal place of a pergunnah, and situate six miles N.W. of the town of Rungpoor. It is the station of the native officer of police, and contains 300 houses, which, according to the usually admitted ratio of inmates to dwellings, would make the population amount to about 1,500. The vicinity of the town has a pleasing aspect, containing several houses of Europeans embosomed in trees. Lat. 25° 46′, long. 89° 10′.

DHAR, in Bussahir, a considerable village, is situate on the declivity of a hill overlooking the valley of the Pabur. The surrounding country is characterized by Fraser as surpassing in beauty and fertility any which he had seen among the mountains. Lat. 31° 6′, long. 77° 46′.

DHAR.—A town in Hyderabad, distant N.E. from Aurungabad 58 miles, N. from Jaulnah 38 miles. Lat. 20° 23′, long. 76° 4′.

DHAR, in Malwa, the principal place of a raj of the same name, is situate on the route from Mhow to Baroda, 33 miles W. of the former, and 183 E. of the latter. The town is nearly three and a quarter miles in length and half a mile in breadth. It is surrounded by a mud wall, and has many striking buildings, especially two large mosques, built of red stone, but fast falling to decay. Water is abundant, being supplied from two small and eight large tanks. There is a fort, built of red stone, situate outside the city, on an eminence rising forty feet above the plain. The rampart, from thirty to thirty-five feet high, has twenty-four round, and two square towers, on the larger of which last the rajah's palace is, built of stone. The gate of the fort is in the western face, and is defended by octagonal towers. The city is represented to have once contained 20,000 houses, an amount which would assign it a population of about 100,000. At present its numbers fall short of that amount to an extent which would make comparison ludicrous. An English and vernacular school has been established here by the present ruler of Dhar.

The raj or petty state of Dhar contains an area of about 1,070 square miles, and has much fertile ground, producing abundant crops of rice, wheat, millet, maize, pulse, oil-plants, sugar-cane, tobacco, opium, ginger, cotton, hemp, turmeric, esculent vegetables, and pulse. The annual revenue is estimated at 475,000 rupees, or 47,500*l.*; the population at 104,860. The rajah maintains a military force, which, inclusive of the police, amounts to about 1,100 men; and a contribution is made by the state of 8,000 rupees per annum in aid of the support of the Malwa Bheel corps. The rajah is a Puar or Pramar Rajpoot, of a very ancient family, but owes his present dignity to the gift of the Peishwa, about a century ago. Towards the close of the last and in the early part of the present century, the state of Dhar was miserably devastated by the troops of Scindia Holkar and other freebooters; and when the British troops, in 1817, advanced to this part of India, the limits of the state were greatly contracted, and its revenue did not exceed 35,000 rupees. By the intervention of the British government, various districts of which Dhar had been dispossessed were restored to the rajah, and Bairseeah, which had been conquered from the Pindarries, was granted to him, subject to the condition that the British government should retain possession of it for a limited period, for the purpose of liquidating a loan; after which period that government was to have the option of holding it, or of letting it, for the benefit of the Dhar state, which was thenceforth to be entitled to the revenue and produce. This arrangement was made in 1819. In 1821, a new engagement was concluded, by which the district of Bairseeah was ceded to the British government from the expiration of the period of retention before stipulated for; in consideration of which, and of the tribute of Allee Mohun also ceded, a specified annual payment was to be made. The bargain, however, was found a losing one, and Bairseeah was in a few years given back to Dhar; but the home authorities regarding this as an illiberal proceeding towards an ally who had no power to resist, annulled the surrender, and directed the engagement of 1821 to be adhered to. Possession of Bairseeah was consequently resumed, and the stipulated payment restored. By the treaty of 1819 the British government undertook to protect the state of Dhar, in return for which the rajah ceded the tributes of Banswarra and Doongerpore, entered into the usual engagements of subordinate co-operation and friendly alliance, and bound himself, at all times when required, to furnish troops in proportion to his ability. Elevation of the town above the sea 1,908 feet. Lat. 22° 35′, long. 75° 20′.

DHAREE DEBEE, in the British district of Kumaon, lieut.-gov. of the N.W. Provinces, a village on the route from Almora to Sireenuggur, and 10 miles S.E. of the latter. Lat. 30° 15′, long. 78° 55′.

DHARMA, in the British district of Kumaon, lieut.-gov. of the N.W. Provinces, a Bhotia mahall or subdivision, lying north of the main range of the Himalaya, and between it and Hiundes, or South-western Tibet. Still some of the summits have a great elevation; Lebong, on the eastern frontier, being 18,942 feet above the sea. The elevation of the Dharma pass, on the northern frontier, leading to Hiundes, is probably about 15,000. The whole habitable portion consists of the narrow and generally very rugged valleys down which flow the river Dhouli and its feeders; the rest consists of rocks or mountains, covered with perpetual snow. The boundaries of a tract so ill peopled and difficult to explore are not very precisely defined, but they may be considered as lying between lat. 30° 5′—30° 30′, long. 80° 25′—80° 45′, and as inclosing an area of about 400 square miles. When Traill drew up his account, it had twenty-four villages, containing 342 houses; and consequently, if six persons be allowed to each house, the population may be estimated at 2,052, or between four and five to the square mile. They are called Bhotias, and are of the Mongolian or Tartar variety of the human race. "In their personal appearance," observes Traill, "the Bhotias are perfect Tartars, and exceed the natives of this province in size and stature, more particularly the Dharma Bhotias, among whom individuals possessing extraordinary strength are by no means uncommon. They are excessively dirty in their persons, using the skirts of their dress to cleanse both their persons and their cooking utensils, yet are in good circumstances, having warm clothing, substantial houses, and abundance of animal food in the flesh of their numerous sheep and goats, used as beasts of burthen in the lucrative carrying-trade with Hiundes. In the course of this commerce, grain, the produce of Lower Kumaon, and cotton broadcloths, hardware, sugar, and other goods, brought from Hindoostan, are sent to Hiundes, and exchanged for culinary salt, tincal or borax, gold dust, and wool; besides some others of less importance.

DHARMDA.—A town in the British district of Midnapoor, lieut.-gov. of Bengal, six miles S.W. of Midnapoor. Lat. 22° 21′, long. 87° 19′.

DHARMKOT, in Sirhind, a small town in the British district of Ferozepore, with a fort, situate about seven miles from the left bank of the Sutlej. Dharmkot is distant 39 miles W. from Loodiana, N.W. from Calcutta 1,140 miles. Lat. 30° 55′, long. 75° 17′.

DHARMSALEH.—A town in the native state of Nepal, on the left bank of the river Kurnalli, and 126 miles N.E. from Almora. Lat. 29° 51′, long. 81° 45′.

DHARWAR, in the presidency of Bombay, a British district, named from its principal place. Previously to 1836, the collectorate of Dharwar consisted of eighteen talooks, stretching nearly 300 miles from north to south. In that year the ten northern talooks were formed into a new district, denominated the Collectorate of Belgaum, those in the south remaining under the control of the collector of Dharwar, and forming the district now distinguished by that name. As at present constituted, the district of Dharwar is bounded on the north by the Belgaum collectorate; on the east by the territory of the Nizam and the British collectorate of Bellary; on the south by the Mysore dominions; and on the west by the Madras territory and the Belgaum collectorate. It extends from lat. 14° 16′ to 15° 50′, and from long. 74° 50′ to 76°. Its greatest length from north to south is 105 miles; its greatest breadth ftom east to west 77 miles. The area is 3,837 square miles. A great part of the collectorate consists of extensive plains. A small portion has an inclination to the south-west, as indicated by the direction taken by the streams, which, flowing towards that point, fall into the Kali Nadi, a river making its way through a deep valley in the Ghauts to the Arabian Sea or North Indian Ocean. The Tumbudra, rising in the territory of Mysore, on the eastern declivity of the Ghauts, flows for ninety-five miles to the southern boundary of the collectorate; thence continuing its course circuitously, but generally towards the north-east, for sixty-five miles, it forms the boundary between this collectorate and that of Bellary. In lat. 14° 56′, long. 75° 46′, this river receives on the left side the Wurda, rising on the eastern declivity of the Ghauts, and flowing north-easterly for a distance of fifty miles. In many parts of the collectorate of Dharwar the soil is fertile, and well suited to the growth of cotton. Various attempts have been made by the Bombay government for the introduction of the New Orleans species. Previous experiments having failed, the last was commenced in 1842, and has been attended with success. In that year twenty-five acres only were sown with American cotton. It was cultivated by the ryots in the midst of their own native products, and much in the same manner, excepting that the American cotton was sown some weeks earlier. The return of the newly-introduced species being found much larger than that of the indigenous article, and the quality considered superior, the cultivation spread with extraordinary rapidity. Small experimental farms were established by government; but these, except in so far as they tended to provide a supply of seed, seem to have been of no value, as it is stated by competent authority, that the cultivation of the ryots themselves excelled that of the farms. These establishments were consequently soon relinquished, and the breadth of land devoted to the cultivation of American cotton continued, without artificial aid, to extend, until, in five years only from the date of the successful experiment, it had reached 25,000 acres; and it is stated that, but for the occurrence of unfavousable weather at the proper time for sowing, it would have amounted to 60,000 acres. The superiority of the New Orleans cotton over the indigenous species is now generally recognised in Dharwar. The principal marts are Hooblee, Havery, Narragoorda, Sircy, Noolgoond, and Balgapoor. Their distances vary from 80 to 130 miles from the Madras port of Coompta, to which a good road for wheeled carriages has been constructed, and where the cotton is shipped for Bombay. The population of this collectorate is for the most part Canarese, the Mahrattas, though once the ruling race, not amounting now to more than a tenth of the whole. Canarese, the language of the people, was, therefore, in 1836, judiciously substituted for Mahratta, in the transaction of official business. The population is given under the article BOMBAY. Dharwar, the principal town, and Hooblee, as well as others of note, are described under their respective names in the alphabetical arrangement. The principal roads are the following:—One leading from south-east to north-west, from the town of Dharwar to Belgaum, and thence eastward, through Sawunt Warree, to the port of Vingorla; another, from south-east to north-west, from the town of Dharwar to Kolapore; and a third, from Dharwar to Hooblee, and thence to Wuddeguttee, on the Canara frontier of the Madras territory, there to join the road constructed by the Madras government for facilitating the inland trade between Dharwar and the port of Coompta.

The territory comprised within the collectorate of Dharwar appears at the earliest recorded period to have formed part of the Brahminical realm of Vijayanagar, and on its overthrow, by the defeat of its rajah at Talikot, in 1565, by a Mussulman confederation, to have become part of the kingdom of Beejapoor. In 1675 it seems to have been overrun and partially conquered by Sevajee, the notorious founder of the Mahratta sway, becoming thereby subject to the power of the rajah of Sattara, and subsequently to that of the Peishwa. In 1776 the province was overrun by Hyder Ali, the usurping sultan of Mysore. The capture by that chief, in 1778, of the fort and town of Dharwar, and their recapture, in 1791, by a British force acting in co-operation with the Mahrattas, are noticed in the article on the town. On the overthrow of the Peishwa in 1818, Dharwar was incorporated with the territory of the East-India Company.

DHARWAR, the principal place of the British collectorate of the same name, in the presidency of Bombay, is situate close to the frontier which divides the Bombay territory from the Madras collectorate of Canara. Duff, describing its condition, says, "The defences of this fortress are principally of mud, and though irregular and now greatly decayed, were then [in 1790] very strong. It is situated in a plain, having an outer and an inner ditch from twenty-five to thirty feet wide, and nearly as many feet deep. Adjoining to the fort on the south side, and outflanking it to the eastward, is a town or pettah, defended by a low mud wall and a ditch of no strength." In 1837, this place was the scene of religious disputes between the Brahmins and Lingayets, which rose to such a height as to render necessary the interference of authority. The principle upon which the British government have acted in such matters, is to allow to the members of every religious persuasion the undisturbed exercise of their own rites and ceremonies so long as they are unattended with danger to the public peace. The Vrayasunthole procession at Dharwar, in the judgment of the Bombay government, was incompatible with this necessary condition, in consequence of the mutual animosity subsisting between the Lingayets and the Brahmins, and it was determined that it should not again take place. Two of the government vernacular schools, the one Mahratta and the other Canarese, are established in this town; as is also one of the government English schools. In 1778, Dharwar was taken from the Mahrattas by Hyder Ali, the sultan of Mysore, and in 1791 retaken by a British force auxiliary to the Mahrattas, who very little furthered the operations. On the final overthrow of the Peishwa, this place, with the other possessions of that potentate, fell to the disposal of the British government. Distant from Bombay, S.E., 288 miles; from Poona, 223; from Sattara, 170; from Goa, E., 70; Hyderabad, S.W., 270; Seringapatam, N.W., 235. Lat. 15° 28′, long. 75° 4′.

DHATA, in the British district of Futtehpore, lieut.-gov. of the N.W. Provinces, a town, the principal place of the pergunnah of the same name, five miles N.E. of the left bank of the Jumna, 36 miles S.E. of the town of Futtehpore. Lat. 25° 32′, long. 81° 20′.

DHATA, in Sirhind, a village on the route from Hansee to Lodiana, 13 miles N. of the former town. It is situate in a level country partially cultivated, and yielding moderate supplies. The road in this part of the route is good. Distant N.W. from Calcutta 989 miles. Lat. 29° 16′, long. 76° 5′.

DHAYABUNG.—A town in the native state of Nepal, on the left bank of the river Bori Gunduk, and 29 miles N. from Khatmandoo. Lat. 28° 3′, long. 85° 3′.

DHEBUROOA, in the British district of Goruckpoor, lieut.-gov. of the N.W. Provinces, a town on the left bank of the river Raptee, 60 miles N.W. of Goruckpoor. Lat. 27° 24′, long. 82° 51′.

DHEEGWAS, or **DHIGONS**, in the district of Ahladganj, territory of Oude, a town 30 miles N.W. of Allahabad, 80 S.E. of Lucknow. Butter estimates the population at 8,000, all Hindoos.

DHEEISMAELPOOR. — A town in the British district of Midnapoor, lieut.-gov. of Bengal, 40 miles S. of Midnapoor. Lat. 21° 50′, long. 87° 21′.

DHEEMAHPOOR, in Eastern India, a town in the recently lapsed territory of Tooleram Senahputtee, situate on the left bank of the river Dhunseeree, and 70 miles S.E. from Nowgong. Lat. 25° 53′, long. 93° 46′.

DHEEPA.—A town in the native state of Singboom, on the S.W. frontier of Bengal, 39 miles S.W. from Chaibassa, and 100 miles N.E. from Sumbulpoor. Lat. 22° 19′, long. 85° 18′.

DHEKULOO, in the British district of Kumaon, lieut.-gov. of the N.W. Provinces, a guardhouse and military station on the route from Moradabad to Almora, and fifty miles north-east of the former. It is situate in the valley down which the river Kosilla flows from the mountains to the plains, on the right bank of the stream, and amidst scenery described by Heber as being as wild and romantic as ever painted by Salvator Rosa. Elevation above the sea 1,221 feet. Lat. 29° 29′, long. 79° 12′.

DHENKANAUL, one of the independent hill tribes known as the Cuttack Mehals, adjoining the British district of Cuttack: it is situated on the banks of the Braminy river, and its centre is about lat. 20° 45′, long. 85° 30′.

DHEN KANAULGUR.—A town in the native state of Dhenkanaul, one of the Cuttack Mehals, 25 miles N.W. from Cuttack, and 62 miles N.W. from Juggernaut. Lat. 20° 40′, long. 85° 36′.

DHERALEE, in Gurhwal, a village on the left bank of the Ganges, or Bhageerettee, as that river is called in the upper part of its course. It is situate in a rocky recess, and commands a fine view of the river, and beyond it of the snow-clad peaks of Jumnotri, towering over forests of cedar. There are on the river side three small temples built of stone, and of good workmanship. Lat. 31° 2′, long. 78° 49′.

DHERGAUM. — A town in the British district of Akraunee, presidency of Bombay, 73 miles E. of Broach. Lat. 21° 53′, long. 74° 10′.

DHERIAGOTE, or **SOEE**.—A small village in Sinde, on the route from Sehwan to Larkhana, and 22 miles S. of the latter place. It is situate in the extensive and fertile island inclosed between the Indus and its great offset the Narra, and is seven miles from the right bank of the former, and three miles from the left bank of the latter. Lat. 27° 10′, long. 68° 4′.

DHI.—A town in a detached portion of the possessions of Holkar, situate 78 miles S.W. from Mhow, and 90 miles E. from Baroda. Lat. 22° 9′, long. 74° 37′.

DHINISA.—A town in the native state of Nepal, situate 50 miles N. from Nepal. Lat. 28° 24′, long. 85° 22′.

DHOA, in the territory of Gwalior, or possessions of Scindia, a town 20 miles S.W. of the fort of Gwalior. Lat. 26° 3′, long. 77° 54′.

DHOBHUNG.—A town in the native state of Nepal, 104 miles S.E. from Khatmandoo, and 90 miles W. from Darjeeling. Lat. 27° 17′, long. 86° 54′.

DHODA, in the Peshawur division of the Punjab, a town situated on the route from Kala Bagh to Kohaut, 14 miles S. of the latter. Lat. 33° 27′, long. 71° 45′.

DHOKI.—A town in one of the recently sequestrated districts of Hyderabad, or dominions of the Nizam, 50 miles N. from Sholapoor, and 102 miles S. from Jaulnah. Lat. 18° 22′, long. 76° 10′.

DHOLARRA, or **DHOLERA**, in the peninsula of Kattywar, province of Guzerat, a town within the British district of Ahmedabad, in the swampy tract extending along the western side of the Gulf of Cambay. The space between the town and the port of Dholera, a distance of about four miles, is traversed by a tramway, constructed by a company of native speculators. The line was opened in May, 1851, and bids fair to be highly profitable to its projectors. Distance from the city of Ahmedabad, S.W., 65 miles. Lat. 22° 11′, long. 72° 11′.

DHOLATGHAT.—A town in the native state of Nepal, 27 miles S.E. from Khatmandoo. Lat. 27° 34′, long. 85° 41′.

DHOLKA, in the British district Ahmedabad, presidency of Bombay, a town situate amidst ruined palaces, mosques, mausoleums, and fine and spacious tanks, embanked and lined with masonry. Though not regularly fortified, it is surrounded by a wall of mud four miles in circuit. Population 25,000. Distance from Ahmedabad, S.W., 22 miles; Baroda, N.W., 60; Surat, N., 110; Bombay, N., 262. Lat. 22° 42′, long. 72° 25′.

DHOLNUH, in the British district of Budaon, lieut.-gov. of the N.W. Provinces, a village on the route from Futtehgurh to Meerut, and 80 miles N.W. of the former place. Lat. 27° 50′, long. 78° 36′.

DHOLPORE.—A small raj or territory on the northern bank of the Chumbul river, named from its principal place, and bounded on the north and north-east by the British district of Agra; on the south-east by the Chumbul, dividing it from the territory of Gwalior; and on the west by the territory of Kerowly. It lies between lat. 26° 30′—26° 57′, long. 77° 32′—78° 20′; is about fifty-four miles in length from north-east to south-west, twenty-three in breadth, and has an area of 1,626 square miles. The large river Chumbul, touching on the territory at its south-west angle, forms its south-eastern boundary for about sixty miles, and subsequently flowing eastward, forms the boundary between the British district of Agra and the territory of Gwalior. The Bangunga, called in this part of its course the Ootungun, after forming the boundary for a few miles, passes to the interior, through which it flows in a direction generally easterly for about fourteen miles, and subsequently, for twenty miles, forms the boundary between this territory and the district of Agra. In its course along the frontier, it on the right or south side, and in lat. 26° 54′, long. 77° 57′, receives the torrent Parbutty, flowing in a direction from south-west to north-east through this territory, which it enters from the territory of Kerowly. The surface of the country in the eastern part is generally level and sandy; the south-western part is hilly, being overspread with low ranges of sandstone, connected with the hills of Gwalior. Notwithstanding the poor quality of the soil, it is rendered fertile by continual irrigation, and in due season is covered with fine crops, interspersed with groves of mango-trees.

The principal towns of the territory—Dholpore, Baree, and Rajahkera—are described under their respective names in the alphabetical arrangement. If the population be assumed at the rate of that of the surrounding British districts, it will amount to 550,000. The revenue is estimated at 700,000 rupees, or 70,000*l.* per annum. The principal route through the country is from north to south, from Agra to Gwalior, by the town of Dholpore. The chief, who is styled Rana, and the majority of his subjects, are Jauts, who, according to the Brahminical notions respecting caste, are a spurious offset of the Rajpoots. Probably the first of the Rana's ancestors who rose into notice was the chief of Gohud, who, about the middle of the eighteenth century, acquired territory by the favour of the Peishwa Bajee Rao, but on the defeat of the Mahrattas at Paneeput, rebelled, and about 1761 made himself master of Gwalior and the adjacent country. The political relations between the Rana and the East-India Company commenced in 1779, when the respective parties formed a treaty of alliance, offensive and defensive, in which it was stipulated, that when peace should be concluded between the Company and the Mahrattas, the Rana should be included in it, and that his then present possessions, and such acquisitions made during the war as it should be agreed to leave in his hands, were to be guaranteed to him, together with the fort of Gwalior, recognised as of old belonging to the family of the Rana, if at the time of the peace he should be in possession of it. In 1780, that fort having been taken by a British detachment under Major Popham, was made over to the Rana, from whom subsequently it was wrested by Scindia, in 1784, the British government having abandoned the Rana, on the ground that he had been guilty of treachery. In 1804, however, that government engaged to establish the Rana in his hereditary dominions of Gohud, and certain districts enumerated in the treaty of that date; but difficulties arising in the way of carrying out this engagement, in consequence of the opposition of Scindia, the Rana agreed, by a new treaty, concluded in December, 1805, to relinquish the possessions thus guaranteed, receiving in their stead those which he now holds, comprising three districts—Dholpore proper, Baree, and Rajahkeri. Hence the chief is sometimes, though rather inaccurately, styled the Rana of Dholpore Baree. The military force maintained by the Rana, inclusive of the quotas of the jaghiredars, consists of about 2,000 men.

DHOLPORE.—The principal place of the small raj or territory of the same name, a town on the route from Agra to Gwalior, 34 miles S. of the former, 37 N. of the latter. It is situate a mile from the north-west or left bank of the Chumbul, here crossed by ferry, but fordable at Keytri, four miles higher up the stream, though the channel is there three-quarters of a mile wide. The river during the rainy season rushes down with a vast volume of water, overflowing the right bank, but restrained by the left, which is high and steep, so that the fort situate on it has a striking appearance. Here are some fine antique mosques and mausoleums. One of the mosques is stated to have been built by Shah Jahan in

1634; and some other of the buildings here are of still earlier date. They "are all elaborately built, and worked out of the fine freestone of the country; and the trellis-work upon some of their stone screens is still as beautiful as when first made." Dholpore is an ancient place, and was founded at a very remote period by a prince called Daula, from whom the name has been derived. Such, at least, is the traditional report of the natives, as recorded by Tieffenthaler. Baber repeatedly mentions the place, and states that it surrendered to him in 1526. He adds, that, seeing a huge solid mass of red stone there, he ordered it to be hewn into a house, if practicable; but finding that it had not sufficient depth for that purpose, he caused the top of the rock to be levelled, and a tank excavated therein. He also caused a palace, a mosque, a pleasure-ground, and a well to be formed near it. At present there is encamping-ground here, and a large bungalow or lodge for travellers, built by a former British resident, and purchased by the Rana for its present purpose. Distant N.W. from Calcutta, by Etawa, 793 miles. Lat. 26° 41′, long. 77° 58′.

DHOLPURI, in the British district of Moradabad, lieut.-gov. of the N.W. Provinces, a village on the route from the town of Moradabad to Almora, and 16 miles N. of the former. Lat. 29° 2′, long. 78° 56′.

DHOOLIA.—A considerable town in the British district of Candeish, presidency of Bombay, situate on the great route from Bombay to the city of Agra, 181 miles N.E. of Bombay. Lat. 20° 54′, long. 74° 45′.

DHOOLIAT.—A town in the native state of Gwalior, or territory of Scindia, 11 miles W. from Asseergurh, and 80 miles S. from Mhow. Lat. 21° 29′, long. 76° 17′.

DHOOM.—A town in the native state of Nepal, 91 miles N.E. from Pilleebheet, and 104 miles S.E. from Almora. Lat. 29° 3′, long. 81° 19′.

DHOOMA, in the British territory of Saugor and Nerbudda, lieut.-gov. of the N.W. Provinces, a town on the route from Nagpoor to Jubbulpoor, 40 miles S. of the latter. Lat. 22° 44′, long. 79° 50′.

DHOONDA, in Gurwhal, a village on the right bank of the Bhageerettee, as the Ganges is called in the upper part of its course. The road to the south is of extreme difficulty and danger, along the face of a precipitous mountain rising over the river on its right side. Dhoonda is in lat. 30° 41′, long. 78° 24′.

DHOONDGUL.—A town in Hyderabad, or dominions of the Nizam, 19 miles N. from Hyderabad, and 60 miles S.E. from Beder. Lat. 17° 38′, long. 78° 30′.

DHOOR.—A town in the British district of Cuddapah, presidency of Madras, 29 miles N. of Cuddapah. Lat. 14° 51′, long. 78° 48′.

DHOORCATEE, the smallest of the protected hill states between the Sutlej and the Tonse, is bounded on the east by Bussahir, and on all other sides by the British district of Kothkaee. Its area is not more than five miles. Its centre is in lat. 31° 8′, long. 77° 40′. The surface has considerable elevation, the district containing the peak of Toongroo, which rises to the height of 10,102 feet above the sea, and whence streams flowing on the west to the Giree, and on the north to the Pabur, become feeders to those rivers. This state comprises only a single pergunnah, with a population of 200 and a revenue of 40*l*. It is free from tribute.

DHOOREE, in Sirhind, a village on the route from Hansee to Loodiana, and 41 miles S. of the latter town. It is situate in a country having a slightly-undulated surface, fertile, and partially cultivated. Distant N.W. from Calcutta 1,062 miles. Lat. 30° 22′, long. 75° 57′.

DHOOREEAPOOR is the principal place of the pergunnah of the same name, in the British district of Goruckpore, lieut.-gov. of Agra, situate three miles to the west or left of the route from Azimgurh to Goruckpore, and distant 34 miles N. of the former, 28 S. of the latter. It is styled by Buchanan a market-town. Distant N. from Ghazeepore 78 miles, N.E. from Calcutta 509. Lat. 26° 23′, long. 83° 18′.

DHOOS, in the British district of Benares, lieut.-gov. of the N.W. Provinces, a town on the route from Benares to Sasseram, 10 miles E. of the former. Lat. 25° 16′, long. 83° 14′.

DHOR, in the Peshawur division of the Punjab, a town situated on the left bank of the river Indus, five miles S. of the town of Attock. Lat. 33° 50′, long. 72° 20′.

DHORAOO.—A town in the British district of Bolundshuhur, lieut.-gov. of the N.W. Provinces, 70 miles S.E. of Delhi. Lat. 28° 7′, long. 78° 14′.

DHORAJEE.—A town in the peninsula of Kattywar, province of Guzerat, 43 miles S.W. from Rajkote, and 52 miles E. from Poorbundur. Lat. 21° 45′, long. 70° 33′.

DHORI, in the British district of Azimgurh, lieut.-gov. of the N.W. Provinces, a village on the route from the town of Azimgurh to Goruckpore cantonment, 31 miles N.E. of the former, 34 S.E. of the latter. It is situate on the right bank of the Ghogra, here a great river, confined to one channel crossed by a ferry. Lat. 26° 14′, long. 83° 33′.

DHOULAGIRI, in Nepal, one of the highest peaks of the great Snowy range of the Himalayas, being 27,600 feet above the level of the sea. Lat. 29° 11′, long. 82° 59′.

DHOULI, a principal head-water or tributary of the great river Ghoghra, has its remotest source at the southern base of the Neo Dhoora Ghat, or pass leading from the Bhotia mahall, or subdivision of Dharma, to Hiundes or South-western Tibet, and at an elevation above the sea of probably about

15,000 feet, and in lat. 30° 28′, long. 80° 33′. Its source is to the north of the main range of the Himalaya, through which it holds its way by the valley of the Dharma mahall or subdivision, and flows at the western base of the great mountain Lebong. About thirty-five miles from its source, and in lat. 30° 5′, long. 80° 40′, it touches on the mahall of Choundans, the western frontier of which it forms for fifteen miles, and falls into the Kalee on the right side, in lat. 29° 57′, long. 80° 38′. Its stream is in general a succession of violent rapids in a rocky channel, amidst awful precipices and ravines. Webb describes it, at twenty-five miles from its source, as "violent, turbid, in continued rapids from six to twenty-five feet; bed rocky, average breadth from sixteen to twenty yards;" and adds, that after rain "the water is so foul and turbid as to be unfit for drinking." The road to Hiundes by the Neo Dhoora Pass proceeds up the course of the river, passing by means of spar bridges from side to side, according to the exigencies of the path, which sometimes winds along the faces of the nearly perpendicular precipices; yet, during the season when the passes are open, this difficult track is crowded by innumerable laden goats and sheep, bearing grain and other merchandise from the lower districts to Hiundes.

DHOUR BOONGA, in the British district of Gurhwal, lieut.-gov. of the N.W. Provinces, a town on the right bank of the river Sanee, 20 miles S. of Sireenuggur. Lat. 29° 57′, long. 78° 52′.

DHOURERA.—A town in the territory of Oude, 80 miles N. from Lucknow, and 73 miles E. from Shahjehanpoor. Lat. 28°, long. 81° 9′.

DHOWLUTNUGUR, in the Jetch Dooab division of the Punjab, a town situated on the route from Wazeerabad to Bhimbur, 20 miles N. of the former. Lat. 32° 47′, long. 74° 9′.

DHUBBOOEE, in Guzerat, or the territory of the Guicowar, an ancient decayed town. It has a nearly quadrangular ground-plan, and is inclosed with a rampart two miles in circuit, made of large hewn stones, and having on the interior side a beautiful and useful colonnade of the same material. Within this inclosure is a large tank of strong masonry, access to the water of which is by means of a grand flight of stairs extending quite round it, and on the well-constructed stone embankment are numerous Brahminical temples. The total circuit of the tank is considerable, it being supplied with water not only from the periodical rains, but also by means of an aqueduct of stone, conveying it from the country outside. Viewed from the country, Dhubbooee has a noble aspect, its ramparts being surmounted by fifty-two towers, besides one at each angle, of superior dimensions to the rest. In each face of the quadrangular rampart is a double gate, with a spacious area between, surrounded by a corridor and guard-rooms. The portal on the eastern side is called the "Gate of Diamonds," and with the temple adjoining, forms a very noble and elegant specimen of Hindoo architecture. It extends 320 feet in length, with proportionate height, and the upper part of the building is supported by rows of figures of elephants sculptured in stone, and represented as richly caparisoned. All parts of these superb buildings are embellished with a profusion of sculptures, representing warriors in combat on horses, on foot, or on elephants, in a very superior style of execution; and there are besides, sculptures innumerable of lions, camels, birds, snakes, and various other animals. A considerable part of the ramparts and other buildings have been destroyed by the hand of time and by invading Mussulmans. According to native tradition, these magnificent structures, including the fortifications, tank, and temples, cost upwards of ten millions sterling. The vast quantity of massive hewn stone used in them, is calculated to excite the greater surprise, as not the smallest pebble is to be met with in this part of Guzerat. The place swarms with monkeys, which are supported, encouraged, and protected by the inhabitants, though very mischievous and troublesome. Distance from Baroda, S.E., 15 miles; Surat, N.E., 78; Bombay, N., 225; Ahmedabad, S.E., 80. Lat. 22° 8′, long. 73° 25′.

DHUJ PEAK, in the British district of Kumaon, lieut.-gov. of the N.W. Provinces, a summit of the Sub-Himalaya, or mountain-system south of the great range, east of Fort Almorah 40 miles, and equidistant from the rivers Ramganga (Eastern) and Kalee (Eastern). Elevation above the sea 8,248 feet. Lat. 29° 38′, long. 80° 20′.

DHUKOWLEA, in the British district of Futtehpoor, lieut.-gov. of the N.W. Provinces, a village on the route from Banda to the town of Futtehpoor, and four miles S.W. of the latter. Lat. 25° 54′, long. 80° 50′.

DHUMDA.—A town in the British province of Nagpoor, 135 miles E. from Nagpoor, and 30 miles N.W. from Ryepoor. Lat. 21° 23′, long. 81° 14′.

DHUMRAH, or DOMRAH RIVER, in Cuttack, the name of the principal outlet of the Byeturnee: its mouth is in lat. 20° 59′, long. 87° 2′.

DHUMRAH.—A town in the British district of Cuttack, lieut.-gov. of Bengal, 71 miles N.E. of Cuttack. Lat. 20° 50′, long. 86° 59′.

DHUMTERRY.—A town in the British province of Nagpoor, distant E. from Nagpoor 150 miles. Lat. 20° 39′, long. 81° 26′.

DHUMTHAN, in Sirhind, a halting-place in the British district of Kythul, on the route from Hansee to Loodiana, and 43 miles N. of the former town. Distant N.W. from Calcutta 1,019 miles. Lat. 29° 42′, long. 76° 5′.

DHUMTOUR, or DUMTAUR, in the

British province of the Punjab, a valley extending nearly in a direction from east to west, in lat. 34°—34° 10′, and long. 72° 55′—73° 15′. It is described by Baron Hügel, who explored it, as giving the impression of having been once the bed of a vast torrent. It is still furrowed by numerous watercourses, discharging themselves into the river Dor, which flows with a scanty stream in a stony channel half a mile wide. Here the traveller, descending from the elevated country lying to the north, finds the vegetation assuming the character of that which prevails in Hindostan. The sugar-cane especially is grown in such abundance, that it forms a principal article of fodder for cattle. The mountains which inclose the valley on the north-west are clothed with dense and luxuriant forests of oak, pine, walnut, wild olive, and plane trees. The valley is populous, and abounds in villages, each defended by a small fort. Dhumtoor, which gives name to the valley and district, is a small and poor place. The inhabitants are Eusufzai Afghans.

DHUMTOUR, in the Punjab, a small town, 16 miles E. of the Indus, lying on the route into Cashmere, by the Dub Pass. It is situate in a beautiful, well-watered, and productive valley, crowded with small forts, erected and maintained on account of the dangerous proximity of the Eusufzais. Lat. 34° 7′, long. 73° 7′.

DHUNAIREE.—A town in the province of Guzerat, or dominions of the Guicowar, 26 miles N. from Deesa, and 140 miles S.W. from Oodeypoor. Lat. 24° 37′, long. 72°.

DHUNCHI.—A town in the native state of Nepal, 42 miles N. from Khatmandoo. Lat. 28° 19′, long. 85° 14′.

DHUNELA, in the territory of Gwalior, or possessions of Scindia, a small town on the route from Agra to the fort of Gwalior, 60 miles S. of former, 11 N.W. of latter. It has a bazar, and supplies may be obtained. Here, on the 24th December, 1843, was the encampment of the Mahratta army, consisting of twenty-two regiments, with a large and well-appointed park of artillery, advancing to give battle to the British, posted at the neighbouring village of Hingona, under Sir Hugh Gough, commander-in-chief. Lat. 26° 24′, long. 78° 8′.

DHUNGAWAN, in the British district of Sohagpoor, territory of Saugor and Nerbudda, lieut.-gov. of the N.W. Provinces, a town 34 miles S.E. of Sohagpoor, 119 miles E. of Jubbulpoor. Lat. 23° 2′, long. 81° 52′.

DHUNGOEE.—A town in the British district of Sarun, lieut.-gov. of Bengal, 39 miles N. of Chupra. Lat. 26° 17′, long. 84° 40′.

DHUNGSURRA, in the Rajpoot state of Joudpore, a village on the route from Jessulmeer, *viâ* Nagor, to Nusseerabad, and 102 miles N.W. of the latter. Lat. 27° 8′, long. 73° 35′.

DHUNGURHEE.—A town in the territory of Oude, 130 miles N. from Lucknow, and 53 miles E. from Pilleebheet. Lat. 28° 41′, long. 80° 47′.

DHUNOWDA, in Sirhind, a small town with a bazar, on the direct route from Hansee to Loodiana, and 30 miles N. of the former place. Provisions may be had in abundance, and water from wells. Distant N.W. from Calcutta 1,006 miles. Lat. 29° 31′, long. 76° 4′.

DHUNSEEREE, a considerable feeder of the Brahmapootra river, rises in lat. 25° 20′, long. 93° 33′, on the southern frontier of Tooleram Senaputtee's country, and, flowing in a northerly direction through that country for twenty-one miles, then forming its boundary for forty-six miles on the side of the Nagor territory, subsequently separating the latter for the distance of thirty miles from the British territory of Nowgong, it traverses Assam for thirty miles, and falls into the Brahmapootra on the left side, in lat. 26° 41′, long. 93° 44′.

DHUNTALAO, in the territory of Gwalior, or possessions of Scindia, a village on the route from Hoshungabad to Neemuch, 93 miles W. of former, 181 S.E. of latter. It is situate at the north-west extremity, or on the crest of a pass leading from the valley of the Nerbudda to the table-land of Malwa. Lat. 22° 44′, long. 76° 32′.

DHUNWA.—A town in the Rajpoot state of Jessulmeer, five miles S. from Jessulmeer, and 62 miles W. from Pokurn. Lat. 26° 50′, long. 71°.

DHUR, in the mahall or subdivision of Dharma, British district of Kumaon, a village a mile from the right bank of the river Doulee. East of the village, a hot spring throws up a dense and powerful stream. The banks of its small channel are tinged of an ochreous hue, partly occasioned by its heat, and partly, perhaps, from a chalybeate quality. Elevation above the sea probably about 8,000 feet. Lat. 30° 5′, long. 80° 37′.

DHURAMPORE.—A town in the native state of Nepal, 70 miles S.E. from Khatmandoo, and 50 miles N. from Durbunga. Lat. 26° 52′, long. 85° 55′.

DHURAVEE.—An island situate to the north-west of Salsette, off the coast of Bombay: it is about seven miles long by two broad, and its centre is in lat. 19° 14′, long. 72° 53′.

DHURKOT.—A town in the native state of Nepal, 162 miles N.W. from Khatmandoo, and 122 miles N.W. from Goruckpoor. Lat. 28° 22′, long. 82° 48′.

DHUROWLEE, or DEROWLI, in the British district of Furruckabad, lieut.-gov. of the N.W. Provinces, a village on the route from the cantonment of Allygurh to that of Futtehgurh, and 39 miles W. of the latter Lat. 27° 30′, long. 79° 7′.

DHURPHUREEPUTTEE. — A town in the British district of Tirhoot, lieut.-gov. of Bengal, 27 miles W. of Mozufferpoor. Lat. 26° 7′, long. 85° 2′.

DHURRUMPOOR, a petty Rajpoot state under the political superintendence of the government of Bombay, is bounded on the north by the petty raj of Bansda; on the east by the Daung; on the south by the district of the rajah of Penth; and on the west by the British district of Surat. The country (which includes an area of about 225 miles), overrun with dense forest, admits of little cultivation. The revenue is estimated at 91,000 rupees, or 9,100*l.* The rana maintains a small military establishment, and the population of his territory is returned at 16,650 inhabitants. In 1831 the rajah's pecuniary embarrassments led him to mortgage to his creditors the revenues of a portion of his villages, he agreeing to abstain from all interference in the revenue or police management of these mortgaged villages until his creditors' claims should be liquidated; but, at a later date, it being found that public inconvenience was occasioned from the suspension of the rajah's exercise of the powers of police, he was authorized by the Bombay government to resume them, but subject to the general control of the British agent. The rajah of Dhurrumpore was formerly tributary to the Peishwa, but by the treaty of Bassein, concluded in 1802, the tribute was transferred to the British, and rated in the schedule of the treaty at 9,000 rupees per annum. The town of Dhurrumpore is in lat. 20° 31′, long. 73° 15′.

DHURUMPOOREE. — A town in the native state of Dhar, in Malwa, 29 miles S. from Dhar, and 35 miles S.W. from Mhow. Lat. 22° 10′, long. 75° 26′.

DHURUMPOOREE.—A town in the British territory of Sattara, presidency of Bombay, 49 miles N.E. of Sattara. Lat. 17° 57′, long. 74° 44′.

DHURUMSAL.—A town in the native state of Cashmere, or territory of Gholab Singh, 39 miles N.E. from Jhelum, and 78 miles S.W. from Sirinagur. Lat. 33° 15′, long. 74° 10′.

DHURUMSALLA. — A village in the native state of Cutch, presidency of Bombay, eight miles S. of Bhooj. Lat. 23° 9′, long. 69° 41′.

DHUTARA, in the British district of Boolundshuhur, lieut. gov. of the N.W. Provinces, a village on the route from Khasganj to Meerut, and 45 miles S. of the latter. Lat. 28° 23′, long. 77° 58′.

DHYWELL.—A town in the British district of Candeish, presidency of Bombay, 41 miles W. of Dhoolia. Lat. 21° 2′, long. 74° 7′.

DIAMOND ISLAND, or LYCHUNE ISLAND, situate at the mouth of the Negrais river: it is low, covered with trees, about a mile and a half in extent, and surrounded with reefs. It is considered unhealthy and dangerous to remain on it during the night. H.M.'s ship *Sibylle* lost several of her men by fever from this cause. Distant 70 miles S.W. of Bassein. Lat. 15° 52′, long. 94° 19′.

DIAMOND HARBOUR.—The well-known port so called is situate in the river Hooghly, 29 miles below Calcutta. The adjacent territory, though interesting from being the first possession of the East-India Company in Bengal, is singularly unhealthy, the whole country round being swampy. There is no town, unless a few native huts are worthy the appellation; but ships are usually lying in the harbour, for the reception or discharge of cargo. The road from Calcutta is excellent. Communication between this place and the capital is also maintained by means of the electric telegraph. Lat. 22° 12′, long. 88° 10′.

DIA SIAWALA.—See DEEHA.

DIBING.—A town in the native state of Cashmeer, or territory of Gholab Singh, 109 miles E. from Sirinagur, and 67 miles N.E. from Kishtewar. Lat. 33° 56′, long. 76° 50′.

DIBONG RIVER rises in lat. 28° 23′, long. 96° 46′, and, flowing for ninety miles west through Thibet, and fifty miles south-west through Sudiya, in Assam, falls into the Brahmapootra river in lat. 27° 50′, long. 95° 28′.—See BRAHMAPOOTRA.

DICHOO.—See DAICHOO.

DIG, in the British district of Cawnpore, lieut.-gov. of the N.W. Provinces, a village on the route from the cantonment of Cawnpore to that of Calpee, and 15 miles N.E. of the latter. Water is abundant here, but supplies must be collected from the surrounding country. Lat. 26° 17′, long. 79° 57′.

DIG, or DIGA, in the British district of Allahabad, lieut.-gov. of the N.W. Provinces, a village on the left bank of the Ganges, 752 miles N.W. of Calcutta by the river route, 56 S.E. of the city of Allahabad by the same. Lat. 25° 15′, long. 82° 18′.

DIGAR.—A town in the native state of Cashmeer, or territory of Gholab Singh, 20 miles N.E. from the town of Le, and 134 miles N.E. from Kishtewar. Lat. 34° 16′, long. 77° 55′.

DIGAROO.—A river in Upper Assam, rises in Thibet, in lat. 28° 10′, long. 96° 13′, and after a course of ten miles through Thibet and fifteen through the Sudiya district of Assam, falls into the Brahmapootra, in lat. 27° 50′, long. 96° 2′.

DIGGEE, or DHIGGI, in the Rajpoot state of Jeypore, a town on the route from Nusserabad to Gwalior, 48 miles E. of former, 193 W. of latter. It is of considerable size, and supplies and water are abundant. Lat. 26° 24′, long. 75° 35′.

DIGNUGGUR, in British district of Burdwan, lieut.-gov. of Bengal, a town four or five miles on the right of the railway now under construction from the town of Burdwan to Raneegunge, 18 miles N.W. of former, 38 S.E. of latter. Jacquemont describes it as having many hundred houses, a considerable number of native gentry, some in the employment of government, others speculating in sugar, which is abundantly produced in the surrounding country. Distance N.W. from Calcutta by Burdwan 70 miles. Lat. 23° 22′, long. 87° 45′.

DIHATRA, in the Rajpoot state of Bikaneer, a considerable village on the route from the town of Bikaneer to that of Jessulmeer, and 40 miles S.W. of the former. The vicinity contains a few fields producing wheat. Dihatra is in lat. 27° 43′, long. 72° 51′.

DIHONG.—A river rising on the northern face of the Himalayas, in lat. 30° 25′, long. 82° 5′, and, pursuing an easterly course through Thibet for upwards of 1,000 miles, during the greater part of which it bears the name of the Sanpoo, it suddenly sweeps round to the south and enters Assam, where, under the name of the Dihong, it falls into the Brahmapootra.

DILLY (MOUNT).—A remarkable headland in the British district of Malabar. In clear weather it may be discerned from sea at a distance of from twenty-four to twenty-seven miles, and as the contiguous land is low, the headland, which is bluff, and has a small ancient fort on the summit, appears at a distance like an island. "The shore here is bold and safe to approach, there being seven and eight fathoms at one and two miles' distance, twenty and twenty-two fathoms at two or two and a half leagues' distance, and at fifteen leagues' distance abreast the mount you lose soundings. This is the narrowest part of the channel between the main and Lacadiva Islands, the distance being twenty-seven leagues between Elicalpeni Bank and Mount Dilly. Abreast of this headland there is frequently a drain of current to the southward, with a short confused swell, the effect of brisk north-westers, which greatly prevail here." Elevation above the sea 804 feet. Some years ago a project was set on foot for the construction of a harbour off this promontory, but in consequence of the enormous expense required for its formation, the scheme was abandoned. Lat. 12° 2′, long. 75° 16′.

DILODE.—A town of Malwa, in the native state of Bhopal, 17 miles N. from Bhopal, and 30 miles W. from Bhilsa. Lat. 23° 30′, long. 77° 22′.

DILSHAPOOR.—See DULSAEPOOR.

DINAGEPORE, under the lieut.-gov. of Bengal, a British district named from its principal place. It is bounded on the north-east by the native state of Bhotan; on the east by that of Coosh Behar and the British district of Rungpore; on the south by those of Bograh, Rajeshaye, and Malda; on the west by Purnea; and on the north by the British territory of Darjeeling. It lies between lat. 24° 53′—26° 38′, long. 88° 2′—89° 16′; is 130 miles in length from north to south, and 75 in breadth. The area is 3,820 square miles. It is a very flat country, the only eminences being mere undulations, not rising more than 100 feet above the ordinary level of the surface. There is, however, a general, though very gradual, slope of the country from north to south, as indicated by the flow of the rivers in that direction. The principal of these is the Teesta, which, flowing southerly from the mountains of Sikkim, touches on the district in lat. 24° 53′, and flowing south-east for thirty-five miles, divaricates into two streams, one, called the Attree, flowing south, the other flowing south-east into Coosh Behar, and retaining the name of Teesta. The Attree communicates with other streams having courses in some measure parallel to its own, and sends from its right side a large offset, called the Pernabada, which, flowing south westerly by the city of Dinagepore, passes the southern boundary of the district into the British district of Malda, and falls into the Mahanunda. The Jamuna, or Jabuna, a considerable stream, holds a course nearly parallel to the Attree, but on an average about fifteen miles to the east of it. With a parallel course, but still farther to the eastward, flows the river Curateea, an offset from the Attree. The Tangon, rising in the northern quarter of the district, and having a course parallel in some measure to the Attree, and on an average about twenty miles west of it, flows through this district for about 140 miles, crossing the southern frontier into the British district Malda. The Coolick, a considerable watercourse, unites the Tangon with an important stream termed the Nagor. Numerous smaller streams traverse the country, communicating with the greater and with each other; the whole tract, in consequence of the propinquity of the Himalaya and the powerful influence of the monsoons, having such redundancy of moisture, that the surface is little but a reticulation of watercourses. Rice is the principal grain of the district. Wheat and barley are raised, but in no great quantities; meruya (Cynosurus coracanus) and various kinds of millet are also articles of cultivation. Peas, and various other kinds of pulse, as well as oil-seeds, are extensively raised. The insipid fare of the bulk of the people peculiarly requiring seasoning, many products are grown for this purpose: ginger, turmeric, capsicum, coriander, anise, and pepper. Of esculent vegetables, there are the potato, sweet potato, begun or egg-plant, esculent arum radish, plantain (Musa paradisiaca), various cucurbitaceous plants, and many others unknown in Europe; most of the vegetables of that quarter of the world, however, thriving here during the cool season. A small quantity of cotton is cultivated: it is generally of poor quality, and is retained for home use. There is, however, a kind denominated son, of superior quality, produced in the eastern part, having a strong staple, well suited for sailcloth and cordage.

The sugar-cane flourishes, having a stem of considerable thickness, and twelve or fourteen feet high. The canes are planted in the beginning of spring, and gathered towards the close of the succeeding winter. The juice is prepared merely by boiling down, either into a thick syrup or a hard dry cake, and in these states sent to market. The tobacco grown is not sufficient for the consumption of the district. Betel (Piper betle) and hemp (Cannabis sativa), yielding an intoxicating extract, are grown to considerable extent. The cultivation of indigo has been tried, but does not appear to prosper. Silk is produced in considerable quantity, the worms being fed on the foliage either of the mulberry or of the castor-oil plant (Ricinus communis).

The majority of the people are wretchedly lodged in huts, the sides of which are of strong coarse matting, the roofs of thatch, the framework of strong bamboos. Persons in easier circumstances have dwellings of mud, and latterly a few of the more wealthy have built houses of brick, in imitation of those of the Europeans. Mosques are numerous in the district. They are generally small, and of simple construction; the form, a cube, covered with a dome, or a parallelopiped covered with several. The most numerous Hindoo places of worship are denominated sthans, and are merely heaps or square terraces of earth placed under trees, having a stone or a rude image of clay painted as an object of worship. A step in advance of this is the mondop, having walls painted with rude, frightful imagery, on subjects drawn from the Hindoo mythology. Such a building, surmounted by a pyramid or a dome, is a still higher effort of devotional zeal, and is reserved for the more revered objects of worship. The most complex and expensive is called a novorotno, or "building of nine ornaments," having a roof of two stages, with an octagonal ground-plan, a central pyramid, and eight others, one at each external angle. Such buildings are costly, as they are cased with expensive tiles elaborately carved. That at Gopalganj is said to have cost 20,000*l*. The population is given in the article BENGAL. The Mussulmans have been estimated to exceed the Hindoos. Among both, marriages take place excessively early, the conjugal union being ordinarily completed before the female has reached the close of her thirteenth year, or the male that of his sixteenth. The effects of these premature marriages are said to be manifested in the physical and intellectual deterioration of the population, and the small increase of their numbers. The inhabitants of Dinagepore are represented by Buchanan as a puny, weak race, and far from having numerous families. They are, moreover, said to be generally short-lived, being cut off in great numbers by fevers and dysentery. The prevalence of these affections does not appear to arise from want of food. Polygamy is very prevalent, especially among the Brahminists. Widows rarely burned themselves with the bodies of their husbands, even when that horrible practice was permitted by law, and not more than one or two instances occurred annually. Only a few Brahmins of superior rank are versed in Sanscrit. Much more extensive is the knowledge of the Prakrit, a dialect corrupted from the Sanscrit, which has supplied most of the words, the syntax and inflexions having sprung from the ordinary tongue of the district. The common people are acquainted only with Bengalee. The number of towns is very small in proportion to the extent and population of the district, the great majority of the people residing in dispersed hamlets. The chief towns—Dinagepore the capital, Hemtabad, Raegang, Damdahah, and Ghonaghat—are noticed under their respective names in the alphabetical arrangement. There are few routes through this district. They are —1. From west to east, from Purneah, through the town of Dinagepore, to Rungpore; 2. from south to north, from Berhampore, through the town of Dinagepore, to Darjeeling; 3. from south-west to north-east, from Maldah to the town of Dinagepore.

Legends respecting the primeval state of the tract comprised in this district abound in the works relating to the early mythology of India; but the commencement of authentic history may be placed at the beginning of the thirteenth century, when Raja Lokhymon or Lakshmanyah was expelled from his dominions by Muhammad Bakhtyar, one of the generals of Kutb-uddin, emperor of Delhi. When Fakhruddin, in 1338, proclaimed himself independent sovereign of Bengal, he appears to have made himself master of Dinagepore at the same time, though its obedience was probably precarious. Eventually it was, in 1538, reduced, with the remainder of Bengal, by Shir Shah, the renowned Afghan, who soon after established himself in the sovereignty of Delhi, from which he had expelled Humayon. After the death of Shir Shah, it was subdued in 1584 by Akbar, the son of Humayon, and appears to have remained a district of the empire of Delhi until the time nearly of its dissolution. In 1765 it was conveyed to the East-India Company by the grant of Shah Alum.

DINAGEPORE.—The principal place of the British district of the same name, a town on the route from Purneah to Rungpore, 85 miles E. of the former, and 43 W. of the latter. It is situate on the river Purnabada. Through the exertions of the British authorities, it is now clean and well watched, which is understood to present a favourable contrast to its former state. There is no public building deserving any consideration, the spacious residence of the rajah having for many years been in a state of ruin, and the ditch and rampart with which it was inclosed being nearly obliterated. There are no Brahminical temples worth notice, and but one mosque, even that being small, and of no architectural pretensions. The public offices of the civil establish-

ment are large, but ill built, and totally devoid of elegance. The population has been estimated at from 25,000 to 30,000 persons. Dinagepore is distant N. from Berhampore 142 miles, N. from Calcutta 261. Lat. 25° 34′, long. 88° 38′.

DINAPOOR, in the British district of Patna, lieut.-gov. of Bengal, a town on the right or south bank of the Ganges. It is an important military station, and remarkable for the fine barracks built by government for the accommodation of the troops. The barracks for the accommodation of the European soldiers are comprised within a magnificent and elegant structure, and those of the officers, though rather inferior, are yet very fine buildings, and of great extent. Many of the officers have built commodious lodges in the vicinity, and the grounds about them are neatly and tastefully laid out. There are also extensive and very handsome barracks for the native troops. The church is capacious and handsome, and the various houses scattered in market-places within the boundaries of the cantonment, and subject to military authority, were stated in 1807 to amount to 3,226; so that if five persons be allowed to each, the population should be estimated at 16,130, exclusive of military. The markets are well supplied, especially with articles suited to European taste. Distant E. from Benares, by Ghazeepore, 145 miles, W. from Patna 10, N.W. from Calcutta 411. Lat. 25° 37′, long. 85° 7′.

DINAREH.—A town in the British district of Shahabad, lieut.-gov. of Bengal, 70 miles S.W. of Dinapoor. Lat. 25° 12′, long. 84° 6′.

DINDARY.—A town in the British province of Nagpore, 175 miles N.E. from Nagpore, and 80 miles N. from Ryepoor. Lat. 22° 20′, long. 81° 33′.

DINDEE RIVER rises in lat. 17° 2′, long. 78°, and flowing in a south-easterly direction for 110 miles through Hyderabad, or the Nizam's territories, falls into the Kistna in lat. 16° 22′, long. 79° 16′.

DINDIGUL, in the British district of Madura, presidency of Madras, a town with a fort, situate at the north-eastern extremity of the valley of the same name. It is built on a gentle declivity, and is in length from north to south 987 yards, and in breadth from east to west 927. The streets are wide, the houses well built, and the bazars plentifully supplied with all the necessaries of life. The number of houses a few years ago was stated to be 1,833, and that of the inhabitants (exclusive of the troops) 6,550. The military lines, situate at the north-west corner of the town, are well drained, and always dry and clean. The Court of Justice and collector's lodge are about a quarter of a mile from the town; and between them and the town are the lodges of the officers, surrounded by groves and gardens, inclosed with hedges of euphorbium and aloes. The water is in general good, but the population give a preference, for drinking, to that obtained from the Brahmin's Baoli, a large public well at the north of the town. Excellent water is also found in a reservoir situate at the bottom of the rock, and replenished by the rains. The fort is situate on a wedge-shaped mass of gneiss 400 feet in length and 300 in breadth, perfectly bare of vegetation, with the exception of a few patches of scanty soil about the summit, in which some stunted trees and shrubs grow. The ascent is on the eastern side by a flight of stone steps, the other sides being nearly perpendicular. Near the summit there is a well of great depth, erroneously supposed by the natives to be unfathomable. The water from it is excellent. Dindigul is the principal place of a subdivision of the same name, forming part of the British district of Madura. Elevation of the town above the sea 700 feet, of the rock 980. Distance from Madura, N., 32 miles; Tanjore, S.W., 88; Trichinopoly, S.W., 60; Cochin, E., 126; Madras, S.W., 247. Lat. 10° 22′, long. 78° 3′.

DINDOOREE.—A town in the British district of Ahmednuggur, presidency of Bombay, 96 miles N.W. of Ahmednuggur. Lat. 20° 1′, long. 73° 50′.

DINGAR, in the native state of Gurwhal, a village in the valley of the Budiar, and on the left bank of the torrent of that name. Elevation above the sea 7,119 feet. Lat. 30° 56′, long. 78° 17′.

DINGARA.—See DEEGAREE.

DINGARH KINER, in Sirmoor, a large village situate on a very picturesque site in the gorge through which the route passes northwards from Nahun to Rajgurh. It has very splendid views,—on the north, of the Chur mountain; on the south, of the valley of the Julal river. Fraser, who thought it the largest place in Sirmoor except Nahun, the capital, describes it as consisting of well-built flat-roofed houses, arranged in rows on the ledges of the solid limestone rock forming the mountain. The country, though very rocky, has some fertile spots, which produce luxuriant crops, especially of wheat. Lat. 30° 44′, long. 77° 21′.

DINGATHUR, in the British district of Kumaon, lieut.-gov. of the N.W. Provinces, a village on the route up the course of the Ramgunga river (Eastern) from Petorahgurh to the Unta Dhura Pass, 16 miles north of Petorahgurh, one and a half east of the left bank of the Ramgunga. It was an important position in the survey of Kumaon by Webb, who remained there fifteen days engaged in trigonometrical and meteorological observations. Elevation above the sea 4,443 feet. Lat. 29° 49′, long. 80° 12′.

DINGEE, in Sinde, a fort between Kheyerpoor and Hyderabad, and 50 miles S. of the former town. It is surrounded by walls fifteen feet high, and has an abundant supply of water from wells. Here, in the beginning of 1843, the ameers of Sinde collected an army, preparatory to their final struggle with the British. Lat. 26° 52', long. 68° 40'.

DINGUR KINGUR.—See DINGARH.

DINGYE, in the Rajpoot state of Joudpore, on the route from Nusseerabad to Deesa, and 123 miles S.W. of the former. The surrounding country is in general level and bare, but occasionally with a few small hills. The road in this part of the route is firm and good. Lat. 25° 37', long. 73° 27'.

DIPAL, or DUTI.—A town in the native state of Nepal, 51 miles S.W. from Jemlah, and 70 miles N.E. from Pilleebheet. Lat. 29° 5', long. 80° 54'.

DIPALPOOR.—A town in the Punjab, situate in the Doab between the Ghara and the Ravee, 21 miles from the right bank of the former, 26 from the left of the latter. In the time of the emperor Acbar, it was the chief town of a district which yielded an income of 3,233,353 rupees. Lat. 30° 37', long. 73° 38'.

DIRAWUL, or DILAWUR (the *l* and *r* being interchangeable).—A fortress of Bhawlpoor, situate in the desert, forty miles from the left bank of the Punjnud. It is strongly fortified, according to the notions of native powers, and with reference to their practical skill in the arts of defence; but its safety principally lies in the difficulty of access to it, the road lying through a parched desert totally devoid of water; so that a besieging army must draw its supply from a distance of fifteen miles. At the time of Atkinson's visit, it contained the treasure of the late nawaub Bhawl Khan, vaguely estimated at 700,000*l*. Here also was his zenana, and thither he retired for relaxation from the fatigues of business, or for security when threatened with invasion. There is here a manufactory of gunpowder for artillery, but the produce is of very indifferent quality. Lat. 28° 44', long. 71° 17'.

DIREEAPOOR, in the British district of Allygurh, lieut.-gov. of the N.W. Provinces, a town with a bazar, on the route from the cantonment of Allygurh to that of Etawah, and 19 miles S. of the former. Lat. 27° 39', long. 78° 12'.

DISANG.—A river rising in lat. 26° 47', long. 95° 25', in the country inhabited by the Naga tribes, through which it flows north for thirty miles to the village of Boorhath, where it turns easterly, and flowing for sixty miles through the British district of Seebpoor, in the territory of Assam, it falls into the Brahmapootra in lat. 27° 4', long. 94° 30'.

DIU.—A seaport town on the south coast of the peninsula of Kattywar, province of Guzerat, belonging to the Portuguese, who obtained possession of the place in 1515. It is situate at the eastern extremity of an island extending in a direction from east to west about seven miles, and having a breadth varying from a mile and a half to two miles. "Off the point on which the town stands, and which projects to the eastward, there is a rocky ledge, extending upwards of a quarter of a mile farther in the same direction, and protecting to the southward the bay formed by the main coast opposite. The bay or harbour is further protected by two small banks, one a quarter and the other three-quarters of a mile to the eastward of the rocky ledge." The general depth of the anchorage is three and four fathoms, and formerly on the east side there was sufficient for a 74-gun ship; but the depth of water is considered to have decreased latterly. The channel between the island of Diu and the mainland is navigable only for fishing-boats and other small craft, the western entrance, which is defended by a fort, having four or five feet of water on the bar when lowest. The water is brackish, except that preserved from the rainy season. Vegetables and other provisions are plentiful, being brought from the mainland, the soil of the island itself being little productive. The town is well fortified, being surrounded by a wall strengthened with towers at regular intervals. Notwithstanding the excellence of the harbour for ships of moderate draught, there is but little traffic. Under orders from the Portuguese government in Europe, the trade in slaves formerly carried on in this island has been discontinued. Diu Head, two miles to the westward of the west end of Diu island, has on its east side a small harbour, where vessels might lie sheltered from the westerly winds in from two to three and a half fathoms. It lies in lat. 20° 42', long. 70° 52'. The town of Diu is distant from Ahmedabad, S.W., 192 miles; Baroda, S.W., 182; Bombay, N.W., 170. Lat. 20° 42', long. 71°.

DIVY POINT.—A low headland on the coast of the British district of Masulipatam, presidency of Madras. Around the point, and between it and the cape known as Divy False Point, several branches of the river Kistna fall into the sea. "The rise and fall of the tide is seldom more than four or five feet in the springs at the mouths of the rivers; but it sometimes happens, when a severe gale of wind blows from the sea, that the low land contiguous to it is inundated, causing great destruction of property and lives." Divy Point is 19 miles N.E. of the mouths of the Kistna, and 13 S. of Masulipatam. Lat. 15° 59', long. 81° 14'.

DIWARNUGGUR.—A town in the British district of Silhet, lieut.-gov. of Bengal, 33 miles W. of Silhet. Lat. 24° 59', long. 91° 20'.

DOA.—A village in Arracan, on the Aeng route, a little to the east of the Yoomadoung Mountains. Lat. 20° 10', long. 94° 17'.

DOAREE, in the British district of Gurhwal, lieut.-gov. of the N.W. Provinces, a town on the route from Rampoor to Sireenuggur, 37 miles S. of the latter. Lat. 29° 41', long. 78° 59'.

DOBBILI, or BOBILEE.—A town in the

British district of Vizagapatam, 62 miles N. from Vizagapatam, and 41 miles N.W. from Chicacole. In 1758 the fort was stormed by a force under the French commander Mons. Bussey. When all hope of maintaining it against the assailants had been abandoned by the garrison, the chiefs put to death their wives and children, and the massacre being performed, "those who accomplished it returned like men agitated by the furies to die themselves on the walls." Lat. 18° 34′, long. 83° 26′.

DOBDUR HAUT.—A town in the British district of Seebpoor, in Upper Assam, 10 miles S. of Seebpoor. Lat. 26° 52′, long. 94° 37′.

DOBOORJEE, in the Baree Dooab division of the Punjab, a town situated on the right bank of the Ghara river, 50 miles S. of the town of Lahore. Lat. 30° 53′, long. 74° 20′.

DODA, in the territory of Gwalior, or possessions of Scindia's family, a town on the route from Neemuch to Baitool, 51 miles S.E of former, 261 N.W. of latter. It is supplied with water from wells, and has a small bazaar with market. Elevation above the sea 1,482 feet. Lat. 23° 46′, long. 75° 10′.

DODA.—A town in the Punjab, amidst the mountains south of Cashmere, situate on the right or north bank of the Chenaub, nearly opposite its confluence with the river of Budrawar. The Chenaub, here sixty yards broad, is crossed by a *jhoola* or bridge, formed by a cable stretched from bank to bank, and traversed by a suspended seat, drawn backwards and forwards by means of a rope. Doda is a neat, well-built town, with a good bazar, and a square fort having a tower at each angle. Lat. 33° 12′, long. 75° 18′.

DODABALLA, or DODA BALAPORE.—A town in Mysore, the name signifying "Balapore the Great," to distinguish between it and Chika Balapoor, or Balapore the Less, which is situate fourteen miles north-east of this place. Dodaballa has a mud fort of great size and strength, but within, nothing is found but ruins and rubbish. The place has some trade, but it is only for the supply of domestic wants. The traders have neither enterprise nor capital. Distant from Bangalore, N., 25 miles. Lat. 13° 14′, long. 77° 24′.

DODAIREE, or DODDERI, in Mysore, a town about eight miles W. of the right bank of the river Vedavutty. Near this place, in 1698, the Mahrattas, commanded by Suntajee, surrounded, defeated, and destroyed a force commanded by Kasim Khan, whom Aurungzebe had appointed governor of the Carnatic. Distant from Chittel Droog, E., 22 miles; Bangalore, N.W., 110; Seringapatam, N., 130. Lat. 14° 18′, long. 76° 46′.

DODHUR.—See DODA.

DODOOKEE.—A town in the British province of Nagpoor, 118 miles S.E. from Nagpoor, and 76 miles E. from Chanda. Lat. 20° 5′, long. 80° 33′.

DOESAH.—A town in the British district of Chota Nagpore, lieut.-gov. of Bengal, 100 miles S. of Shergotty. Lat. 23° 7′, long. 84° 51′.

DOGHINE, a small river of the Amherst district of the Tenasserim provinces, rises in lat. 16° 58′, long. 98° 33′, and flowing west for forty miles, falls into the Gyein river, in lat. 16° 55′, long. 98° 6′.

DOHRA, in the British district of Bareilly, lieut.-gov. of the N.W. Provinces, a village on the route by Nanak Math, from the town of Pilleebheet to Almora cantonment, 25 miles N. of the former. Lat. 28° 57′, long. 79° 49′.

DOHUD, in the territory of Gwalior, or possessions of Scindia's family, a town on the common boundary of Malwa and Guzerat, W. of the former, E. of the latter, on the route from Mow to Deesa, 118 miles N.W. of former, 208 S.E. of latter. It is a place of considerable traffic and importance, the road being the channel of considerable and lucrative commerce between Malwa and Upper Hindostan on the one side, and Guzerat on the other. It commands the principal pass on the north-east of Guzerat by means of its fort, situate at the east extremity of the town. This building, formerly a great caravanserai, said to have been built by Aurungzebe, is of a square ground-plan, measuring each way 450 feet, and has two strong gates, one on the north, the other on the south, and in the interior contains two wells and a mosque, and some other structures of fine workmanship and durable materials. Distant W. of Oojein 100 miles, N.E. of Baroda 77. Lat. 22° 50′, long. 74° 15′.

DOLANUH, in the British district of Meerut, lieut.-gov. of the N.W. Provinces, a town on the southern frontier, towards the British district of Bolundshuhur, 28 miles E. of Delhi. Lat. 28° 38′, long. 77° 43′.

DOLEH, in the Rajpoot state of Joudpore, a group of three villages on the route from Balotra to the city of Joudpore, and 33 miles N.E. of the former. It is important as containing three wells, supplying the only good water obtainable throughout a considerable tract. Lat. 26° 4′, long. 72° 52′.

DOLEHKUN.—A town in the British district of Tannah, presidency of Bombay, 59 miles N.E. of Bombay. Lat. 19° 29′, long. 73° 36′.

DOLLA.—A town in the British district of Sudiya, in Upper Assam, six miles from the left bank of the Brahmapootra, and 12 S.W. of Sudiya. Lat. 27° 42′, long. 95° 36′.

DOMEL, one of the principal islands of the cluster known as the Mergui Archipelago: it is twenty-six miles in length from north to south, and five miles in breadth; its centre is about lat. 11° 40′, long. 98° 20′.

DOMEPARRA.—A town in the British district of Pooree, lieut.-gov. of Bengal, 44 miles N. of Juggurnaut. Lat. 20° 23′, long. 85° 40′.

DOMRAH.—See DHUMRAH.

DOMRI, in the British district of Furruckabad, lieut.-gov. of the N.W. Provinces, a town two miles to the left or west of the route from Futtehgurh to Khasgunj, and 44 miles W. of the former. Lat. 27° 32′, long. 79°.

DOMUS, in the British district of Surat, presidency of Bombay, a town situate on the headland bounding the estuary of the river Taptee on the south-east. Distance from the city of Surat, S.W., eight miles; Bombay, N., 150. Lat. 21° 4′, long. 72° 48′.

DONABUE. — A town in the recently-acquired British district of Pegu, situate on one of the main streams by which the Irawaddy flows into the sea: it is 65 miles N.W. from Rangoon, 54 miles N.E. from Bassein. The place has attained a degree of celebrity in the annals of Burmese warfare, as well from its successful resistance of Brigadier Cotton's attack in 1825, as from its contiguity to the scene of a more recent disaster which befell the British. Here, on the 4th February, 1853, a detachment of sepoys, accompanied by a party of seamen and marines under the command of Captain Granville Loch, of the Royal Navy, suffered a repulse in a struggle with a Burmese force, and lost some of its bravest officers, including its distinguished commander. Lat. 17° 10′, long. 95° 27′.

DONGERPOOR, in the jaghire of Rampoor, lieut.-gov. of Agra, a town on the north-eastern route from the city of Rampoor to Nugina, and 1½ mile N. of the former. Lat. 28° 49′, long. 79° 5′.

DONGUR MULARNEE.—A town in the Rajpoot state of Jeypoor, 66 miles S.E. from Jeypoor, and 98 miles W. from Gwalior. Lat. 26° 16′, long. 76° 41′.

DONGURPOOR, or DOONGERPORE.—A petty native state in the province of Rajpootana, under the political superintendence of the Governor-General. It is bounded on the north and east by Mewar or Oodeypore; on the south-east by Banswarra; and on the south and south-west by the Myhee Caunta district of the province of Guzerat. Its length from east to west is forty miles, its breadth from north to south thirty-five, and it contains an area of about one thousand square miles. It is situate between lat. 23° 35′—24° 3′, long. 73° 40′—74° 18′. Its chief is descended from a branch of the Oodeypore family, whose ancestors became, at an early period, dependent on the emperor of Delhi, and so continued until subjugated by the Mahrattas, from whose oppressive yoke the prince and his territory were rescued by the British. The treaty by which the British connection was established, was concluded in 1818; and the terms and conditions are substantially the same with those of the treaty concluded about the same time with the chief of Banswarra, and which are described in the article upon that state. The population of Dongurpoor, estimated at 100 to the square mile, amounts to 100,000. The revenue is stated at 109,000 rupees, or 10,900*l.* per annum. Under the treaty above referred to, the British government is entitled to tribute not exceeding in any case three-eighths of the actual revenue. The armed force of the state is represented to consist of 125 cavalry and 200 infantry, with a police establishment of 100 men; making a total of 425. The tributary chiefs holding lands on military tenure are only eight in number. Dongurpoor since its connection with the British government has not been free from those disturbances which seem inseparable from the condition of an Indian state. In 1827, the Rawul consented to divest himself of the exercise of the government, and to surrender it to his adopted son Dulput Singh; but the latter was reclaimed by his grandfather, the rajah of Pertaubghur, being his only surviving descendant, and on whose death he was allowed to succeed to the raj of Pertaubghur, still remaining regent of Dongurpoor. On the death of the rawul of the last-named state, however, the question arose whether Dulput Singh should succeed to the dignity by virtue of the adoption. It appeared that the thakoors or nobles of Dongurpoor were greatly averse to the union of the two principalities, and it was therefore agreed that Dulput Singh should adopt a son from among the kindred of the late rawul, who should be placed on the Dongurpoor guddee, Dulput Singh continuing regent during the minority. It seems, however, to have been thought, that in a legal point of view, the reclamation of Dulput Singh by his own family did not annul the rights which had accrued to him by adoption; but for the sake of preserving the peace of the country, he consented to compromise his claim in the manner above described.

DONGURPOOR, in Rajpootana, a town, the residence of the rawul of the petty state of the same name, lies on the route from Neemuch to Deesa, and is 139 miles S.W. of the former, and 121 S.E. of the latter. It is of considerable size, and fortified. Distant direct from Mhow, N.W., 150 miles; from Bombay, N., 345. Lat. 23° 50′, long. 73° 50′.

DONGURTHAL, in the British territory of Saugor and Nerbudda, lieut.-gov. of the N.W. Provinces, a town on the route from Seuni to Nagpoor, 36 miles N.E. of the latter. Lat. 21° 39′, long. 79° 22′.

DON MANICK ISLANDS, situated near the mouths of the Megna, in lat. 21° 55′, long. 90° 43′, and 50 miles S.E. of Backergunge.

DOOAB (THE). — See NORTH-WESTERN PROVINCES.

DOOAB CANAL.—See JUMNA RIVER.

DOOBAH, a small river of Sinde, rises in the southern part of the Keertar Mountains, about lat. 25° 54′, long. 67° 45′. After a course which may be estimated at forty-five miles, generally in a south-easterly direction, it forms a junction with the Damajee river, coming from the south-west; and below the confluence the name is changed for that of Dhurwal. In the commencement of its course, it bears the name of the Pokrun river, and lower down, that of the Kajoor. It is dry for the greater part of the year, but water may always be obtained by digging in its bed.

DOOBAR, in the British district of Mirzapoor, lieut.-gov. of the N.W. Provinces, a town on the route from Rewah to Mirzapoor, 17 miles S.W. of the latter. Lat. 24° 59′, long. 82° 28′.

DOOBDI.—A town in the native state of Sikhim, 24 miles N. from Dargeeling. Lat. 27° 23′, long. 88° 20′.

DOOBKEE, in the British district of Cawnpore, lieut.-gov. of the N.W. Provinces, a village on the route from the cantonment of Etawah to that of Cawnpore, and 41 miles W. of the latter. Lat. 26° 21′, long. 79° 50′.

DOOBLANA, or DUBLANA, in the territory of Boonde, in Rajpootana, a town on the route from Delhi to Mhow, 272 miles S.W. of former, 235 N. of latter. It has a bazar, and water is abundant. Here, in 1744, was fought an obstinately-contested battle between Omeda, the exiled raja of Boonde, and the troops of Jeypore, who had seized his capital, in which conflict the raja was utterly defeated. Distant from the city of Boonde, N., nine miles. Lat. 25° 35′, long. 75° 44′.

DOOBLING.—A town of Bussahir, in the division of Koonawur, on the left bank of the Sutluj, and 96 miles N.E. from Simla. Lat. 31° 44′, long. 78° 40′.

DOOBOWLEEA, in the British district of Goruckpoor, lieut.-gov. of the N.W. Provinces, a town five miles from the left bank of the Gogra river, 53 miles W. of Goruckpoor. Lat. 26° 40′, long. 82° 33′.

DOOBTA.—See DABUTA.

DOOBULHATTEE.—A town in the British district of Rajeshaye, lieut.-gov. of Bengal, 30 miles N.E. of Rampoor. Lat. 24° 45′, long. 88° 53′.

DOODEE, in Sirhind, a village on the route from Hansee to Lodiana, and 57 miles N. of the former town. It is situate in a level, low country, liable to be rendered swampy by the inundation of the river Gagur. When this occurs, the road, though generally good, becomes difficult. Distant N.W. from Calcutta 1,033 miles. Lat. 29° 53′, long. 76° 1′.

DOODEE GHAT.—A village in the Punjab, situate on the right bank of the river Chenaub, and five miles N.W. of Mooltan, from which there is a good road. It is mentioned by Elphinstone under the name of Oodoo-ka-Gote. Here is a much-frequented ferry, by which the great route lies from Mooltan to Dera Ghazee Khan. Lat. 30° 15′, long. 71° 22′.

DOODGAON.—A town in the native state of Sanglee, one of the Southern Mahratta jaghires, 62 miles S.E. from Sattara, and 18 miles N.E. from Kolapoor. Lat. 16° 52′, long. 74° 30′.

DOODGAUM.—A town in Hyderabad, or dominions of the Nizam, 136 miles N.E. from Jaulna, and 67 miles S.E. from Elichpoor. Lat. 20° 17′, long. 77° 58′.

DOODHILI, in the Dehra Doon, on the frontier of Gurhwal, is a summit of the mountains rising above the valley on the north. It is surmounted by a small fort, now in ruins, which was a station of the lesser series of triangles in the trigonometrical survey of the Himalaya. Elevation above the sea 7,254 feet. Lat. 30° 28′, long. 78° 2′.

DOODHOO, in the Rajpoot state of Jeypore, a town on the route from Agra to Ajmer, 186 miles E. of former, 42 W. of latter. It is of considerable size, containing 700 houses, with more than 100 bunyas (shops), and is surrounded by a mud wall, with a thin fausse-braie or renee, its ditch being cut out of a hard kunkur soil, of which the ramparts are also constructed. Lat. 26° 40′, long. 75° 18′.

DOODNA.—A river flowing in a south-easterly direction through the territories of Hyderabad, or territory of the Nizam: it rises in lat. 20° 2′, long. 77° 5′, and falls into the Poorna river, a considerable branch of the Godavery, in lat. 19° 16′, long. 76° 58′, after a course of about 120 miles.

DOODOO, in Bussahir, a village on the route from Mussouree to the Gunas Pass, and five miles N.W. of the former place. It is of inconsiderable size, but before the establishment of the British power was of some importance as the residence of a freebooter, who affected independence, and laid the surrounding country under contribution. Elevation above the sea 8,790 feet. Lat. 31° 11′, long. 78° 8′.

DOODPATLEE, or DOODPUTLEE, in Eastern India, a village of Cachar, and the site of a large cantonment of the Burmese during the war of 1825. The post was strongly fortified, consisting of seven stockades of a most formidable nature, which were destroyed upon the occupation of the place by the British. Lat. 25° 3′, long. 92° 42′.

DOODYALEE.—A town in the Rajpoot state of Joudpore, on the left bank of the Sookree river, and 69 miles S. from the town of Joudpore. Lat. 25° 20′, long. 73°.

DOOGAREE, in the territory of Boondee, in Rajpootana, a town on the route from Delhi to Mhow, 210 miles S.W. of former, 297 N. of latter. It has a bazar, and water is abundant. It is nearly surrounded by hills, and has to the westward a jhil or small lake. On the eastern margin of the lake, and adjoining the village, is an old residence of the raja of Boondee, on a considerable eminence; and on the extremity of a tongue of land projecting into the jhil is a temple, consecrated to Mahadeo. Distance from Boondee, N.E., 19 miles. Lat. 25° 40′, long. 75° 52′.

DOOJANO, in the Rajpoot state of Joudpore, a village on the route from Nusseerabad to Deesa, and 147 miles S.W. of the former. Lat. 25° 17′, long. 73° 14′.

DOOJANUH, in the jaghire of Jughur, a town on the route from Kurnaul to Rewaree, and 73 miles S. of the former. It is the residence of a jaghiredar or grantee of a small territory from the East-India Company. The jaghire was, in 1811, granted to Ubdus Summud Khan, in exchange for a part of Hurreeana, which he had received in 1806 as a reward for his services against the Mahrattas. The small district of Bohoo Nahur Jul, also granted in 1806, has been united with Doojanuh, and these at present form the jaghire of the grandson of Ubdus Summud Khan. The area of the jaghire is about seventy-one square miles; the population is estimated at upwards of 6,000. A small force, consisting of 50 cavalry and 150 infantry, is maintained by the jaghiredar. The town of Doojanuh is situate in lat. 28° 40′, long. 76° 40′. The centre of the small district granted in 1806 is in lat. 28° 25′, long. 76° 27′.

DOOKOO.—A town in the territory inhabited by the Bor tribes, six miles N.E. from the river Dihona, and 40 miles N.W. from Sudiya, in Assam. Lat. 28° 14′, long. 95° 16′.

DOOKYN.—A village situate on the right bank of the Kuladyne river, in Arracan. Lat. 20° 48′, long. 93° 4′.

DOOLABAREE, in the British district of Rajeshahye, lieut.-gov. of Bengal, a town on the river Attree. Distance from Baulea, N., 25 miles; from Berhampore, by Baulea, 55; from Calcutta, by Berhampore, 180. Lat. 24° 42′, long. 88° 42′.

DOOLALGUNJE.—A town in the British district of Purneah, lieut.-gov. of Bengal, 17 miles N.E. of Purneah. Lat. 25° 53′, long. 87° 48′.

DOOLAPOOR, in the British district of Mynpooree, lieut.-gov. of the N.W. Provinces, a village on the route from the cantonment of Allygurh to that of Mynpooree, and 17 miles N.W. of the latter. Lat. 27° 22′, long. 78° 55′.

DOOLA SERA, in the British district of Boolundshuhur, lieut.-gov. of the N.W. Provinces, a village on the route from the cantonment of Allygurh to that of Delhi, and 43 miles N.W. of the former. Lat. 28° 24′, long. 77° 48′.

DOOLEE.—A town in the British district of Tirhoot, lieut.-gov. of Bengal, 41 miles N.E. of Dinapoor. Lat. 25° 59′, long. 85° 38′.

DOOLKOTE.—A village in the British district of Delhi, lieut.-gov. of the N.W. Provinces, on the route from Delhi to Rewaree, and 22 miles S.W. of the former. Lat. 28° 26′ long. 77° 1′.

DOOLOO.—See BUSSUNDAR.

DOOLOORIA, in the British territory of Saugor and Nerbudda, lieut.-gov. of the N.W. Provinces, a town on the route from Hoosungabad to Nurnulla, 11 miles S.W. of the former. Lat. 22° 37′, long. 77° 40′.

DOOLUBA, in the British district of Goruckpoor, lieut.-gov. of the N.W. Provinces, a town on the route from Goruckpoor to the Nepal territory, 46 miles N.W. of the former. Lat. 27° 20′, long. 83° 15′.

DOOMAH, in the British district of Saugor and Nerbudda, lieut.-gov. of the N.W. Provinces, a town on the route from Nurnulla to Baitool, 52 miles S.W. of the latter. Lat. 21° 30′, long. 77° 39′.

DOO MAHAN.—A town in the native state of Nepal, 44 miles S.E. from Khatmandoo, and 76 miles N.E. from Bettia. Lat. 27° 11′, long. 85° 42′.

DOOMALUNG.—A town in the native state of Bhotan, 110 miles E. from Dargeeling, and seven miles from the left bank of river Bagnee. Lat. 26° 52′, long. 90° 3′.

DOOMKOT, in the British district of Gurhwal, lieut.-gov. of the N.W. Provinces, a town on the route from Bijnour to Sireenuggur, 13 miles S. of the latter. Lat. 30° 4′, long. 78° 50′.

DOOMUREEAHGUNJ, in the British district of Goruckpoor, lieut.-gov. of the N.W. Provinces, a small town 52 miles N.W. of the cantonment of Goruckpoor. Buchanan describes it at the time of his survey, forty years ago, as containing 175 huts, very poor, but forming a straight wide street. Distant N. from Allahabad and Benares 135 miles. Lat. 27° 10′, long. 82° 43′.

DOONA GIREE, in the British district of Kumaon, lieut.-gov. of the N.W. Provinces, a town on the route from Almora to Sireenuggur, 19 miles N.W. of the former. Lat. 29° 48′, long. 79° 30′.

DOONARA.—A town in the native state of Joudpore, on the left bank of the Loonee river, and 33 miles S.W. from Joudpore. Lat. 25° 55′, long. 72° 52′.

DOONDA.—A town in Hyderabad, or dominions of the Nizam, situate four miles from the right bank of the Payne Gungah river, and 170 N.W. from Hyderabad. Lat. 19° 50′, long. 78° 15′.

DOONDEE, in the British district of Bareilly, lieut.-gov. of the N.W. Provinces, a considerable village on the route by Nanakmath to Ruderpoor, from the town of Pillibheet, 28 miles N.W. of the latter. It is situate two miles E. of the left bank of the river Sookhee. Lat. 28° 58′, long. 79° 43′.

DOONDIA KHER.—See DAUNDIAKHERA.

DOONEE, in the territory of Jeypoor, in Rajpootana, a populous town, though of moderate size. It is surrounded by a mud wall, and though not provided with cannon, was in 1809 so resolutely defended as to baffle all the ill-directed efforts of Doulut Rao Scindia to take it. Distant from Jeypoor S. 70 miles. Lat. 25° 53′, long. 75° 47′.

DOONGA, or **TUPI DOONGA**, in the British district of Kumaon, lieut.-gov. of the N.W. Provinces, a halting-place on the route by the Unta Dhura Pass, from Almora fort to Hiundes or South-western Tibet, 144 miles N.E. of Almorah. It is a singularly desolate place, about four miles S. of the crest of the pass, and eight miles S. of the Chinese frontier. The elevation above the sea, according to Barron's estimate, from the boiling-water point, is 15,450 feet. Lat. 30° 32′, long. 80° 17′.

DOONGERPORE.—See DONGURPOOR.

DOONGRA, in the British district of Kumaon, lieut.-gov. of the N.W. Provinces, a village with a small Hindu temple, a mile from the left bank of the Lohooghat river, and two from its confluence with the Kalee (Eastern). Lat. 29° 20′, long. 80° 19′.

DOOPUND.—A town in the British district of Cuddapah, presidency of Madras, 120 miles W. of Masulipatam. Lat. 15° 56′, long. 79° 26′.

DOORAMOW.—A town in the territory of Oude, 60 miles S.E. from Lucknow, and 55 miles N.E. from Futtehpoor. Lat. 26° 17′, long. 81° 41′.

DOOREHA.—A town in the native state of Punnah, in Bundelcund, 26 miles S.E. from Punnah, and 96 miles N.E. from Jubbulpoor. Lat. 24° 27′, long. 80° 33′.

DOORGADAS, in the British district of Cawnpore, lieut.-gov. of the N.W. Provinces, a village on the route from Allahabad to Etawah, and 72 miles S.E. of the latter. Lat. 26° 11′, long. 79° 57′.

DOORGEENUGRA, in the jaghire of Rampoor, lieut.-gov. of the N.W. Provinces, a village on the route from Bareilly to Moradabad, and 38 miles N.W. of the former. Lat. 28° 44′, long. 79° 8′.

DOORHATTA.—A town in the British district of Hoogly, lieut.-gov. of Bengal, 32 miles N.W. of Calcutta. Lat. 22° 54′, long. 88° 5′.

DOORUNDA, in the British district of Chota Nagpoor, lieut.-gov. of Bengal, a cantonment on the route from Hazareebagh to Sumbulpoor, 60 miles S. of former, 170 N. of latter. At the cantonment is stationed the principal part of the Ramgurh light infantry and four guns, and two squadrons of local horse. A mile and a half north of the cantonment is the civil station of Kishenpoor, where is the Sudder or head establishment of the Governor-General's agent for the South-West Provinces. Doorunda is in lat. 23° 24′, long. 85° 20′.

DOORWAI, or **DHOORWYE**, in Bundelcund, a small town, the principal place of the jaghire of the same name, which contains an area of eighteen square miles, eight villages, and a population of 3,000 souls. Its chief has an annual revenue of 15,000 rupees, and maintains a small military force of eight horse and 230 foot. The jaghire is held from the East-India Company by sunnud or grant, dated in 1823. This raj was formerly tributary to Jhansi; but in 1821 the jaghiredars were induced to relinquish their claim to certain villages which had been resumed by Jhansi, in lieu of the annual tribute, which was calculated at 3,500 rupees per annum. Doorwai is 63 miles S.W. of Calpee. Lat. 25° 28′, long. 79° 7′.

DOOSTPOOR, in the territory of Oude, a town on the route from the cantonment of Goruckpoor to that of Sultanpoor, 84 miles W. of the former, 26 E. of the latter. Lat. 26° 18′, long. 82° 30′.

DOOVAH.—A town in the British district of Masulipatam, presidency of Madras, 54 miles N.E. of Masulipatam. Lat. 16° 47′, long. 81° 41′.

DOR, a small river of the Punjab, rises in lat. 34° 27′, long. 73° 7′, in the mountains west of Mazufurabad, which divide the valley of the Indus from that of the Jhelum. It holds a westerly course of about fifty miles, and, uniting with the Sirrun, falls into the Indus on the eastern side, near Torbela, in lat. 34° 8′, long. 72° 50′.

DORAHA.—A town in the native state of Bhopal, 18 miles N.W. from Bhopal, and 111 miles S.W. from Saugor. Lat. 23° 21′, long. 77° 10′.

DORAVEED.—A town in Hyderabad, or dominions of the Nizam, 50 miles W. from Hyderabad, and 37 miles E. from Mulkair. Lat. 17° 18′, long. 77° 50′.

DORENALL.—A town in the British district of Cuddapah, presidency of Madras, 139 miles W. of Masulipatam. Lat. 15° 55′, long. 79° 10′.

DOTUNUH.—See DEOTHAN.

DOUBLE ISLAND.—Situated off the coast of the Tenasserim provinces, 14 miles S. of Moulmein. Lat. 15° 52′, long. 97° 40′.

DOUDCANDEE.—A town in the British district of Tipperah, lieut.-gov. of Bengal, 22 miles S.E. of Dacca. Lat. 23° 31′, long. 90° 41′.

DOUDPOOR.—A town in the British district of Beerboom, lieut.-gov. of Bengal, 20 miles S. of Moorshedabad. Lat. 23° 54′, long. 88° 15′.

DOUJA, in the British district of Allahabad, lieut.-gov. of the N.W. Provinces, a village on the route, by Rajapoor ferry, from the cantonment of Allahabad to Banda, and 20 miles W. of the former. Lat. 25° 23′, long. 81° 35′.

DOULANG.—A town in the British district Amherst, in the province of Tenasserim, presidency of Bengal, 38 miles N.E. of Moulmein. Lat. 16° 42′, long. 98° 14′.

DOULEE.—A river rising in a spring on the southern face of the Niti Ghaut, in lat. 30° 57′, long. 79° 54′, leading from the British district of Kumaon to Tibet. The crest of the ghaut, from which the water flows southward, is 16,814 feet above the sea, yet was there no appearance of snow on it in the middle of August, nor even in the middle of October, though the cold was then found very severe. Passing by the village of Niti, it holds a course generally south for nineteen miles, as far as Mularee, in lat. 30° 42′, long. 79° 55′, 10,290 feet above the sea. As it is principally fed by rills running down the sides of the mountains inclosing the valley or vast gorge down which it flows, those supplies are suspended by congelation during the night, and released by the heat of the sun during the day, so that the river is invariably much fuller towards evening than in the morning. From Mularee the Doulee flows south-west about twenty miles to Tupookun, in lat. 30° 29′, long. 79° 42′, and 6,182 feet above the sea. At Tupookun the river turns north-west for eight miles, to its confluence with the Vishnoo at Vishnooprag, in lat. 30° 33′, long. 79° 38′, and 4,743 feet above the sea. The united stream of the Doulee and Vishnoo is named the Aluknunda downwards from the confluence; and the origin of the Doulee in the Niti Ghat is the remotest source of the Ganges, except that of the Jahnuvi.

DOULEE (river of Kumaon).—See DHOULI.

DOULUTPOOR, in the British district of Cawnpore, lieut.-gov. of the N.W. Provinces, a village on the route from Calpee to Pertabgurh, and three miles N. of the former. Water is abundant here. Lat. 26° 9′, long. 79° 49′.

DOULUTPOOR, in the British district of Suharunpoor, lieut.-gov. of the N.W. Provinces, a village on the route from Suharunpoor to Huridwar, and 27 miles E. of the former town. There is a bazar here, and an abundant supply of water. Distant N.W. from Calcutta 938 miles. Lat. 30° 6′, long. 77° 57′.

DOULUTPOOR.—A village in Sinde, situate near the left bank of the Indus. It forms part of the district of Bhoonj Bhara, and was comprised in the transfer of territory made by the British in 1843, from the ameers of Khyerpoor to Mahomed Bhawl Khan, in reward of his steady friendship. Lat. 28° 19′, long. 69° 45′.

DOUNDEEAKEIRA.—A town in the territory of Oude, on the left bank of the Ganges, and 50 miles S.W. from Lucknow. Lat. 26° 11′, long. 80° 45′.

DOUR VALLEY, situated in Bunnoo Murwut, of the Daman division of the Punjaub, is 80 miles W. of Kala Bagh, and 102 S.W. from Kohaut. Lat. 32° 55′, long. 70° 10′.

DOURAHAH SERIE, in Sirhind, a village on the route from Kurnaul to Loodiana, and 14 miles S.W. of the latter. It consists of a few hovels, scattered at the base of a slight eminence, surmounted by a caravanserai; but the remains of temples and tombs prove it to have been formerly more considerable. There is a small bazaar, and water is abundant. The road in this part of the route is good. Distant N.W. from Calcutta 1,075 miles. Lat. 30° 48′, long. 76° 8′.

DOURALA, in the British district of Meerut, lieut.-gov. of the N.W. Provinces, a village on the route from the town of Meerut to that of Suharunpoor, and eight miles N. of the former place. Distant N.W. from Calcutta 938 miles. Lat. 29° 7′, long. 77° 46′.

DOWDAUND.—A town in the British district of Bhagulpoor, lieut.-gov. of Bengal, 44 miles S.W. of Rajmahal. Lat. 24° 39′, long. 87° 17′.

DOWLASERUM.—A town in the British district of Rajahmundry, presidency of Madras, four miles S. of Rajahmundry. Lat. 16° 57′, long. 81° 50′.

DOWLPOOREE.—See DHOLPURI.

DOWLUTABAD, in Hyderabad, or the territory of the Nizam, a town with a celebrated fortress, near the north-west frontier. The fortifications of the town or pettah, which, however, are utterly contemptible, communicate on the east side with those of the stupendous fortress. This stronghold consists of a conical hill, or rather vast rock of granite, scarped all round to a complete perpendicular, for a height of about 150 feet from the base. The summit of this conical rock is a small platform not many feet in width, on which is mounted a brass twenty-four pounder; and there is also a staff, on which flies the flag of the Nizam. The upper and conical part of the hill is not accessible by any stairs or passage externally visible, but at the base of the scarp an opening gives admission into a low narrow passage, hewn in the solid stone, and leading to a large vault, excavated in the interior of the hill. From this chamber, a ramp, or gallery, gradually sloping upwards, and also excavated in the solid rock, winds round in the interior. This ramp, or ascending gallery, which has a height and breadth of about twelve feet, terminates above in a recess on the top of the rock, about twenty feet square. At the base of the hill, throughout its whole circuit, is a ditch, passable throughout its whole extent only by one causeway, constructed of stone, so narrow as to admit the passage of only two men abreast, and defended on the side towards the rock by a battlemented building. At a short distance outside the ditch is a minaret, apparently 100 feet high, said to be erected in commemoration of the first capture of this place by the Mahomedans. On the slope of the hill, and about 100 yards from the summit, is a cistern, hewn in the rock, and holding, it is conjectured, about forty hogsheads. The perpendicular height of the hill above the surrounding plain is about 500 feet. It is altogether isolated, being about 3,000 yards from the nearest hills, which are situate to the north and west. The original name of this place was Deoghur; and it received that of Dowlutabad from the Emperor Mohammed, son of Toghluk Shah, who proposed to make it the capital of the imperial state, to the supersession of Delhi, and who sought to force the inhabitants of the latter city to fix their abode in the former. The attempt, however, was abortive. It may be added, that the present state of Dowlutabad does not exhibit any appearance of the prosperity or good fortune indicated by its name. Dowlutabad is distant from Aurungabad, N.W., 10 miles; Hyderabad, N.W., 280; Bombay, N.E., 170. Lat. 19° 57′, long. 75° 18′.

DOWLUTGUNGE.—A town in the British district of Nuddea, lieut.-gov. of Bengal, 21 miles E. of Kishnuggur. Lat. 23° 25′, long. 88° 50′.

DOWLUTGURH.—A town in the Rajpoot state of Odeypoor, six miles from the right of the Koree river, and 57 miles S.W. from Nusseerabad. Lat. 25° 37′, long. 74° 25′.

DOWLUTPOOR.—A town in the British district of Hydrabad, in Scinde, presidency of Bombay, 10 miles from the left bank of the Indus, and 78 miles N. of Hydrabad. Lat. 26° 29′, long. 68° 5′.

DOWLUTPOOR.—A town of Malwa, in the native state of Bhopal, 41 miles S.W. from Bhopal, and 55 miles W. from Hoosungabad. Lat. 22° 53′, long. 76° 54′.

DOWNA.—A town in the British district of Nagpoor, 133 miles N.W. from Sumbulpoor, and 21 miles S. from Ruttunpoor. Lat. 21° 57′, long. 82° 2′.

DOWSAH, or DEOSUR, in the Rajpoot state of Jeypore, on the route from Agra to Ajmer, 110 miles W. of former, 118 E. of latter. It is of considerable size, and is built on one side of a rocky hill, having a flat summit, "nearly four miles in circumference, which, besides being difficult of access, is surmounted with a wall pierced with loopholes, and having two large bastions at the bottom, on one side of the rock." It is at present used as a state prison by the government of Jeypore. The town is surrounded by a ruinous wall of stone, and contains one fine old Hindoo temple, several smaller ones, a mosque, and some large and richly-carved houses, but all verging to decay. There are also many handsome tombs. Lat. 26° 50′, long. 76° 29′.

DOYANG.—A river of Eastern India, rising on the frontier of the native state of Muneepoor, in lat. 25° 36′, long. 94° 7′, and, flowing in a northerly direction through the British territory inhabited by the Naga tribes, falls into the Dhunseeree river in lat. 26° 7′, long. 93° 59′.

DRAS, or DURAS, in Ladakh, at a short distance north of the northern frontier of Cashmere, is a collection of villages, with a fort, in a valley of the same name, through which lies the route from Le to Cashmere by the Bultul Pass. Through the middle of the valley flows the river Dras, which, rising in the Bultul or Kantal Pass, a little to the south, flows northward to the Indus, which it joins opposite the village of Morol, in lat. 34° 44′, long. 76° 20′. Dras is 9,000 feet above the sea, and in lat. 34° 23′, long. 75° 54′.

DRAUPA, in the peninsula of Kattywar, province of Guzerat, a town situate in the district of Hallar. There are seventeen villages annexed to it, and the total population is estimated at 4,000. An annual tribute of 4,000 rupees is paid to the British government. Distance from Ahmedabad S.W. 170 miles. Lat. 22°, long. 70° 13′.

DROOG.—A town in the British district of Nagpoor, 141 miles E. from Nagpoor, and 22 miles W. from Ryepoor. Lat. 21° 11′, long. 81° 20′.

DROORAJAPATAM, or DOOGOORAUZEPATAM, in the British district of Nellore, presidency of Madras, a town on the Coromandel Coast, on the western shore of the northern inlet forming communication between Pulicat Lake and the Bay of Bengal. Southeast of the outward or seaward mouth of the inlet, "is a space from three to four miles wide, now called Blackwood Harbour, with soundings from four and a half fathoms near the shore, to six or seven fathoms contiguous to the edge" of Armegon Shoal, which shelters it in certain directions, while Pundi Point and shoal, and the mainland, protect it on other points; so that ships may lie here in safety; and it is stated by Captain Maxwell, assistant marine surveyor-general, that "it is the only place on the Coromandel Coast which offers the least protection to ships during an easterly gale." "During the north-east monsoon, or stormy season, the sea breaks very high on the shallow ridge of the shoal, rendering the harbour within comparatively smooth." It has recently been determined to connect this town with the city of Madras, by means of an extension of the navigable line of communication through the Pulicat Lake. Distance from Madras, N., 60 miles; Nellore, S., 34. Lat. 13° 59′, long. 80° 13′.

DUB, in the Punjab, a pass over a mountain on the route from Attock to Cashmere, by the Baramula road. While under the dominion of the Sikhs, it was infested by freebooters, who held possession of the fort of Futighur, and spread terror over the whole vicinity. But Hari Singh, an intrepid and energetic Sikh chieftain, attacked them, drove them out of a jungle where they took refuge, by firing it, and put the whole body to the sword. The Dub Pass is situate on the waterline dividing the feeders of the Kishengunga, and consequently of the Jhelum, on the east side, from those of the Indus on the west. Lat. 34° 17′, long. 73° 21′.

DUBAREE.—A town on the right bank of the Brahmapootra, in the British district of Goalpara, lieut.-gov. of Bengal, 46 miles S.W. of Goalpara. Lat. 26°, long. 89° 56′.

DUBBAR, or DABHA, an estuary of the Indus, being one of the numerous outlets by which the Indus reaches the sea. The mouth of the Dubbar is in lat. 24° 21′, long. 67° 17′.

DUBBOI.—See DHUBBOOEE.

DUBHAE, in the British district of Boolundshuhur, lieut.-gov. of the N.W. Provinces, a town on the route from Buddaon to Delhi, 69 miles S.E. of the latter. Population 7,837 souls. Lat. 28° 13′, long. 78° 21′.

DUBKA.—A river rising in the British district of Kumaon, lieut.-gov. of the N.W. Provinces, on the southern declivity of the Gagur or Ghutgarh mountain, in lat. 29° 27′, long. 79° 26′. It holds a south-westerly course for twenty miles, as far as the village of Burooa, where, in lat. 29° 20′, long. 79° 13′, it finally passes from the mountains into the plain; and for this distance the valley down which it flows forms the direct route from Almora to Moradabad. In this part of its course it is fordable at all seasons. From Burooa it takes a nearly southerly direction for about ninety miles, and falls into the Western Ramgunga in lat. 28° 24′, long. 79° 17′. Below Burooa, it bears the name of Googha, and still lower down, that of Nahul.

DUBOKA.—A town in the British district of Nowgong, Lower Assam, 73 miles E. of Gowhatty. Lat. 26° 6′, long. 92° 53′.

DUBRA, in territory of Gwalior, or possessions of Scindia, a village on the route from the fort of Gwalior to Saugor, 33 miles S. of former, 169 N.W. of latter. There is water from wells and a small stream, and supplies are procurable. Lat. 25° 53′, long. 78° 20′.

DUBWALLEE, in the British district of Bhutteeana, lieut.-gov. of the N.W. Provinces, a town on the route from Hansi to the Punjab, 96 miles N.W. of the former. Lat. 29° 57′, long. 74° 49′.

DUCHO.—A town in the native state of Nepal, on the left bank of a branch of the Bori Gunduk river, and 32 miles N. from Khatmandoo. Lat. 28° 9′, long. 85° 13′.

DUDANA.—A town in the province of Guzerat, or territory of the Guicowar, situate on the left bank of the Bunnass river, 39 miles S.W. from Deesa. Lat. 23° 49′, long. 71° 42′.

DUD COOSY, a river tributary to the Coosy, rises in Nepal, in lat. 27° 59′, long. 86° 31′, and, flowing in a southerly direction for about fifty miles through Nepal, falls into the Coosy, in lat. 27° 20′, long. 86° 30′.

DUDDEE.—A town in the British district of Belgaum, presidency of Bombay, 16 miles N.W. of the town of Belgaum. Lat. 16° 2′, long. 74° 30′.

DUDDIAN.WALLA, in the Daman division of the Punjab, a town situated on the left bank of the Khoorum river, 56 miles N. of the town of Dera Ismael Khan. Lat. 32° 35′, long. 70° 52′.

DUDDUR.—A town in the British district of Hydrabad, in Sinde, presidency of Bombay, 70 miles N.E. of Hydrabad. Lat. 26° 10′, long. 69° 8′.

DUDEROO, in the Rajpoot state of Beekaneer, a village on the route from Rutungurh to the town of Beekaneer, 66 miles E. of the latter. It contains 130 houses, and has a supply of excellent water from a well 196 feet deep. Lat. 27° 57′, long. 74° 24′.

DUDHOA, in the jaghire of Jhujhur, lieut.-gov. of the N.W. Provinces, a village on the route from Hansee to Neemuch, and 52 miles S. of the former. Water is good and abundant. Lat. 28° 28′, long. 76° 17′.

DUDKUNDA.—A town in the native state of Nepal, on the right bank of a branch of the San Coosy river, and 48 miles N.E. from Khatmandoo. Lat. 27° 54′, long. 86° 1′.

DUFFLAPOOR.—A town in the native state of Juth, one of the Sattara jaghires, 87 miles N.E. from Belgaum, and 84 miles S.E. from Sattara. Lat. 17°, long. 75° 8′.

DUG.—A town of the Rajpoot state of Jhallawur, formerly belonging to Holkar, but transferred in 1818, by the treaty of Mundeesor, to the ruler of Kotah, upon the partition of whose dominions it was allotted to the division of Jhallawur. Lat. 23° 55′, long. 75° 55′.

DUGDUGEE, in the British district of Futtehpoor, lieut.-gov. of the N.W. Provinces, a town on the right bank of the Ganges, 882 miles from Calcutta by the river, 74 miles above Allahabad, 22 miles E. of the town of Futtehpoor by land. Lat. 25° 56′, long. 81° 15′.

DUGSHAI, in Sirmoor, a sanatarium for troops, between the rivers Sutlej and Jumna, eight miles S.E. from Sabathu, 16 miles S. from Simla. Lat. 30° 53′, long. 77° 7′.

DUHLEE, in the British district of Etawa, lieut.-gov. of the N.W. Provinces, a town situate in lat. 27° 2′, long. 78° 52′.

DUHLEEA, in the British district of Furrukhabad, lieut.-gov. of the N.W. Provinces, a town on the right bank of the Ramgunga, eight miles N.E. of the city of Furrukhabad. Lat. 27° 26′, long. 79° 45′.

DUHRAON, or DHERAON, in the British district of Boolundshuhur, lieut.-gov. of the N.W. Provinces, a village on the route from Allyghur cantonment to that of Delhi, and 33 miles N.W. of the former. Lat. 28° 18′, long. 77° 53′.

DUKIA, or DUKEEA, in the British district of Moradabad, lieut.-gov. of the N.W.

Provinces, a village on the route from Moradabad to Almora, and 29 miles N. of the former place. Lat. 29° 12′, long. 79° 1′.

DUKKA JEUNG.—A town in the native state of Bhotan, on the right bank of the Guddada river, and 62 miles N.E. from Darjeeling. Lat. 27° 21′, long. 89° 15′.

DUKTOWLEE.—See DEKTOWLI.

DULASSEREE.—The name assigned in the lower part of its course to the Konaie, a great watercourse in Bengal.—See KONAIE.

DULCHIPOOR.—A town in the Boondela native state of Shahgurh, 33 miles S.E. from Tehree, and 34 miles N.E. from Saugur. Lat. 24° 14′, long. 79° 3′.

DULEELUGUNJ.—A town in the territory of Oude, on the left bank of the Ganges, and 91 miles S.E. from Lucknow. Lat. 25° 40′, long. 81° 33′.

DULEEPGUNGE, in the territory of Oude, a village on the route by Shahabad from Lucknow to Shahjehanpoor, 24 miles south of the latter. It has a bazar and abundance of good water. Lat. 27° 31′, long. 80° 2′.

DULEEPGURH, in the Daman division of the Punjab, a fort designed and built by Major Edwardes, and situated on the right bank of the Khoorum, 63 miles N.W. of the town of Dera Ismael Khan. Lat. 32° 41′, long. 70° 41′.

DULEYNUGUR, or DULABNAGAR, in the British district of Etawa, lieut.-gov. of the N.W. Provinces, a village on the route from Calpee to the cantonment of Etawah, and 29 miles S.E. of the latter. Lat. 26° 31′, long. 79° 26′.

DULGANO.—A town in the British district of Durrung, Lower Assam, 62 miles W. of Bishnath. Lat. 26° 34′, long. 92° 12′.

DULSAEPOOR, in the British district of Muttra, lieut.-gov. of the N.W. Provinces, a village on the route from the city of Agra to Bareli, and 38 miles N.E. of the former. Lat. 27° 32′, long. 78° 30′.

DULSING SERAI.—A town in the British district of Tirhoot, lieut.-gov. of Bengal, 51 miles E. of Dinapoor. Lat. 25° 38′, long. 85° 55′.

DUMAJEE.—A village in Sinde, on the route from Sehwan to Kurrachee, and 60 miles N.E. of the latter town. The road near Dumajee is represented as indifferently good, and forage can be obtained to a considerable extent. The supply of water is rather scanty: there are two wells which afford it, but they are liable to fail in the dry season. After rainy weather, a torrent, called the Dumajee river, flows by the village, and falls into the Dhurwal river about twelve miles to the N.E. Dumajee is in lat. 25° 21′, long. 67° 50′.

DUMBA, or DOOMBEH, a small river in Sinde, rises in the southern part of the Keertar range of mountains, about twenty miles north-east of Kurrachee, in lat. 25° 4′, long. 67° 16′, and, after a southerly course estimated at eighteen miles, falls into the river Mularee, in lat. 24° 52′, long. 67° 15′. About ten miles above its mouth it is crossed by the route from Kurrachee to Sehwan, and is at that point, during the rainy season, a small stream. In the dry season, the channel has no stream, though water may be obtained by digging in the bed. The place where it is crossed by the road, as above mentioned, is called the Dumba Camp. The road there is generally good, and forage may be obtained in considerable quantities.

DUMDUHA, in British district of Purneah, lieut.-gov. of Bengal, a town 22 miles W. of the town of Purneah. It is situate on the west or right bank of the river Cosy, is the principal place of a pergana of the same name, and has 1,300 houses. Lat. 25° 41′, long. 87° 11′.

DUMDUM, in the British district called the Twenty-four Pergunnahs, a town, formerly the head-quarters of artillery for the presidency of Bengal. In its vicinity is the cannon-foundry, of which a military writer thus speaks:—"This cannon-foundry is in every respect better contrived than that of Woolwich. It contains a boring-room in which twelve brass guns may be bored at the same time, for the government procures the iron guns from Europe. During the time I was there, six guns were cast; and the arrangements are such, that three times the number might have been manufactured." The church "is a very pretty building, divided into aisles by two rows of Doric pillars, and capable of containing a numerous congregation." Distant from Barrackpore, S.E., 10 miles; Calcutta, N.E., eight miles. Lat. 22° 38′, long. 88° 30′.

DUMDUM.—A valley in Cashmere, with a pass over the mountains which inclose that country to the south. This pass, situate between the mountains Futi Panjal and Pir Panjal, is generally called the Pir Panjal Pass, but sometimes the Nandan Sar Pass. It is 11,800 feet above the sea, and through it lies the route into Cashmere from the Punjab, by Rajawur. The river Rembeara rises about the summit of the pass, and, flowing north-east, falls into the Vehut or Jhelum, which drains the whole of Cashmere. It is called the Huripur river by Vigne. Lat. 33° 45′, long. 75°.

DUMDUMA, in the British district of Allahabad, lieut.-gov. of the N.W. Provinces, a village on the left bank of the Ganges, 788 miles N.W. of Calcutta by the river route, 16 S.E. of the city of Allahabad by the same. Lat. 25° 19′, long. 82° 9′.

DUMDUMA, in the British district of Baraset, lieut.-gov. of Bengal, a village with a police-station, on the Isamutti, an offset of the Ganges. Distance from Calcutta, E., 42 miles. Lat. 22° 28′, long. 89° 3′.

DUMDUMMA.—A town in the British district of Dinajepoor, lieut.-gov. of Bengal, 96 miles E. of Bhagulpore. Lat. 25° 18′, long. 88° 31′.

DUMDUMINEAH.—A town in the British district of Bhagulpoor, lieut.-gov. of Bengal, 20 miles S.W. of Rajmahal. Lat. 24° 55′, long. 87° 31′.

DUMJA.—A town in the native state of Nepal, on the left bank of the San Coos river, and 36 miles N.W. from Khatmandoo. Lat. 27° 25′, long. 85° 46′.

DUMKEIRA.—A town in the British province of Nagpoor, late territory of the rajah of Berar, 173 miles E. from Nagpoor, and 94 miles S.E. from Ramgurh. Lat. 21° 39′, long. 81° 45′.

DUMMOW, in the British territory of Saugor and Nerbudda, a town near the common boundary of Malwa and Gondwana, the principal place of a pergunnah of the same name, on the route from Jubbulpoor to Saugor, 65 miles N.W. of former, 46 E. of latter. It has a large bazar, and water is abundant from wells. The area of this pergunnah is 1,554,058 acres. The total population at the period of the latest return was 363,584. The Hindoos greatly predominate; the numbers being, agricultural, 282,079; non-agricultural, 69,416; total, 351,495; while those of all other denominations amount only to—agricultural, 3,626; non-agricultural, 8,463; total, 12,089. The town of Dummow is distant from Calcutta, *viâ* Allahabad, 775 miles. Lat. 23° 50′, long. 79° 30′.

DUMOH.—See DUMMOW.

DUMPA.—A town in the native state of Bhotan, 146 miles N.E. from Dargeeling, and 130 miles N. from Goalpara. Lat. 28°, long. 90° 27′.

DUMUL.—A town in the British district of Dharwar, presidency of Bombay, 52 miles S.E. of Dharwar. Lat. 15° 18′, long. 75° 50′.

DUNAHAR, in the British district of Mynpooree, lieut.-gov. of the N.W. Provinces, a village on the route from the city of Agra to the cantonment of Mynpooree, and nine miles W. of the latter. The road in this part of the route is in many places laid under water during the periodical rains in the latter part of summer; at other times it is tolerably good. The country is level, and partially cultivated. Lat. 27° 14′, long. 78° 58′.

DUNDEESRUH.—See DERESURA.

DUNDOOKA, in the British district of Ahmedabad, presidency of Bombay, a town 62 miles S.W. of the city of Ahmedabad, 100 N.W. of Surat. Lat. 22° 20′, long. 71° 56′.

DUNDORUH.—See DENDOWRA.

DUNGAVA.—A town in the British province of Nagpoor, situate on the left bank of the Hutsoo river, and 208 miles S.W. from Sherghotty. Lat. 22° 28′, long. 82° 34′.

DUNGHYE, in the British district of Behar, lieut.-gov. of Bengal, a small town on the route from Hazareebagh to Benares, 43 miles N.W. of former, 146 S.E. of latter. It is situate at the north-west extremity of the pass of the same name, at the bottom of the descent by which the road passes from the high land of Ramgurh to the plains of Behar. The road down this descent is, according to Jacquemont, execrable, and indicating great want of care and skill in the government engineers who laid it down. The little town itself has a bazar, and is well supplied with water. Elevation above the sea 660 feet. Lat. 24° 27′, long. 85°.

DUNGKOT.—A town in the native state of Nepal, 84 miles N.E. from Khatmandoo, and 137 miles N.W. from Darjeeling. Lat. 28° 10′, long. 86° 32′.

DUNHORA.—A town in the British province of Nagpoor, late territory of the rajah of Berar, 102 miles S.E. from Nagpoor, and 67 miles N.E. from Chanda. Lat. 20° 14′, long. 80° 21′.

DUNKOUR, in the British district of Bolundshuhur, lieut.-gov. of the N.W. Provinces, a town, the principal place of the pergunnah of the same name, situate on the route from Muttra to Delhi by the left bank of the Jumna, and 28 miles S.E. of Delhi. Lat. 28° 21′, long. 77° 37′.

DUNTOLA.—A town in the British district of Purneea, lieut.-gov. of Bengal, 45 miles N.E. of Purneea. Lat. 26° 9′, long. 88° 6′.

DUNWAR.—A town in the British district of Shahabad, lieut.-gov. of Bengal, 51 miles S.W. of Dinapoor. Lat. 25° 9′, long. 84° 28′.

DUPHA PANEE RIVER, a small stream of the Sudiya district of Upper Assam, rises in lat. 27° 38′, long. 96° 50′, and, flowing in a south-westerly direction for thirty-five miles, falls into the Noh Dihing river near the village of Imjong, in lat. 27° 28′, long. 96° 30′.

DUPHALA. — A tribe inhabiting the country lying between the main range of the Himalaya Mountains and that known as the Sub-Himalaya, and which is situate to the north of the Luckimpoor district of Upper Assam. The centre of the tract is in lat. 27° 35′, long. 93° 45′.

DURA, in the British district of Agra, lieut.-gov. of the N.W. Provinces, a town close to the western frontier towards Bhurtpoor, 19 miles S.W. of the city of Agra. Lat. 27° 3′, long. 77° 48′.

DURABUND, or **DERABUND**, in the tract of territory on the right bank of the Indus, a small town and fort in the Derajat, about 42 miles S.W. of Dera Ismael Khan. It is the place of rendezvous of the Lohani and other caravans, which every spring depart westward with the annual supply of British and Indian wares for Central Asia. These Lohanis descend, with their camels and other cattle, to spend the winter in the mild climate and luxuriant pastures stretching along the western bank of the Indus, and at the same time to furnish themselves with articles suitable for supplying their customers in Afghanistan and the countries north and west of it;

and they assemble at Durabund to muster their strength for resisting the predatory tribe infesting the roads through which they have to pass. The town of Durabund is a small ill-built place, but bearing evidence of having been more prosperous, until ruined by the predatory attacks of the Vaziris and other marauders from the west. The permanent population is scarcely 1,000. Lat. 31° 35′, long. 70° 13′.

DURAJEE, in the delta of Sinde, a small town on the Buggaur, or great western branch of the Indus. When, about 200 years ago, this branch was navigable from the sea to the main channel of the river, Durajee and Lahory-bunder, about two miles lower down, were the principal ports of Sinde, being accessible for vessels of 200 tons burthen. The Buggaur, however, has now for many years ceased to be navigable during the season of low water in the Indus, and goods landed at Durajee are, by means of camels, conveyed to Tatta overland, a distance of thirty miles. Though, during the season of low water, the Buggaur is unnavigable above Durajee, it has at all times a depth of at least twelve feet deep from that place downwards as far as the Pittyanee mouth of the Indus, a distance of twenty-eight miles. This easy access from the sea renders Durajee the port of Tatta and the greater part of the delta, as Kurrachee is the general haven for the upper part of Sinde. The closure of the port of Vikkur, in consequence of the great alteration which took place in the Hujamaree mouth in 1839, will probably cause an increased resort to Durajee. Lat. 24° 30′, long. 67° 30′.

DURALAH, in Sirhind, a village on the route from Kurnal to Lodiana, and 17 miles N.W. of the former town. Distant N.W. from Calcutta 982 miles. Lat. 30° 2′, long. 76° 52′.

DURBUH, or DURBA, in the British district of Bhuttiana, lieut.-gov. of the N.W. Provinces, a small town or village near the south-eastern boundary, towards Hurriana. On the restoration of the canal of Feroz Shah in 1825, a branch, for the purpose of irrigation, was made from it to Durba, a distance of thirty-two miles. It gives name to one of the pergunnahs or subdivisions of the district. Lat. 29° 25′, long. 75° 12′.

DURBUNGA, in the British district of Tirhoot, lieut.-gov. of Bengal, a town on the route from Dinapoor to Purneah, 70 miles N.E. of former, 131 W. of latter. It is situate on the banks of the river Buckea, and supplies for troops may be had here in great abundance. Lat. 26° 8′, long. 85° 58′.

DUREEAGUNJ, in the British district of Furrukhabad, lieut.-gov. of the N.W. Provinces, a town on the north-western frontier, towards Aligurh, 33 miles N.W. of the city of Furrukhabad. Lat. 27° 37′, long. 79° 8′.

DUREEBA.—A town in the Rajpoot state of Jeypoor, 50 miles N. from Jeypoor, and 103 miles N.W. from Bhurtpoor. Lat. 27° 39′, long. 75° 59′.

DUREEPOOR.—See DERIAPOOR.

DURGAON, or DERGAON, in the native state of Gurwhal, a village on the western declivity of a mountain rising from the left bank of the Supin or Tonse, about 2,000 feet above its bed, and a mile above its confluence with the Roopin. Jacquemont, from an observation with the barometer, estimates its elevation above the sea at 7,159 feet. Lat. 31° 4′, long. 78° 11′.

DURGAPOOR.—A town in the British district of Mymensing, lieut.-gov. of Bengal, 75 miles S. of Goalpara. Lat. 25° 4′, long. 90° 41′.

DURGUK.—A town in the native state of Cashmere, or territory of Gholab Singh, 220 miles N.E. from Jamoo, and 189 miles N.E. from Kangra. Lat. 34° 8′, long. 78° 17′.

DURKOTHEE.—See DHOORCATTEE.

DURLAH.—A river of Bengal, rising in Bhootan, in lat. 27°, long. 88° 43′, and, proceeding in a southerly direction for forty miles, reaches the northern boundary of the British district of Dinajepore. Flowing through that district south-east for about ten miles, it passes first into the territory of Cooch Behar, and then into the district of Rungpore, and re-entering a second time each of the two last-mentioned tracts, which it traverses for the aggregate distance of ninety-eight miles, it is finally discharged into the Brahmapootra, on the right or west side, in lat. 25° 40′, long. 89° 45′. Its course throughout is from north-west to south-east, and its total length 148 miles. During the rainy season, it is navigable throughout for craft of about ten tons burthen, but at other times the upper part is not navigable. As far up as Mogulhat, however, about forty miles from its mouth, it is at all times navigable for craft of ten or twelve tons burthen.

DURMAHPOOR.—A town in the territory of Oude, seven miles E. from the left bank of the Gogra river, and 86 miles N.E. from Shahjehanpoor. Lat. 28° 11′, long. 81° 20′.

DURMAWARAM.—A town in the British district of Bellary, presidency of Madras, 196 miles N.W. of Madras. Lat. 14° 25′, long. 77° 48′.

DURRAUNGDRA, in the peninsula of Kattywar, province of Guzerat, a town in the district of Jhalawar, near the northern frontier, towards the Runn or Salt Marsh. It was formerly a place of considerable importance, but is represented now as rather decayed, though still numbering 2,000 houses in good preservation, and having walls erected at a late period. Its chief, of the Jhala tribe, is considered one of the most exalted of that race. The territory to which this place gives name is, in its relations with the British government, considered united to the small tallook of Hulwud, conjointly with which it is returned officially as having a population estimated at 51,709, and paying annually a tribute of 43,909 rupees. In 1828, it was stated that many villages had been deserted, and that from famine and the inroads of freebooters, the population had been reduced to little more than a third of its former amount. There are some manufactures of coarse cloth, carpeting, and other articles. Distance from Ahmedabad, W., 75 miles; Baroda, N.W., 125. Lat. 23°, long. 71° 25′.

DURROOR.—A town situate in one of the recently sequestrated districts of Hyderabad, or dominions of the Nizam, 36 miles N.W. of Kurnool. Lat. 16° 13′, long. 77° 44′.

DURRUNG, in Lower Assam, a town, the chief place of a considerable district of the same name, containing an area of 2,000 square miles, and a population of 80,000 souls. The town is situate on the right bank of the Brahmapootra, 73 miles S.W. of Bisnath. Lat. 26° 25′, long. 92° 2′.

DURSENDAH.—The principal place of the pergunnah of the same name, a town on the river Baghin, a tributary of the Jumna, seven miles S.W. of the right bank of the latter, 39 E. of the town of Banda. Lat. 25° 27′, long. 80° 57′.

DURUK.—A town in the territory of Oude, 70 miles E. from Pileebheet, and 81 miles N.E. from Shahjehanpoor. Lat. 28° 35′, long. 81°.

DURWESHABAD, in the British district of Futtehpoor, lieut.-gov. of the N.W. Provinces, a town on the route from Hummerpoor to the town of Futtehpoor, and 14 miles N.W. of the latter. Lat. 26° 1′, long. 80° 41′.

DURYAH KHAN, in the Sinde Sagur Dooab division of the Punjab, a town situated near the left bank of the Indus, and 11 miles E. of the town of Dera Ismael Khan. Lat. 31° 45′, long. 71° 5′.

DUSERA, in the British district of Boolundshuhur, lieut.-gov. of the N.W. Provinces, a village on the route from Allygurh cantonment to that of Delhi, and 24 miles N.W. of the former. Lat. 28° 10′, long. 77° 58′.

DUSGAON.—A town in the British district of Burdwan, lieut.-gov. of Bengal, 79 miles N.W. of Calcutta. Lat. 23° 30′, long. 87° 42′.

DUSNUGGUR.—A town in the British district of Silhet, lieut.-gov. of Bengal, 36 miles S. of Silhet. Lat. 24° 25′, long. 91° 45′.

DUSPULLA.—One of the Cuttack Mehals, in Orissa, placed under the political superintendence of an agent appointed by the Governor-General of India. It has an area of 162 square miles, containing a population of 7,290: its centre is about lat. 20° 25′, long. 84° 40′. The timber required for the car of Juggernaut is annually supplied from this petty state, where the sal-tree, of which the car is constructed, grows to a prodigious size.

DUSSARA, in Guzerat, or the territory of the Guicowar, a town lying a short distance beyond the northern frontier of the prant or district of Jhalawar, and near the eastern border of the Runn, or great Salt Marsh. With the twenty-five villages annexed to it, this place is shared among several zemindars, members of the same family, called the maliks of Dussara, who pay annually a tribute of 12,000 rupees to the British government. Distance from Ahmedabad, N.W., 55 miles. Lat. 23° 18′, long. 71° 52′.

DUTI, or DIPAL.—A town in the native state of Nepal, on the left bank of one of the branches of the Ghogra river, and 101 miles N.E. from Bareilly. Lat. 29° 5′, long. 80° 54′.

DUTNUGGUR, in Bussahir, a large village on the left bank of the Sutluj. It is situate where the valley of the Sutluj expands, and forms a flat of about two miles in length, well watered by canals, and bearing luxuriant crops of rice. It is inhabited by about fifty families, of whom one-half are Brahmins, holding their lands rent free. Elevation above the sea 3,200 feet. Lat. 31° 24′, long. 77° 38′.

DUTTAEEBOODD, in Orissa, a town in the hill zemindarry of Jeypoor, 15 miles S.E. from Jeypoor, and 102 miles N.W. from Vizagapatam. Lat. 19°, long. 82° 40′.

DUTTAHUR.—A town in the British district of Nellore, presidency of Madras, 137 miles N.W. of Madras. Lat. 14° 50′, long. 79° 22′.

DUTTEEAH, in Bundelcund, a town, the principal place of the territory of the same name, lying on the route from Agra to Saugor, 125 miles S.E. of the former, 148 N.W. of the latter. Like most places in Bundelcund, it has a rocky site. It "is surrounded by a stone wall about thirty feet high, with its foundation on a solid rock; but it has no ditch or glacis, and is capable of little or no defence against cannon." Though the streets are narrow and intricate, the place has altogether a flourishing aspect, there being many good houses, the residences of the principal zemindars or landholders throughout the territory. The residence of the raja is in the town, within the walls of a garden or pleasure-ground, about ten acres in area, "crossed and recrossed at right angles by numerous walks, having rows of plantain and other fruit-trees on each side, and orange, pomegranate, and other small fruit-trees to fill the space between." The inclosing wall, about thirty feet high, with embattled towers at each of its four corners, has, in its eastern face, a fine and large gateway; and surmounting the wall at the opposite side of the pleasure-ground is the pavilion or lodge in which the raja resides. Between the pavilion and the gateway a building rises, in the midst of a fine reservoir, of which the following description is given:—"The shaft presented an octagon of about twenty feet span, surrounded with columned cloisters, and at each angle a figure of an elephant, sculptured in stone, with uplifted proboscis, spouted water to a vast height into the air." Within the wall of the city is another palace, at present untenanted ; and outside, and westward of the city, is a third, of great extent as well as strength, and in a fine style of architecture, but likewise deserted. The population, estimated by Sleeman at forty or fifty thousand, consists almost exclusively of votaries of Brahminism, though three or four miles from the town is a curious cluster of temples of the Jains. The Brahminical temples appear to be not much worth notice. The rocky ground around the town for two or three miles is overgrown with copse or stunted forest, abounding in game. Adjacent to the town is a jhil, or small artificial lake.

The raj or territory of which Dutteeah is the principal place, lies between lat. 25° 32′—26° 18′, long. 78° 15′—78° 54′. It is estimated to contain an area of 850 square miles, and 380 villages, with a population of 120,000. The revenue was estimated, in 1832, at 120,000*l.*, and in 1847, at 100,000*l.* The raja pays no tribute. He maintains a military force, consisting of 1,000 cavalry, 5,000 infantry, and eighty artillerymen. This state was formerly part of the dominions of Oorcha, and its raja appears to be descended from Dewada Bir, who, about the end of the fourteenth century, at the head of a colony of warlike Rajpoots, invaded and conquered a considerable tract of country. Subsequently, Dutteeah, after passing under the overwhelming domination of the Mogul empire, became subordinate to the Peishwa, as appears from the treaty concluded with the raja by Lord Lake, wherein the former "professes his obedience and attachment to the British government, and to that of his highness the Peishwa." By this treaty, the raja "submits to the arbitration of the British government in matters of dispute with his neighbours, promises to join the British forces with his troops, and to act in subordinate cooperation. The ancient territories of his house are guaranteed, also protection against foreign aggression." The Peishwa having in 1817, by Art. XIII. of the treaty of Poona, ceded to the British government all his rights in Bundelcund, the raja of Dutteeah, in acknowledgment of his zealous friendship and active cooperation, was, by treaty in 1818, rewarded by the Governor-General with a considerable addition to his territory. The last hereditary raja died in 1839, and was succeeded by a foundling whom he had adopted, and who was recognised by the British government. Dutteeah is distant W. of Allahabad, by Banda, Chirkaree, and Jhansi, 260 miles; N.W. of Calcutta 755. Lat. 25° 40′, long. 78° 31′.

DUTTODAH.—A town in the native state of Indore, or possessions of Holkar's family, 107 miles S.W. from Bhopal, and 215 miles S.E. from Ahmedabad. Lat. 22° 33′, long. 75° 55′.

DUWARKA, or DOARKA, in the district of Sultanpoor, territory of Oude, a fort on the left bank of the river Goomtee, 32 miles S.E. of Sultanpoor cantonment, 110 S.E. of Lucknow. It is held by Fateh Bahadur, a notorious freebooter, who has 1,000 men under his command. In 1812, it was stormed by a British force commanded by Colonel Faithfull, and for some years was occupied by a detachment of the Company's troops, but evacuated about 1838. It was then repaired by the present occupant, who pays annually 50,000 rupees to the Oude government, and remunerates himself by widely ravaging the neighbouring country. Lat. 26° 2′, long. 82° 28′.

DWARA HATH, or DEWARA HATH, in the British district of Kumaon, lieut.-gov. of the N.W. Provinces, a village on the route from Almora to Sireenuggur, and 25 miles N.W. of the former. Here, according to Traill, are tombs substantially built of large flat tiles, the memorials of Moguls located on the spot in the course of Tamerlane's expedition into Hindustan. Lat. 29° 47′, long. 79° 28′.

DWARKA, or DWARIKA, called also Jigat, in the peninsula of Kattywar, province of Guzerat, a town on the western shore, in the district of Okamundel. The land towards the sea is moderately elevated, and the place is conspicuous, from the commanding appearance of the great temple of Krishna or Dwarkanath, "the Lord of Dwaraka." It is the most celebrated of all the shrines raised to Krishna, and is built on an eminence rising from the seashore, and surrounded by a fortified wall (which likewise encircles the town), from which it is, however, separated by a lofty partition-wall, through which it is necessary to pass to see it to advantage. "It may be said to consist of three parts: the munduff, or hall of congregation; the devachna, or penetralia (also termed gabarra); and the sikra, or spire." "The munduff is square, measuring twenty-one feet internally, and five distinct stories high. Each story is colonnaded, the lower being twenty feet in height, and of the same square form to the last, where the architraves are laid transversely to form a base for the surmounting dome, whose apex is seventy-five feet from the pavement. Four massive pillars on each face of the square form the foundation for this enormous weight; but these being inadequate to sustain it, intermediate pillars to each pair have been added, to the sacrifice of all symmetry. A colonnaded piazza surrounds the lowest story, of about ten feet in breadth, from which to the north, south, and west, portions are projected, likewise colonnaded. Each story of the munduff has an internal gallery, with a parapet of three feet in height, to prevent the incautious from falling. These parapets, divided into compartments, had been richly sculptured." "The sikra or spire, constructed in the most ancient style, consists of a series of pyramids, each representing a miniature temple, and each diminishing with the contracting spire, which terminates at 140 feet from the ground. There are seven distinct stories, before this pyramidal spire greatly diminishes in diameter. Each face of each story is ornamented with open porches surmounted by a pediment, supported by small columns. Each of these stories internally consists of column placed upon column, whose enormous architraves increase in bulk in the decreasing ratio of the super-imposed mass; and although the majority at the summit are actually broken by their own weight, yet they are retained in their position by the aggregate unity." "The entire fabric, whose internal dimensions are seventy-eight feet by sixty-six, is built from the rock, which is a sandstone of various degrees of texture, forming the substratum of the island. It has a greenish hue, either from its native bed, or from imbibing the saline atmosphere, which, when a strong light shines upon it, gives the mass a vitreous transparent lustre." Joined by a colonnade to this temple is a smaller one, dedicated to Deoki, the mother of Krishna; and at the opposite angle of the great temple is another, still smaller, dedicated to Krishna, under his title of Madhu Rae, or the "Prince the intoxicator." The Gumti, a small rivulet which flows by the group, is considered especially sacred, but it is so shallow that it does not reach the ancle. The site of the temple was once insulated; but the sea having thrown up a sandbank across the channel, this sacred spot is now connected with the mainland. About eighteen miles north of Dwarika is Amrara, supposed to be Muldwarka or ancient Dwarka, where Krishna met his death. Others, however, consider Mahadoopoor, ninety-five miles south-eastward of Dwarka, to have been contiguous to Mool Dwarka, which, according to tradition, was swept away by the sea. At this spot, native report declares that a bird annually springs from the foam of the sea, and having perched and sported on the top of the temple, falls down and dies, and from its plumage the Brahmins prognosticate whether the year will be rainy or otherwise. Dwarka is distant from Ahmedabad, S.W., 235 miles; Baroda, W., 270. Lat. 22° 15′, long. 69° 1′.

DWARKA.—A river rising in the British district of Beerbhoom, lieut.-gov. of Bengal, in lat. 23° 57′, long. 87° 21′. Flowing through that district in an easterly direction nearly parallel with the Mor river, which it receives after a course of about sixty miles, the united stream, twenty miles below the confluence, falls into the Bhagruttee, in lat. 23° 43′, long. 88° 10′.

DYAGUNJ.—See Deaganj.

DYALOUNG.—A river rising in lat. 26° 4′, long. 93° 42′, on the southern boundary of the British district of Nowgong, in Lower Assam. Flowing in a westerly direction for ninety-five miles, it falls into the Kullung, a tributary of the Brahmapootra, in lat. 26° 12′, long. 92° 31′.

DYE, in the district of Bainswara, territory of Oude, a village on the route from Cawnpore to Pertabgurh, 56 miles S.E. of the former. Lat. 26° 2′, long. 81° 14′.

DYEHINDIA.—A village situate in one of the recently sequestrated districts of Hyderabad, or the dominions of the Nizam, 36 miles S.W. of Ellichpoor. Lat. 20° 50′, long. 77° 11′.

DYHNWOLEE.—A town in the British district of Tannah, presidency of Bombay, 37 miles N.E. of Bombay. Lat. 19° 3′, long. 73° 25′.

E.

ECHAGUR.—A town in the British district of Pachete, lieut.-gov. of Bengal, 163 miles N.W. of Calcutta. Lat. 23° 6′, long. 85° 59′.

ECHAWUR, in Malwa, a town in the territory of Bhopal, on the route from Hindya to Sehora, 45 miles N. of former, 12 S. of latter. At the commencement of the present century, the district was wrested from Bhopal by the Mahrattas; but being ceded in 1818, with several other possessions, by the Peishwa to the British government, it was with four other pergunnahs granted to the nawaub of Bhopal, in reward of his zeal and fidelity. Lat. 23° 3′, long. 77°.

ECHIBUL, in Kashmir, a fine fountain, discharging a vast quantity of the most beautifully limpid water. It is situate in the eastern part of the district of Bureng, and has four or five orifices, from the principal of which the spring rises with such force as to form what may be termed a mound of water, a foot and half high, and twelve feet in diameter. Vigne, with much probability, supposes it to be the efflux of that portion of the water of the river Bureng which sinks into the ground about ten miles to the south-east. If, however, this opinion be correct, the sunken stream must receive large additions from springs in its subterraneous course, as the volume of water discharged at Echibul far exceeds that which disappears in the bed of the Bureng. According to Vigne, the water is not very good for drinking. Bernier, on the contrary, who describes this vast fountain under the name of Achiaval, states the water to be excellent (*admirablement bonne*); he adds, that it is so cold as to be almost insupportable to the touch. At the time of his visit (1665), it was surrounded by a superb pleasure-ground, belonging to Aurungzebe, having been made by order of his grandfather, Jehangir; but all is now in utter ruin. Lat. 33° 39′, long. 75° 12′.

EDGHEER.—See Eidgheer.

EDMONSTONE ISLAND.—An island at the mouth of the Hoogly river. From a mere half-tide sandbank, it became an island two miles long, covered with shrubs, and affording a supply of fresh water. In 1820 it was adopted as a marine station for affording assistance to ships in distress; but was subsequently abandoned, in consequence of the rapid demolition of the island by the encroachment of the sea. Lat. 21° 32′, long. 88° 20′.

EDMY, in the British district of Mynpooree, lieut.-gov. of the N.W. Provinces, a village on the route from the city of Agra to the cantonment of Mynpooree, and 36 miles W. of the latter. Lat. 27° 7′, long. 78° 35′.

EDUR.—The principal Rajpoot state of the Myhee Caunta, in the province of Guzerat, tributary to the Guicowar, but under the political superintendence of the government of Bombay. This petty state was founded by Anund Sing and Raee Sing, sons of the celebrated Ajeet Sing, rajah of Joudpore. The districts were assigned to them by their elder brother, the viceroy of Guzerat, under the Moguls; and the brothers, accompanied by several chiefs and 5,000 followers, took possession of their territory about the year 1724. The revenues of the state, including those of the recently acquired possessions of Ahmednuggur, and of the feudatories of both districts, were estimated in 1847 at 23,434*l.*; of which the rajah's share was 15,000*l.*, subject to the deduction, on account of tribute to the Guicowar, of 3,295*l.* The political relations of the British government with this state originated in 1820, under an arrangement with the Guicowar, by which it was stipulated that his troops should evacuate the province; and the British government thereupon guaranteed the payment of his dues free of all expense. The districts of Ahmednuggur, already noticed, were formerly comprised within the state of Edur, but were bestowed, about sixty years ago, by the ruling prince, upon his second son, Sugram Sing. The late rajah of Ahmednuggur, Tukht Sing, having, however, been elected to the vacant throne of Joudpore, his possessions in the Myhee Caunta reverted to the senior branch of the family, and are now reincorporated with the state of Edur. In 1848, the military force at the disposal of the Edur state, inclusive of the quotas of the feudal chiefs, consisted of 921 horse and foot. These troops are maintained almost entirely for purposes of police.

EDUR, in the Myhee Caunta division of Guzerat, presidency of Bombay, the principal town of the district. It is a place of little importance, containing about 1,200 houses. Though encircled by hills on three sides, and defended on the fourth by a wall, the position would be one of no strength, even if the defences were completed, as it is commanded by a hill to the right, which forms part of the range. In the rear, and upon the hill, which there rises to the height of between 400 and 500 feet, is a fort, now in ruins, which in former times afforded shelter to the rajahs of Edur when driven from the town below. The hill is ascended by a steep and stony zigzag pathway, having four gateways, in tolerable repair. The eminence on the right of the town is surmounted by several Jain temples, and also by the remains of a palace, built by the former rajahs of Edur. Population 10,000. Lat. 23° 50′, long. 73° 3′.

EEB.—A river rising in lat. 20° 50′, long. 73° 42′, in the territory of the Daung rajahs, on the western slope of the Syadree range, and, flowing westerly for seventy miles through the native states of the Daung, Baunsda, and the British district of Surat, falls into the Arabian Sea, in lat. 20° 43′, long. 72° 54′.

EECHOUREEA, in the British district of Bareilly, lieut.-gov. of the N.W. Provinces, a village situate on the left bank of the Ramgunga, six miles S. of the town of Bareilly. Lat. 28° 17′, long. 79° 29′.

EECTENA.—A town in the British district of Mymunsing, lieut.-gov. of Bengal, 215 miles N.E. of Calcutta. Lat. 24° 30′, long. 91° 7′.

EEKAH, in the Rajpoot state of Joudpore, a village on the route from Phulodee to Pokrun, and six miles N.E. of the latter place. It is situate in an elevated rocky tract, and has a small fort, on a craggy eminence. On the south there is an extensive depression, which after the rainy season becomes a great sheet of salt-water, but is at other times dry. Lat. 26° 56′, long. 72° 4′.

EEKAIREE, or AKHERI, in the territory of Mysore, a decayed town, once the capital of a considerable and flourishing state, is situate amidst the headwaters of the Varada. Its walls are of great extent, and form three concentric inclosures. There are besides a citadel, a great temple of Siva, and a mean building, which was the ancient palace of the extinct dynasty of Sedasiva, a personage whose wonderful adventures are preserved in Hindoo fable. Historically, he appears to have been a gauda or chief of Kilidi, in the neighbourhood of Akheri, who received a grant of some districts from Krishna Rayara, of Vijayanagar, who also bestowed on him the name of Sedasiva Nayaka, he having previously borne that of Bhadraconda. Kilidi continued the seat of his government for about twelve years afterwards, when he removed it to Akheri, which then attained the highest measure of prosperity which it ever reached, and of which most exaggerated reports are preserved by the natives. In 1645 or 1646, the government was removed to the neighbouring town of Bednore, and subsequently Akheri became deserted. At this time, all the buildings except the temple above mentioned are desolate, and the town without inhabitants. In 1763, Hyder Ali, the usurper of Mysore, took Bednore, then governed by the widow of the last actual chief, a profligate and shameless woman, who had caused the adopted son of her deceased husband to be murdered; and who, in conjunction with her paramour, had selected another successor to the first place in the state. All the parties were righteously subjected by Hyder to imprisonment, intended to be perpetual, but from which the chances of war subsequently relieved them. Akheri is distant from Bednore, N., 20 miles; from Seringapatam, N.W., 162. Lat. 14° 7′, long. 75° 5′.

EENDPALSIR-KA-BAS, in the Rajpoot state of Beykaneer, on the route from Ruttungurh to the town of Beykaneer, and 30 miles E. of the latter. It contains fifty houses, and has a supply of brackish water from a well 274 feet deep. It is the largest of seven contiguous villages, with separate wells. Lat. 27° 55′, long. 74° 15′.

EESAEE, or HEESEYEE, in the British district of Mynpooree, lieut.-gov. of the N.W. Provinces, a village on the route from the cantonment of Allygurh to that of Mynpooree, and 16 miles N.W. of the latter. Lat. 27° 21′, long. 78° 55′.

EESAGURH, or ESAUGURH, in the territory of Gwalior, or possessions of the family of Scindia, a town, with a fort, in a hilly and difficult country. It was formerly called Oondee, and belonged to a chief of the Ahir Rajpoots, from whom, at the close of the last century, it was taken by Doorjun Lal, a celebrated chief of the Kaichi Rajpoots, and by him denominated Bahadurghur, or "Hero's Town." It became the capital of his new dominions. Subsequently, in 1803, it was wrested from him by Baptiste, one of Doulat Rao Scindia's officers. It is styled in Malcolm's Index, "the fort of Resum or Esaugurh." Lat. 24° 50′, long. 77° 55′.

EESAH, in the British district of Etawa, lieut.-gov. of the N.W. Provinces, a village on the route from the cantonment of Agra to that of Etawa, and three miles N.W. of the latter. Lat. 26° 48′, long. 79° 2′.

EESOULEE.—A town in the territory of Oude, on the left bank of the Goomtee river, and 69 miles S.E. from Lucknow. Lat. 26° 24′, long. 81° 58′.

EGUTPOORA.—A town in the British district of Ahmednuggur, presidency of Bombay, 71 miles N.E. of Bombay. Lat. 19° 43′, long. 73° 34′.

EIDGHEER, in Hydrabad, or territory of the Nizam, a town on the left or north-west bank of the Beema, a considerable tributary of the Krishna. Distance from Hydrabad S.W. 100 miles. Lat. 16° 45′, long. 77° 11′.

EILGUNDELL.—A town in Hyderabad, or dominions of the Nizam, 81 miles N.E. from Hyderabad, and 123 miles S.E. from Nandair. Lat. 18° 23′, long. 79° 4′.

EINWAH.—A town in the territory of Oude, on the left bank of the Gogra river, and 54 miles W. from Goruckpoor. Lat. 26° 35′, long. 82° 33′.

EJASSON.—A town of Malwa, in the native state of Burwanee, on the left bank of the Nerbudda river, and 205 miles W. from Baitool. Lat. 22° 5′, long. 74° 48′.

EKDIL SERAI, in the British district of Etawah, lieut.-gov. of the N.W. Provinces, a village on the route from Calpee to the cantonment of Etawah, and six miles S.E. of the latter. Lat. 26° 45′, long. 79° 8′.

EKDULLA KHASS, in the British district of Futtehpoor, lieut.-gov. of the N.W. Provinces, a town on the route from Allahabad to Hummeerpoor, 52 miles N.W. of the former. Lat. 25° 38′, long. 81° 9′.

EKHUMBA.—A town in the British district of Purneea, lieut.-gov. of Bengal, 66 miles N.E. of Bhagulpoor. Lat. 25° 56′, long. 87° 40′.

EKOU.—A town in the native state of Nepal, 48 miles S.W. from Khatmandoo, and 52 miles N. from Bettia. Lat. 27° 30′, long. 84° 34′.

EKTALE.—A town in the British district of Midnapoor, lieut.-gov. of Bengal, 88 miles S.W. of Calcutta. Lat. 22° 20′, long. 87° 4′.

ELAMBAZAR, in the British district of Beerbhoom, lieut.-gov. of Bengal, a town on the route from Berhampore to Bancoorah, 63 miles S.W. of former, 52 N.E. of latter. It is situate on the left bank of the river Hadjee, here navigable, and is from this circumstance a great mart for rice, extensively grown in the vicinity. The number of houses was estimated in 1814 at 544, the number of inhabitants at 2,950. Distance from town of Burdwan, N.W., 35 miles; from Calcutta, N.W., 90. Lat. 23° 37′, long. 87° 39′.

ELEPHANTA, in the presidency of Bombay, a small island on the east side of the harbour of Bombay, and distant about five miles from the mainland. It is something less than six miles in circumference, and is "composed of two long hills, with a narrow valley between them. The usual landing-place is towards the south, where the valley is broadest." About 250 yards to the right of the landing-place is a large clumsy figure of an elephant, cut out of an insulated black rock; and from this circumstance the island (which by the natives is called Gara-pori) has derived the denomination by which it is known to Europeans. This huge figure, which is thirteen feet in length, is represented as much mutilated, and rapidly sinking into total decay, its head and neck having, in 1814, fallen from the rest of the body, which was also fast coming to the ground, an extensive fissure having taken place in the back. On advancing farther from the landing-place, the visitor comes suddenly in front of "the grand entrance of a magnificent temple, whose huge massy columns seem to give support to the whole mountain which rises above it," and out of which it is hewn. The geological formation of the rock is probably basaltic. The entrance is by a spacious front, supported by two ponderous pillars and two pilasters, forming three openings, under a thick and steep rock, overhung by brushwood; and the impression on reaching the interior is rendered very deep and solemn, by "the long ranges of columns, that appear closing in perspective on every side; the flat roof of solid rock, that seems to be prevented from falling only by the massive pillars, whose capitals are pressed down and flattened, as if by the superincumbent weight; the darkness that obscures the interior of the temple, which is dimly lighted only from the entrances; and the gloomy appearance of the gigantic stone figures, ranged along the wall, and hewn, like the whole temple, out of the living rock." There are three principal parts in this extraordinary work: the great temple, 133 feet broad and 130½ long; and two smaller temples, one on each side of the principal one. These two appendent temples do not range in a straight line with the front of the principal one, but recede considerably from it, being approached by two narrow passes in the hill, one on each side of the grand entrance, but at some distance therefrom. Each of these passes conducts also to a side-front of the grand excavation, exactly like the principal front, consisting of two huge pillars with two pilasters. These two side-fronts are precisely opposite to each other, on the east and west, the grand entrance facing the north; and the plan is regular, there being eight pillars and pilasters in a line from the northern entrance to the southern extremity, and the same number from the eastern to the western entrances. The only striking deviation from this regularity in the chief temple, is afforded by the occurrence of a small square excavation, observable on the right in passing up the temple. At the further extremity of the temple are two small excavations, facing each other on the right and left. "The pillars, which all appear to run in straight lines, parallel to each other, and at equal distances, are crossed by other ranges running at right angles in the opposite direction; they are strong and massy, of an order remarkably well adapted to their situation and the purpose which they are to serve, and have an appearance of very considerable elegance. They are not all of the same form, but differ both in size and ornaments, though this difference also does not at first strike the eye. They rise to upwards of half their height from a square pedestal, generally about three feet five inches each way, crowned on the top by a broad bandage of the same shape: above this, but divided from it by a circular astragal and two polygonic fillets, rises a short round fluted shaft, forming about a fourth of the column, and diminishing with a curve towards the top, where a circular cincture of beads binds round it a fillet composed of an ornament resembling leaves, or rather cusps, the lower extremity of which appears below the cincture, while the superior extremity rises above, projecting and terminating gracefully in a circle of overhanging leaves or cusps. A narrow band divides this ornament from the round fluted compressed cushion, which may be regarded as the capital of the column, and as giving it its character: its fluted form coalesces beautifully with the fluted shaft below. This cushion has its circumference bound by a thin flat band or fillet, as if to retain it; and above supports a square plinth, on which rests the architrave, that slopes away on each side in scrolls, connected by a band or riband, till it meets the large transverse beam of rock, which connects the range of pillars." Fronting and within the principal entrance, is a "gigantic bust, representing some three-headed being, or three of the heads of some being to whom the temple may be supposed to be dedicated. Some writers have imagined that it is what they have called the Hindu trinity of Brahma, Vishnu, and Shiva." Others consider it a triform representation of Siva alone. This bust, which represents the deity down to the breast, and is consequently a third-length, has been ascertained by measurement to the top of the cap of the middle head to be about eighteen feet high; and a notion of its bulk may be formed from the measurement in an horizontal curved line, embracing the three heads at the height of the eyes, and touching them, which is nearly twenty-three feet. This, though the most remarkable, is but one specimen amidst a profusion of carved figures, representing various subjects of Brahminical mythology, though it is puzzling to observe, that one at least appears to be a representative of Buddh, held in abomination by the Brahmins. The precise nature of the worship to which these temples were consecrated, seems, indeed, to be of very disputable character. There are, in different parts, three sanctuaries or shrines, which, in the opinion of a judicious writer already quoted, were devoted to the adoration of certain emblems, which, though occupying a distinguished place in Hindu mythology, are not fitted to be made the subject of popular disquisition. This opinion is deduced from the position of the emblem in question in various parts of these excavations. The writer above referred to, in explaining the grounds of his belief, observes, that the "use made of temples by the ancient Greeks and Romans, as well as by the modern Hindus, is considerably different from that required of them by Christian nations. A Hindu goes alone, as an ancient Roman would have done, when he finds it convenient, offers his solitary prayers before his idol, prostrates himself in his presence, and leaves his offering: he attempts to bribe his god to prosper him in his trade, whether it be merchandise, or procuration, or theft. There is no stated regular time of teaching, no public prayers said by a priest in the name of a mixed congregation, no gathering of the people to go through a solemn service. Their great festivals are like our ideas of a fair; each man goes in his own time to the temple, makes his offering at the feet of the idol, goes out, and purchases sweetmeats. All teaching or reading of the sacred books is in private houses; or, if it is in the temple, it is in the courts of the temple, never in the consecrated edifice: the verandas or porticos near the temple are used just as any others equally convenient would be. This use, to which the courts of the temple are applied, will throw light on many passages of history and the sacred volumes of the Jews. It is evident that the temples of nations, whose worship is so conducted, need not be large, like our churches, since it is not required that they should contain a multitude. In all very ancient temples, however magnificent, the part of the temple in which the deity is supposed to reside is small, surrounded by numerous buildings, in which the priests and servants of the temple reside. This seems to have been the plan of the first temple of Jerusalem; it was that of the older Grecian temples, as we may observe from the Ion of Euripides; and it is at this day that presented by the temple of Mecca. In the temples of the Hindus the great object of worship is not constantly exposed to view, nor placed in the larger outer building; it is always in an inner, small, dark apartment, usually having only one door, requiring to have lights burning before it in order to be seen, and facing the door, so as to be visible from the further side of an intervening saloon." The arrangements at Elephanta appear, as far as can be judged, to have corresponded precisely with this view, and to countenance the conjecture of the writer quoted. All, however, is wrapped in mystery. Even the period and authors of these extraordinary works are totally unknown; but there seem no good grounds for assigning them a very remote antiquity. The stone is of a mouldering nature, and many parts are far gone in decay. Elephanta is seven miles E. of Bombay. Lat. 18° 57′, long. 73°.

ELEPHANT POINT, on the coast of Chittagong, lieut.-gov. of Bengal, 85 miles S. of Chittagong, and 89 miles N.W. of Akyab. Lat. 21° 9′, long. 92° 8′.

ELEPHANT POINT.—A headland on the southern coast of the British province of Pegue, situate on the west side of the mouth of the Rangoon river, 23 miles S. of Rangoon: it derives its name from a clump of cocoanut-trees, "which, with the help of the imagination, does somewhat resemble that animal." Lat. 16° 28′, long. 96° 25′.

ELLICHPOOR, in the territory of Hyderabad, or the dominions of the Nizam, a town, the principal place of an extensive jaghire or feudal possession. The town is situate on the river Purna, a tributary of the Taptee, and is of considerable size, but slenderly fortified, being only partially surrounded by a stone wall, which, though sixty feet high, is but four feet in thickness. It is surmounted by battlements, and entrance is obtained by means of a highly-ornamented gateway, built, as well as the wall, of sandstone. The palace of the nawaub has no great splendour, but in its vicinity are some handsome houses and bazars built of brick. The nawaub holds his jaghire from the Nizam, on condition of furnishing a contingent of "a brigade of two battalions of infantry, 2,000 horse, and four guns." Of late, the relation between the feudatory and his chief has been disturbed. On the 30th May, 1850, an action took place between the troops of the nawaub of Ellichpoor and a body of those of the Nizam, sent to dispossess the former of his jaghire. Considerable loss was sustained on both sides, but the result seems to have been favourable, on the whole, to the dependent chief. Another action, fought on the 20th July, is reported to have terminated in his defeat. The nawaub, however, rallied, and on the 9th August gained a victory over the troops of his master, which was followed by another on the 28th September. The grounds of the quarrel are not very satisfactorily explained; but the total disorganization of the Nizam's financial arrangements, and the character of the measures to which his ministers have too often resorted to repair their condition, give plausibility to the statement which ascribes the difference to the aggression of the superior ruler. Ellichpoor forms part of the Nizam's territory which has been recently sequestrated to the British, as a provision for the maintenance of his military contingent. Distance from Hydrabad, N., 275 miles; from Madras, N.W., 600; from Bangalore, N., 570; from Nagpore, W., 100; from Bombay, N.E., 345; from Calcutta, W., 700. Lat. 21° 10′, long. 77° 36′.

ELLORA.—A decayed town in Hyderabad, or dominions of the Nizam, situate 13 miles N.W. from Aurungabad, and seven from Dowlutabad. It was formerly a place of some note, deriving its celebrity chiefly from the remarkable excavations in the neighbouring mountain, known as the temples of Ellora. According to Hindoo legend, the date of these temples is carried back for a period of 7,950 years, and their origin ascribed to Rajah Eeloo, the son of Peshfont, of Ellichpore, when 3,000 years of the Dwarpa Yoag were yet unaccomplished. The more rational account of the Mahometans states that "the town of Ellora was built by Rajah Eel, who also excavated the temples. Eel Rajah was contemporary with Shah Momin Arif," who lived 950 years ago. According to Elphinstone, however, the first mention in history of these caves occurs in connection with the Princess Dewal Devi, daughter of the rajah of Guzerat, who was captured by a party who had gone from the camp of Alp Khan to visit the excavations at Ellora. These wonderful productions of human industry and perseverance, "which," says Elphinstone, "have been compared, as works of labour, to the pyramids of Egypt, and which in reality far surpass them as specimens of art," have drawn forth expressions of admiration from all who have studied them. "Whether," says Sir Charles Malet, "we consider the design, or contemplate the execution of these extraordinary works, we are lost in wonder at the idea of forming a vast mountain into almost eternal mansions. The mythological symbols and figures throughout the whole leave no room to doubt their owing their existence to religious zeal,—the most powerful and most universal agitator of the human mind."

From the elaborate notice of a more recent observer, Colonel Sykes, it appears that the hill containing the excavations takes the form of a crescent, presenting its concavity to the west, and rising in its extremities to an elevation considerably above the intermediate level. The sculptures at the two extremities are those of Dehr Warra and Parusnath, the interval, somewhat exceeding a mile, being occupied by other caves at irregular distances from each other, and seldom on the same level. The very minute and complete account of these celebrated caves which is contained in Colonel Sykes's paper, will furnish the inquirer with the fullest information, and leave him nothing to desire further. To this, therefore, the reader is referred. Ellora was ceded, in 1818, by Holcar, under the treaty of Mondesoor, to the British, who transferred it to the Nizam in 1822, by the treaty of Hyderabad. Ellora is in lat. 20° 2′, long. 75° 13′.

ELLORE, in the British district of Masulipatam, presidency of Madras, a town with a military station, situate on the Jummalair, a torrent flowing in a direction south-east from the Eastern Ghats, and which, about three miles below the town, falls into the Colair Lake. On the right bank of the river are the barracks and the cantonment hospital; on the other side, the officers' houses. Communication between all parts of the station is practicable throughout the year, as the torrent is never unfordable. The town is tolerably well built. The sides of the streets and roads in the town and its vicinity are planted with rows of trees, affording very grateful shade, in a place where the heat has been known to reach 110° within-doors, and 120° in tents. The nights, especially during the months of April and May, are very oppressive; and it was in the latter month, when the land-wind blows with much violence, that the great degree of heat above mentioned was observed. The official report styles Ellore a "populous town;" but the number of its inhabitants is not stated. Distance from Bombay, S.E., 565 miles; Hyderabad, E., 180; Mangalore, N.E., 500; Bellary, N.E., 300; Bangalore, N.E., 350; Madras, N., 255; Masulipatam, N., 39; Calcutta, S.W., 620. Lat. 16° 42′, long. 81° 10′.

ELPHINSTONE ISLAND.—An island on the coast of Tenasserim, thirteen miles long and four and a half broad, 65 miles N.W. from the town of Tenasserim. Lat. 12° 21′, long. 98° 10′.

EMANGUNGE, in the British district of Allahabad, lieut.-gov. of the N.W. Provinces, a village on the route from the cantonment of Allahabad to Futtehpoor, and 20 miles N.W. of the former. Lat. 25° 31′, long. 81° 40′.

EMAUM GHUR, in Sinde, was lately a strong fortress in the Thur or Great Sandy Desert, separating that country from Jessulmere. As scarcely a drop of fresh water can be had on the route from Sinde after leaving Choonkee, distant about fifty miles from Emaum Ghur, this fortress was generally considered by the ameers as an inexpugnable place of refuge. On this account, when the disputes between them and the British came to extremity, Sir Charles Napier determined at all risks to attempt its seizure. Setting out with fifty cavalry, two twenty-four-pound howitzers, drawn by camels, and three hundred and fifty European infantry, mounted on animals of the same description—two on each, he, after a very trying march of three days, over a succession of steep sandhills, reached the fort, which was immediately surrendered. The captor describes it as "exceedingly strong against any force without artillery. The walls are forty feet high, one tower is fifty feet high, and built of burned bricks. It is square, with eight round towers, surrounded by an exterior wall of fifteen feet high, lately built. There are some bomb-proof chambers." Twenty thousand pounds of powder were found in various places built up for concealment. These were employed in springing thirty-four mines, which reduced the fort to a mass of ruins, shapeless and irretrievable. The grain found in store had been previously distributed in rations. The British force marched back to the interior of Sinde without any loss. Emaum Ghur is in lat. 26° 35′, long. 69° 20′.

EMENABAD, in the Reechna Dooab division of the Punjab, a town situated on the road from Lahore to Wazeerabad, 33 miles N. of the town of Lahore. Lat. 32° 4′, long. 74° 10′.

EMILEEA, in the British district of Allahabad, lieut.-gov. of the N.W. Provinces, a village on the route by the Kutra Pass from Allahabad to Rewa, and 24 miles S.E. of the former city. Lat. 25° 15′, long. 82° 10′.

EMROKEE, in the native state of Sumpter, in Bundlecund, a village on the route from Gwalior to Saugor, 60 miles S.E. of the former. Here, in the beginning of December, 1817, the British army under command of marquis of Hastings, governor-general, was encamped in its advance towards Gwalior, to intimidate Scindia. Distance S.W. of Calpee 54 miles. Lat. 25° 47′, long. 79° 2′.

ENAYUT-KA-SARAE, in the British district of Allahabad, lieut.-gov. of the N.W. Provinces, a village on the route from the city of Allahabad to Benares, and eight miles S.E. of the former. Lat. 25° 25′, long. 82°.

ENDREESA, in the Punjab, a village situate in the bifurcation where the Beas and Sutluj rivers unite. Burnes sought here in vain for the altars dedicated by Alexander to commemorate his conquests. He found nothing but a brick ruin, unquestionably of Mahometan origin. Were this even the actual locality of those altars which have given rise to so much controversy, the probability of their still existing is perhaps not great; it being unlikely that the natives would allow the trophies of the invader's triumph to remai after his disappearance. Endreesa is in lat. 31° 12′, long. 75° 3′.

ENGLISH BAZAR, in the British district of Maldah, lieut.-gov. of Bengal, a town, th seat of the civil establishment of the district, on the route from Berhampore to Purnea, 62 miles N. of former, 70 S.E. of latter. It i situate on the right or west bank of th Mahanunda. Distant N. from Calcutta 188 miles. Lat. 24° 58′, long. 88° 10′.

ENNORE.—A town in the British district of Chingleput, presidency of Madras, nin miles N. of Madras. Lat. 13° 13′, long. 80° 23′.

ERICH, or IREJ.—A town of Bundelcund, in the British district of Jaloun, situate on the south or right bank of the river Betwa, on the route from Saugor to Gwalior, 65 miles S.E. of the latter. It was formerly a place of importance, and had a considerable population, principally Mahomedan, as is indicated by the numerous mausoleums, surmounted by domes, around it. Here, in the end of November, 1817, the British army, commanded by the marquis of Hastings, governor-general, was encamped in its advance on Gwalior, to intimidate Scindia. It was part of the territory of Jhansi until 1843, when it was ceded by the rao of that place to the East-India Company. At the time of cession, its annual revenue was returned at 7,148 rupees. Lat. 25° 47′, long. 79° 9′.

ERINPOORA.—A town in the Rajpoot state of Serohee, 135 miles S.W. from Nusseerabad, and 78 miles S. from Jodhpoor. Lat. 25° 10′, long. 73° 9′.

ERRIODE.—A town in the British district of Madura, presidency of Madras, 230 miles S.W. of Madras. Lat. 10° 37′, long. 78° 8′.

ERROAD.—See YIRODU.

ERRUCKPOOR.—A town in the British district of Cuttack, lieut.-gov. of Bengal, 196 miles S.W. of Calcutta. Lat. 20° 40′, long. 86° 11′.

ERUNDOLE.—A town in the British district of Candeish, presidency of Bombay, 212 miles N.E. of Bombay. Lat. 20° 56′, long. 75° 19′.

ESANUGGUR.—A town in the Boondela state of Chutterpoor, 84 miles N.E. from Saugur, and three miles E. from the right bank of the Deesaun river. Lat. 24° 52′, long. 79° 26′.

ESEE, in the British district of Allygurh, lieut.-gov. of the N.W. Provinces, a village on the road from the cantonment of Allygurh to that of Muttra, and eight miles S. of the former. Lat. 27° 48′, long. 78° 7′.

ESEEPOORA, in the British district of Allahabad, lieut.-gov. of the N.W. Provinces, a village on the route from Allahabad cantonment to Jaunpore, and nine miles N.E. of the former. Lat. 25° 27′, long. 82° 1′.

ESEWUN, in the territory of Oude, a ruined town on the route by Nanamow Ghat from Futtehgurh cantonment to Lucknow, 25 miles W. of the latter. When Lord Valentia passed it in 1803, it was nearly in ruins, having been deserted for the neighbouring town of Meahganj, recently founded by the eunuch Almas Khan, minister of finance to the Nawaub Vazir of Oude. Its site is, however, pleasant, on a slight eminence, overlooking a small lake. It is mentioned in the Ayeen Akbery under the name of Aseyun. Lat. 26° 48′, long. 80° 30′.

ESSAU KAYLE, in the Daman division of the Punjab, a town situated on the right bank of the Indus, 177 miles N. of the town of Mooltan. Lat. 32° 39′, long. 71° 16′.

ESUN, a small river of the Doab, rises in the British district of Allyghur, in the neighbourhood of Sikundrarow, in lat. 27° 41′, long. 78° 27′. It takes a south-easterly course towards the Ganges, into which it falls on the right side, in lat. 26° 47′, long. 80° 11′. At the town of Mynpooree, it is crossed by a bridge of brick. About twenty miles lower down, the route from Etawa to Futtehgurh crosses it by a ford. It is throughout a mere torrent, and in the dry season the current totally ceases in some parts of its channel.

ESURDA, or ESUNDA, in the territory o Jyepore, in Rajpootana, a town 60 miles S. of the city of Jyepore, and near the left bank of the river Bunas. Broughton, who passed close to it, mentions, "It belongs to a takoor or lord of the Jypoor family; is surrounded by a strong wall and ditch, and has a citadel in the centre of the place, and is apparently by much the handsomest and most commodious town that I have seen in this part of India." Lat. 26° 10′, long. 76° 10′.

ESWUNTGURH.—A town in the British district of Rutnageriah, presidency of Bombay, 164 miles S.E. of Bombay. Lat. 16° 39′, long. 73° 25′.

ETA, in the Rajpoot state of Jessulmeer, a village on the route from the town of Beykaneer to that of Jessulmeer, and 55 miles N.E. of the latter. The road in this part of the route is heavy, lying among sandhills. Lat. 27° 10′, long. 71° 42′.

ETAROLI, in the British district of Etawa, under the lieut.-gov. of the N.W. Provinces, a village on the route from Lucknow in Oude, by Nanamow, to Etawa cantonment, and 20 miles E. of the latter place. Lat. 26° 46′, long. 79° 25′.

ETAWAH.—A British district named from its principal place, and subject to the lieut.-gov. of the N.W. Provinces. It is bounded on the north by the British districts Mynpooree and Furruckabad; on the east by the British district of Cawnpore; on the south by Bundelcund; on the south-west by the Mahratta territories of Gwalior; and on the west by the British district of Agra. It lies between lat. 26° 21′—27° 9′, long. 78° 46′—79° 49′, and contains an area of 1,674 square miles. It was formerly part of Cawnpore, but was formed into a separate zillah under the sanction of the home authorities in 1840. The greater part of Etawah lies in the Doab, a small strip only, forming the pergunnah of Burpoora or Janibrast, being separated from the rest by the Jumna, and lying along the right or south-western bank of that river. The Jumna touches on the north-western extremity of the district, and, flowing in a south-easterly direction, either bounds or traverses it for 115 miles. About 25 miles S.E. of the town of Etawah, the Jumna is joined on the right side by the Chumbul. So considerable is the accession of water from this source, that the Jumna below the confluence has been known to rise in twelve hours between six and seven feet, in consequence of a flood in the Chumbul. The obstacles which formerly presented themselves to the safe navigation of the Jumna in this part of its course, were principally shifting shoals and sandbanks, trunks of trees imbedded in the bottom, and numerous boulders, as well as fixed rocks of kankar or calcareous conglomerate. The sunken trees were removed after a careful search, in 1833, and during the last twenty years, the clearance of other impediments has been in progress, under the directions of various officers of the engineer service. The channel is most obstructed at Kurimkhan, ten or twelve miles below the mouth of the Chumbul. The Seyngur or Kurun runs nearly parallel to the Jumna, but ten or twelve miles more to the eastward, and falls into that river on the left side, about twenty miles south of the southern frontier. The Rind flows across the north-eastern extremity of the district, in a direction parallel to the Seyngur, but about fifteen miles more to the eastward. The Pandwa and some other streams of the district are mere torrents during the periodical rains, and cease to flow during the dry season. All the streams run towards the south-east, indicating the general slope of the country to be in that direction; but there is also a slope from the middle part of the Doab towards the Jumna, all the streams of the district being ultimately discharged into that river. The levels taken in laying down the Etawah branch of the prolongation of the Ganges Canal have shown the elevation of the country above the sea to diminish from about 676 at the northern frontier, to 640 at the town of Etawah.

The principal spring crops are wheat, barley, gram (Cicer arietinum), and other pulse of various kinds. The autumnal crop consists of opium, sugarcane, cotton, indigo, rice, jowar (Sorghum vulgare), bajra (Holcus spicatus), moth (Phaseolus aconitifolius). The government assessment upon the lands of this district has been fixed for a specified period, and is not liable to increase till the year 1871. In the vicinity of the cantonment of Etawah, the seeds of European vegetables are sown after the rainy season, at the close of summer, and peas, cauliflowers, and lettuce are fit for use at Christmas, attaining a high degree of excellence; carrots and other esculent roots are of inferior quality; oranges, citrons, limes, and lemons, are very fine, and grapes succeed tolerably. Melons are abundant, luxuriant, and excellent. The apple, mango, plantain, guava, jak (Artocarpus integrifolia), succeed well; but pomegranates are scarcely worth gathering. The unsheltered situation of Etawah affords ample opportunity for the contemplation of the changes of the atmosphere. In no part of India do the hot winds blow with greater fury. They commence in March, and continue during the whole of April and May. The wind usually rises about eight in the morning, and continuing through the whole day, subsides at sunset, though it sometimes blows throughout the whole night. "Every article of furniture is burning to the touch; the hardest wood, if not well covered with blankets, will split with a report like that of a pistol; and linen taken from the drawers is as if just removed from a kitchen fire. The nights are terrible, every apartment being heated to excess, each may be compared to a large oven." The human constitution suffers great exhaustion from this state of temperature. The hot winds are succeeded by the monsoon or periodical rains, the transition being marked by a furious tornado. Even at midday, darkness as of night sets in, caused by the dense clouds and volumes of dust; and so loud is the roar of the storm, that the incessant peals of thunder can be heard only at intervals, whilst the flashes of lightning seldom pierce through the gloom. The rain then descends in torrents, floods the country, and refreshes the animal and vegetable world. "Before the watery pools have penetrated into the parched earth, so rapid is the growth of vegetation, patches of green appear along the plain, and those who take up their posts in the veranda for an hour or two may literally see the grass grow. In the course of a single day the sandy hillocks will be covered with verdure, and in a very short time the grass becomes high and rank." The rains usually continue from the first or second week in June until the middle of October, and in some seasons are very violent, causing extensive and destructive inundations. The final fall is generally the heaviest, lasting three or four days, and ushering in cool weather. The climate is delightful from October to March; exercise in the open air may be taken with satisfaction on foot until ten o'clock in the forenoon, and all day in carriages; fires are requisite to comfort in the evening, and warm bedding is requisite at night.

The vigorous administration of the laws by the British authorities has of late years much checked the hand of crime in this district, which was formerly infamous as one of the principal haunts and places of refuge of the Thugs and Phansigars, and whose secret and systematic robberies and murders have been carried to an appalling extent all over Hindostan. Some of these wretches were Mahomedans, but the majority were Hindoos; some gangs contained a mixture of all denominations and castes. In some instances these assassins were under the protection of the zemindars or landed proprietors of the eastern part of the district, but the mixed gangs generally lurked in the ravines and jungles of the wild tract of Sindouse, on the right of the Jumna, and in the Doab between that river and the Chumbul. Some ostensibly followed agricultural avocations, or other pursuits equally unsuspected, though they were in reality supported by their nefarious practices; others were mere vagrants, living, when urged by want, on the flesh of jackals and other unclean animals. To so great an extent did the crime of thuggee once prevail, that in one year (1808) sixty-seven dead bodies were taken out of wells in this district. The population in 1853 was ascertained by official return to amount to 610,965. Of this number, 401,367 are returned as Hindoos engaged in agriculture; 176,791 Hindoos engaged in other pursuits; 9,327 Mahomedans and others, not Hindoos, agricultural; and 23,480 of those classes, non-agricultural. Hence it is seen that the Hindoos constitute an overwhelming majority of the population.

The following is a classification of the towns and villages of the district:—

Number containing less than 1,000 inhabitants..	1,313
Ditto more than 1,000 and less than 5,000......	96
Ditto more than 5,000 and less than 10,000	4
Ditto more than 10,000 and less than 50,000....	1
Total........................	1,414

The principal towns will be found noticed in the proper places. The principal routes through the district are—1. From south-east to north-west, from Calpee to Muttra, by Etawah, running parallel to the left bank of the Jumna, and on an average ten or twelve miles from it; 2. from south-east to north-west, from Cawnpore, joining the former route five miles from the cantonment of Etawah; 3. from Lucknow, in Oude, to the cantonment of Etawah, and, subsequently crossing the Jumna, to Gwalior; 4. from north-east to south-west, from the cantonment of Futteghur to that of Etawah; 5. from north to south, from the cantonment of Mynpooree to that of Etawah. The right of the British government to this tract dates from 1801, when it was ceded by the Nawaub Vizier, forming a portion of the possessions alienated by that prince in commutation of subsidy.

ETAWAH, a town, the principal place of the pergunnah and also of the district of the same name, is situate about a mile east of the left bank of the Jumna, here crossed by ferry, or occasionally by a bridge of boats. Access to the water is had by means of numerous ghats or flights of stairs, some in a state of great decay, others recently built by wealthy Hindoos, to afford devotees easy approach for the purpose ot ritual ablution. The sight of the town has a striking appearance, the houses being in many instances insulated on small summits, amongst which deep, narrow, steep-sided ravines wind. These indentations appear to have been formed by the violent torrents caused by the periodical rains washing away the softer parts of the elevated strata, leaving prominent the indurated kankar or calcareous conglomerate, in some instances sixty feet above the river. Hodges, who visited the place in 1783, describes it as then "large, but very wretched, having but two tolerable houses." Tieffenthaler spoke of it, about thirty years before, as "a very ancient and famous town, situate on the east side of the Jumna, and formerly well peopled. At present," he continues, "many old houses have fallen down. The fort, situate on a high sandhill, on the bank of the Jumna, which flows along its southern side, is of moderate size, and has a foundation of brick." In the time of Baber, in the early part of the sixteenth century, it was of much note, and was governed by the son-in-law of that sovereign, by whom it is repeatedly mentioned. At present its prosperity appears somewhat on the increase, in consequence of its favoured commercial position at the junction of the road from Calpee to Agra with that from Cawnpore to the same place. The jail is one of the largest and best secured of any in the North-Western Provinces. The cantonment is a mile north-west of the town. It is little liked by Europeans, who consider it to be "peculiarly desolate, and to exhibit in full perfection the dreary features of a jungle-station. Upon a wide sandy plain, nearly destitute of trees, half a dozen habitable bungalows lie scattered, intermixed with the ruins of others, built for the accommodation of a larger garrison than is now considered necessary for the security of the place, a single wing of a regiment of sepoys being deemed sufficient for the performance of the duties of this melancholy out-station." The population consists of 23,300 persons. Distant N.W. from Calcutta 710 miles, N.W. from Cawnpore 100, S.E. from Agra 73, S.E. from Delhi, *viâ* Allyghur, 183. Lat. 26° 46′, long. 79° 4′.

ETAWEH, in the British district of Saugor, territory of Saugor and Nerbudda, lieut.-gov. of the N.W. Provinces, a town on the route from Saugor to Jeypoor, 40 miles N.W. of the former. Lat. 24° 10′, long. 78° 19′.

ETCHAK.—A town in the British district of Ramgur, lieut.-gov. of Bengal, 218 miles N.W. of Calcutta. Lat. 24° 5′, long. 85° 29′.

ETIMADPOOR, or ATAMADPOOR, in the British district of Agra, lieut.-gov. of the N.W. Provinces, a town on the route from the cantonment of Etawa to that of Muttra, and 39 miles S.E. of the latter. It is of inconsiderable size, and surrounded by an indifferent mud wall. Here is a large tank, inclosed by massive embankments of masonry, and having in the middle a polygonal building two stories high, surmounted by a dome. It is built of stone, and communicates with the land by a bridge of several arches of the same material. Local tradition attributes its construction to a retainer of the imperial court of Delhi, but his name has not been preserved. The town has a bazar, and water and supplies are abundant. Lat. 27° 14′, long. 78° 16′.

ETOUNDA.—A town in the native state of Nepal, 24 miles S.W. from Khatmandoo, and 54 miles N.E. from Bettiah. Lat. 27° 26′, long. 85° 3′.

ETOWLEE, in the British district of Shahjehanpoor, lieut.-gov. of the N.W. Provinces, a village on the route from Bareilly to Lucknow, 56 miles S.E. of the former, 100 N.W. of the latter. Lat. 28° 2′, long. 80° 12′.

EVEREST MOUNT.—A mountain of the Himalaya range, situate between the mountain of Kinchingunga, in Sikkim, and the city of Khatmandoo, in Nepaul, and presumed to be the loftiest summit in the world. Its elevation is 29,002 feet above the level of the sea. The highest summit of the Andes is Sorata, having an elevation of 25,267 feet. Mount Everest is reported to have been recently discovered by Colonel Waugh, and to have been named in compliment to the late surveyor-general of India.

EYTUH, or ETA.—The principal place of the pergunnah of the same name, in the British district of Mynpoorie, under the lieut.-gov. of the N.W. Provinces. It has a bazaar, and is surrounded by a mud wall. In consequence of the lowness of its site, it is nearly encompassed by a jhil or piece of water during the periodical rains in the latter part of summer. Supplies and water are abundant at all seasons. This place lies on the route from Allyghur to Mynpoorie, and is 34 miles N.E. of the latter. Lat. 27° 34′, long. 78° 43′.

F.

FAGU, in the hill state of Keonthul, a halting-place on the route from Simla to Kotgurh, and 12 miles E. of the former. Here is a building of one apartment, erected by government for the accommodation of travellers. The adjacent country is picturesque, and in many places well wooded, and, though rough and mountainous, well suited for the culture of esculent vegetables, especially potatoes, and of the salep misri, a species of orchis, yielding in great abundance a mucilaginous food, both palatable and highly nutritious. Fagu is 8,030 feet above the level of the sea. Lat. 31° 6′, long. 77° 21′.

FALSE ISLAND.—The most southern of a cluster of islands on the coast of Arracan, situate between the island of Cheduba and the mainland. Lat. 18° 39′, long. 94°.

FALSE POINT.—A headland on the coast of Cuttack, at the mouth of the Mahanuddee river, and 30 miles S.W. from Point Palmyras. "It is low and woody." A lighthouse has been erected here, exhibiting its light 120 feet above high water. Lat. 20° 20′, long. 86° 51′.

FARAH, in the British district of Agra, lieut.-gov. of the N.W. Provinces, a town, the principal place of the pergunnah of the same name, lies on the route from the city of Agra to that of Muttra, 22 miles N.W. of the former, 13 S.E. of the latter. It is situate a mile from the right bank of the Jumna. Heber describes it as "built in a great measure within the inclosure of what has evidently been a very extensive serai, whose walls seem to have been kept up as a defence to the village. They have, however, not been its only defence, since, on a little hill immediately above it, is a square mud fort, with a round bastion at each flank, and a little outwork before the gate." The town is well supplied with water, and has a small bazar. The surrounding country is well cultivated and open. Lat. 27° 19′, long. 77° 50′.

FATIABAD, in the territory of Tijarra, under the political management of the Governor-General's agent in Rajpootana, a town on the route from Delhi to the town of Alwar, and 31 miles N. of the latter. Supplies may be procured here, and water is plentiful. Lat. 27° 55′, long. 76° 45′.

FATTEHGAD, in the Peshawur division of the Punjab, a town situated at the entrance of the Kyber Pass, 10 miles W. of the town of Peshawur. Lat. 34°, long. 71° 30′.

FAZILPOOR.—A village in the district of Mooltan, one of the divisions of the Punjab, situate 91 miles S.W. of Mooltan. Lat. 29° 18′, long. 70° 25′.

FEELNUGGUR, in the British district of Shajehanpoor, lieut.-gov, of the N.W. Provinces, a village on the route from Bareilly to the cantonment of Futtehgurh, and 28 miles S.E. of the former. Lat. 28° 1′, long. 79° 44′.

FEEROZAPOOR, in the British district of Furruckabad, lieut.-gov. of the N.W. Provinces, a village on the route from Futtehgurh to Lucknow, and 28 miles S.E. of the former. Lat. 27° 3′, long. 79° 58′.

FENNY RIVER.—A stream rising in the mountains of independent Tipperah, and, flowing south-west, forms for several miles the boundary between Tipperah and the British district of Chittagong, and for thirty-two miles separates the district last named from that of Bulloah, and falls into the Bay of Bengal in lat. 22° 53′, long. 91° 33′.

FEROZABAD, in the British district of Agra, lieut.-gov. of the N.W. Provinces, a town, the principal place of the pergunnah of the same name, on the route from Muttra to Etawa, and 53 miles S.E. of the latter, 25 miles E. of the city of Agra. It is of considerable size, surrounded by a wall, outside which are numerous mounds and shapeless ruins. Jacquemont states that it "displays very beautiful relics of ancient splendour. It must have been a wealthy town, but its fine edifices are in ruins and deserted; and its present inhabitants dwell in good cottages thatched with straw. Still it may in India be considered a town." It has a bazar, and is supplied with water from wells. The population is returned at 12,674. Its present name is of comparatively recent date, and has probably been given in honour of some chief of Afghan or Persian descent, Firoz being a usual appellative among those of that lineage. Under its former name, Chandwar, it is frequently mentioned by Baber as a place of importance. Lat. 27° 9′, long. 78° 28′.

FEROZABAD.—A town in Hyderabad, or dominions of the Nizam, on the left bank of the Beema river, and 114 miles S.W. from Hyderabad. Lat. 17° 4′, long. 76° 50′.

FEROZEPOOR, in the British district of Moradabad, lieut.-gov. of the N.W. Provinces, a town on the route from Allygurh to the town of Moradabad, and 19 miles S.W. of the latter. Lat. 28° 37′, long. 78° 40′.

FEROZESHAH.—A village situate about twelve miles from the left bank of the Sutlej, within the country under the control of the commissioner and superintendent of the Cis-Sutlej states. This place has been rendered memorable by the attack made on the 21st December, 1845, by the British army, under Sir Hugh Gough and Sir Henry (afterwards Lord) Hardinge, on the formidably-intrenched Sikh camp here, which, after two days' hard fighting, was captured, and the enemy put to flight. The triumph was complete; but, as in most of the actions throughout the Sikh war, the loss of the victors was heavy. Lat. 30° 52′, long. 74° 50′.

FEROZE SHAH CANAL runs from the river Jumna, at lat. 30° 20′, long. 77° 38′. One branch discharges itself in the desert, in lat. 29° 16′, long. 75° 16′, and the other rejoins the parent stream at Delhi.

FEROZPOOR, in the British district of Mozuffurnuggur, lieut.-gov. of the N.W. Provinces, a village with a small fort, half a mile from the right bank of the Ganges. Elevation above the sea 848 feet. Lat. 29° 30′, long. 78° 2′.

FEROZPOOR, in the British district of Suharunpoor, lieut.-gov. of the N.W. Provinces, a town on the route from Meerut to Suharunpoor, 45 miles N.W. of the former. Lat. 29° 37′, long. 77° 31′.

FEROZPORE, a British district in Sirhind, deriving its name from the town so called, formerly a place of some note, and now again rising into importance. It forms part of what are called the Cis-Sutlej territories of the East-India Company. The boundary is irregular, and not very well defined, but its centre may be stated to be in lat. 30° 45′, long. 75°. Its area is returned at ninety-seven square miles; but this return, it is explained by the deputy commissioner, refers only to the district of Ferozpore as it stood before the war with Lahore. Subsequently, four pergunnahs, containing a very considerable tract of country, were added to it; and at a still later period, the larger portion of one of them was severed from the district, and transferred to a native chief, the rajah of Furreedkote. Part of the territory thus alienated was granted to the rajah, in consequence of his good behaviour during the war; another part was subject to certain cash payments; and a third portion was in exchange for other territory more conveniently situate with reference to Ferozpore. This latter process gave additional complication to the circumstances of the district, which is again increased by the incorporation with it of certain pergunnahs from Wudnee, abolished as a separate district. The fact that the latest return was made immediately after these changes, and before any sufficient arrangement could be entered into for insuring accuracy, accounts for the presentation of a statement which does not even offer any pretensions to correctness. The circumstances which have rendered the return as to area unsatisfactory, are equally applicable to the return of population, under which the number is given at 16,890. The district, however, is said to be very thinly peopled, not a thirtieth part, it is alleged, being under cultivation. The remainder is either barren or covered with jungle; but the former populousness and prosperity of the country are proved by the existence of several ruined villages and towns, as well as of fine brick-lined wells, now half-filled with rubbish. The wells at a distance from the river are deep, but much of the soil might be irrigated without recourse to them, as the dry bed of a nullah or watercourse, called the Sukri, traverses the country with a sinuous channel, and it would only require a canal a mile in length to admit the water of the Sutlej or Gharrah. In the following extract, the climate is represented as favourable to the European constitution:—"The climate of Ferozepore promises well: it is peculiar to this part of India, and unlike any other, except Loodiana. Continual cloudy weather, occasionally rainy, and a climate particularly advantageous to Europeans, as well as natives. We can ride out all day without the slightest inconvenience, except that sometimes it is rather too cold than otherwise, to be comfortable without a great coat: scarcely any sick in hospital." The condition of the climate here described was in January. The territory of Ferozepore escheated to the British, upon the demise, in 1835, of Sirdarree Luchmun Koonar. The claims of Lahore were subsequently compromised by a division of the territory with Runjeet Singh, the portion then allotted to that potentate again changing masters, as above noticed, upon the conclusion of the Lahore war.

FEROZPORE, in Sirhind, a town and fort

so named because built by Feroze Toghluk, who sat on the throne of Delhi from 1351 to 1388. It is the chief place of a portion of the British possessions in that quarter, and is situate three miles from the left bank of the Sutlej. It must have been formerly a large town, as the extensive ruins around it indicate. The fort is an irregular building, incapable of defence against a regular attack. It is a hundred yards long, forty broad, and has a dry ditch, ten feet wide and ten deep, with one gateway, which is on the east face. The interior is filled with earth to half the height of the walls, and the mound thus formed is crowded with mean brick houses and mud hovels, separated by alleys not exceeding six feet wide. The town is surrounded by a ditch and by a weak mud wall. It is well supplied with water from a hundred and twenty-four brick-lined wells. Before the introduction of artillery, and when in good repair, the fort must have defied attempts to storm it; and even now, according to the report of an eye-witness, when viewed at a distance, its appearance is very striking. "The large, heaped-together, and well-raised round towers of the forts about here," says a visitant, "give more an impression of England than any I have seen in India. At two or three miles distant, in looking on Ferozepore, you might fancy yourself gazing on Arundel, if not Windser Castle." The town, though originally very mean, has been improved since its occupation by the British; bazars have been made, and several good shops established. The population has also greatly increased. Its rapid improvement is thus described by a late traveller:—"When I was at Ferozepore in January, 1839, the streets were narrow, and in the filthiest state imaginable; the houses all huddled together. When I was there in February, 1841, on my return from Affghanistan, a totally new prospect presented itself. The fort and town had been new-modelled, indeed rebuilt of burned brick; wide streets, with colonnaded rows of shops, had been constructed, and the whole exhibited the promise of an extensive mercantile city. For this improvement, we are much indebted to the zeal and exertions of Captain H. Lawrence, assistant political agent. The native merchants of India and the Punjaub, seeing distinctly the dawn of commercial prosperity in that quarter, at once entered into the speculation of erecting long lines of shops and warehouses, and increasing the town; and there can be no doubt that in a very short period Ferozepore will become one of the most important mercantile entrepôts in the north-west part of India." For this purpose it is well adapted, by its situation near one of the great ferries over the Gharrah, and the means of easy communication with the lower part of the Punjaub, Bahawulpore, and Sinde, afforded by that great river, and its recipient the Indus. There is also facility of communication by good roads with all parts of Sirhind. In November, 1838, an interview took place here between Runjeet Singh, then maharaja of the Punjaub, and Lord Auckland, the Governor-General of British India, on which occasion 10,000 men, rendezvoused at Ferozpore previously to their advance to the invasion of Affghanistan, went through the evolutions of a bloodless battle for the amusement of the Seik ruler, as well as to produce on him an impression of the superiority of British discipline and tactics. In the subsequent operations of the Affghan war, it was repeatedly visited by British armies, marching and countermarching. Within the monumental church erected in this town, the names of the gallant officers and men who fell in the Sutlej and Punjaub campaigns will be perpetuated on tablets sacred to their memory. The population of Ferozpore is about 6,000. It is distant W. of Loodiana 79 miles, N.W. of Calcutta 1,181 miles. Lat. 30° 55′, long. 75° 35′.

FEROZPORE.—The principal place of the pergunnah of the same name, in the British district of Goorgaon, lieut.-gov. of the N.W. Provinces, on the route from Delhi to Alwar, and 74 miles S. of the former. Jacquemont describes it as surrounded by a rather strong wall, flanked with small towers, and inhabited principally by Mussulmans. The fort had strong walls and towers, constructed of mud and mounted with cannon, and contained the nawaub's palace, of no great size, but handsomely built, and furnished in the English style. According to the latest official return (1848), the number of inhabitants was 7,989; but this statement was founded on a census made two or three years earlier, and chiefly, if not entirely, through native agency. The jaghire of Ferozpore, containing an area of about 138 square miles, with that of Loharoo, containing 350, were granted, in the beginning of the present century, the former by Lord Lake, the latter by the ruler of Alwur, to Ahmud Buksh Khan; on whose death, in 1827, they descended to his son, Shumsooddeen Khan. The two younger brothers of Shumsooddeen, having well-founded claims on Loharoo, in virtue of an arrangement made by their father Ahmud Buksh, Mr. William Fraser, the British political agent at Delhi, exerted himself to induce the British government to make a partition in their favour. Shumsooddeen, to avert the threatened loss, and in revenge for the proposed measure, as well as for some censure passed, and some coercion exercised, in regard to certain parts of his conduct, caused Mr. Fraser to be murdered, at Delhi, by a hired assassin, in October, 1835. A year afterwards, he was brought to trial for the murder, and, being duly convicted, was hanged. His jaghires being declared forfeited, Loharoo was granted to his brothers, and Ferozpore embodied with the British district of Goorgaon. There are works in the town for smelting iron-ore, raised at a mine three miles distant. The bazar is well supplied, and water is abundant. The road in this part of the route is good. Elevation above the sea about 840 feet. Distance N.W. from Calcutta, by Agra and Muttra, 895 miles. Lat. 27° 47′, long. 77° 1′.

FILOR, or FALOUR. — A town in the Julinder Dooab division of the Punjab, on the route from Amritsir to Loodiana, and about six miles N.W. of the latter place. It is situate on the right bank of the Sutluj, and is defended by a fort, built on the high steep rising from the river. The fort, which was constructed by order of Runjeet Singh in 1809, is small, affording accommodation for a garrison of only 150 men, but it is rendered conspicuous by its large barbican. Here is the ferry over the Sutluj, for the communication of Loodiana and its neighbourhood with Amritsir and Lahore. The Sutluj, in inundation, forms extensive sheets of water round the town, and these remain after the river has shrunk to the confines of its usual channel. Lat. 31° 2′, long 75° 49′.

FIVE SISTERS ISLANDS.—A group of islands on the coast of the Tenasserim province, in lat. 11° 25′, long. 98° 9′, and 82 miles S.W. from the town of Tenasserim.

FLAT ISLAND.—An island, called by the natives Negamale, situate about five miles from the south-eastern shore of Cheduba (Arracan), which island in soil and productions it very much resembles. It is about four miles in length from north to south, has a pool or two of fresh water, and is high towards the centre. Lat. 18° 37′, long. 93° 50′.

FORT ST. DAVID.—A town and fort on the coast of Coromandel, in the British district of South Arcot, presidency of Madras. This place, formerly known as Tegnapatam, was purchased by the East-India Company from a native prince in 1691, and became a station of some importance. Upon the capitulation of Madras to the French in 1746, the Company's agent here assumed the general administration of British affairs in the south of India, and successfully resisted an attack made by Dupleix upon the settlement. In 1756, Clive was appointed governor of Fort St. David. It was attacked by the French in 1758, both by sea and land, and capitulated, when the fortifications were demolished, and were never rebuilt. Distant N. from Cuddalore three miles; from Madras, S., 100. Lat. 11° 45′, long. 79° 50′.

FORT ST. GEORGE.—See Madras.

FORT WILLIAM.—See Calcutta.

FOUL ISLAND, off the coast of Arracan, situate about six leagues from the mainland, is two miles in length, its shape conical, with a gradual declivity from the centre towards the sea. The island is covered with a profusion of trees. Lat. 18° 4′, long. 94° 16′.

FRASERPET, or KOOSHALNUGGUR, in the British district of Coorg, presidency of Madras, a town situate on the left bank of the river Cauvery, here 225 feet wide, fordable in the dry season, but during the monsoon rising from twenty to thirty feet. It is situate close to the ruins of Jaafarabad, a fort built by Tippoo Sultan on the site of the ancient Kooshalnagar, and is the head-quarters of the sappers and miners employed on the roads and other public works in Coorg. The soil is alluvial but well drained, and the air salubrious, though, in consequence of its comparatively depressed site, warmer than in most parts of Coorg. The nights, however, are cool and pleasant at all seasons, and during the monsoon little rain falls, and the temperature is moderate, the heat of the sun being mitigated by continual clouds and light fogs. Elevation above the sea 3,200 feet. Distance from Merkara, E., 14 miles; Mangalore, S.E., 81; Bangalore, S.W., 117; Madras, W., 290. Lat. 12° 28′, long. 76° 1′.

FRENCH ROCKS, in Mysore, a British military station for native troops, at a rocky hill, five miles N. of the river Cauvery at Seringapatam, and 300 feet above it. The cantonment is on a gently rising ground, with a gravelly soil and well drained. There are no jungles nor marshes in the vicinity, nor any stagnant water, except that contained in a fine deep tank with a rocky bottom, which yields an abundant and excellent supply throughout the year. The atmosphere is rather moist; fogs and heavy dues prevail at the close of the winter and the early part of spring. The heat is less than at Seringapatam, a few miles distant, and the thermometer is at no time much above 85°. The monsoon rains generally cease about the middle of September. Notwithstanding the many apparently favourable circumstances of its site, it has been from time to time subject to attacks of severe endemic fever, generally of intermittent type. They appear, however, to be in a great degree confined to the native population, the British generally enjoying good health. Elevation above the sea 2,300 feet. Lat. 12° 31′, long. 76° 45′.

FRENCH SETTLEMENTS.—See Pondicherry.

FULAILEE, in Sinde, is a branch of the Indus, leaving the main channel about nine miles above Hyderabad, and in lat. 25° 31′, long. 68° 29′. It flows southward, after proceeding a short distance to the east of Hyderabad, which it insulates, by sending off to the westward a branch which rejoins the main river about fifteen miles below the town. Below this last divarication it bears the name of the Goonee, takes a south-easterly course, discharging its water eastward into the Purana or Phurraun, and ultimately into the sea by the Koree mouth.

FULJAR TAL, in the British district of Shahjehanpoor, lieut.-gov. of the N.W. Provinces, a small lake, the source of the river Goomtee. Lat. 28° 35′, long. 80° 10′.

FULTA, in the British district known as the Twenty-four Pergunnahs, lieut.-gov. of Bengal, a town on the left bank of the river Hooghly, opposite the mouth of the Damoodah. Distance from Calcutta, S.W., by land, 22 miles ; by the course of the Hooghly, 29. Lat. 22° 18′, long. 88° 10′.

FUREEDABAD, a town in Bulubgurh or Fureedabad, a jaghire under the lieut.-gov. of the N.W. Provinces, is situate on the route from Delhi to Muttra, and 21 miles S. of the former city. The country around is for the most part barren and disagreeable, but groves of tamarinds and other trees enliven the immediate neighbourhood of the town. Here is a bazaar, and also a large tank. The town is surrounded by a wall. At the time of Thorn's visit, fifty years ago, it was noted for the manufacture of bows and arrows. Water is abundant. Lat. 28° 25′, long. 77° 23′.

FUREEDGUNGE, in the British district of Allahabad, lieut.-gov. of the N.W. Provinces, a village on the old route from the cantonment of Allahabad to Futtehpore, and 39 miles N.W. of the former. Lat. 25° 41′, long. 81° 25′.

FUREED KOT, in the British district of Bhutteeana, lieut.-gov. of the N.W. Provinces, a town on the route from Patialah to Bhawulpoor, 116 miles S.W. of the former. Lat. 30° 1′, long. 74° 47′.

FUREED KOTE, one of the protected Sikh states of Sirhind, is bounded on the north, south, and east by the British district of Ferozepore, and on the west by the native state of Mundote : it extends from lat. 30° 40′ to 30° 56′, and from long. 74° 22′ to 75° 9′ ; is forty miles in length from east to west, and nineteen in breadth. The area is 308 square miles, containing a population of 45,892. Fureedkote, the chief town, is 60 miles S.W. from Loodiana. Lat. 30° 40′, long. 74° 59′.

FUREEDPOOR, in the British district of Moradabad, lieut.-gov. of the N.W. Provinces, a village on the route from Allyghur to the town of Moradabad, and four miles S.W. of the latter. It is situate near the right bank of the Gangun, in an open, level, cultivated country. Lat. 28° 47′, long. 78° 49′.

FUREEDPOOR, in the British district of Bareilly, the principal place of the pergunnah of the same name, on the route from the town of Bareilly to Shahjehanpoor, and 12 miles S.E. of the former. It is situate close to a grove of very fine mango-trees, in a flat fertile country, well cultivated, especially under cotton. Heber describes his visit to this place on November 13th as delightful :—"The morning was positively cold, and the whole scene, with the exercise of the march, the picturesque groups of men and animals round me, the bracing air, the singing of birds, the light mist hanging on the trees, and the glistening dew, had something at once so oriental and so English, I have seldom found anything better adapted to raise a man's animal spirits and to put him in good temper with himself and all the world." There is a bazar here, and water and supplies are abundant. The road in this part of the route is good. Lat. 28° 12′, long. 79° 36′.

FUREEDPORE.—A British district under the lieut.-gov. of Bengal, named from its principal place. It is bounded on the north by the British district Mymensing ; on the east by the British district Dacca ; on the south by the British district Backergunge ; and on the west by the British districts Jessore and Pubna : it lies between lat. 23° 3′—24° 5′, long. 89° 30′—90° 15′, and has an area of 2,052 square miles. Fureedpore is altogether an alluvial tract, low and swampy in the southern and north-eastern parts, where it is much subject to inundation ; but in the north and north-western portions, rather more elevated, with a deep soil of fine quality. Few districts more abound in rivers : the Ganges, in this part of its course called the Podda, touches on the western frontier at Juffergunge, where that river receives an offset of the Konaie or Jabuna, by which its volume of water is more than doubled. Thence taking a south-easterly course for fifteen miles to Malapora, it enters the district, through which it flows for forty-five miles, to Kagauta, on the eastern frontier, at which place it sends off eastward a great branch, called the Kirtynassa ; and then taking a southerly course for fifteen miles, it at Hobigunje crosses the southern frontier into the British district of Backergunge. It on the left side receives numerous considerable water-courses, and on the right side sends off many others, especially during the rainy season, when it rolls along with a vast volume of water, four, five, or six miles in width. The Konaie, or Jabuna, from the north, touches on this district at its north-western corner, and flowing southerly for about five miles, forms its western boundary as far as Ameerabad, where it sends off to the left, or south-eastwards, a large stream, called the Dulasseree, and, turning south-westward, it receives, at a distance of five miles, the Oora Sagar, on the right side ; the united stream a few miles lower down falling into the Ganges. The Dulasseree holds a south-easterly course for thirty-five miles to Sabar, on the eastern frontier, towards the British district of Dacca, where it receives the Bunsi, flowing from the north. From the confluence, the Dulasseree holds a course south-east, forming for twelve miles the eastern boundary of Fureedpore towards Dacca, when it passes into that district. The Barashee or Chundna, a large offset of the Ganges, flowing from north-west to south-east, touches this district on the western frontier, at Moodoocallee, and taking a course very sinuous, but generally southerly, for fifty-five miles, to Go- [illegible], it for that distance forms the western [illegible]ndary, towards the British district Pubna and Jessore. Rennell remarks that "the only subordinate branch of the Ganges that is at all times navigable, is the Chundnah river, which separates at Moddapore, and terminates in the Hooringotta ;" and Horsburgh states that ships of 500 tons can enter and load in the Hooringotta estuary. The Barashee or Chundna is the only stream in this district navigable throughout the year; all the others, including the main stream of the Ganges or Podda, during the dry season become in many parts so shallow, that even small boats cannot traverse them.

The soil is in general very rich, particularly in the northern part, producing fine crops of sugarcane, cotton, indigo, oil-seeds, and some others of less value; while the swampy grounds are fruitful in rice. Sugar is probably the most important crop. The manufacturing industry of the district is chiefly employed in the preparation of indigo and sugar, and in the distillation of rum. A considerable quantity of coarse cotton cloth is made for home use. Here are mahajans or merchants, reputed to be considerable capitalists, who drive an extensive and lucrative business, there being a brisk traffic in the import, export, and transit departments. The population is given under the article BENGAL. Mussulmans are more numerous in the southern part, and Brahminists in the remainder of the district. There are some thousands of native Christians of the Romish persuasion, descended from the offspring of the union of Portuguese with native women. The district of Fureedpore passed to the East-India Company by the grant of Shah Alum, emperor of Delhi, in 1765. Fureedpore, the locality of the civil establishment, Hobigunge and Juffergunge, the principal places, are noticed under their respective names in the alphabetical arrangement.

FUREEDPORE.—The principal place of the British district of the same name, situate on the right or south-west side of the Ganges, here called the Podda. According to Heber, "The huts of the natives are in no compact village, but scattered thinly up and down a large and fertile extent of orchard-garden, and paddy (rice) ground." There seems to be little more to be said of Fureedpore, and that little not of the most creditable character, it having formerly been a noted resort of river pirates, who made the navigation of this part of the river very hazardous; but the evil has in a great measure ceased since the place has become the locality of the principal government establishments of the district. Here are various buildings for the accommodation of the different branches of the civil department. Distance from Dacca, W., 38 miles; Calcutta, N.E., 115. Lat. 23° 36′, long. 89° 50′.

FUREEDUH, in the British district of Bolundshuhur, lieut.-gov. of the N.W. Provinces, a town, the principal place of the pergunnah of the same name, situate on the right bank of the Ganges, 60 miles E. of Delhi. Lat. 28° 33′, long. 78° 17′.

FURRA.—A town in the native state of Gwalior, or possessions of Scindia, five miles from the right bank of the Parbutty river, and 113 miles S.W. from Agra. Lat. 25° 57′, long. 76° 59′.

FURRUCKABAD.—A British district, under the lieut.-gov. of the N.W. Provinces, named from its principal place. It is bounded on the north by the British districts Budaon and Shahjehanpore; on the east by the territory of Oude; on the south by the British districts of Etawah and Cawnpore; and on the west by Etawah and Mynpooree. It lies between lat. 26° 46′—27° 43′, long. 78° 57′—80° 2′, and has an area of 1,909 square miles. The general slope of the country is to the south-east, as indicated by the courses of the Ganges, Esun, and Rind, which run in that direction. The other rivers intersecting the district are the Kali Nadi and the Ramgunga. The south-western portion of the district is part of the crest or gentle elevation extending along the Doab at nearly an equal distance from the Ganges and the Jumna.

The soil varies a good deal in quality, much of that on the banks of the Ganges being khadir or marsh, having a deep rich soil, saturated with moisture. The town of Imrutpoor, in this tract, is described as situate in a "country spread for many surrounding leagues with one sheet of luxuriant cultivation, interspersed with beautiful and ancient mango-trees. In the rainy season this rich and fruitful tract is scarcely habitable or passable, the whole country between the Ganges and Bareilly exhibiting one vast lake of water." Even in the driest part of the year, water may be obtained at a very small depth below the surface, and many ponds and watercourses occur. The most important crop on soil of this description is indigo, which is thought to be indigenous, being everywhere observable wild; and the herb thus produced has been said to yield a finer dye than when cultivated. The culture is generally managed by the natives, who dispose of the crop to European capitalists for conversion into a marketable state, a process which is largely carried on in the town of Furruckabad. A considerable part of the country is very sandy and sterile, especially the northern, and there the soil is so little retentive of moisture, that it becomes perfectly dry a few hours after being drenched with rain; yet assiduous culture, and judicious irrigation where water can be obtained from either streams or wells, clothe these unpromising tracts with good crops of grain, pulse, and tobacco. Where unimproved by human industry, the aspect of the country is dismal. In many places in the midland and southern parts of the district, the soil is fertile, producing fine wheat, barley, and pulse, and the crops of maize and sugarcane are so luxuriant and dense, as to attain a height of eight or ten feet, and exclude the rays of the sun. The southern part is so well wooded, as, when viewed from some distance, to have the appearance of a forest. Cotton and tobacco are grown chiefly for home consumption. Many vegetables of usual growth in Europe succeed well here, especially potatoes, which are so much esteemed, that they are sent to many other parts. The land revenue in this district has been fixed by the government for a term of years, and is not liable to be increased until the year 1865. The population of this district is returned at 1,064,607; of which number, 695,567 are classed as Hindoo agricultural; 241,180 as Hindoo non-agricultural; 45,608 as Mohammedans and others, agricultural; and 82,252 as coming under the same general head, but non-agricultural. The Mussulmans are said to be descendants of the Patans or Afghans, who early in the last century established themselves in the tract extending between Oude and the Punjab, and have been reputed to retain some of the sanguinary and turbulent spirit characteristic of their ancestors. Lord Valentia describes the condition of society before the settlement of the district by the British authorities in gloomy terms:—"The state of the country was then most wretched. Murders were so frequent at Furruckabad, that people dared not venture there after sunset, and the workmen who came out to the cantonments always retired to their own houses during daylight." He adds, that seventy persons were in prison to be tried for murder. Tennant also, writing in 1798, complains hearing of the numbers and murderous outrages of the banditti of Furruckabad. Archer, writing thirty years later, and even after the establishment of British rule, says, "No peasant thinks of living out of the village in a cottage by himself: it would not be secure, and would certainly tempt to plunder and murder." Happily, a very different state now prevails. The district is not only tranquil, but prosperous. The recent revenue settlement, effected for a term of thirty years,—a period sufficient to afford opportunity for agricultural enterprise, without surrendering in perpetuity the just rights and interests of government,—has been extended to this district, in common with other portions of the North-Western Provinces. Under it, the rights of all parties being defined and secured, industry is sure of its reward, and consequently flourishes. Honest labour has superseded lawless rapine as an occupation; and person and property are alike safe. The minuter advantages of civilization are in course of introduction, and efforts have been made to communicate to every class some measure of education. The progress of improvement is mainly attributable to the exertions of the late Mr. Thomason, while filling the office of lieutenant-governor of the North-West Provinces. "To him," says a late writer, "is due an improved executive administration, such as we have never had elsewhere in India." The principal routes in the district are—1. From west to east, from Agra to Mynpooree, whence one branch proceeds to Futteghur, and another (the grand trunk road from Calcutta to Delhi) to Cawnpore. 2. From Allyghur to Futteghur, and thence to Cawnpore. 3. From south-west to north-east, from Etawah to Futteghur, and continued thence to Bareilly. The East-Indian Railway intersects the southern quarter of the district. The principal places are Furruckabad, Chubramow, Imrutpoor, Allygury, Kunnoj, Khudaganj, Nawabganj, Jalalabad, which will be found noticed in their proper places.

In the earlier part of the eighteenth century, the Rohilla Patans had established themselves in the tract comprised in the present district. In 1749, Ahmed Shah, of Delhi, urged by his vizier, marched thither, and confiscated the estates of the deceased ruler, who had just fallen in an unsuccessful war with the Rohillas. The country, with the exception of a small portion allotted to the support of the family of the late prince, was bestowed on the vizier, from whom, however, it was wrested by Ahmed Khan, brother of the former ruler, who forthwith proceeded to invade Oude. Expelled from that territory, though not without difficulty, Ahmed sought refuge in the hills, but on his submission was restored to Furruckabad, with a revenue of sixteen lacs of rupees. After being occupied by various classes of adventurers, it appears, however, to have reverted to the vizier of Oude, who, in 1801, transferred his claims to the East-India Company. In 1802 the Company assumed actual possession of Furruckabad, liquidating the claims of the tributary Patan nawaub by a fixed monthly stipend of 9,000 rupees, in addition to which, an annual sum of nearly 180,000 rupees was bestowed in pensions and charitable allowances to his dependants. In 1804, Holkar, at the head of a great body of cavalry, the number of which has been estimated at 60,000, ravaged this tract, and, flying before the British army under Lord Lake, was surprised at the town of Furruckabad, and having lost 3,000 men, the remainder were so reduced by desertions and other causes, that not above half their number ever rejoined the standard of their leader: the loss of the British was only two dragoons killed, and about twenty wounded. In their march to overtake the enemy, and in the pursuit subsequent to the route, the British traversed a distance of above seventy miles in twenty-four hours.

FURRUCKABAD, the principal place of the district of the same name, in the N.W. Provinces, is situate between two and three miles west of the right bank of the Ganges; its Patan founders, from their exclusive addiction to military pursuits, attaching no value to the facilities afforded by the great river, navigable upwards for nearly two hundred miles, and downwards to the ocean. Furruckabad is rather a handsome town, and considered healthy, though many of the streets are shaded by trees, a circumstance usually considered to have in India a tendency to produce malaria. Its population is returned at 56,300 persons. The healthiness of the place may be owing, in a great degree, to its cleanliness, a point more attended to here than in most Indian towns; and the width of the streets and squares no doubt contributes towards this good end. The trade is considerable, and the banking business especially is extensive and important. The surrounding country being fertile and well cultivated, provisions are abundant and excellent. In the town is a mud fort, built as a residence for the nawaub, on a considerable height, commanding extensive views of the Ganges and of the surrounding country. The commercial importance of this town was marked by its having a mint, the coinage of which circulated extensively, especially throughout the North-Western Provinces. The issue continued down to the year 1824, the value of the Furruckabad rupee being to the Sicca rupee as fifteen to sixteen. The British military cantonment of Futtygurh is three miles east of the town, and on the right bank of the Ganges. The elevation of Furruckabad is probably about 570 feet above the sea. It lies twenty miles to the right of the great north-western route from Calcutta to Delhi, by the new line, and distant N.W. from the former 660 miles, S.E. from the latter 160, N.W. from Lucknow 95, E. from Agra 90. Lat. 27° 24′, long. 79° 40′.

FURRUCKABAD.—A town in the British district of Maldah, lieut.-gov. of Bengal, 16 miles S.W. of Maldah. Lat. 24° 49′, long. 88° 4′.

FURRUCKNUGGUR. — A petty Mahomedan chieftainship, comprising a few villages, situate on the south-east corner of the native state of Jhujhur. On acquiring supremacy in the Delhi territory, the British government found Mozuffer Khan in possession of the jaghire, and his rights were respected in the subsequent grant of Jhujhur to the Buraitch family. The chief bears the title of nawaub. The centre of the estate is in lat. 28° 24′, long. 76° 52′. Its area is about twenty-two square miles. The population, assuming the average of the adjacent territories, may be estimated at 4,400. The nawaub maintains a small military force of twenty-five infantry.

FURUKNUGUR, in the British district of Meerut, lieut.-gov. of the N.W. Provinces, a town on the route from Delhi to the town of Meerut, and 14 miles N.E. of the former. It is situate on the right bank of the Hindun, here crossed by ford from two to two and a half feet deep, and in an open and partially-cultivated country. Lat. 28° 44′, long. 77° 26′.

FUTEHGUNGE (WESTERN), in the British district of Bareilly, lieut.-gov. of the N.W. Provinces, a town on the route from Bareilly to Moradabad, and 12 miles N.W. of the former. It is a thriving and populous village, and has a bazar and market, and is abundantly supplied with water from wells. Here, in 1796, the Rohilla Patans were defeated by a British force under Sir Robert Abercrombie. Within view of the action were about thirty thousand native troops, in the service of the nawaub of Oude, ostensibly an ally of the East-India Company; but they kept aloof until the British, after suffering very severely, totally routed their adversaries, when their treacherous auxiliaries rushed in and seized the greater part of the spoil. The cavalry of the British army fled on the first charge of the Patans, who, taking advantage of the opening thus made, got into the rear, and cut to pieces six companies of infantry, but ultimately fell before the unshaken courage of the survivors. Ramsay, the commander of the cavalry, who showed the example of flight, saved himself from the punishment due to his delinquency by taking refuge in America, and ultimately was employed by Napoleon in his commissariat. The East-India Company raised a monument to those of their troops who fell in the action. "It is of obelisk form, and stands on a small mound, the only elevation in this vast plain, on which point of vantage the enemies' guns were ranged, and afterwards taken. The names of fourteen British officers are recorded on the 'storied stone;' among whom were three commanding officers of regiments. Within a stone's throw of this plain and simple monument, rises the carved and minaretted tomb of two illustrious Rohilla chiefs, who fell in the action." A collection of dwellings, the extension of the contiguous village of Betoura, and which were the immediate scene of the conflict, has received the appellation of Futehgunje, or "Victory Market." Lat. 28° 28′, long. 79° 24′.

FUTEHGUNJE (EASTERN), in the British district of Bareilly, lieut.-gov. of the N.W. Provinces, a town on the route from the town of Bareilly to Shahjehanpoor, and 23 miles S.E. of the former. It is situate near the right bank of the river Bhagul, and close to a noble grove of mango-trees, covering between twenty and thirty acres, but is a poor, insignificant place, surrounded by a ruined mud wall, in which, however, are two handsome brick gateways. It has a small bazar, and is well supplied with excellent water. The town was founded by Shujahuddawlat, the nawaub of Oude, in commemoration of a victory which, gained by the British army in 1774, gave him possession of a large portion of Rohilcund. It is probable that the battle was not, however, fought on the site of the present Futehgunje, but at Tessunah, about four miles north-west of it, and marked as a battle-field, with crossed swords, in Rennell's Bengal Atlas. The engagement is sometimes called the battle of Cutterah or Kuttra, from a town three miles to the south-east of Futehgunje. The successive conflicts in an action so obstinately contested, probably took place in localities at a considerable distance from each other. Hafiz Rahmat Khan, the Rohilla commander, was described to Heber "as a noble old warrior, with a long grey beard, who led his cavalry on in a brilliant style against the allied armies. When his nobles, at the head of their respective clans, either treacherous or timid, gave way, he remained almost alone on a rising ground in the heat of the fire, conspicuous by his splendid dress and beautiful horse, waving his hand, and vainly endeavouring to bring his army back to another charge, till, seeing that all was lost, he waved his hand once more, gave a shout, and galloped on the English bayonets. He fell, shot through and through." Colonel Champion, who commanded the British, had his body wrapped in shawls, and sent with due honour to his relatives. Futehgunje is in lat. 28° 4′, long. 79° 42′.

FUTEHPOOR, in the British district of Furruckabad, lieut.-gov. of the N.W. Provinces, a village on the route from the cantonment of Cawnpore to that of Futehgurh, and 25 miles S.E. of the latter. Lat. 27° 5′, long. 79° 53′.

FUTEHPOOR, in the Baree Dooab division of the Punjab, a town situated on the right bank of the Ghara river, 50 miles S.E. of the town of Mooltan. Lat. 29° 41′, long. 72° 10′.

FUTHABAD, in the British district of Agra, lieut.-gov. of the N.W. Provinces, a town, the principal place of the pergunnah of Futhabad, is situate on the right bank of the Jumna. Lat. 27° 2′, long. 78° 22′.

FUTHEPOOR SIKRI, in the British district of Agra, a town on the route from the city of Agra to Jeypore, and 23 miles W. of the former. The place in its present state is an expanse of ruins, inclosed by a high stone wall, about five miles in circuit, and having battlements and round towers. This space is divided by a hilly ridge of considerable elevation, running nearly from south-west to north-east, and extending beyond the inclosure five or six miles on each side. The scene of desolation is the more awful, as Akbar commenced those structures as late as 1571; and the fury of victorious enemies, principally Mahrattas, has in the comparatively brief interval reduced them to their present shattered or prostrate state. The most striking object at present is the great mosque, still in tolerable repair. The aspect of the great front is southwards, "crowning the principal height, and overlooking the low country, the face of its walls terminating in a gigantic causeway, surmounted with domes and minarets. From a distant position, the effect of this enormous structure is to cause the hill on which it stands to dwindle into a mere hillock; but when the traveller arrives at its base, and can estimate the magnitude of the building by that of the eminence on which it is exalted, his admiration is raised to wonder and awe at the startling height to which it rises." The height of the gateway, from the pavement to the summit of the interior outline, is 72 feet, and to the exterior summit, 120. The gateway is reached by a flight of steps of almost unrivalled magnificence; but these are becoming dilapidated, the periodical rains, which sweep down the slope of the hill, annually loosening some and dislodging others, so that, if requisite repairs be not attended to, in a few years the whole of this superb portal must become a heap of shapeless ruins. The interior, to which this noble entrance leads, is a quadrangle nearly 500 feet square, and all around which runs a very lofty and majestic cloister, into which opens a range of cells, intended probably as lodges for dervishes, or for pilgrims. In this quadrangle, and to the left of the entrance, is a large mosque, surmounted by three fine domes of white marble, and opposite the entrance, the tomb of Shekh Selim Cheestee, a Mussulman ascetic, whose intercession by prayer to heaven Akbar had implored, that the imperial couch might be blessed by the birth of a son. The prayer was considered to be answered by the timely birth of a prince, named Selim, in honour of the Shekh, and subsequently emperor of Hindostan, under the name of Jehangir. The outline of the tomb is a square of forty-six feet, the material white marble, elaborately carved with much taste, in a florid style. The sarcophagus containing the body is inclosed within a screen of marble, carved into lattice-work and inlaid with mother-of-pearl. Numbers of women repair to this place to pray at the tomb and implore the saint's intercession in their favour. There is also within the inclosure another tomb of elaborate workmanship, represented to contain the remains of several members of Akbar's family. To the westward of the great inclosure are the massive ruins of the palace. The stables form a long and wide street, with a portico on each side fifteen feet deep, supported with carved stone pillars in front, and roofed with enormous slabs of stone, reaching from the colonnade to the wall. The whole hill on which the palace stands bears marks of terraces and gardens, to irrigate which an elaborate succession of wells, cisterns, and wheels, appears to have been contrived adjoining the great mosque. Numerous other great and remarkable ruins are everywhere scattered over the extensive inclosure of the ancient ramparts of the town. A huge and massive gateway is particularly worth notice, on account of two figures of "astonishing elephants," of the natural size, carved in stone with admirable skill and truth. At no great distance is a tower, forty or fifty feet high, built, according to local report, of elephants' tusks, but actually of composition, moulded and enamelled into a resemblance of those natural substances. Outside the town, and to the north of the hills on which it is built, is the ruined embankment, extending a circuit of twenty miles, and formed by Akbar to dam up the torrent Khari. A lake was thus made, and on its margin was built an amphitheatre with high minarets. Abulfazl continues: "The amphitheatre is used for the game of chowgong; and here also are exhibited the elephant-fights." The wide extent inclosed by the ruined wall of this favourite city of the greatest of the monarchs of Hindostan is now overspread with "ruined houses and mosques, interspersed with fields cultivated with rice and mustard, and a few tamarind-trees." The surrounding country is fine, and its character shows the good taste of Akbar, who chose it as the scene of his gorgeous seclusion. "The scene [from the top of the great gateway] is indeed a lovely one, extending over an immense tract of country, the horizon of which is on all sides thirty miles distant from the beholder on a clear day, such as that which we enjoyed. The low line of hills upon which the place is built is seen creeping through the whole face of the level country from east to west, crowned every here and there with ruined buildings, or a hill fortress. Among these Bhurtpore is just visible. On the opposite side is the Jumna, winding through the distance, and leading the eye to the glittering, though far-off, towers and domes of Agra. The middle distance is richly wooded, and thickly spotted with ruins of every age, and in every style of design." The town, though so ruinous, has at present a good bazar, and is at all times abundantly supplied with good water from wells and tanks. Population 5,949. Lat. 27° 6′, long. 77° 44′.

FUTICKCHERRY.—A town in the British district of Chittagong, lieut.-gov. of Bengal, 23 miles N. of Chittagong. Lat. 22° 40′, long. 91° 54′.

FUTI PANJAL, a mountain in Kashmir, is one of that range which bounds the valley to the southward. According to the estimate of Vigne, its height must exceed 12,000 feet, as its summit rises above the lake Kosah Nag, which has that elevation. Its name signifies the mountain of victory. Its culminating ridge in some measure resembles the arc of a circle, the extremities of which are east and west, and the northern or concave part directed towards Kashmir. Its total length is about forty miles. Lat. 33° 34′, long. 74° 40′.

FUTTEABAD.—A town in the native state of Gwalior, or possessions of Scindia, 134 miles N.W. from Hoosungabad, and 12 miles S.W. from Oojein. Lat. 23°, long. 75° 40′.

FUTTEGHUR.—A fort built by the Sikhs, during the prevalence of their sway, to command the eastern end of the Khyber Pass. It is situate a mile N.E. from Jamrood, and being close to the entrance of the pass, has great command over it. The defences consist of a square of 300 yards, protecting an octagonal fort, in the centre of which is a lofty mass of buildings commanding the surrounding country. The supply of water from the mountain-streams is liable to be cut off by the hostile Khyberees of the adjacent hills. In the hope of providing a remedy for this inconvenience, the Sikhs sunk a well 200 feet deep, but without reaching water. Lat. 34° 2′, long. 71° 25′.

FUTTEGURH. — A town in the Rajpoot native state of Kishengurh, 72 miles S.W. from Jeypoor, and 35 miles S.E. from Ajmeer. Lat. 26° 10′, long. 75° 10′.

FUTTEHABAD, in the British district of Hurreeana, lieut.-gov. of the N.W. Provinces, on the route from Hansee to Bhutneer, and 40 miles N.W. of the former. Lat. 29° 30′, long. 75° 25′.

FUTTEHABAD, in the British district of Hurriana, lieut.-gov. of the N.W. Provinces, a town on the route from Hansee to the Punjab, 41 miles N.E. of the former. Lat. 29° 29′, long. 75° 33′.

FUTTEH ALLY, in the Reechna Dooab division of the Punjab, a town situated on the left bank of the Chenaub river, 72 miles W. of the town of Lahore. Lat. 31° 44′, long. 72° 57′.

FUTTEHGURH, in the British district of Bhutteeana, lieut.-gov. of the N.W. Provinces, a town on the route from Bhawulpoor to Ferozpoor, 51 miles S.W. of the latter. Lat. 30° 27′, long. 73° 59′.

FUTTEHJUNG, in the Sinde Sagur Dooab division of the Punjab, a town situated 24 miles from the left bank of the Indus, and 29 miles S.E. of the town of Attock. Lat. 33° 35′, long. 72° 39′.

FUTTEHPOOR, in the British district of Etawah, lieut.-gov. of the N.W. Provinces, a village on the route from the cantonment of Etawah to Calpee, and 33 miles S.E. of the former. Lat. 26° 30′, long. 79° 28′.

FUTTEHPOOR.—A town in the British district of Mymunsing, lieut.-gov. of Bengal, 212 miles N.E. of Calcutta. Lat. 24° 36′, long. 90° 58′.

FUTTEHPOOR, in the Rajpoot territory of Shekawuttee, a town held by a thakoor or baron of the country, whose annual income, according to Tod, is 64,000 rupees. The town is surrounded by a low weak rampart of stone, but the fort is rather strong, and has a roomy interior, defended by lofty ramparts, a fausse-braie, and a ditch of masonry. This was a prosperous and important place during the life of Rao Raja Luchman Singh, who resided here; but since his death it has been much deserted. Water is brackish and scarce, being drawn from wells ninety feet deep. Distance W. from Delhi 145 miles, N.W. from Jeypoor 90, E. from Bikaner 105. Lat. 27° 58′, long. 75° 5′.

FUTTEHPOOR.—A town in the territory of Oude, 27 miles N.E. from Lucknow, and 96 miles S.E. from Furruckabad. Lat. 27° 8′, long. 81° 18′.

FUTTEHPOOR.—A town in the Rajpoot state of Kerowly, 84 miles S.E. from Jeypoor, and 69 miles S.W. from Agra. Lat. 26° 37′, long. 77° 12′.

FUTTEHPOOR, under the lieut.-gov. of the N.W. Provinces, a British district named from its principal place. It is bounded on the north-east by the Ganges, which divides it from the kingdom of Oude; on the east by the British district of Allahabad; on the south-west by the Jumna, dividing it from the British districts Humeerpore and Banda; and on the north-west by the British district of Cawnpore. It lies between lat. 25° 25′—26° 18′, long. 80° 12′—81° 23′, and has an area of 1,583 square miles. The whole district is comprised within the tract called the Doab, and the two large rivers the Ganges and the Jumna, which bound it on two sides, afford extensive means of inland navigation. The Rind or Urrund, a small river, passes into this district from that of Cawnpore, over the north-western boundary, and, flowing by the town of Korah, holds a course nearly southerly for thirty miles, finally falling into the Jumna on the left side. The Etawah branch of the Ganges Canal will also pass over the north-western boundary into this district, from that of Cawnpore, and, holding a south-easterly course for about fifteen miles, will join the Jumna about twenty miles below the town of Humeerpore.

The climate can differ little from that of southern Oude, situate on the other side of the Ganges, and at the same elevation. According to Butter, the climate of that country is characterized by great dryness, and wide range of variation in the thermometer, which sometimes rises to 112°, at others falls to 28°; the mean daily range being about 30°, and the mean temperature 74°. Heber states, that in 1824, the year in which he passed through this district, no rain had fallen as late as the beginning of October. The statement is, however, made on report, and not on personal observation. As the physical circumstances of the district are so nearly similar to those of southern Oude, the reader may refer to the article on that country for further information. The soil is fertile, and in seasons not afflicted by drought, well repays the tiller's care. Von Orlich, whose journey took place in the beginning of March, observes, "Its peculiar freshness in this dry season was very remarkable. It is a boundless garden, in which sugarcane, indigo, cotton, poppy, wheat, barley, and many vegetables flourish. Beautiful groves of mangoes, tamarinds, and bananas overshadow the village pagodas, mosques, and tanks, and give an ever-varying beauty to the landscape, which is animated by pilgrims, peasantry, travellers on foot and horseback, heavily-laden carts, and camels. Altogether, this district presents one of the most original and picturesque scenes of Indian life." It may be inferred that this part of India has been much benefited by British rule, as Tennant, who travelled through it in 1798, describes it as then a melancholy waste, though exhibiting in its ruined towns, tanks, seraes, and other scattered works of utility, memorials of former prosperity. Under the existing revenue settlement of the North-Western Provinces, the government demand on the lands of this district has been fixed for a term of years, and is not liable to be increased until the year 1870. The population is officially returned at 679,787, of which number the Hindoos form by far the larger proportion; viz., 364,159 agricultural, and 248,278 non-agricultural; while the Mussulmans amount only to 28,006 agricultural, and 39,344 non-agricultural. The number of towns containing less than 1,000 inhabitants, is 1,247; those containing more than 1,000 and less than 5,000, are 145; four towns contain more than 5,000; and there is one containing upwards of 10,000; making a total of of 1,397. The principal towns—Futtehpore, Korah, Kudjooa or Cujwa, Hatgang, and Huswa—are noticed under their respective names in the alphabetical arrangement. The great trunk road from Calcutta to Delhi and the northern Doab, by Allahabad, proceeds through this district, in a direction from south-east to north-west, passing through the town of Futtehpore. From this last town a route proceeds south-westward by Chillatara Ghaut to Banda; another westward to Calpee. The route from Cawnpore to Banda by Chillatara Ghat passes through the north-western part of the district in a direction from north to south. The district is also traversed by the East-Indian Railway.

The tract in which this district is comprised, was conquered, in 1194, by the Afghan Mussulmans, under Shahabuddin Muhammad, ruler of Ghuznee. These invaders so well established their power in this quarter, that they were able to offer an obstinate resistance to Baber, whose son Humayon they expelled, under the conduct of Sher Shah. After Akbar removed the seat of government to Agra, the adjacent part of the Doab became of great political importance, and in 1659, Aurungzebe and his brother Shuja met in conflict for sovereignty and life at Kudjooa or Cujwa, twenty miles north-west of the town of Futtehpore. After a sharp action, Shuja was routed, with the loss of 114 pieces of cannon, and the entire dispersion of his army. By treaty dated 16th August, 1765, between the East-India Company and Shuja ud Dowlah, the nawaub of Oude, this part of the Doab was assigned to the emperor of Delhi, the fourth article providing, that "the king, Shah Allum, shall remain in full possession of Cora, and such part of the province of Allahabad as he now possesses, which are ceded to his majesty as a royal demesne for the support of his dignity and expenses." Shah Allum having in 1772 given up to the Mahrattas his claims on these provinces, that step was regarded by the British authorities as amounting to a forfeiture, and they agreed by treaty of the 1st May, 1775, that this tract should remain in the possession of the nawaub of Oude, in as full a manner as the rest of his dominions. Finally, by treaty of the 10th November, 1801, the nawaub re-conveyed it to the Company, in commutation of the subsidy which he had stipulated to pay for the defence of his territory.

FUTTEHPORE.—The principal place of the district of the same name, a town on the route from Allahabad to Cawnpore, 70 miles N.W. of the former, and 50 S.E. of the latter. It has a spacious serae or lodge for travellers, built of brick, which Heber describes as a "large court, with two gateways opposite to each other, surmounted by towers not unlike those of a college, with a cloister or veranda all round, raised about a foot from the ground, with a pucka (baked brick) floor, and having little fireplaces contrived against the wall, just large enough to hold the earthen pitchers in which all the cookery of the country is carried on; and behind this a range of small and dark apartments, a step lower than the veranda." Contiguous to the serae is a well-supplied bazar. Futtehpore is a large and thriving town, with a population of 20,864 persons. It has some good houses, and a small but very elegant mosque, built by the nephew of Almas Ali Khan, a eunuch, the minister of the nawaub of Oude, farmer of the revenues of the Southern Doab, and "of nearly half of the province of Oude" at the close of the last century and commencement of the present. The environs are crowded with burial-places. Tieffenthaler, writing a century ago, describes it as having a long street, and formerly populous, but at that time much decayed. At its north-east side was a mud fort, of quadrangular outline, with a round tower at each corner. In the Ayeen Akbery, its revenue is stated to be 72,317 rupees. Here is the chief seat of the civil establishment of the district, consisting of a judge, collector, deputy-collector, and other functionaries. In the military distribution, Futtehpore is within the Benares division, and a detachment of infantry is usually stationed here. The Arabic word fath, forming part of the name, shows that it must have been given subsequently to the overthrow of the Hindoos by the Affgan Mussulmans, under Shahabuddin, in the year 1194. The place was certainly in existence previously to the invasion of this region by Baber, as it is mentioned by him. Supplies and water may be had here in great abundance, and the road in this part of the route is good. Distance N.W. from Calcutta 571 miles, and from Allahabad 76; S.E. from Cawnpore 48, from Delhi 267. Lat. 25° 57′, long. 80° 54′.

FUTTIHPOOR, in the Baree Dooab division of the Punjab, a town situated on the left bank of the Ravee river, 92 miles S.W. of the town of Ferozepoor. Lat. 30° 50′, long. 73° 5′.

FUTTOOHA, or FUTWA, in the British district of Patna, lieut.-gov. of Bengal, a town at the confluence of the Poonpoon with the Ganges, and on the right bank of each river. The Poonpoon is here crossed by "a very long and handsome bridge." It is on the route from Berhampoor to Dinapoor, 272 miles N.W. of former, 21 E. of latter. It has a large bazar, and contains 2,000 houses, with a population estimated at 12,000. The Ganges here is considered especially sacred, and at certain times of the year vast multitudes assemble and bathe here. Futwa is 10 miles S.E. of Patna, 21 S.E. of Dinapore; from Calcutta N.W., by Berhampore, 390. Lat. 25° 30′, long. 85° 22′.

FUTTUNPOOR, in the British district of Furruckabad, lieut.-gov. of the N.W. Provinces, a village on the route from the cantonment of Allyghur to that of Futtehgurh, and 20 miles N.W. of the latter. Lat. 27° 26′, long. 79° 24′.

FUTTYGUNGE, in the territory of Oude, a town on the route by Nanamow ghat or ferry from Etawah to Lucknow, eight miles W. of the latter. It has a bazar, and is supplied with water from wells. Lord Valentia, who passed through this place in 1803, describes it as tolerably populous, and consisting of a street, inclosed by a wall of trifling height, and having at each end a gateway, the gates of which were broken. It was built by Shuja ud daulah, nawaub vizier of Oude, in commemoration of a victory gained over the Rohillas; and hence the name. Lat. 26° 48′, long. 80° 49′.

FUTTYGURH, in the British district of Furruckabad, lieut.-gov. of the N.W. Provinces, a military cantonment on the left bank of the Ganges, crossed here by ferry, and three miles E. of the city of Furruckabad. Tieffenthaler describes it as consisting, in his time, about a century ago, of two parts. It is now of somewhat less importance than during the period from the first establishment of the cantonment, in 1777, to the beginning of the present century, when the dubious political relations of the East-India Company with the state of Oude, and the proximity of the Mahratta power under Perron, required considerable military resources to be promptly available in this part of India. It is a favourite station with the military, being healthful, and abundantly supplied with a variety of excellent provisions at a cheap rate. The consequence of this station is likely to be increased on the completion of the projected branch of the Ganges Canal, which, issuing from the main channel on the left side, a little north of Meerut, is continued for the distance of 170 miles to Futtyghur. There is a church at this place. Holcar, in the course of his incursion into the Dooab in 1804, attacked the town, burned the cavalry stables and the officers' bungalows, and was proceeding to attack the defences, when the arrival of the British, and his consequent defeat, drove him into precipitate flight. The cantonment is 25 miles to the E. of the great route from Calcutta to Delhi, and 703 miles N.W. of the former, 184 S.E. of the latter. Elevation above the sea 550 feet. Lat. 27° 22′, long. 79° 41′.

FUTTYPOOR, in the British territory of Saugor and Nerbudda, lieut.-gov. of the N.W. Provinces, a town 20 miles S. of the south or left bank of the river Nerbudda, and on the Unjon, a small stream tributary to that river. Its site is picturesque, among the low hills forming the southern boundary of the valley of the Nerbudda, and it is a place of some importance, as three petty Gond rajas or chiefs reside there. Distant from Saugor cantonment 80 miles. Lat. 22° 38′, long. 78° 38′.

FUTWA.—See Futtooha.

FYZABAD, in the British district of Saharunpoor, lieut.-gov. of the N.W. Provinces, a village in lat. 30° 19′, long. 77° 38′.

FYZABAD, called also BANGLA, in the district of Pachamrat, territory of Oude, a town on the right bank of the Ghoghra, here a great and navigable river, expanding in some places in the rainy season to the breadth of a mile and a half, and crossed at the Rai ghat by ferry. Fyzabad, and the ruins of the ancient Ayodha or Oude, adjoining it on the south-east, extend ten miles along the right bank of the river, and for a distance of two miles from it. Saadat Ali Khan, first nawaub vazir of Oude, and who may be considered the founder of this town, about the year 1730 built here a palace, and adjoining to it laid out a handsome garden, in the Persian style. It was further embellished by his successors Sefdar Jang and Shujah ud daulah with various buildings and pleasure-grounds. The latter enlarged the market-place, strengthened the fort with a wall, a ditch, and round towers, and collected so great a population, that it became a great city. Subsequently, however, on his acquisition of a large part of Rohilcund, he removed the seat of government to Lucknow. This took place in 1775, and since that time Fyzabad has much decayed, the present population consisting almost exclusively of the lower and more indigent classes, the leading men, merchants, bankers, and others, having transferred their residence to Lucknow. The tide of emigration, which is represented as constantly increasing, is accelerated by the exactions practised on the inhabitants. Everything brought into the town is heavily taxed. The chief manufactures at present are cloth, metal vessels, and arms. The population is estimated by Butter at 100,000, but is fast diminishing, from the numbers of those who seek an asylum from oppression, in the Company's territories, or wherever else peace and security may be enjoyed. The military route from Goruckpore cantonment to that of Lucknow passes through this place, crossing the river Gogra by ferry at the Rai ghat, where are usually many boats. To the west of the town is an encamping-ground. Distant E. from Lucknow 89 miles, N. from Allahabad 95. Lat. 26° 47′, long. 82° 10′.

FYZEPOOR.—A town in the British district of Candeish, presidency of Bombay. Some very elegant and expensive houses, belonging to native bankers and cotton-merchants, have of late years been built in this town. Lat. 21° 11′, long. 75° 53′.

G.

GADHWALA, in the Rajpoot state of Bikaner, a village on the route from Ratungurh to the town of Bikaner, and nine miles E. of the latter. It contains forty houses, supplied with very good water from a well 270 feet deep. Lat. 27° 57′, long. 73° 30′.

GAIGHAT, in the British district of Goruckpoor, lieut.-gov. of the N.W. Provinces, a petty market-town on the small river Manaura, on the route from the cantonment of Goruckpoor to that of Sultanpoor, in Oude, 49 miles S.W. of the former, 61 N.E. of the latter. The number of its houses is stated by Buchanan at 115, which, allowing six persons to each house, would give a population of 690. Lat. 26° 35′, long. 82° 47′.

GALAOTI, or GOLAUTTI, in the British district of Boolundshuhur, lieut.-gov. of the N.W. Provinces, a town on the route from Allyghur to the town of Meerut, and 29 miles S. of the latter. It has a bazar. Lat. 28° 36′, long. 77° 51′.

GALKOT.—A town in the native state of Nepal, on the left bank of a branch of the Gunduck river, and 142 miles N.W. from Khatmandoo. Lat. 28° 18′, long. 83° 7′.

GALNA.—See JALNA.

GANDARACOTTAH.—A town in the British district of Tanjore, presidency of Madras, 195 miles S.W. of Madras. Lat. 10° 36′, long. 79° 5′.

GANDAREE.—A town in Hyderabad, or territory of the Nizam, 78 miles N.W. from Hyderabad, and 180 miles S.E. from Jaulnah. Lat. 18° 24′, long. 78° 10′.

GANEROW.—A town in the Rajpoot state of Godwar, 108 miles S.W. from Nusserabad, and 78 miles S.E. from Jodhpoor. Lat. 25° 16′, long. 73° 36′.

GANESPOOR, in the British district of Goruckpoor, lieut.-gov. of the N.W. Provinces, a small town on the river Koyane. According to Buchanan, it contains 200 houses, and consequently, allowing six persons to each, a population of 1,200. Part is surrounded by a rampart of earth. Distant W. from Goruckpoor cantonment 38 miles. Lat. 26° 48′, long. 82° 48′.

GANGAMEIK.—A village in Arracan, situate on the left bank of the Arracan river. Lat. 20° 21′, long. 93° 5′.

GANGAROWL, in the British district of Allygurh, lieut.-gov. of the N.W. Provinces, a town 20 miles S.E. of the cantonment of Allygurh. Lat. 27° 41′, long. 78° 18′.

GANGES.—A celebrated river of India, and of which the Bhageerettee is generally and popularly regarded as the remote feeder. The distinction of originating the great mass of waters subsequently termed the Ganges was some years since proposed to be accorded to the Jahnuvi, a stream which joins the Bhageerettee in lat. 31° 2′, long. 78° 55′. It was then believed that the Jahnuvi took its rise from the north of the culminating range of the Himalayas, within the limits of Chinese authority. This supposition turns out, however, to be erroneous. It has been since ascertained that the remotest source of the Jahnuvi is situate in British territory, on the southern base of the before-mentioned range; and in reference to this discovery, Captain Strachey, to whom its merit is due, contends that the Ganges should be considered to originate in the most distant tributary of the Aluknunda (a feeder of the Ganges having a larger volume of water than the Bhageerettee). But as the distance between the ascertained source of the most remote tributary of the Bhageerettee and the point of confluence of the latter river with the Aluknunda is still believed to be fully equal to the distance between the source of the Doulee, to which the Aluknunda owes its commencement, and the same point of confluence, there seems no reason for depriving the sacred stream of the Hindoos of its ancient title; and it is therefore proposed in this article to regard the Bhageerettee as the true Ganges. The Bhageerettee first comes to light near Gangotri, in the territory of Gurwhal, in lat. 30° 54′, long. 79° 7′, issuing from under a very low arch, at the base of a great snow-bed, estimated to be 300 feet thick, which lies between the lofty mountains termed St. Patrick, St. George, and the Pyramid, the two higher having elevations above the sea, respectively, of 22,798 and 22,654 feet, and the other, on the opposite side, having an elevation of 21,379. "From the brow of this curious wall of snow, and immediately above the outlet of the stream, large and hoary icicles depend. They are formed by the freezing of the melted snow-water at the top of the bed; for in the middle of the day the sun is powerful, and the water produced by its action falls over this place in cascade, but is frozen at night." As in Brahminical mythology, the Ganges is said to flow from the head of Mahadeva or Siva, a Hindoo who attended the English party by whom this place was explored, expressed his belief that these icicles must be the hair of the deity. On the 31st May the mean breadth of the stream was found to be twenty-seven feet; the mean depth was estimated at fifteen inches. From this spot, which has an elevation of 13,800 feet, the stream holds a direction north-west for ten miles to Gangotri, where the mean breadth, on the 26th May, was found to be forty-three feet, the depth eighteen inches, and the current very rapid. On the 2nd June the stream was ascertained to be two feet deep, and wider than previously observed. The elevation of Gangotri is 10,300 feet, and the average descent of the river thereto, from the place where it emerges from the snow-bed, is 350 feet per mile. From Gangotri the Bhageerettee holds a course nearly north-west to Bhairogati, in lat. 31° 2′, long. 78° 54′, the point of confluence with the Jahnuvi, holding its steep and foaming course from the north-east. The latter is considerably the larger river. The distance is seven miles from Gangotri to Bhairogati; and as this latter place has an elevation of 8,511 feet, the average descent of the river in this part of its course is 255 per mile. The united stream holds a course first westerly, and then south-westerly, for thirteen miles, as far as Sookhee, in lat. 30° 59′, long. 78° 45′, where it may be said to "break through the Himalaya Proper." The elevation of the waterway is here 7,608 feet, and consequently, the descent of the stream from the confluence is on an average seventy feet per mile. From Sookhee the river holds a very sinuous but generally a south-westerly course for about thirty-six miles, to Utal, in lat. 30° 43′, long. 78° 25′, where it turns nearly southward for about fifteen miles more to Surota, in lat. 30° 33′, long. 78° 24′. It thence takes a direction south-east, and, at a distance of nine miles, in lat. 30° 28′, long. 78° 29′, receives, on the left side, the Julkar, a considerable torrent flowing from the north-east; and eight miles lower down, on the same side, at Teeree, in lat. 30° 23′, long. 78° 31′, the Bhillung, another tributary of considerable size, also flowing from the north-east. The elevation of the waterway at this confluence is 2,278 feet, and the average descent of the river from Sookhee thereto is seventy-eight feet per mile. Continuing to flow south-east for twenty-two miles, it is, at Deoprag, in lat. 30° 8′, long. 78° 39′, joined on the left side by the Aluknunda, a large stream formed by the union of the Vishnoo and the Doulee. The Aluknunda is a larger river than that whose volume it contributes to swell, bearing to it the proportion of three to two. The elevation at the point of this confluence is 1,953 feet; and consequently the average descent of the river from Teeree to it is fifteen feet in the mile. From Deoprag, the united stream, now called the Ganges, flows southwards eight miles, to Nougaon, in lat. 30° 3′, long. 78° 38′, where, on the left side, it receives the Nyar, a considerable stream flowing from the south-east. From this confluence the river holds a course very sinuous, but generally westerly, for twenty-four miles, to Rikkee Kasee, in lat. 30° 6′, long. 78° 23′, where it touches upon the Dehra Dhoon. Rikkee Kasee having an elevation of 1,377 feet, the fall of the river to that place from Deoprag is on an average eighteen feet per mile. In its passage between the Dehra Dhoon and the province of Kumaon, it receives, opposite the village of Kankur, in lat. 30° 2′, long. 78° 19′, on the right bank, the Sooswa, a considerable stream, draining the valley, down which it flows in a south-easterly direction. This is the only stream of importance which falls into the Ganges on the right side, from the confluence of the Jahnuvi to this part of its course, though it receives numerous small torrents on that side. Its descent by the Dehra Dhoon is rather rapid to Hurdwar, in lat. 29° 57′, long. 78° 14′, a distance from Rikkee Kasee of fifteen miles, in a south-westerly direction. The elevation of Hurdwar is 1,024 feet; consequently, the average descent of the river in passing the Dhera Dhoon is twenty-three feet per mile. The volume of water discharged at Hurdwar when the river is lowest is estimated at 7,000 cubic feet per second; being equal to only a small part of the alleged volume of the Dihong or Sanpoo, the principal feeder of the Brahmapootra.

From Hurdwar the general course of the Ganges is nearly south for about 130 miles, as far as Anopshuhur, in the British district of Bolundshuhur, in lat. 28° 31′, long. 78° 20′, where it turns to the south-east, and 160 miles lower down, in lat. 27° 7′, long. 80° 3′, receives on the left side the Ramgunga, a considerable river flowing from the north-west. Eight miles lower down, it on the right side receives the Kallee Nuddee, flowing likewise from the north-west; and twenty miles beyond, the Eesun Nuddee. One hundred and seventy miles lower down, at Allahabad, in lat. 25° 26′, long. 81° 45′, it is joined, also on the right side, by the Jumna, from the north-west. From Hurdwar to Cawnpore, the distance is about 348 miles: as the descent of the river from the former to the latter place is about 645 feet, the average fall of the river in this part of its course is about one foot ten inches per mile; and as there does not appear to be any marked difference in the declivity of its channel between Cawnpore and Allahabad, the same average descent of the waterway may with probability be assumed for the whole distance from Hurdwar to Allahabad. Throughout the whole of its course above Allahabad, the Ganges is "a stream of shoals and rapids." There are fords across it; as at Sakertal, in lat. 29° 29′, long. 78° 4′; at Ahar, seven miles above Anopshuhur; at Kumuroodeennuggur, in lat. 28° 55′, long. 78° 11′; in the vicinity of Hurdwar; and without doubt in other places at times, when the water is very low. It is, however, navigable for river craft as far as Hurdwar: steamers conveying passengers and treasure, ply as far as Ghurmukteesur, 393 miles above Allahabad; and as far as Cawnpore, 140 miles above Allahabad, the navigation is plied with much activity, the reach of the river at that military station having the appearance of a port on a small scale. From Allahabad, the stream meanders in a direction generally easterly for 270 miles, to Manjhee, near which, in lat. 25° 46′, long. 84° 40′, it is joined on the left side by the Gogra. Between Allahabad and Manjhee, it on the left side receives the Goomtee, and on the right, the Tons and Kurumnassa; besides many smaller streams right and left. The average breadth in this part during the dry season is from 1,200 to 1,500 feet. At Benares, at that season, a section of the river is set down as having a breadth of 1,400 feet, and an average depth of thirty-five feet; and the discharge was estimated at 19,000 cubic feet per second. During the periodical rains, the breadth of the river at the same spot is 3,000 feet, and, rising forty-three feet, its average depth is about fifty-eight feet. The mean discharge at Benares throughout the year is estimated at 250,000 cubic feet per second. The depth of the channel is, however, subject to great inequality, in many places exceeding fifty feet during the periodical rains; while, in the dry season, it was found that near Kutchwa, thirty-five miles above Benares, a shoal extends completely across the river, having only two feet six inches water on its lowest part; so that all craft having a draught exceeding two feet, grounded in attempting to pass; and it is obvious, that at this spot the river must be then fordable. Eighteen miles below the junction of the Gogra, opposite to the town of Cherand, in lat. 25° 39′, long. 84° 53′, it on the right side receives the Sone, a large river flowing from the south-west; and after this addition, "its channel, when clear of islands, is generally about a mile wide; but in spring by far the greater part is a mere dry sand, covered with clouds of dust, which render all objects at any distance invisible; so that, travelling on its channel, one might imagine himself in the midst of a frightful desert." At Hajeepoor, on the left side, twenty miles below the confluence of the Sone, the Ganges receives the Gunduck, a large river from the north-west, and continues to flow eastward for 160 miles, to Kuttree, in lat. 25° 20′, long. 87° 17′, where, on the left side, it receives the Coosy, also a large river flowing from the north, having in its course between the junctions of these two great rivers received right and left several streams of less importance. Below the confluence, for thirty-five miles, to Sikreegali, situate in lat. 25° 10′, long. 87° 43′, numerous tributaries from the north pour their waters into the Ganges; yet such is the enormous loss by evaporation, that, two miles below the above-mentioned place, the river, though a mile wide, has only five feet of water where deepest, with a current of only a mile and a quarter per hour; and so shallow in several places is the stream, that craft should have a "draught little exceeding eighteen inches, to navigate safely and beneficially between Calcutta and Allahabad." At Sikreegali the river turns south-east, a direction which the main stream continues to hold for the remainder of its course; but sixty miles below Sikreegali, and opposite the town of Seebgunge, in lat. 24° 44′, long. 87° 59′, the Bhagarathi, a great watercourse, parts on the right side from the main stream; and seventy miles lower down, the Jellinghee, another watercourse, also of considerable dimensions, diverges on the same side, at the town of Jellinghee, in lat. 24° 9′, long. 88° 40′. The Bhagarathi proceeding southward for 120 miles, is then rejoined by the Jellinghee, after a course of about the like distance, and the united stream, called the Hoogly, continuing to hold the same direction for forty-eight miles, becomes navigable for vessels of considerable burthen at Chandernagore, in lat. 22° 50′, long. 88° 24′, at the distance of 115 miles from the sea, into which it falls about lat. 21° 40′, long. 88°; its estuary being considered by the Brahminists the termination of the sacred stream, which, rising near Gangotri, and issuing from the mountains at Hurdwar, flows by the holy city of Benares. Its total length of course, from the source of the Jahnuvi to its fall into the Bay of Bengal at Saugor, is about 1,514 miles, viz.:—

	Miles.
From the source of the Jahnuvi to the junction of the Aluknunda and Bhageretee rivers	133
Thence to Hurdwar	47
,, Allahabad	488
,, Seebgunge (origin of the Bhagirathi)	563
,, Junction of Bhagirathi with Jellinghee	120
,, Chandernagore	48
,, The Sea	115
	1,514

Below the divergence of the Bhagirathi and the Jellinghee, the main stream is called the Podda or Ganges; and from that point the joint delta of the Ganges and Brahmapootra may be considered to commence. The Podda or Ganges, flowing south-east, receives some considerable streams on the left side; and on the right, besides the Jellinghee, it throws off, five miles lower down, the Martabhanga; forty miles below this latter divergence, the Gorae; and forty miles still further, the Chundni. At the distance of thirty miles lower down, it is joined on the left side, at Juffergunge, in lat. 23° 52′, long. 89° 45′, by an offset of the Konaie or Jabuna, a vast river, the principal channel of the Brahmapootra, and here much larger than the Podda or Ganges. The united stream takes a course south-east for sixty miles, when it throws off the Kirtynassa, and sixty-five miles below that divergence, it joins the Meghna, after which, flowing southwards for thirty-five miles, it is finally discharged into the Bay of Bengal, in lat. 22° 15′, long. 90° 43′; its total length of course, from the issue beneath the snow at Gangotri, being 1,557 miles, or from the source of the Jahnuvi, 1,570 miles. In continuation of what has been already stated as to the slope of the river down to Allahabad, it may be mentioned that Prinsep estimated the fall, in a distance of 139 miles (measured along the continuous course of the stream), from that city to Benares, at six inches per mile; from Benares to Colgong, being 326 miles, at five inches; from Colgong to Jellinghee, being 167 miles, at four inches; from Jellinghee to Calcutta, being 170 miles, also at four inches; from Calcutta to the sea, about 100 miles, at one or two inches, according as the water may be at its highest or lowest state. Access at all seasons for any considerable craft from the sea to that part of the Ganges above the Delta can be attained only through the continuous channel of the Meghna and Podda, or through the Chundna, which, diverging from the Podda or Ganges on the right side, in lat. 23° 55′, long. 89° 6′, takes a direction southwards, and falls into the Bay of Bengal by the Hooringottah estuary. During the dry season, neither the Bhagirathi nor the Jellinghee, forming by their junction the Hoogly, is navigable for craft drawing above eighteen inches water; and at that period the communication by water between the Hoogly below Calcutta and the Ganges above the Delta, is maintained by a circuitous course called the Soonderbund Passage, opening into the Chundna. In the Podda or Ganges the tide is felt as far as Juffergunge, 160 miles from the sea, and in the Hoogly to a distance of about 150 miles from the sea. Besides the principal channels,—the Hoogly, the Podda, and the Chundna, numerous streams of less importance, parting from the main ones, find their way to the Bay of Bengal through the Soonderbunds, a wonderful maze of sea-islands, separated by numerous channels holding every direction, but principally from north to south. There are upwards of twenty of the estuaries of those channels opening into the head of the bay. The water of the Ganges begins to rise towards the end of May, and is usually at its maximum in September. The following table, drawn up by Captain Thomas Prinsep, illustrates the rise of the water in the river at various places:—

	Greatest known Annual Rise. Ft.	In.	Rise in low Seasons. Ft.	In.
At Allahabad	45	6	29	0
Benares	45	0	31	0
Colgong	29	6	28	3
Jellinghee	26	0	25	6
Ditto by observations quoted by Rennell	32	0		
Commercolly & Custee (not quite certain)	22	6	22	0
Agurdeep	23	9	23	0
Calcutta (independent of tide)	7	0	6	7
Dacca, according to Rennell	14	0		

Rennell is of opinion that the rising of the water of the Ganges is not in any considerable degree caused by the melting of the snows of the Himalayas, but results principally from the fall of rain in the less-elevated mountains and over the plain. "By the latter end of July all the lower parts of Bengal contiguous to the Ganges and Burhampooter are overflowed, and form an inundation of more than 100 miles in width, nothing appearing but villages and trees." "Embarkations of every kind traverse the inundation; those bound upwards availing themselves of a direct course and still water, at a season when every stream rushes like a torrent. Husbandry and grazing are both suspended, and the peasant traverses in his boat those fields which in another season he was wont to plough, happy that the elevated site of the river-banks places the herbage they contain within his reach, otherwise his cattle must perish." Many extensive tracts are guarded from being inundated by the river by means of dams, made at an enormous expense, and having collectively a length of above 1,000 miles. With respect to the general breadth of the Ganges, Prinsep states it to be "very unequal, but may be reckoned to average a mile in the dry season on its whole course through the plains, and two miles in the freshes." According to Burnes, the average discharge of the Indus is four times that of the Ganges during the dry season. Like other rivers subject to periodical inundations, the water of the Ganges carries down earth in a state of suspension. The amount of solid matter in bulk in proportion to the quantity of water, is, according to laborious observations and calculations made by the Rev. R. Everest, as follows:—During the rainy season $\frac{1}{858}$th part, or about two cubic inches in a cubic foot; during the winter five months, $\frac{1}{3878}$th part; and during the rest of the year, $\frac{1}{7834}$th part; and following out his data, this writer concludes the total annual discharge of earthy matter to be 6,368,077,440 cubic feet in bulk. The total extent of inland navigation connected with the Ganges is not ascertainable with any degree of accuracy, but is unquestionably very large, and will be considerably increased on the completion of the works now in progress for facilitating the irrigation of the Doab by means of the Ganges Canal, and at the same time adding to the means of water-transit. The first idea of a plan of irrigation for the Doab originated as long since as the time of Lord William Bentinck, by whose orders some steps were taken for ascertaining its practicability; but, upon inquiry, the project did not appear capable of being successfully carried out. Under Lord Auckland the inquiries were resumed, the importance of the subject having been painfully pressed upon the notice of government by the occurrence of severe famine in the districts which the proposed works were designed to benefit. A magnificent plan for irrigation and navigation was laid down by Captain Cautley, comprising a main trunk line, running from the town of Hurdwar, through the centre of the Doab, with a connecting line to Cawnpore, as the inlet and outlet for navigation; the tracts of country lying between the different rivers which run into the Jumna and Ganges being irrigated by branches, extending the benefits of this fertilizing process to every village in the Doab. This project was subsequently referred to a committee of engineer and artillery officers for examination and report. Their testimony was highly favourable. The only serious difficulty to the execution of the project was presented by the tract of low land through which the drainage of the Solani river runs before its junction with the Rutmoo. Two methods of surmounting this were suggested: one by an aqueduct; the other by diverting the line so as to cross the Solani and its tributaries by means of dams. The latter was recommended by its being presumed to be less costly; but the former plan, deemed far better in every other point of view, was finally adopted. An account of this magnificent aqueduct will be found under the article "Solani River." The Ganges Canal is now rapidly advancing to completion. The main line has been constructed from Hurdwar to the vicinity of Allyghur, whence it diverges in two channels, one to Cawnpore, and the other to Humeerpoor, *viâ* Etawa, with three offsets, designated the Futtehghur, Bolundshuhur, and Coel branches. The total length of the canal with all its branches will measure about 810 miles.

	Miles.
Hurdwar to Allyghur........	180
Allyghur to Cawnpore	170
Allyghur to Humeerpoor	180
Branch to Futtehghur	170
Ditto to Bolundshuhur	60
Ditto to Coel	50
	810

The total cost is estimated at a million and a half sterling. No inconvenient diminution of the navigable facilities of the Ganges is anticipated from the abstraction of the larger portion of its waters at Hurdwar for the purposes of the canal, inasmuch as no such result has taken place on the Jumna, where the whole apparent stream has been diverted to feed the two canals diverging from that river. Notwithstanding this, the under-current which percolates the gravelly or sandy bed, together with the drainage of the intermediate country, furnishes a navigable stream of water at Agra, a distance of 290 miles by the river's course; and it is thence inferred that the navigation of the Ganges below Cawnpore will not be injuriously affected; while the navigation above will be carried on by means of the canal. It may be observed, that the discharge of the Ganges at Hurdwar, the place at which it emerges from the hills, is in the dry season in proportion to that of the Jumna as seven to three, the discharge of the Ganges being estimated at 7,000 cubic feet per second, and that of the Jumna at the canal heads at about 3,000.

GANGLUNG.—See GANTUNG.

GANGOONDOUM.—A town in the British district of Madura, presidency of Madras, 274 miles S.W. of Madras. Lat. 9° 28′, long. 78° 47′.

GANGOOROO.—A town in the native state of Gurhwal, on the right bank of the Tonse river, and 60 miles N.E. from Dehra. Lat. 31° 9′, long. 78° 23′.

GANGOTRI, in the native state of Gurhwal, a small temple on the right bank of the Bhageerettee, as the Ganges is called in the upper part of its course, and eight or ten miles N.W. of its source. The river here expands a little, and on the bank of a small bay or inlet the temple is built, about fifteen feet above the water. It is in a small inclosure, surrounded by a wall of unhewn stone, cemented with lime-mortar, and has close to it, and in the same inclosure, a small comfortable house, built for the officiating Brahmins. The temple is a square building, about twenty feet high, and contains small statues of Ganga, Bhagirathi, and other mythological personages, supposed to be connected with this locality. There is no village here, the pilgrims having no other shelter than a few sheds of wood, and caves in the adjoining cliffs. There are several pools, called by the names Brahmakund, Bishnukund, and others of corresponding import. Ablution in these is considered an important part of the ritual to be observed by pilgrims who visit this spot, considered popularly to be the source of the Ganges, as farther progress up the stream is generally, though erroneously, regarded as impracticable. Though this ablution, with due donations to the officiating Brahmins, is considered to cleanse from all offences, the number of pilgrims is not considerable, in consequence of the great length and ruggedness of the journey, and the difficulty of obtaining subsistence by the way. Flasks and similar vessels are filled at Gangotri with the sacred water of the stream, and being sealed by the officiating Brahmin, are conveyed to the plains, where they are highly prized by the superstitious. Gangotri is below the upper limit of forests; cedars growing here, though to no great size, and birch-trees thriving remarkably. The mean breadth of the Bhageerettee or Ganges here was ascertained by Hodgson, on the 26th of May, to be forty-three feet, the depth eighteen inches, the current very swift, and over rounded stones. On the 2nd of June following, he conjectured its volume to be doubled, in consequence of the rapid melting of the snow. Rennell's account of Gangotri would scarcely have been expected from one who usually displays so much information and judgment. "This great body of water [the Ganges] now forces a passage *through* the ridge of Mount Himmaleh, at the distance possibly of 100 miles below the place of its first approach to it, and, sapping its very foundations, rushes through a cavern, and precipitates itself into a vast basin, which it has worn in the rock at the hither foot of the mountains. The Ganges thus appears to incurious spectators to derive its original springs from this chain of mountains, and the mind of superstition has given to the mouth of the cavern the form of the head of a cow." The Brahmin who showed the holy places to Fraser, ridiculed the fancy that the stream issued from a rock like a cow's mouth. Herbert estimates the length of course of the Bhageerettee or Ganges, from its source near Gangotri to its entrance on the plains of Hindostan, at about 203 miles. The elevation of the temple above the sea is 10,319 feet. Lat. 30° 59′, long. 78° 59′.

GANGPORE.—A petty raj within the territory superintended by the political agent for the south-west frontier of Bengal. It is bounded on the north by the British district of Chota Nagpoor; on the east by the native state of Bonei; on the south by that of Samba and the British district of Sumbulpore; and on the west by the native states of Ryghur and Jushpoor. It extends from lat. 21° 50′—22° 37′, and from long. 83° 31′—84° 57′, and is ninety miles in length from east to west, and thirty-five in breadth, with an area of 2,493 square miles. The latest available reports give a very unfavourable account of the state of the country, which is little better than a great jungle, giving shelter to vast numbers of wild animals, and affording admirable sport to the hunter. The soil is naturally rich, but there is little cultivation, and not even the semblance of any administration of justice. The annual revenue was supposed to be about a lac of rupees (10,000*l.*), and the British tribute, which is only 500 rupees, was regularly paid. The prince, at the date of the report, though a young man, was sunk into that condition of sloth and imbecility which almost invariably results from indulgence in opium. The population is believed to be about 112,000. Gangpore, the principal place, is in lat. 22° 3′, long. 84° 43′.

GANISCOTTEE.—A town in Hyderabad, or territory of the Nizam, 85 miles N.E. from Hyderabad, and 204 miles S.E. from Ellichpoor. Lat. 18° 32′, long. 78° 53′.

GANJAM.—A British district under the presidency of Madras, named from the town formerly its principal place. It is bounded on the north-west, north, and north-east, by the territory of Orissa; on the south-east by the Bay of Bengal; on the west by the British district of Vizagapatam; and lies between lat. 18° 13′—19° 52′, long. 83° 50′—85° 15′. The area is stated officially to be 6,400 square miles. The seacoast, commencing at the estuary of the Naglaudi Nadi, or Chicacole river, is bold and rocky, and is marked by a range of rugged hills, running in some parts close to the shore; in others, nearly parallel to it, but a few miles inland. Those near the northern extremity of the coast recede gradually from it, and leave space for an extensive sandy plain, partly occupied by the jhil or lake of Chilka, lying between this district and that of Cuttack, and separated from the sea for many miles by a long narrow strip of sand, seldom more than three hundred yards in breadth. Though coasting vessels may enter the river Rasikoila, in lat. 19° 22′, long. 85° 8′, there is throughout the whole extent of coast no haven for ships of any considerable burthen, which, if trading to places on any part of it, must anchor abreast of them in the open sea. The streams of the district flow from the western hills, and hold a course south-eastward, falling into the Bay of Bengal. The principal are, the Naglaudi or Chicacole river, the Callingapatam river, and the Rasikoila; but all, without exception, are mere torrents, which are dry for a part of the year. The jhil or lake of Chilka, the greater part of which lies within the limits of the British district of Cuttack, touches part of the northern frontier of this district. It is about forty-two miles in length from north to south, and fifteen in breadth; of small depth, its greatest not exceeding six feet, while in most parts it has not more than four. During the hot season, and the close of the rainy one, agues and fevers of very bad type are common; and in

1815 these diseases carried off such great numbers, both of the European and native population, of the town of Ganjam, that the civil and military establishments were removed to Chicacole; and the former place has since been nearly deserted. The level country is in general extremely fertile, producing abundant crops of rice, sugarcane, maize, millet, pulse of various kinds, oil-seeds, and raji (Eleusine coracana); while the hilly country yields wax, lac, gums, dye-stuffs, arrowroot, and great variety of timber and ornamental woods. Cotton is produced annually to a considerable extent; and the local demand is such as to leave scarcely any for exportation. The only manufactures of importance are coarse cotton cloths and muslins, which last were formerly in high esteem and extensively manufactured, but are not now produced to the same extent, on account of the diminished demand consequent on the irresistible competition of British fabrics. The population is given under the article MADRAS PRESIDENCY. The former prevalence, and recent suppression of human sacrifices in a part of Ganjam, are briefly noticed in the article GOOMSOOR. Ganjam occupies the northern portion of the territory known as the Five Circars, the possession of which was an object of fierce contention between the French and English about the middle of the last century. They were obtained by the former in 1753, and continued under their dominion for six years, when Clive transferred them to the East-India Company, to whom they were formally ceded in 1765, by the emperor of Delhi. Chicacole, the principal place of the district, Ganjam and Russelkondah, the towns of note within the district, are described under their respective names in the alphabetical arrangement. The great route from north-east to south-west, from Calcutta to Madras, runs through the whole length of the district parallel to the seacoast, and generally at a short distance from it. The construction of a macadamized road from Berhampore to Russelkondah has been authorized, at the estimated cost of 14,224*l*.

GANJAM, in the British district of the same name, presidency of Madras, a town on the left side of the Rosikoila Nuddee, immediately above its fall into the Bay of Bengal. This town, formerly remarkable for its fine buildings, is now much decayed, the fort and cantonments being in ruins, and the place nearly deserted, in consequence of a deadly epidemic fever, which, in 1815, carried off great numbers of the inhabitants, both Europeans and natives. The civil and military stations were then removed to the town of Chicacole. The insalubrity of the situation has, it is said, passed away; but the establishments which formerly caused its prosperity have not been restored. It has still, however, some coasting trade by means of the river. Distance direct from Chicacole, N.E., 110 miles; Vizagapatam, N.E., 165; Madras, N.E., 536; Cuttack, S.W., 90; Calcutta, S.W., 315. Lat. 19° 23′, long. 85° 7′.

GANJBUR, in the British district of Paneeput, lieut.-gov. of the N.W. Provinces, a village on the route from the city of Delhi to Kurnal, and 16 miles S.E. of the latter. Lat. 29° 29′, long. 77° 2′.

GANTUNG PASS, in Bussahir, over a range of mountains on the north-eastern boundary, between Koonawur and Chinese Tartary. Jacquemont describes it is a vast opening between summits which overtop it about a thousand feet. The highest part of the pass is covered with perpetual snow. To the west, a declivity extends towards the distant Sutluj, with a surface sloping gradually, but inexpressibly rugged. Gerard crossed the pass at the end of July, amidst falls of snow and sleet, which lasted all day, yet so mild was the temperature, comparatively with the enormous elevation, that the thermometer did not sink below 33°. The Rishi Gantung, a snowy peak rising above the pass, has been ascertained trigonometrically to have an elevation of 21,229 feet above the sea; that of the pass itself is 18,295 feet. Lat. 31° 38′, long. 78° 47′.

GAOMUTEE, in Kumaon, a river rising on the eastern declivity of the peak of Budhan Garh, and in lat. 30°, long. 79° 36′. It holds a course, generally south-easterly, through an extensive valley or elevated plain, remarkably level, and above ten miles in diameter. This expanse is fertile, wooded, though not densely, and well watered by the numerous feeders of the Gaomutee; but though having an average elevation of above four thousand feet above the sea, it is extremely unhealthy, from some cause as yet unascertained. The Gaomutee, after a course of about twenty miles, joins the Surjoo, a feeder of the Kalee, at Bagesur, in lat. 29° 49′, long. 79° 49′.

GAPELONG.—A village in Arracan, situate on the left bank of the river distinguished by the same name. Lat. 20° 48′, long. 93° 7′.

GAR.—A town in the Rajpoot state of Boondee, 73 miles S.E. from Nusseerabad, and 74 miles S. from Jeypoor. Lat. 25° 52′, long. 75° 52′.

GARAHUNG.—A town in the native state of Nepal, near the left bank of the Gunduck river, and 102 miles N.W. from Khatmandoo. Lat. 27° 57′, long. 83° 41′.

GARAKOTA, in the British territory of Saugor and Nerbudda, a town, situate in the angle formed by the confluence of the rivers Sonar and Guddari. The fort is at the apex of the angle, and is of irregular ground-plan, being washed on two sides by the confluent streams. In October, 1818, the town was held by a garrison for the raja of Nagpoor or Berar, and being invested by a British force under General Watson, in a few days a practicable breach was made, and the place surrendered. Distant 25 miles E. of Saugor, 206 S.W. of Allahabad. Elevation above the sea 1,345 feet. Lat. 23° 47′, long. 79° 12′.

GARASPOOR, in the territory of Gwalior, or possessions of Scindia's family, a town on the route from Hosungabad to Saugor, by Bhilsa, 88 miles N.E. of former, 49 S.W. of latter. The town has a small fort of masonry on its south-east side, and a tank east. There are some antique buildings, having elaborate sculptures, in the fine sandstone of the neighbouring hills. Lat. 23° 40′, long. 78° 10′.

GAR GUNSA.—A town in the native state of Cashmeer, or territory of Gholab Singh, 177 miles N.E. from Dehra, and 185 miles N.E. from Simla. Lat. 32° 10′, long. 80° 4′.

GARHA, in the district of Sultanpoor, territory of Oude, a fort on the right bank of the Goomtee, 14 miles S.E. of Sultanpoor cantonment, 106 S.E. of Lucknow. It was, in a remote period, built by a sovereign of Oude, of the Bhar race, a low caste of Hindoos, and the stone used in its construction was, according to tradition, brought by water from Nepal. It early fell into the hands of the Patan invaders of Hindostan, who destroyed the upper part of the walls, leaving them standing to the height of eight or ten feet. The ruined portion has been restored, partly in brick, partly in mud. Part of the stone wall rises from the bed of the Goomtee, and exhibits many sculptures, as well as inscriptions, some in the Nagari, some in the Persian character, relating the history of the place. Lat. 26° 10′, long. 82° 19′.

GARIADHAR, in the peninsula of Kattywar, or territory of the Guicowar, a town in the district of Gohilwar, in a fertile tract, well watered, but indifferently cultivated. Distance from Ahmedabad, S.W., 125 miles; Baroda, S.W., 120; Surat, N.W., 90; Bombay, N.W., 195. Lat. 21° 31′, long. 71° 31′.

GARI SADA KHAN, in the Sinde Sagur Dooab division of the Punjab, a town situated near the left bank of the Kishengunga river, 74 miles N.E. of the town of Attock. Lat. 34° 20′, long. 73° 28′.

GAROBIR.—A town in the native state of Nepal, on the left bank of the Jimru river, and 200 miles N.W. from Khatmandoo. Lat. 28° 5′, long. 82° 5′.

GAROTHA, or GUROTA, in Bundlecund, a small town on the route from Banda to Gwalior, 78 miles W. of the former, 126 S.E. of the latter. It has a bazar, and water is plentiful. Lat. 25° 35′, long. 79° 22′.

GAROWKE, or KAROWKE.—A halting-place on the great Aeng route (Arracan), and situate at the foot of Natyagain. The ascent is very steep, but the path being carried in a zigzag manner, the labour is thereby lessened. The encamping-ground is good, and well supplied with water. Elevation 3,165 feet. Lat. 20° 2′, long. 94° 5′.

GARREE.—A town in the British district of Hydrabad, in the province of Sinde, presidency of Bombay, 63 miles S.E. of Tatta. Lat. 24° 18′, long. 68° 51′.

GARROW HILLS.—This group, situate on the north-eastern frontier of the Bengal territory, extends over a tract of country bounded on the north by Goalpara; on the east by the Cossyah hills; and on the south and west by Mymensing. The chief divisions, with the statistical particulars of each, as far as they can be ascertained, are as follows. The Garrows contain by estimation an area of 2,268 square miles; Ram Rye, 328; Nurtung, 360; Muriow, 283; Molyong, 110; Mahram, 162; Osimla, 350; Kyrim and the domains of various petty chiefs, 486. The population of the whole is given at 65,205. The character of the country is wild, as is also that of the people. For some years past the just and liberal policy of the British government has secured the general prevalence of tranquillity; but in 1852 it was deemed necessary to depute Lieutenant Agnew into the Garrow Hills to inquire into a local disturbance.

GAR YARSA.—A town in the native state of Cashmeer, or dominions of Gholab Singh, 202 miles N.E. from Simla, and 177 miles N.E. from Dehra. Lat. 31° 49′, long. 80° 29′.

GASULPOOR, in the British district of Saugor and Nerbudda, lieut.-gov. of the N.W. Provinces, a town on the route from Jubbulpoor to Rewah, 16 miles N.E. of the former. Lat. 23° 20′, long. 80° 10′.

GAUR, or LUCKNOUTI.—A ruined city in the British district of Maldah, presidency of Bengal. It is situate on a range of inconsiderable eminences, extending along the east or left bank of the Bhagruttee, a watercourse formerly the main channel of the Ganges, but now containing a small portion only of its stream. The best description of this vast monument of the industry and resources of India at a remote period is that given by Rennell, who visited the place. "Taking the extent of the ruins of Gour at the most reasonable calculation, it is not less than fifteen miles in length (extending along the old bank of the Ganges), and from two to three in breadth. Several villages stand on part of its site; the remainder is either covered with thick forests, the habitations of tigers and other beasts of prey, or become arable land, whose soil is chiefly composed of brick-dust. The principal ruins are a mosque, lined with black marble elaborately wrought, and two gates of the citadel, which are strikingly grand and lofty. These fabrics, and some few others, appear to owe their duration to the nature of their materials, which are less marketable, and more difficult to separate, than those of the ordinary brick buildings, which have been, and continue to be, an article of merchandise, and are transported to Moorshedabad, Mauldah, and other places for the purposes of building. These bricks are of remarkably solid texture, and have preserved the sharpness of their edges and smoothness of their surfaces through a series of ages. The situation of Gour was highly convenient for the capital of Bengal and Bahar as united under one government, being nearly centrical with respect to the populous parts of those provinces, and near the junction of the principal rivers that compose that extraordinary inland navigation for which those provinces are famed; and, moreover, secured by the Ganges and other rivers on the only quarter from which Bengal has any cause of apprehension."

Gaur is probably a place of great antiquity; the researches of Wilford, however, do not appear to establish it as of any great importance until A.D. 648, when its chief became independent, on the fall of the previously paramount sway of Magadha. The chiefs of Gaur from that time were powerful, until the reign of Lakshmana, from whom it probably received the name of Lucknouti, by which it is frequently mentioned in history. In 1202 the city was taken, and Lakshmana driven into flight, by Bakhtiar Khilji, a commander subordinate to Kutbuddin Eibak, viceroy of Delhi, for Shahabuddin, monarch of Ghor, in Afghanistan. It in A.D. 1212 was made the capital of the kingdom of Bengal, by Ghiyasuddin, who built there a fine mosque, a college, a caravanserai, and made numerous embankments to protect the city against inundations. About a century and a half later, the seat of government was transferred to Pundua or Peruya, but restored to Gaur in 1409, by Jalaluddin. Nasir Shah, in 1450, surrounded it with the vast rampart of which the extent may still be traced. In A.D. 1536, Sher Shah, the Patan rival of Humayun, having overrun Bengal, took Gaur, and drove its king, Mahmood, into flight, but was himself, the year after, dispossessed by Humayun, who resided for some months in the city, and changed its inauspicious name of Gaur to Jennetabad. He, however, found it necessary to retreat to the western part of his dominions, and his rival, Sher Shah, took possession of the city. After the death of Sher Shah, the governors of Bengal assumed the style of independent rulers of that country, until 1574, when Monaim Khan, in command of the troops of Akbar, subjugated it, and made it the seat of local government, but in a few months perished, with nearly all his troops, by the effects of the pestilential climate. From that period commenced the ruin of the city, and on the acquisition of the country by the British, soon after the middle of the eighteenth century, Maldah, and subsequently English Bazar, became the seats of government of the province. Gaur is distant from Burhampoor, N., 61 miles; from Calcutta, by Burhampoor, 179; Rajmahal, S.E., 25. Lat. 24° 55′, long. 88° 8′.

GAURA.—A town in the native state of Nepal, on the right bank of a branch of the San Coos river, and 55 miles E. from Khatmandoo. Lat. 27° 45′, long. 86° 10′.

GAWILGURH, in Hyderabad, or dominions of the Nizam, a stronghold on the southern declivity of the range of mountains bounding the valley of the Taptee to the south. It consists of two forts, one of which, fronting the north, where the rock is inaccessible, is defended by an outer fort, that entirely covers it to the north and west. All the walls are very strong, and rendered more formidable by bastions and towers. It is a post of considerable importance, as it commands a route much frequented across the mountains from south to north. Its strength is greatly increased by the extreme difficulty of transporting guns of sufficient calibre into commanding positions. Gawilgurh was taken by storm in 1803, by the British troops under Colonel Stevenson. Distance from Nagpoor, W., 114 miles; Ellichpoor, N.W., 15; Aurungabad, N.E., 170; Bombay, N.E., 340; Hydrabad, N., 290. Lat. 21° 20′, long. 77° 23′.

GAYAH.—A town, the principal place of the British district of Behar, lieut.-gov. of Bengal. It consists of two parts, one the residence of the priests and of the population connected with them; the other, the quarters of the great bulk of the population. This last, the name of which was originally Elahabad, was much enlarged by Law, and thence denominated Sahibgunj. The streets in Sahibgunj are wide, straight, and have on each side a row of trees, between which is a road for carriages, with a footway on each side. The town is well laid out, but the houses are for the most part merely mud-built huts, though there are a few brick-built, having neat gardens. There is an hospital, principally for the relief of sick or wounded pilgrims. The old town of Gayah, which is inhabited by the priesthood and their retainers, "is a strange-looking place, and its buildings are much better than those of Sahibgunj, the greater part of the houses being of brick and stone, and many of them having two or even three stories. The architecture is very singular, with corners, turrets, and galleries rojecting with every possible irregularity." 'rom this style of building, and the elevated site, the appearance of this portion of the town from a distance is picturesque, but on entering it, the streets are found crooked, narrow, and uneven, and withal so filthy, as to be with difficulty passable. The town and its vicinity abound in shrines and places of pilgrimage, the visits of votaries to which are attended with heavy charges, some persons of high rank having been known to expend 4,000*l.* or 5,000*l.* each. The torrent Phalgu is considered a holy stream, and ghats, or flights of stone stairs, give access to the water, for the purpose of ritual ablution. The best-built and most revered structure is the Vishnupod, a building in an elaborate style of architecture, eighty-two feet in length, and surmounted by an octagonal pyramid about 100 feet high. It was built at a cost of 30,000*l.* by Ahalya Bai, a superstitious Mahratta princess of Indore. The number of pilgrims annually has been estimated at 100,000, though in some years there have been double that number. Between the two towns, on an area once called the Ramna or Game Preserve, is the British civil establishment, consisting of the ordinary European and native functionaries. Buchanan estimated the number of houses at the time of his visit, early in the present century, at 6,400; which, according to the usually admitted ratio of inmates, would give the amount of population at about 32,000 persons. A considerable enlargement of the town, and a proportional increase of its inhabitants, appears to have subsequently taken place, a late return giving the number of houses at 9,165, and the population at 43,451. Gayah is distant 55 miles S. of Patna, 265 N.W. of Calcutta. Lat. 24° 48′, long. 85° 4′.

GAZEEPOOR KHASS, in the British district of Futtehpoor, lieut.-gov. of the N.W. Provinces, a town on the route from Allahabad to Humeerpoor, 73 miles N.W. of the former. Lat. 25° 48′, long. 80° 50′.

GEEABOONG, in Bussahir, a village of the district of Koonawur, is situate in the valley of Ruskulung, and near the right bank of the river Darbung. The site is pleasant, at the north-eastern base of a wooded eminence, and in a dell inclosed by mountains covered with perpetual snow. The population consists of about twenty families of lamas. Elevation above the sea 9,200 feet. Lat. 31° 47′, long. 78° 29′.

GEEDHORE, or GIDHOUR, in the British district of Bareilly, division of Pilleebheet, lieut.-gov. of the N.W. Provinces, a village on the route from Bareilly to Petoragurh, and 48 miles N.E. of the former. Lat. 28° 49′, long. 79° 56′.

GEEDUR GULLEE, in the province of Peshawur, is a pass between Peshawur and Attock, and has received its name—*The Jackal's Pass* or *Neck*, from its being so extremely narrow, that the natives, in exaggeration, say that a jackal only can make its way through it. The defile is not more than ten or twelve feet wide, and is bounded on each side by rather high and rugged hills. Though much frequented, it does not appear to be regarded as important in a military point of view, probably from the facility with which it can be turned. It is five miles N.W. of Attock. Lat. 33° 56′, long. 72° 12′.

GEEDWAS.—A town in the British district of Purneah, lieut.-gov. of Bengal, 64 miles N.E. of Bhagulpoor. Lat. 26° 4′, long. 87° 25′.

GEELATULLEE.—A town in the British district of Silhet, lieut.-gov. of Bengal, 74 miles W. of Gowhatty. Lat. 25° 5′, long. 91° 39′.

GEERWAH, or GIRWAH, in the British district of Banda, lieut.-gov. of the N.W. Provinces, a small town or village on the route from the town of Banda to Rewa, 11 miles S. of the former. Lat. 25° 19′, long. 80° 27′.

GEESGURH.—A town in the Rajpoot state of Jeypoor, 56 miles E. from Jeypoor, and 128 miles S.W. from Delhi. Lat. 26° 52′, long. 76° 49′.

GEHOON, in the Rajpoot state of Joudpore, a village on the route from Pokhurn to Balmer, and four miles N. of the latter place. It lies at the eastern base of a small range of rocky hills, dividing the Great from the Little Desert. The road in this part of the route is sandy and uneven. Lat. 25° 50′, long. 71° 20′.

GEIRAH, or GIRA, in Gurhwal, a village in the valley watered by the Bunal, and about five miles above its confluence with the Jumna. It is pleasantly situate on the southern declivity of a mountain, and contains about a dozen houses and 100 inhabitants. Lat. 30° 52′, long. 78° 15′.

GENORI, or GUNOURI.—A town with a fort, in the British district of Boolundshuhur, lieut.-gov. of the N.W. Provinces, 55 miles S.E. of Delhi. Lat. 28° 20′, long. 78° 4′.

GEORGEGURH, in the jaghire of Jhujhur, lieut.-gov. of Agra, a small fort built by the adventurer George Thomas during his temporary dominion over this part of India. Here, in 1801, Thomas was attacked by the Mahrattas, and being driven into the fort, was there closely invested. His officers now advised unconditional surrender, but Thomas determined, if possible, to effect a retreat to Hansi. Quitting his camp accordingly, at the head of a small body of cavalry, he fell in with a party of the enemy, who attacked him with vigour, and his men, dispirited by constant defeat, giving way on all sides, he made his escape with difficulty to Hansi, the scene of his final discomfiture. Georgegurh is in lat. 28° 38′, long. 76° 37′.

GEORGE TOWN.—See Prince of Wales Island.

GERAPOORUM.—A town in Hyderabad, or territory of the Nizam, on the left bank of the Godavery river, and 150 miles N.E. from Hyderabad. Lat. 18° 28′, long. 80° 29′.

GEROLA, on the south-western frontier of Bengal, a town in the native state of Phooljee, 60 miles W. from Sumbulpoor, and 92 miles S.E. from Ruttunpoor. Lat. 21° 18′, long. 83° 7′.

GEROLI, or GURROWLEE, in Bundelcund, a jaghire or feudal grant named after its principal place, which is situate in lat. 25° 5′, long. 79° 24′. "It is stated to comprise fifty square miles, to contain eighteen villages, with a population of 5,000 souls, and to yield a revenue of 15,000 rupees. The jagheerdar (feudatory) maintains forty horse and 100 foot." The sunnud, or grant of the jaghire from the East-India Company, is dated 1812.

GEROLI, in Bundlecund, the principal place of the jaghire or feudal grant of the same name, a town on the right bank of the river Dhasan, 80 miles S.W. of Calpee. Lat. 25° 5′, long. 79° 24′.

GERWARA, or GIRWAR, in Bundlecund, a village on the route by Rewa from Allahabad to Saugor, 123 miles N.E. of the latter. Elevation above the sea 1,216 feet. Lat. 24° 31′, long. 80° 29′.

GEYGLAH, or GIGELLA, in the British district of Muttra, lieut.-gov. of the N.W. Provinces, a village on the route from the city of Agra to the cantonment of Aligurh, and 17 miles N. of the former. Lat. 27° 22′, long. 78° 6′.

GEYLA.—A river rising in Kattywar, in lat. 22°, long. 71° 20′, and, flowing in an easterly direction, falls into the Gulf of Cambay, in lat. 21° 47′, long. 72° 13′.

GHAGUR, or GHUTGARH, in the British district of Kumaon, lieut.-gov. of the N.W. Provinces, a lofty mountain, forming the most southern brow of the Himalayan system, and rising abruptly over the terai or marshy forest north of Pillebheet. It extends in a direction nearly from south-east to north-west, between lat. 29° 14′—29° 30′, long. 79° 10′—79° 40′; is about thirty-five miles in length, with an average breadth probably of ten or twelve. Though the most southern range of the great Himalayan system, and the most remote from the line of greatest elevation, it exceeds in height some which intervene. The road from Almora to Moradabad passes by Ghagur fort, at the elevation of 7,121 feet above the sea. Budhan Dhoora, a summit of the same range, three or four miles to the north-west, has the elevation of 8,502 feet; Uraka Khan, five miles to the south-east, that of 7,366. The summit of Ghagur is crowned with a noble forest of cypress, toon, fir, and other timber-trees.

GHAIKOOL.—A town in the British province of Nagpoor, late territory of the rajah of Berar, on the right bank of the Wein Gunga river, and 103 miles S.E. from Nagpoor. Lat. 19° 49′, long. 79° 48′.

GHARA.—A town in the British district of Kurrachee, province of Scinde, presidency of Bombay, 22 miles W. of Tatta. Lat. 24° 44′, long. 67° 39′.

GHARA.—A stream in Sinde, flowing by the village of the same name, and falling into a long creek opening into the Indian Ocean, ten miles east of Kurrachee. The mouth of the Ghara creek is in lat. 24° 45′, long. 67° 12′. As the country on each side of the Ghara is low, both westward, to the mouth of this creek, and also eastward, and the stream communicates with the Indus, it seems probable that a ship-canal might be formed to connect Kurrachee with the deep and wide part of the Indus, near Tatta. The country between the Ghara river and the port of Kurrachee, it is to be observed, is also low and suitable for the purpose.

GHARA.—The name by which the united streams of the Beas and Sutluj are known, from their confluence at Endreesa to the confluence with the Chenaub, in lat. 29° 18′, long. 71° 6′. The length of course between these points is about 300 miles. After the confluence last mentioned, the united streams are called the Punjnud. At the ferry of Hurekee, a short distance below the confluence of the Beas and Sutluj, Burnes found "the Ghara a beautiful stream, never fordable," 275 yards wide at the lowest season, and twelve feet deep, running at the rate of two miles and a quarter an hour. In the same locality Vigne found it 200 yards wide. It is remarkably direct in its general course, which is south-west, but tortuous at short intervals. In the lower part of its course, where it forms the boundary, it is a slow muddy stream, with low banks of soft alluvial earth, overflowed to the extent of several miles on occasion of the slightest swell. The confluence with the Chenaub takes place without any turbulence, in a low marshy tract, in which the channels of the rivers are continually changing. Each river is about 500 yards wide, and the united stream about 800 yards. The water of the Chenaub is reddish, that of the Ghara pale; and for several miles downwards, the difference of hue may be observed, the right side of the stream being of a red, and the left of a pale hue.

GHATAMPOOR, in the district of Bainswara, territory of Oude, a town three miles from the left bank of the Ganges, 45 miles S. of Lucknow, 22 S.E. of Cawnpoor. Butter estimates the population at 4,000, including fifty Mussulmans. Lat. 26° 16′, long. 80° 40′.

GHATPILLY.—A town in Hyderabad, or territory of the Nizam, 97 miles N.E. from Hyderabad, and 100 miles S. from Chanda. Lat. 18° 30′, long. 79° 22′.

GHATTA.—A town in the Rajpoot state of Jeypoor, 45 miles S.E. from Jeypoor, and 104 miles S.W. from Agra. Lat. 26° 38′, long. 76° 35′.

GHATUMPOOR, in the British district of Cawnpore, the principal place of the pergunnah of the same name, a town on the route from Calpee to Pertabgurh, and 28 miles E. of the former. There is a small bazar. Lat. 26° 9′, long. 80° 13′.

GHAUTS (WESTERN). — An extensive range of mountains of Southern India. Their northern limit is the valley of the Taptee, of which a branch from the Syadree Mountains (as the upper part of the Western Ghauts is called by the natives) forms the southern inclosing range, about lat. 21°—21° 15′, long. 73° 45′—74° 40′, and is connected with groups which diminish in height towards the east until they sink into the table-land of Berar. The northern side of the valley of the Taptee is inclosed by the Satpura range, having an elevation of about 2,000 feet above the sea. The Syadree range in this part consists of trappean formations, which extend to the seacoast, forming the rocks of Bombay and Salsette, and others in that vicinity. In lat. 21° 10′, long. 74°, this great range (the Western Ghauts) turns south nearly at right angles to that which forms the south inclosing range of the valley of the Taptee. Its elevation increases as it proceeds southwards, and at Mahabulishwar, in lat. 18°, long. 73° 40′, is 4,700 feet above the sea. In this part, as elsewhere, the western declivity is abrupt, and its base depressed nearly to the level of the sea: on the eastern side, though generally undulating, or even rugged, it slopes gradually eastward towards the plains of Hyderabad. In respect to geological structure, it may be observed generally, that the great core of the Western Ghauts is of primary formation, inclosed by alternating strata of more recent origin. These strata, however, have been broken up by prodigious outbursts of volcanic rocks, and from Mahabulishwar to their northern limit, the overlying rock of the Western Ghauts is stated to be exclusively of the trap formation. The face towards the Concan is not uniformly precipitous, but consists of vast terraces with abrupt fronts, such a conformation being characteristic of this kind of rock. The scenery is delightful and grand, "displaying stupendous scarps, fearful chasms, numerous waterfalls, dense forests, and perennial verdure." "The Western Ghauts," says Elphinstone, "present the charms of mountain scenery on a smaller scale" than the Himalayas; "but it is no exaggeration of their merits to say, that they strongly resemble the valleys of the Neda and the Ladon, which have long been the boast of Arcadia and of Europe." Chasms and breaks in the brows or the culminating ridges of the range, give access to the highlands, and are denominated ghauts or passes, a name which has become generally applied to the range itself. The principal elevations between the eighteenth and nineteenth degrees of latitude, are Poorundhur, 4,472 feet; Singhur, 4,162; Hurreechundurghur, 3,894. In consequence of the boldness of the declivities and the precipitous character of the faces of the trap rocks, the summits in many parts of the range are nearly inaccessible. The natural strength of these portions has in many instances been increased by art, and the hill forts in all ages of Indian history have been regarded as the bulwarks of the Deccan. The trap formation terminates southward on the seacoast, in about lat. 18°, and is succeeded by laterite, a ferruginous clay, easily cut when first raised, but by continued exposure to the atmosphere becoming hard as brick. This last-mentioned formation extends southwards as the overlying rock, almost without interruption, to Cape Comorin, covering the base of the mountains and the narrow slip of land that separates them from the sea. South of Mahabuleshwar, and in latitude about 15°, the elevation diminishes, so as not to be more than 1,000 feet above the sea; the slopes are gradual, and the outlines rounded. Still farther to the south, however, the elevation increases, and attains its maximum towards Coorg, where Bonasson Hill is said to be 7,000 feet above the sea; Tandiannole, 5,781; Pupagiri, 5,682. South of those elevations, the Ghauts join the Neilgherry group by means of the Nedimula range, which forms the western buttress of the Neilgherry tableland to lat. 11° 15′, long. 76° 25′, where it rises into the lofty Kunda Mountains, and about twenty-five miles farther south terminates abruptly in high and nearly perpendicular precipices, forming the northern side of that great valley or depression, which, affording an uninterrupted communication in this latitude between the eastern and western sides of the peninsula, is bounded on the south by the extensive range of mountains of which Cape Comorin is the extremity. South of this valley, the mountains are described as lofty, and pouring down cascades of prodigious height. The width of this extensive gap, called the Palghat Valley, from the town of that name, is about twenty miles.

The length of the Western Ghauts, from the northern extremity of the Syadree Mountains, forming the southern side of the valley of the Taptee, to the southern brow, joining the Kunda Mountains on the north side of the Palghat Valley, is about 800 miles. The mountains rising on the south side of Palghat Valley, and which may, with some latitude of expression, be called a continuation of the Western Ghauts, have considerable elevation, a spacious table-land, being 4,740 feet above the sea, a peaked summit 6,000, another 7,000; and there are several peaks not measured, but judged by sight to have elevations not inferior. The length of the chain of mountains extending from Cape Comorin to the valley of Palghat is 200 miles. The western brow of the range is, with little exception, abrupt; on the eastern side of the culminating range, the declivity is in general gradual, the surface in many places being extensive table-land, sloping gently, and nearly imperceptibly, eastward. Such a conformation would seem to indicate a volcanic disturbance of the surface, the disruption taking place along the western precipitous face.

It has been supposed that the steep declivity of the Western Ghauts on the seaward side, by presenting a vast front to the violence of the south-west monsoon, is instrumental in arresting and condensing the abundant moisture borne along by that formidable aerial current from the Indian Ocean, and that the excessive rains which fall in the Concan and in Malabar result from this cause. Such a conclusion, however, is at variance with the fact that Chili and Peru, similarly circumstanced with respect to the Pacific Ocean and the Cordilleras, are amongst the driest countries in the world,—a discrepancy the cause of which does not appear to have been explained. But it is not only the countries intervening between the mountains and the sea that are visited with so great a superabundance of rain: the fall on the west brow of the Western Ghauts is enormous, and perhaps unparalleled. At Mahabulishwar, in lat. 18°, long. 73° 40′, the mean annual fall of rain is 239 inches. There, however, during a considerable portion of the year, the weather is dry. Not so at Bednore, in lat. 13° 49′, long. 75° 6′, situate on the western verge of the table-land of Mysore, and near the western brow of the verge. There "nine rainy months in the year are usually calculated on, and for six of that number it is the practice in most families to make the same preparatory arrangements for provision (water only excepted) as are adopted for a ship proceeding on a six months' voyage." In consequence of this excessive moisture, the low tract between the Ghauts and the sea is traversed by innumerable torrents, which, stagnating as they approach the coast, overspread the depressed levels, and form that extraordinary series of shallow lakes called by the British, Backwaters. The word Ghauts, as already mentioned, is an appellation given by the British to the range which in its northern part is by the natives called Syadree, in its southern Sukhien.

GHAUTS (EASTERN).—A chain of mountains of Southern India, rising in the vicinity of Balasore, in about the same latitude as the Western Ghauts on the opposite side of the peninsula. This chain may be traced in a south-westerly direction, a little to the west of Ganjam, and thence to Naggery Nose, about 56 miles N.W. of Madras, where it forms a junction with the range, "which sweeping irregularly inland, crosses the peninsula in a south-west direction by Chittore, Sautghur, and Salem, and joins the Western Ghauts north of the Gap of Paulghautcherry." The direction of the Eastern Ghauts, south of the point of junction with the transverse range, is marked at intervals along the coast of Coromandel by outliers and detached hills to a point within about twenty miles of Cape Comorin, where the Eastern and Western Ghauts appear united. It is to be observed, however, that the point of junction between the two great ranges of Malabar and Coromandel is not unusually regarded as taking place at the Neilgherries, "which, rising into the loftiest summits of the peninsula, form the southern boundary of the great table-land" of the Deccan. The average elevation of the Eastern Ghauts is stated to be about 1,500 feet. With regard to geological structure, granite is said to constitute the basis of the whole range, and overlying the granite, gneiss, and mica-slate, that form the sides of the mountains, are occasionally found clay-slate, hornblende-slate, flinty slate, and primitive or crystalline limestone. The surface of the level country appears to consist of the debris of granitic rocks, as far north as the Pennar, in approaching which, the laterite or iron-clay formation expands over a large surface. From the Krishna northward, the granite is often penetrated by injected veins of trap and dykes of greenstone. Passing on to Vizagapatam and Ganjam, syenite and gneiss predominate, occasionally covered by laterite.

GHAZEEOODDEENINUGGUR, in the British district of Meerut, lieut.-gov. of the N.W. Provinces, a small town on the route from Delhi to Moradabad, and 18 miles E. of the former. It is surrounded by a weak wall, and situate on the left bank of the river Hindun, navigable for rafts and small boats from this place to the Jumna, a distance of thirty miles, but, notwithstanding this advantage, is much decayed. Lat. 28° 40′, long. 77° 29′.

GHAZEEPOOR.—The principal place of the pergunnah of the same name, a town 10 miles N.E. of the left bank of the Jumna; 10 miles S.W. of the town of Futtehpoor. Lat. 25° 49′, long. 80° 48′.

GHAZEEPORE.—A British district under the lieut.-gov. of the N.W. Provinces, and named from its principal place. It is bounded on the north-west and north by the British district Azimgurh; on the north-east by the great river Ghogra, separating it from the British district Sarun; on the south-east by the British district Shahabad; on the south partly by the British district Shahabad, partly by the British district Benares; and on the west by the British districts Benares and Jaunpore. It lies between lat. 25° 17′—26°, long. 83° 8′—84° 40′; is ninety-six miles in length from east to west, and forty in breadth. It embraces an area of 2,187 square miles. The principal rivers which skirt or traverse the district are the Ganges, Ghagra, Karamnassa, Tons, Bisu, and Manghi. The country on both sides of the Ganges slopes gently, probably in the degree of seven or eight inches in a mile, from north-west to south-east. In the eastern part of the district is one large piece of water, called Surhah Talao; and many jhils or shallow lakes are dispersed over the country. The elevation of the waterway of the Ganges where it is greatest, that is, at the western extremity of the district, is about 260 feet; and as there are no eminences of any importance, probably no point in the district is much more than 350 feet above the sea. Water in some places is to be had by digging to the depth of ten or twelve feet, in others it is not to be obtained at less depth than fifty or sixty feet. From the resources afforded by wells, tanks, jhils, and rivers, the means of irrigation are derived; and the practice is universally pursued, it being indispensable for the success of the rubbee or crop grown in the cool or dry season, commencing in October and ending in the following March. The climate is in general healthy, except at the close of autumn, when fevers are common, but not remarkably malignant in character. The thermometer ranges in the coldest months from 58° to 71°; in April, 86° to 96°; May, 86° to 98°; June, 85° to 98°; July, 86° to 96°. The agricultural produce consists principally of maize, rice, indigo, pulse of various sorts, and oil-seeds, wheat, barley, oats, gram, safflower, opium, cotton, tobacco, and sugar. The sugarcane of this district is greatly esteemed, and fetches a high price. The number of the entire population is returned at 1,596,324 ; and thus subdivided :—Hindoos, agricultural, 984,331 ; non-agricultural, 453,754 ; Mahomedans, and others not Hindoo, agricultural, 35,050 ; non-agricultural, 123,189. It thus appears that the numbers of the agricultural classes nearly double those of the non-agricultural, and that the Hindoos are more than seven times as many as the followers of all other systems. The number of inhabitants to the square mile is about 484. The chief places stand in the following order as to population :—

Number containing less than 1,000 inhabitants..	5,506
Ditto more than 1,000 and less than 5,000....	[illegible]
Ditto ,, 5,000 ,, 10,000....	16
Ditto ,, 10,000 ,, 50,000....	3
Total................	5,793

The language spoken by the common people is Hindee of a very corrupt kind. The principal routes are,—1. From Benares through Ghazeepore to Buxar, crossing this district from west to east ; 2. from the cantonment of Goruckpore to that of Ghazeepore, north to south ; 3. from Azimgurh to Ghazeepore, north-west to south-east ; 4. from Chupra through Ghazeepore town to Jaunpore, east to west ; 5. from Ghazeepore, crossing the Ganges at the eastern extremity of the town, pursuing a direction north to south, and joining at Sawunt the great route from Calcutta to Benares.

The tract comprised within this district probably formed in remote antiquity part of the "territory which in ancient legend is called Maha Kosala," first subject to the sovereigns of Ayodhya, subsequently to those of Kanouj. On the overthrow of the Kanouj dynasty, by the victory gained in 1194, over Jaya Chandra, by Mohammad of Ghor, this tract fell under Patan sway, from which it was wrested by the conquering Baber. On the dissolution of the empire of Delhi, consequent on the invasion of Ahmed Shah Durani in 1761, it formed part of the portion seized by Shujah-ood-dowlah, nawaub-vizier of Oude. In 1764, the emperor of Delhi, Shah Allum, granted the territory of Ghazeepore to the East-India Company, by whom, in the subsequent year, it was relinquished to the nawaub-vizier of Oude. Finally, in 1775, the nawaub-vizier by treaty ceded it, with other districts, to the East-India Company. In the Ayeen Akbery it is styled Sircar Ghazipoor, in soobah of Allahabad. Its military contingent is there stated at 310 cavalry, 16,650 infantry ; and its revenue at 335,782 rupees.

GHAZEEPORE, the principal place of the district of the same name, is situate on the left bank of the Ganges, which is crossed by ferry at the north-eastern extremity of the town. Bishop Heber states the river to be here as wide as the Hooghly at Cossipore. Ghazeepore is surrounded by luxuriant groves of the banyan (Ficus indica) and pipal (Ficus religiosa), enlivened by flocks of nightingales, jays, crested sparrows, and many other birds ; and by crowds of monkeys, unmolested, and familiar as domestic animals. Ghazeepore contains a population of 38,573 persons. Viewed from the river, its appearance is very striking ; but, on closer inspection, the buildings are found to be mostly in ruins. At the eastern extremity of the town is a palace, which, though somewhat disfigured by time and neglect, still retains abundant marks of former beauty. It is said to have been built by Meer Cossim Ali, the nawaub of Bengal, infamous for the massacre in cold blood of his British prisoners. "It is raised on a high bank, and on a point commanding two great reaches of the river, up and down. From the bank, which is full thirty feet from the water, is raised another basement of brick and masonry, fifteen feet high, in which are some apartments ; on this is the building, which is an oblong square (rectangle), with great pavilions at the angles, and in the centre of each side ; the whole is an open space, supported by colonnades surrounding it. Within, on the floor of the building, is a channel for water, about four feet wide, which encircles the floor ; and at equal spaces there were formerly fountains. In the centre of the building is a space sufficient to contain twenty people. Nearly adjoining to this palace is a building for the purpose of raising water for the fountains, and supplying them by means of pipes, which communicate with each other." Heber characterizes the palace as the best and most airy of any eastern building which he had seen, with magnificent verandas, and capable of being made, at no great expense, one of the handsomest and best-situated houses in India. It is at present a custom-house, the numerous apartments being converted into store-rooms and habitations for the guards and officials. There is a jail here, reported to be large, strong, and airy. The bazars are well constructed, and well supplied, the skill of the tailors especially being noted. A few Europeans keep shops, duly furnished with wares in demand with the population from home. Ghazeepore is celebrated for its rose-water, and the rose-fields in the vicinity of the town occupy several hundred acres. Some attar, or essential oil, is also made, and is sold, even after some adulteration as is believed, at the rate of 10*l.* for one rupee-weight. There is a church, represented as a very attractive object, and an hospital. At the south-west end of the town, and separated from it by gardens and scattered cottages, are the bungalows or lodges of the servants of the Company, here employed on civil duties. These consist generally of spacious and handsome apartments, mostly on ground-floors. Beyond these are the military cantonments, the buildings in which are low and unsightly, with sloping roofs of red tiles.

Contiguous is a cenotaph monument to Lord Cornwallis, who died here in 1805, while in progress up the country. It is constructed of excellent stone, but, according to Heber, the style and execution are utterly at variance with good taste. It has been suggested, however, that it might be turned to account by being converted into a belfry, in the event of a church being built in contiguity to it. Two miles inland from the river are the remains of a serai, or lodge for travellers, and nearly adjoining, several tombs, in a handsome style of architecture, and good preservation. Races, held close to the town, are some of the best and most-frequented in India. A stud, which government maintains in the vicinity, supplies the cavalry and horse artillery with many good horses.

From observations on the thermometer, made in the town of Ghazeepore, in the years 1831 and 1832, May appears to have been the hottest month (mean temperature 97°), and January the coldest (mean temperature 56°). Bishop Heber says, "Ghazeepore is celebrated throughout India for the wholesomeness of its air." He ascribes this to the advantages of its locality, "the elevated level on which it stands, and the dryness of its soil, which never retains the moisture, and after the heaviest showers, is, in a very few hours, fit to walk on with comfort." Another favourable circumstance he considers to be, "that it has a noble reach of the river to the south-east, from which quarter the hot winds generally blow." Ghazeepore is distant N.W. from Calcutta, by water 598 miles, by land 431; N.E. from Benares, by water 71, by land 46; E. from Allahabad, by water 210, by land 120. Lat. 25° 32′, long. 83° 39′.

GHAZIKA THANNA.—A town in the Rajpoot state of Ulwar, 47 miles N.E. from Jeypoor, and 110 N.W. from Agra. Lat. 27° 27′, long. 76° 21′.

GHENDY.—A town in the native state of Nepal, situate three miles from one of the branches of the Gunduck river, and 122 miles N.W. from Khatmandoo. Lat. 28° 21′, long. 83° 29′.

GHERGONG.—A town in the British district of Seebpoor, Upper Assam, eight miles S.E. of Seebpoor. Lat. 26° 57′, long. 94° 46′.

GHERIAH, or VIZIADROOG, in the collectorate of Rutnagherry (Southern Concan), presidency of Bombay, a town and fort at the mouth of the river Kunvee, which flows west from the Ghauts. This place "has an excellent harbour, the anchorage being landlocked and sheltered from all winds. There is no bar at the entrance, the depths being from five to seven fathoms, and from three to four fathoms inside at low water. The rise of the tide is about six or seven feet." Gheriah was fortified, in 1662, by Sevajee, the Mahratta chief. It subsequently passed into the possession of the Angria branch of the Bosla family, from whom the Portuguese and English in 1722, and the Dutch two years later, in vain attempted to wrest it. In 1755, it was attacked by a British force, consisting of three ships of the line, one ship of fifty guns, and one of forty-four, with some armed vessels belonging to the Bombay marine, amounting altogether to fourteen sail, commanded by Admiral Watson, and having on board 800 Europeans and 1,000 native soldiers, under Colonel Clive. A bombardment was immediately commenced; Angria's fleet was totally destroyed, and, in the course of a few hours, the place surrendered. It was a few months afterwards given up to the Peishwa, under the treaty concluded with the Mahrattas in 1756, and finally acquired by the British government on the overthrow of that potentate in 1818. The name Gheriah is that by which the fort was denominated by the Mussulmans, Viziadroog being the name more familiar to the Mahrattas. The place is distant S. from Bombay 170 miles. Lat. 16° 32′, long. 73° 22′.

GHIDDORE, in the British district of Monghyr, lieut.-gov. of Bengal, an ancient fort of great extent. Its walls are from twenty-three to twenty-four feet in thickness, and thirty feet high. According to Buchanan, it was built at a very remote period by a Hindoo raja, but repaired by Sher Shah, the Patan chief, in his war with Humaion, about 1539. Distant S. from Monghyr city 35 miles. Lat. 24° 53′, long. 86° 15′.

GHIRDEE.—A town in the British province of Sattara, presidency of Bombay, 89 miles S.E. of Sattara. Lat. 17° 17′, long. 75° 21′.

GHIRGAON, in the British district of Kumaon, lieut.-gov. of the N.W. Provinces, a village on the route up the course of the Ramgunga (Eastern), and subsequently of the Goree, from Petoragurh to the Oonta Doora Pass, 32 miles N. of Petoragurh. It is situate seven miles west of the right bank of the Goree, on a ridge proceeding southwards from the main range of the Himalaya, and consists of cottages scattered over the steep declivity and summit of the ridge. Lat. 30° 2′, long. 80° 13′.

GHISWA, or GHISSOOA.—The chief town of a pergunnah of the same name, in the British district of Jounpore, lieut.-gov. of the N.W. Provinces, distant 17 miles W. from Jounpore, 39 miles N. from Mirzapoor. Ghiswa has a population of 8,868 persons. Lat. 25° 41′, long. 82° 28′.

GHOGHEEA.—A town in the British district of Sarun, lieut.-gov. of Bengal, 93 miles N.W. of Dinapoor. Lat. 26° 54′, long. 84° 38′.

GHOGRA.—A large river, and a considerable feeder of the Ganges. Its remotest headwater, as far as has been hitherto ascertained, is the source of the Kalee (Eastern), on the south-western declivity of the range forming the northern boundary of the British district of Kumaon, towards South-western Tibet. This spot, situate in lat. 30° 28′, long. 80° 40′, was visited by Webb, and is thus described by him: "The Kalee river, two furlongs distant, its breadth reduced to four or five yards. At two and a quarter miles in a north-west direction, it is covered with snow, and no longer to be traced; neither is the road passable beyond this point at the present season. After the middle of July, when the thaw is perfected, it may be traced as a small stream for about four miles more, in the direction last mentioned, and from thence to its head in the snow, north-west two miles farther. The stream scarcely flows in winter, being derived almost exclusively from the thawing snow." The elevation above the sea, of the source, is probably between 17,000 and 18,000 feet. The river takes a south-easterly direction down the valley of Beeans, receiving numerous snow-fed torrents right and left; and at thirty miles from its source, the Kalipani, a considerable stream, flows into it on the left side. Two or three miles below that point, the river turns to the south-west, in which direction it continues to flow twenty-three miles farther, to the confluence of the Dhouli, a large river, which falls into it on the right side, in lat. 29° 57′, long. 80° 38′. The Kalee, which at the confluence appears to be twice the size of the Dhouli, is previously a vast torrent, and in many places a huge cataract tumbling over vast rocks, which in some spots form natural bridges, being wedged together by their pressure against each other, and against the sides of the precipices inclosing the deep gorges down which the stream rushes. In many places the stream for considerable distances is totally hidden under glaciers. Below the confluence the stream is thirty yards wide; but, swelled by numerous mountain-streams received right and left, it soon attains a width of eighty yards. It continues to flow in a south-westerly direction, and twenty-two miles lower down, or seventy-five from its source, it on the right side receives the Gori or Gorigunga, a river equal in size to the Kalee. This confluence is in lat. 29° 45′, long. 80° 25′, and is 1,972 feet above the sea; so that the river has a descent, so far, of about 15,500 feet in seventy-five miles, or 207 feet per mile. Below this place twelve miles, and eighty-seven from its source, the river is represented in the surveyor-general's map as receiving on the left side, from Nepaul, the Chumulea; and three miles lower down, at the Jhula ghat, a ferry from Kumaon to Nepaul, the elevation of the water's edge is 1,789 feet; so that the declivity of the waterway now diminishes to twelve feet per mile. Sixteen miles below this, at Puchesur, lat. 29° 27′, long. 80° 18′, it on the right side receives the Surjoo (Western), the greatest of its feeders. Thenceforward the united stream is no longer called the Kalee, but, variously, the Sarda, the Surjoo, and the Ghogra. At Puchesur it turns a little to the south-east, and ten miles lower down, on the right, receives the Lohoghat river, two miles below the confluence of which a large tributary from Nepaul flows in on the left. Turning southwards at that point, it, at a distance of eighteen miles beyond, receives on the right the Ludheea, a considerable stream. By all these accessions it becomes a great river, and at Birimdeo, twelve miles lower down, in lat. 29° 6′, long. 80° 13′, and 148 miles from its source, it enters the plain of Hindoostan, 798 feet above the sea. Webb found it "about 150 yards broad on an average, bed stony, very deep, and moderately rapid." Herbert estimates the discharge of water here during the dry season at 4,800 cubic feet per second; that of the Ganges at 7,000, at Hurdwar. From within a few miles of its source to this place, according to Art. V. of the treaty of Seegowlee, it forms the boundary between the British district of Kumaon and Nepaul, holding generally in this part of its course a direction nearly from north-east to south-west. From Birimdeo guardhouse, the river, sweeping first for about twenty-three miles in a southerly direction, forms for that distance the boundary between the British district of Pillebheet and the territory of Oude, and subsequently, flowing south-east for forty-five more, forms the boundary between the British district of Shahjehanpore and the territory of Oude. In that interval, according to Buchanan, it becomes navigable for craft of considerable burthen from Mundeya, in lat. 28° 40′, long. 80° 18′, but probably those of lighter description can be brought up as far as the vicinity of the egress from the mountains, or about forty miles higher. One hundred and ten miles below Birimdeo, it on the left side receives the Kurnalli, flowing from the mountains of Nepaul, whence much timber is sent by the stream. Buchanan regards this river merely as a different channel by which the great river Setiganga, descending from the Himalaya of Ne-ul, discharges itself. Wilford considers the tiganga or Swetaǵanga as identical with the Gunduck. According to the surveyor-general's map, at ninety-four miles below the last-mentioned confluence, and in lat. 27° 10′, long. 81° 25′, the Ghogra receives on the right side a considerable tributary in the united streams of the Chouka and Woel; twenty-two miles farther down, it on the left side receives the Eastern Surjoo, and thenceforward is known in Oude by the names Deoha, Surjoo, or Sarayu, as well as Ghogra. Butter describes it as navigable for the largest class of boats in all seasons, and as having an annual rise and fall of thirty feet. Forty-two miles below the confluence of the Surjoo (Eastern), it touches on the British district of Goruckpore, having passed in its course the city of Oude. Thence pursuing a south-easterly direction, it forms for seventy-five miles the boundary between the British district and the territory of Oude. In this part of its course it is considered by Buchanan larger than the Ganges at Chunar, and is from one to three miles in breadth. Like other great rivers traversing low alluvial tracts, it sends off lateral watercourses, communicating in the rainy season by numerous offsets with the parent flood, and with each other. Of these the principal, called the Tons

(North-eastern), leaves the Ghogra on the right side, ten miles above the city of Oude, and, taking a south-easterly course, falls into the Ganges near Bhullea. The Ghogra enters the British territory in lat. 26° 15′, long. 83° 11′, and, still pursuing a south-easterly direction for sixty-five miles, forms the boundary between the British districts of Goruckpore and Azimgurh. In this part of its course, it on the left side, and in lat. 26° 12′, long. 83° 46′, receives the large river Raptee, and at other points a few streams of less importance. Flowing still south-east, it for eight miles forms the boundary between the districts of Azimgurh and Sarun, and for thirty-six miles the boundary between the districts Ghazeepore and Sarun, joining the Ganges, on the left side of the latter river, in lat. 25° 46′, long. 84° 40′. The total length of course of the Ghogra may be estimated at 606 miles. According to Buchanan, an eye-witness of the confluence, the Ghogra certainly exceeds the Ganges in breadth and rapidity, and equally in depth. Though throughout the year navigable nearly to the mountains, the Ghogra is turned to little account in this respect. The navigation is indeed in some places rendered hazardous and intricate by the occurrence of shoals of kunkur or calcareous conglomerate; but engineering skill, with adequate means, could easily remove such obstructions, and render free the navigation of the Ghogra, as well as throw open that of its tributaries the Raptee and the Chouka.

GHOLAB SINGH'S DOMINIONS.—See Cashmere.

GHOONGEE.—A river which has its source beyond the northern frontier of British India, in the Nepaul territory, and in about lat. 27° 50′, long. 83° 20′. It holds a course generally southerly, and at Lotan, about seventy miles from its source, and in lat. 27° 15′, long. 83° 19′, Buchanan found it in January to have a deep channel, along which rolled a wide, rapid, fordable stream. It receives many streams right and left, and by lateral channels communicates with numerous pieces of water, stagnant or running; drains or fertilizes, by means of its many branches, a great extent of country, and, running still in a direction generally south-easterly, joins the Dhumela in lat. 27° 5, long. 83° 12′, and ultimately falls into the Raptee on the left side, in lat. 27° 3′, long. 83° 12′, having altogether flowed about 100 miles.

GHOOROUTUH, or GAROTAH, in the British district of Goorgaon, lieut.-gov. of the N.W. Provinces, a village on the route from Muttra to Delhi, by the right bank of the Jumna, and 55 miles S.E. of the latter city. Lat. 27° 56′, long. 77° 28′.

GHORA TRUP.—An inconsiderable village situate on the right bank of the river Indus, 11 miles S.W. of Attock, and 34 S.E. of Peshawur. The river here has a very dangerous rapid, with a sudden fall of a foot and a half, resulting from the lateral contraction of the high and rocky banks inclosing it, as the depth is no less than 186 feet. Wood describes the passage as very dangerous. "Though the fall was shot with startling rapidity, the boat, when over, seemed spell-bound to the spot, and hung for some time under the watery wall in spite of the most strenuous efforts of her crew. At last she moved, the men cheered, and out she darted into the fair channel." The breadth of the Indus here is only 250 feet, and through this narrow gut the whole of its immense volume of water rushes at the rate of from nine to ten miles an hour, and with the noise of thunder. Ghora Trup is about six miles below Nilab, and for the whole of this distance the river may be described as one immense and irresistible rapid. Lat. 33° 46′, long. 72° 9′.

GHORAWUL, in the British district of Mirzapoor, lieut.-gov. of the N.W. Provinces, a town on the route from Sasseram to Rewah, 78 miles S.W. of the former. Lat. 24° 46′, long. 82° 51′.

GHOSEA.—A town in the district of Azimgurh, lieut.-gov. of the N.W. Provinces, on the route from Ghazeepoor to Goruckpoor, and 47 miles N. of the latter. Distance N.E. from Benares 64 miles. Lat. 26° 5′, long. 83° 36′.

GHOSEEA, or GUSIA, in the British district of Benares, lieut.-gov. of the N.W. Provinces, a village situate four miles north of the left bank of the Ganges, and where the route from the city of Benares to that of Allahabad is intersected by that from Jounpoor to Mirzapoor. Distant W. of the city of Benares 29 miles; from Allahabad, E., 45. Lat. 25° 16′, long. 82° 36′.

GHOSGURH.—A town in the native state of Bhawulpoor, 73 miles S.E. from Bhawulpoor, and 127 miles N.E. from Jessulmeer. Lat. 28° 24′, long. 72° 6′.

GHOSNA, or GUSUNA, in the British district of Muttra, lieut.-gov. of the N.W. Provinces, a village on the route from the cantonment of Aligurh to that of Muttra, and five miles N.E. of the latter. Lat. 27° 32′, long. 77° 48′.

GHOSPOOR, in the British district of Ghazeepoor, lieut.-gov. of the N.W. Provinces, a town on the left bank of the Ganges, 10 miles E. of Ghazeepoor cantonment, 590 miles N.W. of Calcutta by water. Lat. 25° 37′, long. 83° 47′.

GHOTAL, in the British district of Hooghly, lieut.-gov. of Bengal, a town on the river Roopnarain, on the route from Burdwan to Midnapore, 40 miles S. of former, 30 N.E. of latter. Distance from Calcutta, W., 40 miles. Lat. 22° 38′, long. 87° 48′.

GHOTE.—A town in the British province of Nagpoor, late rajah of Berar's dominions, 110 miles S.E. from Nagpoor, and 131 miles N.W. from Jugdulapoor. Lat. 19° 50′, long. 80° 8′.

GHOTIPURTI.—A town in Hyderabad, or dominions of the Nizam, 73 miles N.E. from Hyderabad, and 140 miles N.W. from Masulipatam. Lat. 17° 30′, long. 79° 39′.

GHOUBIPOOR.—See CHOBIPOOR.

GHUGA, or GUGYA, in the British district of Goruckpoor, lieut.-gov. of the N.W. Provinces, a village on the route from the cantonment of Ghazeepoor to that of Goruckpoor, 22 miles S. of the latter. Lat. 26° 20′, long. 83° 30′.

GHULLA.—A town in the native state of Wusravee, 163 miles N.E. from Bombay, and 32 miles S. from Broach. Lat. 21° 15′, long. 73° 5′.

GHUNDAWUL.—See CHUNDAWUL.

GHUNNAPOORA, in Hyderabad, or territory of the Nizam, a town, the principal place of a district of the same name. It is situate on an eminence, is surrounded by a rampart, and contains some good buildings. Distance from the city of Hyderabad, S.W., 60 miles. Lat. 16° 34′, long. 78°.

GHUNSAMPOOR, in the British district of Shajehanpoor, lieut.-gov. of the N.W. Provinces, a village on the route from Bareilly to Setapoor, and 48 miles S.E. of the former. Lat. 28° 6′, long. 80° 6′.

GHUNTAL.—A village in the British district of Goorgaon, lieut.-gov. of the N.W. Provinces. Lat. 28° 14′, long. 76° 53′.

GHURAUNDA, or GUROUNDA, in the British district of Paneeput, lieut.-gov. of the N.W. Provinces, a village on the route from the city of Delhi to Kurnal, and 12 miles S.E. of the latter. It has a bazar. Lat. 29° 32′, long. 77° 2′.

GHURCHOOROOLEE.—A town in the British province of Nagpoor, on the left bank of the Wein Gunga river, and 87 miles S.E. from Nagpoor. Lat. 20° 12′, long. 80° 1′.

GHURIALA, in the Rajpoot state of Bickaneer, a small town on the route from the town of Bickaneer to that of Jessulmere, and 50 miles S.W. of the former. It is situate two or three miles from the frontier towards Jessulmere, and contains a small fort, 180 houses, a few shops, and two wells 210 feet deep, yielding brackish water. On the frontier, close to this place, an interview took place in 1835, between the rulers of Bickaneer and of Jessulmere, and by the arrangement made by a British mission under Lieut. Trevelyan, an amicable adjustment of the common boundary was made. Ghuriala is in lat. 27° 44′, long. 72° 36′.

GHURMUKTEESUR.—See GURMUKTEESUR.

GHUROUT, in the British district of Goorgaon, lieut.-gov. of the N.W. Provinces, a village on the route from Hansee, by Goorgaon, to Muttra, and 54 miles N.W. of the latter. Lat. 28° 5′, long. 77° 16′.

GHURPARRAH, in the British district of Saugur, lieut.-gov. of the N.W. Provinces, a town on the route from Saugur to Tehree, seven miles N.W. of the former. Lat. 23° 55′, long. 78° 47′.

GHUSIPURA, in the British district Bijnour, lieut.-gov. of the N.W. Provinces, a village on the route from Moradabad to Hurdwar, and 33 miles S.E. of the latter. Lat. 29° 35′, long. 78° 25′.

GHUSPUR, in Sirhind, a village on the route from Loodiana to Ferozpore, and 10 miles W. of the former town. It is situate close to the watercourse of Loodiana, an offset of the Sutlej, four miles from the left bank of the main channel, and in an open, level country, scantily cultivated. Distant N.W. from Calcutta 1,112 miles. Lat. 30° 57′, long. 75° 44′.

GHUSUL PASS, in Bussahir, across the range of the Himalaya, forming the southern boundary of Koonawur. It is a quarter of a mile S.E. of the Gunas Pass, and less than half a mile S.E. of that of Nibrung. "These three passes," observes Gerard, "lead from Sungla to Chooara, and although they are so near to each other, they can only be crossed at different times: Neebrung is first open, and it had become practicable only a few days before we arrived (June 21); the other two passes were shut, and had not been attempted this year." Elevation of Ghusul above the sea 15,851 feet. Lat. 31° 21′, long. 78° 13′.

GHUTASUN DEBI PASS, in Sirmor, lies through a low ridge traversing the Kyarda Doon in a direction from north to south, and running from the Sub-Himalaya to the Sewalik range. Its crest forms the division between the waters of the Bhuta, flowing eastward to the Jumna, and those of the Markanda, flowing to the south-west towards the Sutluj. A route from Dehra to Nahun lies through the pass. Elevation above the sea 2,500 feet. Lat. 30° 31′, long. 77° 28′.

GHYBEEPOOR.—A village in the British district of Huriana, lieut.-gov. of the N.W. Provinces. Lat. 29° 25′, long. 76°.

GIDDALOOR.—A town in the British district of Cuddapah, presidency of Madras, 158 miles S. W. of Masulipatam. Lat. 15° 23′, long. 79°.

GIHROR, in the British district of Mynpoorie, a small town on the route from Agra to Mynpoorie, and 17 miles W. of the latter. Elevation above the sea 648 feet. Lat. 27° 11′, long. 78° 51′.

GILGIT, in the dominions of Gholab Singh, a small unexplored country on the southern declivity of Hindoo Koosh, lying between Bultistan or Little Tibet on the east, and Chitral on the west. It consists principally of one large valley, down which the stream called the river of Gilgit flows, and falls into the Indus on the right or north-western bank, in lat. 35° 47′, long. 74° 31′. There is also a village of the same name on the right bank of the stream, in lat. 36°, long. 74° 10′.

GINEEKHERA, in the British district of

Moradabad, lieut.-gov. of the N.W. Provinces, a village on the route from the town of Moradabad to Almora, and 28 miles N. of the former. Lat. 29° 11′, long. 79°.

GINGEE.—A town in the British district of South Arcot, presidency of Madras, 82 miles S.W. of Madras. Its fortress, though originally of some strength, which was extravagantly magnified in the estimation of native opinion, was taken by the French in 1750, with extraordinary facility, but subsequently yielded to a British force under Captain Smith. Lat. 12° 16′, long. 79° 27′.

GIRAEE.—A village in the British district of Hurriana, lieut.-gov. of the N.W. Provinces. Lat. 29° 14′, long. 75° 58′.

GIRAJSIR, in the Rajpoot state of Jessulmere, a small town on the route from the town of Bikaneer to that of Jessulmere, and 50 miles S.W. of the former. Close to this place, under the management of the British mission, in 1835, a conference was held between the ruler of Jessulmere and that of Bikaneer, and an amicable adjustment made of the common boundary, which had been previously disputed. Girajsir is in lat. 27° 42′, long. 72° 36′.

GIRAREE, in the British district of Sohagpoor, one of the divisions of the Saugor and Nerbudda territory, lieut.-gov. of the N.W. Provinces, a town on the route from Ramgurh to Palamow, 39 miles N.E. of the former. Lat. 22° 53′, long. 81° 37′.

GIRAUB.—A town in the Rajpoot state of Joudpore, 62 miles S.W. from Jessulmeer, and 157 miles S.W. from Joudpore. Lat. 26° 5′, long. 70° 40′.

GIRDHEEAE, in the British district of Moradabad, lieut.-gov. of the N.W. Provinces, a village on the route from the town of Moradabad to Almora, and 26 miles N. of the former. Lat. 29° 10′, long. 79°.

GIRHUR.—A town in the British province of Nagpoor, 37 miles S. from Nagpoor, and 110 miles S.E. from Ellichpoor. Lat. 20° 39′, long. 79° 10′.

GIRNA.—A river rising in lat. 20° 37′, long. 73° 45′, on the eastern slope of the Syadree range of mountains, and, flowing through the British district of Candeish, in the presidency of Bombay, first in an easterly direction for 120 miles, and subsequently north for fifty miles, falls into the Taptee on the left side, in lat. 21° 9′, long. 75° 17′.

GIRNAR, in the peninsula of Kattywar, province of Guzerat, or territory of the Guicowar, a remarkable mountain of granite, in the north of the district of Sorath, the summit being, according to native account, about ten miles east of the town of Janagurh. The elevation has been variously conjectured at 3,500 and 2,500 feet above the sea. Distance from Baroda, S.W., 175 miles. Lat. 21° 30′, long. 70° 42′.

GIRREE, a river of the hill state of Kothkaee, and a considerable feeder of the Jumna. It rises in lat. 31° 4′, long. 77° 42′, and at an elevation of 7,400 feet above the sea, on the concave side of a ridge of a horse-shoe shape, which connects Wartu summit with that of the Chur, and which, on the convex or eastern side, throws off numerous feeders to the Pabar. Holding a south-westerly course for about thirty-five miles, during which it receives numerous insignificant feeders, it is joined by the Ushun, in lat. 30° 54′, long. 77° 16′. It thence takes a south-easterly course for fifty miles, and falls into the Jumna in lat. 30° 27′, long. 77° 44′. At the confluence, this river discharges on an average 100 cubic feet of water per second.

GIRWAR.—A town in the Rajpoot state of Seerooee, 57 miles W. from Oodeypoor, and 51 miles N.E. from Deesa. Lat. 24° 36′, long. 72° 45′.

GIRWAREE.—A town in the native state of Gwalior, or territory of Scindia's family, 50 miles S.W. from Gwalior, and 69 miles N.W. from Jhansee. Lat. 25° 48′, long. 77° 37′.

GISREE, in Sinde, one of the mouths of the river Indus, receiving a small torrent flowing from the southern part of the mountain-range called, farther north, the Keertar and Lukkee hills. Lat. 24° 45′, long. 67° 8′.

GIVAROI.—A town in Hyderabad, or territory of the Nizam, eight miles from the right bank of the Godavery river, and 51 miles S.E. from Aurungabad. Lat. 19° 17′, long. 75° 49′.

GNASANQUA.—A town in the native state of Bhotan, 76 miles N.W. from Durrung, and 83 miles N.E. from Goalpara. Lat. 27° 12′, long. 91° 15′.

GNA YOKHYOUNG.—A pass over the Youmadoung range of mountains, from the coast of Arracan to the town of Bassein, in Pegu, 27 miles S.W. from the latter. Lat. 16° 30′, long. 94° 35′.

GNETZAZAKAN.—A small village, with an encamping-ground, on the Aeng pass (Arracan), about five miles from Sarowah, and situate on the edge of a precipitous descent. There is a spring at the bottom of the hill.

GNOPARAWA.—A village of Arracan, situate on one of the connecting creeks between the Arracan and Kuladyne rivers. Lat. 20° 31′, long. 93° 20′.

GOA.—The former capital of the Portuguese possessions in India, once an opulent and powerful city, but now fallen into an apparently irremediable and hopeless state of decay. It is situate in lat. 15° 30′, long. 74°. The territory of the same name lies on the western coast of the Indian peninsula, and is bounded on the north by the native state of Sawunt Warree; on the east by the British districts of Belgaum and North Canara; and on the south-west by the Indian Ocean. It extends from lat. 14° 54′ to 15° 45′, and from long. 73° 45′ to 74° 26′; is sixty-two miles in length from north to south, and forty in breadth, and contains an area of 1,066 square miles. The population has been returned at 313,262. Of this number two-thirds are stated to be Christians, of the Roman Catholic persuasion; but these are not under the direct jurisdiction of the Church of Rome, the throne of Portugal claiming the right of appointing its own bishop, and assuming the control and direction of the Catholic Church in its Indian possessions.

The settlement of Goa is divided into districts, which are again subdivided into parishes, the largest of which is Pangaum, containing the present seat of government, and about 10,000 souls. The harbour, which is a fine one, is formed by an arm of the sea, into which flows a small river, and is distant about five miles from the old city of Goa. The appearance of the harbour is of imposing beauty; but on reaching Pangaum, which is the new town and nearest to the harbour, all agreeable impressions vanish, the situation being low and sandy, and the houses wretched. Goa is connected with this place by a stone causeway about 300 yards long: though containing many fine buildings, churches, and monasteries, it is fast becoming a mass of deserted ruins—miserable and squalid indications that there has been here a great city. Its inhabitants are almost entirely ecclesiastics. The military force of the state of Goa consists of 3,300 fighting men, of whom about 400 are Europeans. The revenues are estimated at 719,200 rupees, an amount stated to be annually exceeded by the expenditure. The chief products are rice, but not in sufficient quantity for the consumption of the inhabitants; pepper, cocoanuts, betelnut, and salt; which latter article is manufactured to a very large extent. The brilliant career of the Portuguese in regard to India, and their achievements in navigation and conquest during the fifteenth and sixteenth centuries, are thus noticed in a modern historical work:—The Portuguese, indeed, have made no durable impression on the country, in which they appeared like a brilliant but destructive meteor; but their unwearied exertions to push the arts and discoveries of navigation beyond the limits within which they had been previously restricted, were too beneficial to the world at large to be passed over without notice. Their discoveries received the first impulse from Henry, the fifth son of John, the first king of Portugal of that name. Under his auspices, several expeditions were fitted out for exploring the coast of Africa and the adjacent seas. The first discovery was not very important, but was sufficient to afford encouragement, and stimulate to perseverance. It consisted of the little island of Puerto Santo, so named from its having been discovered on the festival of All Saints. This was in the year 1418. In the following year the adventurers were further rewarded by the discovery of Madeira. For more than half a century, the voyages of the Portuguese were continued in the same direction, but in general without more important results than occasional additions to the small stock of geographical knowledge then existing. Little progress seemed to have been made towards the attainment of the grand object of these enterprises, viz. the discovery of a new route to India, till the latter end of the fifteenth century, when Bartholomew Dias eclipsed the fame of all preceding navigators, by his success in reaching the southernmost point of Africa, and in doubling the famous promontory called by himself Cabo Tormontoso, the Cape of Storms, but more happily and permanently designated by his sovereign, Cabo de Bona Esperanza, the Cape of Good Hope. Emanuel, the successor of John of Portugal, proceeded in the steps of his predecessor. An expedition was fitted out in furtherance of the object in view, and committed to the care of Vasco de Gama. It sailed from Lisbon on the 9th of July, 1497, doubled the Cape on the 20th of November following, and finally reached Calicut; thus achieving the triumph so long and so anxiously sought. The admiral was forthwith introduced to the native prince, a Hindoo, called by the Portuguese historians Zamorin, by native authorities, Samiri; and after a short stay, marked by alternations of friendliness and hostility, set sail on his return to Portugal, where he was received with the honours which he had so well earned. The Portuguese returned, and received permission to carry on the operations of commerce. But disputes soon arose, and acts of violence were committed on both sides. The power and influence of the Portuguese, however, continued to extend, and the assistance afforded by them to the neighbouring king of Cochin, in his quarrel with the Zamorin, was rewarded by permission to erect a fort for their protection within the territories of the former prince. Thus was laid the foundation of the Portuguese dominion in the East. An attempt to obtain possession of Calicut failed. Against Goa the invaders were more successful. That city was taken by storm; and although subsequently retaken by a native force, was again captured by the Portuguese, and became the seat of their government, the capital of their Indian dominions, and the see of an archbishop, the primate of the Indies. The Dutch supplanted the Portuguese as traders, and with their commerce the latter nation lost their power and grandeur. Thus did Goa become the melancholy spectacle which it is now, and which it will continue to present until some further step in downward progress shall sink it still lower into wretchedness and degradation, or unless by some happy incident it should become absorbed into the British territories.

GOA, or GWA.—A populous village in the district of Sandoway, in the province of Arracan. It was formerly a town of considerable importance, but has for some time been on the decline. It possesses a harbour for vessels of 200 tons burden, but there is an awkward obstruction at its entrance, occasioned by a bar of sand, which renders it highly dangerous. A route from this place to Henzadah, on the *Irawaddy river, is called the Goa route. Lat. 17° 33′, long. 94° 41′.*

GOA ISLAND, or GWA ISLAND.—A small island situate near the mouth of the river in Arracan bearing the same name, and about a mile and a half from the shore. There is a large coral bank three miles to the westward. Lat. 17° 34′, long. 93° 38′.

GOA RIVER.—A small river which empties itself in the sea near the village of the same name in Arracan. Its entrance is broad and deep, sufficiently so for ships of 500 tons burden. Its mouth is about lat. 17° 34′, long. 93° 40′.

GOALGUNGE, in the territory of Bijawur, in Bundelcund, a town on the route from Banda to Saugor, 93 miles S.W. of the former, 79 N.E. of the latter. It has a bazar, and is supplied with water from wells. Lat. 24° 42′, long. 79° 26′.

GOALPARA.—A British district of the Bengal lieut.-gov., bounded on the north by the native state of Bhotan; on the east by the British district of Camroop, in Lower Assam; on the south by the native territory of the Garrow tribes and the British district of Mymensing; and on the west by that of Rungpore and the native state of Coosh Behar. It extends from lat. 25° 40′ to 26° 31′, and from long. 89° 42′ to 91° 8′; is 100 miles in length from north-west to south-east, and seventy miles in breadth, and contains an area of 3,506 square miles, with a population of 400,000. The principal crops of the district are cotton, tobacco, and sugar: mustard, also, is said to be extensively grown. Goalpara, or North-eastern Rungpore, in a geographical point of view, belongs to Bengal proper, having constituted an integral part of that province in 1765, when the British government obtained the grant of the Dewanny from the emperor of Delhi; but from the circumstance of its being placed under the superintendence of the commissioner of Assam, and from its general resemblance in respect of climate and other circumstances to that province, it has sometimes been regarded as one of the districts of Assam. Goalpara, the principal town of the district, suffered severely by fire in 1838. Lat. 26° 8′, long. 90° 40′.

GOAS.—A town in the British district of Moorshedabad, lieut.-gov. of Bengal, 114 miles N. of Calcutta. Lat. 24° 13′, long. 88° 29′.

GOBEENUGUR.—A town in the British district of Dinajepoor, lieut.-gov. of Bengal, 32 miles N.W. of Dinajepoor. Lat. 25° 59′, long. 88° 27′.

GOBINDGUNJ.—A town in the British district of Sarun, lieut.-gov. of Bengal, situate on the left bank of the Gunduck river, 52 miles N.W. of Chupra. Lat. 26° 29′, long. 84° 41′.

GOBINGUNJE, in the British district of Bogra, lieut.-gov. of Bengal, a town 22 miles N. of the town of Bogra. It is a place of considerable trade, and contains about 1,000 *houses, a number which, according to the usually-received average of inmates to dwellings,* would assign it a population of about 5,000. Lat. 25° 10′, long. 89° 22′.

GOBRIA.—A town of Malwa, in the native state of Bhopal, two miles from the left bank of the Betwa river, and 18 miles S.E. from Bhopal. Lat. 23° 9′, long. 77° 37′.

GOCURNUM, in the British district of North Canara, presidency of Madras, a town on the coast of the Arabian Sea, or North Indian Ocean. It is built in a straggling manner among cocoanut-palms, but has some commerce, and is held in high repute among the Brahminists, on account of an image of Mahabalishwar or Siva, said to have been brought to this place by Ravana, the giant tyrant of Lanka. Distance from Mangalore, N., 120 miles. Lat. 14° 32′, long. 74° 22′.

GODAGARI, in British district of Rajeshaye, lieut.-gov. of Bengal, a small town on the left bank of the Podda, or great eastern branch of the Ganges. It is situate on a ridge of stiff clay, mixed with kunkur or calcareous conglomerate, and derives its importance from the stability of its site, many of the places in this district being subject to inundation by the swollen rivers during the periodical rains of autumn. The Podda is here crossed by means of a ferry on the route from Berhampoor to Jumalpoor, 32 miles N.E. of former, 151 S.W. of latter, 150 N. of Calcutta. Lat. 24° 30′, long. 88° 20′.

GODAIRY.—A town in the Khoond state of Purlahkemedy, 118 miles N. from Vizagapatam, and 83 miles W. from Ganjam. Lat. 19° 20′, long. 83° 51′.

GODAR DEOTA, in the British district of Raeen, near Bussahir, a peak surmounted by a curious temple of a tutelary deity of that locality. It is situate near the left bank of the Pabur. Elevation above the sea 8,605 feet. Lat. 31° 10′, long. 77° 50′.

GODAVERY.—A river rising in the Deccan, in the British district of Ahmednuggur, on the eastern declivity of the Western Ghats, near Nassick, in lat. 19° 58′, long. 73° 30′, and 50 miles E. from the shore of the Arabian Sea. Taking a direction south-east for 100 miles, it reaches the western frontier of the territory of the Nizam at Phooltamba, in lat. 19° 48′, long. 74° 40′, and continuing to hold the same direction for ninety miles further, forms the boundary between the collectorate of Ahmednuggur and the territory of the Nizam, to a point ten miles beyond Mongee, in lat. 19° 23′, long. 75° 37′, having previously, at Toka, in lat. 19° 37′, long. 75° 2′, received on the right side the river Paira, flowing from the west. Below Mongee the Godavery enters the Nizam's territory, after which it proceeds in a sinuous, but generally easterly course, for 160 miles, to the vicinity of Lasona, and receives on the left side, in lat. 19° 6′, long. 77° 5′, the Doodna, a considerable stream flowing from the north-west. From that confluence, taking a course *south-east for eighty-five miles, in lat. 18° 48′, long. 77° 55′,* it receives on the right side the Manjara, a large river flowing from the south. The course of the Godavery after this confluence is still sinuous, but generally eastward, for about 170 miles, to the town of Veel Saugor, in lat. 18° 48′, long. 79° 49′, near which the Manair river falls into it: thence flowing for about twenty miles to Kulaisur, in lat. 18° 52′, long. 79° 55′, it receives on the left side the Wain Gunga (there termed the Prauheeta), a large river from the north, which discharges the great drainage of the southern declivity of the Vindhya range. Thence the Godavery takes a direction south-east for 170 miles, to Kottoor, in lat. 17° 29′, long. 81° 34′, where it crosses the frontier into the British district of Rajahmundry, finding its way through a deep chasm in the Eastern Ghats, with a very slight declivity. About twenty-five miles below Kottoor, it issues from the mountains at Polaveram, in lat. 17° 15′, long. 81° 42′. In passing through the great barrier of hills, it is stated by the boatmen who navigate the river, that there are no falls throughout the length of its channel, nor indeed any obstructions of importance; and the testimony of these persons would appear to be confirmed by the fact, that large timber-rafts from the Nizam's territory are floated down when the river is almost at its lowest, and has not more than two or three feet water at the fords in the low country. From Polaveram the river continues to hold a direction south-east for twenty-three miles, to Pechakalunka, in lat. 16° 57′, long. 81° 49′, where, entering the alluvial country which it has itself formed, it diverges into two great branches, the left flowing to the south-east for fifty-five miles, and falling into the Bay of Bengal at Point Gordeware, in lat. 16° 48′, long. 82° 23′; the right taking a southern direction for fifty-five miles, and falling into the bay at Narsipur, lat. 16° 18′, long. 81° 46′.

The alluvial country traversed by the two streams spreads out on both sides, extending on the west till it meets the delta of the Kistnah, at the Colair Lake, a distance of about forty miles; and on the east side spreading for about thirty-two miles, to the shore of Coringa Bay, where the coast runs for some distance nearly north and south. From the hills the river has a very moderate fall. At Polaveram, where, as already stated, it issues from the mountains, the alluvial land forming its banks is eighty feet above the level of the sea at high water. This land has a very regular slope, commencing with a foot and a half per mile, and gradually diminishing to one foot as it approaches the sea. But as the rise and fall of the river at Polaveram amounts to thirty-eight feet, its summer surface at that place cannot exceed forty-two feet above the sea-level, which gives an average fall of seven inches and a half per mile. At the head of the delta, the bed of the ford is twenty-two feet above the sea, and the actual distance being about fifty miles, the fall is little more than five inches *per mile. Besides the slope of the land towards* the sea in the delta, it has another and much more abrupt slope in a direction lateral to the course of the river. The banks of the river on both sides form ridges, rising several feet above the level of the land beyond. This ridge-like character is common to rivers which overflow their banks without restraint, as for instance the Nile, and is well known to arise from the deposit of the heavier matter near to the margin of the river, while the finer and lighter is carried to the limits of the inundation. The delta inclosed between these two great arms is traversed by many smaller branches diverging from them. An offset from the great north-eastern branch flows by the town of Coringa, and admits vessels of ten or twelve feet draught. The branch which disembogues at Narsipur is less suited for the purposes of navigation, admitting only vessels drawing eight or nine feet water. In December, 1846, the sanction of the Court of Directors was given to the construction, at an expense of 47,500*l.*, of a dam or annicut of sufficient height to command the delta of the river, and to supply to the rich alluvial soil of which that tract is composed, the means of constant irrigation. In 1848 the amount had been expended, but the works were far from completion, and a further sum, equal to 13,900*l.*, was assigned for that object. The annicut, 4,200 yards long, has been thrown across the river near the village of Dowlasweram on the east bank, and Wadapillay on the west. For boats and timber that may be required to pass down or up the river when there is neither so much water as to allow of their passing over the annicut, nor so little as to prevent their navigating the river, locks are constructed at the heads of the irrigating channels, by means of which a communication between the upper and lower stream is maintained round the annicut. At the town of Rajahmundry, a few miles above the point where the river divaricates, the channel is of great width, and during the periodical inundations in the close of summer, is filled from bank to bank with a vast and rapid body of water, bearing down great quantities of timber, wrecks of wooden houses, and carcases of animals; but during the dry season the current shrinks so much, that it might in most places be forded. The construction of the annicut already noticed has, however, changed this, by retaining, for the benefit both of agriculture and navigation, a never-failing supply of water, previously suffered to flow in useless abundance to the sea. The long gorge by which the river finds its way through the Eastern Ghats, though having so slight a declivity as to admit of navigation, allows the channel a space of not more than a quarter of a mile, with banks rising on each side into mountains so steep and high, that travelling along the stream by land is altogether impracticable, and communication can be maintained by navigation only. Above the gorge, the volume of water in the upper or more level country expands during inundations to a width of from three to six miles on each side of the river, and on the retiring of the stream, the soil remains covered with a black alluvial mud, which imparts to it great fertility. The total length of the Godavery from its source to Narsipur is 898 miles.

The value of this river as an instrument of communication for commercial and military purposes is perhaps not yet fully appreciated. It appears, that from Mahadepoor to Rajahmundry the voyage in boats properly adapted to the purpose has been performed in fifty-two hours; and it is inferred, with great appearance of probability, that steamers similar to those used on the Ganges might ascend the Godavery to a considerable distance, affording great facility for conveying troops and stores to Nagpore and Jubbulpore, as well as a mode of transmitting to the eastern coast the produce of Berar and the Nagpore territories, far more advantageous than the land route by carts and bullocks. The passage from Chanda, on one of the feeders of the Godavery, to Mahadepoor, has been performed in eighteen hours; and it has been suggested, that by means of this great river and its tributaries an uninterrupted water communication might be obtained from the coast into the heart of the Deccan. The experiment of navigating the Godavery by means of steam has been entertained by the government of Madras, and measures for carrying it into effect are under consideration.

GODHUL.—A town in Hyderabad, or territory of the Nizam, 69 miles S. from Hyderabad, and 34 miles S.E. from Ghunnapoora. Lat. 16° 21′, long. 78° 37′.

GODRA, in the territory of Guzerat, presidency of Bombay, a town on the route from Neemuch to Baroda, 187 miles S.W. of former, 52 N.E. of latter. It was formerly a very important place, the head of a large district of the kingdom of Guzerat, yielding annually 2,000,000 rupees, and is still a considerable town. Lat. 22° 45′, long. 73° 36′.

GOGAON, in the British district of Mirzapoor, lieut.-gov. of the N.W. Provinces, a village on the right bank of the Ganges, 36 miles W. of the city of Mirzapoor, 757 N.W. of Calcutta by water. Lat. 25° 13′, long. 82° 20′.

GOGAREE.—A river traversing the British district of Tirhoot, lieut.-gov. of Bengal. In the upper part of its course it is denominated Kamala or Kumla, and, according to Buchanan, rises in Nepal, in the Sub-Himalaya, about lat. 27° 20′, long. 85° 40′. Taking a course south-east for about seventy miles, it passes through the Terai or marshy forest in the southern part of Nepaul, and in lat. 26° 35′, long. 86° 15′, crosses the British frontier into the district Tirhoot, through which it flows in a southerly and south-westerly direction for about thirty-five miles, and subsequently for fifty miles in a south-easterly direction, when, passing from Tirhoot, it flows for forty miles through the district of Monghyr, and for twenty-five miles through Bhaugulpore; then, forming for fifteen miles the boundary between the districts of Purneah and Bhaugulpore, it falls into the Coosy, on the right side, in lat. 25° 24′, long. 87° 16′; its total length of course being about 235 miles.

GOGGOT RIVER.—An offset of the Attree, quitting it a few miles after its divergence from the Teesta, and in lat. 26° 19′, long. 88° 45′. It maintains a south-east direction, and, flowing through Coosh Behar, Rungpore, and Bograh, falls into the Konaie, a main branch of the Brahmapootra, after a total course of 145 miles, in lat. 24° 55′, long. 89° 41′.

GOGHA, in the British district of Allahabad, lieut.-gov. of the N.W. Provinces, a village close to the route by the Kutra Pass from Allahabad to Rewa, and 29 miles S.E. of the former. Lat. 25° 13′, long. 82° 13′.

GOGHPOOR, in Sirhind, a village on the route from Kurnal to Loodianah, and 32 miles N.W. of the former town. It is situated in a level tract, insulated by two branches of the river or torrent Markunda. Distant N.W. from Calcutta 997 miles. Lat. 30° 5′, long. 76° 49′.

GOGI.—A town in Hyderabad, or dominions of the Nizam, 126 miles S.W. from Hyderabad, and 68 miles S.E. from Beejapoor. Lat. 16° 43′, long. 76° 49′.

GOGO, in the British district of Ahmedabad, presidency of Bombay, a town situate in the peninsula of Kattywar, on the western shore of the Gulf of Cambay. About three-quarters of a mile east of the town, is an excellent anchorage, in some measure sheltered by the island of Perim, which lies still further east. The best Lascars in India are natives of this place, and ships touching here may procure water and refreshments, or repair damages. It is a safe place for vessels during the south-west monsoon, or to run for if they part from their anchors in Surat Road, being an entire bed of mud, three-quarters of a mile from the shore, and the water always smooth. The land about Gogo being generally low, is inundated at high spring-tides, which renders it necessary to bring fresh water from a distance of four or five miles: firewood is scarce. The inhabitants of this town have for many years laudably exerted themselves in promoting municipal improvements by means of self-taxation. Distance from Bombay 190 miles. Lat. 21° 39′, long. 72° 15′.

GOGOOLPULLY.—A town in the British district of Nellore, presidency of Madras, 138 miles S.W. of Masulipatam. Lat. 15° 17′, long. 79° 21′.

GOGRA RIVER.—See GHOGRA.

GOGRI, in the British district of Mongheer, lieut.-gov. of Bengal, a town a mile north-east of the left bank of the Ganges. It is the principal place of a pergunnah of the same name, but is of small size, the population not exceeding 700 or 800. Distant N.E. from Moongheer 10 miles, N.W. from Bhaugulpore 27 miles. Lat. 25° 25′, long. 86° 37′.

GOH.—A town in the British district of Behar, lieut.-gov. of Bengal, 30 miles N.W. of Shergotty. Lat. 24° 58′, long. 84° 41′.

GOH, in the British district of Kumaon, lieut.-gov. of the N.W. Provinces, a town on the right bank of the Dhouli river, and 69 miles N.E. of Almora. Lat. 30° 15′, long. 80° 35′.

GOHADEE, in the British district of Bareilly, lieut.-gov. of the N.W. Provinces, a village on the route from the town of Bareilly to Almora, and 43 miles N. of the former. Lat. 28° 52′, long. 79° 27′.

GOHALA, in the Rajpoot territory of Shekhawutee, a town on the route from Hansee to Nusserabad, 127 miles S. of former, 116 N.E. of latter. It has a large bazar, and water is abundant. Lat. 27° 39′, long. 75° 43′.

GOHANUH, in the British district of Rohtuk, lieut.-gov. of the N.W. Provinces, a town, the principal place of the pergunnah of the same name. It is situate on the Rohtuk branch of the Delhi Canal, and near the northern extremity of a great depression of the soil, extending about fifty miles southwards. In the course of the original formation of the canal by Ali Mardan Khan, the water being introduced as far as Gohanuh, could proceed no farther along the channel, in consequence of an error in the level, and, accumulating at this spot, overflowed and swept away the embankment intended to form the waterway. The great body of water which thus escaped, extensively inundated the country, and destroyed Lalpoor, a considerable town, the ruins of which may still be seen. The town of Gohanuh is 50 miles N.W. of Delhi, with a population of 6,668. Lat. 29° 8′, long. 76° 47′.

GOHAR TULAO, in Sinde, a tank on the summit of a strong pass on the route from Kurrachee to Sehwan, and 34 miles N.E. of the former place. The importance of the place results merely from its having a supply of water; in other respects it offers nothing to the traveller, the country around having a rugged surface of bare rock, and yielding neither forage nor provisions. Lat. 25° 5′, long. 67° 33′.

GOHILWAR, in the peninsula of Kattywar, province of Guzerat, or territory of the Guicowar, a district named from the Gohil Rajpoots, by whom it is principally peopled. It is bounded on the north by the British district of Ahmedabad; on the east and south-east by the Gulf of Cambay and Ahmedabad; on the west by the districts of Babriawar and Kattywar; on the north-west by the district of Kattywar; and lies between lat. 20° 56′—22° 3′, long. 71° 14′—72° 13′. It is eighty-five miles in length from north-east to south-west, and sixty in breadth. The principal towns—Limri, Palitayna, Mowa or Mahowa, and Tulaji or Taloja—are noticed under their respective names in the alphabetical arrangement. The district contains 690 towns and villages, and the aggregate population has been computed to be 247,980. The chief, styled the Rawul Raja, or thakoor of Bhaonagar, has an income estimated some years since at 740,000 rupees annually, and pays a tribute of 81,950 rupees to the British government, and 39,202 to the Guicowar. Bhaonagar, his capital, is within the jurisdiction of the British district of Ahmedabad; and this being regarded as an humiliating circumstance, has sometimes suggested to this affluent chief the removal of his residence to some town within his own.

GOHUD, in the territory of Gwalior, or the possessions of the family of Scindia, a town on the route from Etawa to Gwalior, 55 miles S.W. of the former, and 28 N.E. of the latter. Its fortifications consist of an outer curtain of mud, faced with stone, and inclose an extensive area, between which and the citadel are two other walls. The citadel is lofty, with massive towers, and has spacious and commodious apartments. Around the outermost rampart runs a ditch, which can be filled with water from the small river Besulee. Tieffenthaler, describing the condition of the place seventy years ago, states it to be then populous and rich. It is now, however, much decayed, though there are a few good modern houses, especially that of the Mahratta governor. The rana of Gohud was originally a Jat zemindar or landholder, who, in the early part of the eighteenth century, rose to considerable power by taking advantage of the opportunities for aggrandizement which were common during that troubled period. In 1779, he secured the alliance of the British government, from whom, in the following year, he received most valuable aid against the Mahrattas. Among other services, the fort of Gwalior, previously reputed impregnable, was captured by a British force under Captain Popham, and placed in the possession of the rana of Gohud. Here, however, in 1784, the rana was besieged by Madhajee Scindia, and obliged to surrender. His capital, Gohud, also passed into the hands of the enemy. In 1803, negotiations were opened by the British government with the rana of Gohud, and a treaty was concluded, by which certain territorial possessions were guaranteed to that chief. The right of the British thus to deal with the territory in question was, however, impugned by Scindia, and, in consequence, a new arrangement was effected. Gohud was transferred to Scindia, and the rana received from the British government the territory of Dholpoor, which his descendant still enjoys. Distance S.E. of Agra 60 miles; N.W. of Calcutta, by Etawah, 700. Lat. 26° 25′, long. 78° 26′.

GOHUN, in the British district of Jaloun, lieut.-gov. of the N.W. Provinces, a town on the route from Jaloun to Etawah, 13 miles N.W. of the former. Lat. 26° 19′, long. 79° 20′.

GOHUREE, in the British district of Allahabad, lieut.-gov. of the N.W. Provinces, a village on the route from Allahabad cantonment to that of Pertabgurh, in the Oude territory, seven miles N. of the former, 24 S. of the latter. Lat. 25° 34′, long. 81° 51′.

GOKAK.—A town in the British district of Belgaum, presidency of Bombay, 32 miles N.E. of Belgaum. Lat. 16° 10′, long. 74° 53′.

GOKUL, in the British district of Muttra, lieut.-gov. of the N.W. Provinces, a small town on the left or eastern bank of the Jumna. Here is a ferry across that river to Mohunpur, on the right bank, six miles S.E. of Muttra cantonment. It is a place of some note among the Hindoos, from its association with the memory of one of their revered sages. Wilson observes: "Vallabhi Swami, the son of Lakshmana Batt, a Tailinga Brahman—This Sanyasi taught early in the sixteenth century; he resided originally at Gokul, a village on the left bank of the Jumna, about three cos to the east of Mathura." It is also regarded by some as the place where Vishnu first appeared on earth, in the form of Krishna. Lat. 27° 26′, long. 77° 48′.

GOKUL, a village of Bussahir, on the frontier of Gurwhal, is situate at the south-eastern extremity of a high and massive ridge rising between the valleys of the rivers Tons and Pabur. Elevation above the sea 7,079 feet. Lat. 31° 4′, long. 77° 57′.

GOL, in the Rajpoot state of Joudpore, a village on the route from Balmeer to the town of Joudpore, and 46 miles E. of the former. It is situate in a low swampy country, on the right bank of the Lonee, at the confluence of the torrent called Leek. The surrounding country is extensively overflowed by the inundations of those streams during the rainy season. Gol contains fifty houses. Lat. 25° 52′, long. 72° 9′.

GOL.—A town in the Rajpoot state of Joudpore, on the right bank of the river Sookree, and 76 miles S.W. from Joudpore. Lat. 25° 25′, long. 72° 29′.

GOLA.—A town in the British district of Ramgur, lieut.-gov. of Bengal, 38 miles N.E. of Hazareebagh. Lat. 23° 34′, long. 85° 44′.

GOLAH GHAT.—A village situate on the right bank of the Dhunseree river, in the British district of Seebpoor, Upper Assam, 72 miles E. from Nowgong. Lat. 26° 33′, long. 93° 58′.

GOLCONDA, in the territory of the Nizam, a fortress and ruined city, seven miles W. of the city of Hyderabad. The fortress, situate on a rocky ridge of granite, is extensive, and contains many inclosures. It is altogether very strong, and in good repair, but is commanded within breaching distance by the summits of several of the enormous and massive mausolea of the ancient kings of the place. Being the depository of the treasures of the Nizam, and also used as a state prison, it is very strictly guarded, and entrance cannot be obtained by any but official persons in confidential capacity. The ancient mausolea form a vast group, about 600 yards from the fort, in an arid, desert, rocky ground, the stern features of which heighten the impressiveness and grandeur of those astonishing buildings. "Desolate, and abandoned to the ravages of time, they rear their stately domes and pinnacles on the bare plain, no outward defences now existing to ward off the approaches of any assailant, who, through ignorance or wantonness, may hasten the progress of decay. The most ancient of these tombs is not more than 300 years old; but they have been subjected to so many and such barbarous attacks, that nothing save the great solidity of their walls has preserved them from utter ruin. Each mausoleum stands in the centre of a spacious quadrangular platform or terrace, approached on all sides by flights of steps, entering upon a rich arcade, formed of an equal number of pointed arches on each front, and finished with a lofty balustrade, and a minaret at each angle. The body of the building, also quadrangular, rises about thirty feet above the upper terrace of this arcade, and is also surrounded by a balustrade, flanked with minarets of smaller dimensions than those below. From the centre of this portion of the building springs the dome, forming by its magnitude a distinguished feature in a structure equally remarkable for the splendour and symmetry of its proportions. The principal material employed is grey granite, ornamented in some parts with stucco, and in others with the porcelain tiles for which India was at one time so famous. The colours retain their brilliancy to the present day, and the extracts from the Koran, formed of white characters on a polished blue ground, have all the richness of enamel. There is a mosque attached to each of these tombs, which formerly possessed the privileges of sanctuary; and those religious edifices not only supported a considerable number of priests, but also afforded a daily meal to the neighbouring poor." "These tombs were erected at a great expense, some of them being said to have cost 150,000*l.* The enamelled-work with which they are ornamented is reported to have been the production of artists brought from China for the purpose; but there is every reason to believe that these decorations are of native workmanship, similar ornaments being to be found at Beejapore, Agra, Behar, Bengal, and other places." The diamonds of Golconda have obtained great celebrity throughout the world; but they were merely cut and polished here, having been generally found at Parteall, in a detached portion of the Nizam's dominions, near the southern frontier, in lat. 16° 40′, long. 80° 28′, a place which affords no favourable indication of the wealth to be derived from the avocation of seeking diamonds, as it is in ruins, and the inhabitants ill-clothed, and half-starved in appearance.

Golconda, in former times, was a large and powerful kingdom of the Deccan, which arose on the dissolution of the Bahmani empire, but being subdued by Aurungzebe, was incorporated with the empire under his rule. Even in its extinction, however, it was able to maintain some struggle, and even to venture on an attack upon the imperial army, and to plunder its baggage. The confusion consequent upon the breaking up of the empire almost obliterated the recollection of the once flourishing kingdom of Golconda. The fort is in lat. 17° 22′, long. 78° 29′.

GOLUGONDA.—A town in the British district of Vizagapatam, presidency of Madras, 56 miles W. of Vizagapatam. Lat. 17° 40′, long. 82° 31′.

GOLYGAIRA.—A town in the Mysore, 67 miles N.E. from Seringapatam, and 118 miles W. from Arcot. Lat. 12° 51′, long. 77° 38′.

GOMATI.—A river of the hill state of Kooloo, rising in lat. 32° 2′, long. 77° 34′, and, flowing in a south-westerly direction for fifty-five miles, falls in the Beas river near the village of Hurla, in lat. 31° 49′, long. 77° 12′.

GOMBELA, or TOCHEE, a river of Bunnoo, rising in lat. 32° 53′, long. 70° 1′, on the eastern slope of the Suliman range of mountains, and, flowing easterly for about 100 miles, falls into the Indus near the village of Kafer Kote, in lat. 32° 30′, long. 71° 20′.

GOMUL.—A river, or rather a prolonged torrent, rising in the eastern part of Afghanistan, and making its way through the Suliman range of mountains towards the Indus. After a course of about 160 miles, it is lost in the sands to the east of the Suliman range. Its bed for a great distance forms the Goolairee Pass, or great middle route from Hindostan to Khorasan, by Dera Ismael Khan and Ghuznee, the northern being through the Khyber Pass, and the southern through the Bolan. It crosses the Suliman range about lat. 32° 6′.

GOMUL.—A village in the Daman division of the Punjaub, on the road from Ghuznee to Dera Ismael Khan, and 40 miles W. of the latter place. It is situate near the eastern entrance of the pass of Gomul, and on the river or torrent of the same name. Lat. 31° 58′, long. 70° 8′.

GONDA, in the British district of Sohagpoor, Saugor and Nerbudda territory, lieut.-gov. of the N.W. Provinces, a town on the route from Jubbulpoor to Sirgoojah, 100 miles E. of the former. Lat. 23° 2′, long. 81° 35′.

GONDA, in the territory of Oude, a village six miles N.E. of the town of Pertaubghur. According to Butter, the "population is 2,000, all of the military tribe of Hindoos, except about fifty Mussulman weavers." Lat. 25° 59′, long. 82° 3′.

GONDAGHAON, in the British province of Saugor and Nerbudda, lieut.-gov. of the N.W. Provinces, a town on the route from Bhopal to Aurungabad, 52 miles S.W. of the former. Lat. 22° 31′, long. 77° 10′.

GONDWANA, or the land of the Gond race, an extensive, imperfectly-defined tract of Southern India. It may, however, be considered as lying between lat. 19° 50′ and 24° 30′, long. 77° 38′ and 87° 20′, and as comprising part of the British districts of Saugor and Nerbudda, and also those of Singrowli, Chota Nagpore, and Sirgooja, with the petty native states on the south-west frontier of Bengal, the Cuttack Mehals, and the greater portion of the northern part of the British province of Nagpore. It is throughout a hilly tract, comprising within its limits the eastern portion of the Vindhya and Mahadeo mountains, and having in some places a considerable elevation, stated, though perhaps without sufficient grounds, to be at Amarkantak 5,000 feet above the sea. Its great elevation in some parts is, however, proved by the fact that rivers take their course northward, as the Betwa and others of less importance, which flow into the Jumna or Ganges; eastward, as the Mahanuddy, to the Bay of Bengal; and westward, as the Nerbudda and Taptee, with their tributaries, to the Indian Ocean. The Goonds, who form the greater portion of the population of Gondwana, have been conjectured to be the aborigines of Hindostan, and speak a language radically different from Sanscrit and its dialects, introduced from regions west of the Indus. Many of the Goonds seen by Blunt in his passage through the country were so devoid of any approach to civilization as to live in a state of entire nudity. They appeared, however, to be an athletic, well-looking race.

The history of a race so rude must obviously be scanty and obscure. The Goond rajah Narsing Rae is represented in 1399 to have been powerful and wealthy; but his greatness was overthrown in 1433, by Hooshung, the Mussulman monarch of Malwa, who, having slain him in battle, reduced Kehrla, his capital. Subsequently, in 1513, the Goond chiefs are found forming a powerful confederacy against the king of Malwa. The western part was subjugated by Akbar, and included within the fiscal organization of his empire; Kehrla, the capital of the principal Goond rajah, being mentioned in the Ayeen Akbery as the chief place of a circar of the soubah of Berar. The eastern part, as remarked by Rennell, "was neither reduced by Akbar, nor even known in particulars to the author of the Ayeen Akbery." The rajah of Deogarh, in this part of Gondwana, was, in the latter part of the seventeenth century, induced to profess Mahomedanism by the influence of Aurungzebe; and in 1744, his sons having embroiled themselves with Ragoghee Bhonsla, were by him deprived of their possessions, which he incorporated with his own. Ragoghee in the previous year had overrun and partially subjugated Western Gondwana. There is henceforward little to relate until the operations of the British forces in the Nagpore dominions in 1818-19. Appa Sahib Bhonsla, the rajah of Berar, having fled from Nagpore, his capital, took refuge among the Mahadeo Mountains, in Western Gondwana. The British forces tracked him with unwearied perseverance through those intricate wilds, and, successively gaining his fastnesses and lurking-places, obliged him to fly in disguise. Another British armament overrunning Southern Gondwana, stormed the fortified town of Chanda; a third marching into South-eastern Gondwana, stormed the town of Kompta, and took military occupation of the neighbouring country. By the treaty of Nagpore, in 1818, the British government acquired the extensive tract now denominated the Saugor and Nerbudda territory, with other considerable tracts in the northern portion of Gondwana. It may, however, be observed in conclusion, that the name Gondwana must be regarded as obsolete.

GONDWARA.—A town in the British district of Purneah, lieut.-gov. of Bengal. It is the principal place of an extensive pergunnah or subdivision, yet consists of only three straggling market-places, having a population of about 1,500. Lat. 25° 30′, long. 87° 22′.

GONKOR.—A river of Nepal, formed by the junction of the Ponna and the Mui. The united stream flows in a direction south for twenty-five miles, through the Terai of Nepal; for 100 miles through the British district of Purneah; and for ten miles, during which it forms the boundary between Purneah and Malda, when it falls into the Ganges, near the town of Deatpore, in lat. 25° 10′, long. 87° 51′.

GON MYOO.—A town in the British district of Amherst, one of the Tenasserim provinces, presidency of Bengal, 55 miles S.E. of Moulmein. Lat. 16° 2′, long. 98° 23′.

GONSAINTHAN.—A peak of the Himalaya Mountains, between Nepal and Tibet. Altitude 24,700 feet above the sea. Lat. 28° 20′, long. 86°.

GOODALOOR.—A town in the British district of Coimbatoor, presidency of Madras, 11 miles N. of Coimbatoor. Lat. 11° 9′, long. 77° 1′.

GOODALUS.—A town in the British district of Malabar, presidency of Madras, 81 miles S.E. of Cannanore. Lat. 11° 30′, long. 76° 35′.

GOODAREE.—A town in the British province of Nagpoor, late dominions of the rajah of Berar, 186 miles E. from Nagpoor, and 81 miles S. from Ruttunpoor. Lat. 21° 8′, long. 81° 59′.

GOODHA, in the Rajpoot native state of Jeypoor, a town on the route from Delhi to the city of Jeypoor, 39 miles N.E. of latter. It is situate among isolated rocky hills, rising abruptly from a barren sandy plain. Lat. 27° 4′, long. 76° 31′.

GOODHA.—A town in the Rajpoot state of Boondee, 97 miles S.E. from Ajmeer, and 10 miles S.W. from Boondee. Lat. 25° 20′, long. 75° 39′.

GOODHA.—A town in the Rajpoot state of Shekawutee, 66 miles N.W. from Jeypoor, and 19 miles S.E. from Jhoonjhnoo. Lat. 27° 50′, long. 75° 40′.

GOODHANUH.—A village in the British district Goorgaon, lieut.-gov. of the N.W. Provinces. Distance S. from Delhi 45 miles. Lat. 28°, long. 77° 25′.

GOODICOTTA, in the British district of Bellary, presidency of Madras, a town, the principal place of a subdivision, distant from Chittel Droog, N.E., 44 miles; from Bellary, S.W., 30. Lat. 14° 50′, long. 76° 42′.

GOODOOR.—A town in Hyderabad, or territory of the Nizam, 30 miles N. from Hyderabad, and 165 miles E. from Sholapoor. Lat. 17° 46′, long. 78° 25′.

GOODROWLEE, or CHUK BHAN, in the British district of Futtehpoor, lieut.-gov. of the N.W. Provinces, a village on the route from Cawnpore to the town of Futtehpoor, and 23 miles N.W. of the latter. Lat. 26° 8′, long. 80° 38′.

GOODUH, in the British district of Bhutteeana, lieut.-gov. of the N.W. Provinces, a town on the route from Hansee to Furreed Kot, 72 miles N.W. of the former. Lat. 29° 42′, long. 75° 6′.

GOODYWADA.—A town in the British district of Masulipatam, presidency of Madras, 22 miles N.W. of Masulipatam. Lat. 16° 27′, long. 81° 3′.

GOOGUL.—A town of Malwa, in the native state of Tonk, on the left bank of the Parbuttee river, and 137 miles N.W. from Saugur. Lat. 24° 43′, long. 76° 51′.

GOOJAH, in Sinde, a town on the route from Kurrachee to Tatta, and 10 miles W. of the latter town. Masson describes it as "a small bazaar town, with pools or deposits of rain-water." Situate only 12 miles E. of Garrah, and on a navigable creek debouching into the Indian Ocean close to Kurrachee, it is believed that an inland navigation might easily and advantageously be effected here between that seaport and the main channel of the Indus, the intervening ground being low and level. Lat. 24° 44′, long. 67° 48′.

GOOJERANWALA.—See GUJURUWALLA.

GOOJERAT.—See GUJERAT.

GOOJERBAS, in the native territory of Alwur or Machery, under the political management of the Governor-General's agent in Rajpootana, a village on the route from Mhow cantonment to Delhi, and 88 miles S.W. of the latter. There are a few shops. Lat. 27° 50′, long. 76° 22′.

GOOJRAT, in the Sinde Sagur Dooab division of the Punjab, a town situated on the left bank of the Indus, and 31 miles W. of the town of Mooltan. Lat. 30° 8′, long. 71°.

GOOJUNGGUR.—A town in the British district of Cuttack, lieut.-gov. of Bengal, 55 miles N.E. of Juggurnaut. Lat. 20° 14′, long. 86° 36′.

GOOJUROO, in the British district of Kumaon, lieut.-gov. of the N.W. Provinces, a fort on a ridge of the Sub-Himalaya, bounding the Patlee Doon to the north-east. It is situate three miles to the right of the route, by the course of the Ramgunga (Western), from Moradabad cantonment to Fort Almorah, 80 miles by route N.E. of the former, 26 W. of the latter. Lat. 29° 35′, long. 79° 16′.

GOOLAH.—A river rising in the southern or outer group of the Himalaya, in the British district of Kumaon, lieut.-gov. of the N.W. Provinces. Lat. 29° 23′, long. 79° 44′. It leaves the mountains close to Khera, in lat. 29° 15′, long. 79° 37′, after a tortuous course, generally in a south-westerly direction, for a distance of thirty miles, in which it receives the drainage of Nyni Tal, Bhim Tal, and some smaller lakes. From its entrance on the plain, it takes a further course a little west of south for eighty miles, to its junction, under the name of Sunka, with the Ramgunga, on the left side of that stream, in lat. 28° 17′, long. 79° 27′.

GOOLAIREE.—An important pass across the Suliman range, from the Derajat into Kabool. It holds its course along the channel of the Gomul river, or (in the words of Burnes) "leads by broken rugged roads, or rather the watercourses of the Gomul, through the wild and mountainous country of the Muzarees." It is a pass of great importance, being the middle route from Hindostan to Afghanistan, as the Khyber is the northern and the Bolan the southern. Immense caravans, consisting principally of Lohani Afghans, every spring traverse it westward from the Indus and the adjacent countries, and, returning in autumn, winter in the Derajat. The Goolairee Pass enters the Suliman Mountains at their eastern base, in lat. 32° 6′, long. 70°. Its course is very winding: for about twenty miles from its entrance into the mountains, the direction of the road is north-west; then for about forty miles it proceeds in a westerly direction, though with numerous deviations at short intervals: it then turns to the north-west, in which direction generally it holds a sinuous course to Ghuznee. It is much infested by freebooters of the Vaziri Afghan tribe, and the caravans have often to fight their way with much loss of life and property.

GOOLAM ALIKA TANDA.—A town in the British district of Hydrabad, province of Scinde, presidency of Bombay, 36 miles S.E. of Hydrabad. Lat. 25° 9′, long. 68° 59′.

GOOLEUM.—A town in the British district of Bellary, presidency of Madras, on the right bank of the Hugry, and 19 miles N.E. of Bellary. Lat. 15° 20′, long. 77° 9′.

GOOLUREA, in the territory of Oude, a village on the route from Bareilly to Lucknow, 58 miles S.E. of the former, 98 N.W. of the latter. Lat. 28° 1′, long. 80° 14′.

GOOLUREEA, in the British district of Moradabad, lieut.-gov. of the N.W. Provinces, a village on the route from the town of Moradabad to Meerut, and 22 miles W. of the former. Lat. 28° 54′, long. 78° 31′.

GOOMA.—A town in the British district of Ramgur, lieut.-gov. of Bengal, 33 miles N. of Hazareebagh. Lat. 24° 25′, long. 85° 35′.

GOOMA.—A river of the peninsula Kattywar, presidency of Bombay, rising in lat. 22° 18′, long. 71° 30′, and, flowing in an easterly direction for seventeen miles through the territories of native chieftains, and fifty-three miles through the British district of Ahmedabad, it turns south-east, and after a further course of eighteen miles, falls into the Gulf of Cambay, in lat. 22° 3′, long. 72° 17′.

GOOMANOOR.—A town in the British district of Bellary, presidency of Madras, 23 miles E. of Bellary. Lat. 15° 10′, long. 77° 19′.

GOOMGAWN.—A town in the native state of Bhotan, 57 miles N.W. from Nowgong, and 48 miles N.N.E. from Gowhatty. Lat. 26° 47′, long. 92° 3′.

GOOMGONG, in the British province of Saugur and Nerbudda, lieut.-gov. of the N.W. Provinces, a town on the route from Hoosungabad to Boorhaunpoor, 59 miles S.W. of the former. Lat. 22° 5′, long. 77° 9′.

GOOMLA.—A town in the district of Singboom, on the south-west frontier of Bengal, 106 miles S. from Hazareebagh, and 111 miles W. from Midnapoor. Lat. 22° 30′, long. 85° 41′.

GOOMSOOR, in the British district of Ganjam, presidency of Madras, a town situate 43 miles N.W. of Ganjam. It was formerly the principal place of a feudal possession of the same name, tributary to the British, but the native chief failing in his feudatory obligations, and subsequently rising in rebellion, the zemindary, in 1835, was declared forfeited to the paramount power. A period of disorder ensued, during which atrocious acts of violence and outrage were perpetrated, and at length it was found necessary to appoint a special commission, with a view to the restoration of order and tranquillity. Among the beneficial measures arising from these proceedings, is the suppression in this part of India of human sacrifices. A discovery had been made that this horrible practice prevailed to a considerable extent among the Khoonds, a barbarous people inhabiting the adjacent frontier tracts. Recourse was had in the first instance to conciliatory means, by which it was hoped the civilization of the Khoonds might be effected; but the experiment, though continued through a series of years, failed in presenting any prospect of ultimate success; and in 1845, a commission for the suppression of Meriah sacrifices was appointed by the Indian government. Disturbances again broke out, attended with great destruction of life and property, and it became necessary to call in military aid. The insurgents were defeated, and peace restored. Several chiefs have been induced to enter into formal engagements to abandon the practice of human sacrifices and female infanticide, on condition of British protection; and these barbarous rites are now considered as effectually suppressed. The town of Goomsoor is in lat. 19° 50′, long. 84° 40′.

GOOMTEE.—A river rising in lat. 23° 43′, long. 92° 24′, in the native territory known as Independent Tipperah, and flowing through that state in a westerly direction for eighty miles, and for sixty miles through British Tipperah, falls into the Megna or Brahmapootra river, in lat. 23° 32′, long. 90° 42′.

GOOMTEE.—A river rising in the British district of Shahjehanpore, lieut.-gov. of the N.W. Provinces, in an alluvial tract between the rivers Deohah or Gurrah, and Ghogra. According to the surveyor-general's map, Fuljur Tal, the source of the Goomtee river, is a small lake or morass, in lat. 28° 35′, long. 80° 10′, and nineteen miles east of the town of Pilleebheet. As the elevation of Pilleebheet above the sea is estimated at 517 feet, and the intervening country is remarkably level, the source of the Goomtee may be assumed as about 520 feet above the sea. It takes a course sinuous, but generally to the south-east, for the distance of forty-two miles, when it crosses into the territory of Oude, and according to the surveyor-general's map, it, at the distance of about ninety-four miles from its source, in lat. 27° 28′, long. 80° 27′, receives on the left side a stream flowing from the north, and having a course of about forty miles. From this confluence the Goomtee continues its progress in its previous direction for about eighty miles, to Lucknow, receiving during its course the Suraru. It is at that city navigable, and crossed by a bridge either of brick or of stone. Rennell describes it to be at that place "a small river," and Lumsden, "a paltry and narrow stream;" but according to Von Orlich, a bridge of boats traversing the stream, below that of masonry, is 240 paces in length; and the same traveller states that an iron bridge of three arches, sent out in pieces from England, to traverse the river, was calculated for a width of 200 paces. The river certainly admits of navigation to an important extent; a small steamer belonging to the king of Oude having tested its capability in this respect. Tieffenthaler observes that the breadth of the river is more remarkable than its depth. Though its value for the purposes of navigation and irrigation is great, the water, according to Butter, is often contaminated by gross impurities, and occasionally becomes the source of disease. "During the rainy season, the water of the Goomtee is loaded with an immense quantity of yellow clay, and becomes unfit for drinking; and when any great mortality prevails at Lucknow, or along the banks of the river, a putrid scum forms on its surface, occasioned by the number of dead bodies thrown into it." Fish, however, so abound in it, that Butter estimates that a fifth of the population draws its subsistence from that source. It is greatly affected by the periodical rains, rising and falling annually from that cause about fifteen feet; and according to tradition, the variation formerly was much greater. At all times "it is excellently adapted for navigation, its waters never dispersing themselves over a greater breadth than 140 yards, and having generally a depth of four feet in the driest season; while its excessive windings, which lengthen its course seventy-five per cent., answer the purpose of canal locks in diminishing slope and rapidity. It is, however, intersected at every four or six miles by kankar (calcareous conglomerate) ridges of two or three yards in width, which in the dry season sometimes diminish the depth to two feet. These ridges might be removed at no great expense, were the political condition of the country such as to give its natural importance to the trade between central Oude and the British provinces. At present, the few boats which convey supplies to Lucknow return empty. During the rainy season, boats of 1,000 or 1,200 maunds (forty tons) are sometimes seen proceeding to Lucknow." The river continues its course in a south-easterly direction from Lucknow, and about seventy miles below, it, according to the surveyor-general's map, receives on the left side, in lat. 26° 42′, long. 81° 40′, the Kuliani, a stream flowing from the north-west, and having a course of about eighty miles. Below this confluence, the river's right bank is in general high, and consists of solid kankar; the left, low and sandy. At the station of Sultanpoor, about 170 miles south-east of Lucknow by the river's course, eighty in direct line, the stream is in the dry season 100 yards wide, with a mean depth of four feet, and a current of two miles an hour. About fifty-two miles lower down, and in the same direction, it passes over the frontier into the British district of Jounpoor, and flows through it thirty miles, to the town of the same name, where its breadth is such as to require a bridge of sixteen fine arches. About eighteen miles below that town, on the right side, it receives the river Sai; thirty-three miles lower down, in its course by the district of Benares, on the same side, the Nind; and five miles below the last confluence, and in lat. 25° 29′, long. 83° 15′, it falls into the Ganges on the left side, after a total course of 482 miles. Close above its mouth, it is crossed by means of a bridge of boats from the middle of October to the middle of June, and during the rains by ferry.

GOOMY.—A town in the native mehal of

Purlahkemedy, on the S.W. frontier of Bengal, 54 miles N. from Ganjam, and 66 miles N.W. from Juggernaut. Lat. 20° 10′, long. 84° 58′.

GOONAH, in the territory of Gwalior, or possessions of the Scindia family, a British cantonment on the route from Gwalior fort to Mow, 135 miles S.W. of former, 185 N.W. of the latter. The village in which it is situate is large, and in 1843 was inhabited by plunderers, who, notwithstanding the presence of eighty or 100 men of the Gwalior contingent, connived at and aided the freebooters, who swarmed in the neighbourhood during the disturbances consequent on the disputes at the court of Gwalior. Lat. 24° 40′, long. 77° 20′.

GOONASS PASS, in Bussahir, across the southern range of the Himalaya, which hold a direction from east-south-east to west-north-west. In approaching this pass from the south side, the road first proceeds upwards by the course of the Rupin, a feeder of the river Tons. The valley through which this river flows is terminated abruptly by a steep ridge, down which the stream pours in a cascade above 100 feet high. The ascent is by a path winding up by this stream, and proceeding over an expanse of snow to the crest of the pass, 16,026 feet above the sea. The inclination of the mountain-slope on the northern side is more gradual, but still very difficult, being, as far as the eye can reach, a dreary expanse of snow. The Goonass Pass lies in lat. 31° 21′, long. 78° 13′.

GOOND.—One of the native hill states on the left bank of the Sutlej river, tributary to the chief of Keyonthul. It is bounded on the north by a detached portion of Kooloo and the native hill state of Komharsin, which also bounds it on the east; on the south by those of Bulsun and Mudhan; and on the west by those of Bhugee and Theog. It lies between lat. 31° 4′—31° 15′, long. 77° 22′—77° 32′; is twelve miles in length from north to south, and six miles in breadth.

GOONDAGOLE.—A town in the British district of Masulipatam, presidency of Madras, 46 miles N.E. of Masulipatam. Lat. 16° 49′, long. 81° 20′.

GOONDAOW, in the British district of Muttra, lieut.-gov. of the N.W. Provinces, a village on the route from the city of Agra to Bareilly, and 26 miles N.E. of the former. Lat. 27° 26′, long. 78° 20′.

GOONDAR.—A river in the Madras collectorate of Madura, rising in lat. 9° 57′, long. 77° 45′, and, flowing in a south-east direction for ninety-five miles, falls into the Gulf of Manaar, in lat. 9° 8′, long. 78° 33′.

GOONDEE.—A town in the native state of Cashmeer, or territory of Gholab Singh, on the right bank of a branch of the river Pir Panjal, and 89 miles N.E. from Wazeerabad. Lat. 33° 43′, long. 74° 24′.

GOONDLOOR.—A town in the British district of Cuddapah, presidency of Madras, 47 miles S. of Cuddapah. Lat. 13° 50′, long. 78° 52′.

GOONDOOMREE.—A town in the British province of Nagpoor, late rajah of Berar's dominions, 68 miles E. from Nagpoor, and 67 miles S.E. from Seuni. Lat. 21° 11′, long. 80° 12′.

GOONDREE.—A town in the native state of Guzerat, or territory of the Guicowar, three miles from the right bank of the Bunnass river, and 26 miles N.E. from Deesa. Lat. 24° 32′, long. 72° 17′.

GOONEER, in the British district of Futtehpoor, lieut.-gov. of the N.W. Provinces, a town which, with that of Kootea, gives name to the pergunnah or subdivision of Kooteea-Gooneer. Gooneer is situate a mile from the right bank of the Jumna, 16 miles direct N.W. of the town of Futtehpoor. Lat. 26° 5′, long. 80° 44′.

GOONJE.—A town in Hyderabad, or territory of the Nizam, on the right bank of the Godavery river, and 200 miles N.W. from Hyderabad. Lat. 19° 15′, long. 76° 17′.

GOONJEE.—A town in the British district of Belgaum, presidency of Bombay, 22 miles S. of Belgaum. Lat. 15° 31′, long. 74° 34′.

GOONNOUR, in the British district of Budaon, lieut.-gov. of the N.W. Provinces, a town on the route from Boolundshuhur to Budaon, 44 miles N.W. of the latter. Lat. 28° 15′, long. 78° 30′.

GOONRA.—A town in the territory of Oude, 64 miles N.E. from Lucknow, and 113 miles N. from Allahabad. Lat. 27° 5′, long. 82°.

GOONWARO, in the territory of Saugor and Nerbudda, in the jaghire of Myhir, a village on the route from Mirzapoor to Jubulpoor, 87 miles N.E. of the latter, 158 S.W. of former. Lat. 24° 8′, long. 80° 40′.

GOOR.—A river rising in lat. 19° 8′, long. 73° 36′, on the eastern slope of the Western Ghauts, and, flowing in a south-easterly direction for fifty miles through the British district of Poona, and for fifty through that of Ahmednugur, falls into the Beema river, in lat. 18° 30′, long. 74° 36′.

GOORAH.—A town in Hyderabad, or territory of the Nizam, on the left bank of the Payne Gunga river, and 179 miles N. from Hyderabad. Lat. 19° 55′, long. 78° 11′.

GOORBAN, in Sinde, a village on the route from Sehwan to Kurrachee, and 30 miles N.E. of the latter place. It is situate on the river of the same name, where it receives a small torrent called the Kuttagee. Water consequently may readily be obtained, and even when the rivers have ceased to run, it may be had from pools or wells dug in their beds. The country hereabouts is very rocky and barren, and supplies are scanty. Lat. 25° 4′, long. 67° 28′.

GOORBAN.—A river in Sinde, so called from a village of that name on its bank. It rises in the mountainous tract between Kurrachee and Sehwan, about lat. 25° 14′, long.

67° 36′, and, after a south-westerly course of about sixty miles, falls into the Bay of Kurrachee by the Gisree creek, in lat. 24° 47′, long. 67° 6′. Like most of the streams in this part of Sinde, it is known by different names in different parts of its course; being called Vuddia near its source, Goorban in the middle, and Mulleeree lower down. Though occasionally flooded, and having then a considerable body of water, it is dry for the greater part of the year; but water, as stated in the preceding article, may at all times be obtained by digging in its bed. It is crossed by the route from Kurrachee to Sehwan, at the village of Goorban.

GOORDAH, in the territory of Bhurtpore, a village on the route from Agra to Ajmeer, 48 miles W. of former, 180 E. of latter. It is situate on the Baun or Ootunghun, "where the bed is about three-quarters of a mile wide, and of heavy sand. From November to July there is little water in the river, and from being so much spread out at the Ghat, it is but seldom unfordable any length of time in the rains." Lat. 27° 3′, long. 77° 20′.

GOOREA-TEEKA, or GURIALI, in Gurwhal, a pass over a ridge having a south-easterly direction from Surkanda summit to the right bank of the Bhageerettee, as the Ganges is called in the upper part of its course. It was a secondary station in the trigonometrical survey of the Himalayas. Elevation above the sea 7,041 feet. Lat. 30° 19′, long. 78° 27′.

GOORETHUH, in the British district of Budaon, lieut.-gov. of the N.W. Provinces, a town on the route from Bareilly to Bolundshuhur, 38 miles E. of the latter. Lat. 28° 24′, long. 78° 32′.

GOORGAON, a British district under the lieut.-gov. of the N.W. Provinces, is bounded on the north by the jaghire of Jujhur and the British district of Delhi; on the east by the jaghire of Bullubgurh and the river Jumna, separating it from the British districts of Boolundshuhur and Allygurh; on the south by the British district of Muttra, and by Tijarra and the territory of Bhurtpoor; and on the west by Tijarra and Jujhur. It lies between lat. 27° 40′—28° 30′, long. 76° 21′—77° 35′, and contains an area of 1,942 square miles. The population amounts to 662,486, of whom 322,183 are returned as Hindoo and agricultural; 138,591 Hindoo non-agricultural; 158,371 as Mahomedans and others not being Hindoos, agricultural; and 43,341 of the like classes non-agricultural. There are four towns containing each between 5,000 and 10,000 inhabitants, and three containing upwards of 10,000. The climate is for the greater part of the year dry and hot. The general elevation of the country is about 820 feet above Calcutta, or 840 above the sea; that of the town of Goorgaon being fixed by a scientific observer at 817. Some parts are, however, considerably higher. Jacquemont estimates the height of the hills about Soonah at more than 400 feet above the general level of the country; and Fraser mentions some which rise 600 feet above it. The part extending along the right bank of the Jumna is low, level, and in many places rather fertile, though, long after the cause had ceased to operate, it continued to be overrun with jungle, the consequence of the neglect of cultivation, produced by incessant devastation by the Mahrattas and other freebooters, previously to the conquest of the country by the British. Heber, who passed in 1825, observes, it "is still but badly cultivated; but fifteen years ago it was as wild, I am assured, as the Terrai, as full of tigers, and with no human inhabitants but banditti." The progress of improvement, however, seems to have been rapid, as Jacquemont, five years later, describes the country as rather well cultivated; and more recently a further stimulus has been given to agricultural industry by the revenue settlement of the district, under which the rate of the government assessment on the land has been fixed for a series of years, and is not liable to be increased until the year 1872. In the vicinity of the town of Ferozepore, iron-ore is extracted and smelted; but the quantity diminishes annually, in consequence of the great difficulty of obtaining charcoal, the country being very scantily wooded; and the miners and iron-workers earn but a very wretched subsistence. The surface of the country is furrowed by numerous deep chasms and ravines, usually indicating the course of a torrent. The air in many of those ravines is, in autumn, deadly in the extreme, especially where the course of the torrent is marked by the growth of bamboos, which are invariably signs of the insalubrity of the situation. Yet each generally contains a hamlet of goatherds, now of necessity peacefully dwelling under the powerful but mild restraint of British rule, but until lately the pests of the surrounding districts, which they incessantly harassed with their incursions, sweeping away all moveable property, and seizing the inhabitants, with the view of extorting ransom. This rude people are of the Meo or Mewatti race, for the most part nominally professing Mahomedanism, but intermingling it with innumerable Hindoo superstitions. They are very fond of animal food, especially goat's flesh, and also of spirits, but are not addicted to opium. Jacquemont, who considers them the aborigines of this part of India, describes them as very black, with the lower extremities long, the features in general not strongly marked, but the nose approaching to the aquiline form, lips rather prominent, moderately-sized mouths, and oval eyes, the cast of their countenances altogether resembling that of the North-American Indians. Westward of the first rocky table-land, rising from the valley of the Jumna, and inclosed between it and the rocky range still farther west, is a valley or depressed sandy plain, stretching from north to south, about twenty miles in length and six or eight in breadth. In many places, the ground is so saturated with salt, that in the hot dry weather the surface is covered with an efflorescence of it; the soil is barren, or produces merely a scanty growth of mimosa, and a few other products, common under such circumstances. These tracts are so abruptly defined, that, in the immediate neighbourhood of them the soil will be found free from saline impregnation, and fertile, the wells also yielding fresh water. In many places, by digging to the depth of twenty or thirty feet, fresh water is found; but if the well be sunk ten or twelve feet lower, salt springs are reached, the water of which is less saline than that of the sea, but more bitter, in consequence of containing a large quantity of sulphate of soda and muriate of magnesia. The salt water of each well being raised in a large leathern bucket, worked by rope and pulley, and set in motion by the labour of oxen and buffaloes, is conveyed through a small channel into a reservoir two or three feet deep, and lined with clay or mortar; and the moisture exhaling by the heat of the sun, the crystals are collected for sale. The quantity of salt produced in this way was formerly very considerable, but the article is now almost excluded from the market by the cheaper produce of the Sambhar Lake. In this sandy tract is a jhil or lake, about eight miles in length from north to south, and four in breadth. It is shallow, and its water, though without outlet, is fresh. It is frequented by great numbers of water-fowl, especially pelicans.

The greater part of the district of Goorgaon passed to the British by the treaty of Serjee Anjengum, dated 30th December, 1803, by which Doulut Rao Scindia ceded to the East-India Company his territories "northward of those of the rajahs of Jeypore and Joudpore, and of the ranah of Gohud." Part of it, containing about a hundred and eighty square miles, was held in jaghire by the Kashmirian adventurer Zebal Nisaa, more generally known under the name of the Begum Sumroo, and lapsed to the British on her death in 1836. Another portion of about 200 square miles, termed the jaghire of Ferozepore, from its principal place, was held with Loharoo by Shamsuddin Khan, who took it by descent from Ahmad Buksh Khan, to whom it had been granted by the British government early in the present century, on account of services rendered against the Mahrattas. Shamsuddin Khan having, with the view of defeating some contemplated measures which would affect his jaghire, caused the murder of Mr. William Frazer, the British political agent at Delhi, was hanged at that city, in October, 1835, and his jaghire forfeited. Loharoo was by the British government generously bestowed on the offender's half-brothers; but the territory of Ferozepore was embodied with the district of Goorgaon. The principal places are Goorgaon, Ferozepore, Faridabad, Rewarree, Pulwul, and Hodul, which will be found noticed under their respective names in the alphabetical arrangement.

GOORGAON, a town giving name to the British district so called, is situated near the western base of a range of hills of quartzose formation. Here was formerly a considerable military cantonment, the buildings erected for which are now occupied by the civil establishment. Goorgaon was formerly one of the principal places in the territory of the Begum Sumroo, which, lapsing on her death in 1836, was embodied with that of the British. The elevation of Goorgaon above the sea is 817 feet. Its mean temperature has been ascertained for various months as follows:—May, 104°; June, 98°; July, 85°; August, 84°; September, 89°; October, 87°; November, 75°; December, 66°; January, 70°; February, 72°; March, 80°. Distant S.W. from Delhi 18 miles; N.W. from Calcutta, by the grand trunk road, 918. Lat. 28° 28′, long. 77° 5′.

GOORGAUT.—A town in the native state of Guzerat, or territory of the Guicowar, three miles S. of the Gulf of Cutch, and 100 miles W. from Rajkote. Lat. 22° 12′, long. 69° 19′.

GOORHA, in the British district of Banda, lieut.-gov. of the N.W. Provinces, a village on the route from the town of Banda to Rewa, 24 miles S. of the former. It is situate on the right bank of the river Baghin. Lat. 25° 9′, long. 80° 33′.

GOORHA.—A town of Baghelcund, in the native state of Rewah, 13 miles from the left bank of the river Sone, and 13 miles E. from Rewah. Lat. 24° 30′, long. 81° 35′.

GOORMA, a river in Baghelcund, or territory of Rewah, rises on a plateau in lat. 24° 40′, long. 82° 16′. The elevation of its source above the sea exceeds 1,100 feet, since, at the cascade of Bilotri, about ten miles lower down, the elevation of the stream is 1,128 feet. It is at that cascade precipitated 398 feet over the brow of the Kutra ridge, and continuing in a north-westerly direction for a farther distance of fifteen miles, falls, on the right side, and in lat. 24° 56′, long. 81° 56′, into the Chutenea river, the united stream flowing a few miles further down into the Bilund, a tributary of the Tons.

GOOROO.—A town in the British district of Kurrachee, province of Scinde, presidency of Bombay, 39 miles S.W. of Tatta. Lat. 24° 18′, long. 67° 39′.

GOOROURUH, in the British district of Goorgaon, lieut.-gov. of the N.W. Provinces, a town on the route from Rewaree to Rohtuk, 38 miles S. of the latter. Lat. 28° 21′, long. 76° 42′.

GOORSERAIE, in the British district of Jaloun, lieut.-gov. of the N.W. Provinces, a town on the route from Hummeerpoor to Jhansee, 38 miles N.E. of the latter. Lat. 25° 36′, long. 79° 14′.

GOORSOUTTEE, or **GURSOUTI**, in the British district of Muttra, lieut.-gov. of the N.W. Provinces, a village on the route from the city of Agra to Aligurh, and 18 miles N. of the former. Lat. 27° 23′, long. 78° 7′.

GOORSUHAGUNJE, in the British district of Furrukhabad, lieut.-gov. of the N.W. Provinces, a town on the route from Cawnpore to Futtehgurh, and 19 miles S.E. of the latter. Lat. 27° 7′, long. 79° 47′.

GOORUM CONDA.—A town in the British district of Cuddapah, presidency of Madras, 127 miles N.W. of Madras. Lat. 13° 46′, long. 78° 38′.

GOORWALLUH, in the Daman division of the Punjab, a town situated thirty-five miles from the right bank of the river Indus, and 105 miles N.W. of the town of Mooltan. Lat. 31° 11′, long. 70° 12′.

GOOSUR.—A town in the Rajpoot state of Oodeypoor, 74 miles N.W. from Neemuch, and 58 miles S.E. from Seerooee. Lat. 24° 42′, long. 73° 47′.

GOOTHNEE.—A town in the British district of Sarun, lieut.-gov. of Bengal, 51 miles N.W. of Chupra. Lat. 26° 8′, long. 84° 6′.

GOOTOOHATOO.—A town in the British district of Chota Nagpoor, lieut.-gov. of Bengal, 74 miles S.S.E. of Hazareebagh. Lat. 22° 59′, long. 85° 46′.

GOOTUL.—A town in the British district of Dharwar, presidency of Bombay, 88 miles E.N.E. of Honahwar. Lat. 14° 50′, long. 75° 42′.

GOOTY, in the British district of Bellary, presidency of Madras, a town and military station. The place consists of a cluster of fortified hills, nearly surrounding a lower fort and native town; and outside the chain of fortified summits are the military cantonment and another pettah or town. The summits of the inclosing rocks are connected by a rampart, and the access to the town within is through two openings, secured by fortified gateways, one on the south-east, the other on the south-west; and there are besides two footpaths, affording a communication through sallyports. In the northern part of the circuit of inclosing rocks is an immense smooth rock, which, "fortified by gradations surmounted through fourteen gateways, overlooks and commands the whole of the other works, and forms a citadel which famine or treachery can alone reduce." On the summit of this fortified hill are several tanks and reservoirs for water, and various buildings, in which are detained some state prisoners. About half-way down the northern side of this huge rock is a projecting shoulder of considerable extent, called Maha Gooty, on which are barracks, formerly occupied by part of a European regiment, but now fast falling to decay. External to this circular inclosure of rocky hills, and on the west side, are the present cantonments, with a contiguous pettah, consisting of one principal street, well drained, and having tolerably good houses. The cantonment, once of considerable size, is now in ruins, with the exception of two or three houses. There is a good parade-ground, on the north of which are a place of arms, store-rooms, and huts contiguous, for accommodating native infantry. On the west of the cantonment is a large tank, which is devoid of water during part of the year. This place, formerly the head-quarters of a brigade, including one European regiment, is now garrisoned by two companies of native infantry, who enjoy excellent health, the air being in general salubrious. The population of the town is stated to be 4,386, of whom one-fourth are Mussulmans, the rest Brahminists of various castes, with the exception of about forty Christians. Elevation of highest summit above the plain 989 feet, above the sea 2,171. Distance from cantonment of Bellary 48 miles; from Bangalore, N., 146; Madras, N.W., 215. Lat. 15° 7′, long. 77° 42′.

GOPALGUNJE.—A town in the British district of Jessore, lieut.-gov. of Bengal, 92 miles E.N.E. of Calcutta. Lat. 23° 1′, long. 89° 48′.

GOPALGURH, in the territory of Bhurtpore, a town on the route from Muttra to Ferozpoor, 40 miles N.W. of the former, 12 S.E. of latter. Lat. 27° 40′, long. 77° 7′.

GOPALPOOR, in the British district of Muttra, lieut.-gov. of the N.W. Provinces, a village near the southern frontier, towards the district of Agra, and close to the left side of the route from Muttra cantonment to Bhurtpoor, 13 miles N.E. of the latter. Lat. 27° 21′, long. 77° 39′.

GOPALPOOR, in the British district of Futtehpoor, lieut.-gov. of the N.W. Provinces, a town on the right bank of the Ganges, 898 miles from Calcutta by the river, 88 miles above Allahabad, and 12 miles N.E. of the town of Futtehpoor. Lat. 26° 2′, long. 81° 1′.

GOPALPOOR, in the British district of Goruckpoor, lieut.-gov. of the N.W. Provinces, a town on the route from Azimgurh to Goruckpoor cantonment, 23 miles N. of the former, 33 S. of the latter. It has a bazar, and water and supplies are abundant. This town, though within the limits of Goruckpoor district, gives name to a pergunnah in that of Azimgurh. Lat. 26° 20′, long. 83° 20′.

GOPALPOOR, in the British district of Benares, lieut.-gov. of the N.W. Provinces, a village on the left bank of the Ganges, 16 miles N.W. of Mirzapoor, or higher up the stream; 737 N.W. of Calcutta by the river route. Lat. 25° 15′, long. 82° 26′.

GOPAMAU, in the district of Sandi, territory of Oude, a town situate two miles S.W. of the left bank of the Goomtee, in a plain on the northern verge of a thick forest. It was built by Patans, and contained many houses of brick, surrounded by handsome gardens. Even in the time of Tieffenthaler, a century ago, it was much ruined, having been nearly depopulated in the wars which afflicted the country. Distant 60 miles N.W. of Lucknow. Lat. 27° 32′, long. 80° 21′.

GOPAULPOOR, in the territory of Gwalior, or possessions of the Scindia family, a town 46 miles S.W. of Gwalior fort. Lat. 25° 43′, long. 77° 37′.

GOPEAGUNJ, in the British district of Etawah, lieut.-gov. of the N.W. Provinces, a small town on the route from the cantonment of Etawah to Lucknow, in Oude, and 11 miles E. of Etawah. Supplies and water are abundant. Lat. 26° 47′, long. 79° 16′.

GOPEE, in the British district of Allygurh, lieut.-gov. of the N.W. Provinces, a village on the route from the cantonment of Allygurh to that of Mynpooree, and 20 miles S.E. of the former. Lat. 27° 45′, long. 78° 23′.

GOPEEBULLUBPOOR.—A town in the British district of Midnapoor, lieut.-gov. of Bengal, 29 miles S.W. of Midnapoor. Lat. 22° 11′, long. 87°.

GOPIGANJ, in the British district of Benares, lieut.-gov. of the N.W. Provinces, a town with bazar, on the route from the city of Benares to that of Allahabad, 35 miles W. of the former, 39 S.E. of the latter. Lat. 25° 16′, long. 82° 30′.

GOPUT.—A river rising in Korea, a native state on the south-west frontier of Bengal, and about lat. 23° 40′, long. 82° 27′. It flows circuitously, but generally in a north-westerly direction, for seventy miles, and in lat. 24° 12′, long. 81° 57′, takes a north-easterly course for fifty-five miles, to its fall into the Sone, on the right or southern side, at the small town of Burdhee, and in lat. 24° 33′, long. 82° 26′.

GORA.—A town in the British district of Tannah, presidency of Bombay, 50 miles N. by E. of Bombay. Lat. 19° 39′, long. 73° 6′.

GORA, in the British district of Mirzapoor, lieut.-gov. of the N.W. Provinces, a village on the right bank of the Ganges, 21 miles N.W. of the city of Mirzapoor, or higher up the stream. Lat. 25° 12′, long. 82° 24′.

GORABI RIVER, one of the mouths of the Indus, discharging its waters about 50 miles S.W. of Tatta, in lat. 24° 20′, long. 67° 21′.

GORAE RIVER.—A considerable watercourse diverging from the left bank of the Ganges, in lat. 23° 55′, long. 89° 6′, and, flowing south-east through the British district of Jessore for forty-five miles, falls into the Koomar river, in lat. 23° 33′, long. 89° 32′.

GORAGOT, or GHORAGHAT, in the British district of Bograh, lieut.-gov. of Bengal, a town on the northern boundary, towards the British district of Dinagepore. It is situate on the river Kurateea, an offset of the Teesta, and hence the name, signifying horse-ferry or horse-pass, as Virat, an ancient Hindoo rajah, kept his horses here. The city, at the time of its greatness, extended eight or ten miles in length and about two in width, but appears to have been at all times built in a straggling manner. There are the remains of several small mosques, but no traces of any great public building, except the rampart of a fort, inclosing a space on the bank of the river about a mile in length and half a mile in width. Goragot at present has about 3,000 inhabitants, which continue to carry on some trade; but such altogether is the desolation of the place, that tigers prowl nightly in the streets. Distant S.E. from the town of Dinagepoor 48 miles. Lat. 25° 12′, long. 89° 17′.

GORAOW, in the British district of Etawah, lieut.-gov. of the N.W. Provinces, a village on the route from the cantonment of Agra to that of Etawah, and 20 miles N.W. of the latter. Lat. 26° 59′, long. 78° 51′.

GORBOONJEE.—A town in the native state of Calahandy, 153 miles N. by W. from Vizagapatam, and 153 miles W. by N. from Ganjam. Lat. 19° 50′, long. 82° 51′.

GOREYEE, in the British district of Allygurh, lieut.-gov. of the N.W. Provinces, a town, the principal place of the pergunnah of the same name. Lat. 27° 42′, long. 77° 54′.

GORI, or GORIGUNGA, one of the most considerable feeders of the great river Ghogra, rises within and near the northern boundary of the British district of Kumaon, lieut.-gov. of the N.W. Provinces, about twelve miles from the southern base of the Unta Dhura Pass into Hiundes or Chinese Tartary, and in lat. 30° 34′, long. 80° 16′. It flows from a vast glacier, apparently of very remote formation. This is thus described by Weller:—"The river comes out in a small but impetuous stream, at the foot of apparently a mass of dirt and gravel, some 300 feet high, shaped like a half-moon. This is in reality a mass of dark-coloured ice (bottle-green colour), extending westward to a great distance, and covered with stones and fragments of rock, which in fact form a succession of small hills. I went along this scene of desolation for a long space, but could not nearly reach the end. Here and there were circular and irregularly-shaped craters (as it were), from 50 to 500 feet diameter at top, and some of them 150 feet deep. The ice was frequently visible on the sides; and at the bottom was a dirty sea-green-coloured pool of water, apparently very deep. Into one of these craters I rolled down numerous large stones from off the edge, and in a few seconds huge masses of ice rose from below, seemingly detached by the agitation of the water." Webb found the stream at its exit from the glacier twenty-eight feet wide and four deep, and from its coldness and great rapidity altogether unfordable. There is no passage up the gorge beyond the glacier. The elevation above the sea, of the point of emergence from the glacier, is, by barometer, 11,543 feet. The great accumulation of snow in the gorge results from the fall of avalanches, which Webb observed to cause in a few days an increase in the thickness of the stratum of upwards of forty feet. Hênce, notwithstanding the extraordinary rapidity of the stream, resulting from a fall in some parts of its bed of 800 feet per mile, the river is overlaid with deep snow for a considerable distance below its source. It first takes a south-easterly direction for four miles, to its confluence with the Ghunka, which, rising on the southern declivity of the Unta Dhura Pass, has a course nearly south, and in lat. 30° 24′, long. 80° 12′, joins the Gori on the left side of the latter. Though the Ghunka has a greater length of course by about twelve or fourteen miles, and a greater volume of water than the Gori, the latter gives its name to the united stream. For some miles below the confluence, the stream varies in width from twelve to twenty yards, and runs with such extraordinary violence and rapidity, as in many places to resemble a cascade tumbling down a rugged face of rocks; in others it is hid below a continuous mass of ice and snow. In forty miles, the declivity of the waterway is 6,599 feet, or upwards of 160 in a mile. It receives on the right and left many torrents, none very considerable; and continuing its course in a southerly direction, so as totally to run about sixty miles, falls into the Kalee on the right side. Webb, who crossed it at this place by a sangha or spar bridge, found it unfordable, 102 feet wide, very violent and rapid. A short distance lower down, it is, however, fordable in three and a half feet water. The confluence is 1,972 feet above the sea. Lat. 29° 45′, long. 80° 25′.

GORIHAR, or GOURIAR, in Bundelcund, the principal place of the jaghire or feudal grant of the same name, a small town or village 16 miles S.W. of Banda, 66 S.E. of Calpee. Lat. 25° 16′, long. 80° 15′. The jaghire is stated to comprise an area of seventy-six square miles, and to contain nineteen villages, with a population of 7,500 souls, and yielding a revenue of 65,000 rupees (6,500*l.*). It is held of the East-India Company, under grant dated November, 1807, and the jaghiredar maintains a force of thirty horse and one hundred foot.

GORKHA, in the native state of Nepaul, a town 53 miles W. by N. from Khatmandoo, and 104 miles N.E. from Goruckpoor, and formerly the principal place of the country of the reigning dynasty of Nepaul. Lat. 27° 52′, long. 84° 28′.

GORPOORE.—A town of Assam, in the British district of Luckimpoor, 40 miles S.W. of Luckimpoor. Lat. 26° 53′, long. 93° 39′.

GORUCKNATH, in Sirhind, a village on the route from Pinjor to Malown, and 12 miles N.W. of the former place. It is situate at the base of the Sub-Himalaya, near the right bank of the river Sursa, and on the north-eastern border of the Pinjor Doon. Lat. 30° 54′, long. 76° 54′.

GORUCKPORE, a district under the lieut.-gov. of the N.W. Provinces, is named from its principal place. It is bounded on the north by the territory of Nepaul; on the east and south-east by the district Sarun; on the south by the British district of Azimgurh; on the south-west and west by the territory of Oude. It lies between lat. 26° 7′—27° 30′, long. 82° 12′—84° 30′, and includes an area of 7,346 square miles. The district is in general remarkably level, but at a few spots in the east and south-east, there are some ridges of slight elevation, seldom exceeding sixty feet in perpendicular height above the plain, with a breadth of from 100 to 300 yards. They consist of a light soil, well suited for the growth of trees, but are not cultivable, the steepness of their slopes precluding irrigation. The more southern are visible to those passing up and down the Ganges. Their crest has an uneven outline, and they are rendered the more remarkable by the fact that no similar elevations are visible in navigating the river from the vicinity of the Himalayas. From calculations founded on the slope of river-beds, the average elevation of the central part of the district of Goruckpore above the sea is estimated at about 340 feet. The surface slopes with a general and very gentle declivity from north-west to south-east, as is indicated by the courses of the Ghaghra, Raptee, Gunduck, and divers other streams. The general descent probably does not on an average exceed eight inches per mile; and in consequence of the comparative flatness, many parts are laid under water during the rainy season. From many hollows the abundant rains never entirely evaporate, and hence the country abounds in jhils or shallow lakes. The most important are the Moti Jhil (Pearl of Lakes), or jhil of Bakhira, twelve miles west of the town of Goruckpore, in the dry season seven miles long and three broad; the Ramgarhtal, close to the east of the same town, six long and three broad; and Bherital, in the south-east of the district, and near the left bank of the Ghaghra.

The climate of Goruckpore is sultry in the southern parts, but is considered as healthy as any in India of the same average temperature. In the north, or towards the base of the Himalaya, the heat is not so great, but the air is less salubrious; fever, intermittents, and other complaints generated by malaria, being much more common. The easterly and westerly winds are the more prevalent; and the change to the opposite directions generally takes place after a short intervening calm, without veering through the intermediate points. The west winds prevail from the middle of February to the middle of June, when they are succeeded by those from the east. These continue until the middle of October, and during the remainder of the year the east and west winds blow for nearly equal periods, the north and south winds blowing only occasionally. In the immediate vicinity of the mountains, a current of air rushing down each considerable gorge, produces nearly every forenoon a wind from north to south. The westerly winds are not attended by that searing and pernicious sultriness which causes them in tracts lying more to the westward and south-westward to be emphatically denominated "the hot winds." In winter, indeed, they are accompanied by such a degree of cold as produces thin ice. The periodical rains continue from the middle of June to the middle of October: they are less liable to failure than in places farther south or west, and are more abundant and certain in proportion to proximity to the mountains. The lands liable to inundation are cultivated with rice, which is the staple crop of most parts of this district, though in some, wheat is more extensively grown. A few years since, inquiries were made by the local government as to the probability of the latter becoming a profitable article of export to the United Kingdom, but the results were not such as to afford encouragement to the trial of the experiment. Other crops are barley, millet, maize, the opium poppy, arhar (Cytisus cajanus), gram (Cicer arietinum), peas, and various other kinds of pulse; some species of amaranthus, mustard, and other oil-plants; ginger, turmeric, and betel. Cotton is grown, though not to a sufficient extent for the home demand. In the experimental farms of the government, native sorts were found to succeed well, but the American kinds failed. Indigo is cultivated by grantees of the East-India Company. Tobacco is extensively grown, principally for home consumption. The sugarcane is well suited to the soil and climate, though more remote from the equator than the generality of tracts in which sugar is successfully cultivated. The attention of British capitalists has latterly been directed to the planting of mulberry-trees. The population being very indigent, and in a low state of civilization, the manufactures are few and simple, being nearly restricted to coarse cottons, woollens, tanning, dyeing, rude workings in metals, sugar-boiling, and extraction of soda and nitre from soils impregnated with those substances. The exports are represented to be grain, pulse, oil-seeds, oil, sugar, melasses, ginger, turmeric, tobacco, lac, honey, wax, indigo, cotton cloth, nitre, ghee or clarified butter, elephants, kine, buffaloes, goats, fish, and timber. The imports are said to consist of cotton wool, thread, and cloth, chintzes, silks, broad-cloths, blankets of wool and cotton, hardware, and some other articles of less importance.

The principal routes are—1. from west to east, from Fyzabad, through the town of Goruckpore, to Betiya; 2. from south-east to north-west, from Dinapoor to the town of Goruckpore, and thence continued in the same direction to Sekrora, in Oude; 3. in a direction nearly from north to south, from the town of Goruckpore to Azimgurh; 4. in a direction nearly from north to south, from the town of Goruckpore to Ghazeepore; 5. from north-east to south-west, from the town of Goruckpore to Sultanpoor, in Oude. Great improvements, calculated to develop the resources of the country, have been effected in the district within the last few years, by the Road Fund Committee, resulting in an increase of the government rental, the amount of which was subsequently fixed for a series of years, and is not liable to a further increase until 1859. A plan adopted by the local government for bringing the waste lands into cultivation, which first came under the notice of the home authorities in 1836, did not, when the details came to be understood, secure their approbation. Vast grants of waste land at a progressive rental, increasing from the fourth to the twenty-fifth year, were made to various individuals, four-fifths of whom were Europeans, and the remainder Anglo-Indians. These grants were stated to have amounted to nearly 418,000 British statute acres, or 653 square miles; and it appeared that three individuals were concerned, either directly or indirectly, in no less than 208,480 acres, or 345 square miles; an area exceeding that of the county of Middlesex. These enormous allotments were judged by the home authorities to have been made without due regard either to the circumstances of the country transferred, or to the means possessed by the grantees for effecting the required improvement; and orders were given to cancel the grants as far as might be practicable. For the guidance of the local government in future, certain rules were enjoined, and others recommended, for the purpose of avoiding on future occasions the errors committed in regard to these grants. Among the objects proposed by these rules, were the prohibition of any grant of land without previous survey; the prohibition of any grant to a European, unless he engaged to reside on the land himself, and to bring it into cultivation within a specified period; the prohibition of sale or transfer until the land had been brought into cultivation; the limitation of the extent of grants made under general conditions, and the annexation of special conditions to additional grants; the resort to public competition, by inviting tenders for the purchase of waste land; the admission of natives to a share in the distribution; the preservation of all ancient rights; the maintenance of roads and drains, and the due apportionment of water for irrigation. Some of these points were enforced in orders issued in 1836, and final and peremptory orders on the subject were sent out in 1842.

The population, according to a census taken in 1853, amounts to 3,087,874. Of these, 2,267,513 are returned as Hindoos engaged in agriculture; 449,262 Hindoos employed in other occupations; 262,133 Mahomedans and others, not being Hindoos, agricultural; 108,966 non-agricultural. It will thus be seen that the great majority of the inhabitants of Goruckpore are Hindoos. The Mahomedans of course form the next largest number. There are, it is said, a few Sikhs; and a small number of the rich merchants and tradesmen profess the doctrine of the Jains. Men of all classes and descriptions formerly went armed for the purpose either of outrage or defence; but since the country passed into the hands of the British government, all the strongholds of freebooters have been demolished, and no open resistance is now shown to the ruling authority. The tract constituting this district was formerly part of the possessions of Oude, and was comprised within the transfer of territory made under the treaty of the 10th November, 1801, by the nawaub vizier, to the East-India Company, in commutation of their claims for subsidy and other charges. The district contains four towns having more than 5,000 inhabitants but less than 10,000, and three (Goruckpore, Jungul Purowna, and Birdpoor) having more than 10,000.

GORUCKPORE.—The principal place of the British district of the same name, within the limits of the lieut.-gov. of the N.W. Provinces. It is situate on the left bank of the Raptee, which is here a fine navigable river, with a channel about 200 yards wide, at all seasons containing deep water, and consequently passable only by ferry, there being no bridge. "Only a corner of the town is adjacent to the bank, the extent of high ground being there small, and widening farther back from the river. The situation, however, is good and healthy, and would be more agreeable were the forests and plantations cleared away, as they exclude ventilation, occasion many musquitoes, and harbour great numbers of monkeys, which are exceedingly troublesome. But the natives object strongly to any such measure." This favourable report of the place must, however, be received with some qualification, as there is much marsh in the vicinity of the town, and in the rainy season the whole country southwards for six miles, as far as the river Ami, is often laid under water. Tieffenthaler estimates its circuit at three miles, but mentions that the natives reported it to be seven. A few of the houses are of brick, and tiled; the larger portion of the remainder have mud walls, but are tiled; but a small number are mere hovels of hurdle, and thatched. "When new, like others in this district, the tiled roofs are uncommonly neat, but they are very soon spoiled by the monkeys, who, from their insatiable curiosity and restless mischief, turn over the tiles, and render the roofs the most unseemly and useless in the world." There are two mosques; one completely ruinous; the other, which is in better preservation, and is still frequented, is built of brick, in a remarkably heavy, tasteless style. Both buildings are mentioned by Tieffenthaler, who describes the former as ancient a century ago. The Imam-barah, built by Shoojah-oo-Dowlah, nawaub of Oude, is handsome and spacious, and is kept in excellent repair by a person who has a large endowment. It would have a striking and fine effect, were it not surrounded by a chaos of filth and misery. The fort bears the name of Basantpoor, and is situate close to the left bank of the Raptee. The ground-plan given by Tieffenthaler is a regular square, with a bastion at each corner, and two intermediate, at regular intervals on each face; and consequently twelve altogether. When the English took possession, in 1802, the fortifications had become ruinous, and part of the fort was then demolished, and some rooms built in the European style. Buchanan adds—"But still it is a very sorry place, although it serves the collector as an office and treasury. Round the town the magistrates have made some good roads, and the houses of Europeans are scattered on the east, south, and west sides of the town, especially on the last, where the military cantonments and jail are situated. I have seen no station where the houses of the Europeans have so poor an appearance, or where the grounds about them are so destitute of ornament." The cantonment is at present on the east side of the town, on the highest ground that could be appropriated for the purpose; and from the sandiness of the soil, water seldom lodges on it for more than a day or two. But this high ground immediately rises from the Ramgartal, a jhil or shallow lake situate on its south-east side, which is six miles long and three broad, and from the channels by which this expanse of stagnant water receives the drainage of a great jungle lying on the north, and stretching eastward of the cantonment. When this jhil and the river Raptee rise to a certain height, a communication is formed between them, and the level of the stagnant water is regulated by that of the river. If, however, the communication be long interrupted during hot weather, the whole surface of the jhil becomes a mass of decayed vegetable matter. The cantonment affords accommodation for a detail of native artillery, a detachment of light cavalry, and a regiment of native infantry. The civil establishment consists of the usual European officers and native functionaries. The population of the town of Goruckpore, according to a census taken in 1853, amounted to 54,529. A short distance from the town is the sthan or place of Gorackhnath, near which is a tank intended for ritual ablutions, and said to have been miraculously formed. This town is mentioned in the Ayeen Akbery as having a brick fort. Elevation above the sea between 330 and 340 feet. Distance direct from Calcutta, N.W., 430 miles; from Hazareebagh, 230; from Dinapore, 130. Lat. 26° 42′, long. 83° 23′.

GORUCKPORE, in the British district of Furruckabad, lieut.-gov. of the N.W. Provinces, a village on the route from the cantonment of Bareilly to that of Futtehgurh, and eight miles N.E. of the latter. Lat. 27° 28′, long. 79° 41′.

GORUH, in the British district of Meerut, lieut.-gov. of the N.W. Provinces, a town the principal place of the pergunnah of the same name. Lat. 28° 49′, long. 77° 56′.

GORUH, in the British district of Budaoon, lieut.-gov. of the N.W. Provinces, a village on the route from Agra to Bareilly, and 66 miles N.E. of the former. Lat. 27° 50′, long. 78° 45′.

GOSAINGANJ, in the territory of Oude, a village on the route from Lucknow cantonment to Purtabgurh, 20 miles S.E. of the former, 90 N.W. of the latter. It has a bazar, and is well supplied. Lat. 26° 42′, long. 81° 8′.

GOTEH.—A town in the Southern Mahratta jaghire of Jumkundee, 86 miles N.E. from Belgaum, and 163 miles S.E. by S. from Poonah. Lat. 16° 41′, long. 75° 30′.

GOTELAEE, in the British district of Mynpooree, lieut.-gov. of the N.W. Provinces, a village on the route from the cantonment of Aligurh to that of Mynpooree, and 29 miles N.W. of the latter. Lat. 27° 30′, long. 78° 46′.

GOTKEE, in Sinde, a small town on the route from Subzulcote to Shikarpoor, and 34 miles W. of the former place. It is situate six miles from the left bank of the Indus, in a low, level, alluvial country, much overspread with jungle. Though the houses are meanly built of mud, there is a showy bazar, with numerous verandas, decorated with various fantastic devices. The town also possesses a mosque of considerable size, surmounted by a cupola covered with glazed tiles. The vicinity is infamous on account of the predatory and sanguinary character of its inhabitants. Lat. 28° 2′, long. 69° 20′.

GOTRA.—A town in the native state of Gwalior, or territory of Scindia's family, 83 miles S.W. by W. from Gwalior, and 99 miles W. by N. from Jhansee. Lat. 25° 39′, long. 77° 5′.

GOTTARAO, or SURDHAR GHUR, in Sinde, a fort on the route from Roree to Jessulmair, and 50 miles N.W. of the latter place. It is situate near the eastern frontier, in the Thur or Sandy Desert, the surface of which undulates in a succession of sandhills, not totally barren, as they produce a spare vegetation of stunted bushes and tufted grass. Water in this district is scarcely to be had except during rains, and even then in small pools barely capable of supplying 100 men. The fort of Gottarao is built of brick, and forms a square of about 200 yards. The wall is from twenty to twenty-five feet high, and a keep in the interior is about ten feet higher. On the east and the greater part of the north side is an outer wall of about ten feet high. There are about a dozen round bastions in various parts of the walls. The fort is supplied with water from a depth of 150 feet by five wells. Two of these are within the walls; the remaining three without, but close to them. During the sway of the Talpoor dynasty, this place belonged to the ameers of Khyerpoor, and was defended by two guns and a garrison of 150 matchlock-men. An inconsiderable village is attached to the fort. It is frequently called Sirdar Ghur (the Sudur Ghur of Walker's map). Lat. 27° 16′, long. 70° 4′.

GOUHANEE, in the British district of Banda, lieut.-gov. of the N.W. Provinces, a town three miles left or S.E. of the route from Allahabad to Kallinger, 65 miles W. of the former, 57 N.E. of the latter. Lat. 25° 18′, long. 81° 9′.

GOULLY, in the British district of Bijnour, lieut.-gov. of the N.W. Provinces, a village on the route from Moradabad to Mozuffernuggur, and 37 miles N.W. of the former place. It is situate in an open and partially-cultivated country, in which water and abundant supplies can be obtained. Distant N.W. from Calcutta, by Moradábad, 925 miles. Lat. 29° 7′, long. 78° 23′.

GOUNTIA, in the British district of Furruckabad, lieut.-gov. of the N.W. Provinces, a village on the route from the cantonment of Shahjehanpoor to that of Futtehghur, and five miles N.E. of the latter. Lat. 27° 24′, long. 79° 41′.

GOUR.—See GAUR.

GOURANGHEE.—A river rising in lat. 26° 43′, long. 90° 7′, on the southern slope of the Sub-Himalaya range of mountains, and in the native state of Bhotan, and, flowing south for thirty miles through Bhotan, and eighteen miles through the British district of Goalpara, falls into the Brahmapootra on the right side, in lat. 26° 10′, long. 90° 13′.

GOUREA, in the British district of Cawnpore, lieut.-gov. of the N.W. Provinces, a village on the route from Allahabad to Etawah, and 70 miles S.E. of the latter. Lat. 26° 12′, long. 79° 55′.

GOURIAR.—See GORIHAR.

GOURJEANUH.—A town in the native state of Bhawulpoor, near the left bank of the river Ghara, and 130 miles E.N.E. from Bhawulpoor. Lat. 30° 14′, long. 73° 39′.

GOVARDANGERRY.—A town in the British district of North Canara, presidency of Madras, 93 miles N. by W. of Mangalore. Lat. 14° 11′, long. 74° 42′.

GOVERDHUN, in the British district of Muttra, lieut.-gov. of the N.W. Provinces, a town on the route from the cantonment of Muttra to Deeg, and 15 miles W. of the former. Here, on the night previous to the battle of Deeg, were the head-quarters of General Fraser. It has a bazar, and water and supplies for troops are abundant. The road eastward, or towards the cantonment of Muttra, is generally indifferent, and heavy in parts; westward, towards Deeg, it is good. This vicinity is in the Hindoo mythological legends marked by the fabled miracles and exploits of the divinity Krishna, who at the age of eight years "took up Mount Goovurdhunu in his arms, and held it as an umbrella over the heads of the villagers and their cattle, during a dreadful storm, with which the angry king of heaven was overwhelming them." In the great Indian Atlas, published by authority, the site of the town is represented in an opening in a range of mountains running north-east and south-west, on the western boundary of the district of Muttra; but Garden, in his remarks on the surrounding country, states it to be "flat and cultivated." That this, however, is a mistake, appears from the account of Sleeman, who lately visited this place, and states that "the town stands upon a narrow ridge of sandstone hills, about ten miles long, rising suddenly out of the alluvial plain, and running north-east and south-west." The extremities of this ridge slope gradually to the plain, from which the sides rise abruptly. The population is at present scanty, consisting in a great measure of Brahmins, supported on the endowments annexed to the tombs of the Jat rajahs of Bhurtpore and of Deeg, whose bodies are burned and their ashes inhumated at this town. The tomb of Suraj Mul, the eminent Jat ruler of Bhurtpore, is on the north-eastern extremity of the rocky ridge, about two miles from the town, and is a handsome building, tastefully designed, and elaborately executed in fine white sandstone, little inferior to marble. Connected with this principal building are various subordinate temples, and the whole group extending along one side of a fine tank, full of clear water, and on the other side overlooking a large and beautiful garden. In the middle of the town is the handsome tomb of Ranjit Singh, the rajah who successfully defended Bhurtpoor against British assaults in 1805. On each side of the tomb is a tank, one being full; the other, though deeper, is dry, the contents having been drunk off by Krishna, when heated and thirsty, after dancing with his milkmaids; and never since has it had any water. Lat. 27° 30′, long. 77° 32′.

GOVINDAPOORAM.—A town in the British district of Rajahmundry, presidency of Madras, 82 miles S.W. of Vizagapatam. Lat. 17° 14′, long. 82° 14′.

GOVINDGURH, in the Baree Dooab division of the Punjab, a fortress, built in 1809, by Runjeet Singh, avowedly for the purpose of protecting the pilgrims resorting to Amritsir, but in reality to overawe the dangerous assemblage. Since its occupation by the British, measures have been taken for adding to its security. Lat. 31° 40′, long. 74° 45′.

GOVINDPOOR, in the Baree Dooab division of the Punjab, a town situated on the right bank of the river Beas, 85 miles E. by N. of the town of Lahore. Lat. 31° 44′, long. 75° 33′.

GOW GHAT, in the British district of Allahabad, lieut.-gov. of the N.W. Provinces, a ferry across the Jumna, near the city of Allahabad, and on the south side of it. The bed of the river is here three-quarters of a mile wide, and the stream in the dry season occupies nearly the whole space. The left bank is rather steep, the right sloping. Lat. 25° 25′, long. 81° 55′.

GOWHA.—A town in the British province of Nagpoor, three miles from the left bank of the Wein Gunga, and 38 miles E. from Nagpoor. Lat. 21° 6′, long. 79° 43′.

GOWHATTY.—A town in the British district of Camroop, lieut.-gov. of Bengal, 69 miles E. of Goalpara. Its insalubrity has been brought to the notice of the government, and improvements have in consequence been carried on from time to time, with the view of remedying the unhealthiness of the station. Though much yet remains to be done in this respect, great benefit is stated to have resulted from the measures already adopted. Lat. 26° 9′, long. 91° 45′.

GOWNDUL, in the peninsula of Kattywar, province of Guzerat, a town in the district of Hallar. The talook attached to it contains 156 villages and towns, and has a population estimated at 84,700 persons. A tribute of 53,005 rupees is paid to the British government, and 74,400 rupees to the Guicowar. Distance from Ahmedabad, S.W., 135 miles; Baroda, W., 160. Lat. 21° 57′, long. 70° 50′.

GOWRA, in the British district of Goruckpoor, lieut.-gov. of Agra, a small town on the right bank of the Chota Gunduk river, close to the south-east frontier, towards the British district of Sarun. According to Buchanan, it contains 250 houses; which amount would assign it a population of 1,500 persons. Distant S.E. from Goruckpoor cantonment 36 miles. Lat. 26° 43′, long. 83° 20′.

GOWRA, in Bussahir, a village on the route from Rampoor to Seran, and six miles N.E. of the former town. It is a neatly-built cleanly village, on the flank of a spur of the Himalaya, jutting into the Sutluj. The country in the vicinity is well tilled, and the views are fine. The rajah of Bussahir has here a neat residence; close to which is a handsome Hindoo temple, surrounded with an open trellis of wood, and ornamented with a profusion of carving, executed with much skill and taste. Elevation above the sea 6,042 feet. Lat. 31° 28′, long. 77° 45′.

GOWRA, in the British district of Futtehpoor, lieut.-gov. of the N.W. Provinces, a town seven miles from the left bank of the Jumna, 26 miles W. of the town of Futtehpoor. Lat. 25° 59′, long. 80° 29′.

GRAM.—A town in the Mysore, 50 miles N.W. from Seringapatam, and 94 miles E. from Mangalore. Lat. 12° 59′, long. 76° 17′.

GRAMUNG, in Bussahir, a village of Koonawur, in the valley of Tidung, and near the right bank of the river of that name, here a violent torrent, rushing down a channel having in some places a descent of 300 feet, in others of double that quantity, in a mile. The village of Gramung is pleasantly situate on a slope towards the south, the houses rising above each other, in consequence of the inclination of the ground. There is a small extent of cultivated ground, producing thriving crops of wheat, buckwheat, barley, turnips, and pulse. The whole is neatly laid out, and intersected by watercourses, the banks of which are adorned with walnut, apricot, apple, and poplar trees. The houses are well built, and roofed with birch bark overlaid with clay, and supported by timbers. Each has a pole, bearing a white flag or pennon, inscribed with the sacred sentence, "Um Mane pai me Um," and surmounted by the chouri or tail of a black yak; and the vicinity contains thousands of little temples, shrines, and other structures devoted to the ritual observances of the Lamaic monks and nuns, who inhabit the village. Elevation above the sea 9,174 feet. Lat. 31° 33′, long. 78° 33′.

GRINGAVARPUKOTA.—A town in the British district of Vizagapatam, presidency of Madras, 18 miles W. of Vizianagram. Lat. 18° 6′, long. 83° 13′.

GUASUBA.—The name of one of the channels by which the waters of the Ganges flow into the sea. Though of considerable size, it is "the most difficult to enter of any on the coast." Its mouth is in lat. 21° 35′, long. 88° 55′.

GUDDADA.—A river rising in lat. 27° 52′, long. 89° 8′, on the southern slope of the great Snowy Range of the Himalaya Mountains, and, flowing in a southerly direction for 120 miles through Bhotan, and forty miles through the British district of Goalpara, falls into the Brahmapootra on the right side, in lat. 27° 3′, long. 89° 57′.

GUDDRA.—A town in the British district of Hydrabad, province of Scinde, presidency of Bombay, 139 miles E. by N. of Hydrabad. Lat. 25° 40′, long. 70° 37′.

GUDHEYREE, in the British district of Mynpooree, lieut.-gov. of the N.W. Provinces, a village on the route from the cantonment of Allygurh to that of Mynpooree, and six miles N.W. of the latter. Lat. 27° 15′, long. 79° 2′.

GUDJUNTURGURH.—One of the Southern Mahratta jaghires. The town of the same name, and its principal place, is situate 98 miles E. of Belgaum, and 74 miles N.W. from Bellary. Lat. 15° 43′, long. 76° 2′.

GUDKA.—A town in the province of Guzerat, or territory of the Guicowar, 11 miles S. from the Gulf of Cutch, and 84 miles W. by S. from Rajkote. Lat. 22° 9′, long. 69° 33′.

GUDUK.—A town in the British district of Dharwar, presidency of Bombay, 43 miles E. of Dharwar. Lat. 15° 26′, long. 75° 43′.

GUDURPOOR, in the British district of Bareilly, division of Pilleebheet, lieut.-gov. of the N.W. Provinces, a town, the principal place of the pergunnah of the same name, on the route by Nanakmath and Rooderpoor from the town of Pilleebheet to Kashipore, 21 miles S.E. of the latter. Lat. 29° 2′, long. 79° 17′.

GUERMANDA, in the British district of Kumaon, lieut.-gov. of the N.W. Provinces, a halting-ground on the route from Almora to Sireenuggur, and 48 miles N.W. of the former. It is situate on a considerable stream, crossed here by a sangho or wooden bridge. Lat. 29° 58′, long. 79° 9′.

GUGGUR.—A river or great torrent of Sirhind, and the principal stream of that territory. It rises beyond the north-east frontier, in Pateeala, about lat. 30° 52′, long. 77° 7′. In consequence of the extent of the hilly country which it drains, its volume of water in time of inundation is very considerable. After forming the boundary for a short distance between some of the hill districts and Sirhind, it finally enters the latter in lat. 30° 43′, long. 76° 57′, whence its course is mainly in a south-west direction through a shallow level valley, about twenty-nine miles wide. The Markunda and Sursooty, farther east, flow down the same valley, which, in time of inundation, is deluged with water, forming a close network of streams, and sometimes causing the three rivers to coalesce into one great stream. In the season when lowest, it becomes a "small thread of water." Jacquemont, who crossed it at that time, describes the channel as narrow, but very deep, being, in fact, a ravine scooped by the torrent out o the alluvial soil. The water was then about two feet deep, but appearances indicated that in time of inundation it might be eight or nine. Having received the Sursooty, and some streams of less importance, it, after a course of about 140 miles, generally in a south-west direction, passes into the British district of Hurreeanah, and subsequently into that of Butteeanah; its course through these two provinces measuring about 110 miles. It then crosses the Beekaneer frontier, close to which, near Badhopal, and twenty-two miles south-east of Bhatnir, in lat. 29° 24′, long. 74° 14′, it is joined by a watercourse, the continuation of the celebrated canal of Feroz Shah. Hereabouts it becomes totally exhausted by evaporation, absorption, and diversion for the purposes of irrigation, but formerly reached the Sutlej, about twenty miles north-east of the town of Bahawulpoor, by a channel which, though now devoid of water, can be traced to that extent. In the dry season, however, the water does not flow beyond Dundhal. The country about the lower part of its course, though now quite barren and depopulated, abounds in ruins, the evidence of former prosperity. The river is mentioned by Baber, under the name of Kagar, and by Rennell, under that of Caggur or Kenker.

GUHMUR.—A town on the right bank of the river Ganges, in the British district of Ghazeepoor, lieut.-gov. of the N.W. Provinces, containing a population of 7,420 inhabitants. The place is of comparative importance, there being few towns in the whole district of Ghazeepoor containing a population exceeding that of Guhmur. Distant S.E. from Ghazeepoor 14 miles. Lat. 25° 28′, long. 83° 51′.

GUJELHATTI, or **GAJELHATTI**, in the British district of Coimbatoor, a fort in a pass between the territory of Mysore and the district of Coimbatoor. This fort, formerly looked upon as of great importance, has of late years been much disregarded, and the pass is scarcely frequented, those farther north being preferred, as more convenient for the lines of communication with Madras and Tanjore. The valley through which the pass lies, is the great gorge down the bottom of which flows the Moyaar, a large torrent, and the sides of which are formed towards the south-west by the precipitous brow of the Neilgherries, having an elevation of from 3,000 to 4,000 feet above the torrent, and towards the north-east by the steep declivities of the mountains rising towards Mysore. The fort of Gujelhatti, situate on the left bank of the torrent Moyaar, was, in 1768, taken from Hyder Ali by a British force commanded by Colonel Wood, but was retaken in the same year. It is distant from Seringapatam, S.E., 63 miles; Coimbatoor, N., 38 miles; Madras, S.W., 240. Lat. 11° 33′, long. 77° 4′.

GUJERAT.—A considerable walled town of the Punjab, about eight miles from the right bank of the Chenaub, and on the great route from Attock to Lahore. It was invested by Maha Singh, who sickened and died in the course of the siege. It subsequently fell into the hands of his more fortunate son, Runjeet Singh, early in the course of his career. Near this place, on the 21st February, 1849, a battle was fought between a British force, under the command of Lord Gough, and a Sikh army, under two chieftains, described as Sirdar Chuttur Singh and Rajah Shere Singh, combined with some troops belonging to the ruler of Cabool, the entire number being estimated at 60,000. This apparently overwhelming force was vigorously attacked by the British, greatly inferior in point of numbers, and driven in succession from point to point, until, utterly defeated, the enemy took to disorderly flight, abandoning their camp, artillery, baggage, and magazines. In addition to their numerical strength, the Sikhs brought into the field a larger number of pieces of artillery, fifty-three of which became prize to the victors. Lat. 32° 35′, long. 74° 8′.

GUJNAIR, in the British district of Cawnpore, lieut.-gov. of the N.W. Provinces, a town on the route from Humeerpoor to Russoolabad, and 25 miles N. of the former. Lat. 26° 17′, long. 80° 7′.

GUJNER, in the Rajpoot state of Bikaneer, a village on the route from the town of Bikaneer to that of Jessulmere, and 19 miles S.W. of the former. Here is a hunting-palace of the rajah of Bikaneer. Lat. 27° 57′, long. 73° 10′.

GUJNERA, in the British district of Bareilly, lieut.-gov. of the N.W. Provinces, a village on the route from the town of Bareilly to Setapoor, and 14 miles S.E. of the former. It is situate on the banks of the Punaili, a small stream passable by a good ford. Lat. 28° 20′, long. 79° 41′.

GUJOWLEE, in the British district of Agra, lieut.-gov. of the N.W. Provinces, a village on the left bank of the Jumna, seven miles N. of the city of Agra. Lat. 27° 15′, long. 78° 3′.

GUJPOOR, in the British district of Goruckpoor, lieut.-gov. of the N.W. Provinces, a small town on the right bank of the river Raptee, distant from Goruckpoor cantonments, S.E., 18 miles. Lat. 26° 30′, long. 83° 28′.

GUJROWLA, in the British district of Moradabad, lieut.-gov. of the N.W. Provinces, a village on the route from the town of Meerut to Moradabad, and 40 miles S.E. of the former place. There is a small bazar. Distant N.W. from Calcutta 923 miles. Lat. 28° 51′, long. 78° 19′.

GUJURU-WALLA, or **GOOJERA-WALA**, in the Punjab, a town on the route from Amritsir to Vazeerabad, and 20 miles S. of the latter place. Here is a large square fort with mud walls, surrounded by a ditch. It was the original residence of the family of Runjeet Singh, whose grandfather, born at this place, was a common soldier. The ashes of Runjeet Singh's father and mother are deposited here in tombs of plain appearance. It a few years ago was the residence of the celebrated Hari Singh, the most dauntless of all the Sikh chieftains. The interior of the fort is very highly decorated, and the garden is described by Baron Von Hügel as one of the finest he saw in India. Gujuru-Walla is in lat. 32° 10′, long. 74° 13′.

GUJYNLEE, in Bussahir, a village on the route from Kothkae to the Burinda Pass, and eight miles E. of the former. It is inhabited by miners, who extract and smelt the iron-ore of the neighbouring hills. The elevation probably exceeds 6,000 feet. Lat. 31° 8′, long. 77° 42′.

GULEE BUSSUR, in the British district of Kumaon, lieut.-gov. of the N.W. Provinces, a village on the route from Almora to Sireenuggur, and 12 miles N.W. of the former. Lat. 29° 42′, long. 79° 36′.

GULER, in the Baree Dooab division of the Punjab, a town situated on the right bank of the river Beas, 126 miles E. by N. of the town of Lahore. Lat. 31° 57′, long. 76° 12′.

GULGAOM PIMPRALLA, in the British district of Candeish, presidency of Bombay, a town in which some very elegant and expensive houses have of late years been built by native bankers and the great exporters of cotton. Lat. 21°, long. 75° 37′.

GULLOO RIVER, in Scinde, one of the numerous channels by which the waters of the

Indus disembogue into the sea. It leaves the parent stream in lat. 24° 28′, long. 67° 54′, and, pursuing a south-westerly direction for fifty miles, reaches the sea, under the name of the Hujamri, in lat. 24° 8′, long. 67° 26′.

GULZARGANJ, in the British district of Jounpoor, lieut.-gov. of the N.W. Provinces, a town on the route from Allahabad to Jounpoor cantonment, 53 miles N.E. of the former, 13 W. of the latter. It has a bazar. Lat. 25° 44′, long. 82° 34′.

GUMAR.—A small town in the north-east of the Punjab, and on the southern slope of the Himalaya. The houses are built of stones, cemented with mud, and strengthened with timbers of fir laid horizontally. The roofs are of fir spars, covered with slates; but as these are laid loose, they form a very imperfect protection against the weather. There is here a mine of rock-salt, which is worked to considerable extent, but in a very rude manner. The salt is of a reddish colour, and is very compact and heavy. The rajah of Mundi derives a considerable revenue by its sale. Lat. 31° 57′, long. 76° 24′.

GUMBADEE.—A town in the British district of Kurrachee, province of Scinde, presidency of Bombay, 14 miles S. of Tatta. Lat. 24° 33′, long. 67° 57′.

GUMBHERA, in the British district of Allahabad, lieut.-gov. of the N.W. Provinces, a town on the route from Allahabad to Goruckpoor, 15 miles N.N.E. of the former. Lat. 25° 39′, long. 82° 4′.

GUMBHIR (EASTERN), a stream of Malwa, rises on the north side of the Vindhya range, seven miles S.E. of the British cantonment of Mow, and in lat. 22° 30′, long. 75° 54′. It holds a course generally northerly for about seventy-five miles, and falls into the Seepra on the right side, in lat. 23° 26′, long. 75° 42′. It is crossed about ten miles from its source, by the route from Mow to Indore, "by a good ford; bed forty yards wide, banks steep, and bottom gravelly; water throughout the year." About sixty-five miles from its source, and in lat. 23° 18′, long. 75° 42′, it is crossed, by means of a ford, by the route from Baitool to Neemuch. "The bed is fifty yards wide, stream fifteen, and one foot deep in fair season; bottom sand and rock; banks steep, and cut into ravines, through which the road passes for some distance."

GUMBHIR (WESTERN), or WAG, a river of Malwa, rises 22 miles S.W. of the town of Nimbera, in lat. 24° 20′, long. 74° 40′, and, holding a course of forty-five miles, in a direction generally north-westerly, falls into the river Beris on the right side, about half a mile west of Chittorgurh, and in lat. 24° 53′, long. 74° 44′. It is crossed, on the route from Neemuch to Nusserabad, by means of a stone bridge, close to Chittorgurh, and described by Heber as "the ruins of a long, lofty, and handsome bridge, of eight arches, and one semicircular one in the centre, with a ruined tower and gateway at each end."

GUMHEERPOOR, in the British district of Azimgurh, lieut.-gov. of the N.W. Provinces, a small town, with bazar, on the route from the town of Azimgurh to that of Jounpoor, and 16 miles S.W. of the former, 26 N.E. of the latter. Distant N. from Benares 45 miles. Lat. 25° 54′, long. 83° 3′.

GUMNAIGPOLIAM. — A town in the Mysore, 128 miles N.E. from Seringapatam, and 117 miles N.W. by W. from Arcot. Lat. 13° 50′, long. 77° 59′.

GUMPAPOOL. — A town in the native state of Bhotan, two miles from the left bank of the Monas, and 95 miles N. by W. from Gowhatty. Lat. 27° 30′, long. 91° 34′.

GUMSALEE, in the British district o Kumaon, lieut.-gov. of the N.W. Provinces, a village on the route from Joshimath to the Niti Pass, and 15 miles S. of the latter. It is situate on the right bank of the Doulee. Elevation above the sea 10,317 feet. Lat. 30° 45′, long. 79° 52′.

GUNAI, in the British district of Kumaon, lieut.-gov. of the N.W. Provinces, a village on the route from Almora to Sireenuggur, and 36 miles N.W. of the former. It is situate near the river Ramgunga, which is fordable except in the rains, when it can be crossed, at about a mile from the village, by means of a sangha or wooden bridge. Lat. 29° 50′, long. 79° 20′.

GUNAISGURH.—A town in the Rajpoot state of Beekaneer, 119 miles N. by E. from Beekaneer, and 124 miles E. by N. from Bhawulpoor. Lat. 29° 40′, long. 73° 48′.

GUNBHUR.—A river rising in the south-western declivity of the Himalaya, in about lat. 30° 52′, long. 77° 8′. It takes a north-westerly course, and flows along the south-western base of the height on which Subathoo stands, and 1,300 feet below that station, about five miles beyond which it receives from the north-east its most considerable feeder. It continues its north-westerly course down the deep valley which separates the ridge of Ramgurh from that of Malown, and, after a course of about forty miles, falls into the Sutlej in lat. 31° 17′, long. 76° 47′.

GUNDEVEE, in the district of Broach, presidency of Bombay, a town and port situate on the estuary of the river Eeb, at which the British government possess the right of levying customs-duties. As the port, however, belongs in sovereignty to the Guicowar, the provisions of the British customs-laws have not been introduced therein. Lat. 20° 46′, long. 73° 2′.

GUNDLACAMA, a river of the Madras presidency, rising in lat. 15° 40′, long. 78° 49′, and, flowing in a very circuitous course for 155 miles, through the British collectorates Cuddapah, Nellore, and Guntoor, falls into the

Bay of Bengal thirteen miles west of the town of Ongole, and in lat. 15° 33′, long. 80° 18′.

GUNDLAPETTA.—A town in the Mysore, 42 miles S. from Seringapatam, and 89 miles E. from Cannanore. Lat. 11° 50′, long. 76° 44′.

GUNDOUS, or GOONDOSE, in the Rajpoot state of Joudpore, a town on the route from Nusseerabad to Deesa, and 120 miles S.W. of the former. It contains a good bazar. Lat. 25° 39′, long. 73° 31′.

GUNDUCK, SALAGRA, or NARAYANI.—A large river, flowing from the Himalaya, and falling into the Ganges. The position of its remotest source has probably not yet been indubitably ascertained. Buchanan says: "This is a grand river, the most remote source of which, named Damodarkund, is beyond the Snowy Mountains, in the territories of a chief of Bhotan or Thibet, named the Mastang Raja, and now tributary to Gorkha." The position of the source thus assigned is lat. 29° 40′, long. 83° 14′. Colebrooke, however, expresses a wish "that some traveller may be induced to visit the Himalaya in that quarter, and explore the great Gandhaki river to its source at the foot of Dhawalagiri;" a position laid down from trigonometrical operations in lat. 29° 11′, long. 82° 59′, or about half a degree farther south. After a long and winding course through the immense chasms of the Himalaya and the hills of inferior height south of them, and during which it receives numerous tributary streams, it is joined, at Nayakot, in lat. 27° 31′, long. 84° 5′, by the Trisoolgunga, which comes from the higher parts of the Himalaya north of Kathmandoo, and is considered by Buchanan to have the greater volume of water, though its course is the shorter of the two. From this point downwards it is navigable for canoes; and at Bhelaunji, ten miles below the confluence last named, becomes so for boats of considerable burthen. The length of course from its remotest source down to this point will be 200 miles. A short distance below this, it sweeps round the base of Maddar Mountain, in the Sub-Himalayan range. Buchanan describes the scenery there, as not to be surpassed. "The utmost magnificence, however, of rude nature that I have ever seen, is the view from the Gandaki, in passing up that river by the foot of Maddar. The river is larger, I think, than the Thames at Chelsea, and much finer, being perfectly clear. Its banks are partly abrupt rocks, partly levels covered with very stately forests, while every turn opens a new view of the snowy peaks seen over an endless variety of dark shaggy mountains, which in most countries would be considered as stupendous." He adds, that upon reaching the plains, it appears in the dry season to have quite as much water as the Ganges after the junction of the Jumna at Allahabad. In consequence of the height of the banks, the breadth does not much increase in the rainy season, but the current becomes so rapid as to give rise to danger. In the dry season the water is ten or twelve feet deep, and the current, although equable, is very strong, approaching near, but not reaching, that degree of rapidity which occasions a rippling noise; the water is perfectly clear, and the bottom consists chiefly of large water-worn pebbles. Though navigable continuously through its whole course downwards from Bhelaunji, there are in the part of its channel nearer that place many rapids and passes, where, the course being obstructed by rocks, navigation becomes difficult and dangerous. Near Bhelaunji it first touches the British territory, which for fifteen miles it divides from Nepaul; thence taking a south-easterly direction, forms for twenty miles the boundary between the districts of Goruckpore and Sarun; then for forty miles flows through Sarun, and again for seventeen miles forms the boundary between the two before-mentioned districts, when it again enters Sarun, through which it holds a circuitous course, but generally in a south-easterly direction, for forty-five miles, to lat. 26° 13′, long. 84° 58′, where it touches on the British district of Tirhoot, and continuing its circuitous but generally south-easterly course for sixty miles, during which it forms the boundary between the districts of Sarun and Tirhoot, it falls into the Ganges on the left side, in lat. 25° 39′, long. 85° 16′, at the town of Hajeepore, situate on the left bank, and opposite the city of Patna. According to the view of Buchanan, its length of course should be estimated at 407 miles. At its confluence with the Ganges, the latter is a wide expanse of water, probably not less than four miles in breadth, from Hajeepore on the north bank to Patna on the south, and having two large shifting banks or islands, which much perplex the navigation. It does not appear that the Gunduck, after leaving the mountains, receives any feeder of importance; but during the rainy season it inosculates right and left with many watercourses then traversing that alluvial country. Buchanan, in his report, drawn up above forty years ago, adverts to the great changes which the river-channel had undergone in the thirty years which had then elapsed since Rennell laid down the survey of that part of the Ganges. "The island, when Major Rennell made his survey, which was opposite to the cantonment of Danapur, seems to have been carried away; and that which was then situate east from it, in the middle of the river, now, in a great measure, adheres to the southern bank. In the rainy season, a passage still continues open; but in the fair season, its upper end becomes perfectly dry, and boats can no longer reach the Company's cloth-factory, situated on the former bank of the river. This island is now about six miles long, and where largest, about one broad. The main channel, passing round the north side of the above-mentioned island, does not now receive the Gandaki at Hajipur; a long, wide, and cultivated tongue of land projects from the west side of the Gandaki, and passing east about six miles from Hajipur, separates the stream of the Gandaki from the Ganges; but as in the rainy season a small channel separates this tongue from the northern shore, the union of the two rivers is still supposed to take place where it did formerly, and on the full moon of Kartik (seventh lunar month), the holy spot is frequented by immense multitudes; and at Hariharchhatra, on the west bank of the Gandaki, opposite to Hajipur, there is then held a very great fair, especially for horses." In Tassin's great map of Bengal and Behar (Calcutta, 1841), the tongue of land mentioned above is represented as severed from the northern bank by the main stream of the Ganges restored to its former channel. In lat. 27° 9′, long. 84° 9′, 160 miles above its mouth, the Gunduck is crossed, at the village of Butsura, by the route from Goruckpore to Mullye, the passage being made by ferry. The Gunduck is mentioned by Baber as a line of defence taken up by the Bengalese to resist his invasion.

GUNDUCK CHOTA, or LESSER GUNDUCK, so called in distinction from the greater Gunduck, flowing a little farther to the east. It is called Burha Gunduck, or Old Gunduck, from a notion of the natives that it at one time formed part of the course of the Great Gunduck, though, as Buchanan observes, it is impossible, in consequence of intervening mountains, that there could have been any communication between the streams. The Chota Gunduck rises from a fine perennial fountain at the base of a mountain, near the northern boundary of the district of Goruckpore, and about lat. 27° 20′, long. 83° 50′. It holds a sinuous course, but generally in a southerly direction, and, fifty-two miles from its source, according to Buchanan, is "little sunk below the surface, and towards the end of February (dry season) contained a pretty clear stream, about forty feet wide, and more than knee-deep;" and fifty-six miles lower down, or 108 from its source, "the Lesser Gunduck in some parts is a channel 100 yards wide, which in March contains a clear, gentle stream, thirty yards wide and two feet deep, running on pure sand; in other parts it is much narrower, the channel being clay; and there the water is deep, but even in November (close of the rainy season) nearly stagnant, and rather dirty." At about 150 miles from its source, and seventeen from its mouth, according to the same author, "this river may be 150 or 200 yards wide. At all seasons it may be navigated by canoes, although it has little current and is full of weeds; and in the rainy season boats of 1,000 maunds (thirty-six tons) burden could frequent it." It receives numerous small streams right and left, and communicates by lateral channels with several of the watercourses which abound in this level and alluvial tract, and, having flowed altogether about 170 miles, falls into the Gogra on the left side, in lat. 26° 1′, long. 84° 12′.

GUNDUK (THE LITTLE). — A river rising on the northern boundary of the British district of Sarun, presidency of Bengal, near Fort Soomeysur, in lat. 27° 22′, long. 84° 22′. Flowing in a south-easterly direction for about 120 miles, it, in lat. 26° 16′, long. 85° 18′, leaves the district of Sarun and enters that of Tirhoot, which it traverses in the same direction for about seventy miles, to its junction with the Bagmuttee, in lat. 25° 45′, long. 86° 2′.

GUNGA.—A considerable watercourse of the Ganges, leaving that river in lat. 28° 6′, long. 78° 34′, and flowing in a south-easterly course for fifty miles, during which it divides the Budaon collectorate from those of Allygurh and Mynpooree, enters the district of Furruckabad, which it traverses for forty-five miles, and then rejoins the parent stream, in lat. 27° 26′, long. 79° 39′.

GUNGA BAL.—A small lake in Cashmere, on the Haramuk Mountain, on the north-eastern boundary of the valley. It is a mile and a half long, and two or three hundred yards wide. Its appearance presents nothing remarkable, and its dimensions, it has been seen, are inconsiderable; but it is regarded with a superstitious veneration of the deepest kind by the Hindoos. Pilgrims flock to its banks, and into its waters are thrown such fragments of bone as remain undestroyed by the fires lighted by Hindoo feeling to consume the fleshly habitation from which the spirit has departed. Lat. 34° 27′, long. 74° 58′.

GUNGAPERSAD.—A town in the British district of Purneah, lieut.-gov. of Bengal, 43 miles S. of Purneah. Lat. 25° 10′, long. 87° 38′.

GUNGAPOORA.—A town in the Rajpoot state of Oodeypoor, 92 miles S.S.W. from Ajmeer, and 106 miles S.E. from Jodhpoor. Lat. 25° 13′, long. 74° 21′.

GUNGAVULLY.—A river of Bombay, rising in lat. 15° 45′, long. 75° 10′, a few miles south-east from Dharwar, and, flowing in a south-westerly direction for thirty-five miles through Dharwar, and sixty-five miles through North Canara, falls into the Indian Ocean, in lat. 14° 36′, long. 74° 23′.

GUNGAWUTTEE.—A town in one of the recently sequestrated districts of Hyderabad, or the dominions of the Nizam, situate on the left bank of the Toongabudra river, and 30 miles N.W. from Bellary. Lat. 15° 26′, long. 76° 38′.

GUNGE.—A town in the British district of Cuttack, lieut.-gov. of Bengal, 58 miles E.N.E. of Cuttack. Lat. 20° 45′, long. 86° 46′.

GUNGEEREE, in the British district of Allyghur, lieut.-gov. of the N.W. Provinces, a small town on the route, by Khasganj, from Bareilly to Allyghur cantonment, and 26 miles S.E. of the latter, 54 miles N.E. of Agra. It has a bazar and a market. Lat. 27° 51′, long. 78° 31′.

GUNGEROO, in the British district of Muzufurnugur, lieut.-gov. of the N.W. Provinces, a village in the narrow tract between the Doab Canal on the east and the river Jumna on the west, and four miles W. of the former, three E. of the latter. Lat. 29° 18′, long. 77° 17′.

GUNGHUN.—A river rising in the British district of Bijnour, in lat. 29° 39′, long. 78° 31′, and, after a direct south-westerly course of about seventy miles, falls into the Uril on the left side, in lat. 28° 25′, long. 79° 1′. It has a considerable stream, running between steep banks, and is unfordable in the rains, but fordable in many places during the dry season.

GUNGOH, in the British district of Suharunpoor, lieut.-gov. of the N.W. Provinces, a town, the principal place of the pergunnah of the same name, containing a population of 6,260 inhabitants, and situate in lat. 29° 46′, long. 77° 20′.

GUNGOLEE HATH, in the British district of Kumaon, lieut.-gov. of the N.W. Provinces, a small market-town, or rather village, on the route from Almorah cantonment to Petoragurh, 34 miles N.E. of the former. Water is obtained from a baoli or great well. Lat. 29° 40′, long. 80° 5′.

GUNGPOOR, in the British district of Cawnpore, lieut.-gov. of the N.W. Provinces, a village on the route from Cawnpore to Futehgurh, and 39 miles S.E. of the latter. Lat. 26° 57′, long. 80° 4′.

GUNGRANA.—A town in the Rajpoot state of Jodhpoor, 57 miles E. by N. from Jodhpoor, and 46 miles W. from Ajmeer. Lat. 26° 34′, long. 73° 59′.

GUNGURAR.—A town in the Rajpoot state of Jhalawar, on the right bank of the Chota Kallee Sind river, and 122 miles W.N.W. from Bhopal. Lat. 23° 54′, long. 75° 39′.

GUNJOOLY, in Hydrabad, or territory of the Nizam, a town 60 miles W. of the town of Beeder, 128 N.W. of the city of Hydrabad. Lat. 17° 55′, long. 76° 42′.

GUNJUNSIR.—A town in the native state of Cutch, 45 miles N.W. from Bhooj, and 107 S.E. from Tatta. Lat. 23° 39′, long. 69° 10′.

GUNNAIRY.—A town in Hyderabad, or territory of the Nizam, on the left bank of the Payne Gunga river, and 177 miles N. from Hyderabad. Lat. 19° 54′, long. 78° 33′.

GUNNAPOOR.—A town in the territory of Oude, two miles from the right bank of the river Gogra, and 71 miles N. by E. from Lucknow. Lat. 27° 50′, long. 81° 20′.

GUNNEA GURH.—A town in one of the Cuttack Mehals of Orissa, situate 65 miles W. from Cuttack, on the right bank of the Mahanuddee river. Lat. 20° 24′, long. 85° 6′.

GUNNUPWARRUM.—A town in the British district of Rajahmundry, presidency of Madras, 40 miles W.N.W. of Rajahmundry. Lat. 17° 11′, long. 81° 20′.

GUNOOR GURH.—A town in the native state of Bhopal, 14 miles N.W. from Hoosungabad, and 30 miles S.S.E. from Bhopal. Lat. 22° 50′, long. 77° 32′.

GUNOUR, in the British district of Paneeput, lieut.-gov. of the N.W. Provinces, a village or small town on the route from Delhi to Kurnoul, and 36 miles N. of the former. It is surrounded by a ruined wall, but otherwise has, according to Barr, a pleasing appearance:—"The approach to Gunnour, where we halted, is extremely picturesque; a few huts on a rising ground, overhung by some large and drooping trees, bounding one side of the prospect, the other being formed by a large and handsome caravanserai, with its embattled wall and towers reflected on the surface of a beautifully clear tank." Lat. 29° 7′, long. 77° 3′.

GUNRORA.—A small river, rising in the hill state of Hindoor, amidst the lower range of the Himalaya, about lat. 31° 9′, long. 76° 54′. It takes a north-westerly direction, along the north-eastern base of the high steep ridge of Malown, which separates it from the Gunbhur, holding a parallel course at a distance of about three miles. The Gunrora, after a course of about fifteen miles, falls into the Sutlej, in lat. 31° 17′, long. 76° 48′.

GUNTOOR, a collectorate under the presidency of Madras, is bounded on the north by the Kistna river, which separates it from the Nizam's dominions and the British district of Masulipatam; on the south by Nellore and the Bay of Bengal; on the east by Masulipatam; and on the west by the Cuddapah collectorate and the territory of the Nizam. It lies between lat. 15° 37′ and 16° 50′, and long. 79° 15′—80° 59′, and the area, according to official return, is 4,960 square miles. The seacoast of this district extends from Gollapalem, in a direction from south-west to north-east, for thirty miles, and subsequently in a direction, first eastward, and afterwards south-eastward, for about twenty-five miles more, to the principal mouth of the Kistna. This coast is generally called the Golconda coast, which is understood to commence at about lat. 15° 20′, and to proceed northwards, in contradistinction to the coast of Coromandel, which extends from the limit just named to the vicinity of Adam's Bridge. The coast is so low as not to be easily distinguished at a safe distance, and is, moreover, beset by an extensive and dangerous bank, called the Shoal of Motapilly. In consequence of these dangers and impediments to navigation, this coast, for an extent of fifty-four miles, is scarcely frequented by shipping, especially during the north-east monsoon, which prevails throughout October, November, and December. The principal river is the Kistna. This river, formerly little available for irrigation, has recently, through the liberal efforts of the government, become an important and valuable instrument for diffusing fertility over the adjacent country. To navigation, the violence of its current, and the varying, uncertain depth of its stream, are great impediments. The other rivers are the Gundama, the Nullamuda, the Nagoler, and the Pillaur; but these are merely torrents, nearly or entirely dry during the hot season. Tanks, or artificial lakes, are not numerous, though of importance for irrigation. This district lies within the influence of the south-west and north-east monsoons. The former commences in May, and occasional rains continue till the month of August, moderating the heat of the land-winds, which blow sometimes with great force across this part of the country. A great quantity of rain also falls in the months of September, October, and November. The heat at Guntoor is greatest from the middle of March to the middle of June. The zoology of Guntoor is meagre, there being fewer wild animals in this part of India than in almost any other. Cholum (Holcus sorghum) is the staple alimentary crop of the district, and rice in considerable quantity is grown in the low tracts along the seashore and the courses of the river; bajra (Holcus spicatus) is also grown in considerable quantities; besides oil-seeds, turmeric, onions, capsicum, and various esculent vegetables. The principal commercial crops are betel, tobacco, and cotton. Cotton cloths are manufactured to a considerable extent, and exported to the territory of the Nizam, as well as to the British districts. The cattle of Guntoor are in great repute, and bullocks are exported in great numbers. The population is given under the article MADRAS PRESIDENCY.

Guntoor constitutes the southern portion of the maritime tract known as the Five Northern Circars, which were ceded to the East-India Company, in 1765, by the emperor of Delhi. The grant, however, was not rendered available in respect to Guntoor until 1788, when the Nizam surrendered the circar, and the British thus became possessed of the whole line of coast from Juggernaut to Comorin. The great northern route from Madras to Masulipatam and the Northern Circars passes through this district, and sends a branch to the left, or north-west, to Hyderabad. Guntoor, the principal place, Nizampatam, and Vinukonda, are described under their respective names in the alphabetical arrangement.

GUNTOOR, the principal place of the British district of the same name, in the territory subject to the presidency of Madras, is situate about 18 miles S.W. of the right bank of the great river Kistna, and 30 from the Coromandel coast, or western shore of the Bay of Bengal. The surrounding country is open and flat, but free from swamps or stagnant water; and to these circumstances is owing the salubrity by which it is characterized. The soil of the country around is black, and produces luxuriant crops of gram (Cicer arietinum), cholum (Holcus sorghum), and cotton. The place is divided into what are called the Old Town and New Town, both very irregularly built, and in general much overcrowded, especially in those parts inhabited by the poorer classes. The population is estimated at 20,000. Distance from Bangalore, N.E., 300 miles; Masulipatam, W., 47; Ongole, N., 63; Nellore, N., 133; Madras, N., 225. Lat. 16° 18', long. 80° 30'.

GUNWAN, in the British district of Budaon, lieut.-gov. of the N.W. Provinces, a village on the route from Allygurh to Moradabad, and 40 miles S.W. of the latter. It has a few shops and a weekly market. Lat. 28° 25', long. 78° 25'.

GUNYSH BUL, in Cashmere, a place of Hindoo devotion, at the eastern extremity of the valley, on the route to the celebrated cave of Amur Nath. According to Vigne, the name signifies "the place of Gunysh," or Ganesa, the only son of Siva. The object of superstition is a large fragment of rock lying in the Lidur river, and worn by the current into what the Hindoos fancy a representation of an elephant's head, to which a trunk, ears, and eyes have been added by human art. The superstitious feeling caused by this object results from the belief that Ganesa has the head of an elephant. Here, the pilgrims proceeding to Amur Nath make their preparatory ablutions and prostrations. Gunysh Bul is in lat. 33° 58', long. 75° 31'.

GUOCHNAUT.—A town in Guzerat, or territory of the Guicowar, on the left bank of the river Bunnass, and 50 miles S.W. from Deesa. Lat. 23° 45', long. 71° 31'.

GURANG, in the Daman division of the Punjab, a town situated on the right bank of the Indus, 74 miles N.W. by N. of the town of Mooltan. Lat. 31° 11', long. 70° 46'.

GURDANGERRY.—A town in the Mysore, 80 miles N.N.W. from Seringapatam, and 104 miles E.N.E. from Mangalore. Lat. 13° 29', long. 76° 18'.

GURDEGA.—A town in the native state of Bamra, on the south-west frontier of Bengal, 52 miles N.N.E. from Sumbulpoor, and 95 miles S.S.W. from Lohadugga. Lat. 22° 7', long. 84° 25'.

GURGURREE.—A town in the British district of Bhagulpoor, lieut.-gov. of Bengal, 72 miles S.W. of Rajmahal. Lat. 24° 23', long. 86° 55'.

GURGUZGUR.—A town in the British province of Nagpoor, 64 miles N.W. by N. from Nagpoor, and 48 miles E. by N. from Baitool. Lat. 21° 59', long. 78° 40'.

GURH, in the province of Boghelcund, district of Rewa, a village on the direct route from Mirzapoor to the diamond-mines of Punna, and 65 miles S.W. of the former. Elevation above the sea 1,036 feet. Lat. 24° 50', long. 81° 42'.

GURHEA.—A town in the British district of Beerbhoom, lieut.-gov. of Bengal, 138 miles N.W. of Calcutta. Lat. 24°, long. 86° 59'.

GURHEE DOODHLEE.—See DOODHLI.

GURHOREE.—A town in the British province of Nagpoor, late dominions of the rajah of Berar, 67 miles S.E. by S. from Nagpoor, and 149 miles E.S.E. from Ellichpoor. Lat. 20° 19′, long. 79° 39′.

GURKHOOEEA.—A town in the territory of Oude, on the left bank of the river Gogra, and 44 miles E. from Lucknow. Lat. 27°, long. 81° 41′.

GURMUKTESAR, or GURMUKTESWAR, in the British district of Meerut, the principal place of the pergunnah of the same name, on the route from the town of Meerut to Moradabad, and 31 miles S.E. of the former. The population is returned at 8,781 persons. It is situate on the right bank of the Ganges, four miles below the reunion of the Burha Ganga, or old course of the Ganges, with the present main channel, which, a mile and a half above the town is crossed by a much-frequented ferry, on which fifteen boats constantly ply. It may be regarded as the port of Meerut and the adjoining part of the Doab, as the Ganges is the channel of considerable inland navigation from the sea to this ferry, and in a less degree to Sukurtal, fifty miles higher up. Both banks of the river are for several miles in width overgrown with a thick grassy jungle, infested in the dry season with tigers and other wild beasts, and in the rainy season laid extensively under water by the swollen stream. Even in the dry season, when the larger craft cannot proceed higher than Furruckabad, about 150 miles lower down, Gurmuktesar can be reached by boats admitting of some comfortable accommodation to the traveller. That in which Lumsden proceeded in the dry season from this place to Calcutta, was of about twenty tons burthen, forty feet in length, ten in breadth, and navigated by a master and eight rowers. The road from Gurmuktesar westward towards Meerut is good. Distance N.W. from Calcutta 887 miles. Lat. 28° 47′, long. 78° 10′.

GURNADDEE.—A town in the British district of Bakergunje, lieut.-gov. of Bengal, 120 miles E. by N. of Calcutta. Lat. 22° 59′, long. 90° 15′.

GUROWLEE.—See GEROLI.

GURRA.—A town in the Rajpoot state of Jodhpoor, on the right bank of the Loonee river, and 120 miles S.W. from Jodhpoor. Lat. 25° 11′, long. 71° 42′.

GURRAH, or DEOHA.—A river rising at the northern base of the Sub-Himalaya, in lat. 29° 9′, long. 79° 49′, in the British district of Kumaon, under the lieutenant-governorship of the North-Western Provinces. It takes a southerly course of 240 miles, passing by the towns of Pilleebheet and Shahjehanpoor, and through the British districts of Bareilly and Shahjehanpoor, into the Oude territory, in which it falls into the Western Ramgunga, on the left side, in lat. 27° 12′, long. 79° 58′. At Pillibheet, sixty miles from the source, its bed is 250 yards wide, with a sandy bottom, and the depth so inconsiderable, that it is fordable from December to June; but for the rest of the year it can be crossed only by ferry. Forty-five miles lower down, where crossed by the route from Bareilly to Mahomdy, its dimensions are the same as above mentioned. At Shahjehanpoor, forty-five miles farther, it is fordable at some seasons, but generally crossed by ferry. Fifty miles still lower down, where crossed by the route from Futtehghur to Seetapore, in lat. 27° 32′, long. 79° 55′, it is sometimes forded, sometimes crossed by ferry.

GURRAH, in the British territory of Saugor and Nerbudda, a town situate on the right bank of the Nerbudda, near the town of Jubbulpoor. Fitzclarence states that it "is built in a most singular pass, and extends through and along the face of a mountainous ridge about two miles." With the town of Mandla, farther to the south-east, it gave name to that portion of Gondwana once known by the name of Gurha Mandla. Abulfazl mentions, that in his time, about the middle of the sixteenth century, the adjacent country was under forest, harbouring great numbers of wild elephants, though at present in that region those creatures are not known in a state of nature. Elevation above the sea about 1,400 feet. Distant S.E. from Saugor 90 miles; S.W. from Allahabad 200; S. from Agra 303; N.E. from Nagpoor 145; W. from Mow 273. Lat. 23° 7′, long. 79° 58′.

GURRAWARRA.—See BURRA GURRAWARA.

GURREE, in Sinde, a village on the route from Roree to Jessulmair, and 14 miles S.E. of the former place. It is situate on the northern boundary of the Thurr or Great Sandy Desert, and about three miles east of the left bank of the Eastern Narra, a great offset of the Indus. This stream in time of inundation is here fifty yards wide and twenty feet deep, but it becomes nearly dry at other times. Gurree has about a dozen shops, and is capable of furnishing supplies in moderate quantity. Lat. 27° 31′, long. 69° 4′.

GURREHOO, in the Saugor and Nerbudda territory, lieut.-gov. of the N.W. Provinces, a village on the route from Mirzapoor to Saugor, 211 miles S.W. of former, 76 N.E. of latter. Elevation above the sea 1,131 feet. Lat. 24° 14′, long. 79° 51′.

GURR KOHOOREE.—A town in the British district of Ganjam, presidency of Madras, 38 miles N.E. by N. of Ganjam. Lat. 19° 52′, long. 85° 25′.

GURR KOOSPULLA.—A town in the British district of Pooree, lieut.-gov. of Bengal, 36 miles W.S.W. of Cuttack. Lat. 20° 13′, long. 85° 28′.

GURR TAPPING.—A town in the British district of Pooree, lieut.-gov. of Bengal, 32 miles S.W. of Cuttack. Lat. 20° 5′, long. 85° 40′.

GURRUMAREA.—A town in the British

district of Maldah, lieut.-gov. of Bengal, 14 miles S.E. of Maldah. Lat. 24° 52′, long. 88° 18′.

GURRUSGOAN.—A town in one of the recently sequestrated districts of Hyderabad, or territory of the Nizam, 30 miles E. by S. from Ellichpoor, and 74 miles W. from Nagpoor. Lat. 21° 4′, long. 78°.

GURUDWARA, in the British district of Dehra Doon, a large village, agreeably situate, and having a pleasing appearance. Here is a handsome temple, founded by a Sikh devotee. During the festival of the Holi, an annual fair held here is numerously attended by pilgrims from the Punjaub and other Sikh countries. About half a mile north of the village, was fought, in 1803, the battle which decided the war between the Goorkha invaders and the rajah of Gurhwal, who was slain on the field, and whose death was immediately followed by the submission of the country. Lat. 30° 20′, long. 78° 7′.

GURWAH.—A town in the British district of Palamow, presidency of Bengal, 28 miles N.W. of Palamow. Lat. 24° 10′, long. 83° 46′.

GURWAR, in the British district of Ghazepoor, lieut.-gov. of the N.W. Provinces, a town on the route from Azimgurh to Dinapoor, 57 miles E.S.E. of the former. Lat. 25° 46′, long. 84° 5′.

GURWHAL (BRITISH).—See KUMAON.

GURWHAL, a hill state under British protection, is bounded on the north by Bussahir and Hiundes, or South-western Thibet; on the east by British Gurwhal; on the south by British Gurwhal and the Dehra Doon; and on the west by the Dehra Doon, the pergunnah of Jaunsar, and Bussahir. It is about ninety-five miles in length from north to south, and seventy in breadth from east to west; contains about 4,500 square miles, and lies between lat. 30° 2′—31° 20′, long. 77° 55′—79° 20′. It extends over the south-western declivity of the Himalaya, and is throughout a vast range of mountains of enormous height, intermingled with several valleys, the drainage of the whole ultimately finding its way to the Ganges. The principal channels are those of the Tonse, of the Jumna, and of the Bhageerettee, one of the remote sources of the Ganges. The most elevated part of the country is the north and north-east, where the peaks about the Tonse, the Jumnotri peaks, and several others, are more than 20,000 feet above the sea. The highest summit is probably the peak of Kedarnath, having an elevation of 23,062 feet. Rikkee-Kasee, nearly parallel with the southern boundary, is the lowest spot in the territory, being only 1,377 feet above the sea. It is the point where the Ganges touches upon the Dehra Doon. The confluence of the Tonse and Jumna, which is the lowest point of the aggregate of valleys drained by those rivers, is rather higher than Rikkee-Kasee, being 1,686 feet above the sea. A few small tracts, extending along the lower courses of the Bhageerettee and Aluknunda, and the Jumna previously to its confluence with the Tonse, have elevations less than 5,000 feet; but by much the greater part of the country lies considerably above that height. The rivers of Gurwhal—the Tons, Jumna, Bhageerettee, Bhillung, Mandakini, Aluknunda, Aglar, Pabur, Rupin, Soong, Budiar, and Banal—are separately adverted to in the alphabetical arrangement. The climate of Gurwhal is hot in the low tracts along the banks of the Aluknunda, on the southern frontier, where Raper, in the beginning of May, found the thermometer to reach 101° in the shade. In the lower mountains, having an elevation of from 5,000 to 8,000 feet, the climate is moderate, the thermometer seldom exceeding 75° in the hottest part of the year. In midwinter, frosts are frequent, with occasional falls of snow. The periodical or monsoon rains are very heavy, commencing in the middle of June and ending towards the middle of September. The northern part of the territory, containing the lofty peaks of the Himalayas, rises beyond the limits of perpetual congelation. In the higher mountains bears are common; the lower are infested, in addition to these, by leopards and tigers. Monkeys are numerous, even as high as Sookhee, which has an elevation of 8,869 feet, and is in lat. 31°. According to Skinner, they are not venerated by the inhabitants of the mountains, as in some other parts of India.

The rural economy of the natives of Gurwhal varies with the nature of the soil and the degrees of elevation. Scarcely any fruit-trees are cultivated except the walnut, apricot, and mulberry; but the second is of very indifferent quality, and the last-named is cultivated for the leaves, not with a view to the production of silk, but to be used as fodder for cattle. In the low ground, capable of irrigation and having a warm climate, rice is the principal crop. Besides small quantities of sugarcane and of cotton, there are raised ginger, turmeric, sweet potato, and hemp, the latter cultivated for the supply of bhang, as well as for the fibre. In more elevated tracts, where the surface on the mountain-slopes is generally formed into artificial terraces by embankments, the crops are wheat, barley, buckwheat, battu or amaranthus, mundua or Eleusine coracana, a remarkably prolific plant; pulse of various sorts, and oil-seeds. The poppy is very generally cultivated, either for opium or the seed, which is a favourite food of the natives. The plough is no better than a forked log, drawn by oxen, guided by women; and the ground is rather scratched than ploughed. The ears of corn when ripe are cut off the stalks, which are then eaten down by kine, kept either for their milk or for labour, as the influence of Brahminical prejudices causes their slaughter to be regarded as impious. They are very small, of dark-brown colour, short-horned, and with a hump on the withers like those of Hindostan. The sheep, also small, are of a brown colour and coarsewoolled ; the goats large, and generally white. No family is without a dog, of dark-brown colour, middle size, well covered with strong hair, and of a mongrel aspect. Horses are rare,—even the ghunt or mountain pony ; and asses are unknown. The houses are substantially built of layers of stone and squared beams placed alternately. They have generally three stories, each from six to seven feet high. The lowest shelters the cattle, the middle is used as a granary, and the family resides in the upper story, the accommodation of which is enlarged by a strongly-constructed gallery all round. The roof, nearly flat, is generally of slabs or coarse slate laid on thick beams, and projects over both walls and gallery. The communication between the floors is by steep stairs, or rather ladders.

The natives of Gurwhal are in general below the middle size, their stature (according to one traveller) rarely exceeding five feet. Their complexions are less dark than those of the Hindoos of the plains: on the other hand, while red or brown hair may sometimes be observed among the latter, the hue of the hair and beard in Gurwhal is almost invariably dark. The beard is scanty, especially on the cheeks, not strong on the upper lip, fullest on the chin. It is most deficient in men having the Mongolian aspect, who in some instances show no trace of this appendage of the male. On the contrary, those who have long narrow faces, prominent aquiline noses, and fully-developed foreheads, are best provided with beards. They are, according to Jacquemont, a mild, peaceable, timid race, remarkably devoid of mental energy, and living tranquilly, without any control from fixed law, and very little from authority of any kind. Others, however, do not represent them as so strongly marked with those features of the golden age. Frazer relates, that coming to a village where only women, children, and decrepit men were found, on asking them what had become of the able-bodied part of the population, he received for answer, "that they had gone to buy corn or steal sheep," with a tone and manner indicating that they spoke of nothing extraordinary or requiring apology. Hodgson also states that they plunder their eastern neighbours of the Kedarnath districts, and pride themselves on such exploits. This writer reports them to have neither fire-arms swords, nor war-hatchets ; their only weapons being bows and arrows.

According to the traditional account given to Frazer, Gurwhal was originally divided into above twenty petty states, which, about 500 years ago, were consolidated into one by a bold and rapacious adventurer from the plains. Previously to the Goorkha invasion in 1803, the dominions of the rajah of Gurwhal comprised, in addition to his present territory, the fertile district of Dehra Doon, and the western portion (being about one-half) of the present British province of Kumaon. The Goorkha force which invaded the country, conducted by several veteran commanders, was very inadequately opposed by Purdumin Sah, the rajah, an indolent and unwarlike prince, who, at the head of 12,000 men, was defeated and slain at Gurudwara, in the Dehra Doon. On the occurrence of this event, the inhabitants of Gurwhal discontinued all resistance to the Goorkhas, who made ruthless use of their victory. According to Frazer, they in the course of about twelve years sold 200,000 of the people into slavery ; but this is palpably an exaggeration, as a population not exceeding 300,000 could scarcely have been capable of supplying two-thirds of that number of saleable slaves in twelve years. The number, however, of the unhappy victims of the cupidity of the conquerors was no doubt very great, as Moorcroft found the fertile traot about the Terrai quite depopulated, in consequence of the deportation and sale of the natives as slaves by the Goorkhas. Sheeo Dursun Shah, the son of the slain rajah, had fled the country after the fatal battle which had given it to the Goorkhas. In 1815, when the success of the East-India Company's army had put an end to the Goorkha dominion, this prince was restored to the western portion of the territory formerly enjoyed by his family. The Dehra Doon, on the south, was reserved to the East-India Company, as was also Eastern Gurwhal. The portion of Gurwhal restored to the rajah is divided from the remainder, on the east, by a line which, commencing in lat. 31° 5′, long. 79° 20′, with a south-westerly direction, skirts the great glacier giving rise to the Bhageerettee, and thence continued southward to the source of the Mandakini, follows the course of that river to its confluence with the Aluknunda, along the line of which it proceeds to its junction with the Bhageerettee, and in a westerly direction down the last-mentioned river to Rikkee-Kasee, where it touches upon the Dehra-Doon. The rajah holds his territory subordinate to the East-India Company. The amount of the population of native states can rarely be ascertained with any approach to precision: that of the rajah's portion of Gurwhal probably does not much exceed 100,000. This, however, is an estimate based on grounds purely conjectural ; but if near the truth, it will give a proportion of about twenty-two to the square mile. The annual income is stated by Prinsep at 40,000 rupees (4,000*l.*) ; by Moorcroft, at 60,000 (6,000*l.*) ; by De Cruz, at a lac (10,000*l.*).

GURYS, in Bultistan or Little Thibet, is situate close to the northern boundary of Kashmir : it is an elevated valley, five miles long and one mile wide. The upper part of the Kishengunga flows in a direction from east to west along the bottom of the valley, which, though 7,200 feet above the sea, is surrounded by lofty and very abrupt peaks, chiefly of limestone. Lat. 34° 33′, long. 74° 50′.

GUTNI, in the territory of Oude, a town on the left bank of the Ganges, here crossed by ferry, on route from Banda to Pertaubgurh, 92 miles N.E. of the former, 44 W. of the latter. It is perhaps the Gotini of Butter. Lat. 25° 42′, long. 81° 27′.

GUTPURBA. — A river rising in lat. 15° 50′, long. 74° 3′, on the eastern slope of the Western Ghats, and, flowing in a north-easterly direction for 160 miles through the British district of Belgaum, and intersecting the Southern Mahratta jaghire of Moodhul, falls into the Kistnah, in lat. 16° 20′, long. 75° 52′. The material for a wire-rope bridge, proposed to be thrown across this river, at Sootguttee, by a native gentleman, named Sirdar Sukum Gourab Wunkmoonka, was shipped from England in 1850.

GUZERAT.—This large province, inclusive of the peninsula of Kattywar, and comprehending within its limits, together with several petty independent states, the whole dominions of the Guicowar, and those of his tributaries, is bounded on the north by the Gulf of Cutch and Rajpootona; on the south by the Indian Ocean, the Gulf of Cambay, and sundry collectorates of the Bombay presidency; on the east by Candeish and Malwa; and on the west by Cutch and the sea. It extends from lat. 20° to 24° 45′, and from long. 69° to 74° 20′, and contains an area of 41,536 square miles, as will be seen from the following table :—

	Sq. Miles.
Guicowar's territory, and Kattywar	24,249
Myhee Caunta	3,400
Rewa Caunta	4,879
Pahlunpore	1,850
Radhunpore	850
Balasinore	258
Cambay	500
The Daung	950
Chourar	225
Bansda	325
Peint and Hursool	750
Dhurrunpore	225
Thurraud and other petty states N.W. frontier	2,325
Sucheen	300
Wusravee, and adjacent territory	450
	41,536

Of the extensive region marked out by those boundaries, a considerable portion is occupied by the Gulf of Cambay, and by the British district of Ahmedabad, which, extending about the gulf, is on all sides, except seaward, inclosed by the territory of the Guicowar. Of the whole territory, 19,850 square miles are stated to be comprised within the peninsula, or that part which may be marked off from the continent by a line drawn from the head of the Gulf of Cutch to the head of the Gulf of Cambay. The mainland of Guzerat, as contradistinguished from the peninsula, has some considerable rivers, which intersect or skirt the country. Among them may be enumerated the Saburmuttee, the Bunass, the Myhee, the Nerbudda, and the Taptee.

Of the mountains, the most important are the Western Ghauts, which, running in a direction from south to north, constitute the eastern boundary of the territory, from its southern limit, in lat. 20°, to lat. 21° 28′, where, turning eastward, they form the lofty brow inclosing the valley of the Taptee on the south. The average elevation of these mountains is about 1,200 feet, though the height of some summits is probably not less than 2,000 feet. From the western face of the Ghauts proceed numerous spurs or ridges of inferior elevation, a few of them reaching to the sea; and in some parts they are replaced by isolated hills or rocks, such as those of Parnera, Rola, and several others, the elevation of which seldom exceeds 300 or 400 feet. North of the Taptee, the Satpoora range, dividing the valley of that river from the valley of the Nerbudda, extends for some distance into this territory, terminating to the westward near Rajpeepla. North of the valley of the Nerbudda, is the western extremity of the Vindhya Mountains, expanding into the Barreea Hills, low and irregularly grouped; and still farther north, into those of Loonawara. Beyond these, in the same direction, are those of Dongurpore, becoming ultimately united to Mount Aboo. The overlying formation of the northern section of the Ghauts is volcanic, as is also that of the Satpoora range, and consists for the most part of trap. The trappean formation extends into the peninsula of Kattywar, where it forms the bold mountain of Palithana, celebrated for its numerous Jain temples. Farther westward, granite is met with, rising to an elevation of 2,500 feet, in the celebrated Girnar Mountain, "an immense bare and isolated granite rock, presenting all the gigantic masses peculiar to that formation." The lower parts of the mountain, as well as the vicinity, are overlaid with soft limestone. The island of Perim, in the Gulf of Cambay, formed of sandstone, is remarkable for containing numerous organic remains. The mineral wealth of this extensive tract is but scanty, and calls for little notice; the most important production is iron-ore, raised in the peninsula. The mouth of the Taptee, and probably the whole bed of the Gulf of Cambay, abounds in a black sand, very rich in iron, and containing some platina. At Rajpeepla, the finest cornelians are obtained in great abundance. In the southern districts, the proximity of the sea, and the mountains covered with jungle or forests, moderate and equalize the temperature. The most disagreeable season is during the south-west monsoon, when the atmosphere, loaded with moisture, causes very distressing sensations and maladies, the effects being most severely felt during the night. In the inland districts, in the north of the territory, between the rivers Nerbudda and Saburmuttee, the average temperature is greater than in the southern districts. In this sultry tract, the hot winds blow from about the 20th of March to the 20th of May, and at this time the thermometer in a double-walled tent rises often to 115°, and in the house to 103°. Many, as well natives as Europeans, suffer from coup de soleil, and in parts where the soil is loose, the heat is rendered more annoying by the profusion of fine sand borne along by the wind. Throughout the district, the weather becomes cooler towards the end of October, and in the cold season hoar frosts are not uncommon. The climate of the peninsula, particularly in the Geer, is marked by insalubrity to such an extent as almost inevitably to cause death to those who are so rash as to expose themselves to it in the season following the autumnal monsoon. The shores of the Gulf of Cambay are also generally malarious.

The zoology of Guzerat is varied and interesting. The lion is not uncommon, and equals in size and strength the same description of animal in Africa. It is observed to have a less mane ; but this circumstance is considered to result from its frequenting the thick jungles instead of the open desert, the usual resort of his African fellow. Tigers and leopards are very numerous, and destructive of both men and cattle. There are also the wolf, hyæna, antelope, and deer in great number and variety. The nylgau (Antilope picta) is common in the northern parts, where there are large herds of them. Of birds, there are the flamingo, argala or adjutant-bird, sarus or gigantic crane, and a great variety of aquatic birds. Of domestic animals, the principal are the camel, most common north of the Saburmuttee and in the plains in the vicinity of the deserts of Rajpootana. It is also met with in the western part of the peninsula. The buffalo is everywhere to be met, but in greater abundance and excellence in the south. Kine are numerous, but in the southern part are of inferior quality, while in the northern the breed is very fine, not being excelled by any in Britain. The ass is small and weak ; but in the wilds of the north-west, the wild ass is a creature of great speed, as well as of considerable beauty, and is sometimes tamed for purposes of show and pomp. The horse of Kattywar was formerly highly prized ; but the breed has degenerated, and the Guzerat horse at present bred by the natives is in no esteem, being small, weak, and ugly. In some of the jungly valleys and wilds, there is a breed of wild cattle, different from the bison, and far less fierce.

The crops, alimentary as well as commercial, grown in this territory, are very important. Of the alimentary, rice is more or less common in all districts under the hills, and in the alluvial soil along the seacoast throughout the whole extent of the province. It is also much cultivated about the river Saburmuttee. Wheat is very extensively grown, especially in the northern part, and in the country between the Taptee and the Nerbudda. Barley thrives in many parts, jowar (Holcus sorghum), in the light lands in the north ; bajra (Holcus spicatus) is cultivated on inferior lands throughout the whole territory, and is the staple article of food for the poorer classes of the people. In the peninsula of Kattywar, jowar and bajra are the chief alimentary crops, but wheat is also cultivated to considerable extent ; as are kodra (Paspalum scorbiculatum) and gram (Cicer arietinum). Sugarcane flourishes in every part of the territory : it is one of the principal products in the south, and the quality is considered fine ; but cotton may be regarded as the staple commercial crop. The date-palm (Phœnix dactylifera) and palmyra (Borassus flabelliformis) are extensively planted in the vicinity of the sea, on account of the sap, from which, when fermented, the ardent spirit toddy is drawn by distillation. The mhowa (Bassia latifolia) grows in great abundance, and its flowers are in great request, as the petals when dried afford a pleasant food, resembling raisins, and by distillation yield an ardent spirit, which, though nauseous to Europeans, is consumed largely by the lower classes of the native population. Mango-trees are in great abundance, and produce fine fruit. Towards the coast are many fine specimens of Adansonia, with its grotesque and huge stem, large white flower, enormous fruit, valuable to fishermen, for whom it serves as floats for their nets ; while the wood is so light that a man often carries on his shoulder a large log of it, to be used as a raft in fishing, or in taking water-fowl. The pulp of the fruit also yields a pleasant acid, which is used in medicine and in making sherbet. The jak (Artocarpus integrifolia), with its huge fruit, the tamarind, and the Buchanania latifolia, yielding fruit resembling an almond in taste, abound in this well-wooded country. The great wonder, however, of the vegetable creation is the cubbeer-bur, or great banian-tree (Ficus indica), situate on an island in the Nerbudda, covering an area estimated at from three to four acres. So great is its height, that at a distance it resembles a hill, and so numerous, large, and close its branches, that in the season of inundation, the population dwell amidst them, until the subsidence of the river leaves their usual homes free from water. Esculent products are numerous and excellent, especially the watermelon, considered the best in India ; but the plantain is not abundant, and the produce is of no great excellence. The manufacturing industry for which this territory was formerly noted, has much decayed, and in general has nearly disappeared, from the greater cheapness of the wares thrown into the market by British competition.

Of the population inhabiting these extensive dominions, there are no means of ascertaining the precise numbers. Nothing exists beyond mere estimates, and those estimates probably rest but on vague grounds. According to the best information available, the population may be considered as something less than 3,000,000. They are of various lineage and characters, but no census having been made, the comparative numbers of the respective castes, classes, and tribes, could be assigned only conjecturally. Though the Mahrattas are the ruling race, they appear to be surpassed in number by other tribes, especially in the peninsula. The Rajpoots are very numerous; Brahmins abound, and are mostly landed proprietors or village officers. Mussulmans are to be found principally in the towns, and the Bora sectarians of that faith are in general industrious, wealthy, and influential members of society. The Parsees, though a few are engaged in agriculture, in general resort to the larger towns, where they are distinguished by their industry, quiet demeanor, and commercial sagacity. Coolies, a race settled here from remote antiquity, are especially numerous in the districts north of the river Myhee, and of the tracts about the upper parts of the various rivers in the north. Along the north-west frontier of the territory, they constitute the bulk of the population. They are in general a robust race, and, though professing the Brahminical faith, eat flesh, particularly that of the buffalo, and are much addicted to intoxication, as well by opium and bhang, as by ardent spirits. Many of them are depredators of various classes, some secret plunderers, others highway robbers; yet they are said to be trustworthy when expressly hired, either as guards of property, or to convey money to some destined place. The Koonbies are an agricultural tribe, who exist in great numbers in the south and midland parts of the territory, but to a less extent in the north. Besides those just enumerated, are some anomalous tribes of less importance; such as Dunjas, a small, well-knit, active race, engaged to some extent in cultivation, but by choice deriving their subsistence as far as practicable from the chase, fishing, or the collecting of wild fruits and the marketable produce of the jungles for sale. Their peculiar pursuits, little relished or shared in by the rest of the community, cause them to be viewed with dislike and dread; and the reputation of possessing great power in sorcery subjects them to much cruel treatment. Sometimes, in the true spirit of native barbarity, they are punished for such imputed delinquency by having their noses cut off, or by other mutilations. The Katties, who at a rather remote period emigrated from the banks of the Indus to the peninsula, form a majority of the inhabitants in a considerable praut or district to which they have given their name. They are considered to have been originally from Central Asia, and their northern origin is believed to be evidenced by their fair hair and complexions, blue eyes, tall stature, and athletic frame. Over the population in general, but especially over the Rajpoots, two classes of men, Bhats and Charuns, exercise wonderful influence. The Charuns, who, as well as the Bhats, boast of celestial origin, are divided into two tribes,—the Machilee being merchants, and the Maroo bards; and these two have in the aggregate 120 subdivisions. The men of those numerous subdivisions profess to understand the rites and observances which propitiate Siva and his consort Parvati, the favourite deities of the Rajpoots; and as few of the population except these pretenders to sanctity can read or write, they add to their other means of influence acquaintance with the genealogies of chiefs and tribes, and with laudatory legends, which they chant in their honour. It is represented, that amongst the Rajpoots there is a deep impression that certain destruction results from being instrumental in shedding the blood of a Charun, or of any member of his family. In reference to this impression, one of the class intent on attaining an object which he cannot otherwise bring about, will not scruple to murder a relative; and instances have not been wanting in which, in extreme cases, a Charun has destroyed himself. The aged and the young among the Charuns are taught, not merely to be ready to part with life whenever the honour of their family or the class to which they belong calls for the sacrifice, but it is said that, "from the feeble female of four-score to the child of five years of age, they are eager to be the first to die;" and this, it is added, "is no rare feeling, but one which appears to belong to every individual of this singular community." Under influence, acquired from the dread of the consequences of urging the Charun to such frightful extremities, the members of this community guarantee the performance of contracts entered into by the most faithless freebooters, and also become security for the payment of sums sometimes of very large amount. They also attend travellers as safeguards, and hesitate not to inflict on themselves wounds, or even death, should they fail in insuring protection to those whom they escort. Their influence, however, on such points has latterly been on the wane; probably because it has become less requisite since the establishment of greater security to life and property, by the advance of British power and influence in the dominions of the Guicowar. The Bhats, according to the imperfect information which we have concerning them, appear to differ little from the Charuns, except that they have less influence and fame. The portion of either which they possess results from their officiating as chroniclers, bards, flatterers, or lampooners. "They give praise and fame in their songs to those who are liberal to them, while they visit those who neglect or injure them, with satires, in which they usually reproach them with spurious birth and inherent meanness. Sometimes the Bhat, if very seriously offended, fixes the figure of the person he desires to degrade on a long pole, and appends to it a slipper, as a mark of disgrace. In such case the song of the Bhat records the infamy of the object of his revenge. This image usually travels the country, till the party or his friends purchase the cessation of the ridicule and curses thus entailed." Those singular religionists, the Jains, are rather numerous, especially in the peninsula, where there is scarcely a village of any size which has not several of their families; and their innumerable beautiful temples, shrines, and monastic establishments on the mountains of Geernar and Palithana, are amongst the most interesting architectural works in India. The Bheel tribe exist in considerable numbers in the wilder tracts of the eastern and north-eastern part of the territory, especially about the river Myhee. They are considered a people of remote origin, and formerly possessed of power, and of a considerable degree of civilization, until subjugated and oppressed by both Rajpoots and Mussulmans. At present some of them have settled into habits of fixed residence, and are engaged in agriculture; thus being raised above the savage state of the majority of their fellows.

Hereditary slavery is not uncommon in parts of Guzerat; and those claiming ownership over the unfortunate beings reduced to this state, not only avail themselves of the advantage of their services, but hire them out to others. In deference to the philanthropic views of the British government, the Guicowar has lately, indeed, issued a proclamation, prohibiting, under penalties, the future sale or purchase of children within his dominions, except under express permission of the durbar. This, however, is a very imperfect and unsatisfactory measure, perhaps a merely colourable one; and the home authorities have justly expressed regret that the prohibition was not made absolute. The vernacular language, denominated Guzerattee, is an offset from the great Sanskritic stock, and closely resembles the Hindee. The principal towns—Baroda the capital, Pahlunpore, Cambay, Radhunpore, Chowrar, Baunsda, Peint, Hursool, Dhurrumpore, Thurraud, Sucheen, Wusravee, Deesa, Rajkote, Poorbunder, Dwarka, Loonawarra, Barreah, Daunta, Dongurpore, Banswarra, Jabbooa, Oodepore, Rajpeepla, Saunte, and Beyt—are noticed under their respective names in the alphabetical arrangement. There are scarcely any made roads in this territory; but most parts of the country are very level; so that communication for half the year is easy, and wheeled carriages traverse it in all directions. The country will be traversed by the line of the Bombay and Baroda Railway Company. A railway is also projected from Baroda to Tunkaria.

The early history of Guzerat presents no features of greater interest than those which usually occur in the records of the eastern nations of the like periods. It formed part of the Mahomedan empire of Delhi; but in the reign of Mahmood Toghluk, was separated from it by Mozuffer Khan, previously governor, but thenceforward king. About the year 1572 it was the seat of great confusion, and was re-annexed to the empire by Akbar. When the Mahratta fortune prevailed, the chief officer of the confederacy, the Peishwa, secured a large amount of tribute from it; while another chief, called the Guicowar, became the ruler of the principal state in Guzerat, called Baroda, to the article on which the reader is referred for information on its history.

GUZZLEHUTTY.—See GUJELHATTI.

GWALIOR TERRITORIES, the possessions of the family of Scindia, have a singularly irregular outline, and consist of several detached districts, the principal of which is bounded on the north-east by the Chumbul, dividing it from the British districts of Agra and Etawah; on the east, in a very tortuous direction, by Bundelcund and the British districts of Saugor and Nerbudda; on the south by the native states of Bhopal and Dhar; on the west by those of Rajgurh, Jhalawur, and Kotah; and on the north-west by the Chumbul, separating it from Dholpore and Rajpootana. The extreme points of the Gwalior territory are in lat. 21° 8′—26° 50′, long. 74° 45′—79° 21′. The length of the principal portion above described is 246 miles from north to south, and 170 in breadth. The area of the whole comprises 33,119 square miles, and comprehends part of the ancient province of Agra, most of Malwa, and part of the Deccan. The rivers of the Gwalior country are numerous. The Taptee, flowing west, traverses the most southern part of the territory; and parallel to this, but about forty miles farther north, the Nerbudda flows in a similar direction; but by far the greater portion of the drainage of the territory is discharged into the river Chumbul, which, receiving the waters of the Chumbla, Seepra, Chota Kallee Sind, Newuj, Parbutty, and some others of less importance, flows along the north-west frontier of the country, separating it from the Jeypoor, Kerowly, and Dholpore territories; subsequently turning south-east, it forms the north-eastern boundary, towards the British districts of Agra and Etawa, and joins the Jumna in the latter district, twenty miles distant from the north-eastern course of the Gwalior territory. The Sinde, a considerable river, but less than the Chumbul, flows in some measure parallel to it, but farther to the east, and after forming for a considerable extent the south-eastern boundary towards Bundelcund, intersects for thirty miles the north-eastern corner of Gwalior, and finally falls into the Jumna, a short distance below the confluence of the Chumbul with that river. In the northern part of the territory, forming a tract extending between the Chumbul and the Sinde, rise the Kooaree, Asun, Sank, and some other torrents of less importance, which, flowing east or north-east, fall into the Sinde on the left side.

The northern part of the country, of moderate elevation, and in most places either rocky or sandy, has a climate partaking of the torrid character of the neighbouring tracts of Agra or Rajpootana. In these parts the climate, during the rainy season, and for a short time afterwards, is exceedingly unhealthy, fevers being then very rife, in consequence, according to an intelligent writer, of the moisture imbibed by the superficial diluvial soil being prevented from passing off by an impermeable substratum of sandstone. Hence results great damp, indicated by mouldiness on all substances susceptible of it. During the dry and hot seasons, the climate is not unhealthy. The middle, the southern, and the western parts, or those comprised within Malwa, with little exception, have a mild and rather equable climate, resulting from the elevation of the surface. The range of the thermometer is unusually small, except during the latter part of the year, when great and sudden changes often take place. The cool season comprises the period between the beginning of November and the end of February; the hot season succeeds, and continues to the middle of June, when the periodical rains set in, and last to the close of September, the average fall being about fifty inches. During this season the thermometer has a very moderate range, rarely more than from 72° to 78°. The climate becomes cooler after the rains, and in proportion to the approach towards the winter solstice, when the coldest weather commences, and continues through January and the early part of February, the thermometer sometimes falling three or four degrees below the freezing-point. During the sultry season the hot winds are comparatively mild and of short duration, though the thermometer sometimes rises to nearly 100° during the day; but the nights are invariably cool and refreshing.

The population of the north-eastern part of this territory is of a mixed kind, comprising, besides Mahrattas (the ruling order), Boondelas, Jauts, Rajpoots, with some less distinctly defined divisions of Hindoos, and Mussulmans. Until the Mahratta inroads in the last century, the country was from an early period a possession of the Mahomedan rulers of Delhi; and in no part of the territory, except the small tract south of the Nerbudda, do the Mahrattas form any large proportion of the people. In the greater part of the southern and south-western parts, comprising a portion of Malwa, a very considerable section of the population is Brahminical; and Malcolm remarks: "There is perhaps no part of India where the tribes of Brahmins are so various, and their numbers so great." He however adds, "but there is certainly none where there are so few of them either wealthy, learned, or where there is less attention paid to the religious rites of the Hindoo faith, or to its priests, by the rest of the population." Rajpoots exist in large numbers, and pay little regard to the Brahmins, whose place as to moral and religious influence is supplied by the cognate tribes of Bhats and Charuns. There are many petty Rajpoot rajahs, who yield ostensibly fealty and tribute to the family of Scindia, but display from time to time evidence of a refractory disposition, which would render them perilous subordinates in case of any reverse happening to the paramount power. They are described by Malcolm as an indolent, sensual race, living habitually under the besotting influence of opium; while the atrocious practices of infanticide and suttee find toleration. The Mussulman population is estimated at about a twentieth of the whole. The relative density of the population assumed by Malcolm for Central India is ninety-eight to the square mile; and this ratio, compared with the area, would make the amount 3,228,512. The present military force consists, first, of the contingent, paid by the British government from funds derived from territorial assignments, and numbering 8,400, forty-five of whom are European officers, selected from the Bengal army; and, secondly, of the troops maintained by the Gwalior government, and at its disposal, amounting (cavalry, infantry, and artillery) to upwards of 9,622; thus rather exceeding the maximum fixed by the treaty of 1844, which (exclusively of the contingent) was 9,000.

The founder of the Scindia dynasty was Ranojee Scindia, a Soodra, of the Koombi or cultivator tribe, and hereditary potail or headman of a small rural district. He appears to have first come into notice as a domestic of Balaji Wiswanath, who was Peishwa from 1714 to 1720. Ranojee Scindia, being considered by his master trustworthy in his humble avocation, was advanced to a station in the bodyguard; subsequently rising rapidly, he became a chief of considerable importance, and on his death, about 1750, was succeeded in his position as head of the Scindia family, by Madhaji Scindia, one of his natural sons, who was present at the great battle of Paniput, in 1761, in which Ahmed Shah Dooranee defeated the confederated Mahrattas. Madhaji escaped the carnage with difficulty, and not without a desperate wound, which rendered him lame for life. This great national disaster of the Mahrattas did not, however, operate unfavourably for Scindia; for the shock given to the power of the Peishwa actually removed a principal obstacle out of his way. He recovered some possessions in Malwa, which had been wrested from him after the battle of Paniput, levied contributions very extensively, enforced tribute from the chiefs of Rajpootana and others in the vicinity of his dominions, and maintained a large and effective force in the Deccan, to control the Peishwa and other parties opposed to the growth of his power. He seems to have first come into serious collision with the British forces in 1779, when, in concert with the troops of the Peishwa and of Holkar, he baffled the Bombay army in an attempt to march to Poona, and subsequently, in a convention with the managers of the expedition, exacted a cession of a portion of Broach. The growth of Scindia's power up to this period is thus described by Malcolm:—"Madhaji Scindia took full advantage of the dissensions that occurred at Poona, after the death of B lajee (1761), to usurp, as far as he could, the rights and lands of the head of the empire to the north of the

Nerbudda. The detail of the progress of this system of spoliation of both friend and foe, is not necessary; suffice it to say, this able chief was the principal opposer of the English in the war they carried on in favour of Ragobah. He was the nominal slave, but the rigid master, of the unfortunate Shah Allum, emperor of Delhi; the pretended friend, but the designing rival, of the house of Holkar; the professed inferior in all matters of form, but the real superior and oppressor, of the Rajpoot princes of Central India; and the proclaimed soldier, but the actual plunderer, of the family of the Peishwa." His extensive possessions in Malwa, however, formed the main basis of his power. Mohammed, the weak emperor of Delhi, having, in 1741, granted the province of Malwa in jaghire to the Peishwa, who intrusted its management to Ranojee Scindia, that chief, and subsequently, still more effectually, Madhaji, succeeded, by constantly-repeated encroachments, in acquiring complete dominion over the greater part of the province. Madhaji Scindia having succeeded in making himself master of the strong hill-fort of Gwalior, about 1779, lost it in 1780, when it was surprised in a night attack by a British force under Major Popham, assisted by Captain Bruce. In the following year, Colonel Camac, in command of a British force, having invaded Malwa, and penetrated as far as Seronje, was so beset by Madhaji Scindia, as to be compelled to make a precipitate retreat, in the course of which, however, he succeeded in surprising and defeating his pursuer. Consequent on this defeat, a treaty was concluded, by which the British authorities agreed to evacuate all the territory claimed by Madhaji Scindia to the right of the Jumna, he also engaging to leave the rana of Gohud in unmolested possession of Gwalior and of the adjoining country. By the treaty of Salbye, concluded between the East-India Company and the Peishwa, in 1782, Madhaji Scindia was recognised as a sovereign prince, and declared the guarantee of its conditions. The fort of Gwalior was, in 1784, invested by him, at the head of 70,000 men, and ultimately fell into his hands by surrender. In the succeeding year he entered Delhi, and was, by Shah Allum, made minister, but soon after expelled by a hostile confederacy. In 1788, however, he vigorously pushed his fortune, and, among other successes, acquired Agra. His most formidable force at this time was that commanded by De Boigne, a Savoyard by birth, but trained in the Irish brigade in the service of the king of France. This able soldier, by means of funds supplied by Scindia, kept on foot an army of 18,000 regular, and 6,000 irregular infantry, 2,000 irregular horse, and 600 Persian cavalry, with 200 cannon. By these means, in 1790, were gained, within a few weeks of each other, the battle of Patun, and that of Mairta, in Joudpore, by which its rajah was effectually humbled. Delhi, and its immediate dependencies, had, in 1788, been occupied by Scindia, who expelled and punished with tortures, ending in death, Ghulam Kadir, the brutal oppressor and mutilator of Shah Allum. Madhaji Scindia at the same time maintained a preponderance at the court of the Peishwa at Poona, and at the time of his death, in 1794, his dominions extended from the river Taptee south, to the northern limit of the district of Delhi, and from the Gulf of Cambay on the west, to the Ganges in the east; including Candeish, a portion of the Deccan, the greatest part of Malwa, the districts of Agra and Delhi, and the central and finest part of the Doab. He was succeeded in his possessions by his grand-nephew Dowlut Rao Scindia, then in the fifteenth year of his age. The early years and efforts of Dowlut Rao were expended principally in contests at Poona and its vicinity, for obtaining influence over the Peishwa, or the means for overawing him, with the view of wielding the power derived from his ostensible protection and countenance; thus playing a chief part in "a scene of intrigue, art, and treachery, which is perhaps unparalleled." Dowlut Rao, joining his forces with those of Ragoji Bhonsla, rajah of Berar, the allied chiefs, in 1803, invaded the territory of the Nizam, protected by the East-India Company, and on the 23rd of September in that year, the Mahratta army, unskilfully encamped, was surprised at Assye by a British force of about an eighth of its number, commanded by General Sir Arthur Wellesley, subsequently the illustrious duke of Wellington, and, after a prolonged and fiercely-contested battle, was totally defeated. The overthrow of Scindia's military resources in the Deccan was completed by the defeat which the confederated Mahrattas received from Sir Arthur Wellesley at Argaum, in Berar, on the 28th of November following.

The destruction of the Mahratta power in Hindoostan north of the Nerbudda had, in the mean time, been not less signally effected by General, afterwards Lord Lake, the British commander-in-chief, who having, in the beginning of September, 1803, stormed Allygurh, a few days afterwards, at Patperganj, on the left bank of the Jumna, nearly opposite Delhi, totally defeated Scindia's disciplined army, commanded by the Frenchman Bourquien, and effectually cleared the Doab of the Mahrattas. Delhi was immediately occupied by the victorious army, to which, before the close of the same year, Agra yielded, after a brief attempt at defence. General Lake, indefatigably following up his advantages, destroyed at Laswaree, a few weeks afterwards, the remnant of Scindia's disciplined force. To avert impending ruin, Doulut Rao, at the close of the year 1803, acceded to the treaty of Serji Anjengaum, dictated by the British government, ceding on the left bank of the Jumna "all his forts, territories, and rights in the Doab;" and on the right bank of the river, "all his forts, territories, rights, and interests in the countries which are to the northward of those of the rajahs of Jeypore and Jodepore;" or, substantially, all tracts which, eastward of long. 76°, are situate north of the Chumbul. Ambajee, a feudatory of Doulut Rao, had at his ostensible instance engaged to yield to the British the fort of Gwalior; but it was found necessary to commence military operations against the place, and the Mahratta garrison, rendered tractable by this measure, consented to receive a bribe, and depart. The fort was by the British government transferred to the rana of Gohud; but some difficulties arising, the grant was revoked, and the place, "from considerations of friendship"—such was the phrase—was in 1805 ceded to Doulut Rao Scindia by the second article of the treaty of Mustafapore. The Mahratta prince so highly appreciated the advantages resulting from the strength of the place, that he regarded it as his capital, and fixed his residence in a permanent camp at the base of the rock. In 1817, when the Peishwa confederated with Appa Sahib Bhonsla, of Nagpore, and Holkar, for the overthrow of the British power, the marquis of Hastings, governor-general, took the command of a formidable army, and advancing to the river Chumbul, so far overawed Scindia that on November 5th, 1817, a treaty was executed, binding this chief, among other conditions, to concur with the British in effectually quelling the Pindarries and other freebooters, and for this purpose to furnish a body of 5,000 horse, to act under the control of British officers. Doulut Rao Scindia died in 1827, and as he had no male issue, Mugut Rao, a boy eleven years old, and nearest relation of the late maharajah who could from his age be adopted, was declared sovereign by the name of Ali Jah Junkojee Scindia. This youth displayed a trait of character of no common atrocity on occasion of his marriage, when he discharged arrows among the assembled people, one of whom was killed. He died childless in 1843, when Bhagerut Rao, his nearest male relative, eight years of age, was declared successor, and proclaimed under the title of Ali Jah Jyajee Scindia. The maternal uncle of the deceased maharajah became regent, under the title of the Mama Sahib, but was quickly displaced by court intrigue and military violence, and the reins of government were thrown ostensibly into the hands of the maharanee, widow of the late maharajah, "a passionate girl of twelve years of age." Her ignorance, caprice, and froward petulance accelerated the progress of anarchy inevitable in such a juncture, and the more alarming, as the most active promoters of the turmoil were numerous and determined, well trained to arms, amply equipped with them, and actuated by a Mahratta love of violence and spoil. This state of things naturally and justly excited the apprehension of the government of British India, Scindia's dominions being extensively conterminous with those of the East-India Company, and likely, in case of outbreak, to share in the calamities and suffer from the deeds of rapine and blood sure to be perpetrated by a lawless soldiery, associated with freebooters more lawless than themselves. The actual minister was the Dada Khasji Wala, who was seized by the soldiery, probably less from any hostile feeling than a desire to employ him as the tool of their rapacity. Hence ensued a military conflict between those who seized the minister and those supporting the maharanee and her party; but after a brief and feeble engagement, the soldiers agreed to make common cause, intelligence having arrived that a large British force had been concentrated at Agra. Reinforcements were thereupon called in from every side, ammunition in large quantity was served to the troops of all arms, and extensive preparations of every kind made for war. The Dada Khasji Wala was given up to the British authorities; but all order had now ceased in Scindia's territories; the zemindars refused to pay in the rents, and any semblance of rule that remained, depended altogether upon the will of the soldiery. The British government then resolved upon advancing, for the purpose of obtaining full security for the future tranquillity of the common frontier, for the maintenance of order within the territories of Scindia, and for the conducting of the government of those territories in accordance with the established relations of amity towards the British government. It was required that the army of Gwalior should be reduced within reasonable limits. These objects were avowed in the proclamations issued by the Governor-General on the entrance of the British forces into the Gwalior territory, towards the close of the month of December, 1843. On the 21st December, the British army, led by Sir Hugh Gough, commander-in-chief, accompanied by Lord Ellenborough, governor-general, commenced crossing the Chumbul near the town of Dholpore, and by the 26th of the same month the whole had passed to the right side, and encamped at Hingona, twenty-three miles north-west of the fort of Gwalior. This force advancing on the 29th, came in front of the Mahratta army about fifteen miles north-east of Gwalior, and in a position supported by the neighbouring villages of Maharajpore and Chonda. After an obstinate engagement, in which the British suffered very severe loss from the well-served artillery directed against them, the Mahrattas were dislodged from all points of their position, and the survivors of the carnage retreated to Gwalior, having lost fifty-six pieces of artillery and all their ammunition-waggons. The total loss on the side of the British was 106 killed, 684 wounded, and seven missing. The numbers engaged were probably nearly equal,—about 14,000 on each side. Simultaneous with the march of the commander-in-chief from Dholpore was that of Major-General Grey, with an army probably of about 8,000 or 9,000 men, from Bundelcund. Crossing the river Sinde at Chandpore, this force marched to Puniaur, twelve miles south-west of Gwalior, and there, on the 29th December, encountered a Mahratta army, despatched from the capital, and estimated at 12,000 strong, with twenty-four guns. The Mahrattas, after a severe struggle, were defeated, with the loss of all their artillery and a great number of men. The loss on the part of the British was twenty-five killed, and 189 wounded. On the 4th of January, 1844, the fort of Gwalior was occupied by the contingent force, commanded by British officers; and thus passed into the power of the East-India Company this celebrated stronghold, which effectually commanded the Lashkar, or stationary camp, at its base, where 5,000 refractory troops, amply supplied with artillery, still held out; but all hope of successful resistance having ceased, they accepted the offer made to them of full liquidation of all arrears, with the addition of a gratuity of three months' pay, and, surrendering their artillery and small arms, they quietly dispersed. It has been recently determined that no further repairs shall be made to the fort. On the 13th January, 1844, was concluded a treaty, by which various previously existing treaties were confirmed, except so far as they might be affected by the stipulations of the new one. The contingent force for the protection of Scindia's territory, originally provided for in the treaty of Serjee Anjengaum (1803), by the assignment of certain districts for its maintenance, was to be increased, and the revenues of other districts, in addition to the former, were, by a schedule to the new treaty, appropriated to that purpose, as well as, it would appear, to defray the charges of the civil administration of such districts, which was to be conducted by the British government for Scindia. To meet sundry debts due to the British government, and to cover various charges incurred by the misconduct of that of Scindia, a sum of twenty-six lacs was to be paid within fourteen days from the date of the treaty; in default of which, territory described in another schedule was to be assigned as provision for the payment of the principal debt, and the interest accruing thereon, together with the charges of the civil administration. The military force maintained by Scindia beyond the contingent was not to exceed 9,000 men, of whom not more than one-third were to be infantry. During the minority of the maharajah, all acts of government were to be under the control of the British resident, the administration being vested in a council of regency. Three lacs of rupees were set apart as a provision for the maharanee. Such was the position of the relations under the treaty between Gwalior and the British government. The exemplary character, however, of the young maharajah, and his high promise of qualifications for government, led to his being intrusted with the administration of his dominions before the expiration of his minority. The formal act of coronation was postponed until the attainment of his majority in 1853, when, by its performance, the young rajah was solemnly confirmed in the authority which he had previously exercised.

GWALIOR.—A celebrated hill-fort, the capital of the possessions of Scindia's family. The rock on which it is situate, is completely isolated, though 700 yards to the north is a conical hill, surmounted by a remarkable building of stone; and on the south-east, the south, and the south-west, are similar hills, which form a sort of amphitheatre, at the distance of from one to four miles. Near the place, and on the east of it, runs the small river Soowunreeka, nearly dry, except during the rains. The rock of Gwalior, and the ranges in its vicinity, are of ochreous sandstone, capped in some places with basalt, which appears to have formerly universally overspread them, and the fragments of which lying at their bases, form slopes for a considerable distance up their sides. The sandstone of the hill-fort is arranged in horizontal strata, and its face presents so steep a fracture, as to form a perpendicular precipice, rising above the upper limit of the slope. Where the rock was naturally less precipitous, it has been so scarped as to be rendered perpendicular; and in some places the upper part considerably overhangs the lower. The greatest length of the rock, which is from north-east to south-west, is a mile and a half, the greatest breadth 300 yards. The height at the north end, where it is greatest, is 342 feet. On the eastern face of the rock, several colossal figures are sculptured in bold relief. A rampart runs round the edge of the rock, conforming to the outline of its summit; and as its height is uniform above the verge, its top has an irregular appearance. The entrance within the inclosure of the rampart is towards the north end of the east side; first, by means of a steep road, and higher up by steps cut in the face of the rock, of such a size and of so moderate a degree of acclivity, that elephants easily make their way up. This huge staircase is protected on the outer side by a high and massive stone wall, and is swept by several traversing-guns pointing down it; the passage up to the interior being through a succession of seven gates. The principal gate is called Hatipul, or the elephant's gate, from the figure of that animal sculptured over it. The citadel is at the north-eastern extremity of the inclosure, and has a very striking appearance. The outline of the great masses of the antique palace surmounted by kiosks, is strongly marked against the sky, and adjoining is a series of six lofty round towers or bastions, connected by curtains of great height and thickness. Along the eastern side of those buildings extends horizontally, in the upper part, a course of bricks or tiles of brilliant blue colour, like coarse porcelain; and the effect produced by this great vivid streak is singular, but not unpleasing. There are within the inclosure of the rampart several spacious tanks, capable of supplying an adequate garrison, though, according to a military author, 15,000 men would be required fully to man the defences. The old town of Gwalior is situate along the eastern base of the rock. It is of considerable size, having a street a mile long, and has many good houses of stone; but is very irregularly built, and extremely filthy. It contains a very beautiful building of white sandstone, with a cupola covered with blue porcelain tiles, beneath which lie the remains of Muhammad Ghous, a famous sage, celebrated for his sanctity in the time of Akbar. The Lashkar, or stationary camp of the maharajah, is represented as extending several miles from the south-west end of the rock, and as being a place of considerable traffic and wealth; but the great reduction of the military force of the state must cause a diminution of the prosperity of this establishment. It has been described as a very filthy collection of rude buildings, even the residence of the maharajah being of mean exterior, and those of the rest, in appearance little better than hovels, though much wealth, the proceeds of a long course of rapine, was stored within them. There are scarcely any manufactures in Gwalior, except artillery-founding, and the making of gunpowder and fireworks for the prince and court.

According to the researches of Wilford, the fort of Gwalior was built in 773, by Surya-Sena, rajah of a small territory lying about the rock. Ferishta, however, assigns it a date antecedent to the commencement of the Christian era. In 1023, it was besieged by the celebrated Mahmood of Ghuznee, who found the attempt to capture it hopeless, and marched away, taking a present. After a long siege in 1196, it was taken by Bahauddin, or Kutbuddin Eibak, lieutenants of Shahabuddin, or Muhammad, of Ghor. In 1211, it was lost by the Mussulmans, but recovered in 1231, after a blockade for a year, by Shamsuddin Altamsh, the slave king of Delhi. Narsingh Rae, a Hindoo chief, taking advantage of the troubles produced by the invasion of Tamerlane in 1398, took Gwalior, which was not recovered by the Mussulmans until 1519, when it was retaken by Ibrahim Lodi, the Patan sovereign of Delhi; after whose defeat and death in battle against Baber, it was seized by a Patan adventurer. In 1526, Baber gained it by stratagem, and in 1543, after the expulsion of his son Humayon, it fell into the hands of his successful rival Sher Shah; but, after the return and re-establishment of Humayon, it was, in 1556, recovered by his successor Akbar, who made it the state prison for captives of importance. Here he confined, and subsequently put to death, his first cousin, Abulkasim, son of the ill-fated Kamran. Here also Aurungzebe confined his brother Morad, and shortly after put him to death. The same suspicious and cruel sovereign consigned to this prison the son of Morad, and his nephews Soliman and Sepehr Sheko, the sons of Dara, who here quickly found a grave. In the dismemberment of the empire of Delhi, Gwalior was seized by the Jat rana of Gohud. It subsequently changed hands, and in 1779 was garrisoned by Scindia, from whom it was taken by the forces of the East-India Company, on the 3rd August, with little trouble and small loss. At midnight, ladders and all other auxiliaries for scaling having been prepared, the party for the attack was formed. Two companies of grenadiers and light infantry led the van, under Captain Bruce; Major Popham followed with twenty Europeans and two battalions of sepoys. A battalion, two guns, and a small body of cavalry, were ordered to march at two o'clock, to cover the retreat of the English party, in case of premature discovery, or, in the event of success, to prevent the garrison from escaping. At break of day, the van arrived at the foot of the scarped rock, the spies ascended by wooden ladders, and having made fast ladders of ropes, the troops followed. Some resistance was offered, but the garrison was intimidated by the unexpected attack, and the assailants were soon masters of the place. Transferred by the British government to the rana of Gohud, it was in 1784 recovered by Madhajee Scindia, from whom it was again taken in 1803, but restored in 1805, "from considerations [it was said] of friendship." Finally, in January, 1844, subsequently to the battle of Maharajpoor, it was occupied by the Gwalior contingent, commanded by British officers; and thus has virtually been placed within the power of the British government. It has been determined that no further repairs shall be made to the fort. Distant S. from Agra 65 miles, S. from Delhi 175, W. of Calpee 100, N.W. of Allahabad 277, N.W. of Calcutta, by Allahabad, 772. Lat. 26° 13′, long. 78° 15′.

GYA.—A town in the native state of Cashmere, or dominions of Gholab Singh, 128 miles N.E. from Chamba, and 144 miles N.E. from Kangra. Lat. 33° 39′, long. 77° 50′.

GYCHAN, in native Gurhwal, a hamlet at the confluence of the two great torrents Roopin and Soopin, the united stream of which from this point bears the name of Tons. It is elevated 456 feet above the bed of the Tons, and 5,756 above the level of the sea. Lat. 31° 4′, long. 78° 10′.

GYDER KHAIL, in the Daman division of the Punjab, a town situated 32 miles from the right bank of the Indus, 24 miles S.S.W. of the town of Peshawur. Lat. 33° 40′, long 71° 32′.

GYNDAJOOR, in the British district of Bijnour, lieut.-gov. of the N.W. Provinces, a village on the route from Moradabad to Hurdwar, and 25 miles N.W. of the former. Lat. 29° 10′, long. 78° 40′.

H.

HACKNITWARRA.—A town in one of the recently sequestrated districts of Hyderabad, or territory of the Nizam, 47 miles S. from Ellichpoor, and 111 miles W.S.W. from Nagpoor. Lat. 20° 30′, long. 77° 38′.

HADJEE.—See Aji.

HAFIZGANJ, in the British district of Bareilly, lieut.-gov. of the N.W. Provinces, a small town on the route from the town of Bareilly to Pillebheet, 16 miles N.E. of the former. There is a bazar, and also a weekly market. Lat. 28° 30′, long. 79° 37′.

HAGLEWADDY.—A town in the Mysore, 75 miles N. from Seringapatam, and 137 miles E.N.E. from Mangalore. Lat. 13° 30′, long. 76° 49′.

HAJEEGUNJE.—A town in the British district of Tipperah, lieut.-gov. of Bengal, 24 miles S.W. of Tipperah. Lat. 23° 16′, long. 90° 52′.

HAJEEPOOR, in the Daman division of the Punjab, a town situated 27 miles from the right bank of the Indus, 98 miles S.W. by W. of the town of Mooltan. Lat. 29° 20′, long. 70° 13′.

HAJEEPOOR.—A town in the British district of Mymunsing, lieut.-gov. of Bengal, 36 miles W. by N. of Nusseerabad. Lat. 24° 50′, long. 89° 51′.

HAJEEPOOR, in the British district of Allyghur, lieut.-gov. of the N.W. Provinces, a village on the route from the cantonment of Allygurh to that of Etawa, and 22 miles S.E. of the former. Lat. 27° 37′, long. 78° 14′.

HAJEEPOOR, in the British district of Tirhoot, lieut.-gov. of Bengal, a town at the confluence of the Gunduck with the Ganges, and on the left bank of both rivers. It is on the route from Dinapore to Khatmandoo, 15 miles N.E. of former, 182 S. of latter. The Ganges is here crossed by ferry from Patna, which is immediately opposite. The place is much frequented by pilgrims, and from that circumstance has doubtless received the name, signifying pilgrim's town. Lat. 25° 40′, long. 85° 17′.

HAJIGUNJE, in the British district of Fureedpore, lieut.-gov. of Bengal, a town on the right or south-west bank of the Ganges, described by Heber as here six miles wide during the rainy season. Distance from the town of Fureedpore E. five miles. Lat. 23° 36′, long. 89° 56′.

HALABAK.—A town in the principality of Cashmere, or dominions of Gholab Singh, 163 miles E. from Sirinagur, and 158 miles N.E. by N. from Kangra. Lat. 33° 55′, long. 77° 46′.

HALAN SYUDS, in Sinde, a village on the route from Hyderabad to Sehwan, by way of Kotree, and 32 miles N. of the last-mentioned place. It is situate about a mile and a half from the right bank of the Indus. Lat. 25° 54′, long. 68° 18′.

HALEESHUR, in the British district of Baraset, lieut.-gov. of Bengal, a populous town situate on the left bank of the Hooghly river, and celebrated for the number of Sanscrit colleges, founded by a former rajah of Nuddea. Lat. 22° 55′, long. 88° 23′.

HALIPOOTRA, in Sinde, a village on the route from Sehwan to Larkhana, and four miles N. of the former place. It is embosomed in high trees, and is situate two miles from the right bank of the Indus. Lat. 26° 27′, long. 67° 54′.

HALLA, in Sinde, near the left or eastern bank of the Indus, is situate in a tract of no great fertility, the soil being impregnated with salt. The new town is larger and more wealthy than the old one, which is contiguous to it. There is here a much-frequented shrine of a reputed Mahometan saint. The bazar, which is partially roofed over, is well supplied, and considerable business is transacted there. Sindian caps, the general head-dress of all in the country except the Hindoos, are made here in great numbers, and of excellent quality. Halla new town is celebrated for its earthenware, the coarser kinds of which are manufactured from clay taken from the bed of the Indus. In the finer kinds, this material is mixed in a large proportion with ground flints: the decorations are very showy, and sometimes tasteful; the colours, which are obtained from the oxydes of copper, lead, or iron, being remarkable for brilliancy and richness. A sort of unctuous earth, called "chunniah," is obtained from lakes near the town, and is eaten in considerable quantities, especially by the women. Estimates of the population differ widely, and Burnes upon this point is not consistent with himself. In one place (vol. iii. 264), he states it at 2,000, and in the same volume (p. 227) at 10,000. The latter seems the more probable amount. Lat. 25° 39′, long. 68° 24′.

HALLAR, or **HALLAWAR**, in the peninsula of Kattywar, province of Guzerat, a district named from the Halla tribe of Rajpoots. It is bounded on the north by the Gulf of Cutch; on the north-east by the districts of Muchoo-Kanta and Jhallawar; on the east by the district of Kattywar; on the south by the districts of Kattywar and Soruth; on the south-west by the district of Burda and the Arabian Sea; and on the west by the district of Okamundal, from which it is divided by a small runn or salt-marsh. It lies between lat. 21° 39′—22° 50′, long. 69° 9′—71° 3′; is about 130 miles in length from east to west, and 75 in extreme breadth. Its area may be stated at about 4,960 square miles. The greater part of this district belongs to the thakoors or chiefs of Naunagar, Gondul, Rajkot, Dhurol, and Kotra Sangani. The total population is estimated at 358,560; an amount which, compared with the area, indicates a relative density of seventy-two to the square mile. The annual tribute by the various chiefs and landholders is stated to be 345,778 rupees; of which the sum of 161,598 rupees is paid to the British government, 167,495 to the Guicowar, and 16,685 to the nawaub of Joonaghur.

HALLOWAL, in the Reechna Dooab division of the Punjab, a town situated nine miles from the right bank of the Ravee, 53 miles N.E. of the town of Lahore. Lat. 32° 10′, long. 74° 45′.

HALLWY.—A town in the British district of Bellary, presidency of Madras, 53 miles N. by E. of Bellary. Lat. 15° 52′, long. 77° 10′.

HAMEEDNUGGUR. — A town in the British district of Behar, lieut.-gov. of Bengal, 34 miles N. by W. of Sherghotty Lat. 25° 2′, long. 84° 43′.

HAMEERGURH.—A town in the Rajpoot state of Oodeypoor, 91 miles S. from Ajmeer, and 73 miles W. from Kotah. Lat. 25° 10′, long. 74° 43′.

HANAGHAT.—A town in the British district of Nuddea, lieut.-gov. of Bengal, 44 miles N. by E. of Calcutta. Lat. 23° 11′, long. 88° 33′.

HANGO, or HUNG, in Bussahir, a village of Koonawur, in the Tartar division called Hungrung, is situate near the north-eastern base of the Hungrung Mountains. It consists of three or four hamlets or small subdivisions, and is situate at the head of a fertile and cultivated dell, a mile long, and about half that breadth, bearing luxuriant crops of corn and pulse, and watered by three never-failing streams, which flow down it to the river Li. Hango is noted for a temple, of high repute among the natives, and apparently devoted to a mongrel superstition, half Brahminical and half Lamaic. It is a large building, crowded inside with grotesque idols, the principal of which is a large earthenware figure of a hideous man, wearing a diadem of human skulls, and an enormous necklace of the same, reaching down to the ground, and in his right hand the hilt of a sword, in his left a human skull, cut down to the form of a drinking-cup. An enormous serpent, with protruded tongue, is twined round his neck, and is of such a length as to reach the ground with its head. The idol holds in its arms a woman, whose head is also crowned with a chaplet of skulls, and who bears in her hand a skull, formed into a drinking-cup, the group being apparently intended to represent incarnations of the deities in a state of wrath. The village contains thirty families of Tartars and a few nuns, and, according to Herbert, gives name to the surrounding district of Hungrung. Elevation above the sea 11,400 feet. Lat. 31° 49′, long. 78° 34′.

HANLE.—A town in the native state of Cashmere, or dominions of Gholab Singh, 154 miles N.E. from Simla, and 166 miles E. by N. from Chamba. Lat. 32° 43′, long. 78° 56′.

HANSEE.—A town in the British district of Hurreeanah, lieut.-gov. of the N.W. Provinces. It is situate on the watercourse made, in 1356, by Feroz Toghluk, king of Delhi, who, in some places clearing and deepening the bed of the Chitang torrent, and in others excavating a channel, conducted a branch from the Delhi Canal westward beyond Hissar, until it either disembogued into the Gagur, or was lost by evaporation or absorption in the arid waste. Hansee appears to have been an important place as early as 1036, when Massaoud, the son of the renowned Mahmud of Ghuznee, invaded India ; as, according to Ferishta, "the Hindoos reckoned it impregnable, and were taught to believe that it could never fall into the hands of the Mahomedans. On this occasion, the India soothsayers, like those of other nations, deceived their followers, for, in the space of six days, the king escaladed the place, and took it by storm. Herein he found immense treasure." Tieffenthaler, writing about the middle of the last century, describes it as having a ruinous brick-built fort, situate on a hill. The canal must also, at that time, have been in a ruinous state, as the place suffered from want of water insomuch that there was only one crop in the year, and that dependent on the periodical rains. In 1798, when for a short period it was the capital of the adventurer George Thomas, it was supplied with water from wells, none other being procurable for above a dozen miles. "Here," says Thomas, "I established my capital, rebuilt the walls of the city, which had long since fallen to decay, and repaired the fortification. As it has been long deserted, at first I found difficulty in procuring inhabitants, but by degrees, and gentle treatment, I selected between five and six thousand persons, to whom I allowed every lawful indulgence. I established a mint, and coined my own rupees, which I made current in my army and country ; cast my own artillery, commenced making muskets, matchlocks, and powder." In 1801, Thomas, being besieged here by a vastly superior force of Mahrattas, under the French adventurer Perron, evacuated the place, and took refuge in the territory of the East-India Company. The population has been recently returned at 9,112. The road to the south-east of the town, or in the direction of Delhi, is good ; to the west it is also good, running the whole way to Hissar along the bank of the canal. Hansee is distant N.W. from Delhi 89 miles, N.W. from Calcutta 989 miles. Lat. 29° 6′, long. 76° 3′.

HANSOTE, in the British district of Broach, presidency of Bombay, a town near the south-eastern bank of the estuary of the river Nerbudda. Population 5,000. Distance from Surat, N., 28 miles. Lat. 21° 32′, long. 72° 50′.

HANSOUTEE.—A river rising in lat. 27° 58′, long. 76° 7′, in the native state of Jhujhur, a few miles south of the town of Narnol, and flowing in a north-easterly direction for seventy-five miles, alternately through Jhujhur and the British territory of Goorgaon, and for twenty-two miles through that of Delhi, falls into the Delhi Canal a few miles north of the town of Delhi, in lat. 28° 40′, long. 77° 15′.

HAPOOR.—See Haupur.

HARAMUK.—A lofty summit in the range bounding Cashmere on the north. In a depression on the northern declivity is a small lake, called Gunga Bul,—"the place of the Ganges," which, like many other reservoirs of water, is held in high veneration by the Hindoos. The elevation of Haramuk above the level of the sea is estimated by Vigne at 13,000 feet. Lat. 34° 26′, long. 75°.

HARAPA.—A village of the Punjab, close to the left bank of the Ravee, and seated amid very extensive ruins, the most striking being the relics of a large brick fortress. This is considered by Masson to be the site of the Sangala of Arrian, where the Indians made such an obstinate defence against Alexander; but this opinion is regarded by eminent authority as open to question. Professor Wilson observes, "Whether they [the Macedonians] followed the course of the Iravati [Ravee] to Harapa, may be reasonably doubted." Harapa is in lat. 30° 40′, long. 72° 53′.

HARAWUG.—A castle in the north of the Punjab, on the route from Lahore to Cashmere by the Banihal Pass, and 28 miles S. of the last-mentioned place. It is built of wood, in a ravine on the right bank of a stream which, at a short distance below, falls into the Chenaub. Harawug is in lat. 33° 12′, long. 75° 3′.

HARIHARPOOR, in the British district of Goruckpore, lieut.-gov. of the N.W. Provinces, a petty market-town on the Jamura, a small river, a feeder of the Rapti. According to Buchanan's report, thirty years ago, it contained 150 houses; and allowing six persons to each, consequently a population of 900. Distant S.W. from Goruckpore cantonment 22 miles. Lat. 26° 45′, long. 83° 2′.

HARIKE, in the Punjab, a village situate on the right bank of the Ghara river, three miles below the confluence of the Sutluj and Beas. The name Ghara is in this instance given to the river with some latitude, as it is not usually so called above a spot twelve miles below Harike. The site of the village is on the high bank of the river, and, when the water is low, distant a mile and a half from the ferry. Though a small place, the trade is important, and twenty years ago, nearly the whole traffic with Hindostan, from Afghanistan, Kashmir, and the Punjab, passed through it. There is besides great local traffic between the districts in its immediate vicinity on both sides of the river. Harike is in lat. 31° 10′, long. 74° 59′.

HARIPOOR, in the Punjab, a town on the great route by the Dub Pass into Cashmere, is a populous and thriving place, with a handsome and well-supplied bazar. Von Hügel considers it one of the wealthiest places in the Punjab, the streets being thronged with a busy and cheerful crowd, exhibiting evident indications of prosperity, and the shops supplied with all that can contribute to the gratification of Indian taste. It is situate on the river Dor, which, about ten miles westward, falls into the Indus near Torbela. Lat. 34° 14′, long. 72° 57′.

HARIPOOR, in the north-east of the Punjab, among the lower mountains of the Himalaya, is a fort, surrounded by a small town, which contains a good and well-supplied bazar. The name signifies the town of Hari, one of the incarnations of Vishnu, and Hindoo superstition here flourishes in the highest degree of vigour. Haripoor is in lat. 31° 56′, long. 76° 11′.

HARIPOOR, in the British district of Jaunsar, at the southern frontier, where it joins the Dehra Doon, a village in the bifurcation at the confluence of the Tons and Jumna. Though the Tons loses its name, and the united stream continues to be called the Jumna, the former is the larger, its discharge per second, when surveyed by Hodgson, being 2,827 cubic feet, and that of the latter 1,045. Elevation above the sea 1,686 feet. Lat. 30° 30′, long. 77° 54′.

HARIPOOR, in Cashmere, a small town situate in the Punch Pass from the Punjab into that valley, and near the spot where the pass opens into the low ground of Cashmere. It is close to the right bank of the Rembeara, a considerable feeder of the Veyut or Jhelum. Hence the Rembeara is sometimes called the River of Haripoor. The town is small and mean, remarkable only for its picturesque site beneath the Pir Panjal mountain, which on the south rears its towering summit, covered with snow during the greater part of the year. Lat. 33° 40′, long. 74° 51′.

HARNHULLY.—A town in the Mysore, 64 miles N.W. by N. from Seringapatam, and 96 miles E.N.E. from Mangalore. Lat. 13° 14′, long. 76° 16′.

HAROWTEE.—See KOTAH.

HARREEPOOR.—See AREEPOOR.

HARRIORPOOR.—A town in the Cuttack mehal of Mohurbunge, 30 miles N.W. from Balasore, and 56 miles S.W. from Midnapoor. Lat. 21° 51′, long. 86° 46′.

HARRISON'S ISLAND.—A small island lying off the coast of Arracan, situate about ten miles from the shore, and among the cluster of islands to the south of Ramree. Lat. 18° 40′, long. 94° 2′.

HARU, a small river of the Punjab, rises at the base of the Himalaya, and receiving the Nilab from the north-east, and several smaller streams, flows into the Indus on the eastern side, a few miles below Attock, after a course of about sixty miles. This confluence is in lat. 33° 49′, long. 72° 16′.

HASHTNUGGUR, in the Daman division of the Punjab, a town situated on the left bank of the Lundye, 20 miles N. of the town of Peshawur. Lat. 34° 15′, long. 71° 45′.

HASSAN, in the territory of Mysore, a town on the route from Bangalore to Mangalore. In 1690 it was conquered by Chikka Deo, rajah of Mysore, and incorporated with his dominions. Distant from Bangalore, W.,

102 miles; from Mangalore, E., 88. Lat. 13°, long. 76° 9′.

HASSAN ABDAL, in the Punjab, so called from containing the tomb of a reputed Mahometan saint of that name. It is situate in a delightful valley, watered by numerous springs, which gush from among the rocks. Here are the ruins of a pleasure-ground and small palace, tastefully formed by the Mogul emperor Akbar, and though much decayed, displaying yet an exquisite combination of elegance and refined luxury. Lat. 33° 48′, long. 72° 45′.

HASSAN KE GHURREE.—A town in the British district of Shikarpoor, province of Sinde, presidency of Bombay, 47 miles N. of Sukkur. Lat. 28° 20′, long. 68° 44′.

HASTINGS (FORT), in the British district of Kumaon, lieut.-gov. of the N.W. Provinces. It is a small well-built fort, on the summit of a conical hill, three miles and a half W. of Lohughat or Rikhesur. Water can be obtained only from the bottom of the hill, at a distance of half a mile of steep descent, so that the post, if regularly invested, must speedily fall. The artillery attached to Fort Hastings consists of two field howitzers, two brass six-pounders, four iron twelve-pounders, with an ample supply of ammunition. Elevation above the sea 6,240 feet. Lat. 29° 25′, long. 80° 5′.

HATEE, in Baghelcund, a town in the native state of Rewah, on the route from Mirzapoor to Lohogaon, 110 miles direct S.W. of Mirzapoor, 58 S.E. of Banda. Elevation above the sea 1,070 feet. Lat. 24° 42′, long. 80° 53′.

HATEE OOSTEE.—A town in the British district of Bhagulpoor, lieut.-gov. of Bengal, 63 miles N.N.W. of Bhagulpoor. Lat. 26°, long. 86° 31′.

HATH KA PEEPLEA.—A town of Malwa, in the native state of Dewas, 28 miles E. from Indoor, and 95 miles W. from Hoosungabad. Lat. 22° 45′, long. 76° 17′.

HATIMABAD, in the British district of Bolundshuhur, lieut.-gov. of the N.W. Provinces, a village on the route from Muttra to Meerut, and 48 miles S. of the latter. Lat. 28° 21′, long. 77° 56′.

HATIYA.—A town in the native state of Nepal, on the right bank of the river Arun, and 97 miles E. by N. from Khatmandoo. Lat. 27° 58′, long. 86° 50′.

HATRAS, in the district of Allygurh, lieut.-gov. of the N.W. Provinces, lies on the route from the cantonment of Agra to that of Allygurh, 33 miles N. of the former. It is built in the form of a square of about 500 yards, and is surrounded by a mud wall and a very deep dry ditch. The old fort is situate half a mile due east of the town, and though now a heap of ruins, was once regarded as formidable. When approached by the British troops in 1804, while in pursuit of Holkar's army in the Doab, Thorn describes it as built on a small hill, with a gradual ascent; and he continues: "In the centre of it stands a very high brick building, considerably overtopping the surrounding bastions. The glacis is about 100 yards wide; and a renny-wall (fausse-braie), with a deep, dry, and broad ditch behind it, surrounds the fort." The owner, a talookdar or renter of the surrounding district, on the occasion of Holkar's invasion, as well as at other times, acted with hostility towards the British; and at length his assumption of independence was found so mischievous and alarming, especially in the threatening state of affairs at the commencement of the Mahratta war in 1817, that it was found necessary to dislodge him. Dya Ram, who held the place at that time, was accordingly summoned to surrender the fort, and allow measures to be taken for its being dismantled. Trusting in the defences, which had been strengthened in imitation of those of the neighbouring British fort of Allygurh, by preparing a covered way, raising a glacis, and diminishing the height of the ramparts, the occupant refused compliance; whereupon, on the 23rd February, 1817, the town was breached and evacuated; and on the 1st of March fire was opened on the fort from forty-five mortars and three breaching-batteries of heavy guns. At the close of the same day, a magazine in the fort exploded, and caused such destruction of the garrison and buildings, that Dya Ram, terror-struck, abandoned the place in the course of the night, and it was forthwith dismantled, as well as the neighbouring fortress of Mursan, and some others. The population of this town, always considerable, has much increased since its direct subjection to British sway, the number of its inhabitants in 1853 being returned at 20,504. It is the chief mart for the cotton of the neighbouring tracts, which is forwarded by easy land-carriage to Furruckabad, on the Ganges, and conveyed by that river to the lower provinces. Distance S.E. from Delhi, by Allyghur, 106 miles; N.W. from Calcutta 815. Lat. 27° 36′, long. 78° 9′.

HATTIA RIVER.—One of the principal mouths of the river Megna.—See GANGES RIVER.

HATTIA.—An island lying at the mouth of the Megna river, and comprised within the jurisdiction of the British district of Bulloah, lieut.-gov. of Bengal. Its centre is in lat. 22° 35′, long. 91° 8′.

HATTOD.—A town in the native state of Indore, or territory of Holkar, 10 miles N.W. from Indore, and 129 miles W. from Hoosungabad. Lat. 22° 47′, long. 75° 44′.

HATTUH.—A town in the British province of Nagpoor, 88 miles N.E. from Nagpoor, and 49 miles E.S.E. from Seuni. Lat. 21° 46′, long. 80° 20′.

HAULKOORKY.—A town in the Mysore, 65 miles N. by W. from Seringapatam, and 109 miles E.N.E. from Mangalore. Lat. 13° 19′, long. 76° 26′.

HAUMP, in the Rewa Caunta division of Guzerat, presidency of Bombay, a town situate on the left bank of the Nerbudda river, and 73 miles E. by N. from Broach. Lat. 22°, long. 74° 6′.

HAUNSEE, in the Reechna Dooab division of the Punjab, a town situated on the left bank of the Chenaub, 70 miles W.N.W. of the town of Lahore. Lat. 32° 3′, long. 73° 6′.

HAUPUR, in the British district of Meerut, lieut.-gov. of the N.W. Provinces, a town situate on the route from the town of Meerut to Muttra, and 20 miles S. of the former. It is of considerable size, and has a population of 13,598. The place has been selected as the locality of one of the government studs, which has obtained celebrity for the character of the horses passed into the different branches of the service. Lat. 28° 44′, long. 77° 51′.

HAVALEE, in the Baree Dooab division of the Punjab, a town situated 10 miles from the right bank of the Sutlej, 90 miles S.W. of the town of Lahore. Lat. 30° 26′, long. 73° 34′.

HAVEYLEE, in the Jetch Dooab division of the Punjab, a town situated on the left bank of the Jhelum, 107 miles W. by N. of the town of Lahore. Lat. 31° 48′, long. 72° 23′.

HAWULBAGH, in the British district of Kumaon, lieut.-gov. of the N.W. Provinces. It is situate five miles north of Almora, and on the left bank of the Kosilla, running at a considerable depth below, with a deep, black, and violent current. The site is picturesque and fine, and as the climate is warmer than that of Almora, in consequence of an elevation less by 1,900 feet, it is generally the residence of the civil officers in charge of that town and of the district of Kumaon. There is also here a cantonment for the provincial battalion. Elevation above the sea 3,889 feet. Distance N.W. from Calcutta 963 miles. Lat. 29° 38′, long. 79° 40′.

HAYATNUGAR, in the district of Sultanpoor, territory of Oude, 80 miles S.E. of Lucknow. Butter estimates the population at 100, half of whom are Mussulmans. Lat. 26° 15′, long. 82° 13′.

HAYCOCK ROCK, situate off the shore of Arracan, in lat. 17° 10′, long. 94° 31′.

HAYES ISLAND, off the coast of Tenasserim, 93 miles from Tenasserim: length four, and breadth two miles. Lat. 11° 52′, long. 97° 45′.

HAZAREEBAGH.—A British district subject to the political agent for the south-west frontier, called also Ramgurh, which see.

HAZAREEBAGH, the principal place of the district of Hazareebagh or Ramgurh, a town on the route from Calcutta to Benares, 239 miles N.W. of the former, 189 S.E. of the latter. Jacquemont, who visited it in 1829, styles it a large village. Its principal bazar is regularly built, and some of the shops and houses, which are all of mud, are two stories high. It was formerly a place of more importance than at present, having been for some time the head-quarters for a regiment of the Queen's infantry, when a church was built, on the supposition of the permanent cantonment at that place, of an European regiment. In 1845, the station ceased to be a cantonment for European troops, and now is occupied by a detachment of the Ramgurh native battalion. It is also the station of a principal assistant to the Governor-General's agent for the south-west frontier, and contains a jail for civil and criminal prisoners. Hazareebagh is situate in an extensive and elevated plateau, overspread with forest and jungle, and having in many places the remains of mango-groves and other regular plantations, indicating the country to have been formerly much better peopled and cultivated. Its present desolate state is probably attributable to the devastations of the Mahrattas in the middle of the eighteenth century. Hazareebagh was selected as the residence of the ex-ameers of Sinde. Subsequent arrangements were made, under which two of the four brothers were permitted to remove to Lahore. Elevation above the sea 1,750 feet. Lat. 24°, long. 85° 24′.

HAZOO.—A town in the British district of Camroop, province of Assam, 15 miles W.N.W. of Gowhatty. Lat. 26° 15′, long. 91° 31′.

HAZRUTGUNJ, in the British district of Furruckabad, lieut.-gov. of the N.W. Provinces, a town near the northern frontier, towards Mynpooree, and 30 miles N.W. of the city of Furruckabad. Lat. 27° 39′, long. 79° 16′.

HEEAT.—A town in the Rajpoot state of Jodhpoor, on the left bank of one of the branches of the Rairee river, and 52 miles S.E. from Jodhpoor. Lat. 25° 53′, long. 73° 50′.

HEEPURGEH.—A town in the British district of Sholapoor, presidency of Bombay, 23 miles E. of Beejapoor. Lat. 16° 48′, long. 76° 8′.

HEERAPOOR, in the British territory of Saugur and Nerbudda, lieut.-gov. of the N.W. Provinces, a town on the route from Ramgurh to Baitool, 47 miles S.W. of the former. Lat. 22° 30′, long. 80° 21′.

HEERAPOOR, in the British district of Mynpooree, lieut.-gov. of the N.W. Provinces, a village between the cantonment of Allygurh and that of Mynpooree, and 32 miles N.W. of the latter. Lat. 27° 33′, long. 78° 44′.

HEERAPORE, in Bundelcund, a small town in a district of the native state of Churkharee, on the route from Banda to Saugor, 120 miles S.W. of the former, 52 N.E. of the latter. It has a bazar, and water from wells and a tank. By the Hirapur Pass, half a mile S.W. of the town, the route from Banda to Saugor ascends from the plains of Bundelcund to the plateau on the range styled by Franklin the Panna Hills. The pass "is about a mile in length, and easy." Lat. 24° 23', long. 79° 16'.

HEERIOOR, in the Mysore, a town situate on the right bank of the small river Vedavati, a perennial current of fine water. It once possessed 2,000 houses, an outer and inner fort, and several temples; but the place was ruined by the Mahrattas, and the calamities inflicted by them were completed by a dreadful famine which succeeded, and which swept away nearly all the inhabitants, the small remainder flying, and leaving the town in desolate waste. It recovered very slowly, and has never attained a degree of prosperity at all to be compared with its former state. Distance from Seringapatam, N., 100 miles; Bangalore, N.W., 94. Lat. 13° 57', long. 76° 41'.

HEGGADVENCOTTA.—A town in the Mysore, 33 miles S.W. from Seringapatam, and 56 miles E. by N. from Cannanore. Lat. 12° 7', long. 76° 23'.

HELUJA-KA-GOTE, in Sinde, a small town on the route from Tatta to Hyderabad, by Kotree, and 32 miles S. of the last-mentioned place. It is situate near the eastern extremity of the Kunjur Dund, a considerable expanse of brackish water, abounding in fish, and surrounded by low sandstone hills. Close *Shikarghas*, or "hunting-preserves," intervene between the town and the right bank of the Indus, distant about a mile and a half to the east. Plenty of forage may be obtained, and water is supplied from a small pond near the town. Lat. 24° 54', long. 68° 8'.

HELWANK.—A town in the British territory of Sattara, presidency of Bombay, 30 miles S.W. of Sattara. Lat. 17° 20', long. 73° 47'.

HEMMAUDY.—A town in the British district of South Canara, presidency of Madras, 56 miles N. by W. of Mangalore. Lat. 13° 41', long. 74° 46'.

HEMTABAD, in the British district of Dinajpore, lieut.-gov. of Bengal, a town on the left bank of the river Coolick, 25 miles W. of the town of Dinajpore. That it was formerly a place of importance, appears as well from tradition as from numerous ruins existing in its vicinity. Those of more remote date are considered to be of an era anterior to Mussulman sway. One of the most entire architectural relics of the latter period is a mosque, surmounted by seven small cupolas; the whole building, though of ungraceful construction, manifesting elaborate and costly workmanship. Contiguous is another building, denominated Takhti Husayn Padshah, or "Throne of King Hoseyn," formerly monarch of Bengal. It consists of a truncated pyramid, twenty feet high, having on its summit a considerable area, in the centre of which is a square, on which Husayn sat to witness public spectacles. Several tombs and shrines of deceased persons, regarded by Mussulmans as saints, are dispersed over the area. Hemtabad is in lat. 25° 38', long. 88° 12'.

HENERY ISLAND.—See ONDAREE.

HENNAVUTTY, in the Mysore, a river rising near the western frontier, on the eastern declivity of the Western Ghats, and in lat. 13° 12', long. 75° 44'. It flows for thirty-five miles south-eastward, to Santapoora, where it turns eastward, and thence holds a tortuous course, but generally in the direction last mentioned, for fifty miles, to Sagra. At that place it turns south-eastward, and continues to flow in that direction for thirty-five miles, to its fall into the Cauvery, on the left side of the latter river, near Kistnaraajpoor; its total length of course being 120 miles. It is officially described as a valuable stream, never quite dry.

HENZADA.—A town of Eastern India, in the British province of Pegu, on the right bank of the Irawady, and 65 miles W. from Pegu. Lat. 17° 40', long. 95° 18'.

HEOONLA, a river in the British district of Kumaon, lieut.-gov. of the N.W. Provinces, rises in the most southerly range of mountains of the Himalaya system, and in lat. 29° 55', long. 78° 40'. Its direction is generally north-westerly, and after a course of about twenty-five miles it falls into the Ganges, on the left side, in lat. 30° 6', long. 78° 26'. Webb forded it in April, five miles above its mouth, and found it forty yards wide and sixteen inches deep, with a moderately rapid current.

HERDOSE.—A town in the Southern Mahratta jaghire of Bore, situate on the right bank of one of the branches of the Neera river, and 26 miles S. from Poonah. Lat. 18° 4', long. 73° 42'.

HERRINKAIRO, in the British territory of Saugur and Nerbudda, lieut.-gov. of the N.W. Provinces, a town on the route from Hoosungabad to Ellichpoor, 17 miles S.S.W. of the former. Lat. 22° 30', long. 77° 40'.

HERRUN, a small river, rises in the British territory of Saugor and Nerbudda, and in lat. 23° 30', long. 80° 26'. It holds a sinuous course, but generally south-west, of about ninety miles, and falls into the Nerbudda, on the right side, at Sacar, in lat. 23° 4', long. 79° 26'. At the confluence, the Nerbudda has already attained such magnitude as to be 600 yards in width.

HETTOURA.—See ETOUNDA.

HEWEEKEIR.—A town in one of the recently sequestrated districts of Hyderabad, or dominions of the Nizam, 42 miles W. from Ellichpoor, and 164 miles E. by N. from Malligaum. Lat. 21° 7', long. 76° 57'.

HEWERKAIR, in the British territory of Saugur and Nerbudda, lieut.-gov. of the N.W. Provinces, a town on the route from Gawilgurh to Nagpoor, 70 miles W. by N. of the latter. Lat. 21° 22', long. 78° 6'.

HEWRA, or UHEERA, in the British district of Poona, presidency of Bombay, a village the vicinity of which has been selected for the site of one of the government botanical gardens.

Distant 27 miles N. from Poona. Lat. 18° 52′, long. 73° 45′.

HIDDAGOTE.—A village of Sinde, on the route from Sehwan to Larkhana, and nine miles N. of the former place. The road north and south is rendered inconvenient by numerous watercourses, which aid the cultivation of this fertile and populous tract. The village is situate about a mile from the right bank of the Indus. Lat. 26° 32′, long. 67° 53′.

HIDGELLEE.—A British district situate within the jurisdiction of the presidency of Bengal. It is bounded on the north-east by the Hoogly river, separating it from the British districts of Hoogly and the Twenty-four Pergunnahs; on the south-east by the river Hoogly and the Bay of Bengal; on the west by the Balasore division of Cuttack, and by the British district of Midnapore. It lies between lat. 21° 36′—22° 22′, long. 87° 22′—88° 12′, and has an area of 1,014 square miles. It has a considerable length of coast, commencing at its south-western extremity, in lat. 21° 36′, long. 87° 26′, and washed by the Bay of Bengal for twenty miles, as far as the mouth of the small river Mahona, where the estuary of the Hoogly may be considered to commence. The shore of this estuary continues to form the boundary of the district for eleven miles in a direction north-east, to the mouth of the Russoolpoor river; and, in the same direction, for seventeen miles, to the mouth of the Huldee; thence, still north-east, for twelve miles, to Diamond Point, where it turns north-westward for eighteen miles, to Tumlook. The inside channel, giving access from the Bay of Bengal to the Hoogly, extends along the whole of this coast as far as the mouth of the Roopnarain. This was formerly the deepest and most-frequented channel; and Kedgeree, about eight miles above, or north-east of the Russoolpoor river, was much used as an anchorage for the largest ships; but of late years the channel has become silted up, so as to have not more than two or three fathoms water, and is now frequented only by country vessels. The Roopnarain does not appear to be navigable for large ships, and the flood-tide setting strongly up into it, many vessels making for the Hoogly, on their way to Calcutta, have been swept up the shallow estuary and lost. Besides the Hoogly, the Roopnarain, and the Russoolpoor river, the only stream of importance belonging to the district is the Huldee, which, rising in Midnapore, crosses the north-western frontier of this district, and, holding a course easterly for about thirty-five miles, falls into the estuary of the Hoogly. The streams above mentioned, though nearly dry during the greater part of the year, contribute largely to swell the Hoogly during the periodical rains. A considerable quantity of fine salt is manufactured by a rude but effective process. The sea along the coast is remarkably productive, and the fisheries are pursued with eagerness and success. The climate, especially in the more depressed and moist parts, is very unhealthy even to the natives, who are greatly affected by elephantiasis, dysentery, agues, and fevers. Rice is the principal crop, and is produced of a large size, and in great luxuriance and abundance, but is considered inferior to the average produce of Bengal and Behar. The other crops are sugarcane, tobacco, pulse, cucurbitaceous plants, millet, mustard, castor-oil plant, and other oil-yielding productions, hemp, safflower (Carthamus tinctorius), sweet potatoes, capsicum, and various potherbs. The cocoanut-palm and the toddy-palm (Borassus flabelliformis), from the fermented juice of which an ardent spirit is distilled, grow in the maritime tracts. There are no manufactures of any importance, unless that of salt be considered as such. The population is given under the article BENGAL. The only routes are—1. From north-east to south-west, from Calcutta to the town of Contai or Hidgellee; 2. from south-east to north-west, from the town of Hidgellee to that of Midnapore. This district was included in the grant of the dewanny of Bengal, Behar, and Orissa, made to the East-India Company by the emperor of Delhi, in August, 1765.

HIDGELLEE.—A town in the British district of the same name, under the presidency of Bengal. It is situate on the right or western shore of one of the entrances of the Hoogly, called the Inner Channel, and at the mouth of a small river falling into it. The civil establishment of the district appears to have been removed to the town of Contai. Distance from Calcutta, S.W., 48 miles; from Midnapore, S.E., 82. Lat. 21° 49′, long. 87° 50′.

HIGH ISLAND.—A small island about five miles from the mainland of Arracan, in lat. 17°, long. 94° 30′. There is another of the same name in lat. 16° 38′, long. 94° 20′.

HILSAH.—A town in the British district of Patna, lieut.-gov. of Bengal, 21 miles S.S.E. of Patna. Lat. 25° 17′, long. 85° 22′.

HILL STATES.—Under this name are included a number of small sovereignties or chieftainships in the Cis-Sutlej territory, all of which appear to have possessed some degree at least of independence, till overrun and subjugated by the encroaching power of the Goorkhas. On the breaking out of the war with Nepaul in 1814, Sir David Ochterlony issued a proclamation inviting the various chiefs to co-operate with the British, and promising to such as should satisfactorily comply with the call, confirmation in their hereditary possessions, and protection from future attempts at aggression. A few only entitled themselves to the benefits held out: some had fled from the oppression of their invaders, some kept back from fear, and probably some distrusted the promises of the British government, and were apprehensive that by compliance with the required conditions, they should but exchange one tyranny for another. The success of the British army removed all ground for hesitation, and put an end to the opportunity of choosing between the Goorkhas and their conquerors. All the chieftains now became candidates for the exercise of either the justice or the clemency of the triumphant power, and the liberality of the British government was manifested in admitting claims which had been justly forfeited, and restoring possessions which the fortune of war had placed at its disposal. A part of Gurwhal was restored to its fugitive rajah; the remainder, consisting of the districts situate to the eastward, above the confluence of the Mandakini and the Aluknunda, together with the Dehra Dhoon, the pergunnah of Raeengurh, Subathoo, and Sewah, were retained by the victors, as was also the pergunnah of Sundock, in which is a cantonment for British troops. Burrowlee passed to the rajah of Nalagurh or Hindoor, in exchange for Malown, occupied as a British post. Bughat was dismembered, and a portion disposed of to the rajah of Patteeala; the remainder has since lapsed to the paramount power, from failure of heirs. A claim, however, to the succession has been recently preferred by a first cousin of the last two chiefs. The claim was not allowed, but a discretionary authority was given to the local government either to retain the estate, or, if more expedient, to bestow it on the claimant by a new sunnud: this was in 1849. The former alternative was adopted, and Bughat is now a British possession. Keyonthul, like Bughat, was subjected to the process of dismemberment, and the excised part was transferred to the rajah of Patteeala. In consideration of this alienation, the remainder of the Keyonthul state is excused the payment of tribute. At a later period, Raeengurh, which had been reserved by the British government as a military post, was made over to the ruler of Keyonthul, in exchange for Simla. Kothkai, in consequence of long and irreclaimable misgovernment, was in 1828 annexed to the British dominions. The ruler of Ootrach or Turoch, from the like cause, but more than ten years later, incurred the penalty of confiscation, and the territory was incorporated with Joobul. The states now recognised as having a distinct existence are the following:—Bhagul, Beejah, Beejee, Bulsun, Bussahir, Dhamie, Dhorcatee, Ghurwal, Hindoor or Nalagurh, Joobul, Keyonthul, Koomharsin, Koonyhar, Kothar, Kuhloor or Belaspore, Manee-Majra, Mangul, Muhlog, and Sirmoor Nahun. The area of the whole is 10,054 square miles; the entire population about 581,020. Each will be found noticed in its respective place under the alphabetical arrangement, as will also the portions of territory in these districts originally retained, or subsequently acquired by the British government.

HIMALAYA.—A vast assemblage of mountains, stretching in an irregularly curved line from the defile above Cashmere, on the north-west, through which the Indus penetrates into the plains of the Punjab, and separates the range from the mountains of Hindoo Koosh, to the southern bend of the Sanpo or Dihong on the east, previous to its junction with the Brahmapootra. This stupendous mass extends over 22° of longitude, its western extremity lying in long. 73° 23′, and its eastern in long. 95° 23′.

In so brief a sketch as necessity compels, it is impracticable to go beyond an outline of the more noticeable facts of this remarkable region; and it is necessary to premise, that the view must be restricted in a great degree to the southern slope of the mountains, as that which constitutes the limit of India on the north. To extend inquiry to the Tibetan side, would exceed the proper bounds of the work; while, to carry research into the wide variety of subjects which might be introduced, as into the various branches of natural history, or into the habits, languages, history, and present circumstances of the inhabitants, would swell the article to a length disproportioned to the place which it should occupy in a book embracing so wide a field. Some information on these points will, moreover, be found under other heads; among which, the reader may be referred to the articles Kumaon, Gurwhal, and Bussahir. It would, however, be unjust to refrain in this place from noticing a very admirable, though short tract, by Dr. Hooker, "On the Climate and Vegetation of the temperate and cold regions of East Nepal, and the Sikkim and Himmalaya Mountains;" in regard to meteorology and plants of the parts proposed to be illustrated, it is most valuable, and the more so, as it is the result of the personal observations of the learned author.

About midway between the limits above defined, and in the vicinity of Lake Manasarowar, is the southern extremity of the mountain-range, which, extending from the north-west into Thibet, separates the drainage system of the Indus from that of the Sanpoo (afterwards the Brahmapootra), and is by some regarded as the grand central axis of Asia. From this centre the chain of the Himalayas stretches to nearly an equal distance in a north-westerly direction on the one hand, and a south-easterly on the other, throwing off at right angles lateral ranges sloping southward to the plains of India. Deep narrow valleys, separated from each other by these meridional ranges, contain the sources of the numerous rivers which constitute the drainage system of the Indus, the Ganges, and the Brahmapootra. Among the tributaries of the Indus, may be enumerated the Jhelum, Chenab, Beas, Ravee, and Sutlej; the principal feeders of the Ganges are the Jumna, Gogra, Gunduck, and Cosy: the Teesta and some others fall into the Brahmapootra. The elevation of the culminating range of the Himalaya, observes Dr. Thomson, "is probably at a mean about 18,000 or 20,000 feet; it is nearly uniform at about these elevations throughout a great part of the chain, but gradually diminishes towards both ends. Like all mountain-chains, it presents alternations of high and low portions, the lower parts or passes, as they are called, from their affording the means of passage to travellers from one side to the other, being at the upper extremities of the river-basins. These passes are, with a few exceptions, rarely under 17,000 or 18,000 feet. The lateral chains, starting from the more elevated portions of the central axis between the passes, gradually diminish in elevation as they approach the plains of India, not, however, with any exact uniformity of progression ; for it is not unfrequent to find them rise into lofty peaks, considerably more elevated than any known part of the central axis. The greater part of the giant peaks, which rise to an elevation of 26,000 or 28,000 feet, are situated in this manner, not on the central axis, but to the south of it."

The distribution of the Himalayas, by the authority just quoted, into two grand sections (the eastern and western), is calculated to exhibit with greater perspicuity the leading characteristics of each, and is obviously preferable to the distribution of Herbert, under which the chain is divided into three separate portions ; the section designated the "Indo-Gangetic range," and stretching from the source of the Sutlej, in Lake Manasarowar, to the vicinity of Ropur, on that river, in long. 76° 40′, occupying the central position. A more recent traveller, whose researches extended to those regions, adopts the less complicated of the two arrangements, and in so doing advances additional arguments in its favour. The two sections, he contends, furnish points of resemblance, in presenting almost insurmountable obstacles to communication between the countries which they divide, and both marking the boundaries of nations, by separating the Botis of Thibet from the Hindoo family of India. The distinction of climate he considers not less positively marked than that of nations ; both ranges forming the "lines of demarcation between the cold and dry climate of Thibet, with its dearth of trees, and the warm and humid climate of India, with its luxuriance of vegetable productions." Some analogy, moreover, may be traced between the drainage systems of the two sections ; the one separating the waters of the Sanpo from those of the Ganges and its affluents, and the other intervening between the Indus, flowing at its northern base, and the subsequent tributaries of that river rising on its southern slope.

Major Cunningham, however, appears to be in error in supposing that the two divisions present points of contrast as well as of resemblance. "There is," he observes, "one marked difference between the eastern and western ranges, which can scarcely fail in striking the most casual observer. The inferior mountains of the eastern chain generally run at right angles to its axis ; whereas those of the western chain are mostly disposed in subordinate parallel ranges." This marked difference, however, is not between the eastern and western divisions, but between two separate portions of the latter. The ramifications running "at right angles" to the axis, and the "parallel ranges," are both comprised within the limits assigned by Major Cunningham to his western division ; viz. from the sources of the Sutlej to the banks of the Indus. In allusion to a portion of this division, Captain Strachey observes : "If we examine the structure of the mountains more closely, we shall find that from the sources of the Tonse to those of the Kali, a space which includes the provinces of Gurwhal and Kumaon, all the great rivers, the Bhagerati, Vishnugunga, Douli of Niti, Gori, Douli of Darma, and Kali, run in directions not far from perpendicular to the general direction of the Himalaya. Further, that they are separated one from another by great transverse ranges, on which all the highest of the measured peaks of this region are to be found." From these, moreover, proceeds an intricate ramification of subordinate ridges, giving to the whole area a most irregular and confused appearance. "Even the Snowy chain," says Herbert, speaking of the Indo-Gangetic chain, "though defined to a certain degree by a phenomenon so singular on a first view to the inhabitant of the plain country, loses on a nearer approach all character of continuity and regularity, and appears under the same confused and irregular aspect which the lower elevations are observed to bear."

The length of the western division of the culminating range of the Himalayas, from the source of the Sutlej to the peaks of Dayamur on the Indus (within which limits are comprised the Indo-Gangetic and the Bara Lacha ranges), is nearly 700 miles. The elevations of its summits are as under :—

Peaks.	Height.
1. Monomangli or Gurla......	23,900
2. Kunlas Peak	22,513
3. Gula Ghal Peak	21,258
4. XX.	20,479
5. XIX.	22,707
6. XVIII.	22,511
7. XV.	22,491
8. Nanda Devi..............	25,749
9. XIII.	22,385
10. XII.	22,385
11. A. No. 1	23,531
12. XI.	20,758
13. A. No. 3	23,317
14. N.	23,482
15. L.	22,266
16. K.	22,570
17. I.	23,300
18. Kamet	25,550
19. VIII.	23,236
20. Badrinath Peak	22,954
21. VII.	23,441
22.	22,754
23. H.	21,894
24. G.	22,556
25. U.	21,612
26. Kedarnath	23,062
27. M.	22,792
28. St. Patrick	22,798

	Peaks.	Height.
29.	St. George	22,654
30.	Rudru Himála............	22,390
31.	Swarga	22,906
32.	The Pyramid	21,579
33.	Jaonli Peak	21,940
34.	E. C....................	21,772
35.	F.	21,964
36.	G. Srikanta	20,296
37.	Rock Peak	21,076
38.	Windy Peak (Kyobrang) ..	20,169
39.	Glacier Peak	20,544
40.	Raldang or W. Kailás	21,103
41.	Pyramidal Peak	20,106
42.	Porgyal.................	22,700
43.	Chang-Razing Peak	20,500
44.	Gyu Peak................	24,764
45.	Parang Peaks	19,500
46.	Zanskar Ridge...........	20,000
47.	Ser and Mer.............	20,000
48.	Bal Tal Peak	19,650
49.	Dayamur	20,000
50.	Peak N. of Peshawur......	20,493

The mean elevation, as already observed, is about 20,000 feet, the limits of the snow-line on the southern slope having a height of about 18,500 feet. According to Herbert, the geological structure of these mountains consists of gneiss and a schistose formation, comprising micaceous, chloritic, and talcose schists. Captain Strachey, describing the character of the Indo-Gangetic chain, observes: "Along the lines on which the points of greatest elevation are found in this part of the range, we invariably see, for a breadth of several miles, veins of granite in great abundance penetrating the schists, often cutting through them, but perhaps most frequently following the bedding of the strata, between which they seem to have been forced. The great peaks are, I think, in almost every case, composed of schistose rock, but the granite veins may be most clearly seen on the faces of the mountains to very great elevations. Kamet, one of the highest of the peaks in this region, seems, however, to be among the exceptions to this rule; its summit, which is upwards of 25,500 feet above the sea, appearing to consist of granite alone. This line of granite seems to be subdivided into several branches, distributed generally along the strike, but otherwise not very regularly. In immediate succession to the crystalline schists penetrated by granite veins, we here come at once upon slaty beds overlying them, along the bottom of which, near the mica schists and gneiss, is a line of granite veins, differing somewhat in appearance from those of the larger eruption, and not producing any great alteration in the slaty beds themselves, as is shown by the occurrence of a coarse conglomerate, the component parts of which are perfectly distinct only a few feet above the granite. Above these are slaty beds, in all perhaps 9,000 feet in thickness, consisting of coarse slates, grits, and limestones, all more or less affected by slaty cleavage, and all devoid of fossil remains. It is after reaching the top of these strata, which is rarely done at a less elevation than 14,000 feet above the sea, that we at length enter again a region of fossiliferous rocks, which extends as far as my examinations have been carried. And it is not a little wonderful to find at this immense elevation a regular succession of most of the more important formations, from the silurian to the tertiary periods."

The length of the eastern section of the culminating range of the Himalayas, from the confluence of the Dihong with the Brahmapootra in the east, to the river Kalee, forming the boundary of Nepaul on the west, is about 800 miles. This portion supports the l[illegible] peaks of Kinchinjunga and Dhwalagiri. Seen from Patna, observes Dr. Royle, "at a distance of about 150 miles, these stupendous mountains present a long line of snow-white pinnacles, which, on a nearer approach, are seen towering above the dark line of lower but still lofty mountains." Dhwalagiri, having an elevation of 28,000 feet, is in lat. 29° 10′, long. 83°. Two hundred miles eastward of this, and in lat. 28° 20′, long. 86°, is situate the mountain of Gossainthan, attaining the height of 24,740 feet. After another interval of 140 miles in the same direction, the lofty peak of Kinchinjunga rises to the height of 28,176 feet. This last-named mountain is in the north-east angle of Nepaul. Between Kinchinjunga and the city of Katmandoo another mountain is reported to have been recently discovered, having an elevation of 29,002 feet. It has been named Mount Everest. This is probably the highest mountain in the world, its summit overtopping the principal peak of the Andes by above half a mile of perpendicular altitude. Contiguous to Nepaul on the east, is the petty territory of Sikkim, speaking of which Dr. Hooker says:—"Viewed from a distance on the plains of India, Sikkim presents the appearance—common to all mountainous countries—of consecutive parallel (wooded) ridges, running east and west, backed by a beautiful line of snowy peaks, with occasional breaks in the foremost ranges, through which the rivers debouch. Any view of the Himalaya, especially at a sufficient distance for the distant snowy peaks to be seen overtopping the outer ridges, is very rare, from the constant deposition of vapours over the forest-clad ranges during the greater part of the year, and the haziness of the dry atmosphere of the plains in the winter months. At the end of the rains, when the south-east monsoon has ceased to blow with constancy, views are obtained, sometimes from a distance of nearly 200 miles. The angle subtended by the giant peaks is so low (not a degree), that they appear like white specks very low on the horizon, tipping the black lower and outer wooded ranges, which always rest on a belt of haze, and from the density, probably, of the lower strata of atmosphere, are never seen to rest on the visible horizon. The remarkable lowness on the horizon of the whole stupendous mass is always a disappointing feature to the new comer, who expects to see dazzling peaks towering in the air. Approaching nearer, the snowy mountains sink behind the wooded ones long before the latter have assumed gigantic proportions, and when they increase in size, they appear a sombre, lurid grey-green mass of vegetation, with no brightness or variation of colour. There is no break in this forest caused by rock, precipice, or cultivation; some spurs project nearer, and some valleys appear to retire further into the heart of the first great chain that shuts out all the country beyond. No pines whatever are seen on the outer range of Sikkim, both soil and climate being far too damp in the rainy season; nor are the colours of the foliage so varied and bright as the more perennially humid forests of tropical shores, from the want of any abundance of such palms as caryota, tall arecæ, and of artocarpi, or of orange-groves." Beyond this, extensive tracts of the Himalayas remain unexplored, though it is known that a considerable portion of the Bootan territory, extending to long. 95°, presents a succession of lofty and rugged mountains, frequently rising to an altitude of 20,000 feet above the level of the sea, and covered with snow throughout the year.

Thus it will be seen that the great Himalaya range, from its north-western extremity, where its continuity with the Hindoo-Koosh is broken by the Indus, takes a south-easterly direction, giving rise in its course to the Jhelum, Chenaub, Ravee, and Beas rivers, after which it is penetrated by the Sutlej, previous to its debouch into the plains near Roopur. Further east, it continues its original direction, throwing off in its progress the feeders of the Ganges, and also of the Brahampootra subsequently to its confluence with the Sanpoo or Dihong. The entire chain may be said to have an average breadth of 150 miles; its length is computed at about 1,500. "The noblest scenery in India," says Elphinstone, "is under the Himalaya, where the ridges are broken into every form of the picturesque, with abrupt rocks, and slopes covered with gigantic pines and other trees, on the same vast scale, mixed with the most beautiful of our flowering shrubs, and the best of our fruits in a state of nature. Over the whole towers the majestic chain of the Himalayas, covered with eternal snow, a sight which the soberest traveller has never described without kindling into enthusiasm, and which, if once seen, leaves an impression that can never be equalled or effaced."

HIMMUTGUNGE, in the British district of Allahabad, lieut.-gov. of the N.W. Provinces, a village on the route from the cantonment of Allahabad to Jubbulpore, and four miles S. of the former. It is situate on the left bank of the Jumna, at the Gawghat ferry, and has a small space suited for encamping. Lat. 25° 26′, long. 81° 55′.

HIMUTGARH, in the territory of Gwalior, or possessions of Scindia, a small town 10 miles S.W. of the fort of Gwalior. It is situate at the north extremity of a narrow pass, extending from north to south, through a range of rocky sandstone hills, to the town of Puniar. Close to it was fought, on 29th December, 1843, an engagement, styled the battle of Puniar, between the British detachment led from Bundelcund by General Grey and the Mahrattas. The British lost thirty-six men killed, and 180 wounded; the Mahrattas lost all their artillery, amounting to twenty-four pieces, all their ammunition, some treasure, and a great number of men. Lat. 26° 6′, long. 78° 3′.

HINDIA, or HANDIYA, in the territory of Gwalior, or possessions of Scindia's family, a town on the route from Baitool to Mow, 90 miles N.W. of former, 96 S.E. of latter. It is situate on the left or south bank of the Nerbudda, here a great river, 1,000 yards wide. It is of considerable size, and has a large bazar, and a fort commanding several ghats or passes over the river. This place was, in 1820, occupied by a British force, and by the treaty of 1844, was, with its pergunnah, and that of Hurda, yielding together an annual revenue of 140,000 rupees, placed under British management, the revenue being appropriated to the maintenance of the augmented Gwalior contingent. Distant S. from Gwalior fort 280 miles, S.E. from Oojein 90. Lat. 22° 26′, long. 76° 59′.

HINDOLEE.—A town in the Rajpoot state of Boondee, three miles from the left bank of the Nej Nuddee, and 13 miles N.W. from Boondee. Lat. 25° 35′, long. 75° 34′.

HINDON, a river of Hindustan, rises at the south-west base of the Sewalik range, in lat. 30° 15′, long. 77° 53′. Its course is southerly, and divided from that of the Jumna by a slight elevation of the surface, along which the Doab Canal extends. In the rainy season it communicates by cross channels and branches with various torrents, which then traverse the country. After a course generally southerly of about 160 miles, it falls into the Jumna on the left side, in lat. 28° 27′, long. 77° 30′. It is crossed by the route from Dehra to Saharunpoor, in lat. 29° 58′, long. 77° 43′, and is there fordable during the dry season. It is also crossed by the route from Kurnoul to Mozuffernuggur, in lat. 29° 22′, long. 77° 33′, and is there fordable, except when swollen during the rains; by the route from Kurnoul to Meerut, in lat. 29° 12′, long. 77° 34′, and is there fordable, with a depth of from two to two and a half feet; and by the route from Meerut to Saharunpoor, in lat. 29° 53′, long. 77° 40′, and is there crossed by a bridge and long causeway.

HINDOOR, or NALAGURH.—A hill state at the south-western declivity of the Himalaya Mountains. It is bounded on the north by Kuhloor; on the east by Bhagul and Muhlog; on the south and west by Sirhind. It contains an area of 233 square miles, the centre being in lat. 31° 7′, long. 76° 50′. It is traversed throughout its whole extent by a steep range of hills, which, rising over the left bank of the Sutlej, continues in a south-easterly direction until joining the Sub-Himalaya near Subathoo. Parts of this ridge attain a considerable height; Chumbagarh being 4,400, and Ramgarh 4,054 feet above the sea. The drainage is either by the rivers Gumbur and Gunrora, which flow in a north-westerly direction to the Sutlej, or by the Sarsa, which, rising in the Pinjor Doon, takes also a north-westerly direction, and falls into the Sutlej near Kanoli, after a course of about thirty miles. Moorcroft speaks of part of the country thus traversed in favourable terms:—"The valley of the Gamrora is populous and well cultivated. Along the courses of the different small streams by which it is intersected are rows of pear-trees, which, at the time we passed them, were in full blossom. Villages occurred repeatedly on either side of the road." The Sursa receives several small streams from the north and north-east: of these the most worth notice are the Baladh and the Ruta. The Lohund and the Kalakund, two small rivers, flow down the mountain-tract sloping to the north-west, and fall into the Sutlej. The low grounds on the banks of the Sursa and Sutlej are alluvial, fertile, and, being little more than 1,000 feet above the sea, have a climate and produce resembling those of intertropical regions. The crops are generally maize, rice, wheat, barley, various kinds of millet, cotton, opium, ginger, turmeric, hemp, tobacco, oil-seeds, and esculent vegetables. The fruits are pomegranates, peaches, apricots, plums, apples, pears, walnuts, raspberries, strawberries, and melons. The pulp of the pomegranates is eaten; the husks are dried, and exported for the purposes of dyeing and tanning. The acacia, Indian fig, pine, elm, willow, gentian, geranium, rose, and other shrubs familiar in Europe, adorn the hills. The country is altogether picturesque, beautiful, fertile, well watered, and highly cultivated. The only places of importance are Nalagarh, Ramgarh, and Plassi or Palasi. Nalagarh is at present the residence of the rajah, in place of Plassi, at which he formerly dwelt. The population of the raj is estimated by Moorcroft at 20,000. It is represented to contain 136 villages, and to yield an annual revenue of 10,000*l.*; but according to official report of a recent date (1848), the revenue does not exceed 8,000*l.* The thakooree of Burrowlee, with the exception of a small part, was conferred on the rajah of Hindoor, in November, 1815, in lieu of the fort of Malown, with six villages, retained as a post for British troops. The rajah holds under the East-India Company, from whom he received his raj on the expulsion of the Goorkhas in 1815; and in troublous times his conduct has been characterized by his devotion to British interests.

HINDOSTAN.—See INDIA.

HINDOUL, in the British district of Muttra, lieut.-gov. of the N.W. Provinces, a village on the route from the cantonment of Meerut to that of Muttra, and 17 miles N.E. of the latter. Lat. 27° 42′, long. 77° 49′.

HINDOWN, in the Rajpoot state of Jeypore, a town on the route from Agra to Mow, 71 miles S.W. of former, 344 N.E. of latter. It was formerly a large city, with several extensive buildings, but suffered so much from the devastations of the Mahrattas, that it is much decayed, though still populous. The rampart which once surrounded it is now quite in ruins, but it has a good bazar. Lat. 26° 41′, long. 77° 10′.

HINGLAJGARH, or HINGLAISGARH, in Malwa, a hill fort in the possession of Holkar's family, long deemed impregnable by the natives. It is surrounded by a deep ravine 200 feet deep, 250 wide, and with perpendicular sides, from the edge of which the walls rise, and is accessible only by three causeways, made to form communications across the chasm, with three gates respectively. It was, however, stormed July 3rd, 1804, by a British detachment sent by Colonel Monson, stationed at Sunara, ten miles farther east. The detachment, commanded by Major Sinclair, consisted of a battalion of a native regiment, with six six-pounders and a party of irregular horse. After battering for an hour, the British escaladed the walls, and took the place with little loss, not a British officer being either killed or wounded. It was subsequently restored to Holkar, apparently in conformity to the declaratory article annexed to the treaty of Rajpurghat, 1805. Distant from Indor, N., 130 miles; from Oojein, N., 100. Lat. 24° 40′, long. 75° 50′.

HINGMEE.—A town in Hyderabad, or dominions of the Nizam, on the right bank of the Payne Gunga river, and 168 miles N. by W. from Hyderabad. Lat. 19° 43′, long. 77° 57′.

HINGNAH.—A town in the British province of Nagpoor, 12 miles S.W. from Nagpoor, and 96 miles E. by S. from Ellichpoor. Lat. 21° 2′, long. 79° 2′.

HINGOLEE, in Hydrabad, or territory of the Nizam, a town on the route from the city of Hydrabad to Akola, 185 miles N.W. of former, 72 S. of latter. It is one of the stations of the force denominated the Nizam's contingent, but actually a British force, officered by British, and under the direction and control of the British government. Distance from Madras, N.W., 500 miles; Bangaloor, N., 465; Secunderabad, N.W., 190; Bombay, E., 290; Kampti, S.W., 167. Lat. 19° 42′, long. 77° 11′.

HINGONA, in the territory of Gwalior, a village on the route from Agra to the fort of Gwalior, 47 miles S. of former, 23 N.W. of latter. It is situate on the left bank of the small river Kohari, and has a bazar. Here, in the end of December, 1843, the British army under Sir Hugh Gough, commander-in-chief, accompanied by Lord Ellenborough, remained encamped some days during the abortive negotiation previous to the battle of Maharajpoor and Chonda. Lat. 26° 34′, long. 77° 57′.

HINGUNGHAT, in the territory of Nagpore, a town on the river Wunna, a tributary of the Wurda. It is a place of considerable trade, and is interesting to the geologist, from containing numerous specimens of organized substances in the Vulcanian formation, general in this part of India. They are principally portions of fossilized palm-trees. During the Mahratta war in 1818, it was occupied by a British force, to cut off the communication of the flying Peishwa from the city of Nagpore. Distance from Nagpore, S., 45 miles. Lat. 20° 34′, long. 78° 53′.

HINWA, a river of Nepal, rising in lat. 27° 20′, long. 88° 4′, on the western slope of a spur of the Himalayas which connects the main or Snowy range with that known as the Sub-Himalaya, and, flowing through the district of Chyanpoor, in a westerly direction, for forty-five miles, falls into the Tambur on the left side, in lat. 27° 9′, long. 87° 24′.

HINWA, or EINWAH, in the district of Aldemau, territory of Oude, a village two miles from the right bank of the river Ghaghra, 28 miles S.E. of Fyzabad, 100 E. of Lucknow. Butter estimates its population at 500, all Hindoos. Lat. 26° 37′, long. 82° 25′.

HINWA.—A river of Nepal, rising in lat. 27° 20′, long. 88° 3′, on the western face of an extensive spur of the Himalayas, separating Sikhim from Nepal. It flows in a direction westerly for fifty miles, to its junction with the Tambur, in lat. 27° 8′, long. 87° 27′.

HIRDOEE, in Bundelcund, a town in the British district of Jaloun, on the route by Koonch from Gwalior to Calpee, 32 miles W. of the latter. It has a bazar, and is well supplied with water. Lat. 25° 59′, long. 79° 20′.

HIRNEE.—A town in the British district of Tirhoot, lieut.-gov. of Bengal, 81 miles E. by N. of Dinapoor. Lat. 25° 47′, long. 86° 24′.

HISSAMPOOR.—A town in the territory of Oude, five miles from the left bank of the Gogra river, and 48 miles N.E. by E. from Lucknow. Lat. 27° 13′, long. 81° 39′.

HISSAR, in the British district of Hurreeanah, lieut.-gov. of the N.W. Provinces, a town on the route from the city of Delhi to Bhutneer. It is situate on the branch made by Feroz Shah from the Delhi Canal to supply water for irrigation, as well as for the use of the numerous host of followers brought by him into this arid tract, which was his favourite hunting-ground, the neighbouring wastes harbouring lions and tigers, besides other wild beasts less formidable. This watercourse appears to have been partly made by excavation, partly by clearing the channel of the Chitang, or one of its branches. In 1825 it was, by order of the British government, cleared out as far as Darbah, twenty-five miles north-west of Hissar, to which last place it is navigable for timber-rafts. Previously to this renovation, the town and its vicinity suffered much from want of water, being supplied merely from tanks or from wells, of which last it had 306 in the time of George Thomas. There is a well-supplied bazar, and formerly the East-India Company had here a stud, to furnish a supply of horses for the army; but in 1844 the establishment ceased. The place was likewise selected as the site of a farm for rearing cattle for the ordnance department; but this establishment also has been recently abolished. In the time of Akbar, Hissar had two forts, one of stone, the other of brick. The circar, of which it was the principal place, was rated to furnish 6,875 cavalry, 55,700 infantry, and an annual revenue of 13,75,022 rupees. The road to the east is good; to the west it is in many places good, but occasionally heavy. Distant N.W. from Delhi 104 miles; N.W. from Calcutta 991 miles. Lat. 29° 8′, long. 75° 50′.

HISSULOOR.—A town in the British district of North Canara, presidency of Madras, 126 miles N. by E. of Mangalore. Lat. 14° 42′, long. 74° 59′.

HOBIGUNJE.—A town in the British district of Dacca Jelalpore, lieut.-gov. of Bengal, 40 miles S. by W. of Dacca. Lat. 23° 11′, long. 90° 11′.

HOBRA, in the British district of Baraset, lieut.-gov. of Bengal, a town lying on the route from Calcutta to Dacca. It has a small bazar. The road in this part of the route is in general good, though in some places not free from swamps, the country being low and marshy. Distance from Calcutta, N.E., 28 miles; from Dacca, S.W., 158. Lat. 22° 52′, long. 88° 41′.

HOCHO, or HOPCHO, in Bussahir, a stream of Koonawur, rises near the north-eastern frontier, in lat. 31° 38′, long. 78° 48′, on the western declivity of the Gantung Pass, from the melted snows of which it is supplied. Even near the source, it in some places spreads to a width of 100 yards, and in one part to 200, in another to 300; but is so shallow as scarcely to cover the pebbles in its bed. In other places it is arched over with snow, or buried under the ruins of cliffs, from which it again bursts out and expands over the plain. The fall, which in the upper part of its course is very gentle, lower down is very rapid, as from its source to the confluence with the Sutluj, a distance of less than twelve miles, in a westerly direction, it descends 10,000 feet, and is in general one broken sheet of foam. The mountains bounding its course on each side are precipitous, lofty, and covered with perpetual snow, avalanches of which frequently descend, and, damming the stream, form deep lakes, over the icy embankments of which the river is precipitated with a loud noise.

HODUL, in the British district of Goorgaon, lieut.-gov. of the N.W. Provinces, a town on the route from Delhi to Muttra, and 60 miles S. of the former. Though now a small decayed town, containing a population of only 5,840 persons, the ruins observable prove it to have been once extensive and important. It has a bazar, and there is a large and very fine tank, with water between twenty and thirty feet deep, and accessible by means of a range of stone steps extending all round it. The road in this part of the route is good. Lat. 27° 53', long. 77° 26'.

HOJEENO, in the jaghire of Jujhur, lieut.-gov. of the N.W. Provinces, a village on the route from Rohtuk to Narnol, and six miles N. of the latter. Lat. 28° 8', long. 76° 12'.

HOKYE.—A town in the British district of Northern Cachar, lieut.-gov. of Bengal, 110 miles S.E. of Gowhatty. Lat. 25° 6', long. 92° 57'.

HOLCAR'S DOMINIONS.—See INDORE.

HOLLA HONOOR, in the territory of Mysore, a town situate on the right bank of the river Bhadra, which, a few miles below, uniting with the Tunga, forms the Tungabhadra or Tumbudra. The Bhadra is 250 yards wide, yet fordable except during the monsoon rains. The fort is described, in 1790, as "large, of a square form, with towers at the angles, and two in each face, between the angular ones;" the town as "extensive, tolerably well built, and inclosed by a bad wall and ditch." The fort, in 1791, yielded to a British detachment, acting in junction with the Mahrattas against Tippoo Sultan. Distance from Seringapatam, N.W., 127 miles. Lat. 13° 58', long. 75° 44'.

HOLLAL.—A town in the British district of Dharwar, presidency of Bombay, 150 miles N.N.E. of Mangalore. Lat. 14° 51', long. 75° 47'.

HOLLALGOONDY.—A town in the British district of Bellary, presidency of Madras, 27 miles N.N.E. of Bellary. Lat. 15° 30', long. 77° 9'.

HOLLALKAIRA.—A town in the Mysore, 116 miles N. by W. from Seringapatam, and 122 miles N.E. from Mangalore. Lat. 14° 3', long. 76° 14'.

HONAHWAR, in the British district of North Canara, presidency of Madras, a seaport and town, the principal place of a talook or subdivision of the same name. It is situate on the north side of an extensive estuary, or rather inlet of the sea, forming an expanse of salt-water, which at its south-eastern extremity receives the Gairsoppa or Sheravutty, a considerable river flowing from the Western Ghats, farther eastward.

Of this place there is but little notice before 1569, when it was a rich and beautiful city, with a fort, belonging to the queen of Gairsoppa, a city now in ruins, about fifteen miles farther east, on the river Sheravutty, and was plundered and burned by the Portuguese, who shortly after fortified and garrisoned it. On the decay of the Portuguese power in India, it was acquired by the sovereigns of Bednore, on the conquest of which place by Hyder Ali, this town also submitted to him. It 1783 it was taken by assault by a British force, despatched from Bombay under the command of General Matthews; and, in 1784, obstinately and successfully defended by Captain Torriano, against Tippoo Sultan; to whom, however, in the same year, it was ceded by the treaty of Mangalore. On the overthrow of that prince in 1798, it again came into the possession of the East-India Company. Distance direct from Bombay, S.E., 340 miles; from Mangalore, N.W., 110; from Seringapatam, N.W., 200; from Madras, N.W., 410. Lat. 14° 17', long. 74° 30'.

HONHULLY.—A town in the Mysore, on the right bank of the Tongabudra river, and 144 miles N.W. by N. from Seringapatam. Lat. 14° 15', long. 75° 43'.

HONWAR.—A town in the British district of Belgaum, presidency of Bombay, 20 miles W. of Beejapore. Lat. 16° 49', long. 75° 30'.

HOOBLEE, in the British collectorate of Dharwar, presidency of Bombay, a town situate about 12 miles S.E. of the town of Dharwar. Though ill-built, it is a thriving place, and has some considerable trade, being one of the principal cotton marts of the Southern Mahratta country. In this respect its importance will probably increase, from the improved means of communication with the coast. A cart-road from Dharwar to Hooblee was completed some years ago. In 1847 a further continuation of this road was authorized to Wuddeguttee, on the Canara frontier, there to meet the road constructed by the Madras government for facilitating the inland trade between Dharwar and the port of Coompta.

Hooblee was formerly the seat of an English factory, which, in 1673, was, with the rest of the town, plundered by Sevajee, the Mahratta leader, to the amount of 7,894 pagodas. Moazzim, son of Aurungzebe, sent by his father into this country at the head of an army, took Hooblee. During the decline of the kingdom of Delhi, the town fell into the hands of the Mahrattas, and on the overthrow of the Peishwa, in 1818, was, with the rest of that prince's dominions, taken possession of by the government of the East-India Company. Its population is estimated at 15,000. Distance from Bombay, S.E., 290 miles; from Poona, S.E., 230 miles. Lat. 15° 20', long. 75° 13'.

HOODESARA.—A town in the British district of Camroop, province of Assam, 47 miles N.W. of Gowhatty. Lat. 26° 34', long. 91° 10'.

HOOGHLY.—A British district subject to the lieut.-gov. of Bengal, and named after its principal place. It is bounded on the north by the British district of Burdwan; on the east by the river Hooghly, separating it from the British districts of Nuddea, Baraset, and the Twenty-four Pergunnahs; on the south by the river Roopnarain, separating it from the British districts of Midnapore and Hidjelee; and on the west by the British districts Midnapore and Burdwan. It lies between lat.

22° 13′—23° 13′, long. 87° 34′—88° 30′; is seventy-two miles in length from north to south, and fifty-two in breadth. The area, according to official return, is 2,089 square miles. In its general aspect, the district is low and level in the eastern part, but more hilly in the western and north-western, where it runs towards the high lands of Burdwan. The principal rivers which traverse or skirt the district are the Hooghly, the Damoodah, and the Dalkissore.

The periodical rains set in at the end of June, and last until the end of September or the early part of October. During this period the country is very unhealthy, fevers and agues being especially rife. The cool season lasts from the beginning of November to the end of January, and in the nights ice is sometimes formed to such an extent, that masses may, with due precautions, be preserved to be used during the hot season. February is cool and very pleasant, and is hailed with as high feelings of gratification by the natives, as the finest part of spring is welcomed in Europe. The soil in the south, in some places, is much impregnated with common culinary salt, which was formerly extracted on account of government. Along the courses of the rivers, and generally in the low grounds, it is very fertile, and as irrigation is easily practised, it produces abundant crops. Besides rice, the principal objects of cultivation are the sugarcane, indigo, the mulberry-tree (for the sake of its leaves to feed silkworms), cotton, tobacco, mustard and other oil-seeds, ginger, hemp, potatoes, cucurbitaceous plants of various kinds, peas, onions, cabbages, and various other esculent vegetables. The principal exports are raw silk, indigo, and sugar. A large quantity of plantains is also sent to the Calcutta market, and distillation of rum is greatly increasing, in consequence of the brisk demand for it in the British market. Spirits are distilled in considerable quantities from the sap of the date-palm, and palmyra or toddy-palm. Large quantities of bamboos find a ready sale in the Calcutta market. Hemp is made into ropes, sacking, and coarse canvas. Formerly there was a considerable manufacture of cotton cloths, but the greater cheapness of the fabrics brought from Great Britain has nearly put an end to that branch of industry in this district, as well as in other parts of India. The population is given under the article BENGAL.

The French settlement of Chandernagore is situate within the limits of this district, as are also Chinsura and Serampore, now British possessions, but originally belonging, the one to the Dutch, and the other to the Danes. Hooghly, the principal place, Ampata or Omptah, Boenchie, Jehanabad, Shahbazar, Ghotal, Keerpoy, and the places just mentioned as now or lately held by foreign powers, are described under their respective names in the alphabetical arrangement. The principal routes are,—1. From south-east to north-west, from Calcutta through the town of Hooghly to Burdwan; 2. from south-east to north-west, from Calcutta through Jehanabad to Bancoora; 3. from north to south, along the right side of the river Hooghly; 4. from north-east to south-west, from Burdwan to Midnapore; 5. from east to west, from Calcutta to Midnapore. The tract comprised within the present district of Hooghly appears, according to the remotest historical records, to have formed part of a considerable realm, called Tamaralipta, from its capital of that name, identical with the modern Tumlook. It is reputed to have maintained, or aspired to maintain, extensive foreign relations, and it is said, that in the year 1001, the king despatched an ambassador to the monarch of China. At the time of the invasion of Bengal by the Mussulmans, at the commencement of the thirteenth century, the tract was comprised within the dominions of a rajah residing at Nuddea, on the Bhagirathi, north of the present district of Hooghly. This feeble chief, without an attempt at resistance, deserted his dominions, which were seized by Bukhtyar Khulijy, the Mussulman general, and subsequently incorporated with the state which he founded, and styled the kingdom of Bengal. It was probably united to the kingdom of Delhi by the renowned Sher Shah, when, in 1542, he took the city of Gour, and overthrew the kingdom of Bengal. Wrested from Delhi during the troubles ensuing on the death of Sher Shah, it was reunited to it in 1576, by Khan Jehan, an officer of Akbar. At the commencement of the eighteenth century, it became part of the virtually independent state which, under the denomination of the soobah of Bengal, was founded by Murshid Kuli Khan, during the weakness and distractions of the kingdom of Delhi, ensuing on the death of Aurungzebe. The right of the East-India Company to this tract originated in the treaty concluded with Meer Cossim in 1760, and was confirmed in 1765, by the emperor Shah Allum.

HOOGHLY.—The principal place of the British district of the same name, a town on the line of railroad now under construction from Calcutta to Benares. It is situate on the right bank of the great offset of the Ganges, from it denominated the Hooghly. The river in this part is much contracted in breadth. The civil establishment of the district located here is accommodated in several buildings, of striking appearance, in the Grecian style of architecture, but of frail beauty, being merely overlaid with chunam or stucco. The church, built by the Jesuits, according to the inscribed date, 1599, is a large fine structure, of such durable materials as to appear to have been but recently erected. Here is a college, erected in 1836, upon a site granted for the purpose by the government, and supported by funds derived from the estate of Haji Muhammad Mohsin. Instruction is given both in English and Oriental literature. Connected with this institution are several branch schools.

The civil establishment, of which Hooghly is the chief station, comprises the following European officers :—A civil and sessions judge, a collector, a magistrate, a joint magistrate, and deputy collector; two assistants to the above, an assistant-surgeon, a superintendent of abkarree, an assistant to that officer. Besides these, there is a considerable number of native functionaries, of various grades and denominations. This town is conjectured to have been founded by the Portuguese in 1537. In 1632, it was, after an obstinate defence of three months, stormed by the troops of Shahjehan, 1,000 Portuguese being slaughtered, and 4,400 taken prisoners. Sixty-four large vessels, and 254 of smaller dimensions, were burned, three only escaping to Goa. The place, thus possessed by the Moguls, became the royal port of Bengal. In 1676, the English established a factory here, and about the same time Tavernier mentions a similar establishment belonging to the Dutch. In 1681, the English factory was fortified, and provided with a small guard, consisting of twenty Europeans, which was the first military establishment of the Company in Bengal. Subsequently wrested from the Company by Soorajoo-dowlah, it was, in 1757, retaken by Clive, and has from that time been retained. The population of the town is estimated at about 12,000. Distance N. from Calcutta 27 miles; from Benares, S.E., 394. Lat. 22° 54′, long. 88° 22′.

HOOGHLY.—A large river of Bengal, formed by the junction of two great branches of the Ganges, the Bhagruttee and the Jellinghee, the confluence of which is in lat. 23° 25′, long. 88° 22′, and 125 miles from the sea, reckoned by the windings of the stream to Diamond Point, or, if the estuary be included as far as Saugor Roads, 160 miles. Its mean breadth above Calcutta is three-quarters of a mile, and it was formerly navigable for ships of the line as high as Chandernagore, 115 miles from Saugor Roads, and seventeen above Calcutta. There is indeed a rumour, pretty generally credited, that the river is gradually silting up, and will at some future time cease to afford adequate accommodation to the trade of the capital of British India. This would be a fearful blow to the prosperity of the "City of Palaces," unless a suitable remedy should be provided. Towards this end, it has been suggested that either a ship canal or a railway might be constructed from Calcutta to the Mutwal, a river some distance to the eastward, not unfitted to become the successor of the Hooghly, should it be necessary to abandon that channel; and thus the commerce of the maritime emporium of Bengal be retained. However, "the draught of water for ships departing from Calcutta to proceed down the river, is usually limited to seventeen feet, but the pilots will, for a gratuity presented to them, sometimes take charge of vessels drawing seventeen and a half or eighteen feet; and if a powerful steam-tug be employed, they may be taken from Calcutta drawing nineteen or even twenty feet, when the tides and weather are favourable." When the river is not affected by the annual periodical inundations, which take place at the close of summer, the water is slightly salt at Calcutta, but "in September the freshes are at their height; there is then no visible tide off Calcutta, the ships do not swing up, and the river-water is perfectly sweet, far beyond Saugor, in the open sea." The following general summary of the variations of the tides of the Hooghly is given by the writer just quoted:—"From the point of lowest low water in the dry season, to that of the highest high water in the freshes, is twenty feet ten inches. The greatest mean rise of tide from low to high water-mark takes place in March, April, and May, and is fifteen feet ten inches. The greatest mean rise of tide from low to high water-mark in the freshes is ten feet. The smallest mean rise of tide takes place in the freshes, and is at neap tides only three feet six inches. The smallest mean rise of the tide in the dry season, neap tides, is four feet. From the lowest fall of the river to high-water mark, neap tides, in February, is eight feet. From the lowest fall of the river to low water in the freshes, neap tides, is twelve feet. The river is at its lowest in the beginning of March. The river is swollen by the freshes in July, August, and September, and part of October. The freshes take off about the middle of September, and are generally out of the river by the end of October. At the beginning of November, although the freshes are out of the river, it is upwards of three feet higher at low water than in March. The river is in the most quiescent state during the months of November, December, January, and February. During these months, the night tides are higher and more rapid than the day tides; and there are, on some occasions, bores at night. The strongest flood tides, and the greatest mean rise of the tides, are in March, April, May, and June. The day tides in these months are higher than the night tides. The strongest freshes are in September. In July, the strength of the flood tides is counteracted by the freshes, and this, therefore, is a moderate month as regards tides. The bores also are moderated, as a consequence. In August, the flood tides are overcome by the freshes, and the bores are moderate: should there be a high parallax of the moon, however, the great height of the sea in this month will cause a considerable bore." Though not a mile wide at Calcutta, the river does not at all times afford perfect security to ships, as there have been instances of their being blown ashore there in violent storms. The river has little increase of breadth until after it has received the waters of the Dammoodah and Rupnarain, and passed Diamond Point, fifty miles from Calcutta. Below that point, it rapidly expands, and at Saugor Roads, where the estuary terminates in the open sea, is is about fifteen miles wide. The tides, under circumstances calculated to favour their action, are violent and rapid, running sometimes at the rate of seven miles an hour near Calcutta; and in the south-west monsoon, when a great current is driven into the river from the Bay of Bengal, the extraordinary phenomenon denominated the Bore, which sometimes rises on the sands contiguous to the banks in waves twelve or fifteen feet perpendicular, rushes on at the rate of twenty miles an hour, carrying every floating body along with it. The Hooghly, though the only channel of the Ganges frequented by large ships, is at its mouth much encumbered by shoals, amidst which ships can be steered safely only by much skill and attention. Of the channels between those shoals, the principal are — 1. The Inside Channel, farthest west, stretching from Balasor close along the shore inside, or to the north-westward of all the shoals, with depths generally of from two to three fathoms at low water. This is used only by the small coasting vessels navigated by the natives. 2. Fairway, or the Western Channel, suitable only for ships drawing not more than fourteen or fifteen feet of water. 3. Middle Channel, which is narrow, has not more than three fathoms of water, and is little used. 4. Sagar Channel, or Eastern Channel: this is represented as at present the channel in general use by ships entering or departing from the Hooghly. 5. Thornhill Channel, which has two fathoms and three-quarters at low tide, but commonly three, three and a quarter, or three and a half. 6. The Old Channel, having from three to four fathoms at low water. 7. Lacam Channel, or Channels Creek, called by the natives Baratulla, separates Saugor Island and Clive's Island from the low land of the Sunderbunds. It has a good depth of water, but is rendered somewhat intricate by sands projecting from the land. If these, however, were marked by buoys or beacons, the navigation would not be difficult. Several ships at different times have entered it by mistake, and passed in safety.

The Hooghly is considered by the Brahminists as the real and much-venerated Ganges, having its source at Gangoutri; and the Podda, which takes its course farther east, though having a much larger volume of water, is regarded as a mere branch. The banks of the Hooghly are studded with numerous towns and villages, many of which possess an interest, "from old associations, or have been rendered memorable by historical recollections." A project is under consideration, to connect the city of Calcutta with the suburb of Howrah, by means of a bridge thrown over the Hooghly, in the immediate vicinity of the terminus of the East-Indian Railway.

HOOKEO.—A pass over a lofty range of mountains on the north-eastern frontier of Koonawur, and bounding the table-land of Chinese Tartary westward, and which here has a surface of reddish gravel, swelling into gentle slopes. The rock is calcareous, with occasional quartzose veins, and abounds in shells. Here is a Chinese watch-tower, to exclude obnoxious intruders on the Celestial empire. Elevation above the sea 15,786 feet. Lat. 31° 36′, long. 79°.

HOOKEREE.—A town in the British district of Belgaum, presidency of Bombay, 28 miles N. by E. of Belgaum. Lat. 16° 12′, long. 74° 40′.

HOOLEH, in the Daman division of the Punjab, a town situated 10 miles from the right bank of the Indus, 45 miles W. by S. of the town of Mooltan. Lat. 29° 59′, long. 70° 49′.

HOOLIGEYRI.—A town in one of the recently sequestrated districts of Hyderabad, or dominions of the Nizam, 28 miles W. by S. from Moodgul, and 78 miles E.N.E. from Dharwar. Lat. 15° 57′, long. 76° 8′.

HOOLIORDROOG, in the Mysore, a town, with the ruins of a fort, situate on a rock deemed impregnable except by blockade, and hence formerly regarded as a place of importance. In 1659 it was acquired by Dud Deo Raj, ruler of Mysore: it subsequently passed into the power of Hyder Ali, and in 1791 was surrendered to the British army under Lord Cornwallis, by whom it was dismantled and relinquished. It was subsequently repaired and reoccupied by Tippoo Sultan, but was retaken by the British before the termination of the war. Distant from Seringapatam, N.E., 48 miles. Lat. 12° 50′, long. 77° 5′.

HOOLOOGOREE NUGUR.—A town in the British district of Seebpoor, province of Assam, 30 miles N.E. of Seebpoor. Lat. 27° 16′, long. 95° 3′.

HOOLSOOR.—A town in one of the recently sequestrated districts of Hyderabad, or dominions of the Nizam, 106 miles N.W. of Hyderabad. Lat. 18°, long. 77° 6′.

HOOLY ONORE.—See Holla Honoor.

HOOMNABAD.—A town in Hyderabad, or dominions of the Nizam, 92 miles W.N.W. from Hyderabad, and 109 miles N. from Raichoor. Lat. 17° 45′, long. 77° 13′.

HOONOOMANGUNGE, in the British district of Allahabad, lieut.-gov. of the N.W. Provinces, a village on the route from the cantonment of Allahabad to Benares, and 12 miles S.E. of the former. Lat. 25° 25′, long. 82° 5′.

HOONSOOR.—A town in the Mysore, 13 miles S.W. from Seringapatam, and 114 miles E.S.E. from Mangalore. The place is noted for its manufactures of flannel, blankets, and buff accoutrements. Lat. 12° 15′, long. 76° 28′.

HOONUGOONDA.—A town in the British district of Belgaum, presidency of Bombay, 105 miles E. by N. of Belgaum. Lat. 16° 3′, long. 76° 9′.

HOORHOOREE, in the British district of

Bareilly, lieut.-gov. of the N.W. Provinces, a village on the route from the town of Bareilly to Moradabad, and 19 miles N.W. of the former. Lat. 28° 30′, long. 79° 15′.

HOORINGOTTAH RIVER.—One of the principal mouths by which the Ganges discharges its waters into the Bay of Bengal, in lat. 21° 51′, long. 90°. The entrance is spacious, being about three leagues wide, between the two great banks or shoals which form it, and the depth of water in the great channel is sufficient for the passage of large ships.

HOOSAINPOOR.—A town situate on the right bank of the river Ganges, in the British district of Furruckabad, lieut.-gov. of the N.W. Provinces, contiguous to the military station of Futtygurh. Distant three miles E. from Furruckabad. The population is stated to be 11,698. Lat. 27° 22′, long. 79° 42′.

HOOSHUNGABAD.—See Hoshungabad.

HOOSSEIN BELA, in Sinde, a village on the route from Subzulcote to Shikarpoor, and 15 miles E. of the latter place. It is situate on the left bank of the Indus, here crossed by a much-frequented ferry, generally called the ferry of Azeezpoor, which place, however, is above a mile north-east. The Indus is here divided into two branches: the eastern, called the *Dund*, is about 150 feet broad and twenty-four feet deep; the western branch is very wide, between thirty and forty feet deep, and is separated from the eastern by an island a mile and a half in breadth. At a short distance higher up, there is a good ferry over the undivided stream of the river; and that would be a preferable place for the passage of any considerable number of persons, but the boatmen prefer the lower ferry, as nearer their village. This latter ferry is sometimes called Amil Got, from the village of Amil, on the western side. (See Amil Got.) Hoossein Bela is in lat. 27° 52′, long. 69°.

HOOSUNABAD.—A town in Hyderabad, or dominions of the Nizam, 60 miles W.S.W. from Hyderabad, and 62 miles N. by E. from Raichoor. Lat. 17° 3′, long. 77° 42′.

HOOTEECHENEE.—A town in the principality of Cashmere, or dominions of Gholab Singh, 55 miles S.W. by S. from Sirinagur, and 72 miles N.N.E. from Wazeerabad. Lat. 33° 20′, long. 74° 40′.

HOOVIN HUDDAGULLY.—A town in the British district of Bellary, presidency of Madras, 165 miles N.N.E. of Mangalore. Lat. 15°, long. 75° 59′.

HORTEE.—A town in the British territory of Sattara, presidency of Bombay, 20 miles N. by E. of Beejapoor. Lat. 17° 6′, long. 75° 51′.

HOSANG HAJOO.—A town of Eastern India, in the British district of Cachar, 116 miles S.E. of Gowhatty. Lat. 25° 7′, long. 93° 6′.

HOSHIARPUR, in the Punjab, a small town near the southern base of the Himalaya Mountains, and on the route from Lahore to Nadaun. Lat. 31° 33′, long. 75° 57′.

HOSHUNGABAD, a district or subdivision of that portion of the British possessions known as the Saugor and Nerbudda territory, and now placed under the jurisdiction of the lieutenant-governor of the North-West Provinces. No regular survey has been made, but its area is estimated at 1,916 square miles. The total amount of the population, according to a recent census, is 2[illegible]2,641; but no distinctions of creed, caste, or occupation, were noticed. An attempt was made to supply this deficiency by conjectural means; under which operation the people were thus distributed:—Hindoos, agricultural, 108,468; non-agricultural, 122,685; Mahomedans and others, not Hindoos, agricultural, 654; non-agricultural, 10,834. These proportions derive plausibility from the results of a former census, which probably furnished the chief ground for their assumption, but the total only can be entirely relied on. This district is so remarkable for fertility, as to be commonly styled the garden of Central India. It possesses also one of the elements of mineral wealth, in coal of excellent quality, and it is believed in abundant quantity. On a comparison with some of the coal imported from the northern part of Great Britain, that of Hoshungabad was found to merit a preference. The great distance of the beds from the coast is, however, at present a serious impediment to its being brought extensively into use.

HOSHUNGABAD.—The principal place of the British district of the same name. It is situate on the left or south bank of the river Nerbudda, stated to be here 900 yards wide, and subject, during the periodical rains, to rise to such an extent as to cause very considerable inundations. Here is a fort, of quadrangular ground-plan, and having high walls. The town is irregularly built, and the houses being much dispersed, the population is not dense. The river is not fordable opposite the town, the water at the shallowest part, even in the season when lowest, being between five and six feet deep, and flowing over an irregular rocky bottom. It is infested with alligators, both of the long-snouted and bull-mouthed kinds. There are thirteen ghats or fords over the river, within twelve or fourteen miles of Hoshungabad, becoming passable in the beginning of winter, and continuing so until spring advances. That nearest the town was found, when the water was lowest, to be covered three feet deep. East of the town is a small cantonment of British troops belonging to the Saugor division, and the town itself is the seat of a political agency subsidiary to that of Saugor.

Hoshungabad was founded about the year 1433, by Hoshung Shah, sovereign of Malwa, whose remains were deposited there, but subsequently removed to Mandoo. In 1562 it was, with the rest of Malwa, conquered by Akbar. On the dismemberment of the empire of Delhi, Hoshungabad was appropriated by the nawaub of Bhopal, from whom it was taken by storm by the rajah of Nagpore or Berar, in 1796. It was, however, soon after retaken by the ruler of Bhopal, and again, in 1807, taken by the rajah of Nagpore, by whom it was ceded, in 1818, to the British government. Distant S.W. from Saugor, by Searmow, 114 miles; S. from Agra, by Saugor, 388; S.W. from Allahabad 428; N.W. from Calcutta, by Allahabad, 924; E. from Mhow 144. Lat. 22° 44′, long. 77° 44′.

HOSKOTE, or OOSCOTTA, in the territory of Mysore, a town. It is a considerable place, and has a mud fort, which, in 1761, was besieged by Basalut Jung, of Hyderabad, who, after ineffectually attempting to reduce, received the surrender of it from Hyder Ali, together with three lacs of rupees, in consideration of his investing that adventurer with the title and office of nawaub of Sera, a dignity and country which Basalut Jung had no claim either *de jure* or *de facto* to dispose of. Distant from Bangalore, N.E., 16 miles. Lat. 13° 5′, long. 77° 52′.

HOSPETT.—A town in the British district of Bellary, presidency of Madras, 35 miles W.N.W. of Bellary. Lat. 15° 16′, long. 76° 29′.

HOSSANPOOR.—A town in the Mysore, on the right bank of one of the branches of the Cauvery river, and 18 miles W. from Seringapatam. Lat. 12° 24′, long. 76° 29′.

HOSS DROOG.—A town in the Mysore, 100 miles N. by W. from Seringapatam, and 117 miles N.E. from Mangalore. Lat. 13° 49′, long. 76° 20′.

HOSSDURG, in the British district of South Canara, within the territory subject to the presidency of Madras, a town on the route from Cananore to Mangalore. It has a large fort, well built of laterite, which material abounds throughout the country. It is on a fine rising ground, and, viewed from afar, looks well. Here is a temple, established by the rajah of Ikeri, who built the fort. Lat. 12° 18′, long. 75° 10′.

HOSUNPOOR.—A town in the British district of Mymunsing, lieut.-gov. of Bengal, 31 miles S.E. of Nusseerabad. Lat. 24° 28′, long. 90° 40′.

HOSURU.—A fortified town, formerly within the territory of Mysore, now within the British dominions. Its position has often rendered it the object of obstinate contention between the powers of Mysore and the Carnatic. In 1654, it was taken by the rajah of Mysore; in 1768, it fell into the hands of the British: after various vicissitudes, it returned to the possession of Mysore, but was occupied by the British in 1791, on the advance of Lord Cornwallis against Seringapatam. In the arrangements consequent on the wars with Tippoo Sultan, it was finally annexed to the British possessions, being included in North Arcot. Distance from Seringapatam, E., 80 miles; Bangalore, S.E., 23; Madras, W., 200.* Lat. 12° 45′, long. 78° 54′.

HOWRA, in the British district of the Twenty-four Pergunnahs, forming part of the lower provinces of Bengal, a town on the right bank of the river Hooghly, opposite Calcutta, of which place, indeed, it may be considered a suburb, and with which it is about to be more closely connected by means of a bridge over the Hooghly. It is described by Heber as a considerable place, chiefly inhabited by ship-builders, but containing some pretty villas. The Hooghly, nearly a mile wide, is covered with large ships and craft of all kinds. The town has been selected as the site for the terminus of the railroad from Calcutta to the North-West Provinces. Lat. 22° 36′, long. 88° 23′.

HUBB.—A river forming for a considerable distance the western frontier of Sinde, and dividing it from Beloochistan. It has been traced downwards from Hoja Jamote, on the northern boundary of Lus, in lat. 26° 12′, long. 66° 51′, and is supposed to rise near that place. For about twenty-five miles in the upper part of its course, it flows south-easterly, and then turning due south, holds its way for about fifty miles in that direction. It then turns to the south-west, and, after a total length of 100 miles, falls into the Arabian Sea, on the north side of Cape Monze, in lat. 24° 54′, long. 66° 43′. De la Hoste states, that for a distance of fourteen miles from the mouth, water was in the end of summer found to the depth of eight inches, and that in some places deep pools exist, abounding in fish and alligators. He adds, that the river is said never to fail in the driest seasons. Masson, however, states, that it is only on extraordinary occasions that the water of the Hubb reaches the sea; and in this he is supported by Hart, who crossed it about fifteen miles above the mouth, where the channel was 100 yards wide. Though, in consequence of heavy rains, there was then a large body of running water, he found but a small stream on his return a short time after, and was informed it would soon cease to flow, and that water would then be found only in detached pools. The whole course is described as a succession of rocky or gravelly gorges in the rugged and barren Pubb Mountains.

HUBBEEGUJE.—A town in the British district of Silhet, lieut.-gov. of Bengal, 50 miles S.W. of Silhet. Lat. 24° 19′, long. 91° 23′.

HUBRA.—A town in the British district of Dinajepoor, lieut.-gov. of Bengal, 20 miles E. of Dinajepoor. Lat. 25° 31′, long. 88° 58′.

HUBSHEE.—See JINJEERA.

HUBUNNAGAR, in the British district of Allahabad, lieut.-gov. of the N.W. Provinces, a village on the route from the cantonment of Allahabad to Futtehpoor, and 37 miles N.W. of the former. Lat. 25° 40′, long. 81° 26′.

HUDEEALEE, in Gurwhal, a village on the left bank of the Bhageerettee, as the

Ganges is called in the upper part of its course. Raper describes it as "a very pretty village, with fine cultivation." It is situate opposite the mouth of the Nagur, a torrent which falls into the Bhageerettee on the right side. Hudeealee is in lat. 30° 33′, long. 78° 24′.

HUGRY.—A river rising in the Mysore, in lat. 13° 28′, long. 75° 55′, and, flowing first in a north-easterly, and subsequently in a northerly direction for 125 miles, it passes into the British collectorate of Bellary, through which, maintaining its northerly course, it flows for 100 miles, to its junction with the Toongabudra, on the right side, in lat. 15° 44′, long. 76° 58′.

HUJAMREE, in Sinde, is an offset of the Sata, or great eastern channel of the Indus, and is called in the upper part of its course the Seeahn. The Hujamree mouth is wide, but rapidly narrows inland to about 500 yards: at Vikkur, twenty miles from the sea, it is only about 170 yards wide; and still higher up, near its junction with the Sata, its breadth is found not to exceed fifty yards. In 1831 it was navigable for boats from the sea to the entrance into the Sata, as the small flotilla which conveyed Captain Burnes and his party in that year passed this way. According to the statement of that officer, there were then fifteen feet of water on the bar at high tide, and a depth of four fathoms all the way to Vikkur. He observes, however, adverting to the changing character of the river, "The next season perhaps Vikkur will be deserted." The anticipated change occurred, though not so early as suggested. In 1839, the British troops marching from Bombay to Afghanistan, ascended the Hujamree and landed at Vikkur; and in the course of the same year this branch was closed by a change in its channel, caused by the violence of the current. The Hujamree mouth is in lat. 24° 16′, long. 67° 18′.

HUKUMUTWALA, in Sirhind, a village on the route from Ferozpur to Simla, and 12 miles S.E. of the former town. Distant N.W. from Calcutta 1,159 miles. Lat. 30° 52′, long. 74° 35′.

HULDI, in the British district of Ghazeepore, lieut.-gov. of the N.W. Provinces, a village on the route from Ghazeepore cantonment to Chupra, 52 miles E. of the former. Lat. 25° 45′, long. 84° 15′.

HULDOOG GHAT.—A ferry near the village of Surian, in the British district of Kumaon, lieut.-gov. of the N.W. Provinces, and forming a communication between the East-India Company's territories and Nepal: S.E. of Petoragarh cantonment 11 miles. Lat. 29° 28′, long. 80° 21′.

HULDOUR, in the British district of Bijnour, lieut.-gov. of the N.W. Provinces, a town on the route from Bijnour to Moradabad, 10 miles S.E. of the former. Lat. 29° 17′, long. 78° 21′.

HULDYPOOKRE.—A town in the British district of Pooralia, lieut.-gov. of Bengal, 148 miles W. of Calcutta. Lat. 22° 37′, long. 86° 8′.

HULHALLI.—A town in the Mysore, on the right bank of one of the branches of the Cauvery river, and 25 miles S.S.W. from Seringapatam. Lat. 12° 6′, long. 76° 37′.

HULKANT, in the British district of Agra, lieut.-gov. of the N.W. Provinces, a town on the south-eastern frontier towards Gwalior, and 50 miles S.E. of the city of Agra. Lat. 26° 47′, long. 78° 46′.

HULLAGOOR.—A town in the Mysore, on the left bank of one of the branches of the Cauvery, and 33 miles E. from Seringapatam. Lat. 12° 27′, long. 77° 14′.

HULLEE.—A town in the British province of Nagpoor, 133 miles S.E. from Nagpoor, and 135 miles E. by S. from Chanda. Lat. 19° 38′, long. 81° 25′.

HULLEEA, in the British district of Mirzapoor, lieut.-gov. of the N.W. Provinces, a town on the route from Rewah to Benares, 53 miles S.W. of the latter. Lat. 24° 50′, long. 82° 24′.

HULLEEJEH, in Sinde, a village on the route from Kurrachee to Jurruk, and 50 miles E. of the former place. It is situate among the low hills north-west of Tatta, and near the western shore of a considerable *dund* or piece of water, communicating with the Indus by the Ghara watercourse. Lat. 24° 47′, long. 67° 46′.

HULLEHNOH.—A town in the native state of Bhurtpoor, 51 miles W. from Agra, and 86 miles E. from Jeypoor. Lat. 27° 7′, long. 77° 17′.

HULLIAL.—A town in the British district of North Canara, presidency of Madras, 19 miles W.S.W. of Dhawar. Lat. 15° 21′, long. 74° 50′.

HULLOLE, in Guzerat, or territory of the Guicowar, a town at the north-western base of the mountain of Pawangarh. Distance from Ahmedabad, S.E., 65 miles. Lat. 22° 32′, long. 73° 28′.

HULSUNGEE.—A town in the British territory of Sattara, presidency of Bombay, 36 miles N. by E. of Beejapoor. Lat. 17° 19′, long. 75° 56′.

HULWUD, in the peninsula of Kattywar, province of Guzerat, a town in the prant or district of Jhalawar, near the northern frontier, towards the Runn or Salt-marsh. It was formerly of much importance, but is now rather decayed, yet has eight villages dependent on it. In its relations with the British government, it is considered united with the tallook of Drangdra, and they are officially returned as conjointly having a population of 51,709, and paying an annual tribute of 43,909 rupees. Distance from Ahmedabad, W., 85 miles. Lat. 23°, long. 71° 10′.

HUMAPUKHUR.—A town in the native state of Nepal, 71 miles N.W. from Khatmandoo, and 135 miles N.E. by N. from Goruckpoor. Lat. 28° 24′, long. 84° 28′.

HUMBER, in Sirhind, a village on the route from Lodiana to Ferozepoor, and 10½ miles W. of the former town. It contains a few shops, and is supplied with water from two wells. The road in this part of the route is good, passing through an open and partially-cultivated country. Population about 600. Distant N.W. from Calcutta 1,099 miles. Lat. 30° 57′, long. 75° 46′.

HUMEERPOOR.—A British district under the lieut.-gov. of the N.W. Provinces, deriving its name from its principal town, and forming, with Calpee, a collectorate. The united territory is bounded on the north-east by the river Jumna, dividing it from the British districts Etawa, Cawnpore, and Futtehpore; on the east and south-east by the British district of Banda; on the south by the native states of Churkaree and Chutterpore; and on the west by the territories of Jhansi and the British district of Jaloun. It lies between lat. 25° 7′—26° 26′, long. 79° 20′—80° 25′, and has an area of about 2,240 square miles. The principal rivers are the Jumna, the Betwa, the Dessaun, and the Cane. The average elevation above the sea, of the waterway of the Jumna, at the northern extremity of the district, is probably about 550 feet, and perhaps no point within it is 300 feet above that height. The soil is favourable to the growth of sugarcane, cotton, indigo, the aal-plant (Morinda multiflora), wheat, barley, Holcus sorghum, Holcus spicatus, and every species of the pulse and lentil tribe. In the more sterile parts are grown several species of grain of the millet kind. The cotton, which is produced on the better soil in great abundance and of good quality, is largely transmitted from Calpee and other places on the Jumna, to the lower provinces. Under the last revenue settlement of the N.W. Provinces, the government demand upon the land of this district was fixed for a term of years, and is not liable to increase till the year 1872.

The climate is not favourable to the European constitution, having a tendency to occasion intermitting fevers; but the natives appear to enjoy a full average share of health. During the latter part of spring and commencement of summer the heat is very great. The population consists generally of Boondelas, a spurious tribe of Rajpoots. There are several other tribes of less importance. The number of inhabitants, as ascertained by actual enumeration in 1853, is stated to be, Hindoo agricultural, 380,104; Hindoo non-agricultural, 128,481; Mahomedans and others, agricultural, 14,679; same classes, non-agricultural, 25,340: total, 548,604. The number of towns or villages containing less than 1,000 inhabitants is returned at 663; those containing more than 1,000 and less than 5,000, at 164; those containing more than 5,000 and less than 10,000, at five; and those containing more than 10,000, at two. The principal military routes are—1. From north to south, from Cawnpore to Banda, by Humeerpore; 2. from north to south, a little east of the last-named, from Cawnpore to Banda, by Chilah Tarah ferry; 3. from south-east to north-west, from Banda to Calpee; 4. from north to south, from Calpee to Kitha, and thence to Chutterpore and Saugor; 5. from south-east to north-west, from Banda to Gwalior.

The tract of which this district forms part, seems to have been always of some importance in India, and Ferishta relates that Vasdew, king of Kunouj, about the year 350, founded the fort of Calpee. It was amongst the earliest of the Mussulman conquests in India, having been taken in 1196 by Kutbudin, viceroy of Muhammed of Ghor. It submitted to the Timurian invader Baber in 1527, and was frequently the scene of his military operations. A British force invaded it in 1778, crossing over the Jumna from the Doab, and taking the fort of Calpee. In the same year, General Goddard led his army from that place on the celebrated march which he performed across India to Surat. Towards the close of the last century, it was overrun by the Mahrattas, and subsequently transferred by Hummat Bahadur, one of their chiefs, to the East-India Company, to whom it was guaranteed by the Peishwa, in 1802, by Art. IV. of the treaty of Bassein; and in the following year the British troops took Calpee and occupied the country.

HUMEERPORE, the principal place of the British district, and also of the pergunnah of the same name, a town situate on the tongue of land or doab at the confluence of the Betwa and Jumna, on the right bank of the latter. The Jumna, according to Jacquemont, in February, has a stream of 1,000 feet wide, running in a channel half a mile in breadth, with a rapidity of three or four miles an hour. The town is considerable, consisting originally of several villages grouped together. It is a civil station; the European establishment consists of one magistrate and collector, one joint magistrate and deputy collector, and one assistant to the magistrate and collector. It is on the route from Banda to Cawnpore, 36 miles N. of the former, 39 S. of the latter, 28 S.E. of Calpee, 155 S.E. of Agra, 110 N.W. of Allahabad, 575 N.W. of Calcutta. Lat. 25° 58′, long. 80° 14′.

HUMPASAGRA.—A town in the British district of Bellary, presidency of Madras, 59 miles W. of Bellary. Lat. 15° 9′, long. 76° 8′.

HUNDIA, HINDIA, or HUNDERAH, in the British district of Allahabad, lieut.-gov. of the N.W. Provinces, a small town on the route from the city of Allahabad to that of Benares, and 23 miles S.E. of the former. Lat. 25° 22′, long. 82° 15′.

HUNDOUR, in the district of Pertabgurh, territory of Oude, a town two miles from the right bank of the river Sai, 85 S.E. of Lucknow. Butter estimates the population at 3,000, all Hindoos, except about twenty Mussulman agriculturists. Lat. 25° 55′, long. 81° 52′.

HUNDRY.—A river rising in lat. 15° 16′, long. 77° 25′, in the British collectorate of

Bellary, and, flowing in a circuitous but generally north-easterly direction for fifty miles through that district, and for twenty-eight miles through Kurnool, it falls into the Toongabudra on the right side, near the town of Kurnool, in lat. 15° 49′, long. 78° 6′.

HUNDY ANNANTPOOR.—A town in the British district of Bellary, presidency of Madras, 59 miles N.W. of Bellary. Lat. 14° 41′, long. 77° 41′.

HUNGOO, in the Daman division of the Punjab, a town situated 30 miles from the right bank of the Indus, 36 miles S.S.W. of the town of Peshawur. Lat. 33° 31′, long. 71° 25′.

HUNGRUNG, in Bussahir, a subdivision of the district of Koonawur, is a very elevated region, bounded on the south and west by the lofty limestone range of Hungrung, on the north by Ladakh, and on the east by Chinese Tartary. It lies between lat. 31° 48′—32° 8′, long. 78° 25′—78° 45′.

HUNGRUNG, in Bussahir, a pass in the district of Koonawur, over a range of limestone mountains bounding the district of Hungrung on the south-west. The route from the south-west proceeds up a dell to the crest, which commands an extensive view in both directions; the southern, or Koonawur side, and the northern, or Tartarian. Hutton, who crossed the pass in June, found furze and junipers growing on the south-western side as far as the summit; but on the northern side, the snow reached continuously several hundred yards from the crest. Several travellers have mentioned the strongly-marked change which takes place in the aspect of the country in proceeding northward across this range. "The change in the nature of the country is most sudden: looking from the summit of the range in a northerly direction over Hungrung, the country is seen to wear a sad and sombre air of cheerless desolation; not a tree is to be seen, and the black and crumbling hills are either wholly barren, or clothed with nothing of larger growth than the dwarf willow and the dog-rose. The hills are chiefly of the secondary class, and being more rounded in their outline, want the grand and almost terrific beauty of the towering granitic peaks which so strongly characterize the scenery of Koonawur." "On the southern side of this range lies the thickly-wooded district of Koonawur, where cultivation is often carried in steps nearly to the summits of the mountains, and presenting a rich and cheerful picture, which delights the eye, and imparts a feeling of joyousness and security to the traveller as he wanders on through forests of majestic pines." The adventurous and hardy Gerard, who ascended the pass in August, found it then free from snow, but the cold so intense, that he became quite benumbed; the blood forsook the surface of his body, and he travelled three miles, half-torpid and congealed. The elevation of the crest above the sea is 14,800 feet. Lat. 31° 48′, long. 78° 35′.

HUNNOOMANA, in Baghelcund, or the territory of Rewa, a village on the route by the Kutra Pass, from the cantonment of Allahabad to the town of Rewa, and 74 miles S.W. of the former. It is situate on an elevated table-land, where the prevailing formation of red sandstone is continually exposed to view. Cultivation is consequently scanty, and supplies are scarce at the village. Water is obtained from tanks. Elevation above the sea 1,219 feet. Lat. 24° 47′, long. 82° 9′.

HUNSASIR.—A town in the Rajpoot state of Jodhpoor, 80 miles N. by E. from Jodhpoor, and 42 miles S. from Beekaneer. Lat. 27° 25′, long. 73° 20′.

HUNSGUNJ, in the British district of Muttra, lieut.-gov. of the N.W. Provinces, a village on the left bank of the Jumna, opposite the city of Muttra. Here, on the route from Allygurh to Muttra, is a ferry over the river during the rainy season, and for the rest of the year a bridge of boats. Lat. 27° 31′, long. 77° 45′.

HUNTER'S ISLAND.—A small island near the coast of Arracan, and situate just outside of Andrew's Bay. Lat. 18° 16′, long. 94° 23′.

HURAGAON.—A town in the native state of Gwalior, or dominions of Scindia, 52 miles W. from Hoosungabad, and 70 miles E. from Indore. Lat. 22° 43′, long. 76° 58′.

HURAH, in the territory of Oude, a small town on the route from the cantonment of Cawnpore to that of Pertaubgurh, 10 miles S.E. of the former, and situate close to the left bank of the Ganges. It is styled Harha by Butter, who estimates the population at 6,000. The inhabitants, according to the same authority, are money-changers, dealers in cloth, in grain, and fermented liquors, weavers, pandits or professors of learning, medical men, servants, bird-catchers, raiyats or cultivators, and labourers. Garden, however, merely styles it a small village, affording no supplies. The road is bad to the north-west, or towards Cawnpore; better to the south-east, or towards Pertaubgurh. Lat. 26° 22′, long. 80° 32′.

HURAWUL, in Sirhind, a town fifty miles from the left bank of the Sutluj. It is comprised within the possessions of a Sikh chief under the protection and control of the British. Distant N.W. from Calcutta, by way of Delhi and Munuk, 1,043 miles. Lat. 30° 17′, long. 75° 20′.

HURDA, in the territory of Gwalior, or possessions of Scindia's family, a town on the route from Baitool to Mow, 76 miles N.W. of former, 109 E. of latter. It is the principal place of a pergunnah of the same name, has a bazar, and is well supplied with water from a stream. Its pergunnah, united with that of Handya, adjacent, yields an annual revenue of 140,000 rupees, and, by the peace of 1844, was with it placed under British management for the maintenance of the augmented Gwalior contingent. Lat. 22° 18′, long. 77° 7′.

HURDAGUR.—A town in the British province of Nagpore, 23 miles N.W. from Deogur, and 42 miles E.N.E. from Baitool. Lat. 22° 7′, long. 78° 31′.

HURDANHALLI, in the Mysore, a small fortified town, the principal place of a tallook or subdivision of the same name. It is situate in the immediate vicinity of three considerable tanks. Distant from Seringapatam, S.E., 50 miles. Lat. 11° 52′, long. 77° 1′.

HURDOEE.—A town in the territory of Oude, 38 miles S.S.E. from Lucknow, and 54 miles E. from Cawnpoor. Lat. 26° 23′, long. 81° 17′.

HURDOOAGUNJ.—A town in the British district of Allyghur, lieut.-gov. of the N.W. Provinces, situate six miles E. from Allyghur. The population is stated to be 8,292. Lat. 27° 56′, long. 78° 13′.

HURDWAR.—A town in the British district of Saharunpoor, lieut.-gov. of the N.W. Provinces. It is called sometimes Gangadwara, or the "Gate of the Ganges," being situate on its western or right bank, at the southern base of the Sewalik range, here intersected by a ravine or gorge, by which the river, finally leaving the mountainous region, commences its course over the plain of Hindostan. The stream here is divided by islands into three channels, the principal one being on the eastern side. They are all so shallow in places, that the passage of large unloaded boats through them is not practicable without difficulty. The breadth of the river in the rainy season, from the extreme eastern to the extreme western bank, is represented to be "a full mile." The town, which has an appearance of great antiquity, is situate close to the western bank, and the foundations of many of the houses are in the bed of the river. Raper, who visited it in 1808, describes it, at that time, as very inconsiderable, having only one street, about fifteen feet in breadth and a furlong and a half in length. Most of the houses have the upper part of brick, the lower of stone, which is of good quality. Chiefly, perhaps, from this town being situate close to the point at which the Ganges enters Hindostan, it is beyond all others visited in pilgrimage; the multitudes which throng to it being, however, beyond doubt, increased by the facility of access to it from various parts. Ablution in the river is the great rite practised here by the Hindoo pilgrims, their belief being, that purgation from sin is thus obtained. According to their notions, the orthodox place for bathing is at the ghat or stairs leading down to the river, and called Harika Pairi, or "the stairs of Vishnu." Priority in ablution at the propitious moment is considered to be of great importance in a spiritual point of view, and many persons have formerly perished in the attempt to secure the advantage, being either crushed to death in the rushing crowd, or precipitated into the river, and there drowned. In 1819, "in consequence of a desperate rush made by the infatuated pilgrims to gain a precedency in bathing, 430 persons were squeezed to death; among whom were several British sepoys, placed as guards to prevent this very catastrophe." The propitious moment is laid down by astrologers, according to their alleged calculations and observations, and sometimes happens at midnight. Since the occurrence of the accident above mentioned, the East-India Company's government has caused the old ghat to be replaced by one of sixty steps, and 100 feet wide. The rigidly pious, and those who dread to enter the water unassisted, are supported by a Brahmin on each side. As, however, the depth close to the ghat is not above four feet, the majority plunge in unassisted, men and women bathing together indiscriminately.

The assemblage of pilgrims, which is annual, is attended by people from all parts of India, and from many places far beyond its bounds. "The bathing commences in the month of Chaitra, when the sun is in Mina or Pisces, and concludes on the day he enters Mesha or Aries, agreeably to the solar computation of the Hindoos, and corresponding with the 10th April, on which day the sun has actually advanced 20½° in that sign. Every twelfth year is celebrated with greater rejoicing, and is called the Cumbh-mela, so denoted from the planet Jupiter being then in the sign of Aquarius. Whether this sign be symbolical of the purpose for which they meet, or whether the conjunction be arbitrary or accidental, is not ascertained; but a pilgrimage at those duodecennial periods is considered the most fortunate and efficacious." The 10th of April is the Purbi, or last day of bathing. The Mela or fair, held on this occasion for commercial purposes, is the means of very extensive traffic. From the Punjab, and from the countries west of the Indus, are brought camels, horses, mules, salt, antimony, fine woollens and piece-goods, tobacco, asafœtida, dried fruits (such as apricots, figs, prunes, raisins), almonds, pistachio-nuts, and pomegranates; from Cashmere, shawls and other fine woollen fabrics; from Rajpootana, various fancy-goods, such as chiras or spotted turbans, toys, and other wares in metals and ivory, besides inferior woollens, and a great number of camels; from the British provinces, cotton and silk fabrics, and European goods. There are besides less-important articles of commerce in great quantity and variety; and the food required for the vast assembled multitude constitutes an extensive and lucrative subject of traffic. The number of those who on these occasions resort to Hurdwar from various motives is enormous. Hardwicke, who visited the Cumbh-mela in 1796, and paid much attention to the subject, estimated the number at two millions and a half; and Raper, at the following Cumbh-mela, in 1808, says, "If we estimate the number at two millions of souls, we shall probably fall short rather than exceed the reality." No such number is, however, at any one time assembled; as those who visit the place for the purpose of bathing, arrive in the morning and depart in the evening, or on the next day; so that there is a constant succession of strangers. Such a collection of people, under the influences which bring them together, and rule them, may readily be imagined ripe for any acts which their spiritual leaders may suggest; and the rivalry of conflicting parties has often led to sanguinary conflicts. In 1760, on the Purbi, two rival sects,—the Gosains and the Bairagis, met in battle, which terminated in the defeat of the latter, of whom, according to report, 18,000 were slain. At the time of Hardwicke's visit, in 1796, the Gosains, venturing to resist the better-organized Sikh pilgrims, were defeated with the loss of about 500 men. The latest of the great duodecennial gatherings took place in 1844, and passed off without disturbance.

Hurdwar formerly bore the name of Koupela or Goupela. According to Wilford, it was so named from an ancient ascetic. "Capila, a most religious man, performed for a long time religious austerities near Hurdwar, where they show to this day the place where he lived, under the name of Capila-Sthan; hence the pass of Hurdwar is sometimes called the pass of Capila or Kupeleh." Tamerlane, marching to this place after taking Delhi, massacred a multitude of Hindoos here assembled, and carried off a rich booty. The elevation of Hurdwar above the sea is 1,024 feet; and a little below the town is the head of the great canal of irrigation for the North-Western Provinces, for an account of which see GANGES RIVER. Distant N.W. from Calcutta, by Lucknow and Moradabad, 924 miles. Lat. 29° 57′, long. 78° 14′.

HUREAWALA, in Sirhind, a village on the route from Ferozepore to Simla, and 24 miles S.E. of the former town. Distant N.W. from Calcutta 1,100 miles. Lat. 30° 42′, long. 74° 40′.

HUREERAMPOOR.—A town in the British district of Dacca Jelalpoor, lieut.-gov. of Bengal, 121 miles N.E. of Calcutta. Lat. 23° 39′, long. 89° 58′.

HURNAL, in the Sinde Sagur Dooab division of the Punjab, a town situated 26 miles from the right bank of the Jhelum, 96 miles S.E. by E. of the town of Peshawur. Lat. 33° 19′, long. 73° 8′.

HUROOKEE THAN, in the British district of Kumaon, lieut.-gov. of the N.W. Provinces, a town situate 31 miles N.E. of Almora. Lat. 29° 54′, long. 80° 4′.

HUROONUGLA, in the British district of Bareilly, lieut.-gov. of the N.W. Provinces, a village on the route from the town of Bareilly to Seetapoor, and four miles S.E. of the former. Lat. 28° 22′, long. 79° 31′.

HUROOR.—A town in the British district of Salem, presidency of Madras, 34 miles N.E. of Salem. Lat. 12° 4′, long. 78° 30′.

HUROWRAH, in the British district of Suharunpoor, lieut.-gov. of the N.W. Provinces, a village on the route from the town of Suharunpoor to Dehra, and eight miles E. of the former place. It is situate in a productive and well-cultivated country, on the river Hindon, so that water and other supplies are abundant. Distant N.W. from Calcutta 1,015 miles. Lat. 30°, long. 77° 45′.

HURPUNHULLY, in the British district of Bellary, presidency of Madras, a considerable town, situate amidst tanks discharging their redundant water into a tributary of the Tumbudra. The surrounding country is fertile and highly cultivated. Distance from Bangalore, N.W., 165 miles; Bellary, S.W., 65; Madras, N.W., 380. Lat. 14° 48′, long. 76° 2′.

HURRAH.—A town in the British district of Nuddea, lieut.-gov. of Bengal, 72 miles N. of Calcutta. Lat. 23° 36′, long. 88° 31′.

HURREAH, in the Punjab, a village on the route from Ramnuggur to Pind Dadun Khan, and 14 miles E. of the latter place. It is situate near the left bank of the river Jhelum, in a country described by Burnes as a sterile waste of underwood. Lat. 32° 37′, long. 73° 20′.

HURREEANAH, a British district under the lieut.-gov. of the N.W. Provinces, is bounded on the north-west, north, and north-east by Sirhind; on the east by the British district of Rohtuk and by Dadree; on the south by Dadree and Loharoo; and on the west by the state of Bikaneer and the British district of Bhutteana. It lies between lat. 28° 33′—29° 49′, long. 75° 20′—76° 22′, and comprehends an area of 3,300 square miles. Its soil appears to be for the most part formed of alluvial matter swept down by the Gagur, the Chitang, and other streams flowing from the Sub-Himalaya, and is, as might be expected, very fertile, producing, where duly watered, large crops of rice, wheat, barley, millet, pulse, and various other productions. Their luxuriance, however, depends on the periodical rains falling at the close of summer and early part of autumn, when the inhabitants partially provide for their future wants by preserving the water in numerous tanks lined with masonry. These supplies fail, however, as the hot season advances, and then recourse must be had to wells, of which some are 100 feet in depth, some 120, and some even more. The necessity for this is imposed by the fact of the land-springs lying very far beneath the surface, and the mountain-torrents being lost by absorption or evaporation farther north, in Sirhind. The country is consequently for great part of the year excessively arid; the few springs to be met with are for the most part brackish; and the want of water is a source of distress. This tract was a favourite hunting-ground of Feroz Toghluk, the renowned king of Delhi, the ruins of whose buildings still occupy several square miles, and who, in the year 1356, to obtain a supply of water, as well for his numerous followers as for the purposes of irrigation, made a canal from the Jumna, which, passing by Hansi and Hissar, proceeded westward until it joined the river Gagur. This canal, which had been nearly obliterated, was cleared out in 1825; and by this process, the extension of the main line, and the construction of additional branches, was made largely available for the purposes of irrigation, as well as for rafting timber and navigating small barges.

The jungles and wastes of Hurreeanah still harbour many wild beasts. Tigers are common, and lions are sometimes met with, though generally thought to infest no part of Hindostan, except Guzerat and its immediate vicinity. The population is scanty in comparison with the extent of the district, amounting only to 330,852; of whom 207,144 are Hindoos engaged in agriculture, 40,762 Hindoos non-agricultural, 61,827 Mahomedans and others agricultural, and 21,119 of the like description non-agricultural. The excess in the number of Hindoos over the Mahomedans is, as thus appears, very much greater than in some other districts of this part of India. Hansee and Hissar are the only towns in the district which contain more than 10,000 inhabitants.

Hurreeanah was, at the close of the eighteenth century, the scene of a bold but abortive attempt by George Thomas, an Irish adventurer, to found an independent state under his own rule. He fortified Hurreeanah, and collected there about 6,000 persons, cast cannon, made muskets and other arms, and coined rupees in his own name. He was, however, attacked by a vastly superior force of Mahrattas, commanded by the French adventurer Perron, and being overpowered after a gallant resistance, took refuge in Bengal, where, in 1802, he died on his journey towards Calcutta.

HURREEHURPOOR.—A town in the native state of Nepal, 29 miles S. by E. from Khatmandoo, and 62 miles S.W. from Bettiah. Lat. 27° 18′, long. 85° 23′.

HURREEPOOR, in an outlying district of Puteeala, a village with a fort, on the route from Subathoo to Simla, and five miles N. of the former post. It is situate on a principal feeder of the Gunbur, and is the property of the rajah of Puteeala. Elevation above the sea 3,147 feet. Lat. 31° 1′, long. 77° 3′.

HURRIANA.—See Hurreeanah.

HURRICKPOOGUR.—A town in the British district of Cuttack, lieut.-gov. of Bengal, 49 miles S.E. of Cuttack. Lat. 20° 4′, long. 86° 31′.

HURRIORPOOR.—A town in the native state of Sirgoojah, on the south-west frontier of Bengal, 136 miles S.W. from Sherghotty, and 108 miles W. from Lohadugga. Lat. 23° 30′, long. 83° 5′.

HURRISUNKRA, in the British district of Nuddea, lieut.-gov. of Bengal, a town on the route from Berhampore to Pubna, 35 miles E. of former, 25 W. of latter. The Pudda, or great eastern branch of the Ganges, which formerly flowed through this town, has now deserted its old channel, and flows two miles more to the north. Hurrisunkra is 102 miles N. of Calcutta. Lat. 24° 2′, long. 88° 50′.

HURRUND, or HURROOND.—A small and hilly district, with a town of the same name, in the Daman division of the Punjab, south-westward of the Derajat. The town of Hurrund is situated within the British dominions, on the route from Dera Ghazee Khan to Cutch Gundava. It has a fort and a considerable number of houses. Lat. 29° 28′, long. 70° 1′.

HURRYAL.—A town in the British district of Pubna, lieut.-gov. of Bengal, 133 miles N.N.E. of Calcutta. Lat. 24° 19′, long. 89° 22′.

HURRYE, in the British district of Allahabad, lieut.-gov. of the N.W. Provinces, a village on the route from the cantonment of Allahabad to Rewa, and 17 miles S.E. of the former. It has a few shops, and is supplied with water from wells and a tank: the country is fertile. Lat. 25° 18′, long. 82° 2′.

HURRYE, in the British province of Nagpore, a town on the route from Gurrawarra to Nagpoor, 33 miles S.E. of the former, 122 N. of the latter. It has a bazar, and is supplied with water from wells. Lat. 22° 36′, long. 79° 14′.

HURRYHUR, in the Mysore, a town with a fort, on the right bank of the river Tungabudra or Tumbudra, which, during the periodical rains, washes the western wall of the fort, but at other times flows 300 yards from it, and is not more than mid-deep, though the bed is 700 yards wide. Having been a place of considerable trade, it was repeatedly plundered by the Mahrattas, though rather well fortified. In the fort is a temple dedicated to Harihara, an idol representing a union of Hari or Vishnu and Hara or Siva; and hence was derived the name of the place. The British cantonment here is situate on an extensive plain, 1,500 yards from the river, towards which the ground gently slopes. The water of the river is good, but the distance renders it inconvenient to resort to it for a supply, so that it is generally obtained from wells, being usually found at a depth of about forty feet. The climate is in general exempt from great heat at any season, and during the south-west monsoon is pleasantly cool. The hot season occurs during the months of May and June. The elevation of the cantonment above the sea is said to be about 1,900 feet. Distance from Bangalore, N.W., 160 miles; from Seringapatam, N.W., 132; from Mangalore, N.E., 181; Bellary, S.W., 85; Chitteldroog, N.W., 45; Madras, N.W., 320. Lat. 14° 31′, long. 75° 51′.

HURSANEE.—A town in the Rajpoot state of Jodhpoor, 65 miles S. from Jessulmeer, and 150 miles W. from Jodhpoor. Lat. 26°, long. 70° 49′.

HURSOLE.—A town in the British district of Kaira, presidency of Bombay, 38 miles N.E. of Ahmedabad. Lat. 23° 20′, long. 73° 2′.

HURSOLEE.—A town in the Rajpoot state of Ulwar, situate on the right bank of a branch of the Saubie Nulla, and 20 miles N. from Ulwar. Lat. 27° 50′, long. 76° 40′.

HURSOOL.—A town in the petty native district of the same name, presidency of Bombay, 10 miles S. from Peint, and 93 miles N.E. from Bombay. Lat. 20° 9′, long. 73° 30′.

HURSUKE GURHEE, or GURHEE HURSEORO, in the British district of Goorgaon, lieut.-gov. of the N.W. Provinces, a town on the route from Delhi to Rewari, and 27 miles S.W. of the former. It has a bazar. Lat. 28° 25′, long. 77°.

HURSUR.—A town in the British province of Nagpoor, 153 miles E.S.E. from Nagpoor, and 52 miles S. by W. from Ryepoor. Lat. 20° 31′, long. 81° 23′.

HUSESMOW.—See ASAMOW.

HUSHTNUGGUR (or "the Eight Towns").—A town and fortress of the province of Peshawur, situate north of the Kabool river, and 20 miles N. of the city of Peshawur. The surrounding country is very fertile, beautiful, and well watered, but much exposed to the attacks of the restless and fierce tribes to the northward. Lat. 34° 16′, long. 71° 45′.

HUSSEINGUNJ, in the territory of Oude, a village or small decayed town on the route by Nanamau ghat or ferry from Futtehgurh to Lucknow, 17 miles S.W. of the latter. Tennant styles it a poor village. Lat. 26° 45′, long. 80° 42′.

HUSSEINPOOR GHAT, in the British district of Furruckabad, lieut.-gov. of the N.W. Provinces, a village or station on the left bank of the Ganges, on the route from Bareilly to Futtehgurh, and just below the fort. Here is a ferry over the Ganges, the principal stream of which is stated to be 150 yards wide in the dry season. The passage over the rest of the bed of the river is, during the dry season, intricate, from channels, pools, and quicksands; but during the periodical rains in the latter part of summer, the stream is between three and four miles wide. Lat. 27° 22′, long. 79° 42′.

HUSSUNGURH, in the British district of Allygurh, lieut.-gov. of the N.W. Provinces, a town on the route from Boolundshuhur to Agra, 44 miles N. by W. of the latter. Lat. 27° 48′, long. 77° 57′.

HUSSUNPOOR, in the British district of Moradabad, lieut.-gov. of the N.W. Provinces, a town on the route from Moradabad to Boolundshuhur, 32 miles W. by S. of the former. Population 7,569. Lat. 28° 43′, long. 78° 22′.

HUSSUNPOORA.—A town in the British district of Sarun, lieut.-gov. of Bengal, 37 miles N.W. of Chupra. Lat. 26° 2′, long. 84° 27′.

HUSTINASSORE, the principal place of a pergunnah of the same name, in the British district of Meerut, lieut.-gov. of the N.W. Provinces, is situate close to the right bank of the Boorea Ganges, or old channel of the Ganges, 24 miles W. of the present stream, and on the border of the Kadir or marsh-land. It is now an insignificant, obscure place, but much celebrated in the mythological lore of the Hindoos, as the capital of the Panchala, an ancient race, and the residence of King Bharata, the fifth in descent from Swayambhuva or Adam, and the ancestor of the renowned rival families the Kuroos and Pandoos. According to the legend, it received its name from Hasti, its founder; but it is perhaps more probable, as the name means "elephant's town," and those animals still abound in the forest about fifty miles north, at the south-western base of the Sewalik range, that this circumstance affords the true derivation. It is also called Hastinagara, a word of similar import to its more usual name. In the Ayeen Akbery, it is mentioned under the name of Hustnapoor, and stated to be "an ancient Hindoo place of worship, on the banks of the Ganges," and to yield a revenue of 1,11,672 rupees. It appears to have been the Bastinora of the Greek geographers, and is by Ritter styled (with no great perspicuity) "the Babylon of ancient India." Of its present condition scarcely anything appears to be known; and as it is but twenty miles northeast of the town of Meerut, in an open country, frequented by Europeans, the silence of travellers on the subject seems to indicate that it now contains nothing worth notice. The account given of it by Hamilton, Ritter, and some others, is little more than a repetition of Wilford, who states that there "remains only a small place of worship, and the extensive site of that ancient city is entirely covered with large ant-hills, which have induced the inhabitants of the adjacent country to suppose that it had been overturned or destroyed by the Termites." Lat. 29° 10′, long. 78° 8′.

HUSTNAPOOR.—A town in the British district of Cuddapah, presidency of Madras, 126 miles N.W. by W. of Madras. Lat. 14° 10′, long. 78° 50′.

HUSUNPOOR, in the British district of Meerut, lieut.-gov. of the N.W. Provinces, a village on the route from the town of Meerut to Moradabad, and 13 miles S.E. of the former. Lat. 28° 54′, long. 77° 56′.

HUSWA.—A town in the British district of Behar, lieut.-gov. of Bengal, 44 miles N.E. of Sherghotty. Lat. 24° 50′, long. 85° 30′.

HUSWA, in the British district of Futtehpore, lieut.-gov. of the N.W. Provinces, a town close to the route from Allahabad to the town of Futtehpore, and seven miles S.E. of the latter. Baber mentions it under the name of Aswah. Lat. 25° 51′, long. 80° 53′.

HUTEOUT.—A town in the native state of

Nepal, 54 miles S. from Khatmandoo, and 50 miles W. by S. from Bettiah. Lat. 26° 55′, long. 85° 21′.

HUTGAON, the principal place of the pergunnah of the same name, a town with a bazar, on the route from Allahabad to the town of Futtehpoor, and 19 miles S.E. of the latter. Lat. 25° 52′, long. 81° 11′.

HUTGIA, in the British district of Allahabad, lieut.-gov. of the N.W. Provinces, a village on the route from the city of Allahabad to Lucknow, and eight miles N.W. of the former. Lat. 25° 34′, long. 81° 53′.

HUTNEE.—A town in the British district of Belgaum, presidency of Bombay, 72 miles N.E. of Belgaum. Lat. 16° 43′, long. 75° 8′.

HUTNOOR.—A town in Hyderabad, or dominions of the Nizam, 150 miles N. from Hyderabad, and 120 miles S.S.W. from Nagpoor. Lat. 19° 30′, long. 78° 38′.

HUTSOO.—A river rising in the petty native state of Korea, on the south-west frontier of Bengal, in lat. 23° 18′, long. 82° 32′, and, flowing in a southerly direction for forty-five miles, passes into the Ruttunpoor district of the rajah of Berar's dominions, which it traverses for sixty miles. Subsequently separating for twenty-five miles a detached portion of the Sumbulpoor British territory and the native state of Bootea from Berar, it falls into the Mahanuddy river, in lat. 21° 50′, long. 82° 46′.

HUTTAH.—A town in Hyderabad, or dominions of the Nizam, 170 miles N.W. by N. from Hyderabad, and 80 miles S.E. from Jaulnah. Lat. 19° 20′, long. 77°.

HUTTAH, in the British territory of Saugor and Nerbudda, lieut.-gov. of the N.W. Provinces, a town on the route from Allahabad to Saugor, 170 miles S.W. of the former, 61 N.E. of the latter. It is situate on the right bank of the river Sonar, has a bazar, and is the residence of a principal assistant to the commissioner in the Saugor and Nerbudda district. Elevation above the sea 1,183 feet. Lat. 24° 8′, long. 79° 40′.

HUTTALEE, in the Daman division of the Punjab, a town situated thirty miles from the right bank of the Indus, 138 miles N.N.W. of the town of Mooltan. Lat. 31° 55′, long. 70° 28′.

HUTTEEN, in the British district of Goorgaon, lieut.-gov. of the N.W. Provinces, a town on the route from Delhi to Muttra, 47 miles N.W. of the latter. Lat. 28° 2′, long. 77° 19′.

HUTTIPOOR, in the British district of Furruckabad, lieut.-gov. of the N.W. Provinces, a village on the route from Allygurh cantonment to that of Futtehgurh, and seven miles N.W. of the latter. Lat. 27° 25′, long. 79° 35′.

HUTWASS, in the British territory of Saugur and Nerbudda, lieut.-gov. of the N.W. Provinces, a town on the route from Baitool to Saugur, 70 miles N.N.E. of the former. Lat. 22° 46′, long. 78° 23′.

HUZARA, one of the subdivisions of the Punjab, situate at the north-eastern extremity, between Peshawur and Gholab Singh's dominions, and lately placed under the jurisdiction of the commissioner of Peshawur.—See PUNJAB.

HYATNUGGUR.—A town in Hyderabad, or dominions of the Nizam, 10 miles S.E. by E. from Hyderabad, and 110 miles N. by E. from Kurnool. Lat. 17° 19′, long. 78° 40′.

HYBUTPOOR, in Sirhind, a village on the route from Hansi to Lodiana, and 54 miles N. of the former town. It is situate in a level country, liable to be overflowed during inundations of the river Gagur; and at that time the road in this part of the route is impracticable for carriages or artillery, though at other times good. Distant N.W. from Calcutta 1,030 miles Lat. 29° 51′, long. 76° 2′.

HYDASPES.—See JHELUM.

HYDERABAD, or the territory of the Nizam, an extensive realm of Southern India, the name by which it is thus distinguished being that of the city which is its capital. The territory lies between lat. 15° 10′—21° 42′, long. 74° 40′—81° 32′; is 475 miles in length from south-west to north-east, and about the same distance in breadth. The area is estimated at 95,337 square miles. It is bounded on the north-east by the territory of Nagpore; on the south-east by territory subject to the presidency of Madras, and the territory lately belonging to the nawaub of Kurnool; on the west by territory subject to the presidency of Bombay; on the north-west by territory belonging to the presidency last named, by the territory of Gwalior, or of the family of Scindia, and by the British districts of Saugor and Nerbudda. The principal rivers which skirt or traverse the territory are the Godavery, with its tributaries the Doodna, Manjera, Pranheeta; the Wurda, with its tributaries; and the Kistna, with its feeders the Beema and Toongabudra.

The climate may be considered in general good, and as there are no arid, bare deserts, similar to those of Rajpootana and some other tracts of Northern India, the hot winds are less felt. In the vicinity of the city of Hyderabad, the mean temperature in the house, according to observations made at sunrise, at two o'clock in the afternoon, and at sunset, for one year, "was, in January, 74½°; February, 76¼°; March, 84°; April, 91¼°; May, 93°; June, 88°; July, 81°; August, 80¼°; September, 79°; October, 80°; November, 76½°; December, 74½°: giving as an annual mean 81½°." The south-west monsoon commences about the beginning of June, and ends about the beginning of October, and, as is usually the case, brings heavy rains. After it has ceased, variable weather continues for a few weeks; and this is followed by the north-east monsoon, bringing rains, though less heavy than those accompanying the former. At midwinter the variation of temperature in the northern part of the territory is very great and sudden. The mornings are very cold, and ice is formed; but the days are hot, the thermometer sometimes reaching 80° in the shade. The closing monsoons are considered the most unhealthy periods of the year, producing fevers and agues, but in general not of formidable types, except in the vicinity of extensive marshy jungles. Diseases of the spleen are common in the vicinity of the Godavery. Cholera is not a prevalent disease, and when it does occur, is consequent on famine. Diseases of the eyes are prevalent in the sandstone districts. The wells in general yield impure, unpalatable water, productive of disease, especially the dracunculus or guinea-worm, from which those who use the water from tanks or streams are exempt. There are no returns of the amount of population, but its relative density is probably not very low, as the soil is on an average fertile, the climate good. If the relative density be assumed at 120 to the square mile, the aggregate will be 10,666,080 persons. The revenue of the Nizam is stated at 1,550,000*l*. The cities and places of chief note, viz., Hyderabad the capital, Secunderabad, Jaulna, Jaafarabad, Beder, Janur or Chinur, Ellichpoor, Doulatabad, Golconda, Nirmal, Nander, Palensha, and Warangol, are described under their respective names in the alphabetical arrangement. The military roads are in general good, especially in the granitic tracts, where the prevailing material is easily beaten into a smooth, sound, durable surface. The principal routes are,—1. From north to south, from Nagpore, through the city of Hyderabad, to Bangalore; 2. from south-east to north-west, from Madras and Masulipatam, through the city of Hyderabad, to Poona, and thence to Bombay; 3. from south-east to north-west, from the city of Hyderabad to Aurungabad. A large subsidiary force is maintained by the British government under the terms of the treaty with the Nizam, concluded in the year 1800. The Nizam's military force consists of four separate descriptions of troops:—1. The auxiliary force, organized under British officers, which is composed of regular troops, officered from the Company's army, and paid by the Nizam's government. 2. The irregular troops, consisting of cavalry, infantry, and artillery. 3. A miscellaneous irregular force, composed of Arabs, Scindees, Moguls, and Seiks; and, 4. the troops maintained by ameers and others from revenues assigned by government for their support.

To deduce from the earliest available sources the history of the countries which constitute the dominions of the Nizam, would require more space than could be spared for the purpose in such a compilation as the present. The Nizam himself derives his authority from a chief named Azof Jah, who held high command under Aurungzebe, and who, while nominally bearing allegiance to that sovereign, and administering the government of the Deccan as his viceroy, actually established himself there as an independent prince. This chief, known as Nizam-ool-Moolk (Regulator of the State), died in 1748, at the age of upwards of 100 years, and the right of succession to his power and authority was fiercely contested among his descendants. The claimants most favoured were two. One of these, Nazir Jung, the second son of the deceased ruler, being on the spot when his father died, had seized the treasure, and obtained the support of the army; and, moreover, fortified his claim by an alleged renunciation of the right of succession on the part of his elder brother. The other, named Mozuffer Jung, was a grandson of Nizam-ool-Moolk, by a favourite daughter; and to him it was said the succession was conveyed by testamentary bequest. Each of these two candidates had the good fortune to secure the countenance and support of one of the great European powers then commencing their career of contention for supremacy in the East; the English espousing the cause of Nazir Jung, the French, that of his rival Mozuffer Jung; but after a very brief period, dissensions between the commander, and his officers caused the retirement of the French force from the field; and Mozuffer Jung, deprived of its support, became the prisoner of Nazir Jung. Differences now arose between the latter and his English allies, and their assistance was withdrawn. Nazir Jung subsequently gave himself up to idleness and sensual pleasure; a majority of the officers of his army, seduced by the French, fell from their allegiance, and by the hand of one of them, he perished in a conflict with a body of French troops, which had mustered to attack his camp. Mozuffer Jung was now undisputed viceroy of the Deccan, exercising his authority, however, under the control of the French commander Dupleix, whose will was supreme. But Mozuffer Jung was not destined long to enjoy even the appearance of power. He fell in an affray with some Patan chiefs, who, having been instrumental in placing him on the throne, were disappointed in the amount of reward to which they thought their services entitled. A new occupant of the seat of power was now to be sought; and the French, passing over an infant son of Mozuffer Jung, selected Salabut Jung, a brother of Nazir Jung, to be ruler of the Deccan. A new claimant for the dignity, however, shortly afterwards appeared, in the person of Ghazee-ood-deen, the eldest son of Nizam-ool-Moolk, who advanced to Aurungabad at the head of a large army, to assert the right which Nazir Jung alleged to have been renounced. Salabut Jung, aided by the French, prepared for resistance; but the impending contest between the brothers was averted by the sudden death of the elder, Ghazee-ood-deen, brought about, it has been said, by poison; and though the Mahrattas by whom he was supported, continued for their own purposes to maintain hostilities, their unvarying ill-success disposed them to listen to proposals for procuring their absence on the usual terms. The English and French, however, continued to struggle for power and influence in the Deccan; but the latter were compelled, after a while, by the danger of their own possessions, to withdraw from the support of Salabut Jung, who, thus weakened, and apprehensive, moreover, of the designs of a younger brother, Nizam Ali, entered into an engagement by which he promised to dismiss the French from his country and service, and renounce all connection with them. In 1761, this weak prince was dethroned by his youngest brother, Nizam Ali, whom, contrary to the advice of the most judicious of his French counsellors, he had intrusted with power, which was used to supplant the donor. Two years afterwards, the usurper made further acknowledgment of his brother's favour, by putting him to death. In 1765, he ravaged the Carnatic, exercising in his course a measure of cruelty far beyond what was necessary to his purpose; but he retired on the approach of a British force. Still, the British government was anxious to be on better terms with him, partly from apprehension of his future hostility in alliance with other powers as unscrupulous as himself, and partly from a desire to obtain his concurrence to their retention of a maritime district known by the name of the Northern Circars, formerly possessed by the French, but now occupied by the English, who had fortified their right by the firman of the emperor.

Nizam Ali was straitened for money (an infirmity which has clung to the Hyderabad state to the present time), and, in 1766, a new treaty was concluded, not unacceptable to either party, under which the East-India Company engaged to "have a body of their troops ready to settle the affairs of his highness's government, in everything that is right and proper," subject, however, to withdrawal when their own possessions, or the peace and tranquillity of the Carnatic, might be in danger, and to pay, as a consideration for the free gift of the Circars, a sum of five lacs every year in which the assistance of their troops should not be required. There were other stipulations; and among them one reserving the life-right of Bazalut Jung, a brother of Nizam Ali, in one of the circars, subject to his good behaviour. The aid of British troops was afforded, as provided by the treaty, to enable Nizam Ali to proceed against Hyder Ali Khan, then rapidly rising into power; but, after a good deal of vacillation, Nizam Ali preferred to unite with that adventurer. The allies, however, were unprosperous, and the Nizam was compelled to sue for peace, which was concluded by a new treaty in 1768. By the sixth article, the East-India Company and the nabob of the Carnatic (who was a party to the treaty) were to be always ready to send two battalions of sepoys, and six pieces of artillery manned by Europeans, whenever the Nizam should require them, and the situation of affairs would allow of such assistance being rendered, the Nizam paying the expense during the time such force should be employed in this service. In 1782, Bazalut Jung died; but the Company did not obtain possession of the circar held by him till 1788. The peishcush, or payment to be made to the Nizam on account of the Circars, had fallen into arrear, and was not adjusted till even a later period. These matters, however, having been at length arranged, the British Governor-General, Lord Cornwallis, in 1789, addressed a letter to the Nizam, explaining and interpreting the treaty of 1768, but declining to enter into any new treaty, as had been suggested. This letter of the Governor-General's was subsequently declared, by a resolution of the House of Commons, to have been meant, and to have had the full force of a treaty executed in due form. In this letter, the Governor-General agreed that the force stipulated for in the sixth article of the treaty of 1768 should be granted whenever applied for, provided it was not to be employed against any power in alliance with the Company. In the following year, on the breaking out of the war with Tippoo, son of Hyder Ali, a treaty of offensive and defensive alliance was concluded between the Nizam, the Peishwa, and the British government. Tippoo purchased peace at the sacrifice of half his dominions, and the Nizam had no reason to be dissatisfied with his share of the spoil. At a later period, the Nizam, being engaged in war with the Mahrattas, claimed the assistance of the British government under the subsisting relations between them; but the Governor-General, Sir John Shore, refused to afford it, and the Nizam was consequently obliged to conclude an ignominious peace with his enemy. This refusal, and its results, so incensed the Nizam, that he requested that two battalions, stationed at his capital as a subsidiary force, should be withdrawn. The Nizam now sought safety in the entertainment of a party of Frenchmen, who, however, were dismissed, in accordance with the provisions of a treaty concluded in 1798, under the administration of the earl of Mornington, afterwards Marquis Wellesley, who was most anxious to rid India of all French influence. By this treaty, a subsidiary force, augmented to 6,000 sepoys, with a due proportion of field-pieces, was assigned to the service of the Nizam. On the fall of Tippoo Sultan, and the annihilation of the state of Seringapatam, the Nizam participated largely in the division of its territory, under the partition treaty of 1799, and his share was increased on the Peishwa's withdrawal from the treaty. In 1800, the subsidiary force with the Nizam was further augmented, and the pecuniary payment for its maintenance was commuted for a cession of territory. The territory ceded for this purpose consisted of the acquisitions made from Tippoo allotted to the Nizam, under the treaty of Seringapatam in 1792, and the treaty of Mysore, concluded in 1799, after the destruction of Tippoo's power and government. Thus the Nizam secured the future defence of his person and state, without any sacrifice either of money, or of any portion of his original dominions, the territory assigned for payment of the subsidiary force having been acquired under the protection and influence of the power which now undertook to maintain his authority by means which itself had placed at his disposal. In 1804, on the conclusion of the first Mahratta war, the Nizam obtained further territorial advantages, and at the termination of the second, in 1817, certain exchanges between the Company and himself took place, some of them made for mutual convenience, others to gratify the Nizam's wishes. The precise position of the Nizam, in regard to the British government, is determined by the treaties above referred to, and it does not materially differ from that of other states with which that government maintains subsidiary alliances. Nizam Ali, of whom mention by no means to his honour has been made in the course of this narrative, closed a long and guilty life in 1803. He was succeeded by his son Secunder Jah, with whom the Company confirmed all existing treaties. His feeble and unprosperous rule was terminated by his death in 1829, when he was succeeded by his eldest but illegitimate son, to whom the existing engagements were again confirmed. Under this prince the misgovernment of the country has continued and increased. A host of mercenary troops, entertained by him, so far from contributing to the purpose of defence, have been a terror both to government and people; the administration of justice, or even the semblance of it, was almost unknown, while debt, public and private, was allowed to accumulate to an enormous extent. The British government was at one time creditor for arrears of payments due to it, to the amount of between five and six hundred thousand pounds. This claim, to the continued increase of which there seemed no probable limit, was strongly pressed on the notice of the Nizam's government, and its arrangement was at length effected by a territorial cession, the revenues of the districts thus sequestrated being applicable both to the reduction of the debt and the maintenance of the Nizam's military contingent.

HYDERABAD, the principal place in the territory of the Nizam, is situate on the river Mussi, here between 400 and 500 feet wide. The environs have a wild but highly picturesque appearance, being overspread with granite hills and isolated rocks, some of hemispherical form, others of cubical or columnar. Approached from the west, the appearance of Hyderabad is very striking: "The palace and numerous mosques rising above the surrounding buildings, give it an air of grandeur, which is much strengthened by the very superb pile of buildings erected as the British Residency." The town is feebly fortified by a wall of stone, too weak to stand a moment against battering-guns, though adequate for protection against predatory attacks. The ground-plan inclosed by the wall is a trapezoid, the longest or north-western side of which, extending along the right bank of the river Mussi, is about two miles and three-quarters in length; the south-eastern, two miles; the southern, one mile; the south-western, one and three-quarters. There is a considerable suburb on the left side of the river, and in this quarter is situate the British Residency, the communication between it and the city and palace being maintained by a handsome stone bridge. This fine structure, planned and executed by a British officer in 1831, is built of squared granite stone, and has eight arches, semi-elliptical, each of fifty-six feet span and eighteen feet rise, with piers ten feet wide; the breadth of the bridge being twenty-four feet. There is, besides, on the left or northern side, a land-arch of seventy-seven feet span and sixteen feet rise. The total cost was 10,200*l.* "The city is crowded with buildings of all descriptions, from the stately and stupendous palaces of the nobility and other men of rank and wealth, to the low and dirty hovels of the poor. The construction of the houses of the great is entirely native, displaying little or no taste. They are erected too close to each other, rendering their situations unpleasantly confined, if not unhealthy." The streets, some of which are paved with stone, are in general narrow. In addition to the water of the Mussi, the place is abundantly supplied from numerous wells, in various parts of the town. Besides the palace of the Nizam (a large building in the usual style of native grandeur), the most remarkable structures are the principal mosque and the British Residency. In the environs of the city are many fine gardens, containing gorgeous pavilions. Among them, that of the minister of the Nizam is represented as marvellously beautiful. "It is inclosed, after the Asiatic manner, by high walls, the centre containing a large marble basin filled with water, and fed by numerous fountains, their silvery columns being mingled with stately cypress-trees. The pavilions, galleries, and terraces around are built and ornamented in the richest style of Oriental architecture, that beautiful carved trellis-work, which always produces so exquisite an effect, frequently intervening, while the painting and gilding are equally profuse and striking." The country about Hyderabad abounds with fine tanks or artificial pieces of water of great dimensions. One, called Husain Sagur, four miles north of the city, and close to the British cantonment of Secunderabad, is about three miles in length and two in breadth; another, a few miles to the south, is stated to be twenty miles in circuit. There is no tolerable approximation to a trustworthy estimate of the population, which probably does not exceed 200,000, of whom a large proportion are Mussulmans. Elevation above the sea 1,800 feet. Distance from Mangalore, N.E., 498 miles; Bangalore, N., 373; Bellary, N.E., 229; Madras, N.W., 389; Bombay, S.E., 449; Nagpore, S., 314; Calcutta, S.W., 962. Lat. 17° 22′, long. 78° 32′.

HYDERGURH, in the territory of Oude,

a small town on the route from Lucknow cantonment to that of Pertabgurh, 40 miles S.E. of the former, 70 N.W. of the latter. It has a bazar, and is well supplied with good water. Lat. 26° 37′, long. 81° 17′.

HYDERNUGUR.—A town in the British district of Behar, lieut.-gov. of Bengal, 56 miles W. of Sherghotty. Lat. 24° 30′, long. 83° 59′.

HYDRABAD, in Sinde, was formerly considered the principal town of that country, in consequence of its having been selected as the residence of the chief ameers, or those ruling the southern and principal part of the country. It is situate four miles E. of the eastern bank of the Indus, on an eminence of the low rocky range called the Gunjah Hills, and in an island inclosed between the Indus and the Fulailee, a branch which, leaving the main stream about twelve miles above the town, communicates with it about fifteen miles below. The Fulailee flows about 1,000 yards east of the town, the base of the rampart being washed by a creek from it in the season of inundation, though the whole branch is dry when the river is low. This fortress, which was esteemed very strong by the Sindians, and would no doubt prove so in their mode of warfare, was built nearly on the site of the ancient Nerunkot, by Futteh Ali, the first ameer. The outline is irregular, corresponding with the winding shape of the hill's brow, on the very edge of which the walls, for the greater part of their extent, rise to the height of from fifteen to thirty feet. They are built of burnt bricks, and are thick and solid at the base, but taper so much, and are so greatly weakened by embrasures and loopholes with which they are pierced, that a few well-directed shot would demolish any part, and expose the defenders to the fire of the assailants. The ramparts are flanked by round towers or lofty bastions, at intervals of 300 or 400 paces, which, combined with the height of the hill, give the place an imposing appearance. Where the walls do not rise immediately from the edge of the declivity, the defence is strengthened by a ditch of ten feet wide and eight deep. The rock is too soft to admit of being scarped, and slopes so gently, that if the wall were breached, the rubbish would rest on the face of the hill, and afford footing for a storming-party. The plateau of the hill on which Hydrabad is built is a mile and a half long and 700 yards broad; the height is about eighty feet, and on the southern part are the fortress and the suburbs or pettah. There are about 5,000 houses, meanly constructed of mud, one-half of that number being within the fortress, the rest in the pettah. The fortress contained the residence of the ameers, and a massive tower built as the repository of their treasures. The bazar is extensive, forming one street the entire length of the town; and it displays considerable bustle and appearance of business. The most important manufacture of Hydrabad is that of arms of various kinds,—matchlocks, swords, spears, and shields; and the skill of the workmen is said to be scarcely inferior to that attained in Europe. There is also a considerable manufacture of ornamental silks and cottons. A cemetery, which overspreads the northern part of the eminence, contains the tombs of the deceased members of the Talpoor dynasty, and of the preceding one of the Kaloras. That of Gholam Shah Kalora is a beautiful quadrangular building, with a handsome central dome. It is lined with fine marble, is highly ornamented with mosaic, and inscribed with sentences from the Koran. The tomb of the late Ameer Kurum Ali is also a handsome quadrangular building, surmounted by a dome, and having a turret on each corner. When the Belooches, under the conduct of Futteh Ali, of the Talpoor tribe, overthrew the Kalora dynasty, that successful chieftain gave to one branch of his relatives Khyerpoor, with a considerable district attached; to another, Meerpoor, and allowed his three brothers to share with himself the government of Hydrabad and its dependent territory, comprehending the greater part of the country. Sir C. Napier entered this place on the 20th February, 1843, having previously received the submission of six of the ameers of Sinde. On the 24th he marched out to give battle to Sheer Mahomed of Meerpore, who yet remained in arms, and was posted in great force behind a neighbouring nullah, which had been partially fortified. The ameer was, however, attacked and defeated; the British force being thus enabled to advance upon Meerpore. Hydrabad is supposed to have a population of 24,000. Lat. 25° 22′, long. 68° 28′.—See Sinde.

HYDRAMEYEE, in the British district of Alligurh, lieut.-gov. of the N.W. Provinces, a village on the route, by Khasgunj, from Bareilly to Alligurh cantonment, and 28 miles S.E. of the latter, 49 N.E. of Agra. Lat. 27° 51′, long. 78° 28′.

I.

IBRAHEEMPORE, or IBRAHIMABAD.—A town in the British district of Ghazeepore, lieut.-gov. of the N.W. Provinces. It has a population of 26,582. Distant E. from Ghazeepore town 60 miles. Lat. 25° 48′, long. 84° 38′.

IBRAMPUTNA.—A town in Hyderabad, or the dominions of the Nizam, 16 miles S.E. from Hyderabad, and 103 N.E. by N. from Kurnoul. Lat. 17° 11′, long. 78° 42′.

IDDOOR CONCAUDY.—A town in the British district of North Canara, presidency of Madras, 61 miles N. of Mangalore. Lat. 13° 46′, long. 74° 50′.

IDULABAD.—A town in Hyderabad, or dominions of the Nizam, 11 miles from the right bank of the Payne Gunga river, and 130 miles S.E. by S. from Ellichpoor. Lat. 19° 39′, long. 78° 41′.

IDULABAD.—A town in one of the recently sequestrated districts of Hyderabad, or dominions of the Nizam, 95 miles W. by S. of Ellichpoor. Lat. 21° 1′, long. 76° 8′.

IEEJ.—A town in one of the recently sequestrated districts of Hyderabad, or dominions of the Nizam, 29 miles W.N.W. of Kurnoul. Lat. 16°, long. 77° 43′.

IHUBBHER, in the Reechna Dooab division of the Punjab, a town situated 34 miles from the right bank of the Ravee, 38 miles N.W. of the town of Lahore. Lat. 31° 58′, long. 73° 40′.

IHUNG, in the Jetch Dooab division of the Punjab, a town situated on the left bank of the Chenaub, 104 miles W. by S. of the town of Lahore. Lat. 31° 19′, long. 72° 28′.

IKERI, in the British district of Allygurh, lieut.-gov. of the N.W. Provinces, a village on the route, by Khasganj, from Bareilly to Allygurh cantonment, and seven miles S.E. of the latter. Lat. 27° 53′, long. 78° 14′.

IKERY.—See EEKAIREE.

IKOUNA, or EKOWNA.—A town in the British district of Ghazeepore, lieut.-gov. of the N.W. Provinces, situate three miles from the left bank of the Ganges river. Ikouna has a population of 7,005 inhabitants. Distant E. from Ghazeepore town 43 miles. Lat. 25° 43′, long. 84° 20′.

ILLPOOR.—A town in the British district of Madura, presidency of Madras, situate 20 miles S. from Trichinopoly, and 48 miles E. by N. from Dindigul. Lat. 10° 32′, long. 78° 43′.

IMJONG.—A town of Eastern India, in the British district of Sudiya, province of Assam, 59 miles E.S.E. of Sudiya. Lat. 27° 28′, long. 96° 32′.

IMLAK, in the territory of Oude, a village on the route from the cantonment of Goruckpoor to that of Sultanpoor, and 15 miles N.E. of the latter. The road in this part of the route is good. Lat. 26° 15′, long. 82° 21′.

IMLEA.—See AMILEA.

IMRUTPOOR, in the British district of Furruckabad, lieut.-gov. of the N.W. Provinces, the principal place of the pergunnah of Islamgunge. It is a small town on the route from Shahjehanpore to Futtehgurh, 12 miles N. of the latter, and is situate less than a mile from the left bank of the Ganges, in a country extensively laid under water during the periodical rains in the latter part of summer, but at other times displaying a scene of great fertility, high cultivation, and luxuriant vegetation, interspersed with ancient and fine groves of mangoes. Indigo is the chief crop. There is a bazar in the town, and during the dry season the road is good. It is called Hemratpur by Tieffenthaler. Lat. 27° 32′, long. 79° 40′.

INCHULKURUNJEE, or EENCHULKURUNJEE.—A jaghire or feudal dependency of Colapore, in the territory of Bombay. These possessions, however, are held in enam, and not on surinjam tenure; and the Colapore state has consequently no right to claim military service from their chief. The centre of the jaghire is in lat. 16° 41′, long. 74° 2′. A part of the country, stretching to the Ghauts bordering on the Concan, is rugged and jungly, but the greater portion lies on the plains, and is very productive. The revenue is 75,000 rupees. A late chief was greatly burthened with debt, and his jaghire had become a prey to usurers. He died in 1852, without leaving male issue, when his widow was permitted to adopt a successor, subject to certain conditions; among which was the abolition of transit-duties and other objectionable taxes. The adopted ruler died childless in 1854, and the question whether the estate shall be resumed by the Colapore government has been made dependent on the non-existence of any male relative of the founder of the ruling family. Should the resumption be sanctioned, the estate of Inchulkurunjee will probably be transferred to the British government in liquidation of the debt incurred by the Colapore state for the suppression of the insurrection in the year 1844.

INDAPOOR.—A town in the British district of Poonah, presidency of Bombay, 84 miles E.S.E. of Poonah. Lat. 18° 8′, long. 75° 5′.

INDARUM.—A town in the British province of Nagpoor, situate three miles from the left bank of the Wein Gunga, and 138 miles S.E. by S. from Nagpoor. Lat. 19° 25′, long. 80° 6′.

INDEE.—A town in the British district of Sholapoor, presidency of Bombay, 136 miles N.E. by E. of Belgaum. Lat. 17° 10′, long. 76° 1′.

INDERAOTEE.—A river rising in lat. 19° 56′, long. 81° 50′, in Bustar, one of the districts of Nagpoor, or the rajah of Berar's dominions, and, flowing in a south-westerly direction, falls into the Godavery river on the left side, in lat. 18° 40′, long. 80° 20′.

INDERGARH, in the British district of Furruckabad, lieut.-gov. of the N.W. Provinces, a small town on the route from Calpee to Futtehgurh, and 34 miles S. of the latter. It has a bazar. Lat. 26° 56′, long. 79° 45′.

INDERGURH.—A town of Bundlecund, in the native state of Dutteah, 32 miles N. from Jhansee, and 32 miles S.E. from Gwalior. Lat. 25° 55′, long. 78° 40′.

INDGURH, in Sirhind, a town on the route from Lodiana to Ferozpore, and 33 miles W. of the former place. It contains several shops, and is abundantly supplied with water from twelve brick-lined wells, each about twenty feet deep. The surrounding country, though partaking of the nature of a deep sand, is well cultivated. Lat. 30° 55′, long. 75° 20′.

INDIA, an extensive region of Asia, the main divisions of which, together with the several subdivisions, their towns and villages, lakes and rivers, will be found more particularly described under their respective names in the alphabetical arrangement of this work. India is bounded on the north by the Himalaya Mountains, dividing it from Thibet. The Suliman range, a continuation of the Sufeid Koh Mountains, separates it from Afghanistan and Beloochistan on the west; and parallel offshoots from the opposite extremity of the Himalaya Mountains form its frontier on the east. On all other sides, from the port of Kurrachee on the west, to the southern extremity of the Tenasserim provinces on the east, it has a maritime coast, bordered by the Bay of Bengal on the one hand, and by the Arabian Sea, or North Indian Ocean, on the other. Its greatest length, measured from Cape Comorin in the south, to the extremity of the Punjaub in the north, may be estimated at 1,830 miles, a distance which closely corresponds with its breadth, measured from Kurrachee in the west, to the extremity of Assam in the east. It lies between lat. 8° 4′—36°, long. 66° 44′—99° 30′. Within these limits is comprised an area of 1,399,443 square miles, with a population of 172,399,235. Another chain of mountains, termed the Vindhya range, crosses the continent of India at a lower latitude, from east to west. This range unites at one of its extremities with the Eastern, and at the other with the Western Ghauts, and thus forms the base of the triangle upon which rests the table-land of the Deccan. Such is a general outline of the mountain system of India. Extensive means of inland navigation are presented in the noble rivers by which the country is traversed. These may be conveniently distributed into two classes; the one deriving their chief supplies from the melted snows of the Himalayas, and the other being mainly fed by the rains of the south-west and north-east monsoons. In the one class may be ranked,—1. The Indus and its tributaries, consisting of the Sutlej, Beas, Ravee, Chenab, and Jhelum; 2. the Ganges and its tributaries, the chief of which are the Jumna, Gogra, Gunduck, and Cosy; 3. the Brahmapootra, with its principal feeders the Sanpoo and the Teesta; and, 4. the Irawaddy, traversing Burmah and the recently-acquired province of Pegu. In the second class are ranged the great rivers of the Deccan; among which may be enumerated the Godavery, Kistnah, and Cauvery, together with the Nerbudda, Taptee, Mahanuddee, and various others intersecting Southern and Central India.

For political objects, as well as for administrative purposes, the British possessions in India have been distributed into several principal divisions, which, with their respective areas and population, are stated below:—

	Area. Sq. Miles.	Population.
Bengal, including Assam and the Tenasserim Provinces	235,646	41,186,522
North-Western Provinces	85,651	30,872,766
Saugor and Nerbudda territory	17,543	2,143,599
Punjaub	78,447	9,153,209
Cis-Sutlej territory	4,559	2,311,969
Nagpore	76,432	4,650,000
Pegu	32,250	540,180
Madras	132,090	22,301,697
Bombay	120,065	11,109,067
Total, exclusive of the Eastern Straits settlements, the area of which is 1,575 square miles, population 202,540	782,683	124,269,009

It will thus be seen that more than one-half of the superficial extent of India is strictly British, the remainder, comprising an area of 616,760 square miles, and a population of 48,130,226, is occupied by native states. In some of these, as in Oude and the Mysore, the administration of public affairs has been altogether assumed by the British government; in others the native ruler exercises sovereign power with more or less restriction within his dominions. Among the states of the latter class are included Hyderabad or the dominions of the Nizam, Guzerat or the territory of the Guicowar, Gwalior or Scindia's territory, Indore or Holcar's possessions, Mysore, Travancore, Cochin and Cutch, Nepaul, Bhopal, Cashmere or Gholab Singh's dominions, the Rajpoot states, and a variety of others, forming in the aggregate a number falling little short of 200. If to these be added the petty chieftainships of Kattywar, the number of native states will be more than doubled.

With the exception of Nepaul, and one or two petty governments, the whole of these states have entered into treaties and engagements with the British government, involving the obligation of protection on the part of the paramount power, and allegiance on that of the subordinate. In some instances, the dependent state is subject to the payment of tribute; in others, it is exempt from any pecuniary claim. All have relinquished the right of self-defence, as well as that of maintaining diplomatic relations with each other; and the British government, which guarantees external protection and internal tranquillity, has been constituted the arbiter of all disputes arising between native rulers. But though debarred from the exercise of military power in regard to external aggression, the native governments are not prohibited from maintaining a separate military force; in some cases, they are required to provide such a force, which, in the event of war, is to be available to the British government against the common enemy. In some instances, the number of troops to be maintained is restricted. Under these arrangements, the existing military resources of the native princes comprise a force of little less than 400,000 men. It may be observed, however, that considerable portions of the regular troops of native states are described in the official returns as fitted rather for police purposes than for regular military duties. It will be evident from this view, that the British authority in India is paramount. That of the French is almost annihilated: they still occupy Pondicherry, and one or two other places of small importance; but they no longer dispute with the English the dominion of the East. The Portuguese linger in a few spots, the scenes of their former commercial grandeur; but from neither of these powers has Britain at this time anything to fear. Her rivals have fallen before her, and left her in possession of the most gigantic dominion that ever was appended to a foreign state.

So vast a region, varying, in respect to latitude and elevation, from the sea-level of the lower provinces of Bengal to the lofty summits of the Himalayas, must necessarily embrace various degrees of temperature; and in a general description of the climate of India, it is only the leading characteristics that can be noticed. The year admits of a division into three seasons,—the hot, the rainy, and the temperate. The hot season commences in March, and continues till the beginning of June, when the rains, brought from the Indian Ocean by the south-west monsoon, set in, and last with occasional intermission till October, at which period the temperate weather commences, and continues till the end of February. "In a great part of the country," says Elphinstone, "the sun is scorching for three months in the year; even the wind is hot, the land is brown and parched, dust flies in whirlwinds, all brooks become dry, small rivers scarcely keep up a stream, and the largest are reduced to comparatively narrow channels, in the midst of vast sandy beds. In winter, slight frost sometimes takes place for about an hour or two about sunrise." "At a low level, if towards the south, the greatest cold in winter is only moderate heat."

Considerable interest is attached to the zoology of India. The forests contain a variety of wild animals, the most remarkable of which is the elephant. These animals associate in herds, which, emerging from the jungles, frequently occasion serious injury to the crops. They are often destroyed by parties of hunters, or caught in pits and tamed. The elephant of the Deccan is considered inferior to that of Bengal. The rhinoceros, wild buffalo, and bear, are also inhabitants of the forest. Tigers, leopards, panthers, wild boars, hyænas, wolves, and jackals, pervade both forest and jungle, and sometimes infest patches of underwood in the immediate vicinity of cultivated lands. Lions are met with only in particular tracts, and more especially in the western part of Rajpootana, the province of Guzerat, and its vicinities. Among the remainder of wild animals may be enumerated deer, antelopes, and monkeys. Crocodiles, serpents, and other reptiles are most numerous. The domestic animals are buffaloes, camels, horses, sheep, swine, oxen, and goats. Game and fish are found in abundance, as are also birds of splendid plumage.

Among the principal trees are the teak, considered superior to the oak for purposes of shipbuilding, the sal, the sissoo, and the babul. There is also the cocoanut-tree, every portion of which is rendered available to the wants of man; the fruit being serviceable as food, the husk which envelops the nut affording a fibre from which cordage is manufactured, while the wood is peculiarly adapted to the construction of water-pipes, and also of beams and rafters. Another valuable tree, yielding a fleshy flower, which is important as an article of food, and from which spirit is moreover distilled, is the mahua. Besides the above, may be enumerated the bamboo, largely employed in scaffolding, and also in the manufacture of baskets and mats; the banyan, the tamarind, and the mango, the palmyra and other palms. Sandal and ebony are found in many parts. In the Himalayas, pines abound, including the magnificent deodar; together with oaks and other forest-trees indigenous in Europe, or capable of being naturalized there. On the banks of the Lower Ganges, and all round the seacoast of the peninsula, rice constitutes the staple food of the inhabitants. Wheat is largely consumed in the north-west provinces of Bengal. The peasantry of the Deccan depend for subsistence upon jowar and bajra, or upon a small and poor grain called raggi. The last-named grains are sown at the commencement of the rains, and reaped in autumn. Wheat ripens during winter, and forms a spring crop. But, though there are thus two distinct cultivations, the tropical and temperate crops are seldom sown on the same ground in the same year, except in the rich soil of the lower provinces of Bengal, and in some other irrigated tracts, where the rice crop requires only three months to arrive at maturity. Extensive tracts of land are appropriated to the production of the staple articles of export, consisting chiefly of cotton, sugar-cane, indigo, rice, opium, tobacco, and oil-seeds; pepper and cardamums are largely cultivated on the western coast, and ginger, capsicum, cumin, coriander, and turmeric, are a common field-produce. Among the vegetables, indigenous or exotic, are yams, potatoes, carrots, onions, spinach, radishes, gourds, and cucumbers. The fruits consist of plantains or bananas, mangoes, tamarinds, guavas, jacks, melons, grapes, pine-apples, peaches, strawberries, oranges, &c.; figs are not very general; apples are devoid of flavour; pears and plums do not succeed.

Numerous as are the towns and cities of India, none are remarkable for the amount of their population. That of Calcutta, independently of its suburbs, has been recently returned at 413,182. No census has been yet taken of the population of the city of Madras; but Bombay, with its suburbs, and including also the floating population in its harbour, contains only 566,199 inhabitants. Throughout the whole extent of the North-West Provinces no one city, including its suburbs and cantonment, can boast a population of 200,000; Delhi has only 152,424, Cawnpore 118,000, Benares 171,668, Bareilly 111,332, Agra 125,262, Furruckabad 132,513. The towns are usually composed of high brick houses, and, with some exceptions, the streets are narrow, and badly paved. Many of these are walled, and capable of some defence. Villages vary according to locality; some being defended by walls, others open, or surrounded only by a fence. Each village has its temple and bazar, its annual fair and festivals. In the North-Western Provinces, the houses of the peasantry are usually built of unburnt brick, and are tiled; in Bengal the cottage has its thatched roof and cane walls; and in the Deccan the huts are either of mud or stone, with terraced roofs. Throughout India the dwelling of the peasant is scantily furnished; the principal articles consisting of a few earthen pots and brass vessels, a hand-mill, pestle and mortar, and an iron plate, on which cakes are baked. A mat is the substitute for a chair, and tables are dispensed with.

The enormous population of India is composed chiefly of two leading races,—Hindoos and Mahomedans. The Hindoos, though resembling each other in their religion and in the observances and habits which it involves, are at the same time distinguished by many points of difference. Diversity in appearance, in dress, in the staple articles of food, in the mode of building, and in many other respects, is occasioned partly by local peculiarities, and partly by the nature of their institutions. The natives of Northern India are tall and fair; those of Bengal and the Deccan, small and dark: the former are manly and warlike, the latter timid and superstitious. There are also the aborigines of India, the Bheels and Coles. Some account of the former will be found under the article CANDEISH, and of the latter under ORISSA. Bhats and Charuns, and some other tribes, are noticed under the head of GUZERAT.

According to the latest returns which are available, the gross revenues of the British government in India amount to about 27,000,000*l.*, more than one-half of which is derived from the land. The other principal sources of revenue are customs, stamps, excise, salt, and opium. The revenue from salt is secured by a duty charged upon the prime cost of the home manufacture, and by a customs duty upon the foreign supply; the rate being the same in both cases, and amounting to about three farthings per pound. The annual revenue contributed by this article may be estimated at two millions sterling. Opium, from the poppy cultivated in the British provinces, is manufactured solely on account of government: that produced in native states is subject to a transit-duty on its passage through British territory to the coast. In both cases the tax may be regarded as being paid wholly by foreigners. The annual revenue from opium exceeds three millions sterling: from land, the chief source of revenue, the amount derived is more than fifteen millions sterling.

In so vast an extent of country, it might be presumed that wide diversity of language prevails; and such is the fact. In Upper India, the chief dialects are Hindee, Bengalee, Punjabee, Mahratta, Guzerattee, Cutchee, Boondela, Brig Bhakhur, Ooriya, and Assamese. These are all derivatives from the Sanscrit. The languages of Southern India, Teloogoo, Tamul, Canarese, Malayala, and Cingalese, are also closely dependent upon Sanscrit, the storehouse of the religious ceremonies of the Brahmin, and the language of the laws of Menu, which may be regarded as the basis of the actual civil law of the Hindoo, and the mainspring of his daily avocations. Oordoo, or Hindostanee, is the common language of Mahomedans throughout India, and is in fact Hindee, the primitive tongue of the Hindoos, modified by the chief languages of their Mahomedan conquerors, Arabic and Persian. Pushtoo and Sindhee are also derived from Arabic, the language which is the depositary of the Mahomedan faith, and of the laws and civil regulations of those who profess it. Persian was formerly the language of the law courts of the East-India Company; but, in 1837, its use was abolished, and the vernacular of each district substituted.

Little or nothing deserving the name of education existed in India till a comparatively recent period. Near the end of the last century, the British government established a Mahomedan college at Calcutta, and a Sanscrit college at Benares; but these foundations, however well intended, did little either to inform or to enlarge the minds of those admitted to them, and taught at least as much of error as of truth. Bishop Heber says:—"The Mussulman literature very nearly resembles what the literature of Europe was before the time of Copernicus, Galileo, and Bacon. The Mussulmans take their logic from Aristotle, filtered through many successive translations and commentaries; and their metaphysical system is professedly derived from Plato. Both Mahomedans and Hindoos have the same natural philosophy, which is also that of Aristotle in zoology and botany, and Ptolemy in astronomy, for which the Hindoos have forsaken their more ancient notions of the seven seas and the six earths." From this state of mental thraldom, the native mind could never be expected to emancipate itself without assistance. Early in the present century, more serious and more useful exertions in the cause of education began to be made. The literature and science of the western world were introduced to a great extent; and there can be no doubt that gradually, though perhaps slowly, these will supersede the trifling and deadening studies which for ages have added to the darkness of India, in place of tending to dispel it. The seminaries wherein the higher studies are pursued, may be pronounced to have been generally successful. In the attempt to improve and extend vernacular instruction, the British government, though equally zealous, has not been equally successful. The best results attained have been in the North-Western Provinces, where the new revenue settlement, under which the rights of every individual interested in the land became matter of record, has afforded precisely the stimulus required. The desire to ascertain and to preserve their recognised rights, induces in the people a desire for the acquisition of the arts of reading, writing, arithmetic, and mensuration. A few other of the simpler elements of knowledge are found to be easily added; and perhaps no great number of years will elapse before the mass of the people in the provinces above named will be well instructed in those branches of knowledge which are more immediately necessary; while those who have advanced somewhat farther, will not be few.

Among the great public works which have more recently been undertaken in India, may be mentioned the Ganges Canal, full particulars of which are given under the article GANGES RIVER. Measures are likewise in progress for establishing a comprehensive scheme of railway lines, to constitute the main arteries of communication throughout the country. Commencing at Calcutta, a railroad is now under construction, *viâ* Rajmahal and the valley of the Ganges, to Delhi; to be thence extended to the north-west frontier. A line, from Bombay in a north-easterly direction, will form a junction with the Calcutta line in the vicinity of Mirzapore; while the cotton districts of Berar will be connected with the western coast by a branch from the Bombay line. It is further proposed to connect by railway the presidency towns of Bombay and Madras, in the direction of Poona and Bellary, while the eastern and western coasts of the more southern part of the peninsula will be linked together by a line from Madras to Ponany. Electric telegraph lines have also been constructed, whereby the means of instantaneous communication have been secured, not only between the presidency towns, but between all the principal military and civil stations of the country, from the Punjaub to Pegu.

The early history of India is involved in extreme obscurity, and fable has in consequence usurped the place of fact. Our best information is derived from the Greeks; and until the conquests of Alexander, they were acquainted with India only through vague and meagre reports obtained from the Persians. Alexander passed the different rivers of the Punjaub, and advanced towards the Ganges, which, however, he was not destined to reach. The narratives of his followers are admitted to be, in some respects, discordant; and though, previous to the time of Ptolemy, the spirit of commercial adventure had added something to the stock of information, the knowledge of India possessed by the Greeks must be regarded as both scanty and inaccurate; but though unsatisfactory, it is sufficient to show that the people to whom it relates are almost unchanged by the lapse of centuries. Even the minute features of the national character are at this time the same that they were two thousand years ago.

Previously to the invasion of the Moguls, the Mahometan history of India possesses slender interest, and is, perhaps, little to be relied on. For a considerable time after that event, it offers but a picture of those commotions and crimes which characterize a state of society in which conflicting parties are struggling for the sovereignty. The most remarkable person of this period was Timur or Tamerlane. His conquests extended from the Irtisch and Volga to the Persian Gulf, and from the Ganges to the Archipelago. The death of Timur took place about ninety years before the arrival of the Portuguese in India by the south-east passage, the discovery of which was to effect a revolution in the destinies of the country, compared with which all previous changes were unimportant. The great mass of commerce between India and Europe was carried on by the route of the Red Sea, until the seventh century, when the conquest of Egypt by the Saracens transferred it by the Black Sea to Constantinople. When, however, the Mamelukes became masters of Egypt, they permitted the Venetians to resume the ancient route; and Alexandria was thenceforward the sole entrepôt of Indian trade. The spirit of Portuguese discovery received its impulse from the genius of Prince Henry, youngest son of John I. of Portugal. Under his countenance, naval adventure became popular; but the progress of discovery was greatly impeded by the imperfect state of navigation. The first acquisition was but of small importance, consisting only of the little island of Puerto Santo. It was sufficient, however, to encourage confidence, and stimulate to further exertions, and a subsequent expedition was rewarded by the discovery of the rich and beautiful island of Madeira. After a tedious succession of voyages continued for nearly half a century, Vasco di Gama, an active and enterprising Portuguese admiral, doubled the Cape of Good Hope, and, coasting along the eastern shore of the continent of Africa, sailed from thence across the Indian Ocean, and landed at Calicut, on the coast of Malabar. At the period of his arrival, the west coast of Hindostan was divided between two great sovereigns, the king of Cambay and the Zamorin, each of whom had under him numerous petty princes. The dominions of the Zamorin included the whole coast from Bombay to Cape Comorin; but the attempts of Di Gama to conclude a commercial treaty with this power were frustrated by the jealousy of the Mahometan merchants, and he returned to

Lisbon. His successor, Cabral, was not more fortunate; and in consequence he proceeded to Cochin and Cananore. The kings of these places were dependants upon the Zamorin: a dependency from which they were anxious to be emancipated. By them Cabral was very favourably received; and in an incredibly short time, the Portuguese acquired a paramount influence over the whole coast. Previously, however, to the arrival of Albuquerque in 1508, they were not possessed of a good port. After a violent struggle, they secured and fortified Goa, which from thenceforth became the capital of the Portuguese settlements, and the point from whence they spread their conquests and their commerce over the Eastern seas. Of all their mighty dominion, a miserable remnant is all that now exists, and that remnant depressed, impoverished, and almost in a state of estrangement from the mother country.

The annexation of Portugal to the crown of Spain was fatal to the colonial dominion of the former country, and the Dutch occupy the next conspicuous place in the commercial history of India. In the year 1594 they despatched four ships to India, under the command of Hautman, and a sanguinary war with the Portuguese soon followed. Success was long doubtful; but the Dutch ultimately triumphed. The Portuguese at first lost Malacca and Ceylon; they were subsequently driven from various settlements on the coast of Malabar; and not long afterwards the native princes permitted the Dutch to establish factories at Negapatam, Sadras, Pulicat, and Bimlipatam, on the east coast. From this period the power of Portugal in the East was rapidly approaching to extinction. The spirit of rivalry to the Portuguese was not confined to the Dutch. The splendid results which had followed the discovery of the south-east passage could scarcely fail to excite the emulation of a maritime and enterprising nation like the English. An association was formed and a fund subscribed for the purpose of obtaining a participation in the Indian trade, and a memorial presented to the government, setting forth the places with which the Spanish and Portuguese had established intercourse, and pointing out others to which the English might resort without affording ground of complaint to their predecessors. Some difficulties were interposed by the government on account of a treaty then pending with Spain, but permission was given to make preparations for a voyage, while the patent of incorporation was under consideration, and on the last day of the year 1600, the adventurers were by letters-patent from the queen constituted a body politic and corporate, by the title of "The Governor and Company of Merchants of London trading to the East-Indies." The government of the Company was vested in a committee of twenty-four and a chairman. It was empowered to trade to all places beyond the Cape of Good Hope and the Straits of Magellan for fifteen years, with the exception of places in possession of princes in amity with the queen, whose objection should be publicly declared. From James I. a renewal of the charter was obtained, by which all preceding privileges of the Company were confirmed, and they were constituted a body corporate for ever. The early voyages of the Company were confined to the islands of the Indian Ocean; but after the confirmation and extension of their charter by James, they proceeded to establish a commercial intercourse with the Asiatic continent. Their endeavours were of course opposed by the Portuguese; but the English Company finally succeeded in establishing factories on various parts of the coast. One of their earliest settlements was at Surat, and this factory, with that at Bantam, remained for a long period their principal stations. In the Dutch, the English Company found enemies more formidable than the Portuguese. The Dutch were bent on securing a monopoly of the spice-trade, and they enforced it in the most unscrupulous and vindictive spirit. After a long course of hostility, relieved by some weak and inefficient attempts at pacification, the spirit of the whole British people, with the exception of their sovereign, was roused to the highest pitch of indignation by the atrocious proceedings at Amboyna. The Dutch, having determined on obtaining the exclusive possession of the island, fabricated a plot, to afford them a pretext for effecting their purpose. The plot, it was pretended, was confessed by two soldiers in the Dutch service, one a Japanese, the other a Portuguese, who had been put to the torture. Upon this evidence the English were apprehended, imprisoned, loaded with irons, and their books and property seized. A mock trial followed, in the course of which the prisoners were subjected to the most varied and horrible tortures, for the purpose of extorting confession. It is unnecessary to say that this mode of examination was successful. Confession was of course followed by conviction—conviction by execution; and the commercial interests of the Dutch were cemented by the blood of the accused persons. The pretence of a conspiracy was too absurd to deceive even the most credulous. When the bureaux of the factors were opened and their papers rifled, no traces of such conspiracy were discovered. The number of English on the island did not exceed twenty, while the Dutch had a garrison of three hundred men in the fort, and several other garrisons in the island. The English were not only few in number, but they were unprovided with arms and ammunition. They had not a single ship, whereas the Dutch had eight lying off the town of Amboyna. A conspiracy against the Dutch authorities, under such circumstances, could have been formed only by men labouring under insanity; and those who professed to believe in its existence, had they been sincere, would have justly fallen under the same imputation. It would be idle to say a word in refutation of a mode of trial from which common sense and humanity alike recoil. The torture procured for the Dutch authorities that which they wanted—a legal excuse for the condemnation of their victims; but the courage of the sufferers revived as they approached a more righteous tribunal, and on the awful verge of eternity they solemnly protested their innocence. Those who will deliberately commit the graver crime of murder, will of course not hesitate at the comparatively light one of robbery. Massacre was not unnaturally followed by confiscation, and the Dutch retained English property to an immense amount. Its value has been stated at 400,000*l*. The truckling policy of James deterred him from seeking reparation of this great national wrong, and the disturbed reign of Charles allowed the Dutch a prolonged period of impunity; but the honour of the country was in some degree vindicated by Oliver Cromwell, who required and obtained payment of a large sum in satisfaction of the pecuniary injury inflicted.

At this time all the factories in the tract extending from Cape Comorin to the Persian and Arabian Gulfs were controlled by the presidency of Surat. On the coast of Coromandel the Company had established themselves in the first instance at Masulipatam. Subsequently they left that place for Armegum. Finally they settled at Madraspatam, where, by permission of the native government, they erected Fort St. George, now the seat of one of the British presidencies. The connections of the Company with Bengal were formed gradually. The first privilege which they obtained from the court of Delhi was that of free resort to the port of Pipley, a privilege afterwards much extended, through the intervention of a surgeon named Boughton, who acquired influence at the imperial court by the exercise of his professional skill. Factories were accordingly established at Hooghley, Cossimbazar, Balasore, Patna, and Malda. Of these Hooghley was chief; but the whole of them were subordinate to Fort St. George. The accession of Charles II. to the throne was followed by a renewal of the charter of the Company, by which their former privileges were confirmed, and authority conveyed to them to make peace and war with any people, not being Christians, and to seize unlicensed persons within their limits, and send them to England. From the same prince they obtained a grant of the island of Bombay, which he had received as part of the marriage portion of Catherine of Portugal. This island, now the seat of a presidency, was on its first acquisition subordinate to Surat.

Though the British interest in India was on the whole progressive, its advance was not uninterrupted. A civil war in Bantam was the means of excluding the English from Java, while the factories of Surat and Bombay were disturbed by unremitting war between the Mogul and the Mahrattas. The Mogul empire was established by Baber, a descendant of Timur, already mentioned, and sultan of the Mogul Tartars. Having lost the northern part of his own dominions by the hostilities of the Usbeck Tartars, he attempted the conquest of Hindostan with such success, that, putting an end to the dynasty of Lodi at Delhi, he established an empire, which was raised to the greatest splendour and authority under Aurungzebe towards the end of the seventeenth century. The Mahrattas were a native Hindoo race, little known till the middle of that century, when, under a chief named Sevagee, they became successful rivals to the Moguls. The conflict between these two great powers was necessarily injurious to the English. Both the belligerents had fleets of galliots on the coast; these repeatedly skirmished in the very harbour of Bombay, and the factory was, in self-defence, occasionally driven into hostilities with each party. Surat suffered even more severely, the Mahrattas ravaging up to its very gates. In Bengal, the English, thinking they had reason to be dissatisfied with the conduct of the native powers, resolved to seek redress by arms; but the attempt was unfortunate, and they were obliged to retire from Hooghley and take refuge at Chutanuttee, contiguous to Calcutta. After a succession of hostilities, in which the factories at Patna and Cossimbazar were taken and plundered, an accommodation was effected, and the English were allowed to return to Hooghley. Negotiations for regaining their ancient privileges were commenced, but were interrupted by fresh hostilities. The contest between the Moguls and the Mahrattas had taken a decided turn in favour of the former; and Aurungzebe threatened to drive the English from his dominions. But the revenue derived from the trade was too valuable to be relinquished, and a fresh negotiation for peace terminated favourably. Tegnapatam, on the coast of Coromandel, had been ceded to the English by the rajah of Gingee, while besieged in his capital by Aurungzebe; and on the defeat of the rajah the grant was confirmed by the Mogul chief: the English fortified the station, and it has since been known as Fort St. David. The peace was followed by an event which deserves notice, as having laid the foundation of the future capital of British India. This was the transfer of the agency to Chutanuttee, to which place the British had retired when expelled from Hooghley. It was subsequently fortified, and in 1698, a grant was obtained from Prince Azim, one of the grandsons of Aurungzebe, of the three connected villages of Chutanuttee, Govindpore, and Calcutta, with the justiciary power over the inhabitants. These new possessions were forthwith fortified, and received the name of Fort William; and about the same time Bengal was elevated to the rank of a presidency. For some years the position and relative constitution of the British presidencies had fluctuated considerably; but Bombay at last completely superseded Surat: and from the building of Fort William the established presidencies were those of Madras, Bombay, and Bengal.

From its commencement the Company had been occasionally exposed to the competition of rivals. In the reign of James I. Sir Edward Mitchelbourne, for whose employment the government had vainly interceded, obtained a license to engage in the eastern trade, which was an evident violation of the charter of the Company; he however made but one voyage, and it appears rather for plunder than for traffic or discovery. By Charles I. Sir William Courten was invested with similar privileges, and formed an association which assumed the name of the Assayda Merchants: with this body, after some years of competition, the Company coalesced. In the reign of William III. another company was formed under a charter from the king, which was termed the English Company, the old one being designated the London Company. The rivalry of these two bodies was soon found to be productive of mischievous consequences to both, and the expediency of a union became apparent. This was ultimately effected, and in 1708 the companies were consolidated by Act of Parliament, under the name of the United Company of Merchants of England trading to the East Indies. From this period the British interests in India may be considered as steadily advancing; the amount of trade and shipping increased, and the intercourse and influence of the Company were extended.

A period of quiet prosperity affords slender materials for history; and till the breaking out of the war between England and France, in 1745, nothing occurs worthy of notice. The first appearance of the French in India was nearly 150 years before this period, when a company which had been formed in Brittany sent out two ships; but the voyage was attended with so little success, that on their return the company was dissolved. At later periods the French made some further attempts to trade and establish factories: their chief rendezvous was at Surat; but the Dutch and English uniting against them, they were compelled to abandon it. They next attempted to seize on Trincomalee, but in this also they were unsuccessful. They were more fortunate in an attempt upon St. Thomé, a seaport contiguous to Madras, which they carried by assault. They retained it, however, only two years; but from the wreck of this establishment was formed their celebrated settlement of Pondicherry, where a small district was ceded to them by the native prince. In 1746 Madras was besieged by a French armament, and compelled to capitulate. Admiral Boscawen made an attempt to retaliate upon Pondicherry, which was unsuccessful; but the peace of Aix-la-Chapelle restored Madras to the English.

From this time the history of India rises in interest and importance. We have no longer to detail the advantages of commercial speculation, but to record the transfer of a magnificent empire into the hands of strangers, who, a short time previously, were supplicants for the privilege of defending themselves. The territory of the Carnatic was one of the subordinate principalities immediately governed by nabobs, but subject to the soubahdar of the Deccan, who was himself a feudatory under the Mogul emperor. Nizam ul Mulk, soubahdar of the Deccan, dying in 1748, the succession to the vacant province was disputed between his son Nazir and his grandson Murzafa; at the same time the nabob of the Carnatic was opposed by a rival claimant. The pretender to the province and the pretender to the nabobship made common cause, and succeeded in attaching to their interests M. Dupleix, governor of Pondicherry, a man of great talent, and of still greater ambition and capacity for intrigue. The combined forces of these allies were successful in a battle, in which the lawful nabob of the Carnatic was killed, and his eldest son taken prisoner. His second son, Mahomet Ali Khan, having escaped, implored and obtained the aid of the English. Such was the origin of the Carnatic war between the English and the French; and it is remarkable that these two nations should have been engaged in hostile operations against each other in India at a time when no war existed between them in Europe. As soon as intelligence of these extraordinary events reached the courts of the two countries, orders were sent out to put an end to the contest, and a treaty was entered into, by which the two nations were to possess equal dominion, military force, and advantages of commerce on the east coast of the peninsula. The breaking out of the seven years' war in 1756 prevented the execution of this treaty, and the French and English became principals instead of auxiliaries. The French at first met with some partial success; but the tide of fortune turned in favour of their rivals, who acquired, partly by conquest and partly by negotiation, a considerable increase of dominion as well as of influence. The English were at the same time obliged to have recourse to arms to defend their interests in another part of India. The nabob of Bengal, Surajah Dowlah, attacked, and after a brief resistance, took Calcutta. The event has attained an infamous celebrity by the cruelty which accompanied it. The European inhabitants, 146 in number, were, in the most sultry season of the year, confined for twelve hours within the too-memorable Black Hole, a cube of eighteen feet, having no outlets except two small windows, strongly barred. In this miserable den, all, except twenty-three, perished. The city was in a short time retaken by Colonel Clive, afterwards Lord Clive, who had already exhibited proofs of that talent which raised him to eminence. Peace with the nabob followed; but it was subsequently proved that he was in correspondence with the French. The English resolved to punish his faithlessness, by supporting the pretensions of a rival. This led to the famous battle of Plassy, by which Meer Jaffier obtained the nabobship, and his English allies considerable treasure and accession of territory.

Meer Jaffier, however, became unwilling to fulfil the conditions of his elevation, and he was in consequence deposed. His successor, who was raised by the same influence, was his son-in-law Meer Cossim, and it was stipulated that he should grant to the English, for the pay of their army, the districts of Burdwan, Midnapore, and Chittagong. But he, too, became hostile to the power which had raised him, and it was deemed expedient to restore Meer Jaffier. A war ensued with Cossim, in which the English were completely victorious, and Cossim escaped into the dominions of the vizier of Oude. The same year which witnessed the expulsion of Cossim was signalized by the conclusion of a peace between France and England. The former country was reinstated in the factories which she possessed in 1749; but the latter, in addition to her old settlements, retained the circar of Masulipatam and its dependent districts, acquired from the French, as well as the castle of Surat, the jaghire round Madras, the Calcutta zemindary, and the districts of Burdwan, Midnapore, and Chittagong. The vizier of Oude, Suja Dowlah, with whom Cossim had taken refuge, encouraged by some discontents which existed in the British army, decided on hostilities, and war commenced. The discipline of the British army having been restored, Suja Dowlah was twice defeated; first by Major Carnac, secondly by Major Munro, and was compelled to throw himself upon the generosity of the victors. Such was also the fortune of a more elevated individual, the emperor of Delhi, who had been recently engaged in hostilities with the British, but was now a fugitive and a temporary sojourner with his nominal vassal, the ruler of Oude. Terms were granted to both, and in regard to the vizier, they were certainly not hard ones. The entire territories which the vizier had previously governed were restored to him, with the exception of certain districts reserved to the Mogul emperor, who, in return for the consideration shown for him, conferred upon the British the dewanny of the three provinces of Bengal, Bahar, and Orissa. The word dewanny is derived from dewan, which was the appellation of the officers appointed by the Mogul government for the collection and disbursement of the provincial revenues, and for the administration of civil justice. These officers held their stations during pleasure, and were only stewards for the emperor; but the grant to the Company was in perpetuity, and assigned to them the whole provincial revenue, subject only to the payment of certain specific sums. In addition to this, the emperor granted to the English the maritime districts known by the name of the Northern Circars, though over them his authority was but nominal. They fell within the government of the soubahdar of the Deccan; but having been the seat of hostilities between the English and French, the soubahdar's authority was not well established. By negotiation with him, the Company obtained possession of this disputed territory, with the exception of a small part which became theirs in reversion. This cession, however, involved the British in new wars. It was a condition of their treaty with the soubahdar, that they should assist him with troops when he might stand in need of them; and in 1760 he applied for this assistance against Hyder Ali Khan, the sovereign of Mysore. The required aid was granted; but Hyder Ali, not less skilful as a diplomatist than as a warrior, succeeded in detaching the soubahdar from his English connection, and prevailed upon him not only to conclude a separate peace, but even to enter into an alliance offensive and defensive, for the purpose of extinguishing the British power in the Deccan. Their combined operations were frustrated, and the soubahdar deserting Hyder as he had done his former ally, made peace with the British, and retired to his own dominions. Hyder Ali then prosecuted the war alone, and, entering the Carnatic, committed dreadful ravages. Having diverted the British forces to a distance from Madras, he suddenly appeared before that place with 6,000 cavalry, having accomplished a march of 120 miles in three days. His further progress was arrested by negotiation, and a treaty was concluded on the principle of a mutual restitution of conquests.

Our arms were next directed against the Mahrattas, who had invaded the Rohilla country. The British, acting as the allies of Suja Dowlah, drove them beyond the Ganges. For this service the Rohilla chiefs had agreed to pay Suja Dowlah forty lacs of rupees; but failing in the performance of their contract, the Rohilla country was added to the British conquests. A considerable tract of land was also conquered from the Jauts and other adventurers, by which the boundaries of the province of Oude were considerably advanced. On the death of Suja Dowlah, which took place soon afterwards, the province of Benares was ceded to the Company. A subsequent war with the Mahrattas was distinguished by some movements of uncommon brilliancy. A body of native troops, commanded by British officers, but whose number did not exceed 7,000, traversed with success almost the entire Mahratta territory. Several fine provinces were subdued, and important fortresses taken; but war breaking out with Hyder Ali, peace was made with the Mahrattas, and all the acquisitions given up, except Salsette, and the small islands situate within the gulf formed by Bombay, Salsette, and the continent. The war with Hyder Ali raged until his death, and was continued by his son Tippoo Sultan; but the conclusion of a peace between the English and French depriving Tippoo of the hope of assistance from the latter power, hostilities were terminated by a treaty, which left the affairs of both the belligerents nearly in the same condition as before the commencement of the war. But Tippoo Sultan's restless character would not suffer him to remain at peace, and his invasion of the possessions of the rajah of Travancore, who was under the protection of the English, involved that power in a fresh quarrel with this turbulent prince. The result to him was humiliating. After two years' war, he was compelled by Lord Cornwallis to purchase peace by the payment of a large sum of money, the sacrifice of half his dominions, and the delivery of two of his sons as hostages for the due performance of the conditions of the treaty.

The memorable campaign which terminated in the discomfiture of Tippoo Sultan, was succeeded by seven years of tranquillity. The enemies of British interests were not, however, inactive, but were employed in sowing the seeds of future wars. Among the most insidious and dangerous of these enemies may be reckoned the French, ever on the watch for an opportunity of diminishing the power of the English, and now intoxicated with the doctrines of liberty and equality which they had undertaken to disseminate throughout the earth. Even regions which for ages had patiently submitted to despotic power, were not exempt from the intrusion of these opinions. The French ventured to establish a society in Mysore for the diffusion of the knowledge of the rights of man, and met with very different success to that which awaited the unfortunate Jean Bon St. André in the kindred region of Africa. They received from the sovereign patronage and protection. He even condescended to become an honorary member of the society, and was enrolled among its associates by the incongruous name of *Citizen Tippoo.* The result of these machinations was another war, which terminated with the storming of Seringapatam, the death of Tippoo, and the partition of his dominions. In the division, the English retained the districts of Canara, including all the seacoast of the Mysore, the provinces immediately adjoining the possessions of the British on the coast of Malabar, and the Carnatic; the forts and posts of the passes into the Mysore, and the island and fortress of Seringapatam. Certain districts were given to the Nizam, which, however, were afterwards surrendered by that power to the English, together with other territories which had been acquired by a former treaty. A third portion was reserved to be given, upon certain conditions, to the Peishwa, the actual, though not the nominal, head of the Mahrattas; but he having refused to accede, the reserved territory was divided between the British and the Nizam. The Peishwa, however, was forced ultimately to claim the assistance of the British to deliver him from the state of anarchy by which he was surrounded. A treaty was in consequence concluded, by which the British consented to furnish the Peishwa with a certain number of troops, and he to assign a portion of territory for their payment.

The war which ensued for the protection of the Peishwa was distinguished by the brilliant services of Lord Lake, and of another commander, who in the East commenced that illustrious career which he terminated by the liberation of Europe. The splendour of his Indian campaigns is indeed obscured by the surpassing glory that encircles the head of the conqueror of Napoleon; but no one who adverts to this period of the history of India, however briefly, can be excused if he pass by the name of Wellington without bestowing the tribute of admiration. Space will not permit a detailed recital of the achievements of the British army in these wars: it must suffice to record the results. In a comparatively short space of time, a formidable confederation of French and Mahratta power was broken, and an immense accession of territory gained.

From this period the history of India presents little of importance until 1814, when the British became involved in a war with the Nepaulese, a people of aggressive habits, occupying a mountain country. The nature of the country, the imperfect knowledge which the British possessed of it, the courage of the enemy, and the fortifications by which they were defended, were obstacles to the success of the British, and continued for some time to impede it. Military skill ultimately overcame these difficulties, and the Nepaulese, being subdued, agreed to a treaty, by which the British became possessed of certain districts deemed necessary to the security of their frontier; but endeavouring, in the true spirit of Indian policy, to evade ratification of the treaty, a renewal of hostilities became unavoidable. A war of very brief duration was sufficient to accomplish its object. The constant wars and commotions prevailing among the native powers of India produced in great numbers men trained in habits of rapine and disorder. Gathering strength by degrees, these lawless ruffians became at length associated in bands under recognised leaders, and on the arrival of the marquis of Hastings in India, they mustered a force of not less than 40,000 cavalry. They were termed Pindarries, and in their predatory excursions committed the most shocking excesses. The irruptions of these bandits into the Company's territories compelled the government to take up arms, and they were preparing to take vigorous measures for their expulsion, when the Peishwa, an ally and dependant of the British, revolted against their authority. The rajah of Nagpore, who stood in the same relation to the British, pursued a similar course. Both these powers were subdued, while the war with the Pindarries was prosecuted with vigour. In the mean time the British government became involved in disputes with Scindia and Holkar, two independent chiefs. With the former they made terms; but the treaty forced upon him was executed with extreme reluctance. Holkar resolved to have recourse to war. It ended in his entire defeat; his power was completely broken, and he was compelled to sue for peace. The army being now at liberty to act against the Pindarries, the dispersion of that lawless body was at length effected.

Not many years elapsed between this and the war with the Burmese. That war, like most of those in which the English have been engaged, was occasioned by the aggression of the power with whom it was waged. During the Pindarrie war, the Burmese were in communication with several of the belligerent native chiefs, and were even prepared for an invasion of the frontier of Bengal. This was averted by a stratagem. The marquis of Hastings had received a rescript from the Burmese monarch, requiring the surrender of all provinces east of the Baugrutty. The projected hostility was evidently a measure concerted with the Mahrattas. Lord Hastings sent back the envoy with an intimation that the answer should be conveyed through another channel. It declared that the Governor-General was too well acquainted with his majesty's wisdom to be the dupe of the gross forgery attempted to be palmed upon him, and he therefore transmitted to the king the document fabricated in his august name, and trusted that he would submit to condign punishment the persons who had endeavoured to sow dissension between two powers, whose reciprocal interest it was to cultivate relations of amity. By this proceeding the necessity of noticing the insolent step of the Burmese monarch was evaded, and that sovereign, on hearing of the defeat of his Mahratta allies, was content to remain at peace. But though the expression of hostile feeling was for a while suppressed, the feeling itself was not removed, and the Burmese monarch now gained courage to attack, where before he had been satisfied to threaten. War commenced, and the successes of the British led to the conclusion of an armistice, which was employed in negotiations. These negotiations being unsuccessful, hostilities were resumed. The march of the English, as in Nepaul, was in some degree retarded by the nature of the country; but this obstacle being overcome, the Burmese were completely defeated, and the British advanced towards the capital, when negotiations were recommenced, and a treaty concluded, by which the Burmese secured their existence as a nation, and the English obtained an extension of territory, valuable as affording a secure frontier. During the progress of the Burmese war, the British obtained from the king of the Netherlands, Malacca, Singapore, and the Dutch possessions which remained to that nation on the continent of India, in exchange for the settlement of Bencoolen and other possessions in Sumatra; an event deserving notice, and rendered important from the position subsequently attained by Singapore, as a vast *entrepôt* of commerce. Some years later, the misconduct of the rajah of Coorg, a small principality in Southern India, rendered necessary his deposal from sovereignty, and his removal from the country which he had misgoverned; and there being no one entitled to succeed him, Coorg was unavoidably annexed to the British dominions, of which it has since formed part.

The Affghan war, commenced in 1839, with a view to raising a barrier against the aggressive power of Russia, brought to the British no accession of territory, of power, or, taken on the whole, of glory. It was ostensibly undertaken to restore to the throne a former Affghan ruler, Shah Shoojah, supposed at least to be actuated by friendly feelings towards the British, though doubts on that point may well be entertained. The advance of the forces destined for the conquest of Affghanistan was attended by much difficulty and dreadful suffering; but at length a part of the invading army reached the chief city, Cabool. Here it was thought the object of the expedition was gained; but the commencement of a new and frightful series of calamities was at hand. Insurrection broke out, the British envoy was treacherously murdered, a large part of the British force was destroyed, and the remainder compelled to retire under the most disastrous circumstances, incessant annoyance and fearful slaughter marking its progress. Many deeds of heroism, never surpassed, tended indeed to add fresh lustre to the British name; and, among others, the noble defence of Jelalabad by Sir Robert Sale can never be forgotten so long as Affghanistan is remembered. But the war and its consequences contribute to furnish an awful page in the history of British enterprise in India. Ultimately the country was avenged, and its reputation vindicated, through the vigorous counsels and vigorous acts of Generals Pollock and Nott. The former arrived first at Cabool, and replanted the British colours there: the latter arrived shortly afterwards. The British could now withdraw without discredit, from a country where, for the first time, the *prestige* of their national character seemed endangered. That at least was vindicated and upheld; though, looking at the expenditure of blood and treasure, at the mass of suffering, and the imminent danger of irreparable disgrace which must have followed a premature retirement, every Englishman must wish that the war had never been undertaken.

The chapter in the history of British India which records the annexation of Sinde, is little more consolatory to a sound-hearted Englishman than that on the war in Affghanistan. The ameers or rulers of Sinde were ever opposed to any close connection with foreigners. Various attempts had at different times been made to establish such connection, but they had been met reluctantly and unfavourably. Two or three treaties had been entered into; but they were brief, dry, and to neither party satisfactory. The ameers of Sinde hated the alliance, which the British were anxious to establish, at first for commercial, latterly for political purposes. When the British commenced the march to Affghanistan, a treaty was forced upon the rulers of Sinde, which was more distasteful than any former one. Under this treaty, a British military force was to be permanently stationed in Sinde; and, after some considerable time, Sir Charles Napier, whose career in Sinde has given rise to such a mass of controversy, was appointed to the chief command there. He commenced his course certainly with vigour, but as certainly with little consideration of the existing rulers. Treaties were proposed, which, though rejection must have been looked for, were accepted, whether with sincerity or not;—probably there was little of that quality on either side. But, notwithstanding the acceptance of the treaties, Sir Charles Napier continued to advance. During his progress the British Residency was attacked. It was gallantly defended, but weakness of numbers and deficiency of ammunition soon rendered retreat necessary. This was effected in good order, but at the sacrifice of the greater part of the property within the Residence. The battle of Meeanee followed, in which the British gained a brilliant victory. Another battle, fought near Hydrabad, the capital, may be said to have terminated the contest; and Sinde, in 1843, became a British possession. The conclusion of the contest in Sinde found the British government involved in difficulties in Gwalior, or the dominions of Scindia. The death of the representative of that house without heirs rendered an arrangement for the appointment of a successor necessary. A child, said to be the nearest relative of the deceased prince, was selected, and the British government approved. But every Indian court is a focus of intrigue, and that of Gwalior formed no exception. A rabble army of 30,000 men was a source of weakness, not of strength; and through the influence of a profligate and reckless court, combined with that of a disorganized army, the state appeared rapidly tending to dissolution. Internal war had in fact commenced, when the British government, somewhat tardily, though at the last rather hastily, put in motion a military force towards the disturbed country. It soon came into hostile collision with the enemy; and two victories in one day, gained by two separate portions of the British force, decided the questions at issue. A new treaty followed, dated January, 1844, in which a variety of arrangements for the safety of Scindia's territories and the security of those adjacent were embodied.

By this time, a new cause for apprehension had arisen in the north-western part of India. The death of Runjeet Singh, the "Lion of the Punjab," had been followed by a series of excesses, terminating in a state of things in which the army was triumphant over the government, and was an object of its dread rather than of its dependence. At length a portion of it crossed the Sutlej, and invaded the British territories. This of course was repelled; and, first at Moodkee, subsequently at Ferozeshah, in December, 1845, the Sikhs were defeated. At Aliwal, and at Sobraon, fresh triumphs attended the British forces, who finally crossed the river, and dictated the terms of submission at Lahore, the Sikh capital. Here a treaty was concluded, under which the British obtained a cession of all the territory between the Beas and the Sutlej; the native government of Lahore being retained, with some requisite modifications. But this arrangement proved of short duration. The atrocious conduct of a chief, holding the fortress of Mooltan, where two British officers were murdered, the generally distracted state of the country, the open violation by the government and people of the treaty so recently concluded, and the actual levying of war against their peaceful neighbour, demanded further intervention of a hostile character. One step only remained to be taken, and the success which again attended the British enabled the Governor-General to take it. The Punjab was annexed, and was thenceforward a part of the vast empire of India. In this instance, as in so many others which occur in the history of that empire, the cause of Great Britain was the cause of general humanity.

Another Burmese war followed; rendered necessary by the wrongs, public and private, inflicted by the Burmese government. It was neither long in duration nor brilliant in events; and concluded with the annexation, in December, 1852, of the extensive province of Pegu, in satisfaction to some degree of the injuries sustained, and in aid of the means of defending British territory and property from further aggression.

After all the declamation that has been expended upon the means by which the British dominions have been acquired, probably no conquests were ever made more righteously. This is certainly true with regard to the greater portion of them. Strangers were forced to become conquerors in self-defence. During a considerable part of the last century, the question was, whether India should be subjugated by France or by England. To this question but one answer could be given. The perfidy of the native princes was another source of war, and of British aggrandisement. But the crimes of these rulers have in this respect been beneficial to their subjects, by transferring them to the care of a better and a milder government. No friend to mankind can wish that the natives had remained under their old masters, and none but the most prejudiced can believe that their lot would have been improved by transferring them to the French.

INDMEYEE.—See Edmy.

INDOOR.—A town in Hyderabad, or the dominions of the Nizam, 94 miles N. by W. from Hyderabad, and 162 miles E.N.E. from Sholapoor. Lat. 18° 40′, long. 78° 10′.

INDOORTY.—A town in Hyderabad, or the dominions of the Nizam, situate on the left bank of one of the branches of the Kistna river, and 38 miles S.E. from Hyderabad. Lat. 17°, long. 78° 59′.

INDORE TERRITORY.—From the capital, the name of Indore is extended to the aggregate of the possessions of the Holcar family. These consist of several isolated tracts, some of them lying very remote from others. The area of the whole is estimated at 8,318 square miles. Of these districts, those situate to the north are drained by the river Chumbul and its feeders; those to the south, by the Nerbudda, flowing east and west. Like the rest of Malwa, these districts are fertile, producing in abundance and excellence, wheat and other grain, pulse, sugar-cane, cotton, and especially opium, the poppy producing it being so generally cultivated, that, when in bloom, it gives the country the appearance of a vast garden. Tobacco is also much cultivated, and is of excellent quality. The great Vindhya range traverses the southern or Indore division of Holcar's dominions, in a direction nearly from east to west, a small portion of the territory lying to the north of the mountains, but by much the larger part to the south of them. The part lying south is a portion of the valley of the Nerbudda, bounded on the south by the Satpura Mountains. The summits of the Vindhya vary in height, probably from 1,500 to 2,000 feet; and at one place the crest of the Jam Ghat, lat. 22° 23′, long. 75° 49′, rises to the elevation of 2,328 feet above the sea. The elevation of the Satpura range is somewhat greater, one summit being 2,500 feet above the level of the sea.

Besides the ruling tribe of Mahrattas, the population comprises many other classes of Hindoos, a few Mahomedans, and a considerable number of Gonds and Bheels. It is peculiarly the country of the Bheels, who are considered to have been the earliest occupiers of the soil. This race is one of the most wild and savage found in India, its people living for the most part on wild vegetables and game, the latter the produce of their bows and arrows, or on the plunder of their more civilized neighbours. They are, however, not entirely irreclaimable, but have in some instances been converted into useful and trustworthy soldiers. The population of the whole of Holcar's dominions is estimated at 815,164, which yields an average of 98 to the square mile. The revenue in 1848 was estimated at 22,17,210 rupees, or 221,721*l*. The armed force, including the contingent of cavalry, amounted to about 7,000 men. The principal towns,—Indore, Mundlaisir, Rampoora, Bhanpoora, and others, are described under their respective names in the alphabetical arrangement.

The founder of the family of Holcar was Mulhar Rao, a ryot or cultivator of Hul, a village of the Deccan. His birth is said to have taken place in the year 1693. First a shepherd, and subsequently a soldier, he obtained distinction and promotion in hostilities against Nizam ool Mulk, and being received into the service of the Peishwa, was appointed to the command of 500 horse. In 1728, he received a jaghire of twelve districts north of the Nerbudda; in 1731, he obtained seventy more, being at the same time appointed to the general management of the Mahratta interests in Malwa; and in 1733, Indore was granted to him, with the district appertaining to it. From that time until his death in 1767, he was the most distinguished of the military commanders of the Mahratta race. In addition to the possessions above referred to, he was appointed deshmook or feudatory of Chandore, in Khandeish; while his revenues were further increased by the levy of fixed tributes on several states. He was among the Mahratta leaders at the battle of Paniput in 1761, but fled when it became apparent that the defeat of the Mahrattas was inevitable. Mulhar Rao Holcar had only one son, Koondi Rao, who was killed during his father's lifetime. On the death of Mulhar Rao, the succession devolved on Malli Rao, the son of Koondi Rao. Malli Rao died insane after a few months, and the sovereignty of Indore fell into the hands of his mother Alia Baee, who committed the charge of the military force of her dominions to Tookajee Holcar, a member of the same tribe, but not otherwise related to the family with which the Baee was allied. He appears to have acted strictly in conformity with her wishes during his long command, which was terminated by his death in 1797. This harmony of action and the abilities of both parties brought Indore to a state of high prosperity. Succession to the power of Tookajee was disputed by his two legitimate sons Kasi Rao and Mulhar Rao, the latter of whom was cut off by assassination, through the treachery of his brother, a person weak in intellect, deformed in body, and, as his actions showed, not less deformed in his moral constitution. Tookajee left also two illegitimate sons, Etojee and Jeswunt Rao. Etojee attempted to maintain himself by a course of freebooting, but being seized, was put to a very cruel death by the Peishwa, who looked on unmoved, whilst the wretched man, tied to the leg of an elephant, implored mercy, or shrieked in agony, as he was dragged along until torn in pieces. Jeswunt Rao, who, on the murder of his brother Mulhar Rao, had fled to Nagpore, and besought the rajah's protection, received it in the shape of imprisonment; from which, however, he contrived to escape. He thereupon, like his brother Etojee, commenced a predatory career, and soon assembled an army of about 30,000 men, with above 100 pieces of artillery. But this large force received a signal defeat from the army of Scindia, when Jeswunt Rao Holcar lost nearly all his artillery, and the disaster was followed by the plunder of the capital. He rapidly recovered from the effects of this mischance, and employed European officers to introduce their discipline into his army. In October, 1802, at the battle of Poona, which he gained over the combined forces of Dowlut Rao Scindia and the Peishwa, he had fourteen regular battalions, 5,000 irregular infantry, and 25,000 horse. The distinguished state of Indore at the commencement of the present century, when the British government was engaged in arduous conflict with various enemies, gave opportunity for Jeswunt Rao Holcar to indulge in devastation and plunder to an enormous extent. General Lake despatched against him five battalions of sepoys and 3,000 irregular horse, under Colonel Monson, an officer of extraordinary bravery, but unfortunately destitute of a corresponding degree of judgment. The expedition accordingly terminated disastrously, and the unhappy retreat of this force is characterized as one of the most lamentable events in the history of the British career in India. The apparent success of Holcar caused great numbers of freebooters to join him, and at the end of August, 1804, he advanced at the head of 60,000 horse to the Jumna, and took the city of Muttra. Marching thence, he commenced the siege of Delhi on the 8th of October, but retreated baffled on the 14th; the British under General Lake marching to its relief. Holcar then, at the head of his cavalry, suddenly crossed the Jumna near Paniput, and laid waste the Doab with fire and sword, closely pursued by General Lake, who, on the morning of November 17th, surprised him in his bivouac at Furruckabad, where he was totally routed, leaving about 3,000 dead; and so rapidly did his predatory followers fall off, that it is stated, that of the 60,000 cavalry which he led across the Jumna, less than half that number recrossed it. His infantry, which had been intrenched under the walls of Deeg, had previously been attacked and defeated by a British force under General Frazer, on whose fall, before the fate of the day was determined, the command devolved upon Colonel Monson, who had then the satisfaction of frustrating in some degree the disastrous consequences of his retreat. According to an authority whose means of information were great, Holcar entered Hindostan (or Northern India) with "92,000 men, of whom 66,000 were cavalry, 7,000 artillery, and 19,000 infantry, and 190 pieces of ordnance; and he left it with his whole force diminished to 35,000 horse, 7,000 infantry and artillery, and thirty-five guns." In October, 1805, Holcar, encouraged no doubt by the wavering and imbecile policy of Lord Cornwallis, and subsequently of Sir George Barlow, successively Governors-General, marched from Ajmeer, where he had remained during the rains, and with 12,000 cavalry, 2,500 infantry, and thirty guns, advanced to the Punjab, pursued by the British under Lord Lake, who came up with him at the city of Amritsir, where, in December, 1805, a treaty was concluded, by which Holcar relinquished any claim on Tonk, Rampoora, Bhoondee, and all places north of the Bhoondee Hills, and in possession of the British government; but was confirmed in nearly all his other possessions. In the following year he murdered Kasi Rao, the legitimate son of Tookajee Holcar, and Kundi Rao, the infant son of Mulhar Rao, another legitimate son of Tookajee, assassinated at an earlier period, while contending with his brother Kasi Rao. These atrocities were closely followed by the insanity of the perpetrator, who ultimately sank into a state of utter fatuity, in which he died in the year 1811. A stormy regency succeeded, ostensibly administered by Toolsee Bye, mistress of the deceased Jeswunt Rao, but actually, at many periods of its continuance, by her various paramours. Before the death of Jeswunt Rao Holcar, she had adopted an infant, Mulhar Rao Holcar, an illegitimate son of her protector, and by general consent he was recognised as his father's successor. In 1817, the intrigues and disturbances fomented by the different factions which disturbed the state, came to a crisis. The army seized Toolsee Bye and the young Mulhar Rao, and having murdered the former, commenced hostilities under the ostensible command of the latter; a result long before indicated. These were, however, brought to a speedy termination by the decisive victory which, on December 21st, 1817, was gained at Mahidpore, by the British army over that of Holcar. On January 18th, 1818, a treaty was concluded at Mundesore, with the British government, that power engaging to extend the same protection to the territory of Holcar as to its own, and to maintain a field-force for the preservation of internal tranquillity, and for defence against foreign aggression; disclaiming all concern with Holcar's relatives or subjects, and entering into a stipulation not to permit the Peishwa or any of his heirs or descendants to claim or exercise any sovereign rights over the dominions of Holcar, and to restore to the latter chief the possessions lately conquered from him. On the other part, Holcar engaged to renounce all claims to the possessions guaranteed to Ameer Khan by the British government; to cede certain pergunnahs to Zalim Singh, of Kota; to confirm to Ghuffoor Khan his jaiaad or grant of various districts in Malwa; to renounce all claim to any places north of the Bhoondee Hills; to cede to the British government all claims of revenues and tributes from the Rajpoot states, and all the Mahratta chieftain's territories within and south of the Satpura range, including the fort of Sindwa, as well as all his possessions in the province of Khandeish, and others intermixed with the territories of the Nizam and the Peishwa; to abstain from diplomatic intercourse with other states, except with the knowledge and consent of the British resident; to entertain in his service no Europeans or Americans without similar permission; to permit an accredited minister from the British government to reside with the maharajah; to discharge his superfluous troops, and not to keep a larger force than 3,000 horse, for whose regular payment a suitable arrangement was to be made. Of the effect of this arrangement, Malcolm observes, "This was in fact a new condition to the Holcar state; for twenty years had elapsed since it had enjoyed any regular resources or government, and its same during the greater part of that period had only served as a pretext to plunderers for committing every species of excess and crime."

Mulhar Rao Holcar died in 1833. His mother, known by the title of the Mahjee, thereupon assumed the reins of government; and an adoption took place by Mulhar Rao's widow, of an infant son of Bapoo Holcar, a distant relative of the family. The pregnancy of one of the females in the deceased maharajah's zenana (who subsequently gave birth to a son) having been concealed, the succession of the adopted son, under the title of Martund Rao Holcar, was recognised by the British government, and the birth of the posthumous child was not allowed to disturb the arrangement. Subsequently, public feeling appeared to be decidedly in favour of the superior claims of Hurree Rao Holcar, a former competitor for the guddee, and the nearest male relative of the late maharajah, by whom he had been kept for many years a prisoner in the fort of Maheyseer. An insurrection broke out in favour of the prisoner; the troops sent against him espoused his cause, and the existing government found it necessary to submit. Neutrality was observed by the British government during the contest, and amicable relations were maintained with the new ruler. Hurree Rao Holcar appears to have manifested the full amount of incapacity for government which is ordinarily exhibited by Indian princes. Under his sway the state of the country was so wretched, that it was rapidly deserted by the inhabitants, especially the more respectable and wealthy portion of them. On the death of this imbecile specimen of oriental chieftainship, he was succeeded by a youth named Kumdee Rao Holcar, whom he had adopted with the sanction of the British government. The career of this adopted successor was, however, terminated by an early death, when it appears no person possessed any hereditary claim to the guddee, neither had any one valid title to adopt, and the continuance of the Holcar possessions under a separate form of government became a question for consideration. It being determined that it should be so continued, the choice of a ruler was to be made; and, after weighing the competing claims of various candidates, the guddee was bestowed upon a youth named Mulkerjee, whose elevation it was avowed was not in virtue of either adoption or hereditary claim, but of the express nomination of the British government. The opportunity was taken to limit the succession to lineal heirs, to the exclusion of adoption. The new chief being a minor, the government was carried on, during his legal infancy, under the superintendence of the resident, by a council of regency, composed of the Maee Sahiba (widow of Jeswunt Rao Holcar) and three principal officers of state. Under this arrangement the administration and state of the country greatly improved. The young chief, educated under the auspices of the British government, displayed at an early age great capacity for public business, and drew forth, by his exemplary conduct, the approbation of the Governor-General. In February, 1852, upon the attainment of his majority, the young rajah assumed the reins of government.

INDORE, the capital of the possessions of Holcar's family, a town situate in a plain of no great extent on the left bank of the small river Kutki. It is an ill-built place, the houses, which are disposed in irregular winding streets, being constructed with sundried bricks, and covered with clumsy tiles laid on bamboos. It contains a few mosques, of no architectural pretensions, and numerous Brahminical temples, built of basalt, and whitewashed with lime. Jacquemont, who visited the place in 1832, describes the palace of Holcar as having no claims to notice, but mentions that he was building another, which would be much superior. The house of the British resident is situate east of the town; and as this, as well as the dwellings of his assistants, are well built, surrounded with groves and gardens, and judiciously disposed in a fine park-like expanse, the whole forms a pleasing scene. A strong escort of cavalry and infantry attend the resident, but the principal British force for this part of India is cantoned at Mhow, thirteen miles more to the south-east. The resident at Indore, in addition to his duties connected with that state, is the immediate representative of the British government in regard to various petty states under its protection, but in other respects differing greatly in their circumstances. The Bhopal subordinate agency is also subject to his control.

Jemnah, or old Indore, is situate on the right side of the stream. The present Indore, on the left bank, was built by order of Alia Baee, widow of Mulhar Rao Holcar, immediately after his death, in 1767. The outline of the city is nearly square, each side being about 1,000 yards in length; the area is about 216 acres, or a third of a square mile, and its population may be conjectured not to exceed 15,000. Its elevation, according to Malcolm and Dangerfield, is 1,998 feet above the sea; but Jacquemont, who, however, did not make any barometrical observations on the subject, is of opinion that this estimate errs in excess. Indore was plundered in 1801 by the army of Doulut Rao Scindia, which had previously defeated Holcar, at the head of above 30,000 men. In 1804, it was occupied, without resistance, by a British force under Colonel Murray; but was restored on the subsequent pacification, in 1805. Distance south-west from Agra 402 miles; S.W. from Delhi 494; S. from Neemuch 142; S. from Nusseerabad, by Neemuch, 285; S.W. from Saugor 224; S.W. from Allahabad, by Saugor, 537; W. from Calcutta, by Allahabad, 1,030; N.E. from Bombay, *vià* Maligaum and Nassick, 377. Lat. 22° 42′, long. 75° 50′.

INDOS.—A town in the British district of

Burdwan, lieut.-gov. of Bengal, 62 miles N.W. of Calcutta. Lat. 23° 9′, long. 87° 41′.

INDRAL.—A town in Hyderabad, or dominions of the Nizam, three miles from the left bank of the Manjera river, and 111 miles W.N.W. from Hyderabad. Lat. 18° 12′, long. 77° 6′.

INDREE, in Sirhind, a town on the right bank of the Delhi Canal, and on the route from Kurnal to Boorea, being 15 miles N. of the former. A little above this town it has been proposed to commence a watercourse from the Delhi Canal, to feed the canal in contemplation for uniting the waters of the Jumna and of the Sutlej. Distant N.W. from Calcutta 980 miles. Lat. 29° 52′, long. 77° 8′.

INDURGURH, in the Rajpoot state of Boondee, a fort and town held by a petty tributary rajah, 45 miles N.E. of the town of Kotah. Lat. 25° 41′, long. 76° 19′.

INDURPUR, in the fief or jaghire of Rampore, under the jurisdiction of the lieut.-gov. of the N.W. Provinces, a village on the route from Bareilly to Almora, and 51 miles N. of the former. Lat. 28° 57′, long. 79° 26′.

INDUS.—A great river of Asia. Though the vigilant jealousy of the Chinese, who rule Tibet, has excluded Europeans from that country, the inquiries of Moorcroft, Trebeck, and Gerard, have established, beyond any reasonable ground of doubt, that the source of the longest and principal stream of the Indus is at the north of the Kailas Mountain, regarded in Hindoo mythology as the mansion of the gods, and Siva's paradise; and though over-estimated by Gerard in respect to its altitude, still having an elevation of 22,000 feet above the level of the sea. The locality of the source of the Indus may be stated with some probability to be in lat. 32°, long. 81° 30′. Near its source, it bears the name of *Sinh-kha-bab*, or "lion's mouth," from a superstitious belief that it flows from one. It first takes a north-westerly direction to Tagle, about 160 miles from the place of its reputed source. It is there joined on its left, or south-western side, by the Eekung Choo, or "river of Gartope," which rises on the western base of the Kailas Mountain. The united stream bears the name of the northern confluent, Sinh-kha-bab; and, near the La Ganskiel Pass, about fifty miles below the junction, the river leaves the table-land through which it had previously flowed, and enters the deep gorges of the great depression dividing the Kouenlun or Mooz Taugh from the Himalaya. To this point, five miles from the Chinese frontier, and having an elevation of 14,000 or 15,000 feet, its course has been explored by Trebeck, the companion of Moorcroft. It is situate in lat. 32° 56′, long. 79° 22′, on the border of a sandy plain, or rather wide valley, studded with small lakes, having their edges incrusted with soda. The river was here found to be about sixty yards wide, apparently deep, and in the middle of November frozen over in most parts. Thirty miles below this, the river turns nearly south-west for a short distance, and then takes the direction of north-west. At Ugshi, which is about 330 miles from the source, it was surveyed by Moorcroft, and found to be about fifty yards wide. Close to Le, the capital of Ladakh, and thirty miles below Ugshi, the elevation of its bed is not less than 10,000 feet; and if that of its source be assumed at 18,000, and its length, so far, at 360 miles, its fall will be found to be twenty-two feet per mile. Yet the descent of the bed of the Sinh-kha-bab is far less rapid than that of the Sutluj, which in thirty miles descends 2,300 feet, or about seventy-six feet in the mile. Holding its course in a direction approaching to north-west, the Sinh-kha-bab, about eighteen miles below Le, is joined, opposite to Niemo, by the river of Zanskar, flowing from the district of the same name, and in a direction from south-west to north-east. The Zanskar is a very rapid, turbid river; the Sinh-kha-bab, a clear and placid stream. About thirty miles below this, and 408 from its source, Vigne found the river, at Kulutzi, crossed by a wooden bridge, and only twenty-five yards wide. The small size of the river, after a course of more than 400 miles, can only be accounted for by the excessive aridity of the elevated tract through which it has held its way. Moorcroft estimates the breadth of the river at this place at only twenty yards; but he found that it rose nearly forty feet during the season of inundation. Having flowed about fifty-five miles below this place, in a north-west direction, it receives from the south the river of Dras, which, rising in the mountains forming the north-eastern frontier of Kashmir, holds a north-easterly course of about ninety miles, and, receiving several streams both from the east and west, discharges a considerable volume of water at its confluence. From this confluence the Sinh-kha-bab takes a more northerly direction, for about forty-seven miles, to the fort of Karis, in lat. 35° 11′, long. 75° 57′, where it receives, from the north, the water of the Shy-yok, by far its most important tributary above the river of Kabool. At the confluence of the two rivers, the Shy-yok is about 150 yards broad, the Sinh-kha-bab not more than eighty; but the latter is the deeper, and has a greater body of water. Below the confluence, the river is known by the name Aba Sind (Indus Proper). About twenty-five miles below the point of junction, and westward of it, the Indus, opposite Iskardoh, receives from the north the river of Shyghur. The downward course of the Indus between Iskardoh and Makpon-i-Shagaron, in which interval it runs a distance of about ninety miles, is in a direction west-north-west. At Makpon-i-Shagaron, in lat. 35° 48′, long. 74° 30′, according to Vigne, who viewed the place at the distance of eighteen miles, the river emerges from the mountainous region, and, turning south, a course which it thenceforth continues to keep generally to the sea, takes its way through the unexplored country north of

Attock. Vigne caused the part intervening between Iskardoh and Makpon-i-Shagaron to be explored by his native servants, who found it to flow through a succession of rocky gorges and deep and narrow valleys, rugged and difficult, but presenting nothing else remarkable: more recently this section has been examined by Europeans. About three miles south of Makpon-i-Shagaron, it receives, from the north-west, a considerable stream, called the river of Gilghit. Vigne, who viewed the Indus at Acho, about twenty-five miles below this confluence, describes it there as a vast torrent rushing through a valley six or seven miles wide, and holding a south-westerly course, which might be traced downwards for at least forty-five miles. From thence to Derbend, a distance of about 114 miles, its course lies through countries inhabited by barbarous and fanatical tribes of Mussulmans, and which does not appear to have ever been explored by Europeans. At Derbend, on the northern boundary of the British territory of the Punjab, it was in 1837 surveyed by Lieutenant Leech, of the Bengal Engineers, and there, in the middle of August, about which time it is fullest, he found it 100 yards wide. From this place, about 812 miles from its source, and in lat. 34° 18′, long. 72° 54′, he descended the river on a raft to Attock, a distance of about sixty miles. In this interval, the river, flowing through a plain, has a broad channel of no great depth, containing many islands, and is fordable in five places.

The fords are only available in winter, when the river is lowest, and even then the attempt is perilous, from the rapidity of the current and the benumbing coldness of the water. If the account given by Masson be correct, 1,200 horsemen were swept away and drowned on one occasion when the Indus was crossed by Runjeet Singh at one of these fords. Hough states the number lost at 7,000. Shah Shooja forded the Indus in 1809 above Attock, but his success was considered to be almost a miracle. Where crossed by Forster, about twenty miles above Attock, in the middle of July, and consequently when fullest, it was three-quarters of a mile or a mile in breadth, with a rough and rapid current, endangering the ferry-boat, though large enough to contain seventy persons, together with much merchandise and some horses. Close above Attock, the Indus receives, on the western side, the great river of Kabool, which drains the extensive basin of Kabool, the northern declivity of Sufeid Koh, the southern declivity of Hindoo Koosh and Chitral, and the other extensive valleys which furrow this last great range on the south. Both rivers have large volumes of water, and are very rapid; and as they meet amidst numerous rocks, the confluence is turbulent, and attended with great noise. The Kabool river appears to have nearly as much water as the Indus, and in one respect has an advantage over it, being navigable for forty miles above the confluence, while the upward navigation of the Indus is rendered impracticable by a very violent rapid, immediately above the junction. Both rivers have gold in their sands, in the vicinity of Attock. It is obtained in various places along the upper course of the Indus, or its tributaries; as at Gartope, in Hundes, and also near the confluence of the Shy-yok, and near Iskardoh. Attock, just below the confluence of the Kabool river, about 872 miles from the supposed source of the Indus, and in lat. 33° 54′, long. 72° 16′, is remarkable, as being the limit of the upward navigation of the latter river, and the place most frequented for passage over it from Hindostan to Afghanistan. The passage is, for the greater part of the year, made by bridges of boats, of which there are two: one is above the fort of Attock, where the river is 800 feet wide; the other below, where it is above 540 feet wide. Wood found the depth at Attock, in August, to be sixty feet; the rate of the current six miles an hour; the breadth, where he measured it above the place of the bridge, 858 feet. The inundation affects the depth and speed of the current, rather than the breadth, at Attock. This remarkable point is about 1,000 feet above the sea, and consequently about 17,000 feet below the source of the Indus, which falls, therefore, to that extent in 872 miles. This is at the average rate of about twenty feet per mile. The length of its channel from Attock to the sea is 942 miles, and consequently, in that lower part of its course, it falls little more than a foot per mile. At Attock, the river, flowing generally south-south-west, as it does below Derbend, enters a deep rocky channel in the Salt range, or secondary mountains, which connect the eastern extremity of Sufeid Koh with the base of the Himalaya, in the Punjab. In this part of its course, the river, as well as the fort on its left or eastern bank, is known by the name of Attock, in consequence, as is generally supposed, of the prohibition under which the Hindoos originally lay of passing it westward. For about ten miles below Attock, the river, though in general rolling between high cliffs of slate rock, has a calm, deep, and rapid current; but for above 100 miles farther down, to Kala-Bagh, it becomes an enormous torrent, whirling and rolling among huge boulders and ledges of rock, and between precipices rising nearly perpendicularly several hundred feet from the water's edge. The water here is a dark lead-colour, and hence the name *Nilab*, or "blue river," given as well to the Indus as to a town on its banks, about twelve miles below Attock. At Ghora Trup, about twenty miles below Attock, the immense body of water passes through a channel only 250 feet wide, but having a depth of 180 feet, the velocity being about ten miles an hour.

Wood, describing the course of the river from Attock to Kala-Bagh, says, "It here rushes down a valley varying from 100 to 400 yards wide, between precipitous banks from 70 to 700 feet high." During inundation, the river rises in this part about fifty feet. As the river approaches the plain country below Kala-Bagh, the channel expands nearly to the breadth of 500 yards; just above that town the width is 481 yards. Below Kala-Bagh, in lat. 32° 57′, long. 71° 36′, and about 830 miles from the mouth, the river enters the plain, the east or left bank here becoming low, while on the right the Khussoree Hills rise abruptly from the water, having, as Burnes observes, "the appearance of a vast fortress, formed by nature, with the Indus as its ditch." Along the base of these hills, which stretch south-south-west for about seventy miles, the channel is deep, generally having soundings about sixty feet. On entering the plain, the water loses its clearness, and becomes loaded with mud. In inundation, the depth of the stream is not so much affected in this part of its course as are the breadth and velocity; and here, as well as in the Delta, the river, when swollen, overflows the adjacent country to a great extent. From Kala-Bagh, southwards, to Mittunkote, distant about 350 miles, the banks, either right or left, or both, are in several places so low, that the first rise of the river covers the country around with water, extending, as the inundation advances, as far as the eye can reach. As the inundation originates in the melting of the snows in the Hindoo Koosh and the Himalaya, it commences with spring, and retrogrades as autumn advances; and so regular is this process, that, according to Wood, it begins to rise on the 23rd of March, and to subside on the 23rd of September, its maximum being about the 6th or 7th of August. The average rise of the inundation between Kala-Bagh and Mittunkote is eight feet and a half; the declivity of the water's edge is eight inches per mile. In this part of its course, with the exception of the Koorum, the Indus receives scarcely any accession to its water. Higher up it has a few tributaries, though of no great importance. Thus, on the right, or west bank, in lat. 33° 25′, long. 71° 52′, the Toe, described by Elphinstone as a deep and clear stream, falls into it. On the left, or east side, in lat. 33° 47′, long. 72° 16′, the Indus receives the Hurroo, a small stream; and on the same side, lower down, in lat. 33° 1′, long. 71° 46′, the Swan, also an inconsiderable stream. The Indus, between Kala-Bagh and Mittunkote, in consequence of the great breadth of its channel, is scarcely affected by rain; but in the narrow part, above Kala-Bagh, it sometimes rises eight or nine feet in a short time from this cause. In many places where the river flows through the plain, there is an inner and an outer bank. The outer banks run at a great distance from each other, and between them, during inundation, the vast body of water rolls often in several channels, separated by shifting islands: when the river is low, this great course becomes a shallow valley of very irregular breadth, and the shrunken river meanders along its bottom. If the outer banks were continuous, the river would roll along in a stream varying in breadth according to the greater or less degree of inundation; but at all times, even when fullest, in a defined channel of moderate breadth, though varying greatly in different parts. In many places, however, the outer bank is wanting, and, during inundation, the river expands over the country, converting it into an extensive lake. Between Mittunkote and Bukkur, the inundation extends sometimes twenty miles from the western side of the river, in its low state, and ten or twelve from the eastern side. Wood gives the width of the shrunken river as varying from 480 to 1,600 yards, and the average width at about 680 yards; its usual maxima of depth, at nine, twelve, or fifteen feet: but its bed is so irregular, and so liable to be obstructed by shifting shoals, that though it cannot be regularly and safely forded in any part, except that intervening between Torbela and Attock, its navigation, even below the confluence of the Kabool, cannot be effected at all times, and continuously throughout its whole course, by boats drawing more than thirty inches water. The general velocity of the stream in its shrunken state is estimated by Wood at three miles an hour; but he observes, "it is scarcely necessary to remark, that the three last items (breadth, depth, velocity) are very inconstant. At no two places are the measurements exactly alike, nor do they continue the same at one place for a single week." In fact, the breadth, during inundation, is only 250 feet at Ghora Trup; and below Mittunkote, it in one place amounts to thirty miles; the depth at the same time and place is 186 feet, and in other places only twelve feet: the velocity at Ghora Trup, during the inundation, is ten miles an hour; at other places, not half that, and when the river is low, often not more than two miles an hour.

The general course of the river is a little west of south from Attock to the confluence of the Punjnud, the channel which conveys the collected streams of the Punjab. This confluence is on the left or eastern side of the Indus, two or three miles below Mittunkote, in lat. 28° 55′, long. 70° 28′, and about 490 miles from the sea. Above the confluence, the breadth of the Indus is less than that of the other river, but, in consequence of the greater depth and velocity, the former has the greater volume of water. Wood found the Indus having a breadth of 608 yards, a velocity of about five miles an hour, a depth of twelve or fifteen feet, and discharging 91,719 cubic feet per second. The Punjnud had a breadth of 1,766 yards, a velocity of about two miles an hour, a depth of twelve or fifteen feet, and discharged 68,955 cubic feet per second. Below the confluence, the Indus is in its lowest state 2,000 yards wide. Its aspect in this part is well described by Boileau. "At the place where we crossed the Indus, almost immediately below its junction with the Punjnud, its stream is 2,047 yards, or nearly a mile and a quarter, in breadth, at a place where its width was unbroken either by islands or sandbanks. The banks are very low, and the water very muddy, having just begun to rise, from the melting of the snows at its sources; nor is the stream of very great depth, except in the main channel; but with all these drawbacks, it is a magnificent sheet of water—a very prince of rivers." For a considerable distance above and below Mittunkote, the country is low, and the inundation extensive, reaching to Shikarpoor, and even to some places distant from the river twenty miles to the west, and extending eight or ten miles to the east. Lower down, at Roree, the stream makes its way through a low ridge of limestone and flint, which stretches from the mountains of Cutch Gundava, eastward, to Jessulmair. There are strong indications that the stream, in remote ages, swept far eastward along their northern base, and irrigated the level tract at present desert, but exhibiting numerous proofs that it once was traversed by large streams, and was both fertile and populous. At present, this ridge is cut, not only by the Indus, but, a few miles farther east, by the Eastern Narra, which diverges from the main stream, on the eastern side, a short distance above Roree, and takes a south-easterly course through the desert, in which it is usually lost, though in violent inundations it rolls onward to the sea in a great volume of water, discharging itself through the Koree, or most eastern mouth, which is in general quite deserted by the fresh water. At Roree, there are four rocky islets, the largest of which, that of Bukkur, contains an extensive fort, and divides the river into two channels. Fifty miles below this place, the Western Narra, a great and permanent branch, divaricates from the Indus on the western side, and, after a tortuous course of nearly 120 miles, rejoins the main stream about four miles south-east of Sehwan. A little above that town, the Narra has a large but shallow expansion, called Lake Manchur, varying in circuit from thirty to fifty miles, according to the greater or less degree of inundation. This great watercourse, in the part intervening between Lake Manchur and the Indus, has a name distinct from that of the Narra, being called the Arul. From Sehwan, downwards, to the efflux of the Fulailee, a distance of about eighty miles, the bed of the river is much depressed below the level of the adjacent country, and the banks are elevated from sixteen to twenty feet above the surface in the low season: in this part of the course, inundations rarely overspread the country, and irrigation is effected by raising the water with the Persian wheel. The Fulailee, a large branch, though yearly diminishing, leaves the Indus, on the eastern side, about twelve miles north of Hyderabad, and, flowing south-east, insulates the Gunjah Hills, on which that town is built, as, about fifteen miles below it, an offset running westward rejoins the main stream. At Triecal, where is the point of reunion, in lat. 25° 9′, long. 68° 21′, the Delta commences; all below it, and contained between the Fulailee on the east, and the extreme western branch of the Indus, being, with little exception, alluvial, and obviously deposited by the river. The Fulailee holds a south-easterly course, in the lower part of which it bears the name of the Gonnee, which, communicating, during high inundations, with the Phurraun, is thereby discharged into the sea through the Koree mouth. The Koree mouth may more properly be termed an arm of the sea, as the water is salt, and it receives a current from the Indus only during inundations of unusual height. Burnes found it seven miles wide and twenty feet deep at Cotasir, about twenty miles from the open sea. Some suppose it to have once been the principal mouth of the Indus, constantly discharging the water of the Narra, which they consider to have been the chief branch. It is at present the most eastern of the estuaries connected with the Indus. The Pinyaree, a wide branch, which diverges from the Indus at Bunna, about forty miles below Hyderabad, is navigable, downwards, to within fifty miles of the sea: at that distance the navigation is closed by a bund or dam, thrown across it at Maghribee; but as the water makes its way through small creeks in time of inundation, the navigation recommences below the bund, and continues to the sea. The Pinyaree discharges itself through the Sir estuary, two miles wide at its mouth, with a depth on the bar of one fathom, and of from four to six inside: it is next, westward, to the Koree mouth. At about six miles above Tatta, the Kulairee, a small branch, leaves the Indus on the right or western side, and may be considered to mark the commencement of the Delta on that side. Were not its water lost by absorption and evaporation, it would generally insulate Tatta, as it now does occasionally. At about five miles below Tatta, and sixty miles from the sea, the Indus is divided into two great branches,—the Buggaur, which flows westward, and the Sata, which maintains the previous course of the Indus southward, and is in strictness the continuation of that river. The Mull and the Moutnee, formerly great branches, leaving the left or eastern side of the Sata, are now so diminished as to be almost dry. The estuaries, however, remain: that of the Mull is navigable for boats; it is the mouth next westward of the Sir; and beyond this, in the same direction, is the Kaha, or estuary of the Moutnee, at present unnavigable. A few miles further west is the Kookywarree mouth, now blocked up by a sandbank, but forming, in 1837, when Carless published his account, "the grand embouchure of the Indus," having a breadth of 1,100 yards. Even then, however, the navigation was rendered difficult by an enormous bank stretching across it, and extending five miles out to sea. The Sata now discharges the great bulk of its waters through the Kedewarree, the next mouth proceeding westward, the embouchure of which was considerably diverted during the inundation of

1848. Its channel is well defined, having no less than from seven to eight feet water at low spring tides. Following the line of coast in a north-westerly direction, the next estuary is that of the Hujamree, where the English force, advancing in 1838 on Affghanistan, were landed. Next in succession, in the same direction, is the Jooa mouth, leading by the river of the same name to the Buggaur, and practicable to the junction for river steamers during the floods. During the low season, the estuaries of both the Jooa and Hujamree are safe roads for ingress or egress, independent of fresh-water discharge. The Dubbar and Gorabee, now united, form the next mouth, which has five feet on the bar at low water; beyond which is the Pityanee, also communicating with the Buggaur, by which it was for a time deserted. Further on is the Cooddee mouth, having five feet at low water; and this is succeeded by the Pitty, one of the largest, deepest, and best-defined of the mouths of the Indus, and much frequented by steamers to and from Kurrachee. Next and last is the Gizree, the estuary of a branch of the Indus formerly obliterated, but again rendered navigable for boats, though having but two feet water at its mouth at low tide.

The distance from the Koree estuary, in the south-east, to the mouth of Gizree creek, in the north-west, is about 130 miles, and such is, consequently, the length of the seacoast of the Delta. There are several mouths of less importance, and the enumeration of which is unnecessary. There are also numerous intricate cross-channels, allowing an inland navigation for small vessels between the various creeks and branches. To sum up briefly this involved subject—during the season of low water, the Indus falls into the sea by only one channel of any importance: this, called the Sata, Munnejah, or Wanyanee, has its efflux by the Kedewarree mouth, the entrance of which is very unsafe, and consequently avoided by coasting craft. "Impetuous currents and shifting sands are dangers they are not disposed to encounter. Sharp vessels grounding on such a locality seldom escape serious disaster, a few hours being sufficient to engulf them in a bed of sand, from which no human aid or skill can extricate them." The other mouths, with the exception of the Pitty, are, in the season of low water, little more than creeks silted up and closed at various distances from the sea. The number of these creeks or estuaries at present at all worth noticing, is thirteen, occurring in the following order in proceeding from south-east to north-west: the Koree, Seer, Mull, Kaha, Kookewarree, Kedywarree, Hujamree, Jooa, Durbar, Pitteeanee, Coondee, Pitty, and Gizree. The tide influences the Indus nearly up to Tatta, a distance of about seventy miles. The spring tide rises nine feet.

The description above given of the mouths and lower branches of the Indus is mainly applicable to their state when the river is lowest. When the river is at its height, as Burnes observes, "the great branches of this river are of themselves so numerous, and throw off such an incredible number of arms, that the inundation is general; and in those places which are denied this advantage by fortuitous circumstances, artificial drains, about four feet wide and three deep, conduct the water through the fields." For about twenty miles from the sea, the whole country is nearly submerged. At this season, the water of the sea is fresh for some distance from the land, and discoloured for a still greater. The quantity of water discharged by the Indus is by no means proportionate to the enormous supplies derived from its numerous tributaries: the larger portion seems lost by evaporation, absorption, and employment for irrigation in a sultry climate where rain seldom falls. Wood and Lord state the *maximum* discharge in August, at 446,080 cubic feet per second, and in December, at 40,857 cubic feet per second. The water in the early part of the season of inundation is very unwholesome, in consequence of the great quantity of decayed vegetable and animal matter held in suspension by it. Lord, who made experiments by desiccating the water and weighing the residuum, computes that the quantity of silt annually discharged by the river, during the seven months of inundation, would suffice to form an island or bank forty-two miles long, twenty-seven miles broad, and forty feet deep; but it is clear, that this computation must be received with great allowances, as, according to it, the land of Sinde must have been much farther advanced into the Indian Ocean than it is found to be. After the early part of the season of inundation, if the water be preserved until the earthy admixture has subsided, it is both palatable and wholesome.

The Indus is infested by alligators: they are of the *guryial* or long-snouted kind, the common kind being unknown in the river, though numerous in lagoons near Kurrachee. The *bolun*, a cetaceous animal, the size of a porpoise, is common. Nowhere are fish finer or more abundant, and they form a large portion of the sustenance of the population of the adjacent country. Westmacott enumerates sixteen kinds, some as long as six or seven feet. The *pulla*, a species of carp, is a rich and delicious fish, though bony to a degree dangerous to an incautious eater. It is largely consumed on the spot, and also dried for exportation, forming an important article in the scanty trade of Sinde. The fisherman of the pulla floats, with his breast downwards, on an oblong earthen vessel, closed in all parts except an orifice, which he covers by applying his stomach to it. In this position, he passes along, taking the fish with a net at the end of a long bamboo, and depositing it in the vessel.

Wood observes, that "the population of the banks of the Indus are almost amphibious. The boatmen of Lower Sinde, for example, live, like the Chinese, in their boats. If a native of the Lower Indus has occasion to cross the stream, a pulla-jar wafts him to the opposite shore. At Bukkur, the *mussuk* (inflated hide) supersedes the pulla-jar; and from Mittunkote upwards, every man living near the river has one. Kossids (couriers) so mounted make surprising journeys, and the soldier, with sword and matchlock secured across his shoulders, thus avoids the fatigue of a long march." The leisure time of every description of persons is spent in the water, or floating on it. Such familiarity with the water naturally inclines the population to regard it as the great medium of commercial intercourse, and Hamilton, who visited Sinde at the close of the seventeenth century, found the traffic considerable. Until within the last few years, the trade of the Indus was obstructed, and in many places destroyed, by the oppression and vexatious rapacity of the various petty powers and tribes claiming sovereignty over divers parts of its course. The success of the British arms has led to the restoration of a better state of things. The *doondah*, or boat generally used in Lower Sinde, is a clumsy vehicle, flat-bottomed, of capacity varying from thirty to fifty tons, with bow and stern, each forming a broad inclined plane, having, the former, an angle with the surface of the water of about twenty, the latter of about forty degrees. The *jumptees*, or state barges of the ameers, were of considerable dimensions. Wood measured one 120 feet long, eighteen and a half broad, and drawing two feet six inches water. In the upper part of the Indus, the boat chiefly used is the *zohruk*, in most respects resembling the doondah, except that it is smaller, lighter, and more manageable. The *duggah*, used only in the boisterous part of the current above Kala-Bagh, is very strongly built, with stern and bow greatly projecting, to keep away the hull from the bank, in case of collision with it. It is so heavy and unmanageable, that if brought far down the river, it is usually disposed of there, to save the labour and expense of tracking it back. In proceeding up the stream when the wind is unfavourable, as is generally the case during the half-year between the autumnal and vernal equinoxes, way must be made exclusively by tracking. During the other half-year southerly winds prevail, and the boats run up under sail before it, except where the use of sails becomes dangerous from peculiar circumstances. Steam will doubtless be found highly efficient in navigating the Indus. Communication by its means has indeed been already established between Kurrachee and Mooltan, by government vessels, for goods and passengers; an advantage which it is confidently believed will shortly be extended to Kala-Bagh, on the Indus, and to the town of Jhelum, on the tributary of that name. The principal obstacle to its general employment is the dearness and inferior quality of the firewood of Sinde; but coal has been discovered near the Indus, both in the Punjab and on the western bank of the river, though further investigation is required as to its quality and quantity.

In estimating the advantages to be drawn from the navigation of the Indus, reference should be had, not only to the home consumption of Sinde and the Punjab, but also to the demand of the various marts of those countries through which Affghanistan, Khorasan, and Central Asia are largely supplied; and the best means of advancing this most important branch of trade have been deemed to be the establishment of grand periodical fairs at suitable points on the banks of the Indus, and in affording facilities of communication and protection to the commercial classes. Kurrachee and Sukkur have been selected as sites for this purpose. Communication between Kurrachee and the higher parts of the river is carried on by means of government steam-vessels.

Although some of the particulars following have been already noticed, it may be convenient, in conclusion, to bring them into one view. The length of the navigable part of the river from the sea to Attock has been ascertained, by measurement, to be 942 miles; that of the upper part is about 860 miles; making a total length, in round numbers, of 1,800 miles. The average declivity of the watercourse from the supposed locality of the source to Attock is, per mile, twenty-four feet; from Attock downwards to Kala-Bagh, a distance of about 110 miles, it is twenty inches; from this last place to Mittunkote, a distance of about 350 miles, it is eight inches; and thence to the sea, six inches. The Indus is probably destined to be an important channel of political and commercial communication.

INGEMOOR.—A town in the British district of Nellore, presidency of Madras, 129 miles N.N.W. of Madras. Lat. 14° 49′, long. 79° 39′.

INHOWNA, in the territory of Oude, a small town on the route from Lucknow cantonment to Pertaubgurh, 51 miles S.E. of the former, 59 N.W. of the latter. It has a small bazar, and is well supplied with water. Lat. 26° 33′, long. 81° 25′.

INGLEGHEE.—A town in Hyderabad, or dominions of the Nizam, 104 miles W.S.W. from Hyderabad, and 84 miles E. by N. from Beejapoor. Lat. 17° 2′, long. 77° 1′.

INJADRI.—See SAUTPOORA MOUNTAINS.

INJILLY.—A town in the British district of Ganjam, presidency of Madras, 20 miles W.N.W. of Ganjam. Lat. 19° 29′, long. 84° 50′.

INNACONDA, or VINUKONDA, in the British district of Guntoor, presidency of Madras, a town, the principal place of the talook or subdivision of the same name. Shocks of earthquake have been occasionally felt at this place. Lat. 16° 3′, long. 79° 48′.

INTGAON, in the British district of Bareilly, lieut.-gov. of the N.W. Provinces, a village on the route from the town of Bareilly to Seetapoor, and 29 miles S.E. of the former. Lat. 28° 16′, long. 79° 56′.

IRADUTNUGUR, in the British district of Agra, lieut.-gov. of the N.W. Provinces, a town on the route from Dholpoor to Agra, 15 miles S. of the latter. Lat. 26° 59′, long. 78° 9′.

IRAK RIVER, in Sinde, rises at the base of the Bhool Hills, in the mountainous tract between Kurrachee and Sehwan, and in about lat. 25° 20′, long. 67° 45′. It holds a course of about forty miles in a south-easterly direction, and empties itself, in lat. 24° 53′, long. 68° 6′, into the dund or lake of Kunjur, a considerable body of brackish water, abounding in fish. Though the stream fails in time of drought, water may always be obtained by digging in the bed.

IREJ.—See Erich.

IRLAPAUL.—A town in the British district of Nellore, presidency of Madras, 37 miles S.W. of Ongole. Lat. 15° 12′, long. 79° 40′.

IRON ISLAND, off the coast of the Tenasserim provinces, measuring twenty miles in length from north to south, and two in breadth. The north part of the island terminates in a point with rocks, having close to them from twenty-five to thirty fathoms water. Lat. 12° 45′, long. 98° 28′.

IRRAWADDY.—A river rising at the eastern extremity of the Snowy range of the Himalayas, the source of its principal tributary being in lat. 28° 5′, long. 97° 58′. It flows in a direction from north to south, traversing the heart of the Burmese territories, which it separates into two nearly equal divisions. After a course of 790 miles, it reaches the southern frontier of Burmah, and crossing over into the British province of Pegu, pursues its way for a further distance of 270 miles, reaching the Bay of Bengal by several mouths, which form the delta of the Irrawaddy. At the distance of 540 miles from its source, it passes the Burmese town of Ummerapoora; and a few miles farther, it flows past the capital of the empire, sixty-five miles beyond which it receives, on the right side, its great confluent the Khyendwen, flowing also from the north. The course of the united stream through the Burmese territory continues for the further distance of 180 miles. Fifty miles below the southern frontier of Burmah, as at present defined, it passes the British town of Prome; ninety miles below which it diverges into two principal branches, each measuring about 130 miles in length. The more easterly of these branches is designated the Rangoon or Siriam river, from the cities of those names built upon its banks; and it falls into the Gulf of Martaban, in lat. 16° 28′, long. 96° 24′. The other main branch, intersecting the province in a southwesterly direction, is known as the river of Bassein, and discharges itself into the Bay of Bengal, in lat. 15° 50′, long. 94° 26′. Innumerable watercourses, forming the delta, are thrown off from these two rivers.

From experiments instituted in 1852 across the river at Prome, to ascertain the velocity of the current, it appeared that the fall of the stream from October to February amounted to about twenty feet; the mean depth on the 25th April was found to range from twelve to thirteen feet; and its mean speed was computed at about two miles per hour. The Bassein branch affords a passage for the largest ships for sixty miles from its mouth, and for forty miles further for vessels of 300 tons. No river of similar magnitude, it is stated, presents so few obstructions. According to the theory of M. Klaproth and the Chinese geographers, the Irrawaddy is a continuation of the Sanpo of Thibet; but though absolute proof be yet wanting of the identity of the latter with the Brahmapootra, little doubt appears to be now entertained on this point. A high authority, exploring the Irrawaddy at a spot obviously at no great distance from its source, observes: "The Irrawaddy we were surprised to find but a small river, smaller even than we anticipated, though aware of the proximity of its sources. It was not more than eighty yards broad, and still fordable, though considerably swollen by the melting snows; the bed was of rounded stones, and both above and below where we stood, we could see numerous shallow rapids. As to the origin of the river, I felt perfectly satisfied from the moment I made inquiries at Sadiya; but since further evidence, founded on the report of the natives, might not have satisfied those who had adopted M. Klaproth's opinion, that the waters of the Sanpo find an outlet through the channel of the Irrawaddy, I had resolved, if possible, to have ocular and incontrovertible demonstration; and I could not help exulting, when standing on the edge of the clear stream, at the successful result of our toils and fatigues. Before us, to the north, rose a towering wall, stretching from west to east, offering an awkward impediment to the passage of a river in a cross direction; and we agreed on the spot, that if M. Klaproth proved determined to make his Sanpo pass by Ava, he must find a river for his purpose considerably removed towards or into China." A chart of the Irrawaddy from Rangoon to Yandaboo has been published, and further attempts to explore this river have, it is believed, been successful in adding somewhat to the stock of knowledge on the subject. But at present their results are not available for general use, as no public communication, either official or otherwise, has yet been made of them. A short time will probably throw open the discoveries to all who may take an interest in the matter.

ISAKHANKAKOT, in Sirhind, a village with a small fort, on the route from Loodianah to Ferozpoor, and 46 miles W. of the former town. It is situate in an open, level country, partially cultivated, and capable of yielding supplies for a moderate number of troops. Water is abundant, and the road in this part of the route generally good, though in some places sandy, yet not so much so as to present serious difficulties for guns or carriages. Distance N.W. from Calcutta 1,134 miles. Lat. 30° 57′, long. 75° 16′.

ISHAMUTTEE.—The name of one of the numerous watercourses of the Ganges which intersect the lower provinces of Bengal: it divaricates from the Martabhanga in lat. 23° 24′, long. 88° 42′, and flowing in a southerly direction for seventy miles through the British districts of Nuddea and Barasut, falls into the Bay of Bengal through the Soonderbunds.

ISHAPORE.—A village on the left bank of the Hooghly river, in the British district of Barasut, lieut.-gov. of Bengal. At this place are the powder-works of the government. The manufacture of gunpowder at Ishapore was, however, directed to be suspended in 1852; and though renewed at a later period under a temporary emergency, a desire was expressed by the home government that the future manufacture of this article should be transferred to a station in the upper provinces. Distant N. from Calcutta 13 miles. Lat. 22° 36′, long. 88° 23′.

ISKARDOH, the capital of Bultistan, is situate in an elevated plain, forming the bottom of a valley embosomed in stupendous ranges of mountains. The plain or valley of Iskardoh is nineteen miles long and seven broad. Its soil is formed of the detritus brought down and deposited by the Indus, and by its great tributary the Shighur river; the confluence being at the northern base of the rock on which the fort is built. The killah or rock, the site of the fort, is on the left bank of the Indus, here a deep and rapid torrent, above 150 yards wide. It is two miles long, and at the eastern end, where it is highest, rises nearly perpendicularly 800 feet above the river, from a buttress of sand, loose stones, and broken rocks. The killah has this mural face on every side, except the west, where it slopes steeply to the plain. Vigne considers that it could be rendered as strong as Gibraltar, to which, in appearance, it bears much resemblance. The castle of the former sovereigns of Bultistan stands on a small natural platform about 300 feet above the bed of the river, and is built of stone, with a framework of timber, and numerous strong defences against musketry. It is approached by a steep zigzag path, traversed by gateways and wooden defences, several of which are also disposed in such parts of the sides of the rock as require to be strengthened. There is a look-out house on a peak a little above the castle, and another on the summit above that. Everything in the interior of this stronghold is constructed for defence rather than comfort, the place "being a confusion of break-neck stairs, low doors, and dark passages." There is a splendid view of the valley and the river from the windows. The highest summit of the rock is a small level space of a triangular shape, and here are piled stones, ready to be rolled down for the destruction of assailants. It is scarcely accessible, except on the western side; and there, at a height of about 200 feet, the acclivity is strongly fortified by walls and square towers. The formation of the rock is gneiss. There is no water in the upper part of the killah, but below the castle is a fine spring. The residence of the population attached to the seat of government of this fallen state is on the plain at the base of the rock, and can, according to Vigne, "hardly be called a town, being a straggling collection of houses." The number of these houses is estimated by Moorcroft at 150. Vigne displays the enthusiasm of an ardent admirer of the picturesque in describing the appearance of this singular and secluded place, as viewed by him on his first visit to it from the direction of Cashmere. "I, the first European who had ever beheld them (so I believe), gazed downwards from a height of 6,000 or 7,000 feet upon the sandy plains and green orchards of the valley of the Indus at Iskardo." "The rock, of the same name itself with the rajah's stronghold on the east end of it, was a very conspicuous object. The stream from the valley of Shighur, which joins the Indus, as it washes its foot, was visible from the spot where I stood, but the latter river was hidden by the height of its left bank, whilst on the north, and wherever the eye could rove, arose with surpassing grandeur a vast assemblage of the enormous summits that compose the Tibetian Himalaya." Respecting the origin of Iskardoh, Wade mentions an absurd tradition, which at least has the interest of novelty for those whose knowledge of the exploits of "the great Emathian conqueror" is derived from classical sources. It is, "that Alexander the Great came here on an expedition towards Khata, or Scythia (modern China), and that the Koteli Mustak, or the Mustak Mountains, which lie between Yargand and Khata, being at that time impassable on account of the depth and severity of the snow, the Macedonian halted on the present site of the capital until a road could be cleared for his passage; when, leaving every part of his superfluous baggage, together with the sick, old, and infirm of his troops, behind in a fort which he erected while there, he advanced against Khata. These relics of the army founded a city, which they named Iskandaria, or Alexandria, now pronounced Iskardoh." The tradition received no countenance from Ahmed Shah, the intelligent gylfo or sovereign of the country, to whom Moorcroft applied for information on this curious subject. Neither the gylfo, nor any other inquirer, had been able to find any trace of Greek colonists. Vigne, who at one time maintained the fabulous Greek origin of Iskardoh, in retractation states that "Iskardo, Skardo, or Kardo, as it is sometimes called, is obviously only an abbreviation of Sagara Do, the two floods or rivers." He then mentions, that the people of Ladakh called it Sagar Khood, and adds, "Sagara is an old Sanscrit word for the ocean; and in this case Sagar Khood may signify the valley of the great flood or river: *do*, signifying two in Persian and its cognates, is added to the name Sagar, because the open space is formed by the junction of two streams, the Indus and the Shighur river." The plain or bottom of the valley of Iskardoh is 6,300 feet above the sea, and the summit of the rock is 7,200 above the same level. Ahmed Shah, the late native sovereign, had ruled the country with a moderation and paternal regard for his people little known among Asiatic despots. He made some unsuccessful efforts to become a protected vassal of our Indian government, as he justly dreaded the power, rapacity, and cruelty of the Sikhs. His fears proved true, as, a short time since, Iskardoh, notwithstanding its great natural strength, was seized by Gholab Singh, the present ruler of Cashmere. Iskardoh is in lat. 35° 12′, long. 75° 35′.

ISLAMABAD, in Cashmere, a town situate on the north side of the Behut or Jhelum, here navigable, and running with a gentle current. The river is about eighty yards wide, and is crossed by a wooden bridge. Islamabad is built at the extremity of a long, low eminence, extending from the mountains eastward. At the foot of this eminence is a spacious reservoir, of a triangular shape, supplied by a copious spring of clear water, slightly sulphureous, and from which gas is continually evolved. This spring, called Anat Nag, is supposed to have been produced by Vishnu. The gas does not prevent the water from swarming with fish, which are considered sacred. There are about 300 shops of shawl-weavers at Islamabad, and a considerable quantity of chintzes, coarse cottons, and woollens is also manufactured here. Its name was originally Anat Nag, which, in the fifteenth century, was changed to that which it now bears. Lat. 33° 43′, long. 75° 17′.

ISLAMABAD.—See CHITTAGONG.

ISLAMGURH, or NOHUR.—A fort of Bhawlpoor, on the route from Khanpoor to Jessulmere, and 65 miles N. of the latter place. It is a recent acquisition of the khan of Bhawlpoor, who made himself master of it at the expense of Jessulmere. The fort is a very ancient structure of small bricks, and has an area of about eighty yards square, with very lofty ramparts, varying in height from thirty to fifty feet. At the north-east angle is a high gateway, covered by an outwork. There are numerous bastions on the north and east faces, but few on the others. There is no ditch, and the situation is unfavourable for defence, as it is commanded on every side by sand-hills eighty feet high, and less than a quarter of a mile distant. There are a few buildings in the interior, and some straggling houses outside. Water is supplied from two wells. Islamgurh is in lat. 27° 50′, long. 70° 52′.

ISLAMKOTE.—A fort and village of Sinde, in the Eastern Desert, near the frontier of Cutch. The fort, 350 yards from the village, is seventy yards square, with walls of burnt brick thirty feet high, having a tower at each angle. There is but one gateway, which is on the eastern side. Lat. 24° 42′, long. 70° 10′.

ISLAMNUGGUR, in the British district of Budaon, lieut.-gov. of the N.W. Provinces, a town, the chief place of the pergunnah of the same name, situate on the route from Suhuswan to Moradabad, 18 miles N. of the former, and in lat. 28° 19′, long. 78° 47′.

ISLAMNUGUR, ISLAMGARH, or ISLAMABAD, in the territory of Bhopal, a town on the route from Seronj to the town of Bhopal, 55 miles S. of former, five N. of latter. It is situate at the confluence of the rivers Bes and Patra, the waters of which supply a ditch, extending from one to the other; so that the town, and a fort of masonry within, are by this means completely insulated. It was originally called Jugdispur, and received its present name from Dost Muhammad Khan, the founder of the state of Bhopal, who took it by surprise from a Hindoo zemindar, its previous holder. Lat. 23° 20′, long. 77° 25′.

ISLAMNUGUR.—A town in the British district of Mongheer, lieut.-gov. of Bengal, 32 miles S.S.W. of Mongheer. Lat. 25°, long. 85° 58′.

ISLAMPOOR.—A town in the British district of Dacca, lieut.-gov. of Bengal, 18 miles N. by E. of Dacca. Lat. 23° 59′, long. 90° 21′.

ISLAMPOOR.—A town in the British territory of Sattara, presidency of Bombay, 48 miles S.S.E. of Sattara. Lat. 17° 1′, long. 74° 20′.

ISRANA, in the British district of Paneeput, lieut.-gov. of the N.W. Provinces, a village on the route from Kurnoul to Rewaree, and 34 miles S.W. of the former. Water and supplies are abundant. Lat. 29° 16′, long. 76° 55′.

ITAPALLI, in the territory of Cochin, presidency of Madras, a town situate on a stream flowing from the Western Ghats. Distance from the city of Cochin, N.E., six miles; Bangalore, S.W., 292. Lat. 10° 2′, long. 76° 22′.

ITKHAPOOR.—A town in the British district of Ganjam, presidency of Madras, 32 miles S.W. of Ganjam. Lat. 19° 7′, long. 84° 44′.

ITUHLEE.—See ETAROLI.

IVIKER, or AIBIKA, in the territory of Travancore, a town on the seacoast, at the mouth of a channel by which the sea communicates with the extensive estuary or shallow expanse called by the British the Backwater. The channel or river of Aibika is wide, but admits small craft only, having at its entrance a bar, with only five or six feet of water when highest. A large ship, taking in cargo here, must anchor in the open sea, in six or seven fathoms of water, a considerable distance from the shore. There is here some export trade of timber, pepper, ginger, cardamums, lac, and turmeric. Distance from the city of Quilon, N.W., five miles. Lat. 8° 57′, long. 76° 37′.

IYLOOR.—A town in the British district of Madura, presidency of Madras, 44 miles N. of Madura. Lat. 10° 33′, long. 78° 13′.

J.

JAALPOOR, in the British district of Moradabad, lieut.-gov. of the N.W. Provinces, a village on the route from the town of Moradabad to Almora, and 13 miles N. of the former. Lat. 28° 59′, long. 78° 54′.

JABOOAH, in Malwa, a town, the chief place of a small territory of the same name, lies on the route from Mhow to Deesa, 92 miles W. of the former, 234 S. of the latter. It is inclosed by a wall of mud, with circular bastions of masonry, and is beautifully situate in a valley lying at the eastern base of a ridge of hills. On the north bank of a fine lake, south of the town, is the fortified palace of the petty rajah or chief. The boundaries of his small territory are as follow:—On the north, Banswarra; north-east, a portion of Holcar's territory; south-east, Amjherra; south, Alee Rajpore; and west, a portion of Scindia's territory, and Dohud. The area contains 1,348 square miles. The population consists principally of Bheels, of the more civilized classes, and is returned at 132,104. The annual revenue of the territory, in 1840, was stated at 144,536 rupees, or 14,453*l.* This is inclusive of the income derived from certain territories farmed from Holcar, which is said to amount to about 35,000 rupees (3,500*l.*). It is believed that the Jabooah state derives no pecuniary benefit from this farm, but, on the contrary, sustains some loss; but the districts of which it consists lying intermingled with the territory of Jabooah, the administration of them is a desirable object, with a view to security and the maintenance of order. A small military force appears to be maintained by this state, but, in order that its contribution in aid of the Malwa Bheel corps might be less onerous, it was proposed to incorporate in that corps such of the troops as were disposed to enlist into it.

The rajahs of Jabooah claim descent from the Rhattore princes of Joudpore. Bhunjee, one of their ancestors, commanded 400 horse at Delhi, and his son, Kishen Doss, was placed in attendance on the prince Allah-oo-Deen, to whom, subsequently to his accession to the throne, he rendered considerable service by regaining possession of Dacca, which had been withheld by a rebellious governor. For this service, he was requited by liberal grants of territory. Jabooah was at that time subject to Suka Naiga, a Bheel ruler and notorious freebooter, who, in conjunction with a Rajpoot chief named Chunderbahn, ruler of Dholitah, had plundered and murdered the family and followers of the governor of Guzerat. Kishen Doss was ordered to revenge this wrong, and set about the task in the only way probably in which he was likely to succeed. Disguising himself as a horsedealer, he proceeded to Jabooah with some remarkably fine specimens of the animal in which he professed to deal, and having won the favour and confidence of the Bheel chief, by allowing him to obtain the horses at very low prices, he lured him to a carousal, and taking advantage of the moment when excess had wrought its work, put him and his principal adherents to the sword. The zeal and success with which he had executed his instructions, procured him a grant of the dominions of the slaughtered chief, and henceforth Kishen Doss took a high place among the Hindoo dependants of the throne of Delhi. From this period, the history of the chiefs of Jabooah is not more interesting than that of the petty states around. Their territorial acquisitions were diminished by successive alienations in favour of younger branches of the family; and they shared in the common ruin which the Mahrattas spread over the face of that part of India, until the supremacy of British power and influence restored peace, and led to the introduction of a higher measure of civilization. The means taken by this state, as well as by others, to defend itself from Mahratta domination by the employment of foreign mercenary troops, increased its calamities, and extended their duration; for long after the Mahratta power had ceased to be formidable, the mercenaries, originally called in to assist it, remained a source of danger and alarm. For upwards of three years, down to 1836, the country was kept by them in a state of anarchy, which was finally suppressed only by the armed interference of the British government. Tranquillity was thereby restored, and by the deportation of the foreign troops, the country was freed from the main cause of disturbance. The rajah being a minor, the management of the country was, at the request of the ranee, temporarily assumed by the British, under whose administration it greatly improved. Distance of the town from Neemuch, S., 120 miles; from Oojein, S.W., 80; from Bombay, N.E., 285. Lat. 22° 45′, long. 74° 36′.

JADUN, in the Rajpoot state of Joudpore, a village on the route from Nusseerabad to Deesa, and 97 miles S.W. of the former. It contains a dozen shops, and is supplied with water from a tank and thirteen wells. Lat. 25° 50′, long. 73° 37′.

JAEESA.—A town in the native state of Bhotan, 91 miles N. by W. from Goalpara, and 128 miles E. by N. from Darjeeling. Lat. 27° 25′, long. 90° 20′.

JAFARGANJ, in the British district of Futtehpore, lieut.-gov. of the N.W. Provinces, a town situate one mile from the left bank of the Jumna, and 16 miles W. of the town of Futtehpore. Lat. 25° 55′, long. 80° 34′.

JAFFERABAD, in Hyderabad, or territory of the Nizam, a town near the north-west frontier, towards the British district of Ahmednuggur. It is situate on the river Gurkpoornah, a tributary of the Godavery, and here a large stream. The town is of considerable size, but there does not appear to have been any further information made public concerning it. Distance from Hydrabad, N.W., 260 miles; from Aurungabad, N.E., 45; from Bombay, N.E., 220. Lat. 20° 14′, long. 76° 5′.

JAFFERABAD, in the peninsula of Kattywar, province of Guzerat, a town and seaport in the district of Babriawar, situate on the estuary of the small stream Ranuy. It is "the best river on the coast, there being no bar, and the entrance easy. Although shoal, vessels will receive no damage by lying on the soft mud at low water, as they are well sheltered. The town is about a mile up the river, surrounded by a wall: next to Diu, it is the most considerable place for trade on the coast of Guzerat." It belongs to the Seedee or Abyssinian chief of Jinjira, on the coast of the southern Concan, and is governed by an officer holding under him. Jafferabad, with eleven villages annexed to it, possess a population estimated at 5,680. Distance from Ahmedabad, S.W., 170 miles; Baroda, S.W., 150; Bombay, N.W., 165. Lat. 20° 53′, long. 71° 21′.

JAFURABAD, in the British district of Bijnour, lieut.-gov. of the N.W. Provinces, a town situate on the route from Sireenuggur to Moradabad, and 70 miles N.W. of the latter. Elevation above the sea 1,041 feet. Lat. 29° 41′, long. 78° 30′.

JAGEPETTAH.—A town in Hyderabad, or dominions of the Nizam, three miles from the left bank of the Manjera river, and 44 miles N.W. from Hyderabad. Lat. 17° 50′, long. 78° 6′.

JAGGEE.—A town in the British district of Nowgong, province of Assam, 33 miles E. of Gowhatty. Lat. 26° 10′, long. 92° 17′.

JAGHESUR, in the British district of Kumaon, lieut.-gov. of the N.W. Provinces, a village situate on a nullah or rivulet of the same name, in the Sub-Himalaya, or mountain system south of the great range, 20 miles N.E. of Almorah cantonment. It has a Hindoo temple, and is supplied with water from a baoli or large well. Close to the temple is a confined encamping-ground. Lat. 29° 39′, long. 79° 53′.

JAGNOR, in the British district of Agra, lieut.-gov. of the N.W. Provinces, a small town near the southern frontier, towards Dholpoor, is situate in the pergunnah or subdivision of Sarhendi, among the sandstone hills extending southwards from Futtehpoor Sikri. It is 35 miles S.W. from the city of Agra. Lat. 26° 52′, long. 77° 40′.

JAGUN.—A place in Sinde, 10 miles N.W. of Shikarpoor. It consists of a fort and village, with some lofty square fortified buildings outside. It has a small, but rather well-furnished bazar. Supplies may be procured in moderate quantities, and forage, both for camels and horses, is plentiful. Jagun is eleven miles and a half from Janehdurra, from which place the road lies over a level country with much wood. There is an encamping-ground on the south-east of the village. Lat. 28° 8′, long. 68° 33′.

JAHANPOOR, in the British district of Agra, a village on the route from the city of Agra to Jeypoor, and 24 miles W. of the former. Lat. 27° 5′, long. 77° 42′.

JAHAUTOO.—A town in the British district of Chota Nagpoor, lieut.-gov. of Bengal, 182 miles W. by N. of Calcutta. Lat. 23° 7′, long. 85° 40′.

JAHJUR, in the British district of Agra, lieut.-gov. of the N.W. Provinces, a village on the southern frontier, towards Dholpoor, and 17 miles S. of the city of Agra. It is situate on the north or left bank of the Bangunga, in this part of its course called the Ootunghun, and which in the dry season is here only a small rill of clear water. In the rainy season, however, the stream becomes considerable, running in a sandy bed 130 yards wide, with steep banks cut into deep ravines. Lat. 26° 55′, long. 77° 59′.

JAHNUVI.—A feeder of the Ganges, in the upper part of the course of the latter, where it bears the name of the Bhageerettee. The Jahnuvi has been supposed to derive its origin from the north of the culminating range of the Himalayas, within the limits of Chinese authority; but this conjecture is without foundation, it being now ascertained that the remotest source of this river is situate in British territory, on the southern base of the before-mentioned range. The Jahnuvi rises in Gurwhal, in lat. 30° 55′, long. 79° 14′, and, holding first a northerly, then a westerly course, joins the Bhageerettee near the Sanga of Bhairogathi. At this point the Jahnuvi is from eighty to 100 feet wide, and superior in volume to the Bhageerettee, though the latter was long considered the origin of the holy and celebrated Ganges. The Jahnuvi flowing for the distance of thirty miles from its source, to the point of confluence, is evidently the most distantly derived of all the branches of the Ganges; for if the course of the latter be measured upwards from Deoprag to the source of the Jahnuvi, its length will be found to exceed the distance from the same point to the source of the Doulee. It must, therefore, be admitted that the Jahnuvi is the real origin of that great river, notwithstanding the rival claims of the Doulee.

JAINKEEPOOR, in the British district of Allahabad, lieut.-gov. of the N.W. Provinces, a village on the route by the Rajpoor ferry from the cantonment of Allahabad to Banda, and 21 miles W. of the former. Lat. 25° 24′, long. 81° 38′.

JAIPOOR.—See JEYPORE.

JAIRULA, in the Reechna Dooab division of the Punjab, a town situated 12 miles N. of the Ravee river, and 139 miles S.W. by W. of the town of Lahore. Lat. 30° 40′, long. 72° 10′.

JAITANU, in the Sinde Sagur Dooab division of the Punjab, a town situated on the right bank of the Jhelum, 100 miles N.W. of the town of Lahore. Lat. 32° 40′, long. 72° 59′.

JAITPOOR.—A town in the province of Guzerat, or the dominions of the Guicowar, 40 miles S. by W. from Rajkote, and 63 miles E. by N. from Poorbundur. Lat. 21° 45′, long. 70° 44′.

JAJARCOTE.—A town in the native state of Nepal, 148 miles N. by E. from Lucknow, and 105 miles E. by N. from Pilleebheet. Lat. 28° 56′, long. 81° 33′.

JAJMOW, in the British district of Cawnpore, lieut.-gov. of the N.W. Provinces, a town in the pergunnah of the same name, is situate on the right bank of the Ganges, six miles S.E. of the cantonment of Cawnpore by land, and five by water. It has a bazar, but does not seem of any great importance, not being mentioned by Lord Valentia, Skinner, or Lumsden, in their voyages down the river. In the time of Baber, it was perhaps more considerable: that sovereign, in his Memoirs, mentions that in one of his campaigns against the Afghans, they attempted to make a stand here, but were routed by his son Humaion. It is the Jaujesmow of Rennell's Index. Distant N.W. from Calcutta 620 miles by land, and by water 949, or, going by the Sunderbund passage, 1,125. Lat. 26° 26′, long. 80° 28′.

JAJOO.—A village in the jaghire of Jujhur, lieut.-gov. of the N.W. Provinces. Lat. 28° 29′, long. 76° 14′.

JAKO, in Bussahir, a village on the southern declivity of the outer or most southern Himalaya, and the last inhabited place on that side of the range in the route northwards by the Gunas Pass. It is of no great size, and the inhabitants, who bear the marks of poverty, are supported principally by the carrying-business across the mountains. Elevation above the sea 9,188 feet. Lat. 31° 15′, long. 78° 9′.

JAKO, in Keonthul, a high peak of the Simla range, and overtopping on the east the Simla station. The summit is of clay-slate. It is remarkably bare of trees to the south, though its declivity on the north side is well clothed with oaks, pine-trees, and rhododendrons. It was one of the stations in the great trigonometrical survey of the Himalaya. Elevation above the sea 8,120 feet. Lat. 31° 5′, long. 77° 15′.

JAKODA, in the British district of Rhotuk, lieut.-gov. of the N.W. Provinces, a village on the route from Delhi to Hansee, and 22 miles N.W. of the former place. Lat. 28° 48′, long. 76° 55′.

JALA, in the British district of Kumaon, lieut.-gov. of the N.W. Provinces, a town on the route from Almora to Sireenuggur, 28 miles N.W. of the former. Lat. 29° 52′, long. 79° 21′.

JALALABAD, in the British district of Shahjehanpore, lieut.-gov. of the N.W. Provinces, a small town on the route from Bareilly to the cantonment of Futtehgurh, and 52 miles S.E. of the former. It has a bazar and a ruined fortress "of inconsiderable dimensions, but surrounded by a lofty mud parapet, formidable bastions, and a deep fosse." It was probably built by Hafiz Rahmat Khan, the chief who commanded the Rohilla Pathans at the battle of Tessunah, where he fell. Lat. 27° 43′, long. 79° 43′.

JALALUDDINNAGAR, in the district of Aldemau, territory of Oude, a small town on the right bank of the Ghaghra, 10 miles S.E. of Fyzabad, 78 E. of Lucknow. Butter estimates the population at 1,500, including 500 Mussulmans. Lat. 26° 44′, long. 82° 12′.

JALEEA.—A town in the British district of Belgaum, presidency of Bombay, 84 miles E. of Belgaum. Lat. 15° 50′, long. 75° 50′.

JALHOTREE, in the territory of Oude, a small town on the route from Cawnpore to Lucknow, 25 miles N.E. of the former, 26 S.W. of the latter. It is situate close to a fine circular lake a mile in diameter. Lat. 26° 42′, long. 80° 42′.

JALHPOOR, in the British district of Benares, lieut.-gov. of the N.W. Provinces, a town on the route from Benares to Ghazeepoor, nine miles N.E. of the former. Lat. 25° 21′, long. 83° 10′.

JALHU, or JALHUPUR, the principal place of the pergunnah of Jalhu, a town a mile N.W. of the left bank of the Ganges, and 12 miles N.E. of Benares. Lat. 25° 22′, long. 83° 10′.

JALIHAL.—A town in one of the recently sequestrated districts of Hyderabad, or dominions of the Nizam, 133 miles S.W. by W. of Hyderabad. Lat. 16° 22′, long. 76° 50′.

JALLIAPULLUNG.—A village in Arracan, situate on the south bank of the river Raeezoo, and forming the termination of the first division of the great route from Chittagong to Akyab, from the former of which places it is distant about 105 miles. The country in the vicinity is well cultivated and populous. Lat. 21° 17′, long. 92° 10′.

JALLOR.—A town in the Rajpoot state of Jodhpoor, on the left bank of the Sookree river, and 71 miles S.W. by S. from Jodhpoor. Lat. 25° 23′, long. 72° 40′.

JALNA, or GALNA, in the British district of Candeish, presidency of Bombay, small town with a fort, on an isolated hill, not high, but steep and rocky. The summit is fortified all round, and on the side towards the town, where it is least steep, has in some parts two, in others three walls of good masonry. In October, 1804, it belonged to Holkar, and was invested by a British force under Wallace, who, having breached the defences in two places, prepared for an assault, the necessity for which, however, was superseded by the garrison, amounting to 700 men, evacuating the place. On the subsequent pacification, it was restored to Holkar. It was ceded in 1818, by Mulhar Rao Holkar, to the British government, by the sixth article of the treaty of Mundeesor, and surrendered to a detachment sent by Sir Thomas Hislop to take possession. Distance direct from Mow, S.W., 150 miles; from Bombay, N.E., 165. Lat. 20° 46′, long. 74° 30′.

JALOUN.—A district of Bundlecund, and now a British possession. It is bounded on the west and north-west by the territories of Duttea, Sumpter, and of Gwalior; on the north by Gwalior and the British district of Etawah; on the north-east by Cawnpore; on the south-east by Hummerpore; and on the south by Jhansee and Tehree. It lies between lat. 25° 32′ and 26° 26′, long. 78° 45′ and 79° 53′; its greatest length from north to south is about seventy miles, and its breadth from east to west sixty miles. It was estimated in 1832 to have an area of 1,480 square miles, and to comprise 518 villages. Since that period, the limits of the district have been extended, by the addition of some pergunnahs from the adjacent state of Jhansee, ceded to the British government, and also of a confiscated jaghire called Chirgong. According to more recent returns, the area of the district thus increased is 1,873 square miles, supporting a population of 246,297 persons.

The district of Jaloun came into the possession of the Peishwa early in the eighteenth century, and the management of it was committed to one of his servants. Under the series of arrangements effected with the Peishwa in 1802 and 1803, the sovereign rights of that prince over Jaloun were transferred to the East-India Company. The administrator, Nana Govind Rao, of Calpee, subsequently took up arms against his new lords; but the dispute was brought to an immediate conclusion. In 1817, the British government, by a new engagement, constituted the Nana "hereditary ruler of the lands then in his actual possession." In 1832 the principality passed to a child only six years of age, who was placed under the guardianship of the widow of the former chief. The regent, however, who was herself but a child, being at the time not more than thirteen or fourteen years of age, proved quite unequal to the duty of controlling the refractory spirits in the district. A strong party was formed adverse to her authority; the country became disorganized, the government was involved in debt, and portion after portion of the territory mortgaged to talookars, until at length the regent and her minister, finding the credit of the government at an end, applied to the British agent for his guarantee of a further loan, declaring their inability to carry on the government without it, and exhibiting a statement of revenues and expenses, which showed an annual deficit of two and a half lacs of rupees. In these circumstances, it was deemed necessary that the British government should assume the temporary management of the country, for the purpose of reducing the expenditure, paying off the debt, resuming the mortgaged territory, and restoring order. This step was accordingly taken in 1838. The organization of a local military force being indispensable, to supersede the undisciplined and disorderly troops previously retained, the formation of a legion was authorized, composed of cavalry, infantry, and a gun establishment, with two European officers, as commanding officer and adjutant. Under the British administration, many beneficial changes were effected; cultivation was extended, and the country manifested unequivocal proofs of being in a state of gradual improvement. The infant chief did not live to the period when the propriety of committing the administration of the country to his charge could become a subject of discussion. He died during his minority, and no one surviving of the family of Nana Govind Rao entitled to claim the succession under the engagement by which that chief was constituted hereditary ruler of the district, it lapsed, as a matter of course, to the East-India Company as paramount lord. Since the lapse, the indications of progressive improvement have continued to be satisfactory. A revenue settlement for a term of years was made in 1849.

JALOUN.—A town of Bundelcund, situate 15 miles S.W. of the right bank of the Jumna. It is the chief place of the territory bearing the same name, and is distant W. from Calpee 28 miles, S.E. from Agra 110, N.W. from Calcutta 675. Lat. 26° 9′, long. 79° 24′.

JAM.—A town in the territory of Hyderabad, or dominions of the Nizam, situate 62 miles S.W. by S. of Ellichpoor. Lat. 20° 24′, long. 77° 7′.

JAMALGARHI, in the Daman division of the Punjab, a town situated 40 miles N.N.E. of Peshawur, and 42 miles N.N.W. of the town of Attock. Lat. 34° 29′, long. 72° 1′.

JAMALLABAD, in the British district of South Canara, presidency of Madras, a town founded by Tippoo on the site of a ruined city called Narasingha Angady. Tippoo at the same time built a fort, on a huge rock westward of the town, and wholly inaccessible except by one narrow way; so that it is totally impregnable by assault. It is, however, exposed to the effects of bombardment, by which it was attacked by a British force in 1799, after the fall of Seringapatam. The soldiers of the garrison made their escape; the commandant poisoned himself, and the other officers of the garrison, who submitted to be taken, were hanged. It was shortly after surprised by a freebooter, but retaken, after a blockade of three months, and permanently occupied by a British garrison. Distant from Mangalore, N.E., 34 miles. Lat. 13° 2′, long. 75° 22′.

JAMBO, in the district of Salon, territory of Oude, a town 26 miles W. of Sultanpoor cantonment, 50 S.E. of Lucknow. It has a fort, in which resides a Hindu chief of the Khatri (military) caste, who, according to Butter, is a descendant of the ancient Hindoo sovereigns of Oude, and who maintains 400 armed followers. According to the same authority, the population is 7,000, of whom half are Mussulmans. Lat. 26° 21′, long. 81° 44′.

JAMBOOLPATA.—A town in the British district of Tannah, presidency of Bombay, 37 miles S.E. of Bombay. Lat. 18° 40′, long. 73° 22′.

JAMBOTEE. — A town in the British district of Belgaum, presidency of Bombay, 18 miles S.W. of Belgaum. Lat. 15° 40′, long. 74° 22′.

JAMERAPAL.—A town in the British district of Midnapoor, lieut.-gov. of Bengal, 85 miles S.W. by W. of Calcutta. Lat. 21° 59′, long. 87° 16′.

JAMGAUM.—A town in the British district of Ahmednuggur, presidency of Bombay, 108 miles E. of Bombay. Lat. 19° 4′, long. 74° 31′.

JAMGONG.—A town in the British province of Nagpoor, late the dominions of the rajah of Berar, situate 16 miles from the left bank of the Mahanuddy river, and 184 miles E. from Nagpoor. Lat. 21° 7′, long. 81° 42′.

JAMGURH.—A town of Malwa, in the native state of Bhopal, 59 miles E. from Bhopal, and 60 miles S.W. by S. from Saugur. Lat. 23° 8′, long. 78° 18′.

JAMIDPOOR, or JUMDOA, in the British district of Allahabad, lieut.-gov. of the N.W. Provinces, a village on the route, by Rajapoor ferry, from the cantonment of Allahabad to Banda, and 34 miles W. of the latter. Lat. 25° 27′, long. 81° 28′.

JAMJOONGGA.—A town in the native state of Bhotan, 66 miles N.N.W. from Goalpara, and 122 miles E. from Darjeeling. Lat. 27° 1′, long. 90° 16′.

JAMKA.—A town in the British district of Kurrachee, province of Scinde, presidency of Bombay, 21 miles W. by S. of Tatta. Lat. 24° 40′, long. 67° 40′.

JAMKHEIR.—A town in the British district of Ahmednuggur, presidency of Bombay, 48 miles S.E. of Ahmednuggur. Lat. 18° 44′, long. 75° 22′.

JAMNEIR.—A town in the British district of Candeish, presidency of Bombay, containing a population of 4,000 inhabitants. Distant 83 miles E. by N. of Malligaum. Lat. 20° 48′, long. 75° 44′.

JAMNI.—A river rising in the British territory of Saugor and Nerbudda, and probably about lat. 24° 8′, long. 78° 42′. After a course north of a few miles, it passes the northern frontier, into the Shahgurh district of Bundelcund, through which it flows north twenty miles, and crosses into the Gwalior territory, which it traverses for about fifteen miles, and subsequently, still flowing north, forms the western boundary between Bundelcund and the territory of Gwalior, to its junction with the Betwa, on the right side, in lat. 25° 15′, long. 78° 40′; its total length of course being about ninety miles.

JAMOO, in Sirmor, a limestone peak about four miles from the left bank of the Giri. It was a station of the series of small triangles in the great trigonometrical survey of the Himalayas. Elevation above the sea 6,852 feet. Lat. 30° 37′, long. 77° 34′.

JAMOO, a considerable town in the north of the Punjab, and among the mountains forming the southern range of the Himalaya, is situate on a small river, which, rising about forty miles to the north, takes its course below the town for about twenty miles, in a south-westerly direction, and falls into the Chenaub. The town and palace are built on the right or western bank of the river; on the east is the fort, elevated about 150 feet above the stream, which is here fordable when lowest. The place, with the lofty and whitened palace and fort, has a striking and pleasing appearance when viewed from without. The bazar is large, well built, and well supplied; the streets are extensive, and the population considerable, amounting, according to Vigne, to about 8,000. The palace is a spacious and handsome building. The fort, though built with great cost and labour, is untenable against a regular attack, being commanded by an adjacent height of easy access. There is an extensive and beautiful pleasure-ground, belonging to the rajah. About the town are numerous ruins of great size, the evidence of its prosperity under its hereditary rajahs, before the expulsion of their family by the Sikhs. It is still held by Gholab Singh as part of his dominions, although the position of this prince has been greatly altered by the transfer to him of Cashmere and the adjacent hill country, a consequence of the success of the British arms in the Punjab in 1845. Jamoo is in lat. 32° 44′, long. 74° 54′.

JANEEDERA, in Sinde, a village on the route from Shikarpoor to Bagh, and 18 miles N.W. of the former town. It is situate near the border of the Pat, or desert of Shikarpoor, yet the immediate vicinity is fertile, and was well cultivated before it suffered from the devastations of the marauding Belooches, who some years ago laid the village in ruins. There is a fort of considerable size, containing a good well. There are three other wells outside the fort. Lat. 28° 16′, long. 68° 28′.

JANGI, in Bussahir, a village in the district of Koonawur, is situate on the right bank of the Sutlej, and at the eastern base of a high mountain, the cliffs of which being soft and fissile, are shattered by the expansive force of frost; from which cause vast masses continually tumble down, forming a sloping surface, composed of sand, fragments of mica-slate, and spar, with an admixture of earth, and capable of cultivation wherever a stream from the snows above can be directed over it. By such management those accumulations of apparent rubbish become soon covered with crops of grain and fine vineyards. Jangi is at the elevation of 8,905 feet above the sea. Lat. 31° 36′, long. 78° 29′.

JANJPAT.—A town in the British district of Tirhoot, lieut.-gov. of Bengal, 105 miles N.E. of Dinapoor. Lat. 26° 27′, long. 86° 31′.

JANSUTH, in the British district of Muzuffurnuggur, lieut.-gov. of the N.W. Provinces, a town on the route from Hurdwar to Meerut, 28 miles N. by E. of the latter. Its population is returned at 5,589. Lat. 29° 18′, long. 77° 55′.

JAOLI, in the British district of Mozuffurnuggur, lieut.-gov. of the N.W. Provinces, a town, the principal place of the pergunnah of the same name, is situate in lat. 29° 25′, long. 77° 55′.

JAOLI, in the Rajpoot territory of Alwur, a village on the route from the town of Alwur to Muttra, and 51 miles W. of the latter. Lat. 27° 33′, long. 76° 56′.

JARAILLAH.—A town in the Rajpoot state of Jessulmere, 29 miles S.W. from Jessulmere, and 156 miles W. by N. from Jodhpoor. Lat. 26° 37′, long. 70° 40′.

JARESANG.—A town in the native state of Nepal, situate on the left bank of the Arun river, and 110 miles S.E. by E. from Khatmandhoo. Lat. 27° 9′, long. 86° 57′.

JAR KHASS, in the British district of Futtehpoor, lieut.-gov. of the N.W. Provinces, a town on the route from Futtehpoor to Hummeerpoor, 20 miles W. of the former. Lat. 25° 57′, long. 80° 34′.

JARPURRAH.—A town in the British district of Cuttack, lieut.-gov. of Bengal, 14 miles S.E. of Cuttack. Lat. 20° 20′, long. 86° 4′.

JARRAH.—A town in the British province of Nagpoor, 140 miles S.E. from Nagpoor, and 90 miles E. from Chanda. Lat. 19° 50′, long. 80° 45′.

JASROTA.—A small raj and town in the north-east of the Punjab, among the mountains of the southern range of the Himalaya, within the dominions of Gholab Singh. The residence of the rajah (the last occupant of which fell a victim to the rapacity of Runjeet Singh) is a stately mansion, with four towers. The town has a bazar of small size and inconsiderable business. Lat. 32° 29′, long. 75° 27′.

JATEEA DEEBEE, in one of the hill districts of the rajah of Pateeala, a small temple of the Hindoo goddess Kali, on a ridge betwen Subathoo and Simla, and five miles S.W. of the latter post. Elevation above the sea 5,031 feet. Lat. 31° 6′, long. 77° 9′.

JATEEARA, or JULEEARA, in the Rajpoot state of Joudpore, a village on the route from the town of Joudpore to that of Ajmere, and 35 miles E. of the former. It contains 100 houses, three shops, and nine wells. Lat. 26° 25′, long. 73° 44′.

JATWALA, in the Rajpoot state of Joudpore, a village on the route from the town of Joudpore to that of Ajmere, and 40 miles N.E. of the former. Lat. 26° 25′, long. 73° 40′.

JAULDOE, in the British district of Pachete, lieut.-gov. of Bengal, a small town on the route from Burdwan to Dorunda, in Chota Nagpoor, 125 miles W. of former, 45 E. of latter. Lat. 23° 22′, long. 86°.

JAULNA, in the territory of the Nizam, a British cantonment on the route from the city of Hyderabad to Aurungabad. It is located in a very dreary, barren country, having a surface rendered uneven and rugged by numerous ravines and hills of trap or other volcanic formation, overlaid in many places with laterite. The immediate site of the cantonment is a gently-sloping declivity, in front of which a small range of hills, from one to two miles distant, form a sort of amphitheatre. The lines extend from south-east to north-west, the cavalry lines being at the south-eastern extremity, those of the infantry in the middle, and those of the horse and foot artillery at the north-west. Behind those lines are the officers' quarters, well built, and situate within spacious compounds or inclosures, having good gardens, outhouses, and stabling attached to them. The cantonment is capable of affording accommodation for one troop of horse-artillery, one regiment of native cavalry, and three regiments of native infantry; having barracks, hospitals, and storerooms. They were built in 1827. A place of worship has also been erected for the Roman Catholic soldiers at this station. The climate is admirably adapted for the purposes of horticulture; in the cool season, abundance of excellent European vegetables are raised: pease, beans, cabbages, carrots, parsnips, turnips, celery, cauliflowers, and potatoes; besides many common in India. Figs, grapes, peaches, and strawberries, are also produced; the latter of extraordinary size, but somewhat deficient in flavour. South-west of the cantonment two miles, and on the left bank of the small river Kundulka, is the town of Khaderabad. It is surrounded by a high stone wall, and has about 7,000 inhabitants. On the opposite bank is the old town of Jaulna, formerly large and flourishing, having enjoyed an extensive trade in grain and silks. It yet possesses to some extent a manufacture of silks for native use. The place, however, is much decayed, though having a population estimated at 10,000, of whom about a fifth are Mussulmans. Many of the houses are substantially built of stone, and a fort, well planned and strongly constructed, indicates the former importance of the place. Distance from Secunderabad and Hyderabad, N.W., 240 miles; Nagpore, S.W., 235; Aurungabad, E., 38; Bombay, N.E., 210. Lat. 19° 50′, long. 75° 56′.

JAUM, in territory of Indore, or possessions of Holkar's family, a village with a fort on the route from Mhow to Aseergurh, 14 miles S. of the former, 100 N.W. of the latter. It is situate on the crest of a pass through a ravine of the Vindhya range, descending from Malwa to the valley of the Nerbudda. The ghat or pass is a mile and a half in length, and is so steep, narrow, and zigzag, that, according to Malcolm, it is impassable for wheeled carriages of any sort; but Garden states that six-pounders have been lowered down it. Notwithstanding its great difficulty, it is much frequented by foot-travellers, being the most direct route from Malwa southwards. Elevation above the sea 2,328 feet. Lat. 22° 23′, long. 75° 49′.

JAUMGONG.—A town in the petty native territory of Peint, presidency of Bombay, 100 miles N. by E. from Bombay, and 97 miles S. by E. from Broach. Lat. 20° 20′, long. 73° 15′.

JAUNJMEER.—A town in the peninsula of Kattywar, province of Guzerat, situate on the west coast of the Gulf of Cambay. Lat. 21° 10′, long. 72° 4′.

JAUNPORE.—See Jounpore.

JAUNSAR.—A British hill district officially connected with the Dehra Doon, and which, stretching northward from it, is as it were indented between Gurwhal and Sirmor. It is bounded on the west by Sirmor, from which it is separated by the river Tons; on the north and east by Gurwhal, from which it is for a considerable distance separated by the river Jumna, which river also, on the south, divides it from the Dehra Doon. Jaunsar is about thirty-three miles long in a direction from north to south; its breadth from east to west is twenty-three; and it has an area of 579 square miles. It lies between lat. 30° 30′ and 30° 57′, long. 77° 46′ and 78° 9′. The surface throughout is rugged and mountainous, rising to the middle from the Tons on the west, and the Jumna on the east, and discharging from the elevated and central part numerous small streams into those rivers. Some of the summits are lofty; as Bairat, having an elevation of 7,559 feet; Bhadraj, of 6,043; and Baila, 6,318. The elevation diminishes generally, though irregularly, to the southern frontier, where, at Haripur, at the confluence of the Tons and Jumna, it is reduced to 1,686 feet above the sea. The number of townships within this district is 414. The population, according to official return, amounts to 24,684 persons. Jaunsar was formerly part of the raj of Sirmor, but on the expulsion of the Ghoorkas in 1815, it became subject to the British government.

JAUT, in the British district of Goorgaon, lieut.-gov. of the N.W. Provinces, a village on the route from Delhi to Rewaree, and 48 miles S.W. of the former. It is situate near the left bank of the Sabi, the bed of which is dry from November to July, but for the rest of the year is the course of a torrent discharging water into the jhil or lake of Najafgarh, or of Furrucknuggur, whence it passes ultimately into the Jumna at Delhi. Lat. 28° 15′, long. 76° 44′.

JAVANAGOONDENHULLY.—A town in the Mysore, on the left bank of the Hurry river, and 99 miles N. from Seringapatam. Lat. 13° 51′, long. 76° 48′.

JAWUD, in the territory of Gwalior, or possessions of Scindia's family, a town, the principal place of a pergunnah containing 133 villages. It is surrounded by a stone wall, and has good gateways, but the defences are of no strength. In 1818, it was held by a refractory retainer of Doulat Rao Scindia, and being stormed by a British detachment, was made over to that prince. Population 30,000. Elevation above the sea 1,400 feet. Lat. 24° 35′, long. 74° 55′.

JAYBHOOM.—A town of North-eastern India, in the British district of Goalpara, presidency of Bengal, 26 miles W. by S. of Goalpara. Lat. 26° 4′, long. 90° 14′.

JAYES, in the district of Salon, territory of Oude, a decaying town, 35 miles W. of Sultanpoor, 55 S.E. of Lucknow. It is situate on the left bank of the Naia Nuddy or stream, a tributary to the river Sai, and contains many large brick-built houses, constructed by Mussulmans of former times. According to Butter, the population is 9,000, of whom three-fourths are Mussulmans. Lat. 26° 14′, long. 81° 37′.

JEEAGAON, in the territory of Gwalior, or possessions of Scindia's family, a town on the route from Hoshungabad to Mow, 54 miles W. of former, 90 E. of latter. It is situate on the small river Jamnair, a tributary of the Nerbudda. Supplies are plentiful. Population about 1,800. Lat. 22° 37′, long. 76° 59′.

JEEKA MOUNTAIN, in the island of Ramree, off the coast of Arracan. Its elevation is about 3,000 feet above the sea, and it rises in a very abrupt manner from the range with which it is connected. With the exception of the summit, it is covered with a dense forest. A brown ferruginous sandstone, regularly stratified, with an inclination to the south-west, is the only rock visible on the surface.

JEELAIKE.—A town in the native state of Bhawulpoor, on the left bank of the Sutlej river, and 103 miles N.E. by E. from Bhawulpoor. Lat. 30° 6′, long. 73° 15′.

JEELOO.—A town in Tourwuttee, a dependency of the Rajpoot state of Jeypoor, situate 63 miles N. from Jeypoor, and 100 miles S.W. by W. from Delhi. Lat. 27° 50′, long. 76°.

JEENJUNEE.—A town in the native state of Gwalior, or the territory of Sindhia's family, situate on the right bank of the Kooaree river, and 24 miles N. by W. from Gwalior. Lat. 26° 33′, long. 78° 10′.

JEEOTEE, in the British district of Mynpooree, lieut.-gov. of the N.W. Provinces, a village on the route from the cantonment of Allygurh to that of Mynpooree, and 10 miles N.W. of the latter. There is water from wells. Lat. 27° 18′, long. 79°.

JEERA.—A town in Guzerat, or the dominions of the Guicowar, 71 miles S. by E. from Rajkote, and 132 miles W. by S. from Broach. Lat. 21° 16′, long. 71° 4′.

JEERA.—A town of Baghelcund, in the native state of Rewah, 129 miles S.W. from Sasseram, and 101 miles W. from Palamow. Lat. 23° 50′, long. 82° 27′.

JEEREE.—A river rising in lat. 25° 9′, long. 93° 28′, and, flowing in a south-west direction for forty miles, during which it forms the boundary between Southern Cachar and Muneepoor, falls into the Barak river, in lat. 24° 43′, long. 93° 12′.

JEERUN, in the territory of Gwalior, or possessions of Scindia's family, a town on the route from Neemuch to Baroda, 12 miles S. of the former, 227 N.E. of the latter. It has a bazar, and supplies and water are abundant. The surrounding district, which is of considerable size, bears its name. Elevation above the sea 1,590 feet. Lat. 24° 18′, long. 74° 58′.

JEETEE.—A town in the British district of Ahmednuggur, presidency of Bombay, 54 miles S. by E. of Ahmednuggur. Lat. 18° 20′, long. 74° 56′.

JEHANABAD, in the British district of Shahabad, lieut.-gov. of Bengal, a town on the route from Hazareebagh to Benares, 118 miles N.W. of former, 50 S.E. of latter. It has a bazar, and supplies and water are abundant. According to Buchanan, there are 200 houses; so that, if the usual average be assumed, the population appears to be about 1,000. Lat. 25° 3′, long. 83° 52′.

JEHANABAD, in the British district of Bareilly, lieut.-gov. of the N.W. Provinces, a town on the route from Shahjehanpoor to Almora, 52 miles N. of the former. Lat. 28° 38′, long. 79° 47′.

JEHANABAD, in the British district of Hooghly, lieut.-gov. of Bengal, a town on the route from Calcutta to Bankoora. Distance 45 miles N.W. of the former, 56 W. of the latter. Lat. 22° 52′, long. 87° 50′.

JEHANGEERPOOR.—A town in the native state of Gwalior, or the territory of Sindhia's family, situate on the right bank of the river Chumbul, and 16 miles W. from Oojein. Lat. 23° 11′, long. 75° 32′.

JEHANGEERPOOR.—A town of Malwa, in the native state of Dhar, 61 miles S. by W. from Oojein, and 22 miles S.E. from Dhar. Lat. 22° 19′, long. 75° 33′.

JEHANGEERUH.—A town in the British district of Bhagulpoor, lieut.-gov. of Bengal, 16 miles W. of Bhagulpoor. Lat. 25° 11′, long. 86° 44′.

JEHAUJPOOR.—A town in the British district of Cuttack, lieut.-gov. of Bengal, 42 miles N.E. of Cuttack. Lat. 20° 51′, long. 86° 24′.

JEHWOOR.—A town in the British district of Ahmednuggur, presidency of Bombay, nine miles N.E. of Ahmednuggur. Lat. 19° 11′, long. 74° 50′.

JEITPORE, in Bundelcund, a town, the principal place of a small raj or principality of the same name. It lies on the route from Calpee to Jubbulpoor, 72 miles S. of the former, 197 N. of the latter, and is situate on the western side of an extensive jhil or mere. Here is a bazar. The territory of which this town is the principal place "comprises 165 square miles, and is stated to contain 150 villages, with a population of 16,000 souls, and to yield a revenue of 60,000 rupees: it maintains a force of sixty horse and 300 foot." In 1812, the British government granted the state to Rajah Kesree Singh, a descendant of Chuttur Sal, the founder of the independence of Bundelcund. In 1842, the rajah, becoming refractory and committing depredations against the British possessions, was deposed, and the raj was granted to another descendant of Chuttur Sal, named Khet Singh, who had a few years before submitted a claim, apparently well grounded, to the raj of Chirkaree, which, however, he had ceased to press, on stipendiary provision being made for him. On the death of Khet Singh, in 1849, the raj lapsed to the British government. The town of Jeitpore is situated in lat. 25° 16′, long. 79° 38′.

JEJOOREE.—A town in the British district of Poonah, presidency of Bombay, 28 miles S.E. of Poonah. Lat. 18° 16′, long. 74° 12′.

JELALABAD, or JULLALABAD.—A town in the British district of Shahjehanpoor, lieut.-gov. of the N.W. Provinces. It contains a population of 6,629. Distant 11 miles S.W. from Shahjehanpoor. Lat. 27° 46′, long. 79° 50′.

JELALPOOR.—A town in the Punjab, on the right or western bank of the Jhelum, situate in a narrow valley of great fertility, extending between the river and the eastern extremity of the Kala or Salt range. According to Elphinstone, this was the scene of Alexander's battle with Porus; but Burnes thinks it must have been at Jhelum, higher up, where the river, according to him, is fordable at all times except in the monsoon, but where Hügel found it, at the beginning of January, when lowest, a great stream, larger than the Indus at Attock, and bridged with twenty large boats. It is therefore doubtful whether the river could at that point be forded at the season of inundation (when, as Arrian informs us, it was crossed by Alexander); and where, indeed, the British army lost eleven men in fording it in December, which is the low season. It is, however, said that all the fords in the Punjab are more or less zigzag, and are also subject to variations, not only from season to season, but even from day to day. Jelalpoor is one of the great passages over the Jhelum, on the route from Hindostan to Afghanistan. Lat. 32° 40′, long. 73° 26′.

JELALPORE, in the British district of Jounpoor, lieut.-gov. of the N.W. Provinces, a town on the route from Benares to Jounpoor, 26 miles N.W. of the former. Lat. 25° 35′, long. 82° 51′.

JELGOON.—A town of Malwa, in the native state of Burwanee, situate on the right bank of one of the branches of the Taptee river, and 111 miles E.S.E. from Baroda. Lat. 21° 43′, long. 74° 52′.

JELLALABAD, in the territory of Oude, a town on the route from Cawnpore cantonment to that of Sooltanpoor, 48 miles N.E. of the former, 87 N.W. of the latter, five S. of Lucknow. It has a bazar. Lat. 26° 45′, long. 80° 57′.

JELLASORE, or JALLESUR, in the British district of Midnapore, lieut.-gov. of Bengal, a town on the route from the town of Cuttack to that of Midnapore, 130 miles N.E. of the former, 49 S. of the latter. It is situate on the left or east bank of the Soobaureka river, here a considerable stream, yet fordable during spring, but at other seasons crossed by ferry. Here is an antique mosque, and on the opposite bank of the river is a ruined fortress of great extent, but very rude construction, being merely an inclosure, formed by a ditch and mud rampart, surmounted formerly by a dense prickly hedge, scarcely passable, except during the dry season in spring, when it could be easily fired. Jallesur is in lat. 21° 46′, long. 87° 14′.

JELLINGHEE, in the British district of Moorshedabad, lieut.-gov. of Bengal, a town situate at the point where the river Jellinghee parts from the Podda, or great eastern branch of the Ganges. Elevation above the sea seventy-five feet. Distance E. from Berhampore 25 miles, N. from Calcutta 105. Lat. 24° 8′, long. 88° 40′.

JELLINGHEE.—A river parting from the Podda, or great eastern branch of the Ganges, at the town of Jellinghee, in lat. 24° 8′, long. 88° 40′. It holds a course very sinuous, but generally S.W., for about ninety-five miles, and, at the town of Nuddea, in lat. 23° 25′, long. 88° 22′, joins the Bhagruttee, another great offset of the Ganges, the united stream being designated the Hooghly. Of the three rivers, the Bhagruttee, the Martabhanga, and the Jellinghee, forming the direct channels of navigation between Calcutta and the North-West Provinces, the last is by much the deepest and most important, retaining two feet of water during the dry season in spring, when the others have an average depth of about one foot. Still it cannot at that period be navigated by the craft usual in the Ganges, and they must then proceed through the Soonderbund passage, and thus incur a delay of a week in reaching their destination.

JELLY PUTTY.—A town in the British district of Coimbatoor, presidency of Madras, 38 miles E. by N. of Darapooram. Lat. 10° 49′, long. 78° 8′.

JELOOR, in Sirhind, a village on the direct route from Hansee to Lodiana, and 62 miles N. of the former town. The river Guggur is subject to sudden and great inundations, which sometimes for a considerable distance render the road in this vicinity impracticable. Distant N.W. from Calcutta 1,037 miles. Lat. 29° 56′, long. 76°.

JELPESH.—A town in the British district of Dinajepoor, lieut.-gov. of Bengal, 63 miles N. by E. of Dinajepoor. Lat. 26° 28′, long. 88° 53′.

JELPIGOREE.—A town in the British district of Dinajepoor, lieut.-gov. of Bengal, 62 miles N. of Dinajepoor. Lat. 26° 29′, long. 88° 42′.

JELUNGA.—A town in the British district of Chota Nagpoor, lieut.-gov. of Bengal, 62 miles S. by W. of Hazareebagh. Lat. 23° 7′, long. 85° 10′.

JEMDAH.—A town in the British district of Jessore, lieut.-gov. of Bengal, 80 miles N.E. of Calcutta. Lat. 23° 31′, long. 89° 10′.

JEMLAH.—A town in the native state of Nepal, situate on the right bank of the Kurnalli river, and 123 miles E. by S. from Almora. Lat. 29° 19′, long. 81° 41′.

JENJAPOOR.—A town in the British district of Tirhoot, lieut.-gov. of Bengal, 89 miles E.N.E. of Dinapoor. Lat. 26° 13′, long. 86° 22′.

JEORUHA, in Bundelcund, town of Mahoba, an outlying portion of the British province of Jaloun, situate on the route from Calpee to Ajeegurh, 70 miles S.E. of the former. It has a large Hindoo temple in good repair, and once containing much wealth, which was some years ago carried off by dacoits or gang-robbers, who murdered the officiating priest. Lat. 25° 13′, long. 80° 3′.

JERA, in the British district of Allahabad, lieut.-gov. of the N.W. Provinces, a village on the right bank of the Ganges, N.W. of Calcutta, by the river route, 769 miles; 39 S.E. of the city of Allahabad, by the same. Lat. 25° 13′, long. 82° 15′.

JERDEEKER, a river rising in lat. 27°, long. 88° 53′, on the southern slope of the Sub-Himalaya Mountains, and, flowing through Bhotan in a southerly direction for forty miles, and south-east through Coosh Behar for forty-five miles, falls into the Toresha rivera, feeder of the Brahmapootra, in lat. 26° 15′, long. 89° 26′.

JEROULEE, in the British district of Futtehpoor, lieut.-gov. of Agra, a town on the left bank of the Jumna, 14 miles S. of the town of Futtehpoor. Lat. 25° 44′, long. 80° 55′.

JERRAMULLA.—A town in the British district of Bellary, presidency of Madras, 34 miles S.W. of Bellary. Lat. 14° 48′, long. 76° 35′.

JERRODE.—A town in Guzerat, or dominions of the Guicowar, 14 miles N.E. from Baroda, and 49 miles W. by S. from Cambay. Lat. 22° 24′, long. 73° 22′.

JESARA, in the British district of Gurhwal, lieut.-gov. of the N.W. Provinces, a town on the route from Hurdwar to Hiundes or South-west Thibet, 71 miles E. by N. of the former. Lat. 30° 12′, long. 79° 22′.

JESOOL, in the Punjab, a small town on the route from Mooltan to Leia, and 10 miles S. of the latter place. It is situate near the left bank of the Indus, the water of which of late years has in this part of the course been directed to the right or west side, so that the former bank on the east side now bears the appearance of a low brow or continuous eminence, running in some degree parallel to the main channel, and seven or eight miles distant from it. Jesool is in lat. 30° 49′, long. 71° 2′.

JESSORE.—A British district under the lieut.-gov. of Bengal, named from its principal place. It is bounded on the north-east by the British district of Pubna; on the east by those of Dacca-Jelalpore and Backergunge; on the south by the Soonderbunds; and on the west by the British districts of Baraset and Nuddea. It lies between lat. 22° 28′—23° 46′, long. 88° 44′—89° 55′; is 105 miles in length from south-east to north-west, and forty-eight in breadth. The area, according to official statement, is 3,512 square miles. The surface is, with scarcely any exception, level and depressed, and its appearance tame, uninteresting, and unvaried, except by the interchange of dry ground and swamp; this district having redundant moisture, being traversed by numerous streams, and many offsets from the Ganges, in their course from north to south, from the great parent stream to various estuaries in the Soonderbunds. Of these the Koomar and Barashee are navigable throughout the year, the others only during the inundations caused by the periodical rains of closing summer and autumn, when innumerable cross-streams cause communications between the larger channels, intersecting the country in every direction, and in many parts laying it extensively under water. The climate is bad, the air being tainted with pestilential exhalations from the muddy and weedy tanks and watercourses: hence fevers and ague, severe and often fatal, are rife at all times of the year, but especially in autumn and the close of summer, when the temperature is sometimes above 100°. In December and January it is sometimes at night as low as 55°. So fatal are the epidemics in the season during which they prevail, that whole villages are often depopulated. The zoology of the district, though very inadequately explored or described, is rich and interesting. It comprises, of wild beasts, the tiger, leopard, panther, bear, jackal, fox, ichneumon, wild deer, swine, and porcupine. The botany is very comprehensive and varied, but has received little attention. From the exclusively alluvial character of the country, it contains no minerals; but salt is obtained from the southern frontier. The soil is generally very fertile; in the northern part, however, having considerable admixture of sand and clay. In the south, it comprises a larger proportion of rich alluvial earth or vegetable mould, abundantly productive of rice, indigo, oil-seeds of various kinds, sugar, tobacco, cocoanuts, areca-nuts, gram (Cicer arietinum), rye, pulse, hemp, turmeric, and fruits of various kinds. Mulberry-trees have latterly been planted in great numbers, for feeding silkworms. Indigo is largely exported, as also is rice. The production and export of sugar and rum have latterly been greatly on the increase, large quantities being prepared by inspissating the sap of the palm-tree. The population is given under the article BENGAL. Jessore, the principal place, and the other towns, Khulna and Muhommudpur, are noticed under their respective names in the alphabetical arrangement.

JESSORE.—The principal place of the British district of the same name, on the route by Baraset from Calcutta to Dacca, 77 miles N.E. of Calcutta, 103 S.W. of Dacca. The civil establishment of the district is located here. The jail at this place is a spacious building, capable of holding in safe custody 1,000 persons. The school is a fine building, the cost of erecting it having been defrayed by subscription of the zemindars of the district. The establishment consists of five members, a secretary, a head-master, an assistant, and two pundits or native teachers. The pupils are instructed in English, Persian, and Bengalee. The school was first opened in 1838. This place was formerly reputed an unhealthy station; but within the last few years considerable pains have been taken, and expense incurred, with a view to sanitary improvement; and happily with success. Jessore is in lat. 23° 10′, long. 89° 10′.

JESSULMERE, the most western of the fourteen states of Rajwara or Rajpootana, is bounded on the north by the territory of Bahawulpoor; on the north-east by the territory of Bikaneer; on the south-east and south by that of Joudpore; and on the west by Sinde. This state was formerly much larger, extending to the Indus and Ghara, till the territory of Bahawulpoor was wrested from it by the Daudpootras. It now contains an area of 12,252 square miles. It lies between lat. 26° 8′—28° 28′, long. 70° 3′—72° 51′. According to Tod, a line drawn in a north-west direction from Lowarki, in lat. 27° 5′, long. 71° 50′, to Kharreh, lat. 27° 27′, long. 70° 14′, would divide the territory of Jessulmere into two nearly equal parts, the southern of which is in many places rocky, being traversed by a ridge of hills, which may be considered continuous with the high lands of Cutch. "These barren hills are the only objects which diversify the almost uniform sterility of these regions. No trees interpose their verdant foliage to relieve the eye or shelter the exhausted frame of the traveller. It is nearly a boundless waste, varied only by a few stunted shrubs of acacia or mimosa family, some succulent plants or prickly grapes, as the bhoorut or burr." Macmurdo, however, draws a less repulsive picture of this tract, representing it as abounding with patches of good pasture among the rocks and sandhills, and feeding great herds of cattle. There are no running streams in the territory of Jessulmere, the periodical rains producing merely temporary sars or lakes of salt-water, formed by damming up the streams running down from the sandhills and intervening gulleys. The sars in general last but a few months, though, after very heavy monsoons, some have been known to continue through the year. The largest is the Kanod Sar, so called from the town of Kanod, on its southern border. It is about eighteen miles in length when fullest, and retains some water throughout the whole year. When filled to the greatest extent, a small stream proceeds from its eastern side, and, after a course of about thirty miles in an easterly direction, is lost in the sands of Joudpore. Salt is obtained from the ground left dry in the shrunken state of the lake; and this is a source of revenue to the Rawul or sovereign. Water in Jessulmere is at so great a depth below the surface, that wells in some places must be dug above 300 feet before a steady supply can be obtained. Thus, at Dihatra, on the north-west frontier, the wells are 309 feet deep; at the town of Jessulmere, 304 feet. To provide a sufficiency of that which is everywhere one of the first necessaries of life, but in warm countries pre-eminently so, the natives dig extensive tanks, which, being filled by the periodical rains, supply water during the greater part of the year; but when those supplies fail, which sometimes occurs, many human beings and cattle perish from thirst. Jessulmere is devoid of valuable minerals, but limestone is abundant, and of good quality. The zoology of Jessulmere appears to be neither varied nor important. A few lions are said to haunt the wilds about the southern frontier, and wild hogs are numerous in the same region. Tigers and leopards occur but rarely; wolves and jackals are more common. There are a few antelopes, deer, and nylgaus (Antilope picta). Snakes are so numerous that the people wear leggings of leather as a defence against them. But, in general, little amount or variety of animal life could be expected in a country so barren and of such limited extent. Domestic cattle are numerous and valuable. They consist principally of dromedaries, horses, kine, and sheep; of which last large flocks are kept. The trees are generally stunted: they are the babul (Mimosa), janth, the kurit (Capparis aphylta), the pilu. But one crop is raised in the year, the cultivation consisting in little else than scratching the ground with a small light plough, and scattering the seed in the way of broadcast. As, from the want of streams or large bodies of water, and the depth of the wells, artificial irrigation is impracticable, the weight of the crop depends entirely on adequate falls of rain. The principal crop is bajra or millet; in the more fertile parts, various sorts of pulse are cultivated. The only manufacture of any importance in Jessulmere is that of woollens, of both coarse and fine fabrics, made from the produce of the numerous native flocks. The coarsest part of the wool is made into cordage of various kinds; the next quality into blankets, and the finest into excellent woollen cloths and fabrics.

The ruler, and the influential portion of the population, are of the Bhatti tribe of Rajpoots, according to Tod originally from Zabulistan. They are a dissipated race, debasing and destroying their moral, intellectual, and physical powers by the excessive use of opium, which they imbibe sometimes in an infusion, sometimes by smoking, and not unfrequently till they become quite insensible. The dress and accoutrements of a Bhatti in easy circumstances consist of a tunic of white cloth or chintz, reaching to the knee, trousers loose, and of many folds in the upper part, but tight round the ankles; round the waist a scarf, in which a dagger is stuck; a shield, suspended from the left shoulder by a strap of deer-skin, and a sword, girt on with a belt of the same material. The head is covered by a turban, generally of a red colour, and terminated above by a high peak. The dress of females is of red woollen cloth, very full below; and a scarf is generally worn, which is more or less costly, according to the circumstances of the wearer. All wear rings of ivory or bone on the arms, in such numbers as nearly to cover them from the shoulders to the wrists. The legs above the ankles are also adorned with silver rings; and women will deny themselves the necessaries of life to obtain the means of purchasing these ornaments. The religious strictness of the Bhatti Rajpoots is rather relaxed, in consequence of their continual intercourse with the Mussulmans to the westward. The next class in number and importance to the Rajpoots are the Palliwals, a Brahminical tribe, who nearly engross the commercial business of the community, and the Pokurna tribe, also Brahminical, and exclusively devoted to rural pursuits, which are also followed by the Jat tribe, who constitute a considerable portion of the population. There are also a few Jains.

The population is estimated at 74,400. Unlike many other dialects of India, that of the Bhattis of Jessulmere has no admixture of Persian, that language being nearly unknown there. Their language closely resembles the Marwari, a dialect spoken in Joudpore, Bikaneer, and the neighbouring parts of Rajpootana. The Rawul, and principal people, write in a kind of Nagari character, which, though in some degree differing from the Devanagari, could, with little practice, be fluently read by a Hindee scholar. The citizens of Jessulmere appear to favour learning, and about 1,000 young persons are in course of education there, some by Brahmins, some by other instructors. A short time since, an English schoolmaster formed part of the domestic establishment of the Rawul. The sovereign has an annual revenue of about 8,500*l.*, of which about one-half is from transit-duties, the remainder from khalsa or crown lands, and miscellaneous sources. The military force maintained by the state does not exceed 1,000 men; but Tod states that, if on good terms with his thakoors or vassals, the chief could muster 5,000 infantry, 1,000 horse, and a camel corps. The history of Jessulmere is little else than an apocryphal subject for antiquarian research, previously to 1808, when the Rawul, probably alarmed at the encroachments of the khan of Bahawulpore, made advances to an amicable understanding with the British government. This relation matured in 1818 into an alliance, by which Jessulmere became entitled to British protection, and engaged to act in subordinate co-operation with the British government, and with submission to its supremacy. The principal places are noticed separately in the alphabetical arrangement. Boundary disputes had sprung up from time to time between this state and those of Bahawulpore and Khyrpore; the differences with the latter originating in the cession to Jessulmere, after the conquest of Sinde, of a portion of the desert originally belonging to Jessulmere. Under the auspices of the British government, these differences have been now adjusted, and the boundaries of Jessulmere defined both towards Khyrpore and Bahawulpore.

JESSULMERE.—The capital of the Rajpoot state of the same name. It is situate in a rocky tract, described by Boileau as "a succession of valleys, or inclined planes, several miles long, and three or four miles broad, formed by low ridges of yellow limestone, the strata of which are not quite horizontal, but dip gently to the westward, and crop out on the eastern side, with a tolerably bold profile of ninety or 100 feet in height." The city is built at the base of the south end of one of these ranges, and has ramparts of uncemented stone, with bastions constructed in the same way, and generally much higher than the intermediate curtains. Many of these bastions are, however, in ruins. Inclosed within the ramparts, and in the south part of the town, is the citadel, situate on an insulated eminence, three-quarters of a mile in circumference, and with steep sides, scarped all round, and faced with masonry to the height of about twenty feet, above which distance the surface of the hill recedes, at an elevation of about 40°, to the foot of the renee, which, with a width of six feet, runs quite round the fort. The ramparts of the fort vary in height from fifteen to thirty feet, the top of the parapet being about 130 feet above the town. The palace of the Maha Rawul or sovereign, within the citadel, is a great pile of building, surmounted by a huge umbrella, made of metal, and supported by a stone shaft. This is considered an emblem of high dignity, to which no other Rajpoot prince is entitled, except the chief of Oodeypoor. There are in the citadel, besides the palace, six temples, three for those of the Jain persuasion, and three for the Brahminists. The Jain temples are of great antiquity, built of stone, elaborately carved, and surmounted by gilt spires, towering over the adjacent buildings. Within the citadel, there are eight wells, above 300 feet deep. The water which they furnish is brackish, but not to such an extent as to be undrinkable. Progress has been made in sinking a well close to the gate. The work, at the time of Boileau's visit, had proceeded to the depth of 120 feet; but a much greater depth had still to be attained before reaching the main spring. The city contains about 8,000 houses, including those within the citadel. The domestic architecture is in many instances elaborate and solid. The house of a citizen in moderate circumstances has usually a frontage of about twenty-five feet. The basement story is painted red on the outside, and is quite plain, having one door giving access to the interior, and two or three slits instead of windows, to give light to the lumber-room, which occupies that part of the house. The upper or principal story is very neat, the front having a small projecting balcony, constructed of stone well carved, though rather in a heavy style. On each side is a latticed window about four feet square, and ornamented with framework of limestone, curiously carved. The balcony is surmounted by a massive canopy, the top of which is level with the flat roof, and being, like it, provided with a balustrade or battlement of cut stone, serves as a place for the inmates of the dwelling to enjoy the fresh air and prospect. Each house is raised above the street by a terrace about four feet high and six or seven wide, and has in front of every story a stone spout, to carry off the water into the street below. In the fronts of the terrace, long blocks of stone are bedded, so as to project some distance, and these have knobs at the ends, to which cattle may be tied. The interior of the house has a court a few feet square, into which various water-spouts are discharged, and the drainage passed off into the street by the subterraneous channel. On one side of the court is the cistern, on the other, the rusora or kitchen. One or two narrow and steep staircases of stone lead from the corners of the area to the upper story and roof, where the females of the family take the air. The principal sleeping-room occupies the front side of the square. The back part of the house is laid out in store-rooms, and the two sides of the square are formed into numerous small chambers, with a profusion of odd but convenient little nooks, and cupboards built into the thickness of the wall. Pretty cradles and beds are provided for the children; long wooden pegs neatly painted, project from the wall for the purpose of hanging up clothes, and, in short, everything wears an appearance of comfort, the more pleasing, as it is quite unexpected. The most remarkable building in the town is the house of the ex-minister, a very costly structure of five stories of cut stone, with a sixth of timber, surmounted by five cupolas. There is scarcely anything like a bazar, and the only appearance of traffic is at the custom-house, near the gate of the citadel. The inhabitants of the town are supplied with water from a large tank, 300 yards south-east of the city; and near its banks are several small pits, which collect water from the drainage of the surface, but are not sufficiently deep to reach the springs. Close outside the western gate of the city are two wells, 241 feet deep, with water slightly brackish. They are protected from falling into the hands of an enemy by parapets with loopholes.

According to Tod, Jessulmere was founded in 1156, by Jesul, a Bhatti prince, to replace the more ancient capital, Lodorva, situate 10 miles N.W. of the present. The site of Lodorva had no natural difficulties which might aid its defence, and in consequence of its exposed situation, was sacked by a hostile force; whereupon the surviving inhabitants settled at Jessulmere. The population of Jessulmere is probably about 35,000. It is distant N.W. from Calcutta, by Allahabad, Calpee, Gwalior, and Nusseerabad, 1,290 miles. Lat. 26° 56′, long. 70° 58′.

JETCH DOOAB.—One of the natural divisions of the Punjab, formed by the two rivers Jhelum and Chenaub. It is the smallest of the four dooabs bounded by the Indus and its tributaries, and lies between lat. 31° 10′—33° 2′, long. 72° 13′—74° 48′. Its length from north-east to south-west is 165 miles, and its breadth 33.

JETTOE, in the Sinde Sagur Dooab division of the Punjab, a town situated on the left bank of the Indus, 54 miles S.W. of the town of Mooltan. Lat. 29° 31′, long. 70° 56′.

JEWAHIRGURH, in the British district of Muttra, lieut.-gov. of the N.W. Provinces, a village on the route from the city of Agra to Allygurh, and 20 miles N. of the former. The road in this part of the route is very good, the country well cultivated. Lat. 27° 25′, long. 78° 7′.

JEWALA MUKI, in the north-east of the Punjab, a celebrated Hindoo place of pilgrimage, 10 miles N.W. of Nidaon, situate in an elevated nook, immediately under the mountains of Changa, is frequented by votaries from all parts of Hindostan, anxious to worship the mythological personage called Devi, wife of Mahadeo, her presence being indicated, as they believe, by some inflammable gases which issue from fissures in the rock. The name Jewala Muki is composed of two Sanscrit words,—*Jewala*, flame, and *Muki*, mouth. The flame, according to the legend, proceeds from the fire which Sati, the bride of Siva, created, and in which she burned herself. Siva, finding that this flame was about to consume the world, buried it in the hollow of the mountain. The temple is about twenty feet square, and the principal place of flame is a shallow trough, excavated in the floor, where it blazes without intermission. There are several jets of less importance. The gas also lies on the surface of some small reservoirs of water, and, when ignited, continues to burn for a short time. The roof of the temple is richly gilt, but the interior is blackened by the smoke of burned butter, sugar, and other gross offerings. In 1839, Runjeet Singh, when ill, made an offering of butter to the amount of 1,500*l.*, hoping the renovation of his health from the favour of the deity. The weight of the offering was probably about sixty or seventy tons; and Vigne, who was at the place while the burning was going forward, found "the stench similar to that of a candlemaker's shop." Near the principal temple is one smaller, called Gogranath, and hence concluded by Von Hügel to be of Buddhist origin. The ground adjoining to the group of sacred buildings is crowded with cows, Brahmins, pilgrims, and mendicants, and loaded with filth. The pilgrims, most of whom are paupers, are supported for one day from the funds of the temple. The town is dirty and neglected, but has an extensive bazar, containing great quantities of idols, votive garlands, rosaries, and other trumpery of the like description. The population is about 3,000. Near the town is a mineral spring, the water of which is found to be singularly efficacious in discussing bronchocele. Moorcroft was unable to analyze this water; but it probably contains some form of iodine, now known to possess much efficacy in resolving glandular tumours. Lat. 31° 53′, long. 76° 22′.

JEWUNPOOR, in the British district of Azimgurh, lieut.-gov. of the N.W. Provinces, a village on the eastern route from the town of Azimgurh to that of Goruckpoor, and 12 miles N.E. of the former, 60 miles N.E. of Benares. Lat. 26° 9′, long. 83° 24′.

JEWUR, or JEWAR, in the British district of Boolundshuhur, lieut.-gov. of the N.W. Provinces, a town on the route from Coel to Delhi, 36 miles N.W. of the former. The population is returned at 6,056. Lat. 28° 7′, long. 77° 39′.

JEYPOOR.—A considerable raj or territory of Rajpootana, named from its principal place.

This state, called anciently Amber, lies between lat. 25° 40′—27° 37′, long. 75° 8′—77° 20′; is about 150 miles in length from east to west, and 140 in breadth; having an area of 15,251 square miles. It in general is an extensive plain, though in the northern and north-western parts are insulated peaks, and clusters of dentated hills, here and there rising above the general level. They may be regarded as connected with a similar formation in the vicinity of Delhi. Jacquemont estimates their average elevation above the plain at about 300 feet. Their geological formation is quartz and granitoid rock, intermixed with white calcareous rock or marble, and occasionally mica. The country extending south of those hills is generally a level expanse of fine white sand, nearly devoid of vegetation, except where moistened by a spring or perennial rill, either of which is of very rare occurrence. A large portion of the soil is employed in grazing, and cattle are very numerous. Those parts of the territory which admit of cultivation, produce great crops of grain, pulse, cotton, and tobacco. The periodical rains are light, and confined to the close of summer, and there are few perennial streams. The Banganga, the most considerable of the transient torrents which traverse the country, is in winter and spring devoid of water. There are a few springs, but the water which they afford is soon absorbed by the sands. Water, however, may be obtained at all times by digging in the beds of torrents, and in most places is met with near the surface; so that wells need not be sunk to any great depth. From the naked, arid character of the soil, the temperature, during the prevalence of the hot winds, in the latter part of spring and beginning of summer, is dreadful, the thermometer frequently rising to 130° in the shade, and the heat proving fatal to men and beasts. In winter, however, the temperature is sometimes so low as to produce hoar frost. The population is a collection of various races, of which the most numerous are the Minas, supposed to be the aboriginal possessors of the country. Next, and nearly equal in number, are the Jats, who are extensive holders of land, and the most industrious and skilful agriculturists. Brahmins are numerous, being in greater proportion to the rest of the population than in any other state of Rajwara. Rajpoots, the ruling class, though inferior in number to the Minas and Jats, are conjectured to be still capable of mustering 30,000 men in arms. They are of the Kachwaha or Kashwaha tribe, according to tradition descended from Kash or Kasha, the son of Rama, and supposed to have originally come from Mount Aboo, but they are not considered equal in prowess to the Rahtors, the Haras, or some other Rajpoot tribes. Of less important tribes, the chief are the Banias, Dhakurs, and Gujurs. Tod estimates the relative density of the population of Shekawutti at 80, and the remainder of Jeypoor at 150 to the square mile, giving an average of 124 to the united area; and assuming this, the area being 15,251 miles, 1,891,124 would be the aggregate number of the inhabitants. Of the accuracy of the assumption on which this calculation is based, there are no sufficient means of judging; but it differs considerably from the view of Malcolm, who estimates the relative density of the population of Central India at ninety-eight to the square mile; which would yield an aggregate of only 1,494,598.

The revenue of Jeypoor has greatly fluctuated. It was estimated in round numbers at a crore of rupees, or a million sterling, during the most flourishing condition of the state. This was probably an exaggeration; but, however that may be, various causes combined to reduce the amount in 1802 to 81,83,000 rupees; a sum differing widely from that now realized, which, independent of feudal jaghires and charitable endowments, is returned at 45,83,950 rupees. Under a treaty concluded in April, 1818, Jeypoor became tributary to the East-India Company. For the first year no demand was to be made; for the second year the amount was fixed at four lacs of Delhi rupees; the third year at five lacs; the fourth year at six lacs; the fifth year at seven lacs. Thenceforward the annual tribute was to be eight lacs, until the revenues of the state should exceed forty lacs, when five-sixteenths of the excess was to be paid in addition to the eight lacs. In 1842, however, an arrear had accumulated amounting to no less than forty-six lacs. The whole of this was remitted, and the annual tribute fixed at four lacs. The military strength of Jeypoor and its dependencies comprises 2,096 cavalry, 18,377 infantry, 692 artillery, with 126 police; and with the addition of forces maintained by feudatories, 5,690, and of troops in garrison, 5,267, the total amounts to 32,248. The government is vested in an hereditary rajah; and when that dignity is held by an adult of firm character and talent, he engrosses nearly all power; but, as in most Eastern states, during a minority, or the reign of an imbecile prince, the country may be regarded as partitioned among the thakoors; each then becoming nearly, if not quite, independent in his estate and fort. The principal towns are noticed under their respective names in the alphabetical arrangement. The principal military routes are—1. From north-east to south-west, from Delhi to the city of Jeypoor, and thence to Mhow; 2. from east to west, from Agra to the city of Jeypoor, and thence to Ajmere; 3. from north-east to south-west, from Agra to Neemuch; 4. from east to west, from Calpee to Neemuch.

The Kachwaha Rajpoots, who founded the state of Jeypoor, claim descent from Kush, second son of Rama, king of Ayoda or Oude, whose reign is fixed at a very early period. After many centuries of wars and migrations, they overran the tract at present forming the state of Jeypoor, and, expelling or subjugating the Minas and Bingoogurs, founded the kingdom of Dhoondar or Amber, in 967, under the conduct of Dhola Rae, the first rajah. In the year 1200, Alauddin, the Patan king of Delhi, stormed the celebrated fortress of Rantambor, and put its defenders to the sword. At a later period, the rajah attached himself to the fortunes of Baber, and afterwards, as rajah of Amber, received from Humayon, about the year 1532, a munsab or commission of command over 5,000 men. A subsequent rajah gave his daughter in marriage to Selim, the son of Akbar, and afterwards padshah under the name of Jehangir. The alliance, however, proved unfortunate. Prince Khusroo, the offspring of the marriage, was hated by his father; and some circumstances in their disputes so affected the princess his mother, that she destroyed herself by poison. Khusroo aspired to succeed Akbar, in supersession of his father, but the attempt was unsuccessful, and he passed the rest of his days in captivity. Latterly he was intrusted to the charge of his brother Shah Jehan, another son of Jehangir, and afterwards padshah, in whose custody he died, not without suspicion of having been cut off by order of his brother. Under the reign of Arungzebe, Jey Singh, the rajah of Amber, was one of the most powerful and assiduous courtiers of that monarch, from whom he received a munsab or command of 7,000 men; and, amongst other services, he betrayed to his patron his rival brother, the rightful heir, Prince Dara. He also contrived to place in captivity Sevajee, the celebrated founder of the Mahratta sway, whom, however, he in some degree compensated by subsequently aiding in his escape. Aurungzebe becoming jealous of Jey Singh, caused him, it is said, to be poisoned. The munsab was reduced to Jey Singh's successor to 4,000 men, and to the third in succession to 3,000 men. The next prince, Jey Singh the Second, entered into the contest for the succession, which, on the death of Aurungzebe, arose among his sons. He supported the cause of Azim against his brother Moazzim; and, after the defeat and death of the former, was by the victor subjected to terms much more rigorous than were enforced on other Rajpoot princes. The course of events, however, favoured Jey Singh, and he was subsequently, it is believed, admitted to conditions not inferior to those granted to his most favoured brethren. At a later date, when Ferokshere was raised to the throne of Delhi, Jey Singh held a high command under him. When a powerful conspiracy threatened the ruin of that feeble-minded monarch, the Rajpoot steadily supported him; and having in vain urged him to resistance, on his murder retired to Amber. Jey Singh was high in favour with Mohammed Shah, successor of Ferokshere, and, on account of his great scientific attainments, was by that monarch intrusted with the reformation of the calendar; for which purpose he drew up astronomical tables, which, in honour of the Padshah, he named Zij Mohammadshahi, or "Tables of Mohammad Shah." For furthering astronomical pursuits, he erected observatories, and provided them with scientific apparatus of enormous magnitude, at Jeypoor, Benares, Muttra, Oojein, and Delhi. He also founded the city of Jeypoor, which remains a monument of his architectural skill. The career of Mahratta conquest towards the north and north-east appears to have been at first favourable to the aggrandizement of Jeypoor, which for a time made common cause with the new race of marauders, in seizing the fragments of the falling realm of Delhi, but itself soon became a sufferer from them. Scindia demanded heavy contributions, which being resisted, that chieftain marched with a large army to enforce them. He was, however, signally defeated. The defection and subsequent independence of the chief of Macherry or Alwar, about the year 1790, rent away a large portion of the territory of Jeypoor; and Tukajee Holkar, the Mahratta chief, invading the remainder, extorted an engagement for the payment of a large annual tribute, which was afterwards transferred to Ameer Khan. From this period the country was overrun and desolated by different parties of freebooters, who often fought among themselves for the spoil, till, in 1803, a treaty was concluded between Juggut Singh, rajah of Jeypoor, and the British government, but annulled by Sir George Barlow, governor-general, in 1805, contrary to the earnest remonstrances of Lord Lake. On this occasion, the Jeypoor agent observed to the British general, that this was the first time the English government had been known to make its faith subservient to its convenience. Jeypoor was now left to the mercy of the Mahrattas, whose desolating ravages reduced the finest tracts to the state of deserts. In 1818 another treaty was concluded, by which the British government agreed to protect Jeypoor, that state engaging to acknowledge its supremacy, to yield subordinate co-operation, and to pay tribute. Some hesitation was manifested by the durbar of the Jeypoor state in receiving the overtures of the British; the existence of which was ascribed, and probably with justice, to a fear that the stronger power might, as before, break the engagement when deemed inconvenient, leaving the weaker to the vengeance of the Mahrattas. But though saved from outrages of this kind, the country prospered not. Juggut Singh, the prince with whom the treaty was concluded, died in the same year in which it was executed. After a short interval, a posthumous son of the deceased rajah was acknowledged as his successor; and during his minority his mother assumed the regency. This authority she continued to exercise till her death, which occurred in 1831. Throughout this period, the most scandalous corruption, intrigue, and misgovernment prevailed, and shortly after the ranee's death, the British government found it necessary to move a force into Jeypoor, for the purpose of redressing the wrongs and correcting the abuses which had brought the country to a state which led to its being described by a traveller in 1835, as exhibiting "an empty treasury, desolate palaces, stagnating commerce, a ferocious populace, and a rabble army." The greater part of the country was in the hands of the thakoors or subordinate chiefs, each of whom possessed a military force, and as many retainers as he could keep together, exercising all the powers of government within his own district. These thakoors were in general engaged in quarrels and wars with each other, and frequently in combinations and contests against the ruling powers of the state, while marauders from neighbouring districts ravaged the country, sometimes even with the connivance of the rajah's minister, who closed his eyes to these outrages, and participated in the plunder. This man consummated his villanies by poisoning his master. He followed up the atrocity by attempts on the life of Major Alves, the Governor-General's agent, and his assistant, Mr. M. Blake, and against the latter was unhappily successful. It remains to be added, that the convicted contriver of these vile deeds was permitted to end his days in the fortress of Chunar, an example of lenity ill merited. The measures of the British government speedily introduced a better state of things; a regency during the minority of the infant successor of the murdered prince was appointed; financial reforms were commenced, and an approximation to at least something like the administration of justice made. The effect of the pervading influence of the British government is thus stated by Colonel Sutherland:—"A visible improvement has taken place in the condition of the fine and modern city of Jeypore itself, and generally throughout the country, while everywhere there is a sense of security and the prevalence of order, which, the people say, have been unknown during either of the last two reigns, and which they compare with what existed in the days of Jey Sing, the founder of the city of Jeypore." Subsequently, opportunity was found for the exercise of the charities of life; hospitals and dispensaries were established, of the benefits of which nearly 2,000 patients availed themselves within eight months. Of this number nearly seven-eighths were discharged cured, and only five persons died under treatment. The financial results under the influence of English authority were not less happy. The government, it is needless to add, was in debt; for all Indian governments, however hopeless their credit, contrive to accumulate debt. In 1843-44, 9,39,587 rupees of the public debt was paid off; and only 3,59,545 rupees remained due. Towards this reduction, 7,32,414 rupees, derived from the discovery of treasure formerly concealed by the infamous minister of Jeypoor, was made available. In 1844-45 the revenues exceeded the disbursements by 3,38,138 rupees, and the amount of debt was reduced by 49,777 rupees, leaving a balance of 3,09,768 rupees. In 1845-46 the receipts exceeded the disbursements by 5,14,012 rupees, and the state was free from debt. In 1851 the young chief completed his eighteenth year. He had in some degree been initiated into public business, and the British authorities entertaining a favourable opinion of his general fitness for the duties of his station, he was allowed to assume the reins of government, and exhorted to continue the beneficent system of administration under which his dominions during his minority had attained so high a degree of prosperity.

JEYPOOR.—A large city, the principal place of the territory of Jeypoor or Amber. It is situate in a small plain, or rather basin, conjectured to be the bed of a dried-up lake, having on all sides, except the south, barren stony hills, crowned in many places with forts. On the north, the hill rises above the town several hundred feet, and on this is built the citadel, which "has a very bold appearance when viewed from the town, the south face of the rocks being very precipitous, and totally inaccessible." It is approachable, however, on the north, where the rock slopes gradually towards the antique town of Amber. The town of Jeypoor is about two miles in length from east to west, the breadth about one mile. It "is entirely surrounded by a wall of masonry, with lofty towers and well-protected gateways, but the ramparts are too thin to offer an effectual resistance even to field artillery, and they are so low, that the shifting sands have in some places drifted against the outside of the wall nearly as high as the parapet, totally obliterating the ditch, if ever there was one." There are seven gateways, in no manner differing from each other. Outside the rampart, another wall runs parallel to it, embattled at the top, and having numerous loopholes for musketry. It is considered to be the most handsome and regularly built of the cities laid down by native Indians. A main street, two miles in length, and forty yards in breadth, extends from east to west. This is intersected by several streets of about forty yards in width, and at each point of intersection is a chauk or market-square. "The cross-streets are in their turn intersected at right angles by narrower streets, and the latter are again subdivided in a similar manner by lanes, which are aligned with equal accuracy; so that nearly the whole city is portioned out into rectangular blocks." "The palace, gardens, and royal premises, occupy the whole of the central block, being half a mile long." The front of the royal residence is extremely high, having seven or eight stories, and is flanked at each extremity by a lofty tower, surmounted by a cupola. Within are two spacious courts, and several of smaller dimensions, surrounded by cloisters, with stone pillars. The garden, which is surrounded by a high embattled wall, terraced at top, and cloistered below, is "extremely beautiful, full of fountains, cypresses, palm, and flowering shrubs, with a succession of terraces and alcoves, none of them, singly taken, in good taste, but, all together, extremely rich and striking." Jacquemont states that there are in this vast residence fully a dozen palaces, communicating either by galleries or gardens. The most remarkable apartment is the Diwani Khas, or hall of audience, a splendid oblong room, entirely built of white marble, which material is also profusely employed throughout in the construction of the palaces. The houses in the principal streets are in general finely built of stone; and numerous mosques and temples add to the architectural splendour of the town. The arsenal contains a furnace for casting, and machinery for boring guns; but none have lately been made here. There are some antique cannon of enormous dimensions, constructed of wrought-iron bars, laid longitudinally, and kept together by a coat of gun-metal founded around them; but they are totally unserviceable. The huge observatory, erected here by Jai Singh, is in good preservation, but no pundit of the place has skill to make use of it. Besides the huge dials, azimuth-circles, altitude-pillars, and such other bulky instruments, of masonry, there are some brazen altitude-circles of enormous size and great weight. Jeypoor was built in the early part of the eighteenth century, by the celebrated Sewae Jai Singh, rajah of Dhoondar or Amber, and, having named it after himself, he hither removed his residence and court from the adjacent city of Amber, now desolate. Distant direct from Agra, W., 140 miles; from Delhi, S.W., 150; Allahabad, N.W., 400; Calcutta, N.W., 850. Lat. 26° 56′, long. 75° 55′.

JEYPOOR.—A town in the British district of Seebpoor, province of Assam, 43 miles E.N.E. of Seebpoor. The place some years ago had been selected as a military station, but, in consequence of its insalubrity, the home authorities suggested the removal of the troops. Coalfields abound in the vicinity. Lat. 27° 14′, long. 95° 19′.

JEYPOOR, in Orissa, a town in the native zemindarry of the same name, on the south-west frontier of Bengal, situate 111 miles N.W. from Vizagapatam, and 69 miles W. by S. from Ryaguddah. The territory of which this town is the principal place is bounded on the north by the petty state of Calahandy and the Koond tribes; on the east by the British collectorate of Vizagapatam; on the south by the river Godavery; and on the west by the territory of Nagpore. It lies between lat. 17° 15′—19° 45′, long. 81° 28′—83° 53′. Its length from north-east to south-west is 212 miles, and its breadth 100. The area is computed at 13,041 square miles, and the population at 391,230. The tract is held by a number of chiefs, styled hill zemindars, who collectively pay an annual tribute of 16,000 rupees, or 1,600*l.*, to the British government. The tribute has occasionally fallen into arrear, owing to internal dissensions, in which the British government have declined to interfere. Indeed, from the wild state of the country, access to the interior is scarcely practicable, and a further barrier is imposed, in the pestilential nature of the climate. An alleged instance of human sacrifice in this territory was some time since brought to the notice of the British government, and measures were instantly adopted for the suppression of the barbarous practice. The town of Jeypoor is in lat. 19° 1′, long. 82° 27′.

JEYPOOR.—A town in one of the recently sequestrated districts of Hyderabad, or dominions of the Nizam, 68 miles W.S.W. of Ellichpoor. Lat. 20° 45′, long. 76° 39′.

JEYT, or JYNT, in the British district of Muttra, lieut.-gov. of the N.W. Provinces, a small town or village on the route from the cantonment of Muttra to Ferozpur, and 10 miles N.W. of the former. It has water from wells, and also from a tank. Lat. 27° 35′, long. 77° 40′.

JEYTPOOR, in the British district of Sohagpoor, territory of Saugor and Nerbudda, lieut.-gov. of the N.W. Provinces, a town on the route from Sohagpoor to Sasseram, 25 miles N.E. of the former. Lat. 23° 30′, long. 81° 49′.

JHAJPOOR, in the Rajpoot state of Oodeypoor or Mewar, a town on the route from Nusseerabad to Saugor, 63 miles S.E. of former, 287 N.W. of latter. It has a good bazar, and supplies and water are abundant. Here is a fortress on an isolated oblong hill, guarding the eastern entrance of an important pass from the lowlands of Boondee into the territory of Oodeypoor or Mewar. It is large and strong, and consists of two similar ramparts, one within the other, a considerable space intervening. Each has a good ditch and numerous round bastions. The town lies north-west of the fort, at the foot of the hill, and is large, well built, and fortified. The pergunnah of Jhajpoor, of which it is the principal place, contains 100 townships, inhabited by the indigenous tribe Mina, who muster 4,000 bowmen. Lat. 25° 40′, long. 75° 21′.

JHALLAWAR, in the peninsula of Kattywar, province of Guzerat, a district named from the Jhalla tribe of Rajpoots, who are the principal part of the population. It extends over the north-eastern part of the peninsula, and is bounded on the north by the Runn or Salt-marsh, connected with the eastern extremity of the Gulf of Cutch; on the east by the British district of Ahmedabad; on the south by the British district of Ahmedabad and the prant or district of Kattywar; on the south-west by the prant of Hallar; on the west by the prant of Muchockanta; and lies between lat. 22° 18′—23° 8′, long. 70° 50′—72° 10′. No official return has been made of the area; but, by a probable approximation, it may be stated at 3,000 square miles.

JHALLODE, in the territory of Scindia, a town on the route from Neemuch to Baroda, 181 miles S.W. of former, 108 N.E. of latter. It was formerly of importance, being the principal place of a pergunnah of the kingdom of Guzerat, containing seventeen towns, and it is still a considerable place. It has a bazar, a mosque, a small temple, a large and fine tank, and some well-built houses of brick, two stories high, and covered with tiles. Lat. 23° 7′, long. 74° 9′.

JHALLOWA.—A small raj, formed in the year 1838 by a division of the Rajpoot state of Kota. The circumstances which led to this division (which are of singular character) will be found detailed in the article KOTA. It is divided into three separate portions, the largest of which extends from lat. 24° 6′ to 24° 40′, and from long. 76° 30′ to 76° 58′. The area a little exceeds 2,200 square miles, and the population, according to the rate of estimate usually adopted for this part of India, would be upwards of 220,000. Upon the death of the late chief of Jhallowa, in 1848, a suttee took place; and in consequence of this violation of existing engagements, the British government withheld for a time their formal recognition of the present ruler. Precautions were subsequently taken to prevent a recurrence of the atrocious practice, and friendly intercourse between the two governments was re-established.

JHALOO, in the British district of Bijnour, lieut.-gov. of the N.W. Provinces, a town, the principal place of the pergunnah of the same name. It has a population of 6,551, and is situate in lat. 29° 20′, long. 78° 17′.

JHALRA PATUN, in Rajpootana, a town in the Jhallowa division of the state of Kota, situate on the route from Neemuch to Saugor, 90 miles E. of the former, 216 N.W. of the latter. It is a handsome and well-built town, the modern part of which was laid down by Zalim Singh, the regent of Kota, on the model of Jeypoor. Distant from Oogein, N., 100 miles; from Kotah, S.E., 50; from Agra, S.W., 215. Lat. 24° 32′, long. 76° 13′.

JHANDINOOR, or JENDIPOOR, in the British district of Agra, lieut.-gov. of the N.W. Provinces, a village on the route from the city of Agra to that of Muttra, and 25 miles N.W. of the former. Lat. 27° 22′, long. 77° 49′.

JHANSI.—A British province in Bundlecund. It consists of two parts, lying nearly contiguous to each other, being separated only by a narrow slip of territory belonging to the native raj of Tehree. The western division is bounded on the north by Gwalior and Dutteah; on the east by Tehree; on the south and west by Gwalior. The eastern portion is bounded on the north-west by the British district of Jaloun; on the east by that of Hummeerpoor; on the south and south-west by Tehree. The combined territory lies between lat. 24° 55′ and 25° 48′, long. 77° 53′ and 79° 31′, and extends from east to west about 100 miles, and from north to south about 60. In 1832 it was estimated to have an area of 2,922 square miles, 956 villages, and a population of 286,000. Since that period, however, the limits of the district have been contracted by alienation, and consequently the above-quoted estimates do not, in respect either of extent or population, represent its present condition. Probably 390 miles should be subtracted from the area as above stated, and 86,000 persons from the population.

The tract was formerly part of the possessions of the Boondela rajah of Oorcha. Subsequently, it fell into the hands of the Peishwa, and was assigned to the administration of one of his officers in the character of soubahdar. In 1804 a treaty of defensive alliance was concluded by the British with the then soubahdar, as a tributary of the Peishwa. In 1817, consequent on the cession to the East-India Company of the Peishwa's rights in Bundelcund, a second treaty was concluded by the British government with the soubahdar of Jhansi, by which he was acknowledged "hereditary ruler" of the territory, subject to the payment of an annual tribute of 74,000 rupees (Jhansi currency). In 1832 he was permitted to assume the title of rajah. Ram Ramchund Rao, the ruler on whom this dignity was conferred, died in 1835, without issue. Various claimants to the succession thereupon appeared, but the British government decreed in favour of Rao Rugonath Rao, the uncle and next of kin of the deceased rajah. He died about three years after his accession; his brief period of rule having been rendered unquiet by opposition to his claim, professedly grounded on the fact of his being a leper, which was asserted to be a disqualification for the occupation of the seat of power. Rugonath Rao left no legitimate issue, and the succession became again the subject of contending claims. Some of these were obviously inadmissible, and the propriety of at once sanctioning any of them appeared very questionable, regard being had to the distracted state of the country, which had greatly deteriorated in condition, from continued misgovernment; the revenue (which is said at one period to have been eighteen lacs of rupees) having fallen from twelve lacs, its amount in 1832, to three lacs. Under these circumstances, it was deemed advisable that the Governor-General's agent in Bundelcund should assume the administration, the various claims to the raj being reserved for future adjudication. This step was accordingly taken, though not without opposition; the mother of Ramchund Rao, who espoused the cause of one of the claimants to the succession, having compelled the British government to make military demonstration before she would quit the fort of Jhansi. A commission appointed to investigate the different claims, unanimously rejected all except that of Baba Gunghadar Rao, brother of the late chief, and the only surviving male descendant of Sheo Rao Bhow, with whom, as soubahdar, the first engagement of the East-India Company with Jhansi was concluded. The selection was approved by the home authorities; but the new rajah was not of strong intellect, and was therefore thought unequal to the task of retrieving the principality from the state of disorder into which it had fallen It was thereupon determined to carry on the administration by British agency, giving the rajah a fixed allowance, with the understanding that the administration should be made over to him partially, or entirely, when it should be deemed safe to trust it to his hands. This plan, thus dictated by temporary necessity, was attended with such success, that the revenue, which, as already mentioned, had fallen so disastrously, was in one year considerably more than doubled. To provide for defence, and to maintain tranquillity, the Jaloun force (afterwards called the Bundelcund legion) was increased, and made available for the service of this state, as well as of that for the protection of which it had originally been raised. After a few years of British management, the country having attained that state in which it appeared safe to make the transfer always contemplated, it was given up to the management of its native chief, subject to a cession of territory, in commutation of the annual payment previously made towards the support of the Bundelcund legion, and to other necessary conditions. This took place in 1843. Baba Gunghadar Rao dying in 1854 without lineal heirs, the territory of Jhansi lapsed to the British government.

JHANSI, in Bundelcund, a town, the principal place of the small territory of the same name, lies on the route from Agra to Saugor. Hunter, who visited the place in 1792, says, "It is frequented by the caravans from the Deccan, which go to Furruckabad and the other cities of the Dooab. Hence, an afflux of wealth, which is augmented by a considerable trade in the cloths of Chanderi, and by the manufacture of bows, arrows, and spears, the principal weapons of the Boondela tribe." The town is situate amidst tanks and groves of fine timber-trees, and is surrounded by a good wall. On a rock overlooking the town, is a fortress, or castellated residence of the former rajahs, a lofty mass of building, of stone, more striking from being surmounted by a huge round tower. This fort is said to have between thirty and forty pieces of cannon. It was built by the Mahrattas, from whom it was wrested in 1761, and for some time detained by the nawaub of Oude, who reduced it almost to ruins. The streets and bazars are clean and orderly, great attention having been paid to their due regulation. There is another hill 600 yards south-east of that on which the fort is situate, and of nearly equal elevation to it. Jhansi is 142 miles S. of Agra, 130 miles N. of Saugor, 245 miles W. of Allahabad by Banda, and 740 N.W. of Calcutta by Allahabad. Lat. 25° 28′, long. 78° 38′.

JHARI.—A town in the native state of Nepal, situate on the right bank of the San Coos river, and 20 miles N.E. from Khatmandoo. Lat. 27° 50′, long. 85° 34′.

JHAROWLEE.—A town in the Rajpoot state of Seeronee, 51 miles W.N.W. from Oodeypoor, and 10 miles E.S.E. from Seerooee. Lat. 24° 55′, long. 73° 4′.

JHARSAINTULEE, or JHARSOUTLI, in the jaghire of Bullubgurh, lieut.-gov. of the N.W. Provinces, a village on the route from Delhi to Muttra, and 29 miles S. of the former. Lat. 28° 18′, long. 77° 21′.

JHARSUH, in the British district of Goorgaon, lieut.-gov. of the N.W. Provinces, a town on the route from Rewaree to Delhi, 20 miles S.W. of the latter. It is situate to the south of a rocky range of quartzose formation, and contains a bazar, with a good supply of water. Lat. 28° 24′, long. 77° 6′.

JHEEND.—A small native territory within the limits of the tract of country over which the British government maintains a controlling power, through the commissioner and superintendent of the Cis-Sutlej states. Some years since, the territory lapsed, from failure of direct heirs, and possession was taken of it; but, in 1837, the larger portion was granted to a collateral heir. In 1842, the revenue of the state thus constituted was estimated at three lacs of rupees, or 30,000*l.*; but this estimate is inapplicable to the present condition of the state, as, on the conclusion of the war with Lahore, an accession of territory was bestowed on the rajah, in consideration of his fidelity during that contest. The possessions of this state being made up of scattered portions of territory, there is much difficulty in dealing with them as a whole; but they are returned as having an area of 376 square miles, and a population of about 56,000 persons. The British government, in granting to the rajah an extension of dominion, took advantage of the opportunity furnised by the act of favour, to promote the cause of public improvement, and advance the interests of humanity, by binding the rajah to abolish transit-duties, to make and keep in repair a military road, and to suppress suttee, infanticide, and slave-dealing.

JHEEND, in Sirhind, a town situate on Feroz Shah's canal, in a naturally fertile country, but which, in consequence of deficient cultivation, is extensively overrun with jungle, especially of dakh (Butea frondosa). It is a considerable town, and is the chief place of the native state bearing the same name: there is a good bazar, and a palace, the residence of the rajah. The road in this part of the route, which is in general good, crosses the canal by a bridge. Supplies are abundant. Jheend is distant N.W. from Calcutta 979 miles. Lat. 29° 19′, long. 76° 23′.

JHELUM, or BEHUT.—A river of the Punjab, and the most western of the five great rivers which intersect that region east of the Indus. It rises in Cashmere, the whole valley of which it drains, making its way to the Punjab, through the Pass of Baramula, in the lofty range of Pir Panjal. Its most remote source is the head of what is regarded by some as its principal feeder, the Lidur, which rises in the mountain-range bounding the valley on the north-east, and in lat. 34° 8′, long. 75° 48′; and, having drained the small mountain-lake called Shesha Nag, takes a south-westerly course of about fifty miles, to its confluence with the Breng, flowing from the south-east. About ten miles to the north-west, this united stream forms a junction with a large feeder flowing from the south, and itself formed by the junction of the Sandren, the Veshau, the Huripur, and some other streams of less importance, none having a length of course exceeding forty miles. Of these, the Veshau is the principal, and, according to Vigne, so far exceeds in size the other upper feeders of the Jhelum, that its fountain-head should be regarded as properly the source of that great river. The Veshau flows by a subterraneous passage from Kosah Nag, a small but deep lake, situate near the top of the Pir Panjal Mountain, and at an elevation of about 12,000 feet above the level of the sea. Here, Vigne states, "its full strong torrent is suddenly seen gushing out from the foot of the last and lofty eminence that forms the dam on the western end of the lake, whose waters thus find an outlet, not over, but through, the rocky barrier with which it is surrounded." This remarkable spot is in lat. 33° 35′, long. 74° 43′. The stream thus produced and reinforced, subsequently receives numerous small feeders; passes through the City Lake, the Manasa Lake, and the Wulur or Great Lake, and sweeps through the country, confined by embankments, which prevent it from overflowing the lower part of the valley. Previously to entering the Wulur, it receives a considerable tributary named the Sinde, which rises in the lofty range bounding the valley on the north. The whole course of the Jhelum through the valley, before it finds an outlet through the Pass of Baramula into the lower ground of the Punjab, is about 130 miles, for seventy of which it is navigable. It is the opinion of Vigne, that the river made its way gradually through this pass, and thus drained the lake, which, according to tradition, formerly occupied the site of the valley. At Baramula, where the stream is 420 feet broad, is a bridge of seven arches. At Mozafarabad, about 205 miles from its source, it is joined by the Kishengunga, a stream of nearly equal volume, which rises in Little Tibet, receives a considerable tributary from the valley of Gurys, and subsequently makes its way through the mountains stretching from Cashmere to the vicinity of Attock. The united stream takes a course nearly due south, from Mozafarabad, and about 255 miles from its source, leaves the mountains, and enters on the plain of the Punjab, near the town of Ohind, whence it is navigable to the Indus. It is here a very great stream, though considered by Burnes less than the Chenaub. Von Hügel at the commencement of January, when the rivers of the Punjab are lowest, crossed it at the town of Jhelum, sixty-five miles lower down, on a bridge of twenty large boats, and estimated it to have a greater volume of water than the Indus at Attock. Moorcroft, at the same place, found it in the middle of October 150 yards wide, and from twelve to sixteen feet deep, but 600 yards wide at a short distance both above and below that point, and flowing at the rate of about a mile an hour. At this place the direction of the Jhelum changes from southerly to south-westerly. At Jelalpoor, from which point Burnes descended by a boat to Pind Dadun Khan, the stream was muddy but rapid, with a current of three or four miles an hour. Elphinstone crossed the river at Jelalpoor, in July, when he found it one mile, one furlong, and thirty-five perches wide, with a depth of from nine to fourteen feet, and a current running four miles an hour. It abounds in fish, and is infested by great numbers of crocodiles. Below Jelalpoor, it takes a direction nearly southerly, and joins the Chenaub a little above the ferry of Trimo, in lat. 31° 10′, long. 72° 9′, after a course of about 490 miles. The Jhelum was, at the confluence, when observed by Burnes at the end of June, about 500 yards wide. After the union, the channel of the united waters was a mile broad and twelve feet deep. The Jhelum was unquestionably the Hydaspes of the Greeks. It is still known to the Hindoos of the vicinity by the name of *Betusta*, corrupted by the Greeks, according to their usage with respect to foreign names. The scene of the battle between Porus and Alexander is generally placed at Jelalpoor.

JHELUM.—A town of the Punjab, on the right bank of the river of the same name. Jhelum is a town of considerable extent, with a population mostly Mahomedan. It is, however, rendered unhealthy by the inundation, which extends widely over the eastern bank of the river. The principal crops in the vicinity are wheat, barley, and cotton. During the season when the river is lowest, there is a ford nearly a mile above the town. The passable part of the bed describes two sides of a triangle, the vertex of which is down the river. By this ford the British army crossed in the middle of December, 1839, in its return from Afghanistan; and though this is the low season, several were swept down the stream, and eleven persons, including an officer, drowned. Hough, who was present on the occasion, states, "the ford extended over a line of about 500 yards, and had more than three feet water, and a strong current near the south bank." It is obvious that, for the greater part of the year, the ford must be totally impassable. The elevation of Jhelum above the sea is estimated at 1,620 feet. It is expected that steam communication between Kurrachee and this town will shortly be established by means of government vessels. Lat. 32° 56′, long. 73° 47′.

JHINJANUH, in the British district of Mozuffurnuggur, lieut.-gov. of the N.W. Provinces, a town on the route from Kurnal to Meerut, and 21 miles S.E. of the former. Lat. 29° 31′, long. 77° 17′.

JHIRREE, in the territory of Gwalior, or possessions of Scindia's family, a town on the route from Calpee to Kotah, 187 miles S.W. of former, 134 E. of latter. It has a bazar, and is supplied with water from a jhil or small lake. Lat. 25° 33′, long. 77° 28′.

JHOK, in Sinde, a village on the route from Hydrabad to Meerpoor, and 35 miles S. of the former town. It is situate in the fertile alluvial tract insulated by the Indus and its great offsets the Fulailee and Pinyaree. The adjacent country is described by Pottinger as very fine, and capable of producing rich crops. Lat. 24° 47′, long. 68° 25′.

JHOONEE, in the British district of Kumaon, lieut.-gov. of the N.W. Provinces, a village on the route, up the course of the river Surjoo, from Almorah to the Unta Dura Pass, 40 miles N.E. of Almorah fort. It is situate on the right bank of the Surjoo, five miles below its source. Lat. 30° 7′, long. 80° 3′.

JHOONJHNOO, in the Rajpoot state of Shekawuttee, a town on the route from Delhi to Bikaneer, 120 miles S.W. of former, 130 E. of latter. It is a handsome town, with trees and gardens, the appearance of which is the more agreeable, as they occur in the midst of a dreary sandy desert. Here, during the existence of the Shekawuttee confederacy, each of its five chiefs had a stronghold; but these were subsequently occupied by British garrisons. Lat. 28° 5′, long. 75° 32′.

JHOORH.—A town in the Rajpoot state of Jodhpoor, 18 miles N.N.E. from Jodhpoor, and 103 miles S. from Beekaneer. Lat. 26° 32′, long. 73° 13′.

JHOOSEE, or JHOUSEE.—The principal place of the pergunnah of the same name, a town on the left bank of the Ganges, close to the confluence of the Jumna. It is opposite the city of Allahabad, with which it communicates by a ferry across the Ganges. A more frequented communication between the left bank of the river and the British cantonments, which adjoin the city on the north, is at Daraganj, two miles higher up. The bed of the river is there a mile in width, but in the dry season the stream occupies only a third of it, the remainder being used as a road. It is always heavy, either from sand or mud. This ferry has thirty boats, and troops and stores are passed free of charge. In some seasons the Ganges is impassable here by ferry, in consequence of shifting sands, and the passage must then be made at Papamow, five miles higher up. These sands form a great obstruction to the navigation of the Ganges below Cawnpore. It flows "in a race" over a shifting channel in the dry season, and has a very strong current (in some places seven miles an hour) during the rains. Distant N.W. from Calcutta, by water, 810 miles; by land, 503. Lat. 25° 26′, long. 81° 58′.

JHOOSHARA JHOLE, in Gurhwal, a village on the left bank of the Bhageerettee, as the Ganges is called in the upper part of its course. The river, here about thirty yards wide, is traversed by a bridge made of ropes, with a footway of rude wicker-work. Jhooshara is in lat. 30° 43′, long. 78° 29′.

JHOREGA.—A town in the British district of Candeish, presidency of Bombay, 12 miles N.E. of Malligaum. Lat. 20° 40′, long. 74° 40′.

JHOWANU, in the Rajpoot territory of Alwur, under the political superintendence of the Governor-General's agent for Rajpootana, a village 40 miles S.W. of Delhi. Lat. 28° 10′, long. 76° 54′.

JHOWLYE.—A town in the Rajpoot state of Jeypoor, situate on the left bank of the Bangunga river, and 20 miles E. by N. from Jeypoor. Lat. 27°, long. 76° 13′.

JHUGERPOOR.—A town in the native state of Rygurh, on the south-west frontier of Bengal, 62 miles N.W. from Sumbulpoor, and 124 miles S.W. from Lohadugga. Lat. 22° 10′, long. 83° 25′.

JHUGGEE.—A town of Sinde, in the British district of Hydrabad, presidency of Bombay, 58 miles S.E. of Tatta. Lat. 24°, long. 68° 25′.

JHUJHUR, with DADREE.—A native state within the Delhi agency, and subject to the jurisdiction of the lieut.-gov. of the N.W. Provinces. It is bounded on the north by the British districts of Hurriana and Rohtuk; on the east by Delhi, Goorgaon, and Alwur; on the south by Goorgaon and the territory of the Alwur rajah; and on the west by Shekawutty and the pergunnah of Loharoo. It lies between lat. 27° 55′—28° 55′, long. 75° 55′—76° 58′, and has an area of about 1,230 square miles. The general elevation of the country may be estimated at 820 to 840 feet above the level of the sea, as, in the rainy season, it is pervaded by numerous watercourses having a very slight declivity, and which, about thirty miles to the eastward of the territory, discharge themselves into the Jumna, by a channel close to the north side of the city of Delhi, at an elevation of 800 feet. The south-western part is intersected by numerous low rocky ranges, like those of the adjacent territory of Patun. The jaghire is traversed from north to south by the military route from Hansee to Nusseerabad and Neemuch, and from west to east by the route leading from the town of Dadree to that of Jhujhur. The principal places are Jhujhur, Narnot, Dojana, Dadree, and Kanound. The annual revenue is estimated at 60,000*l*. The nawaub maintains a military force of about 3,000 men, and is bound to furnish 400 cavalry when demanded by the British government. The jaghire being well managed, is in a prosperous condition. If the population be estimated at ninety to the square mile, the average of the adjacent district of Hurriana, it will amount to 110,700. This jaghire was assigned by Lord

Lake to Nijabut Ally Khan, of the Bhuraitch family, in consequence of his services against the Mahrattas, from whom it was taken; and in 1806 the grant was confirmed in perpetuity by the Governor-General. Fyze Ally Khan, the present nawaub, grandson of the original grantee, succeeded in 1835.

JHUJHUR, the principal place of the jaghire of the same name, and the residence of the nawaub, lies on the route from Hansee to Muttra, by Goorgaon, and 60 miles S.E. of the former place. At the close of the last century, it was by the Mahrattas assigned, with some other places, to the adventurer George Thomas, in reward of his services, and was for some time the capital of his short-lived state. Distant W. from Delhi 35 miles. Lat. 28° 35′, long. 76° 43′.

JHULLAEE, or JELLAH, in the native state of Jeypore, in Rajpootana, a town on the route from Nusseerabad to Gwalior, 82 miles E. of former, 160 W. of latter. It is of considerable size, is fortified, and water and supplies are abundant. Lat. 26° 8′, long. 76° 10′.

JHUPUHAO.—A town in the British district of Tirhoot, lieut.-gov. of Bengal, 47 miles N.N.E. of Dinapoor. Lat. 26° 12′, long. 85° 29′.

JHURRIE.—A river rising in the British district of Goruckpoor, lieut.-gov. of the N.W. Provinces, about 18 miles N. of the town of Pudrownan, and in about lat. 27° 5′, long. 84° 3′. "Its source is a channel about thirty yards wide, and sunk very deep. In February the stream might be twenty feet wide, knee-deep, and not rapid." After a course of about six miles, it joins a branch of the Gunduk, and the united streams flow southerly for thirty miles, when, below and east of Pudrownan, they again separate. The Jhurrie takes a southerly course for thirty-six miles, when it crosses over into the British district Sarun, through which it flows in the same direction for about twenty miles. It then forms for ten miles the boundary between the two districts of Goruckpore and Sarun, after which, passing into the latter, and continuing to flow southward through it for twenty-eight miles, it falls into the Ghaghra on the left side, in lat. 26°, long. 84° 11′, having a total course of 130 miles. At Hosipoor, in lat. 26° 24′, long. 84° 12′, it is crossed by the route from Dinapoor to Goruckpoor, and is there so considerable that the passage must be made by a temporary bridge.

JHUSDUM.—A town in Guzerat, or the dominions of the Guicowar, situate on the right bank of the Bhader river, and 30 miles E.S.E. from Rajkote. Lat. 22° 5′, long. 71° 15′.

JIGAT.—See DWARKA.

JIGNEE, in Bundelcund, a town near the right bank of the river Dessaun, is the principal place of the jaghire or feudal grant of the same name, held from the East-India Company, under the political superintendence of the lieut.-governor of the N.W. Provinces. The jaghire is estimated to contain twenty-seven square miles, with a population of 2,800. Its revenue is estimated at 1,500*l.* per annum. The jaghiredar maintains nineteen horse and fifty-one foot. In 1840, the mal-administration of the jaghire having become intolerable, managers responsible to the British authorities were appointed. Jignee is 33 miles S.W. of Calpee. Lat. 25° 45′, long. 79° 28′.

JILLBERAH, in Sirhind, a village on the route from Kurnal to Patiala, and 45 miles N.W. of the former town. It is situate in a level country, which, though fertile, is imperfectly cultivated and overrun with jungle. The road lies westward of the trunk line from Calcutta, and notwithstanding the even surface of the country, is bad, and scarcely practicable for guns or carriages. Distant N.W. from Calcutta 1,010 miles. Lat. 30° 12′, long. 76° 40′.

JILLING SIRRING.—A town in the British district of Chota Nagpoor, lieut.-gov. of Bengal, 71 miles E. by S. of Lohadugga. Lat. 23° 11′, long. 85° 51′.

JIMPOOR, in Sinde, a village near the route from Kurrachee to Hyderabad, and 32 miles S.W. of the latter place. It is situate in the Doab, or tract between the Irak and Rodh rivers, and five miles N.W. of the *Dund*, or small lake of Kunjur, into which they discharge themselves. Lat. 24° 57′, long. 68° 4′.

JIMRU RIVER.—The name of a considerable feeder of the Raptee river, rising in lat. 28° 46′, long. 82° 10′, and, flowing through Nepaul in a southerly direction for eighty miles, falls into the Raptee, in lat. 28° 2′, long. 81° 54′.

JINDALA, in the Reechna Dooab division of the Punjab, a town situated twenty-two miles from the right bank of the Ravee, and 26 miles N.W. of the town of Lahore. Lat. 31° 49′, long. 73° 46′.

JINGERGATCHEA.—A town in the British district of Jessore, lieut.-gov. of Bengal, 54 miles N.E. of Calcutta. Lat. 23° 4′, long. 89° 6′.

JINJEERA, on the coast of Bombay, a district and harbour, sometimes called the Harbour of Rajapoor, from the town of that name situate on the northern point of land forming the entrance of the harbour. "This is an excellent harbour, without any bar, having from four to five fathoms in the entrance, and the same depths inside, at low water, where there is shelter from all winds." Off the mainland is the fortified island of Jinjeera, formerly regarded as a place of high importance. During the existence of the Mussulman monarchy of Beejapoor, it was the principal depôt of the maritime force of the Seedee or African admiral of that state, who held his dignity on condition of maintaining a fleet for the protection of commerce, and conveying pilgrims to the Red Sea. After the rise of the power of the Mahrattas, it was attacked repeatedly, but in vain, by Sevajee. On one occasion, the garrison revolted, and placed the fort in the hands of Aurungzebe. Rajapoor, on the mainland, had previously been taken by the Mahrattas. In 1682, Sambajee, son of Sevajee, besieged the island, which he attempted to connect by means of a mole with the mainland; but the project failed, and in other attempted modes of attack, the assailants were repulsed with great loss. On the decline of the realm of Delhi, the Seedee or chief of Jinjeera assumed independence, which he and his successors maintained more or less effectually, and the petty power still exists, under the protection of the East-India Company. The Jinjeera principality lies between lat. 18° and 18° 32′, and its revenues are computed at 17,500*l.* The title Seedee or Hubshee is one given in India to Abyssinians, and hence the territory is designated that of the "Hubsies."

JINJINEALLA.—A town in the Rajpoot native state of Jessulmeer, 48 miles S. by W. from Jessulmeer, and 148 miles W. from Jodhpoor. Lat. 26° 16′, long. 70° 48′.

JINKIPUDDA.—A town in the Cuttack mehal of Moburbunge, 84 miles N.E. by N. from Cuttack, and 30 miles W. from Balasore. Lat. 21° 32′, long. 86° 33′.

JINSI, in the territory of Gwalior, a village on the route from Gwalior to Saugor, six miles S.E. of the Residency. Here, before the reduction of the military force of Gwalior, was located the Mahratta artillery, well known for the number and excellence of their guns and the skill with which they were served. Lat. 26° 11′, long. 78° 10′.

JINTEA.—A town in the British district of Dinajepoor, lieut.-gov. of Bengal, 17 miles N. by E. of Dinajepoor. Lat. 25° 48′, long. 88° 42′.

JINTOOR.—A town in Hyderabad, or dominions of the Nizam, situate 135 miles E. by N. from Ahmednuggur, and 121 miles S.W. by S. from Ellichpoor. Lat. 19° 39′, long. 76° 43′.

JIRAMEYEE, in the British district of Mynpooree, lieut.-gov. of the N.W. Provinces, a village on the route from the city of Agra to the cantonment of Mynpooree, and seven miles W. of the latter. Lat. 27° 14′, long. 79° 1′.

JITHAREE.—A town of Malwa, in the native state of Bhopal, 82 miles E. from Bhopal, and 87 miles W. from Jubbulpoor. Lat. 23° 14′, long. 78° 40′.

JOA, in the Punjab, a large and flourishing town in the Salt range, about 50 miles E. of the Indus. Here are said to be satisfactory indications of the existence of good coal. Lat. 32° 50′, long. 72° 30′.

JOAGUR. — A town in Hyderabad, or dominions of the Nizam, 81 miles W. from Hyderabad, and 111 miles E.N.E. from Beejapoor. Lat. 17° 23′, long. 77° 20′.

JOAR, or JUWAR, in the British district of Allygurh, lieut.-gov. of the N.W. Provinces, a town on the route from the cantonment of Allygurh to that of Muttra, and 24 miles S.W. of the former. It has a bazar. Joar was plundered in 1805, by the Patan freebooter Ameer Khan, during his inroad into the Doab. Lat. 27° 36′, long. 77° 58′.

JOBNEER, in the Rajpoot state of Jeypoor, a town on the route from Delhi to Nusseerabad, 177 miles S.W. of former, 66 N.E. of latter. It has a bazar, and supplies and water are abundant. Lat. 26° 56′, long. 75° 28′.

JOBUT.—A town of Malwa, situate under the Vindhya Mountains, 23 miles S. from Jabboah. Lat. 22° 25′, long. 74° 40′. The petty Bheel state of which this town is the principal place yields a revenue of about 10,000 rupees, or 1,000*l.*, per annum. Upon the demise of its chief, a few years since, without direct heirs, it was proposed that the state should lapse to the paramount power. Subsequently, however, a new grant was issued by the British government, recognising a native successor to the vacant throne.

JODHPOOR.—See JOUDPORE.

JODKA, in the British district of Bhutteeana, lieut.-gov. of the N.W. Provinces, a village on the route from Hansee to Bhutneer, and 57 miles N.W. of the former. It is a poor place, being ill supplied in every respect, not excepting even water. Lat. 29° 30′, long. 75° 12′.

JOGHEEGURH, or JOOGA, in the territory of Gwalior, or possessions of Scindia's family, a fort on a small island in the river Nerbudda. Here is a rapid, precluding navigation during the season of low water, but allowing the passage of boats during the periodical rains. Lat. 22° 20′, long. 76° 46′.

JOGIGOPA.—A town of Eastern India, in the British district of Goalpara, lieut.-gov. of Bengal, six miles N.W. of Goalpara. Lat. 26° 13′, long. 90° 35′.

JOGI RIDAN, in the Daman division of the Punjab, a town situated 33 miles from the right bank of the Indus, 110 miles N.W. of the town of Mooltan. Lat. 31° 19′, long. 70° 14′.

JOGLIO.—A town in the Rajpoot state of Beekaneer, 72 miles E. from Beekaneer, and 100 miles N. from Ajmeer. Lat. 27° 54′, long. 74° 32′.

JOHANABAD, in the native state of Gwalior, or possessions of Scindia's family, a town situate on the left bank of the Taptee, and 79 miles W. from Ellichpoor. Lat. 21° 16′, long. 76° 22′.

JOHILA, a river a tributary of the Sone, rises, according to native accounts, from a swampy, jungly tract near the famous shrine of Ummurkuntuk, and about lat. 22° 45′, long. 81° 50′. According to report, the Nerbudda, Sone, and Johila rise near each other; the Nerbudda from the kund, or pool of Ummurkuntuk, the Sone three or four miles further east, and the Johila about the same distance north. The Hindoo story runs, that the titular deity of the Sone, a male divinity, became enamoured of the Nerbudda, a female, whose handmaiden Johila attempting to personate her mistress in an interview with the lover, was so severely chastised by the enraged Naiad, that she melted into tears, whence ever since the stream Johila has continued to flow. It holds a course north-west for ninety miles, to the northern frontier of the district, towards the territory of Rewa, in lat. 23° 20′, long. 81° 4′, and a few miles further turns north-east, and falls into the Sone on the left side, in lat. 23° 39′, long. 81° 19′.

JOMBEE.—A town in the hill zemindarry of Jeypoor, territory of Madras, 24 miles E.N.E. from Jeypoor, and 86 miles N.W. by N. from Vizianagrum. Lat. 19° 9′, long. 82° 47′.

JONGAR.—A town in the native state of Bhotan, 70 miles N. from Goalpara, and 91 miles N.W. from Gowhatty. Lat. 27° 8′, long. 90° 50′.

JONKUR, in the territory of Gwalior, or possessions of Scindia, a town of Malwa, on the route from Goonah to Mow, 129 miles S.W. of former, 56 N.E. of latter. It has a bazar, and water is plentiful. It is the principal place of a small pergunnah of the Oojein district. Population about 3,000. Lat. 23° 14′, long. 76° 13′.

JOOALAPOOR, in the British district of Saharunpoor, lieut.-gov. of the N.W. Provinces, a town with a population of 12,162, and the chief place of the pergunnah of the same name, situate in lat. 29° 55′, long. 78° 10′.

JOOBUL.—A protected hill state in the southern or lower Himalayas. Inclusive of Ootrach or Turoch, with which it has been incorporated, this state is bounded on the north by Poondur, a detached district of Keonthul, and Bussahir; on the east by Bussahir and Gurwhal, the Pabur separating it from the former, and the Tonse from the latter; on the south by Sirmour; and on the west by Sirmour and Bulsun. It lies between lat. 30° 48′—31° 6′, long. 77° 32′—77° 54′: it is stated to have an area of 330 square miles. Its northern part lies in the extensive valley of the Pabur, along the right bank of that river; its southern is comprised within the valley of the Shalwee, a tributary of the Tonse. The valley of the Pabur is described by Jacquemont as one of the most delightful tracts he had ever seen, especially that subdivision in which Deohra, the residence of the rana, is situate. The elevation of Joobul in general is very considerable. That of the great peak of Chur, at the south-western frontier, is 12,149 feet; that of Urrukta, in the north, above 10,000. The elevation of the bed of the Pabur at Raingarh, on the north-eastern frontier, is 4,932 feet.

The people of Joobul are said to be distinguished by beauty of person, and some of the natives are nearly as fair as Europeans. The dress of the men consists of a pair of loose trousers, of thick striped woollen stuff; a sort of capote of similar stuff, reaching to the knees, and girt tight round the waist, but having many folds from the hip downwards; a cotton scarf, a shaggy flat woollen cap, and shoes of a sort of close network or twill of woollen thread, with a leather sole. Women appear in public without reserve, but are treated with little kindness or delicacy by their male relatives, who make no scruple in selling them. Mundy relates, that at Deohra "an instance of this was afforded to Lord Combermere's party, a very pretty girl being brought to the camp, and offered for sale, at the moderate price of 150 rupees; more than which sum," adds the writer, "I have seen given for a Scotch terrier at Calcutta." The religion of the people is Brahminism; the language a dialect of the Hindee. The population is believed to amount to about 15,000. The revenue is estimated at 14,136 rupees, or 1,413*l*. The military force consists of 300 infantry. The rana, or ruler, a descendant of a Rajpoot family, was restored to power by the British on the expulsion of the Goorkhas, in 1815. By the same authority, he was excluded in 1833, and an annual pecuniary provision assigned to him, which he, however, pertinaciously refused to accept. On his death in 1840, the raj was restored to his son, an infant. During his minority the territory continued under British management, but upon attaining mature age in 1854, the young chief was placed in possession of his estate. The only places of importance in Joobul are the fort of Chepal and Deohra, the residence of the rana.

JOOGA.—See JOGHEEGURH.

JOOGUL.—A town in the Southern Mahratta jaghiredaree of Sherbal, 58 miles N. by E. from Belgaum, and 84 miles S.E. by S. from Sattara. Lat. 16° 39′, long. 74° 45′.

JOOLKAPOOR.—A town in the British district of Midnapoor, lieut.-gov. of Bengal, 58 miles W.S.W. of Calcutta. Lat. 22° 12′, long. 87° 39′.

JOONAGHUR, in the peninsula of Kattywar, province of Guzerat, a town in the district of Sorath, surrounded by a rampart about five miles in circumference, with numerous massive square towers and crenellated parapet, and is situate advantageously on a ridge of sandstone. Within the rampart, and in the north-east of the area inclosed by it, is the citadel, the ground-plan of which is an irregular trapezium of very great size. The huge rampart of hewn stone is on the outside, strengthened by a deep and wide ditch, hewn in the solid rock. The town is ill built, with narrow filthy streets; and not more than half of the space inclosed within the walls is occupied. There is no appearance of commerce, or of the prosperity resulting therefrom. The palace of the nawaub is an insignificant building, situate in one of the bazars. The population of the town is variously estimated at 5,000, 20,000, and 30,000. The chief, a Mussulman, styled the Nawaub of Joonaghur, holds territory comprising 506 villages, and is joint proprietor of thirty-nine more; the whole estimated to contain a population of about 284,300. He pays annually a tribute of 3,065*l.* to the East-India Company, and 3,700*l.* to the Guicowar. Distance from Ahmedabad, S.W., 170 miles; Baroda, S.W., 180; Surat, W., 150; Bombay, N.W., 235. Lat. 21° 31′, long. 70° 31′.

JOONA NUGGUR.—A name sometimes given to the town of Sirgoojah, which see.

JOONEER.—A town in the British district of Poonah, presidency of Bombay, 70 miles E. by N. of Bombay. Considerable improvements were effected in the streets and approaches of this place, by means of a grant of money sanctioned by the government for the purpose in 1841. Lat. 19° 14′, long. 73° 56′.

JOONGAR, on the south-west frontier of Bengal, a town in the native state of Nowagudda, 143 miles S.W. from Sumbulpoor, and 77 miles N. from Jeypoor. Lat. 20° 9′, long. 82° 20′.

JOONJOOWARRA.—A town in Guzerat, or the dominions of the Guicowar, situate on the Runn of Cutch, and 73 miles S.W. by S. from Deesa. Lat. 23° 20′, long. 71° 32′.

JOONNAGUDDA, on the south-west frontier of Bengal, a town in the native state of Calahandy, 125 miles N. by W. from Vizianagrum, and 144 miles W. by N. from Ganjam. Lat. 19° 51′, long. 83°.

JOONUNGHEE.—A town in the native state of Cutch, situate 15 miles S. from the Great Western Runn of Cutch, and 59 miles W.N.W. from Bhooj. Lat. 23° 33′, long. 68° 51′.

JOORA, in the British district of Furruckabad, lieut.-gov. of the N.W. Provinces, a village on the route from the cantonment of Allygurh to that of Futtehgurh, and 38 miles W. of the latter. Lat. 27° 30′, long. 79° 7′.

JOORIA, in the peninsula of Kattywar, province of Guzerat, a seaport on the south-eastern coast of the Gulf of Cutch. Opposite are several sandbanks, and the water off this part of the coast is too shoaly for ships of any considerable burthen. There is a tradition, most probably little trustworthy, that, not much more than 200 years ago, a footpath at low water completely crossed the gulf from this place to the opposite coast of Cutch. Though not admitting large vessels, this place has a considerable trade. Distance from Ahmedabad, W., 145 miles; Baroda, W., 180; Surat, N.W., 190; Bombay, N.W., 300. Lat. 22° 40′, long. 70° 22′.

JOOTA, in the Rajpoot state of Joudpore, a village on the route from Nusseerabad to Deesa, and 60 miles S.W. of the former. It has a bazar, and is abundantly supplied with water from a tank and wells. Lat. 26°, long. 74° 8′.

JOOTAH, in the British district of Futtehpoor, lieut.-gov. of the N.W. Provinces, a village on the route from Allahabad to the town of Futtehpoor, and 35 miles S.E. of the latter. Lat. 25° 45′, long. 81° 20′.

JORAEE, in the Rajpoot state of Joudpore, a village on the route from Balmer to the town of Joudpore, and 12 miles N.E. of the former. It contains sixty houses. Lat. 25° 54′, long. 71° 39′.

JOREHAUT.—A town in the British district of Seebpoor, province of Assam, 31 miles S.W. by W. of Seebpoor. Lat. 26° 47′, long. 94° 12′.

JOSHIMATH, in Kumaon, a town a mile below the confluence of the Bishenganga and Doulee or Leti, which united, form the Aluknunda. The town is situate on the left bank of the Aluknunda, in a hollow recess, and on a declivity, being sheltered on every side by a circular ridge, and especially to the north, where a high mountain intercepts the cold blasts rushing from the Himalaya, rising in that direction. The entrance to the town is up a bank cut into steps faced with slate or stone, with both which materials the streets also are paved, but very irregularly. The houses are neatly built of grey stone, and roofed with shingles. Amongst them is the residence of the rawal or high-priest of Bhadrinath, who lives here for the six months during which the approaches to the elevated temple that he serves are buried under snow. The building containing the idol Nara Singha is more like a private residence than a Hindoo temple. It is built with gable-ends, and covered in with a sloping roof of plates of copper. Pilgrims halting here, put up in a large square, having a stone cistern, supplied by two brazen spouts, which yield a never-failing flow of water, derived from a stream descending from the Himalaya. A collection of temples, bearing marks of great antiquity, extend along one side of the square, being ranged along a terrace about ten feet high. In the centre of the area is a temple sacred to Vishnu, surrounded by a wall thirty feet square. Several of those temples are much dilapidated, having been partially overthrown by earthquakes. The temples of Vishnu, Ganesa, Surya or the Sun, and the Naudevi, have suffered least. The statue of Vishnu is of black stone, in a very superior style of workmanship. It is about seven feet high, and is supported by four female figures, standing on a flat pedestal. The image of Ganesa is two feet high, well carved, and polished. In the town is a line of water-mills, placed one below the other, at intervals of fifteen or twenty yards, and turned by one stream, which, flowing from the mountain above, is supplied to them in succession by a communication through troughs of hollowed trunks of firs. Joshimath is situate on the route from Hindoostan to Chinese Tartary, through the Niti Pass, and also on that by the Mana Pass. The town contains 119 houses, of which twenty-one belong to Brahmins, fourteen to merchants, sixty-eight to cultivators, and the rest to other classes. Elevation above the sea 6,185 feet. Lat. 30° 33′, long. 79° 37′.

JOTEPOOR, on the south-west frontier of Bengal, a town in the Cuttack mehal of Keunjur, situate on the left bank of the Byeturnee river, and 95 miles N. from Cuttack. Lat. 21° 49′, long. 85° 43′.

JOUDPOOR.—A town of Bundlecund, in the native state of Punnah, 50 miles S.S.W. from Punnah, and 64 miles N. from Jubbulpoor. Lat. 24° 5′, long. 79° 58′.

JOUDPORE, or MARWAR, the most extensive of the Rajpoot states, is bounded on the north-west by Jessulmere; on the north by Bikaneer and Shekhawuttee; on the east by Jeypore, Kishengurh, Ajmeer, and Mewar; on the south by Oodeypoor and Serohee, and the Guicowar's dominions; and on the west by the Runn of Cutch and Sinde. It is 330 miles in length from south-west to north-east, and 160 in breadth in the direction of the opposite angles. It lies between lat. 24° 36′—27° 40′, long. 70° 4′—75° 23′, and has an area of 35,672 square miles. The most marked feature in the physical aspect of the country is the river Lonee, which, rising on the eastern frontier near Pokur, takes a south-westerly course, nearly bisecting the territory, and forming the boundary between the fertile and sterile tracts; the former lying along the south-eastern or left bank, the latter along the north-western. The western part, bordering on the great desert of Scinde, is, throughout, a mere desolate waste. Eastward of this are numerous long ranges of rocky hills, dividing the Great from the Little Desert, which occupies the right bank of the Lonee, and runs up north-eastward between the city of Joudpore and Pokhurn. The Little Desert appears to be covered with sandhills nearly throughout, though low rocks show themselves on each flank towards Joudpore and Mundor on the east, and Pokhurn and Phulodi on the west. On the eastern frontier, the country swells upwards to the Aravulli range, which rises boldly to the height of between 3,000 and 4,000 feet above the level of the sea. The whole of the south part of Joudpore, about Sachor, Jalor, and Siwana, exhibits a succession of rocky hills; the eastern parts, about Pali Nimaj and Merta, are less stony, and there is much arable ground between Balotra and the capital, as well as on the north-east frontier. On the southern frontier are occasional appearances of rocks, generally regarded as volcanic by geologists. Stewart states porphyry to be the prevailing, if not the only rock in that region; "which near the town of Nuggur-Parkur rises in a range of lofty hills to the height of 1,000 feet, assuming, in its rugged features, a regularity equally singular as picturesque."

The climate is very hot in summer, but cold, healthy, and bracing in winter, when severe frosts sometimes occur. Throughout the western part, the generally sandy nature of the country renders the air dry and healthy at all times, so that it is a common native proverb, that neither mud, musquitoes, nor malaria are to be found in those regions. The case is different towards the south-east, where the Lonee occasionally rolls along with a great body of water, and the country is cut up by numerous torrents, which eventually discharge themselves into that river. There is consequently much swamp in that region during the rains, and Joudpore, the capital, itself is then considered unhealthy. Salt abounds in this territory, large quantities being extracted from the waters of the Sambhur Lake, about twelve miles long and five broad, situate on the north-east frontier. Salt is also extracted at Deedwana, 110 miles north-east of Joudpore; at Puchbhudra, sixty miles south-west of that place; and at Phulowdee, seventy miles north-west of it. Boileau considers that the numerous rocky hills in the east and south of this country contain various metals, as the range which passes into Ajmeer from the northward contains lead, iron, copper, and silver; but these promising deposits do not appear to have been worked in Joudpore. There are very fine quarries of white marble at Mukrana, 120 miles north-east of the town of Joudpore, which is itself built on a hill of a hard red freestone, of excellent quality as a building material. The calcareous conglomerate called kankar is abundant in many districts, and burned to make lime for mortar; tin and lead are found at Sojut, alum about Pali, and iron is obtained from the districts adjoining Guzerat. Cotton is cultivated to a considerable extent, but is a precarious crop, being sometimes totally destroyed by frost, as happened during Tod's visit, when every pod was nipped, the cold being so severe as partially to freeze the water in his bags. The districts along the base of the Aravulli being watered by the numerous small streams which flow down from that range, produce every kind of grain except bajra, which thrives best in a sandy soil. On an average for the whole country, the majority of the inhabitants are supported on bajra or moth. The emperor Shir Shah meeting with some reverses during his invasion of the country in the year 1544, declared that he had nearly lost the empire of India for a handful of millet, alluding to the poverty and low produce of Joudpore.

The zoology is neither rich nor varied. The banks of the Lonee are in places infested by lions and leopards, and tigers have been discovered in some dense and secluded jungles; there are, towards Cutch, wolves, hyænas, jackals, and three kinds of foxes: nylgaus, antelopes, and wild asses roam about the southern frontier towards Sinde. According to the account given by Macmurdo, who shot several, the wild ass "is an inhabitant of the salt wastes, so common in the desert, but frequents the cultivated country in the cold season, and does considerable damage to the crops. The wild ass is thirteen hands high; has a back, neck, and body of a light-brown colour, with a belly approximating to white. He has the dark stripe down the back in common with all dun animals. His ears are long, like those of the domestic ass; but his limbs are strong and well formed. His voice is a bray, but is so fine as to resemble that of a frightened deer. The animal is gregarious, being generally seen in herds, from ten to fifty; he is, however, occasionally found singly and in pairs." His food consists of the saline grasses and shrubs of the desert, and he is never seen in bad condition: he prefers brackish water to fresh. The flesh of this animal is said to afford tolerable food. Snakes are so common, that in some places the people are obliged to protect themselves against them by means of thick leggings or gaiters. Camels and horses are bred in great numbers, and fetch good prices. The kine of Nagor are highly celebrated; a pair broken in for draught are worth from sixty to ninety rupees. Great numbers of sheep graze in the wilder tracts of the country, and their fleeces are in large quantities converted into coarse cloths and blankets. Coarse cottons are also manufactured for home consumption. Matchlocks, swords, and other warlike instruments, are fabricated at Joudpore, at Nagor, and at Pali; at which latter places are made tinned boxes of iron, resembling those of Europe. Joudpore is famous for ivory-turning, as well as for ornamental manufactures in leather and glass; and all ordinary works in iron and brass are produced at Nagor. Iron platters, especially, are made in great numbers.

The Jats, a very ancient race, scattered over the great tract extending on the east of the Indus, from the Himalaya to the ocean, were probably the aboriginal population of this country, and still constitute five-eighths of the number of its inhabitants; two-eighths more being Rajpoots of the Rahtor tribe, and the remainder Brahmins or Jains. The Charuns, a tribe of Rajpoots, have among their countrymen unbounded influence, discharging the sacerdotal office, as well as the duties of chroniclers. There is a general impression, that certain and sweeping ruin results from shedding their blood or that of their families, or in being instrumental to its being shed. Hence their influence; and they lose no opportunity of warning their children not to scruple sacrificing their lives, should the measure be necessary for maintaining the claims of their order. Trusting to such influence, one of this class generally becomes the safeguard of travellers dreading the attacks of Rajpoot freebooters. Should robbers approach, he warns them off by holding a dagger in his hand, and if they disregard him, he wounds himself, and throws his blood towards them, denouncing woe and ruin in the most terrific language which he can command. If this have not the desired effect, the operation of wounding himself is repeated with increased severity. In extreme cases, one of the Charun's relatives, often either an aged or an infant female, is put to death, and sometimes the principal actor himself commits suicide, in which he is imitated by his wives and children. Something of similar character to the Charuns, but inferior in pretension and influence, are the Bhats, or bards of the community, whose power is exercised by means of satirical songs, pictures, and effigies. The population, estimated at the rate of fifty to the square mile, which is believed to be tolerably correct, would amount to 1,783,600. All classes in Joudpore are inordinately addicted to opium. They are fit for nothing until they take it, and after its effects have passed, are little better than idiots, until the dose be repeated. Indulgence in this baneful habit is more necessary to the Rajpoot than his food, and to eat opium together is the most inviolable pledge. The burning of women on the funeral-pile of their deceased husbands was formerly frightfully prevalent. In 1728, six queens, and fifty-eight women of inferior position, were burned with the dead body of Maharaja Ajit Sinh. Even at a very recent period, the atrocious practice had not become extinct, as, in 1844, the efforts of the British government to prevent the sacrifice in this way of six lives, on occasion of a deceased rajah's funeral, were unavailing. Happily, however, by the perseverance and well-timed suggestions of the British resident, the maharaja has at length been prevailed upon to prohibit the barbarous rite, and the necessary proclamation has been issued. The language spoken in Joudpore is a peculiar patois, called Marwari, considered to have an affinity to Hindee. Some attention appears to be paid to education, there being, it is said, in the town of Joudpore, above 100 schools for the children of the humbler orders.

The ruler of Joudpore is styled Maharaja. The constitution, if the name can well be given to such an irregular political machine, is feudal, and the authority of the maharaja is checked by the counteracting power of a number of refractory thakoors or chiefs, by whom the greater part of the country is held, on condition of military service, the feudatory being bound to furnish troops in proportion to his estate; but as some of the estates have been exempted from this burden, and the value of others falls greatly below the sums at which they have been estimated, the number of troops has diminished; and it is believed that the maharaja cannot rely upon mustering more than 2,000 men from this source, instead of upwards of 4,000, which the estimates would seem to warrant. The present military establishment consists, first, of the Joudpore legion, in lieu of the Joudpore contingent, amounting to 254 cavalry, 739 infantry, thirty-one artillery and Bheel companies, 222 strong, in all

1,246; and, secondly, of about 5,850 infantry and 2,680 cavalry, at the disposal of the Joudpore state; in addition to what the feudatories maintain. The present amount of revenue is 175,252*l*. Salt is a fertile source of income. According to Tod's account, "this productive branch of industry still employs thousands of hands, and hundreds of thousands of oxen, and is almost entirely in the hands of that singular race of beings called Brinjarries, some of whose tandas or caravans amount to 40,000 head of oxen. The salt is exported to every region of Hindostan, from the Indus to the Ganges, and is universally known and sold under the title of Sambhur Loon, or salt of Sambhur; notwithstanding the quality of the different lakes varies, that of Pachbadra, beyond the Loni, being the most esteemed. It is produced by natural evaporation, expedited by dividing the surface into pans, by means of mats of the sirkunda grass, which lessens the superficial agitation. It is then gathered and heaped up into immense masses, on whose summit they burn a variety of alkaline plants, by which it becomes impervious to the weather." By the author just quoted, the other sources of revenue are stated to be buttae, or corn-rent; angah, or poll-tax; gasmali, or tax on cattle; kewari, or tax on doors; sayer, or commercial imposts. The state pays to the British government an annual tribute of 108,000 rupees, and a contribution towards the expense of the Joudpore legion, amounting to 115,000 rupees. The former payment was originally made to Scindia, on whose account it is still collected by the British government, and applied by that government to the maintenance of Scindia's contingent. The Rajpoot dynasty of Joudpore is supposed to have been established about the year 1212, by Seoji or Sivaji, son of the last Hindoo king of Kannouj, who perished in 1194, on the conquest of his capital by Shahab-ud-din, or Mohammed of Ghor, the subverter of the Ghaznevide empire in India. In 1459, Jodha, the maharaja of Marwar, removed the seat of government from Mundor to Joudpore, a fort and residence which he had built a few miles to the south. About 1569, Akber made himself master of the greater part of the state of Joudpore, which he conferred on Udi Sinh, the son of the late maharaja, whom he had expelled. The power of Udi Sinh was subsequently strengthened by the marriage of his sister to Akber. About the year 1680, Aurungzebe, in one of his ineffectual attempts to enforce the observances of Mahomedanism, attacked and pillaged Joudpore, and most of the other towns in Marwar; defaced and desecrated the Hindoo temples, many of which were totally demolished; erected mosques on their sites, and compulsorily inflicted the outward mark of Islam on such Rajpoots as fell into his power. The yoke of the emperor of Delhi was, however, soon thrown off; but, for upwards of a century, the country was distracted by anarchy and a series of petty wars, till the conclusion of a treaty, ratified in the beginning of 1818, between the maharaja of Joudpore and the British government. For several years subsequently to the conclusion of the treaty, there was little communication between the British government and Joudpore; but a series of disturbances commenced in 1824, which called for interposition, and the unsatisfactory nature of the arrangement then made, having led to their revival in 1828, when a pretender to the throne received the support of a large body of chiefs, eventually led to further interference, to the extent of a requisition from the British government to the pretender for the withdrawal of his claims. In 1829, Appa Sahib, the perfidious ex-rajah of Nagpore, having been expelled from Bikaneer, sought refuge in Joudpore, the ruler of which country was required by the British government to give him up, or at least to cause his departure in a given direction. Great reluctance was manifested towards complying with this demand, and it was withdrawn, on condition that the rajah of Joudpore should be responsible for the safe custody and peaceable conduct of Appa Sahib, so long as he should remain in the country. This act of considerate regard to the alleged feelings of Rajpoot hospitality was, as usual, very indifferently requited. The chief of Joudpore suffered his tribute to fall into arrear; supplied the stipulated military assistance reluctantly and tardily, protected plunderers, and was believed to have entered into political correspondence having objects hostile to British interests and influence in India. These acts of misconduct were submitted to with great forbearance for a long period, during which the misgovernment and distraction of the country were extreme; and at length, from all these causes, it was deemed necessary to instruct Colonel Sutherland to proceed to Joudpore and demand reparation. His mission proving ineffectual, a body of troops was moved to enforce that which negotiation had failed to achieve. Their approach alarmed the rajah, who forthwith displayed tokens of submission. The immediate consequences were, the establishment of a council of regency, with a British agent at its head, to carry on the government in conjunction with the rajah, and the reception of a British garrison within his fortress. A variety of useful reforms followed. The rajah died a few years after the commencement of the system which led to these beneficial steps, but they were pursued under his successor Tukht Singh, of Admednuggur, who was elected to the vacant throne by the thakoors. Under the administration of this prince, various reforms have been effected; among the chief of which must be reckoned, as already noticed, the abolition of suttee.

JOUDPORE, the capital of the Rajpoot state of the same name, is situate at the north-eastern edge of a cultivated but woody plain, which, farther south, passes into the low tract fertilized by the river Loni and its feeders. Its site is striking, being at the southern extremity of a ridge or rock twenty-five miles in length, between two and three in breadth, and rising between 300 and 400 feet above the average level of the plain. The city, inclosed by a rampart five miles in circuit, is built on an irregular surface, sloping upwards towards the base of the rock surmounted by the citadel, the view from which is thus described by Boileau:—"A bird's-eye view of the city from the summit of the upper fort is really magnificent. Perched upon a parapet of the bastion, encircling the pointed pagoda at the southern extremity of the citadel, we gazed with delight upon the fair scene at our feet. The whole of the city lies close to the rock on which the palace stands, surrounding its east, south, and west sides, the north side being occupied by a hilly neck, connecting the citadel with the Mundor range, and too much broken to afford good building-ground. The lively green of the trees, and the quantity of fine white plaster applied to the red stone houses, afforded a pleasing variety of colours, and give the city a gay look. The numerous tanks, now filled with water; the white ramparts, running along the higher parts of the city; the piles of buildings crowded upon each other, and rising tier above tier to the Chandpol gate; and the confused mass of outworks on the west side of the citadel, formed a scene that will not soon be forgotten." On a closer inspection, however, the streets are said by this writer to have been found irregular and ill laid out, the houses mean and badly constructed, the place being inferior in this respect to the other capitals of Rajpootana, but containing some fine temples, especially the Pasbunka Mandir. Tod gives a different and more favourable account. "The streets," he says, "are very regular, and adorned with many handsome edifices of freestone." There are several tanks within the walls. The Pudum Sagur, in the north-western part of the city, is excavated in rock, but is of small dimensions; the Rani Sagur, in the same quarter, is at the foot of the western entrance into the citadel, with which it is connected by low outworks, placing it under the thorough command of the garrison, for whose exclusive use it is reserved, except an extreme emergency requires it to be thrown open to the citizens. The Goolab Sagur, on the east, is of great extent, and finely built of stone throughout. The Bai-ka-talao, recently built, is also extensive, and receives several conduits, conveying the water of many distant torrents. Yet, in long-continued droughts, all fail, except the Rani Sagur. There are above thirty wells of the kind called baoli, in which access is obtained to the water by means of steps: in some of these, the water is carried up to the surface by human labour or by the Persian wheel, though the depth in many instances exceeds forty feet. The Persian wheel is even used in the Tonr-jee-ka-Jhabra, where the depth, from the mouth above to the surface of the water, exceeds ninety feet, the depth of the water itself being also ninety feet. This fine well is cut in the solid rock, and, by the time-worn appearance of the carving in the interior, bears evidence of great antiquity. It is of immense size at the surface of the ground, and of square shape. On three sides, flights of steps lead down to the water, but the fourth side is perpendicular, to allow the working of the Persian wheel. The water is good, and never fails.

The wall about the town was, at Boileau's visit, in 1835, in a very bad state, and in many places some yards of the parapet, and even of the rampart, had fallen down so completely as to allow free passage between the interior and exterior; and on the south side, the sand had in one place drifted to within a few inches of the crest of the parapet. Two steeply-scarped masses of rock, 80 or 100 feet high, form part of the line of defence on the east side of the city, and are crowned with walls and towers on their outer faces. In the whole circuit there are 101 bastions and 70 gates, each bearing the name of the place to which it leads. The fortifications of the town are continuous with those of the citadel, which is, however, divided from it by a rampart on the brow of the ascent, and generally 370 feet above the plain. The elevation at the north-east angle is 382 feet; and the scarp wall, which covers the great gate there, has a sheer face of hewn stone 109 feet high. Other parts of the wall appear to be still higher. These defences are well built of stone quarried from the subjacent rock. In some places, however, the ramparts and bastions are weak and ill-constructed, and would be almost contemptible, but for the stiff section of the rocks on which they are erected. The main entrance is on the north. The road passing through it is practicable for heavy guns; and the access covered by six successive gateways, besides the inner one, opening immediately into the maharaja's palace. The road over the hilly ridge extending northward from the citadel, is practicable for heavy artillery; and the place could not long hold out against an attack conducted according to the rules of European warfare. The whole citadel is 500 yards long, and about half that breadth. The royal palace and buildings attached are situate at the north end, and occupy two-fifths of the area; an equal space is occupied by magazines, granaries, and other public buildings, and the remainder is empty. There are five reservoirs of water within the citadel, but in ordinary times the principal supply is derived from the Rani Sagur. The palace overtops all other buildings, and its highest part is 454 feet above the plain. The state apartments present little to excite admiration, being inferior to those of the humbler ruler of Bikaneer. The most remarkable is the chamber of audience, styled "the thousand-columned hall," a vast apartment, the ceiling of which is supported by a great number of massive columns of no great height, arranged in parallel rows, about twelve feet asunder.

Outside the city, and distant a cannon-shot from the north-east angle, is the large suburb, deriving its name of Mahamandir, or "the great temple," from a building within it, which confers the right of sanctuary on its inclosure and environs. It constitutes a distinct town of 1,000 houses, with 112 shops, inclosed by a thin stone wall a mile and a quarter in circuit, having a few weak bastions, but without any parapet, unless that name can be given to battlements three feet high and five or six inches thick. The area is an irregular quadrangle, having a gateway in each of its faces. The temple above mentioned is surmounted by a spire, conspicuous from afar by the brilliant lime-wash with which it is covered. The interior is richly decorated, and the sacred shrine of the tutelary saint is placed under a canopy of silver, in the form of an umbrella. There is a tank, supplied with water brought from a distance by conduits. A baoli, eighty feet deep, has an inexhaustible supply of good water. A flight of steps reaches to the water's edge, and three Persian wheels raise and discharge no inconsiderable stream for irrigation and domestic purposes. The inclosure of the Mahamandir contains two palaces, one of which is inhabited by the maharaja's gooroo or spiritual adviser, who lives in great state; the other palace has no living occupant, being reserved by native superstition as the residence of the spirit of the last deceased gooroo, whose bed is laid out in one of the state-chambers, with a small golden canopy over the pillow. Five miles north of Joudpore are the striking ruins of Mandor, which was the capital of Marwar previously to the foundation of the present capital by Maharaja Jodha or Joda, in 1459. Hence the name of the town, and also of the eminence of its site, which is called Jodhagir, or "the warrior's hill." A mile and a quarter west of the town are handsome gardens, with a fine tank named Ukhe Rajka Talao, described by Boileau as "a magnificent sheet of water, clear, deep, and extensive, resembling rather a natural lake than an artificial tank." Two or three miles north of this, is Bal Sumundur, a small but beautiful lake, half a mile long and about 200 yards wide, with craggy banks of red sandstone, feathered with picturesque shrubs, and bordered by a fine pleasure-ground, abounding in towering palm-trees. Two miles north of the city, and between the two last-mentioned pieces of water, is the Sur-Sagor, an immense tank, on the southern embankment of which stands the Motimahall, or Pearl Palace, a beautiful building of white marble, from the flat roof of which is a fine view of the citadel. According to the estimate of Boileau, Joudpore city, citadel, and suburbs, contain 30,000 houses, which, at the usually-received average of five persons to each house, makes the population 150,000; an amount scarcely credible. Boileau elsewhere states the amount of the population at 129,150, which reduced number is, however, probably excessive. *Tod says, "The number of families* some years ago, stated to be 20,000, probably 80,000 souls—an estimate far too great for the present day." Joudpore is distant W. from Calcutta 1,128 miles; S.W. from Delhi, by Nusseerabad, 358 miles. Lat. 26° 19′, long. 73° 8′.

JOUNPOOR, under the lieut.-gov. of the N.W. Provinces, a British district, named from its principal town. It is bounded on the north-west by the territory of Oude; on the north-east by the British district Azimgurh; on the east by the British district Ghazeepore; and on the south by the British districts Benares and Allahabad. It lies between lat. 25° 22′—26° 12′, long. 82° 12′—83° 10′; is sixty miles in length from east to west, fifty-five in breadth, and embraces an area of 1,552 square miles. It is a remarkably level tract, with a gentle declivity, probably not exceeding on the average, six inches per mile, from north-west to south-east, as indicated by the course of its numerous streams flowing in that direction. The south-eastern extremity is about 260 feet above the sea; and probably the elevation of no part exceeds 300 feet. The principal rivers are the Goomtee and the Sai. The population was ascertained by census in 1853 to amount to 1,143,749, being at the rate of 737 to the square mile—a high average. Of the above number, 821,163 were returned as Hindoos and agricultural, 210,425 Hindoos non-agricultural, 43,348 Mahomedans and others not Hindoos, but employed in agricultural pursuits, and 68,813 persons not being Hindoos, devoted to other occupations. It thus appears that the preponderance of Hindoos in this district is overwhelming, the disciples of that creed being more than fifteen times as numerous as the followers of all other religions. The numbers of the agricultural class exceed those of the non-agricultural in the proportion of nearly three to one. The townships, villages, &c., are thus arranged according to population:—

Number of towns and villages containing less than 1,000 inhabitants	2,861
Ditto more than 1,000 and less than 5,000	178
Ditto „ 5,000 „ 10,000	2
Ditto „ 10,000 „ 50,000	1
Total	3,042

With the exception of Jounpoor, the towns are unimportant; those most requiring notice,—Singra or Sangrampur, Mureahu, Muchlishahr, Badshahpur, Zafarabad, and Ghissooa, as well as the capital,—will be found in their proper places in the alphabetical arrangement.

The tract comprised within this district was probably first reduced under Mussulman sway by Muhammad Shahabuddin, the Patan ruler of Ghor, who is recorded to have, at the close of the twelfth century, conquered Eastern India as far as the confines of China. During the confusion caused by the invasion of India by Timur, near the end of the fourteenth century, or perhaps something earlier, Jounpoor, *with some adjacent tracts*, was acquired by an officer of the padshah of Delhi. The Purebi Sherki, or Eastern dynasty, thus founded, was of no long duration, being overthrown in 1478, by Behlol Lodi, the Afghan padshah of Delhi, who reannexed Jounpoor to the empire, and made it an appanage of his son Barbik Khan. In 1527, it passed from the Afghans to the victorious Baber, being conquered by his son Humayon, acting under his orders. On the dissolution of the Timurian empire of Delhi, consequent on the invasion by Ahmed Shah Durani in 1760, it formed part of the spoil seized and retained by the nawaub vizier of Oude. In 1764, a firman or grant of this, among other districts, was made by Shah Alum, titular padshah of Delhi, to the East-India Company, who, by the treaty of Allahabad, relinquished to the nawaub vizier the claim thus founded, as well as the military occupancy established by the victory gained at Buxar in the preceding year. In 1775, it was ceded by the nawaub vizier to the East-India Company, and embodied with the dominions of that power. In the Ayeen Akbery, its military contingent is stated at about 915 cavalry and 36,000 infantry, and its revenue at 14,09,853 rupees.

JOUNPOOR.—The principal place of the British district of the same name, a city on the banks of the river Goomtee, here navigable, and generally unfordable. The river divides the city into two unequal parts, the greater on the left, the less on the right bank; and the communication is by means of an antique bridge, considered one of the finest specimens of architectural skill in India, but which, from the diminutive span of its arches, would scarcely be noticed in Europe. The roadway passes from the left or north-eastern bank, over ten arches, called, collectively, the great bridge, to an island in the channel, and, proceeding over it, is thence continued by the lesser bridge of five arches and a land arch, to the right side. A native writer enumerates the spans of the arches and the breadth of the piers of the greater bridge. It is constructed of stone, so well cemented, that it is comparatively unimpaired, though nearly three centuries old, during which period it has resisted the floods, which sometimes sweep over it in such volume, that, in 1774, a fleet of boats conveying a British army, with a numerous train of baggage, camp-followers, and attendant animals, were borne down the stream, right across the line of roadway, without any impediment from the submerged structure. The building is said to have been commenced in the year 1564, and completed in three years, by Fahim, a freed man of Munim Khan, an officer high in the confidence of Akbar: the cost is reported to have amounted to 300,000*l*. The fort, situate on the bank of the river, is a vast massive stone structure, the ground-plan of which is an oblong quadrangle, half a mile in circuit. It is said to have been built A.D. 1370, by Feroz Shah Toghluk, Patan sovereign of Delhi, who named it after his cousin and predecessor on the throne. According to Lord Valentia, there is a gateway in the wall of the castle, "ornamented with mosaic-work of different-coloured varnished tiles. It has been beautiful. The courts are extensive and the verandas on the walls command a very pleasing prospect, particularly on one side, which overhangs the river and the bridge; beyond which are the ruins of the different tombs, raising their cupolas among palms and tamarind-trees. The distant country is rich in cultivation, and well clothed with wood." The fort has been used as a prison. On the east of the town is a large mosque, in very bad repair, but noble even in ruin. It is described by Tieffenthaler as a splendid structure of red stone, with three lofty domes, and a fore-court, surrounded by colonnades. It is stated to be fifty ells high, and adorned with elaborate and tasteful workmanship. A view given of it by Daniell confirms this favourable description. Adjoining it is another mosque of similar character; and the whole town and its vicinity abound in striking ruins of mosques, palaces, and other memorials of its ancient magnificence, confirmatory of the account given by Khairuddin of the grandeur of this capital. The military cantonment is at the eastern extremity of the town, and on the left bank of the river. The civil establishment here consists of the usual European and native functionaries. The population of the town is returned at 27,160. Distant N.W. from Benares 35 miles, N.E. from Allahabad 55. Lat. 25° 44′, long. 82° 44′.

JOUNT GURHEE, in native Gurwhal, a fort on a summit three miles east of the river Jumna. It was formerly occupied by the Goorkhas, and hither, in 1814, during the Nepaul war, Bhulbudur Singh, one of their commanders, retreated, after having evacuated Kalunja, and subsequently been put to flight by Major Ludlow. He was attacked here by Major Baldock, in command of 600 regular and 400 irregular troops, whom, however, he repulsed, and then succeeded in making good his passage across the Jumna to Jaitak. Lat. 30° 36′, long. 78° 9′.

JOURASEE, in the British district of Saharunpore, lieut.-gov. of the N.W. Provinces, the principal place in the pergunnah so called, and from which its name is derived. Lat. 29° 49′, long. 78°.

JOWAH.—A village of the British district of Hurreeana, lieut.-gov. of the N.W. Provinces. Lat. 29° 26′, long. 75° 50′.

JOWAUR.—A town in the British district of Tannah, presidency of Bombay, 68 miles N.N.E. of Bombay. Lat. 19° 51′, long. 73° 14′.

JOWLA.—A town in Hyderabad, or dominions of the Nizam, 94 miles E. of Poonah. Lat. 18° 33′, long. 75° 20′.

JOWNSAR.—See JAUNSAR.

JOWRA, in Malwa, a town on the route from Neemuch to Mhow, 61 miles S. of the *former, and 94 N.W. of the latter.* It is situate on the small river Piria, and has abundant supplies for troops. The river is unfordable during the rains, and is traversed by a bridge handsomely and solidly built of a porphyritic stone. The territory of which this town is the principal place lies between lat. 23° 32′—24° 10′, long. 74° 53′—75° 35′. It has an area of 872 square miles, and belongs to a Patan chief, styled Nawaub of Jowra, the representative of Ghuffoor Khan, to whom, in 1818, the jaghire was secured by the British government, under the treaty of Mondesoor, concluded with Holkar, on condition that the nawaub and his heirs should maintain, independent of the sebundy (armed police) for his pergunnahs, and his personal attendants, in constant readiness for service, a body of 600 select horse; and further, that this quota of troops should be thereafter increased, in proportion to the increasing revenue of the districts granted him. The number of troops, inclusive of the sebundy, in the service of the nawaub, is 850; his annual revenue, in 1848, was 8,00,000 rupees; the population of the territory, including the jaghires of dependants, 85,456. The town, according to Malcolm, in 1820, contained 3,551 inhabitants; but Jacquemont, in 1832, estimated their number at 10,000 or 12,000. It is distant N.W. from Oojein 53 miles, S.W. from Gwalior 260. Elevation above the sea 1,437 feet. Lat. 23° 38′, long. 75° 5′.

JOYNUGGUR.—A town in the British district of Dacca-Jelalpoor, lieut.-gov. of Bengal, 101 miles N.E. of Calcutta. Lat. 23° 29′, long. 89° 41′.

JUALDINNE.—A town in the British district of Nellore, presidency of Madras, 117 miles N. by W. of Madras. Lat. 14° 47′, long. 80° 8′.

JUBBOOGAUM.—A town in the native state of Rajpeepla, territory of Bombay, 36 miles N.E. from Surat, and 115 miles S.S.E. from Ahmedabad. Lat. 21° 28′, long. 73° 18′.

JUBBULPOOR, within the British territory of Saugor and Nerbudda, a town on the route from Allahabad to Nagpore, 222 miles S.W. of the former, 156 N.E. of the latter. It is the principal place of the district of the same name, and is situate at the base of a rocky hill, about a mile from the right bank of the Nerbudda, fordable in that place in the season of low water, when it is three feet deep, with a width of about 300. It is a large, well-built, and thriving place, in consequence of its favourable position in a populous and highly-cultivated country. Around it are several small lakes and tanks, which in the rainy season are so swollen as greatly to strengthen it as a military position. Here is a small cantonment of British troops, belonging to the Saugor division, also a political agency subsidiary to that of Saugor. The small collegiate establishment formerly existing in the town was abolished in 1850. It has been succeeded *by a school of industry, which has been brought to a state of great efficiency, and the advantages* of which have been extended beyond the classes for whose benefit it was originally established. Here, on December 19th, 1817, a British force of 1,100 men, commanded by General Hardyman, defeated 5,000 Mahrattas, the troops of the rajah of Nagpore. The Mahrattas suffered severe loss, and the survivors fled precipitately, abandoning the town, nine pieces of ordnance, and a large quantity of military stores. The loss on the side of the British was only two killed and ten wounded.

The country in the vicinity of Jubbulpoor is highly interesting to the geologist, on account of the variety of its formations. The range of hills overlooking the town is granite, of several kinds; and every formation subordinate to granite is to be found in this neighbourhood, including gneiss, hornblende, schistose rock, dolomite. In a limestone range near the town of Jubbulpoor, are deposits of fossil bones, and about fifteen miles farther west are others still more extensive, including remains of the elephant, or other gigantic quadrupeds. Excellent coal is found in some parts of the pergunnah. The district, of which this town is the chief place, contains an area of 6,237 square miles, and a population of 442,771, which affords an average density of seventy-one to the square mile. Elevation above the sea 1,458 feet. Distant S.E. from Saugor 111 miles; S.W. from Allahabad 222; W. from Calcutta, by Allahabad, 718; S.E. from Agra, by Saugor, 383; N.E. from Nagpore 156. Lat. 23° 10′, long. 80° 1′.

JUBLING.—A town in the native state of Nepal, situate three miles from the left bank of the Dud Coosy river, and 72 miles E. from Khatmandoo. Lat. 27° 40′, long. 86° 28′.

JUCKOO.—A town in the native state of Cutch, 62 miles W. from Bhooj, and 113 miles S.S.E. from Tatta. Lat. 23° 15′, long. 68° 46′.

JUDDENGY.—A town in the British district of Rajahmundry, presidency of Madras, 32 miles N. of Samulkottah. Lat. 17° 30′, long. 82° 12′.

JUFFERGUNJE, in the British district of Dacca-Jelalpore, lieut.-gov. of Bengal, a town at the confluence of the Jubuna with the Ganges, forming a stream described by Heber as not less than four miles wide during the rainy season. Distance from the town of Furreedpore, N., 20 miles; Calcutta, N.E., 120. Lat. 23° 52′, long. 89° 48′.

JUGADREE, in Sirhind, a town on the route from Saharunpoor to Loodiana, and 24 miles N.W. of the former place. It is a populous, thriving town, with a good bazar and a plentiful supply of water. Distance N.W. of Calcutta 983 miles. Lat. 30° 10′, long. 77° 22′.

JUGDEESPORE, in the British district of Shahabad, lieut.-gov. of Bengal, a town 17 miles N.W. of the north-west or left bank of the *river Son. It is the principal place of the pergunnah of Belowtee. The number of houses in Jugdeespoor is estimated at 1,000,* an amount which, according to the usual average of the number of inmates, would assign it a population of 5,000. Lat. 25° 27′, long. 84° 28′.

JUGDESPORE.—See JUSHPORE.

JUGDISPOOR, in the territory of Oude, a town on the route from Lucknow cantonment to Pertabgurh, 60 miles S.E. of the former, 45 N.W. of the latter. It has a large bazar, and is well supplied with water. The road in this part of the route is good, and passes through a jungly country, with occasional patches of cultivation. Lat. 26° 29′, long. 81° 40′.

JUGDISPOOR.—See ISLAMNUGUR.

JUGDULAPOUR.—See JUGDULAPOOR.

JUGDULAPOOR, or BUSTUR.—A town in the British district of Nagpoor, late dominions of the rajah of Berar, situate in the district of Bustur, 85 miles W.N.W. from the hill zemindary of Jeypoor, and 230 miles S.E. from Nagpoor. Lat. 19° 13′, long. 81° 58′.

JUGGANA.—A town in the hill zemindary of Jeypoor, 21 miles N.E. by N. from Jeypoor, and 97 miles N.W. by N. from Vizianagrum. Lat. 19° 16′, long. 82° 39′.

JUGGERNATH DIGGY. — A town in the British district of Bulloah, lieut.-gov. of Bengal, 192 miles E. by N. of Calcutta. Lat. 23° 9′, long. 91° 21′.

JUGGOO.—See AMHERST ISLAND.

JUGGURNAUTH, or POOREE, in the British district of Cuttack, presidency of Bengal, a town distinguished in India as one of the strongholds of Hindoo superstition, and deriving its celebrity from its connection with the famous temple of the same name. The town is situate on the north-western shore of the Bay of Bengal, in that part called the Coast of Orissa. The surf here is very violent, so that landing can be effected only by means of Masula boats, similar to those used on the Coromandel coast. During the south-west monsoon, a refreshing sea-breeze blows with little intermission, rendering the climate in the hot season one of the most agreeable and healthful in India. The beach has been selected as the site for the British military station. The town itself is to the south-west of the station, and on a low ridge of sandhills, to which an attempt has been made to give a factitious grandeur, by styling it Neilgherry, or Blue Mountain. "Every span of it is holy ground; and the whole of the land is held free of rent, on the tenure of performing certain services in and about the temple. The principal street is composed almost entirely of the religious establishments called Maths, built of masonry, having low pillared verandas in front, and plantations of trees interspersed. Being very wide, with the temple rising majestically at the southern end, it presents by no means an unpicturesque appearance; but the filth and stench, the swarms of religious mendicants, and other nauseous objects which offend one's senses in every part of the town, quite dispel any illusion which the scene might otherwise possess. Fine luxuriant groves and gardens inclose the town on the land side, and produce the best fruit in the province." In the vicinity are many fine tanks, considered of great antiquity; and among the sands, between the sea and the south-west face of the town, are numerous ancient and curious-looking edifices, now nearly overwhelmed with sand. The temple of Juggurnauth stands within a square area, inclosed by a lofty stone wall, measuring 650 feet on a side. The inclosure is entered on the east by a grand gateway, from which a broad flight of steps gives access to a terrace twenty feet in height, inclosed by a second wall, 445 feet square. From this platform the great pagoda rises, from a base thirty feet square, to the height of about 180 feet from the platform, or 200 from the ground, tapering from bottom to top, not in the form of a cone, but rounded off in the upper part with an outline approaching to the parabola. The present edifice appears to have been completed in the year 1198, at a cost of nearly half a million sterling. Most of the Hindoo deities have temples within the inclosure; and of those, two, besides the great pagoda, are peculiarly remarkable when viewed from sea, being described as "three large circular buildings, surrounded by several smaller ones: they are of a conical form, decreasing in diameter from their bases to their summits, which are crowned with white domes, and an ornamental globe or urn and wind-vane. The westernmost pagoda is the largest, and the eastern one the smallest of the three." The eastern gate is flanked by griffins and other mythological figures, and in front stands a column of dark-coloured basalt, and of very light and elegant proportions, surmounted by a figure of the monkey-god Hanuman. This temple is dedicated to Krishna, considered as an avatar or incarnation of Vishnu, but is also held in joint tenancy by Balarama, identified with Siva or Mahadeo, and Subhadra, regarded as his sister and also his consort in Hindoo mythology. Krishna is, however, the principal object of worship, and from his title Juggurnauth the great temple is denominated. The three idols, intended to represent those three characters respectively, are three blocks of wood, each surmounted by a frightfully grim representation of the human countenance, the block, with the head, measuring about six feet in height. The block representing Krishna is painted dark blue, that representing Siva white, and Subhadra's yellow. Each is provided with a rath or rude chariot, being a sort of lofty platform mounted on wheels. That of Juggurnauth is 43½ feet high, 34½ feet square, and is mounted on sixteen wheels, each 6½ feet in diameter. The raths of the two other idols are of dimensions somewhat less. "The grand festival occurs in the month of March, when the moon is of a certain age, after the sun has entered Aries;" and at the *Rath Jatra*, as this festival is denominated, the idols are taken on their raths to visit their country-house, about a mile and half distant. Thousands of men, women, and children, draw them along by means of cables fastened to the raths, and Brahmins stationed on the platforms sing and repeat obscene stories, accompanied by appropriately foul gestures, hailed by the multitudes with sounds and movements expressive of applause. Formerly, wretched fanatics offered up their lives in honour of the idols, by throwing themselves down before the moving wheels, which of course crushed them to death; but those horrible deeds have for some time ceased.

The British obtained possession of the place and temple in October, 1803; previously to which occupation, a tax had been levied by the Mahrattas upon the pilgrims resorting thither. This produced a very large sum, out of which a small one was assigned to defray the expenses of the temple. The priests made application to the British commissioner for the usual donation, which was at once granted; but the continuance of the pilgrim-tax was not contemplated. The priests, however, were anxious that the tax should be continued, inasmuch as the government might become tired of making a considerable donation at its own cost, while an accession of revenue from the temple would, it was thought, render the contribution to the priests more secure. The wish of these holy persons was complied with; the government donation was withdrawn, and the collection of money for the support of the temple permitted in substitution. In 1806 a change took place. The government took the superintendence of the temple upon itself, and laid down the most minute arrangements for its management. The pilgrim-tax thus became a regular source of revenue to the state. The measure was proposed before the retirement of the Marquis Wellesley, but he refused it his sanction. Sir George Barlow had no scruple on the subject, and under him the proposal became law; not, however, without a strong protest against it from one member of council, Mr. Udney. At home it was disapproved by the Court of Directors; but the president of the Board, Mr. Dundas, took a different view, and through his influence a despatch was framed, to the effect, that as the tax on pilgrims had been levied under Mahomedan and Mahratta governments, there did not appear any objection to its continuance under the British government. In 1839, under the administration of Lord Auckland, the subject came again under notice, when the tax was abolished, the expenses of the temple fixed at a certain sum, and a donation ordered to be paid from the public treasury, to make up the amount supposed to be required, and for which no other available means of providing existed. This donation somewhat exceeded 30,000 rupees. Subsequently, more careful inquiry was made, and the allowance was fixed at 23,000 rupees. This arrangement, however, was deemed objectionable, inasmuch as it did not disconnect the government from idolatrous worship. To effect this object, orders were recently sent out directing, as a final measure, that government should withdraw altogether from the temple, leaving it to be supported by its own resources, but making such compensation, if necessary, as should suffice to place the establishment in as good a pecuniary position as it enjoyed when the country passed into the hands of the British. According to a statement published a short time since, its condition in this respect is indeed much better. The pilgrim-tax, it may be mentioned, has never ceased, it having been collected by the native authorities after it was relinquished by the government. It is a circumstance for congratulation, that the government has thus purged itself from a foul scandal, which lowered its character and impaired its usefulness.

Here, over a branch of the Mahanuddy, is an antique stone bridge, having eighteen waterways, not arched above, but traversed by "laying horizontal tiers of stone on the piers, the one projecting slightly beyond the other, in the manner of inverted stairs, until they approach near enough at top to sustain a keystone or cross-beam." According to official report, the town of Juggurnauth or Pooree contains 5,741 houses, which, if the usually-received ratio of five inmates to each house be applicable, would indicate a population of 29,705. Distance from Madras, N.E., 595 miles; Cuttack, S., 47; Nagpore, E., 450; Calcutta, S.W., 250. Lat. 19° 49′, long. 85° 53′.

JUGGUTPOOR, in the British district of Etawa, lieut.-gov. of the N.W. Provinces, a village on the route from the cantonment of Etawa to Calpee, and 30 miles S.E. of the former. Lat. 26° 31′, long. 79° 28′.

JUGRAON, in Sirhind, a town eleven miles from the left bank of the Sutlej. It is situate in the British district of Loodiana. Distance N.W. from Calcutta, by Loodiana, 1,124 miles. Lat. 30° 47′, long. 75° 31′.

JUGUR.—A town in the native state of Bhotan, 96 miles N. from Goalpara, and 138 miles E. by N. from Darjeeling. Lat. 27° 31′, long. 90° 28′.

JUGURNATHPOOR.—A town in the British district of Behar, lieut.-gov. of Bengal, 23 miles E. of Sherghotty. Lat. 24° 36′, long. 85° 12′.

JUGUTPOOR.—A town in the territory of Oude, 60 miles S.S.E. from Lucknow, and 30 miles E. by N. from Futtehpoor. Lat. 26° 4′, long. 81° 20′.

JUHANABAD.—A town on the left bank of the Ganges, in the British district Bijnour, lieut.-gov. of the N.W. Provinces. Lat. 29° 15′, long. 78° 11′.

JUHANABAD, in the British district of

Allahabad, lieut.-gov. of the N.W. Provinces, a town on the left bank of the Ganges, 839 miles from Calcutta by the river, and 30 miles above the town of Allahabad. Lat. 25° 36′, long. 81° 40′.

JUHANABAD, the principal place of the pergunnah Juhanabad, in the British district Bareilly, and from the pergunnah deriving its name, is situate in lat. 28° 38′, long. 79° 47′.

JUHANGIRABAD, in the British district of Boolundshuhur, lieut.-gov. of the N.W. Provinces, on the route from Bareilly to Delhi, and 63 miles S.E. of the latter, is described by Thorn as an extensive town, surrounded by a high wall. Its population is returned at 10,247. Supplies and water are abundant. Lat. 28° 24′, long. 78° 10′.

JUHANGIRPUR, in the British district of Boolundshuhur, lieut.-gov. of the N.W. Provinces, a town on the route, by way of Chandaos, from Allygurh to Delhi, and 45 miles S.E. of the latter. Lat. 28° 11′, long. 77° 46′.

JUJJA, in Bhawlpoor, a town on the route from Khanpoor to Mittunkote, and 10 miles N.W. of the former place. It is situate about ten miles from the left bank of the Indus, in the alluvial tract extensively laid under water during the inundation of that river. It contains forty shops, a number which, according to the proportion usually found in such Indian towns, would indicate a population of about 600. Lat. 28° 46′, long. 70° 39′.

JUJURI, or JUGROG, in Hindoor, a fort on the lofty and steep ridge bearing in a south-easterly direction from the left bank of the Sutlej to the base of the Himalaya. At the commencement of the Goorkha war, it was, in the course of the operations preparatory to the investment of Malown, surrendered to the British, by whom it was subsequently dismantled. Lat. 31° 7′, long. 76° 51′.

JUKTIAL.—A town in Hyderabad, or dominions of the Nizam, situate 108 miles N. by E. from Hyderabad, and 160 miles S. by W. from Nagpoor. Lat. 18° 52′, long. 78° 58′.

JULAL, a river of Sirmour, rises near the south-western frontier, about lat. 30° 45′, long. 77° 16′. It is a clear and brisk stream, holding its way through a picturesque country of hill and dale, displaying occasionally considerable cultivation. After a course of about twenty miles in a south-easterly direction, the Julal falls into the Girree, on the right side, in lat. 30° 36′, long. 77° 30′.

JULALABAD, in the British district of Furruckabad, lieut.-gov. of the N.W. Provinces, a town on the route from Cawnpore to Futtehgurh, and 23 miles S. of the latter. It has a small bazar. Lat. 27° 6′, long. 79° 51′.

JULALABAD.—The principal place of a pergunnah of the same name, in the British district of Meerut, lieut.-gov. of the N.W. Provinces, a town on the route from Paneeput to Boolundshuhur, 32 miles N.W. by N. of the latter. Lat. 28° 46′, long. 77° 38′.

JULALEE, the principal place of the pergunnah of the same name, lies on the route from Allyghur cantonment to Bareilly, by Khasgunj, and is 13 miles S.E. of the former. It has a bazar, with a market, and is abundantly supplied with water from wells. Lat. 27° 52′, long. 78° 19′.

JULALPOOR, in the Jetch Dooab division of the Punjab, a town situated six miles from the right bank of the Chenaub, 73 N. of the town of Lahore. Lat. 32° 40′, long. 74° 10′.

JULALPOOR.—See JELALPOOR.

JULALPOOR.—The principal place of the pergunnah of the same name, a town on the route from Banda to Calpee, 48 miles N.W. of the former. It is situate on the right or south-east bank of the river Betwa, which here has "bed 550, and stream in the dry season 180 yards; bottom, sand and gravel; usual depth of water, two and a half feet; right bank steep. Some small ferry-boats at this ghat in the rains." It is probably a place of some importance, represented to have "some hundred large brick houses," and a population estimated by intelligent natives at 10,000. The neighbouring country, to the south, is rather wild and sterile, being much cut up by ravines. Lat. 25° 52′, long. 79° 52′.

JULDROOG.—A town in Hyderabad, or dominions of the Nizam, situate 133 miles E. by N. of Belgaum. Lat. 16° 14′, long. 76° 30′.

JULEYSUR, in the British district of Muttra, lieut.-gov. of the N.W. Provinces, a town on the route from Muttra to Furruckabad, 39 miles E. of the former. Its population amounts to 15,613 inhabitants. Lat. 27° 29′, long. 78° 23′.

JULGAUM.—A town in the British district of Candeish, presidency of Bombay, 147 miles N.E. of Bombay. Lat. 20° 24′, long. 74° 30′.

JULINDER DOOAB.—A tract of country in Upper India, lying, as the word Dooab implies, between two rivers, which, in this case, are the Beas and the Sutlej. It is situate between lat. 30° 57′—32° 5′, long. 75° 4′—76° 38′, and contains an area of about 374 square miles. It came into British possession during the earlier operations against the Seikhs, and was permanently retained as a portion of the British territory, under the third article of the treaty of Lahore, concluded on the 9th March, 1846, whereby the maharaja of the Punjaub ceded to the East-India Company, "in perpetual sovereignty, all his forts, territories and rights in the dooab or country, hill and plain, situate between the rivers Beas and Sutlej." The tract is fertile, and the climate agreeable. Soon after this district came into the hands of the English, some disturbances occurred between the beef-consuming part of the population and those who adhered to a simpler diet, caused by the opening of shops for the gratification of the former. They were, however, speedily suppressed, and quiet restored.

JULINDER, in the Punjab, the chief place of the Dooab, a considerable town near the right bank of the Sutluj, was once the residence of the Lodi-Afghan dynasty. It is situate in a tract of great richness, amidst flourishing orchards of mangoes and other trees. The vast number of large and finely-built mausoleums which are around, bear evidence of its former greatness. It has still a population of about 40,000. Lat. 31° 21′, long. 75° 31′.

JULKAR, in Gurwhal, a feeder of the Bhageerettee river. It rises in lat. 30° 35′, long. 78° 38′, and, flowing southerly for about twenty miles, falls into the Bhageerettee, in lat. 30° 28′, long. 78° 29′.

JULLAH, in the Jetch Dooab division of the Punjab, a town situated nine miles from the right bank of the Chenaub river, 81 N.W. by W. of the town of Lahore. Lat. 32° 12′, long. 72° 59′.

JULLALPOOR, in the British district of Banda, lieut.-gov. of the N.W. Provinces, a town on the right bank of the Jumna, 27 miles N.E. of the town of Banda, 55 W. of Allahabad. Lat. 25° 40′, long. 80° 45′.

JULLALPOOR, in the Baree Dooab division of the Punjab, a town situated seven miles from the right bank of the Ghara river, 43 miles S. by W. of the town of Mooltan. Lat. 29° 31′, long. 71° 22′.

JULLAREE, in the Baree Dooab division of the Punjab, a town situated on the left bank of the Ravee river, 39 miles N.E. of the town of Mooltan. Lat. 30° 29′, long. 71° 59′.

JULLAWGOTE, in Sinde, a village on the route from Sehwan to Larkhana, and 14 miles N. of the former town. It is situate on the right bank of a great watercourse filled by the inundation of the Indus, and a mile and a quarter from the main channel. Lat. 26° 37′, long. 67° 55′.

JULLMOOR.—A town in the British district of Ganjam, presidency of Madras, 92 miles S.W. of Ganjam. Lat. 18° 31′, long. 84° 4′.

JULLUT, in the British district of Kumaon, lieut.-gov. of the N.W. Provinces, a village on the route up the course of the river Goree, and by the Unta Dhura Pass, from Almorah fort to Hiundes or South-western Tibet, 93 miles S.E. of Almorah. It is situate near the right bank of the river Goree. Lat. 30° 5′, long. 80° 17′.

JULOWLEE, in the British district of Furruckabad, lieut.-gov. of the N.W. Provinces, a village on the route from the cantonment of Cawnpore to that of Futtehgurh, and 35 miles S. of the latter. Lat. 27°, long. 80°.

JULUPGURH, in the British district of Mozuffurnuggur, lieut.-gov. of the N.W. Provinces, a village on the route from Kurnal to Meerut, and 15 miles S.E. of the former. Lat. 29° 34′, long. 77° 13′.

JUMALGURH, in the British district of Saharunpoor, lieut.-gov. of the N.W. Provinces, a town the chief place of the pergunnah bearing the same name, is situate in lat. 29° 54′, long. 77° 20′.

JUMALPOOR, in the British district of Allyghur, lieut.-gov. of the N.W. Provinces, a village on the route from the cantonment of Allyghur to that of Moradabad, and one and a quarter mile N.E. of the former. Lat. 27° 57′, long. 78° 6′.

JUMALPOOR, in the British district of Allyghur, lieut.-gov. of the N.W. Provinces, a village on the route by Khasganj from Bareilly to Allyghur cantonment, and 10 miles S.E. of the latter. Lat. 27° 52′, long. 78° 16′.

JUMALPOOR.—A British military cantonment in the district of Mymensing, lieut.-gov. of Bengal, at the point where the Konaie diverges from the river Brahmapootra. Distance from Mymensing or Nusserabad, N.W., 25 miles; Burhampoor, N.E., 123; Dacca, N.W., 86; Calcutta, N.E., 190. Lat. 24° 56′, long. 90° 3′.

JUMARRA.—A town in the British district of Bhagulpoor, lieut.-gov. of Bengal, 27 miles S.W. by W. of Rajmahal. Lat. 24° 50′, long. 87° 28′.

JUMBOO.—A town in the native state of Bhotan, three miles from the left bank of the Monas river, and 124 miles N.E. by N. from Goalpara. Lat. 27° 46′, long. 91° 38′.

JUMBOOSEER, in the British district of Broach, presidency of Bombay, a town situate on the headland projecting between the estuaries of the rivers Nerbudda and Muhi or Mhye. It is the principal place of a pergunnah of the same name. In the vicinity are numerous large tanks, and the soil being of redundant fertility, and teeming with rank vegetation, malaria for a part of the year prevails, diffusing the seeds of disease and death. Tunkaria, a village on the seacoast, 10 miles S.W. of Jumbooseer, is its seaport, through which considerable quantities of cotton, grain, coarse cloths, and the produce of the mowa (Bassia latifolia), are exported. The population of Jumbooseer is estimated at 10,000. Distance from Surat, N., 60 miles; Bombay, N., 212. Lat. 22° 2′, long. 72° 50′.

JUMKUNDEE.—A town in the Southern Mahratta jaghire of Jumkundee, 69 miles N.E. from Belgaum, and 167 miles S.E. by S. from Poonah. The jaghiredar was bound to furnish a military contingent to his feudal superior, the British government, an obligation which has now been commuted for a pecuniary payment. His revenues amount to 2,70,246 rupees, or 27,024*l.*, per annum. Lat. 16° 30′, long. 75° 20′.

JUMLAH.—A town in Guzerat, or the dominions of the Guicowar, situate on the left bank of the Bhader river, and 80 miles S.W. from Rajkote. Lat. 21° 30′, long. 70° 1′.

JUMMULMUDGO.—A town in the British district of Cuddapah, presidency of Madras, 177 miles N.W. of Madras. Lat. 14° 51′, long. 78° 27′.

JUMNA.—The name of a great river of India, and the most important feeder of the Ganges. It rises at the south-western base of the group called the Jumnotri Peaks, at an elevation of 10,849 feet, and in lat. 31°, long. 78° 32′. About 500 feet to the north-west of the hot spring of Jumnotri, the face of the mountain rises very steeply, and is entirely cased in snow and ice. From a rock which projects from the snow, a small rill descends during the daytime. It is about three feet wide, and very shallow, being only a shower of spray produced by the snow melted by the sun's rays, and is, according to Hodgson, the most remote source of the Jumna. This point was found inaccessible by that observer, the snow-bed being intersected by rents and chasms, caused by the falling in of the snow as it became melted by the steam of the boiling springs below it. The rill finds its way through chasms formed in the snow-bed to the ground beneath, out of which gush numerous springs of water of nearly boiling heat, and the steam from those, melting the mass of ice and snow above them, causes a copious shower, which affords the principal supply to the nascent Jumna. The stream holds a course generally south-westerly for about eight miles, when the Berai-Ganga, a stream which down to this point surpasses the Jumna in length and volume of water, joins it on the left side, in lat. 30° 56′, long. 78° 27′. The declivity of the bed of the stream in this part of its course is enormous, as in a distance of sixteen miles, between its source and Kotnur, the fall is 5,036 feet, being at the rate of 314 feet to the mile. About five miles below this, and in lat. 30° 49′, long. 78° 19′, it receives on the right the Budeear, a great torrent, descending from the mountain Kedar-Kanta. On the same side, about three miles farther, the Bunal joins it, and, eight miles beyond, it is increased by the accession (also on the right side) of the Comalda, the largest of its tributaries above the Tonse. About four miles lower down, it receives the Rickna, and ten miles farther, the Khootnee, both on the right side. At the confluence with this last stream, and in lat. 30° 39′, long. 78° 5′, Hodgson found the Jumna, at the end of March, to be ninety feet wide, from three to five feet deep, rapid, and not fordable. About fifteen miles below this, it is joined on the left side by the Aglar or Agilwar, a considerable torrent. In addition to those above enumerated, numerous streams of less importance flow into the Jumna on both sides, between the source and this confluence. At the latter point, in lat. 30° 31′, long. 78° 8′, the course of the river, previously for the most part south-westerly, turns due west, which direction it keeps for thirteen miles, to the confluence of the Tonse, in lat. 30° 30′, long. 77° 53′, and at an elevation of 1,686 feet above the sea. The Tonse is by far the more considerable stream, its discharge being found, when surveyed by Hodgson and Herbert, to amount to 2,827 cubic feet in a second of time, whilst that of the Jumna was only 1,045. About ten miles farther down, on the same side, the Jumna receives the Girree, a small river, discharging 100 cubic feet in a second. At Raj Ghat, immediately below this confluence, Moorcroft describes the river as being 100 feet wide in the middle of February. Garden, however, assigns it greater dimensions here: according to that authority, the channel of the river is 600 yards wide, and the stream usually about 100 during the dry season, clear, deep, and rapid. A mile below this place, it receives on the left side, and at an elevation of 1,470 feet, the Asun, flowing from the south-east, and draining or irrigating the western part of the Debra Doon. Taking from this point a direction first westerly, then southerly, it flows through a ravine in the Sewalik Mountains, and about twelve miles below the confluence of the Asun, at Badshamahal, in lat. 30° 20′, long. 77° 38′, enters the plain of Hindostan. Herbert estimates the length of course, from the source of the Jumna to this place, at 123 miles, its elevation here at 1,276 feet, its discharge, at the beginning of March, at the rate of 4,000 cubic feet in a second. This assigned length of course, however, appears too great, the actual course being only about ninety-seven miles. Thus the fall from the source to this place is about 100 feet per mile. In the vicinity of Badshamahal, the Jumna divides into several branches, and on its right side a canal was, in the year 1356, dug by Feroz Toghluk, king of Delhi. At about eighty miles from the commencement of this canal, the canal of Ali Mardan Khan parted from it, and, taking a southerly direction, made its way to Delhi. This work appears to have been maintained in a state of efficiency till 1760; but in the canal of Feroz Shah the water ceased to flow at Suffeedon in 1740. The restoration of the Delhi Canal engaged at an early period the attention of the marquis of Hastings. In 1817, operations were commenced, and by the end of May, 1820, the water was brought to the city of Delhi, and, passing through the main conduit in the palace, rejoined its parent stream. The supply is drawn from a point in the vicinity of Choocarpore, and conducted along a natural channel to Jhyadri, thence by a new cut into the river Outralla, which it follows to its junction with the river Soumb; and, passing through this last-named river, is carried on, *viâ* Dadoopur, Kurnaul, Rair, and Boanuh, to Delhi; its total length being 185 miles. In 1823, the restoration of the Feroz Shah Canal, passing by Hansi and Hissar, was commenced. The two canals having one common head, the work consisted in the clearance of the old line from

Rair to Bahaderah, 151 miles; the construction of a branch to Rohtuk, forty-five miles long; of another in the direction of Darbah, thirty-two miles; and of the new supply-head, twelve miles: making a total of 240 miles. The water was turned down the canal in 1825. The restoration of the Dooab Canal, parting from the eastern bank of the Jumna near the village of Fyzabad, and rejoining the parent stream opposite the city of Delhi, was commenced in 1824, and the works were completed in 1830. "The original and almost sole object of the government in undertaking these works, appears to have been to convey a large supply of water from the Jumna for the purposes of irrigation of the crops—1st, on lines of country where the natural depth of wells was so great as to render the cost of irrigation from them so heavy as to impede the improvement of the districts, as on the Delhi Canal; 2nd, to supply the means of cheap and easy irrigation to the districts, as on the Dooab Canal, where, although the wells are not so deep, the irrigation from the canal would be comparatively cheap and easy; and, 3rd, as on Feroz's canal, to confer the means of irrigation on districts where, from the excessive depth of the wells, none was heretofore in use, and to convey a supply of wholesome water to a country where generally it is brackish or salt."

From Badshamahal to the point of reunion with the Delhi Canal, a distance of 145 miles, generally in a southerly direction, the Jumna is occasionally available for floating rafts of timber cut in the Sewalik Mountains, though even that rude kind of navigation is attended with danger during inundation, and in hot weather with delay. In addition to the works above enumerated, the construction of a canal from the Jumna, at a point about five miles east of Kurnaul, to the Sutlej at Loodiana, has been suggested, and a survey of the line of level made, the result of which appears favourable to the plan. At Delhi, the river is crossed during the dry season by a bridge of boats, constructed every year at the cessation of the rains. From that city, the course turns a little to the east; but though in many places extraordinarily circuitous, it holds generally a south-easterly direction to its confluence with the Ganges at Allahabad, a distance from Delhi, by the river's course, of 619 miles. Between Delhi and Allahabad, the Jumna receives on the right side the following rivers:—The Baun or Ootunghun, in lat. 26° 59′, long. 78° 31′; the Chumbul, in lat. 26° 30′, long. 79° 19′; the Sind, eight miles below; the Betwa, in lat. 25° 55′, long. 80° 17′; the Cane, in lat. 25° 47′, long. 80° 35′, all considerable streams; besides some others of less importance. The chief streams which fall in on the left side are, the Hindon, in lat. 28° 28′, long. 77° 30′; the Seengoor, in lat. 26° 9′, long. 79° 59′; the Rhind, in lat. 25° 53′, long. 80° 37′. Jacquemont styles the Jumna in the lower part of its course an enormous river; in the rainy season, it is in some places a mile, in others several miles, in width, and with a very rapid current. In consequence, however, of its bed being obstructed by shoals and rocks, navigation was not practicable for craft above Delhi, except by means of the canal. Prinsep thus speaks of the Jumna:—"That river, although of greater length than the Ganges above their confluence, yet much inferior to it in the average volume of its discharge, is the line of communication with some of the principal commercial marts and military stations in India,—Calpee, Etawah, Muttra, and the cities of Agra and Delhi, all situated upon its banks, and with the distant post of Kurnaul, by the ancient canal branching off at Delhi, which has been lately repaired and re-opened. Its banks are lofty and precipitous, and ridges of rock in many places advance into the stream, combining with its general shallowness and strong current to render navigation extremely difficult and dangerous." Much has, however, been done to remedy this inconvenience. At Kurinkhan, near Oryah, lat. 26° 26′, long. 79° 35′, the whole bed was formerly interspersed with kankar rocks, abounding with organic remains and huge blocks of sandstone, which rendered the navigation so intricate and dangerous, that great numbers of boats were lost, and others delayed for several weeks; but those obstacles have, for the most part, been removed by blasting or other means, and a dam made to deepen and give permanence to the channel; other improvements have been effected, and the practicability of navigating by steam the river below Calpee has been established. The Jumna contains crocodiles or alligators in the lower part of its course. The total length of the river, from its source to its confluence with the Ganges at Allahabad, is 860 miles. On the rocky point where the waters meet, stands the fort of Allahabad. The streams at the junction are nearly equal in volume; the Ganges, the deeper, with yellow water; the Jumna, the more rapid, with water as clear as crystal, but considered less palatable and wholesome than that of its fellow. The Jumna or Yamuna is by the Hindoos considered sacred, and its confluence with the still more sacred Ganges is dignified by a legend, according to which the Sarasvati or Sursuti, a stream that is lost in the wilds of Sirhind, flows underground to Allahabad, where it oozes from under one of the towers, and mingles its water with those of the other two rivers. Hence this confluence is called *Tri-veni*, or "three-plaited locks."

JUMNOTRI, a collection of hot springs near the source of the Jumna, is situate at the western base of the most western of three closely adjoining mountains, styled in the trigonometrical survey the Jumnotri Peaks. The mountain-mass formed by this collection of peaks bears the common name of Banderpuch. Fraser, who viewed it from the south-west, says: "Two lofty and massy peaks rise high above the rest, deep in snow, from which all the inferior ridges appear to take their rise: they are connected low down by a sharp neck;

their south and south-east exposure is the least steep, and bears a great depth of pure unbroken snow. Little or no rock is seen, except at a few points in the ridge connecting the peaks, where it is too sharp and steep for snow to lie; and here it appears of a red colour. Here and there lofty precipices are observed in the snow itself, where the lower parts have melted, and the upper masses have given way, sliding down the ravines below, leaving a face of snow of several hundred feet high, and showing the depth of that which has accumulated for ages."

According to native report, Banderpuch has four peaks, situate around a lake, in which Hanuman, the monkey-god, extinguished his flaming tail. In the trigonometrical survey, three peaks are laid down, having the respective heights and technical names,—Black E. 21,155 feet, Great E. 20,916, Lower E. 20,122. The group of hot springs is about 500 yards from the spot where the first water of the Jumna, a small rill, shoots over the brow of a rock projecting from the perennial and unexplored snows which overspread the summit of Banderpuch. The stream quickly finds its way through the mass of snow lying beneath the precipice, and having a thickness of forty feet, and runs beneath it close to the hot springs, receiving the water flowing from them. The steam of the springs melts the lower part of the mass of snow, so as to form a number of excavations, resembling vaulted roofs of marble; and from these incessant showers fall, which yield the principal supply to the nascent Jumna. The hot springs are numerous and extensive, and the water bursts up in them with great ebullition through a granite rock, and deposits a ferrugineous sediment. It is devoid of taste and smell, and has a temperature of 194·7°, nearly that of boiling water at that elevation, which is 10,849 feet above the sea. Lat. 30° 59′, long. 78° 35′.

JUMROOD.—A fort and small village, the former now in ruins, the latter scarcely traceable, in the province of Peshawur, 10 miles, or according to some 14 miles, W. of the city of that name, and a short distance from the eastern entrance into the Khyber Pass. The fort was seized by the Sikhs in 1837, and an attempt of the Afghans to retake it led to a battle, in which the Sikhs were defeated, and their general, Hari Singh, an officer of high reputation, slain. Previous to the acquisition of the Punjab by the British, the Sikhs strengthened their position by building the fort of Futighur, on the east side of Jumrood. The place is 1,670 feet above the sea. Jumrood is described by Forster under the name of Timrood. Lat. 34°, long. 71° 24′.

JUMTHUR, in the British district of Kumaon, lieut.-gov. of the N.W. Provinces, a village on the route, by the course of the Ramgunga, from Petoragurh to the Unta Dura Pass, 10 miles N. of Petoragurh. Lat. 29° 44′, long. 80° 16′.

JUMUNEE BHOJPOOR.—A town in the territory of Oude, 90 miles N.E. from Lucknow, and 120 miles E. from Shahjehanpoor. Lat. 27° 52′, long. 81° 54′.

JUNANABAD, or JEHANABAD, in the British district of Behar, lieut.-gov. of Bengal, a town on the route from Dinapore to Hazareebagh by Gaya, 37 miles S. of Dinapore, 30 N. of Gaya. It has a bazar, and is noted for the manufacture of good cotton cloth. The soil is fertile and highly cultivated, the main crop being rice. The town contains 887 houses, and, according to the usually admitted ratio of inmates to houses, a population of 4,435. Lat. 25° 12′, long. 85° 3′.

JUNGALEE, in the Punjab, a village on the route from Lahore to Ramnuggur, and 50 miles N.W. of the former place. The adjacent country is described by Burnes as sandy, yet rather productive, being irrigated from innumerable wells, which yield water at a depth seldom exceeding twenty-five feet. Lat. 32° 6′, long. 73° 55′.

JUNGLEG, in Bussahir, is the last and highest village in the valley of the river Pabur, on the route from Sirmor to Koonawur, by the Burenda or Broang Pass. It is situate on the right bank of the Pabur, which holds its course down a valley formed by two spurs of mountain running south-westward from the Himalaya. Elevation above the sea 9,257 feet. Lat. 31° 18′, long. 78° 4′.

JUNGROWLEE, in the British district of Bareilly, lieut.-gov. of the N.W. Provinces, a village on the route from Bareilly to Petoragurh, and 38 miles N.E. of the former. Lat. 28° 42′, long. 79° 52′.

JUNGUMCOTTA.—A town in the Mysore, 98 miles N.E. by E. from Seringapatam, and 164 miles W. from Madras. Lat. 13° 16′, long. 77° 55′.

JUNJEERA.—A town in the British district of Rutnageriah, presidency of Bombay, 80 miles S. by E. of Bombay. Lat. 17° 49′, long. 73° 10′.

JUNOH.—A town in the British district of Chota Nagpoor, presidency of Bengal, 191 miles W.N.W. of Calcutta. Lat. 23° 25′, long. 85° 38′.

JUPHA.—A town in the native state of Nepal, on the left bank of the Arun river, and 99 miles E. from Khatmandoo. Lat. 27° 37′, long. 86° 52′.

JUPLA.—A town in the British district of Behar, lieut.-gov. of Bengal, 51 miles W. of Sherghotty. Lat. 24° 33′, long. 84° 3′.

JURAJPOOR.—A town in the territory of Oude, on the right bank of the Goomtee river, and 50 miles N.W. from Lucknow. Lat. 27° 25′, long. 80° 29′.

JUROUNDA. — A town in the British province of Nagpoor, situate 138 miles S.E. from Jubbulpoor, and 187 miles E.N.E. from Nagpoor. Lat. 22° 6′, long. 81° 50′.

JUROWLY, in the British district of

Bolundshuhur, lieut.-gov. of the N.W. Provinces, a village on the route from Allyghur cantonment to that of Moradabad, and 28 miles N.E. of the former. Lat. 28° 17′, long. 78° 17′.

JURRAH, in the British district of Futtehpoor, lieut.-gov. of the N.W. Provinces, a town on the right bank of the Ganges, 874 miles from Calcutta by way of the river, 66 miles above Allahabad, and 28 miles by land S.E. of the town of Futtehpoor. Lat. 25° 50′, long. 81° 19′.

JURROW, or JHUROW, in the Rajpoot state of Joudpore, a village containing 125 houses, on the route from the town of Joudpore to that of Ajmeer, and 32 miles N.W. of the latter. The road in this part of the route is indifferent. Lat. 26° 33′, long. 74° 18′.

JURRUK, a town of Sinde, is situate on an eminence of small elevation, which forms a headland projecting into the Indus on the western side, and rising about thirty feet above the water. The principal manufacture is turnery of a very tasteful and highly-finished kind. Its population is probably about 1,500 or 2,000. Lat. 25° 3′, long. 68° 20′.

JUSHPORE, or JUGDESPORE.—A small raj included within the territory superintended by the Governor-General's political agent for the south-west frontier of Bengal. It extends from lat. 22° 4′ to lat. 22° 50′, and from long. 83° 24′ to long. 84° 10′, and has an area of 617 square miles. The country is a high table-land, much overrun with jungle, but was recently found by the British agent to be improving under the government of the native chief, represented as far surpassing the majority of his class in intelligence and attention. The people appear happier than in many other parts of the political agency. Rice, grain, and oil, are the staple productions. Lak and wild silk are abundant where cultivation has not subjugated the jungle. The country is computed to yield a revenue of 10,000 rupees. The population is estimated at upwards of 27,000.

JUSHPOOR.—A town in the native state of Jushpoor, on the south-west frontier of Bengal, 93 miles N. from Sumbulpoor, and 73 miles S.W. from Lohadugga. Lat. 22° 43′, long. 83° 56′.

JUSHPOOR, on the south-west frontier of Bengal, a town in the Cuttack mehal of Mohurbunge, 153 miles W. by S. from Calcutta, and 67 miles W.N.W. from Balasore. Lat. 22°, long. 86° 8′.

JUSOL, in the Rajpoot state of Joudpore, a ruined town near the left bank of the Loonee, between Balmeer and the town of Joudpore, and 60 miles S.W. of the latter. It is situate at the northern base of a small conical hill about 200 feet high, on the upper part of the rocky side of which was the residence of the thakoor or chief. The river Loonee, abreast of this place, was, when ferried over by Boileau in the rainy season, at the beginning of July, 700 yards wide, and running with a very violent current. The town in the time of its prosperity contained 3,000 houses; but not a tenth of that number are now inhabited. The road in this part of the route between Balmeer and the town of Joudpore is under water during the rainy season, and unsafe. Lat. 25° 47′, long. 72° 23′.

JUSPOOR, in the British district of Moradabad, lieut.-gov. of the N.W. Provinces, a town on the route from Pilleebheet to Suharunpoor, and 100 miles S.W. of the former. It is situate near the southern boundary of the Terai or marshy forest extending along the base of the mountain, and in lat. 29° 17′, long. 78° 53′.

JUSSO, in Bundelcund, a town, the principal place of a jaghire or feudal possession of the same name, containing an area of 180 square miles, with a population of 24,000. The revenue of the raj is returned at 1,300*l.* per annum, and the chief maintains a small military force. The town is distant 26 miles S.E. of Punnah. Lat. 24° 27′, long. 80° 35′.

JUSTWUNTNUGUR, in the British district of Etawa, lieut.-gov. of the N.W. Provinces, a small town on the route from the cantonment of Agra to that of Etawa, and nine miles N.W. of the latter. It has a mosque and a small bazar. The population of the town is returned at 5,239. Lat. 26° 53′, long. 78° 58′.

JUTEEPOOR, in the British district of Bareilly, lieut.-gov. of the N.W. Provinces, a village on the route from Bareilly to Petoragarh, and 26 miles N.E. of the former. Lat. 28° 37′, long. 79° 47′.

JUTPOOL.—A town in Hyderabad, or dominions of the Nizam, 94 miles S. by W. from Hyderabad, and 18 miles N.E. from Kurnool. Lat. 16° 1′, long. 78° 16′.

JUTPOORA, in the British district of Moradabad, lieut.-gov. of the N.W. Provinces, a village on the route from Allygurh to the town of Moradabad, and six miles S.W. of the latter. Lat. 28° 46′, long. 78° 47′.

JUTT.—A town in the Sattara jaghire of Jutt, 95 miles N.E. from Belgaum, and 136 miles S.E. by S. from Poonah. The jaghiredar is bound to furnish a contingent of cavalry to its feudal superior, the British government. A proposal made by the latter for a commutation of the obligation by a pecuniary payment, was met by refusal on the part of the chief. Lat. 17° 1′, long. 75° 16′.

JUTTA KA GOTE, in Sinde, a village on the route from Tatta to Hydrabad, by way of Kotree, and 17 miles N.E. of Tatta. It is situate a mile and a half from the right bank of the Indus, and half-way between that river and the brackish *Dund*, or lake of Kunjur. The adjacent country is plain, and occupied principally by a shikargah or hunting-ground, lately belonging to one of the ameers of Hydrabad. Lat. 24° 56′, long. 68° 12′.

JUTTEEL MOUNTAINS, in Sinde, form a portion of that mountain system which, stretching eastward from the great Hala range, terminates abruptly on the right bank of the Indus, near Sehwan. The Jutteel Mountains run south-west from Sehwan to Dooba, a distance of between sixty and seventy miles. They are steep and of considerable height, probably in few places less than 2,000 feet. The direct road from Sehwan to Kurrachee lies between them and the Keertar range, which is equally high, and holds a parallel course, but more to the west. The Jutteel range extends between lat. 25° 32′—26° 20′, and long. 67° 48′—68° 8′.

JUTTOO, in the Punjab, a village on the route from Mooltan to Dera Ismael Khan, and 18 miles N.W. of the former town. It is situate 10 miles from the right bank of the Chenaub river, in what Elphinstone calls the Little Desert, extending between the Chenaub and the Indus, and which he describes as having a length of 250 miles from north to south, and, in the latitude of Juttoo, a breadth of two days' march, or about forty miles. Lat. 30° 20′, long. 71° 17′.

JUWAHIR, or **JUWAR**, in the British district of Kumaon, lieut.-gov. of the N.W. Provinces, the most considerable of the Bhotia mehals or subdivisions north of the culminating ridge of the Himalaya. It comprises the upper part of the valley drained by the river Goree, together with the lofty mountains rising on each side, and ranges between lat. 30° 10′—30° 35′, long. 79° 50′—80° 20′. The surface throughout has great elevation, the lowest part affording passage to the river Goree, over the southern frontier, at Leepookee Than, in lat. 30° 10′, long. 80° 17′, at an elevation of 9,152 feet above the sea; the head of the Goonka, its remotest feeder, being at the Oota Dhoora Pass into Hiundes, and at an elevation probably of not less than 15,000 feet. The valley drained by the river, extending between these places, is the habitable part of Juwahir; the more elevated tracts, rising on the east and west, being unexplored wastes of perennial snow. Therein are summits of extraordinary height, some rising 22,000, some 23,000, feet above the level of the sea; and one, called Nanda Devi, reaching 25,749. At the fall of the year, the whole surface of the country becomes covered with deep snow, which commences early in October, when the inhabitants migrate to the more southern, lower, and warmer parts of Kumaon. The accumulation is progressive to the beginning of April, and snow continues to fall until late in May. The depth, in open and level situations, varies in different years from six to twelve feet, and is wholly dissipated by the first week in June; but in confined and much-depressed places, successive avalanches sometimes cause accumulations several hundred feet thick, and in many deep valleys and ravines the whole is not melted until late in July. Goats and sheep are the most general beasts of burthen, the former carrying from twelve to twenty-four pounds, the latter from ten to sixteen. These animals journey on an average a distance of five miles daily, being allowed to remain stationary for the greater part of the day for pasture, which affords their only means of subsistence. The inhabitants of Juwahir are supported by the traffic between Hiundes and the countries to the south. The more wealthy, having command of capital, combine commercial speculations in both quarters with the carrying-business, which forms the main resource of the less opulent. The inhabitants of Juwahir are favoured by the Tibetan authorities, in being allowed access to all parts of Tibet, while the other Bhotias of Kumaon are restricted to particular places for trade. They take into Hiundes grain, cottons, broadcloths, hardware, glassware, wooden vessels, coral, pearls, dye-stuffs, spices, sugar, sugarcandy, and timber; and bring back gold-dust, salt, borax, sheep's-wool, goat's-wool or shawl-wool, chauries or yak-tails, coarse shawls, inferior silks, leather tanned in a similar manner to the Russian, dried fruits, and drugs. The Juwaharis are of Tibetan descent, and exhibit the singular anomaly of yielding allegiance both to the mother country and to the government of Kumaon; the latter enforced by military power, the former by the influence resulting from commercial relations. Their religion is a medley of Lamaism and of Brahminism, administered indifferently, according to exigency, by the priests of either faith. They affect the same scruples as the Brahmins with respect to food, and have assumed the designation of Sinh (lion), but are regarded by the Brahminists with abhorrence, as the descendants of a kine-killing race. The Tibetan language has died away and been replaced by the Hindoostanee, now universally used in Juwahir. The people are represented by Traill as an honest, industrious, orderly race, patient and good-humoured, but very filthy in their habits, using the skirts of their dress to scrub both their persons and cooking-utensils. Under the Goorkha sway, the tribute levied was oppressively large. This arose not entirely from fiscal, but partly from vindictive motives, the Juwahirs having frequently baffled the military efforts made to reduce them to submission. Juwahir comprises thirteen villages and 455 houses; and if six be taken as the average for the number of inmates of each, the result would be a population of 2,730.

JWALA MUKHI.—See JEWALA MUKI.

JWITEE.—A town in the hill zemindary of Jeypoor, presidency of Madras, four miles E.N.E. from Jeypoor, and 91 miles N.W. from Vizianagrum. Lat. 19° 3′, long. 82° 30′.

JYE BOORDEE.—A town in the British district of Tannah, presidency of Bombay, 81 miles N. of Bombay. Lat. 20° 7′, long. 72° 45′.

JYGURH.—A town in the British district of Rutnagherry, presidency of Bombay, 118 miles S. by E. of Bombay. Lat. 17° 17', long. 73° 19'.

JYNTEEA.—A district of Eastern India, situate in the Cossya Hills, and extending from lat. 24° 55' to 26° 7', and from long. 91° 53' to 92° 48'. It is eighty miles in length from north to south, and forty in breadth. The tract formerly constituted the northern division of the possessions of a native prince, styled the rajah of Jynteea, between whom and the British government political relations appear to have been first established during the Burmese war in 1824, when the territory of the rajah was secured to him by treaty. This treaty, however, was regarded merely in the light of a personal engagement with the reigning prince, and its conditions were not considered binding on his successor. In 1835, it being proved that the new rajah, while heir-apparent, had ordered or connived at the kidnapping of four British subjects for the purpose of human sacrifice, the British government confiscated his possessions in the plains, upon which the rajah voluntarily relinquished his districts in the hills. A pension of *50l.* a month was assigned for his support, and he retired to Dacca. The forfeited possessions were annexed to the British dominions; those situated in the plains being incorporated with the district of Sylhet, and the remainder (forming the subject of this article) being placed under the jurisdiction of the political agent in the Cossya Hills. Coal is stated to abound in the hills of Jynteea.

JYNTEEAHPORE.—A town of Eastern India, in the British district of Jynteea, 77 miles S.S.E. of Gowhatty. Lat. 25° 7', long. 92° 5'.

JYNUGUR.—A town in the British district of Tirhoot, lieut.-gov. of Bengal, 58 miles N.E. of Mozuffurpoor. Lat. 26° 31', long. 86° 15'.

JYRUNG.—A town of Eastern India, in the Cossya Hills, situate in the native state of Osimlee, 21 miles S.W. by S. from Gowhatty, and 63 miles E.S.E. from Goalpara. Lat. 25° 52', long. 91° 36'.

JYSINUGUR, in the British territory of Saugor and Nerbudda, lieut.-gov. of the N.W. Provinces, a town on the route from Saugor to Hoosungabad, 19 miles S.W. of the former. Lat. 23° 37', long. 78° 38'.

JYTO.—A town in one of the petty Cis-Sutlej jaghires, 77 miles S.W. from Loodianah, and 38 miles S.E. by S. from Ferozepoor. Lat. 30° 28', long. 74° 55'.

JYTPORE.—See Jeitpore.

JYTUK, or JAITAK, in Sirmor, a very steep ridge of clay-slate, rising over the north-western extremity of the Kyarda Doon. A peak of this ridge is surmounted by a stone fort, about seventy feet long and fifty wide, having a small round tower or bastion at each corner, the whole, however, constructed in an unsubstantial manner. During the war with the Goorkhas in 1814, it was occupied by them with a garrison of about 2,200 men, who, on the 27th of December, were attacked by two separate British detachments, one of about 1,000 strong, the other of about 700. The former meeting with a well-conducted resistance, and suffering severe loss, fled panic-struck to camp; the other made good a lodgment in an important position near the fort; but being called off by General Martindell, who commanded the army of which the detachment formed part, it was harassed greatly on its retreat, and narrowly escaped total destruction. The loss to both detachments amounted to four officers killed, and five wounded; seventy-nine non-commissioned officers and privates killed, and 281 wounded and missing. On the 13th of March following, two eighteen-pounder battering-guns were with great difficulty hauled by hand up the nearly perpendicular side of the ridge, and placed in battery against the fort, besides two six-pounders, two eight-and-half-inch mortars, and two five-and-half-inch howitzers. The defences of the Goorkhas were in consequence much damaged, and in a short time the British posts were so arranged as completely to blockade the fort, which, early in May, was surrendered, but not till the stock of provisions for the use of the garrison was reduced to one day's rations. Nearly 1,500 armed men marched out, besides about 1,000 women and children. Jytuk is 4,854 feet above the sea. Distant N.W. from Calcutta 1,014 miles, by Dehra. Lat. 30° 36', long. 77° 24'.

K.

KABILPOOR, in the British district of Shahjehanpoor, lieut.-gov. of the N.W. Provinces, a village on the route from Bareilly to the cantonment of Futtehgurh, and 35 miles S.E. of the former. The road in this part of the route is good; the country open, level, and cultivated. Lat. 27° 55', long. 79° 44'.

KABO.—A town in the British district of Chota Nagpoor, lieut.-gov. of Bengal, 186 miles W. by N. of Calcutta. Lat. 22° 58', long. 85° 35'.

KABOOL RIVER, or JUI SHIR.—The only great tributary of the Indus from the west. It is generally supposed to rise at Sir-i-Chushmuh, in lat. 34° 17', long. 68° 14', where at a height of 8,400 feet above the sea, a very copious spring bursts from the ground, and forms the chief source of the principal stream. But the extreme head is about twelve miles farther west, on the eastern declivity of the Oonna ridge. It is at first an inconsiderable stream, everywhere fordable for sixty miles, as far as Kabool; at a short distance beyond which place it receives the river of Logurh, and thenceforward is a rapid river. About forty miles below Kabool, it receives the Punchshir river, which has a course of 120 miles. About fifteen miles below this, it receives the Tagoa river, having a course of about eighty miles. The united streams of the Alishang and Alingar join the Kabool river about twenty miles farther down, after a course each of about 120 miles. At the distance of about twenty miles more, the Soorkh Rood, or Red River, so called from the colour which its water derives from the earth suspended in it, falls into the Kabool river after a course of seventy miles. Twenty miles further east, the Kabool river receives the river Kama, called also the river of Kooner, which rising in Chitral, flows through Kafiristan. Such is the course of the Kabool river, and thus does it acquire force and volume. Flowing easterly, it drains the valley of Kabool, the Sufeid Koh, and the southern slope of the Hindoo Koosh; and after receiving on both sides several considerable streams, becomes a large river, sweeping with prodigious rapidity and violence along the northern base of the Khyber Mountains, and, in consequence of its boiling eddies and furious surges, not navigable, except on rafts of hides. Eastward of these hills, and in lat. 34° 10′, long. 71° 27′, it enters the British territory of the Punjab, and divides into three branches, which, at Dobundee, twelve miles lower down, reunite, and thence the river is navigable for boats of forty or fifty tons to Attock, near which it joins the Indus. Just below Dobundee it is joined from the north by the Lundye, or river of Panjkora, which, rising in that unexplored region of the Hindoo Koosh lying east of Chitral, passes south-west by Panjkora, receives the river of Sewat from the north-east, and some tributaries of less importance from the west, and has a total course of above 200 miles. After this confluence, the Kabool river continues to flow eastward for forty miles, and falls into the Indus on the western side, nearly opposite Attock, and in lat. 33° 54′, long. 72° 16′, having a total course of about 320 miles. As both rivers are very rapid, and have great bodies of water, the confluence produces turbulent eddies and violent surges.

KACHAURA, in the British district of Agra, lieut.-gov. of the N.W. Provinces, a town on the south-eastern frontier, towards the British district of Etawah. It is situate on the right bank of the Jumna, 55 miles S.E. of the city of Agra. Lat. 26° 50′, long. 78° 48′.

KADASUR, in the British district of Ghazeepoor, lieut.-gov. of the N.W. Provinces, a town on the route from Ghazeepoor cantonment to Hazareebagh, 21 miles S. of the former, 171 N.E. of the latter, is situate on the river Karamnasa. Lat. 25° 19′, long. 83° 32′.

KADIPOOR, in the district of Aldemau, territory of Oude, a village two miles from the left bank of the river Tons (eastern), 42 miles S.E. of Faizabad, 108 E. of Lucknow. The population is estimated by Butter at 1,000. Lat. 26° 22′, long. 82° 43′.

KADIRPOOR.—A village in Sinde, between Subzulcote and Shikarpoor, and 24 miles W. of the former place. It is situate near the left bank of the Indus, in a level country, in some places overrun with jungle, but capable of successful cultivation, in consequence of the facility of irrigation by means of watercourses from the river. Lat. 28° 10′, long. 69° 20′.

KADLOOR.—A town in one of the recently-sequestrated districts of Hyderabad, or dominions of the Nizam, 60 miles N.W. of Kurnool. Lat. 16° 22′, long. 77° 23′.

KADMUH, in the jaghire of Jujhur, lieut.-gov. of the N.W. Provinces, a village near the western frontier towards Lobaroo. Lat. 28° 24′, long. 76° 4′.

KADURGUNGE, in the British district of Buddaon, lieut.-gov. of the N.W. Provinces, a town on the route from Futtehgurh to Buddaon, 16 miles S.S.W. of the latter. Lat. 27° 49′, long. 79° 9′.

KAEELAUN, or **KYLAWUN**, in the British district of Boolundshuhur, lieut.-gov. of the N.W. Provinces, a village on the route from Khasgunj to Meerut, and 53 miles S. of the latter. Lat. 28° 18′, long. 78° 2′.

KAENG, in the island of Ramree (Arracan), a village prettily situated near the sea, at the mouth of a small creek. The neighbourhood consists of extensive plains, which are exceedingly fertile, and rice and indigo are cultivated to a great extent. In the opinion of Lieutenant Foley, who visited it in 1834, "this village is superior to any in the island, both with respect to situation and the general appearance of neatness and comfort that prevails." Lat. 19° 5′, long. 93° 45′.

KAFR KOT, or **THE INFIDELS' FORT.**—A huge, lofty, and massive ruin near the west bank of the Indus, and between that river and the Largee valley. It consists of a number of towers bearing every mark of extreme antiquity, rising on the very summit of the mountain-chain. These are connected with the Indus by a dilapidated wall extending from them to the edge of the water. Wood, who surveyed the spot, expresses his astonishment at the toil and skill which must have been directed to the construction of this stupendous edifice, singularly contrasting with the mean mud hovels which, with this exception, are the only buildings to be found throughout this region. The time and circumstances of its erection are totally unknown. Lat. 32° 30′, long. 71° 22′.

KAGAKAT.—A town in the native state of Nepal, on the left bank of the Gunduck river, and 163 miles N.W. by W. from Khatmandoo. Lat. 28° 57′, long. 83° 3′.

KAGUL.—A jaghire or feudal dependency of Kolapore, of which it forms part, and situate within the jurisdiction of the political agency of the Bombay government. The inhabitants, always engaged in feuds with Kolapore under the native government, yield ready obedience to the British authority, which has assumed the temporary management of the Kolapore territories. The revenue amounts to something more than 70,000 rupees, and the military force to about 700 men. Kagul, the chief town, is in lat. 16° 32′, long. 74° 23′.

KAHA, in Sinde, is a mouth of the Indus, by which the Moutnee, formerly a large offset of the Sata, or great eastern branch of that river, discharged its water into the sea. In consequence of the channel of the Moutnee having been almost entirely deserted by the stream, the Kaha mouth has become little more than a salt-water creek. Lat. 23° 56′, long. 67° 35′.

KAHEREE.—A village of the Daman division of the Punjab, situate on the right bank of the Indus. Here is one of the principal ferries on that river. It is on the route from Hindostan to Afghanistan, by Dera Ismael Khan and the Gomul or Goolairee Pass. Elphinstone, who crossed here at the beginning of January, when the water is lowest, found the main channel 1,010 yards wide; and it is known to be much broader during the swell. Lat. 31° 25′, long. 70° 47′.

KAHGUDIPOOR, in the British district of Ghazeepoor, lieut.-gov. of the N.W. Provinces, a village on the route from Ghazeepoor cantonment to that of Goruckpoor, 15 miles N. of the former, 76 S. of the latter. Lat. 25° 44′, long. 83° 45′.

KAHSEHS.—A town in the native state of Nepal, three miles from the right bank of the Kurnalli river, and 90 miles E.S.E. from Almora. Lat. 29° 12′, long. 81° 8′.

KAILAS.—See Koonlus.

KAIMGUNJ, in the British district of Furruckabad, lieut.-gov. of the N.W. Provinces, a town on the route from Futtehgurh to Budaoon, 20 miles N.W. of the former. Population 8,983. Lat. 27° 34′, long. 79° 25′.

KAIMUR.—A mountain-range in the territory of Rewa or Baghelcund, extending S.W. from about lat. 24° 40′, long. 82°, for about 70 or 80 miles, and dividing the valley of the Tons from that of the Son. It has in one part a remarkable conical shape, and an elevation probably exceeding 2,000 feet above the sea. The formation, according to Franklin, is primitive sandstone, intermixed with schistose limestone. This range is a section of the Vindhya Mountains.

KAIR.—A town in Hyderabad, or dominions of the Nizam, situate three miles from the left bank of the Payne Gunga river, and 176 miles N. by E. from Hyderabad. Lat. 19° 50′, long. 79° 9′.

KAIRA, a British collectorate in the presidency of Bombay, is bounded on the north by the Myhee Caunta division of Guzerat; on the east and south by the river Myhee; and on the west by the collectorate of Ahmedabad and the dominions of the Guicowar. It extends from lat. 22° 12′ to 23° 33′, and from long. 72° 30′ to 73° 27′. The greatest length from north to south is ninety-four miles, and its greatest breadth fifty miles. The area is 1,869 square miles. The principal staple articles of cultivation are tobacco, sugar, indigo, cotton, opium, poppy, and cumin. The district is traversed by the Bombay and Baroda railway; but there are no metalled or macadamized roads in this collectorate, with the exception of the line extending from the southern gate of the town of Kaira to the Seree river, near the village of Ruttunpoor. The highways and crossways throughout the collectorate are for the most part formed by the tracks of carts, and though uneven and narrow, they are generally in other respects pretty good. Among the principal highways which traverse the collectorate, is one from Baroda *viâ* Kaira to Ahmedabad, which crosses the river Myhee northward of the town of Wasud, and another from Malwa and Loonawarra to Ballasinore, Kupperwung, and Ahmedabad. The country being sandy, the roads are somewhat heavy for wheeled carts, and in the rainy season some of them are partially flooded; but a few days' fine weather is sufficient to render them again passable. The population is given under the article Bombay.

The implements used in husbandry by the agricultural classes are of the same description as those employed by their forefathers. No improvements have taken place. A few American ploughs were introduced by the government in 1843, two of which were given to the cultivators for trial. They complained that they were clumsy and unsuited to native management, that the furrows formed by them were too wide, and that additional labour was required to level the surface. It was objected, moreover, that it would cost as much to repair one of these ploughs as to make a new one on the old plan. The cultivators are extremely averse to innovation, and the attempt to introduce these ploughs proved a failure. The principal towns are ten in number,—Kaira, Kupperwung, Borsud, Nerriad, Mehmoodabad, Mahtur, Tansra, Mahoonda, Nepar, and Oomrut, which will be found described in their proper places. Government vernacular schools have been established in various parts of the district. The tract forming the district of Kaira was ceded to the East-India Company by the Guicowar, under different treaties and engagements, commencing with the grant or sunnud dated 3rd May, 1803, under which the British were put in possession of the fort of Kaira.

KAIRA, in the presidency of Bombay, a town, the principal place of the British collectorate of the same name. It is situate near the confluence of two small rivers, the Watruk and Seree, over the latter of which a bridge has been recently erected. The surrounding country is fertile and beautiful, and overspread by fine orchards, or, where those are not to be met with, by thickets of wild fig-trees and other wild-fruitbearers. The town is of considerable size, and is surrounded by a wall with bastions. The streets within are uneven and narrow.

The houses, however, are solid and lofty, with sloping tiled roofs, and a good deal of carving about the woodwork of their gables and verandas. Near the centre of the town are a large Jain temple and school, the former consisting of many apartments, some of them raised, and approachable only by ascending flights of stairs; some on the ground-floor, and some underground. In this building is some fine carving in dark-coloured wood. There is also a subterraneous Jain temple, containing, seated on an altar, four white marble statues of characters considered by the worshippers as sacred. Near the temple is the Adawlut, or court of justice, a handsome building, with pillars in the Grecian style, having its attic story raised high above the town, and containing very convenient apartments for the judge and his family. Contiguous is the prison, a large strong building. There is in the town a church, a large clumsy building. There is also a government vernacular school. The military cantonments are about a mile and a half from the city, and separated from it by a small river. They are extensive, and in most respects well laid out, except that, being built in the form of a square, a large portion is deprived of the benefit of free ventilation. The climate is very hot and unhealthy, producing fever, ague, and other diseases resulting from malaria. The town is distant from Bombay, N., 265 miles; from Ahmedabad, S., 20 miles. Lat. 22° 45′, long. 72° 41′.

KAISLA, in the British territory of Saugor and Nerbudda, lieut.-gov. of the N.W. Provinces, a town on the route from Hoosungabad to Baitool, 42 miles N. of the latter. Lat. 22° 26′, long. 77° 54′.

KAITHAULA, in the district of Salon, territory of Oude, a town 70 miles S.E. of Lucknow, 40 S.W. of Sultanpoor cantonment. It is situate on the right bank of the river Saee, which nearly surrounds the town by its windings. The population is estimated by Butter at 8,000, all Hindoos. Lat. 26°, long. 81° 37′.

KAITI, or KYTEE, in the British district of Benares, lieut.-gov. of the N.W. Provinces, a town on the left bank of the Ganges, just above the confluence of the Goomtee, 645 miles N.W. of Calcutta by water, 24 N.E. of Benares. Lat. 25° 30′, long. 83° 13′.

KAITI, in the British district of Benares, lieut.-gov. of the N.W. Provinces, a village on the right bank of the Ganges, 662 miles N.W. of Calcutta by water, seven miles N.E. of Benares. Lat. 25° 20′, long. 83° 12′.

KAITRI, in territory of Gwalior, or possessions of Scindia's family, a small fort and village on the route from Agra to Gwalior fort, 38 miles S. of former, 31 N.W. of latter. It is situate on the south or right side of the river Chumbul. The bank is bold and lofty, and the channel, three-quarters of a mile wide, is filled by a deep and rapid torrent. In the dry season it is crossed by ford, much frequented, as, opposite Dholpoor, four miles lower down the stream, the passage must be made by ferry or bridge of boats. Lat. 26° 37′, long. 77° 57′.

KAKA.—A town in the native state of Nepal, situate under the mountain Dhoulagiri, and 169 miles N.W. by W. from Khatmandoo. Lat. 29° 8′, long. 83° 4′.

KAKADU, in the British district of Cawnpore, lieut.-gov. of the N.W. Provinces, a village on the route from Calpee to the cantonment of Cawnpore, and five miles S.W. of the latter. The road in this part of the route is metalled or macadamized; the country is well cultivated. Lat. 26° 28′, long. 80° 21′.

KAKEENADA.—A town in the British district of Rajahmundry, presidency of Madras, nine miles S.E. of Samulkottah. Lat. 16° 58′, long. 82° 19′.

KAKHUNDKEE.—A town in the British district of Sattara, presidency of Bombay, 89 miles N.E. of Belgaum. Lat. 16° 37′, long. 75° 37′.

KAKITA.—A town in the British district of Vizagapatam, presidency of Madras, 48 miles W.S.W. of Vizagapatam. Lat. 17° 24′, long. 82° 44′.

KAKRAJEET.—A town in the British district of Midnapoor, lieut.-gov. of Bengal, 78 miles S.W. by W. of Calcutta. Lat. 21° 58′, long. 87° 22′.

KAKTEE.—A town in the Mahratta jaghire of Sanglee, territory of Bombay, nine miles N. from Belgaum, and 56 miles S.S.E. from Kolapoor. Lat. 15° 57′, long. 74° 37′.

KAKUBA, or KAKOOA, in the British district of Agra, lieut.-gov. of the N.W. Provinces, a village on the route from the city of Agra to Gwalior, seven miles S. of former. Here, in December, 1843, the British army, under command of Sir Hugh Gough, accompanied by Lord Ellenborough, governor-general, encamped, in the advance against Gwalior. Lat. 27° 4′, long. 78° 3′.

KALA BAGH.—A town on the right or west bank of the Indus, where it finds a passage through the Salt range, which stretches from Afghanistan into the Punjab. The breadth of the stream, bounded by very lofty and steep banks, is here about 350 yards. The road, a gallery cut in the side of the cliff, and about 100 feet above the edge of the water, is so narrow as not to allow a laden camel to pass. A great part of this excavation is through rock-salt, extremely hard, pellucid, clear, and nearly colourless as crystal. Some specimens are so hard that they are worked into platters. The town rises as though it were stuck against the precipitous eminence overhanging the road and river, and, together with the salt-rock, the stream, and the prospect over the country to the east, forms a striking scene. The heat in summer is here excessive, and the air unwholesome, as well naturally as from the effluvia of alum-works. The alum is obtained from a sort of slate, which is found in vast quantities in the neighbouring mountains. This is placed in layers between wood, and the pile thus formed set on fire; the residuum is then boiled in iron pans, filtered, and, by means of evaporation, rendered solid alum. There are fourteen manufactories for the purification of the mineral. Great quantities of salt are extracted here, for the supply of Western India and Afghanistan. There is also coal in its vicinity, but of poor quality, and in inconsiderable seams. The Indus is navigable to Kala Bagh at all-seasons, and it is expected that the communication by government steam-vessels, which has been established between Kurrachee and Mooltan, will be shortly extended to this town. The population probably does not exceed 2,000. Lat. 32° 57′, long. 71° 35′.

KALAISUR.—A town in Hyderabad, or dominions of the Nizam, situate on the right bank of the Godavery, 139 miles N.E. of Hyderabad. Lat. 18° 51′, long. 79° 53′.

KALAPYNDONG KEON, in Arracan, a small river taking its rise in the Wyllatong Hills, about lat. 21° 8′, long. 92° 51′, and joining the Myoo river about lat. 20° 43′, long. 92° 42′, at the village of Khengkeong.

KALEE RIVER.—See GHOGRA.

KALEEGUNJE.—A town in the British district of Mymunsing, lieut.-gov. of Bengal, 189 miles N.E. of Calcutta. Lat. 24° 36′, long. 90° 29′.

KALEEGUNJE.—A town in the British district of Rungpoor, lieut.-gov. of Bengal, 30 miles E.S.E. of Rungpoor. Lat. 25° 34′, long. 89° 43′.

KALEE KEMAON.—See CHAMPAWUT.

KALEE OUNG.—A town in the British province of Tenasserim, 134 miles S.S.E. of Moulmein. Lat. 14° 39′, long. 98° 22′.

KALEGOUK ISLAND is situate six miles off the coast of Amherst (Tenasserim provinces). Its length from north to south is six miles, and its breadth one mile. Lat. 15° 32′, long. 97° 43′.

KALE MYO.—A town of Burmah, situate on the left bank of the Myithia Khyoung, and 135 miles N.W. from Ummerapoora. Lat. 23° 3′, long. 94° 28′.

KALERAWUN, in the British district of Hurriana, lieut.-gov. of the N.W. Provinces, a village on the route from Hansee to Bhutnair, and 28 miles N.W. of the former. It is a poor place, and even water is scarce. Lat. 29° 18′, long. 75° 35′.

KALE SERAI, in the Punjab, a village and caravanserai on the route from Attock to Rawul Pindee, and 39 miles S.E. of the former place. It is situate on the river Kalee, a tributary of the Hurroo. The Kalee, though of short course, is deep: the passage across it is effected by an old stone bridge. It is the Toomrah of Walker's Map. At a short distance to the north-west of the village is a baoli or great well, the water of which is reached by a descent of 100 steps. The surrounding country is remarkably rocky, rugged, and barren, and the roads are rough and difficult. Lat. 33° 40′, long. 72° 54′.

KALIDUNGA, in the British district of Kumaon, lieut.-gov. of the N.W. Provinces, a village on a mountain of the same name, rising from the right bank of the river Ghagra, 20 miles S.E. of Chumpawut cantonment. Elevation above the sea 1,115 feet. At the base of the mountain, and about a mile from the village, is the Kalidunga ferry across the Kalee, forming a communication between the territory of the East-India Company and that of Nepal. Lat. 29° 7′, long. 80° 19′.

KALI MATH, in the British district of Kumaon, lieut.-gov. of the N.W. Provinces, a temple dedicated to the Hindoo goddess Kali, on a summit sloping westward to the left bank of the river Kosila, and four miles N. of Almora. A stockade was here garrisoned by the Goorkhas during their possession of Kumaon. Elevation above the sea 6,301 feet. Lat. 29° 38′, long. 79° 42′.

KALI NUDDEE.—A river rising in the collectorate of Dharwar, presidency of Bombay, close to the town of Dharwar, and in about lat. 15° 30′, long. 75° 6′. It holds a south-westerly course of about eighty miles, and falls into the Arabian Sea, or North Indian Ocean, at Sedashevagurh, in lat. 14° 50′, long. 74° 10′. Near Barabuti, forty-five miles above its mouth, it is joined on the left side by the river Bidhati, flowing from the south.

KALIPANI, in the British district of Kumaon, lieut.-gov. of the N.W. Provinces, a remarkable spring, regarded as sacred by the natives, and hence considered as the source of the great river Kalee, though this last has its remotest head-water about thirty miles farther to the north-west. The spring is situate on the north-eastern declivity of the great mountain Bians Rikhi, and on the route from Bians Pass to Askot, five miles S.W. of the pass, 45 N.E. of Askot, and in lat. 30° 11′, long. 80° 56′. Its water is discharged into a stream flowing a few hundred feet to the west, and which bears the name of Kalipani river. This river is formed by the union of two streams, one rising close to the western entrance of the Bians Pass, and, holding a westerly course of about four miles, joins the other, rising on the western declivity of the great Kuntas Peak, in lat. 30° 14′, long. 80° 56′, and, flowing five miles southerly, to the confluence, in lat. 30° 11′, long. 80° 55′, and about a mile above the spring. The united stream flows five miles south-westward, to its confluence with the Kali, in lat. 30° 8′, long. 80° 54′, and at an elevation above the sea of 11,413 feet. The spring is resorted to for ritual ablutions and other religious practices, by pilgrims on their route to Manasarovara. The confluence of the branches of the Kalipani is about 150 feet below the limit of perpetual snow, and the streams scarcely flow during the winter season, when the waters of this tract generally are masses of ice.

KALKAPORE.—A town in the British district of Beerbhoom, lieut.-gov. of Bengal, 148 miles N. by W. of Calcutta. Lat. 24° 37′, long. 87° 50′.

KALLACH.—A town in the dominions of Gholab Singh, 163 miles N. by E. from Kangra, and 116 miles E. by N. from Sirinagur. Lat. 34° 19′, long. 76° 57′.

KALLEENJUR.—A celebrated hill fort in the British district of Banda, in Bundelcund, under the lieut.-gov. of the N.W. Provinces. It is situate at the south-eastern extremity of the plains of Bundelcund, where rises the Bindachal range, the first and lowest terraced elevation of the Vindhya Mountains. The rocky hill on which the fort is situate is completely isolated from the adjacent range by a chasm or ravine, about 1,200 yards wide. A modern writer has hazarded a conjecture, that it may be regarded as having been formerly an island, situate in an ocean rolling over the plain of Bundelcund. The sides rise rather steeply from the plain, and in the upper part have a nearly perpendicular face of 150 or 180 feet in height, in most places inaccessible. The lower part of the hill consists of syenite, in vast polyhedral masses, fitting into each other, and on the outer surface forming an accessible slope; but the upper part, consisting of sandstone arranged in horizontal strata, presents externally so bold a scarp as to be for the most part impracticable of ascent. Franklin states that he found indications of coal in the vales about the hill; but the granitoid character of the formations affords grounds for questioning the soundness of his conclusion. The summit of the rock, a sort of table-land slightly undulated, is between four and five miles in circuit. Throughout its whole extent it is fortified by a rampart rising from the very edge, in continuation of the scarp of the rock, and at places where the difficulties of the ascent in its natural state might be overcome, access has been guarded against by a facing of masonry. The fortifications are massively constructed of large blocks of stone, laid generally without cement, and about twenty-five feet thick; but in many places they have been allowed to fall into decay. A few small hamlets are scattered over the table-land, and numerous ruins indicate that there must have been a town of some importance, which was supplied with water from tanks yet to be seen. One, at least, of these still contains water at all seasons, though the quality is bad. There are also several palaces, which, though ruinous, appear to be of no great antiquity. One of considerable size is, however, in such repair as to serve for the abode of the small garrison. Temples are numerous, the place being regarded by the Hindoos amongst the holiest class. The divinity in most repute is Siva, the images of whom are extremely numerous, and all ithyphallic to a degree of the grossest indecency.

Since the capture of the place in 1812, the British soldiers have mutilated many of those hideous and grotesque figures, knocking off their emblems. The principal idol is called Nilkanth, a name of Siva; and the figure is hewed out of the rock on the southern scarp of the hill, the proportions being so huge, that the figure, though represented squatting, is above thirty feet high. Jacquemont describes it as making a most scandalous display of the parts which decency requires to be concealed. At no great distance is a large lingum, three feet high and two in circumference, with a rude resemblance of a countenance having two large silver eyes. In the scarp of the hill is an entrance to a very long flight of steps, penetrating the interior of the rock to a great distance, and terminating at a subterraneous reservoir of clear cool water of great depth, and said by the natives to be unfathomable. Access to the vast circumvallation of this hill is by a pathway sloping up the face of the rock in an oblique manner, at the south-eastern side. It is a rough and narrow passage through jungle, to the lowest gateway, situate a considerable way up the hill; but from that point it is a wide and fine stairway, reaching to the table-land of the fortress, and passing in the ascent successively through seven gates, some of them commanded by fortifications reputed impregnable. There are several rude pieces of artillery lying about dismounted, some formed of bars of iron laid longitudinally, and bound round with a flat band of the same material wound about them. At present, the place is in command merely of a lieutenant of British infantry. As a station, it has the advantages of interesting archæological associations, highly picturesque scenery, and remarkably salubrious climate.

The town is situate at the south-eastern base of the hill, and, though now much decayed, has numerous ruins, which prove it to have been once important. According to Ferishta, Kalleenjur was founded by Kedar Raja, cotemporary with Mahomet, the founder of Islam, and consequently about the commencement of the seventh century. It appears to have subsequently become the capital of a considerable realm, as it is related that its rajah, in the year 1022, marched at the head of 36,000 horse, 45,000 foot, and 640 elephants, to oppose Mahmood of Ghuzni, who subsequently besieged the fort; but, probably despairing of success, allowed himself to be appeased by submission and rich presents, and evacuated the territory. In 1202, it was besieged by Kootb-ood-deen, the lieutenant of Mahomed Sultan, of Ghor, in Afghanistan, and reduced, in consequence of the supply of water failing. In 1532, it was again subjected to siege by Humayun, emperor of Delhi, who, at the expiration of a month, relinquished his attempt, on receiving a large amount of treasure for his forbearance. In 1543, Sher Shah, the Patan ruler, who had succeeded in driving Humayun from his throne and kingdom, besieged Kalleenjur. During the operations, some explosive missile projected against the garrison, rebounded, and, setting fire to some gunpowder, Sher Shah was scorched so dreadfully, that in a few hours he died in great agony, but not before the assault had succeeded. About the middle of the eighteenth century, it was wrested from the sovereign of Delhi by the rajah of Punna, owing, it is said, "to the disorders of the times, the troops which garrisoned it being kept in arrears, mutinied for want of pay, and sold their charge." About 1790, Ali Behadur, a Mahratta invader of Bundelcund, besieged Kalleenjur, but, after a blockade of ten years, died, without making himself master of it. The fort at that time was held by a Brahmin, successor to a killadar or commandant appointed by the rajah of Punna, but who subsequently assumed independence and the exclusive dominion of the place. He had given much trouble to the British authorities, and committed or connived at numerous depredations on their subjects; and in consequence, on January 19th, 1812, it was besieged by a force consisting of about two regiments of cavalry, six battalions and five companies of infantry. The besieging force took possession of a summit situate north of the fort, and though of small dimensions, scarcely inferior in elevation to it. To this summit, estimated to be 780 feet above the surrounding plain, the British, with very severe toil, dragged up four long iron 18-pounders and two mortars, and the surface being bare rock, the earth requisite to make the batteries was carried up in canvas sacks. About two-thirds lower than this upper battery, or 260 feet above the plain, a battery of two 18-pounders and two 12-pounders was erected on a shoulder of the eminence; but its fire was of little avail, as, in consequence of the great depression, the shot, striking the walls in a direction slanting upwards, glanced off, and produced little effect. As soon as the upper batteries were completed, a British detachment occupied the town, which the enemy evacuated without resistance. The fire of the upper battery, which was alone efficient, was directed against the north-east angle of the rampart, distant half a mile, and in three weeks the breach was considered practicable. On the morning of the 20th of February the besieging batteries opened a brisk fire of round-shot, grape, and shrapnell, to clear the breach, and a storming-party making its way up the steep, rocky, and rugged face of the hill, attempted, by means of scaling-ladders, to mount the ill-opened breach and the portions of perpendicular cliffs presenting themselves in many places. Though the assailants pushed their enterprise with amazing vigour and intrepidity, they suffered so severely by the fire of matchlocks, and from large stones rolled down from the higher ground, that the attempt was found hopeless, and after a struggle of thirty-five minutes, the survivors were recalled. The storming-party consisted of a column headed by five companies of the King's 53rd infantry, twelve companies of grenadiers, and nine companies of light infantry. The loss of the British was severe: it included two commissioned officers, one serjeant, and ten other men killed; ten commissioned officers, six serjeants, and 114 men wounded. There were, besides, a commissioned officer and forty-one native pioneers wounded. Mundy, a military officer, states, that twenty men and as many old women, with no other arms than the huge stones piled around, could make the place good against hundreds of thousands. The loss of the defenders, however, was very severe, from the fire of the British artillery. When the assault was deemed inevitable, the rajah's family, and all the women within the garrison, were collected into a large stone building, and arrangements made by the defenders to blow it up in the event of the success of the attack. The chaube, however, who held the fort, surrendered it to the British eight days afterwards, on condition of receiving an equivalent in lands in the adjacent plain. In 1854 orders were issued for the destruction of this celebrated fort. Lat. 25°, long. 80° 32′.

KALLEE NUDDEE (EAST), a river of the Doab between the Ganges and Jumna, has its origin in the British district of Mozuffernuggur, at Untwana, at an elevation of 900 feet above the sea, and in lat. 29° 19′, long. 77° 51′. Near the town of Meerut, twenty-five miles south from its source, it, on the western side, receives the Khodara Nulla, or Aboo Fuquers, which formerly communicated with the Kallee Nuddee (West) by means of a canal, now dry, and which is attributed by tradition to a native of the name of Muhammad Abu Khan. The Khodara *nulla* passes through the British cantonment, and is traversed by two bridges, one built by the East-India Company, the other by the Begum Sumroo. The latter, in consequence of the inadequate waterway allowed by its three diminutive arches, has sometimes caused serious inconvenience by extensively flooding the cantonment during great inundations, though in the dry season the channel is nearly devoid of water. In the dry season, the Kallee Nuddee is crossed by means of ford, on the route from Meerut to Mhow. At the town of Boolundshuhur the elevation of the river above the sea is 764 feet; and as the distance from its source is eighty miles, the fall in its channel so far is little more than a foot and a half per mile. Close to the town of Boolundshuhur, on the route to Bareilly, it is crossed in the dry season by ford, and during the rains by ferry. The fall between this point and the vicinity of Khoorjah, a further distance of ten miles, does not exceed one foot per mile. Here it takes a south-easterly direction, which it holds for the rest of its course of about 220 miles, falling, three or four miles below Kunnoj, into the Ganges, on the right side, in lat. 27° 1′, long. 80° 3′, running altogether a distance of 310 miles. Between the vicinity of Khoorjah and that of Hurduaganj, a distance of forty miles, the inclination of the channel is one foot one and a half inch per mile. The route from Allyghur to Bareilly passes it by a brick bridge, about twenty miles below Hurduaganj, and the river thence continues navigable downwards to its mouth.

KALLEE NUDDEE (WEST), a river of the Doab between the Jumna and Ganges, rises in the British district of Saharunpoor, at an elevation probably of more than 1,000 feet above the sea, and in lat. 30°, long. 77° 47′. It takes a southerly course of about fifty miles, as far as Mozuffernuggur, and a mile west of that town is crossed by the route to Kurnoul, being in that part fordable, except during heavy inundations. About ten miles below Mozuffernuggur it takes a south-westerly direction, and falls into the Hindun, on the east or left side, in lat. 29° 13′, long. 77° 35′, after a total course of about seventy miles. Formerly it communicated with the Khodara Nulla, running through Meerut, by means of the canal of Mohammed Aboo Khan, which passed off six or eight miles north of Sirdhana.

KALLEE SIND, a river of Malwa, rising on the south side of the Vindhya Mountains, and in lat. 22° 36′, long. 76° 26′. It has a course generally northerly, and in lat. 23° 57′, long. 76° 16′, about ninety miles from its source, receives on the left side the Ludkunda, also rising in the Vindhya range; and on the same side, about sixty miles farther down, it is joined by the united streams of the Ahoo and Amjar, at Gagroun, in lat. 24° 37′, long. 76° 19′, close to the pass where the Kallee Sind makes its way through the Mokundara range into the more depressed tract of Harouti. The scene is described by Tod as striking. "The ascent to the summit of the ridge was so gradual, that our surprise was complete, when, casting our eye north, we saw the Caly Sinde sweeping along the northern face of both fort and town, whence it turns due north, ploughing its serpentine passage, at a depth of full 200 feet below the level of the valley, through three distinct ranges, each chasm or opening appearing in this bold perspective like a huge portal, whence the river gains the yielding plains of Harouti." Thirty-five miles lower down, it receives the Newuj, on the right side. After a total course of about 225 miles, it falls into the Chumbul, on the right side, in lat. 25° 30′, long. 76° 23′. At Kundgong, about fifty miles from its mouth, it is crossed on the route from Kotah to Saugor, and at the place of passage has "bed 450 yards wide, and bottom of flat rock-like pavement; banks cut into ravines; water shallow during the fair season, deep and rapid in the rains."

KALLY BHEEL, in the British district of Saugur and Nerbudda, lieut.-gov. of the N.W. Provinces, a town on the route from Baitool to Burwanee, 57 miles W. of the former. Lat. 21° 54′, long. 77° 5′.

KALOO.—A town in the Rajpoot state of Jodhpoor, on the left bank of the river Loonee, and 62 miles E. from Jodhpoor. Lat. 26° 23′, long. 74° 7′.

KALOREE, in the jaghire of Jujhur, lieut.-gov. of the N.W. Provinces, a village on the south-western frontier towards Shekhawati. Lat. 28°, long. 76° 7′.

KALPEE.—See CALPEE.

KALSAMREE.—A town in the British district of Chota Nagpoor, lieut.-gov. of Bengal, 241 miles W. by N. of Calcutta. Lat. 23° 30′, long. 84° 50′.

KALUNGA.—See NALAPANI.

KAMA, in the territory of Bhurtpore, a town on the north-east frontier, towards the British district of Muttra, on the route from the town of Muttra to Ferozepore, in Goorgaon, 39 miles N.W. of the former. Of late years, it appears to have been scarcely visited by Europeans, but, according to Tieffenthaler, who described it about eighty years ago, it was then a small city, fortified with strong walls and towers, and belonging to the rajah of Jeypore. Towards the latter part of the last century, it was taken by Nujuf Khan, the powerful commander-in-chief of the forces of Shah Alum, of Delhi; but subsequently acquired by the rajah of Bhurtpore. Distant N.W. from Muttra 39 miles. Lat. 27° 40′, long. 77° 20′.

KAMALPOOR, in the British district of Allahabad, lieut.-gov. of the N.W. Provinces, a small town on the route from the city of Allahabad to Futtehpore, and 38 miles S.E. of the latter. Close to it is a grove of noble trees, and the surrounding country is a vast field of tombs and ruins, forming, with the intermixed jungle, a very picturesque and romantic scene. The place is named from Kamal, a reputed Mahomedan saint, who, with his son and several of his disciples, lies buried here. Lat. 25° 42′, long. 81° 25′.

KAMARUDDINNAGAR, in the British district of Meerut, lieut.-gov. of the N.W. Provinces, a town in the Kadir or marsh of the Ganges, and on the left bank of its channel, here fordable during the dry season. It is a remarkable and important locality, being one of the very few points at which the Ganges is fordable after leaving the mountains. Amir Khan, the Patan freebooter, on the occasion of his invasion of Rohilcund, in 1805, and when urgently anxious to escape across the river from the British army under General Smith, in active pursuit, searched in vain for a ford for a distance of 100 miles, and was about to march upwards to Hurdwar, where the stream issues from the mountain, until relieved from his embarrassment by a native, who unexpectedly pointed out the ford at Kamaruddinnagar. The amir found the ford not difficult about the 12th of February, at which time, probably, the stream had scarcely risen by any melting of the Himalayan snows; so that he "crossed with all his horse, the girths even not being wetted, so shallow was the water." On the 15th of the same month, the British army in pursuit crossed the river at the same place, but appear to have missed the best line of ford, as the water, which was half a mile wide, was about breast-high, and in the middle even deeper, insomuch that the horses there got out of their depth, and took to swimming, and several women and children of the bazar, who were mounted on ponies and on bullocks, were swept away by the current and drowned. On the 12th of March, the amir recrossed at the same place, pursued on the 15th by the British, who found the ford still more difficult than before. Kamaruddinnagar is 24 miles E. of Meerut, 55 miles N.E. of Delhi. Lat. 28° 56′, long. 78° 10′.

KAMBACHO.—A town in the native state of Nepal, near the left bank of the Kumbachen river, and 51 miles N.W. by N. from Darjeeling. Lat. 27° 37′, long. 87° 52′.

KAMGAUM.—A town in one of the recently sequestrated districts of Hyderabad, or dominions of the Nizam, and a celebrated mart for cotton, 72 miles S.W. by W. of Ellichpoor. Lat. 20° 41′, long. 76° 37′.

KAMMAH.—A town in the British province of Pegue, on the right bank of the Irawady, and 23 miles N. by W. from Prome. Lat. 19° 4′, long. 94° 56′.

KAMONAH, in the British district of Boolundshuhur, lieut.-gov. of the N.W. Provinces, a town near the right bank of the East Kalee Nuddee, 64 miles S.E. of Delhi. In 1805, when Amir Khan, the Patan freebooter, made an irruption into the Doab, the zemindar or proprietor of Kamonah favoured his cause, and for some time defended the mud fort of the place against all the efforts of a British besieging force, but finally submitted. The zemindar subsequently again revolted in 1807, when his fort fell into the hands of the British, after a resistance which cost the lives of Captain Fraser and many others of high character and merit. Lat. 28° 8′, long. 78° 10′.

KAMPTA, in Bundelcund, a village giving name to a small jaghire or feudal grant held of the East-India Company, the jagheerdar being "free landholder and controller of the said villages." It "is possessed by Rao Gopal Loll. It comprises two villages within the area of one square mile, has a population of 300 souls, and yields a revenue of 1,500 rupees." D'Cruz intimates that Rao Gopal Lal holds the jaghire in compensation of his claim as one of the Chaubis or joint Brahminical possessors of the stronghold of Kaleenjur, surrendered on conditions in 1812. The village is very probably the "Compta" of Franklin's great map of Bundelcund, situate on a feeder of the small river Paisuni, 48 miles S.E. of the town of Banda, 65 S.W. of Allahabad. Lat. 25° 11′, long. 80° 55′.

KAMPTEE, in the territory of Nagpoor, a British cantonment on the route from Hazareebagh to the city of Nagpoor, 565 miles S.W. of the former, nine N.E. of the latter. Though the climate is, from its intertropical situation, hot, the thermometer ranging above 100° in April, yet severe hailstorms are sometimes felt, as in April, 1830, when hailstones fell varying from six to nine inches in circumference. A commodious church was built here in 1833. A few years later, the experiment was tried of substituting the arrangements of a coffee-room for those of a canteen for the troops. The result has been highly successful, the sale of spirituous liquors being in a great measure superseded by that of beer, tea, and coffee. Kamptee is in lat. 21° 16′, long. 79° 14′.

KAMRA.—A town in the British district of Moorshedabad, lieut.-gov. of Bengal, 134 miles N. of Calcutta. Lat. 24° 30′, long. 88° 10′.

KAMROIJ.—A town in the native state of Wusravee, presidency of Bombay, on the left bank of the Taptee, and 13 miles N.E. from Surat. Lat. 21° 15′, long. 73° 2′.

KAMTAOL.—A town in the British district of Tirhoot, lieut.-gov. of Bengal, 30 miles N.E. by N. of Dinapoor. Lat. 25° 58′, long. 85° 23′.

KAN, or KAND, a small river of Malwa, rises on the north side of the Vindhya range, eight miles E. of the British cantonment of Mow, about lat. 22° 36′, long. 75° 51′. It takes a northerly course, and, flowing through a very fertile country by the city of Indore, is joined by the Sirsootty; it then takes a north-easterly direction for about nineteen miles, and, winding by the town of Samer, falls into the river Ghutty, its total length being forty-five miles. On the route from Mow to Oojein, it is crossed, about twelve miles from its source, "by a good ford, water about one foot deep during the fair season."

KANACGERRI.—A town in one of the recently sequestrated districts of Hyderabad, or dominions of the Nizam, 129 miles E. by S. of Belgaum. Lat. 15° 34′, long. 76° 29′.

KANADKHAID.—A town in Hyderabad, or dominions of the Nizam, situate on the left bank of the Doodna river, 158 miles N.W. from Hyderabad. Lat. 19° 20′, long. 77° 5′.

KANAR.—A town in Gwalior, or possessions of Scindia, situate on the left bank of the Asun river, and 36 miles W.S.W. from Gwalior. Lat. 26° 1′, long. 77° 43′.

KANARAK.—See CANARAC.

KANASIR, in the Rajpoot state of Jodhpoor, a village on the route from Pokhurn to Balmeer, and 60 miles N. of the latter. It is situate on a sandhill near the western side of an extensive jungle of large bushes of the ber or jujube, from fifteen to twenty feet high. Lat. 26° 19′, long. 71° 45′.

KANDA.—A town in the principality of Cashmere, or dominions of Gholab Singh, situate on the right bank of the Jhelum river, and 130 miles E. from Peshawur. Lat. 34° 14', long. 73° 44'.

KANDA, in the British district of Ghurwal, lieut.-gov. of the N.W. Provinces, a town on the route from Sireenuggur to the Rakus Lake, 38 miles E. by N. of the former. Lat. 30° 19', long. 79° 27'.

KANDAL GHATI, in Gurhwal, a pass over a ridge rising above the right bank of the Bhageerettee, as the Ganges is called in the upper part of its course. It was a secondary station in the trigonometrical survey of the Himalayas. Elevation above the sea 11,893 feet. Lat. 30° 59', long. 78° 43'.

KANDCUTTE.—A town in the British district of Ramgurh, lieut.-gov. of Bengal, 246 miles N.W. by W. of Calcutta. Lat. 24° 19', long. 85° 7'.

KANDLAH, in the British district of Muzuffurnugur, lieut.-gov. of the N.W. Provinces, a village on the right or west bank of the Doab Canal. Population 7,062. Lat. 29° 19', long. 77° 20'.

KANEEMYO.—A town of Burmah, situate on the right bank of the Khyendwen river, and 80 miles W.N.W. from Ava. Lat. 22° 25', long. 94° 59'.

KANEEREE.—A town in one of the recently sequestrated districts of Hyderabad, or dominions of the Nizam, situate 58 miles S.W. of Ellichpoor. Lat. 20° 39', long. 76° 54'.

KANEWARA, in the British district of Saugur and Nerbudda, lieut.-gov. of the N.W. Provinces, a town on the route from Jubbulpoor to Seuni, 18 miles E.N.E. of the latter. Lat. 22° 9', long. 79° 55'.

KANGAL.—A petty fort on a small feeder of the Sutluj, situate two miles from the left bank of that river. Elevation above the sea 6,311 feet. Lat. 31° 16', long. 77° 25'.

KANGAN.—A town in the principality of Cashmere, or Gholab Singh's dominions, 161 miles E. from Attock, and 106 miles N. from Jamoo. Lat. 34° 17', long. 75° 3'.

KANGAON.—A town in the British province of Nagpoor, situate five miles from the left bank of the Warda river, and 54 miles S.W. from Nagpoor. Lat. 20° 31', long. 78° 40'.

KANGCHANG.—See KINCHINJUNGA.

KANGLA.—A town in the native state of Nepal, situate on the left bank of the Dud Coosy river, and 76 miles E. by S. from Khatmandoo. Lat. 27° 30', long. 86° 30'.

KANGRA, in Sirmor, a summit of the mountains between the Giree and Tons, and nearly equidistant, or about three miles from each river. It is composed of limestone. During the great trigonometrical survey of the Himalaya, it was one of the stations of the small series of triangles. Elevation above the sea 6,660 feet. Lat. 30° 34', long. 77° 47'.

KANGRA, or KOT KANGRA, in the north-east of the Punjab, among the mountains in the lower ranges to the south of the Himalaya, is an extensive hill fort situated on the top of an eminence, about 150 feet above the Ban Gunga, near its confluence with the Beas. The eminence is about three miles in circuit, bounded for the most part by precipices nearly perpendicular, and, in places of less declivity, rendered inaccessible by masonry and ramparts. Its position is in all respects such, that Vigne considers that by European engineers it might be rendered impregnable. About the beginning of the present century it belonged to Sansa-Chand, who, being attacked by the Goorkhas, defended it for four years against them, but finally gave it up to Runjeet Singh, who expelled the invaders. Kot Kangra is in lat. 32° 5', long. 76° 18'. Soon after the Punjab became a British possession, the vicinity of Kangra was selected as one of the localities for the culture of the tea-tree. The experiment commenced upon a petty scale, and in 1851 only two small plantations had been made; but the high character of the produce satisfied the government that the soil and climate were admirably adapted to the growth of the plant, and authority was given for the formation of an extensive plantation at the foot of the Chumba range of mountains. Later reports fully confirm the favourable anticipations formed by the government.

KANGRAULI, in the British district of Goruckpore, lieut.-gov. of the N.W. Provinces, a small town near the south-eastern frontier, towards the British district of Sarun. It contains, according to Buchanan, 300 houses, which would assign it a population of about 1,800 persons. Distance S.E. from Goruckpore cantonment 55 miles. Lat. 26° 16', long. 84° 2'.

KANGYAM.—A town in the British district of Coimbatoor, presidency of Madras, 158 miles E.S.E. of Cannanore. Lat. 11°, long. 77° 36'.

KANHAN.—A river rising in the Deogarh Mountains, in the British territory of Saugor and Nerbudda, about lat. 21° 54', long. 78° 11'. Holding a tortuous course, but generally south-easterly, for about 130 miles, it receives on its left side, in lat. 21° 17', long. 79° 13', the Pench, flowing from the north. The joint stream, from the confluence, continues to hold a south-easterly course of about forty-five miles, passing by the British cantonment at Kamptee, and falls into the Waingunga on the right side, in lat. 21° 5', long. 79° 39'. At Kamptee, about forty-three miles above the mouth, the river's bed is 500 yards wide. Timber, both for building and firewood, is floated down the river in considerable quantities, and in smaller quantities is transported upwards, by tracking against the stream. The river is also serviceable for the transport of military stores.

KANHOOR.—A town in the British district of Ahmednuggur, presidency of Bombay, 24 miles W. of Ahmednuggur. Lat. 19° 7′, long. 74° 24′.

KANIKA.—A town in the principality of Cashmere, or dominions of Gholab Singh, 104 miles N.N.E. from Kangra, and 118 miles E.S.E. from Sirinagur. Lat. 33° 29′, long. 76° 49′.

KANJOLE.—A town in the British district of Bhagulpoor, lieut.-gov. of Bengal, 161 miles N. by W. of Calcutta. Lat. 24° 49′, long. 87° 50′.

KANKA, in the British district of Allygurh, lieut.-gov. of the N.W. Provinces, a village on the route from the cantonment of Allygurh to that of Muttra, and 14 miles S.W. of the former. Lat. 27° 43′, long. 78° 3′.

KANKRAULI, in the Rajpoot territory of Oodeypoor, a town on the route from Neemuch to Deesa, 79 miles N.W. of former, 171 N.E. of latter. It is situate at the south extremity of a considerable lake, called Raj Samundar, and is a large town, with a good bazar. Lat. 24° 50′, long. 73° 56′.

KANNEH.—A town in Cashmere, or Gholab Singh's dominions, situate on the left bank of the Jhelum river, and 110 miles E. from Peshawur. Lat. 34° 8′, long. 73° 30′.

KANODE, in the Rajpoot state of Jessulmere, a town north-east of the city of Jessulmere. It is situate at the southern border of an extensive lake of salt water, stretching to the north about fifteen miles, with a breadth of about eight. Such are, however, the dimensions during the periodical rains only, as at other times it nearly disappears, leaving the ground over which it had spread encrusted with salt, which is removed and sold for the benefit of the rawul or ruler of Jessulmere. The lake, when fullest, is discharged on its eastern side by a stream, which, flowing about thirty miles in an easterly direction, is lost in the sands of Jodhpoor or Marwar. Kanode is in lat. 27° 8′, long. 71° 5′.

KANOJE.—See Kunnouj.

KANOOND, in the jaghire of Jujhur, lieut.-gov. of the N.W. Provinces, a town on the route from Hansee to Neemuch, and 70 miles S. of the former. During the troubled period which preceded the expulsion of the Mahrattas by Lord Lake, it was an important place, being one of the principal strongholds of Vavon Rao, an influential chief of that people. It at present has a large bazar, and is abundantly supplied with water, which is, however, rather brackish. The road in this part of the route is heavy and sandy. The surrounding country, though having occasional patches of cultivation, is described by Elphinstone as in general very barren. "On approaching Canound, we had the first specimen of the desert to which we were looking forward with anxious curiosity. Three miles before reaching that place, we came to sandhills, which at first were covered with bushes, but afterwards were naked piles of loose sand, rising one after another, like the waves of the sea, and marked on the surface by the wind, like drifted snow. There were roads through them, made solid by the treading of animals; but off the road our horses sunk into the sand above the knee." Lat. 28° 14′, long. 76° 13′.

KANPOOR, in the Rajpoot state of Jodhpoor, a village on the route from Nusserabad to Deesa, and 159 miles S.W. of the former. Lat. 25° 11′, long. 73° 10′.

KANSBANS, a river of Cuttack, rising in lat. 21° 13′, long. 86° 31′, a few miles S.E. of the town of Koparee, in the British district of Balasore, through which it runs in an easterly direction for thirty miles, and falls into the Bay of Bengal, in lat. 21° 9′, long. 86° 53′.

KANT, in the British district of Shahjehanpoor, lieut.-gov. of the N.W. Provinces, a small town on the route from Futtehgurh to the cantonment of Shahjehanpoor, and 10 miles S.W. of the latter. It has a small bazar and abundance of water. Lat. 27° 49′, long. 79° 51′.

KANTAL, in the north-east of Cashmere, a lofty mountain south of the pass called Bultul by Vigne and modern geographers. Through this pass lies one of the principal routes from Cashmere to Ladakh and Bultistan. Its crest forms a division between the basin of the Indus and that of the Jhelum; the Dras river, which rises here, flowing northwards to the former river, and the Sinde, in a south-west direction, to the Jhelum. The elevation of this pass is 10,500 feet. Lat. 34° 15′, long. 75° 39′.

KANTANAGAR, in the British district of Purnea, lieut.-gov. of Bengal, a town on the south boundary, and on the left bank of an offset from the Ganges, 30 miles S. from the town of Purnea. It contains 700 houses, and, according to the usually-received average of inmates to houses, 3,500 persons. Lat. 25° 22′, long. 87° 28′.

KANTEE, in the jaghire of Jujhur, lieut.-gov. of the N.W. Provinces, a village on the route from Delhi to Narnol, and 14 miles E. of the latter. Lat. 28° 3′, long. 76° 23′.

KANTEE, in the British district of Allahabad, lieut.-gov. of the N.W. Provinces, a small town on the route by the Sohagi Pass from Allahabad to Rewa, and 16 miles S. of the former city. It has a few shops: water is obtained from a tank and wells. Lat. 25° 15′, long. 81° 51′.

KANUM, in Bussahir, a small town, the principal place of the district of Koonawar, is situate on the declivity of a recess embosomed in lofty mountains, and near a feeder of the Sutluj, which flows past at the distance of about a mile. The sloping surface is formed into terraces by means of rough and massive embankments of stone, and the more extensive levels thus made are overlaid with earth and cultivated, those narrower forming the sites of houses rising above each other in such a manner, that the flat roofs of those beneath are platforms in front of the upper. Interspersed through this straggling collection of dwellings, are fine groves of poplar, and flourishing orchards of peach, apple, apricot, and walnut-trees. This prosperity results from the judicious employment of irrigation, the means of which are supplied from the torrent flowing down the valley, as the great aridity of the climate otherwise precludes vegetation. Here is a celebrated Buddhist temple, provided with a library of books, printed in the Tibetan language; one of these is an encyclopædia, in 225 volumes; another a system of theology, in 100. The encyclopædia is considered by Jacquemont a translation from the Sanscrit. The printing is distinct, and done with wooden types. Kanum is the fountain-head of learning and faith for Koonawur, and its lama is the superior of all others in that tract, in fact, the great pontiff of the country. He is elected by the lamas from their own number, but the choice requires the ratification of the lama of Ladakh. The dress of the grand lama of Kanum closely resembles that of a Roman Catholic bishop; the mitre is exactly the same. Jacquemont gives a lively description of one of their grotesque ceremonies. The grand lama bearing a bell, and his followers drums, cymbals, and other noisy instruments, kept time to a slow and solemn chant; whilst three other lamas, masked, danced at first in measured paces, but finally with the wildest and most furious gesticulations and capers, the villagers standing by, and, with the most boisterous mirth, expressing their gratification. The ceremony terminated by the grand lama sipping water from a chalice, and throwing into a fire a cake, decked with sprigs of juniper, which was no sooner done, than the actors departed peaceably, the whole scene being intended to display the efficacy of the prayers and rites of the priests in rendering the malignant demons powerless. Jacquemont, during his brief stay at Kanum, visited Csoma de Koros, the Hungarian traveller, then secluded there, and closely occupied in the study of Tibetan language, theology, and antiquities. Kauum is in charge of an hereditary wazir, who governs it for the rajah of Bussahir, to whom he forwards the trifling revenue. It contains about sixty or seventy families; but as in that inclement climate and sequestered locality the physical exigencies of the population are numerous, and must be supplied principally from domestic resources, each homestead is extensive, and has many inmates; and the commercial character of the inhabitants causes a small warehouse to be a usual appurtenance to a residence. Elevation above the sea about 9,296 feet. Lat. 31° 40′, long. 78° 30′.

KANUNA.—A town in the Rajpoot state of Jodhpoor, situate on the right bank of the Loonee river, and 53 miles S.W. from Jodhpoor. Lat. 25° 50′, long. 72° 30′.

KANUWAH, in the Baree Dooab division of the Punjab, a town situated on the right bank of the river Chukki, 83 miles E. by N. of the town of Lahore. Lat. 31° 55′, long. 75° 30′.

KANWARA.—A town of Malwa, in the native state of Tonk, situate on the right bank of the Ahoo river, and 178 miles W. by N. from Saugur. Lat. 24° 25′, long. 76° 4′.

KAOLAIR.—A town in Hyderabad, or dominions of the Nizam, 137 miles N.N.W. from Hyderabad, and 137 miles S. by E. from Ellichpoor. Lat. 19° 17′, long. 78°.

KAOMALLA.—A town in the Rajpoot state of Jodhpoor, 106 miles S.W. by S. from Jodhpoor, and 54 miles N. by E. from Deesa. Lat. 24° 58′, long. 72° 21′.

KAONDAUR.—A town of Orissa, on the south-west frontier of Bengal, in the native zemindarry of Jeypoor, 22 miles E. from Jeypoor, and 76 miles N.W. from Vizianagrum. Lat. 18° 59′, long. 82° 46′.

KAPALADROOG, in the Mysore, a fort on a steep hill producing sandal-wood. It was selected by Tippoo Sultan for the incarceration of those unhappy persons who incurred his especial displeasure. The choice was probably made with reference to the insalubrity of the place, the air and water being extremely bad, and the quality of the latter being rendered more deleterious by throwing into the wells branches of euphorbium and putrescent animal substances. These sources of death, further aided by unwholesome food, told on the wretched inmates of the place so fearfully and fatally, that it is said "no native prisoner ever returned to detail the horrors of this dungeon." Kapaladroog is situate in the rough mountainous tract N.E. of Seringapatam, from which it is distant 30 miles. Lat. 12° 30′, long. 77° 21′.

KAPOORTHELLA, in the Julinder Dooab division of the Punjab, a town situated eight miles from the left bank of the river Beas, 75 miles E. by S. of the town of Lahore. Lat. 31° 24′, long. 75° 25′.

KAPRAIRA, in the Rajpoot state of Jodhpoor, a village or small town on the route from Nusseerabad to the town of Jodhpoor, and 29 miles E. of the latter. It contains 500 houses. Lat. 26° 17′, long. 73° 36′.

KAPURRA.—A town in the Rajpoot state of Boondee, five miles from the right bank of the river Chumbul, and 29 miles E.S.E. from Boondee. Lat. 25° 22′, long. 76° 10′.

KARAKNARIL.—A town in Hyderabad, or the Nizam's dominions, 60 miles N.N.E. from Ahmednuggur, and 60 miles S.E. by S. from Malligaum. Lat. 19° 52′, long. 75° 7′.

KARANJA, in the presidency of Bombay, an island on the east side of the harbour of Bombay, situate south of the island of Elephanta, and separated by a narrow channel from the mainland. It is four miles long, and nearly two broad, and is low, with the exception of two remarkable hills, called the Great and Little Karanja Hills. Karanja Little Hill is on the north part of the island, and has an irregular outline. The great hill, which is on the south part of the island, is very conspicuous. Its shape is somewhat convex, but with a flat space on the summit, and a steep declivity at each end. The town of Karanja is a small assemblage of low ill-built houses, situate near a tank. On the south hill, and on a site very difficult of access, is the fort, now ruinous, and at no time strong, mounting fourteen guns, but offering no resistance to attack except from its difficulty of approach. The less-elevated part of the island is very fertile, "abounding with rice-fields, cocoanut, palmyra, mango, and tamarind-trees; the trees being filled with monkeys, parrots, owls, and singing-birds of various kinds." Karanja was an early possession of the Portuguese; and in 1661, when Bombay was ceded as part of the dowry of the Infanta of Portugal, on her marriage with Charles II., was retained, notwithstanding the protest of the English authorities that its retention was a violation of the treaty. The Portuguese, moreover, availed themselves of its possession to give every possible annoyance to the settlement of Bombay. It soon after (in 1683) fell into the hands of Sambaji, the Mahratta chief. In 1774, it was taken by the English, and formally ceded by the Mahratta government in 1775, the cession being confirmed by an additional clause in the treaty of Poorunder, concluded in the following year. Karanja is in lat. 18° 51′, long. 73° 2′.

KARANO.—A town in the British province of Nagpoor, 102 miles S.E. by S. from Nagpoor, and 55 miles E. by N. from Chanda. Lat. 20° 8′, long. 80° 14′.

KAREAL.—See KERIALL.

KAREANS.—A town in the British district of Amherst, in the Tenasserim provinces, 58 miles E. by S. of Moulmein. Lat. 16° 20′, long. 98° 34′.

KARENLUR.—A town in the British district of Malabar, presidency of Madras, 51 miles S.E. by S. of Cannanore. Lat. 11° 18′, long. 75° 56′.

KAREPUTTUN.—A town in the British district of Rutnageriah, presidency of Bombay, 174 miles S.S.E. of Bombay. Lat. 16° 32′, long. 73° 41′.

KARGVIL.—A town in the principality of Cashmere, or dominions of Gholab Singh, two miles from the right bank of the river Dras, and 79 miles E.N.E. from Sirinagur. Lat. 34° 32′, long. 76° 15′.

KARHLA, or KARBLA, in the Rajpoot state of Jodhpoor, a village on the route from Neemuch, *viâ* Palee, to the city of Jodhpoor, and 33 miles S. of the latter. Supplies are scanty, but there is good water in tanks. The road to the south is excellent, over an open country; to the north, very sandy, over undulating ground. Lat. 25° 51′, long. 73° 23′.

KARIAN, in the Jetch Dooab division of the Punjab, a town situated 15 miles from the left bank of the Jhelum, 88 miles N. by W. of the town of Lahore. Lat. 32° 47′, long. 73° 54′.

KARICAL.—A French settlement within the limits of the British district of Tanjore, presidency of Madras, situate near the Coromandel coast of the Bay of Bengal, on a small estuary of the river Cauvery. In the dry season, the mouth of this estuary is quite obstructed by a bar of sand, which, during the periodical inundations of the Cauvery, is so far swept away, that the channel is navigable for coasting craft. The French territory, which is completely surrounded by the British district of Tanjore, contains an area of 63 square miles. It was restored at the general pacification in 1814, on condition that no fortifications should be erected thereon. The population is estimated, for town and territory, at—Europeans, 43; East-Indians, 71; natives, 49,193: giving a total of 49,307. By the terms of the treaty, no military are to be retained but such as may be required for purposes of police. The civil establishment consists of a governor, a colonial inspector, a commandant of the troops, a royal judge, and other officers. Distant from Tanjore, E., 47 miles; Madras, S., 150 miles. Lat. 10° 55′, long. 79° 53′.

KARINJA.—A town in the British province of Nagpoor, 46 miles W. from Nagpoor, and 59 miles E. from Ellichpoor. Lat. 21° 10′, long. 78° 28′.

KARINJA, in the British district of Saugor and Nerbudda, lieut.-gov. of the N.W. Provinces, a town on the route from Baitool to Ellichpoor, 44 miles S.S.W. of the former. Lat. 21° 18′, long. 77° 40′.

KARIS, in the British district of Allygurh, lieut.-gov. of the N.W. Provinces, a village on the route from the cantonment of Allygurh to that of Muttra, and 18 miles S.W. of the former. Lat. 27° 39′, long. 78° 2′.

KARKEEKOT.—A town in the native state of Nepal, three miles from the left bank of the Gunduk river, and 131 miles N.W. by W. from Khatmandoo. Lat. 28° 27′, long. 83° 21′.

KARKULL, in the British district of South Canara, presidency of Madras, a town on the stream discharging itself, a short distance below, into a small lake. It is without fortifications, and near it are the ruins of the palace of the Byrasu Wodears, rajahs of the Jain persuasion, and formerly rulers of this country. Here is an image of Gomuta Raya, who, according to tradition, had been once a powerful king. It "is made of one piece of granite, the extreme dimensions of which above-ground are, thirty-eight feet in height, ten and a half feet in breadth, and ten feet in thickness;" and there are probably three feet more under-ground. Karkull is 26 miles N.E. of Mangaloor, 360 W. of Madras. Lat. 13° 13′, long. 75° 3′.

KARLEE.—A village in the British collectorate of Poona, presidency of Bombay, situate on the main road from Bombay to Poona, seven miles E. of the Bhore Ghaut. That which chiefly gives distinction to Karlee, is the cavern-temple, with its accessories of attendant excavations, in conformity with the view taken by Colonel Sykes, who observes, "These monasteries consisted of a chapel or chapels, common halls or refectories, with sleeping-cells around them," and other appendages. Heber describes it as hewn on the face of a precipice about two-thirds up the side of a steep hill, rising with a very scarped and regular talus to the height probably of 800 feet above the plain. Besides the principal temple, the excavations contain many smaller apartments, evidently intended for the lodging of monks or hermits. Some of these are very highly ornamented. The temple itself is approached by a narrow path winding among trees, brushwood, and fragments of rock, and entered by a noble arch. In the front is a pillar surmounted by three lions back to back. Within the portico are several colossal figures of elephants, on each of which is a mohout, very well carved, and a howdah with two persons seated in it. Naked male and female figures in alto-rilievo, and somewhat larger than life, cover the screen on each side of the door. Both as to dimensions and elaborate ornament, this temple merits high distinction among buildings of its kind. It contains no visible object of devotion, except the mystic chattah or umbrella. Buddhist symbols predominate throughout. All the various cave-temples have much in common, as may be seen to a certain extent in the article ELEPHANTA, in this work. Karlee is distant E. from Bombay 40 miles, N.W. from Poona 32. Lat. 18° 46′, long. 73° 31′.

KARMEL, in the Punjab, a village on the route from Ramnuggur to Pind Dadun Khan, and six miles N.W. of the former town. It is situate near the right bank of the Chenaub, and close to the ferry, which is one of great importance, as the river, when fullest, is above a mile broad, and the traffic considerable. Lat. 32° 26′, long. 73° 46′.

KARNAPRAYAG, in the British district of Kumaon, lieut.-gov. of the N.W. Provinces, a village at the prayag or confluence of the Aluknunda and Pindar rivers. It contains a math or shrine of Karna, a mythological personage revered by the Hindoos; and hence is one of the five prayags pilgrimage to which is enjoined in the Shastras. The Pindar is here crossed by a jhula or rude suspension-bridge of ropes. Elevation above the sea 2,560 feet. Lat. 30° 15′, long. 79° 16′.

KAROOMBA.—An island situated in the Gulf of Cutch, four miles from the coast of the peninsula of Kattywar, one and a half mile long, N. to S., and three miles broad, E. to W. Lat. 22° 27′, long. 69° 47′.

KAROORAH.—A town in the British province of Nagpoor, four miles from the right bank of the Soondoo river, and 128 miles W. by S. from Sumbulpoor. Lat. 21° 1′, long. 82° 7′

KAROW RIVER, rising on the south-west frontier of Bengal, in lat. 22° 50′, long. 85° 13′, in the British territory of Singboom, and, flowing in a circuitous, but generally northeasterly course, through the British district of Chota Nagpoor for eighty-five miles, falls into the Soobunreeka river, on its right bank, in lat. 23° 16′, long. 85° 52′.

KAROWKE.—See GAROWKE.

KARRAN.—A town in the native state of Bombra, on the south-west frontier of Bengal, situate on the left bank of one of the branches of the Braminy river, and 61 miles E. from Sumbulpoor. Lat. 21° 27′, long. 84° 59′.

KARTINAAD, in Malabar, a district or raj extending from the seacoast up the western declivity of the Western Ghats. The more level parts towards the sea are very fertile and productive, especially of rice; but the dreadful devastations of Tippoo Sultan threw the country into such a state of confusion and weakness, that the grain produced was not sufficient for the consumption of the inhabitants, who, in 1800, imported from the southern districts as well as from Canara. In the eastern part of the district the hills are much overgrown with wood, which the Nairs, constituting the majority of the population, regard as a protection against invasion. Amongst those woods cardamoms are of natural growth. Those who bring them to market search such places as are thickly covered with bushes, and have many springs and small streams, and they generally succeed in finding some scattered plants of the valued shrub. They then clear away the trees and underwood around the plants, which multiply abundantly during the rainy season, and in the fourth year flower and produce their fruit. Coolness is requisite for the perfection of this plant, which consequently can be successfully managed only on lofty hills. The Nairs of this country exhibit in character and manners all the revolting peculiarities of their caste. The ancestor of the rajah of Kartinad, or Cadutinada as it is called by the natives, was a Nair of eminence, who, about 1564, wrested this tract from the rajah of Cherikal, and exercised absolute power within it; as did his successors, until the invasion of Tippoo Sultan. On the expulsion of that tyrant, in 1792, the then rajah was restored. A tribute is paid to the East-India Company, but in other respects the rajah assumes sovereign sway. He resides at Kuthipuram, in lat. 11° 42′, long. 75° 44′.

KARUB.—A town in the British district of Patna, lieut.-gov. of Bengal, 15 miles S.S.E. of Patna. Lat. 25° 21′, long. 85° 21′.

KARUNJA, in Hyderabad, or territory of the Nizam, a town on the northern declivity of the range of mountains bounding the valley of the Taptee on the south. Distance from Ellichpoor, S., 53 miles; Aurungabad, N.E., 140; Hyderabad, N., 225. Lat. 20° 28′, long. 77° 34′.

KASEENUGUR.—A town in the independent state of Tipperah, presidency of Bengal, situate on the right bank of one of the branches of the Barak, and 32 miles S.S.E. from Silhet. Lat. 24° 32′, long. 92° 10′.

KASEGAON.—A town in the British province of Sattara, presidency of Bombay, 88 miles E. of Sattara. Lat. 17° 36′, long. 75° 22′.

KASHEEPORE, in the British district of Goorgaon, lieut.-gov. of the N.W. Provinces, a village on the right bank of the Jumna. Distance S.E. from Delhi 48 miles. Lat. 28° 1′, long. 77° 33′.

KASHIPOOR, in the British district of Moradabad, lieut.-gov. of the N.W. Provinces, a town on the route from the town of Moradabad to Almora, and 31 miles N. of the former. It is situate in a marshy plain, overrun with gigantic grass, intermixed with bushes and trees. Heber observes, that he had "never seen a more feverish or tigerly country." It is a famous place of Hindoo pilgrimage, having several temples, and a holy tank, where pilgrims bathe, on their way to Badrinath. A short distance to the south-east is a fort, now in ruins. There is a brisk transit-trade in this town, between Kumaon and Chinese Tartary on one side, and Hindostan on the other; and some of the traders are opulent. The natives attribute to it great antiquity, alleging it to have been built 5,000 years ago, by a renowned personage called Cashi. Elevation above the sea 756 feet. Lat. 29° 13′, long. 79° 1′.

KASHMERE.—See CASHMERE.

KASHUNG, or KOZHANG, in Bussahir, a river, or rather torrent, in the district of Koonawur, is crossed by the route from Pangi to Sungnum, in lat. 31° 37′, long. 78° 22′, and at an elevation of 8,240 feet above the sea. Its volume of water is considerable, and is hurried along with extreme violence, noise, and rapidity, forming a complete line of foam. The route crosses it by means of a good sanga or wooden bridge; about two miles below which, flowing in a south-easterly direction, it falls into the Sutlej, in lat. 31° 36′, long. 78° 22′.

KASIMKA.—A town in the native state of Bhawulpoor, four miles from the left bank of the Ghara river, and 91 miles N.E. by E. from Bhawulpoor. Lat. 30° 2′, long. 73° 8′.

KASIMPOOR, or KASIMABAD, in the British district of Allyghur, lieut.-gov. of the N.W. Provinces, a town on the route from Futtehgurh to Meerut, by Khasgunje, and 101 miles N.W. of Futtehgurh. It is situate near the left bank of the Kalee Nuddee (East), in an open country but partially cultivated. Lat. 28° 3′, long. 78° 19′.

KASIN.—A town in the Cis-Sutlej Seik state of Mundote, situate on the left bank of the river, and 33 miles S.W. by W. from Ferozepoor. Lat. 30° 38′, long. 74° 14′.

KASNIKOTA.—A town in the British district of Vizagapatam, presidency of Madras, 22 miles W. of Vizagapatam. Lat. 17° 40′, long. 83° 1′.

KASNUH, in the British district of Boolundshuhur, lieut.-gov. of the N.W. Provinces, a town, the principal place of the pergunnah of the same name, on the route from Delhi to Muttra, by the left bank of the Jumna, and 25 miles S.E. of the former. Lat. 28° 26′, long. 77° 36′.

KASSEHGAON.—A town in the British province of Sattara, presidency of Bombay, 154 miles S.E. by S. of Bombay. Lat. 17° 8′, long. 74° 16′.

KASSIAREE.—A town in the British district of Midnapoor, lieut.-gov. of Bengal, 80 miles W.S.W. of Calcutta. Lat. 22° 8′, long. 87° 17′.

KASSYE GOPANG, in Sinde, a town on the route from Hyderabad to Sehwan, by the way of Kotree, and 25 miles N. of Hyderabad. It is situate on the right bank of the Indus, in a fertile and well-cultivated country. Lat. 25° 46′, long. 68° 22′.

KATELEE.—A town in the British district of Mymunsing, lieut.-gov. of Bengal, 77 miles E. of Dinajepoor. Lat. 25° 27′, long. 89° 50′.

KATHA MYO.—A town of Burmah, situate on the right bank of the Irawaddy river, and 161 miles N. from Ava. Lat. 24° 11′, long. 96° 14′.

KATH KI NAO, in the British district of Kumaon, lieut.-gov. of the N.W. Provinces, a summit in the range dividing the valley of the Western Ramgunga river from that of the Kosilla. On it are a fort and stockade, held by the Goorkas during their occupation of the country. Elevation above the sea 5,001 feet. Lat. 29° 34′, long. 79° 10′.

KATHOJIYA.—A town in the native state of Nepal, three miles from the right bank of the Trisul Gunga river, and 35 miles W.N.W. from Khatmandoo. Lat. 27° 53′, long. 84° 47′.

KATHORI, in the Rajpoot state of Jessulmere, a village on the route from the town of Jessulmere to Bahawulpore, and 16 miles N. of the former. It is supplied with water from a fine tank. There are several wells, but the water is brackish. The village is inhabited by Puliwals, called elsewhere Boras, a tribe of Brahmins engaged principally in commercial pursuits. Lat. 27° 7′, long. 70° 59′.

KATHOURA, in the British district of Rohtuk, lieut.-gov. of the N.W. Provinces, a village on the route from Delhi to Hansee, and 37 miles N.E. of the former. Lat. 28° 50′, long. 76° 45′.

KATI, or KASTEE, in Jaunsar, a village among the mountains on the right of the Jumna, and two miles from its bank. It is situate in a chasm, inclosed on every side by declivities, and hence the air is remarkably close, oppressive, and unhealthy. Lat. 30° 36′, long. 78° 3′.

KATI.—A town in Hyderabad, or dominions of the Nizam, situate 141 miles E. by S. of Poonah. Lat. 17° 58′, long. 75° 58′.

KATKARINJEH.—A town of Orissa, on the south-west frontier of Bengal, in the native state of Keunjur, 185 miles W. by S. from Calcutta, and 110 miles E.N.E. from Sumbulpoor. Lat. 21° 55′, long. 85° 40′.

KATMANDOO.—See KHATMANDOO.

KATNUGGUR.—A town in the British district of Midnapoor, lieut.-gov. of Bengal, 77 miles S.W. by W. of Calcutta. Lat. 22° 1′, long. 87° 22′.

KATOH.—A town in the Rajpoot state of Jodhpoor, 94 miles N.E. by E. from Jodhpoor, and 51 miles N.W. by N. from Ajmeer. Lat. 27° 7′, long. 74° 19′.

KATOLE.—A town in the British province of Nagpoor, situate on the left bank of one of the branches of the Warda, and 35 miles W. by N. from Nagpoor. Lat. 21° 16′, long. 78° 37′.

KATTEREWAH, in the British district of Saugur and Nerbudda, lieut.-gov. of the N.W. Provinces, a town on the route from Jubbulpoor to Ruttunpoor, 76 miles S.E. of the former. Lat. 22° 29′, long. 80° 57′.

KATTYWAR.—A province comprehending the whole of the peninsula of Guzerat, the name of one of the districts having been thus extended. On the north and north-west the peninsula is bounded by the Runn and the Gulf of Cutch; on the south-west and south by the Arabian Sea; on the east by the Gulf of Cambay and the British district of Ahmedabad. It lies between lat. 20° 42′—23° 10′, long. 69° 5′—72° 14′, and has an area of 19,850 square miles. It is divided into ten districts, called prants, named respectively, Jhalawar, Kattywar, Muchoo Caunta, Hallar, Soruth, Burda, Gohilwar, Oond Surweya, Babriawar, and Okamundel. These districts are again subdivided into the separate possessions of a host of Hindoo chiefs, some of whom are tributary to the British government, others to the Guicowar. The Peishwa formerly claimed very considerable tributary rights in Kattywar; and the destruction of his power and sovereignty by the British transferred them to the latter. In this manner did the British government acquire superiority over part of the chiefs above mentioned; and it being found inconvenient that two authorities should exercise the power of levying tribute, all have been placed under the control of that government, by whose agency the entire tribute is now collected; the Guicowar's share being accounted for to that prince. The number of chiefs amounts to 216, their total revenue to 450,172*l.*; of which 104,739*l.* is paid as tribute, leaving a residue of 345,433*l.* The military force maintained consists of about 4,000 cavalry and 8,000 infantry. The chiefs are left in a large degree of independence. A criminal court has been established for the trial of more serious offences, through the agency of the British residents; but the native chiefs of the several states within the jurisdiction of the court sit therein

The surface of the country is generally undulating, with low ranges of hills running in irregular directions. The land in the middlemost part of the district is the highest, and here all the rivers take their rise, disemboguing themselves respectively into the Runn, the Gulf of Cutch, the Arabian Sea, or the Gulf of Cambay. The locality denominated the Gir consists of a succession of ridges and hills, covered with forest-trees and jungle, and with a surface extremely rugged. Towards the south of the peninsula, some of the hills are above 1,000 feet high; but their elevation declines towards the north. Caverns, deep ravines, and other fastnesses, are very numerous, and being extremely difficult of access, afford retreats from which those within cannot be dislodged but with the utmost difficulty. The deadly climate of this wild tract is an additional security against the attacks of strangers, who encounter great risk by attempting to remain in it at the close of the year. The Seedees, a people from the coast of Africa, alone encounter it with impunity. Some of other races are occasionally tempted to brave the danger, as water and forage may be obtained here when they have failed in the plains, from which the cattle are driven up at such times; the water, however, is bad, and few persons drink of it for many days without incurring the penalty of disease. Numbers are cut off by death, and many more linger in a state of suffering from agues, fevers, and visceral complaints. These wooded hills are haunted by lions, leopards, chitas or hunting-leopards, wolves, jackals, foxes, wild cats, wild swine, deer, and antelopes; porcupines are also numerous, and vast bodies of migratory rats sometimes move over the country, none knowing whence they come, nor, on their disappearance, whither they go. They are double the size of the common rat; and their ravages in some years are of frightful extent. In 1814 they produced a famine, and on this account it acquired, and is still referred to, as the "rat year."

Of domestic animals, the Kattywar horse was once celebrated, and considered superior, for military purposes, to any in India; but of late years the breed has much deteriorated. Of kine, the breed called Desam is much prized, both in the peninsula and beyond its limits; and buffaloes are also much valued. There are a few camels; but they are small, and not much valued.

The grains principally cultivated are bajra or millet, joar or maize, and wheat. The sugar-cane is grown to a considerable extent, but want of skill among the people prevents the produce from being brought to any other form than goor or molasses. Cotton is the principal commercial crop. The soil is not fertile, being in general rather sandy, and requiring considerable irrigation for the production of crops; but for this there are ample means, as besides the numerous streams throughout the country, water is in general close to the surface, and wells are very numerous, especially in the southern part of the country. The population is returned at 1,468,900. The principal towns, Amreli, Choteyla, Koondla, Buggusra, Cheetal, are described under their respective names in the alphabetical arrangement. For further information, see the article GUZERAT.

KATUKPOOR, in the British district of Moradabad, lieut.-gov. of the N.W. Provinces, a village on the route from Allygurh to the town of Moradabad, and 30 miles S.W. of the latter. Lat. 28° 33′, long. 78° 32′.

KAULARI, or KOELARU, in the British district of Agra, lieut.-gov. of the N.W. Provinces, a town 12 miles S.E. of the city of Agra. Lat. 27° 3′, long. 78° 14′.

KAUMOORY.—A town in the British district of Madura, presidency of Madras, 40 miles S.S.E. of Madura. Lat. 9° 24′, long. 78° 25′.

KAUNDY, in the British district of Cawnpore, lieut.-gov. of the N.W. Provinces, a village on the route from the cantonment of Etawa to that of Cawnpore, and 43 miles W. of the latter. Lat. 26° 21′, long. 79° 47′.

KAUNKAKOTE, in the Jetch Dooab division of the Punjab, a town situated on the left bank of the Jhelum, 113 miles W. of the town of Lahore. Lat. 31° 31′, long. 72° 16′.

KAUNWUN.—A town of Malwa, in the native state of Dhar, 137 miles W.S.W. from Bhopal, and 174 miles E. from Ahmedabad. Lat. 22° 53′, long. 75° 18′

KAURLOOALLA, in the Sinde Sagur Dooab division of the Punjab, a town situated 24 miles from the right bank of the Jhelum, 142 miles W. of the town of Lahore. Lat. 31° 29′, long. 71° 46′.

KAUTCOT.—A town in the native state of Gwalior, or the territory of Sindhia's family, 103 miles W.S.W. from Hoosungabad, and 120 miles N.W. from Ellichpoor. Lat. 22° 20′, long. 76° 12′.

KAVUDAHALLI.—A town in the British district of Coimbatoor, presidency of Madras, 141 miles E. of Cannanore. Lat. 12° 4′, long. 77° 30′.

KAYBONG.—A town in the British province of Pegue, on the right bank of one of the mouths of the Irawady, and 68 miles W. by S. from Pegue. Lat. 17° 30′, long. 95° 16′.

KAZA.—A town in the British district of Guntoor, presidency of Madras, 10 miles N.E. of Guntoor. Lat. 16° 24′, long. 80° 36′.

KAZIKHERA, in the British district of Cawnpore, lieut.-gov. of the N.W. Provinces, a village on the route from the cantonment of Cawnpore to Futtehpore, and five miles S.E. of the former. Lat. 26° 25′, long. 80° 27′.

KAZURANGA.—A town of Assam, in the British district of Nowgong, 42 miles E.N.E. of Nowgong. Lat. 26° 37′, long. 93° 24′.

KEDA.—See QUEDAH.

KEDAR GUNGA, in native Gurwhal, a river rising at the north-eastern base of the mountain styled in the trigonometrical survey Mount Moira, and in lat. 30° 54′, long. 79° 5′. It holds a very rapid course of ten or twelve miles, generally in a north-westerly direction, and falls into the Bhageerettee, on the left side, about a gunshot below Gangotri, and in lat. 30° 59′, long. 78° 59′. Like other Himalayan streams, it is subject to great and rapid increase, from the melting of the mountain snows by the sun's heat; and this may account for the different descriptions of it by Fraser, and by Hodgson and Herbert. According to the former, it is "a rapid and considerable stream, said to have its rise in the Cedar Mountain, twelve cos distance." According to the latter, "It has no claim to the title of a river, being merely a torrent from the snow, of ten or twelve feet wide, and shallow. It comes out of a rocky gorge, and its course cannot be longer than three or four miles."

KEDAR KANTA, in native Gurwhal, a peak in the ridge separating the rivers Jumna and Tons. The acclivity of its sides is moderate in all parts, so that it can without much difficulty be ascended everywhere, though elevated considerably above the ridges which radiate from it to almost all points of the compass. The summit terminates in an horizontal area of a few square yards; and, according to Hodgson and Herbert, consists of gneiss; but Jacquemont explicitly states that the formation is micaceous schist (micaschiste), which, according to him, forms the whole mass of the mountain. About the base, however, in many places are enormous beds of white saccharoid limestone, veined with yellowish mica, and sometimes upwards of 120 feet thick. The top of Kedar Kanta is above the limit of forest vegetation, which terminates on its sides, at an elevation of about 10,000 feet above the sea, in rather precise demarcation, on soil well suited for the growth of trees; and consequently the cessation of their growth must be the effect of diminished temperature. Below the stated limit, the sides of the mountain are covered with dense forests of oak, pine, yew, maple, holly, horse-chestnut, alder, rhododendron, and thickets of juniper and gooseberry. The character of the forests is quite that of similar vegetation in Europe, the growth of whose mountains and plains is here united. The treeless and higher part of the mountain produces a sedgy sward, intermixed with various sorts of the anemone, ranunculus, iris, corydalis, phalangium, primula, gentiana, saxifraga, and some other Alpine plants. A minute species of euphorbia thrives, but not below 11,000 feet. In the year when this mountain was surveyed by Hodgson and Herbert, "in June, it was deep in snow, but in August had lost it all." Jacquemont, at the end of May, found the summit free from snow, though a patch lay undissolved on the north-eastern declivity. From a barometrical observation, he estimates the elevation at 12,756 feet above the sea. The estimate of Hodgson and Herbert is 12,689; a closer correspondence than usual between those authorities. It was a station of the large series of triangles in the great trigonometrical survey of the Himalaya. Lat. 31° 1′, long. 78° 14′.

KEDARNATH (TEMPLE OF), in Gurhwal, is situate on a lofty ridge, rising on the eastern frontier towards Kumaon. The temple is rather large and handsome, and, according to Traill, was only completed about twenty-five years since. It is frequented by Hindoo pilgrims, a previous visit to Kedarnath being considered a necessary preparation to the pilgrimage of Badarinath. The object of worship is a rock, supposed to represent a portion of the body of Kedarnath, who, flying from some pursuers, took refuge here in the form of a buffalo, and, finding himself overtaken, dived into the ground, leaving, however, his hinder part on the surface an object of adoration. The remaining portions of the body of the god, four in number, are objects of worship at four separate temples, situate along the Himalaya chain, and which, along with Kedarnath, form what is termed the "Panch Kedar," the pilgrimage to which places in succession is considered an achievement of extraordinary merit. In the vicinity of Kedarnath is the peak of "Maha Panth," where, in imitation of the Pandavas, who, according to the legend, devoted themselves, and from whence they were believed to be taken up to heaven, from twenty to thirty wretched victims of superstition annually commit suicide, either by proceeding into the snowy waste until they perish by hunger and cold, or by precipitating themselves from a precipice in the neighbourhood, called Bhyrava Jhamp. These suicides are chiefly from Guzerat and Bengal; the hill people seldom thus devote themselves. The rawal, or chief priest of the temple, is invariably a Brahmin from the Malabar coast. The temple has an annual income of about 6,000 rupees, principally from lands, and eked out by offerings. Elevation above the sea, of the temple, 11,755 feet. Lat. 30° 44′, long. 79° 7′.

KEDER.—A town in the British district of Midnapoor, lieut.-gov. of Bengal, 60 miles W.S.W. of Calcutta. Lat. 22° 19′, long. 87° 31′.

KEDJEREE, in the British district of Hooghly, lieut.-gov. of Bengal, a seafaring place on the western coast of the estuary of the Hooghly, and on the inside or most western channel, formerly the principal approach for shipping destined for Calcutta. The largest ships might then moor here, the depths being six or seven fathoms; but a sand-bank has accumulated in the road or channel, by which the depth has been reduced to two or two and a half fathoms at low water. The first section of telegraphic communication in India extended from this place to Calcutta. Distance from Calcutta, S.W., 40 miles. Lat. 21° 53′, long. 88°.

KEDYWAREE, in Sinde, is the mouth of an offset from the right or western side of the Sata, or great eastern branch of the Indus, by which the great bulk of its waters is discharged. Since the inundation of 1848, the old bed of the Kedywaree has been deserted, and the stream now flows to the sea by a channel inclined six miles more eastward. The new channel is at present tolerably well defined, having six to eight feet water at low tide. Lat. 24° 2′, long. 67° 21′.

KEECHOWLEE, in the British district of Mynpooree, lieut.-gov. of the N.W. Provinces, a village on the route from the cantonment of Allygurh to that of Mynpooree, and 13 miles N.W. of the latter. Lat. 27° 20′, long. 78° 57′.

KEEKAIRY.—A town in Mysore, 29 miles N.N.W. from Seringapatam, and 96 miles N.E. by E. from Cannanore. Lat. 12° 46′, long. 76° 30′.

KEELEEPALEE.—A town of Orissa, on the south-west frontier of Bengal, in the native state of Sonepoor, situate on the left bank of the Mahanuddy river, and 22 miles S. from Sumbulpoor. Lat. 21° 10′, long. 84° 3′.

KEEL KUNDAH.—A town in the British district of Malabar, presidency of Madras, 100 miles S.E. by E. of Cannanore. Lat. 11° 14′, long. 76° 45′.

KEENY.—A town in Hyderabad, or dominions of the Nizam, situate 65 miles S.S.W. of Ellichpoor. Lat. 20° 19′, long. 77° 16′.

KEERPOY, in the British district of Hoogly, lieut.-gov. of Bengal, a town on the route from Burdwan to Midnapore, 40 miles S. of the former, 30 N.E. of the latter, 48 W. of Calcutta. Lat. 22° 44′, long. 87° 41′.

KEERTAR. — A range of mountains of inconsiderable height in the western part of Sinde, being an offset of the great Hala range farther west. Their average height is probably below 2,000 feet, but neither as to dimensions nor in a geological point of view, have they been well explored. They lie between lat. 25° 50′—26° 40′, and about the meridian line of long. 67° 40′.

KEERUTPOOR, in the British district of Mynpoorie, lieut.-gov. of the N.W. Provinces, a town on the route from the cantonment of Etawa to that of Mynpoorie, and six miles S.W. of the latter. Lat. 27° 10′, long. 79° 2′.

KEIM.—A town in the British district of Sholapoor, presidency of Bombay, 171 miles E.S.E. of Bombay. Lat. 18° 11′, long. 75° 22′.

KEIPU, in Bussahir, a pass in Koonawar, over a lofty range of mountains dividing the valley of the Taglakhar river from that of the Hocho. Elevation above the sea 13,456 feet. Lat. 31° 40′, long. 78° 35′.

KEIRNAH.—A town of Orissa, on the south-west frontier of Bengal, in the native state of Mohurbunge, 153 miles W. by S. from Calcutta, and 117 miles N. from Cuttack. Lat. 22° 9′, long. 86° 5′.

KEITHA, or KITHA, in the British district of Humeerpoor, lieut.-gov. of the N.W. Provinces, a town on the route from Calpee to Jubulpoor, 52 miles S. of the former, 217 N. of the latter. It is situate on the small river Bearma, amidst sandstone rocks, and on the border of a plain of black soil, to the effects of which is attributed the deadly malaria which has caused the place to be deserted as a military station. The deleterious influence is aggravated during the rainy season by the inundations which overspread the vicinity, and at other times by a very sultry temperature. Here was a British cantonment, which, in 1828, was occupied by two regiments of infantry and a troop of cavalry. They were subsequently withdrawn, and when, six months afterwards, the place was visited by Davidson, the lodges of the Europeans, and even their tombs, had been partially demolished by the natives, and a force of thirty native soldiers and a European serjeant were all that remained. It has, however, still a small bazar, where supplies may be obtained. Lat. 25° 31′, long. 79° 36′.

KEKAPAR, in the British district of Saugur and Nerbudda, lieut.-gov. of the N.W. Provinces, a town on the route from Baitool to Jubbulpoor, 69 miles N.E. of the former. Lat. 22° 33′, long. 78° 41′.

KEKREE, in the British district of Ajmeer, lieut.-gov. of the N.W. Provinces, a town, the principal place of a pergunnah of the same name, on the route from Nusseerabad to Boondee, 36 miles S.E. of former, and 56 miles N.W. of latter. The population of the town, which is surrounded by a wall, and represented as a place of importance, is 4,025. Distant S.E. from Nusseerabad cantonment 35 miles; S.E. from city of Ajmeer 50. Lat. 26° 1′, long. 75° 20′.

KELEEAREE, in the British district of Kumaon, lieut.-gov. of the N.W. Provinces, a town on the route from Almora to the Nepal territory, 26 miles E. of the former. Lat. 29° 39′, long. 80° 8′.

KELLA CALLE.—A town in the British district of Backergunje, lieut.-gov. of Bengal, 100 miles E. by N. of Calcutta. Lat. 22° 50′, long. 89° 59′.

KELLUKKAMOOREY.—A town in the native state of Travancore, 120 miles W. by N. from Madura, and 131 miles S.E. by S. from Cannanore. Lat. 10° 15′, long. 76° 27′.

KELSAKARREE.—A town in the British district of Backergunje, lieut.-gov. of Bengal, 137 miles E. by S. of Calcutta. Lat. 22° 17′, long. 90° 30′.

KELZUR.—A town in the British province of Nagpoor, 26 miles S.W. from Nagpoor, and 86 miles E. by S. from Ellichpoor. Lat. 20° 54′, long. 78° 51′.

KEMNA.—A town in the British district of Tirhoot, lieut.-gov. of Bengal, 88 miles N.E. of Dinapoor. Lat. 26° 22′, long. 86° 16′.

KENAMOW.—A town in the territory of Oude, 48 miles S. from Lucknow, and 39 miles S.E. from Cawnpoor. Lat. 26° 11′, long. 80° 57′.

KENKAR.—A town in the native state of Bhotan, situate on the left bank of the Monas river, and 65 miles N.N.E. from Goalpara. Lat. 27°, long. 91° 9′.

KENLAY.—A town of Burmah, 48 miles S.E. by E. from Ava, and 212 miles N.N.E. from Prome. Lat. 21° 30′, long. 96° 39′.

KENNERY.—See SALSETTE.

KEN RIVER.—See CANE.

KEOBRUNG, in Bussahir, a pass over a very lofty ridge, forming on the north-east the boundary between Koonawar and Chinese Tartary. It is situate a short distance within the boundary of Chinese Tartary, but the exposure and severity of the climate prevent any piquet of that people from being stationed there, so that it has been repeatedly visited by Europeans, who, on attempting to continue their course to the eastward, have been uniformly stopped and turned back by the authorities of the Celestial Empire. Hence it has been of late years the remotest point reached by European enterprise in attempting to penetrate in that direction to Central Asia. The pass has been found free from snow at the end of July, though at the enormous elevation of 18,313 feet above the sea. Lat. 31° 36′, long. 78° 54′.

KEONGPULA, KEONGPEETA, or KHEOUNGKELA.—A stockade situate near the river Arracan, in the province of the same name, and about thirty miles from the town likewise so designated. It is noticeable only on account of an attempt to reduce it, made in 1825, by a marine force under Commodore Hayes. It was then garrisoned by 1,000 men, and after a severe contest of ten hours' duration, the commander was forced to retire. Lat. 20° 30′, long. 93° 8′.

KEOOKOOCHEE, in Bussahir, a halting-place on the north-eastern declivity of the elevated Charung Pass, which traverses the huge mountain dividing the valley of the Buspa from that of the Tidung. This place is frequented on account of its supply of herbage from thyme, mint, sage, and other odoriferous plants, and of fuel, from junipers and other shrubs, indispensable resources to travellers in those frigid and dreary wastes. The halting-place is on the right bank of the Nungulti, a rapid unfordable torrent, falling into the river Tidung a few miles farther down. Elevation above the sea 12,457 feet. Lat. 31° 27′, long. 78° 37′.

KEOUN NAGAH.—A town of Burmah, situate on the left bank of the Irawaddy river, and 40 miles N. from Prome. Lat. 19° 20′, long. 95°.

KEOW PEA.—A town in the British province of Tenasserim, 37 miles N.W. by N. of Tenasserim. Lat. 12° 33′, long. 98° 49′.

KEPU, in the hill state of Kotgurh, a village situate on the left bank of the Sutluj, and at the northern base of the lofty ridge on which stands the fort of Kotgurh. The village of Kepu is 3,000 feet above the sea, and surrounded by beautiful and luxuriant vegetation. Lat. 31° 20′, long. 77° 31′.

KERAON, in the British district of Cawnpore, lieut.-gov. of the N.W. Provinces, a town three miles N. of the left bank of the Jumna, 20 miles E. of Calpee. Lat. 26° 7′, long. 80° 7′.

KERIAL, KOREN, or BHOKUR.—A raj under the control of the political agent for the south-west frontier of Bengal. The chief districts bordering on it are Bora Samba, Patna, Phooljer, and Calahandy; and it embraces an area of 1,512 square miles. Its centre is in lat. 20° 30′, long. 82° 40′. The country is wild, and the people savage. The tribute, however, amounting with that of Bhokur, which is included in it, to 1,095 rupees, is represented as paid with regularity. The present annual value of the country has been computed at 10,000 rupees. The population is supposed to be about 68,000. Kerial, the capital, is in lat. 20° 19′, long. 82° 50′.

KERIM KHAN, in the British district of Humeerpoor, lieut.-gov. of the N.W. Provinces, a village on the right bank of the Jumna, the channel of which is obstructed by rocks of kankar or calcareous conglomerate, lying in confusion, in consequence of the less-resisting clay, which sustained them, having been washed away by the violence of the stream. The rocks formerly extended in broken masses four or five feet above the water, for two-thirds of the width of the river, and at the season of low water formed so dangerous and difficult an obstruction to navigation, that by the order of government, engineers have for some years been employed in removing them. Lat. 26° 20′, long. 79° 34′.

KEROWLEE.—A small state in Rajpootana, denominated from the city of the same name. It is bounded on the north by Bhurtpore; on the east by the state of Dholpore; on the south-east by the river Chumbul, dividing it from the territory of Gwalior, or the possessions of the Scindia family; on the west by the river Bunass, dividing it from the state of Jeypore; and on the north-west by the state of Jeypore. It lies between lat. 25° 53′—26° 48′, long. 76° 47′—77° 38′. The area is 1,878 square miles. Little or no authentic information as to its physical characteristics or productions appears to exist. The population computed at the rate of 100 to the square mile, would amount to 187,800; and this is believed to be not widely distant from the fact.

From its slight importance, the early history of this district is very obscure, and perhaps the first that is known of it is, that in 1454 it was conquered by Mahmud Khilji, king of Malwa, and, with some neighbouring tracts, assigned as an appanage to his son. After the conquest of Malwa by Akbar, the territory of Kerowlee probably became incorporated with the empire of Delhi, and on the decline of that state, it appears to have been so far subjugated to the Mahrattas, that they exacted from it a tribute of 25,000 rupees annually. In 1817, the right or claim to this tribute, with some others of a similar nature, was, under the fourteenth article of the treaty of Poona, transferred by the Peishwa to the British government, which gratuitously remitted it to the rajah. He was, however, little grateful for the concession, as, though bound by treaty to acknowledge the supremacy of the British government, and to co-operate with it, he in 1825, when that government was engaged in the Burmese war, and the standard of rebellion was hoisted at Bhurtpore by Doorjun Saul, lent his puny aid to sustain the cause of the usurper just named, and on the fall of the fortress, assembled troops for his own defence. Subsequently, however, he made strong professions of attachment, and it was not deemed necessary to take any serious notice of these very foolish but hostile proceedings. Beyond the adjustment of some border differences between the states of Kerowlee and Jeypore, there seems to have been hardly any communication with the rajah of this small principality, from the period of the negotiation of the treaty until recently, when the advice and remonstrance of the British political agent were demanded by the usual causes—mismanagement on the part of the head of the state and his servants; pecuniary difficulties thence resulting, and the existence of faction and insubordination among the military chiefs. Subsequently, the distracted condition of the state induced the rajah to solicit the interference of the British government; and a compliance with his request led to the restoration of tranquillity. Upon the death, in 1852, of the young rajah Nursing Pal, his adopted son Bhurt Pal was recognised by the British government as his successor, and arrangements were made for the administration of the state during the minority of the rajah. Shortly afterwards, however, it was discovered that certain irregularities in the adoption of Bhurt Pal had rendered the ceremony invalid. Upon this being made known to the British government, the recognition of Bhurt Pal as successor to the throne was annulled, and Muddun Pal, the nearest of kin to Nursing Pal, and a chief of mature age, was elevated to the throne. The total revenue of the country is stated at 506,903 rupees; but so much is alienated for various purposes, as to leave little more than two-thirds of that sum for the use of the state. The military force appears greatly disproportioned to the importance or necessities of the state, being returned at 784 (cavalry and infantry), besides nearly 1,100 men in the garrisons of a few forts; making a total of nearly 1,900.

KEROWLEE, in Rajpootana, the principal place of a small state of the same name, is situate on the route from Nusserabad to Gwalior, 152 miles E. of the former, and 89 W. of the latter. Garden gives nearly all that of late years is known of the place in the following passage:—"A large town and capital of the Karowlee state; supplies and water abundant; the town is inclosed by a pucka (masonry) wall, and surmounted by difficult ravines to an extent of nearly two miles." Tieffenthaler, describing its condition about seventy years ago, states that the site of the town was selected by the rajah, when seeking security against Mahomedan invaders, on account of the difficulty of access to it, the road being for two miles narrow and easily defended. The immediate environs of the town he describes as well watered, fertile, carefully cultivated, and containing fine groves; the houses as built of brick, and those of a superior class faced with squared stone, and covered with large thin slabs; but the streets as narrow and filthy. He mentions two forts on two connected hills close to the town. One, the residence of the rajah, is described as a fine building, with very lofty towers, the walls being outside and inside faced with red stone, put together with admirable accuracy and fine finish. The interior is represented as containing fine buildings and agreeable gardens. The walls of the town are stated to be massive, and well built of large slabs, laid in regular layers one over the other; but the whole upper fabric as too frail to bear artillery, and subject to inevitable destruction, if so assailed. Kerowlee is distant S.W. of Agra 80 miles, S. of Delhi 150. Lat. 26° 28′, long. 77° 10′.

KERUTPOOR, in Sirhind, a village in the alluvial tract on the left bank of the Sutlej. It is situate in a beautiful grove of mango-trees, and at the foot of a bank surmounted by an elegant Hindoo temple, approached by means of a finely-proportioned and grand flight of stone steps. The neighbouring alluvial eminences are furrowed and broken up by torrents into numerous abrupt knolls, the resort of innumerable wild peafowl, protected by the superstition of the natives, and enlivening and heightening the beauty of the scenery. Distant N.W. from Calcutta 1,090 miles. Lat. 31° 11′, long. 76° 37′.

KERYCAUD.—A town of Southern India, in the native state of Travancore, situate on the coast, 122 miles W.S.W. from Madura. Lat. 9° 11′, long. 76° 32′.

KESSODE.—A town in the province of Guzerat, or the dominions of the Guicowar, 13 miles N.E. from the coast, and 81 miles S.S.W. from Rajkote. Lat. 21° 16′, long. 70° 18′.

KEST, in the British district of Etawa, lieut.-gov. of the N.W. Provinces, a village on the route from the cantonment of Agra to that of Etawa, and eight miles N.W. of the latter. Lat. 26° 52′, long. 78° 58′.

KETHOR, in the British district of Meerut, lieut.-gov. of the N.W. Provinces, a town on the route from Muzuffurnuggur to Boolundshuhur, 33 miles N. of the latter. Lat. 28° 51′, long. 78°.

KETWAREE, in the territory of Bhurtpore, a village on the route from Muttra to Ferozpore, in the British district of Goorgaon, 35 miles N.W. of former, 17 S.E. of latter. Lat. 27° 37′, long. 77° 12′.

KEUNJUR.—A town of Orissa, on the south-west frontier of Bengal, in the native state of Keunjur, three miles from the left bank of the Byeturnee river, and 82 miles N. by W. from Cuttack. Lat. 21° 39′, long. 85° 41′.

KEUNJUR, in Orissa, one of the Cuttack mehals, on the south-west frontier of Bengal, bounded on the north by Singboom; on the north-east by Mohurbunge; on the east by the British district of Balasore; on the south by the Cuttack mehals; and on the west by the native states of Bombra and Bonei. It extends from lat. 21° 1′—22°, and from long. 85° 7′—86° 23′; is ninety miles in length from south-east to north-west, and sixty miles in breadth. The population is returned at 225,990. The mehal became subject to British supremacy upon the conquest of the province of Cuttack in 1804.

KEUTEE, in Bhaghelcund, or the territory of Rewa, a village on the direct route from Mirzapoor to the diamond-mines of Punnah, and 75 miles S.W. of the former. It is remarkable for a cascade, where the Mohana, a small tributary of the Tons, falls a depth of 272 feet, over a purplish rock overlying a mottled sandstone. Elevation above the sea 923 feet. Lat. 24° 49′, long. 81° 31′.

KEWAIE, or KOT KEWAYI, in the British district of Allahabad, lieut.-gov. of the N.W. Provinces, a small town near the eastern frontier towards Benares, and about eight miles from the left bank of the Ganges, 25 miles E. of the city of Allahabad. Lat. 25° 25′, long. 82° 23′.

KEYALL, in the Sinde Sagur Doosb division of the Punjab, a town situated on the left bank of the river Indus, 78 miles S.W. of the town of Mooltan. Lat. 29° 15′, long. 70° 43′.

KEYONTHUL, a hill state between the Sutlej and the Jumna, is bounded on the north by Simla and by the chieftainships Kothee, Mudhan, Theog, and Goond, all of them tributary to Keyonthul; on the east by Bulsun; on the south by Sirmour and by territory appertaining to the rajah of Pateeala; and on the west by Baghat and a portion of Pateeala. It is about fifteen miles in length from north to south, and about the same distance in breadth. The centre is in lat. 31°, long. 77° 18′. It is throughout a maze of mountains of considerable height, no part of the country having probably an elevation less than 3,000 feet, while one summit, that of Manund, attains the height of 7,800; and another, that of Mahhassu, 9,078 above the sea. The drainage is south-eastward into the river Giri. The principal place is Junug, the residence of the rana, or Hindoo prince.

The territory of Keyonthul was dismembered by the British government, after the conquest of the hills, and a portion sold to the rajah of Pateeala. In consideration of this alienation, the remainder of the Keyonthul state is exempted from the payment of tribute. As at present existing, Keyonthul proper has an area of 139 square miles; but if its tributary dependencies, Kothee, Mudhan, Theog, Goond, and Poondur, be included, the area will be 272 miles. The population of Keyonthul proper is about 14,000; with that of the dependencies, it is estimated at 26,000. The chief state produces an annual revenue of about 2,000*l.*; the dependencies about 1,350*l.*

KEYRAULOO, in Guzerat, or territory of the Guicowar, a town on the route from Neemuch to Deesa, 219 miles W. of former, 41 S.E. of latter. It is situate in a fertile country, and is a flourishing town, with considerable manufactures. Population about 12,000, many of whom are of Sindhian descent, the place being held by chiefs of that nation on feudal tenure from the Guicowar. Lat. 23° 54′, long. 72° 39′.

KEYSOPOOR, in the British district of Allyghur, lieut.-gov. of the N.W. Provinces, a village on the route from Allyghur cantonment to that of Etawa, and 29 miles S.E. of the former. Lat. 27° 32′, long. 78° 18′.

KEYSUMPETT.—A town in Hyderabad, or the Nizam's dominions, 32 miles S.S.W. from Hyderabad, and 80 miles N.N.E. from Kurnool. Lat. 16° 56′, long. 78° 24′.

KHAB, or CHAP, in Bussahir, a village of Koonawar, on the left bank of the Sutluj, which here flows between stupendous cliffs of mica-slate and granite. The site of the village is circumscribed by fragments of rock, amidst which the traveller is surprised to find himself instantly amongst fields, vineyards, and avenues of apricot-trees. It is the highest place in which the grape grows in Koonawar. It does not, however, ripen properly, and is little better than the produce of the wild vine of Koonawar. Elevation above the sea 9,310 feet. Lat. 31° 48′, long. 78° 41′.

KHABILI.—A river of Nepal, rising in lat. 27° 27′, long. 88° 7′, on the western side of the spur of the Himalayas, separating Nepal from Sikhim. It flows in a south-westerly direction for fifty miles, and falls into the Tambur in lat. 27° 13′, long. 87° 27′.

KHABUL, in Bussahir, a village in the valley of the Pabur, and a mile from the right bank of that river, is situate on the route from Subathoo to the Burenda Pass, and 20 miles S.W. of this last place. The surrounding country is described by Lloyd as "well tilled, and the villages large, clean, and delightfully situated amongst shady trees. The sycamore, chestnut, and apricot, the last loaded with green fruit, grew in great luxuriance. Numerous streams likewise rushed down the sides of the mountain, and either turned mills or were conducted to irrigate the fields." Elevation above the sea 8,400 feet. Lat. 31° 15′, long. 77° 58′.

KHACHI.—A town in the native state of Nepal, 154 miles W. by N. from Khatmandoo, and 98 miles N.N.W. from Goruckpoor. Lat. 28°, long. 82° 51′.

KHACHROD, in the territory of Gwalior, or possessions of Scindia's family, a town on the route from Baitool to Neemuch, 231 miles N.W. of the former, 81 S.E. of the latter. It is a large open town. Elevation above the sea 1,638 feet. Lat. 23° 28′, long. 75° 20′.

KHAIRABAD. — A village on the right bank of the Indus, opposite Attock, and at the Peshawur or western extremity of the ferry, or of the bridge of boats which affords the means of communication during the season of low water. Lat. 33° 54′, long. 72° 15′.

KHAIRAH, in the British district of Muttra, lieut.-gov. of the N.W. Provinces, a town in lat. 27° 42′, long. 77° 30′.

KHALBOLEA.—A town in the British district of Nuddea, lieut.-gov. of Bengal, 66 miles N.N.E. of Calcutta. Lat. 23° 30′, long. 88° 43′.

KHALIYANPOOR, in the British district of Futtehpoor, lieut.-gov. of the N.W. Provinces, a town on the route from Cawnpore to the town of Futtehpoor, and 15 miles N.W. of the latter. There is a serai or lodge for travellers here. Lat. 26° 4′, long. 80° 42′.

KHALIYANPOOR (KULEEANPUR), in the British district of Bareilly, lieut.-gov. of the N.W. Provinces, a small town on the route from the town of Bareilly to Almora, and 46 miles N. of the former. It is a wretched place, and, though situate on a plain apparently open and dry, the air for the greater part of the year is very unhealthy, afflicting the inhabitants with severe intermittents and other fatal fevers. The natives call the disease awal, and, with perverse ignorance, attributing it to the quality of the water, take no precautions against the malaria. Lat. 28° 54′, long. 79° 30′.

KHALKA DEBI, called also ATTUK, in the British district of Kumaon, lieut.-gov. of the N.W. Provinces, a ruined village, with Hindoo temple, on the route from Askot to the Bians Pass, 11 miles N.E. of former, half a mile from the right bank of the Kalee river. Lat. 29° 49', long. 80° 32'.

KHALSEE, in Jaunsar, a town, with a fort, at the confluence of the rivers Tons and Jumna. In the Goorkha war it early fell into the power of the British, and was retained, with the rest of Jaunsar, by the East-India Company, when the rajah of Sirmoor was restored to his possessions. It was formerly more considerable and flourishing than at present, yet still remains the entrepôt of the commerce between the plains and the tracts northward. Close to the town a copper-mine was formerly worked, but has been for some time abandoned. As the confluence of the Tons and Jumna is 1,686 feet above the sea, the elevation of Khalsee, situate on a ridge rising considerably above that point, must exceed that amount. Lat. 30° 32', long. 77° 54'.

KHAMARIYA, in the British district of Goruckpore, lieut.-gov. of the N.W. Provinces, a small town 55 miles W. of Goruckpore cantonment, is situate on the Ramrekha, a feeder of the river Koyane. Distant N.W. of Benares 110 miles, N.E. of Allahabad 100. Lat. 26° 50', long. 82° 18'.

KHAMBAT.—A town of Burmah, 19 miles from the right bank of the Khyendwen river, and 173 miles N.W. from Ava. Lat. 23° 46', long. 94° 25'.

KHANAIWALA, in the Baree Dooab division of the Punjab, a town situate 17 miles from the left bank of the Chenaub, 28 miles E.N.E. of the town of Mooltan. Lat. 30° 16', long. 71° 47'.

KHANAPOOR.—A town in the British province of Sattara, presidency of Bombay, 57 miles S.E. by E. of Sattara. Lat. 17° 15', long. 74° 48'.

KHANAPOOR. — A town in the native state of Kolapoor, territory of Bombay, 29 miles S. from Kolapoor, and 40 miles N.W. by N. from Belgaum. Lat. 16° 19', long. 74° 13'.

KHANAPOOR. — A town in the British district of Belgaum, presidency of Bombay, 15 miles S. of Belgaum. Lat. 15° 39', long. 74° 33'.

KHANBAILA, in Bhawlpoor, a considerable town near the left bank of the Punjnud. The neighbouring country is very fertile, and, in the season of inundation, overspread by the waters of the river; so that the dense population, by light labour, draw from it abundant and rich crops, especially of rice, wheat, and barley. When visited by Wood, so early as the end of April, "the surface was often, as far as the eye could range, one continuous corn-field. It was harvest-time, and crops of wheat and barley stood ready for the sickle, dressed in the rich livery of the season." When the waters retire, the seed is thrown down, and the farmer has no further trouble till the harvest calls him forth to husband his crops. Khanbaila is in lat. 29° 4', long. 70° 52'.

KHANDEISH.—See CANDEISH.

KHANGHER.—A town of Sinde, in the British district of Shikarpoor, presidency of Bombay, 25 miles N.N.W. of Shikarpoor. Lat. 28° 19', long. 68° 24'.

KHANGURH.—A town in the native state of Bhawulpoor, 68 miles S. from Bhawulpoor, and 103 miles W.N.W. from Beekaneer. Lat. 28° 16', long. 71° 45'.

KHANGURH, in the Sinde Saugur Dooab division of the Punjab, a town situated on the right bank of the Chenaub, 32 miles S.W. by S. of the town of Mooltan. Lat. 29° 45', long. 71° 13'.

KHANPOOR, in the British district of Ghazeepore, the principal place of the pergunnah or subdivision of the same name, a town on the route from Ghazeepore cantonment to Jounpore, 32 miles W. of the former, 28 S.E. of the latter. Lat. 25° 34', long. 83° 11'.

KHANPOOR, in Bhawlpoor, a flourishing commercial town, with a good roofed bazar, is situate on the Ikhtiarwah, a navigable canal from the Punjnud. There is a ruinous mud fort, 200 yards long and 120 broad. The surrounding country is populous, and, where irrigated, fertile; but in general of lighter quality than the region to the south and west, as the eastern desert here begins to be observable. The route from Islamgurh, situate 55 miles south, is through the sandy desert, in which the characteristic features of such frightful tracts are peculiarly striking. They are well described by Boileau:—"Long and lofty ridges of sandhills follow each other in ceaseless succession, as if an ocean of sand had been suddenly arrested in its progress, with intervals of a quarter or half a mile, or even more, between its gigantic billows; for, after ascending many hundred yards along a gradual slope, we would suddenly come to a steep descent, when our path lay across the line of waves; and on other occasions we would perhaps move parallel to them, with a steep wall of sand on one hand, and a gentle rise on the other." Khanpoor has many symptoms of having been formerly a place of much greater importance than now. Population 10,000. Lat. 28° 35', long. 70° 41'.

KHANPOOR, in the Punjab, a fort 41 miles E. of Attock, is situated at the foot of the low range of mountains forming the first stage of the ascent from the plain to the Himalaya. It is surrounded by a fertile country, containing beautiful gardens. Lat. 33° 52', long. 73°.

KHANPOOR GHAT, in the British district of Goorgaon, lieut.-gov. of the N.W. Provinces, a pass through a low range of hills extending from north-east to south-west. The small town or village of Pingawa is situate a mile east of the pass, which is on the route from Muttra to Ferozpoor, and 52 miles N.W. of the former. Lat. 27° 54', long. 77° 9'.

KHANSRU CHOKI, in the British district of Dehra Doon, a halting-place on the route from Hurdwar to Dehra, and 12 miles N.W. of the former place. Distant N.W. from Calcutta 937 miles. Lat. 30° 5′, long. 78° 11′.

KHANWAH, in the territory of Bhurtpore, a village on the route from Agra to Ajmeer, 31 miles W. of the former, 197 E. of the latter. It is described by Heber as a large but dilapidated village, situate at the foot of a great ridge of rock, surmounted by a small mosque. Here, in the year 1526, commenced the great battle between Baber, the Mogul conqueror of Delhi, and Rana Sanka, of Oodeypore, the head of a confederacy of Rajpoot princes, banded to engage the Mussulmans. Baber was so alarmed respecting the result, that, hoping to gain the favour of heaven by contrition, he renounced the use of wine, or any other strong drink, broke up his drinking-vessels of gold and silver, and distributed the metal as alms. Rana Sanka was totally defeated, and escaped with difficulty, and Baber assumed the title of Ghazi, or "victorious champion of the faith." He also caused a tower of the skulls of the infidels to be erected on a small hill close to the field of battle. The force opposed to Baber is reported to have amounted to 200,000 men, principally cavalry. Khanwah is in lat. 27° 3′, long. 77° 37′.

KHAPALU, or KHOPALU, in the territory of Gholab Singh, a fort built on the summit of a rock, nearly isolated, in an expanse on the left bank of the Indus. This open space is described by Vigne as a sloping bank "of two or three miles in extent, and exhibiting a green and shady confusion of stone walls, cottages, and fruit-trees." The eminence on which the fort stands is more than 1,000 feet above the Indus, and commands a very grand view. Lat. 35° 7′, long. 76° 24′.

KHAPPA.—A town in the British province of Nagpore, situate on the right bank of one of the tributaries of the Wein Gunga river, 21 miles N. by W. from Nagpore. Lat. 21° 25′, long. 79°.

KHAPPOH, in the British district of Saugur and Nerbudda, lieut.-gov. of the N.W. Provinces, a town on the route from Jubbulpoor to Nagpoor, 14 miles S. by E. of the former. Lat. 22° 59′, long. 80° 4′.

KHAPURHA, in the British district of Jounpoor, lieut.-gov. of the N.W. Provinces, a village on the route from Jounpoor cantonment to Purtabgurh, 14 miles W. of the former, 34 E. of the latter, situate on the right bank of the river Saee, here crossed by a fine bridge of masonry. Lat. 25° 45′, long. 82° 33′.

KHARRAH, in the Rajpoot state of Jodhpoor, a village on the route from Bikumpoor to Balmeer, and 67 miles S. of the former. It is situate in a sterile ill-cultivated country. Lat. 27° 1′, long. 72° 12′.

KHARROH, or KHARA, in the Rajpoot state of Jessulmeer, a village on the western frontier, towards Sinde. A line drawn from this village in an easterly direction to the opposite frontier would nearly bisect Jessulmeer, and divide the comparatively fertile tract in the southern part from the thoroughly barren desert in the northern. Khara is in lat. 27° 32′, long. 71° 39′.

KHASGUNJ, in the British district of Furruckabad, lieut.-gov. of the N.W. Provinces, a village on the route, by Nanamow Ghat, from Lucknow to Futtehgurh, and 38 miles S.E. of the latter. The country is fertile, and generally cultivated, though much cut up by ravines and fissures. Lat. 27°, long. 80° 2′.

KHASGUNJE, in the British district of Mynpoorie, lieut.-gov. of the N.W. Provinces, a town on the route from Allyghur to Bareilly, and 38 miles S.E. of the former. It is situate on the Kalee Nuddi (East), here crossed by a handsome brick bridge of five arches, up to the vicinity of which the river is navigable from the Ganges; thus affording a communication by water from the sea to this place. Here was formerly a military cantonment, which was burned during Holcar's incursion into the Doab in 1804. It is now a large town, with a population of 10,752. The road in this part of the route is good generally, but in some parts heavy; the country open, and partially cultivated. Lat. 27° 48′, long. 78° 43′.

KHATAH.—A town in the native territory of Rampoor, district of Bareilly, 25 miles N.W. from the town of Bareilly, and 26 miles E.S.E. from Moradabad. Lat. 28° 40′, long. 79° 14′.

KHATANG.—A town in the native state of Nepal, three miles from the right bank of the Arun river, and 96 miles E.S.E. from Khatmandoo. Lat. 27° 18′, long. 86° 46′.

KHATMANDOO.—A town of Nepaul, situated on the east bank of the Bishnmutty river, and regarded as the capital of the country, not so much in consideration of its superiority in point of size or population, as from its being selected for the residence of the rajah. Its length along the bank of the river is about a mile, and its average breadth scarcely exceeds a quarter of that distance. Access to the town from the westward is obtained by means of two slight bridges thrown over the river, one at its northern, the other at its southern extremity. Though building-stone abounds, edifices of this material, with the exception of some of the ornamental parts of temples, are altogether wanting. The city, however, is adorned by several temples, "constructed of brick, with two, three, and four sloping roofs, diminishing gradually as they ascend, and terminating pretty generally in pinnacles, which, as well as some of the superior roofs, are splendidly gilt, and produce a very picturesque and agreeable effect." But among the most striking objects of the place are its numerous wooden temples, many of them of considerable elevation and proportionate bulk, which are scattered over the environs as well as throughout the body of the town. Like those of most other eastern towns, the streets of Khatmandoo are narrow and dirty. The houses are of brick, with tiled roofs, and though consisting ordinarily of several stories, they are represented, almost without exception, as of a mean appearance. Even the residence of the rajah is entitled to no particular notice. The number of houses has been estimated at 5,000, and the population at 50,000. Khatmandoo is distant 137 miles N.E. from Goruckpore, and 53 E. by S. from Gorkha. Lat. 27° 42', long. 85° 18'.

KHEDRA.—A village in the British district Huriana, lieut.-gov. of the N.W. Provinces, presidency of Bengal. Lat. 29° 21', long. 75° 56'.

KHEEREE.—A town in the territory of Oude, 10 miles from the left bank of the Chowka river, and 72 miles N. from Lucknow. Lat. 27° 54', long. 80° 51'.

KHEERWA.—A town in the Rajpoot state of Jodhpoor, 49 miles S.E. by S. from Jodhpoor, and 93 miles S.W. from Ajmeer. Lat. 25° 41', long. 73° 33'.

KHEGUMPA.—A town in the native state of Bhotan, three miles from the left bank of the Demree river, and 64 miles N.N.W. from Gowhatty. Lat. 27°, long. 91° 24'.

KHEIR.—A town of Guzerat, in the native state of Mhyecaunta, on the left bank of one of the branches of the Saburmuttee, and 87 miles N.N.E. from Ahmedabad. Lat. 24° 9', long. 73° 9'.

KHEIR.—A town in the British district of Poonah, presidency of Bombay, 68 miles E. of Bombay. Lat. 18° 51', long. 73° 55'.

KHEIR.—A town in the British district of Poonah, presidency of Bombay, 76 miles S.E. of Bombay. Lat. 18° 23', long. 73° 53'.

KHEIR.—A town in Hyderabad, or the Nizam's dominions, situate on the right bank of the Godavery river, and 160 miles N.W. from Hyderabad. Lat. 18° 58', long. 76° 50'.

KHEIR.—A town in the British district of Ahmednuggur, presidency of Bombay, 135 miles E.S.E. of Bombay. Lat. 18° 22', long. 74° 51'.

KHEJURWALA, in the British district of Suharunpoor, lieut.-gov. of the N.W. Provinces, a village on the route from Meerut to Suharunpoor, and nine miles S.E. of the latter place. It is situate in a level, open, well-cultivated country. Distant N.W. from Calcutta, *viâ* Kurnaul, 1,000 miles. Lat. 29° 52', long. 77° 41'.

KHELCHEEPOOR, in the territory of Gwalior, or possessions of Scindia's family, a town on the route from Neemuch to Saugor, 138 miles E. of former, 168 W. of latter. It is a thriving town, and is the principal place of a small state tributary to Scindia, and held by a chief of the Kichi Rajpoot tribe, who pays annually a tribute of 13,500 rupees to Scindia, and of 1,050 to the rajah of Kota. The rajah maintains sixty horse and 300 irregulars. Lat. 24° 2', long. 76° 34'.

KHEMANDI, in the Rajpoot state of Jodhpoor, on the route from Nusseerabad to Deesa, and 154 miles S. W. of the former. It contains 150 houses and thirty shops, and is supplied with water from twenty wells. The surrounding country is rather hilly, and the road occasionally rough in this part of the route. Lat. 25° 15', long. 73° 11'.

KHEMLA, in the Rajpoot state of Jeypore, a town on the route from Agra to Nusseerabad, 82 miles S.W. of former, 138 N.E. of latter. It has a bazar. Lat. 26° 41', long. 76° 55'.

KHEMPOOR, in the British district of Moradabad, lieut.-gov. of the N.W. Provinces, a village on the route from Hurdwar to the town of Moradabad, and 15 miles N.W. of the latter. The road in this part of the route is good. Lat. 29° 2', long. 78° 44'.

KHENGUNPOOR, in the Baree Dooab division of the Punjab, a town situate nine miles from the right bank of the Beas, 61 miles S. by W. of the town of Lahore. Lat. 30° 46', long. 74° 8'.

KHER.—A town in the British district of Rutnageriah, presidency of Bombay, 93 miles S.S.E. of Bombay. Lat. 17° 44', long. 73° 30'.

KHERA, in the British district of Agra, a village on the route from the city of Agra to Jeypore, and 19 miles W. of the former. The road in this part of the route is good; the country fertile and highly cultivated. Lat. 27° 7', long. 77° 46'.

KHÉRA, in the British district of Muttra, lieut.-gov. of the N.W. Provinces, a village on the route from the city of Agra to Bareilly, and 37 miles N.E. of the former. The road in this part of the route is good; the country well wooded, and cultivated. Lat. 27° 31', long. 78° 28'.

KHERAH, in the British district of Suharunpoor, lieut.-gov. of the N.W. Provinces, a village on the route from Kurnaul to Suharunpoor, and 12 miles S.W. of the latter town. It is situate in a level country, amidst considerable cultivation. Distant N.W. from Calcutta 995 miles. Lat. 29° 53', long. 77° 26'.

KHERAH, in the British district of Delhi, lieut.-gov. of the N.W. Provinces, a village on the route from the city of Delhi to Kurnal, and eight miles N.W. of the former. The road in this part of the route is good. Lat. 28° 46', long. 77° 11'.

KHEREE, a village with a ruined brick fort in the British district of Suharunpoor, lieut.-gov. of the N.W. Provinces, is situate on the route from the town of that name to Dehra, and 22 miles S.W. of the latter. Here was a secondary station of the great trigonometrical survey of the Himalaya. Lat. 30° 3', long. 77° 52'.

KHERI, in the British district of Muzuffurnugur, lieut.-gov. of the N.W. Provinces, a village on the route from Kurnal to the town of Muzuffurnugur, and 25 miles W. of the latter. Lat. 29° 26', long. 77° 22'.

KHERNI, in the Rajpoot state of Jeypore,

a small town on the route from Boondee to Agra, 70 miles N.E. of former, 120 S.W. of latter. It is surrounded by a rampart of masonry. Lat. 26° 14′, long. 76° 23′.

KHERSIONG.—A town in the British district of Darjeeling, lieut.-gov. of Bengal, 12 miles S. of Darjeeling. Lat. 26° 52′, long. 88° 18′.

KHETI.—A town of Sinde, in the British district of Kurrachee, presidency of Bombay, 53 miles S.W. by S. of Tatta. Lat. 24° 10′, long. 67° 30′.

KHETREE, in the Rajpoot territory of Shekhawutee, a town, the principal place of a district which, with Kot-Pootli, granted by Lord Lake, yields its thakoor or lord an annual revenue of 6,00,000 rupees. Distance S.W. from Delhi 90 miles, N. from Jeypore 75. Lat. 28°, long. 75° 53′.

KHEYRA, in the British district of Mirzapore, lieut.-gov. of the N.W. Provinces, a small town or village which, with Mungror, gives name to the pergunnah of Kheyra Mungror, is situate 21 miles S.E. of Benares, 43 E. of the city of Mirzapoor. Lat. 25° 4′, long. 83° 19′.

KHI, in Sirhind, a small town seven miles from the left bank of the Sutlej, on the route from Ferozpoor to Mandot, and five miles S.W. of the former place. It was formerly comprised within the possessions held by the maharajah of the Punjab on the left of the Sutlej, under British protection and control, but has now been incorporated with the British district of Ferozepore. Distant N.W. from Calcutta, by way of Delhi and Fureedkote, 1,111 miles. Lat. 30° 54′, long. 74° 30′.

KHILPURI, in the British district of Bareilly, lieut.-gov. of the N.W. Provinces, a small town on the route from the city of Pillibheet to Almora, 30 miles N.W. of the former, situate on the Bygul, a small river tributary to the Gurra. Lat. 28° 59′, long. 79° 46′.

KHILPUTEE, in the British district of Kumaon, lieut.-gov. of the N.W. Provinces, a village with small military station, on the route, by Puchesur, from Petoragurh cantonment to Chumpawut, 15 miles S. of Petoragurh, seven N.E. of Chumpawut. Lat. 29° 23′, long. 80° 13′.

KHIRAGARH, in the British district of Agra, lieut.-gov. of the N.W. Provinces, a town on the south-western frontier towards Dholpoor, 22 miles S.W. of the city of Agra. Lat. 26° 53′, long. 77° 56′.

KHIRKA, in the British district of Bareilly, lieut.-gov. of the N.W. Provinces, a village on the route from the town of Bareilly to Moradabad, and 14 miles N.W. of the former. Lat. 28° 28′, long. 79° 16′.

KHIRKA BURNA, in the British district of Bareilly, division of Pilleebheet, lieut.-gov. of the N.W. Provinces, a village on the route from Bareilly to Petoragurh, and 47 miles N.E. of the former. Lat. 28° 48′, long. 79° 56′.

KHIRON, in the district of Bainswara, territory of Oude, a town 25 miles S. of Lucknow. Butter estimates the population at 5,000, a third of that number being Mussulmans. Lat. 26° 30′, long. 80° 50′.

KHOAPOOR, in the British district of Futtehpoor, lieut.-gov. of the N.W. Provinces, a village on the route from Calpee to the town of Futtehpoor, and 10 miles N.W. of the latter. It has a few shops; water is obtained from wells and a tank; and supplies may be collected from the neighbourhood. Lat. 26°, long. 80° 45′.

KHOAPOOR, in the British district of Cawnpore, lieut.-gov. of the N.W. Provinces, a village on the route from Calpee to Futtehgurh, and 14 miles N. of the former. Lat. 26° 17′, long. 79° 47′.

KHODABAD, in Sinde, is a ruined town, 30 miles N. of Hyderabad, and 10 miles E. of the Indus. Little more than thirty years ago, it rivalled Hyderabad in size and population, yet now not one habitable dwelling remains. The ruins cover two square miles. On this, Wood remarks, "How perishable must be the architecture of Sinde!" It had been a favourite residence of the Talpoor chiefs of Sinde, and here the remains of several of them rest in tombs of neat but plain construction. Lat. 25° 48′, long. 68° 32′.

KHODAGANJ, in the British district of Furrukhabad, lieut.-gov. of the N.W. Provinces, a town on the route from Cawnpore to Futtehgurh, and 13 miles S. of the latter. It is situate on the north bank of the Kalee Nadi (East), here crossed by a suspension-bridge, constructed at the expense of the Nawaub Hakeem Mehndee. In the town is a good serai or resting-place for travellers, built of brick and lime-mortar, with vaulted chambers and two high gates. There is likewise a bazar. Lat. 27° 11′, long. 79° 44′.

KHŒTORA.—A town in the British province of Nagpoor, 22 miles N.E. from the river Wurda, and 62 miles S.S.E. from Nagpoor. Lat. 20° 18′, long. 79° 25′.

KHOJAH SARAE, in the British district of Delhi, lieut.-gov. of the N.W. Provinces, a village and caravanserai on the route from the city of Delhi to Muttra, and 14 miles S.E. of the former. Lat. 28° 30′, long. 77° 22′.

KHOJAPHUL, in the British district of Cawnpore, lieut.-gov. of the N.W. Provinces, a town on the route from Calpee to Etawah, and 45 miles S.E. of the latter. Lat. 26° 24′, long. 79° 39′.

KHOLAKOT, in the British district of Kumaon, lieut.-gov. of the N.W. Provinces, a village on a ridge in the Sub-Himalaya, or mountain-system south of the main range, on the route from Chumpawut to Askoth, eight miles N. of the former. Lat. 29° 28′, long. 80° 7′.

KHOLRO, in the jaghire of Loharoo, lieut.-

gov. of the N.W. Provinces, a village on the eastern frontier towards Jujhur. Lat. 28° 30′, long. 75° 55′.

KHONDEAN, or KHOADEAN, in the Sinde Sagur Dooab division of the Punjab, a town situate eight miles from the left bank of the Indus, 168 miles W.N.W. of the town of Lahore. Lat. 32° 26′, long. 71° 30′.

KHONGJUEEKHOOLEL. — A town of Eastern India, in the native state of Munneepoor, 93 miles S.E. by E. from Silhet, and 140 miles E.N.E. from Tipperah. Lat. 24° 20′, long. 93° 10′.

KHONGWA ZAKAN.—A village in Arracan, about five miles from Aeng, on the route which bears the name of that town, and close to where it crosses the river. There is no bridge, but the river is fordable, being only two or three feet deep. Lat. 19° 52′, long. 94° 9′.

KHOODA, in Sirhind, a village in the British district of Umballa, on the route from Loodiana to Suharunpoor, and 50 miles N.W. of the latter place. Distant N.W. from Calcutta 1,008 miles. Lat. 30° 20′, long. 76° 58′.

KHOONDS.—See GONDWANA.

KHOORDAH, or KHORDAGARH, in the British district of Pooree, or southern division of Cuttack, lieut.-gov. of Bengal, a town at one time the capital of Orissa, but now much decayed, the walls of the old palace and some gateways being the only relics of its former importance. It is still the principal place of the zemindary of the rajah of Khoordah, the most opulent landholder in Orissa.

The rajah of Khoordah exercises superintendence over the temple of Juggurnauth and all its affairs, as well as over the priests, officers, and servants attached to that stronghold of superstition; a power continued to him by the British government when it ceased to collect the pilgrim-tax. A donation, fixed in the first instance at something more than 30,000 rupees, subsequently reduced to 23,000, was to be made in compensation of the loss which it was supposed would be sustained by the abolition of the tax; but it has been directed, by orders from home, that government should renounce altogether its connection with the temple, taking care only that it should be placed in a position as good, as to pecuniary means, as it held when it first came within the circle of British rule. Its present position is believed to be much better than this, and there seems good ground for the belief. The act by which the pilgrim-tax was abolished forbade the rajah of Khoordah to receive any payment from pilgrims, or to allow such payments to be received, except such as might be voluntarily offered. It is obvious that such an enactment must be nugatory, as, indeed, it has proved. The pilgrim revenue is as productive as ever, perhaps more so than at any former period; but it is most honourable to the home authorities, that they have repudiated the stain of idolatry, by instructing the local government to sever the last link of the chain by which it was kept in contact with so contaminating an association. Distance from the town of Cuttack, S.W., 25 miles; Calcutta, S.W., 245. Lat. 20° 10′, long. 85° 43′.

KHOORJA. — The principal place of the pergunnah of the same name, in the British district of Boolundshuhur, on the route from Muttra to Meerut, and 54 miles S. of the latter. It is of considerable size, and has a bazar. The population is returned at 22,147. At the time of Lake's campaign in the Doab in 1803, this was a place of importance, having a fort, with large stores of grain, which were relinquished by the garrison evacuating the place. Elevation above the sea 770 feet. Lat. 28° 15′, long. 77° 55′.

KHOORUM.—A river rising in lat. 33° 28′, long. 69° 27′, on the south-eastern slope of the Suffeid Koh range of mountains, and, flowing through Affghanistan in an easterly direction for 45 miles, enters the territory of the Punjab through a gorge in the Suliman Mountains, and shortly afterwards turning south-east, flows for 100 miles through the valley of Bunnoo, and falls into the Indus at the town of Kafer Kote, in lat. 32° 30′, long. 71° 20′.

KHOOSHALPOOR, in the British district of Bijnour, lieut.-gov. of the N.W. Provinces, a town on the route from Moradabad to Hurdwar, and 50 miles N.W. of the former. Lat. 29° 29′, long. 78° 28′.

KHOOTHAR, in the British district of Shahjehanpoor, lieut.-gov. of the N.W. Provinces, a town on the route from Pilleebheet to Lucknow, 41 miles S.E. of the former. Lat. 28° 11′, long. 80° 20′.

KHOOTNEE, in the British hill district of Jaunsar, a stream rising in the mountains in the middle of that district, and in lat. 30° 45′, long. 77° 56′. It has a south-easterly course of about fifteen miles, and falls into the Jumna on the right side, in lat. 30° 39′, long. 78° 5′. Hodgson, who calls it the Cunti, forded it at the confluence, where he found it sixty feet wide and from one and a half to two feet deep. Skinner, who forded it nearer its source, found the water rather deep, and about fifty feet wide.

KHOPA, in the British district of Allahabad, lieut.-gov. of the N.W. Provinces, a town on the route from Allahabad to Banda, 22 miles W. of the former. Lat. 25° 21′, long. 81° 34′.

KHOPA, in Bundelcund, a village of Punnah, on the route from Banda to Jubbulpoor, 99 miles S. of the former, 96 N. of the latter, situate near the left bank of the river Cane, near that place crossed by ford, with a "stony bottom." It has a bazar, and water is abundant. Lat. 24° 19′, long. 80° 20′.

KHOPRA NUDDEE.—A river rising in

the Saugor and Nerbudda territory, in lat. 23° 26′, long. 79° 9′, and, flowing about 55 miles in a north-easterly direction, through the British district of Dumoh, falls into the Sonar on the right side, in lat. 24° 3′, long. 79° 31′.

KHOR, in the jaghire of Jujhur, lieut.-gov. of the N.W. Provinces, a village close to the eastern frontier, towards the territory of Tijara. Lat. 28° 5′, long. 76° 19′.

KHORO, in the jaghire of Doojana, territory of Jujhur, lieut.-gov. of the N.W. Provinces, a village on the route from Dadree to Rewaree, and eight miles S.E. of the former. Lat. 28° 28′, long. 76° 23′.

KHOSALGURH.—A town in the Rajpoot state of Banswarra, 119 miles E. by N. from Ahmedabad, and 22 miles S. from Banswarra. Lat. 23° 10′, long. 74° 27′.

KHOUNGTOUNG MYO.—A town of Burmah, situate on the left bank of the Irawady river, and 166 miles N.N.E. from Ava. Lat. 24° 10′, long. 96° 55′.

KHUDDEE.—See KUDDI.

KHUDRA, in Bussahir, a village of the district of Koonawur, is situate on the right bank of the Sutluj, and on the low circuitous route from Pangi to Lipi. Elevation above the sea about 8,300 feet. Lat. 31° 35′, long. 78° 26′.

KHUJURA, in the British district of Goruckpore, lieut.-gov. of the N.W. Provinces, a small market-town four miles S. of the right bank of the Raptee, 25 miles N.W. of Goruckpore cantonment. Lat. 26° 57′, long. 83° 7′.

KHUJURIA, in the jaghire of Rampoor, lieut.-gov. of the N.W. Provinces, a village on the route from the town of Bareilly to Almora, and 39 miles N. of the former. The road in this part of the route is bad; the country level, open, and cultivated. Lat. 28° 48′, long. 79° 25′.

KHULALA.—See KHUNDALA.

KHULLELGANJ, in the British district of Allygurh, lieut.-gov. of the N.W. Provinces, a village on the route from the city of Agra to Bareilly, and 30 miles N.E. of the former. Lat. 27° 28′, long. 78° 22′.

KHULSA, in the British district of Boolundshuhur, lieut.-gov. of the N.W. Provinces, a village on the route from Muttra to Meerut, and 50 miles S. of the latter. Lat. 28° 19′, long. 77° 55′.

KHUND, or KOOND, in Cashmere, a valley furrowing the northern side of the Panjal, or mountain Barichal. It is three miles long, displays great picturesque beauty, is well cultivated, and contains some villages. The less-cultivated part is covered with wild apricot-trees, "whose blossom," Vigne observes, "in the early spring, yields a perfume so fragrant and powerful, that the Cashmirians come far and near to inhale it." So romantic a spot could scarcely be without one of those legends so rife in Cashmere; accordingly, Vigne was informed "that the place was infested by a serpent, so long, that his tail was perceived at the bottom of a hill when his head might be seen moving on the top of it." It is so embosomed in lofty mountains, that its climate is said to be the coolest in the lowlands of Cashmere. Vigne estimates its elevation above the level of the sea at 6,000 feet. Koond, the principal place, is in lat. 33° 32′, long. 75° 10′.

KHUNDALA, in the Rajpoot state of Jodhpoor, a village on the route from Balotra to the town of Jodhpoor, and 16 miles S.W. of the latter. Lat. 26° 10′, long. 73° 2′.

KHUNDALU.—A lake in the hill state of Hindoor, situate about 2,800 feet above the sea, amidst the hills forming the range extending in a south-westerly direction from the left bank of the Sutlej to the Sub-Himalaya or Sewalic Mountains. It is about a mile and a half in length during the season of low water, but in the rainy season, when fullest, is a mile longer. The natives consider it unfathomable, and in some parts it is actually very deep, requiring a line of 138 feet to reach the bottom. British visitors consider that it has much resemblance to Ullswater, though neither so large nor so clear. The similitude is thought to be in its winding length, in the outline of the inclosing hills, and in the shore being clothed with vegetation to the water's edge. A species of fish, popularly called the Himalaya trout, abounds in it. A village of the same name is situate about a mile from the lake, and on the mountain-top rising above it the British political agent has built a house, the windows of which to the north command a noble view of the fortress of Malown, and the Himalaya rising behind it; whilst to the south the eye can for a vast distance trace the course of the Sutlej through the plain of Hindoostan. Lat. 31° 10′, long. 76° 47′.

KHUNDEH, in the British district of Humeerpoor, lieut.-gov. of the N.W. Provinces, a town on the route from Banda to Calpee, 14 miles N.W. by W. of the former. Lat. 25° 33′, long. 80° 12′.

KHUNDELA, in the Rajpoot territory of Jeypore, a town on the N. frontier towards Shekawuttee. It is the property of the powerful thakoor or baron, who pays annually a tribute of 60,000 rupees to the government of Jeypore. Distant N. of Jeypore 50 miles. Lat. 27° 34′, long. 75° 40′.

KHUNDOWLI, in the British district of Agra, a town on the route from Agra to Allygurh, and 13 miles N. of the former. It has a bazar. Lat. 27° 18′, long. 78° 5′.

KHUNJUR, in the British district of Muttra, lieut.-gov. of the N.W. Provinces, a village on the route from the cantonment of Meerut to that of Muttra, and 21 miles N. of the latter. Lat. 27° 45′, long. 77° 51′.

KHUNNAH, one of the petty Cis-Sutlej states in Sirhind, having an area of about twenty-eight square miles. Upon the death of the ranee, in 1851, without heirs, her possessions, yielding an annual revenue of 4,000*l.*, escheated to the British government. Khunna, the principal place, 8 miles N.W. from the town of Sirhind, is in lat. 30° 42′, long. 76° 20′.

KHUNPOOR, in the British district of Shahjehanpoor, lieut.-gov. of the N.W. Provinces, a village on the route from Bareilly to the cantonment of Futtehgurh, and 36 miles S.E. of the former. Lat. 27° 54′, long. 79° 44′.

KHUR, in the Cis-Sutlej territory of Sirhind, a town situate 25 miles N. of Ambala. Lat. 30° 45′, long. 76° 43′.

KHURAWAR, in the British district of Rohtuck, lieut.-gov. of the N.W. Provinces, a village on the route from the city of Delhi to the town of Hansee, and 36 miles N.W. of the former. Lat. 28° 50′, long. 76° 45′.

KHURCOT.—A town in the native state of Nepal, 46 miles S. from Khatmandoo, and 100 miles N. from Dinapoor. Lat. 27° 3′, long. 85° 22′.

KHUREHLA.—A town in the British district of Hummerpoor, lieut.-gov. of the N.W. Provinces. It has a population of 8,064 inhabitants. Distant S.W. from Hummerpoor 36 miles. Lat. 25° 33′, long. 79° 52′.

KHURENCHA, in the Rajpoot state of Jodhpoor, a village on the route from the town of Jodhpoor to that of Ajmeer, and 38 miles N.E. of the former. It is situate in a rough country, having a gravelly soil, much cut up by ravines; and in consequence the road in this part of the route is indifferent. Lat. 26° 24′, long. 73° 43′.

KHURGAON, in the British district of Bareilly, lieut.-gov. of the N.W. Provinces, a village on the route from the town of Bareilly to Seetapore, and one mile S.E. of the former. Lat. 28° 22′, long. 79° 29′.

KHURIAL, in Sirhind, a village on the route from Hansee to Loodiana, and 74 miles N. of the former town. It is situate in a country of an undulating surface, and which, though in some parts sandy and covered with jungle, has considerable cultivation. Distant N.W. from Calcutta 1,050 miles. Lat. 30° 6′, long. 75° 58′.

KHURKHOUDA, a town in the British district of Rohtuk, lieut.-gov. of the N.W. Provinces, is the principal place of the pergunnah or subdivision of Khurkhouda. Lat. 28° 52′, long. 76° 58′.

KHURKHURRA, in the British district Rohtuk, lieut.-gov. of the N.W. Provinces, a village on the route from Delhi to Hansee, and 29 miles S.E. of the latter. Lat. 28° 56′, long. 76° 25′.

KHURSALEE.—See CURSALEE.

KHURTAPOOR.—A town in the territory of Oude, situate three miles from the left bank of the Ghogra, and 103 miles N. from Lucknow. Lat. 28° 20′, long. 81° 9′.

KHURUK, in Sirhind, a halting-place on the route from Hansee to Loodiana, and 18 miles N. of the former town. Supplies can be collected from the adjacent country, and water is obtainable from two brick-lined wells. Distant N.W. from Calcutta 976 miles. Lat. 29° 21′, long. 76° 4′.

KHUSA.—A town in the native state of Nepal, situate two miles from the right bank of the Bhotiya Coosy river, and 53 miles N.E. from Khatmandoo. Lat. 28° 7′, long. 86°.

KHUSAWARA, or KURSARVA. — A small raj, part of Singhbhoom, and under the control of the political agent for the south-west frontier of Bengal. Its centre is in lat. 22° 50′, long. 85° 49′. Its annual revenue has been estimated at 6,000 rupees.

KHUTA, in the territory of the jaghire of Rampoor, lieut.-gov. of the N.W. Provinces, a village on the route from the town of Bareilly to Almora, and 45 miles N. of the former. Lat. 28° 52′, long. 79° 27′.

KHUTARO.—A town in the British province of Sattara, presidency of Bombay, 137 miles S.E. of Bombay. Lat. 17° 39′, long. 74° 28′.

KHUTKURRIE, in the territory of Rewah, in Baghelcund, a town on the route, by the Kutra Pass, from Allahabad to Jubbulpoor, and 83 miles S.W. of the former. Jacquemont describes it as a populous village of huts, built of mud, thatched with straw, and falling to ruin; and a similar description is given of it by a British traveller. Elevation above the sea about 1,200 feet. Lat. 24° 42′, long. 82° 3′.

KHUTOWLEE, in the British district of Muzuffurnugur, lieut.-gov. of the N.W. Provinces, a town on the route from Meerut to Hurdwar, 20 miles N. by E. of the former. Lat. 29° 17′, long. 77° 49′.

KHUTTEEAR.—A town in the British district of Purneah, lieut.-gov. of Bengal, 21 miles S. by E. of Purneah. Lat. 25° 28′, long. 87° 37′.

KHUTUWAS, in the Rajpoot state of Jodhpoor, a village on the route from Balotri to the city of Jodhpoor, and 18 miles S.W. of the latter. The road in this part of the route is good, and passes through a level and well-wooded country. Lat. 26° 9′, long. 73°.

KHYBER MOUNTAINS, in Eastern Afghanistan, rise west of the plain of Peshawur, and connect the most southern and lowest range of Hindoo Koosh with the Sufeid Koh, the Salt range, and the Suliman Mountains. They at first sight present the appearance of a mass of hills irregularly grouped; but a careful observer will find the distinct arrangement of a chain separating the plain of Peshawur on the east, from the plain of Jelalabad and the uneven surface of Nungnehar on the west. They generally consist of slate and primary limestone, with a small proportion of overlying sandstone. The sanguinary and rapacious character of the population has prevented their mineral deposits from being explored; they are, however, known to abound in antimony, which so strongly impregnates the water at Ali Musjid, as to render it highly deleterious. The Tatara summit is the most elevated in the range, being 8,500 feet above the plain of Peshawur, and 4,800 above the sea. The breadth of the Khyber range may be stated at about twenty miles; the length, from the base of the nearest and lowest range of the Hindoo Koosh to the Sufeid Koh and Salt range, at about fifty. It is cross-cut by two great natural channels—the Khyber ravine or pass, and, further north, the channel of the Kabool river. These, in the opinion of Lord, drained a vast lake, which once occupied the extensive valley of Kabool, an opinion strengthened by the nature of the soil of Peshawur, which, near the pass, for a great depth, consists of fragments of slate and limestone, the constituent substances of the Khyber range. Griffith, however, urges some forcible objections to this hypothesis of Lord. The Khyber Mountains are supposed to be so called from the Khyber tribe who inhabit them; and these are divided into the Afreedees, Shainwarries, and Oruk Zais. As this range is lower than the Hindoo Koosh to the north, and the Sufeid Koh, the Salt, and the Suliman ranges to the south, the most practicable passes from Hindustan to northern Afghanistan lie through it. There are four of these passes, leading from east to west, and lying in the following order from south to north:—First, the Khyber Pass, the most level, and the only one practicable for cannon. Second, the Tatara Pass, commencing near the eastern entrance of the Khyber Pass, taking a circuit northwards, and then running in some degree parallel to it, and finally rejoining it at Duka, at the entrance of the valley of Jelalabad. Third, the Abkhana Pass, by which the Abkhana route proceeds. This crosses the Kabool river at Muchnee, and recrosses it at Abkhana, where it enters the Khyber Mountains, and proceeds along the southern bank of the river to Duka, joining the Tatara and Khyber passes. Fourth, the Carapa route, which crosses the Kabool river above Dobundee, then crosses the Lundye from east to west, and proceeding nearly due west to Lalpoor, recrosses the Kabool river, and joins the main road proceeding westward. The Khyber range lies between lat. 33° 30′—34° 20′, and long. 71° 10′—71° 30′.

KHYBER PASS.—The principal pass in the north between Afghanistan and Hindustan, as the Bolan is in the south; hence it is called the key of Afghanistan. It commences at Kadam, a remarkable collection of caves, about ten miles west of Peshawur, and extends about thirty miles, in a tortuous but generally northwesterly course, to Duka, at the entrance of the plain of Jelalabad. Havelock, considering the pass to commence at Huzarnow on the west, estimates its entire length at fifty miles. It lies for the most part through slate rock, and along the bed of a torrent liable to be filled with a sudden fall of rain, and then so violent as to sweep away everything in its course. At other times the bed is dry, or the water shrunk to a small rill, sometimes disappearing under the gravel, or running on one side. There are two peculiarly difficult portions of the pass. One of these is close to Ali Musjid, where the road is merely the narrow bed of a rivulet, inclosed on each side by precipices, rising to the height of 600 or 700 feet, in some places to 1,000 or 1,200, at an angle of seventy or eighty degrees, and overhung by the small fort of Ali Musjid. This petty fort occupies the summit of a peaked rock, but is of small value as a military position, from want of water, and from being commanded by adjacent heights. Its possession was obstinately contested during the late military operations in Afghanistan. The Afghans in garrison evacuated it as soon as they found it commanded by the hostile artillery, and the British occupied it, but being ultimately in peril from the Khyberees, retreated, though with considerable loss. The air in this gorge, though dry, has been considered remarkably deleterious, as most of the troops posted in it perished by disease. Some, however, with more reason, attribute the mortality to the poisonous nature of the water, which is impregnated with antimony. At Lalabeg, about midway through, the pass expands into a small valley, in which is a great tope or artificial mound, on the north side of the road. Near Landee Khana, the road is for a great distance a gallery of about twelve feet wide, having on one side a perpendicular wall of rock rising to a great height above, and on the other a deep precipice. The pass rises gradually from the eastern entrance, but has a steep declivity westward, though the descent is not so great in that direction, as the plain of Jelalabad is more elevated than that of Peshawur. The height of the summit of the pass is 3,373 feet above the sea, and about 2,100 above Peshawur. As the Khyberees are a predatory and ruthless race, well armed with long rifled matchlocks, jezzails, or jingels, which take effect at greater distance than muskets, it is necessary that those who have occasion to use the pass should purchase their forbearance; and for this purpose the Durani monarchs pay them 130,000 rupees annually. The slender resources of Dost Mahomed Khan obliged him to reduce this allowance to 20,000 rupees, distributed among 26,000 fighting-men. Nadir Shah, is said to have disbursed a sum equal to 100,000*l.* for an unmolested march through the pass; but, according to Masson, he turned it by taking a southern route through Tira. The Khyber Pass was the scene of obstinate and sanguinary conflicts during the war in Afghanistan. It was forced by the British after their first occupation of Kabool. A similar attempt, made after the disastrous retreat from Kabool, failed, with great loss; but subsequently, though obstinately defended by a large body of men, it was again forced in April, 1842. The eastern entrance of the Khyber Pass is in lat. 33° 58′, long. 71° 30′.

KHYENDWEN, the principal feeder of the Irawady, rises in lat. 26° 28′, long. 96° 54′, in the northern part of the Burmese territory, through which it flows, generally in a southerly direction, for 470 miles, and falls into the Irawady, on the right side, a few miles below the town of Amyenmyo, and in lat. 21° 48′, long. 95° 3′.

KHYOUKKALOUNG.—A town of Burmah, situate on the left bank of the Irawady river, and 24 miles W. from Ava. Lat. 21° 55′, long. 95° 40′.

KHYOUK PHYOO.—See KYOUK PHYOO.

KHYOUNGZAH ROUTE commences at a large village of the name, from whence it takes its designation, and leads by a good road, in one march, to Kioungyee, in lat. 16° 49′, long. 94° 48′, a short distance N. of Bassein, in the British territory of Pegue.

KHYR, in the British district of Allygurh, lieut.-gov. of the N.W. Provinces, a town on the route from Muthra to Boolundshuhur, 32 miles N.N.E. of the former. Lat. 27° 56′, long. 77° 55′.

KHYRA, in the hill state of Bhugee, a village on the declivity of a mountain rising from the left bank of the Sutluj. Elevation above the sea 2,613 feet. Lat. 31° 14′, long. 77° 16′.

KHYRA, in the British district of Mirzapoor, lieut.-gov. of the N.W. Provinces, a village on the right bank of the Ganges, 31 miles N.W. of the city of Mirzapoor. Lat. 25° 14′, long. 82° 20′.

KHYRABAD, in the territory of Oude, a town on the route from Setapoor to Sekrora, five miles S.E. of the former, 75 N.W. of the latter. Tieffenthaler describes it, about eighty years ago, as a populous town, in an extensive plain, studded with numerous ponds, productive of great variety of luxuriant crops, and adorned by a vast number of fruit-trees planted in rows. The cultivation was estimated at that time to yield annually 12,00,000 rupees. Two centuries earlier, it, according to the Ayeen Akbery, was 10,91,109 rupees. The principal manufacture was fine cotton cloth. Distant N.W. from Lucknow 62 miles. Lat. 27° 32′, long. 80° 49′.

KHYREEGUR, in the territory of Oude, a town in the north-western extremity, towards Kumaon, is situate on the left bank of the river Ghaghra. Tieffenthaler, describing its condition about eighty years ago, states it to be a fortified place, worthy of note, as well on account of its excellent construction as of its size, being four or five miles in circuit. The defences are built of large blocks of stone below, and above of bricks, of unusual size; but it now lies waste, and infested with tigers and other wild beasts. It was built by an Afghan chief on a site well chosen to check the mountaineers who might threaten Oude from Kumaon or Nepaul. The town is two miles N.E. of this great work, the intervening space being overrun with trees and grassy jungle, the haunts of beasts of prey. Distant 110 miles N. of Lucknow. Lat. 28° 26′, long. 80° 41′.

KHYRGAON, in Sinde, a town on the west bank of the Koodun, a branch of the Western Narra, the great offset leaving the Indus near Bukkur, and terminating in Lake Manchur, from which this town is distant about thirty miles north. Though, as Westmacott observes, it has not yet found a place in the map, it is of considerable importance, having seven mosques, and between 2,000 and 3,000 inhabitants, of whom a fifth part are Hindoos. It has a handsome bazar, well supplied with cottons. Lat. 26° 55′, long. 67° 50′.

KHYROO, in the British district of Hurreeana, lieut.-gov. of the N.W. Provinces, a village on the southern frontier, towards Loharoo. Lat. 28° 41′, long. 75° 58′.

KHYRPOOR, in the British district of Shahjehanpoor, lieut.-gov. of the N.W. Provinces, a village on the route from Bareilly to the cantonment of Futtehgurh, and 30 miles S.E. of the former. Lat. 27° 59′, long. 79° 44′.

KHYRPOOR, in Bhawlpoor, a town situate a mile from the left bank of the river Ghara. The sand-hills of the Thurr, or great sandy desert, are, on the east, so close to the town, that the extremities of the streets in that direction open on a dreary waste of sand-hills, ruined houses, and walls half-buried by the sand, which is continually encroaching on the cultivated ground along the river. The rapidity of the encroachment may be estimated from the fact, that a few years ago the boundary of the desert was two miles east of the town. In time of inundation, the town only intervenes between the water's edge and the desert. The houses are built of unburnt brick, which are found to last long, as rain seldom falls; the round domes of the mosques are generally built of the same material, the great mosque alone being constructed of burned brick. This last edifice is embellished with tiles, varnished. of various colours; but has been allowed to fall greatly into decay. There is a tolerable bazar, containing about 400 shops; but the number of these was greater formerly, all trade having here, of late years, fallen away considerably. It is, however, still a small mart for cafilas or caravans resorting from the desert to obtain various articles of commerce. The neighbourhood abounds in small ruined mud forts, formerly held by petty chiefs, who resisted the authority of the ancestors of the present Bhawl Khan. Khyrpoor is in lat. 29° 36′, long. 72° 12′.

KHYRPOOR, a town of Sinde, is situated about fifteen miles east of the Indus, in a country of alluvial formation, but in which, as bordering on the Thurr, or eastern desert, sand is largely intermixed with the clay deposited by the river. A large canal, called the Merwah, from the Indus, yields water both for irrigation and drinking; that obtained from wells being in general brackish, unpalatable, and unwholesome. One well in the palace yields very fine water. The canal receives its water a few miles below Roree, and in time of inundation, by means of numerous ramifications, overspreads the country. Part of the water finds its way back, in many small streams, to the Indus, in the lower part of its channel; the rest is finally lost by absorption and evaporation. When the river is very low, the canal is sometimes destitute of water. The town, originally a military cantonment, grew into importance in consequence of having been selected as the residence of the chief ameers of Northern Sinde. But notwithstanding this, it is but a large collection of mud hovels, with a few houses of a better description scattered about; destitute of fort or defence, unless the embattled mud wall inclosing the residence of the ameer can be deemed such. This palace is situate amidst the bazars, and presents little worth notice, except a mosque crowned with a cupola covered with gaudy lackered tiles of various hues. The town is very filthy: from this cause, together with the heat of the climate, and the deleterious influence of the stagnant marshes around, it is unhealthy. The population is estimated at 15,000. There is no manufacture, except to a very small extent in weaving and dyeing coarse cottons. During the Talpoor dynasty, the ameers of Khyrpoor held the northern and finest part of Sinde; but as it was much inferior in size to the dominions of their kinsmen, the ameers of Hyderabad, the former were subordinate, though allowed an influential voice in all questions considered to affect the general welfare. The territory subject to the ameers of Khyrpoor was 120 miles long, and of the same breadth. The government, it need scarcely be added, was a military despotism; the power, military resources, and revenue, being divided in various proportions between a great number of the ruling Beloochee family of Talpoor, of whom the eldest in lineage was regarded as the chief. Though mild as affecting life, the rule of this multitude of chieftains was in all fiscal matters so oppressive and rapacious as to be productive of rapidly progressive ruin and desolation. The revenue of the Khyrpoor ameers was estimated at 120,000*l.* per annum. The military force appears to have been based on a rude and ill-compacted feudal system; the chiefs having allotments of lands on condition of bringing forward and supporting a proportionate force of armed men, who were paid partly in money, partly in grain. The number of men which might be raised on emergencies was from 10,000 to 12,000. When Sinde was subjugated by the British forces, a large measure of favour was extended to one of the Khyrpoor ameers, Ali Moorad, on the ground of his early and consistent adherence to the cause of the conquerors; and it was proposed to confirm him not only in his patrimonial lands, but also in others, which had passed into his possession by virtue of a treaty executed in 1842, when he vanquished his brother and nephew, and obtained certain cessions as the price of farther forbearance. The extent of these cessions was open to question, but Ali Moorad, having persuaded Sir Charles Napier to adopt that view which best promoted his interest, was admitted to all he claimed. Suspicion, however, was never altogether lulled, and subsequent inquiry proved the ameer's claim to rest on fraud and forgery. The treaty had been written, according to Mahommedan custom, upon a leaf of the Koran, and the extent of territory transferred being very small, Ali Moorad, by interpolating some words, contrived to convey to himself one much larger; the effect being to invest him with considerable districts, in place of small villages. Fearing, however, that some curious eye might detect the interpolation, he subsequently removed the leaf, and caused its place to be occupied by another, bearing record to the like effect. This was established before a British commission on the 5th of January, 1853, and on evidence which could not be doubted, the instruments and assistants of Ali Moorad being brought forward and confronted with him. But one result could reasonably follow, and Ali Moorad was of necessity deprived of his ill-gotten acquisitions, which were incorporated with the rest of Sinde, as part of the British empire in India. He was, however, permitted to retain the lands allotted to him by his father, an act certainly not of justice, but of that liberality of which so many instances are found in the dealings of the British government with native chiefs. Since his connection with the British government, Ali Moorad has abolished slavery within his territory. Khyrpoor is about 13 miles S.W. of Roree, the road from which place is good. Lat. 27° 30′, long. 68° 48′.

KHYTOOPARA.—A town in the British district of Pubna, lieut.-gov. of Bengal, 112 miles N.E. of Calcutta. Lat. 23° 50′, long. 89° 32′.

KIANTHENGSAH.—A town in the Tenasserim provinces, 158 miles S. by E. of Moulmein. Lat. 14° 17′, long. 98° 18′.

KICHIWARA, in Malwa, a district so named, because inhabited by Kichi Rajpoots. It lies between lat. 23° 40′—24° 16′, long. 76° 16′—77° 11′. Detailed information respecting it is given in the notice, in the alphabetical arrangement of Rajgurh, its principal place.

KIDDERPORE, in the British district called the Twenty-four Pergunnahs, lieut.-gov. of Bengal, a small town almost adjoining Calcutta, of which it may be regarded as a suburb. It is described by Heber as a large village, in the vicinity of which are several considerable houses inhabited by Europeans, and considered to be remarkably dry and salubrious. There is here a dockyard, formerly belonging to Mr. James Kyd, but now the property of government. A factory has also been recently erected, and thus the means are concentrated within the dock establishment for the efficient repair of the government steamers. Distance from Fort William, S.E., four miles. Lat. 22° 30′, long. 88° 24′.

KIDWARRA, or KULWARI, in the British district of Allygurh, lieut.-gov. of the N.W. Provinces, a village on the route from the city of Agra to Allygurh cantonment, and 30 miles N. of the former. Lat. 27° 34′, long. 78° 7′.

KILA DOWLA, in the Sinde Sagur Dooab division of the Punjab, a town situated 43 miles E. from the left bank of the Indus, 142 miles W. by N. of the town of Lahore. Lat. 31° 54′, long. 71° 49′.

KILLADEE.—A town of the Deccan, in the territory of Nagpore, situate nine miles from the left bank of the Wein Gunga river, and 46 miles E.S.E. from Nagpoor. Lat. 20° 56′, long. 79° 49′.

KILNER GHAUT.—A pass on the Bombay and Agra road, constructed over the Vindhya range of mountains, under the superintendence of Captain Kilner, in compliment to whom it has been named. The return of traffic passing over this ghaut exhibits a gradual annual increase, the amount of tolls received having been doubled between the years 1845 and 1852. Later accounts continue to show a progressive increase. Lat. 22° 22′, long. 75° 35′.

KILPOOREE, in the British district of Bareilly, lieut.-gov. of the N.W. Provinces, a town on the route from Pilleebheet to Almora, 27 miles N. by W. of the former. Lat. 29°, long. 79° 47′.

KIMLASA, in the British territory of Saugor and Nerbudda, a town on the route from Tehree to Oojein, 50 miles S.W. of former, 170 N.E. of latter. It is of considerable size, and has a fort on a hill. Lat. 24° 12′, long. 78° 25′.

KIMLIA, in Bussahir, a pass over the range of the outer Himalaya, bounding Kunawur to the south. It is rarely passable but during May, June, and part of July; afterwards, the snow is treacherous, and many flocks of sheep and herds of goats, with the people in charge of them, have sunk in the soft and melting mass, and perished. It is therefore little frequented after the periodical rains have set in. Its elevation above the sea is probably about 17,000 feet. According to local information, this snow-bed could bear a person's weight for the first half of July, early in the morning, before the sun casts a heat sufficient to melt it; but at other times is impassable. A peak two or three miles south-west of the pass, was by the great trigonometrical survey ascertained to have an elevation 19,481 feet above the sea. The pass is in lat. 31° 14′, long. 78° 28′.

KIMSUR, in the Rajpoot state of Jodhpoor, a village on the route from Jessulmere to the town of Nagor, and 123 miles N.W. of the latter. Lat. 26° 58′, long. 73° 27′.

KINCHINGUNGA.—A mountain of the Himalaya range, situate in the territory of Sikhim, and presumed to be the second loftiest summit in the world. Its elevation is 28,176 feet above the level of the sea. That of Mount Everest, recently discovered, exceeds 29,000 feet. Lat. 27° 45′, long. 88° 2′.

KINEYREE, in the Baree Dooab division of the Punjab, a town situated on the left bank of the Chenaub, 41 miles S.S.W. of the town of Lahore. At this place, in May, 1848, the troops of the khan of Bahawulpore having effected a junction with Captain Edwardes and General Courtlandt, sustained an attack from Moolraj (the rebel of Mooltan), which resulted in the complete discomfiture of the latter. Lat. 29° 36′, long. 71° 12′.

KING.—An island situate 10 miles W. from the coast of Tenasserim. Length, north to south, 26 miles; breadth, east to west, 10 miles. Though infested by tigers and snakes, it is inhabited, and affords plenty of large straight timber, fit for masts and several parts of shipbuilding. Lat. 12° 31′, long. 98° 28′.

KINGRI.—A town in the dominions of Gholab Singh, 91 miles N.E. by N. from Kangra, and 147 miles S.E. by E from Sirinagur. Lat. 33° 4′, long. 77° 15′.

KINIKOTE.—A town in the native state of Cutch, seven miles S.E. from the great Western Runn, and 48 miles E.N.E. from Bhooj. Lat. 23° 28′, long. 70° 26′.

KINJUR, in the Sinde Sagur Dooab division of the Punjab, a town situated on the left bank of the Indus, 32 miles S.W. by W. of the town of Mooltan. Lat. 29° 55′, long. 71° 3′.

KINTALEE.—A town in the British province of Aracan, lieut.-gov. of Bengal, 209 miles S.S.E. of Aracan. Lat. 17° 57′, long. 94° 35′.

KINTALEE.—The name of a pass leading over the Youmadoung Mountains, from the town of the same name, on the coast of Arracan, to the interior of the British district of Pegue. Lat. 17° 59′, long. 95° 5′.

KIOWOONG.—A town in the British district of Beerbhoom, lieut.-gov. of Bengal, 83 miles N.N.W. of Calcutta. Lat. 23° 43′, long. 88° 31′.

KIRBASSAH.—A town in Nepal, three miles from the right bank of the Jimru river, and 198 miles W. by N. from Khatmandoo. Lat. 28° 23′, long. 82° 10′.

KIREE, in Sirhind, a village on the route

from Kurnal to Loodiana, and 36 miles N.W. of the former town. It is a small collection of houses, pleasantly situated. Distant N.W. from Calcutta 1,001 miles. Lat. 30° 8′, long. 76° 46′.

KIRREANUGGUR. — A town in the native state of Cutch, 14 miles S.E. from the great Western Runn, and 62 miles E.N.E. from Bhooj. Lat. 23° 30′, long. 70° 40′.

KIRSTNAPATAM.—A town in the British district of Nellore, presidency of Madras, 82 miles N. of Madras. Lat. 14° 17′, long. 80° 11′.

KIRTYNASSA.—A considerable offset of the Ganges river, flowing from the parent stream in lat. 23° 30′, long. 90° 3′, and, holding a south-easterly course for eighteen miles through the British district of Fureedpore, and twenty-five miles through that of Dacca, falls, in lat. 23° 15′, long. 90° 32′, into the Megna, as the Brahmapootra is called in the lower part of its course.

KIRUTPOOR, or KEERUTHPOOR.—A town in the British district of Bijnour, lieut.-gov. of the N.W. Provinces, distant N. from Bijnour 80 miles. Lat. 29° 30′, long. 78° 15′.

KIRWAH, in the territory of Seronj, a possession of the family of Ameer Khan, a small town on the route from Tehari to Oujein, 81 miles S.W. of former, 185 N.E. of latter. Lat. 24°, long. 77° 58′.

KISHENGHUR, or KRISHNA GURH, in the Punjab, a strong fort, about 10 miles E. of the Indus, and on the route to Cashmere through the Dub Pass. It is of a quadrangular form, and regularly built, though the walls are only of mud. Vigne observes, "Krishna Gurh is the finest specimen of a regular square mud fort that I have seen in the Punjab." Lat. 34° 4′, long. 72° 53′.

KISHENGUNGA, or SINDH, in the Punjab, a large river, which, rising in lat. 34° 48′, long. 75° 4′, in the mountains forming the north-eastern boundary of Kashmir, sweeps round the north of that valley, and, after a course of about 120 miles, falls into the Jailum at Mazufurabad, in lat. 34° 23′, long. 73° 22′, being little inferior there to the principal stream. It was formerly crossed by a wooden bridge; but this has been destroyed, and the communication is now kept up by a ferry.

KISHENGUNJE.—A town in the British district of Purneah, lieut.-gov. of Bengal, 31 miles N.E. of Purneah. Lat. 26° 4′, long. 87° 56′.

KISHENGURH, in the Rajpoot territory of Alwur, under the political superintendence of the Governor-General's agent in Rajpootana, a town on the route from Delhi, by Rewari, to the town of Alwur, and 23 miles N.E. of the latter. It is situate near the Kishengurh pass, which lies through a range of low rocky mountains, and is traversed by a bad road. Supplies are procurable in this town, and water may be obtained in abundance from wells. Lat. 27° 49′, long. 76° 47′.

KISHENGURH, in Rajpootana, a small state named from its principal place. It is bounded on the north-west and north by the territory of Joudpore; on the east by the territory of Jeypore and Ajmere; and on the south and south-west by the British district of Ajmere. Kishengurh lies between lat. 25° 50′—26° 50′, long. 74° 50′—75° 15′. The area is estimated at 724 square miles. It is in general a barren country, having a soil of unpromising clay, except where overspread by rocky hills, of which the principal is a range near the middle of the country, extending from south-east to north-west. The cultivation of the lower parts of the district might, however, be much increased, as water is there found near the surface. The wild vegetation is of a repulsive aspect, being principally euphorbias, which overspread the craggy hills. The population, estimated at the rate proposed by Sir John Malcolm, of ninety-eight to the square mile, would amount to upwards of 70,000.

The family of the rajah is Rajpoot, of the Rahtore tribe, and an offset of the family of Joudpore. Kulliam Singh, rajah of Kishengurh in 1818, entered into a treaty with the British government, the latter stipulating to afford protection, the former to acknowledge the supremacy of the British government, and to act in subordinate co-operation with it; to abstain from entering into negotiations with other states without its sanction, to refrain from aggression, to refer disputes to the arbitration of his British ally, and to furnish troops when required, according to his means. The rajah with whom this treaty was concluded, soon manifested eccentricities sufficient to warrant the belief that he was not of sane mind. In 1825, he left his capital, under an alleged impression that the British authorities were about to interfere in the internal administration of his dominions, and proceeded to Delhi, there to represent his case. It was explained to him that no such danger existed, and he appeared satisfied with the explanation. Shortly afterwards, he despatched troops to attack two of his principal dependants, himself proceeding again to Delhi, there to await the result of the movement. The effects of these disturbances were soon felt injuriously in the British district of Ajmere, where depredations were committed by one or both the belligerent parties. It was thereupon represented to the rajah, that the British government would hold him answerable for the conduct of his chiefs and their troops, as well as for his own; an intimation which seems to have caused him some alarm, for upon receiving it, he quitted Delhi with some raw levies, which he had made, demanded the assistance of his remaining dependants, and marched in person to reduce those in arms against him. His nobles had, however, no inclination for assisting in the destruction of members of their own order, whose interests were identified with theirs, and they accordingly deserted him, attempted to gain possession of the capital, and avowed their intention to depose the ruling prince, and set up his infant son. The rajah then fled to Ajmere, and invoked the arbitration of the British government. The chiefs made a similar appeal. The British authorities enjoined an immediate settlement of disputes by arrangement between the contending parties, which, after a time, was apparently effected. But this pacification was not lasting. The rajah, soon after the temporary adjustment, again quitted his territory. On the urgent remonstrance of the representative of the British government, he returned, but never succeeded in effecting a reconciliation with his discontented chiefs, and probably never attempted it in sincerity. Eventually, in 1832, he abdicated in favour of his son, and retired to the British dominions, on an allowance of 36,000 rupees per annum; a sum significant of the small resources of the state in comparison with its extent and population.

KISHENGURH, the principal place of the small native territory of the same name, a town on the route from Nusserabad to Hansee, 21 miles N.E. of the former, 222 S.W. of the latter. It is situate on the south-west side of a range of hills of gneiss and granite, which have a direction from south-east to north-west, and is surrounded by a high and thick rampart of masonry. Within the town is the residence of the rajah, a large and strongly-fortified structure, but in rather a rude style of architecture. Adjoining is a large tank, and there are gardens fenced with hedges of cactus. The town, once considerable, is now in many places ruinous. Lat. 26° 33′, long. 74° 57′.

KISHENGURH, in the Rajpoot state of Jessulmere, a fort and village in the desert, close to the frontier towards Bahawulpoor, and 80 miles N.W. of the town of Jessulmere. Lat. 27° 40′, long. 70° 36′.

KISHENNUGUR.—A town in the British district of Beerbhoom, lieut.-gov. of Bengal, 104 miles N.W. of Calcutta. Lat. 23° 46′, long. 87° 29′.

KISHENPORE.—The chief station of the Governor-General's agent for the south-western frontier, and commissioner for Chota Nagpore. Here is a jail for both civil and criminal prisoners. About a mile and a half south of this place is Dorunda, the present headquarters of the military within the district. An experimental coffee-plantation was formed in the vicinity of the town in 1844, and samples of the produce were sent home and submitted to brokers and merchants, by whom they were highly esteemed. The object of the experiment having been answered, by demonstrating that the climate and soil of the district were well adapted to coffee-cultivation, the plantation was disposed of by the government. Lat. 23° 28′, long. 85° 20′.

KISHNUGUR, in the British district of Nuddea, lieut.-gov. of Bengal, and the seat of the civil establishment of the district, a town on the route from Calcutta to Berhampore, 64 miles N. of former, and 54 miles S. of latter. This town has the advantage of valuable water-carriage, being situate on the navigable river Jellinghee, ten miles above its confluence with the Hooghly, navigable downwards to the sea. It is noted for its manufacture of fine muslins, highly prized even at present, when similar fabrics are produced in Britain in such perfection and cheapness. The price, however, is high, and the patterns, though tasteful, printed in only a single colour. Here also are modelled, in a sort of cement, small "figures, illustrative of the great variety of castes and classes of the population of Hindostan." One of the government colleges has been established here. The town is in lat. 23° 24′, long. 88° 28′.

KISHOONPOOR, or KISHENPOOR, in the British district of Futtehpore, lieut.-gov. of the N.W. Provinces, a village on the left bank of the Jumna, 25 miles S.E. of the town of Futtehpore. Lat. 25° 39′, long. 81° 4′.

KISHTAWAR, in the dominions of Gholab Singh, the ruler of Cashmere, a town situate on the southern slope of the Himalaya, and in a small plain near the left bank of the Chenaub, which here rushes through a ravine having precipitous sides of gneiss rock about 1,000 feet high. A little up the river, and on the opposite side from the town, is the confluence of the Muru Wurdwun, a considerable river from the north. It is a town of ill-built flat-roofed houses, with an insignificant bazar and a fort. There are trifling manufactures of shawls of inferior quality and of coarse woollens. The population, consisting of Mahometans and Hindoos, are proverbially poor, the place having suffered excessively from the oppression of the Sikhs since the expulsion of the rightful rajah, who ruled over the surrounding territory, which bears the same name, and whose power extended northwards as far as Ladakh. Kishtawar is situated 5,000 feet above the sea, and in lat. 33° 18′, long. 75° 46′.

KISHUNEE.—A town in the territory of Oude, on the right bank of the Goomtee river, and 50 miles E.S.E. from Lucknow. Lat. 26° 34′, long. 81° 44′.

KISHUNGURH.—A town in the Rajpoot state of Jeypoor, 36 miles W.N.W. from Jeypoor, and 64 miles N.E. from Ajmeer. Lat. 27° 9′, long. 75° 25′.

KISING.—A town in Nepal, situate three miles from the left bank of the Gunduck river, and 83 miles W. from Khatmandoo. Lat. 27° 46′, long. 83° 56′.

KISRY.—A town in Guzerat, or the dominions of the Guicowar, 82 miles S. by E. from Rajkote, and 163 miles S.W. from Ahmedabad. Lat. 21° 9′, long. 71° 9′.

KISSEN DASKA TALAO, in the British district of Delhi, lieut.-gov. of the N.W. Provinces, a village and halting-place on the route from the city of Delhi to Muttra, and 11 miles

S. of the former. Supplies may be collected from the vicinity, and water is abundant. Lat. 28° 30′, long. 77° 21′.

KISSENGURH.—A town of Bundelcund, in the native state of Chutterpoor, situate 78 miles N.E. by E. from Saugur, and 94 miles N. by W. from Jubbulpoor. Lat. 24° 29′, long. 79° 49′.

KISSERAING.—An island of the Mergui Archipelago, situate off the coast of Tenasserim; length N. to S. 20 miles, breadth 10 miles. Lat. 11° 34′, long. 98° 36′.

KISSUNPUR, in Sirhind, in the British district of Ferozepore, a village on the route from Lodiana to Ferozepore, and 32 miles W. of the former town. It is situate close to the left bank of a large offset of the Sutlej, and in a level, open country, partially cultivated. Distant N.W. from Calcutta 1,134 miles. Lat. 30° 55′, long. 75° 18′.

KISTNAGERRY.—A town in the British district of Kurnool, presidency of Madras, 23 miles S.W. of Kurnool. Lat. 15° 34′, long. 77° 53′.

KISTNAGHERRY, in the British district of Salem, presidency of Madras, a fort situate on a "tremendous rock," 700 feet in perpendicular height, and remarkably bare and steep. It is supplied with water from reservoirs within the fort; and at the base of the rock there are springs, which supply the petta or town. Distance from Salem, N., 60 miles; Madras, S.W., 150. Lat. 12° 32′, long. 78° 17′.

KISTNAH, or KRISHNA, a river rising in the Deccan, at Mahabulishwar, on the eastern brow of the Western Ghats, at the elevation of 4,500 feet above the level of the sea, and in lat. 18° 1′, long. 73° 41′. Though ultimately falling into the Bay of Bengal, its source is only about forty miles east of the western coast of the peninsula, or of the shore of the Arabian Sea. Taking a south-easterly course of about 145 miles through the territory of Sattara, and thence dividing that province from the jaghires of the Southern Mahratta country for the further distance of ten miles, it near Sanglee, in lat. 16° 50′, long. 74° 36′, on the right side, receives the Wurna, flowing from the west. From that confluence flowing south-east for 158 miles, alternately between and through the jaghires of the Southern Mahratta country, Sattara, and the British district of Belgaum, it on the right side receives the Gutpurba, and thence holds a similar course for thirty-five miles, separating the collectorates of Sholapore and Belgaum, to lat. 16° 10′, long. 76° 18′, where it arrives at the territory of the Nizam. Though its source has a considerable elevation, the country through which it flows in the upper part of its course does not appear to have a rugged aspect, being described as "one extensive plain to the south-east and north-west, whilst the ridges of hills on the north and south are barely visible, and at a distance. The banks of the river [Kistnah], which are deep and shelving, are composed of black earth, with mixed sand. The country undulates, and presents here and there hilly ranges of broken basalt. Some parts of it consist of extensive plains, covered by a little stunted grass, serving as pasture to numerous flocks [herds] of antelopes." In its course through Belgaum, it on the right side, as before mentioned, receives the river Gutpurba, and twenty-two miles lower down, the Mulpurba, besides several small torrents on the right and left. The river, skirting the territory of the Nizam for about ten miles, passes into it, and holds through it a course north-east for about sixty miles, to Lekur, in lat. 16° 32′, long. 77° 3′, where it turns south-east, and, flowing in that direction twenty-five miles, on the left side receives, in lat. 16° 24′, long. 77° 21′, the Beema, a large tributary from the north-west; and, continuing to flow in a south-easterly direction eighty miles farther, receives on the right side, in lat. 15° 58′, long. 78° 19′, the Tumboodra, a considerable river flowing from the south-west; and thence flows circuitously, but generally north-east, for 180 miles, through the rocky gorges of the Eastern Ghats, to Reveralah, in lat. 16° 50′, long. 80° 10′, where it turns south-east, and at Chentapily, ten miles lower down, leaves the recesses of the Ghauts, and enters the plain. In this part of its course, between the confluence of the Tumboodra and Chentapily, it receives on the left side, from the territory of the Nizam, some important tributaries; as the Dindee, the Pedawa, the Hullea, the Mase or Musi, the Palair; and a few miles below its entrance into the plain, it receives, on the same side, the Moonyair, a very considerable stream. During its course through the mountains, its tributaries, though numerous, are all unimportant. From the confluence of the Tumboodra to that of the Palair, it forms the boundary between the territory of the Nizam, lying either north or west, on the one side, and on the other the territory of Kurnoul and the British district of Guntoor. The channel of the Kistnah is deep, its banks varying in height from thirty to fifty feet; and Heyne observes, that it "has very steep, indeed almost perpendicular, banks during its whole course, which renders it altogether useless for agricultural purposes, such as watering the countries through which it flows. Both the banks are higher than the adjoining country, as has been ascertained by barometrical observations." From Chentapily, where it enters the plain, it holds a course of seventy miles south-east to Boburlanka, in lat. 16° 5′, long. 80° 56′, where it parts into two arms, the one flowing south-east thirty miles, and falling into the Bay of Bengal at Point Divy, in lat. 15° 57′, long. 81° 15′; the other flowing south twenty-five miles, and falling into the Bay of Bengal, in lat. 15° 45′, long. 80° 53′; inclosing between them a delta, traversed by a third branch sent off from the southern arm, and by some watercourses from the main branches. The total length of course of the Kistnah is 800 miles. It is subject to two periodical inundations annually; the first and principal, caused by the south-west monsoon precipitating its heavy rains on the Western Ghauts, Mysore, and other elevated tracts about the upper parts of the river's course, takes place at the end of summer; the other periodical inundation occurs in October, being caused by the local rains brought by the north-east monsoon, and is comparatively insignificant. The Kistnah, in consequence of the rapid declivity of its waterway and rockiness of channel, cannot be navigated even by small craft for short distances; and the manner of crossing ferries is by means of large, wide, circular baskets made of bamboo, and rendered water-tight by hides sewed on the outside of the framework, and having the seams secured by being overlaid with resin.

An extensive system of irrigation in connection with this river is now in progress, and has been estimated to cost 150,000*l.* The object is proposed to be effected by means of an annicut or embankment thrown across the river at the head of the delta, and by thus accumulating the waters, to extend the benefits of irrigation to large portions of the districts of Masulipatam and Guntoor.

KISTNAPOOR.—A town in the British district of North Arcot, presidency of Madras, 130 miles W. by S. of Madras. Lat. 12° 52′, long. 78° 27′.

KISTNARAAJPOOR.—A town in the Mysore, on the left bank of a branch of the Cauvery river, and 18 miles W.N.W. from Seringapatam. Lat. 12° 31′, long. 76° 30′.

KISUNI, or KISHNEE, in the British district of Mynpooree, lieut.-gov. of the N.W. Provinces, a village on the route from the cantonment of Etawa to that of Futtehgurh, and 25 miles N.E. of the former. Lat. 27° 2′, long. 79° 19′.

KITTOOR, in the British district of Belgaum, presidency of Bombay, a town formerly of great splendour, but now in decay, situate 26 miles S.E. of Belgaum. This town was the scene of a formidable insurrection in 1832, which, however, was happily suppressed by the zeal and intrepidity of two patells, named Linqua Gowah and Krishen Row, whose services on the occasion were acknowledged on the part of government by grants of land. Lat. 15° 36′, long. 74° 51′.

KIU.—A town within the dominions of Gholab Singh, the ruler of Cashmere, situate 149 miles N.N.E. from Kangra, and 135 miles E. from Sirinagur. Lat. 33° 59′, long. 77° 19′.

KIVALUR.—A town in the British district of Tanjore, presidency of Madras, 166 miles S. by W. of Madras. Lat. 10° 47′, long. 79° 48′.

KIVENTHA, in Arracan, a village on the route from Memboo to Aeng, and situate on the Mine river. It is at this village that the road diverges, one branch leading to Shembegiven. Lat. 20° 18′, long. 94° 22′.

KOAHDA, or CHUTENEA.—A small river, rising in the district of Boghelkhand, territory of Rewa, in two branches, the Odda and Silar, on an elevated plateau, the first-named in lat. 24° 35′, long. 81° 50′; the Silar, in lat. 24° 35′, long. 81° 55′. The elevation of the source above the sea must exceed 1,000 feet, as that is the elevation of the stream at the cascade of Bouti, twenty miles lower down. At that cascade it is precipitated a depth of 400 feet over the brow of the Kutra ridge, and continuing a northerly course of about fifteen miles, during which it is joined by the Goorma, is discharged, on the left side, and in lat. 24° 57′, long. 81° 57′, into the Bilund, a tributary of the Sone. Jacquemont, who, in the dry season, crossed it within a few miles of its source, styles it a rather considerable rivulet.

KOANG, a tributary of the Sone river, rises in the Saugor and Nerbudda territory, in lat. 23° 30′, long. 82°, and, flowing in a westerly direction for forty miles, falls into the Sone in lat. 23° 25′, long. 81° 31′.

KOARA FORT, in the Rajpoot state of Jessulmeer, a village on the route from Roree, in Sinde, to the town of Jessulmeer, from which it is distant 38 miles W. It has a small stone fort. Lat. 27° 7′, long. 70° 26′.

KOATPULLY.—A town in Hyderabad, or dominions of the Nizam, situate nine miles N. from the right bank of the Tandoor river, and 53 miles W. from Hyderabad. Lat. 17° 22′, long. 77° 45′.

KOBELASPOOR.—A town in the British district of Silhet, lieut.-gov. of Bengal, 55 miles S. by W. of Silhet. Lat. 24° 9′, long. 91° 37′.

KOCHANG.—A town in the British district of Chota Nagpoor, lieut.-gov. of Bengal, 60 miles S.E. by E. of Lohadugga. Lat. 22° 55′, long. 85° 30′.

KOCHECHOO, in the British district of Humeerpoor, lieut.-gov. of the N.W. Provinces, a village on the route from Banda to Gwalior, 67 miles W. of the former. It is situate on the river Dhasan; and supplies may be obtained. Lat. 25° 34′, long. 79° 29′.

KOCHELAH BOOREEA.—A town in the British district of Durrung, province of Assam, 57 miles N.E. by E. of Durrung. Lat. 26° 55′, long. 92° 47′.

KOCHERLACOTAH.—A town in the British district of Nellore, presidency of Madras, 50 miles W.N.W. of Ongole. Lat. 15° 50′, long. 79° 25′.

KOCHUS.—A town in the British district of Shahabad, lieut.-gov. of Bengal, 76 miles W.S.W. of Dinapoor. Lat. 25° 10′, long. 84°.

KODAMUNGLUM.—A town in the native state of Travancore, territory of Madras, 112 miles N. by W. from Trivandrum, and 68 miles S.S.W. from Coim atoor. Lat. 10° 4′, long. 76° 42′.

KODUMUDY.—A town in the British district of Coimbatoor, presidency of Madras, 64 miles E. of Coimbatoor. Lat. 11° 4′, long. 77° 57′.

KODUNDOOR.—A town in the British district of Coimbatoor, presidency of Madras, 45 miles S.S.E. of Coimbatoor. Lat. 10° 23′, long. 77° 13′.

KODUNGALOOR.—See CRANGANORE.

KODUNGUL.—A town in Hyderabad, or dominions of the Nizam, situate seven miles from the left bank of the Tandoor river, and 60 miles W.S.W. from Hyderabad. Lat. 17° 6′, long. 77° 41′.

KOEL, or KOYLE.—A river rising in the mountainous tract on the southern frontier of the British district of Chota Nagpoor, about lat. 23° 3′, long. 83° 58′. It holds a course generally northerly, and, receiving several torrents right and left, passes into the native state of Sirgooja and the British districts Palamow and Behar, and falls into the river Son on the right side, in lat. 24° 31′, long. 83° 54′, having a total course of about 140 miles. Valuable coal-fields have been discovered at Singra and some other places on its banks.

KOELAOR.—A town in the territory of Oude, situate on the right bank of the Gogra, and 52 miles E. from Lucknow. Lat. 26° 51′, long. 81° 50′.

KOENT, in the British district of Cawnpore, lieut.-gov. of the N.W. Provinces, a village on the route from the cantonment of Etawa to that of Cawnpore, and 34 miles W. of the latter. Lat. 26° 22′, long. 79° 56′.

KOEREEPOOR, in the British district of Jounpoor, lieut.-gov. of the N.W. Provinces, a village situate in a patch of territory surrounded on all sides by that of Oude, 25 miles N. of Allahabad. Lat. 26° 2′, long. 82° 24′.

KOGOON.—A town of Eastern India, in the British province of Pegue, situate 90 miles E. from Rangoon, and 51 miles N. from Amherst. Lat. 16° 50′, long. 97° 39′.

KOH, or CHOIA, a river of the British districts of Kumaon and Bijnour, rises in the most southern range of the Himalaya mountain-system, near Sungoor fort, at an elevation of about 6,400 feet, and in lat. 29° 55′, long. 78° 42′. It takes a course of about eighteen miles, in a south-westerly direction, to the southern frontier of Kumaon, where it passes into the plain of Hindoostan at Kotdwara, having an elevation of 1,342 feet above the sea. From this place it runs in a direction, first southerly, and subsequently south-easterly, a distance of about forty-five miles, to its junction with the Western Ramgunga, in lat. 29° 17′, long. 78° 42′. It was forded by Webb at Kotdwara, in March, when it was two feet deep and fifteen yards wide, with a rapid current.

KOHAT.—A town of Northern India, in the hilly tract north of the Salt range of mountains, and in the valley of Kohat, which is about seven miles in diameter, populous, fertile, well watered by the river Teo and by numerous springs. The town, which is surrounded by a wall, is meanly built, but has a good bazar and a fine mosque. Its beautiful situation, and the luxuriant vegetation of the surrounding country, render it a delightful place. The great route from Peshawur to Kala Bagh passes through Kohat, as does also westward an important route by Bungush to Khorasan. Kohat is the capital, not only of the pergunnah of the same name, but of an extensive and fertile valley, which, for administrative purposes, has recently been formed into a separate district of the Punjaub. At Sheikh, which is situate a few miles east of the town, are springs of naphtha and very rich and extensive deposits of sulphur. The British government are about to construct a chain of fortresses in the Kohat Pass, with the view of controlling the wild tribes in the vicinity. Kohat is in lat. 33° 32′, long. 71° 27′.

KOHNGAM.—An island 20 miles E. from the coast of Siam, two miles long by one and a half broad. It is situate 258 miles S.S.W. of Siam. Lat. 11° 21′, long. 100° 5′.

KOHRAR KHAS, in the British district of Allahabad, lieut.-gov. of the N.W. Provinces, a town on the route from Mirzapoor to Bandah, 36 miles W. of the former. Lat. 25° 8′, long. 82° 4′.

KOI, or KHOEE, in Sirhind, a village on the route from Hansee to Loodiana, and 48 miles S. of the latter town. It is situate in a country slightly undulated, tolerably fertile, and partially cultivated. Distant N.W. from Calcutta 1,064 miles. Lat. 30° 17′, long. 75° 56′.

KOILA, in the British district of Allahabad, lieut.-gov. of the N.W. Provinces, a village on the route from the cantonment of Allahabad to Futtehpore, and 15 miles N.W. of the former. Lat. 25° 29′, long. 81° 43′.

KOILAH, in the jaghire of Jujhur, district of Dadree, lieut.-gov. of the N.W. Provinces, a village on the north-eastern frontier, towards the British district of Rohtuk. Lat. 28° 44′, long. 76° 19′.

KOILCONDAH.—A town in Hyderabad, or dominions of the Nizam, 65 miles S.W. from Hyderabad, and 62 miles N. by W. from Kurnoul. Lat. 16° 41′, long. 77° 50′.

KOILKOONTLA.—A town in the British district of Cuddapah, presidency of Madras, 61 miles N.W. of Cuddapah. Lat. 15° 13′, long. 78° 23′.

KOKREE, a river of Bombay, rising in lat. 19° 22′, long. 73° 57′, a few miles east of the Malsej Ghat, and, flowing for fifty miles in a south-east direction, through the British districts of Poona and Ahmednuggur, falls into the Goor river, in lat. 18° 52′, long. 74° 20′.

KOKREET.—A town in the British province of Tenasserim, situate 60 miles N. of Moulmein. Lat. 17° 20′, long. 97° 42′.

KOKSAL.—A town in the British district of Pubna, lieut.-gov. of Bengal, 98 miles N.E. by N. of Calcutta. Lat. 23° 48′, long. 89° 16′.

KOKUR, in Cashmere, a celebrated spring at the northern base of the Panjal of Banihal, bounding the valley on the south. It gushes with a copious volume of water out of six orifices at the bottom of a limestone cliff. A considerable stream is thus formed, which flows into the Bureng river. The water is celebrated for its excellence, and the Afghan court, when established in Cashmere, drank no other. Koker Nag is in lat. 33° 30′, long. 75° 19′.

KOKUTNOOR.—A town in the British district of Sholapoor, presidency of Bombay, 32 miles E. of Beejapoor. Lat. 16° 49′, long. 76° 16′.

KOKUTNOOR.—A town in the British district of Belgaum, presidency of Bombay, 73 miles N.E. of Belgaum. Lat. 16° 41′, long. 75° 16′.

KOLA, in the British district of Kumaon, lieut.-gov. of the N.W. Provinces, a small fort, built of stone, and surrounded by a ditch, situate on a hill on the right bank of the river Dubha, on the route from Almora to Kosheepoor, 25 miles N.E. of the latter. Lat. 29° 25′, long. 79° 20′.

KOLABAH.—An island; also a portion of territory on the Concan coast, the whole subject to the presidency of Bombay. The island is situate in the Arabian Sea, or North Indian Ocean, half a mile W. of the shore of the Concan, and opposite the town Ali Bagh, in about lat. 18° 38′, long. 72° 56′. It appears to have been long neglected as a barren rock, but the active operations of European commerce, and maritime warfare, having shown the importance of its position, it was occupied and fortified in 1662, by the Mahratta chief Sevajee, who there "practised as a sea attorney." The course of piracy was, after his death, pursued by the Mahratta family of Angria, and became so formidable and ruinous to the commerce of the maritime powers, that, in 1722, an expedition of three British ships of the line and a Portuguese land force attacked it; but the attempt failed, in consequence of the cowardice of the Portuguese. The pirates continued to thrive in their iniquitous avocation, and Forbes, who, in 1772, visited Ragojee, the possessor of Kolaba, describes his palace, treasury, and other public buildings, gardens and stables, "containing a noble stud of Persian and Arabian horses, elephants, and camels;" adding, that "everything about the durbar was in princely style."

The tract of country on the mainland is bounded on the north by the harbour of Bombay; on the east by the British district of Tannah, with which it is now incorporated as a sub-collectorate; on the south by Jhingeera; and on the west by the Arabian Sea. It extends from lat. 18° 26′—18° 48′, and from long. 72° 55′—73° 12′; is thirty miles in length from north-west to south-east, and twelve in breadth; with an area of 318 square miles, and a population of 58,721. After the overthrow and expulsion of the Peishwa, Ragojee Angria in 1822 concluded a treaty with the British government, by which he agreed to acknowledge its supremacy, and was in turn guaranteed protection against external attack. Ragojee Angria died in 1838, leaving one of his widows in a state of pregnancy. She gave birth to a son, who was recognised as chief of Kolaba. The boy died in infancy, when the legitimate line of descent to the Kolaba state became extinct, and the territory lapsed to the paramount power. Pretensions to the succession were put forth by the illegitimate sons of Ragojee; but these, after due consideration, being ultimately rejected, the territory was annexed to the British dominions. The country is rich in teak forests and other timber. The surplus revenue available for the general purposes of the state, after deducting all disbursements, including pensions to the members of Angria's family, amounted, in 1844, to 1,27,355 rupees.

KOLACHEE, in the Daman division of the Punjab, a town situated 40 miles W. from the right bank of the Indus, and 140 miles N.W. by N. of the town of Mooltan. Lat. 31° 51′, long. 70° 53′.

KOLAD.—A town in the British district of Tannah, presidency of Bombay, 46 miles S.E. of Bombay. Lat. 18° 26′, long. 73° 20′.

KOLADYNE RIVER.—The principal river of Arracan. It takes its rise near the Blue Mountains, in lat. 22° 27′, long. 92° 51′, but the highest point to which it has been explored is in lat. 21° 25′, or ninety miles above Akyab, where its stream is narrow, and navigable only for canoes. After traversing for some miles a mountainous and desolate region, it opens upon wide and luxuriant plains, whereon are several villages, having extensive cultivation in their neighbourhood, more especially of rice, for which the soil is peculiarly adapted, from the facilities of irrigation. The inhabitants of these sequestered villages consist of Mughs and Burmese. The town of Arracan is situated on a branch of the river, about fifty miles from its mouth; and up to within a few miles of that place it is navigable for ships of 250 tons burden. For the last twenty or thirty miles of its course, it is connected with the rivers Myoo and Lemyo by innumerable creeks, by means of which much inland communication is carried on. It empties itself into the sea close to the island of Akyab, which is situated between this and the estuary of the Myoo. The breadth at its mouth is about ten miles.

KOLANGODU, in the British district of Malabar, under the presidency of Madras, a town near its eastern frontier, towards the British district Coimbatore. It is situate in a very beautiful country; the mountains on the south pouring down fine cascades, and the cultivated fields being interspersed with forests and plantations of fruit-trees. Each dwelling is inclosed by a small garden, and the number of houses has been stated at 1,000. Distance direct from Calicut, S.E., 75 miles; Cananore, S.E., 125; Coimbatore, S.W., 32; Madras, S.W., 300. Lat. 10° 37′, long. 76° 45′.

KOLAPOOR.—A raj or state under the political management of the presidency of Bombay. It is bounded on the north and north-east by Sattara; on the east and south by the British collectorate of Belgaum; and on the west by Sawunt Warree and the British collectorate of Rutnagherry. It lies between lat. 15° 58′—17° 17′, long. 73° 47′—74° 46′; is ninety-five miles in length from south-east to north-west, and sixty-five in breadth. The area is stated to be 3,445 square miles. It is throughout included within the country popularly denominated the Deccan, and is a tract sloping with a rugged surface from the culminating ridge of the Ghauts, forming the western boundary, towards the east or plain country, in the British collectorate of Belgaum. From that circumstance, the numerous torrents traversing this rough tract have a direction easterly, falling into the Kistnah, by the channel of which great river their contents are ultimately discharged into the Bay of Bengal. The Kistnah itself, flowing southward from Sattara, touches on this raj a few miles below the confluence of the Wurna, in lat. 16° 50′, long. 74° 36′, and, holding a course very tortuous, but generally in a direction south-easterly, for about twenty-five miles, forms for that distance the boundary between Kolapoor and the Southern Jagheerdars. The Wurna rises at the north-west corner of the raj, at Tewra, on the eastern declivity of the Ghauts, in lat. 17° 20′, long. 73° 46′, and, flowing towards the south-east for about thirty miles, forms for that distance the boundary between this raj and the province of Sattara, and falls into the Kistnah on the right side. The other streams are mere mountain torrents. The elevation of the highest summits of the Ghauts, in the western part of the raj, is probably between 3,000 and 4,000 feet; the average elevation of the lowest part, or that farthest east, varies perhaps from 1,500 to 1,800 feet. The geological formation appears to be throughout volcanic, principally trappean, like the rest of the northern section of the Ghauts; and the volcanic formation is generally overlaid by laterite, or cellular ferrugineous sandstone, which, when disintegrated, forms a very fertile soil. The population consists principally of two races,—Mahrattas and Ramooses; these last resembling in some respects the Bheel tribe, so extensively spread farther north. The Ramooses, however, are more intelligent than the Bheels, and though actuated by similar plundering habits, are much superior in a military point of view. The number of the people has been returned at 500,000. This, however, includes the population of the dependencies of Kolapoor; viz., Vishalgur, Kagul, Inchulkurunjee, and Bowda. The chief of Inchulkurunjee having died without male issue, the question of the lapse of the estate to the Kolapoor government has been made dependent on the non-existence of any male descendant of the founder of the ruling family. Should the resumption be sanctioned, the estate of Inchulkurunjee will probably be transferred to the British government in liquidation of the debt incurred by the Kolapoor state for the suppression of the insurrection in the year 1844. Kolapoor, the seat of government, appears to be the only town. The route from Sattara to Sawuntwarree, from north to south, passes by the town, as does that from south-east to north-west, from Dharwar to the South Concan. There is also a route from north-east to south-west, from Sholapoor to the town of Kolapoor.

The rulers of Kolapoor trace their descent from Sevajee, the founder of the Mahratta empire. While Saho, the third in descent from Sevajee, was a prisoner at Delhi, his uncle, Rajah Ram, the second son of Sevajee, assumed the government. Rajah Ram died before Saho's liberation, and was succeeded by his son Sevajee, who contested the Mahratta supremacy with his cousin Saho. Sevajee did not long survive his father, and left his brother Sambajee heir to his pretensions. Sambajee continued the contest for the throne of Sattara with his cousin Saho; at length a compromise was effected, by which Sambajee acknowledged Saho's right to the whole Mahratta country except Kolapoor with its dependent territory, which was assigned to himself, with the title of rajah, and the same dignity as that assumed by Saho; hence the rajah of Kolapoor was addressed as a superior by the Peishwa. Sambajee died in 1760, without issue. His widow adopted, as her husband's heir, a boy named Sevajee, and conducted the affairs of the principality in his name. The piracy which prevailed on the coast induced the government of Bombay to send an expedition against Kolapoor in 1765. The fort of Malwan was captured and retained until certain satisfaction was rendered, when it was restored to the Kolapoor state by treaty, concluded the 12th of January, 1766. In 1804, when Sir A. Wellesley was engaged in settling the Southern Mahratta country, the Kolapoor rajah preferred certain claims against the Peishwa. He was told that the British government would arbitrate his claims, but would not allow him to invade the Peishwa's dominions. The opportunity was taken to propose an agreement for the suppression of piracy, on account of which the Kolapoor ports were then blockaded; but it does not appear to have ever been concluded. The subjects of the rajah's maritime districts never desisted from piracy: when detected, and punishment threatened, apologies were offered, with promises of reparation for the past, and abstinence from future depredations; but the system of piracy was not effectually suppressed until 1812, when the demand against the rajah on account of plunder of British property amounted to fifty lacs of rupees. During the distracted condition of the Poona government, a hostile conflict was maintained by the states of Kolapoor and Sawuntwarree. Latterly, Appa Dessaye, the Peishwa's general, interfered, and was besieging Kolapoor with a view of reducing it to the Peishwa's authority; but the differences were arranged by stipulations contained in a treaty concluded by Mr. Elphinstone with the rajah of Kolapoor, by which the territorial rights of that prince in regard to the Peishwa were defined, and all claims on his part over the dominions retained by the Peishwa, and over the subjects of that chieftain, surrendered. Malwan and its dependencies were ceded in perpetual sovereignty to the British government, the suppression of piracy was decreed; and, in consideration of these conditions, the Company agreed to guarantee the rajah in possession of the territories assigned to him; at the same time the British relinquished all pecuniary demands against the rajah. In 1822, the rajah Abba Sing was murdered. He left an infant son, by Tarra Bai, usually styled the Dewan; but his brother, Bawa Sahib, seized the Guddee, and his nephew, whose right he had usurped, dying soon after, he became the rightful rajah. In 1825, the rajah's maladministration and aggressions on the neighbouring jaghiredars, who were under British protection, compelled the armed intervention of the Company's government. A force was accordingly moved into the Kolapoor country, when hostile proceedings were arrested by the submission of the rajah, with whom a new treaty was concluded; but scarcely had the British force been withdrawn, when the rajah levied troops and renewed his oppression of the guaranteed chiefs. His conduct compelled the British government to take military possession of the country. The rajah at length submitted, and entered into new engagements, contained in a preliminary treaty, concluded towards the end of the year 1827, and a definitive treaty (more favourable to him), concluded in 1829. It was deemed necessary that his proceedings should for some be watched by a corps of observation, a precaution justified by the event; the rajah, under the pernicious advice of the minister appointed by the British government, and who proved faithless to the authority to which he owed his power, having resumed his previous course of violence. The minister being removed and tranquillity restored, the military force was withdrawn. Nothing of importance occurred till 1839, when the rajah Bawa Sahib died, leaving two sons, both young, and by different mothers. He was succeeded by the elder, Sevajee, usually called Baba Sahib. The mother of the rajah assumed the regency during his minority, but it was shortly wrested from her by Tarra Bai, the widow of the former rajah, Abba Sing, and already mentioned as known by the title of the Dewan. This lady was recognised as regent by the British government. She continued to exercise full authority until 1842, when her extreme mismanagement compelled the government, as guardian of the young rajah's interests, to interfere. After the complete failure of milder measures, the regent was set aside altogether, and a minister appointed to act under the immediate control of the British government. The Dewan's party, discontented from the loss of their nefarious gains, excited a general rebellion throughout the country in 1844. The rebellion was put down by force of arms, and the entire management of the Kolapoor state assumed, and thenceforward directly exercised, by the British government, in the name of the rajah, whose authority in the mean time remains in abeyance.

The military force of the state of Kolapoor amounts to between 9,000 and 10,000 men, of various descriptions. If that of the dependent jaghiredars be added, the number will be increased to more than 12,000.

KOLAPOOR.—The principal place and seat of government of the raj or state of the same name. Being in a secluded tract, seldom visited by Europeans, little is known concerning it. When, in 1825, a British force advanced to the place, the reconnaissance gave the information that the defences were weak, and might, without much difficulty, be taken by escalade. On the rampart were many guns of small calibre, from four to twelve-pounders; but there was reason to conclude the garrison had no supply of ammunition. When, in consequence of the rajah having again become troublesome, it was once more necessary to march a force against him, the place was peaceably delivered up to the British troops, the Arabs and Scindians, who constituted the garrison, marching in search of other service, and the rabble, which had collected from various quarters, dispersing in all directions. Under British authority, the physical condition has been scarcely less benefited than the political and civil circumstances of the country of which it is the capital. The town being excessively crowded and unhealthy, a series of measures for its sanitary improvement commenced in 1848; and it has since been officially reported, that the place has been tolerably cleansed from its filthiness, and that a plentiful supply of water has been obtained. Further improvement may reasonably be looked for. Distant S.E. from Bombay 185 miles, S. from Poona 130, S. from Sattara 70. Lat. 16° 42′, long. 74° 18′.

KOLAR.—A town in the British province of Sattara, presidency of Bombay, situate 27 miles S. of Beejapoor. Lat. 16° 26′, long. 75° 44′.

KOLARAS, in the territory of Gwalior, or possessions of Scindia's family, a town, the principal place of a pergunnah of the same name, assessed at the annual land revenue of 90,000 rupees. Distant 79 miles S.W. of Gwalior fort. Lat. 25° 13′, long. 77° 41′.

KOLASHAGARAPURAM.—A town in the native state of Travancore, territory of Madras, situate 51 miles N.W. by N. from Trivandrum, and 83 miles W.N.W. from Tinnevelly. Lat. 9° 6′, long. 76° 35′.

KOLBAREEA.—A town in the British district of Pachete, lieut.-gov. of Bengal, 131 miles N.W. of Calcutta. Lat. 23° 48′, long. 86° 54′.

KOLHUAGAR, in the district of Bainswara, territory of Oude, a village on the left bank of the Ganges, 10 miles S.E. of Cawnpore, 30 S.W. of Lucknow. Butter estimates the population at 1,000, all Hindoos. Lat. 26° 25′, long. 80° 31′.

KOLLAH.—A town in the British province of Sattara, presidency of Bombay, 31 miles S. by E. of Sattara. Lat. 17° 14′, long. 74° 10′.

KOLLATHOOR.—A town in the British district of Tinnevelly, presidency of Madras, 41 miles N.E. by E. of Tinnevelly. Lat. 9° 1′, long. 78° 15′.

KOLRON, in the Kyarda Doon, in Sirmor, a village and halting-place on the route from Dehra to Nahun, and 54 miles W. of the former town. The hills inclosing the Doon are here so close, that they are separated merely by the channel of the Batta. The road in this part of the route is described by Mundy as a rough track; and no supplies can be procured except water from the Batta. This place is called Kolson by Moorcroft, who states it to have been the scene of a severe defeat received by the Rohilla prince Gholam Kader from Jagat Prakas, the rajah of Sirmor. Distant N.W. from Calcutta 1,086 miles. Lat. 30° 30′, long. 77° 29′.

KOLWAR, in the district of Sultanpoor, territory of Oude, a village 70 miles S.E. of Lucknow, 10 miles W. of Sultanpoor cantonment, half a mile from the right bank of the river Goomtee. According to Butter, the population is 1,000, of whom 100 are Mussulmans. Lat. 26° 23′, long. 82°.

KOMARPOOR.—A town in the British district of Purneah, lieut.-gov. of Bengal, 29 miles S. by E. of Purneah. Lat. 25° 23′, long. 87° 41′.

KOMEDPORE.—A town in the British district of Pubna, lieut.-gov. of Bengal, 110 miles N.N.E. of Calcutta. Lat. 24° 3′, long. 89° 9′.

KOMHARSIN, a hill state between the Sutlej and the Jumna, is bounded on the north by Kooloo, from which it is separated by the river Sutlej; on the east by Kotgurh and the British districts of Sundoch and Kothkaee; on the south by Bulsun; and on the west by the district of Goond, one of the tributaries of the state of Keonthul. It embraces an area of about fifty-six miles. Its centre is in lat. 31° 13′, long. 77° 32′. Except a narrow strip along the left bank of the Sutlej, the surface has a considerable elevation; that of the town of Komharsin above the level of the sea, is 5,279 feet; of the cantonment of Kotgurh, on the eastern frontier, 6,634; of Whartoo, in the same locality, 10,656. The drainage is northwards, by a small stream, into the Sutlej; southwards, by two feeders of the river Giree. The principal crops are wheat, barley, various sorts of millet, phaphur, and some other species of buckwheat; various esculent vegetables, tobacco, and, on the banks of the Sutlej, ginger and cotton. The poppy is extensively cultivated for opium, which is of very fine quality, and brings a higher price than that of the plains. The seeds yield a sweet oil, much used as an article of diet, and for burning. Hemp is an important product, on account of its fibres, the intoxicating drug obtained from its resinous secretion, and its seeds, which yield oil, and are parched and used as food. A hardy species of rice is partially cultivated. Oats grow spontaneously, but are not applied to any use. The fruits are apples of indifferent quality, pears, peaches, apricots, cherries, grapes, walnuts, filberts, raspberries, currants, barberries, and mulberries. Bamboos, and some of the tropical fruits, grow on the bank of the Sutlej.

The rana or prince of this state formerly owed allegiance to Bussahir, but was dispossessed of his rights by the Goorkhas. On the expulsion of these aggressors, in 1815, he was reinstated by the British. The grant was in favour of Rana Kehur Sing and his posterity. Kehur Sing died without issue in 1839, and, according to the strict letter of the endowment, this territory lapsed to the British government; but, in consideration of the early attachment of the deceased rana to British interests, and of other circumstances, the grant was renewed in favour of Preetum Singh, a collateral heir. This chief engaged to prevent suttee, and to abolish infanticide. The present annual revenue of the state is estimated at 1,000*l.*, out of which a tribute of 144*l.* is paid to the East-India Company.

KOMHARSIN, an insignificant village, though the principal place of the hill state of the same name, and the residence of the rana or native prince, is situate on a mountain descending precipitously a depth of 2,280 feet to the left bank of the Sutlej. Fraser describes it, at the time of his visit, as "mean and poor," not consisting of "more than a dozen houses, built, like the rest of the hill villages, of dry stone and wood, in the Chinese fashion." It has probably improved under British protection, as Archer, twelve years afterwards, found the rana residing in a large and well-built residence, and the surrounding country well cultivated and luxuriantly productive. Elevation above the sea 5,279 feet. Distance N.W. from Calcutta, by Kurnool and Subathoo, 1,110 miles. Lat. 31° 19′, long. 77° 30′.

KOMTA, in the territory of Nagpoor, a town on the route from Hazareebagh to the city of Nagpoor, 107 miles N.E. of the latter, 467 S.W. of the former. Here, after the deposition of Appa Sahib Bhonsla, in 1818, some of his partisans attempted to make head, manning the defences, which consisted of a wall and partial ditch, inclosing a small fort. The garrison amounted to above 2,000, and had two batteries. After the outer defences had been forced, and the fort attacked, the garrison surrendered, on promise of personal safety. The loss of the besieged was estimated at 400; that of the besiegers at sixty-one. Lat. 21° 32′, long. 80° 21′.

KOMULMAIR, or KUMULMAIR, in the territory of Oodeypoor, in Rajpootana, a pass defended by a fortress, on the route from Oodeypoor to Joudpore, 50 miles N. of former, 90 S.E. of latter. It lies through a succession of deep and rugged ravines in the Aravulli, and forms the communication between the more elevated region of Mewar and the plain of Marwar. The fortress was gained for the East-India Company in 1818, by bribing the garrison of the ruler of Joudpore to give it up; and it was made over to the rajah of Oodeypoor. Elevation above the sea 3,353 feet. Lat. 25° 10′, long. 73° 40′.

KONADAH.—A town in the British district of Vizagapatam, presidency of Madras, 30 miles N.E. by N. of Vizagapatam. Lat. 18° 1′, long. 83° 40′.

KONADOON.—A town in Hyderabad, or dominions of the Nizam, situate 30 miles S.W. from Hyderabad, and 89 miles N. from Kurnool. Lat. 17° 6′, long. 78° 11′.

KONAIE.—A considerable watercourse of Bengal, separating from the Brahmapootra in lat. 25° 10′, long. 89° 43, near the town of Mehindergunje, in the British district of Mymunsing. Flowing first in a southerly direction for 100 miles, and then communicating with the Ganges by means of a considerable offset, it turns south-east, and, taking the name of the Dulasseree, it flows for seventy-five miles, to lat. 23° 13′, long. 90° 33′, at which point it reunites with the parent stream, there denominated the Megna. The Konaie in its course receives several smaller streams and watercourses, such as the Goggot, the Attree, and the Bunsi.

KONAKAGIRI.—A town in the British district of Salem, presidency of Madras, 190 miles S.W. by W. of Madras. Lat. 11° 53′, long. 78° 4′.

KONCHPARA.—A town of Assam, in the British district of Camroop, 19 miles W. of Gowhatty. Lat. 26° 7′, long. 91° 26′.

KONDA, in the British district of Benares, lieut.-gov. of the N.W. Provinces, a village situate on the right bank of the Ganges, 666 miles N.W. of Calcutta by water. Lat. 25° 20′, long. 83° 9′.

KONDELWUDDY.—A town in Hyderabad, or dominions of the Nizam, situate four miles from the right bank of the Godavery river, and 112 miles N.N.W. from Hyderabad. Lat. 18° 48′, long. 77° 45′.

KONDURH, in the British district of Futtehpore, lieut.-gov. of the N.W. Provinces, a town situate 14 miles S.E. of the town of Futtehpoor. Lat. 25° 46′, long. 80° 57′.

KONGOODY DROOG.—A town in the British district of North Arcot, presidency of Madras, 128 miles W. by S. of Madras. Lat. 12° 46′, long. 78° 29′.

KONKAN.—See CONCAN.

KONKEE.—A river rising in lat. 26° 41′, long. 87° 51′, in Nepal, on the southern slope of the Sub-Himalaya range of mountains, and, flowing in a southerly direction for fifteen miles through Nepal, and fifty miles through the British district of Purneah, falls into the Mahananda in lat. 25° 51′, long. 87° 48′.

KONKEIR, or KAKAIR, in the territory of Nagpoor, a town situate between the right or south bank of the river Mahanuddee and a high rocky hill, surmounted by a fortress. It is surrounded by rocky mountains, of which those to the north, the east, and the south, are very lofty. Under the Mahratta government, the zemindary, of which this town is the chief place, was held on condition of furnishing, when required, 500 troops. In 1809, the rajah was dispossessed of his territory; but having joined the rebels in the troubles which arose on the escape of Appa Sahib, he retook Kakair, and was confirmed in his possession, subject only to the payment of a fixed rent of 500 rupees annually. Distant from Nagpoor, S.E., 170 miles. Lat. 20° 15′, long. 81° 33′.

KONKEL NUGGUR.—A town in the British district of Chota Nagpoor, lieut.-gov. of Bengal, 55 miles S.W. of Lohadugga. Lat. 22° 50′, long. 84° 10′.

KONKLY.—A town in the native state of Tatcheer, one of the independent hill tribes of Orissa, on the right bank of the Braminy river, and 112 miles N. from Ganjam. Lat. 21°, long. 85° 10′.

KONNAVERUM.—A town in Hyderabad, or dominions of the Nizam, situate on the left bank of the Godavery, and 187 miles E. by N. from Hyderabad. Lat. 17° 36′, long. 81° 21′.

KONNOOR.—A town in the British district of Sholapoor, presidency of Bombay, 36 miles S.E. of Beejapoor. Lat. 16° 30′, long. 76° 12′.

KONUKPOOR.—A town in the British district of Silhet, lieut.-gov. of Bengal, 36 miles E.S.E. of Silhet. Lat. 24° 42′, long. 92° 22′.

KOOAREE, or KOHARI.—A small river rising in the territory of Gwalior, about 60 miles S.W. of the fort of Gwalior, and in lat. 25° 44′, long. 77° 28′. It flows first north-west, then north-east, subsequently east, and finally south-east, having a course semicircular in its general outline, and of 185 miles in length, and falls into the Sinde on the left side, in lat. 26° 26′, long. 79° 14′. The route from Agra to Gwalior crosses it at Hingonah, lat. 26° 32′, long. 78° 3′, and there it is represented with "little water, banks steep, and cut into ravines; but they slope off gradually at the ghat (passage), and form no impediment." It is crossed, forty-five miles above its mouth, by the route from Etawa to Gwalior, and is no doubt there fordable, except during heavy rains. The lower part of its course is through Sindous, a barren and wild subdivision of the British district of Etawa, and much cut up by deep, steep, and very difficult ravines, formerly the lurking-places of thugs, dacoits, and other heinous malefactors; but of late years cleared by the energetic operations of the British authorities. This river seems to be identical with the Kewari mentioned by Baber.

KOOATHUREE, in the British district of Kumaon, lieut.-gov. of the N.W. Provinces, a town on the route from Almora to the Nepal territory, 38 miles E. by N. of the former. Lat. 29° 42′, long. 80° 19′.

KOOCHAUN.—A town in the Rajpoot state of Jodhpoor, 128 miles E.N.E. from Jodhpoor, and 50 miles N. by E. from Ajmeer. Lat. 27° 10′, long. 74° 53′.

KOOCH BEHAR.—A territory in the northern part of that portion of British India which is subject to the lieut.-gov. of Bengal. It is under the administration of a Hindoo prince, whose ancestor, having been expelled from the raj, was, in 1773, restored by the British government, on condition of rendering annually to the Company one-half of his revenue, the amount to be ascertained and fixed at the time, and to be thenceforth unalterable. The territory is bounded on the north by Bootan; on the east by the district of Goalpara; on the south and south-west by the British district of Rungpore; and on the west by that of Dinajepore. It lies between lat. 25° 58′ and 26° 32′, long. 88° 42′ and 89° 45′; is sixty miles in length from south-east to north-west, and forty in breadth. The area is 1,364 square miles. It is altogether an alluvial and remarkably level country, but sloping gradually to the south-east, as indicated by the rivers flowing in that direction. The principal of these are the Durlah, the Neelcomer, the Manchee, and the Sonkos or Chonnekosh. This country seems to have been a subdivision of the realm denominated Kamroop. Its early history is fertile in the silly fables which supply the place of facts in Hindoo records. Even for some time after the Mussulman conquests, the state of information is little better. Soon after the East-India Company had acquired Bengal by grant from Shah Alum, their assistance was invoked by the rajah of Kooch Behar. The hereditary minister of this state had rebelled against his master, and, forming an alliance with the Der rajah (ruler of Bootan), had agreed to make large cessions of territory to the latter, on condition of being supported in his attempts to overthrow his lord. A battalion of native troops, with two pieces of cannon, commanded by Captain Jones, was thereupon sent by the British authorities, in 1772, to the aid of the rajah; and this force, after routing the rebellious minister, entered Bootan, stormed the hill fort Dalim Koth, and ultimately compelled the aggressive rajah and his associate to sue for peace. Many difficulties occurred in the consequent settlement of affairs, and it seems to be believed that the ruler of Bootan was treated with much favour. Within the now restricted confines of Kooch Behar (for previous encroachments, together with the recent alienations, had greatly reduced its extent), other difficulties presented themselves, arising from claims made by the minister and the commander of the forces to shares of the territory. These claims were not easily susceptible of adjustment, and have remained for a long series of years matter of dispute. Questions of boundaries also arose, but these were settled with comparative ease. Still more recently, the British authorities found it necessary to despatch an officer (Captain Jenkins) to investigate complaints, numerous and strongly urged, of the oppressive conduct of the rajah's servants towards the people. Though having the title of rajah, the position of the chief is rather that of a zemindar, enjoying the surplus revenue remaining after the payment of a fixed amount of tribute.

KOOCH BEHAR, the principal place of the raj or small tributary state of the same name, is situate on the river Toresha, 45 miles N. of the town of Rungpore. Though it appears in the Tibetan legends a place very renowned in Buddhist lore, scarcely anything but the name appears to be known respecting it. Upon the decease of the rajah of Kooch Behar, in 1847, he was succeeded by an adopted son, a boy of six years of age, who has been placed for education in one of the government colleges. Distant N.E. from Berhampore, by Dinagepore, 230 miles; N.E. from Calcutta, by same route, 348. Lat. 26° 16′, long. 89° 29′.

KOOCHUT.—A town in the British district of Burdwan, lieut.-gov. of Bengal, 50 miles N.N.W. of Calcutta. Lat. 23° 14′, long. 88° 9′.

KOODAL.—A town in the British province of Sattara, presidency of Bombay, 13 miles N.W. by N. of Sattara. Lat. 17° 50′, long. 73° 59′.

KOODLIGHEE.—A town in the British district of Bellary, presidency of Madras, 38 miles W.S.W. of Bellary. Lat. 14° 53′, long. 76° 27′.

KOODSOO.—A town in the Rajpoot state of Jodhpoor, 89 miles N. by E. from Jodhpoor, and 112 miles N.W. from Ajmeer. Lat. 27° 32′, long. 73° 20′.

KOODWUL.—A town in the native state

of Bhurtpoor, 40 miles W.S.W. from Agra, and 18 miles S. from Bhurtpoor. Lat. 26° 59′, long. 77° 31′.

KOODYA, in the British district of Azimgurh, lieut.-gov. of the N.W. Provinces, a small town on the route from the town of Azimgurh to Sultanpoor cantonment, in Oude, 12 miles W. of the former, 56 N. of Benares. Lat. 26° 4′, long. 82° 58′.

KOOHIE.—A town of the Deccan, in the territory of Nagpoor, situate on the right bank of one of the branches of the Wein Gunga, and 20 miles E.S.E. from Nagpoor. Lat. 21° 2′, long. 79° 25′.

KOOJOODOO.—A town of Assam, in the British district of Sudiya, lieut.-gov. of Bengal, 24 miles S. of Sudiya. Lat. 27° 30′, long. 95° 45′.

KOOKAY OORNEY.—A town in the British district of Madura, presidency of Madras, 51 miles E.S.E. of Madura. Lat. 9° 43′, long. 78° 53′.

KOOKIWARI, or KOOKYWARREE, RIVER, one of the mouths of the river Indus, formerly "the grand embouchure" of that river, having a breadth of 1,100 yards, but now blocked up by a sand-bank. Lat. 24° 5′, long. 67° 33′.

KOOKOOLOOBAH.—A town in the British district of Ganjam, presidency of Madras, 56 miles N.N.W. of Ganjam. Lat. 20° 8′, long. 84° 46′.

KOOKRESUR, in the territory of Indore, or possessions of Holkar's family, a town on the route from Neemuch to Kotah, 26 miles E. of former, 96 S.W. of latter. It has a good bazar, and is well supplied with water, and contains about 800 houses, and a population of about 4,000 persons. Elevation above the sea 1,412 feet. Lat. 24° 26′, long. 75° 20′.

KOOKSEE.—A town of Malwa, in the native state of Dhar, situate 41 miles S.W. by W. from Dhar, and 150 miles N.E. by E. from Surat. Lat. 22° 15′, long. 74° 50′.

KOOKUNOOR.—A town in one of the recently sequestrated districts of Hyderabad, or dominions of the Nizam, situate 100 miles E. by S. of Belgaum. Lat. 15° 30′, long. 76° 2′.

KOOKURMOONDA.—A town in the British district of Candeish, presidency of Bombay, 73 miles N.N.W. of Malligaum. Lat. 21° 31′, long. 74° 7′.

KOOLAUR, in Sirhind, a village on the route from Hansee to Loodiana, and 56 miles S. of the last-mentioned town. It is situate in a level well-cultivated country. The road in this part of the route is in general good, but liable to become miry during heavy rains. Distance N.W. from Calcutta 1,054 miles. Lat. 30° 10′, long. 75° 56′.

KOOLBURGA, in Hyderabad, or territory of the Nizam, a town on the route from Hyderabad through Sholapoor to Poona, 110 miles W. of former, 210 S.E. of latter. It is one of the stations of the force denominated the army of the Nizam, but actually a British force, disciplined and commanded by British officers, and under the direction and control of the presidency of Madras. Distance from Madras, N.W., 380 miles; Bombay, S.E., 285. Lat. 17° 19′, long. 76° 51′.

KOOLGURRAH.—A town of the Deccan, in the territory of Nagpoor, on the left bank of the Wein Gunga river, and 96 miles S.E. by S. from Nagpoor. Lat. 20° 4′, long. 80° 1′.

KOOLITULLAY.—A town in the British district of Trichinopoly, presidency of Madras, 21 miles W.N.W. of Trichinopoly. Lat. 10° 56′, long. 78° 29′.

KOOLNA, in the British district of Jessore, lieut.-gov. of Bengal, a town on the river Bhoirub, 35 miles S.E. of the town of Jessore, 75 E. of Calcutta. Lat. 22° 48′, long. 89° 46′.

KOOLOO.—See KULU.

KOOLOO.—A town in the Rajpoot state of Jodhpoor, 91 miles W. by S. from Jodhpoor, and 75 miles S.E. from Jessulmeer. Lat. 26° 3′, long. 71° 43′.

KOOLOOHA, in the British district of Allahabad, lieut.-gov. of the N.W. Provinces, a village on the route by the Rajapoor ferry from the cantonment of Allahabad to Banda, and 42 miles W. of former. Lat. 25° 25′, long. 81° 19′.

KOOLPAC.—A town in Hyderabad, or dominions of the Nizam, situate on the right bank of one of the branches of the Kistnah river, and 43 miles N.E. by E. from Hyderabad. Lat. 17° 41′, long. 79° 6′.

KOOMAR.—A watercourse, and one of the numerous offshoots of the Ganges which intersect the lower provinces of Bengal. It divaricates from the Martabhanga in lat. 23° 50′, long. 88° 51′, and, dividing the districts Pubna and Jessore, flows in a south-easterly direction for seventy miles, and in lat. 23° 32′, long. 89° 28′, falls into the Nabogunga, or, as it is afterwards called, the Barashee.

KOOMARKOLL, in Orissa, a town in the native state of Boad, on the south-west frontier of Bengal, situate five miles from the right bank of the Bang Nuddee, and 64 miles S. from Sumbulpoor. Lat. 20° 33′, long. 84° 7′.

KOOMB.—A town in the British district of Shikarpoor, province of Scinde, presidency of Bombay, 92 miles S.W. of Shikarpoor. Lat. 27° 1′, long. 67° 41′.

KOOMBAH, in Sirhind, a village on the route from Hansee to Loodiana, and 24 miles N. of the former town. It is situate in an undulating country of moderate fertility and partially cultivated. The road in this part of the route is excellent. Distant N.W. from Calcutta 1,000 miles. Lat. 29° 25′, long. 76° 5′.

KOOMBAHARLA GHAT, a mountain-pass over the Western Ghats, between Rutnageriah and Sattara districts of the Bombay presidency, 123 miles S.E. by S. from Bombay. It is traversed by the new line of road from Kerrar, in Sattara, to the port of Chiploon. A toll is levied on the passing traffic. Lat. 17° 22′, long. 73° 48′.

KOOMBHER, in the territory of Bhurtpore, a town 11 miles N.W. of the city of Bhurtpore. Tieffenthaler, describing its condition about eighty years ago, states it to be "a considerable burgh, or rather a small city, situate in a plain, and surrounded by a mud wall and a ditch. Most of the houses are of plaster, but several are of masonry, and tiled. Of the last sort is a fine palace of the rajah, situate on a moderate eminence, and whitewashed. It commands an extensive prospect over the plain, and serves as a fortress, being surrounded by strong walls." The soil around this town is much impregnated with common salt, which is extracted for alimentary purposes by washing the earth, and allowing the brine thus obtained to be evaporated in shallow ponds by the heat of the sun. Koombher was founded at the beginning of the 18th century, by the advice and with the assistance of Jai Singh, rajah of Jeypore or Amber. In 1754, it was unsuccessfully besieged by the Mahrattas. After the capture of the city of Bhurtpore by the British, in 1826, Koombher was surrendered to them without resistance. Distant N.W. of Agra 45 miles. Lat. 27° 19′, long. 77° 26′.

KOOMDONG.—A town of Eastern India, in the native state of Muneepoor, 19 miles N.W. from Muneepoor, and 120 miles S.E. by S. from Nowgong. Lat. 24° 56′, long. 93° 47′.

KOOMERI.—A town in the native state of Gwalior, or the territory of Scindia's family, situate 47 miles N. from Saugur, and 64 miles N.W. from Dumoh. Lat. 24° 30′, long. 78° 50′.

KOOMHPOOR, in the British district of Kumaon, lieut.-gov. of the N.W. Provinces, a town on the route from Almora to Suharunpoor, 16 miles W. of the former. Lat. 29° 38′, long. 79° 28′.

KOONA, or KOYANE, a river rising in the territory of Oude, about lat. 27° 22′, long. 82° 11′, and, running south-east about twenty-five miles towards the frontier of the British district of Goruckpore, forms for twenty miles from that point the boundary between the dominions of the Company and those of the ruler of Oude. It here sends out a small branch, called the Jehada, which, after a course of about three miles, joins the Besui, which latter stream, after a course of five or six miles, returns the water of the Jehada, and discharges its own into the Koyane. That river, holding its way through the district of Goruckpore, in a direction circuitous, yet generally south-east, for 110 miles, ultimately falls into the Ghogra, on the left side, in lat. 26° 16′, long. 83° 28′, after a total course of about 155 miles. Buchanan describes it as "a fine little river, which, with its numerous branches, fertilizes all the southern parts of the district." In its course it receives, in addition to the Besui, a number of streams and rivulets: the Batparoya, the Bengwora, the Pawai, the Manavi, the Kathne, the Marora or Manoramar, the Sajai, the Keyane, and the Jhijara; all of them inconsiderable. Previously to its receiving the Besui, the Koyane has a channel of considerable width, and a stream which, though narrow, is of such depth as to be impracticable for loaded cattle. Lower down, Buchanan, in the beginning of January (dry season), found that the Koyane contained a fine stream, which, he continues, "I could not cross on an elephant without boats." Referring to a point still farther towards the mouth of the river, Buchanan says, "In November [close of the rainy season], I crossed the Koyane, where it was about fifty yards wide, but contained much water, being at least six feet deep. In some parts, however, it is said to have only a foot and a half of water; but at all seasons canoes can pass up and down, and in the rainy season it could be navigated by large boats; but, as far as I could learn, it is never applied to the purposes of commerce; and disputes about the property have prevented the produce of the forests on its banks from being brought to market, except in carts." According to Garden, it is crossed by ferry at Lalganj, on the route from the cantonment of Goruckpore to that of Sultanpore, in Oude, and probably about forty-five miles from its source. It has here a channel seventy yards wide.

KOONAWUR, a district of Bussahir, extending over the northern part of that territory, is bounded on the north by the Spiti valley; on the east by Chinese Tartary; on the south by Gurwhal and the Bussahir districts of Chooara and Dussow; and on the west by Kooloo. It is about seventy miles in length from south-west to north-east, forty in breadth; is said to contain an area of 2,100 square miles, and extends between lat. 31° 12′—32° 8′, long. 77° 50′—78° 52′. It is a very elevated and rugged country, consisting of various groups of enormous and lofty ridges, through which the valley, or rather vast ravine of the Sutluj, runs, in a direction generally from north-east to south-west, a distance of about seventy miles from the point where it leaves Chinese Tartary, about lat. 31° 50′, to the vicinity of Seran, where it passes the south-western frontier, in lat. 31° 25′, long. 77° 38′. The principal habitable part of the country lies not so much along the banks of the Sutluj, which are generally rocky and precipitous, as in the valleys drained by its numerous feeders; the principal of which, on the right side, are the Li, or river of Spiti, the Darbung, the Pejur, the Kozhang, the Mulgun, and the Yala; on the left, the Hocho, the Taglagkhur, the Tidong, and the Buspa.

The general elevation of the country may be determined from the fact that the bed of the Sutluj, necessarily the lowest part, as it drains the whole country, slopes from the elevation of 10,000 feet, which it has at the north-eastern boundary, to about 5,000, being that at Spara, Wodar, and Wongtu Jhula, near the south-western frontier.

The climate in summer is hot in the lower part of the valley of the Sutluj, and sometimes oppressively so, in consequence of the radiation of heat from the inclosing rocks, Cheenee and some other places having an elevation exceeding 8,000 feet. The grape attains great excellence, and yields a product resembling raisin-wine, and a very strong spirit. In the southern and lower part of Koonawur, the monsoon rains are rather heavy in July, August, and September; but as they do not fall to the north of about lat. 31° 30′, the rest of the district is, during those months, refreshed only by partial and light showers; so that cultivation is successful only in situations on which streams can be directed from the snowy summits. The winter is generally rigorous; to such an extent in some places, that for a long period there is no leaving the villages, in consequence of the depth of snow.

The population partakes of both the Mongolian and the Caucasian varieties of the human race. The Koonawaris are in general very dark, but sometimes display considerable ruddiness. They are tall, athletic, and well made; and in character are said to be frank, hospitable, generous, and remarkably free from falsehood and suspicion. Of all the hill people, the Koonawaris alone gave effectual resistance to the Goorkhas, whom they defeated in action, and so baffled by breaking down the bridges and defending the fastnesses, that their invaders entered into a convention, by which, in consideration of the annual payment of about 750*l.*, they agreed to abstain from entering the district, and to leave unmolested the rajah of Bussahir, who had taken refuge there. In consequence of that good service, the Koonawaris are peculiarly favoured by the rajah, who chooses most of his officers and supporters from them, and assesses them more lightly than his other subjects.

Polyandry is almost universal; and in the northern part, the total disregard of the laws of chastity renders the country one vast brothel. The religion of Koonawur is Brahminism in the south; in the north, Lamaic Bhuddism; in the middle, a mixture of the two systems. There prevails a regularly graduated transition from one to the other. Thus, Brahmins are not met with beyond Saharun, near the southern boundary, where they officiate at the shrine of the sanguinary female divinity Bhima Kali, to whom, at no remote period, they offered human sacrifices. At Kanum, about half-way between the northern and southern frontiers, the sacred books are in Tibetan, and lamas are there first met with; but kine are venerated, and some attention paid to the distinction of castes; thus partially amalgamating the two creeds. At Hungrung, on the northern frontier, the religion is pure Lamaic Buddhism. There are five distinct dialects spoken in Koonawur. In the north, the language is Tibetan; and the Kanawari or Milchau dialect, of which a vocabulary is given by Herbert, bears a strong resemblance to that language. Gerard, after an elaborate computation, estimates the population at 9,850 persons; being nearly at the rate of five to the square mile. The principal places are Sungnum and Kanum, which are noticed respectively in the alphabetical arrangement.

KOONCH, in the British district of Jaloun, the principal place of the pergunnah of the same name, a town on the route from Calpee to Gwalior, 42 miles S.W. of the former, 82 S.E. of the latter. In May, A.D. 1804, a British detachment engaged in the siege of Aminta Malaya, a small fort, was surprised by a greatly superior force under Ameer Khan, the noted Patan freebooter. On this occasion, two companies of native infantry and about fifty European artillerymen were cut to pieces, and two howitzers, two twelve-pounders, one six-pounder, and a number of tumbrils, were carried off by the Patan, the remainder of the detachment with difficulty making its retreat to Koonch. About a month after, in the same vicinity, however, the Patan's troops were defeated by the British with signal slaughter. It is mentioned in the Ayeen Akbery, under the name of Kownj, as having a fort, and yielding 46,295 rupees annually. The pergunnah of Koonch contains a native jaghire, belonging to Bhuma Baee, which is under British management. Lat. 25° 59′, long. 79° 13′.

KOONDA.—A town in the British district of Ramgurh, lieut.-gov. of Bengal, 45 miles W.N.W. of Hazareebagh. Lat. 24° 12′, long. 84° 44′.

KOONDALLEE.—A town of the Deccan, in the territory of Nagpoor, on the left bank of one of the branches of the Wurda river, and 32 miles W. from Nagpoor. Lat. 21° 7′, long. 78° 40′.

KOONDALLY.—A town in the native state of Travancore, 117 miles N. from Trivandrum, and 60 miles S. by E. from Coimbatoor. Lat. 10° 9′, long. 77° 10′.

KOONDERKEE, in the British district of Moradabad, lieut.-gov. of the N.W. Provinces, a town on the route from Moradabad to Budaon, 11 miles S. of the former. Lat. 28° 41′, long. 78° 52′.

KOONDGUL.—A town in the Southern Mahratta jaghire of Jamkundee, 63 miles S.E. from Belgaum, and 112 miles W. from Ballary. Lat. 15° 15′, long. 75° 19′.

KOONDLA, in Guzerat, or territory of the Guicowar, a town in the district of Kattiwar, situate on the river Naula, a tributary of the Sitronji. Distance from Ahmedabad, S.W., 138 miles; Baroda, S.W., 115; Surat, W., 95;

Bombay, N.W., 190. Lat. 21° 22′, long. 71° 20′.

KOONDUH, in the British district of Meerut, lieut.-gov. of the N.W. Provinces, a village on the route from Delhi to Meerut, and seven miles S.W. of the latter. Lat. 28° 56′, long. 77° 43′.

KOONDULLA.—A town in the Rajpoot state of Jodhpoor, 13 miles N.N.W. from Ajmeer, and 98 miles E.N.E. from Jodhpoor. Lat. 26° 40′, long. 74° 39′.

KOONEEMOONDAH.—A town of the Deccan, in the territory of Nagpoor, 27 miles N.E. by N. from the hill zemindarry of Jeypoor, and 162 miles W. from Ganjam. Lat. 19° 20′, long. 82° 40′.

KOONGA.—A town in the native state of Patna, 74 miles S.W. from Sumbulpoor, and 126 miles N.N.E. from Jeypoor. Lat. 20° 40′, long. 83° 16′.

KOONGMA, or LAKONGMA, in Bussahir, a pass in Koonawur, over a lofty mountain-ridge running from north to south, and forming the boundary between the British and Chinese empires. Elevation of the crest of the pass above the sea 16,007 feet. Lat. 31° 48′, long. 78° 46′.

KOONJBUNGHUR.—A town in one of the native states of the independent hill tribes of Orissa, situate eight miles from the right bank of the Mahanuddy, and 68 miles S. by E. from Ganjam. Lat. 20° 21′, long. 84° 57′.

KOONJERRY.—See Keunjur.

KOONJUH, a village in the British district of Dehra Doon, situate on the left bank of the Asun, near its confluence with the Jumna. Here was a station of the series of small triangles in the trigonometrical survey of the Himalayas. Elevation above the sea 1,618 feet. Lat. 30° 26′, long. 77° 44′.

KOONLUS, in the boundary of the British district of Kumaon, lieut.-gov. of the N.W. Provinces, a ridge of the main range of the Himalaya, on the north-eastern angle of the district, towards Hiundes or South-western Tibet. It is thus named by the Tartars and Tibetans, the Hindus calling it Kailas. There are two peaks on the ridge, both rising far above the lower limit of perpetual snow, the higher having an elevation above the sea of 22,513 feet, the other, a short distance to the south-east, an elevation of 21,669. The former is in lat. 30° 14′, long. 80° 54′; the latter, lat. 30° 13′, long. 80° 58′.

KOONREE.—A town in the territory of Oude, situate five miles W. of the right bank of the Gogra, and 52 miles N. by E. from Lucknow. Lat. 27° 34′, long. 81° 17′.

KOONSALA, in Gurhwal, a village on the left bank of the Jumna, is situate amidst forests of oaks, rhododendrons, maples, and azalias, containing, however, patches of fertile ground carefully cultivated, and producing grain and potatoes, the latter recently introduced into this part of the Himalayan region. Elevation above the sea 7,084 feet. Lat. 30° 54′, long. 78° 24′.

KOONY.—A river in Hyderabad, or the Nizam's territory, rising in lat. 20° 21′, long. 78° 14′, and, flowing in a south-easterly direction for seventy miles, falls into the Payne Gunga river on the left side, in lat. 19° 46′, long. 78° 49′.

KOONYHAR, or KOONEEAR, a small hill state, bounded on the north-west by Bhagul, and on all other sides by the outlying territory of the rajah of Pateeala. It is about five miles in length and three in breadth, and contains an area of twelve square miles. Its centre is situate about lat. 31° 6′, long. 77° 4′. It contains two pergunnahs or districts. The population is estimated at about 2,500, and the annual revenue at the insignificant sum of 350*l.*, out of which a tribute of 18*l.* is paid to the British government. The rana, or petty sovereign, is said to have about 200 armed retainers, no doubt supported on lands assigned to them on feudal principles. He holds his raj by virtue of a grant made to him by the British government on the conquest of the country from the Goorkhas, in 1815. This prince resides at a small town or village of the same name as the state, and occupies a dwelling which, according to Hügel, "scarcely merits the name of house."

KOOPOONG.—A town of Eastern India, in the British district of Aracan, 162 miles S.E. by S. of Aracan. Lat. 18° 41′, long. 94° 32′.

KOORABUR, in the Rajpoot territory of Oodeypoor or Mewar, a town on the route from Neemuch to Baroda, 68 miles W. of former, 202 N.E. of latter. It has a bazar, and supplies and water are abundant. Elevation above the sea 1,272 feet. Lat. 24° 34′, long. 74° 6′.

KOORAH.—A town in one of the recently sequestrated districts of Hyderabad, or dominions of the Nizam, 80 miles W.S.W. of Ellichpoor. Lat. 20° 59′, long. 76° 22′.

KOORAHUREE, in the British district of Muttra, lieut.-gov. of the N.W. Provinces, a village on the route from the cantonment of Meerut to that of Muttra, and 20 miles N. of the latter. Lat. 27° 44′, long. 77° 50′.

KOORALA, in the British district of Moradabad, lieut.-gov. of the N.W. Provinces, a village on the route from the town of Meerut to that of Moradabad, and 38 miles S.E. of the former place. It is situate near the left bank of the Ganges, in an open and partially cultivated country. Distant N.W. from Calcutta 884 miles. Lat. 28° 51′, long. 78° 16′.

KOORALLA, in the Reechna Dooab division of the Punjab, a town situated 16 miles from the right bank of the Ravee, 45 miles N.N.E. of the town of Lahore. Lat. 32° 10′, long. 74° 29′.

KOORANIA, in Sinde, a village on the

route from Sehwan to Larkhana, and 16 miles N. of the former place. It is situate a mile and a half from the right bank of the Indus, in a level, fertile country, mostly covered with grass, but diversified by occasional patches of cultivation. Lat. 26° 38′, long. 67° 55′.

KOORAOWLEE, in the British district of Mynpooree, lieut.-gov. of the N.W. Provinces, a town on the route from Mynpooree to Allygurh, 11 miles N. of the former. Elevation above the sea 648 feet. Lat. 27° 24′, long. 79° 2′.

KOORAR, in Orissa, a town of Nyaghur, one of the petty hill states on the south-west frontier of Bengal, situate 45 miles N. by W. from Ganjam, and 68 miles S.W. by W. from Cuttack. Lat. 20° 1′, long. 85°.

KOORAWAH, in the British district of Muzuffurnugur, lieut.-gov. of the N.W. Provinces, a village on the route from Kurnal to Meerut, and 39 miles S.E. of the former. It is abundantly supplied with water from tanks and wells. Lat. 29° 21′, long. 77° 30′.

KOORDAH.—See KHOORDAH.

KOOREEGAUM.—A town of the Deccan, in the territory of Nagpoor, situate 20 miles N.W. from Jeypoor, and 113 miles N.W. from Vizianagrum. Lat. 19° 14′, long. 82° 13′.

KOOREEJAMPA.—A town in the native state of Bhotan, 68 miles N. by E. from Goalpara, and 83 miles N.W. from Gowhatty. Lat. 27° 5′, long. 90° 57′.

KOOREEPOOR.—A town in the territory of Oude, 52 miles S. by E. from Oude, and 53 miles W. from Azimgurh. Lat. 26° 3′, long. 82° 23′.

KOORELALESAN, in the Sinde Sagur Dooab division of the Punjab, a town situated 11 miles from the left bank of the Indus, 88 miles N.N.W. of the town of Mooltan. Lat. 31° 20′, long. 71° 3′.

KOORIE, in the Rajpoot state of Jodhpoor, a village on the route from Balotra to the city of Jodhpoor, and 12 miles N.E. of the former. Lat. 25° 56′, long. 72° 30′.

KOORKULLO.—A town in Hyderabad, or dominions of the Nizam, situate on the right bank of the Godavery, and 142 miles N.E. by E. from Hyderabad. Lat. 18° 23′, long. 80° 23′.

KOORMAIL.—A town in Hyderabad, or dominions of the Nizam, situate two miles from the right bank of one of the branches of the Godavery, and 96 miles N. by E. from Hyderabad. Lat. 18° 43′, long. 78° 49′.

KOOROODA.—A village in Arracan, situate on the left side of the Mayu river, about ten miles from its mouth. Lat. 20° 20′, long. 92° 52′.

KOOROOL.—A town in one of the recently sequestrated districts of Hyderabad, or dominions of the Nizam, situate 13 miles E. of Ellichpoor. Lat. 21° 10′, long. 77° 48′.

KOOROOTHANEE.—A town in Hyderabad, or dominions of the Nizam, situate two miles from the left bank of the Payne Gunga river, and 90 miles S. by E. from Ellichpoor. Lat. 19° 57′, long. 77° 57′.

KOORSEE.—A town in the territory of Oude, 15 miles N.N.E. from Lucknow, and 60 miles N.E. from Cawnpoor. Lat. 27° 3′, long. 81° 8′.

KOORSEE.—A town of the Deccan, in the territory of Nagpoor, situate 11 miles E. of the left bank of the Wein Gunga, and 92 miles S.E. from Nagpoor. Lat. 20° 17′, long. 80° 11′.

KOORSUNDUH.—A town in the British district of Mutra, lieut.-gov. of the N.W. Provinces. It has a population of 6,325 inhabitants. Distant S.E. from Mutra 21 miles. Lat. 27° 24′, long. 78° 5′.

KOORTHUL, or KURTHUL.—A town in the British district of Meerut, lieut.-gov. of the N.W. Provinces: it contains a population of 7,972 inhabitants. Distant N.W. from Meerut 31 miles, N. from Delhi 40 miles. Lat. 29° 14′, long. 77° 19′.

KOORTHUL, in the British district of Muzuffurnugur, lieut.-gov. of the N.W. Provinces, a village on the route from Kurnal to Meerut, and 49 miles S.E. of the former. Lat. 29° 14′, long. 77° 33′.

KOORTY.—A town in Hyderabad, or dominions of the Nizam, situate on the left bank of the Payne Gunga river, and 180 miles N. from Hyderabad. Lat. 19° 57′, long. 78° 27′.

KOORUNDAH.—A town in Hyderabad, or dominions of the Nizam, situate 167 miles N.W. by N. from Hyderabad, and 122 miles S. by W. from Ellichpoor. Lat. 19° 27′, long. 77° 18′.

KOORUNDWAR.—A town in the Southern Mahratta jaghire of Koorundwar, situate two miles from the right bank of the Kistnah river, and 58 miles N. from Belgaum. Lat. 16° 40′, long. 74° 40′.

KOORUNGHA.—A town of Orissa, in the native state of Jushpoor, on the south-west frontier of Bengal, situate 80 miles N.N.W. from Sumbulpoor, and 92 miles S. by W. from Palamow. Lat. 22° 33′, long. 83° 38′.

KOORUNTADI, in the British district of Ghazeepore, lieut.-gov. of the N.W. Provinces, a town on the left bank of the Ganges. It has a bazar, and a portion of the government stud on the Ghazeepore establishment is located here. Distant 566 miles N.W. of Calcutta by water. Lat. 25° 34′, long. 84° 2′.

KOORWAEE.—A town in Malwa, the principal place of a native state of the same name, on the right or east bank of the river Betwa, on the route from Tehari to Oojein, distant 60 miles S.W. of former, 150 N.E. of latter. It is of considerable size, is surrounded by a wall, and has a large fort, built of stone.

The inhabitants are principally Patans, who settled here in the reign of Aurungzebe. It was founded by Delut Khan, a Patan of the Feroz Khayl tribe, and a native of Khyber, in Affghanistan; and his descendants once enjoyed sovereignty over a territory of five or six thousand square miles in area; but Mahratta conquests have reduced it within the slender limits of 200, with a population not exceeding 20,000 inhabitants. During the predominance of the Pindaries, the nawab or chief of this little territory was stripped of all his possessions, except the small portion commanded by the fort of Koorwaee; but on the expulsion of those freebooters in 1817, he regained what he at present holds. His annual revenue is estimated at 75,000 rupees. On the left bank of the Betwa, opposite to this town, and almost united to it, is Boraso, also a considerable place. Lat. 24° 6′, long. 78° 5′.

KOOSEEL.—A town of Orissa, in the native state of Bombra, on the south-west frontier of Bengal, situate on the right bank of the Maltee Nuddee, and 12 miles E. from Sumbulpoor. Lat. 21° 27′, long. 84° 11′.

KOOSER.—A town in one of the recently sequestrated districts of Hyderabad, or dominions of the Nizam, situate 42 miles S.W. of Ellichpoor. Lat. 20° 45′, long. 77° 8′.

KOOSHALGURH.—A town in the Rajpoot state of Jeypore, situate on the route from Agra to Mow, 98 miles S.W. of former, 317 N.E. of latter. It has a mud fort, with double wall, round bastions, and a ditch, and contains several large buildings of stone. Lat. 26° 30′, long. 76° 47′.

KOOSHALNUGGUR.—See FRASERPET.

KOOSHALPUR, in the British district of Moradabad, lieut.-gov. of the N.W. Provinces, a village on the route from Kasheepoor to Almora, 13 miles N.E. of the former. It is situate on the left bank of the river Kosilla, in the Tarai or marshy forest extending along the southern base of the Sub-Himalaya. Lat. 29° 19′, long. 79° 11′.

KOOSH BEHAR.—See KOOCH BEHAR.

KOOSHTUGI.—A town in one of the recently sequestrated districts of Hyderabad, or dominions of the Nizam, situate 112 miles E. of Belgaum. Lat. 15° 46′, long. 76° 16′.

KOOTKEBUREE.—A town of North-eastern India, situate in the British district of Goalpara, 31 miles W.N.W. of Goalpara. Lat. 26° 20′, long. 90° 11′.

KOOTLAH, in the British district of Futtehpore, lieut.-gov. of the N.W. Provinces, a small town, with fort, on the right bank of the Ganges, 18 miles E. of the town of Futtehpoor. It is the Cooter of Rennell. Lat. 25° 50′, long. 81° 9′.

KOOTOOMBEH.—A town in the British district of Behar, lieut.-gov. of Bengal, 37 miles W. of Sherghotty. Lat. 24° 38′, long. 84° 17′.

KOOTOOR.—A town in Hyderabad, or dominions of the Nizam, situate on the left bank of the Godavery, and 122 miles N.N.E. from Hyderabad. Lat. 19°, long. 79° 14′.

KOOTREE.—A town in the native state of Cutch, situate 30 miles W.S.W. from Bhooj, and 17 miles N.N.W. from Mandavee. Lat. 23° 5′, long. 69° 19′.

KOOTUBDEA, the name of two islands on the coast of Chittagong, lying close to each other, and extending together about twelve miles in length. They are low and woody. At the south end there is fresh water, close to a tope of trees. Creeks are numerous: one, called Pilot Cotta Creek, forming the division between the two islands, has five or six fathoms water at its eastern entrance, and five feet water on the bar, where it joins the sea, on the west side. The centre of the islands is about lat. 21° 50′, long. 91° 55′.

KOOTUBPOOR, in the British district of Muttra, lieut.-gov. of the N.W. Provinces, a village on the route from the cantonment of Allygurh to that of Etawah, and 42 miles S.E. of the former. The surrounding country is open, with a clayey soil rather well cultivated. Lat. 27° 23′, long. 78° 25′.

KOOWANJEE.—A town in the Rajpoot state of Kotah, situate three miles from the left bank of the Ahoo river, and 40 miles S.S.E. from Kotah. Lat. 24° 40′, long. 76° 10′.

KOPAREE.—A town in the British district of Balasore, lieut.-gov. of Bengal, 156 miles S.W. by W. of Calcutta. Lat. 21° 15′, long. 86° 29′.

KOPEELEE NUDDEE, a tributary of the Kullung river, rises in lat. 25° 8′, long. 92° 33′, and, flowing in a northerly direction, during which it forms the boundary between the British districts Jynteah and Northern Cachar, falls into the Kullung, in lat. 25° 50′, long. 92° 50′.

KOPOORTHELLA.—See KAPOORTHELLA.

KOPURGAUM.—A town in the British district of Ahmednuggur, presidency of Bombay, situate 59 miles N.N.W. of Ahmednuggur. Lat. 19° 53′, long. 74° 29′.

KOPURTHELLA.—A town in the Julinder Dooab division of the Punjab, about 10 miles from the left bank of the Beas, and on the route from Loodiana to Lahore. Here Futteh Sing, the half-brother of Runjeet, built a magnificent street, a palace, and a temple, and near the town commenced and almost completed a mansion, in so massive a style that he incurred the suspicions of the maharaja, and was in consequence obliged to fly. Lat. 31° 24′, long. 75° 25′.

KOR, or KOD.—A town in the British district of Dharwar, presidency of Bombay, 72 miles S.W. by S. of Dharwar. Lat. 14° 31′, long. 75° 30′.

KORA, in Sinde, a small town about 15 miles S.W. of Khyerpoor, and on the great route from that town to Hyderabad. The population consists generally of weavers engaged in the manufacture of loongees or scarfs and of coarse cotton cloths. Lat. 27° 22′, long. 68° 36′.

KORACHAH.—A town of the Deccan, in the territory of Nagpoor, situate 115 miles S.E. by E. from Nagpoor, and 132 miles S.E. by S. from Seuni. Lat. 20° 25′, long. 80° 45′.

KORAEEN, in Sinde, a village on the route from Subzulcote to Shikarpoor, and 23 miles W. of the former town. It is situate in a low, level country, overflowed extensively, in time of inundation, by the Indus, from the left bank of which the village is three miles distant. Koraeen is in lat. 28° 11′, long. 69° 30′.

KORAEJEE NA GOTE, in Sinde, a town on the route from Hyderabad to Sehwan, by the way of Kotree, and 22 miles N. of Hyderabad. It is situate about a mile from the right bank of the Indus, in lat. 25° 44′, long. 68° 25′.

KORAH, in the British district of Futtehpore, lieut.-gov. of the N.W. Provinces, a small town or village on the left bank of the Jumna, 19 miles S.W. of the town of Futtehpoor. Lat. 25° 48′, long. 80° 35′.

KORAH KHAS, in the British district of Futtehpoor, lieut.-gov. of the N.W. Provinces, a town on the route from Futtehpoor to Etawah, 30 miles W.N.W. of the former. It has a bazar. The town is mentioned by Baber. Lat. 26° 7′, long. 80° 27′.

KORAI, in the British district of Futtehpoor, lieut.-gov. of the N.W. Provinces, a village on the route from Calpee to the town of Futtehpore, and four miles N.W. of the latter. Lat. 25° 57′, long. 80° 45′.

KORAM, in Sirhind, a town situate in the Cis-Sutlej territory, 27 miles S.W. by S. of Ambala. Lat. 30° 5′, long. 76° 33′.

KORAMBAH.—A town in the British district of Chota Nagpoor, lieut.-gov. of Bengal, 10 miles S. of Lohadugga. Lat. 23° 18′, long. 84° 43′.

KORAR.—A town of Bundelcund, in the British province of Jhansee, situate 20 miles E. from Jhansee, and 86 miles W.S.W. from Humeerpoor. Lat. 25° 30′, long. 78° 59′.

KORD.—A town in the Rajpoot district of Godwar, situate 105 miles S.W. by W. from Ajmeer, and 53 miles S.S.E. from Jodhpoor. Lat. 25° 35′, long. 73° 24′.

KOREA.—A raj within the limits of the territory superintended by the political agent for the south-west frontier of Bengal. Its centre is in lat. 23° 25′, long. 82° 30′; its area is 2,225 square miles. The country, when lately visited by the British agent, was reported to be in a very deplorable state: it is computed to yield about 10,000 rupees annually; but the British tribute of 1,600 rupees is paid very irregularly. The chief products of the country are lac and wild silk. The population is computed to be about 100,000.

KOREA.—A town, the principal place of the native state of Korea, 153 miles N.W. from Sumbulpoor, and 135 miles S.W. by W. from Sherghotty. Lat. 23° 6′, long. 82° 26′.

KOREA GUNJ, in the British district of Allygurh, lieut.-gov. of the N.W. Provinces, a small town on the route from Bareilly to Allygurh cantonment, and 16 miles S.E. of the latter. Lat. 27° 50′, long. 78° 22′.

KOREE, in Sinde, at the south-eastern extremity of the seacoast of that country, is an arm of the sea, the estuary of the most eastern branch of the Indus, and still receiving part of its waters during high inundations. At Cotasir, twenty miles from the open sea, it is seven miles wide. The Koree mouth is in lat. 23° 40′, long. 68° 25′.

KOREE, a river of the Rajpoot state of Oodeypoor, rises in lat. 25° 32′, long. 73° 57′, at the town of Deogurh, and flows in an easterly direction for 115 miles, forming for a portion of that distance the boundary between Ajmeer and Oodeypoor: subsequently traversing a detached portion of Ajmere, it falls into the Banas river, in lat. 25° 53′, long. 75° 30′.

KOREECH.—See KHURENCHA.

KOREEKOLA.—A town of Orissa, in the native state of Bonei, on the south-west frontier of Bengal, situate five miles from the left bank of the Braminy river, and 70 miles E.N.E. from Sumbulpoor. Lat. 21° 50′, long. 85° 1′.

KOREHGAON.—A town in the British province of Sattara, presidency of Bombay, 12 miles E. of Sattara. Lat. 17° 41′, long. 74° 15′.

KORENEE, in the British district of Delhi, lieut.-gov. of the N.W. Provinces, a village on the route from the city of Delhi to Kurnal, and 15 miles N.W. of the former. Lat. 28° 50′, long. 77° 9′.

KORHALEH.—A town in the British district of Ahmednuggur, presidency of Bombay, 50 miles N.N.W. of Ahmednuggur. Lat. 19° 44′, long. 74° 26′.

KORNRA.—A town in the Rajpoot state of Jodhpoor, 23 miles W.S.W. from Jodhpoor, and 122 miles W. by S. from Ajmeer. Lat. 26° 13′, long. 72° 48′.

KOROUND.—A town in the territory of Oude, situate on the right bank of the Goomtee, and 28 miles N.N.W. from Lucknow. Lat. 27° 12′, long. 80° 49′.

KORULL.—A town in Guzerat, or the dominions of the Guicowar, situate on the right bank of the Nerbudda river, and 30 miles S. from Baroda. Lat. 21° 50′, long. 73° 12′.

KORYGAUM.—See CORYGAUM.

KORYNAUR, in the peninsula of Kattywar, province of Guzerat, a town in the district of Soruth, on the estuary of the river Singora, a fine stream, which, about two miles lower down, or farther south, falls into the Arabian Sea. Here is a considerable fort; and there is also a temple of Krishna, worshipped under the singular title of Rinchor, or the Recreant; and at certain times great multitudes of pilgrims resort to it. Distant from Ahmedabad, S.W., 200 miles; Baroda, S.W., 190. Lat. 20° 47′, long. 70° 40′.

KORZOK.—A town in the dominions of Gholab Singh, the ruler of Cashmere, situate 134 miles N.E. by E. from Kangra, and 194 miles E. by N. from Jamoo. Lat. 32° 57′, long. 78° 17′.

KOSAH NAG, in Cashmere, a mountain lake on the north side of the Futi Panjal, one of the mountains bounding the valley on the south. It is three-quarters of a mile long and 500 yards broad, and is replenished from the melted snows of the neighbouring summit, the supply from which is sometimes so abundant as to raise the surface of the water forty feet above its level in the lowest state. It gives rise to the Veshau, one of the principal feeders of the Jailum, which last river is also known in some parts of its course by the name of the Veshau. Vigne thus describes its efflux:—"Its full, strong torrent is suddenly seen gushing out from the foot of the last and lofty eminence that forms the dam on the western end of the lake, whose waters thus find an exit not over, but through, the rocky barrier with which it is surrounded." The inclosing rock is a beautiful amygdaloid, containing spots of quartz in a dull, dark purple-coloured matrix. The lake is held in great veneration by the Hindoos, who call it Vishnu Paudh (the foot of Vishnu), in consequence of a legend that the deity produced it by stamping the ground with his foot. It is, in consequence, visited in pilgrimage by devotees, for the purpose of performing ceremonial ablutions. The elevation above the level of the sea is estimated by Vigne at 12,000 feet. Lat. 33° 30′, long. 74° 52′.

KOSEMURA, in the British district of Mynpooree, lieut.-gov. of the N.W. Provinces, a town on the route from the cantonment of Futtehgurh to that of Etawa, and 28 miles N.E. of the latter. Lat. 27° 7′, long. 79° 21′.

KOSILLA, or KOSI.—A river rising in the British district of Kumaon, lieut.-gov. of the N.W. Provinces, in lat. 29° 52′, long. 79° 34′. The elevation of its source is probably considerable, being in the Central Himalaya, and near Pin Nath, a summit 7,111 feet above the sea. Receiving numerous small feeders right and left, it holds a southerly course for about thirty miles, as far as lat. 29° 33′, long. 79° 39′, where it receives, on the left side, the Sooal, a stream of nearly equal size. It passes from the mountains by a gorge of extraordinarily picturesque beauty and grandeur, and with a course so tortuous, that Heber pursuing his way down it, was obliged to ford the stream twelve times in the course of a day's journey. The stream in the beginning of December, the season of low water, was as high as the middle of the saddle, and very rapid. After a total course of between 140 and 150 miles, it falls into the Western Ramgunga in lat. 28° 41′, long. 79° 1′.

KOSLEE.—A town in the native state of Jhujhur, 50 miles W.S.W. from Delhi, and 57 miles S.E. by S. from Hansee. Lat. 28° 23′, long. 76° 33′.

KOSOOMEE.—A town of the Deccan, in the territory of Nagpoor, 11 miles N.W. from Jeypoor, and 104 miles N.W. from Vizianagrum. Lat. 19° 10′, long. 82° 20′.

KOSY, in the British district of Muttra, a town on the route from Muttra to Ferozpoor, in the district of Goorgaon, and 29 miles N.W. of the former. It has a good bazar, and is abundantly supplied with water. In October, A.D. 1804, it was for a night occupied by the Mahratta chief Holkar, in his precipitate retreat from the British army under General Lake, who, having forced the enemy to continue his flight, took the town. The road in this part of the route is rather good, the country open. Lat. 27° 48′, long. 77° 29′.

KOT, in the Punjab, 10 miles E. of the Indus, is a small and poor town. It contains one spacious and fine house, belonging to a fakir, or religious mendicant. This holy man was the pauper of thirty different villages, the inhabitants of which prided themselves on their benevolence in maintaining their mendicant in such state. Von Hügel met him clothed in silk, and borne in a palanquin. Kot (the fort) is in lat. 33° 59′, long. 72° 48′.

KOTAGERI, or KOTERGHERRY.—One of the minor sanitary stations on the Neilgherry hills, in the district of Malabar, presidency of Madras, situate 6,000 feet above the level of the sea. This station is well protected from the violence of the south-west monsoon by the Dodabetta range, which stands out like a huge wall, to screen it. The annual fall of rain averages fifty inches. Lat. 11° 27′, long. 77°.

KOTAGHEER.—A town in Hyderabad, or dominions of the Nizam, situate five miles E. from the right bank of the Manjera river, and 96 miles N.N.W. from Hyderabad. Lat. 18° 34′, long. 77° 52′.

KOTAGOODEM.—A town in Hyderabad, or dominions of the Nizam, situate on the right bank of the Godavery, and 160 miles E.N.E. from Hyderabad. Lat. 18°, long. 80° 52′.

KOTAH.—A town of Baghelcund or Rewah, situate 51 miles S.S.E. from Rewah, and 44 miles N.N.E. from Sohagpoor. Lat. 23° 51′, long. 81° 45′.

KOTAH, a raj or state of Rajpootana,

named from its principal place. It is bounded on the north-east and east by the newly-formed state of Jhallowa, the territory of Gwalior, and Chupra, a small isolated possession of the noted Patan freebooter Ameer Khan; on the north-west by the Chumbûl, dividing it from the state of Bhoondee; on the west by a detached portion of Gwalior; and on the south by a detached portion of Holcar's territory and Jhallowa. The raj of Kotah lies between lat. 24° 30′—25° 50′, long. 75° 35′—76° 56′; is about ninety miles in length from north to south, and eighty in breadth. The area of the raj, as at present constituted, may be estimated at 4,339 square miles. Its surface slopes gently northward from the high table-land of Malwa, and is drained by the Chumbul and its tributaries, the Kalee Sindh, the Newaj, the Parbaty, and some other streams of less magnitude, all of which take a northerly or north-easterly direction. A range of hills, of moderate height, running from south-east to north-west, formerly bisecting the Kotah territory, now forms the boundary between it and part of Jhallowa. This range is considered to form the boundary between Malwa and Harowtee; and the route through the Mokundurra Pass is the great outlet between the Deccan and Northern India. Though in general a fertile and highly-cultivated country, the climate of Kotah has little to recommend it, being sultry in the extreme during the prevalence of the hot winds at the commencement of summer, and exceedingly unhealthy during the periodical rains. The population of this raj, estimated at the rate adopted generally for Rajpootana (100 to the square mile), would be 433,900.

The raj of Kotah, which, with Bhoondee, forms the district denominated Harowtee, was formerly a fief of Bhoondee. During the reign of Rao Ratan, chief of the territory last named, Kotah was severed from Bhoondee and given to Madhu Singh, the second son of Rao Ratan, by the emperor Shah Jahan, in reward of his valour and conduct at the battle of Burhanpore. Mindful of the favour conferred upon their father, the five sons of Madhu Singh supported their benefactor's cause against his son Aurungzebe, and in the battle of Oojein, where the latter was victorious, four of the brothers were slain, and the survivor left on the field for dead. After the death of Aurungzebe, Ram Singh, then rao or rajah of Kotah, supported the cause of the younger son, Azim, against the elder, Moazzim, and was slain in the battle of Jajau, in which the former prince was defeated, and lost his life. Bhim Singh, son and successor of Ram Singh, rose high in favour with the sovereign of Delhi, and fell in his service, being slain in battle against Nizam-ul-Mulk, who, having revolted against his lord, was intercepted in his march to the Deccan by the Rajpoot rajah. The Mahrattas, confederated with the Jats and the rajah of Jeypore, invaded the territory of Kotah in 1744, and invested the city; but, after a siege of three months, were compelled to retreat with loss. Somewhat later, the internal history of the Kotah state became truly extraordinary. About the year 1771, on the death of a rajah named Goman Singh, the entire powers of the government passed into the hands of a chieftain named Zalim Singh, in the character of regent, the departed rajah having nominated him to this office during the minority of the heir, Omed Singh, then only ten years of age. Zalim Singh, who was originally the hereditary foujdar or commander-in-chief of Kotah, exercised his new powers with extraordinary ability. He established and maintained a commanding ascendancy over all the states of Rajpootana; and, whether from indolence or a distrust of himself, Omed Singh, after the termination of his minority, continued in the hands of Zalim Singh the entire and uncontrolled administration of the country, retaining only the outward pomp and show of sovereignty, which, with the most scrupulous attention and subserviency, were conceded to him by the possessor of the actual power. In 1804, the advance and retreat of the force under Colonel Monson afforded Zalim Singh an opportunity for showing to the British two different aspects of his policy, as modified by circumstances. On the advance of Colonel Monson, he received him with cordiality, and readily afforded supplies and assistance; on the disastrous retreat of that unfortunate commander, Zalim Singh shut his gates against him, influenced by a fear of Holkar, whom, however, this negative manifestation of hostility to the British cause was insufficient to propitiate, the incensed chief exacting 10,00,000 rupees (100,000*l.*) from the government of Kotah, as a penalty for the friendly services rendered the English. In 1817, a treaty was concluded between the British government and the state of Kotah, which, besides the usual stipulations for friendship on both sides, protection on the part of the superior, and subordinate co-operation on that of the dependent state, the freedom of the latter in its internal affairs, and its renunciation of all external relations except with the British, provides that the tribute previously paid by the Kotah state to the Mahratta chiefs shall thenceforward be paid to the British government. This treaty was of course contracted in the name of the reigning prince Omed Singh; but the administration had then been for nearly half a century in the hands of Zalim Singh, and the ostensible ruler took no apparent interest in public affairs. A supplemental article, annexed about two months after the conclusion of the treaty, confirmed the succession to the principality to Keshour Singh, the son and heir-apparent of Omed Singh, and his heirs, in regular succession and perpetuity; but vested the entire administration of affairs in Zalim Singh, by whom it had been so long exercised, and after him, in his eldest son, Madhoo Singh, and his heirs, in like regular succession, in perpetuity. It was thus proposed to perpetuate the extraordinary state of things which had accidentally arisen out of the commanding talents of one man and the supine indifference of another; an experiment little likely to be attended with success. The results which might have been anticipated, followed. The rajah, Omed Singh, died in 1819, and the dissatisfaction of his successor, Keshour Singh, soon became apparent. In December, 1820, the prince left Kotah, and entered into an extensive series of intrigues, directed towards the recovery of the alienated powers of sovereignty. It is the ordinary fate of native princes to trust to agents whose only object is personal advantage; and the wandering rajah of Kotah fell into the hands of one of this class, whom he deputed to Calcutta, and who, by collusion with the principal native servants in the political secretary's office, was enabled to persuade his master that his mission was in a fair train, and that government were well disposed towards him. At Delhi, the intrigues set on foot were more successful. The treasurer of the residency was enlisted in the cause of the disaffected rajah, and by the aid of that functionary large sums of money were raised. Keshour Singh was thus enabled to proceed, with 2,000 followers, towards Rajpootana, where he caused reports to be disseminated to the effect that the measures of the local agent were disapproved by the British government, and that the expatriated rajah had their approval and support. Public feeling was strongly with him, and Keshour Singh soon found himself at the head of 6,000 men. With this force he advanced into Kotah, and on the 30th September, 1821, ventured to risk a contest with a body of British troops which had been marched thither to support the existing state of rule. The event was destructive of the rajah's hopes; he was defeated, his brother killed, and his adherents dispersed. The rajah found shelter in the sanctuary of Nathdwara, in Joudpore; whence, in the December subsequent to the battle, he returned to Kotah, and was again installed in the pageant sovereignty from which he had fled. A fixed allowance was made for his personal expenses and the support of his dignity, and an instrument executed, by which the perpetual administration of Zalim Singh and his heirs was again recognised. In 1824 Zalim Singh died. His son, Madhoo Singh, seems to have inherited no portion of the abilities of his father; and the incongruity of a titular prince and a servant invested with sovereign power was now rendered more glaring, by the fact that the latter was an incompetent administrator. To get rid of a system so anomalous, unpopular, and inconvenient, it was proposed by the British government that Madhoo Singh should resign his pretensions to the administration, and receive in compensation a part of the territory, to be formed into a new principality, and held by him independent of Keshour Singh and his heirs. From this proposal, however, Madhoo Singh recoiled, declaring that he should be infamous throughout Rajpootana, if he consented to dismember the territories of his master. The proposal, therefore, at that time, fell to the ground; but the inconveniences of the existing system continued to manifest themselves so strongly, that the necessity of recurring to it at some time appears to have been constantly before the eyes of government. A few years removed from life both the titular and the actual ruler of Kotah; the former being succeeded by a nephew, whom he had adopted, and the latter by a son. The proposal was now revived, and the difficulties in the way of carrying it out surmounted. The more southern part of the Kotah territory, with a small detached portion on the eastern side, were assigned to the descendant of Zalim Singh, as a separate principality, in supersession of his claim to the administration of the whole country; the remaining portion being thus left to the representative of the ancient rajahs of Kotah, who retains the title of his ancestors, with the larger share of their possessions. The chief of the new state is called rana of Jhallowa. The territory assigned to him was estimated to yield a revenue of twelve lacs; that retained by the rajah of Kotah, twenty lacs. The latter seems to have improved under the change, as, a few years subsequent to the separation, the revenue was estimated at twenty-five lacs, and it is now reported to amount to twenty-eight lacs. An arrangement was made for the assignment of three lacs of rupees annually from Kotah, for the formation of a contingent force, under British officers; but, in 1844, the demand was reduced to two lacs. The charge rather exceeds this sum. The strength of the force in 1846 was 283 cavalry, 66 artillery, and 799 infantry; total, 1,148. The native force consists of about 3,450 men of every description, and 2,000 sebundies for police purposes. Suttee has recently been prohibited in this state. There is a British political agent for Kotah or Harowtee.

KOTAH, in the Rajpoot tract denominated Harowtee, a town, the principal place of a raj or state of the same name, is situate on the right bank of the river Chumbul (here crossed by a ferry), and on the route from Nusserabad to Saugor. East of the town is an extensive tank, on the bank of which is a well-wooded pleasure-ground. The city is inclosed by a strong rampart, with bastions and dry ditch. On the side towards the river, the rampart runs parallel to the bank, and at no great distance from it. At its southern extremity, placed within a fortress, and separated from the town, is the palace, embellished with numerous cupolas and slender minarets. The terminating bastion to the north is a little fort of itself, and commands the surrounding country on both banks. In the Chumbul, abreast of the town, is an islet, containing the summer residence of the rajah, built in a florid style of architecture. The town is of considerable size, and contains many Hindoo temples and some mosques. It is a thriving and rather wealthy place, having considerable traffic both in the transit-trade and for supplying the home markets with manufactures. The climate is extremely sultry during the prevalence of the hot winds in the beginning of summer, and very unhealthy during the periodical rains, when the air and water are equally deleterious. Distant N. from Oojein 140 miles, S.W. from Agra 195, S. from Delhi 260. Lat. 25° 10′, long. 75° 52′.

KOTAKA-SERAE, in the territory of Gwalior, or possessions of Scindia, a town on the route from the fort of Gwalior to Saugor, 10 miles S.E. of former, 191 N.W. of the latter. It is situate on the small river Oomrar. Lat. 26° 9′, long. 78° 11′.

KOTANUH, in the British district of Meerut, lieut.-gov. of the N.W. Provinces, a town on the route from Meerut to Jheend, 33 miles W. by N. of the former. Kotanuh has a population of 6,684 inhabitants. Lat. 29° 6′, long. 77° 15′.

KOTAOOR.—A town in the British district of Tinnevelly, presidency of Madras, 54 miles N.N.E. of Tinnevelly. Lat. 9° 26′, long. 78° 3′.

KOTAR.—A town in the native state of Travancore, 40 miles S.E. by E. from Trivandrum, and 44 miles S.S.W. from Tinnevelly. Lat. 8° 9′, long. 77° 27′.

KOTARGO, in Sinde, a village on the route from Hyderabad to Sehwan, by the way of Kotree, and eight miles S.E. of Sehwan. It is situate near the right bank of the Indus, and close to the southern extremity of the pass formed by the approach of the Lukkee Mountains to the river. Kotargo is in lat. 26° 16′, long. 67° 57′.

KOTARY.—A town in Hyderabad, or dominions of the Nizam, 170 miles N. by W. from Hyderabad, and 106 miles S. from Ellichpoor. Lat. 19° 40′, long. 77° 45′.

KOTAY PEAK.—A mountain in the Western Ghats, at the junction of the boundaries of the British districts Madura and Tinnevelly and the native state of Travancore. Lat. 9° 33′, long. 77° 29′.

KOTAYEM, in the British district of Malabar, a town situate five miles from the seacoast. Distance from Calicut, N.W., 42 miles; Cananore, S.E., 12. Lat. 11° 50′, long. 75° 36′.

KOTBUND, or KOTWUN, in the British district of Muttra, lieut.-gov. of the N.W. Provinces, a village with a fort on the route from the cantonment of Muttra to Delhi, and 32 miles N.W. of the former. The road in this part of the route is good. Lat. 27° 50′, long. 77° 28′.

KOTDWAR, in the British district of Bijnour, lieut.-gov. of the N.W. Provinces, a village at the southern entrance of the gorge in the Sewalik range, where the small river Koh flows southwards from the mountains to the plain of Hindoostan. It is a remarkable locality, as gold is found there in the sands of the Koh, and in that of most of the streams to the westward, as far as Hurdwar, a distance of nearly thirty miles, and, as Herbert observes, "the fact furnishes proof of the actual occurrence of gold in some part of the strata which these rivers traverse;" and the weighty opinion of Prinsep (James) is, that extensive veins of the metal are in that vicinity. Lat. 29° 43′, long. 78° 33′.

KOTE, in the British district of Ahmedabad, presidency of Bombay, a town on the route from the city of Ahmedabad to Rajkot, 32 miles S.W. of former, 90 E. of latter. Lat. 22° 38′, long. 72° 16′.

KOTE, in the Sinde Sagur Dooab division of the Punjab, a town situated on the right bank of the Chenaub, 13 miles N. of the town of Mooltan. Lat. 30° 20′, long. 71° 31′.

KOTEE, in Bundelcund, a town, the principal place of the jaghire or feudal grant of the same name, on the route from Banda to Rewa, 66 miles S.E. of the former, 46 N.W. of the latter. The jaghire is held by an hereditary Bundela chief, to whom it was confirmed by the British government in 1810, after its acquisition of Bundelcund. The sunnud, or instrument of grant, enumerates eighty-two villages, with the lands annexed to them. Lal Madhoo Singh, the late chief, died in 1852, and was succeeded by his brother Lal Abdoot Singh. Kotee is in lat. 24° 45′, long. 80° 49′.

KOTEKUTCHWAH, in Sirhind, a village on the route from Kurnal to Loodiana, and 45 miles N.W. of the former place. Distant N.W. from Calcutta 1,010 miles. Lat. 30° 17′, long. 76° 53′.

KOTELI.—A town in the dominions of Gholab Singh, the ruler of Cashmere, situate on the right bank of the Jhelum, and 140 miles E. from Peshawur. Lat. 34° 7′, long. 74° 1′.

KOTE ODOO, in the Sinde Sagur Dooab division of the Punjab, a town situated nine miles from the left bank of the Indus, 36 miles N.W. of the town of Mooltan. Lat. 30° 28′, long. 71° 4′.

KOTESALBAHAN, in the British district of Budaoon, lieut.-gov. of the N.W. Provinces, a town on the route from Budaoon to Moradabad, 21 miles N.W. of the former. Lat. 28° 15′, long. 78° 58′.

KOTE SOOLTAN, in the Sinde Sagur Dooab division of the Punjab, a town situated on the left bank of the Indus, 55 miles N.W. by N. of the town of Mooltan. Lat. 30° 47′, long. 70° 58′.

KOTEWA.—A town in the British district of Sarun, lieut.-gov. of Bengal, 52 miles N. of Chupra. Lat. 26° 29′, long. 84° 55′.

KOTGURH, a small hill state, bounded on the north by the river Sutlej; on the east by

Bussahir; on the south by the British district of Kothkaee; and on the west by Komharsin. It is seven miles long, about five broad, and contains an area of thirty square miles. Its centre is in lat. 31° 19′, long. 77° 38′. Kotgurh was one of the petty states formerly recognised under the general appellation of the Baru Thakooraee, or Twelve Lordships, occupying the tract between the Sutlej and the Tonse. It would appear to have formerly acknowledged a degree of dependence on the state of Bussahir, but by the terms of the sunnud dated the 6th November, 1815, granting that province to the reigning family after its conquest by the British, the petty chiefs of Kotgurh were declared independent of all but the paramount authority of the British government.

The cantonment for British troops is in the pergunnah or division of Sundoch, and is situate on the brow of the eastern side of a ravine nearly 4,000 feet deep. To the north-west, the surface rapidly sinks to the depth of 4,000 feet to the left bank of the Sutluj, distant about four miles. Lloyd mentions a striking instance of the effect produced on the temperature by this sudden depression of the surface:—"The effect of aspect and elevation upon the cultivation is very remarkable; for while on the uplands the produce is green, it has been reaped and carried at the base of the valley. Indeed, this is extraordinarily exemplified in two gardens which Captain P. Gerard had at Koteghur, one of which is near the house where he resided, and the other in the dell, 4,000 feet below. In the lower one, plantains and other tropical fruits are abundant, while in the upper English fruits are equally plentiful." The climate of this cantonment is pleasant and salubrious. Frost sets in about the middle of October, and continues till March; and during December, January, and February, snow falls, and lies in shaded places to the depth of two or three feet. The winters, however, are by no means intolerable, being said to resemble those of Europe, but to be less severe. During April, May, and June, the climate is agreeable within-doors, and woollen clothing is comfortable; but in places exposed to the direct rays of the sun, they are found very powerful. The pergunnah in which the cantonment is situate was retained by the British government as a military station, after the conclusion of the Goorkha war in 1815. Elevation above the sea 6,634 feet. Distance N.W. from Calcutta, by Kurnal and Subathoo, 1,120 miles. Lat. 31° 15′, long. 77° 34′.

KOTHAR, a small hill state under the superintendence of the Governor-General's agent for the Cis-Sutlej territories, is bounded on the east by Subathoo, and on the remaining sides by the states of Mhilog and Beja. It is about five miles long and three broad: its centre is in lat. 30° 57′, long. 77° 1′: it comprises six pergunnahs. The population is estimated at 4,000, and the annual revenue at 700*l.*; out of which is paid a tribute to the British government of 108*l.* Kothar belongs to a Hindoo raun, who received it from the British government on the expulsion of the Goorkhas in 1815.

KOTHEE, a small hill state, bounded on the north by Bhugee; on the east by Mudhan; on the south by Simla and Keyonthul, and on the west by a portion of the territory of the rajah of Pateeala. Its centre is in lat. 31° 8′, long. 77° 16′. The area of the state is thirty-five miles. It consists entirely of a few ridges of considerable elevation, with intervening valleys. The drainage is northward, to the Sutlej, by the stream termed the Nowla Gad. It is divided into five pergunnahs, is estimated to have a population of 3,000, and an annual revenue of 400*l.* This petty chieftainship is tributary to the state of Keyonthul.

KOTHKHAEE, between the Sutlej and the Touso, one of the hill states in that quarter, and formerly a native possession, is bounded on the north by Bussahir and the British pergunnah of Sundoch; on the east by Bussahir and Turroch; on the south by Poondur; and on the west by Bulsun and Kambarsin. It is about twelve miles from north to south, and six from east to west: its centre is in lat. 31° 7′, long. 77° 37′. It forms the eastern part of a considerable valley, communicating with others of less size, penetrating the great range of mountains extending from Wartu on the north, to the Chur on the south. On the west side of this range, the Giree and its feeders in the upper part of its course have their origin. On its eastern side, it throws off several large feeders to the Sutlej, the Pabar, and the Tons. It is generally composed of gneiss and red and white quartz. The south side of the valley is deeply wooded, and in the highest degree romantic and picturesque, being enlivened by the Giree, which, rising here, pursues its noisy course among huge masses of fallen rocks and precipices, variegated with profuse vegetation. Kothkhaee, on the Giree, was formerly the residence of the rana, or Hindoo chief, placed over this territory by the British government; but the atrocious cruelty and tyranny consequent on the misgovernment of the second prince, rendered it necessary, in 1828, to dethrone him, and to annex the territory to the British possessions. An annual allowance of 130*l.* is made to the degraded chief, and one of 70*l.* to his relatives; and after these deductions, a revenue of 355*l.* is received by the East-India Company.

KOTHKHAEE, in the British hill state of the same name, the principal place of the district, and the residence of the rana previously to his deposition by the British government in 1828. This village has a picturesque site on the right bank of the Giree, and contains two remarkable masses of buildings; one, the residence of the family of the deposed sovereign, the other, of a principal zemindar or landowner; each being situate on a lofty promontory or rock, just affording sufficient area for the houses and offices. Here, also, is a bungalow or stage-house, belonging to the British government. Elevation above the sea 5,515 feet. This little town is thus described by Gerard, who visited it in 1818:—"It is situate on a most romantic spot, upon the point below which two streams unite to form the Giree. On one side, the rock is 182 feet perpendicular, and on the other there is a long flight of stone steps: neither of the streams, which are only twenty feet broad, are fordable; so, by destroying the bridges, the place might be well defended against musketry. The rana's residence is "three stories high, and has a most imposing appearance: each story projects beyond the one beneath, and the top is crowned by a couple of handsome Chinese turrets, beautifully adorned with finely-carved wooden work." Lat. 31° 7′, long. 77° 36′.

KOTI, in Bussahir, a village on a feeder of the Pabur, and about six miles from the left bank of that river. It is situate on an eminence rising in the midst of a dell, opening into the valley of the Pabur. The sanga or wooden bridge over the torrent flowing by the village has an elevation of 5,910 feet above the sea. Lat. 31° 5′, long. 77° 56′.

KOTIUM.—A town in the native state of Travancore, 82 miles N. by W. from Trivandrum, and 103 miles S.S.W. from Coimbatoor. Lat. 9° 35′, long. 76° 35′.

KOT KANGRA.—See KANGRA.

KOT KASSIM, in the British district of the same name, lieut.-gov. of the N.W. Provinces, a town situate on the route, by Rewaree, from Alwar to Delhi, and 69 miles S.W. of the latter. Lat. 28°, long. 76° 48′.

The territory of which this town is the principal place forms one of the non-regulation districts, subject to the superintendence of the lieut.-gov. of the N.W. Provinces. It extends from lat. 27° 59′ to 28° 7′, and from long. 76° 41′ to 76° 55′, and contains an area of seventy square miles. The population is returned at 13,767, of whom 11,719 are Hindoos.

KOTKIPAR.—A town of the Deccan, in the territory of Nagpoor or Berar, situate 141 miles E.N.E. from Nagpoor, and 118 S.E. from Jubbulpoor. Lat. 21° 51′, long. 81° 12′.

KOT KUMALIA, in the Punjab, a small town six or seven miles from the right or west bank of the Ravee. It has an appearance of antiquity, and is built of burnt bricks. There is a fortress, constructed of the same materials, and a bazar. Masson supposes "that Kamalia may have been the fortress at which the great Macedonian hero had nearly become the victim of his temerity." Arrian distinctly states that Alexander was marching through the Doab, or peninsula between the Chenaub or Acesines, and the Ravee or Hydraotes; that he crossed the Hydraotes in pursuit of some Indians who had fled over it; that he again crossed (recrossed) the same river in pursuit of the fugitives, and there attacked this unnamed city, in the storming of the citadel of which he received his wound. This certainly very exactly designates the country in which Kumalia is situated, and affords countenance to Masson's opinion, though he states that he had nothing to rely on but his memory. Still there is no sufficient evidence to fix this very town as the actual scene of the event. Kumalia is in lat. 30° 46′, long. 72° 43′.

KOTKUPPOORA, in Sirhind, a town situate 42 miles from the left bank of the Sutlej. It lies on the route, by Munuk, from Delhi to Ferozpoor, and 40 miles S.E. of the last-mentioned place. There is a small fort at the north of the town. It was comprised in the possessions which the maharaja of the Punjab held on the left of the Sutlej, but is now incorporated with the British district of Ferozepore. Distant N.W. from Calcutta, by Delhi and Munuk, 1,130 miles. Lat. 30° 36′, long. 74° 51′.

KOTLA, in the Baree Dooab division of the Punjab, a town situated on the right bank of one of the branches of the Beas, 124 miles E.N.E. of the town of Lahore. Lat. 32° 13′, long. 76° 4′.

KOTLA, in the British district of Agra, lieut.-gov. of the N.W. Provinces, a town on the route from Agra to Furruckabad, 28 miles E. by N. of the formor. Lat. 27° 17′, long. 78° 32′.

KOTLI, in the dominions of Gholab Singh, the ruler of Cashmere, a small town among the mountains south of Cashmere, and on the route from Lahore to Cashmere, by the town of Punch. It contains 150 houses, and is the post for levying the duties on goods introduced into Cashmere through the Punch Pass. Lat. 33° 28′, long. 73° 59′.

KOTNUR, in Gurhwal, a village on the left bank of the Jumna, is situate at the confluence of a torrent with that river, and about 150 feet above the water. The houses, rudely built of blocks of stone, and covered with slabs of coarse slate, are situate on a small fertile expanse, gently sloping to the foot of a mountain. Altogether the village and its environs have a neat, clean, lively appearance. Lat. 30° 51′, long. 78° 22′.

KOT POOTELEE, in the Toorawuttee dependency of the Rajpoot state of Jeypore, a district so called from kot, or fort, and the adjacent village of Pootlee. The village, with the fort, is on the route from Delhi to Mhow cantonment, and 99 miles S.W. of the former. The fort was an important place at the close of the last century, and was held by the Mahrattas, before their expulsion from this region by Lord Lake, who, on that event, granted it to the Shekhawuttee rajah of Keytri. Lat. 27° 43′, long. 76° 16′.

KOTREE, in Sinde, a village on the right bank of the Indus, nearly opposite Hyderabad, from which it is distant four miles S.W. It is important in a military point of view, as here is the junction of the routes from Kurrachee, from the Delta, and from Sehwan to Hyderabad. It consequently commands, in a great measure, the southern part of Sinde west of the Indus. Here, in the beginning of 1839, was encamped the Bombay division of the British army advancing towards Afghanistan. Kotree is in lat. 25° 22′, long. 68° 23′.

KOTREE.—A town of Sinde, in the British district of Hydrabad, presidency of Bombay, 106 miles S. by E. of Hydrabad. Lat. 23° 54′, long. 68° 46′.

KOTTAUM.—A town in the British district of Rajahmundry, presidency of Madras, 36 miles N.E. by N. of Samulkottah. Lat. 17° 29′, long. 82° 30′.

KOTTOOPAUDEE. — A town of the Deccan, in the territory of Nagpoor or Berar, situate 19 miles N.W. from Jeypoor, in the hill zemindarry of that name, and 112 miles N.W. from Vizianagrum. Lat. 19° 15′, long. 82° 16′.

KOTTOOR.—A town in the hill zemindarry of Jeypoor, on the south-west frontier of Bengal, 123 miles S.W. from Jeypoor, and 94 miles N. by E. from Masulipatam. Lat. 17° 29′, long. 81° 30′.

KOTTOROH, in the Rajpoot state of Jodhpoor, a small town on the route from Pokhurn to Balmer, and 28 miles N. of the latter place. Lat. 26° 7′, long. 71° 11′.

KOTUH, in the British district of Boolundshuhur, lieut.-gov. of the N.W. Provinces, a town situate five miles from the right bank of the East Kalee Nuddee, and 34 miles E. of Delhi. Lat. 28° 32′, long. 77° 50′.

KOTULUH, in the British district of Goorgaon, lieut.-gov. of the N.W. Provinces, a village on the western shore of an extensive fresh-water jhil or lake. Distance S.W. from Delhi 48 miles. Lat. 28° 1′, long. 77°.

KOTYANA.—A town in Guzerat, or the dominions of the Guicowar, situate on the right of the Bhader river, and 67 miles S.W. from Rajkote. Lat. 21° 39′, long. 70° 8′.

KOULSERA, in the British district of Boolundshuhur, lieut.-gov. of the N.W. Provinces, a village on the route from the cantonment of Allyghur to that of Delhi, and 18 miles S.E. of the latter, is situate near the left bank of the Hindon. Lat. 28° 32′, long. 77° 29′.

KOUNG-GOOAH.—A town in the British province of Pegue, situate on the left bank of the Irrawady river, and nine miles N. from Prome. Lat. 18° 52′, long. 95°.

KOWAUN, in the Reechna Dooab division of the Punjab, a town situated on the left bank of the Chenaub, 76 miles N.E. by N. of the town of Mooltan. Lat. 30° 59′, long. 72° 14′.

KOWLAS.—A town in the native state of Indore, or territory of Holkar, situate 10 miles from the right bank of the Nerbudda river, and 89 miles N.W. from Baitool. Lat. 22° 31′, long. 76° 49′.

KOWLASS, in Hyderabad, or territory of the Nizam, a town on the route from Hyderabad to Nandair, 85 miles N.W. of former, 65 S.E. of latter, close to a remarkable hill of granite traversed by a great vein of basalt. Lat. 18° 20′, long. 77° 45′.

KOWPOOM.—A town of Eastern India, in the native state of Muneepoor, 30 miles W.S.W. from Muneepoor, and 112 miles E. by S. from Silhet. Lat. 24° 40′, long. 93° 36′.

KOWRAH.—A town in the native state of Cutch, situate in the Great Western Runn, and 44 miles N. by E. from Bhooj. Lat. 23° 50′, long. 69° 50′.

KOWREEA, in the British district of Azimgurh, lieut.-gov. of the N.W. Provinces, a town on the route from Azimgurh to Oude, 17 miles N.W. by N. of the former. Lat. 26° 13′, long. 83° 7′.

KOWRIA.—A town of Baghelcund, in the native state of Rewah, situate on the right bank of a branch of the Sone, and 80 miles S.W. by S. from Rewah. Lat. 23° 32′, long. 80° 42′.

KOWRI ALI SINGH KE, in Sirhind, a village on the route from Hansee to Loodiana, and 65 miles N. of the former town. Distant N.W. from Calcutta 1,041 miles. Lat. 29° 59′, long. 75° 59′.

KOWROUKIRE, in Arracan, a halting-place on the Aeng route, between Natyagain and Aeng. A fine stream issues from the hills close to it. Lat. 20°, long. 94° 14′.

KOWTA.—A town in the Southern Mahratta jaghire of Sanglee, situate 84 miles N.N.E. from Belgaum, and 72 miles S.E. from Sattara. Lat. 17°, long. 74° 55′.

KOWTALL.—A town in the British district of Bellary, presidency of Madras, 48 miles N.N.E. of Bellary. Lat. 15° 47′, long. 77° 11′.

KOYANDOWNG, the name of a hill in the island of Ramree (Arracan), and in the neighbourhood of the town of Ramree. It has two temples on its summit. It is sometimes called St. George's Hill.

KOYER.—A town in Hyderabad, or dominions of the Nizam, situate on the left bank of the Naringa river, and 55 miles W.N.W. from Hyderabad. Lat. 17° 38′, long. 77° 46′.

KOYLATH, in the Rajpoot state of Beekaneer, a village on the route from the town of Beekaneer to that of Jessulmeer, and 29 miles S.W. of the former. Here is a very large and well-filled tank, where is held every October, at the full moon, a mela or fair, much frequented by the superstitious Hindoos, who attribute high expiatory and sanctifying powers to ablution in the water. Koylath is in lat 27° 48′, long. 73° 1′.

KOYUL.—A town in the dominions of Gholab Singh, the ruler of Cashmere, situate

186 miles E.N.E. from Kangra, and 173 miles N.E. from Simla. Lat. 32° 54′, long. 79° 17′.

KRISHNA.—See KISTNAH RIVER.

KROL, in the hill state of Keyonthul, a peak of the lower and more southerly part of the Himalaya, 12 miles E. of Subathoo. According to Jacquemont, it is formed of schistus and greywacke, having at the summit a saccharoid white magnesian limestone, which yields the lime employed in the buildings at Simla. Elevation above the sea 7,612 feet. Lat. 30° 56′, long. 77° 10′.

KUARA, or POOJALEE, in Bussahir, a village on the route from Musooree to the Gunas Pass, and 15 miles S. of the latter place. It is situate amidst mountains of great height, near the left bank of the Roopin, a deep and rapid river, crossed below the town by a wooden bridge thirty-five feet in length, and above it by one of forty-four. This place is described by Herbert as "a substantial village of about forty houses." The elevation is nearly the same as that of Dudu, situate on the opposite side of the river, 8,790 feet above the sea. Lat. 31° 12′, long. 78° 10′.

KUBARA, in the British district of Allahabad, lieut.-gov. of the N.W. Provinces, a village on the right bank of the Ganges, 11 miles below the city of Allahabad by way of the river. Lat. 25° 20′, long. 82° 2′.

KUBRAEE, in the British territory of Jaloun, in Bundelcund, lieut.-gov. of the N.W. Provinces, a small town on the route from Banda to Saugor, 24 miles S.W. of the former. It has a bazar. Lat. 25° 25′, long. 80° 5′.

KUCHAREEHAUT.—A town of Assam, in the British district of Seebpoor, 50 miles S.W. of Seebpoor. Lat. 26° 31′, long. 94° 3′.

KUCHLA GHAT, in the British district of Budaon, lieut.-gov. of the N.W. Provinces, a ferry over the Ganges, on the route from Agra to Bareilly, and 83 miles N.E. of the former. The channel of the Ganges is uncertain here, the stream being sometimes single and at other times divided into two or more branches. Lat. 27° 56′, long. 78° 56′.

KUCHNAR, in the British district of Moradabad, lieut.-gov. of the N.W. Provinces, a village on the route from the town of Moradabad to Almora, and 15 miles N. of the former. Elevation above the sea 741 feet. Lat. 29° 1′, long. 78° 55′.

KUCHOUNA.—A town in the territory of Oude, 40 miles W.N.W. from Lucknow, and 47 miles N. by E. from Cawnpoor. Lat. 27° 9′, long. 80° 26′.

KUCHRAWUD.—A town of Malwa, in the British district of Mundlaisur, 148 miles W. by N. of Baitool. Lat. 22° 6′, long. 75° 41′.

KUCHRIE, in the Rajpoot state of Jessulmer, a halting-place on the route from Roree, in Sindh, to the town of Jessulmer, from which it is distant 30 miles in a N.W. direction. There are thirteen wells lined with stone, and a tank containing good water. The road in this part of the route is good. Lat. 27°, long. 70° 44′.

KUCHROWLI, in the British district of Paneeput, lieut.-gov. of the N.W. Provinces, a village on the route from the city of Delhi to Kurnal, and 18 miles S.E. of the latter. The road in this part of the route is good. Lat. 29° 27′, long. 77° 1′.

KUCHUHWA, or KUTCHWA, in the British district of Mirzapoor, lieut.-gov. of the N.W. Provinces, a town with a bazar on the left bank of the Ganges, 705 miles by water N.W. of Calcutta, or 882 taking the Sunderbund passage; 35 S.W. of the city of Benares, or higher up the stream. It is on the direct route by land from Benares cantonment to that of Mirzapoor, 19 miles S.W. of the former, eight N.E. of the latter. Lat. 25° 12′, long. 82° 46′.

KUCKRUMPILLE.—A town in Hyderabad, or dominions of the Nizam, situate 20 miles S.E. from the right bank of the Godavery river, and 96 miles N. from Hyderabad. Lat. 18° 43′, long. 78° 20′.

KUDDERPOOR.—A town in the British district of Ahmedabad, presidency of Bombay, 111 miles S. by W. of Ahmedabad. Lat. 21° 29′, long. 72° 12′.

KUDDI.—A petty jaghire in Bundelcund, containing an area of twenty-two square miles, with a population of about 2,800. Upon the demise, in 1850, of Purseram Bahadoor, the original grantee, the territory lapsed, under the conditions of the grant, to the British government. Kuddi, the principal place, is situate in lat. 25° 20′, long. 80° 12′.

KUDDUN.—A town of Sinde, in the British district of Hydrabad, presidency of Bombay, 73 miles S.E. by S. of Hydrabad. Lat. 24° 29′, long. 69° 3′.

KUDJOOA.—See KUJWA.

KUDKA.—A town in Hyderabad, or dominions of the Nizam, situate on the right bank of one of the branches of the Manjera river, and 106 miles N.W. from Hyderabad. Lat. 18° 28′, long. 77° 25′.

KUDSEH.—A town of Eastern India, in the native state of Muneepoor, 37 miles N.N.W. from Muneepoor, and 104 miles S.E. from Nowgong. Lat. 25° 17′, long. 93° 52′.

KUGGUTNAAD.—A town in the British district of Coorg, presidency of Madras, 25 miles S.S.E. of Merkara. Lat. 12° 7′, long. 75° 59′.

KUGNALI, or SACRIFICE ROCK.—A small steep rocky island, lying six miles off the coast of the British district of Malabar. It has been called Sacrifice Rock, "from the crew of an English ship having been massacred there by pirates, at the beginning of the seventeenth century: it is famous for edible birdsnests, found in the clefts in the rocks." Lat. 11° 30′, long. 75° 35′.

KUHLOOR, a small hill state or raj amidst

the Sub-Himalaya, is bounded on the north by the Sutlej, separating it from the Upper Punjab; on the east by the petty states of Mangul and Bhagul; on the south by that of Hindoor; and on the west by a strip of the Sirhind territory. The rajah was deprived by Runjeet Singh of that part of his territory lying on the right side of the Sutlej; and the state at present consists principally of a narrow belt of land of about six miles in breadth and thirty in length, deeply indented by the winding course of the great river which borders it, and lying between lat. 31° 10′—31° 25′, long. 76° 27′—76° 55′. The area is about 150 miles: the general elevation is considerable. At Soonee, about eighteen miles above the frontier of Kuhloor, the bed of the Sutlej is 2,283 feet above the sea; and as its descent in this part of its course averages twenty feet a mile, the elevation of the bed of the river at the frontier must be about 1,920 feet. The left bank of the Sutlej, for a short distance from the water, is tolerably level and fertile as high up as Belaspoor; and lower down, on the western frontier of the district, this flat space expands into the small plain of Makowal, communicating at its southern extremity with the Pinjor Dun. A steep ridge rises at no great distance from the river, in the north-western corner of the district, and holds a south-easterly direction until it joins the Sub-Himalaya. Parallel to this, and separated from it by the Gumbah or Gumbar river, is the ridge of Malown, which, very steep and difficult, rises to the height of 4,448 feet, and at the fort of the same name has a breadth of only twenty-two yards. The country, viewed from this height, is represented as very beautiful. "The terraced fields are like the steps of some magnificent amphitheatre, upon which the produce waves in many hues. These terraces are carried up to the tops of the ranges, and frequently in situations apparently inaccessible. Many elegant little hamlets are scattered up and down the fields, and upon the peaks are several small forts, while here and there large pine-woods sweep down in rich dark-green masses, intersected by thin rills of the whitest foam, or long forky mountain-paths. There is, too, an amenity and perfume in the air, and repose, which soothes the senses, while the immensity of the view expands the mind." The low lands on the bank of the Sutlej are alluvial; the mountains and other high grounds consist of recent sandstone, gravel, or indurated clay. The climate and products in the low tract in some degree resemble the less ardent parts of intertropical regions; and on the high grounds approach to those of the warmest parts of Europe. The rainy season is felt with considerable severity, extending through the later summer months, to the end of September or beginning of October. The crops are maize, rice of various kinds, wheat, barley, various kinds of millet, oil-seeds, pulse, ginger, turmeric, bang or hemp, cultivated on account of its intoxicating qualities, opium, tobacco, chillies or red pepper, and a variety of esculent vegetables. The principal fruits are peaches, apricots, walnuts, apples, pears, pomegranates, raspberries, gooseberries, strawberries, and barberries. Except the Sutlej, the only river of any importance is the Gumbhur or Gumbah, which, flowing in a north-westerly direction by the hill of Malown, crosses the southern frontier in lat. 31° 14′, long. 76° 50′, and, after a course of four or five miles, falls into the Sutlej in lat. 31° 17′, long. 76° 48′. A few other streams,—the Gumrara, the Sir, the Lohund, the Jujur,—are little more than large brooks. The only considerable piece of water is the Khundalu Lake. The rajah of Kuhloor was formerly of much greater importance than at present, having then considerable possessions on the right bank of the Sutlej, which were wrested from him, as already mentioned, by Runjeet Singh. His possessions to the left of the Sutlej, also, were much more extensive than at present, as, besides Kuhloor, they included twelve lordships or small states, yielding an aggregate annual revenue estimated at 13,500*l*. Kuhloor, with the other hill states between the Kali and Sutlej, having been overrun by the Goorkhas, became in 1814 the scene of obstinate struggle between that power and the East-India Company; and here that serious conflict was ultimately decided by the surrender of Ummer Singh, the Goorkha commander-in-chief, who had been cooped up in the fortress of Malown. The territories of the rajah of Kuhloor were included in the subsequent pacification, which transferred the hill states to British protection. It is stated to yield an annual revenue of 11,000*l*. The population is estimated at 64,848: the military force amounts to about 400 infantry. In 1850, Rajah Juggut Chund, chief of Kuhloor, was permitted to abdicate in favour of his grandson and heir, Heer Chund. Besides about ninety villages, the territory contains the towns of Belaspoor, Kuhloor, Anandpoor, and Makowal.

KUHLOOR, a small town in the hill state of the same name, is situate at the south-western base of the Nina Devi Mountain, and five miles from the left bank of the Sutlej. Though bearing the name of the state, whence it might be supposed to be the chief place in it, it is in fact of little importance, Belaspoor being much larger, and the residence of the rajah. Kuhloor is distant from Calcutta 1,103 miles. Lat. 31° 15′, long. 76° 40′.

KUJEENAAD.—A town in the native state of Travancore, presidency of Madras, situate 53 miles S. from Coimbatoor, and 63 miles E.N.E. from Cochin. Lat. 10° 15′, long. 77° 11′.

KUJWA, or KUDJOOA, in the British district of Futtehpore, lieut.-gov. of the N.W. Provinces, a town on the route from Calpee to the town of Futtehpore, and 20 miles N.W. of the latter. Tieffenthaler describes it, a century ago, as a large place (grosser Flecken), with a fine serai of brick, with vaulted apartments, and a lofty and beautiful portal on the west side, and another on the east; and on the north-east a spacious garden, inclosed with a wall having turrets at intervals. It was built by Aurungzebe, to commemorate his victory gained here over his brother Shuja, who "fled from the field, leaving 114 pieces of cannon and many elephants, to the victor." The name of Aurangabad, which the victor gave to this place, in honour of himself, appears to have endured but a short time. It has a bazar. Lat. 26° 8′, long. 80° 35′.

KUKKOR, or KAKORH, in the territory of Jeypoor, district of Ooniara, in Rajpootana, a large town, with a fort, in a very picturesque situation on the southern extremity of a range of hills. Close to it is an extensive jhil or small lake, which, however, becomes dry in prolonged droughts. Distant direct from Boondee, N.E., 40 miles; from Kota, N., 60; Jeypoor, S., 65. Lat. 26° 2′, long. 76° 4′.

KUKRALA, in the British district of Mynpooree, lieut.-gov. of the N.W. Provinces, a village situate on the route from the cantonment of Allygurh to that of Etawah, and 38 miles N.W. of the latter. Lat. 27° 11′, long. 78° 36′.

KUKRALUH, in the British district of Buddaon, lieut.-gov. of the N.W. Provinces, a town on the route from Buddaon to Furruckabad, 11 miles S.S.E. of the former. Lat. 27° 54′, long. 79° 16′.

KUKRUHTEE, or KURETI, in Bundelcund, a village in the district of Punna, on the route from Banda to Jubulpoor, 64 miles S. of the former. It has a bazar; water is abundant, and supplies are procurable. The country here slopes gently from the plateau on the summit of the range styled by Franklin the Pannah Hills. Lat. 24° 34′, long. 80° 21′.

KUKURAH, or KAKARA, in the British district of Allahabad, a town on the left bank of the Ganges, 14 miles above the city of Allahabad by the course of the river. Lat. 25° 30′, long. 81° 49′.

KUKURRAMUTTA.—A town of the Deccan, in the territory of Nagpoor or Berar, situate 146 miles E. from Nagpoor, and 134 miles S. by E. from Ramgurh. Lat. 20° 55′, long. 81° 23′.

KULADGEE.—A town in the British district of Belgaum, presidency of Bombay, 71 miles E.N.E. of Belgaum. Lat. 16° 11′, long. 75° 33′.

KULAIREE, in Sinde, a considerable watercourse, which parts from the right side of the Indus three miles due east of Tatta, and in lat. 24° 46′, long. 68° 2′. It holds a circuitous course, first north, then west, and then south; and in times of inundation, has so great a body of water as to insulate Tatta. At such times as the torrents flow down from the hilly country to the north-west, several of them empty themselves into the Kulairee. At the season of low water in the Indus, the Kulairee becomes completely dry. It holds a course almost due west, and, under the name of the Gharra Creek, falls into the Arabian Sea. Burnes inadvertently states that it is the first offshoot of the Indus on its right bank; but the Western Narra, and many others, leave the right bank far above this place.

KULALPOOR, in the Reechna Dooab division of the Punjab, a town situated on the right bank of the Ravee, 43 miles N.E. by N. of the town of Mooltan. Lat. 30° 40′, long. 71° 58′.

KULAN COTE, KULIA KOTE, or KULLAN KOTE (the Great Fort), in Sinde, is situate near the north or right bank of the Buggaur, or western branch of the Indus, and three miles south of Tatta. To the west are the remains of a suburb, and on the other side the ruined fort is washed by a lake of considerable extent, communicating with the Indus. The site is on a hill of limestone, abounding in marine shells, and everywhere honeycombed with natural cavities. The walls are of mud, faced with kiln-burned brick, and inclose an area three-quarters of a mile long and 500 or 600 yards broad. It appears to have been constructed with much care and skill, and has numerous massy round towers, connected by curtains: among other remarkable ruins, are those of a mosque of spacious dimensions. Lat. 24° 42′, long. 67° 54′.

KULEAGUNJE.—A town in the British district of Dinajepoor, lieut.-gov. of Bengal, 27 miles W. by S. of Dinajëpoor. Lat. 25° 30′, long. 88° 13′.

KULEEAHPOOR.—A town in the British district of Sarun, lieut.-gov. of Bengal, 66 miles N.W. by N. of Chupra. Lat. 26° 31′, long. 84° 10′.

KULEEANPOOR.—A town in the British district of Sarun, lieut.-gov. of Bengal, 47 miles N. by E. of Chupra. Lat. 26° 25′, long. 85°.

KULEGPESE.—A town of Orissa, in the hill zemindarry of Jeypoor, 38 miles W.S.W. from Ryaguddah, and 75 miles N.W. by N. from Vizianagrum. Lat. 19° 4′, long. 82° 56′.

KULELLY.—A town in the native state of Travancore, presidency of Madras, 52 miles N. from Trivandrum, and 63 miles N.W. by W. from Tinnevelly. Lat. 9° 13′, long. 76° 57′.

KULGAUM.—A town in Hyderabad, or dominions of the Nizam, situate on the left bank of one of the branches of the Payne Gunga river, and 98 miles S. from Ellichpoor. Lat. 19° 47′, long. 77° 47′.

KULHOREE, in the British district of Mynpooree, lieut.-gov. of the N.W. Provinces, a village on the route from the city of Agra to the cantonment of Mynpooree, and 14 miles W. of the latter. Lat. 27° 12′, long. 78° 54′.

KULIANEE, in the territory of Gwalior, a village on the route from the fort of Gwalior to Saugor, 21 miles S. of former, 181 N.W. of latter. Lat. 26° 2′, long. 78° 15′.

KULIANPOOR, in the Rajpoot state of Jodhpoor, a large village on the route from Balotra to the city of Jodhpoor, and 28 miles N.E. of the former. It is situate in a level country, rather fertile, and cultivated; but the water, which is obtained from wells only, is very brackish. Lat. 26° 4′, long. 72° 44′.

KULIANPOOR.—A town in the British district of Hijellee, lieut.-gov. of Bengal, 40 miles S.W. of Calcutta. Lat. 22° 10′, long. 88°.

KULIGAM, in Cashmere, a town, the capital of the district of Deosir, is situated near the left bank of the river Jhelum, here called the Veshau. The road from the Punjab, by the Col Narrawa Pass, debouches by Kuligam, and hence is sometimes called the Kuligam Pass. Kuligam is in lat. 33° 37′, long. 75° 5′.

KULIGAM, in Cashmere, a village at the head of the Lolab valley, and near the source of the river of that name, a small tributary of the Jhelum. It is situate at the southern base of the Green Mountains, bounding the valley of Cashmere on the north-west. Close to it on the east is a circular valley, five miles and a half in diameter, inclosed on every side by a verdant range, and having a morass in the centre. Here every evening, an incredible number of birds of the *corvus* genus assemble from all parts of Cashmere, to pass the night in the sheltered and warm valley. Kuligam is in lat. 34° 33′, long. 74° 41′.

KULINJERA, or KANJRA, in the raj or state of Banswara, in Rajpootana, a small town on the route from Neemuch to Baroda, 99 miles S.W. of former, 139 N.E. of latter. It has water and supplies in abundance. Here is a fine spacious antique temple, now quite deserted. Heber, who was informed that it was a Jain temple, describes it as of very complicated and extensive plan, covered with numerous domes and pyramids, divided into a great number of apartments, roofed with stone, crowded with images, and profusely embellished with rich and elaborate carvings. This was formerly a place of considerable wealth and trade, conducted by Jain merchants, who were all ruined or driven away by Mahratta freebooters. Lat. 23° 24′, long. 74° 28′.

KULKEREE.—A town in the British district of Sholapoor, presidency of Bombay, 72 miles S.S.E. of Sholapoor. Lat. 16° 40′, long. 76° 21′.

KULLANOOR, in the British district of Rohtuk, lieut.-gov. of the N.W. Provinces, a village on the route from Hansee to Goorgaon, and 36 miles S.E. of the former. Lat. 28° 50′, long. 76° 27′.

KULLEE KUHAR, in the Sinde Sagur Dooab division of the Punjab, a town situated twenty-three miles from the right bank of the Jhelum, 131 miles N.W. by W. of the town of Lahore. Lat. 32° 49′, long. 72° 28′.

KULLELPOOR, in the British district of Bareilly, lieut.-gov. of the N.W. Provinces, a village on the route from the town of Bareilly to Moradabad, and six miles N.W. of the former. Lat. 28° 24′, long. 79° 26′.

KULLIANEE, in Hyderabad, or territory of the Nizam, a town with a fort, formerly of considerable strength, but now ruinous. Distant from the city of Hyderabad, N.W., 106 miles. Lat. 17° 51′, long. 76° 59′.

KULLIANPOOR, in the British district of Cawnpore, lieut.-gov. of the N.W. Provinces, a village on the route from the cantonment of Cawnpore to that of Futtehgurh, and seven miles N.W. of the former. Lat. 26° 31′, long. 80° 18′.

KULLIANPOOR, in the British district of Allahabad, lieut.-gov. of the N.W. Provinces, a village on the route from the cantonment of Allahabad to Futtehpore, and 32 miles N.W. of the former. Lat. 25° 36′, long. 81° 30′.

KULLOOR.—A town in Hyderabad, or dominions of the Nizam, situate 139 miles E. from Hyderabad, and 52 miles N.W. from Ellore. Lat. 17° 13′, long. 80° 36′.

KULLOOR, in the Sinde Sagur Dooab division of the Punjab, a town situated three miles from the left bank of the Indus, 131 miles S. by W. of the town of Peshawur. Lat. 32° 10′, long. 71° 17′.

KULLOOR, in the Daman division of the Punjab, a town situated on the right bank of the Indus, 92 miles S. by W. of the town of Peshawur. Lat. 32° 44′, long. 71° 20′.

KULLSAPAWA.—A town in the British district of Cuddapah, presidency of Madras, 47 miles N. by E. of Cuddapah. Lat. 15° 8′, long. 79° 1′.

KULLUNG, a river of Eastern India, rises in lat. 25° 4′, long. 93° 5′, on the southern boundary of Toolaram Senahputtee's country, and flows north for sixty-five miles, dividing that territory from the British district of Cachar, when it enters the district of Nowgong, through which it flows in a north-westerly direction for ninety miles, to its junction with the Brahmapootra, in lat. 26° 15′, long. 91° 55′.

KULLUS.—A town in the British district of Poonah, presidency of Bombay, 65 miles E.S.E. of Poonah. Lat. 18° 13′, long. 74° 50′.

KULLYAVA KOORTY.—A town in Hyderabad, or dominions of the Nizam, situate 50 miles S. from Hyderabad, and 64 miles N.E. by N. from Kurnool. Lat. 16° 40′, long. 78° 33′.

KULOONJUR.—A town in the British district of Tirhoot, lieut.-gov. of Bengal, 54 miles N.E. by E. of Dinapoor. Lat. 26°, long. 85° 51′.

KULORA, in Sinde, a village on the western

route from Roree to Hyderabad, and 60 miles S.W. of the former town. It is situate four miles from the left bank of the Indus, in an alluvial country much intersected by watercourses, dug for the purposes of irrigation. Lat. 27° 11′, long. 68° 13′.

KULORAH, in Sinde, a village on the western route from Sehwan to Larkhana, by way of the Arul river, and seven miles south-west of Larkhana. It is situate on the Cheela, a watercourse from the Western Narra river. The road in this part of the route is in general good, though occasionally traversed by small watercourses. Kulorah is in lat. 27° 24′, long. 68° 9′.

KULPANEE, in the British territory of Saugur and Nerbudda, lieut.-gov. of the N.W. Provinces, a town on the route from Jubbulpoor to Nagpoor, 41 miles S.E. by S. of the former. Lat. 22° 40′, long. 80° 23′.

KULPEE, or **CALPEE**, in the British district called the Twenty-four Pergunnahs, lieut.-gov. of Bengal, a town situate on the left bank of the river Hooghly, at the place where it expands into an extensive estuary. Distance from Calcutta, S., 31 miles. Lat. 22° 4′, long. 88° 18′.

KULPUTTY.—A town in the British district of Coimbatoor, presidency of Madras, 38 miles S. of Coimbatoor. Lat. 10° 28′, long. 77° 4′.

KULU, KULLU, or **KOOLOO**, a small raj or state in the north-east of the Punjab, consists of a few rugged valleys on the southern slope of the Himalaya, together with the inclosing ridges. It is consequently rough, barren, and thinly peopled. The chief, a Rajpoot, before the occupation of the country by the British, suffered much from the tyranny of the Sikh government. The capital is sometimes called Kulu, but is better known by the name of Sultanpoor. Kulu lies between lat. 31° 20′—32° 33′, long. 76° 45′—77° 50′.

KULUGA, a village on the right bank of the Gurrah, in the British district of Bareilly, division of Pilleebheet, lieut.-gov. of the N.W. Provinces. Lat. 29° 6′, long. 79° 47′.

KULU SAIYID'S TOMB, in the British district of Bijnour, lieut.-gov. of the N.W. Provinces. It is situate on the crest of that part of the Sewalik range bounding the Patlee Doon on the south, and marks the burial-place of Kulu, a Saiyid, or descendant of Fatima. He fell in command of a Mussulman force, in an unsuccessful invasion of Gurhwal. Lat. 29° 34′, long. 78° 44′.

KULUTZI, KALLACH, or **KHALETSE**, in Ladakh, one of the largest villages in that country, is situate on the right or north bank of the Indus, which has here a rocky channel only twenty-five yards wide. The site is elevated considerably above the stream. Moorcroft observes: "At first sight, the situation appears unfavourable, presenting to the southward a line of towering rocks, and encircled nearly from east to west by a ridge of brown and barren hills. The cultivated ground is, however, of good quality, though rather incommodiously laid out in terraces. The grain sown here ripens in three months, and a second crop of buckwheat, or turnips, is obtained from the same soil." The population, for the most part, are Buddhists, votaries of the Grand Lama of Tibet. At the time of Moorcroft's visit, there was a *sanga* or wooden bridge across the river, three-quarters of a mile from the village. It was "substantially constructed, resting on two scarped rocks, and was about thirty yards long. The river was not more than twenty yards broad, and was rolling, black and impetuously, about twelve feet below it." The depth at this time must have been very great, as, during the season of low water, a few months after, the surface of the stream was forty-five or fifty feet below the bridge. Kulutzi is in lat. 34° 19′, long. 76° 58′.

KULWAH, in Sirhind, a town on the route from Hansee to Kurnal, and 41 miles S.W. of the latter place. There is a bazar here, but water is scarce in the dry season: the surrounding country is scantily cultivated. It is comprised in the possessions of the rajah of Jheend, a Sikh chief under British protection and control. Distant N.W. from Calcutta, by Delhi and Hansee, 1,015 miles. Lat. 29° 20′, long. 76° 35′.

KUMALGANJ, in the British district of Furruckabad, lieut.-gov. of the N.W. Provinces, a village on the route from the cantonment of Cawnpore to that of Futtehgurh, and seven miles S. of the latter. Lat. 27° 16′, long. 79° 41′.

KUMALPOOR, in the British district of Ghazeepoor, lieut.-gov. of the N.W. Provinces, a town on the route from Chunar to Dinapore, 36 miles N.E. of the former, 110 S.W. of the latter. Lat. 25° 23′, long. 83° 27′.

KUMANPILLY.—A town in Hyderabad, or dominions of the Nizam, situate six miles from the right bank of the Godavery river, and 120 miles N.E. by N. from Hyderabad. Lat. 18° 48′, long. 79° 35′.

KUMAON, including Eastern Gurhwal, a British province under the lieut.-gov. of the N.W. Provinces. It is bounded on the north-east by Chinese Tartary; on the east by Nepaul; on the south-west by Rohilcund, comprising the British districts Pillibheet, Moradabad, and Bijnour; on the west by the British district Dehra Doon; and on the north-west by the native raj of Gurhwal. Its form is nearly that of an equilateral rectangle, the diagonals of which lie in a direction nearly from south-west to north-east, and from south-east to north-west; the extreme points being in lat. 29° 5′—31° 6′, long. 78° 17′—80° 56′. No country exhibits more extraordinary diversities of elevation, temperature, and climate, than Kumaon. The southern part is either Bhawar (forest lands), extending over the plain, or else Terrai (marsh). The low region comprising those tracts extends along the whole frontier on that side, with a breadth varying from two to fifteen miles, and is thus described by Herbert :—"Along the foot of the mountains, extends a tract called Bhawar, which has been always, I believe, reckoned an integral part of the mountains, politically speaking. It is of considerable elevation, and is further distinguished by an almost total deficiency of springs or running streams. It is bounded on the southward by a line of springs or waterheads, which is also the northern boundary of the tract called Terrai, one equally distinguished with the former from the southern plain country, but occasionally annexed to it, and occasionally to the hills. This tract is remarkable for its moisture, as the other is for its dryness."

With the exception of these low lands, and a few similar tracts of small extent stretching along the great rivers in the lower parts of their courses, Kumaon is a maze of mountains, some of which, if not the loftiest known, may aspire very nearly to that distinction. The elevation of the surface increases towards the north and north-eastern frontier; the rivers rising respectively, in the Byanse, the Darma, the Juwahir or Juwar, the Niti and Mana passes, flowing south-westerly to pour their waters at various points into the great trunk of the Ganges. The north-eastern frontier is formed by the high ground which divides the drainage-system of the Indus from that of the Ganges, throwing off from the north and north-eastern sides feeders to the Sutlej, and from the other the great feeders of the Ganges just mentioned. The elevation of this dividing range, or succession of heights, is in general very great; thus the crest of the Niti Pass is 16,895 feet above the sea; that of Mana more than 20,000; that of Byanse about 15,000. This range, forming towards the south the boundary of the table-land of Tartary, is itself greatly overtopped by groups of gigantic mountains, situate generally thirty, forty, or fifty miles to the south and south-west of these passes, and attaining heights scarcely surpassed by any in the world. Nanda Devi, one of them, rises to the elevation of 25,749 feet above the sea; and close to it are two others, having the respective elevations of 23,531 and 23,317 feet; two others, farther north-west, respectively measuring 23,441 and 23,236 feet; eleven others, either in Kumaon or a few miles beyond its frontier, have elevations respectively exceeding 22,000 feet; eight others have elevations exceeding 21,000 feet; and ten more reach respectively an elevation of above 18,000 feet; so that there are thirty-four summits rising to elevations exceeding 18,000 feet, in a tract not more than 140 miles in length and forty in breadth. These summits are not situate on one extended ridge, but form groups separated by very deep valleys, determining the course of the several great torrents or rivers, all discharging themselves ultimately by the trunk of the Ganges. These remote feeders of the Ganges are on the declivity of the southern buttress of the table-land of Tartary, and north, or beyond the highest summits of the Himalaya Mountains, amongst which they make their way down valleys of rapid declivity and extraordinary depth. The more remote of these have their sources at an average elevation probably of about 13,000 feet. Enumerated in a direction from east to west, the principal are, the Kalee, the Eastern Douli, the Goonka or Gorigunga, the Western Douli, the Vishnugunga. Of the valleys down which these streams flow, the deepest is that of the Aluknunda river, formed by the united streams of the Vishnugunga and Western Douli, and which, at the confluence, having an elevation of 4,743 feet above the sea, is bounded to the east by the Nandadevi group, rising, in a distance of little more than twenty miles, to the elevation of 25,749 feet; and on the west by the Badrinath group, rising, in a distance of about fifteen miles, to the height of 23,441 feet; thus forming an enormous depression of between thirty and forty miles in width, irregularly defined, with a very varied surface, and having its lowest part more than 20,000 feet below the culminating point on one side, and more than 18,000 below that on the other. Those remote feeders of the Ganges soon become swollen by numerous tributaries descending from the great Himalayan heights; and the rivers thus formed take their way through the mazes of the subordinate ranges overspreading the southern tract, and ultimately pass into the plain of Hindoostan by two great channels; that of the Kalee or Gogra on the east, and of the Aluknunda on the west. Inferior to these, and unconnected with them, are some less extensive and less important drainages of the southern and less elevated high lands. Of such, the principal are the Kosila, and west of this the Ramgunga; but ultimately all are discharged into the Bay of Bengal by the channel of the Ganges.

Kumaon produces gold, which is obtained by searching the sands of the Aluknunda, and of which Captain Herbert obtained particles from a matrix of granite near Kedarnath. The Goorkha government, during its sway, derived a small revenue from the gains of the gold-washers, but it has been remitted by the British, as too trifling for notice. Captain Herbert, however, considers that by encouragement the pursuit might become more beneficial, as well to the rulers as to the labourers; he also has a favourable opinion of the lead-mines, which formerly, it is said, yielded more than the aggregate of the mines of every kind at present. Such views must, however, be received with great caution, as the value of the copper-mines, respecting which very glowing accounts had been given, has been brought to the test of experiment with very unsatisfactory results. Thus it had been asserted that one mine in Pokree yielded in a single year a return equal to 5,000*l.*; but experiments conducted there, under able European management, for several years, afforded a return of 780 rupees, against an expenditure of 8,164 rupees. The object was in consequence abandoned in 1841. The situation of these mines is almost inaccessible, and the vicinity affords no adequate supply of fuel for smelting. From these causes British copper is cheaper in Kumaon than that of native origin. Some arrangements were, however, made in 1852, in view to the working of some of these mines by persons of capital. The principal mines are in the group of Pokree above mentioned, in lat. 30° 20′, long. 79° 15′, and that of Dhunpur and Dhobri, in lat. 30° 14′, long. 79° 5′. The others are Gangoli, Sira, Khori, and Shor Gurarg. Iron abounds in this province. Of all the iron districts in India of which anything is known, Kumaon is said to be the most promising. Within the last year deposits of surpassing richness have been discovered by Colonel Drummond in the Bhabur district of this province, and that officer is now (1856) in England, endeavouring to form a company to work the iron-mines in this quarter of India. In 1850, specimens of plumbago were sent to this country, and subjected to examination, when it was ascertained that the mineral of this description could not be made serviceable as graphite. A specimen of the pure graphite of Cumberland was subsequently forwarded to Kumaon, as the standard of the mineral for which it would be desirable to search, its value being computed at 3,000*l.* per ton.

The climate varies, according to the elevation, from the suffocating and deadly sultriness of the Terrai to the perennial snow of the Himalaya. At Hawilbagh, having an elevation of 3,887 feet, the average height of the thermometer at two P.M. was, for January, 47°; February, 55°; March, 61°; April, 66°; May, 73°; June, 76°; July, 78°; August, 79°; September, 75°; October, 69°; November, 60°; December, 52°. The temperature is subject to great variations. Some years pass without any snow; the natives consider that they have reason to expect a snowy season every third year. When it falls, it never lies but on the mountain-tops and ridges, and not even there except they be very lofty, or densely covered with forests. On the Ghagar range, which rises on the southern frontier to an elevation of between 7,000 and 8,000 feet, snow lies so late as the middle of May. There do not appear to have been any systematically accurate observations respecting the limit of perpetual congelation, except those recently taken by Lieutenant Richard Strachey, in that section of the Himalayas lying between the north-west frontier of Nepaul and the river Sutlej. From these it appears that the heights crowned with perpetual snow extend from the 77th to the 81st degree of east longitude, and are confined within a belt of thirty-five miles in breadth, between the 30th and 32nd degrees of north latitude. The results of this traveller's observations further show that the snow-limit which resists the effect of summer recedes to a higher altitude on the northern or Tibetan slope of the mountains than on the southern or Indian side, having an elevation on the former of 18,500 feet, while on the latter it is permanently maintained at about 15,500 above the sea-level.

Kumaon is subject to earthquakes. McClelland records eight as having occurred from 1831 to 1835. The most severe mentioned in any account that may be relied on as authentic, is that of 1803, which demolished a great number of the temples and other substantial buildings of the territory. According to Heber, scarcely a year elapses without one or two slight shocks; and, as a measure of precaution, the residences of the British are seldom built more than one story high.

Of forest-trees, the most important are the deodar or Himalayan cedar, pines, and firs, of which there are eight varieties; oaks, of which there are six kinds; sal (Shorea robusta), rhododendrons, red and white, horse-chestnut, toon. Adverting to the tree last named, Traill speaks of "an endless variety, some common to the plains, and others peculiar to the hills." Some of the firs and pines are above two feet in diameter, and rise to the height of sixty or seventy feet, free of branches, with a strong clear grain, full of turpentine; and though somewhat more dense and heavy than those used in Europe, well suited for mizen-masts, topmasts, and lower yards of ships of 800 tons burthen. The difficult situation, however, of the forests must ever interfere with their produce being made extensively available. Yew-trees and pines attain great dimensions in the elevated Himalayan regions. Batten saw some on the route to the Niti Pass having a girth of twenty-seven feet. The fruit-trees comprise apple, pear, apricot, cherry, walnut, pomegranate, mulberry, peach, mango, guava, orange, lemon, citron, plantain. There are also grapes, raspberries, barberries, gooseberries, currants, strawberries, melons, and pumpkins. The churi or butter-tree, a production peculiar to the hills, bears a small edible fruit, from which a fixed oil, resembling butter, is obtained.

The zoology of Kumaon is copious and varied. Elephants are numerous in the Terrai, and being now protected by the orders of government from wanton destruction, may be expected to increase so as to supply the commissariat. The tiger is a great scourge to the people of Kumaon. In the cooler season, it haunts the deep valleys and lower grounds, and in hot weather, or during the rainy season, ascends the hills, and prowls about the villages, which it occasionally enters, and carries off any living being which it may pounce upon. These animals every year destroy from 200 to 300 of the limited population of the province, sometimes causing extensive tracts to be deserted. Government pays a pound sterling for every tiger's head brought in; but the number of these animals seems to suffer no decrease.

Leopards are very numerous, and destructive to sheep, goats, and especially dogs, but do not molest human beings, except in self-defence. Bears are numerous and mischievous, devastating the crops; but unless very closely pressed, showing no disposition to attack their pursuers. For the destruction of these devastating animals, rewards are offered by government. In the snowy districts of the Himalayas, there is a large species, of variable colour, tawny in summer and nearly white in winter. The cheang, an equine quadruped frequenting the same region, though often approached and pursued, has hitherto by its cunning eluded the close examination required for a scientific description. The best account of the animal is probably that given by Weller:—"I saw, what with great difficulty and the aid of my telescope, I made out to be a wild horse (cheang); probably 'wild ass' is the more correct term. This animal seemed about twelve hands high, short and compact, and more like a mule, particularly about the tail, which, with the mane and face, was black, the legs and belly white, and the sides and back reddish brown. When feeding, the animal looked much like a small punchy native horse, but when alarmed, he drew the head up so erect, that he looked far more like a burral or neaudh, in which his colour assisted. The head was rather large, and the forehead broad. This animal proved the most cunning I had ever met, though they are said to be easily approached when in herds. He never stopped in a hollow, but always trotted briskly through to the next eminence, whence he could have a clear view of all around. There, if I ran or walked up quickly, he would remain till I came within 150 or 200 yards." The spotted axis (Cervus axis), a species of elk, frequents the higher and more difficult tracts of the mountains.

In the lower, warmer, and more fertile parts, there are annually two successive crops—the rubbee, or that sown in autumn and cut in spring, and the kurreef, or that sown in spring and cut in autumn. The rubbee consists principally of wheat, barley, oats, millet, pease, beans, vetch, tares, chickpeas, pigeon-peas, and lentils; tobacco, safflower, and succory; flax, and plants allied to mustard, and rape to serve as oilseeds; carrot, coriander, cumin, and the esculent vegetables of Europe. The kurreef crop consists of rice, cotton, indigo, maize, Holcus sorghum or Indian millet, joar (Sorghum vulgare), koda (Paspalum scorbiculatum), various tropical legumes, cucumbers and gourds, sesamum for oil, the egg-plant, ginger, turmeric, and sweet potato. The sugarcane is cultivated to a limited extent. The cultivation of hemp is considerable, and the quality excellent. It is raised both for an intoxicating drug and for the fibre, which is either exported to the plain or manufactured at home into cordage or coarse cloth. The common potato has of late years been introduced by Europeans, and is cultivated to considerable extent. The cultivation of the tea-shrub and preparation of the leaf have been introduced into Kumaon by the orders of government. The shrubs have thriven well, and some samples of the tea have been by good judges declared very fine. Jameson observes, "The experiment, as far as it has been tried, has fully realized the most sanguine expectations." On the authority of the Chamber of Commerce of Calcutta, the tea has been pronounced "a very good marketable article;" by experienced tea-brokers in London, "fine-flavoured and strong, and equal to the superior black tea sent as presents, and better for the most part than the China tea imported for mercantile purposes." Mr. Commissioner Lushington sent a small quantity of the tea across the British frontier to the authorities in Tibet, by whom it was declared to be of "superior quality; and many inquiries were made as to the locality of the plant." The green-tea plant is also reported to thrive well. Indeed, the best hopes are entertained of establishing the tea-plant as an article of profitable cultivation; and the merit of this important accession to the resources of the country is attributable to the earnest and truly valuable efforts of Dr. Royle, by whom the cultivation was first suggested. The object has been pursued with great zeal and judgment by Dr. Jameson, under whose care the plantations will probably be extended over a wide extent of country.

As several frequented routes from Hiundes or Chinese Tartary traverse Kumaon, the traffic carried on by its inhabitants is considerable. The most westerly route proceeds up the course of the Aluknunda and its tributary the Bishenganga, by Joshimath, Badrinath, and Mana. East of that, a route proceeds up the Douli river, by the village of Niti, and debouches by the Niti Pass. Then in succession eastwards, are the routes proceeding respectively by the course of the river Gorigunga, and through the Uta Dhura Pass; 2nd, up the course of the Eastern Douli, and through the Dharma Pass; 3rd, up the course of the Eastern Kalee, and debouching by the Byanse Pass. There are likewise some important routes from the plains, penetrating into the interior of the country, and terminating there without any continuation to Hiundes; such is that by Srinagur and up the course of the Mandakini to Kedarnath; the British military route to Lohugat and Petoragurh, and that to Almora and Hawilbagh. The Bhotias, or natives of the mahals or hamlets situate between the culminating ridge of the Himalaya and the frontier of Hiundes, have exclusively the right to traffic with it, the Chinese authorities allowing them the privilege, in consequence of paying tribute and allegiance as well to that state as to the British. Thus, the Bhotias take from the traders of the south the merchandise destined to be transmitted from that quarter to Hiundes, and, receiving the produce of the great table-land, make their returns in it. The merchandise of the south consists of grain of various kinds, coarse sugar, sugarcandy, spices, dyes, broad-cloths, cottons, tobacco, hardware, pearls, coral, glass beads, glassware, cabinetware, wooden vessels, and timber. The returns from Hiundes are goat's-wool for the manufacture of shawls, sheep's-wool, culinary salt, borax, gold-dust, coarse shawls, coarse silks, chauris or tails of yaks, gunts or Tartarian ponies, tanned leather, resembling the Russian, dried fruit, saffron, and some other drugs. Besides this transit-trade, there is a direct one carried on with the plains, by dealers of the district of Kumaon, who are remarkable for intelligence and enterprise. One of this class, with an investment composed of Tartarian goods, acquired by his own capital,—iron, copper, wax, ginger, turmeric, and other hill roots, and drugs, sets out for the plains, often proceeding to Furruckabad or Lucknow, and bringing back cottons, broad-cloths, sugar, manufactures of Hindostan and of Britain, and other goods, which find ready market in the hills. The exports from the Terrai to the south are considerable, consisting principally of timber, ebony, bamboos, firewood, wooden vessels, charcoal, gum, gumlac, ghee or clarified butter, oil, grain, pulse, oil seeds, sweet potatoes, red pepper, and grass for cordage.

The greater part of the population is probably descended from a Hindoo stock migrating from the plains at a remote period, and continually reinforced by pilgrims and other devotees, attracted by the veneration investing numerous shrines and localities in this district. At present the population is mainly divided into Brahmins, the descendants of those of that caste among the Hindoo emigrants, Rajpoots, and Doms or outcasts. These last perform all the menial offices, and exercise the trades considered of inferior character; as that of the coppersmith, blacksmith, carpenter, mason, quarrier, miner, tailor, and musician. They are, for the most part, hereditary slaves, and have been so from time immemorial. In their physical type, they differ from the Hindoo race, as they have black woolly hair, and very black complexions. The Bhotias are another race, distinct in their Tartarian aspect, and their language, which is a dialect of the Tibetan. The general language of the population of Hindoo descent is Hindee, as derived from Sanscrit, without any mixture of Persian, but rude and irregular in its inflections. Brahminism is the generally acknowledged faith; but to it is superadded a variety of local superstitions. To every mountain-peak, cave, forest, fountain, and crag is assigned, in popular belief, its presiding spirit, to which frequent offerings and propitiatory rites are paid by the neighbouring inhabitants, in small temples erected on the spot. This form of superstition is on the increase, whilst regular Brahminism is declining. The principal shrines and places of pilgrimage are Kedarnath, Badrinath, Deoprayag, at the confluence of the Bhageerettee and Aluknunda; Rudraprayag, where the latter river receives the Mundagnee; Kurnaprayag, where it receives the Pindur; Nundaprayag, where it receives the Nandakini; and Vishnooprag, at the confluence with the Doulee. When a marriage is contemplated, the suitor invariably pays to the nearest relative of the damsel a sum of money, the amount of which varies from twenty-five to a thousand rupees, which are disbursed in the expenses attending the ceremony and the commencement of housekeeping. Polygamy is practised, and priority of marriage establishes a right of precedence among the wives. The services of the suitor for a given number of years are sometimes accepted in liquidation of the price of the damsel, who is borne away by the servitor at the termination of the stipulated time of service. Polyandry has long been discontinued, as well as the atrocious cruelty of burning widows with the corpses of their deceased husbands. All dead bodies are, however, still consumed by fire.

The present British district of Kumaon comprises the former raj or state of that name and a large portion of the neighbouring state of Gurhwal, reserved when, on the expulsion of the Goorkhas in 1815, the western part was restored to the hereditary rajah. The reserved territory of Gurhwal and Kumaon proper have been estimated to have each an area of about 5,000 square miles. A more recent estimate gives to Kumaon proper (Gurhwal being excluded) an area of 6,962 square miles. This result was attained by a rough calculation from the parallels of latitude and longitude, and consequently the true superficial area exceeds the statement, the figures therein representing the area of the plain surface covered by the hills. The entire population of Kumaon proper has been returned at 166,755, and that of Gurhwal at 132,744, but these returns are based on very loose premises.

In the year 1379, an army sent by Feroz Toghluk, king of Delhi, overran Kumaon, and reduced 23,000 of the inhabitants to slavery. Timur, in the early part of the fifteenth century, made a transient incursion into the south of Kumaon, and some authorities state that the descendants of certain of his troops located there may still be met with in the Bhotiah district Dharma. According to Buchanan, the family of the last rajah of Kumaon was descended from an adventurer, a native of Jhansi, a village on the left bank of the Ganges, opposite Allahabad, who, about 350 years ago, succeeded in seizing on the sovereignty of the country. Prinsep states that "neither Akbar, nor any of his descendants on the throne of Delhi, made any attempt to add the tract of hills to the Mogul empire;" but Buchanan relates that Akbar sent into Kumaon an invading army, which besieged Almora, but was defeated by the rajah Rudra, who, pursuing his success, advanced into the plain, and made himself master of a considerable tract along the base of the mountains. This was subsequently granted to him in jaghire by Akbar, who treated him with great favour, and, among other privileges, empowered him to strike money. It is difficult to ascertain the precise date of the conquest of Kumaon by the Goorkhas. The following statement is perhaps the most explicit that exists on the point. "So far back as the year 1791, after reducing Kumaon and its dependencies, the Gurchalis made an attempt to subdue the country of Gurwal." In the course of the war which, in 1814, broke out between the Goorkhas and the East-India Company, a British force under Colonel Nicholls penetrated into Kumaon, in the beginning of April, 1815, and, after a series of skilful manœuvres and fierce skirmishes, invested the town of Almora, which, being surrendered by the Goorkha commander, his troops, under a convention, evacuated the whole district of Kumaon, and marched home across the river Kalee. Several competitors set up hereditary claims to the liberated raj, but the government put an end to disputes by constituting it an integral part of the British dominions, under the title of the province or district of Kumaon, having embodied with the raj of that name the reserved portion of Gurhwal, or that part east of the river Alaknunda and Mandakini.

KUMARARA.—A town in the British district of Pooralia, lieut.-gov. of Bengal, 46 miles W. by S. of Midnapoor. Lat. 22° 17′, long. 86° 41′.

KUMAULPOOR.—A town in Guzerat, or the dominions of the Guicowar, situate 80 miles W. from Baroda, and 77 miles E. by N. from Rajkote. Lat. 22° 28′, long. 72°.

KUMBACHEN, a river of Nepal, rising on the south-western face of the great peak of the Himalayas known by the name of Kangchang, in lat. 27° 40′, long. 87° 55′. It flows along the north-western side of a spur of the above-named peak for thirty miles, to lat. 27° 27′, long. 87° 32′, the point of its junction with the Tambur river.

KUMBOOA, in Sinde, a village on the route from Shikarpoor to Larkhana, and eight miles S.W. of the former place. It is situate nine miles from the right bank of the Indus, and in that scantily-cultivated tract where the fertile alluvial soil adjoining the river degenerates into the *Pat* or desert of Shikarpoor. Lat. 27° 54′, long. 68° 34′.

KUMBUR.—A town of Sinde, in the British district of Shikarpoor, presidency of Bombay, 54 miles S.W. by W. of Shikarpoor. Lat. 27° 33′, long. 67° 58′.

KUMEREE, in the British district of Kumaon, lieut.-gov. of the N.W. Provinces, a village on the route up the course of the river Sarju, from Almorah fort to the Unta Dhura Pass. It is situate on the right bank of the Sarju, 35 miles N.W. of Almorah fort. Lat. 30° 2′, long. 79° 58′.

KUMHARPANEE.—A town of the Deccan, in the territory of Nagpoor or Berar, situate 40 miles N. from Nagpoor, and 77 miles E. from Baitool. Lat. 21° 43′, long. 79° 9′.

KUMLA RIVER.—The name given to the Gogaree in the upper part of its course.—See GOGAREE.

KUMLA GURH, or THE FOOL'S FORTRESS, in the north-east of the Punjab, and near the left or south bank of the Beas, a range of forts, constructed partly out of the natural rock and partly of masonry. They are built on several sandstone peaks, which extend, north and south, a distance of about three miles. The principal stronghold among them is an isolated rock, with precipitous sides, rising about 150 feet above the other peaks, about 1,500 feet above the Beas, and having an elevation of 3,000 feet above the sea. This range of forts is situated on the summit of a mountain about eight miles long and five broad, surrounded by deep ravines, with precipitous sides, 80, 100, or 150 feet high. These strongholds belong to the ruler of Mundi. Sansar Chand, the powerful rajah of Tira, and once the rival of Runjeet Singh, attacked them in vain; and they were considered by the people of the country to be impregnable, until taken by the Sikhs under Ventura. Kumla Gurh is in lat. 31° 48′, long. 76° 43′.

KUMLANOOL.—A town in Hyderabad, or dominions of the Nizam, situate 62 miles S. by W. from Hyderabad, and 50 miles N.N.E. from Kurnool. Lat. 16° 29′, long. 78° 22′.

KUMMERGUNJE, in the British district of Bhagulpoor, lieut.-gov. of Bengal, a small town on the route from Bhagulpoor to Moongheer, 20 miles W. of former, 15 S.E. of latter. Lat. 25° 13′, long. 86° 40′.

KUMMUMMETT, in Hyderabad, or territory of the Nizam, a town on the left bank of Moonyair river, a considerable tributary of the Kistna. It is the principal place of an extensive zemindary or nominal raj held under the Nizam, but with so much latitude, that it may be regarded rather in the light of a tributary state. The district is also often called the raj of Paloon Shah, from a considerable town with fort which it contains. Distance from the city of Hyderabad, E., 110 miles. Lat. 17° 15′, long. 80° 13′.

KUMMUR, in the Daman division of the Punjab, a town situated seventeen miles from the right bank of the Indus, 87 miles S.S.W. of the town of Peshawur. Lat. 32° 53′, long. 71° 3′.

KUMORA DUMORA, in the jaghire of Rampoor, lieut.-gov. of the N.W. Provinces, two villages adjoining each other on the route from Bareilly to the city of Rampoor, and six miles S.E. of the latter. Lat. 28° 41′, long. 79° 11′.

KUMPIL, in the British district of Furruckabad, lieut.-gov. of the N.W. Provinces, a town on the route from Futtehgurh to Buddaon, 26 miles N.W. of the former. Lat. 27° 37′, long. 79° 21′.

KUMPIN.—A town in the British district of Bellary, presidency of Madras, 28 miles N.W. of Bellary. Lat. 15° 25′, long. 76° 40′.

KUMROO.—See MOHNE.

KUMUR, in the Daman division of the Punjab, a town situated on the right bank of the Indus, 84 miles S. by W. of the town of Peshawur. Lat. 32° 50′, long. 71° 20′.

KUMURDAH.—A town in the British district of Balasore, lieut.-gov. of Bengal, 86 miles S.W. of Calcutta. Lat. 21° 45′, long. 87° 25′.

KUNADEEA.—A town in the native state of Indore, or territory of Holkar, situate 80 miles W. from Bhopal, and 110 miles W.N.W. from Hoosungabad. Lat. 23° 21′, long. 76° 10′.

KUNAPOOR, in the British province of Sagur and Nurbudda, lieut.-gov. of the N.W. Provinces, a town on the route from Baitool to Omraoutee, 40 miles S. of the former. Lat. 21° 17′, long. 78°.

KUNCHABAREE.—A town in the British district of Purneah, lieut.-gov. of Bengal, 65 miles N.E. by E. of Purneah. Lat. 26° 23′, long. 88° 21′.

KUNCHUNPOOR, or CHANDPOOR, in the British district of Cawnpore, lieut.-gov. of the N.W. Provinces, a village on the route from the cantonment of Cawnpore to that of Calpee, and 29 miles N.E. of the latter. Lat. 26° 24′, long. 80° 6′.

KUNCHUNPOOR, in the British district of Sohagpoor, territory of Saugor and Nerbudda, lieut.-gov. of the N.W. Provinces, a town on the route from Sohagpoor to Nagpoor, 80 miles S. of the former. Lat. 22° 53′, long. 81° 26′.

KUNDA, in native Gurhwal, a village on the left bank of the Jumna, nearly opposite the confluence of its tributary the Budiar. It is situate on a mountain, rising from the base of which is a spring of fine water, from a source choked with lilies. This is by the superstitious Hindoos supposed to be the Ganges, which, at the prayer of an ascetic, made its way beneath a vast mountain intervening between this spot and Gangotri, and thus saved the devotee from the laborious journey which he daily took to bathe in the sacred stream. The name in Sanscrit signifies "drinking-cup," and, according to Hindu mythology, the Ganges takes its course through the Kunda or drinking-cup of Brahma. The village is in lat. 30° 49′, long. 78° 19′.

KUNDAHAR, in Hyderabad, or territory of the Nizam, a town 135 miles north-west of the city of Hyderabad. Lat. 18° 52′, long. 77° 17′.

KUNDAL.—A town in the British district of Bulloah, lieut.-gov. of Bengal, 40 miles N.E. of Bulloah. Lat. 23° 11′, long. 91° 27′.

KUNDALA.—A town in the British district of Poonah, presidency of Bombay, 37 miles E.S.E. of Bombay. Lat. 18° 48′, long. 73° 26′.

KUNDAVELLEE.—A town in the British district of Rajahmundry, presidency of Madras, 20 miles S. of Rajahmundry. Lat. 16° 42′, long. 81° 50′.

KUNDERY.—A town in the native state of Sirgoojah, on the south-west frontier of Bengal, situate 41 miles N.E. from Sirgoojah, and 71 miles W. from Lohadugga. Lat. 23° 28′, long. 83° 40′.

KUNDIAPURRA.—A tract inhabited by one of the independent hill tribes of Orissa. Its centre is in lat. 20° 17′, long. 85° 17′.

KUNDIE.—A town of the Deccan, in the territory of Nagpoor or Berar, situate 152 miles E. by N. from Nagpoor, and 86 miles S.S.E. from Ramgurh. Lat. 21° 39′, long. 81° 26′.

KUNDROWNI.—A town of Bundelcund, in the British province of Jhansee, situate three miles from the right bank of the Mohwur river, and 22 miles W. by N. from Jhansee. Lat. 25° 32′, long. 78° 20′.

KUNEENUH.—A village in the jaghire of Jujhur, lieut.-gov. of the N.W. Provinces. Lat. 28° 18′, long. 76° 22′.

KUNERAH, in the British district of Muttra, lieut.-gov. of the N.W. Provinces, a village on the route from the city of Agra to Bareilly, and 21 miles N.E. of the former. Lat. 27° 23′, long. 78° 15′.

KUNGRA, in the British district of Goruckpoor, lieut.-gov. of the N.W. Provinces, a small lake half a mile in length and 200 yards wide, with high banks, and water free from weeds. It appears to have been a deep part of the channel of a river, the current of which has now taken a different course. This part of the country is yearly extensively flooded by the periodical rains, and, as the waters subside, vast quantities of fish find their way to Kungra, and are pursued thither by many crocodiles. The natives believe it to be unfathomable, and that it was excavated by some god; but Buchanan found the depth of the spot which he sounded to be sixty-two feet. Lat. 26° 35′, long. 83° 22′.

KUNGULL.—A town in Hyderabad, or dominions of the Nizam, situate on the right bank of one of the branches of the Kistnah, and 58 miles S.E. by E. from Hyderabad. Lat. 16° 56′, long. 79° 18′.

KUNGURH.—A town of Bundelcund, in the native state of Punnah, situate 27 miles E. from Punnah, and 47 miles N.W. by W. from Rewah. Lat. 24° 45′, long. 80° 41′.

KUNHER.—A river rising in Bengal, on the southern frontier of the British district of Sirgooja, towards the state of Odeipoor, and about lat. 23° 15′, long. 83° 38′. It has a direction generally northerly, but slightly inclined to west, and falls into the river Son on the south or right side, in lat. 24° 29′, long. 83° 10′, after a total length of course of about

130 miles, forming for the greater part of the distance the boundary between Palamow and the district of Sirgooja.

KUNJUR, or KINJORE, in Sinde, a lake, or, as it is vernacularly called, a *dund*—an extensive and permanent piece of stagnant water, left by the Indus after it has retired to the channel to which it is confined in the season when it is lowest. The dund of Kinjore is about three miles westward of the channel, and is a beautiful expanse of water. It is one of three, which extend north and south about twenty miles, and swarm with fine fish, caught with much skill and in great abundance by the fishing population on the banks, and forming their principal subsistence. Lat. 24° 55′, long. 68° 8′.

KUNJPOORA, in Sirhind, a town close to the south-eastern frontier, in the space insulated between the canal of Feroz Shah and the Jumna, from the right bank of which it is distant two miles. It is the principal place of a small district, the annual revenues of which, estimated at 5,000*l.* sterling, are divided between two sirdars, in the proportion of two-thirds to one and a third to the other; but these chiefs have no independent authority. At the battle of Kurnal, fought in 1739, between the army of Nadir Shah, of Persia, and that of Muhammad Shah, of Delhi, a division of 20,000 Persian matchlockmen and musketeers, concealed among the houses and orchards of Kunjpoora, fell on the flank of the enemy during the height of the engagement, and routed them with dreadful carnage. Kunjpoora is in lat. 29° 43′, long. 77° 8′.

KUNKAS.—A river rising on the south-western slope of the Garrow Hills, in lat. 25° 23′, long. 89° 58′, and, flowing in a south-easterly direction for 130 miles, through the British district of Mymunsing, falls into the Barak river in lat. 24° 16′, long. 90° 56′.

KUNKEEPOOR, in the British district of Mynpooree, lieut.-gov. of the N.W. Provinces, a village on the route from the cantonment of Allygurh to that of Mynpooree, and 15 miles N.W. of the latter. Lat. 27° 21′, long. 78° 55′.

KUNKHUL, in the British district of Saharunpoor, a large town on the route from Saharunpoor to Hurdwar, and three miles S.W. of the latter place. It is situate on the right bank of the Ganges, in a delightful country, and embosomed in trees, crowded with monkeys, regarded by the Hindoos with superstitious favour, and hence so tame, that they intrude into the dwelling-houses and shops, and snatch away any provisions within reach. The town consists principally of a main street, running parallel to the river, and consisting of houses substantially built of brick and mortar, plastered over, and painted in fresco with grotesque and ill-executed groups of men and animals. Those fantastic residences belong to rich Hindoos, from all parts of Hindoostan, it being considered a mark of wealth, as well as of piety, to have a house at this town, which, as well as Hurdwar, is a place of pilgrimage; and in consequence, the holy stream of the Ganges is rendered accessible by numerous ghats, or stairs of cut stone. There are also numerous long, low serais, built of brick, for the accommodation of pilgrims, who lodge there in irregular crowds, interspersed with their cattle, brought to be blessed at the sacred stream. The streets, filthy in the extreme, are so deep with black mud, that it is difficult to make way through them. Kunkhul was a secondary station in the great trigonometrical survey of the Himalayas. Elevation above the sea 1,032 feet. The head of the Ganges Canal is situate a little to the north of the town. Lat. 29° 55′, long. 78° 12′.

KUNKUNWAREE. — A town in the British district of Belgaum, presidency of Bombay, 44 miles N.E. of Belgaum. Lat. 16° 21′, long. 74° 58′.

KUNNAUGOODY.—A town in the British district of Madura, presidency of Madras, 58 miles E. of Madura. Lat. 9° 56′, long. 79° 1′.

KUNNEIJRA. — A town in the native state of Cutch, situate 10 miles N. from Bhooj, and four miles S. of the Great Western Runn. Lat. 23° 21′, long. 69° 46′.

KUNNIGHERRY.—A town in Hyderabad, or dominions of the Nizam, situate 140 miles E. from Hyderabad, and 57 miles N.W. from Ellore. Lat. 17° 21′, long. 80° 39′.

KUNNIGHERRY.—A town in the British district of Nellore, presidency of Madras, 37 miles W. by S. of Ongole. Lat. 15° 25′, long. 79° 33′.

KUNNOJ, or KUNNOUJ, the principal place of the pergunnah of the same name, in the British district of Furruckabad, a decayed town, situate on the Kalee Nuddee, a river which falls into the Ganges about three miles below. The Ganges, represented to have formerly touched the town, now flows two miles east of it. The eastern part of the present site is situate on a gentle eminence, the western in the plain. At present it is little more than an expanse of ruins, as described by an eye-witness:—"For many miles before you enter the present town, you travel through jungles interspersed with small fields of tobacco, that consist of brickdust and mortar. To remove all doubt that the rubbish consists of the remains of a town, walls and broken gateways here and there raise their heads, in defiance of time. The greatest part of the standing buildings are ruinous, uninhabited, rent, and tottering to decay. The few poor people now in the place accommodate themselves under mud huts buttressed up against the old walls. Not a great many buildings are entire; whole mountains of unshapely ruins meet your eye in every direction, upon a space of ground much larger than the site of London."

The principal street is described by Tieffenthaler as half a mile long, straight, of moderate breadth, with some brick-built houses; the whole length of the present town being above a mile, the breadth half that measure. The ruinous fort, situate on a sandhill of slight elevation, rather steep on the west side, but on the others low and easily accessible, has a brick rampart, but is little worthy of notice, and appears, it is said, of no great antiquity. The buildings at present (or lately) most remarkable, are two handsome Mahomedan mausoleums. Some portions of this vast scene of ruins, in themselves not very striking, but highly interesting from their historical associations, are represented finely by Daniell. Though now thus fallen, Kunnoj was formerly one of the chief of Indian cities, as it was also probably one of the most ancient; Elphinstone intimating, that in this respect it ranked next to Ayodha or Oude, which he considers the most early in Hindostan. It is not, however, mentioned in the celebrated ancient poem of the Mahabharat, the era of which is by Elphinstone conjectured to be about 1400 B.C. Hamilton (Francis), however, considers the town to have existed before the first introduction of Brahminism from the west. So remote is its antiquity, that some relics of its language have baffled the multifarious acquirements, acuteness, and perseverance of Mr. Prinsep in his attempts to decipher them; "the characters in which their legends are graven being wholly unknown." In its palmy state, according to a learned writer of easy belief, "the circumvallation covered a space of more than thirty miles," and its sovereign led forth an "army which in numbers might compete with the most potent which, in ancient or modern times, was ever sent into the field. Eighty thousand men in armour, 30,000 horse covered with quilted mail, 300,000 infantry, and of bowmen and battle-axes 200,000, besides a cloud of elephants bearing warriors." Even Ferishta, an author of more sober cast of mind, states that Kunnoj "contained 30,000 shops for the sale of paun [betel-leaf], and 60,000 families of public dancers and singers." The era of this prosperous condition he states to be in the reign of Khoosrow Purvees, king of Persia, about the year 590, shortly after which period, North-western India is represented as divided into the following states:—1. Kunnoj; 2. Meerut; 3. Mahavun; 4. Lahore. Long afterwards, and a century before the invasion by Mahmood of Ghizny, Kunnoj continued to be the chief city of India. Mahmood took it in 1018, but, appeased by the ready submission of the rajah, left it uninjured, after a stay of a few days. More decisive was the attack of Shahabuddin Mohammed, sovereign of Ghoor, who, in 1194, defeated, near Etawa, Jye-Chund Ray, king of Kunnoj, and overthrew that monarchy. The remaining history of the place records only a succession of disasters. In 1340, Mohammed Toghluk, the frantic tyrant of Delhi, "made an excursion towards Kunnoj, and put to death the inhabitants of that city and the neighbourhood for many miles round." It was in the early part of the sixteenth century the subject of fierce contention between Baber and his Patan foes, but ultimately fell into the hands of the former, who here, in 1528, bridged the Ganges, and crossed it at the head of his army invading Oude. Here, in 1540, Humayon, son and successor of Baber, received a decisive defeat from Sher Shah, his Afghan rival, and was in consequence compelled to fly from Hindostan. At present, this once celebrated place contains only 16,000 inhabitants, living in great indigence. Distant S.E. from Futtehgurh 30 miles, N.W. from Cawnpore 52. Elevation above the sea 494 feet. Lat. 27° 3′, long. 79° 59′.

KUNNOUTA.—A town in the Rajpoot state of Jeypoor, situate 11 miles E.S.E. from Jeypoor, and 89 miles E.N.E. from Ajmeer. Lat. 26° 50′, long. 76° 3′.

KUNNOWHEE, in the British district of Allygurh, lieut.-gov. of the N.W. Provinces, a village on the route from the cantonment of Allygurh to that of Delhi, and 13 miles N.W. of the former. Here is a jhil or shallow lake. Lat. 28° 2′, long. 78° 2′.

KUNNUR.—A town in Hyderabad, or dominions of the Nizam, situate 51 miles W.N.W. from Jaulnah, and 53 miles S.E. by E. from Malligaum. Lat. 20° 10′, long. 75° 13′.

KUNOWEE, in Sirhind, a village on the route from Hansee to Loodiana, and 56 miles S. of the latter town. It is situate in a level, fertile, well-cultivated country. Distant N.W. from Calcutta 1,056 miles. Lat. 30° 11′, long. 75° 56′.

KUNPOOR, in the British district of Muttra, lieut.-gov. of the N.W. Provinces, a village on the route from the cantonment of Allygurh to that of Etawah, and 31 miles S.E. of the former. Lat. 27° 28′, long. 78° 19′.

KUNRAJA.—A town on the S.W. frontier of Bengal, in the recently lapsed state of Odeipoor, 12 miles N.E. from Odeipoor, and 96 miles N.N.W. from Sumbulpoor. Lat. 22° 47′, long. 83° 31′.

KUNSA, in the district of Bainswara, territory of Oude, a town six miles N.E. of the left bank of the Ganges, 30 S.W. of Lucknow. Butter estimates the population at 7,000, including fifty Mussulmans. Lat. 26° 22′, long. 80° 40′.

KUNTHOOA, in the British district of Allahabad, lieut.-gov. of the N.W. Provinces, a small town on the right bank of the Ganges, 865 miles by way of the river from Calcutta, 34 miles S.E. by land from the town of Futtehpore. Lat. 25° 47′, long. 81° 25′.

KUNTIL, in the British district of Mirzapoor, lieut.-gov. of the N.W. Provinces, a town on the route from Mirzapoor to Allahabad, three miles W. by N. of the former. This place is the residence of the rajah of the same name. He is considered the head of the Rajpoot tribe of Guhurwars, a numerous and powerful clan, and possessed of great local influence and consideration. Lat. 25° 7′, long. 82° 35′.

KUNTOOL.—A town of Orissa, in the Cuttack mehal of Autgurh, situate 16 miles W.N.W. from Cuttack, and 88 miles N.N.E. from Ganjam. Lat. 20° 32′, long. 85° 41′.

KUNU, in Bussahir, a village of Koonawur, near the right bank of the river Tidung, here in summer furiously rapid, and sweeping along, suspended in its current, a great deal of fine white sand. The noise of large stones hurried along by the torrent is incessant, and, mingled with the roar of the water, produces a sublime effect. The stream is here crossed by a sanga or rude wooden bridge, fifteen feet long. Elevation above the sea 11,727 feet. Lat. 31° 28′, long. 78° 39′.

KUNWARA.—A town in the Rajpoot state of Jeypoor, situate 81 miles S. from Jeypoor, and 86 miles S.E. by E. from Ajmeer. Lat. 25° 46′, long. 75° 50′.

KUNWYE LARKANI.—A town in the Rajpoot state of Jodhpoor, situate 124 miles N.E. from Jodhpoor, and 68 miles N. from Ajmeer. Lat. 27° 27′, long. 74° 39′.

KUNY KAIRY.—A town in Hyderabad, or dominions of the Nizam, situate six miles from the left bank of the Beemah river, and 99 miles S.W. by W. from Hyderabad. Lat. 16° 36′, long. 77° 19′.

KUPASDEE, in the British territory of Sagur and Nurbudda, lieut.-gov. of the N.W. Provinces, a town on the route from Hoosungabad to Boorhaunpoor, 46 miles S.W. by S. of the former. Lat. 22° 11′, long. 77° 20′.

KUPELA SUNGUM.—A town in the British district of Belgaum, presidency of Bombay, 105 miles E. by N. of Belgaum. Lat. 16° 11′, long. 76° 8′.

KUPPASUN.—A town in the Rajpoot state of Oodeypoor, 45 miles N.E. by E. from Oodeypoor, and 43 miles N.W. from Neemuch. Lat. 24° 53′, long. 74° 25′.

KUPPELVOY.—A town in Hyderabad, or dominions of the Nizam, situate on the right bank of the Moonyair river, and 87 miles E. by N. from Hyderabad. Lat. 17° 30′, long. 79° 50′.

KUPPILI.—A town in the British district Vizagapatam, presidency of Madras, 49 miles N.E. of Vizagapatam. Lat. 18° 10′, long. 83° 53′.

KUPPURWUNJ, in the British district of Kaira, presidency of Bombay, a town situate on a tributary of the river Saburmuttee. It is fortified, and has some trade and a few manufactures. Population about 13,000. Distance from the city of Ahmedabad, E., 30 miles; Kaira, N.E., 32. Lat. 23° 2′, long. 73° 9′.

KUPSA, in the British district Banda, lieut.-gov. of the N.W. Provinces, a town on the route from the town of Banda to Calpee, 11 miles N.W. of the former. It has a bazar, and is well supplied with water. Lat. 25° 34′, long. 80° 17′.

KUPURWAR, in the British district of Goruckpore, lieut.-gov. of the N.W. Provinces, a small town on the left bank of the Raptee, four miles above its confluence with the Ghogra. According to Buchanan, it contains 100 houses; an amount which would assign it a population of about 600 persons. Distant S.E. from Goruckpore cantonment 32 miles. Lat. 26° 15′, long. 83° 43′.

KURAI, in the British territory of Sagur and Nurbudda, lieut.-gov. of the N.W. Provinces, a town on the route from Saugur to Nusseerabad, 31 miles W.N.W. of the former. Lat. 24° 1′, long. 78° 22′.

KURAKUT, a town on the route from Ghazeepore cantonment to that of Jounpore, 40 miles N.W. of the former, 18 S.E. of the latter. Lat. 25° 36′, long. 83°.

KURALEE, in the British district of Allahabad, lieut.-gov. of the N.W. Provinces, a small town on the route from the cantonment of Allahabad to Banda, and 31 miles W. of the former. It has a bazar. Lat. 25° 27′, long. 81° 30′.

KURAMBALORE.—A town in the British district of Trichinopoly, presidency of Madras, 31 miles N. by E. of Trichinopoly. Lat. 11° 15′, long. 78° 51′.

KURAOO.—A town in the Rajpoot state of Jodhpoor, 68 miles W.N.W. from Jodhpoor, and 74 miles E. by S. from Jessulmeer. Lat. 26° 39′, long. 72° 6′.

KURARA.—A town of Bundelcund, in the British province of Jhansee, situate on the right bank of the Mohwur river, and 28 miles W. from Jhansee. Lat. 25° 28′, long. 78° 13′.

KURATTEEA, or CURATTEEA.—An offset of the Attree river, quitting the parent stream in lat. 26° 4′, long. 88° 41′. Flowing in a south-easterly direction for eighty miles, it forms the boundary between the British districts Rungpore and Dinajepore. Thenceforward, traversing for 105 miles the districts of Bogra and Pubna, it falls into the Konaie river, in lat. 23° 58′, long. 89° 45′, a few miles before the junction of that river with the Ganges.

KURAYA, in the territory of Gwalior, or possessions of Scindia's family, a town on the Nun, a small feeder of the river Sindh, on the route from Gwalior fort to Narwar, 24 miles S. of the former, 18 N. of the latter. Lat. 25° 54′, long. 78°.

KURCHOLEE, in the British district of Moradabad, lieut.-gov. of the N.W. Provinces, a village on the ronte from Allygurh to Moradabad, and 44 miles S.W. of the latter. Lat. 28° 30′, long. 78° 33′.

KURCUMBAD.—A town of the Deccan, in the territory of Nagpoor or Berar, situate

18 miles E. of the left bank of the Husdah river, and 101 miles N.W. from Sumbulpoor. Lat. 22° 21′, long. 82° 48′.

KURDA.—See KURDLAH.

KURDAWAD.—A town in the native state of Indore, or territory of Holkar, situate 144 miles E. from Ahmedabad, and 101 miles S. from Neemuch. Lat. 23°, long. 74° 50′.

KURDEE.—A town in the British district of Tannah, presidency of Bombay, 57 miles N.E. of Bombay. Lat. 19° 36′, long. 73° 26′.

KURDEH, in the British district of Goruckpoor, lieut.-gov. of the N.W. Provinces, a town on the route from Goruckpoor to Khatmandoo, 45 miles N.E. of the former. Lat. 27° 6′, long. 83° 55′.

KURDLAH.—A town in the British district of Ahmednuggur, presidency of Bombay, situate 61 miles S.E. by E. of Ahmednuggur. In 1795 an engagement took place between the Mahrattas and the Nizam, near this place, to which the latter retreated, and being completely hemmed in by the enemy, was constrained to accede to an ignominious treaty. Lat. 18° 40′, long. 75° 34′.

KURGOON, in the territory of Indore, or possessions of Holkar's family, a decayed town in the tract of Nimaur, of the southern part of which it was the capital. "It is surrounded by a wall, commenced with stone, and carelessly finished with mud;" and has a small citadel, the residence of the amaldar, or officer of the district. It was nearly destroyed during the Mahratta wars, in the early part of the present century, the number of houses being reduced from 5,000 to 800, scattered amongst heaps of ruins. Distant S. from Indore 60 miles, S. from Mow 49. Lat. 21° 50′, long. 75° 45′.

KURHUL, in the British district of Mynpooree, lieut.-gov. of the N.W. Provinces, a town on the route from Etawah to Mynpooree, 17 miles S. by W. of the latter. Lat. 27°, long. 79°.

KURHUS, in the British district of Paneeput, lieut.-gov. of the N.W. Provinces, a village on the route from the city of Delhi to Kurnal, and 31 miles S.E. of the latter. Lat. 29° 16′, long. 77° 4′.

KURIETA, in the British district of Agra, a village on the route from the city of Agra to Mynpooree, and 30 miles E. of the former. Lat. 27° 7′, long. 78° 31′.

KURINGA, in British district Banda, lieut.-gov. of the N.W. Provinces, a town 25 miles E. of the town of Banda, 72 W. of Allahabad. Lat. 25° 30′, long. 80° 46′.

KURKOWDA, or GHURGOUDUH, in the British district of Meerut, lieut.-gov. of the N.W. Provinces, a village with a small bazar on the route from Allygurh to the town of Meerut, and 11 miles S. of the latter. Lat. 28° 50′, long. 77° 47′.

KURKUMB.—A town in the British district of Sholapoor, presidency of Bombay, 41 miles W.N.W. of Sholapoor. Lat. 17° 51′, long. 75° 22′.

KURKUNNEE.—A town in the Rajpoot state of Jodhpoor, 110 miles E.N.E. from Jodhpoor, and 20 miles S. by W. from Ajmeer. Lat. 26° 45′, long. 74° 48′.

KURMODA.—A town in one of the recently sequestrated districts of Hyderabad, or dominions of the Nizam, situate 52 miles W. by S. of Ellichpoor. Lat. 21° 6′, long. 76° 47′.

KURMPOOR, in Sinde, a village on the route from Sehwan to Larkhana, and three miles N. of the former place. It is situate half a mile from the right bank of a considerable offset of the Indus, and near the south-eastern edge of a large *dund*, or piece of stagnant water. The surrounding country is low, level, and fertile. The road in this part of the route is in general good. Lat. 26° 25′, long. 67° 56′.

KURMULLA.—A town in the British district of Sholapoor, presidency of Bombay, 69 miles N.W. of Sholapoor. Lat. 18° 25′, long. 75° 15′.

KURNAL, in the British district of Paniput, lieut.-gov. of the N.W. Provinces, a town on the route from the city of Delhi to Loodiana, and 78 miles N. of the former, situate on the right or western bank of the Delhi Canal, about fifteen miles above the divergence of the canal of Feroz Shah, and surrounded by a ruinous wall. Jacquemont describes it as "in the interior an infamous sink, a heap of every sort of uncleanliness; amongst heaps of dung, brick-rubbish, and carcases of beasts, are winding paths, scarcely passable for horses, and having here and there a few miserable huts. I have seen nothing so bad in India, and it is fair to mention, that amongst the natives its filth is proverbial." It has, however, a handsome mosque overtopping the wall. North of the town, and adjoining it, is a cantonment of British troops. The population of the town is returned at 20,178 inhabitants. Here, in 1739, Nadir Shah, at the head of an army, the strength of which is variously estimated, by some at 160,000, by others at 70,000 men, encountered and routed the forces of Muhammad Shah, the Timurian monarch of Delhi. Kurnal is distant 965 miles N.W. from Calcutta. Lat. 29° 41′, long. 77° 3′.

KURNALLI RIVER rises in Tibet, in lat. 30° 43′, long. 80° 47′, and flows for seventy-five miles in a south-east direction, to the town of Angharah, on the borders of Nepal, ten miles beyond which it first turns south-west for seventy miles, and subsequently south-east for forty miles, to its junction with the Bhyrvee, on the borders of Oude, through which kingdom it flows for thirty miles in a south-westerly direction, to itsj unction with the Gogra, in lat. 28° 17′, long. 81° 5′.

KURNOLEE, in the Sinde Sagur Dooab division of the Punjab, a town situated 17 miles from the left bank of the Indus, 118 miles S. of the town of Peshawur. Lat. 32° 18′, long. 71° 36′.

KURNOOL.—A British district in the presidency of Madras, bounded on the north by the rivers Toongabudra and Kistnah, separating it from the Nizam's dominions; on the east and south by the British district of Cuddapah; and on the west by that of Bellary. It extends from lat. 14° 55′ to 16° 15′, and from long. 77° 47′ to 79° 15′; is 110 miles in length from north-east to south-west, and eighty miles in breadth, and contains an area of 2,643 square miles, with a population of 273,190. The tract is not included within what are termed "the Regulation districts," power being reserved by legislative enactment of modifying, to any extent that may be deemed requisite, the introduction of the ordinary modes of revenue and judicial administration. For the preservation of peace and order, a body of irregular cavalry was raised, upon the acquisition of the province by the British. The corps maintains a high degree of efficiency, and its formation has conferred additional benefits upon the community, by affording employment, which was much wanted by persons of all classes in the country. Kurnool was visited by a tremendous storm in 1851, which occasioned vast injury to works of irrigation, and great destruction of human life. The revenue in 1843 was returned at nine lacs of rupees, or 90,000*l*.

Towards the close of the year 1838, while the British were planning the expedition for the restoration of Shah Shoojah to the throne of Cabool, information reached them that military preparations upon an extensive scale had been carried on for some time by the nawaub of Kurnool. An investigation followed, the result of which left little doubt that the nawaub was one of the originators of a widespread Mussulman conspiracy for the subversion of British rule in India; its development merely awaiting a fitting opportunity, which it was anticipated events in the northwest would afford. Recourse to arms became necessary. "No difficulty was experienced in obtaining possession of the capital; but the nawaub, with some hundred of his followers, withdrew from the place. Lieut.-Col. Dyce, of the 34th Madras light infantry, marched with a force against them, and, after a sharp encounter, succeeded in securing the person of the nawaub, as well as several other prisoners, and much property." An immense quantity of warlike stores was found in the town, the greater part having been deposited under the shelter of the zenana. No satisfactory explanation could be given for the accumulation of so vast a quantity of the *matériel* of war, or for the systematic disguise and concealment under which it had taken place; and as the obvious conclusion was, that the nawaub's proceedings were connected with plans for the subversion of the paramount power, it was justly thought that the chief had been guilty of a breach of allegiance, and his territory was annexed to the British dominions. The nawaub retired to Trichinopoly, where it was remarkable that he frequently attended the service of the Missionaries' church. Upon the last occasion of such attendance, he was mortally stabbed by one of his Mahometan followers. His eldest son, Uluf Khan, received from the British government a stipend of 10,000 rupees per annum, which lapsed upon his demise in 1848. Orders have been given from home for the formation of this province into a separate zillah.

KURNOOL.—A town in the British district of Kurnool, presidency of Madras, 90 miles N.E. by E. of Bellary. The population has been computed at 20,000. Lat. 15° 50′, long. 78° 5′.

KUROD, in the British district of Surat, presidency of Bombay, a town on the left or south bank of the river Taptee, 25 miles E. of Surat. Lat. 21° 9′, long. 73° 16′.

KURONDE.—See CALAHANDY.

KURORA, in the British district of Allahabad, lieut.-gov. of the N.W. Provinces, a village on the route from the cantonment of Allahabad to Futtehpoor, and 30 miles N.W. of the former. Lat. 25° 36′, long. 81° 31′.

KUROULEE, in the British district of Agra, a town on the route from the city of Agra to Jeypore, and 15 miles W. of the former. It is a small place, situate on a low gravelly hill, and surrounded by a ruinous rampart with towers. Around are scattered a few poor gardens. Lat. 27° 8′, long. 77° 51′.

KUROUNTHUH, a village in the British district of Rohtuk, lieut.-gov. of the N.W. Provinces. Lat. 28° 48′, long. 76° 40′.

KURR.—A town of Eastern India, in the British province of Tenasserim, 110 miles N.N.W. of Tenasserim. Lat. 13° 37′, long. 98° 31′.

KURRA.—A town in one of the recently sequestrated districts of Hyderabad, or dominions of the Nizam, situate 29 miles E.S.E. of Ahmednuggur. Lat. 18° 54′, long. 75° 9′.

KURRACHEE is a seaport of Sinde, near the north-western extremity of the coast of that country. It is situate near the base of the southern extremity of the Pubb or Brahooic Mountains, on a level space intervening between them and the sea, and is the only seaport in Sinde for vessels drawing more than ten feet of water. The port is protected from the sea and bad weather by Munorah, a bluff rocky headland, projecting south-eastward from the mainland, and leaving a space of about two miles between the extreme point and the coast to the east. In the harbour and within the entrance are some rocky islets, which are seen from sea over the low isthmus connecting the point of Munorah with the coast to the west. There is a good roadstead outside Munorah, except during May, June, July, and part of August, when the south-west monsoon blows with such violence as to render anchoring there impracticable. At the entrance of the harbour is a bar, having one fathom and a quarter of water when the tide is out, and two and a half or three fathoms at high water spring tides; it consequently cannot be safely crossed by ships the draught of which exceeds sixteen feet. About a mile inside the bar there is an extensive bank, dry at low water; and between this and the western shore is the channel up the harbour. The general depths in the fair track along that side of the bay are from two to four fathoms at low water. The harbour is spacious, extending about five miles northward from Munorah Point, and about the same distance from the town, on the eastern shore, to the extreme western point; but a small part only of this expanse admits large ships. Experiments, however, have been authorized, with the view of ascertaining the practicability of removing the bar at the entrance, and otherwise deepening the harbour. The first voyage from England direct to the port of Kurrachee was made in 1852, by the ship "Duke of Argyle," of 800 tons. The point of Munorah terminating to the eastward the promontory, which landlocks the harbour on the south, is rocky, and about 150 feet high. On it a fort was built in 1797, which has been said to be so placed that the fire of ships could have no effect on it, because their guns would require to be so greatly elevated, to avoid striking the brow of the hill, that most of the shot must pass over and fall into the sea at the opposite side; while at the same time the vessel must approach the headland so close, that musketry protected by the rocks could clear the decks. This opinion, however, was disproved, and that of Lord, that the eleven guns on the fort, owing to their partial depression, could produce no effect on shipping, corroborated, by what occurred in the beginning of 1839, when the fire of the "Wellesley," 74 guns, in an hour dismantled the fort, which was forthwith occupied by the British troops.

The town is three miles from the landing-place when the tide is out; but it has been rendered easy of access by the formation of a mole and road, constructed at a cost of upwards of 80,000*l.* Before the occupation by the British troops, the fortifications were very mean and irregular, being composed chiefly of mud and straw, and in many parts so dilapidated that a horseman might ride to the top of them. In a few places they were found in good repair, and partially faced with masonry. The town, with its extensive suburbs, was ascertained, by census, in 1813, to contain 13,000 persons. Burnes, in 1830, estimated the population at 15,000, about one-half of them Hindoos, who here carry on an extensive commerce. In 1850, the population amounted to 16,773 persons, and was regarded as on the increase. In 1853, the town contained 13,769 inhabitants, and the suburbs 8,458; making a total of 22,227. An English school has been opened in the town by the government, and a church has been erected. The native exports are camels, saltpetre, salt, rice and other grain, ghee or clarified butter, hides, tallow, oil, oil-seeds, fish, bark for tanning, alkalies, indigo, cotton. The transit exports from the adjoining countries are asafœtida and various other drugs, madder and other dyes, alum, wool, silk, Kashmir shawls, dried fruits, lapis lazuli, gems of various kinds, the precious metals, and horses. The imports are metals, hardware, cottons and silks, twist and yarn.

Kurrachee is a position of very great importance, whether regarded in a commercial, a political, or a military point of view. It has been laid down, that a force stationed here, with detachments at Sehwan and Bukkur, might hold Sinde in complete subjection. Kurrachee is the only safe port of Sinde. In a commercial point of view, it may be defined the gate of Central Asia, and is likely to become to India what Liverpool is to England. It is also the terminus of the Sinde Railway, and will consequently be shortly connected with Hydrabad, and indeed with the whole of Northern India, through which some of the extensions of this railway will doubtless be carried. It has a good route westward to Sonmeeanee, and consequently ready access to Beloochistan. To the east there is a route to Tatta, along the seacoast, as far as Garrah creek, then along the course of the Garrah stream, and from the small town of that name directly to Tattah. There is another route from Kurrachee, directly through the hilly country to Tattah. Another route conducts to Kotree, on the Indus, opposite Hyderabad; another, westward of these, through the Lukkee hills, to Sehwan; another, still farther west, through the same hills, to Shikarpoor.

Burnes and Carless state that there is an inland navigation by means of cross channels, from Kurrachee to the Indus; but there is little doubt that this is an error, as Kennedy, who went down the creek in a boat, found that it debouched into the sea nine miles east of the mouth of the harbour of Kurrachee; and in this he is borne out by the manuscript map of the quartermaster-general. The ground, however, between the creek and the port is quite level, so that a canal could, without much difficulty, be made, connecting the two waters. The Garrah creek is navigable as far as Garrah village, about forty miles from the sea, and the land intervening between this last place and the Indus, abreast of Tatta, is level, low, of a soft nature, and only twenty-five miles across; so that the great river might, with little labour and a moderate outlay, be thus rendered accessible from the sea for large vessels. The climate of Kurrachee is cool in proportion to its latitude, and, under British auspices, the town must speedily become a most important place. Lat. 24° 51′, long. 67° 2′.

KURRADIKUL.—A town in one of the recently sequestrated districts of Hyderabad, or dominions of the Nizam, situate 57 miles W. of Raichoor. Lat. 16° 9′, long. 76° 33′.

KURRAH, or KARHA.—A town on the right bank of the Ganges, on the route from Allahabad to Cawnpore, and 40 miles N.W. of the former. It extends about a mile along the bank, on the more elevated part of which is an old fort, now a heap of ruins, and was so in the time of Tieffenthaler, a century ago. This last author mentions that it had a number of ruined houses, from which, and from the multitude of tombs crowded around it, some conjecture may be formed of its former populousness. Its celebrity and importance, in the opinion of the native population, resulted from the vicinity of the tomb of a famous reputed Mussulman saint, named Kamal Shek, who lies buried at the contiguous town of Kamalpur. The ruin of Kurrah commenced when Akbar, towards the close of the sixteenth century, removed the civil establishment to Allahabad, and was completed by Asof ud Daulah, the nawaub of Oude, who destroyed the finest buildings for the sake of the materials, which he used in raising edifices at Lucknow. The surrounding country, however, could not have been very highly cultivated or peopled three centuries ago, as Baber mentions, that at that time it abounded in wild elephants, and the people of thirty or forty villages were mainly occupied in their capture. The town itself, at the same time, had a fort, the residence of an important Mussulman chief. Distant N.W. from Calcutta by land 535 miles. Lat. 25° 41′, long. 81° 28′.

KURRAR.—A town in the British province of Sattara, presidency of Bombay, 31 miles S.S.E. of Sattara. Lat. 17° 17′, long. 74° 16′.

KURREE, in Guzerat, or territory of the Guicowar, presidency of Bombay, a town in a picturesque site in a finely-wooded country. Here is a palace, formerly the residence of Mulhar Row, Guicowar. Population 25,000, many of whom are excellent artisans. Distance from the city of Ahmedabad, N.W., 25 miles; Baroda, N.W., 85; Surat, N., 155; Bombay, N., 310. Lat. 23° 18′, long. 72° 19′.

KURRUCKPOOR, in the district of Sandi, territory of Oude, a town on the western frontier, towards the British district of Furruckabad, on the route from Futtehgurh cantonment to that of Setapoor, eight miles N.E. of the former, 74 W. of the latter. It is situate on the left bank of the Ramgunga (Western), here crossed by ferry. There is a bazar here, and supplies are abundant. Lat. 27° 27′, long. 79° 47′.

KURRUK, in the Daman division of the Punjab, a town situated 23 miles from the right bank of the Indus, 84 miles S.W. by S. of the town of Peshawur. Lat. 32° 57′, long. 71°.

KURRUMBILA.—A town of Orissa, in the native state of Mohurbunge, situate 60 miles W. by S. from Midnapoor, and 60 miles N.W. by N. from Balasore. Lat. 22° 12′, long. 86° 30′.

KURRUMFOOLEE.—A river of Eastern India, rising in lat. 23° 8′, long. 93° 5′, on the western slope of the Youmadoung range, to the north of the Blue Mountain, and, flowing in a south-westerly direction for 130 miles, falls into the Bay of Bengal a few miles below the town of Chittagong, in lat. 22° 20′, long. 91° 56′.

KURRUNG.—A town of Assam, in the British district of Nowgong, 15 miles N.N.E. of Nowgong. Lat. 26° 33′, long. 92° 56′.

KURSANEH, in the British district of Mynpooree, a small town on the route from Allygurh cantonment to that of Futtehgurh, and 44 miles S.E. of the former. Lat. 27° 44′, long. 78° 46′.

KURSAVA.—See KHUSAWARA.

KURSOD.—A town in the native state of Gwalior, or territory of Scindia's family, situate 28 miles W. from Oojein, and 90 miles S.S.E. from Neemuch. Lat. 23° 12′, long. 75° 22′.

KURTUL, in the British district of Banda, lieut.-gov. of the N.W. Provinces, a village on the route from the town of Banda to Adjygurh, 12 miles N. of the latter. Water is obtained from wells. Lat. 25° 2′, long. 80° 24′.

KURTUR.—A town in the British district of Nellore, presidency of Madras, 95 miles N. of Madras. Lat. 14° 27′, long. 80° 13′.

KURUCKDEA.—A town in the British district of Ramgur, lieut.-gov. of Bengal, 60 miles N.E. by E. of Hazareebagh. Lat. 24° 27′, long. 86° 11′.

KURUHEEA, in the British district of Ghazeepore, lieut.-gov. of the N.W. Provinces, a village on the route from Chunar to Dinapoor, 61 miles N.E. of the former, 185 S.W. of the latter. Lat. 25° 26′, long. 83° 50′.

KURUJGEE.—A town in the British province of Sattara, presidency of Bombay, 24 miles N. of Beejapoor. Lat. 17° 9′, long. 75° 39′.

KURULPETTA.—A town of the Deccan, in the territory of Nagpoor or Berar, situate 205 miles S.E. from Nagpoor, and 25 miles N.W. from Jugdulapoor. Lat. 19° 30′, long. 81° 43′.

KURUMBEE.—A town in the British district of Chota Nagpoor, lieut.-gov. of Bengal, 58 miles W.S.W. of Lohadugga. Lat. 23° 10′, long. 83° 55′.

KURUMNASA.—A river rising in the British district of Shahabad, presidency of Bengal, and in lat. 24° 34′, long. 83° 46′, near the "village Sarodag, close by the southern side of the table-land (of South Shahabad), among some stones, above a rice-field. The Kurumnasa issues from a little fountain called Sarmanchuya, and immediately forms a fine rapid streamlet, which, notwithstanding its horrible impurity, is as clear as crystal." The source is about eighteen miles west of the celebrated fort of Rohtas. Its direction is north-west for about fifty miles, and in this part of its course it has a rapid stream, which flows even in the driest weather, and expands into numerous pools, abounding in fish. In lat. 24° 51′, long. 83° 15′, it turns nearly due north, in which direction it flows twenty-six miles, forming, in the first instance, the boundary between the British districts Shahabad and Mirzapoor, and then traversing the latter district. In this part of its course it is precipitated a depth of 100 feet down a vast rock, called Chhanpathar, and in the rainy season forms a noble cascade, but in the dry season the stream in many sandy places disappears, the channel containing at intervals numerous stagnant pools. In lat. 25° 8′, long. 83° 22′, it takes a north-easterly direction, first intersecting Benares for ten miles, then forming for twenty miles the boundary between that district and Shahabad; and finally, dividing for forty miles the last-named district from that of Ghazeepoor, it falls into the Ganges, on the right side, in lat. 25° 28′, long. 83° 58′, having altogether a course of about 146 miles. About twenty-seven miles above its mouth, and in lat. 25° 19′, long. 83° 44′, it is joined on the right side by the Durgawati, the latter having rather the larger volume of water. Where traversed, about a mile or two above its mouth, by the route from Chunar to Dinapoor, it is 100 yards wide, with very deep water and steep banks, and is usually crossed by troops by means of a bridge of boats. At Nowbulpoor, in lat. 25° 13′, long. 83° 32′, and fifty-five miles from its mouth, it is traversed by the great north-western route from Calcutta to Delhi, the passage being made by a fine bridge of stone masonry, which has replaced one 320 feet in length, constructed of ropes, on the suspension principle. The present structure consists of three equal arches, each fifty-three feet in span; piers 30 by 13; roadway twenty-five feet wide and perfectly horizontal. The cost of 10,000*l*. must be regarded as very low; but advantage was taken of an excellent foundation laid in a previous attempt to build a bridge at the same place. This river is subject to violent rain-floods, and has been known to rise twenty-six feet in one night in June, when scarcely any rain had fallen in the plain extending along the Ganges. According to a statement in a late publication, it is navigable during the periodical rains.

KURUNBAS, in the British district of Boolundshuhur, lieut.-gov. of the N.W. Provinces, a village on the right bank of the Ganges, 72 miles S.E. of Delhi. Lat. 28° 16′, long. 78° 23′.

KURUNRUMMA.—A town in the British district of Ramgur, lieut.-gov. of Bengal, situate 38 miles N.N.E. of Hazareebagh. Lat. 24° 30′, long. 85° 40′.

KURUPAM.—A town in the British district of Ganjam, presidency of Madras, situate 107 miles W.S.W. of Ganjam. Lat. 18° 52′, long. 83° 37′.

KURVULLA.—A town in Hyderabad, or dominions of the Nizam, situate 137 miles E.S.E. from Ahmednuggur, and 105 miles S.E. by S. from Jaulnah. Lat. 18° 31′, long. 76° 44′.

KURWA, in the British district of Ajmeer, lieut.-gov. of the N.W. Provinces, a town on the route from Nusseerabad to Beawr, 20 miles W.S.W. of the former. Lat. 26° 14′, long. 74° 32′.

KURWAKHERA, in the British district of Etawa, lieut.-gov. of the N.W. Provinces, a village on the route from the cantonment of Etawa to Calpee, and 10 miles S.E. of the former. Lat. 26° 42′, long. 79° 12′.

KURYAH.—A town in the native state of Nepal, 46 miles S. from Khatmandoo, and 43 miles E.N.E. from Bettiah. Lat. 27° 3′, long. 85° 10′.

KUSBA, in the British district of Purnea, lieut.-gov. of Bengal, a town situate five miles N.E. of the town of Purnea. It contains 1,500 houses, a number which, according to the usually received average of inmates, would assign it a population of about 7,500 persons. Lat. 25° 49′, long. 87° 32′.

KUSBAH SUCHENDEE, in the British district of Cawnpoor, lieut.-gov. of the N.W. Provinces, a town on the route from Cawnpoor to Jaloun, 10 miles W.S.W. of the former. Lat. 26° 27′, long. 80° 16′.

KUSBEH BOLA, in the British district of Ghazeepoor, lieut.-gov. of the N.W. Provinces, a town on the route from Dinapoor to Ghazeepoor, 11 miles E. by N. of the latter. Lat. 25° 34′, long. 83° 49′.

KUSBUH SECUNDRA, in the British district of Allahabad, lieut.-gov. of the N.W. Provinces, a town on the route from Mirzapoor to Lucknow, 49 miles N.W. of the former. Lat. 25° 35′, long. 82° 4′.

KUSEEA, in the British district of Goruckpoor, lieut.-gov. of the N.W. Provinces, a small town on the route from Dinapoor to Goruckpoor, 110 miles N.W. of the former. Within a mile of the town is a conical mound, constructed of bricks, and known among the people by the name of Devisthan,—"place of the goddess;" and near it the ruin of a solid temple, built of brick. The inhabitants have no tradition as to when, by whom, or from what motives, they were raised. At present water and supplies are abundant here. Lat. 26° 41′, long. 83° 56′.

KUSHBIR, in Bussahir, a village, with a small fort, in the district of Koonawur. It is situate on a declivity, sloping gradually eastward to the right bank of the Sutluj, and surrounded by vineyards. Elevation above the sea 9,284 feet. Lat. 31° 33′, long. 78° 19′.

KUSHEY SONDA, in the Saugor and Nerbudda territories, a town situate in the British district of Ramgurh, on the route from Ramgurh to Rewah, 21 miles N. of the former. Lat. 23° 7′, long. 81° 1′.

KUSHYN, in Bussahir, a fort near the right bank of a considerable feeder of the river Pabur. It is of considerable size, with houses neatly built, and well covered with slate, in a site of little beauty, the view from it being confined by surrounding mountains of repulsive aspect. Close to the town are iron-mines, containing specular ore, embedded in mica-slate. This is smelted and rendered malleable at the village; but the produce is not considered abundant. Elevation above the sea 6,875 feet. Lat. 31° 11′, long. 77° 42′.

KUSMIR.—A town in the British district of Sarun, lieut.-gov. of Bengal, six miles N.N.E. of Dinapoor. Lat. 25° 40′, long. 85° 11′.

KUSMORE.—A town in the British district of Shikarpoor, province of Sinde, presidency of Bombay, 71 miles E.N.E. of Shikarpoor. Lat. 28° 22′, long. 69° 41′.

KUSOWLEAH, in the British district of Furruckabad, lieut.-gov. of the N.W. Provinces, a town on the route from the cantonment of Allygurh to that of Futtehgurh, and 42 miles N.W. of the latter. Lat. 27° 31′, long. 79° 4′.

KUSRAON, in the Sinde Sagur Dooab division of the Punjab, a town situated 26 miles from the left bank of the Indus, 58 miles S.E. by E. of the town of Peshawur. Lat. 33° 27′, long. 72° 29′.

KUSSAREE, in the British district of Allahabad, lieut.-gov. of the N.W. Provinces, a village on the route from the city of Allahabad to Lucknow, and 10 miles N.W. of the former. Lat. 25° 33′, long. 81° 50′.

KUSSAUN, in Sirhind, a village on the route from Kythul to Jheend, and 28 miles N. of the latter place. It is situate amidst bush-jungle, so thick that a small force can scarcely find room for encampment. Distant N.W. from Calcutta 1,003 miles. Lat. 29° 39′, long. 76° 29′.

KUSSEAH, in the British district of Allahabad, lieut.-gov. of the N.W. Provinces, a village on the route from the cantonment of Allahabad to Futtehpoor, and 29 miles N.W. of the former. Heber describes it as a large ruinous village, near a grove of neem-trees. Garden describes the surrounding country as well cultivated, but Heber states it to be much wilder, worse cultivated, and worse peopled than any which he had seen in India. Lat. 25° 36′, long. 81° 32′.

KUSSOOR, in the Punjab, a large town nine miles from the right or western bank of the Ghara. It is a place of great antiquity, is inclosed by a wall, and has several divisions, each surrounded by a separate wall strengthened with bastions. According to tradition, there were formerly twelve of these divisions corresponding to the number of the twelve sons of the founder, who assigned one to each. There are several mosques and palaces. The surrounding country abounds in gardens and other well-cultivated spots. The inhabitants are all Mahometans. Hough observes, that at this place "an army might make a good stand, as not only are there heights, but each division of the town might be turned into a fortified position." Lat. 31° 9′, long. 74° 27′.

KUSSOWLEE, a British sanatory station in Baghat, is situate on the route from Pinjor to Simla, nearly due north of the former place, and distant from it about fourteen miles by a circuitous route. This recently-established station is thus described by a correspondent of of the Delhi Gazette:—"Kussowlee itself is a hill of about five miles in circuit, considerably detached from the chain of which it forms a part. Its height is about 7,000 feet, the upper part is an undulating table-land; and the whole hill does not show any abrupt peak. From the plains the ascent is very sudden, that face of the hill presenting a forbidding aspect, intersected by perpendicular ravines, and showing the strata of clay-slate at an angle of 30° or 40°. The road from Pinjor is chiefly cut along this steep hill-side. The northern face of the hill is much less abruptly defined, and runs into the ranges that slope to the river Gumber." In a direct line, it is about 20 miles S.W. of Simla, and nearly on a level with it. The soil overlying the rock is light and porous, except in places where decaying vegetation has accumulated a black mould. The timber consists principally of firs, mixed with which are a few oaks and rhododendrons. The absence of underwood, and the porosity of the soil quickly absorbing rain, render the air dry and healthful. The principal disadvantage is the want of water. The natural springs are at a distance below the station, and the non-retentive nature of the surface precludes the construction of tanks, while from the rocky character of the substratum, it is impracticable to obtain a supply by sinking wells. Hence, during spring and the early part of summer, water must be brought on mules and bullocks from springs a mile and a quarter distant, and 848 feet below the level of the parade-ground. There is no cultivation except in the valleys, where irrigation is practicable; and in such localities the slopes are formed into terraces, supporting successive slips of soil bearing very fine crops of rice and other grain, ginger, turmeric, potatoes, onions, and other vegetables. The writer already quoted describes the scenery as fine:—"West and south, the view of the plain is boundless, and after the rains, the Sutlej winds along in great majesty, its course being clearly traceable from Roopur to Loodianah; while on the other side the Jumna can be seen. Standing on the summit of the hill, looking down the steep declivity of nearly 6,000 feet, there is one vast map spread before you, which, in the different lights of morning and evening, shows a magic variety of tints and shades. The sun is just now dipping into the Sutlej, where it runs due west; turn gradually to the right, and you will have a view of the plains of the Punjab, until you reach the lowest spurs of the mountain-range, just where the river issues from the hills. Then comes a group of beautiful varied hills, the highest of which is Soorujghur, above Belaspoor. Behind these the white peaks begin to appear, and, looking north, you have the whole snowy rampart rising in uninterrupted majesty; for the hills on a level with Simla, or even Whartoo, form but undulations in the foreground of this magnificent panorama. Turn further round, and to the north-east you have another group of nearer hills, the most conspicuous of which is Baghat, and behind them the snow appearing at intervals till you reach the east. In that quarter you have lost the snow, but there is a beautiful sea of undulating hills, with here and there glimpses of the plains, until, looking south, you come again to an unlimited horizon. In all this landscape, there is but one thing wanting, the one deficiency which prevents our hills from being absolutely lovely, and that is, the absence of water. No lake, no stream, enlivens the view; and this makes all the rest like a beautiful face with the eyes shut." A church has been erected here for the accommodation of the Christian community. In 1845, Kussowlee was visited by cholera, which greatly increased the ordinary rate of mortality; but its general salubrity appears well established. Kussowlee is distant N.W. from Calcutta 1,069 miles. Lat. 30° 54′, long. 77° 3′.

KUTCHEGUD.—A town situate on the north-west point of the peninsula of Kattywar, territory of Guzerat, 10 miles S. from the Gulf of Cutch, and 118 W. of Rajkote. Lat. 22° 20′, long. 69° 1′.

KUTCHNAR SURYE.—A town in the native state of Gwalior, or possessions of the family of Scindia, situate 83 miles W.N.W. from Saugur, and 83 miles S. by W. from Bhopal. Lat. 24° 24′, long. 77° 39′.

KUTCHOUDA.—A town of Malwa, in the native state of Amjherah, situate 10 miles S. from Amjherah, and 126 miles E. from Baroda. Lat. 22° 24′, long. 75° 10′.

KUTCHWA, in the British district of Allahabad, lieut.-gov. of the N.W. Provinces, a village on the left bank of the Ganges, and distant N.W. from Calcutta by the river route 756 miles, S.E. from the city of Allahabad 52 by the same. Lat. 25° 12′, long. 82° 20′.

KUTHOTEEA, in the territory of Saugor and Nerbudda, a town in the British district of Ramgurh, situate on the route from Ramgurh to Jubbulpoor, 18 miles W.N.W. of the former. Lat. 22° 53′, long. 80° 46′.

KUTI.—A town in the native state of Nepal, situate six miles S.E. from the left bank of the Bhotiya Coosy river, and 63 miles E.N.E. from Khatmandoo. Lat. 28° 8′, long. 86° 11′.

KUTKA UMROAHA, in the British district of Benares, lieut.-gov. of the N.W. Provinces, a village on the route from Allahabad to the city of Benares, 55 miles E. of the former, 19 W. of the latter. Lat. 25° 16′, long. 82° 45′.

KUTLUNGEE, in the British territory of Sagur and Nerbudda, lieut.-gov. of the N.W. Provinces, a town on the route from Nagpoor to Ramgurh, 62 miles N.E. of the former. Lat. 21° 47′, long. 79° 50′.

KUTOLA, in the Rajpoot state of Jodhpoor, a village on the route, *viâ* Nagor, from Jessulmeer to Nusserabad, and 142 miles N.W. of the latter. Lat. 27°, long. 73° 16′.

KUTOLLEE, in the territory of Kotah, in Rajpootana, a town on the left bank of the river Parbutty, and held by a feudatory of the rajah of Kotah. The residence of the feudatory is a lofty edifice, in a handsome Hindoo style of architecture, situate on the bank of the river. Distant direct N.E. of Kotah 50 miles, S.W. of Gwalior 110. Lat. 25° 39′, long. 76° 35′.

KUTPURI, in the British district of Etawah, lieut.-gov. of the N.W. Provinces, a village on the route from the cantonment of Agra to that of Etawah, and 18 miles N.W. of the latter. Lat. 26° 58′, long. 78° 53′.

KUTRA, in the British district of Allahabad, lieut.-gov. of the N.W. Provinces, a pass on one of the routes from the city of Allahabad to Rewa, and 63 miles S.E. of the former. The surface of the country rises from the valley of the Ganges about Mirzapoor to the elevated tracts of Bundelcund and Boghelcund, lying to the south-west. The ascent takes place in successive plateaus, becoming continually more elevated towards the west, and bounded on the side of the more depressed tracts by ranges of hills of no great relative elevation. The plateau nearest the Ganges is bounded towards it by a ridge traversed by the Tara Pass, and to the south and south-west it is bounded by a ridge which forms the face of the plateau that rises over it, and is traversed by the Kutra Pass. The north-east side of the Kutra range, towards Tara Pass, is rather steep, yet overstrewn with rubbish of disintegrated rock, amidst which grows a stunted forest of trees allied to pines, besides the pipal (Ficus religiosa) and coranthus. The village of Kutra is situate at the north-east side of the pass, on the left bank of the Seoti, a small river tributary to the Bilund. Into the Seoti are discharged several small streams, which tumble in lofty cascades down the face of the overhanging ridge. At that of Bilohi, twelve miles west of the Kutra Pass, the fall is 398 feet, and the escarpment nearly perpendicular. Franklin considers part of the ridge rising above the village to be saliferous; and adds, that salt is manufactured on the banks of the Tons. According to Jacquemont, however, the water of the wells is not salt. The road through the pass is excellent, being carefully laid down from Mirzapoor. Water is abundant, being obtained from the Seoti; but supplies must be collected from the adjacent country. Elevation of summit of ridge above the sea 1,219 feet; of the village, 520 feet. Lat. 24° 51′, long. 82° 11′.

KUTRA.—See MEERANPOOR KUTRA.

KUTSUHEE.—A town in the British district of Balasore, lieut.-gov. of Bengal, 99 miles S.W. of Calcutta. Lat. 21° 39′, long. 87° 16′.

KUTTAJEE, a small river of Sinde, rises in the hilly tract between Kurrachee and Sehwan, and in lat. 25° 7′, long. 67° 28′. After a course of twenty miles in a north-westerly direction, it falls into the river Goorban. Though so inconsiderable in point of size, it is in this arid country important, for affording a constant supply of good water, as even when it has ceased to run, the pools in its bed contain considerable quantities.

KUTTANO, in the British district of Mynpooree, lieut.-gov. of the N.W. Provinces, a village 30 miles N.W. of the town of Mynpooree. Lat. 27° 24′, long. 78° 37′.

KUTTEEGEEREE.—A town in the British district of Belgaum, presidency of Bombay, 76 miles E. by N. of Belgaum. Lat. 16° 4′, long. 75° 41′.

KUTTOSUN.—See MYHEE CAUNTA.

KUTTOWLI, in the British district of Futtehpore, lieut.-gov. of the N.W. Provinces, a village on the route from Banda to the town of Futtehpoor, and 11 miles S.W. of the latter. Lat. 25° 52′, long. 80° 44′.

KUTTREE.—A town in the British district of Bhagulpoor, lieut.-gov. of Bengal, 20 miles N.E. by E. of Bhagulpoor. Lat. 25° 20′, long. 87° 17′.

KUTTUNGEE, in the British territory of Saugor and Nerbudda, lieut.-gov. of the N.W. Provinces, a town on the route from Saugor cantonment to Jubbulpoor, 89 miles S.E. of former, 22 N.W. of latter. It has a bazar, and is well supplied with water. Here is a considerable quantity of iron, manufactured principally into gun-barrels, which are much esteemed and largely exported. Lat. 23° 27′, long. 79° 50′.

KUTTUNGTOLLA.—A town of the Deccan, in the territory of Nagpoor or Berar, situate 70 miles N.E. by E. from Nagpoor, and 101 miles S. from Jubbulpoor. Lat. 21° 41′, long. 80° 4′.

KUTTUNGY.—A town in the territory of Nagpoor or Berar, situate on the right bank of one of the branches of the Wein Gunga, and 88 miles E.N.E. from Nagpoor. Lat. 21° 43′, long. 80° 21′.

KUTUBPOOR, in the British district of Allyghur, lieut.-gov. of the N.W. Provinces, a village on the route, by Khasganj, from Bareilly to Allyghur cantonment, and 20 miles S.E. of the latter, 52 N.E. of Agra. Lat. 27° 51′, long. 78° 25′.

KUTUBUGGA.—A town in the British district of Sumbulpoor, on the south-west frontier of Bengal, situate 19 miles N.E. by N. of Sumbulpoor. Lat. 21° 41′, long. 84° 10′.

KUTULGARH, in the British district of Kumaon, lieut.-gov. of the N.W. Provinces, a fort, formerly garrisoned by the Goorkha troops, situate on the route, by Ramesur, from the cantonment of Petoragurh to that of Champawut, four miles N. of the latter. Webb, who surveyed it at the close of A.D. 1815, thus describes it:—"The shape of Kutulgurh fort is irregular, and fitted, as it were, to the top of the hill on which it stands. The work is oblong; its greatest length from north to south may be about fifty yards, and the breadth half that quantity: each extremity is completed by a species of star fort: the line connecting these has, at short distances, salient angles, which flank each other with tolerable exactness. The wall is of considerable solidity, and is composed of rough stones without cement; it is looped and pierced all round, and is nine feet high on the outside. The whole work is surrounded, about fifteen feet beyond the wall, by a stockade, the stakes of which are about ten feet above the earth. The whole appears to be in good and defensible order. The ascent to the fort is most easy from the eastern side, but is, even here, very steep; and the latter part, by a zig-zag path, is within long musket-shot" of a detached stockade outside the fort. Close to this stockade is a small Hindoo temple. Water must be obtained from a source covered by a fire of musketry from the stockade, distant 400 feet. Lat. 29° 24′, long. 80° 5′.

KUTUMBO, in the raj or protected Rajpoot state of Ulwar, a small town on the eastern frontier, towards Bhurtpore. It was bombarded and laid in ruins October 29th, 1803, by the Mahratta army, which had escaped from the Deccan, and was flying before the British under General Lake. On the 31st the British general reached the smoking ruins of Kutumbo, but found that the enemy had deserted it that morning; and pursuit being continued, the fugitive host was next morning overtaken, and totally defeated at Laswari. Kutumbo is 60 miles W. of Agra, 95 miles S. of Delhi. Lat. 27° 19′, long. 77° 8′.

KUVOY, in the British district of Malabar, under the presidency of Madras, a town on an extensive estuary of a river flowing from the Western Ghauts. The surrounding country is a sandy plain of no great fertility, but suited for the culture of inferior rice and cocoanut-trees. The town is stated to have only about sixty or seventy houses. The inhabitants are Moplahs or Mussulmans. Here the English had a caftory in 1750; and about that time the French built a fort on the south side of the river. This fort, and another of native construction, are now in ruins. Distance N.W. from Cananore 18 miles, S.E. from Mangalore 58. Lat. 12° 6′, long. 75° 16′.

KUWA, in the British district of Futtehpore, lieut.-gov. of the N.W. Provinces, a town on the left bank of the river Jumna, 17 miles S. of the town of Futtehpore. Lat. 25° 42′, long. 80° 52′.

KYAL PYEN.—A town of Burmah, situate 53 miles from the left bank of the Irawady, and 96 miles N.E. by N. from Ava. Lat. 23° 3′, long. 96° 50′.

KYAN NAYAT MYO.—A town of Burmah, situate on the left bank of the Irawady river, 96 miles N. from Ava. Lat. 23° 15′, long. 96°.

KYAR, or KYE RIVER, one of the mouths of the Indus, leading into the Pittyanee. Lat. 24° 34′, long. 67° 13′.

KYARDA, in Sirmor, a village in the Doon or valley of the same name, and on the route from Dehra to Nahun, being 21 miles S.E. of the latter place. It is a small place, described by Mundy as "romantically situated in a dell, completely encompassed by woody heights, on the summit of the nearest of which are the ruins of what appears to have been a petty Goorkah fortress." The lands comprised in the Kyarda Doon were granted to the rajah of Sirmoor by the British government in 1833, subject to certain conditions; among which were the impartial administration of justice, the abolition of transit-duties, and the construction and repair of roads. Elevation of the village above the sea 1,844 feet. Lat. 30° 28′, long. 77° 36′.

KYBYOUN.—A town of Burmah, situate on the right bank of the Irawady river, and 60 miles N. from Ava. Lat. 22° 42′, long. 95° 56′.

KYL.—A town in the north-east quarter of the Punjaub, situate in the British district of Spiti, 107 miles E. by N. of Kangra. Lat. 32° 17′, long. 78° 3′.

KYLASCOTTAH.—A town in the hill zemindarry of Jeypoor, on the south-west frontier of Bengal, situate 79 miles E. by N. from Jeypoor, and 100 miles W. by S. from Ganjam. Lat. 19° 14′, long. 83° 36′.

KYLEE, in the British district of Benares, lieut.-gov. of the N.W. Provinces, a town on the route from Chunar to Dinapore, situate 21 miles N.E. of the former, 125 S.W. of the latter. Lat. 25° 20′, long. 83° 13′.

KYMPROO, a village in Arracan, situate on the right bank of the Lemroo river, near the confluence of one of the feeders of that river. Lat. 20° 35′, long. 93° 33′.

KYNETA, in the British district of Mynpooree, lieut.-gov. of the N.W. Provinces, a village on the route from the city of Agra to Etawa, and 42 miles N.W. of the latter. Lat. 27° 8′, long. 78° 31′.

KYOKOO.—A town of Burmah, situate 20 miles W. from the right bank of the Irawady river, and 145 miles S.W. from Ava. Lat. 20° 24′, long. 94° 23′.

KYOONTHUL.—See KEYONTHUL.

KYOUKDWAIN.—A town of Eastern India, in the British province of Tenasserim, 142 miles N. by W. of Tenasserim. Lat. 14° 7′, long. 98° 38′.

KYOUKKYAH.—A town of Burmah, situate on the right bank of the Irawady, and 173 miles N. by E. from Ava. Lat. 24° 20′, long. 96° 30′.

KYOUKNEMO, in the island of Ramree, in Arracan, a village situate on a large creek, by which it has access to the sea. It was at one time much infested by dacoits, but through the exertions of the magistrates, it has now become a thriving place.

KYOUK PHYOO, the capital town and principal military station of the island of Ramree, province of Arracan, is situated on its north-western extremity. It derives its designation from Kheouk, signifying white, and Pheo, a stone, on account of the number of beautiful white pebbles which cover the beach in its vicinity. It stands upon the extremity of a sandy plain, which is bounded on the south-west by a range of sandstone hills, varying in height from 500 to 2,000 feet. On the east it is bounded by a small creek, which confers upon it superior facility of water-communication with Calcutta, Chittagong, &c. It is a healthy spot, and its salubrity is probably in a great measure owing to the protection it receives from the range of sandhills on the south-west, forming an admirable barrier against the monsoon, which generally approaches with great fury from that quarter. In connection with that of nature, the powerful hand of art has been at work for the last few years, and a great improvement has been effected by removing all the dense jungle in the vicinity of the town, which generated much dampness, and consequent disease. A judicious system of drainage has also been carried out. Its harbour is said to be one of the finest in the world. Its entrance is so deep and wide as to allow of the safe ingress of the largest-sized ships at any season of the year. Lat. 19° 24′, long. 93° 34′.

KYOUKTEGADEYOUNG, a village in Arracan, situate on the left bank of the Coladyne river, a few miles S. of Ferguson's route. Lat. 20° 50′, long. 93° 9′.

KYOUNGTHA, a pass in the British district of Pegue, on the route over the Youmadoung Mountains, connecting the seacoast of the Bay of Bengal with the interior of Pegue. The crest of the pass is 20 miles N.N.W. of Bassein, in lat. 17° 2′, long. 94° 45′.

KYRABAD, in Rajpootana, a town of

Kotah, situate on the route from Neemuch to the city of Kotah, 78 miles N.E. of former, 44 S.W. of latter. It has a bazar, and water is abundant. The number of houses is estimated at 400. Lat. 24° 37′, long. 76°.

KYRAGURH.—A town of the Deccan, in the territory of Nagpoor or Berar, situate 114 miles E. by N. from Nagpoor, and 102 miles S. from Ramgurh. Lat. 21° 20′, long. 80° 53′.

KYRANUH, in the British district of Muzuffurnugur, lieut.-gov. of the N.W. Provinces, a town on the route from Muzuffurnugur to Paneeput, 30 miles W. by S. of the former. It has a population of 15,162 inhabitants. Lat. 29° 23′, long. 77° 16′.

KYRE.—A town of Burmah, situate on the left bank of the Khyendwen river, and 118 miles N.W. from Ava. Lat. 23° 2′, long. 94° 45′.

KYREE DERA, in Sinde, a village on the route from Larkhana to Bagh, and 15 miles N. of the former place. There is a good supply of water from wells and pools about the village. Lat. 27° 44′, long. 68° 7′.

KYREE GURREE, or KEYRA GHURREE, in Sinde, a town on the route from Larkhana to Bagh, and 44 miles N. of the former place. It is situate on the south-eastern border of the *Pat,* or desert of Shikarpoor, is surrounded with a wall, and is supplied with water from wells. Lat. 28° 6′, long. 67° 57′.

KYRIM, in Eastern India, one of the Cossya hill states, bounded north-east and south by the British territory of Jynteah, and west by the other Cossya states: it extends from lat. 25° 10′—25° 58′, and from long. 91° 48′—92° 11′; is 58 miles in length from north to south, and 13 in breadth.

KYTHUL, in Sirhind, a town the principal place of the territory of Kythul. It is situate in a level, fertile country, and is irregularly, but substantially, built of excellent brick. The palace is a lofty building of a striking appearance, rising above a fine grove of trees, overhanging a spacious sheet of water. There are in the town kilns, producing great quantities of sal ammoniac. The last rajah of the country died in 1843, and, leaving no issue, his possessions lapsed to the paramount power in India. At the period of the escheat, in 1843, the territory comprised 516 villages, and was estimated to yield a surplus revenue of 44,000*l.* Kythul is distant N.W. of Calcutta 1,004 miles. Lat. 29° 49′, long. 76° 28′.

KYUAI-THE-TSAKHAN.—A town of Burmah, situate 33 miles E. of the left bank of the Irawady, and 126 miles N. by E. from Ava. Lat. 23° 39′, long. 96° 32′.

KYUNGYAM.—A town in the dominions of Gholab Singh, the ruler of Cashmere, situate 190 miles E. by S. from Sirinagur, and 159 miles N.E. from Kangra. Lat. 33° 39′, long. 78° 11′.

L.

LABADOR.—One of the islands situated at the mouth of the Megna river. Its length from north to south is 11 miles, and its breadth five; the centre being in lat. 22° 22′, long. 90° 48′.

LABEIRA, in the British district of Bareilly, lieut.-gov. of the N.W. Provinces, a village on the route from the town of Bareilly to Pillibeet, and 13 miles N.E. of the former. Lat. 28° 28′, long. 79° 35′.

LABRUNG, in Bussahir, a village of the district of Koonawur, is situate near the right bank of the Zong, a feeder of the Sutluj, and divided by it from the town of Kanum. Gerard describes it as of considerable size; Hutton, as "a small and filthy-looking place, built on the edge of a shelving hill." Here is a small fort, belonging to the rajah of Bussahir. It is square, about forty feet high, and surrounded by a loopholed wall of stones without cement. Elevation above the sea 9,296 feet. Lat. 31° 40′, long. 78° 29′.

LACARACOONDA.—A town in the British district of Beerboom, lieut.-gov. of Bengal, situate 111 miles N.W. of Calcutta. Lat. 23° 48′, long. 87° 20′.

LACCADIVE ISLANDS.—A cluster off the Malabar coast of India. They extend from lat. 1° 50′ to 12° 20′, and from long. 72° 20′ to 74° 25′, and contain a population of 6,800 The greater portion of these islands are under the uncontrolled management of the Beebee of Cannanore, subject to the payment of an annual tribute to the British government of 1,000*l.* This tribute having fallen into arrear, the islands have been attached, and are now under the administration of the British government

LACHOONG.—A town in the native state of Sikhim, situate on the right bank of the Teesta river, and 52 miles N.E. by N. from Darjeeling. Lat. 27° 40′, long. 88° 47′.

LACKREEGONG, in the British district of Allahabad, lieut.-gov. of the N.W. Provinces, a small town, with bazar, on the route, by Rajapur ferry, from the cantonment of Allahabad to Banda, and 16 miles W. of the former. Lat. 25° 25′, long. 81° 46′.

LADAKH, or MIDDLE TIBET.—A very elevated and rugged country north of the Punjab, and included within the dominions of Gholab Singh, the present ruler of Cashmere. Excluding the British districts of Spiti and Lahoul, Ladakh is distributed into five subdivisions, named Nabra, Ladakh, Zanskar, Rukchu, and Purik-Sura-Dras. It is bounded on the north by the unexplored region south of Chinese Turkistan, and the Chinese territory of Khoten; on the north-east by the Chinese territory of Khoten, and Chan-thau and Rodokh, districts of Great Tibet; on the south by the Chinese territory and Spiti; on the south-west by Lahoul, Chamba, and Kishtewar, and on the west by Cashmere and Bultistan. The information obtained by Vigne and Cunningham justifies us in stating the position of Ladakh as being between lat. 32° 20′—35°, long. 75° 30′—79° 30′; and in computing the area at 26,036 square miles. The most important feature in the physical aspect of Ladakh is the great valley of the Indus, which traverses the country through its whole length, from south-east to north-west, and divides the great northern range called variously Kouenlun, Mooz Taugh, or Karakorum, from the stupendous mountains of Rupshu, Spiti, and Zanskar. The most elevated mountains rise to heights little inferior to those of any summits on the face of the globe. The climate is characterized by cold and excessive aridity.

The population is of that variety of the human race called the Mongolian by Blumenbach and his followers, and are classed under the general denomination Tibetan. The amount is estimated by Moorcroft at between 150,000 and 180,000 persons; but a decrease appears to have taken place since Moorcroft's time, and the present amount of inhabitants is presumed to be 125,000. They have the usual features of the Mongolians, but improved by intermixture with the Cashmerian; the women especially, according to Gholaum Hyder, are pretty and fair, with rosy cheeks. In moral character they are mild, good-humoured, peaceable, and honest, but timid, indolent, excessively dirty, addicted to intoxication and sexual immorality. Gholaum Hyder observes:—"They are the most peaceable race of beings in the world, very quiet, honest, and hospitable." In consequence of this disposition, crimes of violence are scarcely known. Polyandry is common among the lower orders, and, according to the last-quoted authority, under peculiarly disgusting circumstances. "In a family of two or more brothers who are poor, only one of them marries, and the wife is common to all, and no jealousies or quarrels ensue." Primogeniture here has such high privileges, that on the marriage of the eldest son, the property of the parents passes to him, and they become dependent on him for maintenance, while the younger brothers are little better than servants. The men wear close dresses of woollen cloth, and large mantles, which, for the rich, are made of European broad-cloth, for the poor of sheepskin, with the wool inwards. The dress of the grand lama or priest is yellow, that of other lamas of superior rank red; and as these dignitaries wear broad-brimmed hats, they closely resemble cardinals in costume. The dress of the women consists of a jacket and petticoat of enormous dimensions, and a sheepskin mantle. When rich, they are loaded with a variety of fantastic ornaments and uncouth jewellery. "A Ladakhi female, in full costume," observes Moorcroft, "would cause no small sensation amongst the fashionable dames of a European capital." The language is Tibetan, according to Klaproth, the primitive dialect of the aboriginal people inhabiting the vast mountain-region between Hindostan and Tartary. It is very rough, and abounds in harsh combinations of consonants, unutterable even by those accustomed to the most rugged tongues of northern Europe. The religion is Lamaism, a form of Buddhism, resembling apparently in its moral and spiritual tenets those entertained by the early ascetics and by the Quietists of later date. In the existence of monastic establishments for both sexes, the acknowledgment of a supreme infallible head of the whole religious community, and the adoption of pageantry in public worship, some seeming resemblance has been traced to the characteristics of the Romish church. Moorcroft describes Lamaism as "a strange mixture of metaphysics, mysticism, morality, juggling, and idolatry." The transmigration of souls is received as a prominent tenet. The Deity is worshipped in the character of a trinity, but adoration is paid to a great number of inferior beings, represented by a variety of curious idols. The general character of Lamaism appears to be more gentle than that of many other superstitions, and under its influence the terrific Moguls and other Tartars have become a comparatively mild and peaceable race.

Previously to the conquest of this country by the Sikhs, the government was a simple despotism, which, during Moorcroft's residence, was administered by the khalum or prime minister of the rajah, who was himself but a mere pageant: at all times the sovereign was liable to be deposed by the intrigues of the influential lamas, and his place supplied by the next in hereditary succession. The revenue was not paid in money, the people being bound to support the rajah and his officers, not only by furnishing provisions, and all other things requisite for subsistence, but serving as domestic as well as agricultural labourers. They were likewise bound to take the field in case of collision with neighbouring states. Gholaum Hyder says, the "troops are mostly horsemen, armed with a few matchlocks, bows and arrows, and swords, and may amount in all to 2,000 men; the infantry may be about 1,200 men, armed with matchlocks, bows and arrows, and swords." They are incredibly cowardly, and so ill armed that, according to Moorcroft, on occasion of a war with their neighbours of Bultistan, the infantry had but one matchlock for ten men, and one sword for six. It is not therefore surprising that Ladakh made no resistance to the troops of Gholab Singh, the present ruler of Cashmere, who took possession of it in 1835, and still retains his acquisition.

LADNO.—A town in the Rajpoot state of Jodhpoor, 126 miles N.E. from Jodhpoor, and 81 miles N. by W. from Ajmeer. Lat. 27° 38′, long. 74° 28′.

LADWA, in Sirhind, a small territory formerly the jaghire of a Sikh chieftain, who, in consequence of the non-performance of his feudatory obligations during the Lahore war, was deprived of his possessions, which were annexed to the British dominions. Ladwa, the principal place, is situate 22 miles N. from Kurnool, in lat. 29° 59′, long. 77° 6′.

LAENADOWN, in the British district of Saugor and Nerbudda, lieut.-gov. of the N.W. Provinces, a town on the route from Nagpoor to Jubbulpoor, 45 miles S.S.W. of the latter. Lat. 22° 34′, long. 79° 44′.

LAGWAN.—A town in the British district of Bhagulpore, lieut.-gov. of Bengal, 58 miles S.W. of Rajmahal. Lat. 24° 22′, long. 87° 14′.

LAHAR, in the territory of Gwalior, or the possessions of the Scindia family, a town six miles E. of the right or E. bank of the river Sindh. In A.D. 1780, Captain Popham, in command of 2,400 infantry, a small body of cavalry, and a detail of European artillery, with a howitzer and a few field-pieces, besieged this fort, which was found to be much stronger than had been fallaciously represented by the rana of Gohud, who was anxious to have it captured from the Mahrattas. It was imperfectly breached, and as the light field-pieces could produce no farther effect on the defences, the British commander determined to make a desperate attempt at storming. By extraordinary efforts, a lodgment was made in the place. "Dreadful slaughter ensued on both sides. The enemy defended themselves with desperation, and it was not until the garrison, which had consisted of 500 men, was reduced to their killadar and a mere handful of his dependants, that quarter was demanded. The British lost 125 men." It appears to have been ceded to Scindia by the second article of the treaty of Mustafapoor, on the 22nd November, 1805. Lahar is 50 miles W. of Calpee, the same distance E. of Gwalior fort, 85 S.E. of Agra. Lat. 26° 12′, long. 78° 59′.

LAHENEE, in the British district of Futtehpoor, lieut.-gov. of Agra, a town on the right bank of the Ganges, 917 miles from Calcutta by the river, 107 miles above Allahabad, N.W. from the town of Futtehpoor by land 15 miles. Lat. 26° 8′, long. 80° 41′.

LAHORE, a large city in the Punjab, is situate about a mile east of the Ravee river. It is surrounded by a brick wall, formerly twenty-five feet high, but which has recently been lowered by the British government. Runjeet Singh ran a good trench around the wall, beyond this constructed a line of works round the entire circumference, mounted them with heavy artillery, and gave orders for clearing away such ruins and other objects as might yield shelter to assailants. The circuit of this line of fortifications exceeds seven miles. The fort or citadel occupies the north-west angle of the city, and contains extensive magazines and manufactories of warlike stores. There are several large and handsome mosques. The Padshah mosque, said to have been built by Aurungzebe, is a massive, lofty structure of red sandstone, of great size, and ornamented with spacious cupolas. It was converted into a barrack by Runjeet Singh. The Vizier Khan mosque is also a fine edifice, ornamented with lofty minarets, and covered with varnished tiles, inscribed with Arabic sentences, which are popularly supposed to comprise the entire of the Koran. These splendid structures have been desecrated by the Sikhs, who killed swine in them, and converted their courts into stables. The Sonara mosque is another splendid building. There are besides many handsome mosques and Hindoo temples. One of the greatest ornaments in the neighbourhood is the tomb of the Mogul emperor Jehangir. It is very extensive and beautiful, of a quadrangular figure, with a minaret at each corner, rising to the height of seventy feet. The principal material is red sandstone, but there is a profusion of ornaments executed in marble, arranged in elegant mosaics, representing flowers and texts of the Koran in Arabic and Persian. These texts consist of a hundred repetitions of the name of God in different modes of expression. This beautiful monument is about three miles west of Lahore. It is separated from the town by the river Ravee, which has lately swept away part of the wall inclosing the tomb, and threatens speedily to engulf the structure itself. Runjeet Singh gave it as a residence to a French officer of the name of M. Amise, who caused it to be cleared out and put in repair, but died shortly afterwards. His fate was considered by the Mahometans as retributive of his impiety in desecrating the sacred pile, which has since been closed up. Another of these huge ornamental tombs is styled that of Anarkalli, a youth, according to tradition, a favourite of one of the emperors, who, instigated by jealousy, having seen him smile at a lady of the imperial zenana, caused him to be put to death, by being built up in a brick cell, and this splendid mausoleum to be raised over him. Unfortunately, the tone of Mahometan morals is not such as to render the story incredible. Three miles north-east of Lahore is the garden of Shah Jehan, the Shalimar, or "House of Joy." It is about half a mile long, with three successive terraces, rising one above the other, and contains 450 fountains, which throw up water, subsequently received into marble tanks. Runjeet Singh barbarously defaced this superb monument of oriental magnificence, by removing a large portion of the marble embellishments to his new capital, Amritsir.

The streets of Lahore, which are very narrow, contain numbers of lofty but gloomy houses, inclosed within extensive dead walls. The bazars, though numerous, and stocked with profusion of costly wares, are in general contracted and mean. There is an abundant supply of water from wells in the town. The vicinity is fertile and well cultivated, being covered with the most luxuriant gardens and orchards. The great extent and size of the ruins scattered over the adjacent country bear evidence of the former greatness of the city.

Von Hügel describes the scene as a huge mass of serais, palaces, and ruins, which must be seen, to form any notion of their multitude and extent. The population is still considerable, the streets being crowded in an extraordinary degree ; yet in this respect, as well as in regard to trade, Lahore, according to Burnes, is greatly excelled by Amritsir, which has recently grown up into a successful rival ; for though Runjeet Singh resided much at Lahore, where he delighted to show his state, Amritsir was both the spiritual and commercial capital of his dominions. The statement of Burnes, however, as to the comparative amount of the population of the two cities, has been disputed, and the superiority claimed for Lahore, which, even in its decay, is a great city. Von Hügel says that it stretches in a semicircular form four or five miles along the branch of the Ravee, and yet that, if we judge from the ruins, it is not one-tenth part the size that it once was. It is very difficult to make even any safe guess at its population ; but from its extent and the multitudes which throng it, the number can scarcely be less than from 94,000 to 95,000. This indeed is a great declension from the amount in the time when it was the residence of the Mogul emperors, and was nine miles in length ; the population then, probably, was eight or ten times the present number.

Lahore partakes to some extent of the advantages of education, and even forms a centre for their diffusion. It is the seat of an establishment which is at once a vernacular school and a college for the study of Hindoo and Mahomedan learning and European knowledge, through vernacular media. A portion of the funds of the institution is contributed by the British government, but it is chiefly supported by subscriptions from Bhopaul and four other native states, the chiefs and people of which regard its maintenance as inseparably connected with British protection and supremacy ; so that, in the language of Major Cunningham, "it is a kind of fashion to contribute to the school." In 1849 the number of pupils was 541.

Lahore appears to have fallen into the hands of Mahmood of Ghiznee in 1009, on his advance to destroy Naugracut ; and in 1152 it became the capital of the Gaznevide dynasty. In 1186 it was captured from the last Gaznevide by Sahub-ud-dein, the Gourian monarch. In 1523 it was taken by Sultan Baber, whose posterity made it a favourite residence, and raised it to its greatest splendour. In 1748 it fell into the hands of Ahmed Shah, the first Durani emperor. In 1799 Runjeet Singh was, by Zeman Shah, invested with the government of Lahore, with the title of rajah. He immediately manifested his determination to possess the substance as well as the ensigns of power, by expelling three Sikh sirdars, who attempted to retain possession ; and he thenceforward made it one of his favourite places of residence. When, after the death of that chieftain, the enormities committed by those who grasped his power, compelled the English to put an end to his dynasty, Lahore became, with the rest of the Punjaub, British. The events connected with its subjugation are related in the historical sketch of the Punjaub. Lahore is in lat. 31° 36′, long. 74° 21′.

LAHOREE BUNDER, in Sinde, a village on the south or left bank of the Buggaur, or western branch of the Indus, 20 miles from the Pittee mouth. When visited by Alexander Hamilton, in 1699, it was the principal port of Sinde, being accessible for ships of 200 tons burthen ; and at the close of the last century it was the seat of an English factory. It has since fallen to decay, in consequence of the contiguous channel having ceased to be navigable. Lat. 24° 32′, long. 67° 28′.

LAHOUL, in the north-east of the Punjab, a British district, bounded on the north-east by Ladak ; on the east by Spiti ; on the south-west by Kulu ; and on the west by Chamba and Kishtawar. It is about sixty-eight miles in length, and thirty-four in breadth, and contains an area of 1,872 square miles. It is situate between lat. 32° 5′—33° 8′, long. 76° 45′—77° 46′. This territory is surrounded by lofty mountains ; the Ritanka Pass, on the south, having an elevation of 13,300 feet, and the Bara Lacha Pass, on the north-west, 16,500 ; some peaks in the vicinity rising 1,000 feet higher, and being covered with perpetual snow. Lahoul is traversed by innumerable torrents, the feeders of the Surajbhaga and the Chandrabhaga, the junction of which forms the river Chenaub. The elevation of the whole territory must be very great, as Kishtawar, above 100 miles lower down the course of the rapid Chenaub, is more than 5,000 feet above the level of the sea. There are no towns in this secluded tract, the only collections of habitations being two small hamlets, one called Gosha, the other Tandi, both situate close to the confluence of the Surajbhaga and Chandrabhaga. Notwithstanding the elevation of the surface, good crops of grain are produced.

LAIDAH.—A town in the British district of Ramgur, lieut.-gov. of Bengal, 52 miles E.N.E. of Hazareebagh. Lat. 24° 12′, long. 86° 11′.

LAIHRAH, in Sirhind, a village on the route from Hansee to Loodiana, and 16 miles S. of the latter town. It is situate in a country having a surface slightly undulated, moderately fertile, and comparatively cultivated. Distant N.W. from Calcutta 993 miles. Lat. 30° 42′, long. 75° 53′.

LAKAHPOOR, in the British district of Mynpoorie, lieut.-gov. of the N.W. Provinces, a village 20 miles N. of the town of Mynpoorie. Lat. 27° 31′, long. 78° 57′.

LAKAHURRAH, in the Punjab, a village on the route from Lahore to Mooltan, 50 miles N.E. of the latter city. It is situate on the left bank of the Ravee, about 30 miles above its confluence with the Chenaub. Lat. 30° 33′, long. 72° 13′.

LAKGWADWA.—A town in the British province of Aracan, situate 93 miles S.S.E. of Aracan. Lat. 19° 30′, long. 93° 58′.

LAKHAJUMOGARI.—A town in the native state of Nepal, situate on the right bank of a branch of the Marachangdi river, and 67 miles N.W. by W. from Khatmandoo. Lat. 28° 14′, long. 84° 26′.

LAKHA MANDAL, in Jaunsar, a ruined town on the right bank of the Jumna, and 300 feet above it. Some celebrity attaches to it in the Hindoo legends, in which it is regarded as one of the temporary residences of the Pandus, so famous in the heroic ages of Hindustan. Lat. 30° 44′, long. 78° 7′.

LAKNAOTI, in the British district of Suharunpoor, lieut.-gov. of the N.W. Provinces, a village on the route from Kurnoul to Suharunpoor, and 15 miles N.E. of the former place. It is situate on the Sendellie, a torrent falling into the Jumna a few miles lower down. Distant N.W. from Calcutta 980 miles. Lat. 29° 46′, long. 77° 16′.

LAKSA, in the British district of Barasut, lieut.-gov. of Bengal, a village, with a police-station, situate on the Golgosi, an offset of the Ganges, which, some miles lower down, or farther south, is lost in the Sunderbunds. Laksa is distant from Calcutta, E., 40 miles. Lat. 22° 44′, long. 89° 4′.

LALDERWAZA.—A pass on the route from Kheree to Dehra, over the Sewalik range, separating the British districts of the Dehra Doon and Suharunpoor. It was a secondary station in the trigonometrical survey of the Himalaya. Elevation above the sea 2,935 feet. Lat. 30° 13′, long. 77° 58′.

LALDHANG, or LALL DONG.—A village on the northern frontier of the British district of Bijnour, towards Kumaon. Thither, in 1774, Fayzullah Khan, the Rohilla leader, retreated after his defeat by the British in the battle of Tessunah, and, being closely pressed by the victorious army, aided by the nawab of Oude, entered into a convention, acknowledging the supremacy of that potentate. Distant 925 miles N.W. from Calcutta. Lat. 29° 52′, long. 78° 23′.

LALEE RIVER.—A small tributary of the Dihong, rising in lat. 28°, long. 95° 1′, in the mountainous territory inhabited by the Abor tribes. Flowing in an easterly direction, it falls into the Dihong river, in lat. 27° 56′, long. 95° 23′.

LALER FORT, or LALLNEIR, in the British district of Bolundshuhur, lieut.-gov. of the N.W. Provinces, a village on the route from Khasgunge to Meerut, and 61 miles S.E. of the latter. Lat. 28° 13′, long. 78° 7′.

LALGLAH.—A river of Orissa, rising in lat. 19° 35′, long. 83° 18′, on the northern boundary of the native state of Jeypoor, through which it flows in a southerly direction for fifty-three miles. Subsequently traversing the British district of Vizagapatam in a southeasterly direction for eighty miles, it falls into the Bay of Bengal, in lat. 18° 12′, long. 84°.

LALGUNJ.—A town in the British district of Tirhoot, lieut.-gov. of Bengal, 18 miles N.N.E. of Dinapoor. Lat. 25° 50′, long. 85° 12′.

LALGUNJ.—A town in the territory of Oude, situate 19 miles N.E. from the left bank of the Gogra river, and 21 miles N.E. from Oude. Lat. 26° 59′, long. 82° 28′.

LALITA PATUN.—A town in the native state of Nepal, six miles S. from Khatmandoo, and 78 miles N.E. by N. from Bettiah. Lat. 27° 38′, long. 85° 17′.

LAL KANYO, in the Punjab, a village situate in the Doab of the two rivers Chenaub and Jhelum, and very near their junction. Lat. 31° 14′, long. 72° 13′.

LALLEE, in the Punjab, a town in the Doab of Jetch, and nearly equidistant from the Chenaub and Jhelum. It is situate in a level desert tract, and at the base of an inconsiderable eminence, the summit of which is occupied by a station of fakirs, and is also a much-frequented place of pilgrimage. The population of the town is about 5,000. Lat. 31° 49′, long. 72° 30′.

LALLGUNGE, in the British district of Goruckpore, lieut.-gov. of the N.W. Provinces, a small market-town on the route from the cantonment of Goruckpore to that of Sultanpoor, in the territory of Oude, 43 miles S.W. of the former, 67 N.E. of the latter. It is situate on the small river Kooanuh, so that water is abundant. Lat. 26° 43′, long. 82° 56′.

LALLGUNGE.—The principal place of the pergunnah of the same name, in the British district of Mirzapore, lieut.-gov. of the N.W. Provinces, a small town on the route from the city of Mirzapore to Saugor, and 20 miles S.W. of the former. It is situate on the plateau, which is slightly elevated above the valley of the Ganges, lying to the north and north-east, and separated from the more depressed tract by the Tara ridge, traversed by the Tara Ghat or pass. Lallgunge has a bazar, and is well supplied with water. An anonymous British traveller describes it as a large place: it is styled by Jacquemont a very large village, in a wonderfully sterile country. Garden states it to be partially cultivated. The road is excellent, having been made under the superintendence of the East-India Company's engineers. Elevation above the sea 504 feet. Lat. 25° 1′, long. 82° 25′.

LALLOO, in Sinde, a village on the road from Bukkur to Hyderabad, 60 miles S. of the former town. Lat. 26° 52′, long. 68° 57′.

LALLPOOR, in the British district of Cawnpore, lieut.-gov. of the N.W. Provinces, a village on the route from the cantonment of

Futtehgurh to that of Cawnpore and 29 miles N.W. of the latter. Lat. 26° 47′, long. 80° 9′.

LALLPORE.—A town in the British district of Purneah, lieut.-gov. of Bengal, 21 miles N.W. of Purneah. Lat. 25° 59′, long. 87° 20′.

LALPOOR, in the British district of Moradabad, lieut.-gov. of the N.W. Provinces, a village on the route from the town of Moradabad to Almora, and 19 miles N. of the former. Lat. 29° 5′, long. 78° 54′.

LALPOOR, in the peninsula of Kattywar, province of Guzerat, a town in the district of Hallar, situate 170 miles S.W. of Ahmedabad, 200 miles W. of Baroda. Lat. 22° 12′, long. 70° 6′.

LALSOAT.—A town in the Rajpoot state of Jeypoor, situate 43 miles S.E. from Jeypoor, and 110 miles E. from Ajmeer. Lat. 26° 32′, long. 76° 29′.

LAMBA.—A town in the Rajpoot state of Jodhpoor, on the right bank of a branch of the Loonee river, and 50 miles E.N.E. from Jodhpoor. Lat. 26° 33′, long. 73° 52′.

LAMBA, or CHOTA LAMBA, in the territory of Kishengurh, in Rajpootana, a town on the route from Agra to Nusseerabad, 203 miles S.W. of former, 20 N.E. of latter. It has a bazar, and water is abundant. Lat. 26° 24′, long. 75° 6′.

LAMEEA.—A town in the Rajpoot state of Jeypoor, situate 35 miles N.W. from Jeypoor, and 75 miles N.E. from Ajmeer. Lat. 27° 19′, long. 75° 33′.

LAMJUN.—A town in the native state of Nepal, situate on the right bank of the Marachangdi river, and 80 miles W.N.W. from Khatmandoo. Lat. 28° 10′, long. 84° 8′.

LANDEE KHANA.—The most difficult part of Khyber Pass, lying about twenty-three miles from Kadam, the eastern entrance, and seven from the western entrance. The pass here descends very steeply to the west, and is both narrow and rugged, so as to be with difficulty practicable for wheel-carriages. It is in one place a mere gallery, twelve feet wide, with the lofty rock rising like a wall on the north side, and a deep precipice on the south. In April, 1842, the British army under General Pollock, when forcing the Khyber Pass, encamped near this spot. The elevation above the sea is 2,488 feet. Landee Khana is in lat. 34° 10′, long. 71° 10′.

LANDOUR, in the British district of Dehra Doon, a sanatory station on the ridge bounding that valley on the north, was founded for the reception of invalids from Meerut and other cantonments in the plains of the North-Western Provinces. It is situate on a ridge running nearly east and west, and is three miles east of the sanatory station of Mussouree, but connected with it by an intermediate straggling series of buildings. Barracks and other public buildings and private residences are scattered over the rugged ridges and slopes, which form a wild and varied scene, rendered more striking by magnificent views of the distant Himalayas, covered with perennial snow. According to the notice in the Bengal and Agra Guide of 1842, the station contained, about that time, a church, post-office, forty-two private dwelling-houses, large hotel, library, temperance-room, hospital, five barracks for invalid European soldiers, seven officers' quarters, mess-room, guard-room, storehouse and magazine, quarter for steward, quarter for hospital sergeant, godown (storehouse) for commissary stores, godown for barrack department, bakehouse, mule-shed. At the same time, the average number of officers doing duty at the depôt was eight; of Europeans annually sent up, the average number was 110; of those who returned cured, 100. In consequence of the rapid increase of elevation, the diminution of temperature is very striking to a visitor from the plains, as the thermometer has been found to fall from 90° to 52° in a journey of two or three hours. The maxima and minima of degrees of temperature during the successive months, the variations being taken between 6 A.M. and 6 P.M., were,—January, 53°—31°; February, 60°—32°; March, 67°—44°; April, 76°—55°; May, 78°—58°; June, 79°—54°; July, 75°—61°; August, 72°—60°; September, 70°—58°; October, 69°—45°; November, 58°—34°; December, 56°—39°. The burial-ground of the united stations is situate on the northern face of the western extremity of Landour. The highest point of the station is 7,579 feet above the sea. Distant N.W. from Calcutta 1,028 miles. Lat. 30° 27′, long. 78° 10′.

LANGCHEN KHABAB.—The name given to the Sutluj river near its source. See Sutluj.

LANGKONG.—A town of Eastern India, in the native state of Muneepoor, 24 miles W. from Muneepoor, and 116 miles E. from Silhet. Lat. 24° 50′, long. 93° 40′.

LANGLO, or NANGLOEE, in the British district of Delhi, lieut.-gov. of the N.W. Provinces, a village on the route from Rohtuk to the city of Delhi, and 10 miles W. of the latter. Lat. 28° 40′, long. 77° 7′.

LANJE.—A town in the British district of Rutnageriah, presidency of Bombay, 23 miles S.E. of Rutnageriah. Lat. 16° 50′, long. 73° 40′.

LANJEE, in the territory of Nagpore, a town on the route from Hazareebagh to Nagpore, 467 miles S.W. of the former, 107 E. of the latter. It is situate in a difficult country, in a range of mountains stretching southward from the Vindhya range, and called the Lanjee Hills, from this town. Lanjee is in lat. 21° 32′, long. 80° 38′.

LARGEE, a dreary valley north of the Derajat, and separated from the Indus by a prolongation of the Salt range of mountains. It is about forty miles in length and eight or ten in breadth, arid, barren, and desert, being visited merely because the great route from north to south, along the western side of the Indus, passes through it. The middle part is in lat. 32° 20′, long. 71° 5′.

LARH, in the British district of Goruckpore, lieut.-gov. of the N.W. Provinces. It is a market-town, and one of the most considerable in that part of the district, having, according to Buchanan, 1,000 houses. It is situate five miles from the left bank of the Ghogra, two from the left of the Chota Gundack, 50 miles S.E. of Goruckpore cantonment. Lat. 26° 10′, long. 84° 2′.

LARKHANA, in Sinde, a town seven miles west of the Indus, situate on a considerable feeder of that river, and into which it falls about twenty-five miles below Sukkur. The surrounding country, which is fertile, populous, and highly cultivated, is probably the finest tract in Sinde. The town is rudely fortified, and has a citadel at its western end, which, during the rule of the Talpoor dynasty, was the head depôt of the artillery of the ameers of Hyderabad. Larkhana is one of the principal grain-marts of Sinde, and has a good bazar, containing 370 shops, well supplied with wares. The principal manufactures are the weaving of silk and cotton, and the place derives some commercial advantages from being situate on the great route from Southern Sinde to Cutch Gundava, Beloochistan, and Kandahar, through the Bolan Pass. The population has been estimated at 10,000 or 12,000. Near the town, on the banks of the Narra, is a large ruined fortress, called Maihota, built on a huge mound. Larkhana is in lat. 27° 30′, long. 68° 10′.

LASUR.—See Losur.

LASWARI, in the Rajpoot territory of Macherry or Alwur, is a village situate on an eminence on the left bank of the Mahnus Nye, a small river, hence by some called the Laswari. This village and its vicinity were, on the 1st of November, 1803, the scene of one of the most obstinately-contested and sanguinary battles recorded, which terminated in the utter defeat of the Mahrattas by the British, under the command of General Lake, afterwards Lord Lake. The Mahratta force, consisting of seventeen of Scindia's regular battalions of infantry, amounting to about 9,000 men, together with 3,000 cavalry and seventy-two pieces of artillery, under the command of Monsieur Dudernaigue, a French adventurer, was in hasty retreat attacked by the British general with his cavalry, which he had by a forced march brought on five hours in advance of his infantry. In this desperate service, the cavalry suffered dreadfully, especially from the powerful and well-served artillery of the Mahrattas; but, after the infantry came up, the fate of the day became no longer doubtful. The British arms steadily advanced, and by four o'clock in the afternoon, the destruction of the hostile army was complete. Of the British, 172 were killed, and 652 wounded. "The enemy left in the possession of the British troops the whole of their bazars, camp equipage, and baggage, with a considerable number of elephants, camels, and upwards of 1,600 bullocks, seventy-two pieces of cannon of different calibre, forty-four stands of colours, and sixty-four tumbrils completely laden with ammunition. Three tumbrils with money were also captured, together with fifty-seven carts laden with matchlocks, muskets, and stores, and some artificers' carts." A medal commemorative of the victory was struck in London in 1851, and presented, with the sanction of her Majesty, to the surviving officers and soldiers who were present at the engagement.

The Mahnus Nye, or stream of Laswari, has its origin near the south-western frontier, towards Jeypore, and, holding a course generally easterly, passes the eastern frontier into the territory of Bhurtpore, where it is probably lost in the marshes about Deeg, after a total course of 100 miles. When crossed by Jacquemont, in lat. 27° 25′, long. 76° 46′, and at about fifty miles from its source, it was found, on the 23rd of February, and consequently in the dry season, a small river with a gentle current. At Laswari, thirty miles farther from the source, it was, on October 21st, and some time after the rainy season, found to be "a rivulet, the banks of which were very high, and difficult of access." The village of Laswari is 128 miles S. of Delhi, by Alwur. Lat. 27° 33′, long. 76° 59′.

LATHEE, in the Rajpoot state of Jessulmere, a town on the route from Pokrun, in Joudpore, to the town of Jessulmere, and 25 miles N.W. of the former. Lat. 27° 2′, long. 71° 39′.

LAUKKNANG.—A town of Eastern India, in the British province of Tenasserim, 164 miles S.S.E. of Moulmein. Lat. 14° 11′, long. 98° 23′.

LAULGOODY.—A town in the British district of Trichinopoly, presidency of Madras, 10 miles N.E. of Trichinopoly. Lat. 10° 53′, long. 78° 53′.

LAUT.—A town in Hyderabad, or dominions of the Nizam, situate 10 miles S. from the right bank of the Godavery river, 137 miles N.W. by N. from Hyderabad. Lat. 18° 58′, long. 77° 21′.

LAWA.—A town of Malwa, in the native state of Tonk, 21 miles N.W. by N. from Tonk, and 63 miles E. from Ajmeer. Lat. 26° 23′, long. 75° 43′.

LAWAEN.—See Lohain.

LAWAH, in the Rajpoot territory of Oodepoor or Mewar, a town on the route from Neemuch to Jodhpoor, 85 miles N.W. of former, 107 S.E. of latter. It has a bazar, and is abundantly supplied with water from wells. Population about 3,000. Lat. 25° 12′, long. 74° 2′.

LAYGEAH.—A town of Burmah, 102 miles E.S.E. from Ava, and 233 miles N.E. from Prome. Lat. 21° 20′, long. 97° 29′.

LE, in Ladakh, or Middle Tibet, of which it is the capital, is situated about two miles from the right or northern bank of the Indus, here called Sin-kha-bab. A narrow sandy plain stretches between the river and a chain of mountains, which rise on the north about 2,000 feet; and on this level space the town is built. It is inclosed by a wall surmounted at intervals with conical or square towers, and extending on each side to the summit of the mountains. The streets are very irregular and intricate; in many places they are covered over. The houses, varying in height from one to three stories, and in some instances extending to more, are built partly of stone, partly of unburned brick: being whitewashed, they have a lively appearance. They generally have wooden balconies in front. The roofs are flat and ill-constructed of the trunks of poplars, covered with a layer of willow twigs, and this with another of straw, a coat of mud overlaying the whole, which at last constitutes a very insufficient defence against rain. The walls taper as they rise, so that the outer surface slopes inwards. The rain and cold are very imperfectly excluded by wooden shutters, or strong curtains drawn across the windows. There are no chimneys, and the wood-smoke is consequently offensive and suffocating, often producing severe and permanent injury to the eyes. The furniture is very rude, and withal very scanty. The floor sometimes serves for bed, chair, and table, while sheep, goats, and other stock, not unfrequently lodge in the same room with the family. The palace of the rajah, though simple in construction, and rude in finish, yet being several stories high, and having a front of 250 feet, is a conspicuous object. There are several temples as rudely built as the houses. The hereditary rajah, a votary of Lamaism, was deposed by Gholab Singh, the present ruler of Cashmere, who now holds the country.

Le is important as the great rendezvous for the intercourse between the Punjab and Chinese Tartary, and the principal mart for the sale of shawl-wool brought from the latter region. It has above 500 houses, and probably 4,000 inhabitants. Its elevation above the sea is stated by Moorcroft to be more than 11,000 feet, and by Vigne to be about 10,000. Lat. 34° 10′, long. 77° 40′.

LEBONG, in the British district of Kumaon, lieut.-gov. of the N.W. Provinces, a lofty ridge of the main range of the Himalaya. It runs in a direction from south-east to north-west, and is crossed by an excessively difficult and dangerous pass over perpetual snow, from the mahall or subdivision of Beeans on the east, to that of Dharma on the west. Webb, who crossed it from Beeans to Dharma, in June, found a "steep, difficult, fatiguing ascent, former [lower] part over beds of ice, latter [higher] deep and perpetual snow, frozen hard. Severe oppression in breathing, unable to proceed twenty paces at a time without halting." Still higher up, he found "steep ascent, recent snow in parts knee-deep;" and after crossing the crest of the pass, "the whole of this distance [1,516 fathoms] excessively steep and perilous descent, the snow nearly knee-deep. The declivity was so great, that it was necessary to employ people with hatchets to make small hollows in the snow where hard, in which the foot might be placed. As in the ascent all had experienced intolerable difficulty in breathing, so in the descent a violent determination of blood to the head, with severe pain, was equally general. The passage of this ghat occupied twelve hours for people who did not carry loads; none of the bearers of baggage came up before the second day, and some loads not till the second evening. The exertions of this day occasioned a general illness in my camp." The crest of the pass is 18,942 feet above the sea. Lat. 30° 20′, long. 80° 39′.

LEELMA.—A town in the Rajpoot state of Jodhpoor, 178 miles W. by S. from Jodhpoor, and 88 miles S.S.W. from Jessulmeer. Lat. 25° 48′, long. 70° 24′.

LEENGRA.—A town in the British province of Sattara, presidency of Bombay, 47 miles S.E. by E. of Sattara. Lat. 17° 20′, long. 74° 41′.

LEIA, in the Punjab, an important commercial town, situate on a small branch of the Indus, about eleven miles eastward of the main stream. It is a place of great business, not only in direct but in transit trade, as it lies on the main road from Hindostan to the west, by the Kaheree ferry, and is, besides, the mart for the abundant and rich produce of the surrounding fertile country. The principal articles of sale are indigo, madder, sugar, silk, cotton, wool, iron, copper, groceries of various kinds, ghee or clarified butter, and grain. The population is 15,000, and must have greatly increased from the time of Elphinstone, who describes it as a poor place, containing 500 houses. Lat. 30° 57′, long. 71° 4′.

LEIPENGA.—A town on the south-west frontier of Bengal, in the British district of Sumbulpoor, 20 miles N. of Sumbulpoor. Lat. 21° 44′, long. 84°.

LELYP.—A town in the native state of Nepal, situate on the right bank of the Tambur river, and 140 miles E. by S. from Khatmandoo. Lat. 27° 24′, long. 87° 30′.

LEMYO RIVER.—See ARRACAN.

LENGLOONG.—A town in the native state of Bhotan, 118 miles N.N.W. from Gowhatty, and 106 miles N. by E. from Goalpara. Lat. 27° 40′, long. 90° 58′.

LEROREE, in the British district of Budayon, lieut.-gov. of the N.W. Provinces, a village on the route from Bareilly to Delhi, and 37 miles W. of the former. Lat. 28° 26′, long. 78° 56′.

LETKHOK, the name of a pass leading

from the Arracan coast of the Bay of Bengal over the Youmadoung Mountains, to the Bassein branch of the Irawaddy river, in the British territory of Pegue. The crest of the pass is about lat. 17° 28′, long. 94° 55′.

LEYRAHGUR.—A town in the native state of Keunjur, on the south-west frontier of Bengal, 31 miles W.S.W. from Keunjur, and 81 miles E. from Sumbulpoor. Lat. 21° 26′, long. 85° 16′.

LI, or SPITI RIVER, the principal tributary of the Sutlej, and at some seasons not inferior to it in magnitude, rises, according to Gerard, on the northern slope of the Paralasa range, which divides its feeders from those of the Chenab, on the south-western side, in about lat. 32° 39′, long. 77° 44′. Near its source it was forded by Trebeck, the fellow-traveller of Moorcroft, and is by him called the Parang La river, "to which frequent supplies were brought by rivulets and rills from the rocks on either hand, originating in the snow-beds, with which every nook and recess was filled. In one part of the defile, a mass of snow formed a complete bridge across the stream." Flowing circuitously, but generally in a south-east direction, for a distance of fifty-six miles, it receives, in lat. 32° 7′, long. 78° 12′, the Peenoo, a considerable feeder, having a course of about thirty-eight miles; and twenty-eight miles lower down, at the distance of ninety-four miles from their remotest source, the collected waters are joined by the Para or Parati, flowing from the wilds of Rupshu. At the confluence, in lat. 32° 4′, long. 78° 38′, the respective streams were measured in August by Gerard, who found the Spiti seventy-two feet wide, and the Para ninety-eight, and more rapid than the other. Their depths could not be ascertained. At Shalkur, about six miles below the confluence, the bed of the river has an elevation of 10,014 feet above the sea; and if we allow the length of course so far to be 100 miles, and the elevation of the source to exceed 17,000 feet, the slope of the channel is not less than sixty-nine feet per mile. J. G. Gerard, in his passage from Kulu to Ladak, came upon the stream at an elevation of 13,500 feet. From the confluence of the Para, the Spiti or Li flows about twenty miles in a direction nearly due south, to its confluence with the Sutlej, receiving in that interval several feeders, of which the principal are the Yoolang and Leepak, from the west; and by these accessions becomes a very considerable stream, measuring in one part of its course, at Leeo, about six miles from the Sutlej, in width 274 feet, the current being very rapid, and the body of water great. The confluence of the Li and Sutlej, in lat. 31° 48′, long. 78° 41′, and at an elevation of 8,494 feet above the sea, is described by Gerard as very striking. "The character of the gulf at the confluence is certainly one of the wonders of the world. The flanks of the passage are solid granite, stratified as before observed, and seem perfectly mural. The contrast between the two streams is striking: the Li issues forth from its almost subterraneous concealment in a calm blue deep body, to meet the Sutlej; but the salutation is scarcely received before it is grasped in the embrace of its impetuous consort." The noise made by the collision of the two streams, and echoed by the surrounding heights, is completely stunning.

LIDUR, a river of Cashmere, is one of the feeders of the Behut or Jhelum, and by some considered the principal of the streams which unite to form its volume. It rises on the southern slope of the mountain bounding Cashmere on the north-east, in lat. 34° 8′, long. 75° 48′, and at an elevation of probably not less than 14,000 feet. Its current is in consequence very rapid until it reaches the alluvial tract in the bottom of the valley, where it becomes a dull and muddy stream. After a course of about forty-five miles in a south-westerly direction, it falls into the Jhelum, about five miles below Islamabad, in lat. 33° 45′, long. 75° 16′. At the confluence, the volume of water of the Lidur is scarcely inferior to that of the Jhelum.

LILAJUN RIVER, a tributary of the Ganges, rises in lat. 23° 35′, long. 84° 21′. Taking a northerly direction for eighty miles through the British district of Ramgurh, sixty miles through Behar, and twenty-five miles through Patna, it makes a bend eastward, and, flowing for sixty-five miles parallel to the Ganges, forms a junction with that river in lat. 25° 16′, long. 86° 10′.

LILHA.—A town in the territory of Oude, situate on the left bank of the Gumtee, 40 miles S.E. of Lucknow. Its principal business is in grain, cotton, and dyeing. Lat. 26° 35′, long. 81° 40′.

LILOKHERI, in Sirhind, a village on the route from Kurnal to Loodiana, and 12 miles N.W. of the former town. It is situate near the right bank of the Chitang river or torrent, and is a meanly-built place, surrounded by a mud wall, within the inclosure of which are two or three lofty watch-towers, which overlook the surrounding country. There is a good supply of water from a tank and wells, and the road in this part of the route is good. This village is the principal place of a small district belonging to a chief of the protected Sikhs, and yielding him an annual revenue estimated at 400*l.* sterling. Distant N.W. from Calcutta 975 miles. Lat. 29° 50′, long. 76° 59′.

LIMRA, in the peninsula of Kattywar, province of Guzerat, a town in the district of Gohilwar, situate on a small river, which, forty miles eastward, falls into the Gulf of Cambay. It is the principal place of a subdivision containing five villages, and paying an annual tribute of 1,139 Ahmedabad sicca rupees to the Guicowar, and of 300 to the nawaub of

Joonagurh. Distance from Ahmedabad, S.W., 105 miles; Baroda, S.W., 110; Surat, N.W., 90; Bombay, N.W., 210. Lat. 21° 47′, long. 71° 37′.

LIMREE, in the peninsula of Kattywar, province of Guzerat, a town situate in the prant or district of Jhalawar, on the river Bogwara, tributary to the Muchu. It was formerly fortified, but the rampart inclosing it is fast going to ruin. The town, however, is extensive, and noted for the number of wealthy capitalists residing in it. The tallook or subdivision annexed to it contains forty towns and villages, a population of 9,040, and pays an annual tribute of about 1,994*l.* to the British government. The chief is a Rajpoot. Distance from Ahmedabad, S.W., 65 miles; Baroda, W., 90; Bombay, N.W., 265. Lat. 22° 33′, long. 71° 47′.

LINGAGERRY.—A town in a detached portion of the British district of Masulipatam, presidency of Madras, 102 miles W.N.W. of Masulipatam. Lat. 16° 53′, long. 79° 52′.

LINGARA.—A town in one of the recently sequestrated districts of Hyderabad, or dominions of the Nizam, situate 54 miles W. by S. of Ellichpoor. Lat. 21°, long. 76° 48′.

LINGAROO.—A town in the native state of Nepal, eight miles from the left bank of the Kalee river, and 77 miles E.N.E. from Almora. Lat. 29° 56′, long. 80° 55′.

LINGASAGOOR.—A town in one of the recently sequestrated districts of Hyderabad, or dominions of the Nizam, situate nine miles N.E. of Moodgul. Lat. 16° 5′, long. 76° 34′.

LINGO.—A town in the native state of Sikhim, situate on the right bank of the Teesta river, and 34 miles N. by E. from Darjeeling. Lat. 27° 30′, long. 88° 30′.

LINGUMPURRO.—A town in the British district of Rajahmundry, presidency of Madras, 18 miles N. by W. of Samulkottah. Lat. 17° 18′, long. 82° 11′.

LINGWAR, in Bussahir, a village close to the right bank of the Pabur, and a little below the confluence of the Sipoon. Elevation above the sea 8,759 feet. Lat. 31° 18′, long. 78° 1′.

LINYA.—A town in the British province of Tenasserim, 48 miles S. by E. of Tenasserim. Lat. 11° 27′, long. 99° 13′.

LINYA, a river of the Mergui district of the Tenasserim provinces, rises in lat. 11° 17′, long. 99° 18′, on the western slope of the mountains forming the eastern boundary of those territories, and flowing first in a northern direction for twenty-five miles, and subsequently north-west for thirty-eight miles, falls into the Indian Ocean, in lat. 11° 44′, long. 98° 56′.

LIO, in Bussahir, a village of the district of Koonawur, is situate on a small rocky eminence, amidst an alluvial expanse of moderate extent, on the right bank of the Li, or river of Spiti, and at the confluence of the Lipak, a considerable torrent flowing from the west. At the east of the village is an isolated rock sixty feet high, and surmounted by a fort, now in ruins. The population of the village consists of Tartar families, votaries of Lamaism, and a few nuns of the same persuasion. The bed of the Li, or river of Spiti, is here 9,000 feet, that of the village 9,362 feet above the sea, from which this spot is, by the continuous course of the Sutluj and Indus, distant above 1,100 miles; yet even here it is a rapid unfordable river, 277 feet wide. Lat. 31° 53′, long. 78° 37′.

LIPI, in Bussahir, a village of the district of Koonawar, is situate in a sheltered recess of a dell, near the left bank of the Titi, a considerable stream, which, about four miles below, falls into the Sutluj. The village has an elevation of 8,700 feet above the sea. Lat. 31° 39′, long. 78° 26′.

LIPU KETHAN, in the British district of Kumaon, lieut.-gov. of the N.W. Provinces, a very difficult pass on the southern frontier of the Bhotia subdivision of Juwahir. The route here is inclosed between the shoulder of one of the Himalaya mountains, rising on the western, and the rapid course of the river Goree on the eastern side; and the painful path lies over large fragments of rocks, the peril of the traveller being heightened by the frequent fall of masses dislodged from the impending cliffs, either by the inclement weather or by earthquakes, not unfrequent in this region. On the right, when Webb passed in the end of May, 1817, a crag, shaken down by a shock of earthquake, destroyed a trading party of men, with a large train of goats. Elevation above the sea 9,127 feet. Lat. 30° 10′, long. 80° 17′.

LITI, in Bussahir, a torrent on the southern declivity of the Burenda Pass, flowing, during the warm season, from a vast mass of snow, nearly filling the glen above the source. It is remarkable for a fine waterfall, where the stream "rolls over a broken ridge of fine-grained gneiss, in a noble cascade, and is immediately buried beneath a bed of snow." Here is a bungalow or hut to shelter travellers: elevation above the sea 11,692 feet. Lat. 31° 21′, long. 78° 8′.

LOAN, in the British district of Kumaon, lieut.-gov. of the N.W. Provinces, a village on the right bank of the Nundeejah, a feeder of the Goree. Elevation above the sea 12,228 feet. Lat. 30° 20′, long. 80° 12′.

LOANAR.—A town in Hyderabad, or dominions of the Nizam, situate 42 miles E. by N. from Jaulnah, and 109 miles S.W. from Ellichpoor. Lat. 19° 58′, long. 76° 35′.

LOAR.—A town in Guzerat, or the dominions of the Guicowar, situate 96 miles S.S.E. from Rajkote, and 170 miles S.W. by S. from Ahmedabad. Lat. 20° 58′, long. 71° 17′.

LOAWUN.—A town in the British district

of Tirhoot, lieut.-gov. of Bengal, 71 miles N.E. by E. of Dinapoor. Lat. 26° 10′, long. 86° 5′.

LOCAPILLY.—A town in Hyderabad, or dominions of the Nizam, situate 22 miles E.N.E. from the left bank of the Beemah river, and 79 miles S.W. by W. from Hyderabad. Lat. 16° 50′, long. 77° 30′.

LODEEKAW.—A town in Guzerat, or the dominions of the Guicowar, situate 17 miles S.W. by S. from Rajkote, and 140 miles S.W. by W. from Ahmedabad. Lat. 22° 8′, long. 70° 41′.

LODELL.—A town in Hyderabad, or dominions of the Nizam, situate 93 miles N.E. by E. from Hyderabad, and 138 miles N.N.W. from Guntoor. Lat. 18° 7′, long. 79° 40′.

LODHO, in the British district of Allygurh, lieut.-gov. of the N.W. Provinces, a village situate on the cross route from Coel to Khyr, and eight miles S.E. of the latter, 55 miles N. of Agra. Lat. 27° 54′, long. 78° 3′.

LOGAON.—A town in Hyderabad, or dominions of the Nizam, situate nine miles S.W. from the right bank of the Godavery, and 117 miles N.W. by N. from Hyderabad. Lat. 18° 49′, long. 77° 38′.

LOGASSI, or LUGASI, in Bundelcund, a town, the principal place of a small raj or principality of the same name. It is on the route from Calpee to Jubbulpore, 86 miles S. of the former, 183 N. of the latter. Supplies may be had, but water is rather scarce in the dry season. Here is a bazar, and a small fort commands the town. The raj of which it is the principal place "yields a revenue of 15,000 rupees; is stated to comprise an area of twenty-nine square miles, and to contain eleven villages, with a population of 3,500 souls. The jagheerdar maintains a force of fifteen horse and 125 foot." According to Spry, the rajah is of ancient Bundela lineage. He was acknowledged by the British government in 1808, by sunnud or written grant, in which he is stated to be "of the Boondelah caste, and one of the chieftains of rank of the province of Bundelcund;" and his possessions are guaranteed to him rent-free, on condition "of obedience and submission to the government." The town of Logassi is in lat. 25° 4′, long. 79° 39′.

LOGHUR.—A hill fort in the British district of Poona, presidency of Bombay, distant N.W. from Poona 26 miles, S.E. from Bombay 43 miles. Lat. 18° 42′, long. 73° 31′.

LOHADUGGA, in the British district of Chota Nagpore, lieut.-gov. of Bengal, a military cantonment on the route from Hazareebagh to the city of Nagpore, 82 miles S.W. of the former, 492 N.E. of the latter. It is the sudder or principal station of an assistant to the commissioner for Chota Nagpore and political agent for the south-west frontier of Bengal. Notwithstanding its importance in this respect, and that it has a jail and some other buildings for the use of the civil power, it is a very inconsiderable place. An annual fair has been established in the district of Lohadugga, on the banks of the Soobunreeka, near the frontier of Hazareebagh and Singhboom, with every prospect of success. Lat. 23° 26′, long. 84° 46′.

LOHAGURRE.—A town in the British district of Jessore, lieut.-gov. of Bengal, 91 miles E.N.E. of Calcutta. Lat. 23° 3′, long. 89° 46′.

LOHAIN, or LOWAN, in the British district of Allahabad, lieut.-gov. of the N.W. Provinces, a village on the right bank of the Ganges, six miles below the city of Allahabad. Abreast of it, the river in the dry season is very shallow, with a rapid current and a sandy bottom, causing great difficulty and obstruction to the navigation, especially to craft proceeding upwards. Distance N.W. from Calcutta, by the river, 802 miles. Lat. 25° 22′, long. 81° 58′.

LOHANEE, in the British district Hurriana, lieut.-gov. of the N.W. Provinces, a village situate on the eastern frontier, towards Dadree. Lat. 28° 42′, long. 76° 8′.

LOHARA.—A town in the British district of Candeish, presidency of Bombay, 70 miles E.N.E. of Malligaum. Lat. 20° 42′, long. 75° 32′.

LOHARAPALLEE.—A town on the south-west frontier of Bengal, in the British district of Sumbulpoor, situate 45 miles W. by S. of Sumbulpoor. Lat. 21° 18′, long. 83° 20′.

LOHAREE.—A town in the British district of Beerboom, lieut.-gov. of Bengal, 171 miles N.W. of Calcutta. Lat. 24° 13′, long. 86° 29′.

LOHAREE.—A village in the British district Hurriana, lieut.-gov. of the N.W. Provinces. Lat. 29° 15′, long. 76° 8′.

LOHAREE NAIG, in Gurhwal, a stupendous rapid or succession of falls on the Bhageerettee, as the Ganges is called in the upper part of its course. At this point the river is more obstructed than in any part of the course, and here the torrent tears its way over enormous masses of rock, that have fallen into it from the mural precipice forming its left bank. That precipice is a huge cliff of solid granite, which appears to have been undermined at its foot by the stream, so that the lower part has fallen into the channel, while the summit overhangs the vacuity thus formed, through which the river rushes. The pile of shattered fragments extends for about a quarter of a mile; and through and over them the river forces its way in a succession of cascades. "The scene," observes Hodgson, "is full of sublimity and wildness, and the roar of the water is astounding." Lower down, on the right bank, has been another slip of the mountain, but of inferior magnitude. Above the fall, the river is crossed by a sanga or wooden bridge, sixteen paces long, and twenty-five feet above the stream. Elevation of the bridge above the sea 7,389 feet. Lat. 30° 57′, long. 78° 44′.

LOHARGAON, in the territory of Bundelcund, a village with bazar, on the route from Allahabad to Sagar, by Rewa, 198 miles S.W. of Allahabad. It is situate on a calcareous formation, in a slightly depressed tract, between two ranges, styled by Franklin the Punna and the Bandair Hills. Adam supposes this depressed tract to have been an extensive basin, at one time filled by the water of the river Cane, which, having worn a way for itself northwards through the Punna range, left the alluvial bed of the lake dry. Here was formerly a British military station, to maintain the communication between Bundelcund and the posts in Nagpoor. When Fitzclarence visited it in 1817, the force consisted of five companies of native infantry, 120 Rohilla irregular horse, and two six-pounders. The troops have been withdrawn, and when Jacquemont passed in 1830, the place was a scene of desolation. Water is obtainable from a tank and two wells of the depth of forty feet, but is rather scanty in the dry season. The jaghiredar of Behut, a town on the river Dhasan, 90 miles to the north-west, holds also the mowza or rural district of Lohargaon from the East-India Company, subject to an annual payment of 1,400 rupees. Elevation above the sea 1,260 feet. Lat. 24° 29′, long. 80° 24′.

LOHAROO.—A jaghire or feudal dependency, subject to the lieut.-gov. of the N.W. Provinces. It is bounded on the north by the British district of Hurriana; on the east by the jaghire of Jujhur; on the south and south-west by Shekhawuttee; and on the west by Beekaneer and Hurriana. It lies between lat. 28° 22′—28° 50′, long. 75° 44′—76°, and has an area of about 200 square miles, with a population of 18,000 inhabitants. On the expulsion of the Mahrattas by Lord Lake from the Delhi territory, in the early part of the present century, Loharoo was, with some other districts, transferred by him to the chief of Alwur, who granted it to his vakeel or agent, Nawaub Ahmud Buksh Khan. At the same time, Lord Lake conferred the district of Ferozepore, south of Delhi, on the vakeel; on whose death those possessions descended to his son Shumsoodeen Khan. That person was, in 1836, hanged at Delhi, for procuring the murder of Mr. William Fraser, the British political agent there; and his possessions being forfeited, the supreme government conferred Loharoo on his brothers Ameen-ood-deen Khan and Zeeaooddeen Khan. The jaghire is ruled by the elder brother, Ameen-ood-deen, who pays his brother an allowance of 1,800*l.* per annum, as an equivalent for half the net revenues of the estate. Loharoo, the principal place, is in lat. 28° 24′, long. 75° 52′.

LOHARSING.—A town in the British district of Darjeeling, in Northern Bengal, 38 miles S.W. by S. of Darjeeling. Lat. 26° 32′, long. 88° 6′.

LOHATEH.—A town of the Deccan, in the territory of Nagpoor or Berar, situate 130 miles E.S.E. from Nagpoor, and 170 miles S. from Ramgur. Lat. 20° 28′, long. 80° 59′.

LOHAWUT, in the Rajpoot state of Joudpore, a village on the route, *viâ* Nagor, from Jessulmere to Nusseerabad, and 178 miles W. of the latter. It has two wells 310 feet deep, the water from one of which is good, from the other indifferent. The road to the east is heavy, passing among sandhills and thin jungle; to the west it is hard and stony. Lat. 26° 59′, long. 72° 42′.

LOHGURH, in Sirhind, a village on the route from Loodiana to Ferozpoor, and 38 miles W. of the former town. It is situate five miles from the left bank of the Sutlej, in an open level country, partially cultivated, and well supplied with water. Distance N.W. from Calcutta 1,127 miles. Lat. 30° 59′, long. 75° 20′.

LOHI, in the British district of Muttra, lieut.-gov. of the N.W. Provinces, a small town or village on the route from the cantonment of Meerut to that of Muttra, and 23 miles N. of the latter. Water is obtained from wells. Lat. 27° 47′, long. 77° 51′.

LOHIA, in the jaghire of Rampoor, lieut.-gov. of the N.W. Provinces, a village on the route from Bareilly to Moradabad, and 29 miles N.W. of the former. Lat. 28° 38′, long. 79° 12′.

LOHSUL.—A town in the Rajpoot state of Shekawutee, 67 miles N. by E. from Ajmeer, and 62 miles N.W. by W. from Jeypoor. Lat. 27° 23′, long. 75° 2′.

LOHUGHAT, or RIKHESUR, in the British district of Kumaon, lieut.-gov. of the N.W. Provinces, a cantonment for troops stationed to defend the frontier towards Nepal. It is situate on the left bank of the Lohu, a small river, which, taking a south-easterly direction, about twenty miles farther down falls into the Gagra or Kalee river, in lat. 29° 20′, long. 80° 21′. Hence the name, signifying ghat, ferry, or pass, of the Lohu. It is open on the west to the extreme extent of the valley in that direction (about two miles), but on the other sides inclosed by mountains rising above it from 1,000 to 1,500 feet high, with very precipitous sides, yet mostly covered with vegetation. There is an abundant supply of fine water from springs and streams. There are here a bazar, stores, and bungalows or cottages for the accommodation of those connected with the cantonment, which was formerly at Champawut, three miles farther south, but removed to its present position, which is much more salubrious. Elevation above the sea, of the cantonment, 5,562 feet. Distance S.E. from Almora 30 miles. Lat. 29° 24′, long. 80° 9′.

LOHURKOT, in the British district of Kumaon, lieut.-gov. of the N.W. Provinces, a town on the route from Almora to Bareilly, 11 miles S.S.W. of the former. Lat. 29° 27′, long. 79° 39′.

LOJAY, in the native state of Korea, on the south-west frontier of Bengal, a town among the mountains of Gondwana, 50 miles W. of the ruined town of Sirjooja, 120 S. of Mirzapoor, 430 W. of Calcutta by Hazaribagh. Lat. 23° 10′, long. 82° 20′.

LOKAPOOR.—A town in the Southern Mahratta jaghire of Moodhull, presidency of Bombay, situate 61 miles E.N.E. from Belgaum, and 56 miles N.E. by N. from Dharwar. Lat. 16° 10′, long. 75° 25′.

LOKMANPORE.—A town in the British district of Bhagulpore, lieut.-gov. of Bengal, 22 miles N.E. by N. of Bhagulpore. Lat. 25° 27′, long. 86° 57′.

LOLL BAZAR, in the territory of Cooch Behar, a town on the north-western route from Rungpoor to Cooch Behar, 26 miles N. of former, and 20 S.W. of latter. The ruined city of Komotapoor, a "most stupendous monument of rude labour," was situate near this place, on the west or right bank of the Dhorla. Loll Bazar is but an inconsiderable place; it is situate in lat. 26° 4′, long. 89° 18′.

LOLL BAZAR, in the British district of Bogra, lieut.-gov. of Bengal, a small town, the locality of a thannah or police establishment, situate on the river Jabuna, near the northern frontier, towards the British district Dinajpoor. Distance from the town of Bogra, N.W., 30 miles; from Calcutta, N.E., 180; from Berhampur, N.E., 90. Lat. 25° 7′, long. 89° 4′.

LOMYNE.—A town of Eastern India, in the British province of Tenasserim, 71 miles S.S.E. of Moulmein. Lat. 15° 30′, long. 98° 2′.

LONEE, in the British district of Meerut, lieut.-gov. of Bengal, a town, the principal place of the pergunnah of the same name, in lat. 28° 45′, long. 77° 21′.

LONERE.—A town in the British district of Candeish, presidency of Bombay, 23 miles E.N.E. of Malligaum. Lat. 20° 29′, long. 74° 10′.

LONEY.—A town in one of the recently sequestrated districts of Hyderabad, or dominions of the Nizam, 83 miles S. by E. of Ellichpoor. Lat. 20° 44′, long. 77° 43′.

LONJEEGOORA.—A town on the south-west frontier of Bengal, in the native state of Calahandy, 31 miles E.S.E. from Joonnagudda, and 81 miles W. by S. from Goomsoor. Lat. 19° 41′, long. 83° 27′.

LOODAOWLEE, in the British district of Mynpooree, lieut.-gov. of the N.W. Provinces, a town on the route from the city of Agra to Etawa, and 26 miles N.W. of the latter. Lat. 27° 3′, long. 78° 46′.

LOODHOWA, in the British district of Allygurh, lieut.-gov. of the N.W. Provinces, a village on the route from the cantonment of Allyghur to that of Mynpooree, and 18 miles S.E. of the former. Lat. 27° 46′, long. 78° 21′.

LOODHUN, in the Punjab, a village situate on a watercourse connected with the river Ghara, from the right bank of which it is distant about four miles, and sixty miles south-east of Mooltan. Lat. 29° 51′, long. 72° 27′.

LOODIANA.—A British district, forming part of what are called the Cis-Sutlej territories, and named after the chief place within it. It is bounded on the north by the Julindeh Dooab, from which it is separated by the Sutluj river; on the east by the British district of Umballa; on the south by the native territories of Patteala and other protected Sikh chiefs; and on the west by the British district of Ferozpore: it lies between lat. 30° 34′—31° 2′, long. 76° 25′, and has an area estimated at 725 square miles. It was, however, the opinion of the deputy commissioner, in 1848, that this estimate was considerably under the fact, though there then existed no adequate means for correcting it. The population is returned at something under 121,000; but here also there appears to have been error committed, the number being that of males only, distinguished into cultivators and non-cultivators.

A part of this district lapsed to the British government on the failure of heirs in 1836. The remainder came into its possession from escheats at different periods, during the years 1846 and 1847. The district also received some increase on the dismemberment of the district of Wudnee, and the transfer of its territory to others lying adjacent.

LOODIANA, a town of Sirbind, the chief place of the British district bearing the same name, is so called in consequence of having been founded and principally inhabited by the Lodi tribe of Afghans. It is situate on the western brow of an abrupt bluff, rising about thirty feet above the nullah or watercourse, which, having its source near Ropur, and running west for about fifty miles, in some degree parallel to the Sutlej, falls into it at Wallipura, fifteen miles below the fort. The greater part of the course of this nullah was formerly the channel of the Sutlej, which now flows between four and five miles farther north. It is an ill-built town, without a wall, but having a fort on the north side, situate on the bluff rising over the nullah. It was built about 1808, but is of no great strength. The population consists chiefly of Mahomedans, but there is no mosque of any note: still it is a thriving place, its residents including several capitalists; among whom are bankers corresponding with Amritsir, Lahore, Jagadri, Delhi, Calcutta, Bombay, Cashmere, Attock, Peshawur, Caubool, and Herat; and as it lies on one of the principal routes from Delhi to Lahore and Northern Afghanistan, a considerable transit-trade passes through it and over the Sutlej at Filor. The greater part of the inhabitants are weavers, who manufacture a coarse and very strong cotton cloth, suitable for the clothing of the lower orders, or for tent-cloths, and brought to market at a very low price. A still more important branch of industry is the manufacture of shawls, conducted by Cashmirians. The quality is greatly inferior to that of the shawls made at Cashmere, and they would not easily find a sale in Europe, but are readily disposed of in India, in consequence of their greater cheapness. The population of Loodiana has been returned at 47,191.

Loodiana, in consequence of its position on one of the great routes from Delhi to the Punjaub, has long been an important place in a military point of view. One of the most formidable hurricanes which had visited the locality within the memory of man, occurred at Loodiana in 1846, causing great loss of life and the total destruction of the barracks occupied by the Queen's troops. Here Shah Zeman Dooranee took refuge for many years, after he had been deposed, deprived of sight, and exiled from Caubul; and his brother Shah Shooja also here found an asylum until his departure in 1838 to attempt the recovery of the sovereignty of Afghanistan. Loodiana is distant N.W. from Calcutta 1,102 miles. Lat. 30° 55′, long. 75° 54′.

LOOMBOOEE.—A town of Eastern India, in the native state of Muneepoor, 23 miles N.E. by E. from Muneepoor, and 146 miles E. from Jynteeapoor. Lat. 25°, long. 94° 21′.

LOONA.—A town in the native state of Cutch, presidency of Bombay, situate two miles S. of the Great Western Runn, and 41 miles N.W. from Bhooj. Lat. 23° 40′, long. 69° 20′.

LOONEE, or LUNI, a river of Western India, has its extreme source in a marshy tract immediately west of Pokhur, a town in the British district of Ajmeer, and about lat. 26° 37′, long. 74° 46′. It takes a south-westerly course nearly parallel to the base of the Aravulli range, from the north-western declivity of which it receives numerous feeders. Tod crossed the Loonee about lat. 26°, and again near Govindgurh, nearer its source, in lat. 26° 29′, long. 74° 31′. "We crossed a stream half a mile west of Govindghur, called the Saburmati, which, with another, the Sarasrati, joining it, issues from the Poshkur lake. The Saburmati is also called the Loonee: its bed is full of micaceous quartzose rock: the banks are low, and little above the level of the country." Boileau crossed it in lat. 25° 51′, long. 72° 20′, in the beginning of July, when, in consequence of the periodical rains, it "was rushing down with a fierce and turbid stream a quarter of a mile wide, but not very deep." Continuing to flow in a south-westerly direction through the fertile and well-watered tract forming the south-eastern part of the territory of Jodhpoor, it, after a course of about 300 miles, passes into the Runn by two mouths, one in lat. 24° 42′, long. 71° 11′, the other about ten miles more to the south-east, and is lost in that dreary waste. Its total length of course is about 320 miles.

LOONEE, in the Damaun, a village on the route from Ghuznee to Dera Ismael Khan, about 35 miles W. of the latter town. It is situate on a branch of the Gomul river. Lat. 31° 50′, long. 70° 12′.

LOONGHEE.—A town of Burmah, situate on the left bank of the Irawaddy, and 60 miles N. from Prome. Lat. 19° 39′, long. 94° 59′.

LOPO, in Sirhind, a village on the route from Ferozpoor to Simla, and 58 miles S.E. of the former town. Distant N.W. from Calcutta 1,087 miles. Lat. 30° 38′, long. 75° 13′.

LORAPELLY.—A town in the territory of one of the independent hill tribes of Orissa, situate 70 miles E.S.E. from Sumbulpoor, and 76 miles N.W. from Cuttack. Lat. 21° 10′, long. 85° 3′.

LORGURKARA, in Bhawlpoor, a village on the route from Khanpoor to Subzulcote, and 26 miles N.E. of the latter place. Lat. 28° 22′, long. 70° 16′.

LOROO.—A town in the native state of Jushpoor, on the south-west frontier of Bengal, 83 miles N. from Sumbulpoor, and 80 miles S.W. from Lohadugga. Lat. 22° 40′, long. 83° 51′.

LOSUR, in the north-east of the Punjab, a village of Spiti, is situate near the confluence of the Losur river with the river of Peeno. It is the last inhabited spot which travellers find in ascending the course of the latter river, and has an elevation of about 13,400 feet. Above this part of the valley, through which the river flows, the mountains rise in mural cliffs so steep that no snow can rest on their faces, though it lies deeply on their tops, which are for the most part flattened, forming table-lands. The general character of the soil and atmosphere is excessive aridity; but in some places patches of fertility, at the bases of the declivities, are rendered productive by means of irrigation. On one of these slips is situated the village of Losur; and the appearance of this singularly secluded place, as described by Gerard, is far from repulsive. "Lofty as the level of Losur is, there is little in the landscape to betray its position, when viewed in summer, embosomed in flourishing crops, and herds of shawlwool-goats. Yaks and horses meet the eye upon the high acclivities of the mountains, and an ardent sunshine keeps the air looming from the effects of mirage." The inhabitants are Tibetans or Tartars, of the Mongolian type, and their complexions are darker than in the low and sultry plains. When the ground is covered with snow, their black figures contrast strikingly and somewhat grotesquely with the dazzling whiteness of the surface on which they move. Losur is in lat. 32° 28′, long. 77° 46′.

LOTOWTEE.—A town in the Rajpoot state of Jodhpoor, situate on the left bank of the Loonee river, and 51 miles E. from Jodhpoor. Lat. 26° 16′, long. 73° 57′.

LOTUL.—A town in the British district of

Ramgur, lieut.-gov. of Bengal, 67 miles W. of Ramgur. Lat. 23° 39′, long. 84° 29′.

LOTUN, in the British district of Goruckpore, lieut.-gov. of the N.W. Provinces, a small town near the northern frontier, towards the territory of Nepal. Buchanan describes it as containing only seventy poor huts. Distance N. from Gorakhpur 36 miles. Lat. 27° 16′, long. 83° 12′.

LOUR, in the territory of Rewa, in Baghelcund, a village on the route, by the Kutra Pass, from Allahabad to Jubbulpoor, and 102 miles S.W. of the former. Elevation above the sea about 1,200 feet. Lat. 24° 40′, long. 81° 45′.

LOURTA.—A town in the Rajpoot state of Jodhpoor, 46 miles N.W. from Jodhpoor, and 136 miles W. from Ajmeer. Lat. 26° 43′, long. 72° 33′.

LOWAIN, or LOOAHN, in the Rajpoot state of Jeypore, a town on the route from Agra to Nusseerabad, situate 121 miles S.W. of former, 102 N.E. of latter. It has a large bazar. Lat. 26° 46′, long. 76° 16′.

LOWAR, in the Rajpoot state of Jessulmeer, a village on the eastern frontier, where it adjoins the territory of Jodpoor. A line drawn from this village in a north-westerly direction on to Khara, on the western frontier, towards Sindh, would nearly bisect the territory of Jessulmeer, and divide the desert tract extending over the northern part from that of comparative fertility in the south. Lowar is in lat. 26° 10′, long. 70° 8′.

LOWJAH, in the British district of Mirzapoor, lieut.-gov. of the N.W. Provinces, a village on the route from the city of Benares to Allahabad, 49 miles E. of the latter, 25 W. of the former. Lat. 25° 15′, long. 82° 39′.

LOWRI.—A town of Bundelcund, in the native state of Chutterpore, situate 119 miles W.S.W. from Allahabad, and 60 miles S. by W. from Humeerpoor. Lat. 25° 8′, long. 80° 3′.

LOWUN, or LOWAH, in the Rajpoot state of Joudpore, a village on the route from Pokhurn to the town of Joudpore, and eight miles E. of the former. Lat. 26° 51′, long. 72° 8′.

LOWUN.—A town of the Deccan, in the territory of Nagpoor or Berar, on the left bank of the Mahanuddy river, and 118 miles W. from Sumbulpoor. Lat. 21° 31′, long. 82° 11′.

LUBOW, or LABAWA, in the British district of Mynpooree, lieut.-gov. of the N.W. Provinces, a village on the route from the cantonment of Allygurh to that of Etawa, and 36 miles N.W. of the latter. Lat. 27° 9′, long. 78° 37′.

LUBSA.—See Laksa.

LUCHAGEER, in the British district of Allahabad, lieut.-gov. of the N.W. Provinces, a small town with bazar, situate on the left bank of the Ganges, 776 miles N.W. of Calcutta by the river route, 32 S.E. of the city of Allahabad. Lat. 25° 19′, long. 82° 15′.

LUCHMEENPOOR, in the British district Moradabad, lieut.-gov. of the N.W. Provinces, a village on the route from Kasheepoor to Chilkia, four miles N.E. of the former. It is situate at the southern edge of the Terai or marshy forest extending along the southern base of the Sewalik range. Lat. 29° 15′, long. 79° 3′.

LUCHMUNGURH, in the territory of Alwar, under the political management of the Governor-General's agent in Rajpootana, a town, with a fort, near the south-east frontier, towards Bhurtpore. Though now little noticed or known, it was formerly an important and strong place, as Pertab Singh, the Rao rajah of Machery or Alwar, successfully defended himself here against Nuju Khan, until the rainy season compelled that powerful chief to raise the siege. Distance S.W. from Delhi 70 miles. Lat. 27° 23′, long. 76° 56′.

LUCHMUNGURH, in the Rajpoot territory of Shekhawutee, a handsome town, built on the regular model of Jeypoor. It has a fort, situate on a lofty eminence, and conspicuous over the country. Luchman Singh, from whom it was denominated, founded it in the year 1806. Distance from Delhi, S.W., 154 miles; from Jeypoor, N.W., 74. Lat. 27° 48′, long. 75° 11′.

LUCHMUNPOOR, in the territory of Oude, a village on the route from Azimgurh to Sultanpoor cantonment, 56 miles W. of the former, 22 S.E. of the latter. Lat. 26° 5′, long. 82° 20′.

LUCHUWALLA, in the British district of Dehra Doon, a village on the route from Hurdwar to Dehra, and 20 miles N.W. of the former town. It is situate a mile from the right bank of the Soang, from which it is supplied with water, by means of a canal. Distant N.W. from Calcutta 945 miles. Lat. 30° 11′, long. 78° 11′.

LUCKEEPOOR. — A town of Eastern India, in the British district of Southern Cachar, situate 18 miles E. of Silchar. Lat. 24° 46′, long. 93° 6′.

LUCKI DWAR. — A town in the native state of Bhotan, situate on the left bank of the Toresha river, and 64 miles E. by S. from Darjeeling. Lat. 26° 52′, long. 89° 19′.

LUCKIMPOOR.—A town of Assam, situate in the British district of Luckimpoor, 46 miles N.W. by W. of Seebpoor. The district of which this town is the principal place contains an area of 2,950 square miles, and a population of 30,000. The town of Luckimpoor is in lat. 27° 19′, long. 94° 3′.

LUCKIPOOR.—A town in the native state of Bhotan, situate on the left bank of the Jerdeeker river, and 40 miles E. by S. from Darjeeling. Lat. 26° 57′, long. 88° 55′.

LUCKIPOOR. — A town in the British district of Bulloah, lieut.-gov. of Bengal, 156 miles E. by N. of Calcutta. Lat. 22° 57′, long. 90° 50′.

LUCKMEEPOOR, in the British district of Mynpooree, lieut.-gov. of the N.W. Provinces, a village on the route from the cantonment of Allygurh to that of Futtehgurh, and 45 miles S.E. of the former. Lat. 27° 43′, long. 78° 47′.

LUCKNOUTI.—See GAUR.

LUCKNOW.—A district in the territory of Oude, named from the capital. It is bounded on the north by the districts Khairabad and Bahraich; on the east by Bahraich; on the south by Bainswara; and on the south-west by the Ganges, dividing it from the British district of Cawnpore.

LUCKNOW, the capital of the territory of Oude, is situate on the right or south-west side of the Goomtee, which is navigable upwards for many miles above the town, and downwards through its whole course to its confluence with the Ganges. Heber, who saw the stream a short time after the close of the rainy season, styles it "broad and rapid;" while Lumsden, at precisely the same time of the year, describes it as "a paltry and narrow stream." It is ill suited for supplying the population with water, as that which it furnishes during the rainy season can scarcely be used, in consequence of the great quantity of yellow clay which it holds suspended; "and when any great mortality prevails at Lucknow, or along the banks of the river, a putrid scum forms on its surface, occasioned by the number of dead bodies thrown into it." At the north-western extremity of the city is a bridge, a substantial structure of masonry; another, to the south-east, is formed of boats. A complete iron bridge was, in 1816, sent out in sections; but the death of the importer having stayed the progress of the undertaking, it long remained suspended, in consequence, it was reported, of the reluctance of the sovereign to complete a project commenced by a predecessor. At length, after the lapse of about thirty years, the bridge was erected, and now forms a conspicuous ornament of the city, as well as a useful addition to the means of transit. The city is represented as displaying a varied, lively, and even brilliant prospect, when viewed from a position elevated above the general height of the buildings. Of the continuous mass of erections which extends for about four miles along the bank, the middle part, being about a third of the whole, is considered to be the ancient city founded by Lakshmana, brother of Rama. It is meanly built, the houses having generally mud walls, with roofs of straw; and many are no better than booths of mats and bamboos, thatched with palm-branches or leaves. The number of brick-built houses is small. With few exceptions, the streets, which are generally sunk ten or twelve feet below the level of the shops on each side, are crooked and narrow.

According to tradition, the stronghold of Lucknow was on an eminence, and was demolished by Aurungzebe, who showed his zeal for Islam by building a mosque upon its site. Adjoining this division, and on the south-east of it, is one more recent, said to have been built principally by Saadat Ali, the Nawaub Vizier, who ruled in Oude from 1798 to 1814. From the division just described, there extends towards the south-east a handsome street, represented to be a mile in length. Heber describes it as "wider than the High Street at Oxford, but having some distant resemblance to it in the colour of its buildings, and Gothic style of the greater part of them." It is called Chinka Bazar, or Chinese Market, and has at each end a handsome gateway. Between this street and the right bank of the Goomtee is the residence formerly occupied by the deposed king.

The part of the city most interesting to a stranger is remote from the palace, being separated from it by the ancient and original city, to the north-west of which it is situate. This north-western quarter is stated to have been principally built by Asof-ud-doulah, Nawaub Vizier from 1775 to 1797. Its great ornament is the splendid Imambarah, which, according to its representation in Salt's beautiful view, can scarcely be surpassed in the light and elegant style of architecture. Lord Valentia observes respecting it, "The Imaumbarah, the mosque attached to it, and the gateways that lead to it, are beautiful specimens of this architecture (light, elegant, but fantastic). From the brilliant white of the composition, and the minute delicacy of the workmanship, an enthusiast might suppose that genii had been the artificers;" and Heber, a critic of high authority on such subjects, observes, "I have never seen an architectural view which pleased me more, from its richness and variety, as well as the proportions and general good taste of its principal features." It opens on the Hasanabad, a broad street, running nearly from south-east to north-west, and parallel to the river. At no great distance is a large mosque, commenced by Saadat Ali, and at his death left unfinished. Three or four miles south-east of the town, and near the right bank of the river, is Constantia, "a strange, fantastical building, of every species of architecture, and adorned with minute stucco fretwork, enormous lions, with lamps instead of eyes, mandarins and ladies with shaking heads, and all the gods and goddesses of the heathen mythology." It was built at an enormous expense by an eccentric French adventurer, named Claude Martin, who arrived in India a private soldier, and died a major-general, in possession of property to the amount of several hundred thousand pounds. His body is deposited in a sarcophagus in one of the lower apartments. Martin had been bred a Romanist, but appears to have retained little of his early creed. A large share, however, of his vast wealth was devoted to charitable purposes, and a college, called after the founder "La Martinère," preserves his memory at the place where his fortune was accumulated and his eccentricities indulged.

Lucknow may be regarded as entitled to an honourable distinction among Indian cities, in possessing an observatory. It was established under the superintendence of Major Wilcox, who succeeded in training competent assistants for its management, the majority of whom were natives. An hospital and dispensary also afford means for the useful application of European science. A church has been built, and a sum of money assigned for its repair. Of the amount of the population of Lucknow, nothing certain is ascertainable; it is estimated at 300,000. There is a large proportion of Mussulmans among the Hindoos, and not a few Christians. The city of Lucknow is probably about 360 feet above the sea. Distant N.W. from Calcutta, by Benares, Juanpoor, and Sultanpoor, 610 miles; N.W. from Allahabad 128; N.E. from Cawnpore 53. Lat. 26° 52′, long. 81°.

LUCKONDA.—A town in the British district of Rajahmundry, presidency of Madras, 30 miles N. by E. of Rajahmundry. Lat. 17° 25′, long. 82°.

LUCKOWULLY.—A town in the Mysore, situate on the right bank of the Budra river, and 111 miles N.W. from Seringapatam. Lat. 13° 41′, long. 75° 42′.

LUCKPUT.—A town in the native state of Cutch, presidency of Bombay, situate on the left bank of the Koree mouth of the Great Western Runn, the depth of which was considerably increased by the effects of the earthquake of 1819. Luckput is 71 miles N.W. by W. from Bhooj. Lat. 23° 50′, long. 68° 48′.

LUCKSHAUM.—A town in the British district of Bulloah, lieut.-gov. of Bengal, 180 miles E. by N. of Calcutta. Lat. 23° 14′, long. 91° 10′.

LUCKWARIE, in Jaunsar, a village built near the summit of a hill on the right bank of the Jumna, and about 1,000 feet above it. The houses are in general neatly built of stone, and covered with slate. The women are fair and well made, and are distributed economically among the male population, several of whom cohabit with one female by a sort of extraordinary perversion of marriage. Skinner observes—"Four seems to be the mystical number; for all that I have questioned on the subject answer, 'We are four, and have one wife between us.'" Here is a temple built of wood, with doors covered with plates of brass, embellished with well-executed sculptures of figures of Hindu mythology. Lat. 30° 33′, long. 78° 1′.

LUDGAON, in the British district of Futtehpoor, lieut.-gov. of the N.W. Provinces, a village on the route from Banda to the town of Futtehpoor, and 12 miles S.W. of the latter. Lat. 25° 51′, long. 80° 43′.

LUDHEEA, a river of the British district of Kumaon, lieut.-gov. of the N.W. Provinces. It rises amidst the mountains, in lat. 29° 25′, long. 79° 50′, and, holding a course generally in a south-easterly direction for about forty-five miles, falls into the Kalee or Surjoo on the right side, in lat. 29° 9′, long. 80° 19′. It is fordable where crossed by the route from Pillibeet to Petoragarh, in lat. 29° 10′, long. 80° 14′.

LUDHONA.—A town in the native state of Gwalior, or possessions of Scindia's family, situate 46 miles S.E. from Neemuch, and 214 miles W. from Saugur. Lat. 24°, long. 75° 27′.

LUDOOAREE.—A town in the British district of Tirhoot, lieut.-gov. of Bengal, 82 miles N.E. by N. of Dinapoor. Lat. 26° 40′, long. 85° 43′.

LUGAREE, in Sinde, a village on the route from Hyderabad to Omercote, and 60 miles W. of the latter place. It is situate on the right bank of the Poorana river. Lat. 25° 13′, long. 68° 48′.

LUHORAH.—A river rising in lat. 31° 34′, long. 69° 48′, in the Suliman range of mountains, and, flowing in an easterly direction for about forty-five miles, is lost in the valley of the Derajat.

LUKA, in the Punjab, a town on the route from Ferozpoor to Mooltan. It is situate in the Doab between the Ghara and the Chinab. Lat. 29° 52′, long. 72° 20′.

LUK BAWAN, in Cashmere, a village situate at the north-western extremity of a long ridge of hills, which, extending from the Snowy Panjal, gradually diminish in height and size, till they terminate on the plain. Though now scarcely containing half a dozen houses, Luk Bawan was once a considerable place. Here are the ruins of a large bath and an extensive stone-built tank. Lat. 33° 36′, long. 75° 16′.

LUKENWAREE.—A town in one of the recently sequestrated districts of Hyderabad, or dominions of the Nizam, situate 75 miles S.W. of Ellichpoor. Lat. 20° 30′, long. 76° 43′.

LUKHNAU, in the British district of Etawa, lieut.-gov. of the N.W. Provinces, a town situate three miles from the left bank of the Jumna, 11 miles S.E. of the town of Etawa, and 73 miles N.W. of the cantonment of Cawnpore. Lat. 26° 39′, long. 79° 13′.

LUKKEE, in the Daman division of the Punjab, a town situated on the left bank of the Gombela or Tochee river, 116 miles S.S.W. of the town of Peshawur. Lat. 32° 30′, long. 70° 51′.

LUKKEE MOUNTAINS, in Sinde, are a considerable range connected with the Hala or Brahooic Mountains of Beloochistan. With the Jutteel, the Keertar, the Pubb, and some other ranges less known, the Lukkee contributes to give character to the singularly wild tract constituting the western part of Sinde, extending between Beloochistan and the alluvial tract on the Indus, and also between the desert of Shikarpore and Kurrachee. The Lukkee is the most eastern of these ranges, and runs from the Jutteel south-eastward, towards the high lands opposite Hyderabad, being known in different parts by the various appellations of the Eeree Lukkee, Daran Lukkee, and Hallar Lukkee. These mountains are in general of recent formation, containing a vast profusion of marine exuviæ. "The organic remains of former ages," observes Burnes, "are innumerable; the asteroid, the cockle, the oyster, the nummulite, and almost all kinds of sea-shells, may be collected on the Lukkee range." Huge fissures, apparently produced by earthquakes, traverse this range, which, in the frequent occurrence of hot springs and sulphureous exhalations, exhibit signs of volcanic action. Some parts appear to be of more ancient formation, as they produce lead, antimony, and copper. The elevation of the highest part of this dreary and sterile range is estimated at from 1,500 to 2,000 feet. Between the town of Lukkee and that of Sehwan, the mountain has a nearly perpendicular face, about 600 feet high towards the Indus, between which and the precipice there was at one time a road, though in some places so narrow, that only a single camel could pass at a time. In 1839, this defile was washed away by the turbulent river, which now sweeps along the base of the cliff. The length of the Lukkee range is about fifty miles. The centre of the range is about lat. 26°, long. 67° 50′.

LUKKEE (NORTHERN), in Sinde, a large town in ruins, on the route from Shikarpore to Sukkur, and 12 miles S.E. of the former place. Under the Durani sway it was wealthy and populous, but since it passed into the power of the ameers of Sinde, it has fallen into decay. In the time of its prosperity it yielded an annual revenue of 100,000 rupees. It is ten miles from the right bank of the Indus. Lat. 27° 52′, long. 68° 42′.

LUKKEE (SOUTHERN), in Sinde, a town situate a short distance south of Sehwan, close to the west bank of the Indus, and adjacent to the entrance of the Lukkee Pass. Its site is picturesque, being near a lake a mile wide and several miles in length, which appears to have been at one time a reach of the Indus. The Lukkee Mountains, sloping down to the west of the town, and a little to the north, abut on that river, which sweeps along their rocky base. Close to the town is a spring of sulphureous water, which has a temperature of 102°, and flows from the base of a calcareous precipice 600 feet high. Lat. 26° 23′, long. 68° 55′.

LUKKHOKI, in the Punjab, a small town in the Doab between the Ghara and the Ravee, is situate about three miles from the right or west bank of the former river, and on the route from Ferozpoor to Mooltan. Lat. 30° 3′, long. 72° 57′.

LUKMESHWUR.—A town in the Southern Mahratta jaghire of Meeruj, situate 39 miles S.E. from Dharwar, and 98 miles W. from Bellary. Lat. 15° 8′, long. 75° 31′.

LUKTAHA, in the British district of Allahabad, lieut.-gov. of the N.W. Provinces, a village on the right bank of the Ganges, 789 miles N.W. of Calcutta by the river route, 20 S.E. of Allahabad by the same. Lat. 25° 19′, long. 82° 8′.

LUKTUR.—A town in Guzerat, or the dominions of the Guicowar, situate 104 miles W.N.W. from Baroda, and 58 miles W. by S. from Ahmedabad. Lat. 22° 50′, long. 71° 44′.

LULLEEANA, in the Punjab, a village 26 miles S. of Lahore. Lat. 31° 14′, long. 74° 28′.

LULOWLEE, in the British district of Futtehpoor, lieut.-gov. of the N.W. Provinces, a small town near the left bank of the Jumna, on the route from Banda to the town of Futtehpoor, and 22 miles S.W. of the latter place. Lat. 25° 48′, long. 80° 36′.

LUM.—A town in the native state of Nepal, situate on the left bank of the Arun river, and 96 miles E. by S. from Khatmandoo. Lat. 27° 29′, long. 86° 49′.

LUMBEEA, in Bussahir, a pass over the range of the Himalaya bounding Koonawur on the south. This and three other passes cross the ridge within the space of little more than a mile. Its elevation above the sea is probably between 16,000 and 17,000 feet. It is seldom passed, except in May, June, July, and August, on account of cracks and the snow sinking. Lat. 31° 16′, long. 78° 20′.

LUMBREE.—A town of Eastern India, in the native state of Osimlee, on the Cossya Hills, situate 46 miles S. from Gowhatty, and 79 miles S.E. by E. from Goalpara. Lat. 25° 30′, long. 91° 39′.

LUNAWAURA, a small state in the Rewa Caunta division of Guzerat. This principality is situated on the confines of Guzerat, and is a continuation of the mountain-tract which forms the north-eastern boundary of that province. It is situate on the left bank of the Myhee, and adjacent to some important passes. The dominions of the nawaub of Balasinore bound it on the west and south-west: to the north is the Myhee Caunta territory; the states of Soauth and Barreah lie to the east; and Godra, one of Scindia's Punch mahals, to the south. It is situate between lat. 22° 50′ and 23° 16′, long. 73° 21′ and 73° 47′. The length is estimated at thirty miles from north to south, and the breadth at nearly the same distance. The Panum, a tributary to the Myhee, on the banks of which some of the villages belonging to the state are situated, flows within a mile of the capital. This small chiefship having co-operated to the best of its ability with the army under Colonel Murray, in the war with Scindia, of 1803, was admitted by treaty to British protection. Sir George Barlow, in 1806, severed the connection; whereupon it reverted to Scindia, who exacted a tribute from it. In 1819, the right of supremacy over Lunawaura was ceded by Scindia to the British government, the latter guaranteeing the payment of the tribute, on condition that Scindia should immediately withdraw from the state all his troops, karkoons, and other officers, and on no account, for the future, exercise any interference, either directly or indirectly, in its affairs.

Prior to that event, and the introduction of our superintendence and control, Baoz Khan, the leader of bands of mercenaries, exercised the chief authority, under the direction and countenance of the rajah's mother. This power, it is scarcely necessary to say, was not used for the benefit of the country; the prince was held in a state of dependence and poverty, and the people subjected to systematic misrule: the cultivators were oppressed and impoverished, and the larger share of the revenue engrossed by the chief and his band. The nominal rajah (Futteh Sing) was too young and too much awed by the presence of the mercenaries, to attempt the exercise of sovereignty, and was, moreover, alarmed lest the threat of the Ranee to denounce him as a supposititious child, should, in the event of his taking any measures to lessen her influence, be carried into effect. On the expulsion of Baoz Khan by the authority of the British government, towards the end of 1819, the rajah was established in possession of the country, which he now holds.

It appears, however, that Futteh Sing was not the rightful heir, the inheritance being vested in his eldest brother, Sheo Sing, who had been excluded by the consequences of female jealousy. Purtaub Sing, the former ruler of Lunawaura, married two wives, each of whom bore him a son. The children were named Sheo Sing and Futteh Sing. The mother of the latter, from family and priority of marriage, was the first in rank and distinction, but the date of her son's birth was eight months later than that of the son of the other princess. The latter consequently became heir to the guddee, the rights of the firstborn not being invalidated by any inferiority of rank on the part of the mother, provided her marriage be lawful and regular. The circumstance of having given birth to an heir of the state excited against the mother of Sheo Sing a feeling of jealousy in the mind of her rival; domestic feuds were the result, and the rajah, apprehensive for the life of Sheo Sing, presented his mother with a sum of money, and removed her, together with the child, to the house of a distant relative in the principality of Dongurpoor. Soon after these events, Futteh Sing was born, and four years afterwards, Purtaub, his father, died. Through his mother's influence, Futteh Sing was placed on the guddee, whilst Sheo Sing remained at Dongurpoor. His name and birth made him a convenient instrument in the hands of a mehlah named Nana, who, some time after Purtaub's death, hired troops, and began to make collections, under pretence of maintaining the cause of the rightful heir of the deceased prince. In the course of the disturbance for which the conflicting claims of the two parties afforded a pretext, success fluctuated. Sheo Sing was at one period placed on the guddee, but after a brief occupation, was dispossessed by his brother Futteh Sing. The nawaub of Balasinore then appeared on behalf of the former, and brought a body of troops against Lunawaura, which he captured, and retained for the space of a few months; during which period Sheo Sing remained in the territories of his ally. The payment of a large sum of money effected the removal of the Balasinore troops, and shortly afterwards, Sheo Sing's principal supporter, Nana, died. Nana's son, with the aid of a party of Bheels and marauders, then plundered in Sheo's name, but, after a time, made peace with Futteh Sing, and took up his residence at Lunawaura. With the defection of this champion, the active struggles for securing the government to Sheo Sing ended. Sheo Sing, however, submitted his pretensions to Sir John Malcolm, through a vakeel, whom he sent to make known his claims to the guddee, and request British interference in his behalf. To this application an answer was returned, to the effect, that our policy was to disturb existing arrangements as little as possible; which policy had consequently led to the recognition of the title of those whom we found in authority. Futteh Sing, thus supported, retained possession of the guddee.

The family of the chief of Lunawaura may be traced to an early period in the last century. In 1739, an ancestor, styled only zemindar, paid a tribute to the authorities in Guzerat. In 1758, his successor, Deep Sing, was besieged by the Peishwa, and after an honourable defence of his fort, obliged to pay down 50,000 rupees, and give hostages for good behaviour. Deep Sing was succeeded by his son Doorjun, and after him came Purtaub, the father of Futteh Sing. The Lunawaura state is for the most part composed of villages which have been either usurped from the neighbouring states or granted by their chieftains. It has little or no other resources than its land-revenue, which yields from 80,000 to a lac of rupees. It is subject to the payment of a tribute to Scindia of 12,000 rupees per annum; a claim which had existed for more than seventy years, and was paid up to the date 1819, when we became mediators, in order to accomplish our object of restoring peace to the country. It pays a Ghaus Dana also to the Guicowar, of 6,000 rupees, and is subject to a similar charge of 1,200 rupees to the neighbouring state of

Balasinore. The military establishments comprise about 200 horse and foot, and the dependent chiefs of the rajah's family, who hold upon feudatory principles, arm themselves when required. An officer, appointed by the Baroda presidency, is maintained at the joint expense of the Soauth and Lunawaura states, for police purposes in their respective districts.

LUNAWAURA, the capital of the principality bearing its own name, and situate on the bifurcation formed by the junction of the Panum with the Myhee river. It is a fortified town, and the fortifications and town together are nearly three miles in circumference. Its situation is favourable for merchants proceeding from Rutlam and other parts of Malwah to Ahmedabad and the interior of Guzerat. Many of that remarkable race of men called Borahs reside in Lunawaura, which also contains many artisans, as smiths and carpenters, of reputed skill in their respective professions. It is situate in lat. 23° 8′, long. 73° 37′.

LUNDYE RIVER, the name given to the Swat river previous to its junction with the Kabool river.

LUNGOOR, a fort in the British district of Kumaon, lieut.-gov. of the N.W. Provinces. It is situate in the southern or outer range of the Himalaya system, on the summit of a lofty conical hill, extremely difficult of access. The inclosing wall is seven feet high, and is built of rough stones without cement, and loopholed for musketry. Within are a few huts for the shelter of the garrison, but all is now in a ruinous state. In a military point of view, it is valueless, as it commands no route of importance, and water cannot be obtained nearer than half a mile. The Gorkhas, during their occupation, made two tanks within the walls; but they are unserviceable, retaining no water. Elevation above the sea 6,401 feet. Lat. 29° 55′, long. 78° 42′.

LUNGRASOO, in Gurhwal, a village on the left side of the torrent Aglar, and 450 feet above the stream, which runs in so steep a channel as to form a succession of cascades. The village is situate on the rugged side of a mountain, amidst a few cultivated patches, on terraces, formed on the declivity by means of embankments constructed of large blocks of stone. The crops of barley and wheat produced on those narrow surfaces suffice for the scanty population. Elevation above the sea 4,393 feet. Lat. 30° 29′, long. 78° 12′.

LUNGTUNG.—A town of Eastern India, in the British district of Jynteah, 40 miles N. of Jynteahpore. Lat. 25° 40′, long. 92° 9′.

LUNMEE, in the British district of Ramgurh, in the Saugor and Nerbudda territory, lieut.-gov. of the N.W. Provinces, a town on the route from Ramgurh to Ruttunpoor, 55 miles E.S.E. of the former. Lat. 22° 32′, long. 81° 49′.

LUREE, in the Punjab, a village situate on the left bank of the Swan river, on the route from Attock to Julalpoor, and 50 miles S.E. of the former town. Lat. 33° 33′, long. 73° 8′.

LURROO, in Cashmere, on the route from the Banihal Pass to Islamabad, and about eight miles S. of the latter place. At the time of Forster's visit, it was a small but very populous town. It does not appear to be mentioned by Vigne or other late travellers, and it is not improbable that it may have been completely ruined in the dreadful depopulation which, within the last few years, has afflicted Cashmere. Wilson conjectures it to be identical with Lolora or Looloo, mentioned in the Ayeen Akbery. Abulfazel, however, states that Looloo was in Kamraj, or the western division of Cashmere; and Lurroo is, according to Forster's account, in the south-eastern part of the valley. Lat. 33° 36′, long. 75° 16′.

LUSHKUREE KHAN KE SERAI, in Sirhind, a village on the route from Kurnoul to Lodiana, and 19 miles S.E. of the latter place. It is situate in an open and well-cultivated country, so that supplies are abundant, and water can be had in large quantities. The road in this part of the route is excellent. Distant N.W. from Calcutta 1,069 miles. Lat. 30° 45′, long. 76° 12′.

LUTSAN, in the British district of Allygurh, lieut.-gov. of the N.W. Provinces, a village on the route from the cantonment of Allygurh to that of Etawa, and 18 miles S. of the former. Lat. 27° 40′, long. 78° 11′.

LUTTAULA, in Sirhind, a small town on the route from Ferozpoor to Simla, and 84 miles S.E. of the former place. It is situate in an open country, with considerable cultivation, and is abundantly supplied with good water from wells. Distant N.W. from Calcutta 1,069 miles. Lat. 30° 40′, long. 75° 53′.

LUTTEEPOOR, in the British district of Mirzapoor, lieut.-gov. of the N.W. Provinces, a town, with fort, 13 miles S.E. of the fort of Chunar. Here, in 1781, Cheyt Singh, the refractory zemindar of Benares, raised his standard against the British authority, but was speedily compelled to fly, having previously, in cold blood, massacred a number of the East-India Company's troops, whom he had made prisoners. Distant S.E. from Mirzapoor 31 miles, N.W. from Calcutta 390. Lat. 24° 58′, long. 83° 7′.

LUTTIPORE.—A town in the British district of Bhagulpore, lieut.-gov. of Bengal, seven miles N. of Bhagulpore. Lat. 25° 17′, long. 86° 59′.

LUTTOODHEE, or LUTHOODEEH, in the British district of Ghazeepoor, lieut.-gov. of the N.W. Provinces, a village on the route from Ghazeepoor cantonment to Chupra, 24 miles E. of the former, 58 W. of the latter. It has water from wells, but supplies are scarce, and must be collected from the surrounding country. The road in this part of the country is rather good. Lat. 25° 40′, long. 83° 58′.

LUTTUMMUR, in the Daman division of the Punjab, a town situated 28 miles from the right bank of the Indus, 92 miles S.W. by S. of the town of Peshawur. Lat. 32° 53′, long. 70° 51′.

LUVVARA.—A town in one of the recently sequestrated districts of Hyderabad, or dominions of the Nizam, situate 38 miles N.E. of Sholapoor. Lat. 18°, long. 76° 23′.

LUXAR, in Jaunsar, a village on a ridge rising above the right bank of the Jumna, and about two miles from that river. Lat. 30° 34′, long. 78° 2′.

LYNE.—A town in the British territory of Pegue, on the left bank of the Lyne river, and 41 miles W. by S. from Pegue. Lat. 17° 33′, long. 95° 40′.

LYNE RIVER.—The name given to one of the principal branches forming the Delta of the Irawady river. It leaves the parent stream in lat. 17° 55′, long. 95° 20′, when, flowing in a south-easterly direction, and passing the town of Rangoon, it takes the name of that place, and falls into the Indian Ocean in lat. 16° 29′, long. 96° 26′, after a total course of 155 miles.

M.

MAAT, in the British district of Muttra, lieut.-gov. of the N.W. Provinces, a town on the route from Muttra to Allygurh, seven miles N.N.E. of the former. Lat. 27° 35′, long. 77° 49′.

MACHERY, in the territory of Alwar, under the political superintendence of the Governor-General's agent for Rajpootana, a town two or three miles S.E. of the route from Nusseerabad to Muttra, and 76 miles S.W. of the latter. Though at present containing only a few houses, it was formerly the residence of the Rao rajah or Rajpoot sovereign of the territory, now better known by the name of Alwar; whence that petty potentate was, in early official documents of the East-India Company, styled the Maha Rao rajah of Machery. Lat. 27° 15′, long. 76° 45′.

MACHEWARA, in Sirhind, a town on the route from Loodiana to Ropur, and 22 miles E. of the former place. It is situate about four miles from the left bank of the Sutlej, which formerly flowed close to the town, but about fifty years ago took a direction more to the north. Distant N.W. from Calcutta, *viâ* Loodiana, 1,110 miles. Lat. 30° 55′, long. 76° 17′.

MACHILPOOR.—A town in the native state of Indoor, or territory of Holkar, situate 156 miles W. by N. from Saugor, and 105 miles N.N.E. from Indoor. Lat. 24° 7′, long. 76° 22′.

MACHROLE, in the jaghire of Jujhur, lieut.-gov. of the N.W. Provinces, a village on the route from Kurnaul to Rewarree, and 24 miles N. of the latter. Water may be had from a tank. Lat. 28° 27′, long. 76° 43′.

MACHUNDEE, in the British district of Bareilly, lieut.-gov. of the N.W. Provinces, a village on the route from Bareilly to Petoragurh, and 43 miles N.E. of the former. Lat. 28° 45′, long. 79° 53′.

MACHURLA.—A town in the British district of Guntoor, presidency of Madras, 70 miles W. of Guntoor. Lat. 16° 28′, long. 79° 29′.

MADAGEESY, in the Mysore, a small but well-fortified town, on the north-east frontier, towards the British district of Bellary. It is situate at the base of a rock very difficult of access, and surmounted by a fortress. It was formerly the stronghold of a polygar or landholder, who possessed the surrounding country to a wide extent. An unhappy woman, of the name of Madageesy, having performed the rite of suttee, by being burned alive with her husband's corpse, the place received its present name in commemoration of the circumstance. Distance from Seringapatam, N., 104 miles; Chitradurg, S.E., 60. Lat. 13°50′, long. 77°15′.

MADANPOOR, in the British district of Goruckpore, lieut.-gov. of the N.W. Provinces, a small town formerly the royal residence of Madan, the chief of the Tharus tribe, but now containing only 150 huts. It is situate on the Mujnuh or Buthooa, a small stream, a feeder of the river Raptee, 30 miles S.E. of Goruckpore cantonment. Lat. 26° 15′, long. 83° 47′.

MADANPOOR, a village of Oude, in the district of Aldemau, situate on the left bank of the river Tons (North-eastern), 40 miles S.E. of Oude. Butter estimates the population at 300, of whom 200 are Mussulmans. Lat. 26° 30′, long. 82° 26′.

MADAPOOR.—A town in the Mysore, 34 miles N.W. from Seringapatam, and 102 miles E. from Mangalore. Lat. 12° 48′, long. 76° 24′.

MADARA MYO.—A town of Burmah, situate eight miles from the left bank of the Irawady, and 29 miles N.N.E. from Ava. Lat. 22° 15′, long. 96° 12′.

MADDAPOLLUM.—A town in the British district of Masulipatam, presidency of Madras, 42 miles E.N.E. of Masulipatam. Lat. 16° 27′, long. 81° 46′.

MADDEHJEE, in Sinde, a considerable village on the route from Sukkur to Larkhana, and 28 miles W. of the former place. It contains about 150 houses and twenty shops. A plentiful supply of water is procurable. Lat. 27° 40′, long. 68° 30′.

MADHARAJPOORA, in the Rajpoot state of Jeypoor, a town on the route from Delhi to Mow, 190 miles S.W. of former, 317 N.E. of latter. Lat. 26° 35′, long. 75° 42′.

MADHOOPOORA, in the Rajpoot territory of Jeypoor, a town on the route from Hansee to Nusseerabad, situate 143 miles S.

of former, 100 N.E. of latter. It has a large bazar, and water and supplies are abundant. Lat. 27° 26′, long. 75° 42′.

MADHOOPOORA.—A town in the Rajpoot state of Jeypoor, situate 39 miles N.N.W. from Jeypoor, and 94 miles N.E. from Ajmeer. Lat. 27° 28′, long. 75° 43′.

MADHOPOOR.—A town in the Rajpoot state of Jeypoor, situate 79 miles S.E. by S. from Jeypoor, and 121 miles E.S.E. from Ajmeer. Lat. 25° 56′, long. 76° 34′.

MADHUPOOR, in the British district of Pubna, lieut.-gov. of Bengal, a town on the route from Berhampore to Dacca, 89 miles S.E. of former, 83 W. of latter. Lat. 23° 48′, long. 89° 22′.

MADHUPOOR, in the British district of Bareilly, lieut.-gov. of the N.W. Provinces, a village on the route from Moradabad to Bareilly, and 11 miles N.W. of the latter. Lat. 28° 27′, long. 79° 23′.

MADIGOLE.—A town in the British district of Vizagapatam, presidency of Madras, 40 miles W.N.W. of Vizagapatam. Lat. 17° 58′, long. 82° 50′.

MADINA, or MODENA, in the British district of Rohtuk, lieut.-gov. of the N.W. Provinces, a village on the route from Delhi to Hansee, and 33 miles S.E. of the latter. Lat. 28° 56′, long. 76° 30′.

MADOOROO.—A town in the British district of Masulipatam, presidency of Madras, 22 miles W.N.W. of Masulipatam. Lat. 16° 17′, long. 80° 53′.

MADRAS.—One of the three presidencies of British India, named from the city which is the seat of its government. It is bounded on the north by the presidency of Bombay, the territory of the Nizam, that of Berar, and the petty native states on the south-west frontier of Bengal; on the east and south-east by the Bay of Bengal; on the south by the Indian Ocean; and on the south-west and west by the Arabian Sea. It extends from Cape Comorin, in lat. 8° 4′, to the northern extremity of the district of Ganjam, in lat. 20° 18′, and from Golamelly, the north-west point of the British district of North Canara, in long. 74° 9′, to Priaghy, in the British district of Ganjam, in long. 85° 15′. Its greatest length, measured from north-east to south-west, from Priaghy to Cape Comorin, is about 950 miles, and its greatest breadth, measured at right angles to the direction of that line, from the city of Madras to Golamelly, is about 450. Its seacoast on one face, measured in a south-eastern direction, and subsequently eastward to Cape Comorin, extends 540 miles, being nearly throughout washed by the Arabian Sea, and for a short distance by the Indian Ocean. On the other face, measured from Cape Comorin north-east to Priaghy, along the shore of the Bay of Bengal, its length is about 1,187 miles; and consequently the total extent of the seacoast of the presidency is 1,727 miles; being much greater than that of the two others combined. In the presidency of Bombay, however, the haven of the same name can receive and shelter fleets of the largest ships; and in the presidency of Bengal, the Hooghly, though in some respects not so eligible as the harbour of Bombay, can receive and shelter as great a number of ships, not inferior in size. But, notwithstanding the great extent of the Madras coast, there is no harbour equal to either: Cochin, on the Malabar coast, which has the greatest depth of water, is, during several months of the year, closed by the south-west monsoon. Its entrance, moreover, is intercepted by a bar, and it does not appear to be adapted for large ships. In the mid-channel, the depth of water varies from about eleven feet to sixteen. The port of Mangalore admits with safety only vessels having not more than ten or twelve feet draught. Small havens and creeks are, however, very numerous along the coast of Malabar, and are generally estuaries of streams flowing from the Western Ghats in such numbers, that there are not less than twenty-nine rivers and ten nullas [streams of inferior size] within a distance of 217 miles. From Golamelly, the north-western extremity of this coast, to Mangalore, a distance of 150 miles, the coast is in general bold and rocky, with soundings increasing fast as the navigator recedes from the shore. From Mangalore for about sixty-five miles, the land near the sea is generally low and woody as far as Mount Dilly, a headland rising from the sea. The Malabar coast, which may be considered to commence at Mount Dilly, and stretch generally south-east as far as Cape Comorin, a distance of 325 miles, is, with little exception, low, and either muddy or sandy, having numerous shallow inlets extending a considerable distance into the land, and called by the British the Backwaters. The Western Ghats, throughout the whole extent of the coast, from Golamelly to the vicinity of Cape Comorin, stretch nearly parallel to it, at an average distance of about forty miles, though in some parts approaching considerably nearer. They are visible from a great distance at sea, and their height, and bold and rugged outline, render them very striking objects. Cape Comorin itself is low and sandy; but a few miles inland, and to the north of the extreme point, the southern summits of the Ghats rise in lofty and majestic peaks. To the north-east of Cape Comorin, the coast is little frequented for 166 miles, as navigation northwards into the Bay of Bengal is obstructed and rendered impracticable for ships by Adam's Bridge, a sand-bank extending from the mainland of India to Ceylon, having only two navigable channels, and neither of them (although of late years considerably deepened) allowing the passage of craft drawing more than eight and a half feet water. The sea, bounded north-west by the coast of India, north and north-east by Adam's Bridge, and east by the west coast of Ceylon, is called the Gulf of Manar, and though little frequented by large vessels, in consequence of the obstruction northwards, has, on its north-west side, or the shore of Tinnevelly district, the roadstead or haven of Tutacorin, where ships may anchor throughout the year in considerable safety, being sheltered towards the sea by several small islands. The whole of the shore of Tinnevelly and Madura is generally low, rocky, and much beset by reefs. North of Adam's Bridge, the shore extends nearly north-east, being the coast of the British districts of Madura and Tanjore, and bounding on the north-west Palk's Bay or Palk's Gulf, which, on the south, is bounded by Adam's Bridge, on the south-east by Ceylon, and to the north-east is open to the Bay of Bengal. The shore in this part has no bold features; "the whole of the coast bounding the west side of the bay is lined with shoal water." At Calymere Point, 130 miles north-east of Adam's Bridge, and in lat. 10° 16', long. 79° 55', the coast of Coromandel commences, and holds a direction due north across the estuaries of the Cavery, which either inclose or traverse a delta, having a base of eighty-two miles towards the sea. Along this base, the places frequented by shipping are Negapatam, Nagore, and Tranquebar; none of them having shelter for large ships, which must be anchored in the open sea at a considerable distance. Nagore is, however, situate on an estuary of the Cavery, admitting vessels of 200 tons burthen. The Coromandel coast continues to hold a northly direction for 297 miles farther, to Gondegam, in lat. 15° 20', where the river Mussy is considered to bound it to the northward, and retains the same character of slight elevation and general sandy formation, with shallow water along shore. Throughout this distance there is no shelter for large ships, except at Blackwood Harbour, in lat. 14° 1', a roadstead, where ships are secure from gales from all points but the north. At Porto Novo, Cuddalore, Pondicherry, Sadras, Madras, Gondegam, and some other less-important seafaring places along the coast, ships must be anchored in the open sea, exposed to the huge roll of the Bay of Bengal. From Gondegam, the seashore is termed the Golconda Coast, and holds a direction north-east for 269 miles, to the southern point of the district of Vizagapatam, in lat. 17° 15'. In the south-western part, it contains the estuaries of the branches of the river Kistnah, and those more numerous of the river Godavery; and in that part is so low, that when prolonged and violent gales from the north-east are simultaneous with great land-floods, the coast is extensively inundated, and great devastation takes place. The most important maritime places on the coast of Golconda are Masulipatam and Coringa, neither affording shelter to large ships, which, as at the places previously named, must be anchored in the open sea. At Masulipatam, the estuary of a branch of the Kistnah receives coasting craft, and at Coringa, a similar outlet of the Godavery receives vessels of 200 tons. The other maritime places along the Golconda coast are Motapali, Narsapoor, Gordawar, and Watara. In lat. 17° 15', the coast of Golconda is considered to terminate, and that of Orissa to commence. From this point the coast becomes bold and rocky, with rugged hills of no great height at intervals, and for the most part retains this character throughout the coast of Orissa for 243 miles, to the north-eastern extremity of the presidency, at Priaghy. Vizagapatam, the most southern place frequented by shipping on the coast of Orissa, is marked by a bold bluff headland, called by seamen the Dolphin's Nose. The other seafaring places are Bimlipatam, Chicacole, and Ganjam. The hills on the Golconda coast are connected in some places with the great range of the Eastern Ghats; and as this range approaches the south-west, its distance from the shore gradually increases, leaving space for the plain comprised in the tract known as the Circars and the Carnatic. About fifty-six miles north-west of the city of Madras, the Eastern Ghats form a junction with the range "which, sweeping irregularly inland, crosses the peninsula in a south-west direction;" and in the vicinity of the Neilgherries joins the Western Ghats, which extend to Cape Comorin on the one side, and to the northern frontier of the presidency on the other. The low land between the base of these last-mentioned mountains and the sea is of less breadth than that lying in the like situation with respect to the Eastern Ghats, being in some places not more than twenty or twenty-five miles in breadth; nowhere more than fifty. It comprises the level part of the territories of Travancore and Cochin, and nearly the whole of the British districts of Malabar and North and South Canara. The seaward faces of both the Eastern and Western Ghats are far more abrupt and more elevated above their bases than the sides which face towards the interior, as the two great ranges form, one on the south-west, the other on the south-east, the buttresses or walls of the triangular table-land of the Deccan. Though this great table-land rises considerably towards the south, it has a general slope of surface to the east or south-east, all the streams of any considerable magnitude flowing in that direction, and being ultimately emptied into the Bay of Bengal. The line of waterheads extends along the culminating ridge of the Western Ghats, and consequently at a short distance from the Western or Arabian Sea; and the three great rivers, the Godavery, the Kistnah, and the Cauvery, flow south-eastward or eastward nearly across Southern India, to their fall into the Bay of Bengal. Of each of these a description will be found in its proper place under the alphabetical arrangement. Numerous feeders from the Western Ghats discharge themselves into those main streams. Other large torrents flow from the table-land, and in the rainy season drain the level country, and fall into the Bay of Bengal. The principal of these are the Northern Penna, the Southern Penna, and the Palar; all of which rise in the territory of Mysore. On the western side of the presidency, the numerous torrents falling into the Arabian Sea have perennial streams flowing from the Western Ghats, and channels with great declivity in the upper part, in the vicinity of the mountains; but towards the sea the declivity becomes slight, and these streams ultimately expand into shallow estuaries of great width, or into extensive and shallow lakes, communicating with the sea, and denominated by British writers backwaters. Of those, the most remarkable is the Backwater of Cochin, which extends from north to south a distance of 120 miles.

The mineral wealth of the presidency is attracting notice. Iron-ore occurs in several parts: it is found in the district of Malabar, near Beypoor, where iron-works have been erected: it exists also in great abundance in South Arcot, in the vicinity of Porto Novo, where extensive foundries have been established by a joint-stock association, called the East-Indian Iron Company, to whom also belong the works at Beypoor. Manganese exists in Mysore, in the Neilgherries, and in Bellary: copper-ore is found in Nellore, in many parts of the Eastern Ghats, and in Bellary; but there are scarcely any regularly continuous lodes of the metal, and miners have generally been baffled in attempting to work according to the usual rules of their art. Perhaps, however, the unsatisfactory results are attributable to their not having penetrated to a sufficient depth. Antimony is found in Mysore, as is also silver-ore, both there and in Madura, generally in the form of a carbonate: corundum, in the form of emery, as well as in other forms, occurs in the valley of the Cauvery; lead-ore in Mysore; beryl in Coimbatore, and in various other places. Diamonds, generally of moderate value, are sometimes met with in the sandstone of Rajamundry, of Guntoor, and of Vizagapatam; and garnets are peculiarly abundant in the same districts. Coal is found on the banks of the Godavery, near Chinnore; and anthracite in considerable quantities in the same vicinity.

The climate is more varied by the different elevations of the surface, and by other local circumstances, than by the latitude. The table-land, or undulating surface on the summits of the Neilgherry group, having an elevation of from 6,000 to 7,000 feet above the sea, enjoys the mild climate of the finest part of the temperate zone; and on the coast of Canara and Malabar the heat is tempered by the vicinity of the Western Ghats, and by the sea-breezes. On the eastern coast, the heat is very great during the early part of summer; and Masulipatam, on the estuary of a branch of the Kistnah, has been often mentioned as one of the hottest places in India. The Carnatic also, especially the districts of Arcot, Chingleput, and Nellore, is noted for the great heat and dryness of the winds rushing from the gorges of the Eastern Ghats, or sweeping over the parched and sultry plains of the Carnatic or the Circars. The most remarkable circumstance in the climate of this part of India is the regular alternation of opposite monsoons. During the prevalence of the south-west monsoon, which commences in the later of the spring months or the earlier of the summer ones, the clouds discharge volumes of rain on the districts of Malabar and Canara, while a considerable proportion, finding their way over the range, fall on the table-lands of Mysore, the Ceded Districts, and the territory of the Nizam, and swell the Cauvery, Kistnah, Godavery, and other rivers, which roll vast fertilizing currents into the Carnatic and Coromandel coast, at a season when those lands receive no water from the heavens. The fall of rain is enormous on the Western Ghats, in some parts of which nine rainy months in each year are calculated on. As the south-west monsoon dies away, the north-east sets in, and continues to blow during October and November, but brings with it a considerably less quantity of rain than that resulting from the other. The average annual rain-fall during the north-east monsoon does not exceed thirty inches.

The most valuable natural product of the presidency is ship-timber, which abounds in the forests of Malabar, Travancore, and Canara, as well as in those of the Eastern Ghats. Upwards of 100 different sorts of fine timber are enumerated as grown there; and amongst them teak, considered inferior to none for hulls of ships, and peon, of equal quality for masts and spars. A large proportion of the sandal-wood supplied to the Chinese market is obtained from the forests of Malabar and Coorg. Of alimentary crops, rice is largely cultivated, and in great perfection, in the alluvial grounds of Canara, Malabar, Tinnevelly, Tanjore, and Rajamundry. Of dry crops, or those which do not require copious irrigation, the staple is ragi (Eleusine coracana): maize and millet of various kinds are also largely cultivated, as well as oil-seeds, pulse, cucurbitaceous plants, yams, and plantains. The cocoanut-palm receives great attention, and is largely cultivated on the sandy alluvial tracts, as is also the palmyra-palm; the former for the food and cordage which it furnishes, the latter for its sap, which, subjected to the processes of fermentation and distillation, yields an intoxicating beverage. Sugar is produced in considerable quantities. Experiments, conducted by the government, for the introduction of the Mauritius cane, are reported to be progressing favourably. One of the more important commercial crops is cotton; and to the improvement of the quality of this staple produce, as well as to its more extended cultivation, government has been successful in drawing public attention. Some good indigo is cultivated; but the finest kinds grow wild. Tobacco is also raised, but principally for home consumption. Pepper is the principal export of the Malabar coast. Cardamoms, which form a less important, yet a considerable article of export, are brought principally from the valleys of Coorg and Cochin.

Madras has participated in the improvements effected by means of useful public works, carried on at the expense of government for some time past, and which, under recent arrangements, will hereafter be greatly extended. Among such works, the annicuts on the rivers Godavery, Kistnah, and Cauvery, deserve especial mention. Private enterprise, moreover, may be expected to co-operate with the efforts of government in placing this part of India in the position which it is entitled to occupy. Railways are rapidly advancing to completion, and ere long Madras will have the advantage of being connected with Bombay by rail passing in the direction of Bellary, Sholapore, and Poona; while farther south, a line from Madras to Ponany will unite the eastern and western coasts of the peninsula. The electric telegraph, too, supplying the means of effecting communications nearly with the rapidity of thought, will shortly confer its almost magical powers upon Madras, by connecting it with the other presidency towns, and with the rest of India.

The presidency is divided into districts, the respective area and population of each, as officially reported, being set forth in the following tabular statement:—

Districts.	Area in Square Miles.	Popu-ion.
Rajahmundry	4,501	1,012,036
Masulipatam	4,711	520,860
Guntoor, including Palnaud	4,752	570,089
Nellore	7,959	935,690
Chingleput	2,717	583,462
Madras	27	720,000
Arcot, south division, including Cuddalore	5,020	1,006,005
Arcot, north division, including Consooddy	6,580	1,485,873
Bellary	12,101	1,229,599
Cuddapah, including Poonganoon	13,298	1,451,921
Salem, including Vomundoor and Mullapandy	7,499	1,195,377
Coimbatore	8,151	1,153,862
Trichinopoly	2,922	709,196
Tanjore, including Najore	3,781	1,676,086
Madura, including Shevagunga and Ramnad	13,545	1,756,791
Tinnevelly	5,482	1,269,216
Malabar	6,050	1,514,909
Canara	7,152	1,056,333
	116,248	19,847,305
Ganjam	5,758	926,930
Vizagapatam	4,690	1,254,272
Kurnool	3,278	273,190
Coorg	2,116	Not known.
Total	132,090	22,301,697

Of the above, the first eighteen, being under the ordinary system of rules and management, are called "regulation districts;" the latter four, not being yet brought within the operation of that system, are termed "non-regulation districts." The majority of the population throughout the whole presidency are Brahmins, but in some places Mussulmans, many of them said to be converts, or descendants of converts, are found in considerable numbers. The annual revenue, according to official authority, is thus rendered for the year 1853-54:—

Land	£3,402,333
Sayer, &c.	249,086
Stamps	52,819
Customs	126,528
Tobacco	8,957
Salt	480,213
Mint	15,012
Post-office	41,392
Marine	6,606
Judicial fees and fines	11,778
Subsidies from Mysore, Travancore, and Cochin	344,643
Interest on arrears of revenue	34,502
Miscellaneous receipts	173,719
Total	£4,947,588

The native states of Travancore and Cochin, and the hill zemindarries adjoining the British district of Vizagapatam, are also under the political and military management of this presidency. Mysore, though under the political management of the government of India, is subject for all military purposes to the jurisdiction of the Madras presidency, by the territories of which it is indeed almost completely surrounded. Their respective areas are stated as follows:—

	Sq. Miles.
Cochin	1,988
Mysore	30,886
Poodoocottah (Rajah Tondiman's dominions)	1,165
Travancore	4,722
Jeypoor and hill zemindars	13,041

And if to their aggregate, amounting to 51,802 square miles, be added 132,090, the area of the territory of the Company in this presidency, and the further quantity of 188 square miles, the area of the French possessions within it, the total area will be found to be 184,080. The military strength of the Madras presidency comprises a body of 57,063 men. In April, 1853, the entire force was distributed as follows: cavalry, 3,280; infantry, 48,351; engineers, 913; artillery, 4,519. This is exclusive of her Majesty's troops, of whom there is usually a considerable body stationed within the Madras presidency. Upon the annexation of the Punjaub to the British dominions, a revised distribution of the armies of the three presidencies was effected, with the view of providing for the defence of the north-western frontier without further addition to the regular native army. Under this arrangement, the Saugor division above the Ghats, including Mhow, has been assigned to the Madras army, while the Rajpootana field-force army has been transferred to Bombay. At present, the force is accordingly thus distributed:—The central division comprehends Fort Guntoor, which comprises North and South Arcot, and Nellore, comprising Chingleput and the northern parts of Salem; the northern division, containing Masulipatam, Rajahmundry, Vizagapatam, Ganjam, and the Bengal districts of Cuttack; the southern division taking in the southern part of Salem, Coimbatore, Trichinopoly, Tanjore, Madura, Tinnevelly, and the Travancore territory; the Mysore division occupying the territory of the rajah of that country; the Malabar and Canara division, stationed in the Malabar and Canara collectorates; the Ceded District division comprising Cuddapah, Bellary, and Kurnool; and the Saugor district embracing the Saugor and Nerbudda territory. In addition to the various places contained in the above divisions, Madras troops are stationed at Dharwar, Kulladgee, and Sholapore, all within the Bombay presidency, and also at Moulmein, Penang, Malacca, Singapore, Labuan, and, together with troops from Bombay, at Aden. The facilities of the Madras presidency for commerce are not great; the generally unfavourable character of the coast, the inadequate number of ports, and the indifferent nature of those which exist, have always been found impediments to any extensive development of mercantile enterprise. The value of the total foreign exports in the year 1853–54 was 1,96,30,200 rupees; that of the imports in the same year, 95,63,776. The principal exports were to the United Kingdom, Ceylon, and China. More detailed information, relating to the various districts and towns under the presidency, will be found in the articles respectively devoted to them.

MADRAS.—The seat of the presidency bearing that name, and the principal place of the territory subject thereto, as also of the district of Madras. The city is on the Coromandel coast, or the western shore of the Bay of Bengal, to the beach of which its buildings extend. Throughout the whole world no place of equal commercial and maritime importance is so disadvantageously circumstanced for maintaining an extensive and regular foreign trade. For two months in the year, during the continuance of the north-east monsoon, that is from the close of October to the close of December, even the crews of ships of the line, with all their appliances and means, can hold no communication with the shore without great danger; and at no time can they visit it in their own boats. The surf is less violent and dangerous with a westerly wind, which, blowing off shore, diminishes the force of the sea setting in towards the beach; but it is at all times sufficient to dash to pieces any boats of European construction. Landing or putting off to the shipping can only be effected, either for goods or passengers, in native craft, the larger sort of which, called by Europeans a massulah-boat, is made of planks, without ribs or timbers, but merely sewed together with cocoanut-twine or coir, so as to yield to shocks without being shattered by them. During the north-east monsoon, however, even in those boats the landing is very dangerous; and many lives have been lost from time to time by rashly attempting it, the horror and danger being increased by sharks ready to devour any persons that may be exposed to their attacks. The other and smaller craft,—the catamaran, consists of three cocoa-tree logs lashed together, and big enough to carry one, or at most two, persons. With the view of sheltering the landing and diminishing the danger and inconvenience which attend going ashore or putting off to the shipping, an attempt was made to construct a breakwater 300 yards from the beach, the dimensions being, extreme length, from N.N.E. to S.S.W., about seventy-six feet; extreme breadth, from E.S.E. to W.N.W., about fifty-five feet. The soundings on it were found to vary from twenty-five to twelve feet. The attempt, however, was unsuccessful, and as the abandoned work was considered a new source of danger, a buoy was laid down on the south end; and the placing another at the north was contemplated. A breakwater to shelter ships would undoubtedly prove a work of enormous cost and difficulty; but the evils arising from the want of some such protection are almost incalculable, vessels being at present obliged to anchor two miles from shore, in nine, ten, or eleven fathoms, exposed to a heavy swell rolling in from seaward, save when the wind blows from the westward or land side. The bottom is in many parts of stiff mud, from which it is sometimes difficult to extricate anchors; and as it is frequently necessary to hurry to sea in bad weather, many anchors remain in the ground; the loss of these to the owners not completing the mischief, since the abandoned anchors rub and destroy the cables of vessels afterwards lying in the roads. Similar damage is caused by wrecks, of which there are some on the bottom. In 1843, a suspension-pier was projected by M. Piron, a French engineer of Pondicherry, to be erected over the surf of Madras, but the proposal was not entertained. Subsequently, the design of constructing a pier at Madras was taken up by a company, designated "The Madras Pier Company;" but the project appears to have been abandoned, and the company has been dissolved. More recently, a proposal was made by Messrs. Saunders and Mitchell, of London, to erect a pier at Madras, and the subject is now under consideration. The dangers of the roadstead during storms being great, their symptoms or premonitory signs are carefully watched for at the Observatory, and signals, on their appearance, are hoisted at the flagstaff of the master attendant, warning ships to proceed to sea. Innumerable losses have occurred from neglecting due precautions. An excellent judge, however, observes, "Gales are not frequent; and if a ship be kept in good condition for proceeding to sea, embracing the opportunity to weigh, cut, or slip, and run out on the first approach of a gale, there is probably little danger to be apprehended." The old lighthouse within the walls of Fort St. George has ceased to be used, and on January 1st, 1844, on a new lighthouse, erected on the Esplanade north of the fort, a light was for the first time exhibited, and has since been continued for the guidance of mariners. It is elevated 128 feet above the mean level of the sea, and is what is called a flashing light, the duration of the flash to that of the dark interval being as two to three.

The earliest British settlement on the coast of Coromandel was at Armegon, about thirty-six miles north of Pulicat. A small grant of territory at Madras, by a native prince, in 1639, induced the chief, Mr. Francis Day, to abandon the old factory, and erect on the new acquisition Fort St. George, which was the nucleus round which have clustered and grown the remainder of the buildings regarded as constituting, with the fort, the city of Madras. The fort is in form an irregular polygon, somewhat in the form of a semicircle, of which the sea face is nearly a diameter, running north and south, and presenting a clear front on that side of 500 yards. The sea flows to within a few yards of the ramparts, which are fenced by an artificial barrier of stone-work, from the influence of the surf and tide. Dilapidations have notwithstanding occurred, occasioned principally by the sinking of the foundations consequent on the encroachment of the sea; but measures are in progress for the recovery of the beach, when the necessary repairs have been ordered to be made. The foundation of the works on this side contains a series of cisterns, supplied with water from wells in the Black Town. On the land side the fort is defended by a double line of fortifications, both bombproof; its sea face is well armed with heavy guns. The inner inclosure is so constructed as to afford accommodation to a large body of troops. In the rest of the space are the offices of the various departments of government, and barracks for European troops. The barracks occupy the north and western extremity of the inclosure, and are of an oblong form, the length being from north to south. This building has a terraced roof, and is two stories in height, the upper one being occupied by the officers, the lower by the privates. There is said to be accommodation for 1,000 men; but it seems, at the least, doubtful whether such a number can be conveniently lodged. Attached to the barracks is a bazar, for the supply of the troops: the other buildings of note are the Old Church and the Exchange. The Black Town is separated from the fort by a wide esplanade, which is now improved by a few ornamental plantations and well-designed watercourses. Its site is very low, being in some places only six inches above the level of the sea at spring tides, against the inroads of which it has been defended by a strong bulwark of stone. There are three broad streets, running north and south, dividing the town into four nearly equal parts. These streets are respectable in appearance, well built, and contain the principal European shops, as well as many houses with upper stories and terraced roofs. On the beach, parallel with these streets, is a line of public offices, including the Supreme Court, the Custom House, the Marine Board Office, and the offices and storehouses of the principal European merchants. These are well-constructed buildings, having colonnades to the upper stories, supported on arched bases, and overlaid with chunam or cement, made of lime burned from shells, and forming a hard, smooth, and polished surface, resembling white marble. In conspicuous situations in the town are the male and female orphan schools, and the jail of the Supreme Court. The other buildings most worth note are—the Mint, the Roman Catholic Cathedral, the Church Mission Chapel, Armenian Church, Trinity Chapel, the General Hospital and Medical School. The numerous minor streets, which are inhabited by the natives, are irregular, crooked, narrow, and ill-ventilated. The houses are generally built of clay, overlaid with cement of chunam, and roofed with tile; and for the most part they consist of continuous apartments, arranged round a small quadrangular court. In 1847, the outlay of a large sum was authorized for improving the drainage of the Black Town, a measure most essential for raising its sanitary condition. It is a favourable circumstance, that the town is well supplied with water of remarkably pure and good quality, derived from wells, varying in depth from twenty to thirty feet. The water obtained from the wells in a certain inclosure near the north wall, known by the name of the Seven Wells, is especially valued for its purity, which it is said by seafaring men to preserve for a length of time at sea. Public waterworks have been erected in this inclosure by government, and two reservoirs have been constructed, one in the fort, the other midway between the fort and the town, which are daily replenished from the wells by means of metal pipes; and a supply is thus furnished for the shipping, as well as for all the inhabitants who choose to send for it. Royapooram, which must be considered a portion of Madras, lies on the north side of the Black Town, and extends for a mile along the beach. It is a wretched assemblage of mud huts, inhabited chiefly by fishermen and boatmen, whose poverty is extreme, as is the filthiness of the place. From these causes the people are wretchedly unhealthy; and it is calculated that two-thirds of the children born die before reaching maturity. The division called Vepery, including Pursewakum, lies to the west of the Black Town. The principal streets are well built and clean, but the cross-streets are close and filthy. Chintadrapettah, separated from Vepery by the river Koom, which almost incloses the former, is for the most part regularly built, and clean: here is a public dispensary. The populous suburbs of Poodoopettah and Egmore lie nearly due west of Chintadrapettah. Another large division of Madras, called Triplicane, runs parallel with the sea, south of the fort, being divided from it by the small river Koom, flowing very circuitously, but in a direction generally from west to east, and falling into the sea about a quarter of a mile south of the fort. About a mile from its mouth, this river divaricates, forming two nearly equal branches, the left or more northern, close to the point of parting, receiving a watercourse running from the north. After this accession, the left branch flows by the southern rampart of the Black Town, and subsequently by the south-west face of the fort. The right branch of the Koom takes a direction first south, subsequently south-east; and both joining, about 300 yards from the sea, inclose an island, three-quarters of a mile in length and of half that breadth, laid out with roads, and ornamented in the centre by a statue of Sir Thomas Munro. On the right or south-west bank of the right branch are the Government Gardens. Government House is a spacious and handsome building; the floors, walls, and pillars, are overlaid with cement of chunam, highly polished, so as to resemble fine white marble. There is an enormous banqueting-room, built in front of the house; but it is considered to be in bad taste and inconvenient. Chepak Garden, the residence of the nawaub of the Carnatic, is situate south-east of Government Garden; and between it and the sea is a mosque, of some architectural excellence, the only Mussulman place of worship of any importance in the city. Royapetta, another extensive and populous suburb, lies westward of Triplicane, and adjacent to it. St. Thomé, which is also comprehended in the limits of Madras, is situate about three miles to the southward of the fort, and close to the sea. It is a straggling place, the continuity of the buildings being broken by uncovered ground; but the portion occupied is generally clean, and in good order. The situation on the beach is considered favourable for European convalescents. The principal church belonging to the English establishment is that of St. George, situate in Royapetta. It is very beautiful. St. Andrew's Church, built for the use of the members of the Church of Scotland, is in the southern part of the Vepery division. It has been regarded as a fine specimen of architecture and engineering skill. The exterior of the body of the church is in the Ionic order, the interior in the Composite. It was finished in 1820, at a cost of about 20,000*l.* St. Andrew's Bridge, over the river Koom, in the vicinity of the church, was finished in 1818, and is considered a good specimen of architecture on a small scale. The erection of an additional masonry bridge over the river Koom, at a point called Ashton's Shop, was sanctioned by the home authorities n 1846. At the southern extremity of the town, the river Adyar flows from west to east, falling into the sea about half a mile south of St. Thomé. To the west of the town, a chain of tanks, or pieces of stagnant water, extends from north to south. Of these, the most southern, called the Long Tank, is, when full, two miles in length from north to south, and half a mile in breadth: there are several others. Though excellent water is obtained by sinking wells in the Black Town, many of those in the other parts of Madras yield only that which is brackish, and scarcely drinkable. The site of the town is remarkably level, and rather low, no part being probably more than about twenty feet above the sea; but the vicinity of the sandy beach, and the influence of the sea ever rolling in and breaking on it, together with the prevalence of the sea-breezes, have a salutary effect. The average mean annual temperature for eight years is stated as follows:—1831, 81°; 1832, 84°; 1833, 83°; 1834, 87°; 1835, 82°; 1836, 77°; 1837, 82°; 1838, 86°. The north-east monsoon sets in with much thunder and lightning and heavy rain, about the close of October, and continues to the close of December, after which it gradually diminishes in force until the middle of February, about which time it ceases. The south-west monsoon, commencing in May, and ending in the beginning of October, is scarcely felt here, its force being intercepted by the Ghats. During the hot months, the sea-breeze sets in about noon, and continues for some time after nightfall. From its refreshing and invigorating influence, the British popularly call it the doctor. It is succeeded by the land wind, a sultry and oppressive current of air, which prevails until the setting in of the sea-breeze on the following day.

The European residents live in garden-houses, or villas situate in compounds or distinct inclosures, dispersed throughout the suburbs, and about the neighbourhood of the city, extending from three to four miles inland. These are generally of two stories, constructed in a pleasing light style of architecture, terraced, with porticos and verandas, supported by pillars. The lower story is often raised several feet from the ground; the doors and windows are large, and provided with Venetian blinds, so as to admit free ventilation; and the apartments are lofty, spacious, and airy. During the prevalence of the hot, dry winds, mats, made of kusha, a fragrant grass, and kept wet, are placed at the doors and windows on the western side of the house, whereby coolness, moisture, and a grateful scent are imparted to the air permeating them. By these means, aided by the use of the punkah, the heat is rendered more tolerable. The compounds, or inclosures in which the houses are situate, are usually so closely planted with trees and shrubs, that even when viewed from a height, the tops only of many of the houses can be seen. Such plantations interrupt due ventilation; but the evil is tolerated in consideration of the protection which they afford from the dust and glare, so distressing in the Carnatic.

The tables of European residents have ample means of supply in the markets, where are offered for sale in abundance, beef, mutton, veal, kid, fowls, turkeys, ducks, geese, fish of excellent quality, potatoes, turnips, peas, carrots, cabbages, beans, sweet potatoes, yams, onions, salad mangoes, plantains, pine-apples, custard-apples, oranges, grapes, guavas, and other fruits less esteemed. Society is much more limited in Madras than in Calcutta, and there is much less of pretension and luxury: there are few handsome equipages; palanquins are used, chiefly by natives. The favourite drive is the beach, extending along the seashore for about a quarter of a mile south of the fort. The Mount Road, leading from the fort to the cantonment of St. Thomas, has for six miles a succession of beautiful villas on each side, and is lined with noble trees, affording ornament and shade.

Madras being the seat of the government of the presidency, the governor, members of council, and principal functionaries, reside here, as do also the judges of the Supreme Court (a chief justice and two puisne judges), and other officers of that institution. The chief establishments of every department of the government are here, and there are various local establishments. Among these may be mentioned the police-office, attached to which are a superintendent and justice of the peace, two police magistrates, two others, called also deputy-superintendents of police, and several subordinate officers; the court for the recovery of small debts, of which there are four commissioners, and the Government Savings Bank. The Bank of Madras, being not only chartered, but in some degree subjected to the control of government, which nominates part of the directoral body, may, in a certain sense, be regarded as a government institution. Other banks have branches here, and the number of agency and mercantile houses is considerable. Various societies for insurance of lives, as well as against fire and marine risk, have establishments or agencies in the city. Madras is the seat of an episcopal see. In addition to the principal church (St. George's), there are about eight churches and chapels of the United Church of England and Ireland: that of St. Mary's, within the fort, has several monuments; and among them one to the memory of the celebrated missionary Schwartz. In the Scottish church of St. Andrew, already mentioned, the worship is conducted by ministers in communion with the Established Church of Scotland, of whom two are chaplains in the service of the Company. The seceding body from the Established Scottish Church, calling itself the "Free protesting Church of Scotland," maintain public worship in the hall of the Free Church Mission Institution. The Romanists have a bishop or vicar-apostolic, with a considerable staff of clergy, performing the ceremonies of their faith in various places. The Armenians have a church, opened so long since as 1712. The Wesleyans have five chapels, the Baptists two, the Independents one, and the American Mission two. Education, or at least that of the highest order, does not hitherto appear to have been much encouraged: a university was some years ago projected, comprehending a college and a high school, but the latter only is in operation. Measures however have been taken for the introduction of a new scheme of state education throughout the presidency, under which it may be hoped that the literature and science, the philosophy and arts of the West, may be imparted to the people of this division of India. The religious and charitable associations are numerous, and education is a leading object with many of these. The military male and female orphan asylums, two most valuable and meritorious institutions, date respectively so far back as 1787 and 1788. The medical school, founded some years since, for the instruction of natives in medicine and surgery, has been most useful, as well in qualifying for the practice of the healing art, as in gradually removing the repugnance felt to the necessary studies. There is an agricultural and horticultural society, of which the governor is the patron. The Madras Literary Society enjoys the same distinguished patronage, and now adds to the title above given, that of Auxiliary of the Royal Asiatic Society. The mention of the Madras Polytechnic Institution (of which the governor is likewise patron) exhausts the list of societies of this class; but the Government Observatory must not be overlooked among the establishments for the advancement of science. About nine newspapers are published at Madras; some three times a week, some twice, and some once only. Two publications are issued twice in each month; seven are published monthly: one of these is commercial, one devoted to the interests of the society of Freemasons; the remainder are of a religious character. Lists of the army and civil service are published quarterly; and six or seven publications, all of them of the description of almanacks, are sent forth annually.

The city of Madras, including the whole of the various divisions of which it is composed, and the jurisdiction of the Supreme Court, extends along the seacoast in a direction nearly from north to south for a distance of nine miles: its extreme breadth may be considered to be $3\frac{3}{4}$ miles, its average breadth $2\frac{1}{4}$: the area is stated officially to be thirty square miles; but a large portion of this space, comprehended within the assigned limits, is occupied by gardens and compounds or inclosures, and in various parts dwellings are thinly scattered. No census has been made to ascertain either the classes or total amount of the population; and the official statement, in which it has been "assumed at 720,000," probably errs in excess. The great majority are Brahminists; Mussulmans are next in numbers; Christians comparatively few, and consist for the most part of those denominated Portuguese Christians, being descendants of persons of that nation, or of proselytes made by their ecclesiastics. Distance from Tanjore, N., 178 miles; Cuddalore, N., 105; Pondicherry, N., 88; Coimbatore, N.E., 270; Calicut, N.E., 330; Cananore, E., 343; Mangalore, E., 370; Bangalore, E., 185; Arcot, E., 73; Bombay, S.E., 640; Poona, S.E., 570; Bellary, S.E., 270; Hyderabad, S.E., 320; Nagpore, S., 565; Masulipatam, S., 220; Calcutta, S.W., 885. Lat. 13° 5′, long. 80° 21′.

MADRUPORE.—A town in the British district of Bhagulpore, lieut.-gov. of Bengal, 22 miles E.S.E. of Bhagulpore. Lat. 25° 5′, long. 87° 20′.

MADURA, under the presidency of Madras, a British district, named from its principal place. It is bounded on the north by the British districts Coimbatoor and Trichinopoly; on the north-east by Tanjore and Rajah Tondiman's dominions; on the east by Tanjore and Palk's Straits; on the south by the Gulf of Manar; on the south-west by the British district Tinnevelly; and on the west by the territory of Travancore. It lies between lat. 9° 5′—10° 54′, long. 77° 15′—79° 15′, and (including Dindigul) has an area of 10,700 square miles. The seacoast of this district comprises the north-west coast of Palk's Straits and of the Gulf of Manar, and extends in a direction from north-east to south-west 115 miles. The Gulf of Manar, formed on the north-west by the seacoast of the districts of Tinnevelly and of Madura, on the east by the western coast of Ceylon, is terminated on the north and north-east by Adam's Bridge, "a narrow ridge of sand and rocks, mostly dry, nearly connecting the island of Ceylon with the continent." This ridge, at its north-western extremity, joins the island of Rameserum, between which and the headland of Tonitorai, on the continent, is the Paumbaum passage. The other end of Adam's Bridge joins the island of Manaar, between which and Ceylon is a narrow passage, navigable only for craft of moderate size. The coast of this district throughout its entire extent, from the south-west extremity to Adam's Bridge, is much beset with dangerous rocks and shoals. From this cause, that part lying to the north of Adam's Bridge, and forming the north-eastern coast of Palk's Bay, can scarcely be frequented by vessels of any burthen. The north-western part of this district, forming the subdivision of Dindigul, extends over part of the undulating rugged plateau and eastern declivity of the Ghats, in this part called the Vurragiri, Pulnai, or Kunundaven Mountains. This group has at Permaulmullay, its highest summit, an elevation of 8,000 feet above the level of the sea. The principal geological formations are gneiss, stratified with quartz; but in some places there are immense precipices of granite. South-eastward of this group is the extensive valley of Dindigul. The average elevation of the plain country of Dindigul and Madura is, at the base of the mountains, about 800 feet above the sea, falling in the maritime tracts to 200. The south-eastern portion of the district, towards Palk's Straits and the Gulf of Manar, is an extensive plain, without a single hill or conspicuous eminence. The undulating formation, where it appears on the coast, is of sandstone.

Though a few rivers hold their course northward and north-eastward towards Coimbatoor, and discharge themselves into the river Cauvery, the general slope of the country is eastward and south-eastwards, towards the Gulf of Manar, Palk's Bay, and the Bay of Bengal, in which direction is the main drainage. The principal river is the Vygah, which rises at the south-western extremity of the valley of Dindigul, and flows seventy miles north-eastward, to Jyempolliam, receiving on its way numerous feeders right and left, streaming down from the ranges inclosing the valley. It at that point turns south-east, in which direction it flows 100 miles, by Madura and Ramnad, below which latter place it expands into a considerable tank; and eleven miles still lower, falls into Palk's Strait, a short distance north-west of the headland of Tonitorai. The other rivers (which are very numerous), though having sometimes considerable volumes of water during rains, are generally destitute of it in the dry season.

The climate of the hills is mild and genial in summer, being seldom below 50° or above 75°. It is said, however, to be cold in January, when the ground is covered with hoar-frosts during the morning; and it is singular, that at this chill period the population are subject to intermitting fevers. February, March, and April constitute the dry season, which is followed by a succession of rainy weather throughout the prevalence of the south-west monsoon. In October, the north-east monsoon sets in, and continues with more or less violence till December. The climate of the plain is a good deal characterized by dryness and heat, the thermometer having been known to reach 115°, and, according to some, 130°. It participates in the vicissitudes of the two monsoons, —the south-west continuing from April till July, the north-east from October to December; yet, notwithstanding this double provision, the district sometimes suffers ruinously from drought. The soil in the vicinity of the sea is generally sandy, but in the interior black and fertile, produced apparently from decayed vegetation, and well suited for the growth of cotton, which is the principal commercial crop. Sugar-cane and betel-nut are cultivated in the valleys. Tobacco is also grown to some extent, both for home consumption and exportation, it being in much demand, and considered the best produced in the southern provinces. In favourable situations, various esculent vegetables known in Europe are cultivated with success, and in considerable quantities; comprising peas, beans, potatoes, cabbages, parsnips, turnips, cucumbers, and other cucurbitaceous plants. Of fruits, there are the orange, citron, guava, mango, jak (Artocarpus integrifolia), and others of less importance. The population of Madura, including Dindigul, will be found under the article MADRAS. A large majority of the inhabitants are Hindoos. The language spoken in the district is the Tamil. The principal route is from north-east to south-west, from Trichinopoly through Madura, to Palamkotta, and thence to Cape Comorin: from this main line a road passes off north-west to the military and civil station of Dindigul, and south-eastward to that of Ramnad; and another south-eastward to the seaport of Tutacorin. Good roads of less importance are numerous in every direction throughout the plain country, except in the district of Ramnad, where they are generally mere sandy tracks, impracticable for wheel-carriages. The principal places are Madura the (capital), Dindigul, Ramnad, Shivaganga, Kamuri, Kilakarai, Autankarai, Devipatnam, Tonde, Tirumangalum, and Malur.

MADURA.—A town, the principal place of the British district of the same name, presidency of Madras, 33 miles S.S.E. of Dindigul. Of late years, considerable improvements have been made in this town, by laying it out with wide streets, market-places, and accommodation for travellers, whereby the public health and convenience have been greatly promoted. Lat. 9° 55′, long. 78° 10′.

MADUTHOOR.—A town in the British district of Tinnevelly, presidency of Madras, 29 miles E. by N. of Tinnevelly. Lat. 8° 49′, long. 78° 8′.

MADUVANALLI.—A town in the British district of Coimbatoor, presidency of Madras, 122 miles E. by N. of Cannanore. Lat. 12° 10′, long. 77° 13′.

MAGAMURCHY.—A river rising in lat. 11° 59′, long. 78° 6′, and, flowing through the British district of Salem for forty-two miles in a south-westerly direction, falls into the Cauvery on the left side, in lat. 11° 30′, long. 77° 47′.

MAGANUND, a pass through the Sewalik ridge bounding Sirhind to the north-east, is situate on the route from Sidowra to Nahun, and five miles S.W. of the latter town. The road lies along the course of the Markanda, which crosses the ridge, flowing from the Kyarda Doon to Sirhind. Maganund, a small village at the northern extremity of the pass, gives name to it. Here was the rendezvous of the British army destined to attack Nahun, at the commencement of the Goorkha war in 1815. The road was then very difficult, so that great numbers of bullocks and camels perished, the elephant being on that, as on other occasions, found the most surefooted and efficient beast of burthen in hilly roads. At the time of Davidson's visit, it appears to have been much improved, as he describes the ascent from Mogee Nun (Maganund) as very gradual. As the elevation of Nahun is 3,207 feet above the sea, and that of Naraingurh, in the plain of Sirhind, and near the southern base of the Sewalik range, is 2,154, the elevation of Maganund may, by a coarse approximation, be taken at 2,600. Distant N.W. from Calcutta 1,030 miles. Lat. 30° 32′, long. 77° 19′.

MAGUEE.—A town of Eastern India, in the native state of Muneepoor, 22 miles N.N.W. from Muneepoor, and 116 miles from Jynteapoor. Lat. 25° 6′, long. 93° 54′.

MAHA NUDDEE.—A river formed in the British province of Saugor and Nerbudda, from several small feeders, the principal of which are stated to be the Kuthna and the Niwar. The source is in lat. 23° 44′, long. 80° 16′, a few miles west of Belhari, whence the river flows in a north-easterly direction for thirty miles, through the Saugor and Nerbudda territory, thirty-seven miles through the native state of Meyhar, and seven miles through that of Rewa, and falls into the Sone in lat. 24° 4′, long. 81° 7′.

MAHABALIPOORAM, or the SEVEN PAGODAS, on the Coromandel coast, and in the British district of Chingleput (presidency of Madras), so called because built in honour of Maha Bala, or the great Bala, the gigantic brother of the deity Krishna. Distant from Madras, S., 33 miles. Lat. 12° 37′, long. 80° 15′.

MAHABULESHWAR, in the presidency of Bombay, a small town or village on the summit of the range of mountains bearing the same name. The range is part of the Western Ghauts, extending from south to north in a direction nearly parallel to the western shore of India, and at the distance of about forty miles from it. This section is bounded on the north by the gorge from which issue the head-waters of the river Kistnah, in lat. 18° 1′, long. 73° 40′; the southern boundary of this part of the range is in about lat. 17° 55′. Its greatest breadth at the northern extremity is about fifteen miles, and about eight at its southern boundary: its extent, taken diagonally from north-east to south-west, is about seventeen miles. Its southern extremity is bounded by a deep depression of the surface, extending nearly across the range, but leaving a small neck of land on the west side, which maintains continuity with the Ghaut further south. The summit of the range thus marked is a sort of undulating and rugged table-land, the western buttress of which rises abruptly from the adjacent Concan: the descent towards the Deccan is more gradual, and less in actual amount. Excellent roads, made in various directions, give access to all the more interesting spots. An abundant supply of excellent water may be had from wells, in which it is found at depths varying in different parts from ten to forty feet. There are also many streamlets traversing the country, and continuing to run at all seasons. One of the most striking characteristics of the climate is the extreme violence of the monsoon, beginning about the middle of June and ending in the commencement of October. During July and August, the country is always covered with fog, and there is scarcely any intermission of rain, which is generally rather light and drizzling, though occasionally drenching showers descend. One report gives the mean annual fall, as deduced from the observations of ten years, at 229 inches, and the number of days on which rain falls at 127. From the dense nature of the soil, however, and the undulating form of the surface, the water quickly drains off, and there is not the slightest appearance of a marsh or swamp. At other times of the year, the humidity of the atmosphere is moderate. The cool season commences early in October, which is the most genial and pleasant part of the year, in consequence of the moderate temperature and the freshness of the air, resembling that of a European spring. Throughout November, December, January, and February, the sky is almost uniformly clear, and the atmosphere cold, bracing, and elastic. During this period slight hoar-frosts sometimes occur. In scarcely any place is there less variableness in the meteorological phenomena. In contrast with most other hill-stations in India, this is totally free from malaria, an exemption attributed to the circumstance, that the Concan, which stretches from the base of the mountain, through a sultry tract, is not a pestilential one. This place, having in so many circumstances affecting health a decided superiority over the more depressed and sultry tracts in its vicinity, was selected as a sanatory station for troops; but the project was abandoned after a short trial, on the ground, as it is understood, of the climate being unsuited to the acute diseases which are most common among the soldiery. It is, however, much frequented by invalid officers, for whose accommodation there is a sanatarium, containing eight sets of quarters and several detached bungalows. There are also about seventy private dwellings, of which upwards of fifty are substantially built of hewn stone. The greater part have thatched roofs, which are said to be better adapted than tiles to resist the monsoon rains. Many persons not in the service of the government seek the restoration of health at this place, and very generally with success. The number of visitors appears to have been steadily increasing. The station is situate at the north-west corner of the table-land, and has a western aspect, favourable for receiving the advantage of the salubrious sea-breezes. It was established in 1828 by Sir John Malcolm, then governor of Bombay, after whom the village of Malcolm Peth was named. The site was ceded by the rajah of Sattara, in exchange for another spot. The bazar is a tolerably large one, and is well supplied. There is a small church, a subscription-library, and an hotel. A detachment of fifty native troops, under the command of a jemadar, is stationed here to maintain the requisite guards: its European establishment consists of a chaplain and a medical officer, the latter being superintendent of the station. The services of the chaplain are shared by other places, which are visited at stated periods. The general elevation of the station above the sea is 4,500 feet; that of the highest summit, 4,700. Distance N.W. from Sattara, by a good carriage-road, 30 miles; S.W. from Poona, by circuitous hilly route, 70; S.E. from Bombay, crossing the haven and subsequently proceeding by Nagotna, 114; or by another route 127; viz. by sea, down the coast to Bancote, 70, thence up the river Sawitri 30, and subsequently by land about 30 more. Mahabuleshwar is in lat. 17° 59′, long. 73° 41′.

MAHADEO MOUNTAINS, denominated from a celebrated Hindoo temple of the same name, a cluster of considerable height in the north part of the Nagpore territory, towards the British province of Saugor and Nerbudda. It is situate at the eastern extremity of the Sautpoora Mountains, where they adjoin the Vindhya, and may be considered as lying between lat. 21° 30′—22° 40′, long. 78°—80°. None of the elevations appear to have been accurately determined; but Dowlagheree is conjectured to be the highest; and the elevation of Ambarmaph, another, is estimated at 2,500 feet; Chindwara, 2,100; and Pachmarhi has been vaguely conjectured to have an elevation of 5,000; but this estimate is very probably an exaggeration. In a publication of very high character, it is mentioned, that Dokgur, one summit of the cluster, "is stated by Captain Franklin to be 4,800 feet high;" and it is farther observed, "There are two other peaks exceeding this in height, viz. Putta Sunkur (above the cave of Mahadeo) and Choura Deo, the highest of all which I conjecture to be about 5,000 feet above the sea." As, however, no specific reference is given to any work of Franklin in support of those points, they must be considered problematical.

MAHADEPOOR.—A town in Hyderabad, or dominions of the Nizam, situate on the right bank of the Godavery river, and 138 miles N.E. from Hyderabad. Lat. 18° 48′, long. 79° 59′.

MAHAGAON.—A town of the Deccan, in the territory of Nagpoor or Berar, situate 69 miles E.S.E. from Nagpoor, and 95 S.S.E. from Seuni. Lat. 20° 44′, long. 80° 7′.

MAHAGAUM.—A town in Hyderabad, or dominions of the Nizam, situate on the right bank of the Araun river, and 75 miles S.S.E. from Ellichpoor. Lat. 20° 10′, long. 78°.

MAHAGAUM.—A town in the British district of Tannah, presidency of Bombay, 60 miles N. of Bombay. Lat. 19° 48′, long. 72° 50′.

MAHANUDDY.—A river having its origin in Nowagudda, one of the native states on the south-west frontier of Bengal. It rises about lat. 20° 20′, long. 82°, and flowing westerly ten miles through Nowagudda, it enters the territory of Nagpore, through which it holds a course in the same direction for twenty miles, to a point a few miles north-east of the town of Konkeir, when it turns north-east for 110 miles, to its junction, in lat. 21° 35′, long. 82° 16′, with its principal and more remote feeder. Forty miles farther, the united stream receives the Hutsoo river, another considerable tributary, flowing from the north, when, turning south-easterly, it holds a course of about 300 miles through the native states on the south-west frontier of Bengal, to the town of Cuttack, where it divaricates into the numerous branches inclosing or traversing the delta, the total length of its course being estimated at near 520 miles. Its principal mouth is in lat. 20° 20′, long. 86° 50′. At Sumbulpoor, 260 miles above its mouth, it is nearly a mile in breadth during the rains, and at the town of Cuttack, just above its divarication, it at the same season is fully two miles in breadth. From July to February it is navigable for boats from the sea as far as Sewnarain, a distance of about 460 miles. At the point of divarication, near the town of Cuttack, is a hill, said to contain promising indications of coal, but which is more probably merely of volcanic formation. Although the navigation is in some places rendered difficult by rapids, it may be rendered materially available as the means of communication between the sea and the interior of the country. The volume of water rolled down by this river during the periodical rains must be enormous, as Kittoe found the bed of the river near Sumbulpoor 4,500 feet wide, and "the highest flood-water mark to be about forty-seven feet above the level of the shallow stream flowing during dry seasons in the centre of the bed;" and Heber during the rainy season observed, three or four miles out at sea, the fresh water of the Mahanuddee floating, in consequence of less specific gravity, on the salt water of the Bay of Bengal, "exactly like a river about half a mile broad, smooth, dimply, and whirling."

MAHANUNDA.—A large river of Bengal, tributary to the Ganges. It rises in the territory of Darjeeling, and about lat. 26° 57′, long. 88° 20′, and flowing south for fifteen miles, it on the right side receives the Balasun, a stream coming from the north-west; and from the confluence, the united stream flows southerly for twenty-five miles, forming for the greater part the boundary between the British districts Purnea and Dinajepore. Subsequently entering the former district, it takes a course south-westerly for sixty miles, and thence turning south-east for fifty more, receives at Jagatnathpur, on the left side, the large stream Nagor; and touching on the British district Dinajepore, and taking a direction southerly, it again forms the boundary between that district and Purneah for twenty miles. At that distance it passes into the British district Maldah, through which it flows in a direction south-easterly for forty miles, to Rahunpoor, in lat. 24° 47′, long. 88° 20′. From that point turning south, it for thirty miles forms the boundary between the British districts Maldah and Rajeshahye; and at Godari, in lat. 24° 30′, long. 88° 20′, it falls into the Podda, or great eastern branch of the Ganges, on the left side; its total length of course being 240 miles. Even within a few miles of its source, its navigation is practicable for canoes and for floating timber; and from Kishengunje, seventy-five miles from its source, it is navigable for craft of about eight tons during the dry season, and for those of much larger burthen during the rains. In the lower part of its course, it is at all times navigable for craft of between forty and fifty tons burthen.

MAHARAJE DROOG.—A town in the Mysore, situate 61 miles N.W. by W. from Seringapatam, and 73 miles E. from Mangalore. Lat. 12° 54′, long. 76°.

MAHARAJGUNJ, in the British district of Goruckpore, lieut.-gov. of the N.W. Provinces, a small town which, according to Buchanan, who surveyed it about forty years ago, had then 125 houses. Distant N.E. from Goruckpore cantonment 28 miles. Lat. 27° 2′, long. 83° 32′.

MAHARAJGUNJE, in the British district of Benares, lieut.-gov. of the N.W. Provinces, a town on the route from the city of Benares to Allahabad, 52 miles E. of the latter, 22 W. of the former. Lat. 25° 16′, long. 82° 40′.

MAHARAJPOOR, in the British district of Cawnpore, lieut.-gov. of the N.W. Provinces, a town on the route from the cantonment of Cawnpore to Futtehpore, and 12 miles S.E. of the former. It has a bazar, and is supplied with water from a tank and wells. Lat. 26° 19′, long. 80° 31′.

MAHARAJPOOR, in Gwalior, or possessions of Scindia, a village or small town 15 miles N.W. of the fort of Gwalior. This place and the neighbouring village of Chonda were the keys of the position of the Mahratta army on the 29th December, 1843, when the battle took place between them and the British army under Sir Hugh Gough, commander-in-chief. The Mahrattas were driven from all points of their position, lost fifty-six pieces of artillery and all their ammunition-waggons, and retreated to the fort of Gwalior. The loss of the British army was severe, amounting to 106 killed, 684 wounded, and seven missing. The numbers on each side appear to have been nearly equal, numbering about 13,000 British and 15,000 Mahrattas. A monument at Calcutta, constructed from the cannon captured on the field, commemorates the victory. Lat. 26° 29′, long. 78° 5′.

MAHASIN.—A town in the territory inhabited by the independent hill tribes of Orissa, situate 104 miles S. from Sumbulpoor, and 86 miles N.W. by W. from Ganjam. Lat. 19° 59′, long. 83° 59′.

MAHASINGPUR, in the British district of Allyghur, lieut.-gov. of the N.W. Provinces, a village on the route from the cantonment of Allyghur to that of Etawa, and 26 miles S.E. of the former. Lat. 27° 34′, long. 78° 16′.

MAHATTIE.—A town of Eastern India, in the British province of Aracan, eight miles S. of Aracan. Lat. 20° 36′, long. 93° 25′.

MAHBUBGANJ, in the district of Aldemau, territory of Oude, a village on the right bank of the Ghaghra, 18 miles S.E. of the city of Oude. Butter estimates the population at 1,000, including 200 Mussulmans. Lat. 26° 40′, long. 82° 22′.

MAHDARA, in the district of Aldemau, territory of Oude, a village a mile west of the right bank of the Tons (north-eastern), 25 miles S.E. of the city of Oude. Butter estimates its population at 400, all Hindoos. It is the Mijhoura of the surveyor-general's map. Lat. 26° 27′, long. 82° 26′.

MAHE.—A French settlement and seaport included within the limits of the British district of Malabar, containing an area of two square miles. It is situate on the south side of the estuary of a small river flowing from the Western Ghauts, but not navigable for vessels of any considerable burthen, which must anchor in the road, in five or six fathoms, and one and a half or three miles from shore. The river is, however, navigable for boats a considerable distance inland, and in fair weather small craft can cross the bar in safety. The site of the town is fine, on a high ground, overlooking the river; and it is a neat place, many of the houses being good. It was long a serious and vexatious source of annoyance to the British, by affording the French a footing in Malabar, and a ready communication with Mysore and its ruler; but in 1779 it was reduced by a force sent from Bombay, and dismantled, and in 1793 formally taken possession of by the British. The British establishment previously stationed at Tellicherry was then removed to Mahe; but it having been restored to the French at the last general pacification of 1815, the British establishment was replaced in its original station at Tellicherry. The Carmelites have a church and a missionary establishment here. The population is stated at 2,616 souls. Distance from Tellicherry, S.E., seven miles; Bombay, S.E., 636; Cannanore, S.E., 16. Lat. 11° 42′, long. 75° 36′.

MAHEIDPORE.—See MEHIDPORE.

MAHESWA, in the Rajpoot state of Jodhpoor, a village on the route from Nusseerabad to Deesa, and 49 miles W. of the former. Lat. 26° 12′, long. 74° 14′.

MAHEWA, in the territory of the rajah of Panna, in Bundelcund, a small town on the route from Allahabad to Saugor, 101 miles N.E. of the latter. It has a bazar, and supplies and water are abundant. Elevation above the sea 1,181 feet. Lat. 24° 24′, long. 80° 12′.

MAHEWA, in the British district of Allahabad, lieut.-gov. of the N.W. Provinces, a village on the right bank of the Ganges. Distant N.W. of Calcutta 762 miles by the river route, and 46 S.E. of the city of Allahabad by the same. Lat. 25° 10′, long. 82° 18′.

MAHGWAY.—A town of Burmah, situate on the left bank of the Irawady, and 103 miles N. from Prome. Lat. 20° 13′, long. 94° 43′.

MAHHASU, in Keyonthul, a peak of one of the lower ridges of the Himalaya, rises amidst picturesque mountains, clothed with forests of towering cedars, noble oaks, and sycamores. On the summit is a small temple, of Chinese architecture, built of wood and stone, and dedicated to the Hindu deity Siva. Elevation of the summit above the sea 9,140 feet. Lat. 31° 6′, long. 77° 20′.

MAHIM.—A town in the British district of Tannah, presidency of Bombay, 50 miles N. of Bombay. Lat. 19° 40′, long. 72° 47′.

MAHIM.—A town at the northern extremity of the island of Bombay. It is situate on the south side of the channel separating that island from Salsette, and at the point where they are connected by a road running partly on arches of masonry, partly on a causeway constructed by government, aided by a munificent contribution from Sir Jamsetjee Jejeebhoy, a Parsee merchant of great wealth, residing in Bombay. The passage is commanded by a fort, originally intended as a defence against the Mahrattas, and still garrisoned by a small force. The town is ill built, and inhabited chiefly by native Christians, of Portuguese descent, who have here a church and some other relics of their former prosperity; in a wood outside the town are the ruins of another church, of a college, and of some other buildings connected with Romish establishments. Distance from the fort of Bombay, N., seven miles. Lat. 19° 1′, long. 72° 54′.

MAHLTEERY.—A town in the British district of Balasore, lieut.-gov. of Bengal, 48 miles S.W. of Balasore. Lat. 21° 6′, long. 86° 23′.

MAHMUDA, in the British district of Furruckabad, lieut.-gov. of the N.W. Provinces, a village on the route from Cawnpore to Futtehgurh, and 30 miles S.E. of the latter. Lat. 27° 2′, long. 79° 56′.

MAHMUDPOOR, in the British district of Moradabad, lieut.-gov. of the N.W. Provinces, a town, with a bazar, on the route from Allygurh to the town of Moradabad, and 14 miles S.W. of the latter. Lat. 28° 40′, long. 78° 43′.

MAHMUDPOOR, in the British district of Allygurh, lieut.-gov. of the N.W. Provinces, a village on the route, by Khasganj, from Bareilly to Allygurh, and eight miles S.E. of the latter, 46 miles N. of Agra. Lat. 27° 52′, long. 78° 15′.

MAHNUS NY.—A small river in the Alwar territory.—(See LASWARI.)

MAHOBA, in Bundelcund, in the British district of Hummerpoor, lieut.-gov. of the N.W. Provinces, a town on the route from Banda to Saugor, 36 miles S.E. of the former. It is situate in a beautiful and picturesque country, amongst numerous striking ruins of mausoleums, palaces, and temples. There are three very beautiful lakes, on the west, south, and east sides of the town respectively; and though each two or three miles in circuit, and of considerable depth, have been formed artificially, by damming up the extremities of valleys with huge mounds of earth faced with stone. Local tradition attributes those works to Parmal Deo, a Rajpoot prince, who ruled in Mahoba about A.D. 1083. Their construction appears to have been intended to secure a copious supply of water for irrigation, the skilful employment of which has converted into a complete garden a tract otherwise rather sterile. They are, however, productive of malaria, which has hastened the depopulation of the place. The town is now an expanse of ruins, amongst which are scattered some houses still tenanted by a population guessed at 5,000 souls. Above the town rises a rocky hill, once strongly fortified, but the defences are now merely piles of massive blocks of stone. Mahoba, according to tradition, is a place of considerable antiquity, as Parmal Deo, who was the last sovereign, and was subdued A.D. 1083, by Pirthiraj, of Delhi, is alleged to have been the nineteenth in lineal descent from the founder. It appears to have been subdued by the Patan Mussulmans about the close of the twelfth century, as Kutb-ood-Deen Eibuk, their commander, in A.D. 1196 overran this part of India, and took the neighbouring fort of Kaleenjar. In the beginning of the eighteenth century, it was wrested from the declining power of Delhi by Chutter Saul, an enterprising Boondela chief, who, being in his turn hard pressed by Muhammad Khan, the Afghan possessor of Furruckabad, called in the aid of the Peishwa; and in remuneration of it willed to him this and some other considerable portions of the country. The Peishwa gave it in jaghire to Govind Pandit, whose successor, Nana Govind Rao, ceded it, in A.D. 1817, to the East-India Company, to whom the whole of his remaining territory subsequently passed in 1840. The town is 147 miles W. of Allahabad. Lat. 25° 18′, long. 79° 55′.

MAHOLA.—A village in the British district of Goorgaon, lieut.-gov. of the N.W. Provinces. Distance S. from Delhi 27 miles. Lat. 28° 16′, long. 77° 19′.

MAHOMEDABAD, in the territory of Oude, a town on the route from Seetapoor to Sekrora, 38 miles S.E. of the former, 42 N.W. of the latter, 32 N.E. of Lucknow. Lat. 27° 16′, long. 81° 3′.

MAHOMED ALI, in Sinde, a village on the route from Sehwan to Larkhana, and 63 miles N. of the former place. It is situate on the right bank of a great offset of the Indus. Lat. 27° 8′, long. 68° 3′.

MAHOMED AMROO, in Sinde, a village on the route from Sehwan to Larkhana, and five miles S. of the last-mentioned town. Lat. 27° 28′, long. 68° 11′.

MAHOMED KHAN KA TANDA, in Sinde, a town on the route from Hyderabad to Cutch, and 20 miles S.E. of the former place. It is situate on the bank of the Fulailee branch of the Indus, and the neighbouring country, though near the border of the desert, is fertile and well cultivated. It is a thriving place, in consequence of its manufactures and of the transit-trade from Cutch. During the Talpoor sway in Sinde, it was usually the residence of one of the subordinate ameers. Lat. 25° 7′, long. 68° 36′.

MAHOMED KHAN TANDA, in Sinde, a village on the route from Sehwan to Kurrachee, and 70 miles N.E. of the latter place. Lat. 25° 28′, long. 67° 55′.

MAHOMEDPOOR, in the British district of Furruckabad, lieut.-gov. of the N.W. Provinces, a village on the route from the cantonment of Allygurh to that of Futtehgurh, and 11 miles N.W. of the latter. Lat. 27° 23′, long. 79° 34′.

MAHOMEDPOOR.—A town in the native state of Indoor, or territory of Holkar, situate 58 miles S. from Indoor, and 139 miles W. from Baitool. Lat. 21° 52′, long. 75° 50′.

MAHON, a river of Sirgoojah, rising in lat. 23° 6′, long. 83° 18′, a few miles E. of the town of Sirgoojah, and, flowing in a northerly direction for seventy miles, falls into the Rehund, near the town of Cohur, in lat. 23° 50′, long. 82° 51′.

MAHONA, in the territory of Oude, a town on the route from Lucknow to Seetapoor, 13 miles N. of the former. It has a bazar, and is abundantly provided with water from wells. Lat. 27° 6′, long. 80° 50′.

MAHONY.—A town of Baghelcund, in the native state of Rewah, situate nine miles E. of the right bank of the Sone river, and 61 miles S. from Rewah. Lat. 23° 39′, long. 81° 28′.

MAHOP, in the British district of Bareilly, lieut.-gov. of the N.W. Provinces, a village on the north-eastern frontier, and on the route from the town of Pilleebheet to Oude, and 11 miles N.E. of the former. Lat. 28° 40′, long. 79° 59′.

MAHOUL, in the British district of Azimgurh, lieut.-gov. of the N.W. Provinces, a town on the route from Azimgurh to Fyzabad, 23 miles W.N.W. of the former. Lat. 26° 6′, long. 82° 53′.

MAHOUNEA.—A town in the kingdom of Oude, situate 10 miles E. of the left bank of the Ghogra river, and 152 miles N. by W from Lucknow. Lat. 28° 58′, long. 80° 20′.

MAHOWLI, in the British district of Etawa, lieut.-gov. of the N.W. Provinces, a village on the route from Calpee to the cantonment of Etawa, and 34 miles S.E. of the latter. Lat. 26° 29′, long. 79° 30′.

MAHRAM, a native state of Eastern India, situate in the Cossya Hills. It is bounded on the north, east, and west by other native hill states, and on the south by the British district of Silhet: its centre is about lat. 25° 12′, long. 91° 24′. It is twenty miles in length from north-east to south-west, and twelve in breadth, and contains an area of about 162 square miles.

MAHUMUDPORE, in the British district of Jessore, lieut.-gov. of Bengal, a town on the route from Calcutta to Dacca, by Baraset, 108 miles N.E. of Calcutta, 72 S.W. of Dacca, situate on a branch of the river Barashee, here crossed by ferry. Lat. 23° 24′, long. 89° 38′.

MAHUR.—See CHOTA OODEPOOR.

MAHUR. — A town in Hyderabad, or dominions of the Nizam, situate four miles from the right bank of the Payne river, and 98 miles S.S.E. from Ellichpoor. Lat. 19° 50′, long. 78°.

MAHUTHWAR, in the British district of Ghazeepoor, lieut.-gov. of the N.W. Provinces, a town on the route from Ghazeepoor to Mozufferpoor, 49 miles E.N.E. of the former. Lat. 25° 49′, long. 84° 23′.

MAHUYADABAR, in the British district of Goruckpore, lieut.-gov. of the N.W. Provinces, a small town on the Manaura, a feeder of the Koyane, and with it ultimately discharged into the Ghaghra. Buchanan describes Mahuyadabar as a straggling place, buried in plantations, and containing 200 houses, many of which are tiled, and some have two stories. Distant S.W. from Goruckpore cantonment 40 miles. Lat. 26° 34′, long. 82° 44′.

MAI, in the British district of Mynpooree, lieut.-gov. of the N.W. Provinces, a village on the route from the cantonment of Allygurh to that of Mynpooree, and 19 miles N.W. of the latter. Lat. 27° 23′, long. 78° 54′.

MAIDOOR GAT.—A town in the British district of Masulipatam, presidency of Madras, 74 miles N.W. by N. of Masulipatam. Lat. 17° 1′, long. 80° 32′.

MAIKER. — A town in Hyderabad, or dominions of the Nizam, situate on the left bank of the Payne Gunga river, and 96 miles S.W. from Ellichpoor. Lat. 20° 10′, long. 76° 40′.

MAILCOTTA, in the Mysore, a town with a fort, situate on a high rocky hill commanding a noble and extensive view southwards. Here is a huge temple of square ground-plan, and entirely surrounded by a colonnade, but all in a rude and mean style of architecture, and overlaid with many thousand coarse images in plaster. It is dedicated to Krishna, and the traditions respecting its foundation are, as usual in such cases, connected with silly and obscene legends. It is viewed with great veneration by the Brahminists, and possesses a quantity of costly jewels, which remained untouched, either by Tippoo Sultan or by the victorious British army; they are lodged for security at Seringapatam, and conveyed to this place only on occasions of high festivity. Here is a very fine tank, mostly resorted to for ritual ablutions, both of the idols and of their votaries, who have the infatuation to believe that on occasion of great festivals the water of the Ganges is miraculously conveyed thither by subterraneous passages. Distant from Seringapatam, N., 18 miles; Bangalore, W., 65. Lat. 12° 40′, long. 76° 42′.

MAILSIR.—A town in the Rajpoot state of Beekaneer, situate 80 miles N.E. by E. from Beekaneer, and 148 miles N. from Ajmeer. Lat. 28° 36′, long. 74° 28′.

MAIMOKE GHAT (or FERRY), in the Punjab, situate on the Ghara river. By this ferry the route from Hindostan passes to the town of Pauk Petten, where is a celebrated shrine of a Mahometan saint. In consequence of this, the ferry is much frequented at the time appointed for his festival. Lat. 30° 13′, long. 73° 13′.

MAINDOO.—A town in the British district of Pegue, on the right bank of the Rangoon river, and two miles S. from Prome. Lat. 16° 44′, long. 96° 17′.

MAINGY, an island of the Mergui Archipelago, situate 23 miles W. of the coast of Tenasserim. Its centre is in lat. 12° 32′, long. 98° 22′.

MAIRPOOR. — A town in the Rajpoot state of Oodeypoor, situate on the left bank of the Saburmuttee river, and 23 miles W.N.W. from Oodeypoor. Lat. 24° 42′, long. 73° 27′.

MAIRWARRA, or realm of the Mairs, in Rajpootana, a mountainous tract, consisting of a number of parallel ridges, extending in a direction from north-east to south-west, and constituting that portion of the Aravulli range which lies between Komulmer and Ajmere, a space of about ninety miles in length, and varying in breadth from six to twenty. Mairwarra is interposed between Mewar, or the state of Oodeypore, and Marwar, or the state of Joudpore. Its north-eastern extremity is in about lat. 26° 10′, long. 74° 30′, its south-western in lat. 25° 25′, long. 73° 50′. In the valleys between the ridges are numerous isolated eminences. The average elevation of the bottoms of the valleys above the sea is probably about 1,600 feet, and the summits, which increase in height towards the south-west, have an elevation in some instances of about 1,000 feet more. The rocks are of primary formation, and probably contain ores of lead, copper, and antimony, though as yet nothing has been done towards making their presumed contents available. Iron of good quality has been discovered in veins, believed to be inexhaustible. Several furnaces have been erected, and the number is increasing.

The Mairs have been from time immemorial the inhabitants of this rugged country, in which they maintained a savage independence, plundering all around them indiscriminately. They are considered to be of the stock of Menas, who are regarded as the aboriginal population of this part of India, and they have received their present appellation, signifying mountaineers, from the character of the localities which they inhabit. Previously to the establishment of the British power in this tract, the inhabitants lived concealed among their rugged hills, wearing hardly any clothing, and practising scarcely any sort of cultivation. The scanty herds of goats, constituting their live stock, were left to the charge of the boys and old men, while the more able spent their time, mounted on their diminutive ponies, in marauding, plundering, and murdering. Of their number, some professed to be Mussulmans, some Brahminists, but neither were very scrupulous in the observance of their respective tenets; they greedily indulged in flesh and strong drinks, feasting on the carcases even of such animals as had died of disease. They appeared to have had no priests or teachers of either denomination, unless a fakir, or professed ascetic, maintained in some villages, might be regarded as supplying the deficiency. Women were considered as slaves, and the unmarried sold to men requiring wives. The price demanded by the father was sometimes so great in proportion to the slender resources of the majority of the population, that many women found it very difficult to meet with husbands; and the deep disgrace attached to disappointment in this respect was so galling, that to avoid it female infanticide was very prevalent. The British authorities, however, succeeded in moderating this as well as many other evils, and female infanticide has ceased.

Dowlut Rao Scindia having, in 1818, ceded Ajmeer to the British government, it claimed Mairwarra as part of the transferred territory; but the states of Oodeypoor and Joudpore having urged pretensions to a considerable portion of it, their validity was hastily and unadvisedly recognised. The inconvenience of three independent states claiming to exercise the powers of government in a country so circumstanced was, however, subsequently mitigated by arrangements, under which the whole was placed under British management, Joudpore and Oodeypoor engaging to pay a certain sum towards the expense of a local corps, and receiving credit for the net revenue. It was, however, much easier to assert authority over such a people as the Mairs than to enforce it; and it required a strong hand to reduce these wild people to anything approaching to obedience and order. One of the measures, however, which appears to have been most efficacious in reclaiming the people from their predatory habits, was the formation of a local corps, to which, as already mentioned, Oodeypoor and Joudpore were bound to contribute. The former freebooters became speedily excellent soldiers, perfect in the British discipline, well skilled in the use of fire-arms, active, trustworthy, and intelligent. The success of these and other judicious arrangements was complete: the inhabitants soon became orderly and peaceable; the revenue statements exhibited a progressive increase in the collections; and the country presented a pleasing picture of a population, reclaimed by judicious treatment from predatory and lawless habits, rapidly advancing in prosperity and in the arts of peace. The latest accounts indicate a continued increase of cultivation and prosperity. A land revenue settlement has been made for a period of twenty years. The principal place in the district is the newly-established town of Nya Nugga, which has been surrounded by a wall, and promises to be the seat of considerable trade. British Mairwarra contains an area of 282 square miles, with a population of 37,715. The portion allotted to Oodeypoor has an area of 305 square miles, and that belonging to Joudpore a superficial extent of about sixty-seven square miles.

MAISELY, in the British territory of Sagur and Nurbudda, lieut.-gov. of the N.W. Provinces, a town on the route from Gawilgurh to Baitool, 12 miles N.E. of the latter. Lat. 21° 45′, long. 77° 50′.

MAITWARRA.—A town of Malwa, in the native state of Bhopal, situate on the left bank of the Newuj river, and 61 miles W.S.W. from Bhopal. Lat. 22° 59′, long. 76° 29′.

MAJGURRA, in the Damaun division of the Punjaub, a village on the route from Dera Ismael Khan to Ghuznee, by the Golairee Pass, and 29 miles W. of Dera Ismael Khan. It is situate at the foot of a pass across the Suliman Mountains, through which the road is difficult to within a short distance of the village. There is water from a subterraneous aqueduct. Lat. 31° 45′, long. 70° 24′.

MAJINDA, in Sinde, a town on the route from Hyderabad to Sehwan, and 45 miles S.E. of the latter place. It is situate two miles from the right or western bank of the Indus, in an alluvial plain but indifferently cultivated. Its population is 2,000. Majinda has an extensive bazar and a good supply of water. The road in this part of the route is good. Lat. 25° 54′, long. 68° 19′.

MAJOGOYA.—A town in the British district of Seebpoor, a division of Upper Assam, 67 miles N.E. of Seebpoor. Lat. 27° 36′, long. 95° 32′.

MAJOORA.—A town in the British district of Tannah, presidency of Bombay, 31 miles N.N.E. of Bombay. Lat. 19° 21′, long. 73° 4′.

MAJRA, in the British district of Rohtuk,

lieut.-gov. of the N.W. Provinces, a village on the route from Rohtuk to Narnol, and 20 miles S. of the former. Lat. 28° 40′, long. 76° 30′.

MAKAVA.—A town in the British district of Vizagapatam, presidency of Madras, 67 miles N. of Vizagapatam. Lat. 18° 40′, long. 83° 21′.

MAKLOR.—A town in the Rajpoot state of Jodhpoor, 13 miles S. of the left bank of the Loonee river, and 62 miles S.W. from Jodhpoor. Lat. 25° 37′, long. 72° 32′.

MAKOWAL, in the hill state of Kuhloor, a small town situate close to the left bank of the Sutlej, in the level, fertile, alluvial tract stretching between the river and the Nina Devi mountain, and which from this place is usually called the Valley of Makowal. It was wrested from the rajah of Kuhloor by Runjeet Singh, who was subsequently compelled by the British to restore it. Distant N.W. from Calcutta 1,100 miles. Lat. 31° 14′, long. 76° 34′.

MAKRAHA, in the district of Aldemau, territory of Oude, a town situate on the river Tons, 62 miles S.E. of the city of Oudh. Butter estimates the population at 6,000, all Hindoos and cultivators. Lat. 26° 14′, long. 82° 52′.

MALABAR, a British district under the presidency of Madras, bounded on the north by Canara and Coorg; on the east by Mysore and Coimbatore; on the south by Cochin; and on the west by the Arabian Sea, or North Indian Ocean, lies between lat. 10° 15′—12° 18′, long. 75° 15′—76° 55′. The area is 6,060 square miles. It has the advantage of an extensive seacoast, measuring 143 miles in length, and which abounds with havens, though for the most part, in consequence of want of adequate depth of water, they are suited only for the coasting craft of the country, or other vessels of small draught.

The most remarkable feature of the country is the great range of the Western Ghats, the culminating ridge of which, in the north part of the district, is nearly parallel to the coast, and on an average about thirty miles from it, dipping westward towards the low lands of Malabar with a bold precipitous face, but eastward becoming depressed more gradually and slightly into the rugged and rocky expanse of Coorg. The elevation of several of the summits is between 5,000 and 6,000 feet, and the ascent from Malabar so steep, that on the invasion of Coorg by the British troops in 1834, but two passes were found practicable for the advance of a military force; and of those one was so difficult, that the column which attempted it was driven back with severe loss by an inconsiderable and undisciplined body of Coorg troops, who defended the intricate ravine. Probably no part of the world exceeds the mountain-tracts of Malabar in the abundance and excellence of its timber-trees, especially teak (Tectona grandis). The impediments in the way of transporting this valuable timber to the seaports are considerable; but so great is the demand for it, that, notwithstanding the difficulty and cost of shipping, the woods were fast becoming exhausted. With the view to the restoration of these forests, extensive tracts of waste land have been converted by the government into teak-plantations. In the latter part of 1843 and the spring of the following year, no less than 50,000 young trees were planted in these nurseries. In the comparatively level tracts about Palaghaut, elephants are employed to drag to the banks of the river Ponany and its various feeders the huge trees, which are thence floated to the coast; but in the elevated and less-accessible valleys, they are committed to the monsoon torrents, which hurry them down cataracts with such violence that most of them are so shattered as to be unsuitable for purposes requiring timber of large dimensions. In a report on this important subject, 120 valuable sorts of timber are enumerated as produced in Malabar. Some trees are of vast size, having been found on measurement forty-five feet in circumference, upwards of 120 feet high, and sixty feet without a branch. Teak has been felled measuring seven feet in diameter at the lower end, and twenty inches at the height of sixty feet. The peon or puna, a light and strong tree, is fit for masts, and has been cut ninety-five feet in length and three feet in diameter. This wood is as light as Riga timber, while it is stronger and more durable.

The climate of the seacoast is warm, but tolerably equable, the temperature being seldom lower than 68° or higher than 88°, and the mean temperature 78°. March, April, and May, constitute the hot season; the south-west monsoon setting in about the beginning of June, when vast masses of clouds rise from the ocean and move towards the north-east, accumulating and becoming more dense as they approach the land, and casting deep gloom and darkness over the sky. The air, previously calm and sultry, is agitated by violent gusts of wind, followed by loud peals of thunder and flashes of vivid lightning; heavy rain succeeds, and continues for several days, renovating, invigorating, and refreshing vegetation, so that the surface of the country, from an arid, naked expanse of hard earth, becomes a sheet of varied and luxuriant verdure, and the air being cooled and purified, animal life is refreshed.

Wild elephants, inferior in size to none in India, harbour in the forests and jungly valleys, and associate in herds of 200 or 300. Tigers of great size are numerous, and dreadfully ferocious. There are wild buffaloes, deer of various kinds, bears, apes, and monkeys innumerable. The gayal, a gigantic bovine quadruped, lurks in the most secluded recesses of the Ghats: it is stated to be ten feet high, and proportionally bulky, with large beautiful horns, silvery-grey coat, and flesh hard and fibrous, but very palatable and nutritious.

Of commercial products, the most important is pepper, proverbially styled the money of Malabar. It requires much moisture, and hence thrives best in the deep valleys of the Ghats, but may with proper culture succeed in any moist ground. The trailing plant which produces pepper, is propagated by planting a cutting at the root of the jak, the mango, or other tree having rough bark, up which the vine climbs. After it has been planted, it requires no great trouble or attention, the cultivator having little more to do than to collect the produce in the proper season. When the fruit is intended for black pepper, it is not allowed to ripen, but is collected green, and becomes black on drying. That which is intended for white pepper is left to ripen thoroughly, in which state the berries are covered with a red pulp, which being washed off, leaves the peppercorn white, and requiring merely to be dried to be fit for market. Cardamoms, a scarce and high-priced article, are produced spontaneously in the woods of the high land, the care given to them being merely the clearing of the ground from trees in those places where they are observed to spring up naturally. This spontaneous growth affords the only product of cardamoms in Malabar. The betel-vine appears to be little cultivated with a view to the demands of commerce; but every one who has a garden, plants for his own use a few vines, trained up the mango or other suitable trees. The cocoanut-tree (Cocos nucifera) is very extensively raised in the alluvial grounds along the seacoast, the soil and air being favourable to its successful culture. Grants of waste land have been made rent-free by government, for a term of years, with the view of encouraging the cultivation of the coffee-plant. The right of private property in the soil is more fully recognised in this district than in any other part of Madras; but even here a man is not allowed to keep his land waste, unless he agree to pay the government the tax they should derive from its cultivation. Should he decline to do this, the land is delivered over to any person who will undertake to till it, a specification being made, that out of the profits deducible from its cultivation a certain portion (about fifteen per cent.) shall be given to the proprietor, as the landlord's share. The principal routes are—1. From south-east to north-west, from Cochin to Calicut and Cannanore, nearly parallel to the coast, and at no great distance from it; 2. from east to west, from Palghat, on the eastern frontier, to Ponany, on the seacoast, by means of which is carried on the traffic in cotton, tobacco, and salt, between the districts of Coimbatoor and Malabar; 3. from east to west, from Ootacamund, on the Neilgherry Hills, to Calicut, on the seacoast; 4. from south-east to north, from Matanadi, in Wynaad, to Calicut; 5. from Bangalore and Seringapatam, through Periyapatam and Coorg, to Cananore, and which has recently been improved. Superior means of transit will shortly be afforded by means of the railroad from Ponany to Madras, connecting the eastern and western coasts of the peninsula. The principal places—Cochin, Cananore, Pennani, and Tellicherry—are described under their respective names in the alphabetical arrangement. The population is given under the article MADRAS.

Throughout this district the prevailing language is the Malayala, which varies considerably from the Tamul, or what, among the Europeans of Madras, is called the Malabar language. They are nevertheless but different dialects of the same language; and those who respectively use either, can in some measure understand each other. The accents are very different; but the Malayala language is considered more perfect than the Tamul, as containing a larger portion of Sanscrit, and of the Pat, or poetical dialect. The character used in the Malayala language is nearly the same with that used among the Tamuls for writing poetry. There are several grammars of the Malayala language, and a dictionary. There are also translations of the Old Testament, and of the book of Common Prayer of the English Church, printed in this language. The population consists of—1st, Brahminists, or followers of the Hindoo system, of divers castes and various denominations; 2nd, Moplays or Mussulmans; 3rd, Christians, either of native descent, and denominated Christians of St. Thomas or Syrian Christians, or of Portuguese origin, and members of the Romish Church; 4th, Jews. Among the professors of the Hindoo creed, the class considered by themselves as highest in dignity are Brahmins, denominated Namburis, reputed to have been the aboriginal proprietors of the soil, which Varuna, the deity of the sea, at the entreaty of Brahma, caused to emerge from the waters. Their hereditary chief, called Tamburacal, before the establishment of British authority, affected to regard himself as superior to the Tamuri or Zamorin, the Nair sovereign of Malabar, but in reality had no power except over the members of his own caste. Other Brahmins, called Puttar, are much more numerous than the Namburis, who, considering their dignity enhanced by the paucity of their race, keep down their number by preventing the younger sons in their families from marrying. The Brahmins of both these descriptions burn their dead, but it does not appear that at any time their women were required to be burned alive with the corpses of their husbands, in conformity with the horrible practice prevailing in many other parts of India.

The Nairs, who rank next to Brahmins, are here a very numerous and influential body, and long held the ruling power. Their habits and manners are marked by those strange peculiarities which elsewhere distinguish this class from all other people. Among these is the utter disuse of marriage; for though a ceremony which consists in a man tying a string round the neck of some young girl, has sometimes been represented as a marriage rite, it has, in truth, no claim to be so regarded, as no cohabitation between the parties follows at any time. The girl, on attaining marriageable age, forms any connection which she may prefer; and her offspring, who have no claim upon their natural father, become the heirs of her brothers. Thus, the connection of the sexes, which, well regulated, is the basis of domestic and social duty, and the main link by which the well-being of the community is maintained, is here perverted into an organized system of shameless profligacy, alike abominable in its exercise, and mischievous in its effects. How so strange and revolting an illustration of the depth of human corruption could have arisen, is matter for pure conjecture. It has been suggested, that it originated with the early Brahmins, who on this view are imagined to have imposed it for the purpose of securing to themselves the means of sensual indulgence, free from the burden of parental duties, and at the same time to secure a race of soldiers more especially devoted to their service, in consequence of being exempt from the incumbrance of families. The Nairs look upon the Tiars (the next class) to be so much beneath them, that if any of them should by chance touch them, they think themselves contaminated, and are obliged to wash their bodies immediately. It formerly often cost the Tiar his life, without notice being taken of it. It requires some acquaintance with human nature in its more debased forms of existence, to admit the credibility of those whose lives were one systematized violation of the most obvious natural obligations, feeling the touch of an inferior contamination to be washed out only by blood. Yet, the perverseness of man, when under no better influence than passion and superstition, is too well authenticated to justify a refusal to believe in the perpetration of almost any enormity, if attested by sufficient evidence. Such practices, however, have of course disappeared before the impartial and wholesome strictness of British authority.

Of the Nair families, the most exalted is the Tamuri, called generally by Europeans that of Zamorin, whose founder, at a period not capable of being very precisely fixed, obtained a small settlement at Calicut. The chief of this family aspires to higher rank than the Brahmins, claiming to be inferior only to the invisible gods; but this assumption, though maintained by his followers, is of course held by the Brahmins to be unwarranted, absurd, and abominable. The descent of the dignity of head of the family, as well as of the Nair class and of the whole district of Calicut, is regulated in an extraordinary manner, the eldest male of the whole lineage succeeding on the occurrence of a vacancy. In conformity with Nair practice, those only possess the claim of lineage, who are born of a Tamburetti, or female of the Tamuri family; and, according to some authorities, if the eldest Tamburetti happen to be older than the Tamuri, she is considered as of higher rank.

The Tiars are considered next in rank to the Nairs, and are freemen engaged in cultivating the ground: next to these are the Maleres, musicians and conjurers, also freemen. The Poliar Chermar, or slaves, were a numerous class before the establishment of British supremacy, and many remained after that establishment, their condition, however, being then stated to have been much ameliorated. But, though their condition was improved, the landlords and proprietors of slaves still retained the power of mortgaging and letting them out for hire, as well as of selling them, with or without land. It has been supposed that the unfortunate persons in this state were the aboriginal population of the country, enslaved by their Brahminical conquerors. However this may have been, it is certain that they were studiously and systematically degraded, regarded with the utmost contempt, and exposed to the last degree of contumely. Happily, the necessity for adverting more minutely to the subject is removed by the provisions of a legislative act of the government of India, by which slavery is abolished. Measures have been adopted for securing the contemplated advantages of the act by efforts to provide employment for the emancipated, and education for their children, and at the same time to create, as far as practicable, a good feeling between the labourers and their masters.

The native Mussulmans, denominated Mapilas, are a numerous and important class. The name is supposed to be contracted from Mahapilla, or "child of Mocha," in Arabia, from which country they originally came, as in the language of Malabar, Maha means Mocha, and pilla, child. Their settlement in Malabar is of very remote date. According to some traditions, the first mosque in the country was founded as early as 642, being only a short period after the commencement of the Mahommedan era. More sober authorities, however, refer this event to a period about two centuries later. It is asserted that, in the vicinity of Calicut, the Moplahs are more numerous than all the rest of the population. Fanatical outbreaks on the part of the Moplahs have unhappily not been uncommon of late years. One occurred in this district at the end of 1843; another, attended with serious loss of life, followed in 1849. Upon the latter occasion, three murders in succession had been committed by a band of these men, who took shelter in a Hindoo pagoda, and set the police at defiance. Upon the arrival of a company of her Majesty's 94th regiment, the Moplahs boldly advanced to the attack, and of the whole band, amounting to sixty-four, all were killed save one (a boy of sixteen years of age), who was severely wounded: they fought with desperation, seeking no quarter. The wounded prisoner stated that they had received an assurance from their priest, that those who died with arms in their hands fighting against infidels would be immediately translated to Paradise. Measures have been taken for the prevention of these outrages. The Moplahs have numerous mosques. Their spiritual chief, denominated Tangul, resides at Ponany, and is maintained by lands which have been allotted for the purpose.

A considerable portion of the population of Malabar are Christians, of whom, as already intimated, there are two denominations; the Syrian Christians, or those who refer their conversion and the foundation of their religious establishment to St. Thomas the Apostle, and the disciples of the Church of Rome, either descendants from the Portuguese or their converts. The total number of Christians in the tract between Cape Comorin and the vicinity of Mangalore has been estimated at 150,000; but there does not appear to be any satisfactory information as to how many of those are in the British district of Malabar. At one time they were very numerous in the Concan, which they left at the instance of the rajah of Akkeri or Bednore, who induced 80,000 Christians, partly Syrian, partly Romish, to migrate into Malabar and Mysore. The liturgy of the Christians of St. Thomas is in Syriac, as is their version of the Scriptures, the date of which is referred to an early part of the fourth century. According to the information which a priest of this persuasion gave Buchanan, this church "is dependent on the Jacobite patriarch of Antioch; but they have a metropolitan, who resides in Travancore, and who is sent by the patriarch on the death of his predecessor." They are settled chiefly in the mauntainous parts of South Malabar, and had formerly an archbishop at Animalaya, a town on the confines of the British district of Coimbatoor. Their doctrines are stated with a wide difference by different authorities. According to Wrede, they maintained the heresy of Nestorius. "They rejected the divine nature of Christ, and called the Virgin Mary only the mother of Christ, not of God: they also maintained that the Holy Ghost proceeded from the Father, and not from the Father and Son. They admitted no images of saints, where the holy cross alone was to be seen. They had only three sacraments, Baptism, Eucharist, and Orders, and would not admit transubstantiation in the manner the Roman Catholics do. They knew nothing of purgatory, and the saints, they said, were not admitted to the presence of God, but were kept in a third place till the day of judgment. Their priests were permitted to marry at least once in their life." There are, however, monasteries amongst them; and those establishments were formerly much more numerous, until the severe and continual persecutions of the Portuguese against the Syrian congregations and communities. An earnest and well-informed inquirer gives an account varying greatly from that above quoted. He represents their doctrines as identical with those of the Episcopal Church of England; viz., 1. Vicarious atonement for the sins of men by the blood and merits of Christ, and justification by faith; 2. Regeneration by the influence of the Spirit of God; 3. Belief in the Trinity, as set forth in the Nicene Creed. A similar account is given by Swanston, a more recent writer:—"Their creed coincides with the articles of faith of Athanasius, but without its damnatory clauses; they deny the tenets of the Nestorian heresy; they believe in God the Father, Son, and Holy Ghost; that Jesus Christ was born of the Virgin Mary, and was incarnate God and man; and that Christ appeared on earth for the salvation of mankind, through whose blood and merits atonement was made for the sins of men: they hold regeneration to righteousness; and they believe that the souls of the blessed will not see God till after the universal judgment." If thus far their tenets might be admitted to be generally the same with those of the Church of England, that which follows appears perfectly irreconcilable with such admission. The writer proceeds to say, "They commonly acknowledge seven sacraments, Baptism and the Lord's Supper, Ordination, Confirmation, Extreme Unction, Penance, and Marriage; they make use of holy oil in baptism; they practise auricular confession, even in children from the age of seven and upwards; they say masses for the repose of the souls of the dead." Their mode of worship appears also to be accompanied by prostrations, crossings, and other ceremonies, little agreeing with the sobriety and decorum of English devotion. The only imaginable mode of accounting for the existence of these opinions and practices among a people whose creed is said to be in accordance with the doctrines of the Church of England, is by adverting to a schism (hereafter to be noticed) which took place among the Syrian Christians about two centuries since, and by supposing that what in the last-quoted extract appears to be said of the entire body, applies, in fact, to only one section of it.

There is some evidence for concluding that the Gospel was preached in Malabar with successful results by St. Thomas, and that, immediately after his martyrdom, it was widely and zealously received there. It is not, however, to be unnoticed, that a large portion of the Syrian Christians attribute the introduction of Christianity into Malabar to a missionary, whom they call Mar Thome, and who appears to have laboured about the middle of the third century. Many Brahmins, and other persons of rank, became converts, and the church so flourished, that, in the tenth century, it is stated that Alfred, the Anglo-Saxon king, sent a mission to inquire after its welfare. At the time of the first arrival of the Portuguese, in the end of the fifteenth century, the Syrian Christians were a prosperous race, highly esteemed and honoured by the native princes. From the Portuguese, who were Romanists, actuated by all the intolerance which prevailed in their own church, the Syrian Christians endured every species of persecution and cruelty which the new-comers had power to inflict, and in 1599 Menezes, the Portuguese archbishop of Goa, convened at Udiamper, near Cochin, a synod, at which the priests of the Syrian Christians, or at least many of them, terrified at the display of military force by the Portuguese and their native supporters, declared their conformity to the Church of Rome. At length the Dutch, having, in 1663, overthrown the Portuguese power in Malabar, the Syrian Christians recovered their religious liberty; but a considerable number of them voluntarily continued to conform to the faith which their ancestors had been forcibly constrained to adopt, and, coalescing with the Portuguese and their native converts, formed a body under the spiritual jurisdiction of the pope, and known by the denomination of Romish Christians of Malabar.

The Jews of Malabar are of two different denominations,—the Black Jews, from time immemorial settled in the country, and the White Jews, bearing, in their comparatively fair complexions, evidence of the recent emigration of their race from a more temperate climate. The principal settlement of the Jews is in the southern part of the district. In the city of Cochin are many white Jews, the black Jews for the most part inhabiting a suburb on the northern side of the city. The number of both denominations is, however, small.

Malabar, the present name of the tract extending along the south-western coast of Southern India, is considered to be a corruption of the name Malayalam, which, in the vernacular dialect, signifies "skirting the hills." Its original Sanskrit name is stated to have been Kevala, and its original occupants the Brahmins, though there is some reason to conclude that they mastered and enslaved a still more ancient race, which, under the denomination of Poliar, groaned until lately under oppressive bondage. The Brahmins, who originally governed, it is said, by an aristocracy of their own caste, became, in consequence of their incessant and ruinous intestine discords, subject to a great potentate, who ruled them by permals (viceroys); a succession of these officers holding the dignity about twelve years each, until towards the commencement of the ninth century, when Cheruma Perumal threw off the yoke, established his independence, and divided his dominions with the Nairs, whom he had invited from the Carnatic. Having subsequently professed Islamism, he repaired to Mecca, and there ended his days. Great obscurity and inconsistency characterize the traditions, forming the only sources from which the history, real or fictitious, of these early periods is to be drawn. Neither dates nor facts can be relied on. The Nairs, however, appear to have maintained their ascendancy until the arrival of the Portuguese at Calicut in 1498, who found that city the residence of the Tamuri rajah, then the greatest potentate on the coast. From their landing, the intercourse of the Portuguese with the natives was characterized by an equal display of valour, fanaticism, and cruelty, until the overthrow of their power by the Dutch, who, in 1663, took from them the city and seaport of Cochin; and thenceforth the native chiefs held their possessions with little molestation until the irruption of Hyder Ali. Influenced by ambition, rapacity, and the prospect of easy conquest from the dissensions of the chiefs, Hyder, in 1763, invaded Malabar from the side of Canara, overcame the obstinate but desultory resistance of the Nairs, and took Calicut, where the Tamuri rajah or Zamorin in despair fired his palace, and destroyed himself and his family in the flames. Calicut was garrisoned by a Mysorean force; but the inhabitants of Malabar continued obstinately, though ineffectually, to resist: 15,000 of them were driven off to people the devastated parts of the Carnatic; but this cruel measure proved abortive, as not more than 200 survived. Hyder Ali having plundered the country to exhaustion, in 1768 evacuated it; but in 1773, with little difficulty, recovered possession. His son and successor, Tippoo Sultan, outdid his father in acts of ferocity and plunder, everywhere treating the population with the greatest cruelty; and, among other outrages, causing such males as could be seized to be forcibly subjected to the initiatory rite of the Mahomedans. The success of the British arms against Tippoo transferred Malabar to the East-India Company, of whose possessions it has ever since formed part.

MALABAR POINT.—The south-western extremity of the island of Bombay. The place contains a residence for the use of the governor of the presidency. Distant W. from Bombay Castle three miles. Lat. 18° 56′, long. 72° 51′.

MALACCA.—A town in the straits of the same name, situate at the entrance of a small river, near the southern extremity of the Malay peninsula. It consists of two divisions, separated by the river, but connected by a bridge. "On the left bank rises the verdant hill of St. Paul, surrounded by vestiges of an old Portuguese fort. Around its base lie the barracks, lines, and most of the houses of the military, the stadthouse, courthouse, jail, church, civil and military hospitals, convent, police-office, school, and post-office. On its summit stand the ruins of the ancient church of our Lady del Monte, erected by Albuquerque, and the scene of the labours and supposed miracles of that apostle of the East St. Francis Xavier. The bazars and by far the greatest part of the town are situate on the right bank of the river." The view of the town from the roads is extremely picturesque. Lat. 5°, long. 100°.

The British territory, of which this town is the chief place, is bounded on the north-west by the Malay state of Salangore; on the south-east by that of Johore; on the east by Rumbowe and Johole; and on the west by the Straits of Malacca. Its length is about forty miles; its breadth, including Naning, twenty-five; and it contains an area of about 1,000 square miles. The products consist principally of rice, sago, jaggery, pepper, timber, poultry, and cattle: fruit and vegetables are abundant, and fish is plentiful and cheap. The climate is noted for its salubrity, the thermometer ranging from 72° to 85°. According to Newbold, "excessive heat and cold are not encountered here as on the peninsula of India, nor any scorching land-winds: hot nights seldom occur. There are regular land and sea breezes." The settlement is but slightly affected by the monsoons that prevail in the Bay of Bengal. A search for coal, conducted under the authority of the British government in different parts of the peninsula, has proved unsuccessful. Tin-mines are worked in various places.

The population of the settlement, inclusive of the military and also of convicts and all other classes, has been officially returned at 54,021. It is of very heterogeneous composition, embracing persons varying greatly as to descent, country, creed, and habits.

Malacca was captured by the Portuguese under Albuquerque in 1509, and remained in their possession till 1642, when it fell to the Dutch, who in their turn were expelled by the British in 1795. At the peace of Amiens, in 1801, it was restored to the Dutch: upon the renewal of hostilities in 1807, it again fell to the British; but was once more restored to the Dutch in 1818, after the general pacification. In 1824 it was finally transferred to the British, among the cessions made by the king of the Netherlands, in exchange for the British possessions on the island of Sumatra. The settlement, previously a dependency of the presidency of Bengal, was, by proclamation, 1st August, 1851, separated therefrom, and the governor of Prince of Wales Island, Singapore, and Malacca, was authorized to exercise within the three settlements, subject only to the government of India, the powers of administration which had previously been intrusted to the government of Bengal.

The peninsula of which Malacca forms part is inhabited by various tribes, chiefly, but not entirely, of Malay origin. In some tracts are found negroes, distinctly marked by the peculiar physical characteristics of that race. The Malay governments, as might be expected, have little or no pretensions to regularity. The chief is usually styled sultan, and between him and the people stand a body of nobles; but obedience, whether from the nobles to the prince, or from the people to both, is yielded only when inclination prompts, or the danger of resistance affrights. The chief points in the character of the Malay,—his violent and uncontrollable temper, his love of gambling, and more especially of cock-fighting, his faithlessness and cruelty, are well known. It is remarkable that his language should be singularly soft, sweet, and musical: it is of mixed origin, and great simplicity of construction. The following account of it is given by Hamilton:—"There is no inflexion of any part of speech to express relative number, gender, time, or mood; and a word is often used without alteration, as a noun, adjective, verb, or adverb. The tenses of a verb are sometimes expressed by auxiliaries, sometimes by adverbs, but not unfrequently both are omitted, and the reader is left to gather the meaning from the context, the sentiment being rather hinted at than expressed. The language, as spoken in the year 1521 in the island of Tidore, when visited by a companion of Magellan, is said to have been precisely that of the present day. The religion professed by the Malays is Mahomedan."

MALAGARH, in the British district of Boolundshuhur, lieut.-gov. of the N.W. Provinces, a town on the left bank of the East Kalee Nuddee, 38 miles S.E. of Delhi. Lat. 28° 28′, long. 77° 53′.

MALA SHEDAO.—A town in the native state of Bhawulpoor, situate on the left bank of the Beas river, and 77 miles N.E. by E. from Bhawulpoor. Lat. 29° 57′, long. 72° 50′.

MALAUN, in the territory of Oude, a town on the route from Cawnpore to Seetapoor cantonment, 38 miles N. of the former, 44 S. of the latter. Heber, who visited it in 1824, describes it as a large town; and Tieffenthaler, about sixty years earlier, styles it "a small town (Städtchen), mostly built of brick, thickly peopled, surrounded by trees. It has a fort, built partly of mud, partly of brick, and having towers." Tennant describes it, at the beginning of the present century, as a "very large village, in length fully two miles. The inhabitants are numerous; but the town is mean and irregular, consisting almost entirely of small mud huts." Lat. 27°, long. 80° 32′.

MALAVELLY, or MALAWALI, in the Mysore, a large mud fort, situate about two miles from an extensive tank or artificial lake, and on the principal route from the Carnatic to Seringapatam. Here, in March, 1799, a battle took place between Tippoo Sultan and the British army under General Harris, advancing to besiege Seringapatam, in which the Mysoreans lost upwards of 1,000 men, while the loss of the British was only sixty-nine. After the latter had marched onwards past Malavelly, Tippoo Sultan caused it to be destroyed; but, after his overthrow, it was partially rebuilt. Distance from Seringapatam, E., 25 miles. Lat. 12° 23′, long. 77° 7′.

MALCOLM ISLAND, in the Mergui Archipelago, situate 33 miles W. of the coast of Tenasserim. Its centre is in lat. 11° 18′, long. 98° 20′.

MALCOLM PEIT.—A village forming part of the convalescent station on the Mahabulishwar Hills, presidency of Bombay. It has several government bungalows for sick officers; the church is about four miles distant from the village and temples of Mahabulishwar, at the source of the Kistna river. The station is well supplied with vegetables from gardens rented of the government. Distant S.E. from Bombay 104 miles. Lat. 17° 56′, long. 73° 41′.

MALDAH, a British district under the lieut.-gov. of Bengal, named from its principal place. It is bounded on the north by Purneah; on the north-east by the British district of Dinajepore; on the south-east by the British district of Rajeshahye; and on the south-west by Moorshedabad and Bhaugulpore. It lies between lat. 24° 30′—25° 25′, long 87° 50′—88° 30′; is seventy miles in length from south-east to north-west, and thirty-seven in breadth: the area is 1,000 square miles. It is throughout a thoroughly alluvial tract, traversed by numerous streams, all of which, flowing towards the south-east, indicate the general slope of the surface to be in that direction; and as they communicate with each other by numerous offsets, they give the country the character of the delta of a vast river, though distant 200 miles in a direct line from the sea. The principal of these are the Ganges, Mahanunda, Purnabada, and Bhagruttee. The elevation of no part of the surface is considerable; it is probably not more than 110 feet at the north-western or highest part.

The principal towns are Maldah, English Bazar, Ruhanpore, and Sivganj. The population is given under the article BENGAL. The routes are—1. From south to north, from Berhampore to Maldah, thence divaricating north-west to Purnea, and north-east to Dinajepore; 2. from west to east, from Rajmahal to Maldah.

The tract comprised within this district, according to Wilford, quoting Puranic authorities, was originally part of the great kingdom of Magadha or Bengal, on the overthrow of which, in the middle of the seventh century, the town of Gaur became the capital of a rajah, the most powerful monarch of the eastern part of India. This state is said to have been overthrown, at the beginning of the thirteenth century, by Bakhtyar Khilji, an officer subordinate to Kutbuddin Aibak, viceroy of Delhi, for Shahabuddin, the Mussulman monarch of Ghor, in Afghanistan. Baktiyar Khilji assuming the title of king of Bengal, it became part of his realm, the seat of government being established at Laknouti or Gaur. In 1538 Gaur was taken, and the kingdom of Bengal conquered, by Sher Shah, the renowned Pathan chief, who subsequently expelled Humayon from Delhi. During the conflict between those rivals, Humayon subjugated this tract, but was quickly obliged to retreat from it. The country was subdued, and restored to the kingdom of Delhi, in 1576, by the arms of Akbar, and thenceforward remained ostensibly part of that realm, until it was granted to the East-India Company by the firman of Shah Alum, in 1765.

MALDAH, a town, the principal place of the British district of the same name, on the route from Burhampore to Purnea, 73 miles N. of the former, 91 S.E. of the latter. It is situate on the left bank of the Mahanunda, at the confluence of a considerable offset from the Ganges, and during the periodical rains is nearly insulated by the inundation. Buchanan describes it as a wretched place, consisting of ruined houses, forming narrow irregular streets, loaded with filth. The manufactures which it formerly had have disappeared before the superior cheapness of those brought from Britain; and the desolation of the town appears to have extended to the surrounding country, as, though fertile, it had become a melancholy desert, from want of cultivation. Besides mosques, the only public building is a large serai or public lodging-house for travellers. Though giving name to the district, it is not the locality of the civil establishment, which is at English Bazar, four miles to the southward. The number of houses has been estimated at 3,000, which, according to the usually received average ratio of inmates to dwellings, would assign it a population of about 15,000. Distant N. from Calcutta, by Burhampore, 191 miles. Lat. 25° 2′, long. 88° 11′.

MALDAH.—A town in the British district of Mongheer, lieut.-gov. of Bengal, 46 miles W.S.W. of Mongheer. Lat. 25° 8′, long. 85° 48′.

MALEBUM.—A town in the native state of Nepal, 143 miles W.N.W. from Khatmandoo, and 127 miles N. from Goruckpoor. Lat. 28° 30′, long. 83° 12′.

MALEEPARA.—A town in the British district of Nuddea, lieut.-gov. of Bengal, 97 miles N.N.E. of Calcutta. Lat. 23° 54′, long. 88° 51′.

MALEKRA, in the north-east of the Punjab, a town in the southern range of the Himalaya, and close to the celebrated fort Kot Kangra. Here is an idol called Bawun, an object of great veneration to the superstitious Hindoos. It is without its head, which is supposed to be at Jewala Muki, and to breathe forth the perpetual fire issuing from the rock there. Malekra is a neat, clean-looking place, built on the side of a hill traversed by the road from Nadaum to Kot Kangra. Lat. 32° 6′, long. 76° 19′.

MALINGAPOOR.—A town in the Southern Mahratta jaghire of Moodhull, 66 miles E.S.E. from Kolapoor, and 58 miles N.E. from Belgaum. Lat. 16° 23′, long. 75° 14′.

MALKAH.—A town in the native state of Nepal, situate on the right bank of the Kurnalli river, and 19 miles W. by N. from Jemlah. Lat. 29° 22′, long. 81° 23′.

MALLA BONNOOR.—A town in the Mysore, 149 miles N.N.W. from Seringapatam, and 120 miles N.E. by N. from Mangalore. Lat. 14° 21′, long. 75° 49′.

MALLIA.—A town in Guzerat, or the dominions of the Guicowar, situate 86 miles S.S.W. from Rajkote, and 111 miles S.E. from Dwarka. Lat. 21° 10′, long. 70° 21′.

MALLIA, in the peninsula of Kattywar,

province of Guzerat, a town in the district of Muchu Kanta, and in the spot where the Runn or Salt Marsh joins the head of the Gulf of Cutch, and on the estuary of the small river Muchu. The tallook or subdivision annexed to it contains nine villages, the whole having a population of 4,293, and paying annually to the Guicowar, and to the nawaub of Joonaghur, a tribute of 1,641 rupees. It belongs to a thakoor or chief, a Jhareja Rajpoot, representative of the elder branch of the family holding the sovereignty of Cutch. The thakoor and his family reside at Kokraji, eight miles west of Mallia: his gross revenue, including the tribute paid by him, is estimated at 17,138 rupees. Distance from Ahmedabad, W., 115 miles; from Baroda, N.W., 160; Bombay, N.W., 315. Lat. 23° 4′, long. 70° 46′.

MALLIAPOORAM.—A town in the British district of Malabar, presidency of Madras, 24 miles S.E. by E. from Calicut. Lat. 11° 4′, long. 76° 6′.

MALLIGAUM.—A town in the British district of Candeish, presidency of Bombay, situate on the trunk road from Bombay to Agra. A church has been recently erected in the town. A proposal was some time since made to transfer the civil station of the district to this place, from Dhoolia, its present locality, 154 miles N.E. of Bombay. Lat. 20° 32′, long. 74° 30′.

MALLIWARRA.—A town of the Deccan, in the territory of Nagpoor or Berar, situate 98 miles S.E. by E. from Nagpoor, and 94 miles S.W. by W. from Ryepoor. Lat. 20° 30′, long. 80° 29′.

MALLOODIE, in Sinde, a village on the route from Subzulcote to Shikarpoor, and 35 miles S.W. of the former place. Lat. 28° 6′, long. 69° 23′.

MALLUNG.—A town in the British district of Silhet, lieut.-gov. of Bengal, 26 miles N.W. by N. of Silhet. Lat. 25° 11′, long. 91° 38′.

MALOD, in Sirhind, a town on the route from Ferozpoor to Simla, and 101 miles S.E. of the former place. It is the possession of one of the Sikh chiefs, under the protection and control of the British. Distant N.W. from Calcutta 1,069 miles. Lat. 30° 38′, long. 76° 3′.

MALOEE, in the British district of Allygurh, lieut.-gov. of the N.W. Provinces, a village 19 miles S.E. of the cantonment of Allygurh. Lat. 27° 42′, long. 78° 17′.

MALOON.—A town of Burmah, situate on the right bank of the Irawady river, and 85 miles N. from Prome. Lat. 19° 59′, long. 94° 49′.

MALOOR.—A town in the British district of Madura, presidency of Madras, 19 miles N.E. by E. of Madura. Lat. 10° 3′, long. 78° 24′.

MALOOR.—A town in the Mysore, 96 miles E.N.E. from Seringapatam, and 158 miles W. from Madras. Lat. 13°, long. 78° 1′.

MALOUD.—A town in the territory of one of the independent hill tribes of Orissa, situate 85 miles S. from Sumbulpoor, and 98 miles N.W. from Ganjam. Lat. 20° 15′, long. 83° 58′.

MALOWN, in the petty hill state of Hindoor, a celebrated fort, situate on a summit of the ridge of the same name, which rises over the left bank of the Sutlej, and has a south-easterly direction until it joins the Sub-Himalaya. The ridge in the part where the fort is situate is only between twenty and thirty yards wide, having on the north-east a steep declivity of 2,000 feet to the river Gumrara, and on the south-west one equally steep and deep to the river Gumbur. The fort is strongly built of masonry, and contains a court-yard, a few small apartments, and a magazine, the whole occupying a space 100 yards long and twenty wide, and surrounded by a strong wall without a ditch. Here, in April, 1815, the Goorkha forces, under their commander-in-chief Ummer Singh, were shut up, when dislodged from all their other posts in the western hill states by the persevering and masterly operations of General Ochterlony, and the British engineers having, with amazing toil and skill, made up those difficult heights a road practicable for heavy artillery, a breaching battery was formed within 400 yards of the fort, which was surrendered on the 15th of May following. By this capitulation, it was provided that the whole of the hill states west of the river Kalee should be evacuated by the Goorkhas, and delivered up to the British. Malown is 4,448 feet above the sea. Distant N.W. from Calcutta 1,095 miles. Lat. 31° 12′, long. 76° 52′.

MALPURA, in the British district of Agra, lieut.-gov. of the N.W. Provinces, a town situate eight miles S.W. of the city of Agra. Lat. 27° 7′, long. 77° 59′.

MALPURA, in the state of Jeypoor, in Rajpootana, a town on the route from Delhi to Neemuch, 216 miles S.W. of former, 155 N.E. of latter. It is of considerable size, and water and supplies are abundant. Lat. 26° 17′, long. 75° 25′.

MALRA, in the jaghire of Jujhur, lieut.-gov. of the N.W. Provinces, a village on the route from Rohtuk to Narnol, and 47 miles S.W. of the former. Lat. 28° 19′, long. 76° 15′.

MALSEIJ GHAUT, a pass over the Western Ghauts, separating the Tannah and Ahmednuggur districts, 68 miles N.E. by E. from Bombay. Lat. 19° 25′, long. 73° 48′.

MALTEE NUDDEE, a small river rising on the south-west frontier of Bengal, in lat. 21° 22′, long. 84° 13′, and, flowing circuitously, but generally westerly, for twenty miles, through the British district of Sumbulpoor, falls into the Mahanuddy, in lat. 21° 25′, long. 84° 1′.

MALWA, or CENTRAL INDIA, a table-land of uneven surface, elevated from 1,500 to 2,500 feet above the level of the sea, bounded on the west by the Aravulli range of mountains; on the south by the Vindhya chain; on the east by Bundlecund; and on the north-east by the valley of the Ganges. Of a country so extensive and so divided as to government, it would be out of place to attempt a description of either its physical or political circumstances; but in the articles devoted to particular portions, the proper information will be found; and to these the inquirer is referred. Malwa formerly constituted a powerful kingdom: it appears to have thrown off the yoke of Delhi at the close of the fourteenth century, in the reign of Feroz Toghluk. Its first king was Dilawar Ghori, whose ancestors were natives of Ghor, in Afghanistan. It preserved its independence through a line of kings for 130 years, when it was subjugated by Akbar, and annexed to the imperial dominions. Malwa continued a province of the empire until the dissolution of that great fabric of power made way for the subjugation of Malwa by the power then rising in India,—the Mahrattas, by whom it was speedily overrun. The condition of the country became unsettled and irregular, and here, as the proper soil for their production, originated the associations of plunderers, infamous in Indian history under the name of Pindaries. These miscreants gradually extended themselves over Malwa, and would soon have occupied the whole, issuing forth but to carry devastation and misery into the adjacent countries, had not the vigorous measures of the Marquis of Hastings put an end to their success, and forced them to resort to more honest means of life than they had been accustomed to. Malwa was thus restored to peace and security, and the great preservative of peace afforded by the paramount power of the British government has been effectual in maintaining those blessings which its energy and perseverance won for the country. It is divided into a number of principalities, held by native chiefs. The peace of the country is in part preserved by a Bheel corps, embodied in 1840. The Bheels were among the most despised outcasts, and were considered among the most hopeless. The experiment of converting them into soldiers did not appear to bear much promise, but it has succeeded to an extent that the most sanguine could scarcely have looked for: they have been trusted, and they have shown themselves worthy of trust. The expense of the corps is supported partly by the British government, and partly by contributions from Holkar, Scindia, Dhar, Jabooa, and Amjherra. In addition to this force, is the Malwa united contingent, supported by Holkar and the petty states of Dewas and Jourah.

MALWAN, also known by the names of Melundy Island and Sindoodroog, is situate off the coast of the Southern Concan, presidency of Bombay. It is little elevated above the water, and the channel being narrow, it at a short distance is not easily distinguished from the mainland, on which, abreast of the island, is a fort. This was formerly a stronghold of Mahratta pirates, but in 1812 it was, under the treaty of Kurveer, ceded to the East-India Company by the rajah of Colapore. Iron-ore of good quality has been found in the vicinity. Distant S. from Bombay 210 miles, S.W. from Sattara 122 miles. Lat. 16° 4′, long. 73° 31′.

MAMADPOOR, in Sinde, a village on the route from Subzulcote to Shikarpoor, and 22 miles S.W. of the former town. Lat. 28° 7′, long. 69° 34′.

MAMKPOONJ.—A town in the British district of Ahmednuggur, presidency of Bombay, 80 miles N. of Ahmednuggur. Lat. 20° 14′, long. 74° 44′.

MAMUN, in the British district of Boolundshuhur, lieut.-gov. of the N.W. Provinces, a village on the route from Muttra to Meerut, and 49 miles S. of the latter. The road in this part of the route is good, the country open and partially cultivated. Lat. 28° 20′, long. 77° 55′.

MANA, in the British district of Kumaon, under the lieut.-gov. of the N.W. Provinces, a town on the Saraswati, called lower down the Vishnuganga or Bishenganga, a tributary of the Aluknunda. It is the chief place of a petty district of the same name, containing, according to Traill, three villages and 700 or 800 inhabitants. A route from the south proceeds by the village and up the course of the river, to the crest of the range dividing Kumaon from Chinese Tartary, on which it debouches by a pass of the same name as the town. The Mana Pass, though very lofty, is one of the easiest into Chinese Tartary from the south, in consequence of the ascent up the course of the river being rather regular and gradual. It is that usually followed by the Hindoo pilgrims in their journeys to Lake Manasarovara, for which they choose the month of July, returning in October by the Nilun Pass. The town of Mana has an elevation of 10,492 feet, the pass of 18,000. Lat. 30° 46′, long. 79° 32′, of town; lat. 31° 5′, long. 79° 34′, of pass.

MANAAR, an island off the coast of Ceylon, and at the eastern extremity of the narrow long sandbank called Adam's Bridge, which stretches in a direction from east to west between Ceylon and the mainland of India. Manaar gives name to a gulf or rather bay indenting the mainland of India: it bears north-east from Cape Comorin, and south-west from Palk's Straits, from which it is divided by Adam's Bridge. A survey of the gulf, conducted at considerable cost, was completed a few years since, and resulted in the formation of the Paumbum Passage, the particulars of which are described under that head in the alphabetical arrangement. The island is in lat. 9° 3′, long. 80°.

MANAMALEGUDI. — A town in the British district of Tanjore, presidency of Madras, situate 53 miles S. of Tanjore. Lat. 10° 3′, long. 79° 18′.

MANANTAWADDY, in the British district of Malabar, presidency of Madras, a town, the principal place of the talook or subdivision of Wynaad, and the head-quarters of the local force stationed in it. Distance from Calicut, N.E., 43 miles; Cananore, E., 50. Lat. 11° 48′, long. 76° 4′.

MANAPARA. — A town in the British district of Madura, presidency of Madras, 55 miles N.N.E. of Madura. Lat. 10° 39′, long. 78° 29′.

MANARGOODY.—A town in the British district of Tanjore, presidency of Madras, 22 miles E.S.E. of Tanjore. Lat. 10° 40′, long. 79° 30′.

MANAR GURR.—A town in the British district of South Canara, presidency of Madras, 26 miles N. by W. of Mangalore. Lat. 13° 13′, long. 74° 47′.

MANASA BUL, or MANOS BAL, in Cashmere, a beautiful lake, which discharges its water into the Jhelum, on the right or north side. It is altogether, according to Von Hügel, one of the most beautiful spots in existence. On the northern bank are the remains of a palace built by Nur Jehan, the celebrated queen of Jehangir, the Mogul emperor. Lat. 34° 13′, long. 74° 48′.

MANCHEE, a river rising in lat. 27°, long. 89° 3′, on the southern slope of the Sub-Himalaya range of mountains, and, flowing in a southerly direction for forty miles through the native state of Bhotan, and for nineteen through that of Coosh Behar, falls into the Jerdeeker river on the left side, in lat. 26° 20′, long. 89° 15′.

MANCHUN, a river rising in lat. 22° 21′, long. 74° 38′, on the northern slope of the Vindhya range of mountains, and in the native state of Barreah, and, flowing in a northerly direction for fifty-five miles through Barreah, Dewud, Jhallod, and Saunte, falls into the river Mhye, in lat. 23° 32′, long. 74° 1′.

MANDALE.—A town of Burmah, situate five miles N. from the right bank of the Irawady, and 34 miles W.N.W. from Ava. Lat. 22° 2′, long. 95° 32′.

MANDAVEE, in the presidency of Bombay, a town, the principal place of a feudal dependency, which, on the demise of Rajah Doorjun Singjee in 1840, and the failure of heirs in the direct line of succession, lapsed to the paramount power, and was subsequently annexed to the British dominions: it now forms part of the collectorate of Surat. The town is situate on the right bank of the Taptee, 73 miles S. of Baroda. Lat. 21° 11′, long. 73° 20′.

MANDAVEE.—A town in the native state of Cutch, situate on the coast of the Gulf of Cutch, and 34 miles S.W. from Bhooj. Lat. 22° 51′, long. 69° 26′.

MANDAWA.—A town in the Rajpoot state of Jeypoor, situate 86 miles N.W. by N. from Jeypoor, and 115 miles N.N.E. from Ajmeer. Lat. 28° 1′, long. 75° 18′.

MANDEYE, in the British district of Mynpooree, lieut.-gov. of the N.W. Provinces, a village situate on the route from the city of Agra to the cantonment of Mynpooree, and 27 miles W. of the latter. Lat. 27° 7′, long. 78° 43′.

MANDGAON.—A town of the Deccan, in the territory of Nagpoor, situate on the right bank of one of the branches of the Wurda river, and 39 miles S.S.W. from Nagpoor. Lat. 20° 40′, long. 78° 55′.

MANDI.—See MUNDI.

MANDOO, in the small raj or state of Dhar, in Malwa, an extensive deserted city, 15 miles N. of the right bank of the Nerbudda. The circuit of its ramparts is, according to Malcolm, thirty-seven miles; but it is not probable that the whole of this great space was inhabited. The greatest and least-injured of the ruined buildings is the Jama Masjit, or great mosque. Its area is raised several yards above the ground, and is reached by a large and handsome flight of stairs: its interior is open to the heavens. The ground-plan is a square, and on each side is a low deep gallery, supported by several ranges of enormous pillars. The size of this building is great, so that, notwithstanding some degree of heaviness and inelegance, its appearance is very striking. Next in importance is the mausoleum of Hoshung Ghori, king of Malwa, who raised this city to great splendour. It is built in massive style, of white marble, and is situate in a square court, from which proceeds a deep gallery, supported by columns elaborately sculptured; and in a chamber roofed with vast slabs is the sarcophagus of the sultan. The ruins of the palace of Baz Bahadur, king of Malwa, and of many other gorgeous buildings, strew the ground to a great extent. According to Malcolm, Mandoo was founded in the year 370 of the Sambat, or A.D. 313, and was at first the residence of the Hindoo rajahs of the state of Dhar. It is mentioned by Ferishta as the occasional residence and seat of government of Dilawar Khan Ghori, the first Mussulman king of Malwa, who reigned from A.D. 1387 to 1405; and that his son, Alp Khan, who succeeded him under the name of Hoshung Ghori, laid the foundations, during his father's life and reign, of the fortifications, which he completed afterwards when on the throne. In 1526 it was taken by Bahadur Shah, sovereign of Guzerat, and was embodied in his dominions, in which it remained comprised until their conquest by Akbar in 1570. The name of Akbar, and the date of his visit to Mandoo, are inscribed on a marble slab over one of the principal gates. Elevation above the sea 1,944 feet. Distant from Mow, S.W., 26 miles; Indoor, S.W., 38 miles; from Oojein, by Indoor, S.W., 70. Lat. 22° 20′, long. 75° 27′.

MANDOUTHEE, in the British district of Rohtuk, lieut.-gov. of the N.W. Provinces, a town on the route from Rohtuk to Delhi, 18 miles S.E. of the former. Lat. 28° 42′, long. 76° 51′.

MANDOWLA.—A town in the Rajpoot state of Jodhpoor, situate on the left bank of the Loonee river, and 100 miles S.W. from Jodhpoor. Lat. 25° 20′, long. 71° 59′.

MANDREL.—A town in the native state of Gwalior, or the territory of Scindia's family, situate on the right bank of the Parbutty river, and 62 miles W. from Gwalior. Lat. 26° 14′, long. 77° 15′.

MANDULGURH.—A town in the Rajpoot state of Oodeypoor, 96 miles N.E. by E. from Oodeypoor, and 96 miles S. by E. from Ajmeer. Lat. 25° 10′, long. 75° 10′.

MANDUNEE, in Koomharsin, a village on the route from Simla to Kotgurh, and 10 miles S. of the latter place, remarkable for two Hindoo temples, constructed partly of stone, partly of wood, ingeniously and elaborately carved. The village is exclusively inhabited by Brahmins. Elevation above the sea 7,428 feet. Lat. 31° 11′, long. 77° 29′.

MANDWA.—A town in Hyderabad, or territory of the Nizam, situate 161 miles N.E. by N. from Hyderabad, and 127 miles S. by E. from Nagpoor. Lat. 19° 24′, long. 79° 40′.

MANDWA.—A town in one of the recently sequestrated districts of Hyderabad, or dominions of the Nizam, presidency of Bengal, situate 89 miles S.E. by E. of Ahmednuggur. Lat. 18° 32′, long. 75° 59′.

MANDWELLA.—A town in the Rajpoot state of Jodhpoor, situate on the right bank of the Sookree river, and 68 miles S.W. by S. from Jodhpoor. Lat. 25° 28′, long. 72° 35′.

MANDYAH, in the British district of Goorgaon, lieut.-gov. of the N.W. Provinces, a village situate on the route from Dadri to Rewari, and six miles N.W. of the latter. Lat. 28° 15′, long. 76° 36′.

MANEGUMBA.—A town in the native state of Nepal, situate on the right bank of the Arun river, and 102 miles E.N.E. from Khatmandoo. Lat. 28° 7′, long. 86° 51′.

MANERUNG.—A pass over the lofty range of Damuk Shu, bounding Koonawur on the north-west, and dividing it from Ladakh. No European, except Alexander Gerard, appears to have visited that scene of terrific wildness; and its passage, and that of the Charung Pass, were the most arduous undertakings of that intrepid and adventurous explorer. The ascent of the pass from the south-east or Koonawur side is up the course of the Darbung river, to its source, in perennial ice and snow, at an elevation of 15,000 feet. This pass is open about four months of the year: it was crossed by Gerard at the end of August. Elevation above the sea 18,612 feet. Lat. 31° 56′, long. 78° 24′.

MANGAHPETT, in Hyderabad, or territory of the Nizam, a small town on the right or south-west bank of the river Godavery, which flows at the base of a range of mountains situate in the territory of Nagpoor. It has a small mud fort; but the remarkable objects there are some structures in the Cyclopean style of architecture, consisting of huge stones above twenty feet high, set upright as pillars, and arranged in circles like those of Stonehenge, and other antique works considered as Druidical monuments. They are cut out of the sandstone, the natural formation of the rocks in that part of the country. Distance from Hyderabad, N.E., 150 miles; from Polenshaw, N., 50. Lat. 18° 13′, long. 80° 35′.

MANGALORE, in the British district of South Canara, presidency of Madras, a town situate on the north side of the estuary formed by the junction of a river flowing from the north-east, and of the Naitravutty, a considerable river, but navigable only by small vessels, there being but ten or eleven feet water on the bar. "Here," says a traveller who visited the place some years since, "are the magazines for sandal-wood, which grows on the Mysore hills, of which," the writer states, the East-India Company had at the time a monopoly from the rajah. The estuary is a fine expanse of water, separated from the sea by a beach of sand, liable to be breached by the waves in different places, and thence the utility of the haven is greatly impaired, as the depth of water at the entrance, at no time great, is liable to vary at short intervals. The town is large, and is washed on east and west by the two streams whose confluence forms the estuary. The houses are generally mean, and there are no public buildings worth notice.

Mangalore, though a bad haven, was the principal seaport of the territory of Hyder Ali, and, subsequently, of his son Tippoo; and here were constructed the ships forming the maritime force of their realm: the fine teak-woods at the base and on the slopes of the Ghats affording abundance of the best materials. A few miles to the north of Mangalore is an extensive deposit of porcelain-clay, very closely resembling that of Limoges, in France, of which the beautiful Sevres ware is formed; and as the beds of this substance are close to the coast, it could advantageously be shipped to Europe as ballast, or, with the aid of Chinese artificers, might be manufactured in India.

Mangalore early and repeatedly suffered from the ferocity of the Portuguese. In 1547 it was desolated by them with fire and sword: being rebuilt in 1555, it was again destroyed by the same nation. Having recovered this calamity, it once more fell into the hands of these people, who destroyed every living being, and burned the town. In 1567 it was finally occupied by the Portuguese, who built there the fort St. Sebastian and a church. In 1617, the Portuguese governor of Mangalore defeated the rajah of the small territory in the vicinity of the town, and compelled him to cede a portion of his possessions. In 1640 this place was still in the hands of the Portuguese; and it does not appear when or how it was wrested from them by the rajah of Bednore, on the overthrow of whose power by Hyder Ali, in 1763, it was seized by that adventurer. In 1768 it was taken by an expedition sent for that purpose from Bombay, and in the same year retaken by Hyder; the British garrison, though ample and provided with means to make a prolonged defence, pusillanimously evacuating the place, and making off to Bombay. In 1783 it was surrendered to a British force under General Matthews, and in the same year it yielded to Tippoo Sultan; on whose final overthrow, in 1798, it was acquired by the East-India Company.

The population was ascertained by census, in 1836, to amount to 11,548 persons, exclusive of the military. The cantonment is situate on the north side of the town, on a level space, gently elevated, well drained, and open to the sea-breezes; and from these circumstances is healthy. Here, in 1784, was concluded the treaty of peace, called the treaty of Mangalore, between the East-India Company and Tippoo Sultan. Mangalore is called also Codyall Bunder, and is the principal place of a talook or subdivision of the same name. An excellent road from Mangalore to Mercara, a distance of eighty miles, was constructed in 1840, at a cost of upwards of 25,000*l*. The town is distant direct from Bombay, S.E., 440 miles; from Bangalore, W., 188; Seringapatam, N.W., 130; Madras, W., 370; Calcutta, S.W., by Bangalore, Ongole, Ellore, Cuttack, and Midnapore, 1,160. Lat. 12° 52′, long. 74° 54′.

MANGLEE.—A town in Hyderabad, or dominions of the Nizam, situate on the left bank of the Payne Gunga river, and 169 miles N. by E. from Hyderabad. Lat. 19° 45′, long. 78° 59′.

MANGLOOR, in the British district of Suharunpoor, lieut.-gov. of the N.W. Provinces, a town on the route from Suharunpoor to Bijnour, 23 miles S.E. by E. of the former. Lat. 29° 47′, long. 77° 57′.

MANGMUTCHA.—A town in the British district of Mergui, one of the Tenasserim provinces. Lat. 13° 10′, long. 98° 43′.

MANGOR, in the territory of Gwalior, or dominions of Scindia, a fortified village 11 miles S.W. of the celebrated fort of that name, and situate at the base of a high range of hills. Here, during the brief campaign at the close of December, 1843, the Mahratta army took post, preparatory to its attack on the British, under General Grey, posted close to the town of Puniar. In the engagement which ensued, on December 29th, the Mahrattas were driven, with heavy loss, from all points of their position, and all their artillery, consisting of twenty-four pieces, was captured, as well as all their ammunition. The British had 35 men killed and 182 wounded. Lat. 26° 7′, long. 78°.

MANGROL, in the peninsula of Kattywar, province of Guzerat, a town in the prant or district of Soruth, on the south-west coast, washed by the Arabian Sea. Though an indifferent port, the town is very populous, and has considerable traffic. Here is a mosque, the finest building of the kind in the peninsula of Kattywar. A tablet in one part of the building records its foundation, A.D. 1383. It belongs to a petty Mussulman chief, styled nawaub of Mangrol. He is tributary to the chief or nawaub of Joonagurh. The nawaub of Mangrol pays to Joonagurh an annual tribute of 11,000 rupees. Distant from Ahmedabad, S.W., 205 miles; Baroda, S.W., 210. Lat. 21° 8′, long. 70° 10′.

MANGROL, in the Rajpoot territory of Kotah, a town on the route from Calpee to Kotah, 274 miles S.W. of former, 46 E. of latter. Here, on the 21st of September, 1821, a battle was fought between the army of Kishen Singh, the maha rao or hereditary prince of Kotah, and the troops of Zalim Singh, the minister of the state, aided by the British, in which the maha rao was utterly defeated, and his brother, Pirthi Singh, killed. Lat. 25° 17′, long. 76° 33′.

MANGUL, a small hill state under the superintendence of the Governor-General's agent for the Cis-Sutlej states, is bounded on the north by Sooket, from which it is separated by the Sutlej; on the east and south by Bhagul; and on the west by Kuhloor. It is about six miles in length from north to south, and four in breadth from east to west: its centre is in lat. 31° 18′, long. 76° 56′: it contains two pergunnahs. The revenue is estimated at 100*l*., and the population at 1,000 souls.

MANGURH, in the British district of Dumoh, Saugor and Nerbudda territory, lieut.-gov. of the N.W. Provinces, a town on the route from Dumoh to Sohagpoor, 21 miles E.S.E. of the former. Lat. 23° 40′, long. 79° 50′.

MANICKDROOG.—A town in Hyderabad, or dominions of the Nizam, 166 miles N. by E. from Hyderabad, and 107 miles S. from Nagpoor. Lat. 19° 39′, long. 79° 17′.

MANIHALA, or MANIALA, in the Baree Dooab division of the Punjab, a town situated 14 miles S.E. from the left bank of the Ravee, 13 miles E.S.E. of the town of Lahore. Lat. 31° 32′, long. 74° 35′.

MANIKPOOR, in the territory of Oude, a decayed town in the district of Ahladganj, on the route from Allahabad to Lucknow, 38 miles N.W. of the former, 90 S.E. of the latter. It is situate on the left bank of the Ganges, here a rapid stream, shallow in the season of low water, when it is about a third of a mile wide, muddy and discoloured. Distance N.W. from Calcutta, by Allahabad, 541 miles. Lat. 25° 45′, long. 81° 30′.

MANIKPOOR, in the British district of Budaon, lieut.-gov. of the N.W. Provinces, a village on the route from Agra to Bareilly, and 44 miles S.W. of the latter. Lat. 28° 1′, long. 79° 4′.

MANJEE, in the British district of Sarun, lieut.-gov. of Bengal, a considerable town on the left bank of the river Ghogra, three miles above its confluence with the Ganges. Distance from Chapra, N.W., 12 miles; from Dinapore, N.W., 36. Lat. 25° 48′, long. 84° 40′.

MANJERA, a river rising in lat. 18° 44′, long. 75° 30′, and, flowing in a south-easterly direction for 170 miles, separates for that distance one of the recently sequestrated districts from the reserved territories of the Nizam. From the termination of this boundary it continues its course through the territory of Hyderabad, and falls into the Godavery river on the right-hand side, near the town of Sungum, in lat. 18° 48′, long. 77° 55′.

MANKAH.—A town in the British district of Palamow, lieut.-gov. of Bengal, situate 12 miles E.S.E. of Palamow. Lat. 23° 45′, long. 84° 11′.

MANKORE, or **MANKAUR**, in the British district of Burdwan, lieut.-gov. of Bengal, a town on the route from the town of Burdwan to Raniganj, 22 miles N.W. of former, 30 S.E. of latter. Jacquemont styles it a considerable village. Lat. 23° 24′, long. 87° 34′.

MANKOT.—A town in the dominions of Gholab Singh, the ruler of Cashmere, situate 18 miles N.W. from the right bank of the Ravee, and 101 miles N.E. from Lahore. Lat. 32° 38′, long. 75° 24′.

MANOKPOOR.—A town in the Rajpoot state of Jodhpoor, 49 miles N.E. from Jodhpoor, and 70 miles N.E. by N. from Ajmeer. Lat. 26° 49′, long. 73° 40′.

MANOOKE, in Sirhind, a village on the route from Ferozpoor to Simla, and 50 miles S.E. of the former town. Lat. 30° 40′, long. 75° 40′.

MANOOR.—A town in Hyderabad, or dominions of the Nizam, situate 141 miles N. from Hyderabad, and 139 miles S.S.E. from Ellichpoor. Lat. 19° 23′, long. 78° 31′.

MANOOR.—A town in the British district of Ahmednuggur, presidency of Bombay, 41 miles E. of Ahmednuggur. Lat. 19° 9′, long. 75° 21′.

MANPOOR, in the Rajpoot state of Jeypore, a town on the route from Agra to Ajmeer, 87 miles W. of former, 141 E. of latter. It is situate on the right or south bank of the Baun or Banganga river or torrent, the channel of which, 600 yards wide, is devoid of water in the dry season, though having a considerable stream during the periodical rains. The town is surrounded by a mud rampart from twelve to sixteen feet high, with eight good semicircular bastions and a dry ditch. Boileau states that it contains 800 houses; an amount which would assign it a population of about 4,000 persons. Lat. 26° 58′, long. 76° 44′.

MANSA, in the north of the Punjab, a small lake in the southern range of the Himalaya, a mile in length, half a mile in breadth, and very deep. Forster styles it "a delicious spot." It is considered sacred by the Hindoos, who visit it in pilgrimage, regarding it as a meritorious act to make the circuit of it, to propitiate the Devi or presiding spirit. Lat. 32° 40′, long. 75° 8′.

MANSOOD, in the British territory of Saugur and Nurbudda, lieut.-gov. of the N.W. Provinces, a town on the route from Ellichpoor to Deogur, 50 miles N.E. by E. of the former. Lat. 21° 38′, long. 78° 10′.

MANSUK, in the native state of Korea, on the south-west frontier of the presidency of Bengal, a small town or village among the mountains of Gondwana, situate 45 miles W. of the ruined city of Sirgooja, 136 S. of Mirzapoor, 440 W. of Calcutta by Hazaribagh. Lat. 23° 12′, long. 82° 25′.

MANTEE, in the British district of Cawnpore, lieut.-gov. of the N.W. Provinces, a village on the route from the cantonment of Cawnpore to that of Calpee, and 21 miles N.E. of the latter. Lat. 26° 20′, long. 80° 1′.

MANTHALIGHOT.—A town in the native state of Nepal, 47 miles E.S.E. from Khatmandoo, and 95 miles N. from Durbunga. Lat. 27° 30′, long. 86°.

MANTHOLY.—A town in Nagpoor or Berar, situate 129 miles S.E. from Nagpoor, and 92 miles W. by S. from Chanda. Lat. 20° 6′, long. 80° 47′.

MANUND, in Keonthul, a peak on a ridge connected with the Jako or Simla range, and throwing off feeders to the river Giri on one side, and to the Ushun on the other. Elevation above the sea 7,800 feet. Lat. 31° 3′, long. 77° 19′.

MANUROO, or **MUNHEIROO**, in the jaghire of Jujhur, lieut.-gov. of the N.W. Provinces, a village on the route from Hansi to Neemuch, and 34 miles S.E. of the former. Supplies may on notice be obtained in moderate quantity, and water is supplied from wells and tanks. The road in this part of the route is good. Lat. 28° 41′, long. 76° 17′.

MAO, in the British district of Furruckabad, lieut.-gov. of the N.W. Provinces, an ancient town 11 miles N.W. of the city of Furruckabad, and a mile and a half W. of the right bank of the Ganges. Lat. 27° 35′, long. 79° 31′.

MAPAN, in the British district of Kumaon, lieut.-gov. of the N.W. Provinces, a village in the Bhotia subdivision of Juwahir, on the route to Hiundes or Chinese Tartary, and 16 miles S. of the Juwahir Pass. It is situate near the right bank of the Goree river, which flows at the depth of about 250 feet below. The country is above the limit of forest vegetation, producing only a few creeping cedars, barberry and gooseberry-bushes, and other shrubs. Elevation above the sea 11,082 feet. Lat. 30° 23', long. 80° 12'.

MARACHANGDI, a river rising in lat. 28° 55', long. 83° 58', in the Snowy range of the Himalayas, and, flowing in a southerly direction for 100 miles, falls into the Nalng, a tributary of the Trisul-Gunga, in lat. 27° 40', long. 84° 11'.

MARANDAHALLIC.—A town in the British district of Salem, presidency of Madras, 161 miles W.S.W. of Madras. Lat. 12° 24', long. 78° 4'.

MAREE, in Sirhind, a town thirty miles from the left bank of the Sutlej. It was comprised in the possessions held by the maharajah of the Punjab, on the left side of the Sutlej, and is now locally situated within the British district of Ferozepoor. Distant S.E. from Ferozepoor 38 miles; N.W. from Calcutta, by way of Delhi and Munuk, 1,068 miles. Lat. 30° 36', long. 75° 7'.

MARHWAS.—A town of Baghelcund, in the native state of Rewah, situate 42 miles S.E. from Rewah, and 60 miles N.N.E. from Sohagpoor. Lat. 24° 6', long. 81° 51'.

MARIAN RIVER.—One of the mouths of the Irawady, falling into the Bay of Bengal in lat. 16° 35', long. 96° 45'.

MARJA, in Bussahir, a pass over the range of the Himalaya bounding Koonawur to the south. This pass and three others cross the ridge within a space of little more than a mile. The elevation of Marja is probably between 16,000 and 17,000 feet. On account of fissures in the ice, and the snow sinking, it is scarcely passable, except in May, June, July, and the first half of August. Marja Pass is in lat. 31° 16', long. 78° 27'.

MARKAPOOR.—A town in the British district of Cuddapah, presidency of Madras, 91 miles N.N.E. of Cuddapah. Lat. 15° 45', long. 79° 20'.

MARKARI, in the British district Malabar, presidency of Madras, a town on the western base of the Western Ghats, on a river flowing from that range, nine miles E. of Cannanore. Lat. 11° 52', long. 75° 38'.

MARKUNDA, a river, or rather torrent, rises in Sirmour, under the name of Murkwata, in the hills about Nahun, in lat. 30° 35', long. 77° 27'. Holding a course of a few miles in a south-westerly direction, it flows into Sirhind, and still proceeding south-west, joins the Sursooty in lat. 29° 29', long. 76° 39', having run from its source to this point about seventy miles. This river, like the Sursooty to the east, and the Gagur to the west, flows through a shallow valley twenty-nine miles wide, and so level that, in time of inundation, the three rivers communicate by means of numerous branches, forming a maze of streams; and in extraordinary floods all unite, the whole country, except the elevated sites of villages, being laid under water: at other times, like the rest of the streams of Sirhind, it becomes "a mere thread of running water."

MAROOT, in Bhawlpoor, a town in the desert extending through the eastern part of that state, is situate on the route from the town of Bhawlpoor to Bhutneer, and 60 miles E. of the former place. It is surrounded with a mud wall of considerable extent, having numerous bastions. Maroot is in lat. 29° 5', long. 72° 40'.

MAROT, in the British district of Bhutteeana, lieut.-gov. of the N.W. Provinces, a small town or village close to the north-east frontier towards Sirhind. Lat. 30° 10', long. 74° 35'.

MAROUT.—A town in the Rajpoot state of Jodhpoor, situate 140 miles E.N.E. from Jodhpoor, and 52 miles N.E. by N. from Ajmeer. Lat. 27° 5', long. 75° 10'.

MAROWA, in the British district of Benares, lieut.-gov. of the N.W. Provinces, a village on the right bank of the Ganges, 659 miles N.W. of Calcutta by water, 10 N.E. of Benares. Lat. 25° 22', long. 83° 10'.

MAROWRA.—A town in Bundelkund, 22 miles W. by N. from Shahgurh, and 37 miles N. from Saugur. Lat. 24° 22', long. 78° 50'.

MARTABAN.—A town in the British province of Pegue, situate on the east bank of the Salween, immediately opposite the British station of Moulmein. It is a place of no strength, and upon the breaking out of the Burmese war in 1852, it was the first of the enemy's possessions which fell before the British arms. On the 4th April, a fire was opened upon the town from her Majesty's steamer *Rattler*, which had taken up a position at a short distance from the defences, and the garrison offering little resistance, the place became an easy conquest. (See also PEGUE.) Lat. 16° 30', long. 97° 40'.

MARTEE KHAN KA TANDA, in Sinde, a town on the route from Khyerpoor to Hyderabad, and 16 miles S.W. of the former place. Lat. 27° 20', long. 68° 36'.

MARUDGEE.—A town in the British district of Dharwar, presidency of Bombay, nine miles E. of Dharwar. Lat. 15° 29', long. 75° 11'.

MARUPOOR, in the British district of Furruckabad, lieut.-gov. of the N.W. Provinces, a town on the route from Etawa to Futtehgurh, and 13 miles S.W. of the latter. Lat. 27° 14', long. 79° 37'.

MARWAR.—See JOUDPORE.

MASHO.—A town in the dominions of

Gholab Singh, the ruler of Cashmere, situate on the left bank of the Senge Khobab or Indus river, and 158 miles E. from Sirinagur. Lat. 34° 1′, long. 77° 44′.

MASIRANI, in Gurhwal, on the southern frontier, a peak on the range bounding the Debra Doon to the north, and stretching along the left bank of the Aglar, a feeder of the Jumna. It is situate about five miles west of the sanatory station of Mussouree. Elevation above the sea 7,888 feet. Lat. 30° 28′, long. 78° 7′.

MASSEY.—A town in the territory of Oude, situate on the left bank of the Goomtee river, and 37 miles N.W. by N. from Lucknow. Lat. 27° 20′, long. 80° 43′.

MASTEE.—A town in the Mysore, 93 miles E.N.E. from Seringapatam, and 158 miles W. from Madras. Lat. 12° 53′, long. 78° 3′.

MASULIPATAM.—A British district, named from its principal place, within the limits of the presidency of Madras. It is bounded on the north by Hydrabad, or the territory of the Nizam; on the north-east and east by the British district Rajahmundry; on the south east by the Bay of Bengal; and on the south-west by the river Kistnah, dividing it from the British district Guntoor. It lies between lat. 15° 45′—17° 13′, long. 80° 5′—81° 49′, and embraces an area, according to official return, of 5,000 square miles. The seacoast commences from the south-western or mouth of the Kistnah, and has a direction north-east for twenty-nine miles, to Point Divy, at the mouth of the great north-eastern branch of that river. The coast between these points is very low, and ships can scarcely sight it in some parts, shoals extending five or six miles seawards. It is conjectured, not without probability, that those shoals have been formed by the earth swept down the branches of the Kistnah during the rains. At Point Divy the shore takes a direction northward for fifteen miles, to the town of Masulipatam, where it turns to the north-east, following that direction for twenty-eight miles, and subsequently turns eastward for fifteen miles, forming an indenture in the coast, called the Bay of Masulipatam. Narsipore, situate just beyond the coast belonging to this district, at the eastern extremity of the bay, and on the eastern side of the mouth of the western branch of the Godavery, though having but eight or nine feet of water on the bar, and four or five fathoms inside, is the only port in the neighbourhood for shipping, even of that small draught, as the Chinnapuram Canal, which joins the sea at Masulipatam, admits boats only, and those but at high water, they being at other times excluded by a hard bar of sand. The low country extends inland and westward for between forty or fifty miles, and at some distance from the sea becomes more depressed than the shore, which is somewhat elevated by the sand thrown up by the waves, and raised by the winds into low ridges and hillocks. In one place the depression is so great that the rains of the mousoons accumulating, form the lake of Colair, having an area of twenty square miles. Into this lake flow the redundant waters of the Kistnah and the Godavery, by channels proceeding from both rivers. As the waterways of these great streams, where they flow into the district, are much above the average level of its surface, probably no tract of equal extent has to a greater degree facilities for irrigation; yet, for ages, such was the disregard of this advantage, that the crops were allowed to depend on the annual amount of rain-fall, which is extremely precarious; and during three years, 1764, 1765, and 1766, so little rain fell, that the country was desolated; and it has been estimated that one-half of the population perished. The British government, alive to the importance of improving the means provided by the bounty of naturo for averting such fearful results, has, at great cost, established an extensive system of irrigation, in connection with the rivers Godavery and Kistnah. In 1849, the sum of 91,000*l.* was authorized to be expended on the former river, and in the following year, 150,000*l.* on the latter. The hilly country commences about fifty miles inland, or westward from the coast, and attains its greatest elevation (about 1,700 feet) in the vicinity of Condapilly. In the geological formation, a variety of gneiss, which contains garnets instead of mica (though the latter sometimes co-exist), is the predominant rock. Sienite, limestone, granite, and other formations occur. At Malavilly, diamonds are found in a detritus consisting of a mixture of disintegrated sandstone, hornstone, iron-ore, and kunkar or calcareous conglomerate. Iron-ore abounds in many places, and roofing-slate, marble, and limestone are also met with. The great river Godavery throws off a branch, which, for a short distance, flows along the eastern boundary of this district towards Rajahmundry. Above the divarication, this river, during the season of inundation in June and July, rolls down in a rapid and deep current a mile wide. The Kistnah, flowing from the west, from the territory of the Nizam, touches on this district at its confluence with the Pallair, and turning south-east for eighty-five miles, separates Masulipatam from the British district Guntoor as far as Boburlunka, where it divides, sending to the southward one branch, which for twenty-five miles continues to separate the two districts as above, and then falls into the Bay of Bengal; and another, which, flowing south-east for twenty-eight miles, falls into the bay somewhat higher. The delta inclosed by these branches is traversed by others of less magnitude, which are numerous during inundations. The Moonyair, flowing from Hydrabad, or the territory of the Nizam, in a southern direction, falls into the Kistnah. The bed of the Kistnah is sandy, its channel deep, and the body of water considerable during inundation, but at other times rather scanty, so that it is of no avail for the purposes of navigation, except at the estuaries of its various branches, which are in some instances navigable for small craft for a few miles from the sea. Its water is remarkably limpid, and free from any unpleasant or injurious admixture; and so considerable is its volume during inundations, that it fills the entire channel, which is at least a mile and a half wide. The seasons may be divided into the hot, rainy, and cold. The hot season commences in March, and ends in the first week in June; the rainy lasts from June until the end of October; the cold commences in November, and terminates about the end of February; and during this period the sky is generally clear, with a sharp wind from the north-east. March and April constitute the most disagreeable part of the year, the wind then setting in from the south-west, and being very relaxing and debilitating. May is the hottest month; but the excessive heat is mitigated by the sea-breeze, which sets in early in the afternoon. The commencement of the rains lowers the temperature many degrees. Of wild animals, there are the bear, hyæna, wolf, jackal, wild swine, wild buffalo, antelope, and hare: tigers infest the jungles and gorges of the hills in great numbers, and are of extraordinary size, one having been killed about fourteen or fifteen feet in length. The soil in the plain is alluvial, and very fertile, except in the vicinity of the seashore, where it is rather sandy. The cultivation of rice was formerly not considerable, though the soil was favourable to it; but with the extensive means of irrigation now available, its production in large quantities, and of a high degree of excellence, may be looked for. Various kinds of millet, maize, gram, and other pulse, oil-seeds, and other dry grain, are abundantly produced. Of commercial crops, the principal are chay-root (Oldenlandia umbellata), indigo and some other dye-stuffs, tobacco, and cotton. Of this last crop the quantity produced is sufficient to render it an article of exportation. A gradual falling off of late years in the revenue of this district tended to excite the suspicions of government, and led to an investigation, which resulted in the discovery of a gross system of fraud and oppression on the part of the native establishment.

Manufactures are few and insignificant, except those in cotton carried on in the town of Masulipatam. A trifling quantity of iron-ore is raised and smelted among the hills; but the diamond-mines, once celebrated, are now but little worked. The population is given under the article MADRAS. Masulipatam, the principal place, Condapilly, and Ellore, are described under their respective names in the alphabetical arrangement. The principal routes are—1. That from Calcutta, from north-east to south-west, along the coast, through Masulipatam and Ongole, to Madras; 2. in the same direction, but more inland, through Ellore, Guntoor, and Ongole, to Madras; 3. from south-east to north-west, from Masulipatam, through Bezawada, to Hydrabad. Masulipatam is one of the five Northern Circars which were obtained by the French in 1753, and remained in their possession till 1759, when Clive transferred them to the East-India Company, to whom they were formally ceded in 1765, by the emperor of Delhi.

MASULIPATAM, the principal place of the British district of the same name, presidency of Madras, is situate on the Golconda coast, or western shore of the Bay of Bengal, and on the north side of the mouth of a branch of the river Kistnah. The shore is flat, and water very shallow, the depth in approaching it being not more than half a fathom for the distance of nearly a mile; consequently ships must be anchored four or five miles from land, and abreast of the town. During the north-east monsoon, from the middle of October to the middle of December, it is unfrequented by shipping. The Chinnapuram Canal, communicating with the sea about a mile and a half south-east of the fort, and passing close on the south side of its rampart, is navigable up to it for small craft, which ply with cargoes of bricks, tiles, and wood, and, proceeding past the town, joins the river Kistnah, about fifteen miles farther to the north-west. It can be entered from the sea, even by boats, only at high water, as at other times it is closed by a bar of hard sand, on which a violent surf beats, so as to dash to pieces any craft exposed to it. The town is situate in an extensive plain, stretching westward to the Ghats, and in an unhealthy marshy situation, the atmosphere having the characteristic odour of such pestiferous places, arising from the putrefaction of the lacustrine plants, the Salicorniæ principally. In the midst of this swamp, which is overflowed by the sea at spring tides, stands the fort, the ground-plan of which is an oblong rectangle, 800 yards in length and 600 in breadth, with high ramparts and a wide and deep ditch. Within this inclosure are the arsenal, the powder-magazine, the garrison hospital, and barracks for one European and one native regiment; a Protestant church and a Romanist chapel; besides several large houses. There is no good water within the fort, that used for drinking being brought from sources outside the walls. Formerly it was conveyed, by means of a covered channel, into a reservoir; but those works have been allowed to fall into decay. The cantonment and the pettah are situate on a slightly elevated ridge a mile north-west of the fort, four miles and a half in length, and one mile in breadth. It is highest near its south-west extremity: towards the native town, it falls so considerably, as to leave the greater part of both that and the cantonment but little raised above the level of the swamps when flooded. The pettah or native town is situate south-west of the cantonment, and has some wide and airy streets, tolerably straight and well built. In the middle of the pettah, at the spot where two principal streets cross each other, are placed erect, and arranged in a circular form, thirty-three large slabs, of a compact limestone, covered with numerous figures, in basso and alto-rilievo, of the most exquisite execution. The delicate skill and taste displayed in the figures, their anatomical correctness, and the nature and freedom in their positions and attitudes, are said to rival the highest efforts of Italian genius. They were brought from the ruins of a pagoda about seven miles from this town; and some, at least, of the sculptured subjects are conjectured to be representations of the ceremonies of the Jain tribe. There is one large square in the native town, tolerably well built, and in which the markets are held. It bears the name of Mr. Robertson, a servant of the East-India Company, through whose exertions, when assistant to the collector here, it was made, and the vicinity much improved. Many of the houses in the town are large, and well built of brick and lime-mortar, with upper stories and tiled roofs; and even most of the dwellings of the poor are commodious and clean, in consequence of the neatness indispensably required for the manufacture of cotton fabrics, in which many of them are engaged. This branch of industry has of late years been somewhat circumscribed by the effects of the competition of British skill and capital, but it is still not inconsiderable. The operations carried on, include weaving, printing, bleaching, washing, and dressing tartans, ginghams, towels, table-linens, and other articles; and the assiduous and provident habits of the people are indicated by their well-dressed creditable appearance. The population, according to the census of 1837, amounted to 27,884; of this number, 24,029 were Hindoos, and 3,855 Mussulmans; which last class comprised many persons from Western India and Persia, engaged in trade. Distance from Bangalore, N.E., 325 miles; Hydrabad, S.E., 195; Nellore, N.E., 135; Madras, N., 215. Lat. 16° 10′, long. 81° 13′.

MATABHANGA.—A large watercourse in the Delta of the Ganges. Issuing from that river in lat. 24° 3′, long. 88° 45′, it takes a circuitous but generally southerly course for 103 miles, through the British district of Nuddea, and falls into the Hoogly river in lat. 23° 9′, long. 88° 26′. Its channel is said to have been formerly much deeper, and to have afforded the means of transit between Calcutta and the eastern portion of Bengal.

MATAN, in Cashmere, a karywa or table-land extending from the town of Islamabad to the base of the range inclosing the valley on the east. On a slight eminence at its western extremity, are situated the ruins of a very ancient building, which excites in all spectators feelings of admiration approaching to awe, by the elaborate skill displayed in its construction, and the simple, massive, and sublime character of its architecture. Hügel supposes that it was dedicated to the worship of the *linga*, and assigns the date of its erection to the period intervening between the waning of Buddhism and the establishment of Brahminism. In common with others who have visited these ruins, he regrets the weakness of language to express the feelings to which they give rise. "My description unfortunately gives little conception of the impression produced by this simple majestic structure, which I class amongst the finest ruins of the world. The forms are throughout noble, and the embellishments often tasteful; but it is peculiarly characterized by the huge masses of which it is constructed; and the effect of these is heightened by the dark hue of the marble, and the desolation in which it stands in the most fruitful valley in the world." These ruins are situate in lat. 33° 42′, long. 75° 21′.

MATCHUACAL.—A town in the British district of Tipperah, lieut.-gov. of Bengal, 27 miles W. by S. of Tipperah. Lat. 23° 22′, long. 90° 46′.

MATEGAON, in the British territory of Saugur and Nurbudda, lieut.-gov. of the N.W. Provinces, a town on the route from Nagpoor to Ramgurh, 62 miles S.W. of the latter. Lat. 22° 8′, long. 80° 21′.

MATHINGUMBO.—A town in the native state of Nepal, 71 miles E.N.E. from Khatmandoo, and 136 miles N. by E. from Durbunga. Lat. 28° 4′, long. 86° 22′.

MATIL, in Keonthul, a village in the district of Poondur, and on the south-eastern declivity of the high ridge forming the greater part of it. Here, during the operations of the invasion of the Goorkhas, a body of about 6,000 of their troops gave a bloody defeat to the natives of Poondur, and utterly broke their power. Lat. 31° 1′, long. 77° 39′.

MATTA BURAILEE.—A town of Malwa, in the native state of Bhopal, 70 miles E. from Bhopal, and 53 miles S.S.W. from Saugur. Lat. 23° 8′, long. 78° 28′.

MAUCLY DROOG, in the Mysore, a hill fort, with a small town at its base, in the tallook or subdivision of the same name, situate amidst the mountains north-west of Nundy Droog, from which it is distant 13 miles; from Bangalore, N., 33. Lat. 13° 26′, long. 77° 34′.

MAUGRY, or MAGERI, in the Mysore, an ancient fortified town, the principal place of a tallook or subdivision of the same name, situate on a rock, amidst dense and luxuriant forests, and separated by a deep rugged ravine, and a stream flowing through it, from the celebrated hill fort Savan Droog, situate four miles to the south-east. At Guttypoor, in its vicinity, is abundance of fine iron-ore, reducible into excellent iron and steel. The forests yield excellent sandal-wood, but its value has caused the trees to be cut with ruinous wastefulness. Maugry has a considerable tank and numerous ruined temples. Distance from Bangalore, W., 23 miles; Seringapatam, N.E., 53 miles. Lat. 12° 57′, long. 77° 17′.

MAULMASEER.—A town in the territory of Oude, situate five miles W. of the right bank of the Goomtee river, and 18 miles N.W. from Lucknow. Lat. 27° 1′, long. 80° 50′.

MAULPOOR, in Guzerat, or territory of the Guicowar, a town on the route from Mow to Deesa, 200 miles N.W. of former, 126 S.E. of latter. It is situate at the base of a low range of hills, has a bazar, and is supplied with water from wells and a tank, and belongs to a petty chief subject to the control of the British resident at Indor. Lat. 23° 20′, long. 73° 28′.

MAUMDOOR. — A town in the British district of North Arcot, presidency of Madras, 47 miles S.W. by W. of Madras. Lat. 12° 45′, long. 79° 45′.

MAUNBHOOM.—See PACHETE and BARABHOOM.

MAUNDEE.—A town in the British district of Burraboom, lieut.-gov. of Bengal, situate 114 miles W.N.W. of Calcutta. Lat. 23° 4′, long. 86° 45′.

MAUNDPOOR.—A town in the native state of Sirgoojah, 40 miles N. from Sirgoojah, and 51 miles W. by S. from Palamow. Lat. 23° 41′, long. 83° 13′.

MAUNDVEE.—See MANDAVEE.

MAUNGUNGE, in the British district of Cawnpore, lieut.-gov. of the N.W. Provinces, a village on the route from the cantonment of Etawa to that of Cawnpore, and 50 miles W. of the latter. The road in this part of the route is good, the country cultivated. Lat. 26° 21′, long. 79° 42′.

MAUNKAIRA, or MUNKERE, in the Punjab, a town situate in the doab between the Jhelum and Indus. It is surrounded by a mud wall, and has a citadel built of burnt brick; but its principal defence is considered to be its position amidst arid sandhills, which afford no water to invaders. Runjeet Singh, when he invested it, at the close of 1821, supplied his troops at first with water carried for a considerable distance by beasts of burthen, and then without delay proceeded to dig an adequate number of wells. The siege was pressed with so much vigour and success, that the nawab, Hafiz Ahmed, surrendered to the Sikh ruler, on condition of being indemnified by a jaghire in the Derajat. Maunkaira is in lat. 31° 18′, long. 71° 24′.

MAUNSA, in Guzerat, or dominions of the Guicowar, a town near the right bank of the river Saburmuttee: population estimated at 7,000. Distance from Ahmedabad, N., 30 miles; Baroda, N.W., 85. Lat. 23° 26′, long. 72° 40′.

MAUVINHOLA.—A town in the Mysore, 151 miles N.W. from Seringapatam, and 79 miles N. by E. from Mangalore. Lat. 13° 58′, long. 75° 10′.

MAYAKOT.—A town in the native state of Nepal, 193 miles W.N.W. from Khatmandoo, and 157 miles N.N.W. from Goruckpoor. Lat. 28° 46′, long. 82° 25′.

MAYAPOOR. — A town in the British district of Palamow, lieut.-gov. of Bengal, 11 miles S.W. by W. of Palamow. Lat. 23° 45′, long. 83° 53′.

MAYENOUNG. — A town in the British district of Pegue, situate on the right bank of the Irawady river, and 38 miles S. from Prome. Lat. 19° 31′, long. 94° 27′.

MAYUNEE. — A town in the British province of Sattara, presidency of Bombay, 40 miles E. by S. of Sattara. Lat. 17° 25′, long. 74° 37′.

MAZAGON.—A small village in the island of Bombay, distant direct from Bombay fort one mile and three-quarters. Mazagon has a dock for small vessels. Lat. 18° 58′, long. 72° 53′.

MAZUFURABAD, in the Punjab, a town at the confluence of the Jhelum and its great tributary the Kishengunga. It is a place of some importance, chiefly on account of its commanding position at the entrance of the Baramula Pass into Cashmere. There are ferries over both the Kishengunga and the Jhelum. The emperor Aurungzebe built a fort here, which was subsequently replaced by one of greater strength, erected by the Afghan governor Ata Mahomed. Lat. 34° 24′, long. 73° 22′.

MEADAY.—A town on the left bank of the Irawady river, in the British district of Pegue, 35 miles N. from Prome. This village was destroyed by fire on the retreat of the Burmese from Prome in 1825, and has been rebuilt near the frontier line separating Burmah from the British province of Pegue. Lat. 19° 17′, long. 95°.

MEAHSOO, in the Sinde Sagur Dooab division of the Punjab, a town situated 12 miles W. from the right bank of the Chenaub, 71 miles N.N.E. of the town of Mooltan. Lat. 31° 2′, long. 72°.

MEAWALLEH, in the Sinde Sagur Dooab division of the Punjab, a town situated on the left bank of the Indus, 70 miles N.N.W. of the town of Mooltan. Lat. 31° 1′, long. 70° 57′.

MEDDUCK. — A town in Hyderabad, or territory of the Nizam, situate on the right bank of the Manjera river, and 51 miles N. from Hyderabad. Lat. 18° 4′, long. 78° 18′.

MEDIRYEN COATA.—A town in one of the recently sequestrated districts of Hyderabad, or dominions of the Nizam, situate nine miles S.E. from the right bank of the Kistnah river, and 20 miles N.E. from Moodgul. Lat. 16° 13′, long. 76° 42′.

MEDNA.—A town in the native state of Sonepoor, on the south-west frontier of Bengal, 20 miles W. by N. from Sonepoor, and 38 miles S.S.W. from Sumbulpoor. Lat. 20° 58′, long. 83° 49′.

MEEAHGUNJ, in the territory of Oude,

a town on the route, by Nanamau ghat or ferry, from Futtehgurh to Lucknow, 77 miles S.E. of the former, 34 W. of the latter. It was built towards the close of the last century, by the eunuch Almas Ali Khan, the able and powerful financial minister of Saadat Ali, nawaub vizier of Oude. Lord Valentia, who saw it in 1803, when inhabited by Almas, states that it contained his house, a large and neat structure, and three convenient seraes; and adds, "It seems populous, and in a thriving condition, forming a complete contrast to the wretched villages we have hitherto met." Heber, twenty years later, found "trees, towers, gates, and palaces, sinking fast into rubbish and forgetfulness;" the park under crops of grain, and a poor bazar in the fort. The river Sace is traversed a little east of the town by a fine bridge, constructed partly of brick, partly of stone, by Almas, and since his death allowed to fall to ruin. Lat. 26° 48′, long. 80° 33′.

MEEAN DOOAB.—A name sometimes given to the Julinder Dooab, which see.

MEEANEE, in the peninsula of Kattywar, province of Guzerat, a town situate in the prant or district of Burda, and lying on the south-western coast. Affording no shelter for shipping, its traffic is inconsiderable. Distant from Ahmedabad, S.W., 220 miles; Baroda, W., 240. Lat. 21° 50′, long. 69° 31′.

MEEANEE, in Sinde, a village on the route from Hyderabad to Cutch, and six miles S. of the former place, is situate on the left or eastern bank of the Indus. This village is in lat. 25° 20′, long. 68° 20′.

MEEANEE, in Sinde, a village on the banks of the Fulailee branch of the Indus, and six miles N. of Hyderabad. It will long be celebrated as the scene of a great victory obtained here by the Anglo-Indian army, under Sir Charles Napier, over a much more numerous force of the Belooches, headed by the ameers of Sinde. The British general, having ascertained by his emissaries that between 20,000 and 30,000 men, the finest troops of the Belooche nation, were drawn up on the banks of the Fulailee in his front, and that the lapse of another day would place nearly 30,000 more in his rear and on his left flank, moved forward to extricate himself from this threatening situation, and gave the enemy battle, on February 17th, 1843, though his own force amounted to but 2,800 men of all arms, and twelve pieces of artillery. The Belooche force actually on the ground amounted to 22,000 men, with fifteen pieces of artillery. After a close and obstinate engagement for above three hours, during which those brave barbarians showed desperate valour, the right of their position was carried by the Anglo-Indian cavalry, and their army totally routed, losing "artillery, ammunition, standards, and camp, with considerable stores, and some treasure." The British lost 256 men killed and wounded, the enemy about 5,000. Six of the principal members of the Talpoor dynasty immediately surrendered themselves. A local monument has been erected over the remains of the British who fell in the battle. Meeanee is in lat. 25° 26′, long. 68° 26′.

MEEANGUNJ.—See MEEAHGUNJ.

MEECHOO.—A tribe inhabiting a portion of the unsurveyed valley to the east of the native state of Bhotan. Lat. 27° 35′, long. 93°.

MEEMBAH.—A town of Burmah, situate on the right bank of the Irawady, and 48 miles N. from Prome. Lat. 19° 28′, long. 94° 57′.

MEENA.—A town in the British district of Dinajepoor, lieut.-gov. of Bengal, 35 miles S.W. of Dinajepoor. Lat. 25° 15′, long. 88° 11′.

MEENAPARA, in the Rajpoot state of Jeypore, a village on the route from Agra to Mow, 107 miles S.W. of former, 318 N.E. of latter, situate on the small river Bunhun. Lat. 26° 30′, long. 76° 47′.

MEENUJ.—A town in the British district of Sholapoor, presidency of Bombay, 47 miles E.S.E. of Beejapoor. Lat. 16° 27′, long. 76° 21′.

MEERANPOOR, in the British district of Mozuffurnuggur, lieut.-gov. of the N.W. Provinces, a village on the route from Daranagur to Khutowlee, and 14 miles E. of the latter. Lat. 29° 17′, long. 78° 1′.

MEERANPOOR KUTRA, in the British district of Shahjehanpoor, lieut.-gov. of the N.W. Provinces, a town on the route from the town of Bareilly to Shahjehanpoor, and 27 miles S.E. of the former. It has a bazar, and is situate at the spot where the road to Futtehgurh passes off to the right from the direct line to Shahjehanpoor. Near this place, in 1774, the British army under Colonel Champion, supporting the cause of Shuja-huddawlah, nawaub of Oude, utterly defeated a greatly superior force of Rohilla Pathans. This engagement is variously named the battle of Cutterah or Kutra, of Futtehgunge, of Tessunah or Tessua, and of St. George. Kutra is in lat. 28° 2′, long. 79° 43′.

MEEREE, in the Daman division of the Punjab, a town situated 48 miles W. from the right bank of the Indus, 120 miles S.W. by S. of the town of Peshawur. Lat. 32° 37′, long. 70° 30′.

MEEREE KHO, or NAMKIOO RIVER.—The name given to the Irawaddy in the upper part of its course.—(See IRAWADDY.)

MEERGUNGE, in the British district of Goruckpore, lieut.-gov. of the N.W. Provinces, a town situate on the route from Goruckpore cantonment to Lucknow, 28 miles N.W. of the former, 138 E. of the latter. It has a bazar, and is supplied with good water. The road in this part of the route is good. Lat. 26° 45′, long. 83° 5′.

MEERGUNGE, in the British district of

Bareilly, lieut.-gov. of the N.W. Provinces, a town on the route from the town of Bareilly to Moradabad, and 21 miles N.W. of the former. It is inhabited by Rohilla Pathans, has a bazar and market, and is well supplied with water. Lat. 28° 32′, long. 79° 16′.

MEERGUNJE.—A town in the British district of Rajeshaye, lieut.-gov. of Bengal, 116 miles N. by E. of Calcutta. Lat. 24° 14′, long. 88° 43′.

MEERGURH, in Bhawlpoor, a town in the desert extending through the eastern part of that state. The town consists of several dwelling-houses and a few shops, defended by a small brick-built fort: there is a good supply of water from wells, to which the cattle from a large tract of the surrounding desert have recourse. Meergurh is in lat. 29° 10′, long. 72° 52′.

MEERHAUSER.—A river rising in Bundelcund, in lat. 24° 39′, long. 80° 23′. It holds a south-easterly course of about forty miles, and falls into the river Cane on the right side, in lat. 24° 26′, long. 80°.

MEERKHAN TANA.—A town in the British district of Kurrachee, province of Sinde, presidency of Bombay, 74 miles N.E. of Kurrachee. Lat. 25° 30′, long. 67° 58′.

MEERPOOR, in the British district of Allygurh, lieut.-gov. of the N.W. Provinces, a village near the northern frontier, 50 miles S.E. of Delhi. Lat. 28° 4′, long. 77° 48′.

MEERPOOR.—A town in the dominions of Gholab Singh, the ruler of Cashmere, 92 miles S.W. from Sirinagur, and 113 miles N. from Lahore. Lat. 33° 9′, long. 73° 50′.

MEERPOOR.—A town in the British district of Hydrabad, province of Sinde, presidency of Bombay, 40 miles E.N.E. of Hydrabad. Lat. 25° 34′, long. 69° 2′.

MEERPOOR, in Sinde, a flourishing town near the left or eastern bank of the Pinyaree, a great branch of the Indus, and on the route from Cutch to Hyderabad. The surrounding country, which is fertile, well cultivated, and productive, yielded annually a revenue equal to 50,000*l.* to the ameer of Meerpoor, the least important and wealthy of the ameers of Sinde. This town is of importance as commanding the line of communication between Cutch and Sinde. Population 10,000. Lat. 24° 41′, long. 68° 20′.

MEERPUR.—See MEOPUR.

MEERUJ.—A town in the Southern Mahratta jaghire of Meeruj, situate 29 miles E.N.E. from Kolapoor, and 72 miles S.E. from Sattara. The revenues of the jaghire are returned at 17,502*l.* Its chief was bound to furnish a small contingent of horse to the British government, but the obligation has been commuted for a money payment. The young chief, Gungadhur Rao Bala, attained his majority some years since, and assumed the administration. Lat. 16° 50′, long. 74° 42′.

MEERUJGAON.—A town in the British district of Ahmednuggur, presidency of Bombay, 145 miles E. of Bombay. Lat. 18° 46′, long. 75° 4′.

MEERUNGLOOA.—A town of Eastern India, in the British district of Aracan, 51 miles W. of Aracan. Lat. 20° 35′, long. 92° 38′.

MEERUT.—A British district under the lieut.-gov. of the N.W. Provinces, named from its principal place. It is bounded on the north by the British district Mozuffurnugur; on the east by the British districts Bijnour and Moradabad; on the south by the British district Boolundshuhur; and on the west by the British districts Paneeput and Delhi. It lies between lat. 28° 33′—29° 17′, long. 77° 12′—78° 15′; is about fifty-seven miles in length from east to west, and forty-eight in breadth: its area is 2,332 square miles. This district forms part of the Doab, and on the east is washed by the Ganges, which is navigable from the sea to Sukertal, a short distance north of the northern boundary; on the west it is separated from the adjacent districts by the Jumna, which, though at its exit from the mountains discharging 4,000 cubic feet of water in a second, is so reduced in volume by the draughts required to supply the canals of Delhi, of Feroz Shah, and of the Doab, that below the dam constructed for effecting that purpose, it can be crossed dry-shod; yet the under-current which percolates the gravelly bed, together with the drainage of the intermediate country, furnish a navigable stream of water at Agra, a distance of 260 miles by the river's course; and it is inferred from this example, that in abstracting the supply required for the Ganges Canal at Kunkul, the navigation of that river will not be injured below Cawnpore. The surface of the country rises in the middle of the Doab, so as to form a ridge of inconsiderable elevation, declining eastward to the Ganges, and westward to the Jumna. Along this high ground proceeds the line of the Ganges Canal, which, drawing its supply from the right side of that river, near Hurdwar, and traversing the middle of the Doab, discharges its redundant volume, or "tail-water," as it is technically termed, into the parent stream at Cawnpore. The line of this canal for about fifty miles passes through the district of Meerut. Besides the lateral slope of the surface east and west, to the two great bounding rivers, there is a general slope from north to south, as indicated by the course taken by the Ganges, Jumna, Hindun, East Kalee-Nudee, West Kalee-Nudee, and some other streams of less importance. From the levels taken for the construction of the Ganges Canal, the inclination of the surface in this district has been ascertained to average, in round numbers, a foot and a half per mile; the absolute elevation above the sea of the most northern and elevated part is about 900 feet. Muhammudpoor, on the northern boundary, is

894 feet above the sea; and the district being remarkably level, probably no spot throughout it is much higher. Faridnagar, close to the southern boundary, is 834 feet above the sea.

The climate is so favourable, that it produces nearly all the vegetables and fruits of Europe, as well as those of the tropics; and the same fields which in the cool season are covered with crops of wheat, are in the wet bearing sugar-cane, indigo, and cotton. The vicinity of the mountains, the comparatively high latitude, and considerable elevation, render the district one of the healthiest parts of the plain of India. The weather for five months, from November to March, is delightfully cool and invigorating. The prevailing winds are westerly and northerly, with little rain. In January, the ground in the morning is frequently covered with hoar frost, and woollen clothing and fires are found necessary to comfort. In April, the hot westerly winds commence, and, sweeping over the great sandy desert of Scinde and Rajpootana, are arid as well as sultry. The time immediately preceding the setting in of the rains, in the latter part of June, is rather unhealthy; but the heat diminishes, and an improvement takes place, after the commencement of the regular rainy season, which continues, with slight intermission, until the commencement of September. The last-mentioned month is cloudy, with little wind; occasionally extremely hot and exhausting, and altogether the most unhealthy period of the year. In October, though the days are very hot, the nights become gradually cool and pleasant. The population, according to the census of 1853, amounted to 1,135,072. Of these there are, Hindoos employed in agriculture, 427,785; Hindoos non-agricultural, 457,453; Mahometans and others, not being Hindoos, employed in agriculture, 82,350; non-agricultural, 167,484. Thus it appears that the majority of the inhabitants are Hindoo in creed and non-agricultural in occupation. The following classification of the towns and villages is drawn from the vernacular Mouzawar returns submitted by the collector of the revenue:—

Number containing less than 1,000 inhabitants..	1,077
Ditto more than 1,000 and less than 5,000......	288
Ditto more than 5,000 and less than 10,000	5
Ditto more than 10,000 and less than 50,000....	
Total........................	1,373

The land-assessment is fixed for a term of years, which will expire on the 1st July, 1865.

After experiencing a full share of the vicissitude and suffering incidental to a state of society where war is the chief occupation, and conquest almost the only object of pursuit among kings and chieftains, Meerut was embodied into the empire of the Timurian sovereigns of Delhi. It was wrested from them by the Mahrattas, and formed part of the tract ceded to the East-India Company by Dowlut Rao Scindia, in 1803, under the treaty of Serjee Anjengaum. In this district the infamous Sumroo obtained a jaghire, which, on his death, fell to his widow, the celebrated, or rather notorious, Begum Sumroo. Sumroo was either a Swiss or a German by birth: he had served in the French army, under the name of Walter Reinhard, but deserted, and in or about the year 1760 arrived in Bengal, where he bore the name of Walter Summers. After taking service under the English, the French, and divers native princes, he found in one of the latter a fitting master and suitable employment. Meer Cossim, known as the occupant of the musnud of Bengal in the interval between the expulsion of Jaffier Ali Khan and his subsequent restoration, thought him a proper instrument for effecting the massacre of a number of British prisoners. Sumroo, "nothing loth," accepted the office, and discharged it with atrocious fidelity. Forsaking Meer Cossim, when the star of that chief was on the decline, he served in rapid succession a variety of masters, from one of whom he received the jaghire in Meerut. The woman with whom Sumroo connected himself in marriage, was not unworthy of being the helpmate of such a man. She was a dancing-girl, of more than ordinary beauty and fascination; and to her blandishments Sumroo yielded himself a willing captive. She was not at once elevated to the rank of his wife. This step was the result of her own artful management; and when achieved, she perseveringly exercised the rights thereby attained, to raise herself to the actual enjoyment of all the powers derived from Sumroo's political station. Subsequently to the death of that respectable individual, she formed a matrimonial alliance with another European, named Vaisseaux or L'Oiseau, who had been an artilleryman in her service. The mode in which one of these husbands surrendered life was of a tragical character. Whether the result of jealousy, satiety, or some other cause, the Begum became anxious to get rid of her lord and master. To accomplish her purpose, she persuaded him that a plan had been laid for murdering both himself and her, and seizing on the jaghire, and urged him, thereupon, to collect without delay all the treasure that could readily be transported, and by flight save both their lives and a portion of their wealth. Having thus far succeeded, she extorted from her intended victim a vow, in which she joined, to the effect that, in case of their flight being intercepted, each party should by death secure escape from the probable consequences; and to enable her to effect this, should it become necessary, the lady, as well as her husband, carried arms. All arrangements being perfected, the fugitives with their treasure departed, under the cover of night; but scarcely had they passed the boundary of their own jaghire, than they encountered a party of troops, placed in the position which they occupied by order of the Begum. Resistance and recourse to flight seemed alike hopeless, and the report of a pistol from the Begum's palki, followed by loud cries from her attendants, assured the husband that his wife had performed her share in their mutual engagement. Portions of her garments stained with blood were exhibited to confirm the impression; and under the influence of terror, more probably than of conscientious regard for his pledge, the entrapped victim followed the supposed example of his wife, and with a pistol terminated his earthly existence. The sanguinary farce was now at an end; the Begum returned, and resumed her usual habits of life. Of the actual occurrence of the catastrophe above detailed, there appears no room to doubt; but it is somewhat strange that the authorities by whom it is recorded, should not agree as to whether it were the first or the second husband who was the suffering hero in the direful drama. Other fearful acts of atrocity stain the name of this wretched woman; and among them the murder of one of her slave-girls stands pre-eminent for cruelty. By some it is said that the girl's crime consisted in her having attracted the favourable notice of one of the Begum's husbands; but whatever the offence, her barbarous mistress visited it by causing her to be buried alive. The time chosen for the execution was the evening; the place, the tent of the Begum; who, causing her bed to be arranged immediately over the grave, occupied it till the morning, to prevent any attempt to rescue the miserable girl beneath. Notwithstanding these and similar deeds, the Begum lived in great power and splendour, secure in her jaghire under all circumstances, and obtained from the English government a recognition of her right, when, by the course of events, the East-India Company became supreme lords of the territory. Remorse, if she ever felt it, did not shorten her days; she lived to be nearly ninety years of age, and on her decease, which took place in 1836, the jaghire, including the town of Sirdhannah, lapsed to the British government.

MEERUT, the principal place of the British district, and also of the pergunnah of the same name, under the lieut.-gov. of the N.W. Provinces, is situated nearly in the middle of the district, being distant twenty-five miles from the Ganges on the east, and thirty from the Jumna on the west. The Kalee Nuddee flows about three miles to the eastward of the town, and a small branch from it passes through the station. The slope of the country is gentle towards the south; and the Kalee Nuddee, the banks of which are low and marshy, is lost in the widely-spread inundation during the rainy season, but at other times it is a small stream. The soil of the surrounding country is sandy, with a subsoil of kunkar or calcareous conglomerate, and it is covered with grass all the year round. The ruined wall of the town is extensive, inclosing a considerable space, throughout which are scattered "some good architectural remains of mosques and pagodas;" but the houses are wretchedly built, and the streets narrow and dirty. The most important structure in every point of view is the English church: Heber considered it much the largest which he had seen in India; and its organ as one of the best. The building is 150 feet long, eighty-four wide, and being galleried all round, can contain 3,000 persons. It has a high and handsome spire, and its appearance is striking; but the materials are very flimsy, being bad brick overlaid with stucco. The expense of its building was partly defrayed by grant from government, partly by funds raised by subscription; among the contributors to which it is for many reasons somewhat remarkable, that the Begum Sumroo was the most considerable, that extraordinary personage professing the Romish faith, while her life was little calculated to reflect credit upon any creed.

The cantonment of the British force stationed here is two miles north of the town, and is divided into two parts by a small branch of the Kalee Nuddee, over which are two handsome bridges, one built by the East-India Company, the other by the Begum Sumroo. On the northern side of the stream are lines for the accommodation of a brigade of horse-artillery, a European cavalry corps, and a regiment of European infantry, respectively separated from each other by intervals of several hundred yards. In front is a fine parade-ground, a mile in width and four miles in length, having ample space for field-battery practice and the manœuvres of horse-artillery. Upon the extreme right is the heavy battery. The head-quarters of artillery for the presidency of Bengal have been lately removed from Dum Dum to this place. Overlooking the parade are the barracks, with stables, hospitals, riding-schools, canteens, and other military offices. In the rear of the barracks and in a continued line three deep, are the bungalows or lodges of the officers, each surrounded by a garden about a hundred yards square. The barracks consist of a series of separate brick-built low-roofed structures, each consisting of one large and lofty room, surrounded by a spacious inclosed veranda, divided into apartments for the non-commissioned officers and the families of married men. On the opposite side of the stream are the cantonments of the native infantry, who have no barracks, but are quartered in mud huts: the officers are accommodated with detached bungalows. There is water at the depth of from eight to fifteen feet in the wells of the station: the quality is brackish, except from a few wells lined with brick, and for the most part constructed by the Mahrattas. Medical authorities consider the air very healthy for Europeans. In three years, a European regiment 1,120 strong lost only sixty men. The establishment of a military prison in this town has been sanctioned as an experimental measure, with the view of ascertaining the practicability of substituting local imprisonment for the present inefficient punishment of transportation. In hot weather, large quantities of ice are consumed, though to obtain a supply, it has been the practice to resort to a very tedious and laborious process. In mid-winter, a number of wide shallow earthen pans, each containing water to the depth of half an inch, are arranged over a layer of straw or sugarcane-leaf, and in chill nights become covered with ice an eighth or a fourth of an inch thick. These laminæ are carefully collected and stored in pits, lined throughout with thick layers of straw and reeds, and the water which drains off is received into a well of greater depth than that of the pit. The ice, when wanted for use, is wrapped in a coarse blanket, and conveyed to the place where required, in large baskets thickly padded with cotton. About 280 labourers and forty water-carriers employed in this way in a winter, produce 160,000 lb. of ice.

Meerut is noted for the hospitality of its residents, both civil and military, its amusements, and varied social enjoyments. At one time there were no less than five theatres, affording to the inhabitants and visitors the pleasure of dramatic performances; four of these Thespian establishments being supported by the privates of the several regiments. The population of the town, according to the latest return, is 29,014 inhabitants.

Probably the first authentic mention of Meerut is by Ferishta, who relates that the town, in the year 1017, capitulated to Mahmud of Ghuzni, and paid him a ransom of 250,000 dinars and thirty elephants. In 1327 it baffled the attack of Tarmasherin Khan, the formidable Mogul invader, from whom the king of Delhi had been obliged to purchase peace. In 1399 it fell before the sanguinary fury of Tamerlane, whose troops took it by escalade, sacked it, and demolished the walls. "The Gabrs were all flayed alive, their women and children made slaves, the houses burned, the walls razed, and the whole place reduced to dust and ashes."

The elevation of Meerut above the sea has not been accurately ascertained; but an approach to a correct estimation of it may be made by reference to the respective heights of Sirdhana, twelve miles to the north-west of Meerut, up the course of a canal, and that of Furreednuggur, sixteen miles south of it, lower down the slope of the country. The former is 882 feet, the latter 834 feet above the sea. Distance from Calcutta, *viâ* Delhi, 930 miles. Lat. 28° 59′, long. 77° 46′.

MEERZAPOOR.—A town in the British district of Shikarpoor, province of Scinde, presidency of Bombay, 11 miles S. of Shikarpoor. Lat. 27° 51′, long. 68° 39′.

MEETANEE.—A town in the British district of Hydrabad, province of Scinde, presidency of Bombay, 106 miles N. by W. of Hydrabad. Lat. 26° 52′, long. 68°.

MEETANEE.—A town in the peninsula of Kattywar, province of Guzerat, 18 miles N. from Rajkote, and 160 miles W. by N. from Baroda. Lat. 22° 32′, long. 70° 46′.

MEETEYEE, in the British district of Allygurh, lieut.-gov. of the N.W. Provinces, a village on the route from the city of Agra to Allygurh cantonment, and 29 miles N. of the former. Lat. 27° 33′, long. 78° 6′.

MEETHEEPOOR, in the British district of Etawa, lieut.-gov. of the N.W. Provinces, a village on the route from the cantonment of Agra to that of Etawa, and 16 miles N.W. of the latter. Lat. 26° 57′, long. 78° 53′.

MEETTEE.—A town in the British district of Hydrabad, province of Scinde, presidency of Bombay, 96 miles S.E. of Hydrabad. Lat. 24° 45′, long. 69° 50′.

MEETYALLA.—A town in the peninsula of Kattywar, province of Guzerat, situate 80 miles S.S.E. from Rajkote, and 100 miles E.S.E. from Poorbunder. Lat. 21° 12′, long. 71° 17′.

MEGANEE, or MEENGANA, in the Punjab, a thriving manufacturing town three or four miles from the left or eastern bank of the Chenaub. Lat. 31° 10′, long. 72° 12′.

MEGNA.—The name by which the Brahmapootra river is known during the lower part of its course. (See BRAHMAPOOTRA.)

MEHANEE.—A river rising in lat. 24° 2′, long. 85° 16′, ten miles W. of Hazareebagh, in the British district of Ramgurh, and flowing in a northerly direction for thirty miles through Ramgurh, and thirty-three through the British district of Behar, falls into the Lilajun river a few miles above the town of Gayah, and in lat. 24° 44′, long. 85° 4′.

MEHDOORA.—A town in the Rajpoot state of Jodhpoor, situate 161 miles W. by S. from the town of Jodhpoor. Lat. 25° 50′, long. 70° 39′.

MEHEDPOOR.—A town in one of the outlying possessions of Indore, or the territory belonging to the Holkar family. It is situate on the right bank of the river Seepra, in the angle formed by the confluence of a small feeder. Abreast of the town, the Seepra is traversed by the route from Neemuch, by means of ferry; but a short distance farther up, or more to the south, by a deep ford. The ground on the left bank of the Seepra was, in 1817, the scene of the decisive victory obtained by the British over the army of Holkar, whose power was in consequence effectually and irretrievably overthrown. The Mahrattas were commanded, at least ostensibly, by Mulhar Rao Holkar, and strongly posted on the left bank, behind batteries containing about seventy guns. The British army, commanded by Sir Thomas Hislop, crossed the river by the ford above the town, and in front of the left of the enemy's position, distant about 800 yards, and advancing under a murderous fire from the numerous and well-served Mahratta batteries, took them at the point of the bayonet, and routed the whole army. The enemy's camp, sixty-three guns, many of large calibre, and the ammunition-tumbrils, fell into the hands of the British, who, however, had 174 killed, including three European officers, and 604 wounded, of whom thirty-five were European officers. The loss of the Mahrattas was estimated at 3,000 men. The victory was decisive; no farther serious resistance was made; and in the treaty of Mundesor, concluded a few weeks afterwards, Holkar submitted to such terms as reduced him to the condition of an insignificant and virtually dependent power. Elevation above the sea 1,600 feet. Distance N. of Indor 53 miles, N. of Oojein 23, W. of Saugor 200, S.W. of Gawlior fort 250, S.W. of Agra 300. Lat. 23° 30′, long. 75° 40′.

MEHINDERGUNJE.—A town in the British district of Mymunsing, lieut.-gov. of Bengal, situate 24 miles N.W. by N. of Jumalpoor. Lat. 25° 11′, long. 89° 52′.

MEHMOODABAD.—A town in the British district of Kaira, presidency of Bombay, eight miles N.E. of Kaira. The streets of this town are level, broad, and clean. Lat. 22° 49′, long. 72° 45′.

MEHOAR, or MEHEWA, in the British district of Allahabad, lieut.-gov. of the N.W. Provinces, a village on the route, by Rajapoor ferry, from Allahabad cantonment to Banda, and 25 miles W. of the former. Lat. 25° 26′, long. 81° 34′.

MEHOONBARA.—A town in the British district of Candeish, presidency of Bombay, 27 miles E. of Malligaum. Lat. 20° 33′, long. 74° 55′.

MEHUM, or MOHIM, in the British district of Rohtuk, lieut.-gov. of the N.W. Provinces, a town on the route from Hansi to Delhi, and 24 miles S.E. of the former. It was formerly a large and important commercial town, but is now ruinous, though having still a good bazar, and a population of 5,660 inhabitants. Here is a very fine baoli or well, 130 feet deep, lined with stone, and having stairs of the same material twenty feet wide, reaching to the surface of the water. Lat. 28° 58′, long 76° 21′.

MEIL GHAUT.—A town in one of the recently sequestrated districts of Hyderabad, or territory of the Nizam, on the left bank of the Taptee river, and 38 miles N.W. from Ellichpoor. Lat. 21° 38′, long. 77° 15′.

MEINAH COTE, in the British district of Shahjehanpoor, lieut.-gov. of the N.W. Provinces, a village on the route from Pilleebheet to Oude, and 16 miles E. of the former. Lat. 28° 41′, long. 80° 8′.

MEINGHEOUNG.—A town of Burmah, situate on the left bank of the Irawady river, and 79 miles N. from Prome. Lat. 19° 54′, long. 94° 54′.

MEINTSTEIN.—A town of Burmah, situate 40 miles E. of the left bank of the Irawady, and 34 miles S.W. by S. from Ava. Lat. 21° 29′, long. 95° 43′.

MEKRAIME.—A town in the British province of Pegue, situate on the right bank of the Martaban river, 35 miles N. from Martaban or Salween river. Lat. 17° 1′ long. 97° 38′.

MELAKERI, in the Rajpoot state of Alwur, under the political superintendence of the Governor-General's agent for Rajpootana, a town on the route from Jeypoor, by Rajgurh, to the town of Alwur, and 15 miles S. of the latter. The soil of the surrounding country is sandy, but not arid, fresh water being everywhere obtainable in shallow wells. Lat. 27° 23′, long. 76° 42′.

MELLYPORE, in the British district of Bhagulpore, lieut.-gov. of Bengal, a town, the principal place of the pergunnah of the same name. It is situate pleasantly on the river Angjana, and contains 300 houses. Distant 28 miles S.W. of city of Monghyr. Lat. 25° 1′, long. 86° 17′.

MELOUN, a river of the Amherst district of the Tenasserim provinces, presidency of Bengal, rises in lat. 17° 9′, long. 98° 27′, and, flowing in a circuitous but generally westerly direction forty-five miles, falls into the Gyein river, in lat. 16° 32′, long. 97° 43′.

MELOWN.—A village in Burmah, situate on the left bank of the Irawady river. Here, on the 2nd January, 1826, were arranged the terms of a treaty between the British and the Burmese, which, on the part of the latter, were never intended to be confirmed. Upon the expiration of the armistice which had been agreed to, in view to the ratification of the treaty, Melown was taken by storm, and the document, which it was pretended had been transmitted to Ava, was found in the lines. Distant S.W. from Ava 105 miles, N. from Prome 148. Lat. 21°, long. 94° 39′.

MENBOO.—A town of Assam, in the British district of Sudiya, 30 miles N.W. of Sudiya. Lat. 28° 10′, long. 95° 26′.

MENDAT.—A town of Eastern India, in the British district of Tavoy, province of Tenasserim, 119 miles N.N.W. of Tenasserim. Lat. 13° 43′, long. 98° 28′.

MENDURDA.—A town in the peninsula of Kattywar, province of Guzerat, situate 72 miles S.S.W. from Rajkote, and 51 miles S.E. by E. from Poorbunder. Lat. 21° 20′, long. 70° 30′.

MENIL.—A town in the British district of North Arcot, presidency of Madras, 50 miles W. of Madras. Lat. 13° 4′, long. 79° 36′.

MEOPUR, in the district of Aldemau, territory of Oude, a village on the south-eastern frontier, towards the British district of Azimgurh, and 55 miles S.E. of the city of Oude. Lat. 26° 11′, long. 82° 43′.

MEOREE, in the British district of Bareilly, lieut.-gov. of the N.W. Provinces, a village on the route from the town of Bareilly to Seetapoor, and nine miles S.E. of the former. Lat. 28° 21′, long. 79° 35′.

MEPRAN.—A town of Eastern India, in the British district of Amherst, province of Tenasserim, situate 51 miles S.E. of Moulmein. Lat. 15° 55′, long. 98° 13′.

MER and SER, in the north of the Punjab, two mountain-summits, which rise to great height and with sublime effect, fifty or sixty miles east of the eastern boundary of the valley of Cashmere. In their regular conical form they as closely resemble each other as though they had been cast in the same mould, but they differ in hue, one being completely white, the other as uniformly black. They seem to be situate close together; and if this be the case, they must be nearly of the same height. No explanation appears to have been given of the singular fact, that, being of the same height, and situate in the same latitude, one is covered with perpetual snow, the other quite bare. Hügel considers them identical with the Kantal Mountain of the early maps of Cashmere; but Vigne is of opinion that the Kantal is the lofty mountain south of the Builtul Pass. Hügel clearly viewed them at Vizirabad, in the plain of the Punjab, overtopping the Panjals of Cashmere, and many other intervening mountains, though the distance is not less than 140 miles. Mer and Ser may be considered situate about lat. 34°, long. 76° 10′.

MERGUI, a town, the capital of the British district of the same name, in the Tenasserim provinces of Bengal, is situate on the principal mouth of the Tenasserim river. It is built along an uneven hill about 200 feet in height, and has a fine commanding position. The town is about three miles in circuit, and inclosed by a stockade fourteen feet high, with bastions at each angle. The houses of the English residents are built at the top of the hill, and face the sea: here also are situate the barracks, hospital, and cantonments, as well as a few pagodas. The streets of the town are wide, but dirty and ill-drained: the houses are built chiefly of wood, and raised on piles from the ground. The bazar is always furnished with a plentiful supply of every necessary article of food and raiment. The soil near the town consists of a reddish loam, lying on a substratum of gravel, composed of quartz and pebble: argillaceous petrifactions are found in the vicinity, and the clay contains lime. Specimens of tin-ore, discovered in the vicinity, have been pronounced to be of superior quality. Coal has been found, but serious objections appear to have been taken to its use. The harbour is spacious, secure, and easy of access and egress for ships of any size: the town is inaccessible for ships of large burthen, as there is a bank which obstructs the stream. Horsburgh, however, says that it commands a good inland navigation. Its exports are sapan-wood and sandal-wood, palm-leaves for roofing, ratans, yams, dried fish, ivory, tortoise-shell, Nipa-palm toddy, and edible birdsnests.

Notwithstanding that the vicinity of the town is low and damp, and the monsoon violent and protracted, the situation is exceedingly salubrious, probably from being exposed to the cool sea-breezes: there is always a bracing elasticity in the air. There is generally a detachment of European soldiers here, and the paucity of deaths among them is striking: between the years 1829—1836, only two died from disease, out of a number of 226. The population of the town amounts to 8,000; consisting of English, Chinese, Burmese, Siamese, and Malays. The place was taken by the British during the war with the Burmese, after a feeble resistance, and confirmed to the conquerors, with other territory, by the treaty of Yandabhoo, concluded in February, 1826. The district of which this town is the principal place will be found noticed under the article TENASSERIM PROVINCES. The town of Mergui is in lat. 12° 27′, long. 98° 42′.

MERGUI ARCHIPELAGO.—The Mergui Archipelago, consisting of a large cluster of islands, fronts the southern extremity of the coast of Tenasserim. They are generally high and mountainous, and, with the exception of those which are mere rock, covered from their summits to the water's edge with rich and varied foliage, presenting altogether a beautiful and pleasing variety of scenery. Their elevation in one or two instances exceeds 3,000 feet. Most of them appear to belong to the same formation, consisting of granite, which is occasionally intersected by veins of quartz. In some, black slate and sandstone prevail; in others, iron-ore is known to exist. The chief production is the edible birdsnest, found generally on the rocky islands, which are collected and sold by the inhabitants of some of the islands, as well as by the Malays and Chinese, who annually visit them for the purpose of procuring this article. Pearls are found on the coasts of many of them, and oysters abound in the numerous rocks about the Archipelago. The wild animals infesting the forests of the islands, are the tiger, elephant, rhinoceros, and deer. The feathered tribe is numerous, and consists of various kinds of pigeons, gulls, and cranes. The channels between some of the islands are dangerous and intricate, while others are very accessible, and have safe anchorage. The inhabitants are a roving race, having no fixed abode, but shifting from one island to another, in the rainy season preferring the inner, and during the fine weather the outer islands: they are uncivilized and ignorant, but timid and inoffensive. The men employ themselves in fishing, and the women in making a kind of mat, which is sold at Mergui: they are healthy and robust, but indolently disposed. The origin of these people has never been ascertained: they carry on a small bartering trade with the people of Mergui, getting in exchange for their mats, birdsnests, and pearls, divers articles of food and clothing. Among the principal islands in the Archipelago are the Great and Little Canister, King's Island, Cabossa, Bentinck, Domel, Kisseraing, Sullivan's, and St. Matthew's.

MERIAHDO.—A town in Bundelkund, 44 miles S. from Chutterpore, and 66 miles E.N.E. from Saugur. Lat. 24° 17′, long. 79° 41′.

MERKARA, in the British province of Coorg, a town the seat of the civil government of the district, and a military cantonment. It is situate at the south-east angle of an oblong table-land, the declivities from which on the north and east are gentle, but on the other sides dip precipitously to the lower country, to the extent of 500 or 600 feet. There are no morasses or lakes in the neighbourhood, but a small river rises near the town. Numerous springs also afford water, which is collected in large stone tanks. The fort of Merkara is situate on an isolated eminence, the summit of which has been levelled for the purpose. The lines for the native troops are on the south and south-west slopes of the hill, and are rather airy and clean, a stream of water running immediately below them. The fort is an irregular heptagon, having at each of six angles a round bastion, and at the other a gateway. The defences consist of a single strong wall of stone, twelve feet high and ten thick, with a parapet of masonry five feet high and four thick. There is no water within the fort, which is in other respects not tenable against an attack, being commanded by many points within breaching distance. Contiguous are a public bungalow or lodge for travellers, a jail, a revenue office, and, in a large handsome square building adjoining, are a cutchery or court-house and the office of the resident. The palace of the deposed rajah, at no great distance, is a large, substantial, castellated building, in a good style, with numerous windows in front. It is now occupied as a public treasury and storerooms, and as quarters for the officers. There is a separate barrack for the small detachment of European artillery of between twenty and thirty men: there is also an hospital. A church has been recently erected, the necessary funds being raised by private subscription, aided by a large contribution from the government. The population is chiefly composed of the British local authorities and military, with the numerous dependants and followers of both: to these must be added a few natives of Mysore, who are generally tradesmen and shopkeepers, brought to the place by the former. The climate is salubrious, and especially favourable to the European constitution. Merkara was built in 1773, by Hyder Ali, who, ill-instructed in fortification, chose a site which no works could render defensible against a regular attack. Given up to the rajah by the British, after it had been ceded by Tippoo Sultan, at the pacification of 1792, it was, on the contumacious conduct of the first-named prince, in 1834, occupied without resistance by a British force under Colonel Lindsay; and, the rajah being soon after deposed and deported to Benares, the present British establishments were formed. Elevation above the sea 4,506 feet. Distance from Cannanore, N.E., 47 miles; from Mangalore, S.E., 130; from Bangalore, S.W., 130; from Seringapatam, W., 64; from Madras, W., 315. Lat. 12° 24′, long. 75° 48′.

MEROO, in Bussahir, a village of the district of Koonawar, is situate about a mile from the right bank of the Sutlej, near the confluence of a feeder called the Joola. The houses have flat roofs covered with clay. This locality is nearly the most southern limit of the maturity of the grape, which, lower down, cannot be successfully cultivated, on account of the periodical rains of summer. At the time of the visit of Jacquemont, in 1830, the rajah of Bussahir had formed a road from Rampoor to this place, at the instance of the East-India Company, who on that consideration had remitted a portion of his tribute. Elevation above the sea 8,580 feet. Lat. 31° 32′, long. 78° 11′.

MERRIWALLEH, in the Daman division of the Punjab, a town situated on the right bank of the Indus, 74 miles S.W. of the town of Mooltan. Lat. 29° 23′, long. 70° 40′.

METAMIO.—A town of Eastern India, in the British district of Tavoy, province of Tenasserim, 151 miles N.N.W. of Tenasserim. Lat. 14° 16′, long. 98° 35′.

METCALF ISLAND, situate 50 miles off the coast of Tenasserim, among the group forming the Mergui Archipelago. Lat. 12° 18′, long. 97° 53′.

METTOOR.—A town in the British district of North Arcot, presidency of Madras, 30 miles W.N.W. of Arcot. Lat. 13° 3′, long. 79°.

METZA.—A town of Eastern India, in the British district of Amherst, province of Tenasserim, 32 miles N. of Moulmein. Lat. 16° 57′, long. 97° 45′.

MEWASSEE, or MOWASSEE.—The chiefs subject to the jurisdiction and political superintendence of the Rewa Caunta agency, in the province of Guzerat, presidency of Bombay, and residing principally on the banks of the Nerbudda, are styled Mewassee. The district they inhabit, lies between lat. 21° 49′ and 22° 5′, long. 73° 30′ and 74° 10′.

When the political control and superintendence over these chiefs became vested in the British government, the supremacy of the Guicowar over them ceased; and thus was abandoned the right of a ruinous interference in their affairs, which had been long cherished as the source of a large though indirect emolument to the superior state and its officers. In proportion, however, as the people betook themselves to cultivation, and waste land was resumed, there was reason to apprehend that boundary disputes would arise, and old dormant claims to land be revived. To meet these evils, the best provision practicable was made; and as, in such a country, crimes attended with violence were most to be apprehended, steps were taken for their suppression with a strong hand, and for the introduction of a regular-administered system of criminal justice, to which the country was previously a stranger. It was decided that all persons charged with capital offences, such as gang-robbery or murder, within the territories of these chiefs, should be tried before a court of justice, to be styled the Rewa Caunta Criminal Court, in which the resident and three or four chiefs should sit as asssessors. This was established in the year 1839; and it is said that the results have been found satisfactory.

MEWHOWN.—A town of Eastern India, in the British district of Amherst, province of Tenasserim, 89 miles S.E. of Moulmein. It is situate on the Zimme, a river which afterwards, under the name of Attaran, flows into the Bay of Bengal. Lat. 15° 32′, long. 98° 37′.

MEYHAR.—See MYHIR.

MEYSANA.—A town in Guzerat, or the dominions of the Guicowar, 105 miles N.N.W. from Baroda, and 42 miles N.N.W. from Ahmedabad. Lat. 23° 35′, long. 72° 21′.

MEYWAR.—See OODEYPOOR.

MEYWASA.—A town in the peninsula of Kattywar, province of Guzerat, situate three miles from the right bank of the Bhader river, and 32 miles S.W. from Rajkote. Lat. 21° 51′, long. 70° 40′.

MHAR, in the presidency of Bombay, a town at the west base of the Ghats, and on the small river Sawitri, navigable from the sea to this place, a distance of thirty miles. Distance from Bombay, S.E., by sea and by the river Sawitri, 100 miles; direct, 75. Lat. 18° 6′, long. 73° 30′.

MHENDAWUL, in the British district of Goruckpore, lieut.-gov. of the N.W. Provinces, a small town three miles from the right bank of the river Raptee, two from the north shore of the Moti Jhil, or Pearl Lake, 20 miles N.W. of Goruckpore cantonment. Buchanan, writing forty years ago, assigns it 500 houses; and assuming six persons for each house, the population may consequently be estimated at 3,000. Lat. 26° 57′, long. 83° 9′.

MHENDEEGUNJ, in the district of Purtabgurh, territory of Oude, a town three miles south of the right bank of the river Saee, 90 S.E. of Lucknow. It is a busy, thriving place, the population of which is estimated by Butter at 20,000. Lat. 25° 53′, long. 82°.

MHIDURGEE.—A town in the British province of Sattara, presidency of Bombay, situate 152 miles E. of Sattara. Lat. 17° 26′, long. 76° 21′.

MHILOG, a small hill state under the superintendence of the Governor-General's agent for the Cis-Sutlej states, is bounded on the north by Hindoor; on the east by the rajah of Pateeala's territory and by Kothar; on the south by Beja; and on the west by the Pinjor Doon and by Hindoor. It is about fifteen miles in length from north to south, and seven in breadth from east to west: its centre is in lat. 31°, long. 76° 57′. This territory is estimated to yield a revenue of 1,000*l.* per annum, out of which it pays a tribute to the British government of 144*l.* The population in 1832 was estimated at 13,000. Mhilog is one of the petty states wrested from the Goorkhas by the results of the war of 1814, and assigned by British authority to the present family.

MHOOL.—A town of the Deccan, in the state of Nagpoor or Berar, situate 82 miles S.S.E. from Nagpoor, and 160 miles S.E. by E. from Ellichpoor. Lat. 20° 5′, long. 79° 42′.

MHOW, in the territory of Indore, a British cantonment 13 miles S.W. of the town of Indore, situate in a clayey tract resting on basalt. It has altogether the appearance of a European town, having a church with steeple on an eminence, a spacious lecture-room, and library well furnished with books, and a theatre. The cantonments are occupied by a considerable force, and the officers are sufficiently numerous to be enabled to form a society independent of external intercourse. The military force was stationed here in pursuance of Art. VII. of the treaty of Mundesor. The town of Mhow is situate on the Gumbir river, on an eminence one and a half mile north-west of the cantonments. Elevation of cantonments above the sea 2,019 feet. Distance S.E. from Neemuch 142 miles, S.E. from Nusseerabad by Neemuch 272, S. from Oojein 42, S.W. from Saugur 215, S.W. from Agra 355, S. from Delhi 435. Lat. 22° 33′, long. 75° 46′.

MHOW, in the British district of Azimgurh, lieut.-gov. of the N.W. Provinces, a town situate on the eastern route from Ghazeepore to Goruckpore, 57 miles S. of the latter, 34 N. of the former. It is described by Garden as a large straggling town on the right bank of the Surjoo (North-Eastern Tons), which is crossed by a very good ford just below the town. Distance N.E. from Benares 55 miles. Lat. 25° 54′, long. 83° 37′.

MHOW, in the British district of Meerut, lieut.-gov. of the N.W. Provinces, a village on the route from the town of Meerut to that of Moradabad, and 11 miles S.E. from the former place. It is situate in an open country, partially cultivated, but not to such a degree as to yield abundant supplies. Distant N.W. from Calcutta by Delhi 930 miles. Lat. 28° 54′, long. 77° 54′.

MHOW, in the British district of Allygurh, lieut.-gov. of the N.W. Provinces, a town on the route from the cantonment of Allygurh to that of Etawah, and 27 miles S.E. of the former. It has a bazar and market, and is supplied with water from wells. The road in this part of the route is good; the country open, with a soil rather sandy, but well cultivated. Lat. 27° 34′, long. 78° 16′.

MHOW, or MUH, in the British district of Allahabad, lieut.-gov. of the N.W. Provinces, the principal place of the pergunnah of the same name, a town on the route from Allahabad to Pertabgurh, and 17 miles N.W. of the former. It has a bazar, and supplies and water are abundant. The road in this part of the route is good, the country level and partially cultivated. Lat. 25° 39', long. 81° 52'.

MHOWLEE KHAS, in the British district of Goruckpoor, lieut.-gov. of the N.W. Provinces, a small town, yet the principal place of the pergunnah of Mohowli. Here is a residence of a native chief, built on a heap of brick-rubbish, the ruins of some great building of remoter date. There is also a rude native fort, consisting of a rampart inclosing a few buildings, and surrounded by dense wood. Lat. 26° 36', long. 83°.

MHUR.—A town in the British district of Poonah, presidency of Bombay, 59 miles N. of Poonah. Lat. 19° 21', long. 73° 50'.

MHUSLA.—A town in the native territory of the chief of Jinjeera, presidency of Bombay, situate 60 miles S. by E. from Bombay, and 80 miles N. from Rutnageriah. Lat. 18° 8', long. 73° 11'.

MHUSWUR.—A town in the British province of Sattara, presidency of Bombay, 51 miles E. of Sattara. Lat. 17° 39', long. 74° 51'.

MHYE.—See MYHEE.

MIANE, in Sirhind, a village on the left bank of the Sutlej, here crossed by a ferry affording communication with the Punjab. The river is here a noble piece of water, and continues so until broken by shoals several miles lower down. Distant N.W. from Calcutta 1,147 miles. Lat. 31° 4', long. 75° 18'.

MIANEE, in the Punjab, a small town on the right or west bank of the Ravee, which is here, when fullest, 513 yards wide and twelve feet deep. It is on the great route from Loodianah, by Amritsir, to Attock, and the Ravee is crossed at this place by a much-frequented ferry. In the cold season, when the river is lowest, it can be forded. Lat. 31° 49', long. 74° 32'.

MICHENKHEYL, in the Daman division of the Punjab, a town situated 20 miles W. from the right bank of the Indus, 111 miles S.S.W. of the town of Peshawur. Lat. 32° 31', long. 70° 58'.

MIDNAPORE, a British district within the lieut.-gov. of Bengal, named from its principal place. It is bounded on the north by the British districts of Paroolia, Bancoora, and Burdwan; on the north-east by that of Hoogly; on the south-east by the British district of Hijellee; on the south by the Balasore division of Cuttack; on the south-west by the Cuttack tributary mehal Mohurbunja; and on the west by Paroolia. It lies between lat. 21° 41'—22° 57', long. 86° 36'—87° 59', and has an area of 4,015 square miles. It is traversed by numerous rivers and torrents, all taking a direction south-east, thus indicating the declivity of the country towards that point, and ultimately discharging themselves into the estuary of the Ganges, or the Bay of Bengal. The principal of these are the Soobunreeka and the Kosai or Cossya. These great streams inosculate with numerous others of less dimensions, and during the monsoons the country is overspread by a reticulation of torrents and watercourses. At the same season, jhils or small lakes abound, but they become contracted, or else totally disappear, during the dry season. On the seashore, salt is an important object of manufacture.

From its intertropical position and slight elevation, the climate of Midnapore is, in the latter part of the spring and early part of the summer, extremely hot, the thermometer ranging from 80° to 95° in the shade; and in that season the country seems a desert. The monsoon rains setting in at the close of June, lower the temperature, and cause luxuriant vegetation. The cool season lasts from October to February, during which interval the average temperature is about equal to that of midsummer in Central Europe. The population is given under the article BENGAL.

The principal routes are, 1. From north to south, from Bancoorah to Cuttack, through the town of Midnapore; 2. from east to west, from Calcutta to Nagpore: the other lines of communication appear to be merely tracks through wilds. The territory comprised in this district was acquired by the East-India Company in 1760, by sunnud or grant from Cossim Ali Khan, nawaub of Bengal.

MIDNAPORE, a town, the principal place of the British district of the same name, is situate on the route from Calcutta to Cuttack, 68 miles W. of former, and 179 N.E. of the latter. Here is a good bazar, well supplied, especially with provisions, and the town being situate on the left bank of the river Kosai or Coossy, water is also abundant. The school established here is under the government of a local committee, composed of the chief official persons resident in the town. It is conducted by a head-master, who is a European, who has under him several assistant-masters. Midnapore is in lat. 22° 24', long. 87° 33'.

MIEMUMMAW.—A town of Eastern India, in the British district of Mergui, in the Tenasserim provinces, 55 miles N.N.W. of Tenasserim. Lat. 12° 50', long. 98° 47'.

MILAPOOR, or ST. THOME.—A town in the British district of Chingleput, presidency of Madras, four miles S. of Madras. Lat. 13° 1', long. 80° 20'.

MILCHIA.—A town in the native state of Nepal, 23 miles S. by E. from Khatmandoo, and 65 miles N.E. from Bettiah. Lat. 27° 23', long. 85° 22'.

MILLICK, in the jaghire of Rampoor, lieut.-gov. of the N.W. Provinces, a village on the route from Bareilly to Moradabad, and 26 miles N.W. of the former. The road in this part of the route is good; the country open, fertile, and highly cultivated. Lat. 28° 37', long. 79° 13'.

MILUM, in the British district of Kumaon, lieut.-gov. of the N.W. Provinces, a small town, the principal place of the Bhotia subdivision of Juwahir, on the route to Hiundes or Chinese Tartary, and 13 miles S. of the Juwahir Pass. Elevation above the sea, of temple, 11,706 feet; of town, 11,430; of bridge across the river Goree, 11,368. Lat. 30° 25′, long. 80° 11′.

MINDAWAR, or MANDOWR, in the British district of Muttra, lieut.-gov. of the N.W. Provinces, a town on the left bank of the Jumna, eight miles N. of the city of Agra. Lat. 27° 17′, long. 78° 2′.

MINDPOORA.—A town of Malwa, in the native state of Dhar, 15 miles S. by W. from Dhar, and 152 miles W. from Hoosungabad. Lat. 22° 48′, long. 75° 22′.

MIRCHA, in the British district of Goruckpore, lieut.-gov. of the N.W. Provinces, a village on the route from Azimgurh to Goruckpore cantonment, 38 miles N. of the former, 23 S. of the latter. It has a few shops, and some supplies may be collected from the surrounding country, though much overrun with jungle. Lat. 26° 28′, long. 83° 14′.

MIREANEE, in the British district of Cawnpore, lieut.-gov. of the N.W. Provinces, a village on the route from the cantonment of Futtehgurh to that of Cawnpore, and 17 miles N.W. of the latter. Lat. 26° 38′, long. 80° 15′.

MIRGAHUN GHAT, in the British district of Muzuffurnugur, lieut.-gov. of the N.W. Provinces, a station on the left bank of the Jumna, at a ferry on the route from Kurnool to the town of Meerut, and six miles southeast of the former. Lat. 29° 38′, long. 77° 6′.

MIRGANJ, in the British district of Furruckabad, lieut.-gov. of the N.W. Provinces, a station on the route from Cawnpore to Futtehgurh, and 40 miles S.E. of the latter. It is situate on the right bank of the Ganges, crossed here by a ferry, formerly much frequented, but now in a considerable degree superseded by that of Nanamow, nine miles lower down the river. Lat. 27°, long. 80° 3′.

MIRHAKOOR, in the British district of Agra, a town on the route from the city of Agra to Jeypore, and 10 miles W. of the former. It has a small bazar. The road in this part of the route is good, the country well cultivated. Lat. 27° 9′, long. 77° 55′.

MIROT, in the jaghire of Jujhur, lieut.-gov. of the N.W. Provinces, a village near the left bank of the Hansouti nulla, a torrent widely spreading during the rains. Lat. 28° 34′, long. 76° 37′.

MIRPOOR, in the British district of Boolundshuhur, lieut.-gov. of the N.W. Provinces, a village on the route from Allygurh cantonment to that of Delhi, and 26 miles N.W. of the former. The road in this part of the route is good: the country open, with a sandy soil, scantily cultivated. Lat. 28° 12′, long. 77° 57′.

MIRTA, in the Rajpoot state of Jodhpoor, a town on the route from the city of Jodhpoor to that of Ajmeer, and 76 miles N.E. of the former. It stands on high ground, and, viewed from without, has a striking appearance. The wall which surrounds it, is on the western side built of mud, on the eastern of good masonry. There are several temples, and in the middle of the town a large and lofty mosque. There is a manufactory of felt here; and the bazar is well constructed, but has an impoverished look, this town having suffered much from the attacks of hostile troops; in consequence of which the number of houses has been seriously diminished. The present number of houses is 8,000, supplied with good water from three large tanks, the first at the north-west angle of the city, the second close to the east of Ajmeer gate, and the third about a quarter of a mile south-east of the second. The water from the wells is brackish. The population, according to Boileau, is 25,950. Lat. 26° 40′, long. 74° 9′.

MIRUN KE SARAE, in the British district of Furrukhabad, lieut.-gov. of the N.W. Provinces, a town on the route from the cantonment of Cawnpore to that of Futtehgurh, and 33 miles S. of the latter. It has a very fine sarae, whence its name, and the tomb of the founder, in a garden on the opposite side of the road. There is a bazar, and water is abundant. Lat. 27° 1′, long. 79° 59′.

MIRYAGUNJE.—A town in the British district of Backergunje, lieut.-gov. of Bengal, 122 miles E. of Calcutta. Lat. 22° 22′, long. 90° 19′.

MIRZA MOORAD, in the British district of Benares, lieut.-gov. of the N.W. Provinces, a village on the route from Allahabad to the city of Benares, 61 miles E. of the former, 13 W. of the latter. The road in this part of the route is excellent; the country level, wooded, and cultivated. Lat. 25° 17′, long. 82° 50′.

MIRZAPOOR.—A town in the British district of Cuttack, lieut.-gov. of Bengal, 30 miles N.E. of Cuttack. Lat. 20° 43′, long. 86° 17′.

MIRZAPOOR.—A town in the British district of Purneah, lieut.-gov. of Bengal, two miles W. of Purneah. Lat. 25° 46′, long. 87° 31′.

MIRZAPORE, within the limits of the lieut.-gov. of the N.W. Provinces, a British district, named from its principal place, is bounded on the north by the British districts Jounpoor and Benares; on the east by the British districts of Shahabad, Behar, and Palamow; on the south by Sirgooja; and on the west by the territory of Rewa and the British district of Allahabad. It lies between lat. 23° 50′—25° 30′, long. 82° 11′—83° 39′, and has an area of 5,235 square miles. The

Ganges, when first touching on the district, sweeps for about twelve miles round the north-western corner, in a direction first southerly, then easterly, when it passes into the district, through which it holds a sinuous but generally easterly course of about seventy miles, and flowing by the city of Mirzapore and the fort of Chunar, reaches the northern frontier, along which it pursues its course for about eight miles farther, and finally leaves the district six miles above the city of Benares. The average elevation of the waterway of the Ganges at the north-western corner of the district, where it is highest, is about 310 feet above the sea; close to Benares, where lowest, 272. Throughout the ninety miles of this part of its course it is navigable at all times, and probably for craft of fifty or sixty tons burthen. In the lower part, its depth, according to Jacquemont, who viewed it in midwinter, when lowest, is about fifty feet; its breadth he states to be great. At the town of Mirzapore, forty-five miles higher, he describes it, at the same season, as half a mile wide, of considerable depth in the middle, and at the margin two or three feet deep. The Sone, flowing from the Rewa territory, after passing the western frontier of the district, flows through it in a direction from west to east for about fifty-two miles, and then crosses the eastern frontier into the British district of Behar. It is described by Blunt as a considerable river even in the dry season, with a bed half a mile wide, and a rapid stream a hundred yards wide, with about three feet water in the deepest part. The Rehund river enters the district at the south-western corner, and flowing in a north-easterly direction for twenty-three miles, subsequently in a northerly direction for twenty-nine miles, finally falls into the Sone. The Kunhur enters the district at the opposite or south-eastern corner, and, flowing in a north-westerly direction for thirty-five miles, also falls into the Sone.

The northern portion of the district, being part of the lower valley of the Ganges, partakes of its alluvial character. There are some exceptions, however, as between the city of Mirzapore and Chunar is a range of rocky and uneven hills of sandstone, rising at the fort of Chunar into an abrupt rock of considerable height. These eminences are no doubt connected with the low sandstone range running nearly east and west, a few miles farther south, and denominated by Franklin the Bindachal Range, from the town of Bindachal, at its northern base. This range is horizontally stratified, micaceous and schistose towards the base, finer-grained towards the summit, where it is of a light colour, and, being well suited for building, is extensively used at Mirzapore and Benares. Its elevation is about 500 feet above the sea, or 250 above the adjacent valley of the Ganges, the upper surface forming a sort of table-land, diversified by numerous small eminences. South of this the land rises, as a sort of huge terrace, into another table-land, having an elevation of probably 800 or 900 feet, being part of the north-eastern extremity of the great Vindhya range, which overspreads the whole southern part of the district, and gives it a rugged, barren, and savage character.

In a country promising in a geological point of view, the mineral wealth does not appear considerable: the sandstone of Chunar and its vicinity is extensively quarried for building; the kunkar or calcareous conglomerate affords excellent lime; native soda is found at the Tara and Kutra passes; iron-ore at Lalganj, sixteen miles south-west of the city of Mirzapore; fine slate south of the Sone; and on the northern bank of that river coal-fields have been discovered.

Amidst the jungly hills and valleys of the southern part of the district, the air is represented to be, during the hot and rainy seasons, so pestilential as to prove inevitably fatal to Europeans and to many natives; yet, in the beginning of February, Blunt experienced a frost of six days, a consequence, without doubt, of the elevation of the country. Even in the city of Mirzapore, on the bank of the Ganges, fires are desirable during the mornings and evenings of the winter season. In the latter part of spring and the early part of summer, before the mitigating effects of the periodical rains have been felt, the heat is dreadful, especially in the vicinity of the rocks of Chunar. It is said that the station and the city of Mirzapore are rather unhealthy, from the circumstance of the land being high toward the bank of the river, and lower at some distance; by which much stagnant water is produced. It is also stated that the soil of the town of Mirzapore, and the land adjacent to it, is so strongly impregnated with saline particles, as materially to injure buildings composed of bricks and mortar.

Respecting the botanical character of the country, Jacquemont observes, "Doubtless the Borassus flabelliformis (species of palm), the palmyra-tree of Europeans, and the tar of the Hindoos, acquires maturity here, though I have not seen it in this tract; the mango predominates; next the tamarind and various sorts of mimosa; oranges do not succeed well; the Casuarina muricata is occasionally met with in the gardens, but tufted, stunted, and distorted. There are various species of the terebinthine family, nearly devoid of leaves: they are probably spondias. The cotton cultivated in the vicinity of the city is probably the Gossypium herbaceum, with short coarse wool. The sugar-canes, which cover a vast extent of ground, are about the thickness of the finger, and a yard in length." The above description of the cotton grown here does not appear to correspond with that given at a more recent period, when it was stated that the cotton of this district is of good quality, strong, rather fine, of long staple, and making a durable cloth. The produce of the vicinity, however, forms but a small part of the cotton brought to market at the town of Mirzapore, which is the greatest cotton-mart in India, and where the cottons of the Doab, Oude, Bundlecund, the Saugor and Nerbudda territory, and even of parts of Malwa and Nagpore, are collected for transmission to the lower provinces. Indigo is produced to some extent, and sugar is a very important article of cultivation, as this part of the valley of the Ganges is the principal sugar district of India. The principal alimentary crops are wheat, barley, bajra (Holcus spicatus), various sorts of millet, maize, pulse, oil-seeds of different kinds, ginger, turmeric, chillies, hemp (which is cultivated for its intoxicating property), melons, cucumbers, and other products. The usual esculent vegetables of Britain succeed well in the cool season, or that comprehending the close and commencement of the year.

The population is almost exclusively Hindoo, the Mahomedans being comparatively few. The latest census gives the total number at 1,104,315; of which 649,120 are enumerated as Hindoo and agricultural, 380,778 as Hindoo non-agricultural; while the Mahomedans and all others not being Hindoos amount only to 15,364 agricultural, and 59,053 non-agricultural. There are some native members of the English church, and a few descendants of native converts to the church of Rome. The principal places are Mirzapore, Chunar, and Lalganj. The chief military routes are—1. From north to south, from Jounpore to the city of Mirzapore, and continued southward to Agori. 2. From north-east to south-west, from Benares to the city of Mirzapore, and continued in the same direction to Rewa and Saugor. 3. From east to west, from Chunar to the city of Mirzapore, and continued in a north-westerly direction to Allahabad. This road, made under the inspection of engineer officers of the East-India Company's service, is represented to be such as would do credit to any country; and it forms the great thoroughfare by which the valuable products of Bundlecund and the Saugor and Nerbudda territories are conveyed to the banks of the Ganges for transport down the river.

The tract forming this district, probably at the remotest period of Hindoo history was part of the realm of Kasi, the capital of which was the neighbouring city of Varanasi or Benares. About the beginning of the eleventh century, it was subjugated by the sovereigns of Gour, from whom it was wrested at the close of the same century, by the sovereigns of Canouj; and on the overthrow of this last state by Muhammad of Ghor, in 1193, it became subject to the Mahomedan sovereigns of Delhi. In 1529 it was subjugated by Baber. On the dismemberment of the empire of Delhi, consequent on the invasion, in 1760, of Ahmed Shah Dooranee, it formed part of the spoil seized by Shujah-ud-daulah, nawaub vizier of Oude, by whom a part was ceded to the East-India Company under the treaty of 1775, and the remainder by the treaty of 1801.

MIRZAPORE, the principal place of the district of the same name, a town situate on a bank of kunkar, on the right side of the Ganges, here half a mile wide, and when lowest, deep in the middle, shallow towards the edges. The communication with the opposite bank is maintained by public ferry at the Naughat, over which troops and stores are passed free of charge. Its appearance to those passing it by water is imposing, from its great extent, numerous mosques and Hindoo temples, excellent houses of Europeans, and handsome ghats or flights of stairs leading to the water's edge. On closer examination, however, the aspect of the place does not improve: the houses of the Europeans, which are the best of the dwellings, occur only at considerable intervals; the native town is of great extent, but consists mainly of three long, wide, straight streets, along the sides of which are rows of trees and of wells. Those wells are surrounded by a circular platform, and have large mouths, so that many persons can draw water at once, without incommoding each other; and several are tasteful specimens of architecture. The houses for the most part are, however, built of mud or of unbaked brick, though the vicinity contains abundance of excellent building-stone: they are seldom more than two stories high. There is no appearance of grandeur or antiquity in this city, though much of business and bustle. Its manufactures of carpets and other strong woollens, of cottons and of silks, as well as some others of less importance, are considered to be on the decline, and it derives its present importance principally from the fact of its being the greatest cotton-mart in India. The city and its vicinity are said to abound with lawyers, drawn thither by the great amount of litigation, resulting from the active commerce of the place. The great wealth in transit and in store here likewise invites the presence of various classes of thieves. The civil establishment consists of a judge, a collector, a deputy-collector, a collector of customs, and other functionaries for the due administration of the public business. The population of this city is returned at 79,526. The military cantonment is situate three miles north-east of the city, in a sort of peninsula formed by the winding of the Ganges. In the distribution of the Bengal army, Mirzapore is included within the Benares division.

The importance, and perhaps the existence of this place seems to be of very recent date: it does not appear to be mentioned in the Ayeen Akbery. Tieffenthaler, who drew up his description of India between 1760 and 1770, mentions it under the name of Mirzapur the Greater, as a mart, and as having two ghats giving access to the Ganges. It is laid down in Rennell's Atlas, published in 1781, but not mentioned in the acconnts of the march of the British army from Buxar to the vicinity of Allahabad, though the route must have lain through or near it. Distant E. from Allahabad, keeping to the right of the Ganges, 61 miles; keeping to the left of that river, and crossing by the ferry opposite Mirzapore, 53 miles; from Benares cantonment, S.W., 27 miles; from Calcutta, N.W., by land 448 miles, by water 721 miles, or if by the Sunderbund passage, 898 miles. Lat. 25° 6′, long. 82° 38′.

MIRZAPORE CHHOTA (THE LESS), in the British district of Mirzapore, a town on the route from Chunar to Dinapoor, 10 miles N.E. of the former. Supplies and water are abundant here, the town being situate on the right bank of the Ganges, in a well-cultivated country, studded with groves of mangoes. Lat. 25° 12′, long. 83° 4′.

MIRZI, or MIRJAN, in the British district of North Canara, presidency of Madras, a town on an inlet of the Arabian Sea, or North Indian Ocean. According to Horsburgh, "the entrance of the river is between two bluff points; that on the south side has the deepest water, close to which is the proper channel over the bar, where are two and three-quarters and three fathoms water between the point and sand-banks in the middle of the entrance, on which the sea generally breaks." But though the depth of water is sufficient for vessels of considerable burthen, the channel is so narrow as to admit only those of small size. Both the town, and a fort which formerly protected it, are now very ruinous, in consequence of the injuries it suffered in a siege by Hyder Ali, and subsequently from the oppressive government of Tippoo, his son. It was formerly called Midijay, corrupted by the Mussulmans into Mirzi and Mirjan. Distance from Mangalore, N., 115 miles; from Bombay, S., 325; Bangalore, N.W., 236; Madras, N.W., 408. Lat. 14° 30′, long. 74° 29′.

MISREEKOTA.—A town in the British district of Dharwar, presidency of Bombay, 16 miles S.S.E. of Dharwar. Lat. 15° 16′, long. 78° 8′.

MISREEPOOR, in the British district of Cawnpoor, lieut.-gov. of the N.W. Provinces, a town on the route from Cawnpoor to Jeitpoor, 38 miles S.W. of the former. Lat. 26° 5′, long. 80°.

MISROWLI, in the British district of Benares, lieut.-gov. of the N.W. Provinces, a village on the left bank of the Ganges, 656 miles N.W. of Calcutta by water; 13 N.E., or farther down the stream, than Benares. Lat. 25° 24′, long. 83° 15′.

MISSERPOOR, in the territory of Oude, a village on the route from Banda to Purtabgurh, 11 miles W. of the latter, 125 E. of the former. Lat. 25° 55′, long. 81° 48′.

MISSIRPOORA, in the British district of Mirzapoor, lieut.-gov. of the N.W. Provinces, a village on the right bank of the Ganges, 31 miles N.W. of the city of Mirzapoor; 750 N.W. of Calcutta. Lat. 25° 16′, long. 82° 20′.

MISSRIK.—A town in the territory of Oude, 47 miles N.W. by N. from Lucknow, and 68 miles N. by E. from Cawnpoor. Lat. 27° 27′, long. 80° 38′.

MITEEGOOREM.—A town of the Deccan, in the state of Nagpoor or Berar, 167 miles S.S.E. from Nagpoor, and 210 miles N. by W. from Masulipatam. Lat. 19° 5′, long. 80° 25′.

MITHA BEREE, a village in the British district of the Dehra Doon, and near the right bank of the Asun. It was a station of the series of small triangles in the great trigonometrical survey of the Himalaya. Elevation above the sea 2,189 feet. Lat. 30° 19′, long. 78° 2′.

MITHUN KOTE, or MITTUN KOTE.—A town in Sinde, near the western bank of the Indus, close to the confluence of the Punjnud, or stream conveying into it the united waters of the Punjab. Burnes found the Indus here, at the latter end of May, before the swell attained its height, 2,000 yards wide. Later in the season, the adjacent country, to a great extent, is overflowed, and becomes one uninterrupted expanse of water, as the land is, for a considerable distance on each side of the river, on a low level. At this time of year the climate is unhealthy. Mithun Kote is admirably situated for commanding the trade of the Indus throughout its whole extent; and hence has by some been recommended as a convenient site for an annual fair, where the traders of Afghanistan and of Central Asia might be supplied with Indian and British goods; but its insalubrity is a great objection to such a selection. It is surrounded with flourishing date-groves. Elevation above the sea 220 feet. Population 4,000. It is 460 miles from the sea, in lat. 28° 57′, long. 70° 29′.

MITPULLY.—A town in Hyderabad, or dominions of the Nizam, 109 miles N. from Hyderabad, and 174 miles S.S.E. from Ellichpoor. Lat. 18° 54′, long. 78° 41′.

MITTAH TOWANAH, in the Sinde Sagur Dooab division of the Punjab, a town situated 20 miles W. from the right bank of the Jhelum, 123 miles W.N.W. of the town of Lahore. Lat. 32° 20′, long. 72° 15′.

MITTANEE, in the Daman division of the Punjab, a town situated 33 miles W. from the right bank of the Indus, 12 miles S.W. of the town of Peshawur. Lat. 33° 46′, long. 71° 35′.

MITTEETOKUR.—A town in the territory of Oude, 33 miles W.S.W. from Lucknow, and 15 miles N.E. by N. from Cawnpoor. Lat. 26° 40′, long. 80° 30′.

MOBEE.—A town of Burmah, situate 142 miles S.S.E. from Ava, and 154 miles N.E. from Prome. Lat. 20° 5′, long. 97°.

MODERAH, in the Rajpoot state of Jodhpoor, a village on the route from Nusseerabad to Deesa, and 155 miles S.W. of the former. It is situate in a country occasionally studded with hills, but generally level, with a gravelly soil, free from jungle, and partially cultivated. Lat. 25° 18′, long. 73° 10′.

MODHORAJPOORA.—A town in the Rajpoot state of Jeypoor, situate 27 miles S.S.W. from Jeypoor, and 66 miles E. from Ajmeer. Lat. 26° 34′, long. 75° 45′.

MODIBENI.—A town in Nepal, situate on the left bank of one of the branches of the Gunduck, and 119 miles W. by N. from Khatmandoo. Lat. 28° 15′, long. 83° 29′.

MODOOPOOR.—A town in the British district of Ramgur, lieut.-gov. of Bengal, 52 miles E. of Hazareebagh. Lat. 23° 56′, long. 86° 13′.

MODUL, in the Rajpoot state of Jodhpoor, a village on the route from Nusseerabad to Deesa, and 134 miles S.W. of the former. The road in this part of the route is firm and good, and passes through a gravelly country, partially cultivated. Lat. 25° 27′, long. 73° 24′.

MOEYONG, one of the Cossya hill states, bounded on the north by that of Muriow; on the east by Osimlee; on the south by Mahran; and on the west by Nustung: it contains an area of 110 square miles, and its centre is in lat. 10° 20′, long. 91° 27′.

MOGLOOR CHIKA (or THE LESS).—A town in the Mysore, near a tank, and close to the source of the Yagachi river, in the rough country forming the east declivity of the Western Ghats. Distance N.W. from Seringapatam 88 miles. Lat. 13° 18′, long. 75° 51′.

MOGOUNG MYO.—A town of Burmah, situate 167 miles E. by N. from Muneepoor, and 190 miles S.S.E. from Sudiya. Lat. 25° 18′, long. 96° 39′.

MOGRA, in the Rajpoot state of Jodhpoor, a village on the route from Neemuch to Jodhpoor, and 11 miles S. of the latter. Supplies are scarce, and must be previously collected. The water is brackish; both that supplied from wells, and that from a small rill. Lat. 26° 8′, long. 73° 10′.

MOGULPOOR, in the British district of Moradabad, lieut.-gov. of the N.W. Provinces, a village on the route from Hurdwar to the town of Moradabad, and seven miles N.W. of the latter. Lat. 28° 56′, long. 78° 47′.

MOGULPOOR, or MUGHALPOOR, in the territory of Oude, a town on the right bank of the Chauka, here called the Ul, a stream tributary to the Ghaghra, 65 miles N. of Lucknow. Lat. 27° 45′, long. 80° 55′.

MOGUL SERAI, in the British district of Benares, lieut.-gov. of the N.W. Provinces, a town on the route from Hazaribagh to Benares, 177 miles N.W. of the former, 12 S.E. of the latter. It has a bazar. Lat. 25° 16′, long. 83° 12′.

MOGUL SURYE.—A town of Malwa, in the native state of Tonk, or territory of Ameer Khan, 11 miles N. from Sironj, and 78 miles W.N.W. from Saugur. Lat. 24° 16′, long. 77° 40′.

MOHAN, in the territory of Oude, a town on the route from Futtehgurh, by Nanamau ghat or ferry, to Lucknow, 17 miles W. of the latter. It is situate on the left bank of the river Saee, here crossed by a permanent bridge. Lord Valentia styles it a village, but observes that it had the appearance of having anciently been of more consequence, the soil being filled for a considerable distance with a mixture of brick and lime. Lat. 26° 46′, long. 80° 45′.

MOHANA, a river in the district of Boghelkhand, territory of Rewa, rises near the village of Rypoor, and in lat. 24° 32′, long. 81° 32′. The elevation above the sea, of its source, must exceed 900 feet, as at Keuti, twenty-five miles farther north, and the same distance lower down the stream, the elevation of the waterway is 923 feet. At that place, passing from the plateau of Rewa, over the brow of the Kutra ridge, to the more depressed country farther north, it is precipitated down a fall of 362 feet. It thence turns to the north-east, and is discharged into the Tons, on the right side, in lat. 24° 57′, long. 81° 35′, after a total course of thirty-eight miles.

MOHANAH.—A town in the British district of Paneeput, lieut.-gov. of the N.W. Provinces, situate on the route from the city of Delhi to Jheend, and 35 miles N.W. of the former. Lat. 29° 2′, long. 76° 55′.

MOHANE.—See Phalgu.

MOHAREE.—A town of the Deccan, in Nagpoor or Berar, situate 39 miles E.N.E. from Nagpoor, and 130 miles S. from Jubbulpoor. Lat. 21° 19′, long. 79° 43′.

MOHGAON.—A town of the Deccan, in Nagpoor or Berar, situate 43 miles N.W. from Nagpoor, and 54 miles E. by S. from Baitool. Lat. 21° 38′, long. 78° 45′.

MOHNE, in Koonawur, a district of Bussahir, is a fortress, with a celebrated Hindoo temple dedicated to Badrinath, and crowned by a ball of pure gold, said to weigh fifteen or twenty pounds. It is situate on the southern declivity of the great Ruldung Mountain, and in a pergunnah or division bearing the name of Kumroo. Lat. 31° 26′, long. 78° 19′.

MOHODA.—A town in Nagpoor or Berar, situate 20 miles E. from Nagpoor, and 110 miles E.S.E. from Baitool. Lat. 21° 9′, long. 79° 29′.

MOHOL.—A town in the British district of Sholapoor, presidency of Bombay, 19 miles W.N.W. of Sholapoor. Lat. 17° 48′, long. 75° 42′.

MOHOLI, or MAHOWLY, in the territory of Oude, a small town on the route from Bareilly to Lucknow, 89 miles S.E. of the former, 67 N.W. of the latter. It has a bazar, and is well supplied with water. Lat. 27° 40′, long. 80° 32′.

MOHON.—A river of Sirgoojah, on the south-west frontier of Bengal, rising in lat. 23° 11′, long. 83° 18′, and flowing for eighty-five miles first westerly, and then northerly, falls into the Rhern or Rehund, on the right side, in lat. 23° 50′, long. 82° 51′.

MOHONA, or MAHONA, in the territory of Gwalior, or possessions of Scindia, a town on the route from Gwalior fort to Sironj, 30 miles S.W. of former, 130 N. of latter. Lat. 25° 54′, long. 77° 45′.

MOHOUREE, or MOWAREE, in the British district of Allahabad, lieut.-gov. of the N.W. Provinces, a village on the route from Allahabad cantonment to Rewah, and 10 miles S.E. of the former. Lat. 25° 21′, long. 81° 58′.

MOHRA DHELA, in the British district of Moradabad, lieut.-gov. of the N.W. Provinces, a village situate at the point where the small river Dhela flows to the south from the Sewalik range. It promises to be an important locality, containing numerous indications of coal, and many seams have been tried for specimens, which, however, as yet have not been obtained of good quality, as they contain much iron pyrites. N. of Moradabad 40 miles. Lat. 29° 24′, long. 79° 4′.

MOHREE, in the British district Moradabad, lieut.-gov. of the N.W. Provinces, a village on the route from Hurdwar to the town of Moradabad, and 16 miles N.W. of the latter. The road in this part of the route is good. Lat. 29° 4′, long. 78° 42′.

MOHRENI, in the British district of Shahjehanpoor, lieut.-gov. of the N.W. Provinces, a village on the route from Bareilly to Seetapoor, and 43 miles S.E. of the former. Lat. 28° 9′, long. 80° 5′.

MOHUMDABAD, in the British district of Azimgurh, lieut.-gov. of the N.W. Provinces, a town on the route from Azimgurh to Mozufferpoor, 14 miles E. of the former. Lat. 26°, long. 83° 28′.

MOHUMDABAD, in the British district of Jaloun, lieut.-gov. of the N.W. Provinces, a town on the route from Jaloun to Bandah, 17 miles S.E. by S. of the former. Lat. 25° 57′, long. 79° 31′.

MOHUMDEE, in the territory of Oude, a town on the route from Bareilly to Lucknow, 61 miles S.E. of the former, 96 N.W. of the latter. It has a large bazar. Lat. 27° 58′, long. 80° 19′.

MOHUN.—A town in Guzerat, or dominions of the Guicowar, situate eight miles N. from the right bank of the Nerbudda, and 52 miles E. by S. from Baroda. Lat. 22° 6′, long. 74° 2′.

MOHUN CHOKI, in the British district of Suharunpoor, lieut.-gov. of the N.W. Provinces, is on the route from the town of Suharunpoor to Dehra, and 26 miles N.E. of the former. It is situate at the south-western base of the Sewalik range, where the pass of Lalldurwaza or Kheree, following the course of the Solani torrent, debouches on the plains of Hindoostan. Distant N.W. from Calcutta 1,030 miles. Lat. 30° 10′, long. 77° 57′.

MOHUNEEA, in the British district Shahabad, lieut.-gov. of Bengal, a town on the route from Hazaribagh to Benares, 147 miles N.W. of former, 42 S.E. of latter. It has a bazar. According to Buchanan, "it contains 200 houses, of which some are very large, being inns [caravanserais], with very numerous chambers, disposed in a long range." Lat. 25° 8′, long. 83° 40′.

MOHUNGUNJE.—A town in the British district of Pubna, lieut.-gov. of Bengal, 124 miles N.E. of Calcutta. Lat. 24°, long. 89° 40′.

MOHUNGURH, in the Rajpoot state of Jessulmer, a fort in the desert, and about 35 miles N.E. of the town of Jessulmer. Lat. 27° 13′, long. 71° 22′.

MOHUN-KE-SURAEE, in the British district of Benares, lieut.-gov. of the N.W. Provinces, a village on the route from the city of Benares to that of Mirzapoor, seven miles S.W. of the former, 20 N.E. of the latter. Water is plentiful, and supplies may be collected in abundance. The road in this part of the route is excellent; the country level, wooded, and cultivated. Lat. 25° 16′, long. 82° 55′.

MOHUN KOTE.—A town of Sinde, in the British district of Kurrachee, presidency of Bombay, 92 miles N.E. of Kurrachee. Lat. 25° 52′, long. 67° 57′.

MOHUNPOOR, in the territory of Gwalior, or possessions of Scindia's family, a considerable town 110 miles S. of Guwaler fort. Lat. 24° 47′, long. 77° 43′.

MOHUNPOOR.—A town of Eastern India, in the British district of Southern Cachar, 11 miles S.E. of Silchar. Lat. 24° 41′, long. 92° 58′.

MOHUNPOOR, in the British district of Muttra, lieut.-gov. of the N.W. Provinces, a village on the route from the cantonment of Allygurh to that of Etawa, and 36 miles S.E. of the former. Lat. 27° 27′, long. 78° 23′.

MOHUNPOOR, in the British district Bijnour, lieut.-gov. of the N.W. Provinces, a village on the route from Moradabad to Hurdwar, and 23 miles S.E. of the latter. Lat. 29° 42′, long. 78° 18′.

MOHUNPOORA, in the Rajpoot state of Jeypoor, a village on the route from Agra to Ajmeer, 128 miles W. of former, 100 E. of latter. Lat. 26° 52′, long. 76° 10′.

MOHURBUNGE, the name of one of the Cuttack mehals, on the S.W. frontier of Bengal. It is bounded on the north-west by Singboom; on the north-east by the British districts Pooralia and Midnapoor; on the south-east by that of Ballasore and the Cuttack mehal Neelgurh; and on the south-west by that of Keunjur. It extends from lat. 21° 24′—22° 35′, and from long. 85° 38′—87° 14′; is ninety-five miles in length from north-west to south-east, and seventy-five in breadth, and contains an area of 2,025 square miles, with a population of 91,125.

MOHURKAPOOR, in the British district of Cawnpore, lieut.-gov. of the N.W. Provinces, a village on the route from Calpee to Futtehgurh, and 18 miles N. of the former. Lat. 26° 20′, long. 79° 45′.

MOHWAR.—A river of Bundelcund, rising in lat. 25° 6′, long. 78° 5′, and, flowing through Jhansee in a north-easterly direction for sixty miles, falls into the Sinde river, in lat. 25° 47′, long. 78° 23′.

MOIRA FORT.—See ALMORA.

MOJGURH, in Bhawlpoor, a town on the route from the city of Bhawlpoor to Jodhpoor, and 37 miles S.E. of the former. It is situate in the desert extending through the eastern part of the state of Bhawlpoor, which has generally a soil of hard tenacious earth, covered in most places with grassy jungle and stunted shrubs, but in some overspread with hills of loose shifting sand. The site of Mojgurh is of firm ground, with low sandy eminences on every side, but at such a distance that light guns cannot command it. The walls are built of brick; they are about fifty feet high (including the parapet, of about seven feet), and two and a half feet thick, with a terreplein four feet broad. On the north side they are in many places perforated with cannon-balls discharged during the siege carried on by the first khan of Bhawlpoor. The place is half a furlong square, with numerous bastions, and an outwork on the east side, to cover the entrance. A mosque conspicuously surmounts the gateway, and a little to the north is a Mahometan tomb, with a cupola profusely ornamented with coloured glazed tiles. There is a large tank outside the walls, and within are several wells, containing abundance of good water at the depth of fifty-eight cubits. Mojgurh is in lat. 29° 1′, long. 72° 11′.

MOJPOOR, in the Rajpoot territory of Alwur, a small town on the route from Nusserabad to Muttra, and 61 miles S.W. of the latter. Lat. 27° 22′, long. 76° 52′.

MOKAMEH.—A town in the British district of Patna, lieut.-gov. of Bengal, 44 miles E. by S. of Patna. Lat. 25° 22′, long. 85° 56′.

MOKAURA.—A town in the British district of Tannah, presidency of Bombay, 74 miles N.N.E. of Bombay. Lat. 19° 54′, long. 73° 23′.

MOKERIAN, in the Julinder dooab of the Punjab, a town situated on the left bank of the Beas, 92 miles E.N.E. of the town of Lahore. Lat. 31° 57′, long. 75° 39′.

MOKHEIR.—A town in the British district of Ahmednuggur, presidency of Bombay, 120 miles N.E. of Bombay. Lat. 20°, long. 74° 20′.

MOKMAI.—A town of Burmah, 140 miles S.E. by S. from Ava, and 176 miles N.E. by E. from Prome. Lat. 20° 17′, long. 97° 16′.

MOKUMPAD.—A town in Hyderabad, or territory of the Nizam, 133 miles E. by N. from Hyderabad, and 94 miles N. from Guntoor. Lat. 17° 40′, long. 80° 30′.

MOKUNDURRA, in Rajpootana, a small town or village in the territory of Kota, on the route from Neemuch to Kota, 90 miles N.E. of the former, and 32 S.W. of the latter. It is situate in a long and narrow valley, formed by two parallel ridges of hills running north-west and south-east, between the Chumbul and the Kalee Sindh rivers. In proceeding from Kota towards the south-west, the road gradually ascends, amidst cliffs and rocks, to the brow of the elevated table-land of Malwa, towards which its extremity is guarded by a small fort. This defile is of great importance, being the only pass practicable for carriages for a considerable distance over the range extending from the Chumbul to the Kalee Sindh. It has been repeatedly the scene of obstinately-contested engagements, and formed the route of Colonel Monson's disastrous retreat before Jeswunt Row Holkar, in July, 1804. According to Tod, the pass was named from having been fortified by Mokund, who commenced his reign as rajah of Kota about the year 1630. Mokundarra has a bazar in a long narrow street, through which the main road passes. Distant N. from Oojein 115 miles, S.W. from Gwalior 165, S.W. from Agra 210. Lat. 24° 50′, long. 75° 59′.

MOLACALMOOROO, in the Mysore, a fort on the north-west frontier, towards the British district of Dharwar. It is situate on the western acclivity of a ridge of mountains three miles south of the right bank of the river Chinna Hugri. Distant N.E. from Chitteldroog 40 miles, N.W. from Bangalore 140, N. from Seringapatam 165. Lat. 14° 44′, long. 76° 48′.

MOLAWUN, in the territory of Oude, a village on the route from Banda to Pertaubgurh, 22 miles W. of the latter, 114 E. of the former. It has water from tanks and wells, but supplies must be collected from the neighbourhood. Lat. 25° 45′, long. 81° 40′.

MOLLUNG.—A town in the British district of Rungpore, lieut.-gov. of Bengal, 10 miles S.W. by S. of Rungpore. Lat. 25° 33′, long. 89° 10′.

MOLOUR, a town in the pergunnah of the same name, is situate three miles N.E. of the left bank of the Jumna, 15 miles S.W. of the town of Futtehpoor. Lat. 25° 45′, long. 80° 57′.

MOMEIL MYO.—A town of Burmah, situate 50 miles E. from the left bank of the Irawady, and 110 miles N.N.E. from Ava. Lat. 23° 20′, long. 96° 47′.

MOMINABAD, in Hyderabad, or territory of the Nizam, a town, one of the stations of the

British subsidiary force, usually denominated the Nizam's army. Distance from Hyderabad, N.W., 175 miles; Madras, N.W., 485; Bombay, E., 240. Lat. 18° 44′, long. 76° 27′.

MONAPALEYAM.—A town in the British district of North Arcot, presidency of Madras. It is situate on one of the islands of the Pulicat Lake, 55 miles N. by W. of Madras. Lat. 13° 54′, long. 80° 16′.

MONAS.—A river rising in lat. 28° 20′, long. 91° 18′, in the range of the Himalayas, and, flowing through Thibet in a southerly direction for forty miles, it passes through a gorge in the Himalayas into the native state of Bhotan, through which it flows south-westerly for 110 miles, receiving in this part of its course the Demree river, a stream of greater length than itself. It subsequently for twenty-five miles forms the boundary between Bhotan and the Assam district of Camroop, and for fourteen miles the boundary between Camroop and Goalpara, when it falls into the Brahmapootra, on the right side, in lat. 26° 11′, long. 90° 41′.

MONASSA, in the territory of Indore, or possessions of the Holkar family, a town on the route from Goona to Neemuch, 162 miles W. of former, 18 E. of latter. It is situate in a valley bounded on the north by the Chitor range of hills, has a bazar, in which a market is held, and is the principal place of a subdivision of the pergunnah of Rampoora. The town contains 1,030 houses and 4,100 inhabitants. Elevation above the sea 1,440 feet. Lat. 24° 27′, long. 75° 13′.

MONAY.—A town of Burmah, situate 138 miles S.E. by S. from Ava, and 190 miles N.E. by E. from Prome. Lat. 20° 26′, long. 97° 24′.

MONDA.—A town in the Rajpoot native state of Jodhpoor, situate 57 miles S.E. from Jodhpoor, and 74 miles S.W. from Ajmeer. Lat. 25° 47′, long. 73° 50′.

MONER, or MANER, in the British district Patna, lieut.-gov. of Bengal, a town on the right bank of the river Sone, four miles west, or above its confluence with the Ganges. It is estimated to contain 1,500 houses and about 7,000 inhabitants. Distant 20 miles W. of Patna. Lat. 25° 37′, long. 84° 50′.

MONFOO.—A town of Burmah, situate on the right bank of the Irawady river, and 193 miles N.N.W. from Ava. Lat. 24° 23′, long. 94° 51′.

MONGHYR.—A British district, denominated from its principal place, the town of the same name, and subject to the lieut.-gov. of Bengal. The extensive thannahs of Sheikpoorah and Dinniapore were, in 1817, transferred from Behar to this district. It is bounded on the north and east by the British district of Bhaugulpore; on the south-west by the districts of Ramghur and Behar; on the west by Behar and Patna; and on the north-west by Tirhoot. It lies between lat. 24° 20′—26° 1′, long. 85° 40′—86° 50′; is about 115 miles in length from north to south, and sixty in breadth. The area is 2,558 square miles. The principal rivers which skirt or intersect the district are the Ganges, the Sukri, the Kyul or Kewli, the Bhagmuttee, and the Gogaree.

The staple crops are rice and wheat; but barley, pulse, opium, oil-seeds, indigo, sugar, and tobacco are largely produced, mainly by artificial irrigation, by which water is distributed with great skill and perseverance over all parts of the surface.

The climate of the northern part of Monghyr, especially about the city bearing the same name, is considered so salubrious as to be a desirable residence for invalids, many of whom accordinly live here. The prevalent winds are either from the east, commencing usually in the middle of June and continuing to the middle of February, or from the west, which prevail during the remainder of the year; and when the wind changes, it does not usually blow from north or south, or any direction intermediate, but veers round at once from east to west, or west to east. The west winds are characterized by dryness, the east by moisture. The rainy season lasts from the middle of June to the middle of October; and in spring there are frequent squalls, with showers, and the fall of hailstones of great size. The air is considered drier here than in the districts farther eastward, and in the highlands drier than in the plains. The heat also is greater in the highlands than in the lower parts, the elevation not being sufficient to produce any sensible diminution of temperature, which, on the contrary, is heightened by the reflection of light and radiation of heat from the rocks. The winters are less severe than in the districts north and north-eastward, the thermometer scarcely ever falling to the freezing-point. The amount of population is given under the article Bengal. The principal towns, Monghyr, the capital, Soorajpore, Ghiddore, and Shekhpoor, are mentioned under their respective names in the alphabetical arrangement. The principal routes are—1. From east to west, from Berhampore to Benares, by Patna and Dinapore; and this is a very important one in a military point of view, being the only route by which the mountainous tract extending southward into the Ramgurh district is avoided; and, from lying along the right bank of the Ganges, having the further advantage afforded by the extensive navigation of that great river; 2. from north to south, from the city of Monghyr to Sonah, and subsequently turning southwest, to Ramgurh; 3. from east to west, from Soorajgurh to Behar; 4. from south-east to north-west, from Sonah to Behar.

Monghyr was acquired by the East-India Company in 1765, by virtue of the firman of Shah Allum, emperor of Delhi, granting the dewanny of Bengal, Behar, and Orissa.

MONGHYR, the principal place of the British district of the same name, subject to the lieut.-gov. of Bengal, is situate on the right bank of the Ganges, and on the route from Dinapore to Berhampore. The town comprises sixteen markets, scattered over a space a mile and a half long from north to south, and a mile wide. The houses are generally small: they have sloping roofs of red tiles, and gables ornamented with earthenware figures. It is a thriving place, having a great number of manufactories and shops for the fabrication and sale of hardware and firearms, but of execrable quality. The view of the town from the river is agreeable; it appears "ornamented with numerous gay Hindoo temples; and the effect of the whole is highly picturesque." The fort, built on a prominent rock, is partly washed by the Ganges, and where this is not the case, its rampart is defended on the outside by a wide deep ditch. The length of the fort from north to south is about 4,000 feet, the breadth 3,500: it contains three large tanks, and many residences and offices of the civil establishment: it is also a military station. It is a favourite place of residence for invalided military men and their families, being considered highly salubrious, and also very agreeable, from the beauty of the surrounding scenery. The rock jutting into the river is considered sacred by the Hindoos; and at certain seasons vast numbers of pilgrims enter the river, for the purpose of ritual ablution. Formerly there was directly above the bathing-place a handsome Brahminical temple, which was converted into a mosque by Shooja, son of Shahjehan. Within the fort is another mosque, beautifully built of black marble. The ruins of a splendid palace, built by Sultan Shooja, may still be traced; and contiguous is a vast well, always abundantly replenished, and believed to have a subterraneous communication with the Ganges.

Buchanan estimated the population, about forty years ago, at 30,000 persons, inhabiting 5,000 houses, and states the town to be a place of great antiquity, originally named Mudgalpur. It probably was at an early period a place of strength, but the construction of the present fort is generally attributed to Husain, styled by Buchanan the greatest of the kings of Bengal. It was repaired and enlarged, about 1660, by Shooja, son of Shahjehan, at the commencement of his unsuccessful struggle for empire and life against his brother Aurungzebe. It was subsequently repaired by Cossim Ali, when preparing for hostilities against the East-India Company. His precautions, however, availed not, as, after a feeble resistance of a few days' continuance, it was captured by the British. It was then considered a place of consequence as a stronghold in regard to its proximity to the north-west frontier; but the removal of that boundary to so great a distance has rendered it of no importance in such a point of view. Distant from Benares, E., by Dinapore, 265 miles; from Calcutta, N.W., by Berhampore, 304, by the Ganges 371. Lat. 25° 19′, long. 86° 30′.

MONGULHAT, in the British district of Rungpoor, lieut.-gov. of Bengal, a town on the right or south-west bank of the river Durlah. Buchanan describes it as a place of considerable trade, containing 800 houses; which number, according to the usually-admitted ratio of inmates to dwellings, would assign it a population of about 4,000. Distant N.E. from the town of Rungpoor 22 miles. Lat. 25° 58′, long. 89° 25′.

MONKHO, in the British district of Allygurh, lieut.-gov. of the N.W. Provinces, a village 10 miles S.W. of the cantonment of Allygurh, 42 miles N. of Agra. Lat. 27° 47′, long. 78° 4′.

MONOHUR THANA. — A town in the Rajpoot state of Jhalawar, situate 44 miles E.S.E. from Jhalra Patun, and 129 miles W. by N. from Saugur. Lat. 24° 13′, long. 76° 50′.

MONZE CAPE, or RAS MOOAREE, a sharply-projecting headland, forming the western extremity of the coast of Sinde, is the termination seawards of the high lands known in different parts by the names of the Hala, Brahooic, and Pubb mountains. Pottinger states that "it springs abruptly to a conspicuous height and grandeur out of the sea;" but Horsburgh describes it as of moderate height; and in this he is borne out by the outline given in Dalrymple's charts of the coast of Sinde. On the north-west of it is the island of Chilney or Churna, the channel of separation being four miles wide, and six or seven fathoms deep in the middle. Lat. 24° 50′, long. 66° 43′.

MOO, a river of Burmah, rising in lat. 23° 33′, long. 95° 27′, and, flowing in a southerly direction for 125 miles, falls into the Irawady, about forty-two miles below Ava, in lat. 21° 56′, long. 95° 24′.

MOOBAREKPOOR. — A town in the native state of Bhawulpoor, situate five miles from the left bank of the Sutlej, and 58 miles E.N.E. from Bhawulpoor. Lat. 29° 43′, long. 72° 38′.

MOOCHURI, in the British district of Etawa, lieut.-gov. of the N.W. Provinces, a town on the route from Mynpoorie to Etawa cantonment, and 12 miles N. of the latter. Water is obtainable from wells. The road in this part of the route is good. Lat. 26° 57′, long. 79° 1′.

MOOD BIDDEREE. — A town in the British district of South Canara, presidency of Madras, 18 miles N.E. by N. of Mangalore. Lat. 13° 4′, long. 75° 3′.

MOODEBEEHAL.—A town in the British district of Sholapoor, presidency of Bombay, 92 miles S. by E. of Sholapoor. Lat. 16° 20′, long. 76° 12′.

MOODGUL.—A town in one of the recently sequestrated districts of Hyderabad, or dominions of the Nizam, situate 68 miles N.W. by N. of Bellary. Lat. 16°, long. 76° 30′.

MOODHULL.—A town in the Southern Mahratta jaghire of Moodhull, situate 62 miles N.E. by E. from Belgaum, and 45 miles S.W. from Beejapoor. Lat. 16° 20′, long. 75° 20′.

MOODHULL.—A town in Hyderabad, or territory of the Nizam, situate nine miles from the left bank of the Godavery river, and 120 miles N.N.W. from Hyderabad. Lat. 18° 59′, long. 77° 53′.

MOODKEE.—A town twenty-six miles south of the left bank of the Sutlej, and within the jurisdiction of the commissioner and superintendent of the Cis-Sutlej states. It is chiefly remarkable on account of the action which took place in its vicinity on the 18th December, 1845, being the first in the war then in progress between the British government and that of the Sikhs. On this occasion, the Sikhs, whose numbers far exceeded those of the force opposed to them, were repulsed, and successively driven from position to position, with the loss of seventeen pieces of artillery. The victory, however, was not achieved without great loss on the side of the British, especially in European officers, more than fifty of whom were returned among the killed and wounded. Distant N.W. from Calcutta 1,140 miles. Lat. 30° 48′, long. 74° 55′.

MOODKHAID.—A town in Hyderabad, or territory of the Nizam, situate six miles from the left bank of the Godavery, and 140 miles N.N.W. from Hyderabad. Lat. 19° 9′, long. 77° 33′.

MOODÑAIKANHULLY.—A town in the British district of Bellary, presidency of Madras, 49 miles S.E. by S. of Bellary. Lat. 14° 33′, long. 77° 20′.

MOODONG.—A town in the British district of Amherst, in the Tenasserim provinces, situate 16 miles S.S.E. of Moulmein. Lat. 16° 16′, long. 97° 48′.

MOOFTUNG.—A town of Eastern India, in the native state of Chirra, in the Cossya Hills, 50 miles S. from Gowhatty, and 31 miles N.W. from Jynteahpore. Lat. 25° 26′, long. 91° 47′.

MOOGETALA.—A town in Hyderabad, or territory of the Nizam, situate on the left bank of the Kistnah river, and 111 miles E.S.E. from Hyderabad. Lat. 16° 50′, long. 80° 9′.

MOOGLEMEERY.—A town in the Mysore, territory of Madras, situate 119 miles N.E. from Seringapatam, and 151 miles W. by N. from Madras. Lat. 13° 29′, long. 78° 9′.

MOOHUMDABAD, in the British district of Furruckabad, lieut.-gov. of the N.W. Provinces, a town on the route from Futtehgurh to Mynpoory, 13 miles W. by S. of the former. Lat. 27° 19′, long. 79° 30′.

MOOJAUTHAPOORUM.—A town in Hyderabad, or territory of the Nizam, situate on the left bank of the Tandoor river, and 46 miles W.S.W. from Hyderabad. Lat. 17° 4′, long. 77° 57′.

MOOKHWAR, in the British district of Muttra, lieut.-gov. of the N.W. Provinces, a town 14 miles N.E. of the city of Agra. Lat. 27° 18′, long. 78° 14′.

MOOKSI.—A town in one of the recently sequestrated districts of Hyderabad, or dominions of the Nizam, situate 14 miles E. by S. of Moodgul. Lat. 15° 58′, long. 76° 42′.

MOOKUTPOOR, in the British district of Ramgurh, territory of Saugur and Nerbudda, lieut.-gov. of the N.W. Provinces, a town on the route from Sohagpoor to Nagpoor, 42 miles S.S.W. of the former. Lat. 22° 47′, long. 81° 7′.

MOOLA, a river rising in lat. 19° 26′, long. 73° 53′, on the eastern slope of the Western Ghats, and a few miles north of the Malsej Ghat, and, flowing in an easterly direction for 100 miles through the British districts of Poona and Ahmednuggur, falls into the Paira river, a tributary of the Godavery, in lat. 19° 32′, long. 74° 51′.

MOOLA MOOTA, the name of a feeder of the Bheema river, deriving its name from the junction near Poona, in the presidency of Bombay, of two streams, the Moola and the Moota, the former rising near the Bhore Ghaut, in lat. 18° 44′, long. 73° 28′, and the latter in lat. 18° 25′, long. 73° 30′. The united stream falls into the Bheema, in lat. 18° 34′, long. 74° 23′.

MOOLEIR.—A town in the British district of Candeish, presidency of Bombay, 35 miles W.N.W. of Malligaum. Lat. 20° 44′, long. 74°.

MOOLGOOND.—A town in the British district of Dharwar, presidency of Bombay, 38 miles E.S.E. of Dharwar. Lat. 15° 17′, long. 75° 35′.

MOOLKY, in the British district of Canara, presidency of Madras, a town on an inlet of the Arabian Sea, or North Indian Ocean, receiving a river descending from the Ghats, situate eastward. The estuary or inlet on which it is situate is too shallow to be navigated by large vessels, but serves as a place of shelter for coasting and fishing craft. Outside the mouth of the inlet is a group o' rocky islets, known by the name of the Mulki or Premeira Rocks. Distant from Mangaloor, N., 15 miles; from Madras, W., 370. Lat. 13° 6′, long. 74° 51′.

MOOLTAEE, in the British district of Baitool, territory of Saugur and Nerbudda, lieut.-gov. of the N.W. Provinces, a town on the route from Baitool to Nagpoor, 22 miles E. by S. of the former. Lat. 21° 47′, long. 78° 17′.

MOOLTAN.—A town of Malwa, in the native state of Dhar, situate 35 miles N. from Dhar, and 99 miles S. by E. from Neemuch. Lat. 23° 4′, long. 75° 14′.

MOOLTAN, an ancient city, stated to be the largest in the Punjab after Lahore and Amritsir, is situate three miles E. of the Chenaub, the inundations of which reach it. Elphinstone, who saw this place in 1809, before it had been stormed by the Sikhs, describes it as "surrounded with a fine wall between forty and fifty feet high." It is built on a mound of considerable height, formed of the ruins of more ancient cities. The bazars are extensive, and are well supplied with all articles of traffic and consumption, and the shops amount altogether in number to 4,600. Its principal manufactures are silks, cottons, shawls, loongees, brocades, tissues: its merchants are considered rich. Banking constitutes a large proportion of the business of Mooltan, in which it has in some measure supplanted Shikarpoor; and the prosperity of the town is in all respects considered on the increase.

The vicinity is covered with an amazing quantity of ruins of tombs, mosques, and shrines, which show the former extent and antiquity of the city. North of the place is the magnificent shrine of Sham Tabrezi, who, according to tradition, was flayed alive here as a martyr, and at whose prayer the sun descended from the heavens, and produced the intense heat from which Mooltan suffers, and for which it is proverbial. The adjacent country, watered by the inundations of the Chenaub, produces fruits, esculent vegetables, grain, and other crops, in great abundance and perfection. Mooltan is said by Burnes to be to this day styled "Mallithan," which he translates *the place of the Malli;* and thence infers it to have been that capital of the Malli taken by Alexander. But Arrian mentions several such cities; and his brevity, and the slender acquaintance which he had of the localities, must render any decision on such points at the present day hazardous and uncertain. Mooltan was taken by the Mahomedans, under Mahomed Ben Kasim, at the close of the eighth century; by Mahmood of Ghiznee, at the commencement of the eleventh; by Tamerlane, at the close of the fourteenth. It has always enjoyed the reputation of a place of great strength. After various fruitless attempts, extending over several years, it was, in 1818, captured by Runjeet Singh, who cut to pieces the Afghan garrison of 3,000, with the exception of a small number admitted to quarter. The booty on that occasion is said to have amounted to four million sterling. The army of the besiegers consisted of 25,000, of whom 19,000 were slain. Subsequently to the death of Runjeet Singh, and during the distracted times which ensued, this place again furnished an object of contention. The atrocious conduct of Dewan Moolraj, who in 1848 held the fortress of Mooltan, where two British officers were basely assassinated, demanded the renewal of hostilities, the earlier of which movements were rendered memorable by the extraordinary energy, enterprise, and judgment displayed by Major Herbert Edwardes, then a subaltern, "who had seen but one campaign," but whose military qualities would have been deemed worthy of distinction in a veteran soldier. The citadel of Mooltan at this time was represented as being more regular in construction than probably any other place laid down in India by native engineers. It stood on a mound, and in form was an irregular hexagon, with its longest side, which measured 600 yards, to the north-west. The wall, substantially built of burnt brick, was about forty feet high outside, but only four or five feet from the ground *inside*, in consequence of the accumulation of the materials of older buildings. It was surmounted by thirty towers, and protected by a ditch faced with masonry. On the 2nd January, 1849, the city was captured by a British force under General Whish, after an obstinate and gallant defence on the part of the enemy. On the 22nd, practicable breaches having been effected, the British troops were about to storm the citadel, when Moolraj, with his whole garrison, surrendered unconditionally. The destruction of the fort, then commenced, was a few months later completed by the elements, when the most violent storm ever remembered occasioned the flooding of the rivers of the Punjaub. "On the 28th August, the celebrated fortress of Mooltan was converted by the rains and floods into a mass of ruins. Owing, it is supposed, to some neglect of the people in charge of the bund up the river, the floods broke through and deluged the neighbouring country, and the water which surrounds the fort forced its way through the counterscarp into the ditch. In a few hours the whole of the outer wall was flat; and the water undermining the towers, they and the guns on them were all hurled into the ditch. Next day the second principal wall fell in, the citadel wall and several of the domes having previously given way." It was not thought advisable to repair the fortress with a view to its being rendered defensible and occupied as a military post. A redoubt, or small fortification, in the rear of the cantonments, it was believed would suffice for all military purposes. An obelisk, erected in the town by order of government, preserves the memory of those who fell in the Sutlej and Punjaub campaigns. The circumstances under which this part of the Sikh territory became a portion of the British dominions will be found detailed in the article PUNJAUB. The population of Mooltan, including the suburbs and cantonment, is given at 80,966. Of this amount 40,140 belong to the suburbs, and 15,853 to the cantonment. Lat. 30° 12′, long. 71° 30′.

MOOLWAGLE.—A town in the Mysore, presidency of Madras, situate 123 miles E.N.E. from Seringapatam, and 130 miles W. from Madras. Lat. 13° 9′, long. 78° 25′.

MOONAGALAH.—A town in the British district of Masulipatam, presidency of Madras, situate 66 miles N.W. of Guntoor. Lat. 17° 3′, long. 79° 53′.

MOONAGUL.—A town in Hyderabad, or territory of the Nizam, 29 miles W.N.W. from Hyderabad, and 148 miles E. from Sholapoor. Lat. 17° 29′, long. 78° 10′.

MOONDAAR, in Bussahir, a cave on the southern declivity of the Burenda Pass, from the crest of which it is distant two miles. It is important as affording shelter to travellers on their way to attempt that much-dreaded pass. Elevation above the sea 12,807 feet. Lat. 31° 23′, long. 78° 12′.

MOONDAGAM.—A town of the Deccan, in the territory of Nagpoor or Berar, situate 140 miles S.W. by S. from Sumbulpoor. Lat. 19° 54′, long. 82° 40′.

MOONDAGE.—A town in the hill zemindarry of Jeypoor, presidency of Madras, situate 34 miles E.N.E. from Jeypoor, and 109 miles N. by W. from Vizagapatam. Lat. 19° 12′, long. 82° 55′.

MOONDAGOOR.—A town in the British district of North Canara, presidency of Madras, 61 miles N.E. of Honahwar. Lat. 14° 58′, long. 75° 8′.

MOONDAL.—A town in the British district of Kaira, presidency of Bombay, 21 miles E. of Kaira. Lat. 22° 47′, long. 73° 1′.

MOONDEE.—A town in the native state of Gwalior, or territory of Scindia's family, situate nine miles W. from the Suktha river, and 88 miles W. by N. from Baitool. Lat. 22° 2′, long. 76° 39′.

MOONDKA, in the British district of Delhi, lieut.-gov. of the N.W. Provinces, a village on the route from Delhi to Hansee, and 12 miles W. of the former. The road in this part of the route is good. Lat. 28° 40′, long. 77° 6′.

MOONDLAPAUD.—A town in the British district of Cuddapah, presidency of Madras, 60 miles N. of Cuddapah. Lat. 15° 20′, long. 78° 58′.

MOONDRA.—A town in the native state of Cutch, presidency of Bombay, situate on the coast of the Gulf of Cutch, and 29 miles S. from Bhooj. Lat. 22° 50′, long. 69° 49′.

MOONDREE.—A town of Malwa, in the native state of Rutlam, situate four miles from the right bank of the Myhee river, and six miles S.S.E. from Rutlam. Lat. 23° 11′, long. 75° 3′.

MOONDURGEE.—A town in the British district of Dharwar, presidency of Bombay, 62 miles E. by S. of Dharwar. Lat. 15° 13′, long. 75° 57′.

MOONDWA, in the Rajpoot state of Jodhpoor, a village on the route from Nusseerabad to Nagor, and 11 miles S.E. of the latter town. It contains 200 houses, supplied with water from a tank. Lat. 27° 3′, long. 73° 55′.

MOONDYPOLLUM.—A town of Southern India, in the native state of Travancore, 29 miles N.E. from Quilon, and 64 miles N.W. by W. from Tinnevelly. Lat. 9° 11′, long. 76° 56′.

MOONGEE.—A town in Hyderabad, or territory of the Nizam, situate on the right bank of the Godavery, and 41 miles S.W. from Jaulnah. Lat. 19° 27′, long. 75° 30′.

MOONGHOM.—A town of Burmah, 117 miles E. from Muneepoor, and 199 miles N. from Ava. Lat. 24° 42′, long. 95° 52′.

MOONGROOL.—A town in Hyderabad, or territory of the Nizam, 63 miles S. by W. from Ellichpoor, and 104 miles E.N.E. from Jaulnah. Lat. 20° 17′, long. 77° 26′.

MOONJPOOR.—A town in Guzerat, or the dominions of the Guicowar, 109 miles N.E. by N. from Rajkote, and 51 miles S.W. by S. from Deesa. Lat. 23° 35′, long. 71° 43′.

MOONUK, in Sirhind, or territory of the protected Sikh states, a village on the route from Delhi to Ferozepoor, 140 miles N.W. of the former place. Water is abundant, as the village is near the river Gagur. Distant N.W. from Calcutta, *viâ* Delhi, 1,027 miles. Lat. 29° 49′, long. 75° 57′.

MOORA.—A town in the British district of Sumbulpoor, on the south-west frontier of Bengal, situate 29 miles W.N.W. of Sumbulpoor. Lat. 21° 38′, long. 83° 38′.

MOORAUDABAD.—A town in the territory of Oude, nine miles E. from the left bank of the Ganges, and 45 miles W. by N. from Lucknow. Lat. 26° 59′, long. 80° 17′.

MOORBAUR.—A town in the British district of Tannah, presidency of Bombay, 46 miles E.N.E. of Bombay. Lat. 19° 17′, long. 73° 30′.

MOORGOOR.—A town in the native state of Kolapoor, territory of Bombay, situate 22 miles S. from Kolapoor, and 43 miles N.W. by N. from Belgaum. Lat. 16° 23′, long. 74° 15′.

MOORHUR, a river rising in lat. 24° 8′, long. 84° 26′, in the British district of Ramghur, lieut.-gov. of Bengal, and, flowing in a northerly direction for twenty-two miles through Ramghur, seventy-nine miles through Behar, and thirty miles through Patna, falls into the Ganges a few miles below the town of Patna, on the right side, in lat. 25° 28′, long. 85° 23′.

MOORIGOORUM.—A town in Hyderabad, or territory of the Nizam, situate on the left bank of the Godavery river, and 154 miles E.N.E. from Hyderabad. Lat. 18° 14′, long. 80° 40′.

MOORJAPETT.—A town in the territory of Nagpoor or Berar, situate on the left bank of the Wein Gunga river, and 91 miles S.E. from Nagpoor. Lat. 20° 10′, long. 80° 2′.

MOORLEE.—A town in Nepal, situate 53 miles S.S.W. from Khatmandoo, and 26 miles N.E. by E. from Bettiah. Lat. 27°, long. 84° 56′.

MOOROOMGAUM.—A town in the territory of Nagpoor or Berar, 110 miles S.E. by E. from Nagpoor, and 200 miles S. by E. from Jubbulpoor. Lat. 20° 21′, long. 80° 36′.

MOOROOSAY, a river of Arracan, rising in lat. 21° 20′, long. 92° 40′, and, flowing in a south-westerly direction for thirty-five miles, falls into an arm of the sea, near Tek-Naf Point, in lat. 20° 47′, long. 92° 23′.

MOORPILLY.—A town in Hyderabad, or territory of the Nizam, 73 miles N. from Hyderabad, and 208 miles S.S.E. from Ellichpoor. Lat. 18° 24′, long. 78° 40′.

MOORSHEDABAD.—A British district within the jurisdiction of the governor of Bengal, deriving its name from its principal place. It is bounded on the north-east by the British districts Maldah and Rajeshahye, from which it is separated by the Ganges; on the east by the British district Rajeshahye; on the south-east, and part of the south, by the British district of Nuddea; on the remainder of the south by the British district Beerbhoom, which also bounds it on the west, with the exception of a very small portion bounded by Bhaugulpore. It lies between lat. 23° 48′—24° 47′, long. 87° 52′—88° 41′: the area is 1,856 square miles. The Ganges may be said to be the only principal stream of this district; for though there are others, they are offsets from that great river. The Ganges is nearly at its greatest size at the north-west corner, not having at that point sent off any of those great branches which, meandering through Eastern Bengal, find their way to the Sunderbunds. It touches on the district near Furruckabad, on the north-west angle, and, flowing south-east for twenty miles, sends off on the right side the Bhagruttee, a large branch, which, pursuing a sinuous course, but generally southerly, traverses the district for seventy miles to Burwa, where it crosses the south frontier, and forms the boundary between the British districts Nuddea and Beerbhoom. It is navigable during the greater part of the year for the largest craft which ply on the Ganges, and forms the principal channel of the route from Calcutta by water to the North-Western Provinces, a week being saved by proceeding through it instead of by the circuitous Sunderbund passage, farther eastward. During the three months of the dry season in spring, the navigation is nearly impracticable, admitting no craft of above a foot draught. Below the divergence, the main stream is denominated the Podda or the Ganges, and, proceeding in a direction south-east for sixty miles, to the town of Jellinghee, at the south-eastern angle of the district, it there sends off, on the right side, a large offset, denominated the river of Jellinghee, and continuing to flow south-easterly, leaves the district. The Jellinghee, following a very tortuous course, but generally south-west, forms the south-eastern boundary of the district for fifty miles, as far as Ballee, where it passes into the British district of Nuddea, and subsequently joins the Bhagruttee, the united stream being denominated the Hoogly. The Jellinghee, though less frequented than the Bhagruttee, in consequence of its being a less direct channel of communication with the North-Western Provinces, is superior in point of facility of navigation, being at all seasons practicable for craft of about two feet draught.

The eastern part of the district is low, remarkably level, subject to extensive inundations during the rains of autumn, and abounding in jhils or small lakes, apparently portions of the beds of streams which have deserted their channels. There are also many tanks or artificial pieces of water. The town of Jellinghee, on the bank of the Podda, at the south-eastern corner of the district, and probably the lowest point in it, is estimated to have an elevation of seventy-five feet above the sea; and Furruckabad, on the bank of the same river, but at the north-western angle of the district, has probably an elevation of 101½ feet above the sea. In the western part of the district are many hills connected with the neighbouring highlands of Rajmahal and Beerbhoom, whence descend numerous torrents, which join the Ganges or its branches, and, besides the important purposes of irrigation, serve to float down the firewood, which is obtained abundantly from the jungles. This western division of the district, locally denominated Rarha, is nearly unproductive without manure, but, treated with that fertilizing aid and due irrigation, it yields moderate crops of rice, sugar-cane, oil-seeds, pulse, cucurbitaceous plants, indigo, and some other articles of less importance. The mulberry is rather extensively cultivated for feeding silkworms.

The climate, formerly regarded as salubrious, is considered to have latterly, from some unknown cause, deteriorated in that respect. The station of Berhampore is regarded as peculiarly unhealthy. According to one traveller, every breath of air which visits it, comes over swamps and marshy lands; it abounds with ditches and stagnant pools, those fruitful sources of malaria; and its too redundant vegetation is rank and noisome.

Before the commercial character of the East-India Company had ceased, this district was one of the principal seats of its silk manufacture, which was conducted principally at the town of Berhampore. The production and manufacture were subsequently carried on with spirit, and in some instances with profitable results, by private persons. In 1840, the quantity produced was estimated at 2,000 maunds, or 160,000 pounds. Indigo is the commercial crop next in importance. The principal silk manufacture is that of corahs. Of other manufactures, the following may be mentioned:—Coarse cotton fabrics, works in brass and iron, blankets, carpets, paper, mats, toys, and carvings in wood and ivory. Berhampore, the seat of the civil establishment Moorshedabad, the ancient capital and largest town; Jeajanj, Jellinghee, Bogwangola, and Suti, are described under their respective names in the alphabetical arrangement. The principal military routes are—1. From south to north, from Calcutta, through Burwa, Berhampore, and the city of Moorshedabad, subsequently diverging north-west to Rajmahal, and north-east to Bogwangola. 2. From south-west to north-east, from Bancoora, by way of Sooree, through Berhampore, to Murcha and Rampore. The population of this district is given under the article BENGAL.

The tract comprised within this district, formed at a remote period part of the great realm of Magadha, and on its fall, at the close of the seventh century, became a province of the kingdom of Gaur. At the commencement of the thirteenth century, when the Patan Mussulmans, commanded by Bakhtyar Khilji, invaded this part of India, it was ruled by a rajah whose government was located at the city of Nuddea, and who fled without making resistance, leaving his dominions to the mercy of the enemy. It was immediately incorporated with the state which arose under the name of the kingdom of Bengal, and shared its various vicissitudes, until its final subjugation in 1584 by Acbar. In the desperate confusion and exterminating wars supervening on the death of Aurungzebe, when the remoter provinces of the kingdom of Delhi became impatient of the control of the paramount power, Moorshud Kuli Khan, appointed in 1701 by Aurungzebe, his dewan or chief financial officer, over the extensive and productive province of Bengal, fixed the seat of his government at the town of Makhsusabad, to which, after himself, he gave the name, still retained, of Moorshedabad. He exercised his sway more as a potentate tributary to a superior, than as a subordinate officer, until the period of his death in 1725, when he was succeeded in his dignity by his son-in-law Shujah-uddin. On the death of Shujah-uddin, in 1739, his power devolved on Serefraz Khan, son of the ruler last mentioned, and grandson of the founder of the state of Moorshedabad. He, after the enjoyment of government for a few months only, was attacked by Ali Verdi Khan, one of his officers, defeated in battle, and slain; whereupon the victor, without meeting any further resistance, took possession of the city of Moorshedabad, and all the treasures and dominions of the vanquished ruler. Ali Verdi struggled with great perseverance against the numerous armies of the Mahrattas, who repeatedly overran the country, and in 1742 partially plundered the city of Moorshedabad, and succeeded in extorting an agreement for the payment of chouth, or a fourth part of the revenue of the province, as black mail. His death took place in 1756, and he was succeeded by his grandson Suraja Dowlah, the rash and sanguinary prince who, in 1757, defeated at Plassy by the British army commanded by Clive, fled from the field, to meet death in a less glorious mode. Clive, immediately after the battle, pushed on to Moorshedabad, and declared as nawaub Muhammad Jaffier Khan. In 1760 this prince was deposed by the English, who raised Cossim Ali Khan to his place; but he, having engaged in war against the British, was in turn deposed, and Muhammad Jaffier Khan reinstated as nawaub. He retained that position until his death in 1764, and was succeeded by his son Najmud-daulah. The dignity, long since become purely titular, is supported by the magnificent allowance of 160,000*l.* per annum. Of this allowance, the sum of between 50,000*l.* and 60,000*l.* per annum is placed at the disposal of the nawaub; from the remainder are paid the stipends of the collateral branches of the family, and the balance constitutes a deposit-fund, from which are defrayed the charges on account of the agency and of the college, together with other expenses incurred on account of the family. The district of Moorshedabad passed to the East-India Company by the grant of Shah Allum in 1765.

MOORSHEDABAD, a town, the principal place of a British district of the same name, lies on the route from Berhampore to Dinagepore, six miles N. of the former, and 100 S. of the latter. It is situate on the Bhagruttee, a great offset of the Ganges, flowing from north to south, and dividing it into two parts—Moorshedabad properly so called, situate on the left or east bank, and Mahinagar, situate on the west or right bank. The aggregate town extends from north to south for a distance of several miles, with an average breadth of four. It is a very indifferent place, consisting chiefly of a rude assemblage of mud buildings, lying confusedly together. The river, however, enlivens the scene, being for a great part of the year covered with boats, for the purposes of trade or amusement. The palace, constructed by Aliverdi Khan, principally of materials brought from the ruins of Gour, is a gloomy, ruinous pile; but a new palace, which had been several years in course of erection, was completed in 1840. It is described by a traveller, who saw it while in progress, as "a fine building, in the European style, of dazzling whiteness, and rising in glittering splendour, amid stately groves of flourishing trees." Its cost was enormous; and the extent and magnificence of the edifice is altogether disproportionate to the dependent position of the nawaub. Moorshedabad is a place of considerable commerce, lying on the most-frequented route by water between Calcutta and the North-Western Provinces. It is subject, however, to the disadvantage of being unapproachable by craft of above a foot draught during the dry months of spring. According to a census taken in 1829, the number of houses was 40,118; of which 14,281 belonged to Mussulmans, the rest to Brahminists: the number of permanent inhabitants was 146,176; of whom the Mussulmans were 56,090, and the Brahminists 90,086. To this number is to be added that of strangers and temporary residents, 787; making a total of 146,963. Whilst the capital of Bengal, Moorshedabad was a place of great trade and wealth; so great indeed as to lead Lord Clive to institute a comparison between it and the city of London. From want of drainage, the place is said to be extremely unhealthy; but the present nawaub is stated to have manifested a strong desire for the improvement of its sanitary condition. A college was some years since founded here, at the expense of the native authority, to which subsequently an English professor was attached. Distance N. from Calcutta, by Berhampore, 124 miles. Lat. 24° 12′, long. 88° 17′.

MOORSUNGONG.—A town in the native state of Bhotan, 57 miles N. by E. from Durrung, and 74 miles N.W. by W. from Bishnath. Lat. 27° 13′, long. 92° 11′.

MOORTAUZPOOR.—A town in one of the recently sequestrated districts of Hyderabad, or the dominions of the Nizam, situate 36 miles S. by W. of Ellichpoor. Lat. 20° 41′, long. 77° 26′.

MOORUD.—A town in the British district of Tannah, presidency of Bombay, 43 miles S. by E. of Bombay. Lat. 18° 20′, long. 73° 2′.

MOORVEE, in the peninsula of Kattywar, province of Guzerat, a town, the principal place of the division of Muchu Kanta. It is situate on the river Muchu, which, twenty-two miles farther north, falls into the Gulf of Cutch. The tallook or subdivision annexed contains 110 towns and villages, having an estimated population of 24,000. It pays to the Guicowar an annual tribute of 6,000*l*. The thakoor or chief of Moorvee is a Jharegha Rajpoot. Tradition represents him as the descendant of the eldest son and lawful heir of the rao of Cutch, who, in the latter part of the seventeenth century, was murdered by a younger brother, and whose family thereupon fled to this place, then a dependency of Cutch; by the ruler of which their possession of Moorvee was subsequently sanctioned. Disputes still exist between the two rulers. Distant from Ahmedabad, W., 115 miles; Baroda, W., 155; Bombay, N.W., 300. Lat. 22° 48′, long. 70° 50′.

MOOSA KHAIL, in the Daman division of the Punjab, a town situated 41 miles W. from the right bank of the Indus, 129 miles S.W. by S. of the town of Peshawur. Lat. 32° 25′, long. 70° 35′.

MOOSERY.—A town in the British district of Trichinopoly, presidency of Madras, 20 miles W.N.W. of Trichinopoly. Lat. 10° 57′, long. 78° 30′.

MOOSIWALLEH, in the Sinde Sagur Dooab division of the Punjab, a town situated 10 miles from the left bank of the Indus, 123 miles S. by W. of the town of Peshawur. Lat. 32° 16′, long. 71° 22′.

MOOSLA.—A town in the native state of Indoor, or territory of Holkar, 24 miles S.E. from Indoor, and 107 miles W. by S. from Hoosungabad. Lat. 22° 27′, long. 76° 8′.

MOOSLEEMUDDOO. — A town in the British district of Kurnool, presidency of Madras, 28 miles E.N.E. of Kurnool. Lat. 15° 59′, long. 78° 30′.

MOOTA RIVER.—See MOOLA-MOOTA.

MOOTOURKHAS, in the British district of Futtehpoor, lieut.-gov. of the N.W. Provinces, a town on the route from Futtehpoor to Bandah, 14 miles S.W. by W. of the former. Lat. 25° 48′, long. 80° 43′.

MOOTUPETTA.—A town in the British district of Madura, presidency of Madras, 66 miles S.E. of Madura. Lat. 9° 17′, long. 78° 54′.

MOOYANLAKHOOLEL. — A town of Eastern India, in the native state of Muneepoor, 31 miles N.W. by N. from Muneepoor, and 111 miles E. by N. from Jynteahpoor. Lat. 25° 13′, long. 93° 50′.

MOPEA.—A town of Eastern India, in the native state of Osimlee, in the Cossya Hills, 26 miles S. from Gowhatty, and 54 miles N.W. by N. from Jynteahpoor. Lat. 25° 47′, long. 91° 40′.

MOPLAHS.—See MALABAR.

MOPOON.—A town in the British district of Amherst, in the Tenasserim provinces, three miles S. of Moulmein. Lat. 16° 26′, long. 97° 42′.

MOR.—A river rising in the British district of Bhagulpore, lieut.-gov. of Bengal, in lat. 24° 31′, long. 87° 1′; it flows in a south-eastern direction for thirty miles through Bhagulpore, and for thirty-five miles through Beerbhoom, and then, turning easterly, it proceeds forty-five miles to its junction with the Dwarka river. The united stream holds a southerly course for twenty miles, when it falls into the Bhagruttee, in lat. 23° 43′, long. 88° 10′.

MORADABAD, a British district in the division of Rohilcund, under the lieut.-gov. of the N.W. Provinces, is named from its principal place. It is bounded on the north-east by the British district Kumaon; on the east by the British district Bareilly and the jaghire of Rampoor; on the south by the British district Budaon; on the west by Boolundshuhur and Meerut; and on the north-west by Bijnour. It lies between lat. 28° 15′—29° 27′, long. 78° 10′—79° 24′: the area is 2,967 square miles. Its frontier on the north and north-east is marked by a range of hills of no great elevation, separating it from the Patlee Doon, a depressed tract, forming the southern part of the district of Kumaon. Chilkea, situate on the right bank of the Kosila, where it issues from the hills, is 1,076 feet above the sea. From that quarter, the surface of the country generally declines to the south, the streams flowing in that direction. The same inclination is proved by actual measurement; thus the town of Moradabad, forty miles south of Chilkea, is 403 feet below it. The north-eastern part of the territory, extending along the base of the hills, consisting of the Terai or marsh-land, is characterized by the prevalence of springs and streams, luxuriant vegetation, and deadly malaria, and overrun with gigantic grasses and rushes, jungle, and forest-trees. The country is in general level, though in some places moderately undulating. The town of Moradabad is built on a ridge running from north-west to south-east, and rising between twenty and thirty feet above the level of the country. Adjacent to it is a tract of sand, from one to two miles in breadth, and forming the depression down which the Ramgunga flows. To the south-west, the land declines towards the left bank of the Ganges, and at length in some places becomes kadir or marsh, the soil having been deposited by that river, and remaining liable to its inundations. There are other alluvial tracts along the various streams, characterized by moisture and fertility, and under cultivation yielding luxuriant crops. In general, however, the country is well drained by its rivers, the Ramgunga, the Gunghun, and the Kosee or Kosila. The Ramgunga, which issues from the hills at some distance from this district, though rather small, is a rapid stream, receiving in its course various tributaries. From the town of Moradabad, on its way to the Ganges, into which it falls, it is navigable for about nine months in the year. It has been conjectured that the whole extent of the ridge upon which the town of Moradabad stands, was washed by the water of the Ramgunga at some former period. The Gunghun runs nearly parallel with the Ramgunga, flowing on the opposite side of the town of Moradabad, where the two rivers are at no great distance from each other: the former ultimately joins the Ramgunga about ten miles below the town. The Gunghun is not navigable, though a considerable stream, for the most part confined by steep banks. It is variable in depth, and in many places fordable, except during the rains. A scheme for improving the irrigation of the northern division of the district by means of this river was sanctioned by the home authorities in 1837. The water of these rivers, but especially that of the Ramgunga, is good, and by some Europeans is preferred for culinary purposes to that of the wells, though the quality of water procured from the latter source is also well reported of. The wells are numerous, and abundant in their supply, few failing even in the driest season. In the central tract, the average depth of the wells is twenty-two feet. The depth increases towards the hills in one direction, and towards the Ganges in the other. As the whole territory is alluvial, it contains no minerals. The climate of the cleared and dry tracts is more congenial and grateful to Europeans than that of almost any other part of India, and the average amount of disease and mortality amongst them is as low as at home. The prevailing winds are east and west: the former are perhaps more frequent here than on the western side of the Ganges. The atmosphere is remarkably dry and clear, fogs being rare. The cold weather may be said to commence about the middle of October; but from the 15th September the nights and mornings are cool and pleasant. The months of December and January sometimes produce a degree of cold that is almost incredible; for instance, in January, 1836, the thermometer fell on two mornings to 22° at sunrise, and for some successive days it did not exceed 28° at that time: many pieces of water were covered with ice. The cool weather continues to the end of March, and often to the middle of April. The hot winds blow very irregularly, sometimes commencing about the 16th of April, at others not until the end of that month or the beginning of May: they are also generally unsteady, alternating with a less strong wind from the east. Severe north-westers occur at short intervals from April to the commencement of the rains. The periodical rains set in irregularly from the 10th June to the early part of July, and cease in the end of August, or early in September: they are heavy, and during their continuance the temperature is moderate.

Elephants are numerous in the forests, and though the breed is less valued for domestication than those produced farther to the east, some are annually captured for that purpose. Tigers infest the jungly tracts. There are, besides, the leopard, bear, jackal, lynx, fox, wild dog, nylgau, spotted deer, antelope, hare, and squirrel. Among the feathered tribe are the peafowl, floriken or bustard, partridge, quail, pigeon, snipe, bittern, jungle-fowl, wild goose, and wild duck. Of reptiles, there are the boa-constrictor, the cobra de capello, and three other venomous sorts of serpents, water-snakes, and some harmless kinds. Scorpions and centipedes infest every building; but, though causing great suffering, seldom produce death. The streams abound with fish, some of which are delicious.

The agriculture of Moradabad is important and varied. The sugarcane succeeds well: it is of a large black kind, abounding in rich saccharine juice. Cotton also thrives. Rice, of very fine quality, is grown in the watered districts. Wheat is produced in great excellence, and in large quantity; but the food of the labouring classes is principally maize and millet. Fruits and esculent vegetables are abundant and excellent. The mango produces great quantities of large fine fruit, but requires to be carefully protected from the cold of winter. Peaches are large, juicy, and well-flavoured; nectarines scarcely ripen, and apricots are rare: neither apples nor pears are fine. There are custard-apples, figs, mulberries, guavas, and plums. Grapes are abundant and fine, but might be improved by better management; flowers and shrubs in great variety have been introduced from the Botanic Garden at Saharunpoor. Of the esculent vegetables usually grown in Europe, many succeed very well. There are peas, beans, cabbages, cauliflowers, turnips, potatoes, carrots, cucumbers, beetroot, celery, and a profusion of herbs. Under the last revenue settlement of the North-West Provinces, the government demand on the lands of this district has been fixed for a term of years, and is not liable to augmentation until the year 1872. The population, according to official return, amounts to 1,138,461; of whom 502,331 are represented to be Hindoo agricultural, 263,663 Hindoo non-agricultural, 182,767 Mahomedans and others agricultural, and 189,700 of the like description non-agricultural. In comparison with the area, the returns show a population of about 422 to the square mile, a proportion which, to all persons familiar with statistical inquiries, will appear enormous. The British collector assigns various causes for the abundance of the population: the facility with which a family may be supported, and the consequent number of marriages; the temperate habits of the people, and their respect for the nuptial engagement, and their general indisposition to emigrate. That the country is for the most part thickly peopled, is indeed obvious, even to the passing traveller. From one end to the other, with here and there occasional exceptions, a broad expanse of rich cultivation meets the eye, broken by luxuriant mango and other groves, at short distances from each other, with generally a village to each. On entering these villages, the number of children playing in front of every door cannot fail to attract the attention of the most unobservant. Of course the forest-tract is an exception to this general rule. The district contains nine towns in which the number of inhabitants exceeds 5,000 but falls short of 10,000; four in which the number ranges between 10,000 and 50,000; and one in which the number exceeds 50,000.

A scheme for improving irrigation in the northern part of the district was sanctioned in 1837, at an estimated cost of 6,000*l.*; and from Major Colvin's report it would appear that the features of the country were peculiarly favourable to the project. The official document describes the tract over which the proposed works were to be carried as one of gentle undulations of the surface, the main ridges being nearly north and south, and falling off east and west into the rivers leading from the mountains. The sloping sides of these ridges were further stated to be intersected by minor watercourses with a strong southerly fall, and having generally a partial supply of water dependent on springs at their sources.

The principal routes through the district of of Moradabad are,—1. from Allygurh, and through the town of Moradabad, northward to Almora, by Chilkea; 2. from Moradabad to Almora, by Rampoor, a little east of the former route; 3. a route in a direction south-east and north-west, from Bareilly, through the town of Moradabad, by Nugina, to Hurdwar; 4. a route from south to north, to Hurdwar, running nearly parallel to the last, but ten or twelve miles more to the west; 5. a route in a direction east and west, from Meerut to Rampoor, through the town of Moradabad. There are besides several routes of less importance.

Moradabad is part of the tract heretofore known by the name of Rohilcund, in consequence of its colonization by Rohilla Afghans, who established themselves here early in the last century. In 1774, the power of the Rohillas was totally broken by a severe defeat which they received at Tessunah, near Kutterah, from a British force subsidized by the nawaub of Oude, who, in consequence, became master of a large portion of their possessions. In 1801, the province, with some other districts, was ceded to the East-India Company, under a re-arrangement of the Company's relations with the nawaub of Oude, rendered necessary by the improvidence and misgovernment of the latter.

MORADABAD, the principal place of the British district of the same name, is situate on a ridge of ground from twenty to thirty feet above the neighbouring country, and forming the right bank of the Ramgunga. Its appearance is not striking, it being very deficient in mosques, tanks, and all other public works. There is one street about a mile long, full of shops, and paved with vitrified bricks set edgewise. This used to be kept clean and in good repair, but the funds formerly employed for the purpose of so preserving it being no longer available, it is at present neglected. There is a spacious serai for the accommodation of travellers, and a market is daily held for the produce of the neighbourhood. The jail is sufficiently large to contain 1,800 native convicts, ostensibly condemned to work in chains on the roads. Mundy conjectures that their labour might be directed to some other objects; "for the roads," he observes, "through which we have jolted for the last three days seem perfect strangers to the spade and pickaxe." The chief duty of the troops is to guard this great assemblage of convicts. Nearly west of the town, and separated from it by the jail, are the cantonments, agreeably situate amid luxuriant trees, and a parade containing forty acres of ground. Moradabad is a civil station, and the cutcherry, or residence of the collector, is a handsome house, surrounded by a mud rampart, with round bastions and a deep ditch. It was built by an official resident named Leicester, who, on the approach of a powerful Mahratta army under Holkar, manned it with such forces as he could collect, and, though a civilian, kept the enemy at bay until Lake advanced and raised the siege. Moradabad had formerly a mint, the rupees of which had a very extensive circulation. In 1835 and 1836, the mean of the thermometer at noon at this place was, for the month of October, 77°; November, 70°; December, 63°; January, 56°; February, 61°; March, 70°; April, 76°; May, 84°; June, 86°; July, 82°; August, 85°; September, 84°. In these years, however, it is stated that the temperature of the rainy months was much above the usual average. The population, according to the latest official return, is 57,414; the majority of which is Mahomedan, and mostly of Patan descent. Elevation above the sea 678 feet. Distance N.W. from Calcutta 838 miles. Lat. 28° 49′, long. 78° 50′.

MORAD I MUNZIL, in the British district of Ajmeer, lieut.-gov. of the N.W. Provinces, a town on the route from Nusseerabad to Boondee, 43 miles S.E. of the former. Lat. 25° 55′, long. 75° 20′.

MORADNAGAR, in the British district of Meerut, lieut.-gov. of the N.W. Provinces, a town on the route from Delhi to the town of Meerut, and 21 miles N.E. of the former. The road in this part of the route is good. Lat. 28° 47′, long. 77° 34′.

MORALKAKANDA, in Bussahir, a lofty mountain-range, which stretches continuously, but with various height and breadth, in a south-westerly direction, from the Himalaya bounding Koonawar on the south, to Urki, in the state of Bhagul, or from between lat. 31° 29′—31° 10′, and long. 77° 50′ and 77°. It forms the south-eastern or left boundary of the valley of the Sutlej in this part of its course, that great river running along its base, and receiving numerous small feeders from its north-western declivity, whilst from its south-eastern side the streams flow into the Giree, Pabur, Tonse, and Jumna.

MORASSA.—A town in the British district of Kaira, presidency of Bombay, 66 miles N.E. of Kaira. Lat. 23° 27′, long. 73° 21′.

MORDEE BAY, on the east coast of the island of Bombay. The site having been pointed out as an eligible locality for the terminus of the Bombay Railway, a project has been sanctioned for its reclamation from the sea. Lat. 18° 56′, long. 72° 54′.

MORNEE.—A summit in a range of mountains of moderate elevation, stretching from Nahun, in a north-west direction, to the south-eastern extremity of the Pinjor Doon. It is surmounted by a fortress, which, though surrounded by the possessions of the Sikhs, is held by a Mahomedan chief, with a small adjacent territory. It was a secondary station in the great trigonometrical survey of the Himalayas. Elevation above the sea 2,413 feet. Lat. 30° 41′, long. 77° 9′.

MOROOM.—A town in one of the recently sequestrated districts of Hyderabad, or dominions of the Nizam, situate 38 miles E. by N. of Sholapoor. Lat. 17° 43′, long. 76° 30′.

MORRISON BAY, formed by several islands composing the Mergui Archipelago, particulary the two larger ones of Domet and Kisserraing, to the south. Its centre is about lat. 11° 53′, long. 98° 29′.

MORUDEA, in the British district of Cawnpore, lieut.-gov. of the N.W. Provinces, a village on the route from the cantonment of Etawa to that of Cawnpore, and 48 miles W. of the latter. The road in this part of the route is good, the country cultivated. Lat. 26° 22′, long. 79° 42′.

MORVEE.—See Moorvee.

MOSCOS.—A chain of islands on the coast of Tenasserim, known as Northern, Middle, and Southern, extending, "parallel to the coast, from lat. 13° 47′ to 14° 28′, long. 97° 53′, and distant from it three to four and five leagues, having a safe channel inside, between them and the coast, with soundings mostly from ten to fifteen fathoms, deepening generally near the islands, and shoaling to eight, seven, and six fathoms near the main."

MOSEH.—A town in the British district of Poonah, presidency of Bombay, 60 miles S.E. of Bombay. Lat. 18° 26′, long. 73° 36′.

MOSULUKUL.—A town in one of the recently sequestrated districts of Hyderabad, or dominions of the Nizam, situate 26 miles W.N.W. of Raichoor. Lat. 16° 22′, long. 77° 3′.

MOTE, in the British district of Jaloun, lieut.-gov. of the N.W. Provinces, a town on the route from Calpee to Goonah, 64 miles S.W. of former, 121 N.E. of the latter. Lat. 25° 43′, long. 79° 1′.

MOTEYE.—A town in the Rajpoot state of Jodhpoor, 72 miles N.N.W. from Jodhpoor, and 64 miles S.W. from Beekaneer. Lat. 27° 18′, long. 72° 46′.

MOTOORA.—A town in the British district of Pubna, lieut.-gov. of Bengal, 121 miles N.E. of Calcutta. Lat. 23° 55′, long. 89° 40′.

MOUDHA, a town on the route from Banda to Calpee, 21 miles N.W. of the former, 47 S.W. of the latter. It has a population of 7,571 inhabitants, contains a bazar, and is well supplied with water. Lat. 25° 41′, long. 80° 10′.

MOULMEIN, in the British district of Amherst, a town, the principal place of the Tenasserim provinces, is situate on a small peninsula, formed by the Salwein, the Gyne, and the Attaran rivers, opposite to the town of Martaban, and 30 miles N. of Amherst. Upon its cession to the British, in 1826, the site was selected for a military station, and the town, which now bears all the marks of civilization, a few years back presented a very different scene; the accumulation of dirty and ill-ventilated alleys, of which it then consisted, having been converted into a fine seaport town, with open streets, quays, markets, churches, and schools. The main street runs parallel with the river, and communicates with different parts of the town by means of others joining it at right angles. The cantonment is considerably raised, well drained, and healthy, and its position is advantageous in a military point of view; but the facilities of communication now provided by means of steam navigation, for the rapid disposal of troops upon any particular point, may be regarded as sufficient to secure the defence of this portion of the British dominions. The population of the town is given at 17,042. Vast forests in the neighbourhood yield an inexhaustible supply of teak timber, which, coupled with other local advantages, has enabled Moulmein to supplant Chittagong and other ports on the eastern coast of the Bay of Bengal, in shipbuilding. The Company's steamer *Tenasserim*, and her Majesty's steam-sloop *Malacca*, were built at this port. Like most eastern towns, Moulmein has suffered severely from the casualty of fire: in 1850 a conflagration occurred, entailing a loss of upwards of 60,000*l.* upon the principal European merchants. A newspaper, entitled the *Moulmein Guardian*, has been established in the town. Lat. 16° 30′, long. 97° 42′.

MOUTNEE, in Sinde, is an offset on the left or eastern side of the great Sata branch of the Indus. Though once a large stream, it has now become a mere shallow rivulet, discharging its water into the sea by the unnavigable Kaheer mouth, in lat. 23° 51′, long. 67° 38′.

MOUTTSHOBOMYO, or MONCHABOO.—A town of Burmah, situate 19 miles from the right bank of the Irawady, and 43 miles N.N.W. from Ava. The town is venerated as the birthplace of Alompra, the founder of the present dynasty, who selected it, on that account, as the seat of empire. Lat. 22° 25′, long. 95° 46′.

MOUZIMPOOR, in the British district of Muttra, lieut.-gov. of the N.W. Provinces, a village on the route from the cantonment of Allygurh to that of Etawa, and 39 miles S.E. of the former. Lat. 27° 26′, long. 78° 24′.

MOW, in the British district of Allygurh, lieut.-gov. of the N.W. Provinces, a town 20 miles S.E. of the cantonment of Allygurh. Lat. 27° 47′, long. 78° 26′.

MOW.—A small town in the British district of Banda, lieut.-gov. of the N.W. Provinces. It is situate on the right bank of the Jumna, and "is remarkable for two isolated hills upon the Doab side of the river, jutting into the middle of the stream. These hills are of red sandstone, which is quarried" for building, and abound in deep caverns and curious recesses. Distant 67 miles S.E. of the town of Banda, 30 S.W. of Allahabad. Lat. 25° 17′, long. 81° 26′.

MOW, or MAO, in Bundelcund, in the British district of Jhansee, a town on the small river Supprar. It was one of the first conquests of Dewada Bir, who established the Boondela dominion in this part of India, and was the first post of Champat Rao, when, towards the close of the seventeenth century, he raised the standard of revolt against the court of Delhi. Sleeman styles it "the large commercial town of Mow," but gives no other information on the subject. Distant 70 miles S.W. of Calpee. Lat. 25° 15′, long. 79° 12′.

MOW, or MAU, in the British district of Allahabad, lieut.-gov. of the N.W. Provinces, a town on the route from Allahabad cantonment to that of Purtabgurh, in the Oude territory, 17 miles N. of the former, 14 S. of the latter. It has a bazar. Lat. 25° 42′, long. 81° 56′.

MOWA, in the Rajpoot native state of Jeypoor, a town on the route from Agra to Ajmere, 70 miles W. of former, 158 E. of latter. It has a tolerably good bazar, supplied with "cutlery, ornaments of gold and silver, and shawls, as well as the more usual rustic commodities of cotton, corn and flour, ghee, and coarse cloth." The town is surrounded by an earthen rampart with bastions, and has at its north-east angle a fort belonging to the Jeypoor rajah. The interior of the fort "is about ninety yards square, and the walls are very high, having a great command over the renee, the parapet of which appears itself to be from thirty-five or forty feet above the bottom of the ditch. The latter is broad as well as deep, the counterscarp being about twenty feet high, and it is protected by a covered way eight feet broad, to which the interior slope of the glacis furnishes a parapet six feet high, but without any banquette." Boileau states that it contains 2,000 houses, an amount which would assign it a population of about 10,000; but this appears to be an exaggerated estimate. Lat. 27° 3′, long 77°.

MOWA, in Guzerat, a town on the south-eastern coast of the peninsula of Kattywar, at the head of a small bay. It is, however, an indifferent port, the anchorage being without shelter towards the south, and with a sandy bottom at from seven to ten fathoms; and with the flood tide a vessel must lie with a reef of rocks right astern: it however has considerable traffic. Distance from Ahmedabad, S., 150 miles; Baroda, S.W., 130; Bombay, N.W., 160. Lat. 21° 3′, long. 71° 43′.

MOWAH, in the British district of Tirhoot, lieut.-gov. of Bengal, a town on the route from Dinapoor to Purneah, 30 miles N.E. of former, 170 W. of latter. Lat. 25° 46′, long. 85° 29′.

MOWAH.—A town in the British district of Tirhoot, lieut.-gov. of Bengal, 48 miles S.E. from Mozufferpoor. Lat. 25° 33′, long. 85° 55′.

MOWAI, in the British district of Banda, lieut.-gov. of the N.W. Provinces, a village on the route from Cawnpore, by Chila Tara ghat, to the town of Banda, four miles N. of the latter. Lat. 25° 32′, long. 80° 24′.

MOWAI, in the British district of Futtehpoor, lieut.-gov. of the N.W. Provinces, a village on the left bank of the Jumna, 30 miles W. of the town of Futtehpore. Lat. 25° 55′, long. 80° 22′.

MOWANUH, in the British district of Meerut, lieut.-gov. of the N.W. Provinces, a village on the route from the town of Meerut to that of Bijnour, and 11 miles N.E. of the former. Population 6,486 inhabitants. Lat. 29° 6′, long. 77° 55′.

MOWASI, in the territory of Oude, a village on the route from Cawnpore to Lucknow, five miles N.E. of the former, 48 S.W. of the latter. Lat. 26° 30′, long. 80° 31′.

MOWGUNGE, or MAUGANJ, in the territory of Rewa or Boghelcund, a town on the route, by the Kutra Pass, from Allahabad to Jubulpoor, and 91 miles S.W. of the former. It is described by Jacquemont as a large village, but the dwellings are miserable mud-built thatched huts. It has a bazar, and is well supplied with water from a tank, a rivulet, and wells. Elevation above the sea about 1,200 feet. Lat. 24° 40′, long. 81° 56′.

MOWHAR, or MOHAR, in the British district of Futtehpore, lieut.-gov. of the N.W. Provinces, a village situate on the right bank of the Ganges, on the route from Cawnpore to the town of Futtehpore, and 18 miles N.W. of the latter. Lat. 26° 6′, long. 80° 40′.

MOWKHAS, in the British district of Cawnpore, lieut.-gov. of the N.W. Provinces, a village on the route from Allahabad to Etawa, and 64 miles S.E. of the latter. Lat. 26° 13′, long. 79° 50′.

MOYAAR, a river rising in the Neilgherries, in lat. 11° 22′, long. 76° 35′, at the foot of the mountain called Makurty Peak. It receives the drainage-waters of the Pichul and Pykara valleys, and, descending the hills at the north-west angle, by a fall near Neddiwuttum, turns due east after reaching the plains, and, flowing round the base of the Neilgherries, on the northern and eastern faces, joins in lat. 11° 28′, long. 77° 10′, near Danaikencotta, in Coimbatore, the Bowany. After a course of seventy miles, the united stream discharges itself into the Cavery. A bridge of masonry has been erected over the river at Tippacandra.

MOYUNDA, in the British district of Jaunsar, lieut.-gov. of the N.W. Provinces, a village on a rocky and bare ridge, about two miles west of the right bank of the Jumna. Lat. 30° 41′, long. 78° 6′.

MOZABAD, or MAWZABAD, in the Rajpoot native state of Jeypoor, a town on the route from Agra to Ajmere, 180 miles W. of former, 48 E. of latter. Heber describes it as a "rather large town, with a ruined wall, mosque, some good gardens, and several temples." A fine temple belonging to the Jains is profusely adorned with elaborate sculptures, and surmounted by a richly-carved dome and three pyramids of sculptured stone. Lat. 26° 40′, long. 75° 25′.

MOZUFFERPORE, in the British district of Tirhoot, lieut.-gov. of Bengal, a town on the route from Dinapore to Mulye, 50 miles N.E. of former, 50 S. of latter, situate on the Little Gunduck, a river so considerable as to be unfordable, and which must consequently be crossed by ferry. A government school has been established in the town, in which an Arabic and Persian teacher is maintained from the revenues of an estate assigned for that purpose by Mahomed Tuckhe Khan, a zemindar of Tirhoot. The population is estimated at 8,945. A destructive fire, attended with great loss of human life, occurred in this town in 1838. Distance N.E. from Benares, by Dinapoor, 173 miles; N.W. from Calcutta, by Hazaribagh and Dinapoor, 426. Lat. 26° 6′, long. 85° 28′.

MOZUFFURNUGGUR, a British district under the lieut.-gov. of the N.W. Provinces, is bounded on the north by the British district Saharunpore; on the east by the British district Bijnour, from which it is separated by the Ganges; on the south by the British district Meerut; and on the west by the Jumna, dividing it from Paniput and Sirhind. It lies between lat. 29° 10′—29° 50′, long. 77° 6′—78° 10′; is sixty miles in length from east to west, and forty in breadth from north to south: its area is 1,617 square miles. The inclination of the surface is very gentle, and is from north to south, which is the direction of the course of the Ganges on the eastern frontier, the Jumna on the western, and of the intermediate streams, the Kalee Nuddee and the Hindon, as well as of the line of slope of the Doab Canal. The surface rises from the Ganges on the one side, and the Jumna on the other, to the interior of the Doab, where there is a prolonged elevation in some measure parallel to the rivers, and nearer the former than the latter. It is marked by a rage of sandhills, not continuous, but disposed in small ridges, of which one for a short distance runs parallel to the next in succession, before it subsides to the level of the plain. The elevation of this range has been ascertained with considerable accuracy, its crest being selected as the line of the Ganges Canal, which is now in progress, and by means of which a portion of the main stream drawn off near Hurdwar will for the purposes of irrigation and navigation be conveyed down the middle of the Doab to Cawnpore, where any redundant water will be reunited to the parent river. Nusseerpoor, on this line, and close to the northern boundary, in lat. 29° 45′, long. 77° 55′, has an elevation of 974 feet; and probably neither sandhill, nor any other eminence throughout the district, is 100 feet above this place. At Kutowlee, close to the southern boundary, the elevation diminishes to 904 feet. A khadir, or low alluvial marshy tract, stretches in a few places along the left bank of the Jumna, and one much more extensive along the right bank of the Ganges. The Ganges khadir is for the most part very fertile, and admirably suited for rice-grounds; but the damp, unwholesome air renders it ill suited for the residence of man. It is thinly peopled and ill cultivated; a portion is made serviceable for grazing, but this portion yields only the wild produce of the jungle. The chief products of the district of Mozuffurnuggur are sugarcane, cotton, tobacco, rice, wheat, barley, maize, millet, pulse of various kinds, oil-seeds, and esculent vegetables. The tract appears to be considerably infested with wolves. In 1840, the rate of rewards for the destruction of these animals was increased, and in 1841 it was found requisite to increase it still further. The value of money in India considered, the scale of rewards seems high, being five rupees for a female wolf, four for a male, and two for a cub.

The population, from a recent census, appears as amounting to 672,861; of which number 241,246 are returned as Hindoos agricultural; 248,925 as Hindoos non-agricultural; 83,943 Mahomedans and others agricultural, and 98,747 under the same head non-agricultural. The proportion of persons to a square mile exceeds 331. The following is a classification of the towns and villages in the district:—

Number containing less than 1,000 inhabitants	717
Ditto more than 1,000 and less than 5,000....	159
Ditto „ 5,000 „ 10,000....	7
Ditto „ 10,000	4
Total................	887

Of the chief towns some notice is taken under their respective names in the alphabetical arrangement. The land assessment is fixed for a term of years, which will expire on the 1st July, 1861.

The tract forming the present British district of Mozuffurnuggur was wrested from the Mogul empire by the Mahrattas, and in 1803 was ceded to the East-India Company by Scindia, under the second article of the treaty of Serjee Anjengaum, which alienated all that chieftain's "forts, territories, and rights in the Doab." A considerable portion of the district was included in the jaghire of the female adventurer Zebulnisa, more generally known as the Begum Sumroo, of whom some account is given in the article on the Meerut district. On her decease, in 1836, the jaghire lapsed to the Company.

MOZUFFURNUGGUR, the principal place of the British district of the same name, under the lieut.-gov. of the N.W. Provinces, is situate on the left bank of the West Kalee Nuddee. It is a large town, having a population of 9,646 inhabitants. Elevation above the sea about 900 feet. Distance N.W. from Calcutta, by Moradabad and Allyghur, 984 miles. Lat. 29° 28′, long. 77° 45′.

MUBARAKPOOR.—A town in the British district of Bijnour, lieut.-gov. of the N.W. Provinces. Lat. 29° 19′, long. 78° 12′.

MUBARAKPOOR, in the British district of Aldemau, territory of Oude, a town on the right bank of the Ghaghra, 35 miles S.E. of the city of Oude. Butter estimates the population at 3,000; half of which number are Mussulmans, generally employed in weaving. Lat. 26° 35′, long. 82° 38′.

MUCHERHUTTA.—A town in the territory of Oude, 41 miles N.N.W. from Lucknow, and 58 miles S.E. by E. from Shahjehanpoor. Lat. 27° 24′, long. 80° 45′.

MUCHKAUTA, in the peninsula of Kattywar, province of Guzerat, a prant or division named from the river Muchoo, which flows nearly through its centre, in a direction from south to north, and falls into the Gulf of Cutch. This division is bounded on the east and south-east by that of Jhalawar; on the south-west and west by the division of Hallar; on the north-west by the Gulf of Cutch; on the north by the Runn or Great Salt Marsh; and lies between lat. 22° 30′—23° 6′, long. 70° 34′—71° 3′. There is no accurate return of the area, which may probably be about 700 square miles. It is held by three thakoors or chiefs; and in the description of their respective territories, all that is known of the constituent parts of this division is stated.—See MOORVEE, UDALA, and MALLIA.

MUCHLEESHEHUR, in the British district of Jounpoor, lieut.-gov. of the N.W. Provinces, a town on the route from Allahabad to Jounpoor cantonment, 45 miles N.E. of the former, 21 S.W. of the latter. It has a large bazar. Lat. 25° 42′, long. 82° 26′.

MUCKUNDGUNGE.—A town in the British district of Ramgur, lieut.-gov. of Bengal, 19 miles N.W. by N. of Ramgur. Lat. 23° 56′, long. 85° 21′.

MUCKUNPOOR, in the territory of Rewa or Baghelcund, a town nine miles S. of the town of Rewa. It appears to be a place of some importance, as its name enters into the title of the ruler of the country, who is styled rajah of Rewa and Muckunpoor, or Mookunpore, as it is spelled in the English copy of the treaty concluded with him. Lat. 24° 24′, long. 81° 19′.

MUCKWANPORE, in the kingdom of Nepaul, a village situate on the banks of the river Kurra, a feeder of the Raptee, whence the fort of Muckwanpore bears about E. by N. The valley of Muckwanpore, of which the ancient rajah was dispossessed by the Goorkhas, is of no great extent, but the soil is fertile, yielding rice in great abundance and variety. Lat. 27° 22′, long. 85° 11′.

MUDBUNI, in the British district of Ghazeepore, lieut.-gov. of the N.W. Provinces, a village on the route from Ghazeepore cantonment to Chupra, 64 miles E. of the former, 18 W. of the latter. Lat. 25° 48′, long. 84° 32′.

MUDDEERA.—A town in Hyderabad, or dominions of the Nizam, 129 miles E. by S. from Hyderabad, and 76 miles N.W. from Masulipatam. Lat. 16° 57′, long. 80° 26′.

MUDDOOR.—A town in the Mysore, 27 miles E.N.E. from Seringapatam, and 102 miles N.W. by W. from Salem. Lat. 12° 36′, long. 77° 6′.

MUDDUCK SERA.—A town in the British district of Bellary, presidency of Madras, 86 miles S.S.E. of Bellary. Lat. 13° 57′, long. 77° 20′.

MUDDUKRRAY.—A town in the British district of Coimbatoor, presidency of Madras, eight miles S. Coimbatoor. Lat. 10° 54′, long. 77° 2′

MUDDUM.—A town in the British district of Tinnevelly, presidency of Madras, nine miles N.W. of Tinnevelly. Lat. 8° 49′, long. 77° 39′.

MUDDUMPULLY. — A town in the British district of Cuddapah, presidency of Madras, 126 miles W. by N. of Madras. Lat. 13° 33′, long. 78° 34′.

MUDDUNPOOR.—A town in the native state of Calahandy, in Orissa, 51 miles N.E. by E. from Joonnagudda, and 78 miles W.N.W. from Goomsoor. Lat. 20° 19′, long. 83° 37′.

MUDGERRY DROOG, in the Mysore, a hill-fort among the mountains on the north-east frontier, towards the British district Bellary. Approached from the east, its view is very fine, both the works and the vast rock on which they stand being very conspicuous and grand. On the destruction of the monarchy of Vijayanagar by a Mussulman confederacy, A.D. 1564, at the great battle of Talikot, it was seized by a poligar or chief of the country, and subsequently came into the possession of the rajahs of Mysore, one of whom replaced the mud fort with the present fortress of stone, and also built a palace and a large temple; and Hyder Ali, after he had become master of Mysore, extended and strengthened the fortifications. In A.D. 1772 it fell into the hands of the Mahrattas, but was recovered in the following year by Tippoo Sultan. From its long series of calamities, the town, once highly prosperous, is now merely a group of ruins. Distance from Bangalore, N.W., 56 miles; Seringapatam, N. 95. Lat. 13° 40′, long. 77° 16′.

MUDH, in the Rajpoot state of Beekaneer, a village on the route from the town of Beekaneer to that of Jessulmere, and 30 miles S.W. of the former. Here, in 1835, Shah Shooja, the expelled monarch of Afghanistan, took refuge in a state of such distress, that he thankfully accepted some trays of dried fruit from the officers of the British mission in Rajpootana. Mudh is in lat. 27° 50′, long. 73°.

MUDHARGARHI, in the British district of Agra, lieut.-gov. of the N.W. Provinces, a village on the northern frontier, towards the district of Muttra, and on the route from Khasganj to the city of Agra, 14 miles N.E. of the latter. Lat. 27° 19′, long. 78° 11′.

MUDHBUNEE.—A town in the British district of Sarun, lieut.-gov. of Bengal, 28 miles W.N.W. of Bettiah. Lat. 26° 57′, long. 84° 10′.

MUDHOOBUNEE.—A town in the British district of Tirhoot, lieut.-gov. of Bengal, 82 miles N.E. by E. of Dinapoor. Lat. 26° 19′, long. 86° 10′.

MUDHPURI, in the British district of Bijnour, lieut.-gov. of the N.W. Provinces, a village on the route by the course of the Ramgunga (Western), from Moradabad cantonment to Fort Almora, 48 miles N. or the former. Lat. 29° 29′, long. 78° 42′.

MUDHUN, or MANDUN, in the British district of Mynpooree, lieut.-gov. of the N.W. Provinces, a town on the route from the cantonment of Muttra to that of Mynpooree, and 10 miles W. of the latter. Lat. 27° 15′, long. 78° 55′.

MUDIPOOR, in the British district of Delhi, lieut.-gov. of the N.W. Provinces, a village on the route from Rhotuk to the city of Delhi, and six miles W. of the latter. Lat. 28° 40′, long. 77° 11′.

MUDLI, in the Rajpoot state of Jodhpoor, a village on the route from Nusseerabad to Deesa, and 111 miles S.W. of the former. Lat. 25° 44′, long. 73° 30′.

MUDMESUR, in the British district of Kumaon, lieut.-gov. of the N.W. Provinces, a village with a Hindoo temple, situate at the southern base of Badrinath Mountain. The river Mudmesur, which flows below the temple, at a short distance to the south-east, has its origin among the snows of Badrinath, and taking a south-westerly course of about twenty-five miles, falls into the river Mandakini, on the left side, opposite Nalaputun, in lat. 30° 32′, long. 79° 8′. The temple of Mudmesur is in lat. 30° 36′, long. 79° 15′.

MUDNOOR.—A town in Hyderabad, or dominions of the Nizam, eight miles W. from the left bank of the Manjera river, and 97 miles N.W. from Hyderabad. Lat. 18° 30′, long. 77° 40′.

MUDOOPORE.—A town in the British district of Mymunsing, lieut.-gov. of Bengal, 170 miles N.E. of Calcutta. Lat. 24° 37′, long. 89° 59′.

MUDRA, or MUNDURA, in the British district of Allahabad, lieut.-gov. of the N.W. Provinces, a village on the right bank of the Ganges, 772 miles N.W. of Calcutta by the river route, 36 S.E. of the city of Allahabad by the same. Lat. 25° 17′, long. 82° 16′.

MUDSAN, in the British district of Allygurh, lieut.-gov. of the N.W. Provinces, a town situate on the left bank of the Jumna, and 28 miles N. of Agra, 85 S.E. of Delhi. Lat. 27° 35′, long. 77° 58′.

MUDURKOOTEE.—A town in the British district of Barasut, lieut.-gov. of Bengal, 41 miles E.N.E. of Calcutta. Lat. 22° 47′, long. 89° 2′.

MUFTIGANJ, in the British district of Jounpoor, lieut.-gov. of the N.W. Provinces, a town on the route from Ghazeepore to Jounpoor cantonment, 39 miles W. of the former, 11 S.E. of the latter. Lat. 25° 41′, long. 82° 55′.

MUFTI KA PURWA, in the district of Allahabad, lieut.-gov. of the N.W. Provinces, a village on the route from the town of Allahabad to that of Futtehpore, and 13 miles N.W. of the former. It has a few shops. Lat. 25° 28′, long. 81° 44′.

MUGGUR TALAO (Alligator's Pool), in

Sinde, a collection of hot springs, eight miles N. of Kurrachee, and swarming with alligators. They belong to several fakirs, who have attached themselves to the tomb of a Mahometan considered by his countrymen to have been a character of peculiar sanctity. Hence is the name *Muggea Peer*, by which the place is popularly known among Europeans, being a corruption of *Magar Peer* or *Pir*, "the alligator's saint." These thermal springs are situate amidst rocky and very barren hills, and spring out of the bottom of a small fertile valley, thickly wooded with date-trees and acacias, over which the white dome of the shrine is visible. Adjacent to the shrine are a few highly-ornamented tombs, the architectural style of which resembles that of some English structures of the age of Elizabeth. Allen says, "The devices were principally scroll and diamond work; the carving, though not very bold, was elaborate in design and neatly executed." The principal spring issues from the rock on which the shrine is built, and has a temperature of about 98°, the water being perfectly clear, and of a sulphureous smell. Another spring, about half a mile distant, has a temperature of 130°. The water, received into tanks, forms a grateful retreat for the alligators. On occasion of a stranger's visit, the fakirs regale these animals with a carcase of a goat, and their struggles and contests to secure the prey constitute a scene at once ludicrous and disgusting. They are very tame, and never seek to injure human beings. It is remarkable that they are genuine alligators, and totally distinct from the *guryal*, or long-snouted crocodile, which abounds in the Indus, a short distance to the east. The fakirs live in a few mud huts, the only human habitations in this vicinity. Lat. 24° 58′, long. 67° 5′.

MUGHS.—See ARRACAN.

MUGHUR, in the British district of Goruckpore, under the lieut.-gov. of the N.W. Provinces, a town in the pergunnah or subdivision of Husainpur Mughur, situate on the route from Goruckpore cantonment to Lucknow, 18 miles W. of the former, and 148 E. of the latter. It is on the river Aumee, here passed by ford or temporary bridge. Buchanan's survey, made forty years ago, describes it as a poor scattered place, containing 370 houses; and consequently, if six persons be allowed to each, the population might be estimated at 2,220. Here is the reputed tomb of Kavir, a personage held in great account amongst religionists, but whose precise opinions seem to be matter of much doubt. It is under the charge of a Muhammedan disciple, whose ancestors, it is said, have held the office ever since the funeral of the saint or teacher, of whose remains the tomb is the supposed receptacle. Mughur is distant from Benares, N., 100 miles. Lat. 26° 42′, long. 83° 11′.

MUGRA, in Gurhwal, a village amidst the mountains on the southern frontier, between Surkanda and the ridge rising north-east of the Dehra Doon. A few miles to the south-west, on the route between this village and that of Nagal, is Sansar Dhara, or "the dripping rock." Mugra is in lat. 30° 24′, long. 78° 16′.

MUGRIBEE.—A town in the British district of Hydrabad, province of Scinde, presidency of Bombay, 75 miles S. by W. of Hydrabad. Lat. 24° 20′, long. 68° 17′.

MUGRIBEE, in Scinde, a town situated on the Piniaree, a branch of the Indus. Below the town a dam has been thrown across the Piniaree about fifty miles from its mouth. It is forty feet broad, and of proportionate height, but the water in the swell makes its way through numerous small openings to the channel below, called the Goongra, which is navigable to the sea, discharging itself by the Sir mouth. The Piniaree is also navigable from the town upwards to the Indus. The traffic is almost exclusively in rice, which, being produced abundantly in Scinde, is exported down this channel to Cutch. Population 5,000. Lat. 24° 10′, long. 68° 17′.

MUGRONEE, or MAGRAUNI, in the territory of Gwalior, or possessions of Scindia's family, a small town with a fort, three miles north of the left bank of the river Sindh. Some iron-ore, raised in the neighbouring sandstone hills, is smelted here. Lat. 25° 42′, long. 77° 56′.

MUGROR, or MUNGRORE.—A place which, with Kera, gives name to the pergunnah of Kera Mungrore, in the British district Mirzapoor. It is situate 25 miles S.E. of the city of Benares, in the mountainous tract in the south-east of the district of Mirzapoor, and 45 miles S.E. of the city of that name. Lat. 25° 1′, long. 83° 20′.

MUHABUN, in the British district of Muttra, lieut.-gov. of the N.W. Provinces, a town on the route from Muttra to Etawah, and eight miles S.E. of the former. A short distance west of it, the Jumna is passable by a much-frequented ford, by which, in November, 1804, Jeswunt Rao Holkar fled from the Doab, after his enormous body of cavalry had been surprised and dispersed with great slaughter by General Lake, at Furruckabad; and here also, in the early part of 1805, Ameer Khan, the Patan freebooter, crossed in his incursion into the Dooab, and subsequently recrossed in his flight from the British army. It formerly was much more important than at present, as in the eleventh century it was held by a special rajah or monarch, who having been, in A.D. 1017, worsted by Mahmood of Ghuznee, slew his own wife and children, and then turned the point of the sword against himself. The place was then surrendered to the conqueror, who gained with it much treasure and other booty, including eighty elephants. Muhabun contains a population of 6,968 inhabitants, and is distant S.E. from Delhi 105 miles. Lat. 27° 25′, long. 77° 49′.

MUHADEWAH.—A town in the territory of Oude, 15 miles N.N.W. from Oude, and 82 miles W. by N. from Goruckpoor. Lat. 26° 59′, long. 82° 6′.

MUHAIR.—A town in the British district of Behar, presidency of Bengal, 25 miles E.N.E. of Sherghotty. Lat. 24° 43′, long. 85° 13′.

MUHAISREE.—A town in the British district of Mongheer, lieut.-gov. of Bengal, 49 miles S. by W. of Mongheer. Lat. 24° 41′, long. 86° 18′.

MUHAMMAD ALIPOOR, in the British district of Bijnour, lieut.-gov. of the N.W. Provinces, a village on the route up the course of the Ramgunga (Western), from Moradabad cantonment to Fort Almora, 42 miles N. of the former. Lat. 29° 25′, long. 78° 43′.

MUHAMYAING. — A town of Burmah, situate 19 miles E. from the left bank of the Khyendwen river, and 122 miles N.W. by N. from Ava. Lat. 23° 19′, long. 95°.

MUHANWAN, or MAHOWA, in the British district of Allahabad, lieut.-gov. of the N.W. Provinces, a village on the route by the Rajapoor ferry from the cantonment of Allahabad to Banda, and 37 miles W. of the former. Lat. 25° 27′, long. 81° 25′.

MUHAR, in the Reechna Dooab division of the Punjab, a town situated 10 miles E. from the left bank of the Chenaub, 112 miles W.S.W. of the town of Lahore. Lat. 31° 9′, long. 72° 24′.

MUHARI, in the British district of Etawa, lieut.-gov. of the N.W. Provinces, a village on the route from Calpee to the cantonment of Etawa, and 23 miles S.E. of the latter. Lat. 26° 35′, long. 79° 20′.

MUHDEWA, or MAHADEOPOOR, in the British district of Allahabad, lieut.-gov. of the N.W. Provinces, a village on the left bank of the Ganges, 770 miles N.W. of Calcutta by the river route, 38 S.E. of the city of Allahabad by the same. Lat. 25° 14′, long. 82° 17′.

MUHEEAIDEENPOOR, or MOHUDYPOOR, in the British district of Allyghur, lieut.-gov. of the N.W. Provinces, a village on the route from the city of Agra to Khasgunge cantonment, and 51 miles N.E. of the former. Lat. 27° 40′, long. 78° 36′.

MUHESPOOR, in the British district of Bareilly, lieut.-gov. of the N.W. Provinces, a village on the route from the town of Bareilly to Moradabad, and five miles N.W. of the former. Lat. 28° 23′, long. 79° 26′.

MUHESUR, in the British district Moradabad, lieut.-gov. of the N.W. Provinces, a village on the route from the town of Moradabad to Meerut, and 30 miles W. of the former. Lat. 28° 52′, long. 78° 23′.

MUHESUR, in the territory of Indore, or the possessions of the Holkar family, a town on the north or right bank of the Nerbudda. It has a fort, containing many houses within its inclosure, but it is in bad repair. The river, which is here about 2,000 feet wide, has a rapid stream of blue water, rushing over a rocky bottom; the banks are sixty or eighty feet high in the dry season, yet even then the stream, though shallow, is still rapid. Access to the water is gained by a ghat or vast flight of stone stairs, which extends below the water at its lowest stage. Jacquemont, at the time of his visit in 1832, found above 1,000 workmen employed on a spacious palace then in the course of construction by order of Holkar. It is built of grey basalt, and is overcharged with sculptures of human beings, and of elephants, tigers, and other beasts. Muhesur was formerly the residence of the celebrated Ahalya Bai, relict of Kunda Rao, son of Maharajah Mulhar Rao. She appears to have been a woman of singular ability and munificent disposition, but deeply imbued with Hindoo superstition, which feeling she gratified by the erection of numerous and costly Brahminical temples and fanes, here and elsewhere. In 1820 this place contained 3,500 houses, which, at the usual average, would assign it a population of 17,500. Distance from Mhow, S.W., 28 miles; from Bombay, N.E., 280. Lat. 22° 11′, long. 75° 39′.

MUHILA.—A town in the British district of Tirhoot, presidency of Bengal, 71 miles N.N.E. of Dinapoor. Lat. 26° 34′, long. 85° 32′.

MUHLOG.—See MHILOG.

MUHOOAREE, in the British district of Benares, a town situate on the right bank of the Ganges, 15 miles to the N.E. of Benares. Lat. 25° 24′, long. 83° 16′.

MUHUDWANEE, in the British district of Ramgurh, territory of Saugor and Nerbudda, lieut.-gov. of the N.W. Provinces, a town on the route from Ramgurh to Jubbulpoor, 21 miles W.N.W. of the former. Lat. 22° 56′, long. 80° 44′.

MUHUL, in Sirhind, a village on the route from Lodiana to Hurreekee Ghat, and 48 miles W. of the former place. It is situate nine miles from the left bank of the Sutlej, in a level country, of no great fertility, scantily cultivated, and generally overrun with grassy jungle. Distant N.W. from Calcutta 1,137 miles. Lat. 31° 5′, long. 75° 10′.

MUI.—A river of Nepal, forming, together with the Ponna, the head-water of the Gonkor river.—See GONKOR.

MUICAL.—A town in the British district of Malabar, presidency of Madras, 49 miles S.E. of Cannanore. Lat. 11° 24′, long. 75° 58′.

MUIKELUNG.—A town in the British district of Amherst, in the Tenasserim provinces, presidency of Bengal, 35 miles E. of Moulmein. Lat. 16° 30′, long. 98° 13′.

MUIRRI.—A town in Guzerat, or dominions of the Guicowar, situate 111 miles W. by S. from Rajcote, and 64 miles N.W. by W. from Poorbunder. Lat. 22° 6′, long. 69° 10′.

MUJAHUN.—A town in the Rajpoot state

of Beekaneer, 60 miles N.E. by N. from Beekaneer, and 137 miles W. by S. from Hansi. Lat. 28° 43′, long. 73° 54′.

MUJEENWAN, or MUNJEEAWAN, in the British district Behar, lieut.-gov. of Bengal, a small town close to the south frontier, towards Ramgurh, and the principal place of a thana or police division of the same name. The town of Mujeenwan is distant S.E. from Benares 85 miles. Lat. 24° 20′, long. 83° 50′.

MUJERI, in the British district of Bijnour, lieut.-gov. of the N.W. Provinces, a village on the route from Moradabad to Hurdwar, and 39 miles N.W. of the former. Lat. 29° 23′, long. 78° 32′.

MUJGAON, in the British district of Furruckabad, lieut.-gov. of the N.W. Provinces, a town on the right bank of the Esun, 25 miles S. of the city of Furruckabad. Lat. 27° 1′, long. 79° 35′.

MUJHOWLEE, in the British district of Goruckpore, lieut.-gov. of the N.W. Provinces, a small town on the left bank of the river termed the "Little Gunduck," connected with Selempoor, opposite to it, on the right. It contains 200 houses, and with Selempoor is usually considered one town, the former the Hindoo, the latter the Mahometan. Here is a brick-built residence belonging to the petty rajah of the country; but his family usually residing on his estates in the adjoining British district of Sarun, he has allowed it to become ruinous. Mujhowlee is 45 miles S.E. of the cantonment of Goruckpore. Lat. 26° 17′, long. 83° 58′.

MUJWAN, in the British district of Allahabad, lieut.-gov. of the N.W. Provinces, a village on the route, by the Kutra Pass, from the cantonment of Allahabad to Rewa, and 18 miles S.E. of the former. Lat. 25° 17′, long. 82° 4′.

MUJHWAR, in the British district of Benares, lieut.-gov. of the N.W. Provinces, a town on the route from Benares to Sasseram, 19 miles E. of the former. Lat. 25° 14′, long. 83° 22′.

MUJJUL.—A town in the Rajpoot state of Jodhpoor, situate on the left bank of the Loonee river, and 41 miles S.W. from Jodhpoor. Lat. 25° 51′, long. 72° 45′.

MUKARARY, in the British district of Malabar, presidency of Madras, a town situate at the western base of the Western Ghats, on a river flowing from that range, and nine miles E. of Cananore. Lat. 11° 52′, long. 75° 34′.

MUKDUMPOOR, in the British district of Moradabad, lieut.-gov. of the N.W. Provinces, a village on the route from the town of Moradabad to that of Mozuffernuggur, and 24 miles N.W. of the former. Distant N.W. from Calcutta 872 miles. Lat. 28° 58′, long. 78° 30′.

MUKEER.—A town in the British district of Sarun, lieut.-gov. of Bengal, 23 miles N.E. by E. of Chupra. Lat. 25° 56′, long. 85° 6′.

MUKIMPOOR, in the British district of Shahjehanpoor, lieut.-gov. of the N.W. Provinces, a village on the route from Bareilly to Lucknow, 58 miles S.E. of the former, 98 N.W. of the latter. Lat. 28° 2′, long. 80° 13′.

MUKIMPOOR, in the British district of Boolundshuhur, lieut.-gov. of the N.W. Provinces, a village on the route from Khasganj to Meerut, and 46 miles S. of the latter. Lat. 28° 22′, long. 77° 59′.

MUKKOO.—A town in the British division of the Cis-Sutlej territory, 33 miles E.N.E. of Ferozepore. Lat. 31° 6′, long. 75° 5′.

MUKKUD, in the Sinde Sagur Dooab division of the Punjab, a town situated on the left bank of the Indus, 61 miles S. of the town of Peshawur. Lat. 33° 7′, long. 71° 50′.

MUKREE, in Bundelcund, a town, the principal place of a jaghire or feudal possession of the same name, containing an area of ten square miles, with a population of 1,600 inhabitants. The town is distant 28 miles N.E. from Punnah, and 30 miles S. by E. from Bandah. Lat. 25° 2′, long. 80° 33′.

MUKRUMGURH.—A town in the British province of Sattara, presidency of Bombay, 30 miles W.N.W. of Sattara. Lat. 17° 50′, long. 73° 39′.

MUKSOODNUGGUR.—A town in the native state of Gwalior, or territory of Scindia's family, situate 161 miles S.S.W. from Gwalior, and 101 miles W. by N. from Saugur. Lat. 24° 7′, long. 77° 14′.

MUKTULL, in Hyderabad, or territory of the Nizam, a town near the southern frontier, towards the British district of Bellary. It is one of the stations of the British subsidiary force, generally denominated the Nizam's army. Distance from Hyderabad, S.W., direct, 90 miles; Madras, N.W., 305. Lat. 16° 29′, long. 77° 31′.

MUKUNPOOR, in the British district of Mynpooree, lieut.-gov. of the N.W. Provinces, a village on the route from the city of Agra to Etawah, and 39 miles N.W. of the latter. Lat. 27° 7′, long. 78° 33′.

MUKUNPOOR, in the British district of Cawnpore, lieut.-gov. of the N.W. Provinces, a town between the cantonments of Futtehgurh and Cawnpore, and 34 miles N.W. of the latter. It is noted on account of a much-frequented annual pilgrimage to the tomb of Mudar, a reputed Mussulman saint, who, according to the legend, died at the age of 395 years. The tomb, covered with a canopy of cloth of gold, and situate in the middle of a square building, with four windows of fretwork, is from time to time perfumed with otto of roses. There is also a mosque, and in front of it a fountain. Lat. 26° 54′, long. 80° 2′.

MULAHUR, in the Rajpoot state of Jodhpoor, a village on the route from the town of Bikaneer to that of Phulodi, and five miles N. of the latter. Lat. 27° 13′, long. 72° 26′.

MULAIR KOTELAH, in Sirhind, a town on the route from Patiala to Ferozepore, and 45 miles N.W. of the former town. It is the principal place of a district held by a Sikh chief, under the protection and control of the British government, and which is stated to have an area of 144 square miles, and a population of above 21,000. The town is distant N.W. from Calcutta, by Delhi and Hansee, 1,100 miles. Lat. 30° 31′, long. 75° 59′.

MULANUH, in the British district of Umballah, in the territory of Sirhind, a town on the route from Suharunpoor to Loodiana, and 41 miles N.W. of the former place. Like most of the towns of this country, it is walled round, and has a small fort. Distant N.W. from Calcutta, by Delhi and Kurnaul, 1,000 miles. Lat. 30° 17′, long. 77° 7′.

MULAREE, in the British district of Kumaon, lieut.-gov. of the N.W. Provinces, a village on the route from Joshimath to the Niti Pass, and 20 miles S. of the latter. The village contains about twenty houses, built of wood and stone intermixed, and cemented with mud. Some of the houses are two or three stories high; in which case, the lower story is used for housing cattle. Large stones are hung by means of ropes from the projecting beams of the roofs, to prevent them from being blown away by the violent storms common here. A wooden veranda projects from the upper story, and is ornamented with carvings of flowers, and of Ganesa and other Hindoo deities. There are no locks to the houses, which, in the absence of the owners, are secured from trespass merely by dogs tied to the doors. The inhabitants style themselves Rajpoots, but have no regard to the observances of caste, eating raw flesh seasoned with a little salt and pepper, and have no repugnance to it even in a tainted state. Their features denote a mixture of the Hindoo and Tartar races: their stature is low, but they are well made, active, and enduring of labour. The fleeces of their own flocks supply their dress, which is of coarse woollen cloth, in the manufacture of which the women are skilful and industrious. Their persons are excessively filthy, and swarm with vermin, and the state of their dwellings is equally disgusting. They inhabit this part of Kumaon only from about the 24th of May to the 23rd of September, when they migrate to less-elevated places. Their principal means of support is the trade which they drive between Tartary and the low country to the south, conveying the merchandise on the backs of goats and sheep. They also cultivate lal sag, a species of amaranth, used as a potherb, and also for the seed, which is ground into meal; and besides this, they grow buckwheat, millet, barley, and other grains suited to an elevated and inclement climate. Batten found, in the beginning of October, the ground, at the elevation of 10,250 feet above the sea, covered with harvest sheaves, though the perennial snow-line was near, and only 3,000 feet higher. In the vicinity are mines of a galena ore, yielding a considerable proportion of silver. Lat. 30° 41′, long. 79° 56′.

MULARNEE.—See DONGER MULARNEE.

MULBA, in the Rajpoot state of Jodhpoor, a village on the route from Balotra to the city of Jodhpoor, and 37 miles N.E. of the former. Lat. 26° 6′, long. 72° 50′.

MULCAULGHERY.—A town in the territory of Nagpore or Berar, situate 124 miles N. by E. from Masulipatam, and 71 miles N. by W. from Rajahmundry. Lat. 16° 57′, long. 80° 35′.

MULGHAT.—A town in the territory of Oude, situate 124 miles E.S.E. from Khatmandoo, and 90 miles N.N.W. from Purneah. Lat. 27°, long. 86° 7′.

MULGOON, in Bussahir, a large torrent of the district of Koonawur, rises about lat. 31° 40′, long. 78° 12′, on the south-eastern declivity of the Damuk Shu, a very lofty range dividing that territory from Ladakh. Gerard describes it as "a large stream descending at a considerable angle, rushing over rocks with rapid force, and forming a series of cascades." It is crossed by the route from Chini to Pungi, in a spot having an elevation of 8,170 feet above the sea, and where the stream, divided by a mass of rock, is traversed by two sangas or wooden bridges. After a course of about fifteen miles in a south-easterly direction, it falls into the Sutlej on the right side, in lat. 31° 35′, long. 78° 21′.

MULHARA, in the territory of Chutterpore, in Bundelcund, a small town on the route from Banda to Saugor, 60 miles S.W. of the former, 112 N.E. of the latter, is situate on the west of an extensive jhil or mere. It has a bazar. Lat. 25° 2′, long. 79° 44′.

MULHARGURH, in the territory of Indore, or possessions of Holkar's family, a town on the route from Neemuch to Mow, 10 miles S. of former, 141 N.W. of latter. It has a bazar, and is supplied with water from wells. The pergunnah of which it is the principal place, contains 49 villages, yields an annual revenue of 81,722 rupees, and is part of the jaghire or feudal grant of the nawaub of Joura, son of Ghufur Khan, the Patan chieftain, to whom they were assigned by the British government on the conclusion of hostilities with Holkar in 1817. Lat. 24° 19′, long. 74° 58′.

MULHEEABAD, in the territory of Oude, a town on the route from Lucknow to Shahjehanpoor, 12 miles N.W. of the former, situate on the small river Betta, a tributary of the Ghaghra. The inhabitants are principally Patans. Lat. 26° 54′, long. 80° 49′.

MULHEPOOR, in the British district of Suharunpoor, lieut.-gov. of the N.W. Provinces, a town on the route from Suharunpoor to Muzufurnugur, five miles S. of the former. Lat. 29° 54′, long. 77° 38′.

MULHOOPOOR, or **MULUPOOR**, in the British district of Agra, a village on the route from the city of Agra to Allygurh, and 11 miles north of the former. Lat. 27° 17′, long. 78° 5′.

MULIKPOOR, in the British district of Boolundshuhur, lieut.-gov. of the N.W. Provinces, a town on the route from Anoopshuhur to Khoorjub, and five miles W. of the former. Lat. 28° 20′, long. 78° 15′.

MULINATH KA THAN, in the Rajpoot state of Jodhpoor, a town on the route from Balmeer to the city of Jodhpoor, and 72 miles S.W. of the latter. It is situate on the right bank of the river Loonee, here a very rapid stream, a quarter of a mile wide during the rainy season. Here are the shrine and sanctuary of Mulinath, a reputed saint, whose memory is by superstition supplied with the usual assortment of Hindoo miracles. Lat. 25° 53′, long. 72° 9′.

MULIPOOR, in Sirhind, a village on the western route from Thanesur to the town of Sirhind, and 48 miles N.W. of the former. It is protected by a small fort, and is situated in a level, fertile, and pleasing country. Distant N.W. from Calcutta 1,036 miles. Lat. 30° 29′, long. 76° 30′.

MULKA, in the Baree Dooab division of the Punjab, a town situated 19 miles N.W. from the right bank of the Sutlej, 105 miles S.W. by S. of the town of Lahore. Lat. 30° 24′, long. 73° 17′.

MULKAIR, in Hyderabad, or the territory of the Nizam, a town on a considerable tributary of the river Beema. Distance from the city of Hyderabad, W., 86 miles. Lat. 17° 10′, long. 77° 19′.

MULKAPOOR.—A town in Hyderabad, or dominions of the Nizam, situate on the left bank of the river Poorna, and 111 miles S.W. from Ellichpoor. Lat. 20° 4′, long. 76° 22′.

MULKAPOOR.—A town in the native state of Kolapoor, presidency of Bombay, 22 miles N.W. by W. from Kolapoor, and 55 miles S. from Sattara. Lat. 16° 53′, long. 74° 1′.

MULKAPOOR.—A town in one of the recently sequestrated districts of Hyderabad, or dominions of the Nizam, situate in the valley of the Taptee, 12 miles S. of the left bank of that river, 92 miles W.S.W. of Ellichpoor. Lat. 20° 51′, long. 76° 14′.

MULL, in Sinde, an offset on the left or eastern side of the Sata, or great eastern branch of the Indus. Though once a large stream, it has now become a shallow rivulet, discharging a scanty body of water through the Mull mouth, in lat. 23° 55′, long. 67° 44′.

MULLANGOOR, in Hyderabad, or territory of the Nizam, a town 85 miles N.E. of the city of Hyderabad. Lat. 18° 20′, long. 79° 23′.

MULLAOW.—A town in Guzerat, or dominions of the Guicowar, 33 miles N.E. from Baroda, and 68 miles E.S.E. from Ahmedabad. Lat. 22° 37′, long. 73° 32′.

MULLAPOOR.—A town in the territory of Oude, on the right bank of the Ghogra, and 63 miles N.N.E. from Lucknow. Lat. 27° 43′, long. 81° 20′.

MULLICKBAG.—A town at the north-western extremity of the British district of Baraset, lieut.-gov. of Bengal, distant from Calcutta, N., 25 miles. Lat. 22° 56′, long. 88° 24′.

MULLUK HARHUR, in the British district of Allahabad, lieut.-gov. of the N.W. Provinces, a village on the route from the city of Allahabad to Lucknow, and six miles N.W. of the former. Lat. 25° 32′, long. 81° 43′.

MULLYE, in the British district of Sarun, lieut.-gov. of Bengal, a town and military cantonment on the north-east frontier, towards the British district Tirhoot. It is situate on the left or east bank of the river Bagmuttee, here crossed by a wooden bridge. Distant E. from Goruckpore 149 miles; from Dinapore, N., 85. Lat. 26° 46′, long. 85° 29′.

MULMULA.—A town in the native state of Nepal, 153 miles W. from Khatmandoo, and 82 miles N.W. by N. from Goruckpoor. Lat. 27° 46′, long. 82° 50′.

MULPURBA, a river rising on the eastern slope of the Western Ghats, in lat. 15° 45′, long. 74° 19′, and, flowing in an easterly direction through the British district of Belgaum for 160 miles, in the course of which it touches upon or traverses some of the Southern Mahratta states situate in that district, falls into the Kistnah river on the right side, in lat. 16° 12′, long. 76° 9′.

MULSEI, in the British district of Allygurh, lieut.-gov. of the N.W. Provinces, a village on the route by Khasganj from Bareilly to Allygurh cantonment, and 28 miles S.E. of the latter, 53 N.E. of Agra. Lat. 27° 51′, long. 78° 32′.

MULTOWN, in the British territory of Saugor and Nerbudda, a town on the south declivity of the Narat Ghat or pass, to the crest of which the ascent is gentle. It has a fort which commands the pass. Lat. 24° 18′, long. 78° 37′.

MULUGI.—A town in the British district of Dharwar, presidency of Bombay, 50 miles S. by E. of Dharwar. Lat. 14° 46′, long. 75° 13′.

MULWAH, in the British district of Futtehpoor, lieut.-gov. of the N.W. Provinces, a village on the route from Cawnpore to the town of Futtehpoor, and 10 miles N.E. of the latter. Lat. 26° 2′, long. 80° 46′.

MUMOREEBUSTEE, in the Baree Dooab division of the Punjab, a town situated on the left bank of the Ravee, 105 miles S.W. of the town of Lahore. Lat. 30° 43′, long. 72° 57′.

MUNAHPAUD, in the British district of Tinnevelly, presidency of Madras, a town on the seacoast, on the south-west side of the estuary of the river Naut. The point is low and sandy; the soundings are irregular round it; there is a shoal projecting four miles northeast of it; there are other dangerous shoals and rocks to the east, and it is altogether a hazardous place for shipping. It is distant from Cape Comorin, N.E., 41 miles. Lat. 8° 23′, long. 78° 7′.

MUNARA.—A town of Sinde, in the British district of Kurachee, presidency of Bombay, 60 miles S.E. by S. of Kurachee. Lat. 24° 11′, long. 67° 40′.

MUNCHUR, in Sinde, a lake formed by the expansion of the Narra, a branch proceeding from the Indus on the western side. The Narra flows into the lake on the north, the redundant water being discharged on the south-east by the river Arul, which has a course of about twelve miles, and, flowing by Sehwan, falls into the Indus about four miles below that town. The lake is nearly of a circular form when the water is low, and is then about ten miles in diameter. During the inundation, it expands so as to be twenty miles long, the breadth remaining much as before. The space left uncovered by the receding water is sown with grain, especially wheat, which yields very heavy crops. Though shallow at the sides, the lake has a considerable depth of water in the middle, and so great is the abundance of fine fish, according to Burnes, that 1,000 boats are employed in the fishery. They are taken by spearing, the great quantity of weeds preventing the employment of nets. In the season when the lotus is in blossom, the lake presents a very beautiful appearance, as its surface, farther than the eye can reach, is covered with an unbroken succession of bloom and leaves. Lat. 26° 26′, long. 67° 43′.

MUNCURRAY.—A town in the British district of Malabar, presidency of Madras, 106 miles S.E. of Cannanore. Lat. 10° 47′, long. 76° 32′.

MUNDAEE, in the Rajpoot state of Shekawuttee, a village situate 80 miles E.S.E. from Delhi. Lat. 28° 13′, long. 76° 3′.

MUNDAGNEE, or MANDAKINI, called also Kalee, a feeder of the Aluknunda, rises on the boundary between Gurhwal and Kumaon, at the south-eastern base of Kedarnath Mountain, and in lat. 30° 47′, long. 79° 8′. It holds a course generally southerly, and in lat. 30° 32′, long. 79° 9′, receives the Jugaroo or Mudmesur on the left side. Continuing to flow in a southerly direction, it falls into the Aluknunda on the right side, at Roodurprag, in lat. 30° 17′, long. 79° 1′, after a total course of about forty-five miles, forming, for its whole length, the boundary between the state of Gurhwal and the British province of Kumaon.

MUNDAHUL, in the British district of Rohtuk, lieut.-gov. of the N.W. Provinces, a village on the route from Delhi to Hansee, and 15 miles S.E. of the latter. Lat. 29° 1′, long. 76° 15′.

MUNDAI, in the British district of Futtehpore, lieut.-gov. of the N.W. Provinces, a village on the left bank of the Jumna, 26 miles S.E. of the town of Futtehpore. Lat. 25° 33′, long. 81° 10′.

MUNDAKE SERAE, in the British district of Futtehpore, lieut.-gov. of the N.W. Provinces, a village on the route from Allahabad to the town of Futtehpoor, and 13 miles S.E. of the latter. It has a few shops. Lat. 25° 54′, long. 81° 4′.

MUNDALIA, in the Rajpoot state of Jodhpoor, a village on the route from the town of Jodhpoor to that of Ajmeer, and 46 miles N.E. of the former. It is of considerable size, containing twenty shops. Lat. 26° 26′, long. 73° 47′.

MUNDALO, in the jaghire of Jujhur, lieut.-gov. of the N.W. Provinces, a village on the route from Rohtuk to Narnol, and 35 miles S.W. of the former. Lat. 28° 29′, long. 76° 18′.

MUNDALOR, in Gwalior, or the possessions of Scindia, a town on the route from Nusserabad to Gwalior, by the town of Kerowly, 174 miles E. of the former, 67 W. of latter. It is situate on a round isolated hill, two miles north of the left or north bank of the river Chumbul, and is surrounded by a wall of masonry. Distant from Jeypoor, S.E., 98 miles; S. from Bhurtpoor 70; S.W. from Agra 80. Lat. 26° 18′, long. 77° 14′.

MUNDANA.—A town in the British district of Candeish, presidency of Bombay, 76 miles N. by E. of Malligaum. Lat. 21° 37′, long. 74° 44′.

MUNDAWUL.—A town of Malwa, in the native state of Jowra, situate on the right bank of the Chumbul river, and 38 miles N.W. from Oojein. Lat. 23° 35′, long. 75° 24′.

MUNDAWUR, in the British district of Bijnour, lieut.-gov. of the N.W. Provinces, a town on the route from Bijnour to Hurdwar, nine miles N. of the former place. Mundawur has a population of 7,737 inhabitants. Lat. 29° 28′, long. 78° 12′.

MUNDESI, in the British district of Muttra, lieut.-gov. of the N.W. Provinces, a town on the route from the cantonment of Muttra to Bhurtpore, and 17 miles N.W. of of the latter. Lat. 27° 24′, long. 77° 42′.

MUNDESOR, in the territory of Gwalior, or possessions of Scindia's family, a town situate on a tributary of the Chumbul. It is the principal place of a pergunnah assessed at the annual revenue of 18,20,000 rupees. It has a large and generally well-supplied bazar.

Here, in January, 1818, was concluded the definitive treaty between the British government and Mulhar Rao Holkar. Distant S.W. from Gwalior fort 250 miles, N.W. from Oojein 80. Elevation above the sea 1,452 feet. Lat. 24° 4′, long. 75° 9′.

MUNDEWATA.—A town in the native state of Gwalior, or territory of Scindia's family, situate 36 miles N.N.E. from Oojein, and 95 miles W.N.W. from Bhopal. Lat. 23° 39′, long. 75° 58′.

MUNDHA, in the Rajpoot state of Jessulmere, a village on the route from the town of Jessulmere to that of Bahawulpore, and 32 miles N. of the former. It is situate at the eastern side of a fine and well-filled tank, and has besides a well 180 feet deep. Close to the village is a large bed of very fine fuller's earth. Lat. 27° 21′, long. 71°.

MUNDHA, in the territory of Oude, a village on the route from Futtehgurh cantonment to that of Seetapoor, 56 miles N.E. of the former, 27 W. of the latter. Supplies may be had here. Distant 75 miles from Lucknow. Lat. 27° 35′, long. 80° 24′.

MUNDI, in the Jullunder Doab of the Punjab, is a small territory, comprising several valleys, with their inclosing ridges, on the southern slope of the Himalaya, and containing an area of 759 square miles, with a population of 113,091. The capital, which is also called Mundi, is situate at the confluence of the Sukyt river with the Beas, which is here 200 yards wide, very deep, and crossed by a ferry. These rivers during summer have, every twenty-four hours, a periodical rise and fall, in consequence of the melting of snow by the heat of the sun, so that they rise towards evening, and continue to do so throughout the greater part of the night, decreasing towards morning and throughout the forenoon. The rajah's palace is an extensive building, with whitened walls, and covered with slate. It is surrounded by a beautiful garden, containing a profusion of the finest fruit-trees and flowers. The bazar is large and well stocked. Mundi seems to be peculiarly under the influence of Hindoo superstition; and the horrible rite of suttee, or burning the sati or widow with the corpse of her husband, was frightfully prevalent during the rule of the Seiks. In the vicinity are productive mines of iron and salt, and the greater part of the revenue of the prince is derived from these sources. The salt, however, is said to be of inferior description. Upon the conquest of the Punjab, Mundi became tributary to the British, and upon the death of the rajah, in 1851, and the succession of his infant son, arrangements were made for the government of this petty state. The town is in lat. 31° 43′, long. 76° 58′.

MUNDI, in the British district of Allahabad, lieut.-gov. of the N.W. Provinces, a village on the route, by the Kutra Pass, from Allahabad to Rewa, and 32 miles S.E. of the former city. Lat. 25° 12′, long. 82° 15′.

MUNDLA, in the Rajpoot state of Jodhpoor, a village on the route from Pokhurn to the town of Jodhpoor, and 20 miles E. of the former. It is supplied with water from four tanks, and five wells ninety feet deep. Lat. 26° 52′, long. 72° 20′.

MUNDLAH, within the British territory of Saugor and Nerbudda, a town situate on the right bank of the river Nerbudda, the course of which here makes an acute angle opposite the mouth of a small tributary stream called the Bunjir. A ditch, communicating with the Nerbudda above and below the town, forms the base of the triangular spot on which it is situate. The fort occupies the apex of the triangle, the town the more expanded part towards the north, or next the open country. The side towards the north is, in addition to the ditch, fortified by a straight line of works, but these are of little strength, having only the common defences of round towers. This line can be taken in reverse from the opposite bank, both above and below the fort, as no works cover the town along the river. At present those fortifications, as well as the town itself, are in a ruinous state, probably in consequence mainly of the effects of the British attack during the Mahratta war having never been repaired. On the 25th of April, 1818, a British force under General Marshall opened batteries against the place, and in the afternoon of the next day the town was stormed, with the destruction of all the troops not within the fort, except about fifty, who were made prisoners; and on the following morning the fort was evacuated by the garrison, in number about 1,100. The loss of the enemy during the operations against the place was estimated at about 500, while that of the besiegers amounted to only three killed and fourteen wounded.

Mundlah in 1742 came into the hands of the Mahrattas, under Balaji Baji Rao, the Peishwa. It appears to have subsequently passed from under their yoke, as in 1799 it was surrendered to the rajah of Nagpore or Berar by the chief of Saugor. The British government, having previously obtained actual possession by the event of war, received a formal cession of it by the treaty of Nagpore, in 1818. Distant S.E. from Jubbulpore 50 miles; S.E. from Saugor 130; S.W. from Allahabad, by Jubbulpore, 245; N.E. from Nagpore 135; W. from Calcutta 510 miles; N.E. from Bombay, by Mow and Jubbulpore, 635. Lat. 22° 43′, long. 80° 35′.

MUNDLAISIR, in the territory of Indore, or possessions of Holkar's family, a town on the route from the British cantonment of Mow to Asseergurh, 30 miles S. of former, 83 N.W. of latter. It is situate on the right or north bank of the Nerbudda, the bed of which is here about 500 yards wide, unfordable, and crossed by ferry during the greater part of the year, but fordable with difficulty in spring. The navigation of the

Nerbudda from this town extends seaward, or to the west, for eighty miles, and eastward, or up the stream, for fifty-three miles, to Dhadree. The town is surrounded by a mud wall, and has a small square well-built fort of masonry, and a bazar. It belongs to the British government, and there was formerly a cantonment of its troops on the north bank of the Nerbudda, close to the town. A body of the Nimar police, with cavalry attached, is posted in the town, for the protection of the establishment of the British functionary stationed here, and who is styled "principal assistant to the resident at Indore." This principal assistant has charge of the British possessions in Nimar, and of the possessions of Holkar under British management. Population about 2,000 ; elevation above the sea 696 feet. Distance N.E. from Bombay 334 miles ; N.W. from Nagpoor, by Baitool and Mow, 327. Lat. 22° 12′, long. 75° 47′.

MUNDOR, in the Rajpoot state of Jodhpoor, was its capital until A.D. 1459, when Joda removed the seat of government to the neighbouring city of Jodhpoor, which he had recently built. The ruined town of Mundor, still retaining a few inhabitants, is situate in a recess on the east side of the rocky range running south to the town of Jodhpoor, from which it is five miles distant. The greater part of the walls has been demolished, and the materials removed to build the new capital ; but enough remains to show the massive style in which they were constructed. According to the decription of those relics by Tod, "the immense blocks are piled upon and closely fitted to each other, without any cement, the characteristic of all the Etruscan cities termed Cyclopean. The walls, following the direction of the crest of the ridge, are irregular; and, having been constructed long before artillery was thought of, the Purihar or Pali engineer was satisfied with placing the palace on the most commanding eminence, about the centre of the fortress. The bastions or towers are singularly massive, and, like all the most antique, their form is square." The interior of this inclosure contains various ruins, replete with all the revolting monstrosities with which the imagination of Indian superstition is haunted. Tod disports himself in a scene so congenial to him :—"A short distance from the foot of the causeway an archway opens into an inclosed court or area, in the retired part of which, and touching the mountain, is an extensive saloon : the roof is supported by a triple row of columns of that light form peculiar to the Jains. Here are displayed, in all 'the pomp and circumstance of war,' the statues of the knights errant of the desert, armed *cap-a-pie,* bestriding steeds whose names are deathless as their riders, all in the costume of the times in which they lived. They are cut out of the rock, but entirely detached from it, and larger than life. Though more conspicuous for strength than symmetry, the grim visages of these worthies, apparently frowning defiance, each attended by his pundoo or squire, have a *singularly pleasing effect.* Each chieftain is armed with lance, sword, and buckler, with quiver and arrows, and poniard in his girdle." Boileau states that those rude figures are formed of plaster. He thus describes the fantastic scene :—"The first objects introduced to our notice at Mundor, were the eighteen gigantic figures in bas-relief, representing the tutelar divinities of the Rahtor Rajpoots. These figures form one long line, facing the north, and are backed by a low rock of red saudstone ; the three figures at the west end representing Gunesh, the elephant-headed god of wisdom, between two effigies of Bhairon, being placed in an open temple, while the others are carefully protected from the weather by a flat roof of masonry, supported on pillars, with a screen-wall in front. The latter indeed require some such shelter, being finished with coloured cements, while the three figures already mentioned seem to be only daubed with red paint, and bedizened with gold-leaf." There are besides gigantic figures in plaster of the Brahminical deities Brahma, Surya, the monkey-god Hanuman, Rama and his consort Sita, Krishna, and Siva. Some ruins of more ancient date are attributed by Tod to the Budhists or Jains. Amongst those of late date, the most important is the palace of Ajit Sinh, murdered, in 1724, by his son Abhay Sinh. It is neatly built of stone, and in perfect repair ; now without human inhabitant, but swarming with bats. Every Monday there is at Mundor a considerable concourse of devotees, who come from Jodhpoor to pay their devotions at the various shrines. Lat. 26° 21′, long. 73° 8′.

MUNDOTE, in Sirhind, a fort about two miles south of the left bank of the Sutlej, in its lowest state, though in time of inundation the water reaches to within half a mile of the walls. It is square, with a round tower at each corner, and one in the middle of each face, and has a gateway on the eastern, and another on the western side. The walls, which are of burned brick, are fifty feet high and ten thick. The earth excavated from the outward moat has been employed to raise the surface of the inclosed space to half the height of the walls. A dense population is crowded into this inclosure, as it is entirely occupied by houses arranged in very narrow streets. The surrounding country is flat, so that the view is very extensive from the towers surmounting the walls. This fort is of modern erection, being built to replace one constructed in the reign of Mahommed Shah III., king of Delhi. It was held by a Patan chief, whom it was found necessary to depose in consequence of the oppressive and tyrannical character of his government. The territory extending about fifty miles along the river, and having an area of about 780 miles, has been annexed to the British dominions. The population is believed to be upwards of 116,000. Mundote is distant from Calcutta, N.W., by way of Loodiana and Ferozepore, 1,180 miles. Lat. 30° 53′, long. 74° 26′.

MUNDOWI, in the British district of Kythul, in Sirhind, a village on the route from Hansee to Loodiana, and 51 miles N. of the former town. It is situate amidst thick jungle, on the left bank of the Gugur. The road in this part of the route is excellent. Distant N.W. from Calcutta 1,027 miles. Lat. 29° 48′, long. 76° 3′.

MUNDRELA.—A town in the Rajpoot state of Shekawuttee, 13 miles N. from Jhoonjhnoo, and 111 miles W.S.W. from Delhi. Lat. 28° 8′, long. 75° 32′.

MUNDROOP. — A town in the British district of Sholapoor, presidency of Bombay, 14 miles S.S.W. of Sholapoor. Lat. 17° 28′, long. 75° 52′.

MUNDSIR, in the Rajpoot state of Beekaneer, a considerable village on the route from Rutungurh to the town of Beekaneer, and 30 miles E. of the latter. It contains 200 houses, supplied with water from three wells 290 feet deep. The surrounding country has a scanty cultivation. Lat. 27° 54′, long. 73° 43′.

MUNDUL.—A town in the British district of Ahmedabad, presidency of Bombay, 51 miles W. by N. of Ahmedabad. Lat. 23° 16′, long. 71° 50′.

MUNDUL.—A town in the Rajpoot state of Oodeypoor, 76 miles N.E. from Oodeypoor, and 75 miles S. from Ajmeer. Lat. 25° 25′, long. 74° 37′.

MUNDUN, in the territory of Alwur, under the political management of the Governor-General's agent in Rajpootana, a town on the route from Rewari to Narnol, and 18 miles N.E. of the latter. Lat. 28° 6′, long. 76° 27′.

MUNEE, in the British district of Boolundshuhur, lieut.-gov. of the N.W. Provinces, a village on the route from Allygurh cantonment to that of Delhi, and 18 miles N.W. of the former. The road in this part of the route is good; the country open, with a sandy soil, partially cultivated. Lat. 28° 7′, long. 77° 59′.

MUNEEMAJRA, in Sirhind, a town on the route from Umballah to Ropur, on the Sutlej, and 25 miles N. of the former place. It is situate near the southern base of the Sub-Himalaya, in a fertile country, producing great quantities of indigo, which is exported to the Punjab and to Khorasan. There is a good bazar, and water and supplies are abundant. The road in this part of the route is good, over an undulating country. This town is the principal place of a small territory belonging to a Sikh sirdar, and comprising fifty-nine villages, having an area of eighty square miles, with a population of 16,720. The annual revenue is estimated at 4,700*l.* sterling. Muneemajra is distant N.W. from Calcutta 1,043 miles. Lat. 30° 43′, long. 76° 54′.

MUNEEPOOR, in Eastern India, a native state, bounded on the north-east, east, and south by the Burmese empire; on the west by the British district of Cachar and Toola Ram Senaputtee's country; and on the N.W. by Upper Assam. It extends from lat. 23° 49′ to 25° 41′, and from long. 93° 5′ to 94° 32′; is 125 miles in length from north to south, and ninety miles in breadth, and contains an area of 7,584 square miles. The territory is intersected by a good road in the direction of Cachar, constructed in 1840, at the joint expense of the British and Muneepoor governments.

Muneepoor consists principally of one extensive valley, situated in the heart of a difficult and mountainous country. The principality was taken under British protection previously to the breaking out of the first Burmese war; and under the treaty of Yandabhoo, concluded in 1826, the king of Ava renounced all claim to the territory. It pays no tribute, but its connection with the British government was at one time deemed of importance, as affording an outpost against the Burmese; and to render it available for this purpose, its rulers were assisted in disciplining a body of troops. The views of the Indian government in regard to the utility of Muneepoor as a military station appear, however, to have subsequently undergone considerable change. Upon the lapse of Cachar to the paramount power, by the death of its rajah in 1830 without heirs, the British government manifested its friendly feeling towards the ruler of Muneepoor, by conferring upon him a portion of its new acquisition; and upon the death of this chief in 1834, his infant son, Kirtee Singh, was recognised as successor to the raj, and a regency appointed, of which the Senaputtee Nur Sing was the head. Nur Sing appears subsequently to have taken possession of the country for himself. He died in the year 1850, having nominated his brother, Deebindro Singh, as his successor, who was recognised by the British. But the ex-rajah, Kirtee Sing, invading Muneepoor, succeeded in regaining his throne, and drove Deebindro into exile. To put an end to these changes, which subjected the country to constant anarchy and insurrection, the British government made a public avowal of its determination to uphold the reigning rajah, and to punish any parties attempting to dispossess him. The ex-rajah Deebindro resides at Dacca.

MUNEEPOOR. — A town in the native state of Muneepoor, in Eastern India, on the right bank of the Nankatha Khyoung river, and 76 miles E. from Silchar. Lat. 24° 49′, long. 94° 1′.

MUNEER.—A town in the British district of Ghazeepore, lieut.-gov. of the N.W. Provinces. The town of Muneer is situate in lat. 25° 57′, long. 84° 19′.

MUNEEREE. — A town in the native

state of Sawuntwaree, presidency of Bombay, situate 16 miles S. from Sawuntwaree, and 40 miles W. by S. from Belgaum. Lat. 15° 42′, long. 74° 1′.

MUNGAON, in the British district of Allahabad, lieut.-gov. of the N.W. Provinces, a small town on the route from the cantonment of Allahabad to Futtehpoor, and 18 miles N.W. of the former. Lat. 25° 31′, long. 81° 40′.

MUNGARA, in the Rajpoot state of Jodhpoor, a village on the route from Balotra to the city of Jodhpoor, and three miles N.E. of the former. Lat. 25° 52′, long. 72° 21′.

MUNGARI, in the British district of Allahabad, lieut.-gov. of the N.W. Provinces, a small town on the route by the Kutra Pass from the cantonment of Allahabad to Rewa, and 15 miles S.E. of the former. Lat. 25° 18′, long. 82°.

MUNGDOO.—A town of Eastern India, in the British district of Aracan, 61 miles W. of Aracan. Lat. 20° 46′, long. 92° 30′.

MUNGLAH.—A town within the dominions of Gholab Singh, the ruler of Cashmere, situate on the left bank of the Jhelum river, and 113 miles N. by W. from Lahore. Lat. 33° 7′, long. 73° 40′.

MUNGLOOR.—A town in the British district of Suharunpore, lieut.-gov. of the N.W. Provinces: it has a population of 5,959. Distance S.E. from Suharunpore 23 miles; from Hurdwar, S.W., 21 miles. Lat. 29° 47′, long. 77° 56′.

MUNGLORA, in the British district of Mozuffurnuggur, lieut.-gov. of the N.W. Provinces, a village on the route from Kurnal to Meerut, and 10 miles S.E. of the former. Lat. 29° 36′, long. 77° 10′.

MUNGOLAH, in the British district of Allygurh, lieut.-gov. of the N.W. Provinces, a village on the route from Allygurh cantonment to that of Moradabad, and 10 miles N.E. of the former. Lat. 28° 2′, long. 78° 11′.

MUNGOWA, or MAJGOWA, in the tract of Boghelkhand, in the territory of Rewa, a small town on the route by the Kutra Pass from Mirzapoor to Jubbulpoor, and 84 miles S.W. of the former. Jacquemont styles it a populous village, the inhabitants of which are wretchedly indigent; and adds his doubts respecting the reported fertility of the country, which Garden describes as "undulating, highly cultivated, and well wooded." There is a large bazar, and water is plentiful. The road in this part of the route is excellent. Elevation above the sea about 1,550 feet. Lat. 24° 40′, long. 81° 39′.

MUNGROTUH, in the Daman division of the Punjab, a town situated 38 miles W. from the right bank of the Indus, 77 miles W.N.W. of the town of Mooltan. Lat. 30° 36′, long. 70° 20′.

MUNGROULEE.—A town in the native state of Gwalior, or the territory of Scindia' family, situate on the left bank of the Betwa river, and 58 miles N.W. from Saugur. Lat. 24° 24′, long. 78° 10′.

MUNGULCOTE.—A town in the British district of Burdwan, lieut.-gov. of Bengal, 71 miles N.N.W. of Calcutta. Lat. 23° 30′, long. 87° 56′.

MUNGULPOOR.—A town in the native territory of Dhenkanaul, one of the independent hill states of Orissa, situate 58 miles N.W. by W. from Cuttack, and 100 miles N. from Ganjam. Lat. 20° 50′, long. 85° 10′.

MUNGULPOOR, in the British district of Cawnpoor, lieut.-gov. of the N.W. Provinces, a town on the route from Cawnpoor to Bhind, 40 miles W. of the former. Lat. 26° 31′, long. 79° 46′.

MUNGULVERA.—A town in the Southern Mahratta jaghire of Sanglee, 31 miles W.S.W. from Sholapoor, and 96 miles E. by S. from Sattara. Lat. 17° 30′, long. 75° 30′.

MUNHYA, in the British district of Allahabad, lieut.-gov. of the N.W. Provinces, a village on the right bank of the Ganges, nine miles below the city of Allahabad by the river, 799 above Calcutta by the same way. Lat. 25° 20′, long. 82°.

MUNIAH, in the native territory of Dholpoor, a village on the route from Agra to Gwalior, 25 miles S. of former, 44 N. of latter. It has a bazar, and water from wells and from a tank. Lat. 26° 50′, long. 77° 59′.

MUNIKYALA, in the Punjab, a village remarkable on account of an antique monument or tope (as such objects are called by the natives), of great dimensions, said by the people of the neighbourhood to have been built by a prince of the name of Manik. Lat. 33° 27′, long. 73° 17′.

MUNJAISHWAR, in the southern part of the British district of Canara, presidency of Madras, a town on an inlet of the Arabian Sea, or North Indian Ocean, and at the mouth of a river descending from the Ghats. It is described as a large straggling town, containing many good houses. Distant from Mangalore, S., 11 miles; Madras, W., 360. Lat. 12° 42′, long. 74° 57′.

MUNJARY.—A town in the British district of Malabar, presidency of Madras, 72 miles S.E. of Cannanore. Lat. 11° 7′, long. 76° 11′.

MUNJERABAD, in the Mysore, a village with a fort on a hill in the mountainous tract on the south-west frontier, towards Coorg. It is surrounded by dense forests of luxuriant growth, abounding in the sago-palm, one of the largest and most beautiful of that tribe. The trunk consists of a thin ligneous coat, inclosing in the interior a pith, which, being pounded and macerated, and the water allowed to subside, yields the fine farina called sago, used as an article of diet. Like other jungly places, it is very unhealthy. A road from Mysore into Canara, by the Ghaut of Munjerabad, was some time since sanctioned by the home government. Distance from Seringapatam, N.W., 72 miles. Lat. 12° 55′, long. 75° 50′.

MUNJH, in the British district of Etawah, lieut.-gov. of the N.W. Provinces, a small town on a mound, nearly a mile to the south-east of the route from the cantonment of Etawa to that of Futtehgurh, and 13 miles N.E. of the former. Lat. 26° 55′, long. 79° 13′.

MUNKAPOOR.—A town in the territory of Oude, 20 miles N. from Oude, and 77 miles W.N.W. from Goruckpoor. Lat. 27° 3′, long. 82° 13′.

MUNKOLAH, in the British district of Goorgaon, lieut.-gov. of the N.W. Provinces, a village on the route from Hansee to Muttra, and 58 miles N.W. of the latter. Lat. 28° 8′, long. 77° 14′.

MUNNADA, a river of Hyderabad, or territory of the Nizam, rising in lat. 18° 40′, long. 76° 45′, and, flowing in an easterly direction for ninety-five miles, falls into the Manjera, on the left bank, in lat. 18° 40′, long. 77° 47′.

MUNNARGOODY.—A town in the British district of South Arcot, presidency of Madras, 134 miles S.S.W. of Madras. Lat. 11° 19′, long. 79° 38′.

MUNNEAREE.—A town in the British district of Purneah, lieut.-gov. of Bengal, 34 miles S. by E. of Purneah. Lat. 25° 18′, long. 87° 41′.

MUNNIPORE.—See MUNEEPOOR.

MUNNOOR. — A town in one of the recently sequestrated districts of Hyderabad, or dominions of the Nizam, situate 27 miles S.E. by S. of Sholapoor. Lat. 17° 19′, long. 76° 9′.

MUNOHURPOOR, in the Rajpoot state of Jeypoor, a town on the route from Delhi to Mow, 132 miles S.W. of former, 375 N.E. of latter. Though much decayed, it has still a large bazar, and is adequately supplied with water from wells. Lat. 27° 19′, long. 76° 1′.

MUNOLEE.—A town in the British district of Belgaum, presidency of Bombay, 42 miles E. of Belgaum. Lat. 15° 52′, long. 75° 12′.

MUNORA.—A town in the British district of Behar, lieut.-gov. of Bengal, 34 miles N.W. of Sherghotty. Lat. 24° 53′, long. 84° 27′.

MUNPOORA, or MONCOORAH.—One of the islands at the mouth of the Megna river. In September, 1822, this island, together with those adjacent, was overflowed, whereby many of the cattle and inhabitants perished. Lat. 22° 20′, long. 91° 3′.

MUNPORA.—A town of Baghelcund, in the native state of Rewah, 47 miles S. from Rewah, and 39 miles N. from Sohagpoor. Lat. 23° 50′, long. 81° 20′.

MUNSEE DEBEE, in Sirhind, a Hindoo temple and village at the southern base of the low ridge bounding the Pinjor Doon on the south-west. Elevation above the sea 1,263 feet. Lat. 30° 43′, long. 76° 56′.

MUNSOORGUNJ, in the British district of Goruckpore, lieut.-gov. of the N.W. Provinces, a small market-town, which formerly gave name to a pergunnah or subdivision. Distant N.E. of Goruckpoor cantonment 20 miles. Lat. 26° 52′, long. 83° 38′.

MUNSORLA.—A town in Hyderabad, or dominions of the Nizam, situate on the left bank of the river Godavery, and 129 miles N.E. by N. from Hyderabad. Lat. 18° 59′, long. 79° 30′.

MUNSURPOOR.—A town in the native state of Narbah, in Sirhind, or the Cis-Sutlej territory, 20 miles W. from Patialah, and 43 miles S.S.E. from Loodianah. Lat. 30° 20′, long. 76° 9′.

MUNTAREDDY.—A town in the British district of Ganjam, presidency of Madras, 24 miles S.W. by W. of Ganjam. Lat. 19° 10′, long. 84° 50′.

MUNTIM. — A town in Hyderabad, or dominions of the Nizam, situate on the right bank of the river Godavery, and 124 miles N.E. by N. from Hyderabad. Lat. 18° 46′, long. 79° 43′.

MURAMKHOOLEL. — A town in the native state of Muneepoor, in Eastern India, 46 miles N. from Muneepoor, and 132 miles E. by N. from Jynteahpore. Lat. 25° 29′, long. 94° 9′.

MURAMKHOORAO. — A town in the native state of Muneepoor, in Eastern India, 34 miles N. from Muneepoor, and 128 miles E. by N. from Jynteahpore. Lat. 25° 19′, long. 94° 6′.

MURANG, in Bussahir, a town of the district of Koonawur, is situate on the left bank of the Sutlej, near the confluence of the Tidung. The dell is encircled by lofty mountains, at an angle of twenty-five degrees, on every side, except on the westward, where it is open to the Sutlej, on the bank of which there is a small fort. The situation is extremely fine, and the approach to it highly picturesque, leading along the bank of a canal, and through an avenue of apricot-trees. Elevation above the sea 8,500 feet. Lat. 31° 36′, long. 78° 30′.

MURANG.— A town in the native state of Bussahir, situate on the left bank of the Sutlej, and 93 miles N. by E. from Dehra. Lat. 31° 35′, long. 78° 27′.

MURAON, in the British district of Futtehpore, lieut.-gov. of the N.W. Provinces, a village on the route from Allahabad to the town of Futtehpore, and 11 miles S.E. of the latter. Lat. 25° 55′, long. 81°.

MURATGANJ, in the British district of Allahabad, lieut.-gov. of the N.W. Provinces, a village on the route from Allahabad cantonment to Futtehpore, and 23 miles N.W. of the former. Lat. 25° 33′, long. 81° 37′.

MURCHAGUNJE.—A town in the British district of Mymunsing, lieut.-gov. of Bengal, 197 miles N.E. of Calcutta. Lat. 24° 30′, long. 90° 45′.

MURDANA.—A town of Central India, in the British district of Mundlaisir, 135 miles W. of Baitool. Lat. 22° 10′, long. 75° 55′.

MURDEE.—A town in one of the recently sequestrated districts of Hyderabad, or dominions of the Nizam, situate 11 miles N. of Sholapoor. Lat. 17° 49′, long. 75° 47′.

MURDLANDA, in the British district of Hurriana, lieut.-gov. of the N.W. Provinces, a village on the route from Hansi to Loodiana, and 22 miles N. of the former town. Distant N.W. from Calcutta 998 miles. Lat. 29° 23′, long. 76° 5′.

MUREAHOO, in the British district of Jounpore, lieut.-gov. of the N.W. Provinces, a town, the principal place of the pergunnah of the same name, on the route from Jounpore to Mirzapoor, 32 miles N. of the latter, 12 S. of the former. Lat. 25° 34′, long. 82° 41′.

MURELAH.—A village on the route from Nusseerabad to Beekaneer, and 51 miles N.W. of the former. It contains about thirty houses, supplied with water from two tanks. Lat. 26° 37′, long. 74° 14′.

MURGAYA, in the British district of Hummerpore, lieut.-gov. of the N.W. Provinces, a small decayed town on the route from the town of Banda to Calpee, 11 miles S. of the latter. It has a bazar, and the ruins of many brick-built houses prove it to have been formerly a place of some importance. Water is obtainable from wells and a jhil or pond. Lat. 25° 58′, long. 79° 50′.

MURHARUH, in the British district of Allyghur, lieut.-gov. of the N.W. Provinces, a town, the principal place of the pergunnah of the same name, is situate close to the north-west frontier of the district. Lat. 27° 45′, long. 78° 38′.

MURIOW, in Eastern India, one of the Cossya hill states, bounded on the north by the British district of Camroop, in Lower Assam; on the east by the Cossya state of Osimlee; on the south by those of Moeyong and Nuotung; and on the west by that of Ramrye. It contains an area of 283 square miles, and its centre is about lat. 25° 37′, long. 91° 23′.

MURJATTA.—The name of one of the mouths of the Ganges. The entrance to the river is wide, but shoals gradually from the land to three or three and a half fathoms outside. On an island four or five miles up the river, is a tank of fresh water. Lat. 21° 53′, long. 89° 34′.

MURLIDUR KE SARAI, in the British district of Mynpoorie, lieut.-gov. of the N.W. Provinces, a village on the route from the city of Agra to Etawah, and 24 miles N.W. of the latter. The road in this part of the route is good; the country is cultivated, and studded with small villages. Lat. 27° 2′, long. 78° 47′.

MURMAGON, or MARMAGOA BAY.—A considerable inlet on the coast of Goa, where ships may find a good shelter from north-west winds. Its entrance is in lat. 15° 26′, long. 73° 51′.

MUROWREE, in the British district of Bareilly, lieut.-gov. of the N.W. Provinces, a town on the route from Bareilly to Oude, 36 miles E. by S. of the former. Lat. 28° 18′, long. 80°.

MURPOOREH, in the British district of Furruckabad, lieut.-gov. of the N.W. Provinces, a town on the right bank of the Esun, 30 miles S. of the city of Furruckabad. Lat. 26° 58′, long. 79° 41′.

MURRAIE MUKAM, in Sinde, a village on the route from Sehwan to Kurrachee, and 75 miles S. of the former place. Water is procurable at all times from pits in the bed of the Murraie river. The road in this part of the route is good. Lat. 25° 30′, long. 67° 55′.

MURREE, in the Punjaub, a sanatarium for troops, situate on a hill between the rivers Indus and Jhelum, and established in the year 1851. The place is already attracting a considerable population: barracks have been constructed, and houses are rising in every direction. Cherries, strawberries, raspberries, currants, apples, pears, and apricots are abundant; and every kind of European and tropical fruit, it is said, may be successfully cultivated here. Elevation of the station above the sea 7,330 feet. Lat. 33° 54′, long. 73° 27′.

MURREI, in the British district of Agra, a village on the route from the city of Agra to Jeypore, and 25 miles W. of the former. Lat. 27° 3′, long. 77° 42′.

MURROWNEE, in the territory of Gwalior, or possessions of Scindia's family, a small town, with fort, on the route from Tehree to Oojein, 12 miles S.W. of the former. Lat. 24° 35′, long. 78° 43′.

MURRUNGAUPOONY.—A town in the British district of Madura, presidency of Madras, 44 miles N.N.E. of Madura. Lat. 10° 29′, long. 78° 28′.

MURRURAI, in the British district of Allygurh, lieut.-gov. of the N.W. Provinces, a village on the route from the city of Agra to Allygurh cantonment, and eight miles S. of the latter. Lat. 27° 48′, long. 78° 9′.

MURRYVAMLA.—A town in the British district of Cuddapah, presidency of Madras, 131 miles N.N.E. of Cuddapah. Lat. 16° 15′, long. 79° 38′.

MURTOLI, in the British district of Kumaon, lieut.-gov. of the N.W. Provinces, a considerable village in the Bhotia subdivision called Juwahir. It is situate on the route to Hiundes or Chinese Tartary, by the Juwahir Pass, from which it is distant 18 miles S., and is built on the right bank of the river Goree, the houses being constructed very low, and in hollows and ravines, with a view to protection against avalanches and the furious gales which continually blow from the south. With a similar view, the roofs are framed with a low pitch, and firmly overlaid with a coat of compact clay. The snows and other effects of winter set in here in October, when the whole population migrates to reside in the more southern and less-elevated parts of Kumaon, returning in the following June, to ply their trade with Hiundes. That lucrative occupation affords them subsistence, and even affluence, which reconcile them to residence in an inclement climate and barren soil. Elevation above the sea 11,352 feet. Lat. 30° 21′, long. 80° 13′.

MURU WURDWUN, in the north of the Punjab, a long, deep valley, with sides of gneiss and mica-slate. Down this valley a river of the same name flows, and joins the Chenaub at Kishtawar. The valley contains a village, also bearing the same name, opposite which the Nabog Nye Pass, 12,000 feet high, leads into Cashmere. Lat. 33° 45′, long. 75° 45′.

MURWUT.—An extensive, beautiful, and fertile valley, on the west side of the Indus, and south of the valley of Bannoo. It has on the west the lofty Suliman range, and on the north the snow-clad peaks of Sufaid Koh. Though exposed to the incursions of the marauders of the neighbouring mountains, it is so productive of grain and other necessaries of life, that it is thickly peopled. The valley was formerly sometimes visited by an expedition of the Sikhs from the Derajat, who levied an enforced tribute from the inhabitants. Murwut, the chief place, is little more than a village. Lat. 33° 10′, long. 71° 15′.

MUSANAGAR, in the British district of Cawnpore, lieut.-gov. of the N.W. Provinces, a town near the left bank of the Jumna, on the route from Calpee to Purtabghur, and 16 miles E. of the former. It has a bazar. Lat. 26° 10′, long. 80° 1′.

MUSCAL ISLAND.—The largest of a group of islands off the coast of Chittagong, being 15 miles in length from N. to S., and seven in extreme breadth. It has some small elevations: the centre is in lat. 21° 35′, long. 92°.

MUSCLA, in the British district of Agra, lieut.-gov. of the N.W. Provinces, a town near the north-western frontier, towards the territory of Bhurtpoor, 18 miles N.W. of the city of Agra. Lat. 27° 14′, long. 77° 42′.

MUSOODA, in the British district of Ajmeer, lieut.-gov. of the N.W. Provinces, a town, the principal place of a pergunnah containing 20,599 inhabitants. Distance S. of the city of Ajmeer 30 miles. Lat. 26° 6′, long. 74° 35′.

MUSOOR.—A town in the British province of Sattara, presidency of Bombay, 23 miles S.S.E. of Sattara. Lat. 17° 23′, long. 74° 15′.

MUSSOULEE, in the territory of Oude, a small town on the route from Lucknow cantonment to that of Sekrora, 28 miles N.E. of the former, and the same distance S.W. of the latter. It has a small bazar. Lat. 26° 58′, long. 81° 24′.

MUSSOUREE, on the northern frontier of the Dehra Doon, towards Gurhwal, is a sanatory station, established by the British to suspend, relieve, or remove the consequences prejudicial to health from the sultry climate of Hindoostan. It is approached from the south, and consequently from the Dehra Doon, by a road which, at Rajpur, situate at the base of the mountain, becomes very steep for three miles; thence, for two and a half miles, the ascent is more gradual, and for the remaining mile nearly level. The road is described by Mundy, in 1828, as difficult and perilous in the extreme: it "sometimes winds down the edge of rocks, sometimes zigzags up the face of the hill; plunges into the dark depths of a ravine, or creeps over the summit of a naked crag;" but as no mention is made of those terrors by Garden, they have no doubt in a great measure disappeared before the labours of the engineer. Jacquemont indeed describes the road as excellent. The rugged ridge on which the station is situate, consists of beds of compact limestone, alternating with others of soft slate, and is analogous to that called the transition limestone of the north of Europe, the mountain limestone of England. It is black, grey, or greyish-white, cavernous and carboniferous, emitting a fetid smell, and appears to have suffered from the action of heat, insomuch that its vesicular structure resembles that of grey lava. The slate, which alternates with the limestone, is wonderfully varied in its colours,—black, grey, green, brown, red, purple, and yellow. A few veins are so hard and fissile, as to serve for roofing-slate. In some places trap rock makes its appearance, composed in some parts principally of compact white felspar and green diallage, in others of hornblende. The slopes are steep, and, as is usual with such formations, covered with vegetation: in some places there are veins of quartzy sandstone. On the adjacent height of Landour, the prevailing formation is quartz. This rugged tract was formerly thickly covered with forests of large timber-trees; but these have nearly all been felled for building purposes, or for burning lime and bricks. It is thought, however, that the injurious effect to the scenery has been more than compensated by increased salubrity, as the dense and luxuriant forests of Simla are considered at certain seasons to be productive of gloom and sickness. There is no level area of any extent at Mussouree; so that the houses are built at considerable distances from each other, on sites which it has been necessary to level, on a ridge, a crag, or on the southern slope of the mountain. The eastern part has been longer settled, and there the houses are disposed more closely together than westward, in which direction the town is at present extending. In 1841 the number of private residences was about 100. The views are very beautiful, comprising on the north the Himalayas, clad in perennial snow; on the south the rich and varied expanse of the Dehra Doon, bounded by the Sewalik Hills; beyond which the prospect extends over the vast plain of Hindoostan, without any other limit than that of the powers of vision, or that caused by the imperfect transparency of the atmosphere. In the later part of midwinter, there are smart frosts, with occasional falls of snow; neither, however, occurring after March, when spring sets in. There are in that season showers of hail and rain, and thunder-storms occurring at intervals even as late as April. Then succeeds delightful weather until the middle of June, which ushers in the periodical rains. These, which are much heavier than in the neighbouring parts of the plains, cease about the middle of September; from which time to the middle of December, the weather is equable, becoming, however, cooler as the season advances, and terminating in sharp frosts. In 1834, for the latter half of May, the mean temperature at ten A.M. was found to be 76°; the highest temperature at any time of the day being 79°. At the same hour during June, the mean temperature was 69°; the highest temperature at any time 71°. July, for same hour, mean temperature, 67°; highest at any time, 69°. August, at same hour, mean temperature, 67°; highest at any hour, 69°. September, at same hour, mean, 66°; highest at any hour, 68°. October, at same hour, mean, 60°; highest at any hour, 62°. November, at same hour, mean, 55°; highest at any time, 57°. The mean of the mean temperatures, from the 15th of May to 21st of November, 66°. A breeze from the south, called on that account "the Doon breeze," sets in before ten o'clock A.M. and blows until late in the evening: at night there are generally light airs from the north. Mussouree is abundantly supplied from the bazar of the adjoining sanatory station of Landour, with wheat, barley, and other grain from the plains; the finest rice from the hill states; which last also furnish honey, turmeric, ginger, potatoes, onions, and other esculent vegetables. Butcher's meat is abundant and good, as are milk and butter, the hill pastures imparting great excellence to the produce of flocks and herds. The wines, liquors, and wares of Europe and Hindoostan are abundant, and of superior description, and, in consequence of the great competition between the native dealers, cheaper than in the plains. Christ Church, built by subscription, and finished in 1837, is a neat slated structure, with a turret. The Himalaya Club had, in 1842, 155 members. The clubhouse contains accommodation for sixteen resident members, who each have a sitting-room, bed-room, and bath. There are besides a handsome ball-room, two billiard-rooms, a dining-room, and coffee-room, with all accommodation suitable for such an establishment. To these it was intended to add a reading-room, supplied with the best periodicals. In this flourishing little settlement there are two well-managed and successful schools for young ladies, and one for boys. Beer is brewed from native barley and English hops, and the result has been so encouraging, that a large brewery is in course of building. A bank was established in 1841, and has been very successful. An humble botanic garden, subsidiary to that of Suharunpoor, is managed here by natives, at the expense of 66 rupees (6*l.* 12*s.*) per month. Of the diseases contracted in the plains, the effects of a residence here are found favourable to fevers of intermittent and remittent type, dyspepsia, dysentery, liver complaint, pulmonary consumption, rheumatism, general debility, or exhaustion of the constitution. Affections of the heart have had invariably a fatal result. Children thrive remarkably here, though there have been some instances of their being affected with bronchocele or goitre, which has, however, been cured by administering iodine. Mussouree is distant N.W. from Calcutta, by Lucknow, Bareilly, Hurdwar, and Dehra, 1,058 miles. Elevation above the sea 6,282 feet. Lat. 30° 27′, long. 78° 5′.

MUSSOWRAH.—A town in the British district of Patna, lieut.-gov. of Bengal, 31 miles S.W. by W. of Patna. Lat. 25° 20′, long. 84° 50′.

MUSTAFABAD, in the territory of Oude, a small town on the route from Allahabad to Lucknow, 52 miles N.W. of the former, 76 S.E. of the latter. It has a bazar. Lat. 25° 56′, long. 81° 13′.

MUSTAFABAD, in Sirhind, a town on the route from Suharunpoor to Loodiana, and 33 miles N.W. of the former place. It is of moderate size, has a bazar, and is surrounded by a brick wall, like most of the towns in that part of the country. It has a citadel, built of burnt bricks, with curtains and round towers at the angles. This is the residence of the Sikh chief or rajah, whose possessions, under the grant of the British government in 1837, comprise thirty-one villages, and yield an annual revenue of 2,400*l.* sterling. The chief, though retaining his revenue, has been deprived of independent authority within his possessions. The surrounding country is fertile and well cultivated, and abounds in fine mango-groves. Water and supplies are abundant, but the road in this part of the route is rough and heavy, especially where it crosses the river Markunda. Mustafabad is distant N.W. from Calcutta 996 miles. Lat. 30° 12′, long. 77° 13′.

MUSTGARH, in Bussahir, a fortress held

by the Goorkhas during their occupation of the country. It is situate on the crest of a lofty ridge, proceeding in a northerly direction from the Moral-ke-kanda, a great range extending south-westward from the Himalaya. The surface descends for three and a half miles steeply, to Nirt, on the left bank of the Sutlej, and having an elevation of 3,087 feet above the sea. The elevation of Musgarh is probably nearly 6,000 feet. Lat. 31° 20′, long. 77° 39′.

MUSTUFABAD, in the British district of Mynpoory, lieut.-gov. of the N.W. Provinces, a town, the principal place of the pergunnah of the same name, is on the route from the cantonment of Muttra to that of Mynpoory, and 26 miles N.W. of the latter. Lat. 27° 18′, long. 78° 38′.

MUSWAH.—A town in the British district of Candeish, presidency of Bombay, 48 miles N.E. by E. of Malligaum. Lat. 20° 53′, long. 75° 7′.

MUTHEEARA.—A town in the territory of Oude, on the right bank of the Ghogra, and 87 miles N. by E. from Lucknow. Lat. 28° 5′, long. 81° 15′.

MUTIANA, in the petty chieftainship of Goond, tributary to the hill state of Keunthal, a small fort on the route from Simla to Kotgurh, and, by the winding mountain-road, 19 miles N.E. of the former station. Elevation above the sea 8,000 feet. Lat. 31° 11′, long. 77° 27′.

MUTKHANI, in the British district of Kumaon, lieut.-gov. of the N.W. Provinces, a village on the route from Pethoragurh to Thakil Peak, two miles S.E. of the former. Lat. 29° 34′, long. 80° 17′.

MUTKOPA, in the British district of Goruckpoor, lieut.-gov. of the N.W. Provinces, a town on the route from Goruckpoor to the territory of Nepal, 30 miles N.E. of the former. Lat. 27°, long. 83° 43′.

MUTLAH.—See MUTWAL.

MUTOWLI, in the British district of Cawnpore, lieut.-gov. of the N.W. Provinces, a village on the route from Calpee to Etawa, and 44 miles S.E. of the latter. Lat. 26° 24′, long. 79° 38′.

MUTSEE, in the Baree Dooab division of the Punjab, a town situated eight miles W. from the right bank of the Sutlej, 45 miles E.S.E. of the town of Mooltan. Lat. 29° 49′, long. 72° 10′.

MUTTEAREE.—A town in the British district of Purneah, lieut.-gov. of Bengal, 36 miles N.N.W. of Purneah. Lat. 26° 16′, long. 87° 23′.

MUTTIA, in the British district of Futtehpoor, lieut.-gov. of the N.W. Provinces, a town three miles from the left bank of the Jumna, 15 miles S.W. of the town of Futtehpoor. Lat. 25° 42′, long. 80° 47′.

MUTTOAD, in the Mysore, a town with a fort, situate in a valley near a fine tank. Here are several manufactures of glass, made to be converted into bangles or rings for the arms and ankles; the siliceous rocks of the hills hereabouts, and the soda with which the neighbouring earth is impregnated, yielding abundant materials. Distance N.W. from Seringapatam 98 miles. Lat. 13° 46′, long. 76° 28′.

MUTTORA, in the Rajpoot state of Jodhpoor, a village on the route *viâ* Nagor from Jessulmeer to Nusseerabad, and 157 miles N.W. of the latter. It is supplied with good water from one well 250 feet deep. Lat. 26° 56′, long. 73°.

MUTTOUNDH, in the British district of Banda, lieut.-gov. of the N.W. Provinces, a town on the route from the town of Banda to Saugor, 13 miles W. of the former. It has a bazar. Lat. 25° 26′, long. 80° 13′.

MUTTRA, within the limits of the lieut.-gov. of the N.W. Provinces, a British district named from its principal place. It is bounded on the north by the British districts Goorgaon and Allygurh; on the east by the British districts Allygurh and Mynpooree; on the south-west and south by the British district Agra; and on the west by the territory of Bhurtpore. It lies between lat. 27° 14′—27° 58′, long. 77° 20′—78° 34′, and includes an area of 1,607 square miles. The Jumna, crossing the northern frontier in lat. 27° 55′, long. 77° 35′, holds a tortuous course, but generally in a south-easterly direction, of about ninety-five miles, within, or bounding the district, until it passes from it in lat. 27° 15′, long. 78° 2′, having, while flowing through Muttra, divided it into two parts, one lying in the Doab, the other on the south-west side of the river. During the dry season, the volume of water in the channel of the river is inconsiderable. Hence at that season the river is not navigable, except for very small vessels, above the confluence of the Chumbul, about 100 miles lower down. The general inclination of the surface of the country is from N.W. to S.E., as is indicated by the descent of the course of the Jumna. A similar direction is also taken by the Karwan, a small river nearly parallel to the Jumna, and a few miles east of it; and by the Isun, still farther eastward. Actual measurement has ascertained the elevation of the town of Nuh, on the north-western frontier, to be 693 feet above the sea, and that of Kuraoli, near the south-eastern, 648. On the left bank of the Jumna, in the north of the district, is the jhil or shallow lake of Nuh, caused by the overflow of that great river during the rains. The district is, with little exception, a plain, though there are a few hills on the western frontier towards Bhurtpore; and amongst them, that of Goverdhun, famous in Hindoo mythology as the scene of the amours, exploits, and pastoral avocations of Krishna. Though the district is situate some degrees outside the tropic, and its atmosphere is, during the summer months, coole a little by the periodical rains, the heat in spring is excessive. In the beginning of March, Jacquemont found the heat so great as to preclude his travelling after nine in the forenoon, the air at the same time being remarkably dry. As the season advances, the temperature increases, becoming everywhere oppressive. The burning wind, "after passing over the great sandy desert, imparts to the atmosphere in these regions an intensity of heat scarcely to be conceived, even by those who have been seasoned to the fury of a vertical sun. In every direction where this pestiferous current has any influence, the effects are painful to those who have the misfortune of being exposed to it; but westward of the Jumna, the fiery blast is still more distressing, from the want of rivers and lakes to temper its severity, the nearest resemblance to which, perhaps, is the extreme glow of an iron-foundry in the height of summer." The water in the wells is for the most part brackish. The country lying west of the Jumna has generally a sandy soil, mixed with kunkur, or calcareous conglomerate; and though in a state of nature overrun with the Capparis aphylla and some species of zizyphus, yet, under proper cultivation, producing abundant crops of wheat. On the east or left bank of the river, the soil is rather light and bare, but improved towards the middle of the Doab, where it is good. The principal alimentary crops are wheat, barley, various kinds of millet, pulse, oil-seeds, cucurbitaceous plants, and sugar; the principal commercial crops, indigo, and some other plants yielding dyes, cotton, tobacco, and opium. Under the last revenue settlement of the N.W. Provinces, the government demand on the lands of this district has been fixed for a term of years, and is not liable to be increased until the year 1871. The chief towns are Muttra, Bindrabun, Muhabun, Juleisur, Rampore, and Koorsundah. These will be found in their proper places under the alphabetical arrangement.

The population, according to official return 1853, was 862,909. Of this number, 506.178 are returned as Hindoos agricultural; 286,781 Hindoos non-agricultural; 25,913 Mahomedans and others agricultural, and 44,037 of the like classes non-agricultural; showing an immense preponderance of the Hindoo population. The district contains seven towns having more than 5,000 inhabitants, but less than 10,000, and four containing upwards of 10,000. Of these latter, none at the period of the return exceeded 30,000, with the exception of Muttra, in which the number was nearly 66,000. The principal routes are,—1. The great one from Agra to Delhi, traversing the district from south-east to north-west; 2. from Muttra cantonment, in a westerly direction, to Alwar by Deeg; 3. from the town of Muttra, north-westerly, to Ferozepore by Kosi; 4. south-westerly, from Muttra to Bhurtpore; 5. south-easterly, from Muttra to Mynpooree; 6. north-easterly, from Muttra to Allygurh. The district is also traversed by the East-Indian Railway.

The tract comprised within this district fell early under the power of the Affghan Mussulmans, having been conquered in 1017 by Mahmood of Ghuzni. Liberated for a short time, on the fall of the Ghaznevide dynasty, it was, at the close of the twelfth century, subdued by the Ghorian Afghans, and remained subject to the various successive dynasties of that people, which ruled Delhi and its dependencies until conquered by the Mogul invader Baber in 1526. On the decline of the Timurian dynasty in the eighteenth century, it was overrun by the Jats, from whom it was wrested by Nujuf Khan, and embodied in his short-lived state. On his death, it was seized by Madhajee Scindia, the Mahratta chief, whose successor in 1803 ceded it to the East-India Company by the second article of the treaty of Serjee Anjengaum.

MUTTRA, a town, the principal place of the district of the same name, is situate on the right or western bank of the Jumna, which is here crossed in the height of the rains by ferry, and at other seasons by a bridge of boats. The town extends in the form of a crescent along the elevated bank of the river, and, with its great ruined fort, has a very picturesque appearance when viewed from the low ground on the opposite side. Of the lofty fortifications which once encircled the town, only a few fragments, including three gateways, now remain. The river being considered sacred by the Hindoos, its banks are every morning and evening crowded by devotees of both sexes and of all ages, to perform their devotions and religious exercises, access being obtained to the stream by numerous ghats, or extensive flights of stone steps, ornamented with little temples. The site of the town is much cut up by ravines, and the streets are described as steep, narrow, winding, and excessively filthy. Heber, however, speaks of it as a striking town, much resembling Benares, its houses being very high, with the same sort of ornaments as in that city. On an elevated site on the bank of the river is a large ruinous fortress, which formerly commanded the place; and in the middle of the town, the mosque of Aurungzebe, also in a ruinous state, its four lofty minarets, overlaid with glazed ware, being much decayed. The fort was built by the celebrated astronomer Jey Singh, or Jaya Sinha, the Rajpoot prince who succeeded to the sovereignty of Amber 1693, and was some years later high in favour with Muhammad, emperor of Delhi. On the roof of one of the apartments is a ruinous observatory, the work of that scientific prince, and containing an equinoctial dial, sundry amplitude-instruments, horizontal circle, with a gnomon, intended for some purpose as yet unascertained, a mural instrument facing westward, and consisting of a segment exceeding a semicircle, with the convex downwards, on the opposite wall to which is a segment with the convex upwards. The population of the town in 1853, according to official report, was 65,749. Some of the traders are considered to be very wealthy.

The place is regarded as sacred in Hindoo mythology, from being the birthplace of the divinity Krishna, the Khrishnavatar or incarnation of Vishnu under that name. In honour of the monkey-god Hanuman, monkeys are here protected and fed, swarming in the ruins, sitting, running, or playing on the tops of the houses, and skipping from roof to roof across the streets, greatly annoying their Hindoo votaries, as well as strangers. There are also numbers of paroquets, peacocks, and sacred bulls at large without owners. In the central part of the town is a beautiful structure, built by the treasurer of the state of Gwalior, who was also the principal partner in a great native banking house. The building, intended to serve the purpose of a temple and a dwelling, is inclosed by a small but richly-carved gateway, with a flight of steps which leads from the street to a square court, cloistered round, and containing in the centre a building also square, supported by a triple row of pillars, all which, as well as the ceiling, are richly carved, painted, and gilt. Here is a military cantonment: the buildings, which are about a mile south of the town, and separated from it by a small space of broken ground, are very extensive.

Muttra, recommended to the Hindoos by associations connected with their mythology, appears, at an early period of their records, to have been much more important than at present; and its wealth and splendour pointed it out as an object for the attacks of the first Afghan invaders. Mahmood of Ghuznee, in his expedition against Kunnouj in the year 1017, "understanding that at some distance stood the rich city of Muttra, consecrated to Khrishna-Vos-dew, whom the Hindoos venerate as an emanation of God, directed his march thither, and entering it with little opposition from the troops of the rajah of Delhi, to whom it belonged, gave it up to plunder. He broke down or burned all the idols, and amassed a vast quantity of gold and silver, of which the idols were mostly composed. He would have destroyed the temples also, but he found the labour would have been excessive, while some say he was averted from his profane purpose by their admirable beauty. He certainly extravagantly extolled the magnificence of the buildings and city in a letter to the governor of Ghiznee, in which the following passage occurs:—'There are here 1,000 edifices, as firm as the faith of the faithful, most of them of marble; besides innumerable temples; nor is it likely this city has attained its present condition but at the expense of many millions of dinars; nor could such another be constructed under a period of two centuries.' Among the temples at Muttra were found five golden idols, whose eyes were of rubies, valued at 50,000 dinars. On another idol was found a sapphire weighing 400 miskals, and the image itself being melted down, produced 98,300 miskals of pure gold. Besides these images, there were about 100 idols of silver, which loaded as many camels. The king tarried in Muttra twenty days, in which time the city suffered greatly from fire, in addition to the damage which it sustained from being pillaged." After these calamities, it sank into obscurity, and does not appear to be mentioned by Baber in his detailed account of his campaigns in the vicinity. In 1757, it was subjected to pillage and massacre by the Afghan troops of Ahmed Shah Dooranee. Ahmed did not in person command the expedition, having intrusted its conduct to Sirdar Jehan Khan, called Zanus by the Jesuits. Tieffenthaler states his army at 25,000 cavalry, and adds, "Muttra is a populous city, abounding in wealthy inhabitants. In this city, and in another town, called Bendroban [Bindraban], very famous throughout India, on account of the incarnation of Khrishna, the Afghans practised great cruelties, and displayed their hatred of idols and idolaters, burning houses, together with their inmates; slaughtering others with the sword and lance; hauling off into captivity maidens and youths, men and women. In the temples of the idols they slaughtered kine, regarded as sacred by the superstitious people, and smeared the images and pavement with the blood." Scindia, the Mahratta chief, who, after the death of Mujuf Khan, seized Muttra, conferred it on the French adventurer Perron, in jaghire, a grant made on condition of military service. In October, 1803, it was without resistance occupied by the British troops, and in the same year permanently ceded to the East-India Company by the treaty of Serjee Anjengaum. Distant N.W. from Calcutta 831 miles; from Agra, N.W., 35; from Delhi, S.E., 97. Lat. 27° 30′, long. 77° 45′.

MUTTUCK, or MUTTRUCK.—See Assam.

MUTTUNI, in the district of Peshawur, a division of the Punjab, a town situated on the road from Kohat to Peshawur, 14 miles S. of the latter. A fort is in course of construction at this town, with the view of obtaining an effectual command over the Kohat Pass. Lat. 33° 48′, long. 71° 37′.

MUTWAL, or ROYMATLA.—The name of one of the rivers in the delta of the Ganges. It divaricates from the Ganges in lat. 22° 33′, long. 88° 23′, a few miles south of Calcutta, and, flowing in a southerly direction for ninety-four miles, falls into the Bay of Bengal, in lat. 21° 44′, long. 88° 46′. It has never less water in it than three fathoms, and a ship of considerable burden could proceed to Tarda, a village close to the salt lake, near Calcutta. The Mutwal is about to be connected with Calcutta by means of a railway under the auspices of a new company, and thus become the successor of the Hooghly, should it be necessary to abandon the latter, from its ceasing to be navigable, in consequence of the silting up of its channel.—See HOOGHLY RIVER.

MUTWAUR.—A town of Malwa, in the native state of Aleerajpoor, 14 miles S. from Rajpoor, and 74 miles E. by S. from Baroda. Lat. 22° 7′, long. 74° 23′.

MUWAR, in the British district of Cawnpore, lieut.-gov. of the N.W. Provinces, a village on the left bank of the river Singoor, and on the route from the cantonment of Cawnpore to that of Calpee, 18 miles N.E. of the latter. Lat. 26° 18′, long. 79° 59′.

MUXOODPORE.—A town in the British district of Dacca Jelalpore, lieut.-gov. of Bengal, 102 miles E.N.E. of Calcutta. Lat. 23° 20′, long. 89° 50′.

MUZUFURABAD, in the British district of Suharunpoor, lieut.-gov. of the N.W. Provinces, a town on the route from Suharunpoor to Debra, 15 miles N.E. of the former. Lat. 30° 8′, long. 77° 48′.

MUZUFFURGURH, in the Sinde Sagur Dooab division of the Punjab, a town situated on the right bank of the Chenaub, 19 miles W.S.W. of the town of Mooltan. Lat. 30° 3′, long. 71° 14′.

MUZUFFURNUGUR.—See MOZUFFURNUGUR.

MYACONDA, in the Mysore, a fort on the north-west frontier, towards the British district of Dharwar. "The situation of Myaconda is important, as being at the entrance of a pass from the north-westward into the valley of Chittel Droog." Though regarded as a strong place by native soldiers, it was in 1790 breached and stormed by the Mahrattas. Here, in 1749, was fought a battle between the forces of the ranee of Bednore and those of the polygar of Chittel Droog, in which the latter were defeated. Myaconda is distant from Chittel Droog 21 miles, Seringapatam 135. Lat. 14° 17′, long. 76° 9′.

MYADOUNG MYO.—A town of Burmah, situate on the left bank of the Irawady river, and 133 miles N. from Ava. Lat. 23° 49′, long. 96° 8′.

MYAPOOR, in Bundelcund, in the territory of Jhansee, a village on the route by Jhansee from Calpee to Goona, 146 miles S.W. of former, 59 N.E. of latter. About a mile S.W. of the village commences the ascent of the Majapoor Pass, short, stony, and of easy ascent. Lat. 25° 8′, long. 78° 7′.

MYAPOOR, in the British district of Saharunpore, lieut.-gov. of Agra, a village on the right bank of the Ganges, about two miles below Hurdwar. At this spot commences the artificial channel of the new Ganges Canal, to which the supply from the river is led by a natural branch. The masonry-works at this place consist of a dam thrown across the branch of the Ganges, and a regulating bridge across the canal bed. The dam is provided with gates and sluices to carry off the superfluous waters of the Ganges during the floods. The supply of water for the canal at this place will be 6,750 cubic feet per second; the whole discharge of the river at Hurdwar being 8,000 cubic feet per second. Lat. 29° 56′, long. 78° 12′.

MYAVERAM.—A town in the British district of Tanjore, presidency of Madras, 41 miles N.E. by E. of Tanjore. Lat. 11° 7′, long. 79° 42′.

MYHEE, the name of two passes known as the Great and Little Myhee Pass, through which roads are carried over the Youmadoung range of mountains, separating Arracan from Burmah. The Myhee Great Pass is in lat. 19° 14′, long. 94° 30′; the Little Pass is a few miles further north.

MYHEE.—A village and police-station in the British district of Arracan. It is situate on a line of road from Sandoway over the Youmadoung Mountains into Burmah, and is 113 miles S.S.E. from Arracan. Lat. 19° 17′, long. 94° 10′.

MYHEE.—A river rising in the native state of Amjherra, in Malwa, in a small plain, in lat. 22° 32′, long. 75° 5′. It holds a course north-west for 145 miles, to lat. 23° 48′, long. 74° 32′, where the mountains of Marwar turn it to the westward for twenty-five miles; and subsequently south-west, which course it continues to hold 180 miles farther, to its fall into the Gulf of Cambay, a few miles below the town of Cambay, and in lat. 22° 10′, long. 72° 30′; its total length of course being about 350 miles. It does not appear to be navigable for more than fifteen miles from its mouth. Opposite the city of Cambay, seven or eight miles from the sea, the width is probably about three miles, and the water is so shallow from side to side, at low water spring tides, that the ground is left almost dry, and navigation is impracticable even for the smallest boats. Fifty miles from its source, and in lat. 23° 9′, long. 75° 1′, it is crossed by means of a ford on the route from Neemuch to Baroda, and is there described by Heber as shallow and broad, but not stagnant. Sixty miles farther down, or more north-west, it is again crossed on the route from Neemuch to Baroda, *viâ* Pertabghur, at Boongra, where it has a "bed 400 yards wide, with a stream of 100, and a depth of one foot." About fifty miles above its mouth, it is crossed by the route from Neemuch to Baroda by Sulumbur. "Its bed is here 500 yards wide, stream 120, average depth a foot and a half." Heber, who crossed it at this place, describes it as a broad, bright stream, wandering in a wide bed of sand and gravel. About eight miles lower down, its breadth is above two miles; and when the tide is out, there is about a third of that width of water unfordable even at the ebb of spring tides. The elevation of the source is about 1,850 feet.

MYHEE CAUNTA.—A division of Guzerat, under the political supervision of the government of Bombay. It lies between lat. 23° 14′ and 24° 28′, long. 72° 41′ and 74° 5′, and is bounded on the north by the mountainous Bheel districts of Mewar or Odeypore, and Serohee; on the south by the Guicowar's district of Balasinore and the British collectorate of Kaira; on the east by Dongurpore; on the south-east by the petty states of Saunte and Lunawara; and on the west by Pahlunpore, and by various pergunnahs belonging to the Guicowar. Its length from south-east to north-west is about 100 miles, and its breadth in the direction of the opposite angles measures about sixty: the area is 3,400 square miles.

The district comprises six zillahs: Nanee Marwar, in which are included the talooks of Edur and Ahmednuggur (which see), with their dependencies of Morassa, Hursole, and Byer; and those of Tintoee, Daunta, and Malpoor, together with the puttas of Pole, Pall, Posuna, Gudwarra, Wullasun, and Hurrole, all more or less subject to Edur. The remaining five zillahs are Rehwur, Sabur Caunta, Kuttosun, Byal or Baweesa, and Watruck. The streams intersecting the country are seven in number: the Sabur Muttee, Haut Muttee, Karree, Meshwah, Majoom, Watruck, and Surruswuttee. The total amount of the revenue of the Myhee Caunta may be estimated at from 45,000*l.* to 50,000*l.* per annum. From this sum the Guicowar receives a yearly tribute of 9,340*l.*, under the head of Ghans Dana, and 4,500*l.* as revenue; making a total of 13,840*l.* No tribute is paid to the British government. A detachment of 1,000 horse from the Guicowar's contingent is placed under the orders of the political agent in this province. The military force at the disposal of the government of Edur is employed almost entirely for police purposes, and consists of about 2,000 horse and foot, inclusive of the quotas furnished by the feudal chiefs.

The political connection of the East-India Company with the Myhee Caunta dates from the year 1820. Among the possessions of the Peishwa which, in 1818, escheated to the British government, were included Ahmedabad and its dependencies. The occupation of these districts brought the British in immediate contact with the lawless tribes of the Myhee Caunta, and it became at once obvious that there could be no security for the preservation of public tranquillity, unless the differences continually arising between the Guicowar and his turbulent tributaries should be adjudicated by an efficient authority capable of enforcing its decisions. An arrangement was accordingly concluded, under which the Guicowar agreed to withdraw his troops, and to abstain from all further interference with the chieftains, while the British government undertook the management of the country, and guaranteed the payment of the Guicowar's tribute. The British government had no further interest in these arrangements than that which accrued to them in their character as conservators of the general peace. Nevertheless, in carrying them out, they have not failed to avail themselves of the opportunity thereby offered to confer important benefits upon the country. By their means, suttee has been abolished; infanticide and bharwuttie prohibited; and at their instigation a criminal court has been established for the trial of all serious offences, through the agency of the political resident, with native chiefs as assessors. The introduction of this tribunal has had a most salutary effect, and has proved a powerful auxiliary not only in the pacification, but in the civilization of this hitherto troubled region. The principal towns in the Myhee Caunta are Edur, Ahmednuggur, and Wurralee, of which some notice will be found in their places under the alphabetical arrangement.

MYHIR, in the territory of Saugor and Nerbudda, a town, the principal place of the thakoorai or small state of the same name, situate on the route by Rewa from Allahabad to Jubbulpore, and 100 miles N.E. of the latter. According to Garden, it is a "large town and bazar, and the chief place in the district belonging to Thakoor Bishen Singh." Water is plentiful, a large jhil or mere being on the N.W., and another S.W. of the town. The thakoorai of Myhir was originally a grant from the rajah of Panna, and in 1814 was confirmed to the thakoor by sunnud or grant from the British government. It contains an area of 1,026 square miles, and a population of 100,000. On the death of the thakoor in 1826, his two sons took arms and disputed the possession, but were tranquillized by the British authorities. Bishen Singh, who appears to have been remarkable for improvidence, voluntarily placed his estate under the management of the British government, for the purpose of liquidating his debts. The estate was continued under British management after the death of Bishen Singh, in view to paying off his debts. The home authorities at the same time suggested the propriety of issuing a proclamation announcing that the estates of thakoors will not be held responsible for debts beyond the life of the thakoor who shall contract them. The present chief is a minor, and arrangements have been made for his education at Agra under the direction of the British government. Myhir is in lat. 24° 16′, long. 80° 49′.

MYHNATHEIR, in the British district of Moradabad, lieut.-gov. of the N.W. Provinces, a village on the route from Allygurh to the town of Moradabad, and 11 miles S.W. of the latter. Lat. 28° 42′, long. 78° 46′.

MYHSEE.—A town in the British district of Sarun, lieut.-gov. of Bengal, 47 miles N. by E. of Chupra. Lat. 26° 20′, long. 85° 11′.

MYITHIA KHYOUNG.—A river of Burmah, rising in lat. 21° 20′, long. 94° 4′, and, flowing in a northerly direction for 170 miles, falls into the Khyendwen river, in lat. 23° 11′, long. 94° 41′.

MYKHINDA, in the native state of Gurwhal, a village on the route from Sireenuggur to Kedarnath Temple, and 12 miles S. of the latter. It is situate on the eastern declivity of a mountain of gneiss formation, and near the right bank of the Mundagnee river. Elevation above the sea 5,545 feet. Lat. 30° 34′, long. 79° 5′.

MYLE, in the British district of Goruckpoor, lieut.-gov. of the N.W. Provinces, a town on the route from Goruckpoor to Chupra, 47 miles S.E. of the former. Lat. 26° 12′, long. 83° 54′.

MYMENSING.—A British district within the limits of the lieut.-gov. of Bengal. It is bounded on the north by Goalpara, on the borders of Assam, and by the country of the wild Garrow tribes; on the east by the British district of Sylhet; on the south by the British districts Tipperah, Dacca, and Furreedpore; on the south-west by the British district of Pubna; and on the west by the districts Bogra and Rungpoor. It lies between lat. 24° 4′—25° 41′, long. 89° 28′—91° 13′, and has an area, according to official return, of 4,712 square miles. In the northern part, towards Goalpara and the Garrow highlands, there are many hills and irregular tracts densely covered with jungle, and in the south-western part, along the right bank of the Brahmapootra, the country is of a similar description. The rest of the district is in general level, rather depressed and marshy, traversed by numerous watercourses, and containing many jhils or shallow lakes. Of the rivers, the principal are the Brahmapootra and the Konaie. These two great streams communicate by means of the Jenaie, a large watercourse which connects them about twenty miles below their divarication. All three are navigable in their course through the district; but on the Brahmapootra, in consequence of the diminution of its volume of water for the supply of the Konaie, the larger class of native boats can only pass during the rainy season. Inferior streams and watercourses are very numerous, and contribute, together with the many jhils, to extensive inundations of the country during the rains. Most of the jhils become dry in the hot season, but every village, and even every dwelling inhabited by a family of superior class, has a tank yielding a perennial supply of water.

The climate is considered superior to that of the southern part of Bengal, as, though damp, the temperature is cooler. During March and the two succeeding months, when heat is most oppressive in general in India, the weather is here unsettled rather than sultry. Violent storms of wind and rain from the north-west are of frequent occurrence, and are accompanied by thunder and lightning, and frequently prove very destructive. The periodical rains commence in the beginning of June, and continue until the beginning of October, when the northerly winds set in, bringing cold weather, during which fogs are very prevalent, when the sun is seldom visible until nine or ten o'clock in the forenoon. The population is given under the article BENGAL.

This district was included in the grant of the dewanny of Bengal, Behar, and Orissa, made by the king of Delhi to the East-India Company.

MYMUTGURH.—A town in the British district of Rutnageria, presidency of Bombay, 143 miles S.S.E. of Bombay. Lat. 17° 4′, long. 73° 47′.

MYNAH.—A town of Malwa, in the native state of Bhopal, 49 miles W. by S. from Bhopal, and 55 miles E. from Oojein. Lat. 23° 9′, long. 76° 40′.

MYNPOOREE.—A British district under the lieut.-gov. of the N.W. Provinces, named from its principal place. It is bounded on the north by the British district of Budaon; on the north-east and west by the British district of Furruckabad; on the south by the British districts Etawah and Agra; and on the west by the British districts Agra, Muttra, and Allyghur. It lies between lat. 26° 54′—27° 50′, long. 78° 30′—79° 30′, and contains an area of about 2,009 square miles. It is a very level, and in general a well-watered tract, the Jumna forming for thirty-five miles its southern boundary, and the Kalee Nuddee (Eastern) first forming its western boundary for ten miles, then flowing through its northern part for sixteen miles, and subsequently becoming its north-eastern boundary for about fifty-five miles more. The country lying between those two rivers is traversed by four small streams,—the Esun, nearest the Kalee Nuddee and most to the north-eastward; next to that, towards the south-west, the Rind or Urrund; further to the south-west, the Seyngur; and the Sirsa next to the Jumna. Besides these watercourses, the projected line of the Ganges Canal, now in course of progress, passes by the town of Mynpooree, and will ultimately form a navigable channel to the Ganges at Cawnpore. The courses of the two greater rivers, and of the four lesser and intermediate streams, are all in some degree parallel to each other, and all flow to the south-east; thus indicating the general slope of the country to be in that direction. The average elevation of the country above the level of the sea is between 600 and 700 feet; that of the town of Gihoor, a few miles west of Mynpooree, is 648 feet; that of Kerowly, near the northern frontier, 648 feet; that of the bed of the Kalee Nuddee (East), below that town, 614 feet. The general slope of the country is 1·138 feet in the mile. Previously to the mitigating effect of the periodical rains, which set in after midsummer, the heat in this district is very great; yet in winter the thermometer in this part of the Doab sometimes falls below the freezing-point. Rice is grown in the northern part of the district; the sugarcane is produced with little trouble, and in great abundance, though inferior both in size and the yield of saccharine matter to that which is cultivated in rich upper lands. Here also indigo of superior quality grows wild, and, it was stated by an eminent authority, "might be grown at half its present cost, of quality very little inferior, and with the same facility that characterizes the cultivation of the sugarcane." Wheat, barley, millet, gram (Cicer arietinum), and some other pulse, are extensively cultivated; cotton and tobacco succeed well in the Boodh Gunga, as also along the course of the Kalee Nuddee. The soil in the middle parts, about the town of Mynpooree, is good. According to census made in 1853, the population amounted to 832,714; of whom are returned 619,659 as Hindoo agricultural; 161,422 Hindoo non-agricultural; 20,093 Mahomedans and others agricultural; and 31,540 of those various classes non-agricultural. It thus appears that the population is almost exclusively Hindoo. The prevalence among the Rajpoots of the horrible practice of female infanticide caused, some years since, the issue of an order, by a local magistrate, that the bodies of all deceased female Rajpoot children should be sent for the examination of the civil surgeon, with a view to ascertain in each case whether death had resulted from other than natural causes; but the order was withdrawn by direction of the government; and the home authorities approved of the withdrawal, deeming that the operation of the order might be offensive. Measures are in progress for putting a stop to the crime. Mynpooree contains no large town, and only one or two of tolerable size. The number of villages in the district is stated to be 1,353.

The district is traversed in its southern quarter by the East-Indian Railway. The other principal routes are—1. From north-west to south-east, from Allygurh to the town of Mynpooree, and thence to Cawnpore; 2. from west to east, from Agra to Mynpooree, and thence to Futtehgurh; 3. from north-west to south-east, from Muttra to Mynpooree, and thence to Lucknow; 4. from south to north, from Etawah to Mynpooree, and thence to Azimghur; 5. from south-east to north-west, from Etawah to Agra. The tract of which this forms part, was included in the Mahommedan empire of the Afghans overthrown by Baber, and was conquered or overrun by that invader. On the dismemberment of the empire of Delhi, it became part of the transient realm of Nujuf Khan, in virtue of a treaty of partition between him and Shuja-ood-dowlah, the vizier of Oude. After the death of the former, it was seized by the Mahrattas, and in 1803 was ceded to the East-India Company by Dowlut Rao Sindia, under the second article of the treaty of Serjee Anjengaum.

MYNPOOREE, a town, the principal place of the district of the same name, is situate on the banks of the small river Esun, which is here crossed by a bridge of brick, near the cantonment. Thorn, who saw this place in 1804, describes it as then "a walled town, of considerable size, and very populous." A few days previously, it had been attacked by the Mahrattas under Holkar, who plundered and burned part of it, but were repulsed from the jail and cantonments by the provincial militia in the service of the East-India Company, and fled precipitately on the approach of a relieving force. According to official report Mynpooree contains 20,921 inhabitants. Here is a Jain temple, with a Buddhistic idol. It is a favourable station for troops, as supplies and water are very abundant and good. Elevation above the sea about 620 feet. Distance N.W. from Calcutta, by Cawnpore, 727 miles; E. from Agra 71¼; S.E. from Delhi 165. Lat. 27° 14′, long. 79° 4′.

MYNTUPPUL, in Sirhind, a village on the route from Suharunpoor to Nahun, and eight miles S.W. of the latter town. It is situate at the south-west base of the low prolongation of the Sewalik range. The road in the direction of Suharunpoor is level and very good, and in that of Nahun has a considerable acclivity, but is well made. Distant N.W. from Calcutta 1,008 miles. Lat. 30° 31′, long. 77° 17′.

MYNWAR.—A town in the territory of Oude, 112 miles N. by E. from Lucknow, and 92 miles E. by S. from Pileebheet. Lat. 28° 27′, long. 81° 21′.

MYRABPOOR.—A town in Scinde, situate in the patrimony enjoyed by Ali Moorad, 46 miles S.W. by S. from Bukkur, and 34 miles S.E. from Larkhanna. Lat. 27° 7′, long. 68° 34′.

MYRWA.—A town in the British district of Sarun, lieut.-gov. of Bengal, 49 miles N.W. by W. of Chupra. Lat. 26° 11′, long. 84° 11′.

MYSORE, in Southern India, a raj or principality under the protection of the British government, by whom, indeed, the entire management of its affairs is at present exercised. This territory is bounded on the north-west by the British collectorate of Dharwar, in the presidency of Bombay, and on all other sides by various districts of the presidency of Madras; North Canara and Bellary bounding it on the north; the districts of Cuddapah, North Arcot, and Salem on the east; Coimbatore and Malabar on the south; Coorg and South Canara on the west. It is about 250 miles in length from north to south, and 238 in extreme breadth; the area is 30,886 square miles. The country is a table-land, considerably elevated; it is of triangular form, having its greatest width at the northern boundary. The eastern, western, and southern limits of the province are skirted by the Eastern and Western Ghauts, which, gradually converging from the north, form a junction at the southern extremity of Mysore, in the vicinity of the Neilgherry Hills. "The elevation of the country varies a good deal; thus,

Paidnadurgum is 1,907; Baitmungalum, 2,519; Bangalore, 3,000; Mysore (town), 2,513; Seringapatam, 2,558; Serah, 2,223; Narsapore, 2,904; Colar, 2,800; Naikennary, 2,221; and Hurryhur, 1,831 feet above the level of the sea, according to barometrical observations." The Swagunga Mountains, twenty-five miles north-west of Bangalore, have an elevation of 4,600 feet above the sea, and the Bababudin, near Bednor, upwards of 6,000. In the northern part of the territory, the Ghauts, receding from each other, leave the intervening country plain and open, and sloping gradually northwards, as indicated by the course of the rivers, which for the most part flow in that direction. A small portion of the surface, however, in the north-west of the country, slopes to the westward. The Ghauts there are lower than in any other part, and the river Sheravuty, rising in the table-land of Mysore, flows westward, and falls into the Arabian Sea, or North Indian Ocean, at Honahwar. In the south-east part of the territory also, the slope of the country varies from the general inclination, being towards the south-east. The drainage of this part is effected by the river Cauvery. The Lechman Teert and Kubbani, flowing from the south-west, fall into this river, which also receives the Hemavati, flowing from the north-west, and the Shimsha and Arkavati, flowing from the north; besides many other streams, which, during the monsoon rains, contribute to swell it into an enormous torrent, which rushes from the elevated table-land of Mysore to the low country extending south-east to the sea, by two falls, that of Gangana Chuki of 370, and that of Birra Chuki of 460 feet. The Toonga and Budra, rising in the north-west of the territory, unite at Halla Honur, and form the Toongabudra or Tumbudra, which, taking a direction north-east, finally falls into the great river Kistnah. The Hugry or Vedavati, rising in the south-west part of the territory, traverses the country in a direction north-east for about 125 miles, and, crossing the north-eastern frontier, falls finally into the Tumbudra or Toongabudra. The Northern Penna crosses the northern, and the southern Penna traverses the southern quarter of the province. There are a great number of smaller streams, but they are in general mere occasional torrents, devoid of water during the dry season. There do not appear to be any natural lakes in Mysore, but tanks or artificial lakes are numerous. Many of them are surrounded with stone embankments, and have regular sluices for letting off the redundant water. The water of the tanks and rivers is considered good, but that of many of the wells, though limpid, is brackish and unwholesome, tending to produce fevers and agues.

Among the most remarkable geological features are the Droogs, being huge isolated rocks, rising abruptly from the generally unbroken surface of the country to heights varying from 1,000 to 1,500 feet, with bases seldom exceeding two miles in circumference, and chiefly composed of masses of granite, gneiss, and hornblende: most of them are surmounted by forts, nearly inaccessible, but which have been allowed to go to ruin since the establishment of British supremacy. Of those, the more remarkable are Nundydroog, having an elevation above the sea of 4,856 feet; Suwarndroog, 4,004; Ubtaradroog and Chittledroog, the respective elevations of which do not appear to have been ascertained. The rocks of Mysore are in general of primitive formation,—granite, gneiss, quartz, sienite, and hornblende,—and in many places they are overlaid by laterite. Gold-dust is found, but there is no metal, except iron, in any degree of abundance. Garnets are frequently to be met with; common salt and carbonate of soda impregnate the soil in many places, and are extracted for domestic or manufacturing purposes. Between Bangalore and Seringapatam, kunker or calcareous tufa exists in considerable quantities.

As the average elevation of Mysore is not less than 2,000 feet above the level of the sea, the temperature is sensibly less than in the low tracts towards the coast. At Bangalore, about 3,000 feet above the sea, the thermometer has been found not to rise to above 82° in the shade; and the general annual average there at noon in the shade is 76°. "The nights are seldom hot, and the mornings and evenings are always cool, if not cold; and there is an elasticity in the air which is truly delightful;" but the range of the thermometer amounting constantly to 40° from sunrise to noon, renders the highest degree of precaution necessary to avoid injurious consequences. After the end of January, the heat of the days fast increases, until the setting in of the Malabar or south-west monsoon, about the beginning of June; and this, in September, is followed by the Coromandel or north-east monsoon; and from the circumstance of the country being exposed to both, more rain falls than in most parts of India. The monsoon from the south-west is the more violent, filling the largest tanks in a few hours, lasting for several days without intermission, and being accompanied by dreadful thunder and lightning.

Among the more destructive wild beasts, the tiger may be mentioned: some villages have been almost depopulated by this animal. Leopards are numerous and destructive; and the cheta or hunting-leopard exists to a great extent. Elephants and bears are also to be classed among the wild animals of Mysore. The ursine sloth (Bradypus ursinus) is sometimes met with. The ravages of wild beasts are very destructive, 337 human beings having perished thereby between January, 1835, and September, 1836. During the same period, the number of cattle destroyed by the wild beasts amounted to 6,769. The number of wild beasts killed within the time was,—elephants 29, tigers 349, leopards 129, chetas 350, bears 118.

The means of internal communication within the province are considerable. From Seringapatam, a road proceeds south-west, through Sidapoor to Coorg. A route proceeds from south to north, from Coimbatore, through the Gujjalhati Pass, to Seringapatam; thence north-west to Dharwar, and ultimately to Bombay. A road from the British sanatory establishments in the Neilgherry group proceeds north through Gundlapetta to Seringapatam, but it is circuitous and difficult. There is a route leading north from Seringapatam by Nundydroog to Hyderabad, the capital of the Nizam's territory; and another proceeding from Nundydroog north-east to Cuddapa. The principal line of communication between Madras and the north-east part of Mysore is through the valley of Ambur, which admits of a tolerably easy ascent. Among the principal passes from Canara, over the Western Ghats, is that of Hyder Ghur or Angady, in the vicinity of Bednore; that of the Bisli Ghat, nearly due east of Mangalore; and that of Munjerabad, a little to the south of the latter pass. In commenting upon an official report, dated in 1849, showing the nature and cost of the principal roads, bridges, and other public works constructed since the country has been under British management, the Court of Directors remark that the "document affords evidence of a great amount of public benefit produced by judicious expenditure." The territory of Mysore contains the following divisions:—1. Bangalore; 2. Mysore Proper, or Astragam; 3. Chitradroog; 4. Beduor. According to official report, the population was taken to be 3,460,696. Mysore, the principal place, as well as Bangalore, Bednor or Nuggur, Seringapatam, Chittledroog, Ooscotta, Nundydroog, and Kolar, are described under their respective names in the alphabetical arrangement.

The Mysoreans in physical constitution are a healthy, robust race of men; and, though not remarkably tall, are rather superior in size to the Indians on the opposite coast of Coromandel. Their features are regular, and their complexions are fairer than those of the natives of less-elevated tracts. The great majority are Brahminists. The Mahommedans, much inferior in number, are for the most part idlers, and eager for a military life, though a few practise some easy handicrafts. The Mysoreans of all classes are characterized as a deceitful, inconstant, profligate race, yet courteous, contented, and patient under misfortunes. The majority fare hardly, their principal food being raghi (Eleusine coracana), a seed of inferior quality, but surprisingly prolific. The dress of the people is fuller than that of the natives below the Ghats. Both sexes wear a combali or woollen blanket wrapped round them, and the women in addition wear the chola, a kind of jacket covering the body and arms. The houses are for the most part built of mud, having low thatched or tiled roofs, and there are seldom any other openings for light or air, except the doorways, which are so low as not to admit full-grown persons unless they stoop.

The ruinous misconduct of the kurtur or sovereign having compelled the British government to remove him from the actual administration of affairs, everything is now managed by a commission appointed by the government of India. The police establishment in the cantonment of Bangalore is under the same regulations as in the East-India Company's territory, but throughout the country the duties of police are discharged by peons or matchlock-men, of whom there are one or two in every village; and there are two distinct classes, one for the revenue, the other for the judicial department. A body of men called the Mysore irregular horse, or Silladars, are also maintained. They amount to 2,700, are commanded by a European officer, and receiving each twenty rupees a month, are bound to be at all times in readiness, with their horses and equipments complete. The Mysore infantry, also under the command of a European officer, form an efficient body of men, amounting to about 2,400. Seringapatam, formerly a British military station, has been abandoned for that purpose, on account of its pestilential atmosphere engendering deadly endemic fevers, which prevailed there for several years, and carried off great numbers both of Europeans and natives. At present the principal military stations are Bangalore, the head-quarters of the force stationed in Mysore, Hurryhur, and the French Rocks, twenty miles north of Seringapatam. The annual revenue, when the country, on the fall of Tippoo, in 1799, was granted to the kurtur or descendant of the ancient rajahs, was estimated at 2,153,607 pagodas, or, estimating the pagoda at 2 rupees and 14 annas, 619,162*l*. The revenue subsequently to that period progressively increased, and for the year 1803-4 was 2,581,550 pagodas, or 742,195*l*. This was attributed to the good management of Purneah, the dewan or minister of finance. After his death, and the assumption of the powers of government by the kurtur or rajah, the reckless profligacy of that prince had ruinous effects on the finances, from which, even under British management, they have not yet quite recovered. It appears from a statement for fifteen years, ending 30th June, 1846, that the average annual revenue was 69,31,870 rupees; and that the average annual disbursements amounted to 66,25,393; leaving a balance of 3,06,477 rupees, applicable to the discharge of incumbrances.

In the mythological period of India, Mysore is represented to have been the realm of Sugriva, who sent his general Hanuman to aid Rama in his expedition against Ravana, the gigantic tyrant of Lanka. In the earliest serious records of this country, it appears to have been part of the dominions of a dynasty bearing the name of Chalukia, which gave way to another called Cadumba. No explicit or authentic history of the country, however, commences until its invasion, in 1310, by the Mussulmans commanded by Kafier, an officer of Alauddin, padshah of Delhi. This invasion, which was transient and merely predatory, was, in 1326, succeeded by an expedition, sent by Muhammad Toghluk III., which destroyed Dhursummuder, the capital, situate about 100 miles north-west of Seringapatam; and the seat of government was subsequently removed to Tonur, twelve miles north of that town. The remainder of the territory was subjugated and incorporated with the realm of Delhi; the affairs of which, however, soon afterwards falling into confusion, these conquests were lost. In 1336, Buka and Aka Harihar, fleeing from the Mussulman captors of Warangal, took their way southwards, and on the banks of the river Toongabudra or Tumbudra founded a city, which they called Vidanagar (the city of science), in compliment to the favourite pursuits of their minister and preceptor; an appellation afterwards changed into Vijayanagar or Bijayanagar—city of victory. This new state rapidly increased in power, and, besides its districts on the Tumbudra, comprised at an early period nearly the whole of Mysore, ultimately extending its dominions to the Coromandel coast. Ram Rajah of Vijayanagar, having, by his arrogance and encroachments, provoked a confederacy of the Mussulman powers of the Deccan, the armies of the states of Beejapore, Ahmednuggur, Beeder, and Golconda, commanded by their respective kings, met Ram Rajah, in the year 1565, at Talikot, in the present British collectorate of Dharwar, where a great battle ensued, in which the Mussulmans were victorious. Ram Rajah perished; his capital was taken, rifled, with shocking circumstances of cruelty and excess, and in fact depopulated. On the defeat and death of Ram Rajah, at Talikot, the polygar or petty rajah of Mysore took advantage of the course of events to prosecute the views which he entertained in connection with his brother feudatories, and his successors pursued the like plans. Progressively extending their dominions and power, they continually encroached on the jurisdiction of the viceroy of the titular rajah of Vijayanagar; and in 1610, one of them, named Rajah Wadeyar, acquired the fort and island of Seringapatam, with its dependencies. The dynasty, continuing its career of aggression and aggrandizement, towards the close of the seventeenth century extended its sway over nearly the whole of the table-land of Mysore, by the purchase of Bangalore and its dependencies from Kasim Khan, the commandant of Aurengzebe. On the death of Kasim Khan, the rajah deputed a splendid embassy to Ahmednuggur, where Aurengzebe then sojourned. It was graciously received, and returned with a variety of presents, including a signet prepared by the emperor's directions, which, after being paraded through the city, and laid at the feet of the idol Snee Runga, in the great temple, were brought in similar state to the palace. Chicki Deo Raj, the prince thus honoured, enjoyed a successful reign, which terminated in the year 1704. He was an assiduous and skilful financier, and drew from his flourishing territory an annual revenue, from which it is recorded that he never failed to lay by daily 2,000 pagodas, to accumulate untouched in his treasury. Those great treasures were exhausted in 1724 and 1726, through the imbecility and indolence of Dud Kishen Raj, grandson of Chicki Deo. Cham Rajah, who succeeded Dud Kishen, was deposed and destroyed by a minister whom he had disgraced, and who, in 1731, infringing the hereditary succession, raised up a pageant rajah but remotely connected with the family which had hitherto reigned. Deo Raj, the minister who made this change, was a man of talent and determination, and in 1737 defeated, and in a great measure destroyed, a numerous Mussulman force which had advanced into Mysore, attracted by the reputed great treasure still believed to be stored at Seringapatam. In 1749, Hyder Ali, subsequently a name of terror in that part of India, first appeared as a volunteer in the army of Mysore, being at that time twenty-seven years of age. In 1750, Hyder commenced his predatory career. In 1752 he held a command in the army of Mysore, and, notwithstanding some untoward events, continued to prosper until at length he succeeded in obtaining the appointment of foujdar or governor of Dindigul and its dependencies. Here Hyder commenced operations with his accustomed vigour, ability, and activity; subjugated or laid under contribution the great feudatories known in this part of India by the name of polygars; with far-sighted sagacity "obtained from Seringham, Trichinopoly, and Pondicherry, skilful artificers directed by French masters, and began to organize a regular artillery, arsenal, and laboratory." Fortune still continued to favour this aspiring leader, who received the fort of Bangalore with its valuable district and dependencies in jaghire. Shortly after, Nunjeraj, who had usurped all the powers of government, and held the pageant rajah in helpless and humiliating dependency, was driven into obscurity by Hyder Ali, who, under various pretences, obtained assignments of the revenues of territory, amounting at length to more than half the entire dominions of the rajah. In 1760, Hyder, virtually become sovereign of Mysore, at the instigation of the French commander Lally, entered into an alliance against the British, and despatched to Pondicherry a corps under his brother-in-law Mukhdroom Ali, who, falling in with a detachment of British troops, succeeded in putting it to rout with heavy loss. Soon afterwards, however, Hyder was obliged to fly precipitately from Seringapatam, in consequence of a well-concerted conspiracy formed against him. In a short time, however, he was again enabled to take the field. At first his success was fluctuating; but reverting to a course from which he never recoiled,—the employment of the most unscrupulous stratagem, he spread dismay through the ranks of the army opposed to him, by exciting in the mind of the general suspicions of the fidelity of his officers, or rather conviction of their faithlessness; and thus leading him, under the influence of alarm, to provide for his personal safety by flight. Taking advantage of the confusion necessarily caused by the sudden desertion of their general, Hyder fell upon the bereaved army in front and rear, obtaining a complete and decisive victory, and capturing the whole of the enemy's guns, stores, and baggage. Having recruited his army and his finances, he in a short time advanced towards Seringapatam, and encamped on the south bank of the Cauvery, opposite to the centre of the island, whereon a large body of cavalry was encamped. There, under pretence of negotiating, he remained several days, every evening after sunset exercising his troops. At last these evolutions received a termination differing from that which had previously followed. Instead of dismissing the troops as usual, Hyder made a sudden dart across the river and carried destruction into the enemy's camp, capturing the whole of their heavy equipments, and most of their horses. From his newly-occupied ground he sent an insolent message to the rajah, who was compelled to make a professedly spontaneous offer to Hyder, which amounted virtually to a surrender of the government; the whole country being made over to the administration of Hyder, who was also made responsible for the public charges. From the operation of this general transfer of territorial power and revenue, certain districts were excepted, but to the amount of only four lacs; three of which were to provide for the personal expenses of the rajah, the remaining one being assigned to the support of the ex-minister, Hyder's former patron, and one on whom, in common with all who fell in his way, he had exercised his powers of dissimulation. Hyder's ambition and cupidity were only sharpened by his exaltation. From Basalut Jung, one of the various competitors for power in the Deccan, he received the title of Hyder Ali Khan Bahadaur, and in consideration of a present of three lacs, the grant of the nabobship of Seror; although over the territory thus summarily bestowed, the grantor possessed neither right nor power. This defect of title, however, mattered not to Hyder: he proceeded to take possession of his newly-acquired territory, and was successful. In 1763 he engaged in the invasion of Bednore, at the head of a powerful army. His progress rarely met resistance, the cruelties with which he visited those who opposed him, deterring, by the influence of terror, from the repetition of such attempts. He penetrated to the interior of the country, took and sacked the capital, long unacquainted with the horrors of war, and which contained such accumulated wealth, that the booty, it is said, "may without risk of exaggeration, be estimated at twelve millions sterling;" all of which the captor appropriated to his own use. Hyder had undertaken this conquest under the pretext of restoring an exiled prince to the throne. The claimant was an impostor, as Hyder well knew; but it suited his purpose to affect belief in the tale. The conquest achieved, the mask was thrown off, the pretender remitted a prisoner to a distant fortress, and the dominions of Bednore annexed to the possessions of Hyder Ali.

In 1766, died the titular rajah of Mysore, who had been allowed by Hyder to enjoy unmolested an annual income of 30,000*l.*, with the barren emblems of royalty devoid of power. Hyder, on hearing of the event while occupied in Malabar, sent orders with all the indifference attached to an affair of ordinary routine, to go through the usual formality of establishing as his successor the eldest son of the departed prince, a young man about eighteen years of age. In the early part of the year 1767, Hyder arrived at the capital, his presence there being rendered necessary by a variety of circumstances. From Poona, and from Hyderabad, troops were advancing, confederated, as was reported, against Mysore. On his arrival at Seringapatam, Hyder proceeded to make vigorous military preparations for the contest which seemed to be impending, and he embraced the opportunity of making a change in the relations which subsisted between the nominal head of the state of Mysore and the successful adventurer, who was its actual sovereign. The youth whom Hyder had placed on a mock throne, and who naturally looked upon himself as entitled to more substantial marks of royalty than he was permitted to enjoy, had manifested some discontent with his humiliating position. The exhibition of such a feeling Hyder determined to repress, probably on grounds both of revenge and precaution. He proceeded to take measures for this purpose with his accustomed coolness and decision. Districts, of the annual value of three lacs, as already mentioned, had been assigned for the rajah's support: these were now resumed; and this act of confiscation was consistently followed by plundering the palace of the unhappy prince of all the cash and valuables which it contained, with the single exception of the ornaments which the female inmates had actually on their persons at the time when the clearance was made. The expenses of the household were reduced to the lowest practicable scale, and none but Hyder's slaves permitted to remain within the palace.

Hyder now turned his attention to the defence of the dominions of which he had usurped the sovereignty. A combined attack by the Mahrattas and the Nizam, in which the British were to participate, was to be expected. The Mahrattas were actually approaching with the avowed object of entirely subverting the power of the usurper. By the treachery of Hyder Ali's brother-in-law, the first attempt made by the invaders upon a fortified place was successful. Hyder was now under the necessity of buying off the enemy, an object which was effected at the cost of thirty-five lacs of rupees; and having thus relieved himself from the Mahrattas, Hyder Ali readily effected an arrangement with the Nizam, who united his arms with those of Hyder Ali against the late ally of the former, the British. The first attack made by the new confederates was to a certain extent successful; but a subsequent, and more important one, had a different result. The army of Hyder was estimated to consist of 13,000 cavalry and 18,000 infantry, with forty-nine guns; and that of the Nizam at 30,000 cavalry and 10,000 infantry, with sixty guns. This great force having, in the beginning of September of 1767, attacked, near Changama, a British detachment, consisting of 1,030 cavalry and 5,800 infantry, with sixteen guns, under the command of Colonel Smith, was defeated, with the loss of 2,000 killed; and towards the close of the same month received a severe and almost decisive discomfiture near Trinomalee, the loss amounting to about 4,000 men, sixty-four guns, and all the ammunition and stores of the combined forces. After a few more bootless efforts, the baffled confederates relinquished further attempts at action, Hyder, with his army, ascending the Ghats, the Nizam ostensibly separating himself from his ally, and entering into negotiation with the British commander. Hyder was now called to Malabar, where his occupation in other quarters had encouraged revolt from his authority. This movement was aided by a British expedition from Bombay, which succeeded with little effort in capturing Mangalore and some other places, but which retired with disgraceful precipitancy on the approach of Hyder, abandoning their sick as well as their stores and field-pieces. Having by the combined force of cruelty and cunning arranged his affairs in this part of his dominions, Hyder Ali retraced his steps, and invading the territories of the British and their allies in the Carnatic, fought his way in two campaigns almost to the gates of Madras, where he presented himself on the 29th March, 1769, and required that a British diplomatist, whom he himself named, should be sent to him to negotiate the terms of peace. His demand was complied with, and a treaty concluded, on the principle of the mutual restitution of all places taken during the war, except Caroor, which had long been in the possession of the nabob of the Carnatic, Mahomed Ali, but which, being an ancient dependency of Mysore, was now to be assigned permanently to the state to which it originally belonged. In the beginning of the year 1770, the greater part of Mysore was overrun by the Mahrattas, and Hyder was obliged to retreat to Seringapatam, where he was followed by the Mahratta leader, who besieged the city. The siege, though protracted, was conducted with little of either energy or ability; and in 1772 Hyder succeeded in negotiating a treaty, by which he ceded to the Mahrattas an extensive portion of the northern part of his dominions. The titular rajah of Mysore having attempted, during the siege, to open communication with the Mahrattas, was strangled, by order of Hyder, who declared Cham Raj, brother of the murdered prince, his successor.

The death of Madhu Rao, the Peishwa, in 1773, gave rise, at Poona, to a long train of intrigues and dissensions, with their usual accompaniments in the East, of assassinations, executions, and massacres. The country became involved in wars, both intestine and foreign, and Hyder Ali, undaunted by his late disasters, took advantage of the opportunity to set about recovering and extending his dominion, and consolidating his power. His son Tippoo was detached to the northward, and Hyder himself assumed the direction of operations preparatory to the recovery of Malabar, where his power was still but imperfectly recognised. Without offering any justification of the attack, he marched into the raj or state of Coorg, a rugged tract on the south-west frontier of Mysore. The invasion was entirely unexpected, and the chief body of the Coorgs, without any previous arrangement, assembled on a woody hill, which Hyder encompassed with his troops. The apparent conquest was of little difficulty; the raja (Divaia) betook himself to flight, and Hyder, whose chief object was to tranquillize the country, erected the fort of Mercara in the most central situation, and confirming the landholders in their possessions at a moderately increased revenue, returned to Seringapatam, whither the fugitive raja was soon afterwards brought, having been discovered in his place of concealment in the territory of Mysoor. A force was immediately afterwards detached, under Seyed Saheb and Sree Nowas Row Berkee, though Wynaad, by the pass of Tambercherry, which descended at once on Calicut. The place soon fell into their hands: the Nair chiefs, who, during their short relief from foreign usurpation, had only increased their misery by intestine broils, were in a fit state to be acted on by the skilful application of political division; and in a short time the greater part of them arranged the terms of their future dependency on Hyder. This important acquisition having been achieved with a success more rapid than even Hyder had anticipated, he moved with his whole force to give efficiency to his son's operations in the north: his approach had its due effect, and before his junction Tippoo had reduced Sera, Mudgery, Chenroydroog, Goorumconda, and their dependencies, leaving nothing for Hyder in person to accomplish but the easy service of reducing Ooscota and Great Balipoor. Thus, in one short campaign, from September, 1773, till February, 1774, he not only completely reconquered every place that had been wrested from him by the Mahrattas, but recovered, with increased stability, the province of Malabar, which he had wisely abandoned, during the pressure of difficulties, in his former war with the English.

His good fortune was not, however, altogether

undisturbed. An insurrection in the newly-subdued territory of Coorg soon demanded his attention. The great mass of his army was at the capital, distant only thirty miles from the frontier of Coorg; and Hyder moved the whole infantry in several columns to penetrate at once into every portion of the territory, and suppress the rebellion at a single blow; the operation was successful, and as his intelligence was always excellent, he was enabled among his prisoners to distinguish the leaders; every man suspected as being above the class of an ordinary soldier was hanged; and for the purpose of overawing the natives, a series of block-houses was erected, pervading every part of the country, and connected with each other, and with the nearest posts in Mysoor. An event followed which must be given in the words of Colonel Wilks: "About this period, the pageant Raja Cham Raj died; Hyder had hitherto professed to hold Mysoor in behalf of the Hindoo house; and amused his subjects on every annual feast of the Dessera, by exhibiting the pageant, seated on his ivory throne, in the balcony of state; himself occupying the place of minister and commander-in-chief. This ceremonial, in most countries, would have excited feelings dangerous to the usurper; but the unhappy Hindoos saw their country everywhere sustaining the scourge of Mahommedan rule; the singular exception of the Mahratta state, a wide-spreading example of still more ruthless oppression, restrained their natural preference for rulers of their own persuasion; and they were soothed with the occasional condescension, which treated them, and their institutions, with a semblance of respect. Hyder saw and indulged the working of these reflections, and determined to have another pageant. The lineal male succession was extinct, and he ordered all the children to be collected from the different branches of the house, who, according to ancient precedent, were entitled to furnish a successor to the throne. The ceremonial observed on this occasion, however childish, was in perfect accordance with the feelings which he intended to delude, and sufficiently adapted to the superstition of the fatalist. The hall of audience was strewed round with fruits, sweetmeats, and flowers, playthings of various descriptions, arms, books, male and female ornaments, bags of money, and every varied object of puerile or manly pursuit; the children were introduced together, and were all invited to help themselves to whatever they liked best; the greater number were quickly engaged in a scramble for the fruits, sweetmeats, and toys; but one child was attracted by a brilliant little dagger, which he took up in his right hand, and soon afterwards a lime in his left. 'That is the raja,' exclaimed Hyder, 'his first care is military protection, his second to realize the produce of his dominions; bring him hither, and let me embrace him.' The assembly was in an universal murmur of applause; and he ordered the child to be conducted to the Hindoo palace, and prepared for installation. He was of the same name as his predecessor, viz. *Cham Raj*, and was the father of the raja, who was placed by the English at the head of the Hindoo house of Mysoor, on the subversion of the Mahommedan dynasty in 1799." In 1775, Hyder attacked and put to flight Basalut Jung, engaged in the siege of Bellary; and, himself then urging the attack against the town, took and retained it, together with its valuable dependencies. He affected to compromise in the same way with Morari Row, the Mahratta commander (then occupying a fort called Gooty), by sending to demand a similar contribution from him, probably expecting that it would be refused. The intercourse was in imitation of the Mahratta style. On entering the territory, Hyder sent a complimentary message to Morari Row, intimating that he had arrived at the house of the latter; that they were ancient friends, and that he would be troublesome to him for gram and forage for his horses, the value of which he estimated at a lac of rupees. Morari Row perfectly understood the message, and replied to it in terms more distinct than had been employed by Hyder, that he also was a general, and was accustomed to levy contributions, not to pay them. The results are thus narrated by the able and intelligent historian of Mysore:—"On Hyder's nearer approach to Gooty, he repeated a message of similar import, with the same result. He therefore sat down regularly before the place; the guns which Monsieur Lally had employed against Bellary, were a convenient resource; and a battering train for this very purpose had also been ordered from Seringapatam. The fort of Gooty is composed of a number of strong works, occupying the summits of a circular cluster of rocky hills connected with each other, and inclosing a space of level ground forming the site of the town, which is approached from the plain, by two breaks or openings, forming fortified gateways to the south-west and north-west, and by two footpaths across the lower hills communicating through small sallyports. An immense smooth rock rising from the northern limit of the circle, and fortified by gradations, surmounted through fourteen gateways, overlooks and commands the whole of the other works, and forms a citadel which famine or treachery can alone reduce. After a siege of about five weeks, the town and lower forts were carried by assault; and a large booty was found, consisting of 2,000 horses, a considerable number of the elephants of state, a vast amount of private property, and a very respectable equipment of garrison and field guns, and military stores. Hyder continued for two months longer the siege of the upper fort; and was repulsed in numerous attempts to establish himself in the lowest division of these works; but the improvident measure had been adopted of admitting within the walls of the citadel, an immense number of followers, of horses, camels, and even horned cattle: and although, with ordinary precautions, the reservoirs of water were numerous and ample, the strange absurdity of the measure which we have noticed, had reduced the besieged to the utmost distress, and Morari Row found himself under the necessity of sending an envoy to Hyder to treat for peace. The conditions were settled after much discussion; namely, the payment of twelve lacs of rupees, eight in cash or valuables, and a hostage for the payment of the remainder. The cash amounted to only one lac, and plate and jewels to the estimated value of the remaining seven were sent by the hands of the hostage, the son of Yoonas Khan, the former commander-in-chief, who had been mortally wounded in the affair near Ooscota, in 1768. Hyder received his hostage with great courtesy, and invited him to dinner; the young man, considering hostilities to be at an end, was induced by the gracious manners of Hyder to be unreserved in his communications; the conversation was purposely turned to the events of the siege, and Hyder took the opportunity of paying some appropriate compliments to the experience of Morari Row, and the conduct of his troops: not omitting to observe that he frequently noticed the exemplary gallantry of the young man himself. This of course induced some corresponding civilities; and, in the warmth of discussing the past, he was so imprudent as to observe, that there was no want of troops or provisions, and nothing short of being reduced to three days' water could have induced Morari Row to agree to such hard conditions. Hyder heard all this with his accustomed command of countenance; and after dinner referred the young man to the proper department for the delivery of his charge. The description of the valuables had been generally stated in the negotiation, and it was understood, that if, on a fair valuation, the amount should fall short of the seven lacs, Hyder would still receive it, and accept the hostage for the remainder. The period of inspection was designedly prolonged; the appraisers on Hyder's part were duly instructed, he himself testified great impatience for the adjustment, and when the appraisers, accompanying the hostage, returned to report the total amount, including cash, to be only five lacs, Hyder affected the greatest disappointment and anger, said that Morari Row was trifling and deceiving him; and ordered the hostage immediately to return with his paltry five lacs, and announce the negotiation to be at an end. He now fitted his operations to the circumstances of the siege, taking more care to prevent a single person from descending to hollows in the rock, which they had been accustomed to risk for a scanty supply of water, than to serve his batteries, or expedite his approaches; and the besieged could not even execute the alternative which he had proposed, of prolonging his defence, by secretly dismissing the greater part of his garrison. On the third day after this mode of warfare had been adopted, Morari Row could no longer restrain his men from exclaiming, even from the parapets, to the besiegers, that they were dying of thirst, and begged to capitulate. Hyder coolly directed them to be informed, that there was abundance of water below; and if they desired to quench their thirst, they must all descend unarmed, with Morari Row at their head; that he would fire at any flag of truce, and reject all advances, except in the form which he had prescribed. In the course of the day, Morari Row, accompanied by his son, and followed by his unarmed garrison, descended, and threw himself on Hyder's clemency. Every individual, before being passed, was separately searched, and plundered, for Hyder's sole benefit, of the trifling sum they possessed. His garrison then ascended the rock, accompanied by a deputation to take an account of all property public and private, and even the apartments, and *persons*, of the women were plundered of their remaining jewels and ornaments, to the amount of 5,000 rupees only. The official servants of revenue were placed in separate custody; and Hyder, whose own experience enabled him to calculate the amount of embezzlement which each could conveniently spare, satisfied himself for the present with levying on them ten lacs of rupees. These operations being completed early in the month of April, he received the whole of the prisoners, civil and military (their chief alone excepted), into his gracious favour and service." Entering zealously into the wars consequent on the disputed Mahratta succession, Hyder extended his dominions in the Deccan to the right or south bank of the great river Kistnah, in 1779. For many years Hyder had regarded the British with coldness, if not absolutely with aversion, in consequence of the latter declining to afford aid in his contests with the Mahrattas. In 1779, in concert with a French force, Hyder commenced hostilities against the British on the coast of Malabar; and in the following year he invaded the British possessions in the Carnatic with an army of 83,000, of whom 28,000 were cavalry, 15,000 regular infantry, and the remainder infantry less rigidly disciplined, but having considerable efficiency for the purposes of Indian warfare; besides a pioneer corps of 5,000 men, an admirably organized commissariat, and a small reserve of 6,000 horse and foot stationed at Kurpa. Hyder then advanced towards Madras, and so rapid was his progress that, with the exception of Madras and a few other places, the whole of the presidential territory north of the Cauvery was subjugated by him; and with great superiority of force, and of military skill, he succeeded in surrounding, and totally destroying, a powerful British detachment, under the command of Colonel Baillie, marching southwards from Guntoor to form a junction with an army under Sir Hector Munro at Conjeveram; about thirteen miles from which last-named place the disastrous event occurred. Hyder's victory was disgraced by acts of the most brutal atrocity. When all was lost, Colonel Baillie went forward waving his handkerchief as a demand for quarter; and, supposing his request complied with, he ordered his troops to lay down their arms; but the savage host arrayed against them continued long afterwards to slaughter their now unresisting foes. Hyder, however, met reverse in turn, receiving in the succeeding year a severe defeat at Porto Novo, on the seacoast, from a British army commanded by Sir Eyre Coote. This officer then effected a junction with a reinforcement despatched to his assistance, and captured Tripassore, a fortress of some importance. A few weeks afterwards, another severe battle between the Mysore army, under the personal command of Hyder, and that of the British under Sir Eyre Coote, took place. On this occasion, the English remained in possession of the field, but the result was not very decisive, each party claiming the victory. In a subsequent conflict between the same armies, under the same commanders, at Sholingarh, Hyder Ali received a very severe defeat, his loss being estimated at 5,000 men, while that of the English was reported not to exceed a hundred. In other quarters, the British were less fortunate, and a force in Tanjore, commanded by Colonel Braithwaite, notwithstanding the highest efforts of gallantry, skill, and perseverance, both in the commander and his troops, received a disastrous defeat. On the whole, however, the following summary of the circumstances of Hyder at this time, drawn by Colonel Wilks, may be regarded as a faithful picture of his situation and views. "Hyder, in reviewing his actual situation, felt himself foiled in every battle with Sir Eyre Coote. Disappointed, and, as he thought, deceived by the French; assailed in a vulnerable part of his western territories, where a detached army was destroyed, and farther reinforcements threatened more extensive operations; a general insurrection of the Nairs over the whole province of Malabar, aggravated by a rebellion in Bullum and Coorg, two districts on the summit of the hills which overlook that province, might be deemed overwhelming in the ordinary course of Indian warfare; but in addition to all these misfortunes, he was now openly threatened with the more embarrassing danger of a Mahratta invasion from the north. Deeply reflecting on this unprosperous aspect of affairs, he determined to concentrate his force, to abandon his scheme of conquest in Coromandel, and to direct his undivided efforts, first for the expulsion of the English from the western coast, and afterwards for the preservation of his dominions, and for watching the course of events. With these views, he commenced, in December, 1781, the destruction of most of the minor posts of Coromandel in his possession, mined the fortifications of Arcot, preparatory to its demolition; sent off by large convoys all the heavy guns and stores, and compelled the population of the country, hitherto well protected, to emigrate, with their flocks and herds, to Mysore."

The projects of Hyder were, however, rapidly approaching to a termination. From the commencement of the year 1782, the health of the Mysorean disturber perceptibly declined, and towards its close the attacks of disease assumed a more alarming character: Hindoo, Mahomedan, and French physicians strove in vain to overcome the fatal visitation; and on the 7th December in that year, Hyder Ali Khan Behaudur, the fortunate adventurer, the energetic soldier, the accomplished dissembler, the unscrupulous usurper, the tyrant ruler, the ruthless invader, the rapacious and cruel extortioner, the achiever of so many conquests, the perpetrator of so many crimes, the author of such countless miseries, drew his last breath, in his camp near Arcot. It was suggested by one of the ablest of his servants, when the recovery of Hyder became improbable, that his death, whenever it might occur, should be concealed until the arrival of his son and successor Tippoo, who was absent in Malabar. The proposal was adopted, and the necessary measures concerted with those officers and domestics to whom the event must necessarily be known. Immediately after the stroke of death, the body was removed, in a chest filled with aromatics, and sent, under an escort, in the manner in which treasure was accustomed to be conveyed; the persons intrusted with the charge being directed to deposit it in the tomb of Hyder's father, at Colar. It was subsequently removed by Tippoo to the superb mausoleum at Seringapatam; and on that occasion 40,000 pagodas were distributed in alms, and in donations to the priesthood, for prayers offered up for the soul of the deceased, the number of whose villanies was almost equal to that of the acts of his life.

Tippoo assumed the government with extraordinary affectation of humility and grief. Hyder at his death had in the field armies numbering 88,000 men, and his treasury at Seringapatam contained cash to the amount of about three millions sterling, besides a great accumulation of jewels and other costly articles. The extent of the territory of which he had military occupation, though in some parts precarious and imperfect, comprehended 90,000 square miles, being nearly three times the area of the present territory of Mysore. The commencement of Tippoo's reign was marked by great success. General Matthews, despatched by the government of Bombay to invade Mysore, having landed at Kundapore, and forced the pass of Hyder Gurh, in the Western Ghauts, succeeded in gaining possession of the town of Bednore or Hyder; but Tippoo, advancing with a greatly superior force, compelled the Bombay general to capitulate. Tippoo found no difficulty in discovering a pretext for violating the capitulation, and incarcerating the British garrison, many of whom he subsequently caused to be murdered. Success produced in Tippoo Sultan its ordinary effects upon minds alike weak and malignant, inflaming him to a pitch of frenzied arrogance and cruelty, which might almost be regarded as indicating insanity. He caused gibbets to be erected for the ostensible purpose of putting to death some British diplomatic agents, who had arrived with the view of concluding a treaty of peace; but after "the submission of the English to nearly every form of derisive humiliation and contempt, and at a period when imagination could scarcely picture an additional insult, he condescended, on the 11th March, 1784, to sign the long-pending treaty." The most important provisions of this document were, that Tippoo Sultan should evacuate the Carnatic, and release the British prisoners, and that, reciprocally, the Mysorean prisoners should be released by the British authorities; that the British government should cause the evacuation of all places occupied by their forces in Canara and Malabar; that rajahs and zemindars, who had favoured the English, should not be molested on that account; that all commercial privileges given to the English by Hyder Ali should be renewed and confirmed. The few British prisoners who, not having been murdered, were released under the provisions of this treaty, gave an appalling account of the dreadful and wanton cruelties which they had endured.

In 1789, Tippoo Sultan, having marched to invade Travancore, attempted to force the military lines constructed by the rajah as a protection against any attack from the northward; but his troops, panic-struck by a sudden assault on their flank, though made by an inconsiderable body of men, fled precipitately, with the loss of 2,000 of their number. In such headlong disorder did the flight take place, that Tippoo was overthrown in the crowd, and sustained some personal injury; while his palanquin-bearers were actually trodden to death. From this invasion resulted a war between Tippoo and the British government, the latter aided by the Mahratta state of Poona and the Nizam. The British forces, commanded by General Medowes, in 1790 entered Coimbatore, and, having taken Dindigul and Palaghat, were opposed by Tippoo Sultan in person; but a busy and intricate campaign, harassing for both parties, terminated without any decisive result. In Malabar, however, the British were uniformly and completely successful; a body of troops under the command of Colonel Hartley defeated and destroyed a Mysorean army; and, subsequently, another under General Abercromby subjugated the whole province. At the opening of the campaign of 1791, the command of the British army was assumed by Lord Cornwallis, the Governor-General, in person; who, evading the defensive arrangements of his opponent by means of a demonstration to the southward, penetrated the Eastern Ghauts by the Mugli Pass, considerably to the north of the usual route, and invested Bangalore, which, after a siege of a fortnight, was, on March 21, taken by storm, under singularly trying circumstances. Lord Cornwallis subsequently advanced upon Seringapatam. On the march he defeated the Mysorean army commanded by Tippoo; but, having merely reconnoitered the fortress, the British commander destroyed his battering-train, marched back in the direction of Bangalore, and formed a junction with the Mahratta force sent by the government of Poona to co-operate in the war. The latter months of the year were employed in the reduction of various forts, some of which had previously been deemed impregnable. In the beginning of February, 1792, Lord Cornwallis, again leading his army to the capital of the country, defeated Tippoo Sultan on the north side of the Cauvery, and, sending a detachment across the river, lodged it in the island on which are situate the city and the fort of Seringapatam. General Abercromby having in the mean time advanced from Malabar to the west of the island and fort, no serious obstacle remained to the complete investment and blockade of the place, and its northern face was already partially breached by the British batteries. Tippoo Sultan, now considering successful resistance hopeless, on the 19th of February, 1792, consented to sign five articles of pacification, as follows:—First, that one-half of the dominions which Tippoo possessed previously to the war should be ceded to the allies from the countries adjacent to theirs; secondly, that Tippoo should pay three crores and 30 lacs (about 3,300,000*l.* sterling), one-half immediately, the remainder by instalments, at intervals not exceeding four months; thirdly, that all prisoners taken by the four powers, the English, the Nizam, the Mahrattas, and Tippoo, from the time of Hyder Ali, should be restored; fourthly, that two of Tippoo's sons should be delivered up as hostages for the due performance of the treaty; and fifthly, that when the hostages should have arrived in the camp, with articles under the seal of Tippoo, a counterpart should be sent from the allies, hostilities should cease, and the terms of a treaty of alliance and perpetual friendship should be agreed upon. Tippoo could not affix his seal to these articles without intense bitterness of feeling; and he manifested his discontent by dishonourably allowing the fire of his troops upon the British to be continued after the preliminaries had been formally accepted. Such conduct would have justified retribution, but Lord Cornwallis abstained, though the army, incensed by the atrocities of which Tippoo was known to have been guilty towards his prisoners, would to a man have rejoiced in the resumption of hostile operations. At length, however, the fire of the enemy ceased, and, on the 26th February, the fourth article of the preliminary was carried into effect, by the departure of the hostages for the British camp. The scene was witnessed with great interest. The elder of the princes was about ten years of age; his brother two years younger. Each was mounted on an elephant richly caparisoned, and their dresses glittered with numerous and valuable jewels. They were attended by the Mysorean vakeels who had conducted the negotiation; several messengers mounted on camels, and seven standard-bearers, carrying small green flags suspended from rockets, preceded the princes; 100 pikemen, with spears inlaid with silver, immediately followed them; and a guard of 200 sepoys, with a party of horse, brought up the rear. Great crowds were collected to witness the scene, whether actuated by the desire of beholding an imposing spectacle, or by some higher motive. The sultan himself was on the rampart above the gateway through which his sons passed. They departed under a salute from the fort; and as they approached the British camp, twenty-one discharges from its park of artillery greeted their coming, while the part of the British line which they passed was turned out to receive them. On arriving at the tents prepared for their reception, they were met by the Governor-General's agent, Sir John Kenaway, and the vakeels of the Nizam and the Mahratta state. The Governor-General had proposed to meet them here; but, at the express desire of Tippoo, this mark of attention was omitted, and it was arranged that they should proceed to the British head-quarters. The procession accordingly advanced, with the addition which it had received from the accession of the diplomatic agents of the allies and their attendants, and was met by Lord Cornwallis, accompanied by his staff and some of the chief officers of the army, at the door of his lordship's principal tent. On the princes alighting, the Governor-General embraced them; and then, extending to each one of his hands, led them into the tent and seated them by his side. The duty of Tippoo's head vakeel, who had been placed in charge of the boys, was now at an end; and he signalized its conclusion by a graceful appeal to the feelings of Lord Cornwallis. "These children," said he, "were this morning the sons of the sultan, my master; their situation is now changed, and they must look up to your lordship as their father." The Governor-General made an appropriate reply, assuring the vakeel, and the princes themselves, that all possible care would be taken for the protection of their persons and the promotion of their happiness. The promise was religiously fulfilled; and the transfer of the paternal character announced by the vakeel "ceased," says Colonel Wilks, "to be an Oriental image, if determined by the test of paternal attentions." A strong interest for the captive youths was indeed prevalent throughout the British army; a feeling which, with regard to the younger, was increased by the affecting circumstance of his mother having recently died from fright, occasioned by the attack on Tippoo's lines. So fully was the sultan contented with the reception of his sons, that he ordered a royal salute to be fired in testimony of his satisfaction.

The arrangement of a definitive treaty was a work not unattended by difficulty. Eastern diplomatists are accustomed to fight every inch of ground where money or territory is in question: and in this case an obstacle to agreement of more than usual importance arose from a demand on the part of the English, that the Coorg territory, which had been conquered by Hyder Ali, should be included among the cessions to them. There were various reasons for demanding this; and among them the importance of Coorg as affording means for holding Tippoo in check, and the feelings of its then prince towards the two chief belligerents. Warmly attached to the English, and bitterly hostile to Tippoo, to leave him at the mercy of the latter would be to surrender him to certain destruction. On the other hand, Coorg could not be brought within the description of territory to which any of the allies could establish a claim without a strained interpretation of the terms of the treaty. Tippoo was frantic at the demand for the surrender of Coorg, and a recurrence to hostilities seemed inevitable. Such a result would at this time have been very ill suited to the circumstances of the besieging army. Their works had been suffered to go to decay, and materials for repairing or reconstructing them were not at hand. Sickness was rife, and little reliance could be placed on the continued fidelity of the allies with whom the British were associated. Happily a threat of the immediate recommencement of hostilities, if any delay occurred in acceding to the required terms, produced the desired effect. On the 1st of March, the treaty, duly ratified, arrived in the British camp, and on the following day it was presented to Lord Cornwallis by the interesting hostages for their father's fidelity. Relieved from the presence of his invaders, the attention of Tippoo was directed to the means of providing the large share of the contribution towards their expenses, which still remained to be defrayed. His will was of course the only rule, and he had determined that one crore and ten lacs should be furnished from the royal treasury: towards the remainder, the army were to contribute a *gift* of sixty lacs, and the civil officers and inhabitants *a gift* of one crore and sixty lacs. The amount of the military *benevolence* was readily secured by measures for appropriating to the purpose of defraying it a portion of the soldier's pay. The distribution of that part of the burden which fell on the non-military population was made by the heads of civil departments, and they, it is stated, were punctilious in determining and duly entering the respective amounts to be paid by themselves. The accounts manifested the most admirable precision and fairness; but it is believed that these qualities extended no further than the accounts. The collectors contrived to escape all personal contribution, though the demands of the state were enforced upon the inhabitants generally with rigorous exactness, the operation of obtaining payment being aided, when necessary, by the horrible practice of torture. If current report is to be credited, the advantages of the high officials extended beyond mere immunity from contribution. It was generally believed that a much larger sum than the required amount was levied from the unfortunate inhabitants, though a much smaller one found its way into the treasury, a heavy balance having remained as a charge upon the country on behalf of the government, when, several years afterwards, the house of Tippoo ceased to reign.

In 1795, Cham Raj, the titular rajah of Mysore, who, since his elevation, had been detained a prisoner in his own palace, died of small-pox, and Tippoo Sultan, who had previously, once in the year at least, manifested some outward show of respect for his nominal lord, did not on this occasion go through even the formal ceremony which it required. The family of the rajah were expelled from the palace, robbed of all they possessed, down even to their few personal ornaments, and lodged in a wretched hovel. The rajah, a child two years old, cried bitterly when about to be deprived of his tiny golden bracelets, and it is alleged that the instruments of Tippoo's tyranny retained enough of human feeling to be affected by his infantine distress, and to allow him to retain his childish ornaments.

At an early period of Tippoo's political career, he had entered into correspondence with the court of France, but without gaining anything by the step. Subsequently, after revolution had swept over that country and its dependencies, he renewed the attempts through the government of Mauritius, but with no better success. He persevered, however; and, encouraged by the master of a French privateer, which put into Mangalore in 1797, he deputed two of his servants ambassadors to the government of Mauritius; at which island they arrived in January, 1798. The local government remitted the overtures of Tippoo to France, but being unable to afford any regular troops, and perhaps not very sanguine as to the success of projects so wildly conceived and prosecuted as were those of Tippoo, restricted their assistance to a proclamation, inviting volunteers to enlist under the flag of Mysore, to aid in driving the English out of India. The invitation was to a small extent responded to; but the volunteers were the mere refuse of the island. With these, however, the emissaries of Tippoo embarked; and though their master could not but feel disappointed with such a reinforcement, he received the adventurers with great cordiality, externally sympathized with their creed of "liberty, equality, and fraternity," and even became a member of a Jacobin club, where he was received and described as Citizen Tippoo. At this juncture, the Earl of Mornington, afterwards Marquess Wellesley, had arrived to succeed Lord Cornwallis as Governor-General. He perceived the dangers to be apprehended from Tippoo's designs, madly as they were undertaken, and proceeded immediately to make preparations for defeating them. These, amid difficulties the most embarrassing, and impediments insurmountable, except by extraordinary genius and energy, were at length completed, and troops put in motion towards Mysore from different points. The force which Tippoo had to resist this invasion "may be stated in round numbers at 33,000 effective firelocks, including the garrison of Seringapatam, but no other garrison; exclusive of officers and a numerous artillery, which, with drivers and other establishments, amounted to 18,000 more, and about 15,000 cavalry and rocket-men; making an effective total, including officers, of about 50,000 fighting men; of which, at the commencement of hostilities, about 5,000 were detached, and eventually not available during the war." The main British army, called the Army of the Carnatic, which was commanded by General Harris, consisted of 2,635 cavalry, 884 of which were European, 608 European artillery-men, 15,076 infantry, of which 4,381 were Europeans, 1,483 gun lascars, and 1,000 pioneers; making a total of 20,802. This was increased by the British subsidiary force, draughted for this service from the territory of the Nizam, amounting to 6,536, and by the regular infantry of the Nizam, numbering 3,621; besides that prince's regular and irregular horse, of about 6,000. The artillery consisted of forty battering-guns, fifty-seven field-pieces, and seven howitzers, as well as the field-train belonging to the Nizam. Besides the force with General Harris, another (that of Bombay), under General Stuart, was advancing, about 6,420 strong. On the 6th of March, Tippoo Sultan, marching westward, at Sidasir, attacked almost simultaneously in front and rear a brigade of the Bombay army; but General Stuart, having effected a junction, the attack totally failed, after a long and obstinately-contested action; and the Mysorean army was hastily led back to defend the capital. On the 27th of March, the British army, under General Harris, was attacked by Tippoo at Malavili, not many miles distant from Seringapatam. The enemy were repulsed, with the loss of about 1,000; and the British general, without delay, crossed the river Cauvery, and encamped before the south-west face of Seringapatam. A few days afterwards, he was joined by the army of Bombay. After a succession of intricate and arduous measures of approach, the batteries, on the 2nd of May, began to form the breach; and so vigorous and skilful was the fire, that on the following day the breach was reported practicable, and the storming party of 4,376, led by General Baird, forded the river, under a heavy fire from the fortress, mounted the breach, and after a fierce and murderous conflict, in seven minutes reached the summit, and thence making their way amidst much desperate fighting, driving the defenders from the ramparts, forced the passage into the inner citadel. During the progress of the siege, various attempts at negotiation had been made; but the haughty temper of Tippoo could not brook the terms, which were the only ones that could be granted. The position to which he had reduced himself seemed to have paralyzed him, and to have deprived him of the power of exercising the moderate share of intellect which he had received from nature. Throughout the operations of the besiegers, he appears to have forgotten that his was the chief command, and that through his military skill and judgment the loss of his capital was to be averted, if averted it could be. Forgetful of the higher duties imperatively demanded of him, he undertook the labour, and exposed himself to the dangers, of a common musketeer. Overwhelmed with despondency, he sought relief in all the miserable devices which superstition has devised to draw off men's reliance, in the hour of struggle, upon the only source of strength. When apprized that the besiegers were about to storm, he sat down to a repast, which was interrupted by the news that the operation had actually commenced. He then hastened to the northern rampart, placed himself before one of the traverses, fired on the assailants, and it is believed killed several of them. The flight of his troops before the victorious besiegers compelled him to retire. His mind was evidently unequal to the performance of his proper duties, but his personal courage did not desert him. Having received a slight wound, he mounted a horse, and made towards the gate of the interior work, apparently without aim or object. There he received a wound in the right side. He rode forward a few paces, when he was again wounded in the left breast, and at the same moment his horse was brought down. He was now placed by a follower in a palanquin under an arch. A grenadier entering, attempted to seize his sword-belt, which was very valuable; and, had he submitted to lose it, the man would probably have pushed on contented with his prize; but Tippoo, faint and helpless as he was, seized his sword, and with a feeble hand made a stroke at the soldier, who thereupon shot him through the head. Thus perished a man who possessed even more than an average amount of the vices of oriental tyrants, without any redeeming qualities; whose name is but a word to indicate the combination of perfidy and cruelty; who owed his place in history solely to his crimes, and whose death was as unlamented as his life had been detestable. His earthly remains were deposited in the mausoleum of his father, with all the pomp which could be bestowed. A storm, not an unsuitable accompaniment to the closing scene of such a man, raged with extraordinary violence on the evening of the ceremony.

With Tippoo terminated the short-lived, barbarous, and desolating dynasty established in Mysore by Hyder Ali Khan. The conquered country was divided into four parts, three of which were allotted respectively to the Peishwa, the Nizam, and the East-India Company; the remainder was formed into a separate state, to the government of which the titular rajah, retained in captivity by Tippoo Sultan, was elevated. The Peishwa, however, withdrew from the treaty, and the territory assigned to him was divided between the East-India Company and the Nizam.

The sons of Tippoo were removed to Vellore, lodged in the fort there, and allotted an ample income, which, in 1806, in the vain hope of overthrowing the British government, and re-establishing the deposed dynasty, they abused, to the purpose of corrupting the native soldiers, who in consequence rose, and massacred the European troops stationed in the place. On the frustration of the attempt, the children of Tippoo Sultan, who were its instigators, were deported to Bengal, and their residence fixed at Russipuglah, where their descendants have so greatly multiplied, that it has been deemed desirable to hold out to them encouragement to engage in useful pursuits and blend with the general population. A proposal has been recently made by the Council of Education, to establish on the foundation of this school a boarding seminary for the junior members of the Mysore family.

The financial concerns of the newly-appointed rajah, while managed by Purneah, a Brahmin who had held a similar trust under Tippoo Sultan, were eminently prosperous; and on the rajah attaining a competent age for taking charge of the government, there was in the treasury an accumulation of 7,500,000 pagodas, or 2,812,500*l.*, which great sum, however, was dissipated, and the annual income so overstepped and anticipated, that, in 1832, confusion, insubordination, and finally open rebellion ensued, and the British government were compelled to undertake the entire administration of the territory and its revenues, managing them by a commission. The advantageous results have been generally adverted to. The Hindoo rite of suttee has been forbidden; the Mahomedan population have settled down steadily to agricultural pursuits; transit-duties no longer exist; and in regard to commercial relations with Great Britain, Mysore has been placed upon the footing of a British possession. In 1847 the rajah preferred a claim to be reinstated in his dominions; but it was deemed inadmissible, on the ground of his incompetency for the duties of government.

MYSORE, a town, the principal place of the territory, and also of the subdivision of the same name, is situate on a declivity formed by two parallel ranges of elevated ground running north and south. The streets are laid out with considerable regularity, the principal one running north and south, and others at right angles to it. There are many good and substantial houses, of two and three stories high, generally tiled, though some of the best are terraced. The timber used in their construction is generally teak, of which a great quantity grows in the neighbourhood. The British residency and church belonging to it are in the north-east of the town. The main supply of water was once drawn from the river Cauvery by means of a canal made with great labour and expense, being in some places cut from fifty to sixty feet in the solid rock, and its length, measured along its sinuosities, being seventy-three miles; but it is at present useless, in consequence of its embankments in some places having been allowed to go to ruin. At present, water is obtained from tanks, which are liable to be exhausted during droughts, and then recourse must be had to wells yielding an impure supply, being much impregnated with soda, which causes fever and bowel complaints in such as use it. The town is surrounded by a rampart, and is further defended by the fort adjoining it on the north, west, and south sides. The fort is of a quadrangular ground-plan, three of the sides being about 450 yards in length, and the remaining, or north side, somewhat longer. The south-east side is washed by a tank, and on all other sides is a deep double ditch, within which is the rampart, built of stone, and having several bastions, and of the height of the buildings withinside, which have two stories. There is a sloping glacis, varying in breadth from 100 to nearly 200 yards, on every side except that washed by the tank. Within the fort is the palace of the titular rajah, an extensive building, forming three sides of a square, and the rest of the inclosed space is crowded with the dwellings of the retainers of the petty yet ostentatious court. Both the fort and town are situate on sloping ground, so that the filth is carried off by the common sewers during the rains, and at other times is removed by scavengers for manure; and hence the place is rather cleanly. In consequence of its elevation, the climate of Mysore, notwithstanding its intertropical latitude, is rather cool, the annual mean temperature in the shade being about 76°. In midwinter, the winds are cold, disagreeable, and very dry, causing furniture to warp, crack, and split. The climate is not considered very healthy; fevers, dysenteries, rheumatism, being common. With the view, probably, of obliterating associations connected with the memory of the ancient dynasty, Tippoo Sultan, in A.D. 1787, destroyed the old city of Mysore, and used the materials for building on a neighbouring height a fortress, which he called Nezerbar. The population was compelled to remove to Seringapatam; but Tippoo Sultan was overthrown before Nezerbar was finished, and its materials were taken back to Mysore, and used in rebuilding the present fort. According to official report, the number of houses in the town of Mysore, including the fort, is 9,558, and the population is estimated at 54,729. Elevation above the sea 2,450 feet. Distant 10 miles S. by W. from Seringapatam, and 92 miles E. by N. from Cannanore. Lat. 12° 18′, long. 76° 42′.

MYTEELA.—A town of Burmah, 70 miles E. from the left bank of the Irawady river, and 104 miles S. by W. from Ava. Lat. 20° 23′, long. 95° 46′.

MYTHOWLEE, in the British district of Mynpooree, lieut.-gov. of the N.W. Provinces, a village on the route from the city of Agra to the cantonment of Mynpooree, and 11 miles W. of the latter. Lat. 27° 13′, long. 78° 56′.

MYWA GOOLA.—A town in the native state of Nepal, situate on the right bank of the Tambur river, and 137 miles E. by S. from Khatmandoo. Lat. 27° 18′, long. 87° 27′.

N.

NAAF RIVER, or rather an arm of the sea, extends in a northerly direction parallel with the coast of Arracan, from the island of Shahpooree, at its mouth, in lat. 20° 42′, long. 92° 25′, to Elephanta Point, and has a good depth of water; but its entrance is dangerous, from the number of shoals and banks. These banks in few places exhibit much cultivation, being for the most part covered with thick jungle; the villages are small and miserable, inhabited only by herdsmen and hunters, who gain their subsistence by entrapping and training the wild elephants which abound in the forests about these parts.

NABAH.—See NARBAH.

NABOBGUNJE.—A town in the British district of Dinajepore, lieut.-gov. of Bengal, 30 miles E.S.E. of Dinajepore. Lat. 25° 23′, long. 89° 3′.

NABOBGUNJE.—A town in the British district of Dinajepore, lieut.-gov. of Bengal, 46 miles N. of Dinajepore. Lat. 26° 14′, long. 88° 40′.

NABOBGUNJE.—A town in the British district of Rungpore, lieut.-gov. of Bengal, two miles N. of Rungpore. Lat. 25° 42′, long. 89° 15′.

NABOBGUNJE.—A town in the British district of Rajeshaye, lieut.-gov. of Bengal, 137 miles N. of Calcutta. Lat. 24° 33′, long. 88° 20′.

NABOBGUNJE.—A town in the British district of Dacca Jelalpore, lieut.-gov. of Bengal, 133 miles N.E. by E. of Calcutta. Lat. 23° 43′, long. 90° 10′.

NABOG NYH, or NABOG NYE.—A pass over the mountain-range bounding Cashmere on the east, and dividing it from the valley of Muru Wurdwun. The range is formed of gneiss and mica-slate, and differs in structure from most of the mountains bounding Cashmere, which consist principally of basalt, trap, or other description of rock generally regarded as of volcanic origin. The height of the pass is 12,000 feet. Lat. 33° 43′, long. 75° 34′.

NACHNA, in the Rajpoot state of Jessulmeer, a small town in the desert, 65 miles N.E. of the city of Jessulmeer. Lat. 27° 30′, long. 71° 45′.

NADAMEYEE, in the British district of Mynpoorie, lieut.-gov. of the N.W. Provinces, a village on the left bank of the Kalee Nuddee (East), 34 miles N.W. of the town of Mynpoorie. Lat. 27° 39′, long. 78° 49′.

NADBAH.—A town in the British district of Purneah, lieut.-gov. of Bengal, 21 miles S.E. of Purneah. Lat. 25° 31′, long. 87° 44′.

NAGA HAUT.—A town of Assam, in the British district of Seebpoor, 36 miles E. by N. of Seebpoor. Lat. 27° 5′, long. 95° 13′.

NAGA TRIBES.—The country inhabited by these tribes is a wild unexplored tract, situate on the south-eastern borders of Upper Assam, from which it stretches to the mountain-range forming the north-western boundary of the Burman empire. The measures adopted by the British government to restrain the outrages committed by these tribes within British territory, have led to their submission. The centre of this tract is about lat. 26° 30′, long. 95°.

NAGAL, on the eastern boundary of the Dehra Doon, where it joins Gurwhal, a village situate on the western slope of a mountain rising above the Doon. The site is pleasant, on the banks of a small river fringed with willows and raspberry-bushes, and in many places cultivated with wheat and barley. The stream turns several mills of simple construction. An upright shaft, a few feet in length, passes through the middle of a horizontal fixed millstone, about eighteen inches in diameter and four in thickness, and is mortised into the middle of an upper one, which is rotatory, and of similar dimensions. The shaft carrying the upper stone is made to revolve by means of eight or ten broad flat radii set obliquely into the lower extremity, like the vanes of a smoke-jack, and motion is given by a stream of water falling nearly perpendicularly. Nagal is in lat. 30° 28′, long. 78° 10′.

NAGANEINPOLE.—A town in Hyderabad, or territory of the Nizam, situate on the right bank of the river Godavery, and 159 miles N.E. from Hyderabad. Lat. 17° 40′, long. 80° 55′.

NAGANOOR.—A town in the British district of North Canara, presidency of Madras, 17 miles N.E. of Soonda. Lat. 14° 53′, long. 75° 5′.

NAGAR.—A town in the Trans-Sutluj native territory of Kullu, situate 116 miles N.E. of Loodianah. Lat. 32° 8′, long. 77° 10′.

NAGAR, or NAGYR, north of the Punjab, a small town or village, the principal place of a petty state also called Nagar. This is situate N.W. of Bultistan and S. of Pamir: it consists chiefly of a valley of about three days' journey in length and six or eight miles broad; and is intersected and drained by a stream, which falls into the Gilgit river. The female sex in this region are remarkable for their attractions. Vigne, who takes a great interest in such topics, adduces the following singular testimony to their charms:—"The women are famous for their beauty, and Nazim Khan used to assure me that their complexions were so fair, delicate, and transparent, that when they drank, the water was perceivable in their throats." The chief place, Nagar, stands on the banks of the river, and is defended by a fort. The name is generic, and signifies town, but, by no unusual appropriation of such terms, it is used in this instance to designate a particular place. Nagar lies in lat. 35° 47′, long. 74° 22′.

NAGARANOW, in the district of Bainswara, territory of Oude, a town 30 miles S. of Lucknow. Butter estimates the population at 6,000, including 100 Mussulmans. Lat. 26° 34′, long. 80° 50′.

NAGARIA, in the British district of Furruckabad, lieut.-gov. of the N.W. Provinces, a town near the right bank of the Ganges, and 18 miles N.W. of the city of Furruckabad. Lat. 27° 38′, long. 79° 30′.

NAGAWARAM.—A town in the British district of Rajahmundry, presidency of Madras, 35 miles N.W. by W. of Rajahmundry. Lat. 17° 15′, long. 81° 23′.

NAGGAR.—A considerable walled town in the plain of Bunnoo, westward of the Indus, and at the foot of the Salt or Kala Bagh range of mountains. It is a commercial place, and has a good bazar, but the walls have been allowed to fall into great decay. The surrounding country is fertile and well cultivated. Lat. 33° 10′, long. 71° 5′.

NAGGERY.—A town in the British district of North Arcot, presidency of Madras, 33 miles N.N.E. of Arcot. Lat. 13° 19′, long. 79° 39′.

NAGHEER.—A town of the Deccan, in the territory of Nagpoor or Berar, situate 54 miles S.E. from the city of Nagpoor, and 100 miles S. from Seuni. Lat. 20° 36′, long. 79° 44′.

NAGKUNDA, in the hill state of Komharsin, an elevated pass over a ridge proceeding westward from Wartu Peak. The ascent from the south is steep, but otherwise pleasant in the fine season, passing through noble woods of cedar (deodar) and oak, crossed by numerous rills of the purest water, and at many points presenting views of the finest mountain scenery. On the summit is a good house for the accommodation of travellers. Elevation above the sea 9,016 feet. Lat. 31° 15′, long. 77° 31′.

NAGMUNGLUM, in the Mysore, a town of square ground-plan, two miles in circumference, having in the middle a citadel also square. In the citadel are two large temples, and some other religious buildings in good repair, a public court of justice, and a mahal or palace of the former rajah. Nagmunglum is the principal place of a tallook or subdivision of the same name. It was acquired in the year 1630, by conquest, by Cham Raj, sovereign of Mysore. Distant from Seringapatam, N., 28 miles; Bangalore, W., 58. Lat. 12° 48′, long. 76° 49′.

NAGNI, in the hill state of Bulsun, a small fort, generally held by a Ghoorka garrison in the service of the East-India Company. It is built of loose stones, and has the shape of an irregular quadrangle, about fifty feet long, and of nearly equal breadth. Elevation above the sea 8,808 feet. Lat. 31° 5′, long. 77° 31′.

NAGODE.—See NAGOUND.

NAGOOLPAD.—A town in Hyderabad, or territory of the Nizam, 81 miles E.S.E. from Hyderabad, and 73 miles N.W. from Guntoor. Lat. 17°, long. 79° 41′.

NAGOR, in the district of Bainswara, territory of Oude, a village on the route from Cawnpore to Pertaubgurh, 30 miles S.E. of the former, situate close to the left bank of the Ganges. Lat. 26° 22′, long. 80° 38′.

NAGOR.—See NAGOUR.

NAGORE, in the British district of Tanjore, presidency of Madras, a town on the Coromandel coast, on the estuary of a small outlet of the river Coleroon. "There are eight feet on the bar at high water during the springs; the rise of the tide about three feet. Several vessels of two or three hundred tons burthen belong to this place, and are navigated by natives, who conduct them to the coast of Sumatra, Acheen, Malacca Strait, and other parts on the east side of the Bay of Bengal, where they have a constant trade." The town is easily distinguished at sea by five pagodas, rendered more conspicuous by their white colour. It is a large populous place, with good bazars, in which considerable business is done in cotton goods and rice, and other country produce. Distance from Negapatam, N., five miles; Tranquebar, S., 13; Tanjore, E., 48; Madras, S., 160. Lat. 10° 49′, long. 79° 54′.

NAGORE, in the British district of Beerbhoom, lieut.-gov. of Bengal, a town 15 miles W. of Sooree, the seat of the civil establishment of the district. Lat. 23° 56′, long. 87° 22′.

NAGORE, a river rising in lat. 26° 39′, long. 88° 24′, in the British district of Dinajepoor, through which it flows southerly for twenty-five miles; then, for eighty miles forming the boundary between Dinajepoor and Purneah, it falls into the Mahananda, in lat. 25° 26′, long. 88° 6′.

NAGOTNA, or NAGATHANA, in the British collectorate of Tannah, presidency of Bombay, a town on the river Amba, which is navigable for boats of considerable burthen as far as this place, twenty miles from its mouth. From this cause, the town is a considerable thoroughfare for persons proceeding from Bombay to the south-east part of the Deccan, as they can, by sailing across Bombay harbour and up the river, reach Nagotna by a single tide, and thence continue their journey by land. A road runs from this town to Mahabulishwar, a distance of seventy miles, but it is of no great width or solidity of construction, and is deficient in drains and bridges. Another road, running north-east, joins the Bombay and Poona road at the foot of the Bhore Ghaut. When the Concan belonged to the kings of Beejapore, Nagotna marked the limit of the district to the north. Distance from Bombay, S.W., 40 miles. Lat. 18° 33′, long. 73° 13′.

NAGOUND, in the native state of Oocheyra, territory of Saugor and Nerbudda, a small town on the route, by Rewa, from Saugor to Allahabad, and the site of a cantonment for British troops. Here is a fort or castle, stated by Jacquemont to have been, at the time of his visit, the residence of a rajah, probably that of Oocheyra, who, in 1830, was deposed by the British authorities for the murder of his brother. It is situate on the Umrun, a tributary of the Tons (South-eastern), and is consequently well provided with water; and supplies may be had from its bazar. Elevation above the sea 1,099 feet. Lat. 24° 34′, long. 80° 39′.

NAGOUR, in the Rajpoot state of Jodhpoor, a considerable town, is situate in a plain overrun with jungle, and is surrounded by a wall. It has four tanks and fifty wells. The kine reared in the surrounding country are fine, and in much request in the neighbouring parts of India. The town belongs to a feudatory of the maharaja of Jodhpoor, and the district of which it is the capital is stated by Tod to have paid to government, in the prosperous times of Jodhpoor, an annual income of 7,500*l.*, from the sayer or commercial imposts alone. Distant N.W. from Nusserabad 84 miles, S.W. from Delhi 250; from the town of Jodhpoor, N.E., 75. Lat. 27° 10′, long. 73° 50′.

NAGPOOR, in the British district of Gurhwal, lieut.-gov. of the N.W. Provinces, a town on the route from Almora to Kunawar, 56 miles N.W. by N. of the former. Lat. 30° 20′, long. 79° 16′.

NAGPORE.—A British province in Southern India, comprising a great part of Berar and Gondwana, as well as several extensive and nearly wild tracts to the south and east. It is bounded on the north by the British territory of Saugor and Nerbudda, and the native state of Korea; on the east by Sirgooja, the British districts of Sumbulpore and Odeipoor, and the petty native states of Ryghur, Nowagudda, Cahahandy, and the hill zemindarry of Jeypoor; on the south-west by Hyderabad, or the territory of the Nizam; and on the west by Hyderabad and the Saugor and Nerbudda territory. It lies between lat. 17° 50′—23° 5′, long. 78° 3′—83° 10′: its extreme length from north to south has been stated to be 368 miles; its extreme breadth from east to west, 278.

Colonel Blacker conjectured that the area did not exceed 70,000 square miles; but by actual survey it appears to be 76,432. It is in general a tract of considerable elevation, the surface sloping from north-west to south-east, and the whole of the drainage being discharged into the Bay of Bengal, except a very small portion which finds its way, by the Taptee, into the Arabian Sea, and another, equally limited, discharged into the Nerbudda. The northern part of the territory, or Deogurh above the Ghats, comprises part of the great Vindhya range of mountains, and has considerable elevation; the highest part of the Mahadeo Mountains, as this part of the great range is called, being about 2,500 feet above the sea; and other summits having respectively elevations of 2,100, of 1,900, and of 1,641 feet above the sea. The surface, as it stretches southward, becomes less rugged, and finally sinks into an extensive plain. The general level of this plain is estimated at 1,050 feet above the sea. The northern portion of the division of Chutteesgurh, in the eastern part of the territory, has also considerable elevation, rising to the Vindhya Mountains, computed to have at Omerkuntuk an elevation of 3,463 feet; and southward from this locality extend the high lands called the Lanjhee Hills, from the town of the same name. The Lanjhee range is but imperfectly explored; but the summit Leela, lat. 21° 55′, long. 80° 25′, has been ascertained to have an elevation of 1,300 feet above the neighbouring plain country, and 2,300 above the sea; and another summit of the same hills, in lat. 21° 40′, long. 80° 35′, has an elevation of 2,400 above the sea. The Lanjhee divides the territory into two extensive basins, one lying to the north-east, the waters of which are discharged through the Mahanuddee into the Bay of Bengal; the other to the south-west, the drainage of which passes into the Godavery, by the Weingunga and Wurda; thus finding a way also into the Bay of Bengal. In the former basin, the elevations of several points have been ascertained; as Rypore, in lat. 21° 12′, long. 81° 40′, 1,747 feet; Ruttunpoor, lat. 22° 12′, long. 82° 8′, 1,538 feet; Konkeir, in the south, lat. 20° 16′, long. 81° 33′, 1,958 feet; Shawa, about lat. 20° 20′, long. 81° 50′, 2,117 feet; Dhumderee, about lat. 21° 25′, long. 82°, 1,720 feet. The south-eastern part of the territory, comprising fully a third of the whole, and forming the raj or extensive zemindarry of Bustar, has not been explored by Europeans. Hence little is known of the country, but that it is both a woody and hilly tract, the valleys of which alone are cultivated, and partially cleared of jungle; and that there are few roads, or even paths, practicable, except for the savage Gonds, the indigenous inhabitants of those wild parts. This state of the country results rather from the habits of the population than the nature of the soil.

The principal rivers of the territory are the Wyne Gunga, the Mahanuddee, the Wurda, the Kanhan, and the Sew. There are a great number of rivers of less importance, for the country is for the most part very well watered. There are no natural lakes, but there are some tanks or artificial pieces of water of great extent. The most remarkable is the Nawagaon Bund, in lat. 20° 55′, long. 80° 10′, which is twenty-four miles in circuit, and is formed by the construction of two small embankments, which dam up, and cause the accumulation of the water flowing into an extensive natural depression. Another, the Seoni Bund, is six miles in circumference; and those of less dimensions are very numerous. The amount and distribution of the population in 1825 are thus given in an official statement:—

Deogarh below the Ghats	572,792
Wainganga	690,770
Chatisgarh	639,603
Chanda......................	306,996
Deogarh above the Ghats	145,363
City of Nagpore and suburbs ..	115,228

This result showed an increase of above 250,000 in five years. In 1842, a writer who had access to official sources, thought it probable that the population then amounted to 3,200,000, and more recently the number has been given at 4,650,000. Of the amount of population in 1825, it was calculated that 2,120,795 were Brahminists, 58,368 Mussulmans, and 291,603 Gonds. Though the numbers are greatly increased, the proportions probably remain nearly the same.

The Gondee language, which is spoken throughout the whole territory, is a rude dialect, having no written character. In some districts, besides the Gondee, the peculiar dialect of the Cole tribe is used. In the northern part, the prevailing language is a mixture of Hindee, Mahratta, and Gondee; in the eastern part, the Ooriya is partially used, as in the southern the Telinga. Mahratta is the language of the city, as it was of the court and of all the functionaries of government throughout the realm; the Mahrattas being until lately the ruling race; the rajah being of that race, which furnished all the officers of state, and a large portion of the army and people. The Gonds appear to be the aboriginal inhabitants, and the relics of a widely-extended population, subjugated by Hindoo invaders. They are distinguishable by their features, having broad flat noses, thick lips, and curly hair. When reclaimed from the savage state, they are represented as being sincere, faithful, intelligent, and less mendacious than the Brahminists or Mussulmans. The territories of Nagpore have been hitherto divided into the following soubahs or districts:—1. Sindwara, or Deogarh above the Ghats; 2. Nagpore, or Deogarh below the Ghats; 3. Bhandara or Wainganga; 4. Raipore or Chattisgarh; 5. Chanda or Chandarpur. The principal towns are Nagpore the capital, Chanda, Ryepoor, Bundara, Sindwara, Oomrait, Hingunghat, Ramteak, Pohonee, Konkeir, Wairagarh, Bustar, and Kamptee. The principal routes through the territory are,—1. East to west, from Calcutta, through Ryepoor to Kamptee, and thence to Nagpore; 2. east to west, from Cuttack to Ryepoor, where this route joins the former; 3. east to west, from Kamptee, through Nagpore, to Ellichpore, where, turning south-west, this route proceeds through Aurungabad to Bombay; 4. south to north, from Kamptee and Nagpore, to Saugor; 5. north-east to south-west, from Hazareebagh, through Ruttunpore, to Kamptee and Nagpore; 6. north to south, from Kamptee and Nagpore, to Secunderabad and Hydrabad.

The rajahs of Nagpore, sometimes called the rajahs of Berar, were the rulers of a state which was a branch of the great Mahratta confederation, and the heritage of a family distinguished by the appellation Bhoonsla. Its founder was a man named Parsojee, who, it is said, was originally a private horseman, but who rose to rank and power through the gratitude of Rajah Saho, son of Sevajee, whose standard he was among the first to join when that chief was liberated from the captivity in which he had been held by the Moguls. In consideration of his services, Parsojee was invested with the right of collecting the Mahratta demands in the province of Berar. Parsojee was succeeded by his cousin Ragojee, who was related to Saho by marriage, and who succeeded in raising his power apparently on the ruins of that of the Goond rajahs. He extended his encroachments farther, and repeatedly invaded Bengal. The soubahdar of that province being unequal to the task of defending himself, and disappointed in his attempt to obtain aid from the emperor, who was unable to afford any, bribed the Peishwa Balajee, by confirming to the Mahrattas the grant of Malwa, to undertake the expulsion of the intruder. This he effected; but Ragojee, taking advantage of his absence, entered into a confederacy against the Peishwa, and made a rapid march in the direction of Poona. From this confederacy he was detached by the Peishwa conceding to him the right of levying the Mahratta chout in all Bengal and Behar. This right Ragojee asserted with varied success. On one occasion, his troops were successful in the field, but their commander was seduced into an interview with the soubahdar and murdered. Subsequently, the treacherous ruler was compelled to make a cession of territory, and to consent to pay twelve lacs annually as the chout of that province. Ragojee dying in 1755, was succeeded by his eldest son Janojee. This prince, who died without issue in 1772, adopted his nephew Ragojee as his successor, appointing his widow regent during the youth's minority, assisted by one of his brothers, named Sabajee. This arrangement was very distasteful to another brother, named Madajee, who, though the father of the infant rajah, was thus excluded from all control over his affairs. Incessant dissensions and plots resulted, and at last the two brothers, Sabajee and Madajee, came to open hostilities, terminated by a battle, in which the former fell by a pistol-shot from the hand of the latter, delivered under circumstances which amounted to assassination. Madajee thereupon assumed the regency. His administration was of a pacific character. In the struggle for the peishwaship he took no active part, but facilitated the march of a British detachment under Colonel Goodard through the dominions of the Bhoonsla rajah. Upon the death of Madajee, which took place in 1788, the Rajah Ragojee came into the uncontrolled exercise of power. His policy for many years was to avoid external war; but in an evil hour for himself, he, in 1803, joined Scindia in the war against the British government, consequent on the treaty of Bassein. The victories of Assaye and Argaum taught him the necessity for peace, and by a treaty concluded in 1804, he surrendered the province of Cuttack (which had been obtained many years before from the soubahdar of Bengal), as well as other portions of territory, to the British government and their allies. Two years afterwards, in the exercise of the policy of conciliation carried out by Sir George Barlow, part of the cessions were restored. Ragojee died in 1816, and his son, labouring under infirmities which rendered him incapable of governing, the administration of affairs was intrusted to the next in succession, a cousin of the reigning rajah, known in Indian history by the name of Appa Sahib, and who, on the death of his relation, succeeded to his title, being previously in possession of his authority. By him a subsidiary treaty was concluded with the British government. This, however, did not restrain him, a few years afterwards, from entering into intrigues with the Peishwa, with whom the British government was then actually at war; and the treachery was consummated on the 26th of November, 1817, by an open attack on the British troops. The disproportion of numbers was great; but the best dispositions which the suddenness of the attack allowed were promptly made, and the resident, Mr. Jenkins, with his first assistant Mr. Sotheby, repaired to the scene of action. The latter gentleman was left dead on the field; the former remained at the post he had chosen, exposed to all its dangers, till, after a contest of eighteen hours, the conflict terminated in favour of the British. The hill of Seetabuldee, the chief post of the victors, was thus rendered a memorable spot by the courage and perseverance of its defenders. After this, Appa Sahib was admitted to terms far more favourable than he had any right to expect; but no stipulations could bind him. Scarcely had he signed the new treaty, than he entered into fresh measures of hostility, and this being discovered, he was placed under arrest. While on the way to Allahabad, he however effected his escape, and never was retaken, though his life was prolonged for many years. He died at Joudpore in 1840. Subsequently to his deposition, it was discovered that he had caused the afflicted prince who preceded him, and for whom he was appointed to act as regent, to be strangled. The vacancy created by the expulsion of the blood-stained and perfidious Appa Sahib, was supplied by the elevation of a youth maternally descended from Ragojee. During his minority, the country was administered by British officers. In 1826, it was formally made over to the rajah, on the conditions mainly of the treaty concluded in 1816 with his predecessor. In 1848, an impostor, named Ragobartee Gossain, pretending to be Appa Sahib, collected troops, and made his appearance in Berar. A military force was despatched to oppose him, but though the insurgents were defeated, the capture of the pretender and the dispersion of his troops were not effected without considerable loss on the part of the victors. The latest engagement made with the late Rajah Ragojee was in 1829. He died on the 11th December, 1853, without issue, and, it is said, altogether without relations. According to the highest authority on the subject, the succession in the Bhoonsla family was "hereditary in the entire male line from the common ancestor, or first founder of the dynasty, to the exclusion of females or their issue." There was no one who could pretend to this qualification; and it would have been unwise for the British government to elevate a stranger to the musnud. Nagpore was therefore incorporated with the British dominions, and now forms a constituent part of them.

NAGPORE.—The principal place of the territory of the same name. It is situate in a low swampy hollow, which, though it has of late years been in some degree improved by the excavation of tanks and watercourses, is still very wet and muddy during the rains. The town is about seven miles in circumference, but very straggling and irregular in its shape. There is but one good street, the others being mean and narrow, and rendered very incommodious by innumerable channels and watercourses, often impassable during the rains. The place at a distance has the appearance of a forest, in consequence of the great number of trees interspersed among the houses, and which interrupt ventilation, and add to the unhealthiness of the site. The greater part of the houses are built of mud, some being thatched, others tiled; but there are a few of large size, built of brick and mortar, with flat terraced roofs. There is throughout the town no specimen of fine architecture; and even the palace of the late rajah, which is the most considerable building, is devoid of symmetry or beauty: it is merely a large pile of stone masonry, completely obscured by the encroachments of mean mud huts built against its walls. A considerable portion of the edifice itself has been allowed to remain unfinished. The only ornamental parts of the palace are the lofty pillars of carved wood which support the roof of the portico at the entrance, and also those of the principal courts. Close to the city on the west is the ridge of Seetabuldee, running from north to south, and having two summits, one at each extremity, the northern being the higher, but the southern the larger, and all parts commanding the city. The geological formation is basalt, surrounded on all sides by gneiss, or slaty granite. The Nag, a small river, flows along the southern side of the town, and falls into the Kanhan some miles to the eastward. Notwithstanding the situation of the city, which is distant in a direct line about 350 miles from the nearest part of the Bay of Bengal, and 420 from the nearest part of the Arabian Sea, the registered annual rainfall is very considerable. In 1826, the fall slightly exceeded sixty-five inches, of which sixty-two fell during the four months of the south-west monsoon,—June, July, August, September; and in 1831 the fall also slightly exceeded sixty-five inches, fifty-four of which fell during the four monsoon months. The greatest registered fall was seventy-two inches, and that was in 1809. The range of the thermometer in the shade is moderate. Prinsep concludes "that the mean temperature of Nagpoor does not differ much from 80° Fahrenheit, which is nearly two degrees higher than that of Calcutta, and one and a half lower than that of Madras." The manufacturing industry is engaged in making cotton cloths, both coarse and fine; chintzes, turbans, silks, brocades, coarse blankets, and other coarse woollens; cotton tent-cloths, and also tent-cloths and sacks of hemp; utensils of copper and of brass, and of other alloys. Jenkins mentions that shawls, silks, muslins, and piece-goods were in one year imported into the city of Nagpore to the amount of 320,000 rupees, or 32,000*l.* The banking business is carried on with skill and much profit. This business, subsequently to the expulsion of Appa Sahib, largely increased; fifteen banking-houses, some of them very wealthy, having been established since 1818. According to the last census, the dwellings were,—matted huts 48, thatched huts of a better description 14,680, tiled houses 11,120, houses of baked brick and mortar 1,301; total 27,149, inhabited by a population amounting to 111,231; of whom about 2½ per cent. were Mussulmans, the rest Brahminists. Elevation above the sea 930 feet. Distance from Bombay, N.E., 440 miles; Poona, N.E., 390; Hyderabad, N., 265; Madras, N., 565; Calcutta, W., 605; Delhi, S., 530. Lat. 21° 10′, long. 79° 10′.

NAGPORE CHOTA.—See CHOTA NAGPORE.

NAGROLAH, in the north-east of the Punjab, a village on the route from Chumba to Cashmere, by the Banihal Pass. It is situate thirty miles north-west of Chumba, in a rugged country between the upper course of the Ravee and that of the Chenaub. Lat. 32° 50′, long. 75° 50′.

NAGULDINNY.—A town in the British district of Bellary, presidency of Madras, 70 miles N.E. of Bellary. Lat. 15° 55′, long. 77° 38′.

NAGULPILLY.—A town in Hyderabad, or territory of the Nizam, 36 miles N. from Hyderabad, and 169 miles E. by N. from Sholapoor. Lat. 17° 50′, long. 78° 29′.

NAGURBUSSEE.—A town in the British district of Tirhoot, lieut.-gov. of Bengal, 33 miles S.E. by E. of Mozufferpoor. Lat. 25° 51′, long. 85° 54′.

NAGURSOGA.—A town in one of the recently sequestrated districts of Hyderabad, or dominions of the Nizam, 143 miles W.N.W. of Hyderabad. Lat. 18° 11′, long. 76° 35′.

NAGWA, in the British district of Muzuffurnugur, lieut.-gov. of the N.W. Provinces, a village on the route from Kurnal to Meerut, and 52 miles S.E. of the former. It is situate on the right bank of the Hindun, here crossed by ford, having the water from two feet to two and a half feet deep, with a sandy bottom. Lat. 29° 12′, long. 77° 34′.

NAGWAN, in native Gurhwal, a village on the Budeear, a considerable feeder of the Jumna, and close to the confluence of the streams. It is remarkable for being surrounded by a profusion of fine orange-trees, which Jacquemont observes he has not elsewhere noticed in the Himalaya. The size of those trees, and the maturity of their fruit in this locality, is the more remarkable, as it has an elevation of 4,000 feet above the sea, and every winter heavy snows fall. The pomegranate is also produced here. An absurd Hindu fiction prevails, that the Ganges, by a subterranean course, reaches this village, and breaks out in a fine spring close to it. Lat. 30° 50′, long. 78° 19′.

NAHANY.—A town in the British district of Chota Nagpoor, lieut.-gov. of Bengal, 23 miles S.W. of Lohadugga. Lat. 23° 12′, long. 84° 30′.

NAHAPARA.—A town in the British district of Beerbhoom, lieut.-gov. of Bengal, 98 miles N. by W. of Calcutta. Lat. 23° 54′, long. 88° 1′.

NAHARGURH.—A town in the Rajpoot state of Kotah, situate eight miles N.E. from the right bank of the Parbutty river, and 66 miles E. by S. from Kotah. Lat. 24° 56′, long. 76° 53′.

NAHGUL, in the British district of Bijnour, lieut.-gov. of the N.W. Provinces, a village on the route from Moradabad to Hurdwar, and 22 miles S. of the latter. It is situate on the left bank of the Ganges, which, at a short distance from it, is crossed by ferry. Lat. 29° 40′, long. 78° 15′.

NAHNDEEA.—A town in the Rajpoot state of Serohee, situate on the right bank of the Bunnass river, and 54 miles W.N.W. from Oodeypoor. Lat. 24° 51′, long. 73°.

NAHRWALLEH.—A town in the native state of Bhawulpoor, 92 miles S. from Mooltan, and 71 miles S.W. from Bhawulpoor. Lat. 28° 31′, long. 70° 40′.

NAHUL, in the British district of Shahjehanpoor, lieut.-gov. of the N.W. Provinces, a town on the route from Bareilly to Setapoor, and 44 miles S.E. of the former. Lat. 28° 8′, long. 80° 6′.

NAHUN, in Sirmor, the residence of the rajah of that small state, and the only town of importance which it contains, is situate on a hill, principally of grauwacke formation, rising at the western extremity of the Kyarda Doon. It is described by Moorcroft as having a cleaner and handsomer appearance than the generality of Indian cities, and commands fine views of the mountains on the north and on the south of the plain of Sirhind, and of the streams which traverse it. The houses are small, built of stone cemented with lime, and having flat roofs of mud, tempered so as to be waterproof. They are arranged on the uneven crest of a rocky eminence, so that the streets are a sort of flights of stairs, the surface being in most places formed into steps by cutting the rock; and where not thus contrived, are well paved, and kept clean. The residence of the rajah, in the middle of the town, is a large edifice of stone; the Zenana is built of cut stone, in an antique Hindoo style, at once simple and beautiful. There are three Hindoo temples, remarkable rather for their fine sites than their architectural excellence. The bazar is large, populous, and well supplied. On the edge of a tank in the centre of the town is a monument to Lieutenant Thackeray and three other officers, killed at the siege of Jaituk. Nahun was occupied by the British in the Goorkha war, at the close of 1814, and restored by them to the rajah of Sirmor. It is on the route from Suharunpoor to Subathoo, and 54 miles S.E. of the latter place, in which direction there is a good road, made by the rajah of Sirmor. The climate in very fine, in consequence of the elevation, which is 3,207 feet above the sea. Distant N.W. from Calcutta 1,065 miles. Lat. 30° 34′, long. 77° 21′.

NAHUR, in the British district of Goorgaon, lieut.-gov. of the N.W. Provinces, a town on the route from Rewaree to Hansee, 20 miles N.W. of the former. Lat. 28° 25′, long. 76° 29′.

NAHUR, in the jaghire of Doojana, territory of Jujhur, lieut.-gov. of the N.W. Provinces, a village on the route from Dadree to Rewaree, and 18 miles N.W. of the latter. Lat. 28° 23′, long. 76° 29′.

NAHURNUDEE, in the Rajpoot state of Jodhpoor, a village on the route from Balotra to Jodhpoor, and 12 miles S.W. of the latter. The city, citadel, and palaces of Jodhpoor form a striking prospect as seen from this place. It has a well and two tanks. Population 730. Lat. 26° 12′, long. 73°.

NAIKRAS (THE).—The country inhabited by this tribe is comprised within a circle of about sixty coss, or 120 miles; bounded on the north by the petty state of Barreeah, and on the south by the Rewa Caunta district of Chota Odeypore. With the exception of a few partially-cultivated spots, the whole of the tract is covered with jungle; in the most impervious parts of which are situated the villages. The number of inhabitants is said to be about 8,000; but no trustworthy estimate can be formed, as the country is never visited but by travellers compelled to pass through it, and who avoid as much as possible the haunts of the freebooters by whom it is peopled. The huts of the lower class of Naikras are composed of the rudest materials; the principal men have habitations constructed in a more durable manner, generally situate in the valleys, at a short distance from each other. These persons are said to be possessed of much wealth, which is kept concealed in caves on the hills. Each chief has several wives, whose residences are scattered over the country: such is the state of suspicion in which they live, that no man of any consequence sleeps at the same place two nights consecutively. It is the usual custom to return to the hills at sunset, the ravines below which afford shelter on the approach of danger. The rude cultivation of this wild tribe is confined to a few fields of grain, their subsistence being generally derived from the produce of plunder. Cattle are the chief objects of their pursuit, on account of the facility with which they can be disposed of in the neighbouring villages; but articles of the most trifling value offer a sufficient inducement to rob, and even to murder. The latter crime indeed is generally the preliminary to the former. Of the cruelty of these people some idea may be formed from the circumstance of its being the general belief that the custom which obtained among the pirates of old, of sacrificing a human being over their secret haunts of treasure, is the general practice among them. When pushed to extremity, the Naikras subsist on the roots of plants. Opium and tobacco are their greatest luxuries; and in these they freely indulge whenever opportunity offers. A few coolies and small traders reside in their principal villages, and retail these articles, as also gunpowder: but they do not deal in grain. The face of the country is strong. The water is good; but the barbarous practice of poisoning the wells on the approach of a hostile force is always adopted. Matchlocks, swords, and bows and arrows, are the arms in general use.

The Naikras had been induced by the British government to enter into engagements binding them to desist from plundering, and these engagements they for some time faithfully observed; but at length they resumed their depredations, which the feeble chiefs to whom most of them were nominally subject, were utterly unable to control. In 1838, the principal offender, Kewul Naik, was prevailed upon to renew his engagement; but almost immediately violated the new settlement by plundering two villages belonging to Chota Odeypore. A large force was sent out against the Naikras, and it succeeded in seizing all the leading men of the tribe. Among those taken was Kewul Naik, who resided in the village of Barre. Further excesses took place in about eighteen months afterwards; the rebels being headed by Nursing, the son of the last named personage, who went out in barwuttee, after murdering his uncle. This criminal and his associates were tried for the offence, and punished; and an example having been made of several others, the tribe have now been reduced to some degree of order. The principal district inhabited by this class, designated the zillah of Sagtalla, is under the immediate superintendence of a thanadar appointed by the British government, who collects the revenues. In the year 1826, a potdaree engagement was entered into between its rajah and Sulloobhay Khaosall Chund, with a view to arrange the financial embarrassment of the state, and redeem the pledges granted to certain creditors. These objects have been effected and the debts discharged. The revenue of the state amounts to 62,700 rupees. On the death of the last chief, Gungadass, claims were preferred to the guddee by the mother of Pritheerajee and two other widows. The result of the inquiry instituted on the occasion terminated in the recognition of Pritheerajee, the present ruler, who has since occupied the place thus attained.

NAIN, in the district of Salon, territory of Oude, a town 60 miles S.E. of Lucknow. Butter estimates its population at 10,000. Lat. 26° 4′, long. 81° 20′.

NAIRS.—See MALABAR.

NAISREE.—A town of Bombay, in the native state of Kolapoor, 46 miles S. by E. from Kolapoor, and 19 miles N.W. from Belgaum. Lat. 16° 2′, long. 74° 24′.

NAJAFGARH, in the British district of Delhi, lieut.-gov. of the N.W. Provinces, a town on the west shore of the extensive jhil or lake formed by the overflow of the Hansouti torrent during the rainy season. Distance 15 miles S.W. from Delhi. Lat. 28° 36′, long. 77° 2′.

NAJAFGURH, in the British district of Cawnpore, lieut.-gov. of the N.W. Provinces, a small town or village on the right bank of the Ganges, nineteen miles by water below the cantonment of Cawnpore, and 16 miles S.E. of it by land. The principal building here is a residence built by General Martin, a French adventurer, who succeeded in accumulating immense wealth. "It is an Hindostanico-European house with small rooms, fortified as usual by strong doors and shutters." Indigo is much grown in the surrounding country, and here manufactured into a marketable state. Lat. 26° 18′, long. 80° 36′.

NAJREH.—A town in the British province of Sattara, presidency of Bombay, 72 miles E.S.E. of Sattara. Lat. 17° 21′, long. 75° 6′.

NAKARIKALLU.—A town in the British

district of Guntoor, presidency of Madras, 35 miles W. by N. of Guntoor. Lat. 16° 23′, long. 80°.

NAKO, in Bussahir, a village of Koonawur, and one of the largest of that district, is situate on the western declivity of the huge mountain of Purkyul, and about a mile from the left bank of the Lee or river of Spiti. It is a collection of thirty or forty small dirty huts, built partly of stone, partly of unbaked bricks, and covered with a roof of mud overspreading a platform made of the trunks of junipers. "This," observes Gerard, "is the highest village that occurs to the traveller who traces round the frontier of Bussahir. Separate measurements, by excellent barometers and the boiling-point of water, indicate an elevation a little above 12,000 feet from the level of the sea; yet there are produced the most luxuriant crops of barley and wheat, rising by steps to nearly 700 feet higher, where there is a lama's residence, occupied throughout the year. The fields are supported and partitioned by dykes of granite. The other grains are phapur (buckwheat) and turnips." Beans are also cultivated, and though very small, ripen perfectly. In consequence of the extraordinary aridity of the atmosphere, the crops are produced by means of water flowing from the masses of ice and snow above. A little below the village is a small lake or pond, shaded with willows and poplars, which are the only trees, except junipers, found in this vicinity, furze alone being used for firewood; and the scarcity even of this adds to the privations to be endured in a climate so inclement. Yet yaks, kine, horses, and asses are reared here in great abundance. Elevation above the sea 11,850 feet. Lat. 31° 52′, long. 78° 40′.

NAKODUR, in the Julinder Dooab of the Punjab, a town situated 11 miles N. from the right bank of the Sutlej, 70 miles S.E. by E. of the town of Lahore. Lat. 31° 10′, long. 75° 28′.

NAKUNAOD.—A town in the British district of Coorg, presidency of Madras, 15 miles N.N.E. of Merkara. Lat. 12° 15′, long. 75° 42′.

NAL, in the Rajpoot state of Beekaneer, a village on the route from the town of Beekaneer to that of Jessulmeer, and eight miles W. of the former. It is a good village, containing 200 houses, thirty shops, and two wells 200 feet deep. Lat. 28° 3′, long. 73° 16′.

NALAGARH, a fort in the hill state of Hindoor, on the south-western declivity of the Sub-Himalaya. It was a place of considerable strength by its site and structure, but at the commencement of the Goorkha war, General Ochterlony having succeeded in bringing battering guns by the difficult road to it, the defences were demolished, and the Goorkha garrison compelled to surrender. It is the residence of the rajah of Hindoor, and considered the capital of that small state. Distant N.W. from Calcutta 1,094 miles. Lat. 31° 2′, long. 76° 47′.

NALAHPUTUN, in the native territory of Gurwhal, a village with a Hindoo temple, on the route from Sireenuggur to Kedarnath temple, and 18 miles S. of the latter. It is situate about a mile from the right bank of the Mundagnee, a tributary of the Alukananda. Elevation above the sea 4,731 feet. Lat. 30° 32′, long. 79° 8′.

NALAPANI, or KALUNGA, in the Debra Doon, on the western boundary of native Gurwhal, was a fort on the range forming the eastern boundary of the valley. The hill is about 600 feet higher than the lowland, and the table-land on the summit three-quarters of a mile in length, being of very difficult access, from the steepness of the ground. The fort, built on the southern and highest part, was, at the commencement of the war with the Goorkhas, garrisoned with between 300 and 400 of that nation, and on the 29th of October, 1814, invested by Major-General Gillespie, who, after a brief cannonade on the defences from two twelve-pounders, four six-pounders, and four five and a half inch howitzers, ordered an assault with 2,737 men. The assailants, however, encountered such a determined and skilful resistance, that they were compelled to retreat to their camp, having lost their general, who was shot through the heart whilst cheering on his men. Four other officers were killed, and fifteen wounded, and twenty-seven non-commissioned officers and privates killed, and 213 wounded. On the 24th of the succeeding November, the attack was renewed, and again repelled with still greater loss to the assailants, of whom three officers were killed, and eight wounded, and thirty-eight privates killed, and 440 wounded and missing. A few nights after, the garrison, reduced to seventy men, evacuated the fort, which was demolished by the British. This spot was, during the trigonometrical survey of the Himalayas, a station of the series of small triangles. It is more generally known by the name of Kalunga, which, however, according to Hodgson and Herbert, means generally a military post or cantonment. Distant N.W. from Calcutta, by Allyghur, Meerut, and Dehra, 1,000 miles. Elevation above the sea 3,286 feet. Lat. 30° 20′, long. 78° 8′.

NALCHA, in the territory of Dhar, in Malwa, a ruinous town on the route from Mow to Mando, 27 miles S.W. of former, six N. of latter. It has a bazar, and is abundantly supplied with water from tanks and wells. The site is beautiful, on the southern verge of the rich open table-land of Malwa, extending northwards. Jacquemont, by no means addicted to exaggeration, styles it, in 1832, a large town; so that it had rapidly improved under British protection, since, in 1820, a year after it was repeopled, it contained but 144 houses. Close to it runs a small stream, according to Jacquemont a feeder of the Chumbul, but in the MS. map of Malwa by

Malcolm, it falls into the Nerbudda. Nalcha contains many fine ruins of splendid edifices, raised principally by Mahmood Khilji, sovereign of Malwa, who reigned from 1435 to 1469. When Sir John Malcolm, some years ago, converted one of those palaces into a summer residence, a tigress and its cubs were driven away from one of the apartments, formerly the scene of regal splendour. Elevation above the sea 2,022 feet. Lat. 22° 25′, long. 75° 27′.

NALGOON, in Bussahir, a pass over the range of the Himalaya bounding Koonawur to the south. It is perhaps the lowest pass over this range, being at the elevation of 14,891 feet above the sea, or 700 feet above the limit of perpetual snow in that region. A considerable stream, called also the Nalgoon, flows from the pass in a north-easterly direction, and after a course of about ten miles falls into the river Buspa. The pass of Nalgoon is in lat. 31° 19′, long. 78° 17′.

NALING RIVER, a feeder of the Trisul-Gunga, rises in Nepal, in the great snowy range of the Himalayas, in lat. 28° 57′, long. 83° 33′, and flows through Nepal in a southerly direction for 110 miles, to its junction with the Trisul-Gunga, in lat. 27° 33′, long. 84° 12′.

NALUTWAR.—A town in the British district of Sholapoor, presidency of Bombay, 101 miles S. by E. of Sholapoor. Lat. 16° 14′, long. 76° 21′.

NALWAR.—A town in Hyderabad, or territory of the Nizam, situate on the left bank of the river Beemah, and 104 miles W.S.W. from Hyderabad. Lat. 16° 56′, long. 77° 3′.

NAMCUL DROOG.—A town in the British district of Salem, presidency of Madras, 31 miles S. of Salem. Lat. 11° 14′, long. 78° 14′.

NAMDING.—A town of Assam, in the British district of Sudiya, 39 miles S. of Sudiya. Lat. 27° 17′, long. 95° 41′.

NAMGIA, in Bussahir, a village of Koonawur, and the most northern on the Sutlej, is situate on the left bank, about a mile above the remarkable confluence of the Lee or Spiti with that great river on the opposite side. The village is between 600 and 700 feet above the bed of the Sutlej, and at a short distance is surrounded by frightful barrenness and desolation; though close to the town, on the opposite bank of a small stream, are fields of barley, buckwheat, turnips, and a few vines and apricots. Namgia is at an elevation of 9,272 feet above the sea. Lat. 31° 48′, long. 78° 42′.

NAMGOH.—A town in the native state of Sikhim, situate on the left bank of the Teesta river, and 40 miles N.E. by N. from Darjeeling. Lat. 27° 31′, long. 88° 40′.

NAMJUNG.—A town in the native state of Nepal, situate on the left bank of the Kalee river, and 72 miles N.W. from Jemlah. Lat. 30° 3′, long. 80° 53′.

NAMKIOO, or MEREE KHO RIVER, the name of one of the feeders of the Irawady river, rises in lat. 27° 51′, long. 97° 28′, and, after flowing southerly for 142 miles, joins another main source, in lat. 26°, long. 97° 19′.

NAMOOKEE.—A town in the native state of Bhawulpoor, situate on the left bank of the Sutlej, and 116 miles N.E. by E. from Bhawulpoor. Lat. 30° 14′, long. 73° 23′.

NAMROOP, a river of Upper Assam, rises in lat. 27° 9′, long. 96° 23′, and, flowing northwest through Sudiya, falls into the Dehing river, in lat. 27° 23′, long. 95° 58′.

NANAH.—A town in the Rajpoot state of Godwar, 91 miles S. from Jodhpoor, and 142 miles N.W. from Ajmeer. Lat. 25°, long. 73° 12′.

NANAMOW, in the British district of Cawnpore, lieut.-gov. of the N.W. Provinces, a village on the route from Futtehgurh to Lucknow, and 49 miles S.E. of the former. It has a small bazar, and is situate on the right bank of the Ganges, crossed by ferry between this place and Nowbutganj, in the territory of Oude. Lat. 26° 52′, long. 80° 10′.

NAND, in the British district of Ajmere, a village containing 150 houses, on the northwest frontier, towards the Rajpoot state of Jodhpoor, on the route from the town of Jodhpoor to that of Ajmere, and five miles W. of the latter. It is situate at the eastern base of a low rocky range, and in a swampy tract, through which the road eastward towards Ajmere is so bad as to be scarcely passable. Lat. 26° 28′, long. 74° 38′.

NANDA DEVI, in the British district of Kumaon, lieut.-gov. of the N.W. Provinces, a mountain, one of a very lofty Himalayan group, near the north-eastern frontier. The view drawn by Heber represents it as a spire of snow white, with sides forming angles of about 70°, and rising far above the similarly-formed snow-clad summits which surround it. The summit is altogether inaccessible; but a mile below it, a mela, or religious festival, is held every twelfth year, though access to the spot is so difficult that it is reached by scarcely fifty of the pilgrims who make the attempt. Further progress is impracticable, in consequence of the mural cliffs of ice which on every side encase the peak. The natives maintain that smoke is sometimes seen to issue from its summit, which they regard as the kitchen of the local deity; but there is no good evidence of volcanic action in the higher masses of the Himalaya, and the appearance probably results from the forms given by currents of air to clouds resting on the mountain. The elevation of Nanda Devi is 25,749 feet above the level of the sea. Lat. 30° 22′, long. 80° 1′.

NANDAIR, in Hyderabad, or territory of the Nizam, a town on the left or north bank of the Godavery. It is a place of pilgrimage for the Sikhs, who crowd to pay their devotions at the tomb of their guru, or spiritual pastor, Govind, who was assassinated here by a Pathan. Here is a college for the instruction of youths of that persuasion. Distance from the city of Hyderabad, N., 145 miles. Lat. 19° 9′, long. 77° 23′.

NANDAN SAR, in Cashmere, a small lake, situate, with four others, on the northern side of the Pir Panjal mountain, and a little north of the pass of the same name, which also is sometimes called the Nandan Sar pass. The collective waters of these form the source of the Dumdum or Huripur river. According to Hügel, the Perhamgalla river flows from Nandan Sar to the south-west, and the Dumdum to the north-east; but this double efflux seems very improbable. Nandan Sar is held in high reverence by the Hindoos, and is visited by them in pilgrimage. Lat. 33° 37′, long. 74° 40′.

NANDAOLI, in the British district of Allygurh, lieut.-gov. of the N.W. Provinces, a town on the route from the city of Agra to Bareilly, and 43 miles N.E. of the former. It has a bazar and a market twice a week. Lat. 27° 35′, long. 78° 33′.

NANDAPOOR.—A town in Hyderabad, or territory of the Nizam, situate on the right bank of the Peyne Gunga river, and 113 miles S.W. from Ellichpoor. Lat. 19° 35′, long. 77° 17′.

NANDGAON.—A town in the British district of Tannah, presidency of Bombay, 40 miles S. by E. of Bombay. Lat. 18° 22′, long. 73°.

NANDGAON.—A town in one of the recently sequestrated districts of Hyderabad, or dominions of the Nizam, situate 30 miles S.E. by E. of Ellichpoor. Lat. 20° 56′, long. 77° 57′.

NANDGAUM.—A town in one of the recently sequestrated districts of Hyderabad, or dominions of the Nizam, situate 47 miles S.S.E. of Ellichpoor. Lat. 20° 35′, long. 77° 53′.

NANDODRA.—A town in the British district of Ahmedabad, presidency of Bombay, 33 miles W.S.W. of Ahmedabad. Lat. 22° 48′, long. 72° 10′.

NANDRA, in the Rajpoot state of Jodhpoor, a village on the route from the town of Jodhpoor to that of Ajmere, and five miles E. of the former. The road in this part of the route, though sandy, is good, as Boileau, on horseback, passed along it by moonlight at the rapid rate of ten miles an hour. Lat. 26° 18′, long. 73° 14′.

NANDUH, in the British district of Goorgaon, lieut.-gov. of the N.W. Provinces, a village on the south-western frontier towards Alwur. Lat. 28° 10′, long. 76° 28′.

NANDUN, in the British district of Agra, lieut.-gov. of the N.W. Provinces, a town on the left bank of the Jumna, 20 miles E. of the city of Agra. Lat. 27° 7′, long. 78° 24′.

NANDUNUJ.—A town in one of the recently sequestrated districts of Hyderabad or dominions of the Nizam, situate 50 miles S.E. of Ahmednuggur. Lat. 18° 38′, long. 75° 21′.

NANKATHA KHYOUNG RIVER, a considerable tributary of the Irawaddy, rises in lat. 25° 16′, long. 94° 10′, in the native state of Muneepoor, through which it flows southerly for 105 miles, and in the same direction for 110 miles through Burmah, and falls into the Myithia Khyoung, in lat. 22° 36′, long. 94° 21′.

NANNING, a division of the British possessions on the Malay peninsula, bounded on the north by the Malay state of Rumbowe; on the east by that of Johole; on the south-east and south by Segamet; and on the south-west by the Straits of Malacca. Its length from north to south is about forty miles, and its breadth ten; giving an area of 400 square miles. Its revenue and population are stated to be on the increase. The centre of the district is in lat. 2° 25′, long. 102° 30′.

NANOON, in the British district of Meerut, lieut.-gov. of the N.W. Provinces, a small town four miles from the left bank of the Jumna. Here, on 31st October, 1804, General Lake, preparing to pursue Holkar through the Doab, concentrated his forces, after fording the Jumna three miles above Delhi. Lat. 28° 49′, long. 77° 20′.

NANOUTUH, in the British district of Suharunpoor, lieut.-gov. of the N.W. Provinces, a town on the route from Suharunpoor to Paneeput, 20 miles S.S.W. of the former. Lat. 29° 42′, long. 77° 30′.

NANOWN, in the British district of Allygurh, lieut.-gov. of the N.W. Provinces, a village on the route from the cantonment of Allygurh to that of Mynpoorie, and 13 miles S.E. of the former. Lat. 27° 49′, long. 78° 19′.

NANPARAH.—A town in the territory of Oude, 80 miles N.N.E. from Lucknow, and 100 miles E. from Shahjehanpoor. Lat. 27° 52′, long. 81° 36′.

NANTHE.—A town of Burmah, situate five miles E. from the left bank of the Khyendwen river, and 141 miles N.W. by N. from Ava. Lat. 23° 30′, long. 94° 47′.

NANTO, in the Rajpoot territory of Kota, a town on the north-west frontier, towards Boondee, on the route from the city of Kota to that of Boondee, five miles N.W. of former, 19 S.E. of latter. The palace of the late Zalim Singh, formerly protector of the state of Kota, is a fine specimen of a Rajpoot baronial residence, and has in front a spacious court, surrounded by cloisters, and ornamented with groves of orange-trees and other odoriferous growths, in the midst of which is a beautiful pavilion, with fountains; whence, by means of small canals, water is dispersed to the surrounding verdure. Lat. 25° 14′, long. 75° 53′.

NANUKMUTHA, in the British district

of Bareilly, division of Pillibheet, lieut.-gov. of the N.W. Provinces, a small town with temple dedicated to Nanuk, on the right bank of the river Gurra, 22 miles N. of the town of Pillibheet. Lat. 28° 57′, long. 79° 53′.

NAPASIR, in the Rajpoot state of Beekaneer, a village on the route from Ratangurh to the town of Beekaneer, and 10 miles S.E. of the latter. It is situate in a level country, tolerably cultivated, and contains 100 houses and six shops. Lat. 27° 57′, long. 73° 38′.

NAPUTA.—A town in the British province of Pegu, situate on the left bank of the Negrais river, and 101 miles S.W. from Rangoon. Lat. 16° 27′, long. 94° 48′.

NARAEENGURH, in Sirhind, a village with a fortress built of mud, and surrounded by a large ditch, is situate on the route from Dehra to Subathoo, by Sidowra and Bahr, and 72 miles W. of Dehra. Here was a secondary station in the great trigonometrical survey of the Himalayas. Elevation above the sea 2,154 feet. Lat. 30° 29′, long. 77° 11′.

NARAINGUNJE, in the British district of Dacca, lieut.-gov. of Bengal, a town, the locality of a thana or police establishment. Distance from the city of Dacca, S.E., six miles; Calcutta, N.E., 155. Lat. 23° 38′, long. 90° 30′.

NARAINGURH.—A town in the British district of Midnapoor, lieut.-gov. of Bengal, 70 miles W.S.W. of Calcutta. Lat. 22° 10′, long. 87° 27′.

NARAINKHAID.—A town in Hyderabad, or territory of the Nizam, situate seven miles from the left bank of the river Manjera, and 67 miles N.W. from Hyderabad. Lat. 18° 2′, long. 77° 49′.

NARAJOLE.—A town in the British district of Midnapoor, lieut.-gov. of Bengal, 49 miles W. of Calcutta. Lat. 22° 33′, long. 87° 40′.

NARASARAVAPETA.—A town in the British district of Guntoor, presidency of Madras, 26 miles W. by S. of Guntoor. Lat. 16° 15′, long. 80° 8′.

NARASINGABILLA.—A town in the British district of Vizagapatam, presidency of Madras, 28 miles W. by S. of Vizagapatam. Lat. 17° 36′, long. 82° 57′.

NARAUL, in the district of Ahladganj, territory of Oude, a town 25 miles N. of Allahabad, 90 S.E. of Lucknow. It is nearly surrounded by the East-India Company's district of Allahabad, and pillars of brick or of stone, from five to ten feet high, mark the boundary. Butter estimates the population at 6,000, almost all Hindoos. Lat. 25° 43′, long. 81° 40′.

NARBAH, in Sirhind, a town with a fort, the residence of a rajah whose possessions comprised 313 villages, with a population of 80,000 inhabitants, and yielded an annual revenue of 40,000*l*. sterling, but who was mulcted of one-fourth of his territory from non-performance of feudatory obligations during the Lahore war. His present possessions are bounded on the north by the British district of Loodiana, and on all other sides by the native state of Patialah; they extend from lat. 30° 17′ to 30° 41′, and from long. 75° 51′ to 76° 21′, and are forty miles in length from north-east to south-west, and seventeen in breadth. This rajah, with those of Patialah, Jheend, and the former rajah of Khytul, were known by the designation of Malooa Sikhs, from the district of that name, which they occupy in the south of Sirhind; and thus are distinguished from the Manjha and other Sikhs of the Punjab, who settled in the country after their conquest of it. Narbah is distant N.W. from Calcutta 1,035 miles. Lat. 30° 23′, long. 76° 15′.

NAREH, in Sinde, a village on the route from Sehwan to Larkhana, and 53 miles N. of the former town. It is of considerable size, with houses built of burned brick. Its situation is in a level alluvial country, about a mile from the right bank of the Indus. Lat. 27° 3′, long. 67° 57′.

NARGANHALI, in the Mysore, a small town on the north-west frontier, towards the British district of Dharwar. Distance from Chitradurg, N.W., 22 miles; from Seringapatam, N., 145. Lat. 14° 20′, long. 76° 9′.

NARGURH.—A town in the native state of Gwalior, or possessions of Scindia's family, situate 80 miles N.N.W. from Oojein, and 30 miles S.E. by E. from Neemuch. Lat. 24° 12′, long. 75° 17′.

NARINJA, a river of Hyderabad, or the Nizam's territory, rises in lat. 17° 30′, long. 77° 45′, and, flowing north-west for seventy-five miles, falls into the Manjera river, in lat. 18° 6′, long. 77° 7′.

NARKI, in the British district of Agra, lieut.-gov. of the N.W. Provinces, a town 25 miles N.E. of the city of Agra. Lat. 27° 18′, long. 78° 28′.

NARNAVERAM.—A town in the British district of North Arcot, presidency of Madras, 40 miles N.N.E. of Arcot. Lat. 13° 25′, long. 79° 38′.

NARNOL, in the jaghire of Jujhur, lieut.-gov. of the N.W. Provinces, a town on the route from Hansee to Neemuch, and 86 miles S. of the former. It has a large bazar, and supplies and water are abundant. The road in this part of the route is heavy. Narnol was acquired by surrender, by the adventurer George Thomas, and was one of the fortresses of his transient government. Lat. 28° 1′, long. 76° 11′.

NARNOUND, in the British district of Hurreeana, lieut.-gov. of the N.W. Provinces, a town on the route from Hansee to Kurnal, and 66 miles S.W. of the latter place. It is situate near the right or north-western bank of the canal of Feroz Shah, and has a good supply of water. Distant N.W. of Calcutta, by Delhi and Hansee, 990 miles. Lat. 29° 13′, long. 76° 13′.

NARONOE.—A town in Hyderabad, or

territory of the Nizam, 116 miles W. from Hyderabad, and 58 miles E. by S. from Sholapoor. Lat. 17° 30′, long. 76° 49′.

NAROO, a river of Sinde, rising in lat. 27° 42′, long. 69° 4′, a few miles E. of the town of Roree. After a southerly course of 185 miles, the stream is lost in the desert, near the town of Oomerkote, and about lat. 25° 23′, long. 69° 34′.

NARRA (EASTERN), in Sinde, a large branch of the Indus, separating from the main stream on the eastern side, a few miles above Roree. Taking a southerly course, it passes by the ruins of Alore, where it is crossed by a bridge, and thence continues to flow in the same direction until its water, in the dry season, is absorbed or evaporated in the desert of Eastern Sinde. In the lower part of its course, about lat. 25° 55′, long. 69° 16′, it is said to throw off during inundation a branch to the south-westward, bearing the name of Phuraun or Purani Deria, "the ancient river," and then, turning to the south-east, flows by the fort of Omercote. Lower down it joins the united stream of the Purana and the Goonee or Fulailee, and falls into the sea by the Koree mouth, after a course of nearly 400 miles. When the inundation of the Indus is at its height, the Narra generally carries a very large body of water. In 1826 it overspread the desert to a great extent, swept away part of the fortress of Omercote, though ninety miles from the main channel of the Indus, and forced its way to the sea by the Runn of Cutch, working for itself a passage through the Ullah-bund, a mound thrown up across its channel by the great earthquake of 1819. But during the low season of the Indus, the Narra ceases to be a stream, and this defect is about to be remedied by the excavation of a new channel in the vicinity of Roree, whereby a constant flow of water will be insured during the period when a supply is indispensable for purposes of irrigation. The project is in course of execution, the cost of which has been estimated at 47,780*l*.

NARRA (WESTERN), in Sinde, a great and important branch of the Indus. It separates from the western side of the river seven miles east of Larkhanna, in lat. 27° 29′, long. 68° 17′, and takes a southerly course, in a direction in a great measure parallel to the main stream. At its extremity, in lat. 26° 28′, long. 67° 45′, it expands into Lake Manchar. From the south-eastern part of this lake, the Arul, a navigable stream, flows, and discharges its water into the Indus. The direct distance from the place where the Narra divaricates from the Indus to the expansion into Lake Manchar is about seventy-six miles; but, measured along its very tortuous course, it will be found to be fully double that distance. The long narrow island, insulated by the Indus, the Narra, Lake Manchar, and the Arul, is one of the most fertile tracts in the world, very highly cultivated, and densely peopled. During the season of inundation, the Western Narra is preferred to the main channel of the Indus for the purposes of navigation, in consequence of the current being less violent. The word *Narra* signifies a snake in the vernacular language; and the name has, without doubt, been bestowed in consequence of the convolutions of the stream.

NARRAINPOOR.—A town in Hyderabad, or territory of the Nizam, 30 miles E.S.E. from Hyderabad, and 120 miles W.N.W. from Guntoor. Lat. 17° 10′, long. 78° 57′.

NARRAINPOOR.—A town in the recently lapsed state of Nagpoor or Berar, situate 169 miles S.E. from Nagpoor, and 120 miles E. by S. from Chanda. Lat. 19° 41′, long. 81° 13′.

NARRAMPATNUM.—A town in the hill zemindarry of Jeypoor, 26 miles S.W. by S. from Ryaguddah, and 82 miles N. from Vizagapatam. Lat. 18° 52′, long. 83° 15′.

NARRAMSIR.—A town in the native state of Cutch, situate on the Koree mouth of the Great Western Runn of Cutch, and 81 miles W.N.W. from Bhooj. Lat. 23° 40′, long. 68° 33′.

NARRAYUNGAUM. — A town in the British district of Poonah, presidency of Bombay, 44 miles N. by E. of Poonah. Lat. 19° 7′, long. 74° 2′.

NARROOKOLE.—A town in Guzerat, or dominions of the Guicowar, 32 miles E. by N. from Baroda, and 86 miles S.E. by E. from Ahmedabad. Lat. 22° 20′, long. 73° 43′.

NARSINGAH.—A town in the territory occupied by the independent hill tribes of Orissa, situate on the left bank of a small tributary of the Braminy river, and 57 miles W.N.W. from Cuttack. Lat. 20° 41′, long. 85° 5′.

NARSINGNUGUR.—A town in the British district of Tipperah, lieut.-gov. of Bengal, 39 miles N. by E. of Tipperah. Lat. 24°, long. 91° 17′.

NARSINGUR.—A town in the British district of Pooralia, lieut.-gov. of Bengal, 120 miles W. of Calcutta. Lat. 22° 34′, long. 86° 34′.

NARSINGURH, in the British district of Dumoh, Saugor and Nerbudda territory, lieut.-gov. of the N.W. Provinces, a town on the route from Saugor to Rewah, 43 miles E.N.E. of the former. Elevation above the sea 1,314 feet. Lat. 24°, long. 79° 27′.

NARSIPOOR.—A town in the Mysore, 39 miles N.W. from Seringapatam, and 86 miles N.E. from Cannanore. Lat. 12° 46′, long. 76° 17′.

NARSIPOOR.—A town in the British district of Rajahmundry, presidency of Madras, 48 miles S. of Rajahmundry. Lat. 16° 20′, long. 81° 47′.

NARWAR, or NERWAR, in the territory

of Gwalior, or possessions of the Scindia family, a town on the route from Calpee to Kotah, 152 miles S.W. of former, 169 N.E. of latter, and situate on the right bank of the river Sindh. It has probably much decayed since it came under the power of Scindia, but Tieffenthaler, describing its condition a century ago, states that it then contained many handsome and substantially-built houses of stone. A broad flight of stone stairs, 360 in number, leads to the fort commanding the town. The ascending way passes through three successive gates to a platform, containing the palace and many other fine buildings of stone. This area, a mile and a half in circumference, is surrounded by a massive rampart, with battlements, all built of squared stone. Within the inclosure are numerous wells and a great tank of squared stone, which yield a supply of water sufficient for a numerous garrison. The hill and some others contiguous to it contain abundance of magnetic iron-ore, which is smelted to a considerable extent. The Sindh, here a rapid stream rushing over a rocky bed, overflows to a great extent during the periodical rains, and causes swamps, which swarm with alligators and other aquatic reptiles. According to Ferishta, the fort was constructed in the middle of the thirteenth century, by Rajah Jahir Dew, a Kachwaha Rajpoot, and a powerful prince; as, according to the exaggerated account of this historian, he led 5,000 horse and 200,000 foot against Nasiruddin, sovereign of Delhi, who, having defeated this immense host with great slaughter, took the place, after a few months' siege. Previously, however, Narwar had long been the seat of the Kachwahas, whose rajah, Nal, migrating from Ayodha or Oude, founded, in A.D. 295, Nishida, on the site of the present Narwar; and in the beginning of the ninth century, the Kachwahas of Narwar are mentioned as marching to the defence of Chitor. It again came into the hands of the Rajpoots at the commencement of the fifteenth century, probably during the troubles resulting from the invasion of Tamerlane; and was, in 1506, taken from them by blockade, by Sikandar Lodi, sovereign of Delhi. It is described as a vast city, fourteen or fifteen miles in circumference; and the captor employed six months in destroying idols and their fanes and temples, and in erecting mosques; and ultimately surrounded the place with a rampart and other defences. Narwar appears to have again fallen into the hands of the Hindoos, as in A.D. 1792 it was in possession of a rajah infamous for rapine and bloodshed, who was soon after expelled by the Mahrattas. It appears to have been guaranteed to Doulut Rao Scindia by the treaty of Allahabad, in 1805. In 1844, Narwar, with its annexed territory, was assessed, by the government of Gwalior, at 2,25,000 rupees annually. Narwar is 44 miles S. of Gwalior, 108 S. of Agra, 210 S. of Delhi, 125 S.W. of Calpee, 800 N.W. of Calcutta, by Calpee. Lat. 25° 39′, long. 77° 58′.

NASAIRAH, in the Reechna Dooab division of the Punjab, a town situated 28 miles N.W. from the right bank of the Ravee, 32 miles N.W. by N. of the town of Lahore. Lat. 31° 55′, long. 73° 58′.

NASSICK, in the British collectorate of Ahmednuggur, presidency of Bombay, a city of high celebrity, situate on the Bombay and Agra trunk road, and regarded by the Brahmins as the peculiar seat of piety and learning. It contains a great number of ancient Brahminical temples and establishments, very flourishing under the Peishwa's sway, and still enjoying great advantages under British rule, though the government has entirely withdrawn from interference with the affairs of the native religious institutions. Nassick is more revered than even Benares; yet it appears to have been once a locality of Bhuddism. "Near Nasik, the very seat of Brahminism in the Deccan, are extensive Bhuddist excavations. They are vulgarly called Dhermraj-lena. They run round a conical hill, five miles from the town, and about 100 yards or more from the base of the hill. They have every character of Bhuddist excavations, without any trace of Hindooism: the long vaulted cave and Dagop, the huge figures of the meditative curly-head Buddh, the inscriptions in the unknown character, the umbrella and snake-headed canopies, the benched halls and numerous cells."

The population of Nassick is estimated at about 25,000. Distance direct from Poonah, N., 105 miles; from Bombay, N.W., 100. Lat. 20°, long. 73° 47′. The district, of which this town is the principal place, was formerly composed of certain subdivisions of the collectorate of Ahmednuggur, which in 1840 were consolidated into the sub-collectorate of Nassick.

NASSIRABAD, in the district of Salon, territory of Oude, a town 52 miles S.E. of Lucknow. Butter estimates the population at 3,000, three-fourths being Mussulmans. Lat. 26° 11′, long. 81° 35′.

NASSREEDA.—A town in the Rajpoot state of Jeypoor, 71 miles S.S.W. from Jeypoor, and 60 miles S.E. by E. from Ajmeer. Lat. 26°, long. 75° 30′.

NASUMON, in the Northern Punjab, situate on the right or north bank of the Chenaub, and on the great route from India to Cashmere, through the Bainhal Pass. It is a small place, remarkable only for one of those bridges of rude ropes, called in the country *jhoolas*, by which travellers pass the Chenaub, here about seventy or eighty yards wide. Nasumon is in lat. 33° 14′, long. 75° 5′.

NATCHENGUON.—A town in the recently lapsed dominions of Nagpore or Berar, situate on the left bank of the Wurda river, and 60 miles S.W. by W. from Nagpore. Lat. 20° 42′, long. 78° 22′.

NATHDWARA.—A town in the Rajpoot state of Oodeypoor or Meywar, 21 miles N. from Oodeypoor, and 73 miles W.N.W. from Neemuch. Lat. 24° 53′, long. 73° 51′.

NATHPORE, in the British district of Purnea, lieut.-gov. of Bengal, a town on the route from Dinapore to the town of Purnea, 152 miles S.E. of former, 50 N.W. of latter. It is situate on the right bank of the Kosee, here divided into three channels, each unfordable and crossed by ferry. There is considerable business here in the transit-trade from Nepal to Hindustan. The town consists of four market-places, having collectively about 1,600 houses, and, according to the usually admitted average of inmates, a population of 8,000 persons. Lat. 26° 18′, long. 87° 10′.

NATOOPALWUN.—A town in the British district of Rutnageriah, presidency of Bombay, 63 miles N. of Rutnageriah. Lat. 17° 54′, long. 73° 20′.

NATTORE, in the British district of Rajeshahye, lieut.-gov. of Bengal, a town on the route from Burhampoor to Jumalpoor, 78 miles N.E. of former, 105 S.W. of latter. It is situate on the river Nurud, an offset of the Ganges, communicating with the river Ataree. The situation is very low, unhealthy, and subject to inundation; and in consequence of those great disadvantages, the civil establishment of the district, formerly located here, was in 1822 removed to Bauleah. Distant N. from Calcutta, by Burhampoor, 196 miles. Lat. 24° 25′, long. 89°.

NAUCHTEEGAON.—A town in the British district of Silhet, lieut.-gov. of Bengal, 36 miles W.S.W. of Silhet. Lat. 24° 44′, long. 91° 20′.

NAUGAULAUNCHARY.—A town in the British district of Tinnevelly, presidency of Madras, 18 miles S. of Tinnevelly. Lat. 8° 28′, long. 77° 42′.

NAUGULWARREE.—A town of Malwa, in the native state of Indore, or territory of Holkar, 72 miles S.S.W. from Indore, and 105 miles N.E. by N. from Malligaum. Lat. 21° 44′, long. 75° 28′.

NAUGUMPILLY.—A town in the British district of Rajahmundry, presidency of Madras, 16 miles N. of Rajahmundry. Lat. 17° 13′, long. 81° 49′.

NAUGUTWARA.—A town of Malwa, in the native state of Jowra, situate on the right bank of the Chumbul river, and 15 miles N.E. from Jowra. Lat. 23° 46′, long. 75° 16′.

NAUN.—A town in the recently lapsed dominions of Nagpore or Berar, situate 35 miles S. by E. from Nagpore, and 118 miles E.S.E. from Ellichpoor. Lat. 20° 40′, long. 79° 19′.

NAUNDODE, in Guzerat, or dominions of the Guicowar, a town near the south bank of the river Nerbudda, at the northern base of the Rajpeepla hills. The surrounding country is rugged, wild, and ill cultivated, inhabited chiefly by Bheels and Coolies. Distance from Surat, N.E., 65 miles; Baroda, S.E., 35. Lat. 21° 52′, long. 73° 27′.

NAUNGAON.—A town in the recently lapsed dominions of Nagpoor or Berar, situate 125 miles E. from Nagpoor, and 118 miles S. from Ramgurh. Lat. 21° 8′, long. 81° 6′.

NAUSHAHAR.—See Nya Shuhur.

NAUTARAUPOLLIAM.—A town in the British district of Salem, presidency of Madras, 53 miles N.W. by N. of Salem. Lat. 12° 17′, long. 77° 47′.

NAUTPOOR.—A town in the British district of Chota Nagpoor, lieut.-gov. of Bengal, 39 miles S. of Lohadugga. Lat. 22° 52′, long. 84° 47′.

NAVOYCOLUM.—A town in the native state of Travancore, 23 miles N.N.W. from Trivandrum, and 61 miles W. from Tinnevelly. Lat. 8° 46′, long. 76° 50′.

NAWABGANJ, in the British district of Allahabad, a town four miles from the left bank of the Ganges, on the route from Allahabad to Lucknow, and 12 miles N.W. of the former. It has water from wells. Lat. 25° 34′, long. 81° 40′.

NAWABGUNJ, in the British district of Furruckabad, lieut.-gov. of the N.W. Provinces, a town on the route from the cantonment of Allygurh to that of Futtehgurh, and 16 miles N.W. of the latter. There is a bazar, and water is obtainable from wells. Lat. 27° 27′, long. 79° 28′.

NAWADA, or NOWABADA, in the British district of Behar, lieut.-gov. of Bengal, a village, the principal place of a thana or police division of the same name. It is a very beautiful country, and in many parts fertile, but much neglected and uncultivated, yet contains 897 villages, and a population estimated at 157,038, of whom the Brahminists are fifteen to one to the Mussulmans. Nawada is an insignificant place, having about 105 houses and 550 inhabitants. Distant from town of Behar, S., 20 miles; town of Patna, S.E., 50. Lat. 24° 54′, long. 85° 30′.

NAWAGARH, or KOT, in Bussahir, a fort on a ridge stretching in a south-easterly direction from the great range of Moral-kakanda. It is situate on a neck of land stretching from and under a high wooded and rocky peak which commands it. This post was, during the war with the Goorkhas, strengthened by two stockades on the side most easily accessible, and being garrisoned by a force of about 1,000 of that people, was their most important position in Bussahir. In the beginning of 1815, when the military operations of the British led the inhabitants of Bussahir to expect liberation from their Goorkha oppressors, Nawagarh was invested by the insurgent natives, and the garrison, under Kirti Rana, attempting to escape, was surrounded and obliged to surrender. There is probably no great difference between its elevation and that of Baji, situate three or four miles' distance on the same ridge, and being, according to Lloyd, 9,105 feet above the sea. Nawagarh is in lat. 31° 15′, long. 77° 40′.

NAWAUBGUNGE, in the territory of Oude, a town on the route from Lucknow cantonment to that of Sekrora, 19 miles N.E. of the former, 37 S.E. of the latter. It has a bazar, and water is plentiful. The road in this part of the route is good. Lat. 26° 57′, long. 81° 5′.

NAWULA-JO-GOTE, in Sinde, a village on the route from Sehwan to Larkhana, and 16 miles N. of the former town. It is inhabited by the cultivators of the adjacent fertile country. The road in this part of the route is straight and level, but not of easy transit for carriages, in consequence of neglect. Lat. 26° 35′, long. 67° 55′.

NAYAKOT.—A town in the native state of Nepal, situate on the right bank of the Naling river, and 78 miles W. by S. from Khatmandoo. Lat. 27° 32′, long. 84° 3′.

NAYAKOT.—A town in the native state of Nepal, 159 miles W. by N. from Khatmandoo, and 110 miles N.N.W. from Goruckpoor. Lat. 28° 10′, long. 82° 48′.

NEACOTE.—A town in the native state of Nepal, 33 miles S.S.W. from Jemlah, and 100 miles E. by N. from Pilleebheet. Lat. 28° 50′, long. 81° 30′.

NEALLA CONDAPULLY.—A town in Hyderabad, or territory of the Nizam, 106 miles E. from Hyderabad, and 62 miles N.N.W. from Guntoor. Lat. 17° 8′, long. 80° 8′.

NEAUNGSHEWAY.—A town of Burmah, 97 miles S.E. by S. from Ava, and 192 miles N.E. from Prome. Lat. 20° 54′, long. 97°.

NEBKHERA, in the British district of Boolundshuhur, lieut.-gov. of the N.W. Provinces, a village on the route from Muttra to Meerut, and 47 miles S. of the latter. Lat. 28° 22′, long. 77° 56′.

NECKLEY.—A town in the British district of Mymunsing, lieut.-gov. of Bengal, 199 miles N.E. by E. of Calcutta. Lat. 24° 19′, long. 90° 57′.

NEECHBO.—A town in the Rajpoot state of Jeypoor, 72 miles N.W. from Jeypoor, and 78 miles N. by E. from Ajmeer. Lat. 27° 34′, long. 74° 59′.

NEEDAPUTTEE, in the British district of Allahabad, lieut.-gov. of the N.W. Provinces, a village on the route from Allahabad cantonment to Futtehpore, and six miles W. of the former. Lat. 25° 28′, long. 81° 50′.

NEELGUDDIR.—A town in Hyderabad, or territory of the Nizam, situate on the right bank of the Godavery river, and 147 miles N.E. by E. from Hyderabad. Lat. 18° 36′, long. 80° 20′.

NEELGURH, in Orissa, one of the Cuttack mehals, is bounded on the north by the native state of Mohurbunge; on the east and south by the British district of Balasore; and on the west by the native state of Keunjur. It extends from lat. 21° 12′—21° 40′, long. 86° 13′—86° 52′; is 42 miles in length from north-east to south-west, and 22 in breadth. Neelgurh, the principal place, is 13 miles S.W. from Balasore. Lat. 21° 29′, long. 86° 48′.

NEELOO, in the Sinde Sagur Doab division of the Punjab, a town situated six miles N.W. from the right bank of the Jhelum, 116 miles N.W. by W. of the town of Lahore. Lat. 32° 34′, long. 72° 32′.

NEELUNGA.—A town in one of the recently sequestrated districts of Hyderabad, or territory of the Nizam, 126 miles W.N.W. from Hyderabad. Lat. 18° 8′, long. 76° 50′.

NEEMAJ.—A town in the Rajpoot state of Jodhpoor, 62 miles E. by S. from Jodhpoor, and 45 miles S.W. by W. from Ajmeer. Lat. 26° 9′, long. 74° 7′.

NEEMAWER.—See NEMAUR.

NEEMHERAH.—See NIMBERA.

NEEMRA, in Sinde, a village on the route from Larkhana to Bagh, and 44 miles N. of the former place. It is situate in a barren country on the south-eastern border of the *Runn* or arid desert of Shikarpoor. Lat. 28° 3′, long. 68° 14′.

NEEMRANEE, in the district of Tijarra, territory of Alwar, under the political management of the Governor-General's agent for Rajpootana, a small town on the summit of a rocky range of hills. Distance S.W. from Delhi 76 miles. Lat. 28°, long. 76° 19′.

NEEMREE, in the Rajpoot state of Jodhpoor, a village on the route from Nusseerabad to Nagor, and 23 miles S.E. of the latter. It contains sixty houses, supplied with water from two wells. Lat. 26° 57′, long. 74° 3′.

NEEM SURAE, in the British district of Allahabad, lieut.-gov. of the N.W. Provinces, a village on the route from the cantonment of Allahabad to Futtehpore, and seven miles N.W. of the former. Lat. 25° 27′, long. 81° 49′.

NEEMUCH, in the territory of Gwalior, or possessions of Scindia's family, a town with a British cantonment, on the north-western border of Malwa, and at a short distance from the boundary which separates that tract of country from Mewar. It has a good bazar. The British territory here was formerly limited to the site of the cantonments and some acres adjoining, and was sold very reluctantly by Dowlut Rao Scindia, as the space was required for stationing a force in 1817, according to the provisions of the treaty of Gwalior, concluded in that year. Consequent, however, on a later treaty, the country in the immediate vicinity, and some other districts, were annexed. Heber describes the cantonment in his time as "a stationary camp of thatched bungalows, and other buildings, open on all sides, and surrounded by a fine plain for the performance of military evolutions." Wallich, a later observer, gives the following account of it: "The cantonment extends on a slightly elevated ridge. running about north-west and south-east: its extreme length is two and a half miles, and extreme breadth one mile. The lines are placed in front, facing to the northward; the regimental officers' quarters behind these, and the Sudder Bazar and staff to the rear of all. Lines have at various periods been built, capable of containing one regiment of native cavalry, one troop of native horse-artillery, four regiments of native infantry, and a regiment of irregular horse." The bungalows or lodges of the officers are seventy or eighty in number, each surrounded by a garden; and as the soil, principally a disintegrated trap, is naturally fertile, it, by adequate irrigation, produces in abundance esculent vegetables, fruits, and flowers. There are here a small theatre, an assembly-room, and a spacious lecture-room. A small fort has been constructed by the British, as a place of refuge for the families of the military, when called to a distance on duty. It is at present used as a magazine. Here is a fine house, built by the late Sir David Ochterlony, whose principal quarters were for a considerable time here. It is now applied to purposes widely different from that for which it was erected. It furnishes a church, the medical storekeeper's office, and an executive engineer's godown. According to the opinion of Jacquemont, Neemuch is one of the healthiest places in the presidency of Bengal. This circumstance, if correctly ascertained, probably results from the nature of the surrounding country, a well-drained plain, studded with a few small stony hills. The winter is mildly cool; the hot winds, in the latter part of spring and early part of summer, moderate, as are the periodical rains succeeding them; and the average mortality is by no means considerable. An authority already quoted, gives, however, the following less favourable view:—"The climate of Neemuch is unquestionably an agreeable one, as far as sensible qualities are concerned. There exists neither the extreme of heat and cold experienced towards the north-western frontier; and the fall of temperature, following after sunset, is almost always sufficient to insure, relatively speaking, a cool night. In fact, the sultry and suffocating oppressiveness frequently felt in other parts of India, between sunset and sunrise, seldom occurs in this province. This is probably consequent on the influence of the sea-breeze extending higher from the Gulf of Cambay. Yet, notwithstanding these ostensible advantages, it cannot be deemed a really healthy climate. There are constitutions that do not suffer under its influence, and, of course, the proportion that these bear to the whole number subject to it is great; but there are many habits which it does affect, and that severely. It is to be remarked, that those on whom it has produced any disagreeable consequences, are seldom such as have been heedless of undue exposure, or addicted to a free style in living. On the contrary, the most abstemious and careful seem to suffer most frequently and severely. These remarks, I would have it understood, refer chiefly to the effects of the climate on European constitutions." In the following passage, the same writer enters more minutely into the peculiarities of the climate:—"The cold weather usually sets in about the beginning of November, but long before that period the evenings and mornings have become bracingly cool. From the end of September till that of October, the relative temperatures of the days and nights are very similar, or, in other words, the difference, for instance, at noon of a day in September and one in October varies generally but by a few degrees. It is during this species of interregnum that the climate is most unhealthy, owing, no doubt, to the effects of vegetable decomposition being in greatest activity, and the salutary influence of the approaching cold season hitherto unappreciable. Intermittent fevers, rheumatic fevers, and other inflammatory attacks, are now most prevalent. Hoar-frost is seldom discernible, and the lowest temperature usually attends strong easterly winds. Fires are scarcely necessary for comfort's sake. The months of December and January are delightfully cold. By the middle of February, or beginning of March, the midday sun becomes again too powerful for outdoor exercise, and a few days, in which a sudden rise of temperature has taken place, usher in the hot winds. The hot winds blow steadily during the day, or rather from about eight A.M. until sunset, rarely, if ever, continuing later: their direction is from the south or north-west. So long as the luxuries of a house and tattie are procurable, the temperature within-doors can be rendered not only bearable, but pleasant: this season is, unquestionably, the most healthy of the whole year. A few of the sultry days again make their appearance betwixt the termination of the hot winds and the commencement of the rains, which show themselves generally in the middle of June, and last till the middle of September. About the end of May, an inch or two of rain usually falls, and produces a pleasant break at the hottest season. In no part of India is the genial effect of the rainy season felt more both by the animal and vegetable world than it is here. Before its advent, not a blade of grass was to be seen, but every leaf and branch appeared parched up and withered. A few hours have only to elapse, however, after the first shower, when the whole country around presents one uninterrupted expanse of the most brilliant green, and each bough is covered with the most luxurious foliage; nor do the insect tribes appear ignorant of the new-born blessing, for ere the first heavy drops have reached the ground, as if by magic, thousands of winged creatures burst from their narrow tenements, and throng both earth and air. Thunderstorms and violent squalls from the north-east are frequent during the rains; in fact, the first fall is ushered in by a tremendous hurricane. Vegetation goes on increasing during the continuance of the wet weather, till, at last, every nook, and actually the very roads, become choked up with the excessive and dense herbage. The grass in the compounds springs up to the height of two or three feet, and requires to be cut down several times." The village of Neemuch occupies a rising ground, about three-quarters of a mile from the right of the cantonment: its population is roughly estimated at 4,000. It has no manufacture. Elevation above the sea 1,476 feet. Distant N.W. of Mow 155 miles; S.W. from Delhi 371; from Agra 312; W. of Saugor 306; W. of Calcutta, by Allahabad and Saugor, 1,114. Lat. 24° 27′, long. 74° 54′.

NEEPANEE.—A town in the British district of Belgaum, presidency of Bombay, 39 miles N. by W. of Belgaum. The jaghire of which this town is the principal place, lapsed to the British government in 1840, upon the demise of its native chief, and was annexed to the empire in 1842. In the following year, the fort was dismantled. Lat. 16° 23′, long. 74° 28′.

NEERA.—A river rising in lat. 18° 20′, long. 73° 36′, on the eastern slope of the Western Ghats, and flowing in an easterly direction for 130 miles, during which it forms the boundary between the British collectorate of Poona, the Sattara jaghires of Bore and Phultun, and the British province of Sattara, falls into the Beemah river, on the right side, in lat. 17° 58′, long. 75° 12′. A bridge has been thrown over the river in lat. 18° 6′, long. 74° 16′.

NEEWUJ, or NEWAZ, called also JAMNEERI, a river of Malwa, rises on the north side of the Vindhya range, and in lat. 22° 53′, long. 76° 28′. It holds a course generally northerly of 190 miles, and falls into the Kali Sindh, on the right side, in lat. 25° 7′, long. 76° 20′. At Bhopalpoor, about seventy miles from its source, and in lat. 23° 48′, long. 76° 46′, it is crossed, on the route from Neemuch to Saugor, by a ford, "which is 200 yards wide, rocky, and bad for cattle and carts; banks steep, and usual depth of water during the fair season one and a half feet."

NEGAPATAM, in the British district of Tanjore, presidency of Madras, a town on the western coast of the Bay of Bengal. Here is a diminutive estuary of the Cauvery, capable of receiving small coasting-vessels, which carry on a considerable trade, and measures have been recently authorized for the improvement of the harbour. It is situate on an open, level, sandy expanse, having a gentle slope to the sea, above which the town is elevated about three or four feet. There is a wide, open, and airy street in the east end of the town, and another parallel to it in the west; and these are connected by a third, communicating with the other two in the centre of each street. From those principal streets, others branch off, which are mere narrow confined lanes, especially in the part occupied by the Portuguese. The bazar consists of four streets at the south-east side, where various kinds of grains, vegetables, drugs, and piece-goods are exposed for sale. The houses in the principal streets are generally of quadrangular ground-plan, large, well built of brick and lime-mortar, and roofed with tiles; and those of the more respectable classes are clean and well ventilated. Besides this native town, the houses occupied by European residents, and by respectable Dutch and Portuguese families, are in an open, airy situation, to the westward of the town, facing the Esplanade, which intervenes between them and the sea. The ruins of the old Dutch fort are surrounded by a ditch, filled up in many places, in consequence of the pestilential exhalations arising from its stagnant putrescent water. The barracks for the small detachment of native infantry stationed here is an old Dutch dwelling-house, situated to the north-west of the Esplanade, on a dry sandy piece of ground. The jail is an old family residence, but lofty, spacious, and commodious, built of brick and lime-mortar. The inhabitants are generally industrious; but the irresistible effects of British competition confine their manufacturing industry to making coarse cotton and silk fabrics, and some few others for country use, and drawing oil from cocoa-nuts and oil-seeds; and this branch of industry is lucrative and extensive. They also have considerable traffic with Ceylon, and the lands and islands lying eastward. It is "estimated to contain a population of 10,000 souls. A large proportion of these are the descendants of the original Dutch and Portuguese colonists, by whom this place was formerly occupied; the remainder is made up of Hindoos, Mussulmans, and Brahmins." A government school has been established in the town, and the last annual report of the progress of the pupils was considered highly satisfactory. A project for connecting this town with that of Trichinopoly, a distance of eighty miles, by means of a low-speed railway, is under consideration. Distance from Madura, N.E., 133 miles; Tanjore, E., 48; Madras, S., 160; Bangalore, S.E., 214. Lat. 10° 46′, long. 79° 54′.

NEGAWAN.—See NYGOWAN.

NEGOHEE, in the British district of Shahjehanpoor, lieut.-gov. of the N.W. Provinces, a town on the route from Shahjehanpoor to Pilleebheet, 17 miles N. by W. of the former. Lat. 28° 8′, long. 79° 55′.

NEGOOG.—A town in the British district of Ahmednuggur, presidency of Bombay, 32 miles W.S.W. of Ahmednuggur. Lat. 18° 59′, long. 74° 19′.

NEGRAIS, in Eastern India, a British

island at the mouth of the Negrais or Bassein river, rendered conspicuous by a hill forming the easternmost high land on the coast. The circumference of the island is about eighteen miles, and its area ten square miles. Water is plentiful, found at the depth of three or four cubits, and of good quality. In 1836, the population consisted of about fifty families. Arrangements for founding a new city on this island are rapidly progressing. Lat. 15° 58′, long. 94° 24′.

NEGRAIS CAPE, in Eastern India, the name given to the south-west extremity of the coast of Pegu. It is in contemplation to erect a lighthouse here, as a dangerous reef runs out four or five miles into the sea; and the furthest point of the reef will be its site. Lat. 16° 2′, long. 94° 16′.

NEGRAIS RIVER.—The name of one of the mouths of the Irawady, which, in the upper part of its course, takes the name of the Bassein river, from a town of that name situate on its left bank. The mouth is in lat. 15° 55′, long. 94° 25′.

NEHTOUR, in the British district of Bijnour, lieut.-gov. of the N.W. Provinces, a town on the route from Bijnour to Pilleebheet, 15 miles E. by S. of the former. Nehtour has a population of 7,587 inhabitants. Lat. 29° 19′, long. 78° 26′.

NEILGHERRIES.—A talook of the British collectorate of Coimbatore, presidency of Madras, deriving its name from the Neilgherry group of mountains. This remarkable range, situate between lat. 11° 10′—11° 35′, long. 76° 30′—77° 10′, is connected on its western side, where its summits bear the name of the Koondahs, with the Siadri branch of the Western Ghats, which here terminates in a southern face of lofty and nearly perpendicular precipices, forming the north side of the great Palghat valley or depression, which, extending east and west, with a breadth of about twenty miles, admits of an easy communication between the Carnatic and Malabar. The general outline of the Neilgherry group approaches to a scalene triangle, having the side which may be regarded as the base extending nearly from north to south, and facing Malabar; its north side extending east and west, facing Mysore; and the remaining side extending from north-east to south-west, towards the British district Coimbatore, of which it forms a subdivision. "Their greatest extent in an oblique direction from south-west to north-east is from thirty-eight to forty miles, and their extreme breadth fifteen. Taking into account the great undulation of the surface, and the circumstance of the breadth above stated being pretty constant throughout, their superficial extent may be fairly estimated at from 600 to 700 square miles." The north side, towards Mysore, rises about 3,500 feet above that table-land, with which it is connected by a neck about fifteen miles in width. The isolation of this mountain territory would be complete, but for this singular, sharp, and precipitous ridge of granite peaks, which projects from the base of a remarkable cone called Yellamullay, on the western crest of the range, and, taking a west by north course, towards the coast, unites itself with the Western Ghauts. From Coimbatore the Neilgherries rise in a vast precipitous mass to the height of from 5,000 to 7,000 feet; and the aggregate of the group is popularly divided into three ranges,—the Neddimulla on the north, the Koondah on the south-west, and the central or principal range, rising to the summit of Dodabetta, the highest in the group, and having an elevation of 8,760 feet above the sea, being the greatest at present ascertained in India south of the Himalaya. The drainage, which is in every variety of direction, indicates the surface of the group to be an undulating table-land, rising towards the middle, and attaining its maximum of elevation at Dodabetta. To the westward, the drainage is into the Indian Ocean, by the river of Beypoor; to the south and south-east, it is by numerous streams, feeders of the Bowany, a considerable river, which, flowing north-east, falls into the Cavery; to the north, it is by the Paikari and other feeders of the Mayar, which, flowing east down the great gorge separating this group from Mysore, unites itself, near Danaikencotta, with the Bowany, and ultimately falls into the Cavery.

The Neilgherries rise from a plain nearly as level as the Carnatic. The following are the principal elevations as yet ascertained:—Dodabetta, 8,760 feet; Kudiakad, 8,502; Bevoybeta, 8,488; Murkurti Peak, 8,402; Davursolabetta, 8,380; Kundah Peak, 8,353; Kundamoya, 7,816; Ootacamund, 7,361; Tamburbetta, 7,292; Hokulbeta, 7,267; Urbeta, 6,915; Kodanad, 6,815; Davebeta, 6,571; Kotagiri, 6,571; Kundabeta, 6,555; Dimhutty, 6,330; Coonoor, 5,886. There is no natural lake in the group, but advantage has been taken of the streams which flow from the hills in the vicinity of Ootacamund, to form there an artificial one of considerable dimensions.

The Neilgherries, for the most part, are by no means densely wooded, the forests occurring in distinct and singularly isolated patches, in hollows, on slopes, and sometimes on the very apex of a lofty hill, becoming luxuriant and extensive only when they approach the crests of the mountains, and run along the valleys into the plains below. This comparative absence of forest in a region in which, from its position between the tropics, from the abundance of moisture, and from the great depth and richness of the soil, the utmost luxuriance in this respect would be looked for, is very remarkable, and leads to the conclusion that vast tracts of primeval forest-land must at some period have been cleared to make room for cultivation.

Elephants are numerous in the jungles at the base of the hills, but are not to be met with on the table-land, where probably the animal would find the climate too cool. The tiger infests the hills, but is less ferocious than in the plains. The cheta or hunting-leopard exists here, as well as the jackal, the wild dog, the marten, the polecat, the wild hog, the bear, the samber, a sort of large deer; as do also the muntjak and a species of ibex (Capra caucasia). Hares are numerous, as are porcupines; otters infest the streams. Jungle-fowl, or wild gallinaceous poultry, are abundant, as likewise are quails; but partridges are rather rare. There are woodcocks, snipes, pigeons of several kinds, blackbirds, thrushes, wrens, larks, and kingfishers. Of predatory birds, there are found a large eagle, an enormous horned owl, a great number and variety of hawks, of which two kinds are peculiarly beautiful, one being milk-white, except on its back, where there is a large black mark between the wings; the other is cream-colour. Venomous snakes are not common, and scorpions and centipedes are altogether unknown. The area of the Neilgherry group, though circumscribed in extent, is inhabited by five distinct races, who, however, in the aggregate, are numerically insignificant. 1st. Erulars, living at the foot of the mountains, and for a short distance in the forests, which extend from the base into the plains; 2ndly, above them dwell the Kurumbars. People answering the general description of these two tribes are to be met with in other mountainous parts of the peninsula of India; but the Erulars of this vicinity differ from them in many particulars; and the Kurumbars, from their connection with the tribes who inhabit the more elevated parts of the mountains, are now quite distinct from the people bearing this name in other parts of the country. Both tribes are utterly unskilled in the arts of life, and little raised above the condition of savages. They speak a jargon compounded of the dialects of the people in their vicinity. The total number of each of these tribes does not exceed 1,000. 3. Kohatars. They are a strange race, have no distinction of caste, and differ as much from the other tribes of the mountains as they do from all other natives of India. They exercise the callings of goldsmiths, silversmiths, blacksmiths, potters, and other handicrafts; being the only persons who follow such pursuits in these mountains. Rejecting the Brahminical traditions, doctrines, and observances, they worship peculiar imaginary divinities, not represented by any visible objects. Their number is about 2,000. 4. Burghers; the most numerous, wealthy, and civilized of the natives of these mountains. They are Brahminists, and divided into eight classes, all worshippers of Siva, and principally using the Carnatic language. They support themselves mainly by agriculture, and are by far the most numerous of the mountaineers, being about 10,000. 5. The Todars, or, as they are more commonly denominated, Toruwars, who are divided into two branches, or two great families, one called Perkis or Terallis, and who are competent to hold all sacred offices; the other, Kutas, who are competent only to hold minor ones within their own families, and who may be considered as the lay class. Until within a few years, the two classes never intermarried; but such connections between them are now of frequent occurrence. The petty tribe of Todars, not exceeding 600 in number, appear to have attracted the notice of European visitors in no ordinary degree. They are described as a well-made athletic race, generally above the middle stature, and displaying a bold, manly carriage. Their physiognomical characteristics are said to be a full expressive eye, a Roman nose, and a countenance habitually grave, but readily relaxing into cheerfulness. The dress of the men consists of a short under-garment girt round, and large upper mantle, or perhaps, to style it more properly, a sort of blanket, which envelops the person, except the head, legs, and right arm, and affords covering both by night and day. They wear no sandals nor other protection for the feet, and carry no weapons, merely bearing in the right hand a small stick, for driving cattle. They usually wear rings in the ears and on the fingers, and a gold chain round the neck. The women are of a stature proportionate to that of the men, and of fairer complexions, with regular features, and beautiful long black tresses flowing luxuriantly over their shoulders. Their demeanour is stated to be modest, but self-possessed, and free from servility. Their ornaments consist of armlets of brass, worn above the elbow, silver bracelets on the wrists, and rings of various kinds on the fingers and thumbs, a zone round the waist, of chain-work, either silver or brass; and necklaces of silver or braided hair, having cowry-shells suspended from them. Those remarkable people dwell in small hamlets, called morts, consisting of a few thatched cottages, in appearance somewhat resembling the tilt of a waggon.

Owing to the great elevation of the inhabited summits of the Neilgherries, and the consequent rarefaction of its atmosphere, aided, without doubt, in some degree by the beneficial influence of the luxuriant vegetation which clothes the land, the district, although distant only eleven degrees from the equator, enjoys a climate famed for its great salubrity and remarkable evenness of its seasons; the temperature, which falls in the coldest month of the year to the freezing-point, seldom, in the hottest, reaches 75° in the shade. The coldest period is during the months of December and January, and the hottest about April and May, though this latter season is not so certain, as it mainly depends upon the character of the south-west monsoon, and the time of its setting in. The hottest period of the day is from two to half-past two P.M., and the average of the extreme ranges of temperature from sunrise to that time is most commonly 16° throughout the year. The variation is the greatest in January and December, when the extreme radiation which goes on during clear nights produces excessive cold towards sunrise, after which the sun's rays, darting with great fierceness through the rarefied atmosphere, speedily restore heat to the earth, and the temperature of the air rises in proportion. Similar causes reversed in their action necessarily produce sudden and great cold after sunset. An observatory has been erected at Dodabetta. The following table shows the average temperature, fall of rain, and other particulars, throughout the year 1847, on the Neilgherry Hills :—

At OOTACAMUND, 7,300 feet above the level of the sea.

MONTH.	Mean Temperature.			Mean range of Therm.	Rain in Inches.
	At Sunrise.	At 2h. 40m. P.M.	At Sunset.	Sunrise to Sunset.	
January....	42°	63°	58°	21°	1″
February .	44	65	60	21	1
March	49	68	63	19	2
April	54	68	63	14	5
May	54	68	63	14	6
June	53	64	59	11	8
July	52	62	57	10	7
August	52	62	57	10	6
September..	52	62	56	10	7
October	51	62	56	11	9
November..	49	61	55	12	5
December ..	45	60	55	15	3
	Total inches of rain				60

At KOTERGHERRY, 6,100 feet above the level of the sea.

MONTH.	Mean Temperature.			Mean range of Therm.	Rain in Inches.
	At Sunrise.	At 2h. 40m. P.M.	At Sunset.	Sunrise to Sunset.	
January....	51·5°	66°	60°	15°	2″
February ..	52·5	67	63	15	3
March	54	67	63	13	6
April	56	68	64	12	10
May	56·5	68	64	12	2
June	58	69	65	11	2
July	60	70	65	10	4
August	60	71	65	11	2
September..	59	69	64	10	2
October	56	68	63·5	12	10
November..	54	67	61	13	2
December ..	52	66	60	14	5
	Total inches of rain				50

During the prevalence of the south-west monsoon, the atmosphere is almost continuously charged more or less with dense mist, enveloping chiefly the mountain-tops, but descending into the valleys as the warmth of the day passes, and spreading in heavy fog in all directions. When not under this influence, the atmosphere overhanging the mountains is brilliantly clear and cloudless, more especially on the eastern side of the range. The great importance of this group is its adaptation for the establishment of sanatory stations for the re-establishment of health in those who have suffered from the heat of the climate in less-elevated regions. The principal of these stations is Ootacamund, the two minor ones Coonoor and Kotageri.

The number of sick visitors on the Neilgherries from 1840 to 1844 were as follows :—1840, 284 ; 1841, 391 ; 1842, 489 ; 1843, 742 ; 1844, 820. In the year 1845 it became reduced to 571 ; in 1846 it rose to 742. Among the whole number of visitors (1,313) in the two years (1845 and 1846), it is stated that only two deaths occurred ; a very favourable rate of mortality, as compared with the year 1843, in which the deaths were in the proportion of 1¾ per cent. upon the whole number, and favourable even as compared with 1844, when the proportion had diminished to one per cent. The Medical Board hereupon observe : "The climate of the Neilgherries may therefore be confidently pronounced to have maintained its character for salubrity in the case of Europeans suffering from the effects of a tropical climate, when disease has not occasioned organic lesion of any of the important viscera." The results of later years fully support the accuracy of this view.

The Neilgherry district communicates with the neighbouring provinces by means of six passes or ghauts, the roads in which have been cut and kept in repair at the public expense. The only one of these passes which is ascended throughout by wheeled conveyances, is that of "Seegoor," the modes of transit on the others being by bullocks, coolies, and, to a small extent, by asses. By the "Seegoor" Ghaut, however, cartloads of 1,000 pounds weight are brought up, an additional pair of bullocks being required to help the cart over the steepest part of the ascent. By this pass the communication is kept up with Bangalore, Madras, and all places to the northward. The pass from Neddiwuttum to Goodaloor forms the communication between the hills and Cannanore, Tellicherry, and the western coast towards Bombay, through the Wynaad country. Another pass is at Kotergherry, communicating with Matepolliem, in the low country, and thence to Coimbatore and the Salem road. A fourth, at Coonoor, leading down to Matepolliem, the lower half being well constructed, can be ascended by laden carts having an extra pair of bullocks. The Mailoor or Soondaputty Ghaut has gone out of general use, and the remaining one, the Sispara or Koondah Ghaut, forms the line of communication between Calicut and the hills. The delineation of the district having been inaccurately mapped, a re-survey has been authorized. This territory was transferred to the British on the overthrow of Tippoo Sultan.

NEIR.—A town in one of the recently sequestrated districts of Hyderabad, or territory of the Nizam, 58 miles S.S.E. from Ellichpoor. Lat. 20° 26′, long. 77° 58′.

NEIR.—A town in the British district of Khandeish, presidency of Bombay, 26 miles N. of Malligaum. Lat. 20° 55′, long. 74° 30′.

NEJ NUDDEE, a river of Malwa, rises in lat. 25° 20′, long. 75° 17′, in the native state of Marwar, and, flowing easterly through Boondee for 100 miles, falls into the Chumbul, in lat. 25° 36′, long. 76° 25′.

NELGOONDAH, in Hyderabad, or territory of the Nizam, a town, the principal place of a district of the same name, situate at the northern base of a granite hill, on the summit of which, about 1,000 feet above the plain, the fortress is erected. Distance from the city of Hyderabad, S.E., 55 miles. Lat. 17° 3′, long. 79° 20′.

NELGOONDLA.—A town in Hyderabad, or territory of the Nizam, situate 11 miles N. from the left bank of the Kistnah river, and 80 miles S.W. from Hyderabad. Lat. 16° 31′, long. 77° 43′.

NELLACOTTAH.—A town in the British district of Madura, presidency of Madras, 28 miles N.W. of Madura. Lat. 10° 11′, long. 77° 54′.

NELLAMUNGLUM. — A town in the Mysore, 68 miles N.E. from Seringapatam, and 17 miles N.W. by W. from Bangalore. Lat. 13° 7′, long. 77° 28′.

NELLIAH.—A town in the native state of Cutch, 54 miles W. from Bhooj, and 113 miles S.E. by S. from Tatta. Lat. 23° 20′, long. 68° 53′.

NELLIALIAM.—A town in the British district of Malabar, presidency of Madras, 70 miles E.S.E. of Cannanore. Lat. 11° 31′, long. 76° 24′.

NELLORE.—A British district under the presidency of Madras, named from its principal place. It is bounded on the north by the British district of Guntoor; on the east by the Bay of Bengal; on the south by the northern division of Arcot; and on the west by the British district of Cuddapah. It lies between lat. 13° 55′ and 16°, long. 79° 8′ and 80° 21′: the area, according to official return, is 7,930 square miles. The general aspect of the coast is that of a sandy plain, with large tracts of jungle, interspersed with cocoanut-trees and palmyras. The country inland is more hilly, and also more fertile, but few eminences have an elevation exceeding 400 feet above the level of the sea. The principal river is the Northern Pennair or Penna, which, rising in the hills of Nundydroog, in Mysore, sweeps first northward, subsequently eastward, and about 285 miles from its source enters this district, through which it holds its course for seventy miles, to its fall into the Bay of Bengal, eighteen miles below the town of Nellore. In the lower part of its course its bed is sandy, but higher up rocky, with many deep pools well stocked with fish, which being swept down the stream during inundations, find their way into the numerous extensive tanks supplied by the river, and form a considerable portion of the diet of the people of this district. For nine months annually, the bed is in most places nearly dry, but during the north-east monsoon, prevailing at the close of the year, it in a few days becomes filled from bank to bank; and at the town of Nellore the volume of water is then 500 yards wide and thirty feet deep. The Soornamookey, the river next in size to the Pennair, rises in the Eastern Ghats, and, flowing eastward, holds a course nearly parallel to the Pennair, but veering more to the north-east, and after a course of about fifteen miles through this district, it falls into the Bay of Bengal. It is completely dry during the greater part of the year, but in the rainy season has a large volume of water, which is drawn off by numerous channels to replenish the tanks, great numbers of which exist in the level part of this district.

The climate of Nellore is in general dry and salubrious, being subject to no sudden changes of temperature. The prevailing winds during the months of January and February are north-easterly; during March and April, north-easterly and south-easterly; in May and June, south-easterly and south-westerly; in July and August, south-easterly and north-westerly; in September and October, the direction of the wind is continually varying; and in November and December it blows steadily from the north-east. The fall of rain during the year is from thirty to forty inches, and it takes place partly during the south-west monsoon in August and September, but chiefly in October, November, and December, under the north-east monsoon. Not more than half the district is believed to be cultivated, the remainder being either irreclaimably barren or overrun with jungle. The southern and eastern parts produce much rice in the vicinity of the tanks and streams, but in the western part the produce consists of what are called dry crops; such as millet of several kinds, ragi (Eleusine coracana), gram (Cicer arietinum), the castor and some other oil-plants. Tobacco is grown in considerable quantities, as are also indigo and some other plants yielding dyes. Cotton is to a small extent produced; but the soil is not considered favourable to it, and its culture is disliked by the agricultural population. In parts of the district are mines of iron and copper ore: the latter, said to have been worked by the natives from a remote period, were until recently regarded, on the strength of appearance, as containing very rich ores in inexhaustible abundance. Experience, however, has not confirmed the accuracy of this view. In 1834 leases of the copper-mines and other privileges were granted to certain individuals, who were prepared to investigate and render available the supposed mineral riches of the district; subsequently, a private association was formed for prosecuting the same object under a regular system; but in 1841 the operations resulted in disappointment.

The population is given under the article MADRAS. The language spoken in the district is the Teloogoo. The general occupation of the people is agriculture, though weaving is carried on to considerable extent. Culinary salt is extracted either from the soil or from sea-water, in large quantities. Rice is the staple article of diet with those who can afford it, but the ordinary food of the working classes is cholum (Holcus sorghum) and ragi (Eleusine coracana). The Yanadis, a wild race lurking in the woods and jungles, use a great variety of roots, fruits, and leaves as articles of diet; and hence they have suffered less in times of famine than the more civilized portion of the population.

The great road from Madras to the Northern Circars, and through them to Calcutta, runs through the whole length of this district from south to north: its course, which is nearly that of a straight line, lies at a short distance from the coast, and over a plain but slightly elevated above the level of the sea. Throughout the greater part of its extent, it is a causeway artificially raised three or four feet above the general level of the country. During the periodical rains, considerable portions are washed away by the force of the water collecting in the west, or landward of it, notwithstanding numerous outlets for its drainage into the sea. The arches for this latter purpose have been frequently burst by the pressure of water from beneath, but the recurrence of this evil has been guarded against by substituting, in place of the destroyed channels, cylindrical tubes of solid masonry. At Ongole, near the northern frontier, the road is divided into two branches, one proceeding north-east to Masulipatam, the other north-west to Hyderabad, the capital of the Nizam's territory. There are no other routes of importance. Nellore, the capital, and Ongole, the only place worth notice in the district, will be found under their respective names in the alphabetical arrangement. Nellore was transferred to the East-India Company, under the treaty with the nabob of Arcot of 1801, vesting in them the civil and military administration of the Carnatic.

NELLORE, the principal place of the British district of the same name, presidency of Madras, is situate on the right bank of the Northern Pennair or Penna river, and eighteen miles from the place where it falls into the Bay of Bengal. "The town is irregularly built, and in places rather crowded and confined; but there are some good streets occupied by the better classes, and on the whole, for a native town, it is tolerably clean and airy." The site of the town is slightly elevated above the surrounding country, which has a red lateritious soil. To the west of the town is a very extensive tank filled with water from the river. The place was formerly defended by a rampart, which has been allowed to fall into ruins, and the fort, once of considerable importance, is in the same condition. Nellore is not a military station, but it is the seat of the civil establishment of the district. The population of the town is estimated at about 20,000. Distance from Bellary, E., 210 miles; Cuddapah, 80; from Bangalore, N.E., 190; Arcot, N., 120; Madras, N., 100. Lat. 14° 27′, long. 80° 2′.

NEMAUR, or NIMAWAR.—A district of Western India, apparently denominated from the town of the same name. It comprises a large portion of the valley of the Nerbudda and of the Vindhya Mountains, inclosing it on the north, and the Satpoora, inclosing it on the south. The limits are laid down in a recent publication as between lat. 21° 28′—22° 25′, long. 74° 48′—76° 45′. Malcolm estimates its length from east to west at 130 miles, its general breadth at from thirty to forty, though in the middle it is about seventy. The area has been estimated at 2,225 square miles. Its western extremity is at the Hiru Pahl, where the Vindhya and Satpoora ranges, in the vicinity of Burwani, approach the banks of the river. The elevation of the lowest part of the valley, or of the course of the Nerbudda through this district, is considerable, being at Mundlesir, situate about equidistant from either extremity, 700 feet above the sea. The navigation of the Nerbudda is, with some intermission, practicable throughout the valley, though much risk and difficulty are occasioned by the great rapidity of the stream and the numerous and steep rocks in its channel.

The relative density of the population has been estimated at thirty-five to the square mile, and the aggregate amount at about 250,000 persons. The proportion in the British part of the district, estimated to comprehend an area of 269 square miles, is much higher, being at a rate exceeding 164 per mile. The gross population in this portion (the British), as ascertained by a recent census, is 25,727, almost entirely composed of Hindoos; 11,299 of whom are set down as agricultural, and 13,965 as non-agricultural. The Mahomedans, and others not Hindoo, amount to only fifty-five agricultural, and 408 non-agricultural. In the remaining portion, nominally under Mahratta rule, but actually managed by the Anglo-Indian government, comprising by estimate 1,956 square miles, the average is upwards of seventy-one persons per mile, the total number being 90,795; of whom 35,792 are Hindoos engaged in agriculture, 49,991 Hindoos following other pursuits, 967 Mahomedans and others agricultural, and 4,045 non-agricultural. It is hence obvious, that those parts of Nemaur which are under British management are by far the most prosperous. The population for the most part consists of Hindoos, intermixed with Mussulmans, Ghoonds, and Bheels; of which latter there is said to be a considerable number. The Bheels, considered a remnant of the aboriginal population, are a wild and lawless race, living, when left to themselves, principally on the spontaneous produce of the soil, such as wild fruits and roots, eked out with game, generally obtained by archery, a

Bheel being seldom seen without bow and arrows. They are mongrel professors of Brahminism, seeking to propitiate the inferior Brahminical deities by sacrifices and offerings; but they neither construct nor frequent any temples, performing their simple rites under the shade of trees. The Barwars, a sort of pretenders to sorcery, appear to be the only persons among them regarded in any respect in the capacity of priests. Previously to the powerful coercion exercised by the British government, they were notorious plunderers, and many still lurk among the nearly impenetrable fastnesses, and subsist in a great degree on the cattle which they steal. They do not, however, appear to be irreclaimable, some having been trained to render good service in the capacity of police.

Nemaur is parcelled out among various possessors, whose respective tracts are in many instances so intermingled, that any attempt here to make their situation and relative position intelligible must be abortive. Beside the British possessions, it comprises territory belonging to Scindia, to Holkar, to the rajah of Dhar, and other chiefs of less importance. The confusion is increased by the fact of a portion of the native territory being under the management of the British government. The interests of that government are intrusted to the care of a political agent stationed at Mundlesir, who is subject to the authority of the resident at Indore.

NEMAUR, or NIMAWAR.—A town situate on the right bank of the Nerbudda (here 1,000 yards wide), and on the route from Baitool to Mhow, being distant 90 miles N.W. from the former, and 95 E. of the latter. It is the chief place of the pergunnah of the same name; and probably the district of Nemaur also derives from it the appellation by which it is known. It is stated by Malcolm to belong to the family of Holkar. Distant 365 miles N.E. of Bombay, 90 S.E. of Oojein. Lat. 22° 27′, long. 76° 58′.

NENKUR, in Sinde, a village on the route from Sehwan to Larkhana, and five miles N. of the former town. It is situate two miles west of a large offset from the Indus, and four miles west of the main channel. The surrounding country is level, alluvial, and fertile, but little cultivated. The neglect of cultivation is more especially remarkable towards the Indus, in which direction the land is, for the most part, overrun with jungle. Lat. 26° 27′, long. 67° 54′.

NEO DHOORA or GHAT, in the British district of Kumaon, lieut.-gov. of the N.W. Provinces, a pass into Hiundes or South-western Thibet, at the head of the Dhouli river, in the mahall of Dharma. It is much frequented by the Bhotias of Dharma, who carry on a brisk trade with Hiundes by means of great flocks and herds of sheep and goats, which they drive before them, laden with grain from Lower Kumaon, broad-cloth, cottons, hardware, and other goods from Hindustan; and bringing back in return culinary salt, gold-dust, borax, wool, and some other goods of less importance. Though the pass is among summits inferior in height to the main range of the Himalaya farther south, it still has considerable elevation, probably not less than 15,000 feet above the sea. Lat. 30° 29′, long. 80° 37′.

NEPAUL, an independent kingdom of Northern India, bounded on the north by Thibet; on the east by Sikkim and the British territory of Darjeeling; on the south by the British districts of Purneah, Tirhoot, Sarun, and Goruckpore; on the south-west by Oude; and on the west by the British district of Kumaon. It extends from lat. 26° 25′ to 30° 17′, and from long. 80° 15′ to 88° 15′; is 500 miles in length from east to west, and 160 in breadth, and contains an area of 54,500 square miles. The principal territorial divisions are Moorung, Chayanpoor, Muckwanee, Khatang, Nepaul, Gorkha, Khachi, and Malebum.

Throughout their southern border, from the river Kalee on the western frontier, to the banks of the Mahanunda on the eastern boundary, the territories of Nepaul are skirted by the Terai, a long narrow strip of land separating them from the Bengal provinces, and from Oude. Ten miles from the frontier commences the great forest of Nepaul, following the same direction as the Terai, possessing an average breadth of from eight to ten miles; and though much overrun in parts with underwood, yet containing a great variety of noble trees; among the chief of which may be enumerated the saul, sissoo, Phullamikhd (iron-wood), kalekaht (a sort of blackwood), the sajh, bhurra, sumni, and multa. The ebony is also found here. Beyond this, in a northerly direction, lies a hilly tract of country, which again is succeeded by two others of increasing elevation, the first of which may be denominated the mountainous, and the second the Alpine region of Nepaul, with its lofty peaks of Dhoulagiri, Gossainthan, Mount Everest, and Kinchinjunga. Full particulars of the nature and character of the Terai will be found under the article KUMAON. The hilly tract, the geological formation of which consists of limestone, hornstone, and conglomerate, rises gradually towards the north, and is traversed by many small rivers having their origin on the southern faces of the first lofty mountains, to which these hills gradually approach. Interposed, as already intimated, between the hills and the Alpine region (some notice of which latter appears in the article HIMALAYAS), is the mountainous region, having a breadth of from thirty to forty miles, consisting of one mountain heaped on another, and rising to a great height, so that when any fall happens in winter, their tops are for a short time covered with snow. The whole of this division is well watered by streams and springs, and the vegetable productions are of most remarkable stateliness, beauty, and variety. It is diversified by several inhabited valleys, varying in elevation from 3,000 to 6,000 feet above the plains of Bengal, and contains Nepaul proper, within which is situated the great valley of Nepaul, with its towns of Khatmandoo, Patn, and Bhatgong. Khatmandoo, the capital, was built by the Ghoorkas, and is comparatively modern: the old Newar town (the Newars being the original inhabitants) is Patn. According to Kirkpatrick, the valley of Nepaul, on all sides surrounded by hills, is "nearly of an oval figure; its greatest extent is from north to south, in which direction it may be computed at twelve horizontal miles. It stretches from east to west about nine miles, and its circuit is roughly estimated by the inhabitants at twenty-five coss, or from forty to fifty miles. It is bounded on the north and south by very stupendous mountains, near the foot of which rise several of those humbler eminences called collines in Switzerland; indeed the bottom of the valley, besides being in general extremely uneven and intersected by deep ravines, occasioned by autumnal inundations, is speckled throughout at various distances with similar little hills. To the east and west the inclosing mountains are much less lofty, the immediate head of the valley to the westward being defined principally by a low steep ridge covered with brushwood, and anciently called Maroor, but at present most commonly Naga-Arjoon, from the name of an idol for which it is famous. This ridge passes close behind Sumbhoo-Nath, and is itself backed by a more considerable one named Dhochoak. To the eastward, the most remarkable hills are those of Ranichoak and Mahabut, or Mahadeopokhra; but they by no means reach the elevation either of Phalchoak (which is the most towering of the summits that illustrate the southern confine of the valley), or of Sheopoori, which constitutes its principal barrier to the northward, and is unquestionably by far the highest of all the mountains that encircle it. The other chief links of this superb chain are Mount Kukunni, which stretches westerly from Sheopoori, being united to Naga-Arjoon by Mount Bheerbundy and Chumpabaidi, which, with one or two more inferior peaks, complete the girdle by joining Chandraghiri to Phalchoak." Viewed from Chanudraghiri, the scene is thus described by the same writer:—"From hence the eye not only expatiates on the waving valley of Nepaul, beautifully and thickly dotted with villages, and abundantly chequered with rich fields, fertilized by numerous meandering streams, but also embraces on every side a wide expanse of charming and diversified country. It is the landscape in front, however, that most powerfully attracts the attention; the scenery in this direction rising to an amphitheatre, and exhibiting to the delighted view the cities and numberless temples of the valley below, and stupendous mountain of Sheopoori; the still supertowering Jib Jibea, clothed to its snow-capped peak with pendulous forests; and finally the gigantic Himaleh, forming the majestic background to this wonderful and sublime picture."

Hindoo records describe the valley of Nepaul as originally an immense lake, which in the progress of time gradually retired between the banks of the Bhagmutty. The statement would appear to be borne out by the physical aspect of the valley, the waving nature of the ground strongly resembling the bed of a large body of water, and the soil, which consists of a rich black mould, being evidently an alluvial deposit.

At the western head of the valley of Nepaul stands the temple of Sumbhoo-nath, an ancient edifice occupying the summit of a hill having an elevation of about 300 feet above the subjacent plain, the ascent to which is gained by a flight of steps cut out of the rock. A colossal figure of the god Boudh, the lawgiver of the Bhootias, stands at the foot of the steps. The temple rises from the centre of a terrace, which completely occupies the summit of the hill, and is discernible at a great distance, from its gilded spires and turrets.

The principal rivers which traverse Nepaul, are the Kurnalli, Gunduck, Trisul-Gunga, Bori-Gunduck, Coosy, and Bhagmutty; these are separately described under their respective heads in the alphabetical arrangement.

Notwithstanding its low latitude, Nepaul, from its great elevation, which is about 4,000 feet above the level of the sea, enjoys a climate resembling in some degree that of southern Europe. Snow lies on the mountain-chain which surrounds the capital for days together in winter, and occasionally falls in the valley below, where hoar-frost is by no means unusual. In the same season ice sometimes covers the tanks and pools of standing water, but the rivers never freeze. During Kirkpatrick's stay in the valley of Nepaul, from the 17th to the 25th of March, the thermometer at noon usually ranged between 81° and 84°: a little after sunrise it stood at from 50° to 54°, but was once so low as 47°; and at nine in the evening it fluctuated between 62° and 66°; upon one occasion within the seven days it rose to 87°; yet by ascending the sides and summits of the inclosing mountains, the heat of Bengal may be speedily exchanged for the cold of Russia. Nepaul is characterized by seasons similar to those of Upper India, the rains commencing a little earlier, and setting in from the south-east. At the foot of the hills in the Terrai, the air is unwholesome from the middle of March to the middle of November, engendering putrid fever, of which those attacked by it, die in a few days.

Several mineral productions are obtainable in Nepaul. A vague belief formerly prevailed, that the country contained gold-mines; but the search for their discovery, conducted under the authority of the native government, proved fruitless. The absence of gold is, however, compensated by the excellence of other metals. Copper and iron mines are worked, and the iron of Nepaul is said to be not surpassed in excellence by that of any other country. Its copper, though of superior quality, does not appear to enter into competition in the western markets with the copper of Europe; but this circumstance may be attributed partly to the expense of transportation through a mountainous country, and partly to the ignorance of the natives in the art of metallurgy. Ores of lead have been met with in several tracts, and the western parts of Nepaul abound in arsenic and pyrites. Stone well adapted to building purposes abounds; but owing to the expense of its transportation, stone edifices are more uncommon than even in Bengal.

Among the wild animals are the rhinoceros and the tiger; herds of elephants also range in the great forest, and large numbers are annually caught on behalf of the government, who claim an exclusive right to them. The mode in which they are caught is not, as elsewhere, by driving the animals into a keddah or inclosure, but by nooses thrown over their necks by a hunter seated on a decoy elephant. Of domestic animals, it may be briefly noticed that the cattle of Nepaul are little superior to those ordinarily met with in Bengal and the upper provinces; but within the last three or four years horned cattle and sheep have been imported from England, with the view of introducing the breed into Nepaul.

Rice is the staple article of food; the other principal crops are wheat and pulse. Esculent vegetables are of inferior description; the potato degenerates rapidly, and can only be grown successfully by the annual importation of fresh roots from Patna and other localities. Among the indigenous fruits are the peach, raspberry, walnut, and mulberry.

The population, amounting to 1,940,000, consists of—1st. Ghoorkas, the conquerors of Nepaul, who are Hindoos; 2nd. Newars, the aborigines, who are chiefly confined to Nepaul proper, and furnish unequivocal signs of their Mongolian origin, in the flat nose, high cheek-bone, small eye, and copper-coloured complexion. Between these two races there subsists, as well in character, manners, and features, as in religious rites and language, the most marked differences. The Ghoorkas make the better soldiers, the Newars the more skilful artisans. Besides these, there are the Bhotias and the Dhanwars and Mhanjees, who are the cultivators and fishermen of the western districts.

Though the commerce of Nepaul is not extensive, it carries on trade with Bengal, Thibet, and Oude. Among the principal exports are elephants, rice, timber, hides, ginger, honey, and fruit. The manufactures of the country consist in the fabrication of cutlery, ordnance, muskets, and other warlike instruments; of utensils of brass, copper, and iron, and the casting of bells. Coarse cottons are made up for home consumption, and the paper manufactured in the capital appears to be of superior quality. Nepaul is likewise famous for the production of a beautiful flat brick used for the fronts of houses.

Little is known of the Ghoorkas prior to their conquest of Nepaul, which appears to have been completed in 1768. In 1790 the Nepaulese invaded Thibet, and pillaged its temples. The Lamas had recourse for aid to the emperor of China, who despatched a force of 70,000 men against the Ghoorkas. The latter were defeated and pursued to Noakote, near their capital, where terms dictated by the victors were accepted, and Nepaul became a dependency of China. The submission, however, was merely temporary. On the 1st of March, 1792, a treaty of commerce was concluded between the British government and Nepaul; and some years later political relations were established between the two governments by the treaty of Dinapoor, concluded in October, 1801. By a separate article of that treaty, the British government guaranteed the payment of the stipend of the ex-rajah of Nepaul, who had been compelled to abdicate in favour of his son, and had retired to Benares. No security had been taken from the Nepaul government for the repayment; and the omission resulted in loss and annoyance to the British government. At length the alliance between the two states was formally dissolved. This took place in 1804, and from that time till 1812 little intercourse seems to have taken place, beyond vain remonstrances on the part of the British against border invasions and encroachments. These at length occurred so frequently, and to such an increasing extent, that it became necessary for the British government to take some decisive mode of vindicating its rights. An attempt was made to settle the matters in dispute by the appointment of commissioners; but the endeavour ended unsatisfactorily, as such measures often do: the rights of the British were established, but the Nepaulese evaded their recognition. Fresh outrages followed, and ultimately war becoming inevitable, preparations for carrying it on were commenced on a somewhat extensive scale. The force destined to act against Nepaul, many thousands strong, and duly provided with ordnance and all other necessary implements of war, was distributed into four divisions, under four commanders, to each of whom was assigned a defined course of action. Various diplomatic arrangements were also made, with a view of assisting the military operations, and rendering the whole conducive to the establishment of the relations of peace. Of the attempts at negotiation, it is enough to say that they were generally defeated by the bad faith and chicanery which almost invariably characterize native diplomacy, and which pre-eminently mark that of Nepaul. The commencement of military operations was also inauspicious. An unsuccessful attack upon the strong fortress of Kalunga was attended with frightful loss, including among the slain the gallant but ill-fated officer by whom it was conducted, General Gillespie. Another attempt, made under another officer, and with increased means of destruction, was equally unsuccessful; and though subsequently the place fell into the hands of the assailants, through the abandonment of its garrison, the conquest must be regarded as dearly purchased. Other mischances also occurred. Some of the divisions of the invading army achieved nothing; and it is to the caution and military talent of Sir David Ochterlony, to whom happily one of the divisions had been intrusted, that the British cause was saved from utter defeat and disgrace. His success alarmed the enemy; and under the influence of such alarm negotiation recommenced, and a treaty was arranged, which was ratified as soon as received at Fort William. Its fate at Khatmandoo was widely different. The desire for war had been only checked, not extirpated; and the repudiation of the acts of its own accredited agents was of course not allowed by the Nepaulese government to act as an impediment to the indulgence of its hostile propensities: the treaty therefore was rejected. A renewal of the war was consequently inevitable, but its continuance was happily short. Sir David Ochterlony advanced through jungle and across mountains; and though the enemy at length found courage to attack him, it was without success. The fears of the court of Khatmandoo revived, and an emissary of that court proceeded to the British camp, with the required ratification of the treaty previously concluded, which thus became the rule of the political relations between the two powers. This took place in March, 1816.

Henceforward the history of Nepaul presents little that can excite interest in a European mind. Eternal intrigue, and occasional resort to rougher means, identify its character with that of most oriental courts. At times, however, events have occurred, which by their unusual atrocity relieve the tameness of the surrounding incidents. Such events have marked the career of Jung Bahadoor, whose name at least is pretty well known in England, which country he visited a few years since. Jung Bahadoor was the nephew of a man who had the good fortune (if such a term may be properly applied) to attain the office of prime minister of Nepaul. His youth was devoted to gambling, and his expertness in the avocation which he chose, repaired the financial dilapidation occasioned by his wild excesses. On his uncle becoming prime minister, Jung Badadoor quitted the obscurity of an outpost for the capital, which he regarded as the only field for the development of genius like his own. There he was the subject of many remarkable adventures, and committed sundry acts not recognised as lawful by the moral codes of the western world. Among the latter was the murder of his uncle, which he undertook and perpetrated at the instigation of the queen, who had previously been the minister's patroness. A new ministry was formed, and Jung became commander-in-chief. The opportunity of slaughter on a larger scale soon awaited him. The new premier was assassinated, and the queen, with whom he was a prime favourite, demanded vengeance. One of the colleagues of the murdered minister was suspected of being concerned in the crime. Jung proposed to another colleague of the unfortunate premier, that the suspected man should be put to death, and the government be administered by the sole survivor, he to whom the proposals were made. Hesitation on his part being displayed, Jung determined to place him in confinement till his object was effected, and gave a signal for his seizure. The son of the intended prisoner, apprehensive for the safety of his father, rushed forward to his rescue, but was forthwith cut down; the father sprung to avenge his son's death, but a bullet from the rifle of Jung Bahadoor laid the former by the side of the latter. This was, however, but the prelude to what was to follow. Fourteen hostile chiefs confronted Jung; but he was prepared to deal with them promptly. Backed by a small force, on which he could depend, he levelled his rifle fourteen times in succession, and at each discharge, excepting one, brought down his selected victim. The man who escaped his aim was he who had been accused of the murder of his colleague; but his reprieve was short; he reached the door, but there met from a sword the death which he had escaped from Jung's rifle. Massacre now raged throughout the palace; but the bodies of the slain were for Jung the stepping-stones to power. Before the dawn of the succeeding day, Jung Bahadoor was invested with the office of prime minister. His future course was not inconsistent with its commencement. A conspiracy was formed for his destruction; but Jung not only escaped, but seized and beheaded all the adherents of the chief conspirator. The queen was ordered to quit the country with her two sons: the king accompanied them, and the heir-apparent was raised to the throne. A feeble attempt was made by the monarch to regain his crown, but the information and energy of Jung baffled it, and the king was made prisoner. He still remains in captivity, but is sometimes, as an indulgence, allowed to occupy a seat on the throne next to his usurping son.

NERBUD.—A town in Guzerat, or the dominions of the Guicowar, situate 86 miles E.S.E. from Rajcote, and 79 miles W.S.W. from Baroda. Lat. 21° 52′, long. 72° 7′.

NERBUDDA.—A river rising in the British district of Ramgurh, presidency of Bengal, on the elevated plateau of Amarakantak or Ummurkuntuk, in the Vindhya Mountains, at an elevation of probably between 3,000 and 4,000 feet above the sea. Though that place is within the British frontier, little is known of it. According to the accounts collected by Tieffenthaler and Blunt, its remotest source is in an inexhaustible pond, inclosed by a wall of masonry, close to the temple of Amarakantak, in lat. 22° 39′, long. 81° 49′. The nascent river is a yard wide at its exit from the pond, and flowing eastward a mile and a half, is precipitated twenty-six yards from the brow of the table-land, and, changing its direction, flows westwards. In the upper part of its course, the declivity must be very rapid, as Jubbulpore, having an elevation above the sea of 1,458 feet, and situate on the right bank of the river, is, if the distance be measured along the channel, 190 miles below the source; and if the elevation of this last be assumed at 3,500 feet, the average descent of the water-way in that interval may be estimated at about ten feet in each mile. About Jubbulpore, it enters on what is generally called the valley of the Nerbudda, or the great depression bounded north by the Vindhya, on the south by the Satpoora Mountains; and the immediate drainage of this supplies nearly the whole volume of its water, as perhaps no river of the same magnitude and length of course receives so few important tributaries. About forty miles below Jubbulpore, and in lat. 23° 4′, long. 79° 26′, it, near Bairkaira, on the right side, receives the Herrun, a small river; and twenty miles lower down, on the left side, the Shair, still smaller. The formations along its banks, in the upper part of its course, appear for the most part to be trappean; lower down, at Jubbulpore, granitic. At Bhera Garh, below Jubbulpore, the channel is contracted between two high perpendicular cliffs of magnesian limestone, white as snow. The river, notwithstanding the great width of its bed in some parts of its upper course, appears to be scarcely anywhere continuously navigable for any considerable distance, in consequence of the innumerable basaltic rocks scattered over its channel; and these obstacles are the more seriously injurious, as at Chandgurh, near Poonassa, and Tendukhera, near Jubbulpore, are inexhaustible mines of iron-ore, of good quality, which, were the navigation available, would prove a most useful resource to that part of Hindustan. A recent report on the state of this river is officially described as "presenting an interesting, but not very encouraging narrative as respects its navigation for purposes of trade." Four or five miles above Hoshungabad, 360 miles from its source, and in lat. 22° 45′, long. 77° 49′, it on the right side receives the Towah, perhaps the largest of its tributaries; and a little below the confluence it is 900 yards wide.

About fifty yards above the junction of the Towah river with the Nerbudda, there is a ledge of black limestone rock, which stretches the whole way across the Nerbudda, connecting the two banks by a causeway, as it were: a fine waterfall is the result, while immediately below it is an exceedingly deep hole, which is literally alive with immense alligators. The ascent, from its steepness and slippery nature, is impracticable to them, and they content themselves with sporting about the deep water at its base. Below Hoshungabad, for about eighty miles, as far as Jooga, in lat. 22° 20′, long. 76° 46′, and 445 miles from the source, the channel is rather free from obstacles; but at that place there is a stony rapid, which, however, is, during the periodical rains, passable for boats of considerable burthen; and about ten miles below this rapid is the fall of Mundhar, of ten feet, causing an insuperable impediment to navigation. This stoppage of the navigation is in lat. 22° 15′, long. 76° 48′, below the source of the river 455 miles; above its mouth 346. Between Mundhar and Hoshungabad, the country on each side of the river is a very wild, woody tract, consisting of a succession of low hills, and deep ravines and watercourses, covered with dense and lofty forests, and scarcely capable of being traversed in most parts for seven or eight miles from the river by any but foot-passengers. Iron-ore abounds. Below Mundhar twenty-five miles, and in lat. 22° 16′, long. 76° 28′, are the falls of Dhardri, of forty feet descent, there being, during the season of low water, four or five channels, but during the periodical rains, an unbroken sheet of water, about a hundred feet in width from the cliff on the left to that on the right side; navigation being totally impracticable. Close below this fall is the rapid of Kal Bhyru, "in forty feet, three feet," the river being only 100 feet wide, and three feet water on the rapid; and here is a ford much frequented at seasons of low water. At the termination of the rapid is the rocky isle of Mundatta, the ruinous pagodas on which are annually much frequented, being sacred to Siva. The geological formations of the banks in this part of the river's course appear to be slate of various sorts. Between the rapids at Mundatta and the British cantonment at Mundlesir, seventy miles lower down, several rapids occur, but none totally interrupting navigation. The estimated elevation of Mundlesir above the sea is 700 feet, or 760 below Jubbulpore, where the stream, descending from the table-land, enters the valley of the Nerbudda; and as the distance between those two towns is 360 miles, measured by the stream, the average descent in that interval is little more than two feet per mile.

Jacquemont describes the river as about 2,000 feet wide at Mundlesir in the season of low water, when it is fordable, though with difficulty, in consequence of the great rockiness of its bed. In the periodical rains, the water rises here from thirty to forty feet above its height in the shrunken state of the river. At Hiranpul, seventy miles below Mundlesir, the navigation is totally interrupted by a rapid, 100 feet in length, and having a fall of six feet. The channel, 150 feet in width, is studded with basaltic rocks, rising above the surface. In a late attempt made to try how far it might be navigated, a very strong canoe, guided by means of two ropes worked by several men on the bank, was several times upset or sunk, though at last hauled out by main strength. The Hiranpul rapid is in lat. 22° 5′, long. 74° 43′, 620 miles from the source, 181 from the mouth. A mile below this, "it [the Nerbudda] finds a single channel of forty yards, bounded on either side by cliffs, into which the stream, 600 yards in width, contracts in volume as it rushes down the declivity of this gorge with extreme fury." From this place the river is unfit for navigation for seventy miles, to Soolpan Mahadeo, or Makri Fall, in lat. 21° 47′, long. 73° 48′, 691 miles from the source, 110 from the mouth. According to Dangerfield, in this part of its course "the stream finds its way, contracted to within half its usual breadth, between two hilly ranges, and its course being much impeded, so as to render navigation impracticable, by large masses and elevated ridges of rock." In one spot, the channel for this vast volume of water "was not ten yards in breadth, the water rushing through it with a slight fall and tremendous force." From Makri Fall to Tullukwara, a distance of twenty-five miles, the navigation is difficult; but, with much care and toil, practicable. From Tullukwara, in lat. 21° 57′, long. 73° 32′, to the sea, a distance of eighty-five miles, it is navigable for boats of considerable burthen. Flowing by the city of Broach, situate on its right or north bank, it falls into the Gulf of Cambay, in lat. 21° 35′, long. 72° 35′; its total length of course being 801 miles. The tide is perceptible only twenty-five miles above Broach, or fifty-five from the sea. Throughout the tidal part of its course, the breadth of the Nerbudda exceeds a mile. At Broach, about thirty miles from the mouth, it is a noble sheet of water two miles wide, even when the tide is out. Ships of burthen can proceed up the river to Broach; but skilful pilotage is necessary, as the navigation is very difficult, in consequence of a bar at the entrance of the river, and numerous sandbanks in its channel. The practicability of improving the navigation by artificial means has been considered; and several years since instructions were sent out for a survey by a competent officer, with a view to this end. An experienced geologist was at the same time directed to examine the coal-fields in the neighbourhood of Hoshungabad, for the purpose of ascertaining their capacity as a source of supply to Bombay, thereby relieving that port from its exclusive dependence upon Europe for coal. The latest results reported are of an encouraging character. Few rivers have a more direct course than that of the Nerbudda, which is nearly due east and west. It is considered to be the boundary between the Deccan and Hindostan.

NERBUDDA TERRITORY. — See SAUGOR AND NERBUDDA.

NERIAD, in the British district of Kaira, under the presidency of Bombay, a town on the route from Baroda to the city of Ahmedabad. Its streets are level, conveniently broad, and clean. It is the principal place of the extensive tobacco tract in that district, and is situate in a thriving, well-cultivated country, abounding in towns and prosperous villages. Population 40,000. Distance from Baroda, N.W., 35 miles; from Ahmedabad, S.E., 30. Lat. 22° 40′, long. 72° 55′.

NEROWLEE.—A town in the Rajpoot state of Jeypoor, situate 69 miles S.E. from Jeypoor, and 130 miles E. from Ajmeer. Lat. 26° 20′, long. 76° 48′.

NEROWLEE, in the British district of Moradabad, lieut.-gov. of the N.W. Provinces, a town on the route from Moradabad to Coel, 25 miles S. by W. of the former. Lat. 28° 29′, long. 78° 49′.

NERRONA.—A town in the native state of Cutch, situate on the Great Western Runn of Cutch, and 12 miles N.N.W. from Bhooj. Lat. 23° 23′, long. 69° 40′.

NEVERDEEPOOR, in the district of Salon, territory of Oude, a town on the right bank of the river Saee, 75 miles S.E. of Lucknow. Butter estimates the population at 3,000 Hindoos, including 100 Bhats. Lat. 25° 59′, long. 81° 38′.

NEWA SHAHER, in the Julindur Dooab division of the Punjab, a town situated 15 miles W. from the right bank of the Sutlej, 130 miles E. by S. of the town of Lahore. Lat. 31° 12′, long. 76° 18′.

NEW HALLA.—A town in the British district of Hydrabad, province of Scinde, presidency of Bombay, 30 miles N. of Hydrabad. Lat. 25° 48′, long. 68° 26′.

NEWSUR.—See NOWSUR.

NEWTAH, in the British district of Dumoh, one of the divisions of the Saugor and Nerbudda territories, lieut.-gov. of the N.W. Provinces, a town on the route from Dumoh to Jubbulpoor, 12 miles S.E. of the former. Lat. 23° 40′, long. 79° 38′.

NEWULGURH.—A town in the territory of Oudh, 60 miles N.N.E. from Oudh, and 81 miles N.W. from Goruckpoor. Lat. 27° 35′, long. 82° 34′.

NEYH.—A town in the native state of Cutch, 68 miles W.N.W. from Bhooj, and 96 miles S.E. by S. from Tatta. Lat. 23° 30′, long. 68° 42′.

NEYPAAR.—A town in the British district of Kaira, presidency of Bombay, 33 miles S.E. by E. of Kaira. Its streets are narrow and uneven. Lat. 22° 28′, long. 73° 7′.

NHOON, in the Sinde Sagur Dooab division of the Punjab, a town situated on the left bank of the Indus, 135 miles S. by W. of the town of Peshawur. Lat. 32° 7′, long. 71° 18′.

NIBRUNG, in Bussahir, a pass across the elevated ridge forming the southern boundary of Koonawar. It has the appearance of a gateway, and lies between two perpendicular rocks, each thirty-five feet high. Gerard remarks that he had nowhere else observed so great a difference in the height of the thermometer exposed to the sun's rays and in the shade; in the former case being 104°, in the latter 35½°. Three hundred yards to the south-east is the Goonas Pass, and a quarter of a mile further, in the same direction, is the Ghusul Pass. Nibrung is 16,035 feet above the sea. Lat. 31° 22′, long. 78° 13′.

NICHLOUL, or NUHLAWALI, in the British district of Goruckpoor, lieut.-gov. of the N.W. Provinces, a small town near the northern frontier towards Nepaul. Buchanan, who surveyed it forty years ago, describes it as a very sorry place, having 200 huts: and if six persons be allowed to each, the population may be estimated at 1,200. Here is a ruinous mud fort, which formerly belonged to the petty rajah of Palpa, in Nepal. Distant N.E. from Goruckpore cantonment 45 miles. Lat. 27° 17′, long. 83° 47′.

NICHOR, in Bussahir, a village of the district of Koonawar, is situate on the northern declivity of a mountain sloping down to the left bank of the Sutluj. Elevation above the sea 6,925 feet. Lat. 31° 33′, long. 78°.

NICKRYE.—A town in the British district of Cuttack, lieut.-gov. of Bengal, 37 miles E. by N. of Cuttack. Lat. 20° 34′, long. 86° 29′.

NICOBARS.—A cluster of islands in the Indian Ocean, lying between lat. 6° 40′—9° 20′, and long. 93° 3′—94° 13′: they are inhabited by about 1,000 Malays. The Danes formed a settlement here in 1756, but abandoned it in 1768. At the latter end of the year 1840, the whaler *Pilot*, of London, was seized by pirates infesting the Nicobars. An English cruiser being despatched to these islands to exact reparation, a quantity of marine stores, not pertaining to the *Pilot*, were discovered, and a suspicion arose that some of the many vessels which had sailed in recent years for China or the Straits, and had never since been heard of, might have fallen victims to the pirates of the Nicobars or Andamans. At this period, the sovereignty of the Nicobars was claimed by the Danes. Evidence subsequently obtained, left little room for doubt that in several instances the crews of British vessels had been murdered, and the vessels scuttled and sunk by the islanders; and it further appeared that the murder of the crew had always been effected by surprise. Measures were taken to give notoriety to these circumstances, and commanders of trading vessels likely to touch at the Nicobars were recommended to employ, during their stay, a portion of the crew as an armed watch. In 1848, the Danish government came to the determination to abandon all claim to sovereignty over the Nicobars; and on the final removal of Danish authority, the chiefs of the island of Car Nicobar hoisted the British flag, and expressed their desire, through a British merchant of Moulmein, to acknowledge the supremacy of the British government. It was not, however, deemed expedient to recognise these proceedings. Some few years later, certain residents of Chittagong made a representation to the British government regarding two brigs which sailed for the Nicobars in 1852. Neither of them had since been heard of, and the presumption was, that both had been cut off by savages. Captain Dicey, of the steamer *Tenasserim*, was thereupon despatched to the Nicobars for the purpose of inquiring into the fate of the missing vessels; and the report of this officer, the home authorities observe, "leaves no doubt that two vessels, one of them English, have recently been destroyed, and their crews murdered by the inhabitants of the Nicobar Islands; and there seems too much reason to fear that these atrocities have been preceded by many similar outrages." These and the adjacent islands termed the Andamans would, it has been suggested, answer admirably for a convict settlement.

NIDAON, or NADAUN, in the north of the Punjab, a small town on the Beas, here a deep, rapid, and clear stream, 150 yards wide, and running at the rate of three miles and a half an hour. The right bank is of sandstone, lofty and abrupt; the left of mould, lower and shelving. Here is a ferry much frequented, being on the route from British India to Cashmere. Nadaun was formerly a flourishing place, and was held by an independent rajah; but the prince was expelled by Runjeet Singh, and since that event the town has fallen into decay. Near Nadaun is Jewala Muki, a celebrated Hindoo temple, surmounted with a richly-gilded roof, and inclosing a fissure in the rock, from which issue jets of inflammable gas, which, when lighted, are considered the breath of the tutelar deity. The assessment of the land revenue, when payable to the Sikh government, was regulated by a curious contrivance, which, according to Moorcroft, "without diminishing the amount, was likely to be satisfactory to the peasantry. This was by a rough analysis of the soil. A given quantity of the earth was put into a fine muslin sieve, and washed with water until all the mould was carried through, and nothing but the sand left; and according to its proportion to the whole, a deduction was made from the assessment." The rate for rich soil was about five shillings an acre. The site of Nadaun is delightful; and during its prosperity it was celebrated for fine gardens, and various other attractions. Vigne mentions a popular proverb—"Who will come to Nadaun, and then leave it?" It is in lat. 31° 46′, long. 76° 23′.

NIDDAGOONDA.—A town in Hyderabad, or territory of the Nizam, 56 miles N.E. by E. from Hyderabad, and 127 miles N.W. from Guntoor. Lat. 17° 43′, long. 79° 19′.

NIDDAVOLE.—A town in the British district of Masulipatam, presidency of Madras, 63 miles N.E. by N. of Masulipatam. Lat. 16° 55′, long. 81° 44′.

NIDIGULL, in the Mysore, a fort and town on the north-east frontier, towards Bellary, garrisoned by Hyder Ali. It in the year 1770 was, after a deperate resistance, stormed by the troops of the poligar or chief of Chitradurg, auxiliary to the Mahrattas.

Distance from Chitradurg, E., 48 miles; Bangalore, N.W., 89. Lat. 14° 10′, long. 77° 9′.

NIDJIGUL.—A town in the Mysore, 67 miles N.E. by N. from Seringapatam, and 146 miles W. by N. from Arcot. Lat. 13° 15′, long. 77° 15′.

NIE SARAE, in the territory of Oude, a village on the route from Cawnpore to Lucknow, 28 miles N.E. of the former, 25 S.W. of the latter. Lat. 26° 41′, long. 80° 42′.

NILAB, in the Punjab, a small town on the left or eastern bank of the Indus, a short distance below Attock, and close to the confluence of the Hurroo river. The name signifies "blue water," and has been assigned to it from the deep blue colour of the water of the Indus at this place. The great river here is narrow, rapid, and 120 feet deep. There is a ferry, at which, according to Wood, Timur crossed on his invasion of India; but Rennell is of opinion that he crossed at or near Attock. Lat. 33° 46′, long. 72° 15′.

NILING, in Chinese Tartary, near the northern frontier of Gurwhal, is situate in the district of Chaprang, being distant south-west from the town of that name six days' journey, by a tolerably good track. It is situate on the right bank of the Jahnevi, a great confluent with the Bhageerettee, called lower down the Ganges. The houses are built very low, in consequence of the great violence of the wind. Besides the road to Chaprang, there is another to Koonawar by the Chungsakhago Pass, situate about lat. 31° 14′, long. 78° 37′. This is probably the most difficult pass in the Himalayas, as Gerard, who had crossed several above 18,000 feet high, could find no guide willing to accompany him across the Chungsakhago; and some years before his arrival in that tract, eighteen people perished in attempting the passage; since which time few loaded travellers venture on it. Elevation above the sea 11,127 feet. Lat. 31° 6′, long. 79° 2′.

NILLEHGAON.—A town in the British province of Sattara, presidency of Bombay, 20 miles E. from Sholapoor, and 69 miles N.N.E. from Beejapoor. Lat. 17° 41′, long. 76° 15′.

NIL NAG, "blue lake," in Cashmere, a great spring or piece of water, which gives rise to a stream falling into the Behut or Jhelum, in the vicinity of Baramula, in lat. 33° 48′, long. 74° 47′. Like most other sources of rivers, it is regarded with superstitious veneration by the Hindoos. It is situate on the north-eastern declivity of the Pir Panjal, and 21 miles S.W. of Serinagur.

NIMAR.—See NEMAUR.

NIMBEH.—A town in the British district of Ahmednuggur, presidency of Bombay, 11 miles N.N.W. of Ahmednuggur. Lat. 19° 15′, long. 74° 41′.

NIMBERA, in Rajpootana, the principal place of a pergunnah, one of the possessions of the noted Patan freebooter Muhammed Ameer Khan, is situate on the route from Neemuch to Nusseerabad, 16 miles N.W. of the former, and 127 S. of the latter. It is surrounded by a rampart with towers, and has a small mosque, some small temples, and a neat cutchery or court of justice. There is a very beautiful baoli or well. It has a noble staircase, and a verandah of rich Saracenic arches round the wall about half-way down. The pergunnah contains 275 villages, and an area of 172 square miles. Of its separate population there is no return, but information on that of the whole of the dependencies of Ameer Khan will be found in the article on Tonk. It is estimated to yield an annual revenue of 1,40,000 rupees, or 14,000*l.* Though forming part of the jaghire of the noted Ameer Khan, its fiscal affairs and police have long been under the management of the East-India Company; an arrangement originating in a great outrage committed on some British subjects from Neemuch, who were attacked, stripped, and some of them killed. The proper British officer having applied to Ameer Khan for redress, that chieftain answered that he had no sufficient army to sustain his authority in so distant a possession, and that he wished that the English would take the district in farm, give him a fair rent, and govern it their own way; which offer was accepted. Tod, who passed through this place in 1820, and a few years before Heber's visit, states it to be a "considerable town, with an excellent stone circumvallation;" and adds that, "being on the high road between Malwa and Hindostan, it enjoys a good share of traffic." Lat. 24° 36′, long. 74° 43′.

NIMBSOR.—A town in the British province of Sattara, presidency of Bombay, 35 miles S.E. by E. of Sattara. Lat. 17° 27′, long. 74° 31′.

NIMKESARAE, in the British district of Muttra, lieut.-gov. of the N.W. Provinces, a village on the route from the city of Agra to Bareilly, and 22 miles N. of the former. Lat. 27° 24′, long. 78° 17′.

NIMKHAR, or NIMKHAR-MISRIK, in the district of Khairabad, territory of Oude, a town near the left bank of the Goomtee, is the principal place of the subdivision of the same name. On a high sand-hill on the bank of the river is a brick fort, of quadrangular ground-plan, half a mile in circuit, having four round towers, one at each angle, but fallen into ruin. Contiguous is a reservoir, regarded sacred by the Hindoos, of octagon outline, surrounded in its circuit of about 180 paces by a wall, sloping towards the water, with ten steps. The water is supplied from hidden springs; is clear, deep, of a skye-blue colour, and is used by the Hindoos as a bath for ritual ablutions. Similar tanks abound in the neighbourhood. This place is mentioned in the Ayeen Akbery as having a brick fort, and yielding an annual revenue of 89,101 rupees. Lat. 27° 21′, long. 80° 32′.

NINA DEVI, in the hill state of Kuhloor, a peaked mountain in the narrow peninsula formed by a remarkable flexure of the Sutlej, and about four miles from the left bank of that river. It rises about 3,000 feet above the town of Anandpoor, or 4,000 above the level of the sea. Its shape is singularly like the peaked turban worn by the Sikhs, which people hold the spot in great veneration, because Guru Govind Singh ascended to its summit, and there, surrounded by a few faithful followers, concerted measures for the propagation of their faith. A small well-constructed temple is situate on the summit, to which there is access by means of a flight of stone steps. Lat. 31° 18′, long. 76° 37′.

NINGROO.—A town in the British district of Sudiya, Upper Assam, 34 miles S. of Sudiya. Lat. 27° 20′, long. 95° 42′.

NIRMUL, in Hyderabad, or the territory of the Nizam, a town nine miles north of the left or north bank of the Godavery, in a country of granatic formation, overlaid with fossiliferous strata, on the route from Hyderabad to Nagpoor, 120 miles N. of former, 150 S.W. of latter. Lat. 19° 7′, long. 78° 25′.

NIRT, in Bussahir, a village on the left bank of the Sutlej, belonging to Brahmins, who hold it rent free. Elevation above the sea 3,087 feet. Lat. 31° 23′, long. 77° 37′.

NISHOWRA.—See NASAIRAH.

NISUNG, in Bussahir, a village of Koonawar, is situate near the left bank of the Taglakhar, a large stream which rises in Chinese Tartary, three or four days' journey to the eastward. The village lies at the northern base of the Tungrug Pass, from which it is accessible by a footpath of steep descent, passing through growths of juniper and thyme. The soil and climate are sufficiently genial to bring to maturity esculent vegetables and small fruit, such as gooseberries, though it has an elevation of 10,165 feet above the sea. Lat. 31° 39′, long. 78° 34′.

NITI, in the British district of Kumaon, under the lieut.-gov. of the N.W. Provinces, a village near a celebrated pass of the same name, across the range or succession of mountains forming the boundary towards Hiundes or Chinese Tartary. The village, thirteen miles south of the pass, is situate on the left bank of the Doulee, and at the foot of a range of eminences, which, sweeping round, defends it on the north and north-west from tempests. The route from the village is up the course of the Doulee, which rises on the southern face, where, in the early part of October, not a speck of snow was to be seen. After the route diverges from the Doulee, the ascent becomes very steep, amidst crumbling crags of blue limestone. The pass opens at the top on the table-land of Tartary, or rather on the slightly depressed basin of the Sutluj, the bed of which there has an elevation of 14,924 feet above the sea. This is considered the easiest and best pass between Kumaon and Hiundes, and in consequence is one of the principal channels of the trade between Chinese Tartary and Hindoostan; and the carrying-business forms the principal means of subsistence of the Bhotias of Niti. The pass becomes open at the latter end of June, and continues so generally to the second week in October. The articles of merchandise are conveyed on yaks, goats, and sheep. The Bhotian sheep carries from ten to twenty pounds weight, the goat from twelve to twenty-four; the Tibetan sheep, which is larger and stronger, carries from thirty to forty. They can, if urged, travel in a day seven or eight miles over the mountain-tracks; but for a continuance not more than five. Grain, borax, salt, and such other goods as can be commodiously divided, are sewn up in saddle-bags, called karbik, made of woollen and cased in leather, and are hung on each side, being secured in place by a crupper and breast-band. Wool, cottons, and goods of similar description, are in the same way arranged in small packages. The sufferings of travellers from disordered respiration, in consequence of the tenuity of the air, are very severe; and though the Bhotias take pains from early age to train themselves to endure it, some can never succeed; and even yaks and other beasts are not exempt from sufferings resulting from it. The most marked symptoms are vertigo, inordinate action of the heart, accelerated respiration, and the most distressing difficulty of breathing. The statement of Batten is conclusive as to the reality of this influence:—"During this walk I was almost killed by mere pain. The rarity of the air along this high road to Daba (nearly 17,000 feet) was perfectly awful. My dandi people would not go on, and returned to the crest of the pass. One man accompanied me; and he and I went groaning along at a snail's pace, on a level, and yet in great agony. Angina pectoris I now consider nothing in comparison. I felt the pain most at my chest, and suffocation seemed to threaten me at every step." The district adjacent to Niti bears the same name, and contains ten villages and 219 houses. Elevation of crest of pass above the sea 16,814 feet; lat. 30° 57′, long. 79° 54′. Elevation of village 11,464 feet; lat. 30° 46′, long. 79° 53′.

NITTERKONAH.—A town in the British district of Mymunsing, lieut.-gov. of Bengal, 45 miles E. of Jumalpore. Lat. 24° 50′, long. 90° 45′.

NIWANS, in the British district of Ramgurh, territory of Saugor and Nerbudda, a town on the route from Ramgurh to Jubbulpoor. 37 miles W.N.W. of the former. Lat. 23° 3′, long. 80° 30′.

NIZAMABAD, in the British district of Azimgurh, lieut.-gov. of the N.W. Provinces, a town, the principal place of the pergunnah of the same name, is situate on the route from the town of Azimgurh to that of Jounpoor, eight miles W. of the former, 32 N.E. of the latter, 50 N. of Benares, and in lat. 26° 5′, long. 83° 5′.

NIZAMOODEENPOOR BUGREH.—A town in the British district of Sarun, lieut.-gov. of Bengal, 56 miles N.N.E. of Chupra. Lat. 26° 42′, long. 85° 25′.

NIZAMPATAM, in the British district of Guntoor, presidency of Madras, a town on the estuary of an inconsiderable stream, and a mile N.W. of the Golkonda coast, or western shore of the Bay of Bengal. Though no vessel of great burthen can approach the place, there is a considerable coasting-trade carried on in the small country craft. It is the principal place of a tallook or subdivision of the same name, which, according to official return, together with the town, has a population of 24,646; of whom there are 13,168 males, and 11,478 females; the number of houses being 7,682. Distance from the town of Guntoor, S.E., 31 miles; Madras, N., 175. Lat. 15° 55′, long. 80° 44′.

NIZAMPOOR.—A town in the British district of Tannah, presidency of Bombay, 51 miles S.E. by S. of Bombay. Lat. 18° 20′, long. 73° 22′.

NIZAM'S DOMINIONS.—See HYDERABAD.

NOACOLLY.—A town in the British district of Bulloah, lieut.-gov. of Bengal, 14 miles E.S.E. of Bulloah. Lat. 22° 49′, long. 91° 8′.

NOACOTE.—A town in Nepal, situate on the left bank of the Bori Gunduk river, and 20 miles N.W. from Khatmandoo. The valley, of which this town is the principal place, is about eighteen miles distant from Khatmandoo, and was visited some years ago by Prince Waldemar of Prussia and his party. According to a recent visitor, "it does not offer much attraction to the traveller; and as I looked into it from the top of Sheopoori, I thought it hardly worth the trip. Not so extensive as that in which Khatmandoo is situated, it lies lower, and is very fertile." Lat. of town 27° 53′, long. 85° 3′.

NOAGONG.—A town in the native territory of Duspulla, one of the hill states of Orissa, situate 72 miles N.W. by N. from Ganjam, and 92 miles W. by S. from Cuttack. Lat. 20° 17′, long. 84° 32′.

NOBRA, or NUBRA.—A division of Ladakh or Middle Tibet, subject to Gholab Singh, the ruler of Cashmere. It is a singularly wild tract, of great elevation, on the south side of the Karakorum Mountains, or eastern part of Hindoo Koosh, and is bounded on the north, the east, and the south sides by the Shy-Yok, or river of Nobra, which, rising in the Nobra Tsuh lake or glacier, embosomed in the mountain, joins the Indus a few miles above, and east of Iskardo. The lowest part of this tract is estimated by Vigne to be more than 11,000 feet above the sea; but though so elevated and very mountainous, it is described by him not only as picturesque, but as having a considerable degree both of culture and population. Deskit, the chief place, is in lat. 34° 35′, long. 77° 37′.

NOBUTTA, in the British district of Agra, lieut.-gov. of the N.W. Provinces, a village on the route from the city of Agra to that of Muttra, and four miles N.W. of the former. Lat. 27° 12′, long. 78° 3′.

NOELGUNJ, in the territory of Oude, a town on the route, by Nanamow Ghat or Ferry, from Lucknow to Mynpooree, 19 miles W. of the former city, 116 S.E. of the latter. Heber describes it, A.D. 1824, as "a large walled village, with gates, and a bazar in a much handsomer style than usual, but the walls bearing marks of decay, and many of the houses roofless, though the shops were neat, and the appearance of the people comfortable and thriving." The road in this part of the route is good. Lat. 26° 45′, long. 80° 45′.

NOEWALA, in the Punjab, a town on the route from Ramnegurh to Lahore, and 55 miles N.W. of the latter place. It is situate in an extensive plain, of great fertility, and well cultivated, producing abundant crops of grain, especially wheat. Lat. 32° 12′, long. 73° 54′.

NOGOAN, in the Rajpoot state of Alwar, under the political management of the Governor-General's agent for Rajpootana, a village on the route from Alwar, by way of Ferozpoor, to Delhi, and 87 miles S. of the latter. Lat. 27° 38′, long. 76° 58′.

NOH, in the British district of Goorgaon, lieut.-gov. of the N.W. Provinces, a village 40 miles S.W. of Delhi. The population of Noh is stated at 6,009. Lat. 28° 7′, long. 77° 4′.

NOHBUT GUNGE, in the territory of Oude, a village on the route, by Nanamow Ghat, from Futtehgurh to Lucknow, 50 miles S.E. of the former, 60 W. of the latter. It is situate on the left bank of the Ganges, here crossed by ferry to Nanamow, in the territory of the East-India Company. Nohbut Gunge has a small bazar, and supplies are abundant. Lat. 26° 53′, long. 80° 11′.

NOH DIHING, a tributary of the Brahmapootra, rises in lat. 27° 9′, long. 96° 56′, and, flowing in a north-westerly direction through the British district of Sudiya, in Upper Assam, for 100 miles, falls into the Brahmapootra, on the left side, in lat. 27° 44′, long. 95° 48′.

NOHUR.—See ISLAMGURH.

NOK, in the Rajpoot state of Jessulmeer, a village on the route from Beekumpoor to Balmeer, and 15 miles S.E. of Beekumpoor. It contains 100 houses, and nine wells fifty feet deep, yielding abundance of fine water. Lat. 27° 34′, long. 72° 20′

NOKEELA, in the British district of Bogra, presidency of Bengal, a town on the route from the town of Bogra to Jumalpoor, 16 miles E. of former, 26 S.W. of latter. It is situate near the river Konaie, a vast offset of the Brahmapootra, and has a thana or police-station, the jurisdiction of which extends over 303 villages. Distant N.E. from Berhampore 144 miles, from Calcutta 262. Lat. 24° 50′, long. 89° 37′.

NOKOREE, in the British district of Kumaon, lieut.-gov. of the N.W. Provinces, a village on the route from Almora fort to Hiundes or South-western Tibet, by the Juwahir Pass, 53 miles N.E. of Almora, 103 S.W. of the latter. Lat. 29° 58′, long. 80° 2′.

NOKRA, in the Rajpoot state of Jessulmeer, a collection of dwellings comprising two small villages, together containing sixty houses, of which four are shops. It is situate on the route from the town of Beekaneer to that of Jessulmeer, and 52 miles S.W. of the former. Water, though of indifferent quality, is supplied from a tank. The road in this part of the route is firm. Lat. 27° 39′, long. 72° 45′.

NOKUR, or **NOUSIR**, in the Rajpoot state of Beekaneer, a town in the desert tract near the northern frontier, towards Hurreeana. Lat. 29° 11′, long. 74° 52′.

NOLBAREE.—A town in the British district of Camroop, Lower Assam, 28 miles N.W. of Gowhatty. Lat. 26° 26′, long. 91° 27′.

NOLYE, in the territory of Gwalior, or possessions of Scindia's family, a town in Malwa, on the route from Mow to Deesa, 46 miles N.W. of former, 255 S.E. of latter. It is of considerable size, and is the principal place of a pergunnah yielding annually a revenue of 265,000 rupees to the Gwalior government. Malcolm observes, "Nolye was built by Raja Nol, from whom its name originated; but its modern one is Burnuggur, the first being thought of bad omen if pronounced before breakfast;" but he gives no explanation of this singular passage. Population about 5,000; elevation above the sea 1,698 feet. Distant 29 miles S.W. from Oojein. Lat. 23° 8′, long. 75° 23′.

NONORE.—A town in the British district of Shahabad, lieut.-gov. of Bengal, 50 miles S.W. by W. of Sasseram. Lat. 25° 16′, long. 84° 43′.

NOOGYHULLY.—A town in the Mysore, 44 miles N.N.W. from Seringapatam, and 111 miles E. by N. from Mangalore. Lat. 13° 1′, long. 76° 31′.

NOOH, in the British district of Muttra, the principal place of the pergunnah of Nooh Jhil, a town situate on the south-eastern border of the jhil, and four miles east of the eastern or left bank of the Jumna. Lat. 27° 51′, long. 77° 42′.

NOOH, in the British district of Allygurh, lieut.-gov. of the N.W. Provinces, a village on the route from the city of Agra to Bareilly, and 36 miles N.E. of the former. Lat. 27° 31′, long. 78° 28′.

NOON, in the jaghire of Jujhur, lieut.-gov. of the N.W. Provinces, a village near the western frontier, towards Loharoo. Lat. 28° 20′, long. 76° 5′.

NOONEE.—A town in the British district of Bhagulpore, lieut.-gov. of Bengal, 52 miles S. of Bhagulpore. Lat. 24° 30′, long. 87° 8′.

NOONGSAEE.—A town of Eastern India, in the native state of Muneepoor, 37 miles S.W. by W. from Muneepoor, and 50 miles W.N.W. from Silchar. Lat. 24° 30′, long. 93° 32′.

NOORABAD, in the territory of Gwalior, or possessions of the Scindia family, a town on the route from Agra to the fort of Gwalior, 60 miles S. of the former, 11 N.W. of the latter. It is situate on the right or south bank of the river Sank, here crossed by a bridge of seven arches, well built of masonry. Adjoining the village is a pleasure-ground of considerable size, inclosed by a wall of stone, built A.D. 1666, by order of Aurungzebe, as appears from an inscription over the gate. Within the inclosure is the mausoleum of Goonna Begum, consort of Ghaziuddin Khan, vizier of Ahmed Shah, and of Alamgir, sovereigns of Delhi from 1749 to 1754, and from 1754 to 1759. The begum was "celebrated for her personal accomplishments, as well as for the vivacity of her wit and the fire of her poetical genius." Her monument bears an inscription, "Alas! Goonna Begum, 1189" (A.D. 1775). Lat. 26° 25′, long. 78° 10′.

NOORJA, in Sinde, a considerable village between Sehwan and Larkhana, and 10 miles N. of the former town. It is situate two miles west of the right bank of a large offset of the Indus, and three miles west of the main channel. The surrounding country is level, alluvial, and in many parts cultivated, but greatly broken up by numerous channels, cut for the purposes of irrigation. Noorja is itself supplied with water from wells. Lat. 26° 34′, long. 67° 53′.

NOORNAGUR.—A town in the British district of Tipperah, lieut.-gov. of Bengal, 20 miles N. of Tipperah. Lat. 23° 45′, long. 91° 10′.

NOORNUGUR, in the British district of Muzuffurnugur, lieut.-gov. of the N.W. Provinces, a town on the route from Muzuffurnugur to Hurdwar, 22 miles N.E. by N. of the former. Lat. 29° 41′, long. 77° 59′.

NOOROODDEN SURRAEE, in the Baree Doab division of the Punjab, a town situated 27 miles S.E. from the left bank of the Ravee, 34 miles E. by S. of the town of Lahore. Lat. 31° 30′, long. 74° 52′.

NOORPOOR.—A town in the territory of

Oude, 34 miles N.N.E. from Lucknow, and 76 miles N.E. from Cawnpoor. Lat. 27° 18′, long. 81° 13′.

NOORPOOR, in the Sinde Sagur Dooab division of the Punjab, a town situated 22 miles N.W. from the right bank of the Jhelum, 131 miles N.W. by W. of the town of Lahore. Population 10,531. Lat. 32° 40′, long. 72° 38′.

NOORPOOR, in the Sinde Sagur Dooab division of the Punjab, a town situated 14 miles W. from the right bank of the Jhelum, 122 miles W. by N. of the town of Lahore. Lat. 31° 57′, long. 72°.

NOORPOOR, in the Daman division of the Punjab, a town situated on the right bank of the Indus, 90 miles S.W. by S. of the town of Mooltan. Lat. 29° 8′, long. 70° 36′.

NOORPORE.—A town in the British district of Dacca Jelalpore, lieut.-gov. of Bengal, 22 miles S.W. of Dacca. Lat. 23° 29′, long. 90° 12′.

NOORPUR.—A town in the British district of Bijnour, lieut.-gov. of the N.W. Provinces. Lat. 29° 9′, long. 78° 28′.

NOOZUDOO.—A town in the British district of Masulipatam, presidency of Madras, 48 miles N.N.W. of Masulipatam. Lat. 16° 49′, long. 80° 55′.

NORAY, in the territory of Oude, a village on the route from Goruckpore cantonment to Lucknow, 95 miles W. of the former, 71 E. of the latter. Water is abundant here, but supplies are scanty. The road to the east, or towards Goruckpore, is much broken and out of order, except near the village, where it is rather good; towards Lucknow, generally good, yet heavy in some parts. Lat. 26° 47′, long. 81° 52′.

NORRIWALLEH, iu the Sinde Sagur Dooab division of the Punjab, a town situated on the left bank of the Indus, 76 miles N.N.W. of the town of Mooltan. Lat. 31° 7′, long. 70° 58′.

NORTHERN CIRCARS.—See CIRCARS.

NORTH-WESTERN PROVINCES.—The great political division of India so called comprehends a vast tract of country, forming a sort of vice-presidency, under the chief government of India. The administration is conducted by an officer bearing the title of lieutenant-governor, appointed by the Governor-General in Council, as hereafter mentioned. The North-Western Provinces proper lie between lat. 23° 51′, the extreme southerly point, and lat. 30° 26′, the extreme northerly point; long. 75° 20′, the extreme western point, and 84° 40′, the extreme eastern point. If, however, the portion of the non-regulation districts connected with the government of the North-Western Provinces be included, the boundaries will extend from lat. 21° 17′ to lat. 31° 6′, and from long. 73° 2′ to long. 84° 40′. The North-Western Provinces proper are bounded on the north by Sirhind, the Deyra Dhoon, Kumaon, and Nepaul; on the east by Nepaul, Oude, and the lower provinces of Bengal; on the south by the lower provinces of Bengal and the native state of Rewah; and on the south-west by Bundelcund, Scindia's territory, and Rajpootana. These provinces are distributed into six large divisions, in which are comprehended thirty-one districts, as stated below:—

Divisions.	Districts.
Delhi	Paneeput. Hurreeanah. Delhi. Rohtuk. Goorgaon.
Meerut	Saharunpore. Mozuffurnuggur. Meerut. Boolundshuhur. Allygurh.
Rohilcund ..	Bijnour. Moradabad. Budaon. Bareilly and Pillibheet. Shahjehanpore.
Agra	Muttra. Agra. Furruckabad. Mynpoorie. Etawah.
Allahabad ..	Cawnpore. Futtehpore. Humeerpore and Calpee. Banda. Allahabad.
Benares	Goruckpore. Azimghur. Jounpore. Mirzapore. Benares. Ghazeepore.

The non-regulation districts under the authority of the lieutenant-governor of the North-Western Provinces comprise the Saugor and Nerbudda territories; the Butty territory, including Wuttoo; the pergunnah of Kote Kasim; Jaunsar and Bawur; the Deyrah Doon; Kumaon, including British Gurhwal; Ajmere, and British Nemaur. The physical characteristics of so wide an extent of country of course differ greatly. These, as well as the chief articles of production, animal and vegetable, and such statistical particulars as are available, are described and enumerated under the names of the respective portions of territory embraced within the limits which circumscribe the authority of the subordinate government, under which the revenue and judicial affairs are administered. The following return of the land revenue, area, population, and other statistical particulars of the North-Western Provinces, has been prepared from information collected during the recent revenue settlement of that portion of India :—

Number of townships		81,908
Area in acres		46,114,514
Land assessed to revenue :—	Acres.	
Cultivated	24,450,228	
Culturable	7,942,491	
		32,392,719
Land unassessed :—		
Rent free	3,267,203	
Barren	10,454,592	
		13,721,795
Total area in acres		46,114,514
Demand on account of land revenue		Rs.4,06,54,410

	R.	a.	p.
Rate per acre on total area	0	14	1
On total assessed land	1	4	1
On total cultivation	1	8	2

Population :—		
Hindoo—Agricultural	17,699,160	
Non-agricul.	8,024,951	
		25,724,111
Mahomedan and others :—		
Agricultural	1,894,270	
Non-agricultural	2,653,501	
		4,547,771
Total population		30,271,882

It may be added, that the area of the six divisions constituting the North-Western Provinces proper, given in the above statement in acres, amounts to 72,054 square miles, British statute measure ; and the total population being 30,271,882, gives an average of something beyond 420 inhabitants to the square mile. The land is held under putteedarree settlement. The government assessment, calculated upon the basis of two-thirds of the net rent, has been fixed for a period of thirty years. By this limitation of the public demand, a valuable and marketable private property has been created in the land ; and every landholder, however petty his holding, is to a certain extent a capitalist. In connection with this admirable system, two servants of the East-India Company merit especial mention. The task of revising the settlement, and reconstructing it upon better principles, belongs to Mr. Mertins Bird ; the duty of carrying it out, and realizing its advantages to the inhabitants, was reserved for Mr. Thomason, who administered the affairs of the North-Western Provinces as lieutenant-govenor for nine years. Neither gentleman lives to contemplate the success of his labours. Mr. Bird died in this country, in August, 1853 ; Mr. Thomason was removed from life in the same year, almost immediately after his appointment to the governorship of Madras, to which presidency it was anticipated that he would render similar benefits to those which he had conferred on the North-West Provinces. The Court of Directors were not unmindful of his merits, and bore to them the following testimony, in the dispatch acknowledging the communication of the melancholy news of his death :—

"Mr. Thomason had obtained distinction in the several stages of his official progress ; and as lieutenant-governor of the North-Western Provinces during a period of nine years, he exhibited all the qualities of an accomplished and successful administrator. He omitted no research, and spared no pains, to make himself master of every subject that came before him, however minute, or however comprehensive. His decisions, founded on results so obtained, were clearly, concisely, and impressively delivered. We seldom dissented from his judgment, and never but with hesitation and reluctance. He inculcated and maintained discipline in the public service by the discernment with which he observed and rewarded merit, by a rare union of conciliation and firmness, by uniform kindness and courtesy to those below him, and by his own marked example of deference to superior authority. In his administration of the territorial revenue, an efficient watchfulness over the just interests of the state was always tempered by a benevolent care for the well-being of the agricultural community. We are persuaded that all classes who lived under his government, from the highest public servant to the cultivator of the soil, must participate in the sorrow which we feel for his loss." Within these provinces are some thriving and populous towns, the chief of which are noticed in their proper places in the alphabetical arrangement. There are also several educational establishments. Those partaking of a collegiate character will be found mentioned under the heads of their respective localities. For the promotion of popular instruction, a comprehensive scheme has recently been devised, and partially brought into operation, in the way of experiment. It contemplates the establishment of schools in each tehsildarree division of the Provinces, the masters of which are to receive small salaries from government, in addition to the fees received on account of the scholars ; the course of instruction to comprise reading and writing the vernacular languages, both Oordoo and Hindee ; accounts, and the mensuration of land according to the native system. Instruction in history, geography, geometry, and other useful subjects, is also proffered ; but the communication of this appears to be dependent on the desire of the people to receive it. The working of the system is to be under the supervision of pergunnah visitors, zillah visitors, and a visitor-general. This system, it is to be observed, is intended not to supersede native schools, but to increase their number and improve their character. The government schools will be in fact central model establishments, exhibiting the advantages of an improved course of teaching, and aiding the efforts of the inhabitants in adopting such means as may tend to secure its benefits to their children.

Under the last general arrangement for the government of India (3 & 4 Wm. 4, cap. 85), the then existing presidency of Fort William was to be divided into two presidencies ; one retaining the previous name, the other to be called the Presidency of Agra. This plan, however, was never acted upon; and by an act subsequently passed (5 & 6 Wm. 4, cap. 52), power was given to the home authorities to suspend its operation, and to the Governor-General in Council to appoint during such suspension a lieutenant-governor of the North-Western Provinces, exercising his powers within an extent of territory defined by the authority from whom he received his appointment, and with such limitations as the same authority might deem fit. Agra is the seat of the government thus established; from which circumstance the officer administering it is often called the lieutenant-governor of Agra.

NOSAREE, in the British district of Surat, presidency of Bombay, a town situate on the left or south bank of the river Poorna, and eight miles above its fall into the Gulf of Cambay. The river "is wide at the entrance, but difficult of access, on account of the winding channel among banks, and has but three or four feet in it at low water spring tides." The town is eligibly situate, and surrounded by much rich cultivation, principally dry. Many of the inhabitants are Parsee weavers, who work to supply the markets of Surat; and there are many artificers in copper, brass, iron, and wood. There is considerable coasting and export trade in grain, coarse sugar, wood, and other articles, the produce of the country. As the port, however, belongs in sovereignty to the Guicowar, the provisions of the British customs laws have not been introduced therein. Population 15,000. Distance from Surat, S., 18 miles; Bombay, N., 140. Lat. 20° 55', long. 73°.

NOSHEHR SERAI, or NAOSHERA.—An extensive caravanserai on the route from Lahore to Cashmere by the Pir Panjal Pass. It is built of brick, faced at the gateways with stone, and was originally of such strength as to serve for a fortress as well as a caravanserai; but it is now in a ruinous state. It is situate on the river Tauhi or Tihoi, which, at thirty-five or forty miles to the south-east, falls into the Chinab. An inscription on one of the gateways records that it was built by the Mogul emperor Akbar. Noshehr Serai is in lat. 33° 9', long. 74° 17'.

NOSHURUH, in the British district of Mynpooree, lieut.-gov. of the N.W. Provinces, a village on the route from the city of Agra to Etawa, and 41 miles E. of the former. Lat. 27° 6', long. 78° 40'.

NOSOOM.—A town in the British district of Cuddapah, presidency of Madras, 45 miles N.W. of Cuddapah. Lat. 14° 58', long. 78° 27'.

NOUBUTPOOR, in the British district of Benares, lieut.-gov. of the N.W. Provinces, a town on the route from Hazarebaugh to Benares, 162 miles N.W. of the former, 27 S.E. of the latter. It has a bazar, and a staging bungalow, or public lodge for travellers, and is situate on the left bank of the river Kurumnassa, here crossed by a bridge of masonry, the material for which is a very hard, fine-grained, light-red sandstone, quarried in hills situate to the east. Supplies are abundant, and the water of the Kurumnasa is as "clear as crystal." The road in this part of the route is good. Lat. 25° 19', long. 83° 29'.

NOUGAON, in the British district of Moradabad, lieut.-gov. of the N.W. Provinces, a small town on the route from the town of Moradabad to Muzuffernugur, and 28 miles N.W. of the former place. It has a bazar. Distant N.W. from Calcutta 916 miles. Lat. 29° 1', long. 78° 29'.

NOUGAWA, in the British district of Allygurh, lieut.-gov. of the N.W. Provinces, a village on the route from the cantonment of Allygurh to that of Muttra, and 16 miles S.W. of the former. Lat. 27° 41', long. 78° 8'.

NOUGMA.—See NOUGAWA.

NOURUNGA, or AURUNGABAD, in the British district of Behar, lieut.-gov. of Bengal, a town, the principal place of a thana or police division of the same name, situate on the route from Hazarebaugh to Benares, 88 miles N.W. of former, 101 S.E. of latter. It has a bazar. The town has 615 houses, which, according to the usually admitted ratio of inmates to houses, would assign it a population of 3,075 persons. Lat. 24° 44', long. 84° 25'.

NOURUNGABAD, in the British district of Muttra, lieut.-gov. of the N.W. Provinces, a village on the route from the city of Agra to that of Muttra, and four miles S. of the latter. Lat. 27° 26', long. 77° 47'.

NOURUNGABAD, in the territory of Oude, a small town on the route from Bareilly to Seetapore, 77 miles S.E. of the former, 28 N.W. of the latter. It is situate five miles E. of the left bank of the Goomtee, crossed by the route from Bareilly, and fordable by cattle from December to June, during which interval the average depth is three feet. At other times it must be crossed by ferry. There is a bazar here. Lat. 27° 46', long. 80° 26'.

NOURUNGABAD, in the British district of Allygurh, lieut.-gov. of the N.W. Provinces, a village on the route from the cantonment of Allygurh to that of Mynpooree, and four miles S.E. of the former. Lat. 27° 52', long. 78° 13'.

NOUSHARA, in the Peshawur division of the Punjaub, a town situate on the banks of the Kabool river, 18 miles N.W. of Attock. Here, in 1823, the Afghans were utterly routed by the Sikhs, commanded by Runjeet Singh. The Sikhs built a fort here, under the direction of General Avitabile; it has four bastions and a double row of loopholes. The vicinity has been selected for the site of a sanatarium for troops in the province of Peshawur. The inundations caused by the heavy rains of 1856 completely destroyed the cantonment at this place. Lat. 34° 3', long. 72° 2'.

NOUSHERA, in the Punjab, a village, with an adjoining fort, on the route from Attock to Kashmir, by Mazufurabad, from which last place it is distant about 20 miles S.W. It is situate at the western base of the mountains inclosing Kashmir on the west. The surrounding country consists of parched uncultivated plains, intersected at different distances by long, rocky, barren ridges. Noushera is in lat. 34° 8′, long. 73° 8′.

NOUVARUNGAPOOR.—A town in the recently lapsed territory of Nagpore or Berar, situate 34 miles E. by N. from Jugdulapoor Bustur, and 107 miles N.W. from Vizianagrum. Lat. 19° 20′, long. 82° 27′.

NOWABAD, or NUWABPOORAH, in the British district of Bijnour, lieut.-gov. of the N.W. Provinces, a village on the route, up the course of the Ramgunga (Western), from Moradabad cantonment to Fort Almora, 44 miles N. of the former. Lat. 29° 28′, long. 78° 45′.

NOWADA.—A town in the British district of Moorshedabad, lieut.-gov. of Bengal, 94 miles N. of Calcutta. Lat. 23° 55′, long. 88° 23′.

NOWA DEYRA, in Sinde, a village on the route from Larkhana to Sukkur, and 12 miles E. of the former town. It contains about 100 houses and five wells. The road in this part of the route is a mere path through jungle. Lat. 27° 38′, long. 68° 19′.

NOWAEE, in the Rajpoot state of Jeypore, a town 50 miles S.E. of the city of Jeypore. Here, in 1804, the grand British army under General Lake was encamped, to give effect to the attack on Rampoora, which was stormed by a detachment under Colonel Don. Lat. 26° 21′, long. 76° 3′.

NOWAGAON.—See NYGOWAN.

NOWAGHAM.—A town in the territory of one of the hill tribes of Orissa, 45 miles N.W. by W. from Goomsoor, and 123 miles W. by S. from Cuttack. Lat. 20° 9′, long. 84° 3′.

NOWAGUDDA.—See NOWAGURH.

NOWAGUDDA, on the south-west frontier of Bengal, a town in the native state of Nowagudda, 133 miles S.W. by W. from Sumbulpoor, and 107 miles N. by W. from the hill zemindarry of Jeypoor. Lat. 20° 33′, long. 82° 13′.

NOWAGUR.—A town in the British district of Palamow, lieut.-gov. of Bengal, 22 miles N.E. by E. of Palamow. Lat. 23° 59′, long. 84° 20′.

NOWAGUR.—A town in the recently lapsed territory of Nagpore, situate 162 miles E.N.E. from Nagpore, and 100 miles S. from Sohagpoor. Lat. 21° 53′, long. 81° 32′.

NOWAGUR.—A town in the recently lapsed territory of Nagpore, situate on the right bank of the Husdah river, and 46 miles S.E. by E. from Ruttunpoor. Lat. 21° 52′, long. 82° 43′.

NOWAGURH.—A town in the Rajpoot state of Oodeypoor, 75 miles N.N.E. from Oodeypoor, and 70 miles S.W. by S. from Ajmeer. Lat. 25° 39′, long. 74° 10′.

NOWAGURH.—A raj subject to the political agent for the south-west frontier. It is of irregular shape, and is bounded on the north, west, and south by the recently lapsed territory of Berar, and on the east by Kerrial. Its centre is in lat. 20° 20′, long. 82° 25′; its area is 1,512 square miles. From official statements, the country seems to be among the worst governed of those within the circle to which it belongs. The *rajah* was at one period reported by the political agent to be under arrest for the attempted murder of three horse-dealers. Many other murders were attributed to him; and it appeared that he was in the habit of offering human sacrifices, in the manner of the Khoonds, but with a difference as to the selection of victims. The Khoonds have no predilection as to origin, but rear from infancy children of any caste for the terrible purpose; while the rajah of this district preferred Brahmins, they being enemies of the caste to which he himself belonged. The country was estimated to produce about 5,000 rupees annually; but the tribute, though only 400 rupees, was obtained with difficulty. The population is estimated at 68,000. Nowagudda, the chief town, is in lat. 20° 30′, long. 82° 12′.

NOWAKOTE.—A town in the British district of Hydrabad, province of Scinde, presidency of Bombay, 76 miles S.E. by E. of Hydrabad. Lat. 24° 51′, long. 69° 31′.

NOWAKOTE, in the Sinde Sagur Dooab division of the Punjab, a town situated 32 miles N.W. from the right bank of the Chenaub, 62 miles N. of the town of Mooltan. Lat. 31°, long. 71° 30′.

NOWANUGGUR, in the peninsula of Kattywar, province of Guzerat, a seaport on a creek indenting the southern shore of the Gulf of Cutch. It is the principal place of the district of Hallar, and is described as a considerable town, and nearly four miles in circuit. It has much trade, and the cloths manufactured here are celebrated for their fine quality. The dyes given to those fabrics are peculiarly admired, and their excellence is attributed to the quality of the water of the Nagne, which washes the walls of the city. Piece-goods are manufactured here for the Arabian and African markets. In the sea north of the town are some beds of pearl-oysters, belonging to the chief of the place; but the pearls are not fine, and from mismanagement the stock is wasting away. The chief, who bears the title of Jam of Nowanuggur, holds the greater part of the district of Hallar in jaghire; his territory comprising 540 villages, with a population estimated at 207,680. He pays to the British government an annual tribute of 47,259 rupees (independently of what is paid for villages occupied by him in the prant or division of Kattywar), and to the Guicowar 77,547 rupees. Copper-ore has been discovered in a range of hills near the town. Distance from Ahmedabad, S.W., 160 miles; Baroda, W., 200; Surat, N.W., 190; Bombay, N.W., 310. Lat. 22° 28', long. 70° 11'.

NOWARRY.—A town in the district of Deoghur above the Ghauts, in the recently lapsed territory of Nagpore, situate 50 miles N.E. from Deoghur, and 71 miles S.W. by S. from Jubbulpoor. Lat. 22° 20', long. 79° 20'.

NOWA THULA.—A village in the Rajpoot state of Jessulmeer, on the route from the town of Beekaneer to that of Jessulmeer, and 48 miles N.E. of the latter. It contains a small fort, 100 houses, thirty shops, and two wells 195 feet deep, yielding brackish water. The road in this part of the route is sandy and bad. Lat. 27° 7', long. 71° 43'.

NOWBUTPOOR.—A town in the British district of Patna, lieut.-gov. of Bengal, 18 miles W.S.W. of Patna. Lat. 25° 27', long. 85°.

NOWGAON, in the British district of Mirzapoor, lieut.-gov. of the N.W. Provinces, a village on the right bank of the Ganges, 18 miles N.W. of the city of Mirzapoor. Lat. 25° 14', long. 82° 26'.

NOWGAON.—See NYAGAON.

NOWGONG. — A town in the British district of Nowgong, Lower Assam, situate 50 miles E. of Durrung. The area of the district of which this town is the principal place is 4,160 square miles, sustaining a population of 70,000 inhabitants. Lat. 26° 21', long. 92° 49'.

NOWGURH, in the British district of Mirzapoor, lieut.-gov. of the N.W. Provinces, a town on the route from Mirzapoor to Ramgur, 50 miles E.S.E. of the former. Lat. 24° 50', long. 83° 19'.

NOWLGOOND.—A town locally situated within the district of Dharwar, presidency of Bombay, 24 miles E.N.E. of Dharwar. The estate of which this town is the principal place has been allowed to descend to an adopted son, the former chief having died in 1838 without issue. In recognising the adoption, the British government insisted upon the fulfilment of certain conditions; among which were the abolition of all duties on trade, and the general assimilation of the administration to the system prevailing in the neighbouring government villages. Lat. 15° 33', long. 75° 25'.

NOWPAUDA. — A town in the British district of Ganjam, presidency of Madras, 79 miles S.W. by S. of Ganjam. Lat. 18° 33', long. 84° 21'.

NOWPOOR, in the British collectorate of Candeish, presidency of Bombay, a town on the route from Surat to Malligaum, 60 miles E. of the former, and 65 N.W. of the latter. Lat. 21° 9', long. 73° 48'.

NOWR, in the British district of Goruckpore, lieut.-gov. of the N.W. Provinces, a tal or small lake, which, during the periodical annual rains, is about three miles long and one broad, but of about a third of the size in the dry season, when it shoals throughout, and is in many parts overgrown with reeds and other aquatic vegetation. Lat. 26° 40', long. 83° 19'.

NOWSARA.—See NOSAREE.

NOWSHARA, in Bhawlpoor, a small town with a good bazar, and surrounded by a wall. It is situate on an eminence at the western edge of a ravine, in a fertile country crowded with villages. Lat. 28° 26', long. 70° 26'.

NOWSHARRA, in the Punjab, a village situate on an offset of the Indus, and five miles from the left bank of the main stream. It is about eight miles north of the town of Leia, on the route from Dera Ismael Khan to Mooltan. Lat. 31° 4', long. 71° 2'.

NOWSHERA.—A town of Sinde, in the district subject to Ali Moorad, 76 miles S.W. by S. from Sukkur, and 88 miles S.S.W. from Shikarpoor. Lat. 26° 51', long. 68° 10'.

NOWSHERA, in the Daman division of the Punjab, a town situated on the right bank of the Indus, 58 miles N.W. of the town of Mooltan. Lat. 30° 42', long. 70° 58'.

NOWSUR, in Sinde, a village on the route from Shikarpoor to Larkhana, and seven miles and a half S.W. of the former town. There are between 200 and 300 inhabitants. The place is supplied with water from two wells. Lat. 27° 54', long. 68° 34'.

NOWSUR, in the Rajpoot state of Jodhpoor, a village on the route, *viâ* Nagor, from Jessulmere to Nusseerabad, and 163 miles N.W. of the latter. It is supplied with water from one well 260 feet deep. Lat. 26° 54', long. 72° 57'.

NOYEL RIVER. — A tributary of the Cauvery, rising in lat. 10° 59', long. 76° 44', on the eastern slope of the Western Ghats, and flowing in an easterly direction for ninety-five miles through the British district of Coimbatore, and past the town of the same name, falls into the Cauvery on the right side, near the town of Kodumudy, in lat. 11° 4', long. 77° 59'.

NOZEED.—An estate or petty territory so called, situate within the British district of Masulipatam, presidency of Madras. This tract acquired some notoriety in this country between twenty and thirty years ago, from the successful issue of a bill then introduced into parliament, for compelling the East-India Company to satisfy the claim of Mr. James Hodges in respect of money advanced on the security of the lands of the zemindarry. The particulars, which are somewhat curious, will be found detailed in the Appendix to Thornton's History of India, vol. v., page 379. Lat. 16° 35', long. 80° 45'.

NUBBEEGUNJ, in the British district of Mynpooree, lieut.-gov. of the N.W. Provinces, a town on the route from Mynpooree to Lucknow, 24 miles E. of the former. Lat. 27° 12′, long. 79° 27′.

NUBBEEPOOR, in the British district of Cawnpore, lieut.-gov. of the N.W. Provinces, a village on the route from the cantonment of Cawnpore to that of Calpee, and 22 miles N.E. of the latter. Lat. 26° 21′, long. 80° 2′.

NUBBEESIR.—A town in the British district of Hydrabad, province of Scinde, presidency of Bombay, 83 miles E. by S. of Hydrabad. Lat. 25° 6′, long. 69° 44′.

NUBEENUGUR, in the British district of Behar, a town at the base of the mountains stretching along the south frontier. It is the principal place of a thana or police division containing, with the neighbouring thana of Mujiainha, 1,085 villages, and a population of 105,833, of whom the Brahminists are fifteen to one to the Mussulmans. The town of Nubeenugur contains 461 houses; and if the usually received ratio of inmates to houses be admitted, the population may be assumed at 2,305. Distant S.W. from Gaya 55 miles; Benares, S.E., 85. Lat. 24° 36′, long. 84° 10′.

NUDDEA.—A British district under the lieut.-gov. of Bengal, apparently thus denominated from a town of the same name, which, however, is situate in the British district of Burdwan. It is bounded on the north by the British district Rajeshaye; on the east by the British districts Pubna and Jessore; on the south by the British district Baraset; on the west by the British districts Hoogly, Beerbhoom, and Burdwan; and on the north-west by the British district Moorshedabad: it lies between lat. 22° 49′—24° 10′, long. 88° 9′—89° 11′; is about ninety miles in length from north to south, and forty-five in breadth: the area is 2,942 square miles. It is altogether comprised within the delta of the Ganges, the branches of which everywhere traverse it. The principal streams communicate with each other by numerous lateral offsets, the whole surface being overspread with a reticulation of watercourses, and extensively inundated during the periodical rains. Considerable progress has been made of late years in facilitating the navigation of the rivers by which Nuddea is traversed. This district, besides the advantages of extensive water-carriage and ample means of irrigation, has a fertile, friable soil, easily vultivated, and producing in abundance rice, various kinds of millet, maize, pulse, oil-seeds, cucurbitaceous plants, sugar-cane, indigo, tobacco, and hemp. The mulberry is grown to great extent, to yield food for the silkworm. Though populous and productive, Nuddea, like most other parts of Bengal, has few towns of any importance. Kishnugur, the seat of the civil establishment, Plassey, and Hurrisunkra, are described under their respective names in the alphabetical arrangement.

The numerous watercourses rendering land routes difficult, and affording ready means of communication by water in every part and direction, preclude, in a great degree, the construction of roads, while they obviate their necessity. There are but two chief routes; one from south to north, from Calcutta to Berhampore, by Kishnugur and Plassey; the other from south-west to north-east, from Calcutta to Jessore, Fureedpore, and Dacca. This last route, however, is so wretched, that it is described by Garden as "no regular road: distances uncertain." The physical circumstances of the district, and its vicinity to the metropolis, obviously denote it to be capable of great advances in general prosperity. The population is stated in the article BENGAL.

At the time of the invasion of Bengal by the Mussulmans, under Bakhtyar Ghilji, 1202, the tract comprehended within this district was ruled by Rajah Luchmunyah, who, though possessing the ancient city of Gaur, resided in Nuddea, at present, as already mentioned, within the British district of Burdwan; and who, being attacked by the Mussulmans, fled, leaving his dominions a prey to the invaders, by whom they were speedily overrun and permanently conquered. Nuddea subsequently followed the fortunes of Bengal, and in 1765 was included within the grant made under the firman of the emperor Shah Alum. The titles of the rajahs of Nuddea had been discontinued for two generations; but in 1849, Srees Chunder Roy, a descendant of the ancient family, received permission from the British government to take the title of maharajah.

NUDDEA, in the British district of Burdwan, under the lieut.-gov. of Bengal, a town on the route from Cutwa to Hoogly, 20 miles S.E. of the former, 34 N. of the latter. It is situate on the right bank of the Bhagruttee, or great western branch of the Ganges, at the point where it is joined by the branch denominated the Jellinghee, the united volume of water acquiring the name of the Hoogly. Here is an antique Brahminical college, now fallen into decay. The town, though within another district, gives name to the district Nuddea, on the opposite or eastern side of the Bhagruttee. It appears to have been, at the remotest period of its history, the residence of a Hindoo sovereign, who was expelled in 1203 by Bukhtyar Ghilji, subahdar or governor of Bengal, who had been raised to that station by Kootb-ood-deen, the sovereign of Delhi. Distant N. from Calcutta, by land, 60 miles; by water, along the course of the Hoogly, 80. Lat. 23° 25′, long. 88° 22′.

NUDDYAGONG, in a detached portion of the native state of Dutteea, a small town on the route, by Koonch, from Gwalior to Calpee, 53 miles W. of the latter. It has a bazar, and being situate on the river Puhuj, is well supplied with water. Lat. 26° 6′, long. 79° 5′.

NUGAON, in the British district of Furruckabad, lieut.-gov. of the N.W. Provinces, a village on the route from the cantonment of Allygurh to that of Futtehgurh, and 25 miles N.W. of the latter. Lat. 27° 27′, long. 79° 20′.

NUGEENA, in the British district of Goorgaon, lieut.-gov. of the N.W. Provinces, a village on the route from Alwur, by Ferozpore, to Delhi, and 65 miles S.W. of the latter. Here is a handsome bungalow, or lodging-house for travellers, which was originally built as a country seat by Shumsuddin Khan, of Ferozpore, who was hanged at Delhi in 1836, for the murder of William Fraser, the British political agent. The road in this part of the route is good. Lat. 27° 55′, long. 77° 2′.

NUGEENAH, in the British district of Bijnour, division of Rohilcund, lieut.-gov. of the N.W. Provinces, a town on the route from Hurdwar to Moradabad, and 48 miles N.W. of the latter. It is situate five or six miles S. of the belt of forest marking the Terai, and is described by Davidson as "a very large, populous town or city, full of brick-built houses and bazars. This is the Birmingham of Upper India, and is known from the attention paid to the manufacture of gun-barrels and detonating-locks for fowling-pieces." The population was stated by Davidson to be above 30,000 souls; but a more recent return gives only 14,001. The surrounding country is open and cultivated, and the road in this part of the route is good. Elevation above the sea 849 feet; distance N.W. from Calcutta 936 miles. Lat. 29° 27′, long. 78° 30′.

NUGGEREE.—A town in the recently lapsed territory of Nagpore, situate on the left bank of the Weingunga river, and 82 miles S.E. from Nagpoor. Lat. 20° 19′, long. 80°.

NUGGRA.—A town of Malwa, in the native state of Rutlam, nine miles N.E. by E. from Rutlam, and 165 miles E. by N. from Ahmedabad. Lat. 23° 20′, long. 75° 8′.

NUGGUR.—A town in the native state of Dholpoor, 11 miles S.W. from Dholpoor, and 46 miles S.S.W. from Agra. Lat. 26° 34′, long. 77° 53′.

NUGGUR.—See BEDNORE.

NUGGURNAUR.—A town in the recently lapsed territory of Nagpore or Berar, situate 10 miles E. from Jugdullapoor, and 26 miles S.E. by E. from the hill zemindarry of Jeypoor. Lat. 19° 13′, long. 82° 7′.

NUGGUR PARKUR.—A town in the British district of Hydrabad, province of Scinde, presidency of Bombay, 154 miles S.E. by E. of Hydrabad. Lat. 24° 22′, long. 70° 38′.

NUGLA, in the British district of Pilleebheet, lieut.-gov. of the N.W. Provinces, a town on the route from Belheri to Nugeena, and 28 miles W. of the former. Lat. 28° 59′, long. 79° 35′.

NUGLEEA, in the British district of Moradabad, lieut.-gov. of the N.W. Provinces, a town close to the north-western frontier, towards the district Bijnour, and four miles E. of the left bank of the Ganges. Lat. 28° 52′, long. 78° 15′.

NUGLUH, in the British district of Muzuffurnugur, lieut.-gov. of the N.W. Provinces, a village on the route from Kurnal to Meerut, and seven miles S.E. of the former. Lat. 29° 18′, long. 77° 8′.

NUGOWLUH, in the British district of Allygurh, lieut.-gov. of the N.W. Provinces, a village on the route from the cantonment of Allygurh to that of Moradabad, and seven miles N.E. of the former. The road in this part of the route is good; the country open, with a clayey soil, partially cultivated. Lat. 28° 1′, long. 78° 10′.

NUGRA, in the British district of Azimgurh, lieut.-gov. of the N.W. Provinces, a town on the route from Azimgurh to Chupra, 45 miles E. of the former. Lat. 25° 56′, long. 83° 56′.

NUGRA, in the British district of Pilleebheet, lieut.-gov. of the N.W. Provinces, a village on the route to Rudopoor from the town of Pilleebheet, 28 miles N.W. of the latter. Lat. 28° 57′, long. 79° 36′.

NUGULSUR.—A town in the British district of Balasore, northern division of Cuttack, lieut.-gov. of Bengal, 20 miles N.E. by E. of Balasore. Lat. 21° 37′, long. 87° 13′.

NUGURBERRA.—A town in the British district of Camroop, Lower Assam, 44 miles W. of Gowhatty. Lat. 26° 5′, long. 91° 2′.

NUGURDA, in the British district of Mirzapoor, lieut.-gov. of the N.W. Provinces, a village on the left bank of the Ganges, 25 miles N.W. of Mirzapoor. Lat. 25° 15′, long. 82° 23′.

NUGUREA, in the British district of Allygurh, lieut.-gov. of the N.W. Provinces, a village on the route from Meerut to Muttra, and 29 miles N.E. of the latter. Lat. 27° 52′, long. 77° 50′.

NUGUR KHAS, a small town, giving name to the pergunnah or subdivision of Aurungabad-Nugur, in the British district of Goruckpore, lieut.-gov. of the N.W. Provinces, is situate on the northern bank of the small lake called Chanda Tal. It contains 100 houses; and consequently, allowing six persons to each, a population of 600. It has defences in good repair, in the native style, as it is the residence of a chief, or petty rajah. Distant W. from the cantonment of Goruckpore 44 miles. Lat. 26° 42′, long. 82° 43′.

NUJEEBABAD, in the British district of Bijnour, lieut.-gov. of the N.W. Provinces, a town on the route from Hurdwar to Moradabad, and 31 miles S.E. of the former. It is called from Nujeebuddowlah, a Rohilla chief, who founded it about the middle of the last century. Its site is not well selected, being low and swampy. Hardwicke, who visited it in A.D. 1796, describes it at that time "about six furlongs in length, with some regular streets, broad, and inclosed by barriers at different distances, forming distinct bazars. In the neighbourhood are the remains of many considerable buildings." Outside the town is the tomb of Nujeebuddowlah, surrounded by a square building, formed into apartments for the accommodation of those engaged in performing ceremonies for the benefit of the soul of the deceased. The town is at present thriving and considerable, having a brisk transit-trade between Kumaon and the south. Two miles south-east of the town is Puthurgarh, a large square brick-built fort, with bastions at the angles, and at the spots equidistant from them in the middle of each face. The road in this part of the route is good. Distant N.W. from Calcutta, *viâ* Moradabad, 950 miles. Lat. 29° 37′, long. 78° 25′.

NUKOOR, in the British district of Suharunpoor, lieut.-gov. of the N.W. Provinces, a town on the route from Suharunpoor to Kurnal, 14 miles W. of the former. Lat. 29° 56′, long. 77° 23′.

NULCHERA, in the British district of Backergunje, lieut.-gov. of Bengal, a town on the right or south-west side of the Ganges. It is the principal port and commercial place of the district, and to it repair, in considerable numbers, river craft from the Arracan coast and other places to the eastward. There is also active communication by means of the river with Calcutta and other places westward or north-westward. The principal imports are teak and iron; the exports are much more considerable, consisting of rice, cocoanuts, and betelnuts. Distance N. from Burisaul 12 miles. Lat. 22° 55′, long. 90° 19′.

NULDROOG, in one of the recently sequestrated districts of the Nizam, a town with a fort on an eminence. Distance from Beeder, W., 81 miles; from the city of Hydrabad, N.W., 150. Lat. 17° 40′, long. 76° 20′.

NULHATTEE.—A town in the British district of Beerbhoom, lieut.-gov. of Bengal, 126 miles N.N.W. of Calcutta. Lat. 24° 18′, long. 87° 50′.

NULKAR.—A town in the native state of Bhotan, situate on the right bank of the Monas river, and 77 miles N.W. by N. from Durrung. Lat. 27° 22′, long. 91° 30′.

NULLACHERLA.—A town in the British district of Masulipatam, presidency of Madras, 56 miles N. by E. of Masulipatam. Lat. 16° 57′, long. 81° 29′.

NULLING.—A town in the British district of Candeish, presidency of Bombay, 24 miles N.E. by N. of Malligaum. Lat. 20° 50′, long. 74° 41′.

NUMBALGERRY.—A town in the British district of Bellary, presidency of Madras, 46 miles S.W. of Bellary. Lat. 14° 42′, long. 76° 26′.

NUNA.—A river rising in the British district of Tirhoot, in a lake 10 miles S.W. of the town of Mozuffurpoor, and in lat. 26° 1′, long. 85° 18′. It flows in a south-easterly direction for sixty miles through the district of Tirhoot, and twenty miles through that of Mongheer, to its junction with the Bagmuttee, in lat. 25° 30′, long. 86° 12′.

NUNDANAWONUM.—A town in the British district of Nellore, presidency of Madras, 73 miles N.W. of Nellore. Lat. 15° 13′, long. 79° 16′.

NUNDANAWONUM.—A town in the British district of Nellore, presidency of Madras, 80 miles N.N.W. of Nellore. Lat. 15° 29′, long. 79° 31′.

NUNDAPORUM.—A town in the hill zemindarry of Jeypore, presidency of Madras, 55 miles S. from Jeypoor, and 71 miles N.W. by W. from Vizagapatam. Lat. 18° 14′, long. 82° 28′.

NUNDEEJAH, a river of the British district of Kumaon, lieut.-gov. of Agra, rises on the eastern declivity of the lofty Nanda Devi mountain, about lat. 30° 22′, long. 80° 8′, and having an easterly course of about eight miles, falls into the Goree, a great feeder of the Kali, at an elevation of 10,514 feet above the sea. It was crossed near its mouth by means of a sangha or bridge of spars, by Webb, in the beginning of June, when it was found to be twelve yards wide, and with a rapid turbid stream. A mile higher up, its course was buried beneath snow-beds.

NUNDGUNJE, in the British district of Ghazeepoor, lieut.-gov. of the N.W. Provinces, a village on the route from the cantonment of Benares to that of Ghazeepoor, 36 miles N.E. of the former, 10 W. of the latter, three N.W. of the left bank of the Ganges. The road in this part of the route is good. Lat. 25° 30′, long. 83° 30′.

NUNDIALLUMPETT.—A town in the British district of Cuddapah, presidency of Madras, 17 miles N. of Cuddapah. Lat. 14° 43′, long. 78° 50′.

NUNDLAPOOR, in the British district of Agra, a village on the route from the city of Agra to Allygurh, and nine miles N. of the former. The road in this part of the route is very good, the country partially cultivated. Lat. 27° 15′, long. 78° 7′.

NUNDOORBAR.—A town in the British district of Candeish, presidency of Bombay, 61 miles N.N.W. of Malligaum. Lat. 21° 22′, long. 74° 12′.

NUNDOUR, in the British district of Goruckpore, lieut.-gov. of the N.W. Provinces, a tal or small lake three miles long and one broad. It is generally shallow, yet in several places tolerably deep; channels of no great width wind among shoals overgrown with reeds, amidst which the water is in some parts not easily perceived by a spectator on shore. Lat. 26° 46′, long. 83° 15′.

NUNDOW, in the British district of Agra, lieut.-gov. of the N.W. Provinces, a village on the route from Agra, by Khasgunj, to Bareilly, and nine miles N.E. of the former. Lat. 27° 16′, long. 78° 16′.

NUNDPOOR.—A town in the recently lapsed territory of Nagpore or Berar, situate 44 miles S. by W. from Nagpore, and 106 miles E.S.E. from Ellichpoor. Lat. 20° 33′, long. 79° 2′.

NUNDRA KHAIL, in the Daman division of the Punjab, a town situate on the right bank of the Gombela Tochee river, 123 miles S.S.W. of the town of Peshawur. Lat. 32° 24′, long. 70° 48′.

NUNDWA, in the British district of Saugur and Nerbudda, lieut.-gov. of the N.W. Provinces, a town on the route from Jubbulpoor to Baitool, 48 miles S.W. by W. of the former. Lat. 22° 44′, long. 79° 25′.

NUNDYAL.—A town in the British district of Kurnool, presidency of Madras, 38 miles S.E. by E. of Kurnool. Lat. 15° 30′, long. 78° 33′.

NUNDY DROOG, in the Mysore, a fort on a huge rock of granite, one of three which rise close to each other to a height exceeding 1,500 feet. When invested in the year 1791, by a British force, the rock was inaccessible, except on one point, where there was a double line of ramparts. Three weeks were expended by the besieging force in regularly working up the steep declivity, and in breaching; and the place was stormed with the loss of thirty killed and wounded on the part of the British, who lost 120 in the whole course of the siege. Hyder Ali and Tippoo Sultan had been at great trouble in fortifying this post. "At one time it was famed for the salubrity of its climate, and was frequently visited by invalids from Madras. It, however, became all at once unhealthy: and has for many years been abandoned as a station." Elevation above the sea 4,856 feet; distance from Bangalore, N., 30 miles; from Seringapatam, N.E., 94. Lat. 13° 22′, long. 77° 45′.

NUNDYGANAH.—A town in the British district of Masulipatam, presidency of Madras, 71 miles N.W. by W. of Masulipatam. Lat. 16° 47′, long. 80° 20′.

NUNEOO.—A town in the Rajpoot state of Jodhpoor, 75 miles N.W. by N. from Jodhpoor, and 146 miles W.N.W. from Ajmeer. Lat. 27° 14′, long. 72° 31′.

NUNGAVELLY.—A town in the British district of Salem, presidency of Madras, 22 miles W.N.W. of Salem. Lat. 11° 47′, long. 77° 56′.

NUNGKLOW.—A town of Eastern India, in the native territory of Osimlee, one of the Cossya states, 36 miles S. from Gowhatty, and 53 miles N.N.W. from Silhet. Lat. 25° 37′, long. 91° 40′.

NUNGSAGOOMA.—A town in the native state of Bhotan, situate on the right bank of the Bagnee river, and 102 miles N.E. by E. from Darjeeling. Lat. 27° 54′, long. 89° 41′.

NUNGUR, in the territory of Bhurtpore, a town on the route from Muttra to Alwar, 39 miles W. of former, 36 E. of latter, 28 N.W. of the city of Bhurtpoor. Supplies and water may be had in abundance. Lat. 27° 25′, long. 77° 10′.

NUNJANGODE, in the Mysore, a town situate on the south or right side of the Cubbany river, which, near this place, is crossed by a bridge, which is here looked upon as a prodigy of grandeur: in Europe it would be considered a disgrace to the architect of the meanest town. The arches are about five feet span; the piers are of nearly an equal thickness, and do not present an angle to the stream. The sides of the arch have scarcely any curvature, but are composed of two planes meeting at an acute angle. The parapet is rude, and the whole is composed of an irregular mixture of brick and stone. The pavement consists of rough and irregular flags, which form a very bad road. The bridge is, however, both long and wide, and is a great convenience for foot-passengers, or merchants conveying their goods on oxen. In and about this place are numerous Brahminical temples, most of them ruinous. The great temple, however, the ground-plan of which is a square of 400 cubits, is in repair. Distance from Seringapatam, S., 22 miles. Lat. 12° 7′, long. 76° 45′.

NUNNENWARRE.—A lofty mountain of Cashmere, in the range which bounds the valley on the north-east. Over it is the Bunderpoor Pass, from Cashmere into Tibet. Von Hügel found the boiling-water point on it to be at 186·8, which, according to the approximation usually adopted, would give about 11,000 feet for the height of the pass. North-west of this, the Nangaparvat attains a much greater elevation, the exact amount of which has not been ascertained. Lat. 34° 31′, long. 74° 50′.

NUNULA, or **NUNEWULAH**, in the British district of Umballa, territory of Sirhind, a small town on the route from Kurnal to Patiala, and 50 miles N.W. of the former place. It is a ruinous town, situate in a level, fertile, and beautiful country, but scantily cultivated, and in consequence, in many places overrun with jungle. The road in this part of the route is bad, and, notwithstanding the level nature of the country, is in many places scarcely practicable for guns or carriages. Distant N.W. from Calcutta 1,015 miles. Lat. 30° 14′, long. 76° 39′.

NUNWAR, in Sinde, a village on the route from Sehwan to Larkhana, and 39 miles N. of the former town. It is situate near the north bank of a piece of stagnant water replenished during inundation by the Indus, the main channel of which is distant about a mile south. Lat. 26° 54′, long. 67° 54′.

NURAICH, in the British district of Agra, a village on the route from the city of Agra to Allygurh, and four miles N. of the former. It is situate about a mile E. of the left or eastern bank of the Jumna, in a sandy spot through which the road is heavy. Lat. 27° 12', long. 78° 6'.

NURAT, in the territory of Saugor and Nerbudda, a village at the north-east base of a range of hills dividing Bundelcund from Malwa, and on the route from Tehree to Oojein, 30 miles S.W. of former. South-west of the village commences the Nurat Ghat or Pass, at first narrow and stony, but after the brow of the hill has been surmounted, there is a good road. Lat. 24° 24', long. 78° 37'.

NURELUH, in the British district of Paneeput, lieut.-gov. of the N.W. Provinces, a considerable village on the route from the city of Delhi to Kurnal, and 16 miles N.W. of the former. The road in this part of the route is good. Lat. 28° 51', long. 77° 10'.

NURGOOND.—A town in the Southern Mahratta jaghire of Nurgoond, presidency of Bombay, 59 miles E. by S. from Belgaum, and 109 miles W.N.W. from Bellary. Nearly all the villages of this estate have been mortgaged to creditors, and the position of its chief is represented as being greatly embarrassed. Lat. 15° 43', long. 75° 27'.

NURHEE, in the British district of Ghazeepore, lieut.-gov. of the N.W. Provinces, a town situate about two miles from the left bank of the river Ganges. It contains a population of 5,803 inhabitants. Distant N.E. from Ghazeepore 29 miles. Lat. 25° 40', long. 84° 6'.

NURHUN.—A town in the British district of Sarun, lieut.-gov. of Bengal, 40 miles W.N.W. of Chupra. Lat. 25° 56', long. 84° 20'.

NURKEIR.—A town in the recently lapsed territory of Nagpore or Berar, situate eight miles E. from the left bank of the Wurda river, and 43 miles N.W. by W. from Nagpore. Lat. 21° 27', long. 78° 36'.

NURKODA.—A town in the native state of Hyderabad, or territory of the Nizam, 13 miles S.W. by W. from Hyderabad, and 158 miles W.N.W. from Guntoor. Lat. 17° 16', long. 78° 23'.

NURNULLA.—A town in one of the recently sequestrated districts of Hyderabad, or territory of the Nizam, situate 31 miles W. from Ellichpoor, and 50 miles E. from Boorhampoor. Lat. 21° 14', long. 77° 7'.

NURPOOR, in the Baree Doab division of the Punjab, among the lower and southern mountains of the Himalaya range, a town of considerable importance, as being on the route from Hindostan to Cashmere. It contains a good and well-stocked bazar, and has 6,000 or 8,000 inhabitants, a large portion of whom are Cashmerians, employed in shawl-weaving. There is a fort built of stones and mud, on an eminence about 200 feet high, at the base of which flows a small river, a feeder of the Ravee, which it joins about thirty miles lower down. It is commanded on every side by higher eminences. Nurpoor was formerly held by the Sikh government, who expelled the hereditary rajah. Elevation above the sea 1,924 feet. It is in lat. 32° 18', long. 75° 57'.

NURRAH.—A town in the recently lapsed territory of Nagpore or Berar, situate 93 miles S. by E. from Ruttunpoor, and 107 miles W.S.W. from Sumbulpoor. Lat. 20° 56', long. 82° 29'.

NURRALAH.—A town in the native state of Calahandy, on the south-west frontier of Bengal, 37 miles E.N.E. from Joonnagudda, and 102 miles S.S.W. from Sumbulpoor. Lat. 20° 4', long. 83° 31'.

NURRIAWUL, in the British district of Bareilly, lieut.-gov. of the N.W. Provinces, a village on the route from the town of Bareilly to Shahjehanpoor, and four miles S.E. of the former. The road in this part of the route is good; the country open, level, and cultivated. Lat. 28° 19', long. 79° 31'.

NURRODIE.—A town in the recently lapsed territory of Nagpore or Berar, situate 137 miles E.N.E. from Nagpore, and 77 miles S. from Ramgurh. Lat. 21° 42', long. 81° 10'.

NURRUNJUNPOOR, in the British district Budaon, lieut.-gov. of the N.W. Provinces, a village on the route from the city of Agra to Bareilly, and 38 miles S.W. of the latter. Lat. 28° 5', long. 79° 6'.

NURSAPOOR.—A town in the British district of Tannah, presidency of Bombay, 38 miles E. of Bombay. Lat. 18° 59', long. 73° 28'.

NURSINGURH.—The principal town of a native state of the same name, 37 miles N.W. by N. from Bhopal, and 109 miles S.W. from Saugor. It is the residence of one of the chiefs between whom the district of Omutwarra is divided, and who exercises his authority under the title of Dewan.—See Omutwarra. Lat. 23° 40', long. 77° 6'.

NURSINGPETTAH.—A town in the native state of Hyderabad, or territory of the Nizam, 52 miles N. from Hyderabad, and 170 miles E. by N. from Sholapoor. Lat. 18° 6', long. 78° 28'.

NURSINGPOOR.—One of the Cuttack Mehals, in the province of Orissa: it lies on the left bank of the Mahanuddy river, and its centre is in about lat. 20° 34', long. 85°. It pays an annual tribute of 1,364 rupees to the British government, and its chief maintains a military force of 1,500 men.

NURSINGPOOR GURH.—A town on the south-west frontier of Bengal, in the hill state of Sursingpoor, in Orissa, situate 52 miles N.E. by N. from Goomsoor, and 51 miles W. from Cuttack. Lat. 20° 27', long. 85° 9'.

NURSINGPORE.—See Saugor and Nerbudda territory.

NURUNGA.—A town in the British district of Tirhoot, lieut.-gov. of Bengal, 49 miles

N.N.W. of Durbunga. Lat. 26° 47′, long. 85° 42′.

NURWUL, in the British district of Cawnpore, lieut.-gov. of the N.W. Provinces, a town eight miles W. of the right bank of the Ganges, 18 miles S. of the cantonment of Cawnpore. Lat. 26° 16′, long. 80° 30′.

NURWUR.—A town of Malwa, in the native state of Bhopal, 41 miles E. from Bhopal, and 62 miles S.W. by W. from Saugor. Lat. 23° 18′, long. 78°.

NURYOOB, in the Daman division of the Punjab, a town situated 49 miles W. from the right bank of the Indus, 63 miles S.W. of the town of Peshawar. Lat. 33° 25′, long. 70° 50′.

NUSRUTHPOOR, in the British district of Ghazeepoor, lieut.-gov. of the N.W. Provinces, a town on the route from Ghazeepoor to Sasseram, 11 miles S. of the former. Lat. 25° 23′, long. 83° 38′.

NUSSEERABAD, or SOWARA. — The principal place of the British district of Mymensing, lieut.-gov. of Bengal, situate on the right or south-west bank of the Brahmapootra. It is the locality of the district civil establishment. Distance from Jumalpoor, S.E. by E., 25 miles. Lat. 24° 44′, long. 90° 23′.

NUSSEERABAD.—A town in the British district of Candeish, presidency of Bombay, 79 miles E.N.E. of Malligaum. Lat. 20° 59′, long. 75° 37′.

NUSSEERABAD, in the district of Ajmeer, lieut.-gov. of the N.W. Provinces, a British cantonment 15 miles S.E. of the city of Ajmeer. It is situate in a vast plain of a soil of sand or gravel, overlying primitive rock, and bounded north-west by the mountains of Ajmeer, but in all other directions stretching farther than the eye can reach. This arid and exposed site, though having many inconveniences, is conducive to salubrity, in which the cantonment is considered to excel any in India. The climate is, however, very hot, the mean temperature in the shade, in July, 1831, being 91°, the maximum of the year 102°, the mean temperature of the year 76°. The cantonments are extensive and commodious, being laid out in wide regular streets. There are several tanks and wells, but the water is rather brackish. Fruit-trees do not thrive, but garden vegetables are cultivated with some success. Timber is excessively scarce and dear, and as the place is very remote from the sea, or any great mart, European wares are probably dearer than in almost any other place in India. When Jacquemont visited this place in 1832, it was occupied by three regiments of infantry, one of cavalry, two parks of artillery, and adequate proportion of sappers and miners, and sixty British officers, who had provided for their recreation a theatre, a ball-room, a racket-court. Heber observes, "I have not in all India met with a better-informed, a more unaffected and hospitable society." It is the head-quarters of the Rajpootana field-force. Elevation above the sea 1,486 feet. Distance (travelling) from Delhi, S.W., 243 miles; from Agra, W., 222; Saugor, N.W., 350; Neemuch, N., 143; Calcutta, N.W., 1,051 miles. Lat. 26° 20′, long. 74° 50′.

NUSSURPOOR.—A town in the British district of Hydrabad, province of Sinde, presidency of Bombay, 19 miles N.E. by E. of Hydrabad. Lat. 25° 30′, long. 68° 41′.

NUSTUNG.—The name of one of the Cossya hill states. The territory is bounded on the north-west by the Garrow territory and the Cossya state of Ramrye; on the east by those of Munriow, Moeyong, and Mahran; on the south by the British district of Silhet; and on the west by that of Mymunsing: it extends from lat. 25° to 25° 28′, and from long. 90° 53′ to 91° 21′; is forty miles in length from north-east to south-west, and fifteen in breadth; and contains an area of 360 square miles.

NUTHOAPOOR, in the British district of Cawnpore, lieut.-gov. of the N.W. Provinces, a village on the route from Allahabad to Etawa, and 71 miles S.E. of the latter. Lat. 26° 12′, long. 79° 56′.

NUTOOTA.—A town in the Rajpoot state of Jodhpoor, 114 miles E.N.E. from Jodhpoor, and 26 miles N.N.E. from Ajmeer. Lat. 26° 49′, long. 74° 51′.

NUTTOOSIR, in the Rajpoot state of Beekaneer, a village on the route from Chooroo to the town of Beekaneer, and 40 miles N.E. of the latter place. Elphinstone found it, in the beginning of November, an unhealthy place, from bad water, and great and sudden changes of temperature, the nights being excessively cold, and succeeded immediately on the rising of the sun by great heats. Out of a force not exceeding 400 men, thirty became sick in one day. Lat. 28° 18′, long. 74° 2′.

NUTWABARA.—A town in the British district of Ramgur, lieut.-gov. of Bengal, 32 miles E. by S. of Hazareebagh. Lat. 23° 53′, long. 85° 53′.

NUVVEE BUNDER, in the peninsula of Kattywar, province of Guzerat, a town on the south-west coast, and in the district of Burda. It is situate at the mouth of the river Bhadur, which, during the monsoon, is navigable by boats for about eighteen miles upwards. The port is available only for small craft. Distance from Ahmedabad, S.W., 209 miles; Baroda, W., 225; Bombay, N.W., 255. Lat. 21° 28′, long. 69° 54′.

NUWABGUNJ, in the British district of Allahabad, lieut.-gov. of the N.W. Provinces, a town on the route from Allahabad to Lucknow, 11 miles N.W. of the former. Lat. 25° 33′, long. 81° 50′.

NUWABGUNJE.—A town in the British

district of Purneah, lieut.-gov. of Bengal, 16 miles E. of Purneah. Lat. 25° 46′, long. 87° 50′.

NUWABGUNJE, in the British district of Bareilly, lieut.-gov. of the N.W. Provinces, a town on the route from Bareilly to Pilleebheet, 20 miles N.E. of the former. Lat. 28° 33′, long. 79° 42′.

NUWWABGUNJ, in the territory of Oude, a town with bazar, on the route from Lucknow cantonment to that of Sekrora, 41 miles N.E. of the former, 15 S.W. of the latter. It is situate on the left bank of the river Ghaghra, here crossed by ferry. Lat. 27° 6′, long. 81° 21′.

NUWWABGUNJ, in the territory of Oude, a village on the route from Allahabad to Lucknow, 63 miles N.W. of the former, 65 S.E. of the latter. Lat. 26° 6′, long. 81° 18′.

NUWADAH, in the British district of Dehra Doon, a village on the declivity of a low ridge running in a direction nearly north and south. Here was a station of the series of small triangles during the great trigonometrical survey of the Himalayas. Elevation above the sea 2,364 feet. Lat. 30° 12′, long. 78° 7′.

NUWARI, in the British district of Cawnpore, lieut.-gov. of the N.W. Provinces, a village on the route from Allahabad to Calpee, and 22 miles E. of the latter. Lat. 26° 9′, long. 80° 9′.

NUWULGURH, in the territory of Shekawuttee, a town belonging to a thakoor or baron, to whom it, with the annexed lands of Mundao, yields an annual revenue of 70,000 rupees. It is a thriving town, fortified with ramparts of masonry. Distance S.W. of Delhi 135 miles, N.W. from Jeypoor 75. Lat. 27° 51′, long. 75° 26′.

NYABAS, in the British district of Boolundshuhur, lieut.-gov. of the N.W. Provinces, a village on the route from the cantonment of Allygurh to that of Delhi, and 10 miles S.W. of the latter, is situate on the left bank of the Jumna. Lat. 28° 35′, long. 77° 22′.

NYAGAON, or NOWGAON, in Bundelcund, and the principal place of a jagheer or feudal grant of the same name, a small town, 50 miles W. of Banda. Lat. 25° 27′, long. 79° 35′. The jagheer is stated to comprise an area of thirty square miles, and to contain fifteen villages, with a population of 5,000 souls, and to yield a revenue of 10,000 rupees (1,000*l.*). The jagheerdar maintains a force of 100 foot. The grant is from the East-India Company, under date 19th June, 1812, to a branch of the Chowbeys of Kalinger, in compensation for the surrender of that fort.

NYAGAON.—A town in Bundelcund, situate on the left bank of the Pysunnee river, 25 miles N.E. from Kalleenjur. Lat. 25° 10′, long. 80° 56′.

NYAGAON.—A town in the British district of Midnapoor, lieut.-gov. of Bengal, 28 miles S.S.W. of Midnapoor. Lat. 22° 2′, long. 87° 14′.

NYAGHUR.—One of the Cuttack Mehals, in the province of Orissa, situate on the eastern border of the British district of Ganjam: its centre is about lat. 25°, long. 80°. Nyaghur pays an annual tribute of 5,179 rupees to the British government, and maintains a body of cavalry and infantry.

NYAGONG, or NYAGAON, in the British district of Banda, lieut.-gov. of the N.W. Provinces, a small town on the route from Adjygurh to Kalleenjur, nine miles N.E. of former, six S.W. of latter. Its situation is beautiful, amidst small well-wooded, fertile valleys, watered by the head-waters of the river Baghin, yet the heat in the early part of summer is almost unsupportable. Lat. 24° 58′, long. 80° 26′.

NYAGONG, in the British district of Suharunpoor, lieut.-gov. of the N.W. Provinces, a town on the route from Suharunpoor to Dehra Dhoon, 20 miles N.N.E. of the former. Lat. 30° 12′, long. 77° 43′.

NYAGURH.—A town of Baghelcund, in the native state of Rewah, 34 miles N.E. by E. from Rewah, and 105 miles N. by E. from Sohagpoor. Lat. 24° 48′, long. 81° 50′.

NYANUGGUR, in the British district of Mairwara, lieut.-gov. of the N.W. Provinces, a town on the route from Nusseerabad to Jallor, 31 miles W.S.W. of the former. Lat. 26° 6′, long. 74° 25′.

NYAR, or SANEE, in the British district of Kumaon, lieut.-gov. of the N.W. Provinces, a river rising at an elevation of between 6,000 and 7,000 feet, and in lat. 30° 5′, long. 79° 13′. It first holds a course generally south-westerly, and then north-westerly, to the confluence of the Chipal Ghat river, in lat. 29° 56′, long. 78° 45′; and thence continuing to flow north-westerly, it falls into the Aluknunda, in lat. 30° 3′, long. 78° 38′, at an elevation of 1,342 feet above the level of the sea. Its total length, upon Herbert's computation, would be about fifty miles. Where crossed by Webb in April, at about five miles above its mouth, the stream was forty yards wide, twenty-six inches deep, and running at the rate of eight or nine miles an hour.

NYA SHUHUR, or MADHUPUR, in the Rajpoot state of Jeypore, a considerable town near the southern frontier, towards the territory of Boondee. No account of it appears to have been given by a European eye-witness; but Broughton, who passed close to it, states that it is larger than any city in the territory except Jeypore, the capital. It is only accessible by two roads among the rocky hills which surround it, and both are strongly fortified. Distance from Jeypore, S.E., 172 miles; from Agra, S.W., 133. Lat. 25° 55′, long. 76° 33′.

NYA SURYE.—A town of Gwalior, or

territory of the Scindia family, situate on the right bank of the Sinde river, and 100 miles N.W. by W. from Saugur. Lat. 24° 49′, long. 77° 39′.

NYATHANA, in the British district of Kumaon, lieut.-gov. of the N.W. Provinces, a small fort formerly held by the Ghoorkas, situate on a summit sloping westwards to the left bank of the Western Ramgunga. Distant 25 miles N.W. of Almorah. Elevation above the sea 5,785 feet. Lat. 29° 48′, long. 79° 21′.

NYERAK.—A town in the dominions of Gholab Singh, the ruler of Cashmere, 124 miles E. from Sirinagur, and 134 miles N.N.E. from Kangra. Lat. 33° 51′, long. 77° 9′.

NYEWAL.—A river of Bhutteeana, which, after flowing through that district, passes into the great desert of Rajpootana, where its waters shortly become absorbed for purposes of irrigation, or by evaporation.

NYGOWAN, or NOWAGAON, one of the petty jaghires in Bundelcund, comprising sixteen square miles, and containing four villages, with a population of 1,800 souls, and yielding a revenue of rupees 10,000 per annum. The town of the same name is in lat. 25° 6′, long. 79° 39′. It is held from the East-India Company, under sunnud or grant dated 19th September, 1807, but not in perpetuity; and upon the death of the present chief, Juggut Singh, the estate will lapse to the British government.

NYIMA.—A town within the dominions of Gholab Singh, the ruler of Cashmere, situate on the right bank of the Senge Khabab or Indus river, and 159 miles N.E. by E. from Kangra. Lat. 33° 12′, long. 78° 42′.

NYKOOL.—A town in the native state of Bombra, on the south-west frontier of Bengal, situate on the right bank of the Braminy river, and 59 miles E. from Sumbulpoor. Lat. 21° 22′, long. 84° 54′.

NYNEE TAL, in the British district of Kumaon, lieut.-gov. of the N.W. Provinces, a town on the route from Rampoor to Almora, 22 miles S.W. by S. of the latter. This new settlement is extensively resorted to as a sanitarium; and a market has thus been opened for the productions of the neighbouring country, which, it is represented, is of considerable advantage to the cultivators. Nynee Tal contains a church, erected by public subscription in 1847. Measures have been taken by the government for introducing order and regularity into the affairs of the settlement. Lat. 29° 20′, long. 79° 30′.

NYNTWA, in Gurwhal, a village situate on the point of land formed by the confluence of the Rupin and Lupin, or Tonse rivers. It is now ruined and nearly uninhabited; but the traces of its former size and population prove that the traffic in this part of the Himalaya must have been once much more considerable than at present, as the inhabitants, in consequence of the barrenness of the country, could have had no other means of subsistence than that derived from conveying travellers across the Rupin. Nyntwa is in lat. 31° 4′, long. 78° 10′.

NYNWAH, in the territory of Boondee, in Rajpootana, a town on the route from Delhi to Mow, 251 miles S.W. of former, 256 N. of latter. It has a large bazar, and water is abundant. Lat. 25° 46′, long. 75° 55′.

NYOUNGBENTHA.—A town of Burmah, situate on the right bank of the Irawady river, and 130 miles N. from Ava. Lat. 23° 43′, long. 96°.

O.

OAMCHOO, a river in the native state of Bhotan, rises in lat. 27° 30′, long. 91° 55′, and, flowing in a westerly direction for thirty miles, falls into the Monas river, opposite the town of Nulkar, and in lat. 27° 23′, long. 91° 31′.

OBEREA, in the British district of Shahjehanpoor, lieut.-gov. of the N.W. Provinces, a village on the route from Futtehgurh to the cantonment of Shahjehanpoor, and 19 miles S.W. of the latter. Lat. 27° 44′, long. 79° 45′.

OCHUTTI.—A village in the jaghire of Jujhur, lieut.-gov. of the N.W. Provinces. Lat. 28° 22′, long. 76° 21′.

OCLISEER, in the British district of Broach, presidency of Bombay, a town on the route from Surat to Baroda, 35 miles N. of the former, and 50 S. of the latter. Population 7,000. Lat. 21° 38′, long. 73° 2′.

ODEIPORE.—A raj within the jurisdiction of the political agent for the south-west frontier of Bengal. It has an area of 2,306 square miles; the centre being in lat. 22° 40′, long. 83° 23′. It is computed to be of the annual value of 15,000 rupees. The population is estimated at 133,000. The chief having been found to be a systematic murderer, the British government assumed the management of this state, and there being no person entitled to succeed, the rajah of Sergoojah being considered to have no right to the estate as a lapse by failure of heirs, the raj has been declared an escheat to the British government.

ODEIPORE.—A town on the route from Hazarebaugh to Nagpoor, 160 miles S.W. of former, 295 N.E. of latter. It is the principal town of the petty state of the same name, which has recently lapsed to the British government. Distant from Patna, S.W., 235 miles; from Benares, S., 183; from Calcutta, W., 320. Lat. 22° 40′, long. 83° 23′.

ODEYPOOR.—See Oodeypoor.

OHIND, in the Peshawur division of the Punjab, a town situated on the right bank of the Indus, 49 miles E. by N. of the town of Peshawur. Lat. 34° 8′, long. 72° 29′.

OIN, in the territory of Gholab Singh, the ruler of Cashmere, a small town near the base of the mountains inclosing Cashmere on the south. It is situate on the river Jhelum, the navigation of which here again becomes practicable after its interruption between Baramula and this place. Oin is in lat. 33° 44′, long. 73° 35′.

OKAMANDAL, in the peninsula of Kattywar, province of Guzerat, presidency of Bombay, a small prant or district at the north-west angle of the peninsula, and separated from the mainland by a runn or salt marsh, extending from the Gulf of Cutch to the Arabian Sea, except by the connecting link of a narrow bank of sand at Mudhe. The Runn extends in a direction from north-east to south-west, and on all other sides the district is washed by the sea, into which it projects in the form of a bold headland, indented on its north side by the Gulf of Beyt. It lies between lat. 22° 5′—22° 30′, long. 69°—69° 17′. There is no official return of the area; but, by probable approximation, it may be stated at 334 square miles. Possibly the district was formerly an island; and even now, at spring tides, the Runn is completely overflowed. Towards the Gulf of Cutch, the coast is in many places beset with shoals, reefs, and rocks; and is indented by the harbour of Beyt, a considerable inlet, at the mouth of which is the island of Beyt, and at its north-western point the island of Soonia. The peninsula of Okamandal, so well adapted from its situation for intercepting and annoying the commerce and navigation of the Arabian Sea, was always a great resort and harbour of pirates, until they were either expelled, destroyed, or constrained to relinquish their lawless pursuits by the overwhelming force of British ascendancy. The total length of seacoast of the district is about seventy-five miles. The district is returned as containing forty-three villages (excluding eleven which are waste), and having a population estimated at 12,590. It is altogether a district of little value: the soil is sterile, and the water bad.

The sankh, or conch shell, which is obtained of large size and in great quantities on the shoals contiguous to the northern shore, forms the only article of export from this barren district. These shells are sent in the first instance to Bombay; but the provinces of Bengal are said to furnish the greatest demand for them. "As the war-shell," says Colonel Tod, "with which he was wont to peal a blast, the onslaught to battle, no longer graces the hand of the Rajpoot in these degenerate days; its use is now restricted to the Brahmin, wherewith to awaken the gods in the morning; to let the world know when he dines; or, what is of far more importance, to form chooris or bracelets for the arms of the Hindoo fair."

OKERAH.—A town in the British district of Bancoora, lieut.-gov. of Bengal, 104 miles N.W. of Calcutta. Lat. 23° 39′, long. 87° 19′.

OKULDOONGA, in the British district of Kumaon, lieut.-gov. of the N.W. Provinces, a village on the route from Moradabad to Almora, and 65 miles N.E. of the former. The picturesque beauty of the scenery is much enhanced by the appearance of the Kosilla, rolling its rapid and clear stream down a deep, tortuous, and craggy channel. The rice produced here is remarkably fine, and on account of its whiteness, firmness, and good flavour, is in great request throughout India, being known by the name of Pilleebheet rice, as it is brought to market chiefly at that town. The air, however, of this vicinity is during the hot season very unhealthy, close, and sultry, in consequence of the exclusion of the breezes by the inclosing eminences. The elevation above the sea is about 2,000 feet. Lat. 29° 31′, long. 79° 16′.

OLIAPORE.—A town in the British district of Rungpore, lieut.-gov. of Bengal, 22 miles E. by S. of Rungpore. Lat. 25° 36′, long. 89° 36′.

OLLAVACONDA.—A town in the British district of Cuddapah, presidency of Madras, 70 miles N.W. of Cuddapah. Lat. 15° 9′, long. 78° 17′.

OMARGURH, in the British district of Boolundshuhur, lieut.-gov. of the N.W. Provinces, a town on the route from Anoopshuhur to Meerut, and 50 miles S.E. of the latter. Lat. 28° 28′, long. 78° 12′.

OMEDUNDA.—A town in the British district of Chota Nagpoor, lieut.-gov. of Bengal, 32 miles E.N.E. of Lohadugga. Lat. 23° 39′, long. 85° 12′.

OMERCOTE, in Sinde, a town and fort in the eastern desert. The fort is situate half a mile from the town, and is 500 feet square, having a mud wall forty feet high, a strong round tower at each corner, and six square towers on each side. There is but one gate, which is on the eastern side, and is protected by an outwork. It was usually garrisoned by 400 men. Though nearly 100 miles from the Indus, a branch of that river finds its way hither in time of inundation, and, in 1826, flowed with such violence as to sweep away the north-west tower. Water is to be had near the surface, and there is a pool twenty feet deep in the channel of this branch of the Indus west of the fort. Omercote was taken in 1813, by the ameers of Sinde, from the rajah of Joudpoor. It is celebrated as the birthplace of the renowned emperor Akbar, his father Humaion having in his exile taken refuge here. Lat. 25° 22′, long. 69° 47′.

OMERKANTAH.—See AMARAKANTAH.

OMER KAYL, in the Daman division of the Punjab, a town situated on the right bank of the Indus, 114 miles S. by W. of the town of Peshawar. Lat. 32° 23′, long. 71° 20′.

OMERKOTE, in the Daman division of the Punjab, a town situated on the right bank of the Indus, 19 miles S.W. of the town of Mithunkote. Lat. 28° 45′, long. 70° 18′.

OMERKUNTUC.—See AMARAKANTAK.

OMETA, within the British district of Kaira, presidency of Bombay, a town on the right bank of the river Myhee. It is the residence of a thakoor or chief. Distance from the city of Ahmedabad, S.E., 60 miles; Baroda, W., 12; Surat, N., 80; Bombay, N., 230. Lat. 22° 17′, long. 73° 6′.

OMLAO, in the British district of Jaunsar, lieut.-gov. of the N.W. Provinces, a river rising in the mountains north-west of Bairat, and in lat. 30° 40′, long. 77° 55′: it has a direction generally southerly, and, flowing by the small town of Khalsee, falls into the Jumna on the right side, a mile east of the confluence of the Tons, and in lat. 30° 30′, long. 77° 54′, after a course of about fifteen miles.

OMPTA.—See AMPATA.

OMRAH, in Bundelcund, a fort on the route from Calpee to Goorah, 72 miles S.W. of the former, 133 N.E. of the latter. It belongs to the rajah of Sumpter, is surrounded by a wet ditch, and is a place of some importance. Lat. 25° 42′, long. 78° 58′.

OMRAOUTTEE.—See OOMRAWUTTEE.

OMUDPOOR, in the British district of Cawnpore, lieut.-gov. of the N.W. Provinces, a village on the route from Calpee to Futtehgurh, and 13 miles N. of the former. The road in this part of the route is good, the country well cultivated. Lat. 26° 17′, long. 79° 47′.

OMUTWARRA, in Malwa, a district lying between lat. 23° 28′—24° 9′, long. 76° 19′—77° 11′. Its length from north to south is sixty miles, and its breadth fifty-five miles. The district derives its name from the Omut Rajpoots, who, having emigrated from Oodeypoor at an early period, succeeded, during the decline of the Mogul empire, in overrunning and subjugating this country, under the command of two brothers, named Mohun Sing and Perseram. The territory thus acquired, with the exception of five districts reserved to the elder brother, as a mark of superiority, was equally divided between the leaders, one of whom assumed the title of rawul or chief, the other that of dewan or minister. These names, however, do not at all indicate the relative positions of the two parties, for each was ruler within his allotted domain. The mode of division was not less remarkable than this assignment of titles; for no compact territory was possessed by either of the sharers in the conquest, but the dominions of both were so intermixed, that in some instances the two authorities held and exercised rights over the same villages. The successors of the rawul fixed their residence at Rajghur, and became tributary to Scindia; those of the dewan chose Nursinghur, and the fort there was erected by one of them, named Alohee Singh. This branch of the ruling family acknowledged dependence upon Holcar. The principal places are Rajgurh, Nursinghur, and Khujnir.

ONAGONG.—A town in the native state of Bhotan, situate on the left bank of the Goddada river, and 56 miles W.N.W. from Goalpara. Lat. 26° 23′, long. 89° 48′.

ONAIL.—A town in the native state of Gwalior, or territory of the Scindia family, situate on the left bank of the Seepra river, and 17 miles N.W. from Oojein. Lat. 23° 18′, long. 75° 35′.

ONDAREE, called also Henery, a small island, situate on the west coast of the Northern Concan, and about twenty miles south of the city of Bombay. The "island lies about a mile from the mainland, opposite to the village of Thull. It is very low, and is fortified by a wall which surrounds it."

ONDOO.—A town in the Rajpoot state of Jodhpoor, 90 miles W. from Jodhpoor, and 60 miles S.E. from Jessulmeer. Lat. 26° 20′, long. 71° 42′.

ONGOL, in the British district of Nellore, presidency of Madras, a town near the northern frontier, towards the British district Guntoor, situate 11 miles N.E. of the left bank of the river Mooshee. It is of considerable size, and has a fort at no time of much strength or size, and now greatly dilapidated. The dwellings in the town are for the most part wretched hovels of mud, and thatched, but the scenery in the neighbourhood has the advantage of being varied and picturesque. The town, with the annexed tallook or subdivision, has, according to official return, a population of 31,666. Distance from Madras, N., 189 miles; Masulipatam, S.W., 132. Lat. 15° 30′, long. 80° 6′.

ONORE.—See HONAHWAR.

ONTIMITTA.—A town in the British district of Cuddapah, presidency of Madras, 15 miles E.S.E. of Cuddapah. Lat. 14° 23′, long. 79° 5′.

OOCH, in the Sinde Sagur Dooab division of the Punjab, a town situated near the junction of the Jhelum and Chenaub rivers, 128 miles W.S.W. of the town of Lahore. Lat. 31° 12′, long. 72° 3′.

OOCHEYRA, in the territory of Saugor and Nerbudda, a native state under the political superintendence of the lieut.-governor of the North-Western provinces. It is bounded on the north-east by the jaghire of Sohawul and by Rewah; on the east by Rewah; on the south-east by Myheer; and on the west by Punnah. It lies between lat. 24° 10′—24° 36′, long. 80° 35′—81° 4′; the area comprises 436 square miles; the population is estimated at 120,000, and the annual revenue at 66,320 rupees, or 6,632*l*. This small state is under British authority and protection, by virtue of a sunnud granted in 1809 to Lal Sheoraj Singh, then its possessor. The eldest son and successor of that personage having been convicted of the murder of his brother, was deposed, banished the country, and placed under restraint at Allahabad. The son of the murderer being a minor, the British government assumed the charge of his person and education, and the management of his estate, until he attained his majority in 1838, when he was formally admitted to the exercise of the rights of the chieftainship. The hopes entertained of his administration were, however, disappointed. Having exhausted his treasury, and become deeply involved in debt, he found himself utterly incapable of preserving order in his territories, and proposed that his estate should be placed temporarily under British administration. To this request the British government acceded; and the speedy restoration of order, and a great reduction of debt, attested the success of their management. The town which gives name to the jaghire lies on the route, by Bisramgunj Ghaut, from Banda to Jubbulpore, 110 miles N.W. of the latter, and in lat. 24° 23′, long. 80° 50′.

OOCHOOLAROO, in Gurwhal, a peak on a ridge between the rivers Jumna and Bhageeruttee. Its sides are clothed with forests, which extend to the height of 11,800 feet above the sea. When surveyed by Hodgson and Herbert, in September, the summit was bare of snow, except one small patch. Elevation above the sea 14,302 feet. Lat. 30° 54′, long. 78° 39′.

OODAGHERRY.—A town in the British district of Nellore, presidency of Madras, 59 miles N.W. by W. of Nellore. Lat. 14° 52′, long. 79° 17′.

OODAGHERRY.—A town in the native state of Purlahkemedy, inhabited by one of the Orissa hill tribes, 62 miles W. by S. from Ganjam, and 114 miles N.E. by N. from Vizagapatam. Lat. 19° 9′, long. 84° 13′.

OODAPEE, in the British district of South Canara, presidency of Madras, a town, the principal place of a subdivision of the same name. It is situate four miles from the coast of the Arabian Sea, or North Indian Ocean, and contains three Brahminical temples, and fourteen matams or convents for devotees of that caste. The temples are rude buildings, roofed with copper, which must have cost much money; but being coarsely wrought, are of no striking appearance. The population of the town is estimated at about 1,200. A large portion of the population of the district consists of Brahmins, but the Corar or Corawar, a caste of slaves by birth, before the abolition of slavery within British India, are also numerous, and, like the Helots of Laconia, they are the descendants of the race that once owned and ruled the country. Rice is the staple produce, but the cocoanut-palm, sugarcane, and pulse of various kinds, are largely cultivated. Distant from Mangalore, N., 34 miles; from Madras, W., 380. Lat. 13° 20′, long. 74° 49′.

OODEEPOOR, in the Rajpoot state of Shekawuttee, a town in an advantageous situation, commanding a narrow and rocky defile, called the Baghora Ghat, the only pass for fifteen miles to the north-east, and the same distance to the south-west, from the eastward through the Shekawuttee Mountains. Though unfortified, except by a few ruinous towers, it is strong by its situation. It is a considerable town, and is close to a torrent descending from the hills, but flowing only during the periodical rains. Distance N.W. from Agra 160 miles, S.W. from Delhi 130, N. from Jeypoor 55. Lat. 27° 42′, long. 75° 34′.

OODEPOOR, in Guzerat, the chief town of a petty state of the same name, situate on the route from Baroda to Mow, 50 miles E. of former, 115 W. of latter, situate on the river Orsung, a tributary of the Nerbudda. Population about 6,000. Distance from Ahmedabad, S.E., 105 miles; Surat, N.E., 110. Lat. 22° 20′, long. 74° 1′.

OODEPOOR CHOTA, a district of the Rewa Caunta province of Guzerat, is sometimes called Mahur, but more commonly by the former appellation. It is bounded on the east by Allee Mohun; on the south by the British district of Akraunee and the Mewassee districts; on the west by the territory of the Guicowar; and on the north by Deoghur Barreea. It lies between lat. 22° 2′—22° 32′, long. 73° 47′—74° 20′, and has an area of 1,059 square miles. It is traversed by the river Orsung, which empties itself into the Nerbudda.

Oodepoor was included in the arrangement with the Guicowar, under which the collection of the tribute from the chiefs within the Myhee and Rewa Cauntas and Kattywar was transferred to the British government. By an agreement entered into on the part of the rawul, he acknowledges that, under the protection of the British government, he has subscribed to the payment of tribute to the Guicowar government, amounting to the sum of 10,500 rupees per annum. The rawul further engages to keep under restraint the Bheels and Mehwassees within his territory, and to answer in the event of their committing depredations in the Guicowar's districts; he also stipulates not to harbour incendiaries or other bad characters in his district; and to refer all cases of dispute with neighbouring talookdars to the British government. The public road he engages to keep open; commerce is to be duly protected, but smuggled opium is to be seized and disposed of agreeably to orders received. The state contributes the sum of 500 rupees annually to the support of a police establishment acting under British superintendence. It maintains within its own limits 368 infantry, and about 70 horse. There are about thirteen Bheel chiefs under this government, who are bound to render military service when required; but the number of their military followers is not known.

The founder of this state was Pritheeraj,

grandson of the common ancestor Prithee Rawul, whose descendants are still in possession of the states of Barreea and Oodepoor. Prithea Singjee, the immediate predecessor of the present chief, inherited the right from his father, Raee Singjee; but, though he is said not to have been deficient in intelligence, the management of affairs was retained in the hands of his mother. Dying without issue, in 1832, he was succeeded by his cousin Gooman Singh, the present occupant of the guddee. He has a son, the heir-apparent to the chieftainship.

In 1855 it was discovered that a general system existed in the Rewa Caunta, of bribing the native establishment of the political agent's office, and the evidence being complete against the rajah, that he had disbursed money for the purpose of bribery, it was resolved to place his possessions under attachment.

OODERAMSIR, in the Rajpoot state of Beekaneer, a village on the route from Nagor to the town of Beekaneer, and six miles S. of the latter. It contains 100 houses, and is supplied with water from a well. Lat. 27° 57′, long. 73° 23′.

OODERPEE DROOG. — A town in the British district of Bellary, presidency of Madras, 40 miles S.E. by E. of Bellary. Lat. 14° 49′, long. 77° 25′.

OODETPOOR, in the British district of Cawnpore, lieut.-gov. of the N.W. Provinces, a village on the route from the cantonment of Futtehgurh to that of Cawnpore, and 20 miles N.W. of the latter. Lat. 26° 40′, long. 80° 12′.

OODEYPOOR, or MEWAR, a Rajpoot state of the first rank, is bounded on the north by the British district of Ajmere; on the east by the native states of Boondee, Gwalior, Tonk, and Purtabghur; on the south by Banswara and Dongurpore and the Myhee Caunta; and on the north-west by Serohee, Godwar, and the British district of Ajmere. It extends from lat. 23° 46′ to 25° 56′, and from long. 72° 50′ to 75° 38′; is 150 miles in length from north to south, and 130 in breadth, and contains an area of 11,614 square miles, supporting a population estimated at 1,161,400, or 100 to the square mile.

A section of the Aravulli range of mountains expands over the south-western portion of this territory, from the city of Odeypore to the frontier of Serohee, whence it stretches in a northerly direction through Komulmair, towards Ajmere, separating the state of Odeypore from that of Joudpore. Northward of Komulmair, this mountain-tract is termed Mhairwarra; its breadth here varies from six to fifteen miles, and its deep and rugged valleys and gorges have in all ages afforded haunts to the Bheels, Minas, and Mairs. Southward of Komulmair the range is inhabited by communities of the aboriginal races, acknowledging no paramount power, and paying no tribute. Its geological formation is in general primitive, consisting of granite, quartz, gneiss, and in many parts abounding in metals and other valuable minerals. The tin-mines of Odeypore were formerly productive, and yielded no inconsiderable portion of silver. Copper is abundant, and supplies the currency. According to Tod, the rana believed that his native hills contained every species of mineral wealth. The remainder of the country, comprehending the valley of Odeypore, has an average elevation of about 2,000 feet above the level of the sea. Its general inclination is from south-west to north-east, as indicated by the course of the principal rivers, the Banas and the Beris, and of their numerous feeders, flowing from the base of the Aravulli.

The historian Mill speaks of "Oudepore as a mountainous district lying between Ajmere and Malwa; the prince of which, though acknowledging subjection to the Mahometans, yet, protected by his mountains, had never been actually subdued." The royal house of Odeypore is the most illustrious among the Rajpoots. It boasts of never having incurred the contamination of a matrimonial alliance with the imperial house of Delhi. Rennell says, "The rana, or prince of Oudipour, has always been regarded as the head of the Rajpoot states. A long-established custom of homage, from those who do not acknowledge his superiority in any other way, seems to prove the existence of real power in the hands of his ancestors; and under whom, probably, Rajpootana constituted one entire kingdom or empire."

According to Rajpoot tradition, the kingdom of Odeypore derives its origin from the Solar dynasty, which reigned in Oude. Its princes claim descent from Loh, the son of Rama, who emigrated to the Punjab, and built the city of Lahore, the ancient Lohkote. During the reign of Samarsi, the Chohan monarch Pirthi Raj had succeeded to the throne of Delhi. Shortly after his accession, he encountered, at Taneseer, in 1191, the Mahometan commander Shahabadin, afterwards Mahomed of Ghor, and routed him with great slaughter. Two years later, Shahabadin having recruited his army, advanced once more to contest the sovereignty of India. In this emergency, Pirthi Raj despatched an embassy to solicit the aid of Samarsi, who had married his sister. Their united armies marched to the banks of the Cuggar, in full confidence of victory. They were met near the field of the former battle by Shahabadin, when a desperate conflict ensued, which terminated in the subversion of Hindoo dominion. Samarsi fell with the bravest and best of his nobles, and Delhi was carried by storm. Throughout the period of anarchy and devastation which ensued, Odeypore maintained in some degree its independence of the government of Delhi, until, in the year 1303, its capital, Chittor, was sacked by the imperial forces. It was, however, almost immediately after recovered by Hamir, who then ruled in Mewar. Hamir marched to meet Mahmood, who was advancing to recover his lost possessions, defeated and took prisoner the emperor, and did not liberate him till he had agreed to the surrender of Ajmere, Rinthumbore, Nagore, and Sooe Sopoor. He received homage from the princes of Marwar, Jeypore, Boondee, and Gwalior, and rendered the power of Odeypore as solid and extensive as it had been previously to the Tartar occupation of Hindostan. From the death of Hamir, for a century and a half the arms of Mewar were successful, until the reign of Sanga, the competitor of Baber, when Mewar reached the summit of its prosperity. The Tartar prince having defeated Ibrahim, and secured Agra and Delhi, turned his arms against Sanga of Chittor. They met in 1527: a successful attack upon the advanced Tartar guard checked the energies of the Mussulmans, and led them to throw up intrenchments for security, instead of advancing with the assurance of victory. Baber remained blockaded in his encampment about a fortnight, when he determined to renounce his besetting sin, and seek superior aid to extricate him from his peril. "I vowed," he says, "never more to drink wine. Having sent for the gold and silver goblets and cups, with all the other utensils used for drinking-parties, I directed them to be broken, and renounced the use of wine, purifying my mind. The fragments of the goblets and other utensils of gold and silver I directed to be divided among dervishes and the poor. The first person who followed me in my repentance was Asas, who also accompanied me in my resolution of ceasing to cut the beard, and of allowing it to grow. That night, and the following, numbers of amirs and courtiers, soldiers and persons not in the service, to the number of nearly 300 men, made vows of reformation. The wine which we had with us we poured on the ground. I ordered that the wine brought by Baba Dost should have salt thrown into it, that it might be made into vinegar." Baber then broke up his camp, and drew up his army in front of his intrenchments. The Hindoos were equally ready for a decisive effort; and on the 16th March, 1527, an attack commenced by a furious onset on the centre and right wing of the Mussulmans. For several hours the conflict was tremendous; but ultimately Baber was triumphant. Sanga retreated with the wreck of his army to the hills, resolved never to return to his capital, except in triumph. He survived his defeat only for a short period; being succeeded by his eldest surviving son, Rana Rutna, in 1530, who, after a reign of five years, lost his life in a personal encounter with the prince of Boondee, who had carried off his affianced bride. Rana Rutna was succeeded by his brother Bikramajeet. This prince, by his haughty demeanour, alienated the attachment of his chiefs. Bahadoor, the sultan of Guzerat, taking advantage of their disaffection, invaded Mewar, defeated the Rana, and laid siege to Chittor. This sacred fortress was long and bravely defended, and when further opposition became vain, 1,300 females were immolated; then, throwing open the gates, the survivors of the devoted garrison rushed upon the enemy and sold their lives at the highest price. The advance of Humayoon, son of Baber, compelled Bahadoor to retire towards Guzerat. Rana Bickramajeet was then restored to his capital, but was shortly after deposed, and put to death by his nobles.

After a short usurpation by Bunbeer, a spurious member of the family, the throne of Mewar was occupied by Rana Oody Sing, the youngest son of Rana Sanga. During his reign, or in 1568, Chittor was taken by the emperor Ackbar. 30,000 Rajpoots and 1,700 of the immediate kin of the prince are said to have fallen in the defence of this sacred place. Nine queens and a great number of females perished in the flames or in the assault; for even the princesses of this illustrious house are said to have fought on this occasion like common soldiers.

On the loss of his capital, the Rana retired to the valley of the Girwo, in the Aravulli, where he founded the city of Odeypore, henceforth the capital of Mewar. Oody Sing survived the loss of Chittor only four years, and was succeeded by his son Pertab, who disdained submission to the conqueror. After sustaining repeated defeats, Pertab fled into the desert towards Scinde. Fortune suddenly turned in his favour. By the help of some money supplied by his minister, he collected his straggling adherents, surprised and cut to pieces the imperial forces at Deweir, and followed up his advantage with such celerity and energy, that in a short campaign he recovered nearly all Mewar, of which he retained undisturbed possession until his death.

Pertab was succeeded by his son Umra, who enjoyed tranquillity during the remainder of Ackbar's reign. But his successor Jehanghir determined upon the entire subjugation of Mewar. In prosecution of this design, he was twice defeated by Rana Umra. Alarmed at these defeats, Jehanghir tried the experiment of setting up in Chittor, Sugra, the brother of the late Rana Pertab, as rana, in opposition to his nephew Umra. After seven years, Sugra, ashamed of his own apostasy from the national cause, put Rana Umra in possession of the ancient capital. Jehanghir equipped an overwhelming force to crush the Rana. This army, which was commanded by Purvez, the emperor's son, got entangled in the pass of Khamnor, and was completely defeated. Jehanghir then despatched Mohabut Khan, the ablest of his generals, to take the command of the army. Mohabut's success falling far short of the emperor's expectations, he removed the imperial camp to Ajmeer, with the avowed intention of placing himself at the head of the army employed against the Rana. The army was, however, really commanded by his son Sultan Khoorum, afterwards Shah Jehan.

Although the Rajpoots had generally been

successful in battle, yet their diminished numbers rendered further opposition to the colossal power of the empire hopeless. In this state of things, Rana Umra made his submission to the emperor in 1613. He was magnanimously received by Jehanghir, who lavished honours and distinctions upon him and his son Kurrun Sing. But Rana Umra's proud spirit could not brook dependence, however disguised, and in 1621 he abdicated in favour of his son Kurrun, who died in 1628, and was succeeded by his son Juggut Sing, who was succeeded by his son Raj Sing in 1654. Shah Jehan's mother having been a princess of the house of Jeypore, he was well disposed towards the Rajpoots, who enjoyed peace during his reign.

Aurungzebe's attempt to impose a capitation-tax on Hindoos was successfully resisted by the Rajpoots, who defeated the imperial armies in several sanguinary conflicts. An accommodation was, however, effected in 1681, by which the emperor relinquished the odious tax. In the same year Rana Raj Sing died, and was succeeded by his son Jey Sing, who reigned in peace twenty years. He was succeeded by his son Umra.

Rana Umra took an active part in the contentions amongst the sons of Aurungzebe, whose intolerance had rendered him obnoxious to the Rajpoots, and led to the formation of a confederacy by the rulers of Mewar, Marwar, and Amber, for the purpose of throwing off Mahomedan supremacy. In 1713, during the reign of the emperor Ferockser, the confederates commenced their operations by expelling the Mogul officers and razing the mosques which had been erected upon the sites of Hindoo temples.

This triple confederacy was but of short duration; Ajit, raja of Marwar, made separate terms with the emperor, to whom he gave a daughter in marriage, and Rana Umra soon after concluded a treaty with the emperor, which, though it admitted subordination, was in all other respects favourable. Umra Rana died in 1716, and was succeeded by Sangram Sing. During his reign, that is, from 1716 to 1734, the power of the empire rapidly declined; the soobadarries of Bengal, Oude, and Hyderabad, rising to all but nominal independence out of its weakness, while the Mahrattas were rapidly rising into power.

Sangrim was succeeded by his son Juggut Sing II. The emperor having ceded the chouth to the Mahrattas, who were already in possession of Malwa and Guzerat, they exacted it from the states of Rajpootana, as being dependencies of the empire. In 1736 Bajee Rao concluded a treaty with the Rana, stipulating an annual payment to the Peishwa of 1,60,000 rupees.

The Odeypore family had ceased to intermarry with the other Rajpoot families who had given daughters in marriage to the imperial family. This exclusion was keenly felt; and the re-admission to the honour of matrimonial connection with the Odeypore family was always stipulated in the coalitions formed by the Rajpoot chiefs against the emperors; and it was further agreed, that the sons of Odeypore princesses should succeed the father in preference to elder sons by other mothers. This led to family dissensions, which the Mahrattas artfully turned to their own advantage.

On the demise of Sawaie Jey Sing of Jeypore, in 1743, his eldest son, Esuri Sing, was proclaimed raja, but a strong party supported the claim of Madhu Sing, a younger son by the Rana's sister. The Rana espoused the cause of his nephew, and Esuri Sing obtained assistance from Scindiah. In an engagement which took place in 1747, the Rana was defeated. He then called in the aid of Holkar, upon an engagement to pay him 64,00,000 rupees on the deposal of Esuri Sing. A dose of poison gave Madhu Sing the guddee and Holkar the sixty-four lacs.

Rana Juggut Sing died in 1752, and was succeeded by his son Pertab, during whose short reign of three years, Mewar was oppressed by the Mahrattas. He was succeeded by his son Rana Raj Sing, who reigned seven years, during which the ravages and exactions of the Mahrattas continued. He was succeeded by his uncle Rana Ursi, in 1762.

This rana made himself unpopular with most of his chiefs, who formed a party to depose him and set up a youth named Rutna Sing, alleged to be a posthumous son of the late rana. A civil war ensued. Both parties applied for assistance to the Mahrattas, who were ever ready to act as armed arbitrators. Scindiah took the part of the pretender. In a severe battle fought near Oojein, about 1768, the Rana was defeated. Scindiah laid siege to Odeypore, which would have fallen, but for the talent and energy of the Dewan Umra Chund Burwa. After a protracted siege, Scindiah agreed to raise it and abandon the pretender, for a payment of 70 lacs of rupees. After the treaty had been signed, Scindiah, believing he could dictate his terms, demanded twenty lacs more. Umra indignantly tore up the treaty, and sent the fragments with defiance to Scindiah, who, alarmed at the resolute spirit thus evinced by the garrison, made overtures for a renewal of negotiations. Umra replied, that he must deduct from the original terms the expense that had been occasioned by the Mahrattas' bad faith. At length Scindiah accepted 63½ lacs; thirty-three of which were paid, and the districts of Jawud, Jeeran, Neemuch, and Morwun were mortgaged for the remainder. These lands were never recovered by Mewar. Morwun was made over to Holkar, who, in 1771, extorted from the Rana the surrender of the district of Neembahaira. The province of Gadwar was about the same time granted on feudal tenure to Jodhpore and last to Mewar. Rana Ursi was murdered by the heir-apparent of Boondee, while on a hunting excursion. Ursi was succeeded by his son Rana Hamir, who was a minor. His mother's ambition for power, and the feuds among the chiefs, had well nigh dissolved the government.

Regardless of previous experience, the queen-mother, in 1775, invited the aid of Scindiah to reduce the Beygoo chief, who had revolted and usurped crown lands. Scindiah exacted for his own benefit a fine of twelve lacs from the refractory chiefs, and took possession of the districts of Ruttungurh, Keri, and Singalli, and made over those of Irmia, Jauth, Beechore, and Nuddomay, to Holkar. Up to this period the Mahrattas had extorted from Mewar 181 lacs of rupees and territory to the annual valuo of twenty-eight lacs.

In 1778 the young rana died, and was succeeded by his brother Bheem Sing, then in the eighth year of his age. The commencement of his reign was marked by sanguinary feuds among his chiefs, which rendered his country an easy prey to the insatiate rapacity of the Mahrattas, who, for their own aggrandizement, identified themselves with all parties by turns, and Mewar was alternately devastated by Scindiah and Holkar, until it was rendered almost desolate.

The suit of the raja of Jeypore for the hand of the princess Kishna Kour had been favourably received by her father, the Rana. But Raja Maun Sing also advanced pretensions to the lady's hand, on the plea that she had been betrothed to his predecessor, and that the engagement was with the throne and not the individual occupant. This led to a ruinous war between Marwar and Jeypore. The minister of Odeypore was induced to persuade the Rana to sacrifice his daughter to the peace of Rajwarra. The wretched father at last yielded, and poison was administered to the ill-fated princess. From this time, 1806, to 1817, Mewar continued to be ravaged by the Mahrattas and the Pindarry Ameer Khan. On the suppression, in 1817, of the predatory system which prevailed in Central India, it was resolved, chiefly with a view to prevent its revival, to extend British influence and protection over the states of Rajpootana. The chiefs were accordingly invited to ally themselves with the British government, on the basis of acknowledging its supremacy and paying a certain tribute, in return for external protection and internal independence. The rana of Odeypore eagerly embraced the invitation, and entered into a treaty.

Bheem Singh died in 1828, and was succeeded by his only son Jowan Singh, who died in 1838, leaving no issue, and was succeeded by Surdan Singh, chief of Bangore, the nearest heir of the family. He died in 1842, and was succeeded by his younger and adopted brother Maharana Suroop Singh. The state of Odeypore has assigned the revenue of Mhairwarra, to the extent of 50,000 rupees per annum, towards the maintenance of the Mewar Bheel corps. This corps was raised in 1841, at the joint expense of the British and Odeypore governments, for the pacification of the Bheel tracts of the latter; and complete success has been the result. Under the treaty of 1818, Odeypore became one of the tributaries of the British government. The amount of annual tribute had been fixed at three-lacs of Odeypore rupees; but in 1848 it was reduced to £20,000, being a reduction of the sum previously paid, to the extent of £2,400 per annum.

OODEYPOOR, in Rajpootana, the principal place of the territory of the same name, or of Mewar. It is situate on a low ridge, in a sort of valley or basin, surrounded on all sides by hills, except on the west, where extends a lake five miles in circuit. The valley is of considerable size, being thirty miles in length and ten in breadth. Besides the great lake close to the city on the west, is another, of inferior but still of considerable dimensions, six miles farther west; and there are, besides, numerous jhils, or small meres and marshes. Hence result frequent attacks of fever, ague, and cholera. The appearance of the town, when viewed from the east, is striking and pleasing, but when viewed more closely, is found to be an ill-built place. The palace is, however, a noble pile of granite, a hundred feet high, situate on the crest of a rocky ridge overlooking the lake, the city, and the valley. The lake is artificial, having been formed by an embankment collecting the water of the stream which feeds it. This dam is 334 yards in length, and at top 110 yards in thickness, but becomes much thicker towards the base. The height of the dam above the water is thirty-seven feet; its face is of marble, embellished with sculptured figures, and small temples and other buildings. Tod states, that in 1818 the number of houses, formerly 50,000, had diminished to 3,000; but the city, as well as the state, seems somewhat reviving under British protection. According to Tod, this city was founded by Oody Singh, rana of Mewar, after the sack of Chitor by Akbar, in 1568; and the city, as well as the Oody Sagur or lake, was named after the founder. Elevation above the sea 2,064 feet. Distance from Neemuch, W., 70 miles; from Mow, N.W., 190; Oujein, N.W., 164; Deesa, E., 110; Nusserabad, S.W., 135; Bombay, N., 395. Lat. 24° 37′, long. 73° 49′.

OODEYPOORA.—A town in the British district of Ghazeepoor, lieut.-gov. of the N.W. Provinces. It contains a population of 5,865 inhabitants, and is distant 15 miles E. from Bulliah. Lat. 25° 44′, long. 84° 25′.

OODGHEER, in Hyderabad, or territory of the Nizam, a small town with a fort, 115 miles N.W. of the city of Hyderabad. Lat. 18° 24′, long. 77° 11′.

OODIPOOR.—A town in the Rajpoot state of Beekaneer, 84 miles N.N.E. from Beekaneer, and 135 miles W. from Hansee. Lat. 29° 7′, long. 73° 53′.

OOGAPORE, in the British district of Mirzapore, lieut.-gov. of the N.W. Provinces, a village on the route from Jounpoor to Mirzapore, 33 miles S. of the former, 10 N. of the latter, situate three miles N. of the left bank of the Ganges. Lat. 25° 17′, long. 82° 37′.

OOJAL.—A river of Kattywar, rising in lat. 21° 31′, long. 70° 51′, and flowing in a circuitous, but generally westerly direction, for 75 miles, falls into the Bhader river, near the town of Nurvee Bunder, in lat. 21° 27′, long. 69° 59′.

OOJEANEE, in the British district of Etawah, lieut.-gov. of the N.W. Provinces, a town on the route from Calpee to the cantonment of Etawa, and 17 miles S.E. of the latter. Lat. 26° 38′, long. 79° 17′.

OOJEIN, in the territory of Gwalior, or possessions of the Scindia family, a city on the right bank of the river Seepra. It is of oblong outline, six miles in circumference, surrounded by a stone wall with round towers. The houses, which are much crowded together, are some of brick, some of wood; but in the construction of the former, a frame-work of wood is first made, and the intervals then filled up with bricks. They are covered either with tiles or lime terraces. The principal bazar is a spacious street, with houses of two stories; the lower of which is built of stone, and occupied by shops; the upper, of brick or wood, furnishes the habitation of the owner and his family. There are four mosques, and a great number of Hindoo temples. The city is well supplied with water both from the river and from two large tanks, one of which is very handsome. The head of the Scindia family has a palace here, spacious and commodious, but with little of exterior magnificence. Near it is an antique gate, said to have originally belonged to a fort built by Vikramaditya, whose reign is placed by chronologists more than half a century prior to the commencement of the Christian era. At the southern extremity of the town is an obervatory, constructed by Jai Singh, the scientific rajah of Jeypoor or Amber, and minister of Mahomed Shah, emperor of Delhi, who reigned from 1719 to 1748. Oojein, says Conolly, is "surrounded on every side but the south with an almost uninterrupted belt of groves and gardens. Their names, had I room for them, would be a history of the place and of its manners. On one side lies the garden of Dowlut-Rao, on the other that of his carpenter; here is the garden of Rajah Mal, whose name has outlived his history; while near, and in contrast to it, is another, which, but a few days ago, gloried in the name of the Baizi Bai, now publishes, by a change of title, the fickleness of fortune. The Maharaj Bagh (Dowlut-Rao's) was formerly the pride of five proprietors; but the modern Ahab coveted his neighbour's vineyard, out of five small gardens made a large one, and deprived the owners of the inheritance of their fathers. The best of the gardens seem to have been planted by Mussulmans, who, we learn from Baber, introduced the fashion into India." About a mile to the north of the present city are the ruins of the ancient capital of Malwa, which, according to Brahminical tradition, connected with a ridiculous fable, was overwhelmed by a shower of earth poured down upon it as a divinely-inflicted punishment. On the cause of the destruction of the ancient city, different opinions have been advanced. It has been suggested that an inundation of the river might have produced the disastrous effect; and the suggestion is countenanced by the fact, that in modern times the river has been known to overflow a great part of the present town, and cause much damage, notwithstanding the shortness of its course, and its comparatively inconsiderable volume of water. Another conjecture has ascribed the catastrophe to an earthquake; but the alleged soundness of the walls is presumed to offer an obstacle to the reception of this view. A third hypothesis assigns as the cause, the operation of a violent wind, carrying with it showers of loose earth or sand. To this, however, the nature of the soil seems opposed. The first of these conjectures is embraced by Malcolm, the last by Hunter.

Five miles north of the city, the river separates into two channels, and surrounds an oval-shaped rocky eminence, crowned by a palace never finished, and now in a state of ruin, though, from the excellence of the materials used in its construction, its decay is far less rapid than might be looked for. It is believed to have been erected on the site, and with the materials, of an ancient Hindoo temple. The island was connected with the left bank of the river by two bridges; one of which has been nearly swept away; the other is little, if at all, impaired. Close to this latter bridge are some curious works, by which the stream has been diverted to purposes of pleasure and ornament. The vicinity of these works is adorned by an arcade, and a walled inclosure at a short distance is suspected to have been once a garden.

Oojein is one of the seven sacred cities of the Hindoos, and the first meridian of their geographers. It appears to be mentioned by Ptolemy under the name of Ozoana. Its period of chief grandeur has been supposed to date from the era of Vikramajit; but previously, it is believed to have been populous and wealthy. According to the Mahawanso, a Ceylonese record, Piyadaso, or Asoka, or Dhanmasoko, grandson of the renowned Chandragupta, was in the year B.C. 325 viceroy of Oojein, being sent thither, as into honourable banishment, by his father Bindusaro, king of Patilipura or Patna, who dreaded his sanguinary and turbulent disposition. The same document states, "that B.C. 157 the Buddhist high-priest Dhammarahkito took with him 40,000 disciples from the Dakkhinagiri temple at Oojein to Ceylon, to assist in lying the foundation-stone of the great temple at Anuradhapura." Later, Vikramaditya, or

Vikramajit, king of Oojein, was so renowned, that the Samvat era, 57 B.C., universally used throughout Hindostan to this day, dates from the commencement of his reign. His son Chandrasen is represented to have possessed himself of all Hindostan. At the commencement of the eleventh century, when Mahmud of Ghuznee invaded India, Oojein was the seat of an independent rajah ruling Malwa. It appears to have fallen into the hands of the Mussulmans in the year 1310; and after the assumption of independence in 1387 by the Dilawar Ghori, the viceroy of the Patan sovereign of Delhi, the seat of the government of Malwa was transferred first to Dhar, and subsequently to Mandu. In 1561 it was with the rest of Malwa subjugated by Akbar. It fell into the hands of the Mahrattas about the middle of the last century, and was regarded as the capital of Scindia's possessions, until Doulut Rao, in 1810, fixed his residence at Gwalior. Oojein, with its annexed lands, was assessed at 1,40,000 rupees annually to Scindia's government; but by a recent arrangement, the town and territory have been assigned to the Baiza Baee, formerly regent of Gwalior, at the same annual rent. Elevation above the sea 1,698 feet. The city is sometimes called Avanti and Visala. Distance S.W. from Goonah 152 miles, from Gwalior 260, S.W. from Allahabad, by Saugor, 598. Lat. 23° 10′, long. 75° 47′.

OOJHANEE, in the British district of Budaon, lieut.-gov. of the N.W. Provinces, a town on the route from Budaon to Allygurh, eight miles W. by S. of the former. Population 6,361. Lat. 28°, long. 79° 4′.

OOJKE CHOKEE, in the British district of Mirzapoor, lieut.-gov. of the N.W. Provinces, a village on the route from the city of Benares to that of Allahabad, 42 miles W. of the former, 33 S.E. of the latter. Water can be obtained but from one well; but within a mile of the village is a jhil or pond, where it may always be had. Lat. 25° 19′, long. 82° 25′.

OOKEE MUTH, in the British district of Kumaon, lieut.-gov. of the N.W. Provinces, a village having a Hindoo temple, and lying on the route from Srinugur to Kedarnath Temple, 18 miles S. of the latter. It is situate on an eminence of gneiss rock, on the left bank of the Mandakini, here crossed by a jhula or rope bridge. Elevation above the sea, of the temple, 4,339 feet; of the jhula, 3,464. Lat. 30° 31′, long. 79° 8′.

OOKLEE.—A town in the British district of Sholapoor, presidency of Bombay, 66 miles S. of Sholapoor. Lat. 16° 42′, long. 75° 56′.

OOLAH.—A town in Hyderabad, or the Nizam's dominions, 129 miles N.N.W. from Hyderabad, and 144 miles S. by E. from Ellichpoor. Lat. 19° 10′, long. 78° 9′.

OOLAUL.—A town in the British district of South Canara, presidency of Madras, three miles S. of Mangalore. Lat. 12° 50′, long. 74° 54′.

OOLOOR.—A town in the native state of Travancore, 55 miles N.W. by W. from Cape Comorin, and five miles N.W. by N. from Trivandrum. Lat. 8° 32′, long. 76° 58′.

OOLOWTEE, a river of Guzerat, rises in lat. 22° 13′, long. 71° 33′, and, flowing in an easterly direction through the British district of Ahmedabad for fifty miles, falls into the Gulf of Cambay, in lat. 21° 58′, long. 72° 14′.

OOLPAR, in the British district of Surat, presidency of Bombay, a town situate on a small river, which, eight miles farther west, falls into the Gulf of Cambay. Population 3,500. Distance N. from Surat 12 miles. Lat. 21° 17′, long. 72° 47′.

OOMDEE.—A town in the British province of Sattara, presidency of Bombay, 108 miles E. by S. of Sattara. Lat. 17° 14′, long. 75° 39′.

OOMERKOTE.—See OMERCOTE.

OOMNEE.—A town in the territory of Oude, 126 miles N. from Lucknow, and 60 miles E. from Pilleebheet. Lat. 28° 40′, long. 80° 51′.

OOMRAIR, in the recently lapsed territory of Nagpore, a town on the right bank of the river Amb, a tributary of the Weingunga. Iron-ore is found in its vicinity. Distance from the city of Nagpore, S.E., 24 miles. Lat. 20° 50′, long. 79° 22′.

OOMRAIT.—A town in the recently escheated territory of Nagpore or Berar, situate 72 miles N.N.W. from Nagpore, and 56 miles E.N.E. from Baitool. Lat. 22° 7′, long. 78° 45′.

OOMRAWAH, in the British district of Shahjehanpoor, lieut.-gov. of the N.W. Provinces, a village on the route from Futtehgurh to the cantonment of Shahjehanpoor, and 16 miles S.W. of the latter. Lat. 27° 46′, long. 79° 50′.

OOMRAWUTTEE.—A town situate on the route from Nagpore to Aurungabad, and in one of the districts of Hyderabad which has been transferred to the British government. It is a place of great commercial importance; several considerable firms are established here, and most of the influential merchants of Upper India, as well as those of Bombay of any note, have either correspondents or branch houses at this place. The subordinates of some of these firms spread themselves over the cotton-growing districts, and make advances to the cultivators, or assist them in paying their kists, on the agreement that the produce shall be at the disposal of their employer. When the crop is ready for picking, the cultivator for the most part has nothing farther to do with it, the speculating capitalist being apprehensive that if the cultivator were permitted to gather it, much would be purloined by him. When picked, it is transferred to Oomrawuttee, where are large warehouses appropriated to its reception, and where it is cleaned and repacked for exportation, either from Bombay or from Calcutta. This place being within one of the districts recently ceded by the Nizam to the British government in satisfaction of arrears of subsidy, it now partakes of all the advantages enjoyed by the dominions of that government in India, and among them, that of freedom from the baleful effects of transit-duties. It will moreover be connected with the port of Bombay by means of a branch from the main line of the Great Indian Peninsula Railway Company. Distance from Bombay, N.E., 350 miles; from Hyderabad, N., 245. Lat. 20° 50′, long. 77° 49′.

OOMREE, in the British district of Allahabad, lieut.-gov. of the N.W. Provinces, a village on the route by Rajapoor ferry from the cantonment of Allahabad to Banda, and nine miles W. of the former. Lat. 25° 27′, long. 81° 48′.

OOMREIT.—A town in the British district of Kaira, presidency of Bombay, 32 miles E. by S. of Kaira. Lat. 22° 40′, long. 73° 10′.

OOMROWREE, in the British district of Futtehpoor, lieut.-gov. of the N.W. Provinces, a village on the route from Cawnpore to Futtehpore, and 14 miles N.W. of the latter. Lat. 26° 3′, long. 80° 43′.

OOMUREE, in the British district of Mynpooree, lieut.-gov. of the N.W. Provinces, a village on the route from the city of Agra to Etawah, and 28 miles N.W. of the latter. The road in this part of the route is good, the country cultivated, and studded with small villages. Lat. 27° 4′, long. 78° 44′.

OOMURGURH, in the British district of Muttra, lieut.-gov. of the N.W. Provinces, a small town on the route from the cantonment of Allygurh to that of Etawah, and 44 miles S.E. of the former. It has a market, and is supplied with water from wells. The surrounding country is open, with a clayey soil, well cultivated. Lat. 27° 22′, long. 78° 25′.

OOMURKEIR.—A town in the native state of Hyderabad, or the Nizam's dominions, situate on the left bank of the Payne Gunga river, and 161 miles N.N.W. from Hyderabad. Lat. 19° 33′, long. 77° 45′.

OONA.—A town in the peninsula of Kattywar, province of Guzerat, situate 102 miles S. from Rajkote, and 96 miles S.E. by E. from Poorbunder. Lat. 20° 50′, long. 71° 2′.

OONCHADEH, in the British district of Allahabad, lieut.-gov. of the N.W. Provinces, a village on the route by the Kutra Pass from Allahabad to Rewa, and 28 miles S.E. of the former. Lat. 25° 14′, long. 82° 12′.

OONCHADEH, in the British district of Allahabad, lieut.-gov. of the N.W. Provinces, a town on the route from Allahabad to Palamow, 38 miles S.E. of the former. Lat. 25° 1′, long. 82° 17′.

OONCHOD.—A town in the native state of Gwalior, or territory of Scindia's family, situate 52 miles S.E. by E. from Oojein, and 71 miles S.W. by W. from Bhopal. The united pergunnahs of Sonkach and of Oonchod, yielding an annual revenue of 90,000 rupees, were, by the treaty of Gwalior in 1844, placed under British management, and allocated for the maintenance of the augmented Gwalior contingent. Lat. 22° 44′, long. 76° 28′.

OONDA.—A town in the British district of Bancoora, lieut.-gov. of Bengal, 87 miles N.W. by W. of Calcutta. Lat. 23° 7′, long. 87° 14′.

OONDRACONDAH.—A town in Hydrabad, or the Nizam's dominions, 82 miles E. by S. from Hydrabad, and 75 miles N.W. from Guntoor. Lat. 17° 5′, long. 79° 44′.

OOND SURWEYA, in the peninsula of Kattywar, province of Guzerat, a small prant or district. It is bounded on the west by the prant of Kattywar, and on all other sides by that of Gohilwar; lies between lat. 21° 18′—21° 30′, long. 71° 38′—71° 55′; is twenty-six miles in length from north-east to south-west, and thirteen in extreme breadth. No official return has been made of the area, but, according to a probable approximation, it may be stated at 174 square miles. It is a level, low district, extending on each side of the river Setronjee, and on the north side of the Wullak hills, and contains fifty-three villages, and a population of 11,373 persons, and held chiefly by Rajpoots. They pay collectively a tribute of 12,878 rupees annually to the Guicowar.

OONDURGAON.—A town in the British district of Sholapoor, presidency of Bombay, 32 miles N.W. of Sholapoor. Lat. 18° 1′, long. 75° 39′.

OONDWA NULLAH, in the British district of Bhaugulpoor, lieut.-gov. of Bengal, a small stream, discharging itself into the Ganges on the right side. It drains an extensive jhil or shallow lake, becoming a morass during the dry season, and in the periodical rains having a great body of water. It gives name to a village with an antique fort, to which, in 1763, the army of Meer Cossim Ali, subahdar of Bengal, then engaged in hostilities with the East-India Company, fled, after being defeated in a general engagement near Sootee. On the intrenchments were mounted about 100 pieces of artillery, and they were manned by a force estimated at 60,000 men. It was, however, taken by the British in September, by a night attack from two different points; one of these movements being intended to divert the attention of the enemy from the other, which, it is stated, was undertaken upon the information of a soldier, who, having deserted from the British army to that of Meer Cossim, had become tired of the latter service, and made his peace with his former employers by affording this assistance. The slaughter of the garrison is represented as great; the surprise having rendered them incapable of defending themselves with effect, though the number of the assailants did not exceed 3,000 men of all arms. Oondwa Nullah is on the route from Burhampoor to Rajmahal, 70 miles N. of former, eight S. of latter, 188 N. of Calcutta, by Burhampoor. Lat. 24° 58′, long. 87° 53′.

OONIARA, in the Rajpoot state of Jeypore, a considerable town, the principal place of the small raj or state held by a junior branch of the reigning family of Jeypore. The rajah resides here, in a fort of masonry. The town is surrounded by a wall, with ditch. Distant S. of Jeypore 70 miles. Lat. 25° 55′, long. 76°10′.

OONTAREE.—A town in the British district of Palamow, lieut.-gov. of Bengal, 45 miles N.W. of Palamow. Lat. 24° 16′, long. 83° 30′.

OONYENEE, in the British district of Bareilly, division of Pilleebheet, lieut.-gov. of the N.W. Provinces, a village on the left bank of the Bhagul river, on the route from the town of Pilleebheet to Nugeena, and 15 miles N.W. of the former. Lat. 28° 46′, long. 79° 41′.

OOPIN UNGADY.—A town in the British district of South Canara, presidency of Madras, 30 miles E. of Mangalore. Lat. 12° 50′, long. 75° 20′.

OOPLANA.—A town in the British district of Hydrabad, in the province of Scinde, presidency of Bombay, 66 miles S.S.W. of Hydrabad. Lat. 24° 30′, long. 68° 5′.

OORAGHUM.—A town in the native state of Cochin, presidency of Madras, 33 miles N. from Cochin, and nine miles S. from Trichoor. Lat. 10° 26′, long. 76° 17′.

OORALWADA.—A town in the British district of Cuddapah, presidency of Madras, 52 miles N. of Cuddapah. Lat. 15° 14′, long 78° 57′.

OORCHA, in Bundelcund, a town, the principal place of a raj or principality known by the name of Oorcha or Tehree. It lies three or four miles to the right or south-west of the route from Agra to Saugor, 142 miles S.E. of the former, 131 N. of the latter, and on the left or west side of the river Betwa. Tieffenthaler, writing eighty years ago, describes it as situate on a rocky eminence; as being about three miles in circuit, surrounded by a wall of unhewn stones piled one upon the other without cement, with three lofty gateways. The fortress, situate within the town, is represented as a fine structure, containing the handsome residence of the rajah, as well as a splendid palace built for the accommodation of the Padshah Jehangir. The communication with the rest of the town the writer states to be by means of a wooden bridge, the fortress during the periodical rains being insulated by a branch of the flooded Betwa. In the town is a temple ornamented with lofty spires.

The raj of which this town is the capital was estimated, in 1832, to contain 2,160 square miles, 640 villages, with a population of 192,000 souls; yielding a revenue of 10,00,000 rupees (100,000*l.*), and maintaining a force of 1,200 cavalry and 4,000 infantry. The revenue appears to be on the decline, as in 1837 it was estimated at only 6,00,000 rupees (60,000*l.*); while the military force in 1847 was computed at between 7,000 and 8,000 men, of whom more than 7,000 were infantry. The rajah pays to the Jhansi chief, through the British government, 3,000 rupees per annum, as quit-rent for the jaghire of Terhowlee.

The rajah of Oorcha is considered the head of the Boondela race, of Rajpoot origin, being descended from a spurious branch of the Gurhwars. According to a recent authority, Hurdeo, one of the Gurhwar family, came into the country with a slave-girl, and took up his abode at Gurh Kurar, in the neighbourhood of Oorcha. He was there invited to give his daughter in marriage to the rajah of Oorcha, but refused, on account of objection to his caste or descent. After much importunity, however, he gave his consent, on condition that the rajah should at the marriage feast partake of the prepared viands, and thus lose all distinction of caste. The rajah consented, was poisoned with all his family, and the Gurhwar obtained possession of the country. His son was called Boondela, because he was the offspring of a bandee or slave-girl; and this name has been given to his descendants. This origin of the family is assigned by Elliott to the beginning of the thirteenth century; but Franklin is of opinion that the event occurred as late as the close of the fourteenth century. The town of Oorcha was built in 1531, by Pretap Hrad, the chief of the Bundelas. Madhikar Sah, his grandson, appears to have advanced his raj to considerable prosperity by gaining the favour of Akbar. Birsing Deo, the son and successor of the last-mentioned rajah, was a notorious freebooter, and thence called Dang, a name equivalent to robber; from which circumstance Bundelcund is also called Dangaya. The desperate character of Birsing Deo pointed him out to Selim, son and declared heir of Akbar, as a proper instrument to cut off the celebrated Abulfazl, his father's favourite and minister, and who was thought unfavourable to the prince's views. Birsing Deo accordingly laid an ambuscade for Abulfazl, at Berkeh Sarae, as he proceeded towards Gwalior in his return from the Deccan, and, notwithstanding a valorous defence, the obnoxious minister was killed, and his head sent to Selim, by whom the murderer was amply rewarded. Jajhar Singh, son and successor of Birsing Deo, revolted against the sovereign of Delhi, but was overpowered, driven to take refuge in Gondwana, and his country seized by the conqueror. Pehar Singh, however, his brother, was reinstated, and the Oorcha rajahs continued feudatories of the padshahs of Delhi until the dissolution of the empire. The raj or principality has been, however, much reduced, Dutteea being formed out of it, probably by partition arising out of family arrangements, as its chief is of the same lineage as the rajah of Oorcha. The territory of Jhansee was wrested from Oorcha in 1733, by the Mahrattas; the small raj of Sumpter was also severed from Oorcha, but the time and cause of the event are unascertained. The rajah, though he received assistance from the Peishwa in 1733, at no time acknowledged that potentate as his sovereign; and in the treaty concluded between the East-India Company and him, in 1812, it is set forth, that by him "and his ancestors his present possessions have been held during a long course of years, without paying tribute or acknowledging vassalage to any other power." By the terms of this treaty, the rajah professed obedience and attachment to the British government, which guaranteed his possessions to him free of tribute, and undertook to protect his territories from foreign aggression; the rajah abstaining from collision with any powers in alliance with the British government, or dependent on it. In 1842 Oorcha assumed such a refractory attitude, that a military demonstration on the part of the British authorities was found necessary.

The rajah Soojan Singh for the most part residing at Tehree, one of his towns, forty miles south-east of Oorcha, was of late years generally styled rajah of Tehree. Soojan Singh died in 1854, leaving no issue, whereupon the neighbouring Boondela chiefs were required to indicate the nearest collateral heir to the late rajah capable of adoption. Humeer Singh being the party selected, was installed as rajah, and a regent appointed during his minority. The town of Oorcha is distant 100 miles S.W. of Calpee, 137 W. of Banda, 248 W. of Allahabad, 743 N.W. of Calcutta. Lat. 25° 21', long. 78° 42'.

OORCHA, in Bussahir, a village and halting-place for travellers in Koonawur, is situate on a mountain-side near the right hand of the Taglakhar river, a considerable feeder of the Sutluj. The vicinity is remarkable for the great number of manes, or peculiar structures devoted to the purposes of the Lamaic religion. These are low tumuli or mounds, of lengths varying from ten to 200 feet, two feet broad, and three or four feet high, constructed of loose uncemented stones, and covered at top with numerous pieces of slate of all shapes and sizes, with sentences carved in the Oochen or sacred character, the most common being the mystic exclamation, Oom mane paemee oom. There is always a path on each side of these erections, and the devotees invariably pass them on the right hand, even though this observance should entail the necessity of taking a circuit of a quarter of a mile, as Gerard has sometimes known to be the case. The road and country are dreary in the extreme, presenting nothing but a rugged surface of rock, bare, and formed generally of the jagged edges of slate strata. A few dwarf deodars spring from crevices, and are almost the last trees in the journey eastward from central Koonawur to the Tartarian table-land, the parching and freezing gusts of which check the growth of all trees, except a few scantily-distributed birches. Here, at the end of July, the thermometer rose in a tent to 99°, and in the open air to 79°, a high temperature for a spot having an elevation of 11,296 feet above the sea. Lat. 31° 38', long. 78° 37'.

OORCHAN.—A town in one of the recently sequestrated districts of Hyderabad, or dominions of the Nizam, 35 miles S.E. by S. from Sholapoor, and 155 miles W. from Hyderabad. Lat. 17° 13', long. 76° 14'.

OORJUAH, in the British district of Etawa, lieut.-gov. of the N.W. Provinces, a town, the principal place of the pergunnah of the same name, situate on the route from Allahabad to Etawa, and 39 miles S.E. of the latter. It has a bazar, and is abundantly supplied with water. Population 5,645. Lat. 26° 28', long. 79° 35'.

OORMEL, or URMAL, a river rising in Bundelcund, and in lat. 24° 50', long. 79° 36'. Its course is first northerly, then sweeps round nearly in a semicircle north-easterly, easterly, and south-easterly. Having run sixty miles, it falls into the river Cane on the left bank, in lat. 24° 56', long. 80° 9'.

OORNEE, in Koonawur, a district of Bussahir, is a village near the right bank of the Joola, which about a mile below falls into the Sutluj, on the right side. It is situate in a rugged and barren country, amidst huge masses and precipices of gneiss. Lat. 31° 32', long. 78° 10'.

OOROOLEE.—A town in the British district of Poonah, presidency of Bombay, 20 miles E. of Poonah. Lat. 18° 30', long. 74° 11'.

OORUN.—A town in the British district of Tannah, presidency of Bombay, 10 miles E.S.E. from Bombay. Lat. 18° 53', long. 73° 1'.

OOSAINEE, in the British district of Agra, a village on the route from the city of Agra to Mynpoorie, and 21 miles E. of the former. The road in this part of the route is good, the country cultivated. Lat. 27° 12', long. 78° 24'.

OOSCOTTA.—See HOSKOTE.

OOSEITH, in the British district of Budaon, lieut.-gov. of the N.W. Provinces, a town, the principal place of the pergunnah of the same name. Lat. 27° 48', long. 79° 18'.

OOSSOOR.—A town in the British district of Salem, presidency of Madras, 82 miles N.N.W. of Salem. A stud establishment is maintained at this place by the government; and it appears from an official statement, showing the average cost of horses passed for the service from the breeding department, that the expense at Oossoor contrasts favourably with the cost of horses purchased at Bombay. Lat. 12° 46', long. 77° 51'.

OOTAKAMUND, a town in the British district of Coimbatoor, presidency of Madras, and the principal sanitary station on the Neilgherry Hills, has an elevation of 7,300 feet above the level of the sea, and is 1,300 feet higher than the minor stations of Kotageri and

Coonoor. It is situated in an open valley almost in the centre of the hills, protected by the Dodabetta range on the north-east and south, but open to the westward. According to the authority already quoted, "the only town on the hills properly so called, is Ootacamund; and even this term can only be applied legitimately to the native portion of the settlement, since the residences of Europeans are too widely dispersed along the slopes of the valley to admit at present of its further extension. So rapidly, however, is the number of houses increasing, that before long the term town will not be inappropriately applied to the whole settlement." The site of Ootakamund was first occupied in 1822. The mean annual temperature is 58°: the rain-fall, on an average of four years, was found to amount to forty-four inches. An elegant church, which has been recently enlarged, is one of the greatest ornaments of the settlement. There are also public gardens, and the site has been selected for one of the meteorological stations of the Madras presidency. Ootakamund is 32 miles N.W. by N. of Coimbatoor. Lat. 11° 24′, long. 76° 47′.

OOTALOOR.—A town in Hyderabad, or the territory of the Nizam, situate six miles S.W. from the left bank of the Manjera river, and 60 miles N.W. from Hyderabad. Lat. 18° 2′, long. 78°.

OOTAMPOLLIAM.—A town in the British district of Madura, presidency of Madras, 54 miles W. by S. of Madura. Lat. 9° 49′, long. 77° 23′.

OOTCH, in Bahawulpoor, a city situate four miles from the left bank of the Punjnud river, amidst beautiful groves. It is formed of three distinct towns, a few hundred yards apart, and each surrounded by a ruinous brick wall. The streets are narrow and meanly built, but the bazars are large, and well supplied with wares, and there is considerable general traffic. These towns are built on mounds, formed by the materials of great cities formerly existing here. In the immediate vicinity are prodigious quantities of ruins, still in such preservation that they could be easily rendered habitable. Ootch is regarded with veneration by Mahometans, in consequence of containing five shrines of deceased *pirs* or saints, *Saiyids*, reputed descendants from Mahomet. Lat. 29° 13′, long. 71° 9′.

OOTERPARA, in the British district of the Twenty-four Pergunnahs, lieut.-gov. of Bengal, a town situate on the right bank of the river Hooghly. In this town an income-tax has been imposed upon the inhabitants for the production of funds for municipal purposes. Lat. 22° 35′, long. 88° 23′.

OOTGIR, or DEOGURH.—A town in the Rajpoot state of Kerowly, situate on the left bank of the Chumbul river, and 28 miles S.S.W. from Kerowly. Lat. 26° 6′, long. 77°.

OOTHA, in the British district of Allahabad, lieut.-gov. of the N.W. Provinces, a village on the route by the Kutra Pass from Allahabad to Rewa, and 30 miles S.E. of the former. Lat. 25° 13′, long. 82° 14′.

OOTRACH, or TUROCH, a district in the lower or southern mountains of the Himalayas, is bounded on the north by Bussahir; on the east by Raeen and Bussahir; on the south by Joobul (of which state indeed it now forms part); and on the west by Poondur and Kothkaee; and has an area probably of between sixty and seventy square miles. It lies between lat. 30° 56′—31° 6′, long. 77° 42′—77° 54′. It consists almost entirely of a portion of the crest and declivities of a lofty range proceeding from Wartoo Mountain in a south-west direction to the river Tons. The general elevation is probably very considerable, as the summit of Tungru Peak, a little above the north-western frontier, is 10,102 feet. The population of Ootrach is estimated by De Cruz at 2,500; the annual revenue at 300*l.*; of which amount, the sum of 28*l.* was paid by the rannee as tribute to the East-India Company. The armed followers of the chief were computed at about 100. On the expulsion of the Ghoorkas in 1815, this state was granted to a claimant alleged to be the heir of the rana dispossessed by those invaders. It was, however, subsequently ascertained that the claim was fraudulently made, to the prejudice of an elder brother, and he was compelled to abdicate in favour of his son, a pecuniary allowance being at the same time assigned to his nephew. But the mal-administration of this petty state subsequently rendered it necessary to depose this prince also; and on account of the insignificance of Ootrach, and the small amount of its revenue, it was deemed advisable to incorporate it with Joobul.

OOTRA DROOG.—A town in the Mysore, 47 miles N.E. by N. from Seringapatam, and 32 miles W. from Bangalore. Lat. 12° 58′, long. 77° 10′.

OOTUNCURRAY.—A town in the British district of Salem, presidency of Madras, 49 miles N.E. by N. of Salem. Lat 12° 16′, long. 78° 35′.

OOTURHEE, in the British district of Cawnpore, lieut.-gov. of the N.W. Provinces, a village on the route from the cantonment of Futtehgurh to that of Cawnpore, and 28 miles N.W. of the latter. Lat. 26° 46′, long. 80° 9′.

OPAH.—A town in the British district of Chota Nagpoor, lieut.-gov. of Bengal, 17 miles E.N.E. of Lohadugga. Lat. 23° 32′, long. 85°.

OPERAI, in Bundelcund, in the territory of Dutteah, a town on the route from Banda to Gwalior, 160 miles W. of the former. It has a bazar, and water is plentiful. Lat. 25° 46′, long. 78° 27′.

OPERBUNDA.—A town in the British district of Beerbhoom, lieut.-gov. of Bengal, 150 miles N.W. of Calcutta. Lat. 24° 10′, long. 86° 56′.

ORAI, in Bundelcund, in the British territory of Jaloun, a small town on the route from Calpee to Jhansee, 22 miles S.W. of the former. It has a bazar, and adequate supply of water. Lat. 25° 59′, long. 79° 31′.

ORAYE.—A town in the British district of Balasore, province of Cuttack, lieut.-gov. of Bengal, 61 miles S.W. by S. of Balasore. Lat. 20° 45′, long. 86° 30′.

ORISSA.—An extensive tract of India, comprising the British district of Cuttack, part of the British district of Midnapoor, and the wild and unsettled region lying to the westward of those, and between them and the territory of Nagpore. It lies between lat. 17° 16′—22° 23′, long. 81° 35′—87° 20′. The area, according to official report, is 52,995 square miles. It is bounded on the north by the British district of Mirzapoor; on the north-east by the British districts Palamow, Pachete, Ramgurh, and Midnapoor, on the south-east by the Bay of Bengal and the Northern Circars; on the west by Nagpore or the territory of Berar, and the British districts denominated the Ceded Territory of Saugor and Nerbudda. The maritime part of Orissa, forming the British district of Cuttack, is described under that name in the alphabetical arrangement.

The scanty notices which we have respecting this extensive tract, represent it as consisting of an extensive range of mountains, the continuation of the Eastern Ghauts. Some of the summits of these attain an elevation considerably exceeding 2,000 feet; and one summit has been estimated by an intelligent traveller to have an elevation of 4,000 feet above the level of the sea. Timber abounds in the vast forest, which extends uninterruptedly from the banks of the Godavery to those of the Ganges, a distance of nearly 600 miles. The geological character of the mountains is primary, being granite, gneiss in large quantities, and mica-slate; and throughout the rocks garnets are interspersed in surprising abundance. In many places the gneiss has a strongly-marked porphyritic character, and elsewhere passes by imperceptible transition into sandstone, or is overlaid with laterite. In the northern part there is much primary limestone, intermixed with quartz and mica-slate. Iron-ore is very abundant in many places; and in the midland parts, in the vicinity of the town of Sumbhulpore, diamonds, gold, and rubies are found in the detritus of rocks; and there is reason to conclude that they exist in situ in the neighbouring mountains. It has been stated that promising indications of coal have been observed; but it has not yet been found in any part of the district. The climate during the hot season, in the close of spring and early part of summer, is extremely sultry, the thermometer reaching 115° in the shade; and this very high temperature acting on decayed vegetation, saturated with moisture, is productive of deadly malaria, rendering the climate one of the most unhealthy in India. This unfavourable circumstance, more than any other, prevents the settlement and adequate cultivation of a country having a vast extent of well-watered and fertile soil, suited for the successfully raising most of the valuable intertropical products. Wild beasts are numerous: there are the wild elephant, the gayal, a huge bovine quadruped, wild buffalo, nylgau (Antilope picta), wild swine, deer of various kinds, the antelope, porcupine, hare, monkey, squirrel, tiger, leopard, bear, wolf, hyæna, jackal, fox, and wild dog. The dhanesa (Buceros indica) or rhinoceros-bird is common; but in general the ornithology of the district has been neglected. Enormous snakes infest every jungle and ravine. Motte, a traveller who visited the country in the latter part of the last century, mentions having seen near Sumbhulpore an immense snake, worshipped as a deity, and alleged to be coeval with the world. It was lodged in a cavern at the foot of a rock, and came out once a week to take his food; consisting of a kid and some fowls, offered to him by his votaries, and picketed on a small plain before his den. After the monster had gone back to its den, the traveller examined its traces in the muddy soil, and concluded its diameter to be about two feet. Kittoe, who visited this locality in 1838, or sixty years later than Motte, states that he was informed that this monstrous snake was still living, and able to enjoy the offerings of his votaries. The boa lurks in every jungle, and attains enormous size; venomous snakes are also very numerous, as are scorpions and centipedes. Fish swarm in the numerous streams and tanks, and form a considerable portion of the food of the population.

The general slope of the surface is eastward, except in the extreme southern part, where a few feeders flow southward to the Godavery. At the northern extremity also, some small rivers flow northwards, and discharge themselves into the Son, a large feeder of the Ganges. The rest of the rivers flow eastward, and discharge themselves into the Bay of Bengal. Of these the principal are the Mahanuddee and the Brahminy. There are a great number of rapid and large torrents, which, during the rainy season, fall either into the greater streams or into the Bay of Bengal.

The population is estimated at 4,534,813. There are four principal divisions of the population:—1. The Urias, Orias, or Odras, being Brahminists, and inhabiting principally the plains and valleys, more especially in the western tracts, towards the British district of Cuttack; 2. the Coles, in the northern part, a race also called Hos, semibarbarous, yet not sunk in the lowest stage of savage brutality; 3. the Khonds, in the middle part; and 4. the Saurias or Sauras, in the south. These three last races are considered the aborigines of the tracts which they now inhabit, and of others much more extensive, of which they have been dispossessed by the encroachments of the more recent population, generally denominated Hindoo. The Coles are rather favourably delineated by a recent writer, who commends their love of truth, honesty, obliging willingness, and happy, ingenuous disposition, the more striking as contrasted with the trickery and falsehood of the wily Hindoo. He represents them as hospitable to strangers, and ready to relieve the indigent; altogether a lighthearted, kind people, but very irascible, and so prone to feel deeply injuries, whether real or imaginary, that they frequently vent their resentment or grief in suicide, to which they are frightfully addicted. In occasional collision with British troops, they have not shown themselves remarkable for courage. These rude people have been won over by proselytizing Brahminists to a certain observance of their rites and festivals, and are besides polytheists, worshipping several imaginary deities, whom they strive to propitiate by sacrifices; they, however, say, that as they have never seen those deities, they cannot assign them shapes. The Khonds, who inhabit the central part of Orissa, are represented as having made some progress in civilization. Agriculture is practised by them with a degree of skill and energy which is rarely surpassed in India, and which has produced a degree of rural affluence rarely paralleled. The same writer, however, represents the population to be so scanty as to suggest grave doubts of his accuracy, either as to the numbers of the people, or to their alleged proficiency in agriculture. As to physical constitution, the Khonds are of the average stature of the Hindoos, muscular, robust, symmetrical, and active. The skin varies in hue in different individuals, from deep copper-colour to yellowish olive. The face is rather handsome, with high expanded forehead, prominent cheek-bones, nose aquiline in some instances, though not in all, but generally broad at the top; lips full, but not thick; mouth rather large. The whole physiognomy is generally indicative of intelligence and determination, blended with good humour. They fight with bows and arrows, slings and battle-axes, and are considered to be brave, neither giving nor taking quarter. Their good qualities are stated to be love of independence, bravery, hospitality, and industry; but they are dreadfully vindictive, and addicted to drunkenness. They are polytheists, believing in the existence of various imaginary divinities, and worshipping the earth, the moon, the god of war, and many other objects, beside the Hindoo goddess Kali. The god of the earth is, however, the most revered, and, under the influence of a detestable superstition, his votaries seek to propitiate him by the sacrifice of human victims, generally children, bought for the purpose from those who steal them from neighbouring people. It appears to be a rule, that no Khond should be sacrificed, and no victim is considered to be acceptable unless bought with a price. This horrible rite is intended to induce the god of earth to favour them with plentiful crops. At the time appointed by their priests, a feast is held, and after it has continued for two days and two nights, a scene of drunken and obscene revelling, the victim is brought out on the third day, and bound to a stake. Its limbs are then broken, and the priest having struck it with an axe, the crowd set upon it, and crying aloud, "We bought you with a price, no sin rests on us," hew the living body into pieces, each carrying away a bloody morsel, which they throw on the earth in some part of their grounds. The number of human beings yearly murdered in this manner was formerly very great. Macpherson states that he found seven victims held in readiness for immediate sacrifice in a valley two miles long, and less than three-quarters of a mile wide. The British government has made strenuous efforts to check the practice, but the Khonds adhere to the sanguinary rite with dreadful pertinacity, and with unflinching ferocity defend their fastnesses, where, for the greater part, malaria would inevitably destroy an invading force. There is reason, however, to hope that ere long the country will be purged from these fearful crimes. By an act of the government of India, passed in September, 1845, the Governor-General is empowered to withdraw the districts where they prevail from the jurisdiction of the ordinary authorities, and to place them under a special officer, called "the agent for the suppression of Meriah sacrifices," who is of course selected with particular regard to vigilance, energy, firmness, and discretion. The Saurias are slaves to the same superstitions as are the Khonds, but are considered much more savage and barbarous. They are represented "as in general a harmless, peaceable race, but so entirely destitute of all moral sense, that they will as readily and unscrupulously deprive a human being of life as any wild beast of the woods, at the orders of a chief, or for the most trifling remuneration." The language of the Urias is a dialect of Sanscrit, closely resembling the Bengalee; and the basis of the alphabet is the Nagari. The Gond language is spoken in some parts towards the western frontier. The Khonds use two distinct dialects, each containing many words of Tamul and Teloogoo. Of the dialects of the Coles we have no information.

Sumbulpoor, the only considerable town in the country, Boad, and Sohnpoor, are described under their respective names in the alphabetical arrangement. The principal routes are, 1. From north-east to south-west, from Calcutta, through Midnapore, to Sumbulpoor; 2. from east to west, from Cuttack, through Sumbulpoor, to Nagpore and Kamptee.

The decline of the ancient royal house of Orissa dates from the death, in 1524, of Rajah Pertab Rudra Deo, an event which the Hindoo monarchy was not destined long to survive. Its downfall may be regarded as consummated in 1592, when a lieutenant-governor arrived from the Mahomedan kingdom of Bengal to assume charge of the administration of Cuttack. With the exception of this province, and a portion of Midnapore, Orissa was acquired by the East-India Company in 1765, by virtue of the firman of Shah Alum, emperor of Delhi, granting the dewanny of Bengal, Behar, and Orissa.

OSIMLEE.—One of the Cossya hill states: it is surrounded entirely by the other hill states, and extends from lat. 25° 20′—25° 59′, long. 91° 26′—91° 41′. It is forty-three miles in length from north to south, and sixteen in breadth, and has an area of 350 square miles.

OSMANPOOR, in the British district of Agra, lieut.-gov. of the N.W. Provinces, a village on the route from the city of Agra to Bareilly, by Khasgunj, and 14 miles N.E. of the former. Lat. 27° 19′, long. 78° 11′.

OSSOOR.—See Oossoor.

OTTAPUDARUM.—A town in the British district of Tinnevelly, presidency of Madras, 28 miles N.E. by E. of Tinnevelly. Lat. 8° 56′, long. 78° 5′.

OUDANULLA.—See Oondwa Nullah.

OUDE, a province so called from the ancient city of the same name, is bounded on the north and north-east by the territory of Nepaul; on the east by the British district of Goruckpore; on the south-east by the British districts Azimgurh and Jounpoor; on the south by the British district Allahabad; on the south-west by the Doab, including the British districts Futtehpoor, Cawnpoor, and Furrukhabad; and on the north-west by Shahjehanpoor. It lies between lat. 25° 34′—29° 6′, long. 79° 45′—83° 11′; is 270 miles in length from south-east to north-west, and 160 in breadth. The area is 23,738 square miles. The north and north-eastern part, lying along the base of the Sub-Himalaya, or continuation of the Sewalik range, has not been well explored by Europeans; it forms part of the Terrai or wooded marsh stretching through that part of Hindostan, and, suffering from a deadly malaria, is scarcely habitable. Tieffenthaler, who penetrated into this tract, states it to be generally a forest, impassable on account of the close growth of trees, underwood, and reeds, and giving shelter to the elephant, rhinoceros, bear, wild kine, wild hog, and deer. The general surface of the Oude country is a plain, declining from north-west to south-east, according to Butter at the rate of seven inches per mile; and hence in that direction is the course of the principal rivers, the Ganges, Chowka, Ramgunga, Raptee, Surjoo or Ghogra, Goomtee, and Saee. The elevation of Birimdeo guardhouse, at the north-western angle, is estimated by Webb at 798 feet above the sea; that of the left bank of the Ganges, at the south-eastern point, may be concluded to be 346½.

The climate of Oude is dry during the greater part of the year, and subject to wide extremes, the temperature sometimes rising to 112°, and at others sinking to 28°. The cool season extends through November, December, January, and February, and is pleasant and salubrious, though occasionally rather chilly, sometimes to such an extent that thin ice appears on shallow water; but in sheltered spots the sun has considerable power throughout the season. March, April, May, and June, are the hot months; noon daily bringing a westerly wind, loaded with fine light greyish sand, which obscures the horizon, gives a sombre hue to the entire atmosphere, and is so sultry and drying as to cause woodwork to crack. The temperature, however, generally diminishes towards sunset, and rarely continues oppressive throughout the night. Occasionally the wind blows from the east all day, and is loaded with oppressive vapour from the swamps of Bengal, or Assam. The power of the hot winds is observed to be steadily on the increase. Sometimes hurricanes, accompanied by thunder, lightning, and rain, set in, and do extensive damage. The annual fall of rain varies greatly in amount, as the rains sometimes commence in the middle of June and terminate in October, while at other times they last only two months. The consequence is, that in some years eighty inches fall, in others not more than thirty.

Besides the huge quadrupeds which haunt the marshy forests of the Terrai, the following wild animals are found in the country:—the tiger, wolf, hyæna, jackal, fox, hare, deer, nylgau or blue antelope, wild hog, porcupine, otter, mongoose, squirrel, rat, musk rat, wild cat, bat, and flying fox. Tigers are so numerous, that, during the visit of Von Orlich to Lucknow, a hunting-party killed forty of them, some of great size, the skin of one having measured nine feet from the head to the tail. Wolves are very abundant, and destroy many persons, especially children, whom they carry off even from the bazars of the towns. These ferocious animals are often spared when in the power of the natives, from a mischievous superstition that their death causes the destruction of the slayer's house. Wolves are not the only devourers of children: hyænas carry off many.

The principal alimentary articles of the spring crop are wheat, barley, gram, called also chana (Cicer arietinum), masur (Ervum lens), mustard, and some other oil-plants. Kusum (Carthamus tinctorius), grown for dye-stuff, is also an article of this crop. Of the crop reaped in autumn, the principal article is rice, sown in those parts liable to inundation. In the Ayeen Akbery the rice of Oude is stated to be "incomparable for whiteness, delicacy, odour, and digestiveness." The other principal articles of this crop are millet of various sorts, maize, makra (Cynosurus coracanus), joar (Holcus sorghum), bajra (Holcus stativus), urdh (Phaseolus maximus), kodu (Paspalum frumentaceum), moth (Phaseolus aconitifolius), urhur (Cajanus flavus), and til (Sesamum orientale). The cultivation of the sugarcane is very circumscribed, and the produce, from mismanagement, execrable; though soil and climate appear rather well adapted for its growth. Potatoes have been introduced, and their cultivation is on the increase, but rather slowly. The growth of opium receives some attention, and might be immensely extended; but the drug, from the slovenly and injudicious manner in which it is prepared, and its bad character from adulteration, scarcely commands a remunerating sale. Hemp is cultivated for the sake of its products in the shape of bang, ganja, charas, and similar powerful inebriants. Generally each village has a patch of ground under tobacco. Most of the esculent vegetables of temperate climates succeed in the cool season. Cotton is raised in many places throughout the country, and is of good quality, though inferior to that of Bundlecund. The quantity, however, is not sufficient for the demand, and much is imported from Bundlecund and the Doab.

Though Oude appears to have ceased to be an independent realm at a very remote period, the population have a highly warlike character; the territory, in proportion to its extent, supplying a surprising number of soldiers to the army of the East-India Company, and to those of Gwalior, Hyderabad, and Alwur. Most of the troops of the last-mentioned power are said to be natives of Oude. Though the kingdom has been for several centuries under Mussulman sway, much the greater portion of its inhabitants are Hindoos. If a judgment may be formed on the relative amount of the different classes stated by Butter in the enumeration of the population of the towns, the Mussulman proportion forms a very insignificant part. The first class of Hindoos, in number and influence, are the Brahmins, who are divided into subcastes, too numerous and intricate to be here enumerated. The next in numbers and importance are the Chhatris, or military caste, in which the Rajpoots rank first, and are divided into a great number of sub-castes. The Brahmins have numerous and preposterously strict regulations respecting intermarriages; the Chhatris, on the contrary, admit intermarriages between all tribes of their own caste. The proposal of marriage is made by the girl's father, who, in proportion to his means, incurs a large expenditure, less in the way of dower than in presents to the youth and his relations, and in feasting the families and acquaintances on both sides. Among most Brahmin tribes, however humble the station of the parties, no marriage can take place without an expenditure of 700 rupees; of which 100 are laid out in trinkets for the bride; fifty for culinary utensils; fifty for clothes; 100 as a present to the youth from the head of the girl's family; 100 similarly presented by the same person to the youth's father; a sum, sometimes amounting to 150 rupees, distributed in presents of four rupees each to the youth's relatives; the remainder being expended in feasting, which continues five days. The matrimonial ceremony is performed when the parties chiefly concerned are about thirteen years of age, sometimes later; but never until they are past the age of nine. Cohabitation commences at fourteen; and there is then a repetition of the same merry-making, but at half the expense. Important characters in society are the Bhats, hereditary bards or minstrels, who perambulate from house to house, sing the praises of the inmates, and are rewarded with presents of money, horses, arms, and clothing. The Mussulmans, probably, are for the most part Shias, or those who reject from the Khalifate the first three successors of Mahommed, revering exclusively his grandson Ali.

The entire population of Oude is understood to be 2,970,000; affording an average of 125½ to the square mile. The dwelling-houses of the people are generally built either of unburned brick, or of layers of mud, each about three feet in breadth and one foot high. The roofs are made of square beams, placed a foot apart, and covered above with planks laid crosswise; over which are mats, and a covering of wet clay, well rammed down, and a foot and a half in thickness. The walls are carried up to six or seven feet above the upper surface of the roof, to afford a concealed place of recreation for the females of the family; and during the rains this small elevated court is covered with a slight roof of bamboos and grass. These thick mud-covered roofs are very durable. Around the houses there are usually verandas, covered with pentroofs of tiles. Inside, the beams and covering are exposed to view, without any ceiling; the floors are of earth, well beaten down and smoothed; and are partially covered with mats, or, on great occasions, with cotton carpets. In the front of the house is a chabutra, or raised platform of earth, open to the air at the sides, and having a roof of tiles or grass supported on pillars. Here the neighbours meet and chat in the evenings.

The language in use in Oude is Hindustanee or Urdu, with a greater admixture of Persian and Arabic, and less of Hindee, than in places more eastward.

The principal routes are — 1. That from Cawnpore, north-east, to Lucknow, being the only regularly-made road in the kingdom. From Lucknow, a route proceeds north-west to Seetapore cantonment, and there diverges, one branch continuing its former direction to Shahjehanpoor cantonment, the other proceeding north by Khairigarh, and thence up the valley of the Ghogra into Kumaon. 2. A much-frequented route proceeds from Mynpooree, being joined by that from Futtehgurh across the Ganges, at Nanamow Ghat, in lat. 26° 52′, and thence in a direction from west to east to Lucknow; 3. from Lucknow, a route lies in a north-easterly direction to Sekrora cantonment, and thence to Buraech, and on to Tulsipore, in the vicinity of the Terai or marshy forest at the southern base of the first range of mountains; 4. from Lucknow also a road proceeds eastward to Fyzabad and the city of Oude, and crossing there the frontier by ferry over the Ghogra, continues to hold an easterly course through the British district of Goruckpore to the cantonment and town of that name; 5. a route proceeds in a north-westerly direction from Fyzabad to Sekrora cantonment; 6. a route proceeds in a north-easterly direction from Sultanpore cantonment, crossing the Ghogra by ferry near Kusba-Tanda, and thence proceeding to Goruckpore cantonment; 7. from Allahabad a route lies northward to Pertabgurh, and thence in the same direction to Sultanpore; 8. a route leads from Allahabad north-west to Lucknow; 9. a route runs in a direction first north-easterly then south-easterly, from Cawnpore to Sultanpore; 10. another proceeds in a south-easterly direction from Cawnpore to Pertabghur; 11. a much-frequented route proceeds from Lucknow south-easterly to Sultanpore cantonment, and thence into the British district of Juanpore, and to the cantonment of that name; 12. another leads from east to west, from Jounpoor cantonment to Pertabgurh. With the exception of the military road from Cawnpore to Lucknow, the ways are wretched tracks, in many places scarcely passable for wheels. A project for the construction of a railway through this province has been laid before the public.

The kingdom contains the following divisions and subdivisions:—I. Chakla Sultanpore, containing pergunnahs: 1. Sultanpore, 2. Jagdispore, 3. Chanda, 4. Isauli, 5. Tappa Asl, 6. Bilahri. II. Chakla Aldemau, containing pergunnahs: 1. Aldemau, 2. Akbarpore, 3. Dostpore, 4. Berhar, 5. Tanda. III. Chakla Pertabgurh, containing pergunnahs: 1. Pertabgurh, 2. Amethi, 3. Dalipore Palti. IV. Chakla Pachhamrat, containing pergunnahs: 1. Manglasi, 2. Rat Haveli or Faizabad, 3. Rampore. V. Chakla Bainswara, containing pergunnahs: 1. Ranjitpurua, 2. Harha, 3. Ateha, 4. Mauhranwa, 5. Kumranwa, 6. Daundiakhera, 7. Hasnganj, 8. Majranw, 9. Haidargarh, 10. Rae Bareli, 11. Dalamau, 12. Sarendi, 13. Bardar. VI. Chakla Salon, containing pergunnahs: 1. Salon Khas, 2. Parsadipore, 3. Jayis, 4. Ateha. VII. Chakla Ahladganj, containing pergunnahs: 1. Ahladganj, 2. Bihar, 3. Manikpur, 4. Rampore. VIII. Chakla Gonda Bahraieh, containing pergunnahs: 1. Bahraieh, 2. Gonda Khas, 3. Muhammadabad, 4. Bari, 5. Atraula. IX. Chakla Sarkar Khairabad, containing pergunnahs: 1. Khairabad, 2. Nimkharmisrik, 3. Khirilahrpur, 4. Bangar, 5. Muhemdi, 6. Bilgiram, 7. Fattehpur Biswa, 8. Sandila, 9. Malihabad, 10. Kakori, 11. Bijnaur, 12. Kasmandi, 13. Malanwa. X. Chakla Sandi, containing pergunnahs: 1. Sandi, 2. Pali, 3. Saromnagar, 4. Shahabad. XI. Chakla Rasulabad, containing pergunnahs: 1. Safipur, 2. Rasulabad or Miyanganj, 3. Asiman, 4. Unnaw or Onaw, 5. Muhan. XII. Chakla Lucknow, containing pergunnahs: 1. Rudauli Daryabad, 2. Goshaenganj, 3. Dewe-Jahangirabad, 4. Kursi, 5. Sidhaur.

Lucknow, the capital, as well as the towns of Fyzabad, Ayodha or Oude, Roy Bareilly, Shahabad, Khyreegurh, Manikpore, Buhraech, Sahganj, Ranjit, Purwa, Tanda, and some others of less importance, will be found noticed in their respective places under the alphabetical arrangement.

In natural advantages, Oude may be justly considered to surpass most parts of India. The defence of its south-western frontier is facilitated for a long distance by the line of the Ganges, fordable only in very few places, and in those but for a short period of the year. The soil of the country is amongst the most fertile; its climate, though rather warm, is favourable both to animal and vegetable life; its means of irrigation and of water-carriage are very extensive, and conveniently distributed for the welfare of every quarter. Accordingly, it need excite no surprise that the most judicious and laborious inquiries should have pointed out this tract, the primitive Kosala, as one of the earliest seats of Indian government and civilization. Buchanan conjectures the settlement to have taken place 1,366 years before the Christian era; the reign of Rama, so celebrated in Hindoo romance and mythology, 775 years; and the restoration of the kingdom destroyed by hostile aggression, he attributes to Vikramaditya, king of Oojein, anno 57 B.C. It is probable that the independence of Oude was lost, and no further separate notice appears to be made of it in Indian record. At the close of the twelfth century, after the conquest of Canouj by the Mussulmans, Oude was subdued by Mohammed Bakhtiar Khilzi, an officer sent for the purpose by Kutbuddin Aibuk, viceroy of India, for Mohammed Ghori, sultan of Ghuznee. It thenceforward became an integral part of the realm of the sovereigns of Delhi, and on the conquest of the empire by Baber, was easily subdued. On the dismemberment of the Mogul empire, it was about 1760 seized by Shuja-ud-dowlah, the vizier of the empire and also viceroy of Oude. The following is the table of the sovereigns of Oude:—

A.D.	
——	Saadat Ali Khan.
——	Sefdarjang.
1756.	Shuja-ud-dowlah.
1775.	Asoph-ud-dowlah.
1797.	Vizier Ali, spurious, and displaced in favour of Saadat.
1798.	Saadat Ali, brother of Shuja-ud-dowlah.
1814.	Ghazee-ood-Deen Hyder, son of Saadat Ali.
1827.	Nusseer-ood-Deen Hyder, son of Ghazee-ood-Deen.
1837.	Mahomed Ali Shah, brother of Ghazee-ood-Deen.
1842.	Umjud Alee Shah, son of Mahomed Ali.
1847.	Wajid Alee Shah, son of Umjud Alee Shah.

Shuja-ud-dowlah having in 1763 made common cause with Meer Cossim in resisting the arms of the East-India Company, was, May 13th, 1764, repulsed in an attack on the British army at Patna, and on the 22nd of the same month was totally routed at the battle of Buxar. In the following year, 1765, the British army, entering Oude, occupied Lucknow, and again defeated Shuja-ud-dowlah, who in the same year was glad to make peace, putting Shah Alum, the titular emperor of Hindostan, or Great Mogul, in possession of the districts of Allahabad and Corah. In 1768 reports reached the government that the Nawaub Vizier was making extensive military preparations with a view to obtain possession of the provinces of Corah and Allahabad. A reduction of his military force was considered necessary; and by the treaty of November, 1768, the Nawaub Vizier stipulated not to "entertain a number of forces exceeding 35,000 men." Of this number, there were to be—cavalry 10,000; ten battalions of sepoys, not to exceed 10,000; the Nujib regiment, consisting of 5,000 men with matchlocks; 500 artillery; and the remaining 9,500 were to be irregulars, neither to be clothed, armed, nor disciplined after the manner of the English sepoys or Nujib regiment. The ill-advised Shah Alum having transferred his claim to the provinces of Corah and Allahabad to the Mahrattas, was considered to have forfeited those possessions; and by the treaty of 1773, they were transferred to the Nawaub Vizier, in consideration of the sum of 50,00,000 rupees. In 1774 the British troops, auxiliary to the Nawaub Vizier, having overthrown the Rohilla power, the greater part of Rohilcund became subject to that potentate. Shuja-ud-dowlah died in January, 1775, and was succeeded by his eldest son Asoph-ud-dowlah, who, at his accession, ceded by treaty to the East-India Company Benares, Jounpore, and some contiguous districts; and in return, the English engaged "to defend the soubah of Oude at all times." It was also stipulated that a brigade of British troops, consisting of two battalions of Europeans, one company of artillery, and six battalions of sepoys, should be stationed in Oude whenever required by the vizier; for the support of which he engaged to pay monthly 2,60,000 rupees, an annual amount of about 312,000*l.* By agreement, 1781, one regiment of sepoys was added, for the purpose of protecting the office, treasury, and person of the resident at Lucknow, at an expense of 30,000*l.* annually; and it was provided that Faizullah Khan, the Rohilla chief, having forfeited his independence, the Nawaub Vizier should occupy his dominions, and pay him a moneyed income. In 1787 the Nawaub Vizier agreed to fix his subsidy at 500,000*l.* per annum; in which sum was included the additional expense on account of troops, the allowance to Saadut Ali Khan, the Rohilla stipend, and the expenses of the British residency. In 1797, a great increase of the Company's military establishment having taken place, the vizier consented to defray the expenses of two regiments of cavalry, one European and one native, the additional charge not exceeding 55,000*l.* per annum; making the total subsidy 555,000*l.* per annum. In 1797 the vizier Asoph-ud-dowlah died, and the British government recognised the succession of his supposed son, Vizier Ali. The spuriousness of Vizier Ali's birth being, however, soon after established, Saadut Ali, the brother of the late vizier, was placed on the musnud.

By existing treaties, the Company were bound to defend the territories of Oude against all enemies. In order to enable them to fulfil this engagement, and at the same time to provide for the protection of their own dominions, they had largely increased their military establishment, by the addition of new-levied regiments both of infantry and cavalry; and, in consequence thereof, Saadut Ali agreed, in 1798, to increase the subsidy to 760,000*l.* per annum. The Nawaub Vizier also ceded the fortress of Allahabad, and gave 80,000*l.* to the Company for its repairs, and 30,000*l.* for those of Futtehgurh. The British troops in Oude were not to consist of less than 10,000 men, including Europeans and natives, cavalry, infantry, and artillery; and should it become necessary to augment the Company's troops beyond the number of 13,000 men, the vizier agreed to pay the actual difference occasioned by the excess above that number. The threatened invasion of Zeman Shah attracted the attention of the Marquis Wellesley (then earl of Mornington) to the state of Oude. It was desirable to substitute efficient troops for the unskilful and undisciplined force maintained by the vizier, and to place the defence of the Oude frontier against foreign invasion upon a more substantial basis. To accomplish these objects, the pecuniary subsidy was commuted for a territorial cession; and by treaty, 10th November, 1801, the Nawaub Vizier ceded the Southern Doab, and the districts of Allahabad, Azimgurh, Western Goruckpore, and some others, estimated to yield in the aggregate an annual revenue of 1,35,23,474 rupees, or 1,352,347*l.* In July, 1814, Saadut Ali Khan died, and was succeeded by his son Ghazree-ood-Deen Hyder. In the month of October of that year, the government of Oude lent the East-India Company 1,000,000*l.* A second loan of like amount was obtained in the following year, in aid of the war against Nepaul; and on its successful termination in the beginning of 1816, the British authorities transferred to Oude the whole of the Terrai, or marshy forest stretching along the north-eastern frontier of that country. This tract had been ceded by the government of Nepaul, and the subsequent transfer to Oude was in liquidation of one million sterling of the loan made by the Nabob Vizier. In 1819, the Nabob Vizier formally renounced his dependence on the Great Mogul, or titular emperor of Hindostan, and assumed the title of king of Oude, the assumption being recognised by the British authorities. The financial exigencies occasioned by the Burmese and Bhurtpore wars led the British government, in 1825, to apply to the ruler of Oude for aid, and another crore of rupees (a million sterling) was obtained as a loan in perpetuity, at an unvarying interest of five per cent. Nusseer-ood-Deen Hyder ascended the musnud in 1827, on the death of his father, Ghazee-ood-Deen. In 1829, the British government agreed to receive as a special loan the sum of 624,000*l.*, the interest of which was to form a provision for certain members of his majesty's family; and in 1833, at the request of the king, the British government consented to receive 30,000*l.*, and to guarantee the appropriation of the interest thereof to the relief of the poor of Lucknow. In 1837 Nusseer-ood-Deen Hyder died, without legitimate issue, and was succeeded by his uncle Mahomed Ali Shah, though not without a sharp but very short struggle; the Begum having raised a disturbance, which, by the promptitude and firmness of the British resident, Colonel Lowe, was suppressed in the outset. In 1842, on the death of Mahomed Ali Shah, his son ascended the musnud, and the opportunity was embraced for pressing the reforms requisite to place the kingdom in a state of tranquillity and security. A limited period was assigned for effecting the required work; and in default of performance, it was distinctly intimated that the country would be placed under British management. The intimation proved totally ineffective. Umjud Alee Shah died in 1847, when his son Wajid Alee Shah ascended the throne. In weakness and profligacy, the new sovereign equalled, perhaps even surpassed, his predecessors. The progress, without intermission, was from bad to worse. At length the home government felt bound to extend its sanction to the adoption of such measures as might be requisite to give effect to the provisions of the treaty of 1801. A new treaty was accordingly prepared for the acceptance of the king, whereby the administration of the territories of Oude would have been transferred to the British government, ample provision being made for the dignity, affluence, and honour of the king and of his family. This treaty the king refused to sign; whereupon the treaty of 1801 was declared to be null and void, and a proclamation was issued, declaring that the government of the territories of Oude was thenceforth vested exclusively and for ever in the East-India Company.

OUDE.—A town in the kingdom of the same name. It is situate on the right bank of the river Ghogra, which Buchanan considers here to be "fully larger than the Ganges at Chunar," and which is navigable downwards to its mouth, upwards to Mundiya Ghaut, in the district of Bareilly. It extends about a mile in a south-east direction, from the adjoining recent city of Fyzabad; the breadth of the town is something less from north-east to south-west, or from the river landwards. The greater part of the site is on gently-swelling eminences; but to the north-west, or towards Fyzabad, is low. Most of the houses are of mud, and thatched, though a few are tiled. Here, in a large building a mile from the river, is an extensive establishment, called Hanumangurh, or Fort of Hanuman, in honour of the fabled monkey-god the auxiliary of Rama. It has an annual revenue of 50,000 rupees, settled on it by Shuja-ud-daulah, formerly Nawaub Vizier. It is managed by a malik or abbot, the spiritual superior; and the revenues are dispensed to about 500 bairagis or religious ascetics, and other Hindoo mendicants of various descriptions; no Mussulman being allowed within the walls. Other establishments of similar character are Sugrimkilla, Ram-Parshad-ka-Kana, and Bidiya-Kund; maintaining respectively 100, 250, and 200 bairagis. Close to the town on the east, and on the right bank of the Ghogra, are extensive ruins, said to be those of the fort of Rama, king of Oude, hero of the Ramayana, and otherwise highly celebrated in the mythological and romantic legends of India. Buchanan observes, "that the heaps of bricks, although much seems to have been carried away by the river, extend a great way; that is, more than a mile in length, and more than half a mile in width; and that, although vast quantities of materials have been removed to build the Mahomedan Ayodha or Fyzabad, yet the ruins in many parts retain a very considerable elevation; nor is there any reason to doubt that the structure to which they belonged has been very great, when we consider that it has been ruined for above 2,000 years." The ruins still bear the name of Ramgurh, or "Fort of Rama;" the most remarkable spot in which is that from which, according to the legend, Rama took his flight to heaven, carrying with him the people of his city; in consequence of which it remained desolate until repeopled by Vikramaditya, king of Oojein, half a century before the Christian era, and by him embellished with 360 temples. Not the smallest traces of these temples, however, now remain; and according to native tradition, they were demolished by Aurungzebe, who built a mosque on part of the site. The falsehood of the tradition is, however, proved by an inscription on the wall of the mosque, attributing the work to the conqueror Baber, from whom Aurungzebe was fifth in descent. The mosque is embellished with fourteen columns of only five or six feet in height, but of very elaborate and tasteful workmanship, said to have been taken from the ruins of the Hindoo fanes, to which they had been given by the monkey-general Hanuman, who had brought them from Lanka or Ceylon. Altogether, however, the remains of antiquity in the vicinity of this renowned capital must give a very low idea of the state of arts and civilization of the Hindoos at a remote period. A quadrangular coffer of stone, whitewashed, five ells long, four broad, and protruding five or six inches above ground, is pointed out as the cradle in which Rama was born, as the seventh avatar of Vishnu; and is accordingly abundantly honoured by the pilgrimages and devotions of the Hindoos. Ayodha or Oude is considered by the best authorities to be the most ancient city in Hindostan; and Prinsep mentions that some of its coins in the cabinet of the Asiatic Society of Bengal are of such extreme antiquity that the characters in which their legends are graven are totally unknown. According to Elphinstone, "from thence the princes of all other Indian countries are sprung." Buchanan conjectures that it was founded by Brahmins, whom he considers as an immigrant race, more advanced in civilization than the indigenous Indians. "These personages came from western Asia, introducing with them the Sanskrit language, generally admitted to be radically the same with the Persian dialect; while the languages spoken among all the rude tribes that inhabit the fastnesses of India, and which are, probably, remains of its ancient tongue, have no sort of analogy to the languages of the West." This author supposes the city to have been founded by Vaiwaswata, one of this race, about 1,366 years before the Christian era. He considers that its renowned ruler Rama perished A.C. 775, involved in the destruction of his city by the hostile confederacy of his sons; that being rebuilt, it suffered a similar fate under the reign of Vridhabala, A.C. 512; and having lain for centuries desolate, was rebuilt A.C. 57, by Vikramaditya, the celebrated king of Oojein. Tod, however, and Wilford, fond of large numbers, place the foundation of Ayodha in an era more than 2,000 years B.C. The former writer states, without comment, a tradition that Lucknow, distant eighty miles from the present city of Oude, was formerly one of its suburbs. The great decline of Oude is of comparatively recent date, as it is described in the Ayeen Akbery as one of the largest cities of Hindostan; and it is farther stated, "In ancient times this city is said to have measured 148 cose [perhaps 200 miles] in length, and thirty-six cose in breadth. It is esteemed one of the most sacred places of antiquity." With the havili or municipal district attached, the city is assessed in the Ayeen Akbery at 50,209 rupees, a sum so moderate as to throw discredit on the previous statement of its being one of the greatest cities of India. The present population, according to Butter, is 8,000, including 500 Mussulmans. Distant E. from Lucknow 75 miles, N. from Allahabad 95. Lat. 26° 47′, long. 82° 11′.

OUDEYPORE.—See OODEYPOOR.

OUDUNPOOR, in the territory of Oude, a town on the route by Shahabad from Lucknow to Shahjehanpoor, 14 miles S. of the latter. It is situate on the north-western frontier, towards the British district of Shahjehanpoor; and, according to Heber, "is what would be called a moderate-sized market-town in England." It is situate close to an extensive grove of mango-trees, in the midst of which is a shrine of Siva. The surrounding country is rather well cultivated, especially under cotton. Lat. 27° 42′, long. 80°.

OUNLA.—See AONLAGANJ.

OUR.—A town in the Rajpoot state of Jodhpoor, situate on the right bank of the Sookree river, and 64 miles S.S.W. from Jodhpoor. Lat. 25° 26′, long. 72° 50′.

OURAD.—A town in Hyderabad, or the territory of the Nizam, 94 miles N.W. by W. from Hyderabad, and 109 miles E.N.E. from Sholapoor. Lat. 18° 14′, long. 77° 29′.

OURAHEE.—A town in the territory of Oude, situate on the left bank of the Ghogra river, and 60 miles N.N.E. from Lucknow. Lat. 27° 39′, long. 81° 26′.

OURLAGONDA.—A town in Hyderabad, or the territory of the Nizam, 92 miles E. from Hyderabad, and 76 miles N.W. by N. from Guntoor. Lat. 17° 14′, long. 79° 54′.

OURUNGA.—A river rising in lat. 20° 37′, long. 73° 33′, on the western slope of the Syadree range of mountains, and flowing in a westerly direction for thirty-three miles through the native states of the Daung rajahs and Bansda, and fifteen miles through the British district of Surat, falls into the Arabian Sea, in lat. 20° 36′, long. 72° 56′.

OWEN ISLAND.—One of the islands forming the Mergui Archipelago. It is about four miles in diameter, and its centre is in lat. 11° 15′, long. 98° 21′.

OWLUHA KHASS.—A town in the British district of Sarun, lieut.-gov. of Bengal, 22 miles S.E. of Bettiah. Lat. 26° 33′, long. 84° 49′.

OWNCHUH, in the British district of Mynpoorie, lieut.-gov. of the N.W. Provinces, a town 13 miles N.W. of the town of Mynpoorie. Lat. 27° 19′, long. 78° 53′.

OWSA.—A town in one of the recently sequestrated districts of Hyderabad, or dominions of the Nizam, situate 59 miles N.E. from Sholapoor, and 145 miles N.W. from Hyderabad. Lat. 18° 16′, long. 76° 34′.

P.

PAAREE.—A town in the Rajpoot state of Seerooee, five miles S.E. from Seerooee, and 93 miles S. by W. from Jodhpoor. Lat. 25°, long. 72° 51′.

PA BANG.—A town of Burmah, 130 miles E. by N. from Prome, and 109 miles N.N.E. from Pegu. Lat. 19° 8′, long. 96° 59′.

PABUL.—A town in the British district of Poonah, presidency of Bombay, 26 miles N.N.E. of Poonah. Lat. 18° 50′, long. 74° 3′.

PABUR, a river of Bussahir, has its source close to the Burenda Pass, in a lake called Charamai, about a mile in circuit, whence the stream rushes forth over a perpendicular rock, forming a fine cascade. Above are enormous banks of snow, 80 or 100 feet in thickness, which have cracked, and partly fallen outward into the lake. This spot is in lat. 31° 22′, long. 78° 12′, and has an elevation of 13,839 feet above the sea. The river holds a southerly course of between ten and eleven miles to the confluence of the Sipoon, at an elevation of 8,354 feet above the sea, and in lat. 31° 18′, long. 78° 4′, and in that distance has the enormous average fall of 545 feet per mile. Continuing its course in the same direction for about eleven miles to Chergaon, it there receives, at an elevation of 5,985 feet, and in lat. 31° 13′, long. 77° 56′, the Andrytee, flowing from the north-west. For this last portion of its course it has an average fall of 254 feet per mile. The valley through which it thenceforth holds its way is the finest part of Bussahir, being beautiful, fertile, and highly cultivated, and, from the amount of its elevation above the sea, enjoying a genial climate. The river flows still in a south-westerly direction between ten and eleven miles to Rooroo, lat. 31° 12′, long. 77° 48′, and at an elevation of 5,100 feet: there it takes a southerly direction of about twenty-five miles to its confluence with the river Tons, in lat. 30° 56′, long. 77° 54′, after a total course of about fifty-eight miles. Fraser describes it as a large, clear, and rapid stream at Raingarh, about fifteen miles above its mouth.

PABYA RIVER.—An offset of the Yennan, one of the branches of the Irawaddy, the chief river of Burmah. The Pabya runs in a south-easterly direction, intersecting a portion of the valley lying between the Irawaddy and the Sitang, and falls into the latter after a course of about fifty miles, in lat. 18° 58′, long. 96° 30′.

PACHAMRAT, a district of the territory of Oude, is bounded on the north-east by the river Ghogra, dividing it from the British district Goruckpore; on the south-east by the district of Aldemau; on the south-west by Sultanpoor; and on the west by Bainswara. Its centre is in about lat. 26° 50′, long. 81° 53′.

PACHETE, a British district in the lieut.-gov. of Bengal, is denominated from the town of the same name. It is under the jurisdiction of the Governor-General's agent for the south-west frontier. It is bounded on the north by the British districts Ramgurh and Beerbhoom; on the east by the British district Bancoora; on the south by the British districts Pooralia, Barabhoom, and Singhbhoom; on the west by the British district Chota Nagpore: it lies between lat. 22° 56′—23° 54′, long. 85° 46′—87° 10′; is 105 miles in length from north-east to south-west, and ninety-five in breadth. The area is 4,792 square miles. The information respecting its aspect and physical geography is very scanty. Jacquemont, who traversed the northern part from east to west, describes the country as marked by hills from 400 to 600 feet high, overrun with forest or jungle, in some places intersected with plains or open vales of limited extent. About lat. 23° 35′, long. 85° 50′, near the town of Pachete, and skirted by the river Damooda, he observed a mountain having, as he conjectured, an elevation of 2,500 or 3,000 feet. About fifteen miles more south-west is Rogonathpore, and near the centre of the district the same traveller examined several hills, the rocky formation of which was of granite; the elevation about 900 feet. In the vales and plains rice is the staple crop, interspersed with oil-seeds and some other products of less importance; but much of the country now covered with jungle or waste, bears marks of having been formerly cultivated. Its present condition probably arises from the injudicious rural economy of the natives, under which the soil is cropped until exhausted, and then neglected until the rest of many years gives hope of its again becoming productive. The geological formation is described by Jacquemont as generally primitive, consisting of either granite, gneiss, or syenite. In the northern part of the district, however, according to the received theories, it appears to be of a later era, coal being found near Jeria, in lat. 23° 44′, long. 86° 25′, and iron-ore existing in great abundance at a short distance. The south-western part appears to be a maze of mountains and ravines, connected with the adjacent highlands of Chota Nagpore. The district is traversed by some considerable rivers, the course of which being to the south-east, indicates the general slope of the country to be in that direction. Among the principal of these may be enumerated the Damooda, the Soobunreka, and the Cossye. Many torrents discharge themselves into those greater streams, the country being fully under the influence of the periodical rains; and the drainage is good, in consequence of the rapid declivity of the surface. This tract is considered to have been considerably improved since its incorporation with the dominions of the East-India Company, villages formerly deserted having become re-inhabited, many more having been built, and culture much extended. An investigation some time since took place into an alleged case of suttee, reported to have been authorized by the rajah of Pachete, a petty potentate of hill jungle in this district; but the inquiry resulted in the acquittal of the rajah. There does not appear to be any collection of residences which can be properly termed a town. Pachete, regarded as the capital, Rogonathpore, Jalda, and Chas, are noticed under their respective names in the alphabetical arrangement. The great trunk road from south-east to north-west from Calcutta to the North-West Provinces, through Burdwan, passes through the northern part of the district; the other route between the capital and the North-West Provinces, through Bancoora and Hazareebagh, lies through the middle of the district. The only remaining route of any importance is from east to west, from Bancoora, through Jalda, to Chota Nagpore. Pachete is within the limits of the dewanny granted to the British in 1765 by Shah Alum, emperor of Delhi.

PACHETE, reputed the principal place of the British district of the same name, a ruined town six miles south-west of the right bank of the river Damooda. It is situate midway between the new and old line of road from Calcutta to the N.W. Provinces, and about ten miles from each line. Distance from Calcutta, N.W., 150 miles. Lat. 23° 36′, long. 86° 50′.

PACHIPONTA.—A town in the British district of Vizagapatam, presidency of Madras, 56 miles N. by W. of Vizagapatam. Lat. 13° 30′, long. 83° 10′.

PACKBURRAH, in the British district of Moradabad, lieut.-gov. of the N.W. Provinces, a village on the route from the town of Moradabad to Mozuffurnuggur, and six miles W. of the former place. It is situate in an open country, partially cultivated. Distant N.W. from Calcutta 890 miles. Lat. 28° 50′, long. 78° 44′.

PACTNA, in the British district of Kumaon, lieut.-gov. of the N.W. Provinces, a town on the route from Almora to Pillibheet, 19 miles S.S.E. of the former. Lat. 29° 21′, long. 79° 49′.

PADRA.—A town in Guzerat, or dominions of the Guicowar, situate eight miles W.S.W. from Baroda, and 36 miles N. by E. from Broach. Lat. 22° 12′, long. 73° 7′.

PADROO.—A town in the Rajpoot state of Jodhpoor, situate 11 miles E. from the left bank of the Loonee river, and 82 miles S.W. from Jodhpoor. Lat. 25° 32′, long. 72° 11′.

PADSHAHGANJ, in the district of Sultanpoor, territory of Oude, a village two miles S.W. of the cantonment of Sultanpoor. Here a foujdar or commandant of police resides in a square building of masonry. Butter estimates the population at 300, of whom 100 are Mussulmans. Lat. 26° 18′, long. 81° 59′.

PADSHAH MAHAL, in the British district of Suharunpoor, a ruined palace, built by Shahjehan, is situate at the spot where the river Jumna enters the plain, and opposite the point where the Delhi Canal passes off to the south-west. Distant N.W. from Calcutta 1,030 miles; elevation above the sea 1,276 feet. Lat. 30° 20′, long. 77° 39′.

PADSHAHPOOR, in the British district of Goorgaon, lieut.-gov. of the N.W. Provinces, a small town on the route from Hansi to Muttra, by Goorgaon; distant 25 miles S.W. of Delhi. It is situate among rocky hills, and has still a bazar, though much fallen away from its state during the time of the Patan sovereigns of Delhi. Lat. 28° 22′, long. 77° 6′.

PADSHAHPOOR.—A town in the British district of Belgaum, presidency of Bombay, 21 miles N.E. by N. of Belgaum. Lat. 16° 5′, long. 74° 46′.

PADSHAHPUR.—See SHAHPUR.

PADUR.—A town in the British district of Coimbatoor, presidency of Madras, 73 miles N.E. of Coimbatoor. Lat. 11° 41′, long. 77° 49′.

PAGHAM MEW.—A town of Burmah, situate on the left bank of the Irawady river, and 99 miles S.W. by W. from Ava. According to Hamilton, this city, in remote times, was the residence of a long dynasty of kings, and is still famous for its numerous temples, to count which is among the proverbial impossibilities of the Burmese. Lat. 21° 7′, long. 94° 42′.

PAGODA POINT.—The southernmost extremity of the district of Bassein, province of Pegue, named from a pagoda standing upon it. Lat. 15° 56′, long. 94° 19′.

PAGODA POINT.—A prominent headland on the coast of Tenasserim, at the entrance of the small river on which is situate the town of Amherst. Lat. 16° 5′, long. 97° 38′.

PAHAREE.—See PUHAREE.

PAHARGURH, in the territory of Gwalior, or possessions of Scindia's family, a town 28 miles S.W. of the fort of Gwalior, situate on a sandstone hill; whence its name. Lat. 26° 11′, long. 77° 44′.

PAHARPOOR, in the Daman division of the Punjab, a town situate on the right bank of the Indus, 136 miles S. by W. of the town of Peshawar. Lat. 32° 8′, long. 71° 3′.

PAHARPOOR, in the British district of Furruckabad, lieut.-gov. of the N.W. Provinces, a village on the route from the cantonment of Bareilly to that of Futtehgurh, and seven miles N.E. of the latter. The road in this part of the route is good; the country level, fertile, and very well cultivated. Lat. 27° 28′, long. 79° 41′.

PAHLADPOOR, in the British district of Budaon, lieut.-gov. of the N.W. Provinces, a village on the route from Agra to Bareilly, and 68 miles N.E. of the former. It is situate in a depressed place, formerly the bed of the Ganges, but now deserted by the stream and dry. Lat. 27° 52′, long. 78° 46′.

PAHLUNPORE.—A petty state under the political superintendence of the presidency of Bombay, comprising the divisions of Dhandar, Deesa, and Dhuneyra. It lies between lat. 23° 57′—24° 41′, and long. 71° 51′—72° 45′. It is bounded on the north by the Rajpoot principality of Serohee; on the south by the Puttun district; on the east by the Guicowar district of Keyralla, and by that of Daunta; and on the west by the petty chieftainship of Thurraid. It contains about 300 villages. The rivers that water the Pahlunpore territory, are the Bunass, Surruswuttee, and Numrodakee, with other small streams. They all take their rise from the mountains in the north-east, and fall into or disappear near the Runn. The principal of them is the Bunass, on the banks of which is the Deesa cantonment. There is but one good road through the district; but it is of some importance, being the route by which most of the commerce from Hindostan, including the great mart of Pallee, finds its way to the different bunders on the Cutch, Kattywar, and Guzerat coasts; and again from those bunders to the north.

The number of inhabitants is about 130,000: of these, one-seventh are Mussulmans, the rest Hindoos. There appears to be a remarkable disparity between the numbers of male and female children; and from the paucity of the latter, it has been suspected that female infanticide is practised. Major Brown, who inquired into the subject in 1845, acquitted the people of this horrible charge, and assigned the following three causes for the disparity above adverted to: first, early marriages, under which female children were regarded as adults; secondly, the marriage of females with foreigners; thirdly, an excess of male births. This statement does not, however, appear altogether conclusive. If the practice of early marriage caused a diminution of the apparent number of female children, by throwing them into the class of adults, it must, at the same time, have unduly increased the latter class, and created therein an apparent disparity of females over males. The second cause, if it existed to any great extent, would to that extent account for the disparity; but its existence is asserted only, not proved; and if proved, would further require to be shown that it operates so as to withdraw a large number of females from the country, not after attained maturity, but during the period of childhood. So, also, with the third alleged cause; it is not proved; and it may naturally be asked, Why should this great preponderance of male over female births occur in Pahlunpore rather than anywhere else? There is certainly no reason *à priori* to conclude that the district is in this respect an exception to the rest of the world. Another British officer, however, Captain Leckie, concurs in the belief that infanticide is not practised; and the result of the latest inquiries (1848) is only the conclusion, that no light can be thrown upon the subject.

The Pahlunpore state pays no tribute of any kind to the British government, but merely the expenses of its agent, amounting to 500 rupees per mensem; but it pays 50,000 rupees yearly tribute to the Guicowar state. The revenues of the state, including land-tax and customs, average nearly 300,000 rupees per annum: the disbursements, including civil, military, and agency charges, allowances to the late Shumshere Khan's family, and relatives of the present chief, amount to about 200,000 rupees per annum. If to this be added the tribute of 50,000 rupees to the Guicowar, there remains a sum of about 50,000 rupees for the expenses of the chief and his household. In 1844, a criminal court for Pahlunpore and the neighbouring petty states was established, on the principle of the political agent's court in Kattywar and the Myhee and Rewa Cauntas.

The only engagement with neighbouring states is with the petty Rajpoot district Daunta, joining the eastern boundary of Pahlunpore. In 1819, that state having suffered severely from the depredations and incursions of the Coolies of the neighbouring districts north and east of it, its chief sought the assistance of Pahlunpore. It was granted, on an agreement between the two states, that for the support to be afforded, Pahlunpore should receive seven annas in the rupee of all the revenue collected in Daunta. The contract was approved and confirmed by the British government, and still remains in force. The native force consists of 115 horsemen and 416 foot-soldiers; they are stationed on the frontiers and in different villages, as police, to protect the district from incursions of the Coolies and Bheels of the neighbouring states, and to afford protection generally. From the tranquillity which has usually prevailed, it is to be inferred that they are efficient. The only troops subsidized by this state, are 150 Guicowar horse and 100 Guicowar foot. They consist generally of foreigners, and are commanded by jemadars, who receive thirty rupees per mensem for each horseman, and ten rupees per mensem for each foot-soldier; all expenses of arms and horses being included in these respective amounts. They were first raised in 1817. They are bound to serve wherever they are ordered, but the foot-soldiers generally remain stationed in the town of Pahlunpore, together with a portion of the horsemen, for the protection of its different gates. The rest of the horsemen are posted in detachments on the frontier most open to the incursions of plunderers. Formerly, an officer, receiving 600 rupees per mensem, was appointed to command them; but they are now under the charge of the political superintendent.

Our first connection with this state was in 1813. For some years previously, the chief power had been in the hands of a faction of Scindee jemadars, who in 1812 murdered the then reigning dewan, Peeroze Khan, when out hunting, under suspicion that he was about to restrict their authority. Having committed this act, they offered the dewanship to his only son, Futteh Khan, the present chief, and then only thirteen years of age. By the advice of his mother he refused the offer, and, through his late father's karbarees, petitioned the Guicowar and British governments for assistance and protection from his father's murderers. In the mean time the jemadars, having seized and placed him in strict confinement, invited his uncle, Shumshere Khan, then chief of the district of Deesa and Dhuneyra, to Pahlunpore, to undertake the management of affairs. This chief, who had been superseded in the dewanship by Peeroze Khan eighteen years before, although he had since constantly waged a petty war with Pahlunpore, and sometimes with success, had no hand in the death of the dewan. He, however, accepted the offer made to him; but in the mean time, interference in favour of the rightful heir being considered necessary by both the British and Guicowar governments, Captain Carnac, then Resident at Baroda, proceeded to Pahlunpore, with a force furnished by those governments, under the command of General Holmes. On the road, information was received that, on the approach of the force to Pahlunpore, the jemadars intended to carry off Futteh Khan, in order that his presence might give a sanction in the country to any lawless measures which it might suit their interest to pursue. In this design, however, Shumshere Khan did not participate, and he was afterwards fully exonerated from all suspicion. In hopes of preventing the meditated act, the force marched with all practicable speed to Pahlunpore, which was threatened with assault, unless Futteh Khan was immediately given up. Thereupon he was sent to the British camp, and Shumshere Khan shortly afterwards surrendered himself. Captain Carnac intimated to the rebellious jemadars, that if they submitted, their personal safety would be insured, and anything they had to urge in defence of their late proceedings would be attended to; but, fearing the displeasure of the British government, they fled, with a few followers, to the hills; whence, from the great strength of the country, and the smallness of the force disposable for the purpose, it was not considered advisable to follow them. The town was given up without resistance.

In consequence of Futteh Khan's youth and inexperience, it became necessary to ascertain if any members of his family were fit to superintend the affairs of the state during his minority. After a strict examination, none were found to whom the trust could safely be committed, all being deficient in intellect, education, or habits of business; or from other causes incapable. Under these circumstances, the choice of a guardian became a point of some difficulty, as the interposition of the Guicowar's authority was a measure which it was most desirable to avert. After some consideration, it was deemed the most advisable course, with a view to the suppression of anarchy and intestine feuds, and to the gratification as far as practicable of the feelings of all parties, to unite the interests of the young chief Futteh Khan with those of his uncle Shumshere Khan. The management of affairs during the minority of the young chief was accordingly offered to Shumshere Khan. He at first refused, and urged his priority of pretension to the guddee over the family of the late chief. Into this claim it consequently became requisite to inquire, and the result of the researches instituted by Captain Carnac was a conviction that it was untenable. Shumshere Khan after a time acquiesced in the decision; and finally, after much discussion, it was agreed that he should be associated with Futteh Khan; and, having no male issue of his own, that he should adopt the latter as his son, and make him heir to all his possessions, including the districts of Deesa and Dhuneyra; with the exception, in the event of a son being subsequently born to him, of a small provision for such offspring. The differences which prevailed having been apparently settled by this compromise, agreements were signed by the respective parties before Captain Carnac; and on the 22nd December, 1813, the ceremony of investing Futteh Khan with the rule of Pahlunpore, and his adoption by Shumshere Khan, took place, in presence of that officer and several other gentlemen, as well as the principal people of the place, to whom the arrangement appeared to be entirely agreeable. To make the tie more binding, it was afterwards agreed that Shumshere Khan should give his daughter in marriage to Futteh Khan. From this date until 1816, although dissensions were not unknown, it does not appear they were considered of sufficient moment to require the interference of the British government; but at the latter end of that year Futteh Khan complained to the resident at Baroda of his uncle's conduct in alienating the revenues of the state, and other malpractices. Lieutenant Robertson was thereupon deputed to inquire into the alleged grievances; and, both parties being summoned to Sidpore (eighteen miles from Pahlunpore), a lengthened investigation of the different charges took place; and it was fully proved that Shumshere Khan had on several occasions departed from his agreement as guaranteed by the British government. It appeared that since he had held the management of affairs the debts of the state had greatly increased; that the Guicowar's tribute of 50,000 rupees had remained unpaid since 1813; and that within three years last preceding, Shumshere Khan had, without the signature or permission of Futteh Khan, given away nearly 100 villages, to wuzedars, distant relations of his own, and to others, in order to attach them to his person; thereby alienating from the state nearly 50,000 rupees, or upwards of one-fifth of its yearly revenue. It was also reported to the agent, on good authority, that Shumshere Khan had threatened to take the life of the young chief, should he be deprived of the management of affairs. Lieutenant Robertson having received his instructions from the resident, then addressed a letter to Shumshere Khan, in the name of the British government, informing him that, in consequence of his having failed in administering the affairs of the state according to his agreement, as shown in the foregoing inquiry, it was deemed necessary, with a view to the security of the rights and interests of Futteh Khan, to divest him (Shumshere) of all authority in the state; and that any resistance to this measure would deprive him of all claim to consideration, and put an end to any chance of retaining his authority over Deesa. On receiving this letter, Shumshere Khan, as a last resource, opened a private communication with Futteh Khan, trying to persuade him that the British government, in interfering between them, merely wished to benefit itself at their joint expense, and that Futteh Khan would thereby become a mere pensioner on that government. He suggested a restoration of the relations of friendship for their mutual benefit, and promised at once to carry into effect the marriage of his daughter with Futteh Khan, a measure long before agreed on, but which had been delayed by the dissensions of the contracting parties. These solicitations and promises seem to have answered their intended purpose, for Futteh Khan secretly left the agent's camp in company with Shumshere Khan, and proceeded with him and his followers to Pahlunpore. On this Lieutenant Robertson returned to Baroda, and a field-force under Colonel Elrington was detached to Pahlunpore to effect a settlement of its affairs; Captain Miles being appointed to accompany it and conduct the negotiations.

On the 10th October, 1817, the force having arrived in the neighbourhood of Pahlunpore, it was attacked by the troops under Shumshere Khan, who, after a slight skirmish, retreated within the walls. The town was then assaulted and carried; Shumshere Khan and all his followers retreating towards the hills northward, taking Futteh Khan with them. Detachments from the British force having followed the fugitives, Shumshere Khan took shelter in the foreign territory of Neemuj, and Futteh Khan shortly afterwards came to Captain Miles and submitted himself to the British government, who, taking into consideration his youth and inexperience, and being aware that he had acted by the advice and influence of others, refrained from visiting his error in the manner which he might reasonably have expected. Of his inability to conduct his own affairs, he, himself, however, soon became painfully conscious; for, a few days after his return, he addressed a letter, through Captain Miles, to the Guicowar, requesting that prince to use his interest with the British government to allow him an English gentleman to superintend his concerns; and also asking that the Guicowar government would depute a respectable native as vakeel, to assist him in his revenue accounts, and make arrangements for the payment of the yearly tribute to that state. Both requests were consented to, and after some negotiation, the villages unlawfully alienated from the state by Shumshere Khan having been resumed, articles of agreement in supersession of all former treaties were sealed and delivered by Futteh Khan to Captain Miles, and afterwards approved and confirmed by the British and Guicowar governments, with the exception of one article; the number of troops to be subsidized was reduced from 250 to 150, the state being considered unequal to bearing the expense of the greater force. Under this agreement, Futteh Khan engaged to hold no communication with Shumshere Khan or his adherents. Captain Miles was shortly after confirmed in his appointment as political agent, to superintend the affairs of Pahlunpore. In 1819, Shumshere Khan having given himself up, nine villages, whose net revenue amounted to 25,000 rupees per annum, were appropriated for his support; to revert to the state at his death. This event happened in 1834, when provision was made for his widows and servants, to the amount of 6,000 rupees yearly, in addition to the revenue of four villages, amounting to 6,000 rupees; making a total of 12,000 rupees. His daughter had been married to Futteh Khan shortly after his submission. By the arrangement which has thus existed with this state since 1817, the British government exercise a control over its finances; the different charges and expenditure being fixed, and no extra disbursement of any heavy amount being admitted without its special sanction. All interference, however, with its internal affairs is limited to recommending measures when called for, leaving the execution of them to the authorities.

The interference of the British government has been of the greatest advantage to this petty state. From the day a British agent was placed in charge of its affairs, it has continued to prosper; instead of being a scene of anarchy and confusion, ruled as it often had been by a band of foreign mercenaries, and overwhelmed with debts, it is now in a flourishing condition, in the enjoyment of perfect immunity both from foreign oppression and internal dissension, and unembarrassed by oppressive debts.

The present dewan of Pahlunpore derives his descent from a tribe of Affghans, who occupied Behar in the reign of Hoomayon, emperor of Delhi. In 1682, Futteh Khan, one of his ancestors, was dewan of Shalore, now a large district of Marwar, adjoining Pahlunpore. During his dewanship he received from the emperor of Delhi, in gift, the districts of Pahlunpore, Deesa, and Sachore: he died in 1688, leaving one only son, by name Peer Khan, whose claim to the dewanship was set aside by his uncle Kumaul Khan, on the plea of incapacity. During Kumaul Khan's reign, and in the year 1698, Shalore and Sachore were resigned by him to Marwar. Pahlunpore and Leesa only were retained in the family, who then came to reside at the former place, which from this date became the seat of government. In 1704 Peeroze Khan succeeded his father Kumaul Khan; Peer Khan's claim having been again passed over, he applied to Delhi, and obtained a sunnud of investiture from the royal court for his patrimonial rights. By some mistake, or through the intrigues of Peeroze Khan's vakeel, who also went to Delhi to support his master's rights (it is said, indeed, that the writer of the sunnud was bribed by him), the name of Peeroze Khan was inserted in the sunnud instead of that of Peer Khan, unknown to the court. This lost the latter his rights; for Peeroze Khan, standing on the letter of the sunnud, refused to resign, and Peer Khan was eventually persuaded not to urge his claim, and remained satisfied with the grant of ten or twelve villages for his maintenance. He died in 1735, leaving an only son, named Futteh Khan, who, at his decease, left three sons—Tej Khan, Peeroze Khan (the present chief's father, who was murdered in 1812), and Mahomed Khan. Peeroze Khan, the second son, some years afterwards laid claim to the chieftainship, but for a long period without effect, the other branch of the family being too powerful.

Peeroze Khan, the son of Kumaul Khan, died in 1721, and was succeeded by his son Kurreen Khan, who, in 1733, was followed by his son Par Khan. In 1743, Par Khan, having died childless, was succeeded by his uncle Bhadur Khan, son of Peeroze Khan and brother to Kurreen Khan. In 1781, Sulleen Khan, his son, reigned; and in 1784 was succeeded by his son Sheer Khan. In 1791, Sheer Khan, having died childless, was succeeded by his nephew Moobariz Khan, through the intrigues of his mother, a sister of Sheer Khan's; but he only reigned for about two years, being superseded by Shumshere Khan, of whom mention has already been made. Shumshere Khan was a grandson of one of the brothers of Bhadur Khan, and was assisted in the usurpation by such of the chiefs of the district as were hostile to Moobariz Khan. During the disturbances which followed, Peeroze Khan, the son of Futteh Khan, whose claims had so long been overlooked, now urged them afresh, and Shumshere Khan having fled to Deesa, his rival was installed in 1794, with, it is alleged, the unanimous voice of the people. The murder of Peeroze Khan in 1812 was followed by the events which have been already recounted.

PAHLUNPORE, in Guzerat, a town, the capital of the petty state of the same name, and situate on the route from Neemuch to Deesa. It is surrounded by a wall, and has some trade and manufactures, there being within it many artificers of various kinds, and shopkeepers. The population is estimated at 30,000. The chief, styled Nawaub, who is also chief of Deesa, is descended from a tribe of Afghans settled in Behar in the time of Humaion, emperor of Delhi, and established in their present possessions in the reign of Aurungzebe. Distance from Neemuch, W., 160 miles; from Deesa, S.E., 18 miles; from Ahmedabad, N., 80 miles. Lat. 24° 12′, long. 72° 23′.

PAHTUN.—A town in the British province of Sattara, presidency of Bombay, 23 miles S.S.W. of Sattara. Lat. 17° 22′, long. 73° 56′.

PAI.—A town in the British territory of Tenasserim, 103 miles N.N.W. of Tenasserim. Lat. 13° 30′, long. 98° 36′.

PAIGA, in the Daman division of the Punjab, a town situated 33 miles W. from the right bank of the Indus, 69 miles W. by S. of the town of Mooltan. Lat. 29° 57′, long. 70° 24′.

PAIK TSOUNG.—A town in the British territory of Tenasserim, 51 miles N.E. by N. of Moulmein. Lat. 17° 5′, long. 98° 8′.

PAIMSAH KA PURWA, in the territory of Oude, a village on the route from Lucknow to Sultanpoor, 70 miles S.E. of the former. It is well provided with good water. Lat. 26° 25′, long. 81° 40′.

PAINTEE, in the British district of Moradabad, lieut.-gov. of the N.W. Provinces, a village on the route from the town of Moradabad to Mozuffurnuggur, and nine miles W. of the former place. There is open ground for encamping, and water can be obtained from a good well. The surrounding country is open and partially cultivated, and the road in this part of the route is good. Distant N.W. from Calcutta 897 miles. Lat. 28° 51′, long. 78° 41′.

PAIRA.—A river rising in lat. 19° 32′, long. 73° 39′, on the eastern slope of the Western Ghats, and, flowing through the Ahmednugur collectorate in an easterly direction for 105 miles, falls into the Godavery on the right side, near the town of Toka, in lat. 19° 36′, long. 75° 3′.

PAKANGGOLO.—A town in Nepal, situate 13 miles E. from the left bank of the Arun river, and 111 miles E. by N. from Khatmandoo. Lat. 27° 59′, long. 87° 3′.

PAK CHAN.—A town in the British territory of Tenasserim, 90 miles S. by W. of Tenasserim. Lat. 10° 51′, long. 98° 42′.

PAKOLIYA, in the British district of Goruckpore, lieut.-gov. of the N.W. Provinces, a petty town on a small feeder of the river Koyane. Buchanan states the number of its houses at 100; and consequently, if six persons be assigned to each, its population may be taken at 600. Distant 46 miles W. of Goruckpore cantonment. Lat. 26° 48′, long. 82° 34′.

PAKUL.—See Bakul.

PAL, in the Rajpoot state of Jodhpoor, a village on the route from Balotra to the town of Jodhpoor, and five miles S. of the latter. It it situate at the north-eastern base of a low rocky ridge. The road in this part of the route is tolerably good, and passes through a wooded tract. Lat. 26° 15′, long. 73° 4′.

PALAKEE, in the Sinde Sagur Dooab division of the Punjab, a town situated 36 miles W. from the right bank of the Jhelum, 106 miles N.W. by N. of the town of Lahore. Lat. 33° 3′, long. 73° 17′.

PALAMOW, a British district of Bengal, is bounded on the north by those of Behar and Ramgurh, or Hazerabagh; on the east by the British district last named; on the south by that of Chota Nagpore; on the south-west by the British district Sirgoojah; and on the west by that of Mirzapoor. It lies between lat. 23° 12′—24° 22′, long. 83° 18′—84° 31′; is eighty-eight miles in length from south-east to north-west, and seventy in breadth: the area is 3,468 square miles. It is an ill-explored country, and little comparatively is known of it, but that it is rough and irregular. Torrents are numerous in the rainy season, and most of them discharge themselves into the river Koel, which, taking a direction north-west, passes into the British district of Behar, and falls into the Son on the right side, in lat. 24° 33′, long. 83° 56′; having a total length of course of about 130 miles. The torrents quickly disappear as the dry season advances. To this, however, the Koel is an exception, retaining a continuous stream at all times. The mountains are everywhere covered with forest or jungle, containing a great variety of trees and shrubs; amongst them the sal (Shorea robusta). The Mimosa catechu, denominated by the natives khair, is very abundant; and the gum-catechu, or terra Japonica, which is largely prepared from it, is regarded the best in India. The jungly valleys and mountains harbour the gaour, a bovine quadruped, greatly exceeding ordinary kine in dimensions, a full-grown bull being above eighteen hands high. It is shy, but when brought to bay very fierce; and though many have been taken young, all attempts to domesticate them have failed. There are also in those valleys the wild buffalo, elk, nylgau (Antilope picta), various kinds of deer and antelopes. Tigers are very numerous, and lions have sometimes been destroyed. The mineral resources of the district are of considerable value and utility. At Singra, on the right bank of the river Koel, in lat. 24° 5′, long. 84° 3′, are extensive fields of good coal, and iron-ore in inexhaustible quantities. Some other parts contain valuable coal-fields and iron-mines; and the Koel might, it is said, be made available for navigation to a considerable extent. The only places which can with any propriety be denominated towns, are Oontaree, near the northern frontier, and Palamow, in the middle of the district. There are, however, numerous villages and hamlets dispersed over it; yet altogether it is very thinly peopled. Nothing has been stated as to its separate population, but the amount, united with that of Chota Nagpore, is computed to be 482,900. Its area is 3,468 square miles.

This district is part of the territory under the administration of the political agent for the south-western frontier and commissioner for Chota Nagpore, to whose jurisdiction it was transferred in 1833, subsequently to an insurrection commencing in the preceding year, and which overspread the whole of this district, and the adjoining one of Chota Nagpore. A strong military force was employed to reduce the disturbed districts to obedience, and subsequently order has prevailed.

PALAMOW.—The principal place of the British district of the same name, situate five miles east from the river Koel, amidst mountains containing coal and iron. Distance S.W. from Patna (Behar) 145 miles. Lat. 23° 50′, long. 84° 1′.

PALAR.—A river rising in the territory of Mysore, in lat. 13° 20′, long. 78° 2′. It holds its course circuitously, but generally in a south-east direction, for fifty-five miles, through Mysore, when it crosses the frontier into the British district of North Arcot, thirty miles below which point it passes through the gorges of the Eastern Ghats, in lat. 12° 41′, long. 78° 36′, about eighty-five miles from its source. Quitting the hills, it holds a course generally east for eighty-seven miles, and passes by Vellore and Arcot, to lat. 12° 48′, long. 79° 42′, where it crosses into the British district of Chingleput, through which it continues its direction south-eastward for forty-eight miles, to its fall into the Bay of Bengal, on the Coromandel coast, in lat. 12° 28′, long. 80° 13′; its total length of course being about 220 miles. The entrance of the river Palar or Paliar, about three and a half or four miles to the southward of Sadras, is contracted by a bar or narrow ridge of sand, inside of which the river becomes of considerable width. During the rainy seasons, it has a considerable volume of water, but at other times is completely dry, though water may always be obtained by digging in its bed. A project has been sanctioned for constructing an annicut or dam across this river in the vicinity of Arcot, for the purpose of insuring a supply of water to the tanks on both sides of the river, in the districts of Chingleput and North Arcot.

PALAVERUM.—A town in the British district of Chingleput, presidency of Madras, 11 miles S.W. of Madras. Lat. 12° 58′, long. 80° 15′.

PALCONDA.—See PALLAKONDA.

PALDEO, in Bundlecund, a small state, or rather jaghire, granted by the East-India Company to the commandant of the fortress of Kalleenjur at the time of its surrender, and still held by his descendant. It is stated to have an area of twenty-eight square miles, fourteen villages, a population of 3,500, and an annual revenue of 10,000 rupees, or 1,000*l.* The jaghirdar maintains a force of 100 infantry. Paldeo, the principal place, is situate in a mountainous tract 67 miles S.W. of Allahabad. Lat. 25° 6′, long. 80° 51′.

PALEE, in the British district of Goorgaon, lieut.-gov. of the N.W. Provinces, a town, the principal place of the pergunnah of the same name, situate at the eastern base of a rocky range, formed of sandstone largely intermixed with quartz. Distance S. from Delhi 18 miles. Lat. 28° 23′, long. 77° 18′.

PALEEKHEYRUH, or PALIKHAIRA.—A town in the British district of Muttra, lieut.-gov. of the N.W. Provinces. Lat. 27° 34′, long. 77° 31′.

PALGHAT, in the British district of Malabar, presidency of Madras, a fort with straggling town on the north or right side of the Palaur, the principal feeder of the river of Ponany. It is situate in a beautiful country, in that great depression in the Western Ghats, about lat. 10° 35′—10° 55′, "which leaves a communication between the two coasts of the Peninsula, covered only with forests of the stately teak." The fort of the Palghat is a fine structure, built by Hyder Ali, when that adventurer, in the year 1757, found footing in Malabar, by marching to the aid of the Nair chief of this place. In the year 1783 it was taken by a British force commanded by Colonel Fullarton, and restored to Tippoo Sultan in the following year, by the treaty of Mangalore. In the year 1790 it was, after a brief but vigorous siege, surrendered to a British force commanded by Colonel Stuart. Distance from Calicut, S.E., 68 miles; Mangalore, S.E., 190; Cananore, S.E., 113; Coimbatoor, S.W., 25; Bangalore, S., 162; Madras, S.W., 290. Lat. 10° 45′, long. 76° 43′.

PALHANPOOR.—A town in Guzerat, or dominions of the Guicowar, 20 miles E. from Deesa, and 83 miles N. by W. from Ahmedabad. Lat. 24° 12′, long. 72° 23′.

PALHANPOOR.—See PAHLUNPORE.

PALHRHAGUDI.—A town in Nepal, situate on the left bank of the Arun river, and 147 miles S.E. by E. from Khatmandoo. Lat. 26° 33′, long. 87° 14′.

PALI, in the district of Sandi, territory of Oude, a town on the route from Futtehgurh to Seetapore, 18 miles N.E. of the former, 64 W. of the latter. It is situate on the right bank of the river Garha, here crossed by ferry during the rainy season, at other times by ford. There is a bazar, and supplies are abundant. Tieffenthaler, describing the condition of this town about a century ago, states that it was formerly populous. Distant 90 miles N.W. of Lucknow. Lat. 27° 30′, long. 79° 44′.

PALI, in the district of Bainswarra, territory of Oude, a large decayed town on the right bank of the river Goomtee, 38 miles N.W. of Sultanpoor cantonment, 42 S.E. of Lucknow. Lat. 26° 38′, long. 81° 33′.

PALI, in Gurwhal, a small town in a sequestered glen, down which flows a stream, falling into the Jumna on the right side. It contains about fifty houses, and probably between 400 and 500 inhabitants, the men of whom are stout and hard-featured, the women generally of light complexions and agreeable countenances. The townsmen and other inhabitants of the glen are noted for a hardy and warlike character, having frequently rebelled against the rajah of Gurwhal, as well as against the Goorkhas during their occupation of the country; and at one time cut off an entire company of those invaders. Lat. 30° 53′, long. 78° 22′.

PALICONDA.—A town in the British district of North Arcot, presidency of Madras, 26 miles W. of Arcot. Lat. 12° 54′, long. 79°.

PALKOTE.—A town in the British district of Chota Nagpoor, lieut.-gov. of Bengal, 38 miles S. of Lohadugga. Lat. 22° 54′, long. 84° 40′.

PALLA.—A town in the British district of Candeish, presidency of Bombay, 39 miles W. by S. of Malligaum. Lat. 20° 29′, long. 73° 55′.

PALLAKONDA.—A town in the British district of Vizagapatam, presidency of Madras, 69 miles N.N.E. of Vizagapatam. The talook of which this town is the principal place has been leased by the government to the European firm of Arbuthnot and Co. for a term of years. Lat. 18° 36′, long. 83° 49′.

PALLAMCOTTAH, in the British district of Tinnevelly, under the presidency of Madras, a town and military station situate a mile from the right bank of the Chindinthoora, here crossed by a good bridge, forming a communication with the town of Tinnevelly, on the opposite side of the river. The fort and town are situate on an extensive plain, varied by a few low hills. The site of the fort is a slightly elevated surface of granite rock, of a mouldering nature; but not having a wet ditch, it is free from a common and active source of deleterious exhalations. There are a few tanks to the northward; but as they are shallow, and the water, in consequence of being quickly drawn away for the purposes of irrigation, does not stagnate, no pernicious results ensue. Within the fort are many wells, in which water is obtained at depths varying from eight to twelve feet below the surface, and which never fails at any time of the year, but it is perceptibly saline, except in such as are much worked. The barrack occupied by the European artillery is on the most elevated ground within the fort, and contains many commodious apartments. Near the barrack, and separated from it by a narrow road, are the houses of the European officers, forming an oblong square on the southern face of the fort. They are large convenient buildings; and attached to them are public baths, affording the means of luxury and health. The place of arms for the native troops is in the middle of the town, and has in front an open space large enough to admit of a regiment being drawn up in line. Within a few yards of the place of arms, and separated from it by a road, is the hospital, a spacious building, and originally commodious, but now old and in bad repair, so that it is contemplated by government to replace it by a structure adequate to the exigencies of such an establishment. The native lines are situate outside the fort, on a rock of slight elevation, but sufficient to insure complete drainage. The establishment of the jail and its hospital were, in 1838, removed from the town of Tinnevelly to this place; but the buildings originally provided for their accommodation were very faulty and inadequate; and though improvements have been made from time to time, they are still liable to considerable objections. Within the last few years a church has been erected here. Elevation above the sea 120 feet; distance from the town of Tinnevelly, E., three miles; from Madura, S., 88; from

Ramnad, S.W., 88; Trichinopoly, S.W., 160; Madras, S.W., 348. Lat. 8° 43′, long. 77° 48′.

PALLASSWARRA.—A town in the British district of Candeish, presidency of Bombay, 69 miles N. of Malligaum. Lat. 21° 31′, long. 74° 28′.

PALLAWUR, in the British territory of Saugur and Nerbudda, lieut.-gov. of the N.W. Provinces, a town on the route from Hoosungabad to Baitool, 36 miles N. of the latter. Lat. 22° 21′, long. 77° 55′.

PALLAYGAUM.—A town in Hyderabad, or territory of the Nizam, 93 miles S. by W. from Ellichpoor, and 173 miles E.N.E. from Ahmednuggur. Lat. 19° 54′, long. 77° 14′.

PALLEE, in the Rajpoot state of Jodhpoor, a town on the route from Nusseerabad to Deesa, and 108 miles S.W. of the former. It is the principal mart of Western Rajwara, being situate at the intersection of the great commercial route from Mandavee, in Cutch, to the northern provinces, and from Malwa to Bahawulpoor and Sinde. Pallee is khalsa, or the crown property of the maharaja of Joudpore, in contradistinction to the numerous places belonging to his feudatories. The sum annually obtained from the duties is estimated by Tod at 7,500*l.* It was formerly surrounded by a wall, and in consequence, its possession was frequently contested by conflicting parties during the civil wars of Joudpore, until, at the desire of the inhabitants, the defences were demolished; and their ruins now give the place an air of desolation, at variance with its actual prosperity. It is an ancient place, and was acquired by the Rajpoots under Seoji, A.D. 1156. Tod states the number of houses at 10,000, which would fix the number of inhabitants at about 50,000. Water and supplies for troops may be obtained here in abundance. Distant S.W. from Delhi 351 miles; S.E. from Joudpore 40 miles. Lat. 25° 48′, long. 73° 24′.

PALLEE.—A town in the British district of Tannah, presidency of Bombay, 39 miles S.E. of Bombay. Lat. 18° 31′, long. 73° 18′.

PALLERA.—A native state on the south-west frontier of Bengal, bounded on the north by the native state of Bombra; on the east and south by that of Talcheer; and on the west by Bheracole. It is twenty-three miles in length from east to west, and fourteen in breadth; and contains an area of about 220 square miles: its centre is in lat. 21° 10′, long. 84° 40′.

PALLYAD.—A town in Guzerat, or dominions of the Guicowar, situate 46 miles E. from Rajkote, and 83 miles W.S.W. from Kaira. Lat. 22° 15′, long. 71° 31′.

PALMYRAS POINT.—The name of a low headland on the coast of Orissa. It is clothed with palmyra-trees, and has on each side of it, at a small distance, the mouth of a river. The lighthouse, formerly situate upon Point Palmyras, was abandoned in consequence of the encroachment of the sea, and False Point selected as the site of a new one. Lat. 20° 43′, long. 87° 6′.

PALOOR, in Sirmor, a stream rising on the southern declivity of the Chour peak, and in lat. 30° 51′, long. 77° 33′. After a course of about twenty miles in a south-westerly direction, it falls into the Giree, in lat. 30° 42′, long. 77° 26′.

PALPA.—A town in Nepal, situate on the right bank of the Gunduck river, and 112 miles W. by N. from Khatmandoo. Lat. 27° 54′, long. 83° 30′.

PALPOOR, in the territory of Gwalior, or possessions of Scindia's family, a town 70 miles S.W. of Gwalior fort. Lat. 25° 49′, long. 77° 10′.

PALREE, in the Rajpoot state of Jodhpoor, a considerable village on the route from Nusseerabad to Deesa, and 163 miles S.W. of the former. It contains 200 houses and forty shops, and is supplied with water from forty wells and two tanks. Lat. 25° 9′, long. 73° 5′.

PALRI, in the jaghire of Jhujhur, lieut.-gov. of the N.W. Provinces, a village on the route from Rohtuk to Narnol, and 40 miles S.W. of the former. Lat. 28° 25′, long. 76° 15′.

PALUM, in the British district of Delhi, lieut.-gov. of the N.W. Provinces, a town on the north-eastern bank of the extensive jhil or shallow lake formed by the overflow of the Hansouti Nullah during rains. Distance S.W. from the city of Delhi 10 miles. Lat. 28° 35′, long. 77° 8′.

PAMBAR.—A town within the dominions of Gholab Singh, the ruler of Cashmere, situate on the right bank of the Chenaub river, and 56 miles E.S.E. from Sirinagur. Lat. 33° 38′, long. 75° 50′.

PAMPUR, in Cashmere, a town about five miles S.W. of the city of Sirinagar, is situate on the north bank of the Jhelum or Behut, in a level tract of great fertility, and presents most delightful views of the mountain-ranges to the north. Here is a bridge of several arches over the river. The town is surrounded by luxuriant orchards and gardens: it contains between 300 and 400 houses, a bazar, and two Mahometan shrines. The neighbouring country is generally cultivated for the growth of saffron, and the produce is considered finer than that of any part of Hindostan. Lat. 34°, long. 75° 3′.

PANCHLA, in the Rajpoot state of Jodhpoor, a village on the route *viâ* Nagor, from Jessulmere to Nusseerabad, and 131 miles N.W. of the latter. It is built in a scattered manner, but is in good condition, and is supplied with water from three wells 200 feet deep. Lat. 26° 58′, long. 73° 20′.

PANCHORA.—A town in the British district of Candeish, presidency of Bombay, 54 miles E. by N. of Malligaum. Lat. 20° 38′, long. 75° 20′.

PANCHU, in the British district of Kumaon, lieut.-gov. of the N.W. Provinces, a village in the Bhotia subdivision of Juwahir, on the route to Hiundes or Chinese Tartary, and 15 miles S. of the Juwahir Pass. It is situate on the right bank of the Goree, a little below the confluence of the Goonka. Elevation above the sea 11,284 feet. Lat. 30° 24′, long. 80° 12′.

PANDEHWARA, or PANDLEWARA, in Guzerat, or territory of the Guicowar, a town on the route from Baroda to Neemuch, 106 miles N. of former, 164 S.W. of latter. Lat. 23° 24′, long. 73° 40′.

PANDHARPUR.—See PUNDERPOOR.

PANDOORNA.—A town in the territory of Nagpoor or Berar, 51 miles N.W. by W. from Nagpoor, and 70 miles N.E. by E. from Ellichpoor. Lat. 21° 36′, long. 78° 33′.

PAN DRAS, in Ladakh, a village on the route from Le to Cashmere, by the Bultul Pass, from which it is distant twenty miles N.E. The land in the vicinity is in general employed for pasture, and produces the *prangos pabularia*, so highly esteemed by Moorcroft for winter fodder. Izzet Ullah, who calls this place Panderras, observes that the road is good in this part of the route. Gholaum Hyder styles the village Paeen-dur-rauz. Professor Wilson, the editor of Moorcroft, considers that it should be called Pain-dras, or "Lower Dras;" but this does not seem justifiable, as the place lies higher up the course of the river, and is more elevated than Dras. The elevation above the sea exceeds 9,000 feet. Lat. 34° 23′, long. 75° 47′.

PANDREE, in the British district of Baitool, territory of Saugor and Nerbudda, lieut.-gov. of the N.W. Provinces, a town on the route from Baitool to Ellichpoor, 37 miles S.W. by S. of the former. Lat. 21° 22′, long. 77° 41′.

PANDRENTON, in Cashmere, an antique temple of small dimensions, standing in a reservoir or tank about four miles S.E. of Srinagur, the present capital of the valley. It is a striking specimen of the simple, massive, and chaste style which characterizes the architectural antiquities of Cashmere. The ground-plan is a square of twenty feet, and the roof pyramidal. In each of the four sides is a doorway, ornamented with pilasters right and left, and surmounted by a pediment. The whole is constructed of blocks of regularly-hewn limestone. The interior is filled with water, communicating with that without, which is about four feet deep; and as the building is completely insulated, it can be reached only by wading or swimming. The purpose of its construction is not known, but it is generally considered a Buddhist relic. It exhibits neither inscriptions nor sculptures, except the figure of a large lotus carved on the roof inside. Lat. 34° 2′, long. 74° 47′.

PANDURE.—A town in one of the recently sequestrated districts of Hyderabad, presidency of Bengal, 21 miles W.S.W. of Ellichpoor. Lat. 21° 5′, long. 77° 15′.

PANEEGONG.—A town of Assam, in the British district of Durrung, 55 miles N.E. by E. of Durrung. Lat. 26° 44′, long. 92° 52′.

PANEEPUT, a British district in the territorial division of Delhi, within the lieut.-gov. of the N.W. Provinces, is bounded on the west and north by Sirhind; on the east by the river Jumna, separating it from the British districts of Mozuffurnuggur and Meerut; and on the south by the British district of Delhi. It lies between lat. 28° 50′—29° 48′, long. 76° 40′—77° 16′; is sixty-five miles in length, in a direction nearly south to north, thirty miles in breadth, in a direction at right angles to the former; and contains an area of 1,279 square miles. The country is level, and intersected by the Delhi Canal and its branches, as well as by numerous watercourses, ramifying in time of inundation between the Jumna and those artificial channels. Where not irrigated by the Jumna, or by canals, the country is generally barren and of repulsive appearance, being in many places a waste of undulating sands, exhibiting a very scanty growth of harsh herbage or stunted shrubs. In many places the soil is covered with a saline efflorescence, so abundant as to look like snow; and this incrustation, though containing a large admixture of sulphate of soda with common salt, is collected and used for culinary purposes.

The population in 1853 was returned at 389,085; of which number there were Hindoos, agricultural, 167,757; non-agricultural, 88,054: Mahomedans and others, agricultural, 37,280; non-agricultural, 95,994. It will be seen from this return, that though the Hindoos greatly preponderate in numbers, the proportion of the other classes (chiefly Mussulmans) is larger than is to be found in many parts of India. The number of persons per square mile is something more than 221. The following classification of the towns and villages of this district, with reference to population, is obtained from very recent official returns.

Number containing less than 1,000 inhabitants	366
Ditto more than 1,000 and less than 5,000....	119
Ditto „ 5,000 „ 10,000....	1
Ditto „ 10,000	2
Total................	488

The chief places will be found noticed in the alphabetical arrangement. The land-assessment has been fixed for a term of years, which will expire on the 1st July, 1872. The district came into the possession of the British from Scindia in 1803, under the treaty of Serjee Anjengaum.

PANEEPUT.—The chief town of the British district of the same name. It is situate in a fertile tract, the resources of which are to a considerable extent developed by cultivation, of which irrigation by water, principally drawn from numerous wells, is a very efficient part. The appearance of the place on approaching it is described by Barr as striking and pleasing. "As we approached Paniput, the whole of the surrounding country was converted into one mass of cultivation, here and there broken by small clumps of trees, through which are to be seen the spires and cupolas of numerous temples, with their white and polished surfaces, starting from the dark foliage in which they are imbedded, with an almost dazzling brilliancy." Jacquemont considered Paneeput the largest town, except Delhi, which he had seen in Northern India. It is surrounded by walls and ramparts, apparently of no great antiquity, and built at different periods and in different styles, the outline being very irregular. The houses, generally built of brick, and in some instances two stories high, have usually balconies, and a few have cupolas. A great number, however, are said to be untenanted; but if this be so, the place has, notwithstanding, an amount of population which may entitle it still to rank as a very considerable town. The number of inhabitants in 1853, as ascertained from official report, was 22,612. The chief source of the busy scenes of life, however, appears to be that created by two caravanserais which the town possesses, one on each side. The environs are overspread with the ruins of tombs, many indicating, by their size and style of building, that they were the memorials of persons of rank. Paneeput is situate on the great military route between Western Asia, Affghanistan, and the Punjab, on the one side, and Central and Eastern Hindostan on the other; and the plains around it have repeatedly been the field of battle for powers contending for the empire of India. Here, in 1526, Baber, at the head of 12,000 men, encountered and utterly routed Ibrahim, the Patan king of Delhi, whose army is usually estimated at about 100,000 men, with 1,000 elephants. According to generally received statements, above 40,000 of the army of Delhi were slain, and among them Ibrahim, whose empire was seized by Baber; thus establishing the renowned Timurian dynasty. In the same locality, in 1761, a battle was fought between the Affghans, commanded by their king Ahmed Dooraunee, and the Mahrattas, under Sedasheo Rao Bhao. The troops of Ahmed Shah are estimated by Elphinstone at 40,000 Affghans and Persians, 13,000 Indian horse, and 38,000 Indian infantry, with thirty pieces of cannon; that of the Mahrattas at 15,000 infantry, of whom 9,000 were regularly disciplined, 55,000 cavalry in regular pay, and 15,000 predatory horse, with 200 cannon, numerous wall-pieces, and a great supply of rockets. After some hours of hard fighting, the Mahrattas yielded to the superior valour of the Affghans and the military talents of Ahmed, and were totally routed; their commander, and nearly the whole of their best troops, being slain either in the battle or in flight.

Paneeput is mentioned in the Ayeen Akbery as situate in the soubah of Delhi, and as having a brick fort. It lies on the route from Delhi to Kurnaul, and the road in this part of the route may be described as good. Distant N. from Delhi 78 miles, N.W. from Calcutta 965 miles. Lat. 29° 23′, long. 77° 2′.

PANEITH.—A town in Guzerat, or the dominions of the Guicowar, situate on the left bank of the Nerbudda river, and 28 miles S. from Baroda. Lat. 21° 51′, long. 73° 18′.

PANGKONG.—A long and narrow lake, 100 miles in length, with an average breadth of three, indenting the eastern frontier of the dominions of Gholab Singh, the ruler of Cashmere. Its waters are clear and salt: elevation above the sea 14,224 feet. Cunningham is of opinion, that "in former ages the Pangkong lake had an outlet at its north-western extremity, through a gorge in the limestone cliffs, into the present scanty stream passing by Muglib, and joining the Shayok river just above the village which gives its name to the stream." Its centre is in lat. 33° 45′, long. 79° 15′.

PANGREE. — A town in the British district of Sholapoor, presidency of Bombay, 45 miles N. of Sholapoor. Lat. 18° 19′, long. 75° 58′.

PANGTOOR.—A town in one of the recently sequestrated districts of Hyderabad, 16 miles N. of Kurnool. Lat. 16° 3′, long. 78° 4′.

PANGULL, in Hyderabad, or territory of the Nizam, a town 80 miles S. of the city of Hyderabad. Lat. 16° 15′, long. 78° 9′.

PANJAL, or PANGLA, in the petty hill state of Hindoor, a village situate on the river Gumber, and in the valley between the ridge of Ramgurh and that of Malown. Lat. 31° 5′, long. 76° 52′.

PANJUR.—A river rising on the eastern slope of the Syadree range of mountains, in lat. 20° 53′, long. 73° 53′, and flowing through the British collectorate of Candeish in an easterly direction for sixty-two miles, and northerly for thirty miles, falls into the Taptee river, on the left side, in lat. 21° 17′, long. 74° 59′.

PANNAH.—See PUNNAH.

PANNALAGURH.—A town in the native state of Gwalior, or possessions of Scindia's family, situate 40 miles S. by E. from Kurgoon, and 107 miles N.E. by E. from Malligaum. Lat. 21° 18′, long. 75° 54′.

PANSAVAL.—A town in the British district of Tanjore, presidency of Madras, 37 miles S. of Tanjore. Lat. 10° 16′, long. 79° 13′.

PANTI, in native Gurwhal, a village pleasantly situate on the right bank of the Jumna, and 400 feet above its bed. Lat. 30° 48′, long. 78° 15′.

PANWARA. — A town in the British district of Bhagulpoor, lieut.-gov. of Bengal, 25 miles S. by E. of Bhagulpoor. Lat. 24° 55′, long. 87° 4′.

PANWELL, in the collectorate of Tannah (North Concan), presidency of Bombay, a small town or village on the route from Bombay to Poona, 55 miles N.W. of the latter place. It is situate on the estuary of a small river, the stream of which fails during the dry season, at which period Panwell is accessible by water only when the tide is full. At this state of the tide, communication with Bombay is practicable across the haven of that place, from which it is distant E., in a direct line, 22 miles. This passage, by which a considerable portion of the intercourse between the capital and the great military station of Poona is carried on, has heretofore been subject to much uncertainty and delay, from the varying depth of water and fluctuating strength of tides and winds; but the introduction of the agency of steam will have tended to abate these inconveniences. Heber describes the place as a "small-sized country town, with a pagoda, and a handsome tomb of a Mussulman saint." This pagoda is dedicated to Mahadeo or Siva. Here is a small fortress, the extent and plan of which may still be traced, though it is now much decayed. There is a bungalow or government lodge for travellers, and the road to Poona is well drained and bridged. Panwell is styled a populous town by the Court of Directors, and provision has been made for improving it. The Powna and Moolah rivers are crossed at Panowlee and Awund by indifferent ferries, both of which may be avoided by the more circuitous route of Dapooree. Distance from Poona, *vid* Dapooree, 70 miles. Lat. 18° 58′, long. 73° 12′.

PAPARGHAT, in the district of Sultanpoor, territory of Oude, a ruined town on the route from the cantonment of Sultanpoor to Jounpore, 47 miles N.W. of the latter, 10 S.E. of the former. Here Asaf-ud-daula, nawaub vizier of Oude, who reigned from 1775 to 1797, proposed to found a capital, and commenced building a palace; but, having visited the work after employing 400 workmen for three years, was deterred from its completion by a pestilence which broke out among his followers. The Hindoos attributed the visitation to the wrath of their goddess Debi, to appease whom the superstitious Mussulman prince erected a temple in her honour. The temple remains; and annually, in the month of Chait (March-April), about 4,000 Hindoos resort thither, to pay their devotions at the shrine, but remain only one night, in consequence of the pestilential air of the place. Here are besides a mosque and the unfinished palace of the nawaub. Lat. 26° 10′, long. 82° 17′.

PA PHOS.—A town of Burmah, 140 miles E. by N. from Prome, and 118 miles N.E. by N. from Pegu. Lat. 19° 12′, long. 97° 7′.

PAPOUSA. — A village in the British district of Hurreeana, lieut.-gov. of the N.W. Provinces. Lat. 28° 59′, long. 76° 3′.

PAPPAMOW.—See PHAPHAMOW.

PAR.—A river rising in lat. 20° 30′, long. 73° 43′, on the western slope of the Syadree range of mountains, and flowing in a westerly direction through the territory of the Daung rajahs, then dividing the petty native states of Dhurrumpore and Peint, and subsequently traversing the British collectorate of Broach, it falls into the Arabian Sea, in lat. 20° 32′, long. 72° 56′.

PARA, a river of Ladakh, rises in lat. 32° 27′, long. 78° 3′, at the north-eastern foot of the Parang pass over the Western Himalaya range, and flows through Rupshu, one of the districts of Gholab Singh's dominions. Subsequently it enters the Thibet valley of Tsotso, through which it flows for eighty-five miles, and finally traverses the district of Koonawur to its junction with the Sutlej, in lat. 31° 49′, long. 78° 41′.

PARADANGA.—A town in the British district of Rungpore, lieut.-gov. of Bengal, 29 miles N.E. by E. of Rungpore. Lat. 25° 55′, long. 89° 40′.

PARAMBALORE.—A town in the British district of Trichinopoly, presidency of Madras, 32 miles N.N.E. of Trichinopoly. Lat. 11° 15′, long. 78° 55′.

PARAMUTTY.—A town in the British district of Coimbatoor, presidency of Madras, 66 miles E. of Coimbatoor. Lat. 10° 57′, long. 77° 59′.

PARANG.—A pass over the western range of the Himalaya Mountains: it leads from the British district of Spiti into Gholab Singh's district of Rupshu. Lat. 32° 27′, long. 78° 3′.

PARBUTTY (EASTERN), a small river in the Mahratta territory of Gwalior, rises close to the town of Sipree, and in lat. 25° 31′, long. 77° 46′. It first holds a northerly course for about forty miles, and subsequently turning to the east for fifty miles, falls into the Sinde, on the left side, in lat. 25° 47′, long. 78° 21′. Wilford styles it "the little river Para," but is in error in stating that it winds round the town of Narwar, which is situate on the right bank of the Sinde, twenty-five miles above the mouth of the Parbutty.

PARBUTTY (WESTERN), a river of Malwa, rises on the north side of the Vindhya range, 20 miles S. of the town of Ashta, and in lat. 22° 45′, long. 76° 33′. It has a winding course of 220 miles, first in a north-easterly direction for eighty miles, and subsequently in a north-westerly, and falls into the Chumbul on the right side, in lat. 25° 50′, long. 76° 40′. It receives in its course some mountain-streams, and during rains swells so as not to be fordable. It is crossed by ford on the route from Kotah to Saugor, at Kukwasa, 150 miles from its source, and in lat. 24° 28′, long. 77° 7′; and "there has a bed 150 yards wide, rocky and stony bottom, and fine clear stream." At Khaliyanpur, sixty miles lower down the stream, and in lat. 25° 7′, long. 76° 42′, it is crossed by the route from Kotah to Calpee, and is there fordable.

PARDUMPOOR.—A town in the native state of Phooljer, on the south-west frontier of Bengal, situate on the right bank of the Aurag river, and 69 miles S.W. by W. from Sumbulpoor. Lat. 21°, long. 83° 5′.

PARE.—A town in the native state of Bhotan, situate on the right bank of the Guddada river, and 75 miles N.E. by E. from Darjeeling. Lat. 27° 35′, long. 89° 23′.

PARELI, in the petty hill chieftainship of Ghoond, tributary to Keonthul, a village situate on the right bank of the Giree, here a shallow, rapid, rocky stream of very clear water. Archer describes it as "a sweet romantic village, surrounded with luxuriant cultivation." Lat. 31° 5′, long. 77° 27′.

PARELL.—A town in the island of Bombay, containing a residence for the accommodation of the governor of the presidency, with a considerable domain attached. Distance N. from Bombay Castle five miles. Lat. 19°, long. 72° 55′.

PARGONG.—A town in the British district of Sumbulpoor, lieut.-gov. of Bengal, 43 miles W.N.W. of Sumbulpoor. Lat. 21° 40′, long. 83° 24′.

PARIMBAUCUM.—A town in the British district of Chingleput, presidency of Madras, 33 miles W. of Madras. Lat. 13° 2′, long. 79° 51′.

PARNEIR.—A town in the British district of Ahmednuggur, presidency of Bombay, 20 miles W.S.W. of Ahmednuggur. Lat. 19°, long. 74° 29′.

PARO.—A town in the native state of Bhotan, situate on the left bank of the Guddada river, and 64 miles E.N.E. from Darjeeling. Lat. 27° 22′, long. 89° 18′.

PARO.—A town in the British district of Chota Nagpoor, lieut.-gov. of Bengal, 56 miles S.S.E. of Lohadugga. Lat. 22° 43′, long. 85° 6′.

PARSIDEYPOOR, in the district of Salon, territory of Oude, a town five miles N.E. of the left bank of the Saee, 60 S.E. of Lucknow. Butter estimates the population at 4,000, almost all cultivators; and of the number, 3,000 Mussulmans. Lat. 26° 4′, long. 81° 34′.

PARUNGALOOR.—A town in the native state of Poodoocottah, or possessions of Rajah Tondiman, situate 28 miles S.E. by S. from Trichinopoly, and 69 miles N.E. by E. from Madura. Lat. 10° 30′, long. 79°.

PARUPUNADA.—The principal place of a tallook or subdivision of the same name, presidency of Madras. The town is also called Vaipur, Veypur, and Beypoor, under which last name it is described in the alphabetical arrangement. Parupanada or Beypoor is in lat. 11° 10′, long. 75° 51′.

PARVUTTIPURAM.—A town in the British district of Vizagapatam, presidency of Madras, 77 miles N. by E. of Vizagapatam. Lat. 18° 48′, long. 83° 30′.

PARYUR.—A town in the British district of Tinnevelly, presidency of Madras, 70 miles N. of Tinnevelly. Lat. 9° 44′, long. 77° 51′.

PASKYUM.—A town within the dominions of Gholab Singh, the ruler of Cashmere, 83 miles E.N.E. from Sirinagur, and 119 miles N. from Kangra. Lat. 34° 29′, long. 76° 20′.

PASLEE, in the British territory of Saugur and Nerbudda, lieut.-gov. of the N.W. Provinces, a town on the route from Seuni to Hoosungabad, 24 miles W.N.W. of the former. Lat. 22° 10′, long. 79° 20′.

PATA.—A town within the dominions of Gholab Singh, the ruler of Cashmere, 178 miles E. by N. from Sirinagur, and 178 miles N.E. by N. from Chamba. Lat. 34° 28′, long. 78°.

PATAN.—See PATUN.

PATAN, in Cashmere, a village 25 miles N.W. of the town of Sirinagur. This seems to have been an important locality during the predominance of Hindooism in Cashmere, as in the vicinity are the remains of two ancient buildings in a style similar to the celebrated temple at Matan. Patan is still a place of pilgrimage for the superstitious Hindoos. Lat. 34° 7′, long. 74° 23′.

PATANAGO.—A town of Burmah, situate on the left bank of the Irawady, and 83 miles N. from Prome. Lat. 19° 58′, long. 94° 51′.

PATAPOOR, in the British district of Cawnpore, lieut.-gov. of the N.W. Provinces, a village on the route from the cantonment of Cawnpore to that of Calpee, and 20 miles N.E. of the latter. Lat. 26° 19′, long. 80° 1′.

PATARI, in Gurwhal, a village five miles from the left bank of the Bhageerettee, as the Ganges is called in the upper part of its course. Lat. 30° 48′, long. 78° 25′.

PATCHMARREE, in the territory of Nagpore or Berar, a town situate among the Mahadeo Hills. In this secluded tract Appa Sahib, the fugitive rajah of Nagpoor or Berar, took refuge after his flight from his capital in 1818, but was expelled by the judicious and persevering operations of the British troops commanded by Col. Adams, who penetrated the most difficult recesses, reduced the strongest fastnesses, and thoroughly established the British power over that part of the Mahadeo Mountains. Distant from Hoshungabad, S.E., 53 miles; S. from Saugor 100; N.W. from Nagpoor 96. Lat. 22° 25′, long. 78° 30′.

PATCHWAREE, in the British district of Beerbhoom, lieut.-gov. of Bengal, a town among the highlands in the north of the district, on the south-west route from Berhampoor to Bhagulpoor, 58 miles N.W. of former, 60 S.E. of latter. Lat. 24° 31′, long. 87° 30′.

PATEETA, in the British district of Mirzapoor, lieut.-gov. of the N.W. Provinces, a town surrounded by rampart and fortress, five miles south of the fort of Chunar. In 1781, when Cheyt Singh, the refractory zemindar of Benares, raised the standard of rebellion against the East-India Company, he garrisoned Pateeta, which was stormed by Major Popham, though with considerable loss to the captors. Distant S.W. from Benares 18 miles; N.W. from Calcutta, by Hazaribagh and Sasseram, 420. Lat. 25° 4′, long. 82° 54′.

PATGAON.—A town in the native state of Kolapoor, territory of Bombay, 44 miles S.S.W. from Kolapoor, and 43 miles W.N.W. from Belgaum. Lat. 16° 8′, long. 74°.

PATGONG.—A town in the British district of Rungpore, lieut.-gov. of Bengal, 44 miles N.N.W. of Rungpore. Lat. 26° 17′, long. 89° 3′.

PATHANKOT (Afghan's Fort), in the north-east of the Punjab, and in the southern range of the Himalaya, 14 miles W. of Nurpur, and on the route to Cashmere. The fort has a fine appearance, is built substantially of brick, has a ditch and glacis, and being situate on level ground, is not commanded in any direction; it consequently admits of an obstinate defence. A lofty citadel in the interior rises above the ramparts. It was built by Shah Jehan, the Mogul emperor, during his attack on Nurpur. Notwithstanding its advantageous position and great strength, it seems to be allowed to fall to decay. Elevation above the sea 1,205 feet. Lat. 32° 18′, long. 75° 42′.

PATHOWLEE, in the British district of Agra, a village on the route from the city of Agra to Jeypoor, and six miles W. of the former. Lat. 27° 9′, long. 78°.

PATIALAH.—See PUTTEEALA.

PATIAR, in the north-eastern quarter of the Punjaub, a town situated 13 miles E.N.E. of Kangra, and 92 miles N.N.E. of the town of Loodianah. Lat. 32° 6′, long. 76° 30′.

PATN.—One of the principal towns in the valley of Nepaul, situate on a rising ground about two miles to the south-east of Khatmandoo, and near the confluence of the Bhagmutty with the Meenuskra and Fookacha. The town is adorned by several handsome edifices, and is said to be a neater town than Khatmandoo. It is also much older than the present capital, having been built by the Newars, the aborigines of Nepaul, before the invasion of the Ghoorkas. Lat. 27° 38′, long. 85° 17′.

PATNA.—A British district under the lieut.-gov. of Bengal, named from its principal place. It is bounded on the north by the Ganges, separating it from the British districts Sarun, Tirhoot, and Monghyr, by which last-named district it is also bounded on the north-east and south-east; on the south it is bounded by the British districts Monghyr and Behar; and on the west and north-west by the river Son, separating it from the British district Shahabad. It lies between lat. 25° 3′—25° 38′, long. 84° 45′—86° 10′; is eighty-five miles in length from east to west, and forty-five in breadth: the area is 1,828 square miles. The Ganges flows along its frontier in a stream fully as large as in any part of its course, being usually a mile wide, with a very rapid current during the rainy season, and at all times crowded with craft. The Son forms the western and north-western boundary of the district for thirty-five miles, and is for that distance navigable for craft of considerable burthen. The Poonpoon and the lesser Poonpoon also traverse the district, which, in the season of the periodical rains, is everywhere intersected by torrents and watercourses. It is altogether a very fertile and highly-cultivated tract, producing abundant crops of fine rice, wheat, and barley, and having its aspect enlivened by numerous orchards and groves of fruit-bearing and other trees. Much opium, of fine quality, is produced about Muneer and Pholwarree, in the western part of the district. The winters here are in general very mild. The hot season commences about the middle of March, and terminates about the end of June: the heat is very great along the banks of the Son and the Ganges, being increased by the radiation from the sands in the beds of those rivers. On the banks of the Ganges, towards the Son, the west winds usually prevail from the middle of January until nearly the end of March. From thence to the middle of June, the prevalence of the east and west winds is nearly equal. From that period to the end of July, the east winds are dominant; after which, until the end of August, the west winds again blow. From thence to the end of October, the east winds return; and subsequently, until the middle of January, the east and west winds are nearly balanced. In the rainy season, near the Ganges, there are occasionally north and south winds, and on the banks of the Son, it is alleged that whatever wind may prevail in the course of the day, every morning the wind blows from the south. The population is given under the article BENGAL. The most considerable towns—Patna, the sudder or chief civil station, as well as Dinapore, the military cantonment, and some others—are noticed under their respective names in the alphabetical arrangement. The routes are—1. From north to south, from Bankipore and Patna to Gaya, and thence continued to join the great north-western route from Calcutta; 2. from east to west, along the bank of the Ganges, from Berhampore, through Bhaugulpore, Bar, Patna, Dinapore, and thence across the Son to Arrah, in the British district of Shahabad; 3. from north-east to south-west, along the right bank of the Son, from Dinapore to Daudnagar, and thence to Hooseinabad; 4. from north-east to south-west, from Bar to the town of Behar. The district is also traversed by the East-India railway.

Patna was included under the grant of the dewanny of Bengal, Behar, and Orissa, made in 1765 by Shah Alum to the East-India Company. The revenue is permanently settled.

PATNA.—The principal place of the British district of the same name, under the presidency of Bengal, situate on the line of the East-India railway. It comprises the city or fort, inclosed by a wall of rectangular ground-plan, and extensive suburbs. The city extends a mile and a half in length from east to west, along the right bank of the Ganges, and three-quarters of a mile landwards from it. Many of the houses are built of brick, but the greater number of mud: they are generally tiled, a few only are thatched; but all, with little exception, look mean and slovenly. The eastern and western ramparts have each a gate in the middle, and a main street, rather wide, runs from one gate to the other; but even this principal thoroughfare is neither straight nor regularly built, and the other streets or passages are narrow, crooked, and irregular. Numerous ghats, or flights of stairs, give access to the water of the Ganges. Within the city is the grave of the British prisoners murdered in 1763 by Sumroo, the German adventurer, in obedience to the order of Cossim Ali, the expelled nawaub of Bengal: it is covered by a pillar of uncouth form, built partly of stone and partly of brick. There are many mosques, but they receive small care, and are regarded with so little reverence, that most of them are let as warehouses. Even the principal mosque, a handsome stone building, is occupied in this manner; and the chief Mussulman place of worship at present is in the western suburb. Adjacent to this last-mentioned mosque, is a much-frequented imambara, where 100,000 persons sometimes congregate. The principal suburb on the eastern side, called Marusganj, contains the chief market, and many storehouses for grain. The buildings being generally constructed of wood and mats, have been often burned down; yet no precaution is taken to prevent a recurrence of the calamity. This suburb is joined by another, denominated that of Giafir Khan. On the other side of the city is a long, narrow suburb, extending to Bankipore, a distance of about four miles. The breadth seldom exceeds half a mile, and there are many interruptions from gardens. This is the quarter of Europeans, whose houses are scattered through it, and principally along the bank of the river; but they are in no great numbers, and of no very imposing appearance. Here is a school, under the control of a committee, consisting of nine members, two of whom are natives. The English language and literature, history, and the mathematics, enter into the course of study, which is conducted by a head master and two assistants. Beside these, there are an Oordoo master and a Hindee master. Within the last few years a penitentiary and house of correction have been erected within the city.

During the hot season, the temperature is very high at Patna, being increased by the heat reflected and radiated from a naked expanse of sand on an extensive island in the Ganges, opposite the city. The population of the town of Patna is stated at 284,132.

Patna is a place of great antiquity, and is conjectured by Wilford to have been identical with Padmavati, the capital of Nanda, who, according to Prinsep, reigned over Magadha or Behar 415 years before the Christian era. Subsequently, it probably formed part of the dominions of the rajah of Kunnouj, on whose defeat, in 1194, by Shahabuddin, sovereign of Ghor, Patna, with the rest of Behar and Bengal, fell to the conqueror, who annexed his acquisition to the empire of Delhi. Patna appears to have for the most part continued, ostensibly at least, a portion of the empire until the death of Shir Shah, the Patan, who deposed and expelled Humayon. Muhamad, a relative of Shir Shah, made himself master of Patna in 1545, but was soon after subjugated by Akbar. Aurungzebe conferred the government of Behar on his son Azim, who resided at Patna, from that circumstance generally named Azimabad by the Mussulmans. The English established factories here at an early period, and carried on an extensive trade in opium, rice, and other articles. In 1763 disputes arose between the Company's servants and Meer Cossim, upon the subject of transit-duties. The former claimed an entire exemption from duty, though a heavy tax was paid by all native traders; and the claim was supported by a majority of the council at Calcutta, who sent a deputation to the nabob at Patna, to request he would confirm it. He was, however, unyielding, but at length gave way to an extent not contemplated or desired. In place of remitting duties on the Company's trade only, he abolished all customs-duties whatever, whether on British or native goods. Mortified, however, at the result of an act which in a moment of exasperation he had committed, and which must have materially diminished his revenue, he took every means to annoy the British, and before long resorted to an act of open hostility, by seizing some English boats which were lying in the river. Mr. Ellis, the chief of the English factory, upon this provocation made a precipitate attack upon the city, and took possession of it. The British were, however, soon driven from it by Meer Cossim, who, following the fugitives to their factory, destroyed many of them, and made prisoners of all the rest who were not so fortunate as to effect their escape. This was on the 24th June, 1763. During the four following months, several actions took place between Meer Cossim's forces and the English, which always ended in the defeat of the former. In the beginning of October, his capital town, Monghyr, was besieged and taken by storm. This so enraged him, that he decided on the perpetration of a deed exceeding in atrocity the murder of the Black Hole. He ordered the execution of all the English prisoners he had in his possession; and thus, in cold blood, 200 defenceless Englishmen, whom he had imprisoned in Patna and other places, were shot or cut to pieces under the direction of a European named Sumroo, who was in the service of the nabob. Among the number was Mr. Ellis; the only one who was spared was Mr. Fullarton, a surgeon, who afterwards effected his escape. The British took Patna by storm on the 6th November following, whereupon the nabob and his army fled to the dominions of the soubahdar of Oude, with whom he had lately entered into a treaty. In May following, the British were attacked by Meer Cossim under the walls of Patna, but after a long day's desperate fighting, the enemy were routed with great loss. Thereupon the English remained in quiet possession. Patna is distant E. from Dinapore, by land, 10 miles, by water 12; E. from Benares, by Ghazeepore, 157, by water 205; N.W. from Calcutta, land route, by way of Gaya and Hazaribagh, 377, by water 464. Lat. 25° 35′, long. 85° 15′.

PATNA, a raj in the country under the superintendence of the political agent for the south-west frontier of Bengal. It is bounded on the north by Bora Samba and Sumbulpoor; on the east by Sonepore and Boad; on the south by the river Tell; and on the west by Keriall. Its centre is in lat. 20° 40′, long. 83° 15′: it has an area of 1,158 square miles. Some years since, the country was officially reported to be continually in a state of the most wretched anarchy, incurable except by placing it under the direct management of the British government. The annual estimated revenue is 25,000 rupees: the tribute, which is small,—only 600 rupees, was paid with regularity. The population is believed not much to exceed 52,000. The principal town, bearing the same name, is in lat. 20° 36′, long. 83° 9′.

PATNA.—A town in the British district of Belgaum, presidency of Bombay, 20 miles W. of Belgaum. Lat. 15° 52′, long. 74° 18′.

PATODEE.—A town in the Rajpoot state of Jodhpoor, 48 miles W.S.W. from Jodhpoor, and 103 miles S.E. by E. from Jessulmeer. Lat. 26° 9′, long. 72° 24′.

PATON, in the British district of Kumaon, lieut.-gov. of the N.W. Provinces, a town on the route from Almora to the Rakus Lake, 53 miles N.E. of the former. Lat. 30° 10′, long. 80° 20′.

PATOWDHI.—A small jaghire inclosed within the territory of Jujhur, subject to the lieut.-gov. of the N.W. Provinces. The grant was made early in the present century, for services against the Mahrattas, by Lord Lake, to Fyze Tullub Khan, brother-in-law to Nawaub Nijabut Ali Khan, who, at the same time, was granted the jaghire of Jujhur. The present jaghirdar is Muhammad Akbar Ali Khan, who derives an annual revenue of 50,000 rupees from his jaghire. Pathowdi, the principal place, is on the route from Delhi to Narnol, and 40 miles S.W. of the former. It has a bazar, and is well supplied with water. The surrounding country is slightly undulated in low irregular swells, with a sandy soil, partially cultivated. The road in this part of the route is sandy and heavy, and bad for carts. Lat. 28° 18′, long. 76° 50′.

PATREE, in Guzerat, or territory of the Guicowar, a town at the south-eastern angle of the Runn or Great Salt Marsh. It has a fine tank, and is surrounded by three walls, the innermost of which has a ditch; but, though formerly of considerable importance and strength, it is now much decayed. The chief, styled the Dessaye, has an annual revenue of 18,000 rupees, of which he pays annually a tribute of 5,652 rupees to the British government. Distant W. from Ahmedabad 52 miles. Lat. 23° 10′, long. 71° 44′.

PATREE.—A town in Hyderabad, situate on the left bank of the Godavery river, and 188 miles N.W. from Hyderabad. Lat. 19° 16′, long. 76° 30′.

PATROOD.—A town in Hyderabad, or dominions of the Nizam, 192 miles N.W. by W. from Hyderabad, and 100 miles E. from Ahmednuggur. Lat. 19° 7′, long. 76° 17′.

PATTARSEE, in Sirhind, a village on the route from Kurnal to Loodiana, and 75 miles N.W. of the former place. It is situate on a small eminence, overlooking a level and fertile country, but in many places swampy, and in general slightly cultivated. Distant N.W. from Calcutta 1,040 miles. Lat. 30° 34′, long. 76° 35′.

PATTERGHATTA.—A town in the British district of Dacca Jelalpoor, lieut.-gov. of Bengal, 54 miles S.W. of Dacca. Lat. 23° 10′, long. 89° 48′.

PATUN, called also BUTISI and TONRAWUTTEE.—A small Rajpoot state bounded on the north-west by Shekawuttee; on the north-east by Jhujhur; on the east by Ulwar; and on the south-east and south by Jeypore. It lies between lat. 27° 31′—27° 56′, long. 75° 48′—76° 12′: it is thirty miles in length from north to south, and twenty in breadth. At the time of Boileau's visit, in 1835, it was ruled by Rao Luchmun Singh, chief of the Tour tribe of Rajpoots, who anticipated the proper period of succession by the murder of his father, but was subsequently so haunted by remorse, that he abandoned his palace, in which the foul crime was committed, and took up his abode in a temporary residence in the vicinity. The spirit of the murdered chief was supposed to inhabit the chamber which he occupied in life; and a couch, rose-water, and a few other articles, were kept constantly in readiness for his use. The country is a tract of barren hills and fertile valleys; it is tributary to Jeypore. The least accessible parts are inhabited by a tribe called Minas, who formerly subsisted by cattle-stealing and other plunder, and who, in the exercise of their avocation, undertook long journeys, either on foot or mounted on small dark-coloured camels of great speed and endurance, united at some settled point, committed their depredations, and returned, sometimes singly, sometimes in small bodies, to their fastnesses, where they divided their spoil. These marauders, however, have been much checked by the British forces, which have destroyed nearly all their forts, so that many from necessity have had recourse to agriculture for subsistence. Patun, the principal town, is rather a considerable place, situate in a strong position, at the foot of a hill surmounted by a citadel. The palace is on the side of the hill, about half-way between the base and summit. Distance S.W. from Delhi 100 miles. Lat. 27° 47', long. 76° 9'.

PATUN, within the limits of the territory of Bhoondee, in Rajpootana, a town situate on the left bank of the river Chumbul, 22 miles S.E. of the town of Bhoondee. It is the principal place of a pergunnah, of which (though locally situate, as above stated, within the confines of the state of Bhoondee) two-thirds belong to the family of Scindia, having been granted by the Peishwa, who himself received it from the rajah of Bhoondee, in remuneration for aid afforded against Jeypore. The other third, which had been wrested from Bhoondee by Holkar, was ceded by him to the British government, under the 4th article of the treaty of Mundissor. The rajah of Bhoondee was especially anxious to secure possession of Scindia's portion of Patun, as it contains his ancestral palace, as well as a magnificent temple built and endowed by his family; and by the treaty concluded with the rajah in 1818, the British government engaged that this portion of the territory should be restored to its original possessor, who in return engaged to pay an annual tribute of 40,000 rupees; but Scindia refusing to give up the possession, those clauses of the treaty were not carried out. By the treaty of Gwalior, in 1844, however, the management of this part of Patun was transferred to the British; and probably this may lead to an arrangement by which the long-cherished wishes of the Bhoondee rulers may be gratified. Lat. 25° 15', long. 76° 2'.

PATUNSAONGEE.—A town in the territory of Nagpoor or Berar, situate 13 miles N.N.W. from Nagpoor, and 98 miles E. by N. from Ellichpoor. Lat. 21° 20', long. 79° 3'.

PATURGHATTA, in the British district of Bhagulpoor, lieut.-gov. of Bengal, a small town or village on the right bank of the Ganges, four miles N. of the route from Berhampoor to Dinapoor, 134 miles N.W. of former, 164 E. of latter. Here are several caves and cells excavated in the rock facing the water. Lat. 25° 19', long. 87° 16'.

PATUS.—A town in the British district of Poonah, presidency of Bombay, 42 miles E. of Poonah. Lat. 18° 28', long. 74° 31'.

PAUDURKAORA, in Hyderabad, or territory of the Nizam, a town near the north-east frontier, towards Nagpoor or Berar. Distance from the city of Hyderabad, N., 178 miles; Nagpoor, S.W., 90. Lat. 19° 55', long. 78° 49'.

PAUGA.—A town in the native state of Bhotan, situate on the left bank of the Guddada river, and 65 miles E. by N. from Darjeeling. Lat. 27° 15', long. 89° 20'.

PAUK PUTTEN (Pure Town), in the Punjab, a town situate ten miles west of the river Ravee, and fourteen miles from Mamoke Ghat, a much-frequented ferry over it. The name of this town is considered to indicate its peculiar sanctity, in consequence of its having been for many years the residence of a celebrated Mahometan saint, Shekh Farid-u-Din, of whose miraculous powers many traditions are recounted by the natives. Pauk Putten is supposed by Masson to have been the site of the colossal altars erected by Alexander to mark the eastern boundary of his conquests. Lat. 30° 17', long. 73° 25'.

PAULY.—A town in the Rajpoot state of Jeypoor, situate on the left bank of the Chumbul river, and 88 miles S.E. by S. from Jeypoor. Lat. 25° 50', long. 76° 37'.

PAULYTANNA, or PALITHANA, in the peninsula of Kattywar, province of Guzerat, a town in the district of Gohilwar. It is situate at the eastern base of the Satrunja, a mountain sacred to Adinath, the deified priest of the Jains. As an instance of the liberal endowments and offerings made to this divinity, it is mentioned that lately a rich banker of Ahmedabad presented a crown of massive gold, studded with sapphires, and of the estimated value of 3,500*l*. The extensive summit of the mountain, surmounted by numerous steep peaks, is crowded with temples, shrines, images, and viharas or monastic retreats, connected with the belief of the Jains. The town itself is walled, and contains many relics of antiquity of various eras. Distance from Ahmedabad, S.W., 120 miles; Baroda, S.W., 105; Surat, N.W., 70; Bombay, N.W., 190. Lat. 21° 30', long. 71° 47'.

PAUMANEE.—A town in the territory of Nagpoor or Berar, 10 miles N.W. from Jugdulapoor, and 162 miles N. from Rajahmundry. Lat. 19° 20', long. 81° 51'.

PAUMBAUM, in Rameswaram, presidency of Madras, a town and the only collection of dwellings on that island, except the town of Rameswaram, is situate at the eastern extremity, near the mainland of Ramnad. The regular inhabitants consist chiefly of boatmen and pilots; and their only occupations are passing vessels through the reef, loading them, and discharging their cargoes. There are no artificers, and the bazar has but a few shops, chiefly for the sale of provisions, being deficient for the most part in regard to other articles, though generally to be obtained elsewhere. Lately the prosperity of the place received a stimulus from the presence of a number of strangers employed in improving the passage between the Point of Paumbaum and the Cape Tonitorai or Ramen, on the mainland, and commonly denominated the Paumbaum Passage. This passage was formerly impracticable for ships, in consequence of the obstructions caused by two parallel ridges of rocks about 140 yards apart; the north ridge being considerably the higher, and termed the first or great dam, in most places visible at low water, though nowhere sufficiently connected to prevent entirely at any time the passage of the water; the line of the south ridge or dam being also distinctly traceable at low water, but only a few detached rocks on it even then appearing above. The whole, or greatest part of the space between these two ridges, was filled up by large masses of rock in various positions, but generally in directions nearly parallel to the principal ridges, and usually several feet lower. Of those rocks, composed of sandstone, the strata, when observed in situ, are found to be horizontal. It has been surmised, on geological and historical probabilities, that at one time there was an isthmus connecting the island of Rameswaram with the mainland. Tradition countenances this belief; and the original disruption by an inroad of the sea, caused by a hurricane, is by some believed to have occurred as late as the early part of the fifteenth century. Across this double ridge of rocks were two channels; one affording passage for the larger craft, the other used by small boats only. A series of operations for improving the passage commenced in 1837, and extended over several years. It necessarily involved a considerable outlay, but the success was commensurate with the expenditure. The cost of the operations, from their commencement in 1837, until 1854, amounted to about 35,000*l*. The result was, that a channel was formed from 10 to 12 feet deep at low water neap tides, and a further outlay has been sanctioned for the prosecution of the work to the depth of 13 feet, so as to enable vessels of 300 tons to pass through in ballast.

Of a place like this, in what may be called a transition-state, it is difficult to furnish statistical particulars that will possess more than a temporary approach to accuracy. In 1843, Paumbaum contained about 200 houses. A European officer, with a detachment of about 100 sappers and miners, and a gang of 150 convicts, were stationed there; the camp-followers amounted to about 300. A considerable influx of money, causing a visible improvement in the condition of the inhabitants, was noticeable; and the advancement of trade, and steady increase in the number of shipping visiting the place, afforded indications favourable to its permanent prosperity. Anchorage and customs are levied by the British government. Lat. 9° 17′, long. 79° 17′.

PAUMBEN.—See PAUMBAUM.

PAUMOOR.—A town in the British district of Nellore, presidency of Madras, 53 miles S.S.E. of Nellore. Lat. 15° 7′, long. 79° 30′.

PAUNDORKAUN.—A town in Nepal, 112 miles W.N.W. from Khatmandoo, and 123 miles N. from Goruckpoor. Lat. 28° 27′, long. 83° 42′.

PAUPUGNEE.—A river rising in the Mysore, in lat. 13° 30′, long. 77° 50′, and, flowing north-easterly for forty miles through the Mysore territories, and ninety miles through the British collectorate of Cuddapah, falls into the Pennar, on the right side, in lat. 14° 36′, long. 78° 45′.

PAUTEPASHACURANELLOOR.—A town in the British district of Madura, presidency of Madras, 33 miles S.E. of Madura. Lat. 9° 35′, long. 78° 31′.

PAVANASI.—A town in the British district of Tanjore, presidency of Madras, 12 miles N.E. of Tanjore. Lat. 10° 55′, long. 79° 19′.

PAWGUR.—A town in the Mysore, 123 miles N.N.E. from Seringapatam, and 77 miles S.S.E. from Bellary. Lat. 14° 6′, long. 77° 20′.

PAYANG YAY.—A town of Burmah, situate on the left bank of the Irawady river, and 120 miles S.W. from Ava. Lat. 20° 40′, long. 94° 39′.

PAYE ISLAND.—One of the numerous cluster of islands known as the Mergui Archipelago. It is situate 13 miles W. from the coast of Tenasserim. Lat. 11° 27′, long. 98° 36′.

PA YECH, in Cashmere, a very ancient ruin, situate at the northern base of the Kariwah, or table-land of No Nagur. It is of small dimensions, but in a tasteful and impressive style of architecture. The building appears to be dedicated to Vishnu, as Surya or the sun-god, small sitting figures of whom are inserted in niches on the cornice outside. Pa Yech is in lat. 33° 50′, long. 74° 45′.

PAYNE GUNGA RIVER rises in lat. 20° 32′, long. 76° 4′, near the eastern boundary of the British district of Candeish, and, flowing through the Hyderabad territory in a very circuitous but generally easterly direction, for 320 miles, falls into the Wurda river, on the right side, in lat. 19° 56′, long. 79° 15′.

PEAK, a river of Berar or Nagpore, rises in lat. 22° 20′, long. 78° 47′, and, flowing south-easterly for fifty miles, falls into the Pench river, in lat. 21° 55′, long. 79° 13′.

PEDDAPULLY.—A town in Hyderabad, or territory of the Nizam, 110 miles N.E. by N. from Hyderabad, and 182 miles N.N.W. from Guntoor. Lat. 18° 43′, long. 79° 26′.

PEEDDA WAG, a river of the Nizam's dominions, rises in lat. 16° 59′, long. 78° 32′, and flowing south-easterly for seventy miles, falls into the Kistnah river, in lat. 16° 33′, long. 79° 18′.

PEELKUCHLA, in the British district of Jounpoor, lieut.-gov. of the N.W. Provinces, a town on the route from Jounpoor to Fyzabad, 19 miles N.N.W. of the former. Lat. 25° 58', long. 82° 37'.

PEEMING, a pass in the district of Koonawur, in Bussahir, traverses a lofty ridge of mountains, which, rising from the left bank of the Sutluj, holds a southerly course, dividing that rugged region from the table-land of Tartary, and at the same time forming the boundary between the British and Chinese empires. At a short distance to the north, the vast Pargeul Mountain rises from the right bank of the Sutluj, to the height of 13,500 feet, or to the total elevation of 22,488 feet above the sea. The elevation of the Peeming Pass above the sea is 13,518 feet. Lat. 31° 49', long. 78° 46'.

PEENOO, or PIM, a river in the valley of Spiti, rises in lat. 31° 40', long. 78°, and, flowing northerly for thirty-eight miles, falls into the Spiti river, in lat. 32° 6', long. 78° 12'.

PEEPAR, in the Rajpoot state of Jodhpoor, a town on the route from the city of Jodhpoor to that of Ajmeer, and 37 miles N.E. of the former. A mud wall incloses the town, and there is a small citadel in the middle of it. There are 3,000 houses, supplied with good water from a fine tank immediately opposite the south gate. The population, according to Boileau, is 14,710. Lat. 26° 24', long. 73° 40'.

PEEPCHOO.—A town in the British district of Ramgur, lieut.-gov. of Bengal, 49 miles N.N.E. of Ramgur. Lat. 24° 21', long. 85° 47'.

PEEPLEA.—See HATH KA PEEPLEA.

PEEPLEOD.—A town in the native state of Gwalior, or territory of Scindia's family, situate on the left bank of the Suktha river, and 67 miles N.W. by W. from Ellichpoor. Lat. 21° 39', long. 76° 40'.

PEEPLEY, in the British district of Balasore, lieut.-gov. of Bengal, a town on the left bank of the river Soobunreeka, ten miles above its fall into the Bay of Bengal, formerly of some commercial importance, but now much decayed. It was the first place in which the English were formally permitted to trade, the privilege being in 1634 granted by Shahjehan, padshah of Delhi. The Soobunreeka is from this town denominated the river of Peepley, and a shoal opposite the mouth is called Peepley Sand. Peepley is distant S.W. from Calcutta 90 miles. Lat. 21° 40', long. 87° 22'.

PEEPRA, in the British district of Goruckpore, lieut.-gov. of the N.W. Provinces, a small town on the south-eastern frontier, towards the British district of Sarun, two miles from the right bank of the river Jharia. Distant S.E. from Goruckpore cantonment 52 miles. Lat. 26° 18', long. 84° 9'.

PEEPRAICH (EASTERN), in the British district of Goruckpore, lieut.-gov. of the N.W. Provinces, a town on the route from Goruckpore cantonment to Mulye, 10 miles N.W. of the former. Lat. 26° 47', long. 83° 36'.

PEEPRAICH (WESTERN), in the British district of Goruckpoor, lieut.-gov. of the N.W. Provinces, a small town 10 miles N. of the left bank of the river Ghaghra. It contains 200 houses, and consequently, allowing six persons to each house, a population of 1,200. Distant W. from Goruckpoor cantonment 38 miles. Lat. 26° 42', long. 82° 48'.

PEEPRAON, in the British district of Allahabad, lieut.-gov. of the N.W. Provinces, a village on the route, by the Kutra Pass, from the cantonment of Allahabad to Rewa, and 19 miles S.E. of the former city. Lat. 25° 19', long. 81° 59'.

PEEPRY.—A town in the peninsula of Kattywar, province of Guzerat, situate 66 miles S. by E. from Rajkote, and 159 miles S.W. from Ahmedabad. Lat. 21° 20', long. 71°.

PEEPULKHEEREE, in the territory of Bhurtpore, a town on the N.W. extremity towards Alwar, 40 miles N.W. of the towns of Muttra and Bhurtpoor. Lat. 27° 38', long. 77° 9'.

PEEPULSANA, in the British district of Bijnour, lieut.-gov. of the N.W. Provinces, a village on the route from Moradabad to Hurdwar, and 41 miles N.W. of the former. Lat. 29° 20', long. 78° 32'.

PEEPULTHON.—A town of Malwa, in the native state of Bhopal, 26 miles S.W. by S. from Bhopal, and 42 miles W.N.W. from Hoosungabad. Lat. 22° 58', long. 77° 10'.

PEERAO.—A town in the Rajpoot state of Jodhpoor, 187 miles W. by S. from Jodhpoor, and 82 miles S.W. by S. from Jessulmeer. Lat. 26°, long. 70° 11'.

PEERGUNJE.—A town in the British district of Dinagepoor, lieut.-gov. of Bengal, 26 miles N.W. by W. of Dinagepoor. Lat. 25° 47', long. 88° 20'.

PEERGUNJE.—A town in the British district of Rungpore, lieut.-gov. of Bengal, 28 miles S.S.E. of Rungpore. Lat. 25° 18', long. 89° 24'.

PEERGUNJE.—A town in the British district of Purneah, lieut.-gov. of Bengal, nine miles S.S.W. of Purneah. Lat. 25° 39', long. 87° 30'.

PEER POINTEE, in the British district of Bhagulpoor, lieut.-gov. of Bengal, a small town on the right bank of the Ganges. It is situate at the foot of a detached hill, and on the summit of a cliff impending over the river is the tomb of Peer Pointee, a reputed Mussulman saint; whence the place has its name. Distant E. from Bhagulpoor by Colgong 34 miles, by the course of the river 37; from Rajmahal, N.W., by Sikrigali, 40; from Calcutta, by the course of the river, 289. Lat. 25° 17', long. 87° 26'.

PEERPOREE.—A town in the British district of Nuddea, lieut.-gov. of Bengal, 77 miles N.N.E. of Calcutta. Lat. 23° 39′, long. 88° 48′.

PEESANGUN, in the British district of Ajmeer, lieut.-gov. of the N.W. Provinces, a town, the principal place of a pergunnah of the same name, having a population of 15,740 persons. Distance 15 miles W. of Ajmeer, N.W. of Nusserabad 22 miles. Lat. 26° 26′, long. 74° 30′.

PEETAR.—A village of native Gurwhal, on a feeder of the Tons, and about five miles from the right bank of that river. It is situate near the crest of the woody range dividing the valley of the Tons from that of the Pabur, and producing the celebrated Pinus deodar, the first of that magnificent species observed by Jacquemont in his progress westward through the Himalaya. Peetar is at the elevation of 6,684 feet above the sea. Lat. 31°, long. 78° 1′.

PEETUMPOOR, in the British district of Cawnpore, lieut.-gov. of the N.W. Provinces, a village on the route from Allahabad to Etawa, and 47 miles S.E. of the latter. Lat. 26° 24′, long. 79° 40′.

PEETUMPOOR, in the British district of Boolundshuhur, lieut.-gov. of the N.W. Provinces, a town on the route from Boolundshuhur to Allygurh, 20 miles S.E. of the former. Lat. 28° 11′, long. 78° 10′.

PEGU.—A British province of Eastern India, recently acquired from the Burmese by the result of war. It is bounded on the north by the Burmese territories; on the east by the river Sitang, separating it from the Tenasserim provinces; on the south by the Bay of Bengal; and on the west by the Bay of Bengal and by the Youmadoung Mountains, separating it from the province of Arracan. It extends from lat. 15° 49′ to 19° 30′, and from long. 94° 11′ to 96° 55′: it is 240 miles in length from north to south, and 170 in breadth. The area and population of the several districts into which the province is divided are given in the subjoined table:—

Districts.	Area in Sq. Miles.	Population.
Rangoon........	9,800	137,130
Bassein	8,900	128,189
Prome..........	5,500	100,000
Henzadee	2,200	103,775
Toungoo........	3,950	34,957
Tharawaddy	1,950	66,129
	32,300	570,180

The principal river is the Irawaddy, which, reaching the southern frontier of Burmah in the latitude of Meaday, crosses into the province of Pegu, and pursues its course in a southern direction for a further distance of between 200 and 300 miles, reaching the Bay of Bengal by several mouths, which form the delta of the Irawaddy. Some distance below the city of Prome, the river diverges into two main branches, the more easterly of which flows by the town of Rangoon, while the western branch passes by the town of Bassein.

The government of India during the late war having determined to annex Pegu to the British empire, it became necessary to make arrangements for the administration of the province. The task was not beset with any extraordinary difficulties. Upon inquiry, it became obvious that the whole social and administrative system closely resembled those of Arracan and Tenasserim; and it was wisely resolved that the details of the administration for the new province, not less than its general form, should be taken from the systems which had long prevailed in the adjacent districts. Accordingly, in the departments of civil and criminal judicature, the regulations nave been assimilated to those of Tenasserim. As a temporary measure, the land revenue is levied on each yoke of cattle, according to the custom of the country; but the regulations to be permanently adopted in the revenue department are those of Arracan. The duties upon imports and exports are levied according to the tariff in use at Calcutta.

The earlier history of Pegu would scarcely repay the reader for the labour of tracing it with minuteness. It may suffice to state, that Pegu was formerly an independent state, and that Ava was subordinate to it. After a time, however, Ava revolted, and succeeded in reducing Pegu to a state of dependency. That country in turn revolted, and reasserted with success its claim of supremacy over Ava. Through the energy of an adventurer named Alompra, this claim was, however, questioned; the Peguers were expelled from Ava, and war carried into their own dominions. It terminated in rendering Pegu a province of the kingdom of Ava, in which condition it remained until it became British territory. The events which led to the conquest of Pegu, and to its final incorporation with the British dominions, will be found noticed in the article BURMAH. The result has been to sever from the Burmese empire the richest and most fertile of its provinces, and to deprive the court of Ava of its principal resources for maintaining an army in the field. Under British rule, the country promises decided improvement; and commerce, which never could prosper under such a government as that of Ava, will now find opportunity for developing the full resources of Pegu.

PEGU.—One of the principal towns in the newly-acquired British province of the same name, situate on the left bank of the river having a similar appellation, and which further south falls into the eastern branch of the Irawaddy. The old city was destroyed by Alompra in 1757, on his final triumph over the Peguers. The plan of the new town is a quadrangle, the main street running east and west, and being crossed by others at right angles. The streets are for the most part spacious, and paved with brick; but the houses are of wood, supported on posts, with roofs lightly covered. The building in the town chiefly attracting attention, is the temple of Shoemadoo, which, according to Symes, "is a pyramidical building, composed of brick and mortar, without excavation or aperture of any sort, octagonal at the base, and spiral at the top." This author gives a rather particular description of the building; but as fifty-four years have elapsed since the publication of his volume, as ruin had at that time begun to invade the walls of the lower terrace, and as on the British visit in 1824 the edifice was found in a very neglected condition, and much injured by the weather, it is probable that the account above quoted would require very considerable modifications to adapt it to present circumstances.

Pegu was captured by the British in 1824, and restored upon the termination of the war. During the second war in 1852, the town, previously taken and abandoned, was a second time occupied. A determined attempt on the part of the Burmese was made once more to recover it, but it was met by the officer in command (Major Hill, of the Madras Fusiliers) with a combination of skill and decision which enabled him to maintain it, though under great difficulties, until relief arrived. Distant N. from Rangoon 62 miles. Lat. 17° 40′, long. 96° 17′.

PEHARI, in Bundelcund, a village on the route from Banda to Gwalior, 88 miles W. of the former, 116 S.E. of the latter. It has a bazar, and water from wells and a tank, but supplies are rather scarce. It is the principal place of a small jaghire or feudal grant, "comprising four square miles, containing 800 souls, and yielding a revenue of 800 rupees." The jaghiredar, who receives a small tribute from lands appropriated by the neighbouring rajah of Jhansee, is stated to maintain fifty infantry. Lat. 25° 33′, long. 79°.

PEHONA.—A town in the territory of Nagpoor or Behar, situate on the left bank of the Wurda river, and 62 miles S.S.W. from Nagpoor. Lat. 20° 20′, long. 78° 47′.

PEINLULLAH, in the British district of Hoosungabad, territory of Saugur and Nerbudda, lieut.-gov. of the N.W. Provinces, a town on the route from Hoosungabad to Seuni, 25 miles E. by S. of the former. Lat. 22° 39′, long. 78° 8′.

PEINT, with HURSOOL, a petty native state within the presidency of Bombay, bounded on the north by the raj of Dhurrumpore and the territory of the Daung rajahs; on the east by the British district of Ahmednuggur; on the south by that of Tannah, which also, with Surat, bounds it on the west. It lies between lat. 20° 1′—20° 27′, long. 72° 58′—73° 40′; is forty-six miles in length from east to west, and twenty-eight in breadth; and contains an area of 750 square miles, with a population of 55,000.

On the death of the rajah of Peint, in 1842, without male heirs, the claim of his daughter to succeed to a Mahomedan chiefship was deemed untenable, and the estate was taken under the management of the British government. An intimation was, however, made to the Begum, that the estate would be transferred to the husband she might marry, provided he were a fit person to be intrusted with the management. Subsequently the Begum was informed that she was at liberty to marry whom she pleased, but that unless her choice was considered by government in all respects unexceptionable, the estate would be continued under British management, in trust for herself and the issue of such marriage; but that her husband, in virtue of his marriage, would acquire no rights over the principality. Its affairs still continue under the administration of the British, and the last accounts state that it enjoys a high state of prosperity. Peint, the principal place, is situate 73 miles S.E. by S. from Surat, and 102 miles N.N.E. from Bombay. Lat. 20° 17′, long. 73° 31′.

PEIRGAUM.—A town in the British district of Ahmednuggur, presidency of Bombay, 39 miles S. of Ahmednuggur. Lat. 18° 33′, long. 74° 45′.

PEITAPOOR, in Guzerat, or territory of the Guicowar, a town on the right or western bank of the river Saburmuttee. Population 7,000. Distance from Ahmedabad, N., 15 miles. Lat. 23° 14′, long. 72° 40′.

PEITHAN.—A town in Nepal, 153 miles W. from Khatmandoo, and 90 miles N.N.W. from Goruckpoor. Lat. 27° 53′, long. 82° 50′.

PEJUR, in Bussahir, a river, or rather large torrent, in the district of Koonawur, rises on the south-eastern declivity of the Lipi Pass, about lat. 31° 47′, long. 78° 18′, and holds a south-easterly course of about twenty miles, to the village of Chalun, near which it is joined by the Munglung, a considerable torrent, and below the confluence has the name of Titi, described by Jacquemont as a very impetuous and great stream, one of the largest feeders of the Sutluj, into which, after a total course of about twenty-five miles, it falls, in lat. 31° 38′, long. 78° 29′.

PELEW GEWEN ISLAND, situate at the entrance of the Martaban river. The means by which the British became possessed of this desirable island are curious and interesting. After the treaty of Yandabo was agreed to by the East-India Company and the Burmese, the river Martaban being decided upon as the northern boundary of the former's possessions, a question arose as to whom the island of Pelew should belong. This it was agreed should be decided by the course a gourd-shell should take, being placed in the river above Martaban; viz., if the shell floated to the west of the island, it should become the property of the Company; but if it took the eastern channel, the Burmese should claim it. The ceremony took place, and the gourd slowly floated down the stream, entering the sea by the western channel, thereby making it the undisputed property of the Company. Lat. 16° 20′, long. 97° 37′.

PELLUR.—A town in the British district of Nellore, presidency of Madras, 72 miles N. of Nellore. Lat. 15° 29′, long. 80° 6′.

PEN.—A town in the British district of Tannah, presidency of Bombay, 25 miles S.E. of Bombay. Lat. 18° 43′, long. 73° 11′.

PENANG.—See PRINCE OF WALES ISLAND.

PENCH NUDDEE.—A river of Berar, rising in lat. 22° 11′, long. 78° 45′, a few miles north of the town of Omrait, and, flowing first easterly for sixty-five miles, and south for fifty-three miles, forms a junction with the Kanhan river, in lat. 21° 18′, long. 79° 12′, near the town of Kamptee.

PENGRA BAZAR.—A town in the British district of Seebpoor, in Upper Assam, 13 miles S.W. of Seebpoor. Lat. 26° 51′, long. 94° 32′.

PENGUGURRAM.—A town in the British district of Salem, presidency of Madras, 38 miles N.W. by N. of Salem. Lat. 12° 6′, long. 77° 55′.

PENNACONDA.—A town in the British district of Bellary, presidency of Madras, 87 miles S.E. by S. of Bellary. Lat. 14° 5′, long. 77° 39′.

PENNAGUNCHYPROLE. — A town in the British district of Masulipatam, presidency of Madras, 81 miles N.W. by W. of Masulipatam. Lat. 16° 56′, long. 80° 18′.

PENNAGUR. — A town in the British district of Chingleput, presidency of Madras, 52 miles S.W. of Madras. Lat. 12° 39′, long. 79° 44′.

PENNAR (NORTHERN).—A river having its origin in the territory of Mysore, about lat. 13° 23′, long. 77° 43′, and deriving its earliest supply from a square stone tank, in the centre of the ruined fort of Chandradroog. The tank overflows in the rainy season, and the redundant water, falling into a deep cleft in the rock, issues in a stream from the side of the mountain, about 200 yards lower down. This source fails during the dry season. The stream, flowing to the north-west for thirty miles, then crosses the northern boundary of the territory of Mysore, and takes a northerly course for ninety-five miles, to Ooderpee Droog, where it turns eastward, and, continuing to flow in that direction for 230 miles, passes in its course by Nellore, and falls into the Bay of Bengal in lat. 14° 38′, long. 80° 13′; its total length being 355 miles. Its principal tributaries on the right side are the Chittrarutty, the Paupugnee, and the Cheyair; on the left side, the Koondaur.

PENNAR (SOUTHERN). — A river of Mysore, rising north of the Nundydroog Hills, and in lat. 13° 32′, long. 77° 45′. Receiving the redundant water of a series of tanks at that place, it flows circuitously, but generally south, for fifty-five miles, to Mootanhalli, where it crosses the south-eastern frontier of Mysore into the Carnatic, through which it holds a south-easterly course of 190 miles, and falls into the Bay of Bengal, in lat. 11° 45′, long. 79° 51′, a mile north of Fort St. David; its total length being 245 miles. Gold is found in its sands, in its passage through the Carnatic. Heyne erroneously states that this river falls into the river Cauvery.

PENT.—A town in the British district of Rutnageriah, presidency of Bombay, 40 miles N.N.E. of Rutnageriah. Lat. 17° 30′, long. 73° 35′.

PENY KYOUNG BENTINCK, or MIDDLE BOLONGO, the centre of three islands at the entrance of the Aracan river. It is about twenty-six miles in length, and six in breadth; mountainous, woody, and rugged; without any appearance of inhabitants or cultivation. The centre of the island is in lat. 20°, long. 93° 4′.

PEORA, in Sirhind, a small town on the route from Thanesir to Kythul, and 15 miles W. of the former town. It is situate on a small river or torrent, access to the water of which is given by several neat ghats or stairs. It rises in a striking manner over the jungle which surrounds it, being situated on a rough mound, formed by the ruins of a more ancient town. The houses are built of good brick, but are confusedly intermixed with ruins in every stage of decay. Distant N.W. from Calcutta 1,003 miles. Lat. 29° 50′, long. 76° 37′.

PEORAH, in the British district of Kumaon, lieut.-gov. of the N.W. Provinces, a village, with a public bungalow or reception-house, on the route from Almora to Bareilly, and nine miles S. of the former. Elevation above the sea 5,238 feet. Lat. 29° 31′, long. 79° 40′.

PEPERGAON, in the British district of Furruckabad, lieut.-gov. of the N.W. Provinces, a town on the route from Furruckabad to Mynpooree, five miles W.S.W. of the former. Lat. 27° 22′, long. 79° 34′.

PERAI, in the British district of Allahabad, lieut.-gov. of the N.W. Provinces, a village on the route by Rajapoor ferry, from the cantonment of Allahabad to Banda, and 18 miles W. of the former. Lat. 25° 26′, long. 81° 34′.

PERANTUREI.—A town in the British district of Coimbatoor, presidency of Madras, 46 miles E.N.E. of Coimbatoor. Lat. 11° 16′, long. 77° 38′.

PERBOOTPORE, in the British district of Ghazepoor, lieut.-gov. of the N.W. Provinces, a village on the left bank of the Ganges, 532 miles N.W. of Calcutta by water; E. of Ghazepoor cantonment 50. Lat. 25° 43′, long. 84° 20′.

PERI, in the British district of Goruckpore, lieut.-gov. of the N.W. Provinces, a small town of about 100 houses, near the south-eastern frontier, towards the British district of Sarun, distant 50 miles S.E. of Goruckpore cantonment. Lat. 26° 20′, long. 84° 12′.

PERIAPATAM, in the territory of Mysore, a town near the south-western frontier, towards Coorg, in an elevated tract on the eastern declivity of the Western Ghats, and about 4,000 feet above the level of the sea. The surrounding country is well watered, containing many small lakes, besides numerous tanks; the latter, however, being in a ruinous state, either from neglect or wilful injury during the frequent wars with which the country has been afflicted. The soil is rich, and the climate rather moist and fertile; hence its name, indicating "favoured town." Formerly a flourishing place, protected by two forts, the inner of mud, surrounded by another of stone, it was utterly wasted by the troops of Tippoo Sultan. When visited by Buchanan in 1800, the inner fort was quite ruinous, in consequence of the defences having been blown up; and the place had become so infested by tigers, as to be dangerous to enter even at mid-day: some families of Brahmins, who had houses in the outer fort, were obliged to shut themselves up at nightfall. There are two temples of the Brahminical, and one of the Jain persuasion, in the town. The mahal or palace consists of a square area, surmounted by a dome and surrounded by apartments. This place was formerly the capital of a petty rajah, who, in 1644, being besieged by Kanthi Rao Marso, the kurtar or ruler of Mysore, in despair destroyed his family, and rushing forward recklessly, died sword in hand in the midst of his enemies. In 1791 it was occupied by the British army of Bombay, under the command of General Abercromby, with the view of co-operating with that of Lord Cornwallis before Seringapatam; but the siege of that place being then relinquished, Abercromby precipitately retreated, leaving behind him part of his battering-train and a large quantity of powder, which Tippoo Sultan caused to be exploded, to destroy the great Jain temple in which it had been stored. In the following year Periapatam was again occupied by the army of Bombay, and subsequently once more in 1799, by the army of that presidency, under General Stuart, marching to join General Harris, then besieging Seringapatam. Just previously to the time of its occupation by General Abercromby, it contained 1,500 houses; which number, according to the usually received ratio of five inmates to each house, would indicate a population of 7,500 persons. Tippoo Sultan not only dismantled and ruined the forts, but destroyed the houses also. After the overthrow of Tippoo Sultan, in 1799, the inhabitants returned, and the place has since been slowly recovering from its disasters. Distance from Seringapatam, W., 43 miles; Bangalore, S.W., 110; Mangalore, S.E., 90; Madras, W., 290. Lat. 12° 21′, long. 76° 9′.

PERIKHALEE.—A town in the British district of the Soonderbunds, lieut.-gov. of Bengal, 83 miles E. of Calcutta. Lat. 22° 30′, long. 89° 42′.

PERIM.—An island in the Gulf of Cambay, off the harbour of Gogo, in Guzerat, on the west side of the gulf, and in the British district Ahmedabad. The island is about two miles in length and half a mile in breadth, and is separated from the mainland of Guzerat by a channel, which in parts is seventy-five fathoms deep, while its breadth, according to one authority, is 500 yards; according to another, two miles. In the island are the remains of a considerable fort, and of an antique temple, containing an image of Buddha. This island has received much attention from geologists, from the great quantity of organic remains found imbedded in the conglomerate. They are those of the elephant, mastodon, hippopotamus, rhinoceros, hog, deer, ox, tortoise, and saurian reptiles. Baron Hügel obtained forty-one pieces of fossil bones, the greater part belonging to the Mastodon latidens, of which the teeth left no doubt. Of these he says, "Some of the bones are of an immense size; one fractured piece of the tusk measuring, from the centre to the outside of the circle, 5¼, which gives 10½ inches diameter, or thirty-four inches in circumference." A lighthouse has been erected on this island. Lat. 21° 38′, long. 72° 19′.

PERIPOLLIAM.—A town in the British district of Chingleput, presidency of Madras, 22 miles N.W. of Madras. Lat. 13° 17′, long. 80° 7′.

PERMACOIL.—A town in the British district of South Arcot, presidency of Madras, 33 miles N. of Cuddalore. Lat. 12° 10′, long. 79° 45′.

PEROWA, in the territory of Tonk, or possessions of Ameer Khan, a town on the route from Ooojein to Kotah, 69 miles N. of former, 72 S. of latter. Lat. 24° 9′, long. 76° 4′.

PERRIMBIRE.—A town in the British district of Chingleput, presidency of Madras, 60 miles S.W. by S. of Madras. Lat. 12° 23′, long. 79° 50′.

PERTABPORE.—A town in the British district of Midnapore, lieut.-gov. of Bengal, 28 miles E. of Midnapore. Lat. 22° 24′, long. 87° 50′.

PERTAUBGHUR.—See PURTABGHUR.

PESHAWUR.—A province of the British principality of the Punjab, occupying the extreme north-western corner of the empire, and lying between the Indus above and below Attock and the Khyber Mountains, through which is the great Khyber Pass. It is bounded on three sides by the Khyber, Mohmund, Swat, and Khuttuk hills: in the east it is open to the Indus. It lies between lat. 33° 42′ and 34° 30′, and long. 71° 35′ and 72° 42′. In the extent here assigned to this territory, it is sixty-five miles long, fifty miles broad, and about 2,324 square miles in extent, with a population amounting to 450,099. Its climate is very hot in summer, the thermometer frequently reaching 110° or 112° in the shade. The heat, however, is occasionally mitigated by the breezes from the neighbouring mountains; and as the country, naturally fertile, is well watered by the Indus, the Kabool river, and its tributaries, the chief of which are the Swat and the Bara, and is, moreover, well cultivated, it is amazingly productive. The water is applied to the purposes of cultivation by means of canals and innumerable small channels, from whence it is drawn up by means of a pole having a fulcrum in the middle and a bucket suspended at one end, which is raised by the hand pressing the other end; or where the depth is too great for this mode of operation, the water is obtained by the use of the Persian wheel, worked by camels or bullocks. Here, water is in general too near the surface to require the use of the draw-well. In consequence of this abundant supply, the country continues verdant during the whole year. The principal crops are wheat, barley, maize, millet, and various other crops suitable to warm climates. Peshawur produces the finest rice in the world. It is called Bara rice, because grown on ground irrigated by that river; and Runjeet Singh, ever watchful to secure to himself the best of everything prized by man, exacted part of his tribute in this valued article. Esculent vegetables are cultivated with much success. Many of them are of the kinds known in England—carrots, turnips, radishes, cabbages, cauliflowers, onions; others are there of common occurrence in India. As a substitute for hay, corn and certain green crops are cut before ripe and dried for fodder. Barley, and sometimes wheat, are cut before they form ears, and used for this purpose; and this treatment does not injure the crop. What is called here *paulaiz,* is a very important portion of the crop, and comprises musk-melons, water-melons, scented melons, and various kinds of cucumbers, pumpkins, and gourds, produced in the greatest luxuriance, and consumed in the hot season in large quantities. The castor-oil plant is cultivated: the oil, however, is not intended for culinary or medicinal purposes, but for any other in which a coarse oil may be required. Sesamum, mustard, and some other plants, are reared for the sake of their oil. The sugarcane is raised to be consumed as a sweetmeat; sugar itself being obtained from Hindostan. Ginger, turmeric, tobacco, and cotton, are also extensively cultivated. The ground is moved by the plough, the spade being little employed. Scythes are unknown, and crops of all kinds are cut with sickles. Oxen are used for ploughing, harrowing, and treading out the corn. Mulberry-trees abound, and silk is produced in moderate quantities. The principal fruits are plums, figs, peaches, pomegranates, mulberries, and quinces; but, though large, all except the last have an inferior flavour. The quince of Peshawur is said to surpass those of all other countries. Elphinstone, who entered the country in March from the great defile through which the route from the south passes, describes the scene formed by the mountains, crowned with eternal snow, surrounding the luxuriant and picturesque plain, as at once grand and beautiful in the highest degree, and he found that a nearer survey increased his admiration. At the time of Elphinstone's visit, the population was so dense, that thirty-two villages were counted within a circuit of four miles. It may be doubted whether the impressions of the European visitors on this occasion were not somewhat over sanguine, but it was their belief, "that never was a spot of ground better peopled." Since its annexation to the British dominions, the province has been held by a regular military force of 10,500 men, in which are comprised two regiments of European infantry and a detail of artillery.

Through this fine province lies the great route from Khorasan and Kabool into India, by the passes of the Khyber Mountains and across the Indus at Attock. It is also traversed by the grand trunk road from Lahore to the city of Peshawur, along which is located the army of the Punjab. The former of these routes being open to the wild inhabitants of the mountains, it was found necessary to adopt a comprehensive plan of defence for the security of the valley.

PESHAWUR, or PESHAWER, the capital of the province of the same name, is situate about eighteen miles east of the eastern extremity of the Khyber Pass. In the early part of the present century, when visited by Elphinstone, it was a flourishing town, about five miles in circuit, and reported to contain 100,000 inhabitants. Twenty years later, Runjeet Singh, after defeating the Afghans in the decisive battle of Noushera, took Peshawer, demolished the Bala Hissar, at once the capital and state residence; destroyed the fine houses of the chief Afghans; desecrated the mosques, and, cutting down the groves and orchards about the city, laid waste the surrounding country. Subsequent exactions and oppressions prevented for a time its revival. The numerous mosques, many built in a splendid style of oriental architecture, were intentionally polluted by the Sikhs, and the commerce of the city languished under their stern rule. The fortress erected by them on the site of the Bala Hissar, is a square of about 220 yards, and is strengthened by round towers at each angle, every curtain having in front of it a semicircular ravelin. There is a fausse-braie all round, of substantial towers and curtains, with a wet ditch. The height of the inner walls is sixty feet, of the fausse-braie thirty, all constructed of mud. Within, are capacious and well-constructed magazines and storehouses. The only gateway is on the northern face, and it is protected by towers. The present population of the city is returned at 53,295; of whom 7,706 are stated to be Hindoos, and the remainder Mussulmen.

Peshawur was built by the Mogul emperor Akbar, who affixed the name, signifying "advanced post," in reference to its being the frontier town of Hindostan towards Afghanistan. Elevation above the sea 1,068 feet. Since its occupation by the British, all restrictions have been removed, and trade is rapidly expanding. The suburbs and environs are also represented as having improved in appearance. Lat. 34°, long. 71° 38′.

PETHORA GURH, in the British district of Kumaon, lieut.-gov. of the N.W. Provinces, a cantonment for troops stationed to protect the frontier towards Nepal. It is situate about 10 miles W. of the right bank of the Kali river, and on a low ridge in the middle of Shore valley. There is a bazar attached to the cantonment, and also a large airy hospital, built of stone, and roofed with slates. A hundred yards west of the lines is Fort Loudoun, a neat and well-arranged structure, which commands the whole place. The elevation above the sea probably does not exceed 1,600 feet. Distance N.W. from Calcutta 1,200 miles. Lat. 29° 35′, long. 80° 16′.

PETRABAR.—A town in the British district of Ramgur, lieut.-gov. of Bengal, 21 miles E. by S. of Ramgur. Lat. 23° 40′, long. 85° 50′.

PETT.—A town in Guzerat, or dominions of the Guicowar, situate 92 miles N.N.E. from Baroda, and 89 miles N.E. by E. from Kaira. Lat. 23° 30′, long. 73° 46′.

PETTAH.—A town in the British district of Masulipatam, presidency of Madras, three miles N.W. of Masulipatam. Lat. 16° 11′, long. 81° 10′.

PETTEE, in the Baree Dooab division of the Punjab, a town situated 11 miles from the right bank of the Sutlej, 45 miles E.S.E. of the town of Lahore. Lat. 31° 17′, long. 74° 54′.

PETTEI.—A town in the British district of South Arcot, presidency of Madras, 40 miles N.W. of Cuddalore. Lat. 12° 7′, long. 79° 26′.

PEYHANNEE, in the territory of Oude, a small town on the route from Futtehgurh cantonment to that of Seetapoor, 48 miles N.E. of the former, 34 W. of the latter. It is situate between the rivers Goomtee and Saee. It has a bazar, and abundance of good water. Distant N.W. from Lucknow 70 miles. Lat. 27° 43′, long. 80° 17′.

PEYNT.—See PEINT.

PEYTAHN.—A town in Nepal, situate on the left bank of the Jimru river, and 206 miles W. by N. from Khatmandoo. Lat. 28° 34′, long. 82° 6′.

PEYZOO, in the Daman, a division of the Punjab, situate 16 miles W. from the right bank of the Indus, 133 miles S.S.W. of the town of Peshawar. Lat. 32° 13′, long. 70° 52′.

PHAGEH.—A town of Burmah, 191 miles N. by W. from Ava, and 96 miles E. by S. from Muneepoor. Lat. 24° 34′, long. 95° 30′.

PHAGGEE, in the state of Jeypore, in Rajpootana, a town, with bazar, on the route from Delhi to Neemuch, 192 miles S.W. of former, 180 N.E. of latter. Lat. 26° 34′, long. 75° 38′.

PHAJUDEE.—A town in the native state of Bhotan, situate on the right bank of a branch of the Guddada river, and 68 miles N.E. by E. from Darjeeling. Lat. 27° 29′, long. 89° 19′.

PHALGU, or PHALGOO, in the British district of Behar, presidency of Bengal, a vast torrent, formed by the junction of two great mountain-streams, the Mehanee and Lilajun, which, rising in the British district of Ramgurh, flow northward, and making their way through the mountains on the south frontier of Behar, flow through this latter district in a northerly direction. From the junction near Gayah, and about lat. 24° 44′, long. 85° 8′, it has an enormous volume of water during the rainy season in the latter part of summer, when it rushes down with great violence and rapidity, filling its channel, from 500 to 800 yards wide, bounded on each side by high and rocky banks. It thence proceeds first through Behar, and finally through Patna, in a course a little east of north, to lat. 25° 25′, long. 85° 30′, where, about 180 miles from its remotest source, it takes an easterly direction, which it generally holds to its fall into the Ganges, on the right side, in lat. 25° 11′, long. 86° 10′, having flowed a total distance of about 246 miles. It sends forth a great number of branches right and left, so that during the rainy season its ramifications everywhere intersect the country, and partially lay it under water. In the lower parts of its course, it bears the name of Mehanee, in the higher parts, Julwara and Kuthor; that of Phulgoo being confined to the middle portion, extending about twenty-five miles, and considered sacred, from its vicinity to Gayah.

PHALIAH, in the Jetch Dooab division of the Punjab, a town situate six miles N. of the right bank of the Chenaub, 73 miles N.W. of the town of Lahore. Lat. 32° 27′, long. 73° 38′.

PHAPAMOW, in the British district of Allahabad, lieut.-gov. of the N.W. Provinces, a town on a small eminence on the left bank of the Ganges, the bed of which is here a mile and a half wide, the stream during the dry season occupying one-sixth of this space. It is on the route from the cantonment of Allahabad to that of Lucknow, and four miles N. of the former. Distance by river, N. from Allahabad, seven miles; N.W. from Calcutta 815. This place is stated to have been selected for the location of the government powder-manufactory. Lat. 25° 32′, long. 81° 56′.

PHENA, in the British district of Bijnour, lieut.-gov. of the N.W. Provinces, a village on the route from the town of Moradabad to that of Mozuffurnuggur, and 34 miles N.W. of the former place. Distant N.W. from Calcutta 922 miles. Lat. 29° 5′, long. 78° 25′.

PHENCHOOGUNJE.—A town in the British district of Silhet, lieut.-gov. of Bengal, 16 miles S.S.E. of Silhet. Lat. 24° 41′, long. 91° 57′.

PHILLOUR, in the Julinder Dooab, a division of the Punjab, a town situate on the right bank of the Sutlej, eight miles N.N.W. of the town of Loodianah. Lat. 31° 1′, long. 75° 50′.

PHIRANDEE.—A town in the native state of Cutch, 22 miles S. from Bhooj, and 18 miles E.N.E. from Mandavee. Lat. 22° 57′, long. 69° 40′.

PHITTI, or PITTY RIVER.—One of the largest, deepest, and best-defined of the mouths of the Indus, and generally frequented by the Indus steamers to and from Kurrachee. On the south side of the entrance, two flagstaff beacons have recently been erected, which may be seen in the offing six or seven miles. The mouth of the Phitti is in lat. 24° 42′, long. 67° 12′.

PHOAH.—A town in the British district of Umballa, in the Cis-Sutlej territory, 32 miles S. by W. of Umballa. Lat. 29° 58′, long. 76° 40′.

PHOBOOM.—A town in the British district of Amherst, one of the Tenasserim provinces, 32 miles S.E. by E. of Moulmein. Lat. 16° 12′, long. 98° 6′.

PHOOKANUH, in the British district of Muzuffurnugur, lieut.-gov. of the N.W. Provinces, a town on the route from Muzuffurnugur to Rohtuk, 22 miles W.S.W. of the former. Lat. 29° 19′, long. 77° 29′.

PHOOL, in Sirhind, a town forty-eight miles from the left bank of the Sutlej, and on the route from Delhi to Ferozepore by Munuk. It forms part of the possessions of a Sikh chief under British protection and control. Distant N.W. from Calcutta, by Delhi and Munuk, 1,045 miles. Lat. 30° 22′, long. 75° 14′.

PHOOLGHUR.—A small raj under the superintendence of the political agent for the south-west frontier of Bengal. Its central point is in lat. 21° 15′, long. 83°; the area is 890 square miles. Great part of the country is flat, but there is a portion considerably elevated, which enjoys the advantage of a cool temperature. The soil throughout is rich, and adapted for successful cultivation; but little is reported to be done to improve its capabilities, and herds of wild buffaloes overrun the neglected territory. The administration of the government was found to be such as might be expected from the idle and lawless character of the people, and security for life or property to be unknown. The country has been computed to produce a revenue of 6,000 rupeees; the amount of the tribute is trifling. The post road from Bombay to Raepore traverses this district for some distance; and in consideration, a deduction of eighty rupees is made from the tribute. The population is estimated at 40,000.

PHOOLMURRY, in Hyderabad, or territory of the Nizam, a town near the north-west frontier, towards the British district Ahmednugur. It is situate on the upper part of the river Gurka Poornah, a considerable tributary of the Godavery. The situation is pleasant, amidst groves of mango-trees, tamarinds, and cocoanut-trees. It is surrounded by a wall, flanked with towers of masonry in stone, and is the residence of a petty nawaub, or, more properly, jaghiredar. Distance from Aurungabad, N., 20 miles; Hyderabad, N.W., 280. Lat. 20° 9′, long. 75° 28′.

PHOOLPOOR, in the British district of Allahabad, lieut.-gov. of the N.W. Provinces, a town on the route from the city of Allahabad to Jounpoor, and 19 miles N.E. of the former. It is situate twelve miles from the left bank of the Ganges, and on the right bank of the small river of the same name. It has a bazar, and is supplied with water from a tank and wells. Lat. 25° 33′, long. 82° 9′.

PHOOLREYEE, in the British district of Etawa, lieut.-gov. of the N.W. Provinces, a village on the route from the cantonment of Agra to that of Etawa, and 14 miles N.W. of the latter. Lat. 26° 56′, long. 78° 55′.

PHOOLTAMBA.—A town in the British district of Ahmednuggur, presidency of Bombay, 50 miles N. of Ahmednuggur. Lat. 19° 48′, long. 74° 40′.

PHOOLTULA.—A town in the British district of Jessore, lieut.-gov. of Bengal, 68 miles E.N.E. of Calcutta. Lat. 23°, long. 89° 24′.

PHOOLWAREE.—A town in the British district of Patna, lieut.-gov. of Bengal, nine miles W.S.W. of Patna. Lat. 25° 30′, long. 85° 8′.

PHOONDA.—A town and pass in the native state of Kolapoor, presidency of Bombay, leading to Viziadroog, in the British district Rutnageriah, distant 34 miles S.W. from Kolapoor. Lat. 16° 22′, long. 73° 57′.

PHOONDI, or COONDEE RIVER.—One of the mouths of the Indus, having five feet at low water. "This stream communicates with the Buggaur, and, during the swell of the Indus, discharges fresh water. People are here employed in pearl fishing." The mouth of the Phoondee is in lat. 24° 38′, long. 67° 13′.

PHUGWARA, in the Julinder Dooab division of the Punjab, a town situated 15 miles N. from the right bank of the Sutlej, 14 miles E.S.E. of the town of Julinder. Lat. 31° 14′, long. 75° 45′.

PHULOWDEE, in the Rajpoot state of

Jodhpoor, a town on the route from Beekaneer to Balmeer, and 147 miles N.E. of the latter. It is built on a rising ground, and appears to have been once surrounded by a wall, of which a ruinous portion remains on the southern side of the town. The number of houses is nearly 3,000. The road in this part of the route is good, lying among scanty cultivation and thin jungle. Distant N.W. from Calcutta, by Agra, Nusseerabad, and Nagor, 1,180 miles. Lat. 27° 8′, long. 72° 28′.

PHULSOOND, in the Rajpoot state of Jodhpoor, a town in the depressed tract near the south-west frontier. Lat. 26° 24′, long. 71° 57′.

PHULTUN.—A town in the Sattara jaghire of Phultun, 56 miles S.E. from Poonah, and 37 miles N.E. from Sattara. Lat. 17° 59′, long. 74° 31′.

PHULUNG.—A town in the native state of Bhotan, situate on the left bank of a branch of the Monas river, and 87 miles N.W. by N. from Durrung. Lat. 27° 28′, long. 91° 20′.

PHUMARA.—A town of Sinde, within the territory of Ali Moorad, situate on the right bank of the Naroo river, and 32 miles S.S.E. from Khyrpoor. Lat. 27° 10′, long. 69° 1′.

PHURSABAHA.—A town in the native state of Jushpoor, on the south-west frontier of Bengal, 73 miles N.N.W. from Sumbulpoor, and 102 miles S. by W. from Palamow. Lat. 22° 25′, long. 83° 32′.

PHURSOO, in the territory of Bhurtpore, a village on the route from Agra to Ajmeer, 45 miles W. of the former, 183 E. of the latter. It is situate on the Bangunga, which, in the periodical rains, is a brisk stream; but when Heber visited the place in the middle of January, its course was indicated merely by a dry sandy channel. "The village contains a fortified house of the rajah's, now empty and ruinous, but built in by no means a bad taste, and having its surrounding court ornamented with a range of handsome stone cloisters, lining the inside of the mud rampart." The surrounding country, though naturally of little fertility, is indefatigably irrigated with water drawn from wells, and is richly cultivated under grain-crops. Lat. 27° 3′, long. 77° 23′.

PHYRIA. — A town in Nepal, 37 miles N.E. from Khatmandoo, and 134 miles N. by W. from Durbunga. Lat. 28° 3′, long. 85° 45′.

PICHAOUREE, in the British district of Muttra, lieut.-gov. of the N.W. Provinces, a small town or village on the route by Muhabun from the city of Agra to the cantonment of Muttra, and 17 miles S.E. of the latter. Lat. 27° 23′, long. 77° 59′.

PICHORE, in the territory of Gwalior, a town near the S.E. frontier, towards Dutteah. According to the description of Tieffenthaler, about a century ago, here was a large fort of masonry, with three gates, battlements, and towers, and situate on a rocky eminence, the town lying below it. The rajah, a Jat, formerly possessed territories in the vicinity of Gwalior yielding an annual revenue of from 33,000*l.* to 40,000*l.*; but they were wrested from the family by Scindia, who left it no more than a jaghire or feudal grant of 1,500*l.* annually. In consequence of the high lineage of the jaghiredar, his daughter was in 1832 married to Bulwunt Singh, son and heir of Baldeo Singh, rajah of Bhurtpore. Pichore is 25 miles S.E. of Gwalior, 85 W. of Calpee. Lat. 25° 57′, long. 78° 30′.

PICKALOW.—A town in the British district of Cuttack, lieut.-gov. of Bengal, 18 miles E. by N. of Cuttack. Lat. 20° 30′, long. 86° 11′.

PILAKOOND, in the British district of Moradabad, lieut.-gov. of the N.W. Provinces, a village on the route from the town of Moradabad to that of Mozuffernuggur, and 26 miles N.W. of the former place. Distant N.W. from Calcutta 914 miles. Lat. 28° 59′ long. 78° 30′.

PILLEEBHEET.—A town, the principal place of the pergunnah of the same name, in the British district of Bareilly, lieut.-gov. of the N.W. Provinces. It is situate on the left bank of the river Gurrah, the bed of which is here 250 yards wide; but the stream in the dry season, from December to June, so shallow as to be fordable, though at other times passable only by ferry. The town is of considerable extent, and the route from Bareilly to Petoragah passes through it. The population was officially returned in 1853 at 26,760. Pilleebheet is the mart of a considerable traffic, by which timber, pitch, wax, honey, wool, borax, metals of various kinds, and other produce of the Terai, or marshy forest of Kumaon, and of Chinese Tartary, are exchanged for goods furnished from the plains. The Pilleebheet rice, much prized throughout India for its whiteness, firmness, and fine flavour, is produced in the south of Kumaon, in the fertile valley down which the Kosilla flows to the plain, and has received the name by which it is generally known in commerce, in consequence of being brought to market here. Elevation above the sea 517 feet; distance N.W. from Calcutta 802 miles. Lat. 28° 38′, long. 79° 52′. The territorial division of which this town is the principal place formerly constituted a separate district: it is now incorporated with the district of Bareilly.

PILLITCH.—A town in the British district of Patna, lieut.-gov. of Bengal, 28 miles S.S.E. of Patna. Lat. 25° 12′, long. 85° 27′.

PILOWDA, in the Rajpoot territory of Jeypore, a town on the route from Agra to Kotah, 90 miles S.W. of former, 130 N.E. of latter. According to Thorn, it is a large town, built on the side of a hill. It is stated to have 1,000 houses; an amount which would assign it about 5,000 inhabitants. Lat. 26° 37′, long. 76° 53′.

PIM RIVER.—See PEENOO.

PIMPULGAUM.—A town in the British district of Ahmednuggur, presidency of Bombay, 17 miles N.E. of Nassick. Lat. 20° 10′, long. 73° 59′.

PIMPULNEIR.—A town in the British district of Candeish, presidency of Bombay, 39 miles N.W. of Malligaum. Lat. 20° 55′, long. 74° 4′.

PINAHT, or PINNAHUT, in the British district of Agra, lieut.-gov. of the N.W. Provinces, a town which with Bah gives name to the pergunnah of Bah Pinnahut. It is situate two miles from the left bank of the Chumbul, 30 miles S.E. of Agra, and contains a population of 7,047 inhabitants. Lat. 26° 51′, long. 78° 28′.

PINAYA.—A town within the dominions of Gholab Singh, the ruler of Cashmere, 70 miles S.S.W. from Sirinagur, and 112 miles N. by E. from Lahore. Lat. 33° 11′, long. 74° 25′.

PIND DADUN KHAN, in the Punjab, a town lying near the right or western bank of the Jhelum, from which it is separated by a narrow verdant plain. It consists of three small collections of houses, situate close to each other, and about four miles from the river. The houses are built of mud, with a framework of deodar or cedar, the materials for which are floated down the river from the mountains to the north. Pind Dadun is a short distance south of the Salt range, and salt is raised in the vicinity for the supply of a great part of the Punjab. Population 13,588. Lat. 32° 36′, long. 73° 5′.

PINDEE PUTHAN, in the Reechna Dooab division of the Punjab, a town situated six miles from the left bank of the Chenaub, 71 miles N.W. by W. of the town of Lahore. Lat. 32°, long. 73° 16′.

PIND MULIK ONLEA, in the Sinde Sagur Dooab division of the Punjab, a town situated 10 miles S.E. from the left bank of the Indus, 54 miles S.E. by S. of the town of Peshawur. Lat. 33° 14′, long. 72° 8′.

PINDRAEE, in the British territory of Saugur and Nerbudda, lieut.-gov. of the N.W. Provinces, a town on the route from Jubbulpoor to the territory of Nagpore, 45 miles S.E. by S. of the former. Lat. 22° 34′, long. 80° 17′.

PINDUR.—A river rising in the British district of Kumaon, in lat. 30° 19′, long. 80° 6′, from three snow-beds on the western declivity of a summit of the Himalaya, having an elevation of 22,491 feet. It takes a course generally south-west for forty-five miles, to Chiringa, where it turns north-westward, flowing in that direction thirty miles, to Kurnprag, in lat. 30° 15′, long. 79° 16′, where it joins the Aluknunda.

PINGERI, in the British district of Agra, lieut.-gov. of the N.W. Provinces, a village on the route from the city of Agra to that of Muttra, and 19 miles N.W. of the former. Lat. 27° 17′, long. 77° 53′.

PINJOR, on the north-eastern boundary of Sirhind, a small ruined town belonging to the rajah of Putteeala, is situate at the confluence of two feeders of the river Gagur. The rajah has here a residence and pleasure-ground, which cannot be better described than in the language of an intelligent visitor:—"We next proceeded to a most delightful place. It is a garden, which has been laid out on the natural slope of the ground in six separate and successive terraces, one below another." It contains about sixty acres, is well stocked with trees, bearing the mango, orange, pomegranate, apple, and some other fruits. The fort of this place was dismantled by Bourquin, a French adventurer in the service of Doulut Rao Scindia. The inhabitants of Pinjor at present are few; but the care displayed in the construction and embellishment of a large baoli or well, and the numerous fragments of Hindoo sculpture and architecture scattered about, bear evidence of former populousness and wealth. Pinjor gives name to a valley or doon teeming with vegetable and animal life. The town is distant N.W. from Calcutta, *viâ* Kurnaul and Umballah, 1,053 miles. Lat. 30° 48′, long. 76° 59′.

PINYAREE, in Sinde, a great branch of the Indus, parting from the main stream on the eastern or left side, at Bunna, in lat. 25° 2′, long. 68° 22′. A little below this place Burnes found the channel of the Pinyaree, during the low season, to be a mile broad, with a large sandbank in the middle. It is navigable downwards as far as Mughribee, where a bund or dam, forty feet broad, was thrown across it by one of the ameers in 1799. At Mughribee this great watercourse is called the Goongroo. Below this dam it is navigable southwards to the Seer mouth, in lat. 23° 41′, long. 78° 11′, at which it is two miles wide.

PIPCHA, or BARDAN PIPCHA.—A town within the dominions of Gholab Singh, the ruler of Cashmere, 124 miles E.S.E. from Sirinagur, and 105 miles N.N.E. from Kangra. Lat. 33° 25′, long. 77° 1′.

PIPELI, in the British district of Bijnour, lieut.-gov. of the N.W. Provinces, a village on the route from Moradabad to Mozuffurnuggur, and 44 miles N.W. of the former. It is situate in an open country, partially cultivated, and from which water and considerable supplies can be obtained. Distant N.W. from Calcutta 932 miles. Lat. 29° 11′, long. 78° 17′.

PIPERA, in Bundelcund, a town situate in the petty raj of Bijawur, on the right bank of the river Dhasan, 90 miles S.W. of Banda. Lat. 24° 46′, long. 79° 24′.

PIPEREAH, in Bundelcund, a ghat or pass by which the route from Banda to Jubbulpore ascends from the more depressed tract of Lobarganow to the plateau on the range called by Franklin the Bandair Hills. It is 105 miles S. of Banda, 90 N.E. of Jubbulpore; and is steep, but neither long nor very difficult. About two miles from the pass, the Cane rolls over the rocky brow of the mountain, and forms the falls of Pipereah. "They are well worthy the notice of the passing stranger, on account of the singular forms presented by the rock, which receives the river and conceals its course for many miles." Lat. 24° 15′, long. 80° 23′.

PIPERENDA, in the British district of Banda, lieut.-gov. of the N.W. Provinces, a small town on the route from Cawnpore, by Chila Tara Ghat, to the town of Banda, 10 miles N. of the latter. It has a bazar and abundance of water. Lat. 25° 38′, long. 80° 28′.

PIPLAYE, in the Rajpoot state of Jeypore, a considerable walled town with fort, situate in an extensive sandy plain 55 miles S.E. of the town of Jeypore. Lat. 26° 31′, long. 76° 35′.

PIPRAGANOW, in the British district of Mirzapoor, lieut.-gov. of the N.W. Provinces, a village on the right bank of the Ganges, three miles N. of the city of Mirzapoor, or lower down the stream; 718 N.W. of Calcutta by the stream. Lat. 25° 12′, long. 82° 39′.

PIPRAH, in the district of Sultanpoor, territory of Oude, a town 80 miles S.E. of Lucknow. It is situate in a dense jungle. Distant N. from Gonda eight miles. Lat. 26° 6′, long. 82° 4′.

PIPRA KHAS.—See PEEPRAICH.

PIPROWL, in the British district of Budaon, lieut.-gov. of the N.W. Provinces, a ferry over the Ganges, on the route from Agra to Bareilly, and 81 miles N.W. of the former. The stream of the Ganges being in some seasons divided into several branches at the ferry of Keuchla Ghat, four miles below Piprowl, the passage is then found preferable at the latter. Piprowl is in lat. 27° 57′, long. 78° 55′.

PIPUREAH, in the British district of Shahjehanpore, lieut.-gov. of the N.W. Provinces, a village on the route from Pilleebheet to Oude, and 35 miles S.E. of the former. Lat. 28° 20′, long. 80° 14′.

PIRII.—A town in Nepal, 53 miles E. by S. from Khatmandoo, and 103 miles N. from Durbunga. Lat. 27° 37′, long. 86° 9′.

PIRKEE, in the British district of Sohagpoor, territory of Saugor and Nerbudda, lieut.-gov. of the N.W. Provinces, a town on the route from Sohagpoor to Ruttunpoor, 44 miles S.E. by S. of the former. Lat. 22° 47′, long. 81° 48′.

PIRNAGAR, in the territory of Oude, a village on the route from Lucknow to Seetapoor, 37 miles N. of the former, 14 S. of the latter. It has a small bazar, and is well provided with water. Lat. 27° 23′, long. 80° 45′.

PIR PANJAL, or the SAINT'S MOUNTAIN, a lofty range, forming part of the south-west boundary of Cashmere, and separating it from the Punjab. Its general direction is from north-west to south-east; its length, from the Baramula Pass, at the former extremity, to the Pir Panjal Pass, or that of Nandan Sar, at the latter, is about forty miles. Its highest point is supposed to be about in lat. 33° 40′, and is estimated to be 15,000 feet above the sea. According to Vigne, the highest part is basaltic, consisting of amygdaloidal trap, which has upheaved; transition rocks appearing on its borders. Quartz, slate, and other primary formations are observable on the northern or Cashmere side. At the south-western extremity is the pass, generally called the Pir Panjal Pass, or that of Nandan Sar, from a lake of that name near its northern extremity. It is about 12,000 feet high, and though devoid of trees, is below the limit of perpetual congelation. The name of Pir Panjal, or the Pir's Mountain, has been given, from one of its summits being the residence of a *Pir*, or Mahometan saint, who gives benedictions to those who travel over the pass, and also supplies them with refreshments. This pass, though so elevated, must remain open to a late period in the year, as Von Hügel traversed it in the middle of November, with a numerous train of porters and other attendants from the plain.

PIR PANJAL, a river in Gholab Singh's territory, rises in lat. 33° 30′, long. 74° 43′, and, flowing first north-westerly for forty-five miles, and subsequently south-westerly for sixty-three miles, falls into the Jhelum, in lat. 33° 16′, long. 73° 38′.

PIRTHULUH, in the jaghire of Bulubgurh, lieut.-gov. of the N.W. Provinces, a village on the route from Delhi to Muttra, and 34 miles S. of the former. Lat. 28° 13′, long. 77° 21′.

PISEENY.—A town in Hyderabad, or territory of the Nizam, 144 miles N.N.W. from Hyderabad, and 128 miles S. by E. from Ellichpoor. Lat. 19° 24′, long. 78° 3′.

PITLAUD, or PITLAWUD, in the territory of Indore, or possessions of Holkar's family, a town in the jaghire or feudal grant of the chief of Jabooa, on the route from Neemuch to Baroda, 117 miles S. of former, 150 N.E. of latter. Lat. 23°, long. 74° 52′.

PITLAUD.—A town in the British district of Kaira, presidency of Bombay, 42 miles S.S.E. of Ahmedabad. Lat. 22° 27′, long. 72° 50′.

PITORIA, in the British district of Saugur territory of Saugor and Nerbudda, lieut.-gov.

of the N.W. Provinces, a town on the route from Saugur to Narwar, 21 miles N.W. of the former. Lat. 24° 3′, long. 78° 37′.

PITTY RIVER.—See PHITTI.

PLASSEE, in the hill state of Hindoor, a small town on the route from Roopur to Belaspoor, and 10 miles N.E. of the former place. It is situate on the right bank of the Sursa, a small river discharging the waters of the Pinjor Doon into the Sutlej. Here, at the close of October, 1814, the British army under General Ochterlony took post on the advance against the Goorkha garrison in Malown. Distant N.W. from Calcutta 1,080 miles. Lat. 31° 2′, long. 76° 44′.

PLASSEY.—A town in the British district of Purneah, lieut.-gov. of Bengal, 39 miles S.E. by E. of Purneah. Lat. 25° 27′, long. 88° 2′.

PLASSY, in the British district of Nuddea, lieut.-gov. of Bengal, a town on the left bank of the Hooghly, or rather, perhaps, the Bhagruttee, and on the route from Calcutta to Berhampore, 96 miles N. of the former, 22 S. of the latter. It was here, on the 23rd June, 1757, that the memorable battle was fought between Clive and Sooraj-oo-Dowlah, soubahdar of Bengal, which ended in the total defeat of the latter. The day before the battle, a council of war had been held by the English commander, which decided against hazarding a conflict. This decision, however, Clive, although he had concurred in it, and had been even the first to deliver an opinion in its favour, resolved, after some deliberation, to set at nought; and, acting on this impression, he gave orders for crossing the river which interposed between his army and the enemy. The English force consisted of about 650 European infantry, 150 artillerymen (including fifty seamen), 2,100 sepoys, and a small number of Portuguese, making a total of somewhat more than 3,000 men, with eight six-pounders and one or two howitzers. The soubahdar's force consisted of 18,000 cavalry and 50,000 infantry, forty or fifty French artillerymen, with fifty pieces of cannon of heavy calibre, and four pieces of light artillery. Clive had been in negotiation with Meer Jaffier, a distinguished commander in the service of Sooraj-oo-Dowlah, who aspired to supplant his master, and a treaty had been concluded with this personage, which was to give effect to his wish. The co-operation of Meer Jaffier was consequently to be looked for, and warlike operations had been commenced in the anticipation of receiving it. Still the general character of native diplomacy, and the individual character of Meer Jaffier, forbade implicit reliance upon his fidelity to his engagements, and down to a late period in the day on which the battle took place, Clive remained in a state of much doubt and anxiety. At daybreak, the army of Sooraj-oo-Dowlah was discovered in motion. The cavalry and infantry were disposed in columns of 4,000 or 5,000 each, and between them were placed portions of the artillery. They marched as if intending to surround the English force as far as the river would permit; but as soon as their rear was clear of the camp, they halted, and the Frenchmen, under an officer named Sinfray, advanced with some guns. A general cannonading commenced from the soubahdar's artillery. This was felt severely by the English, who had quitted a grove in which they had taken their first position, and where they were sheltered by a bank, in front of which they were subsequently drawn up. Clive, on the enemy's guns becoming annoying, withdrew his troops to their former position behind the bank. The enemy thereupon advanced their heavy artillery nearer, and fired with greater rapidity than before, but they produced little effect, the English troops escaping the shots by sitting down under cover of the bank. About noon, a heavy shower so much damaged the enemy's powder, that their fire became feeble; but the English, who throughout the day answered the enemy's guns with their field-pieces, continued firing without interruption. The death of Moodeen Khan, an able and faithful officer of the soubahdar, who fell by a cannon-ball, afforded opportunity for the train laid by Clive to take effect. Upon the occurrence of this disastrous event, the soubahdar, a weak and capricious man, sent for Meer Jaffier, with whom he had been on bad terms, and whose fidelity he strongly suspected, and in almost abject terms conjured him to forget all past differences, and to devote all his energies to the defence of the throne. Meer Jaffier readily promised all that was required of him, and the first instance given of his sincerity was to recommend a suspension of the conflict till the following morning. The soubahdar, after some objection, yielded, and consented to the withdrawal of the troops. A letter was addressed by Meer Jaffier to Clive, intimating this arrangement, and urging the English commander to push on for the camp; but the communication miscarried, and Clive was left to act upon his own impression, derived from appearances. These satisfied him that Meer Jaffier meant to adhere to the English; and with characteristic energy and promptness, he spontaneously took the step which it was the object of the latter to suggest. The result was a general rout of the army of Sooraj-oo-Dowlah, whose camp, baggage, and artillery fell into the hands of the British. The enemy were pursued for about six miles, and it is supposed lost in the action, and during the pursuit, 500 or 600 men: the loss of the English in killed and wounded was about seventy. The immediate effect of this memorable battle was the transfer of the soubahdarship of Bengal from Sooraj-oo-Dowlah to Meer Jaffier; but its eventual consequences were much more important, seeing that in this victory was laid the foundation of the magnificent fabric of the British empire in India. Lat. 23° 46′, long. 88° 15′.

PODANGMEW.—A town of Eastern India, in the British province of Pegu, situate on the right bank of the Irawady river, and nine miles S.W. from Promo. Lat. 18° 41′, long. 94° 58′.

PODYCHAID.—A town in Hyderabad, or territory of the Nizam, 51 miles E. from Hyderabad, and 110 miles N.W. from Guntoor. Lat. 17° 23′, long. 79° 19′.

POGULAPULLY.—A town in Hyderabad, or territory of the Nizam, six miles from the right bank of the Godavery river, and 161 miles E. by N. from Hyderabad. Lat. 17° 33′, long. 80° 58′.

POHONEE, in the territory of Nagpoor, a town on the right or west bank of the Weingunga. After the fall of Apa Sahib, the rajah of Nagpoor, in A.D. 1818, it was occupied by a British force, but subsequently restored to his successor, with whom it remained till the lapse of the territory to the British government. Distance from the city of Nagpoor, S.E., 45 miles. Lat. 20° 47′, long. 79° 42′.

POHOOJ, a small river of Bundelcund, rises from a small lake near the south-west boundary, towards Gwalior, 20 miles S.W. of Jhansi, and in lat. 25° 18′, long. 78° 25′. It holds a course sinuous, but generally north-east, for 125 miles, and falls into the Sinde, on the right side, in lat. 26° 25′, long. 79° 13′. It is crossed by ford on the route from Calpee to Gwalior, ninety five miles from its source, and in lat. 26° 6′, long. 79° 5′.

POHUR.—A town in one of the sequestrated districts of Hyderabad, or dominions of the Nizam, 72 miles W.S.W. from Ellichpoor. Lat. 20° 46′, long. 76° 35′.

POKHURN, in the Rajpoot state of Jodhpoor, a town on the route from Phulodi to Jessulmere, and 66 miles E. of the latter. It is situate close to a deserted town of the same name, and contains 3,000 houses, surrounded by a good wall of uncemented stone, and about fifteen feet high, including a parapet six feet high and two and half feet thick. A very conspicuous temple, in an elevated situation, marks the site of the old deserted city, and near it are the monuments of the deceased members of the chief's family. Pokhurn being on one of the great commercial tracks between Eastern Rajpootana and Sinde, much money is realized by the transit-trade. The country also in its immediate neighbourhood is more fertile than in the generality of Jodhpoor. It is one of the greatest fiefs in Jodhpoor, the thakoor or chief having an annual revenue of 10,000*l.*; though it was formerly three times that amount, until reduced by the seizure of the greater part by the maharajah of Jodhpoor. Distant S.W. from Nagore 134 miles; W. from Nusserabad, by Nagore, 228. Lat. 26° 54′, long. 72°.

POKREE, in the British district of Kumaon, lieut. gov. of the N.W. Provinces, a village situate on the western declivity of a mountain covered with forests of oak, rhododendrons, and pines. Here are copper-mines, once so productive that one is represented to have yielded a return valued at 5,000*l.* per annum; but experiments recently conducted there under European management, afforded a return of 780 rupees, against an expenditure of 8,164 rupees; and the undertaking was consequently abandoned in 1841. The richest ore is the vitreous, lying in dolomite or talcose schist, and yielding about twenty per cent. The main obstacles met with in the working are the great quantity of water and the rottenness of the ground, which requires continual and strong timbering. The village of Pokree, situate in a ravine furrowing the mountain on the west side, contains about 100 inhabitants, chiefly of the Chowdry or mining caste. Its elevation is 3,800 feet above the river Aluknunda, from which it is nine miles west, and 6,100 feet above the sea. Lat. 30° 20′, long. 79° 15′.

POKROURA, in the British district of Kumaon, lieut.-gov. of the N.W. Provinces, a village on the route from Pethoraguih to Askoth, seven miles N. of the former. Lat. 29° 41′, long. 80° 16′.

POKRUN.—See POKHURN.

POKUR, in the British district of Ajmere, under the lieut.-gov. of the N.W. Provinces, a town, the principal place of a pergunnah of the same name. It is situate in a low and swampy valley, and on the south margin of a lake, stated to be in Brahminical eyes the most sacred in India. The surrounding scenery is picturesque and striking. Immediately around the town are numerous sandhills, among which are many shrines and cenotaphs, belonging to the families of various rajahs and great men of India, in various styles of architecture. By far the most conspicuous is the shrine of Brahma; of which Tod says:—"This is the sole tabernacle dedicated to the ONE GOD which I ever saw or have heard of in India." The same writer mentions, that it struck him "as not a little curious," and well it might, "that the sikra or pinnacle is surmounted by a cross. The edifice was erected a few years ago, by a wealthy Mahratta, Gocul Pauk, minister of Scindia, at a cost of about 15,000*l.*, though the materials were at hand, and the labour could be got almost for nothing." Ghats or flights of stairs of stone give access to the sacred water, which is frequented every full moon by great numbers of pilgrims, for the purpose of ritual ablution. The full moon in October is regarded to have peculiar sanctity, and then the concourse is much the greatest: a fair for traffic in horses, camels, and kine, as well as for various wares, is held there on that occasion. The lake is asserted to be artificial, and to have been excavated by a prince of Mandor, to receive the water of a natural fountain, by which it is still replenished: the rivers Looni and Sarasvati carry off the redundant water. The lake is of an oval shape, and above a mile in circuit: it is deep, and never dries up: many alligators harbour in it, and are protected from any molestation. The town, situate on the south margin of the lake, has many good houses. According to Heber, this place "is renowned for its gardens and vineyards: the grapes are said to be by far the best and largest in India, and equal to those of Shiraz." Distance from Ajmer, N.W., five miles. Lat. 26° 30′, long. 74° 40′.

POLACHY.—A town in the British district of Coimbatoor, presidency of Madras, 26 miles S. of Coimbatoor. Lat. 10° 39′, long. 77° 4′.

POLAIR.—A town in the hill zemindarry of Jeypoor, presidency of Madras, 61 miles S. from Jeypoor, and 74 miles W.N.W. from Vizagapatam. Lat. 18° 10′, long. 82° 20′.

POLAWURUM.—A town in the British district of Rajahmundry, presidency of Madras, 23 miles N.N.W. of Rajahmundry. Lat. 17° 16′, long. 81° 41′.

POLE.—A town in Guzerat, or dominions of the Guicowar, 81 miles E. by S. from Deesa, and 83 miles N.E. by N. from Ahmedabad. Lat. 23° 59′, long. 73° 20′.

POLEKUL.—A town in the British district of Bellary, presidency of Madras, 72 miles N.E. of Bellary. Lat. 15° 50′, long. 77° 46′.

POLENSHAW, in Hyderabad, or the territory of the Nizam, a town, with a fort, 13 miles from the right bank of the river Godavery. It is situate in a verdant fertile valley, about four miles wide, which is surrounded on all sides by lofty ranges of hills. The residence of the rajah is a small house, the top of which is visible above the rampart. He is called not only rajah of Polenshaw, but also the rajah of Kammummett, from a considerable town of that name within his zemindarry or feudal grant. Distance from Hyderabad, E., 150 miles. Lat. 17° 35′, long. 80° 45′.

POLLASURRA.—A town in the British district of Ganjam, presidency of Madras, 27 miles N.W. by N. of Ganjam. Lat. 19° 41′, long. 84° 53′.

POLLIAM.—A town in Hyderabad, or territory of the Nizam, situate on the right bank of the Godavery river, and 154 miles N.W. from Hyderabad. Lat. 19° 1′, long. 77° 1′.

POLLOOR.—A town in the British district of North Arcot, presidency of Madras, 33 miles S.W. of Arcot. Lat. 12° 31′, long. 79° 10′.

POLY.—A town in the British district of Cuddapah, presidency of Madras, 31 miles S.E. by E. of Cuddapah. Lat. 14° 14′, long. 79° 15′.

POMOORNA.—A town in the lapsed territory of Nagpoor, situate nine miles from the right bank of the Wein Gunga river, and 95 miles S.S.E. from Nagpoor. Lat. 19° 53′, long. 79° 40′.

PONANY, in the British district of Malabar, presidency of Madras, a seaport town situate on the south side of an estuary of a river of the same name, close to its entrance into the Arabian Sea. The river is shoal, and navigable only for small craft, and three or four miles to sea is a shoal with about four fathoms water on it, but inside, and between it and the mainland, having anchorage in six fathoms. The town is built in a straggling manner, on a sandy plain, and is inhabited principally by Mussulmans, who have forty mosques, and are governed by a chief priest called the Tangul. The population is supported by fishing and by trade, having numerous patemars or sea-going boats, which ply to Surat, Arabia, Bombay, Madras, and even as far as Bengal, exporting principally pepper, betel, rice, cocoanuts, iron, and very fine timber, sent down the river from the Ghats. The imports are wheat, sugarcane, molasses, oilseeds, groceries, and spices. Salt is also imported, though in the vicinity there is some made by evaporating sea-water. At the commencement of this century, when Buchanan visited this place, it had about 500 good houses, built with stone, and two stories high, and 1,000 huts. It had formerly been a much more considerable place, until nearly ruined by the oppression of Tippoo Sultan. Besides the patemars, there are manches, large rowboats, used for navigating the river and for coasting. They are about fifty feet long, ten or twelve wide, and five or six deep, and carry sail at sea. They are rudely constructed, and venture to sea only in fine weather. Under the system of railways by which the Madras territories are about to be traversed, the eastern and western coasts of this part of the peninsula will be united by means of a line from Ponany to the city of Madras. Distance from Bombay, S.E., 600 miles; Mangalore, S.E., 160; Calicut, S.E., 34; Bangalore, S.W., 190. Lat. 10° 48′, long. 75° 58′.

PONANY.—A river, named from the town situate on the south side of its estuary, where it disembogues into the Arabian Sea. It rises in the British district Coimbatoor, in the vicinity of some tanks near Cootichipaitum, and in lat. 10° 19′, long. 77° 6′, and flowing north-west, through the great depression separating the Western Ghauts from the mountains in the vicinity of Cape Comorin, crosses the east boundary of the British district of Malabar in lat. 10° 42′, long. 76° 46′, and about fifty-five miles from its source. Thereabouts turning west, it flows by the fort and town of Palghat, and continuing to hold the same direction for twenty-five miles, it in lat. 10° 45′, long. 76° 32′, becomes the boundary between the raj or territory of Cochin and the British district of Malabar, continuing so for twenty-three miles, to lat. 10° 47′, long. 76° 15′, where it enters the district, and flows westward through it for twenty-five miles, to the fall into the Arabian Sea, in lat. 10° 47′, long. 75° 58′; the total length of the course being 128 miles. It is navigable for canoes as high up as Palghat, sixty-three miles from the sea. Buchanan, who crossed it during the dry season five or six miles above its mouth, found the channel very wide, but most of it occupied by dry sands, the water clear, the stream gentle, but with difficulty fordable, on account of the depth. It can be navigated only by small craft, as well on account of a bar with small depth of water at the mouth, as shoal water inside, but is very useful during the monsoons, when it floats down to the coast great quantities of fine timber, highly valuable for the largest ships of war.

PONASSA, or POMAWA, in the Rajpoot state of Jodhpoor, a village on the route from Nusseerabad to Deesa, and 157 miles S.W. of the former. Lat. 25° 2′, long. 73° 4′.

PONDA.—A town in the Portuguese territory of Goa, nine miles S.E. by E. from Goa, and 66 miles W. from Dharwar. Lat. 15° 25′, long. 74° 5′.

PONDALURIA.—A town in the lapsed territory of Nagpoor or Berar, 165 miles N.E. by E. from Nagpoor, and 74 miles S. from Sohagpoor. Lat. 22° 15′, long. 81° 26′.

PONDICHERRY, on the Coromandel coast, a French settlement included within the limits of the British district of South Arcot. It is situate at the mouth of a small river capable of admitting only coasting-craft of insignificant burthen. "In the fair-weather season, from 1st of January to October, the common anchorage in the road is abreast the town, in seven or eight fathoms, about three-quarters of a mile from it. Small ships may moor in five and a half or six fathoms, but during the season when stormy weather may be apprehended, it is prudent to anchor well out, in twelve or fourteen fathoms, in what is called the outer road." The site of the town is eligible, being to the south-east of a long flat hill, and close to the beach, and having numerous buildings, and a conspicuous and agreeable aspect, viewed from the sea. "Previously to the war in 1756, Pondicherry was perhaps the finest city in India. It extended along the seacoast about a mile and a quarter, and was about three-quarters of a mile in breadth, was well built, and contained many public buildings, and a citadel, then the best of its kind in India, but of too contracted dimensions. This fine city was first taken by the English in 1761, and immediately razed to the ground." During the obstinately-contested wars between the British and French in India, in the course of the last century, Pondicherry, as a military and maritime station, had the advantage over Madras of lying to windward of it during the south-west monsoon, which was the season for hostile operations. At the commencement of the present century, it was described by Lord Valentia as the handsomest town, except Calcutta, that he had seen in India. At present, it is regularly built, and divided into two parts, the White Town and the Black Town, separated by a canal. The White Town, which is situate to the eastward of the other, and close to the beach, has well-built streets, regularly laid out at right angles to each other, with trees along the sides. To the west is the Black Town, inhabited by natives. Boulevards planted with trees are great ornaments to the town. The most remarkable buildings are the church of foreign missions, the government house, and bazars constructed in 1836. In the same year a lighthouse was finished, exhibiting a light eighty-nine feet above the sea, and which, in clear weather, may be seen from a ship's poop distant sixteen or seventeen miles. In consequence of the small depth of water on the bar, and the violence of the surf, landing can be effected only by a sort of rafts or flat-bottomed boats, constructed for the purpose. Pondicherry is the capital of the French possessions in India, and the seat of their supreme government. The remaining possessions are Karical, on the coast of Coromandel; Yanaon and the lodge of Masulipatam, on the Orissa coast; Mahé and the lodge of Calicut, on the Malabar coast; Chandernagore, and the five lodges of Cossimbazar, Jougdia, Dacca, Balasore, and Patna. The possession of these lodges is however nominal, and they have been abandoned by the French. In each of these settlements there is a government agent, who receives the governor's orders direct, and corresponds with him. The territory of Pondicherry consists of—1. The district of Pondicherry properly so called, containing, besides the town, eleven villages; 2. the district of Vallanor, containing forty-five villages; 3. the district of Bahour, containing thirty-six villages. The total area is estimated at 107 square miles, and the population in 1840 was returned at 79,743. In 1856, according to an Indian newspaper, the *Madras Athenæum*, the number had increased to 119,755. The establishment here comprises—1. Executive and legislative, including governor, and council of administration and council-general; 2. judicial, including the Royal Court, the Tribunal in the First Instance, and the Tribunal of Peace and of Police; 3. department of public instruction; 4. marine; 5. military. The population of the town is estimated at from 25,000 to 30,000. Distance from Madras S.S.W. 86 miles. South of the town is the village of Ariancoopan, captured by Admiral Boscawen in 1748, prior to the unsuccessful siege of Pondicherry. The town of Pondicherry is in lat. 11° 56′, long. 79° 54′.

PONDUA.—A town in the British district of Silhet, lieut.-gov. of Bengal, 15 miles N.N.W. of Silhet. Lat. 25° 6′, long. 91° 47′.

PONGA.—A town in the British district of Rungpore, lieut.-gov. of Bengal, 39 miles N.W. of Rungpore. Lat. 26° 5′, long. 88° 52′.

PONPUTTA.—A town in the British district of Malabar, presidency of Madras, 71 miles S.E. of Cannanore. Lat. 11° 12′, long. 76° 15′.

PONWAR.—A town in the British district of Shahabad, lieut.-gov. of Bengal, 51 miles N.E. by E. of Sasseram. Lat. 25° 21′, long. 84° 41′.

POOAREE, in Koonawur, a district of Bussahir, is a village on the left bank of the Sutluj, here about 120 feet wide, and flowing with a gentle but deep current. The village, 200 feet above the river, consists of about thirty houses, from two to four stories high, chiefly built of pine-wood, and has adjacent a level, fertile piece of ground, well cultivated with vines, corn, and esculent vegetables. Here, at one time, was a sanga or wooden bridge, which having been allowed to fall, through decay, has been replaced with a jhula or rude suspension-bridge, consisting of a cable made of hair ropes stretched across, and traversed by means of a curved piece of wood sliding on it, and bearing the passenger suspended on a seat hanging below, and drawn from one side to another by means of a string, as occasion may require. Elevation above the sea 6,008 feet. Lat. 31° 33′, long. 78° 20′.

POOBTHUL.—A town in the British district of Burdwan, lieut.-gov. of Bengal, 32 miles N.E. by E. of Burdwan. Lat. 23° 28′, long. 88° 21′.

POOCH, in Bundelcund, in territory of Jhansi, a village on the route from Calpee to Goona, 55 miles S.W. of former, 150 N.E. of latter. Supplies and water may both be had. Lat. 25° 50′, long. 79° 6′.

POODOOCOTTAH, or RAJAH TONDIMAN'S COUNTRY, is bounded on the north by the British district of Trichinopoly, on the east by Tanjore, and on the south and west by Madura: it extends from lat. 10° 6′ to 10° 46′, and from long. 78° 33′ to 79° 16′; is forty-three miles in length from north to south, and the same in breadth, and has an area of 1,165 square miles, with a population of 61,745. Upon the death of Rajah Ragoonath Tondiman, in 1839, arrangements were made for conducting the administration by the widow during her son's minority. The arrangement, however, was not altogether satisfactory, and it was shortly after so far modified as to admit of the judicious interposition of the British resident; and much benefit appears to have resulted from the exercise of this temporary authority. The young chief upon his assumption of the government was noted for the excellence of his disposition; but the hopes entertained of his successful administration were subsequently disappointed, and disturbances have taken place which were not quelled without much difficulty. Poodoocottah, the principal place, is situate on the left bank of the Vellaur river, 59 miles N.E. by E. from Madura. Lat. 10° 24′, long. 78° 52′.

POOGHY SAWUR.—A town in the territory designated the Daung, within the presidency of Bombay, situate 63 miles W. from Malligaum, and 58 miles S.E. from Surat. Lat. 20° 37′, long. 73° 32′.

POOKAREE, in the British district of Banda, lieut.-gov. of the N.W. Provinces, a village on the route from the town of Banda to Ajegurh, 20 miles N. of the latter. Lat. 25° 7′, long. 80° 29′.

POOKHRAEN, in the British district of Cawnpore, lieut.-gov. of the N.W. Provinces, a small town on the route from the cantonment of Cawnpore to that of Calpee, and 10 miles N.E. of the latter. It has a bazar, and water is abundant. Lat. 26° 14′, long. 79° 54′.

POOLALCHERROO.—A town in the British district of Cuddapah, presidency of Madras, 73 miles N. of Cuddapah. Lat. 15° 31′, long. 78° 59′.

POOLAVAINDLA.—A town in the British district of Cuddapah, presidency of Madras, 40 miles W. by S. of Cuddapah. Lat. 14° 25′, long. 78° 17′.

POOLBADY.—A town in the hill zemindarry of Jeypoor, in Orissa, 44 miles S.E. by S. from Jeypoor, and 68 miles N.W. by N. from Vizagapatam. Lat. 18° 33′, long. 82° 51′.

POOLP, in the British district of Kumaon, lieut.-gov. of the N.W. Provinces, a village half a mile W. of the right bank of the Kalee (Eastern), 13 miles S.E. of Champawut cantonment. Lat. 29° 17′, long. 80° 20′.

POONA.—A British collectorate of the presidency of Bombay. It is bounded on the north by the Ahmednuggur collectorate; on the east by those of Ahmednuggur and Sholapore; on the south and south-west by the territory of Sattara; and on the west by the Tannah collectorate. It lies between lat. 17° 53′ and 19° 26′, long. 73° 20′ and 75° 10′, and has an area estimated at 5,298 square miles. The whole is included within the Deccan. The face of the country is intersected by numerous spurs or ridges, which part from the eastern side of the culminating range called the Western Ghauts, and generally hold a direction south-east, diminishing continually in height, until they sink into the plains of the Nizam's territory.

The Moola Moota, the Goor, and the Yeil, uniting with some other streams of less magnitude, which rise in the vicinity of the city of Poona, form the Bheema, which, taking a course south-east, receives, at about 160 miles from the source of the Goor, its remotest head, the Neera, a considerable stream; and below the confluence, continuing to flow in the same direction for sixty miles, finally passes into the territory of the Nizam. The Neera, which rises within the territory of Sattara, on the eastern declivity of the Ghauts, a few miles north of the British sanatarium of Mahabulishwur, flowing south-east for about eighty miles, forms the boundary between Sattara and this collectorate. Those streams must derive most of their contents from the monsoon rains on the Ghauts, as the climate of the less-elevated table-lands of the Deccan, and of the more depressed expanses in its western part, is characterized by aridity. The amount of annual rain-fall has been stated at 17.83 in. for the year 1830. The easterly winds are characterized by extreme dryness; the lips, and the exposed parts of the skin, are cut, and become harsh and scaly; windows, doors, and joiners' work shrink, and present numerous interstices; and to sleep exposed to the easterly wind, is to risk the loss of a limb, or a whole side. In general, however, the climate is not unhealthy, and the cantonments at Poona are found to be remarkably suited to the European constitution.

The character of the vegetation is indicative of the aridity of the soil and climate. Jacquemont found the country in June a parched waste, and water could nowhere be obtained by digging; yet in a few days moderate falls of rain covered the surface with verdure. Trees are very rare in this tract, there being only the Melia azadirachta, intermingled with cactus and euphorbia. Much attention has been given by government to the culture of the mulberry for feeding silkworms; but the experiment, though conducted by a gentleman from the south of Europe, well versed in the business, proved entirely abortive. The trees attained no reasonable size, many decayed altogether, and the aspect of the remainder was so sickly, stunted, and dwindling, as to forbid all probable hope of success. Heber conjectured that the cultivation of the vine would be successful; but the average annual temperature would probably be too high.

The common cereal grains of the Deccan form the staple products of the collectorate, the surplus of which finds its way to the city of Poona, the great mart of the country, and thence to the coast, where salt and European goods are received in exchange. The potato is grown extensively in the northern parts of the collectorate, and supplies a large portion of the Bombay market, to which easy access is obtained by the excellent road that intersects the Northern Pergunnahs. Cotton is not cultivated to any great extent, Indapore being the only producing district. Throughout the collectorate, the cultivation of the Mauritius sugarcane has greatly diminished, owing, it is stated, to the poverty of the Deccan soil. In some of the districts, but more especially in the pergunnahs intersected by good roads, agricultural stock is on the increase. It is calculated that a pair of oxen are equal to the cultivation of ten acres of land. In some of the districts the proportion of land to stock is greater; and this would seem to indicate a more slovenly tillage in those districts.

The district is traversed by the south-eastern branch of the main line of the Great Indian Peninsular Railway Company. The other principal roads are those from Poona, connecting that city with Bombay, Sholapore, Ahmednuggur, Nassick, Sattara, by the Neera bridge. Metalled roads, with side-drains, have recently been constructed in the Cusba Ghora of the Kheir pergunnah, with funds partly raised by assistance received from government, and partly by the voluntary contributions of the inhabitants; a fact showing that the natives are not altogether insensible to the advantages of improved means of communication, and that the expectation of interesting them in such matters is not hopeless. The line of road of the greatest commercial importance in this collectorate is that which, intersecting the Indapoor and Bheemthurry pergunnahs, leads from Sholapore to Poona. A considerable export from the south-eastern and central provinces of the peninsula, consisting chiefly of cotton-wool, is brought to the coast by this line, much of it in carts, for which description of carriage the metalled road from Poona, by way of the Bhore Ghaut, to the coast, affords great facilities. In this collectorate there are no manufactures for export. In some of the large towns, coarse cotton cloths are produced for consumption in the immediate neighbourhood. Paper is manufactured at Poona.

By far the greater portion of the population is Mahratta. There are, however, a considerable number of families deriving their origin from the Concan, some Guzerattees, and not a few Mussulmans, the descendants of the ruling race, when the country was held first by the sovereigns of Ahmednuggur and Beejapore, and subsequently by those of Delhi. There are also some of that class of Mussulmans denominated Boras. The total amount of population is given under the article BOMBAY.

At the close of the year 1852, there were in this collectorate sundry government vernacular schools, besides the Sanscrit and English college in the city of Poona. The Poorhunder village schools, which were established by way of experiment in 1836, with schoolmasters at very low rates of pay, and principally for the purpose of introducing some little instruction among the agricultural classes, were not attended with successful results, and the Board of Education resolved to avail themselves of every opportunity of closing these district schools, and to apply the funds in support of a few schools of a higher class. The principal towns are described under their respective names in the alphabetical arrangement.

Poona, at the period of its earliest mention in history, appears to have formed part of the Mussulman state of Ahmednuggur; by the sovereign of which state, a jaghire, of which Poona was the chief place, was conferred, in 1604, on an officer named Malolee. A son of Malolee, named Shahjee, after acting a conspicuous part in the closing events of the kingdom of Ahmednuggur, passed into the service of Beejapoor, and was continued in his jaghire, which had fallen to that state in the partition of the Ahmednuggur territories. Shahjee was the father of Sevajee, the founder of the Mahratta dominion, which for a time occupied so important a place in the political system of India. The son of Sevajee, named Sambajee, possessed few of the qualities which contributed to his father's success: he was made prisoner by Aurungzebe, and put to death while in captivity. His son Sevajee, subsequently known by the name of Saho, at the time of his father's death was an infant and a captive; circumstances little calculated to benefit his claims to sovereignty, more especially in Asia. Saho was eventually liberated on the death of Aurungzebe, but found the succession contested by his cousin, as stated in the article on Colapore, where also an account of the mode in which the contest was terminated will be found. A Brahmin, named Balajee Biswanat, held under Saho the office of Peishwa or minister; an office which, though it ultimately became the first in the Mahratta confederacy, and even absorbed the authority of the nominal chief, was originally only the second, the Priti Nidhi, or delegate of the rajah, being superior. By Balajee the affairs of Saho were managed with much address; and by the influence of negotiations conducted by him, a treaty was, in 1717, concluded with Hosen Ali, acting on the part of the emperor, by which the claim of Saho to the whole of the territory formerly possessed by Sevajee, with the addition of later conquests, was acknowledged, the emperor agreeing to restore all the forts in his possession within that tract; to allow the levy of chout, or Mahratta demand of a fourth part of the revenue throughout the Deccan, thus giving a legal title to that which was before a mere extortion; and to make a further payment of one-tenth of the remaining revenue, under the name of Sirdesmuki. In return, Saho was to pay a certain amount of tribute, to furnish a specified quota of horse, and to be answerable for any loss occasioned by depredations; thus acknowledging himself a vassal of the emperor. On the death of Balajee Biswanat, his son Bajee Rao succeeded to the office of Peishwa. Bajee Rao was not only a consummate master of artifice, but a man of great boldness of spirit, and actuated by a restless and insatiable ambition. He had a rival in the Priti Nidhi, by whom the arrangement with the rajah of Colapore was concluded; but the success of this minister did not enable him to supplant Bajee Rao, whose influence continued to extend in proportion to the numerous territorial and fiscal acquisitions which he succeeded in making, nominally for his master, but actually for himself. This course of aggression received a temporary check by the invasion of Nadir Shah; but when the country was relieved by the withdrawal of that invader, he resumed the prosecution of his schemes of aggrandizement with unabated vigour. In 1739 he conquered Salsette and Bassein from the Portuguese. The vicinity of Salsette to Bombay, coupled with the fact of Rajah Saho having granted all countries conquered from the Portuguese to the Peishwa in his own right, alarmed the Bombay government, who began to apprehend that the views of this Mahratta leader might not be restricted to the dominions of the Portuguese, but might extend to the possessions of other Europeans. The Peishwa, moreover, was endeavouring to create a maritime force. All these circumstances prompted the resort to measures of security; and with the intention of avoiding the dangers which seemed to be impending, the Bombay government concluded a treaty of fourteen articles with the brother of Bajee Rao, in which the claims of the contracting parties were defined and confirmed. Not long after the conclusion of this treaty, Bajee Rao died, leaving three sons, of whom the eldest, Balajee Rao, succeeded to the office of Peishwa, though not without serious opposition from various powerful Mahratta functionaries and chiefs, the Priti Nidhi, the rajah of Berar, and the Guicowar. The rajah Saho, always indolent, fell, towards the close of his reign, into a state of imbecility, which placed him entirely at the mercy of those around him. His minister Balajee, and the prince's wife Sawatri Bai, contended for the power of controlling him; and the former was so successful as to prevail on the demented rajah to sign a deed transferring all the powers of his government to the Peishwa, on condition of his maintaining the royal title and dignity in the house of Sevajee, though Ram Raja, a posthumous son of the second Sevajee, whose existence had long been concealed by his grandmother, the Tara Bai; and who accordingly succeeded to the nominal chieftainship on the death of Saho, in 1749. Balajee, now virtually the head of the Mahratta confederacy, continued to exercise his power with varied success, till his death in 1761; an event said to have been accelerated by the result of the battle of Paneeput, so fatal to the interests of the Mahrattas. The power and influence of the Peishwa thenceforth declined. Madhoo Rao, the second son of Balajee, succeeded his father; but being a minor, his uncle Ragoba was appointed regent. A protracted struggle for power succeeded between the uncle and the nephew, which ended in favour of the latter. Ragoba was deprived of authority, and subjected to confinement. Madhoo Rao died in 1772. Under the impression that his dissolution was approaching, he sent for Ragoba, and for his brother and successor, Narain Rao, and conjured them to adhere to each other. For a time, amicable feelings appeared to exist between them; but discord arose, and Ragoba was again placed under restraint. Within a year from his accession, the young rajah was murdered, and the ministerial party and Ragoba mutually charged each other with the crime. Ragoba, however, was proclaimed Peishwa; but his security in the possession of that title was shaken by the widow of the murdered Narain Rao giving birth to a son. Ragoba asserted that the child was spurious; but his title was maintained by a powerful party; and the infant was formally installed as Peishwa. In this state of affairs Ragoba applied to the government of Bombay for assistance. The importance of obtaining possession of Salsette had long and urgently been impressed on that government; and the disputed succession of Poona seemed to afford a favourable opportunity for the attainment of the desired object. The Bombay government accordingly recognised the title of Ragoba, and opened negotiations with him. Pending these negotiations, intelligence arrived that the Portuguese were fitting out an expedition at Goa for the recovery of Salsette and Bassein. To prevent these places falling into the hands of their European rivals, the Bombay government took immediate possession of them, informing Ragoba that the measure was merely precautionary, and not intended to affect his rights.

In 1775, a treaty was concluded at Surat, by which Ragoba, in consideration of a certain amount of military force to be furnished by the Company's government for the prosecution of his claims, ceded to that government in perpetuity certain territories, including Bassein and Salsette. In accordance with the stipulations of this treaty, an English force, under Colonel Keating, joined the army of Ragoba at Cambay. Advantages, though not of a decided nature, were gained; but the government of Bengal disapproved of the treaty, and of the connection with Ragoba, and directed the withdrawal of the British force. The Bengal government also deputed Colonel Upton to Poona, to treat with the party in power there without the intervention of the Bombay government. Colonel Upton concluded a treaty, but the conditions were never fulfilled. The Poona ministry was divided into two parties, one headed by Moraba, the other by Nanah Furnavese. Moraba and his party were disposed to make Ragoba regent; Nanah professed views nearly similar; but as he proposed to carry them out through the assistance of the French, the government of Bengal became alarmed, and not only authorized that of Bombay to support Ragoba, but despatched a body of about 5,000 troops from Hindostan to Bombay for the same purpose. A new treaty was hereupon concluded by the Bombay government with Ragoba, in which it was stipulated that he was to exercise the office of regent with full power, during the minority of his rival claimant; while the Bombay government engaged to apply for orders from the Company to sanction the following extraordinary arrangement: that if Ragoba should be able satisfactorily to prove the child supposititious, he, Ragoba, should become Peishwa; but if the child should appear to be really the son of the deceased Peishwa, then, on his attaining the age of seventeen, the government and country should be equally divided between him and his uncle Ragoba. Without waiting for the Bengal troops, then on the Nerbudda, the Bombay government despatched a force to conduct Ragoba to Poona, and to invest him with the regency. This force advanced to within a few miles of Poona, when those under whose orders the expedition was placed suddenly determined on retreat. The force accordingly fell back on a place called Wargaum, where, being surrounded by the Mahrattas, a convention was concluded, under which it was agreed that Salsette and all the recent acquisitions from the Mahrattas should be restored, and that the Bengal detachment should be ordered back to Calcutta. The terms of the convention, which was concluded by a committee of persons called field-deputies, were such, however, as neither they nor even the Bombay government had power to grant, and it was never ratified. Colonel Goddard, who commanded the Bengal troops, knowing that the convention was of no force, disregarded it altogether, and, though his return had been made one of the conditions, pushed on, and arrived at Surat in February, 1779. He was vested with the full powers of treating with the Mahrattas, which other parties had prematurely exercised before his arrival. The Poona durbar, however, declared that no peace could be made unless Salsette were given up: hostilities were accordingly resolved on. Colonel Goddard took Ahmedabad and Bassein; but subsequently, from the general state of affairs and the want of resources, he was compelled to confine himself to the defensive. At length Scindia concluded a separate treaty for himself: one at an earlier period had been concluded with the Guicowar; and after some delay, a treaty, known as the treaty of Salbye, put an end to the war between the British and those administering the territory of the Peishwa. By the treaty, Bassein and some other conquests were restored to the Peishwa; but the cession of Salsette and some other islands to the British, stipulated for in Colonel Upton's treaty, was confirmed. Various other diplomatic arrangements, calculated to effect particular objects, were subsequently concluded between the Peishwa and the British government; but in this brief sketch it would be superfluous to notice them in detail. In 1795 the Mahrattas became involved in war with the Nizam, a war terminated by the convention of Kurdlah, the conditions of which were highly advantageous to the former. In the same year, the Peishwa, Maderow Narrain, died. The next heir was Bajee Rao, the son of Ragoba; but Nana Furnavese tried to exclude him, in order to secure a continuance of his own power. Scindia, however, arriving at Poona with a large force, placed Bajee Rao on the musnud, and was thenceforward lord of the counsels of Poona. In 1802, Bajee Rao, taking part with Scindia in a contest which had arisen between that chieftain, shared in the defeat of his ally, Holkar having gained a complete victory in a battle fought near Poona, on the 25th October. The Peishwa fled to Bassein, having previously sought to avert the ruin he saw impending, by a communication to the British Resident at his court, expressing a desire to enter into a defensive alliance with the British, on the basis of that which they maintained with the government of Hyderabad. A treaty of defensive alliance, known as the treaty of Bassein, was accordingly concluded: a supplementary treaty was concluded in 1803; another treaty, for the settlement of territory ceded by the rajah of Berar and Scindia, was entered into in 1804. The Peishwa had readily entered into a close alliance with the British government, to avert the entire extinction of his authority; but, from his restoration to his deposition, he systematically pursued a course of policy having for its object the subversion of the British power.

In 1812 and 1813 the British government was called upon to arbitrate an adjustment of the Peishwa's claims upon the chiefs of Colapore and Sawunt Warree, and the Southern Mahratta jaghiredars. The decision, which was fatal to his pretensions of sovereignty over Colapore, strengthened the hostile feelings which he previously cherished towards the power to which he was indebted for the retention of his position as a sovereign prince, and his escape from the ruin which, without British assistance, awaited him; the condition of a close prisoner, or that of a destitute wanderer, being the alternative before him. Trimbuckjee Danglia, a man who, by pandering to the profligate passions of his master, had risen from a very low station to be the most important personage in the court of the Peishwa, fanned these feelings, and was ready to take any step for their gratification. The British government was bound by treaty to arbitrate certain long-standing disputes between the Peishwa and the Guicowar, or ruler of Baroda. In 1816, the Peishwa became pressing for the settlement of the disputed claims, and suggested that Gungadhur Shastry, the Guicowar's minister, should come to Poona, there to assist in the investigation and settlement of them. The Shastry knew that he was hated by Bajee Rao; he knew, moreover, the character of that prince, and that of his minion Trimbuckjee Danglia. It is not therefore surprising that he should have been reluctant to place himself in any degree in the power of such men. But the British government guaranteed the personal safety of the Guicowar's minister, and, thus assured, he ceased to be actuated by apprehensions which probably could have been overcome in no other way. The arrival of the Shastry was welcomed by Bajee Rao with the strongest demonstrations of friendship; he proposed to unite the family of his visitor with his own by marriage; and it is not unlikely that the flattering proposal tended in some degree to throw the stranger off his guard and diminish his fears, though it did not altogether remove them. The Peishwa and the Shastry proceeded together on a pilgrimage to Punderpoor, one of those places which Hindoo superstition has invested with sanctity. While there, the Shastry was invited by Trimbuckjee to repair to a celebrated temple, on some occasion which was regarded as of peculiar solemnity. His just appreciation of the villanous character of the man who proposed the visit was still sufficiently strong to induce him to hesitate; and it was not until after repeated messages that he yielded. He went, performed such devotions as Hindoo delusion prescribed, and on his return was assassinated by ruffians hired by Trimbuckjee Danglia, acting under the atrocious instructions of the master, of whom he thus proved himself so fitting an instrument. The British Resident at the court of the Peishwa of course demanded the instant surrender of the wretch who had contrived the means and superintended the committal of the murder. The Peishwa sought to protect him; but at length the British government obtained possession of his person. He was confined in the fort of Tanna, whence, however, he soon found means of escaping. In the mean time the Peishwa was secretly striving by all the means in his power to induce the Mahrattas to unite in common cause against the English: Trimbuckjee, after his escape, actively promoted the designs of his master, by collecting troops for the meditated contest. These steps compelled the British government to pursue a decisive course, by demanding from the Peishwa such terms as a regard for the peace and security of India required, though by no means such as his crimes merited. He had no choice but to comply, or to be at once involved in war with the most powerful state in India. He was not prepared for the latter, and after a severe struggle, he most unwillingly and ungraciously accepted the terms tendered to him.

On the conclusion of the consequent treaty, the greater portion of the British troops were withdrawn from the Peishwa's territories, preparatory to operations against the Pindarries. This appeared to Bajee Rao to afford him another chance of gratifying his revenge, and he availed himself of the opportunity by concentrating a large force at Poona. The small British brigade left at that place was thereupon removed to Kirkee, four miles distant, for the sake of occupying a better position. At this place they were attacked by the Mahrattas; but though the disparity of numbers was great, the enemy was repulsed at every point with great loss. A tedious course of warfare followed; but in all the actions that took place, the Peishwa's forces were defeated. Towards the end of May, 1818, Bajee Rao, wearied out by constant defeat and hopeless wandering, and perhaps apprehensive of a worse fate than that of falling into the hands of the British, opened a communication with Sir John Malcolm. The result was, the formal renunciation by Bajee Rao of all sovereign power, and his acceptance of a grant of pensionary provision, at the amount of which even he could not fail to be surprised, and which, considering the character of the man, together with the facts of his deposal having been formally proclaimed, and his country almost entirely reduced, the Governor-General, the Marquis of Hastings, was justly warranted in considering unnecessarily large. He, however, ratified the terms. Bajee Rao lived many years to enjoy, or at least to receive and expend, the vast income which had been placed at his disposal. With him ended the dynasty of the Peishwa, begun in usurpation and terminated in treachery. Out of the territories placed at the disposal of the British government by the crimes of Bajee Rao, a dependent principality was assigned to the rajah of Sattara, the representative of the founder of the Mahratta rule; the remainder were incorporated with the British dominions. Latterly, the Sattara line of rajahs has run out its course, and this portion of territory has lapsed to the British government.

POONA.—The principal town of the British collectorate of the same name. It is situate on the small river Moota, immediately above its confluence with the Moola, in a treeless plain, extending eastward from the Ghauts, which, at the distance of a few miles, rise to the height of 1,000 feet above the town. The south-eastern branch of the main line of the Great Indian Peninsular Railway Company passes by the city. Poona was originally an ill-built city, without walls or fort, the bazars were mean, and the streets irregular; but recent and extensive improvements have changed both its character and appearance. In the period intervening between the years 1841 and 1846, no less than 400 new houses were built, and several more were in the latter year in the course of construction. A stone bridge of excellent masonry across the Nagjurree Nullah was also in the last-mentioned year completed, at the private cost of a wealthy courtesan, affording greatly-increased facilities to a large class of grain-dealers for the transport of their grain into the heart of the town. The old Mahratta bridge across the Moota Moola river having fallen into decay, was taken down; and it has been replaced by a bridge of stone, at an outlay of 47,000 rupees, or 4,700*l.*, of which the government contributed 3,600*l.* The road over this bridge, which is at the west end of the city, is on the direct route to Bombay, and by it European imported goods, salt, and other articles, are brought from that port, as well as supplies of provisions and fuel from the neighbouring districts. There is another bridge over the same river, in the vicinity of Poona, called the Wellesley Bridge, which was built by the government. The streets and thoroughfares of the whole of the eastern portion of the city adjacent to the cantonment have been macadamized. The most remarkable building is the palace, formerly the residence of the Peishwa. It is of considerable extent, and contains a handsome quadrangle, surrounded by cloisters of carved wooden pillars. It now serves the various purposes of a prison, an hospital, and a lunatic asylum. The head-quarters of one of the divisions of the Bombay army are at Poona. The cantonments are on an elevated site a mile west of the city, and are perhaps the most extensive and best-arranged in India. The church is spacious and convenient, but in bad architectural taste, and disfigured on the outside by gaudy colouring. Poona is represented to have been long in a declining state. During the height of the Mahratta power, the population is believed to have amounted to 150,000. At the time of the overthrow of the Peishwa, in 1818, it was estimated at 110,000; it was in 1838 rated at 75,170. It is, however, to be observed, that these numbers are but conjectural; and the recent increase of houses, already adverted to, would scarcely seem compatible with any considerable diminution of inhabitants. Measures are in progress for effecting municipal improvements in the city.

An ample supply of water for this city had long been a want of primary importance, as affecting the health and comfort of the inhabitants; and endeavours have been made to obtain this desideratum by the repair and enlargement of the adjacent tanks and aqueducts. These measures, however, proved ineffectual, and it was finally decided to throw a dam across the Moota Moola river, with adequate waterworks for the supply of the city. Sir Jamsetjee Jejeebhoy agreed to defray the cost, which was estimated at 73,945 rupees, or 7,394*l.*, exclusive of the machinery, which this distinguished benefactor of his country also undertook to provide. The dam, which was to be erected under the superintendence of an officer of the government, was commenced in the year 1844, but twice failed, once in 1845, and again during the floods in the following year. Sir Jamsetjee having already expended on this work a sum amounting to 175,000 rupees, or 17,500*l.*, the completion of the work was in 1847 authorized at the public expense. The estimated cost was 37,775 rupees, or 3,777*l.* Late in the year last mentioned, further difficulties were encountered in the construction of the dam, and a third failure ensued. In the year 1850, the works were brought to a termination; but from the want of judgment displayed in the formation of the bund, and in the selection also of its site, it was discovered that the work was unsuited to the purpose for which it was designed. It was necessary, therefore, to abandon the bund as the main source, and to resort to other measures for securing a full supply of water to the mass of the population.

There was a government English school in this city, which, in 1846, contained 118 pupils. Of this number, the large majority (eighty-one) consisted of Brahmins; the remaining number (thirty-seven) was composed of Purvoes, Indo-Britons, Sonars, and nine other castes. A public examination of the school was held in October, 1846, conducted by the bishop of Bombay. With respect to the highest class, his lordship expressed himself in terms of high praise. This school has been recently amalgamated with the Sanscrit College, which was instituted in the year 1821, for the preservation, it is stated, of the ancient literature of the country. It is placed under the special superintendence of a European officer. It consists of three departments, Sanscrit, English, and Normal, and in 1853 contained 497 pupils, of whom 342 were in the English department. An interesting experiment is now in progress for promoting female education in this town. In July, 1851, the first girls' school in Poona was established by a few educated native gentlemen. The number of girls under tuition at the end of the first year was fifty; at the close of the second, the number of schools had increased to three, while the aggregate number of pupils amounted to 237.

With the exception of grain-dealers, and those who trade in the raw products of the country, the mercantile classes in Poona are said to be declining in wealth. No market is now found for jewellery and precious stones, which were much sought after when Poona was the seat of native rule. The introduction of European piece goods has caused the disappearance of native fabrics, which could not compete with them in price, and Poona has now scarcely any manufacture except a very small one of paper. Judging, however, from the annual increase in the number of houses, it is to be presumed that the loss of the trade, consequent on the deprivation of a court and other causes, has been supplied to some extent from new sources.

The first mention of Poona in history seems to have been in 1604, when it was granted by the sultan of Ahmednuggur as jaghire to Mallojee, the grandfather of Sevajee, the Mahratta chief. In 1637 it was confirmed by the sultan to Shahjee, father of Sevajee. In 1663, during the operations conducted against Sevajee, by order of Aurungzebe, the imperial viceroy Shaista Khan took possession of this open town, from which, when surprised a few days afterwards by Sevajee, he had great difficulty in making his escape. His son, and most of his guard, were cut to pieces, and he himself wounded. A powerful force, however, immediately reinstated the discomfited commander. In 1667, Aurungzebe restored Poona to Sevajee; but under the sway of his successor Sambajee, it was occupied by Khan Jehan, an officer of the Padshah. On the Peishwa obtaining supremacy in the Mahratta confederacy, the seat of government was removed from Sattara to Poona. In 1763, Nizam Ali, of Hyderabad, sacked the town, and burned such parts of it as were not ransomed. In the struggle between the successive peishwas and their nominal subordinates Scindia and Holkar, Poona suffered many vicissitudes, until, in 1802, by the provisions of the treaty of Bassein, the Peishwa admitted a British subsidiary force to be stationed there. After the deposal of the Peishwa Bajee Rao (the particulars of which event are narrated in the article on the Poona collectorate), the city became the locality of the British civil establishment, as well as of the principal cantonment of the Deccan. Elevation above the sea 1,823 feet. Distance from Bombay, S.E., 74 miles; from Sattara, N., 58; from Ahmednuggur, S.W., 70. Lat. 18° 31′, long. 73° 53′.

POONAHANAH, in the British district of Goorgaon, lieut.-gov. of the N.W. Provinces, a town on the route from Muthra to Rewaree, 40 miles N.W. of the former. Lat. 27° 51′, long. 77° 16′.

POONAKULLO.—A town in Hyderabad, or territory of the Nizam, situate on the left bank of the Godavery river, and 126 miles N.N.E. from Hyderabad. Lat. 19° 6′, long. 79° 7′.

POONAMALLEE.—A town in the British district of Chingleput, presidency of Madras, 13 miles W.S.W. of Madras. Poonamallee is a military station, and accommodation is maintained for two or three companies of European troops. Lat. 13° 2′, long. 80° 10′.

POONASSA.—A town in the native state of Gwalior, or territory of Scindia's family, 82 miles S.E. by S. from Oojein, and 97 miles W. by N. from Baitool. Lat. 22° 10′, long. 76° 30′.

POONCH.—See PUNCH.

POONDUR.—A district originally subject to the hill state of Joobul, of which it forms the northern part. It extends about eight miles in length, nearly in a direction from south-west to north-east, and five in breadth, in a direction at right angles with the former; lying between lat. 30° 58′—31° 4′, long. 77° 35′ and 77° 42′. This tract consists principally of a main ridge running from south-west to north-east, forming part of the range connecting the peak of Wartu with that of Chur, and having probably an elevation of from 6,000 to 7,000 feet above the sea. The streams flow across the district in a south-easterly direction towards the Tonse. The inhabitants are a hardy, fearless race, who continued to resist the Goorkhas after the other mountaineers had submitted, and until after a bloody conflict at Matteelee, where they were overpowered by a force of 6,000 men. On the march of the English troops into this part of the mountains, the inhabitants again rose in arms against the Goorkhas, exterminated those occupying their country, and, investing the fort of Chepal, farther south, conduced mainly to its surrender. On the expulsion of the Goorkhas, and subsequent pacification of the country, Poondur devolved to the East-India Company, for want of heirs to the former ruling family; and as no advantage appeared likely to result from retaining dominion over its barren soil and rude people, it was, by the advice of Sir David Ochterlony, transferred to the rana of Keonthul, its present sovereign. It is estimated by De Cruz to have an annual revenue of 300*l.*, and a population of 3,000, of whom 400 bear arms.

POONG.—A town in the British district of Amherst, one of the Tenasserim provinces, 11 miles N. of Moulmein. Lat. 16° 38′, long. 97° 42′.

POONGUL, in the Rajpoot state of Beekaneer, a village on the route from the town of Beekaneer to that of Babawulpoor, and 48 miles N.W. of the former. It is described as situate amidst desolation, striking even in that desert region. Lat. 28° 29′, long. 72° 52′.

POONITJ.—A town in the native state of Travancore, territory of Madras, 57 miles N. by E. from Quilon, and 91 miles N.W. from Tinnevelly. Lat. 9° 40′, long. 76° 50′.

POONOO.—A town in the British district of Shikarpoor, territory of Scinde, presidency of Bombay, 32 miles W. of Shikarpoor. Lat. 27° 58′, long. 68° 8′.

POONPOON.—A river rising in Ramgurh, among the mountains on the northern frontier of Behar, about lat. 24° 30′, long. 84° 20′. It holds a course generally north-east, through Behar and Patna, receiving in its course some considerable torrents. At its mouth it has steep banks, about thirty feet high, and a channel 100 yards wide. Its total length of course is about 130 miles. At the distance of a few miles further east, is the course of the Little Poonpoon, holding a direction nearly parallel to that of the larger stream, and ultimately joining it twelve miles above its confluence with the Ganges at Futwa, in lat. 25° 29′, long. 85° 23′.

POONWA, in the British district of Allahabad, lieut.-gov. of the N.W. Provinces, a village on the route, by Rajapoor ferry, from the cantonment of Allahabad to Banda, and 38 miles W. of the former. Lat. 25° 27′, long. 81° 23′.

POOPREE.—A town in the British district of Tirhoot, lieut.-gov. of Bengal, 36 miles N.E. of Mozufferpoor. Lat. 26° 30′, long. 85° 50′.

POOR, in the British district of Mozuffurnuggur, lieut.-gov. of the N.W. Provinces, a town, the principal place of the pergunnah of the same name. Elevation above the level of the sea 963 feet. Lat. 29° 40′, long. 77° 54′.

POORAH, in the British district of Cawnpore, lieut.-gov. of the N.W. Provinces, a town on the route from the cantonment of Futtehgurh to that of Cawnpore, and 26 miles N.W. of the latter. It has a bazar, and is well supplied with water. Lat. 26° 45′, long. 80° 9′.

POORAINUH, in the British district of Goruckpoor, lieut.-gov. of the N.W. Provinces, a town on the route from Goruckpoor to Oudh, 54 miles W. by N. of the former. Lat. 26° 49′, long. 82° 32′.

POORALIA.—A British district in the lieut.-gov. of Bengal, bounded on the north-west by those of Barrabhoom and Pachete; on the east by Bancoorah and Midnapoor; and on the south-west by Singhboom and the native state of Mohurbunge. It lies between lat. 22° 9′—23° 15′, long. 86° 5′—87° 13′; is seventy miles in length from north-east to south-west, and sixty miles in breadth. Pooralia, the principal place, is the station of the assistant to the political agent for the south-west frontier of Bengal and commissioner for Chota Nagpore. It is situate forty miles west of Bancoorah.

POORANDA.—A town in the British district of Purneah, lieut.-gov. of Bengal, 22 miles W. of Purneah. Lat. 25° 46′, long. 87° 10′.

POORANUM, in the Jetch Dooab division of the Punjab, a town situated on the left bank of the Jhelum, 89 miles N.N.W. of the town of Lahore. Lat. 32° 46′, long. 73° 40′.

POORBOONI, in Koonawur, a district of Bussahir, is a village on the left bank of the Sutluj. It is of considerable size, with houses built of hewn stone, bonded with beams of deodar. Poorbooni is 7,318 feet above the sea. Lat. 31° 35′, long. 78° 22′.

POORBUNDER, in the peninsula of Kattywar, province of Guzerat, a town on the south-west coast, in the district of Burda. Though having no shelter for ships of considerable burthen, in consequence of a bar obstructing the entrance, it is much frequented by craft of from twelve to eighty tons burthen, and is the best on the west coast, carrying on brisk trade with the opposite coast of Africa, and with various ports in Sinde, Beloochistan, Arabia, the Persian Gulf, and the coasts of the Concan and Malabar; and about sixty vessels of various sizes belong to the port. Poorbunder belongs to a rana or chief of the Jaitwa tribe of Rajpoots, who also holds the whole district of Burda or Jaitwar, for which he pays an annual tribute of 3,000*l.* to the Guicowar, and also pays annually to the British government the moiety of the duties levied at the seaport of Poorbunder, yielding annually a revenue of from 3,000*l.* to 3,500*l.* Distance from Ahmedabad, S.W., 210 miles; Baroda, W., 230; Bombay, N.W., 275. Lat. 21° 37′, long. 69° 45′.

POOREE.—See JUGGURNAUTH.

POORMAH.—A town in the recently lapsed territory of Nagpoor, 126 miles E.N.E. from Nagpoor, and 87 miles S. from Ramgur. Lat. 21° 33′, long. 81° 3′.

POORNA, a river of Hyderabad, and a considerable feeder of the Godavery, rises in lat. 20° 22′, long. 75° 16′, and, flowing south-east for 190 miles, falls into the Godavery river, in lat. 19° 6′, long. 77° 5′.

POORNA.—A river rising in lat. 20° 59′, long. 73° 44′, on the western slope of the Western Ghats, and flowing through the territory of the Daung rajahs, Wusravee, and the British district of Surat, falls into the North Indian Ocean, in lat. 20° 53′, long. 72° 48′.

POORNAH RIVER, rises in lat. 21° 35′,

long. 77° 41', in the British district of Baitool, and flowing southerly for sixty-five miles through that district, and for ninety-five through one of the recently sequestrated districts of the Nizam's dominions, falls into the Taptee, in lat. 21° 4', long. 76° 8'.

POOROGAON.—A town of Eastern India, in the British district of Northern Cachar, 60 miles E. by S. of Jynteahpore. Lat. 25° 4', long. 93°.

POORSA.—A town in the British district of Dinajepore, lieut.-gov. of Bengal, 39 miles S.E. of Dinajepoor. Lat. 25° 13', long. 89° 5'.

POORUNDHUR, in the collectorate of Poona, presidency of Bombay, "a hill fort, connected with a neighbouring range." The highest point of the mountain of Poorundhur is upwards of 1,700 feet from the plain immediately below, and 4,472 feet above the sea. There are two forts, an upper and a lower, situated from 300 to 400 feet below the summit. The works, like most of the hill forts in that part of the country, are of perpendicular rock, and frequently weakened rather than strengthened by curtains and bastions of masonry, by which the natural defences are generally surmounted. It was one of the first places which the Mahratta chief Sevajee secured, and he obtained it by practising on the weakness of those by whom it was held. In 1665 it was invested by the forces of Aurungzebe, under the command of Dilir Khan, and though the defence was obstinate, and the success of the undertaking doubtful, Sevajee appears to have been so intimidated at the prospect of its fall, that he surrendered the place and himself, and entered the service of Aurungzebe, from whom, however, he soon revolted, and in 1670 recaptured the fort. After the power of the Peishwas had superseded that of the descendants of Sevajee at Poona, it was the usual stronghold to which the former retreated when unable to remain in safety at the capital. In 1818 it was invested by a British force, and, after a brief resistance, surrendered at discretion. The fort commands a passage through the Ghats, denominated the Poorundhur Ghat. Here, in 1776, was concluded a treaty between the British government and the Mahratta states; but its conditions were never fulfilled, the treaty being overruled by a subsequent agreement between the Bombay government and Ragoba.

Poorundhur is one of the sanitarial stations for European officers and soldiers; it is distant 20 miles S.E. of Poona, 40 miles N. of Sattara, and 90 S.E. of Bombay. Lat. 18° 16', long. 74° 2'.

POORUNGURH.—A town in the British district of Rutnageriah, presidency of Bombay, 12 miles S. of Rutnageriah. Lat. 16° 50', long. 73° 22'.

POORUNPOOR, in the British district of Shahjehanpoor, lieut.-gov. of the N.W. Provinces, a town on the route from Bareilly to the Nepal territory, 48 miles E. by N. of the former. Lat. 28° 30', long. 80° 13'.

POORWA.—A town in Bundelcund, situate on the left bank of the Pysunnee river, distant four miles N. from Tirhowan. Lat. 25° 16', long. 80° 56'. The territory of which this town is the principal place belongs to a native chief under the protection of the British government: it contains an area of twelve square miles, and a population of 1,800.

POORWAH.—A town in Oude, 65 miles N.W. from Lucknow, and 37 miles E.N.E. from Furruckabad. Lat. 27° 30', long. 80° 13'.

POORWAH.—A town in Oude, 29 miles S.S.W. from Lucknow, and 30 miles E. from Cawnpoor. Lat. 26° 29', long. 80° 51'.

POORYNHA, in the British district of Shahjehanpoor, lieut.-gov. of the N.W. Provinces, a village on the route from Futtehgurh to the cantonment of Shahjehanpoor, and 18 miles S.W. of the latter. Lat. 27° 45', long. 79° 46'.

POORYNEE, in the British district of Bijnour, lieut.-gov. of the N.W. Provinces, a village on the route from Moradabad to Hurdwar, and 44 miles N.W. of the former. Lat. 29° 24', long. 78° 31'.

POOSA, in the British district of Tirhoot, lieut.-gov. of Bengal, a town on the route from Dinapore to Purneah, 50 miles N.E. of former, 150 W. of latter. It is situate on the banks of the Little Gunduck river, has a good bazar, and supplies are abundant. Lat. 25° 59', long. 85° 41'.

POOT.—A town in the British district of Tavoy, one of the Tenasserim provinces, 110 miles S. by E. of Moulmein. Lat. 14° 56', long. 98° 5'.

POOTH, in the British district of Meerut, lieut.-gov. of the N.W. Provinces, a town on the route from Meerut to Budaoon, 38 miles S.E. by E. of the former. Lat. 28° 40', long. 78° 16'.

POOTLEE.—See Kotpootlee.

POOTLEE.—A town in the Rajpoot state of Ulwar, 28 miles W.N.W. from Ulwar, and 98 miles S.W. from Delhi. Lat. 27° 40', long. 76° 13'.

POOTORAY.—A town in the native state of Travancore, presidency of Madras, 20 miles S.E. from Trivandrum, and 32 miles W.N.W. from Cape Comorin. Lat. 8° 17', long. 77° 11'.

POOTTOOR.—A town in the British district of South Canara, presidency of Madras, 26 miles E. by S. of Mangalore. Lat. 12° 47', long. 75° 15'.

PORAKADY.—A town in the British district of Malabar, presidency of Madras, 55 miles E. by S. of Cannanore. Lat. 11° 41', long. 76° 13'.

PORENAUMLA.—A town in the British district of Cuddapah, presidency of Madras,

39 miles N. by E. of Cuddapah. Lat. 15°, long. 79° 4′.

PORIAN POINT, on the coast of the British province of Pegu, at the mouth of the Negrais river. It lies low, is formed of white cliffs covered with trees. Distant 69 miles S.S.W. of Bassein. Lat. 15° 49′, long. 94° 29′.

PORKA, or PORKAD, in Travancore, a town on the seacoast, having a trade in timber, cocoanuts, pepper, and coir or cocoanut-fibre. Distance from the city of Cochin, S.E., 53 miles. Lat. 9° 20′, long. 76° 25′.

PORTO NOVO, in the British district of South Arcot, presidency of Madras, a town on the Coromandel coast, at the mouth of the river Vellaur, which, rising near the base of the Eastern Ghats, and having a considerable length of course, is small at its mouth, and admits only coasting craft. Ships of superior burthen must anchor two miles off shore, where they have six or seven fathoms of water, with good holding-ground in mud. This town was formerly of considerable importance and prosperity; but having suffered much in the wars between the British and Mysorean governments, sank into decay. Its prosperity is, however, rising, in consequence of extensive ironfoundry-works having been established here by a joint-stock association, called the East-India Iron Company, to whom also belong the works at Beypoor. The ore smelted is in great abundance in the vicinity, and can be reduced by the usual processes into the finest steel.

Porto Novo was burned by Hyder Ali in July, 1780, upon his first irruption into the Carnatic. In the following year, a critical battle was fought at this place, between Hyder and the British, which terminated in the complete discomfiture of the former. Hyder had anticipated a different result. Relying upon his vast superiority of numbers, he trusted that the day had arrived when he might completely annihilate the only army that remained to oppose him, and actually issued an order at the commencement of the action, that no prisoners should be taken. Distance from Tranquebar, N., 32 miles; Madura, N.E., 155; Tanjore, N.E., 63; Madras, S., 116. Lat. 11° 31′, long. 79° 49′.

PORTUGUESE POSSESSIONS. — See GOA, DIU, and DAMAN.

POTAL.—A town in the British district of Mymunsing, lieut.-gov. of Bengal, 44 miles S.W. by W. of Nusserabad. Lat. 24° 21′, long. 89° 50′.

POTALPUTTOO.—A town in the British district of North Arcot, presidency of Madras, 35 miles N.W. by N. of Arcot. Lat. 13° 20′, long. 79° 9′.

POTHEE.—A village in the British district of Rohtuk, lieut.-gov. of the N.W. Provinces. Lat. 29° 5′, long. 76° 20′.

POUDELLAH.—A town in the British district of Nellore, presidency of Madras, 28 miles W.N.W. of Ongole. Lat. 15° 38′, long. 79° 41′.

POUNA, or PONNA.—See GONKOR.

POUNNALY.—A town of Burmah, situate on the left bank of the Irrawady river, and 66 miles N. from Ava. Lat. 22° 49′, long. 96°.

POWAEEN, in the British district of Shahjehanpoor, lieut.-gov. of the N.W. Provinces, a town on the route from Shahjehanpoor to Jemlah, 18 miles N.E. of the former. Powaeen is returned as containing a population of 6,071 inhabitants. Lat. 28° 4′, long. 80° 10′.

POWANGURH.—A town in Guzerat, or dominions of the Guicowar, 22 miles N.E. from Baroda, and 69 miles S.E. by E. from Ahmedabad. Lat. 22° 28′, long. 73° 30′.

POWAR.—A town in the British district of Poonah, presidency of Bombay, 17 miles W. of Poonah. Lat. 18° 31′, long. 73° 39′.

POWNAR.—A town in the lapsed territory of Nagpoor or Berar, 40 miles S.W. from Nagpoor, and 79 miles E.S.E. from Ellichpoor. Lat. 20° 48′, long. 78° 42′.

POWREE, in the territory of Gwalior, a town on the route from Calpee to Kotah, 195 miles S.W. of former, 126 E. of latter. Lat. 25° 32′, long. 77° 27′.

POWTI.—A town of the British district Bijnour, lieut.-gov. of the N.W. Provinces. Lat. 29° 12′, long. 78° 32′.

POWUNGURH.—A town in the native state of Kalapoor, presidency of Bombay, 64 miles S. from Sattara, and 69 miles N.N.W. from Belgaum. Lat. 16° 47′, long. 74° 12′.

PRAIGPOOR, in the Rajpoot state of Jeypore, a town on the route from Delhi to the town of Jeypore, 107 miles S.W. of former, 54 N.E. of latter. It has a bazar, and water is plentiful. Lat. 27° 38′, long. 76° 13′.

PRANHETA RIVER.—See WEINGUNGA.

PRINCE OF WALES ISLAND (called also Penang, from its form resembling that of the areca-nut, for which Penang is the Malay term) is situate near the northern entrance of the Straits of Malacca, off the western coast of the Malay peninsula, being separated from its dependency Province Wellesley, on the mainland, by a channel two miles and a half wide. It lies between lat. 5° 14′—5° 29′, long. 100° 25′; is fifteen miles in length and twelve in its greatest breadth, and contains an area of 160 square miles.

Favoured by nature, not less in its highly advantageous mercantile situation than in the rich and varied produce of its soil, this flourishing island is sheltered from the south-west by the lofty mountains of Sumatra, and on the east by the chain of the Malayan peninsula, so that ships approaching its shores escape the fury of the storms which prevail in this quarter of the globe; and a safe access is at all seasons easily obtained to the harbour, which, formed by the strait separating Penang from the Quedah coast, is deep, with good anchorage, enabling ships of large burden to lie a few hundred yards off the town; and so spacious, as to be capable of containing almost any number of vessels. A considerable commerce is accordingly carried on, which is represented as being on the increase. The coast is bold, and studded with several islands, and on almost every side the shore is lined with groves of the cocoanut. A chain of mountains, having an elevation of from 2,000 to 2,500 feet above the level of the sea, run diagonally across the island from north-east to south-west; on each side, extending from their base to the coast, are fertile plains, which are entirely cultivated, except where interrupted by forests of fine trees and groves of the areca. To the north-east is a level plain, three miles in breadth, called the "Valley." This is the most populous part of the island; Georgetown (the capital), with its forts, barracks, &c., being built on its eastern extremity, and the houses of the principal European inhabitants scattered over its surface. The northern part is generally mountainous, and the summits of many of the hills are studded with residences of European planters. There are no rivers; but numerous streams and rivulets, which find their source in these mountains, serve to irrigate and fertilize the soil.

The climate of Penang varies on the hills and in the valley. In the former it is most delightful: the medium temperature of the year is 70°; the average annual range of the thermometer about 10°. Being exposed at all times to refreshing breezes, the heat in the middle of the day, in the hottest weather, is never oppressive; and from the purity and bracing character of the air, together with the beauty of the scenery, it offers a most agreeable resort for convalescents. At some seasons, morning fogs hang over the summits, which make it cold, and render warm clothing necessary. In the valley, covered with its rich verdure and luxuriant vegetation, the climate is moist. There the temperature in the day rises to 90°, and is seldom lower than 76°; but the nights and mornings are always delightfully cool. January and February are the driest months; April, May, and June are rainy ones; but showers are frequent throughout the year. The diseases which are most common are the cholera, fevers, diarrhœa, dysentery, rheumatism, and ulcers.

The geological formation of Prince of Wales Island is primitive. The mountains consist almost exclusively of granite; mica occasionally occurs in pretty large quantities, and quartz is sometimes found. The subsoil of the hills consists in some places of decomposed rock, varying from one to eight feet in depth; the valley is of alluvial formation, formed by the detritus of the mountain, which has been accumulating for ages. Dr. Ward supposes that the sea at some remote period covered these parts, and washed the base of the mountains; and this opinion is borne out by the appearance of the opposite shore, where Captain Low discovered for some miles inland evidences of the gradual retirement of the ocean, in the ridges which at intervals run parallel with the coast. The only mineral known to exist is tin; and it is said the mountains are rich in this ore, though no mines have been worked.

The soil throughout the island is generally light, but varies in quality: at the foot of the mountains it becomes rich; in the valleys it consists of a vegetable mould, some inches in depth, with a substratum of sand. Towards the sea, where it has been covered with mangroves, the soil is a rich black mould, mixed with small quantities of sand and gravel.

The whole island is covered with a luxuriant vegetation. When first transferred to the English, dense forests and noxious jungle covered its surface: these have been now cleared away, and highly-cultivated fields and smiling gardens occupy their place. The eastern side of the island, consisting of low lands, which are well adapted to the growth of rice, is almost exclusively appropriated to its cultivation. On the south-western side, the soil, being of a different character, is occupied by beautiful plantations of the spice and pepper plants. The cleared summits of the hills are productive in cloves, which are the finest in the world; their sides are clothed with forests and plantations of tea, cotton, and tobacco; and the plains are rich also in coffee, sugarcane, and all descriptions of fruit-trees and vegetables. The nutmeg is a tall tree: the island contains several descriptions, varying in the colour of their leaves and the shape of the fruit. The betel-vine is extensively planted; the natives have a great partiality for the leaf, and are large consumers of it.

So great a variety of races constitutes the population of Prince of Wales Island, that Sir George Leith remarks, "There is not, probably in any part of the world, so small a space in which so many different people are assembled together, or so great a variety of languages spoken." There are Malays, Chinese, Buttas, Bengalese, Europeans, Chuliahs, Siamese, and Burmese. When first taken possession of by the British, it was very thinly populated; a few Malay families, who used to gain their livelihood by fishing, and several bands of pirates, being the only inhabitants. Soon after the settlement of the British, however, Chinese, and people from various countries, congregated here to enjoy the advantages of British protection; and in 1797, ten years after the first establishment of the British, the number of inhabitants amounted to 6,937. In 1801 it had increased to 9,587; in 1828 the population was 37,715; in 1855 it had risen to 45,518. The total population of the Straits settlements at the same period, inclusive of military and convicts, was as follows:—

Prince of Wales Island....	45,518
Province Wellesley........	51,509
Singapore.................	57,421
Malacca	54,021
Total..........	208,469

The British inhabitants are either planters, merchants, or gentlemen holding official situations.

Prince of Wales Island is the seat of government for all the British possessions in the Straits. At the latter end of the last century, the East-India Company deemed it necessary to establish a port in the Straits of Malacca; and after several fruitless endeavours to obtain Acheen, Penang was fixed upon. The Company were at the same time apprised by Captain Light, that the king of Quedah would transfer the island into their hands upon the annual payment of 6,000 Spanish dollars. Terms being drawn up and agreed to, Captain Light was appointed by the government superintendent of their new settlement. Through the indefatigable exertions of Captain Light, forests were cleared, lands distributed, a town built, and port constructed; so that in a few years the island was in a most flourishing condition. In 1791, the king of Quedah seeing its prosperous state, demanded an increase of stipend, and upon refusal, collected a force on the opposite shore for the purpose of attack. This intention, however, was frustrated by the timely operations of the superintendent, who, applying for assistance from Bengal, drove him away, dispersed his troops, and afterwards entered into a treaty with him. Captain Light, after filling his station to the satisfaction of his country and those over whom he was placed, died in 1794. A few years afterwards, the designation of superintendent was changed to that of lieutenant-governor. In 1802, a strip of land on the opposite coast, now known as Province Wellesley, was obtained from the king of Quedah; and in 1807, the judicial administration, previously in the hands of the local government, was vested in a recorder's court. Betore the year 1805, the authorities of Penang were subordinate to the Bengal presidency: at that period they were constituted a separate presidency. This new arrangement lasted till 1830, when Malacca and Singapore were incorporated with Penang, and the eastern settlements were again made subordinate to Bengal. A commissioner or governor was appointed to preside over the three settlements, and a deputy-resident was placed over each. In 1851, this dependency upon the government of Bengal was removed, and the governor of the united settlements was declared subject only to the government of India.

PROME.—A town in the British territory of Pegu, situate on the left bank of the Irawaddy. It is a place of considerable importance, and under British administration will probably advance in commercial consequence, wealth, and prosperity. During the first Burmese war (1825), it was taken possession of by the British without the trouble of firing a gun, the enemy having deserted it, after setting it on fire. The conflagration destroyed one quarter of the town. The captors were rewarded by finding among the spoil a hundred pieces of artillery and a large supply of grain. In the second war with Ava (1852), Prome again fell into the hands of the British, and with almost as little effort on their part. Some resistance was offered as part of the troops, after landing, advanced to the position meant to be occupied for the night; but it was speedily overcome, with very trifling loss, and in the morning the town was found evacuated. Prome is distant from the town of Pegu, N.W., 113 miles. The town was nearly destroyed by fire in the early part of 1856. The district of which this place is the chief town has an area of 5,500 square miles, and a population of 100,000 inhabitants. Lat. 18° 47′, long. 95° 3′.

PROMNA.—A town in the British district of Amherst, one of the Tenasserim provinces, 53 miles N. of Moulmein. Lat. 17° 16′, long. 97° 42′.

PROVINCE WELLESLEY. — See WELLESLEY PROVINCE.

PRUCHITGURH.—A town in the native state of Sawuntwarree, presidency of Bombay, 20 miles N.E. from Vingorla, and 52 miles S.W. by S. from Kolapoor. Lat. 16° 3′, long. 73° 53′.

PRUCHITGURH.—A town in the native state of Kolapoor, presidency of Bombay, 50 miles N.W. from Kolapoor, and 38 miles S.W. by S. from Sattara. Lat. 17° 12′, long. 73° 47′.

PUBB MOUNTAINS, extending southward from the Hala range, and forming a natural boundary between the Belooche province of Lus and Sinde. If we consider their northern limit to be in lat. 26°, where the Hala range becomes contracted to about thirty miles in breadth, and their southern to be Cape Monze, their length will be found to be about ninety miles. In lat. 25° 3′, long. 66° 50′, they are crossed by the route from Kurrachee to Sonmeanee, at the pass of Guncloba, described by Hart as "stony, of trifling ascent, and the descent equally gentle." The highest part appears to be about lat. 25° 30′, where native report represents the elevation as great, though it does not probably exceed that of the mountains of Western Sinde, considered to be about 2,000 feet.

PUBNA. — A British district under the presidency of Bengal, named from its principal place. It is bounded on the north by the British district Bogra or Bagura; on the north-east by the British district Mymensing; on the south-east by the British district Dacca Jelalpore; on the south by the British district Jessore; on the west, and also on the north-west, by the British districts Nuddea and Rajeshahye: it lies between lat. 23° 34′—24° 36′, long. 88° 55′—89° 48′, and has an area of 2,606 square miles. It is a remarkably watery tract, containing many jhils or shallow lakes, and being traversed by the Ganges, and numerous offsets from that river and from the Brahmapootra. The population of this district is given under the article BENGAL.

This tract was acquired by the East-India Company in 1765, by virtue of the firman of Shah Alam, conveying to that authority the dewanny of Bengal, Behar, and Orissa.

PUBNA.—A town, the principal place of the British district of the same name, situate about a mile north of the left bank of the Podda, or great eastern branch of the Ganges, and on the Pubna, an offset from it. Pubna is distant N.E. from Calcutta 130 miles. Lat. 24°, long. 89° 12′.

PUCCOLE.—A town in the British district of Mymunsing, lieut.-gov. of Bengal, 49 miles S.S.W. of Nusserabad. Lat. 24° 9′, long. 90°.

PUCHAK, in the Rajpoot state of Jodhpoor, a village on the route from Nusserabad to the town of Jodhpoor, and 43 miles E. of the latter. Lat. 26° 10′, long. 73° 47′.

PUCHARI.—A village in the district of Shekawuttee, territory of Jeypore, lieut.-gov. of the N.W. Provinces. Lat. 28° 8′, long. 76° 1′.

PUCHBUDRA, in the Rajpoot state of Jodhpoor, a town 60 miles S.W. of the city of Jodhpoor, and eight miles N. of the right bank of the Sonee. It is situate in a fertile but scantily cultivated country, and three miles south of salt marshes, the brine of which is so strong in the dry season, that the salt spontaneously crystallizes into large masses about bushes thrown into the pools for that purpose. The town and the salt-works belong to the khalsa or royal estate of the maharaja of Jodhpur, and the revenue from them is allocated to the maintenance of his zenana. Lat. 25° 57′, long. 72° 21′.

PUCHESUR, in the British district of Kumaon, lieut.-gov. of the N.W. Provinces, a village at the confluence of the rivers Surjoo and Kalee (Eastern), on the left bank of the former, right of the latter, 10 miles S. of the cantonment of Petoragurh. Lat. 29° 27′, long. 80° 18′.

PUCHEWOR, in the Rajpoot state of Jeypore, a town on the route from Agra to Nusseerabad, 183 miles S.W. of former, 40 N.E. of latter. It is of considerable size, has a bazar, and supplies and water are abundant. Lat. 26° 30′, long. 75° 26′.

PUCHGAIN, in the British district of Boolundshuhur, lieut.-gov. of the N.W. Provinces, a village on the route from Allygurh cantonment to that of Delhi, and 35 miles N.W. of the former. Lat. 28° 19′, long. 77° 52′.

PUCHOWREA, in the British district of Bareilly, lieut.-gov. of the N.W. Provinces, a village on the route from the town of Pillibheet to Petoragurh cantonment, 25 miles N.E. of the former. Lat. 28° 57′, long. 80° 4′.

PUCHPERA, in the British district of Allygurh, lieut.-gov. of the N.W. Provinces, a village on the route from the city of Agra to Bareilly, and 52 miles N.E. of the former. Lat. 27° 41′, long. 78° 37′.

PUCHPERA, in the British district of Bareilly, lieut.-gov. of the N.W. Provinces, a village on the route from the town of Pillibheet to Nugina, and 16 miles N.W. of the former. Lat. 28° 48′, long. 79° 40′.

PUCHPERA, in the British district of Mynpoorie, lieut.-gov. of the N.W. Provinces, a village on the route from the city of Agra to Etawa, and 30 miles N.W. of the latter. Lat. 27° 5′, long. 78° 41′.

PUCHROLI, in the Rajpoot state of Jodhpoor, a village on the route from the town of Jodhpoor to that of Ajmeer, and 37 miles N.W. of the latter. Lat. 26° 35′, long. 74° 11′.

PUCHUM SUREEORA, in the British district of Allahabad, lieut.-gov. of the N.W. Provinces, a village on the route by the Rajapoor ferry from the cantonment of Allahabad to Banda, and 39 miles W. of the former. Lat. 25° 26′, long. 81° 22′.

PUCKA BHOOTA.—A town in the native state of Bhawulpoor, situate on the left bank of the Indus river, and 131 miles S.W. by W. from Bhawulpoor. Lat. 28° 26′, long. 69° 59′.

PUCKERPOOR.—A town in Oude, 51 miles N.E. from Lucknow, and 106 miles E.S.E. from Shahjehanpoor. Lat. 27° 22′, long. 81° 35′.

PUDAPADDY.—A town in the British district of Malabar, presidency of Madras, 49 miles S.E. by E. of Cannanore. Lat. 11° 29′, long. 76° 2′.

PUDDOW.—A town in the British district of Tavoy, one of the Tenasserim provinces, 131 miles N.N.W. of Tenasserim. Lat. 13° 53′, long. 98° 22′.

PUDHOR.—See BHUDDUR.

PUDORA, in the British district of Allygurh, lieut.-gov. of the N.W. Provinces, a village on the route from the city of Agra to Bareilly, and 53 miles N.E. of the former. Lat. 27° 42′, long. 78° 37′.

PUDREE.—A town in Scinde, situate in the territory of Ali Moorad, 73 miles S.S.E. from Bukkur, and 106 miles N.E. by N. from Hydrabad. Lat. 26° 40′, long. 69° 19′.

PUDREE.—A town in the British district of Tirhoot, lieut.-gov. of Bengal, 44 miles S.E. of Durbunga. Lat. 25° 38′, long. 86° 23′.

PUDROWNAN.—A town on the route from Goruckpore cantonment to Mullye, and 36 miles E. of the former. It is situate in a beautiful well-wooded country, and when Buchanan surveyed it, about fifty years ago, "contained 700 houses. A few had two stories, and a few were tiled, but by far the greater part consisted of miserable thatched huts. The rajah's castle occupied one corner, and the whole had been surrounded by a ditch and bamboo hedge." He adds, "The town had considerable manufactures of sugar, nitre, and cloth, and advances were made from the Company's factory at Ghazeepore for the two latter." Supplies are abundant here, and the road in this part of the route is good. Distant N.W. from Dinapoor 105 miles. Lat. 26° 50′, long. 84° 1′.

PUGGUR.—A town in the British district of Ramgur, lieut.-gov. of Bengal, 23 miles W. by S. of Hazareebagh. Lat. 23° 54′, long. 85° 3′.

PUGHROOKHEE.—A town in the British district of Behar, lieut.-gov. of Bengal, 33 miles S. of Behar. Lat. 24° 44′, long. 85° 37′.

PUHAREE, or PAHAREE, a native state of Bundelcund, with an area of four square miles, containing a population of 800. The rajah maintains a military force of fifty infantry. Puharee, the capital, is in lat. 25° 14′, long. 80° 50′.

PUHAREE, in the territory of Bhurtpore, a village on the route from Mathura to Ferozpoor, by Deeg, 54 miles N.W. of former, 15 S.E. of latter. Lat. 27° 43′, long. 77° 9′.

PUHASOO, in the British district of Boolundshuhur, lieut.-gov. of the N.W. Provinces, a town on the route from Boolundshuhur to Allygurh, 19 miles S.E. of the former. Lat. 28° 11′, long. 78° 8′.

PUHPOOND, in the British district of Etawa, the principal place of the pergunnah of the same name, is situate near the river Seengur, 32 miles S.E. of Etawa, 56 miles W. of Cawnpore. Puhpoond contains a population of 6,063 inhabitants. Lat. 26° 36′, long. 79° 32′.

PUHRAH, or PAHRAH, one of the native states of Bundelcund, containing an area of ten square miles, with a population of 1,600. The rajah maintains a force consisting of four horse and ninety-nine infantry. Puhrah, the principal place, is in lat. 25° 23′, long. 80° 18′.

PUJOUL, in the hill state of Komharsen, a village on the right bank of the Giree. Elevation above the sea 4,980 feet. Lat. 31° 6′, long. 77° 31′.

PUKHROULA, in the British district of Moradabad, lieut.-gov. of the N.W. Provinces, a village on the route from the town of Meerut to that of Moradabad, and 37 miles S.E. of the former place. Distant N.W. from Calcutta, *viâ* Moradabad, 924 miles. Lat. 28° 51′, long. 78° 15′.

PUKHURA.—A town in Nepal, situate on the right bank of the Naling river, and 102 miles W.N.W. from Khatmandoo. Lat. 28° 15′, long. 83° 47′.

PUKKA SERAI, in the British district of Boolundshuhur, lieut.-gov. of the N.W. Provinces, a village on the route from Allygurh cantonment to that of Delhi, and 14 miles S.E. of the latter. Lat. 28° 32′, long. 77° 26′.

PUKLI, in the north of the Punjab, a small tract east of the Indus: it is very fertile. Runjeet Singh obtained possession of it about twenty years ago, by expelling the Mahometan chief, Poyndu Khan, who took refuge in the island of Chuttoorbye, in the Indus. It is generally supposed to be the Peuceolatis of Arrian, but erroneously, as that (lib. iv. 22) was on the west side of the river, and Pukli is on the east. Lat. 34° 15′—34° 30′, long. 72° 50′—73° 15′.

PUKREE, in the British district of Allahabad, lieut.-gov. of the N.W. Provinces, a village on the right bank of the Ganges, 781 miles N.W. of Calcutta by the river route, and 27 S.E. of the city of Allahabad by the same. Lat. 25° 18′, long. 82° 12′.

PULANA, or PLANA, in the hill state of Goond, tributary to Keonthul, a village on the right bank of the Giree, near the confluence of a feeder from the north. Elevation above the sea 6,133 feet. Lat. 31° 6′, long. 77° 29′.

PULANA.—A town in the Rajpoot state of Oodeypoor, 15 miles N.N.E. from Oodeypoor, and 66 miles W.N.W. from Neemuch. Lat. 24° 48′, long. 73° 55′.

PULANTI.—A town in Nepal, situate on the right bank of the San Coos river, and 28 miles E. from Khatmandoo. Lat. 27° 42′, long. 85° 44′.

PULICAT, in the British district Chingleput, presidency of Madras, a town on an island in an extensive inlet of the sea or salt-water lake of the same name. The lake of Pulicat is thirty-three miles in length from north to south, and eleven in breadth where widest, and contains some large islands besides that on which the town is situate. It seems to have been produced by "the sea's breaking through a low sandy beach, and overflowing the lands within, for its communications with the sea are extremely narrow, like the embouchures of small rivers." From one to two miles off shore is the road called Pulicat Anchorage, where there are six or seven fathoms water. The lake, throughout its whole length, forms the north-eastern limit of the British district of Arcot, south division. An extensive line of water-communication has been established between the city of Madras and the town of Doogoorauzepatam, principally by means of this lake. The town of Pulicat is distant from Arcot, N.E., 76 miles; Nellore, S., 75; Madras, N., 22. Lat. 13° 25′, long. 80° 22′.

PULLA, in the British district of Allygurh, lieut.-gov. of the N.W. Provinces, a village on the route from the cantonment of Allygurh to that of Delhi, and nine miles N.W. of the former. Lat. 27° 59′, long. 78° 3′.

PULLA CHAND, in the British district

of Allygurh, lieut.-gov. of the N.W. Provinces, a village on the route from Meerut to Muttra, and 32 miles N.E. of the latter. Lat. 27° 53′, long. 77° 53′.

PULLADUM.—A town in the British district of Coimbatoor, presidency of Madras, 21 miles E. of Coimbatoor. Lat. 11°, long. 77° 19′.

PULLAGOO.—A town in the British district of Tavoy, one of the Tenasserim provinces, 148 miles S.S.E. of Moulmein. Lat. 14° 24′, long. 98° 16′.

PULLAMPUTTI.—A town in the British district of Trichinopoly, presidency of Madras, 33 miles N. by E. of Madura. Lat. 10° 23′, long. 78° 16′.

PULLANAMAIREE.—A town in the British district of North Arcot, presidency of Madras, 36 miles W.N.W. of Arcot. Lat. 13° 13′, long. 78° 48′.

PULLEA.—A town in Oude, situate on the left bank of the Chowka river, and 112 miles N. by W. from Lucknow. Lat. 28° 26′, long. 80° 37′.

PULLEAPOORAM.—A town in the native state of Travancore, 11 miles N.W. from Trivandrum, and 59 miles W. from Tinnevelly. Lat. 8° 36′, long. 76° 54′.

PULLEE.—A town in the Rajpoot state of Jodhpoor, 49 miles N.N.W. from Jodhpoor, and 122 miles W. by N. from Ajmeer. Lat. 26° 57′, long. 72° 50′.

PULLEHRA.—A town in the Boondela state of Tehree, 32 miles N.E. from Tehree, and 88 miles N.N.E. from Saugur. Lat. 25° 1′, long. 79° 15′.

PULLOK.—A town in the British district of Tavoy, one of the Tenasserim provinces, 88 miles N.N.W. of Tenasserim. Lat. 13° 20′, long. 98 41′.

PULLOW.—A town in the British district of Mergui, one of the Tenasserim provinces, 66 miles N.N.W. of Tenasserim. Lat. 13°, long. 98° 44′.

PULLUSGHUR.—A town in the recently lapsed territory of Nagpoor, 85 miles E.S.E. from Nagpoor, and 105 miles S.S.E. from Seuni. Lat. 20° 40′, long. 80° 20′.

PULLYCOOT.—A town in the British district of Malabar, presidency of Madras, 72 miles S.E. by E. of Cannanore. Lat. 11° 20′, long. 76° 20′.

PULLYPATTI.—A town in the British district of Salem, presidency of Madras, 23 miles N.E. of Salem. Lat. 11° 55′, long. 78° 26′.

PULNEY.—A town in the British district of Madura, presidency of Madras, 59 miles N.W. of Madura. Lat. 10° 30′, long. 77° 33′.

PULRA.—A village in the British district of Mozuffurnuggur, lieut.-gov. of the N.W. Provinces. Lat. 29° 22′, long. 77° 35′.

PULUSGAON.—A town in the recently lapsed territory of Nagpoor or Berar, 29 miles S.W. by S. from Nagpoor, and 92 miles E.S.E. from Ellichpoor. Lat. 20° 49′, long. 78° 55′.

PULWUL, in the British district of Goorgaon, lieut.-gov. of the N.W. Provinces, a small town, giving name to the pergunnah so called, on the route from Delhi to Muttra, and 41 miles S. of the former. It has a population of 12,010 inhabitants. Lat. 28° 9′, long. 77° 23′.

PUNAKHA.—A town in the native state of Bhotan, situate on the left bank of the Bagnee river, and 96 miles E.N.E. from Darjeeling. Lat. 27° 34′, long. 89° 45′.

PUNAMURTHCOTAH.—A town in the British district of Malabar, presidency of Madras, 49 miles E. by S. of Cannanore. Lat. 11° 44′, long. 76° 8′.

PUNAPOOR, in the British district of Bareilly, lieut.-gov. of the N.W. Provinces, a village on the route from the town of Bareilly to Seetapore, and six miles S.E. of the former. Lat. 28° 21′, long. 79° 33′.

PUNAR.—A river of the British district of Kumaon, lieut.-gov. of the N.W. Provinces, rising on the northern declivity of the Sub-Himalaya, or southern and inferior range of the Himalaya, in lat. 29° 28′, long. 79° 48′, and 11 miles S.E. of Fort Almora. It flows circuitously, but generally in an easterly direction, and, receiving many rivulets right and left, falls into the Surjoo, a great tributary of the Gogra, on the right side, in lat. 29° 32′, long. 80° 7′, having a total length of course of twenty-five miles. Buchanan, on hearsay evidence, states that gold is found in its channel; but neither Traill, in his Statistical Account of Kumaon, nor Webb, appears to mention this circumstance.

PUNASSA, in the British district of Allahabad, lieut.-gov. of the N.W. Provinces, a small town on the route by the Kutra Pass, from the cantonment of Allahabad to Rewah, 21 miles S.E. of the former. It is situate on the left bank of the Tons, close to its confluence with the Ganges. The Tons, here crossed by ferry, has a bed 400 yards wide; its left bank steep, its right sloping. Lat. 25° 16′, long. 82° 7′.

PUNCH, in the Northern Punjab, a small town on the southern slope of the mountains bounding Cashmere on the south. It is situate at the foot of the Punch Pass, and on the banks of a river of the same name, discharging itself into the Chenaub. At Punch, two much-frequented routes from the Punjab to Cashmere, that by Koteli and that by Rajawur, meet and proceed thence northward, through the Baramula Pass. Elevation of the Punch Pass 8,500 feet; of the town, 3,280. Punch is in lat. 33° 51′, long. 74° 10′.

PUNCH RIVER, in the Punjab, rises on the south-western declivity of the Pir Panjal Pass, about lat. 33° 38′, long. 74° 43′, and takes a direction generally north-westerly down the valley, dividing the Pir Panjal from the Ratan Panjal. After continuing in that direction for about fifty miles, it, close to the town of Punch, receives a feeder from the north, and below the confluence turns to the south-west. Here it is styled by Moorcroft a rivulet; but Jacquemont, who mentions it under the name of Tchaomok, describes it as a torrent so rapid and powerful, that there is much danger in fording it, insomuch that a horse which loses its footing is swept down the stream, and irretrievably perishes. Holding a south-westerly course of about forty miles, it near Koteli receives a considerable feeder, called the river of Rajour, and after a course of about thirty miles further, falls into the Chenaub, in lat. 33° 12′, long. 73° 41′.

PUNDERPOOR.—A town within the presidency of Bombay, on the north-eastern frontier of Sattara, towards the collectorate of Sholapore. It is situate on the Beema, a tributary to the Kistna, and is highly revered by the Brahmins, as containing a celebrated temple dedicated to an incarnation of Vishnu. Here, in 1815, Trimbuckjee Danglia, the profligate minion of the Peishwa, perpetrated the murder of Gungadhur Shastry, the Guicowar's minister and envoy, who had repaired to Poona under the sanction and protection of the British government. The circumstances under which this atrocious crime was committed are thus related:—As he (Gungadhur Shastry) passed along, one of his attendants heard a man in the crowd ask, "Which is the Shastry?" and another reply, "He who wears the necklace;" but not thinking the inquiry of any importance, he paid no attention either to the person asking the question or to him who made the answer. The Shastry entered the temple, performed his devotions, and after remaining a few minutes in conversation with Trimbuckjee Danglia, returned towards the house which he occupied. He advanced but a short distance from the temple, when three men came running behind him, and as if clearing the road for some person of distinction, calling out, "Make way, make way." Their left hands were folded up in cloths, and each of them in his right hand bore what seemed to be a twisted cloth, such as appears to be commonly used for striking persons in a crowd, to make them stand aside. One of them struck the Shastry a violent blow with the cloth, and it was then discovered that he had a sword in his hand; another seized him by the hair and threw him down; and whilst in the act of falling, a third ruffian cut him on the head. Three of the Shastry's attendants remained with their master; but two more assassins rushing from the front, the whole of them were wounded and disabled. The rest of the Shastry's friends and followers, who do not appear to have been blest with any large share of personal intrepidity, ran away, leaving him in the hands of his murderers. Being thus at liberty to complete their bloody work, they mangled the unhappy man in a dreadful manner, and then departed, one of them exclaiming in the Mahratta language, "We have now finished him."

Three of the Shastry's people had remained at the temple in attendance upon one of his suite. As they approached the spot where the murder had been committed, they saw five men with naked swords running towards the temple. This alarmed them; but not being aware of what had happened, they made their way as quietly as possible to the Shastry's house; not finding him there, they returned to the road, where they discovered his body cut to pieces. The population of Punderpoor is believed not to exceed 20,000 persons. Distance S.E. from Poona 112 miles, and 185 S.E. from Bombay. Lat. 17° 40′, long. 75° 24′.

PUNDOOA, or PURROOAH, in the British district of Hooghly, lieut.-gov. of Bengal, a small town with dak or relay-station for bearers, on the route from Calcutta to Burdwan, 32 miles N.W. of former, 30 S.E. of latter. Lat. 23° 3′, long. 88° 18′.

PUNDOOKESUR, in the British district of Gurhwal, lieut.-gov. of the N.W. Provinces, a town on the route from Sireenuggur to Thibet, 54 miles N.E. by E. of the former. Lat. 30° 37′, long. 79° 36′.

PUNDRAWUL, in the British district of Boolundshuhur, lieut.-gov. of the N.W. Provinces, a village on the route from Khasgunj to Meerut, and 36 miles N.W. of the former. Lat. 28° 7′, long. 78° 15′.

PUNGANORE.—A town in the British district of Cuddapah, presidency of Madras, 79 miles S. by W. of Cuddapah. Lat. 13° 20′, long. 78° 37′.

PUNGI, in Bussahir, a collection of hamlets in the district of Koonawur, on the right bank of the Sutluj, and at the south-eastern base of a range dividing the valley of the Kushang from that of the Mulgun. Elevation above the sea 9,197 feet. Lat. 31° 35′, long. 78° 20′.

PUNGURA, in the British district of Banda, lieut.-gov. of the N.W. Provinces, a village on the route from the town of Banda to Jubbulpoor, 20 miles S. of the former. It has water from a tank and wells. Lat. 25° 13′, long. 80° 31′.

PUNHETTI, in the British district of Allygurh, lieut.-gov. of the N.W. Provinces, a village on the route from the cantonment of Allygurh to that of Mynpoorie, and eight miles S.E. of the former. Lat. 27° 51′, long. 78° 14′.

PUNIAR, in the territory of Gwalior, or possessions of Scindia's family, a town 12 miles S.W. of the fort of that name, the scene of an engagement which took place on the 29th December, 1843 (the date of the victory of Maharajpore), between the British and Mahratta forces. Major-General Grey, leading from Bundelcund a British detachment to co-operate with that marching from Agra under the conduct of Sir Hugh Gough, commander-in-chief, crossed the river Sindh at Chandpur, and proceeding north-west, on the 29th, after a march of sixteen miles, was attacked by the Mahratta army, strongly posted near the village of Mangor. The British army took post at

Puniar, and by a series of attacks drove the enemy from all points of his position and captured all his artillery, amounting to twenty-four pieces, and all his ammunition. The Mahratta army is represented to have been about 12,000 strong, and to have suffered most severely; the British loss amounted to thirty-five killed and 182 wounded. Lat. 26° 6′, long. 78° 6′.

PUNJAB (THE), an extensive territory on the north-west of India, so called from two Persian words, signifying "five waters," the name having reference to five great rivers which flow through it. With respect to the propriety of the designation, it is, however, to be observed, that there are in fact six rivers, the Indus, the Jhelum, the Chenaub, the Ravee, the Beas, and the Sutlej; but as the Beas has a much shorter course than the others, it seems to have been disregarded when the name of the country was bestowed. In semi-civilized states, and especially in those of Asia, the boundaries, at all times ill-defined, are subject to frequent changes; and this holds true in regard to the territory lately acquired from the Sikhs, in consequence of their incessant wars with their neighbours to the north and west. In the present case, the province now designated the Punjab will be regarded as co-extensive with the recent empire of the Sikhs, with the exception of the provinces allotted by the British to Gholab Singh, and which are now comprehended within the newly-constituted kingdom of Cashmere. Regarded in this view, the Punjab will be found to possess natural limits remarkably well defined. They are as follows:—On the north, the lower boundaries of Gholab Singh's dominions; on the west, the Suliman range of mountains; on the east and south-east, the river Sutlej and its continuation the Ghara. The shape in outline approaches that of the sector of a circle, the centre of which is at the confluence of the Punjnud and the Indus, in lat. 28° 55′, long. 70° 31′; the extreme radii, the Suliman range, holding in general a direction not greatly varying from north to south; the Sutlej, and its continuation the Ghara, holding a direction from north-east to south-west; the arc in its highest latitude touching the 35th parallel. The most western point is just below the confluence of the Punjnud and Indus; the most eastern is between the 78th and 79th meridian. The length from east to west is about 550 miles; the breadth, measured at right angles to this, about 420; the superficial extent, 73,535 square miles. No two regions can differ more in physical character than the northern and southern part of this territory. Within the north-east angle is comprehended the Alpine region of Kangra. The north-west angle comprises the Eusofzye country, Peshawur, Kohat, Huzara, and the country thence extending southward to the Salt range; the entire tract being intersected by mountain-ranges, and consisting of a series of valleys, encircled by hills. The remainder includes the plain country of the Punjab, distributed into the five doabs, and stretching south-west with a regularity rarely broken by any eminence of importance. The declivity of the surface from north-east to south-west is proved beyond question by the course of the rivers, which all descend in that direction. Jacquemont considers that the courses of the Soorsutty and Guggur, which, flowing from the Himalaya, are lost in the desert of Bikanir, lie along an elevated tract dividing the basin of the Jumna from that of the Sutlej, and that barometric and other observations prove the plain of the Punjab to be below that of Eastern Hindostan. He thence concludes the bed of the Sutlej, in its course through the plain, to be lower than that of the Jumna; that of the Beas lower than that of the Sutlej; and so in succession westward with regard to the beds of the Ravee, the Chenaub, and the Jhelum, to the Indus, flowing through the lowest part of this extensive basin.

About the town of Mundi, near the north-eastern frontier, and on the upper course of the Beas, in the most southern and lower ranges of the Himalaya, is an extensive tract of rocks and deposits of recent formation, of limestone, sandstone, gypsum, argillaceous slate, amidst which veins of quartz occasionally occur. This formation is important, in consequence of containing inexhaustible beds of fossil salt, very compact and heavy, and of a reddish colour. On the west of the Punjab, and crossing the Doab, between the Jhelum and the Indus, is the Salt range, which is cross-cut by the channel of the Indus, and which, to the north of the Daman, on the western side of that river, joins the Suliman and Khyber ranges. The Salt range, sometimes (on the west of the Indus) called the Kalabagh range, holds a direction a little south of east, between lat. 32° 30′—33°, and terminates rather abruptly on the right bank of the river Jhelum. The elevation is not great, probably in few places exceeding 2,000 feet above the sea. The formations composing it are grauwacke, limestone, sandstone, gypsum, and red tenacious clay, investing enormous deposits of common salt, or chloride of sodium.

Altogether, the ascertained mineral wealth of the Punjab and its dependencies appears scanty in proportion to the great extent of its mountains. Gold is found in the sands of the streams of the Chenaub, the Huroo, and the Swan; graphite or plumbago abounds in the Pir Panjal, bounding Cashmere on the south-west; iron is also raised in Mundi, as well as common salt. The Salt range, besides the mineral from which it is named, produces antimony, alum, and sulphur. Nitre is obtained in abundance from the alluvial plains. Coal exists about the Salt range at Mukkud, on the left bank of the Indus, and in the localities of Joa, Meealee, and Nummul. Scientific inquiries into the mineral resources of the Salt range, and the Alpine portion of the Sindh Sagur Doab, have been authorized by the government.

No country of the same extent probably enjoys more largely than the Punjab the means of irrigation and of inland navigation, by means of its six noble rivers. The most eastern, the Sutlej, has its source in Thibet, in lat. 30° 8′, long. 81° 53′. Holding a south-westerly course of about 550 miles, it receives the Beas, below the confluence of which, taking place near Hurekee, and in lat. 31° 12′, long. 75° 3′, the united stream is called the Ghara for about 300 miles, to the confluence of the Chenaub; thenceforward the aggregate body of water bears the name of the Punjnud for a further distance of about sixty miles, to its confluence with the Indus. Next to the Sutlej, westward, is the Beas, rising in lat. 32° 24′, long. 77° 12′, and holding a sinuous course of about 290 miles, in general to the south-west, to its confluence with the Sutlej. Farther to the west flows the Ravee, the least in the volume of its water, though not in the length of its course. Issuing from a lake embosomed in the Himalaya, in lat. 32° 30′, long. 77° 1′, it holds a very tortuous course, but generally in a south-westerly direction, for about 420 miles, to its confluence with the Chenaub. This last-mentioned river, usually regarded as the largest of the Punjab, flows in general west of that of the Ravee, though its source is more eastward, as it sweeps in a wide flexture round the upper part of the smaller rivers. Rising in Lahoul, in lat. 32° 48′, long. 77° 27′, the Chenaub pursues a circuitous course, but for the most part south-west, and at the distance of about 600 miles from its source, unites with the Jhelum, near Trimo ferry. The united stream, proceeding in the same direction for about fifty miles, receives the water of the Ravee; below the confluence it loses the name of Chenaub, and is called the Trimab for a further distance of 110 miles, to the junction of the Ghara. From that point the river flows about sixty miles, as before mentioned, to its confluence with the Indus, being called the Punjnud, a name derived from its conveying the accumulated water of the Beas, the Sutlej, the Ravee, the Chenaub, and the Jhelum. This last river rises in Cashmere, the whole valley of which it drains. Soon after its issue therefrom, it receives a large tributary, the Kishengunga, or river of Mazufurabad, and after a course of about 490 miles, generally in a south-westerly direction, it unites with the Chenaub near Trimo ferry. The Indus, the most westerly of the Punjab rivers, traverses the country in a direction from north to south for about 500 miles, from Derbend to the confluence of the Punjnud. These noble streams, besides affording means of inland navigation, scarcely equalled, are of inestimable value for the purposes of irrigation. Several of the old canals have been improved and enlarged. A new canal, intended to traverse the entire length of the Baree Doab, is under construction. The central line is to be 247 miles in length. It will commence from that point where the river Ravee debouches from the lowest of the Himalayan ranges, thence, cutting through a high bank, it will cross two mountain-torrents, till it gains the table-lands; then it will traverse the heart of the Manjha, passing near the great cities of Deenanuggur, Buttala, and Umritsir; thence, striking into the deeps of the wildest wastes of the lower Doab, and running past the ruined cities, tanks, temples, and canals, all of which it is to vivify and regenerate, it will rejoin the Ravee fifty-six miles above Mooltan. At the thirtieth mile of its course, a branch diverges to fertilize the most arid lands of the Doab, and reach the ancient city of Kussoor. From this branch again, a smaller channel is diverted to the eastward, and carried on till it nearly meets the Sutlej opposite the battle-field of Sobraon. At the fifty-fifth mile of the grand line, another channel branches off, to spread fertility down to the capital of Lahore. In addition to the main 247 miles, the Kussoor, Sobraon, and Lahore branches, of eighty-four, sixty-one, and seventy-four miles respectively, will make up an aggregate of 466 miles.

The plain of the Punjab is divided by its rivers into five extensive natural sections, described by the native term *doab*, signifying a great tongue of land lying in the bifurcation above the confluence of two rivers. First, the doab of Julinder, between the Sutlej and the Beas; second, the doab of Baree, between the Beas and Ghara on the east, and the Ravee on the west; third, the doab of Rechna, between the Ravee on the east, and the Chenaub on the west; fourth, the doab of Jetch, between the Chenaub on the east, and the Jhelum on the west; fifth, the doab of Sinde Sagur, between the Jhelum, Trimab or Chenaub, and Punjnud on the east, and the Indus on the west. Of these, that of Sinde Sagur is the most extensive, but that of Baree by far the most populous, as well as the most important, containing the three great cities Lahore, Amritsir, and Mooltan. The regular and gradual slope of the great plain of the Punjab has been mentioned: even the upper part is but of moderate elevation. Thus, Amritsir and Lahore are each 900 feet above the level of the sea, the town of Jhelum about 1,600, and the surface slopes regularly to the south-western extremity, where, close to Mittunkote, the elevation is about 220 feet. In consequence of the nearly unbroken flatness of the surface, the great rivers frequently change their courses in an extraordinary degree. "Bands of sand traverse the country in a north and south direction, which point out the old beds of rivers, and prove that all of them have been changed. The Sutlej, which formerly ran close to the town of Loodianah, is now seven miles to the northward; the Ravee, which twenty years ago washed the walls of the city of Lahore, runs in a channel three miles off to the northward; the Chenaub, which ten or twelve years ago ran close to the town of Ramnuggur, is now four miles distant; and the same applies to the Jhelum." So the Ghara, at no great distance of time, held, for above 200 miles, a course considerably westward of the present, and parallel to it.

The climate of the plain of the Punjab is in general characterized by dryness and warmth. Little rain falls, except in those parts extending along the southern base of the Himalaya, and where the south-west monsoon is partially felt, diminishing in its effect in proportion as it proceeds westward. According to the statement of Elphinstone, the rain "in the north of the Punjab exceeds that of Delhi; but in the south of the Punjab, distant both from the sea and the hills, very little rain falls." Still the rains of the monsoon extend as far as Lahore, and fall heavily there in midsummer. In the more southern part of the plain, the soil, where productive, is rendered so by irrigation. In addition to the facilities offered by the rivers and canals, the Persian wheel is employed to draw to the surface the water of numerous wells. The winters are cool, even to the feelings of a European. Elphinstone observes, in regard to his residence in Mooltan, at the end of December: "The weather was delightful during our stay; the thermometer, when at the lowest, was at 28° at sunrise: there were slight frosts in the night." During the march of the English army through this country in 1838, thin ice was formed on the water at the end of December, whilst in the day the thermometer rose to 70°. At the end of December, Elphinstone, marching through the doab between the Chenaub and the Indus, found a very cold wind; but it does not appear that snow falls in this part of the Punjab. Burnes describes the weather in the beginning of February as cold and bleak, frequently rainy, and always cloudy. In January, 1839, the lowest state of the thermometer was found, on different nights of the months, to be respectively 34°, 37°, 38°, 44°. In the day the thermometer, even in midwinter, is seldom below 70°, and in January generally reaches 80°, so that vegetation rapidly proceeds, and the wheat harvest is gathered by the end of April. Such, during winter, is the general temperature of the Punjab south of the Salt range. North of that, and even outside the limits of the mountains, the cold is greater, an effect attributable to a slight increase of elevation rather than to change of latitude. The British, in marching through that tract in December, 1839, found the cold severe, the thermometer during the night sinking to 2° below the freezing-point. The heat in summer is excessive; in the plains at Mooltan it is so great as to be proverbial. At Lahore it was found, in the beginning of June, to raise the thermometer to 112° in a tent artificially cooled. A traveller, who experienced the heat of this season, describes it as "perfectly intolerable: we are unable," he adds, "to eat, drink, or sleep, and support existence by suction alone." Bernier, who had endured the heat of the most sultry part of Arabia, found that of the country between Lahore and Cashmere much more distressing, and each morning entertained a dread of being unable to survive till the evening. He describes his body as having become as it were a dry sponge, and he no sooner took a draught of water than it oozed from all parts of his skin, from which the cuticle had peeled, leaving the surface covered with pustules. Some of his companions died of heat even in the shade.

The indigenous vegetation of the plain of the Punjab closely resembles that of the drier tracts of Eastern Hindostan; trees are scarce, and there occur extensive tracts containing only a few bushes, principally babools of the mimosa species. Even the date-palm is, according to Burnes, an exotic, introduced by the Mahometan invaders. The wild palm, a species which produces no fruit, is in many places abundant; as are the peloo (Salvadora persica), various species of willows, the pepool (Ficus religiosa), divers species of acacias and tamarisk, the byr-apple or jujube (Zizyphus ju-juba), and capparis, called here kureel, juwassi, or camel-thorn; the talee, a tree called sissoo in Eastern Hindostan, and sometimes of twelve feet girth, useful for boat-building; the neem (Melia azadurachta), the mudar (Tropæa), the toolse (Ocymum sanctum), kurmul or wild rue. Fuel is scarce, in consequence of the general absence of trees, and cow-dung is extensively used for the purpose. The towns and villages of the Punjab are, however, generally surrounded by groves; but these are usually of forced fruit-trees artificially cultivated,—date, orange, pomegranate, mulberry, apple, fig, peach, apricot, plum, quince, almond, and a few others of less importance. The mango is cultivated, but does not attain high perfection except about Mooltan, and deteriorates in proportion to the advance northward. Since the occupation of the province by the British, endeavours have not been wanting on the part of the government to encourage the growth of timber. Arrangements have been made for the preservation of the tracts of forest and brushwood which already exist; for the planting of copses near the cantonments; of groves round public buildings, and at intervals along the main roads, and of avenues on the banks of canals.

The zoology of the Punjab is more rich and varied than its botany. No accounts afford authority for concluding that elephants exist there in a state of nature; for though Arrian mentions the hunting of elephants on the banks of the Indus, the animals in question clearly appear to have been some turned loose by the natives in their hasty flight. Tigers lurk in the jungle and forests, and sometimes attain the enormous length of ten feet. Lions are not uncommon. The other beasts of prey are panthers, leopards, hyenas, lynxes, wolves, bears, jackals, foxes, otters, martens, stoats, and divers other small *viverræ;* there are also nylgaus, wild hogs, porcupines, various animals of the deer, goat, and antelope species, monkeys and bats, including the large and hideous vampyre, deemed sacred by the natives. Among the feathered tribes there are peafowl, parrots, jungle-fowl (the wild stock of our common domestic fowl), pheasants, various kinds of partridges, quails, water-fowl in great number and variety, herons, cranes, pelicans, eagles, vultures, hawks, magpies, hoopoes, and doves of various kinds. The bulbul, or nightingale of Cashmere, is inferior in note to that of Europe, but very beautiful. A small species of alligator swarms in the rivers, especially the Jhelum. The porpoise ascends the Indus to a great distance. Among serpents, the more remarkable are the cobra de capello, and a small snake, the bite of which is almost immediately fatal. The rivers abound with fish; the pulla, a delicious species of carp, swarming in the Indus, forms an important article of subsistence. Of insects, the silkworm thrives remarkably, and produces an article of admirable quality; bees also produce wax and honey in great abundance and of the finest kind, and this department of husbandry receives great attention. The more important domestic animals are the camel (especially in the south) and the buffalo, of which great herds are kept in the neighbourhood of rivers, these animals being almost of an amphibious nature. Horses are bred extensively, especially in the plain country in the north-east, and receive great attention, the Sikhs being an equestrian people. Much additional light on the ornithology and botany of the Punjab is about to be afforded by an elaborate report on those subjects by Dr. Jameson.

The more important crops in the low, level, and fertile tracts, are indigo, cotton, sugar, tobacco, opium, wheat, which is abundant and in quality excellent; buck-wheat, rice, barley, millet, juwaree (Holcus sorghum), bajra (Holcus spicatus), moong (Phaseolus mungo), maize, various sorts of vetches, oil-seeds, such as sesamum and mustard; peas and beans, carrots, turnips, onions, melons, cucumbers, and sundry kinds of cucurbitaceous plants. So plentiful is wheat, that it sells at Mooltan at from half a rupee to a rupee per maund. Bang, or hemp, is produced for the purpose of inducing intoxication; saffron, safflower for dyes, and a great number of less-important products. Milk, butter, and wool are very important objects of rural economy, the former being almost the only produce of the numerous herds of kine, as the slaughtering of these animals for food is not allowed by the Sikhs.

The manufacturing industry of the Punjab is considerable. It is exercised principally in the silk and cotton productions of Amritsir, Lahore, Mooltan, Shoojahbad, Leia, and some other places in the south, and in the fabrication of arms in Lahore. Much of the commerce of the Punjab consists in the transit of the goods of Hindostan to the countries west of the Indus. The chief marts are Amritsir, Leia, and Mooltan, Lahore being in this respect of inferior importance. The imports from British India are principally sugar, spices, and other groceries; dye-stuffs, cotton, woollen, and silk cloths; metals, and utensils of various kinds of metal; ivory, precious stones, glass, porcelain, and cutlery. From the west, the imports are gold, turquoises, silver, silk, madder, cochineal, asafœtida, safflower, fruits (fresh and dried), wool, horses, and a few of the more portable manufactures of Russia. The exports, whether in the way of transit or the produce of the country, are grain, ghee or clarified butter, hides, wool, silk and cotton fabrics, carpets, shawls, silk, cotton, indigo, tobacco, salt, and horses.

The population consists of various races, being composed of Jats, Gujurs, Rajpoots, and Patans. A small portion of the country included between the Kishengunga and the Indus, north of the Salt range, is held by the Eusufzye Afghans. Of the races above mentioned, the most prominent are the Jats, who are represented as having formed the "core and nucleus" of the Sikh commonwealth and armies. They occupy the centre portion of the Baree Doab and the vicinity of Amritsur; but they have also extensive colonies in various parts of the Punjab. In the south-west angle of the province, about Mooltan, they are held in indifferent repute, their importance there being merely agricultural. The Gujurs, supposed to be the aborigines of Huzara, are described as an industrious class, devoting much attention to agriculture, and differing in this respect from the Rajpoots. The principal localities of the Patans are Mooltan and Kussoor, in the Baree Doab. From the Beas to the Chenab the Hindoo race predominates; but, in all parts of this region, the Mahomedans are numerously interspersed, and in the south they actually form the majority; but of the Mahomedans a large portion are of Hindoo origin. From the Chenab to the Indus, the population chiefly consists of Hindoo converts to Mahomedanism. Beyond the Indus the pure Mahomedan race prevails. Of the whole population, two-thirds are Mussulmans (both spurious and genuine), the remaining one-third are chiefly Hindoos, and of these half are Sikhs.

For administrative purposes, the province has been distributed into a limited number of territorial divisions, each division comprising several districts. The names of the principal divisions, with their respective areas and amount of population, are stated below.

Divisions.	Area in Sq. Miles.	Population.
Lahore	11,628	3,458,694
Jhelum	16,761	1,762,488
Mooltan......	15,494	971,175
Leia	15,271	1,122,621
Peshawur	7,588	847,695
Jullunder .. / Hoshyapoor / Kangra	6,792	2,273,037
	73,534	10,435,710

The Sikhs are for the most part concentrated about the capitals Amritsir and Lahore. The belief of this sect was originally, according to Malcolm, a pure deism, but has so far degenerated that they now consider their founder entitled to divine honours, and regard him as a saviour and mediator with God. Their faith admits the doctrine of the transmigration of souls, either as a punishment, or a remedial process for moral deficiency, and of a future state of bliss for the good. To kill kine is considered by them a horrible impiety. Tobacco is prohibited, but fermented liquors are allowed, and no kind of food is forbidden except beef. Malcolm lays down the following as the great points by which they are separated from the strict Hindoos: the renunciation of the distinctions of castes, the admission of proselytes, and the rendering the pursuit of arms not only allowable, but the religious duty of all. The sect, though it has but recently become powerful, was founded by Nanac, who was born in 1469, at Raypur, sixty miles west of Lahore, and received the name of *Guru*, or "spiritual pastor," from his votaries, who themselves assumed the appellation of *Sikhs*, or "disciples." His followers were at first peaceable and humble, and remained so until the murder, by the Mahometans, of their fourth Guru in succession from Nanac; on which event his successor, Har Govind, in revenge, drew the sword, which has never since been sheathed. Guru Govind, the fifth in succession from Har Govind, and the tenth from Nanac, is regarded as the founder of the temporal power of the Sikhs. His votaries were instructed by him always to bear arms, or at least steel in some form or other, about them, and to assume the name of Singh, or lion, previously affected only by the Rajpoots. By this name they are distinguished from the other Sikhs, or followers of Baba Nanac. They ceased to have any spiritual leader after the death of Govind, who was killed in 1708; and from that period, until the power of Runjeet Singh became paramount, they constituted a turbulent and irregular republic, holding, in cases of great emergency, a Guru-mata, or general diet, at Amritsir, but at other times engaged incessantly in petty warfare with each other. Runjeet viewed the congregated meetings at Amritsir with great jealousy, and built at that place the great fortress of Govindghur, ostensibly to protect, but actually to overawe and control, the excited followers of Govind, who resorted there. Those Sikhs who adhere to the original doctrines of Nanac are called Khalasa; they are less fanatical and warlike than the Singhs, or followers of Guru Govind. Of these latter, a peculiar class is called Acalis, or immortals, and sometimes Nihungs. Their fanaticism, Burnes observes, borders on insanity, and they seem to be at war with all mankind. They go about heavily armed, frequently bearing a drawn sword in each hand, two other swords in their belts, a matchlock on their back, and on their turbans iron quoits six or eight inches in diameter, with their outer edges sharpened; and these, it is asserted, they throw with such force, as well as precision of aim, as to lop off the leg of a horse, or even of an elephant. Osborne, however, who has frequently seen them try their skill, found them to be very bungling, and the missile in their hands to be very inefficient. They are a lawless and sanguinary class, and would have rendered the country desolate, had they not been vigorously coerced by Runjeet Singh.

The sacred books of the Sikhs are called *Granth* (scripture). The principal of them are the *Adi-Granth*, composed by Nanac, their first Guru, and the *Das Padshah ke Granth*, composed by Guru Govind, their last spiritual guide. They charge in battle to the war-cry, *Wai! Guruji ka Fath*, "O Victory to our master the Guru!"

The Sikhs as soldiers appear in a respectable light. Their repeated and signal successes against the formidable Afghans are conclusive evidence of their valour; they are patient of fatigue and privation, and, in case of reverse, readily rally. Malcolm gives rather a favourable view of their character. "The Sikh soldier," he says, "is, generally speaking, brave, active, and cheerful, without polish, but neither destitute of sincerity nor attachment." But for the occurrence of some recent events, the present race of Sikhs might have claimed exemption from the charge of cruelty. Their celebrated maharaja, Runjeet Singh, rarely shed the blood either of criminals or of his personal enemies, and he appears to have aspired to the praise of clemency.

In person, the Sikhs bear a general resemblance to other people of Hindoo origin, but they are more robust; the result of a more varied and liberal diet: they especially excel others of the Hindoo race in having the lower extremities full, muscular, and symmetrical. Their women are esteemed beautiful.

The general dress of the male portion of the Sikh population consists of a jacket and trowsers reaching to the knee; of late, the chiefs have lengthened the trowsers to the ancles. They also wear shawls and scarfs, and wrap their heads in thin narrow cloths, so as to form a rude turban. The Sikhs are in general remarkably illiterate; Runjeet Singh was unable to read or write, and most of his courtiers were alike destitute of these elementary attainments. This may, perhaps be accounted for from the fact of most of the sect, including Runjeet himself, tracing their origin to the Jats, a Rajpoot tribe of very low order.

The language of the Punjab is called by Malcolm a jargon, compounded of various tongues. As spoken in large towns, it is a dialect of the Urdu or Hindustani: in the villages, the dialect in use is Jatbky, sprung from a cognate root, and originally the language of the country: on the southern frontier, Punjaubi contains a large admixture of Sindhi. There are two characters used,—

Laude, that of common translation, and *Gurmukhi*, or the character of the Granth. Measures have been taken by the government for the promotion of popular education. The indigenous schools are of three descriptions, resorted to by Hindoos, Mussulmans, and Sikhs respectively. A government educational institution, partaking of a collegiate character, has been founded at Amritsir. It is remarkable that female education is to be met with in all parts of the Punjab. The girls and the teachers (also females) belong to all of the three races above enumerated.

In facilities of communication, this province enjoys great advantages. Besides those afforded by its noble rivers, it possesses others in a number of roads constructed since its occupation by the British. Of these the principal is the main road from south-east to north-west, from Lahore to Peshawur, passing the towns of Wuzeerabad, Jhelum, Rawul Pindee, and Attock. From Lahore this road is continued in a south-easterly direction across the Jullunder Doab to Loodiana, where it communicates with the grand trunk road from Calcutta. 2. From north to south, from Lahore to Ferozepore; 3. from north-east to south-west, from Lahore to Mooltan; 4. from east to west, from Lahore to Dera Ismael Khan; 5. from north-west to south-east, from Dera Ismael Khan, passing the town of Jhung, in the Rechna Doab, and traversing the Baree Doab to Ullohur, where it joins the road from Delhi; 6. from south to north, from Amritsir to Sealkote. There are, besides, several routes connecting the great northern cities with the chief southern outlet at Mooltan.

The Sikh realm has many considerable towns: of these, the most worthy of notice are—Lahore, Amritsir, Pind Dadun Khan, Mooltan, Peshawer, Dera Ghazee Khan, Dera Ismael Khan, Julinder, Vazeerabad, Leia, Nurpur, Le, Jelum, Jelalpoor, Shoojabad, and several others, especially noticed under their names in the alphabetical arrangement.

The Punjab was, in remote antiquity, the scene of some of Alexander's most arduous exploits. At the beginning of the eleventh century of the Christian era, it was ravaged, widely and sweepingly, by Mahmood of Ghiznee, "the Destroyer." Lahore for about a century remained in possession of the successors of Mahmood, and was frequently the seat of their government, until 1186, when the Ghaznevide dynasty was uprooted by Mahomed, sultan of Ghore. Subsequently to this event, the Punjab became the prey of a succession of weak, licentious, and turbulent rulers, among whom the Afghans generally predominated, until, in 1526, Baber gained the victory of Paniput, and, ascending the throne, established the sovereignty of the Timurian family. In 1748, Ahmed Shah Durani, finding the power of the Moguls broken by the invasion of Nadir Shah, overran the Punjab with an Afghan army, and made himself master of Lahore; and in 1756 the Mogul emperor of India ceded to him these conquests. Soon after this, the power of the Sikhs began to assume a formidable aspect, and in 1768 they overran the country east of the Jhelum, and, crossing that river, took the celebrated fortress Rotas. In 1797, Shah Zeman Durani invaded the Punjab and took Lahore, but being immediately recalled by an insurrection at home, left the country in greater confusion than he found it. The expulsion of Shah Shooja in 1809, and consequent subversion of the Afghan monarchy, facilitated the rise of Runjeet Singh, a Sikh of the caste of Jats, one of the humblest but most numerous among the Rajpoots. In 1799, this adventurer had obtained from Zeman Shah Durani a grant of Lahore, and in the same year succeeded in expelling three rival Sikh chieftains, who had maintained themselves there. In 1809, having extended his power over the greater part of the Punjab, and some of the petty hill states, he carried his arms across the Sutlej, and attacked the Sikh chieftains under British protection. Negotiations ensued, and were brought to an amicable conclusion by a treaty, providing "that the British government will have no concern with the territories and subjects of the raja to the northward of the river Sutlej," and that Runjeet Singh would not commit or suffer any encroachment on the possessions or rights of the chiefs on the left bank of that river. In 1818, Runjeet Singh stormed Mooltan, and extended his power over the whole southern part of the Punjab, and in the same year marched a force across the Indus, and made himself master of Peshawer. In 1819, the Maharaja of the Sikhs, as Runjeet styled himself, conquered the Derajat, on the west side of the Indus, and Cashmere. In 1831, at Rooper, on the Sutlej, an interview took place, amidst great pomp and display, between Runjeet Singh and Lord Auckland, the Governor-General of British India, and a paper was placed in the hands of the Sikh ruler promising him the perpetual amity of the British government. In 1835, Gholab Singh, a vassal of the Maharaja, reduced to subjection the extensive hill state of Ladakh, or Middle Tibet; and five or six years later, the same chieftain subdued Bulti, or Little Tibet. In 1838 Runjeet Singh became a party in the tripartite treaty with the British government and Shah Shooja, and succeeded in obtaining a stipulation securing to him the right to all the territories which he then possessed on both sides of the Indus. Runjeet Singh died in July, 1839, and was succeeded by his son Kuruck Singh. The latter died in 1840, and, as was generally believed, from the effects of poison. Before the funeral ceremonies for this prince were fully ended, his son and successor was killed by the falling of a beam — a catastrophe not accidental, though intended to have the appearance of being so. A competition for the vacant throne then ensued between the widow of

Kuruck Singh and a reputed son of Runjeet Singh, named Shere Singh, but who, though born in wedlock, had been subjected by his alleged father to the stigma of illegitimacy. Shere Singh finally succeeded; but his triumph was of short duration: near the close of the year 1843 he was assassinated; and this was followed by a widely-spread, frantic, and sanguinary anarchy, which, after raging with a fury that overspread the Punjab with desolation and misery, eventuated in an aggressive movement upon the British dominions. The British government, ever reluctant to interpose in the internal dissensions of neighbouring states, had of course no choice but to resort to arms when its own territories were invaded. The appeal was crowned with success to the righteous cause, although the conflicts of Moodkee, Ferozeshah, Aliwal, and Sobraon, attest the obstinacy of those who, having thrown their own country into confusion, proceeded to extend that confusion, if possible, to the territories of a neighbour anxious only to preserve the relations of peace, but whose power was as great as his disposition was pacific. The insolent foe was driven back; and it was in the Seik capital Lahore, then occupied by the British, that the treaty which was designed to regulate the future position of each government towards the other was concluded. But it was not destined long to command even a nominal acquiescence. Treachery and perfidy, almost unparalleled in the annals of even oriental affairs, provoked a further manifestation of British power, and the Governor-General came to the conclusion that, to use his own language, "no other course is open to us than to prosecute a general Punjab war with vigour, and ultimately to occupy the country with our own troops." It would occupy far greater space than can here be spared to detail the events which followed. The battle of Chillianwallah, which at the time excited much discussion, and the victory of Gujerat, were among the most noticeable. The result was not less triumphant, and was far more decisive than that of the former war.

On the 29th of March, 1849, Lahore was again the scene of a most imposing spectacle, the actors in which were assembled for the same object as on a previous occasion—the settlement of the affairs of the Punjab. In the contest between good faith and treachery, victory had decided for the former. The British, now masters of the Punjab, held the determination of its fate, and that determination was the most happy for the people of the conquered territory that could have taken place. On the day and at the place above named, it was solemnly proclaimed that the family of Runjeet Singh had ceased to reign, and that the country of the Five Rivers was incorporated with the British empire. The effects which have followed the incorporation, so different from the usual results of conquest, may be seen in the remarks addressed by the Court of Directors of the East-India Company to the government of India, on receiving a report of the first two or three years only of British administration.

"In the short period which has elapsed since the Punjab became a part of the British dominions, results have been achieved such as could scarcely have been hoped for as the reward of many years of well-directed exertions. The formidable army which it had required so many battles to subdue, has been quietly disbanded, and the turbulent soldiery have settled to industrious pursuits. Peace and security reign throughout the country, and the amount of crime is as small as in our best-administered territories. Justice has been made accessible, without costly formalities, to the whole population. Industry and commerce have been set free. A great mass of oppressive and burthensome taxation has been abolished. Money rents have been substituted for payments in kind, and a settlement of the land revenue has been completed in nearly the whole country, at a considerable reduction on the former amount. In the settlement, the best lights of recent experience have been turned to the utmost account, and the various errors committed in a more imperfect state of our knowledge of India have been carefully avoided. Cultivation has already largely increased. Notwithstanding the great sacrifices of revenue, there was a surplus, after defraying the civil and the local military expenses, of fifty-two lacs in the first, and sixty-four and a half lacs in the second year, after annexation. During the next ten years, the construction of the Baree Doab Canal, and its branches, and of the great network of roads already in rapid progress, will absorb the greater part of the surplus; but even during this interval, according to the Board's estimate, a balance will be left of more than double the amount of the cost of two corps, at which the Governor-General computes the augmentation of the general military expenses of India due to the acquisition of the Punjab. After the important works in question are completed, the Board of Administration, apparently on sound data, calculates on a permanent surplus of fifty lacs per annum applicable to general purposes.

"Results like these reflect the highest honour on the administration of your Lordship in Council, and on the system of Indian government generally. It is a source of just pride to us, that our services, civil and military, should have afforded men capable, in so short a time, of carrying into full effect such a series of enlightened and beneficent measures. The executive functionaries in the subordinate ranks have proved themselves worthy of the honourable career which awaits them. The members of the Board of Administration, Sir Henry Lawrence, Mr. John Lawrence, Mr. Mansell, and Mr. Montgomery, have entitled themselves to be placed in the foremost rank of Indian administrators."

PUNJNUD, a great stream of the Punjab, discharges into the Indus the collected water of the Ghara and Trimab, and consequently of the Sutlej, Beas, Ravee, Chenaub, and Jhelum. The great channel bearing the name of Punjnud commences at the confluence of the Ghara and Trimab, in lat. 29° 21′, long. 71° 3′, and, taking a south-westerly course of about sixty miles, joins the Indus nearly opposite Mittunkote, and in lat. 28° 57′, long. 70° 30′.

PUNKEEMATH, in the British district of Gurhwal, lieut.-gov. of the N.W. Provinces, a town on the route from Sireenuggur to Thibet, 43 miles E.N.E. of the former. Lat. 30° 27′, long. 79° 30′.

PUNNAGHUR, in the British district of Saugor and Nerbudda, a town on the route from Allahabad to Jubulpoor, 261 miles S.W. of former, and 10 N.E. of latter. To the south-east of the town is a very fine tank. Elevation above the sea 1,477 feet. Lat. 23° 16′, long. 80° 3′.

PUNNAH, in Bundelcund, a town, the principal place of the territory of the same name, lies on the route from Banda to Jubbulpore, 62 miles S. of the former, 169 N. of the latter. It is situate on the north-eastern slope of a barren range, or rather plateau, rising about 300 feet above the Bindachal plateau, stretching towards the north-east, and from this town styled by Franklin the Punnah Hills. The site, which is picturesque, is close to an extensive jhil or tank, formed by embanking the extremity of a deep valley. A palace, formerly the occasional residence of Chuttur Saul, noted as the founder of the short-lived independence of Bundelcund, is situate on the bank of the jhil, and around are many mausoleums of elaborate and tasteful architecture. In the jhil are alligators, considered by the Hindoos sacred. Though now quite in ruins, Punnah was once a fine well-built town, the houses being generally constructed of squared sandstone, and covered with tiles. A pathway of large flags extends down the middle of the streets, which have an air of solidity, cleanliness, and convenience. Whole streets, however, are now desolate, being tenanted only by large troops of monkeys, which, posted on the roofs or at the windows, view passengers without alarm. The palace of the rajah is a spacious, beautiful building, surmounted by high, elegant kiosks, and having its exterior crowded with numerous ornamental carvings; but it is in many places ruinous. The town is crowded with Hindoo temples, in a mixed style of architecture, partaking of the Saracenic, and partly derived probably from the Mussulmans. There does not appear to be any mosque in the town, it being almost exclusively inhabited by Hindoos. There are here, however, some followers of Pran Nath, a Khetriya, who, being versed in Mahomedan learning, as well as in his own, attempted to reconcile the two religions. There is a building consecrated to the use of this sect, in one apartment of which, on a table covered with gold cloth, lies the volume of the founder.

The former prosperity of this place resulted from the diamond-mines in the vicinity. The diamonds are found in several localities, of which one is situate a short distance to the north-east of the town; and hence the mines there are called the Punnah mines. The ground at the surface, and a few feet below, consists of ferrugineous gravel, mixed with reddish clay; and this loose mass, when carefully washed and searched, affords diamonds, but few in number, and of small size. The matrix containing in greater quantity the more valuable diamonds, lies considerably lower, at a depth varying generally from twelve to forty feet, and is a conglomerate of pebbles of quartz, jasper, hornstone, Lydian stone, and some others. The fragments of this conglomerate, quarried and brought to the surface, are carefully pounded, and after several washings, to remove the softer and more clayey parts, the residue is repeatedly searched for the gem. As is common in such seductive pursuits, the return often falls below the outlay, and the adventurers are ruined. The business is now much less prosperous than formerly; but Jacquemont does not consider that there are any symptoms of exhaustion in the adamantiferous deposits, and attributes the unfavourable change to the diminished value of the gem everywhere. The rejected rubbish, if examined after a lapse of some years, has been frequently found to contain valuable diamonds, which some suppose have in the interval been produced in the congenial matrix; but experienced and skilful miners are generally of opinion that diamonds which escaped a former search, in consequence of incrustation by some opaque coat, have been rendered obvious to the sight from its removal by fracture, friction, or some other accidental cause. More extensive and important is the adamantiferous tract extending from twelve to twenty miles north-east of the town of Punnah, and worked in the localities of Kamariya, Brijpur, Bargari, Myra, and Etwa. Diamonds of the first water, or completely colourless, are, however, very rare, most of those found being either pearly, greenish, yellowish, rose-coloured, black, or brown. Franklin conjectures the ferrugineous conglomerate to have been of igneous origin, but Brewster's authority is against this opinion. While admitting the possibility of the diamond having been in a state of igneous fusion, that writer considers it highly improbable that it ever was so. The conglomerate matrix of the diamond rests on sandstone, which Franklin, from observations on the hill-side, and in the deep ravines in the neighbourhood, conjectures to be at least 400 feet thick, and remarks, "that there are strong indications of coal underlying the whole mass." During the prosperity of the mines, a tax of twenty-five per cent. was levied on their produce; but the tax now imposed is stated to exceed this rate. The revenue is divided in proportions between the rajahs of Punnah, Banda, and Chircaree. Franklin, calculating the share of the Punnah state at 30,000 rupees, and the aggregate of the other shares at a fourth of that sum, estimates the value of the diamonds found in three mines at 120,000 rupees per annum. Pogson, who worked one of the mines on his own account, considers "that inexhaustible strata producing diamonds exist here;" and Jacquemont imagines that if the mines were properly worked, their productiveness would be found not to have diminished. None of the great diamonds now known appear to be traceable to the mines in the vicinity of Punnah, and Tieffenthaler mentions it as a general opinion that those of Golconda are far superior.

The territory of which Punnah is the principal place is bounded on the north by the British district of Banda, and by one of the outlying divisions of the native state of Chirkaree; on the east by the Saugor and Nerbudda estates of Sohawul, Oocheyra, and Myheer; on the south by the British territory of Saugor and Nerbudda; and on the west by several of the petty states of Bundelcund. It lies between lat. 23° 52′—25° 5′, long. 79° 50′—80° 45′, and "in 1832 was stated to comprise 688 square miles; to contain 1,062 villages, with a population of 67,000 souls; and to yield a revenue of eight lacs (80,000*l.*);" but the income was supposed in 1848 to be only one-half of the above amount. The state pays a tribute of 10,000 rupees (1,000*l.*), and maintains a force of 250 cavalry and 3,000 infantry.

Early in the eighteenth century, Chutter Saul threw off subjection to the sovereign of Delhi, and assumed the title of rajah of Punnah, but being hard pressed by the Mussulman chief of Furruckabad, had recourse to the assistance of the Peishwa, by whose aid he was, in 1733, rescued from his perilous position. After his death, the succession became disputed, and the country fell into a distracted state, until the Peishwa ceded a portion of his rights in the province of Bundelcund to the East-India Company by the treaty of Bassein in 1802; the cession being confirmed and extended by the subsequent treaty in 1817. In 1807, the British authorities granted the raj or territory of Punnah to Kishor Singh, a descendant and representative of the house of Chutter Saul.

The rajah of Punnah was one of the few Bundelcund chiefs who had not consented to abolish suttee; and upon the occurrence of his death, in 1849, the sacrifice took place. Instructions were thereupon given to the British agent to defer the recognition of the late chief's brother as his successor, in order to make use of the opportunity for inducing him to enter into an engagement for its future prevention.

The elevation of the town of Punnah is 1,300 feet above the sea; distant 130 miles S. of Calpee, by Banda; 173 S.W. of Allahabad; 668 N.W. of Calcutta, by Allahabad. Lat. 24° 44′, long. 80° 15′.

PUNNAIR.—See PUNIAR.

PUNNECOIL, in the British district of Tinnevelly, presidency of Madras, a small town, with roadstead, on the north-west coast of the Gulf of Manar. The approach from the south is dangerous, in consequence of an extensive reef stretching in that direction; but a ship having safely made its way past that danger may anchor securely in seven or eight fathoms, with bottom soft mud, and two miles from the beach. Vegetables are scarce, but water, swine, sheep, and fish, abundant. Lat. 8° 39′, long. 78° 11′.

PUNNEEALA, in the Daman division of the Punjab, a town situated on the right bank of the Indus, 122 miles S.S.W. of the town of Peshawar. Lat. 32° 15′, long. 70° 57′.

PUNNOH, in the territory of Bhurtpore, a small town on the route from Agra to Ajmeer, 43 miles W. of former, 185 E. of latter. Supplies may be had, and water is obtainable from wells. Lat. 27° 4′, long. 77° 24′.

PUNTA DEYRA.—A town in the British district of Shikarpoor, province of Scinde, presidency of Bombay, 27 miles S.W. by W. of Shikarpoor. Lat. 27° 49′, long. 68° 18′.

PUNTI, in the British district of Bareilly, division of Pillibheet, lieut.-gov. of the N.W. Provinces, a village on the route from Bareilly to Petoragurh, and 70 miles N.E. of the former. Lat. 29° 2′, long. 80° 3′.

PUNWAR.—A town in the Rajpoot state of Jeypoor, 81 miles S. by W. from Jeypoor, and 72 miles S.E. from Ajmeer. Lat. 25° 48′, long. 75° 36′.

PUNWAREE, in the British district of Humeerpoor, the principal place of the pergunnah of the same name, a town on the route from Goona to Calpee, 126 miles S.W. of the latter. It has water from a lake. Lat. 25° 26′, long. 79° 32′.

PURAI, in the territory of Oude, a town on the route from Azimgurh to Faizabad, 76 miles N.W. of the former, 10 S.E. of the latter, two S.W. of the right bank of the Ghaghra. Lat. 26° 43′, long. 82° 10′.

PURANEEPOOR, in the British district of Allahabad, lieut.-gov. of the N.W. Provinces, a village on the right bank of the Ganges, 779 miles N.W. of Calcutta by the river route, 29 miles S.E. of Allahabad by the same. Lat. 25° 18′, long. 82° 14′.

PURBANEE.—A town in Hyderabad, or territory of the Nizam, situate on the right bank of the Doodna river, and 174 miles N.W. from Hyderabad. Lat. 19° 17′, long. 76° 50′.

PURGAI, in the British district of Cawnpore, lieut.-gov. of the N.W. Provinces, a village on the route from the cantonment of Cawnpore to that of Futtehgurh, and 10 miles N.W. of the former. Lat. 26° 33′, long 80° 17′.

PURGY.—A town in Hyderabad, or territory of the Nizam, 41 miles W.S.W. from Hyderabad, and 138 miles E. by S. from Sholapoor. Lat. 17° 10′, long. 77° 58′.

PURKUNDEE, in the British district of Gurhwal, lieut.-gov. of the N.W. Provinces, a town on the route from Sireenuggur to the native state of Tibet, 28 miles N.E. of the former. Lat. 30° 30′, long. 79° 10′.

PURKYAL, or TUZHEGUNG, in Bussahir, a peak of the ridge in the district of Koonawur, separating the Spiti from the Sutlej, and rising six or seven miles north-east of the confluence of those rivers. A point on a peak two miles west of the highest summit was reached by Gerard, who on this height, 19,411 feet above the level of the sea, found the thermometer, on the 18th of October, only 10° below the freezing-point, and the ground free from snow. The elevation of the highest peak was ascertained to be 22,488 feet above the sea. Vegetation was observed to reach the height of 17,000 feet; and it is intimated that its farther progress was checked by want of soil. At the highest point reached, the peak was found to be formed of enormous disunited blocks of granite, between which were large lumps of ice, clear as crystal. Lat. 31° 54′, long. 77° 46′.

PURLAHKEMEDY.—A tract inhabited by one of the independent hill tribes of Orissa, bordering on the western frontier of the British district of Ganjam: its centre is in lat. 19° 20′, long. 84° 10′.

PURLAH KEMEDY.—A town in the British district of Ganjam, presidency of Madras, 78 miles S.W. by W. of Ganjam. Lat. 18° 47′, long. 84° 10′.

PURLEY.—A town in Hyderabad, or territory of the Nizam, 165 miles N.W. by W. from Hyderabad, and 123 miles E. by S. from Ahmednuggur. Lat. 18° 51′, long. 76° 38′.

PURMUTTY.—A town in the British district of Salem, presidency of Madras, 37 miles S. by W. of Salem. Lat. 11° 9′, long. 78° 6′.

PURNABADA RIVER.—A large offset of the Attree, from which it separates in lat. 25° 50′, long. 88° 41′, in the British district of Dinajepore. After a course of sixty miles, it passes into the district of Malda, which it traverses for twenty-five miles, and then falls into the Mahananda, in lat. 24° 47′, long. 88° 20′.

PURNEAH.—A British district under the lieut.-gov. of Bengal, named from its principal place. It is bounded on the north by the kingdom of Nepaul, and by Sikhim; on the east by the British district Dinagepore; on the south by Malda and Bhaugulpore; and on the west by Bhaugulpore. It lies between lat. 25° 9′—26° 37′, long. 86° 48′—88° 23′: it is 117 miles in length from north-east to south-west, and 105 in breadth: the area is 5,878 square miles. Though remote from the sea, it is a level and rather depressed tract, traversed by numerous streams, generally descending from the Himalaya Mountains, lying to the north. There are no mountains or hills within Purneah, the chief eminence throughout this extensive tract being a conical peak, about 100 feet high, at Munnearee. The principal rivers which skirt or intersect the district are the Ganges, the Kosee, the Gogaree, and the Mahanunda. Besides these rivers, there are numerous smaller streams, connected with the larger and with each other, and in general admitting craft of considerable burthen; so that few tracts have equal advantages of irrigation and water-carriage. The lowest part of the surface is that contiguous to the bank of the Ganges, at the south-east corner of the district, and it may be estimated to have an elevation of 123 feet above Calcutta. Titaliya, on the north-east frontier, and probably the highest point in the district, has an elevation estimated at 275 feet above the sea. There are no lakes of any magnitude in Purneah, but many jhils or extensive shallow ponds, which, according to all appearance, were formerly the deeper parts of the channels of rivers which have changed their courses.

In the latter part of spring, and the commencement of summer, the westerly winds in the south of the district bring very hot, dry weather. During the periodical rains, from the early part of summer to the middle of autumn, easterly winds prevail. In spring, violent squalls are common, which, setting in sometimes from the north, at others from the north-west and north-east, "are accompanied by uncommon quantities of hail. In one storm, by far the greater part of the stones were as large as walnuts, and vast numbers were like small apples, while several were like ordinary-sized oranges." The cold of winter is in every part of the district sufficient to produce hoar-frosts, and, at times, seriously to damage the more tender crops. Earthquakes are not unfrequent, several shocks usually occuring every year, but so slight as to cause no material injury.

The staple produce of the district is rice, which is cultivated with considerable care. The summer rice (bhadai) is a very important crop, and is usually followed in the cool season by crops of wheat, barley, pulse, or oil-seeds, or sometimes intermixed with other articles. The varieties of winter rice are very numerous. Besides maize or Indian corn, various kinds of millet are raised. The principal esculent vegetables are baygan or egg-plant, spinage, various kinds of amaranthus and of cucurbitaceous plants, sweet potatoes, common potatoes, pease, cabbage, and yams; the condiments, ginger, capsicum, turmeric. The cultivation of the sugarcane was found by Buchanan to be very limited and unskilful, and that of cotton subject to the same remarks. Tobacco, a great favourite with the population, is extensively cultivated, as is hemp, for supplying the powerful stimulant called bang. Betel is also one of the productions of the district. The opium-poppy was believed by Buchanan to be secretly reared to some extent. Indigo is the principal commercial crop. Safflower is represented as an object of some importance towards the eastern part. The mulberry-tree was, in the time of Buchanan, confined to three small divisions of the south-east corner of the district, but there the number was very great. It was, however, found to be a precarious branch of industry, as in some years the crop of leaves totally failed, and in others, the worms, without any ascertained cause, perished, without producing silk. The cultivation appears to have been in many instances slovenly.

Cotton is imported from Mirzapore and other places lying to the west; sugar is imported from the British districts Dinajpur, Tirhoot, and Patna. The only external commerce from the district is to Nepaul. The chief exports are cattle, coarse cotton fabrics, silk, indigo, and grain. Banking is carried on to some extent, especially at the town of Purneah, where there are some considerable capitalists; but so scanty is the circulating medium, that, according to Buchanan, a rupee in this country is a large sum; for, being a ploughman's money wages for two months, it may be considered of as much importance in the circulation of the country as three or four pounds sterling may be considered in England. The amount of the population is given under the article BENGAL.

Purneah, the capital, and the other towns of importance within the district, are described under their respective names in the alphabetical arrangement. The principal routes are—1. From south-west to north-east, from Bhaugulpore, through the town of Purneah to Titaleea, and thence to Darjeeling; 2. from south-east to north-west, from Maldah, through the town of Purneah, to Nathpur; 3. from east to west, from Dinajpore to the town of Purneah, and thence to Mozufferpore, in Tirhoot; 4. from south to north, from Rajmahal to Purneah and Nathpore.

The fabulous history of this tract represents that at a remote period of antiquity it formed part of the primeval realm of Mithila, and was governed by a rajah, whose daughter was Sita, the renowned spouse of Rama; and whose abduction by Rawan, the demon-tyrant of Ceylon, gave rise to the war which is the subject of the Ramayana. The district appears to have been subjugated by the Mussulmans about the year 1541, and was acquired by the East-India Company in 1765, under the firman of Shah Alum, of Delhi.

PURNEAH.—The principal place of the British district of the same name, under the lieut.-gov. of Bengal. It is situated on the banks of the Little Kosi, occupying both sides of the river, and lying on the route from Bhaugulpore to Titaleea, 78 miles N.E. of the former, and 72 S.W. of latter. It includes a space of about three miles square; but much of it is occupied by plantations, gardens, and open places. The best part of the town is on the left side of the river, and consists of one wide and tolerably straight street, half a mile long, the houses in which are pretty well built and tiled. Two inferior streets, parallel to the principal one, run on each side of it. It is surrounded by straggling suburbs, in one of which, called Maharajganj, are situate the buildings for the accommodation of the civil establishment of the district, which consists of a civil and sessions judge, a sudder aumeen, a moonsiff, a collector, a magistrate, an assistant to collector, two deputy magistrates, an assistant-surgeon, and an uncovenanted deputy collector. The above are Europeans; and there are, besides, a principal sudder aumeen and several moonsiffs, who are natives. With respect to the population, Buchanan observes, "This town, which occupies a space equal to more than half of London, most assuredly does not contain 50,000 people, though it is one of the best country towns in Bengal." Purneah is distant N.W. from Calcutta by Berhampoor 283 miles; S.E. from Katmandoo by Nathpoor 200 miles; S.W. from Darjeeling 98. Lat. 25° 46′, long. 87° 30′.

PUROKH, in the British district of Mynpoorie, lieut.-gov. of the N.W. Provinces, a village on the route from the cantonment of Allygurh to that of Mynpoorie, and eight miles N.W. of the latter. Lat. 27° 17′, long. 79° 1′.

PUROWLEE, in the British district of Furruckabad, lieut.-gov. of the N.W. Provinces, a village on the route from the cantonment of Allygurh to that of Futtehgurh, and 44 miles N.E. of the latter. Lat. 27° 31′, long. 79° 2′.

PURRAINDER.—A town in one of the recently sequestrated districts of Hyderabad, 211 miles N.W. from Hyderabad. Lat. 18° 19′, long. 75° 30′.

PURRAUNTAJE.—A town in the British district of Kaira, presidency of Bombay, 50 miles N. by E. of Kaira. Lat. 23° 26′, long. 72° 53′.

PURRAUR.—A town in the native state of Travancore, territory of Madras, 126 miles N.N.W. from Trivandrum, and 82 miles S.S.E. from Calicut. Lat. 10° 9′, long. 76° 16′.

PURROOA, or PARRUA, in the British district of Maldah, lieut.-gov. of Bengal, a town on the route from Maldah to Purneah, six miles N. of former. It is now much ruined, but contains many monuments of antique greatness, especially the Adinah mosque, a vast structure nearly 500 feet in breadth from north to south, and 300 from east to west. The style of architecture is, however, rather complex than grand, consisting of a great number of pillars and domes, diminutive in proportion to the vast dimensions of the ground-plan of the building. Within the precincts are the tombs of Sikandar Shah and some other Mussulmans of rank. Besides this vast structure, there are many others, but all very ruinous. The true appellation of the city is said to be Panduya, or Pandoviya, derived from its having been founded by a rajah of the Pandu family, renowned in the lore of Hindu mythology and romance. It has repeatedly been the seat of the government of Bengal, though Gaur more frequently had that distiuction. Distant N. from Calcutta by Burhampoor 197 miles. Lat. 25° 4′, long. 88° 9′.

PURSA.—A town in the British district of Sarun, lieut.-gov. of Bengal, 25 miles N.W. of Chupra. Lat. 25° 57′, long. 84° 37′.

PURSOEE.—A town in the British district of Mirzapoor, lieut.-gov. of Bengal, 53 miles S.S.E. of Mirzapoor. Lat. 24° 27′, long. 82° 58′.

PURSOOD, in the British district of Muttra, lieut.-gov. of the N.W. Provinces, a village on the route from the cantonment of Allygurh to that of Muttra, and 11 miles N.E. of the latter. Lat. 27° 34′, long. 77° 54′.

PURSUR.—A town in Guzerat, or dominions of the Guicowar, 41 miles N.N.W. from Rajkote, and 60 miles E.S.E. from Bhooj. Lat. 22° 51′, long. 70° 36′.

PURTABGHUR.—A town on the route from Neemuch to Baroda, 33 miles S. of the former, and 206 N.E. of the latter. It is the principal place of a raj or small state of the same name, under the political superintendence of the Governor-General, comprising part of the tract called Bagur, and the whole of that denominated Kantul. The raj is bounded on the north-west and north by the state of Mewar or Odeypore; on the east by Mundesore, Jowra, and Rutlaum; and on the south-west by Banswarra; and lies between lat. 23° 14′—24° 14′, long. 74° 27′—75°. The area is estimated at 1,457 square miles, and the population at 145,700. It is a hilly and ill-cultivated tract, rather elevated, and hence frost is not unknown. The annual revenue of the rajah was, in 1848, estimated at 175,000 rupees, or 17,500*l*. The armed force consists of 250 cavalry and 300 infantry, with a police establishment of 200 men. The ruling family is of a junior branch of that of Odeypore. Before the raj became tributary to Holcar, it formed a dependency of the Mogul empire, and one of its former rulers, Salim Sing, having obtained from Mahomed Shah the privilege of coining money in his own name, struck in the mint of Purtabghur the Salim Shahee rupee. The privilege thus conceded has been grossly abused by the more recent rajahs, who have permitted the fraudulent alteration of the standard; and the debased coin issued from this mint has frequently been made the subject of remonstrance on the part of the British government. In 1818, the rajah concluded a treaty with the East-India Company, under which he became entitled to protection; he binding himself to subordinate co-operation, and to pay annually to the other contracting party a tribute of 72,700 Salim Shahee rupees, which sum is transferred to Holcar, the feudal superior of Purtabghur. A detail of the circumstances under which Dulput Singh, the regent of Doongerpoor, succeeded to the raj of Purtabghur, and relinquished his claim of succession to that of Doongerpoor, will be found in the article upon the latter state. The town of the same name as the district, and the chief place within it, though of considerable size, presents nothing particularly worth notice. Elevation above the sea 1,698 feet. Distance of the town direct from Mhow, N.W., 118 miles; from Oojein, N.W., 80. Lat. 24° 5′, long. 74° 58′.

PURTABGURH.—A town in the lapsed territory of Berar or Nagpoor, 70 miles E.S.E. from Nagpoor, and 92 miles S.S.E. from Seuni. Lat. 20° 49′, long. 80° 10′.

PURTABGURH.—A district of the territory of Oude, named from its principal place. It is bounded on the north-east by the district of Sultanpoor; on the east by the British district Jounpoor; on the south by the British district Allahabad; and on the west by the districts Ahladganj and Salon. It lies between lat. 25° 40′—26° 15′, long. 81° 40′—82° 5′; is forty-five miles in length from south-east to north-west, and twenty in breadth. It contains the following subdivisions: 1. Purtabgurh; 2. Amethi; 3. Dalipur Patti.

PURTABGURH, or BELHAGHAT, in the territory of Oude, a town two miles south of the right bank of the river Saee. It is surrounded by a decayed rampart of mud, and on its west side is a fort of the same material, in a ruinous state, but still inhabited by a foujdar or officer of police. The site is rather elevated, sandy, yet not unproductive, and water is found at from thirty to thirty five feet below the surface. Butter states the population at 10,000, "of whom half are Mussulmans, and almost all cultivators, there being no manufactures." Previously to 1834, one of the Company's native infantry regiments, with two guns, was cantoned three miles north-east of the town, on a very healthy spot on the right bank of the Saee. Tieffenthaler gives a brief notice of Purtabgurh, which he concludes by observing, "in this district much salt and saline earth are obtained." Purtabgurh is distant N. from Allahabad 32 miles, N.W. from Calcutta 534, S.E. from Lucknow 90. Lat. 25° 54′, long. 81° 59′.

PURTABPOOR, in the British district of Meerut, lieut.-gov. of the N.W. Provinces, a village on the route from Delhi to the town of Meerut, and eight miles S.W. of the latter. Lat. 28° 55′, long. 77° 42′.

PURTABPOOR, in the British district of Mynpoorie, lieut.-gov. of the N.W. Provinces, a village on the route from the cantonment of Allygurh to that of Etawah, and 41 miles N.W. of the latter. Lat. 27° 13′, long. 78° 35′.

PURTOOR.—A town in Hyderabad, or territory of the Nizam, situate on the right bank of the Doodna river, and 140 miles S.W. by S. from Ellichpoor. Lat. 19° 36′, long. 76° 18′.

PURTYALL.—A town in the British district of Guntoor, presidency of Madras, 59 miles N.W. by W. of Masulipatam. Lat. 16° 40′, long. 80° 30′.

PURULEA.—See POORALIA.

PURUSGAON.—A town in the escheated territory of Berar or Nagpoor, 71 miles E. by N. from Nagpoor, and 130 miles S. from Jubbulpoor. Lat. 21° 18′, long. 80° 14′.

PURUSPUTI, in the territory of Oude, a village on the route from Azimgurh to Sultanpoor cantonment, 66 miles W. of the former, 12 S.E. of the latter. Lat. 26° 17′, long. 82° 10′.

PURWAN NUDDEE.—A river rising in lat. 26° 31′, long. 87° 2′, in the British district of Tirhoot, and, flowing in a southerly direction for seventy miles, generally through the district of Bhagulpore, falls into the Dhamora, in lat. 25° 38′, long. 86° 49′.

PUSGAW.—A town in Oude, 82 miles N.W. by N. from Lucknow, and 16 miles E. by S. from Shahjehanpoor. Lat. 27° 50′, long. 80° 13′.

PUTAOO, in the Rajpoot state of Jodhpoor, a village on the route from Balotra to the city of Jodhpoor, and 14 miles N.E. of the former. Lat. 25° 57′, long. 72° 30′.

PUTCHPAHAR.—A town in the Rajpoot state of Jhalawar, 32 miles W.S.W. from Jhalra Patun, and 53 miles E. from Neemuch. Lat. 24° 21′, long. 75° 45′.

PUTEANUGLA, in the British district of Moradabad, lieut.-gov. of the N.W. Provinces, a village on the route from the town of Moradabad to Almora, and 20 miles N. of the former. It is situate in an open, low, level country, partially cultivated. Lat. 29° 4′, long. 78° 57′.

PUTEHUR, in the British district of Suharunpoor, lieut.-gov. of the N.W. Provinces, a town on the route from Suharunpoor to Simla, 12 miles N.N.W. of the former. Lat. 30° 8′, long. 77° 32′.

PUTENEE, in the British district of Mozuffurnuggur, lieut.-gov. of the N.W. Provinces, a village on the route from Kurnal to Meerut, and 19 miles S.E. of the former. Lat. 29° 32′, long. 77° 14′.

PUTERA, in the British district of Banda, lieut.-gov. of the N.W. Provinces, a village on the route by Chila Tara Ghat from Cawnpore to town of Banda, 17 miles N. of latter. Lat. 25° 42′, long. 80° 32′.

PUTHIA, in the British district of Mynpoorie, lieut.-gov. of the N.W. Provinces, a village on the route from Allygurh cantonment to that of Mynpoorie, and 37 miles S.E. of the former. Lat. 27° 37′, long. 78° 37′.

PUTHONA, in the British district of Allahabad, lieut.-gov. of the N.W. Provinces, a town on the route from Allahabad to Futtehpoor, 21 miles W.N.W. of the former. Lat. 25° 32′, long. 81° 38′.

PUTHURRIA, in the British district of Saugor and Nerbudda, lieut.-gov. of the N.W. Provinces, a town on the route from Allahabad to Saugor, 286 miles S.W. of former, and 28 N.E. of latter. It is situate at the east extremity of a range of trap hills, at an elevation of 1,395 feet above the sea. Lat. 23° 53′, long. 79° 11′.

PUTJIRWA.—A town in the British district of Sarun, lieut.-gov. of Bengal, eight miles W.N.W. of Bettiah. Lat. 26° 48′, long. 84° 28′.

PUTNEETOLA.—A town in the British district of Dinajepore, lieut.-gov. of Bengal, 40 miles S. of Dinajepore. Lat. 25° 2′, long. 88° 42′.

PUTNI.—A small river rising in the Saugor and Nerbudda territory, in lat. 23° 40′, long. 80° 1′, and taking a northerly course of eighteen miles, it crosses the northern frontier into Bundelcund, through which it flows first north-easterly and then north-westerly, and falls into the Cane on the left side, in lat. 24° 20′, long. 80° 8′, having a total course of about seventy miles.

PUTPURGUNJ, in the British district of Boolundshuhur, lieut.-gov. of the N.W. Provinces, a small town near the left bank of the Jumna, on the route from Allygurh to Delhi cantonment, and eight miles S.E. of the latter. It has a bazar, and is supplied with water from wells. Close to it was fought, in 1803, the engagement more generally styled the battle of Delhi, in which the British army under General Lake totally defeated the Mahrattas commanded by Bourquien, a French adventurer. Lat. 28° 37′, long. 77° 21′.

PUTRA.—A town in the recently lapsed territory of Berar or Nagpoor, seven miles N.N.W. from the hill zemindarry of Jeypoor, and 182 miles W. by S. from Ganjam. Lat. 19° 17′, long. 82° 23′.

PUTRUHUT, in the district of Sohawul, territory of Saugor and Nerbudda, a small town, with bazar, on route from Saugor, by Rewah, to Allahabad, 158 miles S.W. of the latter. It is situate on the right bank of the river Tons (South-eastern), here a great torrent, with channel 200 yards wide, and stream about sixty yards wide in the dry season, and crossed by ford. A ruinous fortress of fine and picturesque aspect, built on a limestone rock, formerly commanded the passage, but is now merely the residence of some humble relatives and domestics of the rajah. Lat. 24° 34′, long. 80° 59′.

PUTSEEN.—A town in the British district of Rajeshaye, lieut.-gov. of Bengal, 32 miles N.E. by E. of Rampore. Lat. 24° 37′, long. 89° 5′.

PUTTACOTTE.—A town in the British

district of Tanjore, presidency of Madras, 29 miles S.S.E. of Tanjore. Lat. 10° 25′, long. 79° 21′.

PUTTA HAT.—A town in the British district of Bulloah, lieut.-gov. of Bengal, 14 miles N.W. of Bulloah. Lat. 23°, long. 90° 46′.

PUTTANAPARAM.—A town in the native state of Travancore, presidency of Madras, 43 miles N. by W. from Trivandrum, and 62 miles W.N.W. from Tinnevelly. Lat. 9° 5′, long. 76° 55′.

PUTTARY, in the territory of Rewah, province of Baghelcund, a small town on the old route from Mirzapoor to the town of Rewah, and 35 miles S.W. of the former. Lat. 24° 48′, long. 82° 5′.

PUTTEEALA.—A native state in Sirhind, and within the jurisdiction of the commissioner and superintendent of the Cis-Sutlej states. It is the most important of those known as the Seik protected states, and the chief is regarded by his neighbours as the head of the Pholkean tribe. The original dimensions of the territory were extended by purchases made of additional dominions, on the dismemberment of the states of Bughat and Keyontbul, subsequently to the expulsion of the Ghoorkas; and further extension more recently accrued from grants made by the British government, in reward of the fidelity displayed by the rajah during the war with Lahore. The area, exclusive of the hill district, is returned at 4,682 square miles, and the population at 1,310,960 persons. The territory is among the most fertile in Sirhind, and exports great quantities of grain across the Sutlej to Lahore and Amritsir. By the manifesto issued by the British government on taking possession of Sirhind in 1809, the rajah is guaranteed the sovereignty within his own possessions, and is bound to furnish a quota of troops in case of war. On one occasion, in 1812, an interference with the independence of the rajah became indispensable, in consequence of his frantic and ruinous extravagance; he having so misapplied his resources, that when called upon to supply troops for the public service, he could furnish no more than 200 horsemen of the worst description. At length his misconduct was considered to amount to insanity, and he was deposed, and placed under restraint.

In conferring the additional territory lately bestowed by the British government on the rajah of Putteeala, in reward of his fidelity during the Lahore war, it was stipulated that the rajah should renounce the right of levying transit-duties; should make and maintain in repair a military road, and abolish suttee, infanticide, and slave-dealing within his dominions.

PUTTEEALA, in Sirhind, the chief place in a native state of the same name. It is situate on the river, or rather torrent, Kosilla. This stream, known also by the name of the Putteeala river, runs past the town in a very deep channel, yet has in time of inundation so large a volume of water, that a great embankment has been found necessary to preserve the walls from its destructive influence. It is a compact town, built of brick, neater and more cleanly than the generality in this part of India, and densely peopled. The citadel is small, and of no great strength: it is the residence of the rajah. Putteeala is distant N.W. from Calcutta 1,023 miles. Lat. 30° 20′, long. 76° 25′.

PUTTEEALEE, in the British district of Furruckabad, the principal place of the pergunnah of the same name, a small town near the north-western frontier, towards the districts of Mynpoorie and Budaon, and 44 miles N.W. of Futtehgurh. Here, in 1749, an engagement took place between Ahmed Khan, the Afghan nawaub of Furruckabad, and Safder Jang, nawaub of Oude and vizier of the empire of Delhi. "During the hottest part of the engagement," says Hamilton, "there suddenly arose a sandstorm (common in those parts of India), which blew with violence directly in the faces of the Moguls, and the Afghans, improving this advantage, rushed on in the bosom of a thick cloud of dust, and charged their enemies with irresistible impetuosity. The vizier's troops being blinded by the sand, could neither judge of the number nor distinguish the attacks of their assailants; their panic was increased by the whirlwind and darkness which surrounded them, and in a few minutes they gave way, and fled with the utmost precipitation. All the vizier's artillery was taken, and his infantry cut off to a man. He himself escaped with difficulty." It is mentioned in the Ayeen Akbery under the name of Puttyaly, and its assessment stated at 46,940 rupees. Lat. 27° 41′, long. 79° 4′.

PUTTEERAM.—A town in the British district of Dinajepoor, lieut.-gov. of Bengal, 21 miles S.S.E. of Dinajepoor. Lat. 25° 18′, long. 88° 47′.

PUTTHRI, in the British district of Suharunpoor, lieut.-gov. of the N.W. Provinces, a river or large torrent, having its origin on the south-western declivity of the Khansrow Ghat or Pass through the Sewalik range, and in lat. 30° 3′, long. 78° 5′. It holds a course of about thirty miles in a direction generally southerly, and falls into the Banganga Nuddee, an offset of the Ganges, in lat. 29° 42′, long. 78° 9′. In the upper part of its course, it flows down a bed of shingle and sand, but for the greater part is a shallow expanse of water with little current. This torrent is crossed by the Ganges Canal, by means of a dam thrown across the river, constructed with ten openings of ten feet each, and flank overfalls.

PUTTUN, or ANHULWAR PATTAN, in Guzerat, or the territory of the Guicowar, a town situate on the small river Saraswati, a tributary of the Banas. Here are extensive traces of the ancient city of Anhulwara:—

"The eye," says Tod, "can trace the course of the walls, which formed an irregular trapezium of perhaps five miles circuit, around which extended, chiefly to the east and south, the suburbs, to which there may have been an external circumvallation." The wall inclosing the present city of Puttun is built half-way up with stones from the ancient city, whether from palaces, temples, or fountains; and these more solid foundations are surmounted by a comparatively flimsy rampart of brick. Here are some manufactures of importance, as of swords, spears, pottery of a very light fine kind, and weaving in silk and cotton. The population is estimated at 30,000. Distance from Ahmedabad N.W. 63 miles. Lat. 23° 46′, long. 72° 3′.

PUTTUNCHERROO.—A town in Hyderabad, or territory of the Nizam, 21 miles N.W. by W. from Hyderabad, and 158 miles E. from Sholapoor. Lat. 17° 31′, long. 78° 19′.

PUTTUN SOMNAUT.—See SOMNATH.

PUWYE.—A town in the Boondela state of Punnah, 32 miles S. by W. from Punnah, and 55 miles N.E. by E. from Dumoh. Lat. 24° 16′, long. 80° 14′.

PYARU. — A village in the jaghire of Bulubghur, lieut.-gov. of the N.W. Provinces, distant S. from Delhi 30 miles. Lat. 28° 16′, long. 77° 22′.

PYENA, in the British district of Goruckpore, lieut.-gov. of the N.W. Provinces, a small market-town on the left bank of the river Ghoghra. Buchanan states that it has 500 houses, which would assign it a population of about 3,000 persons. Distant S.E. from Goruckpore cantonment 45 miles. Lat. 26° 15′, long. 83° 50′.

PYGA.—A town in the British district of Moradabad, lieut.-gov. of the N.W. Provinces. Lat. 29° 8′, long. 78° 59′.

PYKHIA.—A town in the British district of Mergui, one of the Tenasserim provinces, 80 miles N. by W. of Tenasserim. Lat. 13° 14′, long. 98° 50′.

PYKOWLEE, in the British district of Goruckpoor, lieut.-gov. of the N.W. Provinces, a small town on the route from Dinapore to Goruckpoor cantonment, 125 miles N.W. of the former. Lat. 26° 52′, long. 83° 38′.

PYLADY.—A town in the British district of North Arcot, presidency of Madras, 38 miles N. by W. of Madras. Lat. 13° 38′, long. 80° 17′.

PYLANEE, in the British district of Bandah, lieut.-gov. of the N.W. Provinces, a town on the route from Bandah to Lucknow, 23 miles N. by E. of the former. Lat. 25° 46′, long. 80° 30′.

PYNG.—A town of Burmah, 19 miles W. from the right bank of the Irawady river, and 149 miles S.W. from Ava. Lat. 20° 18′, long. 94° 24′.

PYNGAWA, in the British district of Goorgaon, lieut.-gov. of the N.W. Provinces, a village on the route from the cantonment of Muttra to Ferozpoor, and 13 miles N.E. of the latter. It is situate a mile east of the Khanpoor Ghat, a pass through a range of low hills. The village has water from wells, and supplies are procurable. The road in this part of the route is good. Lat. 27° 54′, long. 77° 10′.

PYSUNNEE.—A small river rising in Bundelcund, on the table-land surmounting the Punna range, and in lat. 24° 52′, long. 80° 43′. It first flows north-east, and at Jorai is precipitated over the brow of the ridge by a cascade, the height of which is estimated by Jacquemont to exceed 300 feet. A few miles further on, it passes into the British district of Banda, through which it flows first north, subsequently north-east, and falls into the Jumna on the right side, in lat. 25° 26′, long. 81° 14′; its total length of course being eighty miles. It "is sacred among the Hindoos; and its cataract near Jorai, as well as its romantic course to the plains below, is exceedingly interesting."

PYTHEEA, in the district of Aldemau, territory of Oude, a village four miles S.W. of the right bank of the river Tons (North-eastern), 55 miles S.E. of the city of Oude. Butter estimates its population at 400, of whom 100 are Mussulmans. Lat. 26° 16′, long. 82° 48′.

PYTIANI RIVER.—One of the mouths of the river Indus. It communicates with the Buggaur, the western branch of the Indus, in lat. 24° 36′, long. 67° 21′, and flows into the sea in lat. 24° 24′, long. 67° 13′. Little difficulty would be experienced in entering the creek, it being better defined than most of the mouths of the Indus.

PYTON.—A town in Hyderabad, or territory of the Nizam, situate on the left bank of the Godavery river, and 53 miles N.E. by E. from Ahmednuggur. Lat. 19° 29′, long. 75° 28′.

Q.

QABUR SHAKWALA, in the British district of Bhutteeana, lieut.-gov. of the N.W. Provinces, a town on the route from Mundate to Beekaneer, 71 miles S. by W. of the former. Lat. 29° 50′, long. 74° 8′.

QUEDAH.—A native state on the Malay peninsula, occupying that portion of the mainland which lies opposite the British possession of Prince of Wales Island. Province Wellesley forms its western boundary. Quedah, the principal place, is in lat. 6°, long. 100° 30′.

In 1786 an agreement was entered into with the rajah of Quedah, under which Prince of Wales Island was ceded to the British, in consideration of an annual stipend of 6,000 Spanish dollars. In 1800 a further treaty was concluded with the rajah, under which

Province Wellesley was transferred to the British, and the annual payment to the rajah ncreased to 10,000 dollars. In 1821 the king of Siam invaded Quedah, and expelled the rajah, but was induced, in 1842, upon the submission of the latter, to reinstate him in the most valuable portion of his former territory. At a subsequent date, the rajah of Quedah placed himself in a position of hostility towards the British, who visited his misconduct by withholding payment of his stipend. Upon its restoration, the arrears which had accumulated during the period of suspension were declared forfeited.

QUILON, in the native state of Travancore, presidency of Madras, a town on the seacoast, in a bight where ships may anchor under shelter, at about two and a half or three miles from the fort. A small British force is usually stationed here. "The ground on which the cantonment stands, rises by a gentle ascent from the sea, and includes an area of nearly five miles in circumference." "There is no natural boundary between the military cantonment and the Travancore territory, but a broad road round the cantonment points out the line of demarcation." There is in the cantonment a barrack for European troops, formerly occupied by a company of foot-artillery, but for many years past untenanted, and now fast falling to decay: there is also a European hospital. The site of the cantonment is healthy, being in the highest part about forty feet above the sea. The soil is for the most part sandy; but within its limits is a considerable piece of swampy ground. Water is abundant and good. There is a jail here, under the charge of the Travancore authorities. The roads about the cantonment are of laterite, broken small, and are in excellent condition. With Trivandrum, the capital of Travancore, the communication is carried on almost entirely "by means of canals, dug parallel to the low sandy shore, and connecting the different lakes formed by the backwater." There is also a military road, adapted for wheeled carriages, which, however, is but little frequented, owing to the great facility of water-communication, and which, in 1843, was represented as out of repair. Northwards, towards Allepi and Cochin, there are similar opportunities for communication by water; but horses and cattle can travel by an ill-formed sandy road along the beach. In a direction north-easterly, there is a line of communication with Tinnevelly by a pass through the mountains; but it is only an indifferent route, and is rather a footpath than a road. The vegetable productions of Quilon are timber, cocoanuts, coir or cocoanut-fibre, pepper, cardamoms, ginger, betelnuts, and coffee. The population is stated to be about 20,000. An Episcopal church was some years ago erected at this place. Distance from Trivandrum, N.W., 38 miles; Cananore, S.E., 225; Mangalore, S.E., 303; Bombay, S.E., 740; Bangalore, S.W., 290; Madras, S.W., 385. Lat. 8° 53′, long. 76° 39′.

QUOMOROODENUGGUR, in the British district of Delhi, lieut.-gov. of the N.W. Provinces, a village on the route from Rohtuk to the city of Delhi, and 11 miles W. of the latter. Lat. 28° 40′, long. 77° 6′.

R.

RAAT, in the British district of Humeerpore, the principal place of the pergunnah of the same name, a small town on the route from Jubulpoor by Kitha to Calpee, 46 miles S. of the latter. It has a bazar, and supplies and water are abundant. Davidson styles it "a populous and busy village," though a short time before his arrival the corpses of seventy of the inhabitants had been burned, in consequence of dreadful mortality, caused by malaria, resulting from the numerous swamps, tanks, and the rank vegetation with which the place is surrounded. Raat contains a population of 8,616 inhabitants. Lat. 25° 36′, long. 79° 38′.

RACHERRY.—A town in Hyderabad, or territory of the Nizam, 19 miles from the left bank of the Godavery river, and 158 miles N.E. from Hyderabad. Lat. 18° 59′, long. 80° 13′.

RACHOL.—A town in the Portuguese state of Goa, situate 14 miles S.S.E. from Goa. Lat. 15° 19′, long. 74° 4′.

RACHOOTEE, in the British district of Cuddapah, presidency of Madras, a town situate on the Mundaveer or Chittair, a small stream tributary to the river Northern Pennair or Pennaur. It is the principal place of a subdivision of the same name. Distance from the town of Cuddapah, S., 30 miles; Nellore, S.W., 86; Madras, N.W., 123. Lat. 14° 3′, long. 78° 49′.

RACHUR.—A town in the British district of Guntoor, presidency of Madras, 29 miles S.E. by E. of Guntoor. Lat. 16° 3′, long. 80° 50′.

RACKEE, in the Sinde Sagur Dooab division of the Punjab, a town situated on the left bank of the Swan river, 54 miles S.S.E. of the town of Attock. Lat. 33° 15′, long. 72° 48′.

RACKLING.—A town in the native state of Sikhim, 19 miles N. from Darjeeling, and 116 miles N.N.E. from Purneah. Lat. 27° 18′, long. 88° 22′.

RADHUNPOOR, a petty state in the north-western quarter of Guzerat, including the pergunnahs of Moorjpoor and Summee. It lies between lat. 23° 26′ and 23° 58′, and long. 71° 28′ and 72° 3′; and is bounded on the north by Therwarra; on the south by Mundall and Jurjoowarra; on the east by the Puttun district; and on the west by that of

Warye. Its dimensions are about forty miles by twenty.

During the months of April, May, June, and July, the heat is excessive; in August and September, if rain falls, the weather is agreeable; October and November are again hot; but from December until the return of the heat in April, the climate is delightful. There are three descriptions of soil—sandy, black, and saline. The chief products are wheat, cotton, and all the common grains. Salt is both manufactured and self-produced. The British government rent the Unwerpoora salt-pans of the nawab, at the annual sum of 11,048 rupees.

The district is traversed by the Bunnas river, and by the minor streams of the Surruswutti and Roopan. One of the great roads from Hindostan and Palee to the Mundavie Bunder, in Cutch, passes through Radhunpoor. The population, principally Hindoo, consists of about 45,000 souls. Radhunpoor is not tributary either to the British or any other government, but pays black mail to the surrounding Coolie districts. A police force, consisting of 235 sowars and 320 foot-men, is kept up by the state, and detachments are spread about in the different villages for their protection. In case of foreign invasion, the state is entirely dependent on the British government. The first connection of that government with Radhunpoor was in 1813, in which year Captain Carnac, then Resident at Baroda, concluded an engagement between the nawab and the Guicowar, by which the Guicowar state was empowered, under the advice and mediation of the British government, to control the external relations of Radhunpoor, and to assist the nawab with forces in defending it from foreign invasion, but excluded from any interference in the internal affairs of the country. During the five following years, the Kosas and other marauders having greatly infested the northwest part of Guzerat, and more particularly this petty state, the nawab voluntarily solicited the aid of the British government to expel them, and offered to pay a share of the expenses of the war. The required aid was afforded. In 1819, Colonel Barclay marched with a force and expelled the freebooters from all parts of Guzerat; and an agreement was negotiated with the nawab of Radhunpoor, by which he consented to pay a yearly tribute to the British government, leaving the actual amount to be subsequently decided. In 1822 the tribute was fixed at 17,000 rupees per annum for five years, after which it was to be left to the British government to increase the amount or not. The engagement continued in force until the year 1825, when the home authorities, considering the state unable to bear the amount of tribute imposed, it was, by the order of the Bombay government, remitted in full in the month of July of that year.

The Radhunpoor state is under the management of the British agent at Pahlunpoor, who controls its relations with the neighbouring states, but avoids all interference in its internal affairs. It has enjoyed perfect tranquillity since its connection with the British government in 1819.

The first person of the reigning family of which there is any record is Sheer Khan Babee, who was thannadar of Chowal in 1663. His grandson, Mahomed Khan Jehan, was the first of the family appointed as foujdar of Radhunpoor, in 1715. He left two sons, Kumaboodun and Mahomed Unwar. A few days after their father's death, Moobarigul Moolk, then soubahdar of Guzerat, gave the pergunnahs of Summee and Moorjpoor to the eldest, with the title of Jowan Murd Khan, and appointed the second foujdar of Radhunpoor. In 1765, Jowan Murd Khan died, and was succeeded by his eldest son, Gazeeoddeen, in the pergunnahs of Summee and Moorjpoor, his second son succeeding to that of Radhunpoor. In 1787, the latter died childless. In 1813, Gazeeoddeen died, leaving two sons, Sheer Khan and Kumaloodeen Khan. The former succeeded to the Radhunpoor pergunnah, and the latter to those of Summee and Moorjpoor. In 1814, the latter dying without issue, Sheer Khan succeeded to the nawaubship of the three pergunnahs. Sheer Khan died in 1825, and with the unanimous consent of the people was succeeded by the present chief, Zoorawar Khan, an only son, by a slave-girl. But Zoorawar being at this time only three years of age, Sirdah Bebee, the second wife of the late chief, was appointed regent during his minority. In 1837, he was intrusted with the management of his own affairs. He is now about thirty-two years of age, and has a son, heir-apparent to the chieftainship.

RADHUNPOOR, in Guzerat, or territory of the Guicowar, a town on the route from Ahmedabad to Hydrabad, in Scinde, 85 miles direct N.W. of former, 270 S.E. of latter. Though a considerable and fortified town, and not devoid of trade and manufactures, the majority of its population are cultivators, principally Rajpoots and Coolies. Its principal exports are butter, hides, and grain, and coarse cotton cloths, the local manufacture. The chief, styled nawaub of Radhunpoor, is a Mussulman, of the influential family of Babi, and has an annual income of 1,50,000 rupees. He acknowledges fealty to the Guicowar, by annually presenting to him a horse and clothes. His military establishment consists of sixty horse and 550 infantry. Population 15,000. Lat. 23° 50′, long. 71° 30′.

RAEEBAG.—A town in the British district of Belgaum, presidency of Bombay, 48 miles N.N.E. of Belgaum. Lat. 16° 29′, long. 74° 50′.

RAEEGURH, in the British collectorate Tannah, presidency of Bombay, a fort situate amidst the Northern Ghats. During the last campaign against the Peishwa, it was regarded as one of the strongest fortresses in India, and, in fact, "as impregnable as Gibraltar." It was invested by a British force under Colonel Prother, in April, 1818, and surrendered after a bombardment of fourteen days, by which every building, except one granary, was reduced to ashes. Raeegurh, originally denominated Rairi, in 1648 fell into the hands of Sevajee, who changed its name to Raeegurh, and made it his capital. In 1690 it was taken by the forces of Aurungzebe, and having reverted to the Mahrattas during the decadence of the Mahometan empire, was finally taken by the British forces, as already stated. Rairi, as this fort was originally called, must not be confounded with another place of the same name in Sawuntwarree, on the coast of the South Concan. Raeegurh is distant S.E. from Bombay 65 miles, S.W. from Poona 32, N.W. from Sattara 52. Lat. 18° 14′, long. 73° 30′.

RAEEN.—One of the Cis-Sutluj hill states. It is bounded on the north, east, and south by the native state of Bussahir, and on the west by Turroch and Bussahir. It extends from lat. 31° 2′—31° 12′, and from long. 77° 47′—77° 57′, and is twelve miles in length from north to south, and five in breadth.

RAEEPOOR, in the British district of Minpooree, lieut.-gov. of the N.W. Provinces, a village on the route from the cantonment of Allygurh to that of Minpooree, and 55 miles S.E. of the former. Lat. 27° 39′, long. 78° 54′.

RAEEPOOR, in the British district of Cawnpore, lieut.-gov. of the N.W. Provinces, a village on the route from the cantonment of Cawnpore to that of Calpee, and 16 miles S.W. of the former. Lat. 26° 25′, long. 80° 12′.

RAEGANJ, in the British district of Dinajepore, lieut.-gov. of Bengal, a town on the west boundary, towards the British district Purnea, on the left or east bank of the river Kooluk. It is the principal mart in the district, and nearly engrosses the traffic of an extent of rich country about seventy miles in length and twenty in breadth. Rich merchants have numerous stores here, consisting of large yards, inclosed by fences of straw hurdles or mats, and containing many huts and sheds filled with wares. The streets of the town are narrow, irregular, and filthy, but it is a place of great stir, and crowded with boatmen and drivers of cattle. It contains about 1,000 houses, a number which, according to the usually received ratio of inmates to dwellings, would assign it a population of about 5,000. Distant W. from the town of Dinajepoor 32 miles; N.W. from Calcutta, by Dinajepoor, 292. Lat. 25° 40′, long. 88° 8′.

RAEKOTE, in Sirhind, a town situate thirty miles from the left bank of the Sutlej, having a population of 8,704. It belongs to the petty chief of the surrounding territory. It is under the protection and control of the British. The town is distant N.W. of Calcutta, by Delhi and Hansee, 1,130 miles. Lat. 30° 40′, long. 75° 39′.

RAEPOOR.—A town in the Rajpoot state of Oodeypoor, 61 miles N.N.E. from Oodeypoor, and 82 miles S.S.W. from Ajmeer. Lat. 25° 26′, long. 74° 9′.

RAEPOOR, in the British district of Allygurh, lieut.-gov. of the N.W. Provinces, a village on the route from Futtehgurh to Meerut, and 106 miles N.W. of the former, is situate near the left bank of the Kalee Nuddee (East), in an open country but partially cultivated. Lat. 28° 5′, long. 78° 17′.

RAGAVAPOORAM.—A town in the British district of Masulipatam, presidency of Madras, 68 miles N. by W. of Masulipatam. Lat. 17° 8′, long. 80° 59′.

RAGOOGHUR, in the territory of Gwalior, or possessions of Scindia, a town on the route from Goona to Mow. 16 miles S.W. of former, 169 N.E. of latter. This, which is represented to be a considerable place, is situate on a feeder of the river Parbuttee. It has a bazar and a fort, which though now much dilapidated, was in the early part of the present century so strong as for a considerable time to baffle the disciplined army of Doulut Rao Scindia. It was founded in the time of Shahjehan, who reigned from 1628 to 1658, by Lal Singh, a Rajpoot chief; and after the rest of Malwa had been subjugated by the Mahrattas, his successors long resisted, until Dhokul Singh was, in A.D. 1821, finally defeated by the contingent force of Gwalior, commanded by British officers. By the mediation of the British authorities, he was allowed to retain Ragooghur, with an estate of 55,000 rupees, on condition that some retainers of the family should be always in the service of the maharajah of Gwalior. Distant N.E. of Oojein 130 miles, S. of Agra 200. Lat. 24° 30′, long. 77° 11′.

RAGOONAUTHPOOR, in the territory of Gwalior, or possessions of Scindia's family, a town 77 miles W. of Gwalior, near the south or right bank of the river Chumbul. Lat. 26° 4′, long. 76° 56′.

RAHA.—A town in the British district of Nowgong, in Upper Assam, 20 miles S.W. by W. of Nowgong. Lat. 26° 12′, long. 92° 31′.

RAHAHTAH.—A town in the British district of Ahmednuggur, presidency of Bombay, 47 miles N.N.W. of Ahmednuggur. Lat. 19° 42′, long. 74° 30′.

RAHDINPOOR.—See RADHUNPOOR.

RAHINPUR, in the British district of Allahabad, lieut.-gov. of the N.W. Provinces, a village on the route from the cantonment of Allahabad to Jounpore, and eight miles N.E. of the former. The road in this part of the route is good; the country fertile, well cultivated, and studded with villages. Lat. 25° 28′, long. 82°.

RAHLAI, in the British district of Agra, lieut.-gov. of the N.W. Provinces, a town on the southern frontier, towards the territory of Dholpoor, 17 miles S. of the city of Agra. Lat. 26° 56′, long. 78° 6′.

RAHM GHUR, in the Rajpoot state of Jeypoor, a village, with fort, on the route from Agra to Ajmeer, 72 miles W. of former, 156 E. of latter. The fort "is built of stone, with six round towers, perched on a steep eminence, with a double embattled wall stretching down one side to a wall at its foot." Lat. 27° 3′, long. 76° 58′.

RAHOOREE.—A town in the British district of Ahmednuggur, presidency of Bombay, 21 miles N.N.W. of Ahmednuggur. Lat. 19° 23′, long. 74° 40′.

RAHUN, in the Rajpoot state of Jodhpoor, a town on the route from Nusserabad to Nagor, and 57 miles N.W. of the former. It has a large bazar: water is obtained from a tank and fifty wells. The road in this part of the route is good, and passes over an immense plain, covered with scanty bush-jungle. Lat. 26° 46′, long. 74° 8′.

RAHYGAUW.—A town in Nepal, situate on the right bank of the Bhyroee river, and 21 miles S. by W. from Jemlah. Lat. 29°, long. 81° 37′.

RAICHAO.—A town in the Rajpoot state of Jhalawar, eight miles S.E. from Jhalra Patun, and 89 miles E. from Neemuch. Lat. 24° 27′, long. 76° 20′.

RAICHOOR.—A town in one of the sequestrated districts of the native state of Hyderabad, 111 miles S.W. by S. from Hyderabad. Lat. 16° 10′, long. 77° 24′.

RAIDEE.—A town in the British district of Chota Nagpoor, lieut.-gov. of Bengal, 41 miles S.W. by S. of Lohadugga. Lat. 22° 55′, long. 84° 28′.

RAIDROOG.—A town in the British district of Bellary, presidency of Madras, 31 miles S. of Bellary. Lat. 14° 41′, long. 76° 55′.

RAINGURH.—A fort surrounded by a small district, inclosed by the territory of Bussahir. It is situate on the left bank of the Pabur, and at the time of the expulsion of the Goorkhas, in 1815, consisted of a rampart surrounding a small peak, and having rude houses for the accommodation of the garrison. Jacquemont describes it, at the time of his visit, in 1830, as forty yards long and twenty broad, with a weak rampart about twenty feet high, along the inside of which were ranged the lodgings of the garrison, no better than dogholes. It is commanded from various points even by musketry, and has no regular supply of water, as the Pabur runs below, at the perpendicular depth of 476 feet. The Goorkha garrison, which surrendered to the British, was supplied from tanks, sufficing for about a month's consumption. The Pabur, at about a musket-shot below the fort, is crossed by a sanga or wooden bridge, forty yards long. The river, in that part deep, meanders through a level tract about 200 yards wide, fertile, and bearing fine crops of rice, wheat, and opium poppies. It is one of the most delightful spots amidst the Himalayas, and is held by a small community of Brahmins, who have charge of two temples built in the Chinese style. Hindostanee is spoken in considerable purity, and the inhabitants in easy circumstances resemble in make, complexion, and countenance, the Hindoos of the plains; while the labouring classes differ nothing from the ordinary mountaineers.

Raingurh belonged to Bussahir previously to the invasion of the Goorkhas, by whose garrison, on the 10th June, 1815, it was surrendered to the British. In the subsequent settlement of the hill states, it was reserved, with a small surrounding district about five miles long and three miles wide, but at a later period was transferred to the chief of Keonthul, in exchange for territory now forming part of Simla. Distant N.W. from Calcutta by Kurnaul 1,075 miles. Elevation of the fort above the level of the sea, 5,408 feet; of the bed of the Pabur below the fort, 4,932 feet. Lat. 31° 7′, long. 77° 48′.

RAIPOOR, in the British district of Calpee, lieut.-gov. of the N.W. Provinces, a town on the route from Calpee to Etawah, 16 miles N.W. of Calpee. Lat. 26° 17′, long. 79° 36′.

RAIPOOR, in the British district of Suharunpoor, lieut.-gov. of the N.W. Provinces, a town on the route from Suharunpoor to Sirmoor, 20 miles N. of the former. Lat. 30° 15′, long. 77° 40′.

RAIPORE.—See RAJAPORE.

RAIREE.—A river of Jodhpoor, rising on the confines of Mairwara, in lat. 25° 55′, long. 74° 4′, and, flowing in a westerly direction for eighty-eight miles, falls into the Loonee river, in lat. 25° 54′, long. 72° 51′.

RAIREE, on the coast of Rutnagherry, in the South Concan, presidency of Bombay, a fort, on a rocky eminence at the mouth of a small river, navigable for boats of considerable size. It was built in 1662, by Sevajee; subsequently passed into the hands of the rulers of Sawuntwarree; and, becoming a stronghold of the pirates sent out by that state, was in A.D. 1765 taken by a British force, but restored in the following year. By virtue of a treaty concluded in 1819, it passed back to the English; and their possession was confirmed by another treaty concluded in 1820. This place is also called Yeswuntgurh. Distant S. from Bombay 225 miles. Lat. 15° 45′, long. 73° 44′.

RAISEEN, in Malwa, a strong fort in territory of Bhopal, 23 miles N.E. of the town of Bhopal, in an elevated tract, a peak in its vicinity rising to the height of 2,500 feet. The fort is on the route from Hoshungabad to Saugor, 50 miles N. of former, 87 S.W. of latter. It is built at the eastern extremity of a sandstone hill, and on the most elevated part of it. "It is very conspicuous for many miles around, and said to have been built by the celebrated king (Rama) of Ayodha, as a place of refuge from the temporary anger of his brother (Bharata); and that the hill arose at his desire." According to this tradition, probably conveying some truth mixed with fable, the era of its foundation was about 775 years before Christ. Though little noticed of late years, it was formerly of importance; and when, in 1543, it was besieged by Shir Shah, padshah of Delhi, and one of the most powerful and martial princes who ever ruled Hindostan, the siege was protracted for a length of time. When the place at length capitulated, on condition that the Hindoo garrison should be allowed to march out unmolested with their arms and property, Shir Shah commanded his troops to attack them, and after a desperate resistance they were slaughtered to a ma .. On the dismemberment of the empire, towards the middle of the eighteenth century, the fort was, with the adjacent country, seized by the Mahrattas, from whom it was wrested, about A.D. 1748, by the nawaub of Bhopal. At this place, in 1818, was negotiated the treaty between the British government and the nawaub. Distant E. from Oojein 125 miles, S. from Gwalior 202, S. from Agra 260, S.W. from Allahabad 290, N.W. from Nagpoor 170. Lat. 23° 22′, long. 77° 56′.

RAITPOOR, in the British district of Aligurh, lieut.-gov. of the N.W. Provinces, a village on the route from the cantonment of Aligurh to that of Muttra, and 20 miles S.W. of the former. Lat. 27° 38′, long. 78° 1′.

RAJABETA.—A town in the British district of Beerbhoom, lieut.-gov. of Bengal, 159 miles N.W. of Calcutta. Lat. 24° 8′, long. 86° 40′.

RAJAHAT.—A town in the British district of Twenty-four Pergunnahs, lieut.-gov. of Bengal, 19 miles S.S.W. of Calcutta. Lat. 22° 20′, long. 88° 20′.

RAJAH BELL, in the Daman division of the Punjab, a town situated on the right bank of the Indus, 123 miles S.S.W. of the town of Peshawar. Lat. 32° 14′, long. 71° 11′.

RAJAHMUNDROOG.—A town in the British district of North Canara, presidency of Madras, 15 miles N.N.W. of Honahwar. Lat. 14° 31′, long. 74° 26′.

RAJAHMUNDRY.—A British district named from its principal place, and forming part of the territories subject to the presidency of Madras. It is bounded on the north by Orissa; on the north-east by the district of Vizagapatam; on the south-east by the Bay of Bengal; on the west by the British district of Masulipatam; and on the north-west by the territory of the Nizam. It lies between lat. 16° 18′—17° 38′, long. 81° 7′—82° 40′, and has an area of 6,050 square miles. The seacoast, commencing at the outlet from the Lake of Colair, proceeds eastwards for ten miles to Point Narsipore, at the mouth of the Narsipore river, or southern branch of the Godavery. In this estuary ships of small draught may find shelter, as there are eight or nine feet of water on the bar, and three, four, or five fathoms inside; but ships of considerable burthen cannot be brought nearer to the shore than four or five miles, in consequence of shoals extending out to sea. From Narsipore Point the coast of this district extends in a direction north-east, along the seaward face of the delta of the Godavery, a distance of fifty-seven miles, to Point Gordeware, a low narrow sand-bank, extending north and south several miles, on the west side of which is the estuary of the great northern branch of the Godavery. Opposite to this are several shoals and low-islands, caused probably by the accumulation of silt, swept down by that vast torrent. About seven miles north-west of Point Gordeware is the estuary of another and smaller branch of the same river, generally called Coringa river, from the town of Coringa, situate on its bank. This admits vessels of moderate burthen, having twelve or fourteen feet of water on the bar at spring tides. On Hope Island, a small sand-bank above water, about five miles eastward of the mouth of the Coringa river, is a lighthouse for the guidance of shipping on this intricate and shoaly coast, which is so low, that the sea has, in violent storms, extensively overflowed and devastated the land. A little north of Hope Island, and the shoals lying about it, the coast becomes bolder and more free from dangers, so that large ships can approach within two or three miles of it; and it continues to be of the same nature for thirty-seven miles, to Yamawaram, at the north-eastern extremity of the district; its direction during that distance being nearly north-east. The northern and north-western part of the district is hilly; the ground there participating of the character of the Eastern Ghats, situate farther west. The geological formation of those hills is granite, intermixed with gneiss and amygdaloidal trap, and kunkur or calcareous tufa, with a scanty admixture of fine porcelain clay. East of those hills of primitive formation, are others less elevated, and of alluvial formation, principally sandstone, containing valuable deposits of iron-ore. In the bed of the Godavery are abundance of fragments of chalcedony, cornelians, agates, quartz, and crystals.

Towards the coast, the country for the most part is alluvial, fertile, level, and low, and in the rainy season extensively inundated. The only considerable river is the Godavery, which enters the district at the northern frontier, in lat. 17° 29′, long. 81° 34′, and holds a course, generally southerly, through the gorges of the Eastern Ghats for twenty-five miles, to Poorsaotputnum, where it passes into the plain, through which it continues to hold a southerly course, slightly inclining to east, for twenty miles, to the town of Rajahmundry; about four miles below which it divaricates into two branches, the right flowing first southerly for thirty-two miles, subsequently south-westerly for thirteen miles, to Point Narsipore, where it falls into the Bay of Bengal; the other, or left branch, taking a course south-east and subsequently east for fifty-two miles, falls into the same bay three or four miles south-east of Coringa. The total length of the river's course through this district, measured along the main line and continued by either branch to the sea, is about 100 miles; but if the two branches be included in the measurement (and each during a considerable portion of the year has a large volume of water), the total length of fertilizing stream must be nearly 160 miles. During the greater part of the year, it is navigable for boats in all parts within this district, and large quantities of teak timber are floated down it to the sea. The deltas between the two branches are "known to be the richest and most fertile landscapes in the peninsula." Formerly this enormous torrent during the dry season "dwindled to a small stream, generally fordable;" but since the construction of a dam or annicut across the river at the head of the delta, a never-failing supply of water, previously allowed to flow in useless abundance to the sea, is retained for purposes of irrigation. Numerous small islands or lunkas, as they are vernacularly called, are formed in its course by the deposits of silt; and as they are very fertile, and consequently valuable, their formation is assisted by the proprietors of adjacent lands, who plant in the bed of the river a species of long grass, which, shooting up with great strength and luxuriance, obstructs the sand and mud in their progress downwards, until in successive years they form islands of considerable area, and especially desirable, in consequence of being suitable for producing tobacco (the most lucrative crop) in the highest perfection. During spring and the early part of summer, the climate is very hot; but it does not appear that any exact register of the temperature has been made public. The wind during that period is either westerly or south-westerly, and sweeps along great quantities of very fine white sand, rendering the season very disagreeable and oppressive. The south-west monsoon succeeds, and the river becomes swollen from the rains which fall in the more elevated region west of the Eastern Ghats. In October the north-east monsoon sets in, and from that time until March, the climate is peculiarly healthy in the plains; but throughout the year a deadly malaria broods in the jungly valleys and gorges in the hills in the northern and north-western part of the district.

Of the zoology of the country little has been made public; but it comprehends hyænas, jackals, foxes, antelopes, and hares. The deep jungly valleys of the mountains in the west and north of the district must harbour great numbers of wild beasts, but the pestilential air of those secluded tracts renders it impracticable to explore them. Of domestic animals, sheep, which are numerous, are of small size, but the mutton is good; kine are abundant, but their flesh is indifferent; poultry of all kinds are very plentiful.

The soil in the plain is generally a rich alluvial deposit, and along the banks of the river is the fertile dark-coloured earth known by the name of the black cotton ground. The principal alimentary crops are rice, maize, millet, pulse of various kinds, oil-seeds, and sugarcane. Many European vegetables succeed during the cool season. Of commercial crops, the principal are tobacco, indigo, and cotton. The cocoanut-palm and palmyra-palm grow well in the sandy soil along the seashore. The quantity of cotton produced in one year, according to official return, was 4,150,000 pounds. The population is given under the article MADRAS.

Serious disturbances have occurred from time to time in the hill districts of this collectorate, but by the adoption of conciliatory measures, peace and good order appear to have been re-established. Rajahmundry, the principal place, Samulkotta, and Coringa, the only towns of importance, are described under their respective names in the alphabetical arrangement. The principal routes are—1. From north-east to south-west, from Calcutta, through Vizagapatam and Rajahmundry, to Ellore; 2. from east to west, from Samulkotta, through Rajahmundry, to Hyderabad; 3. from south to north, from Rajahmundry to Nagpore.

Rajahmundry is one of the five Northern Circars which were obtained by the French in 1753, and transferred in 1759, by the results of war, to the British, to whom their possession was confirmed in 1765, by the emperor of Delhi.

RAJAHMUNDRY.—The principal place of the British district of the same name, presidency of Madras. It is situate on ground slightly elevated, on the left or north bank of the river Godavery, here a mile broad, and during inundations having a vast body of water, which fills the channel from bank to bank, and sweeps along in its course from the upper country rafts of wood, trees, and herds of cattle. The town consists of one principal street, about half a mile in length from north to south, and containing the chief bazar. The houses on each side are generally of one story, built of mud and tiled. From the principal street are several narrow lanes, running east and west. Those to the west proceed to the bank of the river in an oblique direction, and consist of mean houses, built of mud and tiled, and containing in some few places a larger description of dwelling with upper stories; and in those reside the zemindars or landholders of the vicinity, and some are inhabited by wealthy traders, principally Brahmins. The streets on the east side of the bazar are narrow and very irregular, and inhabited by people of various denominations, but principally Gentoos. The fort, situate north of the town, has a square ground-plan, with high walls of mud, and a ditch now partially filled up. It contains the barracks, hospital, jail, magazine, and the lines of the garrison. The jail is very substantially built, and fire-proof, there being no wood in its construction except for the doors and windows, and is capable of containing 400 persons. Within the fort are also the court-house and lodges for European officers. The inhabitants are supplied from the river with water for drinking and for culinary purposes, as that of the wells is brackish, and the tanks are an imperfect resource, as they sometimes become dry. The population is estimated at from 15,000 to 20,000; of whom the Mussulmans form but a small and indigent class, though numerous mosques, still to be seen, indicate them to have been formerly numerous and wealthy. Distance from Ellore, N.E., 50 miles; Madras, N.E., 285; Calcutta, S.W., 580. Lat. 17°, long. 81° 50′.

RAJAHPOLLIAM.—A town in the British district of Tinnevelly, presidency of Madras, 51 miles N.N.W. of Tinnevelly. Lat. 9° 27′, long. 77° 31′.

RAJAHPOOR.—A town in Oude, situate on the right bank of the Ghogra river, and 50 miles N.N.E. from Lucknow. Lat. 27° 30′, long. 81° 20′.

RAJAKHAIRA, in the territory of Dholpoor, a town, the principal place of a small district of the same name. The rana or prince of Gohud, having by treaty, in 1804, ceded the fort of Gohud, with the districts dependent on it, to the East-India Company, was granted the small district of Rajakhaira, with that of Baree and Dholpoor; and these now form the raj or territory held by the rana of Dholpoor. Rajakhaira is 23 miles N.E. of the town of Dholpoor, 20 S.E. of Agra. Lat. 26° 55′, long. 78° 15′.

RAJAM.—A town in the British district of Vizagapatam, presidency of Madras, 58 miles N.N.E. of Vizagapatam. Lat. 18° 27′, long. 83° 44′.

RAJAORI, or RAJAWUR, in the north of the Punjab, a town situate on the banks of a stream, which, rising in the Pir Panjal, or mountain bounding Cashmere on the south, falls into the Chenaub. The houses are generally built of mud, strengthened with frames of timber, but a few of those of the wealthier classes are of brick. Elevation above the sea 2,800 feet. Lat. 33° 19′, long. 74° 21′.

RAJAPOOR.—A town on the coast of Bombay, in the district of Jinjeera, or territory of the Hubsies, situate on the northern point of land forming the entrance of the harbour of Rajapoor. Lat. 18° 18′, long. 73° 3′.—See also JINJEERA.

RAJAPOOR.—A town in the British district of Rutnageriah, presidency of Bombay, 30 miles S.E. by S. of Rutnageriah. Lat. 16° 39′, long. 73° 35′.

RAJAPOOR, in the British district of Banda, lieut.-gov. of the N.W. Provinces, a small town, with bazar, on the route from Allahabad cantonment to that of Banda, 15 miles W. of the former, 60 E. of the latter. Here is a ferry across the Jumna, the bed of which is sandy, and about 800 yards wide, with the left bank sloping, the right steep. In the dry season the stream occupies about half the bed. Lat. 25° 24′, long. 81° 14′.

RAJAPORE, in the British district of Goruckpore, lieut.-gov. of the N.W. Provinces, a small town on the left bank of the Ghogra, at the confluence of the Raptee. It contains, according to Buchanan, 150 houses, or rather huts. Distant S.E. from Goruckpore cantonment 35 miles. Lat. 26° 14′, long. 83° 48′.

RAJARAMPORE.—A town in the British district of Dinajepore, lieut.-gov. of Bengal, five miles N.E. of Dinajepore. Lat. 25° 36′, long. 88° 41′.

RAJAURA, in the British district of Agra, lieut.-gov. of the N.W. Provinces, a town on the right bank of the Jumna, immediately below the embouchure of the Baun Ootunghun, and 32 miles S.E. of the city of Agra. Lat. 26° 58′, long. 78° 32′.

RAJBARREE.—A town in the British district of Cuttack, lieut.-gov. of Bengal, 55 miles E.N.E. of Cuttack. Lat. 20° 42′, long. 86° 44′.

RAJEAKA, in the British district of Goorgaon, lieut.-gov. of the N.W. Provinces, a village on the route from Narnol to Rewaree, and six miles S.W. of the latter. Lat. 28° 8′, long. 76° 35′.

RAJEHPOOR, in the British district of Furruckabad, lieut.-gov. of the N.W. Provinces, a village on the route from Calpee to Futtehgurh, and nine miles S. of the latter. Lat. 27° 14′, long. 79° 42′.

RAJEPOORAH, in Sirhind, a town on the route from Umballa to Loodiana, and 13 miles N.W. of the former place. It has grown up about a palace built by one of the Mogul emperors, and hence its name. There is a bazar in the town, which is well supplied with water; and the surrounding country, level and fertile, affords abundant supplies. Rajepoorah is distant N.W. from Calcutta 1,033 miles. Lat. 30° 29′, long. 76° 41′.

RAJESHAYE, a British district within the lieut.-gov. of Bengal, is bounded on the north by the British district of Dinajepore; on the north-east by the British district Bagoora or Bogra; on the east and south-east by the British district Pubna; on the south by the Podda or Ganges, dividing it from the British district Nuddea; on the south-west by the same stream, dividing it from the British district Moorshedabad; and on the west by the British district Maldah. It lies between lat. 24° 6′—24° 58′, long. 88° 18′—89° 20′; is sixty-two miles in length from east to west, and fifty in breadth. The area, according to official statement, is 2,084 square miles. It is a very moist tract, having numerous rivers streaming from the Himalaya, situate north of it. The principal are the Ganges and the Mahanunda. The other rivers traversing the district are the Attree, the Jubuna, the Nagor, the Burrul, and the Narrud, receiving the united drainage of the jhils or swampy lakes of Maunda, Dulabari, and Chilum. During the periodical inundations, the district is intersected by numerous other watercourses, the channels of which are dry for the greater part of the year Many of those watercourses stagnating, give rise to swamps or jhils, of which that of Chilum is the largest, extending during the rains, in a direction from south-east to north-west, about twenty-five miles, with an average breadth of about five, one-half being comprised within this district, the other half within the neighbouring district of Pubna. Two others, the jhil of Dulabari and that of Maunda, are each about eight miles in length and three in breadth, and others of inferior dimensions are numerous; and there are also some tanks, or artificial pieces of water, of considerable dimensions.

Of wild animals, there are the tiger, leopard, deer, wild buffalo, wild swine; which two last cause great havoc in cultivated grounds. The principal domestic animals are the buffalo, kine, goat, and sheep. Rice is the staple crop; but there is considerable cultivation of wheat, oats, barley, pulse of various kinds, oil-seeds, cucurbitaceous plants, sweet potatoes, hemp, yam, onion, garlic, capsicum, turmeric, ginger, sugarcane, pine-apple. Of fruit-trees, there are the mango, jak (Artocarpus integrifolius), tamarind, pomegranate, lemon, and citron. The cocoanut and betelnut are cultivated, but they are neither common nor produced in great perfection. Of articles of commerce, the most important are indigo and silk, of which there are large annual exports. The population is given under the article BENGAL. Baliya, the locality of the civil establishment of the district, and Nator, the only places which can be called towns, are described under their respective names in the alphabetical arrangement. The principal routes are, 1. that from south to north, from Calcutta to Darjeeling; 2. from south-west to north-east, from Berhampoor to Jumalpoor. The district was ceded to the East-India Company by the grant of the dewanny, made by the emperor of Delhi in 1765.

RAJGEER, or RAJAGRIHA, in the British district of Behar, lieut.-gov. of Bengal, a small town denominated from its containing the Rajagriha, or royal palace of the ancient sovereigns of Magadha or Behar. It is situate amidst the summits of the Rajagriha hills, and near the north-western extremity of the range, and on the huge and massy rampart of an old fortress. Within the inclosure of the fort are numerous large mounds, probably the ruins of the residences of Jarasandha and his court, as that monarch, the paramount sovereign of India, is considered to have here had his seat of government. Around the inclosure are several great mounds, probably also the ruins of buildings. In the vicinity of this place is a mound four miles long, 150 feet broad at the base, and twelve feet high. It now serves to dam up the inundation from the periodical rains, and thus form an artificial lake; but, according to Buchanan, its main purpose originally was to serve as a causeway to the royal residence. At a short distance south of the town are numerous hot springs, the water of which has a temperature of about 108°. The number of houses has been computed at 800, which, according to the usually assumed average of inmates to each, would assign it a population of 4,000 persons. Rajagriha is 40 miles S. of Patna. Lat. 25° 2′, long. 85° 29′.

RAJGHAT, in the south-western corner of the Dehra Doon, a village with a ferry over the Jumna, there, when crossed by Moorcroft in the middle of February, about 100 feet broad. The ferry is a short distance below the confluence of the Giree and Jumna. Elevation above the sea 1,516 feet. Lat. 30° 26′, long. 77° 45′.

RAJ GHAT, in the British district of Boolundshuhur, lieut.-gov. of the N.W. Provinces, a village on the right bank of the Ganges, 73 miles S.E. of Delhi. Lat. 28° 14′, long. 78° 25′.

RAJGHUR.—A town in Guzerat, or dominions of the Guicowar, 30 miles N.E. from Baroda, and 72 miles E.S.E. from Ahmedabad. Lat. 22° 31′, long. 73° 35′.

RAJGHUR.—A town in the lapsed territory of Nagpoor, situate on the right bank of the Wein Gunga river, and 88 miles S.S.E. from Nagpoor. Lat. 20° 3′, long. 79° 49′.

RAJGHUR.—A town in the Rajpoot state of Oodeypoor or Meywar, situate on the right bank of the Banas river, and 77 miles S.S.E. from Ajmeer. Lat. 25° 29′, long. 75° 11′.

RAJGUR, in the territory of the rajah of Putteeala, a fort two miles from the right bank of the river Giree, a quadrangle built of uncemented stone, and sixty-six feet long and fifty-five wide. Elevation above the sea 7,175 feet. Lat. 30° 53′, long. 77° 14′.

RAJGUR.—A town of Baghelcund, in the native state of Rewah, situate on the left bank of the Sone river, and 54 miles E. by N. from Rewah. Lat. 24° 35′, long. 82° 13′.

RAJGURH.—A town in the native state of Gwalior, or territory of Scindia, 75 miles S.W. by S. from Gwalior, and 68 miles W. by S. from Jhansee. Lat. 25° 20′, long. 77° 35′.

RAJGURH, in Sirmor, a ruined fort belonging to the rajah of that state. It is situate on a natural terrace or flat projection from the side of a mountain, and is of a square outline, with a tower at each corner about forty feet high and twenty square. Inside, along the inclosing wall, are the remains of buildings to accommodate the inmates, the area in the middle being about forty feet square. The whole structure is of slate rock very neatly cut, and bonded throughout with large beams, put together in a substantial and workmanlike manner. It was fired and nearly demolished by the Goorkhas in 1814. Elevation above the sea 7,115 feet. Lat. 30° 52′, long. 77° 23′.

RAJGURH, in the Rajpoot state of Alwar, under the management of the Governor-General's agent for Rajpootana, a town on the route from Nusserabad to Muttra, and 76 miles S.W. of the latter. It is situate on an eminence surmounted by a large fort, and rising abruptly from the bottom of a valley inclosed by steep hills. Troops can obtain water and supplies here in abundance. The road to the north-east, or towards Muttra, is sandy and stony; to the south-west, or towards Nusserabad, good. Lat. 27° 14′, long. 76° 42′.

RAJGURH, in the British district of Ajmeer, lieut.-gov. of the N.W. Provinces, a village, the principal place of a pergunnah of the same name, according to official return having a population of 12,340 persons. According to Jacquemont, here are the ruins of a fortress, the history of which is altogether unknown. The edifice itself is insignificant, but the inclosing rampart is lofty and massive, constructed of great masses of rough stone, and environing an extensive area. Contiguous is a small lake, apparently artificial, and altogether the site is delightful. Distance S. from Ajmeer 10 miles, from Nusserabad W. six. Lat. 26° 19′, long. 74° 44′.

RAJGURH.—A town in the Rajpoot state of Beekaneer, 140 miles E.N.E. from Beekaneer, and 40 miles S.S.W. from Hissar. Lat. 28° 38′, long. 75° 31′.

RAJGURH.—A town of Malwa, meriting notice only as the residence of the rawul or chief inheriting a share of the tract called Omutwarra. An account of the mode of territorial division, and such other particulars as deserve mention, will be found under the article OMUTWARRA. Recently, the affairs of the rawul fell into that state of confusion not unusual in the East, and after the failure of some milder expedients for restoring them, it became necessary for the British government temporarily to assume the management, and assign a stipend for the support of the chief. Lat. 23° 59′, long. 76° 49′.

RAJHLEE, in Sirhind, a village on the route from Hansee to Loodiana, and 56 miles N. of the former town. It is situate on a branch of the river Guggur, in a low, level country. Distant N.W. from Calcutta 1,032 miles. Lat. 29° 52′, long. 76° 2′.

RAJHPOOR, in the territory of Alwar, under the political management of the Governor-General's agent for Rajpootana, a small town on the route from the town of Alwar to Jeypore, and 55 miles N.E. of the latter. It has a fort situate on an eminence rising abruptly from the plain. Lat. 27° 10′, long. 76° 36′.

RAJKOTE, in the peninsula of Kattywar, province of Guzerat, a town in the prant or district of Hallar. The territory annexed to it contains fifty-five villages, and a population of 20,000. It belongs to a Rajpoot thakoor or chief, who has an annual income of 34,500 rupees, out of which he pays an annual tribute of 17,000 rupees to the British government. A church has been erected in the town for the accommodation of the Christian community. Distance from Ahmedabad, S.W., 125 miles; Baroda, W., 150. Lat. 22° 18′, long. 70° 50′.

RAJMAHAL, in the British district of Bhaugulpore, lieut.-gov. of Bengal, a town situate on the right bank of the Ganges, and on the main line of railway now under construction from Calcutta and the valley of the Ganges to Delhi and the north-west frontier. The site of the town is a bank of considerable elevation and steepness, round which the Ganges, here at its greatest magnitude, sweeps with great violence, and sometimes rends away large portions of the land. The place is principally remarkable for the ruins of a palace, built by Shahjehan's son Shuja, viceroy of Bengal. The Jamamasjit, or principal mosque, built by Man Singh, viceroy of Akbar, is a spacious building of imposing aspect, but of rude execution. It is 188 feet in length, and sixty wide. Another mosque of inferior size was built by Futehjung Khan, a rival of Man Singh. Here, also, are the ruins of a palace built by Cossim Ali, the soobahdar of Bengal, raised and subsequently expelled by the East-India Company. The general aspect of the town is ruinous and dismal, as it is now a collection of wretched houses or huts, dispersed amongst twelve market-places, situate at considerable and inconvenient distances from each other. The permanent population is estimated at about 30,000 persons; and the transitory population is considerable, the number of travellers by land and water being great. The supply of provisions to such passengers is the chief support to the town.

Rajmahal is considered by Wilford as a place of great antiquity, and identical with Rajagriha, built by Balarama, brother of Krishna, who, according to Hindoo chronology, is conjectured to have lived 3,101 years B.C. Buchanan, on the other hand, mentions that the natives consider the place as of very recent date, owing its origin to Man Singh, the Rajpoot viceroy of Akbar; and hence the name of Akbarabad, given to it in honour of

the Padshah, and generally used by the Mussulmans to designate it. In the reign of Shahjehan, his son Shuja held the same high trust, until defeated and expelled by his brother Aurungzebe. It was occupied by the British troops after they had, at Oondwa Nullah, forced the lines of Cossim Ali, in 1763, and was formally ceded to the East-India Company by the firman of Shah Alum in 1765, granting them the dewanny of Bengal. Distant N.W. from Calcutta, by Burhampoor, 196 miles; by water, by the course of the Ganges, 249. Lat. 25° 1', long. 87° 50'. In June, 1855, during a period of profound tranquillity, a fearful insurrection broke out among the tribes of the Rajmahal hills, who suddenly descended into the plains and carried devastation in every direction. In this outbreak the Sonthals appear to have been the prime movers. These people are described as frank and industrious, but at the same time as simple and unlettered. They are stated to have been greatly oppressed by the exactions of the Mahajeens or money-lenders of the plains; and as they are represented as incapable of appreciating the adjustment of a disputed demand except by the most simple mode, they were generally overreached in the local law courts in endeavouring to obtain redress for their wrongs. To such grievances has been ascribed the origin of the insurrection. It was not suppressed until martial law had been proclaimed, and a considerable military force had been called out. Measures have been taken for the better administration of the disturbed districts.

RAJNUGGUR.—A town in the Rajpoot state of Oodeypoor, 39 miles N.N.E. from Oodeypoor, and 107 miles S.S.W. from Ajmeer. Lat. 25° 4', long. 74° 2'.

RAJNUGUR, in Bundelcund, a town in the raj of Chutterpore, hence often called the raj of Rajnugur. It is situate 85 miles S. Calpee. Lat. 24° 52', long. 80°.

RAJNUGUR.—A town in the British district of Silhet, lieut.-gov. of Bengal, 26 miles S. of Silhet. Lat. 24° 32', long. 91° 52'.

RAJOOKONDDU.—A town in Hyderabad, or dominions of the Nizam, 23 miles E.S.E. from Hyderabad, and 108 miles N.N.E. from Kurnool. Lat. 17° 12', long. 78° 51'.

RAJOORA.—A town in Hyderabad, or dominions of the Nizam, situate on the right bank of the Wein Gunga river, and 180 miles N. by E. from Hyderabad. Lat. 19° 49', long. 79° 26'.

RAJOORY.—A town in Hyderabad, or territory of the Nizam, 138 miles N.W. by W. from Hyderabad, and 100 miles N.E. from Sholapoor. Lat. 18° 40', long. 77°.

RAJPEEPLA.—A petty Rajpoot state in the Rewa Caunta division of Guzerat. It is bounded on the north by the Nerbudda river; on the east by the district of Akraunee; on the west by the British collectorate of Broach; on the south by the Guicowar's district of Wusraee, and the district of Mandavee, now incorporated with the collectorate of Surat. It lies between lat. 21° 23' and 21° 59', and long. 73° 5' and 74°. The area is 1,650 square miles, inhabited by a population of 122,100. In 1855, the prime minister of the rajah, having been detected in certain fraudulent practices, was dismissed by the British government, and the rajah refusing to nominate a successor for their approval, his possessions were placed in sequestration.

Many parts of the state are inhabited by a wild race, composed of Rajpoots and Bheels, but the lowlands contain a large population of Koonbees, belonging to the industrious portion of the agricultural peasantry, whose villages indicate, from their flourishing condition, the industry peculiar to that class. It is watered by the river Kurgun, on which is situated the capital, Nandode. The sovereigns of Delhi endeavoured at an early period to impose a tribute upon Rajpeepla. The attempt was made without success, but its rulers agreed to keep up a body of horse and foot, whose services should be available when required. Akbar first established a tribute in lieu of this force, but it was paid only so long as authority was retained in the country by the Mahometan rulers. Subsequently, Damajee Row Guicowar, with the consent of the Peishwa, revived the claim, and the rajah consented to pay annually the sum of 40,000 rupees to the Guicowar state. Thus Rajpeepla was constituted one of the original tributary possessions obtained by the Guicowar family on the establishment of its power in Guzerat; and from the year 1764 to 1780 the Guicowar continued to receive tribute to the amount above stated. From the last-named period the successive rulers of Guzerat availed themselves of various favourable opportunities for increasing the amount, until it finally reached a lac of rupees, a sum altogether disproportionate to the ability of the Rajpeepla state to pay. In 1822, the amount of tribute was fixed at 60,000 rupees. An agreement was also entered into for discharging the arrears; and to secure the fulfilment of the revised engagement, a receiver of all the revenues was appointed under British guarantee, which arrangement still prevails. For many years the state was a prey to internal dissensions, owing to the claims set up by rival candidates to the guddee. Ram Sing, whom his father, Ajeeb Sing, had intended to set aside, was placed on the guddee by the aid of his Arab troops, but becoming unfit to conduct the business of the state, the sanction of the British government was given to an arrangement by which Pertaub assumed the management of affairs in the name of his disqualified parent. The legitimacy of Pertaub was disputed by his uncle Nhar Sing, who established his allegation, and laid claim to succeed as rightful heir, but being blind, his eldest son, Vereesaljee, was proclaimed rajah by the united authority of the British and Guicowar governments. The terms entered into by this chief are, to pay the amount of tribute to the Guicowar government; to restrain his wild tribes; not to harbour offenders escaping from justice, and to abide by the decision of the British government in certain specified cases. Rajah Vereesaljee, who was born in 1810, still continues to administer the affairs of the state. The force maintained by the rajah, for purposes of police and state, consists of 100 horse and 285 sebundies, at an annual cost of 47,000 rupees. The revenue of this district formerly amounted to 3,45,500 rupees, but a gradual falling off has taken place: in the year 1843, it only reached 2,22,783 rupees; and a further decline has subsequently taken place. With a view to the adoption of some remedial measures, the Court of Directors in 1848 called the attention of the Bombay government to the fact that this state, which was delivered to the rajah's management in a prosperous condition, was again falling into difficulties, and that the annual disbursements actually exceeded the receipts. An inquiry was thereupon instituted, and the results disclosed the existence of a gross system of misappropriation and deception on the part both of the rajah and potadar or receiver of the revenue. There also appeared strong ground for suspecting certain inferior officers of corruption; and the oppression of the people by illegal exactions and other nefarious practices, was clearly established. Various modes of removing these evils, and preventing their recurrence, were suggested, and subsequently decided upon. Three miles to the east of Numoodra, in the Rajpeepla district, lie the celebrated cornelian-mines. The stones are conveyed by the merchants to Cambay, where, being cut and polished, they are formed into the beautiful ornaments for which that city is celebrated. The revenue derived from the mines has greatly declined, and they now scarcely yield 1,000 rupees per annum. Within the last few years, the rajah has suppressed suttee, and has likewise abolished burning as a capital punishment.

RAJPEEPLA.—A town in the Rewa Caunta division of Guzerat. A Rajpoot, named Chokrana, having quarrelled with his father, the rajah of Oojein, retired to this country, and fixed his residence in Peepla, situated on the top of a lofty hill, now styled Old Rajpeepla, to distinguish it from the modern village of that name. Having made this spot the seat of government, its old name was abandoned, and that of Rajpeepla, now the general appellation of the whole province, given to it. The place is almost inaccessible, and for carts, or any kind of carriage, altogether so. It was, however, a safe retreat for the rajahs whenever the country was invaded by a powerful enemy. In modern times, Nhar Sing was enabled by local advantages to hold out against a superior force sent against him by the Guicowar government. Lat. 21° 47′, long. 73° 29′.

RAJPEETA.—A town in the British district of Pachete, lieut.-gov. of Bengal, 30 miles N.W. of Rogonatpoor. Lat. 23° 50′, long. 86° 25′.

RAJPOOR.—A town of Allee Mohun, in Malwa, presidency of Bengal, and the present residence of the rajah. It is a large and well-built town, and has a capital bazar, with a market-day on Monday. Lat. 22° 20′, long. 74° 21′.

RAJPOOR, in the Julinder Dooab division of the Punjab, a town situated nine miles from the left bank of the Beas, and 43 miles N.E. of the town of Julinder. Lat. 31° 46′, long. 76° 13′.

RAJPOOR, in the British district of Cawnpore, lieut.-gov. of the N.W. Provinces, a village on the route from Calpee to Etawah, and 16 miles N.W. of the former. Lat. 26° 18′, long. 79° 45′.

RAJPOOR, in the British district of the Dehra Doon, a village on the route from the town of Dehra to the sanatory station of Landour, and six miles and a half S. of the latter. The road to Dehra is very good, having a gentle declivity to that town from Landour: it is for the first three miles very steep, but easier for the remaining part. There is a good bazar, and here are kept the camels and elephants of the visitors to Landour. Lat. 30° 24′, long. 78° 10′.

RAJPOORA, in the British district of Bareilly, division of Pillibheet, lieut.-gov. of the N.W. Provinces, a village on the route by Nanakmath and Ruderpoor, from the town of Pillibheet to Kasheepore, 20 miles S.E. of the latter. Lat. 29° 3′, long. 79° 16′.

RAJPOORA.—A town in the Rajpoot state of Beekaneer, 112 miles N.E. by E. from Beekaneer, and 62 miles S.W. from Hissar. Lat. 28° 33′, long. 75° 4′.

RAJPOOREE.—See RAJAPOOR.

RAJPOOTANA.—An extensive tract of Western India, so denominated from its prevailing population, the Rajpoots. It is bounded on the north-east by the British districts Butteeana and Kurreeana, and the native state of Jhujhur; on the east by the British district of Goorgaon, and by Bhurtpore, Dholpore, and Gwalior; on the south by the province of Omutwara, by the territories of Scindia, of Holkar, and of the Guiçowar, by Jabbooa and the presidency of Bombay; on the west by Scinde; and on the north-west by Bhawulpore and the British district of Butteeanee. Defined by these limits, it lies between lat. 23° 35′—29° 57′, long. 70° 5′—77° 40′; is 420 miles in length from east to west, and 400 in breadth. The detailed areas of the states, as given in an official document, are in square miles as follows:—Oodeypore or Mewar, 11,614; Jeypore,

15,251; Joudpore, 35,672; Jhallawar, 2,200; Kotah, 4,339; Bhoondee, 2,291; Alwur, 3,573; Bickaneer, 17,676; Jessulmere, 12,252; Kishengurh, 724; Banswarra, 1,440; Pertabgurh, 1,457; Doongerpore, 1,000; Kerowlee, 1,878; Serohee, 3,024; giving a total of 114,391 square miles.

The widely-spread sept of Rajpoots are considered offsets from the Kshetriyas, one of the four great castes into which the Hindoos were originally divided. In the dim and uncertain light in which Hindoo history lies previously to the Mahomedan invasion in the tenth century, it is not safe to form any judgment as to the period when the Rajpoots appeared as a distinct race. Their origin is by Hindoo tradition placed in Mount Aboo, bordering on Guzerat. Their power and renown appear to have been at their acme about the close of the twelfth century, when Ajmere and Delhi were held in union by one of their princes, Kunnouj by another, Guzerat by a third; but their power soon fell before the enthusiasm, ferocity, and military qualities of the Mussulmans. Pirthi Raj, the sovereign of Ajmere and Delhi, in 1191 defeated at Tirouri Shahabuddin Muhammad, sultan of Ghor, but was in 1193 defeated by that monarch in a great battle, and being taken prisoner, was put to death. Following out his success, Shahabuddin in 1194 defeated Jain Chandra, the Rajpoot rajah of Kunnouj; and by these shocks, the sway of the Rajpoots was restricted within limits nearly corresponding with those which form their present boundaries. Besides the tract denominated Rajpootana, the race is dispersed over many parts of India; as in Bundelcund, where many of the chiefs are Rajpoots, and in Baghelkhand or Rewa, the rajah of which is a Baghel Rajpoot; also in Gurhwal, and several others of the hill states, and in the territory of Cutch. The able compiler of the Sanscrit Dictionary adverts with much felicity to the "peculiar character of the Rajpoots, arising from their situation as the military class of the original Hindoo system. The other classes," he continues, "though kept together as castes by community of religious rites, were mixed up in civil society, and were under no chiefs except the ordinary magistrates of the country. But the Rajpoots were born soldiers; each division had its hereditary leader, and each formed a separate community, like clans in other countries, the members of which were bound by many ties to their chiefs and to each other. The rules of caste still subsisted, and tended to render more powerful the connection just described. As the chiefs of those clans stood in the same relation to the rajah as their own relations did to them, the king, nobility, and soldiery, all made one body, united by the strongest feelings of kindred and military devotion. The sort of feudal system that prevailed among the Rajpoots, gave additional stability to this attachment, and altogether produced the pride of birth, the high spirit, and the romantic notions so striking in the military class of that period. Their enthusiasm was kept up by the songs of their bards, and inflamed by frequent contests for glory or for love. They treated women with a respect unusual in the East, and were guided even towards their enemies by rules of honour, which it was disgraceful to violate. But although they had so many characteristics of chivalry, they had not the high-strained sentiments and artificial refinements of our knights, and were more in the spirit of Homer's heroes, than of Spenser's or Ariosto's. If to these qualities we add a strong disposition to indolence (which may have existed formerly, though not likely to figure in history), and make allowances for the effects of a long period of depression, we have the character of the Rajpoots of the present day, who bear much the same resemblance to their ancestors that those did to the warriors of the Maha Bharat. With all the noble qualities of the early Rajpoots was mixed a simplicity, derived from the want of intercourse with other nations, which rendered them inferior in practical ability, and even in military efficiency, to men actuated by much less elevated sentiments than theirs." Another intelligent writer, who spent much time among the Rajpoots, gives a less favourable account of them. He says, "The warlike character of the Rajpoot has been very much overrated. There appears to be very little chivalrous feeling in his breast. By nature, Rajpoots are generally powerful, muscular men, active by habit and practising gymnastics (though, when not excited, inclined to indolence to a high degree); those who possess horses are generally good horsemen. Some are, by constant practice, dexterous in the use of lance or sword, and, individually, must be often superior to an enemy trained to act in combination, according to a rigid system of discipline. But amongst a large body of Rajpoot horse, only a few would be found such superior men at arms, or so to venture. The Rajpoots do not possess the cool determinate courage, ready to dare any danger, and requiring no artificial excitement. According to their own accounts, even in their former attacks on caravans and towns, surprise was their object; and if successful, they were equally cruel and rapacious, showing no mercy to their captives; and if they met with much resistance, became as cowardly as they had before been violent, and resorted to flight: fighting was not their object. In all their single combats, and all assaults, they resorted to the excitement of opium before commencing battle: their own bards describe the eyes of their heroes as being red from opium. Among their rajahs, the treacherous murders of each other on record were numerous and long premeditated." There is probably much truth in this latter view. Many gloomy shadows darken the portrait of the Rajpoot character, and contrast painfully with the bright hues depicted in the earlier notice. Among them may be reckoned the practice of suttee under its most atrocious forms, the horrible holocaust being increased in cases where the rank and wealth of the deceased were thought to demand the addition, by forcibly throwing numbers of females, either attendant slaves or retainers, into the flames, together with the chief victim.

As another fearful stain on Rajpoot manners, may be mentioned the once universally prevalent crime of female infanticide. To such an extent was it carried among some tribes, that, in 1818, when Macmurdo wrote, it is stated that among the offspring of 8,000 married Jhareja Rajpoots, not more than sixty females were living; and it was considered probable that the number did not exceed thirty. To such an extent was this cruelty to daughters carried, that they were sometimes destroyed after attaining adolescence; the instinct of affection, even when strengthened by time and habit, being insufficient to overcome the suggestions of pride, or imaginary expediency. In 1810, when the rajahs of Joudpore and Jeypore became suitors for a princess of Oodeypore, and supported their pretensions by waging war against each other, the family of the unhappy girl terminated the contest by putting her to death. Some years ago, the marriageable daughter of the rajah of Bickaneer was put to death under similar circumstances, and from similar motives. A practice, less hideously criminal, but most dangerous to themselves and others, is their addiction to the use of opium, already adverted to, in which they indulge to a degree which first inflames their passions, then impairs their intellects, leading in the last stage to permanent and hopeless fatuity. Before the debilitating drug has effected this dire result, it is to the Rajpoot the source of false courage and insensate desperation. Furious from its influence, Rajpoot armies have in many instances recklessly rushed on certain death, and, neither giving nor receiving quarter, have perished to a man. The most appalling manifestation of this madness is denominated *johar*. It consists in an army or garrison, reduced to despair and inflamed by opium, butchering their families in the first place, and then rushing on the enemy and fighting till destroyed. Notwithstanding, however, their deficiency in steady courage, and their inferiority in discipline and tactics, it is certain that the Rajpoots have succeeded in rendering themselves formidable to some of the greatest military characters of India. Baber, exercised from boyhood in the most varied and fierce scenes of warfare, honestly relates the dismay into which himself and his veterans were thrown by the approach of Rana Sanka, of Mewar, the champion of Brahminism, on whose overthrow the Mussulman sultan assumed, for the first time, the much-desired title of Ghazi, or "champion victorious in defence of the faith." Subsequently, Sher Shah, the Afghan who defeated and dethroned Humayon, the son of Baber, and the padshah of Delhi, having invaded Rajpootana at the head of 80,000 men, was fiercely encountered, and nearly repulsed by Kunbha, a Rajpoot chief, at the head of 10,000 of his clan. The Afghan observed, after his dearly-won victory, that he had almost lost the empire of India for a handful of joar, alluding to a coarse grain forming the staple crop in the barren country, which he found so obstinately defended. In more recent times, the Rajpoots have scarcely sustained their former reputation.

Notwithstanding their many strongholds, their numerous forces, and boasted military prowess, they offered little resistance to the Mahrattas, who at will desolated their lands, until shielded by the British power. Some of the Rajpoot states were brought into connection with the British government early in the present century, by the Marquis of Wellesley. His successor, Sir George Barlow, adopted a different policy; but experience having manifested the wisdom of that of the previous Governor-General, it was resumed by the Marquis of Hastings, and these states became generally subject to British influence, and entitled to the benefit of British protection. The required powers are exercised through an officer called the Governor-General's agent for the states of Rajpootana. The connection appears to have been greatly beneficial to the country. European principles of justice and policy are gradually making way. Arrangements have been introduced for the decision of international questions, as well as for the general administration of justice, and are said to be working well.

RAJULA.—A town in the peninsula of Kattywar, province of Guzerat, in the prant or district of Babriawar. Distance from Ahmedabad S.W. 155 miles, Baroda 145. Lat. 21° 2′, long. 71° 28′.

RAJULDESIR, in the Rajpoot state of Beekaneer, a town on the route from Rutungurh to the town of Beekaneer, and 75 miles E. of the latter. It has four towers for its defence, and contains 283 houses, and six wells 100 feet deep. Lat. 28° 1′, long. 74° 34′.

RAJUMPETT.—A town in Hyderabad, or territory of the Nizam, 66 miles N. by W. from Hyderabad, and 166 miles E. by N. from Sholapoor. Lat. 18° 17′, long. 78° 21′.

RAJUNPOOR.—A town in the native state of Bhawulpoor, situate on the left bank of the Indus river, and 116 miles S.W. by W. from Bhawulpoor. Lat. 28° 31′, long. 70° 10′.

RAJUR.—A town in the territory belonging to Ali Moorad, 27 miles S.E. from the left bank of the Indus, and 27 miles S.E. by E. from Bukkur. Lat. 27° 26′, long. 69° 16′.

RAKCHAM, in Bussahir, a village situate in the valley of the Buspa, on the right bank of the river of that name, and near the confluence of a stream called the Gor. The site of the village is striking and not unpleasing, at the western extremity of a glen, and at the base of a huge mass of bare rocks, which rise abruptly in numerous black spires above the village. Elevation above the sea 10,456 feet. Lat. 31° 22′, long. 78° 27′.

RAKHA.—A town in Nepal, situate on the right bank of the Gunduck or Salagra river, and 145 miles W.N.W. from Khatmandoo. Lat. 28° 37′, long. 83° 13′.

RAKISHBOON.—A town in Hyderabad, or dominions of the Nizam, situate on the right bank of the Godavery river, and 37 miles S. by W. from Jaulnah. Lat. 19° 20′, long. 75° 46′.

RAKRI, in the British district of Aligurh, lieut.-gov. of the N.W. Provinces, a village 12 miles S.E. of the cantonment of Aligurh. Lat. 27° 46′, long. 78° 15′.

RALA.—A town in the British district of Arracan, 22 miles N.W. by W. of Arracan. Lat. 20° 51′, long. 93° 8′.

RALDANG, or WEST KAILAS, in Bussahir, a lofty mountain of Koonawar, separating the valley of the Buspa from that of the Tidung. Gerard, who viewed it from the left bank of the Sutlej, gives the following description:—"Some idea of it may be formed by imagining an assemblage of pointed peaks, presenting a vast surface of snow, viewed under an angle of twenty-seven degrees, and at a distance of not more than five miles in a direct line." The highest peak has an elevation of 21,103 feet. Lat. 31° 29′, long. 78° 21′.

RALEIGAON.—A town in one of the sequestrated districts of the native state of Hyderabad, 85 miles S.E. from Ellichpoor. Lat. 20° 27′, long. 78° 36′.

RALHOOPOOR, in the British district of Benares, lieut.-gov. of the N.W. Provinces, a town on the route from Benares to Sasseram, five miles S.E. of the former. Lat. 25° 14′, long. 83° 7′.

RAMA.—A town in the Rajpoot state of Jodhpoor, 46 miles S.S.W. from Jodhpoor, and 128 miles W.S.W. from Ajmeer. Lat. 25° 41′, long. 72° 54′.

RAMAGIRI, in the Mysore, a town with a fort, the principal place of a tallook or subdivision of the same name. It is situate on the right or west side of the river Arkavati. The fort is situate on a high rocky hill of granite, and is capable of defence, yet it surrendered promptly, A.D. 1791, to the British force which advanced against it. Distant from Seringapatam, N.E., 48 miles; Bangalore, S.W., 25. Lat. 12° 45′, long. 77° 30′.

RAMAREE, in the British district of Kumaon, lieut.-gov. of the N.W. Provinces, a village on the route from Almora to the frontier of South-western Tibet, by the Juwahir Pass, 67 miles N.E. of the former, 89 S.W. of the latter. Lat. 29° 58′, long. 80° 9′.

RAMAS.—A high bluff headland on the coast of Goa, "forming in two level points when seen either from the northward or southward: that called False Cape is highest and first discernible; the other, less elevated, forms the extremity of the true cape, on which is a small fort belonging to the Portuguese." Lat. 15° 5′, long. 73° 58′.

RAMA SERAI, in Gurhwal, a valley extending in a direction from north-west to south-east, between lat. 30° 46′—30° 58′, and long. 78°—78° 12′. It is about a mile wide, fertile, and well watered, and formerly was well cultivated, and contained several good villages; but of late years, in consequence of Goorkha devastation, is nearly desolate, overrun with jungle, and full of wild beasts. The Camalda river, which flows down the valley, falls into the Jumna on the right side.

RAMBUDRAPOOR.—A town in Hyderabad, or dominions of the Nizam, situate on the left bank of the Godavery river, and 168 miles E. by N. from Hyderabad. Lat. 17° 48′, long. 81° 2′.

RAMDOORG.—A town within the territories of Bombay, situate 54 miles E. by N. from Belgaum, and 66 miles S.S.W. from Beejapoor. Lat. 15° 58′, long. 75° 22′.

RAMESUR, in the British district of Kumaon, lieut.-gov. of the N.W. Provinces, a village with a Hindoo temple at the confluence of the rivers Surjoo and Eastern Ramgunga. Elevation above the sea 1,500 feet. Lat. 29° 32′, long. 80° 8′.

RAMESWARAM.—An island at the western extremity of Adam's Bridge, forming the northern boundary of the Gulf of Manaar, and extending in a direction nearly east and west, between Ceylon and the south-eastern coast of the peninsula of India. It is represented to be about fourteen miles in length from south-east to north-west, and five in breadth. It is uncultivated, and principally inhabited by Brahmins and their followers, who are supported by the profits derived from the great pagoda and other temples. The entrance to the principal temple is through a fine gateway about 100 feet high, and elaborately carved, its form being trapezoid. The workmanship is massive and regular, and in a style of architecture resembling the Egyptian. Within is a cloister, having a passage between a triple row of pillars, to a square of about 600 feet, cloistered all round, and into which the sacred temples open. The whole is well built, and is one of the finest structures in India. It appears to be dedicated to the divinity Siva, of whom, according to Brahminical legend, Rameswara or Rama is an avatar or incarnation. According to the Ramayana and other Puranic legends, Ravana, the demon tyrant of Lanka, having abducted Sita, the consort of Rama, the injured monarch pursued the ravisher, who carried off his prize to Lanka; so that pursuit was stayed by the intervening sea, until "Nala, the son of fire, then commenced to make a bridge over the sea, and prayed his father that all the great stones, and other heavy articles necessary for the work, might be deprived of their weight and float on the sea. This prayer being granted, he soon completed the bridge, over which the troops marched to Lanka." Such is the fabled origin of the long bank forming the northern boundary of the Gulf of Manaar, and called by the Brahminists "Rama's Bridge;" by the Mussulmans and Christians, "Adam's Bridge."

Near the town of Rameswaram is a fresh-water lake, about three miles in circumference. The great pagoda is a celebrated place of pilgrimage, frequented by crowds from all parts of India; it is under the guardianship and management of a chief, styled Pandaram, who must observe celibacy through life, and on his death is succeeded by his sister's son, or, should there not be any such, by the next eldest collateral male relative. The image of the deity is every morning drenched with water brought on the shoulders of fakirs from the Ganges, and poured over it, and which, having received additional sanctity by this rite, is sold to devotees at a high price. A splendid view of this pagoda is given by Daniell.

At the western extremity of the island is the small town of Paumbaum, and between it and the mainland of India is a passage, formerly so beset with rocks and shoals as to be nearly unavailable for navigation. Measures for its improvement have recently been taken with success, of which some notice will be found under the article PAUMBAUM. According to local tradition, this island was connected with the mainland of India until the early part of the fifteenth century, when the connecting neck of land was partially swept away by the sea during a dreadful hurricane, and the breakers were brought to their present extent by a succession of similar irruptions. Geological observation lends some support to this. The bottom consists in general of sandstone of the same kind as that on Rameswaram and the neighbouring part of the continent of India. The number of pilgrims visiting annually the pagoda is estimated at 30,000, the fixed population at 4,288, of whom 811 are Brahmins, 620 Mussulmans, 372 native Christians, other classes 2,485. The population would appear to be well lodged, as the number of houses is considerable in proportion to its amount; but these being constructed in a great measure to meet the resort of pilgrims, a judgment framed with reference only to the accommodation thus provided would probably be fallacious. The town of Rameswaram is in lat. 9° 18′, long. 79° 21′.

RAMGHAT, in the British district of Bolundshuhur, lieut.-gov. of the N.W. Provinces, a town on the route from Allygurh to Bareilly, and 30 miles N.E. of the former, situate on the right bank of the Ganges, here crossed by ferry. The bed of the river is about a mile and a half wide, and the stream in the dry season usually occupies one-third of that space, and is sometimes divided into two or more channels. Ramghat is 80 miles S.E. of Delhi. Lat. 28° 9′, long. 78° 30′.

RAMGHERRY, in Hyderabad, or territory of the Nizam, a town 110 miles N.E. of the city of Hyderabad. Lat. 18° 38′, long. 79° 39′.

RAMGUNGA (EASTERN). — A river rising in the British district of Kumaon, on the southern declivity of the main chain of the Himalaya, at an elevation of about 9,000 feet, and in lat. 30° 11′, long. 80° 8′. It holds a course generally southerly for about fifty-five miles, to Ramesur, where it falls into the Surjoo, on the left side. Its descent must be very rapid, as the point of its confluence with the Surjoo is estimated to be only 1,500 feet above the sea. The name of Ramgunga is often given to the united stream as far as its confluence with the Kalee. Webb, who crossed it by a spar bridge, in lat. 29° 48′, long. 80° 12′, about thirty miles from its source, found it to be there unfordable during the rainy season, but ascertained that it could be forded at other times, when it had a depth of four feet. Twelve miles higher up the stream, it is crossed by the route from Almora to the Juwahir Pass into Tibet, and is there "fordable, except in the rains, when a rope bridge is thrown across it."

RAMGUNGA (WESTERN). — A river rising in the British district of Kumaon, amidst the outer or lower group of the Himalayas, and in lat. 30° 6′, long. 79° 20′. The stream is formed by a junction of several small rills, flowing from various directions. The elevation of its remotest source above the sea does not appear to be ascertained, but that of Dewalee Khal, a temple situate on a summit two or three miles from it, is 7,144 feet. At the confluence with the Kothar stream, about five miles lower down, the elevation is 3,338 feet. Its course for the first twenty miles is in a south-easterly direction; it then becomes south-westerly, and so continues to its exit from the hills, in lat. 29° 30′, long. 78° 49′, at the distance of about ninety miles from its source. In this upper part of its course, it receives numerous mountain-streams, on both the right and left sides. A short distance below its entrance into the plain, and about 100 miles from its source, it takes a southerly direction, which it holds for fifteen miles, and in lat. 29° 17′, long. 78° 42′, receives the Koh, a considerable feeder, on the right side. At the town of Moradabad, forty miles below this confluence, the Ramgunga, in the early part of December, when it is probably lowest, is described by Heber as "a sluggish river, as wide nearly in this place as the Severn at Shrewsbury, but shallow and fordable." Garden states that the bed is a mile wide here, and that the stream in the dry season is usually divided into two or three channels, from one to three feet deep, with uneven sandy bottom, and that the passage in the wet season is made by ferry. Fifteen miles below this, it, in lat. 28° 41′, long. 79° 1′, receives on the left side the Kosee, a considerable stream, but continues even after this accession fordable from the month of December to that of June sixty miles lower. Besides some feeders of less size, it receives on the left side the Sunka, and is not usually fordable below Jalalabad, seventy-three miles further, in lat. 27° 44′, long. 79° 40′. Sixty miles still lower, it on the left side receives the Deoha or Gurrah, a considerable stream. Ten miles below this last confluence, the Ramgunga falls into the Ganges on the left side, nearly opposite the ancient city of Kanouj, and in lat. 27° 7′, long. 80° 3′. Its total length of course is about 373 miles.

RAMGUNGE, in the territory of Oude, a village on the route from Cawnpore to Lucknow, 16 miles N.E. of the former, 37 S.W. of the latter. Lat. 26° 37′, long. 80° 37′.

RAMGUNJE.—A town in the British district of Bulloah, lieut.-gov. of Bengal, 12 miles N. of Bulloah. Lat. 23° 3′, long. 90° 57′.

RAMGUR.—A town in the lapsed territory of Nagpoor, 80 miles S. from Bustur, and 76 miles N. by E. from Rajahmundry. Lat. 18° 5′, long. 82°.

RAMGURH, otherwise called HAZAREEBAGH, formerly part of a collectorate of wider dimensions. In 1832 a general insurrection broke out on the south-west frontier of Bengal, and extending to this locality, the disturbed tracts comprised within the present district of Ramgurh were withdrawn from the operation of the ordinary regulations, and annexed to the territory under the administration of the political agent for the south-western frontier of Bengal. Both the names by which the district is designated are derived from towns situate within its limits. It is bounded on the north by the British district Behar; on the north-east by the British district of Mongheer; on the east by the British district Beerbhoom; on the south-east by the British district Pachete; on the south by the British district Chota Nagpore; and on the south-west and west by the British district Palamow. It lies between lat. 23° 20′—24° 50′, long. 83° 50′—86° 38′; is 175 miles in length from east to west, and ninety in breadth: the area is 8,524 square miles. Many groups of hills are dispersed over the district; there is also much undulating ground, consisting of plateaus of moderate extent, separated by gentle depressions. Of these plateaus one of the most extensive and elevated is that of Hazareebagh, nearly in the middle of the district, and having, it is stated, an elevation of 1,800 feet above the sea. Many of the mountains are of primitive formation,—granite, quartz, or gneiss; but others, of later formation, abound in coal and iron: the latter, though smelted to a great extent, is reputed not to be of the best quality. Lead-ore is said to have been discovered in the vicinity of Hazareebagh; and it is conjectured that silver-ore may be obtained in the same mine. There are ores of antimony in many places. In the vicinity of Hazareebagh are beds of very fine mica, from which large transparent laminæ are obtained.

The whole country is very thinly peopled, insomuch that Jacquemont, on one occasion at least, scarcely observed a house in a day's journey, though travelling along the direct road from Calcutta to Benares. As far as the eye could reach, nothing could be seen but thick forests, the lairs of lions, tigers, leopards, bears, hyænas, foxes, jackals, wild dogs, wild buffaloes, wild kine, wild swine, hog deer, and other kinds; monkeys, porcupines, and some other quadrupeds of less importance. Tigers are particularly numerous, and the dread of their ravages so great as sometimes to have impelled the inhabitants to desert their homes. Everywhere in those forests lurk the monstrous boa, and several venomous species of serpents, as the cobra de capello and karait. The timber is fine; and together with the sal (Shorea robusta), are found a great variety of trees and plants unknown to Europeans. In many parts the forests are totally impenetrable, and where of practicable access, the air during a portion of the year is so pestiferous as to cause almost certain death to those exposed to its influence. The winter and beginning of spring are the healthier times, and are, in consequence of the elevation, so cool that ice is formed on stagnant water.

The rivers are numerous, but none of them of great volume. The principal drainage is to the south-east, towards the estuary of the Ganges, by the Damooda, and its tributary the Barrackur, the torrent flowing by Hazareebagh. Other streams flow northward, as the Mohana and Leelajan, passing into Behar; others again westward, discharging themselves into the river Koel; and a few small tributaries find their way southward through the channel of the Soobunreeka river into the Bay of Bengal. This great diversity in the directions of the watercourses indicates that the general elevation of the district is greater than that of the tracts surrounding it.

The inhabitants are in a low state of civilization, and live, thinly scattered over this spacious country, in small villages, consisting of wretched huts of hurdles, mud, and matting, covered with a thin roof of thatch. "The natives of these districts are principally agriculturists; many are occupied in trades of different kinds, and some are engaged as soldiers. They are in general temperate, industrious, and tolerably cleanly in their houses and persons."

There are scarcely any places in this district which can properly be denominated towns. Ramgurh and Hazareebagh, which are the principal collections of dwellings, are described under their respective names in the alphabetical arrangement. The population will be found under the article BENGAL. The main course of communication from south-east to north-west, between Calcutta and the North-Western Provinces, lies through this district, in two distinct lines, nearly parallel, and at an average distance from each other of about twenty miles. That more to the south-west passes through Deigwar, Hazareebagh, Kutkumsandee, and Kanachuttee; the other line, more to the north-east, is the grand trunk road, and passes through Doomree, Dhourara, and Churparun, shortening the route about three miles. The district of Ramghur is within the limits of the dewanny granted to the East-India Company in 1765, by Shah Alum, emperor of Delhi.

RAMGURH.—A town within the district of the same name. As it communicates its name to the surrounding tract of country, it may be presumed to have been formerly a place of some importance; but it is now utterly inconsiderable. Lat. 23° 42′, long. 85° 30′.

RAMGURH, in the British district of Ramgurh, territory of Saugor and Nerbudda, lieut.-gov. of the N.W. Provinces, a town on the route from Sohagpoor to Nagpoor, 45 miles S.W. by S. of the former. Lat. 22° 49′, long. 81° 1′. The territory of which this town is the chief place, forms a subdivision under the jurisdiction of the political agent for the Saugor and Nerbudda provinces. Its population is returned at 41,766. The district was ceded to the British by the rajah of Nagpore, in commutation of subsidy.

RAMGURH.—A town of Malwa, in the native state of Burwanee, 21 miles S.W. from Burwanee, and 67 miles N. from Dhoolia. Lat. 21° 50′, long. 74° 49′.

RAMGURH, in the British district of Ajmeer, lieut.-gov. of the N.W. Provinces, a town on the route from Ajmeer to Oodeypoor, 39 miles S.S.W. of the former. Lat. 25° 59′, long. 74° 32′.

RAMGURH, in the Rajpoot territory of Shekhawutee, a town on the west frontier towards Beekaneer. It is a thriving place, neatly fortified, and contains the residences of several wealthy bankers. Distance W. from Delhi 140 miles, N.W. from Jeypore 100, E. from Beekaneer 108. Lat. 28° 9′, long. 75° 5′.

RAMGURH.—A town in the Rajpoot state of Jeypoor, 41 miles N.W. by W. from Jeypoor, and 68 miles N.E. by N. from Ajmeer. Lat. 27° 15′, long. 75° 21′.

RAMGURH, in the Rajpoot territory of Alwar, under the political management of the Governor-General's agent for Rajpootana, a town on the route from Alwar, by way of Ferozpore, to Delhi, and 95 miles S. of the latter. Lat. 27° 35′, long. 76° 52′.

RAMGURH, in the British district of Baitool, territory of Saugur and Nerbudda, lieut.-gov. of the N.W. Provinces, a town on the route from Baitool to Kurgoon, 54 miles W. of the former. Lat. 21° 49′, long. 77° 8′.

RAMGURH.—A town in the native state of Gwalior, or territory of Scindia's family, 36 miles N. from Gwalior, and 34 miles S.S.E. from Agra. Lat. 26° 44′, long. 78° 12′.

RAMGURH.—A town in the British district of Chittagong, lieut.-gov. of Bengal, 48 miles N. by W. of Chittagong. Lat. 23°, long. 91° 43′.

RAMGURH, in the hill state of Hindoor, a fortress on the steep and high ridge which, rising from the left bank of the Sutlej, has a south-easterly direction, and ultimately joins the Himalaya. In the beginning of November, 1814, at the commencement of the Goorkha war, it was invested by the British army under General Ochterlony, who, by a course of tedious yet wonderfully energetic and laborious operations, succeeded in conveying battering-guns up the precipitous and previously trackless declivity. The defences were in consequence speedily demolished, and the garrison capitulated. Elevation above the sea 4,054 feet. Distant N.W. from Calcutta 1,094 miles. Lat. 31° 5′, long. 76° 51′.

RAMGURH, in the Rajpoot state of Jesulmeer, a fort and village 35 miles N.W. of the town of Jesulmeer, is situate at the termination of a low rocky ridge of recent formation, extending from Cutch in various ramifications, but generally in a northerly direction. Ramgurh is in lat. 27° 16′, long. 70° 42′.

RAMGURH, in the British district of Kumaon, lieut.-gov. of the N.W. Provinces, a village with a bungalow, or public reception-house, on the route from Almora to Bareilly, and 19 miles S.W. of the former. Water is scarce here; supplies, however, are abundant, though Heber was struck by the general indigence of the population. This place had formerly a fort, as the name indicates, but it has been allowed to fall to decay. Elevation above the sea 4,872 feet. Lat. 29° 27′, long. 79° 37′.

RAMGURRAH.—A town of Bundelcund, in the native state of Punnah, situate 48 miles S. by E. from the town of that name, and 69 miles N.N.E. from Jubbulpoor. Lat. 24° 3′, long. 80° 28′.

RAMGURTAL, in the British district of Goruckpore, lieut.-gov. of the N.W. Provinces, a jhil or shallow lake close to the cantonment of Goruckpore. At the close of the rainy season it is about six miles long and three broad, but even at that time is shallow and overgrown with weeds, and in the shoaler parts with aquatic trees. As the hot, dry season advances, the vegetation increases, and the water diminishes, and becomes dirty and crowded with reptiles and insects, the decaying remains of which, and of the vegetation, produce malaria. During the rainy season, when the jhil and the contiguous river Raptee swell, so as to communicate, this malaria is either mitigated or totally suspended. Lat. 26° 46′, long. 83° 24′.

RAMJUNDAH.—A town in the British district of Palamow, lieut.-gov. of Bengal, 24 miles W. by S. of Palamow. Lat. 23° 46′, long. 83° 40′.

RAMKOLA, in the British district of Goruckpore, lieut.-gov. of the N.W. Provinces, a small town on the route from the cantonment of Goruckpore to Betiya, 28 miles E. of the former, 54 W. of the latter. Buchanan styles it a market-town, yet elsewhere states that it does not deserve the name of town. It has, however, a bazar. Distant N.W. from Dinapore 110 miles. Lat. 26° 50', long. 83° 56'.

RAMMAGHERRY.—A town in the British district of Madura, presidency of Madras, 53 miles N. of Madura. Lat. 10° 41', long. 78° 12'.

RAMMESSWUR.—A town in the British district of Pooree, lieut.-gov. of Bengal, 28 miles N.W. by W. of Juggurnaut. Lat. 20° 1', long. 85° 33'.

RAMNAD, in the British district of Madura, presidency of Madras, a town, the principal place of an extensive zemindarry or feudal estate of the same name, is situate five or six miles from the seacoast of Palk's Bay, and about a mile and a half from the right bank of the river Vigai or Vigairu. "It is about two miles and a half in circumference, surrounded by a wall and a ditch, and defended by numerous small bastions; but the works are now in a ruinous condition, and the ditch nearly filled up. Though the streets are narrow and ill contrived, the houses are moderately well built. There are a few mosques, which, though not conspicuous, are by no means inelegant. The fort is contiguous to the town, on the west of it, and between them runs a wide street, with two rows of bazars regularly built. The ground-plan of the fort is an equilateral quadrangle, the sides of which respectively facing the cardinal points, are each half a mile in length, and consist of a single wall twenty-seven feet high and five feet thick, without rampart, but with loopholes, and surrounded by a ditch. There are thirty-two bastions and one gateway, which is on the east side. In the centre stands the palace or residence of the zemindar. This fort was built about two hundred years ago, by Moghava Ragunatha Setupatti, who at the same time constructed the large reservoir or tank on the north side. Contiguous to the palace is a handsome residence, built by Colonel Martinez, who for nearly forty years commanded here, and near it a small but neat Protestant church, kept in good repair. The few principal streets, which are within the fort, are wide and airy. There are, however, several mean streets, with mud-built houses. The number of inhabitants within the fort is about 5,000, principally dependent on the zemindar. The only manufacturing industry worth notice in the town, is that of coarse cloths for native wear; any other business is trade in provisions and wares for the supply of the population. This place is garrisoned by a company of native troops. It is a hot station, but the evenings are usually cool, from the influence of the sea-breeze, and altogether it is a very healthy place. Distance from Palamkotta, N.E., 87 miles; Madura, S.E., 60; Tanjore, S., 100; Madras, S.W., 275. Lat. 9° 24', long. 78° 50'.

RAMNAGAR, in the district of Aldemau, territory of Oude, a village on the route from Pertabgurh to Fyzabad, 45 miles N. of the former, 18 S. of the latter. Butter estimates its population at 400, all Hindoos. Lat. 26° 24', long. 82° 56'.

RAMNAGAR, in the British district of Cawnpore, lieut.-gov. of the N. W. Provinces, a village on the route from the cantonment of Cawnpore to that of Futtehgurh, and 12 miles N.W. of the former. Lat. 26° 35', long. 80° 17'.

RAMNAGHUR.—A town in Oude, situate on the right bank of the Gogra river, and 32 miles E.N.E. from Lucknow. Lat. 27° 3', long. 81° 28'.

RAMNAGUR.—A town in the British district of Nuddea, lieut.-gov. of Bengal, 96 miles N. of Calcutta. Lat. 23° 57', long. 88° 30'.

RAMNEGHUR, or RAMNUGGUR, in the Punjab, a walled town close to the left or east bank of the Chenaub, stands on a spacious plain, where, during the reign of Runjeet Singh, the Sikh troops frequently mustered for campaigns to the westward. There is a ferry here across the Chenaub, which, at its lowest season, was found to be 300 yards wide, and for the most part nine feet deep, running at the rate of a mile and a half an hour. Two miles below the town there is, however, a ford, where the depth does not exceed three feet when the water is low. This place was called Rasulnuggur, or "Prophet's Town," until stormed in 1778 by Maha Singh, the father of Runjeet, when it received the present name, signifying the "town of God." Lat. 32° 20', long. 73° 50'.

RAMNUGGUR.—A town in the dominions of Gholab Singh, the ruler of Cashmere, 95 miles S.S.E. from Sirinagur, and 100 miles N.E. from Lahore. Lat. 32° 45', long. 75° 25'.

RAMNUGGUR, in the British district of Goruckpore, lieut.-gov. of the N.W. Provinces, a small town near the south-eastern frontier, towards the British district of Sarun. Distant S.E. from Goruckpore cantonment 50 miles. Lat. 26° 10', long. 84° 2'.

RAMNUGGUR, in the British district of Minpooree, lieut.-gov. of the N.W. Provinces, a village on the route from the city of Agra to the cantonment of Minpooree, and 25 miles W. of the latter. Lat. 27° 8', long. 78° 45'.

RAMNUGGUR.—A town in the British district of Sarun, lieut.-gov. of Bengal, 30 miles N.N.W. of Bettiah. Lat. 27° 9', long. 84° 23'.

RAMNUGGUR.—A town in the native state of Rewah, situate on the left bank of the Sone river, and 23 miles S. from Rewah. Lat. 24° 10', long. 81° 20'.

RAMNUGUR, in the British district of Futtehpore, lieut.-gov. of the N.W. Provinces, a town on the right bank of the Ganges, 879 miles from Calcutta by way of the river, and 71 miles by water above Allahabad; 24 miles by land E. of the town of Futtehpore. Lat. 25° 55′, long. 81° 15′.

RAMNUGUR, in the British district of Allahabad, lieut.-gov. of the N.W. Provinces, a small town on the route, by the Kutra Pass, from the cantonment of Allahabad to Rewa, and 26 miles S.E. of the former. Lat. 25° 15′, long. 82° 11′.

RAMNUGUR.—A town in Oude, situate on the right bank of the Gogra river, and 55 miles E. from Lucknow. Lat. 26° 47′, long. 81° 53′.

RAMNUGUR, in the British district of Benares, lieut.-gov. of the N.W. Provinces, a town on the right bank of the Ganges, and at present the residence of the titular rajah of Benares. The fort in which the rajah resides is a huge pile of building, rising directly from fine ghats or flights of stairs, giving access to the sacred stream. Ramnugur contains a population of 9,490 inhabitants, and is distant N.W. of Calcutta 673 miles by water, or 850 taking the Sunderbund passage; four miles S. of the city of Benares, 425 from Calcutta by the new line of road. Lat. 25° 16′, long. 83° 5′.

RAMNUGUR, in the British district of Bareilly, lieut.-gov. of the N.W. Provinces, a town on the route from Shahjehanpoor to Pilleebheet, 40 miles N. of the former. Lat. 28° 28′, long. 79° 58′.

RAMOO.—A town in the British district of Chittagong, lieut.-gov. of Bengal, 68 miles S.S.E. of Chittagong. Lat. 21° 24′, long. 92° 13′.

RAMOO SERAI.—A town within the dominions of Gholab Singh, the ruler of Cashmere, 17 miles S. from Sirinagur, and 75 miles N. from Jamoo. Lat. 33° 50′, long. 74° 56′.

RAMPOOR, in the British district of Saharunpoor, lieut.-gov. of Agra, a town, the principal place of the pergunnah of the same name, is in lat. 29° 48′, long. 77° 31′.

RAMPOOR.—A town in the British district of Malabar, presidency of Madras, 71 miles E. by S. of Cannanore. Lat. 11°. 42′, long. 76° 29′.

RAMPOOR.—A town in Guzerat, or dominions of the Guicowar, 64 miles E. by N. from Baroda, and 112 miles E.S.E. from Ahmedabad. Lat. 22° 26′, long. 74° 12′.

RAMPOOR.—A town in the British district of Bellary, presidency of Madras, 63 miles N.E. by N. of Bellary. Lat. 15° 56′, long. 77° 24′.

RAMPOOR, in the British district of Bareilly, lieut.-gov. of the N.W. Provinces, a village on the route from the town of Bareilly to Seetapore, and 32 miles S.W. of the former. Lat. 28° 15′, long. 79° 57′.

RAMPOOR, in the British district of Muttra, lieut.-gov. of the N.W. Provinces, a town on the right bank of the river Jumna, 23 miles N. of Muttra Lat. 27° 50′, long. 77° 38′.

RAMPOOR, in the British district of Mirzapoor, lieut.- gov. of the N.W. Provinces, a village on the left bank of the Ganges, 12 miles N.W. of Mirzapoor, 733 N.W. of Calcutta by water. Lat. 25° 14′, long. 82° 30′.

RAMPOOR, in the British district of Allygurh, lieut.-gov. of the N.W. Provinces, a village on the route from the city of Agra to Bareilly, and 45 miles N.E. of the former. Lat. 27° 43′, long. 78° 28′.

RAMPOOR, in the British district of Suharunpoor, lieut.-gov. of the N.W. Provinces, a town, the principal place of the pergunnah of the same name, is in lat. 29° 48′, long. 77° 31′.

RAMPOOR, in the district of Salon, territory of Oude, a town on the route from Cawnpore to Pertabgurh, 26 miles N.W. of the latter. Butter estimates the population at 4,000, principally cultivators, 1,000 of the number being Mussulmans. Lat. 25° 53′, long. 81° 47′.

RAMPOOR, in the district of Aldemau, territory of Oude, a town near the north-east frontier, towards the British district of Goruckpore. A considerable quantity of sugar is made there. Butter estimates the population at 1,000, including 300 Mussulmans. Lat. 26° 36′, long. 82° 12′.

RAMPOOR.—A town of Bussahir, in the division of Koonawar, situate on the left bank of the Sutlej river, and 36 miles N.E. from Simla. Lat. 31° 27′, long. 77° 41′.

RAMPOOR.—A town of Baghelcund, in the native state of Rewah, situate on the left bank of the Sone river, and 20 miles S.E. from Rewah. Lat. 24° 19′, long. 81° 33′.

RAMPOOR.—A town in Oude, situate on the left bank of the Ghogra river, and 138 miles N.N.W. from Lucknow. Lat. 28° 46′, long. 80° 23′.

RAMPOOR.—A town in the lapsed territory of Nagpoor, 98 miles N.W. from Nagpoor, and 47 miles S.E. from Hoosungabad. Lat. 22° 18′, long. 78° 17′.

RAMPOOR.—A town in Oude, situate on the left bank of the Chowka river, and 40 miles N.E. by N. from Lucknow. Lat. 27° 20′, long. 81° 22′.

RAMPOOR.—A town in Nepal, situate on the right bank of the Gunduck or Salagra river, and 93 miles W. from Khatmandoo. Lat. 27° 46′, long. 83° 49′.

RAMPOOR.—A town in the British district of Rajeshaye, presidency of Bengal, 125 miles N. of Calcutta. Lat. 24° 23′, long. 88° 38′.

RAMPOOR, within the British division of Rohilcund, an extensive fief or jaghire, is bounded on the west and north by the British district of Moradabad; on the north-east and south-east by the British district of Bareilly.

It lies between lat. 28° 30′—29° 11′, long. 78° 55′—79° 30′, and has an area of 720 square miles. It is a level, fertile country, abundantly supplied with water in its northern division by the rivers Kosila and Nahul, both of which hold a course generally southerly, and nearly parallel to each other; the latter on an average about ten miles east of the former. The southern division is irrigated by the Ramgunga, which, after receiving the waters of the Kosila, traverses this quarter of the territory in a south-easterly direction. The northern part of the district adjoins the Terai, or tract of marshy forest which extends along the base of the mountains, and is much overrun with jungle, wood, and grass of such luxuriant growth as to be sufficient to conceal a man on horseback. The air in consequence is dreadfully pestilential, except in the coldest part of winter and the time of the heaviest rains. The malaria acts very unfavourably on the population, who are described by Heber as "a very ugly and miserable race of human beings, with large heads and particularly prominent ears, flat noses, tumid bellies, slender limbs, and sallow complexions; and have scarcely any garments but a blanket of black wool." The general slope of the country is from north to south, as indicated by the descent of the rivers in that direction, as well as from actual measurement; Ruddurpoor, on the northern frontier, in lat. 28° 58′, having an elevation of 630 feet above the sea, whilst at the town of Rampoor, a few miles farther south, in lat. 28° 48′, the elevation is but 546 feet. Davidson describes the country in the vicinity of the town of Rampoor as exceedingly "rich and beautiful. The eye wanders with delight over one continuous sheet of ripening corn, interspersed with groves of mango, clumps of bamboo, and little villages." The general thriving cultivation of the country bears favourable testimony to the industry and intelligence of the Patans, the principal occupants of the soil. The population has been computed at upwards of 320,000. The annual revenue is at present estimated at 100,000*l*. The nawaub maintains a military force of 500 cavalry and 1,447 infantry.

This territory was possessed by Fyzoola Khan, a chieftain who gave considerable trouble both to the Vizier and the British government, during the administration of the latter by Warren Hastings. On the death of that personage in 1794, the pretensions of his eldest son and lawful successor were opposed by a younger brother, who raised a rebellion, made prisoner the rightful heir, and subsequently murdered him. A British force under Sir Robert Abercrombie defeated that of the usurper; an event followed by the deposal of the latter, and the grant of a jaghire to the infant son of the murdered chieftain. On the death of the late chief, in 1840, without direct male heirs, the right of a daughter to the succession was discussed and rejected in favour of the next male claimant, Mahomed Saeed Khan, who had served the British government in the important office of deputy-collector of Budaon. Some disturbances took place previously to the final arrangement of the succession, in which the minister of the deceased chieftain and some of his dependants and followers were murdered. Their families were provided for by the new ruler, who, according to report, exercised his authority mildly and judiciously until the year 1854, when he was succeeded by his heir.

RAMPOOR.—The principal place of the jaghire of the same name. It is situate on the left bank of the Kosila, here 450 yards wide, and from two to two and a half feet deep from December to June, for which time it is fordable, but must during the rainy season be crossed by ferry. It is a large town, densely peopled, irregularly built of mud, and surrounded by a thin belt of bamboos, trees, and brushwood; at the back of which there is a low ruined parapet, the only entrances being by narrow ways, defended by strong wooden barriers. The upper order of inhabitants are for the most part Rohilla Patans, a handsome indolent race. The chouk or market-place is decorated by a lofty mosque. A little north of the town is the tomb of Fyzoola Khan, raised on a terrace of masonry, and shaded by trees. Rampoor is 546 feet above the sea. Distant N.W. from Calcutta 789 miles. Lat. 28° 48′, long. 79° 5′.

RAMPOOR, the capital of Bussahir, is situate on the left bank of the Sutluj, over the bed of which its site is elevated 138 feet. Fraser, who approached it from the south-east, by ascending along the left bank of the Sutluj, describes the way as very rugged. The town is situate at the western base of a lofty and nearly perpendicular mountain, which, on the east, stretches to the outer range of the Himalaya. The cliff surrounds the town in the form of a funnel, which confines the air; and in the hot season the rocks radiate the heat in such a manner as then to render the climate nearly insupportable. The climate in winter, on the contrary, is represented as cold and damp, so that the thermometer is frequently lower than at Kotgurh, which is 3,500 feet more elevated. The expanse on which the town is built is rugged, so that the streets and houses rise in tiers one above another. Some of the houses are well built of stone, commonly two stories high, and covered with slate, which is thick, of a blue colour, and laid on with considerable neatness. The palace of the rajah, situate at the north-east corner of the town, is a collection of buildings, some of three, some of four stories high, covered with very large oblong slates, laid on curved roofs, having the concavity outwards, in the Chinese style. They have wooden balconies, ornamented with neat carvings. The Dewan Khana, or hall of audience, has the remains of grandeur, being spacious and ornamented with carving and fresco, much defaced by the Gorkhas when they held this town. There is another residence usually occupied by the inferior branches of the ruling family. Both the palaces are built of stone, uncemented, but bonded by means of numerous beams of larch. The town, previously to the havoc made by the Gorkhas, was larger than at present, having from 300 to 400 houses, and a large bazar, filled with the wares of Hindostan, the Himalayan regions, and of Tartary. It has begun to recover since it has been taken under British protection. The rajah of Bussahir resides here during winter, retiring from the heat in the summer months to the more elevated station of Saharun. The elevation of Rampoor above the sea is 3,300 feet. Lat. 31° 27′, long. 77° 40′.

RAMPOOR SHAHPOOR, in the British district of Allygurh, lieut.-gov. of the N.W. Provinces, a village on the route from Meerut to Muttra, and 44 miles N.E. of the latter. Lat. 28° 3′, long. 77° 55′.

RAMPOORA.—A town in the native state of Indore, or territory of Holkar, 34 miles E. from Neemuch, and 124 miles N. by W. from Indore. Lat. 24° 26′, long. 75° 26′.

RAMPOORA, in the British district of Cawnpore, lieut.-gov. of the N.W. Provinces, a village on the route from the cantonment of Etawa to that of Cawnpore, and 45 miles W. of the latter. Lat. 26° 21′, long. 79° 46′.

RAMPOORA, in Rajpootana, a town, the principal place of a pergunnah, part of the possessions held by the noted Patan freebooter Muhammad Ameer Khan. It is surrounded by a rampart of great strength, being in some places forty feet in thickness, and where weakest twenty feet. It was on the 15th May, 1804, taken by storm by a British force commanded by Colonel Don. The storming party rushed forward provided with a twelve-pounder, and with it blew open three gates, which in succession lay on the way into the fort. Of the enemy's garrison, above 1,000 strong, forty or fifty were killed; the number of wounded was very great, and about 400 attempting to fly, were cut up by the British cavalry in the adjoining plain. It was subsequently by the declaratory article of the treaty of 1805, restored by the British government to Holkar, and in 1818, when the battle of Mahidpore had placed Holkar's dominions at the disposal of the British government, Rampoora was added as a free gift to the possessions which had been guaranteed in the previous year to Ameer Khan. The area of the territory is 152 square miles. Its separate revenue is not known, but with that of Tonk it amounts to 2,00,000 rupees. The estimate of its population is included in that of the whole of the possessions of Ameer Khan, for which see TONK. The town is distant S. from Jeypore 70 miles, S.E. from Nusserabad 90, W. from Agra 145. Lat. 25° 58′, long. 76° 14′.

RAMPOORA, in the territory of Indor, or possessions of Holkar's family, a town on the route from Neemuch to Kota, formerly the capital and residence of the court, before the selection of the town of Indor. It is situate a mile from the north bank of the river Taloyi, at the base of a ridge of hills. It is of considerable size, surrounded by a wall, and has a good bazar. North-east of the town is a Hindoo temple, a place of pilgrimage in the month of April. Here, in January, 1818, Roshun Beg, in command of a body of infantry with sixteen guns, the relics of the force defeated at Mehidpoor, attempted to make head against the British arms, but was immediately defeated, and his troops dispersed. Rampoora has annexed to it several pergunnahs, containing 500 villages, and yielding an annual revenue of 3,75,000 rupees. Elevation above the sea 1,360 feet. Distance N. from Indor 120 miles, from Oojein 95. Lat. 24° 28′, long. 75° 25′.

RAMPOORA.—A town in the native state of Gwalior, or territory of Scindia's family, 123 miles S.W. by S. from Gwalior, and 120 miles N.W. by W. from Saugur. Lat. 24° 45′, long. 77° 11′.

RAMPOOREA, in the British district of Bareilly, division of Pilibit, lieut.-gov. of the N.W. Provinces, a village on the route from Bareilly to Petoragurh, and 37 miles N.E. of the former. Lat. 28° 41′, long. 79° 52′.

RAMPOOREE, in the British district of Bijnour, lieut.-gov. of the N.W. Provinces, a town five miles S.E. from Nujeebabad. Lat. 29° 34′, long. 78° 29′.

RAMPORA, in the territory of Gwalior, a town five miles south of the confluence of the Sindh with the Jumna. Lat. 26° 22′, long. 79° 6′.

RAMPORE, in the British district of Jounpoor, a town on the route from Jounpoor cantonment to that of Mirzapoor, 21 miles S. of the former, 22 N. of the latter. Supplies and water are abundant and good here, and the road in this part of the route is good. Lat. 25° 29′, long. 82° 38′.

RAMPORE.—A town in the British district of Tipperah, lieut.-gov. of Bengal, 52 miles N. of Tipperah. Lat. 24° 13′, long. 91° 10′.

RAMREE.—A town of Eastern India, in the British district of Arracan. It is situate on the island of Ramree, 31 miles S.E. of Kyouk Phyou. The island is separated from the mainland of Arracan by a narrow but deep channel. Its length is about fifty miles from north to south, and its extreme breadth twenty. After the occupation of Arracan in 1825, a British detachment was sent against Ramree, which, upon approaching, they found to be evacuated; possession of it was accordingly taken on the 22nd April, and since that period it has continued under the government of the East-India Company. Lat. of town 19° 5′, long. 93° 54′.

RAMRYE, one of the Cossya hill states, bounded on the north by the British district of

Camroop; on the south-east by the native states of Muriow and Nustung; and on the west by the territory occupied by the Garrow hill tribes. It is about forty miles in length from north to south, and twelve in breadth, and contains an area of 328 square miles. Its centre is in lat. 25° 35′, long. 91° 13′.

RAMSAHGAON.—A town in the British district of Nowgong, in Upper Assam, 46 miles S.E. by E. of Nowgong. Lat. 25° 59′, long. 93° 22′.

RAMSURRA, in the British district of Bhutteeana, lieut.-gov. of the N.W. Provinces, a town on the route from Hissar to Mooltan, 74 miles W. by N. of the former. Lat. 29° 23′, long. 74° 38′.

RAMTEAK, in the territory of Nagpore, on the route from Saugor to Nagpore, 24 miles N.E. of the latter, a town on an elevated ground, the geological formation of which is primitive, being either granite or gneiss. East of the town is a steep peaked hill, on the summit of which, about 500 feet above the circumjacent plain, is a group of Brahminical temples, access to which from below "is by a broad steep flight of well-laid gneiss steps, with resting-places and seats at intervals. The whole is of the best construction, and promises to last as long as the hill itself." In the valley north of the temples is a large fine tank, round which are several small handsome edifices, dedicated to religious purposes, and communicating with the group on the top of the hill by a noble, easy, and lofty flight of steps formed of gneiss. Lat. 21° 24′, long. 79° 22′.

RAMUREDDYPET.—A town in Hyderabad, or territory of the Nizam, 76 miles N. from Hyderabad, and 174 miles E.N.E. from Sholapoor. Lat. 18° 27′, long. 78° 25′.

RANA, in Gurhwal, a village on the left bank of the Jumna, consists of about twenty houses, neatly built of stone, and roofed with shingles. The sides of the hills sloping to the river are fertile, producing grain and potatoes, the culture of which latter has been recently introduced into this part of the Himalayan regions. Elevation above the sea 7,084 feet. Lat. 30° 55′, long. 78° 26′.

RANAUSUN.—A town in the province of Guzerat, or dominions of the Guicowar, 87 miles S.E. from Deesa, and 48 miles N.E. from Ahmedabad. Lat. 23° 28′, long. 73° 9′.

RANEEBULA, in the British district of Bhuttiana, lieut.-gov. of the N.W. Provinces, a village on the route from Hansee to Bhutnair, and 28 miles E. of the latter. Lat. 29° 32′, long. 74° 49′.

RANEE GODOWN.—A town in the British district of Camroop, in Lower Assam, 14 miles S.W. of Gowhatty. Lat. 26°, long. 91° 35′.

RANEEGUNGE, in the British district of Bancoora, lieut.-gov. of Bengal, a town four miles to the left or S.W. of the route from Calcutta to Benares, 126 miles N.W. of former, 295 S.E. of latter. It is situate on the river Damoodah, amidst the rich coal-measures generally known as the Burdwan Collieries. The state of the coal-measures is thus described by Homfray, an operative miner:—"These collieries have their pits sunk down to the main vein of coal, generally to a depth of ninety feet, the vein varying from seven and a half to eight and a half feet in thickness." "This vein of coal is perceptible for seven or eight miles up this nullah." That the district is rich in coal and iron mines is universally admitted. Some difference of opinion existed on the point whether the latter could be worked at a profit; but the construction of a branch from the Calcutta Railway, diverging in the vicinity of Burdwan, and extending to this town, having been completed, the conditions under which the manufacture of iron could now be undertaken must be materially altered. Distant N. from the civil station at Bancoora 25 miles; from Calcutta, N.W., by line of railroad, 120. Lat. 23° 35′, long. 87° 10′.

RANEEPOOR, in the British district of Azimgurh, lieut.-gov. of the N.W. Provinces, a town on the route from Azimgurh to Ghazeepoor, 17 miles E.S.E. of the former. Lat. 25° 53′, long. 83° 29′.

RANEE SERAE, in the British district of Azimgurh, lieut.-gov. of the N.W. Provinces, a village on the route from the town of Azimgurh to that of Jounpore, eight miles S.W. of the former, 34 N.E. of the latter, 50 N. of Benares. Lat. 26°, long. 83° 7′.

RANEESUNKER.—A town in the British district of Dinajepore, lieut.-gov. of Bengal, 30 miles N.W. of Dinajepore. Lat. 25° 50′, long. 88° 17′.

RANEEUH, in the British district of Bhuttiana, lieut.-gov. of the N.W. Provinces, a town on the route from Hansee to Bhutnair, and 36 miles E. of the latter. It is situate in a country of great natural fertility, but generally unproductive, from want of water, the river Gagur or Cuggur, which formerly inundated it, being so much exhausted by embankments and channels for irrigation higher up, in the possessions of the protected Sikhs, that the stream is, in ordinary seasons, lost before reaching Raneeuh. When those embankments have been cut, and the stream allowed to flow to Raneeuh, luxuriant crops of very fine wheat have been produced in great abundance. The town has a tolerably well-supplied bazar and sufficiency of water. The road to the eastward is very good, though, lying for some distance in the bed of the Gagur, it is liable to be overflowed in the event of extraordinary inundations, when the stream reaches this part of the country. To the west, the road is generally good, though sandy in some places. Lat. 29° 32′, long. 74° 53′.

RÀNEH BEDNORE. — A town in the

British district of Dharwar, presidency of Bombay, 72 miles S.E. by S. of Dharwar. Lat. 14° 37′, long. 75° 41′.

RANGAMUTTEE.—A town in the British district of Chittagong, lieut.-gov. of Bengal. It is situate on the right bank of the Kurrumfoolee river, 44 miles E.N.E. from Chittagong. Lat. 22° 40′, long. 92° 30′.

RANGNA.—A town in the native state of Sawuntwarree, presidency of Bombay, situate 12 miles N.W. from Sawuntwarree, and 49 miles W.N.W. from Belgaum. Lat. 16° 3′, long. 73° 53′.

RANGOON. — A town in the recently acquired British province of Pegu, situate on the great eastern branch of the Irrawaddy known as the Rangoon river. The town was originally built in 1753, by Alompra, the founder of the Burmese monarchy, who named it Rangoon, or the "City of Victory," in reference to his conquest of Pegu. When occupied by the British during the first Burmese war, in 1824, it was built in the form of a parallelogram, extending along the river's bank, about twenty-five miles from the sea, the houses, with the exception of some public buildings, being of wood and bamboo, raised on piles, and thatched. It was entirely destroyed by fire in 1850, when upwards of 2,000 houses were reduced to ashes. The site of the new town by which it was succeeded was thrown back from the original position on the river bank to a distance of about a mile; its ground-plan was that of a square of about three-quarters of a mile, having at its northern side a pagoda as a citadel, which was an artificial mound, ascending in ledges, with terraces, and tapering towards the top. This stronghold was stormed by General Godwin during the second Burmese war, in April, 1852; and the capture of the pagoda was the fall of Rangoon: the town suffered severely by fire from the shipping. In 1853, and again in December, 1855, it was visited by fearful conflagrations; many of the public buildings were destroyed, and the houses, being constructed of hollow bamboo and thatched, offered little resistance to the progress of the fire. In the arrangements for rebuilding the town, conditions have been prescribed by the British government not only for insuring its protection against conflagration, but also for securing its cleanliness, by proper drainage and other sanitary precautions. Distant from Pegu, S., 62 miles. The district of which this place is the chief town has an area of 9,800 square miles, and a population of 137,130. Lat. 16° 46′, long. 96° 17′.

RANGOUTTEE. — A town of Bengal, situate in the native state of Tipperah, 40 miles S. by E. from Silhet, and 80 miles N.E. by N. from Tipperah. Lat. 24° 20′, long. 92°.

RANIGAT, in the Peshawar division of the Punjab, a town situated 15 miles from the right bank of the Indus, 53 miles N.E. by E. of the town of Peshawar. Lat. 34° 20′, long. 72° 30′.

RANIGHAT, in the British district of Nuddea, lieut.-gov. of Bengal, a town 44 miles N. by E. from Calcutta. It is said to be the abode of many rich zemindars. Lat. 23° 11′, long. 88° 33′.

RANIWALA, in the British district of Moradabad, lieut.-gov. of the N.W. Provinces, a village on the route from Allyghur to Moradabad, and 50 miles N.E. of the former. Lat. 28° 30′, long. 78° 29′.

RANJITPURA, in the district of Bainswara, territory of Oude, a town 22 miles E. of Cawnpore, 30 S.W. of Lucknow. It may be considered the capital of the district, and formerly was scarcely inferior to Lucknow. Lat. 26° 30′, long. 80° 40′.

RANJUNGAUM.—A town in the British district of Ahmednuggur, presidency of Bombay, 17 miles S.W. by S. of Ahmednuggur. Lat. 18° 53′, long. 74° 37′.

RANKA.—A town in the British district of Palamow, lieut.-gov. of Bengal, 26 miles N.W. by W. of Palamow. Lat. 24° 2′, long. 83° 42′.

RANMUTSH.—A town in Nepal, situate on the right bank of a branch of the Kurnalli river, and 16 miles E.N.E. from Jemlah. Lat. 29° 22′, long. 81° 56′.

RANNEE CHOKEE. — See BUNNEE CHOKEE.

RANOD, in the territory of Gwalior, or possessions of Scindia's family, a town three miles to the right or N. of the route from Calpee to Goona cantonment, 155 miles S.W. of former, 50 N.E. of latter. It is represented to be "a large town, with a great trade in grain." Measures were taken by the British government in 1847 for exploring the antiquities of the town. Lat. 25°, long. 77° 53′.

RANSEE, in the British district of Kumaon, lieut.-gov. of the N.W. Provinces, a secluded village two or three miles to the right of the route from Sireenuggur to the Temple of Kedarnath, and 15 miles S. of the latter. It is situate about a mile from the right bank of the river Mudmesur. Lat. 30° 34′, long. 79° 10′.

RANSKANDY.—A town of Eastern India, in the British district of Southern Cachar, 10 miles E. of Silchar. Lat. 24° 47′, long. 93°.

RAOLDEE.—A village in the jaghire of Jujhur, district of Dadree, lieut.-gov. of the N.W. Provinces. Lat. 28° 36′, long. 76° 21′.

RAOMAKA BAZAR. — A town in the British district of Hydrabad, province of Scinde, presidency of Bombay, 88 miles S.E. by S. of Hydrabad. Lat. 24° 20′, long. 69° 14′.

RAOTSIR.—A town in the Rajpoot state of Beekaneer, 115 miles N.E. from Beekaneer, and 81 miles W. by N. from Hissar. Lat. 29° 18′, long. 74° 30′.

RAPTEE, called also AIRAWATI, after the white elephant of the god Indra, a considerable river, rising in Nepaul. It does not issue from the main range of the Himalaya covered with perpetual snow, but takes its rise in the Sub-Himalayas, in lat. 29° 10′, long. 82° 45′; whence flowing first in a southerly direction for forty miles, and then north-westerly for fifty-five miles, it enters the plains of Oude, in lat. 28° 3′, long. 81° 55′, which it traverses in a south-easterly direction for ninety miles, and in lat. 27° 17′, long. 82° 32′, forms for about twenty miles the western boundary of the British district of Goruckpoor, which it then enters, and continuing a south-easterly and tortuous course for seventy miles, it receives, on the left side, the Dhumela or Burha Rapti, draining an extensive tract extending southwards from the Sub-Himalaya. Below this junction, the Rapti turns southward for the distance of thirty miles, communicating in this part of its course with the Moti jhil, called also the Lake of Bakhira, and thence turns westward for ten miles, to the town of Goruckpoor. From this place it continues its course, in a circuitous but generally south-easterly direction, for eighty-five miles, to its junction with the Ghoghra, on the left side of the latter, in lat. 26° 13′, long. 83° 46′; its total length of course being, from its remotest source, 400 miles, for eighty-five of which downward from the town of Goruckpoor it is navigable for large boats, and for those of smaller size a considerable distance higher. In its course through the district of Goruckpoor, it receives numerous streams right and left, and by lateral channels communicates with several of the numerous watercourses and lakes or marshes found in this level alluvial country. At the town of Goruckpoor it is crossed by the route from that place to Lucknow, the passage being made by ferry. The channel is there 200 yards wide, and at all seasons contains deep water. About ten miles below the town, it is crossed, at the Bhowapoor ghat, by the route from Ghazeepoor to Goruckpoor cantonment, the passage being made by ferry during the dry season, but the route being scarcely practicable during the rains, in consequence of the extent to which the country is overflowed.

RAPTEE (BURHA). — A considerable feeder of the Raptee. Its sources are in the Sub-Himalaya, in the territory of Oude, and about lat. 27° 34′, long. 82° 10′. Flowing for forty-five miles through the territory of Oude, it touches the frontier of the British district of Goruckpoor in lat. 27° 22′, long. 82° 38′, and holding an easterly direction for nineteen miles, forms the boundary between the two territories. At the point of its entrance into the British territory, it receives on the left side the Arra, a stream descending from the Sub-Himalayas. Eighteen miles below this confluence, at the ruined town of Sanauli, the Burha Raptee becomes navigable in the rainy season, and a good deal of timber is then sent down it. Fifteen miles below this place, and in lat. 27° 13′, long. 83° 1′, it receives on the left side the Bangunga; and from the confluence downwards is often known by the name of that stream, which is considered to have the larger volume of water. Twenty-two miles farther, the Burha Raptee receives on the left side the Dhumela, which thenceforward gives its name to the united stream. Buchanan observes, "The channel immediately below the junction is about 100 yards wide, and in January (dry season) contains a pretty considerable stream, although it is fordable; but oxen cannot pass with loads, and a ferry is therefore employed to transport the goods. Timber comes down both the Burha Raptee and Bangunga." Twelve miles below the last-named junction, the united stream is joined on the left side by the Ghoongee, and three miles lower down is discharged into the Raptee, on its left side, in lat. 26° 58′, long. 83° 17′. The length of course to this point is about 134 miles, in a direction generally from north-west to south-east.

RARUNG, in Bussahir, a village of the district of Koonawar, is situate near the right bank of the Sutluj, on the southern side of a mountain of mica-slate, characterized by dreary barrenness, and producing little but a few stunted pines. Elevation above the sea 9,519 feet. Lat. 31° 36′, long. 78° 24′.

RASEEN.—A town in the British district of Ahmednuggur, presidency of Bombay, 46 miles S.S.E. of Ahmednuggur. Lat. 18° 29′, long. 74° 58′.

RASHMEE.—A town in the Rajpoot state of Oodeypoor, 52 miles N.E. from Oodeypoor, and 103 miles S. by W. from Ajmeer. Lat. 25° 2′, long. 74° 27′.

RASOORY. — A town in Hyderabad, or territory of the Nizam, situate eight miles from the left bank of the Payne Gunga river, and 108 miles S.E. by S. from Ellichpoor. Lat. 19° 59′, long. 78° 36′.

RASULPOOR, in the British district of Cawnpore, lieut.-gov. of the N.W. Provinces, a village on the route from the cantonment of Futtehgurh to that of Cawnpore, and 30 miles N.W. of the latter. Lat. 26° 47′, long. 80° 9′.

RASUNWAS.—A village in the jagheer of Jujhur, district of Dadree, lieut.-gov. of the N.W. Provinces. Lat. 28° 36′, long. 76° 13′.

RATGURH, in the British district of Saugur, territory of Saugor and Nerbudda, lieut.-gov. of the N.W. Provinces, a town on the route from Saugur to Bhopal, 21 miles W. by S. of the former. Lat. 23° 47′, long. 78° 29′.

RATTEE, in the district of Bainswara, territory of Oude, a village on the route from Allahabad to Lucknow, 99 miles N.E. of the former, 29 S.W. of the latter. It has a small bazar, and water and supplies may be obtained. Lat. 26° 32′, long. 80° 53′.

RAUCHERLA.—A town of Madras, in the Mysore, 138 miles N.N.E. from Seringapatam, and 72 miles S.E. by S. from Ballary. Lat. 14° 15′, long. 77° 30′.

RAUJGURH.—A town in the Rajpoot state of Kotah, situate on the right bank of the Neewuj river, and 30 miles E. by S. from Kotah. Lat. 25° 5′, long. 76° 20′.

RAUNPOOR.—A town in the British district of Ahmedabad, presidency of Bombay, 78 miles S.W. of Ahmedabad. Lat. 22° 20′, long. 71° 40′.

RAUNPOOR.—A town in Guzerat, or dominions of the Guicowar, 75 miles W.S.W. from Rajkote, and 16 miles N. by E. from Poorbunder. Lat. 21° 50′, long. 69° 49′.

RAURAH.—A town in Nepal, situate on the left bank of a branch of the Kurnalli river, and 13 miles N.N.E. from Jemlah. Lat. 29° 30′, long. 81° 46′.

RAUS, or RASS, in the Rajpoot state of Jodhpoor, a town on the north-west declivity of the Aravulli range, on the route from Nusseerabad to Deesa, and 38 miles W. of the former. It contains 600 houses, supplied with water from twenty wells. Lat. 26° 17′, long. 74° 16′.

RAUSHPOORAM.—A town in the British district of Salem, presidency of Madras, 15 miles S. of Salem. Lat. 11° 28′, long. 78° 16′.

RAVEE, or RAVI, a river of the Punjab, rises in Kulu, on the declivity of a mountain called Bungall, and a short distance west of the Rotang Pass. The source is situate about lat. 32° 26′, long. 77°. At the distance of about forty miles from the source, in a south-westerly direction, the Ravee is joined by two feeders, the Nye and the Boodhill, the latter taking its rise in a lake called Munee Muhees, regarded as sacred by the superstitious Hindoos. Where surveyed by Cunningham, four or five miles from Burmawur, at an elevation of about 7,000 feet, it was found 116 feet wide. At Chamba, about twenty miles below, and south-west of this place, or 100 miles from its source, according to the statement of Vigne, the Ravee is crossed by a bridge. Forster states that it is there "forty or fifty yards broad, and fordable at most seasons of the year." At Bisuli, to which the downward course is about twenty-five miles due west, Forster found it, early in April, about 120 yards wide, very rapid, and unfordable. The statement of Vigne is less explicit:—"I have been twice ferried over the Ravi at Bisuli, once during the rainy season, when it was swelled to a roaring torrent, and once again in winter, when its stream was far more tranquil. On both occasions the natives made the passage upon buffalo-hides. Its width is about eighty yards." From Bisuli, in lat. 32° 34′, long. 75° 48′, the Ravee takes a south-westerly direction, which it generally holds for the rest of its course. Macartney found it, at Meanee ferry, on the route from Amritsir to Vazeerabad, and about 185 miles from its source, to have, at the beginning of August and at the time of fullest water, a breadth of 513 yards, and a depth of twelve feet, where greatest. The deep channel was between thirty and forty feet in breadth, the rest of the waterway having a depth of from three to five feet. In the cold season, when lowest, the water is in no part more than four feet deep. Moorcroft describes it at Lahore, about twenty miles lower down, as divided into three different streams or branches. These, he states, are "separated, in the dry weather, by intervals of half a mile, but in the rainy season the two most easterly branches are united, and form an expansive and rapid stream." "The two first branches are fordable, but the third, which is the principal one, has a ferry." He remarks, that the boats on the Ravee were the largest and best-built that he has seen in India. Burnes, who navigated the Ravee from its confluence with the Chenaub to Lahore, says it "is very small, and resembles a canal, rarely exceeding 150 yards in breadth in any part of its course. Its banks are precipitous, so that it deepens before it expands. Nothing can exceed the crookedness of its course, which is a great impediment to navigation, for we often found ourselves, after half a day's sail, within two miles of the spot from which we started. The water of the Ravee is redder than that of the Chenaub. It is fordable in most places for eight months in the year." From Lahore, its course south-west, measured according to the main direction of the stream, to its confluence with the Chenaub, is about 200 miles, but along all the sinuosities, 380. This point is in lat. 30° 36′, long. 71° 50′. The Ravee joins the Chenaub by three mouths close to each other. Its total length, measured along the main direction of its course, is about 450 miles. It is considered to be the Hydraotes mentioned by Arrian, and the Iravati of Sanscrit authorities: it is still known by the name of the Iraotee, which might easily be corrupted by the Greeks into that which they appear to have given it.

RAVER.—A town in the British district of Candeish, presidency of Bombay, 121 miles E.N.E. of Malligaum. Lat. 21° 14′, long. 76° 11′.

RAVOOR.—A town in the British district of Nellore, presidency of Madras, 33 miles W.N.W. of Nellore. Lat. 14° 36′, long. 79° 34′.

RAVYPAUD.—A town in the British district of Cuddapah, presidency of Madras, 80 miles N.N.E. of Cuddapah. Lat. 15° 34′, long. 79° 15′.

RAWAH.—A town in the native state of Gwalior, or territory of Scindia's family, 24 miles S.S.E. from Neemuch, and 83 miles N.W. from Oojein. Lat. 24° 8′, long. 75° 1′.

RAWALHEIR, in the British district of

Bijnour, lieut.-gov. of the N.W. Provinces, a village on the route from Moradabad to Hurdwar, and 40 miles S.E. of the latter. Lat. 29° 30′, long. 78° 28′.

RAWDUCOONDA.—A town in one of the sequestrated districts of Hyderabad, 31 miles S.E. from Moodgul. Lat. 15° 41′, long. 76° 50′.

RAWUL, in the British district of Goorgaon, lieut.-gov. of the N.W. Provinces, a village on the route from Rewaree to Alwar, and eight miles S. of the former. Lat. 28° 4′, long. 76° 38′.

RAWUL PINDE, in the Punjab, between the Indus and the Jhelum. It is a large populous town, consisting of mud houses with flat roofs. It contains what is called a palace, a wretched building of brick, constructed by Shah Soojah, on his expulsion from Kabool. There is a large bazar, and a considerable business in the transit-trade between Hindostan and Afghanistan. The town is surrounded by a wall with bastions, and has an old fort, on which a few cannon are mounted. Population 15,813. The district of which this town is the chief place has an area of 5,995 square miles, with a population of 553,750. The town is in lat. 33° 37′, long. 73° 6′.

RAWUNHEREE, in the Rajpoot state of Beekaneer, a village on the southern frontier, and on the route from the town of Beekaneer to that of Jesulmeer, being 45 miles S.W. of the former. It is situate in an open country, scantily cultivated. The road in this part of the route is hard and good. Lat. 27° 40′, long. 72° 49′.

RAWUTSIR.—A town in the British district of Hydrabad, province of Scinde, presidency of Bombay, 147 miles E. by S. of Hydrabad. Lat. 25° 2′, long. 70° 46′.

RAYUH, or RAI, in the British district of Muttra, a town, the principal place of the pergunnah of the same name, is situate on the route from the cantonment of Allygurh to that of Muttra, and nine miles N.E. of the latter. It is supplied with water from wells, and has a small bazar with market. Lat. 27° 33′, long. 77° 52′.

REDANOH.—A town in the Rajpoot state of Jodhpoor, 135 miles W. by S. from Jodhpoor, and 74 miles S. from Jessulmeer. Lat. 25° 51′, long. 71° 3′.

REEAN, in the Rajpoot state of Jodhpoor, a town on the route from the city of Jodhpoor to that of Ajmeer, and 27 miles N.W. of the latter. It is surrounded by a ruinous mud wall, and has a fort, the stronghold of the thakoor or chief of the Merteea tribe of Rahtor Rajpoots. The fort, commanding the whole town, is built of stone, and situate on the top of an insulated rocky hill about 200 feet above the plain, and is fifty yards long from north to south, and thirty yards broad. The gateway is at a corner pointing westward, and is defended by a screen of masonry. The town is situate at the western base of the rocky hill: it contains 700 houses, abundantly supplied with water from numerous wells of the depth of twenty feet. There is besides a fine baoli, or large well, forty feet deep, pleasantly shaded by large trees, and having abundance of fine water, to which access is obtained by flights of steps. The population, according to Boileau, is 5,650. The road in this part of the route is bad. Lat. 26° 32′, long. 74° 20′.

REECHNA DOOAB.—A natural division of the Punjab, situated between the rivers Chenaub and Ravee, and extending from lat. 30° 33′ to 32° 36′, and from long. 71° 49′ to 75° 36′.

REEGA.—A town in the territory occupied by the Abor tribe, on the northern boundary of Upper Assam. It is situate on the right bank of the Dihong river, 51 miles N.W. from Sudiya. Lat. 28° 20′, long. 95° 7′.

REERWEE, in the Rajpoot state of Beekaneer, a village on the route from Rutungurh to the town of Beekaneer, and 50 miles E. of the latter. It is of considerable size and is supplied with water from three wells. Lat. 27° 55′, long. 74° 11′.

REGOWLEE, in the British district of Goruckpoor, lieut.-gov. of the N.W. Provinces, a town on the route from Goruckpoor to Khachi, 21 miles N.N.W. of the former. Lat. 26° 59′, long. 83° 17′.

REGOWLI.—See Adjygurh.

REGULAVALASA.—A town in the British district of Vizagapatam, presidency of Madras, 23 miles N. by W. of Vizianagrum. Lat. 18° 27′, long. 83° 27′.

REH, in the British district of Futtehpore, lieut.-gov. of the N.W. Provinces, a village on the left bank of the Jumna, at the mouth of the small river Rind. Lat. 25° 52′, long. 80° 37′.

REHELU, in the Baree Dooab division of the Punjab, a town situated on the left bank of one of the branches of the Beas, 11 miles N. of the town of Kangra. Lat. 32° 14′, long. 76° 18′.

REHLI, in the British district of Saugor and Nerbudda, lieut.-gov. of the N.W. Provinces, a town on the route from Gurrawarra to Saugor, 60 miles N.W. of former, 26 S.E. of latter. It has a bazar, and water and supplies are abundant. Here is a prison capable of containing from forty to fifty persons. Elevation above the sea 1,350 feet. Lat. 23° 44′, long. 79° 5′.

REHLY, in the territory of Oude, a town on the route from the cantonment of Goruckpore to that of Sekrora, 73 miles N.W. of the former, 39 S.E. of the latter. Lat. 26° 52′, long. 82° 4′.

REHUND.—A river rising in lat. 22° 46′, long. 83° 17′, in the British district of Odeipoor, on the south-west frontier of Bengal. It first takes the name of the Rhern, and flowing in a northerly direction through Odeipoor, Sirgoojah, Rewa, and the British district of Mirzapoor, it falls into the Sone on the right side, near the town of Agoree Khas, in lat. 24° 32′, long. 83° 3′.

REINWAL, in the Rajpoot state of Jeypoor, a town on the route from Delhi to Mow, 181 miles S.W. of former, 326 N.E. of latter. It has a bazar, and is supplied with water from wells. Lat. 26° 41′, long. 75° 45′.

REITAL, in native Gurwhal, a village close to the right bank of the Bhageerettee, as the Ganges is called in the upper part of its course. Its situation is very pleasant, on the eastern side of a mountain, the river flowing at the base below it. The village contains about thirty-five houses. Reital was a secondary station in the trigonometrical survey of the Himalaya. Elevation above the sea 7,082 feet. Lat. 30° 49′, long. 78° 39′.

RELLI.—A town in the British district of Vizagapatam, presidency of Madras, 14 miles N. by W. of Vizagapatam. Lat. 17° 53′, long. 83° 19′.

REMRAH.—A town in the native state of Phooljer, on the south-west frontier of Bengal, 75 miles W. by S. from Sumbulpoor, and 82 miles S.E. by S. from Ruttunpoor. Lat. 21° 18′, long. 82° 52′.

RENEE, in the Rajpoot state of Beekaneer, a walled town near the north-eastern frontier, towards Shekawuttee. The surrounding country is less barren than most other parts of Beekaneer, in consequence of the moisture produced by the Katuri, a small stream which flows from Shekawuttee, and is lost in the sands of Beekaneer. Tod states the number of houses at 1,500. Renee is in lat. 28° 41′, long. 75° 6′.

RENTICHOTA.—A town in the British district of Ganjam, presidency of Madras, 61 miles S.W. of Ganjam. Lat. 18° 49′, long. 84° 27′.

REOTEE, in the British district of Ghazeepoor, lieut.-gov. of the N.W. Provinces, a town situate on the stream which discharges the water of the lake Sooraha into the river Ghagra, and four miles S.W. of the right bank of the latter. It is represented as a place of some trade. Distant N.E. of Ghazeepoor cantonment 55 miles. Lat. 25° 50′, long. 84° 25′.

REOTEEPOOR, in the British district of Ghazeepoor, lieut.-gov. of the N.W. Provinces, a town two miles S.W. of the right bank of the Ganges, 10 S.E. of Ghazeepoor cantonment. Reoteepoor contains a population of 10,055 inhabitants. Lat. 25° 30′, long. 83° 48′.

REPALLE.—A town in the British district of Guntoor, presidency of Madras, 32 miles S.E. by E. of Guntoor. Lat. 16° 3′, long. 80° 53′.

RERIGHAT.—A town in Nepal, situate on the right bank of the Gunduck or Salagra river, and 116 miles W. by N. from Khatmandoo. Lat. 27° 58′, long. 83° 27′.

RESSOOLPOOR NARAINPOOR, in the British district of Bolundshuhur, lieut.-gov. of the N.W. Provinces, a village on the route from Allygurh cantonment to that of Moradabad, and 20 miles N. of the former. Lat. 28° 10′, long. 78° 15′.

REVELGUNJE, in the British district of Sarun, lieut.-gov. of Bengal, a town on the left bank of the Ganges, five miles below the confluence of the Gogra. Here is annually held a fair, much frequented, especially by Hindoos, who throng in great numbers for ritual ablution at the neighbouring confluence. Distance N.E. from Benares, by land, 118 miles, by the course of the river 165; N.W. from Dinapoor 24. Lat. 25° 44′, long. 84° 50′.

REWA CAUNTA.—A division of Guzerat, under the political superintendence of the government of Bombay. It is bounded on the north by the Myhee Caunta; on the south by the British collectorate of Candeish, from which it is separated by the river Taptee, and by the Bheel territory of Wusravee; on the east by the petty states of Banswarra, Dohud, Jabooah, Allee, and Akrauna; and on the west by the possessions of the Guicowar, and the British collectorates of Kaira and Surat. It lies between lat. 21° 23′ and 23° 33′, and long. 73° 3′ and 74° 18′. The Rewa Caunta comprises the states of Rajpeepla and Oodepoor, tributary to the Guicowar; Soauth, tributary to Scindia; Loonawarra, tributary both to Scindia and the Guicowar; and Deoghur Barreeah, tributary to the British. An account of each of these tributary states will be found in its proper place. A court of justice, styled the Rewa Caunta Criminal Court, exists in this province. It was established in 1839, and the result has fully realized all the advantages anticipated from its institution. Originally, the British Resident presided in this court, and three or four chiefs sat as assessors. A slight alteration has recently been made in its constitution, the first assistant political commissioner, instead of the Resident, now presiding; but his proceedings are forwarded to government through the latter, an arrangement by which the supervision of that officer is increased. Though not intended to supersede the authority of the chiefs in the internal administration of their territories, yet when they are too weak to punish their subjects, as sometimes happens, criminals are tried before this court, a representative from the state being invited to assist at the trial. On the other hand, when the head of a village is competent to take cognizance of the case, he is allowed to dispose of it; so that no undue interference takes place with their authority. Some account of the chiefs residing on the banks of the Nerbudda, styled the Mehwassee chiefs, who are subject to the jurisdiction of the Rewa Caunta agency, will be found under the head "Mehwassee," and under that of the "Naikras," some particulars of that wild tribe. The practice of suttee has been interdicted within the Rewa Caunta.

REWAH, called also **BAGHELCUND**, or country of the Baghels, an independent raj or principality, bounded on the north by the British districts Allahabad and Mirzapore; on the east by the British district Mirzapore; on the south-east by the native state of Korea; on the south by the British district Saugor and Nerbudda; and on the west by Saugor and Nerbudda, and by Bundelcund. It lies between lat. 23° 20′—25° 10′, long. 80° 40′—82° 52′; is about 140 miles in length from east to west, and 120 in breadth. The area is 9,827 square miles. The western and north-western parts, comprising a considerable proportion of the whole raj, are covered by mountains, rising in three successive plateaus, or vast terraces, from the valley of the Ganges. Of these, that most to the north-east, and styled by Franklin the Bindachal, or First Range, is the lowest, having an average elevation of from 500 to 530 feet above the sea. It is formed of horizontal strata of sandstone: the upper surface presents an expanse of very great sterility. Little of this plateau, however, is included within the limits of Rewah, the boundary of which on this side lies nearly along the base of the mountain styled by Franklin "the Pannah Hills, or Second Range." The elevation of these averages from 900 to 1,200 feet above the sea. Their formation is sandstone, intermixed with schist and quartz, and to the west overlaid with limestone. Above this plateau, nearly parallel to the brow, but more to the south-east, rises the Kaimur range, of which nothing appears to have been ascertained either as to elevation or formation. The brows of those ranges, especially of the second, are steep, in some parts nearly mural, and the Tons (South-eastern) and its tributaries, which drain the second plateau, descend to the lower grounds in cascades of various degrees of fall, from that of Bilohi, of 400 feet, to that of Chachai, of 200. About a third of the country lying south-east of the Kaimur hills is part of the valley of the Son, a tract as yet nearly unexplored. That great river, flowing north from the British district of Saugor and Nerbudda, crosses the south boundary of this raj in lat. 23° 21′, long. 81° 30′, and, flowing through it circuitously, but generally in a direction north and north-easterly, for 180 miles, crosses, in lat. 24° 37′, long. 82° 50′, over the north-eastern frontier, into the British district Mirzapore. Its principal tributary is the Mahanuddee, flowing into it on the left side, in lat. 24° 5′, long. 81° 6′; and it besides receives numerous torrents and small streams right and left. The Tons, flowing north-east from Bundelcund, first touches the raj in lat. 24° 25′, long. 80° 55′, and, draining the highlands, receives the Beher, the Bilund, and several minor torrents, and, holding a course generally north-easterly, passes, in lat. 25° 1′, long. 81° 51′, into the British district of Allahabad, its course through Rewah being eighty miles. None of the rivers are navigable in this raj. According to Hamilton, "there are few parts of the British provinces more highly cultivated than the higher regions of Rewah;" and Ironside, describing the country sixty years ago, states, that it is "well cultivated, and produces tolerably good crops of grain." The villages are in good order, full of inhabitants, who appear to be industrious. The produce of this country is wheat, barley, and different kinds of pease; and they have also large herds of cattle, and flocks of sheep." Jacquemont's report, however, rather tends to discredit these statements, though he mentions that he saw considerable cultivation on the second plateau, north of the town of Rewah. Much of the surface being rock, is unfit for culture, and produces a scanty growth of stunted wood. This is now in many places yielding to the axe, to supply the demand for timber in the British districts in the valley of the Ganges.

The principal places—Rewah, Simerea, Mowganj, Bandoogurh—are noticed in their places in the alphabetical arrangement.

The military routes are, 1. From north-east to south-west, from Mirzapoor to Saugor, through the town of Rewah; 2. from north-east to south-west, from Allahabad by the Kutra Pass, to Jubbulpore, through the town of Rewah; 3. from north-east to south-west, from Allahabad by the Sohagi Pass, through the town of Rewah to Jubbulpore; 4. from north-east to south-west, from Allahabad to Saugor; 5. from north-west to south-east, from Banda to Rewah.

The revenues of Rewah have been estimated at twenty lacs (200,000*l*.). There formerly existed numerous jaghires, of the value of four or five lacs per annum, held by younger descendants of former sovereigns. About twenty years since, resumption to some extent took place, yielding to the state a considerable accession of revenue.

As the rajah and his subjects are Rajpoots, their religion is Brahminism; and the horrible Rajpoot atrocity of female infanticide prevails, or did prevail, to a great extent. The rajah, however, it is stated, on his own authority some time since issued a proclamation, in which he not only forbade the practice, but promised pecuniary aid, when necessary, for the marriage expenses of daughters; and this proclamation was subsequently repeated. Suttee does not appear to be mentioned by any writer as practised in this territory. The population is stated to be 1,200,000. The military force amounts to upwards of 8,000 men.

The earliest mention of the Bhagels is probably that adverted to by Elliot, who says, "The Baghel chief of Rewa is the descendant of the famous Sid Raee Jye Singh, the ruler of Anhulwara Puttun from 1094 to 1145. His court was visited by the Nubian geographer Edrisi, who distinctly states, that at the time of his visit the chief adhered to the tenets of Buddha." The existence of the raj of Rewah seems scarcely ascertainable in the general history of India, until the early part of the present century, when the Pindarries, in 1812, passing through the territory of Rewah, made an inroad into the British district of Mirzapore. The rajah of Rewah was considered to have abetted this enterprise, and he was required to accede to a treaty, by which the British government acknowledged his sovereign title, and bound itself to amity and protection towards him, on condition that all differences between him and foreign powers should be referred to the arbitration of the British authorities; that British troops might be marched through, or cantoned within, his raj, for the purpose of guarding against the advance, or intercepting the retreat of an enemy; and that on such occasions the rajah should dispose his troops in the manner which might be pointed out by the British commanding officer. As the rajah ill followed out his engagements, the British government in 1813 had recourse to military operations, which enforced the conclusion of a second treaty, confirmatory of the former, and binding the rajah further to receive a permanent agent, and to maintain a vakeel, on his own part, with the British agent in Bundelcund, and with the commanding officer of any British detachment stationed in the Rewah territory. He likewise bound himself to concur in the chastisement of certain offenders, and to pay the expenses of the armament sent against him, to the amount of 45,173 rupees. In 1814, a third treaty was concluded, confirmatory of the two preceding ones. In the English copies of the treaties, the chief is styled rajah of Rewah and Mookundpore, the latter appellation being probably from Muckunpoor, a place of some note eight miles S. of the town of Rewah. The rajah has been recently prevailed upon to abolish the levy of transit-duties on the chief staples of commerce. He succeeded his father in 1854, under the title of Baba Ragho Raj Sing.

REWAH.—The principal place of the raj or territory of the same name, a town on the route by the Kutra Pass, from Allahabad to Saugor, 131 miles S.W. of the former, and 182 N.E. of the latter. It is situate on the banks of the small river Beher, a tributary of the Tons (South-eastern), on a formation of dark-coloured limestone. Around it runs a high and thick rampart, still nearly entire and continuous, flanked by towers, and which, in a state of repair, must have been a strong defence. Within this, a similar rampart immediately environs the town, and still further inward, a third surrounds the residence of the rajah, consisting of a few habitable buildings amidst the ruins of a great decayed structure. The town has an aspect of poverty and barbarism, yet the population is estimated by Jacquemont at about 7,000, principally supported by the expenditure of the rajah, who maintains some degree of barbaric state. Elevation above the sea about 1,200 feet. Lat. 24° 31′, long. 81° 21′.

REWAREE, in the British district of Goorgaon, lieut.-gov. of the N.W. Provinces, a town on the route from Delhi to Jeypoor, 50 miles S.W. of the former. Rewaree contains a population of 26,844 inhabitants. Lat. 28° 11′, long. 76° 41′.

REWASUN, in the British district of Goorgaon, lieut.-gov. of the N.W. Provinces, a village on the route by Ferozpoor from Alwar to Delhi, 66 miles N.E. of former, 44 miles S.W. of the latter. Lat. 28° 10′, long. 77° 8′.

REWDUNDA.—A fort in the British district of Tannah, presidency of Bombay, situate on the coast, 29 miles S. of Bombay. Lat. 18° 33′, long. 73°.

REYJWA, in the British district of Muttra, lieut.-gov. of the N.W. Provinces, a village on the route from the city of Agra to Bareilly, and 34 miles N.E. of the former. Lat. 27° 30′, long. 78° 26′.

RHAMUTGANJ, in the territory of Oude, a village on the route from Cawnpore to Lucknow, 22 miles N.E. of the former, 31 S.W. of the latter. Lat. 26° 40′, long. 80° 41′.

RHOTASGURH, in the British district of Shahabad, presidency of Bengal, a celebrated hill-fort on the left or north-west bank of the river Sone. It is situate in the hilly tract in the south of the district, on a table-land five miles in length from north to south, and four in breadth. The outline is much indented and irregular, and the circuit, including all its sinuosities, is computed at twenty-eight miles. The surface of the table-land is very uneven, and much of it consists of bare rock; but there is likewise a considerable extent of fertile red soil, on which grow many fine trees. It is very difficult of access on every side except the south, in which direction a rocky neck or ridge once connected it with the contiguous table-land; but it has been traversed by a deep trench quarried in the rock with great cost and toil. East of the spot where this ditch is excavated in the rock, are some most stupendous works; and access into the fortress is gained through two fine gateways, one thirty yards within the other; and these, as well as the ditch, are protected by a great number of complicated works. These are pierced with embrasures for archery and matchlocks, but there are none suited for regular artillery; and all the defences in this quarter are completely commanded from a height 200 yards distant, so that a passage could readily be laid open for a storming force to occupy the works, and there is no citadel within. On the verge of the mountain all round is a massive battlement, formed of great stones laid together without cement. When Tieffenthaler's account was written, a century ago, there were fourteen gateways, but ten of them had been walled up. Notwithstanding the general steepness and elevation of the sides of the mountain, there are, besides the principal passage traversed by the trench, eighty-three others in various places; much difficulty would consequently be experienced in guarding so many points against surprises. Within the inclosure are several small pieces of water and perennial springs. Sher Shah, on obtaining possession of this place in 1539, set about strengthening it; but the works which he commenced were abandoned, owing to his having discovered a situation which he considered more favourable, and where he erected Shergar.

The most ancient structures herein were built by the Hindoos: the place, according to their tradition, was founded by Cush, the son of Rama, king of Ayodha, long previously to the Christian era. Ferishta, however, attributes the foundation to Rohut, viceroy of Afra-Siab, the legendary king of Turkestan. Sher Shah took the place from the Hindoo rajah, by a stratagem frequently recurring in Indian history. Having asked the rajah to give refuge to the females of his family, taking with them a large amount of treasure, a great number of dolas or covered litters arrived, the foremost of which being examined and found to contain only women, all were admitted without suspicion. The greater number of the dolas, however, were filled with armed men and weapons for the bearers, also soldiers; and the force thus introduced forthwith attacked and slaughtered the garrison and seized the fort. When the Rajpoot Maun Singh was appointed viceroy of Behar and Bengal, a trust for which he was probably indebted to the alliance of his house with that of Akbar, his cousin being married to Prince Selim, son of that monarch, he selected Rhotasgurh as a place of security for his family and treasure. After his death, the fortress was annexed to the office of vizier of the empire, and at a later period it came into the hands of Cossim Ali, nawaub or soubahdar of Bengal, who, after his defeat at Oondwa Nulla, imitated the example of Maun Singh, by selecting this place for the residence of his family and the depository of his treasure. It was surrendered a short time after the battle of Buxar, in 1764, to the British army under Goddard. .

The air of Rhotasgurh, as many of the hill forts of India, is dreadfully unwholesome, especially for European constitutions. Limestone has been discovered in the vicinity, which will be of great service in bridging the Sone. The elevation above the sea is probably about 700 feet, and above the plain 200. Distance S. from Sasseram 22 miles, S.E. from Benares 75, N.W. from Calcutta 373. Lat. 24° 38′, long. 84°.

RHOTUK.—See ROHTUK.

RHUŃOO, in the British district of Jounpore, lieut.-gov. of the N.W. Provinces, a village on the route from Jounpore cantonment to that of Sultanpoor, in Oude, 12 miles N.W. of the former, 46 S.E. of the latter. Lat. 25° 50′, long. 82° 35′.

RIASI, within the dominions of Gholab Singh, the ruler of Cashmere, a town situate near the left or east bank of the Chenaub, and on the southern slope of the most southern of the Himalaya ranges. Here is a fort considered by Vigne "one of the strongest, perhaps the strongest, and best constructed in the country." It is situated on a conical and rocky eminence south of the town, and is nearly square. The walls are built of stone: they are very lofty, and are rendered still more difficult to be scaled by their rising immediately from the precipitous sides of the hill, which are steeply scarped. There is a tower at each angle, and no pains have been spared to render these, as well as most of the buildings of the interior, bomb-proof. The garrison is supplied with water by means of two large tanks within the walls. The fort is separated, by a deep ravine, from an eminence of sandstone of the same height, about a mile distant. The town itself is an inconsiderable place, having about 1,000 inhabitants. Lat. 33° 5′, long. 74° 52′.

RICHAH, in the British district of Pilleebheet, lieut.-gov. of the N.W. Provinces, a town on the route from Pilleebheet to Rampoor, 18 miles W.N.W. of the former. Lat. 28° 43′, long. 79° 37′.

RICHEL RIVER.—The name of one of the mouths of the Indus river, flowing into the sea in lat. 24° 3′, long. 67° 26′.

RICHOLA, in the British district of Bareilly, lieut.-gov. of the N.W. Provinces, a village on the route from the town of Bareilly to Pilleebheet, and 20 miles N.E. of the former. The country is level, open, and cultivated. Lat. 28° 32′, long. 79° 41′.

RICNAR.—A river rising amidst the mountains of the British district of Jansar, in lat. 30° 53′, long. 77° 59′. It holds a south-easterly course of about twenty miles, and falls into the Jumna on the right side, in lat. 30° 44′, long. 78° 8′.

RIKHESUR, in the British district of Kumaon, lieut.-gov. of the N.W. Provinces, a halting-place and small military station on the left bank of the Lohughat river, on the route from Champawut to Petoragurh, and 16 miles S.W. of the latter. Lat. 29° 24′, long. 80° 8′.

RIKKEE KASEE, in the Dhera Doon, a Hindoo temple at the north-east angle, where the Ganges, leaving the mountains, enters the plains of Bengal. The temple is 1,427 feet above the level of the sea; the bed of the river below it, 1,377 feet. Lat. 30° 6′, long. 78° 22′.

RILAKOT, in the British district of Kumaon, lieut.-gov. of the N.W. Provinces, a village in the subdivision of Juwahir, on the route to Hiundes or Chinese Tartary, by the Juwahir Pass, from which it is 20 miles south. It is situate on the left bank of the river Goree, which runs 250 feet below. The roofs of the houses have a slight pitch, and are firmly coated with compact clay, as a protection against the inclemency of the climate. From the end of October to the beginning of June, the inhabitants totally desert the vicinity, residing in the more southern and lower part of Kumaon. During the summer months they return to this barren and dreary tract, less with a view to the scanty crops and pasturage obtainable here, than to the management of the active and lucrative traffic with Hiundes. Elevation 10,680 feet above the sea. Lat. 30° 19′, long. 80° 15′.

RINGNOD.—A town of Malwa, in the native state of Jowra, situate on the left bank of a branch of the Chumbul river, and eight miles N.N.E. from Jowra. Lat. 23° 43′, long. 75° 10′.

RINJAKHAR.—A town in the escheated territory of Nagpoor, 153 miles E.N.E. from Nagpoor, and 53 miles S.S.E. from Ramgurh. Lat. 22° 6′, long. 81° 20′.

RINTIMBORE, or RANTAMBOOR, in the Rajpoot state of Jeypore, a fortress of great strength, near the southern frontier, towards Boondee. It is situate on a rock, on all sides isolated by deep and nearly impassable ravines, and access to the summit is had only by a narrow pathway, inclosed on each side by high and overhanging cliffs; and in the upper part the steepness so increases, that the ascent is made by flights of stairs passing through four gateways in succession. The summit of the rock, a mile in length, and of nearly equal breadth, is surrounded by a massive stone rampart, conforming to the irregular verge, and strengthened by towers and bastions. Within the inclosure are an antique palace, the residence of the governor; a mosque, the tomb of a reputed Mahomedan saint, and buildings for the accommodation of the garrison. Water is supplied from a perennial spring and tanks within the walls. To the east of the fort is a town communicating with it by means of a long flight of narrow stone steps. The fort, regarded as impregnable before the introduction of artillery, is indefensible against the attacks of modern warfare, being completely commanded by the rocky summits on all sides. According to Tieffenthaler, it was at a remote period founded by Rauhamir, a Rajpoot chief. In A.D. 1291 it was in vain besieged by Julal-ood-deen, the Patan king of Delhi, and in the reign of his successor Alla-ood-deen, it is mentioned as being held by Rajah Bhim Deo, who, A.D. 1297, gave refuge to one of the nobles flying from the wrath of his sovereign. In 1299, Noosrut Khan, the vizier of Alla-ood-deen, besieged the fort, but being killed by a stone thrown from an engine, the rajah marched out and defeated the Patan army with great slaughter. Alla-ood-deen shortly after in person renewed the siege, and having formed a mound from a neighbouring height to the top of the rampart, stormed the place, and put to the sword the rajah, his family, and garrison. It was subsequently wrested from the sovereign of Delhi, probably during the distractions consequent on the invasion of Tamerlane at the close of the fourteenth century, and in 1516 it is mentioned as belonging to the king of Malwa. In 1528, it was surrendered by Bikermajet, its Rajpoot possessor, to Baber, who assigned him Shamsabad and its territory as a remuneration. After the expulsion, in 1553, of Muhammad Shah Sur Adili, the Patan king of Delhi, by Humaion, the governor of Rintimbore surrendered it to the rajah of Boondee, who shortly after transferred it to Akbar, receiving in return extensive districts and high immunities. It probably fell into the hands of the rajah of Jeypore on the dissolution of the empire, consequent on the invasion of Ahmed Shah Dooranee in 1761. It is at present held, partly by the rajah of Jeypore, partly by the thakoors or feudal nobility of the state, each having the honour of defending a particular gate, or portion of the work. Distant S.E. from Jeypore 75 miles, S. from Delhi 195, S.E. from Ajmere 115. Lat. 25° 56′, long. 76° 26′.

RISPE, in Koonawar, a district of the hill state of Bussahir, is a village situate on the left bank of the Sutluj, a short distance below the confluence of the river Tidung. Here Lamaic Buddhism is found to be the general religion, the traveller proceeding northwards perceiving here for the first time the lamas or priests of that belief. The vicinity abounds with manes or tumuli, formed of stones, and from ten to forty feet in length, four in height, and two in breadth, and covered at top with large slates, inscribed with various holy texts in the Tibetan language. Elevation above the sea 8,046 feet. Lat. 31° 34′, long. 78° 28′.

RITHOURA, in the British district of Bareilly, lieut.-gov. of the N.W. Provinces, a village on the route from the town of Bareilly to Petoragurh, and 11 miles N.E. of the former place. It is situate in an open and cultivated country, and supplies and water are abundant. Lat. 28° 28′, long. 79° 34′.

RIXI.—A town in the British district of Palamow, lieut.-gov. of Bengal, 24 miles S.S.E. of Palamow. Lat. 23° 30′, long. 84° 11′.

ROBKRIE, in the Sinde Sagur Doab division of the Punjab, a town situated 10 miles from the left bank of the Indus, 95 miles S. of the town of Peshawar. Lat. 32° 40′, long. 71° 33′.

ROGI, in Bussahir, a village of the district of Koonawar, situate about a mile from the right bank of the Sutluj, which rolls 3,000 feet below it. The fine orchards surrounding it produce peaches, apricots, and apples, of which the last are remarkable for size and excellent taste, though grafting is never practised to improve the stock. The road from this place to Pangi, lying north of it, proceeds along the precipitous side of a mountain overhanging the Sutluj. Rogi is 9,100 feet above the level of the sea. Lat. 31° 30′, long. 78° 17′.

ROGONATHPORE, in the British district of Pachete, a small town or village on the route from Bankoora to Hazareebagh, 35 miles N.W. of former, 103 S.E. of latter. Jacquemont describes it as a small place, situate at the foot of a group of small wooded hills of granite, about 800 feet high. Lat. 23° 31′, long. 86° 44′.

ROH.—A town in the British district of Behar, lieut.-gov. of Bengal, 60 miles E.N.E. of Sherghotty. Lat. 24° 53′, long. 85° 45′.

ROHA.—A town in the native state of Cutch, presidency of Bombay, 30 miles W. from Bhooj, and 50 miles S.E. from Luckput. Lat. 23° 15′, long. 69° 17′.

ROHANA, in the British district of Suharunpore, lieut.-gov. of the N.W. Provinces, a village on the route from Meerut to Suharunpoor, and 42 miles N. of the former. Lat. 29° 35′, long. 77° 46′.

ROHENO, in the British district of Allygurh, lieut.-gov. of the N.W. Provinces, a village on the route from the cantonment of Allygurh to that of Mynpooree, and 12 miles S.E. of the former. Lat. 27° 49′, long. 78° 17′.

ROHERA.—A town in the Rajpoot state of Oodeypoor, 42 miles W. by N. from Oodeypoor, and 76 miles N.E. by E. from Deesa. Lat. 24° 42′, long. 73° 10′.

ROHEYREE, in the British district of Allyghur, lieut.-gov. of the N.W. Provinces, a village on the route from the city of Agra to Allyghur cantonment, and 20 miles S. of the latter. Lat. 27° 39′, long. 78° 7′.

ROHILCUND, an extensive tract so called, lying to the east of the Ganges, and bounded on the north-east by British Gurwhal and Kumaon; on the east by the territory of Oude; and on the south-west and west by the Ganges, separating it from the Dooab. It comprises the British districts of Bijnour, Moradabad, Bareilly, including the subdivision of Pilleebheet, Budaon, Shahjehanpoor, and the native jaghire of Rampoor. Its limits are from lat. 27° 15′—29° 51′, and from long. 78° 3′—80° 30′.

ROHTUK, one of the districts of the great British territorial division of Delhi, under the lieut.-gov. of the N.W. Provinces, derives its name from its principal town. It is bounded on the north-east by the British district of Paneeput; on the east by the Delhi district and the native state of Bahadoorgurh; on the south by Jhujhur; on the south-west by Dadree; and on the west by the British district Hurrianah, and by Sirhind. It lies between lat. 28° 38′—29° 16′, long. 76° 10′—77° 4′; is fifty miles in length in a direction from east to west, and forty-four in breadth, and comprises an area of 1,340 square miles.

The Rohtuk branch of Feroze's canal traverses this district from north to south. The line of the old Delhi Canal lay also through this district to Gohana, where it diverged south-east to Jatola, and thenceforward took a course identical, or nearly so, with the line of the present canal. At Gohana, there is an extensive depression, the scene of a great calamity which occurred in the course of the original construction of the Delhi Canal by Ali Murdan Khan, when the water, escaping from the channel intended to confine it, overspread the country, and destroyed the town of Lalpur. Rohtuk is divided into seven pergunnahs, named severally Rohtuk, Beree, Gohana, Kerthowda, Mundowthee, Mehim, and Bewhanee. By the latest returns (1852-53), the amount of population is stated as follows:—Hindoos, agricultural, 219,443; Hindoos, non-agricultural, 112,380; Mahomedans and others, not being Hindoos, agricultural, 23,949; of the like classes, non-agricultural, 21,241; making a total of 377,013. A classification of the towns and villages, drawn from official records of the same date, shows the following results:—

Number containing less than 1,000 inhabitants	204
Ditto more than 1,000 and less than 5,000....	70
Ditto „ 5,000 „ 10,000....	4
Ditto „ 10,000	2
Total................	280

The land revenue has been fixed for a term of thirty years, which will expire on the 1st of July, 1870.

ROHTUK.—The chief place in the British district of the same name. It lies on the route from the city of Delhi to Hansee, and 42 miles N.W. of the former place: it is situate on a watercourse forty-five miles long, formed by order of the British government in 1825, to convey a supply from the canal of Ferozshah. The population amounts to 13,237, and there is a good bazar. The road in this part of the route is generally good, though in some places sandy and heavy. Lat. 28° 54′, long. 76° 38′.

ROHUD, in the British district of Rohtuk, division of Delhi, lieut.-gov. of Agra, a village on the route from Delhi to Hansee, and 27 miles N.W. of the former. The road in this part of the route is good in dry weather. Lat. 28° 44′, long. 76° 52′.

ROHUNPORE, in the British district of Rajeshaye, lieut.-gov. of Bengal, a town on the western frontier, towards the British district of Malda, on the left side of the river Mahanunda, a short distance below the confluence of the Purnabada. Distant S.E. from town of Maldah 20 miles, N. from Calcutta, by Burhampoor, 168. Lat. 24° 48′, long. 88° 20′.

ROHUT, in the Rajpoot state of Jodhpoor, a village on the route from Neemuch, *viâ*

Palee, to the city of Jodhpoor, and 24 miles S. of the latter. Lat. 25° 59′, long. 73° 14′.

ROIR BAZAAR.—A town in the British district of Pooree, lieut.-gov. of Bengal, 23 miles N.N.E. of Juggurnaut. Lat. 20° 7′, long. 86°.

ROJAN.—A town in the British district of Shikarpoor, province of Scinde, presidency of Bombay, 29 miles N.W. of Shikarpoor. Lat. 28° 18′, long. 68° 18′.

ROLAGAON.—A town of Malwa, in the native state of Bhopal, 49 miles S.W. by W. from Bhopal, and 61 miles E. by N. from Indoor. Lat. 22° 51′, long. 76° 48′.

ROLEE, in the British district of Budaon, lieut.-gov. of the N.W. Provinces, a village on the route from Agra to Bareilly, and 41 miles S.W. of the latter. Lat. 28° 2′, long. 79° 5′.

ROLPAH.—A town in Nepal, 40 miles S. from Jemlah, and 121 miles E. from Pilleebheet. Lat. 28° 45′, long. 81° 51′.

RONCHI, in the British district of Muttra, lieut.-gov. of the N.W. Provinces, a village on the route from the city of Agra to that of Muttra, and five miles S. of the latter. It is situate near the right bank of the Jumna, in a country cut up by ravines, and partially cultivated. Lat. 27° 25′, long. 77° 47′.

RONTAN, a considerable village in Raeen, a small hill district occupied by the East-India Company, among the mountains between the Himalayas and the plains, is situate near the left bank of the Pabur. It was a secondary station in the trigonometrical survey of the Himalayas. Elevation above the sea 7,898 feet. Lat. 31° 6′, long. 77° 50′.

ROODHAMOW.—A town in Oude, situate 10 miles from the left bank of the Ganges, and 51 miles W. by N. from Lucknow. Lat. 27° 7′, long. 80° 13′.

ROODRAR.—A town in the British district of Cuddapah, presidency of Madras, 58 miles N.N.W. of Cuddapah. Lat. 15° 16′, long. 78° 40′.

ROODURPOOR.—A town in the British district of Chota Nagpoor, lieut.-gov. of Bengal, 61 miles S.W. by S. of Lohadugga. Lat. 22° 46′, long. 84° 9′.

ROODURPOOR, in the British district of Goruckpore, lieut.-gov. of the N.W. Provinces, a small town, containing 300 mud-built dwellings, with a population of 5,535 inhabitants, is situate on the Mujhane, a small stream, a feeder of the river Raptee. Roodurpoor is distant S.E. from Goruckpoor cantonment 26 miles. Lat. 26° 24′, long. 83° 40′.

ROODURPOOR, in the British district of Bareilly, the principal place of the pergunnah of the same name, on the route from Bareilly to Almora, and 53 miles N. of the former. It is situate on the bank of a bright rippling stream, a feeder of the Ramgunga, amongst some very fine mango-groves, from which the tops of temples and other buildings appearing, give the place, when viewed at some distance, an appearance of beauty and importance, that quickly vanish on a nearer approach. Heber found "all the usual marks of a diminished and sickly population, a pestilential climate, and an over-luxuriant soil. The tombs and temples were all ruins; the houses of the present inhabitants, some two or three score of wretched huts, such as even the gipsies of the open country would hardly shelter in. The people sat huddled together at their doors, wrapped in their black blankets, and cowering round little fires, with pale faces and emaciated limbs; while the groves, which looked so beautiful at a distance, instead of offering, as mango-groves do in well-peopled and cultivated spots, a fine open shade, with a dry turf and fresh breeze beneath it, were all choked up with jungle and nightshade." The road is good on the north, or Almora side, but bad on the south, towards Bareilly. Elevation above the sea 629 feet. Lat. 28° 58′, long. 79° 28′.

ROOKUNPUR, in the British district of Boolundshuhur, lieut.-gov. of the N.W. Provinces, a village on the route from Allygurh cantonment to that of Delhi, and 23 miles N.W. of the former. Lat. 28° 9′, long. 77° 58′.

ROOL, in Bussahir, a village near the southern base of the Shatul Pass, gives name to a small district in the pergunnah of Chooara. The road rises rapidly to the Buchkal Ghat, through a beautiful wood of oak, yew, pine, rhododendron, horse-chestnut, and juniper. Rool village is 9,350 feet above the sea. Lat. 31° 19′, long. 77° 57′.

ROOMAH, in the British district of Cawnpore, lieut.-gov. of the N.W. Provinces, a village on the route from the cantonment of Cawnpore to Futtehpoor, and 10 miles S.E. of the former. Lat. 26° 21′, long. 80° 30′.

ROONUNG, in Bussahir, a pass in the district of Koonawar, over a range dividing the valley of Ruskulung from that of Pejur. The ridge consists of slate, and the crest of the pass is below the limits of perpetual congelation, as the juniper grows there, and even on the heights above. The pass is closed for four of the coldest months of the year, and the communication is then effected by a circuitous and very dangerous route along the bank of the Sutluj. Elevation of Roonung Pass above the level of the sea 14,500 feet. Lat. 31° 43′, long. 78° 28′.

ROOPGUNGE.—A town in the British district of Dacca, lieut.-gov. of Bengal, eight miles N.E. of Dacca. Lat. 23° 47′, long. 90° 31′.

ROOPGURH.—A town in the Rajpoot state of Jeypoor, 45 miles N.W. from Jeypoor, and 76 miles N.E. by N. from Ajmeer. Lat. 27° 21′, long. 75° 22′.

ROOPNARAIN.—A large estuary extending twelve miles, between the British districts Hoogly and Hedjelee, from Tumlook, in lat. 22° 18′, long. 88°, to Fort Mornington, in lat.

22° 13′, long. 88° 6′. This expanse is formed by the Dalkisore meeting the tide at its entrance into the estuary of the Hooghly.

ROOPNUGUR.—A town in the Rajpoot state of Kishengurh, 26 miles N.E. by N. from Ajmeer, and 61 miles W. by S. from Jeypoor. Lat. 26° 47′, long. 74° 55′.

ROOPOHEE RIVER.—A considerable watercourse formed by the Brahmapootra river: it leaves that stream in lat. 26° 34′, long. 92° 51′, and rejoins it again in lat. 26° 17′, long. 92° 1′, after a course of seventy miles, through the district of Nowgong, in Lower Assam.

ROOPSEE, in the Rajpoot state of Jesulmeer, a small town and fort 10 miles N.W. of the city of Jesulmeer. Lat. 26° 58′, long. 70° 50′.

ROOPYN.—A river of Guzerat, rising in lat. 23° 31′, long. 72° 2′, and, flowing west for forty-two miles, falls into the Runn of Cutch, in lat. 23° 28′, long. 71° 28′.

ROORGAON, in the British district of Cawnpore, lieut.-gov. of the N.W. Provinces, a village on the route from Allahabad to Etawa, and 63 miles S.E. of the latter. Lat. 26° 14′, long. 79° 49′.

ROORKEE, in the British district of Suharunpore, lieut.-gov. of the N.W. Provinces, a town on one of the most elevated sites in the doab between the Jumna and the Ganges. It is on this account that the great Ganges Canal has been made to pass by this place, whence channels of irrigation can be directed to most parts of the Doab. With the view of effecting this project, the river Solani has been traversed by an aqueduct of 920 feet in length. The clear waterway is 750 feet, by fifteen arches of fifty feet span each: the cost of the aqueduct was 158,000*l.* The selection of this place as the head-quarters of the canal operations, and the establishment of the necessary workshops, model-rooms, and offices, have tended to convert a small village into a considerable European station. A college has been established here, for the purpose of affording instruction in civil engineering to Europeans and natives, and which, as a mark of respect to the memory of its founder, has been designated the "Thomason College." Sanction has been given to the erection of a church. Lat. 29° 53′, long. 77° 57′.

ROOROO, in Bussahir, a village on the right bank of the Pabur, near the confluence of a small feeder called the Supil. Elevation of the village above the sea 5,100 feet. Lat. 31° 12′, long. 77° 48′.

ROOSHKATONG.—See DARBUNG.

ROOSTUMPOOR, in the British district of Moradabad, lieut.-gov. of the N.W. Provinces, a village on the route from Hurdwar to the town of Moradabad, and 13 miles N.W. of the latter. Lat. 29° 1′, long. 78° 45′.

ROPA, in Bussahir, a village of the district of Koonawur, is situate in the valley of Ruskulung, and near the left bank of the river Darbung. Three or four miles from this village are numerous extensive and rich veins of copper-ore, situate 13,000 feet above the level of the sea. Access to this locality is obtained with excessive difficulty by climbing up the precipitous side of a lofty mountain, near the summit of which the principal veins have been discovered. These lie in white quartz, running between grauwacke and red sandstone, which are here the chief formations. Elevation of Ropa above the sea 9,800 feet. Lat. 31° 47′, long. 78° 28′.

ROPUR, in Sirhind, a town situate a mile from the left bank of the Sutlej, a short distance below its efflux from the Himalaya. The river is here crossed by a ferry, affording an important communication between the Punjab and Sirhind. It is described to be "a noble stream, thirty feet deep, and more than 500 yards in breadth." Its bed consists of large smooth pebbles, mixed with mud. The low range of the Sub-Himalaya, bounding Sirhind on the north-east, does not reach to the Sutlej, along the left bank of which a narrow plain extends for several miles, and in this the town is situate, on a slight eminence. It was the residence of the rajah of the adjacent territory, which yielded an annual revenue of 6,000*l.*; but he, being one of the protected Sikh chiefs who failed in fidelity to the British government on the breaking out of the war with Lahore subsequently to the death of Runjeet Singh, was compelled to retire on a pensionary provision, and his territory escheated to the British authority. Here, in 1831, an interview took place between Lord William Bentinck, Governor-General of India, and Runjeet Singh; the Sikh ruler first crossing on a bridge of boats, and subsequently receiving in turn the visit of the Governor-General, on the right bank of the Sutlej. On "the 1st of November, 1831, both camps broke ground, and commenced their march in opposite directions, after a week of magnificence and mutual display, reminding one of the days of the field of cloth of gold." On this occasion, Runjeet requested and received from the British authorities a paper, containing a promise of perpetual friendship. Ropur is about 1,100 feet above the level of the sea. The population of the town is returned at 7,110. Distant N.W. from Calcutta 1,120 miles. Lat. 30° 58′, long. 76° 37′.

ROREE, or LOHUREE (the ancient Lohurkot), in Sinde, a town situate on the eastern bank of the Indus, on a rocky eminence of limestone, interspersed with flint. This rocky site is terminated abruptly on the western side by a precipice of forty feet high, rising from the beach of the Indus, which, in inundation, attains a height of about sixteen feet above its lowest level. Westmacott is of opinion that it formerly must have risen to fifty feet, washing the brow of the eminence on which Roree stands, and that then the

neighbouring rocky islets in the Indus were sunken rocks. According to the unanimous testimony of the natives, the level of the river during inundation continually decreases, and this is probably owing more to the wearing down of the rocky bed, than to any diminution of the supply of water in the upper part of the river's course.

Roree, when seen from without, has a striking and pleasing appearance, as the houses are four or five stories high, and of corresponding extent; but when surveyed more closely, they are found to be ruinous, in many instances rudely constructed with a slight timber frame, filled up with wicker-work, and plastered with mud: and as whitewash, though very easily obtainable, is not used, they have a dingy and neglected appearance. The few more costly houses of burned brick were erected by wealthy merchants before the establishment of the dynasty of the late ameers. The streets are so narrow that a camel in passing occupies the entire breadth from side to side. The air, in consequence, is very close and unwholesome. There are forty mosques in which prayers are still recited, and twice that number in a state of ruin and desertion. The great mosque stands on an elevated site in the north-east part of the town, and was built at the commencement of the seventeenth century, by the lieutenant of the Emperor Acbar. It is a massive, gloomy pile of red brick, covered with three domes, and coated with glazed porcelain tiles. In an adjacent shrine is kept a hair in amber, in a gold case set with rubies and emeralds, and inclosed in another of wood enriched with silver. This the pious Mahometan undoubtingly believes to be a hair of the beard of his prophet; and a number of guardians of this precious relic are supported at the public expense.

Roree has a spacious and well-built serai, or lodging-place for travellers, but it has been allowed to fall into great decay. There are two bazars, one for grain, the other for miscellaneous articles, and both are tolerably well supplied; but they are ill-built and ruinous. Manufactures are few and unimportant. They embrace the fabrication of paper of indifferent quality, leather, silks, and cottons, and the dyeing and printing of the last-named article. The population is mixed, consisting of Hindoos, indigenous Sindians, Beloochees, Afghans, and Moguls. All trades and handicrafts, with the exception of works in gold, silver, and jewellery, are in the hands exclusively of Mahometans; the Hindoos devote themselves chiefly to banking, money-broking, and similar traffic. The population is estimated at about 8,000. Lat. 27° 38′, long. 68° 55′.

ROREE MEER SHAH, in the Daman division of the Punjab, a town situated on the right bank of the Indus, 75 miles N.W. by N. of the town of Mooltan. Lat. 31°, long. 70° 46′.

ROSHUNABAD, in the British district of Furruckabad, lieut.-gov. of the N.W. Provinces, a town near the right bank of the Ganges, 10 miles N.W. of the city of Furruckabad. Lat. 27° 30′, long. 79° 32′.

ROSS ISLAND.—A considerable island, forming one of the group known as the Mergui Archipelago. Its centre is about lat. 12° 14′, long. 98° 12′.

ROTANGA PASS, leading through the mountains that separate the British district of Lahoul from Kullu, 32 miles N. of Sultanpoor. Lat. 32° 25′, long. 77° 12′.

ROTAS, in the Punjab, an extensive fort six miles west of the right or western bank of the river Jhelum. The interior is two miles and a half long, and is of an oblong, narrow form, having its two sides and eastern end resting upon the edge of ravines, which divide it from a table-land of elevation equal to that of the hill on which the fort stands. The western face of the plateau is washed by the small river Gham, running at its base. Its works are of immense strength, consisting of massive walls of stone thirty feet thick, cemented with mortar, and strengthened with bastions, all crenated throughout, and provided with a double row of loopholes. Connected with the fortress is an immense well, lined with masonry, and having passages down to the water so numerous that from fifty to a hundred persons may draw water at once.

The present fortress was built about the year 1540, by Shir Shah, the Patan emperor of Delhi, who had driven Humaioon into exile; and he is said to have expended a million and a half sterling in its construction. When Humaioon returned, at the head of an army, to reclaim his empire, the fortress was given up to him without resistance. He demolished the palace raised within the fort by his rival and enemy, but found the massive defences too strong for the limited time and means which he could allow for their destruction. The fortress is at present in a ruinous state, and in one place a huge mass of the wall has tumbled down the precipice, and rendered the interior accessible. It is considered by military men indefensible against modern modes of attack. Lat. 32° 59′, long. 73° 38′.

ROTAS.—See RHOTASGURH.

ROTHINGI, in Bussahir, a pass in the district of Koonawar, over a ridge rising abruptly from the left or south-eastern bank of the Taglakhar torrent. The ascent of the pass from the south-west is a mile in length, at an angle from top to bottom of 43°. The elevation of the crest of the pass is 14,638 feet above the sea, yet the rays of the sun, reverberated from the bare rocks, produced a heat quite oppressive. Above rise hoary summits of incredible height and grandeur, with extensive valleys between them, loaded by prodigious bodies of undissolving snow. Lat. 31° 36′, long. 78° 42′.

ROTUK.—See ROHTUK.

ROTUNDA GHAUT.—See RURTONDA.

ROUDPUR, in the British district of Cawnpore, lieut.-gov. of the N.W. Provinces, a village on the route from Calpee to the cantonment of Cawnpore, and seven miles S.W. of the latter. Lat. 26° 29′, long. 80° 20′.

ROUNAPOOR, in the British district of Azimgurh, lieut.-gov. of the N.W. Provinces, a village on the route from the town of Azimgurh to that of Goruckpoor, and 18 miles N. of the former, 43 S. of the latter. It has a few shops; water is plentiful, and supplies may be had from the surrounding country, which is low, level, and partially cultivated. Distant N. from Benares 70 miles. Lat. 26° 15′, long. 83° 20′.

ROWLI GHAT, in the British district of Bijnour, lieut.-gov. of the N.W. Provinces, a ferry over the Ganges, on the route from Moradabad to Mozuffurnuggur, and 25 miles E. of the latter town. The village of Rowli is situate on the left bank of the Ganges. Distant N.W. from Calcutta 970 miles. Lat. 29° 26′, long. 78° 8′.

ROWRAH.—A town in the British district of Ahmednuggur, presidency of Bombay, 118 miles N.W. by N. of Ahmednuggur. Lat. 20° 29′, long. 73° 42′.

ROWSURA.—A town in the British district of Tirhoot, lieut.-gov. of Bengal, 31 miles S.S.E. of Durbunga. Lat. 25° 43′, long. 86° 7′.

ROXAKANDEE.—A town in the British district of Jessore, lieut.-gov. of Bengal, 50 miles N.E. of Jessore. Lat. 23° 40′, long. 89° 26′.

ROYACOTTAH.—A town in the British district of Salem, presidency of Madras, 61 miles N. by W. of Salem. Lat. 12° 31′, long. 78° 5′.

ROY BAREILLY, in the district of Banswara, in the territory of Oude, a town on the route from Allahabad to Lucknow, and 78 miles N.W. of the former, 55 S.E. of the latter. It is situate on the river Sai, which is crossed by a brick-built bridge, and is navigable so far up, and can bear craft of twelve tons, though there are none except a few ferry-boats at the place, in consequence of the intolerable exactions of the proprietors of lands along the lower course of the river. It is mentioned in the Ayeen Akbery, in the sirkar or subdivision Manikpoor, soobah or province Allahabad. "Roybereyli has a brick fort, and is assessed at 91,274 rupees." Lat. 26° 14′, long. 81° 19′.

ROYBUGGA.—A town on the S.W. frontier of Bengal, in the native state of Gangpoor, situate on the left bank of the Sunk river, and 81 miles N.E. by N. from Sumbulpoor. Lat. 22° 17′, long. 84° 42′.

ROYCHANGA.—A town in the British district of Coosh Behar, presidency of Bengal, 18 miles N.W. of Behar. Lat. 26° 27′, long. 89° 16′.

ROYMUNGUL RIVER.—One of the mouths of the Ganges, falling into the sea in lat. 21° 42′, long. 89° 5′.

RUBOOPOORA, in the British district of Bolundshuhur, lieut.-gov. of the N.W. Provinces, a town on the route from Muttra to Delhi, by the left bank of the Jumna, 35 miles S.E. of Delhi. Lat. 28° 15′, long. 77° 40′.

RUDAULI, in the kingdom of Oude, a town 40 miles E. of Lucknow. It is surrounded by swamp, except on the west side, and is superior to many other places of this country, in having brick-built houses; and there is also a Mussulman mausoleum of the same material. Lat. 26° 54′, long. 81° 27′.

RUDAWAL, in the territory of Bhurtpore, a village on the route from Agra to Mow, 41 miles S.W. of the former, 374 N.E. of the latter. Close to it is encamping-ground, and supplies and water are obtainable. Lat. 26° 59′, long. 77° 29′.

RUDLEGUNJ.—A town in the British district of Rungpore, lieut.-gov. of Bengal, 14 miles W. by S. of Rungpore. Lat. 25° 37′, long. 89° 2′.

RUDOWLEE, in the British district of Goruckpoor, lieut.-gov. of the N.W. Provinces, a small town on the river Ami, 40 miles N.W. of Goruckpoor cantonment. Buchanan, describing it fifty years ago, states the number of houses to be 100; and, assigning six to each house, the population consequently may be estimated at 600. Lat. 27° 3′, long. 82° 48′.

RUDRA HIMALEH, a lofty summit of the Himalaya, rises on the eastern frontier of Gurhwal, towards Chinese Tartary. Fraser, who viewed it from Gangotri, at a distance of eight or ten miles, describes it under that aspect as having five huge, lofty snowy peaks, rising behind a mass of bare rocky spires. The highest summit, as ascertained in the trigonometrical survey, has an elevation of 22,390 feet above the sea. Lat. 30° 58′, long. 79° 9′.

RUDRAPRAYAG, in the British district of Kumaon, lieut.-gov. of Agra, a village at the confluence of the rivers Alacananda and Mandakini. At an inconsiderable height above the water is a small math or temple, and adjacent a few houses of Brahmins. There is also a rock thirty feet high and fifteen in diameter, called Bhim ka Chulha, or the "Kitchen of Bhim," a giant famous in Hindoo lore. It is completely excavated, somewhat in the form of a dome, with apertures at top, in which Bhim is supposed to have placed his cooking utensils. It is one of the five principal prayags or confluences mentioned as holy in the sacred books of the Hindoos. Its elevation above the sea is about 2,200 feet. Distance N.W. from Calcutta, by Lucknow, Bareilly, Almora, and Srinagar, 1,020 miles. Lat. 30° 17′, long. 79° 2′.

RUGONATHGURH.—A town in the Rajpoot state of Jeypoor, 57 miles N.N.W.

from Jeypoor, and 104 miles S. by W. from Hissar. Lat. 27° 40′, long. 75° 31′.

RUGOWLEE, in the British district of Banda, lieut.-gov. of the N.W. Provinces, a lofty rocky eminence, very steep and difficult of ascent, 10 miles N. of the hill-fort of Ajegurh. In 1809, when the British government commenced military operations against Luchman Singh, rajah of Ajegurh, his uncle, Pursaud Singh, took post with about 500 picked men on the hill of Rugowlee, the fortified summit of which was accessible only by narrow zigzag pathways, commanded every twenty yards by strong posts behind large rocks, and manned with matchlockmen. All the lower defences were, however, successively stormed by the British forces, who, for want of scaling-ladders, being unable to make good an entrance within the upper inclosure, were withdrawn. In the course of the night the inclosure was, however, evacuated by the enemy, leaving their chief and between sixty and seventy of their number killed, 150 or 160 being wounded. The British loss amounted to twenty-eight killed and 115 wounded. The summit of the hill is probably about 800 feet above the base, or 1,300 above the sea. Lat. 25° 1′, long. 80° 22′.

RUHEEMPOOR, in the British district of Goorgaon, lieut. gov. of the N.W. Provinces, a town on the right bank of the Jumna, distant S.E. from Delhi 42 miles. Lat. 28° 6′, long. 77° 31′.

RUHOLEE, in the British district of Moradabad, lieut.-gov. of the N.W. Provinces, a village on the route from Bareilly to Delhi, 40 miles W. of the former. Lat. 28° 27′, long. 78° 54′.

RUJGAWA, in the British district of Allahabad, lieut.-gov. of the N.W. Provinces, a village on the route by the Rajapur ferry, from the cantonment of Allahabad to Banda, and 41 miles W. of the former. Lat. 25° 25′, long. 81° 21′.

RUJLA.—A town of Malwa, in the native state of Jabboah, 10 miles S. by E. from Jabboah, and 96 miles E.N.E. from Baroda. Lat. 22° 39′, long. 74° 39′.

RUJORA, in the territory of Dholpoor, a town on the route from Agra to Baree, 30 miles S.W. of former, 14 N.W. of the town of Dholpoor. Lat. 26° 50′, long. 77° 45′.

RUJOU, in the British district of Bareilly, lieut.-gov. of the N.W. Provinces, a village on the route from the town of Bareilly to Shahjehanpoor, and seven miles S.E. of the former. Lat. 28° 17′, long. 79° 33′.

RUMALUH, in the British district of Meerut, lieut.-gov. of the N.W. Provinces, a town on the route from Delhi to Suharunpore, 38 miles N. of the former. Rumaluh has a population of 5,234 inhabitants. Lat. 29° 13′, long. 77° 20′.

RUMYEEPOOR, in the British district of Cawnpore, lieut.-gov. of the N.W. Provinces, a town 10 miles W. of the right bank of the Ganges. Lat. 26° 21′, long. 80° 21′.

RUNDALA.—See KHUNDALU.

RUNEEA, in the British district of Cawnpore, lieut.-gov. of the N.W. Provinces, a small town on the route from the cantonment of Cawnpore to that of Calpee, and 31 miles N.E. of the latter. Lat. 26° 24′, long. 80° 8′.

RUNGAGOORA.—A town in the British district of Muttuck, lieut.-gov. of Bengal, 55 miles N.E. of Seebpoor. Lat. 27° 32′, long. 95° 20′.

RUNGAMUTTEE.—A town in the British district of Goalpara, lieut.-gov. of Bengal, 40 miles W. of Goalpara. Lat. 26° 7′, long. 90° 1′.

RUNGAPOOR.—A town in Hyderabad, or territory of the Nizam, 102 miles N.E. from Hyderabad, and 148 miles N.N.W. from Guntoor. Lat. 18° 17′, long. 79° 44′.

RUNGASAMOODRA.—A town in the British district of Cuddapah, presidency of Madras, 65 miles S.W. by S. of Cuddapah. Lat. 13° 42′, long. 78° 19′.

RUNGELPOOR, in the Baree Doab division of the Punjab, a town situated on the left bank of the Ravee river, 25 miles S.W. of the town of Lahore. Lat. 31° 20′, long. 74°.

RUNGPOOR.—See BELASPOOR.

RUNGPOOR.—A British district under the presidency of Bengal, named from its principal place. It is bounded on the north-east by Cooch Behar; on the east by the Brahmapootra, dividing it from the British districts Goalpara and Mymensing; on the south by the British district Bograh; and on the south-west by the British district Dinajepore. It lies between lat. 25° 16′—26° 21′, long. 88° 26′—89° 50′; is 106 miles in length from south-east to north-west, and sixty in breadth: the area is 4,130 square miles. A great part of the district is low; and it is estimated that in a considerable portion thirty-six parts out of 100 are inundated during the rains. The general slope of the surface is from north-west to south-east, as indicated by the flow of the rivers in that direction, the principal of which are the Kuruttea, Teesta, Dhorla, and Brahmapootra. In addition to these, there are many other streams of less note; the whole country being permeated by watercourses, forming communications between the great rivers. During the rains, the surface having everywhere great equality of elevation, an accidental depression in the waterway of either the Brahmapootra or the Ganges will immediately cause the general drainage of the country to set towards the lower of these great rivers. From some unexplained cause, more permanent alterations have taken place in the direction of the drainage; the great volume of the water of the Teesta, which formerly was, by the Attree, or south-western channel of that stream, thrown into the Ganges, is now, by the south-east channel, still denominated the Teesta, thrown into the Brahmapootra. Though there is no lake of any considerable extent, there are numerous jhils or small stagnant sheets of water, formed either in the deserted channels of streams or by the overflowing of springs. Their numbers and positions vary very much; the old ones becoming obliterated either by silt or the accumulation of decayed vegetation, and new ones being formed by the alterations in the courses of rivers and other causes. Buchanan was of opinion, that between the time of Major Rennell and that at which he wrote, these minute lakes had diminished both in number and in size.

The climate of Rungpore differs considerably from that of places in India farther south and west. The hot winds of spring are but little felt anywhere within it; in the eastern part they are unknown, and even in the western they blow for not more than eight or ten days in the whole year. During May the temperature is rather high; but its effects are modified by the easterly winds, which are comparatively cool. From the beginning of June to the end of October the heat is more felt; but this, in the judgment of Buchanan, is owing to the calmness of the weather, as he never found the temperature exceed 84°. In the northern part hoar-frosts are said occasionally to occur in midwinter.

On the zoology of this district Buchanan is almost the sole guide. Apes and monkeys of various kinds are numerous; lemurs are sometimes, though rarely, to be met with; tigers and leopards are neither very numerous nor very mischievous, as they seldom destroy human beings, and the number of cattle falling a prey to them is not great. There are black bears in the district, but not in large numbers; of otters, foxes, and jackals, there are many. Two other animals, seemingly of the canine tribe,—the bungra and the kuhok, are spoken of, but Buchanan was unable to procure a sight of either. Wild elephants infest the eastern part, and also portions of the north-west: they are very destructive to grain-crops, especially rice. The woods harbour the rhinoceros, which is killed for its horn, to which imaginary virtues are attributed, and for its skin, out of which excellent targets are made: the hunters use the flesh as an article of food. The wild hog exists in different parts, in greater or less numbers; the flesh is eaten, and is considered pure. There are wild buffaloes, as well as various kinds of deer and of antelopes. The porcupine is less numerous than in some other parts, and is less sought after for food. The pangolin is found, though a rare animal, and its flesh is greatly valued. Hares are very abundant. Porpoises are numerous in the Brahmapootra, and are killed for the sake of their oil. River turtles are numerous, and attain great size; some, Buchanan was informed, measuring between seven and eight feet in length. These animals furnish an abundance of food to the inhabitants, though Buchanan found it distasteful.

The principal crops are rice, wheat, barley, pulse, oil-seeds, garden vegetables, sugarcane, tobacco, and indigo: the mulberry-tree thrives. Cotton indeed seems unquestionably to be a failure in the district. There are about fifty large indigo-factories. These are either managed by Europeans, or after the European method. Much of that made by natives is of inferior quality, but some is said to equal that of the Europeans. The number of factories of all sizes and descriptions is about 400.

Commerce appears in the time of Buchanan to have been by no means active. He gives a list of exports, which, however, may be regarded as superseded by a more recent one in another publication, and which comprises both exports and imports. From this, indigo appears to be by far the largest among the exports; silk, gunny-bags, tobacco, sugar, carpets, and paddy are next in order: the remainder are less considerable. Among the imports, piece-goods occupy the first place; cotton, salt, woollens, manufactured silks, and metals, are next in importance; and a number of miscellaneous articles are imported to a small extent. The population of the district is given under the article BENGAL.

The tract comprised within the British district Rungpoor was formerly the western part of the ancient Hindoo country called Camroop. The realm appears to have attained its greatest power and prosperity under Rajah Nilambor, who was conquered about the close of the fifteenth century, by Husain Shah, of Bengal. On the overthrow of the kingdom of Bengal, about 1542, by Shir Shah, the renowned Afghan, subsequently padshah of Delhi, the district appears to have become part of that great empire. During the turbulent period subsequent to the death of Shir Shah, it was severed from the empire, to which it was again annexed by Akbar, about 1584. It passed to the East-India Company in 1765, under the firman of Shah Alum.

RUNGPORE.—The capital of the British district of the same name, under the presidency of Bengal, a town situate on the route from Purneah to Goalpara, 128 miles E. of the former, 105 S.W. of the latter. Though the locality of the civil establishment of the district and the head station of the police, it is represented as a wretched place, consisting of scattered huts with a few brick-built houses. A mosque of considerable size, and two monuments much revered by Mussulmans, having been erected in honour of reputed saints, constitute its principal attractions. The Hindoo places of worship are quite unworthy of notice. Rungpore is 150 miles N.E. of Berhampur by Dinajpur, and 268 N.E. of Calcutta by the same route. Lat. 25° 40′, long. 89° 16′.

RUNKUTTA, in the British district of Agra, lieut.-gov. of the N.W. Provinces, a village a mile from the right bank of the Jumna, on the route from the city of Agra to that of Muttra, and 12 miles N.W. of the former. It has a few shops, and is supplied with water from five brick-lined wells, from forty to forty-five feet deep. Lat. 27° 14', long. 77° 56'.

RUNN OF CUTCH.—See CUTCH.

RUNPOOR.—A tract of Orissa, inhabited by one of the independent hill tribes, situate on the western boundary of the British district of Pooree. Its centre is about lat. 20°, long. 85° 20'.

RUOJAN.—A town in the British district of Chittagong, lieut.-gov. of Bengal, 19 miles N.E. of Chittagong. Lat. 22° 33', long. 92° 5'.

RUPBAS, in the territory of Bhurtpore, a small town 16 miles S.E. of the city of Bhurtpore. The hills here consist, in inexhaustible quantities, of rock of compact durable sandstone, of various hues, much in request for fine building purposes, and hence quarried to great extent. The tasteful and highly-finished buildings of Deeg, in the northern part of the territory, are constructed of this stone. Lat. 27°, long. 77° 39'.

RUPIN, in Bussahir, a pass over the range of the Himalaya bounding Koonawar on the south. The formation of the rocks is partly gneiss, partly granite; but the former is most abundant. Elevation above the sea 15,480 feet. Lat. 31° 21', long. 78° 12'.

RUPSHU, in Ladakh, among the Western Himalayas, in a very elevated and barren plain, or extensive valley, bearing a scanty vegetation of grass and stunted furze, subject, even in the height of summer, to frost and snow, and being swept over by the most impetuous whirlwinds. Its mean elevation is 16,000 feet. The climate is characterized by great aridity; and from this cause, and the intense cold, is peculiarly suited to the constitution of the yak and shawl-goat, which thrive here, notwithstanding the scantiness of pasture. Its centre is about lat. 33°, long. 78° 15'.

RURTONDA GHAT.—A pass by which the road from Nagotna to Sattara is carried over the Western Ghats. Distant 34 miles W.N.W. of Sattara. Lat. 17° 54', long. 73° 38'.

RUSAREH, or RUSRA, in the British district of Ghazeepore, lieut.-gov. of the N.W. Provinces, a town on the route from Bulliah to Azimgurh, 20 miles N.W. of the former. Rusareh contains a population of 7,228 inhabitants. Lat. 25° 50', long. 83° 56'.

RUSHDUN, in the British district of Cawnpore, lieut.-gov. of the N.W. Provinces, a village on the route from Calpee to the cantonment of Futtehgurh, and 20 miles N. of the former. It contains a population of 5,000 inhabitants, has a large bazar, and is well supplied with water. Lat. 26° 22', long. 79° 44'.

RUSKOOND.—A town in the British district of Midnapoor, lieut.-gov. of Bengal, 26 miles N. of Midnapoor. Lat. 22° 47', long. 87° 28'.

RUSKULUNG.—See DARBUNG.

RUSOOLA, in the British district of Bareilly, lieut.-gov. of the N.W. Provinces, a village on the route from the city of Agra to Bareilly, and 25 miles S.W. of the latter. Lat. 28° 14', long. 79° 12'.

RUSOOLABAD, in the British district of Furruckabad, lieut.-gov. of the N.W. Provinces, a town near the left bank of the Esun, 25 miles S. of the city of Furruckabad. Lat. 27° 2', long. 79° 42'.

RUSOOLPOOR, in the British district of Muttra, lieut.-gov. of the N.W. Provinces, a village on the route from Muttra cantonment to Bhurtpore, and 13 miles S.W. of the former. Lat. 27° 20', long. 77° 38'.

RUSSAREH, in the British district of Ghazeepoor, lieut.-gov. of the N.W. Provinces, a town near the northern frontier, towards Goruckpoor, and 25 miles N.E. of Ghazeepoor cantonment. Lat. 25° 51', long. 83° 55'.

RUSSELKONDAH, in the British district of Ganjam, presidency of Madras, a town with military cantonment on the north-western frontier, towards the British territory of Orissa. Its name is compounded of the surname of a British commissioner, who accompanied the army in its operations in this part of India, and kondah, signifying "hill;" the cantonment being situate at the foot of an eminence of moderate height. Two small rivers flow through the cantonment, in a direction south-east, and subsequently uniting, pass by Ganjam, a short distance below which the united stream falls into the Bay of Bengal. They overflow their banks during the rains, but are dry at other times, and then the cantonment is supplied with water from wells. In the cantonment are barracks, and a spacious, well-built, commodious hospital. The climate is very hot and oppressive during March, April, and May, but for the rest of the year pleasant and salubrious. Elevation above the sea 150 feet. Distance from Madras, N.E., 560 miles; Calcutta, S.W., 300; Ganjam, N.E., 50. Lat. 20°, long. 84° 40'.

RUSSELLAWALA, in the Baree Dooab division of the Punjab, a town situated 15 miles from the left bank of the Chenaub, 18 miles E.N.E. of the town of Mooltan. Lat. 30° 12', long. 71° 47'.

RUSSOOLABAD, in the British district of Cawnpoor, lieut.-gov. of the N.W. Provinces, a town on the route from Cawnpoor to Etawah, 33 miles W.N.W. of the former. Lat. 26° 40', long. 79° 56'.

RUSSOOLABAD, in the territory of Oude, a town on the route from Cawnpore to Pertabgurh, 40 miles N.W. of the latter. Lat. 26°, long. 81° 30'.

RUSSOOLPOOR.—A town in the British district of Behar, lieut.-gov. of Bengal, 25 miles N.E. by N. of Sherghotty. Lat. 24° 52′, long. 85° 4′.

RUTBHANPOOR, in the British district of Mynpooree, lieut.-gov. of the N.W. Provinces, a small town on the route from the cantonment of Etawa to that of Mynpooree, and 10 miles S. of the latter. Lat. 27° 6′, long. 79° 4′.

RUTHOWRUH, or RHUTORAH, in the British district of Meerut, lieut.-gov. of the N.W. Provinces, a town on the route from Delhi to Suharunpoor, 37 miles N. of the former. Ruthowruh contains a population of 5,734 inhabitants. Lat. 29° 12′, long. 77° 17′.

RUTLAM, in Malwa, the principal place of a district of the same name. It is a large and well-built town, with good bazars. The district contains eighty-eight villages, and yields an annual revenue of 4,50,000 rupees, or 45,000*l*. The rajah who holds it as tributary to Scindia, is descended from Ruttun Singh, a scion of the Rajpoot family of Joudpore, who, about the middle of the seventeenth century, received a grant of the place from Shah Jehan, the emperor of Delhi. Though now much humiliated, he retains influence over a considerable Rajpoot population, and in 1819 succeeded, on a few days' notice, in assembling 1,200 mounted combatants to resist Scindia's claim of tribute. On that occasion, the British government interfered, and enforced an arrangement, by which it guaranteed the annual payment of 84,000 Salim Shabee rupees (about 66,000 Company's rupees) to Scindia, and freedom from molestation or interference to the Rutlam rajah. The population of the town is about 10,000; that of the district, inclusive of Sillana, is computed at 91,728. The area of the territory, as above, is stated to be 936 square miles. The military force of the state amounts to about 800 men. Elevation of the town above the sea 1,577 feet. Distant 50 miles W. of Oojein, 288 S.W. of Gwalior fort. Lat. 23° 19′, long. 75° 1′.

RUTMOO.—A river, or rather a great torrent, of the British district of Saharunpoor, has its origin on the south-western declivity of the Sewalik range, about lat. 30° 10′, long. 78° 2′. It holds a course of about thirty-five miles in a southerly direction, to its confluence with the Solani, in lat. 29° 50′, long. 78°. The body of water in the Rutmoo in time of flood must be very considerable, as, where the passage of the stream crosses the Ganges Canal, a dam has been constructed, with forty central openings of ten feet each, and two side openings of 100 feet each, with flank overfalls, while a regulating bridge is built across the canal, to exclude the waters of the river during the floods.

RUTNAGHERRY, a collectorate of the presidency of Bombay, is bounded on the north by the Hubsies' territory and the collectorate of Tannah; on the south by Sawunt Warree and the Portuguese territory of Goa; on the east by Sattara and Kolapore; and on the west by the Arabian Sea. It extends from north lat. 15° 44′ to 18° 6′, and from east long. 73° 6′ to 73° 58′. Its greatest length from north to south is 167 miles; its greatest breadth from east to west forty miles. Its area is 3,964 square miles. The population is given under the article BOMBAY. The quantity of arable land in the collectorate is small; and from this cause, as well as from the advantage of water-carriage afforded by the numerous creeks which intersect the country, and enable the ryot to find a ready market for his produce, the comparative breadth of cultivation is considerable. On this account, the extreme of want is seldom experienced in this district: while, however, many facilities exist for internal communication, the Concan labours under the disadvantage of being shut out from the Deccan by the Syadree range, which is a vaste obstacle to traffic. Down various parts of this range, the different ghauts or passes communicate with the seacoast, and these, under the native government, were kept by the farmers of the transit-duties in sufficient repair for the passage of bullocks. The transit-duties being now abolished, there is no person directly interested in the repair, and for the most part these avenues of communication between the upper and lower country from the harbour of Bombay, as far south as Malwan, are in a wretched state. There are two exceptions: the "Rotunda Ghaut," leading from Mhar to Sattara, over the Mahabulishwar range, and the "Koombarlee Ghaut," leading from Chiploon to the Deccan, south of Sattara, which was converted into a good bridle-road in 1824, and has been since kept in tolerable repair. The passes of most importance to the well-being of the Concan, independently of the two above specified, are the "Anus Koora Ghaut," which leads to Rajapoor, the town of greatest trade probably in the collectorate, and the principal ghaut leading to Malwan, that of "Bhowda." The former of these is a very important one, probably the most important of any south of the Bhore Ghaut. Were it passable for carts, it would open to the coast a large district, extending along both banks of the Krishna, as far east as Bagulkote and Beejapoor, a rich district, a large portion of the trade of which still passes by this ghaut. Great as has been the relief to the trade of the country from the abolition of transit-duties in 1837, and of sayer-taxes in 1844, greater relief, and a greater impetus to trade, would, in the judgment of competent authority, have been afforded, as regards this district, had those taxes been retained, and their proceeds expended on roads and bridges between the countries separated by the Ghauts. At present, trade stagnates for want of adequate means of intercourse; the cost of carriage is greatly increased by the necessity of resorting to the use of pack-bullocks. In unfavourable seasons, when forage is scarce, large droves of cattle can scarcely penetrate into the interior, except at a ruinous cost.

The employment of bullocks in draught, did the road permit it, would effect an extraordinary saving, as two bullocks harnessed to a cart on a fair road would draw an amount of goods which it would require five or six to carry on their backs. The district has suffered much from the ravages of tigers.

The chief products of the country are rice and grain. Attempts have been made to introduce superior descriptions of produce, but they have been attended by very little success. The Mauritius sugarcane has been tried, but to a very small extent; its cultivation is languid, and nearly stationary, the advance being too slight to merit notice. One of the experimental cotton farms was established in Rutnagherry; but the failure was complete, and in 1845 the establishment was abolished. Some advance seems to have been recently made in the culture of hemp. To the growth of flax, the soil and climate appear to be uncontrollably opposed. The plant is a miserable dwarf, and the fibres of the stalk too short and too weak to be of any value to the manufacturer. Rutnagherry, the chief town of the district, is in lat. 17°, long. 73° 20′.

RUTSER, in the British district of Ghazeepoor, lieut.-gov. of the N.W. Provinces, a town near the northern frontier, towards Azimghur, and 35 miles N.E. of Ghazeepoor cantonment. Lat. 25° 50′, long. 84° 8′.

RUTTEEA, in the British district of Hurriana, lieut.-gov. of the N.W. Provinces, a town on the route from Hissar to Ferozepore, 37 miles N. by W. of the former. Lat. 29° 40′, long. 75° 41′.

RUTTOLE, in Sirhind, a village on the route from Hansee to Lodiana, and 30 miles S. of the latter place. Distant N.W. from Calcutta 1,082 miles. Lat. 30° 29′, long. 76°.

RUTTUNGUNJE.—A town in the British district of Bhagulpore, lieut.-gov. of Bengal, 23 miles W.S.W. of Bhagulpore. Lat. 25° 4′, long. 86° 56′.

RUTTUNGURH, in Kuhloor, a fort on the crest of the steep ridge of Malown, and a mile and a half N.W. of that stronghold. During the brief but obstinately-contested war with the Goorkhas, it was occupied by the British troops, and though of inconsiderable size, being substantially built, and very strong by its site, formed a very important position in the operations against Malown. Distant N.W. from Calcutta 1,098 miles. Lat. 31° 14′, long. 76° 51′.

RUTTUNGURH KHEREE, in the territory of Gwalior, or possessions of Sindhia's family, on the route from Neemuch to Boondee, 36 miles N.E. of former, 73 S.W. of the latter. It is of considerable size, and has a bazar. Lat. 24° 49′, long. 75° 13′.

RUTTUNPOOR.—A town in Oude, 11 miles from the right bank of the Gogra river, and 13 miles S. from Oude. Lat. 26° 35′, long. 82° 10′.

RUTTUNPOOR, in the territory of Nagpoor, a town, or rather collection of huts, on the route from Hazaribagh to the city of Nagpoor, 330 miles S.W. of the former, 244 N.E. of the latter. Though the capital of the district of Choteesgurh, Blunt describes it, at the time of his visit fifty years ago, as consisting of about 1,000 huts, a great many of which were desolate. Of the tanks, the largest has been formed by collecting the water by means of an embankment nearly two miles in length. The town is situate in "a champaign country, abundantly watered with little rivers, full of villages, and beautifully ornamented with groves and tanks." It was originally called Rajepour; but was named Ruttunpoor, in honour of Ruttun Singh, once rajah of the place. In A.D. 1744, Bhonsla Raghojee, rajah of Berar, having dispossessed the Gond rajah of Deogarh, gave him a jaghire in Ruttunpoor. In A.D. 1761, after Law and his French followers, supporters of Shah Alum, were discomfited by the British at Patna, a remnant of 120 men, attempting to retreat across the country to the Deccan, were entertained here for a few days by the Mahratta commander of the town, and afterwards treacherously massacred by him. Ruttunpoor is distant S. from Allahabad 220 miles. Lat. 22° 14′, long. 82° 8′.

RUTTURSAW.—A town in the British district of Purneah, lieut.-gov. of Bengal, 34 miles N.W. of Purneah. Lat. 26° 5′, long. 87° 9′.

RUTUNGURH, in the Rajpoot state of Beekaneer, a town near the eastern frontier towards Shekhawutee, on the route from Odeypore to the town of Beekaneer, and 86 miles E. of the latter place. It is surrounded by a low stone wall, and has a small citadel on the top of a sandhill at its south-east angle. The bazars are neatly laid out, and look well. It is the private property of the rajah of Beekaneer, or is khalsa, a term in some measure corresponding to our "crown land." According to Tod, the number of houses is 1,000. Lat. 28° 3′, long. 74° 43′.

RUTUNJUN.—A town in the British district of Sholapoor, presidency of Bombay, 29 miles N. of Sholapoor. Lat. 18° 4′, long. 75° 57′.

RUTUNPOOREE, in the British district of Pillibheet, lieut.-gov. of the N.W. Provinces, a village on the route by Nanakmath and Ruderpoor, from the town of Pillibheet to that of Kashipoor, 25 miles S.E. of the latter. Lat. 29°, long. 79° 21′.

RUTWAH, in the territory of Gwalior, a village on the route from Calpee to the fort of Gwalior, 84 miles W. of former, 40 E. of latter. Lat. 26° 11′, long. 78° 40′.

RUTWUL.—A town in the British district of Sarun, lieut.-gov. of Bengal, 24 miles N.W. of Bettiah. Lat. 27°, long. 84° 17′.

RUXAM.—A town in the British district of Goalpara, lieut.-gov. of Bengal, 20 miles

S.S.W. of Goalpara. Lat. 25° 53′, long. 90° 30′.

RYAGUDDAH.—A town in the hill zemindarry of Jeypoor, situate on the right bank of the Lalglah river, and 72 miles N. from Vizianagrum. Lat. 19° 10′, long. 83° 29′.

RYALPETTAH.—A town in the British district of Cuddapah, presidency of Madras, 80 miles S. of Cuddapah. Lat. 13° 19′, long. 78° 48′.

RYEPOOR, in the territory of Nagpoor, a town on the route from Cuttack to the city of Nagpoor, 348 miles W. of former, 180 E. of latter. It has a large bazar. Though remote from the sea, bulky and heavy articles can be conveyed to its vicinity during the rains by the continuous courses of the Mahanuddee and Sew rivers. Distant from Calcutta, S.W., 465 miles. Lat. 21° 11′, long. 81° 40′.

RYEPOOR, in the territory of Gwalior, or possessions of Scindia's family, a town six miles S.W. of the fort of Gwalior. Lat. 26° 8′, long. 78° 4′.

RYGURH.—A raj within the jurisdiction of the political agent for the south-west frontier of Bengal. The area is 1,421 square miles: the centre is in lat. 22° 10′, long. 83° 30′. The country, a plain, is wild; but the native government being a tolerable one, it is improving, and the people are orderly. The town of Rygurh, which is neat and surrounded by agreeable groves, is in lat. 21° 48′, long. 83° 12′. The country is computed to be worth 20,000 rupees annually; the tribute is only 170 rupees. The population is returned at nearly 64,000.

RYKWARA.—A town in the native state of Oocheyra, 41 miles W. from Rewah, and 95 miles N.W. by N. from Sohagpoor. Lat. 24° 30′, long. 80° 44′.

RYPOOR, in the tract of Baghelcund, in the territory of Rewah, a small town on the route by the Kutra Pass, from Allahabad to Jubbulpore, and 95 miles S.W. of the former. Jacquemont styles it a populous village, the inhabitants of which are in a state of deplorable indigence, and expresses his doubts as to the reported fertility of the surrounding country, which is described by Garden as "undulating, well wooded, highly cultivated, and exceedingly beautiful." There is a bazar, and abundance of water from wells and tanks. Elevation above the sea about 1,100 feet. Lat. 24° 34′, long. 81° 30′.

RYPORA.—A town of Punnah, in the province of Bundelkund, 61 miles S. by W. from Punnah, and eight miles E. from Saugur. Lat. 23° 53′, long. 80°.

S.

SAAR RIVER, in Burmah, an offset of the Yennan, one of the branches of the Irawaddy. It runs in a south-easterly direction, and falls into the Sitang, near the town of Tongo, in lat. 19° 2′, long. 96° 20′.

SAAWAN, in the territory of Gwalior, or possessions of Scindia's family, a town on the route by Bhaupoora and the Muckundura Pass, from Neemuch to Kotah, 13 miles E. of former, 109 S.W. of latter. It has a bazar, and supplies and water are plentiful. Population about 1,800. Lat. 24° 26′, long. 75° 10′.

SABALGURH, in the territory of Gwalior, or possessions of Scindia, a town with a fort of great natural strength, on a hill on the right or south bank of the river Chumbul, 45 miles W. of Gwalior fort. Lat. 26° 15′, long. 77° 24′.

SABAR.—A town in the British district of Dacca, lieut.-gov. of Bengal, 18 miles N.W. of Dacca. Lat. 23° 52′, long. 90° 13′.

SABBAYEA.—A town of Burmah, situate on the right bank of the Irawady river, and 144 miles S.W. by S. from Ava. Lat. 20° 10′, long. 94° 43′.

SABHAWALA, in the British district of Dehra Doon, a village on the left bank of the Asun. Here was a station of the series of small triangles in the trigonometrical survey of the Himalayas. Elevation above the sea 1,792 feet. Lat. 30° 22′, long. 77° 51′.

SABURMUTTEE, a river of Guzerat, rises in lat. 24° 44′, long. 73° 30′, near the town of Mairpoor, in the Rajpoot state of Oodeypoor, and after a course in a southerly direction of about 200 miles, it falls into the Gulf of Cambay, in lat. 22° 20′, long. 72° 21′.

SACKEKAMENG.—A town of Eastern India, in the native state of Muneepoor, situate on the left bank of the Nankatha Khyoung river, and eight miles N.E. from Muneepoor. Lat. 24° 52′, long. 94° 9′.

SACRAPATAM.—A town in the Mysore, 88 miles N.W. from Seringapatam, and 84 miles N.E. by E. from Mangalore. Lat. 13° 26′, long. 75° 59′.

SACUN.—A town in the British district of Sumbulpoor, on the south-west frontier of Bengal, eight miles N. by E. of Sumbulpoor. Lat. 21° 34′, long. 84° 2′.

SADEEPOOR, in the British district of Banda, lieut.-gov. of the N.W. Provinces, a town on the right bank of the Jumna, 26 miles N.E. of the town of Banda, 20 miles S.W. of the town of Futtehpore. Lat. 25° 46′, long. 80° 37′.

SADOOLAPOOR.—A town in the British district of Rungpore, lieut.-gov. of Bengal, 26 miles S.E. by S. of Rungpore. Lat. 25° 22′, long. 89° 29′.

SADRAS, in the British district of Chingleput, presidency of Madras, a town on the Coromandel coast, in this part low and wooded, though inland three or four miles is a range of rugged hills of no great height, called the Sadras Hills. The estuary of the river Palar, three miles to the south, is so obstructed by a bar as to admit only insignificant coasting-craft; and at Sadras there is no haven, so that ships must anchor in the open sea. According to Heber, "Sadras is a large but poor-looking town, once a Dutch settlement, and still containing many families of decayed burghers, the melancholy relics of a ruined factory. Some of them have little pensions from the charity of the British government." Here are still the ruins of a fort, a place of some strength during the possession of the town by the Dutch. Distance from Cuddalore, N., 62 miles; Arcot, S.E., 62; Madras, S., 42. Lat. 12° 31′, long. 80° 13′.

SAEE, in the territory of Oude, a river rising in lat. 27° 10′, long. 80° 32′, about mid-distance between the Goomtee and the Ganges. It holds a very serpentine course, in a direction generally south-east, and falls into the Goomtee, on the right side, ten miles below the town of Jounpore, its total length of course being about 230 miles. It is navigable during the rains for craft carrying from ten to twelve tons as far as Rae Bareilly, 130 miles from its mouth. At Mohaun, about forty miles from its source, it is crossed by a stone bridge. Close to Rae Bareilly is a bridge of brick, over which passes the route from Allahabad to Lucknow. At Pertabghur, sixty miles lower down, it is crossed by the route from Allahabad to Sooltanpore, the passage being made during low water by ford, at other times by ferry. Still lower, and about twenty miles from its mouth, it is crossed on the route from Allahabad to Jounpore, by means of a fine brick-built bridge, which has been recently repaired. It now consists of four arches, each of forty-seven feet span. Wilford observes that this river "is called Sambu and Sucti, and in the spoken dialects Sye, because it abounds with small shells. This," he continues, "is really the case, as I have repeatedly observed whilst surveying or travelling along its banks. They are all fossil, small, and embedded in its banks, and appear here and there, when laid bare by the encroachments of the river: they consist chiefly of cockles and periwinkles." He remarks subsequently, "This river is not mentioned in any Sanscrit book that I ever saw, but I take it to be the Sambus of Megasthenes."

SAEL.—A town in the territory of Nagpoor, 51 miles S. by E. from Ruttunpoor, and 110 miles W. from Sumbulpoor. Lat. 21° 30′, long. 82° 20′.

SAENUGURH, in the territory of Punna, in Bundelcund, a town on the route from Banda to Jubbulpoor, 69 miles N. of the latter. The Garhi, or little fort here, "consists of four stone houses, connected by a wall, very capable of defence if not attacked by artillery." Lat. 23° 55′, long. 80° 20′.

SAFAPOOR.—A town in the dominions of Gholab Singh, the ruler of Cashmere, 14 miles N.W. by N. from Sirinagur. Lat. 34° 14′, long. 74° 49′.

SAFTIBAREE.—A town in the British district of Rungpore, lieut.-gov. of Bengal, 14 miles N.E. by N. of Rungpore. Lat. 25° 51′, long. 89° 22′.

SAGGOUR.—A town in the native state of Bonei, on the south-west frontier of Bengal, 86 miles E.N.E. from Sumbulpoor, and 110 miles N.N.W. from Cuttack. Lat. 21° 55′, long. 85° 15′.

SAGOR, in the territory of Indore, or possessions of Holkar's family, a small town on the route from the British cantonment of Mow to Baroda, 12 miles W. of former. Elevation above the sea 1,932 feet. Lat. 22° 36′, long. 75° 40′.

SAHANGURREE.—A town in the territory of Nagpoor, 60 miles E. by S. from Nagpoor, and 78 miles S. by E. from Seuni. Lat. 20° 59′, long. 80° 3′.

SAHAPOOR, in the British district of Moradabad, lieut.-gov. of the N.W. Provinces, a village on the route from the town of Meerut to that of Moradabad, and 36 miles S.E. of the former place. Lat. 28° 50′, long. 78° 18′.

SAHDUREE.—A town in the Rajpoot state of Oodeypoor, 51 miles E.S.E. from Oodeypoor, and 23 miles W. by S. from Neemuch. Lat. 24° 21′, long. 74° 33′.

SAHDUREE.—A town in the Rajpoot state of Oodeypoor, 62 miles E.S.E. from Oodeypoor, and 13 miles S.W. by W. from Neemuch. Lat. 24° 20′, long. 74° 43′.

SAHEB GUNJ.—A town in the British district of Tirhoot, lieut.-gov. of Bengal, 30 miles W.N.W. of Mozufferpoor. Lat. 26° 14′, long. 85°.

SAHEEWAL, in the Jetch Dooab division of the Punjab, a town situated on the left bank of the Jhelum river, 119 miles W. by N. of the town of Lahore. Lat. 31° 58′, long. 72° 21′.

SAHGANJ, or SAEGANJ, in the district of Pachhamrat, territory of Oude, a town three miles S.W. of the right bank of the Tons (North-eastern). It is surrounded by two mud walls, one within the other, a ditch of six feet deep intervening. Distant S.E. of Lucknow 78 miles. Lat. 26° 37′, long. 82° 2′.

SAHI, in the hill state of Hindoor, a village and halting-place on the route from Subathoo to Belaspoor, and 18 miles N.W. of the former. Lat. 31° 7′, long. 76° 56′.

SAHINSPOOR, a village in the British district of Dehra Doon, is situate on the right bank of the Asun. It was a secondary station in the great trigonometrical survey of the Himalayas. Elevation above the sea 1,754 feet. Lat. 30° 24′, long. 77° 52′.

SAHJADPUR, in the district of Aldemau, territory of Oude, a town a mile S.W. of the right bank of the river Tons (North-eastern), 100 miles E. of Lucknow. According to Butter, the population is 3,000 of whom two-thirds are Mussulmans, principally weavers. Lat. 26° 26′, long. 82° 28′.

SAH KHAS, in the British district of Futtehpoor, lieut.-gov. of the N.W. Provinces, a town situate on the route from the town of Futtehpore to Banda, and seven miles S.W. of the former. Lat. 25° 53′, long. 80° 46′.

SAHLAYDAN.—A town in the British territory of Pegu, situate on the right bank of the Irawady river, and 16 miles S.W. by S. from Prome. Lat. 18° 35′, long. 94° 54′.

SAHUNPOOR, in the British district of Bijnour, lieut.-gov. of the N.W. Provinces, a town on the route from Moradabad to Hurdwar, and 64 miles N.W. of the former. Lat. 29° 38′, long. 78° 23′.

SAHUSPOOR.—A town in the British district of Sumbulpoor, south-west frontier of Bengal, 11 miles S.S.E. of Sumbulpoor. Lat. 21° 20′, long. 84° 5′.

SAIDABAD, in the British district of Muttra, lieut.-gov. of the N.W. Provinces, a town on the route from Agra to Aligurh, and 21 miles N. of the former. Lat. 27° 26′, long. 78° 6′.

SAIGURH, in the territory of Oude, a village on the route from Lucknow cantonment to Pertabgurh, 80 miles S.E. of the former, 30 N.W. of the latter. Water and supplies are plentiful: the road in this part of the route is good. Lat. 26° 18′, long. 81° 30′.

SAIN, in Sirmour, a range of mountains stretching in a direction from north-west to south-east, between the river Julal, flowing along its south-western, and the Giri, along its eastern base. It is entirely of limestone, the course of the Giri forming the bounding line between that formation and the slate farther north. Fraser states that its height was usually conjectured to be about 8,000 feet; but he considers that amount too great, and adds that between 6,000 and 7,000 is more probable. The range stretches about twenty-five miles in length, between lat. 30° 37′—30° 51′, long. 77° 15′—77° 29′.

SAINJ, a river of Kuloo, rises in lat. 32° 2′, long. 77° 40′, and, flowing south-west for thirty-eight miles, falls into the Beas, in lat. 31° 43′, long. 76° 16′.

SAINT MARTIN ISLAND, off the coast of Arracan, is formed of two divisions united by a dry ledge of rocks, near the east side of the island. There is anchorage in five or six fathoms, where ships may procure fresh water from the springs on the island. Lat. 20° 36′, long. 92° 25′.

SAINT THOMAS'S MOUNT, in the British district of Chingleput, presidency of Madras, a military station at the foot of a hill, the most northern and least elevated of a small range running parallel to the Coromandel coast, and about five miles west of it. "The cantonment is laid out at the base of the eastern and southern sides of the hill from which it takes its name, and occupies a surface of 750 acres. The barracks and most of the buildings have an eastern aspect, and are open to the genial influence of the sea-breeze." It is the principal station and head-quarters of the Madras artillery. The Adyar river, which in the monsoon season has a considerable body of water, but is nearly dry at other times, is at the distance of a mile north of the cantonment, and there are numerous tanks scattered throughout the neighbouring country. The geological formation of the hill is syenite and greenstone, and its summit, 340 feet above the level of the sea, is surmounted by a small range of buildings, including a Roman Catholic chapel and appropriate establishment, under the jurisdiction of the Portuguese archbishop of Goa. According to tradition, the hill called Little Saint Thomas's Mount was the scene of the martyrdom of Saint Thomas, whose apostolic toils are thought to have extended thus far. The native population of Saint Thomas's Mount, exclusive of the military establishment, amounted in 1837, according to official statement, to 17,720 persons; 3,500 being Mussulmans. Distance from Madura, N.E., 252 miles; Tanjore, N., 170; Cuddalore, N., 95; Bangalore, E., 178; Madras, S.W., 10. Lat. 13°, long. 80° 15′.

ST. THOME, in the British district of Chingleput, presidency of Madras, a town on the Coromandel coast, at the bottom of a small bay. From time immemorial, this town, called by the natives Mailapur, is crowded every year with pilgrims from various parts of Asia, including Syria, Palestine, and Armenia, eager to visit the spot where, according to tradition, St. Thomas the apostle suffered martyrdom. The generally alleged scene of the martyrdom is a small mount near the petty fort of St. Thome or Mailapur, and is now included within the suburbs of Madras, in consequence of the extension of the city in that direction. Others, however, maintain that the apostle was martyred at St. Thomas's Mount, rising over the military cantonment of that name. According to the traditions of the native Christians, St. Thomas, having preached Christianity in Arabia, the island of Socotra, and Malabar, proceeded to the Coromandel coast, and having succeeded in making many proselytes at Mailapur, excited the violent jealousy and resentment of the Brahmins, at whose instigation he was stoned to death by the populace, and buried on the mount. The place was taken in the year 1547 by the Portuguese, who named it St. Thome, instead of Mailapur, or "City of Peacocks." During the ascendancy of this nation in India, it became a place of considerable importance. Lat. 13° 2′, long. 80° 18′.

SAIPOOR, or SHAHIPUR.—A town in the native state of Rewah. It is situate on the river Rhern, a tributary of the Sone, 90 miles S. of Benares, 170 W. of Hazareebagh, 409 W. of Calcutta. Lat. 24° 3′, long. 82° 45′.

SAJAPOOR, in the jaghire of Sumpter, in Bundelkund, a town 12 miles N.W. of the left bank of the river Betwa. Here, in Dec. 1817, the British army commanded by the Marquis of Hastings, Governor-General, encamped, in the course of its advance towards Gwalior, to intimidate Sciudia. Distant S.W. of Calpee 75 miles. Lat. 25° 46′, long. 78° 53′.

SAKKEYMOUN.—A town in the British territory of Pegu, situate on the left bank of the Irawady river, and 52 miles S.S.E. from Prome. Lat. 18° 6′, long. 95° 21′.

SAKOON.—A town in the Rajpoot state of Jeypoor, 49 miles W.S.W. from Jeypoor, and 34 miles N.E. by E. from Ajmeer. Lat. 26° 42′, long. 75° 11′.

SAKOOR.—A town in Hyderabad, 72 miles S. by E. from Ellichpoor, and 31 miles N.W. from Mahur. Lat. 20° 10′, long. 77° 40′.

SAKUM, in the Reechna Dooab division of the Punjab, a town situated 14 miles from the right bank of the Ravee, 18 miles N.W. by N. of the town of Lahore. Lat. 31° 49′, long. 74° 8′.

SALAGRA.—See GUNDUCK.

SALAGRAM.—A town in the Mysore, 32 miles W.N.W. from Seringapatam, and 77 miles N.E. from Cannanore. Lat. 12° 35′, long. 76° 18′.

SALAON, or SALON, the principal town of the district of the same name, in the territory of Oude, is situate close to the right bank of the river Saee. It belongs to a proprietor, who, though denominated fakir, has an annual income of 30,000 rupees; out of which reserving 1,200 for his personal wants, he expends the remainder on the maintenance of Hindoo and Mussulman religious mendicants, without distinction of tenets. The population is estimated by Butter at 4,000, of whom 1,000 are Hindoo cultivators, the rest Mussulmans. Lat. 26° 2′, long. 81° 30′.

SALBY, or SALBYE.—A town in the territory of Gwalior, or the possessions of Scindia's family, 32 miles S.E. of the fort of Gwalior. Here, in 1782, was concluded a treaty between the Mahratta states and the British government, unfavourable on the whole to the latter, but making to them an unqualified transfer of Salsette and two or three islands of minor importance, as well as confirming a previous assignment of the Mahratta claims in regard to the city of Broach. Lat. 25° 50′, long. 78° 16′.

SALEEHATTA.—A town on the south-west frontier of Bengal, in the petty native state of Patna, situate on the left bank of the Aurag river, and 42 miles S.W. by S. from Sumbulpoor. Lat. 21°, long. 83° 39′.

SALEM, a British district under the presidency of Madras, named from its principal place, is bounded on the north by Mysore and the northern division of Arcot; on the east by the northern and southern divisions of Arcot; on the south and south-east by Trichinopoly; on the south-west by Coimbatore; and on the west by the last-named district and by Mysore. It lies between lat. 11° 2′—12° 54′, and long. 77° 32′—79°; the area is returned at 8,200 square miles. The western part of the district, bordering on Mysore and the British district of Coimbatore, is very mountainous, and some of the ranges attain an elevation of between 5,000 and 6,000 feet above the level of the sea. "The Juvenaddy Mountains are situate on the eastern side of the Baramahal, the Sheevaroy near the town of Salem, the Patchamally in the talook of Ahtoor, and the Collemally and Shendamungalum range in the south-eastern corner of the district. All these hills are inhabited and extensively cultivated, and produce abundance of teak, sandal-wood, and black-wood." The river Cauvery touches on this district at its north-western angle, and flowing first south-eastward, and subsequently southward, forms the western and south-western boundary of this district towards Coimbatore for 140 miles. It passes into Trichinopoly, and ultimately falls into the Bay of Bengal. The general drainage of the country is southward and south-westward into the river Cauvery; and of the streams taking this course, the principal is the Tyromany, flowing by the town of Salem. A few streams in the eastern part of the district flow northward or north-eastward, and discharge themselves into the Palar, which flows through a portion of the northern part of the collectorate. There are no considerable lakes in this district, but tanks or artificial pieces of water are very common; and during the rains, much of the country becomes swampy, and productive of malaria. Wells are very numerous, and water is generally found within a short distance of the surface; but it is brackish and not perfectly wholesome. The climate, owing to the great difference of elevations, varies considerably: on the hills it is cold and bracing, and for a great part of the year very salubrious. The qualities of the soil differ much; in the country immediately surrounding the town of Salem, a thin layer of calcareous and red loam generally prevailing, through which quartz rocks appear on the surface in many places. Native carbonate of magnesia is found in a stony barren plain about five miles to the north-west of Salem, and is used in forming an excellent cement, as well as in the preparation of sulphate of magnesia, and also in obtaining pure magnesia. In the southern part of the district there is much iron-ore, which, on reduction, yields sixty per cent. of the metal fit for castings. Cotton is the principal commercial crop, and comprises the indigenous, the Bourbon, the American, and the Nankin. Coffee, indigo, sugar, and tobacco are also cultivated. An experiment, conducted by the authority of government in this district in 1843, for the improvement of the manufacture of sugar from the cane, is stated to have been successful. The population is stated to amount to 1,195,377.

SALEM.—The principal place of the British

district of the same name, under the presidency of Madras. "It lies in the lowest and narrowest part of a valley about seven miles in width, formed by the Sheevaroy hills to the northward, and a smaller and undistinguished range to the southward. This valley is prolonged about five miles from Salem in an easterly direction, when, by the termination of the smaller hills, the country again becomes open. Westward, the country is generally open, the only exceptions being occasional small insulated hills."

The climate is somewhat fluctuating and uncertain, "the thermometer having been found to range in December from 60° to 87°; in January from 58° to 82°; in February from 60° to 91°; and in March from 66° to 95°: in the two succeeding months the variation is less, being in April from 72° to 95°, and in May from 75° to 96°. Early in June, the monsoon from the western coast generally extends to Salem in short but heavy and frequent showers, attended with thunder and lightning, continuing till late in September; by the end of October, rain begins to fall from the north-east monsoon, and showers recur with a very clouded sky till the middle of December. Between June and December, the extremes of the thermometer are 68° and 90°." A north-easterly wind prevails pretty steadily at Salem from the beginning of November to the end of January or middle of February, which is for the first two months after it sets in rather moist, cool, and agreeable; but becomes more and more arid as the season advances, blowing from the mountains which bound Salem on the north. In January the wind becomes disagreeably cold in the morning, and unpleasantly warm at noon, being dry and parching at both periods. It produces even in people in health an annoying dryness of the skin, and exposure to it seems a frequent exciting cause of fever. After the middle or end of February, the wind, which is at times variable with frequent lulls, shifts round to the south and south-west, and blows from that quarter in hot puffs and with much uncertainty during April and May. Cooled by the rains of the south-west monsoon, this wind blows pretty freshly in June and July, and more moderately in the two following months. In October the wind becomes again variable, till the setting in of the north-east monsoon."

The river Tiromany, which holds its course down the valley, sweeps along the north and west sides of the town, and is traversed by a substantial bridge of three arches. On the western bank of the river, and rather to the south of the town, stands the old mud fort of Salem, the ramparts of which have been partially thrown down and the ditch filled up. It is now inhabited chiefly by the peons, or local irregular infantry. The houses of the few Europeans resident here are at some distance west of the fort. The old jail, situate on a slightly-elevated rocky site on the right bank of the river, is a heavy bomb-proof building, with thick and strong walls of brick and chunam: the new jail is situate on the left bank of the river. There is a small military detachment stationed at this place. There are many handsome choultries or public lodges for travellers; and Salem may be considered a well-built town for this part of India, there being two wide principal streets, which run from east to west. The number of houses is 3,821, the population 19,021. Elevation above the sea 1,070 feet. Distance from Bangalore, S.E., 100 miles; Madras, S.W., 170. Lat. 11° 39′, long. 78° 12′.

SALHANA.—A town in the British district of Shikarpoor, province of Scinde, presidency of Bombay, 20 miles S. of Shikarpoor. Lat. 27° 44′, long. 68° 37′.

SALIMPUR, in the territory of Oude, a village on the route from Lucknow cantonment to Purtabgurh, 26 miles S.E. of the former, 84 N.W. of the latter. Lat. 26° 45′, long. 81° 4′.

SALLYMAUN, in the Reechna Dooab division of the Punjab, a town situated on the left bank of the Chenaub, 88 miles W. by S. of the town of Lahore. Lat. 31° 33′, long. 72° 29′.

SALMOORA KAPALEE.—A town in Nepal, situate on the left bank of one of the branches of the Gunduck river, and 144 miles W. by N. from Khatmandoo. Lat. 28° 4′, long. 83°.

SALPEE GHAT.—A town in the British territory of Sattara, presidency of Bombay, 23 miles N.N.E. of Sattara. Lat. 17° 59′, long. 74° 14′.

SALSEE.—A town in the British district of Rutnageriah, presidency of Bombay, 50 miles S.S.E. of Rutnageriah. Lat. 16° 20′, long. 73° 39′.

SALSETTE, in the presidency of Bombay, an island separated by a narrow channel from the island of Bombay on the south, and from the mainland on the east, but connected with the former by an arched stone bridge, and likewise by the Bandora and Makim Causeway, more recently constructed at the joint expense of government and Sir Jamsetjee Jejeebhoy. Communication between the two islands and the mainland is also now afforded by means of the Bombay and Callian railroad. It lies between lat. 19° and 19° 18′, long. 72° 54′—73° 3′; is eighteen miles in length from south-west to north-east, and ten in breadth: the area is about 150 square miles. It is a beautiful, picturesque, and well-wooded tract, its surface being much diversified by hills and mountains, some of considerable elevation, while the lower grounds and valley are very fertile, though in some places inadequately cultivated. The eminence of Keneri, in the middle of the island, "commands an extensive view; the island of Salsette appears like a map around the spectator, presenting a fine champaign of rice-fields, cocoa-groves, villages, and cattle, woody hills, and fertile vales; the surrounding mountains form a foreground of grey rocks, covered with trees, or hollowed into gloomy caverns, the haunt of tigers, serpents, bats, and bees in immense swarms. The horizon is bounded on the south by the island of Bombay, with the harbour and shipping; east by the continent; north by Bassein and the adjacent mountains; and west by the ocean. In various parts of Salsette are romantic views, embellished by the ruins of Portuguese churches, convents, and villas, once large and splendid, but suffered to decay since the Mahrattas conquered the island." According to conjecture of rather recent date, the population amounts to 50,000; an amount which would fix the relative density at 333 to the square mile. Salsette contains several antiquities, especially at Keneri, in the centre of the island.

Salsette was attached to the province of Aurungabad under the Mogul rule, but fell into the hands of the Portuguese at an early period of their Indian career. It was claimed by the English as an appendage of Bombay, under the marriage-treaty with Charles II.; but the Portuguese authorities denied its being a dependency of that island, and refused to surrender it to the expedition which, in 1662, arrived on the western coast of India to receive possession of the territory ceded as the marriage-portion of the Queen Catherine. The British, not being in a condition to enforce their claims, were necessitated to be content with such portion of territory as the Portuguese chose to part with, and to submit to their construction of the terms of the treaty. In 1739, the island was taken from the Portuguese by the Mahrattas. In 1774 it again changed masters, being conquered by the British, who retained possession of it, under the additional clause of the treaty of Poorunder, until 1782, when it was solemnly and finally confirmed to them in perpetuity by the treaty of Salbye.

SALT RANGE.—An extensive group of mountains stretching generally, in lat. 32° 30′—33° 20′, in a direction from west to east, from the eastern base of the Suliman Mountains to the river Jhelum, in the Punjab. This range is, in different parts, known to the natives under various denominations, but is by Europeans comprehended under the general term Salt Range, in consequence of the great extent and thickness of the beds of common salt which it in many places contains. Though the southern part of this group terminates rather abruptly at the west bank of the Jhelum, the more northern part is, according to Jameson, connected with the recent formation constituting the lowest and most southern range of the Himalaya, and runs "on by Bimber, Jummoo, Nurpoor, and down by the south of Belaspoor, crossing the Jumna at Fyzabad, and the Ganges at Hurdwar." The general direction of the range is from north-west to south-east.

This extensive range, of recent formation, may consequently be considered to contain not only the saliferous deposits of Kala-Bagh and Pind Dadun Khan, but also those of Mundi, in the north-east of the Punjab. The salt-mines have been long known, being mentioned in the Ayeen Akbery. At the time of the visit of Burnes, in 1832, the total quantity of salt raised in a year amounted to 80,000,000 pounds. The elevation of the Salt Range is not considerable, and probably no summit attains the height of 2,500 feet above the sea. Burnes states that these mountains contain alum, antimony, and sulphur. Jacquemont, Burnes, and Wood, obtained numerous specimens of coal from various parts of them.

The Salt Range is remarkably barren:—"Vegetation is scanty, and the bold and bare precipices, some of which rise at once from the plain, present a forbidding aspect of desolation." About lat. 32° 50′, long. 71° 40′, the Indus traverses this range, making its way down a deep, narrow, rocky channel, on the sides of which the salt-beds come to light. Those parts of the range which lie on the west side of the river are denominated by Macartney the Salt-hills of Kala-Bagh or Karra-Bagh, from the name of the town where its geological structure is most fully exposed to view. Its appearance there is thus described by Elphinstone:—"As we passed beneath, we perceived windows and balconies at a great height, crowded with women and children. The road beyond was cut out of the solid salt at the foot of cliffs of that mineral, in some places more than 100 feet high above the river. The salt is hard, clear, and almost pure. It would be like crystal, were it not in some parts streaked and tinged with red. In some places salt-springs issue from the foot of the rocks, and leave the ground covered with a crust of the most brilliant whiteness. All the earth, particularly near the town, is almost blood-red, and this, with the strange and beautiful spectacle of the salt-rocks, and the Indus flowing in a deep and clear stream through lofty mountains past this extraordinary town, presented such a scene of wonder as is seldom to be witnessed."

The rocks in this part of the range are—first, magnesian limestone; second, new red sandstone; third, fossiliferous sandstone; fourth, red clay and sandstone, containing coal and mineral sulphur, rock-salt, gypsum, brown and red iron-ore, and alum-slate. The lower beds contain no organic remains, but the upper abound in them. The iron-ore is a red or brown hematite, so rich that in many places the needle of the compass becomes quite useless, even at a considerable distance from the rocks, owing to their being highly magnetic, from the quantity of iron which they contain. The sandstone abounds with the exuviæ of enormous animals, either saurians or sauroid fishes. Most of the torrents of the Salt Range carry down gold-dust in their sands, which are washed, in search of the precious deposit, in numerous places, throughout the greater part of the year. The hills at Kala-Bagh contain great quantities of aluminous slate, from which alum is obtained at various manufactories in that town. The slate, well sprinkled with water, is laid in alternate strata with wood, until the pile reaches a height of from twenty-five to thirty feet; it is then lighted, and the combustion continued for about twelve hours, in which time the colour of the slate is converted from greyish black to dark red. This change of colour indicating that the process has been carried to a sufficient extent, the mass is thrown into a tank holding as much water as it is computed the alum is competent to saturate. After three days, the water, which becomes of a dark-red colour, is drawn off, mixed with a due proportion of potash, and boiled down, the residuum on cooling becoming a solid mass of alum. Dr. Jameson expatiates with the earnestness of sanguine excitement on the mineral wealth of the Salt Range, concluding in these terms:—"Such is a rapid account of the riches of this district; and there are few, if any, districts in the world where iron, gold, sulphur, salt, gypsum, limestone, saltpetre, and coal, are met with in such quantity."

SALUR.—A town in the British district of Vizagapatam, presidency of Madras, 58 miles N. of Vizagapatam. Lat. 18° 32′, long. 83° 16′.

SALWEEN.—The largest river in the Tenasserim provinces. Its source has never been visited by Europeans, but it appears to take its rise about lat. 27° 10′, long. 98° 57′, to the north of the Chinese province of Yunnan, where it is known by the name of Lookeang. It takes a southerly course, passing through the provinces of Laos and Siam, enters the British dominions at the confluence of the river Thon-khan, about lat. 18° 40′, and, after a long course, unites its waters with those of the Gyne and Attaran rivers at Martaban, and enters the sea by two mouths, formed by the island of Belu. The northern mouth is in lat. 16° 25′, long. 97° 29′.

SAMANA.—A town of Sirhind, in the native state of Patialah, 16 miles S.W. from Patialah, and 34 miles S.W. by W. from Ambala. Lat. 30° 10′, long. 76° 20′.

SAMANUGUR.—A town in the British district of Silhet, lieut.-gov. of Bengal, 31 miles W. by S. of Silhet. Lat. 24° 50′, long. 91° 21′.

SAMARSÉE, a river of Central India, rises in lat. 21° 50′, long. 77° 53′, in the territory of Nagpoor, and, flowing north-west for sixty miles, through Nagpoor and the Saugor and Nerbudda territories, falls into the Nerbudda, in lat. 22° 46′, long. 77° 49′.

SAMB, in the British district of Seuni, territory of Saugur and Nerbudda, lieut.-gov. of the N.W. Provinces, a town on the route from Jubbulpoor to the Nagpoor territory, 76 miles S. by E. of the former. Lat. 22° 5′, long. 80° 16′.

SAMBHAM.—A town in the British district of Vizagapatam, presidency of Madras, 49 miles N.N.E. of Vizagapatam. Lat. 18° 20′, long. 83° 40′.

SAMBHUR LAKE, in Rajpootana, partly in the state of Jyepore, partly in that of Joudpore, lies on the western boundary of the former, and on the eastern of the latter. According to Boileau's map of Northern Rajwara, it lies between lat. 26° 52′—27°, long. 74° 49′—75° 18′; is twenty-two miles in length from east to west, six in breadth, and about fifty in circuit; but in times of very great moisture the length is thirty miles, and the breadth ten miles. Those are the dimensions during the periodical rains of autumn, when the saltness of the water is much diminished; but during the hot and dry season the greater part of the water evaporates, and a great quantity of salt is found crystallized on the bottom of the lake. The salt is exposed to the sun, to be perfectly dried and hardened, and though at first of reddish hue, becomes in the course of the process very clear and of fine flavour. The western part belongs to the state of Joudpore, the eastern to that of Jyepore, and its produce is monopolized by those governments, which dispose of it on the spot, at the rate of a rupee, or two shillings, for a bullock-load of 375 pounds, according to regulation. The revenue derived from the Jyepore division of the lake was placed under British management, to defray the expenses incurred by the military operations in Shekhawutee, but was released from sequestration upon the liquidation of the debt. The town of Sambhur is situate on the south bank of the lake. Lat. 26° 53′, long. 75° 13′.

SAMBRANI.—A town in the British district of North Canara, presidency of Madras, 37 miles N. of Soonda. Lat. 15° 14′, long. 74° 49′.

SAMBUL.—A town within the dominions of Gholab Singh, the ruler of Cashmere, 12 miles N.W. from Sirinagur. Lat. 34° 11′, long. 74° 47′.

SAMBURA, in the Rajpoot state of Jodhpoor, a village on the route from Balmeer to the city of Jodhpoor, and 58 miles E. of the former. It is situate three miles N. of the right bank of the Loonee, in a low swampy country, liable to be laid under water by the inundation of that river in the rainy season, when the road becomes heavy and difficult. Lat. 25° 55′, long. 72° 19′.

SAMER.—A town in the native state of Gwalior, or territory of Scindia, 20 miles N. by W. from Indoor, and 14 miles S. from Oojein. Lat. 22° 57′, long. 75° 48′.

SAMIWALA, in the British district of Bijnour, lieut.-gov. of the N.W. Provinces, a village on the route from Moradabad to Hurdwar, and 22 miles S.W. of the latter. The road in this part of the route is good, and passes over a fertile country, much intersected by streams and watercourses. Lat. 29° 42′, long. 78° 18′.

SAMOT, in the Rajpoot state of Jeypore, a considerable town on the route from Delhi to Mow, 143 miles S.W. of former, 364 N.E. of latter. It is situate at the base of a fortified hill, and is surrounded by a rampart. Lat. 27° 13′, long. 75° 54′.

SAMPLUH, in the British district of Rohtuk, lieut.-gov. of the N.W. Provinces, a village on the route from Delhi to Hansee, and 30 miles N.W. of the former. Lat. 28° 46′, long. 76° 49′.

SAMRA, in the British district of Agra, lieut.-gov. of the N.W. Provinces, a town on the route from Agra to Jeypoor, 32 miles W. by S. of the former. Lat. 27° 5′, long. 77° 37′.

SAMULCOTTAH, in the British district of Rajahmundry, presidency of Madras, a town, with military cantonment, situate on the right side of a torrent which falls into the Bay of Bengal ten miles to the south-east. The torrent is devoid of water during a great part of the year, but in the wet season is full from bank to bank, though at all times fordable. The cantonment is situate to the north-west of the village, and contains an area of about three-quarters of a mile in diameter. The barracks and sepoys' lines are stated to be judiciously placed, but the hospital is represented as in an objectionable situation, and the officers' houses are said to be badly arranged and badly built. This place came into the possession of the East-India Company by cession from the Nizam, in 1766. Elevation above the sea seventy feet; distance from Rajahmundry, E., 25 miles; Hydrabad, E., 245; Bangalore, N.E., 410; Ellore, N.E., 75; Madras, N., 300; Calcutta, S.W., 550. Lat. 17° 4′, long. 82° 14′.

SAMUREA, in the British district of Bareilly, division of Pillibheet, lieut.-gov. of the N.W. Provinces, a village on the route from Bareilly to Petoragurh, and 41 miles N.E. of the former. Lat. 28° 44′, long. 79° 52′.

SANAH.—A town in the British district of Mongheir, lieut.-gov. of Bengal, 40 miles S. by W. of Mongheir. Lat. 24° 48′, long. 86° 20′.

SANAULI, in the British district of Ghazeepoor, lieut.-gov. of the N.W. Provinces, a village on the right bank of the Ganges, 25 miles S. of Ghazeepoor cantonment by water, 14 by land; 624 N.W. of Calcutta by water. Lat. 25° 25′, long. 83° 28′.

SANCHORI, in the Rajpoot state of Jodhpoor, a village on the route from Nusseerabad to Deesa, and 132 miles S.W. of the former. It contains eighty-five houses, supplied with water from a tank and twelve wells. Lat. 25° 26′, long. 73° 25′.

SAN COOS RIVER.—The name given to the Coosy in the upper part of its course.—See COOSY.

SANDAH.—A town in the British district of Patna, lieut.-gov. of Bengal, 19 miles S.S.W. of Patna. Lat. 25° 19′, long. 85° 8′.

SANDAIRA, in the Rajpoot state of Jodhpoor, a town on the route from Nusseerabad to Deesa, and 144 miles S.W. of the former. It is abundantly supplied with water from wells. Lat. 25° 17′, long. 73° 17′.

SANDI, in the territory of Oude, a small town on the route, by Shahabad, from Shahjehanpore to Lucknow, 85 miles N.W. of the latter. Tennant, who by a whimsical English corruption calls it Sandy Point, complains of "the bleak, desolate, and dreary aspect of the country; where you are constantly sinking at every step in loose sand, and blinded by showers of dust;" yet he admits, that where irrigation can be practised, good crops of grain could be produced. This tract must have much improved since that description was written (1799), as Heber, who traversed it in 1824, says: "The country through which we passed to-day was extremely pretty, undulating, with scattered groves of tall trees, and some extensive lakes, which still showed a good deal of water. The greater part of the space between the wood was in green wheat, but there were round the margins of the lake some tracts of brushwood, and beautiful silky jungle-grass, eight or ten feet high." Tennant, however, travelled through the country in the dry season, Heber a short time after the close of the rains. This last traveller describes the place itself at present, as "a poor little village," and its neighbourhood infested by a race of very bad character. In the driest season of the year the water of the lake totally evaporates, and its bed then becomes a luxuriant pasture; water is, however, at all times plentiful, and there is a bazar. Lat. 27° 18′, long. 80° 1′.

SANDOWAY.—A town in the British province of Arracan, lieut.-gov. of Bengal, situate on the southern bank of a tide nullah, bearing the same name as the town, and distant ten miles from the sea. The town is comprised within a circular area, open on the east and west, where are the defiles through which the river flows. It contains about 500 houses, and was occupied by the British in 1825. The district of which this town is the chief place, forms one of the three divisions of Arracan; 176 miles S.S.E. of Arracan. Lat. of town 18° 25′, long. 94° 30′.

SANDWA.—A town in the Rajpoot state of Beekaneer, 58 miles E. by S. from Beekaneer, and 93 miles N.N.W. from Ajmeer. Lat. 27° 45′, long. 74° 17′.

SANDY ISLAND.—A small island off the coast of Arracan, 80 miles N. of Cape Negrais. Lat. 17° 11′, long. 94° 31′.

SANEE, a river of Gurhwal, rises in lat. 30° 6′, long. 79° 12′, and flowing southerly for thirty miles, and north-west for thirty-two, falls into the Bhagerettee river, in lat. 30° 4′, long. 78° 39′.

SANGAMOOLASA.— A town in the British district of Vizagapatam, presidency of Madras, 77 miles N. of Vizagapatam. Lat. 18° 48′, long. 83° 27′.

SANGANEER, in the territory of Oodeypore, a town on the route from Neemuch to Nusseerabad, 74 miles N. of former, 69 S. of latter. It is of considerable size, and is surrounded by a wall, and from the account of Garden, its present state appears superior to that in which Tieffenthaler describes it to have been about a century ago, when all there was wretchedness and ruin. Lat. 25° 22′, long. 74° 44′.

SANGANEER.—A town in the Rajpoot state of Jeypoor, nine miles S. by W. from Jeypoor, and 78 miles E.N.E. from Ajmeer. Lat. 26° 49′, long. 75° 53′.

SANGAWARA, in the raj or state of Banswara, in Rajpootana, a town on the route from Mow to Deesa, 136 miles N.W. of former, 165 S.E. of latter. Lat. 23° 37′, long. 74° 5′.

SANGHEE.—A village in the British district of Rohtuk, lieut.-gov. of the N.W. Provinces. Lat. 29° 2′, long. 76° 41′.

SANGIM.—A town in the Portuguese district of Goa, territory of Bombay, 24 miles S.E. of Goa. Lat. 15° 13′, long. 74° 13′.

SANGLEE.—One of the southern Mahratta jaghires, territory of Bombay. It consists of several detached portions, but the centre of the principal tract is in lat. 17° 28′, long. 75° 30′. Sanglee yields an annual revenue of about 46,800*l*. In 1846, a sword was presented to Chintamun Row, chief of this territory, by the East-India Company, in testimony of their respect for his high character, and in acknowledgment of his unswerving fidelity and attachment to the British government during the Kolapore rebellion. Chintamun died a few years after, and arrangements have been made for the administration of the estate during the minority of the present chief.

SANGOD, in the Rajpoot territory of Kotah, a town on the route from Nusseerabad to Saugor, 153 miles S.E. of former, 197 N.W. of latter. It is a considerable place, with a bazar. Distant from the city of Kota, S.E., 33 miles. Lat. 24° 55′, long. 76° 20′.

SANGOLA.—A town in the British province of Sattara, presidency of Bombay, 81 miles E. by S. of Sattara. Lat. 17° 26′, long. 75° 16′.

SANGOLEE.—A town in the British district of Belgaum, presidency of Bombay, 24 miles E.S.E. of Belgaum. Lat. 15° 44′, long. 74° 54′.

SANGROOL.—A town in the native state of Kolapoor, territory of Bombay, 10 miles W.S.W. from Kolapoor, and 63 miles N.N.W. from Belgaum. Lat. 16° 40′, long. 74° 10′.

SANGWA, in the Rajpoot state of Jodhpoor, a village on the route from Nusseerabad to Deesa, and 128 miles S.W. of the former. Lat. 25° 32′, long. 73° 27′.

SANICHARA, in the British district of Goruckpoor, lieut.-gov. of the N.W. Provinces, a small town situate four miles from the left bank of the Ghaghra, and as many from the right of the Koyane. It has a market. Distant S.W. from Goruckpoor 25 miles. Lat. 26° 30′, long. 83°.

SANK, in the territory of Gwalior, a small river rising about lat. 26° 3′, long. 77° 57′. It runs in a north-easterly direction, and falls into the Asun river on the right side, in lat. 26° 30′, long. 78° 16′, after a course of about forty-five miles, the whole of which is through the Gwalior territory. It is crossed thirty miles from its source, and in lat. 26° 28′, long. 78° 9′, by the route from Agra to Gwalior, and has there "water shallow, bed stony and rough, right bank rather steep." At Nurabad, ten miles below, or north-east of the ford, it is crossed by a bridge of seven arches, very well built of masonry.

SANKERRY DROOG.—A town in the British district of Salem, presidency of Madras, 26 miles S.W. by W. of Salem. Lat. 11° 28′, long. 77° 55′.

SANKHA, in the British district of Cawnpore, lieut.-gov. of the N.W. Provinces, a village on the route from Allahabad to Calpee, and 18 miles E. of the latter. Lat. 26° 10′, long. 80° 3′.

SANSAR DHARA, in the Dehra Doon, a remarkable spot, the romantic characteristics of which are thus described by an eyewitness:— "In the commencement of this day's march, we enjoyed a sight of uncommon beauty, which was rendered more striking by being concealed by a jutting point of rock till we approached very near, and ascended a little bank, when it burst suddenly on our view. It was a fall of water from an excavated bank, with a cave or grotto at each extremity, forming together an arch of about 100 feet in perpendicular height, with a subtended base of eighty or 100 yards. Through every part of the impending summit, the water oozed in drops, which fell in showers into a basin, whence it was carried by a small stream into the river below. The lofty trees and luxuriant shrubs which overhung the brow threw a partial shade over the picture, while the sun striking full upon the cascade, was reflected in the sparkling globules, giving a richness and brilliancy to the scene which words are incompetent to express. Upon an inspection of the grotto on the right, we were struck with new and more singular appearances. It is a cavern, about six feet in height, ten in depth, and fourteen or sixteen in length, and is a natural excavation, the walls and roof of which are of rock. The water filters through the top, from which pendent shoots like icicles are disposed in all the different stages of petrifaction. The small ramifications form variegated beds of moss, serving as conductors for the water when it first begins to crystallize; and from a tube or pipe, they become, by repeated incrustations, a firm consolidated mass. The various colours produced by the vegetation, changing with the different shades of light, give to the outer surface the appearance of mother-of-pearl; but when the petrifaction is complete, the inside has a great resemblance to alabaster." The water is very cold and clear, and probably contains much lime that is precipitated upon the various substances on which the shower falls. Sansar Dhara is by the superstitious Hindoos considered sacred to Mahadeva, and, in consequence, visited by them in pilgrimage. It is within a dozen miles of the sanatory station of Mussouree and Landour. Lat. 30° 21′, long. 78° 6′.

SANTIPORE.—A town in the British district of Nuddea, lieut.-gov. of Bengal, 56 miles N. of Calcutta. The town has long been famous for its learning. Lat. 23° 14′, long. 88° 26′.

SANTOO.—A town in the Rajpoot state of Jodhpoor, situate on the right bank of a branch of the Sookree river, and 84 miles S.S.W. from Jodhpoor. Lat. 25° 13′, long. 72° 38′.

SAONKEIRA.—A town in Guzerat, or dominions of the Guicowar, 21 miles E.S.E. from Baroda, and 84 miles N.E. by N. from Surat. Lat. 22° 10′, long. 73° 31′.

SAPE.—A town in the native state of Bhotan, 116 miles N. from Goalpara, and 141 miles E.N.E. from Darjeeling. Lat. 27° 48′, long. 90° 26′.

SARAHUN, or SERAN, the summer residence of the rajah of Bussahir, is situate three miles from the left bank of the Sutluj. Its site is fine, being in a beautifully wooded recess or amphitheatre, formed by the hills advancing round it in a semicircle behind, while in front they slope down to the Sutluj, beyond which the mountains of Kulu rise, barren, steep, and with snow-clad summits. The summits of the mountains round the town to the east and south are covered with snow until June, when the rainy season sets in, under the influence of which it melts away. The buildings of this town may be considered handsome, according to the humble standard of taste in this region. They are all in the Chinese style, with pent-roofs, balconies, and some beautifully-carved woodwork. The most remarkable building is a temple dedicated to the Hindoo goddess Kali, to whom, previously to the establishment of British supremacy, human sacrifices were here offered. The residence of the rajah is extensive, consisting of several houses. Sarahun is the limit of Brahminism towards the north, as none of that caste are established beyond it. Elevation above the sea 7,246 feet. Lat. 31° 30′, long. 77° 50′.

SARANGPOOR, in the district of Aldemau, territory of Oude, a town on the river Tons (North-eastern), 110 miles S.E. of Lucknow. Its population is estimated by Butter at 9,000. Lat. 26° 24′, long. 82° 33′.

SARAOON, in the British district of Bhutteeana, lieut.-gov. of the N.W. Provinces, a town on the route from Sirsuh to the Punjab, 62 miles N.W. of the former. Lat. 30° 12′, long. 74° 25′.

SARAWAH.—A town in the British territory of Pegu, situate on the left bank of the Irawady river, and 64 miles W. from Pegu. Lat. 17° 44′, long. 95° 19′.

SARAYAT, in the British district of Goruckpore, lieut.-gov. of the N.W. Provinces, a village 50 miles N.W. of Goruckpore cantonment. Lat. 27° 20′, long. 82° 53′.

SARDAH, or GHOGRA RIVER.—See Ghogra.

SARENDI, in the district of Banswara, territory of Oude, a town near the right bank of the river Saee, 50 miles S.E. of Lucknow. Butter estimates the population at 6,000, including 100 Mussulmans. Lat. 26° 16′, long. 81° 5′.

SARGAUM.—A town in the British district of Tannah, presidency of Bombay, 53 miles N. of Bombay. Lat. 19° 43′, long. 72° 52′.

SARH, in the British district of Cawnpore, lieut.-gov. of the N.W. Provinces, a town in the subdivision of Sulimpur, hence sometimes called Sarh Sulimpur. Lat. 26° 14′, long. 80° 24′.

SARHAT, in the British district of Beerbhoom, lieut.-gov. of Bengal, a town on the route from Pachete to Monghyr, 45 miles N. of former, 80 S. of latter. Lat. 24° 16′, long. 86° 52′.

SARHENDI, in the British district of Agra, lieut.-gov. of the N.W. Provinces, a town on the route from Agra to Kerowly, 29 miles S.W. by W. of the former. Lat. 26° 56′, long. 77° 46′.

SARHULL.—A town in the Rajpoot state of Jhalawar, 27 miles E. by S. from Jhalra Patun, and 143 miles W.N.W. from Saugur. Lat. 24° 28′, long. 76° 40′.

SARSA, a small river, rises in the valley south of Subatoo, and in lat. 30° 54′, long. 77° 3′. It holds a north-westerly course through the Pinjor Doon, and, receiving several small feeders from the mountains of Hindoor, falls into the Sutlej near Kanoli, in lat. 31° 2′, long. 76° 38′, after a course of about thirty miles.

SARSAP, in the Rajpoot state of Jeypore, a hill fort on the route from Agra to Neemuch, 145 miles S.W. of former. Lat. 26° 10′, long. 76° 10′.

SARSEREE.—A town in the British district of Belgaum, presidency of Bombay, 22 miles E. by N. of Belgaum. Lat. 15° 55′, long. 74° 54′.

SARUN.—A British district under the

lieut.-gov. of Bengal, and named from the town of Sarun, its principal place. It is bounded on the north and north-west by the territory of Nepaul; on the east by the British district Tirhoot; on the south-west by the Ganges, dividing it from the British districts Patna and Shahabad, and the Ghaghra, dividing it from the British district Ghazeepore; and on the west by Goruckpoor. It lies between lat. 25° 40′—27° 29′, long. 83° 55′—85° 30′; is 115 miles in length from north to south, and ninety in breadth. The area is 6,394 square miles. It is throughout a very level tract, having no mountains, and scarcely any hills, or even undulations, but with a general inclination towards the south-east, as indicated by the flow of the rivers in that direction. The rivers and watercourses are very numerous, few tracts being better supplied in this respect. The Ganges flowing south-east, forms the south-western boundary from the confluence of the Ghaghra to the confluence of the Gunduk. The other principal rivers by which the district is either traversed or bounded, are the Ghagra, Gunduk, and Bagmuttee.

The principal products are wheat, barley, rice, gram (Cicer arietinum), millet, maize, pease, and some other pulse, oil-seeds, hemp, opium, indigo, tobacco, cotton. The district in general affords an ample and fruitful field for the cultivation of sugarcane. The esculent vegetables of Europe in general thrive well during the cold season. The forests contain some fine timber-trees. Manufactures are few, and of small note. The commerce of the district consists principally in the export of raw produce, of which the chief articles are timber, grain, sugar, tobacco, opium, indigo, and cotton. The most important import is culinary salt; the remainder is composed of silks, broadcloths, and a few other articles, regarded as luxuries amongst the natives, in general simple in their habits. The principal towns—Sarun or Chupra, Bettiah, Revelgunj, Aliganj—are noticed under their respective names in the alphabetical arrangement. The population is given under the article BENGAL.

This district formed part of the kingdom of Magadha, the monarch of which is represented to have been paramount ruler of India long previously to the Christian era. On the overthrow, in 1193, of the kingdom of Kunnouj, by Shahab-uddin Muhammad, king of Ghor, the victor, following up his success, subdued the kingdom of Behar, of which Sarun formed part. Subsequently, in the early part of the sixteenth century, it was subdued by Baber, and in 1765 it was included in the grant of the dewanny made to the East-India Company by Shah Alum, the padshah of Delhi.

SARUNGHUR.—A town in the native state of Sarunghur, on the south-west frontier of Bengal, 68 miles W. from Sumbulpoor, and 84 miles S.S.W. from Odeipoor. The native state of which this town is the chief place, contains an area of 799 square miles, and a population of 35,955. Lat. 21° 30′, long. 82° 59′.

SARUNGKOT, in the Sinde Sagur Dooab division of the Punjab, a town situated on the left bank of the Swan river, 73 miles S.S.E. of the town of Peshawar. Lat. 33° 5′, long. 72° 13′.

SARUNGPOOR, in Malwa, in the territory of Dewas, a town on the route from Goona to Mow, 97 miles S.W. of former, 88 N.E. of latter. It is situate on the right or east bank of the Kallee Sindh river, here crossed by ford; "bed 400 yards wide; bottom of rock in ledges and sand; water shallow during the dry season." Distant N.E. from Oogein 55 miles. Lat. 23° 31′, long. 76° 30′.

SARWAPALLI.—A town in the British district of Nellore, presidency of Madras, 12 miles S. by W. of Nellore. Lat. 14° 17′, long. 80° 1′.

SARWUR.—A town in the British province of Sattara, presidency of Bombay, 10 miles S.W. of Beejapoor. Lat. 16° 43′, long. 75° 41′.

SASA, a river of the Muttuck country, in Upper Assam, rises in lat. 27° 26′, long. 95° 16′, and flowing westerly for forty-five miles, falls into the Booree Dehing river in lat. 27° 15′, long. 94° 43′.

SASOOKHA.—A town in the native state of Bhotan, 110 miles N. from Goalpara, and 141 miles N.W. from Durrung. Lat. 27° 44′, long. 90° 40′.

SASOORAHULLY.—A town in the Mysore, situate on the right bank of the Toonga river, and 138 miles N.W. by N. from Seringapatam. Lat. 14° 9′, long. 75° 45′.

SASPANEE, in the British territory of Saugur and Nurbudda, lieut.-gov. of the N.W. Provinces, a town on the route from Jubbulpoor to Nagpoor, 39 miles S.S.W. of the former. Lat. 22° 39′, long. 79° 49′.

SASRAN.—A town in the native state of Gwalior, or territory of Scindia, 42 miles S.W. by W. from Gwalior, and 70 miles W.N.W. from Jhansee. Lat. 25° 55′, long. 77° 40′.

SASSERAM, in the British district of Shahabad, lieut.-gov. of Bengal, a town on the route from Hazareebagh to Benares, 117 miles N.W. of former, 72 S.E. of latter. It has a bazar, and is of considerable size; but the greater part of its extent is occupied by ruinous mosques and tombs of Mussulmans. The town has a few rude manufactures in hardware and jewellery, and there are many weavers, principally Mussulmans. There is an endowed school, supported by lands formerly granted for the purpose. The population is estimated by Jacquemont at 10,000; but according to Buchanan, the number of houses is 3,600; and assuming the usually-received average of inmates, the number of inhabitants would appear to be 18,000. Lat. 24° 57′, long. 84° 4′.

SASSOOR.—A town in the British district of Poonah, presidency of Bombay, 16 miles S.E. of Poonah. Lat. 18° 20′, long. 74° 3′.

SASUNEE, in the British district of Allygurh, lieut.-gov. of the N.W. Provinces, a town on the route from Agra to the cantonment of Allygurh, and 14 miles S. of the latter. It has a large bazar. In 1803, the conduct of a refractory zemindar rendered necessary the employment of force for the reduction of the fortress, which was consequently attacked by the British, under General Lake, and captured, though not without severe loss on the part of the victors. Sasunee contains a population of 5,524. Lat. 27° 42′, long. 78° 9′.

SATA, or SETTA, in Sinde, the greatest eastern branch of the Indus, or rather the continuation of the main stream, which formerly sent off to the west a large arm called the Buggaur. This last, however, is now almost completely closed during the season when the river is low, becoming then little else than a succession of *dunds*, or fresh-water pools. The Sata below the divarication is generally about 1,000 yards wide. It sends off, on the left or eastern side, two branches,—the Mull and Moutnee, once great streams, but now, during the dry season, shallow rivulets. At the time that Carless wrote, in 1837, the Hujamree and Kedywaree mouths, which gave exit to two other branches sent off by the Sata on the right side, were navigable; but in 1839 the Hujamree mouth was closed by a great alteration in the course of the stream. Having thrown off these branches on the right and left side, the Sata, still the main stream of the Indus, and known in the lower part of its course by the names Munnejah and Wanyanee, falls into the Indian Ocean by the Kookewaree mouth, in lat. 24° 2′, long. 67° 32′.

SATAHUNG.—A town in Nepal, 102 miles W.N.W. from Khatmandoo, and 102 miles N. by E. from Goruckpoor. Lat. 28° 7′, long. 83° 44′.

SATAK.—A town within the dominions of Gholab Singh, the ruler of Cashmere, 160 miles E.S.E. from Sirinagur, and 100 miles N.E. from Kangra. Lat. 33° 8′, long. 77° 30′.

SATHEEKA.—A town in the Rajpoot state of Jodhpoor, 53 miles N. by E. from Jodhpoor, and 97 miles W.N.W. from Ajmeer. Lat. 27° 2′, long. 73° 18′.

SATHWALY.—A town in Hyderabad, situate on the right bank of the Manjera river, and 64 miles N.W. by N. from Hyderabad. Lat. 18° 9′, long. 78° 3′.

SATIGHAT.—A town in Nepal, situate on the right bank of the Marachangdi river, and 70 miles W. from Khatmandoo. Lat. 27° 46′, long. 84° 10′.

SATKOONEEA.—A town in the British district of Chittagong, lieut.-gov. of Bengal, 27 miles S.E. of Chittagong. Lat. 22° 1′, long. 92° 9′.

SATPOORA, in the territory of Indore, or possessions of Holkar's family, a small town on a tributary of the Nerbudda, 75 miles S.E. of Indore. It gives name to a range of mountains, which, running east and west, divides the valley of the Taptee from that of the Nerbudda. This range may be considered as extending between lat. 21°—22°, from long. 73° 40′ to long. 78°, where it becomes confounded with the Vindhya range. The south declivity towards the Taptee is abrupt, the north towards the Nerbudda very gentle. Its elevation does not appear to have been accurately determined. Aseergurh, one of its summits, is probably about 1,200 feet above the sea. Fraser, an eye-witness, estimates the elevation of the highest points at about 2,500 feet above the sea. "The Satpoora differ extremely in appearance from the Vindhya mountains, being bold and romantic in the outlines, rising into lofty peaks, and swelling into shapes that would induce the beholder from a distance to consider them as primitive." They, however, consist of amygdaloid and greenstone, and on the summits, of overlying trap, and are altogether of volcanic formation. Satpoora is in lat. 21° 48′, long. 76° 27′.

SATTARA, so denominated from the fort of that name, is a British province within the presidency of Bombay. It is bounded on the north by the British collectorate of Poona; on the north-east and east by that of Sholapore; on the south by the collectorate of Belgaum, the southern Mahratta jaghires, and the state of Colapore; and on the west by the collectorates of Rutnagherry and Tannah. It lies between lat. 16° 22′—18° 32′, long. 73° 24′—76° 25′; is 215 miles in length from south-east to north-west, and ninety in breadth: the area is about 10,222 square miles. The culminating range of the Siadri Mountains, or Western Ghauts, extend along its west frontier for about ninety miles, separating it from the Concan. Those mountains, which rise so precipitously on the west side, or towards the Concan, have a more gradual declivity on the Deccan side, or towards the east; and in that direction, though the surface is generally very rugged, and diversified by many considerable ranges and isolated mountains, it sinks gradually to the plains of Hyderabad, or territory of the Nizam. All the streams hold a south-easterly direction, and ultimately joining the Kistna, which rises in this territory, are conveyed by the channel of that great river to the Bay of Bengal. Of the remaining rivers, the chief is the Neera. In addition to the Kistna and the Neera, are the Mar, the Yena, the Nandhur, the Yerla, the Wurna, and the Quina, over which last-mentioned river a bridge is about to be constructed.

The climate of the higher parts in the west of this territory is characterized by extreme moisture, the annual fall of rain exceeding that registered in many other places, and having been known to amount to nearly 300 inches in the year. On the eastern declivity of the Ghats in the Deccan, and in the lower parts still farther east, "the rains are light, uncertain, and in all years barely sufficient for the wants of the husbandman; and a slight failure occasions much distress." The mean annual fall of rain in the less-elevated parts is stated not to exceed twenty-three and a half inches. In the upper parts of the Ghats, the heat is much moderated by the elevation; the mean annual temperature being 66°. April is found to be the hottest month, the mean temperature being 74°; the extreme maximum also occurred in the same month, reaching, in 1836, 90°. In the Deccan, at an elevation of 1,700 or 1,800 feet, the maximum temperature of the whole year is stated to be 94°, the minimum 37°. In the upper part of the Ghats, the monsoons during autumn are violent in the extreme; in the less-elevated parts eastward of the Ghats, they are in general scarcely felt, though the extreme east is sometimes slightly visited by the monsoon from the north-east, or that from the Coromandel coast. The climate is considered very salubrious.

The great majority of the population is Mahratta; and this part of India appears from time immemorial to have been the head-quarters of that race, which held the widely-extended region of Maharashtra. In the hills adjoining the Ghats southward of Sattara, there are a considerable number of Ramooses, a predatory tribe, in physical aspect resembling the Bheels, but more subdued and civilized. They have no language of their own, and in dress and manners are more like the Mahrattas. The total population of Sattara has been returned at 1,005,771, which affords ninety to the square mile. Such assumed density may be regarded as ample for a mountainous tract, in general barren, and subject to frequently-recurring droughts. The principal towns—Sattara the capital, Punderpoor, and Beejapoor—are noticed under their respective names.

During the administration of the country by the last rajah, a good carriage-road had been made from Sattara to Mahabulishwar, a distance of thirty miles, which was continued for twenty-seven miles to Mahar, on the navigable river Savitree. There was also a good road continued from the Neera bridge to Sattara, thus completing the communication between that city and Poona. Since the lapse of the territory to the British, many excellent roads have been added. Among them may be noticed one connecting Beejapoor with Sattara; another from the town of Kurar, over the Koombarlee Ghaut, to the Concan; a third over the Pusurnee Ghaut, between the town of Waee and Malcolm Peth, on the Mahabulishwar Hills.

Sevajee, who founded the state of Sattara and the Mahratta confederation, was the second son of Shahjee, a Mahratta leader of some note, under the Nizam Shah dynasty of Ahmednuggur, and subsequently under that of Bejapoor. Sevajee began his predatory career about 1644, and in 1646 acquired his first stronghold, the hill-fort of Torna, by the treachery of the governor holding it on the part of the king of Beejapoor, against whom he, in 1648, openly revolted. From that time his course of successful aggression against both Aurungzebe, then king of Delhi, and the king of Beejapoor was rapid. In 1659 he in person assassinated the general of the army of Beejapoor, and attacked the forces, which, thus surprised and deprived of a leader, were for the most part slain, the Mahrattas among the survivors entering the service of their conqueror. In 1662 he had acquired a tract of country 250 miles in length northwards from Goa, and at its widest part 100 miles in breadth; and "in this small territory the hardiness and predatory habits of his soldiers enabled him to maintain an army of 7,000 horse and 50,000 foot." In 1664 he extended his predatory expeditions so far that he plundered the rich city of Surat, and with his spoil returned unmolested to his fastnesses. In 1665 he collected a fleet, and commenced a course of piratical depredations against the Mussulmans, who were especially enraged by the capture of the ships which, according to annual usage, were conveying pilgrims from India to the Red Sea. In the same year, however, Sevajee accepted service in the army of Aurungzebe, by whom he was soon after placed in confinement. From this durance he escaped, and returned to his fastness at Raeegurh, after an absence of nearly a year. He there became so formidable, that Aurungzebe admitted him to terms, or rather concluded with him a treaty, by which he was acknowledged as jaghiredar or subordinate proprietor of a territory much larger than that which he had formerly held. An attempt, made by order of Aurungzebe, to seize Sevajee, caused him to recommence hostilities, in which he was eminently successful, ravaging to a great extent the territories of the sovereign of Delhi, exacting the chouth or black-mail of a fourth of the revenues from such districts as were spared, and in a field action defeating an army of 20,000 men. In rivalry of the king of Delhi, he was, in 1675, crowned at Raeegurh, with great splendour, adopting, in all their extent, the ceremonies used by that gorgeous court on such occasions. He soon after marched towards the Coromandel coast, and, passing by Madras, took the strong fort of Jinji, one of the possessions of Beejapoor; but in the midst of his triumphs and greatness he was cut off by illness, in 1680, in the fifty-third year of his age. His son Sambajee succeeded to his possessions, but being devoid of talent, energy, and perseverance, and becoming incompetent from drunkenness and debauchery, was, in 1688, made prisoner by the Moguls, and in the following year cruelly put to death, by order of Aurungzebe. Notwithstanding, however, all the talents, resources, and perseverance of the emperor, the Mussulman cause rapidly waned, and that of the Mahrattas prospered: they "seemed to multiply as the Mogul armies decayed. After reducing the Deccan to a desert, they had spread over Malwa, and made a powerful inroad into Guzerat, leaving their traces everywhere, in pillaged towns, ravaged fields, and smoking villages." Aurungzebe, after many campaigns, in which he vainly attempted to retrieve his sinking affairs, died in 1707, at Ahmednugur, whither he had with difficulty led the shattered relics of his ruined host. The rapid decay of the kingdom of Delhi accelerated the progress of the Mahratta power: the officers of the king left in charge of the Deccan, first faintly opposed and then conciliated the Mahrattas; a truce was concluded about 1710, by which they yielded the chouth; and this, or the confirmation of the agreement, together with a formal grant of their territorial possessions by the emperor (Padshah) in 1719, may be considered as the final establishment of the Mahratta government, after a struggle of at least sixty years. The office of Peishwa, "leader" or "prime minister" of the Mahratta empire, had always been a place of importance, and Balajee Rao, who attained that dignity, succeeded in 1749 in engrossing the whole powers of the state. Thenceforward the descendants of Sevajee were mere pensioned captives. From that humiliating state Pertaub Singh, the titular rajah, was released in 1818, when the army of the Peishwa, in its rapid flight, was surprised and routed by a British force at Ashti. On that occasion the rajah, with his mother and brothers, were rescued and set at liberty, after the family had been nearly seventy years in durance. To the rajah was assigned the territory of Sattara, producing an annual revenue of 137,500*l.*, besides jaghires or feudal grants, and other alienations from the rent-roll, making in the aggregate about 200,000*l.* for the gross annual income of the raj. The sovereignty of the territory thus assigned was to be held by the rajah, "in subordinate cooperation with the British government," which engaged to defend the rajah's territories, and give him protection from all injury and aggression. The Mahratta prince having been always retained in a state of pupilage, it was apprehended that to invest him at once with the full measure of power which he was ultimately to enjoy, might be mischievous; the following stipulation therefore formed part of the treaty:—"The rajah shall ultimately have the entire management of the country now ceded to him; but as it is necessary, on account of the recent conquests of the country, that it should at first be governed with particular care and prudence, the administration for the present will remain in the hands of the British political agent. That officer will, however, conduct the government in the rajah's name, and in consultation with his highness; and in proportion as his highness and his officers shall acquire experience, and evince their ability to govern the country, the British government will gradually transfer the whole administration into their hands. He will, however, at all times attend, as above agreed, to the advice which the British political agent shall offer him for the good of his state, and for the maintenance of general tranquillity." The management of the raj remained with the British political agent until April, 1822; and an official report of that date records "the general prosperity and good order that prevailed throughout the rajah's districts, and the satisfaction which was shown by all classes of the people towards his highness's government and the existing system of management." At this prosperous time the government was transferred to the rajah, then twenty-four years of age, and the British functionary, hitherto denominated political agent, was thenceforth styled Resident. Coolness, however, subsequently arose between the rajah and the government of Bombay, which soon increased to alienation. The rajah made demands which the government thought unwarranted by the treaty; and being led into proceedings inconsistent with the position which he occupied, he was, in 1839, deposed, and his brother elevated to his place. The deposed rajah was sent to Benares, where he died in the month of October, 1847. A treaty was concluded with the new rajah, under which a competent revenue was secured to Pertaub Singh, and certain modifications of the terms of the original treaty were effected in regard to certain jaghiredars of the Sattara raj, who, to obviate dispute, were formally declared under the direct control of the British government, though their contingents and pecuniary payments were reserved to the rajah, as previously fixed. Under this arrangement, capital sentences passed by those jaghiredars are made subject to confirmation by the British government.

Under the rule of the new rajah, the condition of the country was highly satisfactory. The British authorities, ever anxious for improvement, found in the prince a willing coadjutor. Not only were substantial reforms introduced, but matters little heeded for the most part by native rulers received some measure of attention. Steps were taken to repair and preserve the fine relics of Mahometan architecture at Beejapoor, while the great interests of humanity were advanced by the encouragement of vaccination, the abolition of suttee, and the suppression of trade in slaves.

The second rajah under the protection of the East-India Company died in 1848, without issue, but adopted, a few hours previously to his death, a boy distantly related to his family. It was obvious, however, that by the general law and custom of India, a dependent principality could not pass to an adopted heir without the consent of the paramount power; yet, plain as this was, the decision of the British government was not given without deliberation. That government was under no pledge, direct or constructive, to give such consent, and it was deemed expedient, in reference to the general interests committed to its charge, to withhold it. The territory accordingly lapsed, by the extinction of the race of Sevajee, to the power which bestowed it, and was formally annexed to the British dominions. The revenue derived from all sources in 1850 amounted to 271,304*l.*

SATTARA.—The principal place of the British province of the same name, in the presidency of Bombay. It is situate amidst the highlands of the Deccan, east of the culminating range of the Ghats, and where the country, though very rugged, inclines generally to the eastward. The site of the fort is the summit of a mountain having an area extending about 1,100 yards in its greatest length, and 500 in breadth. The mountain is of no great height, but very steep. "Its defences consist of a scarp, upwards of forty feet in perpendicular black rock, on the top of which is a stone wall;" and besiegers of it have suffered dreadfully from huge stones precipitated on them from the fort above. Its most striking feature is "the north-east angle, which assumes nearly the shape of a tower, and is one of the strongest points, the rock being forty-two feet high, and the bastion now on the top of it consists of twenty-five feet of masonry, making a total of sixty-seven feet." The "town of Sattara lies immediately under the fort, in a deep hollow, nearly surrounded on three sides by hills; cut off from the west by the Syhadri Mountains (Western Ghats), and from every other quarter by the Yena, Kistna, and Oormooree rivers." When the fort was attacked by the British at the close of the war with the Peishwa in 1818, it mounted only twenty-five guns, of various calibre, and was garrisoned by 400 men, who surrendered, having made scarcely any resistance, after a few shells had been thrown into the place. The British colours were immediately hoisted, but next day lowered, and the standard of Sevajee raised in their place, proclamation being made of the restoration of the titular chief to his dignity, and a portion of the territory held by his ancestors. Previously to the rise of Sevajee, this place had been held by the Mussulman government of Beejapoor; it was taken by that celebrated chieftain in 1673, and made the seat of government by his successors in 1698. In 1700, being besieged by Aurungzebe in person, it was taken by blockade after a vigorous resistance of about two months. In 1705 it was retaken by the Mahrattas by stratagem; and during the ascendancy of the Peishwa, was used ostensibly as the state residence, but actually as the prison of the rajah. After the deposal of the Peishwa, the titular rajah continued to reside here, under the protection and control of the British authorities, till the race of Sevajee failed, by the death of his last descendant in 1848. A new church has been erected in the town by the British government. Distance from Bombay, S.E., 115 miles; from Poonah, S., 55. Lat. 17° 45′, long. 74° 4′.

SATTAVADE.—A town in the British district of North Arcot, presidency of Madras, 33 miles N.W. of Madras. Lat. 13° 27′, long. 80° 1′.

SATTENAPATTI.—A town in the British district of Guntoor, presidency of Madras, 21 miles W.N.W. of Guntoor. Lat. 16° 25′, long. 80° 12′.

SATTENWARREE, in the territory of Bhopal, a fort on the northern frontier, towards the Gwalior territory. In 1818 it was held by a garrison on the part of the rajah of Nagpoor or Berar, and on the 8th of June was invested by a British force under Major Lamb, and on the 9th, the rampart having been breached, an attempt was made to storm; but the advancing party was received with so destructive a fire, that thirty-two men of those near the head of the advancing column were unhappily cut down. The rear thereupon fled in panic to seek shelter, and were of necessity followed by the rest. All efforts to bring the men to renew the attack were unsuccessful, and under cover of darkness, the party retired from the spot, having suffered the loss of eighty-six of their number in killed and wounded. On the following night, however, the garrison evacuated the fort, somewhere about half their number effecting their escape, the remainder being killed or made prisoners. Sattenwarree appears to have been granted with other possessions by treaty of 1818 by the British government to the nawaub of Bhopal, "in order to mark its approbation of his conduct, and to enable him to maintain the stipulated contingent." Distant N.W. of Bhopal 30 miles, N.E. of Oojein 95. Lat. 23° 36′, long. 77° 10′.

SATTIYAMANGALAM.—A town in the British district of Coimbatoor, presidency of Madras, 40 miles N.N.E. of Coimbatoor. Lat. 11° 30′, long. 77° 18′.

SATULA, in the British hill state of Kotgurh, a village on a mountain rising steeply over the left bank of the Sutlej. Elevation above the sea 6,771 feet. Lat. 31° 19′, long. 77° 31′.

SAUBIE NULLA.—A river rising in lat. 27° 12′, long. 76° 19′, and, flowing in a northerly direction for eighty miles through Alwar and Kot Kassim, and for thirty through the British district of Goorgaon and the native territory of Jhujhur, falls into the Hansoutee river on the right side, in lat. 28° 28′, long. 76° 38′.

SAUCKRA.—A town on the south-west frontier of Bengal, in the British district of

Sumbulpoor, 84 miles W. by S. of Sumbulpoor. Lat. 21° 19', long. 82° 43'.

SAUDERVEIL.—A town of Bombay, in the territory of the Daung rajahs, 50 miles E. by S. from Surat, and 66 miles N.W. by W. from Malligaum. Lat. 21°, long. 73° 37'.

SAUEELA.—A town in Guzerat, or dominions of the Guicowar, 42 miles E.N.E. from Rajkote, and 83 miles W.S.W. from Ahmedabad. Lat. 22° 31', long. 71° 25'.

SAUGOR AND NERBUDDA TERRITORIES.—The country thus designated comprises an extensive tract, bounded on the north by Bundelcund and the British districts of Banda, Allahabad, and Mirzapore; on the east by Mirzapore and Korea; on the south by the territory of Nagpore or Berar, and the territory of the Nizam; and on the west by the territory of Gwalior, or the possessions of the Scindia family, and the territory of Bhopal. It lies between lat. 21° 16' and 25° 15', long. 76° 53' and 82° 51'; is 380 miles in length from east to west, and 190 in breadth from north to south, and has an area of 32,114 square miles. Within these boundaries are comprehended the independent state of Rewah, whose rajah is bound to the British government by a treaty of alliance. The other native chieftains are mere feudatories of the East-India Company, under whose grants they hold their possessions; within which, however, they exercise all the powers of government, subject to the interference, when necessary, of the paramount authority. Of the petty states thus situate, there are four—Kotee, Myhir, Oocheyra, and Sohawul; but the larger portion of the country known as the Saugor and Nerbudda territory is directly British. This portion comprises the districts of Saugor, Jubbulpore, Hoshungabad, Seoni, Dumoh, Nursingpoor, Baitool, Ramghur, and Sohajpore. Its outline is very irregular, but it may be described generally as extending from lat. 21° 16' to 24° 30', and from long. 76° 53' to 82° 15', and comprehending an area of about 20,000 square miles.

The Saugor and Nerbudda is, with little exception, a considerably elevated tract, its limits embracing a portion of the ranges of the Vindhya and of the Mahadeo Mountains. The eastern part is an elevated table-land, having at its south-eastern angle the summit of Amarakantak, 3,463 feet above the sea, but declining towards the west into the more depressed tract called the valley of the Nerbudda, that great river holding its course along it westward towards the Indian Ocean. The Mahadeo Mountains form the southern inclosing range of this valley; the Vindhya, the northern. At the distance of about thirty miles south of the Nerbudda, the culminating ridge of the Mahadeo Mountains forms the line of water-heads, dividing the streams flowing northward towards the Nerbudda from those flowing southward and south-eastward towards the Godavery. The Mahadeo range appears to have an average elevation of about 2,000 feet above the sea; one summit is judged to rise as high as 2,500, and two or three others are vaguely conjectured to have a still greater altitude. The elevation above the sea of the Vindhya forming the northern inclosing range of the valley of the Nerbudda, is but moderate. This range is little more than the southern brow of a sort of plateau, of very irregular surface, but for the most part declining northward, and sending off numerous streams in that direction. Few elevations exceed 2,000 feet; that of the Residency at Saugor, one of the most considerable ascertained, is only 2,050. Down this declivity, towards the north and north-east, flow the numerous feeders of the Betwa, the Cane, the Tons, and many others in their course towards the Jumna and the Ganges. The Sone, rising two or three miles east of the source of the Nerbudda, flows eastward; the Taptee, rising in the Mahadeo range, in the south-west of the territory, flowing westward, holds a course parallel to the Nerbudda, but on an average fifty miles more to the southward, and, like that river, it falls into the Arabian Sea. The mineral productions do not present many varieties, but they are highly important, consisting principally of iron and of coal. Iron-ore is found to the north-eastward of Sohagpoor and the eastward of the river Sone, but the most important site is a tract extending from twenty to thirty miles north-east of Jubbulpore, where it is largely raised and smelted. A considerable quantity is manufactured at Poonassa, Chandgurh, and some other places in this district. At Tendukheri also, fifty miles south of Saugor, and ten miles north of the right bank of the Nerbudda, is abundance of iron-ore of excellent quality, which has been fully tested, as it is the material used in the construction of the excellent suspension-bridge over the Beosi, near the town of Saugor. The inexhaustible supply of iron-ore is the more important from there being abundance of excellent coal at many places in the vicinity; as in the Riwan pergunnah of Chandia-Kanria, which adjoins Kumbi on the north-east; and again in the Hoshungabad district, on the south bank of the Nerbudda; also about seven or eight miles below Jubbulpore, and at Sohagpore, on the left bank of the Sone. Limestone abounds in many places, and the sandstone of the northern part of the district is remarkably fine-grained, strong, and may be quarried of any scantling desired. Little mention appears to be made of any other mineral produce in this district.

A considerable portion of the population appear to be of the stock of the Ghonds, perhaps the aboriginal race of this part of India. Some of the Ghond tribes are nearly in what is called a state of nature, lurking in the gloomiest recesses of the thickest forests, and subsisting for the most part on wild roots and fruits, wild honey, and game, which they kill with their arrows. It is even alleged that they are cannibals, cutting the throats of such of their number as they consider irrecoverably ill, and devouring their bodies. However this may be, it is beyond doubt that they offer human sacrifices to their idols. Notwithstanding their barbarism, they are, however, allowed to class themselves under the second caste of Hindoos. Allied in origin and habits to these savages are the Koles, Palis, and Panwars, inhabiting the eastern part of the district. The remaining Hindoo population are Brahmins, Bundelas, various tribes of Rajpoots, and Mahrattas. The Mussulman population, consisting of Patans and others, is not inconsiderable. This territory belonging to what are called the non-regulation provinces, the statistical information regarding it is somewhat loose; but under the names of the several districts—Saugor, Jubbulpore, Hoshungabad, Seonee, Dumoh, Nursingpore, and Baitool—will be found such as is available.

The British territory is under the superintendence of the lieut.-gov. of the N.W. Provinces. The principal towns are Saugor, Jubbulpore, Hoshungabad, Seoni, Baitool, Sohajpur, Belhary, Mandla, Dumoh, and Dhamouni. Of the earlier history of this territory little is known: it was probably long ruled by princes of the Ghond race. It seems to have been at least partially conquered by Akbar, about the year 1599. On the dismemberment of the empire of Delhi, this tract became nominally subject to the Peishwa; but in the latter part of the eighteenth century, Raghojee Bhonsla, rajah of Berar or Nagpore, having received from that potentate grants of the greater part of the territory, made himself master of it. In 1818 this portion was ceded to the British government, in commutation of subsidy and contingent stipulated for by the treaty of 1816; and the cession was confirmed by the treaty of 1826. The claims of the Peishwa in Saugor had been previously surrendered, being included in the "rights, interests, and pretensions, feudal, territorial, and pecuniary," ceded by that prince to the East-India Company, under the thirteenth article of the treaty of 1817. Serious disturbances continued in several portions of these provinces after the termination of the Affghan war, which it was found necessary to quell by concentrating a military force in the disaffected territory.

SAUGOR, the principal place of the British district of the same name, is situate in a hilly tract, considerably elevated above the surrounding country. The town is built along the west, the north, and the north-east sides of a lake nearly a mile in length, and three-quarters in breadth, which occupies the lowest part of a valley, or rather a basin, surrounded by hills of trap formation, interspersed with a few of sandstone. Here are military cantonments, situate on an undulating plain north-east of the lake, and extending from north to south in a continuous line about a mile and a half. The ground, however, it is said, has been injudiciously selected, being in many places low, swampy, and consequently unhealthy. The parade-ground is in front of the lines, and adjoining it is the European burial-ground, the extent and crowded state of which give an unfavourable impression as to the qualities of the atmosphere. The mint occupied a handsome building, situate about a mile to the east of the lake; and here, formerly, 400 men were employed; but the establishment was some years since broken up, and its business transferred to Calcutta. There is a large fort here, which now serves as an ordnance depôt.

In consequence of the considerable elevation of the site, the temperature at Saugor is rather moderate in proportion to the latitude; the thermometer rarely falls below 50° in the cold season, or rises above 95° in the hot. "The quantity of rain which falls during the year, varies from thirty-four to forty-six inches." Here is a sort of collegiate school, under the management of three members, a secretary, a head master, an assistant master, and a Hindee master. There is an English and vernacular department. In the latter, instruction is given in Persian, Hindee, and Mahratta. The scenery of the beautiful lake, well suited for pleasure-boats, and the abundance of fish and wild-fowl on its waters, or on its shores, render it a great source of recreation to the European residents. Saugor is the station of the civil establishment. The European population of the town and its vicinity, vaguely stated as "numbering some hundreds," have the services of a chaplain; and a convenient church has recently been erected in the Gothic style. The total population of the town has been conjectured to amount to 50,000, the majority being Mahrattas.

Over the Bessi or Bes, a river running near the town, was constructed, in 1830, an iron suspension-bridge of the metal obtained at Tendukheri, about fifty miles to the southward. The bridge is 200 feet in span, and was erected by native workmen, at a cost of 4,800*l.*, increased by a gratuity of 500*l.* to Major Presgrave, assay-master of the Saugor mint, under whose superintendence the work was carried on. Elevation above the sea 1,940 feet; distance N.W. from Jubbulpore 90 miles, N. from Nagpore 185, S.W. from Allahabad 223, S. from Agra 233, W. from Calcutta, by Allahabad, 808, N.E. from Mhow 215, N.E. from Bombay 500. Lat. 23° 50′, long. 78° 49′.

SAUGOR ISLAND bounds the great entrance of the river Hoogly on the east side. It is seven or eight miles in length, and half that in breadth. On the east side is an ancient pagoda, and a large tank of fresh water, held in great veneration by the Hindoos, who go there in great numbers once every year to sacrifice. The island is held under a lease of ninety-nine years from government by a company, which engaged at the end of twenty years to pay land-tax to the government on the cleared lands. It was subsequently found necessary to extend the term of rent-free tenure. The population in 1832 was estimated at 10,000. The system of manufacturing salt formerly carried on here by individuals under a system of excise, has been discontinued. An iron lighthouse, to be erected on Middleton Point, was shipped from this country some few years ago. Lat. 21° 42′, long. 88° 8′.

SAUMUND.—A town in the British district of Ahmedabad, presidency of Bombay, 17 miles W. by S. of Ahmedabad. Lat. 22° 59′, long. 72° 20′.

SAUNGI, in the district of Sultanpoor, territory of Oude, a town 90 miles S.E. of Lucknow. Butter estimates the population at 4,000, all Hindoos, of the military class, and cultivators. Lat. 26° 5′, long. 81° 58′.

SAUNTE.—See SOAUTH.

SAUTNAIR, in the British district of Baitool, Saugur and Nurbudda territory, lieut.-gov. of the N.W. Provinces, a town on the route from Baitool to Ellichpoor, 22 miles S.S.W. of the former. Lat. 21° 33′, long. 77° 50′.

SAUTURRA.—A town in the territory of Nagpoor, 166 miles E. from Nagpoor, and 135 miles S.S.E. from Ramgurh. Lat. 20° 59′, long. 81° 41′.

SAVAN DROOG, in the territory of Mysore, a celebrated hill-fort, situate on a vast and bare rock of granite, amidst dense forests and thickets. A small river rushing through a deep ravine, washes the south base of the rock, which is divided by an intervening chasm into two great summits, each surmounted by a fortress independent of each other, and both abundantly supplied with water. The circuit of the base is about eight miles, and the sides are so precipitous as to appear inaccessible when viewed from below. In the year 1791 it was invested by the British army under Lord Cornwallis, and the defences, though formidable by position, were soon breached. The garrison also appears to have been weak and pusillanimous, and both forts were carried by assault without the loss of a single life on the part of the British. After the final overthrow of Tippoo Sultan in 1799, it was garrisoned by a small native force, which was subsequently withdrawn on account of the insalubrity of the place. Elevation above the sea 4,004 feet; distance from Bangalore, W., 19 miles; Seringapatam, N.E., 53. Lat. 12° 55′, long. 77° 21′.

SAVANOOR.—A town in the British district of Dharwar, presidency of Bombay, 39 miles S. by E. of Dharwar. Lat. 14° 55′, long. 75° 19′.

SAVANTANCUTTA.—A town in the Mysore, 172 miles N.W. from Seringapatam, and 86 miles N. from Mangalore. Lat. 14° 6′, long. 74° 51′.

SAVITREE, a river in the collectorate of Rutnagherry, Southern Concan, presidency of Bombay, rises on the western declivity of the Mahabulishwar range, about lat. 18° 17′, long. 73° 27′. It flows west by the town of Mhar, and falls into the Arabian Sea at Bankote, in lat. 17° 58′, long. 73° 5′; its total length of course being about seventy miles. It is navigable as far as Mhar, thirty miles from its mouth, and was formerly accessible at all times for large ships; but a sandbank at the mouth constantly increasing during the south-western monsoon, its facilities for navigation are greatly diminished. The bar has ten feet of water at low tide, and twenty-one at high water, spring tides; and ships may anchor inside in five fathoms. It swarms with fish, and abounds with alligators and other reptiles.

SAWA.—A town in the Rajpoot state of Oodeypoor, 55 miles E.N.E. from Oodeypoor, and 26 miles N.W. from Neemuch. Lat. 24° 45′, long. 74° 39′.

SAWAN.—A river of the Damaun division of the Punjab, rising in lat. 31° 41′, long. 69° 40′, and, flowing easterly for fifty-five miles, loses itself in the desert, about lat. 31° 41′, long. 70° 20′.

SAWAR, in the British district of Ajmeer, lieut.-gov. of the N.W. Provinces, a town on the route from Goona to Nusseerabad, 177 miles N.W. of former, 52 S.E. of latter. The town of Sawar has a good bazar, and water is plentiful. Lat. 25° 49′, long. 75° 21′.

SAWNAIR.—A town in the territory of Nagpoor, 21 miles N.W. from Nagpoor, and 91 miles E. by N. from Ellichpoor. Lat. 21° 23′, long. 78° 57′.

SAWOTTEE.—A town of Burmah, situate on the right bank of the Irawady river, and 59 miles N. from Prome. Lat. 19° 37′, long. 94° 55′.

SAWUNTGURH.—A town in the Rajpoot state of Boondee, 19 miles N.E. by N. from Boondee, and 94 miles S.E. from Ajmeer. Lat. 25° 39′, long. 75° 52′.

SAWUNT WARREE.—A small state under the political management of the presidency of Bombay. It forms the southern part of the tract known by the name of the "Concan," or the territory lying between the Syadree range of ghauts and the sea. It is bounded on the north by the Gar river; on the east by the line of ghauts; on the south by the Tiracole creek and the Portuguese territory of Goa; and on the west by the Vingorla mehal and the Salsee mehal of the Malwan talooka, in the British collectorate of Rutnagherry. It lies between lat. 15° 38′—16° 15′, long. 73° 40′—74° 22′: its greatest length from north to south is nearly fifty miles, its greatest breadth rather more than thirty, and it contains an area of 800 square miles.

The physical character of the country, like that of the Concan in general, is "remarkably rugged and broken, interspersed with huge mountains and thick jungles, intersected by rivers and numberless rivulets, rocky and clear until they descend on the level, where they are affected by the tide, when they are very deep and muddy." The more eastern part, consisting of a strip of land of no great width, extends along the western side of the Ghauts, and over their ridges into the Deccan. Of the scenery which presents itself from the summit of these passes, some idea "may be formed by imagining mountains succeeding mountains, 3,000 or 4,000 feet high, covered with trees, except in places where the huge black barren rocks are so solid as to prevent the hardiest shrub from finding root in their clefts." The monsoon rains on the declivities and ridges of the Ghauts are heavier, perhaps, than in any other part of the world, and 297 inches of rain have been known to fall in this elevated region in one year. Tigers, leopards, hyenas, and other wild beasts lurk in the more fertile tracts, where the great number of torrents and brooks give rise to luxuriant vegetation. Snakes and other reptiles also abound ; and the rivers near the sea swarm with alligators, which prey on the fish, that exist in vast numbers. The staple crops are rice and jowar (Holcus sorghum) ; but wheat, gram (Cicer arietinum), and other pulse, as well as esculent vegetables, thrive well in the milder season of the year. The soil is principally a light sand, full of stones and gravel, and incapable of yielding the superior kinds of produce, such as cotton, tobacco, and sugarcane. Cocoanuts are exported largely. The principal manufactures are gold and silver embroidery, worked on saddle-cloths and horse-appointments, native guns, swords, and spear-heads.

The principal road through this state is the great military route made by the British government from Belgaum down the Ram Ghaut to the port of Vingorla. Besides this, there are native roads from the Deccan, by the Tulkut Ghaut, to Banda and the Goa territory ; down the Parpolee Ghaut, to Warree and Vingorla, with a branch road through Bowlut and Banda, into the Portuguese possessions ; down the Hunmunt Ghaut, by Neroor, Waroos, and Mangaon, to Vingorla and Path ; and by the Gotgha Ghaut to the port of Malwan. There are also cross-roads leading into the Goa territory on one side, and the Company's on the other ; and numerous small passes in the line of ghauts from the upper to the lower country.

The chief rivers are the Gundnuddee, the Karlee, the Banda, the Tullowra, the Tillaree, called also Koodassee, and the Kulna. There are also a number of small streams, which in the rainy season swell into considerable rivers.

The annual revenues of the Warree state amount to about 2,25,000 rupees ; the expenditure is fixed at something under 2,00,000 rupees ; leaving a small surplus revenue for the liquidation of debt. The Warree state is not tributary to the British government or to any foreign power ; but in 1836, the customs leviable on the military road passing through this state from the port of Vingorla to the Ram Ghaut, were transferred to the British government ; and in 1838 an agreement was concluded with the chieftain, under which the whole of the customs of Sawunt Warree became the property of the British government, and the levy of transit-duties was abolished.

A corps was raised in 1839, by order of the British government, for service within the limits of this principality. It received the name of the "Sawunt Warree local corps," and is officered from the line. It is paid from the revenues of the state, and is not bound to serve in foreign territory. This levy consists of 520 rank and file, eighty native officers, and two European commissioned officers. It is disciplined, armed, and clothed in the same way as the Company's irregular corps, and is maintained at an annual cost of about 45,620 rupees, which forms a debit on the revenues of the state.

A census of the population of Sawunt Warree state was taken in 1844. From this it appears that the total population of the district amounted to 143,733, in the proportion of 74,562 males to 69,171 females.

The Mahratta family Sawunt, from whom, as possessors of Warree, the name of the territory originated, appears to have first come into notice in the person of Sawunt Bahadur, the deshmook or chief of the town and district of Warree, under the Mussulman monarchy of Beejapoor, and a member of the Bosla family. In the year 1659, the Sawunt deshmook of Warree formed a treaty with the renowned Mahratta leader Sevajee, by which he agreed to transfer his allegiance from the monarch of Beejapoor to that chief, to whom he engaged to pay half the revenue of the district, and on his account to garrison the forts, and maintain a force of 300 infantry ; but this treaty proving unsatisfactory to both parties, it was soon broken, and the deshmook resumed his allegiance to Beejapoor. In 1662, however, he was subjugated by the Mahratta chief, who subsequently restored to him his deshmookee rights, and found in him a faithful ally.

In the reign of Phoud Sawunt, the first treaty with the East-India Company was negotiated. It appears to have been occasioned by the piracies on British commerce committed by Kanojee Angria and his successors on the guddee of Colaba, and bears date 13th April, 1730. It consists of seven articles ; and after stipulating for perpetual peace and friendship between Phoud Sawunt Bhonslah, the Sir Dessayee, and the Company, and providing for their mutually assisting each other's ships at sea, proceeds to conclude an offensive and defensive alliance against the son of Kanojee Angria, who is characterized as the mutual enemy of both powers, and engages on behalf of the East-India Company to give up all the conquests made during the war to the Sir Dessayee (the ruler of Sawunt Warree), with the exception of Gheriah (the fort of Viziadroog) and the island Kennery, which are to be retained by the British government.

British commerce having suffered much from the pirates of Sawunt Warree, an expedition was despatched from Bombay early in the year 1765, under the command of Major Gordon and Captain Watson, of the Bombay marine. They took the fort of Estwuntghur or Rairee, and changed its name to Fort Augustus; but on the 7th April of the same year, a treaty was concluded with the chieftain of Sawunt Warree, by which the British government agreed to restore the fort of Rairee, on conditions. These conditions do not appear to have been fulfilled; the result was the renewal of negotiation, terminating in another treaty, concluded 24th day of October, 1766, by which the restoration of the fort of Rairee was confirmed, subject to a certain payment. The consequences were natural and obvious: depredations continued to be perpetrated; and, as Duff observes, "it is no slight stigma on the British administration that this system of piracy was not finally suppressed until the year 1812." In that year a treaty was concluded between the chief of Sawunt Warree and the East-India Company, whereby the fort of Vingorla was surrendered to the latter, and very stringent clauses for the suppression of piracy were agreed to. The aggressive and predatory spirit of the rulers of Sawunt Warree was, however, not subdued. Remonstrance having failed, armed interference became necessary, and in 1819 the state was reduced by a British force, but given up again with certain exceptions, the forts of Estwuntghur (Rairee) and Newtee, together with the lands round those forts and belonging to their jurisdiction, comprehending the districts of Panti and Ajgaum, and the whole line of seacoast from the Carlee river to Vingorla, and from Vingorla to the Portuguese territory, being ceded to the English. The treaty under which this cession took place was modified by another, concluded in 1820, by which the inland villages were restored, the British government retaining only the forts and villages forming the line of the seacoast. These two treaties proved equally inefficient with those formerly concluded, and a succession of blundering diplomacy and unskilful military arrangements ensued, which appear to have left the country, as before, a thorough social and political chaos.

This state of things continued until 1838, when, on the breaking out of another formidable rebellion, it was considered inexpedient again to employ British troops in merely suppressing resistance to a chief to whom like aid had already frequently been afforded, and who had proved himself utterly unfit to rule. The removal of the Sir Dessayee from all authority was therefore considered to be an indispensable part of the new arrangement now rendered necessary. The country was temporarily placed under British management, to be hereafter restored to the Sir Dessayee or his family, when there should appear a sufficient prospect of good government. Two invasions of the Warree territory, organized by certain malcontents who had found shelter in the Goa territories, followed; but on both occasions the disturbances were with little difficulty put down. But in 1844 a more formidable insurrection broke out, and Anna Sahib, the heir-apparent, having joined the insurgents, his right to the succession was declared forfeited. The country was taken under the permanent management of the British government, and upon the death of its chief will be at the disposal of the paramount power. Since this period, the tranquillity of this principality has not again been disturbed; suttee has been abolished, and measures have been adopted to afford to all classes of the community protection from oppression, and the ready redress of grievances.

SAWUNTWARREE.—A town of Bombay, in the native state of Sawuntwarree, 38 miles W. by N. from Belgaum, and 22 miles E. by N. from Vingorla. Lat. 15° 56′, long. 74° 1′.

SAWUR, in the Rajpoot state of Jeypoor, a hill-fort and large populous village on the route from Agra to Neemuch, 147 miles S.W. of former, 182 N.E. of latter. Lat. 26° 8′, long. 76° 9′.

SAWURDE.—A town in the British district of Rutnageriah, lieut.-gov. of Bombay, 33 miles N.N.E. of Rutnageriah. Lat. 17° 24′, long. 73° 34′.

SAWURGAUM.—A town in the British district of Ahmednuggur, presidency of Bombay, 47 miles E. by N. of Nassik. Lat. 20° 7′, long. 74° 30′.

SAWUTSIR, in the Rajpoot state of Beekaneer, a village on the route from Rutungurh to the town of Beekaneer, and 33 miles E. of the latter: it contains sixty houses. Lat. 27° 54′, long. 73° 52′.

SAYGEWUN.—A town in Hyderabad, or territory of the Nizam, 61 miles N.W. by W. from Jaulnah, and 47 miles E. by S. from Malligaum. Lat. 20° 24′, long. 75° 11′.

SEAL, a river of Sumbulpore, rises in lat. 21° 33′, long. 84° 18′, and, flowing south-westerly for twenty-six miles, falls into the Mahanuddy river, in lat. 21° 28′, long. 84° 1′.

SEALKOTE, in the Reechna Doodb division of the Punjab, a town situated on the left bank of the Chenaub, 63 miles N.N.E. of the town of Lahore. The population amounts to 19,249. A church has been recently erected here. The district of which this town is the chief place has an area of 1,350 square miles, and a population of 641,782. Lat. 32° 29′, long. 74° 33′.

SEATAKOOND.—A town in the British district of Sarun, lieut.-gov. of Bengal, 36 miles S.E. by E. of Bettiah. Lat. 26° 30′, long. 85° 4′.

SEBBEAN.—A town of Burmah, situate on the left bank of the Irawady river, and 79 miles S.W. by W. from Ava. Lat. 21° 13′, long. 94° 59′.

SECROLE, in the British district of Benares,

under the lieut.-gov. of the N.W. Provinces, a small town adjoining the city of Benares on the west. It contains the civil establishments, the military cantonments, and the residences of the British population whose avocations are connected with the great city in the vicinity. The bungalows or lodges of the British engaged in civil pursuits are rather widely scattered outside the military cantonment, or to the west of it, and among numerous groves and gardens, the only ornaments of a scene otherwise not very attractive. The residences, however, are substantial, well finished, and well appointed, and rank among the best possessed by Europeans in this part of India. In the midst is the church, surmounted by a steeple, and well fitted up in the interior. There is besides a neat chapel, built by subscription, and open for divine service in Hindostanee. The other principal establishments are the Courts of Justice, the Treasury, and the Jail, plain brick-built structures. The best of the government buildings is the Mint, erected under the superintendence of Mr. James Prinsep, formerly manager of that department at Benares. It was scarcely finished, however, when the process of coinage within it was stopped, and the entire business removed to Calcutta.

The military cantonment is traversed by the small stream the Burnah Nuddy, which, in the middle of the assemblage of lodges and regimental buildings, is crossed, by means of a bridge, by the route from Allahabad to the city of Benares. The cantonment is the head-quarters for the Benares division of the Bengal army. Lat. 25° 18′, long. 83° 2′.

SECUNDERA, in the British district of Agra, lieut.-gov. of the N.W. Provinces, a village on the route from the city of Muttra to that of Agra. Here is an asylum for the children of natives who perished in the dreadful famine of A.D. 1837-1838. The number, originally 350, was in 1841 reduced by death to less than 300 boys and girls, in nearly equal proportion: the former are taught gardening and handicrafts; the latter, spinning, sewing, and similar pursuits suitable to their sex; and both are educated in the Christian faith. When of age, they intermarry, and are located in a contiguous village, formed of houses provided for their accommodation. Secundera is celebrated for containing the mausoleum of Akbar, who, with great prosperity and renown, reigned over India and Afghanistan from A.D. 1555 to 1605. The mausoleum is situate in the midst of a square embattled inclosure, said to contain forty acres, and entered by four vast and superb gateways, one being in the middle of each side of the square. They are built of red sandstone, each surmounted by four minarets, with numerous tablets, mouldings, and other ornaments of white marble, and inscriptions in black marble. That on the west side is in tolerable preservation, the rest are in ruins. The remains of Akbar lie in a deep vault, under the centre of the building, and beneath an unornamented slab of marble. This building is generally supposed to have been erected by Akbar for the reception of his own body. However, Akbar's son and successor Jehangir states that he himself built it, in honour of his father's memory. Lat. 27° 13′, long. 78° 1′.

SECUNDERA, in the Rajpoot state of Jeypore, a town on the route from Agra to Ajmeer, 93 miles W. of former, 135 E. of latter. It is situate on the right or south bank of the Bangunga, a torrent having a channel several hundred yards wide, devoid of water in the dry season, but having a wide and rapid stream during the periodical rains. The town is surrounded by a mud rampart. Lat. 26° 57′, long. 76° 38′.

SECUNDERABAD, in the territory of the Nizam, a British military cantonment, advantageously situate on the north-east side of the Hoosain Sagur, a tank or artificial piece of water, about three miles in length from north to south, and two in breadth, lying amidst a number of smaller tanks, with which the surrounding country singularly abounds. To the west, and distant three miles, is a range of hills, consisting of granite rocks, heaped on each other in a variety of strange and fantastic shapes; and two miles to the north-east are two very remarkable and large granitic hills, of an hemispherical shape, each completely isolated. Their summits, which are considerably elevated above the adjacent country, are surmounted by the tombs of Mussulman ascetics regarded as saints, and hence numerous pilgrimages are annually performed to them. The cantonment extends in a line from east to west nearly three miles, forming a curved irregular street, having the officers' houses ranged on either side, in moderately-sized inclosures. This street is intersected in different parts by others, running north and south, which afford a facility of communication with the bazars, the sepoys' lines, and the parade-ground. The sepoys' lines face the north, and behind them are the bazars, extending three-fourths of the length of the cantonment. At the right, or eastern extremity of the cantonment, are the European infantry barracks, and a short distance to the north of Saint John's Church, a large and handsome building, situate on the highest ground in the cantonment; in consequence, however, of the unhealthiness of the spot, orders have been issued for the erection of new infantry barracks on a more eligible site. North of the sepoys' lines are the hospitals and arsenal. On the western extremity of the barracks are the horse-artillery lines, and north of it, and separated from it by the spacious parade, are the foot-artillery barracks. The cavalry lines are two miles north of the cantonment, at Bowenpilly, in an open country, on a rising ground, remarkably healthy. In the town, around the bazars of the cantonment, the streets are crooked, narrow, and irregular, and, the ground being uneven, pools of dirty water, and accumulations of filth are formed, causing during the hot season noisome and pestilential exhalations. Much attention, however, has latterly been given to remedy these evils by the formation of sewers, and the inhabitants are held responsible for the clearing and cleansing of the streets before their respective houses. There is an abundant supply of good water, from numerous wells and fountains. "The south-west monsoon commences generally at Secunderabad in the beginning of June, and continues at intervals till about the middle of October. During November and December the sky is frequently cloudy, and the winds easterly; and sometimes also in the north-east monsoon a considerable quantity of rain falls. From the beginning of January to the end of May the sky is generally clear, and the weather dry. Dews are not unfrequent in January and the early part of February, and in some years light showers of rain occur during these months. The annual fall of rain is estimated at thirty-two inches, but in years when the monsoon fails, it does not amount to half that quantity. The mean temperature in the house for one year, deduced from observations made at sunrise, at two o'clock in the afternoon, and at sunset, was, in January, 74½°; February, 76¼°; March, 84°; April, 91⅓°; May, 93°; June, 88°; July, 81°; August, 80½°; September, 79°; October, 80°; November, 76°; December, 74½°; giving as the annual mean 81⅓°." The most sickly times of the year are the wet and cold seasons. The prevalent diseases are fevers, dysenteries, and rheumatism. According to the latest accounts, there are in the town 5,000 houses, containing a population of 34,357. Elevation above the sea 1,837 feet. Distance from Mangalore, N.E., 498 miles; Madras, N.W., 398; Bombay, S.E., 449; Calcutta, S.W., 962. Lat. 17° 26′, long. 78° 33′.

SECUNDERPOOR, in the British district of Azimgurh, lieut.-gov. of the N.W. Provinces, a town on the route from Azimgurh to Mozufferpoor, 56 miles E. of the former. Lat. 26°, long. 84° 6′.

SECUNDERPOOR.—A town in Oude, situate on the left bank of the Ganges river, and 38 miles S.W. by W. from Lucknow. Lat. 26° 34′, long. 80° 29′.

SEDASHEVAGHUR, in the British district of North Canara, presidency of Madras, a town on the north side of the Cauly Nuddy, and a mile east of its mouth. The Cauly Nuddy, descending from the Ghats, here discharges itself into an inlet of the sea opposite the town, about a mile wide and twenty-five feet deep at high tide; but the entrance is hazardous and intricate, and ships frequenting this part of the coast anchor outside in Carwar Bay, a roadstead sheltered by several islets, of which the principal are Karmaguda and that by the British sailors called Oyster Rock. Sedashevaghur, as the name indicates, has a fort, founded by Sedashwa Rao, one of the rajahs of Soonda, who grew into importance on the overthrow of the great kingdom of Vijayanagar at the battle of Talikote, in the year 1564. Distance N.W. from Mangalore 145 miles, S.E. from Bombay 290. Lat. 14° 52′, long. 74° 12′.

SEEALPUNT, in the British district of Kumaon, lieut.-gov. of the N.W. Provinces, a town on the route from Almora to Tibet, 60 miles E.N.E. of the former. Lat. 29° 58′, long. 80° 39′.

SEEANUH, in the British district of Boolundshuhur, lieut.-gov. of the N.W. Provinces, a town on the route from Boolundshuhur to Moradabad, 20 miles N.N.E. of the former. It contains a population of 5,841 inhabitants. Lat. 28° 37′, long. 78° 9′.

SEEAUL KA GUR, in the Sinde Sagur Dooab division of the Punjab, a town situated 10 miles from the right bank of the Chenaub, 53 miles N.N.E. of the town of Mooltan. Lat. 30° 54′, long. 71° 50′.

SEEBGUNJE, in the British district of Bograh, lieut.-gov. of Bengal, a town on the river Curratten, a considerable stream flowing from north to south, and navigable throughout the year for small craft, and during the periodical rains for those of great burthen. Lat. 25°, long. 89° 20′.

SEEBGUNJE.—A town in the British district of Maldah, lieut.-gov. of Bengal, 26 miles S. of Maldah. Lat. 24° 40′, long. 88° 10′.

SEEBPOOR.—A town in the British district of Midnapoor, lieut.-gov. of Bengal, 46 miles S. by E. of Midnapoor. Lat. 21° 47′, long. 87° 30′.

SEEBPOOR.—A town of Assam, in the British district of Seebpoor, 46 miles S.E. by E. of Luckimpoor. Lat. 27°, long. 94° 40′.

SEEBSAGUR.—A town of Assam, in the British district of Seebpoor, two miles N. of Seebpoor. Lat. 27° 2′, long. 94° 39′.

SEEDUM.—A town in the lapsed territory of Odeipoor, on the south-western frontier of Bengal, 20 miles N. from Odeipoor, and 72 miles S.W. by S. from Palamow. Lat. 22° 57′, long. 83° 24′.

SEEHA, in the British district of Goorgaon, lieut.-gov. of the N.W. Provinces, a village close to the western frontier, towards the jaghire of Jujhur. Lat. 28° 15′, long. 76° 29′.

SEEINGHOU.—A town of Burmah, situate on the left bank of the Irawady river, and 109 miles S.W. from Ava. Lat. 20° 51′, long. 94° 41′.

SEEKAR, in the Rajpoot territory of Shekawutee, a town, the residence of a thakoor or chief, one of the five principal leaders of that country. His revenue, according to Tod, amounts to 8,00,000 rupees annually. On the invasion by the British troops in 1835, it was occupied by them, having been surrendered without resistance. Distance S.W. from Delhi

143 miles, N.W. from Agra 180. Lat. 27° 36′, long. 75° 20′.

SEEKREE, in the British district of Budaon, lieut.-gov. of the N.W. Provinces, a town on the route from Bareilly to Delhi, and 35 miles W. of the former. It has a bazar, and is supplied with water from wells. Lat. 28° 26′, long. 78° 59′.

SEELDHURRUMPORE.—A town of Assam, in the British district of Nowgong, 30 miles S.E. by E. of Nowgong. Lat. 26° 7′, long. 93° 10′.

SEENA.—A river rising in the British collectorate of Ahmednuggur, in lat. 19° 8′, long. 74° 37′. It flows south-east through this collectorate and that of Sholapore, and falls into the Beemah river in lat. 17° 22′, long. 75° 58′.

SEENGURH, in the British district of Mozuffurnuggur, lieut.-gov. of the N.W. Provinces, a village on the route from Kurnal to Meerut, and 17 miles S.E. of the former. Lat. 29° 33′, long. 77° 14′.

SEEPAH.—A town in the British district of Sarun, lieut.-gov. of Bengal, 30 miles S. by W. of Bettiah. Lat. 26° 21′, long. 84° 30′.

SEEPOW.—A town in the native state of Dholpoor, 13 miles N.W. from Dholpoor, and 33 miles S.W. by S. from Agra. Lat. 26° 47′, long. 77° 50′.

SEEPRA.—A river of Malwa, rising on the north side of the Vindhya range, 11 miles E. of the small town of Peepulda, and in lat. 22° 37′, long. 76° 12′. It has a winding course, generally north-westerly, through a fertile country, and forty miles from its source receives on the left side the small river Kaund, and passing subsequently by the towns of Oojein and Mahidpoor, falls into the Chumbul on the right side, in lat. 23° 54′, long. 75° 29′, after a total course of 120 miles. So sinuous is its progress, that in a distance of twenty-six miles it is thrice crossed by the route from Mhow to Mahidpoor, by Oojein, being in each instance fordable in fair weather. At the point of passage, six miles north of Oojein, or lower down the stream than that city, and fifty-five miles from the source, the passage is made by "a rugged rocky ford, of about 100 yards in width." Higher up the stream, and four miles south of Oojein, it is crossed on the route from Agra to Mhow, and there has "a bed rocky for 100 yards; banks steep, and cut into ravines at the ghat (ford); width of the stream in dry season twenty yards, and from one to one and a half feet deep." Still higher, at Bowlea, about twenty miles from the source, it is crossed, on the route from Mhow to Saugor, by a ford "fifteen yards wide, with little water, and a sandy bed." Close to Mahidpoor, it is crossed, on the route from Neemuch to that town, "by ferry, or otherwise by a deep ford higher up." During the rains, the river swells and overflows many places on its banks. In 1821, it rose to such a height as to wash away part of the town of Mahidpore. In the Ayeen Akbery it is gravely stated, "It is astonishing that sometimes this river flows with milk." A similar belief, according to Jacquemont, is still entertained by devotees respecting the water of a small deep tank close to the bank of the river, at Oojein. "The water of this basin, notwithstanding its uninviting appearance, has, for devotees of competent faith, varied and delicious tastes, according to the various seasons of the year. In summer, the taste is that of sherbet; in autumn, of milk; in winter, of honey, &c. &c. It is not drunk unless it has passed through the hands of the Brahmins who frequent the place, and live by the credulity of the devotees."

SEER, in Sinde, the mouth of the Goongroo or Pinyaree branch of the Indus, which in its lower part is, in consequence of the dam thrown across it at Maghribee, deserted by the stream, except during the highest state of the inundation. This estuary is navigable for boats of forty tons. The Seer mouth is in lat. 23° 46′, long. 68° 7′.

SEERAMPOOR.—A town in the territory inhabited by the independent hill tribes of Orissa, 49 miles W. from Goomsoor, and 120 miles S. from Sumbulpoor. Lat. 19° 45′, long. 83° 57′.

SEERHUTTEE.—A town in the native Mahratta jaghire of Sanglee, presidency of Bombay, 41 miles E.S.E. from Dharwar, and 90 miles W. from Bellary. Lat. 15° 13′, long. 75° 39′.

SEERMOW, in the territory of Bhopal, a town on the route from Hoshungabad to Saugor, 76 miles N.E. of former, 38 S.W. of latter. It is situate at the south base of a ghat or passage over a ridge of trap, amidst stupendous hills and cliffs of the same formation. It has a bazar, and is supplied with water from wells. Lat. 23° 24′, long. 78° 34′.

SEERMOWA, in the British district of Furruckabad, lieut.-gov. of the N.W. Provinces, a village on the route from the cantonment of Allygurh to that of Futtegurh, and 14 miles N.W. of the latter. Lat. 27° 26′, long. 79° 29′.

SEEROOEE.—See Serohee.

SEERPAHDEE.—A town in the native state of Mohurbunge, on the south-west frontier of Bengal, 70 miles W. by S. from Midnapoor, and 57 miles S. from Burraboom. Lat. 22° 16′, long. 86° 20′.

SEERPOOR.—A town in Hyderabad, or territory of the Nizam, 164 miles N.N.E. from Hyderabad, and 128 miles S.E. from Ellichpoor. Lat. 19° 30′, long. 79° 38′.

SEERPORE, in the British district of Patna, lieut.-gov. of Bengal, a town on the right or south bank of the Ganges. It has about 1,000 houses, and a population of 5,000. The town is distant W. from Patna 15 miles,

E. from Benares, by way of Ghazipoor, 140. Lat. 25° 40′, long. 85° 2′.

SEERPORE.—A town in the British district of Moorshedabad, lieut.-gov. of Bengal, 18 miles W. by S. of Moorshedabad. Lat. 24° 8′, long. 88° 1′.

SEERPORE, in the British district of Bograh, lieut.-gov. of Bengal, a town near the south frontier, towards the British district of Pubna. It is situate on the right bank of the great river Curatteea, and is of rather considerable size. Distant S. from the town of Bogra 12 miles, N.E. from Burhampoor 82, from Calcutta 200. Lat. 24° 40′, long. 89° 24′.

SEERSOONDEE.—A town in the territory of Nagpoor, 100 miles S.E. by E. from Nagpoor, and 122 miles S.E. by E. from Seuni. Lat. 20° 27′, long. 80° 30′.

SEETABULDEE.—An eminence in the outskirts of the town of Nagpoor, the chief place in the British territory of the same name. This spot has been rendered memorable by an action which took place there on the 26th November, 1817, when a treacherous attack upon the British, made by order of the rajah of Nagpore with a body of 20,000 men, was gallantly met and defeated by a force of not more than 1,400. A noble charge, made by Captain Fitzgerald with a small party of cavalry upon a large body of the enemy's horse, decided the fortune of the day. The resident, Mr. Jenkins, was on the field throughout the day, as was also his assistant Mr. Sotheby, who was there killed. Distant 102 miles E. from Ellichpoor, and 90 miles S.E. by E. from Baitool. Lat. 21° 10′, long. 79° 9′.

SEETA MOW, in Malwa, a town, the principal place of a small raj of the same name. It is held by a petty rajah, a descendant of a scion ot the family of Joudpore. The annual revenue paid to the rajah is estimated at 90,000 rupees, out of which he pays 60,000 Salim Shye rupees, or 47,250 Company's rupees, to Scindia. The rajah some time since claimed a reduction of tribute, on the ground of the insufficiency of the resources of the country to meet the claim; and compliance with his requisition has been made dependent upon the result of a survey of his territory. Population of the town about 10,000. Distant N.W. of Oojein 66 miles, S.W. of Gwalior fort 230. Lat. 24° 3′, long. 75° 27′.

SEETE LEKH, in the British district of Kumaon, lieut.-gov. of the N.W. Provinces, a peak of the main range of the Himalaya, on the right bank of the Kali (Eastern), and forming part of the ridge separating the mahall or subdivision of Bians from that of Dharma. Elevation above the sea 15,833 feet. Lat. 30° 8′, long. 80° 52′.

SEETULGUREE, in the British district of Muzuffurnugur, lieut.-gov. of the N.W. Provinces, a village on the route from Kurnal to Meerut, and 11 miles S.E. of the former. Lat. 29° 35′, long. 77° 10′.

SEEWANA.—A town in the Rajpoot state of Jodhpoor, nine miles S. of the left bank of the Loonee river, and 62 miles S.W. from Jodhpoor. Lat. 25° 40′, long. 72° 29′.

SEGAON.—A town in the territory of Nagpoor, 58 miles S. from Nagpoor, and 123 miles S.E. by E. from Ellichpoor. Lat. 20° 20′, long. 79° 13′.

SEGOR GUNGE.—A town in the jaghire of Rampoor, lieut.-gov. of the N.W. Provinces. Lat. 28° 40′, long. 79° 1′.

SEGOWLEE, in the British district of Sarun, lieut.-gov. of Bengal, a town on the route from Goruckpoor cantonment to that of Mulye, 98 miles E. of former, 51 W. of latter. Supplies and water are abundant. Lat. 26° 44′, long. 84° 47′.

SEGU.—A village in the British district of Boolundshuhur, lieut.-gov. of the N.W. Provinces, 45 miles E. of Delhi. Lat. 28° 35′, long. 78° 1′.

SEHAR, in the British district of Futtehpore, lieut.-gov. of the N.W. Provinces, a town on the right bank of the Ganges, nearly opposite Dalmau, and 18 miles N.E. of the town of Futtehpore. Lat. 26°, long. 81°.

SEHARI KA SARAE, in the British district of Agra, a village on the route from the city of Agra to Jeypore, and eight miles W. of the former. Lat. 27° 9′, long. 77° 58′.

SEHMBILL.—A town in the Rajpoot state of Oodeypoor, 38 miles N.W. from Oodeypoor, and 90 miles S. by E. from Jodhpoor. Lat. 25° 3′, long. 73° 30′.

SEHOOR.—A town in Hyderabad, or territory of the Nizam, 30 miles W.N.W. from Dowlutabad, and 68 miles N. from Ahmednuggur. Lat. 20° 3′, long. 74° 50′.

SEHORE.—A town in the British district of Ahmedabad, presidency of Bombay, 103 miles S.S.W. of Ahmedabad. Lat. 21° 40′, long. 71° 55′.

SEHORE, in Malwa, a town of Bhopal, on the route from Saugor to Asseergurh, 132 miles S.W. of former, 152 N.E. of latter. It is situate on a boldly-rising rock of quartz, and is a considerable town, the residence of the British political agent for Bhopal. Around it is a large grove of mangoes and other trees. There is a considerable manufacture of printed muslins. There is a good bazar, and water is abundant, the town being situate on the right bank of the Saven, a small river tributary to the Parbutty. Distant S.W. of Bhopal 22 miles, N.W. of Hoshungabad 66. Lat. 23° 12′, long. 77° 3′.

SEHRA.—A town within the dominions of Gholab Singh, the ruler of Cashmere, situate on the left bank of the Pir Punjal river, and 57 miles S.W. by W. from Sirinagur. Lat. 33° 38′, long. 74° 6′.

SEHUL, in the British district of Moradabad, lieut.-gov. of the N.W. Provinces, a village on the route from the town of Moradabad to Almora, and five miles N. of the former. Lat. 28° 54′, long. 78° 58′.

SEHUREE, in the British district of Goruckpoor, lieut.-gov. of the N.W. Provinces, a town on the route from Goruckpoor to Buraech, 62 miles N.W. by W. of the former. Lat. 27° 8', long. 82° 31'.

SEHWAN, in Sinde, a town situate on an eminence at the verge of a swamp on the right or south-west bank of the Arul, which flows from the Lake Manchur into the Indus, and which abreast of the town is about 100 yards wide, and when lowest twelve feet deep. The Indus, a few years ago, flowed close to the town, but is now two miles distant from it. Ruined houses, mosques, and sepulchres cover here a wide space, and bear evidence of the greatness of this city before it was ruined by the Kalora princes of Sinde. The houses of the present town are of mud, often several stories high, and arched. They are superior to those usually to be seen in the towns of Sinde; but the bazar, long, crooked, narrow, and covered with mats to exclude the scorching beams of the sun, is ill supplied with goods, and has little trade. The manufactures are inconsiderable, consisting of caps, shoes, and petty silken fabrics. The inhabitants are chiefly fishermen or beggars, which last class are supported by the pilgrims who flock to the shrine of Lal Shah Baz, whose memory stands high for sanctity, not only with Mussulmans, but also with Hindoos. The remains of this reputed saint, who was originally from Khorasan, lie in a tomb inclosed in a quadrangular edifice, covered with a dome and lantern, ornamented with smaller domes and spires, and with glazed porcelain tiles, bearing numerous inscriptions in Arabic characters. The gate is of hammered silver, as is the balustrade round the tomb, which is covered with rich cloths. The sepulchre is reputed to contain a considerable treasure, and its keepers are endowed with the gardens of Sehwan and several villages. Great numbers of pilgrims flock to this spot from all parts of Sinde and the neighbouring countries; but neither the possession of so sacred a deposit, nor the example of so much devotion, has any beneficial effect on the morals of the population, who are remarkable for idleness and profligacy. North-west of the town, and separated from it by a deep channel, is an eminence about eighty feet high, having its sides cased with a brick wall. The summit is oval, and is 1,200 feet long and 750 wide. It is covered with ruins and fragments of pottery; the remains of towers are visible along the circuit of the wall, and two fine arched gateways are in tolerable preservation. The population of Sehwan is estimated by Burnes at about 2,000. Lat. 26° 24', long. 67° 55'.

SEIK STATES.—See SIRHIND.

SEILGOMNA.—A town in the native state of Korea, on the south-west frontier of Bengal, 68 miles E.N.E. from Sohagpoor, and 101 miles W. by S. from Palamow. Lat. 23° 40', long. 82° 26'.

SEIBSA.—A town in the British district of Midnapoor, lieut.-gov. of Bengal, 61 miles W. by N. of Calcutta. Lat. 22° 40', long. 87° 30'.

SEKAYGAHDO.—A town of Burmah, situate on the left bank of the Irawady river, and 66 miles S.W. by W. from Ava. Lat. 21° 22', long. 95° 8'.

SEKKAYBEEN.—A town in the British territory of Pegu, situate on the left bank of the Irawady river, and 69 miles W. by N. from Pegu. Lat. 17° 48', long. 95° 16'.

SEKRORA, in the territory of Oude, a British cantonment three miles E. of the left bank of the Eastern Surjoo, a feeder of the Ghaghra, 56 miles N.E. of Lucknow, 115 N. of Allahabad. The Surjoo is crossed by a ferry: the road towards Lucknow is good in dry weather. Lat. 27° 7', long. 81° 44'.

SEKSURA.—A town in Nepal, situate on the left bank of the Arun river, and 101 miles E. by N. from Khatmandoo. Lat. 27° 54', long. 86° 55'.

SEKUNDRA, in the British district of Cawnpoor, lieut.-gov. of the N.W. Provinces, a town on the route from Cawnpoor to Jalloun, 46 miles W. of the former. Lat. 26° 22', long. 79° 41'.

SELA GUNGA, a river of independent Tipperah, rises in lat. 23° 55', long. 92° 8', and flowing first westerly for thirty-five miles, then south for eighteen, falls into the Goomtee river, in lat. 23° 34', long. 91° 37'.

SELIMABAD.—A town in the British district of Burdwan, lieut.-gov. of Bengal, 11 miles S.E. by S. of Burdwan. Lat. 23° 4', long. 88° 1'.

SELLEEGOREE.—A town in the British district of Dinajepore, lieut.-gov. of Bengal, 77 miles N. by W. of Dinajepore. Lat. 26° 39', long. 88° 23'.

SELON.—A town in Oude, situate on the right bank of the Saee Nuddee, and 68 miles S.E. by S. from Lucknow. Lat. 26° 1', long. 81° 31'.

SEMARA.—A town in Nepal, situate at the source of one of the branches of the Raptee river, and 153 miles W. from Khatmandoo. Lat. 27° 40', long. 82° 50'.

SEMARREEA.—A town in the territory of Nagpoor, 156 miles E.N.E. from Nagpoor, and 77 miles S.S.E. from Ramgurh. Lat. 21° 49', long. 81° 29'.

SEMBEW GHEWN.—A town of Burmah, situate on the right bank of the Irawady river, and 123 miles S.W. from Ava. Lat. 20° 38', long. 94° 36'.

SEMKUR.—A town of Eastern India, in the territory lately belonging to Toola Ram Senahputtee, 74 miles E. from Jynteahpore, and 89 miles S.S.E. from Nowgong. Lat. 25° 12', long. 93° 14'.

SEMOWLEE.—A town in the native state of Gwalior, or territory of Scindia, situate on the right bank of the Asun river, and 19 miles N.W. from Gwalior. Lat. 26° 23', long. 78°.

SEMULBAREE.—A town in the British district of Purneah, lieut.-gov. of Bengal, 20 miles N.E. of Purneah. Lat. 25° 57', long. 87° 47'.

SENDHAT.—A town of Burmah, situate on the left bank of the Irawady river, and 46 miles W. from Ava. Lat. 21° 54', long. 95° 20'.

SENEE.—A town in the native state of Bhotan, situate on the left bank of the Monas river, and 103 miles N. by W. from Gowhatty. Lat. 27° 38', long. 91° 37'.

SENGE KHABAB, or INDUS RIVER. —See INDUS.

SENOWRA, in the British district of Mynpooree, lieut.-gov. of the N.W. Provinces, a village on the route from the cantonment of Aligurh to that of Etawa, and 40 miles N.W. of the latter. Lat. 27° 12', long. 78° 36'.

SENTULGURH, in the Rajpoot state of Jeypore, a small town on the route from Delhi to the town of Jeypore, 26 miles N.E. of latter. It is surrounded by a mud rampart, and is situate in a sandy plain little capable of production, and consequently scantily cultivated. Lat. 27° 5', long. 76° 23'.

SEOGURH.—A town in Oude, 83 miles N.E. from Lucknow, and 120 miles E. from Shahjehanpoor. Lat. 27° 43', long. 81° 55'.

SEOHARA, in the British district of Bijnour, lieut.-gov. of the N.W. Provinces, a town on the route from Dehra to Moradabad, and 29 miles N.W. of the latter. The surrounding country is in general sandy, and overrun with jungle. Elevation above the sea 701 feet; distance N.W. from Calcutta 917 miles. It contains a population of 6,414 inhabitants. Lat. 29° 13', long. 78° 39'.

SEONDA, in the British district of Banda, lieut.-gov. of the N.W. Provinces, a small town on the route from the town of Banda to Kalleenjur, 25 miles N.W. of the latter. Lat. 25° 18', long. 80° 25'.

SEONDARA, in the British district of Moradabad, lieut.-gov. of the N.W. Provinces, a town on the route from Moradabad to Budaoon, 19 miles S. by E. of the former. Lat. 28° 33', long. 78° 56'.

SEOTIE.—A river rising in Mirzapoor, about lat. 24° 44', long. 82° 15', close to the Bujhut Ghat, and at an elevation above the sea of probably about 1,000 feet. It holds a northerly course of about fifteen miles, and then turning to the north-west, flows by the northern base of the Kutra Pass, and receiving several small streams, falls into the Bilund, on its left side, in lat. 24° 55', long. 82° 8', having flowed altogether a distance of about forty miles.

SEOWLA, in the British district of Futtehpore, lieut.-gov. of the N.W. Provinces, a village on the route from Cawnpore to the town of Futtehpore, and nine miles N.W. of the latter. Lat. 26° 2', long. 80° 44'.

SERA, in the British district of Bijnour, lieut.-gov. of the N.W. Provinces, a village on the route from Moradabad to Hurdwar, and 43 miles N.W. of the former. Lat. 29° 24', long. 78° 31'.

SERA, in the territory of Mysore, a town situate on a tributary of the river Vedavati. It has a fort, well built of stone, of considerable size, and regular construction. Within are the remains of the residence of the former nawaub or Mussulman governor. There is likewise a large mosque, besides some others of less importance, this having been formerly a very populous place; but it suffered dreadfully from the predatory attacks of the Mahrattas, and Tippoo Sultan further urged its ruin, by taking away 12,000 families to replenish the town of Shahar Ganjam, which he built on the island of Seringapatam. It has, however, since the establishment of British supremacy, in some degree revived, and contains a few good streets, 2,000 houses having been built in the first year after the overthrow of Tippoo Sultan. Here are two extensive tanks, but in few years is the rain sufficient to replenish them, the climate of this part of Mysore being very dry. The overthrow of the monarchy of Vijayanuggur by a Mussulman confederacy, at the great battle of Talikote, took place in 1564, and about eighty years later Sera was subjugated by the king of Beejapoor, and granted in jaghire to Shahjee, the father of Sevajee. The town became the seat of an extensive provincial government. On the overthrow of the state of Beejapoor by Aurungzebe, it appears to have become part of the soobah or province of the Deccan, and was held as a sort of fief, ostensibly subordinate to the Nizam, after that officer had attained independence. In 1757 it was captured by the Mahrattas; and though still in their possession, it was, in 1761, nominally conferred on Hyder Ali, the formidable adventurer of Mysore, by Basalut Jung, the brother of Nizam Ali. Hyder found little difficulty in making himself master of the place. In 1767 it came into the possession of the Mahrattas, but was immediately restored for a pecuniary compensation. In 1772 it was again wrested from that potentate by the Mahrattas, but retaken in the following year by his son Tippoo Sultan. In 1791, when Lord Cornwallis advanced into Mysore, it was occupied by the British. Its elevation above the sea has been estimated at 2,223 feet. Distance from Seringapatam, N., 92 miles; Bangalore, N.W., 73; Madras, W., 234; Mangalore, N.E., 150. Lat. 13° 45', long. 76° 57'.

SERAEN.—A town in the British district of Pooree, one of the divisions of Cuttack, presidency of Bengal, 17 miles N.W. by N. of Juggurnaut. Lat. 20°, long. 85° 45'.

SERAI, in the British district of Bundelcund, lieut.-gov. of the N.W. Provinces, a town on the route from Tehree to Saugur, 30 miles S. of the former. Lat. 24° 7′, long. 78° 50′.

SERAI GUNGOH, in the British district of Suharunpoor, a village on the route from Kurnal to Suharunpoor, and 23 miles N.E. of the former town. Distant N.W. from Calcutta 988 miles. Lat. 29° 46′, long. 77° 20′.

SERAMPORE, in the British district of Hoogly, lieut.-gov. of Bengal, a town on the right or western bank of the river Hoogly. Heber describes it as "a handsome place, kept beautifully clean, and looking more like a European town than Calcutta, or any of its neighbouring cantonments;" and, viewed from the opposite side of the river, it has a peculiarly pleasing appearance. Here are a court-house, and a large building which was the government house during Danish rule. The place acquired some celebrity as being the spot where, in the latter part of the last century, the Baptist missionaries established themselves, and where they prosecuted their labours for the advancement of Christianity in India, and for the acquisition by Europeans of a knowledge of the languages of the East. The institution which they reared attracted to the place a degree of attention which otherwise it certainly would never have commanded.

Serampore was at one time the Alsatia of Calcutta, and afforded refuge to schemers, insolvent debtors, and reckless adventurers, who had found it prudent to disappear from that metropolis. It was in consequence a bustling, lively, gay, dissipated place; but the state of affairs has been changed by the loss of its immunities, which having been found very troublesome to the jurisdiction of the East-India Company, the place has been purchased from the Danes, and formally transferred to the British: the pecuniary equivalent was calculated at twenty-five years' purchase of the net revenue. Serampore is noted for its manufacture of paper. The supply required for the impressions of the *Calcutta Gazette* is furnished from hence; and the coarser quality, denominated cartridge-paper, is said to be equal in every respect to that of England. Population of town, exclusive of that of the suburbs, 13,000; distant from Calcutta, N., 18 miles. Lat. 22° 46′, long. 88° 24′.

SERAMPORE.—A town in the British district of Ramgur, lieut.-gov. of Bengal, 61 miles E. by N. of Hazareebagh. Lat. 24° 8′, long. 86° 20′.

SERAN.—A town in the native hill province of Koonawar, situate on the left bank of the Sutlej river, and 46 miles N.E. by E. from Simla. Lat. 31° 30′, long. 77° 51′.

SERAO, in Gurwhal, a small town in the valley of the Budeear, and on the left bank of the river of that name. It is situate amidst a large extent of terraces, formed on the declivity of the mountain rising behind it, and carefully cultivated. Serao is 7,885 feet above the sea. Lat. 30° 57′, long. 78° 17′.

SERGOONG.—A town in the native state of Bhotan, 62 miles N. by E. from Durrung, and 73 miles N.W. from Bishnath. Lat. 27° 18′, long. 92° 17′.

SERIEKALA. — A town in the British district of Singboom, on the south-west frontier of Bengal, 18 miles N.E. from Chaibassa, and 36 miles S.W. by W. from Burraboom. Lat. 22° 46′, long. 85° 58′.

SERINAGUR.—See SIREENUGGUR.

SERINGAPATAM, a celebrated fortress and town, formerly the capital of the territory of Mysore, is situate on the western extremity of an island in the river Cauvery. The island is about three miles in length and one in breadth, and the writer by whom these dimensions are furnished, describes it as having "a most dreary, ugly appearance, inasmuch as naked rock and dirty mud walls are its most predominant features." The town of Seringapatam is an ill-built, mean place, with narrow streets, and houses ill ventilated, hot, and excessively inconvenient for Europeans: it is described by the author already quoted as altogether "a sink of nastiness." Water is, however, abundantly supplied from the river Cauvery, which washes the walls on the northern and south-west sides. The ramparts rising from the banks on those sides were the weakest parts of the defences, Tippoo Sultan injudiciously confiding in the difficulties which the river presented to assailants, though it may be forded during the dry season. In the rainy season, however, it is a great torrent, utterly unfordable; and at all times, the rapidity of the current and roughness of the bed, filled with rocks and fragments of granite, render the fording it a matter of some difficulty. The ground-plan of the inclosed space is an irregular pentagon, measuring in diameter, from south-east to the north-west angle, about one and a half mile, and three-quarters of a mile in breadth. On the east and south sides, which are not washed by the river, Tippoo Sultan erected defences, very massive and heavy, and, though not skilfully planned, offering such resistance to an attack, that the final and conclusive one in 1799 was made across the Cauvery, in preference to an attempt to breach those enormous masses. The palace of Tippoo Sultan is within the fort, and is a very large building, formerly surrounded by a strong and lofty wall of stone and mud. It is, however, of very mean appearance, but has some spacious apartments, which, after the place was taken, were used for barracks; but, in consequence of defective ventilation, they were but indifferently suited for the purpose. The inclosing rampart of this inner work has been destroyed, and the space has been planted with trees. Contiguous is the fine and lofty temple of Sriranga, the tutelar deity; and at no great distance the ancient palace of the Hindoo rajahs of Mysore.

The Shehr Ganjam, a considerable suburb detached from the fortified town, and east of it, was demolished by Tippoo Sultan on the eve of the investment of the place, lest it might afford shelter to the besiegers; but after the capture it was rebuilt with considerable regularity. The population of the island in the reign of Tippoo has been conjectured to have amounted to 150,000, all supported by the court and army, scarcely any manufactures having been established. This estimate can hardly, however, be assumed as approaching to correctness, as in 1800, the population, exclusive of the garrison and its followers, was taken to be only 31,895. The number is now only 12,744, the place "having been abandoned as a military station, in consequence of the deadly character of an endemic fever which prevailed there, and which for several years carried off vast numbers both of Europeans and natives; and it is now fast falling into decay, and becoming every year more and more deserted." Srirangapatna, the name of which has by British usage passed into Seringapatam, is said to have been founded by Sri Rang, an ancient prince, who called it Sri Rang Patna, or the town of Sri Rang; but, according to another account, it was founded as late as 1454, by a devotee, who named it the city of Sri Ranga, or the Holy Ranga, which is considered to be one of the names of Vishnu. Native legends again ascribe its foundation to the wives of Ravana, the giant tyrant of Lanka or Ceylon, who, foreseeing his approaching destruction by Rama, caused the females of his family to escape by flying northward. No historical records, however, trace its existence earlier than 1610, when it was acquired by the Raj Wadegar, a chief of Mysore, and made the seat of his government; though there is some reason to believe it to have been previously the residence of the viceroy of the great rajah of Vijayanagar. In 1697 it was besieged by a tumultuary army of Mahrattas, who were repulsed with great slaughter. In 1755 it was besieged by the army of M. Bussy, acting on behalf of Salabut Jung, claiming to be soubhadar of the Deccan, whose hostility was bought off by the payment of a large sum as arrears of tribute. In 1765 it was chosen by the formidable adventurer Hyder Ali as the seat of his government. In 1772 it was again besieged by the Mahrattas, who departed on receiving from Hyder Ali 15,00,000 rupees, with the promise of a like sum at a future period. In 1791, the British government being engaged in war with Tippoo Sultan, son and successor of Hyder Ali, Lord Cornwallis, governor-general and commander-in-chief, after having, without opposition, ascended the ghats by the Mugh Pass, and stormed Bangalore, arrived before Seringapatam, but from want of provisions he was obliged to relinquish the siege, and retrace his course in the direction of Bangalore. Resuming his operations in the beginning of 1792 with an army better appointed and provisioned, he signally defeated the forces of Tippoo Sultan on the north bank of the Cauvery, and having succeeded in establishing a considerable force on the island, the town and fort were nearly invested on all sides, when further hostilities were averted by the arrangement of a treaty, under which the ruler of Mysore ceded one-half of his dominions, paid 3,300,000*l.* to defray the expenses of the war, and gave up to the custody of Lord Cornwallis two of his sons, to be detained as hostages till the conditions were fulfilled. In 1798 Tippoo Sultan was so infatuated as to seek the aid of France to overthrow the British power in India. Thereupon, in the following year, a British army, amounting to 26,802 men, with the addition of the subsidiary force of the Nizam of 10,157, and 6,000 irregular horse in the service of the same potentate, proceeded to chastise the insolent contriver of this insane design. On the 5th April, Seringapatam was invested with an ordnance train of forty battering-guns, fifty-seven field-pieces, and seven howitzers. On the 3rd of May, the British batteries had made a practicable breach; and at one in the afternoon of the succeeding day, a storming party of 4,376 men mounted the rampart, and wheeling, one party to the right, the other to the left, after a long and desperate conflict, accompanied with dreadful carnage, became masters of the place, Tippoo Sultan himself falling by the hand, it is believed, of a private soldier. The territory of the fallen despot, already greatly diminished by the results of the former war with the English, was divided, and a portion allotted to the titular rajah of Mysore, the representative of the race which Hyder Ali had supplanted. The island, town, and fort of Seringapatam were retained by the British as a military station, but, being found unsuitable, the place was subsequently, on account of malaria, abandoned for that purpose, but still remains a possession of the British government. Elevation above the sea 2,412 feet; distance from Madras, W., 248 miles; from Bangalore, S.W., 70; Mangalore, E., 130; Bombay, S.E., 515; Hyderabad, S., 360; Calcutta, S.W., 1,045. Lat. 12° 25′, long. 76° 45′.

SERINGHAM.—A town on an island formed by the division of the river Cauvery into two streams. The island is fourteen miles long from east to west, and nearly two in breadth; the town is one mile and a half N. from Trichinopoly. Lat. 10° 51′, long. 78° 46′.

SERNAL, in Gurwhal, a village on the left bank of the Budiar, a feeder of the Jumna. It is situate amidst groves of mulberry and apricot-trees, on a fertile expanse rising gently up the side of a mountain. Elevation above the sea 7,255 feet. Lat. 30° 54′, long. 78° 18′.

SEROHEE.—A small raj or state of Rajpootana, named from its principal place. It is bounded on the north-west by the territory of Joudpore; on the north-east by Godwar; on the east by the territory of Mewar or Odeypore; and on the south by the dominions of the Guicowar. It lies between lat. 24° 23′—25° 16′, long. 72° 10′—73° 12′, and the area is estimated at 3,024 square miles. The eastern and north-eastern parts of the territory are hilly, extending over the north-western slope of the Aravulli, and inclining towards the desert of Marwar, towards which numerous streams flow in a north-westerly direction, pursuing their course to the river Loni, by the channel of which they find their way into the Gulf of Cutch. The southern and south-eastern part is very mountainous and rugged, containing the lofty mountain Aboo, and the various ridges branching from it. The elevation of the summit of Mount Aboo has been estimated at nearly 5,000 feet above the sea. Many splendid ruins, especially at Chandravati and on Mount Aboo, indicate the former prosperity and civilization of this state, now greatly declined. An important commercial route lying through this country from Guzerat to the great mart of Palee, in the territory of Joudpore, contributes to its reviving welfare. The annual revenue of the rao or prince is estimated at 70,000 rupees, out of which a tribute has been claimed by the state of Joudpore. The military force consists of 200 cavalry and 600 infantry, exclusive of the feudal troops of the jaghiredars; but the whole population, consisting principally of the predatory tribes Minas, Grasias, and Bheels, are armed. The rao is of the Deora subdivision of the Chauhan tribe of Rajpoots.

This state was for some time considered a district of Joudpore. Tod says, "For a few thousand rupees annually paid to the British government by Serohee, who, however, protested against being a party to its ultimate disposition, which might otherwise at some future period have again involved her independence, she was enfranchised for ever from the claims of Marwar, and now looks to the British government alone." A treaty was formally concluded, October 31st, 1823, between that government and the rao of Serohee. The country has been greatly misgoverned; and in compliance with the solicitations of its ruler the administration has been assumed for a term of years by the British government.

SEROHEE.—A town of Rajpootana, on the route from Nusseerabad to Deesa, 183 miles S.W. of the former, and 67 N.E. of the latter. The present town is supposed to have been founded in 1424, and to have been named originally Sheopooree. It superseded the original city of Serohee; the ruins of which are still observable at no great distance. Since taken under British protection, Serohee has become a place of some commerce and wealth, though not many years ago it was merely an expanse of ruins. The extent of the town is rather considerable; the houses are good, and built of brick, but many are still untenanted. The palace of the rao or chief, which stands on a slightly-elevated site, has no architectural beauty to attract notice. The sword-blades manufactured at Serohee are celebrated for their excellence now as formerly. On this point, Ali Mohammed Khan affirms "the swords of Sirohi are celebrated everywhere;" and adds, "there are no better reeds than such as are procured in this country; so that they are carried to Hindoostan, Persia, and other countries for the manufacture of arrows." Distance from Mhow, N.W., 243 miles; from Oojein, N.W., 220; from Neemuch, W., 130; Agra, S.W., 360. Lat. 24° 59′, long. 72° 56′.

SEROHEE.—A town in the British district of Tirhoot, lieut.-gov. of Bengal, 59 miles N.W. of Purneah. Lat. 26° 25′, long. 86° 57′.

SERONCHA.—A town in Hyderabad, or the Nizam's dominions, situate on the left bank of the Wein Gunga river, and 142 miles N.E. from Hyderabad. Lat. 18° 55′, long. 79° 56′.

SERONGE.—See Sironj.

SEROOR.—A town in the British district of Ahmednuggur, presidency of Bombay, 30 miles S.W. by W. of Ahmednuggur. A road connecting the two towns was constructed in 1836, at a cost of 1,200 rupees per mile. Lat. 18° 50′, long. 74° 25′.

SEROWLEE, in the British district of Bareilly, lieut.-gov. of the N.W. Provinces, a town on the route from Bareilly to Moradabad, 20 miles W.N.W. of the former. Lat. 28° 30′, long. 79° 10′.

SERRAW, in the peninsula of Kattywar, province of Guzerat, a town in the prant or subdivision of Rajkote, situate 41 miles N.E. by N. from the town of Rajkote, and 94 miles S.W. from Ahmedabad. Lat. 22° 47′, long. 71° 10′.

SERRUVIAL.—A town in the British district of Madura, presidency of Madras, 38 miles E. of Madura. Lat. 9° 58′, long. 78° 43′.

SERRYAH, in the peninsula of Kattywar, province of Guzerat, a town with a fort, in the prant or division of Hallar, on a stream called the River of Serryah. The town and fort are two miles and a half from the mouth of the river, which not admitting large ships, they are compelled to anchor in a channel between two reefs about three miles off. Notwithstanding this unfavourable circumstance, it is a place of considerable traffic. Distance from Ahmedabad, S.W., 190 miles; Baroda, W., 220. Lat. 22° 18′, long. 69° 47′.

SERUMOGAY.—A town in the British district of Coimbatoor, presidency of Madras, 23 miles N. by E. of Coimbatoor. Lat. 11° 20′, long. 77° 4′.

SERWA, in Bundelcund, a small town on the route from Banda to Saugor, by the Hirapoor Pass, 110 miles S.W. of the former, 62 N.E. of the latter. It has a bazar, and water from wells, but supplies are rather scarce. Lat. 24° 28′, long. 79° 20′.

SESSARUH.—A town in the native state of Bhawulpoor, 67 miles S.E. from Bhawulpoor, and 70 miles N.W. from Beekaneer. Lat. 28° 46′, long. 72° 37′.

SETAPOOR, in the territory of Oude, a British cantonment on the route from Bareilly to Lucknow, 105 miles S.E. of the former, 51 N.W. of the latter. Supplies and water are abundant. The road in this part of the route is good; the country open, and but partially cultivated. Lat. 27° 35′, long. 80° 44′.

SETROONJEE, a river rising in the peninsula of Kattywar, province of Guzerat, in lat. 21° 15′, long. 70° 45′, and, flowing easterly for sixty miles, falls into the Gulf of Cambay, in lat. 21° 16′, long. 72° 5′.

SEUNI, in the British district of Saugor and Nerbudda, lieut.-gov. of the N.W. Provinces, a town on the route from Jubbulpoor to Nagpoor, 82 miles S. by W. of the former. The district of which this town is the principal place is inhabited by Goonds, and appears to have been less skilfully managed than the other districts of the Saugor and Nerbudda territory. Measures have been suggested for its amelioration. Lat. 22° 1′, long. 79° 40′.

SEVERNDROOG.—See SOOWURNDROOG.

SEVUR.—A town in the British district of Coimbatoor, presidency of Madras, 25 miles N.E. of Coimbatoor. Lat. 11° 15′, long. 77° 16′.

SEWAGANJ, in the jaghire of Myhir, territory of Saugor and Nerbudda, a village on the route from Mirzapoor to Jubbulpoor, 171 miles S.W. of former, 74 N.E. of latter. It has water from wells and tanks, but supplies must be collected from the surrounding country. Lat. 24° 2′, long. 80° 32′.

SEWALIK MOUNTAINS.—A low but extensive range, bounding on the north-east the plain of Sirhind and that of the doab between the Jumna and the Ganges. The name Sewalik is applied to that series of summits or ridges which extend in a north-west direction from the right bank of the Ganges. Hills, however, of similar character to the Sewalik, rising on the left bank, are continuous with the mountains of Kumaon, and, diverging from them a little farther south-east, inclose the Patlee Doon. Trail describes this part, south-west of Patlee Doon, "as a low range of hills, which contains numerous passes, some of them practicable for wheel-carriages." Royle, indeed, states that this low range of recent formation may be traced from Roopur, on the Sutlej, in lat. 30° 58′, long. 76° 36′, to the bottom of the Sikkim hills, in lat. 26° 30′, long. 88° 30′, a distance of about 800 miles. It decreases in elevation to the east of the Ganges; and, as already observed, the name Sewalik is applied to that portion which, at its south-eastern extremity, near Hurdwar, in lat. 29° 58′, long. 78° 14′, forms the right side of the gorge through which the Ganges flows into the plain of Hindoostan. Its length from Hurdwar to Roopur, in a direction from south-east to north-west, is about 155 miles; in breadth, where widest, about ten. In the northern part, towards the Sutlej, the range is little more than a succession of sandhills. According to Jacquemont, "the Pinjor valley is separated from the plains by a sort of downs, from sixty metres to eighty in height, and composed of sand scarcely consolidated." The highest part is about lat. 30° 17′, long. 77° 50′, between the Timli and Lal Derwaza passes, and in that vicinity some of the peaks have an elevation of about 3,500 feet above the sea. The Sewalik hills have a direction parallel to the great chain of the Himalayas, with nearly a similar dip, the slope being towards the north, and the abutment to the south. In this part they rise at once in an abrupt mural front from the plain, extending to the south-west, but slope gradually on the north-east side towards the Dhoons, or valley lying between them and the base of the Himalaya, the strata of which they are composed dipping in that direction at an angle of from 20° to 38°. As they run in a direction from south-east to north-west, the numerous gorges by which they are crossed have a direction generally from south-west to north-east. Those gorges cut the ranges into a succession of parallel ridges, the ends of which are steep towards the plain, and sloping towards the Doons. They are thus described by Dr. Royle:—"In many places each hill, if separated, might be represented by a right-angled triangle, the base resting on the pass, the perpendicular facing towards the south-west, and the hypothenuse sloping towards the north-east, and corresponding in dip with the strata. This side is sometimes continued to the level of the pass; at others, another hill, with its perpendicular side, seems to arise from the middle of the last, and is itself in like manner succeeded by a third, forming a succession of abrupt and sloping sides like the teeth of a saw." In the phraseology of geologists, they are of tertiary or alluvial formation, consisting of subordinate beds of clay, loose-grained sandstone, with much mica interposing, conglomerate cemented by calcareous matter, beds of gravel and rolled stones, consisting of various kinds of rock, granite, trap, limestone, clayslate, gneiss, micaceous schists, and all other formations which enter into the composition of the Himalayas; thus offering an explanation plausible at least of the origin of the range, in the supposition that it was originally the debris swept down from the Himalaya, and subsequently upheaved by an earthquake of great extent and force. Parallel in some degree to the Sewalik Mountains, and inclosed between them and the Himalayas, is a succession of valleys,—north-west the Pinjor Doon, south-east that of the Kyarda Doon, and south-east of this last the Dehra Doon. The line of direction of the range is crossed by the Ganges, the Jumna, the Markunda, an offset of the Soorsutty, the Gagur, and some other streams of less importance; but in general the drainage of the Doons is parallel to the direction of the range, and either to the north-west or south-east. Thus the Pinjor Doon is drained by the Sursa, flowing north-west; the Kyarda Doon by the Batta or Bhuta, flowing south-east; the Debra Doon by the Asun, flowing north-west, the Suswa flowing south-east. The geology of the Sewalik is characterized by the occurrence of enormous quantities of fossil remains of animals, especially mammalia. Of those the most remarkable is the Sivatherium, an extinct ruminant of gigantic dimensions, exceeding those of the rhinoceros: it was horned, and provided, like the tapir, with a short trunk. Here also have been discovered fossil remains of the family of quadrumana, the existence of which in a fossilized state had previously been generally denied. The Sewalik is in many places covered with forests of saul, fir, cotton-tree, and various other kinds. Jacquemont represents it as presenting a very varied field of research to the botanist, but of uninteresting appearance, being little more than an extensive copse, dense with underwood and herbage of large growth, above which timber-trees grow at considerable intervals.

SEWAR.—A town in the British district of Sarun, lieut.-gov. of Bengal, 41 miles S. by W. of Bettiah. Lat. 26° 11′, long. 84° 25′.

SEWARRA.—A town in the Rajpoot state of Jodhpoor, 127 miles S.W. by S. from Jodhpoor, and 42 miles N. from Deesa. Lat. 24° 50′, long. 72°.

SEWEHUT, in the British district of Allahabad, lieut.-gov. of the N.W. Provinces, a small town on the route from Allahabad cantonment to that of Purtabgurh, in Oude, eight miles N. of the former, 23 S. of the latter. Lat. 25° 36′, long. 81° 55′.

SEWNA.—A town in the British district of Poonah, presidency of Bombay, 24 miles N.W. by W. of Poonah. Lat. 18° 42′, long. 73° 35′.

SEWNEE, in Hyderabad, or territory of the Nizam, a town near the north-east frontier, towards Nagpore, situate on a small river tributary to the Peingunga. Distance from the city of Hyderabad, N., 200 miles; from the city of Nagpoor, S.W., 80. Lat. 20° 15′, long. 78° 28′.

SEWUNGAON.—A town in one of the sequestrated districts of Hyderabad, 36 miles E.S.E. from Ellichpoor, and 20 miles N.E. from Omraouttee. Lat. 20° 58′, long. 78° 3′.

SEWUNWARRAH.—A town in the territory of Nagpoor, 111 miles E.S.E. from Nagpoor, and 145 miles S. from Ramgurh. Lat. 20° 45′, long. 80° 50′.

SEYHUJ.—A river of Malwa, rising in lat. 24° 27′, long. 78° 25′, and, flowing through Scindia's territory for about forty miles, falls into the Betwa, on the right bank, in lat. 25°, long. 78° 23′.

SEYLOO.—A town in the territory of Nagpoor, 34 miles S.W. from Nagpoor, and 81 miles E.S.E. from Ellichpoor. Lat. 20° 50′, long. 78° 45′.

SEYMREE, in the British district of Muttra, lieut.-gov. of the N.W. Provinces, a village on the route from Muttra cantonment to Delhi, and 18 miles N.W. of the former. Lat. 27° 40′, long. 77° 36′.

SEYNGUR, called also Kuroon, a small river of the Doab, rises in the British district of Allygurh, lat. 27° 50′, long. 78° 12′. As its source is on the south-western side of the crest or slightly-elevated tract which stretches down the middle of the Doab, its course, though very tortuous, generally in a south-easterly direction, tends towards the river Jumna, into which it falls, on the left side, about fifteen miles below Calpee. About sixty miles from its source, it is crossed by the route from Etawah to Futtehgurh, and is there fordable. It is also fordable where it is crossed, about thirty miles lower down, by the route from Etawah to Cawnpore; and also fifteen miles still farther down, where it is crossed by the route from Calpee to Futtehgurh, in lat. 26° 28′, long. 79° 34′; and is also fordable where crossed, thirty-six miles lower down, by the route from Calpee to Cawnpore. Its total length of course is about 210 miles.

SEYRAH, in Guzerat, or the territory of the Guicowar, a town on a small river tributary to the Muhi or Mhi. Distance from the city of Ahmedabad, E., 65 miles. Lat. 22° 55′, long. 73° 37′.

SHABAZPORE RIVER. — One of the mouths of the Megna, flowing east of the island of Deccan Shabazpore into the sea, in lat. 22° 27′, long. 91° 3′.

SHADAUTPOOR, in Sinde, a town on the route from Larkhana to Gundava, and 25 miles N.W. of the former place. It is situate in a barren tract, nearly destitute of population, and described by Kennedy as "more like the bed of a salt lagoon, in an interval of spring tides, than an inland district." To the north-west stretches the dreary tract called the *Pat* or desert of Shikarpoor, noticed by the same writer as "a boundless level plain of indurated clay of a dull earthen colour, and showing signs of being sometimes under water. At first a few bushes were apparent here and there, growing gradually more and more distant, until at last not a sign of vegetable life was to be recognised." Lat. 27° 46′, long. 67° 55′.

SHADEEABAD, in the British district of Ghazeepore, a town situate on the Bisu, a small river tributary to the Ganges, distant 12 miles N.W. from Ghazeepore cantonment, 32 N.E. from Benares. Lat. 25° 40′, long. 83° 22′.

SHADIPOOR.—A town within the dominions of Gholab Singh, the ruler of Cashmere, nine miles N.W. from Sirinagur, and 112 miles N.E. from Jhelum. Lat. 34° 7′, long. 74° 53′.

SHADOWRA.—A town in the native state of Gwalior, or territory of Scindia, 117 miles S.S.W. from Gwalior, and 92 miles N.W. by N. from Saugur. Lat. 24° 37′, long. 77° 40′.

SHAGURH.—A town of Sinde, in the territory belonging to Ali Moorad, 86 miles S.E. by E. from Bukkur, and 53 miles W. by N. from Jessulmeer. Lat. 27°, long. 70° 6′.

SHAHABAD, in Cashmere, a town formerly a favourite residence of the Mogul emperors, but now ruinous and neglected. It is situate in a long narrow valley, bounded on the south-west by the Panjal of Banihal, and on the north-east by a ridge of green hills several miles in length, dividing it from the valley of Bureng or Breng. The valley in some places has a width not exceeding 1,000 yards. It is watered by a stream flowing from the celebrated spring of Vernag, and which lower down, where increased by several small feeders, is called the river Sandaren. Accounts received by Vigne represented the valley to be very rich in mines of iron and copper.

The neighbourhood of Shahabad is celebrated for its fruits, especially apples, and for its wheat, considered the finest in Cashmere. The town, when visited by Moorcroft, had a bazar and a few shops, at which provisions, coarse cloth, and very fine honey were sold. It was formerly the residence of the most powerful of the seven hereditary maleks, or wardens appointed by the emperor Akbar to watch over the passes of Cashmere. The malek of Shahabad had charge of the pass of Banihal, and enjoyed a considerable income from lands held in jaghire. Shahabad has an elevation of 5,600 feet above the sea. Lat. 33° 32′, long. 75° 16′.

SHAHABAD, in the Rajpoot territory of Jhallowa, a town on the route from Calpee to the town of Kotah, 225 miles S.W. of former, 96 E. of latter. It has a good bazar, and water and supplies are abundant. Lat. 25° 13′, long. 77° 12′.

SHAHABAD, in Sirhind, a town on the left bank of the Sursooti, here nearly devoid of water in winter, but sometimes in summer a deep and violent torrent. It is described by Jacquemont as a heap of filth and ruins. The population is returned at 10,852. There is a bazar, and supplies are abundant, as the neighbouring country is fertile and well cultivated. Distant N.W. from Calcutta 1,002 miles. Lat. 30° 10′, long. 76° 56′.

SHAHABAD.—A town in the jaghire of Rampoor, lieut.-gov. of the N.W. Provinces. Lat. 28° 34′, long. 79° 4′.

SHAHABAD, in the territory of Oude, a town on the route from Lucknow to Shahjehanpoor, 15 miles S. of the latter, and 30 miles N.E. of Futtehgurh. Tieffenthaler describes it, about A.D. 1770, "of considerable circuit; and nearly in the middle is a palace of brick, strengthened with towers like a fortress, with a vestibule and spacious covered colonnade. Most of the houses are of brick, and there is a fine mosque built of the same material, and inclosed by a wall. The town extends a mile from north to south, its breadth is something less, but of its flourishing state little remains." When visited by Tennant, A.D. 1799, it was an expanse of ruins, "that appeared in the form of hills and broken swells crumbling to dust;" yet Heber found it, 1824, "a considerable town, or almost city, with the remains of fortifications, and many large houses." According to Tieffenthaler, it was founded by Angot, the nephew of Rama, king of Oude; and if so, must be of high antiquity, as Rama is considered to have reigned 1,600 years B.C.: hence it is sometimes called Angotpur. It was renovated by Dilawar Khan, an Afghan chief contemporary with Aurungzebe. At present it has a bazar and encamping-ground, close to which are two tanks lined with brick. The road to the north, or towards Shahjehanpoor, is good; to the south-east, or towards Lucknow, very bad. Lat. 27° 39′, long. 80° 1′.

SHAHABAD, in the lieut.-gov. of Bengal, a British district, bounded on the north by the British districts of Ghazeepoor and Sarun; on the south-east by the British districts of Patna and Behar; on the south by the British district of Behar; on the west by the British district of Mirzapore; and on the north-west by the British districts of Benares and Ghazeepoor. It lies between lat. 24° 30′—25° 46′, long. 83° 20′—84° 56′; is 106 miles in length from north-east to south-west, and fifty-six in breadth: the area is stated at 4,403 square miles. About a third of the entire district, situate in its south-western part, is rough and elevated, forming a sort of highland, rising on the surface into small detached hills, nearly equal in height. The average elevation of this irregular plateau is probably about 500 feet above the more depressed country on the banks of the Ganges or the Sone, or about 700 feet above the level of the sea.

The climate is very sultry in the latter part of spring and the early part of summer, and the succeeding rains are usually heavy. The winters are generally mild, yet frosts are not unknown. West winds prevail for half the year, from the middle of October to that of April. There are some peculiarities in parts of the district as to winds, the notice of which would require too much minuteness.

The Carumnassa rises a few miles from the southern frontier of the district, of which it forms the western boundary for ten miles, and subsequently the north-western for sixty miles, dividing it from the districts Mirzapoor, Benares, and Ghazeepoor: it does not appear to be navigable. The Ganges forms the north-western and northern boundaries for eighty-eight miles, dividing the district from those of Ghazeepoor and Sarun. It is navigable for craft of considerable burthen, and in the lower part of its course in this district is generally a mile wide. The Sone, flowing eastward from the district of Mirzapore, touches on this district at its south-western extremity, and, taking a direction north-easterly, forms for 110 miles its southern and south-eastern boundary, dividing it from the district of Behar; and for twenty-five miles more its eastern boundary, dividing it from the district of Patna. In the rainy season, it is too rapid for navigation above the mouth of its tributary the Kiyul, 108 miles from its confluence with the Ganges; and in the dry season is too shallow in that part of its course for boats of any considerable burthen, though floats are then conveyed downwards, being pushed over the shoals. Below the mouth of the Kiyul it is navigable for boats of ten or twelve tons burthen. Thus the total river navigation of the district is about 200 miles. Those principal rivers receive numerous small streams and torrents, flowing during the rainy season, but dry in some parts at other times of the year. The low country, forming the greater part of the district, is very level, especially to the north and west; and parts are liable annually to be inundated. The portion of soil unfit for the plough is very trifling; close to the hills it is excellent. The soil may be divided into two kinds, one consisting of fine sand mixed with loose mould, the other of a tenacious clay intermixed with coarse sand: the latter, on the whole, is reckoned the most valuable, producing wheat, barley, and all winter crops, without irrigation. In the northern portion of the district the soil is of the utmost richness, and consists of land regularly flooded by the Ganges. It forms the most valuable part of the district, and the crops there never fail. The river deposits a fine mould, and scarcely ever covers a field with sand.

The lands best suited for irrigation are cropped with rice, which is considered the staple crop where it can be successfully cultivated. It is both a rubbee, or crop sown at the commencement of winter and reaped in spring, and kurreef, or that sown in the beginning of summer and reaped in autumn. Besides those already mentioned, crops of various kinds are produced for aliment or condiment; as maize, millet, maruya (Eleusine coracana), gram (Cicer arietinum), lentils, various sorts of kidney-beans or phaseoli, till or sesame, ricinus or castor-oil seed, and some other oil-seeds, melons and other cucurbitaceous plants; most of the European garden vegetables, which thrive well in the cool season; ginger, turmeric, and capsicum. Sugar is raised to considerable extent. Of commercial crops, an important one is cotton, though attempts to introduce the profitable culture of American cotton have not been successful. Of the rest, the chief are indigo, opium, tobacco, and betel-leaf. There are several hundred square miles of jungle and forest, but the trees are stunted; and Buchanan states that in the whole district there are not ten fine trees of natural growth. Hence, timber cannot be obtained of sufficient size for houses suited for accommodating Europeans; and in the large buildings constructed by the natives, stone is exclusively used. The principal manufactures are cotton cloths, threads, tapes, strings, fabric of silk, and of mixed silk and cotton, paper, spirits, oil, the extraction of salt from brine drawn from wells, sugar, and the extraction of sulphate of iron from native mineral. The exports are principally silk, paper, cotton, and cotton cloths, wheat, millet, rice, barley, pulse, bamboos, paper, oilseeds, opium, and some other articles of less importance; the imports are tobacco, sugar, iron, copper, lead, tin, zinc, salt, cocoanuts, and betel-leaf. The population is given under the article BENGAL.

The principal towns, Arrah, Sasseram, Jehanabad, Buxar, and Bhojpoor, are noticed under their respective names in the alphabetical arrangement. The route from Calcutta to Allahabad traverses this district in a direction from south-east to north-west. The only other important route is from east to west, from Dinapoor to Ghazeepoor.

The district of Shahabad, formerly part of the great empire of Magadha, appears to have been subjected to the sway of the Patan Mussulmans towards the close of the twelfth century, as it is recorded that Shahabuddin Muhammad, sultan of Ghor, subdued the country as far as the confines of China; and his lieutenant, Muhammed Bakhtyar, consolidated the Mussulman power in Behar. Shahabad subsequently acquired some note in consequence of being the scene of the early military operations of Sher Shah, who wrested the empire of India from Humayun, the son of Baber. It afterwards became a part of the soubah of Behar, according to the division of the empire of Delhi laid down in the Ayeen Akbery. The right of the East-India Company to the southern part of this district is derived from Shah Alum, emperor of Delhi; to the northern part, from Azoof-ud-Dowlah, vizier of Oude, under a treaty dated 21st May, 1775. This treaty was the consequence of a memorable engagement which took place at Buxar, in the north-eastern part of this district, when a decisive victory was gained by the British forces, commanded by General Munro, over the combined armies of Cossim Ali and the Vizier.

SHAH ALUM, in the Sinde Sagur Dooab division of the Punjab, a town situated on the left bank of the Indus river, 176 miles W. by N. of the town of Lahore. Lat. 32° 2′, long. 71° 17′.

SHAHAPOOR.—A town in the British district of Poonah, presidency of Bombay, 32 miles W.N.W. of Poonah. Lat. 18° 40′, long. 73° 26′.

SHAHBAZAR, in the British district of Hoogly, lieut.-gov. of Bengal, a town near the north-west frontier, towards the British district of Burdwan, four miles from the right or east bank of the Damooda. Distance from Burdwan, S.E., 16 miles; Calcutta, N.W., 36. Lat. 22° 59′, long. 88° 4′.

SHAHBAZGARHI, in the district of the Peshawar division of the Punjab, a town situated 26 miles N.W. from the right bank of the Indus, 35 miles N.E. of the town of Peshawar. Lat. 34° 15′, long. 72° 12′.

SHAH BUNDER, in Sinde, in the delta of the Indus, a small place on the east bank of the channel which discharges its water into the sea by the Mull mouth. Hither the English factory was removed from Aurungabunder or Dehrajamka, in consequence of this latter place being deserted by the water of the Indus. Previously to the dissolution of the factory here in 1775, its establishment for navigating the Indus consisted of fourteen small vessels, each of about forty tons burthen. Subsequently, this place also was deserted by the stream, and, on the re-establishment of the factory in 1799, Lahoreebunder, thirty-five miles north-west, on the Buggaur, or western branch of the Indus, was selected as its site. Shah Bunder is in lat. 24° 6′, long. 67° 57′.

SHAHDERA, in the British district of Agra, a village and halting-place on the left bank of the Jumna, on the route from the city of Agra to Mynpooree, and five miles N.E. of the former. Lat. 27° 12′, long. 78° 8′.

SHAHDERAH, in the British district of Meerut, lieut.-gov. of the N.W. Provinces, a town on the route from Delhi to Meerut, and six miles E. of the former. It is situate near the left or eastern bank of the Doab Canal, there crossed by a brick-built bridge. Lat. 28° 40′, long. 77° 21′.

SHAHEE, in the British district of Bareilly, lieut.-gov. of the N.W. Provinces, a small town on the route from the town of Bareilly to Almora, and 19 miles N. of the former. It is situate near the right bank of the river Bhagul, here having a bed 220 yards wide, with steep banks and a sandy bottom, and in the dry season a stream sixty yards wide, and two and a half to three feet deep. There is a bazar, with a market. Lat. 28° 33′, long. 79° 23′.

SHAHGARH, in the British district of Bareilly, lieut.-gov. of the N.W. Provinces, a town on the route from the town of Pillibheet to that of Nugeenah, and 25 miles N.W. of the former. Lat. 28° 47′, long. 79° 34′.

SHAHGHUR. — A town, the principal place of a raj or petty native state in the province of Saugor and Nerbudda. The territory has an area of 676 square miles, and a population of 30,000. The chief maintains a military force, consisting of 150 cavalry and 800 infantry. Lat. of town 24° 19′, long. 79° 10′.

SHAH GUNJ.—A town in the British district of Mirzapoor, lieut.-gov. N.W.P., 41 miles S.E. of Mirzapoor. Lat. 24° 41′, long. 83° 1′.

SHAHGURH, in the British district of Bareilly, lieut.-gov. of the N.W. Provinces, a town on the route from Bareilly to Almora, 30 miles N. of the former. Lat. 28° 49′, long. 79° 35′.

SHAHJEHANABAD.—A name given to the city of Delhi by Shahjehan, its founder.—See DELHI.

SHAHJEHANPOOR, in the territory of Gwalior, or possessions of the family of Scindia, a town of Malwa, on the route from Goona to Mow, 114 miles S.W. of former, 72 N.E. of latter. Malcolm, who designates it a large city, mentions that a considerable degree of civilization, refinement, and domestic comfort has been introduced into this place from the European settlements in Guzerat, by the Borahs, an intelligent and wealthy class of Mussulman merchants. It is situate on the left bank of the river Tilir, and just above the town is ground for encampment: supplies are abundant. It received its name from its founder Shahjehan, emperor of Delhi, who reigned from the year 1628 to the year 1658. Distance S.W. from Agra 285 miles. Lat. 23° 24′, long. 76° 18′.

SHAHJEHANPOOR, in the British district of Meerut, lieut.-gov. of the N.W. Provinces, a town on the route from the town of Meerut to Moradabad, and 21 miles S.E. of the former. It has a bazar, and a small mud-built fort, now fallen to decay. Lat. 28° 52′, long. 78° 1′.

SHAHJEHANPOOR, in the British district of Cawnpore, lieut.-gov. of the N.W. Provinces, a town on the route from Calpee to Etawa, and 12 miles N. of the former. There is a bazar, and water is obtained from wells. Lat. 26° 16′, long. 79° 49′.

SHAHJEHANPORE.—A British district under the lieut.-gov. of the N.W. Provinces, deriving its name from its principal place. It is bounded on the north-east, east, and south-east, by the territory of Oude; on the south by the district of Furruckabad; and on the west by the British districts Budaon and Bareilly. It lies between lat. 27° 15′—28° 45′, long. 79° 23′—80° 30′, and contains an area of 2,483 square miles. The shape is very irregular, but partially resembles a crescent, the concavity being towards the west. The north-eastern frontier is formed by the river Surju or Gogra, the south-western for a short distance by the Ganges; and the descent of both rivers towards the south-east proves the inclination of the surface in that direction, towards which also flow the intervening rivers, the Goomtee, Gurrah, Ramgunga, and some others of less magnitude. The greatest elevation is at the most northern point; Burindeo, twenty miles above that point, and situate on the right bank of the Gogra, having an elevation above the sea of 798 feet, and Bilheri, about ten miles lower down, 741. The southern part of the district is considerably below this, being traversed by the Gurrah, the stream of which, at Pilleebheet, sixty miles higher up, has an elevation of only 517 feet. The elevation of the bed of the Ganges, where it washes the southern frontier, in all probability falls short of 500 feet.

The most northern part, adjoining the base of the Sub-Himalaya, forms a strongly characterized portion of the Terrai, or tract of marshy forest and jungle stretching along the foot of the mountains. Numberless small streams, oozing from the hills, or rising from beneath, stagnate, in consequence of the inclination of the surface being too slight to allow the escape of their waters, and their own want of force to cut channels. These, saturating the deep and fertile soil, give growth to gigantic trees, woven together by immense creepers, encumbered above with air-plants, and below with impenetrable underwood. Grasses and other herbage, attaining a height of ten feet, overrun the more open parts, and are annually fired, to allow the spring of a more succulent growth, which is depastured by numerous herds of kine and buffaloes for about two months, after which they cease to be penetrable or suitable for grazing. Throughout the entire region broods a malaria, almost inevitably fatal to the human race and to domestic animals, but not incompatible with the constitution of the elephant, the rhinoceros, wild buffalo, stag, tiger, panther, leopard, and other wild creatures, which in the densest recesses of the forest and jungle attain extraordinary size and vigour. This tract gives rise to the Goomtee, a large river, which, pursuing a southerly course, crosses the frontier into the territory of Oude. As there is a general slope to the south-east, this "region of death" might obviously be made productive by drainage and cultivation; but the first steps in the operation would be marked by a frightful sacrifice of human life. At present the tract is available only for pasturage during a very brief period, as already mentioned, or to yield timber and other forest and jungle produce.

Bishop Heber states that, including the wooded part of the Terrai, there is "a large forest along the whole eastern, southern, and northern frontiers." He found the southern part of the district to have a fine climate, little incommoded by the hot winds, with a well-wooded, fertile, and highly-cultivated soil, producing in profusion rice, maize, wheat, cotton, sugar, tobacco, pulse, mangoes, dates, plantains, walnuts, strawberries, grapes, apples, and pears. The people, though in general skilful and industrious agriculturists, are much annoyed by a set of "landless resolutes," the descendants of Rohilla chiefs, and at once too lazy to work, and too proud to enlist in the East-India Company's service. The land revenue of this district has been fixed for a term of years, which will expire in 1868. The latest official returns (1848) give to this district a population enumerated as follows:—Hindoo, agricultural, 436,166; non-agricultural, 124,420; Mahomedan and other classes, agricultural, 134,520; non-agricultural, 117,482: total, 812,588. The relative proportion of the two great divisions, therefore, is between three and four Hindoos to one of any other class. Of the whole population, 812,588, the children numbered 279,392, leaving an adult population of 533,196; the children having been counted as such up to twelve or thirteen years of age, if unmarried; if married below that age, they were considered as adults. The number of houses was stated to be 150,481; which gives an average per house, on the total population, something above five persons.

The principal towns are Shahjehanpore, Powain, Tilher, and Jalalabad, which will be found noticed in their proper places. The following is a classification of the towns and villages in the district:—Number containing less than 1,000 inhabitants, 2,062; ditto more than 1,000 and less than 5,000, 108; ditto more than 5,000 and less than 10,000, 3; ditto more than 50,000, 1.

Shahjehanpore formed part of the possessions of the Rohilla Patans previously to 1774, when their dominion was overthrown by the signal defeat which they received at Tessunah from the British army supporting the cause of Shooja-ud-Dowlah, the nawaub of Oude. The country about Shahjehanpore, with a much more extensive portion of Rohilcund, was then transferred to the nawaub, and ultimately, in 1801, ceded in commutation of subsidy to the East-India Company.

SHAHJEHANPORE.—The principal place of the British district of the same name. It is situate on the left bank of the Gurrah, which, near the town in dry weather, may be forded, but in the rains can be crossed only by ferry. Bishop Heber describes this town as a "large place, with some stately old mosques and a castle. These are mostly ruinous, but the houses are in good plight. The bazars show marks of activity and opulence." The population, according to a recent census, amounts to 62,785. Shahjehanpore is in lat. 27° 52′, long. 79° 58′.

SHAHJUHANPOOR, in the British district of Goruckpoor, lieut.-gov. of the N.W. Provinces, a town, the principal place of the pergunnah of the same name, on the route from Goruckpoor to the Sarun collectorate, 30 miles E. of the former. Lat. 26° 40′, long. 83° 53′.

SHAHJUHANPOOR, in the British district of Goorgaon, lieut.-gov. of the N.W. Provinces, a town, the principal place of a pergunnah of the same name, situate 62 miles S.W. of Delhi. Lat. 28°, long. 76° 32′.

SHAH JUMAUB, in the Daman division of the Punjab, a town situated on the right bank of the Indus, 56 miles S.W. of the town of Mooltan. Lat. 29° 37′, long. 70° 49′.

SHAHLIMAR.—A splendid pleasure-ground, about three miles east of Lahore, made by order of the Mogul emperor Shah Jehan. Here were numbers of pavilions and other buildings for ornament and pleasure, but many of them were demolished or defaced by Runjeet Singh, to obtain the marble materials for the embellishment of his residence in Lahore, and the construction of his religious capital of Amritsir, and of the neighbouring fortress of Govindghar. Still there is much to cause admiration. Lat. 31° 35′, long. 74° 23′.

SHAH NUHUR CANAL flows out of the Ferozeshah Canal in lat. 29° 28′, long. 76° 54′, and joins it again in lat. 28° 50′, long. 77° 4′.

SHAHPOOR, in the British district of Allahabad, lieut.-gov. of the N.W. Provinces, a town on the left bank of the Jumna, 40 miles W. of the city of Allahabad. Lat. 25° 23′, long. 81° 15′.

SHAHPOOR, in the Baree Dooab division of the Punjab, a town situated on the left bank of the Ravee, 16 miles S.S.W. of the town of Lahore. Lat. 31° 24′, long. 74° 12′.

SHAHPOOR, in the Punjab, a town situate on the left bank of the Jhelum. The district of which this town is the chief place has an area of 3,500 square miles, and a population of 261,692. The town is in lat. 32° 20′, long. 72° 10′.

SHAHPOOR.—A town within the dominions of Gholab Singh, the ruler of Cashmere, eight miles E. of the left bank of the Jhelum river, and 93 miles S.W. from Sirinagur. Lat. 33° 5′, long. 73° 53′.

SHAHPOOR in Sirhind, a village on the route from Suharunpoor to Subathoo, and 31 miles N.W. of the former place. Here was a secondary station in the trigonometrical survey of the Himalaya. Elevation above the sea 1,228 feet. Lat. 30° 17′, long. 77° 22′.

SHAHPOOR, or PADSHAHPUR, in the British collectorate of Belgaum, presidency of Bombay, a town situate on the river Gutpurba, 50 miles N.W. of the town of Dharwar. The population is estimated at between 6,000 and 7,000. Lat. 16° 8′, long. 74° 45′.

SHAHPOOR.—A town in the native prant of Rajkote, in the peninsula of Kattywar, province of Guzerat, 84 miles N.E. by E. from Rajkote, and 42 miles W.S.W. from Ahmedabad. Lat. 22° 51′, long. 71° 59′.

SHAHPOOR, in the British district of Goruckpoor, lieut.-gov. of the N.W. Provinces, a town on the route from Goruckpoor to Azimgurh, 25 miles S. by W. of the former. Lat. 26° 21′, long. 83° 17′.

SHAHPOOR, in the British district of Ramgurh, lieut.-gov. of the N.W. Provinces, a town on the route from Ramgurh to Rewah, 18 miles N. by E. of the former. Lat. 23° 3′, long. 81° 3′.

SHAHPOORA, in the Rajpoot state of Jeypore, a town on the route from Delhi to Mhow, 125 miles S.W. of former, 382 N.E. of latter. It is of considerable size, and is surrounded by a rampart. Lat. 27° 25′, long. 76° 12′.

SHAHPOORAH, in the British district of Ramgurh, lieut.-gov. of the N.W. Provinces, a town on the route from Ramgurh to Bijawur, 32 miles N.W. of the former. Lat. 23° 11′, long. 80° 45′.

SHAHPOOR KUBRA, in the British district of Goruckpoor, lieut.-gov. of the N.W. Provinces, a town on the route from Goruckpoor to Azimgurh, 12 miles S. of the former. Lat. 26° 31′, long. 83° 23′.

SHAHRUH.—A town in the native state of Gwalior, or territory of Scindia, 100 miles S.E. by S. from Oojein, and 82 miles N.W. by W. from Ellichpoor. Lat. 21° 51′, long. 76° 31′.

SHAHZADAHNUGAR, in the British district of Budaon, lieut.-gov. of the N.W. Provinces, a town on the route from Agra to Bareilly, and 34 miles S.W. of the latter. There is abundance of water from the river Yarwuffadar or Sot, and from wells. Lat. 28° 7′, long. 79° 7′.

SHAHZADPOOR, in the British district of Cawnpore, lieut.-gov. of the N.W. Provinces, a village on the route from the cantonment of Etawa to that of Cawnpore, and 26 miles W. of the latter. Lat. 26° 22′, long. 80° 2′.

SHAILGAON.—A town in Hyderabad, or territory of the Nizam, 124 miles N.W. from Hyderabad, and 122 miles E. from Ahmednuggur. Lat. 19° 4′, long. 76° 38′.

SHAIRMADAVY.—A town in the British district of Tinnevelly, presidency of Madras, 10 miles W.S.W. of Tinnevelly. Lat. 8° 40′, long. 77° 36′.

SHAKAPORE, in Sinde, a town on the great route from Cutch to Hydrabad. About a mile north-east of the town are the ruins of a large city, built of excellent burnt brick, and still in such a state of preservation that the walls and bastions are plainly discernible. To the north-east of these ruins is the large bed of a great branch of the Indus, now completely devoid of water. Lat. 24° 34′, long. 68° 24′.

SHALKUR, in Bussahir, a fort near the northern boundary of Koonawar, where the valley of the Spiti river has a less inclination of slope. It is situate on the right bank of the Lee, or river of Spiti, the site being the summit of a diluvial deposit, and elevated 400 feet above the stream, which here, 92 feet wide, is crossed by a sango or rude wooden bridge, made of trunks of the fir-tree. Inside are houses all round the walls, with a small space in the middle. The population consists of Tartar families, and a few monks and nuns of the Lamaic mode of belief, residing in their respective communities. Elevation above the sea 10,413 feet. Lat. 32°, long. 78° 34′.

SHALLEE, in the hill state of Bhuggee, a lofty peak about four miles south of the left bank of the Sutluj, is very difficult of access on account of its steepness. On the summit is a wooden temple, in which human sacrifices were formerly offered to the Hindoo goddess Kalee; and some maintain that the horrible rite is secretly continued, notwithstanding its prohibition by the British government. Elevation above the sea 9,623 feet. Lat. 31° 11′, long. 77° 20′.

SHALWI, in the hill state of Joobul, a river having its sources on the south-eastern declivity of the great range stretching from the peak of Chur to that of Wartu, and in about lat. 31° 3′, long. 77° 36′. Holding its way in a south-easterly direction through an elevated and densely-wooded valley, and being swollen with numerous feeders right and left, it, after a course of about twenty-five miles, falls into the Tonse river, in lat. 30° 48′, long. 77° 49′. In the upper part of its course, where it is called the Koti Nala, it is described by Fraser as a fine copious stream.

SHAMGHUR, in Sirhind, a village on the route from Kurnal to Loodiana, and five miles N.W. of the former town. It is situate on the edge of a jungle, which stretches the whole distance to Kurnal. Though the greater part of the population are Mussulmans, or Hindoos of the Jat denomination, the village with the surrounding country belongs to a chief of the protected Sikhs, to whom it yields an annual revenue estimated at 550*l.* sterling. Shamghur is distant N.W. from Calcutta 970 miles. Lat. 29° 45′, long. 76° 57′.

SHAMGURH, in the British district of Mairwara, lieut.-gov. of the N.W. Provinces, a town on the route from Nusseerabad to Jallor, 24 miles S.W. by W. of the former. Lat. 26° 8′, long. 74° 32′.

SHAMLEE, in the British district of Muzuffurnugur, lieut.-gov. of the N.W. Provinces, a town on the route from Muzuffurnugur to Jheend, 22 miles W. of the former. Shamlee has a population of 11,816 inhabitants. Lat. 29° 26′, long. 77° 23′.

SHANDAMANGALUM.—A town in the British district of Salem, presidency of Madras, 24 miles S. by E. of Salem. Lat. 11° 19′, long. 78° 18′.

SHAPOOREE.—An island off the coast of Arracan, fronting the entrance of the Naaf river. The centre of the island is in lat. 20° 46′, long. 92° 24′. This island in 1823 was in the occupation of the British, when the Burmese, who then possessed Arracan, demanded its surrender. The requisition was followed up by the despatch of troops under the rajah of Ramree, who attacked and captured the island on the 24th September. This, with other encroachments on the part of the Burmese, led to the first British war with that nation, in 1824.

SHAPORAH.—A town in the Rajpoot state of Oodeypoor, 104 miles N.E. from Oodeypoor, and 62 miles S.S.E. from Ajmeer. Lat. 25° 37′, long. 75°.

SHARA.—A town within the dominions of Gholab Singh, the ruler of Cashmere, situate on the right bank of the Senge Khabab, or Indus river, and 192 miles N.E. by E. from *Jamoo. Lat. 33° 50′, long. 77° 57′.*

SHARGODA.—A town in the British district of Ganjam, presidency of Madras, 32 miles W.N.W. of Ganjam. Lat. 19° 32′, long. 84° 40′.

SHATUL PASS, in Bussahir, on the route from Chooara to Koonawar, over the most southern ridge of the Himalaya, here running in a direction from east-south-east to west-north-west. It is excessively dangerous, not only on account of the deep snow from which it is never free, but also the furious cold winds, which so refrigerate the surface of the body and the lungs, as to cause the death of many who attempt the passage. The formations at the summit are chiefly mica-slate, gneiss, and granite. Gerard, who encamped on the crest of the ridge, found the thermometer there at sunrise, on June 9th, eight degrees below the freezing-point. The snow was covered with a species of musquito, apparently dead, but restored to life and activity when exposed to the rays of the sun. The elevation of the pass is 15,555 feet above the sea. Lat. 31° 23′, long. 78° 3′.

SHAWCOTTA.—A town in the British district of Madura, presidency of Madras, 44 miles E.N.E. of Madura. Lat. 10° 7′, long. 78° 47′.

SHAWPOOR.—A town in the British district of Tannah, presidency of Bombay, 46 miles N.E. of Bombay. Lat. 19° 27′, long. 73° 21′.

SHAWPOOR.—A town in Hyderabad, or territory of the Nizam, 119 miles S.W. by W. from Hyderabad, and 93 miles S.E. from Sholapoor. Lat. 16° 40′, long. 76° 56′.

SHAYAK.—A town within the dominions of Gholab Singh, the ruler of Cashmere, 187 miles E. by N. from Serinagur, and 186 miles N.E. by N. from Kangra. Lat. 34° 13′, long. 78° 17′.

SHAYLODE.—A town in the British district of Malabar, presidency of Madras, 50 miles E.S.E. of Cannanore. Lat. 11° 34′, long. 76° 6′.

SHAZADAPOOR, in the British district of Allahabad, lieut.-gov. of the N.W. Provinces, a town on the route from the city of Allahabad to that of Futtehpore, and 35 miles N.W. of the former. It is half a mile from the right bank of the Ganges, and is described by Tieffenthaler, a century ago, as consisting of one long street, and having at its north-western extremity a serai or public lodging-house for travellers, strongly and well built, resembling a quadrangular fort, with a tower at each corner. Lat. 25° 40′, long. 81° 28′.

SHAZADPORE, in the territory of Oude, a town on the route from the cantonment of Goruckpore to that of Sultanpoor, 73 miles S.W. of the former, 37 N.E. of the latter. It is situate on the river Tons (North-eastern), here crossed by a brick-built bridge 400 yards long. Lat. 26° 24′, long. 82° 28′.

SHAZADPORE.—A town in the British district of Pubna, lieut.-gov. of Bengal, 28 miles N.E. by E. of Pubna. Lat. 24° 12′, long. 89° 36′.

SHEALBA, in Gurhwal, a village on the right bank of the Jumna, is situate near the confluence of the Budesar, a feeder of that river. Lat. 30° 50′, long. 78° 20′.

SHEALLY.—A town in the British district of Tanjore, presidency of Madras, 51 miles N.E. of Tanjore. Lat. 11° 15′, long. 79° 48′.

SHEANKRA.—A town of Malwa, in the native state of Tonk, 11 miles S.S.W. from Tonk, and 81 miles E.S.E. from Ajmeer. Lat. 26°, long. 75° 54′.

SHEBEE, in Bussahir, a village of the district of Koonawar, is situate in the valley of Ruskulung, near the left bank of the river Darbung. Close to the village is a copper-mine, but it has not been worked for some years. The village is inhabited by a few monks and nuns of the Lamaic religion. Elevation above the sea 9,800 feet. Lat. 31° 47′, long. 78° 29′.

SHEDBAL, one of the southern Mahratta jaghires, the centre of which is in lat. 16° 38′, long. 74° 47′. Its chief derives from it a revenue of 12,359*l*., and maintains a force consisting of sixty-eight cavalry and 212 infantry. He was formerly bound to furnish a contingent of cavalry for the service of the British government, but has now commuted the obligation for a money payment. His request for permission to adopt an heir has been rejected.

SHEEKUR, in the Rajpoot state of Jessulmere, a village on the route from the town of Beekaneer to that of Jessulmere, and 75 miles N.E. of the latter place. It is situate in a wooded undulating country, and contains fifty houses, supplied with water from a well 220 feet deep. The road in this part of the route is alternately stony and sandy. Lat. 27° 6′, long. 72° 10′.

SHEELGANWA.—A town in the Rajpoot state of Jodhpoor, 58 miles N.E. by N. from Jodhpoor, and 70 miles W.N.W. from Ajmeer. Lat. 26° 56′, long. 73° 42′.

SHEEMOGA, or SIMOGA, in the territory of Mysore, a town on the left or north-west bank of the river Toonga, here broad and navigable downwards during the rainy season. In 1792 it was besieged by the Mahrattas, aided by an auxiliary force of the Bombay army, commanded by Captain Little. As a Mysorean force, commanded by Muhammed Reza, a relative of Tippoo Sultan, was posted in the vicinity ready to attack the besiegers as soon as engrossed by active operations, Captain Little advanced against them at the head of 750 sepoys, and completely defeated them, though very strongly posted, and greatly superior in force, which was estimated at 10,000 foot, 1,000 horse, ten guns, and thirteen elephants. The Mysorean army was quite dispersed, having lost a great number of men and all their guns, ammunition, baggage, and quantity of small arms, and in a few days the town and fort surrendered. At this period the east side of the fort was during the rains washed by the Toonga, and the other three sides had an indifferent ditch, twenty feet wide and twelve deep, the other defences being likewise injudiciously constructed. The town was then estimated to contain 6,000 houses, and, according to the usually-received ratio of inmates to houses, above 30,000 inhabitants. The town was destroyed by the Mahrattas. At the time of Buchanan's visit, the town was estimated to contain 500 houses, and was said to be increasing fast. Distant from Bangalore, N.W., 150 miles; from Seringapatam, N.W., 130; Mangalore, N.E., 90; Madras, W., 325. Lat. 13° 56′, long. 75° 37′.

SHEERGURH, in the British district of Muthra, lieut.-gov. of the N. W. Provinces, a town on the route from Muthra to Delhi, 20 miles N. by W. of the former. Lat. 27° 46′, long. 77° 40′.

SHEERWUL.—A town in the British province of Sattara, presidency of Bombay, 32 miles N. of Sattara. Lat. 18° 9′, long. 74° 1′.

SHEESGURH, in the British district Bareilly, lieut.-gov. of the N. W. Provinces, a small town on the route from the town of Bareilly to Almora, and 34 miles N. of the former. It is situate on an inconsiderable eminence, seen afar in this level country, and rendered more conspicuous by a ruinous fort on its summit. It is well supplied with water, and has a bazar and market; the country open and well cultivated. Lat. 28° 43′, long. 79° 23′.

SHEEVAROY HILLS.—See SALEM.

SHEIKHBUDEEN, in the Daman division of the Punjab, a town situated 15 miles W. from the right bank of the Indus, 130 miles S.S.W. of the town of Peshawar. Lat. 32° 18′, long. 70° 58′.

SHEIKPOORA, in the British district of Monghyr, lieut.-gov. of Bengal, a town situate at the foot of a hill, on the route from the city of Monghyr to that of Behar, 40 miles S.W. of former, 20 E. of latter. Here is a thana or station for a police-division of the same name. It is a filthy, ugly place, inhabited by a very bad set of natives, who commit crimes and wickedness of every kind. Lat. 25° 10′, long. 85° 57′.

SHEKAWUTTEE, in Rajpootana, a state, or rather collection of small states, dependent upon Jeypore. It is bounded on the north-west by Bikaneer; on the north-east by Loharoo and Jhujhur; on the south-east by Jeypore and Patun; and on the south-west by Joudpore. It lies between lat. 27° 20′—28° 33′, long. 74° 52′—76° 10′. It is ninety-five miles in length from north-east to south-west, and sixty-three in breadth in the direction of the opposite angles: the area is 3,895 square miles. It is an arid, barren tract, consisting, with little exception, either of sandy wastes, or rocky hills and mountains. The latter are in the south and south-eastern parts of the territory, being a continuation of the hills commencing a short distance south-west of Delhi. They are in some parts metalliferous, especially in the vicinity of Singhana, where copper-mines have been worked from time immemorial. The sands are not totally unproductive, being sprinkled with tufts of babul (Acacia vera), kuril (Capparis aphylla), and phok. The Katuree, which is almost the only river, crosses the south frontier from the territory of Jeypore, traverses Shekawuttee from south to north, flowing into the territory of Bikaneer, and is there lost in the sands. The most productive parts of the territory are the valleys among the rocky hills in the south-eastern part. There the soil is rather fertile, and the wells being of no great depth, the rubbee, or crop reaped in spring, is abundant. It consists of wheat, barley, and some other grain, pulse, red pepper, and bhang or hemp, yielding an intoxicating resin. The sandy part of the country produces so little vegetation suitable for human sustenance, that great numbers of the people are obliged to subsist occasionally on the seeds of bhurt, a species of strong bur.

The population, though of Rajpoot descent, appear to follow a mongrel religion, and to have engrafted some Mahomedan points of belief, or at least of observance, on their original Brahminism. Hog's flesh is considered unlawful food, and on the birth of every male child the Mussulman profession of faith is repeated; but on the same occasion a goat is sacrificed, and the infant sprinkled with the blood. This hybrid and semi-barbarous population have been inveterate freebooters; and the avocation seems to have thriven with them, as, though their country is little productive, it contains several towns. The most important of these are Sikur, Khundhaila, Futtehpoor, Lutchmangah, Khetri, Goodah, Jhunjhuna, and Singana. The revenue of Shekawuttee, according to Tod, was 23,00,000 rupees.

Before the firm and regulating influence of British authority was recognised here, there appears to have been little or nothing deserving the name of government. The territory was partitioned among many thakoors or petty chiefs, the highest influence being exerted by five, who claimed to be descended from Shekji, a scion of the Rajpoot family reigning at Amber. Shekji, about the beginning of the fifteenth century, succeeded in wresting the greater part of Shekawuttee from the ruler of Amber, to whom it had previously belonged; but in the early part of the eighteenth, it was recovered by the celebrated Jey Singh, founder of the city of Jeypore. Subsequently, the disturbed state of the country required the intervention of the British government, and after some movements of less importance, an adequate force was, in 1834, sent into the country, the most important forts and posts taken, and efficient means adopted for enforcing order. Towards the close of the year, the British force having effected its object, was withdrawn, but the freebooters again proving occasionally troublesome, further measures became necessary; and with a view to the preservation of order, as well as of providing honest employment for part of the predatory population, a body of irregular cavalry was raised, and for some time maintained at the expense of the chiefs. This body, known as the Shekawuttee brigade, is now a British force, and the native chiefs have been for some years relieved from any charge on account of it. Its cavalry and artillery branches have been disbanded.

SHEKHASIR, in the Rajpoot state of Jesulmeer, a decayed village on the route from the town of Beekaneer to that of Jesulmeer, and 95 miles N.E. of the latter. It is important merely on account of a good supply of water from a tank. The road in this part of the route is good, through an open country. Lat. 27° 12′, long. 72° 14′.

SHEKHPOOR, in the British district of Cawnpore, lieut.-gov. of the N.W. Provinces, a village on the route from Calpee to Etawa, and nine miles N. of the former. Lat. 26° 13′, long. 79° 48′.

SHEKOABAD, in the British district of Mynpoorie, a town on the route from Agra to Etawa, and 32 miles N.W. of the latter. It has a good bazar, and is supplied with water from wells. Lat. 27° 6′, long. 78° 39′.

SHEKUL.—A town in the British district of Madura, presidency of Madras, 60 miles S.E. of Madura. Lat. 9° 15′, long. 78° 43′.

SHEMAR, in the British district of Kumaon, lieut.-gov. of the N.W. Provinces, a village on the route up the course of the Ramgunga (Eastern), from Petorahgurh to the Unta Dhura Pass, 14 miles N. of Petorahgurh, half a mile E. of the left bank of the Ramgunga. Lat. 29° 47′, long. 80° 12′.

SHEM DEO, in the British district of Kumaon, lieut.-gov. of the N.W. Provinces, a Hindoo temple on a summit of the Sub-Himalaya, or mountain system south of the main range, east of Almorah cantonment 11 miles. Elevation above the sea 6,760 feet. Lat. 29° 37′, long. 79° 52′.

SHENCOTTA.—A town in the British district of Tinnevelly, presidency of Madras, 49 miles N.E. by N. of Tinnevelly. Lat. 9° 17′, long. 78° 10′.

SHEO, in the Rajpoot state of Jodhpoor, a town on the route from Jessulmere to Balmeer, and 36 miles N. of the latter. It is the capital of an extensive but barren district, subdivided among numerous thakoors or feudatories, who pay little deference to the rajah of Jodhpoor's governor, stationed here with four guns and a small detachment of soldiers. There are 200 houses, and a thanah or police-office. Water is obtained from a fine tank on the north-west side of the town, and from seven wells forty feet deep. Lat 26° 12′, long. 71° 14′.

SHEOGANGUNJE, in the British district of Jounpoor, lieut.-gov. of the N.W. Provinces, a town on the route from the cantonment of Jounpoor to Purtabgurh, 26 miles W. of the former, 22 E. of the latter. It has a bazar, and is well provided with water. Lat. 25° 46′, long. 82° 14′.

SHEOPOOR, in the British district of Benares, a town on the route from Benares to Jounpoor, three miles N.W. of the former, 34 S.E. of the latter, five N.W. of the left bank of the Ganges. Lat. 25° 21′, long. 83° 1′.

SHEOPOOR, in the territory of Gwalior, or possessions of Scindia's family, a town near the western boundary, towards the Jeypore territory. It is the principal place of a pergunnah, the annual revenue of which is estimated at 3,25,000 rupees. It was formerly the capital of a small Rajpoot principality, but in the early part of the present century was subjugated by the forces of Doulut Rao Scindia. In 1816, when garrisoned by Scindia's general Baptiste with 200 men, it was surprised and taken by escalade by the celebrated Rajpoot chief Jey Singh, who had only sixty men. The captor seized a large amount of treasure, and made the family of Baptiste prisoners. Lat. 25° 38′, long. 76° 48′.

SHEOPOOR DEAR, in the British district of Ghazeepoor, lieut.-gov. of the N.W. Provinces, a town two miles from the northern bank of the Ganges, and five miles S.E. from Bulliah. Sheopoor contains a population of 6,382. Lat. 25° 40′, long. 84° 18′.

SHEOPORE, in the British district of Benares, lieut.-gov. of the N.W. Provinces, a town on the route from Benares to Jounpoor, three miles N.W. of the former. Lat. 25° 21′, long. 83° 1′.

SHEORAJPOOR, a small town, with a bazar, on the route from Cawnpore to Futehgurh, and 21 miles N.W. of the former. Lat. 26° 41′, long. 80° 12′.

SHERADONE.—A town in one of the sequestrated districts of Hyderabad, 172 miles W.N.W. from Hyderabad, and 60 miles N. from Sholapoor. Lat. 18° 31′, long. 76° 13′.

SHERBAL.—See SHEDBAL.

SHERECOTE, in the British district of Bijnour, lieut.-gov. of the N.W. Provinces, a town situate on the river Koh. Elevation above the sea 653 feet; distance N.W. from Calcutta 920 miles, from Moradabad 40. It contains a population of 12,084 inhabitants. Lat. 29° 20′, long. 78° 38′.

SHEREGURH, in the British district of Bareilly, lieut.-gov. of the N.W. Provinces, a town on the route from Bareilly to Almora, 20 miles N. of the former. Lat. 28° 40′, long. 79° 27′.

SHERGHOTTY, in the British district of Behar, a town, the principal place of a thana or police-division of the same name. It lies on the route from Hazareebagh to Benares, 58 miles N.W. of former, 131 S.E. of latter. It is situate on a small island formed by a tributary of the river Poonpun. There are several bungalows or lodges, formerly occupied by officers of the government when the place was a civil station. The number of houses is estimated at 1,019; and admitting the usually-received ratio of inmates to houses, the population may be assumed at 5,100 persons. The town is distant 20 miles S.W. of Gayah. Lat. 24° 33′, long. 84° 51′.

SHERGURH.—A town in the Rajpoot state of Jeypoor, 74 miles S.E. by S. from Jeypoor, and 121 miles E. by S. from Ajmeer. Lat. 26° 2′, long. 76° 35′.

SHERGURH (Fort of), in the British district of Shahabad, lieut.-gov. of Bengal, 20 miles W.S.W. of Sasseram. Lat. 24° 50′, long. 83° 49′.

SHERKHANWALA, in Sirhind, a village on the route from Lodiana to Ferozpoor, and nine miles E. of the latter town. It contains a few shops, and has an abundant supply of good water from three brick-lined wells, each about thirty feet deep. The surrounding country is barren, wild, and overrun with jungle. Distant N.W. from Calcutta, by Delhi and Munuk, 1,159 miles. Lat. 30° 56′, long. 74° 42′.

SHETTYKAIRA.—A town in the Mysore, 62 miles S. by E. from Chittel Droog, and 66 miles N. from Seringapatam. Lat. 13° 21′, long. 76° 38′.

SHEU, in Bussahir, a pass on a ridge projecting northwards from the most southerly range of the Himalaya, and subordinate to it. The route from the Burenda Pass, northwards, into Koonawur, lies over the Sheu. The extreme elevation at which birches were found to grow was 12,800 feet, and pines 12,000. The highest cultivation, which was that of buckwheat, was 10,650 feet above the sea. The elevation of the pass itself is 13,350 feet. Lat. 31° 24′, long. 78° 13′.

SHEVAGUNGA.—A town in the British district of Madura, presidency of Madras, 26 miles E. by S. of Madura. Lat. 9° 51′, long. 78° 33′.

SHEVLY.—A town in Hyderabad, or territory of the Nizam, 130 miles S.W. from Ellichpoor, and 111 miles E.N.E. from Ahmednuggur. Lat. 19° 46′, long. 76° 18′.

SHEWAR, in the British district of Benares, lieut.-gov. of the N.W. Provinces, a village on the left bank of the Ganges, 666 miles by water N.W. of Calcutta, or 843 by the Sunderbund passage; three miles N. of the city of Benares, or lower down the stream. Lat. 25° 21′, long. 83° 8′.

SHEWE ZUTO.—A town of Burmah, 18 miles W. from the right bank of the Irawady, and 151 miles S.W. from Ava. Lat. 20° 14′, long. 94° 25′.

SHEWHUR.—A town in the British district of Sarun, lieut.-gov. of Bengal, 28 miles N. by W. of Mozuffefpoor. Lat. 26° 30′, long. 85° 21′.

SHEWLIE, in the British district of Cawnpoor, lieut.-gov. of the N.W. Provinces, a town on the route from Cawnpoor to Mynpooree, 21 miles W.N.W. of the former. Lat. 26° 36′, long. 80° 7′.

SHEYL, in Bussahir, a village at the south-eastern base of the Wartu Mountain. Its site is very pleasant, amidst much cultivation, and surrounded by picturesque mountains. Here is a mine of excellent iron-ore, easily extracted and smelted with the charcoal of the surrounding forests. Elevation 8,000 feet above the sea. Lat. 31° 14′, long. 77° 37′.

SHIAR, in Bussahir, a pass over a ridge proceeding southwards from the great range of the Himalaya bounding Koonawar on the south. On the highest part of the pass is a small piece of level ground about 100 feet across, consisting of a swampy turf yielding to the foot. The prospect from this spot is vast and magnificent, comprehending the Chur Mountain to the south-west; on the east the flanks of Boorendo, but not the pass itself; to the south-east the peaks of Jumnotri, rising one above the other in majestic disorder, and covered with perpetual snow; and beyond, the Goonass Pass, one of the huge Ruldung peaks, upwards of 21,000 feet high. Shiar Pass has an elevation of 13,720 feet above the sea. Lat. 31° 19′, long. 77° 58′.

SHIKARPOOR.—A town in the Mysore, 156 miles N.W. by N. from Seringapatam, and 102 miles N.N.E. from Mangalore. Lat. 14° 16′, long. 75° 25′.

SHIKARPOOR, in the British district of Boolundshuhur, lieut.-gov. of the N.W. Provinces, a town on the route from Boolundshuhur to Mynpooree, 14 miles S.E. of the former: it contains a population of 11,065 inhabitants. Lat. 28° 16′, long. 78° 6′.

SHIKARPOOR, in the British district of Muzuffurnuggur, lieut.-gov. of the N.W. Provinces, a town on the route from Muzuffurnuggur to Rohtuk, 14 miles W.S.W. of the former. Lat. 29° 22′, long. 77° 33′.

SHIKARPOOR, in Sinde, a town, the most important in the country in a commercial point of view, and probably the most populous, though not possessing the distinction of being regarded as the capital. It is situate 20 miles due W. of the Indus, in a country so low and level, that, by means of canals from that river, it is, during the inundation, extensively flooded, and so completely is the soil saturated with moisture, that, by digging to the depth of twelve or fifteen feet, water may at any time be obtained in quantity almost without limit. A branch from the Sinde canal, dug from the Indus, passes within a mile of the town, and is navigable for large boats during four months of the year. Though the inundation leaves extensive tracts covered with stagnant water, and the heat is excessive, the climate is not considered insalubrious, except towards the end of September, when agues prevail. The soil is alluvial, being the deposit of the waters of the canals and channels. It is so rich as to require no manure, producing very great crops, in return of culture and irrigation. The town is surrounded by flourishing groves and orchards, yielding in abundance dates, mangoes, oranges, mulberries, and other fruits the usual produce of this country. Sugarcane is cultivated more with a view to its consumption as a sweetmeat than for producing sugar. The wall by which Shikarpoor was once fortified is now in ruins, but eight gates may still be traced: the circuit of the wall is 3,831 yards. The approaches to the town are bad, and when reached, it exhibits nothing attractive. Much waste ground is interspersed among the houses in the inhabited part, the streets are narrow, and the houses in general small. The mansions of the opulent Hindoo merchants are large, massy, gloomy piles, inclosed and secluded by high brick walls. Shikarpoor contains no public edifice worthy of notice. The character of the place is thoroughly commercial, almost every house having a shop attached to it. The bazar extends for about 800 yards through the centre of the city, and is covered with rafters thatched with palm-leaves. This arrangement is intended to afford protection against the rays of the sun, but it renders the air stagnant, oppressive, and injurious to health. Improvements in the town are, however, about to take place, under the proposed application of the provisions of the Legislative Act of the government of India, No. 26 of 1850. Trade meanwhile appears to thrive. Conolly observes, that "the shops seemed to be well filled with the necessaries of life and various merchandise, and the people had that busy air which characterizes men engaged in active trade." Burnes states the number of the shops in the bazar in 1837 at 884; Postans, in 1841, represents the number of Hindoo shops as 923. The laborious trades and handicrafts are followed exclusively by Mahometans. The transit-trade is important, as the town is situate on one of the great routes from Sinde to Khorasan and Afghanistan, through the Bolan Pass, and also on that which leads northward to the Derajat, by the western side of the Indus. There is likewise a route to Kurrachee, by way of Sehwan, and one to Hindostan and the eastern side of the Indus, by the ferry at Roree and Sukkur, besides others of less importance. "The direct trade of the town of Shikarpoor itself," Burnes observes, "is not extensive; its port is Kurrachee." The trade with Khorasan and Kandahar is considerable, but there is scarcely any with Northern Afghanistan, that being conducted through the Punjab and Bhawlpoor. The transit-trade is principally that from Marwar and the adjacent parts of Hindostan to Khorasan and Persia; but banking and other branches of monetary traffic constitute the more important departments of the commercial operations of Shikarpoor. There are several Hindoos possessing large capitals, which appear to have been accumulated under the supremacy of the Afghans. The improvidence of the latter left the management of money matters to these acute financiers, who, by farming the revenue, and exacting exorbitant interest on loans, public and private, have amassed immense wealth. These capitalists are represented as enterprising, vigilant, and ravenous for gain; living impersonations of heartless avarice, but at the same time specious, civil, and intelligent to an extraordinary degree. Their lingual acquirements are extensive, as they usually understand Persian, Belooche, Pushtoo, Hindostanee, and Sindee. Their credit stands so high that their bills can be negotiated in every part of India and Central and Western Asia, from Astracan to Calcutta. In every important town throughout this vast extent they have agents, whose families remaining at Shikarpoor are a sort of hostages for their fidelity. The commerce and general prosperity of the town, which had rapidly declined under the power of Scindian rulers, are reviving under the lately established supremacy of the British. So much disorganized had society become when Masson visited the place a few years ago, that to pass the walls was almost to incur the certainty of being robbed.

The population of the town is estimated at 30,000. Of these, 20,000 are Hindoos, characterized by great laxity in respect to their peculiar tenets. The remaining 10,000 are Mahometans, of whom 1,000 are Afghans. These share in the general bad character of the population, being considered ignorant, crafty, contentious, and cowardly. It may be hoped that the prevalence of evil is but the result of the long course of oppression, extortion, and cruelty to which the people have been subjected by their rulers, and that under better auspices the tone of morals will be raised, while increased security will be afforded to life and property. Shikarpoor is the principal place of one of the three territorial divisions of Sinde, having an area of 6,120 square miles, and a population of 350,401. The town was founded in 1617. Lat. 28°, long. 68° 39′.

SHINGE.—A town of Eastern India, in the British province of Tenasserim, 116 miles S.S.E. of Moulmein. Lat. 14° 50′, long. 98° 10′.

SHIPKEE, in Chinese Tartary, lies close on the north-eastern boundary of Bussahir, and is usually the limit of the exploratory travels of Europeans in the Clestial Empire, all beyond being guarded from intrusion with the most vigilant jealousy. In proceeding to it from Dabling, there is a choice of two routes; one by Peeming Ghat, having an elevation above the sea of 13,518 feet, the other, a little to the south of the former, by the Kungma Pass, having an elevation of 16,000 feet, but, notwithstanding its greater height, easier than the former. The village is situate a mile from the left bank of the Sutlej, and three miles south of its great flexure, where, having thus far from its source held a north-westerly course, it turns to the south-west. The ridge traversed by the passes just described, stretches in a direction from north to south about three miles west of the town, and forms not only the boundary between the British and Chinese empires, but also the physical limit between the craggy wilds of Koonawur and the more open waste of Chinese Tartary. "Here," observes Gerard, "the scene was entirely changed: a more marked difference can scarcely exist. The mountains to the eastward were quite of another nature from those we before met with; they are of granite, broken into gravel, forming regular slopes, and neither abrupt nor rocky. The country in that direction has a most desolate and dreary aspect, not a single tree or blade of green grass was distinguishable for nearly thirty miles, the ground being covered with a very prickly plant, which greatly resembled furze in its withered state. This shrub was almost black, seeming as if burnt; and the leaves were so much parched from the arid wind of Tartary, that they might be ground to powder by rubbing them between the hands. The brownish tint of the furze, together with the bleakness of the country, have the appearance of an extensive heath, and would strongly remind a Scotch Highlander of his native land." The wind, during the visit of the Gerards, blew a hurricane; and it is said to blow with almost equal violence throughout the year: its aridity is great, and everything exposed to its influence is dried up. The collection of dwellings called Shipkee consists of six hamlets, scattered over the declivity of a bare and brown mountain, sloping northwards to the Sutlej, and presenting everywhere a surface of rocky barrenness, except in the immediate vicinity of the houses, where persevering industry has succeeded in establishing some extent of cultivation. The crops are wheat, barley, buckwheat, and turnips, besides the never-failing apricots. The houses are built of stone, flat-roofed, and have a neat appearance; gardens, hedged in with gooseberry-bushes, appear in front of each, and the scene is enlivened by herds of huge yaks, and of shawl-goats and flocks of Tartar sheep, unrivalled for size, beauty, and the fineness of their wool. These animals are guarded by large native dogs, which, like one of the objects of their charge, the shawl-goats, have fine wool under their coat of hair, affording a defence against the rigour of the climate. The Gerards found the Chinese officers determined to stop their further progress by withholding provisions, the most effectual mode that could be adopted; but they were courteous, either out of regard to the numbers which followed in the train of the travellers (nearly 100 persons), or from a better motive. Gerard says of the inhabitants, "The Tartars pleased us much. They have none of that ferocity of character so commonly ascribed to them. They have something of the Chinese features, and their eyes are small; they go bareheaded, even in the cold weather, and have their hair plaited into a number of folds, ending in a tail two or three feet long. Their dress consists of a garment of blanket, trowsers of striped woollen stuff, resembling tartan, and stockings or boots of red blanket, to which are sewed leather shoes; most wear necklaces, upon which are strung pieces of quartz or bone. They have also knives in brass or silver cases, and all carry iron tobacco-pipes, of the same shape as those used by labourers at home, and the higher classes have them ornamented with silver. In common with the inhabitants of Koonawur, the greater part of them have a flint and steel for striking fire, attached to their apparel by a metal chain. The women, whose dress resembles that of the men, were literally groaning under a load of ornaments, which are mostly of iron or brass, inlaid with silver or tin, and beads round their necks, wrists, and ankles, and affixed to almost every part of their clothes. The elevation of Shipkee above the sea is 10,597 feet. Lat. 31° 48′, long. 78° 48′.

SHIPOOR, in Gurwhal, a lofty peak on the north-east frontier, towards Chinese Tartary, is situate six miles N.E. of Gangotri, and in the bifurcation between the rivers Bhageerettee and Jahnevi. Elevation above the sea 18,681 feet. Lat. 31° 1′, long. 79° 4′.

SHITTARGURH, in the Baree Dooab division of the Punjab, a town situated 16 miles N.W. from the right bank of the Sutlej, 39 miles E. by S. of the town of Mooltan. Lat. 29° 57′, long. 72° 8′.

SHIVANASUNDRUM.—An island in the British district of Coimbatoor, presidency of Madras, formed by the river Cauvery: it is three miles in length by one in breadth, and upon it are the ruins of an ancient city of the same name. Lat. 12° 17′, long. 77° 14′.

SHIVILPUTUR. — A town in the British district of Tinnevelly, presidency of Madras, 55 miles N. of Tinnevelly. Lat. 9° 30′, long. 77° 39′.

SHOEDOWN.—A town in the British territory of Pegu, situate on the left bank of the Irawady river, and 10 miles S. by W. from Prome. Lat. 18° 38′, long. 95°.

SHOLANGHUR. — A town in the British district of North Arcot, presidency of Madras, 14 miles N.N.E. of Arcot. Lat. 13° 4′, long. 79° 29′.

SHOLAPADI.—A town in the British district of Salem, presidency of Madras, 27 miles N.W. of Salem. Lat. 11° 53′, long. 77° 56′.

SHOLAPOOR.—A town in the British district of the same name, in the presidency of Bombay, 124 miles E. of Sattara. Lat. 17° 40′, long. 75° 58′.

SHOLAPORE, a British collectorate in the presidency of Bombay, is composed of three separate divisions, the two largest lying north and south of each other, and the smaller division situate to the north-east of the other two. These districts are bounded on the north by the collectorate of Ahmednuggur and the dominions of the Nizam; on the south by Sattara and the Belgaum collectorate; on the east by the Nizam's dominions; and on the west by the collectorates of Ahmednuggur, Poona, and by Sattara. The collectorate extends from lat. 16° 10′ to 18° 34′, and from long. 75° to 76° 28′: its greatest length, from north-west to south-east, is 170 miles; its greatest breadth, from east to west, fifty miles. In 1838, this district, then a portion of the principal collectorate of Poona, was formed into a separate collectorate.

The general face of the district is described as undulating, and presenting a succession of upland and valley, and, with the exception of some mango-topes and other plantations in the talooks of Barsee, Mungolee, and Moodebehall, the country is stated to be nearly devoid of trees. The Kistna forms the southern limit of the district, which is also traversed by the Bheema, and its confluent the Seena. The climate is dry and healthy; the average fall of the monsoon rains averaging twenty-two inches.

Cotton is the staple product. The experimental cotton-farms are stated to have succeeded beyond expectation, and the soil to be admirably adapted to the growth of the New Orleans species; but the district is represented as suffering from the want of roads. There is no metalled or made road through any part of this collectorate: all traffic and communication are carried on by means of the ordinary country roads, which are nothing more than tracks, hardened by long use to a degree that, especially in the hot season, renders them quite sufficient to answer all the purposes of the best cross-roads. There is a cleared road from Sholapore through Wyrag, Barsee, and Kurmulla, to Patus, within forty miles of Poona, which has been rendered passable for all kinds of carriage since 1844; and a continuation of the whole line to Poona, as a fair-weather road, was sanctioned by the home authorities in 1847; but a more substantial road from Sholapore to Poona is highly desirable. The amount of traffic which passes in this direction is exceedingly large; and as the produce of the whole of the western part of the Nizam's dominions is brought to Barsee for transmission to Bombay, there are few lines where a good made road would be more desirable. There are no passes or ghauts in this collectorate. The two rivers, Seena and Bheema, are the only natural obstacles to regular internal communication, and it is only during the monsoon that they offer any serious impediment. The population is given under the article BOMBAY. Compared with their former condition, the people are said to possess a larger amount of competence among them: great wealth is more rare than formerly, but a medium degree of easy circumstances is also much more common. Many attempts have been made to introduce European implements of husbandry in this collectorate, but with little success. Agricultural skill is by no means at a low standard, and many estates give proof of the greatest care having been taken in their cultivation; but the means of performing many of the most ordinary operations are exceedingly defective; and the same may be said of the mechanical arts, in which the productions are out of all proportion superior to the means of producing them.

The lands of this collectorate have been surveyed, classified, and assessed, and the government demand thereupon fixed under the new settlement for a term of thirty years. The district was acquired by the East-India Company in 1818, on the fall of the Peishwa.

SHOLAPORE, in the British collectorate of the same name, presidency of Bombay, a town in the level tract at the eastern extremity of that collectorate. Its ground-plan is an oblong of a considerable area, with a wall and fausse-braie of substantial masonry, flanked by capacious round towers. A broad and deep wet ditch surrounds the place, and the north and east sides are covered by an extensive pettah or exterior town, surrounded by a good wall, and divided in the same manner into two parts. To the southward, communicating with the ditch, is a tank, surrounded on three sides by a mound, which, on occasion of the attack by the British force, formed a good breastwork to the Peishwa's army, posted outside the place. Sholapore, though having no natural strength, was early a fortress of importance in the Deccan, being mentioned in 1478 as one of the principal strongholds of the Bahmani sovereigns. Long afterwards, its possession was a frequent subject of contest between the sultans of Ahmednuggur and Beejapoor, and so continued until it was taken by Aurungzebe in 1685. During the dismemberment of the empire of Delhi, in the early part of the eighteenth century, Sholapore fell into the hands of the Mahrattas, and after the defeat of the Peishwa and his flight from Poona, in 1818, was invested by a British force under General Pritzler. At that time the number of guns in the fort amounted to thirty-seven, including eleven field-guns; besides which, there were thirty-nine wall-pieces. The defending force consisted of 850 horse and 5,550 foot, stationed in the town, outside the fort, besides the garrison, estimated at 1,000 men. The town was taken by escalade, and the defences of the fort being breached, the place surrendered in four days. A church has been erected in the town. Distance from Poona, S.E., 165 miles; from Sattara, E., 125; from Bombay, S.E., 220. Lat. 17° 40′, long. 76°.

SHOLAVANDAN.—A town in the British district of Madura, presidency of Madras, 12 miles N.W. of Madura. Lat. 10° 2′, long. 78° 2′.

SHOOGOONG.—A town of Eastern India, in the native state of Muneepoor, situate on the left bank of the Nankatha Khyoung river, and 39 miles S. from Muneepoor. Lat. 24° 15′, long. 93° 59′.

SHOOJUL.—A town in the Rajpoot state of Jodhpoor, situate on the left bank of the Rairee river, and 46 miles S.E. by E. from Jodhpoor. Lat. 25° 56′, long. 73° 44′.

SHOOK.—A town in Nepal, 146 miles N.W. by W. from Khatmandoo, and 145 miles N. from Goruckpoor. Lat. 28° 47′, long. 83° 18′.

SHOOKRABAD.—A town within the dominions of Gholab Singh, the ruler of Cashmere, situate 43 miles W. from Sirinagur, and 78 miles N.N.E. from Jhelum. Lat. 33° 59′, long. 74° 14′.

SHORAPORE.—A small subordinate raj situate in the south-west angle of the territory of the Nizam. It is bounded on the south by the river Kistnah, separating it from the Raichoor Doab, and on the north by the territories of Hyderabad. In 1842, the rajah of Shorapore having fallen into pecuniary difficulties, found himself unable to fulfil his engagements to the Nizam, his superior. This necessitated the interference of the paramount power, by whose authority an arrangement was effected, under which the rajah ceded certain possessions south of the Kistna, in commutation of the Nizam's tribute. Rajah Kistnapah Naick dying shortly after, an arrangement was made by the British government for the conduct of the administration during the minority of his successor, by his uncle, Pid Naick. It was, however, unsuccessful, and the British government found it necessary to assume the direct management of the raj. Through their agency, a thorough reform was effected in every department of the previous vicious system of administration, and the country handed over to the young chief in a flourishing condition. Its revenue in 1843 was estimated at five lacs of rupees. The withdrawal of the British agency took place in 1853. No sooner, however, was the government made over to its native ruler, than a system of maladministration recommenced, and the consequences of the relinquishment of British control over the affairs of this petty state are stated to have proved most disastrous. Shorapore, the principal place, is in lat. 16° 32′, long. 76° 52′.

SHORE KOTE, in the Punjab, a small town situate on the route from Jung to Tulumba, and 26 miles N.W. of the latter town. Here are some ruins, which Burnes states to be similar to those of Sehwan, but more extensive. In the Ayeen Akbery, mention is made of Syalkote and of Shoore, two towns in this part of the Punjab; and Shorkot may, perhaps, be the ruins of one of these. Lat. 30° 50′, long. 72° 7′.

SHOREPUR CHOKI, in the British district of Dehra Doon, lieut.-gov. of the N.W.

Provinces, a halting-place on the route from Dehra to Suharunpoor, and seven miles S.W. of the former town. It is situate on the crest of the Khera Pass, across the Sewalik Mountains. Distant N.W. from Calcutta 1,040 miles. Lat. 30° 14′, long. 78° 1′.

SHORON, in the British district of Muzuffurnugur, lieut.-gov. of the N.W. Provinces, a town on the route from Muzuffurnugur to Rewaree, 13 miles S.W. of the former. Lat. 29° 19′, long. 77° 39′.

SHOULAH, or BURA SHOULAH, in the British district of Bijnour, lieut.-gov. of the N.W. Provinces, a village on the route from the town of Moradabad to Mozuffurnuggur, and 81 miles N.W. of the former place. It is situate in an open country, partially cultivated, and supplies and water are plentiful. Distant N.W. from Calcutta 918 miles. Lat. 29° 3′, long. 78° 26′.

SHOYLAGOODY.—A town in the British district of Madura, presidency of Madras, 57 miles S.S.E. of Madura. Lat. 9° 10′, long. 78° 30′.

SHUBERNAGHERRY.—A town in the territory inhabited by the hill tribes of Orissa, 51 miles W. from Goomsoor, and 113 miles S. from Sumbulpoor. Lat. 19° 50′, long. 83° 54′.

SHUBKUDIR, in the Peshawar division of the Punjab, a town situated on the right bank of the Lundye river, 18 miles N. of the town of Peshawar. Lat. 34° 15′, long. 71° 40′.

SHUFEEABAD, in the British district of Paneeput, lieut.-gov. of the N.W. Provinces, a village on the route from the city of Delhi to Kurnaul, and 18 miles N.W. of the former. Lat. 28° 53′, long. 77° 8′.

SHUHUR, in the Rajpoot state of Jeypore, a town on the route from Agra to Nusseerabad, 92 miles S.W. of former, 129 N.E. of latter. It has a hill fort; water is plentiful, as well as supplies of all kinds except wood. Lat. 26° 37′, long. 76° 47′.

SHUJAGANJ, in the territory of Oude, a town on the route from Goruckpore cantonment to Lucknow, 110 miles W. of the former, 56 E. of the latter. Provisions and water are plentiful and good, but firewood rather scarce. Lat. 26° 50′, long. 81° 35′.

SHUJANPOOR.—A town in the Jullunder Doab of the Punjaub, situate 74 miles N.E. by N. of Loodhianah. Lat. 31° 50′, long. 76° 33′.

SHUJAWULPORE.—See SOOJAWULPOOR.

SHUKURPOOR, in the British district of Meerut, lieut.-gov. of the N.W. Provinces, a town on the route from Meerut to Rewaree, 38 miles S.W. of the former. Lat. 28° 37′, long. 77° 21′.

SHUMSABAD.—A town in the native state of Gwalior, or territory of Scindia's family, 29 miles N.W. from Bhilsa, and 81 miles W. by S. from Saugur. Lat. 23° 49′, long. 77° 31′.

SHUMSGURH.—A town of Malwa, in the native state of Bhopal, 12 miles W.S.W. from Bhopal, and 37 miles N.W. from Hoosungabad. Lat. 23° 5′, long. 77° 20′.

SHUMSHABAD, in the British district of Furruckabad, the principal place of the pergunnah of the same name, is situate in the marshy tract on the right of the Ganges, and eight miles from its western bank. It must have been formerly more important than at present, as Baber, who wrested it from the Patans, estimated the annual revenue derived from it at nearly 20,000*l*. In the Ayeen Akbery the revenue derived from it is estimated at 7,138,453 dams, or 1,78,460 rupees. Distant N.W. from Furruckabad 12 miles, N.E. from Agra 88 miles. A recent return gives Shumshabad a population of 6,920 inhabitants. Lat. 27° 32′, long. 79° 30′.

SHUMSHUR NUGGUR.—A town in the British district of Behar, lieut.-gov. of Bengal, 41 miles N.N.W. of Sherghotty. Lat. 25° 4′, long. 84° 31′.

SHUNKERNACOIL.—A town in the British district of Tinnevelly, presidency of Madras, 32 miles N. by W. of Tinnevelly. Lat. 9° 10′, long. 77° 37′.

SHUNTHAPA.—A town in the British district of Tinnevelly, presidency of Madras, 10 miles N. E. by E. of Tinnevelly. Lat. 8° 47′, long. 77° 53′.

SHUPIEN.—A town within the dominions of Gholab Singh, the ruler of Cashmere, situate 26 miles S. from Sirinagur, and 84 miles N.E. by E. from Jhelum. Lat. 33° 43′, long. 74° 56′.

SHUREEARE.—A town in the Rajpoot state of Jodhpoor, 62 miles S.E. from Jodhpoor, and 78 miles S.W. from Ajmeer. Lat. 25° 40′, long. 73° 53′.

SHURUFOODEENPOOR.—A town in the British district of Tirhoot, lieut.-gov. of Bengal, nine miles E. of Mozufferpoor. Lat. 26° 5′, long. 85° 35′.

SHUSHABAD, in the British district of Agra, lieut.-gov. of the N.W. Provinces, a town 14 miles S.E. of the city of Agra. Lat. 27° 1′, long. 78° 12′.

SHUTENEE, in the British district of Cawnpore, lieut.-gov. of the N.W. Provinces, a village on the route from the cantonment of Cawnpore to that of Calpee, and 14 miles N.E. of the latter. Lat. 26° 16′, long. 79° 57′.

SHWAYGEEN.—A town in the British province of Pegu, situate on the left bank of the Sittang river, and 44 miles N.E. from Pegu. Lat. 18° 6′, long. 96° 46′.

SHWELY, a river of Burmah, rises in lat. 23° 51′, long. 98° 30′, and flowing westerly for about 180 miles, falls into the Irawady, in lat. 23° 59′, long. 96° 10′.

SIAM.—An independent kingdom of Eastern India, bounded on the north by Laos;

on the east by Laos, Camboja, and the Gulf of Siam; on the south by the Gulf of Siam and the Malay peninsula; and on the west by the Bay of Bengal and the Tenasserim provinces. It extends from lat. 6° 30′ to 18° 2′, and from long. 98° 25′ to 103° 45′; is about 800 miles in length from north to south, and 370 in breadth. The principal rivers are the Menam and the Me-Ping, flowing north and south. The chief products are rice, sugar, pepper, tobacco, and teak-wood. The earliest connection between this state and the British government appears to have taken place towards the close of the seventeenth century, when the Siamese envoys who had been deputed on an embassy to Louis XIV., visited London, and concluded a commercial treaty with the government of Charles II. This treaty was superseded by one dated in 1715; and from this time to the year 1821, little intercourse seems to have subsisted between the two governments. During this long interval, Siam had been subjected to frequent revolutions, and had carried on constant war with Burmah. In the last-mentioned year (1821), Mr. John Crawfurd was deputed from India by the Marquis of Hastings on a mission to Siam, the chief object of which was the establishment of commercial intercourse, but it was received with distrust. On the breaking out of the Burmese war in 1824, the Siamese volunteered their alliance against their hereditary enemies, but substantially rendered little assistance. The war being terminated, a new treaty was concluded with Siam, in June, 1826, and an arrangement agreed to for the regulation of British trade with its ports. An amicable understanding between the two countries has been the result. In the year in which the treaty was concluded, the Siamese had invaded Queda, and expelled the rajah, who took refuge in Penang, where his residence was permitted, on condition of his abstaining there from any hostile proceeding against Siam. The condition was violated, and on the failure of all attempts to effect a reconciliation between the parties, an article was inserted in the treaty above mentioned, binding the English government to exclude the ex-rajah from his place of refuge, and from certain other localities. By the same article, the English government engaged to prevent any attack upon Queda, or any part of the Siamese territory, from the exiled rajah or his followers; and it was compelled twice to interfere for this purpose. In 1842, however, the king of Siam reinstated the rajah, on his submission; and at the request of the king, the clause of the treaty relating to the rajah was annulled. The death of the king of Siam occurred in 1851. A new treaty has been recently concluded with his successor, which promises to open an extensive sphere for British commerce and enterprise.

SIANEYGUA.—A town in the British district of Tavoy, one of the Tenasserim provinces, presidency of Bengal, 139 miles N.N.W. of Tenasserim, and eight S. of Tavoy. Lat. 13° 59′, long. 98° 21′.

SIAPRI.—A town in Nepal, situate at the foot of the Himalaya Mountains, and 64 miles N.N.E. from Khatmandoo. Lat. 28° 35′, long. 85° 37′.

SICKINDRABAD, in the Baree Doab division of the Punjab, a town situated on the left bank of the Chenaub, 13 miles S.S.W. of the town of Mooltan. Lat. 29° 58′, long. 71° 26′.

SIDDAPOOR.— A town in the British district of North Canara, presidency of Madras, 31 miles E. of Honahwar. Lat. 14° 21′, long. 74° 58′.

SIDDAWATTAM.—See SIDHOUT.

SIDHAM, or SIDHUAN, in Sirhind, a small town on the route from Loodianah to Ferozpoor, and 30 miles W. of the former place. It is situate in a level fertile country, partially cultivated, and about half a mile from the left bank of the Sutlej, crossed here by a ferry. It is within the British district of Loodianah. Population about 1,500. Distant N.W. from Calcutta 1,105 miles. Lat. 30° 55′, long. 75° 26′.

SIDHOUT, in the British district of Cuddapah, presidency of Madras, a town on the north or left bank of the Northern Penna or Pennar river. Here are the remains of the fort, which, though of inconsiderable strength, was the place of refuge of the Patan chief of Cuddapah, who was here obliged to surrender to Hyder Ali, the adventurer who succeeded in acquiring the sovereignty of Mysore. It subsequently was the locality of a British civil establishment; on the removal of which to the town of Cuddapah, this place sank into insignificance. Distance from the town of Cuddapah, E., 10 miles; Madras, N.W., 130. Lat. 14° 28′, long. 79° 2′.

SIDHPOOR, in Guzerat, or the territory of the Guicowar, a town on the route from Mhow to Deesa. It is eligibly situated on the river Saraswati, which being esteemed a sacred river, many rich Brahmins and Gossaens have fixed their dwelling-places here. There is a Math or sacred college, where instruction is given to disciples and hospitality afforded to travellers qualified to receive it. Weaving is carried on extensively; many Mussulman merchants of the denomination called Boras are engaged in trade here. Distance from Deesa, S.E., 32 miles; from Ahmedabad, N., 58; from Baroda, N.W., 125; from Mhow, N.W., 230. Lat. 23° 50′, long. 72° 20′.

SIDNOWAH, in the jaghire of Loharoo, lieut.-gov. of the N.W. Provinces, a village on the route from Hansee to Churu, and 31 miles S.W. of the former. Lat. 28° 42′, long. 75° 49′.

SIDOWRA, in Sirhind, a town on the route from Booreah to Nahun. It is situate near the base of the Sub-Himalaya, and close to the left bank of the Markunda, a torrent descending from that range. It is a large town, well fortified with a brick wall and tall towers of the same material, pierced with three or four tiers of loopholes for musketry. There is a good bazar, and supplies and water are abundant. Part of it belongs to the East-India Company, and the rest to a Sikh sirdar. Sidowra is distant from Calcutta, N.W., 1,047 miles. Lat. 30° 23′, long. 77° 16′.

SIKHUR, in the British district of Benares, a small town with fort on the left bank of the Ganges, nearly opposite Chunar, but a little higher up the stream. In A.D. 1781 it was garrisoned by the refractory rajah of Benares, Cheyt Singh, with 2,000 matchlockmen and 150 cavalry, but was stormed by the British under Lieutenant Polhill. Distant N.W. from Calcutta, by water, 693 miles, or 870 taking the Sunderbund passage; 23 S.W. of Benares by water, 17 by land. Lat. 25° 8′, long. 82° 53′.

SIKKIM, a petty native state in North-Eastern India, is bounded on the north and east by Thibet; on the south-east by Bhotan; on the south by Darjeeling; and on the west by Nepal. It extends from lat. 27° 5′ to 28° 3′, and from long. 88° 2′ to 89°; it is sixty-six miles in length from north to south, fifty-two in breadth, and contains an area of 1,670 square miles, with a population of 61,766. Sikkim became tributary to the Goorkhas in 1789. During the Nepal war in 1814, the rajah co-operated with the British, and upon the termination of hostilities, his safety and independence were guaranteed by the treaty of Segoulee, and his dominions increased, in acknowledgment of his attachment, by the grant of certain tracts which had been ceded to the British by the Nepaulese. In 1836, the rajah made an unconditional cession to the British of the territory of Darjeeling, but shortly after an annual grant of 6,000 rupees was agreed to be made to him as compensation. This, however, he forfeited, together with the territory bestowed on him at the close of the Nepaul war, in consequence of outrages committed by him against British subjects. In 1853 the rajah abdicated the throne in favour of his son.

SIKLEBUN.—A town in Nepal, situate on the left bank of a branch of the Taptee river, and 104 miles W. by S. from Khatmandoo. Lat. 27° 30′, long. 83° 38′.

SIKREE, in the British district of Ghazeepore, lieut.-gov. of the N.W. Provinces, a town on the route from Ghazeepore cantonment to Azimgurh, situate on the river Munghee, 30 miles S.E. of the latter. Lat. 25° 43′, long. 83° 29′.

SIKREEGULEE, in the British district of Purneah, lieut.-gov. of Bengal, a town on the route from Berhampore to Dinapore, 97 miles N.W. of former, 197 E. of latter. It is situate on the right bank of the Ganges, in a difficult pass, where the Rajmahal hills close upon the river. The eminence above the town is surmounted by the picturesque tomb of a Mussulman, regarded by his co-religionists as a saint. Distant N.W. from Calcutta, by Berhampur, 215 miles; by the course of the river, 268. Lat. 25° 10′, long. 87° 43′.

SIKRI, within the territory of the British district of Goorgaon, lieut.-gov. of the N.W. Provinces, a small town on the route from Delhi to Muttra, and 31 miles S. of the former. It is the principal place of a small jaghire containing ten villages, the owner of which, a Mussulman, styled Nawaub, received this recompense for his military services during Lord Lake's campaigns against the Mahrattas in this neighbourhood. Lat. 28° 17′, long. 77° 21′.

SIKUNDERPOOR, in the British district of Goruckpore, lieut.-gov. of the N.W. Provinces, a small town 62 miles W. of Goruckpore cantonment. Buchanan states the number of its houses at 100. Lat. 26° 51′, long. 82° 21′.

SIKUNDRABAD, in the British district of Boolundshuhur, a town on the route from Bareilly to Delhi, and 36 miles S.E. of the latter. It is of considerable size, has a bazar, and supplies and water are abundant. Elevation above the sea 792 feet; population 14,843. Lat. 28° 27′, long. 77° 46′.

SIKUNDRAROW, in the British district of Allygurh, lieut.-gov. of the N.W. Provinces, a town on the route from Coel to Mynpooree, 23 miles S.E. by E. of the former. Lat. 27° 40′, long. 78° 29′.

SIKUNDURPOOR, in the British district of Suharunpoor, lieut.-gov. of the N.W. Provinces, a village on the route from Suharunpoor to Hurdwar, and 13 miles E. of the former town. There is a small bazar. Distant N.W. from Calcutta 1,000 miles. Lat. 29° 57′, long. 77° 50′.

SIKWADANRA.—A town in Nepal, 184 miles W. by N. from Khatmandoo, and 40 miles N.W. from Khachi. Lat. 28° 26′, long. 82° 26′.

SILCHAR.—A town of Eastern India, in the British district of Southern Cachar, 63 miles E. by S. of Silhet. Lat. 24° 48′, long. 92° 51′.

SILDAH.—A town in the British district of Midnapoor, lieut.-gov. of Bengal, 39 miles W.N.W. of Midnapoor. Lat. 22° 40′, long. 86° 51′.

SILHET.—A British district in the lieut.-gov. of Bengal, named from its principal place. It is bounded on the north by the hilly jungly tract inhabited by the wild Garrows, and by Jynteah; on the east by the British district of Cachar; on the south by independent Tipperah; on the west by the British districts Mymensing and Tipperah. It lies between lat. 24° 3′—25° 12′, long. 91°—92° 38′; is 102 miles in length from east to west, and eighty in breadth. The area, according to official report, is 3,532 square miles. In the northern part the country is rugged, rising into jungly eminences towards the Cossya hills, which farther north, beyond the limits of the district, attain an elevation of from 4,000 to 6,000 feet. On the east, the country rises in a similar manner towards the mountains of Cachar, and on the south towards those of Tipperah. The district is described as a vast semi-basin, inclosed by mountains on the northern, eastern, and much of the southern side. The part of this hollow "to the westward, extending nearly to the Brahmapootra, is in most parts always marshy; and the whole is subject to periodical inundations of long duration, being in general under water from April to the middle of November. The towns and villages, which in some parts, more especially to the southward, are numerous, are built on mounds raised with earth dug during the dry season. The houses are in clusters; huts, temples, mosques, and sheds for cattle being huddled together in a manner that gives them the appearance rather of the temporary abode of fugitives than the settled residence of a people." "The eastern division is on a higher level, and rises gradually towards the mountains on either side. Notwithstanding this, the marshes which occasionally occur might lead to a different belief; but these are very limited in extent, and occupy distinct hollows; and the fact of general rise is proved by the course of the rivers, which without it could never exhibit those strong currents for which they are remarkable." In this semi-basin, however, there is considerable irregularity towards the mountains, in consequence of numerous alluvial ridges, having elevations of from 100 to 300 feet above the adjacent country. The valleys between those ridges, and the alluvial tracts along the courses of the rivers, are the most fertile, and best suited for cultivation of any parts of the district. The principal river is the Soormah, which, formed in Cachar by two mountain-streams, the Jeeree and Barak, flows westerly, and touches on the eastern boundary of this district in lat. 24° 50′, long. 92° 39′. The Soormah, a few miles below this point, where it first touches the frontier, divaricates into two branches, one retaining its westerly direction and the name of Soormah; the other turning south-westward, is called the Kusia or Kusiori, and subsequently the Barak. The Soormah, taking a direction generally westward and north-westward, forms for the distance of forty miles the boundary between this district and those of Cachar and Jynteah, until near Rajagunge, at a point about ten miles east of the town of Silhet, it crosses into this district, which it traverses for the distance of 120 miles, passing from the district in a nearly southerly direction, and subsequently forms the boundary between the British districts Mymensing and Tipperah. The Kusia, taking a direction generally south-west, but very sinuously, for about 110 miles, falls into the Soormah on the left or south-eastern side, fifteen miles above its passage from this district. Except in the driest part of the year, the Soormah is navigable as high as Silhet for craft of considerable burthen. The climate of Silhet is damp and cool in proportion to its latitude. During the spring months, which in most parts of India constitute the dry season, the weather is variable, and violent thunder-storms are frequent: the periodical rains set in about the beginning of June, and continue until the middle of September, inundating a great extent of country; so that river craft, instead of being obliged to keep the regular channels, are enabled to hold their course right across the country, as it is deeply under water. The extreme dampness of that season gives rise to cholera, dysentery, agues, and fevers, which are peculiarly fatal to those visiting the district from other quarters. Europeans, however, suffer less from such unfavourable circumstances than Hindoos not natives of the district. There is much jungle in the hilly parts on the eastern, northern, and southern frontiers, but the valleys and banks of the rivers are very fertile and beautiful. "Vast sheets of cultivation, extending for miles along the banks of the Soorma and other streams, intersected by splendid groves of trees and bamboos, forming shelter for extensive villages, and occasionally by low ranges of wooded hills, and backed always by mountains, either near or distant, form an endless succession of gratifying scenes." It appears, however, that the soil, from its low and swampy nature, is not calculated for the production of cotton or tobacco of superior quality. The cultivation of wheat, oats, and indigo, has been tried, but considered to have failed; that of the sugarcane, it is believed, might be increased and improved, if plants of superior quality could be procured. The pastures, which are luxuriant in the low tracts, are the chief resource of the rural population, as they support great numbers of cattle, yielding large quantities of butter, cheese, and hides, for exportation, and bullocks for burthen and draught. Grain is also extensively exported, especially to places eastward and northward. Of fruit-trees, there are the mango, lime, orange, lemon, plantain, apricot, betelnut. The manufacturing industry is insignificant, producing only a few coarse cotton cloths, mats, baskets, and some other articles too insignificant to enumerate. The population is returned officially at 380,000; an amount which, compared with the area, indicates a relative density of about 100 to the square mile. Of this number it is conjectured that three-fifths are Brahminists; the remainder are Mussulmans, as there are scarcely any Christians. Silhet, the locality of the military cantonment and of the civil establishment, is the only place in the district which can be considered a town; it is described in its place in the alphabetical arrangement. The routes are, — 1. From south-west to north-east, from Calcutta through Dacca to Silhet; 2. from west to east, from Silhet to Marajpoor; 3. from south to north, from the town of Silhet to Chirra Poonjee.

SILHET, the principal place of the British district of the same name, lieut.-gov. of Bengal, is situate at the southern base of the Cossya hills, and on the river Soormah, a tributary of the Brahmapootra. It is described to be a mean place, merely a large straggling village, having a bazar, where only the most common articles of native use are to be obtained. The civil establishment of the district is located here. Silhet is the head-quarters of the eastern division of the Bengal army. Distance from Jumalpoor, E., 110 miles; Dacca, N.E., 120; Calcutta, N.E., 260. Lat. 24° 54′, long. 91° 50′.

SILLAY MEW.—A town of Burmah, situate on the left bank of the Irawady river, and 116 miles S.W. from Ava. Lat. 20° 45′, long. 94° 38′.

SILLEE.—A town in the British district of Chota Nagpoor, lieut.-gov. of Bengal, 71 miles E. of Lohadugga. Lat. 23° 23′, long. 85° 53′.

SIMBOLONG.—A town of Eastern India, in the native state of Muneepoor, 37 miles W. from Muneepoor, and 40 miles E. from Silchar. Lat. 24° 48′, long. 93° 28′.

SIMBULKET, in the British district of Kumaon, lieut.-gov. of the N.W. Provinces, a village in the Patlee Doon, on the route, by the course of the Ramgunga (Western), from Moradabad cantonment to Almorah. It is situate on the north-eastern declivity of the Sewalik range, bounding the Doon on the south; distant 56 miles N. of Moradabad. Lat. 29° 36′, long. 78° 45′.

SIMERIA, or SIMRIA, in the territory of Gwalior, a village on the route from the fort of Gwalior to Saugor, 29 miles S. of former, 184 N.W. of latter. Lat. 25° 55′, long. 78° 21′.

SIMIREEAH, in the raj or principality of Rewah, a town on the table-land surmounting the mountain styled by Franklin the "second or Panna range," and 62 miles S.E. of Allahabad. It is the principal place of a jaghire held under the rajah of Rewah, on annual payment of a tribute of 2,500 rupees. The jaghiredar, considering himself obnoxious to the persecution of the rajah, in consequence of his good services towards the British authorities, they guaranteed his possessions to him. The benefit of this guarantee was spontaneously relinquished in 1828, by the jaghiredar, who was immediately expelled by the rajah, and his nephew placed in his stead; but the British government subsequently interfered so far as to have a provision made for his widow. Elevation above the sea 1,009 feet. Lat. 24° 45′, long. 81° 16′.

SIMLA.—A British station in the lower or more southern part of the Himalayas, between the rivers Sutlej and Giree, celebrated as a retreat for those seeking renovation of health, or relief from the oppressive heat of the plains of Hindostan. It is situate on the route from Soobathoo to Kotgurh, 22 miles N.E. of the former post. The houses built for the accommodation of residents or visitors at this place, are irregularly scattered over a narrow ridge of mountain, advantage being taken of every level spot, or moderate slope, for building. A few dwellings are erected on a spur of hills running north at right angles to the Simla range. The eastern extremity of what may be properly called the Simla ridge, is abruptly terminated by the peak of Jako, rising about 400 feet above it. At the western base of this eminence is the bazar of the settlement. The sides of the Jako Peak were originally thickly clothed with wood, and the quantity is still considerable; but the demands for the purposes of building may be expected to cause a rapid diminution. At the western extremity of the ridge of Simla is another eminence, inferior in height to Jako, and devoid of timber, the summit crowned by a mouldering ruin. The scenery within view from the town is very noble. Immediately south is a dark, deep, precipitous valley, which, as well as the neighbouring mountains, is thickly covered with pine-forests; beyond, to the south-west, are seen the mountains about Soobathoo; and still farther, the vast plain of Hindostan, traversed by the meandering Sutlej. To the north, successive mountain-ranges rise in proportion as the distance increases, and are terminated with surpassing grandeur by the snowy crescent of the Himalaya, the peaks of which, in fine weather, have so distinct an outline against the dark-blue sky, that their real distance of sixty or seventy miles seems not more than eight or ten. The following description of this scene, and of its impressions on the observers, occurs in a modern work. "The general appearance of this mass of snow is that of a wide undulating plain, from which peaks rise in every imaginable shape. Upon reaching the crest of the ridge at Simla, the vastness of the scene became oppressive. The lofty snowy range shone from the dense azure of the heavens; its giant flanks were broken with black mural precipices and profound ravines, which were purple from their depth: below was heaped a shattered mass of mountains, peaks and glens, ridges and valleys, some aridly bare, others luxuriantly rich."

The trees in the neighbourhood are, the deodar or Himalaya cedar, pine, oak, and rhododendron; the last-named glowing with bunches of rich scarlet blossoms. Of four-footed animals, the most commonly occurring are the kacker or barking deer (Cervus muntjac), so called from its cry resembling a short bark; the antelope, the wild goat, and the marmot: there are also the wild hog, the flying squirrel, musk, and other kinds of deer, and monkeys, both the hanuman or langoor (Semnopithecus entellus), and the bundur (Simia rhesus). The carnivorous quadrupeds are leopards and leopard-cats, bears, jackals, hyænas, and foxes: sometimes, though rarely, a tiger makes its way to these elevated regions. There is no great variety or abundance of game: the principal of the feathered kind are pheasants, chukars and black partridges, quails, and woodcocks. Eagles, vultures, and crows are very numerous. The fruits and esculent vegetables of Europe in general thrive well here; potatoes especially are grown in great abundance and excellence, and are sent in large quantities to the plains. The climate is considered highly salubrious, and in consequence of its lower temperature, appears in favourable contrast with that of the plains. The winter is sometimes very severe. In 1836 snow lay in the month of February to the depth of six or eight feet, and did not melt away in shady places until the end of May.

In 1841 there were at Simla upwards of 100 houses built in the English style, and varying in rent from 40*l.* to 150*l.* a year. The position and habits of those resorting to the place cause it to be abundantly supplied with the luxuries as well as the necessaries of life, though most sorts of provisions have to be borne three or four days' journey over mountain-roads. The population is very fluctuating. In a recent publication it is thus prospectively estimated: "Should the Governor-General and the Commander-in-Chief come up next season, it will consist of British subjects, 200; natives, 8,000: and when the tributary chieftains and followers come in, it will be nearly 20,000. Again in winter, when but few remain, it will probably not exceed, British subjects, 20; natives, 2,000." Measures have been taken for providing funds for the purpose of carrying out public improvements. The first British dwelling erected in this place was that of Lieutenant Ross, in 1819. It was thatched over, and its walls were composed of spars, grass, and mud. In 1822, the first permanent cottage of the usual materials, stone and timber, roofed with pinewood shingles, was erected by Captain Kennedy. Simla is the seat of an observatory, at which a series of magnetical and meteorological observations were commenced on the 19th January, 1841. A church has been provided, at an expense of 16,000 rupees; of which amount the government contributed 5,000 rupees, the remainder being raised by private subscription.

The district known as Simla is composed of territory acquired partly from the rajah of Putteeala, and partly from the rajah of Keonthul; in both cases by exchange. It is under the civil jurisdiction of the board of administration in the Punjab, and contains a population of 31,858. Elevation of encampment above the sea 7,866 feet. Distance N.W. from Calcutta, *viâ* Kurnal and Soobathoo, 1,097 miles. Lat. 31° 6′, long. 77° 14′.

SIMMURIA, in Bundelcund, a village or small town on the route from Allahabad to Saugor, 230 miles S.W. of the former, 83 N.E of the latter. It is situate in the depressed tract or basin of Lohargaon. Lat. 24° 16′, long. 79° 58′.

SIMONBONG.—A town in the British district of Darjeeling, lieut.-gov. of Bengal, six miles N.W. by W. of Darjeeling. Lat. 27° 4′, long. 88° 13′.

SIMONG.—A town of Eastern India, in the territory inhabited by the Bor Abar tribe, 46 miles N.W. by N. from Sudiya, and 105 miles N.E. from Luckimpoor. Lat. 28° 22′, long. 95° 20′.

SIMONGELPOOR.—A town in the British district of Silhet, lieut.-gov. of Bengal, 45 miles S. by W. of Silhet. Lat. 24° 18′, long. 91° 42′.

SIMOOLBARIA.—A town in the British district of the Twenty-four Pergunnahs, lieut.-gov. of Bengal, 40 miles S. by W. of Calcutta. Lat. 22°, long. 88° 21′.

SIMOWNEE, in the British district of Banda, lieut.-gov. of the N.W. Provinces, the principal place of the pergunnah of the same name, a small town on an insignificant stream tributary to the Jumna, eight miles S. of the right bank of the latter, 20 N.E. of the town of Banda, 78 W. of Allahabad. Lat. 25° 36′, long. 80° 40′.

SIMRA, or SIMORE, in the British district of Goruckpore, lieut.-gov. of the N.W. Provinces, a small town in the pergunnah of Sidhoa Jobhuna, which contains no other, except the principal place, Paraona. It contains about 100 wretched dwellings. Buchanan does not state its precise position, but it must be about forty-five miles east of the town of Goruckpore, and is perhaps the Simore of Garden, who states that it is 93 miles N.W. of Dinapore. Lat. 26° 35′, long. 84° 7′.

SIMRABAS.—A town in Nepal, 44 miles S.W. by S. from Khatmandoo, and 35 miles N.E. from Bettiah. Lat. 27° 10′, long. 84° 56′.

SIMRAUTA, in the district of Salon, territory of Oude, a town 50 miles S.E. of Lucknow. It belongs to a brother of the Tiloi rajah, a reputed descendant of the ancient Hindoo monarchs of Oude. The proprietor is styled by courtesy rajah, and resides in a mud fort, having in the interior buildings of masonry, and defended by 500 of his armed followers. The population is estimated by Butter at 8,000. Lat. 26° 17′, long. 81° 20′.

SIMRAW.—A town in Nepal, 141 miles S.E. by E. from Khatmandoo, and 66 miles N.N.W. from Purneah. Lat. 26° 40′, long. 87° 13′.

SIMREE.—A town in the British district of Behar, lieut.-gov. of Bengal, 36 miles W. of Sherghotty. Lat. 24° 32′, long. 84° 19′.

SIMTOKA.—A town in the native state of Bhotan, 73 miles E.N.E. from Darjeeling, and

120 miles N.W. from Goalpara. Lat. 27° 25′, long. 89° 25′.

SIMULEA.—A town in the British district of Dacca, lieut.-gov. of Bengal, 21 miles N.N.E. of Dacca. Lat. 24° 2′, long. 90° 40′.

SINAWUD.—A town in the native state of Indore, or territory of Holkar, 43 miles S.E. by S. from Indore, and 112 miles N.W. by W. from Ellichpoor. Lat. 22° 8′, long. 76° 10′.

SINCHUL. — A mountain of Sikhim, having an elevation of 9,000 feet, upon a spur of which stands the British settlement of Darjeeling.

SINDE, a river rising in Malwa, "from the small range of mountains about 12 miles S.W. of the town of Seronge," and in lat. 24° 1′, long. 77° 29′. It first has a course north for about 130 miles to Narwar, at the north-west corner of Bundelcund, and thence turning north-east, generally forms, for about 130 miles, the boundary between that district and Gwalior, and falls into the Jumna on the right side, in lat. 26° 26′, long. 79° 18′, flowing altogether about 260 miles. It right and left receives during its course many small streams, the principal being the Parbati and the Pohooj, the first falling into the Sinde on the left side, about twenty-five miles below Narwar, and the other on the right side, four or five miles above its mouth. The Sinde is crossed twenty miles from its source by the route from Nusserabad to Saugor, and is there "100 yards wide, rocky bottom, low banks, and depth of water two feet in fair season." About 150 from its source, and in lat. 25° 50′, long. 78° 28′, it is crossed by route from Agra to Saugor, and there the bed "is about 200 yards wide and sandy; breadth of stream, in dry season, about forty yards, and from one and a half to two feet deep; banks steep, and cut into ravines." It is subject to great inundations during the periodical rains.

SINDE. — An extensive and important province of Western India, so called probably from the river Sinde or Indus. Others consider that the name both of the river and the country is derived from the word Sindhi, synonymous with Hindi, as the inhabitants from the first dawn of recorded knowledge have principally been of the great Hindoo family. It is bounded on the north by Beloochistan, the Daman, and Bhawlpoor; on the east by Jessulmere and Marwar; on the south by Cutch and the Indian Ocean; on the west by Beloochistan; and is situated between lat. 23° 37′—28° 32′, and long. 66° 43′—71° 3′. It is 360 miles long, from north to south, 270 miles in its greatest breadth, from east to west, and contains a surface of 52,120 square miles. Its seacoast, washed by the Indian Ocean, extends a distance of 150 miles in a north-west direction, from the Koree or greatest mouth of the Indus (long deserted by the stream), situate in lat. 23° 38′, long. 68° 25′, to Cape Monze, or Ras Mooarree, in lat. 24° 51′, long. 66° 43′. This whole extent of coast, except the part intervening between Kurrachee and Cape Monze, which are distant from each other about fifteen miles, is very low, being merely a series of mud banks deposited by the Indus, or, in a few places, low sand-hills, blown in from the sea-beach. Exclusive of those few sand-hills, "the shore," observes Carless, "is low and flat throughout, and at high water partially overflowed to a considerable distance inland. With the exception of a few spots covered with jungle, it is entirely destitute of trees or shrubs, and nothing is seen for many miles but a dreary swamp. Whenever this occurs, the land is scarcely discernible two miles from the shore." Wood also observes—"The coast-line is submerged at spring tides, when the delta of the Indus resembles a low champagne tract of verdure." Burnes, too, states that the coast of Sinde is not distinguishable a league from the shore. Westward of the Garrah estuary, and between it and Kurrachee, the southern extremity of the Hala or Pubb Mountains approaches the shore, the point of Munoora, which forms the southern shelter of the harbour of Kurrachee, being rocky; but with the exception of this point, the coast itself is like that eastward, low and alluvial, and so continues westward to Cape Monze, or Ras Mooarree, which rises from the sea to a moderate height. The capability of the coast of Sinde for the purpose of navigation is thus summed up by Wood:—"It is plain to all who are conversant with nautical affairs, that Kurrachee is the only safe seaport for the valley of the Indus. When the season is favourable, the merchant may indeed send his goods direct to the mouth of the Indus; but everything here is subject to such constant change—the weather, the depth of water, the channels, and the very embouchure itself,—that this voyage, even in February, is not without hazards." He then observes, that as the danger of entering the river is greater than of leaving it, exports may be sent from the mouths in November, December, and January, but that all imports should be brought by Kurrachee. It should be observed, however, that though sea-going ships of 400 or 500 tons can at no time safely enter the river, yet smaller vessels, if their draught do not exceed six or seven feet, may do so. An inland navigation, or even a ship canal, could probably be easily made from Kurrachee to the deepest and most navigable part of the Indus below Hyderabad, as the Garrah, a small stream communicating with the Indus, falls into the sea at that port, and is navigable from it for boats as far as Garrah Kot, a distance of forty miles.

Kurrachee, the only port in Sinde for sea-going ships of burthen amounting to 400 or 500 tons, has, at high water, a depth of two fathoms and a half, and at spring tides of three fathoms; but, during the south-west monsoon, the swell is so great on the bar, that it is highly dangerous to cross. The Kookewarree, called the Gora by Burnes, was formerly the principal mouth of the Indus, having a width of 1,100 yards, but it is now blocked up by a sandbank; the Kedewarree has a well-defined channel, with seven or eight feet water at low spring tides; the Hoojamree and Jooa, during the low-water season, are safe roads for ingress and egress for vessels drawing not more than six feet water; the Pittee is the largest, deepest, and best-defined mouth. The Koree mouth is the most eastern, forming the boundary of Sinde towards Cutch: it has long been deserted by the stream, except in very great inundations, when sometimes the Poorana and Fulailee branches pour their waters into it. Burnes states its breadth at Cotasir, twenty miles from the sea, to be seven miles, and that it increases, proceeding downward, until neither shore can be seen. He, however, adds, very justly, that it is nothing more than an arm of the sea.

The base or seaward line of the delta of the Indus measures, from the Garrah mouth, in lat. 24° 43′, long. 67° 12′, to the Koree mouth, in lat. 23° 38′, long. 68° 25′, about 125 miles. If it be regarded as having the shape of a triangle, to which it in some degree approximates, the perpendicular, measured from the seashore to the vertex, near Tatta, where the great branches of the Indus—the Sata or eastern, the Buggaur or western—divaricate, is about fifty miles, and its surface is about 3,000 square miles; but as the river has in some degree deserted a considerable portion of the south-eastern part, the present delta proper does not probably contain more than 2,500 square miles. Unlike the densely-wooded delta of the Ganges, it is nearly destitute of timber, resembling in this respect that of the Nile. It is almost level, of alluvial soil, apparently brought down by the Indus, and consisting of vegetable mould, clay, and sand, which becomes hard soon after being deposited, even in the channels of the river. There are, however, even within the limits of the delta proper, and eastward of the Buggaur, or western branch of the Indus, some rocky hills, known by the name of the Mukali Hills. Near the Pittee, or western mouth of the river, is a dangerous rock, the only point in the delta south of the range just described which is not alluvial.

In some degree similar to the delta, but superior to it in scenery, soil, cultivation, and climate, is the alluvial tract extending on each side of the Indus for a distance varying from two to twelve miles. One of the finest parts is a long narrow island, extending from north to south a distance of about 100 miles, with an average breadth of about eight, inclosed by the Indus on the east, and on the west by the Narra. The greatest extent of this alluvial land in the upper part of Sinde appears to be about Khyerpoor, Shikarpoor, and Larkhana, where canals and watercourses, communicating with the Indus, during inundation cover the surface to a wide range with water, which both irrigates the ground and deposits on it a fertilizing slime. According to Postans, the soil is so rich, that no manure of any kind is used, though it regularly produces two crops every year, and sometimes three; and Macmurdo states, that "the fertility of this province in those parts which are exposed to the floods of the Indus is exceeded by that of no tract of country on the earth." Throughout the alluvial tracts of Sinde, the soil contains saltpetre in great abundance, and it is largely extracted both for home consumption and for exportation.

An extensive alluvial region stretches eastward of the fertile tract along the Indus, but having been generally deserted by the water of the river, it became a desert, yielding a scanty pasture to camels or horned cattle, and in the less-frequented parts occupied only by the fleet goorkhur, or wild ass. Through it, however, flows the Eastern Narra during the height of the inundations of the Indus, for a distance of 300 miles, and a project has just been sanctioned for securing to its channel a permanent supply of water by means of a cutting near Roree. The great doab contained between this branch and the Indus is on an average about seventy or eighty miles wide, the soil consisting generally of a hard sun-baked clay, like the rest of the alluvial soil of Sinde where devoid of water. In this doab are two low ranges of recent limestone; the more southern, that of Hyderabad, about 100 feet high, and on one part of which that city is situate; the more northern running north-westward from the vicinity of Jessulmere, and towards the Indus attaining an elevation of 150 feet, and abounding in flint, which forms, almost exclusively, the rocks on which Roree and Bukkur stand. These ranges are not, however, completely continuous, being cut by valleys, through one of which the Narra, already mentioned, holds its course; through another, the Fulailee branch, insulating Hyderabad.

The stiff nature of the deposit of the river is probably owing to its course in the upper part generally lying through a very mountainous region, principally of primitive formation. In the more southern part of Sinde, the soil has a very large admixture of sand, and is sometimes so impregnated with common salt, that, as Lord observes, "it is not uncommon to see the same soil which, during the season of irrigation, had yielded crops of grain, transferred afterwards to the salt-pan, and furnishing, by the simple process of pouring water over it, which is subsequently evaporated, an abundant supply of salt." The moisture, so indispensable to the productiveness of the soil, is altogether supplied by the water of the Indus, rain in Sinde being very scanty and uncertain. In consequence, the country, where destitute of the means of irrigation, becomes a desert. Of this nature, on the north-east, is the *Pat*, or desert of Shikarpoor, lying between that town and the Bolan Pass, and apparently consisting of the clay deposited by the Bolan, the Nari, and other torrents which flow down from the Hala Mountains, and which are all lost in this dreary tract. It is about ninety miles across, and, according to Kennedy, in some places resembles "the dry bed of a salt lagoon in an interval between spring tides;" in others, it is a level plain of indurated clay, of a dull earthy colour, and having the appearance of being occasionally under water; but during the dry season exhibiting, at long intervals, a few wretched, parched, and stunted shrubs, but without a single blade of grass or other herbage. In the eastern part, and in general reaching to within twenty miles, or even a less distance of the river, is a region called the *Thur*, or desert, having considerable resemblance to that just described, except that it is much more sandy, extensive tracts being covered with sand-hills, varying and shifting under the influence of the tempests of the wilderness; yet, in many places, there is a considerable growth of low shrubs, coarse herbage, and prickly saline or aromatic plants, affording pasturage for camels, buffaloes, kine, sheep, and goats, all in continual motion in search of water, or its concomitant, vegetation. Numerous beds of rivers long dried up intersect this arid tract, appearing to indicate that the waters of the Indus, or of some of the Punjab rivers, once found their way through it. Vestiges of ancient towns also may be observed, in great quantities of fragments of bricks and pottery in some places strewed over the surface. That the Indus, which now finds its way through the limestone rocks at Roree, might at one time have poured its waters in many branches over this waste, at present parched, is by no means improbable, as there are unequivocal indications that it formerly flowed fifty feet above its present level, in the channel between Sukkur and Roree, and that the country on both sides of the river along the base of the limestone range was at that time under water. The old course of the river may also be traced along the northern base of that rocky range, which, stretching nearly 100 miles to the south-eastward, must have sent the water of the Indus over the surface of the country now become the Eastern Desert, since it has been deserted by the stream.

The climate of Sinde is remarkably sultry and dry. As Lord observes,—"Situated on the verge of two monsoons, it is unrefreshed by the waters of either. The south-west monsoon," he proceeds, "terminates at Lucput Bunder (on the western coast of Cutch), as accurately as though it covenanted not to violate the Sindh frontier." At Kurrachee, the annual fall of rain does not exceed six or eight inches; at Hydrabad, the rain of an entire twelvemonth amounted only to 2·55 inches; and farther north, at Larkhana, three years had elapsed continuously without rain, at the time of Hamilton's visit in 1699. The consequence was a pestilence, which cut off one-half of the population. But Burnes, in travelling through the delta on the 10th of April, experienced very heavy showers and a severe fall of hail; and in June, 1809, during the visit of the British mission, the rain fell so heavily there, that the streets frequently resembled rivulets, and none could stir abroad. In the following August, the rains were again excessively heavy during the stay of the mission at Hydrabad. But, notwithstanding the discrepancy in our information on the subject, there can be little doubt that, throughout Sinde, the climate is generally too dry for the purposes of agriculture, except in the parts irrigated by means of the river. On this subject, the ameer of Khyerpoor remarked to Burnes, that rain always brought disease, and that they were better without it. The temperature is very high in summer. Lord states the mean maximum of the temperature of the atmosphere at Hydrabad, during the six hottest months, to be 98·5° in the shade, and considers it the greatest hitherto registered in an authenticated form. The water of the Indus at that time attains the temperature of 92° or 93° when highest, and consequently very nearly blood-heat. There appears reason for concluding that the temperature is still higher in Northern Sinde, where the cooling influence of the ocean cannot extend. Burnes states it at 96° at Khyerpoor in the beginning of April. In Northern Sinde, however, frost is not unknown, and ice has been observed in February. In January, the difference of the temperature at night, and during the day, has been found as much as 40°, the thermometer ranging to 84° and upwards. So high, however, in general, is the temperature in Lower Sinde, that there is, in fact, no winter.

The natural history of Sinde is only now receiving the attention due to so important a subject. An extravagant addiction to field-sports characterized the ameers of Sinde, who sacrificed to it the welfare and even the existence of their subjects, laying waste and inclosing extensive cultivated tracts to form their *shikargahs*, or hunting-jungles. One of the ameers, some years ago, depopulated, near the capital, an extensive tract of fertile ground, and converted it into a shikargah, though this foolish and monstrous act of tyranny caused a loss of revenue equal to 20,000*l*. or 30,000*l*. a year. Another razed a village to the ground, because the noise of the population and domestic animals was considered to disturb the game of a neighbouring preserve.

There are generally two harvests in Sinde; the rubbee, or spring harvest, reaped from seed sown in autumn, and the kureef, or autumn harvest, which is sown in spring. The rubbee crops in general consist of wheat, barley, oil-seeds, millet (Holcus sorghum), the durra of the Arabians, and called here bajra, opium, hemp, tobacco; the kureef crop consists of those productions which require considerable heat to bring them to maturity; such as rice, sugarcane, cotton, indigo, maize. The results of the experiments made for the cultivation of the American cotton and Mauritius cane were not encouraging. Pulse and pumpkins, cucumbers, melons, and esculent vegetables, are sown for both crops, and some products are sown indifferently for either. Rice appears to be the staple crop, and, with maize and wheat, forms the principal article of diet, besides being exported in great quantities. Much importance is attached to the culture of flax. The fruits are dates, mangoes, plantains, pomegranates, limes, citrons, figs, apricots, apples, plums, tamarinds, mulberries, pistachio and some other kinds of nuts, and melons. They, in general, are of inferior quality; the grapes especially are small and sour. The plantations of date-palms are very general and extensive, and the fruit is used largely for food and for distillation; by which process a strong spirit is drawn from it. As food, it is found to be of a very heating nature.

Camels are bred in great numbers in the salt-marshes of the Indus; and though such tracts might seem very uncongenial to the nature of that animal, those reared there are considered very hardy, strong, and enduring, especially of thirst, in consequence of the scanty supply of fresh water in their original soil. The value of the camel is not confined to its virtues as a beast of burden: its milk is a favourite article of diet (though it spoils if not used very fresh), and its hair is woven into coarse cloths. Buffaloes are kept in great numbers in the swampy tracts, where they may be seen wallowing in the mud with their heads only above water. Their flesh is excellent, and their milk is preferred to that of cows, yielding better butter, which, when clarified, forms, under the name of *ghee*, a great article of commerce. A considerable trade is also driven in the hides of these animals. Sheep and goats abound in Upper Sinde, especially on the borders of the *Pat* of Shikarpoor, and of the *Thur*, or Eastern Desert.* The former district, called Boordgah, produces the best wool in Sinde, both of goats and sheep; and both animals are kept throughout Upper Sinde, as well for their fleeces as for their milk and flesh. The wool is taken from the carcase of the animal only when slain for food, as the heat would cause its death after losing its fleece. The coarser wool is manufactured into bags, ropes, and strong cloths; the finer might be obtained in such quantities as to be an important branch of commerce, for which, however, there has been hitherto but little encouragement. The horses of Sinde are small and of mean appearance, but hardy, active, and enduring. They are mostly used for the saddle, the beasts of burden being the camel, the mule, and the ass. The camel is the dromedary or one-humped variety, and the finer descriptions are used for the saddle, carrying generally the rider and his attendant. The breed of asses is small, but they are neatly made, strong, active, capable of enduring great fatigue, and of living and thriving on the coarsest fare. The mules are large, strong, handsome, and quick in pace.

The Sindians of the present day are a mixed race, consisting partly of the Juts, probably aboriginal Sindians, of Hindoo extraction (many of whom have been converted to Mahometanism), and the Beloochees, who have settled here in recent times. Those Hindoos who have adhered to their original religion and manners are divided into Bhattias and Lohannas, with their respective gurus or pastors, and the Pokarna and Sarsat Brahmans. They deviate much in their mode of life from the Hindoos of Hindostan proper, and this laxity is more particularly observable in the Lohannas, who are the most numerous. These last decline no means of subsistence, and readily entered into the service of the ameers, in which case they were obliged to wear their beards like the Mahometans. Compulsory conversions to Mahometanism were not unfrequent, the helpless Hindoo being forcibly subjected to circumcision on slight or misconstrued profession, or the false testimony of abandoned Mahometans. It is still more remarkable, that this forcible conversion was sometimes inflicted as a punishment, and in all instances operated as an irreparable loss of caste. The Mahometan population sprung from the converted Hindoos are a peaceable race, generally engaged in agriculture, and are despised by the Belooches, who affect a bold and martial character. In this, the latter have been encouraged by the ameers, of the same descent as themselves. Besides these distinctive races, there is a large part of the population the offspring of their intermarriages. The Hindoos, however, in many places, form a very large proportion of the population; at Shikarpoor, for instance, they are estimated at two thirds. There are likewise a few Afghans, especially in the north-western part of the country. The Sindians, collectively, are described as handsome, though of dark complexions, well limbed, but inclined to corpulency, and above the middle size. The beauty of their women is proverbial, and Pottinger remarks that among the numerous sets of dancing-girls whom he saw, there was not one who did not display loveliness of face or symmetry of figure. The Belooches, and the mixed race between them and the Hindoos, are considered the finest part of the population. Sinde is supposed by Sir William Jones to have been the original country of the gipsies, who, according to Adelung, fled from India to escape the massacres of the ruthless Tamerlane. The Sindian language is a branch of the Sanscrit or Indo-Germanic stock, merely a little differing in spelling and inflexion from the pure Hindi of Upper India, and is by some considered the elder of the two, being more elaborate and regular in the inflexions of its nouns and verbs. Macmurdo states, on the authority of native scholars, that "it has fewer modern innovations, and a greater number of Sanscrit words, than the Gujarati, which is a pure Hindoo dialect." It has a character peculiar to itself, which is written from left to right. Belochee, another of the Indo-Germanic tongues, is of course largely spoken, especially in the hilly country; and Persian may be regarded as the language of the court and of the higher order of the people.

From the period when Sinde was visited by the Greeks under Alexander, its history is in a great degree a blank. Native annalists appear to be magniloquent in regard to the grandeur, power, and resources of some of its princes; and, on the event of a revolution, brought about through the criminal passion of a queen for a young Brahmin, who was enabled by her favour to ascend, first to the office of chief minister, and subsequently to the throne, the historian who records the facts indulges in the following burst of mingled grief and admiration:—"Such was the close of the race of Rajah Sazee, which had governed the kingdom of Sinde for upwards of 2,000 years; whose princes at one period received tribute from eleven dependent kingdoms, and who had set the threats of the greatest monarchs of the world at defiance." In the sixth century of the Christian era, the country was invaded by the Persians, and to this invasion probably refers the allusion of the enthusiastic chronicler above quoted to the defiance offered by the royal house of Sinde to "the greatest monarchs of the world." The result, however, was disastrous to the reigning prince, though unproductive of any permanent change in the relation of the two countries. The Persians defeated the rajah in a pitched battle, in which the prince fell. But the object of the invaders appears to have been not so much conquest as plunder, and having secured as much booty as they had the means of carrying away, they departed. Among the spoils which they bore from Sinde were some thousands of its most beautiful women.

At an early period of the Khalifate, the reputed wealth of Sinde seems to have excited the cupidity of the representatives of the Prophet; but their attempts, for a time, were unsuccessful. A subsequent invasion was attended by a different result. The Khalifs were in the habit of importing slave-girls from Sinde, and a party of the followers of the Khalif Abool Mulik, in charge of a selection of Hindoo beauties, destined for the harem of their master, were attacked by the rajah's troops, some of them killed, and the remainder made prisoners. This occurrence provoked a hostile visit from a Mahometan army. The rajah was permitted to remain quiet in his capital while the enemy were ravaging his dominions with fire and sword; and when, at last, he left the city with his army, it was but to encounter disaster, defeat, and death. The events of the battle transferred the kingdom to Mahometan rule.

Some centuries later, Sinde became a tributary to the empire of Ghuznee. On the dissolution of that empire, the Sindian chiefs asserted their independence against the Ghorian during many years, and with various success. Ultimately they were compelled to yield, and Sinde became a constituent part of the imperial dominions. In the time of Baber, it was invaded and conquered by the prince dispossessed by that emperor at Kandahar. The invader was subsequently compelled to yield the larger portion of his conquest. His son made an effort to regain what his father had lost, but found new enemies, to whom he was compelled to make large sacrifices. Sinde then, for a time, maintained a claim to independence, but was the scene of great disorders, two successive princes being afflicted with insanity in its most outrageous form. Late in the sixteenth century it yielded to the emperor Akbar, and for about 150 years it remained in the usual condition of Oriental dependencies; its chiefs usually professing unqualified submission to the emperor, paying tribute when they could no longer postpone it, but scrupulously evading that acknowledgment of supremacy whenever their fears were not sufficiently active to prompt to a different course. In 1739, Sinde fell to the Persian conqueror Nadir Shah. On his death, and the consequent dismemberment of his empire, it seems to have reverted to its nominal subjection to the imperial throne of Delhi. In 1756, Sinde was included in certain territories forming part of a dowry bestowed by the reigning emperor upon Tymur, son of Ahmed Shah Durani. It is thenceforward to be regarded as an appendage of Kabool, the new relation being maintained precisely in the same mode as that previously existing with the sovereign of Delhi. In 1779, a rebellion was raised by the Talpoor tribe of Belooches against the reigning nawaub, of the Kooloora tribe, who was defeated and forced to fly. He was reinstated in his dominions by the aid of the ruler of Kabool, and the insurgents retired. They soon, however, returned, deposed the Kuloora prince once more, and took possession of his throne and power. The ruler of Kabool again advanced to maintain the rights of his dependant, but the usurpers had collected an army superior to that of the Afghans, which they totally defeated. This was in 1786. Fortune being against the Afghan prince, it only remained for him to make the best terms he could. The battle was followed by negotiation; in virtue of which, the Talpoor chief engaged to discharge all arrears of tribute, and to meet the accruing payments in future with punctuality. Within little more than three years, presuming on the inability of the nominal emperor to coerce them, the rulers of Sinde signified their indisposition to paying tribute at all, and the weakness of the Duranie government insured to them for a time impunity. Zeman Shah approached their frontier in 1794, to enforce the demand of his house, but was prevailed on to return with a small portion only of the arrears due. A similar result attended the advance of Shoojah-ool-Moolk in 1809: he received a sum equal to something more than one-third of the amount which had accumulated, and returned, perhaps not altogether indisposed to congratulate himself on his good fortune in obtaining anything. The disturbances which subsequently prevailed in Afghanistan were admirably calculated to gratify the dislike of the ameers to dispensing any part of their treasures in the shape of tribute.

The government of Sinde, under the Talpoor dynasty, has been quaintly described by Kennedy, as "a tailor-like personification of royalty, requiring precisely nine ameers or princes to make up one sovereign." In 1786, when Meer Futteh Ali, the Beloochе chief of the Talpoor tribe, succeeded in expelling the Kulora dynasty, and was recognised by the Durani monarch, he assigned large tracts of country to those of his relatives who had aided his enterprise: to Sohrab, Khyrpoor and Northern Sinde; to Thara, Meerpoor, in the south-east, with the adjoining country; at the same time investing them with independent powers. He reserved Hyderabad and the greater part of the country for himself and his three brothers, residing with them in the same palace, and publicly administering the government with them in the same common durbar (hall of audience). Thus the country became divided into three states—Hyderabad, Khyrpoor, and Meerpoor,—each having their little knot of ameers or rulers. In 1839 there were four ameers of Hyderabad, the sons of the first who enjoyed the dignity. There were, at the same time, three ameers at Khyrpoor, and one, or according to Kennedy two, at Meerpoor.

The government under the Talpoor ameers appears to have been a military despotism, unchecked, except by a regard to the dogmas of Islam. The ameers held courts of justice every Friday, and reserved to themselves the right of deciding in cases of life and death. Those potentates, in time of peace, had no more standing army than was sufficient to guard their persons and treasury, to collect the revenue, and retain the forts. Their avarice made them keep the regular military force so low in point of number, that it probably did not exceed 1,500 men. For great and important occasions of national warfare, the army consisted of a feudal soldiery, maintained by the respective chieftains, to whom had been allotted jaghires or grants, on condition of bringing into the field a proportionate number of men, for whom they were responsible, incurring forfeitures in cases of serious misconduct.

The relation of the British government with Sinde was at no time very close or very friendly. It was always characterized by coldness and suspicion on the part of the Scindian authorities, and sometimes by stronger marks of dislike. The agents of the East-India Company resorted thither for the purposes of trade; but early in the present century the commercial resident of the Company was violently expelled, and a large amount of property in his custody seized. According to Pottinger, an attempt was made to murder the Resident. That author deems it matter for regret that on that occasion the ameers were not "made to feel the force of our arms within their dominions: had that been the case," he continues, "their conduct would doubtless have been of a very different nature towards the late missions to their court." Those missions were treated in various instances with great indecorum, and attempts were made to cast indignity on them in matters of etiquette and ceremony. In 1809, however, a treaty was concluded, the most important article of which was the following:—"The government of Sinde will not allow the establishment of the tribe of the French in Sinde;" it being then an important point to exclude from the vicinity of our Indian possessions an enemy who had long been desirous of attacking them. In 1820, another treaty was concluded, the chief object of which seems to have been the exclusion of European and American adventurers from the dominions of the ameers. A new treaty was formed in 1832, the most important provisions of which are those relating to the opening of the roads and the river of Sinde to the merchants of India. This privilege is stipulated for by the third article; and by the fifth, fixed and moderate duties are to be levied; but the concession was shackled by three conditions: First, that no military stores should pass; second, that no armed vessel or boat should come by the river; and third, that no English merchants should settle in Sinde, but should come as occasion might require, transact their business, and return to India. The third restriction was a step in retrogression, it having been stipulated in the treaty of 1820, that "if any of the subjects of either of the two states [the British and the Sindian] should establish their residence in the dominions of the other, and should conduct themselves in an orderly and peaceable manner in the territory to which they may emigrate, they will be allowed to remain in that situation." The change sufficiently marks the jealous feeling of the ameers towards the British government, while the first and second of the restrictions operated materially to diminish the value of the opening of the Indus. A commercial treaty was concluded in the same year, and thus rested the relations of the Anglo-Indian government and Sinde till 1836, when Runjeet Singh prepared to carry into effect a design which he had long meditated, of reducing Sinde to subjection to himself. By the interposition of the government, however, he was prevailed upon to suspend his progress, and the opportunity being thought favourable for establishing a closer connection with Sinde, Colonel Pottinger was despatched to negotiate for the purpose. After a measure of delay proportioned to the practice of Eastern courts, a treaty was concluded in April, 1838, which possessed at least the merit of brevity. It contained only five articles; by the first of which the British government engaged its good offices to adjust the differences between the ameers and Runjeet Singh; by the second, it was stipulated that an accredited British minister should reside at the court of Hyderabad, and that the ameers should be at liberty to depute a vakeel to reside at the court of the British government.

The British government was now engaged in a series of measures designed to erect a barrier to the Anglo-Indian empire, by settling Afghanistan under a prince believed to be friendly to British interests, and an invasion of that country was meditated, for the purpose of restoring Shoojah-ool-Moolk to the possession of the dominions then held by Dost Mahomed Khan and his relations. With a view to this, a tripartite treaty was concluded in July, 1838, the parties thereto being the British government of India, the exiled Shah Shoojah-ool-Moolk, and the Sikh chieftain Runjeet Singh. Preparatory to carrying out its object, it became necessary to establish some more satisfactory relation with Sinde, and measures were taken accordingly, on which the treaty above mentioned was signed. A copy of it, with other papers illustrative of the existing policy of the British government, was transmitted to Colonel Pottinger, who was instructed to the following effect:—He was to apprise the ameers of the conviction of the Governor-General, that a crisis had arrived at which it was essentially requisite to the security of British India that the real friends of that power should unequivocally manifest their attachment: he was to inform them of the intentions of the British government with regard to the westward, and to point out articles in the tripartite treaty, by which that government engaged to arbitrate on the claim of Shoojah-ool-Moolk, as sovereign of Afghanistan, upon the ameers of Sinde; and proposed to bring also to a final settlement the claims of Runjeet Singh, as connected with the Shah and with the territories along the course of the Indus, formerly included within the dominions of the Afghan kingdom. Colonel Pottinger was also to intimate the approach of Shah Shoojah, supported by a British force, to express a hope, on the part of the Governor-General, in the friendly dispositions of the ameers, and to warn them that the disappointment of that hope would render necessary the temporary occupation of Shikarpoor, and of as much of the adjacent country as might be required to afford a secure basis to the contemplated military operations, while, by neglecting to avail themselves of the proffered mediation in regard to the claim of Shoojah, they would become exposed to the full effect of any measures which he might deem proper for the enforcement of his claim, which, under such a supposition, the Governor-General could not interfere to control. The instructions advert to some other points, but the above are the chief.

Colonel Pottinger, in the discharge of his duty, had to encounter a full share of the impediments usual in oriental diplomacy, and the general conduct of the ameers of Hyderabad was such as to lead to an unqualified suspicion of their hostile feelings; the British army, however, passed without molestation, and the members of the British mission were compelled to take their departure. Alexander Burnes's was somewhat less difficult, though here a great obstacle to the conclusion of terms existed in the demand of the British government for the surrender of the fortress of Bukkur. The ameers at length gave way, and signed a general treaty of alliance, together with the most unpalatable article, conveying to his ally the right of occupying the strongest hold in his dominions. The Hyderabad ameers also finally gave way, and after various unsuccessful attempts at agreement, ratified a treaty originally consisting of twenty-one articles, but which had been cut down by the Governor-General, Lord Auckland, to fourteen. Among the articles expunged were several prescribing the manner in which intercourse should be carried on with the port of Kurrachee. Hostile possession of that place had previously been taken by a British force, and the Governor-General regarded this fact as placing in the hands of the captors the power of dictating the terms on which intercourse with the port should be carried on. The general effect of the treaty was to place the territory of the ameers of Hyderabad in a state of subsidiary dependency on the British government. A treaty, nearly corresponding with that entered into with the Hyderabad chiefs, was subsequently concluded with Mere Shere Mohamed Khan, ameer of Meerpoor.

These arrangements did not prevent the recurrence of disputes. The disasters encountered by the English in Afghanistan were calculated to call forth the latent particles of enmity to that power wherever they might lurk, and some of the ameers at last were confidently believed to have passed beyond hostile wishes, and to have committed themselves to acts inconsistent with their relations of perfect amity and alliance with the British government. These circumstances were thought to call for some considerable changes in the existing treaties, and Sir Charles Napier was intrusted to negotiate new treaties, his diplomatic functions being sustained by a considerable military force, to act against the ameers in case of necessity. The ameers hesitated, but ultimately the treaty was signed by those of Lower Sinde, amidst the clamours of a host of infuriated Belooches, who openly insulted the officers of the British residency and their servants. On the following day the residency was attacked, and its inmates were obliged to seek safety elsewhere. Sir Charles Napier immediately advanced, gave battle to the enemy on the 17th February, 1843, and though the Belooches fought bravely, succeeded in achieving the signal victory of Meeanee,—a result greatly aided by the superiority of the arms of the British forces over those of their opponents. Triumph continued to attend the career of the victorious general.

He was again successful in defeating the army of the ameer of Meerpoor, and the result was the complete subjugation of Sinde. Of the conquered territory, a small portion was added to Bahawulpore; a tract far more considerable was conferred upon Ali Moorad, of Khyrpoor; but of this the ameer has been recently dispossessed, under circumstances which will be found narrated in the article KHYRPOOR; and he now retains only the territory which he had inherited. With these exceptions, the province has been annexed to the British dominions: stipends have been granted to the ameers, amounting in the aggregate to 46,614*l.*; of which the sum of 18,264*l.* is allotted to the Khyrpoor branch; 25,290*l.* to the Hydrabad branch; and 3,060*l.* to the Meerpoor branch.

Since its annexation to the British dominions, Sinde has been distributed into three collectorates; those of Shikarpore, Hydrabad, and Kurrachee. The province is traversed by a railway running in a north-easterly direction from the seacoast, and which, with its extensions, will probably, at no distant period, connect every part of Northern India with the flourishing port of Kurrachee. The last census gives a population of 1,087,762. A new system of revenue administration bas been introduced; annual fairs have been established at Kurrachee and Sukkur, and customs duties, previously levied on the land frontier and on the river Indus, have been altogether abolished. The country is represented as rapidly improving; according to official report, lands which have lain waste for half a century are now under cultivation; old canals, long choked up, are reopened, and fresh ones are constructed; new villages are springing up; and people go about everywhere unarmed and in perfect safety.

SINDE CANAL, flowing from the Indus, at lat. 27° 59′, long. 69°, through the British district of Shikarpoor.

SINDE SAGUR DOOAB.—A division of the Punjab, situated between the river Indus to the west, and the Chenaub and Jhelum rivers to the east. Its limits are from lat. 28° 27′ to 34° 39′, and from long. 70° 31′ to 73° 39′.

SINDKHAID.—A town in Hyderabad, or territory of the Nizam, 54 miles E. from Aurungabad, and 111 miles N.E. by E. from Ahmednuggur. Lat. 19° 55′, long. 76° 11′.

SINDOODROOG.—See MALWAN.

SINDOORNEE.—A town in the British district of Candeish, presidency of Bombay, 72 miles E. of Malligaum. Lat. 20° 38′, long. 75° 37′.

SINDOUSI, in the British district of Etawa, lieut.-gov. of the N.W. Provinces, a fort and village in the pergunnah or subdivision of Burpoora. It was until lately a fearful den of thieves, the inhabitants, who are Rajpoots, intermixed with a few Brahmins, being a wild race, and until roughly handled by the British authorities, the principal harbourers of thugs in that part of India; and "it was at Murna, adjoining Sindouse [Sindousi], that Lieutenant Maunsell was killed, on duty with Mr. Halhed, then in pursuit of the thugs." This enforced honesty has been more beneficial to the neighbouring districts than to the lawless occupants of the wilds of Sindousi, since the resources of the zumeendars have been greatly straitened by the expulsion of the thugs, and they have since much declined in prosperity. It contains nineteen mouzahs or hamlets. Sindousi, the principal place, is eight miles W. of the right or west bank of the Jumna, 22 miles S. of the cantonment of Etawa. Lat. 26° 29′, long. 79° 10′.

SINDRAPA.—A town in the native state of Pallera, on the south-west frontier of Bengal, 53 miles S.E. by E. from Sumbulpoor, and 90 miles N. from Goomsoor. Lat. 21° 9′, long. 84° 44′.

SINDREE, in the Rajpoot state of Jodhpoor, a town on the left bank of the river Sonee, and 90 miles S.W. of the town of Jodhpoor. Boileau, who passed near Sindree, states merely that it is "a place of some consequence;" and nothing more appears to be known about it. Lat. 25° 32′, long. 71° 59′.

SINDUNOOR.—A town in one of the sequestrated districts ot Hyderabad, 28 miles S.E. by E. from Moodgul, and 43 miles W. from Bellary. Lat. 15° 46′, long. 76° 50′.

SINDWA, in the presidency of Bombay, a village with a fort on the route from Mow to Bombay, 90 miles S.W. of former, 274 N.E. of latter. It is situate nine miles outside and north of the Sindwa Ghat, or pass across the Satpoora range of mountains. The ghat is a descent moderately steep from the highlands, amidst the Satpoora range, to the valley of the Taptee, in Candeish; and being traversed by the Bombay and Agra road, it has become a much-frequented channel of communication and trade. The fort, which is of masonry, about a mile in circumference, was, with a glacis of 2,000 yards, ceded in 1818 to the British government by Holkar, by the treaty of Mundeesor; but has been recently restored to Holkar, upon the condition of his building a bridge over the Gohee river. Lat. 21° 40′, long. 75° 20′.

SINDWAH, in the British territory of Saugor and Nerbudda, a small town on the route from Tehree to Oojein, 20 miles S.W. of former, 246 N.E. of latter. It has a fine tank, embanked with masonry, and is situate in a remarkably fine country. Lat. 24° 30′, long. 78° 40′.

SINDWARA.—See CHINDWARA.

SINGA, in Bussahir, a pass crossing the range of Himalaya bounding Kunawur on the south. This pass, and three others, traverse the crest of the ridge within a space of little more than a mile. It is open during May, June, July, and the first half of August, but nearly impracticable at other times, on account of the snow, which either sinks under the traveller, or parts into deep fissures. Its elevation above the sea is between 16,000 and 17,000 feet. Lat. 31° 15′, long. 78° 29′.

SINGAPORE.—A town in the Rajpoot state of Jeypoor, situate on the left bank of the Lalglah river, and 71 miles E.N.E. from Jeypoor. Lat. 19° 30′, long. 83° 23′.

SINGAPORE.—An island situated in the Straits of Malacca, at the southern extremity of the Malay peninsula, from which it is separated by a narrow strait, which, though not exceeding half a mile in breadth at some points, was formerly the channel of navigation between India and China, now carried on by a more southward course. According to a statistical report, prepared by order of the government, the island appears to be twenty-six miles in length, and thirteen in its greatest breadth, and to contain an area of 275 square miles. The physical aspect of the island is characterized by a low and undulating surface, rising in parts into rounded hills. "From a view taken from one of the most elevated spots about the town, the whole island appears to be pleasingly diversified with hill and dale, and covered with luxuriant foliage to the water's edge, presenting to the eye a scene that has repeatedly excited admiration. There appears to be only one hill of any considerable elevation in the island, namely, Buket Temah, which is situated near the old straits, and which seems to be about 500 feet in height." The climate of Singapore, though hotter than that of Malacca, is noted for its salubrity; the thermometer ranges from 71° to 89°; frequent tropical showers tend to keep vegetation in a state of perpetual verdure, and the island continues to attract invalids seeking the removal of the prejudicial effects of the sultry climate of Hindostan. The soil, except on the hills, is generally alluvial, producing fine crops of sugar, cotton, coffee, nutmegs, and pepper. Attempts have been made to cultivate the clove, but these have proved unsuccessful. For rice the island is dependent upon external commerce. The population of Singapore has rapidly increased from the date of its occupation by the British in 1819. At that period it consisted only of about 150 fishermen and pirates, living in a few miserable huts. In 1824, when the first regular census was taken, the number of inhabitants amounted to 10,683; twelve years later they numbered 29,984, and according to the latest return (1848), the total population of the island, inclusive of military and convicts, had then increased to 57,421.

Singapore owes its prosperity to the freedom of its port, which has rendered it the great entrepôt for the goods of Europe and Asia. The number of European or American vessels arriving or departing from its port amounted in one year (1853-54) to 1,028, of which 644 were British: the aggregate tonnage was 346,997 tons. The arrivals of native vessels in the same period numbered 2,310, with a tonnage of 75,859 tons. The value of the trade for the same year was as under:—

Imports	£4,481,454
Exports	3,748,939
Total........	£8,230,393

Singapore is one of the penal settlements for India. Setting aside the cost of its convict establishment, the revenues of the island are represented as nearly equalling the expenditure; and thus, at a trifling cost, this great commercial depôt is maintained, with an annual commerce valued at from six to seven millions sterling. Singapore has no fortress, and its defenceless state has recently occupied the attention of the government. It has been well observed, however, that in the event of a European war, the only defence upon which reliance could be placed would be a British fleet, and that any other should be calculated only for the repulse of privateering attacks, or for resistance against assault, in the event of the temporary absence of men-of-war. In accordance with this view, it has been determined to limit the fortifications of Singapore to a few batteries, which have been erected on commanding positions within the island. The harbour affords a safe anchorage to vessels at all seasons; its position is also favourable for commanding the straits; and from the great and growing importance of the settlement, the eligibility of the locality as a naval rendezvous has been strongly urged.

In regard to the promotion of commercial interests, the British government in 1818 were desirous of establishing a settlement in the Eastern Archipelago. Its accomplishment was confided to Sir Stamford Raffles, and the result was an arrangement, made in 1819, with the tumongong or governor of Johore, for the transfer of Singapore to the British, in consideration of a pecuniary equivalent. Subsequently, the absolute cession of the island in full sovereignty was effected by a formal treaty with the sultan of Johore, dated August, 1824, and the territory was recognised as part of the British empire, under the twelfth article of the treaty concluded with the king of the Netherlands in the same year. It now forms one of the British possessions termed the Eastern Settlements, which embrace this island, Malacca, Province Wellesley, and Penang, or Prince of Wales Island, the last named being the seat of the government, which is directly responsible to the government of India.

The town of Singapore "is built on both sides of the embouchure of a small river, that empties itself into the sea at the western head of a deep bay, and which is navigable for small craft." Lat. 1° 16′, long. 103° 53′.

SINGARENY.—A town in Hyderabad, or territory of the Nizam, 120 miles E. from Hyderabad, and 86 miles N. by W. from Guntoor. Lat. 17° 31′, long. 80° 20′.

SINGARPOOR.—A town in the British district of Sarun, lieut.-gov. of Bengal, 23 miles N. of Bettiah. Lat. 27° 6′, long. 84° 31′.

SINGARUPATTI.—A town in the British district of Salem, presidency of Madras, 52 miles N.E. by N. of Salem. Lat. 12° 15′, long. 78° 42′.

SINGAWALA, in Sirhind, a small town twenty miles from the left bank of the Sutlej. It was comprised in the possessions which the maharaja of the Punjab held to the left of the Sutlej, under British protection and control, but has since been incorporated with the British district of Ferozepore. Distant N.W. from Calcutta 1,146 miles. Lat. 30° 46′, long. 75° 11′.

SINGGAH, in the British district of Tirhoot, lieut.-gov. of Bengal, a town on the route from Dinapur to Katmandoo, 29 miles N.E. of former, 176 S. of latter. At Salganj, closely contiguous to it, is the thana or police-station of the police division of the same name. Lat. 25° 50′, long. 85° 15′.

SINGHA, in the British district of Shahjehanpore, lieut.-gov. of the N.W. Provinces, a town on the route from Futtehgurh to Shahjehanpoor, and 18 miles N. of the former. Lat. 27° 38′, long. 79° 40′.

SINGHANA, in the Rajpoot territory of Shekawutee, a town near the eastern frontier, towards Jhujur. Elphinstone describes it as a handsome town, built of stone, on the skirts of a hill of purplish rock about 600 feet high. In a rocky hill two miles S.W. of the town is abundance of copper-ore, which is worked to considerable extent, the subterraneous galleries being in the aggregate nearly two miles in length. The miner's occupation, in every case painful, here is peculiarly so, from deficient skill and capital; and most sink under their labours before they have attained forty years of age. The ore is of very poor quality, yielding from two to seven per cent.; and the miners pay to the Ketri raja, the proprietor, a sixth of the produce, besides a fixed rent of 14,000 rupees annually. There are two kinds of ore,—a sulphate and a sulphuret. The scoriæ or khangar, that have been accumulating for ages, form a line of small hills several hundred feet in length, and from thirty to sixty feet high. There are four isolated stone bastions, built on those artificial hills. Distance of Singhana from Agra, N.W., 148 miles, S.W. from Delhi 95, N. from Jeypoor 80. Lat. 28° 6′, long. 75° 55′.

SINGHAPOOR, in the British district of Shahjehanpoor, lieut.-gov. of the N.W. Provinces, a village on the route from Bareilly to Seetapoor, and 41 miles S.E. of the former. Lat. 28° 9, long. 80° 4′.

SINGHARPOOR, in the British district of Agra, a village on the route from the city of Agra to Jeypore, and 17 miles W. of the former. Lat. 27° 7′, long. 77° 48′.

SINGHBHOOM.—A district of British India, under the superintendence of the political agent for the south-west frontier, comprehending within its limits Colehan, Surakella, Khursawa, and another petty native state bearing the name of the district. It lies between lat. 22°—22° 58′, long. 85° 7′—86° 12′; is sixty miles in length from east to west, and fifty in breadth from north to south. The area of the portion strictly British is stated to be 2,944 square miles. The population of the British part is returned at 200,000. The only place probably to which the name of town can justly be applied is Chaibassa, where the civil establishment is located. There also a detachment of the Ramgurh light infantry and some local horse are stationed, and there is a jail for criminals. The rajah of the petty state called Singhbhoom pays a tribute of 107 rupees, the computed annual value of the estate being only 4,000. The other small states comprehended within this district will be found noticed under their respective names in the proper places in the alphabetical arrangement.

SINGHEASUR.—A town in the British district of Bhagulpoor, lieut.-gov. of Bengal, 51 miles N. by W. of Bhagulpoor. Lat. 25° 55′, long. 86° 51′.

SINGHLA, in Sirhind, a village on the route from Hansee to Loodiana, and 34 miles S. of the latter town. It is situate in a country with a slightly undulating surface, moderately fertile, and partially cultivated. Distant N.W. from Calcutta 1,055 miles. Lat. 30° 27′, long. 75° 59′.

SINGHPOOR.—In the British district of Sohagpoor, territory of Saugor and Nerbudda, lieut.-gov. of the N.W. Provinces, a town on the route from Sohagpoor to Ruttunpoor, 10 miles S.S.E. of the former. Lat. 23° 11′, long. 81° 30′.

SINGIMAREE.—A town of North-Eastern India, in the British district of Goalpara, 56 miles S.W. by W. of Goalpara. Lat. 25° 41′, long. 89° 53′.

SINGOLA, in the British district of Budaon, lieut.-gov. of the N.W. Provinces, a village on the route from Allygurh to Moradabad, and 36 miles S.W. of the latter. Lat. 28° 27′, long. 78° 26′.

SINGON.—A town in the native state of Indore, or territory of Holkar, 52 miles S.S.W. from Indoor, and 122 miles N.E. from Malligaum. Lat. 21° 59′, long. 75° 34′.

SINGORA.—A town in the native state of Phooljer, on the south-western frontier of Bengal, 50 miles W.S.W. from Sumbulpoor, and 96 miles S. from Odeipoor. Lat. 21° 18′, long. 83° 15′.

SINGOWLEE.—A town in the Rajpoot state of Oodeypoor, 100 miles E.N.E. from Oodeypoor, and 46 miles N.E. by N. from Neemuch. Lat. 25°, long. 75° 20′.

SINGPOOR, in the British district of Mirzapoor, lieut.-gov. of the N.W. Provinces, a town on the route from Mirzapoor to Sirgoojah, 73 miles S. by E. of the former. Lat. 24° 7', long. 82° 55'.

SINGPOOR, in the British territory of Saugor and Nerbudda, lieut.-gov. of the N.W. Provinces, a town on the route from Saugor to Seuni, 68 miles S.S.E. of the former. Lat. 22° 58', long. 79° 13'.

SINGPOOREAH, in Sirhind, or the Cis-Sutlej territory, an estate formerly held by one of the protected Seik chiefs. Upon the decease of Umur Singh, in 1848, a collateral branch of the family was admitted to the inheritance; but the chief no longer exercises independent powers within his possessions. Lat. 31° 2', long. 76° 40'.

SINGRAMOW, in the British district of Jounpore, lieut.-gov. of the N.W. Provinces, a town on the route from Jounpoor cantonment to that of Sooltanpoor, in Oude, 25 miles N.W. of the former, 33 S.E. of the latter. Lat. 25° 57', long. 82° 28'.

SINGROUR, in the British district of Allahabad, lieut.-gov. of the N.W. Provinces, a town on the left bank of the Ganges, 27 miles above the city of Allahabad by the river, and 835 miles from Calcutta by the same way. Lat. 25° 35', long. 81° 42'.

SINGROWLEE.—A tract of country, of which a portion (termed the Saipore or Shahpore division) now belongs to the rajah of Rewah, and the remainder (styled Singrowlee Proper) to the British government, forming a pergunnah of the district of Mirzapore. The boundaries of the entire tract are as follow:—North, the Mirzapore pergunnah of Agoree; east, the British district Palamow; south-east and south, Sirgooja, in Gundwana, subject to the British; west, Rewah; and north-west, Burdee. It lies between lat. 23° 44'—24° 24', long. 82° 18'—83° 17': its length from east to west is seventy miles, and its breadth from north to south thirty-five. The British portion consists of the tract lying eastward of long. 82° 49', and comprises about one-half of the whole territory. The rajah of Singrowlee was dependent upon the British government for one part of his zemindary, termed Singrowlee Proper, and upon the Rewah rajah for the remaining portion, named Shahpoor. Of this last, however, he was, in 1840, dispossessed by the rajah of Rewah; and the rest has been since incorporated with the district of Mirzapore, of which, as above stated, it forms one of the pergunnahs.

SINGUR, in the Rajpoot state of Jodhpoor, a village on the route, *viâ* Nagor, from Jessulmeer to Nusserabad, and 101 miles N.W. of latter. The only water obtainable is from a very brackish well, and from a tank, which becomes dry in hot weather, when the inhabitants have recourse to a well four miles distant. The road is good, passing over a large plain. Lat. 27° 10', long. 73° 40'.

SINGURH, in the British collectorate of Poona, presidency of Bombay, a fort among the mountains south of Poona. It was originally called Konaneh, and received its present name from Sevajee, the founder of the Mahratta sway, who, in 1647, obtained it by bribing the commandant. In A.D. 1665, Sevajee, hoping to make his peace with Aurungzebe, surrendered this place to his general Jai Singh, but subsequently revolting, recovered it by surprise in the year 1670. After a lapse of more than thirty years, Singurh again appears as an object of contention between the Mahrattas and the Mahomedans. Between 1701 and 1705, Aurungzebe laboured incessantly to annihilate the Mahratta power, and in that period was successful in reducing many of their forts, of which Singurh was one. The emperor did not long retain his prize, it being retaken by one of the Mahratta leaders, to the great annoyance of Aurungzebe, who forthwith despatched one of his generals to recover possession of the place; a mission in which he succeeded, from the failure of supplies in Singurh. From the same cause it was almost immediately retaken by the Mahrattas, who continued to hold it during the remaining period of their ascendancy. In 1817 it was surrendered by the Peishwa to the British troops, and restored to him at the close of the same year. After the expulsion of that chieftain from Poona, in 1818, it was invested by a considerable British army, and having suffered much from shells and shot, the garrison, at the end of ten days, capitulated. This took place on the 1st of March. The natural strength of Singurh is very great, from its situation among the Western Ghauts. With these hills it only communicates on the east and west, by very high, narrow ridges, while on the south and north it presents a huge rugged mountain, with an ascent of half a mile, in many parts nearly perpendicular. After arriving at this height, there is an immense craggy precipice of black rock, upwards of forty feet high, and surmounting the whole there is a strong stone wall, with towers. The fort is of a triangular shape, its interior upwards of two miles in circumference, and the exterior presents on all sides the stupendous barrier already mentioned, so that, except by the gates, entrance seems impossible. Elevation above the sea 4,162 feet. Distant from Poona, S.W., 11 miles; from Bombay, by Poona, S.E., 70 miles. Lat. 18° 24', long. 73° 50'.

SINGWARUH, in the British district of Sohagpoor, territory of Saugor and Nerbudda, lieut.-gov. of the N.W. Provinces, a town on the route from Sohagpoor to Dumoh, 28 miles W. by N. of the former. Lat. 23° 26', long. 81° 1'.

SINGY.—A town in Oude, situate on the left bank of the Ghogra river, and 101 miles N. from Lucknow. Lat. 28° 19', long. 80° 57'.

SINNUR.—A town in the British district of Ahmednuggur, presidency of Bombay, 73

miles N.W. of Ahmednuggur. Lat. 19° 51′, long. 74°.

SION.—A village in the island of Bombay, situate at its northern extremity, and near the point where the island of Salsette is united with that of Bombay by a causeway, and also by the railway-bridge. Lat. 19° 2′, long. 72° 56′.

SIPOON, a river of Bussahir, rises at an elevation of 15,000 feet, in lat. 31° 24′, long. 78° 6′, on the southern declivity of the Yusu Pass, whence it is sometimes called the Yusu River. In the upper part of its course, it is a violent torrent, making its way, with difficulty, under snowbeds, and amidst huge masses of rock. "The further we went," observes Gerard, "the glen became more contracted, till at last it was bounded by mural rocks of granite, with the Seepon forcing its passage between them in impenetrable obscurity, under immense solid heaps of indestructible ice, running in ridges, and studded with tumuli of snow, shaped like inverted bottles. The fall of the torrent here appears to be above 20°." After a precipitate course of about five miles in a south-west direction, it receives a considerable torrent, flowing from the north-east, and about two miles below falls into the Pabur, the confluence having an elevation of 8,300 feet, and being in lat. 31° 18′, long. 78° 4′.

SIPPREE, in the territory of Gwalior, or possessions of Scindia's family, a town on the route from Calpee to Kotah, 162 miles S.W. of former, 159 E. of latter. It is now much decayed, but eighty years ago, according to Tieffenthaler, it was, after Narwar, the principal town in the district of that name. East of Sippree, and between it and the town of Narwar, the Sindh was traversed by a good bridge of squared stone, now ruined by the monsoon floods. Distant 65 miles S. of Gwalior fort. Lat. 25° 24′, long. 77° 46′.

SIRA, in the Baree Dooab division of the Punjab, a town situated on the left bank of the Ravee river, 49 miles S.W. of the town of Lahore. Lat. 31° 7′, long. 73° 41′.

SIRAKOT, in the British district of Kumaon, lieut.-gov. of the N.W. Provinces, a fort with a Hindoo temple, nine miles N.W. of the confluence of the Goree and Eastern Kalee. It is situate on a rocky ridge, projecting from the northern slope of a mountain, and having two of its sides craggy scarps to the depth of about 2,000 feet, and the part most remote from the mountain terminated by a chasm 700 feet deep. The point where it joins the mountain is traversed by five trenches of considerable depth, cut in the body of the ridge, and formerly crossed by drawbridges, but now in some degree obliterated. The path from Almora to Nepal winds round one of the steep sides, and is so narrow and broken, that it might be rendered impassable in an hour. The temple is situate on a conical rock, which rises nearly perpendicularly from the crest of the ridge, along which the decayed fortifications extend. Water can be obtained only from a small spring and reservoir, three-quarters of a mile distant from the fort, the garrison of which could readily be reduced by cutting off the supply; and accordingly, on its investment by the Gorkha invaders, it at once surrendered, since which time it has remained unoccupied, and has gradually fallen to ruin. Elevation above the sea 6,924 feet. Lat. 29° 49′, long. 80° 17′.

SIRAWUH, in the British district of Meerut, lieut.-gov. of the N.W. Provinces, a town on the route from Meerut to Boolundshuhur, 16 miles S. of the former. Lat. 28° 47′, long. 77° 49′.

SIRCI, in the subdivision of Soonda, in the British district of North Canara, presidency of Madras, a town with a small mud fort, situate on the declivity of a ridge, one of the undulations of the rugged plateau into which the Ghats expand in this latitude. It is the station of the teshsildar or collector for the district. Though not centrically situated, Sirci, according to Buchanan, appears to have been selected for that purpose in consequence of its great thoroughfare and large custom-house. Distant from Mangalore, W., 120 miles; from Bombay, S.E., 320; from Madras, W., 385. Lat. 14° 36′, long. 74° 54′.

SIRDARNUGGUR, in the British district of Cawnpore, lieut.-gov. of the N.W. Provinces, a village on the route from Calpee to Etawa, and 52 miles S.E. of the latter. The road in this part of the route is rather good, the country partially cultivated. Lat. 26° 20′, long. 79° 43′.

SIRDHANA, in the subdivision of the same name, district of Meerut, lieut.-gov. of the N.W. Provinces, a town on the route from Kurnal to the town of Meerut, and 11 miles N.W. of the latter. It is surrounded with a weak mud wall, and has within it a citadel, built of the same material, but latterly allowed to fall to decay. The principal building is the palace of the late Zeb ul Nissa, more generally known by the name of the Begum Sumroo, a spacious and handsome structure, profusely ornamented with paintings. At no great distance is the church, built by the same personage, who professed herself a proselyte to the Roman Catholic faith. It is, on a small scale, an imitation of St. Peter's at Rome, and has an altar ornamented with a beautiful piece of mosaic, enriched with precious stones. The population amounts to 12,481, about 1,200 of whom are professed Christians, having become proselytes, to recommend themselves to the favour of the Begum, and notoriously an idle, profligate race. The remarkable woman of whose petty dominion this small town was the capital, is generally reported to have been a native of Cashmere, originally a dancing-girl, subsequently concubine of Walter Summers, a desperate adventurer, of German origin, and ultimately, by a course of unscrupulous intrigue and fearless sanguinary measures, possessor of three considerable jaghires or principalities, one immediately around Sirdhana, another fifty miles south of it, and a third a few miles south-west of Delhi. In 1803, when Doulut Rao Scindia ceded to the East-India Company the Doab, and some adjacent tracts, the claims of the female adventurer to the jaghires above mentioned were recognised by the supreme government, and confirmed by convention in 1805; and on her death, in 1836, all her territory having lapsed, was embodied into the adjacent British districts, Sirdhana and the contiguous country being made a pergunnah of Meerut. Sirdhana is situate in an open level country, and has water and supplies for troops in abundance. The road in this part of the route is good; the encamping-ground is on the east side of the town, near the church. Elevation above the sea 882 feet. Distance N.W. from Calcutta 897 miles. Lat. 29° 9′, long. 77° 40′.

SIRDHURPOOR.—A town in Oude, situate on the left bank of the Ganges river, and 49 miles W. from Lucknow. Lat. 26° 56′, long. 80° 12′.

SIRDILLA.—A town in the British district of Behar, lieut.-gov. of Bengal, 41 miles S. by W. of Behar. Lat. 24° 39′, long. 85° 29′.

SIREENNUGGUR, in British Gurwhal, under the lieut.-gov. of the N.W. Provinces, a town now much decayed, though once the capital of Gurwhal. It is situate on the south or left bank of the Aluknunda, a great feeder of the Ganges, and in the midst of a valley about four miles long in the direction from east to west, and two miles broad. Viewed from above, the hollow in which the town is situate has the appearance of a double valley, one on a level with the river, the other on its banks, elevated above the water about forty or fifty feet, and extending along the base of the inclosing mountain. The lower valley, in which the town is situate, has apparently been excavated by the river, and left dry by the stream flowing further to the northward, and leaving between its present margin and the original bank a space of land stretching three or four furlongs south of the town, and now laid out in small fields and inclosures, among which mango-trees are thinly scattered. The aspect of the surrounding mountains is very barren, and in the dry season their scanty vegetation is soon parched up, with the exception of a few trees. On an island in the Aluknunda, close to the town, are ruins of buildings formerly connected with it; and on the opposite side are several hamlets, situate along the base of the mountain. The city has somewhat the shape of the segment of a circle, of which the river's bank is the chord. The principal street, which contains the bazar, is about half a mile long, and tolerably broad, but the others are so narrow that two persons can scarcely pass abreast. The houses are built of large rough stones, laid generally in mud instead of mortar, and are usually two stories high, with shelving roofs, covered with slates or shingles. The lower stories are allotted for stores or shops, the families occupying the upper. The houses of the higher orders are little distinguished from those of others, except by a narrow balcony. A gloomy air is given to the town from this uniformity, which probably resulted in former times from the desire of the wealthier inhabitants to avoid attracting the notice of extortionate rulers. The palace of the rajah must have once displayed architectural pretensions and extent, wonderful in a community so rude and poor. It was built of large blocks of black stone laid in mortar, and had three grand fronts, each four stories high, with projecting porticos, and profusely ornamented in the lower part with elaborate sculptures. The porticos still remain, but the rest of the building has been laid in ruins by earthquakes. There are many Hindoo temples, none, however, meriting much notice. At one time the town was in a very flourishing condition, being the residence of the rajah of Gurwhal, and the channel of a brisk trade between the highlands and Tartary on the one side, and the plains on the other. The larger portion of this trade is now conducted through the eastern part of Kumaon, and the place has ceased to be the residence of the rajah since 1803, when he was expelled, and subsequently slain by the Goorkha invaders. In the same year an earthquake nearly destroyed the town, so that when Raper visited it in 1808, not above one house in five was inhabited, the rest being heaps of ruins. At the time of Moorcroft's visit in 1820, it had a few manufactures of coarse linens and woollens. The number of the houses in 1821 was 562, of which 438 were inhabited by Hindoos, ninety-six by Doms or outcasts, and twenty-eight by Mussulmans. The number of inhabitants is probably about 3,000. The native establishments for the revenue and police of the western part of the province have been stationed at this place, and cause some improvement. The Aluknunda has here a channel 250 yards wide, but the breadth of the stream in the dry season does not exceed 100 yards. At the western extremity of the valley in which the town is situated, the current strikes with violence against the rocky base of the mountain. Near that part it is crossed by a jhula, or rude suspension-bridge of ropes, and in the immediate vicinity of the town is a ferry. The river, according to Hardwicke, is navigable for rafts or canoes. On the right bank of the river, and opposite to the town, is the village of Ranihath, containing a temple sacred to Rajah Iswara, at which the dancing-girls, who form the majority of the population, devote themselves to prostitution, by abjuring their kindred and anointing their heads with oil from a lamp placed before the altar. At a short distance beyond it is the fane of an idol, styled by Raper Rassee Devi, or "the god of love." In the hot season the temperature at Sireennuggur is high, as the elevation is not considerable, being probably little more than 2,000 feet above the sea. Distance N.W. from Calcutta, by Lucknow, Bareilly, and Almora, 1,007 miles. Lat. 30° 13′, long. 78° 49′.

SIREENUGUR, in the British district of Ajmeer, lieut.-gov. of the N.W. Provinces, a town on the route from Ajmeer to Tonk, 10 miles E. by S. of the former. Lat. 26° 27′, long. 74° 52′.

SIREY, or SIRSA, in the British district of Allahabad, lieut.-gov. of the N.W. Provinces, a small town on the route, by the Kutra Pass, from the cantonment of Allahabad to Rewah, and 25 miles S.E. of the former. It is situate on the right bank of the Ganges, close to the confluence of the Tons, and on the right bank of the latter, which has here a bed 400 yards wide, and in the dry season a stream 150 yards wide, running under the left bank. Distant N.W. from Calcutta by land 490 miles, by the river 785. Lat. 25° 16′, long. 82° 10′.

SIRGOOJAH. — A raj of British India, named from its principal place, and under the control of the political agent for the south-west frontier of Bengal. It lies between lat. 22° 34′—23° 54′, long. 82° 40′—84° 6′; is 90 miles in length from north to south, and 85 in breadth: the area is 5,441 square miles. The surface is rugged and mountainous, rising from 500 to 600 feet above the table-land of the adjoining district of Chota Nagpore. It is drained by the rivers Kunher and Rhern, with its feeder the Mohan, flowing in a direction generally northerly. These rivers are mostly shallow, except during the rains, when they become rapid torrents.

Besides the ruined town of Sirgoojah, giving name to the district, the only place of the least importance is Sarnuda, and this is little more than a village. The population of the district is stated at 316,252.

The forests contain elephants, leopards, tigers, deer, and hogs: buffaloes come down in large numbers from Benares and Mirzapore to graze here. The timber is of the same species which abounds in Chota Nagpore.

The tract called Sirgoojah was nominally part of the possessions of the Bhoosla sovereign of Berar or Nagpore, but in 1802, in consequence of the frequent predatory inroads made by its insubordinate population into the British territory, Major Jones proceeded at the head of a detachment to the residence of the petty rajah or local chief; and the awe produced by this measure appears to have in a great degree checked further attempts at annoyance. By treaty with the rajah of Nagpore in 1818, the supreme control of this district was ceded to the East-India Company, with some other territorial rights. The country, a few years since, was reported by the Governor-General's agent to be worth annually four or five lacs, and to be in an improving state. The tribute was paid with regularity: it amounted originally to 3,200 rupees per annum; but upon the lapse to the British of the small raj of Odeipoor, a deduction was made of the amount which had previously been annually credited to Sirgoojah from the revenues of that petty state. On the death of the rajah in 1851, the elder son and successor being of infirm intellect, an arrangement was made, by which the administration was placed in the hands of his younger brother, Bindaseree Pershaud. For the relation of the state to the British government, see SOUTH-WEST FRONTIER OF BENGAL.

SIRGOOJAH, the place giving name to the district so called, is a ruined town 140 miles S. of Mirzapore, and 340 W. of Calcutta. Hamilton states that in 1822 scarcely a vestige existed of it. Lat. 23° 8′, long. 83° 8′.

SIRHIND.—An extensive territorial division of Hindostan, bounded on the north by the Punjab; on the east by Sirmoor and other hill states, and by the British districts of Saharunpoor, Paniput, and Rohtuck; on the south by Rohtuck and Hurreeana; and on the west by the state of Bahawulpore. It is about 220 miles in length from east to west, and 160 in breadth; and lies between lat. 29° 3′—31° 24′, and long. 73° 50′—77° 39′: the superficial extent is probably about 17,000 square miles. Sirhind in nearly its whole extent is a level plain, except where the surface, at the north-east, rises into the lower ranges of the Himalaya. This small extent of elevated surface terminates at the north-east frontier in a low range, which stretches seventy-five miles in a south-east direction, from near the left bank of the Sutlej, a little above Ropur, to the right bank of the Jumna, close to its efflux from the Dehra Doon. This range consequently extends from about lat. 30° 22′, long. 77° 38′, to lat. 31° 2′, long. 76° 40′. It is the lowest step of that hill tract described by Dr. Royle in the following passage: "The low range of hills, frequently separated from the true Himalaya by diluvial valleys or doons, such as that of Deyra, seldom attains an elevation of more than 3,500 feet, or 2,500 above the plains of Northern India. The principal passes across this range were 2,339 and 2,935 feet before they were cut down."

The plain which forms the rest of Sirhind, slopes very gradually from north-east to south-west, and is unbroken except by depressions swept by watercourses, or sandhills, especially in the more barren tract which extends over the west and adjoins the territory of Bahawulpoor, and of that of Bhutteeana. A few years ago, a survey was made by order of government, and a line of levels taken for ascertaining the practicability of connecting the Sutlej and Jumna by canal, at the points on those great rivers where the downward navigation commences for vessels of any considerable burthen. The south-eastern extremity of the line contemplated is on the right bank of the Jumna, six miles east of Kurnaul, and at an elevation of about 1,000 feet above the sea; and it held a course in a right line nearly due north-west to Loodiana, on the left bank of a navigable channel of the Sutlej. This line, 112 miles long, crosses all the watercourses flowing from the Himalaya, and probably traverses the roughest part of the country. The inequalities result either from ridges rising to small elevation above the average level of the country, or from shallow valleys, apparently formed by the numerous streams. The country, however, in proceeding westward, has a general and gradual rise, which attains its maximum elevation of sixty-seven feet at Kuddoo, ninety miles from the Jumna, whence, in twenty-two miles, it falls to the Sutlej, the level of which is two feet lower than that of the Jumna. Thus the whole of Sirhind may be regarded as a low ridge, rising between the Jumna and the Sutlej, as the bed of every watercourse between these two rivers is invariably several feet higher than that of either.

In the course of the survey, the depth of 156 wells was taken. By this, the surveyor wished "to ascertain whether, as some supposed, measurements of the level of springs would give data for an approximate calculation of the profile of the country." "In this respect," the author remarks, "my present observations, as well as those made with the same view in other localities, show that the level of springs is too much affected by the vicinity of streams, the degree of permeability of soils, and other local circumstances, to admit of any accurate conclusion being drawn from them regarding the profile of the surface." The water drawn off from the projected canal by the expenditure for lockage, or by evaporation or absorption, could be replaced on the eastern slope at the highest level, by means of a feeder from the Delhi Canal, communicating with the Jumna, and on the western, by one from the Sutlej, above Ropur. Such a canal would connect the extensive and highly important navigation of the Ganges and its tributaries with that of the Indus.

The Jumna, where it issues from the mountains, touches on this territory, in lat. 30° 25′, long. 77° 39′, and forms its south-eastern boundary for about seventy miles. The Sutlej, from the point of its egress from the mountains, about thirty-five miles above Ropur, forms the northern and north-western boundary of Sirhind; the course of the river being for the upper part, first from north to south, then from east to west; for the lower, from north-east to south-west. The country between the Jumna and the Sutlej is traversed by above a dozen considerable torrents. Of these the principal are the Sursooty, the Markanda, the Gagur or Cuggur, the Putteeala Nullah, and the Khan-poorkee-Nuddee. These torrents generally communicate with each other during the season of inundation. On this subject a recent accurate observer says: "From near Thanesur to Konaheree the whole tract of country (with the exception of village sites) is liable to inundation from the Sub-Himalayan torrents, diffused over its surface by means of a network of natural and artificial watercourses, of which some are supplied from more than one of the rivers above named; others again flow from one river into another, and during great floods (as I was given to understand), all three are frequently united. The inhabitants avail themselves largely of the inundation for rice-cultivation, though, during the present season at least, little advantage appeared to have been taken of the facilities afforded for irrigating rubbee (spring) crops, which, where they existed, were generally watered from wells. I had not leisure to ascertain by personal examination whether the first diffusion of these rivers (which I have myself seen nearer the hills in single and separate streams) were caused by natural or artificial means, but it is probably attributable to both. The slope and evenness of the country are calculated to favour even the rudest attempts to divert the streams from their original beds; and the same circumstances would also render it easy, were it desirable, to confine them again to one or two principal channels." Far more important than those streams is a system of artificial watercourses, which in the eastern extremity of Sirhind run in some measure parallel to the Jumna, but to the west of it, and conveying a volume of water nearly equal to that of this river. This great work originated with Firoz Toghluk, Tartar king of Delhi, who ascended the throne 1351, and died 1388. He commenced it at the right bank of the Jumna, in lat. 30° 19′, and turning into it several of the torrents which traverse Sirhind, conducted it 100 miles in a south-westerly direction to Dhatrat, where, according to the opinion of Colvin, he took advantage of the natural bed of the Chittung torrent, flowing in the same direction thirty-five miles farther to Hansi; beyond which the watercourse is continued about eighteen miles, in a direction a little north of west, to Hissar. The total length, consequently, of the canal of Firoz to this place is 150 miles. A few miles beyond Hissar all traces of excavation cease, but a natural channel in time of inundation conveys the redundant water westward, until lost in the sands of Bikanir, or probably, in case of very great floods, discharged into the Gagur, and ultimately into the Sutlej. The canal of Firoz having, after the death of its constructor, been allowed through neglect to become choked up, was, early in the seventeenth century, cleared out by Ali Murdan Khan, who, at Mudloda, about eighty miles from its commencement, formed a channel proceeding due south, and consequently diverging there from the original watercourse. This new channel has a south-easterly direction for about seventy miles, to Delhi, whence it is generally known by the name of the Delhi Canal, sometimes by that of Ali Murdan Khan, and sometimes is styled Shah Nahr (King's River), probably in honour of the royal master of the projector, or perhaps of Ahmed Shah Dooranee, who, during his brief possession of Delhi, expended a lac of rupees in repairing the work. Both those canals were by command of the supreme government put into adequate repair, in the years intervening between 1817 and 1826. The extent of the Firoz Canal, with its various branches, is 240 miles.

The territory is held by native chieftains, with the exception of such portions of it as have escheated to the East-India Company, in virtue of its paramount authority over the country. The descent of the three principal chieftainships, of Putteeala, Jheend, and Nabha, has been formally determined to be to heirs male only; and on failure of such in a direct line, the estate passes to the next of kin. In the minor possessions, the right of inheritance, as established by the custom of each family, so far as it can be ascertained, is invariably respected by the superior government. The customs are not only widely different, but appear to be in their origin and character exceedingly capricious. Captain Murray, formerly superintendent of the hill territories, thus speaks of them:—"The rules of succession to landed property in the Sikh states are arbitrary, and are variously modified, in accordance to the usages, the interests, and prejudices of different families; nor is it practicable to reduce the anomalous system to a fixed and leading principle." Among some tribes female succession is recognised; by others it is disallowed. Succession by adoption has never been practised; and in one or two instances in which attempts were made to obtain the sanction of the British government to the adoption of an heir, it was, with reference to the utter want of precedent, refused. The Sikhs in general, in obedience to an injunction of their religion, eschew smoking tobacco; but considering the use of fermented drinks not forbidden, they exercise the liberty supposed to be allowed them, by indulging in the copious use of ardent spirits; insomuch that sobriety is rare among these people, and numbers shorten their days by excess in this indulgence. They also use opium freely, as well as bang, the intoxicating drug extracted from hemp. Every sort of food is allowed by their religion, except the flesh of the cow, the slaying of which is punished with cruel death. The Sikhs, however, may, on the whole, be considered tolerant, though they treat both Hindoos and Mussulmans with contempt, and prohibit the latter from delivering from their mosques the azan, or solemn call to prayers.

The establishment of the Sikh modification of Brahminism, in many respects a highly important event, is especially so as being perhaps a step to the abrogation of a vast system of superstition, probably the most influential, as well as the most tyrannical and mischievous, that has ever enthralled and depraved human nature. Nanac, the founder of this faith, was born 1469, at Talwandi, a village on the river Beas. Being of a contemplative disposition, and it is said devout and benevolent, he became an ascetic, remarkable for his austerities, even among the Hindoos. Subsequently he is said to have preached the unity and omnipresence of God, the necessity of good works, of peace and of good-will towards men. His successors, however, have greatly departed from the first principles of their faith, if the above statement of the tenets of their founder be correct. He was a very moderate innovator, according to the following account, in which, however, the original purity of the Hindoo creed seems rather needlessly and groundlessly assumed. He "made," it is said, "no material invasion of either the civil or religious usages of the Hindoos; and as his only desire was to restore a nation who had degenerated from their original pure worship into idolatry, he may be considered more in the light of a reformer than of a subverter of the Hindoo religion; and those Sikhs who adhere to his tenets, without admitting those of Guru Govind, are hardly to be distinguished from the great mass of Hindoo population, among whom there are many sects who differ much more than that of Nanac from the general and orthodox worship at present established in India." His followers were called Sikhs, or "disciples;" himself, Guru, or "spiritual guide." He died at seventy years of age, having bequeathed his spiritual supremacy to a favourite disciple. Ram Das, the third guru in exclusive succession from Nanac, formed a celebrated tank, which he called Amritsur, or "lake of ambrosia;" and the great city which has grown up about it bears the same name. Arjunmal, the fourth guru, compiled the Adi Granth, one of the sacred books of the Sikhs, from the various effusions of his predecessors. This last guru having fallen a victim to the persecution of the Mahomedans, his successor, Har Govind, ordered his followers to arm and take vengeance on their persecutors; he also permitted his adherents to eat the flesh of all animals except kine, whereas Nanac had prohibited that of hogs. Guru Govind, the ninth in exclusive succession from Nanac, was a bold innovator, and a brave but ferocious soldier, who, furiously exasperated at the fate of Tegh Bahadur, his father and predecessor, executed by order of the Mogul emperor Aurungzebe in 1675, took up arms, and, mustering his followers, gave them institutions calculated to inspire fierce nationality and unconquerable military ardour. They were to bear the name of Singh, or lion, which had hitherto been exclusively arrogated by the Rajpoots; were always to have steel in some form about their persons, as an emblem of their devotion to war and its duties; while, as external marks of distinction, they were to allow their beards and the hair of their heads to grow in undiminished luxuriance, and to wear blue clothes. At the same time all distinctions of caste were abolished, and every one was invited to receive the initiatory rite, and, becoming a member of the Singh Khalsa or commonwealth, to participate in its advantages. These institutions of Guru Govind caused the division of the Sikhs into two great sects,—the Khalasa, or those who rejected these innovations, and the Singhs, who adopted them, and are actually the great influential body of the nation. Initiation into the community of the Singhs is celebrated by five of their number, who administer to the candidate five draughts of sugar and water, making him at the same time repeat a rhyming liturgy. According to Prinsep, the sacred beverage is made with the water in which the initiators and the neophyte or candidate have washed their feet. Forster, however, states that it is merely touched with the toe. Wilson says, "The Sikhs are still to a certain extent Hindoos. They worship the same deities as the Hindoos, and celebrate all their festivals; they derive their legends and literature from the same sources, and pay great veneration to the Brahmins. The impress of their origin is still, therefore, strongly retained, notwithstanding their rejection of caste, and their substituting the Das Padshah ki Granth, the compilation of Guru Govind, for the Vedas and Puranas." This view of the doctrines and practices of the Sikhs is obviously inconsistent with that which assigns to them the belief in a creed of pure theism, and the practice of a spiritual and benevolent devotion. Probably this palmy state never existed; if it ever did, it is certain that it did not continue long.

Guru Govind, at the head of his followers, whom he had succeeded in transmuting into a host of sanguinary and desperate fanatics, gained repeated victories over the armies of the Mogul emperors; but being at length overpowered, he was obliged to flee, leaving his mother and his two children in the hands of the Mahomedans, who cruelly put them to death at the town of Sirhind. He sank under the weight of his misfortunes, and died in obscurity. He was the last of the gurus, and thus was luckily fulfilled a prophecy which limited their number to ten. Such prophecies are easily manufactured. Sometimes they follow the event; and when they precede it, they conduce to their own fulfilment. After the death of Govind, the military force of the nation was successfully wielded by Banda, a brave but ferocious leader, who, in revenge for the slaughter of the wife and children of Guru Govind, stormed the town of Sirhind, demolished the mosques, exterminated the inhabitants, tore the bodies of the dead from their graves, and cast them forth to birds and beasts of prey. He then overran the whole of the district of Sirhind, and threatened to conquer all Hindostan, until, being defeated in a decisive engagement, he was made prisoner, and about the year 1710 put to death with studied cruelty at Delhi. The Sikhs continued prostrate and obscure until the power of the Mogul empire was broken up by the invasion of Nadir Shah, whose army they harassed and plundered in his return homewards. Subsequently, in their predatory expeditions they overran the Punjab, and on the flight of Timur, the son of Ahmed Shah, in 1758, made themselves masters of Lahore. In 1762, Ahmed Shah Dooranee, after the battle of Paniput, razed Amritsir to the ground, filling up the sacred tank with the ruins, and moreover polluting it with the blood of kine; erected pyramids of the heads of the slain Sikhs, and washed the walls of the mosques with their blood, in revenge for their previous desecration of those edifices. In the following year, when Ahmed Shah had marched home to Cabul, the Sikhs made themselves masters of both Lahore and Amritsir, and retaliated on the Mussulmans the disgrace and cruelties which they had endured. "During the year 1764 they had overrun and seized on an extent of territory reaching from the borders of the Indus to the districts of Delhi;" and throughout this extensive region firmly established their power and religion.

The British power first came into collision with the Sikhs in 1805, when Lord Lake marched into the Punjab in pursuit of Jeswunt Rao Holkar, the Mahratta potentate, who, discountenanced by the wily Runjeet Singh, then in an early stage of his career, was constrained to make peace with his conquerors. In 1809, the aggression of Runjeet Singh on the Sikh chiefs on the left bank of the Sutlej exciting the apprehension of the Anglo-Indian government, a British force was marched across the Jumna, whereupon the ambitious but politic adventurer speedily, and with a good grace, concluded a treaty, by which he restricted himself from all hostile operations in the country lying left of the Sutlej; the number of his troops there being limited to so many as should be required for government purposes in the districts over which his supremacy extended. The British government then issued and circulated, among the remaining sirdars or chiefs, a general declaration that they were under its protection.

Several portions of this territory have at different periods lapsed to the Company's government, from failure of heirs; and when that government was forced into war with Lahore, further alienations took place, from a different cause. The penal measures which it became just and expedient to inflict on several of the Sikh chiefs, for acts of hostility or non-performance of their feudatory obligations during the Lahore war, led to considerable changes in the state of territorial possessions in the Cis-Sutlej territories. In addition to the territory of Ladwa, that of Roopur was wholly confiscated; and the chief having been pensioned, resides at Saharunpore. The Cis-Sutlej possessions of the Allowalleea chiefs were also confiscated, and Nabah, one of the principal of the protected states, has been mulcted of one-fourth of its territory. The British government availed itself of these acquisitions to reward the fidelity of the rajahs of Putteeala, Jheend, and Furreedkote, to each of whom an addition of territory was granted. New sunnuds were granted to the rajahs of Putteeala and Jheend, in which clauses have been inserted, binding them to renounce all transit-duties, to make and keep in repair a military road, and to abolish suttee, infanticide, and slave-dealing. The British police jurisdiction has been introduced into most of the protected Sikh states, and the levy of customs has been abolished in the whole, compensation being granted to the chiefs.

The British possessions in the Cis-Sutlej Sikh territory have been divided into four districts,—Ferozepore, Loodianah, Umballah, and Kythul: the aggregate revenue is between eighteen and nineteen lacs of rupees (180,000*l.* to 190,000*l.*). A civil and sessions judge for the Cis-Sutlej territory has been appointed, and also a commissioner.

Sirhind, situate between the Himalaya on the north and the desert of Bikaneer on the south, has repeatedly been traversed by armies advancing to the invasion of India, and hence has been the scene of many conflicts and other memorable events. As it was saved from the threatened invasion of Alexander by the mutiny of his troops, probably the first great military operation recorded to have taken place on its soil was the capture of Thanesur, in 1011, by Mahmud of Ghuznee, who plundered the city, broke the idols, and carried the fragments of that called Jugsoma to Ghuznee, to be trodden under the feet of Mussulmans. After the death of Mahmud, the Hindoos, in 1043, recovered possession of this place and the rest of Sirhind. In 1191, Mahomed, the Affghan prince of Ghor, attempting to recover the Mussulman conquests in Sirhind, received a severe defeat near Thanesur, and fled to Ghuznee, but returned in the following year, and having on the same field routed a great Hindoo army, made himself master of the whole country, which continued subject to the Mussulmans until the Sikh outbreak. It escaped the horrors of the invasion of Tamerlane in 1397, as the route of that prince in marching from Batnir, which he had laid in ruins, to Delhi, only touched the southern frontier; and having proceeded to Cupeli or Koupelah, to exterminate the Hindoos assembled there, he returned to Khorasan, through the Sewalik Mountains, by Jamoo and the southern boundary of Cashmere, probably crossing the Indus above Attok. In 1525, Baber, in his advance against Ibrahim, the Patan king of Delhi, overran and seized the greater part of Sirhind. In 1554, the vicinity of the town of Sirhind was the scene of an action, in which Humayon, the son of Baber, gained a decisive victory over the far more numerous army of his Patan rival, and gave peace to the Mogul empire. Sirhind appears from that time to have tranquilly enjoyed the imperial favour, until the outbreak of the Sikh insurrection, of the progress and result of which a sketch has been given under the article PUNJAB.

SIRHIND.—A town in the native state of Patiala, 23 miles N. from Patialah, and 27 miles N.W. from Ambala. Lat. 30° 38′, long. 76° 29′.

SIRHOORPOOR, in the territory of Oude, a village on the route from Azimgurh to Sultanpoor cantonment, 46 miles W. of the former, 32 S.E. of the latter. Lat. 26° 15′, long. 82° 43′.

SIRINAGUR, "the town of Surya or the Sun," the capital of Cashmere, and at present more generally known by the same name as that of the valley at large. The town extends about four miles along both banks of the Jhelum or Behut, which here, deep and sluggish, winds in a very picturesque manner through the town, and adds much to the prospect, by the enlivening effect of the numerous and variously constructed vessels by which it is navigated. The north-west part of the town is the principal, and is situate on the right bank of the river; on the south-east and south is the suburb of Sher-Gerh, which has fortifications of no great strength, and contains the usual residence of the governor. This seat of government has two stories overtopping the ramparts, and a principal entrance communicating with the river by broad wooden stairs. On the north of the city rises a hill, called the Kohi Maran, Hari Parbat, or Hirney Parvat, of trap formation, and having an elevation of about 250 feet above the Jhelum: on the summit is an ill-constructed fort of slight strength, though, according to Hügel, it might easily be made impregnable. According to the statement of Vigne, the Mogul emperor Akbar caused a wall to be built round the base of the hill, a circuit of about 4,000 paces. Of the five gates in this wall, one bears an inscription, stating that the tower Naginagur, thus inclosed, was built A.H. 1006, cost 11,000,000 of rupees, and that 200 master-builders were employed on it. Of this great undertaking nothing remains but a handsome mosque; the rest has been reduced to a vast extent of shapeless ruins, at present totally uninhabited. Moorcroft draws a very repulsive picture of the city of Sirinagur. "The general character of the city of Cashmere is that of a confused mass of ill-favoured buildings, forming a complicated labyrinth of narrow and dirty lanes, scarcely broad enough for a single cart to pass, badly paved, and having a small gutter in the centre, full of filth, banked upon each side by a border of mire. The houses are in general two or three stories high; they are built of unburnt bricks and timber, the former serving for little else than to fill up the interstices of the latter. They are not plastered, are badly constructed, and are mostly in a neglected and ruinous condition, with broken doors or no doors at all, with shattered lattices, windows stopped up with boards, paper, or rags, walls out of the perpendicular, and pitched roofs threatening to fall. The roofs are formed of layers of birch-bark covered by a coating of earth, in which seeds, dropped by birds or wafted by the wind, have vegetated, and they are constantly overrun with grass, flowers, and seeds. The houses of the better class are commonly detached and surrounded by a wall and gardens, the latter of which often communicate with a canal. The condition of the gardens is no better than that of the buildings, and the whole presents a striking picture of wretchedness and decay."

The public buildings of this city are not in much better style than the private dwellings. The oldest structure is the tomb of the mother of a Cashmirian king, who reigned in the middle of the fifteenth century. It is built, in an octagonal form, of brick, the walls being seven or eight feet thick, and surmounted by a dome constructed with great strength and solidity, but altogether devoid of architectural beauty. The Jama Musjid, or "great mosque," is the most celebrated building of the city; and native estimate, which is probably exaggerated, represents it capable of containing 60,000 persons. The foundation and lower part of the walls are built of stone, the upper of brick. The whole is surmounted by a dome and spire rudely constructed of timber, and partly supported on pillars of the same materials; and of these there are 384. Every pillar is a pile of square deodar logs, each about a foot thick, and laid one over another, as beams are usually stored in a timber-yard, so that each face presents a succession of butts and sides. These pillars are about ten feet high, and seem to have been devised with a precautionary view against earthquakes, which are here of frequent occurrence, and have damaged the rest of the structure without shaking them, or causing them to deviate from the perpendicular. The deodar is a timber so durable, that though these pillars have stood nearly two centuries, they exhibit no symptoms of decay. The ground-plan of this spacious building is a square of about 400 feet. The mosque of Shah Hamedan is built of deodar, in a singular style of architecture, resembling the Chinese, but less fantastic and meretricious. The Jhelum is crossed by seven bridges. The piers of these are formed of deodar logs, arranged as in the pillars of the great mosque, the road being formed by beams of the same timber stretching from one pier to another. There are no parapets, nor side-rails of any kind, and as the beams are in most places some distance asunder, the passage of these singular bridges is not altogether free from danger. So durable is the material, so gentle the current of the Jhelum, and so exempt the climate of Cashmere from storms, that some of these apparently frail structures have lasted for several centuries. Houses are built on some of them, and in many places trees have spontaneously grown up. Close to the east of Siranagur is the city Dal or lake, described by Vigne as five miles in length from north to south, and two and a half miles in breadth from east to west. The water is very clear and not deep, in few places exceeding eight or ten feet. The lake is divided into two nearly equal parts by an artificial causeway, made across it in the direction from south-west to north-east. This is covered with rushes, and has the appearance of a green lane traversing the water. A single opening, bridged over, admits the passage of boats from one part of the lake to the other. Various tongues of land divide the Dal into inlets or basins, which have distinctive names. It is supplied with water by a stream called the Tybul, but which descends from the mountains bounding the valley on the north-east. This beautiful lake communicates with the Jhelum by a canal having floodgates, which remain open when the current sets from the lake towards the river. During inundations of the Jhelum, the floodgates are closed by the first rush of water towards the lake, which is thus prevented from overflowing the lower part of the city. That part of the city situate between the Jhelum and the lake is in several places intersected by canals, which, with proper care, would serve important commercial purposes, and contribute to salubrity and cleanliness, but in their present neglected state they must rather be classed amongst the deformities and disadvantages of this fallen city.

The Mar Canal is described by Vigne as a singular monument of the ancient prosperity of the city. "Boats pass along as at Venice. Its narrowness, for it does not exceed thirty feet in width; its walls of massive stone; its heavy single-arch bridges and landing-places of the same material; the gloomy passages leading down upon it, betoken the greatest antiquity, whilst the lofty and many-storied houses that rise directly from the water, supported only by thin trunks of deodar, seem ready to fall down upon the boats with every gust of wind. It could not but remind me of one of the old canals in Venice, and although far inferior in architectural beauty, is perhaps not without pretensions to equal singularity." The verdant and level margin of this beautiful piece of water was the favourite resort of the Mogul emperors and their courtiers, and is still in many places overspread with the relics of their pleasure-grounds and palaces. Of these, the most celebrated is the Shahlimar, where Moore's imagination has pictured the closing scene of Lalla Rookh. This pleasure-ground, laid down by the emperor Jehan Gir, is shaded by noble chunars or plane-trees, now, from age, verging to decay. It is, according to Vigne, 700 or 800 yards in length by 280 in breadth. The principal building is placed at the upper end of this inclosure, and is thus described by Vigne in rather singular terms:—"It is of polished black marble, and consisting of two rooms on either side of a passage, which runs through the centre of the building. On the east and west sides of it there is a corridor, six and a half yards wide, formed by a range of six polygonal pillars, about thirteen feet in height, and of the same material. They are said to have been taken from the ruins of a Hindoo temple, but the capitals and bases appear to have been the work of a Mahomedan architect, and the latter in particular are most beautifully scalloped and polished. The building itself is twenty-four yards square, the north and south sides being ornamented with Saracenic reliefs. It stands in the centre of a square reservoir, which is also lined with black marble, whose sides are about fifty-four yards long, and in its whole circumference contains 147 fountains, which are made to play on holidays, the reservoir being filled by the stream, which enters it in the shape of a cascade. The height from the stone floor to the roof is about twenty feet. The latter may originally have been pointed like the Tuscan roof, but as it is now covered with thatch, its original shape cannot be determined. The stream thence descends from the reservoir by a shallow canal cut through the centre of the gardens, and lined with marble, and it falls over an artificial cascade at each of the three lodges through which it passes in its way to the lake. A broad causeway or walk runs on each side of it, overshadowed by large chunar-trees, and here and there a few turfed walks branch off at right angles into the shrubberies, in which are little else than wild plum-trees, planted for the sake of their white blossoms. At the end of one of these is a decayed bath, built of brick, and the walls around are covered with ivy." The view of the lake from the vicinity of the city is very beautiful, the entrance lying between two striking eminences —Huri Parbut on the west, and on the east the Tukhti Suliman, of greater elevation and more imposing aspect. Between these, a magnificent crescent of mountains rises on the north, the east, and south-east, and on the north-west the huge summit of Haramuk towers in the distance with great grandeur. The foreground is formed by the expanse of the clear water of the lake, in many places mantled with the rich green leaves and brilliant blossoms of the water-lily (Nelumbium speciosum), and studded with green islets, in many instances tufted with trees. The beauty of this delightful scene is heightened by the appearance of the shore, teeming with the richest verdure, and ornamented with groves of noble plane-trees and poplars. The floating gardens formed of matted reeds, weeds, and sedge, overlaid with earth, and bearing abundant crops of melons and cucumbers, though on account of their singularity attracting the notice of the traveller, form no feature in the landscape, being at a short distance nearly undistinguishable from the contiguous bank. The scene is, however, enlivened by the numerous boats employed in taking the fish with which the lake abounds. Formerly many persons lived by taking the countless water-fowl which frequent the lake, but these are now unmolested, in consequence of the strictly enforced orders of the Sikh rulers. The appearance of the antique city falling piecemeal into ruin, when viewed at some distance, is no unpleasing feature in the prospect. "The aspect of the city itself is curious, but not particularly striking. It presents an innumerable assemblage of gable-ended houses, interspersed with the pointed and metallic tops of musjis or mosques, melon-grounds, sedgy inlets from the lake, and narrow canals fringed with rows of willows and poplars. The surface of the lake itself is perfectly tranquil, and the very vivid reflections which cover its surface are only disturbed by the dabbling of wild-fowl, or the rippling that follows the track of the distant boat." In the more prosperous ages of Cashmere, this lake was the scene of the frequent pleasure-parties of the volatile and voluptuous Cashmirians. According to Foster, "when a Kashmirian, even of the lowest order, finds himself in the possession of a few shillings, he loses no time in assembling his party, and, launching into the lake, solaces himself until the last farthing is spent." This fondness for festive pleasures is especially displayed at the "Feast of Roses," which flowers are produced in Cashmere of unrivalled beauty and fragrance. "The season when the rose first opens into blossom is celebrated with much festivity by the Kashmirians, who resort in crowds to the adjacent gardens, and enter into scenes of gaiety and pleasure rarely known among other Asiatic nations." As oppression and consequent misery have "frozen the genial current of the soul" in the Cashmirians, that romantic festival has degenerated into the feast of Singaras or water-nuts, celebrated on the 1st of May, by ascending to the summit of the Tukhti Suliman, and feasting there, "eating more particularly of singaras." Sirinagur was formerly much celebrated for its manufacture of shawls, paper, leather, firearms, and attar of rose; but these have nearly disappeared under the oppression which has long crushed the energies of a people naturally ingenious, industrious, and persevering. Moorcroft, who visited the city in 1823, estimated the population at 240,000; the judicious and cautious Elphinstone, in the early part of the present century, at "from 150,000 to 200,000." By another authority the population of Sirinagur was subsequently computed not to exceed 40,000. Vigne, as well as Cunningham, estimates the population at 80,000. This appalling reduction of the population in so brief a period has been the combined effect of oppression, pestilence, and famine. Sirinagur is generally considered to have been founded by Pravarasena, who reigned in Cashmere from A.D. 128 to 176. It is supposed to have succeeded to a more ancient city of the same name, the ruins of which are conjectured by some to be observable at Wentipur, by others at Matan. The elevation of Sirinagur above the sea has been the subject of much controversy, though stated by several intelligent Europeans who have resided at the city for a considerable time, and made this point the specific object of their notice. There can be little doubt that it exceeds 5,000 feet, and falls below 6,000, and 5,500 may be taken as the mean and probable amount. Lat. 34° 5′, long. 74° 57′.

SIRKUN FORT, in the district of British Gurhwal, lieut.-gov. of the N.W. Provinces, a town on the route from Almora to the native state of Gurhwal, 43 miles N.W. by N. of the former. Lat. 30° 10′, long. 79° 20′.

SIRMOUR, a hill state under British protection, is bounded on the north by the hill states of Bulsun and Joobul; on the east by the Jhaunsar Bawur pergunnah of the Deyra Dhoon, from which it is separated by the rivers Tons and Jumna; on the south and west by Sirhind, the territories of the rajah of Putteeala and Keonthul. It lies between lat. 30° 25′—31° 2′, long. 77° 5′—77° 53′, and has an area of 1,075 square miles. Except a very small tract about Nahun, on the south-western extremity, where a few streams rise, and flow south-westward to the Soorsutti and the Gagur rivers, the whole of Sirmour lies in the drainage or basin of the Jumna, which receives from this tract the Giree, and its feeders the Jalal and the Paloor. The river Tons, the great western arm of the stream, called lower down the Jumna, flows along the eastern boundary of Sirmour, and on the right side receives from it two small streams, the Minus and the Naeraee. The surface generally, though irregularly, declines in elevation from the north to the south; the elevation of the Chur Peak, and station, on the northern frontier, being respectively 12,150 and 11,689 feet above the sea, and that of the confluence of the Giree and Jumna, on the southern, being 1,516. From that confluence the Kyarda Doon stretches westward, forming the southern part of Sirmour, and extending about twenty-five miles in length from east to west, and six in breadth, terminating to the west at the eastern base of the Nahun ridge. Its surface rises gradually to the westward from the Jumna to the Ghatusun Pass, a distance of fourteen miles. From Ghatusun, having an elevation of 2,500 feet above the sea, the country falls both eastward, as already stated, and westward, the streams in the former direction flowing to the Jumna, in the latter to the Markunda and other streams holding their course to the Soorsutti and Gagur. The Kyarda Doon is bounded on the south by the Sewalik range. These are of recent formation, and abound in fossil remains of animals, marine and terrestrial. They have probably an average elevation of about 2,500 feet above the sea, and are crossed by the river Markunda at the pass of Maginund. On the north, the Doon is bounded by the Sub-Himalaya, the formation of which is thus described by Fraser:—"Apparently of a hard stone, very apt to crack and break in sharp irregular ridges, which, on exposure to the air, easily bursts in small fragments, and then falls into dust. It consists, I think, of clay and sand, and is generally of a dusky brown colour, or of a brownish grey." The formation is probably the same as that in the vicinity of Bahr, a short distance farther north, and described with more precision by Jameson, as consisting of "sandstone, slate, clay, and trap." Govan describes this portion of the Sub-Himalaya as from 4,000 to 5,000 feet above the level of the sea, and consisting principally of a very compact and hard sandstone of light bluish-gray colour, and spotted with dark purple. In some places the formation becomes slaty, or rests on clay-slate; in others, limestone of an earthy fracture, graywacke, and graywacke slate. The Sain ridge rises to the north-west of the range bounding the Kyarda Doon; on the north, it stretches along the right bank of the river Giri, and has a massive contour, rising at its south-eastern extremity into the summit of Thundu Bhawanee, having an elevation of 5,700 feet above the sea; at its north-western, into that of Sursu Debi, of 6,299. Its formation is of limestone, which extends generally to the bed of the Giri, where the slate rock commences. Beyond the Giri, and at the northern extremity of Sirmour, is the remarkable peak of Chur, 12,150 feet above the sea, connected by a transverse ridge with the outer Himalaya, and itself a central point, from which subordinate ranges ramify in every direction. Of the subordinate ridges, some summits attain a considerable height: Rajgarh and Chitirown Debi, west of the Chur, have respectively elevations of 7,115 and 7,048 feet above the sea; the elevation of Jamu Peak, to the south-east of these, is 6,852 feet; that of Chundpore, near the right bank of the Tons, 8,561; and that of Kangra, little farther south, 6,6 60. The summit is composed of vast tabular masses of granite, which, though compact, is readily decomposed by the weather. Sirmour, though its rocks consist of formations usually metalliferous, at present yields little mineral wealth. At Kalsi a copper-mine was formerly worked, but has been for some years abandoned. A lead-mine is worked profitably, and gives employment to above 100 men. Iron-ore is abundant, and smelted with charcoal on the spot, where it is sold at the rate of about a penny a pound. The extensive slate strata are in some places worked to supply roofing, and in situations admitting of easy transport to the plains, might be found a source of great wealth. The climate varies, from that of Chur, where the surface is under snow the greater part of the year, to the stifling malaria of the Kyarda Doon, of which the greater part is a mere desert, untrodden by human beings, except by woodcutters and collectors of gum catechu, yielded in great abundance by the mimosa, which flourishes there. The shape of the Kyarda Doon, resembling a deep narrow trench, shut in on every side except to the east, where it opens to the Jumna, and having a deep alluvial swampy soil, teeming with rank vegetation, confers on it an aspect and climate similar to those in most intertropical tracts. The air is from these causes fatal to the human constitution, so that in 1815 there were only 600 inhabitants in a tract which, if fully cultivated, would probably maintain thirty times that number. Prior to the Ghoorka invasion, however, the Kyarda Doon is said to have contained eighty-four populous villages. At present, extensive thickets of bamboos indicate the character of the climate. So dense are the forests, that the sportsman finds difficulty in making his way through them in search of wild elephants, tigers, leopards, bears, and hyænas, with which they abound. Wild peafowl are in many places very numerous, being unmolested, in consequence of the superstitious regard of the natives. Rice, cotton, tobacco, opium, capsicum, turmeric, ginger, and all the pulse and esculent vegetables of the plains, are cultivated in the Kyarda Doon, and in the lower valleys along the banks of the rivers, where the heat is sometimes as great as in the lowlands of Hindoostan, and to which the periodical rains of the monsoons extend. In the northern part, according to Blane, "it is said that rain never falls;" but as the rainy monsoon is in some degree felt in Koonawur, so much farther north, and behind the lofty barrier of the outer Himalaya, such a statement seems extraordinary. Wheat and barley are successfully cultivated, but the principal crop is marwa, a small black seed produced by the Eleusine coracana (Cynosurus coracanus of Linnæus, or "thick-spiked dog-grass"), a most prolific vegetable, as, according to Dr. Royle, the ordinary produce is 120 fold, and in one variety 500. Bang or hemp, for narcotic intoxication, is also cultivated. In many places there are two crops in succession annually; the first of wheat, barley, poppy, oilseeds, or marwa; the second of rice, cotton, and tobacco. The rice is very fine, and cultivated in situations suited for irrigation, the ground being arranged in terraces. The natives are indefatigable, repeatedly turning up with the plough their naturally sterile soil, and aiding its productive powers by manuring or fallowing. The grain is trodden out by kine in inclosures floored with slate slabs: the straw is used for fodder, and, being insufficient in quantity, is eked out with dried grass gathered from the jungles, and the leaves of trees, especially pines, oaks, and mulberries. Men and women share the labours of agriculture with equal industry and perseverance. The kine are humped, generally black, and for the most part well tended, fat, handsome, and larger than those of the plains. They are kept for their milk, most of which is used to yield butter or ghee: the Hindoo superstition of the natives preserves them from slaughter. The houses are frequently three stories high, built of stone. bonded with timber, of which there is great abundance, as forests of fine firs, oaks, rhododendrons, horse-chestnuts, and some other trees, overspread the mountains. The roofs are generally of slate, but sometimes of shingles. The family inhabits the upper story, which is surrounded with an inclosed balcony six or eight feet beyond the wall, and the villages, usually situate on the slopes or tops of hills, have a picturesque and pleasing effect in the landscape. Sometimes the houses are slender and lofty, so as to have the form of towers fifty or sixty feet high. These, like the others, are formed of uncemented stone, bonded with wood, on the decay of which, the whole fabric becomes ruinous and untenantable; and as the natives find it less costly to build new houses than repair the old ones, the country abounds with the relics of former habitations in every stage of decadence.

The manufactures of this poor territory are limited to the smelting of a trifling quantity of iron, and the working up of wool and other raw native produce for home consumption. There is no commerce, unless a very trifling carrying-business be considered as such. The state of the roads, or rather paths, as described by Blane, is incompatible with any considerable transit. "The communications through the country are imperfect, and totally unfit for the marching of troops exceeding a few companies. A path of a foot and a half in width, with the mountain rising precipitously on one side, and a deep glen on the other, if not very rugged, is esteemed by the natives a good road. Beasts of burthen are never used beyond Nahun, or Kalsi; and it is with difficulty that a led horse, even of the indigenous breed, accompanies the traveller." The natives of Sirmour are of the physical type called Caucasian by physiologists, and obviously of a race allied to the Hindoos of the plains: on the north-east there is an admixture of the Mongolian race. Goitre is very prevalent amongst all classes, and is sometimes extirpated by the knife. The stature of these mountaineers is low; but they are active and strong, carrying over their rugged roads loads of sixty or seventy pounds weight twelve or fifteen miles in the course of the day. The dress of the middling classes consists of a simple tunic or frock, reaching down to the knees, trousers, and a scarf usually worn across the shoulders, but when the sun is hot thrown over the head: the lower orders content themselves with a blanket girt round the waist: the higher classes dress after the fashion of Hindoostan, and wear the Sikh turban. The women enjoy an unfortunate notoriety for indelicacy and total want of chastity. Polyandry is universal, several brothers cohabiting by a sort of legalized union with the same woman. As this hateful practice leads to what political economists would term a "surplus female population," the occurrence of an inconvenient excess is staved off by the provident arrangements of selling the superfluous stock to the inhabitants of the plains, where they are held in esteem. The price of the "helpmeet" of man varies from five to twenty pounds, the rate rising or falling according to the degree of beauty or other attraction possessed by the object of sale. The British government has prohibited this traffic, which is, however, still covertly practised. The general character of these mountaineers has been variously delineated. Fraser's picture is a dark one. He says, "All are bad. They are revengeful and treacherous, deficient in all good qualities, abandoned in morals, and vicious in their habits. Female chastity is here quite unknown; and murder, robbery, and outrage of every kind, are here regarded with indifference." It is to be remarked, that the juncture at which Fraser visited the country was likely to give scope to the worst passions of a people long subject to the cruel oppression of the Goorkhas, and then at once given up to anarchy, in consequence of the expulsion of that people by the success of the British arms. Gerard, writing fifteen years later, describes the people as liberal and obliging. "Private stealing," he says, "is almost unknown; and of all the many Europeans who have visited the part of the hills of which I am treating, none of them ever lost a single article. I have often travelled over this tract without a guard, and had I occasion to go through it again, I would never take a single sepoy." Possibly the statements of all travellers as to the moral characteristics of a strange people should be received with caution, as their stay is rarely of sufficient length to enable them to perceive and appreciate either all the good or all the evil which longer and closer acquaintance might detect. The religion prevailing in Sirmour is mainly Brahminism, to which is added the superstitious adoration and dread of innumerable local divinities, with which the imagination of the natives has peopled every hill, dell, or grove. The lives of kine are sacred. The people are divided into two castes, as in the plains, and Brahmins abound. The suttee, or practice of burning women alive with the dead bodies of their husbands, was formerly frequent; and in the instances of the death of men of rank, not only the favoured wife, but a whole host of females, were doomed to blaze on the pyre of their deceased lord. The strong disapprobation of the British government has caused the diabolical rite to disappear throughout the hill states. The language of the natives is a dialect of Hindostanee.

Sirmour is governed by a rajah, who claims a Rajpoot descent: indeed, nearly all classes make the claim, except the lowest, who style themselves either coolies or labourers, or chumars, persons who flay cattle and work in leather. The rajah holds his possessions by a grant made on the expulsion of the Goorkhas by the British government, and dated 21st September, 1815. The Kyarda Doon was granted by the same power on the 5th September, 1833: the rajah, however, ill repaid this liberality by fomenting in Kuhloor an insurrection against the East-India Company, who, in consequence, punished him by fine. The annual revenue is estimated at 10,000*l.*; by Moorcroft at 4,000*l.*; but this was before the annexation of Kyarda Doon. Nahun, at the western extremity of the Kyarda Doon, is the residence of the rajah, and the only town in his dominion, as Kyarda is a mere village, and Kalsi has latterly so dwindled as to be no better. The whole territory is divided into twenty-seven pergunnahs or districts: the aggregate population is estimated at 75,595. According to Francis Hamilton, the ruling family has held Sirmour fifteen generations since its acquisition by the first rajah, a scion of the house of Jessulmeer. In 1379 it was made tributary by Firoz Shah, of Delhi, and that prince and several of his successors frequently visited it in their hunting excursions. In 1809 the Goorkhas conquered the country, and in 1815 were conquered by the British, who restored the rajah, as has been already mentioned. His military force is not great: it appears to consist of about 400 infantry and two guns.

SIRONJ, in Malwa, a town lying within the territory possessed by the noted Patan freebooter Ameer Khan, is situate on the route from Nusseerabad to Saugor, 272 miles S.E. of the former, 78 N.W. of the latter. It is built at the base of a ghat or descent from the elevated table-land farther north. The country towards the east, south, and west, is open, fertile, and well cultivated. Sironj, though still a large town, is much decayed from the prosperity in which Tavernier found it in the seventeenth century, when it was crowded with merchants and artisans, and famous for its fine muslins and chintzes, the highly-prized objects of an extensive traffic. The walls which surrounded the town in the time of Tieffenthaler have disappeared, but the fine bazar which he describes remains. There are two caravanserais and many mosques, but no Hindoo temples; though outside the town is the huge black head of an idol, which the Hindoos anoint with oil and butter. West of the town is a rectangular fort, with a square tower at each angle, and to the south a tank of good water. Water of good quality is also supplied in abundance by a small stream flowing from an eminence west of the town: that obtained from wells is brackish. Sironj, with the appertaining pergunnah, was, in 1798, granted to Ameer Khan, by Jeswunt Rao Holkar; in 1809, the threatening attitude assumed towards Nagpore by Ameer Khan led to the advance upon Sironj of a British force under Colonel Close: subsequently, in 1817, this town and district, with other territories, were guaranteed by the British government to the ameer. The territory is estimated to yield an annual revenue of 2,00,000 rupees, or 20,000*l.*: its area is 344 square miles. The estimate of its population is included in that of the entire possessions of Ameer Khan, for which see the article on Tonk. Distance of the town from Oojein, N.E., 140 miles ; S.W. from Allahabad 280, S. from Agra 213, S. from Delhi 310. Lat. 24° 6′, long. 77° 42′.

SIROTE, in the Rajpoot state of Jeypore, a town on the route from Agra to Mow, 62 miles S.W. of former, 350 N.E. of latter. It is inclosed by a mud rampart, and has within a square mud fort with double wall and ditch. There is a bazar here, and supplies and water are abundant. Lat. 26° 49′, long. 77° 12′.

SIRPOOR.—A town in the British district of Candeish, presidency of Bombay, 64 miles N.N.E. of Malligaum. Lat. 21° 20′, long. 75°.

SIRPOORUH, in the British district of Mynpoorie, a small town or village on the route from Allygurh to Futtehghur, and 57 miles S.E. of the former. It has a small bazar, and is supplied with water from wells and tanks. Lat. 27° 38′, long. 78° 56′.

SIRRINUGGUR, in the British territory of Saugur and Nerbudda, lieut.-gov. of the N.W. Provinces, a town on the route from Dumoh to Seuni, 63 miles N. of the latter. Lat. 22° 57′, long. 79° 40′.

SIRRUD, in the Rajpoot state of Jessulmeer, a group of villages on the route from the town of Beekaneer to that of Jessulmeer, and 70 miles S.W. of the former. It is situate in a woody plain, and has an abundant supply of good water from a tank, and from wells about ninety feet deep. The road in this part of the route is in some places hard and good, in others sandy and deep. Lat. 27° 25′, long. 72° 33′.

SIRSA, in the British district of Bareilly, division of Pillibheet, lieut.-gov. of the N.W. Provinces, a village on the route from Bareilly to Petoragurh, and 36 miles N.E. of the former. Lat. 28° 40′, long. 79° 52′.

SIRSAH, in the British district of Bhutteeana, lieut.-gov. of the N.W. Provinces, a small town on the route from Hansee to Bhutnair, and 60 miles N.W. of the former. Lat. 29° 31′, long. 75° 5′.

SIRSALLA.—A town in Hyderabad, or territory of the Nizam, 179 miles N.W. by W. from Hyderabad, and 111 miles E. from Ahmednuggur. Lat. 18° 59′, long. 76° 28′.

SIRSAWA, in the British district of Suharunpoor, lieut.-gov. of the N.W. Provinces, a town on the route from Suharunpoor to Ambala, 10 miles W.N.W. of the former. Lat. 30° 2′, long. 77° 29′.

SIRSEE, in the British district of Moradabad, lieut.-gov. of the N.W. Provinces, a town with a bazar, on the route from Allygurh to the town of Moradabad, and 16 miles S. of the latter. It is situate near the small river Sote, in a level, open, cultivated country. Lat. 28° 38′, long. 78° 42′.

SIRSEEAH, in the British district of Goruckpoor, lieut.-gov. of the N.W. Provinces, a town on the route from Goruckpoor to Nepal, 46 miles N. by E. of the former. Lat. 27° 20′, long. 83° 32′.

SIRSEEGHURREE, a small fortified place in the jaghire of Dadree, lieut.-gov. of the N.W. Provinces. Lat. 28° 49′, long. 76° 20′.

SIRSOO, in the British district of Goruckpoor, lieut.-gov. of the N.W. Provinces, a town on the route from Goruckpoor to Jounpoor, 22 miles S.W. of the former. Lat. 26° 29′, long. 83° 9′.

SIRSOUL, in the British district of Cawnpore, lieut.-gov. of the N.W. Provinces, a town on the route from the cantonment of Cawnpore to Futtehpoor, and 15 miles S.E. of the former. Lat. 26° 18′, long. 80° 33′.

SIRSOUL, in the British district of Allyghur, lieut.-gov. of the N.W. Provinces, a village on the route from the cantonment of Allyghur to that of Delhi, and three miles W. of the former. Lat. 27° 55′, long. 78° 6′.

SIRZA, in the British district of Agra, lieut.-gov. of the N.W. Provinces, a town situate in lat. 27° 21′, long. 77° 43′.

SISAHEE.—A village in the British district of Hurriana, lieut.-gov. of the N.W. Provinces. Lat. 29° 10′, long. 76° 6′.

SISSANDY.—A town in Oude, 18 miles S. from Lucknow, and 49 miles N. by E. from Futtehpoor. Lat. 26° 37′, long. 80° 59′.

SISSERY, in the district of Bainswara, territory of Oude, a town 15 miles S. of Lucknow. It was lately purchased by the chukledar, or governor of the district, who expended considerable sums on the repairs of the defences. The chukledar pays to the government of Oude an annual quit-rent of 1,32,000 rupees, which sum is only six-tenths of what he himself collects from his ryots or tenants. Lat. 26° 38′, long. 80° 50′.

SISSORAH, in the territory of Oude, a village on the route from Bareilly to Lucknow, 59 miles S.E. of the former, 96 N.W. of the latter. Lat. 28° 2′, long. 80° 13′.

SISWAL, a village in the British district Hurriana, division of Delhi, lieut.-gov. of Agra. Lat. 29° 12′, long. 75° 25′.

SITAKUND, in the British district of Bhagulpore, lieut.-gov. of Bengal, a celebrated hot well four miles S.E. of the city of Mongheer. It is much revered by the Brahminists, in consequence of a legend concerning Sita, the wife of Rama, the renowned legendary king of Ayodha. Sita had been abducted by Ravan, tyrant of Lanka or Ceylon ; but when restored to her husband, she asserted that her conjugal purity had remained inviolate. The gods, however insisted on her undergoing the fiery ordeal ; whereupon, at the spot where the spring now is, she threw herself "into a pit filled with fire, and when she came pure from its flames, warm water flowed from the rock, as it continues to do at this day." The water rises in the bottom of a basin inclosed with masonry, and is too hot to admit the immersion of the person uninjured. It is perfectly tasteless, and when cold is esteemed remarkably fine, and conveyed to the very great distances for the use of wealthy and fastidious water-drinkers. The temperature varies from 92° to 138°. Lat. 25° 20′, long. 86° 31′.

SITLAH.—A town in the British district of Bancoora, lieut.-gov. of Bengal, 14 miles N.E. ot Bancoora. Lat. 23° 22′, long. 87° 15′.

SITOONDA.—A town in Hyderabad, or territory of the Nizam, 48 miles N. by E. from Aurungabad, and 62 miles E. from Malligaum. Lat. 20° 32′, long. 75° 29′.

SITTANG.—A town of Burmah, situate on the left bank of the Sittang river, and 72 miles N.N.E. from Rangoon. Lat. 17° 42′, long. 96° 49′.

SITTANG, a navigable river, rises in lat. 21° 40′, long. 96° 50′, and, flowing south for 230 miles through Burmah, and for about 190 miles forming the boundary between the Tenasserim provinces and Pegu, falls into the sea, in lat. 16° 50′, long. 97° 15′.

SITURWALA, in the British district of Bijnour, lieut.-gov. of the N.W. Provinces, a village on the route from Moradabad to Hurdwar, and 40 miles S.E. of the latter. Lat. 29° 30′, long. 78° 28′.

SIVAGANGA, in the Mysore, a town inclosed with a rampart, situate at the east base of a lofty mountain. Distance from Bangalore, N.W., 28 miles; Seringapatam, N.E., 65. Lat. 13° 11′, long. 77° 18′.

SIWANEE, in the British district of Hissar, lieut.-gov. of the N.W. Provinces, a town on the route from Hissar to Jhoonjhnoo, 19 miles S.S.W. of the former. Lat. 28° 53′, long. 75° 44′.

SLICKEEALEE, in the Jetch Dooab division of the Punjab, a town situated 12 miles from the right bank of the Chenaub, 51 miles N.N.W. of the town of Lahore. Lat. 32° 33′, long. 73° 52′.

SOAMWARPETT.—A town in the British district of Coorg, presidency of Madras, 70 miles E.S.E. of Mangalore. Lat. 12° 34′, long. 75° 53′.

SOANG, in Bussahir, a village of Koonawar, situate near the left bank of the Buspa. The vicinity is pleasant, abounding in apricot and walnut-trees, and producing pines of great size; one of them, measured by Gerard, was thirty feet in girth. The crops are poor, and consist of wheat, barley, buckwheat, amaranthus or cockscomb, pease, and some other pulse. The climate has little to recommend it; snow lies for five months, and, during summer, the periodical rains prevail, though not so heavy as in Hindoostan. Elevation above the sea 9,100 feet. Lat. 31° 26′, long. 78° 15′.

SOANGIER.—A town in the British district of Candeish, presidency of Bombay, 40 miles N.N.E. of Malligaum. Lat. 21° 3′, long. 74° 45′.

SOAUTH, or SAUNTE, a small district of the Rewa Caunta, in the province of Guzerat, presidency of Bombay, bounded on the west by Loonawarra; on the north by the Myhee Caunta; on the east by Jhallode, belonging to Scindia, and by Banswarra; and on the south by Barrea. It is situate between lat. 22° 55′ and 23° 33′, long. 73° 45′ and 74° 10′. It is sometimes called Soauth Rampoor, from a village of the latter name on the Sookee, which unites with the Cheboota, a tributary to the Myhee. The fort and town of Soauth stand three or four miles from the open country to the westward, from which it is separated by a continuance of jungly hills of moderate elevation. The fort is built on the western face of a high rocky hill, which it crowns, but the lower walls commence from the base, where there are some tolerably well-built small houses, forming a village in which the rajah's palace is situated. The country of Soauth is strong, difficult to penetrate, troublesome to subdue, and but indifferently productive, yielding only a revenue of about 70,000 rupees.

In the year 1803 the chief entered into an alliance with the British government, and agreed, in lieu of the tribute paid to Dowlut Row Scindia, to maintain at its own expense, devoid of every claim to remuneration, a military force for the defence of his territories, and to oppose any attempt of a hostile power to effect a passage of troops through it. This treaty was similar to that made with the neighbouring state of Loonawarra, and it continued in force only for a similar period, viz. till the year 1806. In 1819 Soauth was included in the arrangement made with Scindia, and it is now one of the protected states. It is subject to a tribute of 7,000 rupees to Scindia, the payment of which is guaranteed by the British government.

Soauth was formed, like its neighbour Loonawarra, into a raj by usurpation or grants from other states. The present rajah, named Bhowan Sing, was born in the year 1833. During his minority, the affairs were conducted by his mother, the Baee, whom it was found necessary to assist in the administration of affairs by stationing a thannadar to report all matters of importance, and carry into effect the orders of the Rewa Caunta agency, under whose political superintendence this state has been placed. Under this arrangement, tranquillity has been preserved, the audacity of the Bheels checked, and the feudatory chiefs reduced to obedience.

The father of Bhowan Sing was Kullian Sing, the uncle of his predecessor Kesree Sing. The rana derives descent from the ancient Powars of Dhar, who, beyond all others, are celebrated in the ancient history of Central India. They were subdued by the Mahometans in the general conquest of the country, when this family took refuge in the wilds of Soauth, and are now represented by the petty rajahs of that district. Soauth, the principal place, is in lat. 23° 10′, long. 73° 47′.

SOBADAH.—A town of Eastern India, in the British district of Northern Cachar, 73 miles S. by E. of Nowgong. Lat. 25° 20′, long. 92° 59′.

SOBORAH.—A town in Scinde, situate in the territory belonging to Ali Moorad, 61 miles E.S.E. from Bukkur, and 74 miles W.N.W. from Jessulmeer. Lat. 27° 21′, long. 69° 51′.

SOBRAON.—The name of a small village on the left bank of the Sutlej, and within the country under the management of the commissioner and superintendent of the Cis-Sutlej territories, near which, on the 10th of February, 1846, an obstinate battle was fought between the British army, under Sir Hugh Gough, and a Sikh force of great strength, formidably intrenched. By the exercise of extraordinary courage and perseverance on the part of the assailants, the intrenchments were in succession forced, and the enemy ultimately driven across the river with immense slaughter. The Sikh army was estimated at 30,000 strong; the British force did not exceed half that number. The event of the battle entirely cleared the left bank of the Sutlej of the Sikh force, and the victors immediately afterwards crossed the river and entered the Punjab. Lat. 31° 8′, long. 74° 54′.

SODAKHOR, in the Rajpoot state of Jessulmeer, a village on the route from the town of Beekaneer to that of Jessulmeer, and 34 miles N.E. of the latter. It has a small fort, fifty houses, four shops, and a well yielding a good supply of water. The road in this part of the route is tolerably good. Lat. 27° 3′, long. 71° 31′.

SOEGAUM.—See SOORGAUM.

SOFAHUN, in Cashmere, a small town at the south-eastern extremity of the valley. Here are the only iron-mines in the province; and the works have greatly fallen away. The iron is considered inferior to that obtained from Bajour and Chinese Tartary. Sofahun is in lat. 33° 32′, long. 75° 12′.

SOGAM.—A town within the dominions of Gholab Singh, the ruler of Cashmere, situate on the left bank of the Jhelum river, and 37 miles N.W. from Sirinagur. Lat. 34° 30′, long. 74° 35′.

SOHAGI GHAT, in the tract of Boghelcund, in the territory of Rewa, a pass on the route from Allahabad to the town of Rewa, and 36 miles S.W. of the former. The village of Sohagi is situate five miles from the right bank of the Tons. "At five furlongs from the village of Sohagi, the ascent commences, and continues for about a quarter of a mile very steep and rugged, path winding, and practicable for laden cattle with difficulty; remainder of the road rugged and rocky, but comparatively level, passing through jungle. Two easy ascents of about 100 yards each, near the end of the stage; no village; water from tank in the jungle." This pass is an indenture in the brow of the Kutra range, forming the north-eastern buttress of the second plateau, by which the elevated region of Bundelcund rises above the valley of the Ganges, lying to the north-east. The village of Sohagi, situate at the base or northern extremity of the pass, has about 130 houses, including twelve shops, and is supplied with water from a never-drying tank and a pucka or brick-lined well. Four miles north-west of the village, the river Tons falls over a rock the depth of 200 feet; and as the elevation above the sea, of the waterway, at that point is 890 feet, that of the crest of the pass probably exceeds 900. Lat. 24° 58′, long. 81° 45′.

SOHAGPOOR.—A town in the British district of Saugor and Nerbudda, lieut.-gov. of the N.W. Provinces. Little more than the name and locality have been made public respecting it, though it is the principal place of a large district, and the station of a small civil establishment. Sohagpoor, originally possessed by a Gond chief tributary to the rajah of Garha Mandla, was, after a long period of anarchy and devastating warfare, subjugated, A.D. 1798, by Ragojee Bhonsla, rajah of Nagpore, and subsequently ceded by that state to the British government, in 1818, by the eleventh article of the treaty of Nagpore. Sohagpoor is distant E. from Saugor 170 miles, E. from Jubbulpoor 90, S. from Allahabad 150. Lat. 23° 20′, long. 81° 28′.

The territory of which this town is the chief place, forms a subdivision under the jurisdiction of the political agent for the Saugor and Nerbudda provinces: it has an area of 2,896 miles, and a population of 78,225.

SOHAGPOOR, in the British district of Saugor and Nerbudda, lieut.-gov. of the N.W. Provinces, a town on the route from Hoshungabad to Goona, 32 miles E. of former, 75 W. of latter. It has a bazar. Elevation above the sea 1,515 feet. Lat. 22° 40′, long. 78° 15′.

SOHAWUL, in the Saugor and Nerbudda territory, lieut.-gov. of the N.W. Provinces, a town, with bazar, in the jaghire of the same name. It is situate on the route, by Rewah. from Allahabad to Saugor, 168 miles S.W. of Allahabad, and on the river Sutni, here crossed by ford fifty yards wide. It was formerly defended by a fort, of massive proportions but rude construction, and now in ruins. Elevation above the sea 1,059 feet. The jaghire of which this town is the chief place, contains an area of 179 square miles, with a population of 80,000. With the view of relieving its chief from pecuniary embarrassment, the British government has consented to undertake the management of the raj. Lat. of town 24° 35′, long. 80° 50′.

SOHERPUR, in British district Banda, lieut.-gov. of the N.W. Provinces, a village on route by Chila Tara Ghat, from Cawnpore to town of Banda, 18 miles N. of the latter. Lat. 25° 44′, long. 80° 32′.

SOHNPOOR.—See SONEPOOR.

SOHOLA.—A town in the British district of Sumbulpoor, on the south-west frontier of Bengal, presidency of Bengal, 40 miles W. by S. of Sumbulpoor. Lat. 21° 18′, long. 83° 28′.

SOHROH.—A town in the British district of Balasore, one of the divisions of Cuttack, lieut.-gov. of Bengal, 22 miles S.W. of Balasore. Lat. 21° 16′, long. 86° 46′.

SOHUREEA.—A town in the British district of Sarun, lieut.-gov. of Bengal, 53 miles N.W. of Bettiah. Lat. 27° 20′, long. 84°.

SOKINDA, one of the Cuttack mehals, situate on the western border of the British district of Cuttack, presidency of Bengal. Sokindagur, the chief town, is in lat. 20° 54′, long. 85° 50′.

SOLAGEERY.—A town in the British district of Salem, presidency of Madras, 71 miles N. of Salem. Lat. 12° 40′, long. 78° 7′.

SOLANI.—A river rising at the south-western base of the Sewalik range, in about lat. 30° 13′, long. 77° 55′. It is crossed by the route from Dehra to Suharunpore, in lat. 30° 4′, long. 77° 51′. It holds a course of about fifty-five miles, generally south-westerly, and falls into the Ganges on the right side, in lat. 29° 3′, long. 78° 1′.

This river is crossed by the Ganges Canal, and to effect the passage, works of extraordinary character became necessary. Across the valley through which the river flows, the canal is conducted generally by means of an earthen embankment, protected by walls of masonry. But this could not be continued throughout, as no provision would have existed for passing the waters of the Solani. To provide this, the river has been bridged by an aqueduct of stone, the bed of which affords transit to the canal. This magnificent work rests upon fifteen arches, each having a span of fifty feet; thus giving a clear waterway of 750 feet for the passage of the river. The strength of this work is enormous, and its duration almost appears destined to be co-existent with that of the earth on which it rests. It is supported by a series of blocks of masonry, sunk twenty feet below the bed of the stream, most of them measuring twenty feet also in length and breadth, the full depth (twenty feet) being never departed from. Vast masses of piles and stones protect every part from being injured by the force of the current; and a full description of all the contrivances, multiform and ingenious almost beyond conception, by which it has been sought to secure the fabric from every accident which the imagination could anticipate, would fill a moderate volume. The expense of the aqueduct has been great,—not less than thirty lacs of rupees (300,000*l.*); but the work is not only the greatest on the line of the canal, but probably the greatest of its kind in the world. A section of the canal of which this noble aqueduct forms part, was recently opened, and is now diffusing fertility throughout its course.

SOLEGONG.—A town in Hyderabad, or territory of the Nizam, 16 miles S.W. from Aurungabad, and 52 miles N.E. by N. from Ahmednuggur. Lat. 19° 44′, long. 75° 10′.

SOMADGANJ, in the British district of Jounpore, lieut.-gov. of the N.W. Provinces, a village on the route from Allahabad cantonment to that of Jounpore, 49 miles N.E. of the former, 17 S.W. of the latter. It has a bazar. Lat. 25° 42′, long. 82° 32′.

SOMANHULLY.—A town in the Mysore, presidency of Madras, situate on the left bank of the Chittravutty river, and 114 miles N.E. from Seringapatam. Lat. 13° 39′, long. 77° 53′.

SOMAWARRUM.—A town in Hyderabad, or territory of the Nizam, 124 miles E. by S. from Hyderabad, and 61 miles N. from Guntoor. Lat. 17° 10′, long. 80° 25′.

SOMEESIR.—A town in the Rajpoot native state of Jodhpoor, 63 miles W. by N. from Jodhpoor, and 78 miles E.S.E. from Jessulmeer. Lat. 26° 31′, long. 72° 10′.

SOMEREA PASS.—See KOMULMAIR.

SOMIEEGOOL.—A town of Eastern India, in the native state of Muneepoor, 63 miles W.S.W. from Muneepoor, and 35 miles S.E. by S. from Silchar. Lat. 24° 23′, long. 93° 9′.

SOMNAGANJ, in the British district of Allygurh, lieut.-gov. of the N.W. Provinces, a town on the route from the cantonment of Allygurh to that of Delhi, and 16 miles N.W. of the former. It is supplied with water from wells, and has a bazar and market. Elevation above the sea 752 feet. Lat. 28° 3′, long. 78°.

SOMNATH PATTAN, in the peninsula of Kattywar, province of Guzerat, a town situate on the south-west coast, washed by the Arabian Sea. The ground-plan of the town is an irregular quadrangle, inclosed by a wall nine feet thick, one mile and six furlongs in circuit, with two gateways, thirty-six square towers, and two round towers. The defences are on three sides strengthened by a ditch: on the west, the base of the wall is washed by the sea. The walls and towers are constructed of uncemented square stones, and are throughout massive and of great solidity and strength. They are everywhere adorned with Brahminical sculptures on mythological subjects, though much decayed by time and the defacing hands of zealous Mussulmans. The site of the place is fine, commanding the view of the Arabian Sea, of a beautiful bay, and of the headland and seaport of Billawul, fortified as a defence against pirates. The population of the town is at present chiefly Mussulman, and there are many mosques, among which the most remarkable is the Jooma Musjid, described by Burnes as "in the Jain style of architecture, of an oblong square figure, with pillars on the great sides, and four domes, resting on pillars at the end which faces the entrance: the shafts of all these pillars are low." The great temple of Somnath is finely situate on an eminence at the north-west of the town, so advantageously, that it can be seen at the distance of twenty-five miles. The accounts of this celebrated temple are numerous, but very confused, and in many instances discrepant. According to Postans, it "consists of one large hall, in an oblong form, from one end of which proceeds a small square chamber or sanctum. The centre of the hall is occupied by a noble dome over an octagon of eight arches, the remainder of the roof terraced and supported by numerous pillars. There are three entrances; the sides of the buildings face the cardinal points, and the principal entrance is on the eastern side. These doorways are unusually high and wide, in the Egyptian style, decreasing towards the top: they add much to the effect of the building. Internally, the whole presents a scene of complete destruction; the pavement is everywhere covered with heaps of stones and rubbish, the facings of the walls, capitals of the pillars, in short every portion possessing anything approaching to ornament, having been removed or defaced." "Externally the whole of the building is most elaborately carved and ornamented, with figures single and in groups of various dimensions. Many of these appear to have been of some size, but so laboriously was the work of mutilation carried on here, that of the larger figures scarcely a trunk has been left, whilst few even of the most minute remain uninjured. The front entrance is ornamented with a portico, and surrounded by two slender minarets." The dimensions are stated to be—extreme length inside (not including the small chamber or sanctum) ninety-six feet; extreme width sixty-eight feet; extreme height twenty-eight and a half feet. If the subject be cleared from the clouds of grandiloquent verbiage with which it has been so profusely overcast, it must appear that the structure, of which the ruins are still to be seen at Pattan, was a gloomy, massive, and rather rudely-built temple, of diminutive size, overlaid externally with a prodigious quantity of mythological sculptures. Of the linga, of historical celebrity, there does not appear to remain a trace, and scarcely a tradition; but near the temple is a multiform symbol of Siva, called Koteswara, meaning "with a million of lingas." It is a huge cylinder of red freestone, covered with miniature lingas. The splendour of Somnath, when greatest, is described (no doubt with much exaggeration) by Mirkhond. "Somnath was an idol in a temple situate on the seaside; which idol the Hindoos worshipped, especially at times of eclipse. More than a lakh of people used to come to it on nights when the moon was under eclipse; and they believed, too, that the souls of the deceased came to Somnath on first leaving the bodies they had occupied, and were there assigned fresh bodies. They also believed that the sea worshipped Somnath, and the rise and fall of the tides were considered to be proof of this. From the most distant parts of India pilgrims used to come to worship at this shrine; 10,000 villages were assigned for its support, and there were so man jewels belonging to it as no king had ever one-tenth part of it in his treasury: 2,000 Brahmins served the idol, and a golden chain of 200 muns supported a bell-plate, which being struck at stated times, called the people to worship; 300 shavers, 500 dancing-girls, and 300 musicians were on the idol's establishment, and received support from the endowment and from the gifts of pilgrims."

This temple was taken by storm by Mahmood of Ghuznee, after repeated attacks, it being desperately defended by its fanatical guardians. It has been said, and the assertion has obtained pretty general belief, that the celebrated "destroyer of idols" carried away as a trophy of his success a pair of gates, which subsequently adorned his own tomb. Ferishta, however, makes no mention of this; and for various reasons, the truth of the story seems open to question. On the retirement of the British army, however, from Affghanistan, in 1842, this reputed trophy was considered of so much importance that its recovery, and consequent restoration to Hindostan, were announced in a proclamation distinguished by remarkable elevation of language, as avenging "the insult of 800 years;" and the chiefs and princes of Sirhind, Rajwarra, Malwa, and Guzerat, were invited to transmit the gates, "with all honour," to the place from which they had been violently removed. That destination, however, they never reached: the home authorities altogether disapproved of the intended re-erection of the gates in their original place, if such it were, regarding such a proceeding as calculated to stimulate religious animosity, to identify the British government with one of the two great parties of religionists into which India is divided, and to give deep offence to the other. The gates were said to be composed of sandal-wood; but less costly materials have been named as more probable; and even an opinion has been expressed that they were nothing better than "rotten old deal."

Ahelia Bhae, a superstitious old lady of the Holkar family, has recently caused a temple to be built for Somnath, in the vicinity of the ancient edifice. The present town contains about 900 houses and 5,000 inhabitants; Billawul, or Vairawull, two miles west of Somnath Pattan, is its seaport, and is a good haven for trading vessels, the traffic being considerable. Distance from Ahmedabad, S.W., 210 miles; Baroda, S.W., 210; Surat, W., 163; Bombay, N.W., 210. Lat. 20° 55′, long. 70° 23′.

SOMURA.—A town in the Rajpoot state of

Jodhpoor, 89 miles N.E. from Jodhpoor, and 70 miles E. by S. from Beekaneer. Lat. 27° 12′, long. 74° 4′.

SONADAH.—A town in the British district of Nuddea, lieut.-gov. of Bengal, 80 miles N. of Calcutta. Lat. 23° 43′, long. 88° 30′.

SONAEE.—A town in the British district of Ahmednuggur, presidency of Bombay, 22 miles N. by E. of Ahmednuggur. Lat. 19° 24′, long. 74° 50′.

SONAHAUT.—A town in the British district of Chota Nagpoor, lieut.-gov. of Bengal, 66 miles E. by S. of Lohadugga. Lat. 23° 13′, long. 85° 45′.

SONAKHODA.—A town in the British district of Purneah, lieut.-gov. of Bengal, 58 miles N.E. of Purneah. Lat. 26° 18′, long. 88° 16′.

SONAMGUNJE.—A town in the British district ot Silhet, lieut.-gov. of Bengal, 30 miles W.N.W. of Silhet. Lat. 25° 3′, long. 91° 24′.

SONAPUSSEE.—A town in the native state of Mohurbunge, on the south-west frontier of Bengal, 100 miles W.S.W. from Midnapoor, and 98 N. from Cuttack. Lat. 21° 51′, long. 85° 58′.

SONAR.—A river rising in the Saugor and Nerbudda territory, about lat. 23° 23′, long. 78° 46′, and at an elevation of 1,950 feet above the sea. It holds a north-easterly course of 110 miles, and receives the Bearma on the right side, and eight miles lower down falls into the river Cane, on the left side, in lat. 24° 22′, long. 79° 59′. The fall of its channel from its source to the confluence is about 950 feet.

SONARA, in the territory of Indore, or possessions of Holkar's family, a town on the route from Neemuch to Kota, 70 miles N.E. of former, 52 S.W. of latter: it is of considerable size, and has a good bazar. It was on his march to this place, whither he had despatched his baggage and stores, that the ill-fated Colonel Monson, in July, 1804, received intelligence that the irregular horse under Lieutenant Lucan, who had been left to watch and report the motions of Holkar, had been attacked by that chieftain with his entire cavalry; the communication being almost immediately followed by the still more afflicting news, that the party thus assailed was beyond the reach of succour, having been totally routed, their gallant commander wounded and made prisoner. Colonel Monson, who was preparing to support them, consequently pursued his march to Sonara. Lat. 24° 34′, long. 75° 55′.

SONDWARA, in Malwa, a district lying between lat. 23° 10′—24°, long. 75°—76° 15′, is a fine, fertile, well-watered tract of diversified surface: it has received the denomination from its inhabitants, the Sondis. "They are often called Rajpoots, but are a mixture of all classes, or rather descendants of a mixed race. In their origin they were probably outcasts, and their fabulous history (for they consider themselves as a distinct people) traces them from a prince who, in consequence of being born with the face of a tiger, was expelled to the forests, where he seized upon women of all tribes, and became the progenitor of the Sondees, or, as the term implies, mixed race." At the conclusion of the treaty between the British government and Holkar, at Mundissor, in 1818, the Sondis were estimated in number at 1,249 horse, 9,250 infantry, all subsisting by plunder. They were, however, quickly reduced to obedience by a force formed of the troops of the East-India Company, of Holkar, and of the rajah of Kota; and at present the territory belongs partly to the last-mentioned chief and partly to Scindia.

SONE, a river rising in Gondwana, in the territory of Nagpore, and on the elevated table-land of Ummurkuntuk, in lat. 22° 41′, long. 82° 7′, and four or five miles E. of the source of the Nerbudda. Flowing north for thirty miles, it crosses the frontier into the British district of Saugor and Nerbudda, through which it holds a course sinuous, but generally north-west, for fifty miles, after which it constitutes the boundary between that territory and Rewa for thirty miles, passing into the latter at the confluence of the Johila, which joins it on the left side. Thence pursuing its course in a northerly direction for forty miles, it receives the Mahanuddee, which falls into it on the same side, in lat. 24° 5′, long. 81° 6′. From this point it turns north-east, and flowing along the south-eastern base of the Kymore range, through the territory of Rewa, or that of its dependencies, for 125 miles, crosses the eastern frontier of the raj in lat. 24° 37′, long. 82° 51′, into the British district of Mirzapoor. At the town of Burdhee, it on the right side receives the small river Goput. Its course through the district of Mirzapoor is east for thirty-five miles, to the east frontier, in lat. 24° 31′, long. 83° 33′; and in this interval it on the right side, near Agoree, receives the Rehund, and twelve miles lower down, on the same side, the Kunher. From the place where it leaves the district of Mirzapoor, it forms the south-east frontier of the British district of Shahabad, being for 120 miles the boundary between it and the British district of Behar, and for fifteen more the boundary between it and the British district of Patna. Its tributaries of any importance in this part of its course are all on the right or south-east side. Of these, the greatest is the Kiyul, Koel, or Koyl, joining nearly opposite the celebrated fort of Rohtas, and in lat. 24° 31′, long. 83° 54′. The Sone falls into the Ganges on the right or south side, ten miles above Dinapore, and in lat. 25° 37′, long. 84° 55′, after a total length of course of 465 miles. There appears reason to think that it formerly joined the

Ganges by some other channels besides the present one. A nearly effaced channel may be still traced opening on that of the Ganges at Bankipoor, below Dinapore, and another still farther down the stream, below Patna. In the time of Abulfazl, in the commencement of the seventeenth century, and in that of Baber, a century earlier, it flowed near to Munir. Blunt, who viewed the stream in lat. 24° 35′, long. 83°, about 280 miles from its source, found that there "the bed of the river was about half a mile wide and full of quicksands, but the stream was not more than a hundred yards broad, and flowed rapidly, with about three feet of water in the deepest part." It rapidly increases in size, as, forty or fifty miles lower down, after it has entered the British district Shahabad, the width of the channel is nowhere less than 600 yards, and in many parts is 1,000. In the end of December the stream is 300 or 400 yards wide, not rapid, but rather clear, generally deep, and scarcely anywhere having fords, though in spring these are numerous; yet even then, when lowest, though boats of burthen can scarcely pass, vast quantities of bamboos are conveyed down in floats. Below the mouth of the Kool, the width of channel increases variously from 600 to 2,000 yards, which great extent is during the periodical rains filled for several days together, and the stream is at such junctures navigable for craft of ten or twelve tons, though the passage is intricate, precarious, and tedious: altogether, it may be regarded as a vast torrent. In lat. 24° 52′, long. 84° 15′, and seventy miles above its month, it is traversed by the route from Hazareebagh to Benares; and in that part, according to Jacquemont, its bed, two miles wide, is during the periodical rains filled by the stream; but in early spring, or the dry season, there were only two streams, each as large as the Seine at Paris, one near the left bank, the other half a mile nearer the right. The passage was made by ferry, but Garden states that it may also be forded. With the view of testing the feasibility of throwing a bridge over this river, the construction of a causeway was some time since intrusted to the superintendent of the grand trunk road, and the effect of the stream during the rainy season was thus ascertained. Measures are now in progess for the construction of a bridge over the Sone, in connection with the East-Indian Railway. The navigation of the river is not considered available for purposes of important utility higher than Daudnagar, sixty miles from the confluence with the Ganges.

SONEGURH, in Guzerat, or the territory of the Guicowar, a town 45 miles E. of Surat. Lat. 21° 8′, long. 73° 33′.

SONEPORE.—The name of a native raj subject to the political agent for the south-western frontier of Bengal: its centre is in lat. 21°, long. 84°, and it contains an area of 1,467 square miles. The country is generally flat and pretty well cultivated, but when last visited by the political agent, the people complained greatly of oppression. The heat here is intense. The southern part of the raj is inhabited by Khoonds, and human sacrifices are represented as of frequent occurrence. The country was estimated by the agent to be worth about six lacs, and the annual tribute (6,400 rupees) was regularly paid. The population is believed to be about 66,000.

SONEPOOR.—A town in the raj of the same name, subject to the political agent for the south-west frontier. It is situate on the right side of the Mahanuddy river, navigable by large river-craft from the sea to this place, a distance of 200 miles. It is distant 39 miles S. from the town of Sumbhulpore. Lat. 20° 55′, long. 84° 8′.

SONEYEE, in the British district of Muttra, lieut.-gov. of the N.W. Provinces, a town on the route from Muttra to Buddaoon, 13 miles E.N.E. of the former. Lat. 27° 33′, long. 77° 58′.

SONEYRA, in the territory of Gwalior, or possessions of the family of Scindia, a small town in Southern Malwa, on the route from Goona to Mow, 107 miles S.W. of former, 78 N.E. of the latter. It has a bazar, and supplies may be obtained. Lat. 23° 27′, long. 76° 23′.

SONG, a river of the British district of Gurhwal, rises on the southern declivity of the Surkanda peak, and in lat. 30° 24′, long. 78° 22′. It first flows in a south-westerly direction for about twenty miles, to Nalapani, and washes its eastern base, from which it takes a southerly course of about twenty miles to the confluence of the Sooswa, where it turns south-east, and after a further course of about eight miles, falls into the Ganges, in lat. 30° 2′, long. 78° 19′, and at an elevation of 1,200 feet above the sea. Its volume of water is in winter inconsiderable, as Moorcroft, who saw it in the middle of February, styles it a rivulet.

SONGDEE.—A town in Hyderabad, or territory of the Nizam, situate on the right bank of the Payne Gunga river, and 166 miles N. from Hyderabad. Lat. 19° 42′, long. 78° 58′.

SONHAT, in the native state of Korea, on the south-western frontier of Bengal, a town among the mountains of Gondwana, 50 miles N.W. of the ruined town of Sirgoojah, 120 S. of Mirzapoor, 420 W. of Calcutta by Hazareebagh. Lat. 23° 20′, long. 82° 23′.

SONK, in the British district of Muttra, lieut.-gov. of the N.W. Provinces, a town on the route from Kombher, in Bhurtpoor, to the cantonment of Muttra, and 15 miles S.W. of the latter. Lat. 27° 23′, long. 77° 34′.

SONKUTCH, in the territory of Gwalior, or possessions of Scindia's family, a large and populous town, the principal place of a pergunnah of the same name, is situate on the east or right side of the river Kalee Sindh.

This pergunnah, with Ouchod united to it, yielding an annual revenue of 90,000 rupees, was by treaty, 1844, placed under British management, for the maintenance of the augmented Gwalior contingent. Distant 40 miles S.E. of Oojein. Lat. 23°, long. 76° 21′.

SONMEANEE, properly SOUMEANEE, in Beloochistan, a small town on the shore of the Arabian Sea. It is situate at the northern extremity of an inlet, called the Bay of Sonmeanee, and described, probably in too favourable terms, by Pottinger, as "a very noble sheet of water, said to be free from rocks or shoals, and is capable of affording anchorage to the largest fleet." This bay is formed by the projection of Cape Monze on the east. According to the competent authority of Carless, "the harbour, which has been formed by the Poorally river, is a large irregular inlet, spreading out, like that of Kurrachee, in extensive swamps, and choked with shoals. The channel leading into it is extremely narrow, and has a depth of sixteen or seventeen feet at high water in the shallowest part; but it shifts its position every year, and vessels of any size could not navigate it without great difficulty until it has been buoyed off inside. There are six or seven, or even ten, fathoms in some places; but towards the town the channels become shallow, and the trading boats cannot approach it nearer than a mile. At the spot where they anchor, they are always aground at low water. During the south-west monsoon the harbour cannot be entered, for the bar at the entrance is exposed to the whole force of the swell, and the breakers on it are heavy." This bar, according to Horsburgh, has two fathoms of water when the tide is out, but the depth is every year diminishing, and will probably be soon too little to admit vessels; at the same time the sea is encroaching on the land, and threatens soon to sweep away the present site of the town. Sea-going vessels in general anchor outside the bar, at the distance of about two miles from the town, and are much exposed to the sea and the weather. The cargoes are discharged into small boats, and so landed; horses for exportation are made to swim to the vessels. The town is mean and dirty, and has about 500 houses, built of mud, and each surmounted by a *badgeer*, or small turret or flue, open on one side to the sea-breeze, which it sends downwards in the interior of the building, for the purpose of mitigating the excessive heat. It was formerly surrounded by a mud wall, which is now so decayed that scarcely a vestige of it remains. Water can be obtained only by digging in the sand a little above high-water mark, and is so brackish as to be scarcely drinkable, insomuch that the British vessels, when stationed here, were supplied from Kurrachee. The inhabitants live principally by fishing, and are extremely poor, except a few Hindoos, who have the whole trade in their hands. The imports from Bombay are silk, cloths, iron, tin, steel, copper, pepper, sugar, and spices; from the Persian Gulf, dates and slaves; from Sinde, coarse cotton cloths. The exports are horses, butter, wool, hides, oil, grain, dried fruits, and gum. In 1808 this place was burned by Arabian pirates, and the trade has much decayed since that time. Its traffic is at present much injured by the predatory Belooches, who interrupt the communication with the interior. The population is estimated by Carless at about 2,000. Lat. 24° 27′, long. 66° 39′.

SONNEL, in the territory of Gwalior, or possessions of Scindia's family, a town on the route from Oojein to Kotah, 85 miles N. of former, 55 S. of latter. It is of considerable size, of square outline, and has a rampart of stone. There are two broad streets, which cross each other at right angles, and at their intersection is a chauk or market-place. Lat. 24° 20′, long. 76° 2′.

SONOREE.—A town of Bundelkund, in the native state of Dutteah, 13 miles N. from the town of that name, and 30 miles S.E. by S. from Gwalior. Lat. 25° 50′, long. 78° 30′.

SONUH, in the British district of Goorgaon, lieut.-gov. of the N.W. Provinces, a town on the route from Delhi to Alwar, by Ferozpore, and 39 miles S.W. of the former. It is situate in a long valley, stretching from south-west to north-east, the bottom of which is quite level, and inclosed by chains of hills of quartzose or sandstone formation, and from 300 to 400 feet high. Here is a hot sulphureous spring, of the temperature of 108° Fahrenheit. The water is received into a reservoir: it gushes from a shaft cut out of the solid rock, and about thirty feet deep, in the centre of a basin, also cut in the rock, and sixteen feet square, with steps leading down to the water, for the convenience of bathing. The whole is covered by a beautiful dome of ancient architecture, and surrounded by apartments with open verandas, occupied by thirty or forty Brahmins, who levy small contributions on those who have recourse to the reservoir, which is used as a warm bath, the inhabitants, Mussulmans and Hindoos, every morning remaining immersed in it for several minutes. This bath is found very sanative in leprosy and other cutaneous affections, in scrofula, chronic rheumatism, and liver complaints, and is much frequented by the afflicted with such disorders; but Jacquemont considers its habitual use by the inhabitants of Sonuh as highly injurious to their health, as, notwithstanding the purity and salubrity of the air, they have all a thoroughly cachectic look. On a hill above the town is a sort of fortress, large enough to contain the inhabitants and their moveable property, and built by them as a place of refuge from freebooters, who much infested the country previously to its conquest by the British. There is a bazar in the town, which is well supplied with water. The road in this part of the route is good;

the population amounts to 8,513. Lat. 28° 14', long. 77° 7'.

SONUND.—A town in the British province of Sattara, presidency of Bombay, 81 miles E.S.E. of Sattara. Lat. 17° 15', long. 75° 13'.

SOOA, in the British district Bareilly, division of Pillibheet, lieut.-gov. of the N.W. Provinces, a village on the route from Bareilly to Petoragurh, and 76 miles N.E. of the former. It is situate on the right bank of the Gogra or Surju, about five miles below its exit from the mountains. Lat. 29° 4', long. 80° 10'.

SOOAL, in the British district of Kumaon, lieut.-gov. of Agra, a small river rising close to Shem Deo temple, at an elevation of 6,760 feet above the sea. Lat. 29° 37', long. 79° 52'. It takes a south-westerly direction, flowing at the south-eastern base of the mountain on which Almora stands, four miles below which place it falls into the Kosila, on the left side, in lat. 29° 33', long. 79° 39', after a course of about twenty miles. Webb, who crossed it in lat. 29° 36', long. 79° 46', and about ten miles from its source, found it between fifty and sixty feet wide and two feet deep, with a stony bed.

SOOBATHOO.—See SUBATHOO.

SOOBHAGDESIR.—A town in the Rajpoot state of Beekaneer, 87 miles E. by S. from Beekaneer, and 89 miles N. from Ajmeer. Lat. 27° 44', long. 74° 44'.

SOOBRAMUNNY.—A town in the British district of South Canara, presidency of Madras, 55 miles E. by S. of Mangalore. Lat. 12° 40', long. 75° 40'.

SOOBU SHEREE.—A river rising in Thibet, in lat. 28° 47', long. 92° 57', and, flowing through Thibet, the territory of the Abor tribes, and Luckimpoor, falls into the Booree Lohit river, in lat. 27° 10', long. 94° 16'.

SOOE, in the British district of Kumaon, lieut.-gov. of the N.W. Provinces, a village in a fine deodar-grove, on a ridge in the Sub-Himalaya, or mountain-system south of the main range, on the route from Champawut to Askoth, seven miles N. of the former. Lat. 29° 26', long. 80° 7'.

SOOEEGAUM.—See SOORGAUM.

SOOGANHULLY.—A town in the British district of Bellary, presidency of Madras, 18 miles N.W. by W. of Bellary. Lat. 15° 17', long. 76° 46'.

SOOJABAD, in the Punjab, a town about four miles from the east bank of the Chenaub, and 20 miles S. of Mooltan. Its size is considerable, and at a distance, with its lofty and irregularly-built fortifications, it has a striking and picturesque appearance. There is a good and well-supplied bazar. Its principal manufactures are cottons and wood-turnery; the excellence of the latter is much celebrated. The gardens belonging to the town are extensive and luxuriant, and the surrounding country is fertile, as well as highly cultivated, yielding great crops of sugarcane, cotton, grain, and indigo. Lat. 29° 53', long. 71° 21'.

SOOJAWULPOOR, in the territory of Gwalior, or possessions of Scindia's family, a town situate on the right or east bank of the river Jamneir. It is of considerable size, and consists of a walled post or fort, and, outside the rampart, of a suburb, having a bazar and many good houses. There is a considerable market for muslins and other cotton fabrics, and for opium. The annual revenue, stated at 2,55,000 rupees, has been transferred to the British authorities, for the maintenance of the increased Gwalior contingent. Distant E. of Oojein 62 miles, S.W. of Gwalior fort 215. Lat. 23° 21', long. 76° 42'.

SOOKEIT.—See SUKHET.

SOOKEY SIR, in the Sinde Sagur Dooab division of the Punjab, a town situated 27 miles S.E. from the left bank of the Indus, 96 miles S. by E. of the town of Peshawar. Lat. 32° 38', long. 71° 59'.

SOOKHEE, in Gurhwal, a village on the right bank of the Bhageerettee, as the Ganges is called near its source. It is situate on the western declivity of a lofty mountain, and surrounded on all sides by rocky precipices of the Himalaya, crowned with snow. At the depth of about 1,000 feet below, the river rushes along, foaming in a narrow channel. The village is now nearly ruined, and contains few inhabited houses. The scenery along the course of the river in this part of the route is very striking, "wall-like precipices of compact granite bounding the river on both sides, to the immediate height of 2,000 or 3,000 feet." The elevation above the sea, of the mountain-top, is 12,000 feet; of the village, 8,869; of the bed of the river below it, 7,608. Lat. 31°, long. 78° 45'.

SOOKLY.—A town in Hyderabad, or territory of the Nizam, 14 miles N. from Mahur, and 86 miles S.S.E. from Ellichpoor. Lat. 20° 1', long. 78°.

SOOKREE RIVER rises in lat. 25°, long. 73° 24', and flowing westerly for 130 miles, through Godwar and Jodhpoor, falls into the Loonee river, in lat. 25° 2', long. 71° 41'.

SOOKSAGUR.—A town in the British district of Nuddea, lieut.-gov. of Bengal, 35 miles N. by E. of Calcutta. Lat. 23° 4', long. 88° 33'.

SOOLEEAY.—A town in the British district of South Canara, presidency of Madras, 44 miles S.E. by E. of Mangalore. Lat. 12° 34', long. 75° 27'.

SOOLGAUNA.—A town in the native territory belonging to the Daung rajah, 56 miles W. from Malligaum, and 65 miles S.E. from Surat. Lat. 20° 33', long. 73° 39'.

SOOLOO.—An island in the Malay Archipelago, situate in lat. 6°, long. 121°. A treaty has been recently concluded by Sir James

Brooke on the part of the British government with the sultan of this place.

SOOLOON.—A town in the Mysore, 25 miles W.N.W. from Bangalore, and 58 miles N.E. from Seringapatam. Lat. 13° 4′, long. 77° 17′.

SOOLPAN MAHADEO.—A town in the British district Akraunee, collectorate of Candeish, 50 miles E. by N. from Broach, and 98 miles N.N.W. from Malligaum. Lat. 21° 48′, long. 73° 48′.

SOOLTANPOOR.—A town in the British district of Candeish, presidency of Bombay, 84 miles N. by E. of Candeish. Lat. 21° 43′, long. 74° 40′.

SOOLTANPOOR.—A town in the Rajpoot state of Kotah, situate eight miles S.E. from the right bank of the Chumbul river, and 31 miles E.N.E. from Kotah. Lat. 25° 19′, long. 76° 20′.

SOOLTANPOOR IN BENARES, so called in contradistinction to Sooltanpoor in Oude, a town with bazar, on the route from the city of Benares to Chunar, 12 miles S.W. of the former, three miles N. of the latter. Here is a cantonment of cavalry. Supplies may be had in abundance, as well as water, the place being situate on the left bank of the Ganges. Distant N.W. of Calcutta, by water, 687 miles, or 864 if the Sunderbund passage be taken; by land, by way of Benares, 433. Lat. 25° 11′, long. 82° 57′.

SOOMAIRPOOR, in the British district of Humeerpoor, lieut.-gov. of the N.W. Provinces, a town on the route from Humeerpoor to Bandah, 11 miles S. of the former. Lat. 25° 50′, long. 80° 13′.

SOOMEYSUR FORT, in the British district of Sarun, lieut.-gov. of Bengal, 45 miles N.N.W. of Bettiah. Lat. 27° 22′, long. 84° 21′.

SOONAMOOKEE, in the British district of Bancoora, lieut.-gov. of Bengal, a town on the route from Berhampoor to Bancoora, 91 miles S.W. of former, 24 N.E. of latter. Lat. 23° 18′, long. 87° 31′.

SOONA MUDAN.—A town in Nepal, situate on the right bank of one of the arms of the Gunduck river, and 126 miles N.W. by W. from Khatmandoo. Lat. 28° 37′, long. 83° 33′.

SOONDA, in the British district of North Canara, presidency of Madras, a town, the principal place of a tallook or subdivision of the same name. It is situate on the Soonda Nulla, a small river tributary to the Baidli Nulla, and was formerly a place of great extent, the outermost wall being forty-eight miles in circumference. Within it are two other lines of fortifications; the innermost, being a square of three miles, was once fully occupied by dwellings, and even when taken by Hyder Ali, of Mysore, in the middle of the last century, contained 10,000 houses. In the spaces between the inner and middle inclosures, and between the middle and the outer, the houses were formerly dispersed in small groups, with gardens, groves, and orchards between them. The surrounding country is rather rugged, being intersected by many deep valleys and gorges, drained by rivulets. The entire tallook or subdivision of Soonda is rough and mountainous, extending over the summit of the Ghats, here expanding into a sort of rugged table-land, traversed by the Baidli Nulla, the Cauly Nuddy, and numerous small torrents. Those well-watered dells are in the lower part fertile, producing, in great perfection, betel-nut, betel-leaf, black pepper, cardamoms, and plantains, and capable of yielding a much greater quantity of these commodities, but that the country has not yet recovered from the desolation to which it was reduced by the Mahrattas and the troops of Mysore. The climate in the western part, towards the brow of the Ghats, is extremely wet during the monsoon; but this excessive moisture diminishes as the country recedes towards the east.

Besides Soonda, the only places within the tallook which can be denominated towns, are Sersi, Banawasi, and Yelapur.

Soonda, called by the natives Sundha, and in Sanscrit Sudhapura, appears to be a place of very remote antiquity. Within the territorial division to which it gives name, there are traces of three several languages having followed each other in a succession commencing with a very early period. The tract formed part of the possessions of the Cadumba dynasty, which ruled as far as the eastern coast of the Peninsula, or that washed by the Bay of Bengal. Its subversion has been conjectured to have occurred in the second century of the Christian era, but neither history nor conjecture furnishes a cause. Thenceforward centuries of total darkness succeed. Probably the irruptions of the Patan sultans of Delhi extended hither; but ultimately the territory formed part of the vast realm of Vijayanagar, remaining so until its total overthrow in A.D. 1565, by a great Mussulman confederacy, when its fate was decided under the general partitioning process that followed. In 1763 it was conquered by Fuzzul Oolla Khan, an officer of Hyder Ali, of Mysore; and the rajah, flying to the Portuguese at Goa, surrendered to them his possessions below the Ghats, in consideration of a fixed stipend: these possessions still form part of the Portuguese territory. The territory of the rajah of the country east of the culminating ridge of the Ghats, which became the prey of Hyder, on the overthrow of Tippoo, in 1799, was incorporated with the dominions of the East-India Company.

The town of Soonda is distant from Mangalore, N., 130 miles; from Bombay, S.E., 318; from Bangalore, N.W., 220; from Madras, N.W., 390. Lat. 14° 45′, long. 74° 52′.

SOONDERBUNDS.—See SUNDERBUNDS.

SOONDERPOOR.—A town in the British district of Silhet, lieut.-gov. of Bengal, 57 miles S.S.W. of Silhet. Lat. 24° 11′, long. 91° 24′.

SOONDICOOPA.—A town in the Mysore, 13 miles W.N.W. from Bangalore, and 63 miles N.E. from Seringapatam. Lat. 13°, long. 77° 27′.

SOONDOO RIVER, a feeder of the Mahanuddy, rises in lat. 20° 12′, long. 82° 6′, and, flowing northerly through Nowagudda and Berar for seventy-three miles, falls into the Mahanuddy, in lat. 21° 4′, long. 81° 56′.

SOONDOOR.—See SOUNDOOR.

SOONDRA.—A town in the Rajpoot state of Jodhpoor, 182 miles W. by S. from Jodhpoor, and 71 miles S.W. from Jessulmeer. Lat. 26° 9′, long. 70° 15′.

SOONDRAPANDYPATAM.—A town in the British district of Madura, presidency of Madras, 69 miles E. of Madura. Lat. 9° 51′, long. 79° 10′.

SOONDURSEE.—A town of Malwa, in the native state of Dewas, situate on the right bank of the Kallee Sinde river, and 61 miles W. from Bhopal. Lat. 23° 16′, long. 76° 28′.

SOONDY.—A town in the British district of Nellore, presidency of Madras, 31 miles S.W. of Ongole. Lat. 15° 11′, long. 79° 46′.

SOONEYRUH, in the British district of Mynpoorie, lieut.-gov. of the N.W. Provinces, a village on the route from the cantonment of Aligurh to that of Futtehgurh, and 50 miles N.W. of the latter. Lat. 27° 37′, long. 78° 57′.

SOONKERODEPETTA.—A town in the British district of Vizagapatam, presidency of Madras, 106 miles S.W. of Ganjam. Lat. 18° 15′, long. 84° 3′.

SOONPUT, in the British district of Paneeput, lieut.-gov. of the N.W. Provinces, a town on the route from Paneeput to Delhi, 27 miles S. of the former. Soonput contains a population of 16,870 inhabitants. Lat. 29°, long. 77° 4′.

SOONTH.—See SOAUTH.

SOOPA, in the tallook or subdivision of the same name, in the British district of North Canara, presidency of Madras, a town on the rugged plateau formed by the expansion of the Ghats towards the east. The tallook of which it is the principal place, has an average elevation of from 1,000 to 1,500 feet above the sea, and though in many places rugged and rocky, has several well-sheltered and watered valleys, producing rice, pepper, betel-nut, sugarcane, gram (Cicer arietinum), raggi (Cynosurus coracanus), and sesame; and the uncultivated parts are overgrown with noble forests of teak, palms, and various other trees. Those forests may be easily traversed, in consequence of being free from underwood; but they are generally avoided, the atmosphere being very unhealthy, and tigers and leopards being numerous and ferocious. The torrents swell during the monsoon rains, so that timber can be floated down to Karwar and other places on the coast. The tallook has an area of 2,052 square miles, and a population of 36,254, indicating a relative density of eighteen to the square mile; but this is incredibly low, and so much less than that of the adjacent tallooks, under similar physical circumstances, that doubtless some error must have entered into the return. The town of Soopa is distant direct from Mangalore, N., 170 miles; Bombay, S.E., 280; Bangalore, N.W., 260; Madras, N.W., 410. Lat. 15° 16′, long. 74° 35′.

SOOPEH.—A town in the British district of Poonah, presidency of Bombay, 38 miles E.S.E. of Poonah. Lat. 18° 20′, long. 74° 26′.

SOOPEH.—See CHANEE SOOPE.

SOOPOLE.—A town in the British district of Bhagulpore, lieut.-gov. of Bengal, 71 miles N.N.W. of Bhagulpoor. Lat. 26° 10′, long. 86° 42′.

SOORADAH.—A town in the British district of Ganjam, presidency of Madras, 48 miles N.W. by W. of Ganjam. The zemindarry of which this town is the principal place having long continued in a state of violence and disorder, was excepted, in 1836, from the operation of the general regulations, and its civic and criminal administration intrusted to an agent of the governor of Fort St. George. Lat. 19° 45′, long. 84° 30′.

SOORAHEE, in the British district of Hurriana, lieut.-gov. of the N.W. Provinces, a village on the route from Delhi to Hansee, and 11 miles S.E. of the latter. Lat. 29° 3′, long. 76° 12′.

SOORAJGUNG, in the British district of Mymensing, lieut.-gov. of Bengal, a town on the right or south-western bank of the Konaie, a great offset of the Brahmapootra. It is the principal mart of the district, between 1,000 and 2,000 river craft of considerable size being usually anchored here, to receive or discharge cargoes. The principal exports are rice, butter, cattle, hides, and timber. Distance from the town of Nusseerabad, S.W., 45 miles; Dacca, N.W., 69; Calcutta, N.E., 153. Lat. 24° 26′, long. 89° 43′.

SOORAJGURH, in the British district of Monghyr, lieut.-gov. of Bengal, a town on the right or south bank of the Ganges, on the route from Dinapoor to the city of Monghyr, 90 miles N.E. of former, 20 W. of latter. It is the principal place of a thana or station of a police division, but otherwise is insignificant. Distant N.W. from Calcutta, by Burhampoor and Patna, 318 miles, by the course of the Ganges 389. Lat. 25° 12′, long. 86° 19′.

SOORAPOOR.—See SHORAPORE.

SOORAUNA.—A town in the Rajpoot state of Jodhpoor, situate on the right bank of the Sookree river, and 97 miles S.W. from Jodhpoor. Lat. 25° 20′, long. 72° 10′.

SOOREE.—A native state on the south-west frontier of Bengal. It is bounded on the north by the British district of Sumbulpore and by Berar; on the east by Burgurh; on the south by Sarunghur; and on the west by Bootea. It is fifteen miles in length from north to south, and ten in breadth: its centre is about lat. 21° 53′, long. 82° 58′.

SOOREE.—A town in the British district of Beerbhoom, lieut.-gov. of Bengal, 109 miles N.W. by N. of Calcutta. Lat. 23° 53′, long. 87° 31′.

SOORGAUM.—A petty district of Chooan Rajpoots, in the north-western part of the province of Guzerat. It is bounded on the west by the Runn of Cutch; on the east by Baubier; on the north by Mow; and on the south by Charchat. It is ten miles long and ten broad, and contains an area of sixty-four square miles. The country is flat and open; the soil is both sandy and saline, producing but poor crops, and those of the commoner grains. Ghussya salt is produced on the Runn side in large quantities: the water is brackish, and not plentiful. The great road from Nuggur Parkur and Sinde, across the Runn, passes through the district. The cold weather lasts during the months of November, December, January, and February: the heat is excessive during the months of April, May, and June: the rains in July, August, and September, are generally very light. No tribute is paid to any government. The population amounts to about 4,500.

The connection of Soorgaum with the British government first occurred in 1819, upon the expulsion by the latter of the numerous bands of plunderers from Guzerat; and a subsequent engagement was entered into in 1826. The policy observed towards it is that of non-interference with its internal affairs, but of control in its external relations. The district is divided amongst five petty chiefs, of the Chooan Rajpoot caste, the principal of whom are Bugwanjee and Fezmuljee, who succeeded their fathers in the authority which they possess, and which they will probably transmit to their sons. The town of Soorgaum is in lat. 24° 9′, long. 71° 18′.

SOORGUL, in the hill state of Bulsun, a lofty peak on a range connected with that of Chur. It is stated by Lloyd to have an elevation greater than that of Wartoo, which is 10,673 feet above the sea. Lat. 31° 5′, long. 77° 33′.

SOORLA, a river of Bombay, rises in lat. 19° 54′, long. 73° 24′, and flowing through the British collectorate of Tannah west for thirty-five miles, and south for thirty-three, falls into the sea at lat. 19° 30′, long. 72° 55′.

SOORNAMOOKY, a river of Madras, rises in lat. 13° 26′, long. 79° 11′, and flowing north-east for seventy-eight miles through North Arcot, and twenty-one through Nellore, falls into the sea at lat. 14° 8′, long. 80° 11′.

SOOROODONGUR.—A town in the territory of Nagpoor, 66 miles N.N.W. from Bustur, and 176 miles E.S.E. from Nagpoor. Lat. 20° 5′, long. 81° 35′.

SOOROUL, in the British district of Allahabad, lieut.-gov. of the N.W. Provinces, a village on the route by the Sohajee Pass from Allahabad to Jubbulpore, and 27 miles S.E. of the former city. Lat. 25° 7′, long. 81° 48′.

SOOROW.—A town in the Rajpoot state of Jodhpoor, situate on the right bank of the Sookree river, and 87 miles S.W. by S. from Jodhpoor. Lat. 25° 20′, long. 72° 20′.

SOORSAH.—A town in Oude, 57 miles N.W. by W. from Lucknow, and 34 miles E. from Futtehgurh. Lat. 27° 20′, long. 80° 14′.

SOORSUTTY.—A river rising in Sirmour, a short distance south-east of Nahun, and about lat. 30° 30′, long. 77° 29′. It takes a south-westerly direction, and after a course of about thirty miles it joins another torrent, the Kharakee, holding nearly the same direction, and then divides into two branches, the more easterly being called the Chittung, the more westerly the Soorsutty. In consequence of the evenness of the surface, and the great body of water sent over it in heavy rains, it sometimes unites with the Markunda, and even with the Guggur. "The whole tract of country," observes Baker, "with the exception of village sites, is liable to inundation from the Sub-Himalayan torrents, diffused over the surface by means of a network of natural and artificial watercourses, of which some are supplied from more than one of the rivers above named; others again flow from one river into another, and during great floods all three (the Guggur, Markunda, and Soorsutty rivers) are frequently united." Having held a south-westerly direction for about thirty-five miles, as far as Thannesur, it there turns to the west, and seventeen miles lower down receives the Markunda, and after a farther course of about forty miles, joins the Guggur, in lat. 29° 52′, long. 76° 10′. Like the other streams of Sirhind, it is, unless during inundation, merely "a small thread of running water." It is regarded with great veneration by the Hindoos, being in their extravagant mythology considered identical with the Sarasvati, the consort of Brahma, and goddess of wisdom, fabled to pass under ground to the confluence of the Jumna and Ganges, and there to mingle her stream with theirs. "It is the famous Sarasvati, which comes out of the hills to the west of the Yamuna [Jumna], passes close to Thaneser, loses itself in the great sandy desert, and reappears at Prayag, humbly oozing from under one of the towers of the fort, as if ashamed of herself. Indeed she may blush at her own imprudence, for she is the goddess of learning and knowledge, and was then coming down the country with a book in her hand, when she entered the sandy desert, and was unexpectedly assailed by numerous demons with frightful countenances, making a dreadful noise. Ashamed of her own want of foresight, she sank into the ground, and reappeared at Prayaga or Allahabad."

SOORUJ GURH, in the hill state of Hindoor, a height on the ridge of Malown, and four and a half miles S.E. of that fort. During the war with the Goorkhas, it was surmounted by a fort occupied by a garrison of that nation, until Colonel Thompson having established himself at the intermediate post of Deontul, and cut off the communication with Malown, the fort of Sooruj Gurh was evacuated, and fell into the hands of the British, by whom it was subsequently demolished. Elevation above the sea 4,927 feet. Lat. 31° 9′, long. 76° 54′.

SOORUJGURH.—A town in the Rajpoot state of Joypoor, 95 miles N. from Jeypoor, and 97 miles W.S.W. from Delhi. Lat. 28° 17′, long. 75° 49′.

SOORUJPOORE.—A town of Bundlecund, in the native state of Punnah, 57 miles W.S.W. from Punnah, and 61 miles N.E. from Saugur. Lat. 24° 30′, long. 79° 26′.

SOORUNG.—See SOANG.

SOORUTGURH.—A town in the Rajpoot state of Beekaneer, 101 miles N.N.E. from Beekaneer, and 108 miles W. by N. from Hissar. Lat. 29° 19′, long. 74° 3′.

SOOSNEER, in the territory of Gwalior, or possessions of Scindia's family, a considerable town, with a good bazar, 200 miles S.W. of Gwalior fort, 55 miles N. of Oojein. Lat. 23° 55′, long. 76° 6′.

SOOSWA.—A river in the British district of Deyrah Dhoon, formed by the confluence, in lat. 30° 15′, long. 78° 5′, and at an elevation of 2,148 feet above the sea, of two rivers, the Ruspunna and the Bindhal Rao, flowing from the south-western declivity of the mountains of Gurwhal. It takes a south-easterly direction, and, receiving several feeders, joins the Song Nuddy in lat. 30° 4′, long. 78° 14′, having previously parted with an offset, which, retaining the name of Sooswa, falls into the Ganges a little below the confluence with the Song.

SOOTEE, in the British district of Moorshedabad, lieut.-gov. of Bengal, a town on the route from Berhampore to Dinapore, 42 miles N.W. of the former, 251 S.E. of the latter. Here, in July, 1763, was fought a battle between a British army and the troops of Meer Cossim Ali, nawaub of Bengal, in which, after a contest of extraordinary severity, the former totally routed their opponents, taking all their cannon and 150 boats laden with grain. The thana or police-station of Sootee has jurisdiction over a small tract containing 128 villages, 4,816 houses, and a population of 34,662; of which the Mussulman proportion is 28,499, the Brahminist 6,163. Sootee is distant N. from Calcutta by land, by way of Berhampore, 160 miles, by water 210. Lat. 24° 35′, long. 88° 6′.

SOOURPOUR.—A town in the British district of Chota Nagpoor, lieut.-gov. of Bengal, 48 miles S.E. of Lohadugga. Lat. 22° 59′, long. 85° 18′.

SOOWURNDROOG, in the presidency of Bombay, a fort on a small and slightly-elevated island close to the coast of the collectorate of Rutnagherry (South Concan). It was made defensible in 1662, by Sevajee, the Mahratta chief; in 1713 it passed by treaty from Shao, rajah of Sattara, to Kanhojee Angria, who had originally been a commander in the Mahratta fleet, and acquired great power and wealth by piracy; in 1755 Tulaji, a successor of Kanhojee, having carried on a prolonged and destructive course of piracy against British commerce, a small force, consisting of "a forty-four gun ship, a ketch of sixteen guns, and two bomb-vessels," was despatched, under the command of Commodore James, against the fort, which was captured after a feeble resistance of a few hours, and without the loss of a man on the side of the captors. On this success Duff observes, "An achievement which, from the previous idea entertained of the pirate Angria, and the strength of the fortifications, was a matter of surprise even to those who accomplished it." It was transferred to the Mahratta government in exchange for Bankote and Fort Victoria, and acquired finally by the East-India Company on the overthrow of the Peishwa in 1818. Distance S. from Bombay 78 miles. Lat. 17° 50′, long. 73° 8′.

SOPUR.—A town within the dominions of Gholab Singh, the ruler of Cashmere, situate on the left bank of the Jhelum river, and 23 miles W.N.W. from Sirinagur. Lat. 34° 15′, long. 74° 40′.

SORAON, in the British district of Allahabad, lieut.-gov. of the N.W. Provinces, a town on the route from Allahabad to Oude, 14 miles N. of the former. Lat. 25° 38′, long. 81° 55′.

SORAWN, in the British district of Allahabad, the principal place of the pergunnah of the same name, is situate on the route from the city of Allahabad to Partabgarh, and 12 miles N. of the former. Lat. 25° 36′, long. 81° 55′.

SORON, in the British district of Budaon, lieut.-gov. of the N.W. Provinces, a town on the route from Coel to Budaon, 25 miles S.W. of the latter. Population 10,395. Lat. 27° 53′, long. 78° 49′.

SORUBA.—A town in the Mysore, 173 miles N.W. from Seringapatam, and 45 miles E. by N. from Honahwar. Lat. 14° 23′, long. 75° 9′.

SORUTH, in the peninsula of Kattywar, province of Guzerat, a district, the most southern of the peninsula. It is bounded on the north by the district of Hallar; on the north-east and east by that of Kattywar; on the east by Babriawar; on the south and south-west by the Arabian Sea, and on the west by the district of Burda; and lies between lat. 20° 41′—21° 50′, long. 69° 58′—71° 12′. There is no official return of the area, but by probable approximation it may be stated at 3,300 square miles. Nearly the whole of this fine district is held by a Mussulman, the nawaub of Joonagurh, so called from his capital of that name, situate among the hills in the north-east part.

The principal places—Joonaghur the capital, Somnath Pattan, Mangroal, Korynaur, Chorwaur, as well as Diu, the Portuguese island and seaport lying off the coast—are described under their respective names in the alphabetical arrangement.

SOSILLA.—A town in the Mysore, 21 miles S.E. by E. from Seringapatam, and 88 miles N. from Coimbatoor. Lat. 12° 16′, long. 76° 59′.

SOTE, or YARWAFADAR.—A river rising in the British district of Moradabad, lieut.-gov. of the N.W. Provinces, about lat. 28° 54′, long. 78° 33′. It holds a south-easterly course of about 130 miles, and falls into the Ganges on the left side, in lat. 27° 41′, long. 79° 29′. About thirty miles from its source, it is crossed by the route from Bareilly to Meerut, and is in that place fordable in the dry season, but during the rains becomes so swollen as to be passable only by ferry. A little lower down, the route from Bareilly to Delhi crosses it by a bridge of fascines, and there it is ten yards wide, and very deep. Forster describes its waters as salubrious, and flowing in a beautifully winding course, and mentions that the name Yarwafadar, or "trusty friend," by which it is generally known in the lower part of its course, was given by Mohammed Shah, of Delhi, in enthusiastic recognition of the advantages derived from it by his army during his invasion of Rohilcund in 1745.

SOTEH.—A town of Eastern India, in the native state of Muneepoor, 28 miles E. by S. from Muneepoor, and 102 miles E. from Silchar. Lat. 24° 41′, long. 94° 27′.

SOUAR, in the jaghire of Rampoor, lieut.-gov. of the N.W. Provinces, a village on the north-eastern route from the town of Rampoor to Nugeena, and 18 miles N. of the former. Lat. 29° 2′, long. 79° 6′.

SOUDAPULLY.—A town in the British district of Cuddapah, presidency of Madras, 72 miles S. by W. of Cuddapah. Lat. 13° 26′, long. 78° 45′.

SOUDRA, in the Rajpoot state of Jessulmeer, a village near the route from Roree, in Sindh, to the town of Jessulmeer, and 11 miles N.W. of it. There are a few shops, and water is obtainable from wells. The road in this part of the route is stony. Lat. 26° 57′, long. 71° 7′.

SOUMB, or SUMBE, a mountain torrent rising at the southern base of the Sewalik Mountains, in lat. 30° 24′, long. 77° 28′, and described by Colvin as "nearly dry, except in rains, when it receives the drainage of the mountains south-east of Nahun, and of the plains east of its course nearly to the Jumna; from which, and a strong fall, its floods are most violent and sudden in their effects."

SOUNDA, or SEUNDA, in the native state of Dutteea, province of Budlecund, a town on the route by Kooneh from Gwalior to Calpee, 72 miles W. of the latter. It is situate on the right bank of the river Sindh, which here has "steep banks, sandy bottom, and usual depth of water during the dry season two feet." Here, in the beginning of November, 1817, were the head-quarters of the British army under the Marquis of Hastings, Governor-General, advancing towards Gwalior to intimidate Scindia. Lat. 26° 9′, long. 78° 50′.

SOUNDA.—A town of Bundlecund, in the native state of Dutteah, 40 miles N.N.E. from Dutteah, and 36 miles W. from Jaloun. Lat. 26° 10′, long. 78° 51′.

SOUNDOOR.—A town in the British district of Bellary, presidency of Madras, 24 miles W. by S. of Bellary. A small portion of the district of which this town is the principal place, belongs to a native chief, styled the rajah of Soundoor. Lat. 15° 5′, long. 76° 36′.

SOURUJPOOR.—A town in Nepal, 113 miles W. by S. from Khatmandoo, and 56 miles N. from Goruckpoor. Lat. 27° 30′, long. 83° 29′.

SOUSA, in the British district of Muttra, lieut.-gov. of the N.W. Provinces, a town on the route from Muttra cantonment to Kombher, in Bhurtpore, and 15 miles N.E. of the latter. Lat. 27° 27′, long. 77° 37′.

SOUTHERN MAHRATTA JAGHIRES.—By this name are indicated the following petty terriorities in the Southern Mahratta country:—Hablee, Jhumkundee, Koonwar, Meeruj (under two chiefs), Moodhole, Nurgoond, Sanglee, Savanore, and Shedbal. They are under the protection of the British government, and locally are within the limits of the Bombay presidency. The area of the whole is returned at 3,700 square miles, and the entire population is stated at 410,700.

The Sattara jaghires, dependencies of the late raj of Sattara, and included within it, are named Akulkote, Bhore, Juth, Ounde, Phultun, and Wyhee. With the state to which they belonged, they have passed under the British government. Most of the jaghires above mentioned are noticed separately in the alphabetical arrangement.

SOUTH-WEST FRONTIER OF BENGAL.—This agency comprehends a large tract of country under the administration of an officer called the Political Agent for the South-west Frontier, and who is also the commissioner of Chota Nagpore. He is aided in the discharge of his duties by several European assistants. In addition to these, there is a native judicial establishment, consisting of a sudder aumeen and nine moonsiffs. The tract of country subject to the commissioner of Chota Nagpore, comprises that province, called also Lohardugga, Maunbhoon, Ramgurh or Hazareebagh, and Sumbhulpore; but the authority of that officer as political agent extends over several native states subject to British control, in most of which the government of the chiefs is of a very loose character, the land but imperfectly cultivated, and the people but slightly reclaimed from natural wildness. The principal of these native domains are Sirgooja, Patna, Sonepore, Korea, Nowagurh, Bora Samba, Sarungurh, Phooljee, Bombra, Bonei, Gangpore, Jushpore, Sucktee, Ryegurh, Burgun, Keriall, Serickala, Kursava, and Colehan. In these states the administration of civil justice rests with the chiefs, subject to an appeal to the political agent. In criminal matters, the rajahs may pass sentence to the extent of fourteen years' transportation, under the approval of the agent; but sentence of death cannot be passed until the case comes before the British agent for trial. In minor cases, the rajahs and chiefs may carry out their own orders at once; but they are expected to make monthly reports, and transmit copies of all proceedings.

The places named in the course of this article will be found noticed in the alphabetical arrangement.

SOWARA.—See NUSSERABAD.

SOWDA.—A town in the British district of Candeish, presidency of Bombay, 108 miles E.N.E. of Malligaum. Lat. 21° 8', long. 76°.

SOWLEEGURH, in the British territory of Saugor and Nerbudda, lieut.-gov. of the N.W. Provinces, a town on the route from Baitool to Indoor, 34 miles N.W. by W. of the former. Lat. 22° 7', long. 77° 31'.

SOWNEE, in the British district of Saugor and Nerbudda, lieut.-gov. of the N. W. Provinces, a town, the principal place of the pergunnah of the same name. It is situate on the route from Hoshungabad to Asseerghur, 30 miles S.W. of former, 111 N.E. of latter. It is described as one of the best-looking and cleanest towns in Central India, with one very wide street of new and well-built houses. Lat. 22° 28', long. 77° 30'.

SOWRICK, in the British district of Furruckabad, lieut.-gov. of the N.W. Provinces, a town on the route from Furruckabad to Jaloun, 25 miles S. by W. of the former. Lat. 27° 3', long. 79° 34'.

SOWUREAH, in the British district of Benares, lieut.-gov. of the N.W. Provinces, a village on the route from the city of Benares to Allahabad, 27 miles W. of the former, 47 E. of the latter. Lat. 25° 16', long. 82° 38'.

SPANZEIK.—A town of Burmah, situate on the left bank of the Irawady river, and 134 miles S.W. from Ava. Lat. 20° 19', long. 94° 43'.

SPITI.—A valley so called, forming the north-eastern angle of the Punjab; it extends from lat. 31° 40'—32° 40', and from long. 77° 43'—78° 33', and is seventy miles in length from north to south, and forty-seven in breadth. The valley is traversed throughout by the river of Spiti, a feeder of the Sutluj. The mean elevation of the inhabited parts is stated to be 12,986 feet. In 1846, the district was leased by the British for three years to the rajah of Bussahir, and after the expiration of that period a revenue settlement was made with the cultivators, which is still in force.

SPITI RIVER.—See LI.

SRAVANA BELGULA, in the Mysore, a village, one of the few places in which the Jain tenets and worship, formerly so prevalent over India, continue to hold their place. Here is a colossal image of Gomuta Raya, one of the great pastors or coryphæi of the Jains, being regarded by them as deified on account of his merits. The statue represents the personage naked; it is of very massive proportions, being seventy feet three inches in height, and consisting of one solid stone. Hence it is supposed to have been formed by hewing away the original mass of rock, until the statue alone remained.

Though the Jains have been nearly extirminated in this part of India, by the persecution of the Brahmins, the votaries of their faith in other quarters regard this place with high reverence, and lately an opulent Jain merchant of Seringapatam evinced his devotion by the construction here of a fine tank. Distance N.W. from Seringapatam 33 miles. Lat. 12° 51', long. 76° 33'.

SREE MUTTRA, or SARMATHURA, in the Rajpoot territory of Kerowly, a town near the western frontier, towards the territory of Jeypore, 35 miles W. of the town of Dholpoor, 62 S.W. of Agra. Lat. 26° 31', long. 77° 29'.

SREEVURDHUN, in the presidency of Bombay, a town in the territory occupied by the Hubsies, 62 miles S.W. by W. from Poonah, and 62 miles S. by E. from Bombay. Lat. 18° 3', long. 73° 5'.

SRIGARTH.—A town in the north-eastern quarter of the Punjaub, in the small raj of Kullu, situate 43 miles S.E. by S. of Sultanpoor. Lat. 31° 24', long. 77° 30'.

SRI KANTA, in Gurwhal, a lofty peak of that part of the Himalaya in the space lying in the great flexure of the river Bhageerettee, where it changes its direction from north-west to south-west. Fraser, who had a transient glimpse of this summit while temporarily free from clouds, designates it as "an enormously lofty and sharp peak." It is visible from Suharunpoor, in the plains of Hindoostan, though many lofty ranges intervene, and the distance in a direct line is 105 miles. The summit of Sri Kanta is 20,296 feet above the sea. Lat. 30° 57′, long. 78° 51′.

SRINAGAR, in the British district of Cawnpore, lieut.-gov. of the N.W. Provinces, a village on the route from Allahabad to Calpee, and 21 miles E. of the latter. Lat. 26° 9′, long. 80° 6′.

SRINUGUR, in the British territory of Jaloun, in Bundelcund, lieut.-gov. of the N.W. Provinces, a town on the route, by the Hirapoor Pass, from Saugor to Banda, 47 miles S.W. of the latter. It has a large bazar, and water and supplies are abundant. Lat. 25° 11′, long. 79° 50′.

SRIRAMAPURAM.—A town in the British district of Vizagapatam, presidency of Madras, 54 miles S.W. by W. of Vizagapatam. Lat. 17° 19′, long. 82° 39′.

STREEMUNTGURH.—A town in the Southern Mahratta jaghire of Sanglee, 47 miles S.E. by E. from Dharwar, and 89 miles W. from Ballary. Lat. 15° 7′, long. 75° 40′.

STREEVY GOONDUM.—A town in the British district of Tinnevelly, presidency of Madras, 17 miles E.S.E. from Tinnevelly. Lat. 8° 39′, long. 77° 59′.

STRIMUSTRUM.—A town in the British district of South Arcot, presidency of Madras, 31 miles S.W. of Cuddalore. Lat. 11° 24′, long. 79° 28′.

SUAGARHI, in the petty hill state of Kothar, the remains of a fort on a high ridge shutting in the Gumbur river. The supply of water is from a tank supplied merely by rain, as there is no spring within a considerable distance. Elevation above the sea 5,620 feet. Lat. 30° 56′, long. 77° 2′.

SUBANRIKA.—A river rising in the British district of Chota Nagpore, about lat. 23° 9′, long. 84° 50′. It takes a direction north-east for fifty miles, and subsequently turning due east, becomes the boundary for thirty miles between the district of Chota Nagpore and that of Ramgurh. At the end of that distance it takes a direction south, and for a like distance forms the boundary between the districts Chota Nagpore and Pachete, and, entering this last-named district, traverses it in a direction south-east for a distance of about twenty-five miles. Continuing in the same direction, it for about six miles forms the boundary between the last-named district and Singbhoom, and then for nine miles the boundary between Barrabhoom and Singbhoom, and for twelve miles between Barrabhoom and Pooralia, through which it flows for fifty miles, and subsequently forms the boundary between it and the territory of Orissa for twenty-five more. Finally entering the district of Midnapore, it holds its course for eighty miles to the sea, disemboguing a few miles below Peepley, in lat. 21° 35′, long. 87° 23′. Its direction after entering district Midnapore is south-east: its total length of course is about 317 miles. Stirling styles it a "respectable river," but its mouth is obstructed by a dangerous bar. It is called Peply or Pipli river by Horsburgh, who mentiones that Peply sand stretches three leagues from the shore, and in some part, four miles from land, is nearly dry at low water; and that there is on the east side of the bank a road where ships may anchor in five fathoms water.

SUBATHOO.—A fort and cantonment, the principal place of a small pergunnah of the same name, reserved by the East-India Company, on the settlement of the hill states at the conclusion of the Ghoorka war, in 1815: previously it was within the thakoorai or lordship of Keunthal. The district is bounded on the west by Kothar, and surrounded on all other sides by Burroulee. It is a sort of table-land, having in its vicinity mountains varying in height from 4,600 to 8,000 feet above the sea, but southwards, or towards the plains, it is rather open, and exposed to the winds blowing from them, though overtopped by some high lands in that direction. The fort is situate on an eminence rising about 1,100 feet from the right bank of the river Gumbur. The surrounding country is populous, being studded with many villages, the number of which has continually been on the increase since the establishment of British supremacy, in consequence of the refuge afforded to persons oppressed in the neighbouring hill states, and the extended demand for labour and produce to supply the consumption of the British troops stationed there. Agriculture is carried on with great industry and skill, the sides of the mountains being formed into successive terraces, like huge steps. The level spots on the banks of the streams are irrigated and cultivated for rice, which is produced in great abundance, and of a quality superior to that of the adjacent plains. The other crops are wheat, barley, maize, millet of various kinds, ginger, cotton, opium, tobacco, oil-seeds, red pepper, hemp, and a variety of esculent vegetables. The fruits are generally excellent; and among them are apricots, peaches, walnuts, a few apples, wild pears, raspberries, and melons; the strawberries are small and without flavour. The high grounds in the immediate vicinity of the station are almost destitute of wood, except on their northern declivities, which are covered with pines. The climate is altogether agreeable, and very healthy, the mean temperature of the whole year being from 65½° to 66°: the heat in May and June is considerable, but not oppressive. The periodical rains are heavy, commencing about the 20th of June and continuing to the close of September: hoar frosts commence in November, and cease about the beginning of March. During December and January, in severe seasons, ice of considerable thickness is produced on standing water. Snow sometimes falls to the depth of four or five inches, but seldom lies above three or four days, as the direct rays of the sun are powerful. The supply of water for the cantonment appears to be sufficient only in ordinary seasons. During periods of drought, recourse must be had to springs three-quarters of a mile distant, and 400 feet below the level of the barracks. The old fort has been converted into a jail for delinquents convicted at the cantonment and at Simla. Subathoo is in the Cis-Sutlej division of the territories subject to the jurisdiction of the commissioner of the Punjaub. The fort is distant N.W. from Calcutta 1,075 miles; elevation above the sea 4,500 feet. Subathoo was some time since selected as the site for a sanatarium for troops. Its salubrity has been satisfactorily tested; the special committee appointed to inquire into the relative healthiness of different stations, having arrived at the conclusion that at least two soldiers die at stations on the plains for one on the hills. Lat. 30° 58′, long. 77° 3′.

SUBBULGARH, in the British district of Bijnour, lieut.-gov. of the N.W. Provinces, a ruinous town and fort on the route from Nujeebabad to Hurdwar, and 10 miles N.W. of the former. It is described by Captain Hardwicke as "a very extensive line of fortification, inclosing the town; both which exhibit little more than naked walls falling to decay. Much of the ground within the fort is in cultivation; in the south-east curtain or face of the fort is a lofty brick-built gateway. The high road leads close past the north-east bastion, and continues along the north face the whole length, within thirty or forty yards of the ditch." Lat. 29° 44′, long. 78° 15′.

SUBHAPUR, in the British district of Futtehpore, lieut.-gov. of the N.W. Provinces, a village on the route from Banda to the town of Futtehpore, and 10 miles S.W. of the latter. It is probably identical with that called by Rennell Shahbazpoor, or "falcon's town." Lat. 25° 56′, long. 80° 36′.

SUBTERMOOKEE RIVER.—One of the mouths of the Ganges, discharging itself into the sea in lat. 21° 34′, long. 88° 26′.—See SUNDERBUNDS.

SUBULKA SAREE, in the British district of Delhi, lieut.-gov. of the N.W. Provinces, a town on the route from the city of Delhi to Rewaree, and 14 miles S.W. of the former. There is a good bazar, and water is abundant. Lat. 28° 33′, long. 77° 10′.

SUBZULCOTE.—A town in the native state of Bahawulpore, situate 14 miles S.E. from the left bank of the Indus, and 76 miles N.E. by E. from Bukkur. The town and district of Subzulcote were conferred upon the khan of Bahawulpore in 1843, in reward of the support afforded by him to the British troops during the war in Sinde and Affghanistan. Lat. 28° 12′, long. 69° 57′.

SUCHANA.—A town in the peninsula of Kattywar, province of Guzerat, situated in the prant or subdivision of Hallar, on the southern shore of the Gulf of Cutch. Distance from Ahmedabad, S.W., 150 miles. Lat. 22° 34′, long. 70° 22′.

SUCHEEN.—A town with a small territory included within the limits of the British district of Surat, presidency of Bombay, though in a great measure independent of the British government. It contains an area of 300 square miles, with a population of 22,260. The chief, styled the Nawaub of Sucheen, possesses, it is stated, seventeen villages and an annual income of 89,000 rupees. Loans to the nawaub, to enable him to discharge his Arab mercenaries and for other purposes, have been granted by the British government. These debts have not yet been liquidated; and it has been suggested that certain villages should be sold to relieve the chief from his embarrassments. The town of Sucheen is distant from Surat city, S.E., 10 miles. Lat. 21° 4′, long. 72° 58′.

SUCHENDEE, in the British district of Cawnpore, lieut.-gov. of the N.W. Provinces, a town on the route from Calpee to the cantonment of Cawnpore, and 14 miles W. of the latter. It has a bazar, and supplies and water are abundant. The population amounts to 5,441. The road in this part of the route is bad, the country partially cultivated. Lat. 26° 25′, long. 80° 14′.

SUDDASHEEPET.—A town in Hyderabad, or territory of the Nizam, situate six miles S.W. from the right bank of the Manjera river, and 41 miles W.N.W. from Hyderabad. Lat. 17° 37′, long. 78°.

SUDIYA.—A town of Assam, in the British district of Sudiya, 34 miles N.E. of Seebpoor. The district, of which this town is the chief place, forms one of the divisions of upper Assam, and contains (inclusive of Mutruck) an area of 6,942 square miles, with a population of 30,000. Lat. 27° 50′, long. 95° 42′.

SUDJUN.—A town in the British district of Tannah, presidency of Bombay, 86 miles N. of Bombay. Lat. 20° 10′, long. 72° 50′.

SUDULPUR JEHUR, in the British district of Bareilly, lieut.-gov. of the N.W. Provinces, a village on the route from the town of Bareilly to Shahjehanpoor, and nine miles S.E. of the former place. It is situate near a large piece of water, in an open, level, cultivated country. Lat. 28° 15′, long. 79° 35′.

SUDURKHANKAKOT, in Sirhind, a village on the route from Loodiana to Ferozpoor, and 44 miles W. of the former town. It is situate seven miles from the left bank of the Sutlej, in a level open country, partially cultivated. The road in this part of the route is generally good, but in some places heavy and sandy, yet not so much as to have serious difficulties for guns or carriages. Distant N.W. from Calcutta 1,146 miles. Lat. 30° 56′, long. 74° 39′.

SUFDARGANJ, in the territory of Oude, a town on the route from the cantonment of Goruckpoor to Lucknow, 137 miles W. of the former, 29 E. of the latter. Here is encamping-ground on an extensive plain. Lat. 26° 56′, long. 81° 15′.

SUFEID KOH, or "THE WHITE MOUNTAIN," is a lofty range bounding the valley of the Kabool river on the south, as the Hindoo Koosh does on the north. These two ranges are about seventy miles apart, and this distance may be considered as the extreme breadth of the valley of the Kabool river. The Sufeid Koh range runs nearly east and west along the parallel of lat. 33° 50′, commencing eastward near Attock, in long. 72° 16′, and terminating westward in long. 69° 36′. Its western extremity sinks into a maze of hills, stretching like network to the Kohistan of Kabool. The Sufeid Koh is generally of primary formation, consisting of granite, quartz, gneiss, mica-slate, and primary limestone. There are three ranges running nearly parallel, and rising in height as they recede from the river: the two lower are covered with pine-forests; the highest and most distant has a very irregular outline, is steep and very rocky, yet furrowed by many beautiful and fertile vales. The highest part is between the meridians of 69° 40′ and 70° 30′, and attains the elevation of 14,100 feet, being covered with perpetual snow. The Soorkh Rood, the Kara Su, and many other shallow but impetuous streams, rush down its northern face, and are discharged into the river of Kabool, which conveys their water to the Indus. The Khyber mountains connect the eastern extremity with the Himalaya, as the Kurkutcha do the western; and between them lies the plain of Jelalabad.

SUFFEEDUN, in Sirhind, a small town on the right bank of the canal of Ferozshah, where it changes its direction from south-west to west. The vicinity, formerly but slightly cultivated, has been much improved in consequence of the irrigation introduced by the repair and cleansing of the canal, which, previously nearly useless, has now become a channel for conveying a large body of water from the Jumna to the south of Sirhind. Distant N.W. from Calcutta 960 miles. Lat. 29° 24′, long. 76° 44′.

SUGEN.—A town in the native state of Bamra, on the south-western frontier of Bengal, situate on the right bank of the Braminy river, and 61 miles N.E. by N. from Sumbulpoor. Lat. 22° 12′, long. 84° 30′.

SUGGUR.—A town in Hyderabad, or territory of the Nizam, 124 miles S.W. by W. from Hyderabad, and 95 miles S.E. from Sholapoor. Lat. 16° 36′, long. 76° 51′.

SUGLA, in Bussahir, a pass over the outer range of the Himalaya, forms a communication between Koonawar and Gurhwal. The road through it is bad, but has the advantage of being practicable for six months of the year, and is passable for loaded sheep and goats: Gerard estimates its elevation above the sea at 16,000 feet. Lat. 31° 13′, long. 78° 29′. A peak about three miles north-east of this pass was, in the great trigonometrical survey of the Himalaya, ascertained to have an elevation of 21,178 feet above the sea.

SUGREE, in the British district of Azimgurh, lieut.-gov. of the N.W. Provinces, a town on the route from Azimgurh to Goruckpoor, 13 miles N.E. of the former. Lat. 26° 7′, long. 83° 23′.

SUHAR, in the British district of Muttra, lieut.-gov. of the N.W. Provinces, a town on the route from Muttra to Delhi, 15 miles N.W. of the former. Lat. 27° 38′, long. 77° 33′.

SUHARUNPORE, a British district under the lieut.-gov. of the N.W. Provinces, is bounded on the north-east by the Sewalik range, dividing it from the British district of Dehra Dhoon; on the east by the Ganges, dividing it from the British districts of Gurhwal and Bijnour; on the south by the British district of Mozuffurnuggur; and on the west by the Jumna, dividing it from Sirhind. It is about sixty-eight miles in length from north to south, and sixty in breadth from east to west, with an area of 2,165 square miles; and lies between lat. 29° 28′—30° 26′, long. 77° 13′—78° 15′. The surface is in general remarkably uniform, sloping gently towards the south; the numerous torrents which rush from the Sewalik range flowing generally in that direction, and ultimately finding their way either to the Jumna or the Ganges. There is little elevation towards the base of the Sewalik hills, which rise precipitously from the plain, the level of which is scarcely broken, except by two long ranges of sandhills running from north to south, in some degree parallel with the Ganges and with each other, and by another similar range near the western frontier, running in like manner from north to south, in a line corresponding generally with that of the Jumna. Between the most easterly of these ranges and the Ganges, lies the Khadir or marsh-land of that river, amounting probably to one-sixth of the whole area of Suharunpore. It is thus described by Cautley:—"The low tract of country lying at the foot of the Sewalik hills, and receiving the drainage which ultimately falls into the Ganges river, is that which is designated by the natives the Ganges Khadir. It consists of a triangular portion of the country, bounded on the north-east by the chain of hills called the Sewalik; on the south-west and south by a high steppe or bank; and on the south and east by the Ganges river. The Sewalik on the north, and the high bank which lies on the south, terminate in an acute angle at the Shahjehanpore pass, in the former range, the bank increasing in abruptness up to this point, near which it is lost entirely. The Khadir receives the whole of the hill drainage from Hurdwar up to this angle, which may be considered as the water-head separating the valley of the Jumna from that of the Ganges." The extent of depression of the surface of the Khadir below the highlands of Suharunpore, it is said, "varies, decreasing in depth from the south-eastern angle upwards, the extreme depth being eighty-four feet. This depression, however, is not universal: in the northern portion there is an isolated tract considerably elevated, on which are situated the towns of Kheri, Inli, and numerous villages. This tract is much intersected and cut up by channels, and is separated, or nearly so, in its centre, by a large ravine, receiving a portion of the Shah Munsoor drainage. In addition to this main insular tract of high land, there are other smaller mounds, upon which villages are built." The entire drainage of this tract is into the Ganges, by means of the Solani and Rutmu, the Putthri, and some torrents of less importance. The two ranges of sandhills already mentioned as rising to the west of the Khadir, form the high land dividing the valley of the Ganges from that of the Jumna. The drainage of the latter is effected principally by the Hindon and its tributaries, the discharge of which is into the Jumna, on the left side. An approximate estimate of the elevation of the northern part above the sea may be formed from the ascertained elevations of the Padshamahal, at the north-western extremity, where the Jumna enters the plains; of Hurdwar, at the north-eastern extremity, where the Ganges enters the plains; and of Suharunpore, lying between them. Those elevations are respectively 1,276, 1,024, and 1,013 feet. Bailra, on the south-eastern frontier, and probably the lowest part of the district, is 940 feet above the sea. The climate is cooler than that of the plain of Hindostan in general, in consequence of the higher latitude and greater elevation. From November, the weather becomes progressively colder until Christmas; in March, a rapid rise takes place in the temperature; and about the beginning or middle of April the hot winds begin to blow. Their effects are thus described by Jacquemont:—"The country, which I had left two days before verdant and smiling, had become covered with dust; in a week the herbage will be entirely withered, and the trees have already a uniformly dull hue. Very near objects appear through the dusty air as if by the false and lurid light of the sun penetrating through storm-clouds, and also seem nearer than they actually are; but at no great distance their outlines are quite effaced." The periodical rains commence in the middle of June, and terminate about the middle of September.

The soil is generally clayey, with a proportion of sand, having in many places a substratum of hard retentive clay, and not unfrequently kankar, or lime in nodules, is imbedded in the earth. The very wide range of temperature gives a corresponding extent to the botany of Suharunpore, which, according to the season of the year, matures in the cooler the productions of the temperate; in the hotter, of the intertropical climes. The elephant, common in the Dhoons north of the Sewalik range, may probably be found; and there are certainly tigers, leopards, lynxes, bears, the piju, a species of viverra (Ratelus mellivorus), otters, jackals, stags, hog-deer, spotted deer, antelopes, wild hogs, and monkeys.

The crops consist of wheat, barley, oats, millet, pease, beans, vetch, tares, lentils, mustard and rape as oil-seeds, carrot, coriander, cumin, tobacco, flax, safflower, and succory. Almost all the esculent vegetables of Europe succeed well in the cold season: hemp grows wild in great abundance and luxuriance. The autumnal crop consists of rice, cotton, indigo, maize, different kinds of millet. The government demand on the lands of this district has been fixed for a term of years, which will expire on the 1st July, 1857.

The means of extensive irrigation are supplied by the Doab Canal, which has its head-water from the Jumna on the left side, a short distance above the Padshahmahal, in lat. 30° 22′, long. 77° 39′. The construction of this canal is attributed to Ali Mardhan Khan, minister of the emperor Shah Jehan, a nobleman to whose wealth and public spirit the execution of various great works is ascribed by popular tradition. The canal is conducted, with considerable knowledge of hydraulics, along the crest of the high ground between the Jumna and the Hindon, so as to admit of its water being thrown, for the purposes of irrigation, over the country on both sides. There are, however, scarcely any traces of lateral offsets or of bridges; whence it has been supposed that the great difficulty of preserving it from the ruinous effects of torrents in the upper part of the course, caused it at an early period to be allowed to lapse into ruin. Its general course is in a southerly direction, nearly parallel to the Jumna, and, on an average, about fifteen miles east of it. Near Delhi it flows into the valley of the Jumna, and passing partly through the grounds of a royal preserve, rejoins the Jumna opposite the city. The length of the main branch is 135 miles. It was, by direction of the supreme government, cleared out, put in thorough repair, and reopened in the beginning of 1830, for the various purposes of irrigation, of affording water-power, and of navigation. Rafts of timber can thus be conveyed from the forests about the base of the Sewalik to Delhi, and boats of from four to eight tons burthen, and drawing two feet water, can also be navigated for the same distance. Another work of a similar character, but on a much larger scale, is in course of completion, with a view to the benefit of the eastern part of the Doab. It consists in the formation of a canal for purposes of irrigation, from the right side of the Ganges, at Kunkhul, about three miles below Hurdwar, to flow through the Doab.

The chief rivers of Suharunpore—the Ganges, Jumna, Hindon, Rutmoo, Solani—are separately described in the alphabetical arrangement.

The population of the district is returned at

801,325. The following official return distinguishes the towns and villages of the district into classes according to their population :—

Number with less than 1,000 inhabitants........	1,328
Ditto with more than 1,000 and less than 5,000	144
Ditto with more than 5,000 and less than 10,000	5
Ditto with more than 10,000 and less than 50,000	4
Total	1,481

On the dismemberment of the Mogul empire, subsequently to the victory gained by Ahmed Shah Durani, the circar of Suharunpore was, about the year 1757, given by the conqueror to Najib-u-doula, a Rohilla chief. He was succeeded by his son Zabetakhan, on whose death, in 1785, the territory devolved to his son Gholam Kaudir, infamous for his cruelties at Delhi, when, a few years afterwards, he obtained possession of that city and of its miserable sovereign, whom, after subjecting to every insult which malice and insolence could devise, he deprived of sight by the point of his dagger; thus consummating a series of excesses, which a cautious historian has pronounced to be "almost without parallel in the history of the world." The Mahratta chief Scindia subsequently dispossessed the wretch of his conquest, and avenged the wrongs of the unhappy ruler of Delhi upon the person of his brutal enemy; for though Gholam sought safety in flight, he was not destined to find it, being pursued and taken by the Mahrattas, loaded with irons, and exposed in a cage. Subsequently he was deprived of his eyes, nose, ears, hands, and feet, and thus horribly mutilated was ordered to be sent back to Delhi. He, however, never reached the scene of his atrocities, having died on the road. Scindia could scarcely add to the calamities of the imperial prisoner, but he still retained him in durance, making use of the emperor's name for his own purposes, till the English, by the capture of Delhi, deprived him of the custody of the pageant prince. With the British government Scindia continued obstinately, though vainly, to contend. The vigorous policy of the Marquis Wellesley, enforced by the extraordinary military ability which that profound statesman had at his disposal, ultimately left the Mahratta no choice but submission; and in the sweeping cessions made by him to the British in 1803, by the treaty of Surjee Anjengaum, the district of Suharunpore was included.

SUHARUNPORE.—The principal place of the British district of the same name, under the lieut.-gov. of the N.W. Provinces. It is situate on the small river Dumoulao, and about a mile E. of the Doab Canal, in an open, level country, rendered fertile by the irrigation derived therefrom, though naturally rather sandy. The immediate environs are rendered pleasing by numerous groves of mangoes and palms, and inclosures of cactus and euphorbia. Altogether the scene displays the results of care and intelligence not usual in this part of India; and those agreeable features, with the dwellings of the British residents arranged about the town, give the place a European air. Jacquemont styles it one of the handsomest English stations in India. Here is a celebrated botanic garden belonging to the East-India Company, arranged and matured by the successive care of two eminent botanists, Dr. Royle and Dr. Falconer. The former thus describes the success attained in acclimating and cultivating the productions of various countries:—"We have collected in one place and naturalized in the open air the various fruit-trees of very different countries; as of India, China, Cabul, Europe, and America." This variety of vegetation is attributed by Dr. Royle to the great range of temperature, which extends from the freezing-point to about 100°, combined with the influence of the periodical rains; and from those causes he considers the botanical capability of this locality "as being nearly the northern limit of the flora of India, as well as the southern boundary of that which is called the oriental or Persian region." The choice of situation for the purpose of forming the garden was made with great judgment. The tropical situation of a botanical garden maintained at Calcutta was found, as might have been expected, very unfavourable for realizing many of the advantages which it was established to promote. Suharunpore offered a more temperate locality; and the comparative proximity of the Himalaya Mountains added greatly to the strength of its claims to selection, while an old endowment afforded means for making so hopeful an experiment at a reduced rate of cost. The garden was formed in 1817; in 1826 a medical garden was annexed to it, and a nursery in connection with it was formed in the adjoining hill district of Mussoorie; but a few years afterwards the charge for the medical garden was abolished, and sundry other reductions enforced, by the minute frugality of Lord William Bentinck. The effect of this cutting down was subsequently found to be a diminution of the utility of the establishment. Lord Auckland manifested great anxiety for the success of the institution, and a strong desire to restore its efficiency; deeming this important, as well because the garden was an object of great interest to the inhabitants, as on the ground of its obvious tendency to the extension of knowledge, and to the promotion of the benefit both of Asia and Europe. Steam navigation was at this period beginning to display its advantages as a connecting link between Great Britain and her possessions in India, and thus were opened facilities previously unknown for the interchange of the seeds, plants, and trees of the two quarters of the world; to the advancement of agricultural, horticultural, and botanical science, and to the probable increase of the comforts and gratification of the tastes of the inhabitants of countries widely separated by distance; thus making them mutually contributory to the wants of each other, and co-labourers in diffusing the elements of enjoyment, physical and intellectual. To effect the necessary improvements involved a small additional expense; but the representations of the Governor-General were effectual, and in 1840 the Court of Directors gave their sanction to the requisite measures for placing the establishment of the garden in such a state as should insure its efficiency for the purposes for which it was maintained. By this, and by retaining at home the services of Dr. Royle, to attend to the promotion by all practicable means of the development of the vegetable resources of India, an impetus was given to the very important objects in view, which cannot fail to issue in a large amount of benefit. The garden of Suharunpore, 680 yards in its greatest length, and 470 in its greatest breadth, is an object of much beauty as well as utility, being tastefully laid out with many delightful walks and carriage-roads.

At Suharunpore is a fort, and also a military cantonment: it has also been selected as the locality for a government stud depôt. Here, in the great trigonometrical survey of the Himalaya, was the principal station, where all the most valuable observations, whether of latitude, longitude, or azimuth, were made.

The population of the town is 37,968, as shown by official return prepared in 1848; elevation above the sea 980 feet; distant N.W. from Calcutta 1,007 miles. Lat. 29° 58′, long. 77° 36′.

SUHAWAR, in the British district of Mynpooree, lieut.-gov. of the N.W. Provinces, a town on the route from Mynpooree to Moradabad, 40 miles N. of the former. Lat. 27° 48′, long. 78° 55′.

SUHEELA, in the British district of Goruckpoor, lieut.-gov. of the N.W. Provinces, a town on the route from Goruckpoor to Khachi, 38 miles N. by W. of the former. Lat. 27° 13′, long. 83° 16′.

SUHESPOOR, in the British district of Bijnour, lieut.-gov. of the N.W. Provinces, a town on the route from Bijnour to Pilleebheet, 33 miles S.E. by E. of the former. Lat. 29° 8′, long. 78° 41′.

SUHESPOOR, in the British district of Bijnour, lieut.-gov. of the N.W. Provinces, a town on the route from Moradabad to Hurdwar, and 22 miles N.W. from the former. It is a very filthy place, remarkably crowded with hogs. Davidson remarks, "Pork ought to be cheap, for the neighbouring fields, roads, ravines, and pools, were covered with these filthy untutored animals." There is a bazar, and water is plentiful. Suhespoor contains a population of 6,442 inhabitants. Lat. 29° 7′, long. 78° 41′.

SUHESPOORA, in the British district of Mirzapoor, lieut.-gov. of the N.W. Provinces, a town on the route from Mirzapoor to Patna, 27 miles E. of the former. Lat. 25° 9′, long. 83° 2′.

SUHPOO, in the British district of Muttra, lieut.-gov. of the N.W. Provinces, a town on the route from Muttra to Futtygurh, 30 miles E. by N. of the former. Lat. 27° 27′, long. 78° 13′.

SUHUSWAN, in the British district of Budaoon, lieut.-gov. of the N.W. Provinces, a town on the route from Budaoon to Rewaree, 23 miles W. of the former. Lat. 28° 4′, long. 78° 50′.

SUJNAIR.—A river rising in the British district of Saugor and Nerbudda, in lat. 24° 22′, long. 78° 35′, a few miles south of the town of Sindwah, and flowing about sixty miles through the territory of Scindia, falls, on the left side, into the Jamnie, a feeder of the Betwa, in lat. 25° 8′, long. 78° 42′.

SUKEET, in the British district of Mynpoorie, the principal place of the pergunnah of the same name, a town on the route from Allygurh to Mynpoorie, and 24 miles N.W. of the latter. There is a bazar, and water and supplies are abundant: the country is flat, open, and but partially cultivated. Immediately north and east of the town is an extensive waste plain, which would form an excellent exercising-ground for 20,000 men. The road in this part of the route is good. Lat. 27° 26′, long. 78° 50′.

SUKHET.—A native state in the north side of the Sutlej, which separates it from the Cis-Sutlej hill states. It is about fifty-two miles in length from east to west, and twenty in breadth, having an area of 420 square miles, containing a population of 44,552, and yielding to the rajah a revenue of 80,000 rupees. Sukhet, the principal place, is in lat. 31° 33′, long. 76° 56′.

SUKKRUND.—A town in the British district of Hydrabad, province of Scinde, presidency of Bombay, 50 miles N. of Hydrabad. Lat. 26° 7′, long. 68° 24′.

SUKKUR, in Sinde, a decayed town on the west or right bank of the Indus, and opposite Roree, on the eastern bank, the island fortress of Bukkur lying between them. It is situate where a low limestone range slopes down to the river's bank, clothed in the neighbourhood of the town with luxuriant groves of date-palms. These groves, combined with the ruined but picturesque town of Sukkur, the river, the huge fortress of Bukkur, and the town of Roree, situated on the bold precipice opposite, form a very noble landscape. In 1839, a British cantonment was made at Sukkur, which became converted from a scene of desolation and wretchedness to one of activity and prosperity. Sukkur has still several towers, mosques, and minarets standing. One minaret is in a state of considerable preservation, and, according to Kennedy, is 100 feet high, and may be ascended by a winding stone staircase, affording access to the summit, whence is a noble prospect. It is a heavy, ill-proportioned column, without ornament. In a commercial point of view, Sukkur is a position of some importance. With the view to the promotion and encouragement of trade, the British government, in 1851, resolved to establish commercial fairs in Sinde. Sukkur was selected as the site of one of these, which is appointed to take place annually on the 1st of January, and to continue for the space of forty-five days. Lat. 27° 40′, long. 68° 54′.

SUKRANEH, in the British district of Furruckabad, lieut.-gov. of the N.W. Provinces, a town on the route from Furruckabad to Jaloun, 30 miles S.S.W. of the former. Lat. 27°, long. 79° 29′.

SUKREEA.—A town in the British district of Shahabad, lieut.-gov. of Bengal, 38 miles N.E. by E. of Sasseram. Lat. 25° 13′, long. 84° 33′.

SUKROUDUH, in the British district of Suharunpoor, lieut.-gov. of the N.W. Provinces, a town on the route from Suharunpoor to Hurdwar, 18 miles E. of the former. Lat. 30°, long. 77° 55′.

SUKTEE.—A small raj, computed by the political agent for the south-west frontier of Bengal, within whose jurisdiction it is included, to be of the annual value of 4,000 rupees; the tribute is 240: the area is 268 square miles. Its centre is in lat. 21° 52′, long. 82° 52′. It appears to be well managed: the tribute is regularly paid, and the people are represented to be quiet and contented. The population is about 12,000.

SUKTEESGURH, in the British district of Mirzapore, a village, with fort, 30 miles S.W. of Benares, 20 S.E. of Mirzapoor. Lat. 24° 58′, long. 82° 53′.

SUKTHA, a river of Malwa, rises in lat. 21° 38′, long. 76° 18′, and, flowing northerly for seventy miles through the territory of Scindia, falls into the Nerbudda river on the left side, in lat. 22° 11′, long. 76° 41′.

SUKULDEAH, in the British district of Benares, lieut.-gov. of the N.W. Provinces, a town on the route from Chunar to Dinapore, 28 miles N.E. of the former, 118 S.W. of the latter. Supplies and water are abundant. Lat. 25° 21′, long. 83° 20′.

SUKULPUR.—A village on the right bank of the Goulah, in the British district of Bareilly, division of Pillibheet, lieut.-gov. of the N.W. Provinces. Lat. 29° 4′, long. 79° 38′.

SUKURTAL, in the British district of Muzuffurnugur, lieut.-gov. of the N.W. Provinces, a small fort and assemblage of dwellings, about half a mile from the right bank of the Ganges, which is navigable from the sea to this point, where, according to Forster, the channel shoals so as to become fordable. Adjoining the place on the west are ruined fortifications, erected by Zabitah Khan, a Pathan chief. Lat. 29° 29′, long. 78° 3′.

SUKUTPOOR, in the British district of Furruckabad, lieut.-gov. of the N.W. Provinces, a town on the route from Furruckabad to Jaloun, 31 miles S. by W. of the former. Lat. 26° 57′, long. 79° 36′.

SULANA, in the territory of Indore, or possessions of Holkar's family, a town, the principal place of a district in the immediate possession of a petty Rajpoot rajah, descendant of a scion of the Jodhpoor family, who, about the middle of the seventeenth century, received an extensive grant of lands in this part of India from Shahjehan, the padshah of Delhi. The rajah is tributary to Scindia. In 1819, some disputes respecting tribute having arisen between the parties, the British government interposed, guaranteeing an annual amount of 42,000 rupees to Scindia, and non-interference and freedom from molestation to the rajah. The administration of the territory has been intrusted to a regency during the minority of the present chief, and the country is said to be improving. Distant N.W. from Oojein 60 miles, S.W. from Gwalior fort 285. Lat. 23° 28′, long. 74° 55′.

SULE.—A town within the dominions of Gholab Singh, the ruler of Cashmere, situate 136 miles E.S.E. from Sirinagur, and 95 miles N.E. by N. from Kangra. Lat. 33° 14′, long. 77° 9′.

SULEEMPOOR, in the British district of Paneeput, lieut.-gov. of the N.W. Provinces, a village on the route from the city of Delhi to Jheend, and 40 miles N.W. of the former. Lat. 29° 5′, long. 76° 56′.

SULEEMPOOR, in the British district of Boolundshuhur, lieut.-gov. of the N.W. Provinces, a village on the route from Khasgunj to Meerut, and 58 miles S. of the latter. Lat. 28° 20′, long. 78° 1′.

SULEMPOOR, in the British district of Cawnpoor, lieut.-gov. of the N.W. Provinces, a town on the route from Cawnpoor to Futtehpoor, 11 miles S.E. of the former. Lat. 26° 21′, long. 80° 32′.

SULEMPOOR, in the British district of Goruckpoor, lieut.-gov. of the N.W. Provinces, a small town in the pergunnah of Selempoor Majhowli, situate on the right bank of the Little Gunduck. Its original denomination was Nagar, which was changed to Islampoor, in honour of a rajah who, on his conversion to Mahometanism, took the name of Islam Khan, and subsequently, by corruption, the name became Sulempoor. It contains only eighty houses; but Majholi, on the opposite or left side of the Gunduck, contains 200; and the two places are usually considered as forming one town, the former being the Mahomedan, the other the Hindu part. Distant S.E. from Goruckpoor cantonment 45 miles. Lat. 26° 15′, long. 83° 57′.

SULEYMPOOR, in the British district of Budaoon, lieut.-gov. of the N.W. Provinces, a town on the route from Budaoon to Shahjehanpoor, 18 miles E. of the former. Lat. 28° 1′, long. 79° 30′.

SULIMAN MOUNTAINS.—An extensive and lofty range, forming the western boundary of the British empire in India. They may be considered to commence in lat. 33° 50′, and from that quarter stretch due south, in nearly the seventieth meridian of longitude, to the mountains about Hurrund and Kahun, and to lat. 29°, attaining their greatest height in lat. 31° 35′, where the Takht-i-Suliman, or "Suliman's seat," called also Khaisa Ghar, is 11,000 feet above the sea. This summit does not enter within the limit of perpetual congelation, being devoid of snow during the height of summer. Of its geological structure scarcely anything is known: Vigne only states that "it consists of recent formations, principally sandstone and secondary limestone, abounding in ammonites and other marine exuviæ, the strata being much shattered and contorted, and often overlaid by shingle." The eastern declivity dips rather steeply to the valley of the Indus, giving rise to numerous watercourses, which fertilize the Derajat, and are expended by absorption or irrigation. The western declivity is much more gradual, to the desert table-land of Sewestan. It is remarkable that no stream rising in this range is known to reach the sea in any direction, or by any channel, except the Kurum, which discharges a scanty volume of water into the Indus, above Kala Bagh. The greatest dimension of the range is from north to south, and is a little more than 350 miles. The Suliman range is generally considered the peculiar seat of the aboriginal Afghans. Nowhere is vegetation more vigorous and varied. The sides of the mountain nearly to the summit are clothed with dense and lofty forests, and the valleys overgrown with a great variety of indigenous trees, shrubs, and flowers.

SULKEA.—A populous suburb of Calcutta, situate on the opposite or western side of the river Hooghly. The government have here extensive godowns or warehouses for the reception of salt. Lat. 22° 34′, long. 88° 24′.

SULLAN, in the Jetch Dooab division of the Punjab, a town situated 13 miles S. from the left bank of the Jhelum, 60 miles W.S.W. of the town of Gujerat. Lat. 32° 23′, long. 73° 7′.

SULLIVAN'S ISLAND.—One of the group forming the Mergui Archipelago, situate about 12 miles W. of the coast of Tenasserim. It is thirty-six miles in length and three in breadth. Lat. 10° 50′, long. 98° 20′.

SULOOMBUR, in the territory of Oodeypore or Mewar, a town on the route from Neemuch to Baroda, 94 miles S.W. of former, 176 N.E. of latter. It is of considerable size, is walled, and has a bazar. Elevation above the sea 876 feet. Lat. 24° 7′, long. 74° 9′.

SULTANGUNJ, in the territory of Oude, a small town on the route by Shahabad from Lucknow to Shahjehanpoor, 58 miles N.W. of the former. Tennant, who saw it at the close of the last century, states, "The village of Sultangunge consists of mud houses wholly, but all neat, and in full repair. It is one of the few towns in India which does not exhibit marks of decay. Even here, however, are the ruins of far more durable and extensive cities, whose only vestige is to be traced by large mounts of brick-dust." It has a small bazar, and is well supplied with water. Lat. 26° 58′, long. 80° 15′.

SULTANKHANWALA, in Sirhind, a small town on the route from Ferozpoor to Simla, and 11 miles W. of the former place. It is abundantly supplied with water from three good wells; the surrounding country is level, and has a rich soil, bearing luxuriant crops of grain in the few cultivated places. It belongs to a Sikh chief under British protection and control. The road in this part of the route is good. Distant N.W. from Calcutta, by Loodiana, 1,157 miles. Lat. 30° 55′, long. 74° 42′.

SULTANPOOR, or KULU, in the north-east of the Punjab, and on the southern slope of the Himalaya, is the capital of the raj, or small state, of Kulu. It is situate on a triangular tongue of land between the river Beas and a feeder flowing into it on the right side. The southern, or lower part, which is next the river, contains the residence of the rajah; and north of this, and separated from it by a small bazar, is the upper part of the town, consisting of the houses of traders, shopkeepers, and artificers. The principal imports are chintzes, coarse cottons, and woollens, and the returns are made in opium and musk, the traffic being conducted by wandering mendicants, of whom great numbers arrive here on their route to various places of pilgrimage in the mountains. The place is, as Moorcroft observes, "of no great population or extent." Lat. 31° 57′, long. 77° 9′.

SULTANPOOR, in the British district of Agra, a village on the route from the city of Agra to Jeypore, and two miles W. of the former. The road in this part of the route is rather heavy, the country well cultivated. Lat. 27° 10′, long. 78° 3′.

SULTANPOOR, or SULTANPOOR-OUDE, in the kingdom of Oude, so named in contradistinction from Sultanpoor-Benares, the principal place of the district of the same name, is situate on the left bank of the Goomtee river. It was formerly the capital of the Bhars, a tribe of low caste, who once possessed "the whole tract from Goruckpore to Bundlecund and Saugor, and the large pergunnah of Bhudoee, in Benares." At that time it was named Kosbhawanpur; was situate amidst an immense jungle, harbouring tigers and wild elephants, and had a rampart eight miles in circumference, strengthened by bastions. It was taken by one of the early Ghorian invaders of India, supposed by Butter to have been Kai Kubad, who reigned from 1286 to 1289. The city, with its walls, was destroyed: on the ruins, now forming a shapeless heap of bricks, the conqueror constructed a fort, still remaining, but partially ruined, though containing habitable residences, occupied by the foujdar, or commandant of police, and his followers. North-west of the fort is an antique mosque, built by the sultan; and there are a few smaller mosques, built by Saiyids, or reputed descendants of Mahomet, the founder of Islam. The town having neither trade nor manufactures, is decaying, and consists for the most part of old brick houses, though there are a few new ones; among others, a large residence built by the vakeel or envoy of the Lucknow durbar. The population is estimated by Butter at 1,500, including 1,000 Mussulmans. The British cantonment is on the right of the river, and communicates with the left bank by ferry, being, even in the dry season, 100 yards wide, four feet deep, and navigable for large boats. Remote hydraulic action of the stream has excavated a small valley, extending along its course, from ten to 100 feet in breadth, on each side from the present banks, and with brows rising about ten feet above the height of the present stream when lowest, and half that height during the rains. The site of the cantonment is sixty feet above the brow of the valley, and preserved from malaria east and west by dry, barren, and undulating ground. On the north is the river; on the south cultivated ground, set off by a range of stone pillars. The station has the inestimable advantage of perfect drainage, occasioned by its proximity to a great stream, that never overflows the brows of the narrow valley down which it holds its course. There are, consequently, no marshes in the immediate vicinity, and none of any considerable size within such distance as to contaminate the atmosphere. The climate is generally characterized by dryness, comparative coolness and salubrity, with the exception of epidemic and contagious affections. In persons recently arrived from damper places, the excessive dryness produces catarrhs, toothache, earache, acute rheumatism, chapped hands and feet, and elephantiasis; still, the station is free from all endemic diseases of an important nature, and altogether is one of the healthiest localities in the plains of Hindoostan. The westerly winds, which prevail from November to June, produce dryness, accompanied by considerable cold, until March, and increasing in temperature for the remaining period of their prevalence, towards the close of which they are so sultry as to resemble the blast from a powerful furnace. Easterly winds prevail during the rainy season, from the latter part of June to the early part of October, and are always loaded with damp, disagreeable to the sensations and oppressive to the spirits. For a few days at the close of the rainy season, the air is so clear, that Dhoulagiri, one of the highest summits of the Himalaya, is visible, though at the distance of nearly 200 miles to the north. The wells of the cantonment, from forty to seventy feet deep, are cut through firm kunkar at little expense, and yield good water, notwithstanding the calcarious nature of the soil, and the copious efflorescence of nitrate, carbonate, and sulphate of soda, which appears on the surface. Snakes are numerous, particularly the two deadly species karait and cobra di capello; but the effects of their bites are generally found to yield to prompt treatment by brandy and laudanum. The communication by water, by the course of the Goomtee, is easy, though tedious, with Lucknow, Ghazeepore, Juanpore, and Benares. The roads in every direction are very bad. The cantonment, originally built to contain an entire brigade, was occupied at the date of the last returns by a regiment of irregular cavalry. Distant S.E. from Lucknow 92 miles, N. from Allahabad 59, from Calcutta, by Allahabad, 562. Lat. 26° 16′, long. 82° 8′.

SULTANPOOR SIVALA, in the British district of Suharunpoor, lieut.-gov. of the N.W. Provinces, a town on the route from Saharunpoor to Simla, 10 miles N.N.W. of the former. Lat. 30° 5′, long. 77° 32′.

SULTANPORE.—A town in the British district of Purneah, lieut.-gov. of Bengal, 30 miles N. by W. of Purneah. Lat. 26° 10′, long. 87° 23′.

SULTANWAH GAM.—A town in the Rajpoot state of Jessulmeer, 41 miles N. from Jessulmeer, and 126 miles E. by S. from Bukkur. Lat. 27° 29′, long. 70° 56′.

SUMBALKAH, or SUMALKA, in the British district of Paneeput, lieut.-gov. of the N.W. Provinces, a small town on the route from the city of Delhi to Kurnal, and 45 miles N.W. of the former. It has a small bazar, and a large caravanserai, once a fine structure, but now much dilapidated. Water is obtained from wells. Lat. 29° 14′, long. 77° 5′.

SUMBHUL, in the British district of Moradabad, lieut.-gov. of the N.W. Provinces, a town on the route from Moradabad to Allygurh, 22 miles S.W. of the former. Population 10,356. Lat. 28° 35′, long. 78° 39′.

SUMBULHERUH, in the British district of Muzufurnugur, lieut.-gov. of the N.W. Provinces, a town on the route from Muzufurnugur to Moradabad, 18 miles S.E. by E. of the former. Lat. 29° 19′, long. 77° 59′.

SUMBULPORE, the chief place in the district of the same name, is situate on the left bank of the Mahanuddy, in lat. 21° 29′, long. 84°. Little information is available as to this place; but it is stated to extend for about two miles along the bank of the river, and to contain some pagodas and other buildings of solid character. There is a fort, which, when the place was visited by the British agent in 1844, was in ruins. There is little or no trade, though the river, affording the means of water-carriage to Cuttack and the sea, is open for small boats throughout the year, and for large ones during six or eight months. The climate is said to be most fatal to the European constitution.

SUMBULPORE, formerly a raj, now a British district, within the range of territory subject to the control of the political agent for the south-west frontier of Bengal. With the exception of two small detached portions, it is bounded on the north by the native states of Ryghur and Gangpoor; on the east by Bonei and Bombra; on the south by Sonepoor and Patna; and on the west by those of Phooljee, Sarunghur, and Burgurh. It extends from lat. 21°—22° 5′, long. 83° 6′—84° 51′; is 112 miles in length from east to west, and sixty in breadth; and it embraces an area of 4,693 square miles. The river Mahanuddy flows through it, and divides it into two unequal parts, the larger lying on the right bank of the river. The eastern portion of this district is mountainous and woody, the northern and western parts generally of a more level character, and at some places greatly depressed. The valley of Sumbulpore, according to Dr. Royle's observations, is only 410 feet above the level of the sea. The soil of this valley is alluvial, and produces in great abundance and perfection, rice, wheat, and sugarcane. The first of these productions is reported to be of the finest quality, and the latter two grow with a luxuriance not surpassed in any part of India. According to the natives, the soil is well suited to the cultivation of the poppy, and they allege that it was formerly grown with advantage. Indigo, it is believed, might be cultivated with success, as the wild plant abounds. Swamps and jhils exist in this district, as in others within the limits of the agency to which it belongs. These become dry in April or May, and fill again on the commencement of the rains. Stagnant water is not by the natives deemed injurious; and so far from making drains for the purpose of carrying it off, they reserve it carefully for irrigation, and seem quite insensible to the disagreeable effluvia which it sends out. It is said that they do not suffer to any great extent from its effects; and it has been suggested, that the surface, being generally covered with plants, which give out a large proportion of oxygen, this provision of nature may tend to counteract the results which might otherwise arise from such deleterious accumulations. The hot winds begin to blow about the 20th March, and continue till the commencement of the rains, which in this district is usually about the 1st July.

The animal and vegetable productions of Sumbulpore are similar to those of the adjacent districts. Extensive forests of teak furnish an abundant supply of that valuable wood. In minerals, the district does not appear to be rich, except in that production, which in popular estimation ranks as the most valuable. Sumbulpore has universally been celebrated for the finest diamonds in the world. These gems are occasionally found in the bed of the Mahanuddy, and at the mouths of other rivers which terminate in it. Gold, but not in large quantities, is also found in the same situations. The quality of the diamond is characterized by a classification bearing the names of the four chief Hindoo castes, the most valuable being called a Brahmin. The diamond-searchers are employed in their occupation from the month of November to the rainy season. They are said to be a very dissipated race.

The population of Sumbulpore, including that of the hill forts, is estimated at 274,000. The great mass is composed of Hindoos of the lowest castes, but the chiefs and principal landholders claim the dignity of Rajpoots. There is no commerce worth notice. The raj was gratuitously conferred by the British government on a chief named Sahi, without "words of inheritance." It was, however, continued to two successors; but on the death of the latter of them without male issue, in 1849, it was annexed to the British dominions. Measures were immediately taken for the abolition of the transit-duties, and for effecting other improvements.

SUMBUR.—See SAMBHUR.

SUMBURPUR, in the British district of Cawnpore, lieut.-gov. of the N.W. Provinces, a village on the route from the cantonment of Futtehgurh to that of Cawnpore, and 18 miles N.W. of the latter. Lat. 26° 39′, long. 80° 13′.

SUMDO, in Bussahir, a village in the district of Koonawar, is situate on a small level space near the south-eastern base of the Manerung Pass, and six miles distant from it. The village has been formed here in consequence of the pasture yielded by the ground, irrigated from the snows above, and the abundant fuel from a forest of birches, the highest in locality to be met with on the vast mountain-range rising to the north-west. Elevation above the sea 12,915 feet. Lat. 31° 52′, long. 78° 25′.

SUMDUN, or SUMJUN, in the British district of Furruckabad, lieut.-gov. of the N.W. Provinces, a small town on the route from Cawnpore to the cantonment of Futtehgurh, and 18 miles S. of the latter. Lat. 27° 7′, long. 79° 46′.

SUMJOK.—A town of Burmah, 13 miles W. from the right bank of the Khyendwen river, and 206 miles N.W. by N. from Ava. Lat. 24° 28′, long. 94° 40′.

SUMMAHN.—A town of Burmah, situate on the left bank of the Irawady river, and 70 miles N. from Prome. Lat. 19° 48′, long. 94° 56′.

SUMMEE, in Guzerat, a town near the left bank of the river Saraswati. Its chief, a Mussulman, and member of the influential family of Babi, being also chief of Radunpoor, is styled Nawaub of Radunpur and Summee.

His annual income has been stated to be 1,50,000 rupees; and he yearly tenders a horse and clothes as acknowledgment of fealty to the Guicowar. Lat. 23° 40′, long. 71° 40′.

SUMMEI-KOUM.—A town of Burmah, situate on the left bank of the Irawady river, and 61 miles W. by S. from Ava. Lat. 21° 44′, long. 95° 5′.

SUMNAPOOR.—A town in the territory of Nagpoor, 91 miles N.E. by E. from Nagpoor, and 39 miles E. from Seuni. Lat. 22°, long. 80° 15′.

SUMODUTTEE.—A town in the British district of Belgaum, presidency of Bombay, 41 miles E. by S. of Belgaum. Lat. 15° 46′, long. 75° 11′.

SUMPTER, in Bundelcund, a small raj or principality under the political superintendence of the lieutenant-governor of the North-West Provinces. It lies between lat. 25° 42′—25° 57′, long. 78° 51′—79° 11′: it is estimated "to comprise 175 square miles, and was supposed in 1832 to contain seventy-two villages, with a population of 28,000 souls. The revenue was then estimated at five lacs (50,000*l.*), and in 1837 at 4,50,000 rupees (45,000*l*)." This state maintains a disproportionate force; namely, 300 horse, forty-five artillerymen, and 4,000 infantry. It was originally severed from the territory of Oorcha or Tehree, but the time and causes of the event do not appear to be ascertained. The rajah, in compliance with his repeated solicitations, was in 1817, by treaty, placed under British protection. The town of Sumpter is situate in lat. 25° 51′, long. 78° 58′.

SUMROO BEEGUM.—See SIRDHANA.

SUMSER, or SONAIR, in the British district of Meerut, lieut.-gov. of the N.W. Provinces, a village on the route from Delhi to the town of Meerut, and 15 miles N.E. of the former. Lat. 28° 44′, long. 77° 28′.

SUNA, in the British district of Allygurh, lieut.-gov. of the N.W. Provinces, a village on the route from the cantonment of Aligurh to that of Mynpooree, and 42 miles N.W. of the latter. Lat. 27° 36′, long. 78° 40′.

SUNASSEE COTTAH.—A town in the British district of Dinajepore, presidency of Bengal, 70 miles N. of Dinajepore. Lat. 26° 33′, long. 88° 23′.

SUNDEEP.—An island at the mouth of the Megna river: it is fertile, abounding with cattle, but free from tigers and other wild beasts which infest the neighbouring continent. Its length is about eighteen miles, and six broad. Lat. 22° 30′, long. 91° 32′.

SUNDELLA, in the territory of Oude, a town on the route from Lucknow to Shahjehanpoor, 30 miles N.W. of the former, 65 S.E. of the latter. It is situate on a level expanse, is half a mile in length, and has many brick-built houses, and a small mud fort, little capable of resisting attack. The inhabitants are principally Patans. Lat. 27° 4′, long. 80° 34′.

SUNDERBUNDS.—A maritime tract of British India, within the jurisdiction of the government of Bengal. This tract may be described as a crowded cluster of small marshy islands, separated by narrow channels, in some places containing brackish, in others fresh water, and generally under the influence of the tide. These islands have obviously been formed by the deposition of the enormous quantity of earth swept down by the Ganges during its periodical inundations. This alluvial archipelago, measured from the mouth of the river Hoogly, the most western of the estuaries of the Ganges, in lat. 21° 40′, long. 88° 3′, to the island of Rabanabad, in lat. 22°, long. 90° 30′, extends about 158 miles; and, thus defined, the Sunderbund district is bounded on the south by the Bay of Bengal; on the east and north-east by the British district of Backergunge; on the north by the British districts Jessore and Baraset; on the north-west by the British district of the Twenty-four Pergunnahs; and on the west by the estuary of the Hoogly. It is about seventy-five miles in breadth; the area is 6,500 square miles. The principal channels by which the water of the Ganges at present reaches the Bay of Bengal, occur in the following order, from west to east, from the Hoogly towards the Meghna:—1. The Moree Gunga, or channel creek; 2. the Subternookhi or Surseni; 3. the Thakooran, Hulluri, or Jumerah; 4. the Mutwal; 5. the Bangadooni; 6. the Guasuba; 7. the Roymungal; 8. the Mollinchoo; 9. the Baypunga; 10. the Murjatta or Kagga; 11. the Pussur; 12. the Bangarah; 13. the Hooringottah; 14. the Rabnabad channel. Though these channels are navigable for the largest craft used for inland navigation, they are in many parts so narrow, that the rigging of the vessels plying through them is entangled in the branches of the trees growing on the banks. Though there is some fine timber, the greater part of the wood is of small growth, suitable only for building boats, or for fire-wood, and for making charcoal for the supply of Calcutta. As the islands are everywhere covered with woods, they afford covert to numerous tigers, wild buffaloes, wild swine, monkeys, and deer. Tigers are peculiarly numerous and daring, preying on the woodcutters and the Molunghees, or those employed in extracting salt from the sea-water. The quantity of salt obtained in this way is very great, and supplies the demand of the lower provinces of Bengal. A large portion of these wastes is totally irreclaimable, the soil being a loose sand, and the surface liable to be overflowed either by unusually high tides or the periodical inundations of the river. In 1823 the extensive island of Saugor was totally submerged by the effects of a prolonged and violent gale. However, notwithstanding many great obstacles, improvement is making a steady though slow progress. The tract has been divided into estates to the number of 264, with an aggregate area of 1,800,000 acres, which, on certain conditions, are granted to applicants by government. The first scheme for bringing the waste lands under cultivation was promulgated in 1825 : this was superseded in 1830 by one more favourable to the grantees ; but in 1853 the government came to the conclusion that "the paramount object in devising rules for the disposal of lands in the Sunderbunds is to effect a clearance of that pestilent jungle in the shortest possible period, and to remove the stigma which most justly attaches to the existence of such a nuisance almost within sight of the capital. Lying," the Governor-General adds, "between the Bay of Bengal and the inhabited parts of the delta, its accumulated and perpetually exhaling malaria, urged by the south-west monsoon, spreads disease and death over the whole country ; the tract swarms with tigers and other wild beasts, whose ravages cause wide destruction both of life and property. The improvement of the revenue is an object of secondary importance." The home authorities concurred with the local government in regarding the clearing of the Sunderbunds as a most desirable object, irrespective of the improvement of the revenue ; and a revised scheme is under consideration. The importance attached by government to the improvement sought, and the liberality which it is disposed to exercise, are shown by its renunciation of almost all immediate or proximate revenue, it being proposed, on the conditions of clearance being duly fulfilled, to subject the land to payments little more than nominal, for a period extending to within one year of a century. Rice is the staple article, but one crop only in the year can be obtained. Besides this, the sugarcane and the indigo-plant have been introduced by the grantees ; and mulberry-trees, for feeding silkworms, have been planted to some extent. Wild honey is produced in great quantities in this tract, and the markets of Calcutta are abundantly supplied with fish from the numerous channels and watercourses. The occupation of the fishermen is, however, not devoid of danger, from the vast number of large and fierce alligators.

SUNDLEE.—A town in the Rajpoot state of Jodhpoor, situate on the left bank of the Loonee river, and 76 miles W.S.W. from Jodhpoor. Lat. 25° 49′, long. 72° 5′.

SUNDLEEPOOR, in the territory of Indore, or possessions of Holkar's family, a small town on the route from Baitool to Mow, 96 miles N.W. of former, 89 S.E. of latter. It has a good bazar, is provided with water from a well and a small stream, and supplies are abundant : population about 1,500. Lat. 22° 32′, long. 76° 57′.

SUNDLIPUR, in the British district of Moradabad, lieut.-gov. of the N.W. Provinces, a village on the route from the town of Moradabad to Hurdwar, and 10 miles N.W. of the former. Supplies for troops are obtainable, and water from wells. Elevation above the sea 690 feet. Lat. 28° 58′, long. 78° 45′.

SUNDOOA, in the British district of Hurriana, lieut.-gov. of the N.W. Provinces, a village close to the southern frontier, towards Shekhawutee. Lat. 28° 45′, long. 75° 54′.

SUNDRU, in Koonawar, a pass across the Himalaya range, extending from east to west, in the southern part of that district. This pass is so difficult, that the adventurous travellers the Gerards could not induce any of the natives to guide them over it. "The people represented it as crossing two ranges, and said it was very seldom attempted, and was never open more than two months in the year ; so it is probably little below 16,000 feet." Lat. 31° 24′, long. 78° 2′.

SUNDUN SERAI, in the British district of Moradabad, lieut.-gov. of the N.W. Provinces, a village on the route from Aligurh to the town of Moradabad, and 32 miles S.W. of the latter. Lat. 28° 32′, long. 78° 30′.

SUNEH, in the district of Salon, territory of Oude, a town near the right bank of the river Saee, 65 miles S.E. of Lucknow. The population is estimated by Butter at 6,000, of whom half are Mussulmans. Lat. 26° 5′, long. 81° 24′.

SUNERAMPOOR.—A town in the British district of Tipperah, lieut.-gov. of Bengal, 46 miles N. by W. of Tipperah. Lat. 24° 6′, long. 91° 2′.

SUNEYA MUNDI, in the British district of Bareilly, division of Pillibheet, lieut.-gov. of the N.W. Provinces, a village on the route from Bareilly to Petoragurh, and 64 miles N.E. of the former. There is a bazar here in the cool season, between November and April, in which interval the mountaineers descend to exchange the products of the more elevated regions for those of the plains. Lat. 28° 54′, long. 79° 58′.

SUNGLA, in Koonawar, a small town on the right bank of the Buspa. It has a fine appearance, and is built on a slope, with the houses rising one above the other, the scene being closed by the gigantic Ruldung peaks towering behind. The town has about fifty families, and is a place of some business, being the mart for traders from Gurwhal and Chooara, which districts send grain of various kinds, and receive in return salt from Chinese Tartary. Elevation above the sea 8,600 feet. Lat. 31° 25′, long. 78° 19′.

SUNGNUM, in Bussahir, a small town of the district of Koonawar, is situate on the left bank of the river Darbung, at the confluence of a torrent (the Bonkeeo) running from the north-east. Those streams yield water for the abundant irrigation of the fertile dell in which the town is situate, and which, in consequence, is for the length of three miles one cultivated area, enlivened with groves and rows of apple, walnut, and apricot trees, and vineyards yielding the finest grapes. The grape does not ripen farther north on this side the Sutluj, and its maturity here is owing to the summer's heat, caused by the reverberation of the sun's rays from the mountains inclosing the dell on every side, except towards the south-east, where it is open, and slopes down to the Sutluj. Apricot-trees bear a profusion of fruit, which is, however, poor and acid, in consequence of the neglect of grafting. They are, however, collected in great quantities, and, being dried in the arid air on the housetops of the villagers, form a considerable article of their winter stock of provisions, and the kernels yield, by expression, a large quantity of fragrant oil. Sungnum is 9,350 feet above the sea. Lat. 31° 45', long. 78° 31'.

SUNGROOR, in Sirhind, a village on the route from Hansee to Loodiana, and 51 miles S. of the latter town. It is situate in a level, well-cultivated country: the road in this part of the route is in general good, though, from the nature of the soil, in some places miry during heavy rains. Distant N.W. from Calcutta 1,061 miles. Lat. 30° 14', long. 75° 56'.

SUNGUM.—A town in Hyderabad, or territory of the Nizam, situate on the left bank of the Manjera river, and 109 miles N.N.W. from Hyderabad. Lat. 18° 49', long. 77° 53'.

SUNGUM.—A town in the British district of Nellore, presidency of Madras, 19 miles N.W. by W. of Nellore. Lat. 14° 35', long. 79° 49'.

SUNGUMESHWAR.—A town in the British district of Rutnageriah, presidency of Bombay, 21 miles N.E. by E. of Rutnageriah. Lat. 17° 9', long. 73° 36'.

SUNGUMNEIR.—A town in the British district of Ahmednuggur, presidency of Bombay, 49 miles N.W. of Ahmednuggur. Lat. 19° 35', long. 74° 14'.

SUNGURH.—A valley in the Daman division of the Punjab, about ninety miles W.N.W. of the town of Mooltan. Lat. 30° 44', long. 70° 6'.

SUNJA.—A town in the Rajpoot state of Jodhpoor, situate eight miles W. from the right bank of the Loonee river, and 92 miles S.W. by W. from Jodhpoor. Lat. 25° 42', long. 71° 51'.

SUNJAIT, in Malwa, a town in the native state of Jowra, situate on the small river Rithum. It is the principal place of a pergunnah containing forty-nine villages, held in jaghire by Nawwab Ghuffur Khan. Distance N. from Indore 115 miles, N.W. from Oojein 85, S.E. from Neemuch 27. Lat. 24° 18', long. 75° 18'.

SUNJULEE.—A town in the British district of Purneah, lieut.-gov. of Bengal, 12 miles S.E. of Purneah. Lat. 25° 39', long. 87° 41'.

SUNK RIVER.—The name given to the Byeturnee river during a portion of its course.

SUNKAR, a river of Arracan, rises in lat. 22° 10', long. 92° 40', and, flowing seventy miles through the district of Chittagong, falls into the sea in lat. 22° 10', long. 91° 58'.

SUNKAR NARAIN.—A town in the British district of South Canara, presidency of Madras, 51 miles N. of Mangalore. Lat. 13° 36', long. 74° 56'.

SUNOUT.—A town in the British district of Behar, lieut.-gov. of Bengal, 39 miles S.W. of Behar. Lat. 24° 50', long. 85° 10'.

SUNPOOR.—A town in the British district of Ramgur, lieut.-gov. of Bengal, 17 miles N. of Hazareebagh. Lat. 24° 13', long. 85° 29'.

SUNTA, in Sirhind, a small town on the route from Kurnal to Putteeala, and 39 miles N.W. of the former place. It is pleasantly situate on the Umla nuddi or torrent, in a level, fertile country, but imperfectly cultivated, and consequently much overrun with jungle. The road in this part of the route, notwithstanding the level nature of the country, is very bad, and scarcely practicable for guns or carriages. Distant N.W. from Calcutta 1,004 miles. Lat. 30° 10', long. 76° 44'.

SUNTOUR GURH, in the British district of Dehra Doon, lieut.-gov. of the N.W. Provinces, a town on the route from Dehra to Koonawar, eight miles N. of the former. Lat. 30° 25', long. 78° 5'.

SUNWARRA, in the British district of Saugur and Nerbudda, lieut.-gov. of the N.W. Provinces, a town on the route from Jubbulpoor to Baitool, 18 miles S.W. by W. of the former. Lat. 23°, long. 79° 49'.

SUPI, in the British district of Kumaon, lieut.-gov. of the N.W. Provinces, an extensive village on the route up the course of the river Surjoo, from Almorah fort to the Unta Dhura Pass, 38 miles N.E. of Almorah. Abreast of the village is a ford over the river, the elevation of the bed of which in that place is 5,659 feet above the sea. Lat. 30° 4', long. 80° 1'.

SUPPAHA, in the British district of Aligurh, lieut.-gov. of the N.W. Provinces, a village on the route from the city of Agra to Aligurh cantonment, and 27 miles N. of the former. Lat. 27° 30', long. 78° 7'.

SUPUHEE, in the British district of Goruckpoor, lieut.-gov. of the N.W. Provinces, a town on the route from Goruckpoor to Bettiah, 47 miles E. of the former. Lat. 26° 42', long. 84° 9'.

SURAGONG.—A town in the British district of Sumbulpoor, lieut.-gov. of Bengal, 97 miles W.N.W. of Sumbulpoor. Lat. 22° 3', long. 82° 40'.

SURAJA, in the Reechna Doab division of the Punjab, a town situated on the right bank of the Ravee, 90 miles S.W. of the town of Lahore. Lat. 30° 50', long. 73° 3'.

SURAJPOOR, in the British district of Boolundshuhur, lieut.-gov. of the N.W. Provinces, a town on the route from Aligurh to Delhi, and 22 miles S.E. of the latter. It has a bazar, and is abundantly supplied with water from wells. Lat. 28° 31′, long. 77° 32′.

SURAJPOOR, in the British district of Futtehpore, lieut.-gov. of the N.W. Provinces, a town with bazar, on the right bank of the Ganges, 117 miles by the river above Allahabad, and 925 above Calcutta. It is described by Lord Valentia as "pleasingly situated on the right bank of the river, with several Hindoo temples and ghats to the edge, for ablution, some of which were in ruins, but others were building." Viewed from the river, it has a pleasing yet ruinous appearance, resulting not so much from actual decay as from the irregular style of building and finishing usual in many Indian towns. Distant 22 miles N.W. from the town of Futtehpore. Lat. 26° 9′, long. 80° 39′.

SURAKELLA, or SERIEKALA, a raj situate within Singbhoom, and subject to the political agent for the south-west frontier of Bengal. Its centre is in lat. 22° 46′, long. 85° 55′. It was lately, during the minority of the rajah, in charge of one of the agent's assistants. The country is reputed to yield 10,000 rupees; the people are said to be wild; and, beyond this, little is known.

SURANDEE.—A town in the British district of Sarun, lieut.-gov. of Bengal, 38 miles S. of Bettiah. Lat. 26° 14′, long. 84° 37′.

SURANEE.—A town in the British district of Hydrabad, province of Scinde, presidency of Bombay, 67 miles S.S.E. of Hydrabad. Lat. 24° 30′, long. 68° 53′.

SURAT, the principal town of the British collectorate of the same name, presidency of Bombay, is situate on the left or south side of the river Taptee, here fordable when the tide is out, but at high tide navigable for boats of forty or fifty tons burthen. Sea-going vessels can only anchor off the bar, fifteen miles lower down. The road outside the bar is very dangerous in the spring, when southerly and westerly winds prevail; and when such set in violently, it is expedient to run up the river, should the draught be sufficiently small, or otherwise to stand out towards the west of the Gulf of Cambay, where shelter may be obtained from the reef and island of Perim. The outline of the town is an arc nearly semicircular, the river forming the chord, and the circuit being about six miles. The castle is situate about the middle of the chord, and though small, has bastions, covered way, and glacis. Surat is an ugly town, with narrow winding streets and high houses, constructed with frames of timber filled in with brick, and having the upper stories projecting beyond the base. It is surrounded by a wall in good repair, with semicircular bastions and battlements. The house formerly occupied by the nawaub of Surat is a plain building of moderate size. Most of the houses of the British inhabitants are in the vicinity of the fort, and are usually of good size, with spacious inclosures. Without the walls of the city is the site of the old French factory, containing some handsome and commodious buildings, now quite deserted: such also is the state of the ancient Dutch factory, once the most regular and best-built mansion about Surat. Surat, in the latter part of the eighteenth century, stood high as a commercial, and, though in a less degree, as a manufacturing place. Then the bazars were "filled with costly merchandise; picturesque and interesting groups of natives on elephants, camels, horses, and mules; strangers from all parts of the globe in their respective costumes; vessels building on the stocks, others navigating the river; together with Turks, Persians, and Armenians, on Arabian chargers; the European ladies in splendid carriages, the Asiatic females in hackeries, drawn by oxen." That vivid and bustling scene has faded away before the great superiority which Bombay has attained, alike in a political, commercial, and maritime point of view, and the competition of British wares, cheaper than those of India; and the commerce of the port is now in a great measure confined to the export of cotton, and of grain for the supply of the less-productive Concan, lying further south. Even now, however, Surat is a place of some importance, being the station of a considerable force, and of the civil establishment of the collectorate. Hence the British society is unusually numerous, and its tone agreeable. There is a very neat and convenient church, as well as an extensive and picturesque burial-ground, full of large ruinous tombs of the former servants of the East-India Company.

The city of Surat has suffered occasionally from the inundations of the river Taptee. In 1837, two of these visitations occurred, causing great damage to the city walls, public and private buildings, and bridges. Some immediate preventive steps were taken to defend the town from the recurrence of such irruptions, which were attributed to the combined effects of a supposed gradual elevation of the bed of the river, an alteration in its channel, and the obstruction of its mouth by a bar of sand. But the more recent reports of the engineer officers throw doubt upon this opinion, and the selection of final measures for affording to the town security from injury by inundation, has been postponed until more complete information shall have been attained. The irruptions drew attention to the general state of the town, and on the occasion last referred to, authority was given for an annual expenditure of 40,000 rupees on the streets, draining, and public works connected with the health and convenience of the inhabitants. The population of the town in 1838 was 133,544. Surat has been conjectured to be a place of great antiquity;. but this conclusion perhaps results from confounding the name of Sorath or Sourashtra, a district of Guzerat, with Surat, the name of the town which is the subject of the present article. The earliest authentic notice respecting this town is probably the mention of its discovery and sack by the Portuguese in 1530, at which time it is described as "containing 10,000 families, mostly handicrafts. An army attempted defence outside the town, but quickly took to flight, and then the city was entered without any further resistance, and nothing left in it that had life, or was of value. Then the city and some ships that lay in the arsenal were burned." In 1531, the town having in some measure recovered from this calamity, was again burned by the Portuguese.

In 1612, permission was granted by Jehangir to establish an English factory at Surat, and in 1657 all the possessions of the Company in the East Indies were placed under the control of the president and council of Surat; but from the subsequent acquisition of Bombay, the importance of Surat progressively declined until 1692, when the seat of the presidency was transferred. In 1664, Sir George Oxenden being governor, Surat was plundered by Sevajee, the Mahratta leader; but the English successfully defended their factory, and having also afforded protection to many of the citizens and their property, Aurungzebe, in recognition of that assistance, granted the East-India Company exemption from the duties levied on others trading at Surat.

During the early part of the eighteenth century, while the empire of Delhi was crumbling into ruins, Surat fell into a state of utter confusion, there being within it a number of conflicting authorities,—Mogul, Mahratta, and others. The Bombay government, greatly interested in the restoration of order at Surat, were zealous to effect this object, either with or without the co-operation of the Mahrattas; but their designs were frustrated, sometimes by the feebleness and vacillation of their own counsels, sometimes by the difficulty of securing the fidelity and stimulating the exertions of the wayward and treacherous people to whom they looked for co-operation. At length taking courage to act vigorously for themselves, they in 1759 attacked the castle of Surat, and succeeded in gaining possession of it. Thenceforward, though order was preserved, a divided authority continued to exist in Surat, the English being charged with the defence of the place, while a portion of the civil power was in the hands of a nawaub, both parties professing to act under the authority of the emperor, though that authority soon became but a name; and the nawaub, in fact, held his office at the pleasure of his British coadjutors. After a continuance of about forty years, a favourable opportunity occurred for terminating a state of things productive of many evils. On the death of the nawaub, in 1799, the British government, with the earnest wishes of the inhabitants of Surat, assumed the entire administration, civil as well as military, conceding to a relative of the deceased the title of nawaub, with a large pensionary provision. This arrangement was settled by treaty concluded in 1800. In 1842 the titular dignity of nawaub became extinct, by the death of its last possessor without male heirs; but certain privileges have been continued to his family. An attempt, made on the part of the government, in 1847, to introduce a uniform system of weights and measures into this city, resulted in failure. The government directed that only mild and conciliatory means should be employed to overcome the aversion of the shopkeepers to the measure, and remove the obstacles to its introduction. Surat is distant from Bombay, N., 150 miles; from Ahmedabad, S., 130. Lat. 21° 10′, long. 72° 52′.

The district of Surat, of which this town is the principal place, is bounded on the north by the collectorate of Broach; on the east by Guzerat; on the south by Guzerat and the British collectorate of Tannah; and on the west by the Portuguese territory of Damaun and the Arabian Sea. It extends from lat. 20° 15′ to 21° 11′, and from long. 72° 45′ to 73° 24′; and contains an area of 1,629 square miles. The population is given under the article BOMBAY. Its boundaries were formerly more extended, and comprised within their limits the contiguous collectorate of Broach, which, in 1843, was placed under a separate jurisdiction. The two districts bear a close resemblance to each other, no less in their chief physical characteristics than in their statistical and social circumstances; and as minute details on these points are given in the article BROACH, which are generally applicable to Surat, the reader is referred to the former head for further information.

SURAWALA, in the British district of Bhuttiana, lieut.-gov. of the N.W. Provinces, a village on the route from Hansee to Bhutnair, and 14 miles E. of the latter. Lat. 29° 35′, long. 74° 38′.

SURAWUL, in the British district of Mynpoorie, lieut.-gov. of the N.W. Provinces, a village on the route from the cantonment of Aligurh to Futtehgurh, and 49 miles N.W. of the latter. Lat. 27° 35′, long. 78° 59′.

SURBURI SUROREE, in the Rajpoot state of Jodhpoor, a village on the route from Balotra to the city of Jodhpoor, and 21 miles N.E. of the former. Lat. 25° 54′, long. 72° 43′.

SURDA, in the British district of Rajeshaye, lieut.-gov. of Bengal, a town situate on a ridge of clay and kunkur, or calcareous conglomerate, on the left bank of the Podda, or great eastern branch of the Ganges, in a country "very populous, well cultivated, and as beautiful as verdure, shade, water, and the splendid variety of Indian shrubs and trees can make it." Here was formerly an extensive filature, or silk establishment, belonging to the East-India Company. Distance N. from Calcutta, by Berhampore, 153 miles. Lat. 24° 18′, long. 88° 42′.

SUR DEOTA.—A peak near Subathoo, so called because sacred to Sur or Mahadeo. Elevation above the sea 5,419 feet. Lat. 31° 3′, long. 77° 6′.

SURDHAUR, in the peninsula of Katteewar, province of Guzerat, a town belonging to a Rajpoot thakoor or chief, who once resided here, but removed to Rajkote, another town belonging to him. Distance from Ahmedabad, S.W., 118 miles; Baroda, W., 140. Lat. 22° 8′, long. 71° 1′.

SUREELA, in Bundelcund, a small raj or principality, named from its principal place, is inclosed on all sides by the British district of Humeerpoor, and lies between lat. 25° 43′—25° 51′, long. 79° 41′—79° 48′. It is "stated to comprise thirty-five square miles, and to contain only eleven villages, with a population of 4,500 souls. Its revenue is estimated at 45,000 rupees (4,500*l.*) per annum, and it maintains a force of twenty-five horse and seventy-five foot." The town is 25 miles S. of Calpee, 45 N.W. of Banda. Lat. 25° 46′, long. 79° 48′.

SUREYA, in the British district of Goruckpoor, lieut.-gov. of the N.W. Provinces, a village on the route from Goruckpoor cantonment to Lucknow, eight miles W. of the former, 158 E. of the latter. Lat. 26° 45′, long. 83° 15′.

SURGONG.—A town in the territory of Nagpoor, 47 miles N.N.E. from Ryepoor, and 91 miles S.E. from Ramgurh. Lat. 21° 50′, long. 81° 58′.

SURGOOR.—A town in the Mysore, situate on the right bank of the Cauvery river, and 36 miles S.W. by S. from Seringapatam. Lat. 12°, long. 76° 26′.

SURHA, in the British district of Banda, lieut.-gov. of the N.W. Provinces, a village on the route from Allahabad to Kalleenjur, 104 miles S.W. of former, eight N.E. of latter. Lat. 25° 6′, long. 80° 36′.

SURHUCHEEA.—A town in the British district of Tirhoot, lieut.-gov. of Bengal, 14 miles N.N.E. of Mozufferpoor. Lat. 26° 17′, long. 85° 33′.

SURHUD.—A town of Sinde, in the presidency of Bombay, situate seven miles S.E. of the left bank of the Indus, and 46 miles N.E. from Bukkur. Lat. 28° 5′, long. 69° 29′.

SURJOO (EASTERN).—A river tributary to the Ghogra. It rises in the kingdom of Nepaul (where it is known by the name of the Relang), in lat. 28° 15′, long. 81° 57′, and flowing in a direction north-westerly for forty miles, it, in lat. 28° 26′, long. 81° 24′, enters the plains of Oude. Its course is then generally from north to south for about 120 miles, when it falls into the great river Ghogra, on its left side, in lat. 26° 58′, long. 81° 46′. At its mouth it expands into a sort of morass; at Burraech, forty-five miles from its mouth, and in lat. 27° 34′, long. 81° 40′, it is described, rather indefinitely, by Tieffenthaler, as "a stone's throw in breadth, and in December [season of low water] two Indian ells deep;" but he adds that it occasionally becomes fordable.

SURJOO, or SURJU (WESTERN), a considerable tributary of the great river Ghogra, rises in the British district of Kumaon, in a gorge on the southern face of the main range of the Himalaya. Eight miles from the source, according to Webb, "the breadth of the Surjoo below Soopee is about fifteen yards, and at this time [early in May] may be forded in twenty inches water. The hills across [beyond] the river [or to the eastward], rise gradually to a lofty chain, the summit of which is yet covered with snow, and its eastern base is washed by the [Eastern] Rangunga river." The great elevation of the source is indicated by the snow, which lies about it so late in the year. At Soopee, already mentioned, the bed of the river is 5,659 feet above the sea. A few miles lower down, Webb forded it in two feet of water, with a breadth of twelve yards; and a few miles still lower, or about fifteen miles from its source, the same traveller found it, in the middle of May, forty-five yards wide, and twenty-seven inches deep. It holds a south-westerly direction, receiving many streams; and one of considerable volume (the Phoongur) falls into it on the left side, thirty-one miles from the source, and in lat. 29° 52′, long. 79° 49′. Flowing five miles further in the same direction, it, at Bagesar or Bageswar, receives, on the right side, the Gaomutee, a considerable stream running from the north-west. From that point it takes a south-easterly direction, receiving several small streams, and thirty-five miles below the confluence of the Gaomutee it receives, on the right side, the Punar, a considerable river flowing from the south-west. About ten miles above this confluence, sixty miles from the source, and in lat. 29° 38′, long. 80° 3′, Webb found "the average breadth about fifty yards, the drift four and a half to five miles per hour. The depth at present [probably in May] is about eight feet, but it becomes fordable about December." Flowing from the confluence with the Punar still in a south-easterly direction, it at Ramesur, three or four miles farther down, receives, on the left side, its greatest feeder, the Ramgunga (Eastern), flowing from the north. This confluence is 1,500 feet above the sea; and as the elevation of the source of the Surjoo may with probability be assumed to be 7,000 feet, its average fall throughout its course to Ramesur, a distance of seventy-four miles, will be above seventy feet in the mile. It is accordingly there "a most impetuous and rapid torrent, dashing over the rocks with the greatest force, causing a deafening noise, and casting the spray about in all directions." Below the confluence it is indifferently called the Surjoo or the Ramgunga. Near the confluence it is crossed by an iron suspension-bridge 180 feet in span. Continuing to flow in a south-easterly direction for twelve miles farther, it, at Puchesur, in lat. 29° 27′, long. 80° 18′, falls into the Kalee (Eastern), or principal head-water of the great river Ghogra. Six furlongs above this confluence, Webb found the river fordable in the season of low water; "the breadth of the stream about eighty yards; transparent, bed stony, depth of the ford about four and a quarter feet; drift of current four miles per hour or more." The total length of course is between eighty and ninety miles. Herbert reckons the continuous courses of the Surjoo and Kali or Ghoghra, from the source of the former river to the entrance of the latter on the plain of Hindoostan, at Bhirm-Deo, to be 143 miles. The united stream, more generally called the Ghoghra, but also known by the name of the Surjoo throughout the whole length of its course to its junction with the Ganges, and under the kindred names of Siru, Sirwu, or Sirjoo, is repeatedly mentioned by Baber. In this river is found the highly esteemed fish the mahasur.

SURKANDA, in Gurwhal, a high mountain near the southern frontier, and overlooking the Dehra Doon. It forms part of the ridge separating the Jumna from the Bhageerettee, as the Ganges is called in the upper part of its course. There is a Hindoo temple on the summit, the formation of which is characterized by Hodgson and Herbert as "composed of a dull greyish stone, coarsely granulated, and having a conchoidal fracture. It is semi-hard." It was a station of the large series of triangles in the trigonometrical survey of the Himalaya. Elevation above the sea 9,271 feet. Lat. 30° 25′, long. 78° 21′.

SURKARA, in the British district of Allahabad, lieut.-gov. of the N.W. Provinces, a village on the route from the cantonment of Allahabad to Futtehpore, and 24 miles N.W. of the former. Lat. 25° 34′, long. 81° 35′.

SURKUNDA, in the British district of Futtehpoor, lieut.-gov. of the N.W. Provinces, a town on the left bank of the Jumna, 18 miles S. of the town of Futtehpore. Lat. 25° 42′, long. 80° 53′.

SURMALEE.—A town and stockade in Nepal, 80 miles W. from Jemlah, and 46 miles E.S.E. from Almora. Lat. 29° 21′, long. 80° 23′.

SURMOTE.—A town within the dominions of Gholab Singh, the ruler of Cashmere, situate 54 miles S. from Sirinagur, and 81 miles E.N.E. from Jhelum. Lat. 33° 23′, long. 74° 45′.

SUROLI, in the British district of Goorgaon, lieut.-gov. of the N.W. Provinces, a village on the route from Alwar, by Ferozpoor, to Delhi, and 16 miles S.W. of the latter. Lat. 28° 28′, long. 77° 8′.

SURREY KONDAH.—A town in Hyderabad, or territory of the Nizam, 31 miles S.S.E. from Hyderabad, and 88 miles N.E. by N. from Kurnool. Lat. 16° 56′, long. 78° 41′.

SURROOL, in the British district of Beerbhoom, lieut.-gov. of Bengal, a town on the route from Burhampoor to Bancoora, 55 miles S.W. of former, 60 N.E. of latter. It is situate two miles N. of the north or left bank of the Aji river. Lat. 23° 40′, long. 87° 42′.

SURRUKPOOR, in the Reechna Dooab division of the Punjab, a town situated on the right bank of the Ravee river, 18 miles S.W. of the town of Lahore. Lat. 31° 27′, long. 74° 4′.

SURRUNGURH.—See Sarunghur.

SURSAWA.—A town in the British district of Sumbulpoor, on the south-west frontier of Bengal, 88 miles W. of Sumbulpoor. Lat. 21° 30′, long. 82° 40′.

SURSEEA.—A town in the British district of the Twenty-four Pergunnahs, lieut.-gov. of Bengal, 26 miles S.S.W. of Calcutta. Lat. 22° 15′, long. 88° 16′.

SURSODA.—A town in the British district of Balasore, lieut.-gov. of Bengal, 54 miles S.W. of Balasore. Lat. 20° 56′, long. 86° 26′.

SURSU DEBI, in Sirmoor, a summit of the Sain range, near its north-western extremity, rises from the right bank of the river Giree. It is surmounted by a small white temple, a secondary station in the great trigonometrical survey of the Himalaya. Elevation above the sea 6,299 feet. Lat. 30° 51′, long. 77° 16′.

SURTOONA.—A town in Guzerat, or territory of the Guicowar, 90 miles N.N.E. from Baroda, and 81 miles N.E. from Kaira. Lat. 23° 30′, long. 73° 39′.

SURUGTHAL, in the British district Bijnour, lieut.-gov. of the N.W. Provinces, a village on the route from Moradabad to Hurdwar, and 34 miles N.W. of the former. Lat. 29° 16′, long. 78° 36′.

SURUMNAGAR, in the territory of Oude, a small town on the route from Lucknow to Shahjehanpoor, 103 miles N.W. of the former. It is situate on the left bank of the Lesser Goomtee, and has an old fort, described by Heber as "pretty much like a large serai, surrounded by a high brick wall, with round towers at the flanks, and two Gothic gateways opposite to each other." Within is "a narrow street of mud houses, some looking like warehouses, and the whole having more the air of a place where the peasantry of a small district were accustomed to secure their stores, than the usual residence of any considerable number of people." Outside are a little straggling bazar and a few huts, with a Hindoo temple, but no mosque. Lat. 27° 33′, long. 80° 2′.

SURWANNEE SURAE, in the British district of Benares, lieut.-gov. of the N.W. Provinces, a town with a bazar on the route from the city of Benares to Jounpoor, nine miles N.W. of the former, 29 S.E. of the latter.

Supplies and water may be had in abundance. Lat. 25° 25′, long. 82° 57′.

SURWAR, in the Rajpoot state of Kishengurh, a town on the route from Goona to Nusseerabad, 204 miles N.W. of the former, 25 S.E. of latter. It has a good bazar, and water is abundant. Lat. 26° 5′, long. 75° 8′.

SURWUN.—A town of Malwa, in the native state of Rutlam, 20 miles N.W. from Rutlam, and 70 miles S. by W. from Neemuch. Lat. 23° 29′, long. 74° 49′.

SURWUN.—A town in the British district of Mongheer, lieut.-gov. of Bengal, 60 miles S. of Mongheer. Lat. 24° 30′, long. 86° 20′.

SUSOLAR, in the British district of Humeerpore, lieut.-gov. of the N.W. Provinces, a town on the route from the town of Banda to that of Humeerpore, 15 miles N. of the former. Lat. 25° 40′, long. 80° 19′.

SUSRAL, in the Sinde Sagur Dooab division of the Punjab, a town situated 13 miles W. from the right bank of the Jhelum, 118 miles N.N.W. of the town of Lahore. Lat. 33° 12′, long. 73° 32′.

SUSTWAR, in Bussahir, a village in the pergunnah of Pekha, and hence sometimes called by that name. It is situate in a delightful country, in many places well wooded, and in general carefully and successfully cultivated. Lloyd observes, "Many of the women were very handsome; their complexions are fair and blushing." Elevation above the sea 8,759 feet. Lat. 31° 15′, long. 78° 2′.

SUTGARH, in the British district of Kumaon, lieut.-gov. of the N.W. Provinces, a village on the route from Petoragurh to Askoth, six miles N.E. of the former. Lat. 29° 40′, long. 80° 19′.

SUTI.—A town within the dominions of Gholab Singh, the ruler of Cashmere, situate on the right bank of the Kishengunga river, and 57 miles N. from Sirinagur. Lat. 34° 55′, long. 75° 1′.

SUTJORA.—A town in the British district of Sarun, lieut.-gov. of Bengal, 30 miles N. by E. of Chupra. Lat. 26° 10′, long. 84° 56′.

SUTLUJ.—The most easterly of the rivers of the Punjab, "the rise of which in the holy lakes of Manasarovara and Rawan Hrad, has been satisfactorily ascertained by the adventurous journeys of Captain H. Strachey and Lieut. R. Strachey." Its most remote sources are the eastern feeders of the lakes, in lat. 30° 8′, long. 81° 53′. Moorcroft, in his journey to Manas Sarovara, seems to have approached near to the source, having come upon the Sutoodra or Sutluj. It subsequently issues from the north-western extremity of this lake, being there in the dry season thirty feet broad, and takes a north-westerly course of about 188 miles through a country of awful and even terrific sublimity, as far as Khab, in lat. 31° 48′, long. 78° 40′. Close to this it receives the river of Spiti from the north-west. Above the confluence, the Sutluj is seventy-five feet wide; its bed 8,600 feet above the level of the sea. Gerard observes, "It is not easy to form an estimate of the water contained in the Sutluj; for although the breadth can be determined, yet within the mountains there is scarcely a possibility of sounding it, on account of its great rapidity." The depth at this spot must be very great, as the volume of water is considerable even eighty miles further up, where, at Ling, the river is too broad to admit of a rope-bridge, and is crossed by one of iron chains; the breadth thereabouts being 120 yards; the depth, at the lowest season, one foot and a half; the rapidity seven or eight miles an hour; the impetus of the stream such as that it can be forded only by yaks or Tartarian kine, if the depth exceed two feet. The bed of the river, a short distance below Ling, is 10,792 feet above the sea. Here the river is by the natives called Langzhing-Khampa, or the river of Langzhing; lower down, Muksung; then, Sanpoo; lower still, Zeung-tee; lower down, Sumeedrung; in Busehar, Sutoodra, or "hundred-channelled," whence the names Zadadrus and Hesudrus of the classical writers; lower down, it is generally called the Sutluj, by which name it is also known up to its source. Though the river is in the upper part of its course a raging torrent, falling in several places 100 or 150 feet per mile, with a clamorous noise and displaying heaps of white foam, yet so severe is the climate, that for 200 miles it is completely frozen for two months every winter. Where not fordable, it is crossed either by a sango, or wooden bridge; by a jhoola, or rope-bridge, which the traveller passes on a seat suspended by a loop made to slide along the rope, by means of a long string, pulled by men stationed on the further bank; or by means of a suzum, or foot-bridge, formed of cables, stretched parallel to each other. These frail suspension-bridges sometimes give way, and the passengers are dashed to pieces. There are also a few chain bridges. At the confluence of the Spiti and Sutluj, the scene is described as awfully sublime; according to Lloyd and Gerard, "the character of the gulf is certainly one of the wonders of the world." The Lee, or river of Spiti, issues forth from a rocky channel, so narrow and deep as almost to seem subterranean, with a calm, blue, deep current. The Sutluj is muddy, and breaks violently on the rocks with a tremendous roaring. The Spiti has probably a larger body of water than the Sutluj. The former river averages from 250 to 300 feet in breadth; the latter, a short distance above the confluence, is seventy-five feet broad. Below the confluence, the stream is so deep and rapid that no bottom could be found with a ten-pound sounding-lead. From this remarkable point its general course is south-west, with a very rapid declivity. At Namptoo the height of its bed is 8,220 feet, its breadth 106; at Wangtoo (lat. 31° 32′, long. 78° 1′) the height of its bed is 5,200 feet, the breadth is ninety-two; at Rampoor (lat. 31° 26′, long. 77° 40′), the height of the bed is 3,360, the width 211. These measurements were made at the narrowest places, where bridges have been constructed; but in other places it is 150 yards wide. From Rampoor to Bilaspoor, in lat. 31° 21′, long. 76° 48′, its course is generally west-south-west. Forster, who crossed it here, describes it as a very rapid stream, about 100 yards broad. A short distance below this it makes a sudden sweep to the north-west, and then back again to the south-east to Ropur, in lat. 30° 58′, long. 76° 35′, where it makes its way through the low sandstone range of Jhejwan, and enters the plain of the Punjab. It is here thirty feet deep, and more than 500 yards wide in its season of greatest fulness, and is crossed either in boats or on floats of inflated buffalo-hides. As is the case with all the rivers descending from the Himalaya, it is far fullest in June, July, and August. At the ferry of Filor or Faloor, in lat. 31° 1′, long. 75° 50′, it was found, in the season when lowest, to be 250 yards wide, seven feet deep, and moderately rapid. Burnes, who crossed it here in August, when fullest, found it 700 yards wide, with a depth, where greatest, of eighteen feet, but on an average of only twelve. Up to this point it is navigable at all seasons for vessels of ten or twelve tons burthen. Its confluence with the Beas is a little above Hurekee, and in lat. 31° 11′, long. 75° 4′. According to Macartney, the Beas has the larger body of water. The whole length of the river, from the point where it issues from Lake Manasarovara to its junction with the Beas, is 550 miles. Below this confluence, as far as the confluence with the Chenaub, a distance of 300 miles, the united stream bears the name of Ghara. Thenceforward the aggregate body of water, until its confluence with the Indus, bears the name of Punjnud, a name derived from its conveying the accumulated waters of the Beas, Sutluj, Ravee, Chenaub, and Jhelum. As before mentioned, the Sutluj is considered to be the Zaradrus, Zadadrus, or Hesudrus of the ancients, and the Hypanis mentioned by Strabo.

SUTNA, or SUTANI, a small river rising in Bundlecund, on the southern declivity of the Panna range of hills, about eight miles south-east of the town of Panna, and in lat. 24° 42′, long. 80° 23′. The elevation above the sea, of its source, cannot be much less than 1,100 feet; as at Sohawul, forty miles to the east, or down the stream, the elevation is 1,059 feet. About that place the course turns rather to the south-east, and twelve miles lower down it falls into the Tons, on the left side, in lat. 24° 30′, long. 80° 56′. The route from Allahabad to Saugor crosses "the Sutnee close under Sohawul—bed fifty yards wide; stream two and a half feet deep; banks rather steep." The passage here was formerly defended by a fort, now in ruins.

SUTRALI, in the British district of Kumaon, lieut.-gov. of the N.W. Provinces, a village with a temple on the route from Almora fort to Juwahir Pass, or Unta Dhura, and 17 miles N. of Almora. Lat. 29° 46′, long. 79° 44′.

SUTTAI, a town of Bundelkund, in the native state of Punnah, 39 miles W. from Punnah, and 84 miles N.E. from Saugur. Lat. 24° 42′, long. 79° 40′.

SUTTALUREE.—A town in the British district of Backergunje, lieut.-gov. of Bengal, 126 miles E. of Calcutta. Lat. 22° 40′, long. 90° 11′.

SUTTEHGEEREE.—A town in the British district of Belgaum, presidency of Bombay, 39 miles E.N.E. of Belgaum. Lat. 16° 1′, long. 75° 7′.

SUTTICUL.—A town in the British district of Coimbatoor, presidency of Madras, 89 miles N. by E. of Coimbatoor. Lat. 12° 15′, long. 77° 13′.

SUTULANU.—A town in the Rajpoot state of Jodhpoor, situate on the right bank of the Loonee river, and 24 miles S.S.W. from Jodhpoor. Lat. 26°, long. 73°.

SUTWARAH.—A town in the native state of Indore, or territory of Holkar, 65 miles S. by E. from Indore, and 16 miles S.E. from Kurgoon. Lat. 21° 44′, long. 75° 59′.

SUTWAS.—A town in the native state of Gwalior, or territory of Scindia's family, 70 miles S.E. from Oojein, and 76 miles W.S.W. from Hoosungabad. Lat. 22° 29′, long. 76° 37′.

SWALI, in the collectorate of Surat, presidency of Bombay, a small town at the entrance of the river Taptee. A spot denominated by our sailors Swallow Point, and projecting south from the town, is the northern point of the entrance of the Taptee, or road of Surat, from which city it is distant by water 18 miles west. During the early part of the seventeenth century, when Surat was the seat of the presidency for managing the affairs of the East-India Company in Western India, Swali was a place of considerable importance, and the roads the scene of some actions between the ships of the English company and those of their rivals the Dutch. Distance N. from Bombay 150 miles, S. from Baroda 90, S. from Ahmedabad 135. Lat. 21° 4′, long. 72° 44′.

SWAN, a river of the Punjab, rises in a subordinate range of the Himalaya, west of Cashmere, and in lat. 33° 45′, long. 73° 7′. It holds a south-westerly course of 120 miles, and falls into the Indus on the left side, about ten miles below Mukkud, and in lat. 33° 1′, long. 71° 46′. Elphinstone, who crossed it in lat. 33° 37′, long. 73° 3′, and about thirty miles from its source, describes it to be, where forded, "a large rivulet, which, though only up to our horses' girths, was so rapid as to be scarcely fordable. Several of our camels were swept down by the stream." Hough, who crossed the Swan when the water was low, describes it as having "a stony bed, not broad, and one foot of water." Burnes, who crossed this stream in lat. 33° 6′, long. 72° 12′, found it there "rapid, red, and swollen," and stirrup-deep.

SYARA.—A town in the Rajpoot state of Jodhpoor, 42 miles E.N.E. from Jodhpoor, and 59 miles W. from Ajmeer. Lat. 26° 29′, long. 73° 48′.

SYDABAD, in the British district of Allahabad, lieut.-gov. of the N.W. Provinces, a town on the route from the city of Allahabad to that of Benares, and 18 miles S.E. of the former. It is four miles from the left bank of the Ganges, has a bazar, and water and supplies are abundant. Lat. 35° 22′, long. 82° 10′.

SYDAPOORUM.—A town in the British district of Nellore, presidency of Madras, 25 miles S.W. of Nellore. Lat. 14° 11′, long. 79° 49′.

SYDOPRE, in the British district of Ghazeepoor, lieut.-gov. of the N.W. Provinces, a town with a bazar, on the route from Benares to the cantonment of Ghazeepoor, 23 miles N.E. of the former, and as many W. of the latter. It is situate on the left bank of the Ganges, near the confluence of the Goomtee, which last river is traversed by the route from Benares by means of ferry during the rains, and during the rest of the year by bridge of boats. Distant N.W. from Calcutta, by water, 641 miles. Lat. 25° 30′, long. 83° 18′.

SYJERAH, in the Baree Dooab division of the Punjab, a town situated nine miles from the right bank of the Sutlej, 35 miles S.E. by S. of the town of Lahore. Lat. 31° 6′, long. 74° 30′.

SYLHET.—See SILHET.

SYMBRAMKUM, in the British district Chingleput, presidency of Madras, a town close to a tank twenty miles in circuit, formed by an embankment between two natural ridges of ground, and irrigating an extent of land giving employment to 5,000 cultivators. Distance from Madras, W., 17 miles. Lat. 13° 4′, long. 80° 3′.

SYNJUNA, in the British district of Shahjehanpoor, lieut.-gov. of the N.W. Provinces, a village on the route from Bareilly to the cantonment at Futehgurh, and 43 miles S.E. of the former. Lat. 27° 48′, long. 79° 43′.

SYREE, in that portion of the hill state of Koonear bestowed upon the rajah of Putteeala, is the name of a pass over a ridge between Subathoo and Simla, and 12 miles N.E. of the former post. Here is a small village with a good house, built for the accommodation of travellers by the British authorities. Elevation above the sea 4,971 feet. Lat. 31° 6′, long. 77° 6′.

SYRIAM.—A town in the British province of Pegu, situate on the right bank of one of the branches of the Irawady river, and 11 miles E.N.E. from Rangoon. Lat. 16° 50′, long. 96° 26′.

T.

TAAKLY.—A town in one of the recently sequestrated districts of Hyderabad, or dominions of the Nizam, 52 miles S.W. from Ellichpoor. Lat. 20° 33′, long. 77° 8′.

TAHNAO.—A village of Gurwhal, on the right bank of the Jumna, here about 100 feet wide, and crossed by a sango or wooden bridge. The houses, narrow, gloomy, and covered with slabs of schist, reminded Jacquemont of those of the Upper Alps. He considered that he could trace a resemblance between the architecture and sculpture of some ruined temples in the village and those of the sacred buildings of Benares. Tahnao is 4,752 feet above the sea. Lat. 30° 49′, long. 78° 19′.

TAHNOOT.—A town in the native state of Kareal, on the south-west frontier of Bengal, 41 miles N.W. by N. from Kareal, and 109 miles W.S.W. from Sumbulpoor. Lat. 20° 49′, long. 82° 30′.

TAHURPOOR, in the British district of Moradabad, lieut.-gov. of the N.W. Provinces, a village on the route from Allygurh to the town of Moradabad, and eight miles S.W. of the latter. Lat. 28° 44′, long. 78° 47′.

TAIMBAH.—A town in the territory of Nagpoor, situate on the left bank of the Wurda river, and 62 miles S. by W. from Nagpoor. Lat. 20° 16′, long. 79° 1′.

TAINGAPATAM, in the territory of Travancore, under the political superintendence of the presidency of Madras, a town on the coast of the Indian Ocean. It is situate on the mouth of a river of the same name. The population here and in the neighbourhood comprises many native Christians of the Syrian church, or that of St. Thomas; and some of these ancient churches may be observed at intervals along the shore from this place to Cape Comorin. Lat. 8° 14′, long. 77° 14′.

TAJPOOR, in the territory of Gwalior, or possessions of Scindia's family, a small town on the route from Goona to Oojein. It has a bazar. Lat. 23° 12′, long. 75° 56′.

TAJUL.—A town of Sinde, in the state of Ali Moorad, 52 miles S. from Bukkur, and 118 miles W. from Jessulmeer. Lat. 26° 55′, long. 69° 4′.

TAK, in the Daman division of the Punjab, a town situated 34 miles from the right bank of the Indus, 150 miles S.S.W. of the town of Peshawur. Lat. 32° 7′, long. 70° 30′.

TAKAL, in the Peshawar division of the Punjab, a town situated on the left bank of the Bahreh river, three miles W.S.W. of the town of Peshawar. Lat. 33° 59′, long. 71° 35′.

TAKALLY.—A town in the territory of Nagpoor, situate on the left bank of the Wurda river, and 60 miles S.S.W. from Nagpoor. Lat. 20° 21′, long. 78° 50′.

TAKAM.—A town in Nepal, situate on the right bank of one of the branches of the Gunduck river, and 166 miles W.N.W. from Khatmandoo. Lat. 28° 36′, long. 82° 49′.

TAKEA.—A town in the British district of Silhet, lieut.-gov. of Bengal, eight miles S. of Silhet. Lat. 24° 48′, long. 91° 51′.

TAKEE, in the British district of Baraset, lieut.-gov. of Bengal, a village on the right bank of the Isamutti, a large offset from the Ganges, and close to the southern frontier towards the Sunderbunds. Distance E. from Calcutta, by Baraset, 50 miles. Lat. 22° 35′, long. 89°.

TAKMHALL.—A town in Hyderabad, situate on the left bank of the Manjera river, and 51 miles N.W. from Hyderabad. Lat. 17° 58′, long. 78° 6′.

TAKWARAH, in the Daman division of the Punjab, a town situated 26 miles from the right bank of the Indus, 155 miles S.S.W. of the town of Peshawar. Lat. 32°, long. 70° 36′.

TALABURA, in the British district of Budaon, lieut.-gov. of the N.W. Provinces, a village on the route from Allygurh to Moradabad, and 36 miles S.W. of the latter. Lat. 28° 29′, long. 78° 28′.

TALAK.—A town in the British district of Aracan, lieut.-gov. of Bengal, situate 68 miles S.E. of Aracan, on the banks of the river of same name, navigable thus far for boats of considerable burthen. Lat. 20° 2′, long. 94° 6′.

TALA KHAR, in Bussahir, a river of Koonawur, falls into the Sutlej on the left side, in lat. 31° 40′, long. 78° 32′. It rises in Chinese Tartary, about lat. 31° 36′, long. 78° 54′, and has a course of about thirty miles, generally westerly. It is described by Gerard as a large stream.

TALAMANCHI.—A town in the British district of Nellore, presidency of Madras, 11 miles N. of Nellore. Lat. 14° 37′, long. 80° 3′.

TALCHEER.—A town giving name to a Cuttack mehal on the south-west frontier of Bengal: it is situate on the right bank of the Braminy river, and 61 miles N.W. from Cuttack. Lat. 20° 56′, long. 85° 9′.

TALGRAM, or **TALIGRAM**, in the British district of Furruckabad, a small town on the route from the cantonment of Etawa to that of Futtehgurh, and 24 miles S.W. of the latter. Lat. 27° 2′, long. 79° 43′.

TALIKOTE.—A town in the British district of Sholapoor, presidency of Bombay, 89 miles S.S.E. of Sholapoor. This place obtained celebrity from the battle fought in its vicinity in 1564, when the power of the Brahminical realm of Bijayanagar was destroyed by a confederacy of the Mussulman kings of the Deccan. Lat. 16° 27′, long. 76° 22′.

TALKA KONEE, in the British district of Mirzapoor, lieut.-gov. of the N.W. Provinces, a town on the route from Mirzapoor to Palamow, 71 miles S.E. of the former. Lat 24° 24′, long. 83° 24′.

TALKHAIR.—A town in Hyderabad, or territory of the Nizam, 19 miles N.E. from Bheer, and 90 miles E. by N. from Ahmednuggur. Lat. 19° 11′, long. 76° 7′.

TALKONAH.—A town in the British district of Mymunsing, lieut.-gov. of Bengal, 31 miles N.N.W. of Jumalpoor. Lat. 25° 17′, long. 89° 51′.

TALKOONDEE.—A town on the south-west frontier of Bengal, in the native state of Bomra, situate on the left bank of a branch of the Braminy river, and 45 miles E. from Sumbulpoor. Lat. 21° 30′, long. 84° 41′.

TALL, in the territory of Jowra, in Malwa, a town, the principal place of a pergunnah containing forty-two villages, a population of 12,308, and yielding an annual revenue of 5,328 rupees to the nawaub of Jowra, son of the Patan chief Ghufur Khan, to whom it was in 1818 secured by the British government, by treaty with Mulhar Rao Holkar. The town contains 641 houses and 2,648 inhabitants. Distance N.W. from Oojein 44 miles. Lat. 23° 42′, long. 75° 22′.

TALLAJA, in the peninsula of Kattywar, province of Guzerat, a town in the district of Gohilwar. It is situate at the base of a conical hill, on the river Setroonjee, called also the river of Sultanpoor, from a seaport distant six miles south-east from Tallaja. Distance from Surat W. 60 miles. Lat. 21° 20′, long. 71° 59′.

TALLAKAD.—A town in the British district of Malabar, presidency of Madras, 79 miles S.S.E. of Cannanore. Lat. 10° 53′, long. 76°.

TALLAMALLA.—A town in the British district of Coimbatoor, presidency of Madras, 45 miles N. of Coimbatoor. Lat. 11° 38′, long. 77° 4′.

TALLAPOOLA.—A town in the British district of Cuddapah, presidency of Madras, 42 miles W.S.W. of Cuddapah. Lat. 14° 13′, long. 78° 18′.

TALMONDA.—A town on the south-west frontier of Bengal, in the British district of Sumbulpoor, 42 miles N.E. by N. of Sumbulpoor. Lat. 22°, long. 84° 20′.

TALNERE.—See Thalneir.

TALWUNDEE NOUBAHAR, in Sirhind, a village on the route from Lodiana to Ferozpur, and 45 miles W. of the former place. Distant N.W. from Calcutta 1,147 miles. Lat. 30° 57′, long. 75° 13′.

TAMBA.—A town in the British district of Sholapoor, presidency of Bombay, 48 miles S. of Sholapoor. Lat. 16° 59′, long. 76° 3′.

TAMBARAVARI, in the British district of Tinnevelly, presidency of Madras, a river rising on the western frontier, on the eastern declivity of the Eastern Ghats, and in lat.

8° 52′, long. 77° 20′. It holds a tortuous course, in some parts eastwards, in others south-eastward, for eighty miles, and falls into the Gulf of Manar in lat. 8° 38′, long. 78° 10′, close to the small town of Punnakoil. It has a bar at its mouth, preventing the entrance of shipping; and thirty-five miles higher up it is crossed by a fine bridge, connecting the towns of Tinnevelly and Palamkottah. It receives on the left side, in lat. 8° 48′, long. 77° 5′, the Chetura torrent, of considerable size.

TAMBUR.—A river of Nepal, rising on the southern face of the Himalayas, and flowing first in a southerly direction for about sixty-five miles, during which course it receives the Yangma, Kumbachen, Yalloong, Khabili, and Hinwa rivers, and afterwards in a westerly direction for thirty miles, falls into the Coosy, in lat. 26° 57′, long. 87° 1′.

TAMOILAH.—A town in the British district of Burraboom, lieut.-gov. of Bengal, 143 miles W. by N. of Calcutta. Lat. 22° 52′, long. 86° 13′.

TAMPEE.—A town in the Rajpoot state of Jodhpoor, situate on the right bank of the Loonee river, and 150 miles S.W. from Jodhpoor. Lat. 24° 52′, long. 71° 23′.

TAMSA.—A town in Hyderabad, or territory of the Nizam, 40 miles S.W. by S. from Mahur, and 153 miles N.N.W. from Hyderabad. Lat. 19° 23′, long. 77° 39′.

TANASSERIM.—An island forming one of the Mergui Archipelago. In coming from the sea, the hills upon it have the appearance of separate islands. Its centre is about lat. 12° 35′, long. 97° 57′.

TANBENGOONG.—A town of Burmah, situate on the left bank of the Khyendwen river, and 174 miles N.W. by N. from Ava. Lat. 24° 2′, long. 94° 47′.

TANDA, or TARAH, in the British district of Bareilly, lieut.-gov. of the N.W. Provinces, a station on the route from Bareilly to Almora, 62 miles N. of the former, and 58 of the latter. It is situate close to a brook, and in a small cleared place in the Terai or marshy forest, the air of which, during the hot season, is so deadly as to cause a fearful loss of life among travellers, as well as those more permanently located in connection with the police-station here. The supply of water here appears to be the only inducement to retain it as a station. The road in this part of the route is good. Lat. 29° 5′, long. 79° 30′.

TANDAH, in the territory of Oude, a town on the route from the cantonment of Goruckpore to that of Sultanpoor, 57 miles S.W. of the former, 53 N.E. of the latter. It is situate three miles from the left bank of the Ghaghra. Butter states the population at 6,000, of whom 4,000 are Mussulmans, chiefly weavers, this being the seat of the largest manufactories of cloth in Oude. Lat. 26° 34′, long. 82° 40′.

TANDAULI, in the district of Aldemau, the territory of Oude, a town near the north-eastern frontier, towards the British district of Goruckpoor. The population, according to Butter, is 3,000, but was formerly double that amount, until diminished by the flight of inhabitants, through dread of the oppression of the government. Lat. 26° 34′, long. 82° 26′.

TANDENKY.—A town in the British district of Masulipatam, presidency of Madras, 22 miles N.W. by W. of Masulipatam. Lat. 16° 21′, long. 80° 57′.

TANDI, in the Punjab, a village of the district of Lahoul, is situate at the point where a considerable feeder of the Chenaub falls into that river, which, immediately below the confluence, is 200 feet wide, with a steady current. Buckwheat is the principal crop, though barley and wheat are cultivated; but the great elevation, probably exceeding 8,000 feet, and consequent lowness of temperature, frequently render the crops of these two last sorts of grain abortive. Lat. 32° 35′, long. 77°.

TANDOOR.—A town in Hyderabad, or territory of the Nizam, 24 miles W. from the right bank of the Wein Gunga river, and 141 miles N.N.E. from Hyderabad. Lat. 19° 11′, long. 79° 29′.

TANDOOR, a river of Hyderabad, rises in lat. 17° 3′, long. 77° 58′, and flowing westerly for eighty-five miles, falls into the Beemah river, in lat. 17° 1′, long. 76° 58′.

TANDUH, in the British district of Meerut, lieut.-gov. of the N.W. Provinces, a village on the left bank of the Jumna. Lat. 29° 16′, long. 77° 13′.

TANGAN, in the district of Bainswara, territory of Oude, a town nine miles N.E. of the left bank of the Ganges, 55 S. of Lucknow. Butter estimates the population at 8,000, all Hindoos. Lat. 26° 3′, long. 81° 20′.

TANGNO, in Bussahir, a valley on the south side of the great range of the Himalaya, bounding Koonawur on the south. It is well wooded with pines and oaks, and contains five villages. Elevation above the sea 8,800 feet. Lat. 31° 20′, long. 78° 3′.

TANGON RIVER.—One of the numerous watercourses traversing the district of Dinajepore: it rises in lat. 26° 43′, long. 88° 31′, and flowing in a southerly direction for 140 miles, falls into the Mahananda, in lat. 24° 57′, long. 88° 14′, having in its course thrown off numerous offsets right and left.

TANGREAH.—A town in the native state of Keunjur, on the south-west frontier of Bengal, 80 miles W. by N. from Balasore, and 118 miles E. by N. from Sumbulpoor. Lat. 21° 44′, long. 85° 49′.

TANJORE.—A British district in the presidency of Madras, named from its principal place. It is bounded on the north-west by the Coleroon, separating it from the British districts of South Arcot and Trichinopoly; on the east and south-east by the Bay of Bengal;

on the south-west by the British district of Madura; and on the west by the British district of Madura, the native state of Poodoocottah, and Trichinopoly. It lies between lat. 9° 52′ and 11° 23′, long. 78° 55′—79° 55′; is 120 miles in length from north-east to south-west, and seventy-five in breadth; the area, according to official return, is 3,900 square miles. Its seacoast extends 165 miles, from lat. 9° 52′ to 11° 23′; but from its southern extremity to Point Calymere, in lat. 10° 16′, long. 79° 54′, a distance of seventy-five miles, the coast cannot be visited by ships of any considerable burthen, in consequence of the shoalness and dangerous nature of Palk's Bay, which washes it. There is, however, much coasting trade carried on by the small craft of the country. The coast, which from its southern extremity to Calymere has a direction either north-east or east, at that point turns due north, which direction it continues to hold to the northern extremity of the district. Point Calymere is low, sandy, and covered with coconut-trees, but from projecting so far into the sea, has much of the advantage of an insular situation; and the air being refreshed and cooled by the sea-breezes, it is frequented as an agreeable retreat during the hot season. Farther north, in lat. 10° 45′, long. 79° 55′, lies Negapatam: it has no port capable of receiving ships, being situate at the mouth of a small branch of the Cauvery, admitting only country boats of inconsiderable burthen. From Negapatam to the mouth of the Coleroon, the great northern branch of the Cauvery, the shore of the delta of that river extends; and though there are many estuaries and inlets, there is no haven capable of receiving ships of any considerable burthen. The best is Nagore, which, having eight feet of water on its bar at spring tides, has belonging to it vessels of from 200 to 300 tons, which ply to the Eastern Archipelago, and to places on the eastern shores of the Bay of Bengal. At Tranquebar (formerly a Danish, now a British possession), in lat. 11° 1′, long. 79° 55′, ships must anchor in the open sea in six or seven fathoms water, the inconsiderable branch of the Cauvery, at the mouth of which it is situate, admitting only small coasting craft. Through its whole extent the coast is low and sandy, the sea shoaly, and the difficulty of communicating with the shore heightened by the violent surf which incessantly beats on it. The Coleroon river, the principal estuary of the Cauvery, and terminating the coast-line of this district towards the north, has at its entrance a bar, dry at low water, from which proceeds a shoal, projecting four or five miles into the sea south-eastward; an impediment which is not, however, without use, sheltering from the southerly winds the anchorage of Porto Novo farther north. The extensive delta of the Cauvery is almost entirely comprised within this district, of which it forms the northern and larger part. This district, besides the moisture derived from the rains of the north-east monsoon, receives the benefit of the superfluous waters of the river Cauvery, which, swelled by the heavy rains precipitated by the south-west monsoon on the remote ghats and the table-land of Mysore, rolls down an abundant volume of water, to irrigate and fertilize the low, level, alluvial region of Tanjore. The inundation of this great torrent is at its height about the middle of July, when it is a mile wide above the head of the island of Seringham, where it parts into two great branches: the northern and larger branch, called the Coleroon, forms the north-western boundary of Tanjore for eighty miles, falling into the sea by an estuary of no great size, near Chillambarum, in lat. 11° 22′, long. 79° 48′; the other branch, continuing to be denominated the Cauvery, takes a south-east direction, and is subdivided into a great number of watercourses, traversing and fertilizing the district, until most of them disappear, from the effects of absorption and evaporation, a few only reaching the sea by small and nearly imperceptible outlets. The principal of these channels is the Vennar, which sends off several large watercourses to the southern part of the district; the next in importance are the Kodamurti and Verashalen. The channel of the Coleroon becomes in its progress far more depressed than that of the Cauvery, and vast embankments have been formed to prevent the water of the more elevated channel from deserting it, and making its way into the lower. At various intervals there are vents, that allow the water of the Cauvery to escape into the lower parts of the delta, and, if redundant, to pass into the Coleroon. Considerable expense has been incurred, and much ingenuity shown, in the construction of the works requisite for dispensing this extensive and intricate system of irrigation. Altogether, probably, this district is excelled in fertility and productiveness by none in India, and equalled by few, except some rich tracts in the valley of the Ganges. The population is given under the article MADRAS. Little appears to be known concerning the political existence of Tanjore before the middle of the seventeenth century. About the year 1678, Vencajee, a Mahratta chief, and brother of the famous Sevajee, obtained possession of the province; and it is from him that the present rajah is descended. From this period a tolerably connected history of the country can be obtained; but it is barren of any information concerning its political relations with other states, its strength, and comparative importance. In 1749 a British expedition was despatched into this principality; and this was the first instance in the Carnatic of the English being engaged against the forces of a native prince. The object of the expedition was the restoration of a deposed rajah of Tanjore, who had applied for assistance to the governor of Fort St. David, promising as a reward the absolute possession of Devi Cottah, exempt from the payment of tribute. The attempt to restore the exiled rajah proved unsuccessful; but the British government, thinking it dangerous to lie under the reproach of defeat, undertook a second expedition, which was attended with better results. The reigning prince consented to buy off the invaders by confirming them in the possession, and granting the immunity which his rival had promised; and engaged to make a small provision for the person whose real or supposed wrongs had given rise to the war, the English undertaking for his peaceable behaviour. From the time of the conquest of the country by Vencajee, to the reign of Rajah Pretaub Sing, in 1764, the descendants of the former personage appear to have exercised authority uncontrolled by the nabob of the Carnatic, and altogether independent of him. During the reign of Tooljajee, the son and successor of Pretaub Sing, Mahomed Ali, the nabob of Arcot, laid claim to tribute from the state of Tanjore. In the prosecution of this claim he was supported by the Madras government, who commenced hostilities on his behalf, took the fort of Tanjore in 1772, and having removed the reigning prince from the throne, delivered over the country to the management of the nabob. The home authorities did not approve the measures adopted by the Madras government, and directed the reinstatement of Tooljajee on the throne of his ancestors, on the condition of his engaging to pay the tribute claimed by the nabob, together with a stipulated sum of money for the maintenance of a subsidiary British force in the fort of Tanjore. On his undertaking to comply, a treaty was concluded between the British government and the rajah in 1781, by which the latter was bound to pay annually the sum of 114,286 star pagodas, as a tribute, and 400,000 as subsidy. This was the first alliance entered into by the British with the rajah of Tanjore. On the death of Tooljajee, there were two claimants to the throne,—the one Ameer Sing, the half-brother of the deceased rajah; the other Serfojee, the son of a distant relative, who had been adopted by Tooljajee a short time before his death. The governor of Madras thereupon proceeded in person to Tanjore, and there laid the claims of the rival candidates before twelve pundits versed in Hindoo law. They unanimously gave it as their decision, that the adoption of Serfojee, to the exclusion of Ameer Sing from the throne, was at variance with that law, and that the claim of Ameer Sing was just. The British government determined to act on this decision; and in April, 1787, Ameer Sing was placed on the throne, and invested with regal authority. A treaty was concluded between him and the British government, augmenting the tribute and subsidy, and containing provisions for securing a regular payment of the same. After a reign of twelve years, it was said to be discovered that the decision given in 1787, by the assembled pundits, was wrong; that the claims then urged by Serfojee, the adopted son of Tooljajee, were supported by the principles of Hindoo law, and consequently that Ameer Sing had no right to the throne. Thereupon, in 1798, he was deposed, and Serfojee elevated in his place. In the following year another treaty was concluded, by which Serfojee gave up the country to the permanent possession of the East-India Company, on condition of receiving annually the sum of a lac of star pagodas, or 3,50,000 rupees (which was to be considered the first charge on the net revenues of Tanjore), and a proportion of one-fifth, to be calculated on the remainder of the net revenue. The reasons for the new arrangements under this treaty, were the *misgovernment of the country*, the *inability* of the state to liquidate the enormous debts contracted by Ameer Sing, which were therefore transferred to the Company, with the territory on the security of which they were contracted. Under the treaty, the rajah had no right of interference with the revenue, or judicial administration of the country: he possessed sovereign authority only in the fort of Tanjore, though, by sufferance, it was subsequently extended to a small degree. Serfojee died in 1832, and was succeeded by his only son Sevajee, whose conduct manifested little of either prudence or regularity. Sevajee died in 1855, without leaving a son by birth or adoption; and there being no law or usage under which the daughter of a Hindoo rajah had any right of succession to the raj. the dignity of the rajahs of Tanjore was declared to be extinct. The extent of Tanjore was formerly greater than at present, parts of the original kingdom having been alienated from it at dates long antecedent to that at which the larger portion of the remainder was transferred to the British.

Negapatam, with Nagore, ranked among the possessions of the Portuguese, from whom they passed to the Dutch in 1660, and were held by the latter till 1781, when they were taken by the British. The transfer of Devi Cottah to the British has been already noticed. The small seaport of Tranquebar, formerly a part of the Tanjore state, and four villages adjacent to it, were purchased from the reigning rajah in the year 1616, by the Danish East-India Company, subject to the payment of an annual tribute of about 4,000 rupees. In 1624 this territory was surrendered by the purchasers to the king of Denmark, subject to the payment of the tribute, and by him ceded to the British government in 1845, for a pecuniary consideration. The district of Karical, situate between Tranquebar and Negapatam, was purchased by the French in 1739 from the rajah, and still remains in their possession free from tribute.

TANJORE, a town, the principal place of the British district of the same name, under the presidency of Madras, is situate in an extensive plain, and on the banks of a branch of the river Cauvery. It consists of two forts, the greater and the less, and several suburbs: the greater "fort, which is about four miles in circumference, is surrounded by a lofty fortified wall, and a ditch, in some parts dry, in others half full of stagnant water. The streets within this fort are irregularly built, and there are various alleys and courts in every direction, without any regard to arrangement: a wide space has, however, been left between the ramparts and the houses. The fort contains also numerous pagodas, elevated considerably above the surrounding buildings. The houses of the respectable portion of the inhabitants are substantially built of brick and chunam, and in many cases are tastefully decorated. Those of the poor are built of mud, which, from the tenacious quality of the soil, is well adapted for the purpose, and are tiled. The villages outside the fort are, with but few exceptions, built of mud, and thatched, the streets being narrow and irregular." Adjoining is the smaller fort, a mile in circuit, very strong, with lofty walls built of large stones, a broad ditch excavated out of the solid rock, and a well-formed glacis. Within it is the great pagoda, considered to be the finest of the pyramidal temples of India. In the front is a colossal figure of a bull in black granite, regarded as being "one of the finest specimens of the arts as practised under the direction of the Brahmins." A fine view of the pagoda and image is given by Daniell, who, however, is alleged in some particulars to have deviated from perfect accuracy. Within the old fort is the palace of the rajah, a spacious structure, inclosed by a high wall, and though of ancient date, never finished. The durbar, or "hall of audience," of the Chola family, the primitive dynasty, which preceded that at present ruling, is in good preservation: being, however, held to be unlucky, it is now never used for the purpose for which it was destined; but, though unoccupied, it far exceeds in splendour the actual residence of the rajah. The roof, formed of vast slabs of black stone, is supported by lofty massive pillars of the same material. The musnud, or throne, is a huge mass of black granite, eighteen feet long, sixteen feet broad, and two feet thick. It is elevated three feet above the floor of the apartment.

The barracks for the small force of native infantry stationed here, are situate on an open, dry, and elevated piece of ground, a mile south-east of the fort. The population of the town of Tanjore is estimated at 80,000 persons. The inhabitants for the most part use water from wells, that from the river being so impregnated with iron as to be unfit for domestic purposes. Tanjore is a place of considerable business, having manufactures of silk, muslins, and cottons. Distance from the town of Trichinopoly, E., 30 miles; from the town of Madura, N.E., 90; from the town of Coimbatoor, E., 150; from Bangalore, S.E., 180; from the city of Madras, S.W., 180. Lat. 10° 47′, long. 79° 12′.

TANK POORBEEA, in the territory of Gwalior, or possessions of the family of Scindia, in the ancient province of Malwa, a small town on the route from Goona to Mow, 137 miles S.W. of former, 48 N.E. of latter. It is situate on the south-west or left bank of the river Lukunda. Lat. 23° 7′, long. 76° 11′.

TANKARIA.—See TUNCARIA.

TANKTSE.—A town within the dominions of Gholab Singh, the ruler of Cashmere, situate 163 miles N.E. from Chamba, and 188 miles E. from Sirinagur. Lat. 34° 2′, long. 78° 19′.

TANLADY.—A town in the British district of Amherst, one of the Tenasserim provinces, 20 miles E.N.E. of Moulmein. Lat. 16° 37′, long. 97° 59′.

TANNAH.—A collectorate of the presidency of Bombay. Including its sub-collectorate of Colaba, it is bounded on the north by the Portuguese territory of Damaun, the collectorate of Surat, and the territory of the Guicowar; on the south by the collectorate of Rutnagherry; on the east by the collectorates of Ahmednuggur and Poona, and the territory of Sattara; and on the west by the Arabian Sea. It extends from N. lat. 17° 56′ to 20° 20′, and from E. long. 72° 42′ to 73° 48′; its greatest length from north to south is 175 miles, and its greatest breadth from east to west sixty-five miles: the area comprises 5,477 square miles.

The great Bombay and Agra road intersects this collectorate from Colsette ferry, opposite the island of Bombay, to the Tull Ghaut, a distance between sixty and seventy miles; as does likewise the road from the north, connecting the capital of Bombay with Surat and Baroda. The district is also traversed by the Indian Peninsular Railway, the first section of which, extending to the town of Tannah, was opened on the 16th April, 1853. The population is given under the article BOMBAY.

The district in 1844 was the scene of extensive gang-robberies and daring outrages. Vigorous measures were rendered necessary for their suppression; and these being taken by the government, the country has now for some years continued in a state of order and tranquillity. Tannah, the chief town, is distant 24 miles N.E. from Bombay. Ten years ago, its population was estimated at about 9,000; but an increase has doubtless taken place since the completion to this town of the railroad from the city of Bombay. Lat. 19° 10′, long. 73° 3′.

TANNOOR, in the British district of Malabar, presidency of Madras, a town and seaport at the mouth of a small river falling into the Arabian Sea. In the year 1782, the British army, under the command of Colonel Humberstone, acting against the forces of Hyder Ali, took refuge here from a storm and rain of five days' continuance, which dispersed the boats, spoiled the provisions, and damaged the ammunition of the expedition. It was formerly a prosperous place, but is now much decayed.

Distance from Calicut, S.E., 22 miles; Mangalore, 170; Bombay, 546. Lat. 10° 58′, long. 75° 56′.

TANWAS, in the jaghire of Jujhur, lieut.-gov. of the N.W. Provinces, a village on the route from Hansee to Neemuch, and 98 miles S. of the former. There are a few shops here, and there is good water from wells. Lat. 27° 52′, long. 76° 16′.

TAOOROO, in the British district of Goorgaon, lieut.-gov. of the N.W. Provinces, a town on the route from Rewaree to Boolundshuhur, 20 miles E. of the former. Lat. 28° 12′, long. 77°.

TAPOO.—A town in the Rajpoot state of Jodhpoor or Marwar, 40 miles N. by E. from Jodhpoor, and 80 miles S. from Beekaneer. Lat. 26° 53′, long. 73° 13′.

TAPTEE.—A river rising within the Saugor and Nerbudda territory. Its source is near Mooltaee, 22 miles S.E. of the town of Baitool, in about lat. 21° 46′, long. 78° 21′. It takes a circuitous but generally westerly direction of 120 miles, to the western boundary of the district, where, in lat. 21° 27′, long. 76° 50′, it passes into the territory of Gwalior, or the possessions of Scindia. Following a south-westerly course along the southern base of the Satpoora range, it flows by the city of Boorhaunpoor, where it has a mean width of 300 feet, and during the periodical rains acquires a great volume of water, but in winter and spring it is easily fordable, the depth seldom exceeding one foot. At that season, the alligators, with which it sometimes swarms, take refuge in the deep pools in the river channel. At the distance of about 161 miles from its source, and in lat. 21° 17′, long. 76° 20′, it passes from the territory of Gwalior, and forming for forty miles the boundary between the Nizam's dominions and the district of Candeish, through which it pursues a westerly course, and subsequently flowing through the southern portion of the Guicowar's dominions and the British district of Surat, it falls into the Bay of Cambay, in lat. 21° 3′, long. 72° 42′, having a total length of course of 441 miles. It can scarcely be deemed a navigable stream, as at Surat, seventeen or eighteen miles above its mouth, it is fordable when the tide is out, and only small craft of about forty or fifty tons burthen can ascend so far from the sea. It is said to be navigable in the dry season for boats of light draught throughout its whole extent in Candeish. The mouth is obstructed by numerous shifting sands and a bar, through which, according to the latest accounts, there is but one channel, which at low water spring tides is so shallow as to allow the passage of only small boats; and even they frequently touch the bottom. Outside the bar is the anchorage, called Surat Roads, at no time very safe, but particularly dangerous in April and May, when south winds prevail. Serious loss of life and property has sometimes been occasioned by the overflow of the river. In 1837, sixty-nine villages are stated to have been ruined, the majority of them being entirely swept away, 2,204 houses destroyed, 112 lives lost, and agricultural stock and property carried off to the value of 2,19,622 rupees, or 21,962*l*.

TARA, in the Rajpoot state of Jodhpoor, a village on the route from Pokhurn to Balmeer, and 29 miles N. of the latter. Lat. 26° 8′, long. 71° 12′.

TARA, in the British district of Moradabad, lieut.-gov. of the N.W. Provinces, a village on the route from the town of Moradabad to Almora, and 30 miles N. of the former. Lat. 29° 12′, long. 79°.

TARA.—See CHILLAHTARA.

TARAGARH, in the hill state of Hindoor, a hill fort on the ridge which, rising from the left bank of the Sutlej, has a south-easterly direction until it joins the Sub-Himalaya. During the Goorkha war, in the operations preparatory to the investment of Malown, Lieutenant Lawtie succeeded, after vast toil and perseverance, in bringing battering-guns over the rugged surface; and the defences being quickly demolished, the Goorkha garrison evacuated the fort, which was found to be one of the strongest places in the country. Distant N.W. from Calcutta 1,090 miles. Lat. 31° 10′, long. 76° 50′.

TARA GHAT, in the British district of Mirzapoor, lieut.-gov. of the N.W. Provinces, a pass on the route from the town of Mirzapoor to Rewa, and six miles S.W. of the former. Here an excellent road, made under the superintendence of British engineers, crosses the brow of the Tara, a low range of sandstone hills rising above the alluvial valley of the Ganges, and forming in that direction the first or lowest buttress of the succession of plateaus constituting the elevated tract of Bhogelcund. Elevation of the crest above the sea 510 feet. Lat. 25° 5′, long. 82° 34′.

TARAGURH, in the Baree Doab division of the Punjab, a town situated on the right bank of the Chakki river, 110 miles N.E. by E. of the town of Lahore. Lat. 32° 25′, long 75° 59′.

TARAGURH.—See AJMERE.

TARAKOTE.—A town in the British district of Cuttack, lieut.-gov. of Bengal, 42 miles N.E. by N. of Cuttack. Lat. 20° 59′, long. 86° 15′.

TARAPOOR, in the collectorate of Tannah, presidency of Bombay, a town situate on the south side of a small bay, and north-west of a mountain called the Peak of Terrapore, which is surmounted by rugged rocks, resembling at a distance a huge fortress. North-west of the town is anchorage, but not very good, the bottom being full of rocks. It was strongly fortified by the Portuguese: in 1739 it was stormed by the Mahrattas, who, having blown up the defences by mines, encountered a desperate resistance until nearly the whole garrison was slaughtered, the few who remained asking and receiving quarter. Distant N. from Bombay 60 miles. Lat. 19° 50′, long. 72° 45′.

TARAPOOR, in the British district of Meerut, lieut.-gov. of the N.W. Provinces, a town on the route from Meerut to Bijnour, 27 miles N.E. by E. of the former. Lat. 29° 14′, long. 78° 8′.

TARAPOOR.—A town in the British district of Sholapoor, presidency of Bombay, 27 miles W. of Sholapoor. Lat. 17° 40′, long. 75° 33′.

TARECHER, in Bundlecund, a small town in the district of Tehree, on the route from Banda to Gwalior, 110 miles W. of former, 94 S.E. of latter. Lat. 25° 25°, long. 78° 58′.

TARGAON.—A town in the British province of Sattara, presidency of Bombay, 16 miles S.E. of Sattara. Lat. 17° 30′, long. 74° 13′.

TARIWALA, in Sirhind, in the British district of Ferozpore, a village situate on the left bank of the Sutlej, which at this point divides itself into two channels, the main stream making a great circuit to the north-west, and sending a branch to the left, nearly west; thus insulating a space of ground about eight miles long and two wide. Tariwala is distant N.W. from Calcutta 1,145 miles. Lat. 31° 2′, long. 75° 14′.

TARKAGHAT.—A town in Nepal, situate on the right bank of the Marachangdi river, and 71 miles W.N.W. from Khatmandoo. Lat. 28°, long. 84° 13′.

TARLA.—A town in the British province of Sattara, presidency of Bombay, 13 miles S. of Sattara. Lat. 17° 30′, long. 74° 1′.

TARLA.—A town in the native state of Kolapoor, 23 miles S.W. from Kolapoor, and 53 miles N.W. from Belgaum. Lat. 16° 27′, long. 74° 4′.

TAROLI.—A town in the British province of Jhansee, territory of Bundelkund, situate on the right bank of the Betwa river, and 26 miles E.N.E. from Jhansee. Lat. 25° 34′, long. 79° 3′.

TAROOR.—A town in Hyderabad, or dominions of the Nizam, situate on the left bank of the Godavery river, and 150 miles N.E. by E. from Hyderabad. Lat. 18° 39′, long. 80° 20′.

TARSA, in the north-east of the Punjaub, a town in the British district of Lahoul, 72 miles N.E. of Kangra. Lat. 32° 43′, long. 77° 13′.

TASGAON.—A town in the British district of Belgaum, presidency of Bombay, 85 miles N. of Belgaum. This town was the chief place of a jaghire of the same name, which a short time since lapsed to the British government. Lat. 17° 2′, long. 74° 40′.

TASSANGSEE.—A town in the native state of Bhotan, situate on the right bank of a branch of the Monas river, and 145 miles N.W. by N. from Durrung. Lat. 27° 34′, long. 91° 17′.

TASSISUDEN.—A town with citadel in the native state of Bhotan, situate on the right bank of the Goddada river, and 127 miles N.W. from Goalpara. Tassisuden is the capital of Bhootan, and the residence of the Deb rajah. Lat. 27° 30′, long. 89° 22′.

TATARPOOR, in the British district of Aligurh, lieut.-gov. of the N.W. Provinces, a village on the route from the city of Agra to Bareilly, and 42 miles N.E. of the former. Lat. 27° 34′, long. 78° 33′.

TATTA, in Sinde, a town formerly very famous, but now much decayed, is situated about three miles west of the right or western bank of the Indus, and four miles above the point where the Buggaur or western, and the Sata or eastern, branches of the river separate. Its site is consequently close to the vertex of the delta of the Indus, the channel of which is here about a mile and a quarter wide, with a muddy stream, in the low season occupying only a third of this space. The present city is built on a slight eminence, composed of the rubbish of former buildings, in an alluvial valley at the foot of the Mukali hills. It is in consequence exceedingly unhealthy. The British troops stationed here in 1839 suffered dreadful loss from diseases, resulting from the pestilential air and bad water, which last is not only unwholesome, but fetid and offensive to the senses. The town appears to have been formerly insulated by the water of the Indus, and is still nearly so during the season of inundation: when this passes away, it leaves numerous stagnant pools which infect the air. Dr. Burnes states that it was once thirty miles in circuit, judging no doubt from the vast space in the vicinity overspread by tombs and ruins; but these are with much probability considered by Wood to be the relics of successive cities, built on various but contiguous sites, to avoid the ravages, or take advantage of the navigation, of the shifting currents of the Indus. These extensive ruins are scattered from Peer Puttah, about ten miles south of Tatta, to Sami-Nuggur, three miles north-west of it. The ruins of the great fortress of Kulancote show it to have been constructed with much labour and skill, in a massive style of building. "The vast cemetery of six square miles," observes Kennedy, "may not contain less than a million of tombs—a rude guess; but the area would admit of four millions." In these ruins the masonry and carving, both in brick and stone, display great taste, skill, and industry; the bricks especially are of the finest sort, nearly equalling porcelain. Kennedy observes, "The finest-chiselled stone could not surpass the sharpness of edge and angle, and accuracy of form." Tatta, viewed at some distance from the outside, presents a very striking and picturesque appearance, as its lofty houses rise over the numerous acacias and other trees, everywhere interspersed, and which, says Kennedy, "formed altogether as fine a picture of city scenery as I remember to have seen in India." But the illusion is dissipated on entering the town, where the houses are everywhere falling into ruin, to which they are prone, being constructed for the most part of a timber framework, on the outside of which are nailed laths, which are plastered over with mud of a grey colour, so as when new to have the appearance of a solid wall of masonry. These structures are sometimes three or four stories high, and covered with flat roofs of earth. From the fragility of the materials, they can last but a short time; and this work of ruin is continually in progress in the town. All the houses are surmounted by *badgeers,* a sort of ventilator, built somewhat in the shape of a windsail, and conveying, even in the most sultry weather, a current of cool and refreshing air. The streets are deserted, the bazars in ruins, and everything indicates depression and poverty: the inhabitants are dirty, squalid, and of unhealthy appearance. The only building worth notice is the brick-built mosque of Shah Jehan, itself crumbling into ruins. Of the decayed manufactures of Tatta, the principal is that of *loongees,* a thick, rich, and variegated fabric, having a warp of silk and a woof of cotton, with (in the more costly kinds) much gold thread interwoven. The silk is imported from Persia, Kabool, and Turkestan; the cotton from Eastern India. Coarse cotton fabrics, both plain and coloured, were formerly manufactured in considerable quantity, but have lately been superseded by those of England. British woollens are greatly prized. It is said that in 1742, when Nadir Shah entered this city at the head of his army, there were 40,000 weavers, 20,000 other artisans, and 60,000 dealers in various departments. Alexander Hamilton, who visited Tatta in 1699, calls it a very large and rich city, about three miles long, and one and a half broad; and states that 80,000 persons had, within a short time previously, died of the plague, and that one-half of the city was uninhabited. This would lead us to the conclusion, that previously to that calamity the population was above 150,000. The present population is variously estimated—at below 2,000, at less than 10,000, at 12,000, 15,000, 18,000, 20,000, and 40,000. The number of artisans and traders ascertained (as mentioned above) by Wood, affords grounds for estimating the population at about 10,000. Tatta has been supposed to be the Pattala of the ancients. Pottinger states that the earliest mention he has found of it is in the ninety second year of the Hegira, but he does not give any reference to the place of such mention: Burnes says, "the antiquity of Tatta is unquestioned:" Outram assigns its foundation to 1445, but does not cite his authority: Macmurdo states, from native authorities, that it was founded 900 of the Hegira, or A.D. 1522. In 1555 it was pillaged and burned by some Portuguese mercenaries; in A.H. 1000, it was, according to this last authority, again destroyed in the Mogul invasion by Akbar, and never completely recovered. In 1758 a British factory was established there, and withdrawn in 1775: in 1799 an abortive attempt was made to re-establish it. In the beginning of 1839, the house belonging to the factory was occupied by a British garrison. Tatta is in lat. 24° 44′, long. 68°.

TAUDAMURRY.—A town in the British district of Bellary, presidency of Madras, 79 miles S.E. by E. of Bellary. Lat. 14° 33′, long. 77° 57′.

TAUDAPURTEE.—A town in the British district of Bellary, presidency of Madras, 79 miles E. by S. of Bellary. Lat. 14° 54′, long. 78° 5′.

TAUNDLA, in the territory of Jabooah, in Malwa, a town near the west frontier, towards Guzerat. It is represented as a considerable place, distant 80 miles W. of Oojein. Lat. 23°, long. 74° 32′.

TAUNGINE.—A town in the British district of Amherst, in the Tenasserim provinces, 16 miles N. of Moulmein. Lat. 16° 42′, long. 97° 41′.

TAUNSA, a river of the British district of Tannah, rises on the western face of the Western Ghats, in lat. 19° 41′, long. 73° 29′, and flowing westerly for fifty-eight miles, falls into the sea at lat. 19° 30′, long. 72° 50′.

TAURSA.—A town in the territory of Nagpoor, 19 miles E.N.E. from Nagpoor, and 57 miles S. by W. from Seuni. Lat. 21° 15′, long. 79° 26′.

TAUSRAH, in the British district of Kaira, presidency of Bombay, a town on the route from Neemuch to Baroda, 38 miles N. of the latter. Distance S.W. of Neemuch 156 miles, E. of Kaira 40. Lat. 22° 48′, long. 73° 18′.

TAVOY.—One of the Tenasserim provinces. It is bounded on the north by Amherst; on the south by Mergui; on the east by Siam; and on the west by the Bay of Bengal: it extends between lat. 12° 44′ and 14° 50′; has an average breadth of about fifty miles, and an area of about 4,920 square miles. Its general character is mountainous, intersected by valleys, through which flow numerous streams. Some of the mountains attain considerable height: the range which separates the low lands round Tavoy from the interior in some parts reaches a height of 3,000 feet: the highest range is about thirty or forty miles from the coast. Thick forest and impenetrable brushwood cover the mountains, and jungle exists over a great part of the province.

Rice is the staple production of the province, and the country is well calculated for its cultivation. A failure in the crops is unknown. By more care and attention than is at present given to the subject, and by converting the swamps and overgrown wilderness into paddy-lands, that commodity might be made an important article of export, and a source of revenue. The cotton-plant is cultivated, but not to any considerable extent. The same may be said of tobacco and indigo, both of which are of good quality. Yams are in great abundance, also potatoes : red pepper, ginger, oranges, limes, citrons, tamarinds, pine-apples, plantains, are good, but scantily produced : the teak, the mango, the papaya, and palms of all kinds, are found in great abundance.

Tavoy is the most valuable of all the Tenasserim provinces in regard to mineral productions. "Of all the iron-ores," says Dr. Helfer, "that of Tavoy is the most important." It is found in many parts of the province, but the best, in point of quantity and quality, is that a short distance to the north of the town. It occurs there in two forms : "Octohedral, common magnetic iron-ore ; massive, in granular concretions, crystallized, splendent, metallic, highly magnetic, with polarity." Though the existence of the ore has been long known to the Burmese, it had not been worked. The locality of these mines is unrivalled with respect to advantageous situation, being a few miles from a part of the river which is accessible to vessels of 200 tons burthen. The province is also rich in tin-ore, which is found generally in hills, or at the foot of mountains.

The population in 1847, of the province and town inclusive, amounted to 37,354 souls ; the greater part consisting of Burmese and Talains, the remainder being Siamese, Chinese, Malays, &c.

TAVOY, the principal place of the province, is situated on the eastern bank of the river of the same name, about thirty-five miles from its mouth, and though inaccessible for vessels of large burthen within some miles of the town, its course being obstructed by shoals and sand-banks, it can be reached by ships of 120 tons. It is in the midst of a rich alluvial plain, which is bounded on the west, three miles distant, and on the east at six miles, by a range of precipitous and thickly-wooded hills, varying in height from 200 to 400 feet. The valley is subject to inundations during the wet season, and rice is cultivated extensively in the vicinity of the town. Notwithstanding, however, this great moisture, which is in most other cases the frightful cause of disease, the place is considered very healthy, and is proved to be so by the few deaths which occur among the troops stationed here, as well as the natives. The shape of the town is that of an irregular square. It is surrounded on three sides by a ditch, the other facing the river : a deep nullah runs through the midst. The town consists of two parts : the inner, which is inclosed by a wall fifteen feet high ; and the outer, which is surrounded by one eight feet high, and now partially in ruins. There is a good bazar, from which any description of provision may be procured at a cheap rate. The streets are open, and in good order. The population in 1847 was upwards of 10,000 souls ; consisting chiefly of Chinese, Malays, Malabars, and Burmese. There is a trade carried on between this place and the ports on the Mergui Archipelago. Lat. 14° 7′, long. 98° 18′.

TAVOY ISLAND extends from lat. 12° 55′—13° 15′, long. 98° 23′, twenty miles south of Tavoy Point. It is of moderate height, six leagues in length, and two miles in breadth : it is the most northern of the chain of islands forming the Mergui Archipelago. There is a pagoda at the south end. In the driest weather, fresh water is procurable on its eastern shore.

TAVOY RIVER has its source in some hills about lat. 14° 50′, long. 98° 30′, and runs in a southerly direction for a course of about 100 miles, entering the sea in lat. 13° 30′, long. 98° 20′. The upper part is much interrupted, but it is navigable for boats of large burthen fifty miles above the town of Tavoy, and at that place ships of 120 tons burthen can approach. It is here 300 yards broad, but in its further progress is swelled by so many streams that at its mouth it exceeds a mile in width. In its lower course it is studded with numerous islands, which, however much they may add to the beauty of the scenery, greatly detract from its commercial advantages, as they materially impede the navigation. There is a good harbour ten miles from the entrance, but the approach to this is rendered intricate from the above-named causes.

TAWURUGERRI.—A town in one of the recently sequestrated districts of Hyderabad, or territories of the Nizam, 17 miles S. from Moodgul. Lat. 15° 46′, long. 76° 29′.

TEBBHEE, in the Baree Doab division of the Punjab, a town situated on the right bank of the Sutlej river, 131 miles S.W. by S. of the town of Lahore. Lat. 30° 6′, long. 72° 55′.

TECTOVA.—A town in one of the recently sequestrated districts of Hyderabad, or dominions of the Nizam, 52 miles S.E. from Ellichpoor. Lat. 20° 36′, long. 78° 4′.

TEEGOOLA.—A town in Hyderabad, or territory of the Nizam, 37 miles N.E. by N. from Hyderabad, and 152 miles N.W. from Guntoor. Lat. 17° 48′, long. 78° 50′.

TEEGURM, in the territory of Nepal, on the eastern boundary of the British district of Kumaon, a village on the left bank of the river Kalee, on the route from Askot to the Beans Pass, 18 miles N.E. of Askot. Lat. 29° 55′, long. 80° 38′.

TEEKREE, in the British district of Delhi, a village on the route from Delhi to Hansee, and 16 miles W. of the former. The road in this part of the route is good. Lat. 28° 40′, long. 77° 1′.

TEEKREE.—A town in the British district of Meerut, lieut.-gov. of the N.W. Provinces, a town situate 27 miles N.W. of the city of Meerut. Population 9,882. Lat. 29° 14′, long. 77° 25′.

TEEMBA.—A town in Guzerat, or dominions of the Guicowar, situate on the left bank of the Taptee river, and 73 miles S. from Baroda. Lat. 21° 11′, long. 73° 10′.

TEENJINNA.—A town in the British district of Chota Nagpoor, lieut.-gov. of Bengal, 55 miles S. of Lohadugga. Lat. 22° 40′, long. 84° 46′.

TEENMOHONEE.—A town in the British district of Jessore, lieut.-gov. of Bengal, 53 miles E.N.E. of Calcutta. Lat. 22° 54′, long. 89° 10′.

TEERA, in the Daman division of the Punjab, a town situated 21 miles from the right bank of the Indus, 46 miles S. by W. of the town of Peshawar. Lat. 33° 21′, long. 71° 29′.

TEERAH.—A town in the native state of Cutch, situate 25 miles S.W. from the Great Western Runn, and 50 miles W. by N. from Bhooj. Lat. 23° 21′, long. 69°.

TEEREE, in Gurhwal, the principal place of that raj, and residence of its rajah. It is situate on the left bank of the Bhageerettee, as the Ganges is called in the upper part of its course, and just below the confluence of the Bhilling, which falls into it on the left or eastern side. Webb, who visited this locality in 1808, describes Teeree as a village; and when Moorcroft passed, in 1819, it contained only the residence of the rajah, a very humble mansion, and the dwellings of his followers. The Bhilling abounds in a sort of fish called a trout by Moorcroft, which is snared in great numbers. Elevation above the sea, of the town, 2,328 feet; of the level of the Bhageerettee, below it, 2,278. Lat. 30° 23′, long. 78° 31′.

TEERNEE, in the British district of Allahabad, lieut.-gov. of the N.W. Provinces, a village on the route, by Rajapoor ferry, from the cantonment of Allahabad to Banda, and 22 miles W. of the former. Lat. 25° 24′, long. 81° 38′.

TEESGAUM.—A town in the British district of Ahmednuggur, presidency of Bombay, 23 miles E.N.E. of Ahmednuggur. Lat. 19° 11′, long. 75° 6′.

TEESTA, a great river traversing part of Bengal, rises, according to the account of the Nepaulese, in Tibet, and, as is conjectured, in about lat. 27° 59′, long. 88° 50′. Flowing westward for twenty miles through Tibet, and southward through Sikkim for ninety-seven miles, it then forms for ten miles the boundary between Bhotan and Sikkim, and for twenty-three miles that between Bhotan and Darjeeling, passing eastward of the sanatarium of the latter place. Subsequently dividing the British district of Dinajepoor from Bhotan for ten miles, it enters Dinajepoor, and thirty miles below that point divides into two branches of nearly equal size: one, proceeding south-westerly, is denominated the Atree; the other, flowing south-easterly, continues to be called the Teesta. About five miles below the point of divarication, it passes into a projecting portion of the territory of Cooch Behar, through which it flows eight miles farther; and then passing into the district of Rungpoor, proceeds through it in a south-easterly direction for 110 miles, to its confluence with the Brahmapootra, on the right side, in lat. 25° 14′, long. 89° 41′; its total length of course being 313 miles. The gorge east of Darjeeling, by which the Teesta flows from the mountains, is one of the two passes from Bengal into Sikkim, and is denominated the Sabuk Gola Pass. The river is deep enough in this gorge to be navigated upwards five or six miles. The body of water is very great, and on reaching the plain, the channel is 700 or 800 yards wide; but the navigation is difficult and precarious, from the rapids, and from numerous rocks and large stones in the bed; so that it is available only for floating timber, and for canoes, used for guiding it. However, as high up as Puharpore, fifteen miles above the divergence of the Attree, it is at all times navigable for craft of six or seven tons, and during the monsoon rains for those of forty or fifty tons. Though the Teesta, or south-eastern branch of this great stream, is now the larger, formerly the Attree, or south-western branch, had a much superior volume of water, and discharged the great drainage of the Snowy Mountains of Sikkim and of Bootan, as well as of the plain at their base, into various tributaries of the Ganges. For the last fifty years, however, the drainage has taken an easterly direction to the Brahmapootra, into which it is discharged principally by the channel of the Teesta.

TEETABURHAUT.—A town of Assam, in the British district of Seebpoor, 40 miles S.W. of Seebpoor. Lat. 26° 36′, long. 94° 10′.

TEETLAKOT, in the British district of Kumaon, lieut.-gov. of the N.W. Provinces, a stockade formerly held by the troops of Nepal. It is situate two miles W. of the right bank of the Kali, on a spur of mountain running southwards from the main range of the Himalaya, on the route from Askot to the Beans Pass, 24 miles N.E. of Askot. Lat. 29° 58′, long. 80° 40′.

TEETROUN, in the British district of Suharunpoor, lieut.-gov. of the N.W. Provinces, a town on the route from Suharunpoor to Paneeput, 26 miles S.W. by S. of the former. Lat. 29° 40′, long. 77° 23′.

TEGHOOR.—A town in the British district of Dharwar, presidency of Bombay, 13 miles W.N.W. of Dharwar. Lat. 15° 32′, long. 74° 54′.

TEGRA.—A town in the British district of Mongheer, lieut.-gov. of Bengal, 33 miles W. by N. of Mongheer. Lat. 25° 27′, long. 86°.

TEHARA, in Sirhind, a small town on the route from Loodiana to Ferozpoor, and 29 miles W. of the former. It is situate close to the left bank of the Sutlej, and exhibits evidence of former importance, its present mud houses being built amongst numerous ruins of edifices constructed substantially of burnt brick. It, with the adjacent territory, was conquered by Runjeet Singh, who conferred it on the Allowalla chief, by whose defection during the Lahore war it has passed into the possession of the East-India Company. Distant N.W. from Calcutta 1,133 miles. Lat. 30° 57′, long. 75° 25′.

TEHER, in the Baree Dooab division of the Punjab, a town situated 10 miles from the right bank of the Sutlej, 86 miles S. of the town of Lahore. Lat. 30° 26′, long. 73° 51′.

TEHREE, in Bundelcund, a town of late years generally the residence of the rajah of Oorcha, thence frequently styled the rajah of Tehree. It is on the route from Agra to Saugor, 201 miles S.E. of former, 72 N.W. of latter. Garden styles it "a large walled town;" but according to Sleeman, it "is a wretched town, without one respectable dwelling-house tenanted, beyond the palace, or one merchant, or even shopkeeper, of capital and credit. There are some tolerable houses unoccupied and in ruins; and there are a few neat temples, built as tombs or cenotaphs, in and about the city." On an adjoining height is a fort. Water and supplies for troops are abundant here. Lat. 24° 42′, long. 78° 52′.

TEHRWARRA.—See THERWARRA.

TEIMBOORNEE.—A town in the British district of Sholapoor, presidency of Bombay, 53 miles W.N.W. of Sholapoor. Lat. 18° 1′, long. 75° 15′.

TEINGHA, in the territory of Oude, a village on the route from Lucknow cantonment to Purtabgurh, 95 miles S.E. of the former, 15 N.W. of the latter. Lat. 26° 7′, long. 81° 45′.

TEKEAH, in the territory of Oude, a small town on the route, by the Nanamau Ghat or ferry, from Futtehgurh to Lucknow, 66 miles S.E. of the former, 45 W. of the latter. It has a bazar. Lat. 26° 51′, long. 80° 24′.

TEKERAPURRA.—A town in the Rajpoot state of Jeypoor, 86 miles N.E. by E. from Jeypoor, and 103 miles W. by N. from Ganjam. Lat. 19° 38′, long. 83° 34′.

TEKKREE.—A town of Malwa, in the native state of Dhar, situate six miles S. of the left bank of the Nerbudda river, and 37 miles S. from Dhar. Lat. 22° 2′, long. 75° 27′.

TEKMAH, in the British district of Azimgurh, lieut.-gov. of the N.W. Provinces, a village on the route from the town of Azimgurh to that of Jounpoor, 21 miles S.W. of the former, and 22 N.E. of the latter. It has a small bazar; distant 40 miles N. of Benares. Lat. 25° 53′, long. 83°.

TEK MYOO.—A town in the British district of Aracan, 50 miles S.W. by W. of Aracan. Lat. 20° 18′, long. 92° 46′.

TEK NAAF. — A town standing on a low point of land at the entrance of the Naaf river, in the British district of Aracan, lieut.-gov. of Bengal, 68 miles W. by N. of Aracan. Lat. 20° 49′, long. 92° 23′.

TEKRA, in the Rajpoot state of Jesulmeer, a village on the route from the town of Bekaneer to that of Jesulmeer, and 70 miles N.E. of the latter. Lat. 27° 10′, long. 72° 2′.

TELIAPUR, in the British district of Moradabad, lieut.-gov. of the N.W. Provinces, a village on the route from the town of Moradabad to Muzufernugur, and 16 miles W. of the former place. Distant N.W. from Calcutta 902 miles. Lat. 28° 54′, long. 78° 36′.

TELL RIVER rises in lat. 19° 54′, long. 82° 41′, and flowing north-west for 130 miles, through the native states on the south-west frontier of Bengal, falls into the Mahanuddy river, in lat. 20° 55′, long. 84° 9′.

TELLICHERRY, in the British district of Malabar, presidency of Madras, a seaport town and British military station. Abreast of the fort is a ledge of black rocks, between which and the land small craft may anchor, being in some degree sheltered from the sea; but large ships touching here, when "there is a chance of unsettled weather, should anchor well out in seven or eight fathoms; for H.M.S. *Superb*, of seventy-four guns, was lost at Tellicherry in November, 1781. The fleet having anchored in five and five and a half fathoms, a heavy sea began to roll, which made that ship strike on the *Sultan's* anchor, she being moored inside the *Superb*." A double light is exhibited from the flagstaff all night throughout the year. For moderate-sized vessels the anchorage is one and a half or two miles off the town, with a bottom of soft mud. The site of the town is very beautiful, open to the sea on the west, and on the opposite side backed by wooded hills interspersed with valleys, and watered by a fine river. The neighbouring country is highly productive, the low lands producing annually two, and in some places three, crops of rice in the year. The cocoanut-tree also grows in great abundance and perfection, and is applied to various uses: the trunks are worked up for small boats, and frames and rafters for houses; the leaves are used for thatch, mats, and baskets; the nut affords food and oil, and in its unripe state an agreeable beverage; and the sap drawn off by incision into the trunk, on fermentation, is converted into the intoxicating beverage toddy, which, when distilled, yields the spirit called arrack. "The citadel or fort, in which are situated the jail and hospital, is built on a rising ground close to the sea, and about forty feet above its level. It is of an oblong shape, being 117 yards in length and thirty-four in breadth: its length runs parallel to the sea-shore. The whole of the north-west side of the citadel is occupied by a lofty building, the upper part of which is appropriated to the criminal court and offices, and the lower part forms the jail," which is calculated to contain

300 persons. The climate, though very wet during the monsoon, the average annual fall of rain being from 120 to 140 inches, is found healthy. On account of its salubrity, it has been denominated the Montpellier of India. The houses of the majority of the population are of unbaked brick, and thatched; but those of a better sort are built of laterite, of which there are great quantities in the neighbouring hills. The population is estimated at 20,000, the majority of whom are Moplahs or Mussulmans; the rest Brahminists, with a few Christians. In the year 1782 it was besieged by the forces of Hyder Ali, and relieved upon the arrival of a British force under Major Abington. At that time it was a place of much importance. In the year 1790 it is described by Bartolomeo as "a city belonging to the English, where they have a considerable settlement, a council, and an arsenal. They employ this city as a military post, where they collect troops brought from Bombay, in order to keep in subjection the inhabitants of Malayala. A brisk trade is carried on at Tillicherry: pepper forms one of the principal articles of commerce; the other exports consist of cardamoms, ginger, arrow-root, cinnamon, sandalwood, and other Malabar productions, which they transport to Bombay, aud thence to England." Distance from Seringapatam, S.W., 95 miles; Madras, S.W., 340. Lat. 11° 45′, long. 75° 33′.

TELTAREE.—A town of North-Eastern India, in the British district of Goalpara, 44 miles W.S.W. of Goalpara. Lat. 25° 52′, long. 90°.

TEMI.—A town in the native state of Sikbim, situate on the right bank of the Teesta river, and 18 miles N.E. from Darjeeling. Lat. 27° 14′, long. 88° 30′.

TENASSERIM.—The provinces of Tenasserim, comprehending Amherst, Tavoy, Ye, and Mergui, extend along the eastern coast of the Bay of Bengal, between lat. 10° 48′—18° 25′, long. 96° 35′—99° 30′. The length is about 500 miles; the breadth is very irregular, varying as the seacoast approaches the range of mountains forming the landward boundary of the territory, or recedes from it: probably it nowhere exceeds eighty miles. The area may be estimated at 30,000 square miles. The area of these provinces has been recently enlarged by the annexation of that portion of the territory acquired from the Burmese in 1852, which lies to the east of the Sitang river; and their northern frontier has thus been extended from the Salween river to the Sitang: on the east they are bounded by the Siamese range of mountains, whose height varies from 3,000 to 5,000 feet; on the south by the river Packshan, and on the west by the sea. These provinces are under the immediate jurisdiction of the supreme government.

The seacoast, though of great extent, presents little variety of character: it is generally bold and rocky, and in many places bordered by numerous islands. Towards the south, opposite Mergui, are a cluster, differing in size, shape, and height, bearing the name of the Mergui Archipelago. The coast is indented by numerous creeks and small streams; several rivers of some magnitude also empty themselves into the bay, affording good anchorage and harbourage for ships of large burthen. With the exception of the deltas of such rivers, which furnish many acres of alluvial soil, peculiarly fit for rice-cultivation, the coast vegetation is confined in a great degree to vast forests and almost impenetrable jungle. Between Ye and Tavoy the coast consists of large tracts of swampy land, called Sunderbunds, where the mangrove, and other trees which thrive in brackish water, grow luxuriantly and in abundance.

The physical aspect of this territory is much diversified: it may be characterized generally as a mountainous country, but having also large plains or valleys, intersected by many fine and fertilizing rivers. The mountains are clothed from the base to the summit with thick forests and brushwood; the valleys are appropriated to the cultivation of the various productions raised within the provinces. Towards the north, the country is more level, consisting of vast alluvial plains, highly fertile, being watered by the Salween and the Sitang; further to the south, the aspect changes to that of a more elevated country. Here the mountains run in three parallel ridges, in a direction from north-north-west to south-south-east, varying in height from 3,000 to 4,500 feet, and gradually diminishing as they approach the shore, till their elevation does not exceed 500 feet. In the lower parts of the province, the interior still continues mountainous, but less elevated, and towards the shore terminates in low plains or swamps; and the only communication here is by boats, which navigate the nullahs and creeks.

The principal rivers have tides flowing a considerable distance up the country: they are all wide, and generally deep at their mouths; and though their navigation is sometimes intricate and interrupted, all can be safely traversed. They are subject to annual inundations, which render the proximate soil amazingly fertile. But besides fertilizing the soil, these rivers afford great facilities for foreign and internal trade; and the villages in the provinces being for the most part situate on their banks, the transit of merchandise from one to another is easily effected by canoes. The chief rivers are the Salween, Sitang, Attaran, and Tenasserim, which will be found described under their respective names.

Almost all the ground that is not subject to inundations is occupied by dense forests, containing gigantic and valuable timber. They occupy, it is said, two-thirds of the whole extent of the province: one-fifteenth only is under cultivation; and when the British first became possessed of the country, it presented a complete wilderness. Rules for the grant of uncleared lands, framed with the utmost moderation and liberality, were in due time drawn out.

One of the most important mineral productions is coal: the quality has been described as excellent, and the quantity considerable. The localities in which it exists, it has also been said, present advantages of transport. "Iron," says Helfer, "is found in one or the other form almost everywhere." It occurs in beds, in veins, and in rocks: it is most abundant between Ye and Tavoy, approximating the seacoast. In the territory between the Salween and Gyne rivers, it is found in sandstone hills, which vary from forty to 200 feet in height. Its quality improves towards the south, near Tavoy; and this situation would be very advantageous for works, being only four-and-twenty miles from the river, which distance might be traversed by a canal or railroad. The ore found here would, Dr. Helfer asserts, furnish from seventy-four to eighty per cent. of raw iron. Mines are nowhere at present worked; in several places, however, are to be found the remains of furnaces and pits long neglected. Next to iron, tin is the metal most generally diffused through the province. It is confined, however, in a great degree, to the southern parts. The richest mines exist near the Packshan river, which forms the southern boundary of the provinces. "The range of mountains in which the tin-ore is found is a continuation of the Siamese tin territory of Rinowng. The tin is found in the debris of primitive rocks, like in all other parts of Tenasserim; but the grains or crystals are much larger, and the soil in which they are buried yields eight to ten feet of tin, while at Tavoy the utmost is seven feet." At Mergui also tin is very prevalent, the hill on which the town stands containing much ore in the form of black sand and oxide. At some remote period, it is evident that the ore has been extracted in considerable quantities, as a large extent of surface remains upturned in the localities where it exists. The Burmese method of working is very rude and unscientific. Gold is frequently to be met with in various parts of the province, but nowhere in any considerable quantities. When found, it is generally in the sands of rivers; but its primary source has not been discovered. It is supposed to lie on the foreign side of the mountain-chain, as it is most prevalent in the streams which flow into Tenasserim from the eastward. An analysis of sundry particles found in the streams of the Tavoy district was considered so satisfactory as to induce the government to order an examination of the rocks in the vicinity of the auriferous streams. Copper has lately been discovered in two islands of the Mergui Archipelago, viz., Sullivan's Island and Callagkiauk; in the former in veins of quartz, in the latter in gneiss. Lead and antimony have been met with in some parts of the Amherst territory, but in very small quantities.

The only manifestation of the existence of volcanic agency appears in the numerous hot springs to be met with in many parts of the country. On the Attaran river, and near Amherst, these exist in great numbers: they are sometimes as much as fifty feet in circumference, and near their banks thirty-five feet deep. The quality of the water is that of a sulphureous mineral, tinged slightly with chalybeate.

The year is divided into the wet and dry season; the former commencing with the approach of the south-west monsoon, about June, and lasting till October, when the latter sets in. The natives on the coast divide the year into three seasons; viz., the hot, the rainy, and the cold; the first commencing in February, the second in June, and the third in October. The temperature, however, hardly varies sufficiently to justify the adoption of this division. The greatest heat prevails during the month of April, and then the thermometer is sometimes above 100°, and the weather very oppressive. Notwithstanding these provinces extend over a distance of seven degrees of latitude, there is little diversity of temperature throughout; and when a difference is perceptible, it is occasioned more from disparity in the fall of rain than any other cause. In the northern parts, the monsoon makes its appearance with great violence, and continues till the end of October or beginning of November. During the five or six following months, no rain takes place. In Mergui, on the contrary, the monsoon comes in mildly, and though it rains more at one time than at another, showers are common all the year. The climate was considered a subject of such importance, that, by order of government, a report was made to parliament concerning the health and mortality of her majesty's troops serving in these provinces; and this investigation has led to the knowledge of the fact that there is less sickness and fewer deaths here, among both Europeans and sepoys, than in almost any other part of the territories of the East-India Company. This appears the more remarkable from the prevalence of that active generator of disease, excessive moisture, caused by the abundance of marshes, jungle, and dense forests which exist in the vicinity of the most populous districts. But clear and undeniable facts are adduced in proof of the healthfulness of the provinces; and it is said that the exhalations, instead of proving pernicious consequences, tend to cool the atmosphere, and promote its salubrity. "So beneficial," says this report, "has the climate of this coast been deemed for invalids, that in November, 1826, in consequence of the favourable result of some previous experiments, the commander-in-chief gave instructions to the medical board at Madras for the establishment of a sanatarium either at Moulmein or at Amherst." The complaints that are most common and dangerous are fevers of the intermittent type, inflammation of the lungs and liver, catarrh, and dysentery. These at times prove fatal, but in the majority of cases are subdued by timely care and attention; and from a table appended to the above-mentioned report, it is shown, that during the ten years from 1827 to 1836 inclusive, out of 10,819 admissions into the hospitals at Moulmein, 305 deaths only occurred.

Cotton is grown to a small extent, but it is not indigenous, and was probably introduced from the continent of India. The plantations are generally situated on the banks of rivers; but little attention is paid to the culture, and the quality of that produced is not high: Dr. Helfer thinks that the Manilla plant, and also the Egyptian, might succeed better. Rice is one of the most important productions, but its cultivation is confined in a great measure to the northern districts, where the alluvial soil is so general. Sugarcane, though it thrives well throughout the provinces, is cultivated to a very limited extent, being almost confined to gardens; but there is every reason to suppose, from the character of the soil and climate, that an extension of this branch of agricultural industry would amply remunerate any person undertaking it. Tobacco is in very common use among the natives; and not only men, but women and children, either smoke or chew it. Much care is bestowed upon its culture, but it is raised only for home consumption: it is also imported from Cheduba. The betel flourishes in some parts, especially about Mergui, where it is extensively produced. The plantations resemble those of hops in England: the young plants require to be placed in a rich soil, where they must be treated with much care, and be screened from the scorching rays of the sun. The planting takes place in March, April, and May; and five or six months after, the leaves may be gathered continuously for fifteen months: fifty from each vine can be collected monthly. The production of the areca-nut is confined to the southern provinces, commencing about the latitude of Tavoy, and flourishing vigorously in Mergui. The cocoanut is found to thrive well, especially near the seacoast, and yet its cultivation is not carried to the extent which its importance would justify; and "the natives," Dr. Helfer observes, "have a great reluctance to plant it." This reluctance may be attributed to the circumstance of its not yielding fruit for eight years after it is planted; or, perhaps, the people may suspect, that as the Burmese considered cocoanut-trees the property of government, the English would take the same view. It is largely imported from the Nicobar Islands. Coffee is not grown, but the soil and climate are both suited for it. The Nauclea Gambir, or Terra Japonica, occurs chiefly on the banks of the Tenasserim river, where it attains the height of six feet. It is uncertain whether or not it is indigenous: the natives chew it, as well as the betel. The fruits are the pineapple, mango, orange, shaddock, lime, citron, melon, gourd, and guava.

The vast forests which cover the greater part of the provinces, and clothe the mountains from their base to their summit, contain an immensity of trees. Dr. Helfer estimates the number of trees in the province at 638,000,000. The same author says that there are no less than 377 different species, each at least attaining a diameter of seven inches. The heights are greater in proportion to the circumference than those in Europe. The wood has the character of being firm and elastic. Teak forests abound in the upper course of the Attaran river, and yield an inexhaustible supply of timber, which is exported in large quantities. On these possessions coming into the hands of the British, prompt steps were taken for rendering the forests a source of revenue; licenses to cut timber were offered, but private speculators appeared to decline engaging in the business; government thereupon led the way by an experiment upon a very small scale. As a pecuniary speculation it failed, as such matters in the hands of government usually do; but the object probably having been rather to call attention to the forests than to realize profit, it may be considered as having been to some extent successful. Private parties took up the trade, which it was clear government could not pursue beneficially; many tons of teak-wood were exported within a few years; and by 1833 shipbuilding had made some progress at Moulmein. In that year the receipts of government from the forests were 13,457 rupees; in 1845–46, they had risen to 1,07,048 rupees. The advance, however, had not been regularly progressive, but had fluctuated considerably. Great abuses, moreover, had existed; and various plans for their suppression had been adopted with more or less success. Numberless disputes and squabbles grew out of the attempt to enforce rules on the one hand, and the desire to evade them on the other; and even yet it cannot be said that they are at an end. Besides the teak, there are several other forest-trees. Bamboo grows naturally, and in great profusion, the best occurring between Tavoy and Ye, in the interior, and on the slopes of the elevated ridges. The jack grows both to the north and south: it is one of the most valuable trees in the province. Every part is applied to some use: the fruit for food, the wood is excellent for furniture, the leaves wholesome for cattle; from the bark exudes a species of caoutchouc; the sawdust, when boiled, yields a yellow dye; and from the kernel oil can be extracted. The sapan-tree is also very valuable, but its growth is confined to the country east of Mergui, near the Siamese frontier: it is felled in August, and floated down the river in rafts. Sandal-wood occurs in the southern parts, and on some of the islands in the Mergui Archipelago. The wood-oil tree grows to a good size. There are other oil-yielding plants: the sesamum is the most common, which all classes use for culinary purposes. Caoutchouc is produced from many trees in the country, and ought to become a source of revenue, as the quality is good, and it exists in abundance. The camphor-plant, the gamboge, and the castoroil-plant all occur. Spices of all descriptions—cloves, cinnamon, nutmegs, peppers—grow in abundance.

From the extensive forests which abound throughout the province, and the vast tracts of land uninclosed and uncultivated, it might be expected that the number of wild animals would be large, and their variety great. Elephants are numerous, and of great size, occupying more particularly the tracts near the eastern frontier. The inhabitants but seldom hunt them, but a few gain a livelihood by catching these animals. This operation is performed by two men, mounted on a trained elephant, and carrying a spear and a lasso. The work is attended with much danger, not only from the elephant sought to be ensnared, but also from tigers, who frequently carry off the elephant-hunters while watching in the jungle. Several species of the rhinoceros exist, and these are hunted by the natives for their horns, which form an article of exportation.

At the period when the British became possessed of Tenasserim, the population, it has been said, did not exceed 30,000 souls; it has been estimated indeed as low as 10,000. More recently, these numbers have been regarded as greatly below the fact, and the people at the time of the British conquest estimated at 90,000. It is probable that all these estimates err, though the more liberal may be regarded as being nearer the truth; but however that may be, the numbers certainly increased under the occupation of the British, and in 1839 exceeded 112,000. In 1847 the population was given at 150,415; and by the latest returns it appears to be 191,476. The people who were the first inhabitants has not been clearly ascertained. The Talians, according to a recent authority, now form the larger portion of the population. This, however, seems open to doubt. Another portion sometimes supposed to be the original occupants of the country, are called Kareans. "To judge from the Kareans inhabiting the interior," says Mr. Helfer, "who seem to have outlived all revolutions of the successive conquests, and following analogy, whatever inhabitants there were, they seem to have belonged to Mongolic races. Burmah, as well as Siam and Cambogia, seem to have been originally peopled from the north; and it is very improbable that the inhabitants of Tenasserim were ever mixed with Malay blood. The comparatively late arrival of that race from Menamcaboo, in Sumatra, in the Malay peninsula, in the districts of Jabor, Malacca, and Queda, where they formed colonies, is now almost universally adopted as a fact approaching to certainty; and if so, they had no time to disperse themselves towards the north." The province has undergone many changes with regard to its inhabitants, each conqueror being followed by new settlers. All the villages are built either on the seashore or on the banks of rivers. There is a headman to each, whose duty it is to collect the revenue, to superintend the police force, and to decide all petty disputes. The language adopted in the courts of law, and in all public transactions, is the Burmese; but that of the Talian inhabitants (sometimes said to form a majority) is their own vernacular tongue, and which is very different from the language of Burmah.

The chief pursuits of the people are hunting and husbandry: the women weave a species of cloth, and assist in beating out the rice, by means of mills, for daily use. Both men and women are fond of music and dancing; and a species of stage performance somewhat resembling the earlier attempts of Europe in the drama, is highly popular. Athletic games and amusements are also practised; as football, wrestling, pugilistic encounters, and boat-races. In the month of April, which is the commencement of the year by their computations, there are great festivities and rejoicings. The most popular amusement consists in throwing water from vessels over each other. Marriage is considered quite a civil contract, and can be annulled without much difficulty: the ceremony observed is that employed by the Burmese. The parents of a youth desirous of forming an alliance employ friends to gain the consent of the girl's relations, who then fix upon the time, and the parties are allowed to see each other. On the day of the ceremony, the bridegroom goes to the house of his intended with his relations and friends, and takes his seat on the right of the party there assembled, the bride being on the left. The ceremony is then performed, which is thus described by Captain Low:—"The elder now gives the bride a nosegay, and makes her repeat some Bali sentences, first directed to her father, again to her mother, next to the parents of the bridegroom, and lastly to her husband. The bridegroom goes through the same ceremony, beginning with his parents and relatives, but does not address the bride. The elder then takes the flower from the bride and places it on the wall of the house; she takes a little rolled-up betel-leaf and presents it to the bridegroom, who exchanges the flower for it. They then both sit on one mat, the bridegroom on the right; a feast ensues, and they finish the ceremonies by eating out of the same dish." A newly-married couple do not proceed to the husband's house, but remain for a period of from one to three years in that of the father and mother of the bride. The results are said to be protective of the rights of the wife, but rather unfavourable to the authority of the husband. The dead are generally burned, with the exception of persons under seventeen years of age, who are buried. It is the custom, if a woman die in childbed, to burn the body on the bank of a river. The obsequies of a phoongee or priest are attended with much display: the corpse, clothed in finery and placed upon a richly-ornamented coffin, is laid on the pile, which is fired by rockets, and utterly consumed.

The Bhuddhist religion is the faith universally held by the Burmese and by the Talians, but they are not such faithful or rigid observers of its precepts as the Peguers and Siamese. The priests are numerous; they live generally in monasteries, and employ a portion of their time in teaching the children to read and write. The Kareans have no prescribed form of worship: they entertain a faint idea of the existence of one supreme being, but do not seem to have any notion of a future state. They are said to have some traditions of the creation of man, his fall, the deluge, the subsequent peopling of the earth, and the growth of idolatry amongst its inhabitants, which appear to have a Mosaic origin. They have a strong dread of a set of supernatural beings somewhat resembling fairies, a belief in whose existence and powers extends also to other classes. The habits of this race are said to be extremely filthy, and they have an almost superstitious aversion to the use of water for the purpose of ablution. Another tribe, called Toungthoos, are found in Amherst: they differ in many respects from all the other classes of inhabitants; but little appears to be known of them, except that they are the best cultivators in the province. The attempts made to introduce Christianity have not been altogether without success. A great difficulty existed from the indifference of the natives on the subject of religion generally; but the American Baptist Missionary Society have built churches and established stations throughout the province, through which they have been able to effect considerable improvement in the moral condition of the people.

The courts of justice, which, during the sway of the Burmese, were open to corruption and bribery, and tended more to the perversion than the administration of justice, are now under the jurisdiction of officers appointed by the government of Bengal, who are under the control and superintendence in civil cases of the court of Sudder Dewanny Adawlut, and in criminal cases of the court of Nizamut Adawlut. These functionaries consist of a commissioner, two assistant-commissioners, and some other officers.

The history of Tenasserim till the commencement of the eighteenth century is involved in obscurity. The country appears always to have been in a state of disorder and agitation, and subject to frequent changes in its possessors; at one time belonging to the Siamese, at another subject to Pegu, and at another to the Burmese. In the year 1760, the last-mentioned nation gained a firm, and, comparatively speaking, lasting possession, retaining it under their harsh and imperious yoke until the termination of hostilities with the British, when, by the treaty of Yandaboo, it was ceded to the last-named power. When first occupied, the province presented a truly deplorable aspect. The inhabitants were few; it yielded no revenue, and in every respect offered nothing but discouragement. Its rapid growth to its present improved condition, therefore, is in the highest degree satisfactory, and calculated to awaken the deepest interest for its future welfare. The fact, however, is unquestionable, that there is still great room for improvement. The advantages which these provinces enjoy over many others of the British possessions in the East are manifold. Nature, with overflowing bounty, has bestowed on the land vast and varied powers of production; the rice-fields yield an increase unrivalled in India; the rivers, besides fertilizing the soil by the periodical inundations, and offering great advantages for commerce, afford large supplies of fish, which furnish an article of food for the inhabitants: the climate is salubrious. The vast amount of physical capabilities, then, are manifest; but with all these advantages the population is so scanty, that it is clear, for the proper development of these resources, an increase is necessary. It is also requisite that such increase should comprise men of vigour and enterprise, possessed of capital, and able to command labour. The greater part of the land is in the hands of government; and from the progress which has already been made, it may be anticipated, that by its judicious efforts, the country may be brought to the condition which it evidently is capable of attaining.

TENASSERIM TOWN.—Formerly the capital of the province so called, but now a place of no importance, containing only 100 houses and 400 inhabitants. It is situate on the river of the same name, at the confluence of the Little Tenasserim. The river is navigable up to the town for vessels of 120 tons burthen. The town was once surrounded by a brick wall, which is now so much in ruins that its remains can be traced only at intervals: it also had two or three pagodas. It is about forty miles from the town of Mergui by the river, and in lat. 12° 6′, long. 99° 5′.

TENASSERIM RIVER.—The most considerable and important river in the province so called. Its source is supposed to lie in the mountains to the north-east of Tavoy, between the fourteenth and fifteenth degree of latitude. For some distance it has a course due south: it here bears the name of the Kamaun-Khiaung river. Upon arriving at the village of Metamio, in lat. 14° 13′, it is joined by the Baing-Khiaung, and the united streams are called the Tenasserim River, which then takes a south-easterly direction, but turns afterwards to the south again, till it reaches the old town of Tenasserim, where it receives the Little Tenasserim. From this it takes a north-westerly direction, and empties itself into the sea by two mouths, which form an island, on which the town of Mergui is situated. The upper part of its course is through a wild and uncultivated tract, sometimes between high and perpendicular banks, at others through a low and barren country. It afterwards opens upon extensive alluvial plains, which are in some places highly cultivated. On many parts of its banks exist forests of fine teak, and the valuable sapan-wood; and some districts have been found to contain minerals and coal. It receives many feeders, but they are generally insignificant, with the exception of the Little Tenasserim, the Baing-Khiaung, and Kamaun-Khiaung. There are few villages on its banks, and none of the slightest importance but Metamio and Tenasserim.

TENDUKHERI, in the British district of Saugor and Nerbudda, a town situate at the base of a remarkable conical hill of trap, the summit of which was once crowned by a cluster of greyish-green basaltic columns, which now lie overthrown about the base, shattered probably by the shock of an earthquake. Close to this place are rich mines of iron-ore, which are worked to considerable extent, and furnished the metal of which a suspension-bridge 200 feet span was constructed at Saugor cantonment. In the vicinity is an extensive forest, in which lions have been recently killed. Distant S. from Saugor 50 miles, N. from Nagpoor 108. Elevation above the sea 1,338 feet. Lat. 23° 10′, long. 78° 58′.

TENDWARRA, in the British district of Banda, lieut.-gov. of the N.W. Provinces, a village on the route from the town of Banda to Rewah, four miles S. of the former. Lat. 25° 25′, long. 80° 25′.

TENGA PANEE, a river of Upper Assam, rises in lat. 27° 38′, long. 96° 20′, and flowing westerly for forty-five miles through the district of Sudiya, falls into the Brahmapootra river, in lat. 27° 46′, long. 95° 49′.

TENGERICOTTA.—A town in the British district of Salem, presidency of Madras, 29 miles N.E. by N. of Salem. Lat. 12° 1′, long. 78° 26′.

TEPPEIN.—A town in the British district of Amherst, in the Tenasserim provinces, 42 miles N. of Moulmein. Lat. 17° 6′, long. 97° 40′.

TERDUL.—A town in the Southern Mahratta jaghire of Sanglee, situate on the right bank of the Kistnah river, and 59 miles N.E. from Belgaum. Lat. 16° 30′, long. 75° 9′.

TEREN TAREN, in the Baree Doaab division of the Punjab, a town situated 25 miles from the right bank of the Beas river, 35 miles E. by S. of the town of Lahore. Lat. 31° 28′, long. 74° 57′.

TEREPUNYTHORAY.—A town in the native state of Travancore, presidency of Madras, 110 miles N.N.W. from Trivandrum, and 84 miles S.W. by S. from Coimbatoor. Lat. 9° 56′, long. 76° 25′.

TERHA, in the district of Bainswara, territory of Oude, a town five miles N.E. of the left bank of the Ganges, 40 S.W. of Lucknow. Butter estimates the population at 6,000, including 100 Mussulmans. Lat. 26° 24′, long. 80° 35′.

TERHA, in the British district of Agra, lieut.-gov. of the N.W. Provinces, a village on the route from the city of Agra to that of Gwalior, and 12 miles S. of the former. It has a bazar. Lat. 27°, long. 78° 1′.

TERIKOT.—A town within the dominions of Gholab Singh, the ruler of Cashmere, situate 47 miles E.S.E. from Jamoo, and 44 miles N.W. by W. from Kangra. Lat. 32° 26′, long. 75° 43′.

TERRAON.—See TIROWAN.

TERRUVUMPET.—A town in the British district of Madura, presidency of Madras, 47 miles E. by S. of Madura. Lat. 9° 51′, long. 78° 51′.

TESSUNAH.—See TISSOOA.

TETOWLEE, in the British district of Muzuffurnugur, lieut.-gov. of the N.W. Provinces, a village on the route from Kurnaul to Meerut, and 25 miles S.E. of the former. Lat. 29° 28′, long. 77° 20′.

TEWAREEPOOR, in the British district of Cawnpore, lieut.-gov. of the N.W. Provinces, a village on the route from the cantonment of Cawnpore to Futtehpoor, and 18 miles S.E. of the former. Lat. 26° 15′, long. 80° 34′.

TEWREE, in the Rajpoot state of Jodhpoor, a small town on the route from Pokhurn to the town of Jodhpoor, and 24 miles N.W. of the latter. Lat. 26° 33′, long. 73°.

TEZGONG.—A town in the British district of Dacca, lieut.-gov. of Bengal, five miles N.N.W. of Dacca. Lat. 23° 46′, long. 90° 23′.

TEZPORE.—A town of Assam, in the British district of Durrung, 46 miles E. by N. of Durrung. Lat. 26° 35′, long. 92° 45′.

THADGAON.—A town in the territory of Nagpoor, 41 miles S. from Nagpoor, and 118 miles E.S.E. from Ellichpoor. Lat. 20° 35′, long. 79° 16′.

THADZENG.—A pass through the range of mountains separating the district of Aracan from the province of Pegu, 16 miles W.S.W. of Bassein. Lat. 16° 38′, long. 94° 38′.

THAIMAH, in the British district of Seuni, territory of Saugur and Nerbudda, lieut.-gov. of the N.W. Provinces, a town on the route from Seuni to Ramgurh, 51 miles E.N.E. of the former. Lat. 22° 20′, long. 80° 22′.

THAIR.—A town in one of the recently sequestrated districts of Hyderabad, or dominions of the Nizam, 50 miles N.E. from Sholapoor. Lat. 18° 20′, long. 76° 13′.

THAIRNA.—A river of Hyderabad, rising in lat. 18° 29′, long. 75° 54′, and, flowing easterly for 100 miles, falls into the Manjera river, in lat. 18° 4′, long. 77° 2′.

THAKIL, in the British district of Kumaon, lieut.-gov. of the N.W. Provinces, a mountain in the bifurcation formed by the rivers Kalee and Surjoo, and about five miles N.W. of their confluence. Its summit consists of bluish-black slate rock, in some places fissile, in others compact, and cropping out from beneath limestone, with which the acclivities are covered. Elevation above the sea 8,221 feet. Lat. 29° 31′, long. 80° 15′.

THAKOOR.—A town of Assam, in the British district of Durrung, 62 miles E.N.E. of Durrung. Lat. 26° 44′, long. 92° 59′.

THAKOORDWARA. — A town in the British district of Moradabad, lieut.-gov. of the N.W. Provinces. Lat. 29° 12′, long. 78° 55′.

THALNEIR.—A town with fort in the British district of Candeish, presidency of Bombay, 64 miles N.E. by N. of Malligaum. The place was ceded to the British by Holkar in 1818, under the treaty of Mundisore; but resistance being offered by the killedar upon receiving a summons for its surrender, the fort was taken by storm by a force under Sir Thomas Hislop. Lat. 21° 15′, long. 75° 6′.

THALOO.—A pass through the range of mountains which separate the Aracan and Pegu districts, 48 miles S.S.W. from Prome. Lat. 18° 6′, long. 94° 50′.

THALWAN, in the Julinder Dooab, a village on the right bank of the Sutlej, which is here crossed by a ferry affording a much-frequented communication from Sirhind with the Punjab. It is distant 21 miles W. from Loodiana. Lat. 31°, long. 75° 33′.

THAMBA, in the British district of Allahabad, lieut.-gov. of the N.W. Provinces, a village on the route by Rajapoor ferry, from the cantonment of Allahabad to Banda, and 29 miles W. of the former. Lat. 25° 26′, long. 81° 30′.

THAMEIN.—A town of Burmah, situate on the left bank of the Irawady river, and 196 miles N. by E. from Ava. Lat. 24° 38′, long. 96° 53′.

THAN.—A town of Burmah, situate on the left bank of the Irawady river, and 33 miles N. from Ava. Lat. 22° 20′, long. 96° 4′.

THANA, in the state of Boondee, in Rajpootana, a village on the route from Nusserabad to Boondee, 74 miles S.E. of former, 18 N.W. of latter. Here is the fortress of the feudatory of the place, a small but strong structure of masonry, on the crest of a low hill. Lat. 25° 34′, long. 75° 29′.

THANA BAOHAN, in the British district of Suharunpoor, lieut.-gov. of the N.W. Provinces, a town on the route from Suharunpoor to Delhi, 28 miles S.S.W. of the former. Lat. 29° 35′, long. 77° 30′.

THANA CHOWKEE, a police-station in the British district of Shahabad, lieut.-gov. of Bengal, 31 miles S.S.W. of Sasseram. Lat. 24° 33′, long. 83° 50′.

THANAPOOR, in the British district of Cawnpore, lieut.-gov. of the N.W. Provinces, a village on the route from the cantonment of Etawa to that of Cawnpore, and 38 miles W. of the latter. Lat. 26° 21′, long. 79° 53′.

THAN-MAU.—A pass through the range of mountains separating the district of Aracan and the province of Pegu, 37 miles S.W. by S. of Bassein. Lat. 16° 20′, long. 94° 30′.

THANNESUR.—See THUNNESUR.

THANOT, in the Rajpoot state of Jesulmeer, a small town in the desert, 54 miles N.E. of the city of Jesulmeer. Lat. 27° 41′, long. 70° 41′.

THARAWADDY, one of the divisions of the province of Pegu, having an area of 1,950 square miles, and a population of 66,129.

THARET KONG.—A town of Burmah, 48 miles S.E. from the left bank of the Irawady river, and 26 miles E.S.E. from Ava. Lat. 21° 46′, long. 96° 24′.

THAUT, in the Rajpoot state of Jodhpoor, a village on the route from Nusserabad to Beekaneer, and 41 miles N.W. of former. It contains twenty houses and ten wells. Lat. 26° 34′, long. 74° 22′.

THEE BO.—A town of Burmah, 88 miles E. from the left bank of the Irawady river, and 94 miles E.N.E. from Ava. Lat. 22° 20′, long. 97° 26′.

THEKA VULLIOR. — A town in the British district of Tinnevelly, presidency of Madras, 25 miles S. by W. of Tinnevelly. Lat. 8° 22′, long. 77° 40′.

THELLAR.—A town in the British district of North Arcot, presidency of Madras, 70 miles S.W. of Madras. Lat. 12° 24′, long. 79° 36′.

THENKAUSHEE.—A town in the British district of Tinnevelly, presidency of Madras, 30 miles N.W. by W. of Tinnevelly. Lat. 8° 58′, long. 77° 22′.

THEOG.—A small fort on the route from Simla to Kotgurh, and by the winding mountain road 14 miles E. of the former post. During the occupation of the country by the Goorkhas, this post was held by one of their garrisons. It gives name to a small thakoorai or lordship tributary to the state of Keonthal, containing eight pergunnahs, and having a population estimated at 4,423 persons. Elevation above the sea 8,018 feet. Lat. 31° 6′, long. 77° 26′.

THERAI, in the British district of Agra, lieut.-gov. of the N.W. Provinces, a town 10 miles S. of the city of Agra. Lat. 27° 3′, long. 78° 7′.

THERWARRA.—A small district inhabited by Coolies, on the north-western part of the province of Guzerat. It is bounded on the north by Deodur; on the south by Rahdunpore; on the east by Kankrej; and on the west by Baubier. It is about ten miles long and eight broad; the country is flat and generally open, but with patches of low jungle: the population is about 800. Therwarra pays no tribute to any state, but looks for protection to the British, with which government its connection commenced in 1819, upon occasion of the expulsion of the bands of plunderers from Guzerat. A subsequent agreement was entered into in 1826. The policy observed towards it is that of non-interference with its internal affairs, but the maintenance of control in its external relations. The town of Therwarra is in lat. 24° 3′, long. 71° 38′.

THINDOOA.—A town in the territory of Oude, situate on the right bank of the Chowka river, and 87 miles N. by W. from Lucknow. Lat. 28° 6′, long. 80° 50′.

THOBA.—A town in the Rajpoot state of Jodhpoor or Marwar, 30 miles N. from Jodhpoor, and 100 miles W. by N. from Ajmeer. Lat. 26° 44′, long. 73° 10′.

THOBAL.—A town of Eastern India, in the native state of Muneepoor, 13 miles S.S.E. from Muneepoor, and 81 miles E. by S. from Silchar. Lat. 24° 39′, long. 94° 7′.

THOGAON.—A town in the territory of Nagpoor, 106 miles S. by E. from Nagpoor, and 176 miles N.N.E. from Hyderabad. Lat. 19° 41′, long. 79° 34′.

THONGHOO.—A town of Eastern India, in the British district of Aracan, 139 miles S.S.E. of Aracan. Lat. 18° 55′, long. 94° 18′.

THOOMIEEOLKHOOLEL.—A town of Eastern India, in the native state of Muneepoor, 22 miles N. from Muneepoor, and 81 miles W.S.W. from Silchar. Lat. 25° 9′, long. 94° 4′.

THOREE.—A town in Nepal, 47 miles S.W. by W. from Khatmandoo, and 40 miles N. from Bettiah. Lat. 27° 20′, long. 84° 40′.

THORLA.—A town in the British district of Tipperah, lieut.-gov. of Bengal, 18 miles N.W. of Tipperah. Lat. 23° 40′, long. 90° 59′.

THOUNG YIN MYIT.—A river rising in lat. 16° 10′, long. 99° 9′, and, flowing northwest for 160 miles, separates the British district of Amherst from the native state of Siam, and falls into the Thaluayn Myeet river in lat. 17° 35′, long. 97° 43′.

THOUREE.—A town in the territory of Oude, situate on the right bank of the Goomtee river, and 60 miles E.S.E. from Lucknow. Lat. 26° 28′, long. 81° 50′.

THREE PAGODAS, in the British district of Amherst, one of the Tenasserim provinces, 92 miles S.E. by E. of Amherst. Lat. 15° 20′, long. 98° 48′.

THULASEEREE.—A town in the British district of Tannah, presidency of Bombay, 79 miles N. of Bombay. Lat. 20° 4′, long. 73°.

THULENDI, in the district of Bainswara, territory of Oude, a small town on the route from Allahabad to Lucknow, 86 miles N.W. of the former, 42 S. of the latter. It has a bazar. Lat. 26° 25′, long. 81° 1′.

THULLEE.—A town in the Rajpoot state of Jeypoor, 24 miles S. from Jeypoor, and 79 miles E. from Ajmeer. Lat. 26° 35′, long. 75° 57′.

THUNDOO BHAWANI, in Sirmor, a summit of the Sain range, and near its south-eastern extremity. It is crowned by a small Hindoo temple, which was a secondary station in the great trigonometrical survey of the Himalaya. Elevation above the sea 5,700 feet. Lat. 30° 40′, long. 77° 26′.

THUNNESIR, in Sirhind, a town on the route from Kurnal to Loodiana, and 23 miles N. of the former place. It is situate on the left bank of the Sursooty, in a level, fertile, well-cultivated country, abounding in groves of mango-trees. The site is a great irregular mound, formed of the ruins of the former city, over which, amidst crumbling walls, are scattered the present habitations. Most of these are wretched huts; but the natives in easy circumstances have handsome houses, on the walls of which are depicted, in gaudy colours and of large dimensions, the grotesque figures of their monstrous idols. The place is surrounded by a ruinous wall, formerly of considerable height: connected with it is a dilapidated fort with numerous towers; there is also a large tank, and a temple of Mahadeo. Outside the town is a ruinous Mussulman tomb, of considerable height and octagonal form, having a turret at each angle, and being surmounted by a large and very elegant cupola of white marble. Its appearance is rendered more striking by its picturesque situation amidst palm-trees, embosomed in a thick mango-grove. Notwithstanding the ruinous state of the buildings, the environs are represented as very pleasing. "We had our tents pitched," says Lloyd, "to the north of the town, upon a green turf shaded by lofty trees. It was a delightful spot, and the tanks, mausoleums, and ruins formed a beautiful picture before us." At a short distance from the town is the lake of Khoorket, famous and revered among the Hindus on account of a great battle, which, according to the Mahabarat, was fought on its banks in the mythological period of the Hindoo records. This lake is thus described by Lloyd:—"As well as I can judge, it is about one mile in length, and half a mile in width. In the centre is an island 235 paces in breadth, connected with the shore on each side by two ancient bridges 235 paces in length each, which, I was informed, are during the rainy season covered with the water of the flooded lake. There is a third bridge also, which leads to the island, said to have been built by Aurungzebe; but it is now useless and broken. There are no temples here, but at the most hallowed spots flights of steps run down to the water's edge, for the convenience of those desirous of performing the usual ablutions." The district of which Thunnesir is the chief town contained ninety-nine and a half villages, and was estimated to have an area of 2,336 square miles, with a population of

496,748, and an annual revenue of 7,600*l.* sterling. A moiety of the territory escheated to the British government in consequence of the failure of heirs in 1833 and in 1851, and the remaining portions have been confiscated, in consequence of the failure of the chiefs in their allegiance. In 1011, Mahmood of Ghuznee crossed the Indus, with the avowed intention of destroying Thunnesir, though his ally, the rajah of Lahore, offered, in case the town were spared, that the amount of its revenues should annually be paid to the invader, in addition to all the expenses of the expedition, besides fifty elephants and a large amount of jewels. Regardless of the intercession and the proffered gifts, Mahmood continued his march, and took and sacked Thunnesir, and, destroying the idols, sent the fragments of Jugsoma, the principal one, to Ghuznee, to be there trodden under foot. Ferishta relates that on this occasion "the Mahomedan army brought to Ghuznee 200,000 captives and much wealth; so that the capital appeared like an Indian city, no soldier of the camp being without wealth or without many slaves." The population has been returned at 12,103. Thunnesir is distant N.W. from Calcutta 988 miles. Lat. 29° 58′, long. 76° 54′.

THURORA.—A town in the territory of Nagpoor, 58 miles E.N.E. from Nagpoor, and 46 miles S.E. by S. from Seuni. Lat. 21° 27′, long. 80°.

THUROWLEE, in the British district of Goruckpoor, lieut.-gov. of the N.W. Provinces, a town on the route from Goruckpoor to Khachi, 42 miles N.N.W. of the former. Lat. 27° 14′, long. 83° 9′.

THURRAUD.—A petty independent state on the north-western frontier of Guzerat, bordering on the Runn, north of the river Bunnas. It extends from north to south about thirty-five miles, and from east to west about twenty-five, and has an area of 600 square miles. It is bounded on the north by the Marwar district of Sachore; on the south by that of Baubier and that of Therwarra; on the east by Pahlunpore; and on the west by the petty state of Wow. Thurraud pays no tribute. The territory appears to have been badly administered, and at the request of its chief it has been taken under British management. The chief town is in lat. 24° 23′, long. 71° 36′.

THUTHA, in the Sinde Sagur Dooab division of the Punjab, a town situated 18 miles S.E. from the left bank of the Indus river, 52 miles S.E. of the town of Peshawar. Lat. 33° 34′, long. 72° 23′.

THUTTEEA, in the British district of Furruckabad, lieut.-gov. of the N.W. Provinces, a town near the southern frontier towards Cawnpore, and on the right bank of the river Esun, a short distance to the left of the route from Etawa to Lucknow, by Nanamow Ghat. Lat. 26° 55′, long. 79° 58′.

THYLOOSA.—A town in the British district of Northern Cachar, lieut.-gov. of Bengal, 60 miles E. of Jynteahpore. Lat. 25° 11′, long. 93°.

TIACOTAY.—See AIKOTA.

TIAGUR.—A town in the British district of South Arcot, presidency of Madras, 46 miles W. of Cuddalore. Lat. 11° 43′, long. 79° 8′.

TIBBEE, in the Daman division of the Punjab, a town situated 11 miles from the right bank of the Indus, 77 miles N.W. of the town of Mooltan. Lat. 30° 57′, long. 70° 39′.

TIBEE, in the British district of Bhuttiana, lieut.-gov. of the N.W. Provinces, a village on the route from Hansee to Bhutnair, and nine miles E. of the latter. Lat. 29° 33′, long. 74° 32′.

TIDONG, in Bussahir, a river, or rather large torrent, of Koonawur, rises on the south-east frontier, towards Gurwhal, and about lat. 31° 23′, long. 78° 42′, and holding a north-westerly course along the north-eastern base of the huge Ruldung range, falls into the Sutlej in lat. 31° 35′, long. 78° 29′. The valley, or rather ravine, down which it flows, is a singular scene of savage grandeur, being inclosed generally by mountains of slate, of a vast height, bare, and of shattered outlines. A fearful pathway proceeds along the course of the river. "In some parts of the road there were flights of steps, in others framework of rude staircases, opening to a gulf below, and embracing ruin from above. In one place is a construction still more dreadful to behold; it is called a rapeea, and is made with great difficulty and danger. I never saw anything of the kind to such an extent. It consisted of six posts, driven horizontally into the clefts of the rocks, about twenty feet distant from each other, and secured by wedges: upon this giddy groundwork a staircase of fir spars was formed, of the rudest nature; twigs and slabs of stone connected them together, just as in the sangas. There was no bar or support of any kind on the precipice side, which was deep and perpendicular to the Tidong, a perfect torrent." For six or seven miles the fall of the stream is 300 feet a mile, and in some places nearly double, where it displays an entire sheet of foam and spray, thrown up and showered upon the inclosing rocks with loud concussions, echoed from one side to the other with a noise like thunder.

TIERRO, in the Sinde Sagur Dooab division of the Punjab, a town situated nine miles from the left bank of the Indus, 69 miles S.W. by S. of the town of Mooltan. Lat. 29° 20′, long. 70° 53′.

TIGGAREAH, or TIGGREAH.—One of the Cuttack Mehals, on the south-west frontier of Bengal: it pays a tribute of 826 rupees to the British government, and the rajah maintains a force of 300 cavalry and infantry. Its centre is in lat. 20° 30′, long. 85° 25′.

TIGHURA, in the district of Punna, in Bundelcund, a village on the route from Allahabad to Saugor, 225 miles S.W. of former, 88 N.E. of the latter. It is situate on the river Cane, here crossed "by a rocky ford, bed 160 yards wide, stream thirty, and two and a half feet deep; banks steep." Elevation above the sea 1,093 feet. Lat. 24° 17′, long. 80° 1′.

TIGREE LUTTERA, in the British district of Moradabad, lieut.-gov. of the N.W. Provinces, a village on the route from the town of Meerut to that of Moradabad, and 34 miles S.E. of the former place. It is situate near the left bank of the Ganges, in an open and partially cultivated country. Distant N.W. from Calcutta 888 miles. Lat. 28° 50′, long. 78° 14′.

TIHANAGANJ, in the British district of Azimgurh, lieut.-gov. of the N.W. Provinces, a small town on the route from the town of Azimgurh to that of Ghazeepoor, 10 miles S.E. of the former, 34 N.W. of the latter, 50 N.E. of Benares. Lat. 25° 57′, long. 83° 14′.

TIHLURA, in the British district of Jounpoor, lieut.-gov. of the N.W. Provinces, a town on the route from Jounpoor to Futtehpoor, 27 miles W. of the former. Lat. 25° 46′, long. 82° 20′.

TIJARA, in the territory of Alwar, under the political superintendence of the Governor-General's agent in Rajpootana, a town 55 miles S.W. of Delhi. The district within which it is situate was overrun by the Mahrattas at the close of the last century, and by one of their chiefs conferred on the adventurer George Thomas, who burned the town, to chastise some predatory aggressions of the inhabitants. In the course of the Mahratta war, the town and district came into the possession of the British government, by which power, in 1803, they were, with other pergunnahs, granted to the rao-rajah of Alwar. On the death of that prince in 1815, the succession was contested, the competitors being Benee Singh, a nephew, and Bulwunt Singh, an illegitimate son of the deceased rajah, both minors. The difficulty was temporarily evaded by an extraordinary arrangement, under which the nephew was to enjoy the dignity of rajah, and the son to possess the power and resources of the state. A few years afterwards, on the approach of the nephew, Benee Singh, to manhood, he seized the entire authority, and made his cousin a prisoner. An attempt to assassinate the guardian of Bulwunt Singh, while on a visit to the British Resident at Delhi, was attributed to the instigation of the rival party at Alwar; and by the interference of the British government, the clumsy arrangement by which it had been sought to reconcile the pretensions of the rival claimants was brought to an end. The nephew of the late rajah was permitted to retain the authority of which he had possessed himself, but he was compelled to provide for Bulwunt Singh, partly in territory, and partly in money, an equivalent for Tijara and other districts bestowed by the British government on that person's father; the territory and property thus ceded, to descend to the heirs of the body of Bulwunt Singh only, and not to any adopted son; but to revert to the principality of Alwar on the failure of natural descendants. Tijara is reported to have been badly administered since its severance from Alwar. The town is situate in lat. 27° 56′, long. 76° 55′.

TIKAPAR, in the territory of Saugur and Nerbudda, lieut.-gov. of the N.W. Provinces, a town on the route from Hoosungabad to Jubbulpoor, 66 miles E. by N. of the former. Lat. 22° 58′, long. 78° 44′.

TIKAREE.—A town in the British district of Behar, lieut.-gov. of Bengal, 24 miles N. of Sherghotty. Lat. 24° 54′, long. 84° 54′.

TIKERI, in the British district of Allahabad, lieut.-gov. of the N.W. Provinces, a village on the route by the Kutra Pass from Allahabad to Rewa, and 35 miles S.E. of the former city. Lat. 25° 10′, long. 82° 17′.

TIKHUR, in Bussahir, a small fort on a mountain projecting eastward from the ridge connecting Wartu with the Chur. It is garrisoned by a British detachment from the cantonment of Kotgarh. Elevation above the sea 7,735 feet. Lat. 31° 11′, long. 77° 41′.

TIKOOREE, in the British district of Budaon, lieut.-gov. of the N.W. Provinces, a village on the route from the city of Agra to Bareilly, and 29 miles S.W. of the latter. It is situate in a well-watered, fertile, and well-cultivated country. Lat. 28° 11′, long. 79° 9′.

TIKOORI FORT, in the native state of Rewah, in Bundelcund, 46 miles S.W. by S. from Rewah, and 51 miles N.W. by N. from Sohagpoor. Lat. 23° 57′, long. 81° 1′.

TIKREE, a village in the British district of Bareilly, lieut.-gov. of the N.W. Provinces, on the route from Pillibheet to Beesulpoor, and 16 miles S. of the former. Lat. 28° 23′, long. 79° 51′.

TIKREEALA JILE.—A town in the native state of Cutch, situate on the Great Western Runn, and 36 miles N. from Bhooj. Lat. 23° 42′, long. 69° 52′.

TILBEGUMPOOR, in the British district of Boolundshuhur, lieut.-gov. of the N.W. Provinces, a town on the route from Boolundshuhur to Delhi, 14 miles W.N.W. of the former. Lat. 28° 29′, long. 77° 42′.

TILCHEE, in the British district of Bareilly, lieut.-gov. of the N.W. Provinces, a village on the route from Bareilly to Seetapoor, and 39 miles S.E. of the former. Lat. 28° 11′, long. 80° 2′.

TILHUR, in the British district of Shahjehanpoor, lieut.-gov. of the N.W. Provinces, a town on the route from Shahjehanpoor to Bareilly, 12 miles W.N.W. of the former. Lat. 27° 58′, long. 79° 49′.

TILJUGA.—A river of Nepal, rising in lat. 26° 51′, long. 86° 39′, and, flowing in an easterly direction for forty miles, falls into the Coosy on the right side, in lat. 26° 40′, long. 87° 12′.

TILLAURAH.—A town in Nepal, 129 miles W. by S. from Khatmandoo, and 54 miles N. by W. from Goruckpoor. Lat. 27° 28′, long. 83° 15′.

TILOI, in the district of Salon, territory of Oude, a town 55 miles S.E. of Lucknow. It is the property and residence of a Hindoo chieftain, styled rajah of Tiloi, the lineal representative of the ancient kings of Oude, and the head of a family which, as late as the middle of the last century, held the whole of the south-eastern part of Oude, from Fayzabad to Manickpoor. The rajah lives in the town, in an ancient mud fort, having within its inclosure many good buildings of masonry. Butter estimates the population at 10,000, of whom a third are Mussulmans. Lat. 26° 8′, long. 81° 30′.

TILOTHOO, in the British district of Shahabad, lieut.-gov. of Bengal, a town a mile N.W. of the left or north-west bank of the river Sone. It is described by Buchanan as a good country town, containing 700 houses. Tilothoo is in lat. 24° 47′, long. 84° 3′.

TILWARA, in the Rajpoot state of Jodhpoor, is situate on the left bank of the Lonee, between Balmeer and the town of Jodhpoor, and 65 miles S.W. of the latter place. Boileau, who was ferried over the river here in the beginning of July, during the rainy season, found the Lonee "rushing down with a fierce turbid stream a quarter of a mile wide, but not very deep." Annually, about the time of the vernal equinox, a great fair is held here, principally for the sale of live stock, and on such occasions it is said that 8,000 people are collected. The road in this part of the route, between Balmeer and Jodhpoor, is overflowed in the rainy season, and becomes unsafe for travelling. Lat. 25° 52′, long. 72° 8′.

TILWARA, in Sirhind, a village on the route from Lodiana to Ferozpoor, and 30 miles W. of the former town. It is situate on the left bank of the Sutlej, in a level open country, with a sandy soil partially cultivated. Distant N.W. from Calcutta 1,132 miles. Lat. 30° 57′, long. 75° 23′.

TILWUN.—A town in the British district of Candeish, presidency of Bombay, 30 miles W. of Malligaum. Lat. 20° 34′, long. 74° 3′.

TIMBOONREE.—A town in Malwa, in the native jaghire of the same name, 59 miles N.W. by W. from Baitool, and 43 miles S.W. from Hoosungabad. Lat. 22° 21′, long. 77° 14′.

TIMBOORNEY.—A town in one of the recently sequestrated districts of Hyderabad, or dominions of the Nizam, 66 miles S.E. from Ellichpoor. Lat. 20° 23′, long. 78° 10′.

TIMERY.—A town in the British district of North Arcot, presidency of Madras, six miles S. of Arcot. Lat. 12° 49′, long. 79° 23′.

TIMLA FORT, in the British district of Almora, lieut.-gov. of the N.W. Provinces, a town on the route from Almora to Khyreegurh, 43 miles S.E. of the former. Lat. 29° 9′, long. 80° 10′.

TIMLA GURHI, in the British district of Kumaon, lieut.-gov. of the N.W. Provinces, a stockade, now in ruins, on the most southern or outer range of the Himalaya, rising over the plain of Pilleebheet. Elevation above the sea 3,821 feet. Lat. 29° 9′, long. 80° 9′.

TIMLI, a village of the British district of Dehra Doon, is situate on the north-eastern declivity of the Sewalik range. Elevation above the sea 2,509 feet. Lat. 30° 21′, long. 77° 46′.

TIMLI PASS, so called from the village of that name about a mile north of it, leads from Suharunpoor to Dehra, over the Sewalik Mountains, bounding the Dehra Doon on the south-west. Elevation above the sea 2,339 feet. Lat. 30° 20′, long. 77° 46′.

TIMMAPOORAM.—A town in Hyderabad, or territory of the Nizam, 112 miles E.N.E. from Hyderabad, and 122 miles N. by W. from Guntoor. Lat. 18° 1′, long. 80° 5′.

TIMMERYCOTA.—A town in the British district of Guntoor, presidency of Madras, 69 miles W. by N. of Guntoor. Population about 3,000. Lat. 16° 33′, long. 79° 30′.

TIMMEROWN.—A town in the native state of Bhopal, situate on the right bank of the Nerbudda river, and 88 miles E. by S. from Bhopal. Lat. 23° 3′, long. 78° 42′.

TINARA, in the British district of Seuni, territory of Saugur and Nurbudda, lieut.-gov. of the N.W. Provinces, a town on the route from Jubbulpoor to Seuni, 20 miles N.E. by N. of the latter. Lat. 22° 15′, long. 79° 50′.

TINDEVANUM.—A town in the British district of South Arcot, presidency of Madras, 38 miles N.N.W. of Cuddalore. Lat. 12° 14′, long. 79° 41′.

TINNEVELLY, in the presidency of Madras, a British district, named from its principal place. It is bounded on the north, north-east, and north-west, by the British district of Madura; on the east and south-east by the Gulf of Manaar, dividing it from Ceylon; and on the west and south-west by the raj or territory of Travancore. It lies between lat. 8° 9′ and 9° 56′, long. 77° 15′—78° 26′: its greatest length from north to south is 122 miles, its greatest breadth from east to west seventy-four miles: the area is estimated at 5,700 square miles. Its seacoast commences at Cannakapoor, lat. 8° 9′, and proceeds, in a direction generally north-east, for about ninety-five miles, to Vaimbaur, forming the north-west side of the Gulf of Manaar. It has few places of any note in a maritime point of view. The coast is generally low and level; the sea near the shore is shoaly and unsafe, and in the north-east part abounds in dangerous reefs and rocks. Proceeding north-east, the navigator discerns, seventeen miles from Cape Comorin, a headland, called East Cape, having on its east side the Bay of Kovolam; and twenty-seven miles farther north-east, Munahpaud, a point on which is situate a town, at the south side of the estuary of the river Naut, but in a situation dangerous for shipping. Farther north-east is the small town of Pinnacoil, the approach to which from the south is also dangerous, from an extensive reef stretching from it in that direction, but affording shelter to small vessels between the town and the reef. North-east of Pinnacoil twelve miles is Tuticorin, the most considerable place on the coast: abreast of it, with a channel between them and the mainland, are several islets, forming a petty archipelago, extending from north to south about eight miles, and there is a safe roadstead, with good anchorage, in which vessels can ride at all seasons of the year. A pearl-fishery is carried on along this part of the coast, but it is not very productive. The western part of Tinnevelly is the most elevated, as the surface rises there towards the Ghauts, attaining in the vicinity of Courtallum an elevation of 4,300 feet above the sea. At the base of the mountains, the elevation of the country is estimated at 800 feet, and eastward it descends to about 200, the average elevation of the plain of Tinnevelly. The mountains are stated to consist of hypogene schists, penetrated and broken up by outbursts of plutonic and trappean rocks. The general slope of the surface is eastward, as indicated by the courses of the rivers; the chief of which are the Tambaravari, the Chittaur, the Vipar. These principal streams are joined right and left by numerous feeders during the monsoons, when the country is in many parts laid under water, and everywhere in the plains contains innumerable small lakes or ponds. That part of the district to the north of the river Tambaravari is the more level and fertile, and is very productive, being extensively irrigated by canals from that river: the south-eastern part is barren, having a light stony soil. The soil throughout the district is generally of a deep red or rusty colour, from the presence of iron, and contains a large quantity of sand, forming a friable mould. In the maritime tract on the south-eastern coast, are extensive salt-marshes, liable to spread greatly during the rainy season. The climate along the seacoast, and generally in the eastern and southern part, is characterized by aridity and heat, the thermometer having been registered at 115°; "some say that they have observed it at 130°." This state of weather prevails in the latter part of summer and throughout autumn, when the coast of Malabar experiences all the violence of the south-west monsoon, which is intercepted by the Ghats, and thereby prevented from affecting the Coromandel coast or the plains of Tinnevelly. During the north-east monsoon, "that is, from October to March," the wind blows from the Bay of Bengal, and moderates the temperature; and at that season Tritchindoor, on the seacoast, is found to be remarkably salubrious. Courtallum, on the western frontier, towards Travancore, presents perhaps greater advantages in point of climate than any part of the Carnatic. There the mountains are of much less elevation and breadth than in other parts, and the chain being divided quite across by a narrow pass, leading from the Carnatic to Malabar, the south-west monsoon finds admission through the opening, and agreeably modifies the climate of Courtallum, and of the neighbouring parts. Early in June, when the south-west monsoon sets in, it brings with it to this tract thick clouds and strong winds, so that the rays of the sun are intercepted, and the air put in violent motion; from which causes, combined with the heavy fall of rain, the temperature is lowered much below the standard in the adjacent tracts.

In regard to the zoology of Tinnevelly, little information is on record. Wild elephants appear sometimes to occasion annoyance, as in 1842 the collector was authorized to grant rewards to persons assisting in the destruction of a large herd of these animals which infested the district.

The natural vegetation in this favoured tract comprises timber-trees of enormous size, date-palm and sago-palm, various twiners, such as the Cocculus indicus, pepper-vine, ferns of enormous magnitude, comprehending the total number of species within the indigenous flora. Many valuable intertropical productions, such as clove, nutmeg, cinnamon, have been introduced, and have thriven well, though it does not appear that in a commercial point of view they have afforded any adequate return. Of all the products of the district, cotton is the most important; but the cultivation is restricted to the native plant of India. The government experiments for the introduction of the American species commenced in Tinnevelly, but the planters were not satisfied with the soil and climate, and in the following year they were removed to Coimbatore. Rice is the principal alimentary crop, but it sometimes fails to a considerable extent, when the amount of rain is below the usual average. The population of the district of Tinnevelly is given under the article MADRAS.

Tinnevelly, the principal town, Pallamcottah, and Tuticorin, the only places of note in the district, are described under their respective names in the alphabetical arrangement.

TINNEVELLY, the principal place of the British district of the same name, is situate near the left bank of the river Chindinthoora, over which is a good bridge, forming a communication with the town and military station of Pallamcottah, near the opposite bank. Here were formerly a jail and an hospital, which have been removed to Pallamcottah; but this place is still the station and residence of the revenue collector. The population, according to the official return, is about 20,000. Distance from Madura, S., 86 miles; from Madras, S.W., 350. Lat. 8° 44′, long. 77° 45′.

TIOKLA.—A town in the British district of Amherst, in the Tenasserim provinces, 23 miles N. of Moulmein. Lat. 16° 50′, long. 97° 41′.

TIPPACANDRA.—See MOYAAR RIVER.

TIPPACHATTRAM.—A town in the British district of Nellore, presidency of Madras, 29 miles S.S.E. of Nellore. Lat. 14° 4′, long. 80° 11′.

TIPPERAH, including Bulloah, a British district of Bengal, bounded on the north-west by the Megna river, separating it from the British districts Dacca and Mymunsing; on the east by those of Sylhet and Chittagong, and by the native territory of Tipperah; on the south by the Bay of Bengal; and on the west by the British districts Backergunge and Dacca. Excluding the islands at the mouth of the Megna, it is 110 miles in length from north to south, and sixty-eight in breadth: it contains an area of 4,850 square miles, with a population of 1,406,950.

TIPPERAH.—A town in the British district of Tipperah, 48 miles E.S.E. of Dacca. Lat. 23° 28′, long. 91° 10′.

TIPPERAH (Independent).—An extensive tract of mountainous country, bounded on the north by the British districts Silhet and Cachar; on the east by the territory of Burmah; on the south by Burmah and Chittagong; and on the west by the British district of Tipperah. It is 130 miles in length from east to west, and eighty in breadth, and contains an area of 7,632 square miles. In 1850 daring outrages were reported to have been committed by the hill tribes upon the British population occupying the frontier of this state. It was proved, however, upon inquiry, that these affrays occurred within the territory of the rajah, and that the violence offered was to persons not subject to the British government. The late rajah dying in 1850, was succeeded by his son, who has declined to accede to the decision of the arbitrators appointed to fix the boundary-line between independent and British Tipperah.

TIRA, or SHAH JEHANPUR, a town and stronghold, in the north-east part of the Punjab, is situate on a rock of sandstone, several miles in circumference and flat at top. The Beas flows along its base on one side, and on every other it is surrounded by precipices eighty or 100 feet high. It was formerly the residence of Sansar Chand, the independent rajah of Kotoch. After the death of Sansar Chand, his descendants were dispossessed by Runjeet Singh, who took possession of Tira, and annexed it to the Punjab. Lat. 31° 36′, long. 76° 26′.

TIRHOOT.—A British district in the presidency of Bengal, bounded on the north by the dominions of Nepaul; on the east by the British district of Bhaugulpore; on the south-east by Monghyr; on the south by the Ganges, dividing it from Patna; on the south-west and north-west by the district of Sarun. It lies between lat. 25° 26′—26° 42′, long. 84° 58′—87° 11′; is 140 miles in length from east to west, and ninety-five in breadth: the area is 7,402 square miles. Though containing no mountains, the surface of the country is considerably varied by undulations, and its general aspect beautiful, from the groves, orchards, and woods which abound, especially on the banks of the lakes and rivers. The drainage of that part of the Himalayas situate to the north, passing through this district in its course to the Ganges, gives rise to numerous rivers and watercourses. Of these, the principal are the Ganges, Gunduck, and Bagmuttee.

The climate of Tirhoot is characterized by mildness and moisture. In December, 1832, the mean of the maximum of temperature through the first half of the month was found to be 72°, through the second half 68°; the mean of the minimum during the first half 57°, during the second 48°. In the succeeding June, the mean of the maximum for the first half of the month was 102°, for the second half 95°; the mean of the minimum for the first and second divisions of the month was 79°. The average means for the whole year were, maximum 87°, minimum 69° 1′: the general mean for three years was 75°. For Europeans, the climate is undoubtedly one of great salubrity, which is attributed to the moderate range of the thermometer, and to exemption from the extreme and sultry moisture of Bengal, and the parching dry heat of the upper provinces. For natives, however, who have not the same sanative means at command, the climate is unhealthy, from malaria, especially in the vicinity of jhils. The northern part of the district, in the vicinity of the Terrai, or swampy forest at the base of the Sub-Himalaya, is the most unhealthy. The results of the malaria are usually dysentery, cholera, fever, ague, biliary affections. The soil is rich, especially in the low grounds, when the inundations have retired; but in some parts it is so saturated with muriate of soda or culinary salt, sulphate of soda, saltpetre, and some other mineral salts, as to be barren and white, as if covered with snow. Those salts are extracted through the means of simple but effectual processes by the natives, who drive a considerable trade in them; and the application of European capital and skill would doubtless greatly increase the beneficial results from this source of commerce. The natives are industrious and persevering cultivators, though not remarkable for skill: they, however, raise good crops of wheat, rice, barley, maize, millet, ginger, turmeric, sweet potato, yam, oil-seeds; and in the cool season the esculent vegetables of Europe. Sugar-cane, tobacco, and cotton are produced to considerable extent, and indigo so largely, that it may be regarded as the staple commercial crop of the district. The following are enumerated as the fruits:—Mango, grapes (green and black), lichi, loquat, citron, shaddock, lemon, lime, guava, plantain, custard-apple, koranda, wampee or Brazilian currant, love-apple, melon, pine-apple, strawberry, cocoa-nut, jaik, baila, tamarind, sola or soap-nut, pumpkin.

The manufacturing industry is rude and of small extent: it is principally directed to producing fabrics of coarse cotton and woollen, sacking, ropes, earthen utensils; extraction of saltpetre and other mineral salts; indigo, sugar-boiling, and lime-burning. The population is given under the article BENGAL.

Tirhoot at a period of remote antiquity was denominated Maithala, and probably formed part of the kingdom of Magadha or Behar, the monarchs of which are said to have been paramount rulers of India long previously to the Christian era. The towns—Muzuffurpoor the capital, Karnal, Durbunga, Hajeepore, Mowah, and Singgah—are noticed under their respective names in the alphabetical arrangement. The principal routes are, 1st, from south-east to north-west, from Monghyr, through Muzuffurpore, to Bettiah, in the district of Sarun; 2nd. from north to south, from Mullye, through Muzuffurpore and Hajeepore, to Gya. According to Stewart, it was first invaded by the Mussulmans about 1225, under the command of Ghiyas-ood-deen Bulbun, sovereign of Delhi. The same writer mentions that about 1240 it was invaded by Toghan Khan, who ruled Bengal under Masaud, sovereign of Delhi, and adds, that in 1324 it was, by Ghiyas-ood-deen Toghlak, sovereign of Delhi, subjugated, and incorporated with that realm. During the weakness of the empire of Delhi, consequent on the inroad of Tamerlane, Nusrit Shah, an ephemeral sovereign of Bengal, seized Tirhoot; but it was again, in 1538, subdued, and brought under the rule of Humayon, padshah of Delhi. The right of the East-India Company appears to have accrued from the grant which, in 1765, Shah Alum made of the provinces of Bengal and Orissa.

TIRIPUNAITORAI, in the raj or state of Cochin, a town about two miles N.E. of the Backwater, an extensive shallow lake, the reservoir of numerous streams flowing from the Western Ghats. Bartolomeo states, in A.D. 1787, that it was the residence of the rajah of Cochin; and it probably continues to be so at present. Distant from Cochin, S.E., seven miles; from Calicut, S.E., 105; Bangalore, S.W., 303. Lat. 9° 57′, long. 76° 24′.

TIRIT.—A town within the dominions of Gholab Singh, the ruler of Cashmere, situate 158 miles E. by N. from Sirinagur, and 167 miles N.E. by N. from Chamba. Lat. 34° 34′, long. 77° 42′.

TIRJOOGA RIVER, rising in lat. 26° 39′, long. 86° 38′, in the Terai of Nepal, through which it flows for eighteen miles, to the boundary of the British district of Tirhoot, and thence pursuing a course generally southerly for sixty miles, during which it bounds or intersects the districts of Tirhoot, Bhagulpore, and Mongheer, falls into the Gogaree on the left side, in lat. 25° 41′, long. 86° 29′.

TIRMIUM.—A town of Madras, in the native state of Poodoocottah, or Rajah Tondiman's country, situate 40 miles S. from Trichinopoly, and 50 miles N.E. by E. from Madura. Lat. 10° 15′, long. 78° 50′.

TIROHA.—See TIROWAN.

TIROOA, in the British district of Furruckabad, lieut.-gov. of the N.W. Provinces, a town on the route from Furruckabad to Cawnpoor, 33 miles S.S.E. of the former. Population 5,865. Lat. 26° 59′, long. 79° 51′.

TIROURI, in Sirhind, or territory of the protected Sikh states, a town on the route from Kurnal to Thunesur, eight miles N. of former, 15 S. of latter. In A.D. 1193, Muhammad Shahabuddin, sultan of Ghor and of Ghuznee, invading India, was here encountered by Pritwi Rajah, sovereign of Delhi and Ajmer. After a desperate conflict, the Hindoos were defeated with great slaughter, and Pritwi Rajah being made prisoner, was put to death after the battle. Lat. 29° 47′, long. 77°.

TIROWAN, or TURAON, in Bundelcund, a small state, or rather jaghire, granted by the East-India Company to a Chaube descendant of one of the proprietors of Callinger, who received it by treaty, on the surrender of the last-named place, in 1812. It is situate within the district of Banda, its centre being in lat. 25° 12′, long. 80° 55′, and is estimated to comprise only twelve square miles, five villages, and a population of 2,000. The annual revenue is given at 10,000 rupees (1,000*l.*), and the native force amounts to about fifty men. Tirowan, the principal place, is situate on the river Pysonee, on the route from Allahabad to Callinger, 38 miles N.E. of the latter, 74 S.W. of the former. It is rather a considerable place, with a large bazar. Lat. 25° 14′, long. 80° 52′.

TIROWAN.—A town in the British district of Banda, in Bundlecund. In 1816, a tract of land situate near this town was granted by the British government to Maharajah Imrit Rao, as an independent jaghire. Benaik Rao, son of Imrit Rao, died in 1853, and the jaghire lapsed to the paramount authority. The town is in lat. 25° 12′, long. 80° 58′.

TIRPAVAUNIUM.—A town in the British district of Madura, presidency of Madras, 10 miles S.E. by E. of Madura. Lat. 9° 50′, long. 78° 17′.

TIRRUPUR. —A town in the British district of Coimbatoor, presidency of Madras, 28 miles E. by N. of Coimbatoor. Lat. 11° 6′, long. 77° 24′.

TIRSOON, in the British district of Boolundshuhur, lieut.-gov. of the N.W. Provinces, a village on the route from Khasgunj to Meerut, and 49 miles S. of the latter. Lat. 28° 21′, long. 78°.

TIRUKOVALUR.—A town in the British district of South Arcot, presidency of Madras, 38 miles W.N.W. of Cuddalore. Lat. 11° 57′, long. 79° 20′.

TIRU VADI. — A town in the British district of South Arcot, presidency of Madras, 13 miles W.N.W. of Cuddalore. Lat. 11° 47′, long. 79° 39′.

TIRUVALUR. — A town in the British district of Tanjore, presidency of Madras, 34 miles E. of Tanjore. Lat. 10° 47′, long. 79° 41′.

TISAR, in the British district of Muttra, lieut.-gov. of the N.W. Provinces, a town near the south-east frontier, towards the British district Mynpooree. Lat. 27° 25′, long. 78° 29′.

TISSOOA, in the British district of Bareilly, lieut.-gov. of the N.W. Provinces, a village on the route from the town of Bareilly to Futtehgurh, and 18 miles S.E. of the former. Here, in 1774, the British army under Colonel Champion, and supporting the cause of Shujahuddawlah, nawaub of Oude, utterly defeated a far more numerous force of Rohilla Pathans, and broke the power of that people. A village four miles south-east of this place was named Futehgunje, or "Victory Market," by the nawaub, who kept aloof during the action, and was then probably posted there. The engagement is also sometimes called the battle of Cutterah or Kuttra, from a small town of that name a few miles to the south-east; and sometimes, "the battle of St. George." Tissooa is in lat. 28° 8′, long. 79° 40′.

TITALIYA, in the British district of Dinajpoor, lieut.-gov. of Bengal, a small town on the route from Purneah to Darjeeling, 72 miles N.E. of former, 45 S. of latter. It is situate on the left bank of the river Mahanunda, here having a channel 300 yards wide, but with a small body of clear water in the dry season, and during the rains navigable only for canoes, in consequence of its varying depth. Craft, however, of from twenty to thirty tons burthen can ascend to within a few miles of the town. The site of the town is a level country, about twenty-five miles south of the south base of the Sub-Himalaya, or first range of mountains. Here was formerly a British cantonment, abandoned in 1829 in consequence of the alleged insalubrity, attributed to malaria from marshes situate east, south, and south-west of the place. The country to the north is, however, salubrious, and provisions are abundant and excellent; population 2,500. An annual fair is held at this place, the establishment of which is officially stated to have been eminently successful. Elevation above the sea 275 feet; distance from Dinajpoor, N., 66 miles; from Burhampoor, by Dinajpoor, N., 359; from Calcutta, by Burhampoor and Dinajpoor, 477. Lat. 26° 27′, long. 88° 20′.

TITULLA.—A town in the British district of Sumbulpoor, on the south-west frontier of Bengal, 59 miles W.N.W. of Sumbulpoor. Lat. 21° 44′, long. 83° 10′.

TOCHEE, or GOMBELA.—A river rising on the eastern slope of the Suliman Mountains, in lat. 32° 53′, long. 70° 1′, and, flowing through the Damaun for ninety miles, falls into the Indus river, in lat. 32° 36′, long. 71° 20′.

TODA.—A town in the Rajpoot state of Jeypoor, 63 miles S. by W. from Jeypoor, and 65 miles E.S.E. from Ajmeer. Lat. 26° 4′, long. 75° 39′.

TODDICOMBIT.—A town in the British district of Madura, presidency of Madras, 39 miles N.N.W. of Madura. Lat. 10° 27′, long. 78° 1′.

TOGA, in the district of Peshawar, division of the Punjab, a town situated 11 miles from the right bank of the Indus, 36 miles S.S.E. of the town of Peshawar. Lat. 33° 30′, long. 71° 38′.

TOHANUH, in the British district of Hurriana, lieut.-gov. of the N.W. Provinces, a town on the route from Hissar to Loodiana, 42 miles N. by E. of the former. Lat. 29° 41′, long. 75° 58′.

TOHREE FUTTEHPOOR, in Bundlecund, a town on the route from Banda to Jhansi, 85 miles W. of the former, and 40 E. of the latter. It is the principal place of a jaghire or feudal grant, which contains an area of thirty-six square miles, fourteen villages, and a population of 6,000 souls. It yields a revenue of 3,680*l.*, and the chief maintains twenty horse and 250 foot, with a few artillerymen. This jaghire was made "subject to a tributary payment of 2,650 rupees, or 265*l.*, conditionally on relinquishment by Jhansi of the village Kesirpoora, resumed by that state." It is held of the East-India Company by sunnud or grant, dated April, 1823. Tohree Futtehpoor is in lat. 25° 27′, long. 79° 10′.

TOKA.—A town in the British district of Ahmednuggur, presidency of Bombay, 41 miles N.N.E. of Ahmednuggur. Lat. 19° 37′, long. 75° 2′.

TOKSELGHAT. — A town in Nepal, situate on the left bank of the San Coos river, and 61 miles E.S.E. from Khatmandoo. Lat. 27° 24′, long. 86° 12′.

TOLA, in the British district of Kumaon,

lieut.-gov. of the N.W. Provinces, a village in the Bhotia subdivision of Juwahir. It is situate on the left bank of the river Gori, 400 feet above the stream, and on the route to Hiundes by the Juwahir Pass, from which it is distant 20 miles S. Elevation above the sea 11,122 feet. Lat. 30° 20′, long. 80° 15′.

TOLJAPOOR. — A town in one of the recently sequestrated districts of Hyderabad, or dominions of the Nizam, 28 miles N.E. from Sholapoor. Lat. 18°, long. 76° 10′.

TOLTA.—A town in the British district of Jessore, lieut.-gov. of Bengal, 30 miles S.S.E. of Jessore. Lat. 22° 44′, long. 89° 20′.

TONDIMAN'S COUNTRY. — See POODOOCOTTAH.

TONGANUR. — A town in the British district of South Arcot, presidency of Madras, 61 miles W.N.W. of Cuddalore. Lat. 12° 6′, long. 79°.

TONGDE.—A town within the dominions of Gholab Singh, the ruler of Cashmere, situate 124 miles E.S.E. from Sirinagur, and 88 miles N.E. by N. from Chamba. Lat. 33° 32′, long. 77° 3′.

TONGHO.—A town of Eastern India, in the British territory of Pegu, and formerly the capital of an independent kingdom, which was subdued by the Peguers, and subsequently annexed to Ava. It is situate on the right bank of the Sittang river, 83 miles E. by N. from Prome. A British officer, describing the place upon its acquisition by the English in 1852, observes, "A few ruined pagodas, scattered over a vast quadrangle, inclosed by a massive wall, and surrounded by a broad ditch, are all that now remain to tell of the former magnificence of ancient Tongho." Since its occupation by the British, great improvements have been made, and there is every prospect that in a few years "Tongho will surpass in wealth and importance all the glories of a barbaric age." The district of which this place is the chief town has an area of 3,950 square miles, and a population of 34,957 inhabitants. Lat. 19°, long. 96° 18′.

TONGLO.—A mountain of Sikhim, having an elevation of 10,000 feet. Lat. 27° 3′, long. 88° 8′.

TONGSO.—A town in the native state of Bhotan, situate on the left bank of the Champamuttee river, and 100 miles N.N.W. from Goalpara. Lat. 27° 30′, long. 90° 9′.

TONK, in Rajpootana, a town in a small district forming one of the possessions of the family of the Patan freebooter Ameer Khan. It lies on the route from Delhi to Mhow, 218 miles S.W. of the former, 289 N. of the latter, and on the right bank of the river Bunass, here crossed by ford, the water being usually only about two feet deep. The town, which is of considerable size, is surrounded by a wall, and has a mud fort. A mile south of it was the site selected for his residence by Ameer Khan, noted during the latter part of the eighteenth century, and the early part of the present, for his restless activity, and distinguished no less by talents for intrigue and war than by treachery and disregard of human life and suffering. Born in an humble station at Sumbhul, in Rohilcund, this notorious freebooter commenced his career in the service of the state of Bhopal, about the year 1794. Soon after he joined the ex-chiefs of Ragoogurh, who were subsisting by plunder, and subsequently he attached himself to the fortunes of Jeswunt Rao Holkar, who, in 1806, granted to him Tonk, with its territory, wrested from the rajah of Jeypore. Having made it his place of abode, the ameer embellished it with various public buildings: he had previously, in 1798, received from Holkar the grant of Seronje. In 1817, he held, in addition to these territories, Perawa and Chupra, in Malwa, with Nimbera and some other pergunnahs in Mewar. All those possessions were in that year by treaty guaranteed to Ameer Khan by the East-India Company, and the fort and district of Rampoora were added as a free gift by the British government. The area of the whole amounts to 1,864 square miles. The population has been estimated at 182,672; the revenues at 8,20,000 rupees, or 82,000*l.*, derived from six provinces, in the following proportions:—Tonk, including Rampoora, 2,00,000 rupees; Chappra, 1,00,000; Perawa, 1,00,000; Allygurh, 80,000; Seronje, 2,00,000; Nimbera, 1,40,000. Total, 8,20,000. Those scattered territories are separated from each other, at distances varying from 100 to 250 miles. The reigning chief, who succeeded his father Ameer Khan in 1834, has contracted debts of large amount, for the payment of which he has mortgaged several districts, together with an annuity of 15,000*l.*, granted to Ameer Khan by the British government as indemnity for the revenue of Pulwul, a district which had been conferred upon the ameer for two generations. The town of Tonk is in lat. 26° 10′, long. 75° 56′.

TONRWUTTEE.—See TOORAWUTTEE.

TONS (SOUTH-WESTERN), a river rising in the native state of Myher, in the territory of Saugor and Nerbudda, lat. 24°, long. 80° 30′. The elevation of the source must considerably exceed 900 feet, as at a cascade ninety-five miles to the north-east, or down the stream, the elevation of the waterway is 890 feet. Here the river, flowing through a ravine in the Kutra range, is precipitated over a fall 200 feet in depth: it continues its course north-easterly over the more depressed tract in that direction. Fifty miles below the fall, it passes through the Tara range into the valley of the Ganges, and twenty miles farther, in the same direction, falls into that river on the right side, between the village of Punasa and that of Sirsa, in lat. 25° 15′, long. 82° 8′, having held a total course of 165 miles. The route from Jubbulpore to Allahabad lies along its left bank for a distance of twenty-six miles from its source, and then crosses the stream at the town of Myher, lat. 24° 16′, long. 80° 50′. Garden says of this point, "Cross the Tonse by an indifferent ferry; bed 250 yards wide; stream, in dry season, sixty yards wide, and from one to two feet deep; right bank steep, left shelving." At a place twenty-four miles north-east of this, fifty from the source of the river, and in lat. 24° 30′, long. 80° 55′, it on the left side receives a small stream, called the Satni or Sutna, and five miles lower down, the route by the Kutra Pass from Allahabad to Saugor crosses it, "close under Puttrahut, by a bad rocky ford, bed 200 yards wide, and stream, during the dry season, about thirty yards wide, and knee-deep." Jacquemont assigns to the bed the inferior width of 150 or 180 feet, but adds (on this point corroborating the former account), that it was not without water even when he passed, in the latter part of January, the driest season of the year. Below this sixty miles, still to the north-east, in lat. 25° 2′, long. 81° 44′, the river is crossed by the route leading from Allahabad to Jubbulpore by the Sohagi Pass, the passage being made by ford; and here the bed is rocky, and the banks steep. Its course from this point to its junction with the Ganges is very sinuous, but generally in a north-eastern direction: it is about fifty miles in length. About a mile above the mouth, it is crossed, between the villages of Punassa and Sirsa, by the route from Allahabad to Mirzapore, and, according to Garden, "the bed of the Tonse at the Punassa ferry is about 400 yards wide, and the stream in the dry season usually runs under the left bank, and is 150 yards wide." He describes the left bank as steep, and the right as sloping. Besides the Satni, falling into it on the left side, the Tons receives on the right side the following tributaries, in the order down the stream in which they are here enumerated:—the Beher, Mahana, Seoti, and Belun.

In the march from Allahabad to Chunar, the Tons was crossed, probably at Punasa, by the army of Baber, who describes it, under the name of Tus, as "a muddy, swampy river," which it doubtless is near its mouth. It is the Tounse of Rennell's map.

TONS (NORTH-EASTERN), a stream of the territory of Oude, is a large offset of the Ghogra or Deoha: leaving that river on the right side, about ten miles above the city of Oude, and in lat. 26° 47′, long. 82° 1′, it takes a south-easterly direction, and about twenty-five miles from its commencement sends northward an offset, by which it communicates with the original stream. During the dry season, the stream is in many places embanked, to collect the water for irrigation; and the stagnation thus produced causes extensive malaria. Proceeding in a south-easterly direction, it passes the town of Azimgurh, and uniting with the Surjoo, another offset of the Ghogra, the joint stream falls into the Ganges on the right side, in lat. 25° 41′, long. 84° 11′; its total length of course being about 240 miles. It is navigable upwards from its mouth as far as the town of Azimgurh, a distance of about 120 miles, but its volume of water is represented as on the decline. By Buchanan, it is called the Sota, or "branch;" by Baber, Tousin.

TONSE, or SUPIN, a river of Gurhwal, rises in lat. 31° 2′, long. 78° 33′, at the north of the Jumnotri peaks, and but a few miles from the source of the Jumna, flowing from the southern base of the same mountains. The source of the Tonse appears to have been first ascertained in October, 1819, when it was visited by Herbert, who found the stream to issue, thirty-one feet wide and knee-deep, from a snow-bed 12,784 feet above the sea, and extending as far as the eye could reach. The course of the river is generally westerly for thirty miles, to the confluence of the Roopin, on the right side, in lat. 31° 3′, long. 78° 10′, and at an elevation of 5,300 feet. The declivity of the channel in that distance must be above 250 feet per mile; so that the stream is almost a cascade. It is from its source to this confluence with the Roopin called the Supin; but downwards the united stream is called the Tonse. The Supin is the larger of the confluents, though the Roopin is described by Jacquemont as deep, nearly fifty feet wide, furiously rapid, and rushing along with a tremendous roaring. The united stream called the Tonse is about 120 feet wide: it holds a south-westerly course of about nineteen miles to the confluence of the Pabur, on the right side, in lat. 30° 56′, long. 77° 54′. The Pabur is a large stream, though somewhat inferior in size to the Tonse. From the confluence, the united stream, still called the Tonse, leaves Gurhwal and takes a generally southerly direction, forming for the rest of its course the line of division between the British pergunnah of Jaunsar and the hill states of Joobul and Sirmoor. Thirteen miles below the confluence of the Pabur, the Tonse receives the Shalwee, a considerable stream, which flows into it on the right side, in lat. 30° 48′, long. 77° 49′. It thence flows about forty miles, in a course generally southerly, but very tortuous, through a succession of rugged ravines of limestone, to its junction with the Jumna, in lat. 30° 30′, long. 77° 53′, and at an elevation of 1,686 feet above the sea. As its total course is about 100 miles, it has the enormous fall of above 110 feet in a mile. Though below the junction the united stream bears the name of the Jumna, the volume of the Tonse is much the greater, as, when surveyed by Hodgson and Herbert, it discharged 2,827 cubit feet in a second of time, while the amount discharged by the other river was only 1,045.

TOOBKEBAUGRA.—A town in the British district of Bulloah, lieut.-gov. of Bengal, 30 miles N.W. of Bulloah. Lat. 23° 10′, long. 90° 37′.

TOODURPOOR, in the British district of Bareilly, division of Pilleebheet, lieut.-gov. of the N.W. Provinces, a village on the route from Bareilly to Petoragurh, and 45 miles N.E. of the former. Lat. 28° 47′, long. 79° 55′.

TOOLA RAM SENAHPUTTEE'S COUNTRY, bounded on the north by the British district of Nowgong; on the south-east by the territory inhabited by the wild Naga tribes, and by that of the Muneepoor rajah; on the south by Cachar; and on the west by Cachar and Nowgong. It is seventy-three miles in length from north to south, fifty in breadth; contains an area of 2,000 square miles, with a population of 30,000: its centre is in lat. 25° 35′, long. 93° 18′. Upon the recovery, in 1834, by Rajah Govind Chunder, of the throne of Cachar, of which he had been deprived by the princes of Muneepore, Toola Ram resisted the authority of the restored prince.. In order to terminate the contest and secure the pacification of the country, Govind Chunder was induced to bestow upon Toola Ram the hill territory of which the latter held possession. Subsequently, when Cachar was annexed to the British dominions, the hilly tract assigned to Toola Ram formed an exception, and a small stipend was assigned to its chief. The government having been badly administered both by Toola Ram and his successors, an intimation was made to the chiefs in 1852, that unless the conditions of the treaty were fulfilled, they would not be allowed to retain the country. The warning failed to have the desired effect, and the administration of the country has been assumed by the British government.

TOOLAVA.—See CANARA.

TOOLSEA.—A town in the British district of Bhagulpore, lieut.-gov. of Bengal, 41 miles N. of Bhagulpore. Lat. 25° 46′, long. 87° 2′.

TOOLUMBA, in the Baree Dooab division of the Punjab, a town situated on the left bank of the Ravee, 50 miles N.E. by E. of the town of Mooltan. Lat. 30° 32′, long. 72° 18′.

TOOMADY.—A town in the British district of Masulipatam, presidency of Madras, 18 miles N.N.E. of Masulipatam. Lat. 16° 24′, long. 81° 19′.

TOOMBGEE.—A town in the British district of Sholapoor, presidency of Bombay, 81 miles S.S.E. of Sholapoor. Lat. 16° 34′, long. 76° 21′.

TOOMBUDRA.—See TUMBUDRA.

TOOMCOOR.—A town in the Mysore, 70 miles N.N.E. from Seringapatam, and 44 miles N.W. by W. from Bangalore. Lat. 13° 20′, long. 77° 9′.

TOOMSUR.—A town in the territory of Nagpoor, situate on the right bank of the Wein Gunga river, and 43 miles E.N.E. from Nagpoor. Lat. 21° 23′, long. 79° 46′.

TOOMULLAGOODIUM.—A town in Hyderabad, or territory of the Nizam, 33 miles E. from Hyderabad, and 118 miles N.W. by W. from Guntoor. Lat. 17° 20′, long. 79° 7′.

TOOMULTHULPOOR.—A town in the British district of Nellore, presidency of Madras, 21 miles W.S.W. of Nellore. Lat. 14° 18′, long. 79° 46′.

TOONEE.—A town in the British district of Rajahmundry, presidency of Madras, 33 miles N.E. of Samulkottah. Lat. 17° 21′, long. 82° 35′.

TOONGA, in the Rajpoot state of Jeypore, a town situate 22 miles S.E. of the city of Jeypore. Lat. 26° 41′, long. 76° 16′.

TOONGA, or TUM.—A river of the Mysore territory, rising in lat. 13° 15′, long. 75° 14′. It holds a tortuous but generally northward course for forty-five miles to Hallamutta, in lat. 13° 40′, long. 75° 16′, whence it flows north-east fifty miles to its confluence with the Budra, in lat. 14°, long. 75° 43′. Below the confluence, the united stream bears the name of Toongabudra. It is merely a great torrent, having a scanty stream during the dry season, and in the monsoon rushing along with vast volume and great rapidity.

TOONGABUDRA.—See TUMBUDRA.

TOONGHAWALA, in the Reechna Dooab division of the Punjab, a town situated 40 miles from the right bank of the Ravee, 40 miles N.W. by N. of the town of Lahore. Lat. 32° 7′, long. 73° 55′.

TOONGLA.—A town in the native state of Bhotan, six miles from the right bank of the Monas river, and 80 miles W.N.W. from Durrung. Lat. 26° 55′, long. 90° 54′.

TOONGROO, in Bussahir, a peak in the range stretching between the Wartu and Chur mountains. From its western side the river Giri takes its rise, and from its north-eastern, feeders pass off to the Pabur. It was one of the stations of the large series of triangles in the trigonometrical survey of the Himalaya. Elevation above the sea 10,102 feet. Lat. 31° 8′, long. 77° 41′.

TOONOOR, in the territory of Mysore, a city, once of great extent, subsequently reduced to a few temples and a small number of dwellings, and now again growing into importance. Here is a vast tank or reservoir, called the Yadavi Nadi, formed by damming up the lower extremity of a rocky valley, by means of a mound seventy-eight cubits high, 150 cubits long, and 250 thick at the base. In A.D. 1798, Tippoo Sultan caused an opening to be made in the mound, and the great rush of water so enlarged the passage as to sweep away a large portion of the mound, and drain the whole reservoir. As the final and successful invasion of the British was then imminent, it has been supposed that he was impelled to this extraordinary act by a desire to deprive the invaders of this supply of water: others attribute the step to an ebullition of bigotry, which was his ruling passion. The lake is generally by Mussulmans called Moteetalab, or Pearl-tank, a name which, on account of its beauty, it received from Nasir Jung, when, in A.D. 1746, he advanced to Mysore to enforce payment of arrears of tribute. After the overthrow of Tippoo Sultan, the reservoir was repaired by order of the British authorities. Distance from Seringapatam, N.W., 10 miles. Lat. 12° 33′, long. 76° 42′.

TOORAVAKIRA.—A town in the Mysore, 51 miles N. from Seringapatam, and 63 miles W. by N. from Bangalore. Lat. 13° 10′, long. 76° 44′.

TOORAVANOOR.—A town in the Mysore, 136 miles N. from Seringapatam, and 60 miles S.W. by S. from Ballary. Lat. 14° 22′, long. 76° 30′.

TOORAWUTTEE, or BUTEESEE. — A district of the Rajpoot state of Jeypore, the management of which during the distracted state of Jeypore was assumed by the British, who, however, in 1837, again restored it to the rajah of Jeypore. Its centre is in lat. 27° 42′, long. 75° 58′.

TOORKEIRA.—A town in the British district of Candeish, presidency of Bombay, 64 miles N. by E. of Malligaum. Lat. 21° 27′, long. 74° 43′.

TOOSHAM, in the British district of Hurriana, lieut.-gov. of the N.W. Provinces, a town on the route from Hissar to Rewaree, 22 miles S.E. by S. of the former. Lat. 28° 51′, long. 76°.

TOOTOO, in the Rajpoot state of Jessulmeer, a village on the route from the town of Bekaneer to that of Jessulmeer, and 55 miles N.E. of the latter. Lat. 27° 12′, long. 71° 49′.

TORA, in the district of Peshawar, division of the Punjab, a town situated 20 miles from the right bank of the Indus, 30 miles N.E. of the town of Peshawar. Lat. 34° 9′, long. 72° 8′.

TORAGUL.—A town in the British district of Belgaum, presidency of Bombay, 48 miles E. by N. of Belgaum. Lat. 15° 56′, long. 75° 17′.

TORBELA.—A small town in the north of the Punjab, and on the left or eastern bank of the Indus, a little below where it issues from the mountains and flows over the plain in a broad and shallow, yet still very rapid current. Below Torbela, and between it and Attock, are the five fords of the Indus. These are dangerous at all times, from the icy coldness and extraordinary rapidity of the stream ; and in summer they are, in consequence of the swell of the stream, totally impracticable. The river is here smooth, rapid, and about 200 yards wide. Lat. 34° 7′, long. 72° 50′.

TOREE.—A town in the Rajpoot state of Jeypoor, 52 miles S.S.W. from Jeypoor, and 56 miles E. by S. from Ajmeer. Lat. 26° 16′, long. 75° 34′.

TOREE.—A town in the British district of Ramgur, lieut.-gov. of Bengal, 46 miles W.S.W. of Hazareebagh. Lat. 23° 40′, long. 84° 46′.

TOREESHA RIVER rises in lat. 26° 57′, long. 89° 14′, in the territory of Bhotan, and, flowing south thirty-eight miles through Bhotan, and forty miles through Coosh Behar, falls into the Durlah river, in lat. 25° 56′, long. 89° 31′.

TORIORE.—A town in the British district of Trichinopoly, presidency of Madras, 23 miles N.N.W. of Trichinopoly. Lat. 11° 9′, long. 78° 39′.

TORRA.—A town in the territory of Nagpoor, 152 miles E. from Nagpoor, and 122 miles S.S.E. from Ramgurh. Lat. 21° 8′, long. 81° 30′.

TORRES.—Two islands in the Mergui Archipelago, situate 72 miles from the coast of Tenasserim. They are about lat. 11° 47′, long. 97° 36′.

TOUDAN.—A town of Eastern India, in the British territory of Pegu, situate on the right bank of the Irawady river, and 30 miles N. by W. from Prome. Lat. 19° 12′, long. 94° 56′.

TOUNGHOO.—See TONGO.

TOUTOULI.—A village in the British district of Rohtuk, lieut.-gov. of the N.W. Provinces. Lat. 28° 58′, long. 76° 37′.

TOUVERAMCOORCHY.—A town in the British district of Madura, presidency of Madras, 20 miles N.E. by N. of Madura. Lat. 10° 20′, long. 78° 27′.

TOWANG.—A town in the native state of Bhotan, situate on the left bank of the Demree river, and 77 miles N. by E. from Durrung. Lat. 27° 30′, long. 92° 19′.

TOWARUM.—A town in the British district of Madura, presidency of Madras, 58 miles W. of Madura. Lat. 9° 55′, long. 77° 20′.

TOWRA, in Sirhind, a village in the British district of Umballa, on the route from Kurnal to Patiala, and 46 miles N.W. of the former place. Distant N.W. from Calcutta 1,011 miles. Lat. 30° 14′, long. 76° 40′.

TOWRAJ, a river of Hyderabad, rises in lat. 18° 22′, long. 76° 18′, and, flowing easterly for thirty-five miles, falls into the Manjera river, a feeder of the Godavery, in lat. 18° 22′, long. 76° 44′.

TRANDA, or TURANDA, in Bussahir, a village in the district of Koonawar, is situate near the left bank of the Sutluj, and at the confluence of the Chonda torrent. Elevation above the sea 7,089 feet. Lat. 31° 33′, long. 77° 55′.

TRANQUEBAR. — A town within the limits of the British district of Tanjore, presidency of Madras. There is a slight curvature in the shore here, concave towards the sea, so that a small bay is formed, causing the surf to be less violent here than in the more exposed part of the coast. It is surrounded by walls, and protected by the fort called Dansborg, which, being white, as well as most of the houses, the place is conspicuous when viewed from the sea. Besides the defence of the fort, the town is surrounded by a wall with bastions. Of public buildings, the most remarkable are a few Lutheran churches, a Roman Catholic place of worship, and the fort, containing the offices of government. The territory extends six miles from north to south, and three miles inland, and has an area of fifteen square miles. The soil is in general under cultivation, though in some places marshy, and throughout impregnated with salt. The greater part produces rice, and much of the remainder is planted with fruit-trees, especially the cocoanut-palm, and other species of palm, the mango, and jak. The climate is considered healthy, in consequence of the prevalence of sea-breezes, which moderate the temperature, so that the thermometer is stated not to range higher than 100°, its lowest limit being about 70°. The settlement of Tranquebar was ceded to the British government in 1845 by the king of Denmark, for a pecuniary consideration. The town, with its district, was stated in 1844 to contain 23,426 inhabitants, of whom 166 were Europeans and their descendants. No later census of the population is available, but the superiority of British over Danish administration is attested by the growing prosperity of the district, and the large increase in the amount of the government revenue. Distance from Negapatam, N., 18 miles; Tanjore, E., 51; Madras, S., 147. Lat. 11° 1′, long. 79° 55′.

TRAVANCORE.—A native state in the south of India, under the political superintendence of the presidency of Madras. It is bounded on the north by the territory of Cochin and the British district of Coimbatoor; on the east by the British districts of Madura and Tinnevelly; and on the south and west by the Indian Ocean. It lies between lat. 8° 4′—10° 21′, long. 76° 14′—77° 38′: it has an area of 4,722 square miles. The most marked physical feature of the country is furnished by the Western Ghauts, or Sukhein, as that great range is called in its southern part. Divided from the northern part by the great gap or valley of Palghat, it expands into a mazy group, overspreading the country to the eastward, and attaining in some places an elevation of 7,000 feet above the sea. The formation of these mountains is such as is referred by geologists to the earliest periods,—hypogeneschists, penetrated and broken up by prodigious outbursts of plutonic and trappean rocks. With these occur occasionally granite, gneiss, and hornblende, the primitive rocks being in some places overlaid extensively with laterite. The termination of the Western Ghats in the bold hill near the Amboli Pass, a little above Cape Comorin, is stated to be of granite. The line of waterheads forms, with little exception, the boundary to the east and north-east, and the drainage is effected by a great number of torrents, passing to the south-west, the west, and the north-west, which discharge their contents either into the Indian Ocean or into the Backwaters, as the British denominate an extensive series of shallow lakes running parallel with the coast, and communicating with the sea at certain places. The Perryaur, the most considerable of the torrents above mentioned, rises on the eastern frontier of Travancore, in a deeply secluded and nearly unexplored part of the Western Ghats, and about lat. 9° 15′, long. 77° 20′. Its course is very tortuous, but generally in a direction north-west, and ultimately expanding into a broad estuary communicating with the Backwater, it is discharged into the sea, in lat. 9° 58′, long. 76° 18′; its total length of course being about 140 miles. After it has reached the plain country, it is called the Alwye, and is subject to enormous floods; so that though the channel is broad, it has been known during the monsoon to rise sixteen feet in twenty-four hours, and continue at that height for some months. Its mouth, called by seamen Cranganore river, or Aycotta river, flows between the south-west boundary of the territory of Cochin and north-west boundary of Travancore. The latter state has here a very short line of seacoast detached from the remainder, lying further southward. This detached piece of coast extends about four miles, to lat. 10° 10′, where commences the seacoast of a detached portion of the territory of Cochin, which continues towards the south-east for about twenty-five miles, to Undarally. There the seacoast of Travancore recommences, and stretches in a south-easterly direction for 155 miles, to Cape Comorin, where it turns to the north-east for six miles, and then terminates at Cannakapoor. Throughout this whole extent of coast, there is no safe harbour for ships of any burthen; the shore is in general low, sandy, and covered with trees; but there are several roads having safe anchorage in favourable weather. The principal resorts of shipping along the coast are Aulapolay or Aleppi, which, though a small place, carries on a considerable trade in teak, cocoanuts, coir or cocoanut-fibre, betel-nut, and pepper; but there being no harbour, ships of any considerable burthen must anchor in the open sea, four miles from the shore: Porca or Poracaud, a town exporting timber, coir, and pepper, where ships may anchor two miles from the shore, in six fathoms water: Iviker or Aibika river, an estuary by which the Backwater communicates with the sea, but so shallow (there being but five or six feet on the bar at high water) that only boats can pass, large ships being compelled to anchor three miles off shore: Quilon, a town the north side of a small bight open to the south and south-west, but on other points sheltered by land and a projecting reef: Anjengo, where there is merely an open road, in which ships may anchor two miles off shore; but their boats are seldom available, on account of the violent surf, and consequently communication with shore is effected by means of the country boats: Pondera, a small town, where the land is bold to approach, so that large ships can anchor near the shore: Taingaputnum, at the mouth of a river of the same name, which, in consequence of a bar, is accessible to none but small boats, except in the rainy season; but within the bar the navigation is practicable at all times, and is of considerable extent: Cuddeaputnum, having an unsafe anchorage between the shore and two rocky islets, a short distance from the shore. Cape Comorin is the next place deserving notice, but it is entitled to this distinction only as being the most southern point of India: it is a low, sandy spot. The whole extent of coast is indeed generally low, nowhere presenting anything more aspiring than a few cliffs of slight elevation; and this adds to the striking effect which the Ghats, about fifteen or twenty miles inland, must under any circumstances produce, from their extent and grandeur. The trading stations along this coast are little frequented during the south-west monsoon, which commences late in May, or early in June, and prevails till September. During June and July, there is a succession of severe squalls, accompanied with heavy rain, and on the coast by high seas; but the weather rather moderates towards the end of the latter month. The violence diminishes in August, and still more in September, though the weather in that month is often cloudy and threatening, and heavy showers of rain sometimes descend. The fair season succeeds, when the weather is occasionally rather close. In November, the north-east monsoon sets in, with far less intensity than that from the south-west, but still bringing rain, and cooling the air. March, April, and May are the hottest months of the year, and also the most unhealthy. In December, January, and February, the nights are comparatively cool, and the dews are heavy: exposure to them is dangerous, being apt to produce fever.

Notwithstanding the nearly equatorial position of Travancore, the high lands, in consequence of their great elevation, enjoy a moderate temperature, and even the lower part of the territory is cooled by the great fall of rain, and by the proximity of the mountains and of the sea. The thermometer at Trivandrum seldom rises above 90° in any season, nor above 75° during the south-west monsoon. In a series of observations made at Quilon during the years 1835 and 1836, the highest range of the thermometer was 88°, and the lowest 69°; the former in April and May, in the afternoons; the latter in December and January, immediately before daybreak. The climate is moist, and the average fall of rain considerable. Though to European constitutions somewhat enervating, it is not considered positively unhealthy. As there is never any cold bracing weather, the recovery of invalids is usually slow; and in rheumatic cases, or where there exists a tendency to pulmonary disease, the dampness of the atmosphere is decidedly injurious.

Notwithstanding the great mountain masses, and the prevalence of primary or early rock formations in Travancore, its mineral resources appear to be very scanty, no metal of importance except iron being reported to be found in it. Its zoology is varied and important. Elephants are very numerous among the wooded valleys and table-lands of the Ghats, where tigers of enormous size are also common: bats as large as chickens abound: the wild buffalo, the wild swine, the elk, the leopard, the black leopard, and the ant-bear are found: monkeys exist in great numbers and variety: the antelope, the civet cat, the jackal, the hare, the ichneumon or mongoose, the otter, and a seal of diminutive size, are also to be reckoned among the animals known in Travancore. Of birds, there are the hawk, the raven, the vulture, the peafowl, the jungle-fowl (Gallus gallinaceus), the pied bird of Paradise (Picus orientalis), parrots and paroquets innumerable, and extremely destructive to the crops; and lastly, aquatic birds of divers species and in great numbers. Of reptiles, there are snakes, various in kind and numerous in quantity, many of them of deadly venomous character; scorpions and centipedes: alligators of great size swarm in the rivers and lakes, and are very voracious and destructive; human beings, as well as inferior animals, occasionally becoming their prey. Their principal food, however, is fish, of which there is great abundance in the rivers and lakes, in addition to that afforded by the sea.

The soil on the more elevated surfaces is light and gravelly, but in the low grounds it is a deep black mould, formed either by deposits from inundations or decayed vegetation. In such soils rice of excellent quality is produced in great plenty: the sago-palm thrives well, and yields an excellent product. Many plantations of mulberry have recently been made by the rajah, in the hope of producing silk on a large scale. A great variety of vegetables congenial to the climate are cultivated; and many European esculents may by care be brought to maturity.

The communication between the lower parts of the territory is much facilitated by inland navigation through the Backwaters; and a trifling outlay in their improvement would open a channel from Trivandrum, the capital, to Trichoor, a distance of 200 miles. The rajah of Travancore some years since formed on his eastern frontier, towards Tinnevelly, a double line of works, extending from a place on the seashore, about half a mile to the west of Cape Comorin, in a northerly direction, to a point where the Western Ghats become impassable for an army. Horsburgh viewing this work, thus notices it:—"The low country seems divided by a wall or trench stretching from the shore to the mountains, and fortified by mounds of earth." The same rajah also constructed a line of works on his north-western frontier, "as a northern boundary towards Calicut, running east and west from a point of the hills [the Western Ghats] deemed inaccessible, chiefly behind or south of a river which discharges itself into the estuary" falling into the Indian Ocean between Kodungaloor and Ayacotta. In 1789 "this miserable wall," as it is styled by a military writer, was forced and partially destroyed by Tippoo Sultan; and as the rajah was under British protection, the aggression gave rise to the war with Mysore in the same year. As the whole country is now subject to British supremacy, those feeble defences have been left to the natural but speedy progress of decay.

The population of Travancore consists of Brahminists, Mussulmans, and Christians, besides a few Jews. Its amount is returned at 1,011,824. Brahmins are very numerous, and are either settlers from other countries or Namburis, considered to be aboriginal Brahmins, highly regarded by the rest of the Brahminist population, over whom they have a more powerful influence than even in other parts of India. The most numerous and important class are, however, the Nairs, who, although of the Sudra or labouring caste by descent, are at present found engaged in various occupations, and from among whom the rajah's troops are recruited. As is the case with the Nairs elsewhere, they do not marry, but select a young girl, and having performed the idle ceremony of tying a band round her neck, and making her some small present, send her back to reside in the house of her father or brother, where she is at liberty to live in licentious intercourse without restraint. The Namburis are said to be the most-favoured lovers of the women placed in these extraordinary circumstances. The male portion of the Nair population live in a course of profligacy similar to that followed by the women; and as none know their own offspring, they regard their sisters' children as their heirs. The rajah appears to belong to this singular class. The Mussulmans comprise the Moplahs, descendants of Arabs settled on this coast, and the Lubbis, a mixed race between the Arabs and Hindoos, besides a few of Pathan descent. Christians probably form a more numerous proportion of the population here than in any other part of India, if the Portuguese dominion of Goa be excepted. They are of three classes: first, the ancient Christians of St. Thomas, or of the Syrian or Jacobite church, who regard the patriarch of Antioch as their spiritual head. These Christians are perpetually at war among themselves, and have appealed to the British government, which has, however, declined to interfere in their disputes: second, Romanists, descendants from Christians of the last-mentioned denomination, but forcibly made to acknowledge the supremacy of the pope: third, Portuguese Romanists, and descendants of heathen natives, converted by missionaries of that nation. The pope is of course acknowledged as the head of the followers of the Church of Rome, the chief local authority being exercised by a vicar-apostolic residing at Verapoli. The Christians in the aggregate are stated to amount to an eighth of the whole population; and in sailing close to land, their churches may be observed occurring at short intervals along the shore of Travancore. Besides the denominations of Christians already mentioned, there are a few Protestants, descendants of converts made by the Dutch, and now under the spiritual care of a British missionary. According to a clerical authority, who appears to have given much attention to the subject, the number of Syrian Christians in Travancore is about 70,000; that of the Romish or Papal Christians about the same; and the entire number of professed Christians, including the Protestants, about 150,000.

In the secluded parts of the mountains is a wild race, extremely rude and savage in their habits, but not ferocious, living on game or the spontaneous produce of the forest. Slavery no longer exists in Travancore. By the introduction and general promulgation of well-defined regulations, the law upon the subject has been placed on precisely the same footing as that on which it stands in British India. There is now no compulsory service, which is the essence of slavery; the courts of justice no longer recognise that status, nor can anything be lawfully done to any one on the ground that he is a slave, which cannot lawfully be done to a free person. Thus it will be seen that, owing to the unremitting exertions of the British government, a recognition has been obtained of the right of slaves to be dealt with as human beings.

The higher ranks of the people of Travancore are stated to be intelligent, especially the Nairs, "who have a quick apprehension, are admirable accountants, and perform the operation of writing with a rapidity and adroitness quite peculiar to themselves." They are, however, in general a listless, unimpassioned race, little characterized by atrocious criminality (except in regard to one branch of the moral code), but addicted to lying; and from their depraved notions respecting the union of the sexes, steeped in the grossest licentiousness. Such a course of life is, as might be expected, attended by the diseases which are its usual penalties, and which nowhere are more general or more virulent than in Travancore.

There are two passes through the hills to Tinnevelly, lying to the east of the Western Ghauts. Of these, the Arungol Pass, situate in lat. 8° 55′, can be traversed only during the rains, from June to December, without incurring great hazard of contracting deadly fever. The Arambooli Pass, seventy miles farther south, is considered to be perfectly safe at all times. The principal places, Trivandrum the capital, Quilon, Aibika, Aulapolay or Alippee, and Anjengo, are noticed under their respective names in the alphabetical arrangement.

The early history of Travancore is too obscure and too unimportant to justify the bestowal of any notice upon it except in a work purely antiquarian. Its first political or commercial relation with the East-India Company was in 1673, when that great corporation, by permission from the government of Travancore, established a factory at Anjengo, on the seacoast. During the prolonged warfare waged by the British with Hyder Ali and his son Tippoo Sultan, the British invariably found the rajah of Travancore a steadfast ally; and in that relation he was, in 1784, included in the treaty between the East-India Company and the sultan of Mysore. In 1789, Tippoo Sultan, under the double impulse of resentment and ambition, attacked the rajah of Travancore, and after a smart repulse, forced the lines which had been erected for the defence of the country on its northern frontier, towards Cochin, overrunning and cruelly devastating the Travancore territory. Lord Cornwallis, then Governor-General, regarding this attack on an ally as an act of hostility against the British government, commenced military operations, which ended in Tippoo Sultan being deprived of half his dominions, and compelled to restore all that he had wrested from the rajah of Travancore. In 1797, the rajah concluded with the East-India Company a treaty, by which he engaged to pay an annual subsidy adequate to maintain three battalions of native troops, with proportionate artillery, to be stationed within his territory. By a subsequent treaty in 1805, the rajah agreed to pay annually, in addition to such subsidy, a sum adequate to maintain one regiment of the East-India Company's native infantry; and in case an additional force should be required for the defence of his territory against attack or invasion, to contribute jointly with the Company towards the discharge of the increased cost such a sum as should appear, on an attentive consideration of the rajah's means, to bear a just and reasonable proportion to his net revenues. It was further agreed, that in case the Governor-General in Council should consider that there were grounds for apprehending failure of funds to defray the expense of the permanent military force, or the extraordinary charges that might arise under the terms of the treaty, he was to have the power to introduce at his discretion such regulations and ordinances, fiscal or otherwise, as might appear necessary for the due administration and government of the state under the management of the servants of the East-India Company; and after due notice, such portions of territory as might be required were to be placed under the exclusive authority and control of the said officers. It was, however, provided that the rajah's actual receipt from his territorial revenues should not be less than two lacs of rupees, together with one-fifth of the net revenues of the whole of his territories; the Company engaging to secure the said amount, and cause it to be paid for the rajah's use at all times and in every possible case. The rajah was to hold no communication with any foreign state without the previous knowledge and sanction of the Company, nor without such to admit any European foreigner into his service; nor to suffer any European to remain within his territories. This treaty, although declared to be binding on the contracting parties "as long as the sun and moon shall endure," failed in securing permanent amity and good faith: the ill government of Travancore was extreme, and the financial position of the state deplorable: retrenchment was indispensable; and to relieve the treasury during the time necessary for performing it effectually, the payment of half the additional subsidy was remitted for two years. No adequate reform, however, took place; the rajah would take no effective steps for reducing his expenditure; a part of the arrears of subsidy was tardily liquidated, but a very large portion still stood undischarged: all power was centred in the hands of a corrupt minister, and the remonstrances of the British Resident were unheeded alike by him and his master. At length it became evident that something more than what, in more modern times, has been called "passive resistance," was intended. Preparations for direct hostility were made, almost without an attempt at concealment; and so serious did the state of affairs appear to the government of Madras, that two bodies of troops were ordered to be put in motion for Travancore. These vigorous measures were, however, suddenly suspended, in order to try the effect of negotiation, which proceeded in the usual style of oriental diplomacy, till broken off by an attack on the house of the British Resident, and an attempt to murder him. That functionary succeeded in escaping on board a British ship, which fortunately arrived just in time to afford the means of his deliverance. Nearly coincident in time with the attack on the Resident was an atrocious outrage committed on a small party of British soldiers, who being on board a vessel which put into Alleppi for water, were treacherously induced to land, and then brutally murdered. An attack on the subsidiary force stationed at Quilon seems to have determined the Madras government to substitute arms for negotiation, which latter had been persevered in even after the attempt to assassinate the Resident. The war thus tardily commenced, was, however, vigorously carried on, and consequently was but of brief duration. The dewan fled, and after wandering for some time, subjected to much privation and suffering, terminated his life by his own hand. His brother, who was involved in the guilt of the murders at Alleppi, was apprehended and publicly executed. This took place early in 1809. On the restoration of peace, the British Resident, at the solicitation of the rajah, assumed the entire management of the state, as provided in the treaty of 1805, and exercised the power so judiciously, that in a few years its finances were freed from embarrassment, and various useful reforms effected. A feeble attempt to destroy the British authority was made in 1812, but immediately suppressed. Soon afterwards an infant rajah succeeded to the throne, to the full enjoyment of the rights of which he was admitted on the completion of his sixteenth year. The country being surrounded by British possessions, excepting that portion bounded by the sea, was considered safe from external attack; and internal peace appearing to be firmly established, the continued presence of the subsidiary force was deemed unnecessary. It was accordingly withdrawn, and in 1832 the entire responsibility of preserving the peace of the country was intrusted to the rajah; but the British government is still bound to afford protection and assistance, should occasion demand its interposition. The rajah died in 1846. During the last few years of his administration the country was allowed to deteriorate, notwithstanding the vigorous remonstrances of the British Resident. Extravagance wasted the accumulations of former years of careful management; and a decreasing revenue, coincident with a lavish expenditure, led to the neglect of nearly all public works, however important or necessary. The roads and bridges were left to go to decay, and even the works for irrigation, so essential to the prosperity of the people, and so closely connected with the immediate interests of the revenue, were not kept in repair. The rajah last mentioned was succeeded by his brother, the Eliah rajah, who, under the able administration of his dewan, corrected the improvident expenditure of his predecessor. This improved system, however, prevailed only for a time: a passion for expense of an alleged religious character seized the mind of the prince, and has been indulged to an extent which has called forth repeated remonstrance from the Resident.

TRAVANCORE, or TERAVANKODE, in the territory of Travancore, a decayed town, formerly the capital of the state, and giving name to it, but nearly deserted since the rajah has transferred his residence to Trivandrum, on the seacoast. Lat. 8° 14′, long. 77° 19′.

TRIBENNEE.—A town in the British district of Jessore, lieut.-gov. of Bengal, 40 miles N. of Jessore. Lat. 23° 42′, long. 89° 9′.

TRICHANGODE.—A town in the British district of Salem, presidency of Madras, 29 miles S.W. of Salem. Lat. 11° 22′, long. 77° 58′.

TRICHINOPOLY.—A British district under the presidency of Madras, named from its principal place. It is bounded on the north and north-east by the collectorate of South Arcot; on the south-east by the river Coleroon, which separates it from Tanjore; on the south by the native state of Poodoocottah (Rajah Tondiman's territory), and by the British district of Madura; on the west by Madura and Coimbatore; and on the north-west by the British district of Salem. It lies between lat. 10° 37′—11° 31′, long. 78° 13′—79° 37′, and is ninety-four miles in length from north to south, and sixty in breadth: the area is, according to official return, 3,243 square miles. It is a flat tract, the surface being diversified only by some high ground to the south of the town of Trichinopoly, and in many places by granite rocks, some tabular, others with rounded summits, which seldom rise to any considerable height. The rock on which the fort of Trichinopoly stands is an exception, rising to an elevation of between 500 and 600 feet, and in the same part of the district there are some other large rocks of similar character. Besides those of granite, there are rocks of secondary trap and greenstone. The granite has externally a dark or dull earthy colour; internally it is variegated, and contains a large proportion of felspar, with some quartz and mica. It is a hard and very durable stone, forming an excellent building material. Quarries of it are worked by the natives. It is hewn out into pillars, and steps for staircases, and the walls of the forts and gateways are built of it. In the high tract to the south of the town of Trichinopoly the soil is sandy or gravelly, and generally barren and uncultivated; but with this exception, the cantonment is surrounded by rice-lands several square miles in extent. In the low grounds along the courses of the rivers, the sub-soil is a stiff, tenacious, red-coloured clay, with an intermixture of sand, from which excellent bricks and tiles are made. The overlying cultivable soil is a deep black mould, very fertile, and, under proper management, producing two crops annually. The mean annual fall of rain is considerable, though not excessive, amounting to from thirty to forty inches; still the district is characterized by aridity, and without the irrigation effected by means of the rivers and torrents flowing from the Ghauts and Mysore, the country would be a parched desert. A steady high temperature, cloudless sky, a dry and close sultry atmosphere, with much glare and intense radiation of heat, are the characteristics of the climate of Trichinopoly. The heat, drought, and glare are often very intense for months together; the hot weather is, however, a good deal broken and varied by high westerly winds; and whirlwinds, often accompanied by clouds of sand and dust, recur at short intervals, often for a week or two at a time. The high winds and dusty weather, which prevail chiefly during May, June, and July, render those months the most disagreeable part of the year, the atmosphere being obscured during the day by clouds of dust. The monsoons are not well marked, except by a change in the direction of the wind. The climate of this part of the southern division may, with tolerable accuracy, be divided into three seasons, viz., the hot and dry, the hot and windy, and the cool and showery; or more simply, into eight months hot and dry, and four showery. March, April, and May are always exceedingly sultry, with much thunder and lightning, and occasionally heavy thunder-showers occur; but from nine A.M. until four P.M. it is always disagreeably hot; June and July are also hot, although in a less degree, the heat being generally at its maximum about the middle of May. When the westerly wind sets in, the heat is moderated, but when accompanied by dust, it is, as already remarked, particularly unpleasant. Thunder-showers occasionally occur during a week or two in the months of August, September, October, and November, which are cool, cloudy, and pleasant. December, January, and the greater part of February are dry, cold in the mornings and evenings, but sultry and close during the forenoon. Fogs and dews are rarely known in the months of March, April, and May, when the country presents the appearance of a vast desert. The rivers and tanks become dried up; the trees shed their leaves, and vegetation is completely at a stand; the respiration of animals at this time panting and oppressed,—in short, all nature, both animal and vegetable, seems to droop and shrink from the raging mid-day heat. When the rains succeed, nature soon revives; vegetation bursts forth with new life and vigour, and the eye is relieved from the oppressive glare and barrenness. The soil being so arid and sandy, there are scarcely any fogs, vapours, or noxious exhalations; and in this respect the climate is salubrious, the atmosphere being seldom damp or humid.

The Cauvery, the principal river, enters the district at its western extremity, in lat. 10° 58′, long. 78° 15′, and flows through it in an easterly direction to Seringham, three miles north of the town of Trichinopoly, in lat. 10° 52′, long. 78° 44′, near which locality it divides into two branches; the northern, called the Coleroon; the southern retaining the name of the Cauvery. The principal feeders of the Cauvery are the Bhavani, the Noyel, and the Ambrawutty, flowing from the Western Ghauts, the Neilgherry group, and the table-land of Mysore; and the Jyaur, which, descending from the eastern declivity of the Eastern Ghauts, falls into the principal stream on the left side, just at the head of the island of Seringham. The Cauvery, having its principal feeders close to the Western Ghauts, is fully under the influence of the south-west monsoon, and conveys, to fertilize the Carnatic, an abundant portion of the rains driven from the ocean by that vast aërial current. The Cauvery is generally nearly empty during March, April, and the early part of May, towards the close of which a scanty stream frequently comes down; about the middle of June, the regular periodical inundation, caused by the south-west monsoon, reaches Trichinopoly; and by the beginning of July, the volume of water is sufficient not only to fill all the tanks and canals, but to afford a redundance of water, which finds its way to the sea by the two channels, the Coleroon and the Cauvery. At the height of inundation, the Cauvery is a vast torrent, for miles wide. The river continues to have a considerable quantity of water during August, but in the two months succeeding becomes very low, until replenished in the course of November by the rains of the north-east monsoon. During winter, it continues to fall, and by March, as already observed, is generally nearly dry. After the divergence of the Coleroon, the Cauvery sends forth on its right or south side a great number of branches, which traverse and intersect the delta of Tanjore. Of those branches, the most important is the Vennar, which diverges about eight miles below the town of Trichinopoly. The Cauvery is used to a considerable extent at certain seasons, as a means of communication and traffic, when cotton piece-goods, saltpetre, and some other wares are floated down from the British districts Coimbatore and Salem, and conveyed to the towns on the seacoast. The communication, however, is only practicable during the inundations; even then it is hazardous and uncertain, and can be effected only by means of circular baskets, ten or fourteen feet in diameter, and covered with buffalo-hides. As soon as those rude craft have reached their destination, the wicker is abandoned, having been previously stripped of the hides, which are transported back either by human labour or on bullocks.

Of the zoology of this district there is scarcely any authentic information. Its general aridity and barrenness are probably unfavourable to the multiplication of animals. The dry ground is infested with great swarms of white, black, and red ants, and other destructive insects, which commit great ravages both in the fields and in houses: water-snakes are very common in rice-fields, and scorpions; the cobra de Manilla and cobra de capello are occasionally met with: common striped squirrels are very numerous, noisy, and troublesome, frequenting the roofs of houses, and plundering the gardens: frogs swarm in the pools and tanks after heavy showers, and at night cause great annoyance by their loud and incessant croaking: eyeflies and musquitoes abound, especially after rain.

There are plantations of cocoanut-trees, made principally on account of the oil obtained from their fruit; but the chief alimentary crops are rice, ragi (Eleusine coracana), various kinds of millet, maize, and plantains. Sugarcane is little cultivated, but tobacco is grown in considerable quantities and of very fine quality. Everything in husbandry depends on irrigation, manure being scarcely used. Cotton is a product of some importance. The population is given under the article MADRAS. The language spoken in the district is the Tamul. The military station of the district is at the fort of Trichinopoly, the force stationed at which furnishes detachments to Negapatam, Tanjore,

Combaconum, and Coimbatore. The district is divided into eight talooks. The principal routes are—1st, From north-east to south-west, from Madras, through the town of Trichinopoly, to Madura and Palamcotta; 2nd. from east to west, from Tanjore, through the town of Trichinopoly, to Coimbatore; 3rd. from east to west, from Combaconum to Trichinopoly. The principal places (Trichinopoly and Seringham) are described under their respective names in the alphabetical arrangement. Trichinopoly was included in the territory styled the Carnatic, the civil and military government of which was vested in the British government, under the provisions of the treaty with the nabob, dated in 1801.

TRICHINOPOLY.—The principal place of the British district of the same name, under the presidency of Madras, a town, with a celebrated fort. The rock on which the fort is built is of sienite, estimated to be 600 feet above the alluvial plain from which it rises, and is a very striking object viewed from a distance at any point of the compass, and commands a very extensive and fine prospect over the surrounding country, including the island of Seringham, with its numerous pagodas, and the meanderings of the Cauvery, and its branch the Coleroon. The fort is situate on a part of the rugged declivity of the rock, and two furlongs from the right bank of the Cauvery, which is embanked; but from want of skill, or of adequate expenditure on the works, they sometimes give way, thus admitting the inundation to lay the neighbouring country under water. The fort, with its strong and massy walls, constructed of solid masonry (which are in general still in a good state of repair, though in some parts rather dilapidated), bears the appearance of having been strongly and regularly built. The walls, which are in some places double, are from twenty to thirty feet in height, of very considerable thickness, and upwards of two miles in circumference. Within them is a very extensive petta or native town. The houses and huts are generally of the ordinary Indian construction, being low, small, and very closely huddled together, with small courts in front of them. They are without windows, and almost all present to the eye the appearance of being filthy, dark, ill-ventilated, and, according to English notions, extremely uncomfortable, being, what they cannot fail to be, decidedly unhealthy, with little prospect of improvement. They are, however, arranged in tolerably straight, wide, and regular streets, which are usually crowded at all hours of the day with multitudes of passengers, carriage-bullocks, and cattle of various kinds. Most of the streets have bazars, for the sale of native goods and wares of every description. The flagstaff is placed on the summit of the rock, and there is an easy access to it by means of a spacious flight of stone steps, which, about halfway up, passes through the site of an old magazine, accidentally blown up in 1772. On the rock is a pagoda, forming a very striking object, and regarded with deep reverence by the Brahminists. The fort contains the arsenal, commissariat, ordnance stores, medical stores, pay-office, garrison hospital, and jail. It has been observed, that from the crowded streets, numerous buildings, and the proximity of the rock, the temperature of the fort is generally higher than that of the immediate neighbourhood or cantonment. The jail erected in 1806 was in a confined situation near the eastern extremity of the fort, and has been replaced by one of recent erection, in which due provision has been made for the separation of the several classes of prisoners, as well as for ventilation, drainage, and cleanliness.

The natives of this town are famed for their skill in the manufacture of hardware, cutlery, and jewellery; their harness and saddlery are also excellent in workmanship and materials, and very moderate in price. Large quantities of cheroots are manufactured, from tobacco of superior quality, grown in this and the neighbouring districts.

The cantonment, in which the troops composing the garrison are quartered, is at the distance of from two to three miles south-west of the fort, on an extensive open plain, studded with masses of granite. It is very extensive, its various buildings and establishments being scattered over an area of not less than from six to seven miles in circuit. Many of the bungalows or lodges occupied by the civil and military officers are spacious and well constructed, and have large and well-stocked gardens. The troops there are generally one regiment of native cavalry, one company of European foot artillery, one regiment of her Majesty's foot, and four regiments of native infantry, forming a force of between 4,000 and 5,000 men: the native infantry corps furnishes detachments to several British military stations. The cantonment is healthy, and has abundance of excellent water, from a considerable branch of the Cauvery, which flows through it. In a central part of the cantonment are public rooms, built and supported by voluntary subscription: they contain a reading-room and good library. In the south of the cantonment, and three miles from the fort, is Saint John's Church, a handsome building, affording ample accommodation for the European inhabitants and troops. In the western part of the cantonment there is a small Romish chapel, at which a Portuguese priest officiates. In the fort is a large missionary chapel.

The mean annual temperature of Trichinopoly is about 85°, the maximum in the shade being 102°, the minimum 68°. The population, exclusive of the troops and other government establishments, is estimated at 30,000, of whom about a fifth are Mussulmans.

Trichinopoly figures rather conspicuously in the history of India during the early part of the eighteenth century. Its Hindoo rajah died without issue in the year 1732. Three wives survived him, two of whom dutifully submitted to con-

flagration; the remaining one preferred to live, and succeeded to the government. A party being raised to oppose her pretensions, she solicited the aid of the Mussulman nabob of Arcot, who sent a force to her assistance, commanded by his son, with whom was associated a man named Chunda Sahib, who occupies a distinguished place in the records of that period. The ranee was sufficiently well acquainted with the average character of the good faith of Indian princes, to entertain some misgivings as to the ulterior designs of those whose aid she had been compelled to invite; to allay them, Chunda Sahib took an oath on the Koran, as it was believed, that the foreign troops should be employed for no other purpose but the establishment of the ranee's authority; and that when that should be secured, they should be withdrawn. To avoid profanation of the holy volume of the Mahometans, it is usual to wrap it in a covering when used for the administration of an oath. When Chunda Sahib thus solemnly attested the pure intentions of himself and his master, the covering was such as was usually employed, but it enveloped only a brick, and the deponent did not feel his conscience bound by an engagement made on so vile a material: accordingly, the first use he made of his power was to subvert the authority of the ranee, and subject her to imprisonment. This distinguished service seemed to entitle Chunda Sahib to the office of administering the government of the place which he had so honourably won, and he was without hesitation appointed thereto. But Chunda Sahib had enemies in the court of his master, which, like all other eastern courts, was a hotbed of intrigue. Failing in their endeavours to prejudice the nabob against one of his favourite servants, these persons had recourse to the Mahrattas, who, ever on the watch for opportunities to acquire either wealth or power, readily assented to do the work of those who envied Chunda Sahib's good fortune, but in reality, as on all other occasions, were bent only on performing their own. The result was the alienation of Trichinopoly from the rule of the nabob of Arcot, under which it had so recently been brought, the Mahrattas succeeding in reducing the fortress, and making its perjured conqueror prisoner. This event took place in 1741. The Mahrattas did not long retain possession of Trichinopoly; and throughout the wars urged between the English and French for supremacy in India, this place continued to be a frequent object of attack or intrigue. One of the latest and most memorable events connected with its history, is the march of Captain Calliaud to its relief, when besieged by the French in 1757. Captain Calliaud was before Madura, which he was preparing to attack, when he was informed of the danger of Trichinopoly, which had then sustained bombardment for several days, an assault being hourly expected to follow. He did not receive the news till three o'clock in the afternoon of the 21st May, and at six he was on his march, which movement was commenced without tents, baggage, or artillery. The men bore their own food; a few bullocks only were taken, and these were laden with ammunition. At six o'clock in the evening of the 25th, the relieving force was within twelve miles of Trichinopoly, having advanced thus far without annoyance; but the great difficulty,—that of entering the town, remained to be overcome. The march of Captain Calliaud was not unknown to the enemy, and troops had been so disposed as to command every line by which, under ordinary circumstances, the place could be approached from the direction of the expected relief. It was discovered, also, that some spies had mixed with the English troops, for the purpose of ascertaining the precise route which would be taken. This precaution, devised for his destruction, Captain Calliaud converted into the means of safety. The spies were suffered to exercise their office undisturbed and apparently unsuspected, until the commander had apparently fully made up his mind as to the route by which he would seek admission to the town, and having pursued it undeviatingly for about six miles, the spies dropped off to communicate the information of which they thought themselves possessed to their employers. Thus rid of these persons, Captain Calliaud, as soon as such a step could with safety be taken, changed his track for another, which, being naturally regarded as unlikely to be selected, had been left by the enemy altogether unguarded. This extraordinary route for the passage of troops lay across rice-fields under irrigation, which were thereby converted into one continuous morass. Every step had to be taken knee-deep in mud and water. The march occupied seven hours, although the distance was less than that number of miles: thus was occupied the night. By break of day firmer ground was obtained, and the labours of the troops were rewarded and cheered by the sight of the city and fort of Trichinopoly at no great distance. A part of the garrison was drawn out, accompanied by two field-pieces, to protect the reinforcement, if any attempt were made to intercept them; but the only duty to which they were called was to give welcome to their deliverers, who marched into the fort amidst universal shouting. Captain Calliaud's attention had been required at so many points during this extraordinary night march, that he had undergone more fatigue than any man among those whom he commanded, and he was in a state of perfect exhaustion. Notwithstanding this, however, he marched at the head of his troops when they entered the fort, though obliged, from weakness, to be supported on each side by a grenadier. The enemy continued anxiously to watch for the approach of the English party by the expected route, till a triumphant salute assured him of their being beyond the reach of his arms. The immediate consequence of this admirably-performed movement was the precipitate retirement of the French from before the place.

Distance of Trichinopoly from Madura, N.E., 75 miles; Coimbatore, E., 120; Tanjore, W., 29; Bangalore, S.E., 165; Madras, S.W., 190. Lat. 10° 50′, long. 78° 46′.

TRICHOOR, in the territory of the native state of Cochin, under the political superintendence of the presidency of Madras, a town, the principal place of a tallook or subdivision of the same name. Of the towns in the territory, it is next in importance to Cochin: the site is advantageous, being close to the eastern coast of the Backwater, an extensive estuary or shallow lake, by which it communicates with Chaugat and the city of Cochin; but by land the only route is that proceeding north-east to Palghat, and being a defile through jungles infested with wild elephants and other dangerous animals, and very unhealthy from November to March. Among the Brahminists it is much celebrated for its sanctity. The fortifications which formerly encompassed the town have been destroyed, and excellent barracks, with an hospital, stores, and magazine, have been built. The sepoys, of whom there are about 150, have dry, airy, and commodious dwellings, and the station is considered very healthy. There are here a native police-station, a court, and jail. Distance from the city of Cochin, N., 41 miles; Bangalore. S.W., 190. Lat. 10° 32′, long. 76° 16′.

TRICOLUM.—A town in the British district of Malabar, presidency of Madras, 69 miles S.E. by S. of Cannanore. Lat. 11° 2′, long. 75° 59′.

TRICOTA, a lofty mountain in the north of the Punjab, and on the south of the valley of Cashmere, has such an elevation as to be covered with snow the greater part of the year. North of it is a remarkable spring, from which the water gushes at very short and regular intervals, as if expelled by pulsations, and is received into a spacious reservoir. During December, January, and the beginning of February, the water is too warm for the hand to bear immersion in it, but at other times cold. According to Von Hügel, this is caused by the water produced by the melting of snow on the heights cooling that yielded by the fountain, which being heated by subterranean fire, has this naturally high temperature during the winter months, when the snows and ice-bound streams withhold their cold admixture. This natural wonder causes the place to be considered holy by the Hindoos, and consequently to be visited as a place of pilgrimage. Lat. 32° 58′, long. 74° 37′.

TRILOKNATH.—A town within the dominions of Gholab Singh, the ruler of Cashmere, situate on the left bank of the Chandra river, and 140 miles S.E. from Sirinagur. Lat. 32° 43′, long. 76° 43′.

TRIMALROYENPATAM.—A town in the French territory of Karical, situate within the British district of Tanjore, presidency of Madras, 47 miles E. by N. of Tanjore. Lat. 10° 53′, long. 79° 53′.

TRIMBUK.—A town in the British district of Ahmednuggur, presidency of Bombay, 16 miles W. by S. of Nassik. Lat. 19° 58′, long. 73° 32′.

TRIMUNGALUM.—A town in the British district of Madura, presidency of Madras, 11 miles S.W. of Madura. Lat. 9° 50′, long. 78° 3′.

TRINOMALEE, in the British district of South Arcot, presidency of Madras, a town at the base of a hill surmounted by a lofty pagoda, which commands all parts of it. Here, in the year 1767, a British force under Colonel Smith defeated an army far superior in numbers and artillery, commanded by Hyder Ali and Nizam Ali. It was besieged in the year 1791 by Tippoo Sultan, and obliged to surrender, in consequence of the cross-fires from a neighbouring hill which commanded it. At present Trinomalee is a considerable and rather well-built place, having a numerous population, including a large proportion of Brahmins. Distance from Cuddalore, N.W., 58 miles; Madras, S.W., 103. Lat. 12° 14′, long. 79° 7′.

TRIPATOOR.—A town in the British district of Madura, presidency of Madras, 36 miles E.N.E. of Madura. Lat. 10° 7′, long. 78° 40′.

TRIPETTY.—A town in the British district of North Arcot, presidency of Madras, and the seat of one of the most celebrated Hindoo temples south of the Kistnah river, situate 51 miles N. by E. of Arcot. Lat. 13° 38′, long. 79° 29′.

TRIPPATUR.—A town in the British district of Salem, presidency of Madras, 63 miles N.N.E. of Salem. Lat. 12° 29′, long. 78° 36′.

TRIPUNAITORAI, in the raj or state of Cochin, a town about two miles N.E. of the Backwater, an extensive shallow lake, the reservoir of numerous streams flowing from the Western Ghats. Bartolomeo states, in the year 1787, that it was the residence of the rajah of Cochin, and it probably continues to be so at present. Distance from Cochin, S.E., seven miles; Calicut, S.E., 105; Bangalore, S.W., 303. Lat. 9° 57′, long. 76° 24′.

TRISUL GUNGA, a river, called in the upper part of its course the Bori Gunduk, rises in the Himalayas, in lat. 28° 57′, long. 85° 48′, and, flowing in a south-westerly direction, forms a junction with the Gunduk in lat. 27° 31′, long. 84° 5′.

TRITCHINDOOR.—A town in the British district of Tinnevelly, presidency of Madras, 35 miles E.S.E. of Tinnevelly. Lat. 8° 30′, long. 78° 10′.

TRITRAPUNDI.—A town in the British district of Tanjore, presidency of Madras, 40 miles E.S.E. of Tanjore. Lat. 10° 33′, long. 79° 42′.

TRITTANY.—A town in the British district of North Arcot, presidency of Madras,

26 miles N.E. of Arcot. Lat. 13° 10′, long. 79° 39′.

TRIVALUM.—A town in the British district of North Arcot, presidency of Madras, eight miles N.W. of Arcot. Lat. 12° 59′, long. 79° 18′.

TRIVANANELLUR.—A town in the British district of South Arcot, presidency of Madras, 29 miles W.N.W. of Cuddalore. Lat. 11° 52′, long. 79° 24′.

TRIVANDRUM, in the territory of Travancore, under the political superintendence of the presidency of Madras, a town situate a mile and a half N.E. of the shore of the Indian Ocean, and on the right bank of a small river or torrent flowing from the Western Ghats. The town is of considerable size, having its greatest length north and south. At the southern extremity is the fort, about half a mile square, without a ditch, with walls of mud cased with stone at some parts of the north and west faces. It is for the most part an ugly, ill-built pile; but the rajah's palace, within its precincts, is a large handsome edifice in the European style. At the north of the town are the barracks and the old cantonment, formerly occupied by a regiment of native infantry and a detachment of artillery, and at present the head-quarters of the Nair brigade. On an eminence outside the town, and 195 feet above the level of the sea, the rajah in the year 1837 built an observatory. Elevation of the town above the sea 135 feet; distance from Cannanore, S.E., 255 miles; Madras, S.W., 395. Lat. 8° 28′, long. 77° 2′.

TRIVATOOR.—A town in the British district of North Arcot, presidency of Madras, 22 miles S.E. of Arcot. Lat. 12° 39′, long. 79° 36′.

TRIVELORE.—A town in the British district of Chingleput, presidency of Madras, 25 miles W. of Madras. Lat. 13° 8′, long. 80°.

TRIVUR.—A town in the British district of Masulipatam, presidency of Madras, 76 miles N.N.W. of Masulipatam. Lat. 17° 8′, long. 80° 40′.

TROMBAY.—An island, named after the town of that name, situate between the island of Bombay and the mainland of the British district of Tannah: the town is nine miles N.E. of Bombay, and in lat. 19° 1′, long. 73°.

TRUNULVAUSEL.—A town in the British district of Tanjore, presidency of Madras, 57 miles N.E. by E. of Tanjore. Lat. 11° 13′, long. 79° 56′.

TSAGAING.—A town of Burmah, on the right bank of the Irawady river, and three miles N.N.W. from Ava. Tsagaing, or Chagain, was formerly the seat of imperial residence: it is situate "partly at the foot and partly on the side of a rugged hill, that is broken into separate eminences, and on the summit of each stands a spiral temple." Lat. 21° 55′, long. 96°.

TSALENG.—A town in the native state of Bhotan, 101 miles N.W. by W. from Durrung, and 72 miles N. from Goalpara. Lat. 27° 10′, long. 90° 40′.

TSHOMORIRI.—See CHAMORERIL LAKE.

TSINGUH MYO.—A town of Burmah, situate on the left bank of the Irawady river, and 49 miles N. from Ava. Lat. 22° 34′, long. 96° 2′.

TSTALONTSKEIK.—A town of Burmah, situate on the left bank of the Khyendwen river, and 69 miles W.N.W. from Ava. Lat. 22° 14′, long. 95° 4′.

TUAVEE, in the British district of Muzuffurnugur, lieut.-gov. of the N.W. Provinces, a village on the route from Kurnal to the town of Muzuffurnugur, and 39 miles S.E. of the former. Lat. 29° 28′, long. 77° 35′.

TUBAH.—A town in the hill zemindarry of Jeypoor, in Orissa, 50 miles S. by E. from Jeypoor, and 69 miles N.W. by W. from Vizagapatam. Lat. 18° 20′, long. 82° 33′.

TUDRI HARBOUR.—See CANARA.

TUDURU, in Mysore, a village on the river Tunga, 14 miles S.E. of Bednore. Lat. 13° 38′, long. 75° 14′.

TUGRA.—A town in the British district of Backergunje, lieut.-gov. of Bengal, 100 miles E. of Calcutta. Lat. 22° 30′, long. 90°.

TUKHT-I-SULIMAN, or "Solomon's Seat," in Cashmere, a lofty hill close to the city of Sirinagur or Cashmere, on the eastern side. Its rocks are of trap. On the summit is a massively-built Buddhist temple, having every mark of extreme antiquity: it is now converted into a mosque. Elevation above the sea 6,950 feet. Lat. 34° 4′, long. 74° 59′.

TUKHWA, in the British district of Furruckabad, lieut.-gov. of the N.W. Provinces, a village on the route from the cantonment of Cawnpore to that of Futtehgurh, and 38 miles S.E. of the latter. Lat. 26° 58′, long. 80° 3′.

TULEHGAON.—A town in the British district of Poonah, presidency of Bombay, 22 miles N.E. by E. of Poonah. Lat. 18° 40′, long. 74° 10′.

TULLAGAON.—A town in Hyderabad, or the Nizam's dominions, situate on the left bank of the Godavery river, and 126 miles N.W. by N. from Hyderabad. Lat. 18° 59′, long. 77° 41′.

TULLAJA.—See TALLAJA.

TULLEGAON.—A town in Nagpoor, situate on the left bank of the Wurda river, and 61 miles W. from Nagpoor. Lat. 21° 8′, long. 78° 12′.

TULL GHAT.—A pass in the mountains dividing the Tannah and Ahmednuggur districts, through which is a road leading from Bombay to Nassik, and continued thence to Agra. The pass is 65 miles N.E. by N. of the town of Bombay, and in lat. 19° 43′, long. 73° 30′.

TULLODA.—A town in the British district of Candeish, presidency of Bombay, 76 miles N. by W. of Malligaum. Lat. 21° 36′, long. 74° 14′.

TULLODEE.—A town in Nagpoor, situate on the left bank of the Wein Gunga river, and 110 miles S.S.E. from Nagpoor. Lat. 19° 41′, long. 79° 48′.

TULLUCK, in the Mysore, a town, the principal place of the tallook or subdivision of the same name, near the north frontier, towards the British district of Bellary. In the year 1790 it was stormed and sacked by the Mahrattas. Distance from Chitteldroog, N.E., 25 miles. Lat. 14° 26′, long. 76° 44′.

TULLUCKWARRA, in Guzerat, or territory of the Guicowar, a town on the right bank of the river Nerbudda, which is navigable to the sea. The place is rudely fortified. Distance from Baroda, S.E., 30 miles; Broach, N.E., 40. Lat. 21° 58′, long. 73° 32′.

TULSIPOOR, in the territory of Oude, a town near the northern frontier, towards Nepal, on the route from Goruckpoor to Kumaon, 80 miles N.W. of the former, 115 N.E. of Lucknow. Lat. 27° 30′, long. 82° 24′.

TULWANDEE, in the Reechna Dooab division of the Punjab, a town situated 13 miles from the left bank of the Chenaub, 45 miles N. of the town of Lahore. Lat. 32° 15′, long. 74° 12′.

TUMACHABAD, in the British district of Benares, lieut.-gov. of the N.W. Provinces, a village on the route from the city of Benares to Allahabad, 56 miles E. of the latter, 18 W. of the former. Lat. 25° 16′, long. 82° 45′.

TUMBONG KHA.—A town of Burmah, 47 miles E. from the left bank of the Irawady river, and 197 miles N.E. by N. from Ava. Lat. 24° 19′, long. 97° 44′.

TUMBUDRA. — A river of the Mysore territory, formed by the junction of the rivers Toonga and Budra, in lat. 14°, long. 75° 43′. Thence it flows sinuously, but generally in a northern direction, for forty-five miles, to Headagatry, in lat. 14° 26′, long. 75° 42′, whence it turns to the north-east, and flows in that direction for fifteen miles, to Hurryhurr, in lat. 14° 30′, long. 75° 52′. There it again takes a course generally north (but not without many sinuosities) for forty-five miles, to the confluence of the Wurda, which joins it on the left side, in lat. 14° 55′, long. 75° 45′. From that confluence it turns north-east, and subsequently east, and then flows for 220 miles, to its fall into the Kistnah, on the right side, in lat. 15° 58′, long. 78° 19′, having a total course of 325 miles. The length of the course of the Budra, the longest of the feeders of the Tumbudra, is ninety-five miles; so that the course of the continuous stream from the source of the Budra to the mouth of the Tumbudra is 420 miles. Ritter, quoting Cullen, states the confluence to be 952 feet above the sea. On the banks of the Tumbudra are teak-forests, the timber of which might, if rendered more buoyant by floats of bamboo, be sent down the Kistnah during the monsoon floods. The river "at all times contains water, but in the dry season, the channel being full of rocks, will not admit floats. In the rainy season it swells prodigiously, and is said to be in most places eight or ten feet higher than the top of the rocks. Its stream is there exceedingly rapid and muddy, and filled with large trees swept away by the flood, while in some places rocks come very near the surface." There is reason, however, to think that those great obstacles to navigation are only in the upper part of its course.

TUMLOOK, in the British district of Midnapore, subject to the lieut.-gov. of Bengal, a town on the right bank of the river Cossye, in this part of its course called the Roopnarayn. The site and vicinity are low, and protected by embankments, with a view to security from inundations, which, however, notwithstanding these precautions, sometimes occur, and cause much injury. Tumlook is the head-quarters of an agency for the manufacture of salt on government account. According to Wilford, it was originally called Tamraliptas, and was the capital of a realm of some note. There does not appear to be any direct route from Calcutta to this place, the absence of such accommodation being probably attributable to the nature of the intermediate country, which is marshy and cut up by watercourses. The direct distance is thirty-five miles; circuitously, by water, down the river Hoogly and up the Roopnarayn, or lower part of the Cossye, 48; travelling distance from Midnapore, E., 40 miles. Lat. 22° 18′, long. 87° 59′.

TUMLOONG.—A town in the native state of Sikhim, situate on the left bank of the Teesta river, and 32 miles N.E. by N. from Darjeeling. Lat. 27° 24′, long. 88° 37′.

TUMOO. — A town of Burmah, 19 miles W. from the right bank of the Khyendwen river, and 191 miles N.W. by N. from Ava. Lat. 24° 8′, long. 94° 29′.

TUNCARIA, in the British district of Broach, presidency of Bombay, a town on the northern side of the estuary of a small river falling into the Gulf of Cambay; distance from Baroda, S.W., 43 miles. The Guicowar has it in contemplation to connect his capital of Baroda by railway with this town. Lat. 21° 59′, long. 72° 40′.

TUNDA, in the British district of Dumoh, territory of Saugor and Nerbudda, lieut.-gov. of the N.W. Provinces, a town on the route from Dumoh to Hoosungabad, 61 miles S.W. by W. of the former. Lat. 23° 24′, long. 78° 40′.

TUNGABUDRA.—See Tumbudra.

TUNGEE, in the district of Peshawar, division of the Punjab, a town situated on the left bank of the Lundye river, 20 miles N. of the town of Peshawur. Lat. 34° 18′, long. 71° 42′.

TUNGRUNG, in Bussahir, a pass in Koonawar, over a lofty ridge separating the valley of the Buspa from that of the Taglakhar. Elevation 13,739 feet above the sea. Lat. 31° 38′, long. 78° 32′.

TUNGUDA.—A town in the British district of Guntoor, presidency of Madras, 49 miles N.W. by W. of Guntoor. Lat. 16° 40′, long. 79° 54′.

TUNGUL.—A town in the native state of Sikhim, situate on the left bank of the Teesta river, and 60 miles N.N.E. from Darjeeling. Lat. 27° 52′, long. 88° 37′.

TUPOOKRA, in the territory of Alwar, district of Tijara, under the political superintendence of the Governor-General's agent in Rajpootana, a town 44 miles S.W. of Delhi. At the close of the last century, when this region was overrun by the Mahrattas, Tupookra with its vicinity was, along with some other districts, granted by one of their chiefs to the adventurer George Thomas; and at the close of the war in 1803, was by the British government transferred to the Rao rajah. Lat. 28° 7′, long. 76° 54′.

TUPPUL, in the British district of Allygurh, lieut.-gov. of the N.W. Provinces, a town on the route from Allygurh to Rewaree, 31 miles W. by N. of the former. Lat. 28° 2′, long. 77° 39′.

TUPURANUH, in the British district of Muzuffurnugur, lieut.-gov. of the N.W. Provinces, a village on the route from Kurnal to Meerut, and 24 miles S.E. of the former. Lat. 29° 29′, long. 77° 19′.

TURANNA, in the territory of Indore, or possessions of Holkar's family, a town on the route from Goona to Oojein, 129 miles S.W. of the former, 22 N.E. of latter. It is situate on the east or right bank of the Chota Kalee Sindh river. Population about 10,000. Lat. 23° 18′, long. 76° 3′.

TURAON.—See TIROWAN.

TURIVAKARAY, in the Mysore, a town, the principal place of a tallook or subdivision of the same name. Here is a fortress, consisting of an outer and an inner fort, strongly defended by a ditch and mud wall: the town is uninclosed. There is here a very fine tank, built, according to tradition, with a treasure, the concealment of which was pointed out by the divinity Ganesa. Distance from Seringapatam, N.W., 54 miles. Lat. 13° 10′, long. 77° 44′.

TURKANAMBI.—A town in the Mysore, 46 miles S. by E. from Seringapatam, and 58 miles N. by W. from Coimbatoor. Lat. 11° 48′, long. 76° 51′.

TURKOD.—A town in the British district of Dharwar, presidency of Bombay, 12 miles N.W. by N. of Dharwar. Lat. 15° 36′, long. 74° 59′.

TURKOOAH. — A town in the British district of Midnapoor, lieut.-gov. of Bengal, 34 miles S. of Midnapoor. Lat. 21° 56′, long. 87° 26′.

TURKOOLWA, in the British district of Goruckpoor, lieut.-gov. of the N.W. Provinces, a town on the route from Goruckpoor to the Sarun district, 34 miles E. by S. of the former. Lat. 26° 36′, long. 83° 55′.

TURMA. — A town on the south-west frontier of Bengal, in the native state of Keunjur, 81 miles E. by N. from Sumbulpoor, and 90 miles N.W. by N. from Cuttack. Lat. 21° 35′, long. 85° 16′.

TUROWLEE. — A town in the British district of Muttra, lieut.-gov. of the N.W. Provinces. Lat. 27° 40′, long. 77° 39′.

TURPOONGY.—A town in the territory of Nagpoor, 160 miles E. by N. from Nagpoor, and 98 miles S.S.E. from Ramgurh. Lat. 21° 30′, long. 81° 35′.

TURRAH, in Guzerat, or the territory of the Guicowar, a town near the right bank of the river Bunass, in a rugged, ill-cultivated country, thinly inhabited by Bheels, Coolies, and similar semi-barbarous tribes. Distance from Ahmedabad N.W. 85 miles. Lat. 23° 58′, long. 71° 43′.

TURRANNA.—A town in the native state of Indore, or territory of Holkar's family, situate on the right bank of the Chota Kallee Sind river, and 44 miles N.E. from Indoor. Lat. 23° 17′, long. 76° 4′.

TURROCH.—See OOTRACH.

TURRYE.—A town in the British district of Hydrabad, province of Scinde, presidency of Bombay, 52 miles S.S.E. of Hydrabad. Lat. 24° 40′, long. 68° 43′.

TURRY KAIRA.—A town in the Mysore, 52 miles E. by S. from Bednore, and 107 miles N.W. by N. from Seringapatam. Lat. 13° 43′, long. 75° 52′.

TURYA. — A town in the territory of Nagpoor, 160 miles E. by N. from Nagpoor, and 108 miles S.S.E. from Ramgurh. Lat. 21° 21′, long. 81° 36′.

TURYA SOOJUN, in the British district of Goruckpoor, lieut.-gov. of the N.W. Provinces, a town on the route from Goruckpoor to the district of Sarun, 56 miles E. of the former. Lat. 26° 36′, long. 84° 17′.

TUTICORIN, in the British district of Tinnevelly, presidency of Madras, and the only important port in the district, is situate on the north-west coast of the Gulf of Manar. It has a safe roadstead, with good anchorage, sheltered on the west, north, and south by the mainland of Tinnevelly, and on the east by a group of islets, extending about eight miles from north to south. The trade of this place was once considerable, the exports having formerly in one year amounted to 365,000*l.*; subsequently a decrease appears to have taken place, but latterly the increased briskness in the cotton trade has caused a great improvement. No fewer than 3,000 bales of cotton have been in less than fifteen months shipped from it to England direct; 3,000 more, intended for the China market, were sent from it to Madras by coasters, to be finally shipped there; while 1,000 were sent by land from Tinnevelly, for transmission to England. The measures adopted for deepening the Paumbaum passage, through the reef between Ceylon and the mainland, have vastly increased the traffic of this port, by opening a direct passage for shipping between it and the Bay of Bengal, thus obviating the tedious and hazardous voyage round the island of Ceylon. Pearl-banks exist in the vicinity of the town, which the government have authorized to be examined. Distance from Tinnevelly, E., 33 miles; Madras, S.W., 325. Lat. 8° 48′, long. 78° 12′.

TUTTABAR.—A town in the British district of Ramgur, lieut.-gov. of Bengal, 56 miles W. by N. of Ramgur. Lat. 23° 51′, long. 84° 40′.

TUTWAS.—A town in the Rajpoot state of Jodhpoor or Marwar, 66 miles N. by E. from Jodhpoor, and 54 miles S. from Beekaneer. Lat. 27° 14′, long. 73° 19′.

TUWARA.—A town in the native state of Gurhwal, situate on the right bank of the Bhageruttee river, and 53 miles N.E. from Dehra. Lat. 30° 51′, long. 78° 41′.

TUZHIGUNG, in Bussahir, a village of Koonawar, at the northern base of the lofty Purgeul, hence sometimes called the Tuzhigung mountain. Lat. 31° 50′, long. 78° 43′.

TWENGNGAGE.—A town of Burmah, situate on the left bank of the Irawady river, and 83 miles N. from Ava. Lat. 23° 4′, long. 96° 1′.

TWENTY-FOUR PERGUNNAHS.—A British district under the lieut.-gov. of Bengal. Its name is derived from its formerly containing twenty-four divisions, called pergunnahs in the vernacular language. It is bounded on the north-east by the British district Baraset; on the east, south-east, and south by the Sunderbunds; on the south-west and west by the river Hoogly, separating it from the British districts of Hoogly and Hidgelee. It lies between lat. 21° 55′—22° 48′, long. 88° 6′—88° 43′: it is sixty miles in length from north to south, and thirty-two in breadth: the area, according to official return, is 1,186 square miles. The whole country is throughout a plain, little elevated above the level of the sea, and traversed by numerous streams and watercourses. The river Hoogly, considered by the Brahminists as the revered Ganges of mythological celebrity, touches on the district at its north-west corner, at Pulta Ghat, and flowing southward ten miles, is the boundary between the British district Hoogly and this district, into which it passes at that distance, and taking a course tending to south-west for twenty miles through the district, flows by Calcutta. Passing out of the district at Bhujbhuj, it continues to flow southward for twenty-four miles, to the mouth of the Roopnarain, in lat. 22° 14′, long. 88° 5′, for that distance forming the boundary between this district and Hoogly. At the confluence of the Roopnarain, the Hoogly turns south-eastward, and for twenty-four miles forms the south-western boundary of the district, passing finally away from it in lat. 22°, long. 88° 12′. Throughout the whole course of seventy-eight miles for which the Hoogly is connected with this district, it is navigable for the largest ships as far as Calcutta. The Pali, a watercourse connecting the Salt Lake, in the environs of Calcutta, with the inlets of the Sunderbunds, extends about ten miles in a direction from west to east; and though rapid and deep, yet does not appear to be navigated. A considerable offset from the Hoogly, immediately south of the city of Calcutta, takes a direction south-east, and flowing through this district twenty-eight miles, to Budurtulla, passes the eastern frontier into the Sunderbunds, through which it winds, and subsequently, by very sinuous channels, opens a communication with the main stream of the Ganges, in the vicinity of Commercolly. This navigation, though circuitous and tedious, being 177 miles longer than that directly upwards through the Hoogly, is very important, being at all times navigable for large craft, and affording a route by water to the North-Western Provinces when the more direct channel can scarcely be navigated by small boats.

In this district there are three seasons, as in other parts of Bengal. The hot season commences in the early part of March, and during its continuance the temperature is very high, in some instances reaching 112° in the shade, and 140° in places exposed to the direct rays of the sun. The hot season is terminated early in June by the periodical rains brought by the south-west monsoon, and which continues to the middle of October. The annual rain-fall is considerable, amounting frequently to eighty inches. In November the weather becomes clear, settled, and comparatively cool, though the days are often rather warm. December, January, and the early part of February constitute the most agreeable and salubrious part of the year, though the weather in the close of the last month becomes variable, and sometimes rather unpleasant from warmth.

There is a considerable quantity of jungle in the eastern part of the district, harbouring tigers, tiger-cats, hyænas, wild swine, wild buffaloes, and deer: jackals are everywhere numerous. The domestic animals are chiefly small horned cattle, sheep, and goats. Horses are not numerous, and are probably for the most part imported. Bullocks are generally used by the natives both for draught and for bearing burthens.

The cocoanut-palm is cultivated to considerable extent, as well as the toddy-palm, from the fermented sap of which a spirit is obtained by distillation. Of other fruits, there are the mango, the jak (Artocarpus integrifolia), guava, tamarind, mulberry, custard-apple, and many others indigenous, besides a variety introduced from foreign countries.

The articles of commerce are native cotton cloths and coarse silk cloths, a small quantity of cotton, hemp, coir or rope made of cocoanut-fibre, cocoanuts, betel-nuts, teak and some other timber, ginger, turmeric, yams, sugar and melasses obtained by inspissating the sap of palms, honey, wax, oil of mustard-seed, rice, a small quantity of indigo, hides, salt-fish, sugar, and rum. The amount of population is given under the article BENGAL. Barrackpore, a cantonment of native troops, is situated within the district, as is also Dumdum, formerly the head artillery station for Bengal. Calcutta, though included locally within the limits of the district, is a separate and exclusive jurisdiction. Alipore, where the civil establishment is located, Kidderpore, as well as Barrackpore and Dumdum, are noticed under their respective names in the alphabetical arrangement.

The district of the Twenty-four Pergunnahs was the earliest territorial possession of any considerable extent obtained by the East-India Company, to whom it was granted in the year 1757, by the Nabob Jaffier Ally Khan.

TYOOR.—A town in the Mysore, situate on the right bank of the Cauvery river, and 18 miles S.E. by S. from Seringapatam. Lat. 12° 13′, long. 76° 53′.

U.

UBDOOLPOOR, in the British district of Ghazeepore, lieut.-gov. of the N.W. Provinces, a town with a population of 6,634 inhabitants, 20 miles N. from Ghazeepore. Lat. 25° 50′, long. 83° 44′.

UBHOO, in the British district of Bhutteeana, lieut.-gov. of the N.W. Provinces, a village near the north-western frontier. Lat. 30° 9′, long. 74° 10′.

UCHARA.—See OOCHEYRA.

UCHARA.—A town in the native state of Rewah or Baghelcund, 34 miles W. by S. from Rewah, and 44 miles S.E. by E. from Punnah. Lat. 24° 23′, long. 80° 51′.

UCHNERA, in the British district of Agra, lieut.-gov. of the N.W. Provinces, a town on the route from the city of Agra to that of Bhurtpore, and 16 miles W. of the former. Lat. 27° 10′, long. 77° 49′.

UCHRA.—See ACHERA.

UDELLEE.—A town in the British district of Ahmedabad, presidency of Bombay, 78 miles S.S.W. of Ahmedabad. Lat. 22°, long. 72° 6′.

UDEPOOR, in the territory of Gwalior, or possessions of Scindia's family, a town situate at the base of a remarkable conical hill. There was formerly a fort on the hill, and its ruins, as well as those of very many others scattered around to a great extent, indicate that it was once a place of much greater importance than at present. Distant S. of Gwalior 160 miles. Lat. 23° 52′, long. 78° 9′.

UDHUR, in the British district of Goorgaon, lieut.-gov. of the N.W. Provinces, a village on the route from Alwar, by Ferozpoor, to Delhi, and 52 miles S.W. of the latter. Lat. 28° 6′, long. 77° 5′.

UDIAMPER, in the territory of Cochin, under the political management of the presidency of Madras, a town celebrated as the place where, in A.D. 1599, Menezes, the Portuguese archbishop of Goa, compelled the Syrian Christians of St. Thomas ostensibly to conform to papacy, and judicially burned their ritual and doctrinal books. Bartolomeo observes, that it has become a very poor place, which, however, retains a church of the Syrian Christians. Distance from city of Cochin, N.E., 10 miles. Lat. 10° 2′, long. 76° 29′.

UDUMPOOR, in the British district of Bareilly, lieut.-gov. of the N. W. Provinces, a village on the route from the town of Bareilly to Almora, and 38 miles N. of the former. Lat. 28° 47′, long. 79° 25′.

UETHAM, in the British district of Kumaon, lieut.-gov. of the N. W. Provinces, a village on the route from Fort Almora to the Juwahir or Unta Dhura Pass, 43 miles N.E. of Almora. It is situate close to the river Surjoo, on the left bank of which is encamping-ground, and supplies are obtainable. Lat. 29° 57′, long. 79° 57′.

UFZULGURH, in the British district of Bijnour, lieut.-gov. of the N. W. Provinces, a fort and town on the route from Pilleebheet to Nugeena, and 15 miles S.E. of the latter. Distance N.W. from Calcutta, *viâ* Moradabad, 938 miles. Lat. 29° 24′, long. 78° 44′.

UGOOHULLY.—A town in the Mysore, 81 miles W.N.W. from Seringapatam, and 58 miles E. by N. from Mangalore. Lat. 13° 3′, long. 75° 44′.

UHEAN.—A town in the British district of Amherst, one of the Tenasserim provinces, 20 miles S.E. by E. of Moulmein. Lat. 16° 20′, long. 97° 57′.

UHEERA.—See HEURA.

UHROW, in the British district of Bareilly, lieut.-gov. of the N.W. Provinces, a village on the route from the town of Bareilly to Almora, and 35 miles N. of the former. Lat. 28° 46′, long. 79° 23′.

UJEETPOOR, in the jaghire of Rampoor, in Rohilcund, a village on the route from Bareilly to Moradabad, and 41 miles N.W. of the former. Lat. 28° 45′, long. 79° 4′.

UJI, in the British district of Goruckpoor, lieut.-gov. of the N.W. Provinces, a small town three miles N. of the left bank of the Gogra. It contains 100 houses, and consequently, allowing six persons to each, a population of 600. Distant W. of Goruckpoor cantonment 42 miles. Lat. 26° 44′, long. 82° 37′.

UKBURPOOR, in the British district of Cawnpoor, lieut.-gov. of the N.W. Provinces, a town on the left bank of the Jumna, 24 miles E. of Calpee. Lat. 26° 4′, long. 80° 10′.

UKBURPOOR, in the British district of Cawnpoor, lieut.-gov. of the N.W. Provinces, a town on the route from Cawnpoor to Jalloun, 26 miles W.S.W. of the former. Lat. 26° 23′, long. 80°.

UKHALIYA.—A town in Nepal, situate on the left bank of the San Coos river, and 116 miles E.S.E. from Khatmandoo. Lat. 27° 6′, long. 87°.

UKHTA.—A town in the British district of Sarun, lieut.-gov. of Bengal, 48 miles E. by S. of Bettiah. Lat. 26° 40′, long. 85° 20′.

UKLEEMPOOR, in the British district of Goorgaon, lieut.-gov. of the N.W. Provinces, a village on the southern shore of an extensive fresh-water jhil or lake. Distance S.W. from Delhi 50 miles. Lat. 27° 58′, long. 77° 2′.

UKPA, in Bussahir, a village in the district of Koonawar, on the right bank of the Sutlej, along which the route proceeds, about a mile from the stream, over a rocky surface, and amidst pine-forests. Ukpa is at the elevation of 8,450 feet above the sea. Lat. 31° 35′, long. 78° 26′.

ULAYI, in the British district of Budaon, the principal place in the pergunnah so called, is situate on the right bank of the Ganges. Lat. 27° 51′, long. 79°.

ULLAEE, in the Rajpoot state of Jodhpoor, a village on the route from Nagor to Beekaneer, and 14 miles N.W. of the former. It contains eighty houses, supplied with water from two tanks and three wells. Lat. 27° 20′, long. 73° 40′.

ULLAGAUVERY.—A town in the British district of Tinnevelly, presidency of Madras, 34 miles N. of Tinnevelly. Lat. 9° 13′, long. 77° 41′.

ULLAH BUND, on the southern frontier of Sinde, a ridge of earth of slight elevation, thrown up by the earthquake of 1819, across the Phurraun or Poorana branch of the Indus. The name signifies "the mound of God," and was given to it by the natives, in allusion to the fact of its not having been made by human efforts. It is thus described by Burnes: "The Ullah Bund, which I now examined with attention, was, however, the most singular consequence of this great earthquake. To the eye it did not appear more elevated in one place than another, and could be traced both east and west as far as it could reach. The natives assigned it a total length of fifty miles. It must not, however, be supposed to be a narrow strip, like an artificial dam, as it extends inland to Ramoaka Bazar, perhaps to about a breadth of sixteen miles, and appeared to be a great upheaving of nature. Its surface was covered with saline soil, and I have already stated that it consisted of shells, clay, and sand." In 1826, a great inundation of the Indus poured such a stream over the desert, that it cut through the Ullah Bund, forming a channel thirty-five yards wide and about thirty feet deep, and immediately below that bank expanded into a lake, covering a surface of 2,000 square miles. This watery expanse received from Burnes the name of the Lake of Sidree, being that of a small fort which it overwhelmed. The place where the Ullah Bund was intersected by the Phurraun is in lat. 24° 21′, long. 69° 11′.

ULLEEGUNGE, or ALLEEGUNGE, in the British district of Bareilly, lieut.-gov. of the N.W. Provinces, a town on the route from the city of Agra to the town of Bareilly, and 13 miles S.W. of the latter. Supplies may be had here in abundance. Lat. 28° 20′, long. 79° 19′.

ULLEEGUNGE, or ALLEEGUNGE, in the British district of Furruckabad, lieut.-gov. of the N.W. Provinces, a town on the route from the cantonment of Allygurh to that of Futtehgurh, and 32 miles N.W. of the latter. It is surrounded by a mud wall, and has a bazar; water is plentiful from wells: the town contains a population of 8,429 persons. Lat. 27° 29′, long. 79° 14′.

ULLEHPOOR.—A town in the British district of Bijnour, lieut.-gov. of N.W. Provinces. Lat. 29° 19′, long. 78° 43′.

ULLYNUGGURH.—A town in the British district of Madura, presidency of Madras, 44 miles W. by N. of Madura. Lat. 10° 3′, long. 77° 33′.

ULTAFGUNJ, in the territory of Oude, a village on the route from Azimgurh to Fyzabad, 56 miles N.W. of the former, 30 S.E. of the latter, situate two miles S.W. of the right bank of the Deoha or Gogra. Lat. 26° 39′, long. 82° 28′.

ULTEAH.—A town in the native state of Kolapoor, presidency of Bombay, 14 miles E.N.E. from Kolapoor, and 66 miles N. from Belgaum. Lat. 16° 47′, long. 74° 30′.

ULUKDEO, in the British district of Bareilly, division of Pillibheet, lieut.-gov. of the N.W. Provinces, a town on the route from the town of Pillibheet to Nugena, and 40 miles N.W. of the former. Lat. 28° 59′, long. 79° 20′.

ULWAR.—See MACHERY.

UMARAWUTTY.—A town in the British district of Guntoor, presidency of Madras, 20 miles N. of Guntoor. Lat. 16° 34', long. 80° 26'.

UMARPOOR, in the British district of Mynpooree, lieut.-gov. of the N.W. Provinces, a town lying on the route from the cantonment of Aligurh to that of Futtehgurh, and 47 miles S.E. of the former. It has a bazar. Lat. 27° 42', long. 78° 48'.

UMBALLA. — A British district of Sirhind, within the Cis-Sutlej division of territory: its centre is in lat. 30° 23', long. 76° 44': its area is stated at 1,832 square miles, and its population as amounting to 782,017. Umballa is one of those possessions which, previously held by a Sikh sirdar, has escheated to the East-India Company in default of rightful heirs. This district was seized by Runjeet Singh during one of his marauding expeditions to the left of the Sutlej; and that aggression occasioned in 1809 the movement of British troops, which resulted in the conclusion of a treaty with Runjeet Singh, by which he was required to withdraw his army from the left bank of the Sutlej, and to relinquish his recent conquests in Sirhind. The climate of Umballa is very hot: in 1838 the thermometer reached 112° in the shade, in June; and in January of the same year it at no time fell lower than 33°.

UMBALLA.—A town, the chief place of a British district within the tract of country called Sirhind. It lies on the route from Kurnoul to Loodiana, 55 miles N. of the former, 69 S.E. of the latter. It is a large walled town, situate in a level and highly-cultivated country, well supplied with water, and capable of furnishing abundant supplies. The houses are built of burnt brick, but the streets are in general so narrow as scarcely to admit the passage of an elephant. The population of the town is given at 21,962. There is a fort at the north-east of the town, and under its walls the encamping-ground of the British troops. Height of the town above the sea 1,040 feet; distant from Calcutta, N.W., by Lucknow, Delhi, and Kurnoul, 1,020 miles. Lat. 30° 24', long. 76° 49'.

UMBARI, in the British district of Dehra Doon, a village on the route from Dehra to Kalsi, and 18 miles N.W. of the former place, situate close to the left bank of the Jumna. Lat. 30° 29', long. 77° 52'.

UMBUD.—A town in Hyderabad, or territory of the Nizam, 17 miles S. by W. from Jaulnah, and 84 miles N.E. by E. from Ahmednuggur. Lat. 19° 37', long. 75° 54'.

UMBUHTUH, in the British district of Suharunpoor, lieut.-gov. of the N.W. Provinces, a town on the route from Kurnaul to Suharunpoor, 16 miles W.S.W. of the latter. Lat. 29° 51', long. 77° 24'.

UMILEA, or UNULEA, in the British district of Cawnpore, lieut.-gov. of the N.W. Provinces, a village on the route from the cantonment of Cawnpore to that of Futtehgurh, and 14 miles N.W. of the former. Lat. 26° 36', long. 80° 16'.

UMLAH.—A town of Malwa, in the native state of Bhopal, 33 miles W.S.W. from Bhopal, and 73 miles E.N.E. from Indoor. Lat. 23° 7', long. 76° 54'.

UMLYALLA, in Guzerat, or the territory of the Guicowar, a town situate on a small river tributary to the river Saburmuttee; distance from Ahmedabad, N.E., 34 miles. Lat. 23° 11', long. 73° 4'.

UMMERAPOORA.—A town of Burmah, situate on the left bank of the Irawady river, and nine miles N.E. from Ava. Lat. 21° 57', long. 96° 7'.

UMMURKUNTUK.—See AMARAKANTAK.

UMRAPOOR.—A town in Hyderabad, or territory of the Nizam, situate on the left bank of the Payne Gunga river, and 90 miles S.W. from Ellichpoor. Lat. 20° 23', long. 76° 30'.

UMREYLEE.—See AMREELI.

UMROHAH, in the British district of Moradabad, lieut.-gov. of the N.W. Provinces, a town on the route from the town of Moradabad to that of Mozuffurnuggur, and twenty miles N.W. of the former place. It is of considerable size, having a population of 72,677 inhabitants, and is situate in an open country, partially cultivated. Distance N.W. from Calcutta 908 miles. Lat. 28° 54', long. 78° 33'.

UMROUDA, in the British district of Cawnpore, lieut.-gov. of the N.W. Provinces, a village on the route from Calpee to Etawa, and seven miles N. of the former. Lat. 26° 12', long. 79° 51'.

UMUR SAGUR, in the Rajpoot state of Jesulmer, a village on the route from Roree, in Sindh, to the town of Jesulmer, and two miles N.W. of the latter. It contains about twenty shops, and water is obtainable from tanks. Lat. 26° 55', long. 70° 57'.

UMURGURH.—A town in the native state of Narbah, Cis-Sutlej territory, 40 miles W. from Ambala, and 34 miles S.S.E. from Loodianah. Lat. 30° 29', long. 76° 9'.

UMURKHERA.—See ANWULKHERA.

UNA, in the Julinder Dooab division of the Punjab, a town situate eight miles from the right bank of the Sutlej, 46 miles E.N.E. of the town of Jullinder. Lat. 31° 28', long. 76° 19'.

UNAO, in the territory of Oude, a small town on the route from Cawnpore to Lucknow, 10 miles N.E. of the former, 43 S.W. of the latter. It has a bazar, and is well provided with water. Lat. 26° 33', long. 80° 33'.

UNCHAGANW, in the British district of Pillibheet, lieut.-gov. of the N.W. Provinces, a village on the route by Nanakmath to Ruderpoor, from the town of Pillibheet, 35 miles N.W. of the latter, situate one and a half miles west of the right bank of the river Goula. Lat. 28° 58', long. 79° 36'.

UNCHAPAHAR, in the Rajpoot territory of Shekawuttee, a lofty hill five miles S.E. of the town of Seekar. The whole surface of the hill is covered with jungle, chiefly of cactus, except the summit, which is a platform or small table-land, about a mile in length and a hundred yards in breadth. Distance S.W. from Delhi 140 miles, N.W. from Jeypoor 55. Lat. 27° 32′, long. 75° 20′.

UNCHGANO, in the district of Aldemau, territory of Oude, a village three miles S.W. of the right bank of the Tons (North-eastern), 14 S. of Fyzabad. Butter estimates the population at 400, all Hindoos. Lat. 26° 38′, long. 82° 9′.

UNDERA, in the British district of Muzuffurnugur, lieut.-gov. of the N.W. Provinces, a village on the route from Kurnal to Meerut, and nine miles S.E. of the former. Lat. 29° 38′, long. 77° 9′.

UNDERSOOL.—A town in the British district of Ahmednuggur, presidency of Bombay, 53 miles E. of Nassik. Lat. 20°, long. 74° 36′.

UNGHHA.—A town in the British district of Behar, lieut.-gov. of Bengal, 41 miles N.W. of Shergotty. Lat. 25°, long. 84° 26′.

UNGOOL.—See ANGOOL.

UNGOTHA, in the British district of Agra, lieut.-gov. of the N.W. Provinces, a village on the route from the city of Agra to that of Bhurtpore, and 11 miles W. of the former. Lat. 27° 10′, long. 77° 57′.

UNJENGAUM.—A town in one of the recently sequestrated districts of Hyderabad, or dominions of the Nizam, situate 14 miles W.S.W. of Ellichpoor. Lat. 21° 6′, long. 77° 21′.

UNJUNVEL.—A town in the British district of Rutnageriah, presidency of Bombay, 39 miles N. of Rutnageriah. Lat. 17° 31′, long. 73° 15′.

UNKARJEE MAHARAJ, or MUNDATTA, in territory of Gwalior, or possessions of Scindia's family, a small town with bazar, on the south side of an island in the river Nerbudda. Lat. 22° 12′, long. 76° 15′.

UNKOLA.—The principal place of the subdivision of the same name, in the British district of North Canara, presidency of Madras, a town two miles from the coast of the Arabian Sea, or North Indian Ocean. It has a ruinous fort and a bazar, but few inhabitants, as in this part of the country the population does not settle in numbers in any spot, but is dispersed in hamlets and farms. Distant from Mangalore, N., 130 miles; Bombay, S., 310. Lat. 14° 40′, long. 74° 22′.

UNNOOSOORA.—A town in the British district of Pooree, lieut.-gov. of Bengal, 42 miles S.S.E. of Cuttack. Lat. 19° 56′, long. 86° 11′.

UNOULA, in the British district of Goruckpore, the principal place of the pergunnah of the same name, a small town on the route from the town of Azimgurh to that of Goruckpoor, 48 miles N. of the former, 13 S. of the latter. The road in this part of the route is much cut up, the country level, much overrun with forest and jungle. It is situate near the river Ami, the channel of which is in that part thirty or forty yards wide, and even in the dry season filled from side to side with a deep, though nearly stagnant, body of water: the route from Azimgurh to Goruckpoor crosses it by a bridge. Distant N. of Benares 90 miles. Lat. 26° 32′, long. 83° 21′.

UNOWAH, in the British district of Allahabad, lieut.-gov. of the N.W. Provinces, a village on the route from the cantonment of Allahabad to Futtehpoor, and 33 miles N.W. of the former. Lat. 25° 37′, long. 81° 29′.

UNRAWATTY RIVER, a tributary of the Taptee, rises in lat. 21° 26′, long. 75° 39′, and flowing for thirty-three miles westerly, through a portion of Holkar's territory, and south-westerly for thirty miles, through the British district of Candeish, falls into the Taptee river, in lat. 21° 20′, long. 74° 55′.

UNTA DHURA, on the northern frontier of the British district of Kumaon, lieut.-gov. of the N.W. Provinces, a pass on the northern frontier towards Hiundes, or South-western Tibet. It lies over a ridge, which is to the north of the main chain of the Himalaya, and though inferior as to its summits than the greater range, has such continuity of elevation as to render it necessary to ascend considerably in proceeding towards Hiundes from the deep gorges of Kumaon. The crest forms the water-line dividing the streams flowing southwards into the basin of the Ganges from those taking a northerly direction towards the Sutlej, as the Louka, a small river rising on the northern declivity of the pass, has a due northerly course, and the Gunka, rising on the southerly declivity, proceeds southwards to the Goree, by which its water is conveyed to the Kalee, and ultimately to the Ganges. The view towards Thibet is little striking: the actual elevation is, however, very great, Weller's observations by the boiling-water point causing it to come out at 18,540 feet above the level of the sea; but he considers this to be probably a good deal in excess; and Manson estimates it at 17,500. In the end of May, Weller found a dreadfully cold wind blowing, and was informed that it becomes awful at the end of the rains, sometimes sweeping down the precipices numbers of the laden sheep and goats, which are the beasts of burthen usually employed in the trade between Kumaon and Hiundes. Even in the end of May, in 1841, Batten found the pass closed by heavy snow, and encountered imminent danger in attempting it: Webb also found it completely closed with snow in the beginning of summer. It is sometimes called the Juwahir Pass, as the route lying over it passes up the Juwahir valley by the courses of the rivers Gooree and

Gunka. According to Garden, there is "encamping-ground on the bank of a stream at the northern base of the Himalaya range: a few stunted bushes to be found for firewood; no supplies. The Thibet frontier is distant four miles north, marked by a low wall." He adds, that snow lies on the pass eleven months in the year. Distant N. from Fort Almorah 156 miles. Lat. 30° 35′, long. 80° 17′.

UNTOOR.—A town in Hyderabad, or territory of the Nizam, 38 miles N. from Dowlutabad, and 50 miles E. from Malligaum. Lat. 20° 29′, long. 75° 16′.

UPKOT, in the British district of Kumaon, lieut.-gov. of the N.W. Provinces, a village on the route by the course of the Surjoo from Almorah fort to the Unta Dhura Pass. It is situate on the right bank of the Surjoo, 42 miles N.E. of Almorah. Lat. 29° 57′, long. 79° 54′.

UPNI and KILANSIR, in the Rajpoot state of Beekaneer, two contiguous villages on the route from Rutungurh to the town of Beekaneer, and 45 miles E. of the latter. They contain 170 houses, supplied with water from two wells 120 feet deep. Lat. 27° 54′, long. 74° 5′.

UPPAEL, in the British district of Ghazeepore, lieut.-gov. of the N.W. Provinces, a town with a population of 5,946 inhabitants, 37 miles N.E. of Ghazeepore. Lat. 25° 49′, long. 84° 10′.

UPSUNG, in Bussahir, a stream of the district of Koonawar, takes its rise in lat. 31° 46′, long. 78° 43′, on the western declivity of a lofty mountain running in a direction from north to south, and forming the boundary between the British and Chinese empires, and after a very rapid course of about five miles, generally in a northerly direction, falls into the Sutlej, on the left side. Gerard describes the ravine down which it flows as peculiarly wild and rugged:—"Before is the abyss of the Oopsung; the rocks are grouped together, and menace the traveller with horror, and he expects to be annihilated at every step. The deep indentations, formed by rushing torrents, must be followed into their darkest windings; and it is in such situations, when the footsteps are tardy and insecure, that the frail outline of the cliffs presses on the imagination." The bed of the Upsung where crossed by Gerard, about a mile above the confluence with the Sutlej, was found to have an elevation of 10,989 feet above the sea.

URDAPOOR.—A town in Hyderabad, or territory of the Nizam, eight miles from the left bank of the Godavery river, and 151 miles N.W. by N. from Hyderabad. Lat. 19° 17′, long. 77° 27′.

URDUN.—A town in the peninsula of Kattywar, province of Guzerat, 47 miles S. by E. from Rajkote, and 63 miles N. from Diu Fort and Island. Lat. 21° 39′, long. 70° 56′.

UREREAL.—A town in the British district of Purneah, lieut.-gov. of Bengal, 22 miles N. by E. of Purneah. Lat. 26° 4′, long. 87° 39′.

URIDACHELLUM.—A town in the British district of South Arcot, presidency of Madras, 31 miles W.S.W. of Cuddalore. Lat. 11° 32′, long. 79° 23′.

URJUNPUR, in the British district of Mynpooree, lieut.-gov. of the N.W. Provinces, a village on the route from the cantonment of Aligurh to that of Futtehgurh, and 51 miles S.E. of the former. Lat. 27° 41′, long. 78° 52′.

URKI.—A fort of the hill state of Bhagul, situate amidst the steep and lofty ridges on the eastern frontier. It was garrisoned by the Goorkha army during the war between that power and the British, who acquired possession of it by the capitulation which preceded the treaty of 1815. Lat. 31° 9′, long. 77° 2′.

URMULLA.—A town in the British district of Balasore, lieut.-gov. of Bengal, eight miles W. of Balasore. Lat. 21° 30′, long. 86° 52′.

URNIA.—A town in the native state of Indore, or territory of Holkar, 47 miles N. from Indoor, and 93 miles S.E. by S. from Neemuch. Lat. 23° 21′, long. 75° 44′.

URROUL, in the British district of Cawnpore, lieut.-gov. of the N.W. Provinces, a town on the route from the cantonment of Cawnpore to that of Futehgurh, and 42 miles S.E. of the latter. In 1803, the British army encamped on the spacious plain around the town, preparatory to the expedition under General Lake against the Mahrattas. Lat. 26° 54′, long. 80° 6′.

URRUKTA, in the hill state of Joobul, a mountain forming part of the great range connecting Wartu peak with that of Chur. It is covered at the top with deep and lofty forests of pines, oaks, and sycamores, with which are intermixed birches, hollies, and yews. The formation of the rock is mica-slate, mixed with veins of quartz. The route from Chepal to Deohra passes by a good mountain-road over the crest of the mountain, between two summits, each about 11,000 feet. The highest point of the route has the elevation of 9,729 feet above the sea. The pass is styled that of Puthur Nulla in the trigonometrical survey. Lat. 31° 3′, long. 77° 44′.

URRUNDE, or RIND, a small river of the Doab, rises in the British district of Mynpoorie, about 35 miles N.W. of the town of that name, and in lat. 27° 27′, long. 78° 34′. Its headwaters are on the south-west or Jumna side of the crest or slightly-elevated tract which marks the interior of the Doab, nearly equidistant from the Ganges and Jumna. The course is tortuous, but generally in a south-easterly direction, to its discharge into the Jumna on the left side, in lat. 25° 54′, long. 80° 37′, after a total length of about 245 miles. It is fordable where crossed by the route from Etawah to Futtehgurh, seventy-five miles from its source, measured along the river banks. Where crossed by the route from Calpee to Futtehgurh, 135 miles from its source, its channel is forty yards wide, with steep banks, and in the dry season the stream is not more than knee-deep.

URRUR, in the native state of Travancore, a town near the coast of the Northern Indian Ocean, among the numerous salt-water lakes and islets in that part of the country. Distance from Cochin, S.E., nine miles; Trivandrum, N., 122; Madras, S.W., 440. Lat. 9° 52′, long. 76° 22′.

URSEEMAREE.—A town in the territory of Nagpoor, 56 miles N.E. by E. from Ruttunpoor, and 118 miles N.W. from Sumbulpoor. Lat. 22° 43′, long. 82° 48′.

URUBA, in the Rajpoot state of Jodhpoor, a village on the route from Balotra to the city of Jodhpoor, and 30 miles N.E. of the former. The road in this part of the route is good, and lies through a level country, rather fertile and cultivated. Lat. 26° 3′, long. 72° 45′.

URWUL, in the British district of Behar, lieut.-gov. of Bengal, a small town on the right bank of the river Sone. Though an insignificant place, it has an indigo-factory, and good paper is manufactured here. It is the principal place of a thana or police-division, well cultivated in general, and producing largely opium and grain, though a few parts have been impoverished by sand blown from the wide bed of the Sone. The thana contains 313 villages, and a population of 50,554 persons, of whom the Brahminists are three to one to the Mussulmans. The town contains 196 houses, and a population of 1,000. Distant S.W. from Patna 41 miles, E. from Benares 103. Lat. 25° 11′, long. 84° 42′.

USABAD, in the British district of Agra, a village on the route from the city of Agra to Mynpooree, and 29 miles E. of the former. The road in this part of the route is good; the country cultivated, and studded with small villages. Lat. 27° 8′, long. 78° 30′.

USEGAH, or ASEEGHA, in the British district of Ghazeepoor, lieut.-gov. of the N.W. Provinces, a town with a population of 7,807 inhabitants, 10 miles N.E. of Ghazeepoor. Lat. 25° 53′, long. 84° 13′.

USHUN, a small river of Keonthal, rises a few miles east of Simla, at the southern base of the mountain of Mahhasu, in lat. 31° 6′, long. 77° 18′, and holding a course first in a south-westerly, and then in a south-easterly direction, falls into the Girree, in lat. 30° 54′, long. 77° 17′, after having run a distance of about twenty-five miles.

USIL, in Gurhwal, a village on the right bank of the Supin, here a powerful and amazingly rapid torrent. It was a secondary station in the great trigonometrical survey of the Himalaya. Elevation above the sea 8,936 feet. Lat. 31° 7′, long. 78° 25′.

USLANA, in the British district of Dumoh, territory of Saugor and Nerbudda, lieut.-gov. of the N.W. Provinces, a town on the route from Dumoh to Tehree, 13 miles N.W. of the former. Lat. 23° 57′, long. 79° 22′.

USNI, in the British district of Futtehpoor, lieut.-gov. of the N.W. Provinces, a town on the right bank of the Ganges, nearly opposite Dalmau, and 15 miles N.E. of the town of Futtehpoor. Lat. 26° 3′, long. 81° 6′.

USUDPOOR, in the British district of Buddaon, lieut.-gov. of the N.W. Provinces, a town on the route from Boolundshuhur to Buddaon, 42 miles W. by N. of the latter. Lat. 28° 11′, long. 78° 32′.

USURI, in the Mysore, a town on the south-east bank of an extensive tank; distance N.W. from Bangalore 52 miles. Lat. 13° 35′, long. 77° 30′.

USYA MUT.—A town in the native state of Sawuntwarree, 29 miles N.W. from Sawuntwarree, and 59 miles S.S.E. from Rutnageriah. Lat. 16° 14′, long. 73° 46′.

UTGHOR, in the British district of Banda, lieut.-gov. of the N.W. Provinces, a village on the route from the town of Banda to Gwalior, 11 miles W. of the former. Water is plentiful from wells. Lat. 25° 30′, long. 80° 13′.

UTREE.—A town in the British district of Behar, lieut.-gov. of Bengal, 28 miles S.W. of Behar. Lat. 24° 55′, long. 85° 20′.

UTTARI, in the jaghire of Bulubghur, lieut.-gov. of the N.W. Provinces, a village situate near the right bank of the Jumna. Distance S.E. from Delhi 28 miles. Lat. 28° 18′, long. 77° 29′.

UTTUR.—A town in the British district of Coimbatoor, presidency of Madras, 64 miles N.N.E. of Coimbatoor. Lat. 11° 51′, long. 77° 20′.

UTURHUT, in the British district of Banda, lieut.-gov. of the N.W. Provinces, a village on the route by Chila Tara ghat, from Cawnpore to the town of Banda, 13 miles N. of the latter. Lat. 25° 40′, long. 80° 31′.

V.

VADARNEAM.—A town in the British district of Tanjore, presidency of Madras, 56 miles S.E. by E. of Tanjore. Lat. 10° 24′, long. 79° 54′.

VADASUNDOOR.—A town in the British district of Madura, presidency of Madras, 44 miles N. by W. of Madura. Lat. 10° 32′, long. 78° 2′.

VAIMBAUR.—A town in the British district of Tinnevelly, presidency of Madras, 53 miles E.N.E. of Tinnevelly. Lat. 9° 6′, long. 78° 25′.

VAIPU, in the territory of Cochin, under the political superintendence of the Madras presidency, a town at the southern extremity of a long narrow island, bounded south-west by the Arabian Sea, and on all other sides by the Backwater, as the British denominate the extensive shallow lake or estuary formed by the streams flowing westward from the Western Ghats. Distance from the city of Cochin, E., two miles; Cannanore, S.E., 145; Bangalore, S.W., 225. Lat. 9° 58′, long. 76° 18′.

VAIPUR.—A river in the British district of Tinnevelly, presidency of Madras, rises near the western frontier, on the eastern declivity of the Eastern Ghats, and in about lat. 9° 25′, long. 77° 20′. Taking an easterly, and in some places south-easterly, course of about eighty miles, it falls into the Gulf of Manar, in lat. 9°, long. 78° 20′.

VAIRAWULL.—A town in the peninsula of Kattywar, province of Guzerat, situate on the seacoast, 40 miles W. by N. from Diu Island, and 102 miles S. by W. from Rajkote. Lat. 20° 55′, long. 70° 21′.

VALAL.—A town in Hyderabad, or territory of the Nizam, situate on the left bank of the Tandoor river, and 59 miles W. by S. from Hyderabad. Lat. 17° 11′, long. 77° 40′.

VALAM.—A town in the British district of Tanjore, presidency of Madras, six miles W.S.W. of Tanjore. Lat. 10° 45′, long. 79° 7′.

VALAMPUTTU.—A town in the British district of Salem, presidency of Madras, 32 miles E. by N. of Salem. Lat. 11° 47′, long. 78° 41′.

VALENGOODY.—A town in the British district of Madura, presidency of Madras, 40 miles N.E. by E. of Madura. Lat. 10° 13′, long. 78° 40′.

VALLARAPULLAI, in the territory of Cochin, under the political superintendence of the presidency of Madras, a town in a small portion of territory isolated amidst the dominions of the rajah of Travancore. Distance from the city of Cochin, N.E., 18 miles. Lat. 10° 18′, long. 76° 28′.

VALOOCURRAY.—A town in the native state of Cochin, 14 miles S. from Trichoor, and 26 miles N. from Cochin. Lat. 10° 20′, long. 76° 18′.

VALOOR.—A town in the British district of Salem, presidency of Madras, 18 miles E.N.E. of Salem. Lat. 11° 44′, long. 78° 29′.

VALOOR.—A town in Hyderabad, or territory of the Nizam, situate on the left bank of the Doodna river, and 127 miles E. by N. from Ahmednuggur. Lat. 19° 29′, long. 76° 39′.

VAMILAPOORA.—An ancient town of Kattywar, in the province of Guzerat, the ruins of which still exist. It is situate on the river Karree, not far from the town of Wulleh, a considerable portion of which is built of materials brought from the ruins of Vamilapoora. The site of the ancient town is about lat. 21° 50′, long. 71° 53′.

VAMULCONDA.—A town in Hyderabad, or territory of the Nizam, 44 miles E. from Hyderabad, and 116 miles N.W. from Guntoor. Lat. 17° 23′, long. 79° 11′.

VANDIVASH.—A town in the British district of North Arcot, presidency of Madras, 34 miles S.E. by S. of Arcot. Lat. 12° 30′, long. 79° 40′.

VANIAMBADDY.—A town in the British district of Salem, presidency of Madras, 78 miles N.N.E. of Salem. Lat. 12° 41′, long. 78° 40′.

VANKEELUPADU.—A town in the British district of Guntoor, presidency of Madras, 31 miles S.S.W. of Guntoor. Lat. 15° 56′, long. 80° 17′.

VARDHA CHATRA.—A town in Nepal, situate on the left bank of the San Coos river, and 124 miles E.S.E. from Khatmandoo. Lat. 26° 57′, long. 87° 4′.

VARIGUNTAPADU.—A town in the British district of Nellore, presidency of Madras, 41 miles W. by N. of Nellore. Lat. 14° 34′, long. 79° 26′.

VAULRAMPOOR.—A town in the native state of Travancore, 44 miles N.W. by W. from Cape Comorin, and seven miles S.E. from Trivandrum. Lat. 8° 26′, long. 77° 5′.

VAZIRGANJ, in the territory of Oude, a ruined town on the route, by Nanamau Ghat or ferry, from Futtehghur to Lucknow, seven miles S.W. of the latter. According to Lord Valentia, who visited it in 1803, "Viziergunge consists only of the two gateways, and about three houses in the centre between them. It seems as if it had been built as an ornamental approach to Lucknow, a large avenue extending thither from it." Tennant, however, attributes its want of population to a frightful instance of despotic vengeance. "The cause of its destruction is said to have been the refusal of the cutwal [municipal magistrate] to deliver up some thieves who had molested passengers going through it. On being threatened with the nawab's vengeance, it, unluckily for the town, happened that some persons were again robbed there that same day. On the next, three battalions were ordered to ransack the town and destroy the inhabitants; an order which they obeyed with such fatal exactness, that not a single hut nor inhabitant was left within the walls. The distance between the two gates is more than a mile, and that constituted the length of the principal street. The rows of trees on each side are still standing, having escaped the flames by which the houses were destroyed." Lat. 26° 46′, long. 80° 53′.

VEBOO.—A town in the British district of Amherst, one of the Tenasserim provinces, 41 miles E. of Moulmein. Lat. 16° 33′, long. 98° 19′.

VEDAVATI.—A name sometimes given to the river Hugry, which see.

VEEJOVA.—A town in the Rajpoot state of Godwar, 63 miles S.S.E. from Jodhpoor, and 110 miles S.W. from Nusseerabad. Lat. 25° 26′, long. 73° 26′.

VEERAGANOOR, in the British district of Salem, presidency of Madras, 33 miles E. by S. of Salem. Lat. 11° 29′, long. 78° 50′.

VEERAJENDERPETTA, in the British province of Coorg, presidency of Madras, a town situate on a small feeder of the Cauvery. It is the largest town in the district, and is principally inhabited by native Christians. In the year 1834, a British column under command of Colonel Foulis, proceeding from Cannanore eastward, after a succession of some days' hard fighting in the defiles of the Western Ghats, penetrated to this town, and forming a junction with the eastern column under Colonel Lindsay, who, proceeding from Mysore, had occupied Merkara, the capital, effectually subdued the country. Elevation above the sea 3,399 feet; distance from Merkara, S., 16 miles; Mangalore, S.E., 80; Bangalore, S.W., 130. Lat. 12° 13′, long. 75° 52′.

VEERAPULLY.—A town in the British district of Cuddapah, presidency of Madras, 23 miles S. of Cuddapah. Lat. 14° 9′, long. 78° 55′.

VEERAVASANUM.—A town in the British district of Rajahmundry, presidency of Madras, 35 miles S. by W. of Rajahmundry. Lat. 16° 31′, long. 81° 41′.

VEERAWOW.—A town in the British district of Hydrabad, province of Scinde, presidency of Bombay, 153 miles E.S.E. of Hydrabad. Lat. 24° 30′, long. 70° 41′.

VEERUMGAUM, in the British district of Ahmedabad, presidency of Bombay, a town near the south-eastern angle of the Runn, or Great Salt Marsh. It is now a thriving place, though but recently revived from a state of great poverty and decay: population 17,000; distance from the city of Ahmedabad 35 miles W. Lat. 23° 7′, long. 72°.

VEESAWUDUR.—A town in the peninsula of Kattywar, province of Guzerat, situate 74 miles S. from Rajkote, and 40 miles N.N.W. from Diu Island and Fort. Lat. 21° 15′, long. 70° 48′.

VEESHALGURH.—See VISHALGURH.

VELAPOOR.—A town in the British district of Sattara, presidency of Bombay, 70 miles E. by N. of Sattara. Lat. 17° 47′, long. 75° 8′.

VELLACOIL.—A town in the British district of Coimbatoor, presidency of Madras, 50 miles E. of Coimbatoor. Lat. 10° 57′, long. 77° 45′.

VELLARY KYEN.—A town in the British district of Malabar, presidency of Madras, 124 miles S.E. of Cannanore. Lat. 10° 30′, long. 76° 38′.

VELLAUR.—A river of the Madras presidency, rising in lat. 10° 28′, long. 78° 21′, and, taking an easterly direction through Madura, Poodoocottah, and Tanjore, falls into the sea, in lat. 10° 6′, long. 79° 17′.

VELLAUR.—A river of the Madras presidency, rising at the base of the Eastern Ghauts, within the British district of South Arcot, and, taking an easterly direction, falls into the sea just below the town of Porto Novo, in lat. 11° 29′, long. 79° 50′. The river is small at its mouth, and admits only coasting craft. The waters of the Vellaur are economized for the purpose of irrigation, by means of a dam or annicut thrown across the river.

VELLORE, in the British district of Arcot, north division, presidency of Madras, a town, with strong fort, on the south or right side of the river Palar. The fort is extensive, with ramparts built of very large stones, and having bastions and round towers at short distances. Between the bastions is a covered way, with embattled wall, and small projecting square towers, which have a striking and pleasing appearance. A deep and wide ditch, cut in the solid rock, surrounds the whole fort, and is filled with good clear water of considerable depth. Within the compass of the ramparts are barracks, hospitals, magazines, and some other buildings, occupied from time to time by state prisoners. East of the fort are some rocky hills, which so completely command it, that a six-pounder could throw a shot over it. The town, situate between the hills and the fort, is rather clean and airy, and has an extensive and well-supplied bazar. The heat at Vellore is very great, as is thought from the radiation from the rocky hills in the neighbourhood; yet the station is considered one of the healthiest in the Carnatic, and regiments arriving from unhealthy quarters in debilitated states have recovered here very quickly. The most remarkable public building at Vellore is a splendid pagoda, apparently dedicated to Krishna, whose adventures with the gopis or milkmaids are represented in a series of spirited and elaborate sculptures. On the inside of the gateway are numerous figures of Rama, the renowned king of Ayodha or Oude, with Hanuman, the martial monkey leader, and his numerous troop of monkey-shaped warriors. There are also numerous sculptures representing Nandi, the bull-shaped attendant of Siva. The erection of a church within the fort was sanctioned by the British government in 1846.

Upon the fall of Seringapatam, the fortress of Vellore had been chosen for the future residence of the sons of Tippoo. The selection was injudicious, as the neighbourhood swarmed with the adherents of the deposed family. On the morning of the 10th July, 1806, the native troops rose against the European part of the garrison, consisting of two companies of the 69th regiment. The attack was totally unexpected; but upon the arrival from the cantonment of Arcot of Colonel Gillespie, with a party of the 19th dragoons, the mutineers were quickly overcome, and order re-established in the fortress. The number of Europeans massacred by the insurgents amounted to 113. Among them were Colonel Fancourt and thirteen other officers. Three hundred and fifty of the mutineers fell in the attack, and about five hundred were made prisoners. Two of the sons of Tippoo were stated to be implicated in the revolt, and the family of that chieftain were forthwith removed to Bengal. The population is returned at 51,500. Vellore is distant from Madura, N., 220 miles; Tanjore, N., 147; Bangalore, E., 104; Arcot, W., 16; Cuddalore, N.W., 94; Madras, W., 79. Lat. 12° 55′, long. 79° 11′.

VELUNGOOR.—A town in the native state of Travancore, 114 miles N.N.W. from Trivandrum, and 14 miles E.N.E. from Cochin. Lat. 10° 3′, long. 76° 29′.

VENCÂTIGERRY.—A town in the British district of North Arcot, presidency of Madras, 59 miles W. by N. of Arcot. Lat. 13°, long. 78° 32′.

VENCATIGERRY.—A town in the British district of North Arcot, presidency of Madras, 72 miles N. by E. of Arcot. Lat. 13° 55′, long. 79° 34′.

VENCATIGHERRY DROOG.—A town in the British district of North Arcot, presidency of Madras, 75 miles N. by E. of Arcot. Lat. 13° 57′, long. 79° 31′.

VENKATREDDYPOLLIAM.—A town in the British district of Cuddapah, presidency of Madras, 113 miles N. by E. of Cuddapah. Lat. 16° 3′, long. 79° 17′.

VENKITAGHERRY.—A town in the British district of North Arcot, presidency of Madras, 36 miles N.W. by W. of Arcot. Lat. 13° 11′, long. 78° 58′.

VENTIPUR, or WANTIPUR, in Cashmere, a village containing ruins, considered by some to be those of the original capital of the valley. It is situate near the right bank of the Jhelum, on the route from Sirinagur to Islamabad, and 16 miles S.E. of the former town. According to the chronicles of Cashmere, it was founded about A.D. 876, by Avanti Verma, king of the valley, who, after his own name, called it Avantipur. Here are the ruins of two great buildings, resembling in plan and character those described in the notice on Matan. The greater ruin is called Vencadati Devi, the less, Ventimadati. They are in a state of extreme dilapidation, yet, according to the detailed account of Moorcroft, are still striking monuments of early architecture. Ventipur is in lat. 33° 54′, long. 75° 9′.

VEPERY.—A suburb of the city of Madras. —See MADRAS.

VERABUDR DROOG.—A town in the British district of Kurnool, presidency of Madras, 30 miles N.E. by E. of Kurnool. Lat. 16° 3′, long. 78° 30′.

VERALLIMALLI.—A town in the British district of Madura, presidency of Madras, 58 miles N.E. by N. of Madura. Lat. 10° 38′, long. 78° 37′.

VERAPOLI, in the territory of Cochin, under the political superintendence of the presidency of Madras, a town on a small island in the extensive shallow lake or estuary called by the British the Backwater. Here is the residence of the pope's vicar-apostolic for Malabar, who superintends sixty-four churches, exclusive of forty-five governed by the archbishop of Cranganore or Kotunglur, and exclusive of the large dioceses of the bishops of Cochin and Quilon, whose churches extend to Cape Comorin, and are visible from the sea. Verapoli is seven miles N.E. of the city of Cochin, 220 S.W. of Bangalore. Lat. 10° 5′, long. 76° 20′.

VERNAG, in Cashmere, in the south-eastern extremity of the valley, is celebrated for a magnificent spring, which rises with a great volume of water, in a basin about 120 yards in circumference, built by the order of the Mogul emperor Jehangir, and forms one of the feeders of the Jhelum. Lat. 33° 29′, long. 75° 15′.

VEYLOOR.—A town in Hyderabad, or territory of the Nizam, 31 miles N. by E. from Hyderabad, and 140 miles N.N.E. from Kurnool. Lat. 17° 47′, long. 78° 37′.

VEYUL.—The name given to the Jhelum in the upper part of its course.—See JHELUM.

VICTORIA FORT, in the collectorate of Rutnagherry, presidency of Bombay, near the town of Bankote. It is situate on a high barren hill, of reddish appearance, on the south side of the entrance of the river Sawitri, "formerly navigable for large ships; but the sandbank at the mouth constantly increasing during the south-west monsoon, it now only admits a passage for small vessels." This place is one of the early acquisitions of the East-India Company within the present limits of the presidency of Bombay, having been ceded in 1756 by the Mahrattas, in exchange for Gheriah, then recently taken by Admiral Watson. Distant S. from city of Bombay 65 miles, S.W. from Poona 65. Lat. 17° 58′, long. 73°.

VIERAVANDY.—A town in the British district of South Arcot, presidency of Madras, 28 miles N.W. by N. of Cuddalore. Lat. 12° 3′, long. 79° 36′.

VIJAYAP.—A town in the native state of Nepal, 134 miles S.E. by E. from Khatmandoo, and 80 miles N.N.W. from Purneah. Lat. 26° 54′, long. 87° 14′.

VIKKUR.—A town in the British district of Kurachee, province of Scinde, 60 miles S.E. by S. of Kurachee. Lat. 24° 11′, long. 67° 40′.

VINCHOR.—A town in the British district of Ahmednuggur, presidency of Bombay. Under the rule of the Peishwa, it was the jaghire or fief of one of the principal Mahratta chiefs, then styled the Vinchorkur or Vinchor jagheerdar. This powerful chief also held in Malwa the five districts of Ashta, Ichawar, Sihor or Sehora, Doraha, and Devipoora, which being ceded by the Peishwa by the treaty of Poona, in 1817, were by the British government granted to the nawaub of Bhopal as a reward for his zeal and fidelity. Vinchor is distant direct from Bombay, N.E., 120 miles. Lat. 20° 8′, long. 74° 12′.

VINDHYA MOUNTAINS.—A chain of mountains crossing the peninsula of India from east to west, forming the northern boundary of the valley of the Nerbudda; and "uniting the northern extremities of the two great lateral ranges (the Eastern and Western Ghauts), forms as it were the base of the triangle which supports the table-land of Southern India." They extend from Guzerat on the west to the basin of the Ganges on the east, and are comprised between the twenty-second and twenty-fifth degrees of latitude. The geological formations are the granitic and sandstone, overlaid by trap rock. Under the Moguls, the country north of the Vindhya range was called Hindostan, and that lying to the south the Deccan.

VINGORLA, in the collectorate of Rutnagherry, presidency of Bombay, a petty town and fort, situate at the mouth of a small river of the same name. Abreast of it, and about two miles from the mainland, are the Vingorla rocks, some of which are about twenty feet above high-water mark, white, and remarkable when the sun shines; while others are even with the water, and very dangerous for shipping. The little bay of Vingorla is completely sheltered from every point of the compass, the south alone excepted. When it blows fresh from that quarter (a rare occurrence, and always of short duration), the little traders make a fair wind of it, and run to Malwan (eighteen miles north), where they remain until the wind changes. There is a road from Vingorla to the interior, proceeding to Belgaum, and thence diverging, one branch leading to Kullogee and Bogulcote, the other to Dharwar, Hooblie, and thence to Sircy, in the Madras territory; but for some distance from Vingorla it is but of an indifferent description. The evil, however, has attracted the attention of both the local and the home authorities, and there is the fullest reason for believing, that as soon as circumstances permit it will be remedied. Vingorla has been conjectured to contain about 5,000 inhabitants: it has a tolerably good bazar, and an increasing number of merchants.

Vingorla was a retreat for the numerous sanguinary pirates who infested this coast, until, in 1812, it was ceded by the chief of Sawuntwarree to the East-India Company. Vingorla is 215 miles S. of the town of Bombay in a direct line; the travelling distance is about 280 miles. Lat. 15° 50′, long. 73° 41′.

VINGUR.—A town in the British district of Hydrabad, province of Scinde, 102 miles S.E. of Hydrabad. Lat. 24° 20′, long. 69° 35′.

VINJAN.—A town in the native state of Cutch, situate 46 miles W. by S. from Bhooj. Lat. 23° 9′, long. 69° 2′.

VINJORAEE, or BINJORAI, in the Rajpoot state of Jessulmer, a town on the route from Balmer, in Joudpore, to the town of Jessulmer, and 30 miles S.E. of the latter. Lat. 26° 30′, long. 71° 10′.

VINUKONDA, in the British district of Guntoor, presidency of Madras, a fort on an eminence of rock composed of quartz and mica. On this hill are two tanks, which afford an excellent supply of water all the year round. It has been supposed to be an extinct volcano; but Heyne observes, that in no part of it can the slightest traces of lava be observed. Distance from the town of Guntoor, S.W., 52 miles; Madras, N., 205. Lat. 16° 4′, long. 79° 48′.

VIRAGHOTTAM.—A town in the British district of Vizagapatam, presidency of Madras, 72 miles N.N.E. of Vizagapatam. Lat. 18° 41′, long. 83° 40′.

VIRDUPUTTY.—A town in the British district of Tinnevelly, presidency of Madras, 62 miles N.N.E. of Tinnevelly. Lat. 9° 36′, long. 78° 1′.

VIRGNAJUNG, in the British district of Kumaon, lieut.-gov. of the N.W. Provinces, a town on the route from Almora to Tibet. Lat. 30° 10′, long. 80° 46′.

VIRSUNDA, in the Peshawur division of the Punjab, a town situated 16 miles from the right bank of the Indus. Lat. 33° 17′, long. 71° 30′.

VISHALGHUR.— A jaghire or feudal dependency of Kolapore: the centre is in lat. 16° 52′, long. 73° 50′, situate in the Ghauts: the country is jungly and rugged. The inhabitants are more hardy and warlike than their neighbours of the plains, and have not unfrequently shown that they participate in the disposition for plundering, which marks the occupants of similar tracts in the vicinity. The revenue of Vishalghur is 1,23,000 rupees; the military force numbers about 170 men. The military service due from the jaghiredar to the government of Colapore has been commuted for a money payment. A proposal is under consideration for the transfer to the British government, of that portion of the possessions of this chief which is situated below the Ghauts.

VISHNOO.—A mountain-torrent rising in the Himalayas, in lat. 31° 4′, long. 79° 28′. It flows in a southerly direction for a distance of forty-three miles, to its junction with the Doulee at Vishnooprag, in lat. 30° 33′, long. 79° 38′; whence the united stream is named the Aluknunda.

VISHNOOPRAG, in the British district of Gurwhal, a town on the route from Sireenuggur to Tibet, 54 miles E.N.E. of the former. Lat. 30° 34′, long. 79° 39′.

VIZAGAPATAM.—A British district named from its principal place, and forming part of the territory subject to the presidency of Madras. It is bounded on the west, north-west, and north by the British territory of Orissa; on the north-east by the British district of Guntoor; on the south-east by the Bay of Bengal; and on the south-west by the British district of Rajamandry: it lies between lat. 17° 15′—19° 3′, long. 82° 24′—84°, and, according to official return, has an estimated area of 7,650 square miles. The seacoast, which throughout has a direction north-east, is comprised within that large extent of shore generally denominated the Orissa Coast. It is remarkably contrasted with the Coromandel coast, farther south, which is with slight exception low and sandy, the coast of this district being bold, steep, and marked by a ridge of rocky hills, which extends along it. The climate on the coast is hot, moist, and relaxing, and more inland, equally sultry, but drier: the land winds, however, so oppressive in many parts of the Carnatic, are here not felt, being intercepted by the vicinity of the hills. Iron is the only metal mentioned to be found in the district: kankar, or calcareous tufa, is abundant, and in many places the soil is largely impregnated with saltpetre. No information has been made public respecting the zoology or botany of the district. The manufacturing industry is scanty, being confined principally to coarse cottons and a few less-important branches, carried on at the town of Vizagapatam. The principal crops are rice, maize, millet, oil-seeds, pulse of various kinds, sugar-cane, indigo, and cotton. The Pallakonda talook, a considerable portion of this district, has been leased by the government for a term of years to the European firm of Arbuthnot and Co.

The population is given under the article MADRAS. Vizagapatam occupies a portion of the territory known as the Five Circars, the possession of which was fiercely contested about the middle of the last century by the French and English. They were obtained by the former in 1753, and retained by them until 1759, when they were transferred by Clive to the East-India Company, to whom they were confirmed in 1765 by the emperor of Delhi. The former prevalence and recent suppression of human sacrifices in this and the contiguous district of Ganjam, will be found noticed in the article GOOMSOOR. Certain portions of this district have, in consequence of their disturbed state, been excepted from the operation of the general regulations, and placed under special supervision.

The military stations—Vizagapatam and Vizianagram—are described under their respective names in the alphabetical arrangement. The most important route of the district is that from north-east to south-west, from Calcutta, through Chicacole and Vizagapatam, to Madras. The cross-roads have recently been put into thorough repair.

VIZAGAPATAM.—The principal place of the British district of the same name, presidency of Madras, a seaport on the Orissa coast, or western shore of the Bay of Bengal. It is situate in the centre of a spit of land projecting from the mainland into the estuary of the Veragapatam river. The bar at the entrance of the river is passable by vessels of from 150 to 200 tons burthen, having eight or ten feet of water at spring tides. South of the estuary, the Dolphin's Nose, a remarkable and bold rocky hill, rises abruptly from the sea, and about 1,500 feet above its level. In the south-west monsoon, ships anchor south of the Dolphin's Nose; in the north-east monsoon, a safe anchorage is found one and a half or one mile and three-quarters from land, where there is a bottom of sand and mud, with eight fathoms water. The fort, which is situate nearly in the extremity, or south-western part of the spit of land, is now dilapidated, its defences having been allowed to fall to decay, and the rampart on the eastern side partly undermined by the sea. Within its precinct are the barracks for the European invalid soldiers, the arsenal, the officers' quarters, and various public buildings, comprising those for the accommodation of the civil establishment. The pettah or native town immediately adjoins the fort on its north and west sides: it contains many good streets, and numerous well-built houses, but is much crowded, from the space on which it stands being shut in by a range of sandhills intervening between it and the sea, and by the extensive swamp already mentioned on the land side. The climate is considered unfavourable to the constitutions of Europeans, who often find it expedient to remove, for the renovation of their health, to localities more elevated and remote from the coast. Distance from Hyderabad, E., 320 miles; Madras, N.E., 380; Masulipatam, N.E., 180; Calcutta, S.W., 470. Lat. 17° 41′, long. 83° 21′.

VIZAYROYE.—A town in the British district of Masulipatam, presidency of Madras, 49 miles N. of Masulipatam. Lat. 16° 50′, long. 81° 3′.

VIZIADROOG.—See GHERIA.

VIZIANAGRAM, in the British district of Vizagapatam, presidency of Madras, a military cantonment, situate on ground sloping gently to the north. It contains twenty-six officers' houses, barracks, hospital, and other suitable offices. Here is a fort, the residence of the zemindar of Vizianagram, separated from the village by a large tank. The present zemindar is a young man, and the estate being large and burdened with debt, it has been deemed necessary to appoint a special agent to undertake its administration for a limited time. The inhabitants of the village are chiefly weavers and agriculturists. The surrounding country has a deep fertile and alluvial soil, highly cultivated, and very productive; in consequence, provisions are abundant and good. The roads about the station are well laid down, and kept in good repair by private contribution. The climate is very salubrious from September to March, and many Europeans at that time repair thither to recruit their health, which may have suffered from the relaxing effect of the air on the coast. In April the weather becomes warm, and towards the middle of the month the thermometer sometimes rises as high as 100° throughout the whole night and day, and seldom falls below 96°. Towards the end of May, rain falls and cools the air; and early in June, after considerable atmospheric changes, the south-west monsoon sets in, causing general coolness, though the nights are occasionally warm. A good deal of rain falls in September and October, and towards the end of the latter month, cold northerly winds commence. The weather during the rest of the year is cold to a degree which some find disagreeable. Distance from Hydrabad, E., 329 miles; Bellary, N.E., 478; Bangalore, N.E., 528; Masulipatam, N.E., 200; Vizagapatam, N.E., 30; Madras, N.E., 400; Calcutta, S.E., 438. Lat. 18° 7′, long. 83° 28′.

VOLCONDAH.—A town in the British district of Trichinopoly, presidency of Madras, 38 miles N.N.E. of Trichinopoly. Lat. 11° 20′, long. 78° 59′.

VOODAGOONY.—A town in the Mysore, 164 miles N.W. from Seringapatam, and 56 miles E. from Honahwar. Lat. 14° 20′, long. 75° 19′.

VUDDACACURRAY.—A town in the native state of Travancore, presidency of Madras, 34 miles N.W. by N. from Trivandrum, and 82 miles S.S.E. from Cochin. Lat. 8° 52′, long. 76° 43′.

VULLARAPULLAI, in the territory of Cochin, under the political superintendence of the presidency of Madras, a town in a small portion of territory isolated amidst the dominions of the rajah of Travancore. Distance from the city of Cochin, N.E., 18 miles. Lat. 10° 18′, long. 76° 28′.

VULLUPULUM.—A town in the British district of South Arcot, presidency of Madras, 13 miles S.W. of Cuddalore. Lat. 11° 35′, long. 79° 40′.

VURRAGHERRY HILLS.—A range of mountains of Southern India, situate between lat. 10° 10′—10° 44′, and long. 76° 21′—77° 52′.

VUZEERPOOR, in the British district of Mynpooree, lieut.-gov. of the N.W. Provinces, a village on the route from Allygurh cantonment to that of Futtehgurh, and 42 miles S.E. of the former. Lat. 27° 45′, long. 78° 45′.

VYGAH, a river of the British district of Madura, presidency of Madras, rises in lat. 10° 17′, long. 77° 37′, and flowing south-east 130 miles, falls into the sea, in lat. 9° 20′, long. 79° 4′.

VYTURNA, a river of the British district of Tannah, presidency of Bombay, rises in lat. 19° 44′, long. 73° 31′, and flowing circuitously, but generally in a south-westerly direction, for seventy miles, falls into the sea, in lat. 19° 36′, long. 72° 55′.

W.

WADONA.—A town in Hyderabad, or territory of the Nizam, situate on the left bank of the Koom river. Lat. 20° 3′, long. 78° 45′.

WAEE.—A town in the British province of Sattara, presidency of Bombay, 20 miles N. by W. of Sattara. Lat. 17° 56′, long. 73° 59′.

WAEE.—A town in the British district of Ahmednuggur, presidency of Bombay, 62 miles N.W. by N. of Ahmednuggur. Lat. 19° 50′, long. 74° 12′.

WAGEIRA.—A town in the native state of Peint, province of Guzerat, 16 miles S. from Peint, and 18 miles W. by N. from Nassik. Lat. 20° 4′, long. 73° 31′.

WAGOOLEE.—A town in the British district of Poonah, presidency of Bombay, 10 miles N.E. by E. of Poonah. Lat. 18° 35′, long. 74°.

WAGOTUN.—A town in the British district of Rutnageriah, presidency of Bombay, 36 miles S. by E. of Rutnageriah. Lat. 16° 30′, long. 73° 30′.

WAGRU.—A town in the British district of Amherst, one of the Tenasserim provinces, 34 miles S. by E. of Moulmein. Lat. 16°, long. 97° 50′.

WAHN I BUCHUR, in the Sinde Sagur Dooab division of the Punjab, a town situated 24 miles from the left bank of the Indus. Lat. 32° 28′, long. 71° 48′.

WALAJAHBAD, in the British district of Chingleput, presidency of Madras, a town with military cantonment 500 yards N. of the north or left side of the river Palar. Distance from Madras, S.W., 38 miles. Lat. 12° 48′, long. 79° 53′.

WALLABHIPOOR.—See VAMILAPOORA.

WALLAJANUGGUR.—A town in the British district of North Arcot, presidency of Madras, 16 miles E. of Vellore. Lat. 12° 56′, long. 79° 25′.

WALLANCHOONG.—A town in Nepal, situate on the left bank of the Tamur river. Lat. 27° 44′, long. 87° 31′.

WALLEE.—A town in the Rajpoot state of Godwar, 74 miles S. by E. from Jodhpoor. Lat. 25° 15′, long. 73° 21′.

WALWA.—A town in the native state of Kolapoor, presidency of Bombay, 49 miles N.W. by N. from Belgaum. Lat. 16° 29′, long. 74° 13′.

WAMBOOREE.—A town in the British district of Ahmednuggur, presidency of Bombay, 14 miles N. of Ahmednuggur. Lat. 19° 19′, long. 74° 45′.

WANCANEER.—A town in the province of Guzerat, situate on the left bank of the Mhye river, and 20 miles N. by W. from Baroda. Lat. 22° 31′, long. 73° 10′.

WANDIPOOR. — A town in the native state of Bhotan, situate on the left bank of the Bagnee river. Lat. 27° 25′, long. 89° 49′.

WANGA BAZAR. —A town in the British district of Hydrabad, province of Scinde, 74 miles S.E. of Hydrabad. Lat. 24° 39′, long. 69° 19′.

WANGEE.—A town in the British province of Sattara, presidency of Bombay, 42 miles S.E. by S. of Sattara. Lat. 17° 12′, long. 74° 28′.

WANGTOO, in Koonawar, a district of Bussahir, is a village on the left side of the Sutluj, here ninety-two feet wide, and confined between banks of solid granite. Lat. 31° 32′, long. 78° 3′.

WANGUR, in Koonawur, a district of Bussahir, is a large torrent, formed by the junction of two others flowing from the eastern declivity of the Damuk Chu. It falls into the Sutlej on the right side, in lat. 31° 33′, long. 78° 10′.

WANJEE.—A town in the British district of Sholapoor, presidency of Bombay, 63 miles N.W. by W. of Sholapoor. Lat. 18° 13′, long. 75° 11′.

WARDAWAN.—A town within the dominions of Gholab Singh, the ruler of Cashmere, situate on the left bank of the Wurdwun river. Lat. 33° 51′, long. 75° 42′.

WARI, or SOONDUR WARREE.—The principal place of the small state of Sawunt Warree. It was probably at no time a place of any great strength, and when invested, in 1819, by the British forces, was easily reduced. Distance from Bombay, S., 220 miles. Lat. 15° 54′, long. 73° 54′.

WARI.—A river of Scinde, rises in lat. 24° 10′, long. 68° 3′, and flowing south for twenty-five miles, falls into the sea, in lat. 23° 51′, long. 67° 56′.

WARNA.—See WURNA.

WARNAIR.—A town in the Rajpoot state of Jodhpoor, 167 miles S.W. from Jodhpoor, and 162 miles E. by S. from Hydrabad. Lat. 24° 58′, long. 71°.

WARRAGAUM.—A town in one of the recently sequestrated districts of Hyderabad. Lat. 20° 32′, long. 76° 52′.

WARRAKUNCHAIRY.—A town in the British district of Malabar, presidency of Madras, 65 miles S.E. of Calicut. Lat. 10° 37′, long. 76° 32′.

WARSA.—A town in the British district of Candeish, presidency of Bombay, 47 miles N.W. by W. of Malligaum. Lat. 20° 54′, long. 73° 54′.

WARUNGUL, in Hyderabad, or the territory of the Nizam, a town, the ancient capital of Telingana, of which little now remains to denote its former grandeur, save the four gateways of the Temple of Siva, which still continue in a state of tolerable preservation. Distance from the city of Hyderabad, N.E., 86 miles. Lat. 17° 58′, long. 79° 40′.

WARYE.—A petty protected state in the north-western quarter of the province of Guzerat, traversed by the river Bunnass. The population, consisting chiefly of Jutts, is estimated at 20,000. The town of Warye is in lat. 23° 47′, long. 71° 29′.

WASEEOTA.—A town in the British province of Sattara, presidency of Bombay, 20 miles W. of Sattara. Lat. 17° 40′, long. 73° 47′.

WASHISHTEE. — A river of the Rutnagherry collectorate of Bombay, rises in lat. 17° 50′, long. 73° 36′, and falls into the sea at lat. 17° 33′, long. 73° 16′.

WASTARA.—A town in the Mysore, 88 miles N.W. by W. from Seringapatam, and 66 miles E.N.E. from Mangalore. Lat. 13° 16′, long. 75° 46′.

WATAR.—A town in the British province of Sattara, presidency of Bombay, 31 miles N.E. of Sattara. Lat. 17° 56′, long. 74° 27′.

WAULOR.—A town in the British district of Surat, presidency of Bombay, 31 miles E. by S. of Surat. Lat. 21°, long. 73° 20′.

WAUNCANEER, in the peninsula of Kattywar, province of Guzerat, a town in the district of Jhallawar, situate on the Bidee or Mutchoo river. Distance from Bombay, N.W., 275 miles. Lat. 22° 36′, long. 70° 59′.

WAUNDIA.—A town in the native state of Cutch, 58 miles E. from Bhooj, and 66 miles N. by W. from Rajcote. Lat. 23° 14′, long. 70° 39′.

WAZEERABAD, a town in the Punjab, is situate about three miles from the left or eastern bank of the Chenaub, here half a mile broad. The country immediately about it is exceedingly fertile, and the view of the Himalaya probably the most extensive and magnificent anywhere. It is one of the handsomest towns in India; General Avitabile, a European officer in the service of Runjeet Singh, having caused it to be rebuilt in the European style, with wide streets and a handsome and commodious bazar. Runjeet Singh made here a pleasure-ground, and palace of singular construction, and covered outside with rude full-length figures of the ten *Gurus*, or spiritual leaders of the Sikhs, painted in fresco. Population 16,846. Lat. 32° 27′, long. 74° 10′.

WAZIRGANJ, in the territory of Oude, a town on the route from Goruckpoor cantonment to that of Sekrora, 84 miles W. of the former, 28 S.E. of the latter. Lat. 26° 58′, long. 82° 5′.

WAZIR GARH, in Gurhwal, a village on

the right bank of the Jumna. Its site is striking and picturesque, being on a slope over the river, and in view of the snowy peaks of the ranges running southward from Jamnotri. Elevation above the sea 5,813 feet. Lat. 30° 54′, long. 78° 23′.

WEAMUNGALUM.—A town in the British district of Malabar, presidency of Madras, 16 miles N.N.W. from Calicut. Lat. 11° 28′, long. 75° 42′.

WEER, in the territory of Bhurtpore, a town on the route from Agra to Ajmeer, by Jeypore, 55 miles S.W. of the former. In A.D. 1826, after the capture of Bhurtpore by Lord Combermere, Weer was, without resistance, surrendered to the British. Distant N.W. of Calcutta, *viâ* Allahabad, 900 miles. Lat. 27°, long. 77° 14′.

WEINBOKE.—A town in the British district of Amherst, one of the Tenasserim provinces, 48 miles S.E. by E. of Amherst. Lat. 15° 44′, long. 98° 17′.

WEINGO, a river of Amherst, one of the Tenasserim provinces, rises in lat. 15° 20′, long. 98° 26′, and, flowing northerly for sixty-five miles, falls into the Attaran river, in lat. 16° 8′, long. 98° 9′.

WEIN GUNGA.—A river of the Saugor and Nerbudda territory, rising in lat. 22° 25′, long. 79° 8′. Its source is among the Mahadeo Mountains, at an elevation of 1,850 feet above the sea. Taking a direction easterly for a distance of eighty miles, and subsequently southerly for thirty-four, to lat. 22° 1′, long. 80° 11′, it at that point becomes the boundary between the Saugor and Nerbudda territory and that of Nagpore; and still flowing in a southerly direction for the further distance of twenty-five miles, continues to be so to lat. 21° 47′, long. 80° 16′. At that point it enters the Nagpore territory, and shortly after turning south-west for eighty miles, it receives, near Ambora, in lat. 21° 5′, long. 79° 39′, and at the distance of 219 miles from its source, the river Kanhan, which joins it on the right side. One hundred and twenty miles farther down the stream, or more to the south, it receives, on the same side, the Wurda, in lat. 19° 38′, long. 79° 51′. Continuing to flow circuitously, but generally southwards, for 100 miles farther, during which it is sometimes called the Pranheeta, it falls into the river Godavery, on its north or left side, in lat. 18° 52′, long. 79° 55′; its total length of course being about 439 miles.

WELAUP.—A town in the British district of Amherst, one of the Tenasserim provinces, 22 miles S.E. of Amherst. Lat. 15° 49′, long. 97° 51′.

WELLESLEY PROVINCE is a dependency of Prince of Wales Island, and comprises a narrow strip of land on the western coast of the Malayan peninsula, immediately opposite the island. It is thirty-five miles in length and four in width, with an area of 140 square miles. "Province Wellesley," says Newbold, "presents a gently undulating superficies, sloping gradually to the sea, with a few narrow strips of sandy soil, well adapted for the cultivation of the cocoanut, from which protrude a few hills of granite." The general appearance of the province in 1822 is thus described by Finlayson, who visited it about that period :—"The country here, to the distance of seven or eight miles from the sea, is low, flat, and swampy, covered for the most part with almost impenetrable jungle, the secure haunts of tigers, leopards, rhinoceroses, and occasionally of elephants; its vast swamps being unfavourable to the latter." Such was the condition of Province Wellesley when transferred to the British. For some years it appears to have been allowed to remain in much the same state: lately, however, cultivation has been making rapid strides; and in 1836, according to Captain Low, the extent of land under cultivation was about 120 square miles, being six-sevenths of the whole province. The staple production is rice, which is cultivated to a great extent, the low swampy lands of the province being well suited for its culture. Sugar is also extensively cultivated in the central and southern portions of Province Wellesley. Several species of indigo exist, but it is not of the first quality; and its manufacture is so crude as to render it only fit for home consumption. The sandy soil, which frequently occurs in the province, is generally appropriated to the cocoanut, which thrives here exceedingly well. Province Wellesley was ceded to the British for a pecuniary consideration by the king of Queda, in 1802. The population is returned at 51,509.

WENRA.—A town in the British district of Amherst, one of the Tenasserim provinces, 36 miles E. of Amherst. Lat. 16° 1′, long. 98° 11′.

WER.—A town in the British district of Boolundshuhur, lieut.-gov. of the N.W. Provinces, 36 miles S.E. of Delhi. Lat. 28° 21′, long. 77° 46′.

WERAH, in the British district of Agra, a village on the route from Agra to Muttra, and 27 miles N.W. of former. Lat. 27° 28′, long. 77° 48′.

WERANG, in Bussahir, a pass in the district of Koonawar, over a range separating the valley of the Pejur from that of the Sutluj. Elevation above the sea 13,000 feet. Lat. 31° 38′, long. 78° 23′.

WESEERPOOR, in the Baree Doab division of the Punjab, a town situated 10 miles from the right bank of the Sutlej. Lat. 30° 34′, long. 73° 43′.

WHARTOO, in Bussahir, a peak of considerable elevation in the lower or more southern part of the Himalaya. It was the most westerly of the stations employed in the great trigonometrical survey of the Himalaya by Hodgson and Herbert. They found it wooded to the very summit, which is surmounted by a ruined fortification, formerly occupied by the Gorkhas. Elevation above the sea 10,673 feet. Lat. 31° 14′, long. 77° 34′.

WODIARPOLLIUM.—A town in the British district of Trichinopoly, presidency of Madras, 48 miles N.E. by E. of Trichinopoly. Lat. 11° 11′, long. 79° 21′.

WODNAPOOR.—A town in Oude, 62 miles N. by W. from Lucknow. Lat. 27° 45′, long. 80° 51′.

WOJERABAD.—A town in Hyderabad, or territory of the Nizam, situate on the left bank of the Kistnah, and 92 miles S.E. by E. from Hyderabad. Lat. 16° 42′, long. 79° 43′.

WOMOLUR.—A town in the British district of Salem, presidency of Madras, 11 miles W.N.W. of Salem. Lat. 11° 44′, long. 78° 5′.

WON, or WUNN, in the territory of Indore, or possessions of Holkar's family, a decayed town situate in the fertile tract of Nimaur, in a slight hollow amidst low hills. In the present ruined town are everywhere to be seen fragments of images and other elaborate sculptures, neglected and prostrate, or built into walls and fences, to serve the purposes of the present poverty-stricken inhabitants. Throughout a great extent of country around, vestiges of temples are of frequent occurrence. Won formerly contained a population of above 10,000 persons: it is at present a collection of ruins, about three furlongs in length and one in breadth, with only seventy inhabited houses. Distant N.E. from Bombay 270 miles, S.W. of British cantonment Mow 51, S.W. of Indor 61. Lat. 21° 51′, long. 75° 31′.

WOODUNTA RIVER rises in Orissa, and flowing easterly, falls into the Tell river, in lat. 20° 11′, long. 83° 12′.

WOONY, in Hyderabad, or territory of the Nizam, a town on the right bank of the river Godavery, on the route from the city of Nagpoor to that of Hyderabad, 81 miles S. of the former, 185 N. of latter. Lat. 20°, long. 79° 3′.

WOREGAUM.—A town in Hyderabad, or territory of the Nizam, 73 miles E.S.E. from Ahmednuggur. Lat. 18° 49′, long. 75° 50′.

WOW.—A petty native district on the north-western frontier of Guzerat. It extends from north to south about thirty miles, and from east to west fifteen, and is traversed by the route from Palee to the Dholera and Mundavie ports. The population, consisting principally of Chooan Rajpoots, amounts to about 10,000; the revenues average only about 5,000 rupees per annum, the district being much divided amongst different kinsmen of the chiefs: the disbursements are about equal to the revenue. Wow pays no tribute to any government. The chief entertains about twenty horse and foot for his personal guard, trusting entirely to the British government for protection from foreign invasions. Lat. of town 24° 22′, long. 71° 30′.

WOZUR.—A town in the British district of Ahmednuggur, presidency of Bombay, 10 miles N.E. by E. of Nassik. Lat. 20° 4′, long. 73° 54′.

WUDDAKURRY, in the British district of Malabar, presidency of Madras. It is rather a considerable place, and well built, on the north side of one of those backwaters or extensive shallow estuaries receiving the waters of several streams descending from the Western Ghauts. The population consists of Moplah Mussulmans. Distance from Cananore, S.E., 22 miles; from Callicut, N.W., 28. Lat. 11° 36′, long. 75° 37′.

WUDDAMURRY.—A town in Hyderabad, or territory of the Nizam, 23 miles N.E. by N. from Hyderabad. Lat. 17° 37′, long. 78° 44′.

WUDJAR CURROOR.—A town in the British district of Bellary, presidency of Madras, 36 miles E. by S. of Bellary. Lat. 15° 1′, long. 77° 28′.

WUDOO.—A town in the British district of Bellary, presidency of Madras, 18 miles W. by N. of Bellary. Lat. 15° 10′, long. 76° 42′.

WUDWAN, in the peninsula of Kattywar, province of Guzerat, a town in the district of Jhalawar, situate on a small river, which, a few miles farther eastward, is lost in the Runn or Salt-marsh dividing the peninsula of Guzerat from the mainland. It is the principal place of a subdivision of the same name, containing thirty towns and villages, and a population of 32,220. The tallook is kept in a state of high cultivation, producing the finest cotton in Kattywar: it consequently yields a considerable revenue in proportion to its area; and in 1828 the rajah was reported to draw from it an annual revenue of 1,00,000 rupees; of which he pays to the British government an annual tribute of 27,831 rupees. Distance from Ahmedabad, S.W., 68 miles; Baroda, N.W., 105. Lat. 22° 40′, long. 71° 39′.

WUEEKCHONG.—A town of Eastern India, in the native state of Muneepoor, situate on the left bank of the Mythia Khyoung river, and 29 miles S. from Muneepoor. Lat. 24° 23′, long. 94°.

WUGGUN.—A town in the British district of Shikarpoor, province of Scinde, 21 miles W.S.W. of Shikarpoor. Lat. 27° 54′, long. 68° 20′.

WUHOAH, in the Daman division of the Punjab, a town situated 44 miles W. from the right bank of the Indus, 103 miles N.W. by W. of the town of Mooltan. Lat. 30° 58′, long. 70° 2′.

WULEEPOOR, in Sirhind, a village situate on the left bank of the Sutlej, at the spot where it is joined by the navigable nulla or watercourse flowing by Loodianah. It contains from thirty to forty mud-built houses. Distant N.W. from Calcutta 1,107 miles. Lat. 30° 56′, long. 75° 42′.

WULENDURPETT.—A town in the British district of South Arcot, presidency of Madras, 31 miles W. of Cuddalore. Lat. 11° 42′, long. 79° 21′.

WULLEH.—A town in the province of Guzerat, situate 71 miles E.S.E. from Rajkote. Lat. 21° 50′, long. 71° 50′.

WULTAIR.—A town in the British district of Vizagapatam, presidency of Madras, three and a half miles N.E. of Vizagapatam. Lat. 17° 44′, long. 83° 24′.

WULUR, in Cashmere, is the largest lake in the valley, and may be regarded as a dilatation of the river Jhelum. It is, according to Hügel, twenty-one miles long from west to east, and nine wide from north to south. In the lake is a small island, which contains the extensive ruins of a Buddhist temple of great antiquity, destroyed by the fanatic Mahometans. The lake is subject to violent squalls. The centre is in lat. 34° 20′, long. 74° 45′.

WUNN.—A town in the British district of Ahmednuggur, presidency of Bombay, 25 miles N. by E. of Nassik. Lat. 20° 20′, long. 73° 52′.

WUNVARLY.—A town in Hyderabad, or territory of the Nizam, 87 miles S. from Ellichpoor. Lat. 19° 58′, long. 77° 30′.

WURDA.—A river rising in the Saugor and Nerbudda territory, near the town of Mooltaee, and about lat. 21° 44′, long. 78° 25′. Taking a southerly course for a few miles, it leaves the district, and becomes the common boundary of the territory of Nagpore and of the dominions of the Nizam, or territory of Hyderabad, to its fall into the Wein Gunga, on its right side, in lat. 19° 37′, long. 79° 51′. The total length of course of the Wurda is about 250 miles, and it flows throughout generally from north-west to south-east. At about 180 miles from its source, and in lat. 19° 57′, long. 79° 15′, it, on the right side, receives the Payne Gunga, a stream little inferior to itself in magnitude. It has many fine pools in the hottest weather, but is generally fordable at all seasons, except at the height of the rains, when it is so full as to be navigable for moderate-sized boats 100 miles above its mouth.

WURNA, a river of Bombay, rises on the eastern declivity of the Western Ghats, in lat. 17° 18′, long. 73° 46′, and flowing south-east for eighty miles, during which course it divides the territory of Sattara from the native state of Kolapoor, falls into the Kistna river, in lat. 16° 50′, long. 74° 36′.

WURNEIR.—A town in the British district of Ahmednuggur, presidency of Bombay, 24 miles N.E. by N. of Nassik. Lat. 20° 16′, long. 74°.

WURR.—A town in the native state of Cutch, 28 miles N. from Bhooj, and 63 miles E. by S. from Luckput. Lat. 23° 37′, long. 69° 46′.

WURRODAH.—A town in one of the recently sequestrated districts of Hyderabad, 64 miles W. by S. of Ellichpoor. Lat. 21° 2′, long. 76° 38′.

WURWANEA, in the peninsula of Kattywar, province of Guzerat, a town in the subdivision of the Mucho Canta. Here is a ferry across the gulf to the opposite shore of Cutch. Distance from Ahmedabad, W., 120 miles. Lat. 23° 4′, long. 70° 44′.

WUSRAVEE.—A native Bheel state in Guzerat, under the protection of the British government. It is bounded on the north by that of Raj Peepla; on the east by the British territory of Khandeish; on the south by the territory of the Daung rajahs; and on the west by the Gulf of Cambay and the British districts of Surat and Broach. It extends from lat. 20° 55′ to 21° 33′, and from long. 72° 46′ to 73° 51′; is sixty miles in length from east to west, and forty-one in breadth: its area is 450 square miles, with a population of 33,300. Wusravee, the chief town, is in lat. 21° 25′, long. 73° 12′.

WUTATUR.—A town in the British district of Trichinopoly, presidency of Madras, 20 miles N.N.E. of Trichinopoly. Lat. 11° 5′, long. 78° 54′.

WUZEERGUNJE, in the British district of Buddaon, lieut.-gov. of the N.W. Provinces, a town 14 miles N. by W. of Buddaon. Lat. 28° 14′, long. 79° 8′.

WUZERA.—A town in the British district of Ahmednuggur, presidency of Bombay, 53 miles N.W. by W. of Ahmednuggur. Lat. 19° 30′, long. 74° 4′.

WYNAAD.—A tallook or subdivision of the British district of Malabar, presidency of Madras, an elevated, mountainous, and wooded tract, separated from the low country of Malabar by the culminating ridge of the Western Ghats, from which it slopes eastward and north-eastward towards Mysore. The area is 1,188 square miles. Though rugged, and overrun by forest and jungle, it is less difficult in a military point of view than Coorg, farther north; and hence the Mysorean invaders of Malabar have usually taken their route through it. Though at the head of an insignificant population, the chief or petty rajah gave much trouble to the British government after the cession of the country by Tippoo Sultan at the pacification of 1792; but for some years there does not appear to have been any serious disturbance in that quarter, a military force being stationed for its control at Manantoddy.

WYRAGUR, in the territory of Nagpoor, near the left bank of the river Waingunga. Diamonds were formerly found in its vicinity, in yellow earth, forming small hills; but the mines have not latterly been worked, as the number and value of the gems obtained were not found to afford a remunerating return. Traces of the former workings are, however, observable in several places. It is a place of some trade, and contains about 300 houses, and a population of 2,000. Distance from the city of Nagpore, S.E., 80 miles. Lat. 20° 27′, long. 80° 10′.

Y.

YAILAGHERRY.—A town in the British district of Salem, presidency of Madras, 73 miles N.N.E. of Salem. Lat. 12° 37′, long. 78° 39′.

YAINUR, in the British district of South Canara, presidency of Madras, a small town, containing eight temples of votaries of the Jain persuasion, one of the Brahminical. Here "is an immense colossal image of one of the gods worshipped by the Jains. It is formed of one solid piece of granite, and stands in the open air." Distance from Mangalore, N.E., 22 miles; from Madras, W., 350. Lat. 13° 2′, long. 75° 13′.

YAJGO.—A town of Burmah, 16 miles W. from the right bank of the Khyendwen river, and 150 miles N.W. from Ava. Lat. 23° 23′, long. 94° 26′.

YAKOOTGUNJ, in the British district of Furruckabad, lieut.-gov. of the N.W. Provinces, a village situate in lat. 27° 19′, long. 79° 40′.

YAKOOTPOOR, in the British district of Allygurh, lieut.-gov. of the N.W. Provinces, a village situate in lat. 27° 52′, long. 78° 11′.

YALLOONG.—A river of Nepal, rising in lat. 27° 35′, long. 88° 5′, on the southern face of Kangchang, a peak of the Himalayas. It flows in a south-westerly direction for forty miles, and in lat. 27° 21′, long. 87° 31′, falls into the Tambur river. The town of the same name is in lat. 27° 32′, long. 87° 56′.

YAMBEESEE. — A town in the British district of Hydrabad, province of Scinde, 68 miles N. by E. of Hydrabad. Lat. 26° 20′, long. 68° 43′.

YAMETHEN.—A town of Burmah, situate 124 miles S. from Ava. Lat. 20° 5′, long. 95° 53′.

YANAON, or YANAN.—A French settlement within the limits of the British district of Rajahmundry, presidency of Madras, situate near the bifurcation of the Godavery and the river of Coringa, and about nine miles above the embouchure of the former. The mouth of the Godavery is obstructed by sand-banks, which preclude the entrance of ships, but the Coringa river has a deep channel, which admits of vessels of 200 tons burthen proceeding as high as Yanaon. The French territory dependent on the factory stretches along the banks of the two rivers for the distance of six miles, and contains an area of 8,147 acres, which, in 1836, were classified as under:—

	Acres.
Land under cultivation	4,310
Woods and forests	862
Barren land	215
Public estates	2,760
Total	8,147

The population in 1840 consisted of 6,881 inhabitants. The town of Yanaon is in lat. 16° 44′, long. 82° 16′.

YANDABOO.—A town of Burmah, on the left bank of the Irawady river, 63 miles W. by S. from Ava. Here, on the 26th February, 1826, was concluded the treaty with the Burmese, in which it was provided that the coast of Tenasserim, together with Arracan and its dependencies, should be retained by the British, and that the king of Ava should renounce all claims upon Assam and the adjoining states of Cachar, Jynteea, and Muneepore. Lat. 21° 38′, long. 95° 4′.

YANG.—A town of Eastern India, in the native state of Muneepoor, 99 miles S.E. from Nowgong. Lat. 25° 31′, long. 94°.

YANGMA.—A river of Nepal, tributary to the Tambur, with which it forms a junction in lat. 27° 38′, long. 87° 32′.

YARDWAR.—A town in the British district of Belgaum, presidency of Bombay, 52 miles N.E. by E. of Belgaum. Lat. 16° 13′, long. 75° 15′.

YAROO, in the Daman division of the Punjab, a town situated 25 miles from the right bank of the Indus. Lat. 30° 10′, long. 70° 30′.

YARWUFADAR.—See Sote.

YATLAKEE.—A town in the British district of Bellary, presidency of Madras, 69 miles E. by S. of Bellary. Lat. 15° 2′, long. 77° 58′.

YAVENESUREN.—A town in the British district of Madura, presidency of Madras, 42 miles S.E. of Madura. Lat. 9° 31′, long. 78° 38′.

YAYGEE.—A town in the British province of Pegu, situate on the right bank of one of the arms of the Irawady river. Lat. 17° 14′, long. 95° 14′.

YE.—The province of Ye is the smallest in extent of the Tenasserim provinces. It is bounded on the north by Amherst; on the south by Tavoy; on the west by the Bay of Bengal; and on the east by the Siamese range of mountains. It is a mountainous district, and, with the exception of a few places which are appropriated to the cultivation of rice, it is overspread with thick forests, brushwood, or jungle. Besides a profusion of excellent timber, the province yields no production of any value; and the district is of less note than any other on the coast. The Ye is the only river in the province, and its mouth is so unprotected, and at the same time obstructed, as to render it unsafe for ships of much burthen. The town of Ye, which is the capital, is situate on its banks, and about six miles from its mouth. Lat. 15° 15′, long. 98° 4′.

YEAVAN GHEOUN.—A town of Burmah, situate on the left bank of the Irawady river, 122 miles S.W. from Ava. Lat. 20° 31′, long. 94° 43′.

YEDDAPAUDY.—A town in the British

district of Salem, presidency of Madras, 24 miles W. by S. of Salem. Lat. 11° 33′, long. 77° 53′.

YEDDAPULLEY.—See ITAPALLI.

YEDDIACOTTAH.—A town in the British district of Madura, presidency of Madras, 50 miles N.N.W. of Madura. Lat. 10° 35′, long. 77° 52′.

YEDTORRA.—A town in the Mysore, situate on the Cauvery, 22 miles W. by N. from Seringapatam. Lat. 12° 29′, long. 76° 26′.

YEHVAPOOR.—A town in the British district of Sarun, lieut.-gov. of Bengal, 41 miles S.W. of Bettiah. Lat. 26° 22′, long. 84° 7′.

YEKALI.—A town in Hyderabad, or territory of the Nizam, 63 miles W.N.W. from Hyderabad. Lat. 17° 40′, long. 77° 40′.

YEKTHOON.—A town in Hyderabad, or territory of the Nizam, 18 miles W.S.W. from Jaulnah. Lat. 19° 44′, long. 75° 41′.

YELBOORGA.—A town in one of the recently sequestrated districts of Hyderabad, 69 miles W.N.W. of Bellary. Lat. 15° 38′, long. 76° 4′.

YELDOORTY.—A town in the British district of Kurnool, presidency of Madras, 21 miles S.S.W. of Kurnool. Lat. 15° 32′, long. 77° 59′.

YELJAL.—A town in Hyderabad, or territory of the Nizam, 40 miles S. by W. from Hyderabad. Lat. 16° 49′, long. 78° 24′.

YELLAGODE.—A town in the British district of Kurnool, presidency of Madras, 36 miles E. by S. of Kurnool. Lat. 15° 44′, long. 78° 38′.

YELLANOOR.—A town in the British district of Bellary, presidency of Madras, 86 miles E.S.E. of Bellary. Lat. 14° 40′, long. 78° 8′.

YELLAPOOR, in the British district of North Canara, presidency of Madras, a small town, distant from Madras, N.W., 400 miles. Lat. 14° 58′, long. 74° 46′.

YELLUANDER.—A town in the Mysore, 36 miles S.E. from Seringapatam, and 72 miles N. from Coimbatoor. Lat. 12° 3′, long. 77° 4′.

YELWALL.—A town in the Mysore, nine miles S.W. from Seringapatam. Lat. 12° 20′, long. 76° 40′.

YEMHATTI.—A town in the British district of Coimbatoor, presidency of Madras, 92 miles N.E. by N. of Coimbatoor. Lat. 12° 10′, long. 77° 40′.

YEMWUNTOUNG.—A town of Burmah, situate 100 miles N.W. from Ava. Lat. 23°, long. 95° 9′.

YENGBINE.—A river of the Tenasserim provinces, falling into the Thaluayn Myeet river, in lat. 17° 22′, long. 97° 48′.

YENNAN RIVER, an offset of the Irawady, falling into the Sittang river in lat. 19° 54′, long. 96° 6′.

YENNICUL GOOTA.—A town in the Mysore, 111 miles N. from Seringapatam. Lat. 14° 1′, long. 76° 52′.

YEOWAH.—A town of Burmah, situate on the right bank of the Irawady river, 108 miles S.W. from Ava. Lat. 20° 56′, long. 94° 40′.

YERNAGOODEM.—A town in the British district of Masulipatam, presidency of Madras, 63 miles N.N.E. of Masulipatam. Lat. 17°, long. 81° 33′.

YERRUMAOOR.—A town in the British district of Malabar, presidency of Madras, 68 miles S.E. by E. of Calicut. Lat. 10° 40′, long. 76° 38′.

YESWANTGURH.—See RAIREE.

YEWUR.—A town in the native territory of the Daung rajahs, 52 miles S.E. by E. from Surat. Lat. 20° 40′, long. 73° 30′.

YEY MULLAY, or MOUNT DELLY, in the British district of Malabar, presidency of Madras, 18 miles N.W. of Cannanore. Lat. 12° 2′, long. 75° 15′.

YINKOLU.—A town in the British district of Guntoor, presidency of Madras, 36 miles S.S.W. of Guntoor. Lat. 15° 50′, long. 80° 15′.

YIRODU.—A town in the British district of Coimbatoor, presidency of Madras, 56 miles E.N.E. of Coimbatoor. Lat. 11° 20′, long. 77° 46′.

YOOLA, in Koonawar, a district of Bussahir, is a considerable stream rising on the eastern declivity of the Damuk Chu Mountains, forming the boundary towards Ladakh. It holds a course nearly southerly for about fifteen miles, and falls into the Sutlej on the right side, in lat. 31° 31′, long. 78° 11′.

YOOLANG.—A torrent in the district of Koonawar, in Bussahir, falls into the Li, or river of Spiti, on the right side, in lat. 31° 55′, long. 78° 37′, after a course of about eight miles in a south-easterly direction.

YOOMADOUNG MOUNTAINS.—A long range of mountains stretching from lat. 16° to lat. 22° 20′, in a direction N.N.E., and forming a natural barrier between Arracan and Ava, and thence stretching southerly, through the British province of Pegu, to Cape Negrais. It is a continuation of the great mountain-chain commencing at the south of Assam, in lat. 26° 30′, and extending southwards, running parallel with the river Irawaddi. This range has received, and been known under, various designations, but the one above mentioned is that generally adopted. The mountains vary in height, according to Crawford, from 200 to 8,000 feet. The loftiest point is the Blue Mountain, in lat. 22° 37′, long. 93° 11′. From this peak, proceeding southward, the mountains gradually decrease in height.

There are several rivers which water the province of Arracan, flowing from these mountains, but none are large, and they derive their importance only from the towns situate on heir banks. The chief are the Arracan or Kuladyne river, the Talak, Aeng, and Sandoway rivers.

YOOSOO (so called from a village of the same name at its southern base).—A pass in Bussahir, over the range of the Himalaya forming the southern boundary of Koonawar. Elevation of the pass above the sea 15,877 feet. Lat. 31° 24′, long. 78° 9′.

YOUNGAI.—A town in the British district of Tavoy, one of the Tenasserim provinces, 114 miles S.S.E. of Amherst. Lat. 14° 30′, long. 98° 18′.

YOUN ZERAY.—A town in the British province of Pegu, situate on the Irawady river, 18 miles S. by W. from Prome. Lat. 18° 31′, long. 95°.

Z.

ZAFFARGHUR.—A town in the territory of the Nizam, 72 miles E.N.E. from Hyderabad. Lat. 17° 46′, long. 79° 31′.

ZAFURABAD, in the British district of Jounpoor, a town situate on the right bank of the river Goomtee, six miles S.E. of Jounpoor cantonment. It is mentioned by Ferishta as early as 1595. Lat. 25° 42′, long. 82° 47′.

ZAHOORABAD, in the British district of Ghazeepoor, lieut.-gov. of Agra, a town, the principal place of the pergunnah of the same name, is 14 miles N.E. of Ghazeepoor cantonment. Lat. 25° 41′, long. 83° 48′.

ZANSKAR, in Ladakh, or Middle Tibet, an elevated region lying between the Indus on the north, and the Chenaub on the south. It is about eighty miles long from south-east to north-west, sixty wide from south-west to north-east, and lies between lat. 33°—34° 30′, long. 76° 20′—77° 40′.

ZEBUEBEEN.—A town of Burmah, situate on the Irawady river, 121 miles S.W. from Ava. Lat. 20° 41′, long. 94° 34′.

ZEEMANIA.—See NUSRUTHPOOR.

ZEERAPOOR.—A town in the territory of Holkar, 108 miles N.N.E. from Indoor, and 100 miles E.S.E. from Neemuch. Lat. 24° 3′, long. 76° 26′.

ZILLAHPUR, in the British district of Cawnpore, a village on the route from Allahabad to Etawa, and 57 miles S.E. of the latter. Lat. 26° 16′, long. 79° 46′.

ZIMNIE RIVER.—See ATTARAN.

ZOIYA.—A town in the British district of Amherst, one of the Tenasserim Provinces, 54 miles E. by N. of Moulmein. Lat. 16° 33′, long. 98° 30′.

ZONGRI.—A town in the native state of Sikhim, 36 miles N. by W. from Darjeeling, and 182 miles E. from Khatmandoo. Lat. 27° 31′, long. 88° 11′.

ZOORHUR GHAUT, in the British territory of Saugor and Nerbudda, lieut.-gov. of the N.W. Provinces, a town on the route from Hoosungabad to Nagpoor, 31 miles S.E. of the former. Lat. 22° 26′, long. 78° 6′.

ZOPHALING.—A town of Assam, in the British district of Suddiya, lieut.-gov. of Bengal, 48 miles E. by N. of Suddiya. Lat. 27° 58′, long. 96° 29′.

ZORAWURGUNJE.—A town in the British district of Bulloah, lieut.-gov. of Bengal, 46 miles E. by S. of Bulloah. Lat. 22° 40′, long. 91° 39′.

ZUMMAWALA, in the Sinde Sagur Dooab division of the Punjab, a town situated nine miles from the left bank of the Indus, 80 miles S. of the town of Peshawar. Lat. 32° 52′, long. 71° 48′.

ZURKEYL.—A town in the British district of Shikarpoor, province of Scinde, 10 miles N. of Shikarpoor. Lat. 28° 9′, long. 68° 40′.

ZUTO.—A town of Burmah, nine miles W. from the Irawaddy, and 145 miles S.W. from Ava. Lat. 20° 15′, long. 94° 34′.

ZUZ NAR.—A town within the dominions of Gholab Singh, the ruler of Cashmere, situate 34 miles S.W. by S. from Sirinagur, and 81 miles N. from Sealkote. Lat. 33° 38′, long. 74° 43′.

ZYNPORE, in the British district of Cawnpore, lieut.-gov. of the N.W. Provinces, a small town on the route, by Nanamow Ghat, from the cantonment of Etawah to Lucknow, in Oude, and 58 miles E. of Etawah. Lat. 26° 58′, long. 79° 56′.

Published by

Facsimile Publisher
Ashok Vihar, Delhi-110052 (India)
Website: www.facsimilepublisher.com

Distributed by

Gyan Books Pvt. Ltd.
5, Ansari Road, Daryaganj, New Delhi-110002 (India)
E-mail: books@gyanbooks.com, Website: www.gyanbooks.com

2 222000 000363